CONTENTS

EDITOR'S NOTE

The present volume is a concise version of the original *Encyclopedia of Mexico: History, Society, and Culture*. It was far from easy for us to decide which essays to omit and retain. This volume includes most of the essays on particular events and many of the broad, synthetic overviews, particularly those dealing with questions of greatest concern to a nonspecialist audience (such as politics, religion, the military, and arts and letters). We have omitted most essays aimed at a higher-level or more specialized readership, and we also have excluded most of the shorter articles on people already discussed in the longer synthetic essays. Throughout this difficult process we have made every effort to preserve the scope, depth, and rigor of the original edition. All essays in this volume appear unabridged and in their original form. We hope that readers will consult the larger version when gaps appear in this more modest text.

The *Concise Encyclopedia of Mexico* seeks to provide students, policy makers, and the general public with convenient access to basic bibliographic and factual data on Mexican history. All topical articles have been extensively cross-referenced, although in the interest of space cross-references generally are confined to topical essays dealing with subjects specifically addressed in the original essay. We also encourage readers to consult the general synthetic essays. We have organized bibliographies around works that we believe are most useful to nonspecialist readers; bibliographies in this concise edition include only English-language works, including translations into English.

The *Concise Encyclopedia of Mexico* is primarily historical in scope, emphasizing the development of broad themes, structures, and processes over time. Not only does this focus allow a more richly contextual understanding of specific events, institutions, and figures in Mexican history, but it also helps foster a deeper understanding of Mexican history. As in the original encyclopedia, we emphasize broad synthetic essays, which allow authors greater freedom to question the very categories that inform the organization of this project. Nonetheless, many of the most difficult and important questions will have to be asked by the readers themselves.

MICHAEL S. WERNER
Austin, Texas
June 2001

ADVISERS

William O. Autry
Elizabeth Bakewell
John H. Coatsworth
Thomas Cummins
Guillermo de la Peña
Ben Fallaw
Jean Franco
Peter F. Guardino
Gilbert M. Joseph
Friedrich Katz
Alan Knight

Claudio Lomnitz
Daniel Nugent
Roger Rouse
Susan Schroeder
Patricia Seed
Emily Socolov
Eric Van Young
Mary Kay Vaughan
Brígida von Mentz de Boege
Richard Warren

CONTRIBUTORS

Mariclaire Acosta
Rolena Adorno
Javier Aguilar García
Maureen Ahern
Salvador Alvarez
Arthur James Outram Anderson
Rodney D. Anderson
Christon I. Archer
Electa Arenal
Israel Arroyo García
Maricela Ayala Falcón
Shannon L. Baker
Elizabeth Bakewell
Clara Bargellini

Eli Bartra
Jean-Pierre Bastian
William H. Beezley
Thomas Benjamin
Frances F. Berdan
Suzanne Bilello
Viviane Brachet-Márquez
Stanley Brandes
Keith Brewster
John A. Britton
Jonathan C. Brown
Kathleen Bruhn
Samuel Brunk
Jürgen Buchenau

Jane Bussey
Melchor Campos García
Enrique Cárdenas
Barry Carr
Fernando Cervantes
John F. Chuchiak IV
Sarah L. Cline
George A. Collier
John F. Crossen
Margarita Vera Cuspinera
Sandra M. Cypess
Sophie de la Calle
Luz María de la Mora
Guillermo de la Peña
Jesús F. de la Teja
Blanca de Lizaur
Aurelio de los Reyes
Kelly Donahue-Wallace
Ingrid Elliott
Romana Falcón Vega
Seth Fein
María Fernández
Martin V. Fleming
José Z. García
Alejandra García Quintanilla
Paul Garner
Richard L. Garner
Luis Javier Garrido
James A. Garza
Marilyn Gates
Courtney Gilbert
Adolfo Gilly
Pilar Gonzalbo Aizpuru
Manuel González Oropeza
Virginia Guedea
Matthew C. Gutmann
Paul Lawrence Haber
Diana Hadley
Nora Hamilton
Brian R. Hamnett
John Mason Hart

Neil Harvey
Ross Hassig
Joy Elizabeth Hayes
J. León Helguera
Timothy J. Henderson
Raymond Hernández-Durán
Lawrence A. Herzog
Josiah McC. Heyman
Frances Karttunen
Benjamin Keen
Norma Klahn
Cecelia F. Klein
Alan Knight
John Koegel
Sandra Kuntz Ficker
Luis Fernando Lara
Thomas Legler
Laura A. Lewis
Stephen E. Lewis
Sonya Lipsett-Rivera
Bernardita Llanos
Soledad Loaeza
Cinna Lomnitz
David E. Lorey
Nora Lustig
Carlos Macías Richard
Rodolfo Mata
Álvaro Matute
Robert McCaa
Emily McClung de Tapia
John Holmes McDowell
Corynne McSherry
Donald McVicker
Mary Frech McVicker
Elinor G.K. Melville
Jean Meyer
Virginia E. Miller
Carl J. Mora
John Mraz
Harley D. Oberhelman
Monica I. Orozco

Rubén Osorio Zuñiga
Erika Pani
Helen Rand Parish
Max Parra
Michael D. Phillips
Charmaine Picard
Jeffrey M. Pilcher
Stafford Poole
Susie S. Porter
Cristina Puga
Jennie Purnell
Eloise Quiñones Keber
Karen Racine
Laura Randall
Kay A. Read
Douglas W. Richmond
Edward A. Riedinger
G. Micheal Riley
Ricardo Romo
Jorge Ruffinelli
Terry Rugeley
Craig H. Russell
Vania Salles
Ricardo J. Salvador
Pedro Santoni
Alex M. Saragoza
William Schell Jr.
Arthur Schmidt

Samuel Schmidt
Michael Schreffler
Susan Schroeder
Friedrich E. Schuler
John F. Schwaller
Ilán Semo
Mónica Serrano
John W. Sherman
Leslie Sklair
Lynn Stephen
Claire T. Stracke
J. Richard Stracke
Clara Elena Suárez Argüello
Paul Sullivan
Angela T. Thompson
Guy P.C. Thomson
María Celia Toro
Yolia Tortolero Cervantes
Rodolfo Tuirán
Esperanza Tuñón Pablos
John Tutino
Martín Valadez
Eric Van Young
Jesús Vargas Valdez
Stacie G. Widdifield
Elliott Young
Francisco Zapata

LIST OF ENTRIES

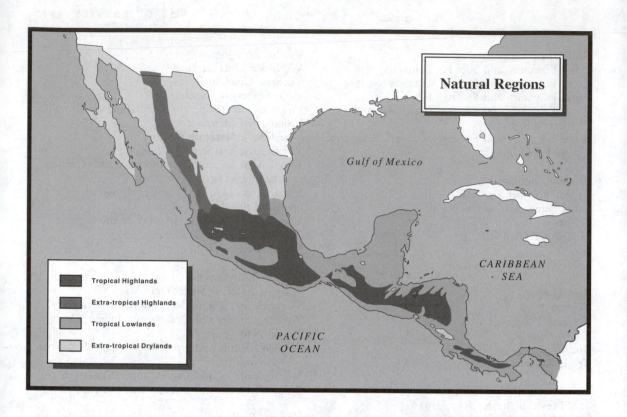

Natural Regions

Tropical Highlands

Extra-tropical Highlands

Tropical Lowlands

Extra-tropical Drylands

Gulf of Mexico

CARIBBEAN SEA

PACIFIC OCEAN

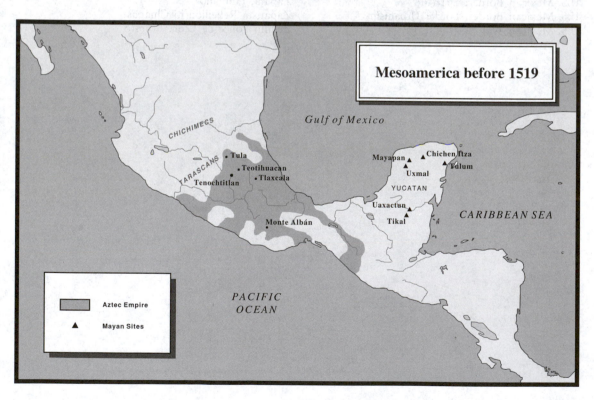

Mesoamerica before 1519

Gulf of Mexico

CHICHIMECS

TARASCANS

• Tula

• Teotihuacan

• Tenochtitlan

• Tlaxcala

• Monte Albán

Mayapan ▲ ▲ Chichen Itza

▲ Uxmal ▲ Tulum

YUCATAN

Uaxactun ▲

Tikal ▲

CARIBBEAN SEA

Aztec Empire

▲ Mayan Sites

PACIFIC OCEAN

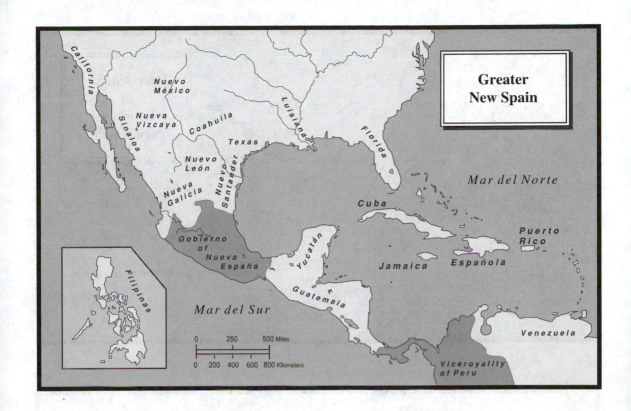

Greater New Spain

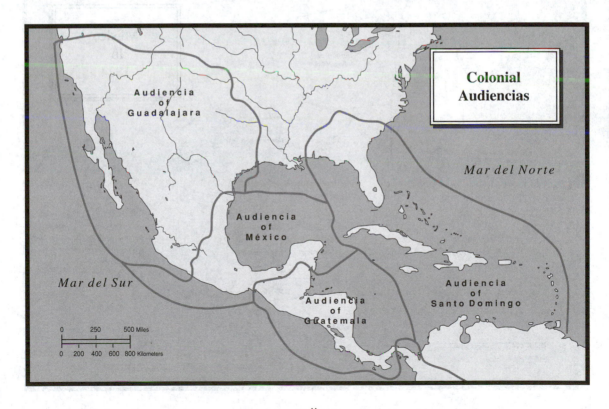

Colonial Audiencias

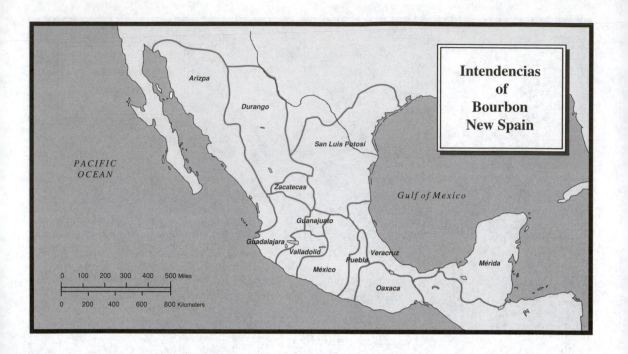

Intendencias of Bourbon New Spain

Arizpa

Durango

San Luis Potosí

PACIFIC OCEAN

Zacatecas

Gulf of Mexico

Guanajuato

Guadalajara

Valladolid

Puebla

Veracruz

Mérida

México

Oaxaca

0 100 200 300 400 500 Miles

0 200 400 600 800 Kilometers

Mexico in 1824

Territory of Alta California

Sonora and Sinaloa

Territory of Nuevo México

Coahuila and Texas

Chihuahua

Territory of Baja California

PACIFIC OCEAN

Gulf of Mexico

Durango

Nuevo León

Zacatecas

Tamaulipas

San Luis Potosí

Guanajuato

Querétaro

Jalisco

Yucatán

Tlaxcala

Michoacán

México

Veracruz

Territory of Colima

Puebla

Tabasco

Oaxaca

Chiapas

Soconusco

0 100 200 300 400 500 Miles

0 200 400 600 800 Kilometers

A

African Mexicans

Scholars generally agree that the first person of African descent to come to the Americas arrived with Columbus on his second voyage in 1493. He was free. Yet African slave labor, which already was established in a limited way in Spain, quickly spread to the Americas, where indigenous peoples, many also enslaved by Spanish colonists, were being decimated by the mistreatment and diseases brought by Spaniards. As these people were felled and the pressure for labor from settlers grew, so did the demand for enslaved Africans. Between 1501, when the Atlantic slave trade to the Americas began, and 1518, the year prior to Fernando (Hernán) Cortés's arrival off the coast of Veracruz, the Spanish Crown permitted Africans who had been "Hispanicized" in Spain to be brought as slaves to the first Spanish colonies. By 1518, however, pressure from the colonies had forced the Crown to begin permitting direct importations from Africa of enslaved Africans.

At least one free "black" (as they were known), a man named Juan Garrido, apparently accompanied the first conquistadors to Mexico, who also brought with them several slaves. Arriving in 1519 or 1520, Garrido might have taken part in the conquest of Tenochtitlan. He most definitely was involved in post-Conquest expeditions organized by Cortés to control outlying lands, and later became the first person to farm wheat in Mexico. As a free man, Garrido was the exception rather than the rule, however. Most blacks came to Mexico already enslaved. Between 1519 and 1580, the earliest period of the slave trade, about 36,500 such persons were brought to Mexico. Mortality rates were high on board slave ships and in the Americas. Moreover, since two-thirds of the slaves were men, many of whom were destined for hard physical labor, sex ratios generally were imbalanced. Therefore, the replenishment of the slave population depended more on the transatlantic trade than on domestic reproduction.

During most of the colonial period, the trade to the Spanish colonies was regulated by the Crown, which granted licenses to individual traders. These traders depended for supplies principally on the Portuguese, who controlled access to the African coast. Between 1580 and 1640, the heyday of the slave trade to Mexico and a period of union between the Spanish and Portuguese Crowns, Portugal dominated the trade. At various points during the late seventeenth and late eighteenth centuries Holland, France, and England also were involved in supplying slaves to the Spanish colonies, both legally and as contraband. Over the course of this later period, however, Mexico's slave importations slowed dramatically.

By the mid-to-late sixteenth century the enslavement of most indigenous peoples had been made illegal. Through the first decades of the seventeenth century, as Mexico's indigenous population followed that of the Caribbean to a precipitous decline and settlers' demands for imported labor accelerated, Mexico's African and African-descended population grew to be the largest in the Americas. In fact, until importations reached their peak in 1640, Mexico was receiving on average two-thirds of all Africans brought legally to Spanish America and many who were brought illegally. Estimates place the African-descended population of Mexico at about 140,000 in 1650, a figure that included men and women, free persons and slaves, African-born slaves known as *bozales* (a word that scholar Gonzalbo Aguirre Beltrán translates as "brutes" or "savages"), Hispanicized slaves known as *ladinos,* and the mulatto offspring of blacks and Spaniards or blacks and Indians (the latter sometimes called *zambos* or *zambaigos*). Since the status of children followed their mother, mulattoes with slave mothers were also subject to enslavement.

Although requests for enslaved blacks continued beyond the seventeenth century, the slave trade to Mexico steadily declined over the rest of the colonial period as the indigenous population recovered and the "mixed" population of mestizos and mulattoes grew. By the end of the eighteenth century slave importations were occurring mostly in sparsely inhabited districts of the Yucatán, and the Mexican population included only about 9,000 enslaved blacks and mulattoes. In 1817 the slave trade was halted, and in 1821 fewer than 3,000 people were still enslaved in Mexico. When slavery was legally abolished with Independence, it had all but ended. Nevertheless, over the 300-year course of the colonial period, approximately 200,000 slaves had been brought to Mexico.

African slaves first came principally from West Africa, specifically from Guinea-Bissau, Senegal, Gambia, and the coast of Sierra Leone. Later the source shifted to Angola and to the Congo in Central Africa. An internal domestic trade flourished alongside the international trade. With the exception of the northern zones (where Chichimec Indians still were sometimes enslaved), black slaves were concentrated in areas of Spanish settlement. Most were in Mexico City and the surrounding Valley of Mexico. But large slave populations also could be found in the eastern Veracruz-Pánuco coastal region, the Bajío silver mining regions and ranches to the north and west of Mexico City, and the sugar plantations, ranches, and mines that followed the southwestern belt running from the city of Puebla to the Pacific.

The decline in the indigenous population, legislation that protected indigenous peoples from certain arduous occupations, and the widespread Spanish belief that Africans were superior workers were all factors leading to the intensive use of enslaved Africans in New Spain's sugar industry, textile workshops, silver mines, and pearl fisheries. In many situations, however, Indians remained the dominant labor force despite laws of protection, and black slaves filled positions as specialized workers. Household slaves also were quite common; slaveholders often hired slaves out for a daily wage (jornal), most of which was to be paid to the slaveholder. Slave ownership extended to a few Indians of high rank and to some aspiring free blacks.

As property, slaves had few rights. They were bought and sold with other property and given names that marked them as their masters' possessions or by their place of origin. Branding was used at ports of entry to identify slaves. It also could be employed as a form of punishment along with other physical tortures, such as the amputation of arms, hands, or ears; the use of leg irons; and a practice known as *pringar*, which consisted of hot pork fat, candle wax, or pitch dripped onto the skin.

Slaves were routinely, if nominally, converted to Christianity through baptism and indoctrination upon capture or during their passage to the Americas. Religious education for both African-born and American-born slaves was expected to continue throughout their lives. Yet religious freedoms granted to blacks, such as the right to form mutual aid societies (cofradías), were sometimes curtailed as fear of organized rebellion grew. In addition, the clergy focused most of its efforts on indigenous peoples. Ultimately, while the Catholic Church played a prominent role in protecting Indians and challenging Spaniards' rights to enslave them, debates over the fate of blacks were few and far between.

Nevertheless, to a certain extent both church and state protected slaves. Laws guaranteed them the right to marry and freedom from excessive punishment. The medieval Spanish legal code, the Siete Partidas, also provided several routes to manumission (freedom). Slaveholders could free their slaves, slaves could purchase themselves for an agreed upon price (which they sometimes paid in installments), and third parties could purchase slaves and free them. Slaveholders could not be forced to give up slaves against their will, however. In addition, even legal statutes meant to give slaves certain rights did not necessarily translate into social practice, since the slaveholders' interests usually came first. Some provisions of the Siete Partidas also were changed to fit conditions in the Americas. For instance, since sexual imbalances in the black and Spanish populations made marriages between black men and Indian women common, and those between black women and Spanish men a possibility, as early as the 1520s Crown and local officials disallowed legislation permitting slaves who married free persons to be freed. Status continued to follow the mother, however, so children born of free women were also free.

Slaves had some access to the courts, where their limited rights to decent care, to a family and, under certain circumstances, to freedom, were recognized and sometimes even enforced. The Inquisition, in particular, oversaw slaveholders' obligations to see to the "Christian" treatment of their charges. But it also persecuted free and enslaved blacks for blasphemy, witchcraft, and other anti-Catholic acts. Other courts oversaw their punishment for secular crimes.

Although slave revolts never produced a substantial change in slave conditions or in the fact of slavery itself, they occurred with frequency throughout the colonial period and were brutally put down. Runaway slaves (cimarrones) also were punished severely when caught, often with mutilation and even, occasionally in the case of male slaves, with castration. Fugitive slaves who were not caught often banded together and sometimes established independent communities. Most of these were overrun quickly by colonists, but several groups of *cimarrones* won the legal right to autonomy during the seventeenth and eighteenth centuries. The most famous and successful of these groups was centered in the Orizaba region of Veracruz and led by an African named Yanga. After years of conflicts with settlers and officials, it was granted a charter as a free settlement in 1612. Over a century later in the same general vicinity slave uprisings in sugar mills produced new *cimarrón* activity. Through negotiations with colonial authorities these *cimarrones* came to aid Spaniards in their mid-eighteenth-century war against Great Britain, and were granted autonomy at the war's conclusion. On the Pacific coast during the same period slaves escaped the ports of Acapulco and Huatulco, setting up their own communities in Guerrero and Oaxaca. While in general blacks' freedom was restricted by legislation that persecuted any hint of independence, it is possible that in the relatively autonomous *cimarrón* communities aspects of ancestral cultures could be maintained successfully.

Mexico's free African-descended population grew substantially as the colonial period progressed. Much of that population consisted of women and children, which probably reflected Spanish slaveholders' favorable treatment of their slave mistresses and mulatto offspring. Freed slaves often were no better off than slaves themselves, since discriminatory laws worked to keep them from improving their social and economic status. For instance, all blacks and mulattoes were forbidden from dressing like Spaniards or Indians, unless they were married to them, from bearing arms, gathering in groups, joining certain craft guilds, and even from living without Spanish supervision. Most blacks and mulattoes remained in the lower echelons of the socioeconomic scale, where they toiled as domestic workers, laborers, shoemakers, itinerant traders, and ranch hands. Some, however, held positions as skilled workers (as did many slaves), and despite restrictions on guild membership, guilds became one of the principal ways in which black men advanced as labor shortages eventually forced their integration. Other blacks, such as a woman named Adriana de Cabrera, who was a native and resident of Veracruz in the middle of the seventeenth century, owned their own businesses (in this case, a boarding house) as well as their own slaves.

As populations intermixed over the course of the colonial period, "caste" boundaries became increasingly obscured. By the late eighteenth century an elaborate caste nomenclature had expanded to include dozens of categories of persons classified by fine "racial" distinctions. At the same time, the Crown attempted to forestall "unequal" marriages through the Pragmatic Sanction, which stipulated parental control over marriage partners. In Mexico the determination of marriages as socially unequal rested on genealogy, with black ancestry the principal determinant of low status.

The abolition of slavery was part of the Independence movement of the early nineteenth century. Leaders such as Miguel Hidalgo and José María Morelos, both insurgent priests, challenged the elite by calling for slave emancipation and the dismantling of the caste system as it was written into law. Nonwhites were drawn to the insurgent movement led by these two men, and later by Vicente Guerrero, one of the new nation's first presidents. Guerrero, who was apparently of partial African ancestry, was frequently indicted by the elite during his political ascent for goading nonwhites to insurgence.

Independence brought significant changes at the level of national and local politics as slavery and the caste system were legally abolished and all but Spaniards were permitted to vote and hold public office. Yet whites gained control of the Independence movement and continued to monopolize economic and political power. Nonwhites, therefore, still possessed a lower social status as whites "held the color line" and in many ways even modeled the new government on the colonial one.

Caste classifications were no longer a standard part of Mexican census data following Independence. As the legal and administrative codes based on caste ceased identifying people by ancestry, blacks disappeared from the official record. Between the late colonial period and the post-Revolutionary period in the twentieth century, the mestizo—the biological and cultural product of Spaniard and Indian—became the Mexican national emblem. Although blacks were a substantial presence during the colonial period and beyond, they were excluded consciously from mestizo ideology by nationalist thinkers. For example, the exiled late colonial Jesuit Francisco Javier Clavigero carefully established the place of the ancient Mexicans, ancestors of the exalted mestizo, in Mexican national ideology, but eliminated black slaves and their descendants from his idea of the Mexican nation, declaring that blacks had "damaged blood and a disorderly physical constitution." "What could be more contrary to the idea we have of beauty and human bodily perfection," he asked, "than a pestilent man, whose skin is dark like ink, head and face covered with black wool in place of hair, eyes yellow or the color of blood, thick, blackish lips and flattened nose?"

Such commentaries speak to eighteenth- and nineteenth-century racism, which was crystallizing around the alleged cultural, biological, and even aesthetic inferiority of blacks. Throughout the late nineteenth and early twentieth centuries African-descended immigrants were discouraged from settling in Mexico, as well as in other parts of Latin America, while European immigrants were courted. During this period veneration of the Mexican mestizo culminated in the Revolutionary-era writings of José Vasconcelos, who explicated the "constructive miscegenation" of *mestizaje* based on a "spiritual eugenics," while promoting the idea that the "Negro race" would vanish on its own as "beautiful and healthy" specimens of the Indian and white "races" spawned the new mestizo. "The inferior types of the species," wrote Vasconcelos, "will be absorbed by the superior type," and blacks soon would become "extinct" as the "ugliest races" made way for the "most beautiful."

The intentional exclusion of blacks from Mexican national ideology during this period perhaps prompted their wider exclusion from the historical and anthropological scholarship on Mexico, as well as from the national consciousness. With few exceptions, little research on Mexico's African-descended population was done until the 1940s and 1950s, when Gonzalo Aguirre Beltrán, the foremost scholar of Mexico's African-descended population, produced two full-length historical and ethnographic works. More recently, several major historical studies have focused on Mexican blacks, for example the works of Colin Palmer and Patrick Carroll.

But in general, blacks have been neglected in Mexican studies. This neglect cannot be attributed to their small numbers. Although those numbers never reached the levels of later Spanish and Anglo-American colonies, and estimates placed Mexico's African-descended population in the latter half of the twentieth century at less than 1 percent, there were even fewer Spaniards than blacks in colonial society. Nevertheless, many works of scholarship focus on Spaniards, as well as on the indigenous majority.

Aguirre Beltrán offers a partial explanation for the disappearance of blacks from national and scholarly discourse. He suggests that they were "integrated" into the wider society through processes of biological and cultural "mixing" dating from the colonial period and continuing through the present. In his estimation, the exceptions to this assimilating process were blacks from the Pacific Coast region known as the Costa Chica. Indeed, while there are self-identified "blacks" in other parts of Mexico, principally in the gulf coast state of Veracruz, the Costa Chica today is widely considered to be the "blackest" part of the country. Costa Chican *negros* or *morenos,* as they are identified by their mestizo and indigenous neighbors, are probably descendants of slaves brought to the coast to work on sugar plantations as well as of runaway slaves from the shipping ports of Acapulco and Huatulco. Mostly peasant cultivators, they tend to occupy a socioeconomic niche between those locally identified as "white" or "Indian." Today, scholars are coming to understand the complex cultural, socioeconomic, and historical ties between these three groups.

Recently the Mexican government also has expressed a new interest in Mexico's African-descended population through support of the project known as Nuestra Tercera Raíz (Our Third Root), which was inaugurated in 1991 to uncover and disseminate knowledge about the African presence in Mexico. In the 1980s and 1990s, research by Mexican, U.S., and European scholars, in conjunction with and independently of this project, has resulted in historical and anthropological studies focused on the presence of African and African-descended peoples on the Mexican landscape. Currently, anthropologists, historians, linguists, ethnomusicologists, and others continue to explore African Mexican culture and history, and knowledge about African-descended peoples in Mexico is therefore increasing.

Select Bibliography

Aguirre Beltrán, Gonzalo, "The Integration of the Negro into the National Society of Mexico." In *Race and Class in Latin America,* edited by Magnus Mörner. New York: Columbia University Press, 1970.

Bowser, Frederick, "Colonial Spanish America." In *Neither Slave nor Free: The Freedmen of African Descent in the Slave Societies of the New World,* edited by David Cohen and Jack P. Greene. Baltimore: Johns Hopkins University Press, 1972.

Carroll, Patrick, "Mandinga: The Evolution of a Mexican Runaway Slave Community, 1735–1827." *Comparative Studies in Society and History* 19:4 (1977).

——, *Blacks in Colonial Veracruz: Race, Ethnicity and Regional Development.* Austin: University of Texas Press, 1991.

Davidson, David, "Negro Slave Control and Resistance in Colonial Mexico, 1519–1650." In *Maroon Societies,* edited by Richard Price. Baltimore: Johns Hopkins University Press, 1979.

Gerhard, Peter, "A Black Conquistador in Mexico," *Hispanic American Historical Review* 58:3 (August 1978).

Graham, Richard, editor, *The Idea of Race in Latin America: 1870–1940.* Austin: University of Texas Press, 1990.

Lewis, Laura, "Blackness, Femaleness and Self-Representation: Constructing Persons in a Colonial Mexican Court." *PoLAR: Political and Legal Anthropology Review* 18:2 (November 1995).

Palmer, Colin, *Slaves of the White God: Blacks in Mexico, 1519–1650*. Cambridge, Massachusetts: Harvard University Press, 1976.

Rout, Leslie B., Jr., *The African Experience in Spanish America*. Cambridge: Cambridge University Press, 1977.

Seed, Patricia, *To Love, Honor and Obey in Colonial Mexico*. Stanford, California: Stanford University Press, 1988.

—LAURA A. LEWIS

Agustín I (Emperor of Mexico)

See Iturbide, Agustín de

Alamán, Lucas 1792–1853

Politician and Historian

Lucas Alamán was born on October 18, 1792, in the province of Guanajuato. While growing up Alamán became a close friend of the mayor of the city of Guanajuato, Juan Antonio de Riaño. A broad circle of physicists, mathematicians, architects, and humanists would gather in Riaño's house. Alamán took classes in French with Riaño's wife, and through Riaño he also made the acquaintance of the priest Antonio Lavarrete, who put his library at his disposal. In Lavarrete's library Alamán was able to read books in English on world history. In the house of his cousins Septien he met two of the most important leaders of the Mexican Independence movement, Miguel Hidalgo y Costilla and the bishop Manuel Abad y Queipo. Alamán later witnessed the sack of Guanajuato by insurgent forces, which would have a lasting impact on him. As the Wars of Independence wracked Guanajuato, Alamán moved to Mexico City, and in 1812 he entered the Royal Seminary of Mining, where he studied mining and chemistry. In the same year his house was raided by the Holy Inquisition, which confiscated several of his books.

Shortly after the restoration of Fernando VII, who had been deposed by the Napoléon, Alamán left for Spain, later traveling to several other countries in Europe. While in Europe Alamán made the acquaintance of such luminaries as Servando Teresa de Mier, José María White, Benjamin Constant, Fouché, Chateaubriand, and Madame Stäel. In February 1820 Alamán returned New Spain—and to his study of classical authors such as Homer and Euripides; Spanish American authors such as Bartolomé de Las Casas, Solis, Francisco Javier Clavigero, Lorenzo Zavala, and Carlos María Bustamante; and European authors such as Shakespeare, Bossuet, Pascal, Voltaire, Montesquieu, and Rousseau.

Alamán entered public life shortly following the restoration of the liberal Spanish Constitution of Cádiz in 1820. In August the viceroy Juan Ruiz de Apodaca appointed him secretary of the Superior Health Council, although he did not have the opportunity to accomplish much in this post. Between October 1820 and February 1821 Alamán served as the representative for the province of Guanajuato in the Cortes of Cádiz, the parliamentary council of Spain and its overseas possessions mandated by the new constitution. Alamán was part of the American faction in Cádiz, which believed that the relationship between Spain and its American possessions should be one of *asociación política*—that is, Spain's overseas possessions and the various regions of Spain should have equal representation in the Cortes, and Spanish Americans should be recognized as full citizens of the Spanish Empire. Although Alamán had important disagreements with much of the American faction, he participated in the final drafting of the American position and was later nominated to be secretary of the Cortes.

The promulgation of General Agustín Iturbide's Plan of Iguala, which called for an independent Mexican empire ruled by a European monarch, and the subsequent capitulation of the Spanish viceroy Juan O'Donojú in the Treaties of Córdoba divided New Spain's representatives at the Cortes. Alamán returned to Mexico just as Iturbide entered Mexico City and proclaimed the independence of Mexico. In April 1822 Alamán was named secretary of state, although he was able to remain in the post for only two years. Nonetheless, he was named secretary of state once again in May 1824 and continued to serve intermittently until 1831. The instability of Mexican government in the first decades following Independence prevented Alamán from ever serving as secretary of state for more than a few months at a time. Nonetheless, his ideas regarding Mexican foreign policy (at least until Mexico's humiliating defeat by the United States in 1847) were marked by a certain political idealism. Between May and July 1823 he gave instructions to Guadalupe Victoria to negotiate an end to military hostilities with Spanish authorities but never to cede on the question of Independence.

During the secession crisis in Texas in August 1823 his instructions were similar, as he hoped to return to the treaty signed between the United States and New Spain in 1819. The capstone of his first term as secretary of state was the signing of a treaty between Mexico and Colombia establishing a confederation between the two countries; Mexico also sought similar ties with other Spanish American countries, hoping that this new confederation, like the confederation of American states formed by England's former colonies in North America, would make each country more secure against foreign invasion. In March 1825 Alamán was able to obtain recognition from England, and in 1829–30 he traveled to Europe for a series of extremely delicate negotiations with Spain. Alamán was able to open Mexican territory to Spanish citizens in 1830 and also attempted to reestablish trade with Spain.

Despite his political idealism, Alamán is remembered most for his role in the foundation of the Conservative Party following Mexico's loss of half its national territory to the United States in 1847. The Conservative Party sought to transform Mexico into a constitutional monarchy with a European prince. Nonetheless, Alamán's monarchism was more an attempt to achieve some degree of equilibrium between Mexico and the United States than a negation of the Mexican political system. Moreover, Alamán's conservatism needs to be taken in historical perspective. Alamán participated in the federalist liberal governments of Guadalupe Victoria and Anastasio Bustamante as well as the centralist governments. His role in the drafting of the centralist Constitution of 1835–36 is quite relevant in this regard. On the one hand, Alamán played a key role in the drafting of the constitution as a member of the Conservative Council; on the other, Alamán continued to draft legislation protecting civil rights in the liberal sense of the term.

Although there were clear conservative tendencies in Alamán's thought in the 1820s and 1830s, they did not crystallize until the 1840s with the foundation of the conservative newspaper *El Tiempo* and his completion of the magisterial *Historia de México*. In the *Historia de México* Alamán combined his long-standing advocacy of centralism with a more radical conservatism. Calling for a sort of "historical constitutionalism," Alamán argued that the foundations of the Mexican nation could be found in the institutions of New Spain. He also called for a Mexican monarchy ruled by a European prince to unify Mexico against further U.S. expansionism.

Like many liberals of his time, Alamán never wanted to be a democrat. His preference for corporate political organizations and the preservation of corporate privileges were a centerpiece of his political thought. Nonetheless, his pragmatism would never allow him completely to reject representative democracy. As a young man Alamán was an enthusiastic supporter of the Constitution of Cádiz. In the 1830s Alamán rejected his earlier liberalism and advocated a more restricted franchise based on property and merit. Even in the 1850s Alamán did not reject representative government but only sought to impose further restrictions—a constitutional monarchy with a unicameral legislature with one representative per state.

As an economic theorist, the creator of economic institutions, and businessman Alamán also played a key role in the economic life of Mexico. Alamán's economic ideas tended to parallel his economic thought. He believed that the creation of a strong nation-state rested on an effective national treasury and the development of the country's national wealth. In his brief participation in the government of Guadalupe Victoria in 1823, Alamán was able to obtain a loan from the Casa Staples to alleviate the government's financial difficulties; he also unsuccessfully sought a loan from English banking houses. He also sought to separate the mining industry from the state (the mining industry had been subject to tight state control as a corporate body), but this initiative was rejected by congress. In January 1824 Alamán was named the delegate for the mining industry of Guanajuato before the Tribunal General del Cuerpo de Minería (General Tribunal of the Corporation of Mining). Later that year he organized a mining company with Mexican and English investment.

The 1830s marked an important rupture in Alamán's economic thought, as his mercantilist vision of the Mexican economy based largely on mining changed to an industrialist vision based largely on manufacturing. This new vision would continue until Alamán's death. Between August and October of 1830 Alamán dedicated himself to the creation of the Banco de Avío (Loan Bank) to promote manufacturing and agricultural production. Funds came from the government (as direct loans) and from taxes on imported cotton cloth. The bank was managed by a committee named by the government and chaired by the secretary of foreign relations—at that moment in the hands of Alamán. Alamán organized the Compañía Industrial de Celaya (Industrial Company of Celaya) to promote the cotton textile industry. When the Banco de Avío shut its doors in 1840 Alamán helped organize the Junta de Fomento Industrial (Industrial Promotion Committee) to group together Mexican entrepreneurs independently from government authorities. Within a short period of time approximately 56 committee were formed in the interior of Mexico and a Seminario de la Industria Nacional (Seminar of National Industry) to promote a "modern" vision of Mexican business and publicize the latest advances of Mexican industrialists. Alamán also unsuccessfully sought to establish vocational schools for workers and promoted trade and tariff policy that would protect vulnerable industries while lowering trade barriers for areas that needed imported machinery and raw materials.

Between November and December of 1842 Alamán drafted a law at the behest of President Nicolás Bravo regulating the Dirección General de la Industria Nacional (General Office of National Industry). Alamán based the law on the old colonial mining ordinances, although he did mandate the independence of the mining industry from the state. In the same year Alamán also was named director of the administrative committee of the department of the Federal District. President Mariano Paredes y Arriallga later asked him to create the superior council of the treasury, which would organize and safeguard state income. Nonetheless, he soon resigned that post to take up other responsibilities—congressional representative for the state of Guanajuato, director of industry for the Federal District, and director of the treasury commission. Alamán later returned to his hacienda to begin work on the *Historia de México*. He would not occupy another economic post until 1853, when he founded the ministry of public works, colonization, industry, and commerce.

Alamán also distinguished himself as a historian, and his journalistic writings in *El Universal* and *El Tiempo*, the three volumes of his *Disertaciones sobre la historia mejicana* ("Dissertations on Mexican History"; 1844–46), and the five volumes of his *Historia de México* (1846–52) are considered key in the development of Mexican historiography. The eight volumes of the *Disertaciones* and the *Historia de México* are the work of a consciousness shattered by the bloody Wars of Independence and later by the loss of half of Mexico's national territory in 1847. However, they also are a sort of epic screenplay on "the conservation and continuity of the Nation." The *Disertaciones* and *Historia de México* include Alamán's reflections on politics, social mores, forms of government, and the institutions of New Spain. However, they also are works of narrative history, including descriptions of landscapes and heroic figures in Mexican history.

In the *Disertaciones* and *Historia de México* the politician and historian are fused. For Alamán history was a way to provide an ideological foundation for the Conservative Party and formulate his political project of nation-building. Indeed, the *Historia de México* was written as a counterpoint to the *Cuadro Histórico* of Carlos María de Bustamante. If Bustamante founded his vision of Mexico in pre-Hispanic myth and the insurgent Independence movement, Alamán saw the Mexican nation as emerging from its Hispanic heritage and the harsh realities following 1847. Lucas Alamán died in Mexico City on June 2, 1853.

—Israel Arroyo García

Architecture

This entry contains three articles that discuss the development of Mexican architecure from the colonial era through the twentieth century:

Architecture: Colonial
Architecture: Nineteenth Century
Architecture: Twentieth Century

For a discussion of pre-Conquest architecture in Mesoamerica, see Mesoamerica; Visual Arts: Mesoamerica. *See also* Urbanism and Urbanization

Architecture: Colonial

Monumental architecture is an art that develops out of and around institutions. In New Spain the two fundamental institutions capable of commissioning substantial building projects were the monarchy and the Catholic Church. The Spanish monarchy was present through its viceroy and the various instances of secular government. The church went further still in dominating life in New Spain. The mendicant friars were fundamental for the evangelization efforts of the sixteenth century, as well as later in frontier areas. They also established themselves in the colonial cities. Other religious orders were equally active in New Spain, while the bishops and secular clergy (those who did not belong to a regular order such as the Franciscans), working out of cathedrals and parish churches, ministered throughout the viceroyalty and prevailed over the regular orders in the seventeenth and eighteenth centuries. Although private patrons built large residences throughout the viceregal period, it was only in the eighteenth century that they commissioned palaces on a truly grand scale.

The religious institutions active in New Spain built a complex web of institutions—and their buildings—

that covered all of what is today modern Mexico, as well as the other territories that were then governed from Mexico City and now extend into the United States and Central America. The variety and wealth of religious architecture largely is the result of the fact that, unlike the government institutions whose buildings were erected out of bureaucratic or utilitarian needs, the church was involved in many different areas of social culture and action and enjoyed the support not only of the Spanish Crown, but also of countless individuals and groups for whom religious projects represented solace and pride in this world and guaranteed salvation in the next.

Of course, this process must be seen within its spatial and chronological dimensions to be better understood. Not all the institutions arrived or established themselves at the same time, nor developed at the same rhythm or in the same place. They often competed, sometimes cooperated, and always had to accommodate to one another as the Spanish and Indian societies that initially made up New Spain evolved and developed ways of mixing and coexisting with each other and with other groups, notably black slaves from Africa.

In architectural terms, it can be said that the Spanish monarchy, in the sixteenth century, established the conditions for all the building, both secular and religious, that was to come thereafter. The coasts and frontiers were fortified and schemes were developed for the layout of new settlements of various types. In other words, there was a program to keep out invaders and control rebellions on the margins, while at the same time, within the viceroyalty, new building was regulated with a view to permanent and continued successful settlement.

As far as fortifications were concerned, the ports of New Spain, like others from Florida to Argentina, were protected by bastioned walls against external invaders, generally in the guise of pirates who could also be agents of foreign powers. Italian military engineering tradition was behind such coastal projects as the fortresses of San Juan de Ullúa in Veracruz, of San Diego in Acapulco, and the walls of Campeche, as well as many others throughout Spanish America. These fortifications, fully established by the early seventeenth century, were constantly renovated and amplified. In the eighteenth century, when New Spain underwent a process of militarization, partly in response to the threat of English naval power, they were complemented by fortifications in the interior, such as the fort at Perote, inland from Veracruz.

Defense at the inland limits of New Spain, the northern frontier, was a more flexible and less monumental affair. Boundaries moved and changed as Indian groups rebelled and were repressed. The "presidios" of the north could be wooden palisades, as we know from written and visual documents, or they could be more permanent structures. Little survives of this architecture, and what does has been rebuilt or integrated into later buildings and is thus difficult to assess without archaeological work. Also, the word "presidio" indicates as much a function as a particular building type, a function that could be fulfilled by almost any kind of enclosure.

Another area of architectural activity for which directives emanated from Spain for all of its dominions was that of town planning. The orthogonal grid plan, of ancient and Renaissance traditions, was applied to all new settlements throughout Spanish America. Although formal ordinances were not promulgated until the reign of Felipe II, in 1573, the practices it codified were in use from the earliest period of the Conquest. In New Spain, orthogonal town planning found a parallel native tradition that had associations with time and ritual cycles. In Mexico City-Tenochtitlan itself, the European scheme was superimposed on the previously existing Indian city. The central square or *plaza mayor*, surrounded by the cathedral and the houses of the principal Spaniards, replaced the ceremonial and government center of the former Indian city. The Indians were relegated to barrios at the margins.

Of course, the European grid scheme was followed most closely in Spanish towns, such as Puebla, founded in 1531, which were not superimposed on pre-Columbian urban sites. The grid plan continued to be the founding scheme into the eighteenth century, as new settlements were established in outlying areas. Only in the case of mining towns, which typically grew quickly and without initial planning, was the orthogonal scheme weakened, generally in favor of development along a river or stream, since water was necessary for the processing of mineral ores. However, even there the heart of the grid pattern eventually would come to dominate the whole, when the mines were rich enough to warrant permanent residence; that is, the central square, bounded by a parish church and the houses of government *(casas reales)* and of the principal citizens, almost invariably constituted the easily identifiable core of any town in the viceroyalty.

Smaller towns at previously established Indian sites in central New Spain also were superimposed on existing settlements in the sixteenth century, with the church and monastery of the mendicant friars taking the dominant place on the central square and the Indian inhabitants distributed in barrios within the orthogonal overall plan. More research

Franciscan Convent, Huejotzingo, Puebla
Photo courtesy of Archivo Fotográfico, Instituto de Investigaciones Estéticas de la UNAM

needs to be done to understand these Christian Indian towns and their relationships to spatial and social organizations of the period immediately preceding the Spanish Conquest as well as their development during the first decades of Spanish rule. The historiography has tended to telescope all of sixteenth-century monastery architecture and treat it as a single post-Conquest phenomenon. The situation was much more complex, and important changes must have taken place between the initial monastic establishments of the 1520s and 1530s and the buildings we see today that date from the middle to the late century. This has recently been proven to be the case at Huejotzingo, one of the first Franciscan establishments, where archaeology has uncovered the buildings that preceded the surviving structures.

Issues of siting and basic distribution seem to follow certain general principles in the great sixteenth-century monastic complexes that rightly have been considered one of the major architectural achievements of Spanish rule in New Spain. Again, it was the Crown that established the conditions that made the monasteries possible by giving first the Franciscans, and then the Dominicans and Augustinians, authority in matters of evangelization and the settlements of newly converted Indians. The friars often chose to replace the ceremonial sites of the pre-Columbian religions with their churches and monasteries, thus making an absolutely clear statement about the substitution of the new religion for the old cults. This is easily seen at the Franciscan complex of Izamal, Yucatán, just to cite one obvious example.

A monastery complex in a Christian Indian sixteenth-century town almost invariably included an ample, four-sided, walled open space, called an atrium ("patio" in the sixteenth century), with a large cross at the center and small *posa* chapels at the corners, where processions around the atrium might make pauses. The atrium generally had a main entrance and at least one side entrance. Opposite the main entrance rose the principal buildings of the complex: the open chapel, the church, and the monastery. The element that has attracted the most attention is the open chapel or the *capilla de indios*. This is a covered space, open toward the atrium, which fundamentally served the function of an apse where mass could be said before enormous congregations of Indians who occupied the chapel itself and the open space before it. The fact that there are so many variations for this part of the monastic complexes is proof that, despite possible European precedents, the open chapel was an American invention, built to fulfill a particular need unique to the New World situation. The situation was that of huge Christian congregations who themselves or whose pre-Hispanic parents and grandparents had been accustomed to worshipping in the open in a benign climate. At the beginning, open chapels were simple grass- or branch-covered spaces *(enramadas)*, but the ones which survive took many forms. There are basilica (Cuilapan, Oaxaca) and many aisled plans (Cholula, Puebla), as well as numerous variations on rectangular and polygonal schemes. They could be barrel vaulted (Actopan, Hidalgo) or covered with complex Gothic vaulting (Teposcolula, Oaxaca). They were usually at ground level, but examples of chapels open to the atrium from the upper story of the monastery also exist (Huaquechula, Puebla).

The church buildings were either basilical or, more frequently, rectangular in plan with wooden or vaulted roofs. In the latter case, the vault of the bay in front of the apse was generally somewhat raised and more richly decorated. It is interesting that the earliest church at Huejotzingo was basilical in plan, suggesting the possibility of references to early Christian architecture, since the friars were explicitly conscious of their role as new apostles in a pagan world. However, most surviving buildings are massive rectangular structures with decorated portals and details, such as merlons, that remind one of fortress construction. Indeed, much of the historiography refers to these buildings as "fortress churches". However, recent scholarship tends to

Catedral de México y Sagrario, Mexico City, by Cristóbal de Medina Vargas, c.1680
Photo courtesy of Archivo Fotográfico, Instituto de Investigaciones Estéticas de la UNAM

consider the defensive elements as symbolic of the heavenly Jerusalem and as allusive to the utopian and apocalyptic ideas of the friars. Interior decoration consisted of sculpted architectural details, wall paintings, and in important churches, at least one monumental gilded altarpiece or retablo, with paintings and sculptures. Exterior decoration was sculptural, particularly around the main entrance portal.

The monasteries themselves, where the friars lived, were generally of two stories around a cloister. In the lower story were spaces for communal life (refectory, chapter hall), as well as a monumental entryway *(portería)* from the atrium, since public access to the lower cloister, though regulated, was permitted. The upper level was restricted to the friars. On comparing these cloisters to those of European monasteries, their reduced size becomes obvious; there were rarely more than four to six friars at any one monastery in New Spain, and they spent much of their time traveling to nearby towns to attend to congregations at smaller churches *(visitas)*. Accessory buildings associated with agricultural work, animals, and storage completed the monasteries.

The vocabulary of the decoration of churches and other buildings might be Gothic (Yecapixtla, Morelos), classicizing—that is, in a Renaissance mode, be it Plateresque (Acolman, State of Mexico) or Mannerist (Tecali, Puebla)—and include Mudejar elements (Tlaxcala, Tlaxcala). Another term, *tequitqui*, defines sculpture executed in a style that recalls the planarity of pre-Columbian treatment of stone (the *posa* chapels of Huejotzingo and Calpan, and the portal at Tepoztlán). Most of this work, the construction as well as the decoration, painting as well as sculpture, was done by the Indians, who quickly became adept at European techniques, under the supervision of the friars and some European masters. European architectural treatises, particularly *Tutte l'opere d'architettura* (1537–75) by the Italian Sebastiano Serlio, and prints often served as models, especially for ornamental elements.

Basilica of Guadalupe, Mexico City, by Pedro de Arrieta, 1695–1709
Photo courtesy of Archivo Fotográfico, Instituto de Investigaciones Estéticas de la UNAM

The initial evangelization process, whose ultimate outcome in architecture were the Christian Indian towns with their great monastery complexes, was over before the end of the sixteenth century. As disease decimated the Indian population and the utopian spirit gave way to the moralizing concerns that emanated from the Council of Trent, and the friars lost their ecclesiastical primacy to the bishops and secular clergy.

The architectural accomplishments of the secular clergy and their congregations can first be seen in the cathedrals built in the principal cities of the viceroyalty beginning in the sixteenth century. As seats of bishops who had extensive territories under their jurisdiction, the cathedrals were the most important buildings of their cities. No other single architectural project attracted the same quality and scale of attention. It helps to understand the colonial cathedrals of New Spain, as well as of the rest of Spanish America, to realize that they were begun a short time after the Reconquest of Spain itself. This makes them almost contemporary to the cathedrals of Andalusía and explains their formal characteristics. As one would expect in the late sixteenth century, the projects are Renaissance in character with strong Gothic reminiscences. All of these Spanish cathedrals are rectangular in plan with an inscribed cross, evident in the nave and transept elevations. Side aisles and side chapels accompany the central nave. Usually there are three portals on the facade and a portal on each side of the building. Two towers generally frame the facade.

The central role of cathedrals made these buildings paradigms of monumental church architecture and the sites of innovations in both structure and ornament, which then passed on to parish and other churches. Furthermore, cathedral projects enjoyed direct financial support from the Spanish Crown and had an architect, known as the *maestro mayor,* assigned to them. Although this post has been studied in depth only for Mexico City (by Martha Fernández), it is clear that these individuals were generally the most renowned architects of their time and were responsible for other projects as well. One of the most important structural innovations established at a cathedral was the dome on a drum at the crossing. The model, set at the cathedral of Puebla, which was dedicated in 1649, was repeated in many variations in countless churches throughout the viceroyalty in the seventeenth and in the eighteenth centuries. Because of the strong accent of light that the dome provided in the interior, it became a basic component of Mexican Baroque architecture.

In portal design, also, cathedral architects played an important role. At the cathedral of Mexico City the twisted "Solomonic" column was used by Cristóbal de Medina Vargas in permanent stone on the lateral portals around 1680. It quickly became an almost universal feature in the Baroque architectural ornament of the entire viceroyalty. Another element of the vocabulary of Mexican Baroque architecture also began at the cathedral of Mexico City: the *estípite* column. This support, in the shape of an inverted obelisk, narrower at the base than at the top, and crowned by a cube and a series of capitals, was first seen in monumental form in Jerónimo de Balbás's *Retablo of the Kings* in the apse of the cathedral, begun in 1718. In the 1740s it was used by the architect Lorenzo Rodríguez on the facade of the Sagrario (the church adjacent to the cathedral where parish functions are carried out) and became an identifying element of Mexican Estípite Baroque. This is the phase that in the past often was called Ultrabaroque and sometimes still is known as Churrigueresque.

The religious architecture of the seventeenth and early eighteenth century in New Spain, after the principal cathedrals were practically finished, included the codification of a few specialized church types and their regionalization. These buildings are either parish churches or the work of different religious orders within cities and towns. Other sites for monumental religious architecture were developed around sanctuaries, generally on the outskirts of important urban areas. As in the sixteenth century monasteries and also in the cathedrals, one often can detect the impact of illustrations in European treatises, especially in the portals of these buildings. It also has been shown that architects continued to plan according to medieval geometric traditions well into the eighteenth century.

By far the most widespread type of church preserved from this period is the cruciform vaulted building with a dome over the crossing and a choir loft inside, above the entrance bay. This is the type most often used for parishes and by all male religious orders, with the frequent exception of the Jesuits and sometimes the Dominicans. It is by no means clear, however, precisely how or when the diffusion of this scheme occurred. The type is so common that it has been taken totally for granted. It is also usually repeated that all these churches are alike, differentiated only by their ornament. Although it is true that these buildings were conceived as fairly simple shells to be complemented by elaborate interior decoration in the form of great gilded retablos, they are, in fact, not all alike. There are important and interesting variations in the proportions of buildings, in the relationships among the nave, the

Church of La Soledad, Oaxaca
Photo courtesy of Colección Luis Márquez, Archivo Fotográfico,
Instituto de Investigaciones Estéticas de la UNAM

crossing and lateral chapels and in the handling of fenestration and, of course, in the manipulation of the vaults and dome. All these buildings generally have a tower at one side of the façade that permits access to the choir loft and provides a place for the bells that mark the time.

In Mexico City the architect Pedro de Arrieta (active 1691 to 1738) or someone very familiar with his work was responsible for at least one building of the type just described: the parish of San Miguel. However, Arrieta was also the architect of churches with a central nave and side aisles, akin to the plans of the earlier cathedral projects. One of these was the sanctuary church of the Virgin of Guadalupe (built 1695–1709), north of Mexico City, and the other was the Jesuit church of the Profesa (1714–20). In the first of these buildings, Arrieta combines a central plan, appropriate for housing the miraculous painting of the Virgin of Guadalupe, with a longitudinal scheme. On the exterior, he made effective use of narratives in relief over the portals of the building. Two towers frame the facade, as is often the case in sanctuary churches.

The cathedral tradition was taken up as well in a few, important parish churches elsewhere in the viceroyalty. This is the case of the parish of San José in Puebla, and of a group of parish churches in the northern towns of San Luis Potosí (1701–30), whose architect Nicolás Sánchez Pacheco (active 1678–1717) certainly knew Arrieta's work in Mexico City, Zacatecas, and Chihuahua. These three buildings, in turn, became the inspiration for attempts later in the eighteenth century to enlarge existing parishes in other northern towns.

The convent church also became an established type in New Spain in the second half of the seventeenth century. This was a simple, single nave building set longitudinally next to the street. Two contiguous portals permitted access to the public on this street side, while the convent extended to the other side of the church. The entire end of the church opposite the altar, where normally one would expect the entrance to be located, was set aside for the nuns who participated in the liturgy from behind screens. Convents were concentrated exclusively in the cities, with almost none north of San Luis Potosí; the only exception being a single convent in Durango. In general, convent churches, although often richly ornamented inside, were not particularly conspicuous buildings. A famous exception is the church of Santa Rosa de Viterbo in Querétaro (finished in 1752), with its two freestanding buttresses on the street side, possibly the work of Ignacio Mariano de las Casas (c. 1719–c. 1785).

Throughout this period a process of regionalization in architecture was taking place. Fundamentally, this meant that the basic schemes were adapted by local masters using local materials. A few of these masters began their careers in Mexico City, but, with time, more and more masters were working in their places of origin.

Important regional variations include the Mexico City area where *tezontle,* a dark reddish pumice, very light in weight, was combined with gray limestone, which defined lines and was appropriate for carved details. In the Puebla-Tlaxcala region, builders made frequent use of brick and glazed tiles, as well as exterior and interior plaster work. Glazed tiles on domes spread to other parts of the viceroyalty; they often were used on the exteriors of domes. Plaster work was used extensively, especially to the south, into Central America. These materials made it possible to include bright colors in architecture. Early-twentieth-century historiography was fascinated by this trait and transformed it into a "national" characteristic. Colonial architecture in Oaxaca and to the west and north of Mexico City was able to take advantage of abundant local limestones. This resulted in rich sculptural decoration both on the exteriors and, in the north, in the interiors of buildings as well. Of course, all these limestones were of different colors, thus tinting Oaxaca in greenish-yellow tones, Zacatecas in rose and ochre, Guadalajara in beige and tan, and so on. Other local variations are related to seismic conditions. Thus, churches in the north could be built with tall towers, whereas in Oaxaca, for example, they have squat towers and very thick walls, and their domes are encased in buttressing. Finally, in small towns everywhere, but especially in the northern reaches of the viceroyalty, adobe was used extensively for church architecture. This architecture has been studied seriously only in New Mexico, where adobe construction achieved monumental proportions.

An important development of this time is the retablo facade. Mention already has been made of how elements first used extensively in retablos, namely the Solomonic and *estípite* supports, began to be used in church portals. However, the retablo facade also implied movement in plan at the entrance of the building. Thus, some portals were developed within niches, such as at San Juan de Dios in Mexico City (1729), the work of Miguel Custodio Durán, while others combined recession and protrusion, as in the facade of Arrieta's Basilica of Guadalupe. Given the close relationships between wood retablos and facade design, it should be no surprise that retablo makers were directly involved in architectural projects. This is the case of Jerónimo de Balbás, who came from Spain to construct the *Retablo of the Kings* in Mexico City cathedral and defined himself as an architect.

Prior to the middle of the eighteenth century it is clear, from documents and extant buildings, that considerable discussion and tensions must have existed around the problem of architectural design and its relationship to ornament, as well as around the role of the architect. For one thing, new ordinances for the Architects' Guild, which insisted on the gentlemanly status of architects, were promulgated in 1736. At the same time, in their buildings, architects seem to have been debating about facades based on the classicizing designs derived from treatises and designs derived from Solomonic and *estípite* retablos. An important case in point is the facade of the Jesuit church in Zacatecas (1746–49), relatively severe in its decorative elements, yet movemented in plan. Only a block away is the contemporary parish church with its elaborate Solomonic flat screen portal. At Taxco, Cayetano de Sigüenza, who also may have been the creator of the Zacatecas Jesuit facade, took into account the breakdown of classicizing restrictions that *estípite* designs permitted, but insisted nevertheless on using columns in the facade of the parish of Santa Prisca (1748–58). A treatise identified by Ignacio González Polo as probably having been written by Lorenzo Rodríguez, indicates that some architects favored leaving facade design to painters or sculptors altogether and insisted on mathematics and planning as the proper domains of their profession.

The emphasis on planning and project supervision is borne out by a good number of buildings erected in the eighteenth century. For one thing, the designs of facades and the internal decoration of some major buildings was thoroughly integrated both in iconographic as well as in formal terms, as can be seen, for example, at Zacatecas and Tepotzlán (finished around 1762). Especially as regards the details of iconography, the desires of patrons, especially clerical patrons, must certainly have played an important role. However, architects were taking iconographic needs into account by varying the contours of nave walls, probably to accommodate retablos that were becoming more voluminous, as at the Carmelite church in Querétaro, the work of Juan Manuel Villagómez, finished in 1759.

More radical experimentation with plans was not frequent, and it is significant that an important early example was the work of a military engineer, that is, of someone with mathematical training. The elliptical convent church of Santa Brígida in Mexico City,

Church of Santo Domingo, Zacatecas
Photo courtesy of Archivo Fotográfico, Instituto de Investigaciones Estéticas de la UNAM

irresponsibly destroyed in 1933, was built from 1740 to 1744 by the Spanish engineer Luis Díez Navarro, who later went to Guatemala. Among architects of New Spain, Francisco Guerrero y Torres (1727–92) was the one who most experimented with plans, while never using the *estípite* in portals. Although as yet no document has been found that relates him directly to the building of the church of the convent of the Enseñanza (1772–78) in Mexico City, there can be little doubt that he designed the unique elongated polygonal plan, crowned by a central dome. He also was responsible for the Chapel of the Pocito (1771–91) near the Basilica of Guadalupe. He based this work, which was his personal donation to the Virgin, on a Roman temple plan, published by Serlio, to create a principal centralized space, entered via a smaller centralized narthex that is matched by a similarly shaped sacristy on the opposite side of the building. The exterior presents a compact and colorful form of red *tezontle* walls with gray limestone detailing, crowned by a large dome and two smaller ones, all three covered by blue and white tile decoration in a zigzag pattern. The building is unified by the blue and white tiles which spill

Cathedral of Zacatecas
Photo courtesy of Archivo Fotográfico, Instituto de Investigaciones Estéticas de la UNAM

Chapel of the Pocito, Mexico City, by Francisco Guerrero y Torres, 1771–91
Photo courtesy of Colección Luis Márquez, Archivo Fotográfico,
Instituto de Investigaciones Estéticas de la UNAM

Palacio de Minería, Mexico City
Photo courtesy of Colección Luis Márquez, Archivo Fotográfico,
Instituto de Investigaciones Estéticas de la UNAM

over onto the drums of the domes and by the motif of star-shaped windows that punctuate both the drums of the domes and the *tezontle* walls below. The preciousness of the whole is appropriate for the chapel's commemorative function at the site of a sacred well.

The insistence by important Mexico City architects of the eighteenth century on a relatively sober classicizing ornamental vocabulary is a complex phenomenon. As mentioned above, its roots are in the treatise tradition of architecture in New Spain. However, it also can be related to the Neoclassical movements of eighteenth-century art, against the background of the Enlightenment. Mixed as it is with elements of Mexican Baroque and even of Rococo vocabulary, the language of architects like Guerrero y Torres represents a uniquely New Spanish strain of Baroque Neoclassicism, for which Jorge Alberto Manrique coined the term "Neóstilo," in reference to the renewed use of columnar supports

that the *estípite* phase of Mexican Baroque had largely eliminated. The Neóstilo is not merely an ornamental style, because it corresponds on the interiors to taller proportions and to the use of greater and more diffuse lighting.

The growth of Mexico City and other urban areas and the trends toward secularization in society in the eighteenth century created an expanding need for secular buildings. The plans of grand, civil architecture hardly varied throughout the entire colonial period and recall European Renaissance schemes. Early examples have survived especially in Puebla. Palaces usually were constructed around four-sided central courtyards, with ancillary blocks, also around courtyards, added as need might dictate. The ceremonial quarters were on the first floor, the piano nobile of Renaissance tradition, and the principal entrance was generally on the central axis of the main courtyard. The exception in New Spain is the corner facade of Pedro de Arrieta's Palace of the

Inquisition (1733–37) in Mexico City, with its hanging keystone arches at the corners of the inner courtyard. This type was adopted in a number of other civil buildings in New Spain. The hanging keystone proliferated in convents and monasteries as well. In Mexico City, in the later eighteenth century, several truly monumental palaces were built by Francisco Guerrero y Torres. The most interesting is that of the Condes de San Mateo de Valparaíso, with its central courtyard enframed by four great, lowered arches and its double spiral interior staircase.

The official establishment in 1785 of the Royal Academy of San Carlos in Mexico City closes the architectural history of New Spain. The Neoclassicism of the Spanish teachers who staffed the new academy was much more orthodox and closer to Roman precedents than the indigenous Neóstilo. As a consequence, Guerrero y Torres himself had projects rejected by Academy architects and important commissions began to go to the recently arrived Spaniards. The irony was that the artists of New Spain had long wished for an academy, so as to improve themselves and their professional standing. Criollo patrons also were supportive of the establishment of the academy, because it promised to place New Spain on an equal footing with European nations in matters of art and taste. Of course, such matters were related directly to the production of the artisans of New Spain and thus to economic concerns. For the Crown, art academies were also a way to weaken the guild system and exercise control over guild and even over church revenues; all proposed construction projects now had to be approved by the academy.

The major building projects of New Spain around 1800 were taken over by academy architects, especially by Manuel Tolsá of Valencia, who, although trained principally as a sculptor, was responsible for the most impressive Academic Neoclassical buildings raised in New Spain. The most famous of these is the Palace of the School of Mines. Built on the traditional courtyard scheme, its classical vocabulary is sober and free of almost all ornamentation. Column shafts are smooth, pure forms, and pediments are unbroken. Among Tolsa's clients were important criollo families, such as the wealthy Fagoagas, for whom he designed a palace in Mexico City, known as the Casa del Apartado from their title. It is a further irony of history that the Fagoagas were among the principal promoters of the movement for political independence from Spain, which was to result in the war that ended the existence of New Spain and of many of its institutions, including the Royal Academy.

Select Bibliography
Baird, Joseph Armstrong, *The Churches of Mexico, 1530–1810.* Berkeley: University of California Press, 1962.
Early, James, *The Colonial Architecture of Mexico.* Albuquerque: University of New Mexico Press, 1994.
Kubler, George, *Mexican Architecture of the Sixteenth Century.* 2 vols., New Haven, Connecticut: Yale University Press, 1948.
_____, and Martin Sebastian Soria, *Art and Architecture in Spain and Portugal and their American Dominions, 1500–1800.* Baltimore and London: Penguin, 1959.
_____, *The Religious Architecture of New Mexico in the Colonial Period and Since the American Occupation.* 5th edition, Albuquerque: University of New Mexico Press, 1990.
McAndrew, John, *The Open-Air Churches of Sixteenth Century Mexico: Atrios, Posas, Open Chapels and Other Studies.* Cambridge, Massachusetts: Harvard University Press, 1965.
Schuetz, Mardith, editor, *Architectural Practice in Mexico City: A Manual for Journeyman Architects of the Eighteenth Century.* Tucson: University of Arizona Press, 1987.

—CLARA BARGELLINI

Architecture: Nineteenth Century

Much has been written about the search for national identity in Mexican architecture, but few scholars explain what is meant by either nation or identity, the terms that presumably define the discourse. Part of the difficulty in clarifying these terms is that they are elusive and constantly changing, since both "nation" and "national identity" are cultural and historical constructs. As early as 1928, José Carlos Mariategui, a Peruvian writer and activist remarked: "The nation . . . is an abstraction, an allegory, a myth that does not correspond to a reality that can be scientifically defined." In a now classic book, Benedict Anderson defined the nation as "an imagined political community—and imagined as both limited and sovereign." The notion of identity is equally problematic because it assumes authenticity and continuity despite multiple ruptures in history. Because of their sociohistorical determination, both nation and identity must be defined as always shifting and never completed. National identity has the dual function of achieving internal cohesion and separating the nation from the outside. Nationalism and national identity are closely related, for the formulation of national identity is a prerequisite for nationalism, and nationalism is the performance or the activation of national identity.

The construction of national identity is based on historical narratives that support the interests of specific groups. This presupposes that multiple versions of national identity can compete and coexist. With the formation of nation states in the nineteenth century, officially sanctioned versions of the nation were created. Although these versions change through history, there is, at any one time in any one place, a dominant version of the nation. This version is the one disseminated through state and state-affiliated institutions such as schools and the mainstream media. It is, in fact, the one that most citizens learn as young children. Alternative versions of the nation offer the potential of challenging, altering, and replacing the official versions.

Architecture takes part in the construction of national identity insofar as it creates or reinforces specific images and narratives of the nation. Because traditionally the history of architecture focuses on monuments commissioned by states and wealthy patrons, it affirms identities constructed by dominant groups. Studies of the representation of identity in architecture are important because they reveal power relations and strategies essential to the construction of nationhood as well as contradictions that the dominant representations of the nation obscure.

The representation of national identity in architecture has been a subject of debate for Mexican architects since the late nineteenth century. Although scholars tend to equate the representation of identity with indigenous building traditions, international styles of architecture have also been used to represent aspects of Mexican identity. By international styles we mean those that had origins in Western Europe and in the United States and subsequently were exported or adopted elsewhere. In fact, if there is one constant in the history of Mexican architecture it is the confluence of indigenous and imported elements.

International styles in architecture are defined by politically or economically influential nations. Thus, the presence of these styles in Mexican architecture indicates an ongoing power relation between the nation and influential outsiders. The representation of locality is frequently achieved through a reintepretation of construction methods, design, and decorative elements from historical or regional architecture. As most professional architects in Mexico fully partake of contemporary international culture, the representation of national identity in architecture often involves the appropriation of traditions from cultures far removed from the direct experience of the designers. In Mexico, ancient historic architecture was built by indigenous civilizations whose descendants were marginalized and dispossessed. Often, these descendants were also the "anonymous builders" of

regional architecture. The incorporation of historical and regional architecture into an ideal construct of the nation frequently functions as a strategy to conceal the state's and the elites' abusive and often violent treatment of marginalized citizens in the nation.

The writing of the history of nineteenth century Mexican architecture is still in its formative stages. Although several scholars have documented and classified numerous buildings from that era, much needed sociohistorical and interpretive work is still wanting. The work of Israel Katzman is the only extensive study, as he photographed and documented over 5,000 buildings and researched the biographies of significant architects of this period. Without his efforts subsequent studies would not have been possible. Other scholars have examined specific stylistic tendencies or focused on the development of specific parts of Mexico City.

Traditional methods of art historical analysis prove unhelpful in the study of nineteenth-century Mexican architecture. Eclecticism is the rule of the period. Yet, despite evidence of a myriad of styles, often practiced by the same architect, sometimes in the same building, scholars have attempted to classify the architecture of the period into discreet categories, such as Classical, Gothic, Romanesque, and Islamic revival. As a result, many buildings fit into more than one category, and specialists are constantly pressured to create additional denominations for buildings that elude classification, such as *ecléctica integrada*, or simplified traditionalism. This situation is not unlike the one created by the classification of colonial Mexican architecture using European stylistic frameworks. European architecture of various periods is similarly eclectic. Perhaps it is time to realize that the notion of style begs for serious revisions, as the purity of style may be a myth, not unrelated to notions of racial purity and stable identities. In the words of Demitri Porphyrios, classifying a building according to style means to focus on the features it shares with others, cleansing it of all impurities. The historian thus elevates the consistencies of the building to the status of principles while silencing or neglecting the building's contradictions. This process resembles the construction of national identity, which favors specific aspects of the nation while excluding others.

For most of the nineteenth century there were no efforts to define a Mexican architecture. Architects and patrons, including the Mexican state, imported European and U.S. architecture to Mexico in an attempt for the country to rival the great world capitals. In other words, international building styles were used to demonstrate the country's participation in modernity. The question of what form a Mexican architecture should take was not even asked for the first half of the century. It was not until the 1860s and most notably in the 1880s and 1890s that the creation of a Mexican architecture employing local architectural traditions as a basis entered architectural debates. Even then, the architects concerned with such questions were few.

During the nineteenth century, Mexico demonstrated no preference for the stylistic currents of one country over another. While various regimes proved fond of Classical styles, which filtered through the Academia de San Fernando in Madrid during the early years of the century and through the Beaux Arts Academy in Paris during the Porfiriato—the era of Porfirio Díaz (president 1876–80, 1884–1911)—stylistic currents from all the developed nations were adopted. This eclecticism parallels the economic policies of the late Porfiriato, when lenders and investors were chosen from various nations in order to prevent dominance of any one country over Mexico.

The history of nineteenth-century Mexico reveals that Mexican elites sought to transform Mexico into a modern nation capable of competing with industrialized European nations and the United States. During this period a series of foreign interventions menaced Mexico's autonomy. By the last third of the century, statesmen and intellectuals were actively searching for forms of indigenous expressions that would symbolically unify the nation and differentiate it from the outside.

One of the few attempts to represent the local took place in the form of pre-Columbian revival buildings inspired by ancient Mexican art and architecture. Although proposals and commissions of works in this tendency were few, these projects signaled Mexico's individuality and resistance to assimilation by another nation and the first attempts by the Mexican state to construct a national identity through architecture.

The City in Nineteenth-Century Mexico

For the first two-thirds of the nineteenth century, Mexico was ravaged first by the Wars of Independence and later by civil wars and foreign interventions such as the U.S.-Mexican War (1846–48) and the Wars of Reform (1858–61). From 1821 to 1876, Mexico had a variety of governments including two empires: one ruled by a criollo (native-born American of Spanish descent), Emperor Agustín de Iturbide I (1822–23), and another one established under French protection with Maximilian von Hapsburg as emperor (1864–67). This climate of unrest was not propitious for large urban projects or for architecture. Little building took place between 1810 and 1887, despite a few short periods of peace. In addition to the restrictions placed by the political climate, the appropriation of church properties during La Reforma (the period of Liberal rule and influence, 1856–76) put an end to sumptuous commissions by the church that had enriched the urban environments of the colonial period. The most important work of architecture during the rule of Maximilian was the renovation of the castle of Chapultepec by the architect Vicente Manero, who transformed the old colonial building into a veritable palace.

The most stable period for politics, economics, and architecture was the government of Porfirio Díaz. Don Porfirio's regime was characterized by an open door policy to foreign investments and industrialization. Díaz surrounded himself with a group of advisers who became known as the Científicos, technocrats who based their policies on the positivist philosophies of Auguste Comte and Herbert Spencer, equating industrialization with progress. The Porfirian administration introduced to Mexico technological innovations such as electric lighting, telephones, automobiles, movies, and water utility systems. Between 1876 and 1910 railroad tracks increased from 400 to 15,000 miles. In order to make these developments possible, the government confiscated thousands of acres of lands owned by indigenous communities and granted them to powerful landowners and industrial companies. Mexico's stability also was achieved through powerful mechanisms of repression, which included the army and a rural police force who became known as the Rurales.

Because of the introduction of new technologies and the positivist emphasis on hygiene, the physical appearance of cities changed during the nineteenth century, and especially during the Porfiriato. Between 1790 and 1910 the population of Mexico tripled and the population of Mexico City quadrupled. Projects of public hygiene, such as the Obras de Aprovisionamiento de Agua Potable and the Ensanche del Desagüe del Valle de México, were inaugurated in 1907. Cities were reorganized; streets and avenues were paved and widened, efforts were taken to clean the city of garbage and to facilitate the circulation of air. Aqueducts gradually were replaced by lead pipes, and the first electric streetcars cruised the city in 1899. By 1890 numerous states including Aguascalientes, Orizaba, Guadalajara, Hermosillo, Puebla, and San Luis Potosí had adopted electric lighting for plazas and streets. Between 1891 and 1900, 1,570,000 square feet (146,000 square meters) of streets were paved with asphalt in Mexico City.

The latter year, two U.S. companies were contracted to pave the streets with concrete and asphalt.

In 1864 Maximilian ordered the Calzada del Emperador, later named Paseo de la Reforma, to be built from the Castle of Chapultepec to the Monument of Carlos IV. Juan and Ramón Agea were responsible for the design. The avenue was 180 feet (55 meters) wide, the widest street in Mexico at that point. The Paseo de la Reforma was later widened under the presidency of Sebastián Lerdo de Tejada, and once more during Díaz's administration.

During the Porfiriato, wealthy districts concentrated on the west and southwest of the historic center of the city. Luxurious *colonias* such as the Colonia del Paseo and the Colonia Juárez developed along the Paseo de la Reforma. Poorer neighborhoods were concentrated on the east and southeast, where the ground was lower, wetter, and more unstable than in the west. This division seems to have been planned by the Porfirian administration. It is not coincidental that new jails inaugurated during the celebration of the centennial of Mexican independence in 1910 were located in the poor neighborhoods.

International Tendencies and the Academy

During most of the Porfiriato upper-class Mexicans wore French and English clothes, danced the minuet, listened to French and Italian operas, and even preferred English to Mexican food. Exclusive neighborhoods with sumptuous Neoclassical homes resembled sections of Paris and Brussels. The owners of these houses often purchased architectural designs in Europe and had them executed in Mexico. Since its founding in 1783, Mexico's Academia de San Carlos de Nueva España (later named Escuela de Bellas Artes) hired mostly European and European-educated instructors. The first director of the section of architecture at the academy was Antonio González Velázquez, a Spanish exponent of Neoclassicism who arrived in Mexico in 1778.

The academy was closed between 1821 and 1824 because of economic difficulties brought about by the Wars of Independence. After 1824, it was of decreasing significance. During this period many of the academy's former students transferred to engineering. The institution reopened in 1843 under orders of President Antonio López de Santa Anna. During his regime, several Mexican architects, including the brothers Juan and Ramón Agea, were sent to study in Europe. On their return to Mexico from Rome in 1846, the Ageas practiced architecture in a Renaissance style; Juan, in particular, introduced to Mexico the theories of Eugéne-Emmanuel Viollet-le-Duc.

In 1856, the academy unified the disciplines of civil engineering and architecture under the directorship of the Italian architect Javier Cavallari, an internationally renowned academic, historian, archaeologist, and former director of the Imperial and Royal Academy of Milan. The study plan was of eight years, including *preparatoria,* or high school. During his stay in Mexico, Cavallari republished a translation of a book he previously had written, with the title *Apuntamientos sobre la historia de la arquitectura* (1860), and he remodeled the building for the Academy of San Carlos. He taught several notable architects, including Eusebio and Ignacio de la Hidalga, Eleuterio Méndez, Manuel F. Álvarez, Antonio Torres Torija, and Manuel Téllez Pizarro. Cavallari returned to Italy in 1864 and Eleuterio Méndez took over the directorship at the academy.

In 1867 the administration of President Benito Juárez mandated the separation of the careers of architect and engineer. The Special School for Engineers was established at the former College of Mining; the career of architect remained confined to the former Academy of San Carlos, renamed theNational School of Fine Arts. Despite various attempts to separate architecture and engineering, the two disciplines remained intimately related until the end of the century. For instance, in 1869 the section of architecture at the National School of Fine Arts closed owing to economic difficulties, but the degree of Engineer and Architect continued to be granted at the School of Mines. Persons working for such title had to learn artistic subjects with sculptors and painters at the National School of Fine Arts and technical subjects with civil engineers.

In the beginning of the twentieth century, the faculty of the school of architecture included Maxime Roisin (French), Adamo Boari (Italian), Antonio Rivas Mercado (a Mexican who had studied in England and at the Ècole des Beaux Arts in Paris), Carlos M. Lazo, Carlos Ituarte, Emilio Dondé, and the brothers Federico and Nicolas Mariscal. Rivas Mercado became director of the National School of Fine Arts in 1903. The French architect Émile Bénard, who came to Mexico to work on the Legislative Palace in 1903, founded an architectural studio where he took Mexican students, including Jesús Acevedo and Eduardo Macedo y Arbeau.

Taking into consideration Mexico's welcoming of imported talent, it is not surprising that the most important architectural commissions of the Porfiriato were given to foreigners. Adamo Boari (an Italian) designed the Post Office built by Gonzalo Garita (1902–07) and the National Theater (1904);

Central Post Office Building, Mexico City, by Adamo Boari, 1902–07
Photo courtesy of Archivo Fotográfico, Instituto de Investigaciones Estéticas de la UNAM

Silvio Contri (another Italian) was responsible for the Secretariat of Communications and Public Works (1902–11); Émile Bénard and Maxime Roisin, both French, designed the Legislative Palace in 1905. This building was never completed because of the outbreak of the Revolution in 1910, but the importance of the Legislative Palace for the Porfirian regime is evident in the ceremonial laying of the first stone of the building during the celebrations of the centenary of Independence in 1910, although work on the building had begun a few years earlier.

Stylistic Tendencies

As in Spain, academic education in Mexico was based on the model of the Ècole des Beaux Arts in Paris, an institution that traditionally favored architecture based on Classical traditions. Neoclassicism became firmly established in Mexico at the end of the eighteenth century, some decades after it had become an international style. The statutes enacted by Carlos III to the Academy in 1784 prohibited any tribunal to employ anyone who was not an academician to measure or direct architectural projects.

Neoclassicism

In nineteenth-century Mexico, Neoclassicism must be understood as a tendency to base the features of buildings on the architecture of Classical antiquity or on later buildings derived from that tradition. This implies neither a desire to be archaeologically correct on the part of architects nor exclusive use of these sources in the architecture. The architectural styles represented in nineteenth-century Mexican architecture refer more to decoration than to spatial characteristics, so much so, that to consider a work as Neoclassical it is sufficient that it has Classical columns. During the first half of the nineteenth century the dominant stylistic tendencies of the school of architecture continued to be Classical. Other tendencies became increasingly important during the period of Cavallari's directorship and thereafter.

Most of the influential academic designers during the first half of the century were Spanish. Miguel Constansó, a military engineer born in Barcelona in 1741, went to Mexico in 1764. Antonio González Velázquez was director of the section of architecture at the Academy of San Carlos until 1794. Manuel Tolsá initially went to Mexico as director of the section of sculpture in the Academy of San Carlos and was appointed director of the section of architecture in 1810. Lorenzo de la Hidalga, born in Álava, Spain, worked in Paris in 1836 under the direction of Henri Labrouste and Viollet-le-Duc and went to Mexico in 1838.

Francisco Tresguerras was one of few active Mexican designers of this period. Born in Celaya, Guanajuato, he was self-educated. In 1794 Tresguerras requested from the academy the degree of Arquitecto de Mérito, a title intended for persons who already had experience in architecture; it is unknown if he received it. Tresguerras exemplifies the confluence of local and international tendencies during the early nineteenth century. Although he regarded himself as a Classicist, many of his works, including his own tomb, align him with the Baroque decorative tradition dominant in colonial Mexican architecture. Because of his eclectic, idiosyncratic style, later scholars variously judged Tresguerras as either a genius or a fraud.

In the West, powerful nations adopted Neoclassical architecture for official buildings in various historical periods. Because Neoclassicism is based on the art of ancient civilizations, its use in later periods is part of a process of validation. Neoclassical styles are ritualistic gestures of empowerment, for they suggest an identification of the nation that commissions them with the great civilizations of Western antiquity. The significance of Neoclassicism in Mexico was double-edged. On one hand, its arrival through Spain signaled a colonial relation; on the other, it was an attempt to legitimize Mexico's independent regimes and to define Mexico as a member of the modern nations. The status of Neoclassicism as an international style during the nineteenth century further problematizes this reading, since the emulation of international tendencies in Mexican architecture suggested Mexico's postcolonial relation of subalternity to Europe and the United States. A chronological listing of notable works in Neoclassical architecture from the nineteenth century includes the Royal Cigar Factory in Mexico City by Antonio González Velázquez and Miguel Constansó (1792–1807); the College of Mining by Manuel Tolsá (1797–1813); the Palace of Government of San Luis Potosí designed by Miguel Constansó (1798–

1827); the Church of El Carmen, Celaya, by Francisco Tresguerras (1802–07); the Church of the Teresitas in Querétaro by Manuel Tolsá, Pedro Ortíz, and Francisco Tresguerras (1803–07); the interior of the Cámara de Diputados in the National Palace in Mexico City by Agustín Paz (1824–29); the National Theater, or Santa Ana Theater, in Mexico City by Lorenzo de la Hidalga (1841–44); the Degollado Theater by José Galvéz in Guadalajara (1856–80); the Academy of San Carlos renovations by Javier Cavallari (1863); the Juárez Theater in Guanajuato by José Noriega and Antonio Rivas Mercado (1873–1903); the Palace of Government in Monterrey (1895–1908); the Project for the Legislative Palace by Émile Bénard (1905); and the Monument to Benito Juárez in Mexico City by Guillermo de Heredia (1909–10).

In his book *Arquitectura del Siglo XIX en Mexico,* Israel Katzman discusses five tendencies related to Neoclassicism: integrated eclecticism, semiclassic eclecticism, Baroque, very simplified traditionalist style, and the French style. As mentioned earlier, these categories overlap and are sometimes indistinguishable from one another. According to Katzman, since in nineteenth-century Mexico there is no pure architectural style, the assignation of buildings to specific stylistic categories is a matter of "degrees of kinship." The usefulness of this classification is debatable, but an alternative is yet to be developed.

In Katzman's view, integrated eclecticism is a current that incorporates traces of classical architecture but includes Baroque and eclectic architectural elements. There is no intention on the part of the architect to return to a specific architectural style. Buildings in this tendency include the Neptune Fountain in Querétaro by Francisco Tresguerras (1797); the Arbeau Theater in Mexico City by José Téllez de Girón (1874–75); the Hospital Concepción Beístegui in Mexico City (1886); and details such as column capitals in the interior of the Juárez Theater in Guanajuato by José Noriega and Antonio Rivas Mercado (1873–1903).

Semiclassic eclecticism is one in which a building's classical elements have greater weight than elements deriving from other styles. Buildings such as the Juárez Theater in Guanajuato, the Palace of Government in Chihuahua (1882–92), and the Palace of Government by Luis Long in Guanajuato (1897–1900) are included in this tendency.

"Very simplified traditionalism" refers to buildings of various stylistic tendencies with a minimal amount of ornamentation. Examples include the Hercules Spinning Mill and Textile Factory in Querétaro (1836–64); the Bella Unión Hotel in Mexico

City (1840), designed by José Besozzi, a military architect; a project for a penitentiary in Mexico City by Lorenzo de la Hidalga (1848); the Iturbide Theater, later the Cámara de Diputados (1851–56) by Manuel Méndez; the San Francisco Market in Morelia, Michoacán (1872–1910); the Maternity Hospital by Eduardo Tamaríz in Puebla (1879–85); and the Agriculture School in the Hacienda de San Antonio Chautla, Puebla, built at the turn of the century. While the first four buildings are based in the classical tradition, a series of gabled roofs placed at various levels give the halls of the San Francisco Market an orientalized aspect. The last two buildings were inspired by Romanesque architecture. The light, open structures of the Buen Tono Factory in Mexico City (1896–97) by Miguel A. de Quevedo and Ernesto Canseco, both engineers, and the building of the Universal Factories in Mexico City by Miguel A. de Quevedo (finished in 1909) prefigure modern architecture.

Baroque and the French Style

Although in Mexico the Baroque is presumed to have ended in the late eighteenth century, Baroque buildings continued to be built in the nineteenth century. For many Mexicans, after the Wars of Independence, the Baroque came to symbolize Mexico's colonial past. Buildings in this tendency completed in the nineteenth century include the Oratory of San Felipe Neri in Guadalajara, Jalisco (finished in 1812); the Naples Chapel in the Villa de Gualoupe, Zacatecas (1845–66), designed by Fray Diego de la Concepción Palomar and redecorated by the *maestro de obras*, Refugio Reyes; the tower of the parish church in Lagos de Moreno, Jalisco (finished in 1871); and the Spanish Casino in Mexico City by Emilio González del Campo (1901–03). As in Mexican colonial Baroque, the majority of these buildings exhibit rich surface decoration but lack structural dynamism. In various buildings the placement of columnated porticoes and engaged columns projecting from the facade produce the impression of movement. This technique is used instead of complex geometries in plan and elevation to produce the same effect. Katzman attributes this trait to turn-of-the-century French Classicism. Yet, this characteristic is found in earlier French and other architecture.

The French "style" is recognized by the presence of mansard roofs and dormer windows in addition to elements of Classical architecture and profuse sculptural decoration of surfaces, including busts, caryatids, angels, and vegetation in vertical arrangements. According to Katzman, the taste for heavy surface decoration is of French Classical origin; but similar characteristics and decorative elements can be found in Mexico since the beginning of the colonial period. An important example of the French tendency is the House of the Braniff family in Reforma Avenue, built by Carlos Hall in 1888.

Gothic, Romanesque, and Islamic Revivals

In addition to variants of Classicism, numerous styles were represented in nineteenth-century Mexican architecture, including Gothic, Romanesque, and Islamic revivals, Art Nouveau, and Neoindigenista (or pre-Hispanic revival). None of these currents existed in isolation but often were mixed with other tendencies. The presence of this variety of styles has been explained as a result of Mexico's search for identity. In his book, *Arte del Siglo XIX en México*, Justino Fernández suggests that Mexico's eclecticism meant not only that Mexico admired foreign styles in architecture but that it was involved in a search for its own authentic and unique expression. Although Fernández's interpretation is correct, it does not explain the presence of eclecticism in Europe and the United States during the same time period, nor does he discuss the implications of this search for "authentic and unique expression." The use of foreign models to represent the Mexican nation suggests an implicit acceptance on the part of Mexicans of the cultural superiority of outsiders, an acceptance typical of many postcolonial nations.

The Gothic revival, practiced primarily by *maestros de obras* in the provinces, included works such as the Portico of Medellín in Colima, by Lucio Uribe (1860); the facade of the Church of San Miguel de Allende in Guanajuato by Ceferino Gutiérrez (1880); the Guadaloupe Sanctuary in Zacatecas begun by Refugio Reyes in 1891 (a combination of a Gothic and Classical facade); the chapel of the French Cemetery in Mexico City by E. Desormes (1891–92); the Episcopal Church of Christ, in Mexico City (1895–98); and the Central Post office Building in Mexico City by Adamo Boari (1902–06). This last building has been identified as representing various styles owing to the presence of Romanesque, Byzantine, Isabelline, and Renaissance elements in the facade.

Romanesque revival buildings include the Chapel of the Spanish Cemetery in Mexico City by Ignacio and Eusebio de la Hidalga (c.1880); the Church of San Felipe de Jesús in Madero Street in Mexico City by Émile Dondé (1886–97); the Church of the Sagrada Familia in Mexico City by Manuel Gorozpe (1910–12); and the Church of Santa Ana in Toluca, Mexico.

Sumptuous houses modeled after foreign catalogs of country houses combined the above mentioned

Church of San Miguel de Allende, Guanajuato,
by Ceferino Gutiérrez, 1880
Photo courtesy of Archivo Fotográfico, Instituto de
Investigaciones Estéticas de la UNAM

styles with elements from medieval English architecture. Katzman calls this tendency *campestre romántica*. Examples include the House of the Braniff family in Chapala (c.1905); the House of Alberto Terrazas in the Calzada del Nombre de Dios, Chihuahua (c.1906); and the House in the Paseo de la Reforma 365, Mexico City (1911–12).

Islamic architecture had active representatives in Puebla. Between 1880 and 1884 Eduardo Tamaríz executed several works in this tendency, including the reconstruction of the San Francisco Mill or "El Marqués de Monserrat" (c.1880) and a Kiosk in the Plaza Constitución (1882–83). Several interiors decorated by the Arpa Brothers in the same city exhibit elements characteristic of Islamic architecture such as pointed, horseshoe, and polylobed arches as well as intricate abstract patterns as decoration. The best-known examples of Islamic architecture in nineteenth-century Mexico, however, are the Mexico Pavilion designed by José Ramón Ibarrola for the

New Orleans Exposition of 1884–85 and the interior of the Juárez Theater in Guanajuato by José Noriega and Antonio Rivas Mercado (1873–1903). The history of the design by Ibarrola illustrates the eclecticism of the epoch, as the architect submitted two projects to the competition for the building: one inspired by English wooden architecture, and the other, the Islamic pavilion.

Art Nouveau

Most of the Art Nouveau architecture built in Mexico has been destroyed. Yet, Mexico achieved extraordinary buildings in this style, including Porfirio Díaz's arms' room on Mexico City's Cadena Street, decorated by Antonio Fabrés (before 1905); the staircase of the Mercantile Center, later the Great Hotel, of Mexico City (destroyed); and various rooms and furniture in the spectacular house of don Luis Requena in Santa Veracruz no. 43, designed by the Catalan artist Ramón Cantó (1901–12). A member of a cosmopolitan Mexican aristocracy, Requena informed his requests for the design of this house on examples of architecture he saw in his frequent travels to Europe. In addition to Art Nouveau music room, dining room, bedroom, and children's room, the house included a Mozarabic patio, a Louis XV living room, and Renaissance and Pompeiian rooms.

There has been controversy regarding the designation of the National Theater, also known as Palacio de Bellas Artes (1904), by Adamo Boari as an example of either Art Nouveau or Neoclassicism. This controversy has emerged because scholars have attempted to fit it into a single stylistic category, when in fact it is a hybrid that includes both. This building is important not only because it fuses various currents but because it exemplifies both the Porfiriato's preference for imports and an attempt by Mexican elites at self-representation. Don Porfirio's administration gave the commission for the building design to Adamo Boari. The Italian artists Leonardo Bistolfi, A. Boni, and Gianetti Fiorenzo, the Hungarian sculptor Geza Marotti, and Agustín Querol, a Catalan sculptor, were responsible for the sculptural decorations. Iron works for the exterior were the creation of the Italian artist Alessandro Mazzucotelli. The great stage curtain was designed by Dr. Atl (whose real name was Gerardo Murillo, a well-to-do Mexican painter who was later instrumental in the development of Mexican muralism). Two German firms, the Vereignitemaschinenfabrik and the Maschinenbaugesellshaft, received the commission for its steel structure. This structure would be covered by crystal plates made by Tiffany Studios in New York. The company Milliken Brothers from Chicago was

Pavilion of Mexico, Universal Exposition of 1889, Paris, by Antonio Peñafiel and Antonio M. Anza
Photo courtesy of Archivo Fotográfico, Instituto de Investigaciones Estéticas de la UNAM

in charge of the buildings's foundations and W. H. Birkmire from New York was to direct most of the construction. The edifice was designed to have a steel structure covered with concrete, in turn covered with marble. Marble architectural details such as columns and pilasters, as well as the reproductions of models for marble and copper sculptures were made abroad by the companies Walton Goody and Triscornia and Hereaux. Machinery, including elevators for the upper and lower stages of the theater, were made by the two German houses mentioned above; the Allgemeine Elektricitats Gesellshaft from Berlin was in charge of the electrical infrastructure for the entire theater.

Despite the predominance of foreign artists and consultants, the National Theater integrated indige-nous themes and decoration into a building of inter-national character. Among the sculptural decorations for the facade, Boari included eagle warriors and feathered serpents based on Aztec prototypes; the stage curtain designed by Dr. Atl depicted the Mexican volcanoes Popocatépetl and Iztaccíhuatl. The government's approval of Boari's design indi-cates an interest on the part of the Porfirian admin-istration to claim a place for Mexican culture next to the cultural heritage of Europe. Similar attitudes clearly were expressed by contemporary architects such as Luis Salazar, Nicolás Mariscal, and Jesús Acevedo, who searched for solutions to create a modern architecture with a national character. While Salazar advocated a Mexican architecture based on ancient indigenous building traditions, Mariscal and

Palacio de Bellas Artes, Mexico City, by Adamo Boari, 1904
Photo courtesy of Archivo Fotográfico, Instituto de Investigaciones Estéticas de la UNAM

Acevedo proposed a national architecture based on colonial buildings.

The image of Mexico represented in the Palace of Fine Arts was primarily one of wealth and sophistication. The state-of-the-art construction techniques, building materials, and infrastructure implied economic power; the international character of the related artworks suggested cultural refinement. Only the references to the landscape and local antiquity identified the building as Mexican. This image of the nation was representative of a very small section of the population: the cosmopolitan upper class. The references to local antiquity recognized Mexico's ancient past as the national heritage, but no reference was made to contemporary indigenes who comprised a significant part of the population. The construction of the National Theater was interrupted from 1917 to 1929 by the Mexican Revolution. Work on the theater finally was resumed in 1930 and completed in 1934 under the direction of Federico Mariscal.

Neoindigenismo

The nineteenth century witnessed the development of pre-Hispanic revival, or Neoindigenista, buildings, a new genre in Mexican architecture. Although it is tempting to regard this tendency as one more example of eclecticism and taste for exotic tendencies that dominated the period, such a judgment is simplistic. In Mexico, pre-Hispanic subject matter had been linked strongly with representations of the local since the colonial period.

The first monument to represent pre-Hispanic themes in a public building was a triumphal arch designed by Carlos de Sigüenza y Góngora for the welcoming reception of a new viceroy to Mexico City in 1680. Built in a traditional style, the paintings of the arch featured the Mexica god Huitzilopochtli and 11 Mexica rulers as the protagonists in allegorical paintings illustrating the virtues of good government. The arch represented a Mexican criollo nation built upon the appropriation of indigenous antiquity by a privileged group. No buildings celebrating indigenous antiquity were constructed in the eighteenth century, although writings such as *Due antichi monumenti di architettura messicana* by Padre Pedro José Marquéz (Rome, 1804) exalted the cultural value of pre-Hispanic monuments.

In the nineteenth century, Neoindigenista architecture played an active part in the representation of national identity as constructed by the Porfirian regime. As wealthy criollos had done in the colonial period, Porfirian elites created an image of the nation embracing ancient indigenous civilizations as the common heritage of all Mexicans. This was a problematic proposition in view of the nation's colonial history and the influx of immigrants to Mexico during the nineteenth century. More importantly, the references to Mexican antiquity without any acknowledgment of contemporary indigenous peoples suggested the extinction of Mexican natives, since archaeological cultures implied a past long gone. In Neoindigenista buildings, Mexican natives represented in paintings and sculptures often appeared as mestizos, suggesting the sacrifice of specific ethnic identities to an ideal image of the nation.

These visual constructs of the nation had roots in attempts to unify the Mexican population. Because of Mexico's growing industrialization during the second half of the nineteenth century, Mexican elites thought of the indigenes as a national "problem." Attempts to deal with this problem ranged from outright annihilation of Native Mexicans—as in the "pacification" campaigns in the north of the country—to proposals for integration of the indigenous population to the nation through education and intermarriage. These proposals had in common the cultural negation and extermination of the natives.

Like buildings in other "neo" styles, no Neoindigenista building was faithful to ancient prototypes, but rather unified various stylistic tendencies. Official commissions of these buildings were few but significant. The first building based on ancient Mexican motifs built in the nineteenth century was the Monument to Cuauhtemoc executed by the engineer Francisco Jiménez and the sculptor Miguel Noreña (1878–87). The monument consisted of a sculpture of Cuauhtemoc resting on a tall pedestal. This pedestal incorporated elements from various pre-Hispanic buildings and sculpture. Cuauhtemoc, the last Mexica ruler, was famous for his resistance to Spanish colonization and later became a symbol of resistance to foreign intervention in general. The placement of this monument in the Avenida de la Reforma, an artery connecting luxurious neighborhoods housing most of Mexico's foreigners, implied Mexico's opposition to foreign intervention. This was a powerful statement given that in the nineteenth century, Mexico suffered substantial territorial losses during the U.S.-Mexican War and later confronted the French Intervention of 1862 to 1867.

The next important Neoindigenista commission was the Pavilion of Mexico in the 1889 Paris World Exhibition designed by Antonio M. Anza and Antonio Peñafiel. Like Boari's National Theater, this building manifested the dual goal of integrating Mexico into modernity and exalting local traditions. The pavilion's plan was based on the Beaux Arts tradition of design, emphasizing regularity and symmetry; but the decorations celebrated Mexico's ancient past. The main entrance was based on various Classic and Postclassic central Mexican buildings, particularly the Temple of Xochicalco. Relief sculptures on the front facade of the building represented mythological figures and Mexica rulers. Although these figures were based on the *Florentine Codex,* the final products took on the classical features and dramatic gestures of French academic sculpture. Constructed with an iron structure and glass, marble, cement, iron, and zinc decorations, the pavilion united two different images: a preindustrial past and a technologically sophisticated present. The use of industrial materials suggested that Mexico was as capable of building as the most powerful lands; the indigenous decorations pointed to Mexico's distinctiveness, implying its resistance to assimilation by another nation.

The choice of ancient Mexican architecture to represent the Mexican nation was influenced at least in part by the great interest that Europeans—particularly the French—demonstrated for Mexican archaeology. In 1864, along with the French intervention, Napoleón III sent an archaeological commission to study Mexican ruins. For the Paris World Exhibition of 1867, the French exhibited a model of the Temple of Xochicalco. During the late Porfiriato, the Mexican government aggressively sought French investment in Mexico with the hope of counterbalancing U.S. influence. The final design for the 1889 pavilion of Mexico was chosen with the help of French critics at the request of a Mexican delegate to the exposition. Thus, in addition to nationalistic concerns, Mexico's representation of itself in architecture was intimately linked with its goals in international politics.

In addition to exemplifying pre-Hispanic revival architecture during the Porfiriato, the Pavilion of Mexico in the 1889 Paris World Exhibition was important because of the theory it generated. At the beginning of the twentieth century, Luis Salazar, an architect and engineer who participated in the government-sponsored competition for the building's design, enthusiastically encouraged architects to create a national style of architecture based on the study of pre-Hispanic ruins (Salazar 1898). His writings would be influential for the nationalistic tendencies in Mexican architecture which developed during the second and third decade of the twentieth century. Other nineteenth-century buildings incorporating pre-Hispanic decorative motifs include the Monument to Benito Juárez in Paseo Juárez, Oaxaca (1899), and a triumphal arch commissioned by the state of Yucatán for the visit of Porfirio Díaz to Merida in 1906.

New Materials

During the second half of the nineteenth century, new building materials including glass, iron, and reinforced concrete were introduced to Mexican architecture. Metallic architecture included buildings in various stylistic tendencies. Iron and reinforced concrete structures frequently were covered with other materials and made to look like buildings in traditional styles.

Students of architecture in Mexico first became familiar with the use of iron as a structural material during Cavallari's term as director of the academy. Initially, iron was used only for discrete parts of the building such as the roof, decorative elements, and outdoor furniture. Iron details often imitated the forms of architectural elements in traditional styles. During the Porfiriato, iron was employed for the whole structure of buildings. At first, this was more common in undecorated utilitarian structures, which in Mexico as in the rest of the world provided important precedents for modern architecture. These utilitarian buildings include the railway station Mexico-Veracruz in Buena Vista, Mexico City (1878); the Metepec-Atlixco Factory in Puebla (c.1889–99); the Slaughterhouse San Lucas in Mexico City by Antonio Torres Torija (1893–95); the glass workshop and warehouse at the factory of Pellandini and Son in Mexico City (begun 1898); and the Mexican Cigarette Factory in Mexico City (1900). Buildings of various stylistic tendencies with iron structures include the Legislative Palace (1905); the National Theater (Palacio de Bellas Artes, 1904); the Central Post Office Building (1902–07); the Secretariat of Communications (1902–11); La Esmeralda Jewelry Store by Eleuterio Méndez (1890–92); the Mercantile Center (1896–97); and the Casa Boker (1898) and La Mutua (1900), both designed by the American firm De Lemos y Cordes. It shall be noted that the iron used for most of these buildings was imported. This meant that in order to be able to con-

Church of the Sagrada Familia, Mexico City, by Manuel Gorozpe and Miguel Rebolledo, 1910–12
Photo courtesy of Archivo Fotográfico, Instituto de Investigaciones Estéticas de la UNAM

struct a cosmopolitan image of itself, Mexico made itself dependent on other countries, reduplicating the colonial relation.

Reinforced concrete was introduced to Mexico by an association formed by the engineers Miguel Rebolledo, Fernando González, and Angel Ortiz Monasterio, a brigadier who previously had worked with Hennebique in Paris. The first constructions with these materials took place in 1903, but commissions were few because the system was thought to be inappropriate to Mexico's elevation. Later buildings in reinforced concrete include the Church of the Sagrada Familia by Manuel Gorozpe and Miguel Rebolledo (1910–12) and the Monument to Benito Juárez by Guillermo de Heredia (1910), both in Mexico City. The Juárez Monument exemplifies the tendency to cover iron and reinforced concrete structures with other materials, as marble was used to cover the concrete.

Conclusion

The history of nineteenth-century Mexican architecture is in need of serious revision. So far, investigators have focused on the Porfiriato, when building was most abundant. Although these studies have been basic to the discipline, architecture from the first two-thirds of the century, the period of instability, might illuminate the processes through which buildings are allowed to come into existence. More attention needs to be given to the social and institutional context of the production of specific buildings, as stylistic classification is of little value in the context of eclecticism.

During the Porfiriato, patrons and practitioners of architecture manifested two impulses: to create an architecture that would indicate Mexico's participation in modernity and to emphasize Mexico's difference from other countries through the incorporation of local characteristics into the architecture. The first goal took precedence over the second during most of the nineteenth century.

A brief examination of the Palace of Fine Arts and the Pavilion of Mexico in the 1889 Paris World Exhibition revealed that the Porfirian regime chose to represent Mexico as an independent, wealthy, and powerful country. This representation obscured painful realities of the nation, since despite growing modernization, Mexico was economically dependent on the industrialized nations, and most of the Mexican population lived in poverty.

The representation of the local in Mexican architecture was achieved mainly though themes and decorative motifs inspired by pre-Hispanic antiquity. These representations were essential to the construction of a common heritage by which the nation might be unified. This emphasis on the ancient past distracted the public's attention from the elites' and the government's contemporary mistreatment of indigenous peoples.

Attempts during the nineteenth century to represent national identity through architecture laid a groundwork for further experimentation. After the Mexican Revolution, successive Mexican regimes would use the pre-Hispanic past to represent the nation. Later architects also took inspiration from the architecture of the colonial period and regional architecture as the creation of a genuinely Mexican architecture became a pressing issue during the twentieth century.

Select Bibliography

Anderson, Benedict, *Imagined Communities*. London: Verso, 1983.

Burns, Bradford, *The Poverty of Progress*. Berkeley: University of California Press, 1980.

Fernández, Maria, *In the Image of the Other: A Call for Re-evaluation of National Identity*. Austin: Center for the Study of American Architecture, School of Architecture, University of Texas, 1992.

_____, "The representation of National Identity in Mexican Architecture: Two Case Studies (1680 and 1889)." Ph.D. diss., Columbia University, New York, 1993.

Hall, Stuart, "Old and New Identities, Old and New Ethnicities." In *Culture, Globalization, and The World System,* edited by Anthony King. Binghamton: State University of New York at Binghamton, 1991.

Mariategui, Carlos, *Seven Interpretative Essays on Peruvian Reality*. Austin: University of Texas Press, 1971.

Porphyrios, Demitri, "Notes on a Method." *On the Methodology of Architectural History. Architectural Design Profile* 96–104 (1981).

Reese, Thomas F., and Carol McMichael Reese, *Revolutionary Urban Legacies: Porfirio Díaz's Celebrations of the Centennial of Mexican Independence in 1910*. Mexico City: UNAM, 1994.

—María Fernández

Architecture: Twentieth Century

During the first three decades of the twentieth century, Mexican architects became preoccupied with the creation of a national architecture expressive of the new society brought about by the Revolution. Some of the stylistic tendencies explored as solutions were revivals of local historic building traditions. It was soon discovered that these did not meet the needs of contemporary life, however, and modern architecture became the preferred idiom. The dialectic between the local and the international already present in nineteenth-century Mexican architecture continued. The tensions and interactions between local and international currents would be at the forefront of architectural debates and practice during the entire century.

Throughout the century, the Mexican state played a crucial role in the development and representation of Mexican national identity in architecture. Successive governments encouraged architects to create nationalist buildings and commissioned grandiose projects that functioned as symbols of the nation. In the beginning of the century various administrations favored the colonial revival style; later, with the exception of a brief period of functionalism, a synthesis of pre-Hispanic decorative traditions and modern architecture was preferred. By the 1950s these developments resulted in a synthesis of international and local styles that earned Mexican architecture international acclaim. During the last four decades of the century, private capital increasingly participated in the construction of Mexican national identity, as individuals and corporations commissioned important buildings.

In contrast to the study of architecture of the previous century, the study of twentieth-century Mexican architecture is less concerned with the classification of buildings than with the role of specific architects in the development of a national architecture. This approach originates in the history of Western architecture, where the architect is traditionally cast in the heroic role of genius. Such rendering contrasts with the presumed anonymity of builders in regional and pre-Hispanic architecture.

Despite a wealth of scholarship on twentieth-century Mexican architecture, various writers agree on the necessity for a more critical approach to the field. As in other parts of the world, in Mexico the job of the architectural historian is often conceived as documenting the works of great architects, or in a revisionist historian mode, giving deserved recognition to figures excluded from the canon. Critical discussion of the work is often unwelcome to both architects and critics.

A critical approach should be concerned not only with the evaluation of aesthetics and the architectural function of buildings but also with the relation of architecture to Mexico's social, political, and economic structures. The writing of such a history is a difficult project for various reasons. Contemporary scholars writing about the latter part of the century often lack the historical and critical distance to identify the relation between architecture and relevant contexts. A contextual analysis of a building is usually more time consuming than a formal analysis, as the former is dependent on archival information that is not always readily available. In addition, it is risky for scholars to write critically about both living architects and those who occupy iconic positions in the history of Mexican architecture. The following essay should be seen not as an example of such a history, but as an outline of significant movements in twentieth-century Mexican architecture that raises questions basic to future criticism.

The history of twentieth-century Mexican architecture exemplifies the construction and affirmation of national identity and nationalism. Various scholars have written about the quest for identity during this period, but many of these studies are limited to identifying the elements and forms that make the buildings "quintessentially Mexican." In addition to recognizing visual constructs of nationhood, a critical history must investigate how these images fit with the everyday reality of the nation. To begin a critical appraisal of nationalist architecture one may ask: Are the images representative of the diversity within the nation? Which groups do the buildings represent? What aspects of the nation are emphasized? What aspects are consistently excluded? To what end? What institutions and individuals benefit from these representations? At what and whose expense are these symbols of nationhood constructed?

Although it is important for historians to recognize the accomplishments of individual architects, the writing of history in a contextual mode entails the possibility that architects and intellectuals contribute to agendas other than their own, knowingly or unknowingly. In any historical period, social and cultural imperatives are achieved through the collaboration of individuals and institutions (governmental, educational, commercial). Individuals work for the advancement of private and institutional objectives but ultimately they may contribute to further more complex projects, often the goals of the state, and more recently, of international corporations.

Various cultural theorists have noted that nationalism is primarily a masculinist project. The existing history of nineteenth- and twentieth-century Mexican architecture supports this idea since it has been almost exclusively a history of men. Recent publications on Mexican architecture credit women collaborators in a few buildings, but the examples are scarce. Photographic illustrations in books on Mexican architecture attest to the education of women in the profession. Women appear among the men in architecture classes and meetings at various institutions, but little is known about the practice of these women as professionals. The erasure of women is characteristic of other regions and periods of architecture history and is indicative of the discipline's focus on elites, usually white and male. To correct this omission, historians might have to engage in a study of struggle, modest achievements, and perhaps even failure, a far cry from documenting the development of genius in the dominant tradition of architecture history.

Revivals

Between 1911 and 1934 Mexico experienced several revolts and seven changes of government, but the promise of the Revolution, the determination to forge a new society, persisted. Influential intellectuals of the period believed that the development of a new Mexican nation and consequently of a national character or identity, depended at least in part upon the creation of a homogeneous culture. The homogenization of the population was thought to be important not only in matters of art. Influential politicians and intellectuals including Manuel Gamio, Andrés Molina Enríquez, and José Vasconcelos proposed *mestizaje,* the mixture of Native Americans and European, as the mark of a new society, a new nation, and ultimately, a superior race. In architecture, the nationalism of this era was manifested as revivals of pre-Hispanic and colonial traditions. Although mixture of these two tendencies occurred infrequently, many architects designed buildings in each current simultaneously.

Neocolonial architecture was established and supported by various post-Revolutionary regimes. Venustiano Carranza (1917–20) decreed the exemption of federal tax to all citizens who constructed their houses in neocolonial style. Álvaro Obregón (1920–24) and Plutarco Elías Calles (1924–28) also commissioned buildings in this style.

One of the most influential theoreticians in the formulation of a Mexican architecture was Federico Mariscal. In his book *La patria y la arquitectura nacional* (1915), Mariscal proclaimed the colonial home as the most truthful expression of "the Mexican character." He justified this choice on the basis of *mestizaje.* Since the majority of the Mexican population was a mixture of Spanish and indigene, national architecture should be the one developed during colonial period, the era where the mestizo, "the true Mexican," originated. As professor of architecture at the National University, Mariscal influenced many architects during the second and third decades of the century.

Carlos Obregón Santacilia worked in both the colonial and pre-Hispanic revivals for a short period of time. The Pavilion of Mexico in the International exposition for the Centenary of the Independence of Brazil, designed by Obregón Santacilia in collaboration with Carlos Tarditi, included a number of colonial motifs including a profusely decorated central retablo around the main entrance. As a complement for the pavilion, the same architects designed a monument to Cuauhtemoc (the last Mexica/Aztec ruler) in which they incorporated pre-Hispanic sculptural motifs such as plumed serpents into the sculpture's pedestal. Favorably impressed with the pavilion, José Vasconcelos commissioned Obregón Santacilia to design the Benito Juárez Primary School (1923–25) in neocolonial style. As secretary of public education, Vasconcelos was instrumental in introducing neocolonial architecture in official buildings. Later buildings in this style include the Renovation of the National Palace by Augusto Petriccioli (1926) and the Departamento del Distrito Federal by Federico Mariscal and Fernando Beltrán y Puga (1934).

In the Secretaría de la Salubridad (1925–27), Obregón Santacilia utilized the figure of an eagle above the entrance, arcades fashioned after colonial buildings, and local materials such as gray stone from Xaltocan. The eagle was a symbol of the sun for late Postclassic central Mexican cultures. Geometrically defined volumes and the scarcity of applied decoration align this building with early modernism. The architecture does not emulate any historically accurate style; it is clear that the architect was more interested in suggesting his sources for ideological reasons than copying or making exact reproductions of traditional architecture.

In 1926, the Mexican government sponsored a contest for the pavilion of Mexico in the Iberoamerican Exposition in Seville. Both neocolonial and pre-Hispanic revival projects were submitted. The winner of the first contest was Ignacio Marquina, but owing to complaints by the other participants, two additional competitions were held. The commission was finally given to Manuel Amabilis. In both Marquina's and Amabilis's projects, ancient Mexican and specifically Maya decorative elements were used to cover structures derived from Western European architecture. As in the Secretaría de la Salubridad, neither building exemplifies any known style of ancient Mexican architecture. The unification of Western and ancient Mexican architecture was more important than archaeological correctness. In Amabilis's building the references to modernity and pre-Hispanic antiquity are striking even in relatively minor aspects, such as two reliefs set before the entrance: one representing physical labor and the other intellectual work. Partially derived from Maya dynastic stelae, the sculptures depict traditionally attired Maya lords among industrial elements such as cogs and pulleys. The images suggest Mexico's roots in a civilized antiquity and its power as an industrial nation in the present.

In the Yucatán, pre-Hispanic revival buildings were constructed at various times during the nineteenth and twentieth centuries. In the late nineteenth century, pre-Hispanic motifs were used to suggest the independence of Yucatán from Mexico by making reference to a glorious local past. This was primarily in the interest of local merchant elites eager to evade state control. After the Revolution, references to local antiquity were used to express socialist ideals and solidarity with the new Mexican state. Pre-Hispanic revival buildings of this period in Mérida include the Sanatorium Rendón Peniche (1919) attributed to Manuel Amabilis, La Casa del Pueblo by Angel Bachini (1928), the Building of the Diario del Sureste by Manuel and Max Amabilis in collaboration with the sculptor Rómulo Rozo (1946), the Parque de las Américas by Manuel and Max Amabilis (1945), and the Monumento a la Patria designed by Manuel Amabilis in collaboration with Rómulo Rozo (1945–56).

Colonial and pre-Hispanic revival buildings have in common the construction and affirmation of a normative "Mexicanness" based on a celebration of the past and the erasure of the contemporary indigene from the nation. Pre-Hispanic revivals proclaim ancient Mexican civilizations, primarily the Mexica and the Maya, as archetypal Mexicans. Pre-Hispanic architecture and decoration usually establish no links between ancient civilizations and contemporary indigenous peoples, although references to mestizos are present in various buildings. Colonial revivals uphold the mestizo as the quintessential Mexican. Indirectly, this establishes the middle-class individual as a model citizen. As in other areas of Latin America, in Mexico people of European heritage are traditionally associated with the upper class, mestizos with the middle class, and indigenes with the lower class. Gamio was explicit in this respect, since in his opinion the economic improvement of the Indian was a precondition for the ethnic unity of the population. Furthermore he regarded the middle-class individual, not the indigene, as the agent of change.

Modern Architecture

Modern architecture first became known in Mexico through foreign publications introduced by progressive practitioners. Around 1915, Eduardo Macedo y Arbeau educated his students in the architecture of Otto Wagner through the magazine *Moderne Bauformen.* During the 1920s, contemporary European and American architecture was known in Mexico through foreign magazines such as *Moderne Bauformen, L'Architecte, Architecture Vivant,* and *Architectural Record.* Soon, Mexican publications began to feature the new architecture. In 1924, *Excélsior* newspaper began a modern architecture section under the direction of Juan Galindo Pimentel and Bernardo Calderón. In 1925, the Tolteca Cement Company began publishing *Cemento,* a magazine that illustrated works by modern architects including Willem Marinus Dudok, Mallet Stevens, Erich Mendelsohn, Joseph Hoffmann, and Le Corbusier. In addition to illustrating works of modern architecture, the magazines featured adds for new materials and modern appliances such as vacuum cleaners and washing machines. *Cemento* was distributed in massive numbers, and hence was influential in educating the public in the properties of cement and in

creating desire for electric devices. Between 1929 and 1932, 30,000 copies of the magazine were issued and circulated.

The hybridity exalted as the key to Mexico's new identity, *mestizaje,* was also evident in the architecture of the period. Perhaps as a result of architects learning mainly from architectural magazines, the first modern buildings in Mexico exhibited a mixture of styles and local variations of established design ideas. In these respects, the buildings were comparable to Spanish colonial buildings in New Spain, which often were conceived from the study of European pattern books. Manuel Monasterio's house in Reforma (1922) and the National Treasury designed by Ortíz Monasterio in collaboration with Vicente Mendiola (1926) exemplify these tendencies. The house is basically a chalet from which ornamentation has been stripped in order to modernize it. The habit of eliminating the external ornaments of a building, regardless of style, was a common interpretation of modern architecture at this time. In the National Treasury, dark lines painted on each architectural member indicate corresponding parts of the building's iron skeleton as a sign of architectural honesty.

During the third decade of the century, José Villagrán García emerged as an influential theorist and practitioner. In 1925 he began teaching at the Escuela de Bellas Artes, later Escuela Nacional de Arquitectura, where his most acclaimed course was the theory of architecture (1926–76). Like the French theorist Julien Guadet, he emphasized the architectural program as the determining element of a composition. In Villagrán's view this prevented the architect from falling into the dangers of formalism, since a building resulted directly from an analysis of its functions. He stressed honesty and integrity in the use of architectural elements and materials as well as the idea that architecture should serve a social function. In the context of post-Revolutionary Mexico this meant that buildings should meet the necessities of the working classes. Despite his functionalist agenda, Villagrán also recognized the importance of spiritual or emotional aspects of architecture.

Starting with Villagrán García's Health Center (begun in 1926), and the Sanatorium at Huipilco, also by Villagrán (1929–36), buildings by Mexican architects manifested more sober interpretations of modern architecture. Nonetheless, it was an eclectic modernism that looked for source material in both turn-of-the-century European architecture, especially Austrian and German, and contemporary work. In the Sanatorium at Huipilco, Villagrán employed pilotis, a flat roof, and no applied decorations, but contrary to the international style the building's surface was broken by a weighty structure and sunshades. The use of rough concrete for the walls added to the building's impression of heaviness.

Modern architecture became established during the early 1930s when, with the support of the minister of education, Narciso Bassols, several young architects occupied state positions and were given important commissions. Villagrán worked as architect of the Department of Public Health from 1924 to 1935, Juan O'Gorman served as director of Construction for the Public Education Department from 1932 to 1935, and Juan Legarreta worked in the Section of Construction for the Department of Communications and Public Works. Between 1934 and 1940, Villagrán completed the Health Center, the Sanatorium at Huipilco, and the National Institute of Cardiology. Juan O'Gorman executed a great number of public schools, and Juan Legarreta designed low-cost housing projects. Best-known among these works are the developments at Balbuena (1932), La Vaquita (1934), and San Jacinto (1934). The two latter complexes were built after Legarreta's death but according to his plans.

The rise of modern architecture in Mexico coincided with the populist, progressive administration of President Lázaro Cárdenas (1934–40), which brought the first period of stability in Mexican politics since the rule of dictator Porfirio Díaz. During this period, O'Gorman, Legarreta, Álvaro Aburto, Enrique Yáñez, Augusto Pérez Palacios, and Carlos Tarditi, among others, adopted and radicalized Villagrán's teachings, giving more emphasis to the social function of buildings than to aesthetics. These architects were instrumental in establishing functionalism as the official expression of the Mexican state. The Cárdenas period was typified by attempts to bolster domestic production and curb the importation of foreign goods; nevertheless, in this case European imports—modern architecture and the philosophy of functionalism—were appropriated and transformed in the service of Mexican nationalism.

The success of the rhetoric of functionalism in Mexico was linked to economic limitations. In the opinion of Narciso Bassols, in functionalist architecture "not even a meter of land is wasted, nor the value of one peso nor a ray of sunshine." Functionalist buildings from this period exhibit unfinished materials, uncovered structural elements, and few luxury materials such as glass and aluminum.

Despite state support, many Mexican architects rejected the new architecture, favoring instead European and U.S. currents of art deco. In 1933, Alfonso Pallares, president of the Society of Mexican Architects (SAM), invited his colleagues to a debate with the purpose of determining the position that Mexico should take in respect to modern architecture. The participants were invited to consider the nature and relevance of functionalism, the role of the architect, and the importance of beauty in architecture. Progressive architects, including Legarreta, O'Gorman, and their colleague Álvaro Aburto, argued for a scientifically driven, technical architecture designed to meet Mexico's social needs. In their view, aesthetic considerations were superfluous in the design of buildings. Legarreta voiced the most radical opinion: "A people who live in *jacales* (shacks) and round rooms cannot SPEAK architecture. We will build the houses of the people. Estheticians and rhetoricians, I hope they all die! They will later have their discussions."

Silvano Palafox disagreed with the idea that meeting the needs of the poor should be the primary function of architecture: "There is no doubt that in Mexico there are poor people, there are many poor people, but there are not only poor people. We have other social classes which are worthy of our attention . . . and we have no right to disregard them and much less to ostracize them only because . . . they do not have the misfortune of belonging to the destitute." In addition, the opposition criticized modern architecture for imposing foreign habits on Mexican people and "sterilizing" the personality of the user since formal simplification of the architecture was only a pretext for lack of imagination. The work of Federico Mariscal, Antonio G. Muñoz, and Silvano Palafox exemplify the design attitudes of established professionals during this period.

Functionalism in Mexico began as a socialist, utopian, and humanistic movement. It had as its main goal the solution of urgent housing needs of the majority of the Mexican population. It had as its basis the belief that every person, regardless of class or race, had the right to shelter and to a decent living. Yet, based on European theories, specially the early writings of Le Corbusier, it was oblivious to the legitimacy of indigenous building traditions.

Despite his claim that he designed architecture only according to technical and social considerations, O'Gorman produced some of the most aesthetically minded houses of the period, including the house/studio for Diego Rivera and the house for Frances Toor, both realized between 1929 and 1934. These works were characterized by small spaces, exposed structures, lack of external decoration, and emphasis on the sculptural values of specific elements such as staircases. In subsequent decades, particularly during the 1960s, functionalism in Mexico was to become academic and formalist, devoid of the humanitarian ideals that first inspired its development.

The populist philosophies of O'Gorman, Legarreta, and Villagrán were tremendously influential in Mexican architecture of the 1940s and 1950s, as functionalism became state policy. In 1938 a group of architects including Alberto Arai, Enrique Guerrero, and Raul Cacho founded the Union of Socialist Architects. In 1939 Hannes Meyer, director of the Bauhaus from 1928 to 1930, went to reside in Mexico at the invitation of the Secretariat of Education to create an Institute of Planning and Urbanism. Although his residence in Mexico was marked by problems caused by professional rivalries, Meyer's contribution to the development of functionalism in Mexico has been underestimated. He held influential positions including secretary of the Commissión de Planeación de Hospitales (1944), technical director in the Secretariat of Labor and Social Security (1942), coordinator of the Administrative Committee of the Federal Program for the Construction of Schools (1945–47). Enrique Yáñez, Raul Cacho, and José Luis Cuevas count among his followers.

Integración Plástica

The integration of art—especially mural painting—into architecture became established during José Vasconcelos's term as minister of education. This tradition continued to be important and became known as the "movement for plastic integration" during the 1950s. Some scholars believe that this movement was as short-lived as the architecture of the Mexican Revolution, but others hold that it continued to thrive in succeeding decades and still characterized much of Mexican architecture in the 1990s, particularly state commissions.

During the 1940s, Mexican architects employed the international style for popular and private housing, institutional, commercial, and religious buildings. As in previous Mexican architecture, functionalism was modified to meet national imperatives. Two important state commissions of popular housing were the Centro Urbano Presidente Alemán designed by Mario Pani and Salvador Ortega Flores (1947–49), and the Centro Urbano Presidente Juárez designed in 1950 by the same architects. These projects initiated many proposals for family apartment buildings (multifamiliares) sponsored by the state throughout Mexico. In these buildings, along with the Hospital de la Raza no. 1 (1945) and the Centro Médico Nacional (1954–58), both designed by Enrique Yáñez, the severity of functionalist architecture was modified to include mural paintings and sculptures. Carlos Mérida designed murals and sculptural

elements for the Multifamiliar Juárez; David Alfaro Siqueiros and Diego Rivera painted murals for the Hospital de la Raza; and José and Tomás Chávez Morado, Siqueiros, and Francisco Zúñiga, among others, contributed art works for the Centro Médico Nacional.

In the next decade, some Mexican architects designed fine buildings in the so-called international style, whereas others renewed their interest in the country's native architectural traditions. Regardless of style, however, most buildings employed modern building materials. Mexico's airport designed by Augusto Álvarez, Enrique Carral, and others (1953); the Secretariat of Labor and Social Prevention by Pedro Ramírez Vázquez and Rafael Mijárez (1953); Juan Sordo Madaleno's Calle Lieja Office Building (1956); as well as the Torre de Seguros Latinoamericana by Manuel de la Colina, Augusto Álvarez, and Adolfo Zeevaert (1950) exemplify transparent, seemingly weightless edifices achieved through the use of glass, steel, aluminum, and technical devices such as elevators and mechanisms to slide windows. The Torre Latinoamericana, a skyscraper of 40 floors, was the tallest building in Mexico at the time. During this period, tall office buildings became a sign of prosperity and proclaimed the triumph of capitalism in Mexico.

A few Mexican artists and architects denounced the International Style as a colonialist strategy and built works inspired by local traditions. The Anacahualli Museum (1943–57) designed by Diego Rivera, and Juan O'Gorman's house (1958, now destroyed) resulted from these attitudes. The Anacahualli Museum is a massive building reminiscent of the monumentality of pre-Hispanic architecture. It incorporates a variety of pre-Hispanic decorative and architectural motifs, including mural painting, but like previous pre-Hispanic revival buildings it is archaeologically faithful to no particular tradition. O'Gorman's house was planned around a natural cave, like the Pyramid of the Sun at Teotihuacan, and covered with stone mosaic. O'Gorman turned against modern architecture during the late 1930s because he came to regard it as a capitalist movement. Along with Rivera, he advocated a national modern architecture that incorporated pre-Hispanic building traditions and decorative elements including mural painting and polychrome sculpture as well as respect for the natural environment. Consequently, in buildings of this period he brought together modern architectural elements such as pilotis and flat roofs with nativistic motifs. The combination of styles in his buildings followed his belief that, for Mexico's survival as a culturally and economically

Torre de Seguros Latinoamericana, Mexico City,
by Manuel de la Colina, Augusto Álvarez, and
Adolfo Zeevaert, 1950
Photo courtesy of Archivo Fotográfico, Instituto de
Investigaciones Estéticas de la UNAM

independent nation, it was necessary to preserve cultural values while meeting modern needs.

The preceding discussion makes apparent that in Mexican architecture of the modernist period, the differentiation of international from nationalist and regionalist currents is not straightforward. The search for a national architecture that first flourished during the second and third decade of the century continued during the 1940s and 1950s. Like the nationalistic architecture built in the 1920s, these attempts to create a Mexican architecture often incorporated elements from colonial and pre-Hispanic art and architecture. The unification of art and architecture into a total work of art characterized these latter searches. While the tendency known as *integración plástica* had antecedents in architecture of the Porfiriato and of the 1920s, it became an acknowledged movement when a collaboration of architects and artists took the magazine *Espacios* as their forum in the 1950s.

Integración plástica was not restricted to a single period of Mexican architecture; rather, it is the hallmark of twentieth-century Mexican architecture. In addition to the Multifamiliar Juárez and the projects directed by Enrique Yáñez mentioned above, innumerable buildings successfully integrate art and architecture. Masterpieces built prior to 1960 include the Capilla de la Purísima in Monterrey by Enrique de la Mora (1948), the Capilla de la Medalla Milagrosa by Félix Candela (1954) , El Museo del Eco by Mathías Goeritz (1953), and Ciudad Universitaria (1950–56).

The ambitious Ciudad Universitaria (University City) project, made possible by postwar prosperity and liberal market economies, presents an image of the country simultaneously nationalistic and modern. Directed by Mario Pani and Enrique del Moral, University City was the work of many architects, and consolidated the movement of *integración plástica*. Some critics regard it as the culmination of 20 years of modern architecture in Mexico. It was indeed a project of tremendous importance because it unified diverse tendencies such as functionalism, nationalism, as well as intermediate and unique positions. In the same way that the notion of *mestizaje* foreshadowed by a century the postmodern celebration of hybridity, so the eclecticism and proclivities towards historicism and appropriation apparent in University City predate postmodernism in architecture.

Built on a site covered by volcanic lava 1,500 hundred years ago, University City presented an image of the national through the use of local materials including volcanic stones from the site and from other regions of Mexico; the incorporation and integration of pre-Hispanic architectural and decorative motifs; and the integration of artworks representative of Mexican Revolutionary art, such as mural paintings. While international style buildings embodied the image of prosperity that Mexican rulers were interested in projecting, references to local building traditions and the use of local materials aligned these buildings with nationalistic and Revolutionary ideals.

The Central Library at University City, designed by Juan O'Gorman, Gustavo Saavedra, and Juan Martínez de Velasco, became the best-known edifice in the complex. Like O'Gorman's house, the exterior is covered with stone mosaics. At the library these mosaics illustrate the history of Mexico. The images are arranged in a narrative plan reminiscent of some of the great murals of the post-Revolutionary period. Pre-Hispanic cosmogony is represented on the building's north side, Western cosmogony on south, and the Mexican Revolution and the modern world on the lateral facades.

The front facade of University City's stadium is ovoid, with a giant *talud* built of earth and volcanic stone. A *talud* is a sloping element that in

Mesoamerican pyramidal structures usually supports an overhanging element. In the stadium, the *talud* displays a mosaic by Diego Rivera. The building was designed by Augusto Pérez Palacios in collaboration with Raul Salinas Moro and Jorge Bravo Jiménez.

In the *frontones* (ball courts) by Alberto T. Arai, modern materials wear traditional dress. Designed as pyramidal forms, the structures are made of concrete covered with volcanic stone to suggest the solidity of pre-Hispanic buildings and to integrate the buildings to the local landscape.

The Pabellón de Rayos Cósmicos, by Félix Candela, represents an idiosyncratic tendency in Mexican architecture: the architecture of shells or *cascarones* for which Candela is best known. A disciple of the Catalan engineer Eduardo Torroja, Candela frequently relied on hyperbolic paraboloids to achieve organic forms in his structures. Candela's architecture is the physical realization of mathematical logic, as he seldom drew a building before its construction but simply described it with an equation. During the 1950s Candela designed shell-shaped, reinforced concrete covers for various marketplaces in Mexico City. The Pabellón de Rayos Cósmicos is conceived as a membrane; its hyperbolic vault is both wall and roof.

Ironically, buildings with nativistic motifs such as the Central Library served both as tourist attractions and as a propaganda tool for the government. Since the buildings were unique to the country, they were likely to attract foreigners. Indeed, it was foreigners who wrote the most about this architecture, particularly about O'Gorman's work. Thus O'Gorman may have helped the Mexican state to achieve an end that was opposite to his own intentions. After 1950 tourism became Mexico's greatest source of income, as well as the county's most important area of dependence on the United States.

During the administrations of Manuel Avila Camacho (1940–46), Miguel Alemán Valdés (1946–52), and the first two years of Adolfo Ruiz Cortines's term (1952–54), economic recovery was facilitated both by petroleum revenues and by the regimes' renewed interest in foreign investments. In addition, the aftermath of World War II favored the demand of Mexican products abroad and the reduction of foreign competition in the domestic market.

The great building projects, including University City, were constructed to signal Mexico's affluence. Yet Mexico's development was compromised. Despite various administrations' attempts to substitute Mexican-made products for imports, the value of imports continued to surpass the value of exports.

Ironically, the high quality of modern architecture built in Mexico during these years depended upon relaxed restrictions on imported construction materials. Only under such conditions could Mexicans obtain the materials required for the new building styles. Despite the claims that University City was economical owing to its utilization of local materials and workforce, its architects relied heavily on expensive imports.

The construction of University City was not a celebratory occasion for all Mexicans, as 65 million square feet (6 million square meters) of communal lands were expropriated for the project with the stipulation that the owners be given new homes. Of this land, 22 million square feet (2 million square meters) were used for the construction. Previous Mexican governments had taken similar measures. The Porfirio Díaz administration expropriated communal lands to renovate archaeological sites that later became tourist attractions. As late as 1922, some of the owners of these lands had not been remunerated. This suggests that the representation of national identity in Mexican architecture has an underside not frequently discussed in architectural history: the dispossession of common citizens for the construction of the spectacle of nationhood.

The integration of pre-Columbian forms and qualities into contemporary architectural idioms typified by the Central Library of O'Gorman, Saavedra, and de Velasco continued through the century, particularly in state commissions. In the Museo de Antropología by Pedro Ramírez Vázquez and others (1963), the wall around the patio is finished with a band or abstract ornament that is a translation of the so-called "Chac noses" found in Maya Puuc architecture to an abstract form. The Heróico Colegio Militar (1975) designed by Agustín Hernández and Manuel González Rul resembles pre-Hispanic ceremonial centers in the placement of buildings in large open spaces connected with avenues and in the monumentality of the edifices. Independent buildings within the complex are inspired by pre-Hispanic architecture and decoration. The armory and the covered swimming pool are pyramidal structures, the Edificio de Govierno forms a large, abstracted Chac mask. In Hernández's Hospital San Gerónimo (1975), each floor was designed to resemble a pyramid profile from Monte Albán. Other architects, including Abraham Zabludowsky, Teodoro González de León, Alejandro Zohn, Francisco Serrano, and Augusto Quijano Axle have incorporated characteristics of pre-Hispanic architecture such as monumentality, durability, solidity, and the preference for

Central Library, Ciudad Universitaria, Mexico City, by Juan O'Gorman, Gustavo Saavedra,
and Juan Martínez de Velazco, 1950–56
Photo courtesy of Archivo Fotográfico, Instituto de Investigaciones Estéticas de la UNAM

enclosed spaces. These architects have received numerous and important governmental and institutional commissions. Zabludowsky and González de León are responsible for Infonavit (1973), the Museo Rufino Tamayo (1975), El Colegio de Mexico (1975), the Universidad Pedagógica Nacional (1979), and the Central Edifice and financial centers for Banamex; Juan Francisco Serrano, Rafael Mijares, and Pedro Ramírez Vázquez were responsible for the Universidad Iberoamericana (1981–87).

Alejandro Zohn designed the Archives of the State of Jalisco and the Unidad Deportiva y Parque 14 de Febrero in Guadalajara, Jalisco (both in 1992). Teodoro González de León, Francisco Serrano, and Carlos Tejeda were responsible for the Palacio de Justicia Federal in Mexico City (1992). Such works indicate that monumental buildings that allude to the pre-Hispanic past still form the official image of Mexico. In addition, there is a tendency among contemporary architects to incorporate the landscape into architectural design. This tendency is related, although indirectly, to ancient Mexican cultures, as respect for the natural environment characterized pre-Hispanic architecture. The landscape architect Mario Schjetnan, whose most representative work is the Parque Tezozomoc in Azcapotzalco designed in collaboration with J. L. Perez and Jorge Calvillo, exemplifies this tendency.

Regionalism

An imprecise differentiation often is made between nationalist and regionalist architecture. In the opinion of Fernando González Gortázar, the difference between these two categories in one of scale and pretension: where nationalist architecture imitates monumental architecture from the past, often without the intention of reestablishing the original culture, regionalist architecture is closer to vernacular, anonymous architecture. Regionalist architecture seeks to master the local climate and use local materials and construction methods. Still, a hard distinction between nationalist and regionalist architecture is difficult to maintain. In the nationalist project of University City, local materials and construction methods were incorporated. On the other hand, Luis Barragán and Ricardo Legorreta, masters of regionalist architecture, occasionally have engaged in design projects involving the translation of pre-Hispanic traditions into modern forms.

Born in 1908, Barragán studied civil engineering at the Escuela Libre de Ingenieros in Guadalajara and undertook additional studies to qualify as an architect. In a trip to Europe from 1924 to 1925, he visited the Alhambra in Seville and became acquainted with Ferdinand Bac's books *Les Jardins Enchantés* and *Les Colombieres*. These works were to have a profound influence on his ouvre. Barragán's early works—two houses for Robles Castillo (1927–28), Enrique Aguilar's house (1928–31), and especially the house for Efraín González Luna (1928)—synthesize lessons learned from Hispano-Morisque architecture. Barragán was not alone in his interests. During the second and third decades of the century, Guadalajara-based architects including Ignacio Díaz Morales, Pedro Castellanos, and Rafael Urzúa designed buildings incorporating Spanish colonial and Mediterranean traditions. This was part of a larger movement of Spanish revival and Mediterranean architecture in Mexico and in the Western United States.

In 1936 Barragán moved to Mexico City and from that year to 1940 he worked on about 20 buildings in a stark rationalist style. Again, Barragán was working in harmony with the dominant movement of his time. Although little of it remains, Barragán's work from this period is important because it provided the basis for the stark simplicity of his later buildings. Barragán's mature works are characterized by minimalism and a masterful synthesis of multiple architectural and artistic traditions. This synthetic eclecticism makes his architecture both regional and at the same time "universal," or to use a more precise term, modern.

Barragán's buildings differ markedly from international style architecture because—along with the influences of Ferdinand Bac, Mies van der Rohe, Le Corbusier, the Bauhaus, De Stijl, Frederik Kiessler, and Richard Neutra—he combines ancient Mexican, Mexican vernacular and monastic architecture, Mediterranean traditions, Japanese and Islamic gardens, and the work of his friend and contemporary, the painter Chucho Reyes. Barragán's best-known works include the Jardines del Pedregal (1945–50); Antonio Galvéz's house in San Angel (1955); his own house in Francisco Ramírez street (1947); the Chapel for the Capuchinas Sacramentarias del Purisimo Corazón de Maria (1952–55); Satellite City Towers, designed in collaboration with Mathías Goeritz (1957); Las Arboledas residential subdivision (1958–61); Los Clubes Residential subdivision (1963–64); the San Cristóbal Stables and the Folke Egerstrom House at Los Clubes (1967–68); and Francisco Gilardi's house in Mexico City (1976).

In the Jardines del Pedregal, Barragán designed an elite residential area on a landscape of volcanic rock interspersed with small green valleys. The complex is reminiscent of pre-Hispanic ceremonial centers in the respect for the natural landscape, the use of solid stone walls as defining elements, and the interconnection of plazas, causeways, and buildings. The arrangement of rocks, native plants, water, and fountains echoes pre-Hispanic, Mediterranean, Islamic, and Japanese gardens, while the orthogonality of the buildings affirms the presence of modern architecture. It is difficult however, to attribute any one architectural element to a single tradition.

His own house brings together the simplicity, placidity, and privacy of Spanish colonial monasteries with powerful color harmonies and tensions, and constructivist geometries. Also present are surrealistic details such as the sculpture of a white galloping horse inside an otherwise empty courtyard. This motif is reminiscent of the paintings of Giorgio De Chirico and Leonora Carrington.

The Chapel for the Capuchinas Sacramentarias, considered to be his masterpiece, is a succession of severe, unadorned spaces that seem to emanate light. This effect is achieved through the use of stained glass panels and lattices. Colored and filtered by the glass, light is the principal design element. While stained glass was commonly used in Gothic cathedrals, latticework is an element of Islamic and Hispano-Morisque architecture.

At Los Clubes, a residential estate developed and designed by Barragán for horse riding enthusiasts, water becomes a primary element of the design. The Lover's Fountain within the complex serves a practical function—a drinking trough for horses and riders—but at the same time it is a mirror and part of an elaborate stage set through which the riders can parade.

With exception of his brief involvement in the design of the gardens of University City, Barragán was not offered any state commissions. Most of his buildings were small-scale, low-tech, and designed for specific individuals. This fact does not exclude a strong nationalist component in his architecture, however, since to a large extent his work was inspired by vernacular traditions. Profound love for the architecture and artistic traditions of his native land are evident throughout.

When Barragán received the Pritzker Architecture Prize in 1980, he described the guiding lights of his architecture: religion, beauty, silence, solitude, serenity, joy, death, gardens, fountains, architecture (including the architecture of Mexican villages and provincial towns and Mexican monasteries), the art of seeing, and nostalgia. He stated, "Underlying all that I have achieved—such as it is—are the memories of my father's ranch, where I spent my childhood and adolescence. In my work I have always striven to adapt the magic of those remote nostalgic years to the needs of modern living."

Illustrated in catalogs or observed in isolation within their specific settings, Barragán's buildings offer a quaint, tranquil, romantic and colorful image of Mexico. Viewed within the context of Mexico City after 1940—the accelerated population growth, the deterioration of the city's center, the stratification of the population in *fraccion-amientos* or *colonias* according to economic and racial affiliations, the confinement of the working classes and the poor to ever sprawling *villas miseria* (shantytowns), and the flight of the rich to fortress homes in the suburbs—Barragán's architecture takes on a different character. The "architecture of silence" that he lovingly designed were havens for the privileged, eager to leave the increasing pollution, traffic problems, overcrowding, and noise of the decaying city. George Bataille thought of the slaughterhouse as the necessary complement of the museum. In the history of twentieth-century Mexican architecture, Mexico's shanties are the repressed, the ghostly other of Barragán's exquisite work and others like it.

On the other hand, many Mexican architects continued to spend at least part of their careers designing low-cost popular housing, although this work is infrequently included in the history of Mexican architecture. Since the Revolution, the government has sponsored numerous projects for low-income housing. These steadily decreased during the last three decades of the century as a result of budget cuts in social services. In their place, self-made shelters proliferated in urban areas. It is estimated that in 1990 20 million Mexicans lived in self-made houses. By the year 2000, this number is expected to increase to 25 million.

Barragán was not alone in his attempts to incorporate local vernacular tradition into modern architecture. During the 1940s and 1950s in Mexico City, a number of architects including as Enrique del Moral, Juan Sordo Madaleno, and Max Cetto welded functionalist architecture with a sensibility for local building materials and landscape. Since its foundation in 1948, the School of Architecture at the University of Guadalajara has encouraged an architecture based on the functionalist precepts of Villagrán, but with attention to the local climate, materials, and craft traditions. Like the work of Barragán, this architecture makes ample use of patios, plazas, terraces, solid walls and lattice windows. Architects from this school, known as the Escuela Tapatía, include its founder, Ignacio Díaz Morales, Fernando González Gortázar, Gabriel Chávez de la Mora, and Andrés Casillas.

Ricardo Legorreta learned his basic vocabulary from Barragán but went on to elaborate it and to apply it in a new form. While Barragán preferred small-scale residential projects, often in a wild landscape or in a rural context, Legorreta has favored elaborate monumental projects inserted into urban contexts. It is not accidental that his most successful projects are factory complexes and hotels.

Organized around patios and plazas, Legorreta's monumental buildings suggest the placidity of Mexican monastic architecture. Like Barragán, he employs color, light, and water as structural elements and translates elements of various architectural and artistic traditions into a modern idiom. In the Centro Banamex in Monterrey spaces are arranged around patios and plazas. Light penetrates the building through small windows reminiscent of North African architecture. The design of Solana, Westlake/Southlake, Texas (1986)—a complex of office buildings, village center, hotel, and recreation facilities developed by IBM in partnership with Maguire Thomas—consists of a series of compounds defined by walls. The scheme is inspired by Mexican haciendas and by the Convent of the Desierto de los Leones near Mexico City. Legorreta designed the complex in collaboration Peter Walker, Barton Myers, and Romualdo Giurgola. For Legorreta the wall is the ultimate expression of Mexican culture: "We live and see Mexico in the walls, tragedy, strength, joy, romance, peace, light, and color . . . the day the wall dies, Mexico will die."

In Legorreta's Casa de Rancho, California (1987), water runs all though the house, serving different functions: lap pool, swimming pool, jacuzzi, and fountain. A similar concept is discernible in Barragán's Francisco Gilardi House (1976), where the pool is placed next to the living-dining area without any divisions between the two spaces.

Faithful to the tradition of *integración plástica,* Legorreta views a building as a total work of art. His first important work, the Hotel Camino Real in Mexico City (1968) incorporates murals, numerous sculptures, fountains, and graphic design. The inclusion of these artworks in the design delayed the completion of the building by many months but added significantly to its visual appeal.

Legorreta differs most markedly from Barragán in the inclusion of humorous elements in his architecture. In addition to adding a personal touch, these motifs fit within a tradition in Mexican culture of delight in the unexpected and the absurd. At the pool of the Hotel Camino Real in Cancún (1975), for instance, the bartenders operate in an area literally submerged within the water, and clients order drinks sitting on underwater stools.

Like other Mexican architects, Legorreta demonstrates interest in integrating architecture to its natural surroundings. In the Hacienda Cabo San Lucas in Baja California (1972) and the Hotel Camino Real at Ixtapa (1981), the buildings are arranged tightly in the terrain and painted in colors similar to the natural colors of the earth. The buildings are literally buried in the sandy landscapes. In the Hacienda Cabo San Lucas, access to the building is gained by stairs to interior patios as in Native American kivas. Reference to vernacular architecture is also evident in the Chrysler Factory in Automex, Toluca (1964), designed in collaboration with Mathías Goeritz. The complex is inspired by a series of granaries near Santa Mónica, Zacatecas.

In Barragán's architecture references to the vernacular stimulate memory; in Legorreta's hotels, vernacular allusions give the user, especially tourists, a taste of the local within safe boundaries. In vacation resorts, cultured versions of regional architecture may be the visitors' only experience of Mexican architecture. Legorreta's commissions abroad indicate the increasing internationalization of Mexican architecture. The architect's works in the United States suggest the increasing cooperation between Mexican and U.S. elites and business interests, which made possible the North American Free Trade Agreement.

Various critics have noted that Mexican regionalism became formulaic as many architects follow lessons from Barragán and Legorreta without paying attention to regional and climatic differences. Toward the end of the century, a tropical architecture developed, primarily in private residences in the coastal areas of the country. This architecture is characterized by open spaces, local materials, and architectural elements including thatched roofs, and tree trunks in their natural state used as support members. Although these elements have been described as belonging to colonial architecture, they form part of long-standing indigenous traditions in various areas of Mexico. Marco Aldaco and Diego Villaseñor are the two most important exponents of the tropical tendency.

Postmodernism

For many years Mexican architects were unenthusiastic about postmodernism. In the opinion of González Gortázar, Mexican architects owe a debt to Barragán for giving them the tools to fight this tendency: "He proved unnecessary the systematic and sterilizing exhumation of prestigious cadavers, the misnamed 'historical references,' so enthusiastically and unsuccessfully undertaken in other places. Only those who do not have parents look for their parents or invent them." Subsequently, various Mexican architects including Juan Palomar, Carlos Petersen, Ricardo Padilla, Jorge Estévez, Juan Carlos Name and Associates, Antonio Attolini Lack, and the firm of Gustavo Eichelmann Nava and Gonzalo Gómez Palacio y Campos have built work in a postmodern vein.

During the late 1980s and early 1990s, Mexico became increasingly integrated into transnational capitalism, with the reduction of nationalized industry, intensified foreign investments, and the proliferation of foreign-owned assembly plants in the north part of the country. At the same time, postmodernism arrived as a theory and a style. This is a suitable match, since like multinational capitalism, Postmodernism appropriates elements from diverse traditions. Multinational capital has not been wholly beneficial for Mexican architecture. Seeking to receive optimum return for their land investments, foreign investors have sometimes disregarded the seismic conditions of Mexico City and proposed huge projects more appropriate to other regions. In the 1990s, as a response to developers' and investors' pressure, the Mexican authorities relaxed building controls in the center of Mexico City, a seismically fragile zone. The tendency toward monumentality in Mexican architecture of the 1990s ignores the destructive regularity of earthquakes in Mexico City, the most recent of which took place in 1985.

Since the late 1950s, the representation of identity in Mexican architecture has been increasingly defined by private capital. But the Mexican state still plays a part in the representation of national identity. During the regime of President Carlos Salinas de Gortari (1988–94), for instance, Mexican elites dreamed of the integration of Mexico into the First World by virtue of the North American Free Trade Agreement. To some, this integration implied a need for greater technical quality in Mexican architecture, since it meant that Mexican buildings would have to compete with the architecture of the developed countries.

This sentiment coincided with the construction in Mexico of a number of buildings that favored international currents and technologically sophisticated materials. Practitioners who built work in this vein between 1989 and 1995 include Luis Vicente Flores; TEN Arquitectos: Enrique Norten y Bernardo Gómez-Pimineta; and the partnerships Óscar Bulnes Valero and Bernardo Lira López; Agustín Landa Verléz and Jorge Alesio Robles; Francisco López Guerra and A. López-Guerra; and Aurelio Nuño and Associates.

One of the most impressive commissions of the Salinas de Gortari government was the Centro Nacional de las Artes, an extensive complex in which each building was assigned to a prestigious Mexican architect. Legorreta was entrusted the Escuela Nacional de Artes Plásticas, the Edificio Central, and the Torre de Investigación Artística. As usual, he drew from a variety of traditions. The Escuela Nacional de Artes Plásticas includes a round building that recalls the Caracol at Chichen Itza and a multidomed structure reminiscent of both the Monastery of San Francisco at Cholula and the Great Mosque at Córdoba. Legorreta previously employed multiple domes in the Cathedral of Managua, Nicaragua (1993).

The Conservatorio de Música by Teodoro González de León and Ernesto Betancourt takes a surprising postmodern character. Groups of inclined pilasters supporting a frieze in the building's courtyard give the building the appearance of imbalance. This feigned instability recalls aspects of Bernard Tschumi's Parc de la Villete in Paris.

The Teatro de las Artes by Grupo LBC (by Alfonso López Baz and Xavier Calleja) includes references to Classical architecture and a moving Baroque facade. The Escuela Nacional de Danza by Luis Vicente Flores and Associates, and the Escuela Nacional de Arte Teatral by TEN Arquitectos: Enrique Norten y Bernardo Gómez- Pimienta, both exhibit sophisticated steel structures and glass membranes.

The Centro Nacional de las Artes is more than a collection of masterful buildings. The architecture houses advanced teaching, research, and production facilities. On site is the national cultural television channel, Estudios Churubusco, the largest film studio in Mexico, and the Centro Nacional Multimedia, a research center for artists that is the best equipped facility of its kind in the Americas. It includes, among other things, computer, video, sound, virtual reality, and robotic studios as well as exhibition spaces. The center's educational projects include documentation of Mexico's museums on CD ROM and virtual reality simulations of archaeological sites such as Tenochtitlan and Monte Albán.

The architecture of the Centro Nacional de las Artes evidences two concerns that have been at the heart of the representation of national identity since

Escuela Nacional de Artes Plásticas,
Centro Nacional de las Artes, Mexico City,
by Ricardo Legorreta, 1994
Photo courtesy of Archivo Fotográfico, Instituto de
Investigaciones Estéticas de la UNAM

the nineteenth century: the representation of the local and the expression of Mexico's international character. In contrast to nineteenth-century pavilion builders, an architect such as Legorreta does not have to choose between international architecture and historic regionalism, as his work incorporates both tendencies. As in the era of Porfirio Díaz, at the end of the twentieth century Mexico defines its identity in terms of its culturally rich past and its capacity to achieve economic and technical development at the same level as the United States and Western Europe.

Conclusions

For all but a brief period during the 1930s, the representation of national identity in Mexican architecture during the last two centuries supports a narrative or glorious antecedents, unproblematic *mestizaje*, modernity, and affluence. Where pre-Hispanic revival architecture and its elaborations affirm the foundations of the country's greatness in the pre-Hispanic past, architecture based on the colonial period celebrates the hybridity resulting from colonization. During the first two decades of the twentieth century, colonial revival architecture upheld the mestizo as the ideal representative of the Mexican nation. International currents of architecture have been employed to indicate Mexico's participation in modernity and international commerce. These constructions of Mexican national identity have been created by Mexican urban and intellectual elites and have been supported and appropriated by the state and, more recently, by private capital.

That there is some validity in these representations is undeniable. Pre-Hispanic cultures including the Maya and the Mexica were indeed complex civilizations that flourished in Mexican soil and whose significant contributions to world heritage continue to be revealed. Just as the mixture of Spanish and Native Mexican gave rise to the mestizo, the Spanish Conquest of Mexico resulted in new types of architecture. Simultaneously, by virtue of its colonization, Mexico became integrated into the culture of the Western European world and has partaken in western intellectual and architectural currents since the sixteenth century.

During the 1930s Mexico felt the international wave of socialism. In the next two decades, aided by postwar prosperity, the Mexican state invested in impressive social service projects including housing, and public health and educational facilities. Since the colonial period, Mexico has had its share of wealthy families. During the early 1990s Mexico boasted to have at least quadrupled its number of resident millionaires. This wealth, combined with national aspirations to industrialization, resulted in a continuous but partial "modernization" parallel with that of Europe and the United States.

Because the nation is rooted in history, no representation of national identity is ever complete. The pre-Hispanic and colonial past, affluence, and modernity are aspects of the Mexican nation that are constantly reinterpreted and reconstituted. Representations of the nation in architecture omit allusions to conflict and contradiction. Consistently mining from the architecture and from its documentation are narratives or at least indications of alternative ways of experiencing the nation.

Inconsistencies in the traditional narratives of nationhood are exposed not through individual buildings but through fissures that open between the monuments to the viewer traveling the city. Pollution, poverty, destitution, and desperation are evident everywhere. The state offers little help and has no answers. Elites benefit from the traditional representations of the nation precisely because they cover up what is important to repress. The state supports homogeneous and harmonic representations of nationhood since to admit dissonance is threatening to the social order and to state control. In some cases, accepting contradictions is tantamount to admitting responsibility for the marginalization and dispossession of a large part of the Mexican population.

Architects in various countries have shown that it is indeed possible to represent inconsistencies. The problem is to obtain commissions to materialize such projects, since more often than not architects depend on the state and affluent patrons for commissions. More appropriate than a proposal on how best to represent the nation is to question the appropriateness and the relevance of representing the nation in architecture today. In recent years, in many parts of the world, private interest represented by transnational corporations take precedence over public interest, and the traditional roles of the state, particularly those of the welfare state, become the province of private enterprise.

In Mexico, as in other Latin American countries, individuals' alliances to the nation are increasingly replaced by identification with ethnic and class-based consumer identities as well as with smaller communities and interest groups. Consumer identities transcend national boundaries, as does the economic order in global capitalism.

It has been argued that in the late twentieth century it has become problematic to identify culture, nation, and ethnicity because traditional signifiers of these constructs now floated in an undefined geographical space. One can find McDonald's, Guatemalan textiles, Navajo and Persian rugs in any corner of the globe. It is difficult to define the nation geographically as migration and nomadism increasingly characterize contemporary human experience. It is more difficult to maintain the distinction between First and Third World as we find Third World enclaves in First World settings, and vice versa.

In view of these developments, the representation of national identity in architecture is fatally compromised. Now more than ever, it is crucial for architects and critics to invent critical practices to subvert and reconfigure the idea of nation. As Gyan Prakash said in another context, "the urge to fashion a strategic response to the prevailing configuration of knowledge and power requires that we think along differentiated, interpolated, mobile, and unsettling lines.

Select Bibliography
Born, Esther, *The New Architecture in Mexico*. New York: The Architectural Record, 1937.

McClintock, Anne, *Imperial Leather*. London: Routledge, 1995.

Rispa, Raul, editor, *Barragán: The Complete Works*. Princeton, New Jersey: Princeton Architectural Press, 1996.

Ruíz Barbarín, Antonio, "Rationalist Stage." In *Barragán: The Complete Works,* edited by Raul Rispa. Princeton, New Jersey: Princeton Architectural Press, 1996.

—María Fernández

Ayutla, Revolution of

The Revolution of Ayutla is, in scholar Edmundo O'Gorman's words, a "paradox" for the historian. It has been hailed as the starting point of the Reforma, allegedly one of the most profound transformations in the nineteenth century, which supposedly finally broke with the "old régime" and ushered "modernity" into Mexico. Nevertheless, its origin, and what has given the movement its name, is the Plan of Ayutla, proclaimed on March 1, 1854, in a small town in the state of Guerrero, by an obscure colonel, Florencio Villarreal, whom the scholar Felipe Tena Ramírez describes as the typical praetorian with no convictions. The plan's vague content was far from innovative: it demanded the impeachment of the current government, in this case, Antonio López de Santa Anna's dictatorial regime, which had held power since April 1853; the convocation of a national congress, which would constitute the nation as a "popular, representative republic" (Article 5); the

lowering of commercial tariffs (Article 6); and the protection of the army, as the "mainstay of order and social guarantees" (article 6). Thus, the plan placed itself in a long list of vaguely liberal military *pronunciamientos* that riddled the first half of the nineteenth century in Mexico. Also in typical fashion, the plan offered the leadership of the armed movement to men of privilege and political and military clout, in this case, Juan Álvarez and Nicolas Bravo, both of whom had fought in the War of Independence. Álvarez would soon become the movement's supreme commander, even though it would be recently retired colonel Ignacio Comonfort, Álvarez's protégé, who would direct most military operations outside Guerrero.

The plan would be reformed by Comonfort a few days later (March 11, 1854) in Acapulco. The term "departments," which implied a centralist system, replaced that of "states." The reformed plan stated that only "liberal"—instead of "republican"—institutions were convenient to the country, but added that the Republic had to be preserved from becoming a "ridiculous monarchy . . . contrary to our character and customs." These modifications reflected both Comonfort's legalistic convictions—the country was in fact divided into departments at the time—and his desire to attract the more moderate elements among both Liberals and Conservatives. His stated objective was to avoid imposing any single system of government on the "national will," which would be known only when expressed through the constituent congress. But by ruling out monarchy as a possibility, and thereby imposing limitations on the national will, Comonfort's reforms in fact reflected the real fear of many political men at the time that a monarchical system could be spawned legally, by a popularly elected congress.

Thus, the Plan of Ayutla, in both its original and reformed versions, was hardly an earth-shattering document. It reflected, as noted by the scholar Edmundo O'Gorman, not a rebellion against a system, but against the person of the dictator. Although "liberal" and republican in broad terms, it did not in fact propose a "modern" state project: it aimed to protect the privileges of one of the state's constituent groups—the army—that challenged the authority of the embryonic nation-state, and it did not touch on the issue of church-state relations, which was to preoccupy subsequent reforms. Nevertheless, it sparked a series of nation-wide armed movements, which culminated with the fall of the dictatorial government. Santa Anna, who during the first half of the century had been hailed regularly by different political groups as the country's only possible savior, was never to return to power again. Adding to the paradox, the Ayutla Revolution has become a historiographical watershed because it seemingly inaugurated the Reforma, a period that traditional historiography has exalted as one of three "key" moments—with Independence and Revolution—in Mexico's national history. The official state rhetoric that aims to describe Mexican history as a shining, unbroken struggle between the unequivocally good, progressive Liberals and the unequivocally bad, reactionary Conservatives has enthroned Ayutla as a heroic, radically "liberal" movement, on par with the actions of José María Morelos, Miguel Hidalgo y Cotilla, Emiliano Zapata, and Venustiano Carranza, and the ideological wellspring for the political and socially activity of the post-Revolutionary Partido Revolucionario Institucional (PRI, or Institutional Revolutionary Party).

Even though seldom as exaggerated and blatantly adulatory as the preceding, such traditional presentations cloud our understanding of the very complex, multifaceted movement that was the Ayutla Revolution. Despite the vagueness of the principles under which the struggle against the dictatorship was fought, and despite the disunity of the movement itself, Ayutla does seem to usher in a new era in nineteenth-century Mexican politics. The pervasive presence of Santa Anna was permanently exorcised. Ayutla also brought to the forefront of public life a group of men who have been called a "generation of giants": military leaders such as Ignacio Comonfort, Santos Degollado, Santiago Vidaurri, Epitacio Huerta, and Manuel García Pueblita; and radical intellectuals such as Melchor Ocampo, Ponciano Arriaga, Guillermo Prieto, and Benito Juárez. Under the auspices of the government born of the Ayutla movement, Congress promulgated the 1857 Constitution, which would become, under the fire of the Reforma and Intervention Wars, not only the banner of the Liberal Party, but that of the nation. From 1867 to 1910, the 1857 Constitution—the "most liberal code on earth," according to Prieto—was to provide the practically unquestioned formal legal framework of Mexican political life.

What, then, was "the Ayutla Revolution"? If we were to be less romantic and more accurate, we would describe the events as the Ayutla rebellions. For while it is true that the arbitrary, spendthrift government of Santa Anna had managed to alienate the large majority of the political class, while high taxes—compounded by bad weather and crop failures—had ignited popular resentment against the dictator, the image of the nation rising as one against

tyranny, its sights set on a definite goal, is exaggerated. By early 1854, the Santa Anna dictatorship, rejected outright by the more radical Liberals and especially by the logically federalist regional strongmen, also had disappointed many Conservatives and even some moderate Liberals—men such as Teodosio Lares and Antonio de Haro y Tamariz, and some of the writers for *El Siglo XIX,* who had hoped a strong, centralized government finally would be able to provide Mexico with a rational, efficient administrative machinery to ensure "regular order" in the state's actions. Initially, the Plan de Ayutla was probably just the localized, angry reaction of Juan Álvarez and his men to the unwanted military intrusion of Santa Anna, who had sent troops into Guerrero under the excuse of helping Álvarez against a possible attack by the French adventurer Rassouet de Boulbon. Nevertheless, the plan was seen as the first open challenge to the dictatorship, and we can say that the nation was perceptive to it: the movement spread to all of Guerrero and Michoacán, while similar movements were started in the northeast, by the young lawyer Juan José de la Garza in Tamaulipas and by Santiago Vidaurri in Nuevo León and Coahuila. In the words of observer and Comonfort apologist Anselmo de la Portilla, the plan "produced a magical effect" throughout the nation.

Nevertheless, it would take over a year for the movement to acquire national dimensions and a pretense of unity. The Ejército Libertador (Liberating Army) of the south was mainly made up of *pintos,* poor peasants from Guerrero, loyal to Álvarez. These men formed guerrilla bands that were successful in disrupting order and, eventually, destabilizing the regime, but were consistently beaten by Santa Anna's army (in the Battles of Coquillo and el Peregrino, for instance). They abandoned the revolution for three to four months in order to harvest their crops. Furthermore, this rag-tag army and the perceived radicalism of Juan Álvarez struck fear in the hearts of all but the most radical of political men. Manuel Doblado, governor of Guanajuato; Generals Leonardo Márquez and José López Uraga; and Antonio de Haro y Tamariz, Santa Anna's old minister of finance, all refused to accept the Plan de Ayutla, even though all opposed Santa Anna. Others, like Santiago Vidaurri, were not willing to submit to anyone's authority but their own.

With the fall of Santa Anna's government in August 1855, the divisions within the revolutionary forces became painfully obvious. As the dictatorship crumbled and Santa Anna fled the country, Haro y Tamariz raised the Conservative flag against Ayutla in San Luis

Potosí, while in Piedra Gorda and Monterrey, Doblado and Vidaurri fostered their own counter-revolutions. In Mexico City, Romulo Díaz de la Vega, commander of the city's garrison, was astounded by the popular support shown for the Plan of Ayutla; a throng of people had gathered at the Alameda and had spent six hours signing a document demanding the city's adherence to the plan. In accordance with Article 1 of the plan, he formed a junta of departmental representatives in order to elect an interim president, who would in turn issue the convocation for a constituent congress. The junta, made up mostly of moderate Liberals such as Mariano Riva Palacio and Miguel Buenrostro, elected General Martín Carrera, thus angering Ayutla supporters who felt the presidency should go to Álvarez. Valentín Gómez Farías, president of the *ayuntamiento* (city council), resigned in protest. The situation was at an impasse: amid such disturbances, Carrera resigned. The nation would be without government between September 12 and October 4.

The issue of the presidency finally resolved thanks to the careful negotiations of Ignacio Comonfort. On September 16, 1855, Comonfort, Haro y Tamariz, and Doblado signed the Lagos Convention, recognizing Álvarez as the general in chief of the revolution. Vidaurri accepted the situation but refused to sign and did not officially recognize the Álvarez government until early November. Álvarez became president, elected by the Cuernavaca Convention, whose members he named himself, on October 4. His cabinet was to include the biggest names among the radical Liberals: Ocampo as minister of foreign relations; Juárez as minister of justice, Prieto as minister of finance; Degollado as minister of public works; Arriaga as minister of the interior. Comonfort was named minister of war. The new, "legitimate" government notwithstanding, the country was hardly at peace. Disagreements within the cabinet made it impossible for it to issue a program of government. After Arriaga's resignation, no on wanted to accept the post of minister of the interior. In the Sierra Gorda, Tomás Mejía and José López Uraga headed a rebellion that aimed at protecting religion and property, and destroying Álvarez's "rude despotism." After two months of ingovernability, Álvarez—well into his sixties and this point—decided to retire, naming Comonfort substitute president. Álvarez's decree would be ratified by Congress in February 1865. The real engineer of the Ayutla triumph was finally sitting in the presidential chair.

What, then, can one conclude about the historical significance of the Ayutla movements? As we have mentioned, they provided the arena into which came forth a new generation of public men, whose influence on the second half of the Mexican nineteenth century would be decisive. It set the stage for the reforms of the 1857 Constitution. But we consider that the nature of the movement itself is perhaps as meaningful as it accomplishments: the "triumph" of Ayutla was possible only because the movement's principles were watered down; because regional leaders such as Doblado and Vidaurri were cajoled into cooperating; and because moderates from both political tendencies were frightened by the presence of the masses (whose involvement in the Ayutla movements was felt acutely, at least in Mexico City) and by the more extreme political possibilities of monarchy on the one side and demagoguery on the other. Ayutla paints a vivid picture of Mexico's "state-building" process in the middle of the nineteenth century, highlighting the obstacles to the birth of a modern nation-state: the nonexistence of a consensual model of government, the tensions between geographic center and periphery and the autonomy of the different regions, and the dilemma between the political class's wariness of the "people" at its avowed republicanism and respect for the "national will." These were issues that would not be resolved until the advent of the Restored Republic, or even the rule of dictator Porfirio Díaz. More than the harbinger of modernity, the Revolution of Ayutla is a showcase of the heterogeneous ideological and political elements that would have to be dealt with before modern Mexico could be consolidated.

—ERIKA PANI

Aztecs

See Mesoamerica: Mexica

Azuela, Mariano 1873–1952
Physician, Soldier, and Writer

Mariano Azuela's name is inseparable from what has become known as the novel of the Mexican Revolution, the narrative trend largely responsible for modernizing national literature in the first half of the twentieth century. He wrote over twenty novels, dozens of short stories and sketches, and several plays and biographies, covering a wide spectrum of topics on Mexican society and history.

Born to a petty bourgeois family in the state of Jalisco, Azuela studied medicine in the city of Guadalajara and returned to establish a practice in his native Lagos de Moreno in 1900. While practicing medicine, Azuela's literary inclinations, evident since his early school years, led him to join a local group of bohemian literati, among them Francisco González León, José Becerra, Antonio Moreno y Oviedo, and Bernardo Reina. Some of Azuela's writings appeared in the group's collected volumes of *Ocios literarios* (1906, 1908).

A keen observer of Mexico's social life, Azuela followed the steps of José Joaquín Fernández de Lizardi, Luis G. Inclán, and José T. Cuéllar, recorders of popular life in the *costumbrista* tradition, and of the novelist *par excellence* of turn-of-the-century small town life, Rafael Delgado. His literary models, however, were the French and Spanish masters of nineteenth-century romanticism and realism, albeit a *modernista* quality is at times also perceptible in his prose. His positivist medical education made him receptive to the influence of Emilé Zola and naturalism, and the penchant to portray characters in terms of physiological and moral decay.

Azuela's prolific literary production underwent several phases. His early novels, of which *Mala yerba* is perhaps the most accomplished, revealed a socially concerned writer that used realistic techniques to portray social types. His most celebrated works were written during the Revolutionary period, when he took as his subjects the politics of self-interest during the war and the popular upheaval itself. *Andrés Perez, maderista* (1912) is a diatribe against political opportunism in the early phase of the Revolution. In *Los caciques* (written in 1914 and published three years later), Azuela denounces wealthy caciques' (local strongmen's) abuses and attacks on middle-class merchants and intellectuals, which ultimately lead to the Revolutionary uprising. Both novels can be seen as research for the author's most serious undertaking: the war itself. Determined to experience and record the everyday life of "genuine Revolutionaries," Azuela joined a faction of the Villista army in late 1914 and stayed with them for several months. Based on this military venture, a year later he published *Los de abajo,* a novel he began writing on the campaign trail and hastily finished in the border town of El Paso, Texas, after the devastating defeats in the Bajío region of north-central Mexico forced the Villista army to flee north.

An amnesty in 1917 allowed the novelist to move to Mexico City, where he would live the rest of his life, and open a consultant office. Two years later, he published three novels about the revolution: *Las moscas,* a series of sketches that canvasses, in a parodic way, social types during the Revolution; *Domitilo quiere ser diputado,* a political satire against unprincipled politicians and government corruption during the Revolution; and *Las tribulaciones de una familia decente,* a novel about the social dislocation of a provincial middle-class family.

By the early 1920s Mariano Azuela had published eight novels and several short stories and sketches, but he was still virtually unknown. Despaired by his literary anonymity, he turned to the avant-garde narrative trend of the day in hope of gaining critical and readership acceptance. Three novels would come out of this experimental phase: *La malhora* (1923), *El desquite* (1925), and *La luciérnaga* (1927). The latter, one of his most accomplished novels, combines interior monologue and an omniscient narrator to produce a vivid and gruesome description of slum life in Mexico City, a theme that would reappear in *Nueva burguesía* (1941).

It was not his experimental novels, ironically, but those of the previous period, that caught the eye of the critics in the mid-1920s. A debate on the existence or non-existence of a Revolutionary literature lead to the "discovery" of *Los de abajo* by Mexico City's cultural elite. The novel recounts the deeds of the small-time regional *"cabecilla"* Demetrio Macias, a "pure blooded" Indian, and his men who join the Villista army and bravely participate in the crucial battle of Zacatecas, in which the federal army was defeated. Unrestrained and intoxicated by their unopposed military power, the troop falls into a state of primitivism in which plunder, earthly pleasures, and abuse against the civilian population reign. When they finally return to their home region amid dwindling support from their own people, they are surprised and killed in an ambush. Although Azuela claims peasants were the true Revolutionaries, he implies that their lack of clear political objectives and overwhelming ignorance prevented them from being able to bring to a satisfactory end the armed conflict.

Azuela's formal accomplishments in this novel were considerable. Through an innovative combination of direct style, spatial and story shifts, fast tempo, vigorous descriptions, and brilliant recreation of popular speech, he was able to capture the popular, epic dimension of the Revolution. The novelist, however, never relinquished the positivistic belief that social unrest was the result of moral deviation. Ultimately, he could only frame a peasant revolution that went far beyond the liberal principles he stood for (i.e., the inviolability of private property) in terms of the moral degeneration of the masses. This vision notwithstanding, from this point on he was labeled the "true" purveyor of Mexico's Revolutionary spirit, and his vision of peasant defeat provided the master narrative for interpreting popular rebellion in Mexico's literary discourse.

Selected Bibliography

Leal, Luis, *Mariano Azuela.* New York: Twayne, 1971.
Robe, Stanley, *Azuela and the Mexican Underdogs.* Berkeley: University of California Press, 1979.

—MAX PARRA

B

Borders

See Foreign Policy; Migration to the United States; Politics and Government; U.S.-Mexican Border

Bullfighting

The practice of bullfighting in Mexico was imported from Spain immediately after the Spanish Conquest. The first official bullfight, or *corrida*, took place on August 13, 1529, celebrating the feast of St. Hippolito, on whose saint's day Tenochtitlan (site of present-day Mexico City) was conquered by Fernando (Hernán) Cortés. Two of seven selected bulls were killed and the meat was distributed to "monasteries and hospitals." An infrastructure supporting local *corridas* was laid when Juan Gutierrez Altamirano, cousin of Cortés, imported fighting bulls and cows from Navarra, Spain, in 1552, an event that caused a group of Indians two years later to petition the viceroy to intervene on their behalf, since the bulls were damaging their crops and menacing farmers. The Atenco ranch founded by Gutierrez Altamirano still sells fighting bulls today.

Until the eighteenth century bullfighting in Spain and Mexico was a chaotic affair. Several bulls were penned into an enclosed area; men on horseback, usually nobles, would incite them, try to outrun or sidestep them, and eventually kill them with lances. Enthusiastic audiences watched. In Mexico these spectacles were held on the feast of St. Hippolito and to celebrate the arrival of a new viceroy, the signing of peace treaties affecting Spain, the canonization of a saint, or the birth or marriage of a member of the royal family of Spain. On such occasions the Plaza Mayor in Mexico City would be fenced in and box seats would be constructed for dignitaries.

When Felipe V, grandson of Louis XIV, acceded to the Spanish throne in 1700, his antipathy for bullfights caused much of the Spanish nobility to shun *corridas* altogether. It continued among the lower classes, but its form changed from an exercise primarily on horseback—the prerogative of nobles—to one by men on foot. This development gave rise to the advent of professional *toreadores,* and to the evolution of cape work to control the bull's charge. While horsemanship continued in bullfights, action on the ground predominated. Joaquin Rodríguez, known as Costillares, a Spaniard, revolutionized the killing of the bull in the late eighteenth century with a technique known as the *volapie* (flying feet), in which the matador charges the bull head-on, thrusting a sword deeply between the shoulder blades, severing the aorta and producing a rapid death. This technique can be executed with relative safety only when the bull's neck is lowered, and after Costillares the use of lances *(pics)* thrust from horseback into the bull's neck muscles to produce the desired lowering became widespread.

With these innovations, bullfighting became a popular and lucrative activity, resulting in the construction of the first single-purpose bullrings in Spain, Mexico, and other parts of Latin America, and in standardization of the spectacle. In 1769 in Mexico City, for example, the bullfight season, under control of the viceroy, lasted for two weeks in November and December, with 12 distinct *corridas,* bringing in 35,000 pesos in total ticket sales (for an audience of about 2,000) and profits to the state of 25,000 pesos after expenses. The most expensive matador, a Spaniard named Tomás Vanegas "El Gachupin Toreador," was paid 240 pesos for his participation in eight *corridas.* Two hundred and ten bulls were purchased at a cost of 10 pesos each and were fought by *cuadrillas* (teams) of bullfighters including two matadors, six *banderilleros,* and seven horsemen. The first permanent bullring in Mexico was constructed in Mexico City in 1788 and the *corrida* spread rapidly throughout Mexico. By 1790, to celebrate the accession of Carlos IV to the Spanish throne, *corridas* were held in Mexico City, Durango, Paplantla, Veracruz, Pátzcuaro, Guanajuato, Tehuantepec, Aguascalientes, Tabasco, Valladolid, Real del Catorce, Chilapa, Zamora, and San Luis de la Paz.

After Independence bullfighting in Mexico declined. But the spectacle was invigorated in 1829 when the Mexican national government began sponsoring *corridas* and again in 1835 when Bernardo Gavino Rueda, a Spanish bullfighter not fully accredited at home, traveled to Mexico to become "director of *corridas* and teacher of bullfighters." He established a bullfighting school that incorporated the Spanish tradition, although he did not teach the *volapie* technique. Jesús Villegas "Catrin," his student, fought in Spain in 1857, probably the first Mexican to do so. Bullfighting was forbidden during the presidency of Benito Juárez, beginning in 1867, initiating another period of decline that lasted until the prohibition was rescinded in 1887. Bullfighting resumed in all states except Oaxaca, where it still is forbidden today. In 1889 one of the best Mexican bullfighters, Ponciano Díaz, traveled to Spain, where modern styles were evolving rapidly, and he fought for a season with the finest matadors there, including Frascuelo and Guerrita, from whom he learned techniques he carried back to Mexico. For some time thereafter bullfighting in Mexico flourished as native and Spanish matadors fought side by side in the largest bullrings of both countries. Rodolfo Gaona became the first Mexican matador to achieve first-ranking status shortly after his arrival in Spain in 1908, where he remained for much of his career until his retirement in 1925. One of the passes he invented, the *gaonera*, in which the matador holds one end of the cape behind his back while the other hand guides the cape, has become part of the standard vocabulary of passes.

The Mexican Revolution decimated the cattle industry in Mexico, from which the breeding of fighting bulls did not recover until the early 1920s. In 1916 President Venustiano Carranza forbade bullfighting in Mexico, a prohibition that coincided with part of Gaona's bullfighting career and lasted until May 1920. In 1927 Fermin Espinosa "Armillita" replaced Gaona as the top Mexican matador when he traveled to Spain at the age of 17, quickly becoming one of the most popular bullfighters there until his retirement in 1949. He, in turn, was replaced by Carlos Arruza, who fought frequently in Spain from the time of his first arrival in 1944 until his retirement in 1953. His career in Spain, like Armillita's before him, coincided with another decline in Mexican bullfighting, this time caused by a severe loss in the stock of fighting bulls, product of an epidemic of hoof-and-mouth disease lasting from 1946 to 1952. After Arruza, no Mexican matador has reached top ranking in Spain, a status still considered the pinnacle of achievement.

The relationship between Mexican and Spanish bullfighting during most of the twentieth century has been complex. During the first decades Mexican *corridas* prospered from the introduction of new styles from Spain. The period between the high point of Joselito's career and the retirement of Juan Belmonte (top Spaniards who fought during the 1920s and 1930s), known as the "golden age" of bullfighting, was one in which bullfighting changed from a relatively static, more "heroic" event for the matador, who waited head-on for the bull to charge, to a more fluid and dynamic event. Belmonte proved that a matador could stand much closer to the bull, from an oblique angle requiring a good deal more movement with the arms to guide the bull's charge. This permitted the linking of one pass to another in a series of fluid motions usually capped off by a *pase de pecho,* in which the matador reverses the direction of the pass across his body, stopping the action. This style favors a smaller, more predictable bull and as it became popular in Spain, breeders began providing smaller bulls. Matadors in Mexico, already accustomed to the smaller, more agile bull bred there, quickly adapted to the new style, and by the mid-1930s more than 300 contracts per year were being issued to Mexican bullfighters in Spain, 50 of these to Armillita alone. But in 1936 the Spanish government, lobbied by an association of native matadors, prohibited the entry of Mexican bullfighters to Spain except under difficult conditions. Mexico reciprocated, and the mutual boycott lasted until 1944 and then was renewed from 1947 to 1951. It has been invoked intermittently since then. By the time Mexicans matadors could return to Spain in 1944, the Spanish Civil War had ruined herds there, and relatively small bulls were fought for a number of years, further enhancing the Spanish careers of Mexican matadors. There is little cross-breeding between the herds of the two countries, owing in great part to stringent veterinary health regulations in each country.

Since the end of the Spanish Civil War, interchange of matadors between Mexico and Spain has been influenced by disparities in fees paid to matadors. During the 1940s, 1950s, and 1960s top-flight matadors in Spain were paid lower fees than they could command in Mexico or other Latin American countries where bullfighting is practiced (Peru, Ecuador, Colombia, and Venezuela). This encouraged Spanish matadors to contract in those countries. From the 1970s to the present, however, the relationship has reversed, and bullfighters can command fees two, three, or more times higher in Spain (sometimes above $50,000 per fight) than they can in comparable bullrings in Mexico. In contrast a Mexican matador near the low end of the top 20 rankings will typically earn about $3,000 to $5,000 per *corrida,* fight 20 to 30 times per year, and must pay travel costs and share his earnings with his *cuadrilla* of four. By the mid-1990s only two or three among the top bullfighters from one country fought in the other in any given year, and the administrative agreement governing exchanges of matadors between Mexico and Spain remained problematic.

Thus, with the bulls of each country bred separately, and with only intermittent and infrequent interaction among matadors, Mexican bullfighting has developed a personality of its own, despite nearly identical regulatory statutes. Mexican bulls continue to be slightly smaller than Spanish bulls, but they are faster and they tend to have more stamina, enabling a matador to extract more passes from them during the last part of the bullfight. They are said to be highly tenacious and fierce but also more "collaborative," in that their charges tend to be more smoothly articulated and more predictable. While this latter quality makes the bull less dangerous, and hence less exciting, it permits a matador, when facing an excellent bull, to execute a rich variety of lively, close passes, complete with flourishes and "adornos," such as posing (briefly) in front of a standing bull with an elbow on its nose. In comparative terms, the Mexican bullfight tends toward something of a cross between the flashy, elegant Sevillian style in which the bull is dazzled by the matador, and the more "classic," slow-moving tempo of the Ronda style, in which the tragic character of the bull is emphasized.

Bullfighting in Cultural Context

The *corrida,* an asymmetrical encounter between humans and a dangerous bull, takes place within a rigorously structured set of norms leading to the death of the bull. Since the bull is a major protagonist, the *corrida* can be viewed as a tragic metaphor, not unlike the Greek conception of tragedy, in which it is precisely the bull's nobility that leads to its death; indeed, one of the major qualities hoped for in a fighting bull is *nobleza.* Certain bullfighting styles,

such as the "classic" style of Ronda, lend themselves to this bull-oriented interpretation. Emphasis on the matador as protagonist, on the other hand, suggests the triumph of intelligence, skill, and human organization over brute force, and is readily apparent in certain bullfighting styles, such as the intensely athletic manner of Carlos Arruza. Since *corridas* evolved in societies with highly developed concepts of authority, the bullfight also can be seen as an illumination of two distinct conceptions: the animalistic, physical authority posed by the raw brute power of the bull versus the more subtle authority of the matador, whose skill ultimately places him in a lethally dominant position. The sexual symbolism of the bull as a masculine figure is nearly universal, and some observers have seen in the modern *corrida* an intricate interplay of masculine and feminine qualities in the actions of the matador with the bull. Bullfighting clearly has its origins in ritual sacrifice, an element that distinguishes it from contemporary sports events or theater, linking it to ancient practices such as those found in the Old Testament or in Mesoamerican civilizations, and on the Iberian Peninsula. Fascination with wild bulls in the Mediterranean region is ancient—the caves of Altamirano in Spain, estimated to be 20,000 years old, contain vivid images of bulls.

Although it has roots in the Spanish and Mexican colonial aristocracies, modern bullfighting in both Spain and Mexico is an urban entrepreneurial activity that developed simultaneously in large, industrializing cities, appealing to large sectors of the middle classes while still remaining popular among the upper classes. The development of nationalistic feelings, cutting across highly unequal class structures in Spain and Mexico during the first half of the twentieth century, may in fact have been assisted by the popularity of the *corrida,* one of the few public spaces outside of politics available simultaneously to various social classes. Little, however, has been written on the subject. Likewise, few studies exist on the social contexts in which bullfighting takes place in the smaller bullrings in Spain or Mexico. The statistics of bullrings in Mexico, however, are suggestive. There are about 200 bullrings throughout Mexico, but only in 37 of these are there at least 4 bullfights per year. By far most bullfights take place in small towns with only one *corrida* per year, and it is unclear whether the phenomenon is different in these settings: whether ethnic and social correlates surrounding bullfights differ in largely indigenous communities, for example, or whether the element of ritual or religious symbolism accompanying *corridas* is stronger in these communities. It is also possible that, as is the case in Spain, informal *corridas* may be held in small communities, with local villagers acting as impromptu bullfighters to demonstrate their courage.

Although bullfighting has prospered in Mexico more than in any other Latin American country, it is still not relatively as important as it is in Spain, where one bull is killed (in novice or regular bullfights) for approximately every 5,000 inhabitants. In Mexico the figure is roughly one per 19,000. Mexico, with more than double the population of Spain, had only about 750 bullfights in 1996, compared to about 1,450 in Spain. And while the number of novices and fully accredited matadors in each country is roughly the same (419 in Spain and 455 in Mexico in 1996), Spanish matadors have far more engagements, a factor particularly important to young matadors trying to hone an individual style through "live" practice.

Women and Bullfighting

From the time it was institutionalized in Mexico until the present women have participated as bullfighters, although far less frequently than men. In November 1779, for example, a *cuadrilla* of four women fought bulls in Mexico City, and the next day six women fought. In December 1791 María García fought with two male matadors, each earning 50 pesos per fight. A royal decree issued in Spain in 1908 expressly forbade women from bullfighting; the decree was enforced until the death of General Francisco Franco. A Peruvian woman, Conchita Cintron, was well known as a *rejoneadora* (fighter of bulls on horseback) throughout the bullfighting world during the 1950s. During the 1980s one Spanish woman, Maribel Atienzar, known as La Espanolita, and Raquel Martínez, a Mexican, fought bulls. As of 1996 the only accredited female bullfighter from Spain was Cristina Sánchez, and the only female bullfighter from Mexico was the novice Monica Hernández.

The Bullfight Described

All aspects of the bullfight—minimum weights of bulls and horses; sizes of the *pic* and *banderillas* (spears about 30 inches—75 centimeters—long, with small, sharp, harpoon-like points), the provision of clinics at bullrings, maximum time limits to kill the bull—are regulated by detailed government statutes, and each bullring has a designated judge empowered to enforce them. Normally six bulls are killed by three matadors who alternate in highly structured three-part performances for each bull. In the first

tercio the bull enters the ring, charging one or more bullfighters fending with large capes; then two horses with protective covering and ridden by *picadores* enter the ring and incite the bull to charge. While the bull is engaged with the horse the *picador* shoves the point of a lance about two inches (five centimeters) into the back of the bull's muscular neck. Bulls that continue to charge while feeling the *pic* are admired for their bravery. The *pic* may be repeated up to three times until the bull is deemed by the judge to be sufficiently punished for it to be fought and killed but still strong enough to provide spirited challenge to the matador. The horses leave the arena, beginning the second *tercio* in which a bullfighter holds two short *banderillas* with raised arms and, using one of several standard techniques, drops them sharply onto the muscular part of the bull's back as it passes by. This may be repeated up to three times, after which the final *tercio* begins. The matador, holding a red cape *(muleta)* incites the bull to charge at close range, guiding the bull as gracefully as possible through a series of linked passes. After a few minutes —in Mexico the bull must be killed within 16 minutes of the beginning of this *tercio;* otherwise its life will be spared—the matador profiles directly in front of the bull, aims his sword in his right hand while trying to divert the bull's charge with the *muleta* in his left hand, and charges, attempting to insert the sword between the shoulder blades while going over the bull's horns. If he succeeds the first time, and the crowd has been pleased by the capework, the matador may be awarded with one or both ears, and, for an extraordinary performance, the tail, taken from the dead bull. During moments of well-executed action a band will play music, usually in the *pasodoble* form associated with bullfighting. The great Mexican popular songwriter Agustín Lara (author of "Grandada") composed a number of highly popular *pasodobles,* some still played today.

Although each bullfight is structured identically, the quality varies considerably, and *aficionados* often have reasons to be less than fully satisfied. The bull can be overly punished by a *picador,* rendering it too weak to charge gamely; or under-punished, making it too dangerous for close passes or the kill. Occasionally the bull refuses to charge at all, or hooks too dangerously to handle at close range. The *banderillas* may be placed badly, causing much pain. The matador may have difficulty executing close passes or the kill. These defects are frequent, and audiences are likely to protest loudly at perceived abuses to the bull or other incompetent behavior. Although unusual, sometimes all six bulls are killed without the granting of a single ear to a matador, and rarely are more than two or three ears granted in an afternoon. However, when the bull exhibits tenacity, vigor, and stamina; when it has been handled skillfully by *picadors* and *banderilleros;* and when the matador has executed close, linked passes with sculptural grace, audiences are sometimes moved to tears at the moment of a bull's death.

Select Bibliography
Marvin, Garry, *Bullfight.* Oxford and New York: Blackwell, 1988.

—JOSÉ Z. GARCÍA

C

Calderón de la Barca, Fanny 1804–82

Writer

Fanny Calderón de la Barca was the author of *Life in Mexico during a Residence of Two Years in That Country*. The book recounts her experiences in Mexico from 1839 to 1841, when her husband, Angel Calderón de la Barca, was Spain's first envoy to Mexico.

Frances Erskine Inglis, who was always called Fanny, was born in Scotland on December 23, 1804, the fifth of ten children. Her father was moderately prosperous, and the children were well educated. When Fanny was 23 her father was forced into bankruptcy. This destroyed his health, and he moved to Normandy with his wife and several of his children. Two years later he died. In 1831 Fanny, her mother, three sisters, and four nieces emigrated to Boston to open a school. The school began well but soon incurred problems. The family split up; Fanny and her mother stayed in Boston while the others moved to Pittsburgh to teach. In 1837 Fanny and her mother moved to Staten Island.

When and where Calderón met Fanny is not clear, but they courted while she was in New York. Calderón seems to have been a man of wide interests. Calderón, like Fanny, had a scholarly aptitude and was very personable. Fanny was perhaps the more open and less conservative of the two. Fanny and Calderón were married on September 24, 1838.

Life in Mexico begins October 1839 onboard the ship sailing to Havana en route to Mexico. The book is based on Fanny's extensive journal-like letters to her family, supplemented by Fanny's private journal. Fanny's letters had been shared with relatives and friends, including the historian William Prescott. Prescott urged Fanny to publish the letters, and he wrote the preface to the book. Prescott later utilized Fanny's descriptions in his *Conquest of Mexico* (1843). The first edition of *Life in Mexico* has a publication date of 1843, although it was published by December 1842. The reviews in the United States were favorable; reviews were less enthusiastic in Mexico. Prescott also assisted in arrangements for a British edition. Reviews in the British press were largely favorable.

Fanny was a critical observer, but less judgmental than many travel writers. She was curious and welcomed opportunities for new places or new experiences. Her tone is sometimes ironic. She is not always complimentary, but neither is she spiteful or mean-spirited. Fanny did not spare her acquaintances or the society they moved in, which may account for the unfavorable reception her book received in Mexico.

After returning to the United States, Calderón and Fanny spent a year in Madrid. Calderón was then reappointed Spanish minister to the United States, and they lived in Washington for nine years. In 1853 they returned to Madrid; when the government fell they fled to France. Fanny began writing again, first a translation from Italian of Father Daniel Bartoli's book on the life of St. Ignatius Loyola, then, anonymously, *The Attaché in Madrid*, recounting their recent turbulent experiences in Spain.

Fanny and Calderón returned to Spain in 1856, where Calderón died of a fever five years later. Shortly after, Fanny was asked to become teacher to the Infanta Isabel. She stayed with the royal family for most of the remainder of her life. In 1876 she was named Marquesa de Calderón de la Barca. She died after a short illness in 1882, at age 77.

Today, the most complete edition of *Life in Mexico* is the one edited and annotated by Howard T. Fisher and Marion Hall Fisher, published in 1966. The editors restored material that had been deleted in earlier editions, replaced the customary initials and dashes with full names, and supplemented the material with information from Fanny's journals. *Life in Mexico* is still lively and entertaining to read, surprisingly undated in style. Fanny's careful descriptions capture the place and time for the reader. Her book remains an invaluable source of information about life in and around Mexico City at that period.

Select Bibliography
Fisher, Howard T., and Marion Hall Fisher, editors, *Life in Mexico: The Letters of Fanny Calderón de la Barca*. New York: Doubleday, 1966.

—MARY FRECH MCVICKER

Calles, Plutarco Elías 1877–1945
President

Plutarco Elías Calles was born in 1877 into one of the oldest farming and cattle ranching families in northern Sonora. His parents were Plutarco Elías Lucero and María Jesús Campuzano. Orphaned at the age of three, he went to live with his father's sister, Josefa Campuzano, and her husband, Juan Bautista Calles. In gratitude for his adoption, Plutarco took the last name Calles.

Although his birth was registered in Guaymas, he spent his formative years in Hermosillo. In the years leading up to the Mexican Revolution, Calles was particularly interested in teaching, agriculture, and business. He was among the first teachers at the prestigious Colegio Sonora, and he occasionally published articles on the educational shortcomings of the time. In Guaymas he published a short-lived monthly review, *La Revista Escolar*, and he published a few love poems in *El Correo de Sonora*, one of the most influential publications in Guaymas. He later resigned his teaching duties because—as he confessed years later—he found the profession too "conformist."

It was not until his adulthood that Plutarco met the family of his biological father. He adopted the family's name, Elías—although he did not renounce the name of his adoptive family, Calles—and inherited some of his father's land. From 1898 to 1909 Calles devoted himself to farming, with disappointing results, on the family estate of Santa Rosa near the U.S. border, and then to managing the Excélsior mill near the town of Fronteras. As sympathy for Francisco I. Madero waxed in Sonora, Calles returned to Guaymas, where he made contact with Madero's supporters and attended several meetings called by José María Maytorena, one of the most important figures in the Sonoran opposition to the dictatorship of Porfirio Díaz.

Like many other Sonorans, Calles became deeply involved in politics only after Madero came to power. He was mayor of the border town of Agua Prieta until Madero was ousted from the presidency, and he then led the resistance to the military dictatorship of Victoriano Huerta in northeast Sonora. Together with other figures who later would become important in the region—Manuel M. Diéguez, Pedro Bracamonte, and Estéban Baca Calderón—Calles published the Manifesto of Nacozari, in which he urged Sonorans to fight by all means possible the "criminal" Huerta and his accomplices.

During the anti-Huerta campaign in Sonora Calles proved to be better suited for politics than military battles. Nonetheless, Calles remained connected with the upper echelons of the Revolutionary military forces. When long-simmering rivalries among the various Revolutionary factions finally erupted, Calles became the head of the forces loyal to Venustiano Carranza. In the second half of 1915 he defeated the forces of Maytorena, who had allied with Pancho Villa. As interim and later constitutional governor of Sonora, Calles implemented an ambitious program of social reform. Like his friend Salvador Alvarado in Yucatán, Calles introduced a minimum wage. He also introduced a number of educational reforms, founding the state teachers' training college and establishing a technical school for children who had been orphaned during the Revolution. Many of his reforms were controversial, however, particularly his decision to expel Catholic priests (whom he considered bastions of conservative thought) from Sonora and his excessive punishment of those who produced, distributed, and consumed alcoholic beverages. He even directed his ire at the interim governor Cesáreo Soriano, whom he expelled from his post, accusing him of covering up alcohol sales in Navojoa. Calles also directed a war without quarter against the Yaqui Indians of Sonora.

In period leading up to the presidential campaign of 1920 Calles rejected at least two offers of cabinet posts from President Carranza before accepting the position of minister of industry, trade, and labor in 1919. Carranza clearly hoped to neutralize a conspicuous ally of the Sonoran presidential candidate Álvaro Obregón. However, Calles left the ministry only a short time later, distancing himself from the Carranza administration and openly supporting Obregón.

The final break between Carranza and the Sonorans came in April 1920 when Calles published the Plan de Agua Prieta, calling for the overthrow of Carranza. Even once the Sonorans seized power, however, Calles continued to jockey for political advantage. His political influence was briefly contained when he was appointed minister of war during

Adolfo de la Huerta's presidency, but during his three-year tenure as minister of the interior under Obregón, Calles began forming political alliances with such political and labor leaders as Felipe Carrillo Puerto, Saturnino Cedillo, Aarón Sáenz, and Luis N. Morones, paving the way for his own bid for the presidency. He eventually clashed with his old friend de la Huerta over the presidential candidacy, obtaining the support of Obregón. When de la Huerta formed a broad coalition of army officers opposed to his presidency, Calles himself led an efficient military campaign against them in the states of San Luis Potosí and Coahuila. Calles was elected president in 1924.

During his campaign and presidency, Calles sought to explain the fundamental ideas girding the reconstructive phase of the Mexican Revolution. Between 1923 and 1925 elements in Mexico and the United States accused Calles of being a radical or even a Bolshevik. Nonetheless, Calles's vague (if emphatic) laborism contrasted, particularly during the early years of his presidency, with his norteño vision of the Mexican countryside, which saw the small farmer—and not the *ejido* (communal village) or collective farm—as the key to economic prosperity. In this sense he insisted on developing the countryside in a "nondestructive" way, assisting small landowners with irrigation, seeds, practical education, and credit. With the advice of seasoned politicians such as Manuel Gómez Morín, Luis L. León, José Manuel Puig Casauranc, and Luis Cabrera, Calles set up commissions for irrigation and road works, an agricultural bank, and technical schools. Assisted by politicians in the treasury who had benefited from the defeat of de la Huerta, Calles organized a modern banking system, most notably the Bank of Mexico, and reorganized the federal treasury.

Calles also sought to implement the secularist and anticlerical provisions of the 1917 Mexican Constitution (Articles 3, 5, 27, and 130), campaigning against the Catholic clergy with the same energy he had earlier directed against them as governor of Sonora. Calles managed to alienate not only the Catholic hierarchy, but also broad sectors of Mexican society, which exploded in the Cristero Rebellion that wracked western and central Mexico from 1926 to 1929. Backed by a large number of Obregón's supporters in Congress, Calles rewrote Articles 13 and 82 of the constitution, allowing presidents to be reelected. The assassination of President Elect Obregón in 1928 prevented these amendment from being put in to practice.

Faced by one of the most grave political crises of twentieth-century Mexico and almost at the end of his presidential term, Calles decided to renounce the power conferred upon him by his leadership and abolish the old-style model of government, which he called "a one-man nation." Faced with a vacuum in the political system caused by Obregón's death and the imminent collapse of the fragile Revolutionary coalition, Calles promoted the formation of the Partido Nacional Revolucionario (PNR, or National Revolutionary Party), the antecedent of the current ruling party, the Partido Revolucionario Institucional (PRI, or Institutional Revolutionary Party).

During the period from 1929 to 1935 politicians and the press referred to Calles as the "*jefe máximo* (commander-in-chief) of the Revolution." On the one hand, despite Calles's stated intention to hold Mexico to the straight and narrow of laws and institutions, the absence of mature political institutions lead to the growth of political structures centered on Calles, and hence the weakening of the presidency; this was particularly clear during the administration of Pascual Ortiz Rubio (1930–32), probably due largely to his lack of political experience and support from any particular social group. On the other hand, Calles clearly used his skill as a power broker and his wide range of alliance with groups in Congress and the armed forces as well as cabinet members in successive administrations to increase his influence and to control policy.

In 1934 Calles supported the presidential candidacy of General Lázaro Cárdenas, who had been one of his officers during the 1915–18 military campaign against the Villistas. However, his relationship with President Cárdenas deteriorated after Calles made statements to the press in June 1935 criticizing the president's excessive sympathy for labor mobilizations and the "inconvenient" formation of a left wing in Congress. Calles's huge influence on Mexican politics declined when Cárdenas removed his supporters from key military and government posts. Street demonstrations against Calles, particularly by the emerging labor organizations, played an important part as Cárdenas dismantled the Calles machine. Calles himself was deported in April 1936, when he was accused (among other things) of setting up an independent political party. He spent his exile in San Diego, maintaining a regular correspondence with prominent opponents of the Cárdenas administration. He returned to Mexico at the invitation of President Manuel Avila Camacho in 1944 and took part in official meetings to solidify national unity during the final days of World War II. He died in Mexico City on October 19, 1945.

—CARLOS MACÍAS RICHARD

Campobello, Nellie 1900–

Dancer and Writer

Nellie Campobello, registered at birth as María Francisca Moya Luna, was born in Villa Ocampo, a small town in Durango, which her ancestors helped to settle in the seventeenth century. Her father, Jesús Felipe Moya, a supporter of Francisco I. Madero and a Villista general, died in the Battle of Ojinaga in 1914, leaving her mother Rafaela Luna to care for the family. The widow remarried Stephen Campbell, a doctor from Boston whose last name Nellie assumed and altered to Campobello. Never marrying and preferring "freedom to love," Campobello engaged actively in the nationalist cultural renaissance of the post-Revolutionary period as writer and ballerina. Seen as a precursor of Mexican modern dancing, and called the Isadora Duncan of Latin America, she established her reputation as ballerina, choreographer, and teacher of dance. She founded and directed the National School of Dance (1932–53), the Folkloric Ballet of Mexico (1937), and the Ballet of Mexico City (1943). Recognized as an authority on indigenous and folk dance, she coauthored *Ritmos Indígenas de México* (Indigenous Rhythms of Mexico) with her sister Gloria Campobello. They studied and recorded the dances of the first Mexicans as illustrated in codices and sculptures, integrating them to contemporary movements.

Campobello's contribution in the field of dance was recognized early on. Her status as writer, however, has taken longer to establish and is still growing. A contemporary of Frida Kahlo, Leonora Carrington, Remedios Varo, Nahui Olin, and María Izquierdo, her work has received increasing critical attention from feminists and literary revisionists. Nellie's first book, *Yo,* a collection of 15 coming of age poems, was published in 1929 under the name of Francisca. Some of these poems were translated by Langston Hughes, whom she met in Cuba, and they appeared later in Dudley Pitts's *Anthology of Contemporary Latin American Poetry* (1942). Although Campobello did not publish more verse, a poetic sensibility marks her two novels, *Cartucho: Relatos de la lucha en el norte de México* (1931) and *Las manos de mamá* (1937).

The publication of *Cartucho,* in particular, situates Campobello generationally with Mariano Azuela, Martín Luis Guzmán, and José Ruben Romero, among others, who experienced, witnessed, and wrote about the armed phase of the Mexican Revolution. Her original and innovative nonfiction novel was the only female vision and version of the Revolution to appear amid the many memoirs and testimonial novels published at the time. It anticipated and is now studied in dialogue with other women's rendering of the Revolutionary period, such as Elena Garro's *Los recuerdo del porvenir* (1963) and Elena Poniatowska's testimonial novel *Hasta no verte, Jesús mio* (1972), whose historically real protagonist disagrees with Campobello on Francisco "Pancho" Villa's image.

Campobello was a staunch Villa supporter and anti-Carrancista when the official discourse was erasing or maligning Villa's participation. Seen as ideologically out of line, Nellie spoke against the promotion of a nationalist and centralizing discourse as historically inaccurate or as depoliticized folklore. In interviews she declared that she wrote to counteract the obliteration of the Northern Revolution, its territory and peoples, with whom she strongly identified. Structured as a series of short narrative portraits, soldiers such as Cartucho, the prototype of the revolutionary, are immortalized as their heroic deaths are recorded. Written as epitaphs or eulogies, the narratives, as remembered by the child or collected by the adult from popular memory, ballads, and legends, pay tribute to the everyday struggles of towns in the north, and the men and women who sacrificed their lives for a cause. The romantic nostalgia for a time of heroes and heroism is readily displaced by the violence depicted. Seen from the female sphere, the horrors of war elude glorification. The chaos disrupting the domestic and private abode of family life is exacerbated as this smaller and injured unit becomes the microcosm of the nation. *Cartucho*'s epic quality has not diminished as it renders homage, not to the Revolution being institutionalized, but to the northern popular movement and the men who died fighting for their beliefs.

The positive and extensive critique of *Cartucho* from her life-long friend and supporter Martín Luis Guzmán, who had published his novel on Villa, *El aguila y la serpiente,* in 1928, was not a surprise since both believed that the Revolution had been betrayed by those who came to power after the fighting ended. In 1940 and from a more objective stance, Nellie herself took up the theme in *Apuntes sobre la vida militar de Francisco Villa* (Notes on the Military Life of Francisco Villa), a researched account of the military campaigns of the "Centauro del Norte." Guzmán followed it with *Las memorias de Pancho Villa* (1951), for which Nellie provided documents and information she held from Villa's private archives. Villa's place in history, still debated today, was officially recognized in 1966 when the government erected a monument in his honor in the Glorieta de Riviera in Mexico City.

Las manos de mamá (1937) is a poetic tribute to her other lifetime model, her mother, who mitigated the brutal world surrounding the child. In this fictionalized testimony the mother is representative of the valor Campobello attributes to the women from the north, who transcended their traditional roles as their familiar world collapsed. It is also a tribute to the northern terrain and the Raramuni (Tarahumaras), its original settlers. Her admiration for this indigenous group persuaded André Bretón to visit their territory during his visit to Mexico in 1937. A second edition of *Las manos de mamá* appeared in 1949, illustrated by José Clemente Orozco, a friend of the family.

In 1960, a compendium of all her works was published with the title *Mis libros*. A long introduction provides an excellent glimpse into her life and era. Campobello disappeared from the literary scene, but was still Director of the National School of Dance in 1983 when she was honored by a special performance at a celebration of the School's fiftieth anniversary. In 1988, a translation into English of her two works *Cartucho* and *Las manos de mamá* appeared in one volume with an introduction by Elena Poniatowska. She confirms that Campobello, who never received the necessary recognition to stimulate her vocation as a writer, still lived isolated in Tlaxcala at the age of 87.

Select Bibliography

De Beer, Gabriella, "Nellie Campobello's Vision of the Mexican Revolution." *The American Hispanist* 4:34–35 (1979).

Meyer, Doris, "Divided against Herself: The Early Poetry of Nellie Campobello." *Revista de Estudios Hispánicos* 20:2 (May 1986).

_____, "Nellie Campobello's *Las manos de mamá*: A Rereading." *Hispania* 68:4 (December 1985).

Parle, Dennis J., "Narrative Style and Technique in Nellie Campobello's *Cartucho.*" *Romance Quarterly* 32:2 (1985).

Poniatowska, Elena, "Introduction." In *Cartucho and My Mother's Hands,* by Nellie Campobello, translated by Doris Meyer and Irene Matthews. Austin: University of Texas Press, 1988.

Verlinger, Dale E., "Nellie Campobello: Romantic Revolutionary and Mexican Realist." In *Latin American Women Writers: Yesterday and Today,* edited by Yvette E. Miller and Charles M. Tatum. Pittsburgh: Latin American Literary Review, 1977.

—NORMA KLAHN

Cantinflas

See Moreno Reyes, Mario (Cantinflas)

Cárdenas, Cuauhtémoc 1934–
Governor and Presidential Candidate

Born in Mexico City on May 1, 1934, Cuauhtémoc Cárdenas lived his first years in the presidential residence as the only son of one of Mexico's greatest and most revolutionary presidents, General Lázaro Cárdenas. He spent much of his adult life in his father's enormous shadow. However, at the age of 54, Cuauhtémoc Cárdenas made his own mark, ironically by leaving the Partido Revolucionario Institucional (PRI, or Institutional Revolutionary Party), which his father had helped create, and running the most successful opposition presidential campaign in Mexican history. After the election, Cárdenas played a leading role in the foundation of a new leftist party that unified many of the diverse groups that had supported his 1988 candidacy. He became the first president of the Partido de la Revolución Democrática (PRD, or Party of the Democratic Revolution) and guided it for the first four years of its existence before resigning to participate as the PRD's candidate in the 1994 presidential election. He remains one of the most influential figures on the modern Mexican left.

The political career of Cuauhtémoc Cárdenas began almost before he could walk. As Lázaro Cárdenas's only son, Cuauhtémoc acted as his father's aide de camp in many political ventures. He knew or met virtually every important figure in the Mexican elite and on the independent left at that time through his father. From his early experiences, he absorbed much of his father's political style, thought, and objectives.

At the age of 17, he participated in the early stages of the presidential campaign of General Miguel Henríquez Guzmán. Lázaro Cárdenas had encouraged his fellow leftist, close ally, and friend to run as an independent candidate in order to put pressure on President Miguel Alemán Valdés (1946–52) to select a less conservative successor at the end of his term. Henríquez and Lázaro Cárdenas asked that the PRI accept more open participation within the party in the designation of the next presidential candidate. While Alemán refused to democratize candidate selection, he did choose a candidate more acceptable to Cárdenas, and Cárdenas abandoned Henríquez Guzmán. This was the first serious attempt by the Cárdenas family to move the PRI towards the left by demanding internal democratization of the PRI and threatening an elite split.

In 1961, Lázaro Cárdenas sponsored a second such effort, in the Movimiento de Libración Nacional (MLN, or Movement for National Liberation). At 27, Cuauhtémoc Cárdenas represented his father on the first National Committee of the MLN. This political experience reinforced many of the political themes that would characterize his presidential campaign in 1988. The MLN grew out of an international movement to support Cuba against the United States, but quickly turned to domestic issues of national sovereignty and economic independence in Mexico. Specific goals included independence from the International Monetary Fund, internal democratization in the PRI and its affiliated unions, municipal autonomy, decentralization, and support for agrarian reform.

In the MLN, Cuauhtémoc Cárdenas also built or strengthened personal relationships that would prove useful in 1988, with such leftist intellectuals and Communist Party activists as Gilberto Rincón Gallardo, Arnoldo Martínez Verdugo, Ricardo Valero, and Heberto Castillo. Castillo also had been his instructor in the engineering department at the Universidad Nacional Autónoma de México (UNAM, or the National Autonomous University of Mexico), where Cárdenas received his degree. In 1988, Castillo would resign as the presidential candidate of the Mexican Socialist Party in order to support the candidacy of his former student. He remained a strong ally—and critic—of Cárdenas within the PRD.

The MLN eventually split over whether or not to participate in elections. Lázaro Cárdenas felt that electoral involvement would weaken the MLN's ability to influence policy. When communist activists in the MLN formed a Frente Electoral del Pueblo (FEP, or People's Electoral Front) to run candidates in the 1964 presidential election, the MLN split. Lázaro Cárdenas withdrew, and Cuauhtémoc Cárdenas began to distance himself. By early 1967, Cuauhtémoc had joined the PRI.

In the PRI, Cuauhtémoc Cárdenas participated in a newly created Technical Advisory Council, part of the Confederación Nacional Campesina (CNC, or National Peasant Confederation), to study agrarian problems. Other participants included economist Ifigenia Martínez, his childhood friend Janitzio Múgica, and a former university acquaintance, Leonel Durán. All of these PRIistas later participated with Cárdenas in the internal dissident group he helped create in 1986, the Democratic Current. Other future Democratic Current members worked together with him at different times on a commission studying development projects in the Las Balsas River basin from 1963 to 1974.

Lázaro Cárdenas died in 1970. From him, Cuauhtémoc Cárdenas had learned to value popular mobilization as a tool. Mobilization made oil expropriation possible. It tried to pull the PRI toward the left during the 1952 Henríquez campaign, and in the MLN period. Coalitions with leftist parties and social activists were constructed in both cases. And in both cases, democratization of the PRI became a central demand. Cuauhtémoc Cárdenas also learned much of his political philosophy from his father, and from the movements in which they both participated. Across more than 60 years, this philosophy stressed national sovereignty, economic independence, and the state's role as an ally in popular struggles. Cuauhtémoc's personal style often reflected his father's, including Lázaro's emphasis on indefatigable small-town campaigning. Perhaps most important, Cuauhtémoc Cárdenas inherited from his father a deep reservoir of popularity and public goodwill that helped him in 1988. Without the Cárdenas name, his candidacy might never have materialized, and it certainly would have attracted far less electoral support.

After his father's death, Cárdenas broke PRI ranks for the first time as an independent agent when he publicly sought the PRI's nomination for governor of Michoacán in 1974. When the PRI ignored him, Cárdenas withdrew, accusing the PRI of forcing members to surrender themselves unconditionally to the party leaders. Yet for the next 12 years, his career followed a fairly typical PRI pattern. In 1976, he became a federal senator, but only served three months. He resigned to become subsecretary of forestry and fauna in the Ministry of Agriculture. In 1979 he finally was tapped by the PRI to run for governor of Michoacán. Apart from some minor clashes, Cárdenas was relatively uncontroversial and even popular for most of his term, from 1980 to 1986.

However, as his term came to an end, Cárdenas embarked on a course of action that led to his leaving the party he had served for 20 years. As Mexico's economic crisis dragged on, President Miguel de la Madrid turned to policies that many on the left in the PRI found unacceptable. These critics argued that the government should not put debt payments ahead of social welfare, because the debt had resulted from the irresponsible behavior of creditors as well as the Mexican government. They objected to deepening budget cuts, accelerating privatization, and dismantling Mexico's traditional model of protectionist import substitution. They expressed concern that the government's apparent indifference to suffering caused by the crisis would lead voters to reject the PRI. And finally, they had fewer and fewer options for influencing policy within the system, owing to their gradual exclusion from policy-making posts.

Within Michoacán, Governor Cárdenas began to sponsor discussion groups to consider ways of putting pressure on the government to change its direction, and he began to make public statements criticizing federal policy. These statements marked him as someone willing to oppose the PRI publicly. By the spring of 1986, his contacts extended to Rodolfo González Guevara, Mexico's ambassador in Spain, and Porfirio Muñoz Ledo, a former PRI president who recently had been relieved as United Nations representative. González Guevara suggested that to influence economic policy, they might copy the example of the "Critical Current" in the ruling Spanish Socialist Workers' Party (PSOE), which opposed certain policies of the PSOE from within the party. However, attempts to influence policy increasingly focused on the presidential succession. According to tradition, Mexican presidents chose their own successors. Left to himself, de la Madrid probably would choose someone with similar policy preferences, prolonging the isolation of leftist PRIistas. Cárdenas and Muñoz Ledo called for potential PRI presidential candidates to declare their interest in running for president and engage in public debates.

They also began to organize the "Critical Current" that González Guevara had proposed. González Guevara proposed nominating Cárdenas as a "precandidate of sacrifice" in the PRI, in the hope that his participation would force public debate over economic policy and the nomination of a more socially oriented candidate, although probably not Cárdenas himself. In the midst of these early discussions, a press leak revealed the group's existence in August 1986 and dubbed it the Corriente Democrática (Democratic Current). For more than a year Democratic Current members used public pressure and negotiation to influence the PRI nomination process from within the party. During this period, the role of Cárdenas became increasingly significant. He became a de facto "candidate," conducting "campaign tours" to raise the issues that concerned the Democratic Current. Only Cárdenas had the public recognition to attract the curious to rallies, as well as an extensive organizational network from his term as governor. It was also Cárdenas who took the first steps toward a split when he sent a public letter to newspapers after the PRI's March 1987 National Assembly, accusing the party's leaders of

antidemocratic, intolerant, and un-Revolutionary behavior that prevented any respectful collaboration. His refusal to accept party "discipline" deepened the confrontation between the Democratic Current and the PRI.

Ultimately, the Democratic Current had to recognize complete defeat when de la Madrid named Carlos Salinas de Gortari—architect of most of the detested neoliberal economic program—as the PRI's presidential candidate. Within days, Cárdenas accepted the nomination of the first of four parties that would support his candidacy for president. In January, three of these parties and an assortment of popular movements and unregistered parties formed the Frente Democratico Nacional (FDN, or National Democratic Front), to support his candidacy.

By the spring of 1988, several surprisingly well attended rallies had converted Cárdenas into the candidate of those who sought to punish the PRI for the economic crisis. He attracted support from protest voters in developed areas such as Mexico City and rural states such as Morelos and Michoacán. His relationship to Lázaro Cárdenas was a significant campaign advantage, because it reminded people of a time when they felt the PRI served social interests. Personally, Cuauhtémoc Cárdenas was known as a singularly uncharismatic speaker. However, he also was seen as honest, and he focused on issues that targeted the major complaints of many Mexicans. The combination of these factors led him to receive, on July 6, 1988, the largest official vote for any opposition presidential candidate: 31 percent.

Nevertheless, considerable evidence suggests that the 1988 elections were marred by electoral fraud, including suspiciously high PRI votes in rural states such as Chiapas, where the opposition had few pollwatchers, and stacks of partially burned ballots marked in favor of the FDN. Most believe Cárdenas did much better than 31 percent, and Cárdenas himself claimed victory. Neither the Partido de Acción Nacional (PAN, or National Action Party) nor the FDN supported the confirmation of Salinas in the Electoral College.

At the same time, Cárdenas refused to call for aggressive mobilization or acts of civil disobedience (like the seizure of public buildings) to defend his claim. He did not want to take responsibility for behavior that had a high probability of ending in violent repression. He did not think that the FDN had sufficient organization to communicate directions effectively to local supporters, and he did not want to risk uncontrolled escalation. Meanwhile, he hoped that public opinion would force Salinas to resign. Others in the FDN argued in favor of much more aggressive action. The refusal of Cárdenas to support such policies therefore played an important role in the decision of the FDN not to go in that direction. Salinas succeeded in winning confirmation and took office in December 1988.

Still, the confrontation over electoral results set the tone for relations between the government and the PRD, the party founded by Cárdenas after the 1988 election. Dominated by his conviction that Salinas had stolen the election, Cárdenas encouraged his party to reject any cooperation with the government that might strengthen the political position of Salinas. This resulted in policies that effectively punished PRD-allied movements or politicians who negotiated with the state in order to meet constituent demands. Later, the party became more willing to support such negotiations, but throughout the Salinas administration, Cárdenas himself refused to meet with Salinas or engage in negotiations without a specific agenda. Only with perfect transparency, he argued, could people be assured that he had not sold out their votes for his own benefit.

The personal influence of Cárdenas had a complex and contradictory effect on the party. On the one hand, his position on negotiation tended to pull the party toward confrontation, mobilization, and intransigent defense of principles, often frightening swing voters. Moreover, his overwhelming presence often circumvented party procedures and encouraged rebellion against decisions made by committee, inhibiting party institutionalization. On the other hand, the PRD might never have been created without the unifying consensus among former PRIistas and socialists that his unique authority provided. He was elected the PRD's first president without opposition and had considerable influence over the composition of its first Executive Board. He remained the key arbiter of conflicts during his term as president, and in some ways continued this function afterward. The party might well have fallen apart without the legitimacy that his approval brought party decisions, the electoral help that his campaign presence provided, and the constant expectation that Cárdenas would again run for president in 1994.

Not until after the 1994 election, when he failed to attract more than 17 percent of the popular vote, did his influence begin to decline. Under the leadership of his old PRI colleague Porfirio Muñoz Ledo, the PRD sought full participation in negotiations with the PRI and PAN on institutional reform, culminating in a 1996 agreement.

Nevertheless, many in the party remained unsatisfied with the results of negotiation. In the 1996 internal election to pick Muñoz Ledo's successor, the winning candidate was Manuel López Obrador, a close ally of Cárdenas who shared many of his tactical and political preferences. Both supported a political alliance with the Zapatista rebels in Chiapas, favored the use of mobilization as a prenegotiation tactic, and saw the PRD's mission as much in terms of support for "popular struggles" as in electoral terms. Cárdenas pressured López Obrador to run for the party presidency and actively campaigned on his behalf. López Obrador's election therefore marked a resurgent influence of Cárdenas within the PRD. In 1997, Cárdenas himself was elected as mayor of Mexico City. As much as any man in the late twentieth century, Cuauhtémoc Cárdenas shaped the modern Mexican left.

Select Bibliography

Bruhn, Kathleen, *Taking on Goliath: The Emergence of a New Left Party and the Struggle for Democracy in Mexico.* University Park: Pennsylvania State University Press, 1997.

Carr, Barry, and Steve Ellner, editors, *The Left in Latin America: From the Fall of Allende to Perestroika.* Boulder, Colorado: Westview Press, 1993.

Castañeda, Jorge, *Utopia Unarmed: The Latin American Left after the Cold War.* New York: Knopf, 1993.

—KATHLEEN BRUHN

Cárdenas, Lázaro 1895–1970
General and President

Lázaro Cárdenas was president of Mexico from 1934 to 1940, a period distinguished by a high level of peasant and labor mobilization, an extensive agrarian reform, the expropriation and nationalization of the foreign-owned petroleum companies, and the creation of an enduring government party structure incorporating labor, peasant, and popular sectors. The Cárdenas administration has also been subject to extensive debate regarding its long-term impact and the original intentions of Cárdenas himself.

Cárdenas was born on May 21, 1895, in Jiquilpan de Juárez, Michoacán. His trajectory to the presidency began in 1913 when he joined the Constitutional Army, serving under both Álvaro Obregón and Plutarco Elías Calles. He advanced to the rank of division general by 1928 and held several positions in the new post-Revolutionary government during the 1920s and early 1930s, including secretary of government, secretary of national defense, and governor of his home state of Michoacán, as well as president of the new Partido Nacional

Revolucionario (PNR, or National Revolutionary Party). His experience in those tumultuous years of military revolts, attempted coups, and religious rebellion undoubtedly shaped his belief in the importance of a strong, centralized state that could maintain some control over the heterogeneous forces unleashed by the Revolution. He thus shared the state-building orientation of the post-Revolutionary leadership.

In other respects, however, his principles diverged from those of many of these leaders, including his mentor and former commander Calles, who was becoming increasingly conservative during this period. As governor of Michoacán, Cárdenas antagonized traditional landowners by carrying out an agrarian reform, even arming the peasants when they were threatened with retaliation by armed guards of the landlords. Cárdenas became a leader of a radical *agrarista* faction that opposed the efforts of the more conservative faction within the government, led by Calles himself, to end agrarian reform in order to reassure commercial landowners and increase agricultural investment and production. The *agrarista* faction nevertheless gained control of the 1934 PNR nominating convention, approving a radical six-year plan for the next government and nominating Cárdenas as presidential candidate.

When he assumed the presidency in 1934, Cárdenas began to assert his independence by supporting labor in a series of labor disputes, resulting in an open break with Calles. He encouraged labor organization, including the formation of industrial unions and federations that could bargain collectively with employers in a given industry, and the establishment of a national labor confederation, the Confederación de Trabajadores de México (CTM, or Confederation of Mexican Workers). His continued support for labor, including tolerance and indeed encouragement of strikes, antagonized many business groups who were concerned not only about his radical stance but also the growing power of the mobilized workers. Labor conflicts were to have a prominent role in the two most significant initiatives of the Cárdenas period, the agrarian reform and the expropriation of the foreign-owned petroleum companies.

The most important phase of the agrarian reform began with a labor dispute on the cotton estates of the Laguna region in the states of Coahuila and Durango. Prior to the Cárdenas administration, the *agrarista* goal of land distribution had been regarded as incompatible with developmental goals of increasing agricultural production and productivity; the distribution that did occur targeted only traditional haciendas. Large commercial estates such as those of the Laguna region, regarded as the most productive form of agricultural holding, generally were exempt from expropriation.

The decision of the Cárdenas government to resolve the Laguna conflict through the expropriation of the estates therefore established a precedent that subsequently was followed, with variations, on the henequen plantations in Yucatán, wheat and rice estates in the Yaqui Valley of Sonora, rice and cattle haciendas in Michoacán, and several large sugar estates in the state of Puebla. Drawing on the experience of several state governments during the 1920s, which in turn drew from communal traditions of the precolonial period and influences from the Soviet Union, especially the Soviet *kolkhoz*, the government distributed the estates as collective *ejidos*, or village cooperatives, that would be farmed by the new owners as a unit, thus maintaining the economies of scale thought to be necessary for high levels of productivity.

The expropriation of commercial estates, their conversion to collectives, and the level of mobilization of peasants and rural workers evoked considerable opposition. In the traditional agricultural areas of west-central and southern Mexico, opposition to land reform was combined with resistance to Cárdenas's promotion of "socialist" education, designed to undermine the control traditionally exercised by the Catholic Church by emphasizing secular and Revolutionary values. Attacks in the press condemned the "communist" policies of the government; in some areas the landowners took up arms or hired mercenaries to attack the new *ejidatarios*. As was the case with attacks on the church in the previous decade, Cárdenas's promotion of socialist education was opposed by many peasants as well, some of whom joined the Sinarquista Rebellion in many of the same areas where the pro-Catholic, peasant-based Cristero Rebellion had erupted a decade before.

Less violent and more indirect efforts to undermine agrarian reform may have been more successful in the long run. In several cases, commercial landowners were able to retain much of the infrastructure of the previous estates, including processing facilities. In Puebla, for example, some landowners retained control of the sugar refineries that peasant owners and *ejidatarios* were obliged to use. The landowners often had allies among officials at the local and state levels who were able to delay or undermine the process of implementation. Although the Cárdenas government created the Ejidal Bank to provide loans to the *ejidatarios*, funds were insufficient to meet the need even during the Cárdenas administration, and subsequent administrations provided little support for the bank or more generally for the agrarian reform sector.

Nevertheless, the achievements of the agrarian reform were significant. The Cárdenas government distributed more land to more peasants than all of his predecessors: 4.5 million acres (18 million hectares) were given to 800,000 peasants during his administration. The proportion of agricultural land in *ejidos* increased from 15 percent of the total cultivated land to nearly 50 percent between 1930 and 1940; and traditional "feudal" relations of production in the countryside were reduced greatly. Despite their problems, some of the collective *ejidos* achieved relatively high levels of productivity, comparable to those of the private sector. Over the next 30 years the agricultural sector was able to satisfy the food demand of the growing urban sector and to support industrialization through exports of agricultural products.

The labor dispute that culminated with the expropriation of the U.S.- and British-owned petroleum companies began with a demand by petroleum workers for a collective contract and for increased wages and benefits. The owners protested that they were unable to meet the wage and benefit requests, and following extensive negotiations as well as a temporary strike the dispute was referred to the Federal Labor Board. The decision by the board in favor of the workers was contested by the owners, who took the issue to the Mexican Supreme Court. When the companies refused to abide by the Supreme Court ruling upholding the decision of the Federal Labor Board, Cárdenas, after consultation with his cabinet, decreed their expropriation.

The decision had both immediate and long-term repercussions. Within Mexico, where the oil companies were regarded as representative of foreign economic imperialism at its worst, the expropriation resulted in a massive outpouring of support for Cárdenas. The oil companies pressured their respective governments to take measures against Mexico: Britain broke diplomatic relations, and the U.S. State Department insisted on immediate indemnification, boycotted Mexican petroleum exports to the United States, and established an embargo on the exports of petroleum equipment to Mexico. The expropriation was also a factor in substantial capital flight, which, in the context of decreased export earnings, led to a devaluation of the peso and severe constraints on government expenditures in the remaining years of the Cárdenas presidency.

In the longer term, the expropriation, and the shifting of the Mexican petroleum companies from foreign to state ownership and management, definitively established the role of the state as a major economic actor and validated its claim as guarantor of national interests in relation to foreign powers. Subsequently the government would gain control of other key industries under foreign control, including electric power, mining, and communications.

Despite frequent conflicts with business and landowning sectors, the Cárdenas government promoted economic development, including support for both national and foreign business interests. Government investments in infrastructure, particularly roads and highways, and in agricultural irrigation (which benefited the large private estates as well as new collective *ejidos* in the north) increased substantially during this period; government banks provided loans to private industries and financial institutions; tariffs and tax exemptions were implemented to protect and encourage "new and necessary" industries; foreign investment in manufacturing (as opposed to extractive industries) was encouraged. Government support for agrarian reform and for higher wages in the urban sector increased the market, another factor in business growth, and thousands of new manufacturing firms and dozens of new financial institutions were established during the Cárdenas administration.

Nevertheless, the last years of the Cárdenas administration were marked by increased concern regarding the tenor of reforms and the growing strength of the labor movement, not only on the part of business groups but also more conservative groups within the government and the governing party. To this was added the uncertainty of the international situation given the outbreak of war in Europe and pending U.S. involvement in war in both Europe and Japan. In the last years of the administration, the reforms were checked, and Cárdenas attempted to consolidate his support through restructuring the government party to incorporate various constituencies.

The party was restructured on a corporatist basis, with four sectors incorporating labor, the peasantry, popular groups, and the military. Apart from the military (which subsequently was dropped), the sectors were comprised of organized groups: the CTM and other confederations and independent unions in the case of labor; the major peasant organizations, which would be grouped in the Confederación Nacional Campesina (CNC, or National Peasant Confederation) established later in the year; and, in the popular sector, organizations of government workers, as well as women, youth, and other groups excluded from the labor and peasant sectors. The sectoral structure allegedly would enable each constituency to have greater input in the new party, which was now called the Partido de la Revolución Mexicana (PRM, or Party of the Mexican Revolution).

The limited input of the respective sectors in party decisions became quickly evident, however, with the nomination of the PRM candidate for the 1940 presidential elections. Progressive groups within the government and party supported General Francisco Múgica, the secretary of communications under Cárdenas, who could be expected to continue the reforms of the Cárdenas administration. However, in an effort to appease conservative groups within the party—and reflecting his own concerns regarding the polarizing effects of a continuation and perhaps expansion of reforms on conditions of internal instability and international uncertainty—Cárdenas chose General Manuel Avila Camacho, a more conservative and certainly less controversial candidate. Although the various sectors within the party were supposed to nominate the candidate, the candidacy of Avila Camacho was in effect imposed on them, and the respective nominating conventions simply ratified the decision.

The Avila Camacho candidacy succeeded in uniting the leadership and most of the rank and file of the party (excepting some of the labor and peasant organizations that supported Múgica and walked out of their respective conventions). However the PRM would face serious opposition in the form of another conservative general, Juan Andreu Almazán, who was supported by a heterogeneous mix of business groups and labor and peasant dissidents who had favored Múgica, as well as the Partido de Acción Nacional (PAN, or National Action Party), formed in 1939 by a group of conservative businessmen and Catholic intellectuals opposed to Cardenista reforms and particularly to socialist education.

Official and highly suspect election returns gave Avila Camacho a resounding victory, reinforcing a pattern of government party control of the electoral process that would continue to ensure the dominance of the PRM (and that of its successor, the Partido Revolucionario Institucional, or PRI—Institutional Revolutionary Party) within the Mexican political system in succeeding decades. The conservatizing trend that began during the last years of the Cárdenas administration was reinforced by the subsequent administration of Avila Camacho and particularly by his successor, Miguel Alemán Valdés.

Cárdenas subsequently held several positions within the government, including secretary of defense (1942–45), executive director of the Tecalpatepec Commission in Michoacán for the Secretariat of Hydraulic Resources (1947–58), executive director of the Río Balsas Commission of the Secretariat of Hydraulic Resources (1969–70), and president of the board of the Las Truchas Steel complex (1969–70). He became unofficial leader of the left or progressive wing of the PRM/PRI and continued to oppose U.S. intervention in the hemisphere, condemning the U.S.-supported invasion of Guatemala in 1954 and the 1961 invasion of Cuba. His efforts on behalf of nonintervention and peace included participation in the Latin American Conference for National Sovereignty, Economic Emancipation, and Peace, held in Mexico in 1961; in the International Tribunal against War Crimes in Vietnam (Russia Tribunal) in 1966; and in efforts to bring about an understanding between the Soviet Union and China on behalf of the people of Vietnam. Cárdenas died on October 19, 1970.

In retrospect, many of those groups that had most strongly opposed the Cárdenas reforms ultimately benefited from them. The expansion of the domestic market through wage hikes and agrarian reform served the interests of industrial capitalists, as did Mexico's ability to support imports of industrial inputs through agricultural exports; businesses also were subsidized through reduced prices for inputs from nationalized firms formerly under foreign control. Perhaps most important, Cárdenas had in effect "resolved" the problem of popular mobilization through an extensive agrarian reform that brought "social peace" to the countryside and the construction of a party system facilitating control over urban and rural labor and the peasantry.

Given this outcome, some revisionist interpretations have taken a cynical view of the Cárdenas era, suggesting that Cárdenas deliberately manipulated workers and peasants in order to bring them under the control of the state. In this sense, he allegedly shared the goals of his predecessors but was much more astute in recognizing the need to organize the workers and peasants and even encourage their mobilization in order to control them more effectively, whether to serve the interests of capitalist development or to reinforce the hegemony of a monolithic state.

Other studies have recognized the distinction between initial intentions, implementation, and long-term effects. The development of regional historical studies has revealed the complexity in the implementation of post-Revolutionary reforms at the local and state levels. Among other aspects, they have demonstrated the resistance by local officials who often identified with the landlords or business interests and who supported reforms only for reasons of political expediency. Regional studies also have provided a new understanding of the role of the would-be beneficiaries or victims of reforms (peasants, indigenous populations) in supporting, resisting, or negotiating different elements of the Cárdenas program (e.g., accepting land reforms but opposing "socialist" education). In short, the actual implementation of the Cárdenas program involved the interaction and negotiation among a plethora of federal government bureaucrats, landowners, state governors, local strongmen, business interests, peasants, workers, and other interests, leading to varying results across different regions and localities.

Among the Cardenistas themselves, policy goals and strategies were formulated in a highly charged context in which both national and international events and intellectual perspectives gave primacy to the state in promoting economic development—whether capitalist or socialist—and in protecting the interests of labor and other popular sectors. Cárdenas and his associates could claim to be determined state builders and dedicated *agraristas* without apparent contradiction. They also could see the state as a vehicle for economic development, a means to control the excesses of capital, and a benevolent, if paternalistic, instrument to secure the rights of peasants and workers.

Finally, the achievements of the Cárdenas government should not be minimized. Hundreds of thousands of peasants received land under the agrarian reform, and the nationalization of petroleum represented a turning point in economic relations with foreign interests, not only for Mexico but other countries of the hemisphere. While controversy undoubtedly will continue to characterize interpretations of the Cárdenas administration, Cárdenas and his associates seized the opportunities provided in that chaotic period to carry reforms further than any of their predecessors in Mexico or their counterparts in other Latin American countries.

Select Bibliography

Becker, Marjorie, *Setting the Virgin on Fire: Lázaro Cárdenas, Michoacán Peasants and the Redemption of the Mexican Revolution.* Berkeley: University of California Press, 1995.

Hamilton, Nora, *The Limits of State Autonomy: Post-Revolutionary Mexico.* Princeton, New Jersey: Princeton University Press, 1982.

Joseph, Gilbert M., and Daniel Nugent, editors, *Everyday Forms of State Formation: Revolution and the Negotiation of Rule in Modern Mexico.* Durham, North Carolina: Duke University Press, 1994.

Knight, Alan, "Cardenismo: Juggernaut or Jalopy?" *Journal of Latin American Studies* 26 (1994).

—NORA HAMILTON

Carranza, Venustiano 1859–1920

General and President

Carranza rose to power by means of social and economic reforms that attracted significant popular support and allowed him to dominate Mexico during the turbulent years of the Revolution and the early post-Revolutionary era. A statesman who articulated nationalism in order to define his international policy, Carranza failed when he lost sight of his original goals and promises.

Carranza's nationalistic convictions merged with his early ambitions. Born in 1859 to Colonel Jesús Carranza in Cuatro Ciénegas, Coahuila, Venustiano Carranza received a good education in Mexico City before returning to Coahuila, where he excelled at farming and ranching. An avid reader, Carranza was interested in Latin American rather than European history. Elected as *presidente municipal* of Cuatro Ciénegas, Carranza earned popularity for his educational improvements. He also defied the Porfirio Díaz–appointed governor and in 1893 led a successful revolt, forcing Díaz to allow Carranza and his brothers to exercise considerable influence throughout Coahuila. As a senator in the national Congress, Carranza inserted new provisions into laws to regulate foreign investors. Although Carranza disapproved of the Científicos (influential intellectuals and policy advisers), he supported the nationalistic tendencies of the late Porfiriato. Nevertheless, Carranza yearned for substantial change. Initially, he backed Bernardo Reyes and then Francisco I. Madero when the 1910 presidential campaign began. Carranza also participated in Madero's revolt against Díaz; in return, Madero permitted Carranza to control Coahuila.

As governor of Coahuila from 1911 to 1913, Carranza pursued reform with a zeal that won him the loyalties of most of the northern state's inhabitants. Carranza introduced firm regulation of economic concessions, progressive taxation, improved working conditions, and dramatic educational reforms, and he encouraged unionization and insisted upon improved health facilities. Taken as a whole, these actions positioned Carranza not as a liberal but as a populist who became a nationalist.

A new phase of the Mexican Revolution began when Carranza assumed leadership of the forces that fought Victoriano Huerta's dictatorship, which had been established after Madero's assassination in February 1913. Within weeks, Carranza received support from northerners willing to preserve reforms by siding with Carranza's national insurrection. At this time, Carranza urged caution because he felt that this movement could be snuffed out easily by larger federal forces. His Plan de Guadalupe avoided appeals to social revolution; it merely outlined the procedure for toppling Huerta and united temporarily Carranza's supporters. Now the "First Chief," however, Carranza began responding to popular grievances. The Carrancistas' ability to feed hungry people by means of bringing in food to hard-hit areas became a particularly popular policy. Carranza's officers forced merchants to sell their goods at low prices, which they listed on the doors of these mercantile establishments.

Carranza's land policies had a direct bearing upon his early success. Those who opposed him often had their lands seized for being "enemies of the people." Seized land remained usually in the hands of loyal supporters, who administered it for the Carranza movement. Hence the term *carrancear*, which means "to swindle." Yet the masses received modest numbers of provisional land titles after they occupied properties or received awards from sympathetic army officers.

Most of the famous women *soldaderas* (female soldiers and/or camp followers) were Carrancistas. What encouraged women to support Carranza? Carranza attracted females because he decreed divorce legal, encouraged feminist groups to organize, and subsidized their publications and speaking tours. In a country long dominated by traditional relations between sexes, this represented a risky political venture. But it was a legitimate social demand that Carranza did not deny.

Pressured by the forces of Carranza, Francisco "Pancho" Villa, Emiliano Zapata, and invading U.S. troops who captured Veracruz, Huerta finally resigned and left the country on July 15, 1914. Carrancista forces under General Álvaro Obregón entered Mexico City on August 15, and Carranza himself entered the capital on August 20. Under the Treaties of Teoloyucan, the various Revolutionary factions were to form a National Junta. On October 10, in the town of Aguascalientes in neutral territory, leaders from the civil war gathered for the Sovereign Revolutionary Convention. The convention's early calls for unity soon gave way to an irreconcilable split between the Carrancista (whose spokesman there was Obregón) and the more radical factions of Villa and Zapata. Ultimately, the Carrancistas lost control of the proceedings, and Eulalio Gutiérrez was chosen as provisional president, an office Carranza himself assumed he would possess.

When news of the events reached him, Carranza withdrew his forces from Mexico City and set up a separate Constitutional government in Veracruz, with himself as president; Villa, meanwhile, installed Gutiérrez as president of the Conventionalist government in Mexico City. Even these political divisions soon became more complex, as Gutiérrez abandoned Mexico City for Nuevo León, the Zapatistas threw their support behind Roque González Garza as president, and Villa governed independently from Chihuahua. The new phase of the Mexican Revolution soon devolved into anarchy, with independent civil wars ranging in various states. Eventually, however, the Constitutionalists began to gain the upper hand, in large part because of the military victories of General Obregón.

But Carranza's political and economic policies were a major contributor to his ultimate triumph as well. Carranza regulated the banks tightly and stopped inflation by the end of 1916. As a nationalist, Carranza increased governmental authority over foreign investments; he forced foreign investors to renounce formal diplomatic protection and consider themselves Mexican citizens. To the delight of many, taxes on oil companies increased seven-fold from 1917 to 1920. Taxes on the Guggenheim mining interests were eight times higher than the Villista taxes on the same firm. Carranza also seized the railroads, telegraphs, and telephones; moreover, the regime's administration of communications became surprisingly efficient. To encourage local entrepreneurs, Carranza raised tariff protection. Despite such restrictions on foreign trade, exports doubled from 1916 to 1920.

Land and labor reforms clinched Carranza's victory. His January 6, 1915, decree gave land taken from peasants by Liberals and Porfirians back to villages and petitioners. It also authorized temporary land seizures by the government. Carranza reduced foreign land ownership considerably. Eventually, a decline in food production, common to nations engaged in land reform, forced the regime to curtail land distribution. Yet Carranza also supported the working class. Carrancistas outlawed debt peonage and the *tienda del raya* company store. The eight-hour day and minimum wages became the norm in areas controlled by Carrancistas. Carranza also allied with the Casa del Obrero Mundial in February 1915. These anarchosyndicalists furnished Carranza six "red" battalions in return for permission to strike and unionize. Carrancistas placed the Casa del Obrero Mundial headquarters in the elite Jockey Club; they backed Carranza until a 1916 general strike led to a parting of the ways. But Carranza allowed laborers to form a moderate labor confederation, the Confederación Regional Obrera Mexicana (CROM, or Regional Confederation of Mexican

Workers) in 1918. In general, Carranza did not interfere with the general growth of working-class organizations.

As president, Carranza soon became the precursor of the strong executives that were to characterize twentieth-century Mexico. Carranza interpreted his authoritarian approach as a form of democracy in which he enjoyed the support of the majority in defining public policy. Embracing egalitarianism meant that upper-class political traditions declined after 1915. The Carrancistas clamored consistently for industrialization, economic growth, education, land reform, and an expanded role for Mexico in world affairs. Self-made leaders now controlled regional and local governments. Military *caudillos* (strongmen) also enjoyed political legitimacy, particularly when they championed themselves as reformers. Eager for status and material gain, many of the new leaders worked to reestablish friendly ties with older elites. But political parties struggled with little success to compete with Carranza and his cohorts because the legislature played a minor role in reforming the country after 1913. A new form of personalistic populism tended to define the political tempo.

Carranza was not a classic dictator. Carranza was a patrician, but this did not prevent him from walking casually through Mexico City's Merced Market. Citizens looked up to Carranza because he exuded idealism and toughness. His personal charisma had limits, but Carranza's quest for greatness was a mixture of humility and grandeur that remains an unmistakable part of the civil war years. Carranza's error was his attempt to convince Mexicans that class demands were sectarian and that his new order would balance the interests of all within the context of a well-run political machine that usually carried out the president's wishes.

Carranza's relations with governors meant that his decisions had to be respected. Carranza encouraged his subordinates to overhaul judicial, tax, electoral, and public service policies so that they came in line with Carranza's usually progressive views on civil reform. It became a fact of life that by late 1914, governors had to check with Carranza before carrying out important proposals. Despite their subordination to Carranza, the governors played a significant role in solidifying a regime constantly under attack. Governors such as Gustavo Espinosa Mireles in Coahuila, Cándido Aguilar in Veracruz, and Salvador Alvarado in Yucatán became instrumental in aiding the national government. In general, those states ravaged by warfare were usually ones in which local reforms were at a minimum. A fair amount of

democracy existed, but Carranza failed to establish a ruling political party.

Wishing to give his regime greater political legitimacy, Carranza called for a constitutional convention to be held in Querétaro in November 1916. Although Carranza viewed the document produced by this convention—the Constitution of 1917—as too radical, he ultimately accepted it. Under the authority of this constitution he was officially elected president in special elections held in March 1917, and on May 1 he took the oath of office.

The 1917 Constitution continues to be the Mexican Revolution's repository of goals. Three items represent the most well-known provisions: Article 3 proclaimed that education was secular and free and that the Catholic Church could no longer teach in secondary and primary schools. In general, Carranza protested such extreme anticlerical measures as outdated relics from the Liberal past. But he supported Article 27, which contained his land reform decree and maintained that land always must have a social function. Resting its legitimacy on this concept of public utility, Article 27 further states that the state can nationalize land to benefit the people and promote economic development. Finally, Article 27 insists that Mexico's subsoil wealth belongs to the state, not private concessionaires. Article 123 provides labor with an eight-hour day, minimum wages, and the rights to strike and to organize for collective bargaining.

Education yielded promising but eventually disappointing results under Carranza. Although he sincerely desired educational progress, Carranza's plans were undermined by his conviction that local governments should control school policies; he believed that all would benefit by casting off the tightly centralized Porfirian system. Carranza based his plans upon the success that decentralized municipal education enjoyed in Coahuila. But state governments often found it difficult to spend the necessary amounts to improve education; as a result, the illiteracy rate changed little. Still, other achievements took place. Schools for the deaf, blind, and retarded appeared, as well as a string of industrial and technical schools. New textbooks drilled students with Carranza's nationalism by emphasizing racial unity, mestizo contributions, and an appreciation for Mexico's indigenous heritage. Beginning in 1917, the government carried out large-scale excavations of the Mexican ruins at Teotihuacan under the direction of Manuel Gamio.

The most consistently nationalistic feature of the Carranza regime was its strident diplomacy. Carranza asserted Mexican sovereignty to an unusual degree, partially because his diplomacy endeavored to protect domestic reforms. An outstanding diplomat, Carranza usually got what he wanted.

Diplomatic relations with the United States ranged from tense to violent. Carranza and his advisers discovered early that Woodrow Wilson was determined to protect U.S. interests in nearly every phase of the U.S. State Department's dealings with Mexico. Because Wilson would not extend de facto recognition to Carranza's regime in 1915, Carranza decided to support a Mexican-American uprising in Texas known as the Plan de San Diego Revolt. Hundreds of troops disguised as *tejanos* crossed the Río Bravo (Rio Grande) to fuel the fighting until Wilson gave in and recognized Carranza in October 1915.

The following year, the Pershing expedition sparked renewed conflict along the border. Launched shortly after Villa's surprise attack upon Columbus, New Mexico, in March 1916, the arrival of U.S. troops into Chihuahua surprised and infuriated Carranza, who ordered that U.S. troops not advance further. After Carranza ordered his forces to fire on advancing U.S. troops, a battle resulted in a Mexican victory at Carrizal in June 1916. Carranza's resistance provided mass support for about two years. A U.S.-Mexican conference in Atlantic City centered upon Wilsonian attempts to force Carranza to curtail his reforms. But Carranza resisted stoutly; weary U.S. negotiators gave up and Pershing's forces withdrew from Mexico empty-handed on the day that Carranza proclaimed the 1917 Constitution.

Neutrality during World War I represents a defiance of Wilson that also appealed to national pride. Carranza's courting of the Germans resulted in the infamous Zimmermann telegram, an offer of territory lost in 1848 as well as financial aid in return for a military alliance with the kaiser. Carranza's public silence on the matter added to Wilson's apprehension about Mexican aims. Yet the shrewd Carranza resisted overtures from Germany because Berlin hoped merely to distract the U.S. government rather than aid Mexico significantly.

Carranza's relations with other nations yielded tangible dividends. Germany, Spain, and other European nations sent Mexico war matériel secretly. Japan supported Carranza actively, particularly when the Japanese constructed a munitions factory in Mexico City. Carranza's overtures to Latin America focused upon pleas for stronger unity to oppose economic imperialism and dollar diplomacy. Carranza's diplomacy was quite successful in central America, where he secured a strong alliance with El Salvador that kept Guatemala from intervening into Chiapas.

Carranza's decline resulted in part from a slackening of social reforms by 1919. The sympathetic but legalistic land reform bureaucrats could do little when land awards came to a virtual end. Eager to find political allies and increase food production, Carranza returned properties to large landowners such as the Terrazas family. While Carranza himself prospered and his estate expanded to 125,000 acres (50,000 hectares), the 1919 restrictions on the distribution of communal village lands stated that *campesinos* (peasants) had to pay taxes on and indemnify the government for land awards. A fall in rural wages also angered the rural population; in a further setback to their cause, the *campesinos* of south-central Mexico lost their most powerful leader when Carranza laid a trap for Zapata, leading to his assassination on April 10, 1919. Meanwhile, falling wages also affected urban workers, who proceeded to strike in large numbers. The educational system also became a source of discontent when cutbacks began in 1918. A shortage of competent teachers exacerbated the problem of educational frustration.

On the international level, the end of World War I meant that Carranza could not resist the United States and count upon substantial European aid. Oil companies began fomenting dissident groups to attack Carranza on the northern border or deep within Mexico itself. Nationalists protested Carranza's last-minute courting of U.S. investors.

Yet the spark that set off the successful revolt that toppled him was Carranza's disastrous decision to impose a colorless successor during the 1920 elections. Many generals attempted to persuade the stubborn president to allow them to elect one of their own. General Álvaro Obregón decided to oppose Carranza. Obregón expected the presidency; he had never been defeated in battle and enjoyed popularity. When Sonora revolted in April 1920, most of the army joined Obregón. Carranza attempted to flee to Veracruz but instead died at the hands of an assassin on May 21, 1920.

Carranza's vision was not revolutionary, but his all-embracing nationalist ideology changed Mexico significantly. By 1920, however, political mobilization had reached the point at which concern over the threatened loss of political rights overrode the success of Carranza's earlier nationalist triumphs. Mexico did not acknowledge Carranza's legacy until the Cárdenas regime revived Carranza's image in the 1930s. Amid tremendous ceremony, Carranza's remains were deposited in the crypt of the Monument to the Revolution in 1942, when Mexico entered World War II. Although U.S. historians of Mexico are usually more critical of Carranza than

Mexican scholars, there is no doubt that the Carranza regime represents a major transition in Mexican history.

Select Bibliography

Katz, Friedrich, *The Secret War in Mexico: Europe, the United States and the Mexican Revolution.* Chicago and London: University of Chicago Press, 1981.

Knight, Alan, *The Mexican Revolution.* Lincoln and London: University of Nebraska Press, 1986.

Richmond, Douglas W., *Venustiano Carranza's Nationalist Struggle, 1893–1920.* Lincoln and London: University of Nebraska Press, 1983.

—Douglas W. Richmond

Castellanos, Rosario 1925–1974

Writer

"It isn't enough to discover who we are. We have to invent ourselves," a character shouted in a radical play written by Rosario Castellanos in 1973. The novels, short stories, poems, essays, and plays that Castellanos wrote between 1948 and 1974 respond to her lifelong inquiry into women's place in creativity and culture in Mexico. Today we continue to read her as a writer and thinker who was decades ahead of her time, not only in terms of pioneering the discussion of relationships among gender, race, and class in her writing by and about women in Mexico, but particularly in terms of her keen insights into the conflicts between indigenous peoples and landholding families in her native region of Chiapas.

Castellanos was born on May 25, 1925, and grew up on her family's ranch in Comitán, Chiapas, near the border with Guatemala. She was educated in Mexico City, where she graduated from the National Autonomous University with a master's degree in Philosophy in 1955. There she became part of the group of young Mexican and Central American writers known as the Generation of 1950. From 1951 to 1957 Castellanos worked in cultural programs for the National Indigenist Institute in San Cristóbal de las Casas, Chiapas, and traveled throughout the region. Those experiences are reflected in her writing, which explores two areas of experience long overlooked in Mexican letters: the critique of racial and cultural oppression of indigenous peoples in Chiapas and the status of women in provincial and urban Mexico. Her fiction focuses on women's struggles to assert their authentic selves during the period of rapid change that followed the land reforms of the Lázaro Cárdenas administration in 1941 and the rapid industrialization and urbanization of Mexico.

Her first novel, *Balún Canán* (1957), winner of the Mexican Critics' Prize for best novel in 1957 and the Chiapas Prize in 1958, drew on her memories of Tzotzil world and myth as seen through the eyes of a solitary child. The short stories in *Ciudad Real* (1960) examine conflicts between Indians, mestizos, and landholders in terms of power relationships between the conquerors and the colonized. Her second novel, *Oficio de tinieblas* (1962), which used the historical events of a Chamula Indian uprising in San Cristóbal in 1867 to recast the struggle of a woman leader against modern colonialism, is still considered to be one of the very best examples of neoindigenist writing in Latin America, marking a break with lurid representations of indigenist cultures as exotic worlds populated by poetic victims. The stories in *Los convidados de agosto* (1964) focused on women's relationships with each other within the patriarchal society of provincial Chiapas. *Album de familia* (1971) shifted its attention to the alienation of women in modern Mexico City who struggle to develop professional vocations. For example, "Lección de Cocina" uses the metaphor of a cookbook and a cooking lesson to satirize middle-class marriage in Mexico. In her play *El eterno femenino: farsa,* published posthumously in 1975 and staged in 1976, ironic humor demolished the myths and stereotypes that have oppressed women in Mexico for centuries.

From 1960 to 1974, Castellanos wrote hundreds of short chronicles for *Excelsior, Novedades, ¡Siempre!* and other Mexican periodicals, which have been partly collected in *Juicios sumarios* (1966), *Mujer que sabe latín* (1973), *El uso de la palabra* (1974), and *El mar y sus pescaditos* (1975). Her reading of Simone de Beauvoir, Simone Weil, and Virginia Woolf inspired her to explore the cultural myths of la Malinche, the Virgin of Guadalupe, and Sor Juana. These archetypal figures provided Castellanos with a rich cluster of metaphors to explore gender, sexuality, and inequality in Mexico throughout all her writing.

Poesía no eres tú (1972) collected the twelve books of poetry that Castellanos had written since 1948. In *Mujer que sabe latín* she describes "the cardinal points" of her verse as "humor, solemn meditation and contact with my carnal and historical roots." "I am a wide patio, a great open house: a memory," shouts the female speaker of "Toma de Conciencia." Yet her concept of otherness transcends gender, becoming the passage to creativity itself. In "Poesía no eres tú" she writes, "The other. With the other, humanity, dialogue, poetry, begin." "Hablando de Gabriel" considered pregnancy in terms of a changing relationship between body, self and other. Many poems and essays examined how language or silence shut women out of power structures, a decade before U.S. and French feminists began discussing these issues. "We have to find another language, we have to find another starting point," she wrote in 1973 in her essay on "El lenguaje como instrumento de dominación." After contemplating female characters and writers whose existence led to suicide, silence, and self-denial, her poem, "Meditación en el umbral" searched for "another way" of living and writing for women that was beyond madness, muteness, or penance. "Another way to be human and free. Another way to be." In 1995 her letters to her former husband, Ricardo Guerra, were published in *Cartas a Ricardo,* an intimate chronicle of that anguished relationship.

From 1960 to 1970 Castellanos was press and information director for the National University of Mexico, where she also held a chair of Comparative Literature. In 1971 President Luis Echeverría Álvarez named her Mexican ambassador to Israel, where she became a popular diplomat and occasionally taught at Hebrew University in Jerusalem. On August 7, 1974, at age 49, she was electrocuted in her home in Tel Aviv, leaving an only son, Gabriel Guerra Castellanos. Mexico paid tribute to her at a state funeral in Mexico City, where she is buried.

Select Bibliography

Ahern, Maureen, editor and translator, *A Rosario Castellanos Reader.* Austin: University of Texas Press, 1988.

O'Connell, Joanna, *Prospero's Daughter: The Prose of Rosario Castellanos.* Austin: University of Texas Press, 1995.

—Maureen Ahern

Caste War of Yucatán

Few episodes in Mexican history were as dramatic as Yucatán's Caste War. The largest and most successful rural rebellion in nineteenth-century Mexico, the Caste War began in July 1847, when Maya peasants rose up against local authorities. Rebels conquered over half the Yucatán Peninsula by the following May, only to be pushed back to the eastern rain forests. The rebellion decimated Yucatecan society. The provincial criollo (Spanish-descended, American-born) elites withdrew to the north and west, where they dedicated themselves to the lucrative henequen industry. Maya rebels carved out an independent state in eastern Yucatán and constructed a new religion based on the worship of a speaking cross. Hostilities between the two worlds flared for decades. More than any other event, the Caste War defined southeast Mexico.

Origins

The lurid mythology surrounding the Caste War of Yucatán obscures its real origins. Far from being the loin-cloth clad *huits* who populate much of the historical literature, the Yucatecan Maya had played an active role in the peninsula's economy and political struggles in the decades preceding the Caste War. Although subsistence farming remained the bedrock of the peasant economy, Mayas gradually had entered the market economy as wage earners and petty entrepreneurs, and actively defended their interests through lawsuits and other forms of resistance. Maya peasants depended on patronage ties outside of the immediate community. Prominent Mayas shared the ambitions of local criollos, while certain marginal criollos and mestizos understood the customs, language, and ambitions of rural Mayas. Intra-elite conflicts mobilized the Maya peasantry in what amounted to dress rehearsals for the Caste War itself.

Isolated from central Mexico, Yucatán had remained a backwater throughout the colonial period. Even as a boom in the region's agricultural economy in the mid-eighteenth century brought new prosperity to the region's criollo elite, Yucatecans maintained a sense of isolation from Mexico. After Mexico achieved independence in 1821, Yucatecans continued to govern their own affairs, and in 1839 the caudillo (local strongman) Santiago Imán launched a revolt that formally separated Yucatán from Mexico. Although Imán mobilized peasants around the issue of tax abolition, his revolt ignited almost millenarian expectations among the Maya peasantry. Moreover, Imán's triumph sparked a cycle of internecine violence as everyone from wealthy Mérida planters to village peasants and mestizos struggled for power. By 1847 Maya peasants from through-out the peninsula had taken part in two wars against pro-Mexican centralists, as well as innumerable local revolts.

Even as many Maya entered into cross-ethnic alliances, however, other factors had heightened interethnic tensions. Mayas chaffed under forced military conscription, heavy tax burdens, and excessive moral scrutiny by the Catholic church. Although some Maya entrepreneurs were able to benefit, a boom in the agricultural economy of Yucatán had a devastating effect on many communities. In the two decades preceding the outbreak of the Caste War in 1847, conflicts over land and other resources had become desperate: the Maya population had been growing steadily for over a century, non-Mayas were flooding the countryside, and criollo elites privatized large amounts of national land previously available to peasant cultivators.

The region's network of social mediators also had begun to break down. Although Maya communities still governed themselves through the *pueblos de indios* instituted during the colonial period, they scarcely existed in isolation. Maya elites were bound to their communities by language, culture, and kinship, but they were also part of a complex system of middlemen and cultural brokers who negotiated Yucatán's rural tranquillity. During the early national period privileged Mayas, particularly the *batabs* (village headmen or caciques), were active in local politics and often became relatively affluent; by the 1830 and 1840s, however, their situation had become increasingly untenable. By disrupting the rural tax system, criollo caudillos disrupted an important key to the batabs' livelihood, and resignations became ever more frequent. Moreover, criollos often dragged Maya elites into their own political quarrels, exposing them to a level of political violence that they had not experienced since the Conquest. The crisis of the Maya elites went beyond their local communities. It disrupted the entire social fabric of rural Yucatán.

Far from being isolated primitives, then, Maya peasants were part of a complex series of social, political, and economic networks. Indeed, the villages of eastern Yucatán that formed the backbone of the Caste War were bound together by a commercial network linked to the British colony of Belize, trading local commodities for sugar, staple foods, distilled alcohol, and contraband (including arms). As the people of these communities came to know each other, they developed a regional identity that set them apart from the other subregions of the peninsula dominated by Mérida and Campeche. Most of the Caste War's soldiers and virtually all of its leaders came from a single 30-mile (50-kilometer) string of villages, and the early stages of the rebel-lion drew in a number of whites, mestizos, and other non-Mayas from this region as well.

The War to 1863

The Caste War erupted in the early morning hours of July 30, 1847. Some days earlier, criollos had gotten wind of a conspiracy among the village leaders in the aforementioned string of communities. They executed one of these—Manuel Antonio Ay—and immediately began a roundup of purported accomplices. Chief among these were Jacinto Pat and Cecilio Chi, the *batabs* of villages along the contraband trade lines. But would-be insurgents were now ready. Chi raided his home village of Tepich, killing the non-Mayas and thus sparking the war. Thereafter, Chi's forces dominated in the north, while Pat, a prosperous landowner and distiller, dominated southern insurgents and maintained access to the Belizean arms merchants. By March 1848 they controlled approximately half of the peninsula.

Complex forces conditioned the fortunes of the war. On one hand, the rebels suffered all the weaknesses of peasant revolts. Perhaps the most important of these were the rebels' ill-defined aims. Despite their public rhetoric of exterminating *"españoles,"* the leaders had far more limited and specific goals. From the beginning, a series of abortive peace negotiations focused on tax relief, with land, debt, and the curtailment of administrative abuses as related issues. Rebels also demanded that the execution of criollo caudillos who apparently had betrayed their trust. By spring 1848 it became clear that the rebels could not achieve these goals under the current political arrangement, and their goals shifted toward complete political independence.

Also problematic were the rebels' inadequate arms and supplies, poorly trained forces, and general lack of cohesion. Although the rebels obtained some materials from Belizean merchants, they often had to make do with improvised munitions. In place of lead bullets, many used small, sharpened sticks known as *palenquetas;* others relied on the trusty machete. Rebels repeatedly had access to sophisticated weapons such as cannon and mortars, but for various reasons failed to take advantage of them. There was no single Maya army, but rather a loose confederation of bands under the command of their own caudillos, each profoundly jealous of the others. Discipline remained scant. These factors ultimately caused the revolt to break down into feuds and intrigues, particularly when the rebellion's momentum stalled and Maya peasants returned home to complete their spring plantings.

On the other hand, the criollo elites suffered their own problems. The rebellion initially panicked them into a retreat that left the field open to rebel advances. But the situation was never as dire as accounts have suggested. The rebels had overextended themselves long before reaching the apogee of their conquests. Campeche in particular was impregnable, and throughout early 1848 arms and supplies continued to pour into the Yucatecan ports from Havana. In mid-1848 the army took the offensive. At the same time Yucatecans rejoined the Mexican Republic, which sent General Manuel Micheltorena to organize a massive counterinsurgency; his campaign proved effective but highly expensive, and in May 1851 he ceded command to General Rómulo Díaz de la Vega, who operated by more flexible methods. By 1853 the Yucatecan government had retaken the bulk of its lost territory.

The rebels were now desperate. They suffered crippling shortages of arms, salt, meat, and even simple clothing. Ambitious subordinates assassinated the original caudillos and assumed command. Disappointed by reality, the caste warriors retreated to the supernatural, rallying around the commands of a Speaking Cross, a device that, although patently controlled by the generals, nonetheless addressed deep-seated concerns and symbols of the rural folk. Rebels now became *cruzob* (cross people) who obeyed their oracle's call for a war without compromise. The remote settlement of Chan Santa Cruz (Little Holy Cross) became their capital.

Fortune smiled on the *cruzob*. In 1853 Yucatán's criollo elite embarked on a decade of coups, revolts, and civil wars as various factions—partly political, partly military—vied for supremacy. Campeche split off as a separate state in 1858. Yucatán's bloody factionalism owed partly to the region's poverty (much of the struggle revolved around control of two scant commodities: customs receipts and political patronage). In part it stemmed from the political instability of Mexico itself in the 1850s; and in part it reflected tensions and havoc generated by the war itself. These internecine conflicts erupted just as rebel fortunes had reached their nadir, and they gave new authority to the Speaking Cross. The *cruzob* now regrouped under a previously unknown leader, Venancio Puc, an iron-willed revolutionary consolidator in the mold of Joseph Stalin. Ruling in concert with a junta of generals, Puc imposed severe discipline on the rebels. He maximized the cult of the Speaking Cross, centralized the partition of spoils, declared his own monopoly on distilling alcohol, expanded trade with Belize, and established rents on farming and logging within *cruzob* territory. In 1857 Puc launched a renewed offensive that culminated in the capture of Bacalar in February of the following year. The Cross now controlled the entire east coast from Tulum to the Belize border. A related policy of intermittent raids helped to intimidate and fragment the Yucatecans. Puc's creation was a harsh militarized society, but it was strong enough to survive into the twentieth century.

Aftermath and Reorganization

The war wrought economic havoc on Yucatán. Whole regions of commercial agriculture collapsed for years. The peninsula's sugar industry recuperated, only to perish under competition from the increasingly mechanized sugar giant, Cuba. Until the henequen boom of the 1870s, Yucatecan estate owners had to content themselves with supplying grain and cattle products to Havana. Moreover, estate owners were profoundly ambivalent toward the war itself. Eager for an army victory, they also used all means in their power to avoid furnishing men and resources for the effort. Prominent locals resented the intrusion of the politically powerful military officers, and the struggle between war polity and municipal society remained a defining feature of the 1850s and 1860s.

Another consequence of the Caste War was the relocation of peoples. From a prewar high of 500,000 to 600,000, the population declined to some 300,000 by 1850. An undetermined number perished, less from battle than from the scarcities and disease that came in its wake. In 1853, for example, a cholera epidemic tore through towns and *ranchos* alike. But if many died, the majority simply changed address. Refugees of all races fled outward to Tabasco, to northern Guatemala, and to the sparsely populated islands of Yucatán's eastern coast. The most important exile community took shape in northern Belize. Here, the survivors from Yucatán's sugar belt reconstructed their old lives as property owners, cultivators, and merchants of alcohol. Still others became internal refugees. Countless Mayas fled into the Yucatecan forests to eke out subsistence. In the process of reconquest the army routinely swept the backlands, capturing and relocating these people whom its officers called "presenters" on the pretext that they had "presented" themselves for removal to the pacified zone.

Not every Maya became a caste warrior; in fact, it is doubtful that more than a minority actually revolted. Peasants of the north and the west had less connection with the socioeconomic lines that had spawned the revolt. They had little exposure to the people and issues outside of their territory, and the aims of the eastern rebels made little sense to them. For this nonradicalized majority the Caste War was a terrifying event. More joined the rebellion than is commonly realized; but most found themselves caught between insurgent armies and a rabid criollo paranoia. Many fled. Other peasants were dragooned into the army as porters and road-clearers, military corveé laborers that the Yucatecans called *hidalgos* after an old colonial term for privileged

Mayas who had aided in the conquest. In the pacified zones the peasants, faced with starvation, violence, or conscription, accepted onerous labor contracts that bound them to the land for periods as long as 15 years. Most evidence suggests that the average peasant lived in mortal terror of the *cruzob,* who made periodic violent raids throughout the 1850s and 1860s, and who were known for killing peaceful Mayas or abducting them as slave labor.

Beginning in 1851 certain rebel communities—the so-called *pacíficos* of the deep south—made peace. These were rag-tag collections of Mayas, deserted soldiers, Belizean blacks, and refugees from Central America's ongoing wars. The *pacíficos* signed treaties with the Mérida governments in which they promised to aid the war effort in exchange for amnesty, tax exemption, and the right to keep their arms. They supplemented a subsistence economy by trade with Belize and Campeche. The arrangement amounted to a near-total political autonomy. The *pacíficos* had no interest in serving the Yucatecan state, only in being left alone. Social structures were anarchic; titular leaders had little real control over their "followers." The *pacíficos* simply ignored political obligations such as extradition. Moreover, while they reveled in small skirmishes with the *cruzob,* they shunned systematic and extended military mobilization. The many criollo plans for some united crusade against the Speaking Cross were thus fantasies.

One of the most sordid features of the war was the return of human slavery. Criollo politicians and military officers, finding themselves with minimal resources and innumerable prisoners, sold *cruzob* prisoners as slaves to the insatiable Cuban sugar estates. Given the psychosis of war, it was inevitable that these same traders, finding captured rebels in short supply, began to enslave peaceful Mayas and mestizos as well. The trade became integral to Yucatán's political instability, as exile groups living in Havana financed their own invasions on the returns from this nefarious enterprise.

The French Empire in Yucatán

The years of the French empire in Yucatán (1863–67) formed a brief but important period of peninsular history. The imperialists momentarily quieted Yucatán's revolts. They also presided over a short-lived cotton boom, a byproduct of the U.S. Civil War. But the empire also escalated hostilities again with Chan Santa Cruz and in so doing provoked the last true episode of caste warfare.

A combination of forces led to this turn. Renewed warfare against the *cruzob* was partly an attempt to strike a nationalist posture. The imperialists hoped that a crusade of reconquest would earn them the support of Yucatán's notoriously quarrelsome elite. But the *cruzob* helped provoke the decision, since the months surrounding the arrival of imperial power were a time of energetic rebel sorties into the pacified zones. By 1864, then, the empire committed itself to a war almost as large as the one it was waging against Benito Juárez and his Liberal government.

The new masters of Yucatán soon stumbled over the realities of a bitterly conflicted peninsula. Imperial commissar José Salazar Ilarregui tried to imitate Spanish colonial methods by moderating the draconian 1847 labor code and appointing a full-time legal defender for the Mayas. But these mild checks on the prerogatives of the landed class merely provoked outrage. At the same time, Yucatecans were more reluctant than ever to mobilize for war. Desertion was endemic, and the populations of the *pacífico* communities swelled with runaway soldiers. Ironically, the imperial war also reinvigorated Chan Santa Cruz, which in 1864 was bordering on fragmentation (a coup eliminated Venancio Puc in January, and although military hard-liners managed to regain control, the threat of internal divisions was clear). In October 1866 the imperial-led army narrowly escaped annihilation at the hands of the *cruzob.* Subsequent army mutinies, combined with a strong nationalist resistance pressing in from Tabasco, doomed the empire in Yucatán.

Peninsular affairs eventually stabilized. With the empire out of the way, the *cruzob* ravaged their hated enemies, the *pacíficos.* The last *pacífico* to challenge seriously the *cruzob*'s southern trade routes was the bellicose Marcos Canul, who died in an abortive raid on Orange Walk, Belize, on September 1, 1872. The Cross at last enjoyed uncontested control of the southeast. Yucatecans, meanwhile, had fought themselves into exhaustion. They contented themselves with the burgeoning profits from henequen, a maguey plant whose fiber provided twine for mechanized wheat-binders. Tightly interlinked with U.S. monopoly capital via secret purchasing agreements, the criollo elites now assumed their role as Yucatán's infamous *casta divina,* an oligarchy that worked its Maya peons like so many slaves and built homes of marble opulence along the grand avenues of Mérida. The only lingering symptoms of warfare were occasional raids, along with a general aura of fear and taboo surrounding the southeastern forests.

The Reconquest of the Southeast

Between 1880 and 1930 the Mexican nation-state reclaimed its control over the storied kingdom of the Cross. Mexican president Porfirio Díaz initially abided the peninsular situation, since it provided a check on the fractious Yucatecans. Over time, however, an economic reconquest swept through the southeast. Mexican fortune-hunters entered the rain forest, lured by resources such as chicle and precious woods. The *cruzob* chiefs alternately resisted and joined forces with the new entrepreneurs, at times even providing their own soldiers as labor gangs.

Eventually the forces of economic and political modernity overwhelmed the *cruzob*. As Mexico's Revolutionary government consolidated itself after 1920, the People of the Cross found it hard to resist the incursions of anthropologists, archaeologists, political agents, and rain forest entrepreneurs. The last of these holdout villages accepted government land titles in the 1920s, hence placing themselves within national political authority. The southeast territory, now renamed Quintana Roo, remained relatively underdeveloped until the 1970s; statehood arrived in 1974, along with a boom in tourism. The effects of this last influence were mixed. Confined largely to the coast, tourism caused little direct incursion into the interior villages. But it raised local prices, and as Mexico's agricultural economy declined throughout the petroleum years following 1976, many villagers migrated to Cancún or Cozumel for construction work. The cult of the Speaking Cross outlived its war-torn origins, but after 1899 it permanently fragmented into rival communities, each with its own Cross.

Mayas of the henequen region also experienced a problematic evolution. The 1910 Revolution abolished debt peonage and ultimately brought agrarian reform. It also helped legitimate Maya culture and bring peasants into politics at the local and state level. But over time residents of the rural *ejidos* (collective farms) became reconstituted peons to an agrarian bureaucracy. To compound problems, the world markets for henequen slid into uninterrupted decline after World War II. By the 1990s the industry was dead. Rural Yucatecans now struggled with subsistence farming, migrated to the cities in search of jobs, and continued to search for viable nontraditional exports. Life in the countryside was difficult indeed. However, in all parts of the peninsula the memory of the Caste War remained a source of pride, the historical emblem of a people's search for dignity and self-determination.

Select Bibliography

Angel, Barbara, "The Reconstruction of Rural Society in the Aftermath of the Mayan Rebellion of 1847." *Journal of the Canadian Historical Association* 4 (1993).

Dumond, Don E., "The Talking Crosses of Yucatán: A New Look at Their History." *Ethnohistory* 32 (1985).

Farriss, Nancy M., *Maya Society under Colonial Rule: The Collective Enterprise of Survival*. Princeton, New Jersey: Princeton University Press, 1984.

Konrad, Herman W., "Capitalism on the Tropical-Forest Frontier: Quintana Roo, 1880s to 1930." In *Land, Labor, and Capital in Modern Yucatán: Essays in Regional History and Political Economy*, edited by Jeffery T. Brannon and Gilbert M. Joseph. Tuscaloosa: University of Alabama Press, 1991.

Patch, Robert W., "Decolonization, the Agrarian Problem, and the Origins of the Caste War, 1812–1847." In *Land, Labor, and Capital in Modern Yucatán: Essays in Regional History and Political Economy*, edited by Jeffery T. Brannon and Gilbert M. Joseph. Tuscaloosa: University of Alabama Press, 1991.

Reed, Nelson, *The Caste War of Yucatán*. Stanford, California: Stanford University Press, 1964.

Rugeley, Terry, *Yucatán's Maya Peasantry and the Origins of the Caste War*. Austin: University of Texas Press, 1996.

Sullivan, Paul, *Unfinished Conversations: Mayas and Foreigners Between Two Wars*. New York: Knopf, 1989.

Villa Rojas, Alfonso, *The Maya of East Central Quintana Roo*. Washington, D.C.: Carnegie Institute, 1943.

Wells, Alan, *Yucatán's Gilded Age: Haciendas, Henequen, and International Harvester, 1860–1915*. Albuquerque: University of New Mexico Press, 1985.

—TERRY RUGELEY

Catholic Church

This entry includes five articles that discuss the Catholic Church:

Catholic Church: Colonial Structure, Divisions, and Hierarchy
Catholic Church: Hapsburg New Spain
Catholic Church: Bourbon New Spain
Catholic Church: 1821–1910
Catholic Church: 1910–96

See also Popular Catholicism; Virgin of Guadalupe and Guadalupanismo

Catholic Church: Colonial Structure, Divisions, and Hierarchy

The hierarchical structure of the Catholic Church in New Spain was the result of one and one-half millennia of development. This article will consider the finished product of this evolution as it was found in Spain and New Spain, beginning in the fifteenth century and reaching its completed form in the sixteenth.

Holy Orders

The structure of the Catholic Church was based on the various levels of ministry globally known as Holy Orders, of which the most important were priesthood and episcopate.

The first step taken by an aspirant to the clerical state was known as tonsure, a ceremony whereby part of his hair was cut to symbolize renunciation of the world and entrance into the status of cleric (clérigo) or of the clergy (clerecía), terms derived from the Greek *kleros,* meaning "lot," that is, one who has cast his lot with the Lord. In its widest sense clérigo meant any person who had entered the clerical state via tonsure. In the sixteenth century it also was synonymous with the diocesan priest—that is, a priest who served as a member of a diocese under a bishop rather than in a religious order. As a sign of their state, clerics in that century wore a small shaven area on the back of the head, which in English is called a tonsure (in Spanish corona).

After this the aspirant passed through eight orders or stages. Four were called minor orders: porter (doorkeeper), lector (reader), exorcist (one who cast out demons), and acolyte (assistant at liturgical ceremonies). The other four were called major orders and were subdiaconate, diaconate, priesthood, and episcopacy. Each of these steps conferred more responsibility than the preceding one. The first of the major orders, the subdiaconate, carried with it the obligation of celibacy and the daily recitation of the canonical hours, also called the divine office or the breviary. The four minor orders and subdiaconate were not considered sacraments.

The order of deacon carried with it the obligation and right to preach, perform solemn baptisms, and conduct funerals. After this came the priesthood and episcopate, the latter in the sixteenth century being considered the fullness of the priesthood because it carried with it the power to impart orders to others.

Territorial Administration

The lowest geographical division of ecclesiastical administration was the parish (parroquia), which was under the direction of a priest called a pastor (párroco). The term cura was also used, although it had the more generic meaning of any priest carrying out a parochial ministry. Above the parish was the large grouping called the diocese (diócesis, obispado) ruled by a bishop (obispo), who had genuine legislative, executive, and judicial power. The bishop's immediate assistant was his vicar general (gran vicario) or his chief ecclesiastical judge (provisor), who sometimes ruled the diocese in the absence of the bishop and were his delegates for all kinds of business, especially that involving ecclesiastical trials. Sometimes a bishop's successor would be appointed in the lifetime of the incumbent and would be called coadjutor with the right of succession (coadjutor cum iure successionis). The practice of having auxiliary or assistant bishops was unknown in New Spain during the colonial period.

The administration of a diocese was shared by the cathedral chapter (cabildo eclesiástico or, in archdioceses, metropolitano). It had a twofold function: first, to act as a board of consultants and advisers to the bishop, and, second, to recite the canonical hours in public in the cathedral. This latter function was carried out with varying degrees of liturgical ceremony. The chapter usually ruled the diocese in the interim between bishops (sede vacante), often through an elected representative called the vicar capitular. In some dioceses the cabildo had the right to nominate the new bishop, but this was not done in the Spanish dependencies.

The cabildo had four ranks: five dignitaries (dignidades), ten canons (canónigos), six racioneros; and six medio-racioneros. The five dignidades had other functions in addition to the two mentioned above and enjoyed the honorific title of don. The dean (deán), usually the senior member of the cabildo, was its president and presided over its meetings in the absence of the bishop. He was in charge of all ceremonies and divine worship and acted more or less as the pastor of the cathedral church. The archdeacon (arcediano) originally was the head of the deacons who participated in the cathedral ceremonies. By the sixteenth century he was examiner of those who presented themselves for ordination. He sometimes acted as administrator of the diocese in the bishop's absence and was ordinarily expected to have at least a bachelor's degree in canon law. In the sixteenth century this was the most powerful position on the cathedral chapter of Mexico. The schoolmaster (maestrescuelas) was in charge of the cathedral school. He was required to offer Latin classes to all clerics and aspirants who asked for them, and he was ordinarily required to have a bachelor's degree in canon law or philosophy. The choirmaster (chantre) was in charge of the cathedral choir and had to do some of the singing personally. The treasurer (tesorero) was in charge of the administration of the physical plant and the revenues from the patrimony, or foundation, of the cabildo. These included the fábrica, or income for the upkeep and maintenance of buildings, and the *superávit,* or surplus funds, at the end of each year. The *canónigos, racioneros,* and *medio-racioneros* had descending levels of importance and income.

Any ecclesiastical office to which a salary *(frutos)* was attached, such as pastor or administrator of a hospital, was called a benefice *(beneficio).* Consequently a *beneficiado* was any cleric who lived by an income attached to an ecclesiastical office. Benefice is a wider term than prebend *(prebenda),* which meant the right to receive a share of the income *(mesa)* from the cathedral. All *prebendados* were *beneficiados,* but not all *beneficiados* were *prebendados.* The matter of cleric's having an income or means to live was very important in the sixteenth century, and even until recent times no one could be ordained to the subdiaconate who did not have a guaranteed means of sustenance *(título).*

Dioceses were grouped into larger territorial units called provinces *(provincias eclesiáticas,* not to be confused with the provinces of religious orders to be mentioned below), of which the chief bishop, whose diocese was called the archdiocese *(arquidiócesis),* had the title of archbishop *(arzobispo)* or metropolitan *(metropolitano).* There was only one archdiocese in a province, the others being called suffragans *(sufragáneos).* The metropolitan had no jurisdiction over the internal administration of his suffragans, although in some cases his courts could hear appeals from theirs.

The terms patriarch and primate are honorary, although ordinarily the primatial diocese or see *(sede,* meaning seat) was the oldest one in a particular country. There is no indication of the term being used in Mexico before or after Independence. The term Patriarch of the Indies was, however, secured for some bishops by the Spanish Crown. The title had a confused history, having been used by the Crown as a means of augmenting its control over the church in the Indies and by the papacy in an attempt to restrict that same control. The title, however, was totally honorary and carried with it no jurisdiction or authority.

A meeting of the bishop of a diocese with his priests to resolve problems and enact legislation was called a synod *(sínodo).* A meeting of all the bishops of an ecclesiastical province was called a provincial council *(concilio provincial).*

Religious Orders

A religious order *(religión* or *orden)* was one whose members took public vows and lived together in community under a rule (for which reasons they are also sometimes called *regulares).* A monastery *(monasterio)* was a religious house in which the members were monks *(monjes)* who lived all their lives in the monastery, which was an autonomous or semiautonomous unit. The best-known of the monastic orders are the Benedictines. It should be noted that in the sixteenth century the term monastery had come to be used loosely for any religious house of men or women. Similarly a convent *(convento)* could be a religious house of either men or women.

The friars *(frailes),* on the other hand, did not commit themselves to life in an individual house but belonged to international groupings with a different form of administration. Some of these orders had originated in the Middle Ages and were called mendicants *(mendicantes)* because they originally had lived by begging. The best-known of these orders were the Franciscans (Order of Friars Minor), the Dominicans (Order of Preachers), the Augustinians, and the Mercedarians (Orden de la Merced Redención de Cautivos). The Jesuits were neither monks nor friars but were originally clerks regular. However, after 1583 they were canonically religious, while remaining distinct from the mendicants.

Mendicant administration existed side be side with that of the bishops and frequently in competition with it. By a privilege called exemption, most male religious orders composed predominantly of clerics were free of the bishop's jurisdiction in regard to their internal affairs while working in a diocese. Geographically, the orders were divided into provinces (not to be confused with the ecclesiastical provinces mentioned above) ruled by a provincial superior *(provincial),* assisted by a council (whose members sometimes were called *definidores).* Individual houses of religious were ruled by superiors or priors, who among the Franciscans were called guardians. The parallel administrations of bishop and religious caused dissension and controversy throughout the sixteenth century. In these struggles the religious relied heavily on the various privileges and exemptions granted them by the papacy, of which the most important was the papal bull *Exponi nobis,* known as the *Omnímoda,* of 1522. In the process of evangelization, the mendicants made use of the mission/presidio system, that is, mission stations protected by a sufficient number of Spanish soldiers. Eventually the mission would become stabilized and become a *doctrina,* a quasi-parish of newly converted Indians. Throughout the sixteenth and a good part of the seventeenth centuries, the *doctrinas* were a bone of contention between bishops and friars.

The term ordinary *(ordinario)* was applied to any office or officeholder with true jurisdiction exercised in his own name and not in that of another. It is the opposite of vicar or vicarious. Although in strict canonical terminology it could be applied to the provincials of a religious order, in everyday speech it more often indicated a bishop, especially in the phrase local ordinary. Anyone who held ordinary power, whether bishop or religious provincial, was called a prelate *(prelado)*, though the term was ordinarily used for bishops alone.

Church Structure in New Spain

The Catholic Church in New Spain has been called a "church of friars" because the first missionary work was carried on by the mendicants, prior to the arrival of any bishop. The first diocese was that of Tlaxcala, with the Dominican Julián Garcés as bishop. Mexico City was made a diocese in 1530, with the Franciscan Juan de Zumárraga as the first bishop. Until 1547 it was suffragan to the archdiocese of Seville, but in that year an independent ecclesiastical province of Mexico was established. Even after that, however, diocesan structure and practice in New Spain tended to follow the model of Seville.

The church in New Spain was entirely supported by the Crown through a system of tithes *(diezmos)*. Theoretically the tithe was a 10 percent tax on agricultural production, although in practice the percentage fluctuated. In the sixteenth century there was a strong debate on whether the Indians should count as part of the tithe. Eventually they paid a tithe on wheat and cattle. They also contributed to church support through labor, often of a forced nature. A royal *cédula* of 1501 defined which items were subject to tithing and the amounts for each. Although church authorities collected the tithe, the money went to the Crown, which redistributed it to the church according to a complex formula. In addition the church received donations and bequests and eventually became a major source of money, land, and financing for capitalist ventures in the colony.

Two important institutions in New Spain did not belong to the hierarchical structure of the church: confraternities *(cofradías)* and convents of nuns. Bishops rather consistently attempted to extend their control over the former, not always successfully. Orders of nuns did not enjoy the privilege of exemption, and so the internal or disciplinary life of a convent was subject to the jurisdiction of the local bishop.

The Patronato Real

Relations between church and state in New Spain under the Hapsburgs were governed by a complex series of laws and privileges collectively called the *patronato real*. It was codified in 1574 in the Ordenanza de patronazgo, which sharply restricted the rights of both mendicants and bishops. No church or monastery could be founded without royal permission The king had the right to found all ecclesiastical offices and to draw the boundary lines of dioceses. Archbishops and bishops were nominated by the king, who presented their names to the pope, while he had the right of immediate appointment for many lower offices.

At the conclusion of the War of the Spanish Succession, the Bourbon Dynasty was established as the ruling house of Spain. Under the monarchs of the Enlightenment, especially Carlos III (1759–88), state control of the church became virtually absolute. Royal policy took on overtones of anticlericalism and even a certain hostility toward traditional religious practices that it had not had before. This hostility reached its climax in the expulsion of the Jesuits from Spanish dominions (1767). The Crown also extended its control over ecclesiastical finances.

Church structure in New Spain followed that of the mother country very closely, with relatively few adaptations, such as the *doctrinas*. This structure was characterized by an intrinsic tension between the diocesan and mendicant elements and by an encroaching state control that eventually made the church a virtual department of state. The difficulties caused by this state control carried over into the national period.

See also Inquisition; Missions

Select Bibliography

Padden, Robert, "The *Ordenanza del Patronazgo*: An Interpretive Essay." *The Americas* 12 (April 1956).

Poole, Stafford, *Pedro Moya de Contreras: Catholic Reform and Royal Power in New Spain, 1571–1591*. Berkeley: University of California Press, 1987.

Ricard, Robert, *The Spiritual Conquest of Mexico*, translated by Lesley Byrd Simpson. Berkeley: University of California Press, 1966.

Schwaller, John Frederick, "The Cathedral Chapter of Mexico in the Sixteenth Century." *Hispanic American Historical Review* 61:4 (November 1981).

———, "The *Ordenazgo del Patronazgo* in New Spain, 1574–1600." *The Americas* 42 (January 1986).

———, *Origins of Church Wealth in Mexico: Ecclesiastical Revenues and Church Finances, 1523–1600*. Albuquerque: University of New Mexico Press, 1985.

—STAFFORD POOLE

Catholic Church: Hapsburg New Spain

In the colonial period, church and state were deeply intertwined institutions, both headed by the Spanish monarch. With the bull Inter Caetera (1493), Pope Alexander VI granted the Spanish Crown title to lands 100 leagues west of the Azores, essentially dividing spheres of control between the Spanish and Portuguese in their overseas activities. The motivation for the Spanish Crown to petition the pope on this matter was to prevent the Portuguese from infringing on territories Spain was claiming. However, Queen Isabel's wish to extend Christian faith to new lands doubltess was also a powerful reason to pursue the matter with the papacy. With this papal bull, the Spanish monarchs became "apostolic vicars" over the New World, since they exclusively were entrusted with its evangelization. In a separate bull (Eximae Devotionis), Alexander VI granted the Spanish Crown the "right of presentation"—the right to present the names of candidates for ecclesiastical posts to the pope for final appointment. In effect it was the power of patronage.

A third major papal concession was made in 1501, by granting the Crown the use of tithes. Tithes were theoretically a 10 percent tax on agriculture and mining for support of the Catholic Church. By granting the tithe income to the Crown, the papacy provided a means to compensate it for the expenses of conquest and evangelization. The power granted the Crown for its overseas holdings exceeded that on the Iberian Peninsula, where tithes went directly to the church rather than first into Crown coffers for later allocation to the church.

The absolute right of *patronato real* (royal patronage) for church affairs in the New World was granted to the Spanish Crown by Pope Julius II in 1508, with the bull Universalis Ecclesiae. Construction of churches, demarcation of dioceses, power of appointment, and the tithe revenues were all under Crown control.

Taken together, these papal bulls gave the Spanish Crown absolute control over the Catholic Church in the Indies. Some scholars assert with good cause that this was the most important of the Crown's powers. Although the Spanish monarchs were not granted power to make religious doctrine, a right reserved to the papacy, nevertheless the Crown could speed or delay the proclamation of doctrine in its overseas colonies, or suppress it entirely.

Although the monarch had absolute control over the Catholic Church in New Spain, there was ecclesiastical intrusion in civil and political affairs. Civil law had religious or spiritual justification; in fact, the Crown based its right to rule on the papal bulls naming the Crown as the agent to evangelize the Indians.

In terms of institutional structure, church and state hierarchies were parallel in many ways. The viceroy was the highest local authority of both church and state, being patron of the church and head of state in New Spain. When the office of viceroy was vacant, the archbishop served as interim viceroy, which happened on more than one occasion. Both the viceroy and the archbishop were based in the capital, while secondary cities, such as Guadalajara and Oaxaca were the seats of civil high courts *(audiencias)* and bishoprics. At the local level, civil jurisdictions were headed by *corregidores* (the civil representative of the Crown), with priests overseeing parishes. Because the Crown had the power to determine the boundaries of both civil and ecclesiastical jurisdictions, they usually coincided.

There was cooperation between church and state on fundamental questions: that civil and moral order be maintained, royal authority be respected, and the "True Faith" (i.e., Catholicism) be the only religious belief permitted. In practice, however, there was considerable friction between civil and religious institutions over primacy of authority and jurisdiction. A standard feature of colonial Mexico was rivalry between the archbishop and the viceroy, or between the bishop and the *audiencia*. The Crown was ultimately the arbiter of these disputes, since it had authority over both hierarchies. In the Hapsburg period the Crown did not subordinate one hierarchy to the other, but nonetheless there were tensions between the two.

At times, jurisdictions or functions of the two hierarchies were overlapping, a clear example being the extension of Spanish sovereignty to new realms by the Catholic Church. The regular clergy (those belonging to a religious order)—especially the Franciscans, Dominicans, and Augustinians—divided territory in the central regions during the immediate post-Conquest period, establishing a permanent Spanish presence in existing native polities. Later the regular clergy established missions on the northern frontier. This was done mainly by the Jesuits during the Hapsburg era, but with their expulsion during the Bourbon period (1767), missions were established by the Franciscans. Although the church's primary goal was to convert the native populations to Christianity, its very presence in regions with no other Spaniards meant the establishment of Spanish royal authority.

In the Conquest period in central Mexico, the mendicant orders were a prime agent of Spanish expansion, following closely the military conquest of central Mexico in 1521. Fernando (Hernán) Cortés invited the Franciscans and Dominican orders to the newly conquered lands. These two orders had undergone a reform in Spain in the late fifteenth and early sixteenth centuries, and it was argued that they would be superior to the secular clergy (those not belonging to a religious order) as agents for converting the natives. There was a practical side to Cortés's invitation as well, since the regular clergy were less firmly under the control of the Crown than the secular clergy, and could therefore be potential allies in his own conflicts with the Crown over jurisdiction and authority. In order to fulfill the function of conversion in its fullest manner, the mendicant orders were granted power by Pope Adrian VI in 1522 to act as parish priests, dispensing the sacraments to the laity, a responsibility that previously had been reserved for the secular clergy.

Although the regular clergy served the Crown's purposes well during the early phases of the colony, the Crown moved to install the secular clergy as parish priests, their traditional role. This was formally done in 1574 with the Ordenanza del Patronazgo, which placed the regular clergy exercising powers of the secular clergy under the authority of the bishops. This was in keeping with edicts from the Council of Trent in the mid–sixteenth century, which placed all clergy with parochial powers under the authority of bishops. Implementation of the *ordenanza* was uneven. As with much colonial legislation that had an impact on civil and ecclesiastical institutions, standard regulations were modified to fit local conditions. Thus, through legislation the Crown could set priorities and goals, but how those were met depended on local powers.

The *ordenanza* marks the Crown's assertion of control over the clergy, particularly aiming to replace mendicants with the secular clergy as the primary spiritual ministers to the Indians. In its efforts to assert control over the ministry to the Indians, the Crown set educational standards for secular clerics and ordered that they learn the Indian languages. The requirement that clerics learn indigenous tongues gave an edge to criollo clerics (those born in the Americas). In the late sixteenth century, criollo clerics came to dominate cathedral chapters, as the Crown in this period clearly favored more local control.

Both church and state agreed in the goal of achieving moral behavior in society. The Inquisition in New Spain became a prime tool of regulation in matters of faith and religious practice, and formally was constituted as a separate office in 1571. The Inquis-

ition criticized both secular and regular clergy, and inquisitors often were arrogant in their actions toward clerics not part of the Inquisition. Although the Inquisition had considerable authority to arrest, imprison, and try individuals (both lay and clerical, but not Indians), it did not formally carry out sentences of execution. Those sentenced to die were "relaxed to the secular arm"—that is, were released to civil custody. Autos de fe, the elaborate ceremonies in which the Inquisition's victims were publicly humiliated or executed, were events of high religious content, but were under the jurisdiction of civil authorities.

Since the Crown had been granted the use of tithes by the papacy, it could enjoy considerable income and power. In fact, the Crown gave the bulk of the revenue to religious institutions and officials. Crown officials had the task of collecting the tithes. Where there were shortfalls from tithe income to support the clergy, the remainder was to be supplied from the royal coffers. The tithe income was divided into four parts. One-quarter of each went to the bishop and to the cathedral chapter. The remaining half was divided into nine parts (*novenos*): two went to the king (this part usually was spent on churches), four to the lower secular clergy (parish priests), one and one-half to hospitals, and one and one-half on "temporalities" (i.e., the material property of the church). Everyone was subject to the tithe, although there was some debate in the early period as to the Indians' obligation. The Jesuits strenuously resisted payment of the tithe, arguing the order was exempt due to pontifical privileges. Jesuit intransigence on this point produced tension between the state and the order (also between the Jesuits and other religious orders, which did pay the tithe), but was not a direct cause of the order's expulsion from the Spanish realm in 1767.

Spanish colonial society was corporate in nature, ensuring special status via *fueros*, rights and privileges granted to specific groups. Clergy were protected by the *fuero eclesiástico*. Separate ecclesiastical courts had jurisdiction over clerics who committed minor criminal offenses or where a cleric was a party in a civil suit. Clerics who committed major crimes were subject to royal courts. In cases of heresy or violation of the sacraments, Inquisition courts had jurisdiction. Such protection for the church as an institution and its personnel lasted through the Hapsburg era, but under the Bourbon monarchs, these privileges came under attack, with the church increasingly subordinated to the state.

During the Hapsburg period, the dual role of the monarch (and by extension, the viceroy) as the head of state and patron of the church gave him power in both the spiritual and temporal spheres. Although tensions existed between the hierarchies of the state and the church, the essential order of colonial rule was not questioned. Some scholars see the Bourbon kings' attempts to subordinate church power to that of the state as a major factor undermining the legitimacy of the Spanish monarch's role, easing the way for overthrow of colonial rule.

See also Inquisition; Missions

Select Bibliography

Gibson, Charles, *Spain in America*. New York: Harper and Row, 1968.
Mecham, Lloyd, *Church and State in Latin America*. Chapel Hill: University of North Carolina Press, 1966.
Ricard, Robert, *The Spiritual Conquest of Mexico*. Berkeley: University of California Press, 1966.
Schwaller, John Frederick, *The Church and Clergy in Sixteenth-Century Mexico*. Albuquerque: University of New Mexico Press, 1987.

—SARAH L. CLINE

Catholic Church: Bourbon New Spain

Although the Bourbon monarchs ascended the Spanish throne after victory in the War of the Spanish Succession (1713), there were no substantial changes in church-state relations until approximately 1760. With the accession to the throne of Carlos III in 1759, in the wake of Spain's defeat by England in the Seven Years' War, the Spanish Crown initiated a sweeping program of change, generally known as the Bourbon Reforms. Until the mid–eighteenth century, the relationship between church and state shifted from a generally coequal status to one of primacy of state power.

Since the establishment of Spain's overseas empire in the late fifteenth and early sixteenth centuries, the papacy ceded control over the church affairs in the New World to the Spanish monarch. This included the right of the *patronato real*, giving the monarch power of appointment of all clerics in the Americas; control over collection and disbursement of the tithe; and de facto veto over the promulgation of papal decrees. The viceroy during the Hapsburg period was both head of state and patron of the church. Although there was not perfect cooperation between church and state, their status and powers were equal and complementary.

The Bourbon Crown, under Carlos III, initiated major changes in institutional structures and functions, aimed at expanding regal power and developing economic prosperity. In terms of church-state relations in the Bourbon period, the Crown (1) redefined the *fuero eclesiástico* (ecclesiastical privileges and immunities); (2) undermined the status and function of parish priests; (3) expelled the Jesuits (1767); (4) secularized missions founded by the regular clergy; (5) sought control of church wealth; (6) refocused the duties of the Inquisition, and (7) entered the regulation of marriage. Taken together, these constituted a revolution in church-state relations that increasingly alienated the church hierarchy from support of the Spanish monarchy.

In its move to redefine church-state relations, the Crown undermined the *fuero eclesiástico*. The *fuero* was a legacy of Iberian practice, giving special privileges to the church and individual priests in legal matters. Ecclesiastics and the institutional church were entitled to have legal disputes of all kinds adjudicated before canonical rather than civil courts. These included lawsuits over property, be the church either a plaintiff or defendant, which effectively gave the church enormous leverage in the economic sphere. In addition, clerics who committed criminal offenses were protected from trial before any but canonical courts and were granted immunity from corporal punishment. Such *fueros* were part of the corporate organization of society, giving members of corporations more rights and privileges than those who were not. Ecclesiastics were but one group with such privileges, miners and merchants being other corporations holding them. In undermining the ecclesiastical *fuero*, the Crown was especially targeting church power, for it established at the same period a *fuero* for members of the newly established institution of the military.

With the Crown's limitation on the coverage of the *fuero eclesiástico*, the church's control over its property and personnel was undermined and the status of clerics reduced significantly. For the absolutist monarchy, this accomplished two purposes. First, it gave the Crown economic power at a point when it was attempting to revivify stagnating economies on the peninsula and in the colonies. Second, it undercut churchmen's privileged status, putting religious personnel on an equal footing with commoners in both civil and criminal proceedings. In a status-conscious society, this was a severe blow to the religious. Some scholars have argued that by undermining the institutional church, the Crown was eroding its own power, authority, and legitimacy.

Under the Bourbon Reforms, parish priests' functions were increasingly confined to a solely spiritual sphere. In many remote areas of New Spain, the parish priest was sometimes the only representative of Spanish power. In other cases the friar and the *corregidor* (the civil representative of the Crown) were the only Europeans among the indigenous population, so that the two officials of Crown and clergy equally represented the Monarch's authority. With the political reorganization of New Spain from *corregimiento* (a system of indirect rule based on purchased offices) to the creation of new jurisdictions known as intendancies, the cooperation that had existed between civil and religious personnel virtually disappeared. The subdelegates (officials in charge of subunits of the intendancy) were to function as the sole representative of Crown power. For parish priests, the special status accorded them as representatives of the Crown was eliminated, placing the priests more on a par with their parishioners and in an adversarial relationship with the subdelegate. Increasingly, parish priests and rural parishioners came to see the Crown not only as despotic, but as an illegitimate power.

One of the most decisive and far-reaching exercises of state power over an ecclesiastical corporation was the expulsion in 1767 of the Jesuits from all Spanish realms. The Jesuits had been under attack by several European monarchies, so their expulsion by the Spanish Crown was not unprecedented. However, more so than in France, Portugal, or their respective colonies, their expulsion from Spain and its empire left a significant vacuum in the spheres of education and missionization of the native peoples. The Crown had intervened in the affairs of the regular clergy (those belonging to particular orders) during the Hapsburg era, and expulsion of individual clerics was within the Crown's power, a tool that could keep ecclesiastics in line. Nothing so sweeping as the Jesuit expulsion had been enacted previously, however.

With the expulsion of the Jesuits on June 25, 1767, the Crown cited its "supreme economic authority" to protect its citizens and the rights of the Crown. Although the expulsion was nominally justified in economic terms, the Crown's motives were more politically charged. There was widespread perception that the Jesuits were less controllable than other religious orders since the Jesuits' organization was not only more centralized but also under the direct influence of the papacy. In the Crown's view, the Jesuits as "soldiers of the pope" could not be depended on to pursue purely Spanish interests.

Their expulsion, however, had unintended consequences for the Crown. Since the Jesuits were the key educators of the sons of the elites as well as the order of choice for elites following a vocation in the regular clergy, criollo (those of Spanish descent born in the Americas) families felt the impact of the order's abrupt expulsion. Many criollo elites were sympathetic to the Jesuits, for the men of the family were educated by them. More directly for elites was the loss of their kin who were Jesuits, for those religious spent the rest of their lives in Italian exile. The Crown's action resulted in alienation by criollo elites toward the increasingly regalist state, making independence from the Spanish monarchy a more possible course for them. Another unintended consequence was the weakening of the Spanish presence on the northern frontiers, since Jesuits had been the successful and virtually sole agents of sovereign expansion. Jesuits in frontier missions obeyed the order of expulsion, which left their mission outposts devoid of personnel. The neophyte native-converts did not linger on the mission sites, awaiting replacement religious personnel.

On the frontier, the Crown continued to rely on the regular clergy, mainly the Franciscans, to extend areas of Spanish presence, mainly Alta California with a string of missions from San Diego north. However, the Crown moved in more central areas to limit the regular clergy's control by placing under the secular (non-order) clergy parishes that previously had been in the hands of the orders. The secular clergy was more directly answerable to the Crown via the episcopal hierarchy than regular clerics organized via their religious orders.

Access to church wealth was a Crown goal. Expulsion of the Jesuits for "economic reasons" meant that the order's rich and extensive estates came into the Crown's hands. More interested in liquidity than real estate, the Crown sold the estates, which had funded the Jesuits' educational institutions and northern missions. The estates generally passed into lay hands, with the purchase price going to the Crown. Another effort to gain control of church wealth was the short-lived attempt to place collection of the tithe, a tax on agricultural production for the support of the church hierarchy, entirely in the hands of royal treasury officials. Vociferous protest by clerics was successful in returning tithe collection to church hands.

Church dominance in the adjudication of testaments was a more successful target of state initiative. Most final wills and testaments included bequests to the church. Because the church had exercised its *fuero* to claim that any dispute to which it was party would be adjudicated in canonical courts, in effect the church had tremendous power to affect the distribution of wealth and enforce its claims. Maintaining that church property was "spiritual" not "temporal," the church had a powerful control of its economic resources. Bourbon legal theorists fundamentally changed the concept of property from a division of spiritual and temporal nature of property to a solely temporal interpretation. Thus, the sovereign monarch in his temporal role had jurisdiction over property, no matter that the church might have an interest in that property. Thus, civil rather than canonical courts gained control over property, virtually eliminating the church's advantage in this sphere. This was an important move by the Crown, since it increasingly viewed the church's hold on the economy as a major stumbling block to economic development.

The state sought to place barriers in the way of further church accumulation of property through elimination of tax exemptions, the levy of 15 percent tax on property passing into mortmain (perpetual church holding), and finally, in 1804, the order abolishing property belonging to *capellanías* (chantries) and *obras pías* (pious works), another form of donation to the church for charity.

These changes, particularly the order to eliminate *capellanías,* had a direct impact on the lower secular clergy. Many lower secular clerics had meager incomes, even if they served as parish priests with an ecclesiastical stipend. A good number of secular clerics received income from *capellanías,* whereby families set aside untaxed income from property to employ a priest to say masses for the soul of the founder of the *capellanía.* In fact, this was a standard way for families to keep a portion of their wealth for their kin. Quite often one of their own relatives held the post of *capellán.*

The funds for pious works and chantries not only supported many secular clerics, but they also were used for the charitable work of the church and a source of capital for mortgages. Thus the Act of Consolidation of 1804, which was designed to take money away from the church and place it in Crown control, had the effect of destroying credit for criollo elites. The church was required to call in all its debts, which meant that long-term loans to criollo elites came due immediately, ruining many financially. What was intended as an attack on the economic power of the church by the state had the effect of dispossessing criollo elites.

The Holy Office of the Inquisition became active in the Bourbon period in a new sphere, that of persecuting political dissent against the Crown and the monarch himself. Statements questioning the right of the monarch could result in their authors being brought before the Inquisition. Thus, that institution was drawn into the political sphere as an instrument of state power rather than dealing exclusively with the moral and doctrinal lapses of the non-Indian population of New Spain.

Another sphere in which the state began to assert itself was in the regulation of marriage, traditionally in the hands of the church. Concerned about the obvious evidence of racial mixing and perceived lowering barriers between white elites and the mainly darker lower classes, the state forbade unions between unequal partners. Although the canonical courts continued to have formal jurisdiction over regulation of marriage, these new state-mandated policies were enforced by canonical courts. The state strengthened the control of parents over their children's marriage choices, with parents instigating suits before canonical courts to block unions to which the parents objected. The traditional position of the church was that marriage was by the consent of the couple wishing to marry, if there were no canonical impediments to the union. The church sanctified the union in a ceremony that could be secret if some outside party sought to prevent the union. However, the new state-mandated marital policies asserted the state's interest as a fundamental aspect of social organization. Evidence is that the church continued to enable couples to sanctify their unions, but that parents attempted to exercise new rights over their children, empowered by the state.

The Bourbon period was one of fundamental change in church-state relations. Scholars have argued that the leading role of the lower secular clergy in the first phase of the Wars of Independence, such as Miguel Hidalgo and José María Morelos, directly followed from their alienation from the Crown because of its actions. The Crown was no longer able to draw on the spiritual loyalties of its colonists, having spent half a century implementing policies that weakened the church as an institution and distanced the monarch as the spiritual head of the church. Thus, when the government of Spain was set to implement the liberal, anticlerical elements of the Constitution of 1812, the clerics in Mexico saw political independence from Spain as New Spain's best course to preserve and expand the power of the church. Mexico's independence from Spain in 1821 had strong support from the episcopal hierarchy, for Agustín de Iturbide's Plan of Iguala had guaranteed that Catholicism would be the only religion tolerated in the independent country and that the clergy would retain their rights and privileges. Parish priests preached support of the plan and its political arm, the Army of the Three Guarantees. The church had much to gain in asserting itself in the new order, emerging from the struggles for independence as a much stronger power than the state.

See also Inquisition; Missions

Select Bibliography

Farriss, Nancy M, *Crown and Clergy in Colonial Mexico, 1759–1821: The Crisis of Ecclesiastical Privilege.* London: Athlone Press, 1968.

Mecham, Lloyd, *Church and State in Latin America: A History of Politicoecclesiastical Relations.* Revised edition, Chapel Hill: University of North Carolina Press, 1966.

—SARAH L. CLINE

Catholic Church: 1821–1910

In the last years of the Spanish American empire, serious church-state conflicts arose from the Bourbon monarchy's attempts to limit the religious orders, eliminate the ecclesiastical *fuero* (or immunity from civil prosecution), and appropriate the debts owed to charitable funds in America. Nevertheless, the Wars of Independence were by no means anticlerical or anti-religious. Indeed, the extent and contradictory character of clerical participation in the wars, and the pervasiveness of Christian symbolism, are indicative of the intricate ways in which religion and the Catholic Church were involved at every level of Mexican politics, economics, and society.

At the heart of the nineteenth century church-state conflict was the Catholic Church's special relationship with the poor and the dispossessed of Mexico, that is, the Indians and *castas* (those of mixed blood) who accounted for as much as 90 percent of the population. For these people, the local parish priest often seemed the only bulwark protecting them from the exploitative powers of the state and of local elites. Parish priests interceded not only between the people and the divine, but they were vital brokers to the temporal world of Mexico as well. They would tend to the sick, help communities plead cases in court, and defend community interests against rapacious outsiders. Moreover, the lives of the poor—urban and rural alike—centered on the Catholic Church. For such communities, church ceremonies and fiestas provided practically the only relief from an otherwise grim and monotonous existence, while church *cofradías* (lay brotherhoods) provided for a measure of welfare and mediated social life in general.

The parish priest, then, became a figure of some controversy. Liberal purists were suspicious of his exaggerated power and authority among the poor, supposing that he used his position to inculcate superstition and possibly subversion. Others—liberals and conservatives alike—argued that the parish priest typically received few rewards beyond the gratitude and veneration of his flock. His salary was invariably miserable, even while royal policies often prevented him from engaging in lucrative commercial enterprises. The only tangible benefit he received from the state was his exemption from civil prosecution, a key element of his authority with the masses. Apologists for the Catholic Church argued that only the parish priest stood between Mexico's tiny, white-skinned elite and a general explosion of popular wrath. Their worst fears were confirmed when Father Miguel Hidalgo, the parish priest of the small town of Dolores (Guanajuato), rallied his Indian and mestizo parishioners in the name of religion and independence, setting off what scholar Nancy Fariss called a "spark . . . that ignited the whole kingdom."

The degree of popular devotion to church and clergy was a decisive factor not only in the course of the Wars of Independence, but it placed definite limits on policy making in the post-Independence era. Liberals who dreamed of transforming Mexico into a progressive, egalitarian nation by breaking up latifundia (great landed estates), ending corporate privilege, promoting private enterprise, and enhancing the power of the central government, would have to negotiate a minefield of clerical special interests. Despite the yawning gulf in income and standards of living between the parish priests and the church notables, there was to be no class struggle within in the Catholic Church in independent Mexico: nearly all clerics and their allies formed a ready pool ripe for political mobilization by the hierarchy. And the hierarchy, early on in Mexico's national life, formed a staunch alliance with conservatives who felt that church wealth and clerical privilege were simply necessary to restrain the base and unruly impulses of the masses. Liberals, for their part, tended to be suspicious of Catholic Church, seeing in it a potential alien power in their midst that inevitably would obstruct the successful consolidation of a modern nation-state. They also resented the Catholic Church's wealth and blamed its lending policies for the continued existence of the great latifundia, which they identified as a key obstacle to the modernization of agriculture.

Although independence was achieved by conservatives who guaranteed clerical privilege and official protection for Roman Catholicism, conflict was not long in coming. An early focus of conflict was the *patronato real*, or extensive political control of the American church that the papacy had granted to the Spanish monarchy in 1508. Most of Mexico's new rulers believed that such political control over the church was necessary to the smooth functioning—and perhaps to the very survival—of the state, and they argued that the right of patronage was inherent in sovereignty. They explicitly claimed that right in the Constitution of 1824. The papacy, meanwhile, was unwilling to offend Spain by recognizing Mexico's new government and granting it patronage over the church. It argued that the right of patronage was abrogated when imperial ties were severed. Although the papacy recognized Mexico's independence in 1836, following the death of Fernando VII, the dispute never was definitively resolved.

The patronage issue had a major impact on the Catholic Church's fortunes. Given the sweeping nature of the patronage, the colonial Mexican church had tended to depend more upon Madrid than upon Rome, and the end of the empire had set off a crisis of legitimacy and a scramble for power that mirrored developments in the civil realm. The struggle eventually favored radically intransigent fringe elements within the church. While the patronage dispute dragged on many church benefices went unfilled. Indeed, with the death of the bishop of Puebla in 1829, not a single resident bishop remained in Mexico, and the archbishopric would remain vacant until 1840. Lacking bishops to perform ordinations and confirmation, the number of priests and faithful fell dramatically, irrevocably damaging church authority and weakening its hold on the masses.

The early governments of the republic generally upheld clerical privilege and were at least circumspect in their attacks on the wealth of the Mexican Catholic Church. The government of Anastasio Bustamante (1830–32) renounced the right of patronage, even while unleashing intemperate repression against liberal rivals. That, in turn, provoked a liberal reaction in 1833 under the leadership of the powerful caudillo Antonio López de Santa Anna, who upon his election to the presidency retired to his Veracruz estate. The government thereupon fell into the hands of Santa Anna's ultraliberal vice president, Valentín Gómez Farías. Gómez Farías, backed by a zealously liberal congress, passed a series of sweeping anticlerical measures, including the confiscation of the resources of the wealthy Catholic missions, secularization of the entire educational system, an end to government support for the collection of tithes, resumption of the right of patronage, and a declaration that monastic vows no longer were to be considered binding. The liberals of 1833 erred in supposing that profound reform could be accomplished by government fiat. Not only was society at large unprepared for such sweeping reform, but the government hardly was strong enough to step into the void left by the sudden dispossession of the Catholic Church. The reaction of late 1834, taking up the durable battle-cry of "religión y fueros," was swift, decisive, and headed by none other than President Santa Anna himself. The new dictator dissolved Congress and decreed most of the anticlerical laws invalid.

The liberal experiment of 1833 showed that Santa Anna, heretofore a reputed liberal, in fact was possessed of shallow as well as endlessly flexible political principles, and considerable deftness in turning popular sentiment to his advantage. The episode also demonstrated just how polarized the church-state issue had become. In particular, the first decades of independence led to such a hardening of clerical intransigence that even the archconservative, pro-clerical Anastasio Bustamante—restored to the presidency in 1837—was subject to clerical reprisals when he sought a loan from church coffers. Not even conservatives, in those days of severe government penury, could fail to take notice of the apparent opulence of the Catholic Church. This opulence was simply too tempting for anyone governing in an age of chronic deterioration in the national economy and treasury, and it blinded statesmen to the fact that such sumptuousness was not an accurate reflection of the Catholic Church's actual holdings, which never were as endless as generally rumored.

The attack on church wealth and property was more often a practical than an ideological matter. It was the one area where liberals and conservatives coincided, if not with respect to means then certainly with respect to ends. The need for the government to appropriate a share of church wealth became especially imperative when the government of Santa Anna and Gómez Farías (restored to power in 1846) needed funds to prosecute the war with the United States. After heated debate, they passed a bill in Congress authorizing the government to demand a loan of 15 million pesos from the Catholic Church, which would be secured by a mortgage on church property. Since this amounted to the de facto nationalization of nearly a tenth of all church wealth, the hierarchy responded with predictable vehemence, threatening with excommunication any who dared to enforce the law. Santa Anna eventually rescinded the law in exchange for a large cash payment from the clergy—in effect, a bribe to restrain him from further attacks on church property. This marked the start of yet another period of ascendancy of church interests in Mexico. Under the auspices of a reconstituted conservative Santa Anna, some anticlerical legislation was repealed and the Catholic Church received some guarantees for its property. But the wily old dictator by now had lost touch with popular sentiment. Under a storm of accusations of absolutism, treason, and corruption, Santa Anna was overthrown for the last time in 1854.

This liberal Revolution of Ayutla marked the ascendance to power of a new generation of dogmatic and doctrinaire liberals, who were fairly quick to undertake the most sweeping and devastating attack on the Catholic Church yet seen in Mexico. These liberals aimed once and for all to liberate the country from clerical and military domination and to create an egalitarian civil society founded upon values of private property, freedom of conscience, the free circulation of capital, secular education, and nationalism. Nearly all of the outstanding figures in the new liberal government were freemasons and staunch anticlericals.

The legislative assault began in November 1855 with the passage of the so-called Ley Juárez (Juárez Law), named for Justice Minister Benito Juárez. This decree stripped the ecclesiastical and military courts of jurisdiction in civil matters. While this was a moderate measure that did not seek to interfere with ecclesiastical jurisdiction in ecclesiastical matters, it aroused a storm of protest. The church and the military, both having been attacked by the same measure, united and revived the old battle cry of "religión y fueros." The Ley Juárez was followed shortly (June 25, 1856) by the so-called Ley Lerdo, which barred all civil and ecclesiastical corporations from owning or acquiring real property except that for the immediate purposes of worship. Church land was to be portioned off and sold at prices equal to those currently being charged in rent. The law was formally defended as a purely economic measure, designed to take land out of the "dead hands" of the Catholic Church and of Indian communities—which hitherto had held their lands in mortmain, a system the liberals deemed wasteful and unproductive—and make that property mobile. Specifically, the Catholic Church would benefit from collecting mortgage payments on property sold, the government would benefit from a 5 percent sales tax on all transactions, and Indians and small farmers would benefit from the impetus to improve and make profitable their private holdings. Although not formally stated, the law would bring the residual benefits of weakening the Catholic Church and helping to remove a major obstacle to the liberals' own economic and political ambitions.

The decree had a powerful negative impact not only on the Catholic Church but also on the Indian villages. The village-based cofradías, or lay brotherhoods, owned properties that now were slated for disentailment. Moreover, the extensive landholdings of the villages, although theoretically exempted from the initial Ley Lerdo, began to be portioned off and sold. And while the erstwhile property owners or tenants were supposed to get first consideration in the bidding for the new plots, in practice the distribution of the land was uneven and often corrupted by the machinations of the wealthy and powerful. Dispossessed villagers once again became natural allies of the church in a dispute with civil authority. Shared grievance overcame the badly diminished role of the church in popular everyday life, which was most clearly evidenced in the scant numbers of parish priests resident in the republic (barely one per 3,000 souls in the mid–nineteenth century).

Further injury to the Catholic Church came with the Iglesias Law of 1857, which limited the amounts parish priests could collect in fees they charged parishioners for sacraments and other services. The final blow came with the promulgation of the Constitution of 1857, which declared public education to be free, nullified the compulsory observance of religious vows, incorporated the Juárez and Lerdo Laws, barred ecclesiastics from holding high public office, and granted the federal government the right to intervene "in matters of religious worship and outward ecclesiastical forms" in accordance with the laws. The Constitution stopped short of formally separating church and state and declaring religious liberty, but neither did it uphold the traditional relationship of church and state. In fact, it was altogether silent on the subject. For champions of the church, that silence was ominous indeed.

Upon its promulgation on February 12, 1857, the Constitution was greeted with open hostility by the clergy. Mexicans suddenly found themselves caught between civil and religious power; the government demanded that public officials swear allegiance to the document, even while the clergy threatened excommunication and denial of sacraments to any who did so. The liberal legislation was denounced roundly in broadsides, books, and pamphlets, which often urged civil disobedience and rebellion against the government. By December, an alliance of church and army under the leadership of General Félix Zuloaga declared war on the Constitution and called for a full return to the status quo ante, including return of church property, protection and guarantees for church and clergy, religious intolerance, and if possible the establishment of a monarchy.

The ensuing war was, in effect, a civil war fought in the name of religion. Perhaps because both sides viewed it as something of a holy war, the extent of brutality exceeded anything Mexico yet had experienced. Tales were rife of prisoners massacred in cold blood, doctors and nurses slaughtered, churches sacked. The contending sides were roughly equal in numbers and strength, and ironically both found themselves obliged to finance their operations by preying on church property. While the conservatives nominally made good their promise to return church property, they at the same time solicited loans from the church, which normally were paid in bonds guaranteed by church property. These bonds were then sold at a discount to financiers with ready cash, who eventually came into full possession of the properties when the church was unable to redeem the bonds. The liberals, for their part, often financed their efforts through outright confiscation of church property, or by promising handsome amounts of real estate to creditors, which would be delivered in the event of a liberal victory. In this fashion, foreigners and financiers came into large amounts of real estate at bargain prices, and both church and state fared poorly.

The inevitable polarization attending civil war led the liberals to carry their anticlerical legislation to its logical conclusion. Decrees ordered the suppression of the religious orders, the complete separation of church and state, religious tolerance, prohibitions against religious ceremonies and the wearing of clerical garb in public, and nationalization of virtually all ecclesiastical holdings. The liberal victory in December 1860 led to further reprisals against conservative enemies, including the expulsion of the archbishop and four other bishops from the republic and the suppression of all cathedral chapters.

The nationalization of church property, however, was so compromised by the exigencies of wartime financing that its benefits to the national treasury were slight. The government of Benito Juárez defaulted on its foreign debts in 1861, providing the pretext for the French Intervention, an intervention aided and abetted by disgruntled clergy for whom an end to national sovereignty seemed a small price to pay for the return of their traditional privileges and properties. Invading French troops were hailed with Te Deum masses as they marched on Mexico City, but the outcome of the intervention was decidedly disappointing to the clergy. The French emperor, Napoleon III, determined to support those who had

bought nationalized church property in good faith. His appointed puppet-emperor, the Austrian archduke Maximilian von Hapsburg, proved to be of a liberal persuasion and not amenable to the importunings of extremist clerics. Pope Pius IX did not, as Maximilian had hoped, support a conciliatory policy. He demanded instead that the emperor nullify all reform laws, decree religious intolerance, restore the religious orders, return education to clerical supervision, and lift all remaining government restrictions on the Catholic Church. Maximilian, alive to the inflammatory potential of such proposals and eager to negotiate, was stunned by the pope's intransigence, which had the effect of driving him further into the liberal camp, at least in religious matters. Far from abrogating the reform laws, Maximilian ratified most of them.

Maximilian's efforts were unproductive; as far as the liberals were concerned, they could not atone for his role in the violation of national sovereignty, even while these moves simultaneously lost him any support he might have desired from the clergy. When Napoleon III withdrew his troops, Maximilian was abandoned by both parties to the conflict, a victim of the century's most intractable conflict. He was executed upon the triumph of the liberals, who immediately set about resurrecting and enforcing their anticlerical legislation.

By the last quarter of the nineteenth century, the Mexican Catholic Church was battered and bitter, possessing only a shadow of its former prestige and grandeur. Pius IX did nothing to help the situation when he intensified his war against liberalism and democracy with the promulgation in 1869 of the famous Syllabus of Errors, which made clear that the Catholic Church would in no way compromise with the modern world. Nor were the liberals disposed to compromise on the issue. The objectionable anticlerical laws, which until now had been largely hypothetical elements in the Constitution, were made more immediate by enabling legislation passed in 1874.

The Catholic Church may have been beleaguered, but it still retained some wealth, primarily in the form of properties held for it by proxies. More importantly, it retained the faith and adherence of the majority of the Mexican people, which made it a force to reckon with and a potential menace to the peace of the republic. The dictator Porfirio Díaz (1876–80; 1884–1911) determined that the church was too formidable to suppress, and that continued government efforts in that direction could only undermine the "order and progress" that were the watchwords of his regime. He proposed, then, to subdue the issue through a policy of conciliation. This meant simply that, while anticlericalism remained the law of the land, for the most part it went unenforced so long as Catholics and clergy recognized Díaz's supreme political authority and tempered their criticism of civil government. The Catholic Church fairly easily accommodated itself to such minor annoyances as civil baptisms and marriages. The hierarchy generally acquiesced, too, in the suppression of the religious orders. Restrictions on religious education were enforced only mildly: private religious schools continued to function, and on occasion religious instruction was offered even in public schools, albeit after hours. Somewhat more conflict was generated by the constitutional restrictions on wearing clerical garb, bell ringing, public religious ceremonies, and other outward manifestations of religiosity. In many cases, such restrictions simply were ignored and the Catholic Church practiced its ceremonial life quite publicly and unimpeded. In other cases, zealous local officials took it upon themselves to uphold the letter of the law, and considerable friction resulted, especially when the occasion was one of great popular resonance such as Holy Week. The most serious source of conflict was the official policy of religious tolerance. Popular hostility toward Protestants and freethinkers often was abetted by the hierarchy, who feared that religious liberty was the first step in a descent into immorality and atheism. Attacks on Protestants and Protestant missionaries were frequent, and often quite vicious.

Under the conciliation policy, the Catholic Church managed to regain some of its economic power and much of its prestige. Donations from well-to-do Catholics made some parishes quite wealthy. Tithes were sometimes collected surreptitiously and illegally, with collectors going from house to house threatening ostracism for nonpayers. Clergymen once again became moneylenders, landlords, and businessmen. Some, like the ultrawealthy Archbishop Eulogio Gillow y Zavalza, were close personal friends of the dictator and moved in the inner circles of his regime. According to one estimate, the value of church property doubled in the years from 1874 to 1910.

This apparent resolution of the church-state conflict in Mexico was superficial, if not wholly illusory. The Catholic Church depended upon the dictator for the maintenance of its special privileges, and accordingly much of the wrath directed toward Díaz found its way, by association, to the church. Wealthy and conservative clerics were identified easily with the class of oppressors. Zealous liberals, meanwhile,

never reconciled themselves to the conciliation policy and became more vocal in their denunciations once the policy became more overt after 1890.

Perhaps the most dangerous development of all was the rise of Social Catholicism following the promulgation by Pope Leo XIII of the encyclical *Rerum Novarum* in 1891. A direct response to the rise of socialism in Europe, *Rerum Novarum* was a fundamentally conservative document in which the Catholic Church gave its attention to the "social question." In place of class conflict, the encyclical urged class harmony, devotion to the commonweal, and corporatism. This new orientation coincided with certain renovations in the Mexican Catholic Church, notably the replacement of the monarchist archbishop Pelagio Antonio Labastida with the more moderate and nationalistic Próspero María Alarcón. At the same time, Catholic administration was revamped with the creation of seven bishoprics and three archbishoprics. With its new social orientation and more responsive administration, the Catholic Church was shaken out of its old traditionalism and passivity and became more activist and enterprising, offering its flock something more than promises of celestial rewards. The hierarchy began urging the faithful to involve themselves directly in their communities through the media of press, schools, theater, political parties, and labor organizations. This movement struck a nerve with the popular classes, who had borne the brunt of certain Porfirian trends such as the dramatic population increase and consequent surplus labor force, the fall in real wages, the expansion of haciendas, the increasing proletarianization of the peasantry, and the decline of artisanry with the massive introduction of imported manufactures. In accordance with the postulates of *Rerum Novarum*, Catholic labor unions were formed to push for shorter hours, an end to child labor, improvements in the status of women, improved and more extensive education and medical care, and better pay—all, presumably, to be achieved without recourse to open class warfare. Catholic organizations and press also mounted a major moralization campaign, denouncing alcoholism, concubinage, and other vices. In 1908, under the energetic leadership of Father José M. Troncoso, numerous "Catholic workers circles" united to form the Catholic Workers Union. By 1911, this organization, under the name National Confederation of Catholic Workers' Circles, claimed a national membership of 14,366.

The church had thus become a serious competitor in the political arena, a circumstance that was violently resented by its rivals. As the virulent anticlericalism of the revolutionary years proves, the church-state conflict had undergone only a relatively brief hiatus during the Porfiriato. It had by no means been resolved.

See also Conservatism; Liberalism; Reform Laws; Wars of Independence; Wars of Reform

Select Bibliography
Bazant, Jan, *Alienation of Church Wealth in Mexico: Social and Economic Aspects of the Liberal Revolution, 1856–1875.* Cambridge: Cambridge University Press, 1971.
Fariss, Nancy, *Crown and Clergy in Colonial Mexico, 1759–1821: The Crisis of Ecclesiastical Privilege.* London: Athlone, 1968.
Mecham, J. Lloyd, *Church and State in Latin America.* Chapel Hill: University of North Carolina Press, 1934.
Schmitt, Karl M., "The Díaz Conciliation Policy on State and Local Levels, 1876–1911." *HAHR* 40:4 (November 1960).

—TIMOTHY J. HENDERSON

Catholic Church: 1910–96

After the struggles for Independence and the civil wars of the nineteenth century, the Liberal state tried to use the Catholic Church, which maintained control at a social rather than a political level, in its program of national construction. Although the state occasionally expressed a desire to destroy the church, it was decided to take control of the institution in order to control and unify civil society. This variant of republican regalism lasted until 1990. The Revolutionary state (1914–40) rejected the church as a social institution and aimed to take it apart with the help of Freemasonry, Protestants, and the "reds." It was not a process of secularization, whereby the autonomy of secular society was affirmed in the context of the church as representative of religious society and sacramental power, but rather a process whereby one group achieved political hegemony over society in general. The church was treated as an obstacle in the way of progress, science, and modernization. Those in power became both antipopular and anticlerical, as revealed during the "rational" and "socialist" education campaign that affected the popular sector during the 1930s.

The Catholic Church reacted to this state of affairs in three ways. In terms of historical continuity, it defended its traditional rights, gambling on education and the family, the development of pedagogical institutions, the Catholic press, and devout practices.

The church also attempted to win over the elites and also keep control over the masses, in the hope of taking over the state at some future date. Finally, the church obtained considerable help from Rome as well as French, Spanish, German, and Belgian churches.

Between 1880 and 1914 the polemic between Liberals and Conservatives, church and state, and positivism (loosely, empiricism and scientific inquiry) and clericalism, disguised deep problems within society. Social Catholicism and the workers' movement emerged discretely, almost without being noticed. Posivitism as the dominant ideology stimulated a reaction that was nationalist and Catholic, socialist and cultural (through such movements as modernism and idealism); this reaction to positivism appeared in Mexico earlier than in other countries. This dynamic period witnessed for the first time the emergence of important Protestant groups that would play a role in the Mexican Revolution. Although under Liberal rule from 1859 to 1910, the Catholic Church also had carried out a second evangelization that evolved through civic and social action movements in the spirit of Leo XIII's encyclical *Rerum Novarum*. The church was thus in a highly expansive period when the Revolution broke out. The initial three years favored the church as well as the ephemeral Partido Católica Nacional (PCN, or National Catholic Party, 1910–13).

The fall of the democratic president Francisco I. Madero in February 1913 renewed the revolutionary violence, and the triumphant faction turned against the Catholic Church. The victors were men from the north of the country, white men stamped by the U.S. frontier and imbued with the values of Anglo-Saxon Protestantism and capitalism, unknown in the old Mestizo, Indian, and Catholic Mexico. For these individuals the church was the incarnation of all they opposed. The Constitution of 1917 gave the state the right to legislate over the "clerical profession," whose power it detested and against whom it frequently clashed, particularly in the areas of education and the union movement. While a moderate president such as Álvaro Obregón (1920–24, reelected in 1928 but immediately assassinated) was in power, none of the numerous small incidents that occurred unleashed a crisis. But scarcely had his successor, General Plutarco Elías Calles, taken sides with some violence when events started a downward spiral. Calles was the representative of a group of politicians in Mexico, Spain, and other countries who believed that Catholicism was incompatible with the state and that a Catholic cannot be a good citizen if his first loyalty is to Rome. Having tried unsuccessfully to create a schismatic (i.e., non–Roman Catholic) church, the government elaborated legislation that considered infractions in matters of worship as violations of common law, obliging the priests to register with the Ministry of Internal Affairs for the right to practice their profession. The law took advantage of the potential for limiting the number of priests. The church responded on July 31, 1926, by suspending the performance of public worship. When the bishops attempted to seek an agreement with the government on August 21, Calles informed them that they could choose between submitting to the force of law or taking up arms.

The church did not choose war, since the Vatican never considered Calles as a Nero—even if it did, it also never forgot that he was also Caesar, and it was more advisable to negotiate. Talks extended over three long years during which certain foreign diplomats and U.S. and Mexican bankers took on the role of intermediaries, and the peasantry took up arms in a pro-Catholic uprising known as the Cristero Rebellion. The conflict, not expected by either church or state, was a pleasant surprise for certain young Catholic militants who dreamed of taking power by force of arms.

Immediately after the tentative schism of 1925, the militants of Acción Católica (Catholic Action), in particular those of the Associación Católica de la Juventud Mexicana (ACJM, or Catholic Association of Mexican Youth), had started up a great political organization, La Liga (the League) and realized an intense campaign of civil resistance and legal action. The first revolts had occurred spontaneously in the moment of the suspension of church services. In August 1926 these events convinced the organizers of La Liga that the conflict would end in rapid victory owing to the unpopularity of the government and the predominant Catholicism of the people. The war lasted for three years, mobilizing 40,000 rebels known as *cristeros*. Dwight Morrow, U.S. ambassador to Mexico, noted on May 3, 1929, that all possibilities of returning to normality were extremely slight if the government did not arrive at an agreement with the church that allowed the resumption of worship.

When the Cristero Rebellion was at its height, the state decided to come to an understanding with the church. Matters were quickly settled in June 1929, just prior to the presidential elections, to avoid a possible alliance between the urban political forces, the revolutionary factions of the opposition, and the *cristeros*, who could have assumed the role of armed support. According to the "Arrangements," as the agreements became known, the law was not changed but its application was suspended. Amnesty was guaranteed between the combatants, as was the restitution of the churches and the priests.

The Peruvian scholar José Mariategui commented in 1928 that in the Latin American countries, the extreme development of liberalism during the nineteenth century led to the approval of Protestantism and the national church as logical necessities for the modern state. This logic never went beyond speculation except in Mexico, where it took concrete form between 1926 and 1938. The policies of President Calles between 1926 and 1934 and of President Lázaro Cárdenas until at least 1938 aimed at integrating the Catholic Church into the state machine. Catholics who traditionally had been kept outside the political camp until 1910 now had become dangerous rivals; the attack on the church was thus a measure of its influence. The incomplete nature of the nation (prior to the Revolution the state was still in the process of creation) pushed the Revolutionary president-generals toward control, centralism, and constriction.

Mexican bishops, insecure as to which path to follow and divided over whether or not to encourage Catholic unionism (at its height 1920–26) and political participation, in the majority accepted with a certain relief their return to the line traditionally dictated by Rome for Mexico: the restriction of the lay members within tightly controlled Acción Católica groups. The encyclical *Paterna Solicitudo Sano* of February 2, 1926, clearly specified this but could not avoid the imminent collision between church and state that resulted in the Cristero Rebellion. The encyclical's application was strictly enforced after June 1929, and the rebellious Catholic organizations were dissolved, beginning with the ACJM. Thus, 40 years prior to emergence of the Latin American left (of both Catholic and non-Catholic persuasion), Mexican Catholics experienced the problem of choosing between an armed or peaceful road to power. The political Catholics of the PCN, Acción Católica, Catholic unionism, and La Liga prefigured the Christian Democracy of the 1960s in other Latin American countries.

Later, Catholics were able to locate their interests in a stable political party—the Partido de Acción Nacional (PAN, or National Action Party)—and in a movement—the Union Nacional Sinarquista (National Sinarquist Union, also known as *sinarquismo*). Both were founded at the end of the 1930s at a moment when the modus vivendi signed in 1929 was about to become a reality. Both party (of urban character, drawing followers from the Catholic middle classes) and movement (which attracted a mass following of mostly rural and provincial origin) were linked to the Catholic Church, although the latter always took care not to give an official seal of approval. Both were opposed and indeed hostile to the state that emerged from the Revolution, but both had learned that the time for revolutions had come to an end in Mexico and that rebellion was no longer a political solution.

The Cristero Rebellion left a deep scar on the country and the Mexican Catholic Church. It explains many differences between Mexico and other Latin American countries. Mexico's church became more cautious than those elsewhere in Latin America, but at the same time it became far more national, practically without a foreign priesthood and backed by numerous members of religious orders. Institutionally, the Mexican Church was the first to create its own episcopal conference, in 1925–26. It also became a church linked to the papacy, symbol of the faith during the uprising; the cristeros' battle cry had been "Long Live the Pope!"

State-church cooperation after the 1920s consisted largely of the latter's acceptance that the social field was the exclusive monopoly of the state in Mexico. This modus vivendi continued until the beginning of the 1950s. The abandonment of control over social movements to the state in the wake of the Cristero Rebellion, the permanent renunciation of Catholic unionism, and the freezing of Catholic "political" activities led the church, without realizing it, to destroy the integral vision of Catholicism. In exchange, the church's victory was that Catholicism came to be seen as one of the essential elements of Mexican nationality. Later there were other moments in which the church appeared to approve the social policy of the state, especially between 1963 and 1965, and 1970 and 1976. In both cases the church seemed to have inclined toward support of government policies that coincided with its own reformist project for society. Such support was neither unconditional nor absolute, since important differences existed over issues such as birth control and education. It was a conditional cooperation. The church played no part in the state's "apparatus of ideological domination." It is not possible to describe the relationship between church and state as "mistaken complicity." The absence of open conflict should not be confused with the existence of an agreement or complicity.

After 1940, three developments marked the Catholic Church in Mexico: an expansion of activities in social and economic affairs, the increasing role of the laity, and the positive, immediate, and generalized response to Rome's directives regarding the material condition of man. Thus was posed the problem of knowing what role the church could and wished to play in the economic and political development of the country. Regardless of events in Mexico, the spectacular commitment of the church and its lay congregation in worldly affairs undoubtedly would have been stimulated and accelerated by the Vatican Council II of 1962 to 1965 and the general evolution of the Roman Church, among the most important events of the twentieth century. This evolution implied renewed confrontation both inside and outside the church as well as the resumption of the old conflict between church and state on different terms, since both powers had changed radically in the meantime.

The scholar Roberto Blancarte has stated that throughout the second half of the twentieth century, two social and political currents were present within the church: the "integral/intransigent" and the "conciliatory/pragmatic." At least two further currents can be added, which became more defined after Vatican Council II: the "integrist" and the "neo-intransigent." These latter were in large measure offshoots of the first two. The "integral/intransigent" current included all those opposed to a commitment to the state and who fought against the imposition of the social model of the Mexican Revolution. The "conciliatory/pragmatic" tendency opted for cooperation with the Mexican state without reneging on the doctrine or principles of the Catholic Church; members of this group also have displayed a burning desire for justice. The "integrist" current was a product of the "integral/intransigent" tendency and has developed to the degree that the latter lost ground to the other currents; this current was made up of the most stubborn elements, resistant to any change or adaptation of the church to the modern world. Finally the "neo-intransigent" tendency, risen from the rank and file of the "intransigent" as much as the "conciliatory" groups, has defended theses of accommodation that aim to modernize the Catholic Church in order to spread their social program more effectively in the contemporary world.

Since the first visit of the pope to Mexico in 1979, the church has manifested its dislike of being confined to the sacristy and has increasingly entered the public arena, solidifying its role as one of the key institutions of civil society at a time when society had become more secularized than ever. As such, the church has exercised a role of counterweight to state authoritarianism. This attitude was accompanied by a radical change on the part of the government, presided over by Carlos Salinas de Gortari. From the start of his mandate at the end of 1988, Salinas showed his willingness to put an end to a modus vivendi that had been current for 50 years but that no longer corresponded with reality. In May 1990 Pope John Paul II made a second tour of Mexico, and the president pointed out that even the Soviet Union had reestablished diplomatic relations with the Vatican. Nevertheless, the old anticlerical lobby continued to resist these moves toward reconciliation. In July 1991 Salinas visited the pope, and in November of the same year in his State of the Union Address declared that the time had arrived to put an end to a situation, to "reconcile the clear secularization of our society with effective freedom of belief . . . whereby making a further step toward internal concord within the framework of modernization." In December the Congress received an initiative for constitutional reforms that were quickly approved. The new Article 3 allowed religious instruction in private schools; the revised Article 5 authorized the existence of religious orders; Article 24 permitted cultural demonstrations outside the churches; Article 27 allowed religious associations to own property; and Article 130 recognized the legal existence of religious associations and gave religious ministers the right to vote (although not to be elected). Nevertheless, the Constitution maintained important restrictions, and the regulations attached to Article 130 in 1992 allowed for an interpretation that has angered the churches. In fact, its uneven application has drawn criticism, provoking for example in 1996 a serious confrontation between the secretary for internal affairs and the Catholic Church, supported by Protestant churches, on the topic of ecclesiastical participation in the political life of the nation. In September 1992 diplomatic relations were established between Mexico and the Vatican. In August 1993 the pope visited Mexico for the third time, but for the first time in an official capacity. Thus after 150 years the Catholic Church and the Mexican state achieved "the separation of the two kingdoms" in a positive way.

See also Constitution of 1917; Cristero Rebellion; Partido de Acción Nacional (PAN); Protestantism

Select Bibliography

Levine, Daniel, editor, *Churches and Politics in Latin America*. Thousand Oaks, California: Sage, 1980.
Pike, Frederick, *Church and State in Mid-century Latin America*. New York: n.p., 1965.
Schmitt, Karl, *The Roman Catholic Church in Modern Latin America*. New York: n.p., 1972.

—JEAN MEYER

Cedillo, Saturnino 1890–1939
Guerrilla Leader, Soldier, and Governor

Saturnino Cedillo was born in 1890 in the small farm community of Las Palomas, located in the Valle del Maíz, a region in the southeast of the state of San Luis Potosí, which has a long tradition of agrarian conflicts. In June 1912, while the state was the scene of considerable social unrest, Alberto Carrera Torres emerged as a central leader of the agrarian movement. Apparently influenced by the Plan de Ayala issued by the followers of Emiliano Zapata in the state of Morelos, this educated advocate of the region's farmers formulated a radical program that called for the return of expropriated lands to the traditional and collectively managed farm communities called *ejidos,* and for the distribution of land to landless *campesinos* (peasants).

A small rebel band emerged that was closely allied to Carrera and led by a poor but well-known family in the region: the Cedillo brothers—Cleofas, Magdaleno, and Saturnino—who worked a goat farm that also produced *ixtle* (a tough vegetable fiber). Their parents owned a modest plot of land and operated a small general store while their closest relatives were mule drivers. The family had begun having major conflicts with the owners of neighboring haciendas since 1909. By the summer of 1912 the Cedillo brothers were leading an armed rebellion by a group of *campesinos* who had been brutally repressed by the local authorities, and in November they took over the town of Ciudad del Maíz and read the Plan of Ayala to the local population.

In the following years of armed conflict they tended to put forward demands reflecting the interests of the poorest *campesinos* of the state, whose support they enjoyed. As a result, they not only were obliged to fight those who identified with the old power structures from the dictatorship of Porfirio Díaz, but also against those hacienda owners who became leading figures in the Mexican Revolution, including the Barragán family. Both the Carrera and Cedillo families fought against the dictatorship of Victoriano Huerta that overthrew the government of Francisco I. Madero, but by no means were close to opposition leader Venustiano Carranza, opting instead to ally themselves with the most radical factions who were eventually defeated during the Revolution. In 1914 and 1915 they openly broke with Carranza by supporting the Convention of Aguascalientes, and later allied with the forces led by Francisco "Pancho" Villa. While they exercised control over the southeast region of San Luis Potosí, their regime was marked by radical and freewheeling policies focused on class struggle. They intervened in a number of landed estates and frequently reacted violently against hostile landowners and administrators, including the execution of one of the region's most affluent and powerful hacienda owners, Javier Espinosa y Cuevas.

Following the defeat of Pancho Villa's forces by Carranza's troops, the Carrera and Cedillo families and their followers returned to their humble existence while continuing to sustain small-scale guerrilla war in the inhospitable and sparsely populated Valle del Maíz. Suffering a series of defeats, desertions, and betrayals, they were also subject to deteriorating living conditions marked by extreme hunger and disease. During this period Cleofas and Magdaleno Cedillo lost their lives, as did Alberto Carrera Torres. The last of the guerrilla band was on the verge of starvation and living in caves when their luck took a dramatic turn for the better in 1920: their old nemesis Carranza was defeated by the forces led by Álvaro Obregón, who recognized their authority over the Valle del Maíz. The federal government allowed them to form what were designated as Military Agrarian Colonies and to remain armed, taking their orders from Saturnino Cedillo rather than from the federal army. This allowed Cedillo officially to reaffirm his credentials as a champion of agrarian reform, guarantee the peaceful well-being of his followers, establish a working relationship with the new leaders of the federal government, and shore up his own personal power. His guerrilla band, converted into a semi-official militia, would be the key element in Cedillo's personal power structure for the rest of his life.

The generals and regional commanders who emerged out of the Revolution played a key role in allowing federal officials to consolidate the political life of the country. In this, Cedillo proved to be paradigmatic figure. He was able to keep the territories under his command in relative peace by playing a mediating role between the federal authorities and the various social forces and regional interests in San Luis Potosí, while combating those who tried to rebel against the new system. Later given the official post of chief of military operations in San Luis Potosí, Cedillo successfully defeated the local supporters of a series of uprisings throughout the 1920s, beginning with the rebellion led by Adolfo de la Huerta in 1923. When the Cristero movement took up arms from 1926 to 1929 in the central states of Mexico, Cedillo captured and executed one of the movement's main leaders and cut off his forces from the regions where they enjoyed support among the population. He was similarly successful in combating the local supporters of José Gonzalo Escobar, who rose in 1929.

These military successes allowed Cedillo to strengthen his ties with the federal government and parlay that relationship into a greater degree of autonomy in exercising control over the state. He consolidated his iron grip on the state beginning in 1925, when he defeated his former ally, the radical agrarian reformer Governor Aurelio Manrique, and by 1927 he had established his own position as governor of the state. While he served only one term (1927–32), he continued to exercise control by placing a series of loyal followers in the governorship during the succeeding years.

However, it was his native Valle del Maíz that remained the focus of his personal and political attention. The Palomas ranch, where he was born, became his private fiefdom and the heart of his political operation. Acting virtually as a feudal lord, his home was open night and day, providing food and shelter to all who asked for help and, when possible, monetary assistance and jobs. In exchange for the military and political support of the people of the region—who also were asked to render other services to Cedillo, his family, and closest circle of aides, and followers—he made sure their basic needs were met. Those who had taken up arms under his command during the Revolution, and the widows and orphans of those who had fallen in battle, were provided with land, water, schools, loans, jobs, and protection. The resulting paternalistic ties survived the passing of years and the effects of modernization that dramatically changed the social and political life of many other regions of Mexico. It was as if time had come to a halt in the Valle del Maíz, and the personal authority of Saturnino Cedillo proved so powerful that many years after his death he continued to be a major reference point in the region, regarded with a mix of gratitude and admiration.

Outside of the region, however, his intense forms of personal control gradually waned. His initial success in extending his patronage-based system of control over the rest of the state was entirely dependent on the aid he received from the federal government, and on his ability to offer material compensations to his supporters and to punish those who questioned his authority. His relationship with unionized workers in the state and elsewhere in the country always proved conflictive.

Although he was not primarily interested in national policies, he did manage to play a role in the political life of the country. He twice served as minister of agriculture, once under the brief presidency of Pascual Ortiz Rubio (September–October 1931) and later under Lázaro Cárdenas after supporting Cárdenas in his fight against former president Plutarco Elías Calles. However, Cedillo later abandoned his cabinet post when he developed serious ideological, political, and personal differences with Cárdenas.

Cedillo's particular brand of *cacicazgo,* or patronage-based political machine, had many features in common with many other post-Revolutionary fiefdoms that emerged throughout the country. Real legal and administrative power was exercised by Cedillo's relatives and most loyal followers rather than by those who formally held office. Key issues such as fiscal policies and agrarian reform were implemented based on the personal criteria of Cedillo and his closest associates rather than in line with the letter of the law. This system, which was based on the loyalty of Cedillo's traditional followers, his agrarian militias, and the peasantry of the region, proved more resilient than other *cacicazgos* to efforts by federal authorities to dismantle such regional power structures. To a certain extent, it was a prototype of the *cacicazgos* that played a central role in the political life of the country in the 1920s and 1930s.

However, the days of semi-autonomous and armed *cacicazgos* were drawing to a close. As federal officials consolidated a national state structure and pacified the country, the agrarian militias in San Luis Potosí began to outlive their usefulness and be seen as a hindrance and affront to the new regime. The state was busy building a professional army, establishing civilian channels for resolving differences between the Revolutionary generals and caudillos (strongmen) who comprised the ruling elite, and developing corporatist labor and peasant unions as a means of assuring the control by the presidency and the ruling party over the political and social life of the country. This latter development led to the establishment of sectoral power structures that replaced the regional structures key to the existence of *cacicazgos* like that of Cedillo.

This objective conflict between cacique-based and sectoral structures combined with a growing ideological conflict between Cedillo and the federal government. Cárdenas proved much more radical than Cedillo, who maintained a more moderate attitude toward the Catholic Church and who had come to oppose the system of collectively managed *ejidos,* which was not only the centerpiece of the agrarian revolution but Cárdenas's preferred vehicle for modernizing Mexican agriculture and achieving social justice in the countryside.

By 1937 tensions between Cárdenas and Cedillo reached their limit as the latter increasingly emerged as a major figure in the conservative opposition to the president. After Cedillo was dismissed as minister of agriculture, the federal government began to suspend the agrarian funding that was key to the cacique's support from the *campesinos* in the Valle del Maíz. Cárdenas drew on the new muscle of the official labor and peasant unions to establish loyal state and municipal officials and finally undercut Cedillo's military might by deposing his old ally Francisco Carrera Torres as the head of military operations in the region.

Owing to his ideological conflict with Cárdenas, Cedillo was approached by many right-wing groups, including the fascist organization known as the "gold shirts." However, such links have been exaggerated by official and left-wing versions of the Cedillo rebellion, who have tried to portray him as an ally of the foreign oil companies whose Mexican holdings were expropriated during the zenith of Cárdenas's Revolutionary nationalist measures in March 1938. While the oil companies undoubtedly were pleased by any efforts to overthrow Cárdenas, the aging, increasingly ill, and militarily weak Cedillo never enjoyed any concrete support from Washington, the oil companies, or even the fascist governments in Europe, who saw little to be gained from such an adventure.

Cedillo's rebellion was virtually stillborn. The federal government had made certain that it possessed all the necessary elements to defeat the caudillo from Palomas before forcing Cedillo to rebel by demanding that he leave his base in the Valle del Maíz. When he was forced to take up arms in 1938, it was basically a suicidal gesture in defense of his personal honor and a refusal to recognize that his days as the caudillo of San Luis Potosí and his local project in the Valle del Maíz were a thing of the past. In a display of the depth of the personal loyalty Cedillo enjoyed, the doomed rebellion had the support of former guerrilla fighters and *campesinos,* particularly in the agrarian colonies concentrated in the same region from which he had operated since 1912. Since he viewed the rebellion as a personal conflict with Cárdenas, however, Cedillo declined the offer of support by many groups of armed *campesinos* and instead opted to take to the hills along with a small band of relatives and close supporters. Their participation in the rebellion was not based on any illusion of success but on the deep gratitude and affection they felt for Cedillo and the fact that their way of life depended on the system he had built in the region.

The old caudillo repeatedly declined various amnesty proposals from the government, which included an offer to send him abroad for medical treatment.

Despite Cárdenas's apparent wish that Cedillo not be killed, many of his closest relatives, including his sister Higinia, were tortured and murdered. Saturnino and his son Suyo were killed by federal troops on January 11, 1939, after associates reported where they were hiding. Nevertheless, many followers remained loyal to his cause, and the last Cedillo rebel did not put down his arms until 25 years later.

Saturnino Cedillo was the last of the great military caciques of the Mexican Revolution who maintained his own quasi-private army. He preferred to die rather than see his legend and honor tarnished before the eyes of those who had served under him during decades of fighting and in the construction of his *campesino* fiefdom.

—ROMANA FALCÓN VEGA

Chiapas Zapatista Rebellion

See Zapatista Rebellion in Chiapas

Conquest

This entry contains six articles that discuss the Spanish conquest of the territory that eventually would become New Spain:

Conquest: Spanish Background
Conquest: Central Mexico
Conquest: Yucatán
Conquest: Northern Mexico
Conquest: Demographic Impact
Conquest: Ecological Impact

See also Catholic Church; Conquistadors; Family and Kinship: Colonial; Malinche and Malinchismo; Mesoamerica; Mestizaje; Politics and Government; Rural Economy and Society

Conquest: Spanish Background

Spain and Portugal, the two great peninsular kingdoms of the modern age, were notable for their precocious colonizing impulse. Placed at the *finis terrae* of the known world, naval powers by necessity, Christian powers by both conviction and convenience, the peninsular nations flung themselves eagerly into enterprise on the high seas. Tacked to the back of Europe like a watchtower over the Atlantic,

first line of fire in the battle against Islam, they aspired to a leadership that had little to do with their position on the geographical sidelines. A long history of colonizations and invasions had branded the peoples of the Iberian Peninsula with a peculiar distrust toward the outside. Moreover, their medieval past had been quite distinct from that of other Europeans, marked by rivalry and war more often than by peace and harmony.

The various ethnic groups long settled in Spain found their differences exacerbated by the geographical characteristics of the terrain they inhabited, as by their contacts, cordial or otherwise, with unfamiliar peoples and cultures. The south and east, opening on the Mediterranean, had assimilated Graeco-Roman cultural patterns centuries before the advent of the Christian age; these regions subsequently maintained trade relations with and even political sway over Italy, Greece, southern France, and northern Africa. The north and west, on the other hand, remained attached to vestigial pagan cults while facing a far more perilous sea. Thus they remained entrenched in isolation until the Lower Middle Ages (eighth through eleventh centuries), when they began to court maritime adventure along Europe's Atlantic seaboard. The central plateau—a land short on natural resources, supporting a people insensible to the finer points of classical civilizations—fought to maintain its independence, making war into a way of life and adopting a readily fanatical, uncompromising brand of religiosity that frequently took the upper hand.

From the Roman presence onward, there were repeated attempts to unify the whole peninsula, each so shaky that it immediately failed. The barbarian groups that conquered the Hispanic provinces after the fall of the Roman Empire were hard-pressed to sustain their own precarious unity under the Wisigoth command, established in the central region, but preceded in Hispania by the Vandals (settled in modern-day Andalusia), the Sweves (in Galicia), and the Alani (in Lusitania, today's Portugal). There were other peoples who had not been Romanized and still others, of Latin language and culture, who only accepted the Teutonic yoke under duress.

The Muslims, goaded by the preaching of a holy war, routed the Wisigoth army in 711 and within seven years spread their dominion over virtually the whole peninsula. However, the disproportion between their moderate numbers and the extensive lands beneath their control prevented this from being a wholesale occupation, especially since armed resistance was immediately launched by rebellious enclaves of Hispano-Romans who had retreated from the Crescent Moon to the highlands of Asturias and the Pyrennees. Thus began the slow wresting back of territory, celebrated as the Reconquista. Until that moment, the ideal of unity always had come hand in hand with invasion; but now, a mystique of national regeneration took hold, built around religious faith inasmuch as Islam and Christianity were the two forces pitted against one another on Iberian soil.

The war between Spanish Christians and African Muslims (who were dubbed Moors, though not all came from Mauritania) lasted almost eight centuries, from 718 (the Battle of Covadonga) until 1492 (the fall of Granada). By the thirteenth century, Spanish kingdoms had obtained papal recognition for their Crusade, with all attendant privileges for those who fought under such a banner.

The movement of reconquest crept from north to south, in campaigns separated by intervals of peace and conducted with varying intensity, according to the strength of the enemy and the level of squabbling among the Christian realms. As a rule, the spells of peaceful coexistence were longer than those of struggle and intolerance. The powerful Caliphate of Cordova splintered into small kingdoms that gave way one by one before the defenders of the Cross. In a series of pacts and treaties, the advancing peninsular rulers partitioned the territories assigned to each, right down to the southern coast. The kingdom of Aragon, linked since the thirteenth century to the county of Barcelona, accomplished its share of the Reconquista in good time and proceeded to pursue its interests in the Mediterranean. This policy led it to dominate parts of France, Italy, and Greece and brought it into conflict with the sultanates of North Africa.

The realms of Castile were joined and parted several times in wills and in wars, until Portugal won its independence and Asturias, Galicia, León, and the original county of Castile were definitively united in the kingdom of that name. Castile completed the expulsion of the Moors from Granada in 1492 and its monarchs were henceforth called Catholic—unlike their predecessors, whose title had been "Of the Three Faiths," since both Muslims and Jews had been their vassals. Shortly afterward, the kingdom of Navarre was united with Castile in the person of Fernando the Catholic, to create the largest, richest, and most populous kingdom in the peninsula.

The marriage of Isabel I of Castile to her cousin Fernando II of Aragon in 1469 amalgamated two very different realms in terms of territorial extension, economic potential, demographic numbers, ethnic composition, political aspirations, and social relations. The Aragonese regarded the power of Castile

with understandable misgivings, fearing that such a union might prove counter to their interest. Indeed, under the Hapsburg monarchs in the sixteenth and seventeenth centuries, the court sat either at Toledo, Madrid, or Valladolid, all in Castile; only exceptionally, and for brief periods, did it move to Barcelona, Zaragoza, or Valencia, the most important cities of Aragon.

The experience of war with a religious justification, the experience of living side by side with other religions, and the missionary urge produced by both had become part and parcel of the mental makeup of the Spanish people at the time of the discovery of America. The chronological coincidence between the termination of any Arab presence in Spain and the appearance of new lands over the ocean spurred the religious ardor of the Catholic monarchs and many of their servants, for none could doubt the perpetuation of Castile's destiny as God's instrument for the expansion of the true faith. When Elio Antonio de Nebrija presented Isabel with his *Gramática castellana* at the camp in Santa Fé de Granada, he still assumed that southward expansion would be directed across the straits toward Morocco. His phrase "language has ever been the handmaiden of empire" encapsulated a fundamental aspect of colonial policy. The opening of a New World unexpectedly broadened the possibilities of expansion; now that the whole of Spanish soil was safely under the Cross, the hour had come to carry it into infidel territory.

The memory of a lengthy but triumphant war against Islam was never far away at the moment of elaborating governmental dispositions concerning the New World. The attempts to evangelize the Muslims of Granada, the boarding schools for the sons of Moorish noblemen, the rules of dress and personal adornment, and the tireless vigilance for signs of heresy—all these were the model for subsequent missions to the Americas. Even more useful was the familiarity with Arabic text transcribed into Latin characters, an adaptation that had been current for several hundred years among Mozarabs, or Spanish Christians living under Muslim rule. By the end of the fifteenth century, the conquest and colonization of the Canary islands, a Spanish bridgehead in the Atlantic near the African coast, constituted the immediate precedent for the American undertaking.

Ever since the Turks mopped up the remains of the Byzantine Empire, trade with the Far East had become difficult, expensive, and occasionally impossible. Goods and spices from China and Southeast Asia were highly prized by Europeans, who could no longer do without them. Portugal led the quest for a southern naval route to Asia, and its sailors explored the African coasts, drew maps, defined the most practical itineraries, and embarked on massive slave-trading to pay for it all. This human commerce was to reach its peak with the high demand for labor in American sugar and cotton plantations. Ten years after Columbus landed at Guanahaní, Vasco da Gama reached India, marking the culmination of the Portuguese journeys.

In search of a western approach to the coveted Spice Islands, Christopher Columbus came across lands that were called the Indies from then on, although by 1505 it was clear that this was not Asia but an unknown land mass. From the outset, the conquest of the new continent fell to Castile, and the great majority of explorers, conquistadors, settlers, and officials who traveled to the Indies were natives of that kingdom. They negotiated with Pope Alexander VI the concession of rights over all lands discovered or awaiting discovery. Both the Portuguese and the Spaniards claimed their conquests justified by the barbarity of African and American peoples, and sanctified by the duty to save their souls; both clamored to the Holy See for approval of what they considered to be their rights. In response to these demands, an imaginary line was drawn dividing the world into two hemispheres, the east for Portugal and the west for Castile. On the basis of this ambiguous papal verdict, a discussion of actual borders was conducted in the town of Tordesillas. The meridian traced on that occasion enabled the Portuguese to occupy, as well as their Asian colonies, a portion of the new continent corresponding to modern Brazil. Castile had the Pope's blessing to appropriate the rest of America, and also managed to plant its flag in the Philippine Islands of southeast Asia. Portuguese and Spanish fleets thus had multiple occasion to cross one other on the high seas, with resulting in frequent showdowns and skirmishes. The first circumnavigation of the globe was completed by a Castilian, with a fleet that began its voyage under Portuguese command.

Early explorations of the West Indian islands and mainland coastlines proved disappointing in terms of profit, for neither jewels nor precious metals were found, neither spices nor artistic treasures such as those described by Marco Polo in his accounts of Cipango and Cathay (Japan and China). The subjugation of Mexico inaugurated a new stage, in which silver became both the motive for conquest and the means of financing costly campaigns and cumbersome bureaucracies; the entire world economy was affected by the plentiful production of this metal and consequent decline in its price, which destabilized the anterior equilibrium. The Spanish empire encompassed a vast territory that it never explored or measured with precision. The riches it yielded promptly vanished into the coffers of the Royal Treasury, to be squandered on interest payments against the king's debts or on all kinds of goods that were no longer manufactured in Castile. Even humble households indulged in bedlinen from Holland, hangings from Rouen, carpets from Turkey, and velvet or silk cushions from Italy, France, or China, as we know from dowry agreements involving quite modest sums of money.

The precarious alliance of the "Spains," as the joined provinces were called in some documents, was almost broken by the death of Queen Isabel la Católica and her husband's new nuptials with Germaine de Foix. But Fernando's second marriage was childless and the kingdom of Aragon remained permanently wedded to Castile with the accession of Queen Juana, whose madness prevented her from ruling. With the premature death of her husband Felipe, Cardinal Ximénez de Cisneros was appointed regent until Carlos should come of age—the young grandson of the Catholic Kings who was brought up in Flanders and years later would fulfill his aspiration to the imperial throne of Germany.

The reign of Carlos I of Spain (also crowned Emperor Charles V of Germany) was distinguished by its involvement in European politics. This activity befitted Carlos not only as German emperor but also as the tireless antagonist of Francis I of France, as the champion of Aragon's territorial ambitions in Italy, the bulwark of papism against Protestantism, and the instigator of the Council of Trent, in which Spanish theologians played a prominent role. During the early years of his reign he had to deal with serious movements of revolt, among the nobility (the so-called Communities of Castile) and among the artisans of Valencia (the "Germanías" of Aragon). These protests found an echo among the many who were angered by the young monarch's moves to curb seigneurial privilege and undermine common law, his imposition of new taxes, his authoritarianism, and those European enterprises that struck many Castilians as ill-advised. The rebels were put down by force, popular discontent found other targets and Spain, like the rest of European countries, stepped into a new historical epoch on the brink of modernity.

Castilian politics were only temporarily and superficially modified by Carlos's imperial adventurism. His marriage to a Portuguese princess favored the interests of Castile, soothing its yearning for an undivided peninsula with the hope that future matches between the heirs of both realms might culminate sooner or later in unification. Such hopes were short-lived. After 1580, Felipe II held on to both crowns through force rather than by any legitimacy of parentage; Felipe III kept them yet more precariously together and Felipe IV was forced to separate them, granting Portugal its independence in 1640.

It was under Carlos I that Fernando (Hernán) Cortés struck out for Mexico and found himself conquering the Mexica Empire. Carlos, busy as ever with wars and treaties, was nonetheless struck by the potential of this new conquest as soon as he laid eyes on samples of the Mexica lords' treasures, including fine pieces of worked gold and silver ingots corresponding to the king's portion, the Royal Fifth. Mines were being discovered in quick succession: first Taxco, Zacualpan, Sultepec, Temascaltepec y Pachuca; soon after, Zacatecas; and in the following century, Guanajuato. Meanwhile, Peruvian gold and the contents of the "silver hill" at Potosí were poured into sustaining the imperial pomp clung to by a permanently debt-ridden and bankrupt metropolis.

Aragon was sufficiently on the margins of Castilian undertakings to devote some energy to its economic development, and maintain steady population growth; this suffered a severe setback at the beginning of the seventeenth century, when political expediency inspired an order to expel all the moriscos (converted Moors) from the territories under Spanish rule. The Mediterranean tradition of smallholding agriculture and many crafts and trades were shattered by this measure.

Meanwhile, Castile was being drained of its life-blood: American emigration was taking its toll on the population, while the lavish unearned income from overseas was not only a disincentive to consolidate what had been a budding but prosperous textile industry; it also was thrown away consistently on the importation of luxury goods.

Although Felipe II could boast that the sun never set over his dominions, Spanish power was already sinking into twilight. Incessant war, state debts, neglect of production, and endemic corruption at every level of government were eroding the foundations of the empire. The ills of the metropolis had repercussions in the farthest outreaches of the colonies, for American silver was financing no more than an artificial prosperity, enough to maintain Spain's ostentatious court and its hitherto invincible regiments, which now began to taste defeat.

Throughout the reigns of the last three Hapsburg kings in the seventeenth century, Spain maintained the appearances of a spurious grandeur: neither the infantry nor the navy, neither financial nor human capital sustained this fiction. At the same time, local elites were gaining strength in the colonies, networks of regional influences were being created, and new, economically powerful groups emerged, ready to defy the representatives of the metropolis.

—PILAR GONZALBO AIZPURU

Conquest: Central Mexico

On April 21, 1519, a Spanish fleet led by an obscure Spaniard named Fernando (Hernán) Cortés reached San Juan Ulúa on the Veracruz coast of the Gulf of Mexico. The expedition came officially on behalf of the governor of Cuba, Diego Velázquez, who was eager to conquer new lands in his own right, but who was still a mere deputy of Christopher Columbus's heir and admiral of the Indies, Diego Colón. For at least two years now Velázquez had been trying to break free from Colón's jurisdiction: he had sent out the exploring and trading expeditions of Hernández de Córdoba and Juan de Grijalva in 1517 and 1518, and he had dispatched personal agents to Spain to urge the Crown to grant him the title of adelantado of Yucatán, with the right to conquer and settle the region. Clearly, Velázquez's initiative to send Cortés in search of Grijalva's fleet and of any Christians held captive in Yucatán was intended to keep his claims alive while he awaited the Crown's decision. What remains somewhat of a mystery is his choice of Cortés to lead the new venture; the future conqueror had no experience, although he might have had the financial means to secure his appointment as captain by contributing substantially to the cost of the expedition.

There is, in fact, enough evidence to suggest that Velázquez himself was having second thoughts about the wisdom of his choice, and that he was becoming apprehensive about Cortés's increasing power and even tried to prevent him from being supplied with provisions. In these circumstances, it is not surprising that when Cortés heard that Grijalva's fleet had returned safely to Cuba, he decided to leave swiftly, before Velázquez had time to prevent him. From this moment he found himself in a delicate and highly dubious position, both in relation to Velázquez and to the Spanish Crown, and it is no great surprise that as soon as he learned about the existence of a powerful ruler called Moteuczoma II, his mind was set firmly on reaching him and somehow persuading him to acknowledge the sovereignty of Queen Juana and her son Carlos, for this was the one sure way to justify and legitimate his original act of rebellion.

The existence of Moteuczoma II was confirmed by a group of Indians sent by Tentil, the Mexica (Aztec) governor of the region, who came to meet Cortés at San Juan Ulúa. On subsequent days the Indians returned loaded with lavish gifts from the Mexica, among which were found objects commonly offered to the gods.

The gesture can be interpreted as an open acknowledgment that the Spaniards were gods, and it is often used in support of the legend that Muteuczoma might have thought that Cortés was Quetzalcoatl, the ancient deity who had left for the east and promised to return. There is, however, no contemporary evidence to support this, and it is almost certainly a later reinterpretation of the events. To insist on it, moreover, obscures the more significant fact that, to Cortés and his followers, the presentation of gifts would have appeared as an admission of conditional subservience and subordination. Through the gifts, in other words, the Mexica were acknowledging Cortés's superior rights; but at the same time they demanded that he not go to the Mexica capital of Tenochtitlan and that he move his camp away from San Juan Ulúa. When, a few days later, five Totonac Indians came to offer their services to Cortés, the reasons why Tentil had expressed concern about the Spanish presence in the area became clearer: Cortés now realized that the Mexica had enemies, and this made the prospect of conquest feasible.

In all these exchanges Cortés had the invaluable help of two interpreters: the Spaniard Jerónimo de Aguilar, who had been shipwrecked in Yucatán around 1511 and had lived among the Maya until he managed to escape and join Cortés's fleet as it passed by on its way to Veracruz in 1519; and doña Marina, one of the 20 Indian women that the people of Coatzacoalcos presented to Cortés in March 1519. She was bilingual in Nahuatl and Maya, and would soon learn Spanish and become Cortés's main interpreter. In the early stages, however, the collaboration of Aguilar was essential: Nahuatl messages were translated by doña Marina into Maya and by Aguilar into Spanish.

Once his mind was made up about conquest, Cortés's priority was to consolidate the support of his followers and to set it firmly upon legal grounds. Given his highly equivocal legal position the issue was especially delicate, but Cortés's solution was masterly. His first step was to found the town of Villa Rica de la Vera Cruz, with its own legal structure and town council. According to Spanish legal tradition, this meant that the new town could function as a political entity directly under the authority of the king. After deciding that the authority granted by Velázquez had lapsed, since the expedition had now fulfilled the governor's mandate, the town council —which had been appointed by Cortés himself— elected their leader as captain. The initiative freed Cortés from the legal restraints placed on him by Velázquez, but it also made it essential for him to succeed in his plan for conquest; for if he failed he would still be liable to the charge of treason against one of the king's governors.

It was in this state of mind that Cortés marched to Cempoala, the nearby town of the Totonacs who had come to the Spanish camp to offer their services. At Cempoala, where he arrived on June 3, Cortés confirmed that the Totonacs were eager to support him against the Mexica, to whom they paid allegiance out of fear rather than loyalty. Cortés would be careful to exploit such political cleavages and grievances among the Mexica tributaries. Accordingly, from now on he adopted a consistent policy of "divide and rule," forging an alliance with the Totonacs and enlisting their much-needed support for the march to Tenochtitlan, while sending persistent signals of friendship to the Mexica.

At this stage, it seemed as if Cortés's plans for conquest would face more opposition from the Spanish than from the Indian side. Upon his return to Veracruz, Cortés learned that King Carlos I (Emperor Charles V) had given Velázquez authority to trade and to found settlements. Cortés responded by sending the king, on July 26, all the gold collected so far, in addition to the royal fifth to which Spanish monarchs legally were entitled. Rumors of Cortés's intention reached Velázquez, who failed to capture the ship and then began preparations for a large fleet under Pánfilo de Narváez to capture Cortés. The situation became especially urgent for Cortés when it was discovered that there were a number of supporters of Velázquez among Cortés's followers, some of whom were conspiring to sail to Cuba. Cortés could afford to take no chances. Swiftly he had the two principal conspirators hanged, the pilot's feet cut off, and the sailors lashed. He then stripped the ten remaining ships of their anchors, sails, and cables and sank them. With no hope of returning to Cuba, Velázquez's potential supporters had no choice but to side with Cortés, who then put Juan de Escalante in charge of Veracruz with about 100 soldiers and, with the vital help of the Totonacs, began the slow march to Tenochtitlan.

Progress was smooth until the Spaniards approached Tlaxcala in early September. The Tlaxcaltecs were well known for their hostility to the Mexica, and Cortés naturally hoped to enlist their support. Yet the fact that the bulk of Indians traveling with Cortés were Mexica tributaries made the Tlax-caltecs suspicious, and accordingly they attacked the Spaniards with unprecedented ferocity and determination. The Tlaxcaltecs were skilled soldiers who attacked in unison using both shock and projectile weapons with great expertise. They posed a much greater threat to Cortés's forces than he had imagined. In normal circumstances, the most prudent policy from the military point of view would have been to withdraw.

The threat to Cortés, however, was not merely military but, above all, strategic. Withdrawal would inevitably have been seen as a sign of weakness that would have done irreparable damage to the fragile alliance with the Totonacs. Under the circumstances, Cortés was wise to adopt a defensive stance from where he could make use of Spanish crossbows, har-quebuses, and rapid-firing artillery to beat back Indian attacks. The tactic was successful; but given the Tlaxcaltec's overwhelming numerical superiority and the rapid dwindling of Spanish provisions and projectiles, it was a precarious and emphatically short-term solution.

Cortés knew that a continuing defensive strategy soon would degenerate into a war of attrition that the Tlaxcaltecs inevitably would win. He therefore wisely combined his defensive strategy with messages of peace, threats, and quick attacks on neighboring villages with the purpose of obtaining provisions and terrorizing the local populations. Gradually, the Tlaxcaltecs began to reconsider their position. Since Tlaxcala was governed jointly by the rulers of four confederated kingdoms, support for the war depended upon reaching a consensus among these rulers. As the war wore on, and as Tlaxcaltec casualties increased, support for the war waned. Once the Spaniards were recognized as a major military force, the Tlaxcaltecs gradually were persuaded by the obvious advantages of seeking an alliance with them. The decision was made in the hope of being able to shift the balance of power against the relentless advance of the Mexica.

The Tlaxcaltec decision to seek an alliance was a momentous triumph for Cortés. He had had enough problems trying to keep the peace in his own camp, where many of his men were near mutiny. Once in Tlaxcala, Cortés learned that the Mexica ruler Moteuczoma II had not been able to conquer his newly acquired allies, despite repeated attempts. This lead him to suppose that the Mexica military power was roughly comparable to the Tlaxcaltec. This impression, he was later to realize, was based on a gross misunderstanding of Mexica military tactics and of their puzzling reluctance to attack the

Spaniards, which Cortés at the time interpreted as a sign of weakness. For the moment, however, the misunderstanding meant that the slow march to Tenochtitlan would continue.

The Spaniards stayed in Tlaxcala for two weeks before resuming their march on October 10. For reasons that probably will never be entirely clear, they decided to go via Cholula, a city traditionally allied to Tlaxcala and Huejotzingo but which recently had become an ally of the Mexica. There they were housed and fed for two days. Then Cortés made one of his most puzzling decisions: he ordered a massacre of unarmed Cholultecs, including the king, the cream of the army, and a number of important leaders, whom he had asked to assemble in the main courtyard.

The Spanish accounts are unanimous in their agreement that the massacre was necessary because the Cholultecs were planning to attack them with the help of a Mexica army, but there is no clear evidence to support this. It seems more likely that the attack was suggested by the Tlaxcaltecs, who had a much better understanding of the internal divisions of the Cholultec system, and attempted to exploit the situation in order to open the field for a pro-Tlaxcaltec successor to the massacred king. Although the attack inevitably would put the Spaniards in opposition to Moteuczoma, it also cemented Cortés's friendship with the Tlaxcaltecs and served as a lesson to Cholula for its recent change of allegiances, a lesson that, from Cortés's point of view, might also shake the confidence of other Mexica allies. More importantly, Moteuczoma now was aware that the new king of Cholula had assumed power with Spanish help. So, too, he must have been acutely sensitive to the potentially dissident groups within his own region. Any opposition to Cortés might easily turn these groups against him and endanger his own position. In the circumstances, his choice to welcome the Spaniards into Tenochtitlan, where he greeted them on November 8—a mere six-and-one-half months after they had landed in San Juan Ulúa—was not a sign of weakness or ineptitude, but a carefully considered and logical decision.

Even as they entered Tenochtitlan, the precariousness of their situation must have begun to dawn on the Spaniards. The Mexica capital was a formidable city by any standards, far beyond anything that the Spaniards had encountered before, either in America or in Europe. Its location on an island, moreover, meant that it would not take much effort for the Mexica to trap the Spaniards. It is no surprise that many of Cortés's followers began to suspect that Moteuczoma had allowed them in as part of a dubious strategy to finish them off in the easiest possible way. Soon after their arrival, moreover, news reached Cortés that a Spanish force sent by Escalante to defend the Totonacs against a Mexica attack had been defeated. Fearing that the news would entice other allies to defect, yet unable to leave Tenochtitlan to deal with the situation himself, Cortés again deployed his remarkable instinct for leadership by taking what is perhaps his most memorable and momentous initiative: on November 14, he approached Moteuczoma and seized him.

The ease with which Moteuczoma submitted to Cortés continues to puzzle historians, and understandably so. It often has been seen as yet another sign of indecision and weakness. From Moteuczoma's point of view, however, the situation was rather more delicate. A refusal to cooperate with Cortés would have brought the Mexica political system to a standstill and threatened Moteuczoma's authority against the claims of the many contenders to the throne in the region, especially those who had opposed the Spanish entry into the city. Cortés tried to use Moteuczoma's friendship and willingness to cooperate to the best possible advantage; but he could not have understood the intricacies of the way in which the Mexica tributaries were integrated into the Mexica state, and of the nature and limits of the king's power. Control of the tributaries, for instance, depended on cooperation rather than on coercion. Such cooperation, moreover, required confidence in the Mexica king's authority and ability to act effectively. Although Cortés controlled Moteuczoma, he often persuaded him to take decisions that were actually contrary to Mexica interests. This led to a marked erosion of support for Moteuczoma among the people and the nobility, and to a consequent rise in the vulnerability of the Spanish position, a situation about which the Spaniards themselves were not fully aware.

Meanwhile, Pánfilo de Narváez's expedition from Cuba had been making slow progress and eventually landed at San Juan Ulúa in late April 1520. As soon as the news reached Cortés, he placed Pedro de Alvarado in charge of Tenochtitlan and marched to the coast. He reached Cempoala in late May, launched a surprise attack after midnight, captured Narváez, had him imprisoned, forced his men to surrender, and persuaded them to join him. He then began the march back to Tenochtitlan with an army of approximately 1,300 men. On their way they were joined by some 2,000 Tlaxcaltec warriors.

The renewed Spanish army entered Tenochtitlan unopposed on June 24. Cortés's confidence was partly the result of precedent. After all, he had entered Tenochtitlan before, and with a much smaller army. Now, however, the situation had changed quite dramatically. During Cortés's absence, Pedro de Alvarado had massacred thousands of Mexica nobles during the May festival of Toxcatl in honor of the god Hitzilopochtli. His motive was that he thought the Mexica were about to attack the Spaniards. The massacre caused disarray and confusion among the Mexica: their forces had been decimated and their very best soldiers had been killed. Although it could be said that in strictly military terms the massacre was a coup for the Spaniards, politically it proved an irreparable mistake. Not only did it turn the tide definitively against them, but it led to the complete withdrawal of support for Moteuczoma. Cortés was aware that the situation had deteriorated, but he was still confident that he could control the situation with Moteuczoma's assistance. His decision to reenter Tenochtitlan thus was taken on the basis of a very inadequate understanding of the mechanisms of Mexica kingship, and it proved to be his most disastrous tactical mistake.

Tenochtitlan had become a trap, and by the time of Cortés's return the Spaniards had been besieged in Moteuczoma's quarters for about three weeks. Their reinforced military power proved useless against the relentlessness of Mexica resistance. Having failed to negotiate a withdrawal, Cortés persuaded Moteuczoma to order the Mexica to stop the attack and brought him out onto the roof, but he was struck down and died. Whether Moteuczoma was killed by the stones thrown by the Mexica, as Spanish accounts aver, or killed by the Spaniards, as Indian testimonies would have us believe, probably will never be known with certainty. The Spanish version seems the most probable; but the Indian account is plausible, given that the Spaniards by now would have realized that Moteuczoma had become a liability. Besides, the official period of mourning for a dead king would have given them a welcome respite.

However that may be, it was now blatantly clear to Cortés that the only option was to flee. He also must have been painfully aware that such a display of weakness would inevitably affect his political alliances, but now the only alternative was death. So in the middle of a heavy rainstorm, late in the evening on June 30, the Spaniards began their escape. They were attacked and many Spaniards were killed along with most of the Tlaxcaltecs and Huejotzincas and some horses. Many were trapped and forced to return to their quarters where they were later killed. All the cannons were lost.

Cortés finally reached Tacuba. From there, he began the march to the north and round the lakes toward Tlaxcala. Mexica assaults continued, but the fighting was now relatively light by comparison, and the Spaniards resumed their defensive formations to maximize the effectiveness of the weapons they still possessed. More important were the horses, since cavalry charges created gaps that could be exploited easily by troops with swords. By the time they reached Tlaxcala, however, Cortés had lost nearly 900 Spaniards and over 1,000 Tlaxcaltecs, and his remaining 440 Spaniards, 20 horses, 12 crossbowmen, and 7 harquebusiers all were wounded.

Cortés was second to none in his ability to learn from his mistakes. It was now clear to him that Tenochtitlan never could be conquered without first establishing a secure line of communications with the coast, which was his only source of supply for reinforcements. Additionally, he needed to reestablish firm alliances with the Indians, especially Mexica tributaries, in order to secure a steady supply of food. For the purpose, Cortés could take advantage of some recent developments he had been studying with care, foremost among which was Mexica factionalism. Even while under assault from the Mexica, Cortés had noticed that many of their tributaries were only too willing to lend him their support. This suggested that allegiance to the Mexica was effective only insofar as a mutual interest existed. Beyond that, loyalty was entirely dependent on fear of Mexica reprisals. Aware of this, Cortés adopted a policy of gradual, piecemeal conquests of Mexica tributaries, a policy that he was careful to combine with promises of protection against Mexica reprisals to facilitate quick shifts in allegiance. A key moment in this strategy was the conquest of Tepeyacac, where Cortés founded and fortified the town of La Villa de la Segura de la Frontera, which he used as a base for Spanish reinforcements and for retaliation against Mexica allies. From Tepeyacac, too, Cortés engineered a number of regional conquests that gradually secured him control of most major towns from Cholula to Ahuilizapan, where the road descended to Veracruz.

In late December, Cortés felt confident to begin the slow march back to the Valley of Mexico. He had 8 cannons, 550 Spanish soldiers (including 40 horsemen), and 10,000 Tlaxcaltec soldiers. Near the great city of Texcoco, Cortés was approached by a group of nobles who invited the Spaniards into the city. Their motive was to take advantage of Cortés's presence in order to shift the political balance against Tenochtitlan and end years of political divisions and dynastic crises. The new alliance, engineered by Ixtlilxochitl, gave Cortés an ideal base for his attack, and it brought with it the automatic allegiance of some adjacent subordinate towns, such as Otompan, that depended on support from Texcoco.

Gaining the loyalty of other areas proved more difficult. The area around Chalco, for instance, long had been antagonistic to Tenochtitlan, and it was of enormous strategic importance to Cortés, since it lay on the road to the coast. Quick to realize this, the Mexica subjected the area to repeated assaults.

Although the Spaniards were generally successful against Mexica attacks—particularly when they could face the Mexica on open ground—there were so many towns on the eastern side of the lakes that Cortés could not possibly hope to defend them all. Paradoxically, therefore, Spanish expansion only served to compound Cortés's problems. The only solution was to take the offensive and strike directly at Tenochtitlan. Yet, any such action would bring the Spaniards closer to the lakes; and there, the Mexica would use the great mobility of their canoes to force the Spanish back, as they consistently had done. If the conquest was to succeed, therefore, Cortés needed to gain control of the lakes. It was no doubt with this in mind that, early in February, he ordered the construction of 13 brigantines.

The ships were launched on April 28, 1521. Each could hold 12 oarsmen, 12 crossbowmen and harquebusiers, a captain, and artillerymen to control a cannon mounted in the bow. The launching was coordinated with the mainland offensive, which was divided into three armies. The first one was lead by Pedro de Alvarado and went to Tacuba with 30 horsemen, 18 crossbowmen and harquebusiers, 150 Spanish soldiers, and 25,000 Tlaxcaltecs. A second army, lead by Cristóbal de Olid, was sent to Coyoacan with 20 crossbowmen and harquebusiers, 175 Spanish soldiers, and 20,000 Indians. Finally Gonzalo de Sandoval was sent to Ixtapalapa with 24 horsemen, 25 crossbowmen and harquebusiers, and over 30,000 Indians. The choice of these cities was not by chance. Each of them controlled access to a major causeway linking them to Tenochtitlan, and their control allowed Cortés to initiate a calculated strategy of starving out the defenders by cutting off the Mexica capital's supplies of food and water.

Their first mission accomplished, Sandoval and Olid returned to join Alvarado at Tacuba and began the slow march to Tenochtitlan along the causeway. Despite their technological superiority, the sheer mass of Mexica defenders was overwhelming, and the initial assault was forced back with heavy losses. Meanwhile Cortés had had the chance to prove the superiority of his brigantines against the Mexica canoes in a naval engagement just off the fortified island of Tepepolco. Their effectiveness greatly complicated the Mexica defensive strategy, which hitherto had been concentrated along the narrow fronts where causeways ran. Now the Spaniards could land forces virtually anywhere around the Valley of Mexico and bring artillery into range of many areas of Tenochtitlan that the Mexica had assumed safe.

With this new advantage, the Spaniards began to make more progress along the causeways. The Mexica responded with a number of tactics that still managed to keep the Spaniards off balance. Foremost among these was the astute use of feigned withdrawals and ambushes, whereby the Spaniards would be drawn forward and then cut off and counterattacked. On June 30 the Mexica feigned one such withdrawal against Cortés, who pursued them, neglecting to fill a breach before he crossed. The Mexica then sent their war canoes into the breach and caught the Spaniards between the two forces. Eight horses and many men were killed, and 68 Spaniards were captured alive, taken to the great temple, sacrificed, flayed, and their faces tanned and sent to allied towns as proof of Spanish mortality and as a warning against betraying the alliance.

Mexica attacks continued during the next few days. For a while it must have seemed as if the tide of battle had turned against Cortés, because most of his Indian allies began to defect and to return home. The most notable exception to this trend was Ixtlilxochitl, who remained at Cortés's side, advising him to continue blocking food and water supplies to Tenochtitlan with the brigantines.

Gradually, Indians began to return from allied towns as the Spaniards took the offensive once again. Yet, news of recent Mexica successes and Spanish vulnerability had led some Mexica allies to attack cities that had allied with the Spanish. Aware of the political consequences that such developments could have on the balance of power, Cortés was quick to act. As soon as he heard that troops from Malinalco had started an attack on Cuauhnahuac, he sent a force under Andrés de Tapia to rout them. Two days later, Sandoval was sent to the Valley of Toluca to rout the Matlanzincas, who were planning an attack on the Spaniards. The policy was successful in consolidating the support of Cortés's Indian allies and regaining that of those who were beginning to waver; but it ran the danger of diverting attention from Tenochtitlan at a time when men were being lost and gunpowder almost exhausted. Just then, in mid-July, a fleet of Spanish ships reached Veracruz with fresh supplies of ammunition and reinforcements. The event, which Cortés saw as a clear sign of God's favor, allowed the Spaniards to make their final advance into Tenochtitlan.

As they entered the great Mexica capital the Spaniards were attacked from the buildings lining the streets. In response, Cortés ordered his allies to send their farmers to Tenochtitlan to raze the buildings on both sides of their advance. The rubble then was used to fill the breaches to facilitate the troop's access into the city. The Mexica then retreated north to Tlaltelolco, where the causeways were still intact and the brigantines would be less of a threat. But the Spanish advance continued, and eventually reached the great market of Tlaltelolco in early August. Meanwhile, Ixtlilxochitl had captured his brother, Coanacoch, and forced the Texcocans to shift their loyalty to Cortés. On August 13, at the final land assault, the Mexica surrendered. Then the inhabitants of Tenochtitlan were massacred for four days. Cortés had conquered the Mexica with a surviving force of 900 Spaniards, but the crucial role had been played by his 200,000 Indian allies.

Cortés's achievement was remarkable by any standards, but it should be remembered that it was as much a triumph for European disease as for Spanish military prowess. The part played by epidemics, smallpox in particular, in sapping the Indians' ability and will to resist, especially in densely populated areas like central Mexico, is fundamental for understanding the thoroughness of the Spanish success. So too, the internal weaknesses in the structure of the Mexica political system, particularly the repressive nature of their domination, facilitated a revolt by the subjugated peoples against their overlords without which the Spanish conquest would have been unthinkable. As we have seen, however, Cortés's military tactics and political genius played a fundamental and decisive role at every step.

Even more important in the long run was Cortés's conviction that "without settlement there is no good conquest," as Francisco López de Gómara put it. This was a conviction that derived from Cortés's experience in the Antilles, where the absence of a policy of settlement had lead to massive destruction and exploitation. In his desire to prevent a similar development in Mexico, Cortés repeatedly tried to turn soldiers into citizens by creating new towns wherever possible. The first instance of this practice, as we have seen in the foundation of the town at Veracruz, was a purely legal act; but it nevertheless provided the pattern for a similar process of municipal incorporation, which led to the proliferation of cities and towns intended for Spaniards and based on the model of the Spanish town. In this, Cortés displayed unusual foresight and common sense, and the initiative set an important precedent for the pattern that Spanish settlement of the New World would take. It is true that in order to attract Spanish settlers Cortés had to favor the introduction of the system of *encomienda*, an idea to which he was initially hostile, having witnessed the destruction that it had occasioned in the Antilles. But Cortés's *encomienda* was to be an improved and reformed institution, which was part of the conqueror's vision of a settled society in which Crown, conqueror, and Indian were linked in a chain of reciprocal obligation sanctioned in practice by the mendicant orders. When, eventually, the New Laws of 1542 attempted to abolish the *encomienda*, even the Dominicans declared themselves in its favor in New Spain. The contrast with other regions of Spanish America is immediately evident, and a large proportion of the credit for the relative stability and prosperity that ensued in central Mexico after the conquest must be given to Cortés.

See also Virgin of Guadalupe and Guadalupanismo

Select Bibliography

Cortés, Hernán, *Letters from Mexico,* translated and edited by Anthony Pagden. New Haven, Connecticut, and London: Yale University Press, 1986.

Elliott, John H., "The Mental World of Hernán Cortés." *Transactions of the Royal Historical Society* 17 (1967).

Hassig, Ross, *Mexico and the Spanish Conquest.* London and New York: Longman, 1994.

León Portilla, Miguel, *The Broken Spears: The Aztec Account of the Conquest of Mexico.* Boston: Beacon Press, 1966.

Sahagún, Bernardino de, *Florentine Codex: General History of the Things of New Spain.* Salt Lake City: University of Utah Press, 1981.

Thomas, Hugh, *The Conquest of Mexico.* London: Pimlico, 1994.

—FERNANDO CERVANTES

Conquest: Yucatán

In two short years Fernando (Hernán) Cortés toppled the mightiest empire in Mesoamerica and was rewarded with treasure, tribute, and bountiful Indian labor. Francisco de Montejo's conquest of the Yucatán Peninsula was vastly more prolonged and difficult, and much less bountiful in its reward. From Montejo's first invasion of the peninsula in 1527 to the founding of his capital at Mérida in 1542, Spaniards twice had to abandon Maya territory completely. Even with the suppression of the Great Rebellion of 1546 to 1547, Mayas continued periodically to rebel and resist over the next 150 years, greatly limiting the spread of Spanish control across

large parts of what are now the Mexican states of Yucatán, Campeche, and Quintana Roo; the Guatemalan department of the Petén; and the nation of Belize. The last independent Maya redoubt—Tah Itza in the Péten—finally was conquered in 1697, though by then prolonged Maya resistance and the growing intrusion of pirates and a rival European power had ensured that much of the peninsula would remain only lightly administered by the Spanish and little known to outsiders until well into the twentieth century.

When Montejo landed with 300 men on the east coast across from Cozumel Island in 1527, he could not have taken the Maya completely by surprise. Long before his arrival they knew that Spaniards were coming. Columbus probably made contact with Maya during his final New World voyage in 1502; a shipwreck in 1511 or 1512 dumped Spanish survivors on the peninsular coast; Ponce de Léon seems to have touched there while traveling between Cuba and Florida in 1513; and Indian canoes from the mainland reportedly made periodic contact with the suffering indigenous population of Spanish-ruled Cuba. In those early years Maya prophets began to speak of the coming of bearded strangers who would bring a new religion. Some, like the famed Chilam Balam of Mani, exhorted his Maya audiences to accept the strangers and the new life they brought. Most Maya, however, were not ready to do so, as Hernández de Córdova found when bested in bloody battles in 1517. Subsequent Spanish visitors such as Juan de Grijalva (1518) and Cortés (1519) enjoyed peaceable receptions, as long as they made their stays brief and continued their westward voyages. Montejo, however, armed with a royal commission and the soldiers, horses, and firearms that his own capital and that of his colleagues could finance, came to Yucatán to conquer, to settle, and to rule over a Maya people made loyal subjects of the Spanish Crown.

The east coast of the peninsula was a poor place to begin. Naum Pat, the Maya lord of Cozumel Island, was friendly to the Spaniards, and more than once lent valuable aid. But coastal forests were unhealthful for the Spaniards, and New Spain, from which supplies and new recruits would come, was too far away. Having established a nascent settlement called Salamanca there in 1527, Montejo marched the bulk of his force to the north and then west, searching for a better site to make his capital. The rulers of some of the Maya provinces through which he passed received him peaceably, and those who did not were defeated in battle. Spanish horses, arms, and organization proved time and again effective against vastly superior numbers of Maya warriors wearing cotton armor, wielding nonmetal blades, and hurling light projectiles. Still, by the summer of 1528 Montejo's men had suffered severe attrition to wounds and illness, and dreams of quick riches were fading. What is more, Montejo had discovered how decentralized Maya society was. The capture of a single prize or target would not ensure submission of the entire land, as the capture of Tenochtitlan did for the invaders of central Mexico. Rather, the peninsula was divided into at least 16 separate provinces, each one of which would have to be courted or forced into submission, and any one of which, as long as it remained independent, would provide a refuge and rallying point for the culturally and linguistically homogenous indigenous population of the peninsula. Understanding now the magnitude of the tasks ahead, Montejo returned to New Spain for supplies and soldiers, eventually abandoning altogether the eastern approach to the conquest of Maya lands.

After pausing to pacify Tabasco, which fell (along with parts of modern-day Guatemala and Honduras) within the domain that the Crown had authorized Montejo to conquer and rule, Montejo returned to the peninsular campaign. This time he approached from the west. Moving from their base in Tabasco, Spanish forces received peaceable receptions from the Maya rulers of the western provinces of Couoh, Canpech, and Ah Canul, and Montejo founded a Spanish settlement near the present-day city of Campeche. By 1531 the conquest of the peninsula seemed well progressed, as Maya rulers around Campeche pledged loyalty and supplied Spaniards with food and labor, though it was slowly dawning upon Mayas that such gifts were in fact tribute that they would be expected to provide in perpetuity. To expand his control of the peninsula, Montejo sent soldiers under his trusted lieutenant, Alonso Dávila, back overland to the east coast to subdue and settle in the Maya province of Chetumal. Soon after Dávila's force set out, however, Mayas around Campeche launched a massive assault upon Montejo's diminished army, while on the other side of the peninsula Dávila was locked in what became months of desperate fighting and siege at Chetumal. Dávila was forced into an extraordinary seven-month retreat down the coast to Honduras, but Montejo managed to defeat the Maya around Campeche and to send his son, also named Francisco de Montejo, to extend the conquest deeper into the interior.

Montejo's son, aided by Maya auxiliaries from friendly western provinces, established a second settlement in the hostile territory of the Cupul amid the ancient Maya ruins of Chichen Itza. There, as had happened before and would happen again, the defeat of initial Maya resistance, pledges of future loyalty from local Maya rulers, and the provision of food and labor deluded the Spaniards into thinking their domination of the Maya was firm. As quickly as possible the Montejos christened their soldiers citizens of the new settlements, assigned houselots and estates, and divided the local indigenous population into *encomiendas* (native settlements "commended" to the care of a Spaniard—an *encomendero*—who, in return for the Indians' labor, had the duty to protect the Indians, maintain missionaries in the villages, and contribute to the military defense of the region). However, around Chichen Itza, as earlier around Campeche, months of quiescence and colonial life was shattered when the Maya attacked in astonishing numbers. After many weeks of destructive warfare, Montejo's son was forced to evacuate Chichen Itza, heading first toward the north coast and eventually linking with his father. Before the Montejos could renew their conquest of hostile Maya provinces, however, the progressive disillusionment and desertion of their colleagues and subordinates forced the would-be conquerors to abandon the peninsula once again. After many months of combat, Spaniards really controlled little more than the immediate environs of their encampments. Protestations of loyalty from Maya rulers could change to deadly hostility without warning. Finally, the peninsula offered little immediate treasure to conquerors who had financed their own participation and that of their subordinates, and the sale of numerous Indian captives into slavery in New Spain or the West Indies was blocked by royal edicts. So when news arrived of the fabulous wealth to be had in the conquest of the Incas and opportunities for lucrative adventure elsewhere in Mesoamerica, only the Montejos and their most die-hard supporters would continue to sacrifice in the war against the Maya. For the time being, they were too few.

Montejo's son led the third invasion of the Yucatán Peninsula, greatly aided by his cousin, also Francisco, while his aged father oversaw the enterprise and occupied himself in the pacification and administration of other parts of his vast domain. This younger Montejo returned to the west coast at the end of 1540, joining a smaller Spanish force that had been sent ahead. Circumstances on the peninsula had changed to favor this latest attempt at permanent conquest. Maya around the Spanish foothold at Champoton—their numbers greatly reduced from flight and probably disease, consequences of earlier episodes in the conquest—were offered perpetual release from tribute and service in return for their cooperation with the Spaniards. Thus the Spanish began to solidify Maya cooperation with the conquest. Maya rulers of other western provinces had other reasons for offering more vigorous support of the Spanish cause this time, as conflicts between western and central Maya provinces had grown more bloody and bitter since the last Spanish invasion, partly in consequence of the seeming collaboration of western Maya with the earlier Spanish forays. This internal conflict aided the conquest. Defeats the Montejos had suffered during the earlier invasion also had taught them valuable lessons, such as not to send expeditions to found settlements deep in hostile territory. This time, instead, they would extend their conquest gradually up the coast and then toward the east in more methodical fashion, subduing each Maya province in turn, founding settlements or strong bases, and ensuring adequate means of communication and supply between them before proceeding on their slow march across the peninsula. Spanish arms always would win the day in pitched battle, although Maya resort to guerrilla war and siege could strain Spanish resolve severely. During the earlier invasions, when the Mayas abandoned their indefensible settlements, plugged up wells, destroyed their own food supplies, and fled into the forest, the Spanish would raid, take captives, steal food, but eventually hunger and the attrition of numerous small skirmishes took their toll on the invaders, as happened to Montejo the son at Chichen Itza or to Dávila around Chetumal. On this, their third attempt to conquer the Maya, Spaniards were better poised to endure such prolonged and bitter resistance, having ensured their own supply from friendly stations in the west. So one by one the Maya provinces fell, Maya returned to their settlements, and tribute of food, cloth, wax, honey, cacao, and more began to flow.

A broad Maya coalition lead by Nachi Cocom failed to drive the Spaniards from their new capital in 1542, and the Maya suffered heavy casualties that crippled their ability to launch subsequent grand assaults. Maya priests and rulers were able to organize one final, massive attempt to expel the Spaniards, attacking them on the night of November 8–9, 1546. A score of Spaniards caught on their estates were killed, along with hundreds of their Maya supporters, although the main Maya attacks on the Spanish settlement of Valladolid failed and the uprising around Mérida never got properly underway. Months of fighting was necessary to suppress the Maya again, and the alleged leaders of the uprising were executed. The Spaniards emerged from the Great Rebellion as secure rulers of a devastated land. During the conquest up to two-thirds of the Maya of the Yucatán Peninsula may have perished in battle, or to starvation and disease. The Spaniards suffered early, too, with only some 160 of the 700 to 800 who fought with the Montejos surviving to enjoy final victory.

The voice of defiant Maya leaders had not been entirely silenced, and much of the southern portion of the Yucatán Peninsula still lay beyond effective Spanish control. Montejo had sent an expedition back to Chetumal province in 1543 under the command of Gaspar Pacheco and his son and nephew, and that expedition succeeded with the usual difficulty in subduing the Maya of that region. The Pachecos were so brutal and destructive (by the judgment even of their peers) that the land along both sides of the present international boundary between Mexico and Belize, once populous and prosperous, was left sparsely populated and tribute poor, and the local Spanish settlement at Bacalar never became more than a remote and precarious colonial backwater. Meanwhile the focus of resistance to further conquest shifted to the Maya center at Tah Itza on a lake in the Péten, and to allied centers in western Belize (Tipu) and what is today southern Quintana Roo (Ixpimienta). Mayas who found Spanish exactions in the north too onerous, or who otherwise saw opportunity in life on the margins of colonial rule, fled south into those areas. Several efforts to court or force the Itza into submission failed. An uprising in 1638 destroyed most of the still-fragile Spanish colonial structure in the south.

Throughout the seventeenth century colonial authorities periodically sent expeditions to round up the fugitive and independent Maya, and Tah Itza was finally subdued in 1697. By that time, however, pirate attacks along the Caribbean coast and increasing British interest in the forests of the Caribbean rim made permanent Spanish presence in that region untenable, and the Spanish colony that the Montejos established remained largely based in the west, north, and central regions of the peninsula conquered in the third invasion led by Montejo's son. A Maya uprising in the mid–nineteenth century again clearly divided the Yucatán Peninsula along that old colonial line, with much of what is presently the state of Quintana Roo and part of Campeche resorting to independent or semi-independent Maya rule, until British forces could subdue the troublesome Maya of western Belize and a Mexican army at the turn of the twentieth century once again could pacify the Maya of Quintana Roo. While the Maya of the Yucatán Peninsula could not resist forever the force of Europeans wielding superior weapons, their prolonged, dogged, costly, and often religiously inspired resistance to conquest profoundly shaped the society in which they would live alongside the descendants of the bearded men come from the east; as a result, the Yucatán Peninsula to this day is home to one of the most vital indigenous cultures in the Western Hemisphere.

See also Caste War of Yucatán

Select Bibliography

Chamberlain, Robert S., *The Conquest and Colonization of Yucatán, 1517–1550*. Washington, D.C.: The Carnegie Institution, 1948.

Clendinnen, Inga, *Ambivalent Conquests: Maya and Spaniard in Yucatán, 1517–1570*. New York: Cambridge University Press, 1987.

Farriss, Nancy, *Maya Society Under Colonial Rule: The Collective Enterprise of Survival*. Princeton, New Jersey: Princeton University Press, 1984.

Jones, Grant, *Maya Resistance to Spanish Rule: Time and History on a Colonial Frontier*. Albuquerque: University of New Mexico Press, 1989.

—PAUL SULLIVAN

Conquest: Northern Mexico

One of the most surprising aspects of the great conquests of the sixteenth century is the enormous mobility of the conquistador armies. The conquest of northern New Spain effectively began in 1524, when Francisco Cortés Buenaventura explored the Pacific coast north of Colima, penetrating as far north as the so-called provinces of Xalisco and Tepique, the present-day states of Jalisco and Nayarit. In 1530, Nuño de Guzmán led a long, bloody campaign of conquest, passing through the provinces of Michoacán, Xalisco, and Tepique and arriving as far north as Culiacán, in the present-day state of Sinaloa. In 1531 a new province, Nueva Galicia, was established in the region with its capital in the town of Compostela.

Nonetheless, these conquests were precarious at best. In 1536 Nuño de Guzmán, who had long had a stormy relationship with Spanish authorities, was taken prisoner and sent into exile. Many of his soldiers fled Nueva Galicia, and the indigenous population plunged under the twin onslaught of disease and European avarice. The weak Spanish towns of Compostela, Chiametla, and other coastal settlements practically disappeared in a very short period of time, and much of the Spanish population retreated to the highlands of the present-day state of Jalisco. After several years of inactivity, however, the exploration of northern New Spain gained a new impetus with the expedition of Francisco Vásquez de Coronado, who pushed up the Pacific coast in an ultimately fruitless quest for the fabled Seven Cities. As the remnants of Coronado's troops retreated south, they met an army personally commanded by Viceroy Antonio de Mendoza, which had been dispatched north in 1541 to quash the indigenous revolt known as the Mixtón War. The combined forces of Coronado and Mendoza helped strengthen the Spanish population of Nueva Galicia, making Guadalajara the new capital of the province.

In 1546 a small group of explorers pushed past Guadalajara toward the mountain pass of the Sierra Madre Occidental, crossing it and discovering what later would be the royal mines of Zacatecas. One of the explorers, Diego de Ibarra, established an encampment on the site. Shortly after several of the most important *encomenderos* of Nueva Galicia joined him in the first Spanish exploitation of the region's rich silver deposits (*encomenderos* were trustees of *encomiendas*, or native settlements, the labor of which the *encomendero* was to receive in return for the responsibility of protecting the Indians, maintaining missionaries in the region, and defending the area militarily). The fame of Zacatecas quickly spread as far as Mexico City. Hoping that Zacatecas would become a new version of Potosí, the fabulously rich silver mine in Peru, many of the leading figures in New Spain—among them Martín Cortés, the marquis of the Valley of Oaxaca—arrived in the region, bringing labor and equipment to intensify mining activity. By 1554 approximately 300 Spaniards and 1,500 Indian peons had settled in Zacatecas, making it the most important population center in northern New Spain. In 1586 the mines received the title of *ciudad* (city), giving it added status and important legal privileges.

With the opening of Zacatecas, the exploration and conquest of the north accelerated. Until then, the exploration and settlement of the region had been concentrated almost exclusively in the Pacific coastal region, while the plateau north of Querétaro remained terra incognita. With the opening of a direct road from Mexico City to Zacatecas, however, new, larger groups of migrants headed north, forming new groups of conquistadors.

One of these groups, led by Francisco de Ibarra, nephew of the founder of Zacatecas, explored the

territories north of Zacatecas in search of the mythical kingdom of Copala. Although the group never
found Copala, it did find silver deposits and sites for
agricultural haciendas that later would be settled.
During his second campaign, begun in 1562, Francisco de Ibarra received from Viceroy Luis de Velasco
the title of governor and captain general of all the
lands he discovered north of Zacatecas. That same
year he created a new province, Nueva Vizcaya,
establishing its capital in the town of Durango.
Despite its status as capital of a new province, the
Spanish population of Durango grew slowly. Between 1563 and 1564 Francisco de Ibarra resumed
his exploration of northern New Spain, eventually
settling with many of his people in the region around
Chiametla (near the present-day city of Mazatlán,
Sinaloa). With the reconquest of the region a large
part of the northern Pacific coast, particularly the
region that today forms the states of Sinaloa and
Sonora, ended up in the territory of Nueva Vizcaya,
with only a small enclave around Culiacán remaining under the jurisdiction of Nueva Galicia. For a
brief period Chiametla, with its rich silver deposits
and abundant supply of Indian labor, had the largest
Spanish population and was the greatest producer
of silver in all of northern New Spain outside of
Zacatecas. In 1563 the mining settlement of Indé was
established in the north of the present-day state of
Durango, and in 1567 Santa Bárbara was established
in the southern part of present-day Chihuahua.
Until the end of the sixteenth century Santa Bárbara
was the northernmost Spanish settlement in the
Americas.

Much as had happened in the case of Nueva
Vizcaya, other regions of northern New Spain were
settled by expeditions that departed from Zacatecas
as well as Nueva Vizcaya itself, generally in search of
silver deposits. Among the most important expeditions were those led by Alberto del Canto in the
1570s, which discovered mines in what later would
be Monclova, as well as the Valleys of Extremadura
(near what later would be the city of Monterrey) and
Saltillo. In 1579 Luis de Carvajal received royal
authorization to settle the regions explored by del
Canto, extending his domain as far as the region of
Pánuco. In 1581 the new governor finally established
himself in the Valley of Extremadura. In 1587,
however, he was denounced by the Inquisition as a
crypto-Jew and arrested, spurring an almost total
abandonment of the region by Spanish settlers.
Many of these settlers fell back to the recently
founded town of Saltillo, which remained under the
jurisdiction of Nueva Vizcaya. The settlement of
Saltillo received an additional boost when a group of

Tlaxcalteca colonists settled nearby in 1591, founding the town of San Esteban de la Nueva Tlaxcala.
In 1596 the new province of Nuevo León was
founded in the region originally settled by del Canto,
and a new capital was established in Monterrey.

The Spanish settlements north of Zacatecas during
the last third of the sixteenth century suffered for a
lack of one basic resource—people. Given the sparse
settlement of the region, the new towns in northern
New Spain depended on the arrival of new immigrants and only to a far lesser degree internal growth.
As the period of great conquests came to an end,
what had been a series of rapid territorial advances
became a long and sporadic process of colonization.
An important case in point is the conquest and foundation of New Mexico. Given the title of *adelantado*
in 1598, Juan de Oñate organized a large expedition
to conquer the region beyond the Rio Grande.
Toward the end of 1598 the army of Oñate had
managed to install itself in San Juan de los Cab-
alleros, in the heart of the territory of the Pueblo
Indians. After several years of consolidating their
presence, the colonists founded the town of Santa Fé,
which served as the capital of the new province.

During the following decades New Mexico
became an authentic Spanish enclave, with minimal
contact with the major population centers of New
Spain. Although in 1609 the viceregal authorities
instituted triennial caravans of wagons to bring
goods to and from New Mexico, the Spaniards of the
new province frequently could go six or seven years
without receiving news from the rest of New Spain.
Nonetheless, other settlements such as Santa Bárbara, Saltillo, and Nuevo León were even more isolated. In 1601 the bishop of Culiacán remarked that
the Spanish settlers in the region could be compared
with the first children of Adam, "because they do
not think or understand that there are other people
in the world."

From the 1580s through the eighteenth century,
the occupation of northern New Spain became a
slow process of colonization. Nonetheless, this did
not prevent the newly settled regions from being
incorporated into the Spanish Empire. A key zone of
colonization was Santa Bárbara. From 1580 until
the end of the 1620s the Spanish population of the
region took refuge in agricultural haciendas, practically abandoning its mining activities. During this
period the indigenous population of the region was
pacified and eventually settled in *reducciones*
(roughly, reservations or ghettos) administered by
Jesuits and Franciscans. By 1620 Santa Bárbara had
become one of the principal granaries of the north.
By 1631 the workforce had expanded enough to

begin exploitation of the mines of El Parral. Parral was the first lasting mine established in the north since Zacatecas. By 1635 approximately 500 Spaniards had settled in the region; by the subsequent decade it had become the capital and most important population center of Nueva Vizcaya, with approximately 10,000 inhabitants.

Under the influence of Parral, a new extension of the main north-south road in New Spain, the Camino Real de Tierra Adentro, was constructed linking Zacatecas and Parral via the Bolsón de Mapimí. Able to handle carts and mule trains, the Camino Real intensified travel and commercial links between the north and central New Spain. However, it did not lead directly to the opening of new territories. Rather, zones already settled by Spaniards saw their populations grow. The Pacific coastal region, including the provinces of Sinaloa and Sonora, was slowly settled until the first decades of the seventeenth century. Aside from tenuous Spanish settlements in Sonora, Culiacán, Chiametla, and the Fuerte River, the only colonial presence in area was the Jesuit mission to the Yaqui and Mayo Indians.

Between the end of the 1630s and the beginning of the 1640s, however, several important transformations took place. In 1636 a captain by the name of Pedro de Perea solicited a charter from the Spanish Crown to settle Spaniards in Sonora, until then terra incognita called Nueva Andalucía. In 1640 the charter was granted, but Perea died soon after. Nonetheless, the charter inspired other colonists to settle the region, establishing such mining and agricultural settlements as San Pedro de los Reyes, San Juan Bautista, Nuestra Señora del Rosario de Nacozari, and shortly after San Ignacio de Ostimuri, which later would be the namesake for the entire Yaqui River basin. This second wave of colonization was linked indirectly to the new prosperity of Parral. Sinaloa and Sonora became the principal source of forced Indian labor in the mines of Parral. Moreover, the only road linking Sonora with the rest of New Spain was a route following the Papagochic River as far as Parral. In 1651 a second road to Sonora from Parral was constructed, which passed through the settlements of Casas Grandes and Janos. Nonetheless, during the rainy season the roads linking the Pacific slope to Parral were virtually impassable, increasing the isolation of the region. By the end of seventeenth century, however, Spanish colonization had pushed as far north as Fronteras, in the north of the present-day state of Sonora, opening the road for the Spanish expansion into the Pimería Alta and Alta Sonora, the present-day state of Arizona.

Other regions that had been terra incognita to Spaniards were settled in the seventeenth century as well. An important landmark in this process of colonization was the establishment of missions, reductions, and agricultural settlements from 1650 to 1680 north of the Río Conchos in the present-day state of Chihuahua. Until the middle of the seventeenth century the Río Conchos had marked the limit of Spanish colonization, increasing the isolation of New Mexico. The growth of the agriculture in the valley of San Bartolomé near Parral, however, sparked new waves of migration that could be channeled toward the pacification and colonization of the Tarahumara region around the Papagochic River; the mines of Cusihuiriachi later were established in the region. A similar series of events occurred around the present-day city of Chihuahua. Thanks to the solid agricultural colonization of the region in the late seventeenth century, by the beginning of the eighteenth century several important grain haciendas had been established. In 1707 the Santa Eulalia mine was established, and in 1709 San Francisco de Cuellar. The Chihuahua region soon displaced Parral as the most important silver-producing region in Nueva Vizcaya. In 1718 on the site of the present-day city of Chihuahua, the town of San Felipe el Real de Chihuahua was established (although local historiography identifies San Felipe el Real with San Francisco de Cuéllar, in reality they are separate towns). One of the most important effects of the settlement of Chihuahua was the establishment of regular trade and travel with New Mexico, breaking much of the isolation of the region.

Chihuahua was the last great town founded in northern New Spain. According to eighteenth-century sources, by 1725 the Chihuahua region had 25,000 inhabitants, making it one of the most important populations of New Spain. There were a few other processes of colonization during the eighteenth century, much of which emerged out of processes of migration to the northern frontier in the seventeenth century. Among these was the province of Texas, settled from the zone of Coahuila. Aware of French efforts to colonize the region, viceregal authorities sent a series of colonizing expeditions to Texas in the 1690s. Nonetheless, these initiatives only bore fruit in the following century. The most notable settlement in Texas was San Antonio de Béjar, founded in 1715. San Antonio later was reinforced by the opening of missions such as Nuestra Señora de Pilar and Nuestra Señora de Loreto. Nonetheless, Spanish settlement in Texas always was tenuous at best.

A similar process occurred in Alta California in the mid–eighteenth century, although the numbers involved were greater. Spurred by the *visitador* José de Gálvez, who had made a tour of inspection in northern New Spain, several advance posts were established in Alta California in 1769, including the ports of San Diego and San Francisco. In the following decades San Diego, San Francisco, and other enclaves were settled largely by people from Sonora, although we cannot speak of well constituted society in Alta California until the nineteenth century. Alta California was the last territory settled from New Spain. Nonetheless, the wave of settlements in the seventeenth century and the last few settlements in the eighteenth century only gave rise to weak local societies.

See also Missions

Select Bibliography

Alvarez, Salvador, "Agricultural Colonization and Mining Colonization: The Area of Chihuahua during the First Half of the Eighteenth Century." In *In Quest of Mineral Wealth: Aboriginal and Colonial Mining and Metallurgy in Spanish America,* edited by Alan Kraig and Robert C. West. Baton Rouge: Department of Geography and Anthropology, Louisiana State University, 1994.

Gerhard, Peter, *The North Frontier of New Spain.* Norman and London: University of Oklahoma Press, 1993.

Mecham, John L., *Francisco de Ibarra and Nueva Vizcaya.* New York: Greenwood, 1968.

Spicer, Edward H., *The Cycles of Conquest.* Tucson: University of Arizona Press, 1962.

—SALVADOR ALVAREZ

Conquest: Demographic Impact

How many people lived in Mesoamerica when Europeans first invaded? How large was the ensuing demographic disaster, and what were its principal causes? What were the effects of Spanish Conquest and colonization on Mesoamericans, on the quality of life, family, and settlement patterns? What was the demographic legacy of European colonialism? In 1810, was Mexican demography more akin to that of 1520 or 1990? Answers to these questions are important for understanding the transformation of economy, society, and culture of colonial and postcolonial Mexico. Explanations remain contentious, notwithstanding more than four centuries of research, writing, and debate. Now there are signs that consensus is emerging on some of these issues, in turn stimulating new insights and scholarly dialogue.

There is consensus that the sixteenth century was a demographic disaster for Mesoamericans. Figure 1 displays 10 authoritative estimates of population decline for the native population of "Mexico" (and diverse parts thereof) during the first century of Spanish Conquest and colonization. Although the range is wide, from less than 25 to more than 90 percent, the graph reveals three broad schools or interpretations: catastrophists, moderates, and minimalists. Catastrophists place the scale of demographic disaster at 90 percent or more and postulate large populations at contact. Moderates project decreases of "only" 50 to 85 percent—disasters nonetheless. They favor smaller populations at contact but agree with catastrophists on population totals at their nadir (1600–40). Minimalists sees the scale of the disaster as much smaller, on the order of 25 percent. The principal proponent of this position, Angel Rosenblat, is the catastrophists' most determined critic. Rosenblat sees a decline from 4.5 to 3.4 million inhabitants (24 percent), with stabilization beginning within one-half century of initial contact with Europeans. It seems to the present author that the population of central Mexico at contact must have been no less than the minimalist estimate of 4 to 5 million and was likely double and possibly even triple that figure.

The "war over numbers" continues because population estimates for any large region of the Mexican subcontinent prior to 1895, when the first national census was taken, are unavoidably crude. For the sixteenth century, the data are dreadfully crude: often derived from gross tax allotments, not actual receipts, or numbers of taxpayers, not total population. Methods for working these data are more numerical than demographic, and at best the results point to orders of magnitude. The fact remains that most places existent in 1519 were never counted. Yet today there survives a surprisingly large corpus of population-like numbers for an exceedingly diverse array of administrative units: such as hamlets, barrios, subject boroughs, towns, district capitals (*cabeceras*), and provinces. Many of these places ceased to exist within decades of first contact, some changed names, and not a few were relocated through the Spanish policy of *congregación*. Natives preferred a dispersed pattern of settlement, to be near a cornfield (*milpa*), following the rules of ecology rather than political geography. After Conquest, successive *congregaciónes* attempted to reduce the natives to settlements conducive to Spanish political, economic, and religious control. By 1650 wherever these efforts were successful, *milpa* dwellers, formerly clustered around cornfields, were forced into Spanish-style

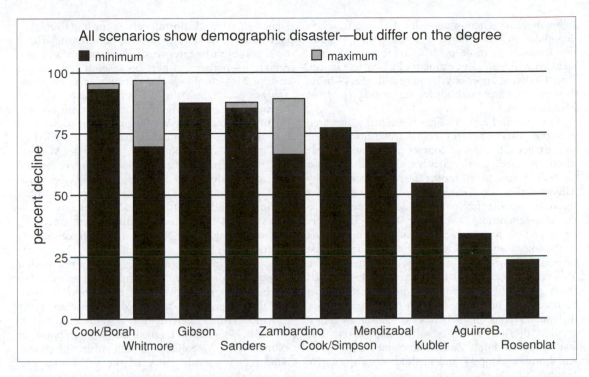

Figure 1
Percentage of depopulation in Mexico, 1519–95

hamlets. Then, when authorities relaxed their grip, many natives drifted back to prior settlements. (Nevertheless, rural settlements in twentieth-century Mexico, with housing clustered around a central plaza, reflect colonial rather than pre-Hispanic origins.) Sporadic censuses—and there are a few remarkably detailed enumerations from the sixteenth century that still survive—or tax surveys of small areas capture only a fraction of this movement and are scarcely sufficient for estimating population totals for large areas. Baptism and burial registers, which might fill the gap, do not become available in large numbers until the late seventeenth century. The paucity of evidence has spawned much research and controversy.

The catastrophist position is best represented by Sherburne F. Cook and Woodrow Borah, the most tenacious researchers and prolific writers in the field of Mexican population history. Their point estimate of 25.2 million inhabitants for 1519 has become a talisman for many, while their more prudent range estimate of 18 to 30 million goes largely ignored. This range takes into account just two of the many sources of variation: a spectrum of average family sizes—3.6 to 5.0—and alternative frequencies of tribute collection—4 to 4.5 times per year. Cook and Borah scoured libraries and archives in Mexico and Spain to develop the largest database of population figures extant for "central Mexico," a region of one-half million square kilometers (0.2 million square miles) bounded in the north and west by a line connecting Tampico and Tepic and in the south and east by the Isthmus of Tehuantepec. Relentlessly quantitative, Cook and Borah standardized and converted taxes—from such diverse units as turkeys, blankets, cotton, and corn—first into tax-payers *(tributarios, casados)*, then into total population—with whopping adjustments for tax-exempt classes, tax-free towns, omissions, errors, and lost records. They concluded that their research documented a demographic catastrophe, "one of the worst in the history of humanity." Their point estimates show the native population decreasing from 25.2 million in 1519 to 7.6 million by 1545, 2.5 million in 1570, and bottoming out at 1.2 million in 1620. Their reconstruction is widely accepted; indeed, it has become a paradigm to explain the collapse of populations elsewhere in the Americas and the Pacific islands following first encounters with Europeans. Their depopulation ratios of 10–25:1 (suggesting population losses of 90 to 96 percent) are in general agreement with independent estimates by Charles Gibson, Peter Gerhard, Thomas Whitmore and others—using different data and methods for varying subregions of Mesoamerica.

As Cook and Borah's figures gradually appeared over the years, often revising sharply upward their own earlier estimates of contact population, a great dispute ensued, particularly with specialists closest to field. Prior, more moderate reconstructions by Miguel Othón de Mendizábal and George Kubler received support from independent analyses by a younger generation of scholars. William T. Sanders developed a formidable challenge to maximalist methodology and conclusions. His systematic sample of more than 3,600 archaeological sites in the Valley of Mexico point to contact populations half those proposed by Cook and Borah, yet it must be noted that his reconstruction (projected to 1595 in Figure 1) sustains the thesis of enormous demographic disaster for the native population. The statistician Rudolph Zambardino questioned Cook and Borah's numbers and methods on quantitative grounds, urging researchers to apply ranges for each conversion factor rather than relying on point estimates alone. Zambardino favors figures of 5 to 10 million at the beginning of the sixteenth century and 1 million at the end, a reduction of 80 to 90 percent. Case studies of specific villages, such as Tomás Calvo's population history of Acatzingo (1973), point to contact populations as little as one-fifth Cook and Borah's estimates.

Gonzalo Aguirre-Beltrán, seemingly a champion of the minimalist camp because he upholds Rosenblat's figures for 1519 and 1570, is instead a moderate in my view. Although the Mexican historian's figures imply "only" a 33 percent decline by 1595, in fact, his series places the nadir at 1645 with scarcely 1.3 million natives and a total decrease of 70 percent, well within the moderate camp's 50 to 85 percent decline.

A third position is staked out by Angel Rosenblat. He proclaims himself a "moderate," but more accurately may be described a minimalist. He defends his reconstruction as follows: "If in fact I did derive moderate and even low figures for the 1492 population, it was not because I had intended to do so. The data I had about the Conquest allowed no other choice, unless one were to assume vast and horrible killing, which requires a macabre imagination and which I found unacceptable given the known extermination techniques of the sixteenth century" (in

Denevan, 1976). Unfortunately, according to Rosenblat himself, in more than three decades of writing on this subject he rarely revised a figure or an interpretation—perhaps in part because, at least in the case of Mexico, no scholar critically scrutinized his analysis of sources. After a comprehensive review of Mexican population figures from historians writing in any of five European languages, he developed his own series using numbers for 1570 compiled by the royal cosmographer Juan López de Velasco. Rosenblat settled on 4.5 million as a "reasonable probability" for the native population of Mexico at contact, declining to 3.5 million by 1570 and to 3.4 million around 1650 (then, slowly rising to 3.7 million by 1825). Unfortunately, the pattern traced by Rosenblat's numbers for the sixteenth century is contradicted by his source narrative. López de Velasco concludes his own assessment of population change in Mexico with the following words: "in the beginning the natives were many more in number than there were afterward, because in many provinces, where there used to be a great multitude of them, they have reached almost the point of extinction." Rosenblat, writing after historians almost unanimously espoused the thesis that epidemic disease was the principal cause for the decline of native populations, insisted on directing his attack against the Black Legend, that the "extermination" of Indians was principally the result of "vast and horrible killing."

The catastrophists' critics' greatest contribution is their detailed assessment of quantitative sources and methods, which emphasizes the difficulties—even the impossibility—of obtaining satisfactory estimates from tax records alone. The catastrophist position is further weakened by a studied refusal to reply to challenges posed by their critics.

The thesis of demographic disaster does not rest solely on numbers. The many extant narratives provide a sound foundation for a qualitative view of the scale and causes of the calamity. That the coastal and tropical regions suffered the greatest losses is widely accepted, as is the thesis that the highlands had fewer fatalities. Colony-wide losses over the course of the sixteenth century reached at least 50 percent, and perhaps as much as 90 percent over wide areas. War mortality, limited primarily to Tenochtitlan (Mexico City), Cholula, the Mixtón in the 1540s, and a few other sites, was of decidedly secondary importance, unlike in Peru and elsewhere in the Americas where prolonged fighting was required to subdue the natives. In Mexico overwork, disruption of the native economy, ecological distress, and forced relocation were much more significant than war in causing demographic disaster, but disease remains the principal explanation for most historians, just as it was four centuries ago for the first chroniclers.

There is consensus that smallpox struck central Mexico in 1520, the first of a series of devastating, multiyear epidemics that erupted in the sixteenth century. As Fernando (Hernán) Cortés prepared to retake Mexico City, smallpox killed the Mexica (Aztec) emperor Cuitlahuatzin, many caciques (chiefs) and warriors, and many women and children. The epidemic was particularly severe because, unlike in Europe, where smallpox was a childhood disease, in Mexico it found "virgin soil," striking in one blow both adults and children. With almost everyone ill at once, there was no one to provide food, water, or care so that many who fell ill died, not of smallpox, but of hunger, dehydration, or despair. The Franciscan Toribio de Benavente (Motolinía) in his *Memoriales* recounts the lethal effects of this horror: "because they all fell ill at a stroke, [the Indians] could not nurse one another, nor was there anyone to make bread [tortillas], and in many parts it happened that all the residents of a house died and in others almost no one was left."

Measles hit for the first time in 1531. When smallpox returned in 1532 and 1538, mortality was reduced because many adults, now immune from having survived an earlier attack, were available to provide care to those who fell ill. A second great multiyear epidemic struck in 1545 (recorded as *cocoliztli,* which might mean typhus, or hemorrhagic fever—the identification of sixteenth-century epidemics is almost as contentious as the dispute over the size of native populations at contact), and a third in 1576 (*matlazahuatl,* perhaps typhus carried by human lice). Although a lively debate continues over which was most severe, it is clear that the effects of each were catastrophic. The founder of New World ethnohistory, Bernardino de Sahagún, writing while the third great epidemic of the century was underway, recalled that because of the epidemic of 1545 "when the entire population wasted away; large pueblos were left depopulated, which afterward were never resettled. Thirty years later the pestilence that now reigns appeared, and many pueblos were depopulated, and if this business continues, and if it lasts for three or four months, as it now is, no one will remain."

Some catastrophists project these epidemics willynilly to encompass the length and breadth of the Americas, but the evidence for such pandemics is thin. For example, the smallpox epidemic of 1520 is alleged to have raged northward to the Great Plains, eastward to the Atlantic seaboard, and south through Central America down the Andes to Peru and beyond. Daniel Reff judiciously reviewed much of the evidence for northern Mexico and concluded that there are few signs of it sweeping beyond the Tarascan-speaking peoples of north-central New Spain.

Lesser crises of mumps, influenza, and others vaguely described as "plague" or "sickness" also occurred, often in tandem with famine. Peter Gerhard lists 14 outbreaks in New Spain for the sixteenth century, 11 for the seventeenth, and 9 for the eighteenth. Lourdes Marquez Morfín lengthens the list, particularly for later centuries, and adds primary source citations. She logs 3 smallpox epidemics in the seventeenth century and 6 in the eighteenth (1711, 1734, 1748, 1761–62, 1779–80, and 1797). If we leave aside the virgin soil epidemic of 1520–21, smallpox seems to have increased in frequency and intensity until the introduction of vaccination in 1804.

Some historians explain demographic recovery of the native population by means of natural selection and Darwinian evolutionism, but there is little evidence to support this hypothesis and much science that negates it. Smallpox mortality was much too low to play a role in human evolution, either in the Americas or in Europe (or in the Middle East, Asia, or Africa). For example, in London, after 500 years or more of experience with the virus, more than 2,000 smallpox deaths were recorded annually from 1710 to 1800, amounting to 7 percent and more of total deaths. Indeed, the horrors of the disease drove Europeans to extraordinary efforts, such as quarantine, inoculation, and ultimately vaccination, to staunch its spread. Mexicans were somewhat fortunate because in the Americas the disease remained epidemic, instead of endemic as in London, recurring at intervals of 15 to 20 years. When smallpox did strike, 1 in 10 might die from it, as happened with the epidemic of 1779 to 1780, which caused 12,345 deaths in Mexico City. What is striking about this epidemic is that four times that number fell ill, received public charity, and recovered. With the succeeding outbreak in 1797, smallpox mortality was halved thanks to timely, systematic, block-by-block assistance for more than 75,000 of Mexico City's residents. Meanwhile in Guanajuato, authorities pursued more drastic measures, hurriedly inoculating some four-fifths of the children in the district with pus from dangerous, live virus; only 1 percent of these children died, in contrast to the 20 percent of the 3,000 who went untreated.

Matlazahuatl (typhus?), another of the big killers of the sixteenth century (in this case probably of pre-Hispanic origin), did not recur with the same intensity for more than one and one-half centuries, until 1736–39, when it decimated much of Mexico. In the archbishopric of Puebla, for example, almost one-third of the inhabitants died from the disease. A recurrence in 1761–62 was preceded by an outbreak of smallpox, and although less severe it still ranked as one of the great terrors of the eighteenth century. Five decades later, in June 1813, while the War for Independence raged in central Mexico, the last great typhus epidemic erupted, killing one-tenth of the population of Mexico City within two months. By 1815, the epidemic had reached Nueva Vizcaya (Parral) in the north and Chiapas (Teopisca) in the south.

Recovery of the native population began, nonetheless, by the middle of the seventeenth century according to most accounts. Rosenblat places the nadir at 3.4 million Indians around 1650, but, as noted above, Aguirre-Beltrán reckons the figure at only 1.3 million (plus 400,000 non-Indians; Cook and Borah favor a total of 1.4). It is surprising that Rosenblat's figures are more than double those of Aguirre-Beltrán, even though both cite the same source, Juan Diez de la Calle.

Aguirre-Beltrán crafted the only comprehensive series of figures for socioracial categories and regions for the entire colonial period, and it is his estimates that are reproduced in Figure 2. His numbers always add up, but they do not always make sense. It seems likely, for example, that the scale of population disaster was greater before 1570 than after, contrary to what his series (following Rosenblat) implies. Likewise, the notion that the growth of the mixed groups was six times greater before 1650 than after seems unfounded. The apparent ever-accelerating growth of population for all socio-racial groups in the eighteenth century may be owing more to improvements in census taking (and adjustments) than to demography. The Villaseñor "census" of 1742 failed to cover the entire colony and reported numbers of families—often crudely eye-balled—rather than inhabitants. For example, the town of Guadalajara is listed with "eight to nine thousand families of Spaniards, mestizos and mulatos, not counting Indians." More common is the degree of inexactitude expressed for the town of Actopan, which reports 50 Spanish families (almost all of whom would be in Aguirre-Beltrán's terms "euro-mestizos"), 2,750 Indian families, and 20 of other *castas* ("indomestizos," "afromestizos," and perhaps an African or two).

The best census of the colonial era was that ordered by the Viceroy Conde de Revillagigedo (1789–93), the first to use a standard format for listing individuals by name, age, sex, race, and marital status. Nevertheless, this effort left large expanses of New Spain wholly unenumerated. Alexander von Humboldt complemented the census with tribute data to produce a comprehensive set of figures, adjusted for growth to 1803. A decade later Francisco Navarro y Noriega increased the Revillagigedo numbers by 20 percent for underenumeration (Humboldt favored 10 percent), obtained figures for districts that had not reported earlier, and estimated growth to 1810 at 25 percent (1.5 percent per year for 17 years using arithmetic rather than geometric cumulation). For almost two centuries now, Navarro y Noriega's results remain the most widely cited, yet they surely exaggerate the true population in 1810 by 10 to 20 percent. This is evident in Figure 2 by the identical steeply sloped curves from 1793 for all groups. The graph shows that the totals for each group in 1810 were computed mechanically. Unfortunately, the royal accountant estimated demographic growth from parish records, by subtracting burials from baptisms and without recognizing that in Mexico baptisms were always more faithfully recorded than burials (this was true until civil registration undermined the parish system toward the end of the nineteenth century). The exercise convinced Mexico's first statistician that annual growth was 1.5 percent per year—probably double the actual value. Thus, 5 to 5.5 million seems a more likely figure for total population in 1810 than Navarro y Noriega's 6,128,238. Or, if this number is accepted, then figures for both earlier and later years would have to be similarly corrected for errors and omissions—a forbidding task. In any case, population growth in the closing decades of Spanish rule was much less than Navarro y Noriega, Humboldt, or many others surmised. In part owing to migration, the population of Michoacán increased fivefold over the century, but there was a noticeable slowing of growth in the final decades, owing to pestilence and famine. Precisely when increase was accelerating elsewhere in America and western Europe, successive calamities from 1736 to 1813 doomed most regions of Bourbon Mexico to slow demographic growth.

There is consensus that demographic recovery meant transformation as well as growth. Infusions of European and African stocks were slight (and predominantly male), as Figure 2 shows. If the Aguirre-Beltrán series is sound, foreign stocks peaked in 1646 with 35,000 Africans (2 percent of total population), mostly slaves, and 10,000 Europeans, mainly Spanish speakers. The most dramatic change was the growth of mestizos, or people of mixed stock, which,

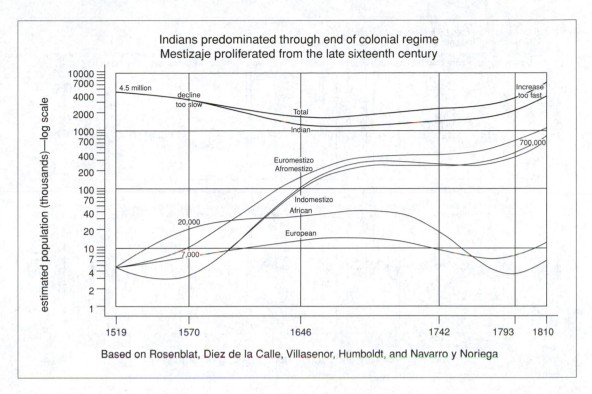

Figure 2
Aguirre-Beltrán's Ethno-races of New Spain

according to Aguirre-Beltrán, constituted almost 25 percent of the population as early as 1646, rising to 40 percent in 1810. Historians agree that in colonial Mexico racial categories were fluid (documents usually speak of *calidad* instead of *raza*—character or reputation, instead of race), and that passing was common. Thus, the rapid growth of the mixed population was mainly a matter of economics and sociology, but demography was also important. Among Europeans and Africans the shortage of females ensured much interbreeding, if not intermarriage. Then too, racial identity had its advantages, for undermining as well as upholding the social order. The onerous head tax levied on Indians encouraged some to abandon their villages (particularly where land was scarce or made scarce by land-grabbing Spanish-speakers) for nearby haciendas or towns and adapt to a non-Indian *calidad*. In Michoacán the native population tripled over the eighteenth century, but the increase in the population as a whole was fivefold (Morin, 1979).

For those of African roots (perhaps 200,000 slaves were imported into Mexico over three cen-

turies), slavery gradually withered away. By the beginning of the eighteenth century, free labor was already too abundant—that is, too cheap—for slavery to compete. Slaves helped destroy slavery, by fleeing, extracting concessions, demanding freedom, taking advantage of civil and church law, and forming communities of free people.

Demographic recovery may be estimated from trends of baptismal series, once parish registers achieve a degree of consistent coverage. Cecilia Rabell's regression analysis of baptism trends for nine parishes shows rapid growth in the north at least from the late seventeenth century (as high as 1.5 percent per year in León and 1 percent in San Luis de la Paz, Valladolid, Charcas, and Marfil), but decelerating growth in the center. The year 1693 is the point of inflection in several center parishes, with negative rates emerging after 1737 or 1763 in others (Rabell, 1990).

Burial series for 10 parishes from Chihuahua to Chiapas illustrate the regional and racial instability of year-to-year population change in eighteenth-century Mexico (Figure 3). Burial registers offer a

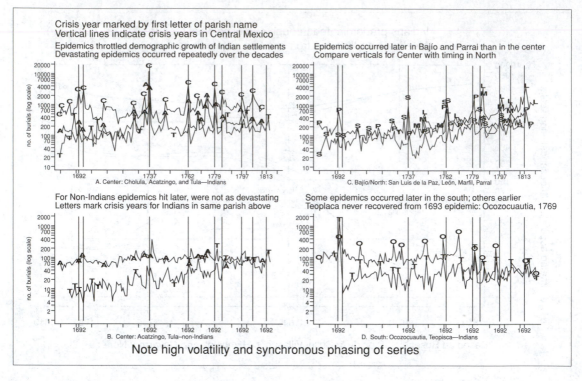

Figure 3
Region and Race in a Long Century of Epidemics

somber view of the "long" eighteenth century (1690–1820), with deaths in crisis years exceeding the norm by four- to fourteenfold, such as in 1692, 1737, 1762, 1779, 1797, and 1813. These graphs illustrate the classic workings of *ancien régime* demography, in which epidemics undercut the enormous growth potential of high fertility populations. Cholula, the site of one of the first, large-scale published studies in modern Mexican historical demography, is a well-known example. In normal years burials in the Cholula region numbered 500 to 1,000, but in 1737 they skyrocketed to 16,926. The disaster roared through the heartland of New Spain, but only faint echoes were heard in the northern parish of San José de Parral or in the southern community of Teopisca (in 1739), and none at all in neighboring Ocozocuautla. The south had its crises as well. In 1693, before the epidemic of that year struck, the Chiapan parish of Teopisca numbered some 2,000 souls. Then, in the month of May, burials surged fourteenfold to 265. For the year 1,510 burials were recorded in the parish, and the priest reported that scarcely 350 people survived the devastation. A

century later Teopisca still numbered much less than 1,000. Nearby Ocozocuautla escaped much of the destruction of 1693 with only a fourfold increase in burials, but in 1769–70 almost half the parish died, and recovery remained elusive one-half century later. These stories challenge the thesis that widespread recovery of the native population occurred around the middle of the seventeenth century.

Demography is a science of rates—of numerators (demographic events) and denominators (population at risk of experiencing an event). Because we lack the makings of good rates, primarily denominators, much of the demographic history of colonial Mexico remains unknown and unknowable. Only where registration is relatively accurate, and reliable population censuses available, can series of baptisms and burials be converted into birth and death rates. Everywhere in colonial Mexico many deaths went unrecorded. High fees encouraged surreptitious burials, as did the widespread belief that final rites were not required for *angelitos*, innocent infants and children unsullied by sin. In high-pressure demographic systems babies and the young often account for 50 percent or more of deaths, but not according to colonial Mexican parish registers, which yield implausibly low infant and child mortality rates.

Baptisms were more faithfully performed, but even then, not necessarily recorded. Catholic priests in the Americas were often responsible for 10 times as many souls as in Europe, and here their parishioners procreated and died with what must have seemed demonic haste, in much higher proportions than in western Europe. Here, to expedite record keeping, priests often used scraps of paper to jot the bare details of baptisms, burials, and other sacraments for subsequent transcription to the corresponding books, as time permitted, perhaps weeks, months or even years later—if at all.

Consequently, the "royal road to historical demography," as Romero Rabell calls the French "family reconstitution" method, proved to be a dead end in Mexico. The five conditions required for a pleasant journey on the royal road—a small parish, stable family names, vital events faithfully recorded for a century or longer, low illegitimacy, and little migration—do not seem to characterize even one of the more than 1,000 parishes of colonial Mexico. Only two Mexican family reconstitution studies have been published since the method was invented in the mid–twentieth century (Calvo, 1984; Klein, 1993). Both offer intriguing insights into colonial demography, but neither is entirely faithful to the method. Lacunae in the records make for truncated studies and, in the case of Tomás Calvo's genealogies from Guadalajara, worrisome error rates. Herbert Klein's history of Amatenango, Chiapas (1785–1816), reveals a high-pressure demographic system persisting through the waning years of colonial rule—in my opinion closely akin to pre-Hispanic patterns, although the author suggests that this may have been a recovery strategy adopted to regain the demographic losses accompanying Spanish Conquest and colonization. In Amatenango during the last decades of colonial rule, Tzeltal women married at very young ages, averaging 16.1 years at first union (in 1990, the figure for non–Spanish speaking women in Chiapas was 19.7 years), and scarcely any remained unmarried to age 20. Frequent widowhood was quickly resolved by rapid remarriage for women as well as men. Fertility was high. Birth intervals averaged 36 months, and the total fertility rate was 8.5 children. Klein concludes that early marriage and high fertility were demographic responses to an environment rich in resources, which permitted unrestricted expansion, but he may have uncovered, instead, the tenacious survival of time-tested pre-Hispanic patterns.

The family reconstitution method, a rigorous procedure for constructing and analyzing demographically valid family genealogies, provides valuable clues about legitimate fertility, but because of technical limitations does not measure extramarital fertility. Where nonmarital fertility is common but variable, as in Mexico, other methods are required.

The handful of parishes in central Mexico for which crude birth rates can be computed average 52 baptisms (births) per thousand population (Rabell, 1990), remarkably close to Cook and Borah's figure of 51 for several dozen Oaxacan parishes from the same period. Child-to-woman ratios also point to high fertility, averaging 750 children under five years of age per thousand women aged 15 to 44 (Cook and Borah, 1974; data are for 91 Oaxacan parishes in 1777), compared with 500 to 600 children per thousand women in late-eighteenth-century England. The total fertility rate in Tacuba (1623–1630) was eight children, just as it was 150 years later in San Luis de la Paz (my estimates from the age distribution of deaths for Tacuba and from Rabell, 1990). Reliable fertility data are too sparse to construct time series or compare social or racial groups. Range of error is likely to exceed any credibly measured differences. "Natural" fertility, without the slightest hint of birth control, characterizes all reliably measured populations in colonial Mexico. Calvo argues that the 256 Guadalajaran families that he "reconstituted" for the years 1666 to 1730 practiced birth control, but the analysis apparently does not take into account children lost to the church registry.

While natural fertility was the rule in colonial Mexico, actual fertility did not reach its biological limits. Marriage made the difference. "Marriage-ways," access to stable unions (including those lacking sanction by church or state), were socially constructed and differed over time and by social or racial group. Stable coupling was the key to regulating fertility and reproduction in colonial society.

For rural Indians three features of the *feria nupcial* (nuptial fair or marriage market) stand out from the small number of studies completed to date. Marriage occurred at an early age, was nearly universal, and accounted for 85 to 90 percent or more of births to Indian parents. The most extreme may be two rural communities in Morelos—Huitzillan and Quauhchichinollan—in the 1530s, where the average age for initiating cohabitation for females was 12.7 years, with all in unions by age 25. Illegitimacy was well below 5 percent (McCaa, 1996). Near Puebla in the village of Acatzingo, average marriage age for women rose from 14 to 15 years in the seventeenth century, to 17 or 18 years by the end of the eighteenth, with all females married by age 25 (Calvo, 1973). The age gap between spouses also narrowed over time from 5 to 6 years in the sixteenth century to only 2 or 3 years in the eighteenth. In Oaxaca, a slow, sustained rise in marriage age has been documented for the last century of Spanish rule (Cook and Borah, 1974).

Early marriage left little time for pre- or extranuptial couplings. In rural areas, illegitimate children, including *"hijos naturales," "hijos de la iglesia,"* or *"hijos de padres noconocidos,"* amounted typically to 10 percent or less of Indian baptisms, with a surprising tendency to decline as marriage age rose toward the end of the colonial period. These patterns did not hold in the city, but only 5 to 10 percent of Indians resided in urban settlements. In the handful of colonial towns—in 1750 there were only 10 with 10,000 or more inhabitants—urban Indians married much later than in the countryside, perhaps, in part owing to the delay occasioned by migration itself. Illegitimacy was also more common in the city, particularly in the demographic black-hole that was Mexico City, where migration more than compensated for the losses owing to appalling mortality (Arrom, 1985).

For European-born Spaniards *(peninsulares),* whose nuptial proclivities stood at the opposite extreme from rural Indians, migration certainly delayed marriage. Male *peninsulares* (there were few female immigrants) married very late, often in their thirties or forties. Many never married at all. They probably sired more than their share of illegitimate children, although the demographic evidence for this is scarce because baptism books usually omit the names of unmarried parents.

Españoles, Mexican-born Spaniards, evolved cultural patterns that by the end of the eighteenth century were akin to the practices of rural Andalucía in southern Spain, where women typically married in their early twenties but as many as 20 percent never married at all. The age gap between spouses was substantial. Men married five to seven years older than women. In New Spain, illegitimacy rates are typically placed at 10 percent for *españoles* (several points greater than in Andalucía), but racial identification at baptism is particularly problematic for illegitimate children, many of whom are listed as complete orphans of unknown parentage.

Intermediate between *españoles* and *indios* in terms of marriage age were mestizos and *castas,* who also were distinguished by unique marriage patterns. Illegitimacy set these groups apart. In San Luis de la Paz at the beginning of the eighteenth century, for example, 20 percent of mestizo births were not legitimate, compared with 33 percent for *castas,* but only 13 percent for Indians and 10 percent for Spaniards—differences that wore thin by the end of the century (Rabell, 1990).

Fertility in colonial Mexico was constrained by both marriage and remarriage. On average, most unions were disrupted by the death of a spouse, usually the male, within 15 or 20 years of first union. Widowers readily remarried, regardless of social or racial origins, but this was not the case for widows, particularly non-Indians. *Españolas* who became widowed faced poor prospects in the nuptial fair, especially as they neared or exceeded the thirtieth birthday. The full reproductive potential of Indians was least likely to be curtailed owing to widowhood, because Indian widows remarried quickly. (Were differences in remarriage prospects for widowed *españolas* and *indias* a matter of wheatbread versus corn tortillas, that is, in the time required to prepare the daily bread). Over the eighteenth century, marriage and remarriage patterns converged in mixed-race communities throughout New Spain, but large contrasts in nuptial practices remained between Hispanicized settlements and Indian villages. The cultural and material conditioning of marriage, and family and household, implied by soci004racial differences is yet to be fully mapped for colonial Mexico.

The history of life expectancy also remains largely unwritten, but not for a lack of effort. The task is made onerous by the poor quality of burial registers. The classic technique of computing mortality rates from registered ages at death (numerator) and a population census (denominator) yields implausible results for colonial Mexico. At best, clues emerge from the inventive analysis of odd bits of data: proportions of orphaned children or age distributions of skeletons, burials, or populations (see Table 1). These straws in the wind all point to the brevity of life in New Spain, near or even below the worst levels recorded for agrarian populations. Model life tables —with mortality patterns that cover the range of experiences of historical populations with life expectancies at birth from 20 to 80 years—serve as useful benchmarks for places and periods with poor data, such as colonial Mexico. Level 1 tables describe the age pattern of death associated with a life expectancy at birth of 20 years. At age 15, level 1 mortality points to a life expectancy of 31 additional years (i.e., with death occurring at age 46 for those who survive to the fifteenth birthday). In 1940, the figure for all of Mexico was an additional 43 years of life after age 15, or death at age 58.

Table 1
Life expectancy at age 15 in colonial Mexico

Place, Period	Years	Author, Method, Data
Model table West, Level 1	31	[2]Coale and Demeny, stable populations
Morelos, 1530s	<30	[3]McCaa, orphanhood, children
Teotihuacan, 1580–1620	13	[2]Storey, mean age at death, skeletal remains
Cholula, 1642–90	29	[3]Hayward, age at burial
San Luis de la Paz, 1745–94	33	Rabell, mean age at death, burials
males	35	(Level 5)
females	31	(Level 1)
Oaxaca, 1700–77	33	Cook and Borah, population age structure, census
Parral, 1808	<30	[1]McCaa, orphanhood, newlyweds
Mexico, 1939–41	43	[2]Camposortega, deaths, census

Example: In 1939–41, Mexicans aged 15 years could expect to live 43 additional years on average, to age 58, given the mortality experience of that period.

Sources: Cook and Borah, 1971; [1]McCaa, 1993; [2]McCaa and Marquez Morfín, 1995; [3]McCaa, 1996; Rabell, 1990; Storey, 1992.

Empirical estimates for New Spain often indicate level 1 conditions (Table 1). An exceptionally detailed Nahuatl census from the 1530s reveals that 15.6 percent of the fathers of 261 children aged 5 to 9 were dead. This figure is three points worse than level 1 rates, suggesting a life expectancy at birth of 15 years or less (McCaa, 1996). In Teotihuacán one-half century later, mortality conditions were so terrible as to imply extinction (a 15-year-old could expect to live only 13 additional years, to age 28) if we accept the results obtained by conventional paleodemographic methods (Storey, 1992). Written records suggest sustainable conditions but little variation over time or space (a 15-year-old could expect to live an additional 29 to 33 years). There is evidence that 15-year-old women could expect to live four fewer years than men (who died on average at age 35), at least in the parish of San Luis de la Paz (Rabell, 1990). On the northern frontier, in 1808, only 46 percent of fathers of grooms were alive when their underage sons married. To attain level 1 conditions (life expectancy at birth of 20 years), the figure should be bumped up five percentage points, or, to reach national levels in 1940, when life expectancy at birth was 40 years, increased by one-half, to 70 percent (McCaa, 1993).

When Independence was finally won in 1822, the result was a political victory, not a social or demographic one. The demographic legacy of the paleolithic past and three centuries of colonial rule remained. The *ancien régime's* high-pressure system—high fertility checked by high mortality—left a small, yet meaningful, margin for population increase. Indeed, some scholars see demographic growth, heightened poverty, and inequality, and the discontent spawned by an inflexible colonial order as the roots of rebellion and the struggle for independence. Enrique Florescano's evidence of price hikes in corn and wheat preceding epidemics suggests positive demographic checks at work, but others find colonial grain price series less persuasive and favor epidemics as the autochthonous regulator of demographic change in Bourbon Mexico. Questions of whether population growth led to misery and social crisis, to agricultural innovation and expansion, or to social and cultural transformation remain unanswered.

A demographic revolution was in the making in late-colonial Mexico, but would not erupt full blown until the 1930s. In Europe, the transition was well underway one and one-half centuries earlier. Already by 1780, England's death rate was probably half that of Mexico, and its growth rate likely doubled Mexico's. Epidemics in Bourbon Mexico were at least twice as devastating as those in western Europe. Grain price fluctuations no longer governed the European mortality regime, unlike in Mexico, where in 1786, the "year of hunger," 15 percent of the population of Michoacán died of starvation and related causes (Morin, 1979), and Indian mothers sold their small children for a couple *reales,* the daily wage of an unskilled laborer. First steps toward demographic revolution were taken under Spanish colonial rule: quarantine to prevent the spread of infectious disease, reforms to discourage elaborate public burial for victims of epidemics and to prevent the sale or rental of victims' clothing, mobilization of massive social relief in times of crisis, vaccination against smallpox. But many steps remained, indeed remain today, as Mexico moves into the twenty-first century.

Select Bibliography

Arrom, Silvia Marina, *The Women of Mexico City, 1790–1857*. Stanford, California: Stanford University Press, 1985.

Brading, D. A., *Haciendas and Ranchos in the Mexican Bajío: León, 1700–1860*. Cambridge: Cambridge University Press, 1978.

Carroll, Patrick J., *Blacks in Colonial Veracruz: Race, Ethnicity, and Regional Development*. Austin: University of Texas Press, 1991.

Cook, Sherburne F., and Woodrow Borah, *Essays in Population History: Mexico and the Caribbean*. 3 vols., Berkeley: University of California Press, 1971.

Denevan, William M., editor, *The Native Population of the Americas in 1492*. Revised edition, Madison: University of Wisconsin Press, 1992.

McCaa, Robert, "The Peopling of 19th-Century Mexico: Critical Scrutiny of a Censured Century." *Statistical Abstract of Latin America* 30 (1993).

_____, "Spanish and Nahuatl Views on Smallpox and Demographic Catastrophe in the Conquest of Mexico." *Journal of Interdisciplinary History* 25:3 (Winter 1995).

Prem, Hanns J., "Disease Outbreaks in Central Mexico during the Sixteenth-century." In *"Secret Judgments of God": Old World Disease in Colonial Spanish America*, edited by Noble David Cook and W. G. Lovell. Norman: University of Oklahoma Press, 1991.

Reff, Daniel T., *Disease, Depopulation, and Culture Change in Northwestern New Spain, 1518–1764*. Salt Lake City: University of Utah Press, 1991.

Storey, R., *Life and Death in the Ancient City of Teotihuacan: A Modern Paleodemographic Synthesis*. Tuscaloosa: University of Alabama Press, 1992.

Van Young, Eric, *Hacienda and Market in Eighteenth-Century Mexico: The Rural Economy of the Guadalajara Region, 1675–1820*. Berkeley: University of California Press, 1981.

—Robert McCaa

Conquest: Ecological Impact

Mesoamerican ecosystems reflect millennia of interaction between humans and nature. Until the sixteenth century, the relations between humans and American ecologies evolved in virtual isolation from the rest of the world. At this time, indigenous patterns and processes were interrupted by invading Europeans, who introduced exotic animals and plants, new systems of land management, and alien understandings of what a landscape should look like. These European transplants interacted with native species and local processes, and with indigenous land management systems and world views, and set in motion processes that resulted, ultimately, in the formation of the modern Mexican environments.

The following discussion does not pretend to cover all the possible permutations of the environmental changes put in motion by the Conquest process, or the associated social and cultural processes. Rather, it reflects the somewhat limited scope of research on the immediate ecological consequences of the European invasion; and hence, it focuses primarily on the impact of Old World diseases and grazing animals, changing patterns of forest exploitation, and the consequences of the introduction of Spanish systems of land management.

The best-known and best-studied aspect of the European impact on the Mesoamerican environments is the introduction of Eurasian and African disease organisms. Indeed, researchers such as Woodrow Wilson Borah and Sherburne Friend Cook pioneered the new field of environmental history in Latin America in studies that demonstrated the course of the diseases and, most especially, the consequences for human population demographics. They found that the introduction of diseases such as influenza, small pox, bubonic plague, measles, chicken pox, whooping cough, typhus, typhoid fever, cholera, scarlet fever, malaria, yellow fever, and diphtheria resulted in almost universal infection in populations that were without defenses. Because Mesoamerican populations (in common with the rest of the Native American populations) had effectively been isolated from the rest of the world's population for millennia, they had never been infected with these diseases and thus had not acquired immunity to them. The alien diseases swept through the populations in terrible epidemics that were repeated regularly over the first 100 years until the indigenous populations acquired some immunity, a process that appears to have taken from four to six generations. The repetition of several distinct infections with very high mortality rates resulted in the demographic collapse of the indigenous populations. The demographic collapse, in turn, played a major role in shaping colonial land-labor regimes.

Disease organisms enter a population in various ways. Some of the new diseases, small pox and measles for example, depended entirely on human carriers for propagation in the American populations. Others were introduced along with the Old World animal species: plague came with the fleas of the domestic rat, swine flu with pigs, malaria with mosquitoes. Yet other diseases took advantage of circumstances that developed in the course of European invasion to extend their range into the Mesoamerican environment: the yellow fever virus, for example, is carried by a mosquito that prefers to breed in water carried in manufactured containers, and the virus was transmitted along with stores of water on board slave ships sailing to the Americas; malaria spread with the expansion of sugar plantations and the consequent increase in standing water.

The very limited variety of domestic animal species in the Americas meant that the indigenous human populations were not accustomed to sharing their domestic environments with a wide range of animals. This situation contrasted markedly with Eurasia, where human populations lived in close association with an extraordinary array of domestic animals. The introduction of alien animal species, along with all their micro-flora and fauna, transformed American disease environments.

When the Spaniards began to settle in Mesoamerica, they brought the animals necessary to reproduce their world in these new lands. They brought grazing animals such as cattle, sheep, goats, horses, donkeys, mules, and pigs in order to produce familiar foods (e.g., milk and meat), material for manufacture (e.g., wool and hides), and muscle power for carrying and traction (e.g., for plowing and drawing wheeled vehicles). They also brought birds of various types, such as chickens, ducks, and geese for their eggs and meat. They introduced animals that were not crucial for subsistence or manufacture, but that were part of their daily life and culture, such as cats and dogs. And they introduced species they would probably far rather have left behind: pests such as lice and fleas, and all the other parasites and plagues that coexist with humans and their domesticated species. And indeed, the sudden introduction of these alien species into the immediate physical environment of the Mesoamerican communities resulted in an increase in the microbial flora and fauna and the development of gastrointestinal infections; and Indians complained bitterly of the contamination of their water supplies by all these animals. The pollution was increased by the effluent from tanning establishments, slaughter houses, and woolen mills, and possibly caused even more illness.

The introduction of this array of domesticated species also may have increased the virulence of the diseases that accompanied the Europeans and Africans into the Americas by producing a situation in which new diseases could evolve. We already have noted the propensity of disease organisms to take advantage of environmental disruption and to move into human niches. The diversion of animal viruses into humans also can lead to the development of "new" viruses (composed of reshuffled genes of familiar viruses) that demonstrate enhanced virulence when they move into human hosts. Hence, the introduction of alien animals into the Americas, and the environmental disruption associated with the invasion, meant not only the introduction of alien diseases such as the swine flu that struck the Caribbean in 1493, but also the possibility of new strains of increased virulence as they evolved in their new setting.

The number of new species introduced into the Mesoamerican environments by the Spaniards was extraordinary: as well as the animals already mentioned, the Spaniards planted wheat, grape vines, and olive trees in order to have the bread, wine, and olive oil so necessary to the Mediterranean diet; and they planted fruit trees, herbs and flowers, grains such as barley, and all the other plants that were necessary to provide the flavors and foods familiar to them. As in the case of the domestic animals, the plants were associated with "useless" species, such as dandelions and thistles, that thrived in the new environments. The success or failure of the portmanteau biota (scholar Alfred Crosby's term for the totality of the species carried into the Americas) depended on the ability of these Old World species to adapt to New World climates, soils, vegetation, and water resources. The adaptation depended, as well, on the ability of the Spaniards, and those Mesoamericans who added the new species to their cultural repertoire, to develop the systems of land management specific to each species, thereby providing the specialized ecosystems necessary for their survival.

Judging by the unexpected consequences of the introduction of alien species into foreign ecosystems in the present day, and given the implications of unanticipated ecological change for modern human communities, all these additions must have changed the intersection between biological and social process (e.g., deforestation and erosion) in Mesoamerica. On this point there is not much disagreement. But, given the paucity of research aimed at distinguishing causal relations between human activity and environmental change in the early Conquest era, it is not an easy matter to demonstrate how and to what extent these introductions influenced indigenous biological and social processes. As a preliminary ordering of events and processes, we can state that in some cases the introduction of alien species initiated entirely new biological processes and resulted in the transformation of certain ecosystems. In other cases, processes already in place when the Spaniards arrived were accelerated; in yet others indigenous processes were decelerated. Further, because we find examples of all these changes occurring in the same space, we can state that Spanish landscapes did not simply replace indigenous landscapes, nor that indigenous landscapes persisted unchanged; rather, the processes by which the colonial landscapes evolved were underlain by extremely complex and mutually influencing processes of environmental and social change. All of this may appear obvious, but it is apparently necessary to state clearly, given popular notions of the power of the Europeans to destroy indigenous landscapes and environments.

The complexity of the environmental impact of the Spanish invasion is exemplified by changes in patterns of forest use and the location and causes of erosion. It is difficult to discern a clear pattern either to deforestation or erosion in the sixteenth century, let alone demonstrate a causal link between specific examples of these processes. Shifting patterns in human and animal demographics, and shifting patterns in land use and consumption, were reflected in changing patterns of tree cover and soil structure. But rather then the simple replacement of one pattern by another—the replacement of indigenous patterns by Spanish, for example—we find a far more fluid situation that is not easily predicted by either indigenous or Spanish experience.

Prior to the arrival of the Spaniards, Mesoamerica was a densely populated region with perhaps as many as 25 million inhabitants. Vast areas of land were given over to agriculture to feed this population, and sometime in the past these lands had been cleared, to a greater or lesser extent, of trees, That is to say, deforestation the pre-Hispanic era was associated with high human population densities.

This pattern changed with the arrival of the Spaniards. Land clearance during the Conquest era was no longer carried out to accommodate a huge human population; indeed the indigenous human population declined by around 90 percent over this period, and the immigrant population of Spaniards and Africans was not large enough, nor did it increase sufficiently quickly to fill the space left by the demographic collapse. Land was now cleared for domestic grazing animals, and trees were cut for lumber needed in the silver mines and in the construction of Spanish cities, and for wood used to manufacture lime and charcoal. Such shifts in land use and in the destination of forest products meant that forests and woodlands that had survived the pre-Hispanic clearance, because they were far from the centers of population or because they were protected by pre-Hispanic legal codes, were cut. Deforestation in the Conquest era, therefore, occurred in regions of low population densities and in regions that were not cleared at contact. At the same time, however, the demographic collapse of the indigenous populations was reflected in an increase in fallow lands, and hence the possibility of forest regrowth—and in some places forests did grow back.

Patterns of erosion also shifted with the changing patterns in land use and tree cover. Not too surprisingly, pre-Hispanic patterns of erosion were primarily associated with dense human populations. Erosion in the Conquest era, by contrast, appears to have been associated with accelerated tree cutting for mining and the manufacture of charcoal and lime, with land clearance for grazing, and with overgrazing. That is, erosion in the Conquest era often occurred in areas that were characterized by very low or falling densities of human populations, where cutting, burning, and/or overgrazing put unusual pressure on the soils by removing the vegetative cover and opening the soils to the erosive forces of wind and rain. But the likelihood of erosion also appears to have increased with the spread of plowing. The European plow disturbed the soil far more deeply than the indigenous foot plow, thereby loosening the soil and making it more liable to increased wind erosion. As well, plowing formed rows that channeled rainwater in ways that the mounds made by the indigenous farmers did not, thereby increasing water erosion. That is, erosion also occurred in agricultural regions near population clusters, as it had in the pre-Hispanic era.

The picture of vegetative change is further complicated by the fact that Spanish invasion and settlement not only resulted in changing patterns of tree cover and soil loss, it also had consequences for the structure and composition of the vegetative communities. The introduction of pastoralism, for example, led to quite spectacular shifts in the composition of the vegetative cover as a result of the processes by which ungulates (hard-hooved herbivores) expand into new ecosystems. When ungulates are introduced into a new ecosystem, and are successful in adapting to the local climate and vegetation, they begin a process of rapid population increase that continues until their population density exceeds the carrying capacity of the range; the population crashes from lack of sufficient food, then adjusts to the reduced range. The vegetative cover goes through a reciprocal trajectory of decrease, recovery, and adjustment to the changing herbivoral population. As well, animals selectively browse the vegetation, eating those species they prefer and leaving unpalatable or "armed" (e.g., spined) species of plants alone.

By the time an introduced animal population and the native vegetative communities have adapted to each other, the composition of the vegetative cover has been modified—quite drastically so in some places. The most common changes are reduction in the height of the vegetative cover and increase in the spaces between plants, and hence an increase in asolation (drying) of the soils. The development of arid microclimates leads in turn to the invasion by arid-zone species with a high proportion of wood to foliage. As the composition and structure of the vegetation changes, so do the associated faunal populations. The end result is a transformed biological regime, and a transformed landscape.

Such changes are not necessarily permanent, and if the ungulate population is removed, the original vegetative cover with its complement of fauna will return. When, however, the ungulate population is managed and maintained by humans, the results are often permanent. Because humans manage grazing animals by controlling breeding patterns, birth rates, eating habits, migrations, and death rates, they have the capacity to influence the relationship of the animal populations with the vegetation. When pastoralists hold the animals in very high densities, for example, they amplify the vegetation changes to the point of total loss of vegetation cover, thereby increasing the possibility of the permanent loss of floral and faunal species and soil erosion. Since their goal is to increase the extent of grasses available for forage, pastoralists also practice deforestation to open the land for grazing, and burning to stimulate grasses; both practices reduce the soil cover and hence increase the likelihood of erosion.

The extent of the changes brought about by the Spanish invasion, and conversely, the persistence of indigenous environments, depended on many variables: biological factors such as the climate, soil, and vegetation; political-economic factors such as the distance from the centers of Spanish power, the presence (or absence) of resources attractive to the Spanish, and access to the markets where new products were sold; and cultural factors such as the acceptability of the new cultural items, knowledge of their use, and practice in their application. Many animal species were accepted and became an integral part of the village economies and the Mesoamerican ecosystems, changing the biological regime as they expanded into these ecosystems, and, in turn, being changed by this process. In fact, variants of the original species developed that were highly adapted to the local environments, the so-called criollo breeds. These ecotypes are so important to local economies and ecologies that it is now often necessary to cross-breed the

scientifically "improved" breeds with the criollo breeds so that the newcomers are not rejected by the local ecosystems. Plant species were not always and everywhere accepted. Some plant species like fruit trees became part of the cultural and environmental repertoire of the indigenous peoples. Other such as wheat were not accepted so easily, apparently because they did not provide any perceived advantages over indigenous species, such as maize.

The process of adaptation and acceptance was not all one-way, however, and the Spaniards were forced to adapt to American realities, often at quite significant expense and dislocation of settled routines. Wheat growing provides a clear example of the need to adapt, not only to new climates and soils, but also to indigenous systems of production. At first wheat was planted in the mounds typical of indigenous maize agriculture; and it was planted to take advantage of the summer rains. When it became clear that wheat production on a commercial scale competed with Indian work schedules, most especially maize cultivation, and that the best grains for bread could not be grown successfully during the summer rainy season, the Spaniards changed their scheduling: from spring sowing of rain-fed wheat and a fall harvest, to fall sowing of irrigated wheat and spring harvest. The shift to a spring harvest meant that threshing was postponed to the following fall, when traditional methods of threshing with the *trilla,* or with large numbers of mares on a flat area of hardened ground, was not threatened by early rains and did not use animals needed for preparing the ground for maize.

A further example of Spanish adaptation to and use of indigenous infrastructure is the use and adaptation of indigenous water management practices. The Spaniards made extensive use of indigenous irrigation systems, and they expanded and modified canals and dams. It is interesting to note, however, that they left the extremely sophisticated systems of wetland agriculture in the hands of the Mesoamericans, making little or not attempt either to adopt the technology or take over these lands—they might have left them alone because of a lack of understanding of the principles involved in this method of soil-water management.

In other areas of water management, the Spaniards applied technologies developed in Europe, and not always with felicitous results. The technology applied to the Basin of Mexico illustrates the problems faced by the Spaniards in their attempts to develop a familiar landscape in this new world, and the consequences of the application of European technology in alien ecologies. The Basin of Mexico is an inland basin with no natural external drainage, and there were constant problems with floods in the city of Mexico-Tenochtitlan in the sixteenth century. But instead of working with the wetlands as the Mesoamericans did and regulating the water levels with dikes as had been done quite successfully in the pre-Contact era, the Spaniards attempted to resolve the problem of flooding by draining the basin. They began the ill-fated *desagüe* (drainage), a process that has had drastic and long-term consequences for both Mexico City and the extensive wetlands that ringed the lakes. The production of dry lands fit for plow agriculture was an added incentive for the drainage of the basin and reflects the entirely different approaches to soil-water management of the Spaniards and Mesoamericans.

The changes that took place in the Conquest era would seem to imply that each region—perhaps each village—was shaped by different processes, or at least by different groupings and arrangements of similar processes. But perhaps this confusion is a factor of the current state of environmental history, or historical ecology as it is known by anthropologists. Our understanding of the implications of the Spanish invasion, and the strength of indigenous ecosystems to persist, is very much at an early stage. Interest in this topic is such, however, that an increasing number of scholars is studying the mechanics of "ecological imperialism," and we can look forward to clarification of some of the problems posed by this topic in the near future.

Select Bibliography

Borah, Woodrow Wilson, *The Population of Central Mexico in 1548: An Analysis of the Suma de Vistas de Pueblos*. Berkeley: University of California Press, 1960.
____, *The Aboriginal Population of Central Mexico on the Eve of the Spanish Conquest*. Berkeley: University of California Press, 1963.
Cook, Sherburne Friend, *The Population of Mixtec Alta, 1520–1960*. Berkeley: University of California Press, 1968.
Crosby, Alfred, *Ecological Imperialism: The Biological Expansion of Europe, 900–1900*. Cambridge and New York: Cambridge University Press, 1986.
Licate, Jack A., *The Creation of a Mexican Landscape: Territorial Organization and Settlement in the Eastern Puebla Basin 1520–1605*. Chicago: University of Chicago Press, 1981.
Melville, Elinor G. K., *A Plague of Sheep: Environmental Consequences of the Conquest of Mexico*. Cambridge and New York: Cambridge University Press, 1994.
Simpson, Lesley Byrd, *Exploitation of Land in Sixteenth Century Mexico*. Berkeley and Los Angeles: University of California Press, 1952.

—ELINOR G. K. MELVILLE

Conquistadors

The immense body of writings on the Spanish Conquest presents varied images of the conquistador, ranging from the heroic to the villainous. These discordant images reflect the different ideological lenses through which historians and others have viewed the subject. The long dispute over the conquistador's character and conduct forms part of a larger debate over Spain's work in America. Two highly polemical phrases coined in the early twentieth century, "Black Legend" (Leyenda Negra) and "White Legend" (Leyenda Blanca), sum up the issues in the debate. The phrase "Black Legend" implied that critics of Spain's colonial record had defamed it with exaggerated, tendentious, and factually wrong charges of Spanish cruelty and bigotry; the phrase "White Legend" implied that defenders of that record had utterly distorted it by their stress on the relative mildness and benefits of Spanish colonial rule. In recent decades, with the rise of a supposedly more dispassionate, objective scholarship, the fires lit by that debate have died down, but they still smolder, kept alive by the publication of books such as *Dogs of the Conquest* (1983) by J. G. Varner and J. J. Varner, with its evidence that some conquistadors committed cruelties of a "grotesque fiendishness"; and by charges such as historian Joseph P. Sanchez's recent claim that the defamatory "Black Legend sentiment survives within the very backbone of our educational system—the monograph and the textbook."

It would be naive to deny that many conquistadors were hard, ruthless men—hard in dealing with each other and harder still with the Indians. We do not have to rely for proof on defenders of the Indian such as the famous Bartolomé de Las Casas. The evidence comes from official chroniclers such as Gonzalo Fernández de Oviedo and Antonio de Herrera; Oviedo, an ardent imperialist who shared the typical contempt of the colonists for the Indian, wrote that some conquistadors could more accurately be called "depopulators or destroyers of the new lands." Official reports and letters provide a mass of testimony on the subject. A report to Felipe II by Alonso de Zorita, a Spanish judge of great integrity who spent 18 years in New Spain and the Caribbean (1548–66), contains this striking phrase: "When the Spaniards discover a new mine, vultures gather."

Spain's economic backwardness and immense inequalities of wealth, which sharply limited opportunities for advancement or even a decent livelihood for many Spaniards, help explain the desperate valor of the conquistadors as they roamed the New World in quest of golden kingdoms; they also suggest one reason for the conquistadors' harsh, intensely exploitative treatment of the Indians. By no accident, many great captains of the Conquest—Fernando (Hernán) Cortés, Francisco Pizarro, Pedro de Valdivia, Basco Núñez de Balboa—came from Extremadura, Spain's poorest province. We should note, too, the climate of violence that prevailed in contemporary Spain, a legacy of the Reconquest—the long struggle to expel the Moors from Spain—and the social and economic conditions it created.

In the Indies, this propensity for violence found a large new field of action. In the first phase of the Conquest, in the absence of a strong Crown presence, it generated incessant feuding among the early conquistadors, culminating in almost three decades of murderous civil wars in Peru; it also contributed to a barbarous mistreatment of Indians that sometimes assumed the proportions of genocide. The semifeudal values and ideals of the conquistadors, who were determined to *valer más* (rise in the world) and achieve a life of ease by whatever means were necessary, who regarded gold as the prime symbol of wealth, also contributed to the Conquest's predatory character, often abetted by the impotence or complicity of royal officials. After plundering and melting down the available stock of Indian gold and silver objects, the conquistadors turned to other means for extracting wealth from the natives: the imposition of intolerable tribute burdens on the Indians, the destructive, wasteful exploitation of Indian labor in enterprises like mining and pearl-fishing, and in some areas a large-scale traffic in Indian slaves. These practices led to the almost complete extinction of the Indians in the Caribbean islands, the adjacent fringes of South America, and parts of Central America. In heavily populated Mexico and Peru the Indian population suffered a decline of perhaps 90 percent in the sixteenth century. Most recent studies agree that diseases of European origin to which the Indians had no acquired immunity—smallpox, measles, yellow fever, malaria, among others—were the major factor producing this demographic catastrophe. But overwork, malnutrition, social disorganization, and loss of will to live contributed to the terrible mortality associated with the great epidemics and even with epidemic-free years.

Finally, we should note the brutalizing effects of a colonial war waged by Europeans against a people of different race, color, and culture, many of whose traits, especially their religious practices, these Europeans found abhorrent. The encounter bred an intense chauvinism and racism in the invaders, and helped transform some ordinary Spaniards who once may have lived peacefully in their native villages into killers and torturers. The epithet "dogs" *(perros)*, commonly applied by the conquistadors to the Indians, served to dehumanize them, contributing to the atmosphere in which the massacres and other well-verified horrors of the Conquest took place.

Not until 1542 did the Crown, fearing the rise of a powerful conquistador feudalism in the Indies and alarmed by the rapid decline of the Indian population, promulgate the reformist New Laws that—although often weakened by the Crown's retreat under pressure from the conquistadors—put some checks on tribute burdens and the exploitation of Indian labor. The New Laws came too late to save the Indians of the Caribbean, but improved the condition of the Indians of New Spain and Peru enough to prevent a repetition of the demographic disaster that occurred in the islands.

To concede the barbarous, rapacious character of the Spanish Conquest is not to ascribe to the conquistadors a unique capacity for cruelty or deviltry. Every colonial or imperialist power has its own Black Legend that is no legend but a dismal reality. The brutality of the Spanish Conquest is matched by that of the genocidal Indian wars waged by the United States in the nineteenth century. What distinguishes Spain from many other colonial or imperialist powers of history is that it produced a minority of men who denounced in the face of the world the crimes of their own countrymen and did all in their power to stop what Bartolomé de Las Casas called "the destruction of the Indies." Jean-François Marmontel, author of the best-selling novel *Les Incas* (1777), a lachrymose account of the destruction of the Inca Empire that usually is regarded as a source of the Black Legend, paid generous tribute to this Spanish trait. "All nations have had their brigands and their fanatics, their times of barbarism, their fits of fury. The finest peoples are those which accuse themselves of their crimes. The Spaniards have this proud trait, worthy of their character."

That Spanish dissident minority included some conquistadors who were transformed by their experiences, were taught humility and respect for Indian values, or even came to concede the moral superiority of the Indian over the Spaniard. Alvar Núñez Cabeza de Vaca learned that lesson in the course of his immense eight-year trek from the Gulf Coast of Texas to Mexico (1528–36), which he survived thanks to the generosity of the Indians. In his account of his adventures he reverses the roles of the Indians and the Spaniards; the Spaniards are presented as savages and the Indians as humane and civilized. Another conquistador, Pedro Cieza de León, the "prince of chroniclers," criticized the cruelties of the conquest of Peru and clearly sympathized with the ideas of Las Casas. Yet another conquistador, Alonso de Ercilla, author of the finest Spanish epic poem of the sixteenth century, *La Araucana,* dealing with the struggle of the Araucanian Indians of Chile against the Spaniards, reverses the customary roles; he praises and even glorifies the Indians who appear throughout the poem as a heroic people determined to be free, while the victorious Spaniards are often portrayed as cowardly, greedy, and selfish.

Granted that not all thought or acted alike, what sort of men were the conquistadors? The Conquest of America attracted a wide variety of types. There was a sprinkling of professional soldiers, some with backgrounds of service in the Italian wars and some with pasts that they preferred to forget. The old conquistador Gonzalo Fernández de Oviedo had such men in mind when he warned the organizers of expeditions against "fine-feathered birds and great talkers who will either slay you or sell you or forsake you when they find that you promised them more in Spain than you can produce." In one of his *Exemplary Tales,* Cervantes describes the Indies as "the refuge and shelter of the desperate men of Spain, sanctuary of rebels, safe-conduct of homicides." No doubt men of this type contributed more than their share of the atrocities that stained the Spanish Conquest.

But the background of the conquistadors was extremely varied, running the whole gamut of the Spanish social spectrum. Few, however, came from its extremes: high-ranking, wealthy nobles who did not need to leave and paupers who generally lacked the means to leave. The majority were commoners: artisans, peasants, tradesmen, seamen (who often jumped ship on arrival in an American port), and professionals or semiprofessionals like notaries or apothecaries and barbers (who sometimes doubled as doctors). In this *Historia verdadera de la conquista de la Nueva España,* the conquistador Bernal Díaz del Castillo claims he and most of his comrades were nobles, but modern-day scholar Fernando Benítez observes that "the beings he paints are men who have not yet shed their smell of earth and onions. . . . One can almost see their callused hands and hear their mule bells, their country songs, and their nicknames." We should note, however, that the terms *hidalgo* (a member of the lower nobility) and "peasant" and "artisan" were not mutually exclusive. Earning one's living may have been ideally incompatible with the nobility's values and way of life, but, as the scholar Ida Altman notes in her study of sixteenth-century emigration to the Indies from Extremadura, the region's villages were filled with humble *hidalgo*-farmers "who worked land with a pair or two of oxen," and some *hidalgo*-artisans held honored posts in town councils.

Many conquistadors were marginal *hidalgos* of a different type, poor gentlemen who wished to improve their fortunes; some were *segundones* (second sons), disinherited by a tendency among the Spanish nobility to entail the family estate in the eldest son: others, like the famous conqueror of Peru, Francisco Pizarro, were illegitimate sons of nobles. Of the 168 men who captured the Inca emperor Atahualpa at Cajamarca in 1532, 38 were *hidalgos* and 91 plebeians, with the background of the rest unknown or uncertain. According to James Lockhart, who has studied the men of Cajamarca, 51 members of the group were definitely literate and about 76 "almost certainly functioning literates." The group included 19 artisans, 12 notaries or clerks, and 13 "men of affairs."

Of the Spanish kingdoms, Castile provided by far the largest contingent of emigrants, with natives of Andalusia dominating the first, or Caribbean, phase of the Conquest, and men from Extremadura the largest single group in the second, or mainland, phase. Foreigners were not absent from the Conquest. Oviedo, in an attempt to clear Spain of sole responsibility for the crimes committed in the Indies, assures us that men had come from every part of Christendom: there were Italians, Germans, Scots, Englishmen, Frenchmen, Hungarians, Poles, Greeks, Portuguese, and men from all the other nations of Asia, Africa, and Europe.

An institution inherited from the Spanish Reconquest, the *compañía* (warrior band), whose members shared in the profits of the enterprise according to certain rules, provided a model for the organization of the American expeditions of conquest. At its head stood a military leader who usually possessed a royal *capitulación* (contract), which vested him with the title of *adelantado* (commander) and with governing powers in the territory to be conquered. Some leaders were wealthy in their own right and contributed large sums or incurred immense debts to finance the expedition. Cortés contributed a substantial portion of the financing of the Mexican venture from his own resources, and also went into debt. Much of the capital needed to fit out ships, acquire horses and slaves, and supply arms and food was provided by Italian, German, and Spanish merchant capitalists and royal officials grown wealthy through the slave trade or other means.

In principle the warrior band was a military democracy, with the distribution of spoils carried out by a committee elected from among the entire company. After subtracting the *quinto* (royal fifth) and the common debts, distribution was made in accordance with the individual's rank and contribution to the enterprise. Despite its democratic aspect, the leaders, captains, large investors, and royal officials dominated the enterprise of conquest and took the lion's share for themselves. Describing the distribution of spoils after the fall of Tenochtitlan, Bernal Díaz recalls in his *Historia verdadera* the grumbling of the cavalrymen and foot soldiers who complained how little was left for them after deducting the royal fifth, another fifth for Cortés (29,600 pesos), and shares for each of the captains, priest, and royal officials. The sums received by some 750 common soldiers, ranging between 80 and 50 pesos, at a time when a sword cost 50 pesos and a crossbow 60, were so paltry that some suggested, ironically or in earnest, that the whole should be distributed among their comrades who had lost their limbs, or were lame or paralyzed or had suffered powder burns, or among the families of the dead. Many had contracted large debts for the purchase of arms and other needs, and naturally resented such meager rewards for their hardships and suffering; they vented their anger at Cortés, claiming that he had hidden part of the gold and making other scurrilous remarks; some of the things they said, Díaz writes, were not fit to repeat in his history.

At a later stage of each conquest came the distribution of *encomiendas* (assignments of Indians who were to serve the grantees with tribute and labor). Craftsmen and other plebeians received *encomiendas* after the Conquests of Mexico and Peru; later, however, only the leaders and *hidalgo* members of expeditions were rewarded with such grants. As a rule, the military leaders and captains received much more populous and valuable *encomiendas* than those granted to rank-and-file conquistadors. After the Conquest of Mexico, Cortés reserved for himself the tribute of rich towns in heavily populated areas, forming a huge feudal domain. The *encomienda*, supplemented by a land grant, typically small, became the principal source of wealth or livelihood for the former conquistadors. If gold or silver could not be obtained directly, the *encomenderos* sought to obtain them by sale in local or distant markets of the tribute goods produced by the Indians. In time the *encomienda* became the basis of great landed estates and their owners a colonial seigneurial class whose power challenged that of the Crown.

The Spanish Conquest was, among other things, a conquest of women. From the time of the Discovery, Indian women were frequently subjected to rape, enslavement, and other brutalities. In Mexico, the fall of Tenochtitlan was followed by the enslavement of both Mexica (Aztec) men and women. A native account, the *Florentine Codex,* tells that "the Spaniards seized and set apart the pretty women, the fair-skinned ones. And some women, when they were robbed, covered their faces with mud and put on old mended shirts and rags for their shifts. . . ." Cortés had ordered that all the slaves taken by the soldiers should be branded so that he could take the royal fifth and his own share of the captives. Bernal Díaz relates that when they returned the next day to take their shares of the remaining slave women they discovered that Cortés and his officers had "hidden and taken away the best looking slaves so that there was not a single pretty one left. The ones we received were old and ugly. There was much grumbling against Cortés on this account. . . ." Much casual sexual intercourse accompanied the Conquest, contributing to the swift rise of a mestizo class. Spanish authorities sometimes required that Indian women be baptized before intercourse. In 1538 the commander of an expedition in present-day Colombia was ordered to see to it that "no soldier slept with any Indian who was not a Christian," but the conquistadors do not seem to have taken such injunctions very seriously. After the Conquest, the *encomienda* provided former conquistadors with a large pool of Indian female servants who often became their concubines.

Bravery, tenacity, and an incredible capacity for enduring hardships were among the conspicuous virtues of the conquistador. The legendary Castilian austerity prepared the conquistador for the difficulties he encountered in the New World. The Spanish common soldier of the War of Granada ate only once a day, fortifying himself with swigs of the thin, sharply bitter wine he carried in a leather bottle. His single meal was a salad of onions, garlic, cucumbers, and peppers chopped very finely and mixed with bread, crumbs, olive oil, vinegar, and water. Soldiers with such traditions were capable of marching a day's journey on a handful of toasted corn.

A fierce nationalism and a religious fanaticism, more often manifested in a brutal contempt for the Indian than in a desire for his or her conversion, were essential elements in the conquistador's psychological make-up. Add to these traits the quality of romanticism. The Reconquest, filled with a thousand combats, raids, and ambushes, had heated the Spanish imagination to an incandescent pitch. Spanish romanticism found expression in a rich literature of romances, popular ballads that celebrated the exploits of the frontier wars against the Moors and that were frequently on the lips of the conquistadors.

The literate soldiers of the Conquest were also influenced by their reading of classic literature, especially of the romances of chivalry with their prodigious line of perfect knights and their mythical islands, Amazons, and giants, which the fantasy of the conquistadors placed in one or another part of the Indies. Some conquistadors were romantically conscious of their historical role. When some of Cortés's soldiers boasted to him that neither the Romans nor Alexander had ever performed deeds equal to theirs Cortés replied that "far more will be said in future history books about our exploits than has ever been said about those of the past."

Of the trinity of motives (God, Gold, and Glory) commonly assigned to the Spanish conquistador, the second was certainly uppermost in the minds of most. "Do not say that you are going to the Indies to serve the king and to employ your time as a brave man and an *hidalgo* should," observed Oviedo in an open letter to would-be conquistadors, "for you know the truth is just the opposite: you are going solely because you want to have a larger fortune than your father and your neighbors." Pizarro put it even more plainly to a priest who urged the need of spreading the faith among the Indians. "I have not come for any such reasons. I have come to take away from them their gold," The chronicler of the Conquest of Mexico, Bernal Díaz del Castillo, ingenuously declared that the conquistadors died "in the service of God and of His Majesty, and to give light to those who sat in darkness—and also to acquire that gold which most men covet." But Díaz wrote with the self-serving end of gaining additional rewards for his "great and notable services to the king," and his book was meant for the eyes of their grave worships, the members of the Royal Council of the Indies.

Most conquistadors dreamed of eventually returning to Spain with enough money to found a family and live in a style that would earn them the respect and admiration of their neighbors. Only a minority, chiefly large merchants and wealthy *encomenderos,* acquired the capital needed to fulfill that ambition, and not all of them returned to Spain. The majority, lacking *encomiendas* or other sources of wealth, remained and often formed ties of dependency with more powerful Spaniards, usually *encomenderos,* whose service they entered as artisans, military retainers, or overseers of the *encomiendas* or other enterprises.

After 1535 more and more would-be conquistadors came to the Indies, opportunities for joining profitable conquests diminished, and disillusioning failures abounded. The problem of a large number of unemployed and turbulent Spaniards, many of whom wandered about, robbing and abusing the Indians, caused serious concern to royal officials and to the Crown itself. One viceroy's proposed solution to rid Peru of the plague of unemployed conquistadors was to send them off on new conquests, "for it is well known that they will not work or dig or plow, and they say that they did not come to these parts to do such things." In 1555 King Carlos I (Emperor Charles V) agreed; permission for new conquests, he wrote, would serve to "rid and cleanse the country of the idle and licentious men who are there at present and who would leave to engage in that business. . . ."

Carlos therefore revoked a decree of 1549, issued at the urging of Las Casas, which prohibited new Indian conquests, and in 1559 the viceroy of Peru authorized an expedition to search for a golden kingdom rumored to exist in the heart of the Amazon. If one aim of the project was to rid Peru of "idle and licentious men," it backfired, for its abject failure produced a mutiny led by a veteran conquistador, Lope de Aguirre. He as been variously described as a forerunner of Latin American independence and a bloodthirsty madman and rebel, but in his own way he typifies the underdogs of the Conquest, the conquistadors who had lost out in the struggle for gold and *encomiendas.* Aguirre devised an audacious plan that called for the conquest of Peru, removal of its present rulers, and rewards for old conquistadors like himself who had "won those Indians with our persons and effort, spilling our blood at our expense, [but] were not rewarded." Accordingly he launched a "cruel war of fire and sword" against King Felipe II of Spain; his revolt caused many deaths, including his own, before it collapsed.

Of the many captains and their followers who rode or marched under the banner of Castile to the Conquest of America, few lived to enjoy in peace and prosperity the fruits of their valor, suffering, and cruelties. "I do not like the title of *adelantado,*" wrote Oviedo, "for actually that honor and title is an evil omen in the Indies, and many who bore it have come to an evil end." Of those who survived the battles and the marches, a few received the lion's share of spoils, land, and Indians; the majority remained in modest or worse circumstances, and frequently in debt. The conflict between the haves and the have-nots among the conquistadors, exemplified by the Aguirre revolt, contributed significantly to the explosive, tension-ridden state of affairs in the Indies in the decades following the great conquests.

See also Conquest

Select Bibliography

Altman, Ida, *Emigrants and Society: Extremadura and America in the Sixteenth Century.* Berkeley: University of California Press, 1989.

Cerwin, Herbert, *Bernal Díaz: Historian of the Conquest.* Norman: University of Oklahoma Press, 1963.

Himmerich y Valencia, Robert, *The Encomenderos of New Spain, 1521–1555.* Austin: University of Texas Press, 1991.

Kelly, John E., *Pedro de Alvarado, Conqueror.* Princeton, New Jersey: Princeton University Press, 1932.

Lockhart, James, *The Men of Cajamarca: A Social and Biographical Study of the First Conquerors of Peru.* Austin: University of Texas Press, 1972.

Thomas, Hugh, *Conquest: Montezuma, Cortés, and the Fall of Old Mexico.* New York: Simon and Schuster, 1993.

—BENJAMIN KEEN

Conservatism

Almost at the end of his life Lucas Alamán, the most organized intelligence behind Conservatism in Mexico, said of himself: "I am a dry leaf that the wind of adversity has driven to and fro." Alamán never imagined that these same words he borrowed from the Book of Job would presage the oblivion into which his political work would fall in the long term, as his "party," the Conservatives, became labeled as reactionary. This was a misleading label, however, because in its origin, Conservatism was created in reaction to the destructive and wide-ranging effects of the French Revolution, whose Mexican variant was the War of Independence. Conservatism was not, as is commonly conceived, a negation of the idea of change or progress, nor did it decry political freedom, republicanism, or the bases of elective representation. Conservative thought in Mexico, as in other countries, was just another branch on the flourishing tree of modernity, taking the English version and the writings of Edmund Burke as the best exemplar. The ancien régime (the political system in France before the Revolution) and Conservatism were terms that ended up being linked together, but they never shared the same meaning.

In Mexico a false dichotomy was soon established, with the Liberals as "the party of progress" and the Conservatives as the "reactionary party." Furthermore, a Manichean historiography soon predominated, which saw Liberalism as synonymous with federalism and Conservatism as synonymous with centralism. Nothing could have been further from reality of the Mexican historical process. Both Liberalism and federalism and Conservatism and centralism have very different doctrinal and historical backgrounds. In the post-Revolutionary France of 1789, for example, Liberalism was frequently compatible with centralism. In Mexico at the beginning of the nineteenth century, a definite pragmatism distinguished the leaders of political groups rather than a clear difference between the groups per se. Lucas Alamán was an enthusiastic Liberal in the Cortes de Cádiz (regent parliamentary council of the Spanish Empire) and secretary of foreign and state affairs in the federalist administration of the 1820s. Valentín Goméz Farías, the radical Liberal vice president (1833–34) and president (1846), was one of the 46 deputies who initially encouraged the proclamation of Agustín de Iturbide's First Mexican Empire (July 1822–March 1823). Servando Teresa de Mier was the main leader of the American group of the Constitución de Cádiz and an unimpeachable Liberal and republican in the first independent Mexican Congresses; at the same time he never stopped being either doctrinally or in practice a fierce defender of centralism. Carlos María Bustamante, a zealous defender of the heterogeneous insurgent movement and author of *Cuadro histórico*, was pro-Iturbide and Liberal in the 1820s, but by the next decade had become a partisan of centralist government and member of the Supremo Poder Conservador (Conservative Supreme Authority) of the centralist republic of 1836.

Francisco Manuel Sánchez de Tagle, who along with José María Luis Mora was one of the founders of *El Observador de la República Mexicana*, had read the works of Jeremy Bentham, the baron of Montesquieu, and Gaspar Melchor de Jovellanos from an early age. Despite this record, he later was the principal coauthor of the centralist Constitution of 1836 and secretary of the Supremo Poder Conservador of the same government. José María Gutíerrez Estrada was a republican and a Liberal in the 1820s; two decades later he had become the most obvious sponsor of a foreign constitutional monarchy. José Joaquín Pesado, author of the novel *Año nuevo* that criticized the Inquisition, a poet and government man, was also cofounder of the federalist Liberal periodical *La Oposición* (1833–34) and keen partisan of the suppression of the monasteries and confiscation of possessions belonging to religious communities in Veracruz (1833–34); nevertheless the same individual was later foreign secretary in the centralist administration of Anastasio Bustamante (1837–39), and during the short-lived "promonarchist" government of Mariano Paredes Arrillaga (1846) he was chief editor of the Catholic journal *La Cruz* (1855–58) and member of the governing council in the Félix Zuloaga–Miguel Miramón administration (1858–60).

The list could be enlarged further, but it is important to point out the lack of a simple dichotomy between federalism-liberalism, on the one hand, and centralism-conservatism, on the other. If this is the case, and if pragmatism or opportunism is evident, then why is there a problem discussing Conservatism in Mexico? Did a Conservative Party really even exist?

The answer in general terms is yes. Nevertheless, the existence of a Conservative philosophy and a Conservative political "protagonist" requires, in the first instance, temporal specificity. Conservatism in Mexico, like Liberalism, did not always remain the same; it was characterized by various protagonists and various specific features that depended on the political circumstances of the time. The study of Conservatism also makes sense in the context of a political "protagonist," rather than a political party, the former made manifest by various generations, plural ways of thinking, and above all the promotion of a national political project different from that of other political "protagonists" in the Mexican historical process. On the other hand, the notion of Conservatism becomes fragile or useless when it is explained as a monolithic and immovable entity.

The First Stage of Centralist Government

Traditional historiography has qualified the centralist republic of 1836 to 1841 as the first stage in Conservative government. The roots of this position can be found both in the automatic association between centralism and Conservatism that was assumed to counter the performance of the previous government, as well as in the political group (the names of Alamán, Sánchez de Tagle, and Gutíerrez Estrada all appear in this context) that encouraged a constitutionalism by the proclamation of the Siete Leyes (Seven Laws). Despite this theory, the events of the time indicated another course of action.

At the end of 1834, Antonio López de Santa Anna made an alliance with the political forces of Anastasio Bustamante. The reaction was basically against the structure of federalist government, but had no intention of annulling republicanism. This reaction is registered in the "Bases" (charter) for the new government of 1835, authored by Lucas Alamán. The new group in power proposed that the previous Congress took on the powers of a constituent assembly. José Ignacio de Anzorena, José María Cuevas, Antonio Pacheco Leal, Francisco Manuel Sánchez de Tagle, and Miguel Valentín were put in charge of the Constituent Commission. Even though it is evident

that there was a clear relationship between the "Bases" of Alamán and the Siete Leyes, Sánchez de Tagle is recognized as being mainly responsible for drawing up the latter.

The final result of the new Constitution was not Conservative; instead, it instituted a centralist republic with proportional and Liberal representation. The document opens with the first declaration of the rights and duties of the Mexican and foreign inhabitants of the Independent Republic of Mexico. This is in great contrast with the federalist constitution of 1824, which is more concerned with the kind of government than the preservation of the Rights of Man.

Sánchez de Tagle started from the idea that these rights and obligations emerged from a rational and social pact, in that these concrete rights of man were born in the moment that individuals associated within a collective identity. The essential point was to forge and protect through the Constitution and the relevant guarantees that which is known today as negative freedom, or the "freedom from," given that the rights of man did not need to be named. They were prescriptives, ahistorical, and inherent in man himself.

As the preservation of the rights of the Mexican citizen was the most important concern, the Constituent Commission did not eliminate the division of powers and instead modified the "classical" form. Inspired by the constitutionalist treaties of Bentham, they established a fourth power, that of the Supremo Poder Conservador (Conservative Supreme Authority). This body not only would limit the abuses of the executive and legislative powers, but also provide security and guarantee the citizenry against sudden changes in authority. The Constituent Commission also guaranteed the rights of the Mexican citizen by means of the division of powers and a certain kind of limited right of *amparo* (which loosely can be translated as a writ of habeas corpus from the executive branch).

The most obvious breaks with the Constitution of 1824 were in the projection of a centralist Republic, evidenced by variations in the electoral system and public representation. The first issue in the new Constitution divided the states into political departments with the intention of putting an end to local rule through a delicate accommodation that would follow the natural divisions of the colonial past. In reality the move was not extremist, serving only to further concentrate the administrative functions and create government councils within the political departments. In the second area the change was more radical. The democratic Liberalism adopted by the Constitution of Cádiz since 1813 and adhered to with brief interruptions ever since, was damaged gravely. An electoral system of proportional representation was set up that had not existed in the previous constitution. The number of inhabitants necessary to constitute a municipality was increased from 1,000 to 8,000, and the vote was restricted, although not immediately, to those citizens who could read and write. It was all very clear. Just like the English tradition of the eighteenth century and greater part of the nineteenth century, the constituents of 1835 to 1836 were "liberals" of the Enlightenment, not democrats.

This brings to mind the idea that if there were differences of principle between the protagonists concerning the structure of federalist and centralist government, then there also were elements of similarity between the political groups of the 1820s and 1830s. Among these points of agreement were respect for individual rights, rejection of despotic government, the permanence of a representative system, the division of public power, written constitutionalism, republicanism (as opposed to any derivative of colonial monarchism), and the pragmatism or opportunism of the Mexican political class.

Faced by this constellation of facts, the existence of a Conservative "party" in the 1830s is inconceivable in the strict sense of the word. It is not, however, in doubt that the various members, writers, governors, or assessors of the Constituent Commission of 1836 would become the future founders of the Conservative group. Alamán himself in his *Historia de México* confesses that links existed between the Conservative group of the period and the thinkers and politicians that adhered to the Scottish Masonic Rite of the 1820s and 1830s. Nevertheless, he decreed that they were not the same; these groups had gone through various alterations and changes of thought, and in the Conservative epoch of the 1840s things did not work according to the logic of the old Masonic lodges.

The Alamán Period, Apogee of Conservatism

It must be emphasized that the Conservative political protagonist with a real identity, although it still was not black-and-white, was a phenomenon of the late 1840s. If there were various thinkers of that group who could be characterized for their support of Enlightenment concepts and practical governing ability, none could touch Lucas Alamán. Alamán was the only thinker and statesman that had conceived a political project at the state level in the widest sense of the phrase. In economic matters Alamán placed his confidence in the shift from trade to manufacturing as the new basis of Mexican wealth. Government

protectionism and the private industrial enterprise were the main means of generating social progress. Alamán considered that education was a basic condition for the social and political evolution of the Mexican people. His means of achieving this was a "total education system" that would strategically place specialized colleges throughout the country.

He regarded Catholicism as being the only unifying link in the structure of Mexican society. As a result the establishment of the agreement on mutual respect between the state and the church was essential. From Alamán's perspective, this implied the protection of the privileges and economic corporativism of the church hierarchy, the nonintervention of the state in matters connected with *patronato real* (appointment of clerical positions), and the maintenance of freedom of conscience.

Alamán's *Historia de México* does not mention art and culture as a specific responsibility of government. Nevertheless Alamán the statesman was an assiduous promoter of theater groups and scientific magazines, and the founder of museums and national archives.

Alamán was the first creator of a Mexican foreign policy in support of independence and against U.S. expansionism. The line of his political romanticism did not vary: he stood for sovereignty (independent of the type of government), Catholicism, and economic self-sufficiency.

The most delicate issue at stake was the change in government structure. When Alamán wrote the fifth volume of the *Historia de México,* he was a broken man. The loss of Texas and other territories as a result of the war with the United States and the instability of the previous governments could have done no less. The mature Alamán forgot his enthusiasm for democratic Liberalism of the 1820s and the centralist republicanism of the 1830s to return to the history of Mexico and his old teacher, Edmund Burke, and his political vision. From this Alamán adopted and adapted a preference for reforms made with "pious fear and trembling solicitude," indicative of his preference for gradual as opposed to radical change as inherent in the concept of revolution. Political problems were seen in intimate relationship with issues of morality and religion; the defense of social and political differences in the citizenry were contrasted with the liberal uniformity of the French and the universalist democracies; the defense of constitutionalism and proportional representation was set against unlimited monarchism; political romanticism was contrasted with foreign universalist or expansionist concepts, and political pragmatism as opposed to paper governments;

variety and pluralism of the historical traditionalism was favored instead of French liberal uniformity and abstractionism; the defense of the "organized freedom" (associated with security of property) was contrasted with "unchained liberalism."

To sum up, the government structure favored by Alamán led him away from his clean federalist republicanism and centralism, and at the same time brought him closer to constitutional monarchy and some of the centralizing emendations of the centralist Constitution of 1836.

Federalism in Alamán's opinion favored local abstentionism and the sacrifice of "the general good for the particular." Nor was it possible to establish a system of general taxation or a national army under the federalist system. For the moment he had to strengthen the executive. As he had announced himself as being very strongly against dictatorship, he proposed first of all to restore the old colonial injunction against the viceroys. Second, even though he again restricted election of public authorities, Alamán did not eliminate political representation. He fought to change the make-up of the Congress by symmetrical and uniform systems in the provinces or political departments. This would have implied the breaking up of the large states and the rearranging of smaller ones to avoid all attempt at separatism or confederatism. At the national level the Congress would have had a single chamber—one deputy for each department—or two chambers if it was considered necessary. Alamán nevertheless allowed elective proportional representation, notably the weakening to a degree of the indirect electoral system by the holding of direct elections for the posts of deputy and president. The task of the Congress would be to legislate, approve the budget, declare war or peace, and regulate tariffs. The other chamber would be smaller than that of the deputies and not participate in the traditional elective system. It would be filled, in brief, by the representatives of governing councils of each department and the ministries of finance and justice to create the "General Council of the Nation." Alamán proposed to install a constituent congress composed of a few members for the reform of the constitution, which would operate the system of commissions and subcommissions with the participation of government agencies according to the theme and branch of business.

The Conservative group had matured by the 1840s and forged its own identity. It was necessary "to accommodate political institutions to events" and not vice versa. Historical constitutionalism supported the remaining characteristics or general principles that had made the Conservatives a political protagonist. It is worth enumerating them briefly. First, they favored gradual rather than revolutionary change. This did not imply the disappearance of the use of violence as a last resort to sustain the existence of the collective and traditions. Second, they favored political pragmatism and realism over uncontrolled abstractionism or idealism. Third, they preferred the provincial interpretation of history as the ultimate explanation of events, as opposed to secular visions. This did not imply the negation of the European Enlightenment; on the contrary there were notable connections with the movement as evidenced in the concept of freedom and property as inseparable entities. Fourth, they had faith in everyday structures instead of uniformity and liberal equality. Fifth, they viewed order and stability as the most important values for collective existence. They exchanged hierarchy for what was most prized by the Liberals: freedom.

The Conservative group participated as an organized political protagonist in the elections for the Mexico City Council in 1849. Alamán was the winning candidate, backed by the newspaper *El Universal*. Changes in government were initiated again in 1853 when Alamán invited the exiled Santa Anna to take up the Presidency once more on the condition that the two would adjust the "Bases" of the administration of the republic that had been drawn up by the Conservative leader. These "Bases" pronounced in favor of a centralist republican government and a reduced legislative council; Conservative principles were reiterated, while distance was established from the dangers of projecting a monarchical regime. Lucas Alamán and José María Tornel y Mendívil died shortly after Santa Anna took possession. Antonio de Haro y Tamariz was deposed from the presidential cabinet. These events gave way to the tyranny of 1853 to 1855 that had no connection with what had been the first exercise in Conservative government, in the strict sense of the word.

The Monarchist Period

Monarchism was without a doubt a further vein of Conservatism in Mexico, but paradoxically not all monarchs had a conservative identity. The political survival of monarchism both preceded and accompanied the creation of the Mexican state. The Spanish Empire, of which New Spain formed a part, lasted three centuries; the Empire of Iturbide only seven months. Prior to the declaration of the federalist Constitution of 1824, there were different prmonarchist factions in the various constituent congresses. In January 1827 Father Joaquín Arenas created a chimerical plan to reestablish Spanish dominion over Mexico and restore the old relationship with the Vatican state. The same luck befell the plan of the curates Carlos Tepisteco and Epigmenio de la Piedra (February 1834) to establish a constitutional indigenous monarchy and maintain the Catholic faith.

Even so, the true association between Conservatism and monarchism arose parallel with the political existence of the latter. The most outstanding figure of this Conservative tendency was José María Gutiérrez Estrada. In 1840 he sent an open letter in which he proposed the formation of a new Constituent Congress. In his opinion, republicanism, be it centrist or federalist, had led only to oppression and anarchy. The party struggle had made necessary a third element to balance the forces. From his perspective, liberty and monarchy were not incompatible terms, nor were despotism and monarchy synonymous. For this reason the constitution should not be suppressed, nor the elective office. The monarch tended to act as protector of the people and the chosen electoral system. Gutiérrez Estrada imagined a proportional system like that proposed in the Constitution of 1836. His preference for a foreign sovereign with royal blood was based both on the three-century-old colonial tradition and the defense of Catholicism against Protestantism as well as his prophetic anticipation of territorial expansionism of the United States. He knew, as an avid reader of Montesquieu, that the best way of governing was not the most modern but that which "best accommodated the customs, morality, and particular circumstances of each country." Disheartened, he believed in the 1840s that monarchy would be the best system to preserve Mexican independence. On a rational basis Gutiérrez Estrada adopted the monarchic system but his "heart," as he himself said, "was purely and sincerely republican."

The monarchic possibility annoyed the military partisans, who preferred to conspire in secret. The scandal was so great that Gutiérrez Estrada was exiled and obliged to depart for Europe. Even so, the promonarchists returned to take power in 1846 with the coup d'état of Mariano Paredes y Arrillaga. The participation of the plenipotentiary of Spain, Salvador Bermúdez de Castro, and that of Manuel Sánchez de Tagle and Lucas Alamán in their capacity as journalists for the periodical El Tiempo are noteworthy in this case. Both of them publicly declared themselves to be sympathizers of constitutional monarchy. The reasons they gave were not substantially different from those voiced by Gutiérrez Estrada. What they did not count on was that the U. S. intervention would weaken their hopes for a monarchy. When the Constituent Congress reunited in June 1846 no one dared to defend monarchism as a form of government. The Constitution of 1824 was redeclared, and the presidency handed over to Santa Anna. Paredes y Arrillaga was banished, never to make any further substantial contribution to Mexican politics.

The return of the Conservatives would not occur until the Catholic opposition to the Constitution of 1857, the War of the Reform (1858–61), and the French Intervention (1862–67). This was in fact the historical period, the Reform especially, in which the antagonism between Liberals and Conservatives is most clearly seen. Paradoxically, the Conservatism defended in this period lacked a serious program. It explored Catholicism (Clemente de Jesús Munguía, José Joaquín Pesado, and José María Roa Bárcena), militarism (Félix Zuloaga and Miguel Miramón), and monarchism (Gutiérrez Estrada, Father Francisco Javier Miranda, Emperor Maximilian von Hapsburg, and Miramón) but never proposed a wide-ranging national program as had Lucas Alamán in his time. Moreover, the search for a foreign prince in 1863 ended with a counter-productive measure for the Conservatives. Maximilian was, in many senses, a Liberal. The alliance between the government of the United States and Juárez simply annihilated them. At the end of the Restored Republic (1867–77), the Conservatives tried to make a comeback in the elections of 1877 but were roundly defeated. From then on Conservatism in Mexico transformed into a socio-religious phenomenon or the political stance of isolated individuals that gradually became diluted in the first stage of the Porfirio Díaz's rule.

See also French Intervention; Liberalism; Wars of Reform

Select Bibliography
Pascal Gargiulo, Jeanne G., "Lucas Alamán, Mexican Conservatism, and The United States: A History of Attitudes and Policy, 1823–1853." Ph.D. diss., Fordham University, 1992.

—ISRAEL ARROYO GARCÍA

Constitution of 1917

The Plan of Guadalupe of December 26, 1913, which laid the foundations of the Constitionalist faction headed by Venustiano Carranza, was the product of the Mexican Revolution and the banishment of Victoriano Huerta. Although established according to the Constitution of 1857, the Additions to the Plan of Guadalupe were to promote substantial reforms to that document. Promulgated in Veracruz on December 12, 1914, they saw the need to legally adopt social measures and to reorganize governmental authority, given the events of the Revolution. Government in its turn was reformed explicitly to summon a constitutional congress on September 14, 1916.

These reforms would comprise what would be known henceforth as the Constitution of 1917. Of course the form or procedure of reforming the text of the 1857 Constitution by means of an ad hoc Constitutional Congress provoked tremendous criticism from the detractors of the Constitutionalists. Among the latter were Jorge Vera Estañol, the minister of justice under Victoriano Huerta, who in exile wrote *Al margen del la Constitución,* published in Los Angeles in 1920. Such men considered that these reforms to the 1857 Constitution were not in agreement with the procedure laid out in that very document. It must be recalled that many constitutional reforms had followed different procedures to those laid down by constitutional law in the political history of Mexico. The Reform Act of 1847 did not stick to the procedure laid down by the Constitution of 1824, and the Constitution of 1857 itself had been passed by an Extraordinary Congress, without following any regular procedure at all. All this proved that in exceptional circumstances, such as the American invasion in the first instance or the Revolt of Ayutla against Antonio López de Santa Anna in the second example, a congress had been convened to make substantial reforms that did not stick to procedures established by the previous constitution.

Once summoned, this new Constitutional Congress differed from preceding ones in various particulars. First, it took place in Querétaro, rather than Mexico City, to avoid any accusation of being centralist. Second, only reform projects would be debated by the Congress, and no other matter, contrary to what had occurred with other Congresses. Finally, the election of the deputies to the Congress was made directly and their election verified on October 22, 1916, in accordance with the convocation of September 19, of the same year.

Membership of the Congress was various, as evidenced in the results of the debates. There were 232 landowning deputies with their respective aides. Chihuahua only had one deputy since the territory was largely occupied by Francisco Villa, at that time in opposition to Carranza, but there was adequate representation for the remaining states. Among the membership were close collaborators of Carranza such as Pastor Rouaix, Gerzayn Ugarte, and Cándido Aguilar. Luis Manuel Rojas, who was also collaborating in the Federal Public Administration, presided over the Congress, while José Natividad Macías was president of the Constitutional Commission.

The process of certifying representatives to the Congress lasted from November 21 to December 1, 1916. Despite some individual cases, the matter was considered to be advanced by December. On December 6, the projected reforms to the Constitution were made known and decisions began to be issued three days later. The commissions within the Congress distributed their decisions by title. The first commission, composed of Francisco J. Múgica, Alberto Román, Luis G. Monzón, Enrique Rocio, and Enrique Colunga, dealt with human rights or individual guarantees. The second commission, dealing with the government, the form it should take and its powers, was composed of Paulino Machorro Narváez, Heriberto Jara, Agustín Garza González, Arturo Méndoza, and Hilario Medina.

The most notable debates were those on education, agrarian reform, and work. There is no doubt that the most dramatic contribution was the inclusion within the Constitution of social guarantees for the protection of industrial and agricultural labor. Such guarantees fell outside the traditional bounds of Constitutional subject matter—primarily the establishment of individual rights and the organization of political power—as had been determined from the eighteenth century with the Declaration of the Rights of Man. What previously had been considered as belonging to the realm of legal regulations was regarded by the Constitution of Querétaro as mandatory within the the new constitutional arrangements. Changes were less spectacular in the area of governmental powers, since the Senate already had been reestablished in a reform of 1874. The presidential succession had been transformed in 1882, and the clause prohibiting reelection had been imposed in the reform of 1911. Nevertheless, aspects such as the strengthening of the presidential system over the parliamentary system (as originally conceived in 1857) and the suppression of political bosses to free up the municipalities were notable changes in the reformed Constitution.

The sessions continued until January 12, 1917. To commemorate the Constitution that they were so substantially altering, the new one was promulgated on February 5, 1917; it was published exactly one week later and became law on May 1.

As a result of the Constitution of 1917, the fifth term of the *Semanario Judicial de la Federación*

(Weekly Gazette of the Federal Judiciary), which began on June 1 the same year, presented new constitutional interpretations elaborated by the federal judiciary. Even though the previous four terms, the first of which was initiated in 1871, were decided by the federal courts at top level, they now were consulted and occasionally cited but generally considered as historical anachronisms since they were interpreting the Constitution of 1857; the reforms of 1917 generally were considered to be so substantial as to create a new Constitution entirely.

From July 8, 1921, until mid-1996, there have been 102 decrees that have legally reformed the 136 articles that make up the Constitution of 1917, not including the temporary clauses. Only 38 articles have not suffered a single alteration since 1917. In a long history of modifications, the article that has been altered the most, 34 times to be precise, is number 73, which dealt with the powers wielded by Congress. Given that Mexico has a rigid system of competition between the federal government and the individual states, according to Article 124, which is more appropriate for a confederation than a federation, each time that the federal government wishes to take up an additional responsibility, the Constitution has to be reformed to include the new jurisdiction. This has been the situation since 1883, when for the first time the exclusive power of the federation to legislate on commercial matters appeared. Form this moment the federal government has continued to exclusively take on the regulation of topics of greater consequence.

From the 1970s one can see a tendency towards cooperative federalism, which now operates through education, health, ecology, and urban housing. Areas of competence in these topics, which are expressly discussed within the Constitution, are divided according to congressional law between the federal government, the states, and the municipalities.

The Constitution also imposed a concurrent system on state and federal government, given that the municipalities do not have legislative powers, which provides the federal government with two means of taxation. First, it can impose all those taxes or contributions it judges sufficient to satisfy public expenditure (Article 73, Section 7); second, it can reserve exclusively certain taxes such as those derived from foreign trade and petroleum, thus excluding state government from being concurrent in tax imposition in important materials (Article 73, Section 29).

The Congress of the Union is unique in having a Senate; this mechanism disappeared at the state level at the same time as it originally was eliminated on a federal level in 1857. Although the Senate was restored within federal government in 1874, this did not occur at state level.

The Mexican legislative process has peculiar constitutional characteristics, since a hierarchy of laws has not been totally defined in the country. The presence of exclusive and excluding power for the federal government in tandem with reserve powers for the states means that federal and state laws cannot clash given their separate areas of competence. If some of these laws appear to enter into conflict, it is only necessary to determine their constitutionality to the extent that they have overrun the strict distribution of competence.

According to Article 72 of the Constitution, legal reform must coincide with the procedure followed to make the law in the first place (in other words by the same legislative organ and observing the same process). Thus in the case of an international treaty, which always is ratified by the Senate without the participation of the Chamber of Deputies, the approving decree does not follow the same agenda as a regular law, since treaties and laws cannot modify each other within the Mexican constitutional system.

The federal executive power was strengthened by the Constitution of 1917; it made the president politically not responsible to the Congress of the Union and unable to be prosecuted other than for transgressions against the law, betrayal of his country, and serious crimes. This Constitution suppressed the vice presidency, which had been reestablished in 1904, in a reform to the previous Constitution, stating that in the case of total absence of a vice presidential successor, the Congress of the Union would take over. The six-year presidency was abolished in 1917, only to be reestablished in 1928. From 1824 the executive power was unified and absolutely free to nominate and remove secretaries of state and those responsible for public agencies that participate within the administration. The power held by the president of the United States as regards the military and international relations is very similar to that established for Mexico in the 1917 Constitution.

No reelection has been a principle since 1833, for which reason the president cannot be reelected. Nevertheless the Mexican president is intimately linked to the destiny of the political party that promoted him, and through this position his limited constitutional powers are increased to control the political life of the nation. Mexico differs from the old socialist countries in that the president of the Republic in turn controls the political party when in power and not the reverse.

The power of the federal judiciary has evolved through a ruling of varied nature: the decision of *amparo* (legal protection). From its creation in 1847, this legal ruling protected the people's human rights and individual guarantees from executive or legislative acts as well as decisions of the judiciary at the state level. Nevertheless, the ruling of *amparo* has become a control mechanism of constitutionalism. From 1869 the law of *amparo* could change the sentences of higher courts in every state when these overstepped an individual guarantee, for example when the letter of the law is not applied "exactly," according to Article 14. The organization of the judiciary is very similar to that of the United States, with 11 ministers in the Supreme Court, collegiate and circuit courts (established since 1950), as well as district juries.

In December 1994 the Council of Judicature was created by means of the corresponding constitutional reform that put the administrative functions of the federal judiciary and the appointment of federal judges within the ambit of the Supreme Court.

—MANUEL GONZÁLEZ OROPEZA

Corridos

The *corrido* is a narrative song genre, a ballad form, that has served as a popular commentary on the events shaping Mexican history over the last hundred years. Related to similar song traditions among Mediterranean peoples and their American offshoots, the Mexican *corrido* has taken root in the imagination of Mexico as no other member of this cluster has in any other setting, attaining in Mexico something of the prominence of its progenitor, the Spanish *romance*, during its heyday in sixteenth-century Spain. Pervaded by an attitude of indifference towards death, the *corrido* evidently draws as well on a backdrop of indigenous Mexican sentiment, belief, and expression.

The term *corrido* derives from a label applied in Spain to a particular sort of *romance,* the broad term used at first to designate any poem in the vernacular language, and later to encompass the diversified tradition of Spanish narrative poetry and song. A *romance corrido* was a through-sung ballad that became popular at the height of the Spanish exploration and settlement of the colonies. Later, in New Spain and eventually Mexico, the term *romance* was dropped and the off-shoot of the tradition became known simply as the *corrido*.

The European antecedents of this narrative song tradition were brought to the Americas by Spanish soldiers, missionaries, and settlers. The chronicles of the Conquest provide evidence of the importance the ballads held in the imagination of this first wave of Europeans in the Americas. In several passages the chroniclers call to mind lines and verses from the *romances* as they contemplate events or scenes encountered in New Spain. For example, Bernal Díaz del Castillo, loyal witness of the Conquest of what was to become Nueva Espana and later, Mexico, cites a number of dramatic moments and incidents that brought lines from the "old romances" to the minds of Fernando (Hernán) Cortes and the soldiers in his retinue. The Spanish authority Ramón Menéndez Pidal views these instances as part of a general pattern:

> Surely in the memory of every captain, of every soldier, of every merchant, went along something of the extremely popular Spanish romancero, as a reminder of a revered childhood often to sweeten the sentiment of loneliness for the home country, to lessen the boredom of those endless trips or the fear of the adventures awaiting them in the unknown world they set foot on.

Remnants of the old ballads are reported in every niche of Spanish America, from Argentina and Chile to New Mexico, and variants in Portuguese have been found in most regions of Brazil.

But the Mexican *corrido* is not a regional vestige of a European ballad tradition. In Mexico, to a degree unrivaled elsewhere in the Americas, these narrative roots produced what the Mexican-American scholar Américo Paredes calls "a living ballad tradition," a practice of creating and performing narrative song in response to events affecting local communities. In the living ballad tradition, the singers no longer focus on the old stories about the Spanish nobility, of exploits in the Reconquest of the peninsula. They sing instead about the heroes and villains of their own time and place, of contemporary events that leave a mark on the community or the nation. The term *corrido* has been reported elsewhere in Latin America, notably in Colombia, Argentina, Cuba, and Venezuela, and there is evidence of narrative song approximating the *corrido* in these and other areas, but only in Mexico does this narrative potential flourish into a tradition so prevalent as to be almost atmospheric.

The first substantial evidence of *corridos* in Mexico traces to the middle of the nineteenth century. A few ballad-like lines and stanzas are preserved from the early decades of that century, but the earliest texts that exhibit the *corrido* style date to the 1860s and 1870s. Scholars have puzzled over this hiatus, the barren years between the arrival of the *romance* and the emergence of the *corrido*. The dean of Mexican ballad scholars, Vicente T. Mendoza, imagined a continuous line of ballad production in Mexico in forms such as the *décima,* and saw the *corrido* as evolving out of this tradition of narrative song during the second half of the nineteenth century.

If the *corrido* is hard to detect in the historical record until the closing decades of the previous century, it comes squarely into its own as a popular chronicle of the Mexican Revolution and the ethnic conflict along the Texas-Mexican border at the outset of the twentieth century. During the Revolution, *corridos* were produced by those close to the fighting as well as by hacks working from newspaper accounts in Mexico City. They were circulated through performances by wandering troubadors and musicians tied to particular factions in the struggles, and through a broadside ballad industry that manufactured and distributed *ojas sueltas* or "loose sheets" with ballad lyrics and emblematic woodcarvings. The broadsides issued by Antonio Vanegas Arroyo with the collaboration of the artist José Guadalupe Posada, many of them preserved in modern collections, testify to the vitality and reach of this publishing venture. There are numerous accounts of blind singers and other troubadors performing these ballads and selling the broadsides in the squares, markets, and plazas of Mexican cities, towns, and villages. The poetic activity of local composers as well as city interpreters assured a diversified stylistic profile for the genre, in which the local ballads stand out for their simple strength of language.

In the aftermath of the Revolution, the popular *corrido* persisted as a running narrative of conflict and violent confrontation associated with outlaw bands and local strongmen. At the same time, the newly nationalistic literati discovered in the *corrido* the authentic voice of the Mexican people, and during the 1920s and 1930s the genre inspired pictorial, poetic, and musical treatments by the artistic elite of the nation. Thus the circle surrounding Frida Kahlo and Diego Rivera held *corrido* evenings, and the mural movement associated with Rivera, José Clemente Orozco, and David Alfaro Siqueiros drew its epic sweep in part from the powerful *corrido* narratives. Under the spell of this post-Revolutionary nationalism, the dean of Mexican composers, Carlos Chávez, wrote in 1934 *El Sol,* a Mexican *corrido* for mixed choir and large orchestra.

As the twentieth century reached its midpoint, the *corrido* had evolved into a new phase in its development as the ballad of contemporary Mexico. The second half of this century saw the *corrido* retain considerable importance as a body of national history commemorating the deeds of the heroes, as a resource for political messages from both the government and its opponents, and as a local chronicle of violent encounters in several *corrido* pockets around the country. Most recently, the genre has experienced a revival through popular and commercial renderings of events tied to the trade in illegal drugs. Commercial recording groups such as Los Tigres del Norte routinely include *corridos* of this ilk on their new releases, and even *banda* music, the dance sensation of the early 1990s, includes newly composed *corridos*. This body of commercial releases dispenses with some of the formalities but remains clearly oriented to the *corrido* tradition as it depicts the clash of federal forces with the *traficantes* (drug traffickers), the accumulation of fortunes, and the early deaths of those involved in this business.

Corrido as Expressive Form

The *corrido* can be characterized broadly as a genre of narrative song, but within the confines of the genre there is room for a great deal of diversity in style, form, and content. Perhaps the most typical *corrido* is the *corrido trágico*, often consisting of stanzas of eight-syllable lines exhibiting assonance or rhyme on the even-numbered lines, and telling in third-person narrative discourse of events involving mortal danger or loss of life. These *corridos* normally open with an introductory stanza in which the singer requests the indulgence of the audience:

> Voy a cantar un corrido
> para los que me están oyendo. . . .
> (I will sing a *corrido*
> for those who are listening to me. . . .)
>
> . . .
>
> Para cantar un corrido
> pido permiso primero. . . .
> (In order to sing a *corrido*
> I ask permission first. . . .)
>
> . . .
>
> Voy a cantar un corrido
> sin agravio y sin disgusto. . . .
> (I will sing a *corrido*
> without malice and without anger. . . .)

These polite opening formulas establish a zone of safe social interaction for the ensuing performance of the song. The *corrido* normally closes with the singer's *despedida*, or farewell, using phrases such as *Ya con esta me despido* (Now with this I take my leave) and *Ya me voy a despedir* (Now I am going to say farewell). Between these framing stanzas, the typical tragic *corrido* sets the scene for the action, often providing the names of protagonists, place names, and dates and times of action, and then moves on to narrate the action, often featuring the exchange of words among protagonists in a state of mortal conflict. In these ballads, the heroes are men of action and of words, and in many instances the *corridos* place primary emphasis on the defiant statements of the protagonists.

But many other kinds of *corridos* are recognized and accepted by the Mexican public as valid members of the genre. One prominent sub-form is the *bola suriana*, cultivated in Morelos and Guerrero, a narrative song consisting in specific combinations of eight- and twelve-syllable lines. *Corridos* need not deal with violent encounters at all; there are first-person narratives of prisoners and drunkards, lyrical songs of love and love lost, tales of memorable horse races, and even humorous *corridos* making fun of pretentious language or telling tales about enormous fleas and other exaggerations. At one extreme, virtually any popular song with a narrative component can be included within the *corrido* genre. In various contexts, people will make finer distinctions, and at the heart of the genre one finds the *corrido trágico*, with its evocation of heroes confronting scenes of mortal danger.

The music of the *corrido* is also open to a range of forms and styles. Some *corrido* tunes are *paso-dobles,* set to the lively rhythm of the bullfighting arena; others are in triple rhythms like the waltz or double rhythms similar to those found in many popular *ranchero* or *norteño* tunes. The melodies are in major keys except on the Costa Chica of Guerrero, where minor keys also appear, giving these *corridos* the aura of dirge or lament. There are several families of *corrido* melodies, with new melodies formed by minor alterations of existing melodies, and existing melodies often reused with new *corrido* lyrics. The instrumentation also varies, although the basic requirement is a guitar. From this minimal unit, the singer and guitar accompaniment, instruments can be added in accordance with the regional taste in ensemble playing: in the north, the ubiquitous accordion, often with electric bass and rhythm guitar; in the central mesa, the mariachi orchestra; in the south, the harp. In rural settings *corrido* singers even will hold forth against the raucous background of a brass-band accompaniment.

Corridos are composed by individuals recognized for this ability and are learned and to some degree recomposed by the musicians who perform them. It is interesting to follow the fate of a local *corrido*, composed by someone in the community and performed by this person or passed on to singers known to him. Some local *corridos* perish without achieving further recognition. Others become part of a local repertoire and may persist in a recognizable form through two or more generations of singers. Occasionally a local *corrido* arrives at the national level, as in the case of "Simón Blanco," a ballad about the assassination of a gentleman in a town on the outskirts of Acapulco, Guerrero, probably in the 1930s. A few old-timers recall the original ballad that must have begun to circulate shortly after the event. From this original a standard ballad has emerged, shorn of local names and details and reduced to less than half its size, but preserving the core element of *compadre* murder. Influential in this process has been the release of recorded versions fixing the shortened ballad in people's memories.

The *corrido* today is a major treasure of the Mexican people, recognized throughout the nation as a body of narrative song commemorating the heroes of the Revolutionary past. Ballads about Pancho Villa and Emiliano Zapata and a host of lesser figures enjoy the status of national balladry, performed at local venues, recorded on commercial records, tapes, and disks, and even celebrated in Mexican cinema. Concurrent with this national presence is the persistence of the *corrido*-making tradition in specific pockets of the nation, mostly in rural areas with a *ranchero* background, and in urban areas among working-class males. *Corridos* are heard in cantinas, in public spaces, on the radio, and at private homes. There is a checkered pattern to the distribution of interest in the *corrido*. Some regions, especially those dominated by the presence of indigenous communities, evince little interest in the genre; others display a historical *corrido* tradition that is now largely inactive; and others exhibit a continuous *corrido* trajectory from the Revolutionary period to the present. In active *corrido* areas, some individuals are deeply involved with the genre, while others are indifferent or even hostile to it. Women are less involved than men, although there are female performers of *corridos,* and women are active as audience members during *corrido* performances in homes and in public venues.

Controversies and Issues

The *corrido* has spawned a number of controversies, both among the general population and among scholars of Mexican culture and politics. Perhaps the most dramatic controversy has revolved around the argument that the *corrido* is of indigenous rather than

European origins. The highly respected scholar and author, and also composer of *corridos,* Celedonio Serrano Martínez, has forcefully argued against tracing the *corrido* to the Spanish *romance.* Correctly pointing out that the *corrido* cannot be reduced to one of its major prototypes, the *romance*-derived octosyllabic quatrain with assonance on the even lines, Serrano Martínez argues for an origin in the narrative poetry and song of the indigenous cultures of Mexico. There is, of course, ample evidence for narrative song traditions among the Mexica (Aztecs) and other major groups, although the available examples do not closely resemble *corrido* discourse. At the same time, for all the similarity in form and content between *corridos* and *romances,* there is a distinctive flavor to the *corrido,* evident in the defiant attitude of the hero, his indifference toward death, that could derive from indigenous sources. The wisest position to adopt in this crossfire is a probable and difficult to decipher conjoining of Europe and America in the *corrido,* a conclusion that seems reasonable in assessing the origins of most of Mexico's cultural forms.

Another interesting controversy lies in the overall function of the *corrido.* Scholars have tended to view the *corrido* as a kind of oral newspaper, spreading word of catastrophic events in its stanzas about accidents, acts of nature, and violent confrontations. It is likely that at some times and in some places the genre has operated to this effect. But another, deeper role can be discovered through an inspection of the *corrido* in its local settings, that of commemorating significant heroes and episodes affecting the community. In these settings, news of violent confrontations, deadly accidents, or devastating acts of nature, circulates by word of mouth before the *corridos* arrive. The narratives in such *corridos* are often dependent on prior awareness of these core events. The *corridos* enter the scene not to inform but to commemorate, to propose in the artistic guise of poetry set to music an interpretation of events already widely known to the public. This commemorative intent is evident in the sometimes intermittent quality of narrative, presupposing and building upon local knowledge. In this process ordinary events often are assimilated to the heroic archetype of the hero standing firm in the face of mortal danger.

The *corrido trágico* raises interesting issues regarding the association of poetry and violence. The genre flourishes in areas where violence has remained endemic, and it takes this violence as the centerpiece of its narratives. The distinguished Mexican scholar Gonzalo Aguirre Beltrán saw in the *corridos* of Guerrero's Costa Chica the manifestation of an aggressive ethos, and he saw the heroes in these Costa Chica *corridos* as role models for the young men of the region. There is evidence to suggest that some men do attempt to imitate the life of these heroes, a life of fast living and early death. On inspection, however, another editorial posture can be detected, one that seeks to impose on the narrated events a moral consciousness, a sense of destiny based on the consequences of actions taken in a world presided over but not closely managed by a just God. Thus, when Simón Blanco is killed by his *compadre* and the Martínez boys, it is not surprising that in a short time these assassins themselves perish, for to kill a *compadre* is "to offend the Eternal":

> A los tres días de muerto
> se fallecieron los Martínez,
> decían en su novenario
> que eso encerraba un misterio,
> porque matar a un compadre
> es ofender al eterno.
> (When he was dead three days
> the Martínez boys passed away,
> they were saying at their wake
> that this thing held a mystery,
> for to kill a *compadre*
> is to offend the eternal one.)

Likewise, when Nicho Esteven is killed, his own mother has to admit that it was God's will:

> Estaría de Dios que pagaras
> la muerte de dos criaturas.
> (It would be God's will you repay
> the death of two little children.)

These interpretive touches offer another dimension to the *corrido*'s handling of violence, one that seeks to understand it, to place it in a larger interpretive framework, rather than simply to promote it.

In areas where *corridos* still are being composed, the attitude of the general public is that the *corrido,* unlike other resources such as newspaper and official accounts, delivers the real truth. One is frequently told to disregard the stories in the newspapers and wait for the true story in the *corridos.* Expressions such as *dice la pura verdad* (it tells the pure truth) and *son verídicos* (they are really true) are used in assessing the truth value of the *corrido.* Thus it is interesting to hear composers explain things rather differently. Composers stress their efforts to secure reliable information from first- or second-hand sources; they read the newspaper accounts and listen in on the public discussion of events in formulating their poetic narratives. But within this commitment to accuracy there is also a recognition that the whole truth can rarely be presented, for fear of offending one party or another, of stirring up additional trouble, even out of concern for one's own security. Specifying in public verse the perpetrators of murder can fan factional disputes, and direct allegations of cowardice or villainy can arouse a desire for vengeance. Moreover, in the politically charged climate of contemporary Mexico, the authorities do not react kindly to *corrido* composers who fashion narratives presenting the government in an unflattering light. *Corrido* composers tread a fine line between two conflicting goals, telling the truth as far as possible while guarding against unwanted complications.

The *corrido* always has gravitated toward expressing the viewpoint of *los de abajo,* the underdogs, the marginalized classes. The *corrido* hero is typically a revolutionary fighting the power of the state, a border hero resisting the onslaught of the *americanos,* a local man standing up against the encroachment of the national or state authorities, a drug runner hoping to make a quick fortune. There are *corridos* written as overt protest song, but their ideological language sets them apart from the typical *corridos* wherein opposition is expressed indirectly and implicitly. The paradigm is the hero of the Revolution, taking up arms against an abusive central government. *Corridos* from the Revolutionary period assimilate their protagonists to the heroic archetype, leaving unstated the often barbaric activities for which they were responsible. The contemporary *corrido* hero acquires something of the luster of these Revolutionary figures owing to a common motif of standing against the government in a context where national and state authorities have yet to establish their legitimacy in the eyes of the general public.

Select Bibliography

Herrera, Hayden, *Frida: A Biography of Frida Kahlo.* New York: Harper and Row, 1983.

McDowell, John, "Folklore as Commemorative Discourse." *Journal of American Folklore* 105 (1992).

Paredes, Américo, "The Ancestry of Mexico's *Corridos*: A Matter of Definitions." *Journal of American Folklore* 76 (1963).

Simmons, Merle, "The Ancestry of Mexico's *Corridos.*" *Journal of American Folklore* 76 (1963).

—JOHN HOLMES MCDOWELL

Cortés, Fernando (Hernán)
1484 or 1485–1547

Conquistador

Fernando Cortés (better but erroneously known as Hernán or Hernando Cortez) was a greedy entrepreneur who sought and found personal aggrandizement for himself and his progeny; he was also a faithful, if ruthless, crusader who sought and found greater glory for his God and his monarch. Cortés was born in Medellín in the kingdom of Castile in 1484 or 1485, when Desiderius Erasmus was probably 18 or 19 and Martin Luther was a babe of one or two. He died in Castilleja de la Cuesta in Castile on December 2, 1547, as infamous in his Catholic world as Luther who died the year before, and more famous than Erasmus who died 21 years earlier.

His parents, Martin Cortés de Monroy and Catalina Pizarro Altamirano, were of modest circumstance but of noble and honorable Castillian families. Fernando Cortés himself had four legitimate heirs, the children of his second wife, Juana de Zúñiga: Martín, María, Catalina, and Juana. He also had five illegitimate but recognized heirs: Martín, son of doña Marina (La Malinche), his indigenous American translator; Luís, son of a Spanish woman named Antonia Hermosillo; Leonor, daughter of Techiupo (Isabel Moteuczoma), sister of the Mexica (Aztec) chieftain, Moteuczoma II; Catalina, daughter of a Cuban Indian woman called Leonor Pizarro; and another daughter born of an Indian woman, neither of whose names are known.

Following a childhood of which we know little, Fernando Cortés was sent to Salamanca in Castile when he was thirteen or fourteen to study grammar and law and to live with his aunt, Iñez de Paz, and her husband, Francisco Nuñez de Valera. Although some combination of restless ambition, lack of funds, adolescent amorousness, and re-occurring illness brought him back to Medellín after two years, the education he received in that well-known university town served him very well in later years as a notary, chronicler, governor, and captain general. At age 19 or 20 he set out to seek his fortune, and before him were two enterprises that promised great adventure and fortune.

Outfitting for major expeditions to Naples and to the West Indies ordered by their monarch, Fernando II, were two tried and trusted royal officers, *el gran capitán* Gonzalo Fernández de Córdoba and fray Nicolás de Ovando, newly appointed governor of the Spanish Indies.

Distantly related and well known to the latter and apparently at least known to the former, Cortés joined Ovando's group in Seville but, felled by an amorous adventure, he failed to sail with it. He then set out for Valencia to join the Naples venture, but for unknown reasons did not do so. After traveling in Castile and another sojourn in Medellín, he left again for Seville in 1506 with funds provided by his father to join a merchandise fleet of five ships preparing to sail to the West Indies. This time he sailed to the island of Hispaniola (modern-day Haiti and the Dominican Republic). There his familial relationship to Ovando soon led to participation in several campaigns on the island, directed at subjecting the native Arawak peoples to Spanish colonial authority.

For his services Cortés received an assignment of Indians in *encomienda,* which provided him a labor force to which no wages had to be paid, some land, and an appointment as *escribano,* or notary, for the newly founded town of Azúa. These emoluments provided the basis for his first entrepreneurial activities, which included trade, livestock, and perhaps sugar cane, all of which apparently were profitable. His services also placed him among Ovando's chief lieutenants, such as Diego Velázquez, a former companion of Christopher Columbus and one of Hispaniola's wealthiest citizens.

In 1511, Ovando's replacement as governor of the West Indies, Diego Colón (son of Christopher Columbus), commissioned Velázquez to undertake a punitive expedition to Cuba to bring that island under Spanish control. Cortés accompanied as chief deputy to the royal treasurer for the expedition. During the eight years that followed, Cortés secured additional *encomienda* grants as well as lands including some in the newly established towns of Baracoa and Santiago de Cuba. Using some of his *encomienda* laborers he successfully panned the rivers in eastern Cuba for gold, and he may have established a foundry and developed a sugar plantation. Although he and Velázquez, now governor of Cuba, had differed often, in 1518 they were allies and Cortés was serving as *alcalde,* or chief magistrate, of Santiago. He was married to Catalina Suárez, had an illegitimate but recognized daughter and was a leading citizen of the Spanish Indies. That year Velázquez selected Cortés to lead an expedition to follow those dispatched in 1517 and 1518 under the commands of Hernández de Córdoba and Juan de Grijalva to explore along the Gulf Coast of today's Mexico. Velázquez chose him in part because Cortés had the necessary wealth to finance a major part of the effort and sufficient status in the colonial community to command it.

Using personal and borrowed funds, Velázquez and Cortés, evidently as equal partners, assembled an expeditionary force that ultimately composed 11 ships, 530 men, 16 horses, a large supply of armaments including some cannons, and a larder of foodstuffs. In mid-November 1518 as the expedition prepared to sail, Velázquez, having grown suspicious once again of Cortés's reckless independence and growing popularity, tried to relieve him of its command. Cortés, warned about Velázquez's intentions, stealthily hastened the expedition to sail on November 18, 1518.

The events that took place from 1518 to 1521 demonstrated Cortés's audacious and effective leadership, his military prowess, his superior political skills, and his uncanny luck. Foremost among these events were his acquisition of two interpreters of the primary languages and cultures of the Maya, Mexica, and neighboring Indian states: the Spanish castaway, fray Gerónimo de Aguilar, and the formerly enslaved indigenous noble woman, doña Marina; the astute founding of the town of Veracruz and use of its town council, or *cabildo,* to legitimate his leadership and to communicate directly with his monarch in Spain; the burning of all of his ships save those sent back to Spain to prevent the mutiny and retreat to Cuba threatened by the followers of Velázquez in his expeditionary force; his use of the fragmented character of the Mexica state and the presence around it of peoples who had successfully resisted domination by it to garner allies who helped force the Mexica to accept domination; his manipulation of the indigenous people's beliefs and traditions; his decisive conversion of the forces sent by Velázquez into allies and much-needed reinforcements, even though Velázquez had dispatched these forces precisely to take control of the Mexican expeditionary effort out of Cortés's hands; and his imaginative besiegement of Tenochtitlan after his forces had been driven from its temples and causeways (Cortés's besiegement techniques included the construction of ships and use of his principal Indian allies, the Tlaxcaltecans, to cut off the city's waterway avenues to supplies and reinforcements).

Emerging from the struggles with the Mexica not only as their master and a hero among his countrymen but as a brutally destructive and greedy conqueror suspected of a disregard for established authority, Cortés set about the establishment of Spanish colonial agencies and sent several of his lieutenants outward from Tenochtitlan–Mexico City to bring other areas of what are today central, northeastern and southern Mexico and Guatemala under his control. He undertook these talks from the fall of 1521 until the tall of 1527, first as a self-anointed governor and captain general and, the, after October 25, 1522, as a formally appointed official with both of those titles. Despite the fact that the Spanish monarch had forbade any further use of the *encomienda* system (by which the indigenous population was forced to labor for European overlords) because the system appeared to have been a major contributor to the decimation of the Indian populations and because the system was vilified as un-Christian by such Spanish missionary clergy as Bartolomé de Las Casas, Cortés began making *encomienda* assignments of Mexica and other subjected peoples of the central Mexican area and using those assignments to reward himself and his followers. As he did so, he used the Mexica and other tribal systems of tribute or taxes in goods and required labor service systems he discovered during the Conquest. His *encomienda* grants, therefore, provided entitlement to both tribute goods (such as cotton textiles, foodstuffs, and some minerals) and labor services from specified numbers of Indians delivered at stipulated intervals. His grants were perceived as indefinite in term and, therefore, transferable.

Cortés also began making grants of lands taken from conquered Indian rulers, nobles, and priests to himself and his followers, and he began to rebuild Tenochtitlan–Mexico City as a Spanish colonial center. He established town governments for it and other Spanish colonial towns he and lieutenants founded, and he formed a provincial government with himself at its head. In his request of his monarch that he be made governor and captain general of the territory that he called New Spain, he asked that missionaries, preferably Franciscans who were not opposed to agencies of colonization such as the *encomienda* (as were many of their counterparts in the Dominican and other orders), be sent to convert and "civilize" the peoples he was conquering. In response, the Spanish Crown in 1524 dispatched the first twelve of what would become hundreds of missionaries. He assisted the first twelve "Mexican apostles" with the establishment of the first of many of missions placed in Indian towns and provinces. As he did so he also created an Indian governance structure comparable to that in Spanish towns and provinces, and he charged Indian officers with functions and powers similar to those of their Spanish counterparts.

In 1524, as he surrendered his royal tax collecting authority to four treasury officials sent to the colony by his monarch, King Carlos I (Emperor Charles V), Cortés made his ill-fated decision to proceed to Guatemala and Honduras to take control of the conquest efforts in those areas, which appeared to be slipping into the hands of ambitious lieutenants such as Cristóbal de Olid. Leaving two of the royal treasury officials and two trusted associates to govern New Spain, Cortés set off with several captives, former Mexica and other Indian chieftains whom he felt could not be left behind safely and from whom he sought directions, and a considerable force of Spanish conquistadors and Indian allies. He was to be absent for nearly two years, during which time he was rumored dead, robbed of many of his newly acquired lands and *encomiendas,* and denied the extensive political and military authority he had enjoyed during the preceding five years.

Jealous rivals and unsatisfied former allies, committed clerics who saw his treatment of the Indians as viciously brutal, and Carlos I himself, combined to relieve him of his titles as governor and captain general, to subject him to investigation of his conduct as a royal governor and captain general, and to seize and embargo a substantial share of his properties. From his return to New Spain in 1526 until he sailed for Spain in 1528, Cortés spent much of his time and remaining liquid resources attempting not altogether unsuccessfully to defend himself and to recoup his property losses.

His efforts in Spain were of like character but included the astute use of his still sufficient funds, prestige, and connections among family and allies to obtain rewarding recognition from his king and a marriage with a member of a noble family, doña Juana de Zúñiga. He returned to New Spain in 1530 as a member of the Spanish nobility, marquis of the Valle of Oaxaca, with a formal title to 22 *encomienda* towns and with the restored (and extended) title of captain general of New Spain and the Mar del Sur (the latter was the fruit of his Honduras enterprise and his dispatch of ships from New Spain's Pacific coast to the Malacca Islands). These rewards and restorations, all in the form of royal *cedulas* (orders), included, in addition, the right to entail as an estate his *encomiendas,* his landholdings, and his trading, mining, and milling properties as the Marquesado del Valle de Oaxaca. Restored to him as well were a number of embargoed or seized properties, and released to him was compensation he was due for exploratory and other services. Not restored to him, however, was his title as governor.

For a decade, 1530 to 1540, the conquistador gave his time and energies to developing the Marquesado, founding a legitimate and noble family, and expanding his trading and related investment interest. At the same time, as captain general, he sought with some initial success (but after 1535 with increasingly less success) to command and participate in the continuing extension of Spanish colonial authority into the northern and southern portions of today's Mexico and into Central America. His efforts to the northwest of the central valleys of Mexico led to discovery of the Baja California peninsula, the nearby "sea" that bears his name, and the long gulf it forms. His exploratory and trading enterprises also took his agents south to Panamá and the northern Pacific perimeters of the vast Inca state that his countryman and probably distant relative, Francisco Pizarro, was bringing under Spanish domination, and across the Mar del Sur (the Pacific) to the Philippines and southeast Asia.

These years were increasingly frustrating for the conquistador, however, as his powers and privileges were circumscribed incrementally by royal officials and royal policies directed at reducing the influence of the conquistadors as well as bringing the *encomienda* system to an end and the Indian peoples of the Indies under direct royal supervision and control. Among the new royal officers, the most difficult for Cortés and other conquistadors like him was the first viceroy appointed in the New World, Antonio de Mendoza; among the most difficult of the new royal edicts were the ordinances reducing *encomienda* tribute payments and reducing and regulating the labor services due *encomenderos* from their Indian *encomienda* charges. Equally vexing for Cortés were the continuing legal battles into which he was drawn by competitors, dissatisfied former followers, and envious Crown officials. In 1540, having just been rebuffed again by Viceroy Mendoza as he sought to exercise what he felt were his rights and powers as captain general in advancing Spanish authority far to the north into the land of Cíbola, just reported by Cabeza de Vaca, Cortés decided to return to Spain to again seek relief and more appropriate recognition. He also returned to arrange marriages for his legitimate children and to secure appointments for his sons in the service of Prince Felipe II, Carlos I's heir.

Cortés's experiences in Spain during, as it turned out, the last seven years of his life, were not unlike those of the preceding decade in New Spain: frustrating and unrewarding. Although his wealth increased in these years and his children secured the recognition due them as young members of Spain's nobility and—in the case of his illegitimate children—its upper-class gentry, he was denied the recognition he felt was his due. He felt particularly neglected when he used his own funds to accompany Carlos I and his army into Tangiers in North Africa to regain Spanish domination in that area, and he was not afforded the opportunity he sought to lead Carlos's forces in the same fashion as he had led his conquistadors against Moteuczoma's imperial troops, Finally, ill and preparing for his death in a small town not far from Seville, he prepared a will that sought to right some of the wrongs he felt he had perpetrated against some of his Indian followers, servants, and slaves, and against his God. His will also passed his title, marquis of the Valle of Oaxaca, and his estate, the Marquesado, to his first-born legitimate son, don Martín Cortés y Zúñiga, and made financial and property provisions for all of his other children, his wife, his servants, and his God.

Founder of the Spanish colonial system on the mainland of the Americas, peerless conquistador, creator for better or worse of the Mexican tradition of "La Malinche," and forerunner of a host of Mexican leaders most of whom were desperately inferior replicas, Cortés was less insensitive and brutal than most of his ilk and was a great deal more effective as a leader and colonizer. He was at the same time very much a man of his times, a crusader who brooked no competition in the advancement of his beliefs and his mercenary interests. Unlike most of his conquistador peers, he was amply rewarded for his services to his Spanish monarch, although not as handsomely as he thought was his due. Unlike many of them he left heirs who for centuries after his time enjoyed a privileged place in Euro-American society. Like many of them, however, he was contrite and disillusioned as he met his end at home again in Spain where in many circles he was, as he is today, both infamous and famous.

For a detailed discussion of Cortés's role in the conquest of central Mexico, see Conquest: Central Mexico

Select Bibliography

Díaz del Castillo, Bernal, *The Discovery and Conquest of Mexico, 1517–1521.* New York: Farrar, Strauss and Cudahy, 1956.

Gómara, Francisco López de, *Cortés: The Life of the Conqueror by His Secretary Francisco López de Gómara,* translated and edited by Lesley B. Simpson. Berkeley: University of California Press, 1964.

Riley, G. Micheal, *Fernando Cortés and the Marquesado in Morelos, 1522–1547.* Albuquerque: University of New Mexico Press, 1973.

Scholes, France V., "The Spanish Conqueror as a Businessman." *New Mexico Historical Quarterly* 27 (1958).

Thomas, Hugh, *Conquest: Montezuma, Cortés and the Fall of Old Mexico*. New York: Simon and Schuster, 1994.

Wagner, Henry Raup, *The Rise of Fernando Cortés*. Los Angeles: Cortés Society, 1944.

—G. MICHEAL RILEY

Cristero Rebellion

Between 1926 and 1929, tens of thousands of peasants throughout central-west Mexico rebelled against the new Revolutionary regime in what came to be called the Cristiada or the Cristero Rebellion. The immediate cause of the rebellion was a conflict between church and state over the anticlerical provisions of the Constitution of 1917. When President Plutarco Elías Calles issued the legislation necessary to implement these constitutional measures at the national level, the Mexican Episcopacy responded with a clerical strike, ordering that all churches be closed and public worship suspended as of July 31, 1926. Sporadic uprisings in support of the Catholic Church erupted almost immediately throughout the republic, from Chihuahua in the north to Oaxaca in the south, involving both peasants and urban lay Catholics. After a period of several months, however, large-scale rebellion was sustained only in the central-west states, particularly within the ranchero villages. The great majority of *cristero* rebels were peasants who opposed the anticlericalism of the new regime, as well as the highly politicized application of the Revolutionary agrarian reform program, and the displacement of local religious and political authorities with allies of Revolutionary officials. Neither the federal army nor the thousands of pro-regime peasants organized in *agrarista* militias were able to defeat the *cristeros* militarily. The rebellion ended only when the Mexican Episcopacy reached an agreement with the administration of Emilio Portes Gil in June 1929, and the hierarchy condemned any further rebellion in support of the Catholic Church.

Antecedents

Anticlericalism had become a dominant feature of Revolutionary ideology and practice by 1914, when generals supporting Venustiano Carranza celebrated military victories by confiscating ecclesiastical property, placing restrictions on religious worship, and expelling foreign priests. The vigor with which the Carrancistas attacked the Catholic Church was in part due to the Mexican Episcopacy's support of the regime of Victoriano Huerta. But anticlericalism was much more deeply rooted in the thinking of Revolutionary elites, as it had been in nineteenth-century liberal ideology: even though it had lost much of its landed wealth through the liberal reforms of the 1850s, the Catholic Church still was seen as a central obstacle to Mexico's social and economic development, insofar as it was perceived as encouraging superstition, fanaticism, and the squandering of economic resources on religious practice. Furthermore, the Catholic Church was viewed as an obstacle to the consolidation of the Revolutionary state: promoting its own unions, rural cooperatives, and political associations, the Catholic Church and its affiliated lay organizations were, after the military defeat of the Zapatistas and the Villistas, one of the Carrancistas' main rivals in the construction of the new order. Revolutionary orthodoxy held that the church was monolithically reactionary, but official anticlericalism was at least in part the result of Revolutionary elites' desire not to compete with a Catholic political opposition capable of drawing considerable popular support.

Carrancista anticlericalism was codified in the Constitution of 1917, which placed strict limits on the social, political, and religious activities of the Catholic Church as an institution, and on the clergy and lay Catholics as individuals. The constitution denied the juridical status of "religious institutions known as churches," thus leaving the Catholic Church without legal standing; required that all primary education, both private and public, be purely secular in nature; denied the clergy the right to vote as well as freedom of speech in political matters; prohibited political parties from adopting names with religious references; and required that all religious practice be confined within church buildings, which were, along with all ecclesiastical real estate, declared to be the property of the nation. One of the most contentious provisions was that granting the state the right to administer the clergy as it would any other "profession," including the right to limit the number of priests and to require their registration with state authorities.

Neither President Venustiano Carranza (1915–20) nor President Álvaro Obregón (1920–24) made much of an attempt to enforce the anticlerical provisions of the Constitution at the national level. Between 1917 and 1924, conflict between anticlerical and Catholic forces was largely the product of efforts by state-level authorities to impose limits on church activities and religious practice. In Michoacán, for example, dozens of people were killed in 1921, when the police opened fire on some 10,000

Catholics protesting the desecration of the Morelia Cathedral by supporters of the anticlerical governor Francisco Múgica. In Jalisco, a boycott of all nonessential goods was declared by lay Catholic organizations in 1918, in response to a decree that limited the number of priests permitted to officiate in the state; in addition, the archbishop of Guadalajara, Francisco Orozco y Jiménez, suspended all public religious worship. The success of organized Catholic resistance in forcing the state government in Jalisco to rescind the anticlerical decrees led Catholics at the national level to adopt a similar strategy when first confronted by the anticlericalism of the administration of Plutarco Elías Calles (1924–28).

In contrast to Carranza and Obregón, Calles was intensely anticlerical; as governor of Sonora, he had imposed strict limits on religious practice. In February 1925, shortly after taking office, Calles directed a memorandum to the state governors, reminding them that it was the responsibility of all state and municipal authorities to oversee church activities and to ensure that they were within the narrow limits allowed by the constitution. That same month, he encouraged the formation of a schismatic movement; churches throughout the republic were seized by members of the Regional Confederation of Mexican Workers (CROM), Calles's main base of political support, in the name of a new Mexican Catholic Church, independent of the authority of the Vatican. Soon after the seizure of the churches, and in response to Calles's memorandum, several states began to place severe restrictions on religious worship. With this intensification of official anticlericalism, urban lay Catholics from the former National Catholic Party (PNC), the Catholic Association of Mexican Youth (ACJM), and other Catholic Action organizations joined in March 1925 to form the National League for the Defense of Religious Liberty (LNDLR). By June, the LNDLR claimed a membership of 36,000, with local chapters in almost all states of the republic.

At the national level, the conflict between church and state came to a head with the publication on July 2, 1926, of what became known as the Calles Law, the legislative package necessary for the implementation of the anticlerical constitutional provisions. Municipal authorities were charged with enforcing the law, and local neighborhood committees were to be appointed to administer all church property. The government declared its right to decide which church buildings might be used for religious practice, and which were to be converted for use by Revolutionary schools, peasant leagues, and unions. The law was to go into effect on July 31, 1926.

Bearing in mind the success of organized Catholic resistance in Jalisco, the Mexican Episcopacy and the LNDLR initially advocated nonviolent opposition to the Calles Law, including the nonpayment of taxes, a boycott of all nonessential goods, and a petition drive to overturn the relevant constitutional provisions. The Vatican, meanwhile, attempted, without success, to negotiate a compromise with the Calles administration. On July 25, shortly after those negotiations collapsed, the episcopacy announced that all priests would withdraw from their churches on July 31, the day that the Calles Law was to go into effect. Thus began the three-year clerical strike that closed Mexico's churches and sparked the popular uprisings that would, after a period of several months, coalesce as the Cristero Rebellion.

The Rebellion of 1926 to 1929

During the second half of 1926, the Cristero Rebellion was characterized by sporadic, disorganized, and short-lived violence, often connected to the seizure of churches by federal troops. The LNDLR had begun to discuss the possibility of rebellion as early as September, but urban lay Catholics directed most of their activities toward the economic boycott declared in response to the Calles Law. Reports of sustained rural uprisings in support of the Catholic Church in Colima and Jalisco began to reach Mexico City, however, and encouraged the LNDLR leadership to contemplate the armed overthrow of the Revolutionary regime. LNDLR leaders met with the episcopacy in November to request official ecclesiastical approval of the rebellion; the hierarchy declined to openly support the LNDLR's plans, but agreed in principle that rebellion against political authorities was, in some cases, justified. The LNDLR proceeded to create a military command structure, and, in a manifesto published in both the United States and Mexico in December, called for a mass insurrection on January 1, 1927, to overthrow the Revolutionary regime and establish a new constitution with guarantees of religious freedom.

The LNDLR's attempt to generate and lead a mass rebellion led to a complex and sometimes conflicting alliance between peasant villagers and Catholic elites, both lay and clerical. The Cristero Rebellion entailed far more than the defense of the institutional prerogatives of the Catholic Church by the clergy and organized lay Catholics: at the popular level, it was essentially an antistate movement, rooted in the defense of community institutions and autonomy vis-à-vis a rapidly encroaching central state. The anticlerical policies of the 1920s entailed a fundamental assault on peasant values, culture, and local political autonomy. These policies certainly limited the role of the Catholic Church in education and the clerical duties of the parish priest, but they also outlawed religious festivities and practices that, while they often had very little to do with the institutional Catholic Church, were at the very heart of community economic, social, and political organization. For many communities, this attack on local institutions was reinforced by the Revolutionary agrarian reform program, and the often top-down *agrarista* mobilization of the period: while the agrarian reform might well increase access to land, it also entailed a radically increased role for the state in the peasant community and a subsequent loss of local autonomy in the regulation of community resources and civil-religious authority. In some regions, particularly those in which there were few haciendas, the highly politicized application of the reform actually threatened community access to land, as when *agrarista* minorities, allied with state officials, made claims on either peasant smallholdings or communal property.

The vast majority of *cristero* rebels, therefore, were far more concerned with defending community institutions and practices against the intrusions of the Revolutionary state than they were with the political ambitions of the LNDLR leadership or the institutional concerns of the episcopacy. The tacit approval of the Catholic hierarchy lent legitimacy to the rebellion, and the LNDLR was able to provide the peasant rebels with logistical support and some military leadership. But peasants, unlike urban lay Catholics, did not rebel in direct response to the LNDLR's manifesto, nor did they readily accept the LNDLR's notions of military discipline, much less the often inept military leaders appointed in Mexico City. With a few exceptions, the peasant rebels recognized the authority of local leaders, be they parish priests, village elders, caciques (local strongmen), or fellow peasants. The *cristero* villagers of the center-west generally did ally themselves in some fashion with the Mexico City–based LNDLR, but the timing, evolution, and nature of the rebellion were much more a product of local conditions and organizations than they were of LNDLR decisions and orders.

Until August 1927, *cristero* rebels operated in small and uncoordinated groups, without a centralized leadership or a coherent military strategy; poorly supplied with arms and ammunition, most *cristero* rebels stayed close to home, engaging in sporadic guerrilla warfare rather than larger-scale and strategic attacks on federal garrisons or major towns. Nearly all of the uprisings that occurred in response to the LNDLR's call for mass insurrection were easily repressed or dispersed, particularly when they entailed members of the LNDLR and ACJM acting on their own or in conjunction with small groups of workers or peasants. Even in areas where the LNDLR was particularly well organized, including the Federal District as well as the states of Chihuahua and Puebla, sustained rebellion proved impossible in the absence of widespread popular support and participation. With the easy suppression of these early uprisings, many urban lay Catholics, particular those in the ACJM, quickly defected from the rebel ranks. By mid-1927, the rebellion was sustained only in the central-west states of Jalisco, Michoacán, Guanajuato, Colima, Zacatecas, and Nayarit. In these states, the strength of the rebellion came from high levels of popular support, as well as the organizational density and military effectiveness of two lay Catholic organizations based in Jalisco: the Popular Union (UP), led by Anacleto González Flores until his execution by federal troops in April 1927; and the U, a clandestine organization with cells throughout much of Jalisco and Michoacán.

Beginning in August 1927, two LNDLR-appointed leaders began to reorganize and coordinate the various local and regional groups operating in the center-west. Jesús Degollado y Guízar was appointed chief of operations in southern Jalisco, Colima, Nayarit, and western Michoacán. Enrique Gorostieta was placed in charge of organizing the rebels in central and northeastern Jalisco; his scope of authority gradually increased over the following year, and in August 1928 he was appointed the position of first chief of the Liberation Army. Gorostieta was unusually successful in gaining the respect of the *cristero* rebels, in part because of his military experience as a general in the federal army under Huerta (1913–14). A much more important factor, however, was his recognition of the authority of the local and regional leadership; one of his first steps in taking command of the *cristeros* was to officially recognize what had always been the de facto leadership of the rebellion.

By late 1927, the *cristeros* began carrying out larger-scale attacks that involved rebels from different regions and states. This was in part the result of improved organization and coordination under Gorostieta's leadership. Another important factor, however, was the military rebellion of Generals Arnulfo Gómez and Francisco Serrano, sparked by Obregón's decision to run for the presidency a second time. The Gómez-Serrano Rebellion was short-lived, lasting only a few weeks in October and November, but it did require the withdrawal of federal troops from the center-west, leaving a military opening for the *cristero* rebels. It was at this point that the regime began to rely more heavily on the *agrarista* militias: some 5,000 to 20,000 pro-regime peasants fought alongside of, or instead of, federal forces throughout the course of the rebellion; the numbers fluctuated in accordance with changing military requirements. Many of the *agrarista* peasants came from the neighboring state of San Luis Potosí, where they constituted the military base of the Revolutionary cacique Saturnino Cedillo. Many others, however, came from the region of the center-west itself, and particularly from the state of Michoacán, where popular support for both the *cristero* and the *agrarista* movements was quite strong.

The situation might have remained one of a military stalemate had it not been for two events. First, Gorostieta was killed in an encounter with federal troops on June 1, 1929; Degollado y Guízar took his place as supreme commander of the Liberation Army, but never was able to command the same respect as his predecessor. Second, the episcopacy explicitly condemned the rebellion at the end of month, having reached its own agreement with the regime on June 29, 1929, after two years of negotiations mediated by U.S. ambassador Dwight W. Morrow. The key stumbling block on both sides had been whether or not there would be any actual revisions of the Constitution of 1917: as Morrow carefully pointed out to Calles, the requirement that priests register with the state, and the right of governors to establish limits on the number of priests practicing within their jurisdiction, did, in fact, represent a real threat to the integrity of the Catholic Church as an institution. After considerable effort, Morrow finally produced an agreement acceptable to both the Catholic hierarchy and to Calles. On June 21, 1929, representatives of the episcopacy and the administration of Emilio Portes Gil issued a joint statement to the press, declaring, among other things, that the requirement that priests register with state officials did not mean that the government could recognize members of the clergy not designated as such by ecclesiastical authorities. Once the agreement was reached, the episcopacy explicitly condemned the rebellion, ordered the LNDLR to cease its political and military activities, and commanded all of the *cristero* rebels to surrender themselves and their arms.

The agreement reached between church and state did not, in fact, reform or modify any of the existing anticlerical laws or constitutional provisions. The state gave no guarantees that religious practice would be tolerated even within the narrow confines of the existing body of law, even as the Catholic Church agreed to register priests with the government, the one provision it had declared itself unable to abide three years earlier. The church's explicit condemnation of the rebellion brought the Cristero Rebellion to an end, however; slowly, and often with great bitterness toward the Catholic Church, the rebels surrendered to federal forces throughout the summer of 1929. Sporadic uprisings continued to occur throughout much of the center-west during the 1930s, in what some authors have called La Segunda, or the Second Cristiada. These uprisings lacked the legitimacy of church approval, however, and were, in fact, condemned by the episcopacy. According to a 1932 statement by Archbishop Maximino Ruíz y Flores of Michoacán, the pope explicitly had forbidden armed struggle, and if the episcopacy had said or written anything in favor of rebellion in 1926, such thinking no longer held.

Interpretations of the Cristero Rebellion

The central controversy in the literature on the Cristero Rebellion concerns the relative importance of the episcopacy, urban lay Catholic organizations, and the peasantry in defining the course and the nature of the rebellion; a corollary to this issue concerns the motivations of the center-west peasants who rebelled in the context of the crisis between church and state at the national level.

Early accounts of the Cristero Rebellion tend to treat it as one episode in a much longer conflict between church and state in Mexico: beginning in the late colonial period, with the expulsion of the Jesuits, this conflict came to a head during the liberal reform period of the 1850s and 1860s, subsided temporarily during the era of Porfirio Díaz (1876–1910), broke out again in full force during the Mexican Revolution (1910–20), and then culminated in the Cristero Rebellion of 1926 to 1929. In this view, the rebellion was part of a last-gasp effort by the Catholic Church to assert its institutional and political prerogatives vis-à-vis the Revolutionary state. Once that state was consolidated under President Lázaro Cárdenas (1934–40), secular elites had little to fear from the politically weakened church, and the long-standing conflict all but came to an end, with church and state coexisting in an at times uneasy but essentially durable modus vivendi. Given this basic understanding of the Cristero Rebellion as one episode in a long-standing intra-elite conflict, the orthodox approach has focused almost exclusively on urban elites and national institutions. The issue of peasant partisanship in the rebellion seldom arises in this literature, the rural rebels most often are subsumed under the general category of "Catholics," thus erasing any distinctions between countryside and city, and between elites and popular-sector groups. When peasant participation in the rebellion is recognized, it generally is attributed to religious fanaticism.

Revisionist studies of the Cristero Rebellion, such as the works by scholar Jean Meyer, differentiate between elite and popular interests in Revolutionary Mexico, particularly during the decade of the 1920s, when, in Meyer's view, a new elite consolidated the Revolutionary state in part by running roughshod over peasant values and institutions. In contrast to the orthodox account, Meyer argues that in terms of motivations, leadership, and organization, the *cristiada* was first and foremost a popular rebellion against a tyrannical state bent on destroying and recreating Mexican society according to a new Revolutionary ideology. More recent work continues to treat the *cristiada* as a popular antistate rebellion but is more explicitly concerned with the question of peasant partisanship, and thus focuses on the local and regional characteristics of the rebellion and the divisions within the peasantry with respect to the policies of the new Revolutionary regime, particularly those policies affecting property rights, religious practice, and political authority.

Select Bibliography

Bailey, David C., *¡Viva Cristo Rey!: The Cristero Rebellion and Church-State Conflict in Mexico*. Austin: University of Texas Press, 1974.

Foley, John, "Colima, Mexico and the Cristero Rebellion." Ph.D. diss., University of Chicago, 1979.

González, Luis, *San José de Gracia: Mexican Village in Transition*. Austin: University of Texas Press, 1974.

Jrade, Ramón, "Counter-revolution in Mexico: The Cristero Movement in Sociological and Historical Perspective." Ph.D. diss., Brown University, 1980.

———, "Inquiries into the Cristero Insurrection Against the Mexican Revolution." *Latin American Research Review* 20:2 (1985).

Meyer, Jean, *The Cristero Rebellion: Mexican People between Church and State*. Cambridge: Cambridge University Press, 1976.

Purnell, Jennie, "The Politics of Identity: Cristeros and Agraristas of Revolutionary Michoacán." Ph.D. diss., Massachusetts Institute of Technology, 1993.

Quirk, Robert E., *The Mexican Revolution and the Catholic Church, 1910–1929*. Bloomington: Indiana University Press, 1973.

Tutino, John, *From Insurrection to Revolution in Mexico: Social Bases of Agrarian Violence*. Princeton, New Jersey: Princeton University Press, 1986.

—Jennie Purnell

Cruz, Sor Juana Inés de la 1651–95

Nun and Writer

If Shakespeare is synonymous with Renaissance England, Sor Juana Inés de la Cruz is synonymous with Baroque Latin America. She lived and worked at the end of the so-called Siglo de Oro, a nearly two-century golden age marked by extraordinary literary, artistic, and musical brilliance, in the metropolitan and colonial centers of the Spanish-speaking world.

Regardless of sex, class, or age, millions of people in Latin America are familiar with Sor Juana's portrait and a few lines from the poem that begins "You foolish and unreasoning men/who cast all blame on women" *(Hombres necios que acusáis/a la mujer sin razón)*. The most often reproduced image of Sor Juana—it appears on Mexican currency—was painted in 1750 by Miguel Cabrera. Its idealized elegance has contributed to her fame as "peerless," *"rara avis"* (rare bird), "Phoenix of Mexico," and "Tenth Muse." The last label was used also for Anne Bradstreet (1612–72), inaugural poet of the Anglo-American colonies, with whom Sor Juana has been compared and contrasted, and for other women poets as far back as Sappho. In the twentieth century, scholar Dorothy Schons called Sor Juana's *Respuesta a Sor Filotea de la Cruz* (Answer to Sister Filotea de la Cruz, 1691), a women's declaration of intellectual emancipation; in Mexico, in 1974, the poet was ceremoniously awarded the title "First Feminist of the Americas."

The extraordinary sweep of both Sor Juana's literary art and of her consciousness of gender are now being more fully understood and appreciated. Lack of biographical documentation, combined with the "worship" and "envy" stirred by her talent gave rise to a distorting mythography. She was not, for instance, either saintly or a mystic; as a sage she was at once daring and humble, but her expressions of humility were largely conventional and tactical. Although she suffered persecution and outrage, and was pressured or convinced to greatly modify her worldly intellectual life about two years before she died, she was not under direct threat of punishment by the Inquisition; the Catholic Church had a less drastic mechanism for instilling compliance. Nor did she die in an ascetic cell while nursing her sister nuns during an epidemic as has been claimed since publication of the first biography by the Spanish Jesuit Diego Calleja (1700). An inventory of her belongings when she died, made public in 1995, lists books, art works, and other possessions. Review of death records at the convent shows no indication of a plague.

Sor Juana was born almost certainly in Nepantla —not far from the two dormant volcanoes, Popo- catéptl and Iztaccíhuatl, mentioned in her verses—in 1651 as noted by Calleja and registered in the con- vent annals. Her mother Isabel Ramírez, who though unschooled efficaciously managed lands leased from the church, had six children, perhaps with three part- ners, none of whom she married; Juana Inés, the prodigious second child, was probably the daughter of a Basque, as she states, about whom little is known. (Many people, including Octavio Paz, her most recent and influential biographer, had been convinced that the baptismal record witnessed in 1648 by family members at the church of Chimal- huacán for a natural child, named Inés, was hers.) She rhymed before she could speak in prose, she tells us, and strove uncommonly hard to master Latin in a short time. At 10 she was taken to Mexico City, where she lived with a well-connected aunt and uncle, wrote her first poem, and attracted attention and a job at court.

Sor Juana represented herself as an insatiably curious reader, a solitary, hard-working learner and an innately gifted poet. She wrote that her real voca- tion was the silent, arduous, and sacred one of the scholar. Her great passion was study. First her grandfather's sizable collection of books, then the viceregal palace's, and finally her own convent library, which held hundreds of volumes, but was not the largest in Mexico (as has been claimed), fed her appetite for knowledge.

After living for approximately five years at the royal court (1664–69) as Juana Inés de Asbaje y Ramírez de Santillana, favorite servant-companion to the vicereine, Leonor Carreto, Marquise de Man- cera, she became Madre Juana Inés de la Cruz, nun of the order of St. Jerome. Before leaving the palace, Calleja tells us, she stunned the most knowledge- able men in the realm with her brilliance in a public examination organized by the viceroy (c. 1668). That such events were not unknown is evidenced by the fact that several decades earlier another scholar, Juliana Morel, born in Barcelona, later an abbess and translator of St. Augustine into French, was sim- ilarly examined in Lyon and Avignon. Sor Juana depicted an analogous performance in writing of the legendary St. Catherine of Egypt, who along with two other mothers of wisdom, Isis (Mother of the Gods), and the Virgin Mary, was her intellectual and spiritual model. Quintilian, Ovid, and Virgil could head the list of her Latin influences; Luis de Gón- gora, Pedro Calderón de la Barca, and Baltasar Grac- ián were first among her Spanish literary mentors. About Egyptology and the natural and physical

sciences she learned most in books by the German Jesuit encyclopedist Athanasius Kircher. St. Teresa of Avila and María de Agreda she mentioned and implicitly debated.

At court and in the convent as well, Sor Juana was a professional writer: much of her literary pro- duction was commissioned, some paid for, some exchanged for favors and gifts. The two volumes published during her lifetime (in Madrid, 1689, and in Seville, 1692) and the third (with Calleja's biogra- phy and many poems of praise, shortly afterward, 1700), were so popular they went through several editions. Yet she had to guard her time for study and writing from the demands of monastic life. Recent research has confirmed that as treasurer of her convent of St. Paula (now a university and museum, dedicated, in part, to promoting studies of the great author's work and her times), Sor Juana was for many years in charge of finances, managing sizable sums of money and making investments beneficial both to the convent and herself.

Sor Juana's privileged intellect evolved in kaleido- scopic New Spain, festively effusive on one hand, ascetically reserved on the other. She absorbed much from books but also from her variegated social milieu. Some of her poems echo popular songs and dances, their images as colorful as market-places, filled with fruit, vegetables, and clothing; others are as elegantly ornate as the cathedrals where her *villancicos* were sung and the aristocratic salons where her plays were performed.

Sor Juana utilized many tonalities and styles of language in her plays, poems, and prose: the accent of non-native speakers of Spanish (Portuguese, Nahua, African, and Basque); the erudite cadences and classical rhetoric of clerics in the Latin church; the tradition of dramatic authors and the poetry "academies" of Madrid and Seville. Her vernacular and cultivated nuances reveal both the elite pages of the enormous number of books she read and the idiomatic turns of phrase she heard from people in every strata of Mexican society (servants, priests, enslaved laborers, aristocrats). Humorous, witty, and ironic, Sor Juana's mature works reflected so richly the viceroyalty's artistic and religious visions, and were so deftly crafted, that their coded critical and revisionary dimensions long escaped many of her readers.

Sor Juana's complete works include 65 sonnets (some 20 of them love sonnets, deemed by many to be among the most beautiful of the seventeenth century); 62 *romances* (similar to ballads); and a profusion of poems in other metrical forms. For dra- matic performance, Sor Juana wrote 3 sacramental *autos* (1-act dramas) and 2 comedies (1 a collaboration); 32 *loas* (preludes to plays, sometimes sung and performed separately for religious and viceregal celebrations); 2 *sainetes* (farces) and a *sarao* (celebratory song and dance), performed between the acts of one of the plays; and 15 or 16 sets of *villancicos* (carols—8 or 9 songs on religious themes such as the Nativity, Assumption, Immaculate Conception, and legends of Sts. Joseph, Peter, and Catherine of Alexandria).

The 12 years of Sor Juana's most intense literary labors began in 1680 when she was chosen by the outgoing viceroy, Archbishop Payo de Rivera, patron of the arts and a friend, to design one of two triumphal arches to be set up in Mexico City, culmination point of pomp and ritual-filled ceremonies to welcome the new head of state and his wife. (Don Carlos de Sigüenza y Góngora, entrusted with the other, may have supervised the execution of both). The colorful paintings were addressed to the massive crowd gathered for the occasion in Mexico City's main plaza. The text included the poems performed at the ceremony held in front of the arch, and for the initiated, an erudite explanation and description of the 14 paintings and emblems she had devised, together with the Latin mottoes and the Spanish verses (two in Latin) that framed the top and bottom of each image. Considered modern in its day, it required a familiarity all educated people of the time had with emblematic literature, books of myths, and the iconographies prepared for use by artists. As far as we know Sor Juana is the only woman in history to receive such an assignment. The arch, titled *Neptuno alegórico* (*Allegorical Neptune*, 1680) brought her glory and scandal—such a public presence was considered forbidden for women, let alone nuns.

About two years later Sor Juana dismissed her confessor Antonio Núñez de Miranda in a sharp letter (1681 or 1682) in which she contests his censure of her having undertaken to design the arch, and his decade of public complaint against her "scandalous" literary activity. Although most scholars believe she wrote it, the letter cannot be authenticated definitively because the copy is from the eighteenth century. Until 1980, when it was discovered, biographies stated that she had been dismissed by Núñez, and that he agreed to serve as her confessor again two years before her death.

The 975-verse *Primero sueño* ("First Dream," also known simply as *Sueño,* or "Dream," c. 1685), celebrated as the most important philosophical poem in the Spanish language, is at once Sor Juana's most abstract and personal work. Long read as a poem of intellectual disillusionment, more recent readings comment on its exploration of quests for knowledge, inductive, logical, intuitive; of the anatomy and functioning of the human body; of the geometrical movements of the stars; of mechanics and medicine; of the human (female) spirit's need for unfettered growth. Its autobiographical vision, not unlike Descartes's, fuses poetry and science.

Finally, Sor Juana wrote two prose essays, the unauthorized publication of the first of which, the *Carta atenagórica* (1690), prompted the writing of the second, the already mentioned *Respuesta a Sor Filotea de la Cruz.* The author stated that at the request of the bishop of Puebla, Manuel de Santa Cruz, and for his eyes only, she prepared and sent a manuscript of her spoken critique, a magnificently logical disagreement with a sermon written 40 years earlier by Antonio Vieira, a well-known Portuguese-Brazilian Jesuit. Santa Cruz had it printed as *Carta atenagórica* (Letter Worthy of Athena; it is also known as *Crisis sobre un sermón*—Critique on a Sermon), adding an admonitory prologue in the form of a letter signed "Sor Filotea de la Cruz." Surprised and angered by the attacks against her critique, within three months Sor Juana had penned her most extraordinary prose work, the *Respuesta,* a response to three major churchmen, "Sor Filotea" (Fernández de Santa Cruz), Núñez de Miranda, and Aguiar y Seijas (the ascetic and woman-phobic archbishop of Mexico), and to all those who would silence her and prevent women from learning, teaching, and writing.

The *Respuesta,* often referred to as a spiritual autobiography, mimics nuns' *Lives,* but is actually structured according to classical judicial and epistolary rhetoric, as a legal document. Praising scientific and pluridisciplinary inquiry, Sor Juana's tour de force defends the legacy of women's contributions to culture, and her own life in letters. Priding herself on being "as much daughter of the Company" as the Jesuit Vieira, she produced a self-defense, a wily and witty 33-page essay on silence and speech, religion and history, on language, knowledge, and interpretation.

In 1995 Elias Trabulse made public as Sor Juana's a short verse satire signed by Serafina de Cristo, and also written in 1691, a mocking retort that implicates Núñez de Miranda rather than Vieira as a main target of the theological critique and emphasizes Sor Juana's capacity to jest. *Enigmas* (Riddles), prepared at the request of a group of Portuguese nuns, discovered around 1970, but not published until 1994, echoes Sor Juana's inveterate playfulness and offers proof of contacts, however indirect, with European religious women. Lost are a treatise on music, *El caracol,* and her reputedly voluminous correspondence, which might tell us more about her self-fashioning. Some scholars underline Sor Juana's doubt, conflict, and melancholy, others her mocking confidence in waging the unending struggle to continue writing despite her ambiguous and often embattled position.

Sor Juana's staunch refusal of marriage and the dynamism of her treatment of love relationships in many works, sacred and profane, may in part be attributed to her mother's relative autonomy, as well as to mythological readings and acquaintance with art; unsettled family life and observations of the fickleness of courtly behavior could also have influenced her elaborations on the classical myths of sexual strife between goddesses, gods, and humans. Nothing is known about the poet's own possible human loves, although much has been invented over the centuries—marking the romantic and unfailingly sexist fashions of the moment.

Critics and scholars generally agree that Sor Juana's most vividly ardent love poetry is found in verses directed to the two vicereines most supportive of her genius and to the Virgin Mary. Drawing upon the wealth and development of reverence for the Virgin of Guadalupe, she made of Mariolatry a foundation that authorized and profoundly inspired her writing. She identified divinity with wisdom and exceptional human beings with godliness.

One of the keenest minds and scintillating pens of an era, Sor Juana helped create Mexican identity, with its intricate linguistic usages. As a Mexican nun of the second half of the seventeenth century, she was famous as an anomaly; as a poet, playwright, and feminist intellectual of the early modern period, Sor Juana forms part of what we now know to have been a formidable tradition of female thinkers and artists in the Western world.

Select Bibliography

Arenal, Electa, and Amanda Powell, editors and translators, *The Answer/La Requesta: Including a Selection of Poems.* New York: The Feminist Press at the City University of New York, 1994.

Bénassy-Berling, Marie-Cécille, *Humanismo y religión en Sor Juana Inés de la Cruz,* translated by Laura López de Belair. Mexico City: UNAM, 1983.

Daniel, Lee A., *The Loa of Sor Juana Inés de la Cruz.* Fredricton, New Brunswick: York Press, 1994.

Flynn, Gerard C., *Sor Juana Inés de la Cruz.* New York: Twayne, 1971.

Merrim, Stephanie, editor, *Feminist Perspectives on Sor Juana Inés de la Cruz.* Detroit: Wayne State University Press, 1991.

Montross, Constance M., *Virtue or Vice?: Sor Juana's Use of Thomistic Thought.* Washington, D.C.: University Press of America, 1981.

Paz, Octavio, *Sor Juana Inés de la Cruz, o las trampas de la fe.* Mexico City: Fondo de Cultura Económica, 1982. As *Sor Juana or the Traps of Faith,* translated by Margaret Sayers Peden. Cambridge, Massachusetts: Bel Knap Press, 1988. Retitled as *Sor Juana: Her Life and World.* London: Faber and Faber, 1988.

Tavard, George H., *Juana Inés de la Cruz and the Theology of Beauty.* Notre Dame, Indiana: Notre Dame University Press, 1991.

—Electa Arenal

Cuisine

Connections between cuisine and identity—what people eat and who they are—reach deep into Mexican history. The native inhabitants of Mesoamerica worshiped their staple crop maize as a god and even may have equated this plant physically with human flesh. Spanish conquistadors assigned great significance to the Mediterranean staff of life, wheat, the only grain acceptable for Catholic communion according to an eleventh-century papal decree. Within the hierarchical society of New Spain, food served along with clothing and language as a status marker, distinguishing criollo (Spanish-descended) patricians with their crusty wheat bread from Indian and mestizo plebes who ate corn tortillas. Following Independence, Mexican leaders abolished legal distinctions within society, but cultural differences continued to impede their efforts to forge a united nation. Cuisine, in particular, offered a promising space for all Mexicans, not just the leaders, to define their national identity.

Scholars have largely agreed on the modern origins of nationalism, rejecting the nineteenth-century idea that nations possess essential characteristics determined in the distant past. Benedict Anderson described nations as "imagined communities" that emerged in the eighteenth century as a product of the Enlightenment. The standardization of vernacular languages through the spread of print and literature allowed people from different ethnic groups to imagine "national" communities that had not previously existed. Anderson emphasized the role of newspapers and novels in establishing a uniform language, but other forms of literature can perform the same service. Arjun Appadurai has shown that cookbooks in contemporary India opened a medium for middle-class women to communicate with one another, helping to dissolve regional, ethnic, and caste boundaries, and thus to foster Indian nationalism. In Mexico, women relegated to the domestic sphere always had assigned meaning to their lives by feeding their families. Culinary literature therefore offered them a natural language to imagine a national community in the kitchen and to define for themselves *lo mexicano.*

Mexican cuisine developed from two quite separate culinary traditions, the indigenous and the Spanish. Native Americans created a highly sophisticated cuisine based on maize, beans, squash, and chilies. This essentially vegetarian diet arose of necessity, for most large mammals had become extinct in North America 10,000 years ago. Nevertheless, the four staples satisfied human nutritional needs for carbohydrates, protein, minerals, and vitamins. Pre-Columbian cooking techniques maximized the value of these foods; for instance, the method of boiling corn in lime (calcium oxide) multiplied available nutrients, while the complementarity of corn and beans provided a complete amino acid chain, allowing the full utilization of vegetable proteins, although either food alone would be deficient. Indeed, Mesoamerican agriculture may have been productive enough to support 25 million people.

In addition, cuisine held a central place in pre-Columbian society and culture. To demonstrate the grandeur of the Aztec Empire, Mexica rulers such as Moteuczoma (Montezuma) dined on spectacular banquets filled with the finest delicacies including turkey, duck, pheasant, fish, rabbit, and venison. Special foods such as tamales also provided communion with the gods during the many religious and civic festivals in the Mexica calendar. Finally, cuisine provided a way for the Mexica to distinguish themselves from neighboring societies. According to the *Florentine Codex,* the Otomis, a northern tribe considered barbaric by the Mexica, picked their corn before it ripened, while the Toluca, a similarly marginalized group on the western slopes, did not eat chilies. The Purépecha, a people living farther to the west, supposedly cooked with neither skill nor sanitation. These imperial rivals, who regularly defeated Mexica warriors in battle, received the ultimate snub: in a land where fresh tortillas were the height of culinary excellence, the Purépecha ate leftovers. These chauvinistic accounts demonstrated the importance of food as an identifying social trait among the Mexica. People who ate tortillas freshly made of golden corn and spiced with chili peppers could claim the Toltec mantle of civilization; all others still wandered the Chichimec wilderness of savagery.

Meanwhile across the Atlantic, Spanish cuisine developed from a long series of invasions. Three thousand years ago, Iberian people introduced wheat cultivation and sheep herding methods from Syria and Egypt. Over the next millennium, successive Celtic, Phoenician, Greek, and Carthaginian settlers planted grapes, olives, and chickpeas. The Mediterranean staples of wheat bread, olive oil, and vinifera wine thus were established firmly when Roman armies conquered Hispania. This culinary trilogy persisted long after the empire's collapse, for Catholic priests could use only wheat bread and wine for the Holy Eucharist, while olive oil was essential for baptizing children. Nevertheless, fifth-century Visigoth invaders had revived the Iberian pastoral economy and medieval Spaniards consumed a carnivorous diet including sheep, cows, pigs, goats, and chickens. Finally, the Muslim occupation (711–1492) imparted to Spanish cuisine an Asian flavor from spices such as pepper, ginger, cinnamon, clove, cardamom, mace, nutmeg, saffron, and sugar. The Arab's heavy hand with spices later influenced the Mexican creation of *mole poblano,* a fragrant deep brown sauce served with turkey.

This long history of exchanging foods made the introduction of European crops a natural step in the conquest of America, but the natives clung stubbornly to their corn-based cuisine. The *Florentine Codex* recorded their initial reaction to wheat bread as being "like famine food . . . like dried maize stalks." Indians found wheat not only distasteful, but also expensive. The European grain required large capital investments in iron plows, oxen teams, grist mills, and brick ovens, none of which were needed for making corn tortillas. Moreover, wheat yields fell significantly below those of corn. As a result, Indians generally needed to be compelled to grow wheat, except for some entrepreneurial farmers who sold the grain to urban markets. Most rural dwellers ate wheat only at communion or in special loaves purchased for religious festivals at the behest of Spanish priests. Indians living in urban areas consumed more wheat—many were drafted into working as bakers—but their preference for corn tortillas remained strong, if only because wheat prices ran as much as ten times higher than corn. While wheat compared unfavorably to maize, many other Old World plants and animals found ready acceptance among the Native Americans. European livestock such as pigs, sheep, and chickens offered significant gains to their largely vegetarian diet, although cattle met with some disapproval because of the damage caused by grazing in corn fields. Indian gardeners also grew European vegetables including cabbages, cucumbers, onions, garlic, and lettuce.

Spanish cooks meanwhile adapted Old World techniques to New World ingredients, creating a criollo cuisine. Immigrants insisted on eating wheat bread and only the most impoverished subsisted on corn tortillas. Nevertheless, American game such as turkey fit readily into recipes for stewed chickens, and indigenous beans proved superior to Iberian chickpeas. Other culinary changes resulted from the inability to obtain traditional ingredients such as grapes and olives, neither of which grew in New Spain for reasons of both climate and imperial policy. Criollos learned to fry with pork fat instead of olive oil, but found no universally accepted substitute for wine, and drank whatever they could afford: imported sherry, sugarcane brandy, native *pulque,* or sweetened chocolate.

Criollo cuisine acquired its most distinctive tastes from Native American chili peppers. The addition of various red and black chilies transformed fragrant Arabic stews into uniquely Mexican *moles.* Peppers likewise imparted a delicious new piquancy to *chorizo,* an already-spicy smoked sausage from Extremadura, and to Iberian *adobos,* vinegar marinades used to preserve meats. Perhaps the most interesting twist given by criollo cooks to European cuisine was the creation of *chilies en nogada,* a green chili pepper stuffed with minced meat, covered with a pure white walnut sauce, and garnished with bright red pomegranate seeds. The green, white, and red of the Mexican flag have made this a modern national icon, but historical texts demonstrate its roots in Renaissance Italy. Diego Granado in his 1599 *Libro del arte de cocina* (Book of the Art of Cooking) gave a comparable recipe for stuffed cabbage in "a composition called *nogada."*

The distinctiveness of criollo cuisine became all the more prominent as European cooking styles changed in the eighteenth century. French chefs began this transformation about 1700 by replacing the sugar and spices prominent in medieval foods with the salt and herbs characteristic of modern European cooking. Enlightenment ideals dictated that a cook should reveal rather than distort the true nature of foods. Medical literature meanwhile banished spicy foods as a positive health hazard, leaving Mexican cuisine as a self-conscious anachronism. José Luis Juárez, in a study of eighteenth-century manuscript cookbooks, has shown that criollo chefs responded to this attack with some ambivalence, adopting French names but not their techniques. A typical recipe for *sopa francesa* insisted on French bread, but also included many spices that had disappeared from continental cooking. After Independence, the distinction provided by chilies constituted a central theme in the construction of a national cuisine.

Mexico's first published cookbooks appeared in 1831 as part of a broader instructional literature providing women with standards of proper domestic behavior. These first two works, *El cocinero mexicano* (The Mexican Chef) and the *Novísimo arte de cocina* (New Art of Cooking), were followed by at least a dozen other volumes spaced relatively evenly over the course of the century. Multiple editions bring the number up to nearly 40, with a few thousand copies for each run, for a total of as many as 100,000 cookbooks. Additional recipes printed in domestic manuals, calendars, and newspapers assured that cooking instructors reached a broad audience, at least among the middle and upper classes. The authors of these works generally remained anonymous, but most were probably men. Only one book printed before 1890 claimed a female author, the 1836 *Nuevo y sencillo arte de cocina, repostería y refrescos, dispuesto por una mexicana, y experimentado por personas inteligentes antes de darse a la prensa* (New and Simple Art of Cooking, Baking, and Refreshments, arranged by a Mexican woman, and tested by intelligent people before being sent to the press).

These published cookbooks reinforced the ideals of a patriarchal society and patriotic behavior. Gender roles that evolved over the course of the nineteenth century established an inherently unequal relationship, placing women under the authority of men, yet assigning mothers responsibility for the family's moral order. Jacinto Anduiza elaborated this theme in an 1893 cookbook that attributed many of the worst domestic calamities to failures in the kitchen. He warned that men dissatisfied with their wives' cooking would seek their pleasures in taverns and bordellos. Moreover, cookbooks contained explicitly nationalist language to help ensure that women raised patriotic sons. The Mexican Chef began this insistence on culinary patriotism, praising "truly national" spicy dishes and deriding delicate European palates unaccustomed to chili peppers. His successors likewise differentiated the national cuisine from foreign foods and advertised recipes specifically accommodated to Mexican palates.

While emphasizing national unity, cookbook authors also recognized the regional diversity of Mexican cuisine. Common references appeared to the *moles* of Puebla and Oaxaca, the black beans and seafoods of Veracruz, and the grilled meats of Guadalajara and Monterrey. Yet compared with modern works, nineteenth-century cookbooks included within the national cuisine only a handful of regional traditions, essentially those with heavy Hispanic settlements. The virtual monopoly of criollo kitchens becomes apparent in the comparative treatment of *mole.* Oaxaca is known today as "the land of seven *moles*," but nineteenth-century works ignored the more indigenous versions such as *verde,* a green stew perfumed with the incomparable anis-like fragrance of *hoja santa.* They focused instead on a black version, *negro,* which like Puebla's dish, contained the spices characteristic of medieval stews.

By defining regional cuisines in criollo terms, authors ignored a gastronomic geography dating back to the pre-Columbian times. Native culinary traditions centered around civilizations such as the Maya, Mexica, Zapoteca, Mixteca, and Totonaca— ethnic groups that rarely corresponded to Mexican political boundaries. The Huasteca, for example, split between the states of San Luis Potosí and northern Veracruz, contained only a small Hispanic population with little national significance. Nevertheless, large numbers of native communities thrived in the area and developed an enormously sophisticated cuisine. Modern ethnographers have counted 42 distinct varieties of tamales, including the meter-long *zacahuil.* Other regional dishes such as the Pacific Coast hominy stew *pozole* likewise received little notice because of their indigenous associations.

Elite cooking manuals gave little attention to the lower-class cuisine of corn. Many cookbooks contained no recipes at all for tamales, *gorditas,* or *quesadillas,* and books that did mention them consigned them to a ghetto labeled "light brunches." Of course, a lack of written recipes does not prove that elites never ate popular foods. The servants who did the cooking hardly needed instructions for making enchiladas, and most were illiterate anyway. Nevertheless, cookbooks often contained positive censures against the derogation of serving Indian foods. One volume explained that the wealthy had virtually no use for the popular corn drink *atole.* The *Diccionario de cocina* (Dictionary of Cooking), published in 1845, pointedly questioned the morals of any family that ate tamales, the food of "the lower orders."

By the time of Porfirio Díaz's dictatorship in the late nineteenth century, the nascent national cuisine, already divided along regional and class lines, had split further according to gender. As Científico elites sought to develop Mexican society by emulating all things European, French haute cuisine prepared by male chefs became de rigueur for fashionable Mexicans. To supply this demand, translations appeared of classic French volumes such as a cookbook by the Paris Jockey Club's celebrated chef Jules Gouffé, and Mexican kitchen manuals included recipes for continental entrées including veal blanquette and chicken cardinal. Aspiring gourmets indulged their appetites for continental cuisine in Mexico City restaurants and social clubs such as the Tívoli of San Cosme and Sylvain Daumont. Banquet menus from these establishments testify to the cosmopolitan tastes of the country's leaders. A dinner for 500 held in the National Theater to celebrate President Porfirio Díaz's birthday in 1891 featured French food, wines, and cognac. Only men were seated for this banquet; their wives had to view the proceedings from a balcony, a significant indication of their exclusion from full citizenship in the patriarchal nation. The quest for imported civility reached its pinnacle in 1910 at the centennial of Independence in a series of banquets honoring President Díaz, cabinet members, and foreign dignitaries. Not a single Mexican dish appeared at any of the score of dinners dedicated to this patriotic occasion. Even the Mexican colony in New York commemorated the centennial with French food.

But at the same time, women began to write their own manuscript and community cookbooks in which they defined an alternate vision of the national community and its cuisine based on Hispanic and even pre-Columbian traditions. By the 1880s foreign travelers already had noticed a growing number of women who filled notebooks with recipes, many copied from family and friends. These manuscripts often served as albums recording family traditions, with dishes handed down from mothers and grandmothers. The fact that the older women often were illiterate added further to the value of their daughters' books. The exchange of cooking tips also reached beyond the extended family to become the focus for Catholic charities, which were one of the few legitimate female activities outside the home. A group of matrons in Guadalajara prepared a recipe manual to support the local orphanage, and several community cookbooks from Mexico City were dedicated to works such as cathedrals for Saint Rafael and Saint Vincent DePaul.

In 1896, Vicenta Torres de Rubio extended this community of cooks throughout the Republic in her *Cocina michoacana,* a serialized guide to the cuisine of Michoacán. Printed in the provincial town of Zamora and sold by subscription, it began with local recipes submitted by women within the state. Nevertheless, she soon expanded her audience to reach cooks from all over the country. A woman from Celaya sent her a recipe for "Heroic Nopales," from Guadalajara came a green chili lamb stew, a Mexico City matron offered her favorite meat glaze, and a reader in the border town of Nuevo Laredo even presented her "Hens from the Gastronomic Frontier." By printing recipes from throughout Mexico, Torres provided the first genuine forum for a national cuisine. Contributors exchanged recipes with middle-class counterparts they had never met and began to experiment with regional dishes, combining them in new ways that transcended local traditions. Thus women began to imagine their own national community in the familiar terms of the kitchen, rather than as an alien political entity formulated by men and served up to them in didactic literature.

This exchange of recipes in community cookbooks even began to cross established class and ethnic lines. Unlike the usual practice of segregating enchiladas and other corn dishes into a section of "light brunches," the community cookbooks tended to integrate these with other recipes for meats and vegetables. One volume prepared by a charitable women's organization in Mexico City gave more recipes for enchiladas than for any other type of food. Vicenta Torres made a virtue of including recipes of explicitly Indian origin, assuring readers that these "secrets of the indigenous classes" would be appropriate at any party. Along with tamales, she included *gordita* cordials, *pozole* de Quiroga, and *carnero al pastor* (Shepherd's mutton), but out of deference to her Porfirian audience, she set them apart with the label *indigenista*.

Care must be taken in interpreting this acceptance of native food as an indication that ties of gender were breaking down lines of class. Even middle-class women, after all, generally could count on a household servant to do the difficult work of grinding corn and chilies. Moreover, these same women shared with elites an admiration for French haute cuisine. Yet they also embraced a genuinely Mexican national cuisine based on colonial *moles* and even pre-Columbian tamales that were rejected by Eurocentric male elites. Being excluded from power themselves, perhaps women simply had less motivation to maintain the distinctiveness of criollo culture. After all, they based their image of the nation on the Virgin of Guadalupe, a symbol shared with the Indian masses, rather than on the trappings of western industrial society idealized by elite men.

This Porfirian faith in imported progress was replaced in the Revolution of 1910 by *indigenismo*, a somewhat misleadingly named nationalist ideology that revalued the indigenous past yet looked to the mestizo for Mexico's future. The search for modern Mexico's roots in the pre-Columbian past, which inspired the mural renaissance led by Diego Rivera and the restoration of Teotihuacan by Manuel Gamio, also gave new legitimacy to Native American foods. Liberal intellectual Andrés Molina Enríquez, in his prophetic book *Los grandes problemas nacionales* (1909), stated that maize "represented

in an absolutely indubitable manner the national cuisine." Folklorist Virginia Rodríguez Rivera searched the country, interviewing everyone from poor indigenous cooks to wealthy criollo matrons, to record traditional Mexican recipes. Artist Frida Kahlo and her avant-garde friends meanwhile recreated pre-Columbian banquets of tamales garnished with Quetzalcoatl figures as an expression of their national identity.

More conventional middle-class women of the post-Revolutionary era likewise explored domestic representations of *lo mexicano*. Community cookbooks, first produced at the turn of the century, became ever more common. These social gatherings of women sharing family recipes developed into organized cooking classes, and successful teachers in turn provided recipes to women's magazines and published cookbooks of their own. The most prolific of these teachers, Josefina Velázquez de León, traveled throughout the republic, holding cooking classes and collecting regional recipes. Her most important work, *Platillos regionales de la República mexicana* (1946), gathered for the first time in a single volume the distinctive dishes of each state. Upon her death in 1968, she had published more than 150 cookbooks exalting tamales and enchiladas as culinary manifestations of Mexican nationalism. Her audience came from the rapidly growing middle class, the wives of businessmen and professionals who shared her vision of the mestizo nation.

These cookbooks portrayed an image of Mexico quite different from the official ideology of the ruling party. Middle-class female cookbook authors paid little attention to traditional heroes of Mexican history such as Benito Juárez and Emiliano Zapata. Instead, they centered their culinary history on the legendary seventeenth-century nuns credited with inventing *mole poblano*, on Emperor Agustín Iturbide, the conservative Independence leader who reputedly inspired the creation of *chiles en nogada*, and on the ill-fated French-imposed emperor Maximilian and empress Carlota, who supposedly introduced French cooking to Mexico. Conservative, religious figures thus formed the pantheon of domestic, middle-class patriotism. The inclusion of tamales and enchiladas within the national cuisine represented not the radicalism of Frida Kahlo but rather an effort to assert hegemony by appropriating Native American symbols and sanitizing them of their former lower-class associations.

Twentieth-century Mexican authors have imagined cuisine to be a symbol of their national identity, a mestizo blend of Native American and Spanish influences. Virtually every dish in the modern kitchen betrays this mixed heritage, from European sausages and stews infiltrated by American chili peppers to the indigenous beans and tamales now cooked with fat from the conquistadors' pigs. Nevertheless, Mexican elites accepted this blending only with great reluctance, preferring the more fashionable culture of Europe. The creation of Mexico's national cuisine is therefore a story of contributions to society made by subordinate groups, both the wealthy women who handed down recipes for colonial *moles* and the poor ones who preserved the pre-Columbian art of making tamales. These culinary traditions, once scorned by a Eurocentric elite, now provide lasting symbols of *lo mexicano*.

See also Maize

Select Bibliography

Appadurai, Arjun, "How to Make a National Cuisine: Cookbooks in Contemporary India." *Comparative Studies in Society and History* 23 (1988).

Coe, Sophie D., *America's First Cuisines*. Austin: University of Texas Press, 1994.

Lomnitz, Larissa Adler, and Marisol Pérez-Lizaur, *A Mexican Elite Family, 1820–1980: Kinship, Class, and Culture*. Princeton, New Jersey: Princeton University Press, 1987.

Ross, Oliver D., "Wheat Growing in Northern New Spain." *North Dakota Quarterly* 45 (Summer 1977).

Super, John C., *Food, Conquest, and Colonization in Sixteenth-Century Spanish America*. Albuquerque: University of New Mexico Press, 1988.

—JEFFREY M. PILCHER

D

Day of the Dead

The Day of the Dead has long been one of Mexico's richest, most varied, and famous annual holidays. Foreign visitors flock to Mexico during the last days of October and first days of November to witness a fantastic, original, and creative cultural display. Candies, breads, paper cutouts, and toys fashioned of plastic and clay, all playing humorously on the theme of death, are evident everywhere. Miniature sweets in the form of skulls, skeletons, and caskets give evidence of an almost irreverent confrontation with mortality. During November 1 and 2, Mexicans visit cemeteries to clean and adorn the tombs of deceased relatives. *Ofrendas,* or offerings, consisting of flowers, candles, and food, are arranged artistically on graves in honor of the deceased. In some parts of the country, including celebrated places like Mizquic immediately south of Mexico City and Purépecha villages around Lake Pátzcuaro in the state of Michoacán, family members hold an all-night vigil at the graves of the departed. Throughout the country, people erect home altars, usually made of plain wooden tables elaborately adorned with offerings of candles, flowers, food, and drink, especially comestibles that the deceased was known to enjoy.

Some Mexicans claim that the souls of the departed watch over their living relatives during the Day of the Dead. Negligent family members await punishment, whether on earth or in the afterlife. Throughout Mexico, this belief is invoked to explain the substantial outlay of time, money, and energy invested in the two-day ceremony. At the same time, it is clear that the holiday provides a boost to local economies, through its promotion of tourism and the lucrative sale of sweets, candles, and flowers. Increasingly, Day of the Dead iconography is employed by small businesses and large department stores to augment the sale of industrial, mass-produced products. Lively drawings of animated skulls and skeletons adorn bakeries, candy stores, and supermarkets throughout large Mexican cities. Reproductions of the *catrina*—the famous female dandy, sporting fleshless face, billowy scarf, and wide-brimmed, plumed hat—are used by salespeople everywhere to attract customers from all social classes and ethnic backgrounds. If the Day of the Dead was ever restricted to a particular social class or ethnic group, the holiday is now celebrated in every geographic region and stratum of Mexican society. It has become among the most salient Mexican national symbols.

It is essential to note that, although the Day of the Dead is associated with Mexico and Mexico alone, its celebration coincides with pan–Roman Catholic feast days, specifically All Saints' Day on November 1 and All Souls' Day on November 2. The term *Día de Muertos* is essentially Mexican, although perhaps the earliest use of this term comes from a Catalan document produced on October 15, 1671, by the Barcelona silversmith's guild in which reference is made to the *Diada dels Morts.* Throughout the Spanish-speaking world outside of Mexico, All Saints' Day is generally called *el Día de Todos Santos,* while All Souls' Day is referred to variously as *el Día de Animas* (Souls' Day) or *el Día de los Fieles Difuntos* (the Day of the Faithful Deceased). In the state of Michoacán, the most popular term is *la Noche de Muertos* (the Night of the Dead), which emphasizes the importance of the all-night candlelight vigil on November 1–2 to the celebration of the holiday in this region.

To the Vatican, only one thing counts in the celebration of All Saints' and All Souls' Days: the observance of special masses on November 1 in honor of the saints and on November 2 in honor of the souls in purgatory. Special masses date from medieval times. During the first third of the eighth century, Pope Gregory III set aside November 1 as a sacred occasion for the Christian faithful to commemorate all the saints. All Souls' Day, November 2, is liturgically the more critical day of the two. On this date, the Office for the Dead and Requiem Masses are celebrated in sympathy with the deceased in order to help them achieve final purification. The choice of November 2 is generally attributed to St. Odilo (d. 1048), the fifth abbot of Cluny. By the fourteenth century, both these dates had assumed a permanently important place in the liturgical calendar. Nowadays, the Catholic Church requires that parish priests recite one special mass on November 1 and another on November 2, although three masses on November 2 are more common: one in honor of the departed souls, a second in honor of a cause designated each year by the pope, and the third in recognition of a cause designated by the parish priest himself.

These special masses constitute what might be called the official celebration of these two feast days. Most observers of Mexico would agree, however, that masses are not the most salient parts of the celebration. The majority of the activities and artistic displays connected with the Day of the Dead represent a folk elaboration, a deviation from orthodox religious practices. Halloween is the U.S. version of this popular celebration, a version so secularized that only the centrality of sweets, the incorporation of ritualized begging, and the prevalence of skeleton costumes and skull-like Jack-o-Lanterns connects it to the contemporary Mexican event.

Scholars have engaged in an ongoing debate about the origins of the Day of the Dead. Because the Day of the Dead is a flamboyant, colorful holiday of considerable renown, it is often cited as expressing a uniquely Mexican view of death, one that demonstrates, in Octavio Paz's words, that "The Mexican . . . is familiar with death, jokes about it, caresses it, sleeps with it, celebrates it; it is one of his toys and his most steadfast love." The alleged Mexican lightheartedness toward death often is contrasted with U.S. denial of death and Spanish lugubriousness. The Day of the Dead is taken as the epitome of Mexican attitudes toward death and dying. Perhaps for this reason, the Day of the Dead, more than any other Mexican ritual, is often said to be either a basically pre-Conquest Indian concept with a European Catholic veneer or a near-seamless fusion of pre-Conquest and Roman Catholic ceremonial practices. The celebration has become a marker of Mexican identity. Consider for example the opinion of scholars Robert V. Childs and Patricia B. Altman, who claim that

the beliefs and practices associated with contemporary observances of Día de Muertos, although not a direct and simple survival of pre-Hispanic ritual, have their roots in the ancient religions of Mesoamerica. . . . However

successful the Spanish church may have been in the destruction of state cults, it is apparent on close scrutiny that much "Catholicism" of contemporary Indian communities is pre-Hispanic in origin, especially the beliefs and customs related to death and the dead.

True, the ancient Mexica (Aztecs) expressed an inordinate concern with death. They celebrated a number of feast days in honor of the dead, among the most prominent being Miccailhuitontli, or the "Feast of the Little Dead Ones," and Miccailhuitl, or "Feast of the Adult Dead." In contemporary Mexico, in fact, November 1 is generally the day in which people mourn the death of children, while November 2 is the day set aside for mourning those who died in maturity. To this extent, there is a probable correspondence between ancient Mexica practices and those today. Further, the Mexica displayed an elaborate iconography of death. Rows of human skulls lined the four sides of the rectangular *tzompantli*, or skull rack, atop which countless sacrificial victims died. Several Mexica deities, including the death god Mictlantecuhli and the earth goddess Coatlicue, are portrayed with fleshless faces.

Much of the justification for claiming pre-Columbian antecedents derives from such ancient Mesoamerican iconography, with its undeniable plethora of skulls and skeletons, corresponding to the equally plentiful presence of similar motifs during the Day of the Dead today. Then, too, the Mexica, like contemporary Mexicans, incorporated anthropomorphic sweets into their religious ceremonies. Periodically, throughout the ritual year, the Mexica fashioned images out of wood, which they covered with *tzoalli*, or amaranth seed dough, shaped in human form. The images, usually representing deities, were distributed for consumption among certain social classes. It of course has been tempting for scholars to interpret these *tzoalli* as ancient precursors of the special breads known as *pan de muerto* as well as of the skull-shaped sugar candies widely sold during late October and early November in Mexico today.

And yet, it is important to refine our comparisons and recognize critical distinctions between ancient and contemporary skulls and skeletons. For one thing, skulls today tend to be humorously decorated sugar confections that are named after and given as presents to living friends and relatives. No contemporary Mexican death ceremony utilizes a real human skull. By contrast, the Mexica used real skulls as decorative motifs. Although these might be adorned with eyes, noses, or other features made of semi-precious stone, the basis of the statuary was actual bone. Anthropomorphic candies like *tzoalli*, on the other hand, represented full-fleshed supernatural beings, not live humans. Moreover these figures were serious in intent and, insofar as we know, completely devoid of the playfulness that characterizes contemporary Day of the Dead sweets. In fact, there is no evidence that the Mexica cult of death even remotely approximated the humorous tone that characterizes the Day of the Dead as we know it.

For the historical record as well as for defining Mexican national identity, it is important to analyze precisely what, if anything, is unique about the Day of the Dead. To begin, consider several ritual elements that usually are considered traditional in the popular celebration of this holiday. First comes the graveside vigil at cemeteries. Family visits to the graves of the departed are absolutely critical to the Mexican celebration of the Day of the Dead. Visits to the graves occur throughout Spain and parts of Latin America, although they almost always take place during the daytime. Most of Mexico in fact follows this general pattern. However, in specific regions of rural and urban Mexico, the graveside vigil, normally called *la velación* (after the candle lighting), occurs principally at night.

Where nighttime visits to the graves occur, the event has become a major tourist attraction for both foreign tourists and urban Mexicans. Scholar Jesús Angel Ochoa Zazueta, who has studied the impact of tourism on the Day of the Dead in Mixquic, says that visitors are required to pay an entrance fee to observe the cemetery vigil. "The visitors on this day pay for everything," he adds. In Tzintzuntzan, on the shores of Lake Pátzcuaro, the enormous influx of outsiders to the cemetery on the night of November 1–2 has induced some mourners to insist that tourists pay for taking photographs. Without doubt the nighttime vigil is an expression of sincere concern for the ongoing spiritual presence of the departed. Nonetheless, it also assumes a theatrical dimension in which mourners enact what they know to be an exotic performance in exchange for cash. In urban Mexico, an opposite process occurs: mourners actually pay performers, specifically musicians, to sing at the gravesides. At Panteón Dolores, the municipal cemetery in Mexico City, mariachis and other musicians wander among the graves seeking work. Mourners hire these musical groups to sing to the departed.

A second important element in the Mexican celebration of the Day of the Dead is the erection of altars in homes, commercial establishments, and public institutions. Altars in honor of the saints are, of course, an integral feature of homes, stores, hospitals, and schools throughout Spain and Latin America. But altars of extraordinary elaborateness and exuberance erected in honor of the departed are a special feature of the Mexican celebration of All Saints' and All Souls' Days. The simplest home altars consist solely of candles and flowers, almost always the yellow *cempasúchil* (from the Nahuatl *cempoaochitl*). Most include bread and fruit, sugar and *mole*; beer, tequila, and other liquor; and pictures of saints and of the deceased.

The decoration of home altars is increasingly replicated on tombstones and in public urban settings. The grave site of Pedro Infante, at the Panteón Jardín in Mexico City, is replete with head shots and photographs showing the movie idol in his most famous roles. Taped recordings of his singing blare from a loudspeaker resting to one side of his tomb. At the Plaza Río de Janeiro in the Colonia Roma, Mex-ico City, the gay community erects dozens of altars in honor of AIDS victims. In addition to candles, flowers, photographs, and sugar skulls, these altars display condoms and informational pamphlets. Schoolchildren create altars to decorate school entrances and hallways, and supermarket employees use store products to create elaborate Day of the Dead altars, which greet customers at store entrances.

A third critical element of the Day of the Dead celebration is ritualized bell ringing and begging. Traditionally, both in Spain and Latin America, the night of November 1–2 has been one in which the church bells should *doblar,* that is, toll in lugubrious indication of mourning, precisely in the manner that occurs when an individual in the community dies. In Mexico, religious brotherhoods or male youth typically have been in charge of the bell ringing. It has been characteristic of All Saints' and Souls' Days, too, that charity is dispensed. Hence, in both traditional Spain and Mexico, needy members of the community would walk from grave site to grave site, asking for the right to pray in honor of the deceased; in return they receive bread, fruit, or other foodstuffs from the mourners. In communities of the state of Michoacán, the youth who are in charge of bell tolling traditionally have had the right to go from house to house, begging for food and drink. On the night of November 1–2, they stay up taking turns ringing the church bells, while others built a fire in the churchyard, which they would use to stay warm and cook the food collected on this occasion. Children throughout Mexico have long used the Day of the Dead as an opportunity to beg passersby for *mi muertito* (little dead one)—the term used to refer to any sweet or item of food the targeted adult is willing to donate. Nowadays children walk through grave sites and city streets with small plastic Jack-o-Lanterns, begging for *"mi Halloween,"* which denotes any small coin or candy.

Ritualized begging and bell ringing, graveside vigils, altars with simple or elaborate offerings—all of these elements are associated elsewhere than Mexico with the celebration of All Saints' and All Souls' Days. Nonetheless, it would be difficult to find another country that celebrates this holiday with the color, exuberance, and sheer outlet of money and effort that can be found in Mexico. To this extent, the Mexican Day of the Dead is unique.

There are two additional ways in which the Day of the Dead is unique. First is the prevalence of humor. As befits any extensive mortuary ritual, the Day of the Dead certainly has its serious, mournful side. However, this annual celebration is and has long been used to poke fun not only at death itself but also at political leaders and public figures. The traditional vehicle for ridicule, and one that seems to grow in prominence with every passing year, is the *calavera*, literally, skull. *Calaveras* come in the form of sugar, chocolate, and amaranth seed sculptures molded as skulls. Candy *calaveras* come in all sizes; they are whimsically decorated with multicolored designs and the name of a living person, to whom the item is presented as a gift.

The term *calavera* refers also to satirical poetry composed to highlight the shortcomings of the person to whom it is dedicated. Friends and relatives write *calaveras* for one another, thereby demonstrating a important social tie; the assumption is that poet and recipient are so close that the bond between them can withstand the shock of ridicule. More prominent, however, is the *calavera* in the public domain, mainly newspapers and magazine supplements, in which artistic caricatures of politicians and well-known literary figures, screen stars, singers, and other celebrities are accompanied by often biting, satirical poems. The poetic *calavera* provides a safe, predictable outlet for the expression of hostility against the privileged and wealthy. Just as the sugar *calavera* implicitly communicates the idea that none of us is immune from death, so the poetic *calavera* shows that the wealthy and powerful are no better than the mass of humanity. The *calavera* is a brilliant social leveling mechanism. It, together with the rest of the humor and whimsy that characterize the Day of the Dead, is unique to Mexico.

A related feature unique to the Mexican Day of the Dead is the pervasiveness of sugar skulls, caskets, cadavers, and other mortuary figurines. To be sure,

people in different parts of Spain, Italy, and other European countries eat sweets specially fashioned for All Saints' and All Souls' Days; on the island of Mallorca, they sell *panetets de mort* (little dead breads); in Spain *ossos de sant* (saints' bones); and in Portugal, *maminhos do preto* (little dark breasts). All of these utilize sugar but have a base of some other substance, be it nuts or flour. Only in Mexico are the figurines actually fashioned from sugar in a paste known as *alfeñique*. The earliest evidence of this practice comes from the Capuchin friar Francisco de Ajofrín, who in the mid-eighteenth century wrote,

> Before the Day of the Dead they sell a thousand figures of little sheep, lambs, etc. of sugar paste, which they call *ofrenda,* and it is a gift which must be given obligatorily to boys and girls of the houses where one has acquaintance. They also sell coffins, tombs, and a thousand figures of the dead, clerics, monks, nuns and all denominations, bishops, horesmen, for which there is a great market.

Sugar figurines have been a unique and central part of the Mexican Day of the Dead for at least the past 250 years.

The Day of the Dead, in the form we know it today, probably dates from colonial times. It shares much with All Saints' and All Souls' Days traditions elsewhere in the West and Latin America, but is sufficiently elaborate and unique to be considered essentially Mexican. There is very little evidence—with the notable exceptions of the iconography of skulls and skeletons and the separation of days devoted to the mourning for youth and adults—that the holiday derives from pre-Conquest ritual practices. More likely, it is a product of colonial circumstances, in which death through disease and warfare was so rampant that conditions were ripe for an elaborate mortuary ritual to take firm hold. It is possible, too, that both the humor and sugar figurines operated in the past as a psychological defense against the heartbreaking reality of extraordinarily high mortality rates.

Nowadays, the Day of the Dead operates principally as a marker of Mexican national identity. Fifty years ago, along the vast northern border of Mexico with the United States, it was uncommon—even exotic—for Mexicans to celebrate the Day of the Dead. The Day of the Dead was associated in the minds of these northerners with central and southern Mexico, while these *norteños* themselves dressed their children in scary costumes and went trick-or-treating in celebration of Halloween. Slowly, from the 1960s on, the Day of the Dead spread throughout the entire Mexican republic, as this holiday became increasingly identified with Mexico. Halloween, by contrast, became associated in Mexican minds with the United States. Especially since the 1980s, however, Halloween has begun to take hold in Mexico, as Sanborns, Superama, Aurora, and other large and powerful commercial chain establishments use sophisticated advertising techniques to sell Halloween masks, costumes, candy, and plastic Jack-o-Lanterns. Many Mexicans, especially the intellectual and artistic elite, express resentment of this incursion of Halloween into central Mexico. They detect in this trend a threat to what they consider to be the survival of pre-Hispanic customs as represented by the Day of the Dead. And yet, most of the Mexican bourgeoisie and working class seem to have adopted this American holiday with fervor.

At the same time, the Day of the Dead has crossed the border into the United States, where Chicanos and other citizens of Mexican ancestry have made the holiday an expression of national identity. Throughout the southwestern United States, elaborate Day of the Dead altars are erected. Increasingly, too, family members visit and adorn the graves of their departed relatives on November 1 and 2. Schoolchildren in California and states as far away from Mexico as New Jersey learn not only about Halloween but also the Day of the Dead. The Day of the Dead has thus become transnational, a holiday that expresses Mexican identity, to be sure, but also a celebration that increasingly belongs to citizens of both Mexico and the United States.

Select Bibliography

Brandes, Stanley, *Power and Persuasion: Fiestas and Social Control in Rural Mexico*. Philadelphia: University of Pennsylvania Press, 1988.

Brodman, Barbara, *The Mexican Cult of Death in Myth and Literature*. Gainesville: University Presses of Florida, 1976.

Carmichael, Elizabeth, and Chloë Sayer, *The Skeleton at the Feast: The Day of the Dead in Mexico*. London: British Museum, 1991; Austin: University of Texas Press, 1992.

Childs, Robert V., and Patricia B. Altman, *Vive tu Recuerdo: Living Traditions in the Mexican Days of the Dead*. Los Angeles: Museum of Cultural History, 1982.

Ingham, John M., *Mary, Michael, and Lucifer: Folk Catholicism in Central Mexico*. Austin: University of Texas Press, 1986.

Nutini, Hugo, *Todos Santos in Rural Tlaxcala: A Syncretic, Expressive, and Symbolic Analysis of the Cult of the Dead*. Princeton, New Jersey: Princeton University Press, 1988.

Paz, Octavio, *El laberinto de la Soledad*. Mexico City: Cuadernos Americanos, 1950; 2nd edition, Mexico City: Fondo de Cultura Económica, 1959; as *The Labyrinth of Solitude: Life and Thought in Mexico*, New York and London: Grove, 1961.

—STANLEY BRANDES

De la Huerta, Adolfo 1881–1955

President

A key figure in the Mexican Revolution, Felipe Adolfo de la Huerta Marcor was born in the port city of Guaymas, Sonora, on May 26, 1881. His father was a merchant who had established good relations with the Yaqui Indians of the region, and the family's comfortable middle-class status enabled it to send Adolfo to Mexico City to study. He made good use of his time there, studying bookkeeping as well as singing (he had a very good tenor voice) and the violin. His father's death abruptly ended his studies, and he was forced to return to Guaymas. He found work as an accountant for a local bank and later as an administrator in a tannery, although he also found time to develop his artistic talents.

De la Huerta's political doubts were first awakened by the propaganda of the Jacobin Partido Liberal Mexicano (PLM), and he subscribed to its newspaper, *Regeneración*. De la Huerta was alienated by the PLM's radicalism, however, and in 1909 he supported the failed presidential bid of Bernardo Reyes. He later supported Francisco I. Madero in his campaign to oust the dictatorship of Porfirio Díaz, and he was part of the reception committee that welcomed Madero to Guaymas.

De la Huerta was an active Madero supporter during the Revolution of 1910, presiding over the Revolutionary Party of Sonora, and after Madero's victory he was elected as local representative in the state legislature. As a state representative he supported Plutarco Elías Calles in his bid for commissioner of the border town of Agua Prieta and clinched Álvaro Obregón's bid for the municipal presidency of Huatabampo. He participated in the fight against Orozquista rebels and proposed solutions to the endemic problems with the Yaqui Indians.

De la Huerta happened to be in Mexico City during the coup d'état against the Madero government, and he returned north to organize opposition to the coup's leader, Victoriano Huerta. He made contact with the governor of Coahuila, Venustiano Carranza, and provided a link between him and Revolutionary forces in Sonora. He attended a meeting in Monclava, Coahuila, in which the Revolutionary forces accepted (provisionally at least) Carranza's leadership. Following defeat of Huerta in October 1914, de la Huerta was named chief of staff in the Ministry of the Interior under Carranza, and in August 1915 he was promoted to secretary of the interior. In May 1916 he assumed the post of interim governor of Sonora.

During his tenure as interim governor, de la Huerta implemented a number of important social reforms. He attempted to broker a peace settlement with the Yaqui Indians and, on a somewhat more sour note, issued decrees against Chinese immigrants in Sonora. One of his most important reforms was the establishment of a state "chamber of workers" to represent workers and mediate labor disputes. At the end of his term de la Huerta handed the governorship to General Plutarco Elías Calles and returned to Mexico City as chief of staff in the Ministry of the Interior; he later served as consul general in New York. In 1919 he was nominated as the official governor of Sonora, and the good impression he had made as interim governor helped him win the election handily.

Nonetheless, de la Huerta's relationship with the federal government during his term as constitutionally elected governor would be far less amicable. In June 1919 the Sonoran Álvaro Obregón was named a candidate for the presidency, and Carranza's opposition to his candidacy alienated the people of Sonora. De la Huerta's first direct confrontation with Carranza was over a seemingly minor technical matter. The federal government declared that the Sonora River belonged under its jurisdiction, while the state government insisted that it belonged under local jurisdiction, since it did not flow into the ocean. In fact, the Carranza administration was looking for an excuse to drop de la Huerta and thus decrease the influence of Sonora. General Manuel M. Diéguez was sent to Sonora as a new military commander for the region. As military commander Diéguez posed a grave threat to the constitutional government of Sonora, attempting to provoke a confrontation with the Yaquis and gain control of the state. With his characteristic diplomatic acumen, de la Huerta armed a contingent of volunteers and was able to convince the officers at Diéguez's operations headquarters to ally with him and not obey Diéguez. Realizing that he had lost control of his own army, Diéguez returned to Guadalajara.

Meanwhile, the national political crisis had begun to heat up. In February 1920 Calles resigned as secretary of industry, commerce, and labor to help lead the Obregón campaign. Following his return to Sonora in April, de la Huerta named him state military commander. Tensions between Sonora and the Carranza administration continued to mount, and when Obregón narrowly avoided capture at the hands of federal authorities in Mexico City a rebel plan was drawn up in Sonora. Titled the Plan of Agua Prieta, the plan was published on April 23 and began a broad national movement of not recognizing Carranza or the governors of the states that supported him. In what has been termed a "generals' strike," the majority of officers in the Mexican army refused to support Carranza; Diéguez, one of Carranza's last military supporters, was taken prisoner in Guadalajara. Carranza attempted to move his government to Veracruz as he had done in 1915, but railway lines had been cut and Carranza and his entourage were forced to retreat on horseback into the Sierra of Puebla, where he was attacked and killed on May 21. Congress named de la Huerta interim president of Mexico until presidential elections could be held and a new president sworn into office on November 30, 1920.

De la Huerta traveled from Sonora to Mexico City to assume the presidency on July 1. The major accomplishment of the de la Huerta administration was, after almost a decade of civil war, to achieve the pacification of Mexico. Carranza had clashed with numerous groups: the Revolutionary followers of Emiliano Zapata and Pancho Villa, counterrevolutionaries such as Manuel Peláez and Félix Díaz, states' rights movements in Oaxaca and Chiapas, and many others. Now that Carranza, their old enemy, was dead, de la Huerta was able to convince the rebels to lay down their arms. Some were integrated into the new government; others, such as Pancho Villa, retired to private life. Only Félix Díaz was forced into exile.

In contrast to the harder line taken by his fellow Sonorans Obregón and Calles, de la Huerta developed a more conciliatory style of government. He formed a cabinet that represented a wide range of anti-Carranza groups. He named José Vasconcelos, who had been living in exile, rector of the national university, and he presided over a veritable educational revolution. De la Huerta's six-month term of office saw considerable labor unrest, but he was able to contain the conflicts. De la Huerta's greatest problem was the United States' refusal to recognize his government. All of de la Huerta's overtures failed, and the problem remained unresolved when he handed the reigns of government to Obregón in 1920.

During the Obregón administration de la Huerta was named secretary of the treasury. De la Huerta,

Obregón, and Calles—who had been named secretary of the interior—formed the so-called Sonoran Triangle, which was seen as the pinnacle of power in Mexico. De la Huerta was able to regain control of the federal budget, as taxes from Mexico's burgeoning petroleum production helped fill depleted government coffers. He also was able overcome problems with Mexico's external debt, signing an agreement with Thomas Lamont of the International Banking Committee in 1922.

Obregón still needed to obtain recognition from the United States, and in 1923 a bilateral commission composed of two representatives from each country was established to work toward a new trade and friendship treaty. Although Obregón did not name de la Huerta as one of the members of the commission, he did ask him to intervene at particularly tense moment when the U.S. representatives threatened to walk out. Nonetheless, de la Huerta opposed the final agreement, the so-called Bucareli Accords, believing that they reversed many of the achievements of the Revolution.

De la Huerta's opposition to the Bucareli Accords came at a moment when candidates were being named for the next presidential election. Although de la Huerta was considered one of the most viable potential candidates, he threw his support behind Calles. Nonetheless, when the president of the Partido Nacional Cooperatista (National Cooperatist Party) was defeated in his bid for the governorship of San Luis Potosí, he named de la Huerta as the party's candidate for the presidency, and de la Huerta resigned as secretary of the treasury. The Cooperatistas also opposed the Bucareli Accords, and Senator Field Jurado was assassinated in the dispute.

The situation between September and December 1923 was quite tense. Although Calles was supported as the candidate of the Partido Laborista (Labor Party), the Cooperatistas were attacked and persecuted. A number of generals, chiefs of military operations, and other officers allied themselves with de la Huerta, and after receiving the support of General Guadalupe Sánchez of Veracruz in December, de la Huerta led a rebellion against the government. The rebellion extended along two fronts, the eastern front, which comprised the states of Puebla, Veracruz, and Tabasco, and the western front, which was centered in the state of Jalisco. As much as 60 percent of the army supported the rebellion; some generals who had been living in exile, including Salvador Alvarado and de la Huerta's old enemy Diéguez, returned to Mexico to support the uprising. Nonetheless, the rebel forces lacked a unified leadership that could coordinate their activities; the uprising has been dubbed *la rebelión sin cabeza* (the headless revolt). Obregón was able to maintain lines of communication between Mexico City and the U.S. border, preventing the two fronts of the rebel forces from uniting. Fighting continued until the first months of 1924, when the eastern front was defeated in the Battle of Esperanza and the western front at Ocotlán.

Many of the generals who had supported the rebellion were executed, but de la Huerta, Prieto Laurens, and other members of the civilian leadership were able to escape to the United States. De la Huerta spent most of his exile in Los Angeles, where he earned a living as a singing instructor. In 1935 President Lázaro Cárdenas granted him amnesty, naming him inspector general of Mexican consulates in the United States and later director general of civil retirement pensions. He died in Mexico City on July 9, 1955.

Select Bibliography

Dulles, John W. F., *Yesterday in Mexico: A Chronicle of the Revolution, 1919–1936.* Austin: University of Texas Press, 1961.

—ÁLVARO MATUTE

De Las Casas, Bartolomé

See Las Casas, Bartolomé de

Díaz, Porfirio   1830–1915
General and President

This entry contains two articles that discuss the life of Porfirio Díaz:

Díaz, Porfirio: Biography
Díaz, Porfirio: Interpretive Discussion

Díaz, Porfirio: Biography

Born in the city of Oaxaca on September 15, 1830, Porfirio Díaz was the son of José de la Cruz Díaz and Petrona Mori. He lost his father at age three and worked odd jobs to help support mother and family while attending private and public school. In 1843 he began attending Conciliar Seminary in Oaxaca, but the U.S. invasion in 1846 interrupted his studies, leading him to drill with a local battalion. Díaz saw little action and returned to the seminary but abandoned it again to pursue legal training at the Institute of Arts and Sciences of Oaxaca in 1849. He studied law until 1854 but did not receive a degree.

Liberal leaders in 1855 appointed Díaz *jefe político* (political boss) of the Ixtlán District because of his support of the Plan de Ayutla, which led to the overthrow of Antonio López de Santa Anna. He joined the Oaxaca National Guard in 1856 and fought on the Liberal side during the Wars of Reform (1858–61), attaining the rank of brigadier general in 1861. After briefly serving as a federal deputy from Oaxaca, Díaz joined the forces of Benito Juárez during the French Intervention and led a successful attack against the French army at Puebla on May 5, 1862, helping achieve the great Mexican victory celebrated annually as Cinco de Mayo. Afterward, he commanded the Army of the East in more than 25 battles, including the liberations of Oaxaca, Puebla, and Mexico City. Díaz retired in 1867 following the victory over the French, but he later accepted command of the second division of Tehuacán, Puebla. He invested in a telegraph line between Oaxaca and Puebla and presided over its inauguration on January 19, 1868.

When Juárez chose to run for a fourth term as president in 1871, Díaz and Sebastián Lerdo de Tejada ran against him. When no clear winner emerged, the constitution threw the election to Congress. Juárez, whose supporters held the most seats, carried the day. Díaz, unlike Lerdo de Tejada, refused to accept the results and declared a rebellion against Juárez, the Plan de la Noria, on November 8, 1871. The revolt failed and Juárez died afterward, leaving Lerdo in the presidency. Díaz retired to Tlacotalpan, Veracruz, to build furniture and plan a new political campaign.

Díaz issued the Plan de Tuxtepec on January 10, 1876, against Lerdo, charging him with violating state sovereignty. Díaz led a military force against government troops in Tlaxcala, and reinforced by Manuel González, triumphed and took Mexico City on November 21, 1876. After submitting to Congress a no-reelection amendment to the Constitution, Díaz successfully ran for president, assuming office on May 5, 1877. During his first term, various revolts of political and agrarian origin plagued him. The most serious rebellions occurred along the U.S. border, led by supporters of exiled president Lerdo de Tejada. Not only did Díaz put down uprisings such as these with brute force, he often ordered the execution of the participants. One example occurred in Veracruz, when Díaz sent a telegraph containing the order *Mátalos en caliente* (Kill them on the spot) to Governor Luis Mier y Terán concerning various prisoners. Díaz centralized political and economic power, decreasing the power of the regional governors and reorganizing finances. The increased strength of the government led to new debt and border security agreements with the United States.

Díaz chose not to run for reelection in 1880 despite pressure from supporters. Instead, he tapped Manuel González, who easily won the office. Díaz briefly remained in government as head of the Department of Development and later as governor of Oaxaca, serving in the post from December 1881 to October 1883. His wife, Delfina Ortega y Reyes, died in 1880. The following year Díaz married Carmen Romero Rubio, daughter of Manuel Romero Rubio, a cabinet member and prominent Positivist. She was 18 and he 51. In 1884, he successfully ran again for president, ushering in a period of increased development while consolidating his rule. In fact, Díaz was elected for five additional terms between 1888 and 1910. The government, under the guidance of Treasury Minister José Yves Limantour, improved credit and reorganized the banking system. In addition, Díaz presided over the modification of Mexico City's drainage system and the dedication of numerous public buildings, monuments, parks, and statues.

Under Díaz, the philosophy of Positivism permeated the upper echelons of government. The Científicos, as those who advocated the application of the scientific method to government became known, were rarely optimistic in their belief that Mexico could educate the Indian masses. Most Científicos believed the nation's future lay with the upper classes and advocated a paternalistic attitude toward the indigenous population. Regarding the nation's economy and foreign trade, during the 1880s and 1890s Díaz presided over a government program that lowered or eliminated most import duties and negotiated a series of loans with favorable rates of interest. Most important, Mexico moved from the silver to the gold standard. Although these measures resulted in a positive image abroad, poverty increased among the poor in Mexico.

Díaz advocated increased industrialization, especially railroad expansion. In 1876, 400 miles (650 kilometers) of track existed in all of Mexico. By 1911, 15,000 miles (25,000 kilometers) were in use. Major lines were completed from Mexico City to outlying border regions and ports, including one from the capital city to Laredo, Texas, in 1888. Financed with mostly U.S. and British capital and using foreign technology, the railroads opened the

Mexican countryside to development. Agricultural production in outlying areas such as the Laguna region in northern Mexico allowed domestic textile mills to use Mexican cotton instead of imported stock. Sugar planters in Morelos imported technology to modernize their facilities. Overall, the railroads allowed Mexican industry to ship raw materials to factories and move finished goods to domestic markets and port facilities.

The use of force to pacify the countryside made industrial expansion possible. Díaz strengthened the *rurales,* a rural militia, into a powerful force to be used to put down revolts. In the urban sector, Díaz expanded police forces, projecting an image of safety to potential foreign investors. Occasionally the inner reality of police corruption revealed itself, as on September 16, 1897, when Arnulfo Arroyo, a known drunk, assaulted Díaz during a military procession. Díaz was unharmed, but agents, acting under the orders of the inspector general of police, murdered Arroyo in his cell. Perhaps the most ingenious method used by Díaz to maintain regional control involved playing off one powerful group or leader against the other. Díaz appointed judges and replaced provincial leaders who had grown too independent.

As Mexico neared the centennial year of Independence, 1910, Díaz grew confident that the system of control he devised would keep the peace. In a 1908 interview with U.S. journalist James Creelman, Díaz said he would retire in 1910. Encouraged by the news, Francisco I. Madero, a northern industrialist, began to campaign for free elections. Soon, Madero joined the Anti-Reelectionist cause and ran for president when it became apparent Díaz would not step down. Briefly imprisoning Madero, Díaz won the presidency for the eighth time. The regime, however, could not squelch the fires of opposition. On November 20, 1910, the first phase of the Mexican Revolution began with a series of regional revolts that spread throughout the country, culminating in the surrender of Ciudad Juárez in May 1911. Díaz, faced with a successful rebellion, resigned the presidency and left Mexico on May 31, 1911, for exile in Paris. During his last years he received accolades from world leaders and toured other nations. He died on July 2, 1915.

Select Bibliography

Beals, Carleton, *Porfirio Díaz: Dictator of Mexico.* Philadelphia: Lippincott, 1932.
Beezley, William H., and Colin M. MacLachlan, *El Gran Pueblo: A History of Greater Mexico.* Englewood Cliffs, New Jersey: Prentice-Hall, 1994.
Camp, Roderic, *Mexican Political Biographies, 1884–1935.* Austin: University of Texas Press, 1991.
Meyer, Michael C., and William L. Sherman, *The Course of Mexican History.* 4th edition, Oxford and New York: Oxford University Press, 1991.

—JAMES A. GARZA

Díaz, Porfirio: Interpretive Discussion

Porfirio Díaz is a vitally important but also a thoroughly controversial figure in the history of modern Mexico. As president for a total of 31 years (1876 to 1880 and 1884 to 1911), he holds the record, and the dubious honor, of being the country's longest-serving constitutional leader during Mexico's often painful evolution as a modern nation-state. His contribution to the construction and evolution of the Mexican nation is often overlooked and frequently has been denigrated in the post-Revolutionary era, since official historiography after 1910 toppled him from his pedestal in the pantheon of Liberal patriots, a position that Díaz himself and his closest associates had attempted to cultivate in his lifetime. As a consequence, Díaz became vilified as a despot, a villain, and traitor to his country by those who sought to legitimize both the Revolution and the political system that emerged from it. Only in recent years has there been an attempt to reevaluate the image of Díaz, first in the light of the growth and sophistication of historical research, especially in Mexico, and second, in accordance with the reformist, cosmopolitan, and neoliberal preoccupations during the presidential administrations of the 1980s and 1990s, especially those of Carlos Salinas de Gortari (1988–94) and Ernesto Zedillo Ponce de León (1994–). These factors, in combination with the political and economic uncertainties unleashed by the North American Free Trade Agreement and *neozapatismo,* have fostered a wave of nostalgia for and revisionism of the Porfirian era (also known as the Porfiriato), most clearly demonstrated by the creation of more than 100 episodes of the historical soap opera (enigmatically titled *El vuelo del águila,* the Eagle's Flight) based on the life of Díaz shown by Televisa, the national television network in 1994.

One of the principal problems in the interpretation of Díaz and his regime is the fact that too much attention has been paid to the final period of presidential office (1906–10), a period in which the regime struggled unsuccessfully to find an adequate response to the economic, social, and political problems engendered by the rapid transformation of the Mexican economy in the 1880s and the 1890s. The years immediately preceding 1910 can be seen, ironically, as a period in which the regime became a victim of its own economic success, since during the Porfiriato Mexico had vastly increased the scale of its mineral and agricultural exports to international markets, attracted ever-increasing levels of foreign investment, and embarked upon an ambitious project of railway construction and public works that transformed the economic and social infrastructure of much (but certainly not all) of the country. This developmentalist economic strategy had made a significant contribution to the consolidation of the regime, but, at the same time, had created a growing number of problems related to the uneven distribution of land and economic resources and the failure to broaden the scope of political participation and democratic legitimacy.

The regime's response to the growing crisis after 1906 was hesitant, inconsistent, internally divided, and, on certain notorious occasions (such as the repression of the mining and textile strikes of 1906 and 1907), highly repressive. It was, in addition, obviously unsuccessful, as demonstrated by the rapid momentum gained by the Madero Revolution after November 1910. In the succinct metaphor of historian Alan Knight, the regime on the eve of the Revolution resembled a creature which could no longer adapt to the changed surroundings of its environment: "like some saurian monster, the regime lacked a political brain commensurate with its swollen economic muscle: hence its extinction."

But to interpret the entire regime largely on the basis of its character and conduct in these last years would be a mistake, since the image clearly would be distorted. All too often the regime has been examined from the perspective of the Revolution and its aftermath: in order to comprehend the regime more fully, it must be seen from the perspective of the nineteenth century.

The political longevity of the Díaz regime was founded upon the construction of a modus vivendi between the three most important components of nineteenth-century Mexican and Latin American politics. First, the traditions of patriarchal authority and the complex network of patronage represented by *caudillismo* (the exercise of personal, authoritarian, noninstitutional power so common in the Hispanic world); second, the diverse and often contradictory traditions within nineteenth-century Mexican Liberalism (constitutionalism, the supremacy of civil power and the secular state, the effective expression of popular sovereignty and representation, and the conflict between centralism and federalism over the distribution of political power between central and regional government); and third, the emergent conservative ideology of Positivism, with its emphasis on "scientific" politics (organic political harmony, social order, and industrial progress). This is not to suggest, however, that the balance was equal between the component parts of the regime. If we examine each of these in turn, then it is clear that the first two elements were far more significant than the third in the origin, structure, and evolution of the regime.

Most historians of *caudillismo* would acknowledge the difficulties of generalization in describing a phenomenon that affected the whole of the continent of the Americas for much of the nineteenth century (and beyond). Most would agree, however, that the "classic" caudillo who dominated the early post-Independence period in Spanish America was a combination of warrior, patriot, and *patrón*, who rose to political power and prominence from a local or regional base. There can be little doubt that Porfirio Díaz demonstrated all of these attributes to a greater or lesser extent both before and after his ascent to the presidency, although his powers of patronage did not result from personal wealth, landed estates, or business acumen, but rather from the military status and political offices he enjoyed from a relatively early age—by the age of 31 he had become both a brigadier general and a *diputado* (member of the National Congress).

There were very early indications of his future development as both warrior and patriot. At the tender age of 16 (in 1846), the young Porfirio, who was preparing under the guidance of his uncle (and future bishop of Oaxaca), José Agustín Domínguez, for a career in the priesthood, volunteered his services to the Trujano Battalion of the National Guard, formed in his native Oaxaca to defend the country in the wake of the invasion of Mexico by U.S. troops. Even though the battalion never saw active service, Díaz's interest in and affinity for military matters lasted throughout his lifetime, and his personal correspondence shows a long-standing interest in military affairs in general and especially in the latest developments in weaponry and military technology. This does not mean, however, that Porfirio Díaz was another in a long line of authoritarian Spanish American military caudillos who represented the interests of the army in the struggle with civil authority. During his long tenure of office, not only did Díaz demonstrate that he was the only nineteenth-century Mexican president able to control the military, but he was also most successful in removing the threat of the frequent military interventions into politics that had characterized the post-Independence period.

Díaz also must be distinguished clearly from the archetypal caudillo in terms of his Liberal political convictions. Whereas "classic" caudillos were characterized by an absence of personal ideological commitment, or, more frequently, were the agents, allies, or subordinates of Conservative interests, Díaz was an ardent supporter of the Liberal cause. At the age of 18 he gave up his studies at the seminary to study law at the liberal Institute of Arts and Sciences in the city of Oaxaca. In fact, when Díaz did eventually take up arms in December 1854, he did so not in pursuit of a professional military career, but, significantly, in response to the dictates of his Liberal political convictions.

The broader, national context for the launch of Díaz's political and military career in 1854 was the political challenge from dissident liberalism to the regime of Antonio López de Santa Anna, a challenge embodied in the Plan de Ayutla of March 1854. After the initial persecution and arrest of its most prominent Liberal enemies (which in Oaxaca included Benito Juárez, and Díaz's liberal *padrino*, the lawyer Marcos Pérez), the regime called for a national plebiscite in December 1854. In Oaxaca, despite the official claim that the vote was to be a free expression of the popular will, voting took place in public in the central square of the city under the watchful gaze of the governor and the military commander of the state, General Ignacio Martínez y Pinillos. Díaz, following the completion of his studies at the institute, had been appointed as a temporary professor of natural law in that same institution. When it was publicly announced that the staff of the institute unanimously supported the continuation of Santa Anna in office, Díaz asked to register a vote of abstention, but, following a public accusation that he had failed to register his vote out of fear, Díaz responded by openly declaring his support for the leader of the Ayutla Rebellion in the state of Guerrero, General Juan Álvarez. An order was issued for Díaz's arrest, and he was obliged to flee the city and to find refuge with a rebel band in the *sierra*.

The drama of this event—which confirmed the image of Porfirio Díaz as committed Liberal, determined rebel, the resolute and fearless leader who possessed the courage of his convictions—has without doubt been embellished for posterity, especially in the proliferation of biographies of Díaz that appeared during the last years of his presidency, when his cult of personality was at its height. Nevertheless, it is tempting to see in the events of 1854 and 1855 the encapsulation of vital elements that would be central to his rise to presidential power in 1876: the tenacity and self-confidence, the thirst for power, the qualities of leadership, and his patriotic liberalism. These attributes would be demonstrated frequently during his subsequent military career between 1855 and 1867, especially during the Wars of Reform (1858 to 1861) and the French Intervention (1862 to 1867). His military career gave him the status of national hero, associated above all with the liberation of Puebla on April 2, 1867. It also enabled him to broaden his network of contacts, subordinates, allies, and admirers, and to pursue his relentless quest for presidential office, whether by means of election (when he stood unsuccessfully against Benito Juárez in the presidential elections of 1871), or by insurrection (unsuccessfully in the Rebellion of the Noria in 1871, and, successfully, in the Tuxtepec Rebellion of 1876).

In the phase of political consolidation that followed his ascent to the presidency for the first time in 1876, the political base that had been nurtured over the previous two decades was fostered and extended. As a consequence, political power in the Díaz system was exercised through a wide network of formal and informal personal relationships carefully cultivated across a broad social spectrum (from peasants to cabinet ministers), and based upon negotiated rather than enforced exchanges of deference and loyalty to the patriarchal figure of Porfirio Díaz. His personal correspondence shows that Díaz adopted a variety of strategies that were skillfully employed to maintain control over the political life of the nation, ranging from the overt use of flattery, discretion, personal appeals to loyalty, patriotism, and self-sacrifice to the covert, but no less effective use of duplicity, manipulation, and, in the last resort, the threat of force or federal military intervention. This political apparatus also was fueled by the provision of multiple opportunities for profit (and graft) to individuals who acted as agents, partners, or intermediaries in foreign enterprises, which proliferated in the wake of the considerable success the regime enjoyed in attracting foreign investment. In short, the political style was fundamentally pragmatic, emphasizing the practice of realpolitik, not only in the conduct of everyday politics, but also with regard to the key political triumphs and successes of the regime: the manipulation and control of regional elites, the reconciliation between church and state, the professionalization (and political emasculation) of the army, the control of the press, and the restoration and extension of diplomatic relations after very inauspicious beginnings in 1876. Díaz's political skills were much in evidence in each of these areas of policy, all of which were vital to the consolidation and survival of the regime.

In spite of the emphasis placed here on pragmatic politics, and in spite of the clear manipulation of liberal ideology and rhetoric by the regime, the basic tenets of political liberalism never were relinquished (personal and political freedom; a secular, republican state without corporate structures or privileges; a society posited upon economic progress; social mobility; and private property). Díaz's commitment to liberalism, however, remains controversial and ambiguous, despite his repeated declarations of loyalty to its principles (as in, for example, his famous declaration to the U.S. journalist James Creelman in 1908, that "I believe democracy to be the only true, just principle of government," before going on to declare—falsely, of course—that he would retire from office in 1910).

Nevertheless, it is increasingly clear that liberalism, traditionally interpreted as an esoteric ideology espoused by and for the benefit of a minority elite, enjoyed considerable popular support among rural communities throughout Mexico in the nineteenth century. As a consequence, liberalism provided both a popular political base for Porfirismo, especially in its early years, as well as a constitutional and ideological framework around which the regime was constructed.

However, while the regime claimed legitimacy through the adherence to the Constitution of 1857 and to constitutional practices (such as elections), in practice it blocked the creation of institutions (i.e., political parties, institutions of government, or an independent judiciary) that would have restrained presidential or personal authority. As an advocate of pragmatic politics, Díaz himself openly admitted his skepticism of constitutional or ideological purity, if we are to believe an anecdote recounted by one of his biographers (J. F. Iturribarria). In response to a request from a journalist as to how to respond to accusations in the opposition press (made in the newspaper *El Partido Liberal*) that the regime had violated the principles of the 1857 Constitution, Díaz chose to draw an analogy with the practice of religion:

The answer is simple: Catholics violate the 10 Commandments every day, because it is impossible to comply rigorously with every one of them: it is equally impossible for the government to adhere strictly to the letter of the law as laid down in our Constitution.

Díaz's natural pragmatism and cynicism were given further endorsement by a third component that provided ideological justification for the regime, particularly in its latter years: Positivism. A powerful faction within the ruling elite warmly embraced this fashionable ideology because it provided them with a political theory that advocated economic progress and social planning under the control of a technocratic elite and bolstered by an authoritarian government. Despite his resolute support of pragmatism rather than ideology as the basis for political action, and despite his claims to be a Liberal, Díaz endorsed the Positivist view that the practice of politics should not concentrate, as liberalism demanded, on the protection of individual freedom, the equality of the individual before the law, or on a guarantee of effective suffrage or democratic representation, but on the protection of social order and the promotion of material (or scientific) progress. As he explained to James Creelman in 1908:

We have preserved the republican and democratic form of government. We have defended the theory and kept it intact. Yet we adopted a patriarchal policy in the actual administration of the nation's affairs, guiding and restraining popular tendencies with full faith that an enforced peace would allow education, industry and commerce to develop elements of stability and unity.

As Díaz himself admitted in the same interview, however, the political situation of 1908 demanded a new form of popular representation. Unfortunately for the regime, the factional divisions within the elite made it impossible to reform the system from within, and no alternative or successor could be agreed upon. The political reforms promised in 1908, which had aroused considerable expectations and political activity throughout the country, failed to materialize.

The indifference with regard to the maintenance of the content as well as the form of Liberal constitutional practice became one of the regime's greatest shortcomings. While the restrictions on the development of political institutions and parties helped to keep opposition to a minimum, it deprived the regime of both institutional forms of succession and of a means of channeling the demand for wider political participation in a society that had undergone a profound transformation by 1910. In addition, the adherence to Positivism, by widening the ideological and factional divisions within the Porfirian elite, narrowed the ideological base as well as the constituency of support for the regime. It was also obvious to many observers that Díaz, as he approached his eightieth birthday in 1910, no longer possessed the capability nor the energy to sustain the necessary degree of control over a personalist system under increasing strain.

As a consequence, the regime's response to the growing political crisis was inadequate, inept, and counter-productive. As the anti-reelectionist movement gained steady momentum after 1908, the regime attempted to repress and erradicate opposition, and, in desperation, persuaded the old caudillo to stand for another term of office in the elections of 1910. Less than a year later, the Maderista Revolution had forced Díaz to relinquish power and go into exile in Paris, where he died in 1915.

For nearly two generations following the death of Porfirio Díaz, his regime was associated in the popular imagination with the worst of excesses of tyranny: the willful violation of Mexican sovereignty, the abuse of constitutional authority, dictatorship, repression, and elitism. In the 1980s and 1990s, however, there have been encouraging signs, however, that official anti-Díaz satanization is increasingly moribund. As the Mexican historian Enrique Krauze stated in a biographical sketch of Díaz in 1987,

> a more generous interpretation—which has always been absent in Mexico—would concede, without distorting the truth, that Porfirio Díaz made a decisive contribution to the material construction and the national consolidation of his country.

Select Bibliography

Katz, Friedrich, "Liberal Republic and Porfiriato." In *Mexico Since Independence,* edited by L. Bethell. Cambridge and New York: Cambridge University Press, 1991.

Knight, Alan, *The Mexican Revolution.* 2 vols., Cambridge and New York: Cambridge University Press, 1986.

—PAUL GARNER

Díaz del Castillo, Bernal c.1495–1584

Conquistador and Chronicler

Bernal Díaz del Castillo is acclaimed today as the author of the most popular and comprehensive eyewitness account of the conquest of Mexico. Despite the extravagance of some of his claims and the inaccuracy of some of his data, his *Historia verdadera de la conquista de la Nueva España* (True Account of the Conquest of New Spain) remains the most rich and compelling version available, eclipsing even Fernando (Hernán) Cortés's famous *Cartas de relación* (1519–26).

Born in Medina del Campo in Old Castile, Bernal Díaz declared that he arrived in the New World in 1514 on Pedrarias Dávila's voyage to Tierra Firme (Nombre de Dios in Panama) and that he participated in the first three expeditions to Mexico, which were those of Francisco Hernández de Córdoba (1517), Juan de Grijalva (1518), and Hernán Cortés (1519). Although it is doubtful that he took part in the second of these expeditions, he is widely acknowledged to have participated as a foot-soldier in Cortés's first overland march to the Mexica (Aztec) capital of Tenochtitlan in 1519 as well as the second major offensive that resulted in the fall of that island capital (the site of today's Mexico City) in August 1521 and subsequent events in Mexico up to 1524. He accompanied Cortés on the disastrous expedition to Hibueras (Honduras) in 1524–26 and spent the remainder of his life in New Spain, sustained by titles of trusteeship *(encomienda),* whereby the labor and goods produced by Indians inhabiting the area held in trust were granted to the trustee *(encomendero)* as tribute. With early grants in the 1520s near Coatzacoalcos in Tabasco and in Chiapas (which he lost in the 1530s), Bernal Díaz settled permanently in Guatemala in the 1540s after the first (1539–41) of his two trips to Spain to secure greater reward for his conquest efforts. The second trip, which either awakened or confirmed his worst forebodings about the future prospects of the *encomendero* class, occurred in 1550–51. He died an octogenarian in Santiago de Guatemala on February 3, 1584.

Bernal Díaz began to write his *Historia* around 1550, some 30 years after the fall of the Mexica capital; in 1568 he finished a version of the work, which he sent to Spain in 1575 for publication. In the meantime he continued to work on the manuscript in his possession, adding the last touches close to the time of his death. During his lifetime, other historians of Mexico, such as Alonso de Zorita (1560s) and Diego Muñoz Camargo (1576), mentioned Bernal Díaz's writings in their own; at least one local resident in Santiago de Guatemala, the municipal official Juan Rodríguez del Cabrillo, stated in 1579 that he had read Bernal Díaz's chronicle.

Bernal Díaz's work thus had at least a limited local circulation in manuscript during his lifetime, but the version sent to Spain was not published until 1632, when it suffered the emendations of Fray Alonso de Remón and Fray Gabriel Adarzo y Santander, who sought to highlight the work of their Mercedarian order and the Christian mission in general in the conquest of Mexico. The manuscript that remained in Guatemala was transcribed and published in Mexico by Genaro García in 1904–05 and now is regarded as the authoritative version of the work.

Although Bernal Díaz's *Historia* concentrates on the events of the Mexican conquest from 1519 to 1521 (chapters 19–156), the work covers events in Mexico from 1517 through 1568 (chapters 1–18, 157–212); it includes the discussion of affairs pertinent to the well-being of the viceroyalty of New Spain that occurred at court in Spain as well as in the seats of governance of Hispaniola and Cuba. Broader in scope than the 1519–21 conquest of Mexico that is the heart of the work, Bernal Díaz's objective was to place New Spain in the context of the Spanish Empire at the time and to ensure that the importance of Mexico was not eclipsed by the subsequent discovery of Inca Peru and its spectacular mineral wealth in the South American Andes.

Equally if not more pressing was his desire to claim for the common conquistador (himself and his remaining peers and their heirs) the privileges and prestige that he understood to be their due and to ensure that those rewards would endure in perpetuity. His trips to Spain taught him that the interests of the *encomenderos* were being eroded by a series of royal decrees that had begun with the New Laws of 1542 as well as by competing claims for royal recognition from others, not the least of which was a developing royal bureaucracy dedicated to managing the Crown's resources at home and abroad. Politically, the conquests in America had come under increasingly severe pressure from Fray Bartolomé de Las Casas and his colleagues, who persuaded the emperor, in the name of Christian evangelization and justice, to curtail the prerogatives of private citizens and their access to the native populations of the Indies.

Even the writing of history had dealt the conquistadors a severe blow. Cortés's published letters (1522–26) effectively attributed the victory over the Mexica to his own brilliance as a military strategist and faith in Divine Providence, and Francisco López de Gómara (1552) and other historians likewise emphasized Cortés's role to the detriment of that of his men. Additionally, these authors inadvertently but effectively undermined the conquistadors' interests by complacently assuming the justice of the conquests at the very time they came under political and legislative attack. This attack was vividly realized in Las Casas's tract the *Brevíssima relación de la destrucción de las Indias,* which appeared in print in Seville in 1552 and which was rebutted by Bernal Díaz in his *Historia* with the same or greater vehemence and scorn that he heaped on López de Gómara's work.

Bernal Díaz's *Historia* is thus of great interest today not only for its inimitable account of the conquest of Mexico, written several decades after the fact, but also for its compelling dramatization of how an old conquistador struggled year by year to keep pace with the events that threatened his economic and political well-being. His greatest achievement was his attempt to grant to the soldiers-conquistadors of Mexico the glory he thought ought to be theirs in accordance with the long Castilian tradition of the Christian warrior who fought against pagans and infidels in the name of his Christian faith.

Select Bibliography

Brooks, Francis J., "Moteuczoma Xocoyotl, Hernán Cortes, and Bernal Díaz del Castillo: The Construction of an Arrest." *Hispanic American Historical Review* 75:2 (1995).

Díaz, Bernal, *The Conquest of New Spain,* translated and with an introduction by J. M. Cohen. Baltimore: Penguin, 1963.

Pastor Bodmer, Beatriz, *The Armature of Conquest: Spanish Accounts of the Discovery of America, 1492–1589,* translated by L. L. Hunt. Stanford, California: Stanford University Press, 1992.

—ROLENA ADORNO

Doña Marina

See Malinche and Malinchismo

Drug Trade

The illicit production of and commerce in drugs in Mexico is oriented toward exports. Most of the marijuana and heroin produced in Mexico, as well as the cocaine traversing the country, is smuggled to the U.S. market. The use of these drugs has not yet become a significant public health problem in Mexico. The only available national household survey on drug abuse (published by *Encuesta Nacional de Adicciones* in 1989) showed that in 1988, of the total Mexican population between 12 and 65 years of age, living in urban areas, 2.99 percent had used marijuana at least once in their lifetime, 0.33 percent had tried cocaine, and 0.11 percent had experimented with heroin. The prevalence of drug use in Mexico, according to this survey, was less than one-tenth that in the United States in 1990, and among the lowest in Latin America.

More important than users as a determinant of the drug trade in Mexico has been the relationship between the price of drugs in this country and their price in the United States, which is largely the result of antidrug law enforcement in both nations. In this market, the costs of producing and exporting drugs reflect the risks of engaging in these illicit activities, which in turn depend on more or less stringent levels of enforcement. Historically, the Mexican drug market has reacted to changes in U.S. antidrug policy, which has followed an increasingly punitive trend. By and large, U.S. efforts to stop drugs (marijuana, heroin, and cocaine) before they enter U.S. territory have worked against domestic Mexican efforts to fight drug trafficking. Furthermore, largely unsuccessful Mexican attempts to curb this illegal market have, over time, had a severe impact on Mexican society and institutions, as well as on U.S.-Mexican relations.

Origins of the Drug Trade

Drug smuggling became a lucrative activity in Mexico at the beginning of this century when the United States approved laws that prohibited the import of opium and cocaine, which had been legal until then. As a result of restrictions on production and trade in drugs, a large part of the American drug market went underground. The U.S. government decision to limit vice markets, drugs and alcohol in particular, resulted in an overnight increase in the prices of these goods, an increase that had a direct effect on Mexico. The enactment of the Opium Exclusion Act of 1909, outlawing the importation and use of opium, of the Harrison Narcotic Law in 1914, prohibiting over-the-counter sale of opium and cocaine in the United States, and of the 1922 Narcotic Drug Import and Export Act, further restricting the import of crude opium and coca leaves, effectively created a profitable market for narcotics in the United States and provided an incentive for Mexicans (and others) to ship drugs into the United States and take advantage of the high prices.

Mexican exports of opium and heroin for U.S. consumption flourished in the 1910s and 1920s. Something similar happened with Mexican exports of marijuana, as more and more states in the United States regulated its use, production, and sale. The cannabis plant, which had been produced legally in Mexico and exported since the late nineteenth century, if not earlier, mostly for industrial and medicinal purposes, quickly reached the U.S. market in larger quantities in the 1920s and 1930s. Thus, a significant contraband along the U.S.-Mexican border emerged after 1910, basically prompted by prohibition in the United States.

Opium coming from other countries also was introduced into Mexico, apparently in large quantities, to be smuggled later into the United States. As a result, Mexico became not only a more prominent producer and exporter of opium and its derivatives, and of marijuana, but a temporary importer too, since its territory offered an attractive transit point for opium smugglers (and later for those carrying cocaine) on their way to the United States.

As opium, morphine, heroin, cocaine, and marijuana dealers became federal or state offenders in the United States, Mexico also became a safe haven for those engaging in illegal transactions across the border, since transgressors could cross the frontier to escape from U.S. law-enforcement authorities. It was not unusual for U.S. officers to cross the border in "hot pursuit" of Mexican or American criminals.

It should not be surprising then that Mexico's first legislation against drugs, introduced by President Venustiano Carranza in 1916, prohibited the import of opium, the use of which was practically nonexistent in Mexico. By banning opium imports Carranza was trying to counter the impact of American antiopium laws on Mexico, that is, the growth in Mexican opium imports and exports, the flight of drug dealers into Mexican territory, and the ensuing U.S. law enforcement raids across the border.

At the same time, Mexican law enforcers and politicians (such as Esteban Cantú, strongman and local governor of Baja California Norte) offered protection to or became active organizers of opium contraband into the United States. In 1917, only a year after banning the importation of opium, Carranza outlawed opium transactions in Baja California Norte, where Cantú ostensibly was contravening the prohibitory statutes.

In response to the proliferation of opium poppy production, President Álvaro Obregón instructed governors in the northern states to ban cultivation and to destroy existing fields before they could be harvested, and in 1923 he promulgated a new decree prohibiting the importation of opium, cocaine, and heroin, and mandating harsher penalties for drug growers and manufacturers. The federal government had already prohibited the cultivation and sale of marijuana in 1920. By the mid-1920s, most of the drug trade in Mexico was illegal.

Yet efforts to enforce antidrug laws only led to the creation of a persevering smuggling business. To the extent that antidrug laws proved to be unenforceable both in Mexico and the United States, more forceful attempts to prohibit the drug trade led to the creation of an ever more lucrative market, largely organized around the use of violence and corruption. By 1927, when President Plutarco Elías Calles signed yet another decree banning the export of marijuana and heroin, it was clear that Mexico was no longer an important transit point for international drug smugglers, but that drug production and trafficking had become entrenched in certain areas of the country. As the 1930s came to an end, Mexican officials had learned that the drug trade could not be stamped out by decree and that efforts to enforce antidrug laws invariably resulted in the corruption and killing of numerous officials. Marijuana and opium poppies were readily available, and their cultivation had expanded beyond northern Mexico. Although presumably the bulk of the drug contraband still originated in Baja California, Sinaloa (by 1943 opium had become the largest cash crop in the state), Sonora, and Chihuahua, large smuggling operations also were organized, for the first time, in states located farther south, such as San Luis Potosí.

Mexican Drug Trade from 1945 to 1980

In 1948 the Mexican government tried to confront a thriving drug market by organizing La Gran Campaña. This program became the first national crop eradication campaign to cover virtually the whole country; a specialized unit of antinarcotic police and a small number of soldiers (no more than 400, according to official accounts) were assigned to the campaign. Since then, these forces have participated in antidrug programs on a permanent basis.

The end of World War II, as well as the subsequent increase in the use of heroin—notorious in the 1950s and 1960s in the United States—had a negative impact on the Mexican drug market. The scant information available indicates that the traditional heroin routes were disrupted as a result of the war, and as traffic from the Far East and Europe through Central America was interrupted, Mexico became an attractive alternative for international heroin traffickers to reorganize their smuggling of heroin into the United States. Apparently, the Mexican government was able to postpone with U.S. assistance (mostly from agents of the Federal Bureau of Investigation) the relocation of heroin trafficking organizations in Mexican territory. However, after heroin manufacturing in Italy and France was banned in the 1950s and 1960s, and after Turkey enforced a draconian program against the cultivation of opium poppies in the late 1960s, Mexico finally became the primary source country for heroin bound to the U.S. market

(according to the President's Commission on Organized Crime, 1986). It is possible that up to 10 tons of heroin were processed every year in Mexico during the mid-1970s, 6.5 tons of which probably were smuggled into the United States.

In the case of marijuana, a considerably larger market in terms of users, Mexican producers and smugglers took perhaps the lead, although often aided by U.S. traffickers, in supplying the heavily expanding demand among the American population in the 1960s. With the exception of a few years, Mexico has been the most important foreign supplier of marijuana for the U.S. market.

Figures on the size of the Mexican drug market can vary considerably, as a result of both political interests and technical difficulties in estimating illegal markets. All sources, however, indicate that by the early 1970s Mexico was supplying more than 80 percent of the heroin and marijuana available in the United States, and was already an important transit point for cocaine (still a small market in those years).

As Mexico emerged as a major producer and exporter of heroin and marijuana, the U.S. government became interested in organizing a joint U.S.-Mexico drug law enforcement program to improve the effectiveness of Mexican policy against the illicit narcotics business. Practically all authors consider U.S. pressure the most important factor explaining the launching, at the end of 1975, of a major antidrug campaign in Mexico—a turning point in Mexico's history against drugs. The typical example of those pressures (and universally considered evidence of the new, more forceful U.S. antidrug policy) is Operation Intercept, which virtually stopped border crossings for a few weeks in September 1969 by meticulously inspecting millions of cars and individuals every day. More important, however, than this exercise in coercive diplomacy was Mexico's evaluation of the risks for Mexican society and institutions of the notorious increase in drug trafficking activities and, equally important, Mexico's perception of the threat that U.S. antidrug policy and agents could represent for the autonomy of its own law enforcement programs.

Drug trafficking organizations had acquired considerable power in traditional drug producing and exporting areas, such as Durango and Sinaloa. The Mexican military, then basically relying on manual destruction of plants, had to fight not only the increase of illegal crops throughout the country but, more significant, a growing number of peasants and smugglers armed and organized for the defense of their illicit activities.

For years, the U.S. government had been fighting for a more stringent enforcement of antidrug laws in Mexico. But by 1973–74, the newly created Drug Enforcement Administration (DEA) was concentrating its efforts on the Mexican case and was ready to fight drug traffickers on its own or through a joint law enforcement program, in which the Mexican government refused to participate, fearful of entering into negotiations with foreign police—technologically and organizationally superior to the Mexican police—for the improved enforcement of its antidrug laws.

Thus, in order to regain control over areas of intense drug trafficking and to maintain antidrug law enforcement as a national affair, the Mexican government opted for a major change. Effective implementation of its new antidrug policy, however, had to rely on U.S. cooperation. The U.S. government offered financial and technical assistance (aerial photographic equipment, telecommunications, helicopters and other aircraft, spare parts, etc.), but most important, police training and support. DEA agents trained a special antinarcotics police unit in Mexico, assisted in the identification of fields, and compiled and shared intelligence with their Mexican counterparts in order to build conspiracy cases against drug traffickers. Three different programs were organized following the DEA's advice: a massive aerial eradication campaign with defoliant chemicals, which seemed adequate under the circumstances (large extensions of land covered with marijuana and opium poppy plants, and powerful, armed traffickers organizing their defense); a program for the interdiction of drugs in transit (including cocaine); and a program oriented toward the dislocation of major drug trafficking organizations. This three-pronged policy remained unaltered for more than 20 years, although resources committed to any one of the programs, as well as targets and tactics, varied over this period.

The results of Operation Condor, the core program, were astonishing. Mexican authorities were able to destroy most of the clandestine production of marijuana and opium poppy in a few years; thousands of hectares were defoliated (between 1975 and 1978, an annual average of 6,000 hectares of marijuana and more than 11,000 of opium poppy). The amount of heroin and marijuana seized reached the highest levels ever, except for 1984. Major drug traffickers were incarcerated (Sicilia Falcón, members of the Herrera family, Jorge Favela Escobar, and others). Mexico's share of U.S. heroin and marijuana imports, usually taken as a proxy for the size of the Mexican drug market, tumbled to around 25 percent or less by 1980, the lowest percentage since the 1940s.

The 1980s Drug Boom and Its Consequences

The "wars on drugs" launched by the Ronald Reagan and George Bush administrations in the 1980s represented a major change in U.S. antidrug policy and diplomacy that had far-reaching effects on the Mexican drug market and on U.S.-Mexican relations regarding the contraband of drugs.

The U.S. government decided to assume a larger responsibility in stopping the traffic of drugs by financing a major domestic interdiction program oriented to halt the illegal import of narcotics at traditional U.S. ports of entry. At the same time, the U.S. government decided to increase its capacity to assert extraterritorially its criminal laws by changing antidrug legislation and heavily expanding federal expenditures to control drugs.

The U.S. interdiction program resulted in an elevation of risks and costs for drug smugglers, and consequently in an unprecedented increase in the price of drugs in the United States. The Mexican government was unable to counter this major change in the relative price of narcotics.

Thus, Mexican drug production and exports effectively boomed in the 1980s. As the smuggling of cocaine, mostly from Colombia and entering the United States via Florida, encountered new obstacles, traffickers reorganized and began sending their merchandise through Mexican territory, eventually striking alliances with local drug smugglers. By the mid-1980s Mexico was again the main supplier of both marijuana and heroin for U.S. consumers, and had become the most important transit point for cocaine.

This new generation of drug traffickers, however, was considerably more powerful than those of the 1970s. The wealth amassed by drug trafficking organizations in very short periods of time and the institutional weaknesses of the Mexican police and criminal justice system explain why drug trafficking became such a formidable challenge for state authority in the 1980s and 1990s. Starting in the mid-1980s, the autonomous enforcement of Mexican antidrug laws became increasingly difficult, as DEA agents began to fight drug traffickers in Mexico more and more frequently on their own, that is, without the consent of Mexican authorities, and as Mexican institutions were increasingly unable to counter not only the economic incentives to smuggle drugs into the U.S. market but the deleterious political effects of the booming drug trade.

In 1987 President Miguel de la Madrid declared narcotics trafficking a national security problem and completely reorganized Mexican antidrug policy, a reorganization that, on similar grounds and with even larger funding, was furthered by the Salinas administration. Notwithstanding a considerable growth in financial and human resources (more than 25,000 soldiers engaged year-round in the eradication program, one-third of the nation's defense budget, and over half of the Attorney General's Office's funds), the viability of the new antidrug programs required, again, U.S. support, especially in police training and intelligence sharing.

The refurbished policy obtained historically unprecedented figures regarding the seizure of cocaine—largely the result of the joint U.S.-Mexican Northern Border Response Force, organized for the aerial interdiction of cocaine smuggling at the border. The Mexican eradication program, nevertheless, has showed increasingly diminishing returns over the 1980s and 1990s. The renewed fight against drug trafficking in Mexico also led to the incarceration of major drug lords, such as Rafael Caro Quintero (held responsible for the torture and murder of DEA agent Enrique Camarena in Mexico in 1985, which unleashed a severe U.S.-Mexican diplomatic crisis), Miguel Angel Félix Gallardo, and Ernesto Fonseca Carrillo. Others, such as "El Güero" Palma, "El Chapo" Guzmán, and Humberto and Juan García Abrego, were detained.

By and large, the Mexican government proved unable to control the illegal drug business. To the extent that drug policies raise the price of drugs, and consumers continue to number several million people capable of financing an expensive habit, prohibition results in a permanent incentive to produce and smuggle drugs. Moreover, trying to suppress such a large and lucrative market has taken a heavy toll on the traditionally weak Mexican criminal justice system. The expansion and persistence of this illegal market has damaged Mexican society and institutions in unanticipated and unpredictable ways.

The conspicuous impact of drug trafficking on the Mexican economy and political system is, however, difficult to evaluate. Estimates in 1987 and 1988 of total Mexican drug revenues (i.e., export earnings) oscillated between US$2 billion and US$6 billion a year, not all of which was invested or spent in Mexico. These figures probably had increased by the mid-1990s, but not dramatically. What changed was the amount of drug trafficking money entering the Mexican financial system as the country became a major money laundering center in the early 1990s.

Considering that Mexico's Gross Domestic Product was $288 billion in 1991, one could argue that drug-related income did not modify the Mexican economy at the macroeconomic level. However, after the mid-1980s, it had an important influence on rural areas, small towns, and even large cities such as Guadalajara, where traffickers successfully established their operations. Drug profits were invested in different economic activities: cattle ranching, real estate, restaurants, shopping centers, the stock market, vacation centers, currency exchange houses, small retail businesses, and local banks; much, of course, also was spent on luxury cars and ostentatious homes.

It has been reckoned that by the mid-1990s between 40,000 and 50,000 peasants in Mexico were involved in or made a living from the cultivation of marijuana and opium poppies. The economic incentives are appalling: growers would need to sell one ton of corn in order to earn as much as they make from one kilogram (2.2 pounds) of marijuana. Yet this should not obscure the fact that many people in the countryside are "talked into" illicitly growing the drug plants: traffickers have a considerable capacity not only to pay, but also to coerce and intimidate peasants (and others, including governmental authorities). They offer seeds, fertilizers, money, weapons and, equally important, protection from law enforcers, who may also intimidate peasants and even collude with traffickers.

The number of participants in this illegal market is, of course, much larger than the peasant population mentioned: pilots, drivers, middlemen, gunmen and people hired for protection—in certain cases, small private armies—money launderers, and other professionals offering a variety of legal and financial services. Starting in 1987 and continuing through the mid-1990s, more than 17,000 persons were apprehended every year on drug trafficking charges.

And yet, the economic consequences of the drug trade in Mexico pale compared with the political costs, in particular the extent to which the impossibility of enforcing antidrug laws undermined the rule of law and thus profoundly affected citizens' confidence in the state. Rumors and scandals became the standard means of learning and informing about drug trafficking.

Drug-related corruption affected the police more than any other state agency. The Mexican police, despite continuous professionalization efforts, sooner or later became involved—offering protection or actively participating in the illicit drug business. To a lesser extent, drug money also bought favors from the military, local politicians, prison custodians, pilots participating in eradication programs, and middle-level officers and officials. Many more, including journalists, prosecutors, and judges, were bribed, intimidated, or killed by drug lords.

Corruption and the use of violence—among traffickers; of traffickers against authorities; of traffickers against possible witnesses; and at times, simply to establish or reinvigorate a reputation for the effective use of violent means—unfortunately were the most infamous results of the illegal drug trade and efforts to curb it. Killings among traffickers as well as the assassination of police and other government authorities at the hands of traffickers increased to unprecedented levels in Mexico during the 1980s and 1990s. The private organization of violence by drug traffickers, to deter and even kill both law enforcers or their rivals, represents a major challenge to the monopoly of the state as the ultimate guarantor of law and order. In this sense, drug trafficking has seriously undermined political legitimacy.

Select Bibliography

Craig, Richard, "Human Rights and Mexico's Anti-Drug Campaign." *Social Science Quarterly* 60 (March 1980).
_____, "Operation Intercept: The International Politics of Pressure." *The Review of Politics* 42 (October 1980).
Lupsha, Peter A., "Drug Trafficking: Mexico and Colombia in Comparative Perspective." *Journal of International Affairs* 35:1 (1981).
Musto, David F., "Patterns in U.S. Drug Abuse and Response." In *Drug Policy in the Americas,* edited by Peter H. Smith. Boulder, Colorado: Westview, 1992.
Nadelmann, Ethan A., *Cops Across Borders: The Internationalization of U.S. Criminal Law Enforcement.* University Park: Pennsylvania State University Press, 1993.
President's Commission on Organized Crime, *America's Habit: Drug Abuse, Drug Trafficking, and Organized Crime.* Washington, D.C.: Government Printing Office, 1986.
Reuter, Peter, and David Ronfeldt, *Quest for Integrity: The Mexican-U.S. Drug Issue in the 1980s.* Santa Monica, California: Rand, 1992.
Toro, María Celia, *Mexico's "War" on Drugs: Causes and Consequences.* Boulder, Colorado: Lynne Rienner, 1995.
Walker, William O., III, *Drug Control in the Americas.* Revised edition, Albuquerque: University of New Mexico Press, 1989.
White Paper on Drug Abuse: A Report to the President from the Domestic Council Drug Abuse Task Force. Washington, D.C.: Government Printing Office, 1975.

—María Celia Toro

E

Earthquake of 1985

On the morning of September 19, 1985, an earthquake measuring 8.1 on the Richter Scale struck central Mexico, causing massive loss of life, injury, and destruction of property. Fatality figures range from under 5,000 to over 20,000, with 10,000 emerging as the most commonly cited figure. Fortunately, the quake occurred at 7:19 A.M., before most people were at work, and children had not yet gone to school. If the quake had hit several hours later, the human toll would have been much higher because large public office buildings collapsed at alarming rates.

While a number of localities suffered human and material damages, the downtown area of Mexico City bore the majority of casualties and physical damage. The quake, which lasted 90 seconds, wreaked havoc on a city constructed on unstable landfill in which many buildings, including many buildings owned by the government, did not meet internationally recognized earthquake standards. Another serious earthquake occurred the following evening, measuring 7.3 on the Richter Scale, which complicated rescue efforts, caused additional damage, and added to the level of anxiety and terror that gripped the city.

Mexico City is divided into political jurisdictions known as delegations. The delegations of Venustiano Carranza, Cuauhtémoc, Benito Juárez, and Gustavo A. Madero received 80 percent of the material damage. Among these, Cuauhtémoc, which is located in the heart of the downtown area, received the most damage: 258 buildings completely crumbled, 143 partially collapsed, and 181 were seriously affected. In Venustiano Carranza, the numbers were 83 completely destroyed, 128 partial collapses, and almost 2,000 individual dwellings were damaged. According to official figures, approximately 250,000 people were left homeless as a direct result of the earthquake. Unofficial figures are often much higher.

The earthquake resulted in a host of political difficulties for the ruling Partido Revolucionario Institucional (PRI, or Institutional Revolutionary Party) and a huge political opportunity for independent popular movements. Attention focused primarily on mobilizing and organizing the homeless, or *damnificados*. Three major groups of *damnificados* organized on a territorial basis in immediate response to the earthquake and in resistance to state's emergency response and initial reconstruction plans: 1) residents from Tlatelolco and Colonia Roma, who were mostly middle class; 2) families of *Multifamiliar Juárez,* a public housing project constructed in the 1950s and 1960s that housed retired state bureaucrats and the middle class; and 3) the *colonias* of El Centro, Morelos, Guerrero, Doctores, Obrera, Peralvillo, Asturias, Nicolás, Bravo, and other *colonias* located in the downtown area that housed workers and the urban poor.

On October 24, 1985, over 20 territorially based urban popular movements, along with the Sindicato Nacional de Costureras 19 de Septiembre, which itself had been constituted only four days earlier, joined together to form the Coordinadora Única de Damnificados (CUD). By November 9, when the CUD held its II Foro de Damnificados de la Ciudad de México, 42 organizations were in attendance. For the next year and one-half, the CUD served as the primary coordinating body for earthquake victims and the most dynamic expression of popular urban militancy between 1985 and 1987. The CUD itself built upon and incorporated existing organizations dedicated primarily to housing issues. Of them, perhaps the most important was the Coordinadora Inquilinaria del Valle de México. The leadership of the Coordinadora came from two well-known radical left organizations, the Asociación Cívica Nacional Revolucionaria (ACNR) and Punto Crítico. One of the points of dispute within the literature on the CUD concerns the balance of power within the CUD, with some arguing that power rested essentially with the popular movements and others arguing that the CUD was dominated by middle-class interests.

The drive to mobilize and organize collectively was encouraged by the fact that the government's response to the earthquake was widely criticized by a cross-section of Mexican society, and the fact that recognizing their inability to deal with the crisis through "official channels," government agencies were willing to open up the process to "opposition groups." Certainly the earthquake presented a crisis of such proportion that even governments of more wealthy nations would have had difficulty responding. Nonetheless, the response of the PRI, from the local neighborhood political machine bosses to President Miguel de la Madrid himself aggravated the political implications of the earthquake in ways not directly related to the lack of material resources. For example, de la Madrid's devotion to stabilization policies was so great that he did not take the opportunity to cut debt payments after the quake, despite public outcries to do so and political fallout for failing to explain his reasoning.

The government exacerbated political problems for itself from the outset, by announcing through the Secretariat of Urban Development and Ecology (SEDUE) that there already existed sufficient housing to absorb all those left homeless from the earthquake. Subsequent statements regarding the need to relocate downtown residents to the periphery (which is where the new housing for those left homeless from the earthquake supposedly already existed or would be constructed) was widely perceived by the CUD and large sectors of public opinion (including middle-class opinion) to be a shallow attempt by the government to use the disaster to implement a long-term goal, namely the gentrification of the downtown area.

Popular movement representatives met on September 27, 1985, with the head of SEDUE, Guillermo Carrillo Arena. Movement leaders present at the meeting have described Carrillo Arena as maintaining a very "despotic" attitude, insisting that the movements incorporate themselves into corporatist channels before expecting government concessions. Movement demands that SEDUE not give preference to PRIista demands were met with scorn, as were requests that the director assist the petitioners in their efforts to repel the eviction plans of powerful landlords.

The government began the process of reconstruction with repeated reference to *concertación* (consensus building) as the operative means by which the program could best take place. Critics responded from the outset that *concertación* required

coordination between citizen's groups and the state, which was being undermined by the state's preference for working with PRI organizations and the exclusion of popular movements from the decision-making process. The fact that the government was widely perceived to have been both authoritarian *and* incompetent in its immediate response to the emergency (with tensions already running high owing to the economic crisis and governmental austerity measures) provided for the opposition an ability to favorably shape public opinion in a manner and to a degree perhaps not seen since the Revolution. Organizations such as the CUD were populated with radical leaders who had long dreamed of just such an opportunity. They moved swiftly to politicize reconstruction to the greatest degree possible.

On October 2, more than 15,000 people marched in support of demands put forward by one of the first coalitions of *damnificados,* the Comité Popular de Solidaridad y Reconstrucción (COPOSORE). They demanded that the reconstruction be "democratic" (i.e., that it include non-PRIista popular movements), that the military pull out of neighborhoods severely affected by the quake in which popular movements were attempting to take political control despite contrary efforts by PRI organizers and the military, that the rights of tenants be respected, and that the state ensure an end to evictions. De la Madrid granted a seven-minute audience to about one dozen urban popular movement leaders, which turned into a 45-minute meeting in which the president was given a document outlining what were to remain core popular movement demands throughout the reconstruction process: expropriation of all condemned buildings and the land upon which they were situated, followed up by a "popular" and "democratic" reconstruction project, which would include the active participation of popular movements. On October 11, the president announced the expropriation of 5,500 properties, covering an area of 550 acres in the delegations of Cuauhtémoc, Venustiano Carranza, Gustavo A. Madero, and Benito Juárez. The presidential decree led to a landslide of expropriation demands by other *colonias* and their representatives.

The administration recognized very early that existing organizational arrangements were inadequate for managing both the technical and political dimensions of the crisis. On October 14, a presidential decree was issued that established the Programa de Renovación Habitacional Popular (PRHP), which was to operate under the direction of the Departamento del Distrito Federal (DDF). These new governmental locations thus became the site of many political contests between groups competing for resources and decision-making influence.

Public protest and mass mobilization designed to reform and expand official reconstruction efforts characterized the months following the earthquake. On October 26, the CUD (which had only formed two days earlier) held its first march, attended by 30,000 people. Protesters did not limit their demands to reconstruction: they insisted that the government declare a unilateral debt moratorium and channel the savings into the reconstruction effort, along with the resignation of the head of the department of the Federal District, Ramón Aguirre, and the head of SEDUE, Carrillo Arena. The protesters emphasized the need for "honest and impartial experts" to administer a reconstruction plan based on an expanded expropriation decree. Scholar Sergio Tamayo notes that the first stage of reconstruction was characterized by "political contention" and suggests that the mix of popular resistance and administration of government programs resulted in "political frictions" at the highest levels of the PRI/government over how to best manage the political fallout resulting from the crisis.

The first task of the PRHP was to produce a census, intended to identify *damnificados* and issue authorizations regarding the rights of individuals to be incorporated into the program. Renovation Councils (Consejos de Renovación) were established to facilitate this process. They quickly became locations of political conflict, particularly on those not infrequent occasions in which receiving rights under the renovation program became contingent on joining or previously belonging to the PRI. Parcero López, ex-secretary of the "third leg" of the PRI, the Confederación Nacional de Organizaciones Populares (CNOP, or National Confederation of Popular Organizations) and then federal deputy from a downtown district, was at the center of the stormy controversy regarding the politicization of reconstruction programs. CUD leaders attended these meetings and defended their memberships' right to receive impartial treatment under the program, regardless of political affiliation. While the president consistently emphasized the importance of participation from urban popular movements, officially referred to as "citizen groups," many of those in charge of implementing those programs, particularly during the early stages, made this promise a hollow one, as those not affiliated with the PRI were treated to bureaucratic run-arounds, paper trails, and other obstacles while those more willing to comply with the PRI's wishes were more promptly attended to. According to the scholar Susan Eckstein, this had

the effect of encouraging some *vecindad* (neighborhood) associations "to affiliate with the party because they thought their prospects of getting state assistance would thereby be improved."

Tensions ran high between the CUD and government officials during the period of October 1985 to February 1986. It became increasingly apparent to both sides that they needed each other if they were to make any substantial progress in the realization of their respective goals. This reality led to the alliance between state reformers and popular movements that was to follow. Certainly, not all popular movements representing *damnificados* belonged to the CUD, but a majority of the most important did. Owing to the multiclass nature of the CUD, it was impossible for the government to respond only to the CUD's middle-class interests while ignoring the interests of the popular classes, also represented by the CUD. So, while the government was learning that they could not ignore the CUD, or deal with them effectively in traditional clientelistic fashion, the CUD was learning that it would have to bargain with the federal government if it was to gain concessions. Most accounts of earthquake politics agree that the replacement of Carrillo Arena of SEDUE with Manuel Camacho Solís was a decisive turning point in the reconstruction effort.

Carrillo Arena had a number of political liabilities. His ineffectiveness during this period resulted primarily from his unshakable belief in the continued feasibility of clientelistic practices as the sole means of relations between the state and civil society, despite changes in the political context that allowed popular movements to resist such an attitude and participate more on their own terms. Furthermore, Carrillo Arena was a key architect for both the Hospital Juárez and the Multifamiliar Benito Juárez, both of which had collapsed during the earthquake, causing hundreds of deaths. On February 18, the CUD sent a telegram to de la Madrid congratulating him on the sacking of Carrillo Arena.

Immediately upon taking office, Camacho Solís reformed the political atmosphere by announcing what amounted to an open-door policy with the CUD and other popular movement representatives. In March, only weeks after taking office, the Programa de Reconstrucción Democrática de Tlatelolco was announced, thereby defusing one of the most important political hot spots in the city. Camacho recognized Tlatelolco citizen groups as legitimate interlocutors. On March 12, 1986, Camacho announced that only 11 buildings would require demolition, in place of the 27 that Carrillo Arena previously had announced. According to a CUD pamphlet, Camacho also admitted that the previous Carrillo Arena estimate contained "diagnostic errors." By discrediting and distancing himself from "people's enemy" Carrillo Arena, Camacho built on his credibility not only with the CUD but with the media, which had become more of an ally to popular movements following the earthquake than at any other time since the 1968 Massacre of Tlatelolco. While this change in policy content and the way in which policy was designed, announced, and administered did not completely reverse the political liabilities associated with reconstruction, it certainly was an important instance of damage control. The success reformers such as Camacho had in dealing with this political crisis contributed not only to the continued professional mobility of the reformers into the administration of President Carlos Salinas de Gortari but also directly bore on the tack taken by the Salinas administration in dealing with popular movements.

In early March, PRHP distributed 39,000 certificates of housing rights to be administered under the program, a substantial percentage of the total number of units to be constructed. Repairs and reparations, which had been long delayed, began finally to be carried out with increased regularity. On April 1, Parcero López was replaced with Manuel Aguilera Gómez, who immediately upon taking office, guaranteed that the PRHP would implement no program without first consulting the intended beneficiaries.

On May 16, political ace Manuel Camacho Solís met with all the significant groups representing the *damnificados*. In return for what turned out to be a truly extraordinary commitment of government resources to construct 48,000 units in a little over a year, Camacho obligated each of the movements to sign the *Convenio de concertación democrática para la reconstrucción de vivienda*. The document committed the PRHP to provide "housing actions" that would benefit 250,000 people. In direct response to popular movement demands, this *convenio de concertación* put in writing that the new housing units would respect the "urban characteristics and cultural identity" of the inhabitants from the city's center. The document also stated that beneficiaries would not be expected to pay back loans at rates beyond their means and recognized the importance of public participation in the design and implementation of the projects. As to credit terms, the document was very specific: the total cost of the loan would be repaid in a period from five to seven years at a monthly interest rate of 16 to 17 percent, which would require beneficiaries to pay between 25 and 30 percent of the minimum salary. Eckstein, in reference to the *convenio,* notes that

> safe provisional housing was to be provided for families during the reconstruction period, close to their original homes, or families were to receive economic assistance, if they found their own temporary accommodations; . . . beneficiaries would only have to repay the direct building costs; and a committee, comprised of representatives of the organizations participating in the agreement, would evaluate proposed alternative projects in terms of the norms of the agreement and existing building codes.

Not unexpectedly, the meaning and desirability of this highly publicized *convenio de concertación* was widely discussed and debated. There were 106 signatories, including the directors of SEDUE, DDF, and PRHP on behalf of the federal government; and la Federación de Comités de Reconstrucción del PRI, el Directorio de Damnificados del PST, and independent *damnificado* movements (of which CUD was the most important but certainly not the only one). The response of Cuauhtémoc Abarca, a key CUD leader, was representative of most popular movement leaders. He understood the *convenio* to be a concession by the state that the reconstruction could not happen without the independent movements, as well as an acknowledgment (however late in coming) by the government of the contribution these same organizations had been making since the beginning of the earthquake crisis. He emphasized the extent to which the *convenio* included the "immense majority" of CUD demands and saw the *convenio* as a testament to the fact that persistent mobilization and organization is capable of achieving the rights of those without significant resources.

Eckstein offers an interpretation that is quite different from that of Abarca:

> *Damnificados* did not need to belong to a group that signed the *convenio* to get housing, but the principal groups that had actively mobilized for housing all had to sign; in so doing, they agree, in effect, to work with and not against the state. The accord therefore included all relevant groups in the resolution of the political crisis. . . . The state as well as the slum-dwellers benefited from the housing reform. To get housing, defiant groups had to agree to quiescence and to accept the terms of housing imposed by the government. Meanwhile, the government allocated housing in a manner that

undermined the social base of the "new social movement" type groups.

The political implications of the *convenio* are not adequately or accurately captured by either Eckstein or Abarca. Abarca misses the fact that the *convenio* is, by definition, a mutual concession on the part of all signers. *Convenios de concertación* of both the de la Madrid and Salinas administrations should be understood as political bargains based on the exchange of valuable concessions on the part of all participants.

A review of CUD activities after the *convenio* signing suggests that the CUD in fact did alter its radical stance, in part because once the implementation of housing programs began, individual movement organizations within the CUD had their hands full overseeing the implementation of programs that were in constant threat of being sidetracked or more completely derailed by local PRI elites, real estate interests, and state employees who felt their interests threatened by specific housing projects and/or the increased popular movement influence in the political affairs of particular barrios and Mexico City politics more generally.

While Eckstein is correct that both state and popular movements benefited from the agreement, she is wrong to imply that by signing the agreement defiant groups became quiescent. Some did, others did not. In general, although the political tone of at least some popular movement activities was moderated, there is ample evidence to support the CUD's insistence that they remained anything but quiescent. Furthermore, while the government certainly endeavored to allocate housing in a manner that undermined the social base of the new social movements, it did not succeed. Many of these same signers continued to participate openly in acts of collective dissent. In fact, on May 13, 1986, when SEDUE formally submitted the signed *convenio* in a public act, upon taking the microphone, CUD representatives reiterated their insistence that the CUD would need to maintain a critical stance vis-à-vis the implementation of the program so as to ensure that the rightful demands of the *damnificados* were fulfilled to the fullest extent possible. On September 11, the CUD held a mass rally to protest a declaration made the previous day by the president of the Mexico City PRI in which he commended his party's role in the immediate emergency earthquake response and then again in the reconstruction process. The CUD declared that such comments "concealed" the true character of the PRI response, which was an effort to immobilize the *damnificados*. They were specific in their charges

by reminding the PRI that their own federal deputies had judged the September 24, 1985, expropriation proposal made by independent representatives of Colonias Guerrero, Morelos, Roma, and Tlatelolco "as adventurous, radical, and an effort to exploit an emergency situation for their own unjust reasons." This, and numerous other similar occasions in which the CUD and other *convenio* signers were to speak out against PRI and government officials, received considerable media attention and contributed in no small way to a growing disenchantment in Mexico City with the PRI, later capitalized on by opposition candidate Cuauhtémoc Cárdenas in the 1988 presidential election.

By July 1986, the Programa Emergente de Vivienda (PEV)-PRHP had assigned, repaired, and constructed nearly 80,000 housing units, to the benefit of 400,000 habitants. This level of commitment to the reconstruction, and the way in which the reconstruction had been implemented, would have been very different if not for the presence and skillful political maneuvering of popular movements. At the same time, the second phase (Fase II) of the PEV was announced with the intent of meeting the needs of the 8,000 eligible people under this program who had not had their rights fulfilled in the first stage of implementation. Fase II, which sought to provide housing to *desdoblados* (persons who live in the homes of others, sharing space and often expenses) and to those who had lost housing that existed on properties exempted from expropriation, is widely perceived to be a direct result of the persistent pressure applied by CUD and other relevant popular movements. While the movements failed to expand the number of expropriated properties, they were insistent in their call that the government was morally obligated to respond to the needs of the remaining *damnificados*. Based on official PRHP figures, Tamayo recorded that only 18 months after expropriation, the PRHP had itself reconstructed 44,500 units. While the CUD had experienced many internal divisions based on both personal and ideological differences as well as struggles for organizational control, it had been successful in presenting a unified front in dealings with the government. As observers of popular movements will appreciate, this was no small feat.

Even as Mexico City's urban popular movements involved in the reconstruction expanded their political agendas to include multiple aspects of a broad-based democratization project, most have not lost sight of the goal of providing basic housing and services to their rank-and-file. There are few periods in Mexican history during which such dramatic public works projects have been implemented with, and to a significant degree because of, independent popular movements.

Select Bibliography

Da Cruz, José, *Disaster and Society: The 1985 Mexican Earthquakes*. Lund, Sweden: Lund University Press, 1993.
Haber, Paul Lawrence, "Collective Dissent in Mexico: The Politics of Contemporary Urban Popular Movements." Ph.D. diss., Columbia University, 1992.

—Paul Lawrence Haber

Ecology

The post–World War II period in Mexican ecological history has been marked by three interrelated but often apparently contradictory currents. First, responding to broad changes in the global political economy, the Mexican government downplayed its economic strategy of replacing imported goods with domestic manufactures ("Import Substitution Industrialization," or ISI) in favor of an export-driven model of economic development. Second, this shift occurred even as Mexico faced an environmental crisis of unprecedented size and scope. Third, the environment increasingly became an arena for state intervention and popular contestation.

Article 27 of the 1917 Mexican Constitution established that all lands and waters are part of the national patrimony subject to control by the state for the public good. Specifically, the state claimed the right, in the words of scholars José Luis Zaragoza and Ruth Macías, "to regulate use of exploitable natural resources in order to make an equitable distribution of public wealth and to care for its conservation." Despite this early assertion of eminent domain, the federal government has been slow to create effective environmental legislation both because of the government's economic development models and its belated recognition of how deeply these models have degraded the environment.

By the mid-1980s, however, the environmental crisis was widely acknowledged. Media attention focused on horror stories about health hazards from border *maquiladoras* (export manufacturing plants), massive oil spills, factory and pipeline explosions, toxic waste dumping, and the asphyxiated capital, Mexico City, arguably the world's most polluted city. Meanwhile, millions of Mexicans have to cope routinely with more mundane irritants such as bad water, tainted food, open sewers, urban congestion, mountains of garbage, and the pollution that is poverty itself. At the same time they are faced both with the ongoing depletion of natural resources —massive destruction of ecosystems, poisoned or eroded soils, contaminated lakes and rivers, desertification, and rapidly vanishing forests—and with increasing pressures internationally from lending agencies and trading partners, and domestically from the government and environmentalists, to arrest this degradation.

Paradoxically, Mexico's environmental crisis has come to a head at a time of impressive achievements with respect to environmental legislation, mitigation, and conservation initiatives. These actions can be seen as part of an ongoing preemptive reform strategy aimed at co-opting the rapidly growing environmental movement and smoothing Mexico's path to a neoliberal economic model (i.e., economic liberalization, diversification, and fiscal austerity). The gap between environmental policy and practice remains vast, however, because of incompatibility with cultural mores, social structural conditions, fiscal austerity, and other political and economic factors at odds with enforcement of and compliance with environmental regulations.

Roots of the Environmental Crisis

The structural roots of Mexico's contemporary environmental crisis lie in the import-substitution strategy adopted after World War II. Until the late 1950s, a rough balance between agricultural and industrial development was maintained, contributing to the "Mexican miracle" of unprecedented growth and diversification. There was a net transfer of value from agriculture to industry, however, through production of cheap food for the new urban areas, where low wages also could be sustained. Mexico City became the national growth pole, as its population doubled between the 1940s and 1960s, while that of the surrounding federal district tripled.

By the late 1960s, critical economic bottlenecks began to emerge as the strategy of rapid industrialization at all costs exacerbated preexisting problems such as rural-urban migration, skewed income distribution, increasing regional disparities, and inefficient, overprotected industries. Agricultural growth rates declined and market forces reshaped production as staple crops increasingly were replaced by export, industrial, and forage crops. From 1970 on, Mexico was forced to import large quantities of basic foods as a consequence of technological modernization, the fruit of the internationalization of the economy.

The consolidation of the shift toward an export-led economy in the 1970s and 1980s reinforced development imbalances and accelerated ecological decline. The increasingly large role of petroleum in the national economy during the late 1970s contributed to the 1982 debt crisis and the transition to free-market policies. Mexico joined the General Agreement on Tariffs and Trade (GATT) in 1986, and the North American Free Trade Agreement (NAFTA) with the United States and Canada was implemented in 1994. Ongoing austerity measures, including social spending cuts and wage and price controls, together with the December 1994 peso crisis followed by soaring interest rates, cumulatively had a severe impact on many sectors of the population and the milieus within which they live and work. The continuing decline in living standards together with frustration over the apparent failure of political reform engendered an unprecedented level of popular protest, including a growing focus on environmental issues. At the same time, the structural adjustment required by the neoliberal transition reduced the resources available for protection of the environment at a time when it was under most pressure because of the imperative of economic competitiveness. Modernization has been achieved at high economic, social, and environmental costs. Yet, the public will to promote economic diversification, foster civil empowerment, and protect resource renewability appears to be on the upsurge.

Environmental Policy

The articulation of formal environmental policy in Mexico was prompted by the widespread international concern (fomented by United Nations initiatives in the late 1960s and early 1970s) over the impact of industrialization on the global resource base. In 1971, the first comprehensive Mexican environmental legislation was enacted, establishing principles for avoiding contamination of air, water, and soil, together with the corresponding penalties. The legislation did not, however, stipulate the norms and standards necessary for implementation, and it lacked effective regulatory authority. Consequently, throughout the 1970s environmental enforcement was negligible.

A more focused environmental law was proclaimed in 1982, prompted by growing public concerns about rising levels of smog in Mexico City, domestic nuclear power development, and the impact of oil exploitation. In 1982, the incoming president Miguel de la Madrid established Mexico's first cabinet-level environmental agency, the Secretaría de Desarrollo Urbano y Ecología (the Ministry of Urban Development and Ecology, SEDUE). In addition, the president encouraged the formation of environmental organizations via an extended national campaign to promote public awareness of the impact of human actions on the natural surroundings. The onset of the debt crisis and ensuing fiscal restraints reduced SEDUE's budget, however, and the ministry was criticized heavily for its failure to confront Mexico City's air pollution, for its response to the 1985 earthquake and other environmental disasters, as well as for generalized corruption and patronage. The de la Madrid government's commitment to environmental protection remained largely symbolic until the end of its term, when a new environmental law with more juridical teeth and greater regulatory capacity was enacted.

The 1988 Ley General del Equilibrio Ecológigo y el Protección al Ambiente (General Law of Ecological Equilibrium and Environmental Protection) differs from its predecessors in its integral ecological approach to the goal of environmental "preservation, restoration, and improvement." The law underscores the connections between rapid economic modernization, population growth, and environmental deterioration, and the fallacy of presuming that industrialization and urbanization automatically improve quality of life. The law assumes that greater sensitivity to the socioeconomic causes of ecological problems, clarification of institutional responsibilities, decentralization of protection functions, and increased social collaboration will permit environmental amelioration "without interrupting or interfering excessively in productive processes." In other words, the law opts for ecological politics based on the possibility of continuing economic development on an environmentally sustainable basis.

The next president, Carlos Salinas de Gortari (1988–94), emphasized environmental protection early in his term of office, through a widely publicized campaign to address pollution and water supply problems in Mexico City, as well as the identification of several areas of the country as domestic policy priorities, including the U.S.-Mexican border region, several river basins, and southern Mexico. After 1990, however, Salinas's environmental policy focused on concerns related to NAFTA raised by environmental groups and other interested parties in the United States and Canada and by domestic critics. In May 1992, SEDUE was replaced by the Secretaría de Desarrollo Social (the Ministry of Social Development, SEDESOL) in an attempt to improve policy implementation. Factory inspection rates, fines and other penalties, and closures of some of the worst sources of industrial pollution increased, while public relations exercises directed at the appearance of environmental sensitivity proliferated.

Other significant actions by the Salinas regime to improve Mexico's environmental image at home and abroad included the elaboration of the Integrated Border Environmental Plan (IBEP) in collaboration with U.S. agencies, measures to protect endangered species and biodiversity, and the decree of a variety of national parks, wildlife preserves, heritage sites, and biosphere reserves, in part as a result of energetic actions by environmentalists. At the same time, however, land reform legislation was revised and new national forestry and water laws proclaimed in order to open previously protected sectors to private investment. While neoliberals maintained that these reforms would improve management efficiency and economic competitiveness, critics argued the likelihood of accelerating resource depletion under diminished state stewardship.

Overall, these initiatives constituted a substantial conservation and protection package, at least on paper. This strategy seems to have succeeded in reassuring the international financial community that Mexico will respect environmental concerns in the process of opening the country to free trade. The government's role in encouraging the formation of largely urban-based environmental interest groups in the early 1980s also was successful initially in facilitating their political manipulation to legitimize reforms. This strategy may have backfired, however, in that a number of these groups have broken with their original sponsors and have begun to act as independent lobbies for environmental policies, often in direct conflict with government interests. Such independent action has been particularly evident in the recent period of transition to neoliberalism as social, economic, and environmental concerns appear to be coalescing in an unprecedented popular challenge to the Mexican government.

Urban Pollution

Competing with Tokyo for the rank of the world's largest city, Mexico's capital also vies for the dubious honor of being the world's most polluted city. As a result of the acceleration of the rural exodus after 1945, reinforced by the government's policy of concentrating investment, industrial infrastructure, and political power in the metropolis, the population reached 15,048,000 in 1990 (as counted by the Dirección General de Estadística). The ensuing extreme pollution; congestion; shortages of housing, service, and water; and administrative paralysis are a dismal testimony to the repercussions of unchecked industrially based urban growth.

According to the United Nations Environment Program and World Health Organization, more than 30,000 industries and 12,000 service facilities operated in the Valley of Mexico in 1994, and almost 3 million motor vehicles were on the streets engaged in an estimated 30 million journeys daily. Atmospheric emissions from these sources are compounded by Mexico City's location in a high-elevation basin on a former lake bed surrounded by mountains; as a result, air drainage is poor and surface as well as upper-air temperature inversions occur frequently. Urban sprawl and associated energy consumption have caused microclimatic changes, reflected in heat anomalies owing to replacement of natural by artificial surfaces, warmth from combustion, and atmospheric alteration from the emission of gaseous and solid pollutants. As a result of these climatological and topographic factors, pollutant emissions are trapped close to the city. National and international air quality standards for sulfur dioxide, ozone, nitrogen dioxide, carbon monoxide, lead, and total suspended particles regularly are exceeded. Health repercussions include chronic respiratory illnesses, cardiovascular diseases, child development disorders, and gastrointestinal infections and hepatitis transmitted by inhalation of fecal dust consequent on poor sanitation facilities.

Shortly after assuming office, President Salinas announced an agenda for improving environmental conditions in the Federal District, including the regulation of vehicle emissions, the introduction of lead-free gasoline, and a traffic revision system. This announcement was followed in 1989 by an innovative program called *un dia sin auto* (a day without a car), whereby drivers must leave their cars at home one day a week in an effort to curtail commuter traffic. Although this program apparently was well received both by environmentalists and the general public, many affluent commuters have been able to circumvent it by purchasing an extra car, while the government continues to encourage the production and consumption of motor vehicles. Other innovative approaches include debt-for-nature swaps, mobilization of neighborhoods to restore or expand green space, and the proposed construction of a 30,000-foot (9,000-meter) "ecological wall" as part of the Metropolitan Area Preservation Project. More conventional measures include the conversion of power plants and vehicle retrofitting to run on natural gas, the closure of an antiquated petroleum refinery, and the lowering of fuel sulfur content. A contingency plan has been developed to cope with prolonged episodes of high air pollution levels as measured by the automatic monitoring network completed in 1985. This plan includes curtailing the activity of the most polluting industries and closing schools or rescheduling classes in periods of extreme atmospheric contamination.

In 1990 a comprehensive pollution control program was announced, *el Programa Integral Contra la Contaminación Atmosférica de la Zona Metropolitana de la Ciudad de México* (The Integral Program Against Atmospheric Contamination in the Metropolitan Zone of Mexico City, PICCA). PICCA focuses on the following strategic actions: improvement in fuel quality; rationalization and restructuring of urban transport; modernization of production technologies and pollution emission control, including prohibition of new contaminating industries and relocation of industries unable to comply with environmental regulations; rescue, protection, and rehabilitation of sensitive or degraded ecological areas; improved solid waste control and disposal, including extension of the sewer network; and education, communication, and citizen participation.

The last area, citizen participation, was central to the environmental policy of the Salinas administration, placing the ultimate responsibility for environmental improvement on the public at large. Obviously, such a Herculean task as cleaning up Mexico City cannot be achieved without active collaboration between state and society, but even the most comprehensive environmental reforms on paper have little chance of success without an effective implementation and enforcement capacity. During the economic and political restructuring and austerity of the mid-1990s, it seemed unlikely that this would be achieved unless a near-lethal threshold of livability should prompt a radical reallocation of priorities.

Cleaning Up the U.S.-Mexican Border

Perhaps even more intractable than the environmental predicament of Mexico City is that of the U.S.-Mexican border region, which extends some 2,000 miles from Tijuana–Metropolitan San Diego to Matamoros-Brownsville. Much of this area constitutes an environmental disaster zone, where rivers contain raw sewage, industrial discharges, dead animals, and domestic garbage; water tables are mined and contaminated by agrochemicals and other toxins; hazardous wastes are dumped; fish and wildlife species are endangered; air pollution is widespread, and so forth.

Most of these problems relate to the influx of migrants intent on a better life on *el otro lado* ("the other side") in the United States, or attracted by the prospect of better-paid jobs in the new industries established in the border free-trade zone, as well as by the increasing dynamism of the northern Mexican

economy overall. Border population on the Mexican side grew from 2.89 million in 1980 to an estimated 3.9 million in 1988 (according to scholars Robert A. Pastor and Jorge G. Castaneda); such growth rates were twice the national average, far exceeding the provision of infrastructure and services. The combined urban population on both sides of the border was 6.5 million in 1980, with growth projected of at least another 43 percent by 2000, up to 9.2 million (Rich, 1992).

Although the *maquiladora* assembly plant program was established in 1965, many environmental problems did not get out of hand until the second-wave boom of urban and industrial growth after 1982, promoted yet unrestrained by national policy. The economic liberalization, diversification, and fiscal austerity required by the International Monetary Fund (IMF) as a condition of debt restructuring created a favorable climate for increased investment in *maquiladoras* by foreign corporations attracted by large, unskilled pools of cheap labor, lax environmental regulations, and low taxes. The number of *maquiladoras* expanded rapidly from 620 in 1980 to nearly 1,900 in 1990, while the *maquiladora* labor force grew from 100,000 to 450,000 (Gereffi, 1992). Tariff relaxation in preparation for NAFTA facilitated the construction of new, more advanced export operations in Mexico's interior in cities such as Saltillo, Hermosillo, and San Luis Potosí, and even as far away as the Yucatán Peninsula. The border zone remained an investment magnet, however, as NAFTA stimulated the growth of additional *maquiladoras* and new transborder service industries on the Mexican side and a proliferation of low-wage subcontracting plants on the U.S. side.

The environmental impacts of this rapid and uncontrolled urban and industrial expansion on the sensitive ecology of the mainly arid borderlands obviously extend across the international boundary regardless of the points of origin. By the early 1980s, it became evident that the border's twin-city metropolitan regions such as El Paso–Ciudad Juárez and Tijuana–San Diego were verging on environmental crisis.

In 1983, the Mexican and U.S. governments signed the La Paz agreement, the first comprehensive border environmental cooperation accord. This agreement was useful as a means of generating international dialogue, but it focused mainly on pollution associated with *maquiladoras* and did not address other pressing problems such as the region's growing shortage of fresh water, the illegal dumping of toxic and hazardous wastes generated mainly by U.S. companies operating in Mexico, and infrastructural deficiencies. Communities, environmental agencies, and nongovernmental organizations looked to the proposed NAFTA as a possible alternative way to deal with natural resource depletion and environmental degradation in the border zone by integrating these concerns into the free-trade debate. The 1990 joint presidential resolution ensued, resulting in the Integrated Border Environmental Plan (IBEP) produced in collaboration by SEDUE and the U.S. Environmental Protection Agency (EPA) in 1992.

IBEP has been criticized for its lack of specifics on implementation, compounded by the considerable difference between the United States and Mexico in the legal and regulatory framework. The lack of attention to budgetary constraints was also a concern, as estimates of the cost of cleaning up the border ranged from $5 billion to $15 billion. IBEP also has been criticized for the shortcomings of the public participation process on both sides of the border. Nevertheless, the very act of community consultation in planning via public hearings was unprecedented in Mexico, and the plan served to focus the attention of both federal governments on a sorely neglected region and a previously under-acknowledged linkage, that between trade and the environment.

As a result of the NAFTA environmental side agreements, the Border Environmental Cooperation Commission (BECC) was established in 1994. The principal concerns of this joint commission were wastewater, drinking water, and municipal solid waste projects on both sides of the border. The BECC's main function was to certify projects to the North American Development Bank (NADBANK), a binational creation also deriving from the NAFTA side agreements, to provide US$2 billion to US$3 billion in financing for border environmental projects. Together, the BECC and NADBANK were intended to offer a different strategy from conventional development banking, with a bottom-up approach to lending to individuals, cities, corporations, and governments on a binational basis.

In October 1995, Border XXI, the successor to IBEP, was announced. Border XXI, in response to the lessons learned from IBEP, was a more open-ended long-range plan to coordinate federal, state, and local government agencies to deal with sustainable development, public participation, decentralization, and local empowerment. As such, it was intended to constitute a reflexive process emerging from the concerns of border residents rather than a top-down plan. At the time of its creation, its likely priorities included air, water, hazardous and solid waste, energy generation, pollution planning, emergency response, and environmental health.

It remains to be seen whether grassroots input and targeted funding are sufficient to offset the economic forces that continue to concentrate population and industrial growth in fragile borderlands ecosystems. Two years after its inception, it appeared that contrary to the predictions of its proponents, NAFTA has exacerbated environmental degradation in this area. In a context of a weakened Mexican economy, public-sector budget cuts on both sides of the border, and continued enforcement problems, prospects of environmental mitigation look dim.

Agriculture: The "Industry of Disasters"
In many respects, Mexico's current environmental crisis derives from the longer-standing agricultural crisis, which emerged in the late 1960s but was rooted in the post-1945 development strategy privileging industry and urban development over agriculture and rural development. Despite the early emphasis after the Mexican Revolution on land redistribution to peasants in *ejidos,* a unique form of communal land tenure, the subsistence sector was neglected by the government in favor of private investment in large-scale commercial agriculture, propelled by rapid advances in agricultural techniques and technologies worldwide—the so-called Green Revolution. As the internationalization of Mexico's economy prompted the increasing emphasis on export crops in this sector, the onus of basic foods production shifted to the peasantry. After 1970, the government initiated a massive and expensive campaign to modernize agricultural production on *ejidos.* Rather than promoting an efficient, expanded productive base, however, this interventionist approach resulted in the institutionalization of an *industria de siniestros* (industry of disasters) in which crop failure, corruption, and chronic indebtedness have been the norm. The economic, social, and environmental costs of agricultural modernization in both the peasant and the private sectors have been devastating.

In the arid regions of northern Mexico, where the government invested heavily in rural infrastructure to foster private irrigated agriculture, salinization has caused the abandonment of thousands of acres. Mining of groundwater for irrigation and to support increasing settlement is reaching critical levels in some regions, such as Baja California Norte and Sonora. Decades of monoculture (the use of farmland to grow single crops, such as fruits and vegetables for export, or cotton, sugar, and rice for both domestic and foreign consumption) have resulted in soil exhaustion and pesticide-resistant plagues. Meanwhile ever-increasing and often indiscriminate use of agrochemicals, including a number of highly toxic pesticides banned or restricted in the United States, has engendered a wide range of health hazards. Other areas suffer from increasing soil erosion and desertification as a result of over-cultivation or over-grazing of marginal lands.

Perhaps the worst environmental degradation incurred by agricultural modernization has been in the tropical forests of southeastern Mexico. According to scholar Ivan Restrepo, tropical forest acreage overall declined from 170 million in 1975 to 47 million in 1980. The Lacondón region of Chiapas has lost 70 percent of its original forest cover. Twenty-five years ago, almost two-thirds of the state of Campeche was forested. At least 1.5 million acres have been cleared in the interim for frontier colonization and logging, mechanized agriculture, or pasture, often in that sequence with cattle as the end phase in the cycle of destruction now typical of the tropical forests of Central and South America.

Mechanized agriculture has been particularly destructive of diverse and complex tropical ecosystems. One hectare (2.5 acres) of forest may contain as many as 200 different species of trees and innumerable smaller plants, animals, and insects, each adapted to a very specific ecological niche. Once large areas have been cleared for agriculture and settlement and the delicate natural equilibrium has been upset, many of these species are unable to survive and reproduce. In particular, direct transfer of agricultural technologies from temperate zones has caused incalculable damage ecologically and has failed to achieve production goals. Attempts to turn the tropical lowlands into a granary have proven especially destructive in that unnecessary expanses of land have been clear-cut; heavy machinery, fertilizers, and monocultures have destroyed fragile tropical soils; and the introduction of crops unsuited to the climate, soils, and terrains has had disastrous results. The predominant solution for these failed agricultural development projects for peasants has been "cattle-ization" by design or by default, at an incalculable cost in terms of the loss of biodiversity.

The environment is likely to be under increasing stress as a consequence of the opening of agriculture to international competition under NAFTA. Currently, Mexico is competitive only in a handful of agribusiness enclaves while the basic foods sector remains stagnant. In this context, the revitalization of agriculture requires a reversal of traditionally paternalistic and protectionist state policies involving long-standing explicit and implicit subsidies, extensive restructuring of inefficient government agencies, intensification of production, and the development

of a climate conducive to the expansion of investment, both foreign and domestic. The amendment of the previously sacrosanct Article 27 of the 1917 Mexican Constitution in 1992 to end land redistribution and permit the legal sale or rental of *ejido* plots seems particularly problematic in terms of potential environmental repercussions, such as another massive rural-urban migration of peasants dispossessed for a pittance. In this scramble for the survival of the fittest farmers, official concerns for conserving resources for the future seem to have been eclipsed by the imperative of free market forces.

Sustainable Development or Developing Sustainability?

The preamble to the 1988 General Law of Ecological Equilibrium and Environmental Protection maintains that the solution to Mexico's environmental problems is not to abandon the pursuit of development, given the country's pressing needs with respect to food, employment, and housing. Rather, the answer lies in continuing but more environmentally aware economic growth following the neoliberal path to prosperity, on the assumption that it is easier for rich nations to be green. Unfortunately, the adjustments required by neoliberal transition has been at odds with this conception of sustainable development. The government's priority of opening the Mexican economy preempts effective environmental legislation, and fiscal austerity reduces resources available for environmental protection.

Another approach to sustainable development calls for a radically different economics, producing much lower rates of growth, if any, to ensure future ecological stability by fully recognizing the processes and limits of the biosphere. This approach, with an additional emphasis on the importance of cultural as well as biological diversity, the right to democracy, and the satisfaction of basic human needs, has been embraced by a number of rural communities, citizen groups, ecological organizations, and segments of the Mexican intelligentsia. In this view, sustainable development becomes more than a core concept in environmentalist rhetoric and a fashionable "buzz term" within the political and economic mainstream. Instead, it constitutes a direct challenge to neoliberalism, voiced by those segments of the population that have been marginalized by the dominant model of development.

It has been suggested that, paradoxically, a key opportunity to promote this type of sustainability may arise from the current crisis in the Mexican countryside, resulting from development policies that have degraded the resource base, promoted inefficient land use, created massive unemployment and under-employment, and prompted ongoing out-migration. These crisis conditions could provide a starting point for sustainable development via small-scale, diversified production to meet basic needs and stimulate local economies in combination with employment of the surplus workforce in environmental reconstruction. An emphasis on the *process* of developing sustainability rather than on the *product* could act as a bridge between the government's commitment to confronting environmental problems and spontaneous, bottom-up initiatives. Such an approach is likely to involve new forms of both policy and practice, with priorities given to community initiative, building knowledge about ecosystems, and holistic planning and management, emphasizing mediation of environmental, economic, and social goals at local and regional levels.

This scenario may not be unrealistic, whether or not free trade promotes significant economic growth and increased employment in Mexico, especially if the hemispheric trading partners see a common interest in breaking the linkages between economic restructuring, environmental degradation, poverty, and social unrest. The January 1994 Chiapas uprising may have provided some incentive in this direction. The financial setbacks Mexico experienced in 1995 underscore the imperative of promoting local environmental solutions rather than relying on government actions in a time of extraordinary economic, political, and social adjustment.

See also Industry and Industrialization; Mesoamerica: Agriculture and Ecology; Urbanism and Urbanization

Select Bibliography

Barkin, David, *Distorted Development: Mexico in the World Economy.* Boulder, Colorado: Westview, 1990.
Barry, Tom, *Zapata's Revenge: Free Trade and the Farm Crisis in Mexico.* Boston: South End Press, 1995.
Berry, Brian J. L., and Frank E. Horton, *Urban Environmental Management: Planning for Pollution Control.* Englewood Cliffs, New Jersey: Prentice-Hall, 1974.
Carley, Michael, and Ian Christie, *Managing Sustainable Development.* London: Earthscan, 1992; Minneapolis: University of Minnesota Press, 1993.
Davis, Diane E., *Urban Leviathan. Mexico City in the Twentieth Century.* Philadelphia: Temple University Press, 1994.
Gates, Marilyn, *In Default: Peasants, the Debt Crisis, and the Agricultural Challenge in Mexico.* Boulder, Colorado: Westview, 1993.
Gereffi, Gary, "Mexico's Maquiladora Industries and North American Integration." In *North America Without Borders? Integrating Canada, the United States, and Mexico,* edited by Stephen J. Randall, Herman Konrad, and Sheldon Silvermann. Calgary: University of Calgary Press, 1992.
M'Gonigle, R. Michael, and Ben Parfitt, *Forestopia: A Practical Guide to the New Forest Economy.* Madeira Park, British Columbia: Harbour, 1994.
Pastor, Robert A., and Jorge G. Castaneda, *Limits to Friendship: The United States and Mexico.* New York: Knopf, 1988.
Rich, Jan Galbreath, *Planning the Border's Future: The Mexican-U.S. Integrated Border Environmental Plan.* Austin: U.S.-Mexican Policy Studies Program, LBJ School of Public Affairs, University of Texas, 1992.

—MARILYN GATES

Ejército Zapatista de Liberación Nacional

See Zapatista Rebellion in Chiapas

Elías Calles, Plutarco

See Calles, Plutarco Elías

EZLN

See Zapatista Rebellion in Chiapas

F

Family and Kinship

This entry includes three articles that discuss household structures and kinship relations, family strategies and life course, and the relations among law, family, and the state:

Family and Kinship: Hapsburg Colonial Period
Family and Kinship: Bourbon Colonial Period and
  Nineteenth Century
Family and Kinship: Twentieth Century

See also Gender; Women's Status and Occupation

Family and Kinship: Hapsburg Colonial Period

The family was the central feature of colonial Latin American society. It was in the family that the first implications of the new forms of colonial life were manifested. The study of the family gives tremendous insights into every aspect of colonial life. In general one can approach the family from three different perspectives. First are internal considerations: relationships between family members, family strategies, and the life course of individuals in the family. Second are forces from the society at large, which have repercussions on the family: household structure, kinship, and the family as part of a larger social network. Last are the state-imposed normative requirements on the family through law and custom; these norms in turn influenced the internal and external forces on the family.

The essence of the family traditionally has been the couple and their offspring. In both native society and Spanish society, the nuclear family also was merely the starting point for the broader institution of the family, which included the extended family of parents, siblings, offspring, and affines (relatives by marriage). The household and the family largely were considered to begin at the common point of the nuclear family. Both societies then expanded the definition of the household to include nonrelated individuals living with the nuclear family.

Several important early colonial documents give us insights into the nature of the family in the late pre-Columbian period, and as such offer suggestions about changes that occurred in native families with the Conquest. The two most important of these are the *Florentine Codex* and the *Codex Mendoza*. The latter provides fairly detailed information about the life cycle, with observations on moral issues and the rearing of children. The former provides many insights into the pre-Columbian family structures among the Nahua. Nevertheless, for the colonial period we must rely on more tangential sources of evidence. These include census data, wills and testaments, religious tracts, sermons and confessionaries, and various types of lawsuits.

One of the most important changes brought by the Conquest was the imposition of Christianity on the native peoples of Mexico. Christianity brought with it European models, out of the Judeo-Christian tradition, of the family, which were often in conflict with the native traditions. Perhaps in no other realm than marriage choice did the two cultures collide with such force. Christianity had adopted monogamy as the sole and unique acceptable matrimonial form. The native peoples of Mexico recognized several other models, with polygamy being the one most often singled out for attack by the missionaries.

A census of villages in what is today the state of Morelos made in the 1540s shows how ineffective the missionaries had been in imposing the new family order on the natives. Even some two decades after the Conquest, Christian marriage was a relatively rare event in some communities. In others as many as half of the marriages had church sanction. Concubinage and polygyny were still evident as well, especially among households headed by men of power and wealth. Although Christian monogamy was extolled as the norm for the natives, it never seems to have been fully implemented. Throughout the colonial period, preachers inveighed against concubinage. Likewise there are indications that some men openly maintained multiple spouses in spite of church opposition.

While the nuclear family was undoubtedly the core feature of Nahua society following the Conquest, the household was the functional core institution. Each nuclear family, or adult married couple, occupied a single house, but these house structures frequently were built around a common courtyard to form a compound. The residents of this compound were considered the household insofar as they shared many important duties with one another, including food preparation and consumption. The household normally consisted of a nuclear family along with various consanguineous (descended from the same ancestor) and affinal kin. A household consisting exclusively of a nuclear family was not the most common household in those that have been studied. Most common were what are called "joint families." In the joint family more than one nuclear family, with various dependents, share a household compound. Of the joint families, the most common type was for brothers with their wives, children, and dependents to share the household. Families and households among the Nahua remained dynamic and flexible in order to adapt better to rapidly changing circumstances. Even the extreme mortality rates that nearly destroyed native communities were unable to rupture the traditional family units. In fact the Nahua were relatively slow in adopting Spanish terminology for family members, preferring to continue to use the indigenous system and terms well into the late seventeenth century.

The point at which the Spanish and native family systems intersected was in the realm of mixed marriages. These marriages more often were conditioned by colonial demonstrations of power than by equality in family roles. The overwhelming majority of such unions were between Spanish men and native women. The family system brought to bear was uniformly that of the Spanish. Even the presence of offspring, in the form of individuals of mixed ethnic heritage, called mestizos, did not bridge the gap existent in colonial power relationships, but in fact often raised them in high relief. Children of irregular or casual unions normally were raised in the family of the mother and took on her ethnic identity. Children of recognized unions, especially where there was a formal recognition of the colonial power relationship between husband and wife, would be raised in the Spanish household and reflect that ethnic identity. Thus in the early decades following the Conquest,

the mestizo population did not threaten the existing dichotomous social order, since the mestizos tended to identify with one or the other of the two ethnic groups. It was only in the late sixteenth and early seventeenth century, when there was a critical mass of mestizos who identified with neither group, that a truly new ethnic entity came into existence.

The acceptance of racially mixed marriages, and the fact of racially mixed children, ran counter to the nominal Spanish policy of dividing society into racially distinct castes. As the racial mixing continued through the colonial period, it was necessary to recognize each mixture officially and to define it legally. By the end of the seventeenth century the system of castes began to break down because of its complexity and owing to the fact that the racial differentiation became a mostly subjective exercise. Evidence has shown a great discrepancy in the racial categorizations made by various colonial officials depending on the ultimate purpose for the information. The same individual would be categorized in one way for a baptismal record and in another for a census.

There was a tendency for the native nobility to marry into Spanish society. While there was a general social stigma attached to Spaniards who married natives, if the native were a member of the elite that stigma was lessened. Such marriages carried with them the economic potential of control over the lands of the ancestral native lords. As a result of these advantageous intermarriages, many of the native lords by the beginning of the seventeenth century were in fact mestizos.

The Spanish family can be seen as consisting of three different groups. The nuclear family constituted the irreducible minimum. Beyond that was the larger household, which, like the native society, contained both consanguineous and affinal kin. In addition there were individuals who did not reside with the family but who were related by ceremonial ties. Principal among these are the baptismal sponsors of children, known as godparents, and sponsors at other religious acts such as confirmation and marriage. The godparents were considered to be legal kin of the family. The biological parents of the child were linked by ceremonial and customary ties to the godparents, each respecting the others as a co-parent or *compadre*. With the passage of time, and the greater incorporation of the native peoples in Christian ritual, *compadrazgo* also took on an important role in native families. Often economic and social considerations went into the selection of godparents. It was not uncommon for humble Spaniards to choose members of the elite to serve as godparents. This assured that the child would have a powerful patron when he or she grew to maturity. Likewise the child's parents then had ties of *compadrazgo* with an influential individual who potentially could benefit them.

There was a wide range of members of an extended household. Among the Spanish elite this might include native servants, slaves, Spanish retainers, and many others. When families immigrated to the Americas, they frequently brought their servants from Spain. Likewise, when establishing households in New Spain they would look to people from their home village or region for their first social ties. In this manner entire villages frequently were reproduced in New Spain. Slaves and Indian servants also were important household members. Many members of the criollo (American-born Spaniard) elite learned native languages at the breast of their wet nurses. Slaves were ubiquitous in Spanish and criollo households.

More humble Spanish residents also maintained complex households in which both affinal and consanguineous kin resided. Mixed family households were also not uncommon; in such a household, two or more families might inhabit the same general residence, mutually supporting one another. A large number of single men in the early colonial period also meant that uniquely male households existed alongside family and complex family households. Even in later periods this would be true of frontier regions and mining districts.

Affinal kin were no less important in the scheme of family and kinship. The role of the church in the family was important. Among the Spanish, residence was patrilocal, with a newly married couple often residing in the house of the groom's family. During the early colonial period it was the church, and not the state, that regulated marriage. Marriage is one of seven sacraments of the Catholic Church. As a sacrament it is believed to have validity only when the parties enter into it through the exercise of free will. A marriage could be declared null if either partner were coerced into it. Consequently, marriage choice was one way in which children could take an active role in determining their own future. The state assisted the church in enforcing decisions over marriage choice. The act of marriage created important ties between the two families. Parents might seek alliances with other families for economic or political reasons. This choice might be at odds with the choice of the young person. In cases of outright conflict, the church normally sided with the young person, although by the early eighteenth century this had changed, and the church began to reflect cultural values rather than theological principles.

Marriage was the linking of two different families. The economic importance of this was recognized in the giving of gifts. At the time of marriage, the father of the bride normally gave money or real property to the groom, a dowry or *dote,* ostensibly to protect the economic position of the bride. Although the dowry was administered by the husband, it was legally the property of the woman. Any decision to sell or alienate the property was subject to the approval of the woman. Likewise, at the time of marriage the groom would often give a gift *(arras)* to the bride. Like the dowry, the *arras* remained the possession of the woman. The basic principle with regard to the administration of these funds was that they would not be lost or diminished, but conserved. The wife also might control her own personal property, especially goods brought into the household at the time of the marriage, aside from those explicitly part of the dowry. Beyond this she also had a claim to wealth generated by her husband during the course of the marriage. This normally would be divided equally between the spouse and any other heirs, such as children.

Inheritance laws played an important role in the colonial Mexican family. Contrary to what one might believe, colonial Hispanic inheritance laws were remarkably egalitarian. Codified in the early sixteenth century, the Laws of Toro governed inheritance. Simply put, children shared equally in the estates of their parents. Parents could designate up to approximately 40 percent of their estate, called an "improved share," to a single heir, often going to the eldest son. Nevertheless, in general, equal distribution was the rule. The rules concerning inheritance placed a tremendous obstacle to the transmittal of concentrated wealth from generation to generation, since the rules tended to break up large estates.

The colonial inheritance system did provide for the creation of entailed estates *(mayorazgos)* formed from the "improved share" of one heir. To create an entailed estate it was necessary also to receive royal permission and pay annual taxes, but once created the estate could not be sold, mortgaged, fragmented, or alienated in any way. The *mayorazgo* had to pass wholly from generation to generation. It was an effective means of transmitting wealth but exceptionally cumbersome. In times of economic downturn it was extremely difficult to turn the estate into cash. Clearly it was only reasonable to entail large estates in this manner, since the costs involved made the practice unreasonable for smaller holdings.

In order to secure some of the advantages of the entailed estate without so many of the difficulties, many colonial families used chantries *(capellanías)* in a similar fashion. The chantry was an ecclesiastical endowment normally invested in a lien on a piece of real property. The interest paid for the services of a priest, usually to say masses for the benefit of the founder and his family. The lien often would be extended to another family member, while yet another family member was the titular beneficiary, a priest who enjoyed the fruits and performed the masses. The chantry could be used as the basis upon which the priest would be ordained. The operation of the chantry was subject to the scrutiny of the church but otherwise could be administered to maximize benefits for an extended family. Like the *mayorazgo*, the *capellanía* was inalienable, but it usually consisted of a smaller capital investment.

Another means whereby families attempted to avoid the destructive effects of inheritance laws was to practice careful career planning of their children. By limiting the number of children who eventually married, a family could concentrate wealth by jumping a generation. If, for example, of several children, only two married and had offspring, the portion of the parents' estates that would have gone to the others could be inherited by the offspring or the siblings who married, upon the death of the siblings who did not. Part of the inheritance might go the church in the form of dowries for daughters who became nuns, part might go to religious orders to support the male members of the family who became friars, but normally enough would remain to be inherited by the second and third generations to allow for some reconcentration of wealth.

Families were linked in marriage. Wealth could be concentrated in the hands of a few through the judicious use of marriage. Brothers from one family might marry sisters from another, thereby increasing the possibility that the wealth of two families might be held in the second generation by only two households. The Spanish elite also were concerned with nobility. Marriage alliances for the sake of acquiring nobility were not uncommon. Wealthy merchant families frequently married into the ranks of the older landed elite. The landed elite, often with ties to the conquistadors and early settlers, would enhance the nobility of the merchants, while the merchants might improve the wealth of the elite family.

The colonial Mexican *encomienda* was an important institution that determined early marriage and kinship relationships. *Encomiendas* were native settlements "commended" in trust to a Spaniard —the *encomendero*—who, in exchange for receiving the Indians' labor, had the duty of protecting the Indians, maintaining missionaries in the villages, and contributing to the military defense of the areas.

Initially one could pass an *encomienda* to an heir. As the Spanish Crown tightened control over the institution, inheritance became limited to three "lives." Yet the definition of "life" included the lives of both the husband and wife. In several instances elderly *encomenderos* married young women to extend the "life" of the *encomienda*. The spouse, upon the eventual death of the older partner, could then remarry, and the *encomienda* would still be considered in the first life. For example, the *encomienda* granted to "la Malinche," doña Marina, passed to her husband, Juan Jaramillo, upon her death. He remarried and the grant then was enjoyed by him and his second wife, doña Beatriz de Andrade. When Jaramillo died the grant was split between Jaramillo's and doña Marina's children and doña Beatriz de Andrade. In this manner a grant that dated from the Conquest continued on until the close of the sixteenth century still in its first "life."

Certain colonial public offices, such as notary public and town councilman, were subject to public sale. By the end of the sixteenth century these offices also were sold with the right to pass the office to one heir, upon the payment of one-third the current value. Subsequent inheritance was not allowed, and upon the death of the heir the office would be resold at public auction. Nevertheless, this became an important means of ensuring family wealth and social status.

The familial naming system used in the colonial period differed from the patterns observed in Mexico today. Parents exercised a much freer reign in the naming of their children. A child might receive the mother's surname rather than the father's or might use a surname of a valued uncle or other affinal relative. Often, in order to inherit a *mayorazgo* or benefit from a chantry, the recipient would need to take the surname of the founder. Consequently, tracing families over time is complicated by the lack of stability in the use of surnames. For example, one of the legitimate sons of the famous conquistador of Mexico, Bernal Díaz del Castillo, was named Bartolomé Becerra.

Among the colonial elite one can see two basic marriage practices. The group tended to marry from within its own ranks. Because of the relatively limited number of suitable spouses, the children of the conquistadors tended to marry children of conquistadors. This developed a rather easily identifiable colonial elite group. Yet new arrivals from Spain provided a secondary source of spouses, especially government officials, merchants, and others with established wealth or social standing. Nearly all of the titled nobles who emerged in Mexico in the seventeenth century could trace their lineage to both the group of conquistadors and early settlers and to more recent immigrants, especially government officials.

Marriage choice for criollos and Spaniards outside of the elite did not differ dramatically. Marriage partners usually came from roughly the same social group. Most marriages used some form of broker, an individual to introduce the two partners. Clearly the likelihood of someone meeting a suitable partner from one's own social group was far more likely than meeting one from a distinct group. While the choice of a marriage partner was reserved to the individual contracting marriage, family and friends could, and did, play an important role. Marriage for love was not an alien concept in early colonial New Spain. Both the Catholic Church and the state accepted the right of the individual to choose a marriage partner, in spite of interference from family members and others.

The elite tended to get married at a slightly older age than did natives or Africans in the society. Research suggests that Spanish women as a whole married at about 25, with criollos marrying slightly younger, nearer to 21. While data are very sketchy on native marriages, the average seems to be much younger, perhaps 16.

The institution of marriage was regulated by both canon and civil law. Yet, most cases dealing with irregularities were heard in either the church courts or by the Holy Office of the Inquisition. In general, church courts dealt with cases of concubinage, incest, and adultery. On the other hand, the Inquisition heard cases of bigamy and clerical solicitation. Concubinage and adultery were similar offenses. Concubinage consisted of unmarried people engaging in sexual relations, or of a married man having sexual relations with an unmarried woman. Two unmarried persons engaging in sexual relations were expected to be married, and could be considered married under most circumstances, if neither had a preexisting obligation to marry another. A woman who engaged in premarital sex was placed in a difficult situation if the male partner did not eventually marry her, since others would not be inclined to do so. According to the norms of the time, adultery was defined only as a married woman engaging in extramarital sexual relations. Adultery was seen as an affront to the woman's husband, and a potential attack on his personal property, since the adulterous union might produce a child who would inherit from the legal, but not biological, father. Incest consisted of sexual relations between those related by blood or marriage within the fourth degree. Consequently, it was illegal for a man to engage in sexual relations either with his sister, or sister-in-law, or blood relatives as near as second cousins, for example. While all of these offenses were serious, each was dealt with by local clerical judges and resulted in minor ecclesiastical and civil punishments. Far more serious offenses were those of bigamy and solicitation. In each instance the guilty party consciously had ruptured the permanence of a holy vow, a vow of marriage or of clerical celibacy. As such these offenses were subject to the scrutiny of the Inquisition. Punishments were far more severe, including long incarceration prior to trial, exile, corporal punishment, heavy fines, and banishment.

The family in colonial New Spain was a complex and multivaried institution. It included blood kin, kin by marriage, kin established during church rituals, and persons affiliated with the household as slaves, servants, retainers, or hangers-on. Native households were equally complex, encompassing the biological family, family networks, and others associated with the household. Natives had an influence on Spanish households, owing to their presence in them as servants. The colonial elite frequently were bilingual and commonly used words from the native tongues in everyday speech. Their foods were prepared by native cooks, using local foodstuffs. Their cloth was woven by native artisans. The native contribution was ubiquitous. The native households frequently were forced to comply with Spanish notions of household and family. In short, while the exchange was far from being an equal one, exchange there was.

Select Bibliography

Boyer, Richard, *The Lives of the Bigamists: Marriage, Family and Community in Colonial Mexico.* Albuquerque: University of New Mexico Press, 1995.

Cline, S. L., editor and translator, *The Book of Tributes: Early Sixteenth Century Nahuatl Censuses from Morelos.* Los Angeles: UCLA Latin American Center, 1993.

Gibson, Charles, *Aztecs under Spanish Rule.* Stanford, California: Stanford University Press, 1964.

Lavrin, Asunción, editor, *Sexuality and Marriage in Colonial Latin America.* Lincoln: University of Nebraska Press, 1989.

Lockhart, James. *The Nahuas after the Conquest.* Stanford, California: Stanford University Press, 1992.

Seed, Patricia. *To Love, Honor, and Obey in Colonial Mexico.* Stanford, California: Stanford University Press, 1988).

—JOHN F. SCHWALLER

Family and Kinship: Bourbon Colonial Period and Nineteenth Century

From the middle of the eighteenth century until the 1870s, Mexico experienced significant political and economic upheaval resulting in its independence from Spain and in its emergence as a republic. Even as the nation adopted republicanism and tried to move toward the ideal of social equality, the authoritarian ideology rooted in a strong patriarchal family tradition prevailed and worked as a powerful force in shaping the politics and culture of the nation. Despite the persistence of patriarchalism, however, by the 1870s and 1880s the family as a basic social and political unit was being transformed by changing economic conditions and by educational and legal reforms that slowly eroded traditional relations of authority within the family and, in turn, in society.

The eighteenth-century administrative and economic reforms of the Spanish empire, known collectively as the Bourbon reforms, attempted to make Spain's American colonies more economically efficient and productive in a world experiencing rapid demographic growth and accelerated economic and diplomatic activity. Indeed, reforms stimulated changes and kindled crises throughout the colonies, for Spain sought to improve the imperial economy by imposing greater control over all aspects of social, political, and economic life. In New Spain, the Crown's efforts in this regard can be seen in new laws, taxes, monopolies, bureaucratic organization, military conscription, and in the expulsion of the Jesuits. Some of these reforms precipitated swift and violent reaction throughout the colony in the 1760s and ultimately contributed to the political ferment that resulted in Mexico's independence in 1821.

The global demographic and economic processes that propelled the eighteenth-century state to seek greater economic productivity impacted the family because the state aggressively promoted the secularization and reorganization of society through reforms in education and health and in family and property law. After Independence in 1821, reforms in these areas accelerated, and, in concert with economic and demographic change, they affected families in all social and ethnic groups, both positively and negatively.

Family Law and the State

The *patria potestad,* or power of the father, served as a fundamental concept in Spanish family law and practice. Although not in complete agreement about the reach of the *patria potestad* (particularly over marriage of children), secular and ecclesiastical authorities generally recognized and protected paternal prerogatives. Most of the diverse racial, ethnic, and social groups of Spain's American colonies accommodated it in one form or the other. The Catholic Church also insisted upon marital monogamy and the permanence of the marital bond. Legal insistence upon paternal authority, monogamy, and protected inheritance of children favored the predominance of the nuclear family of parents and children, but cultural traditions among all ethnic groups and economic conditions made other kinship ties also important. In New Spain, as Spanish authorities and Catholic fathers assumed control over Indian communities, resulting in their increasing Hispanicization by the eighteenth century, Indian families accepted the basic concept of paternal power, which was similar to their own beliefs in male superiority. The major change for Indian families was the Catholic Church's attempt to prohibit polygamy in Indian communities. This was not entirely successful, since many couples, Indian and non-Indian alike, resorted to a variety of informal relationships that undermined the church's insistence on monogamy and its restrictions against absolute divorce.

Beginning in the 1770s, changes in marriage, divorce, and property laws, and the abolition of slavery impacted the *patria potestad* in various ways; some legal changes strengthened it while other laws undermined it. Additionally, Catholic doctrine toward free will in marriage often had created tensions between parents and children over marriage choice and, over time, in concert with other developments probably helped to undermine the *patria potestad*. In fact, the Spanish monarch Carlos III, realizing that paternal authority had weakened to the point that both the authority of the state and the corporate social order were threatened, determined that the Crown's interests were best served by protecting parental power in conflicts over marriage choice and by reducing the Catholic Church's influence in these matters and thus its influence in society. To this end, the Spanish Crown promulgated the Royal Pragmatic on Marriage (Real Pragmática-Sanción de Matrimonios) on March 23, 1776.

Earlier Spanish canon and civil law codified in the Siete Partidas recognized both church and state interests in marriage, considering it both a sacrament and a contract. Church and state interests did not always coincide, however. Because church doctrine privileged marriage as a sacrament in which the main purpose was to bring a woman and man together to procreate and educate offspring, the church considered its responsibility was to maintain the viability, harmony, and permanence of this union. To maintain a marriage in harmony required that the couple enter into it of their own free will. The canon law of the Siete Partidas governed this aspect of marriage. The Council of Trent confirmed the church's support of free will in marriage and strengthened priests' role in protecting against forced marriage, but in prohibiting clandestine marriage, the council also gave leverage to parents.

For its part, the state tended to privilege the contractual role of marriage in order to preserve the social order and to protect and distribute property to support family members. This concept, also contained in the Siete Partidas and developed further in the Laws of Toro of 1505 and the Recopilación de Leyes de las Indias, was manifest in community property rights of spouses, in equal, partible inheritance rights of legitimate children, and in preserving the communal and collective landholding traditions of Indian communities. These rights could not be abrogated easily, because the family, in both its nucleated and extended form, was recognized as the basic institution of social welfare (even illegitimate children had the right to seek basic support from their families for food, clothing, and shelter, called *alimentos*). The potential contradiction between church and state interests arose when parents attempted to force children into undesirable marriages, in which case the church was obligated to protect the children.

The Royal Pragmatic, promulgated in New Spain in 1778, was intended to cement parents' control over their children's marriages to preserve the social order and protect property by preventing marriage between unequals: "the indecency of children entering into inequal marriages without the counsel or consent of their parents" *(el abuso de contraer matrimonios desiguales los hijos de familia, sin esperar el consejo y consentimiento paterno)*. All children under age 25 were required to have their father's permission to marry or, in his absence, that of their mother, grandparent, relative, guardian, or local judge, in that order; children over 25 also were supposed to seek consent. Parents could disinherit children who married in violation of this law, not easily done previously under Spanish law. The Royal Pragmatic provided some protection for children in that parents or relatives were not supposed to force children into marriages against their will. The ultimate decision in disputes was left to royal judges, not priests or ecclesiastical judges. In this respect the Crown undermined the prerogatives of ecclesiastical courts in handling conflicts over marriage choice: "the Royal authority must conform exactly to canonical law" *(la potestad Real debe dispensar al mas exacto*

cumplimiento de las reglas canónicas). A decree that accompanied the Royal Pragmatic charged prelates and ecclesiastical judges to comply with the Pragmatic. Certainly the law intended to privilege the *patria potestad* in these acts, but ambiguities in the Pragmatic opened it up to interpretations that had the potential of undermining parental wishes.

Because the Pragmatic did not precisely define what constituted an unequal marriage *(matrimonio desigual)*, except that it concerned the status, quality, and condition of the two people involved, unequal was interpreted differently in different places within the Spanish empire, especially by the last decades of the eighteenth century, when the basis of social status was increasingly determined by economic condition and individual reputation rather than by condition of birth or association. Although the attempt to preserve the hegemony of white Europeanized elites threatened by a growing Indian and *casta* (mixed-race) population may have been part of the motive for promulgating this law in the colonies, clearly many local officials interpreted the law to mean that as long as a couple could support themselves and both parties were good, reputable people, then a marriage, even between people of different races, was acceptable, although parents or relatives may have strongly objected. Other limits to parental control over marriage were that many children were orphaned before they reached the age of marriage and that a majority of parents had little or no property with which to threaten disinheritance if their children disobeyed. Most parents and guardians, then, had to use other family and community pressures to force compliance on unruly offspring.

The broad and varied interpretations of the Pragmatic in the late-eighteenth- and early-nineteenth-century Mexico not only demonstrated the changing basis of social status but also the decreasing importance of honor as defined by family *limpieza de sangre,* which meant blood or racial purity (determined by the sexual purity of a family's women). By the nineteenth century, especially after Independence in Mexico when racial categories were dropped in all official records, honor and reputation were increasingly dependent upon individual virtue, based upon an individual's decent behavior that could be learned through education and earned through economically productive activity. It no longer depended only or necessarily on birth or association. Illegitimacy continued to be stigmatized, but legitimization (which could only be granted by governmental decree) was more easily obtained. As a result, by the late eighteenth century, people of illegitimate birth could seek positions in the government, church, and military that previously had been denied to them.

Following Independence in 1821, Mexico generally recognized Spanish family law and the concept of *patria potestad* with the 1804 modifications that extended some of the rights of the *patria potestad* to widowed mothers and grandmothers, a recognition of the significant percentage of families with children headed by women. As motherhood became more important in the nineteenth century, married women increasingly were permitted some of the prerogatives of the *patria potestad* over their own children. Also, adult children, especially adult single daughters, were emancipated from parental authority. All of these changes slowly eroded the legal power of fathers and parents over children, but changes in the law often followed social practices that already had changed.

For several decades after Independence, the new Mexican state continued to recognize church control over birth, marriage, death, and ecclesiastical divorce (divorce that only separated the parties and eliminated the marriage obligation but that did not allow remarriage). Until the 1850s, Mexican law also recognized community property, equal, partible inheritance, and communal rights of Indian communities.

The civil conflicts of the 1850s and 1860s had a more profound impact on family law than did Independence. The Reform Laws, the culmination of the process of economic liberalization and secularization of social policy, were passed as a result of these conflicts. Their purpose was to limit church and corporate control over family and community life in order to give impetus to economic renewal by making more property available to individuals and by encouraging the free movement of wealth and capital.

The Ley Lerdo (1856) required towns, church institutions, and other corporate bodies to sell real property holdings not needed to carry out their missions and required Indian communities to sell communal holdings. It also suppressed entailed property. Supposedly meant to increase production by providing more families and individuals with land, over time privatization of landholdings actually facilitated the concentration of land in fewer hands, forcing many families and individuals to become dependent peons or wage laborers on haciendas and in cities. Indian communities were especially hard hit as some of them lost former communal property to non-Indians.

In 1857 state governments were charged with taking control of records of births, marriages, and deaths, and of local cemeteries, breaking the church's monopoly control over these basic family concerns. The Law of Civil Matrimony of July 1859 shifted control over divorce from the church to the state and codified the process of liberalization of divorce under way since the 1820s, especially in regard to simplifying the procedure for seeking divorce. This law did not, however, allow a marriage to be completely dissolved; thus, the parties were not allowed to remarry as long as they both lived. Whereas the 1859 marriage law recognized the equal right of either party to seek divorce if the other committed adultery, the 1870 Civil Code allowed women to seek divorce on this ground only if the husband's adultery was committed in the conjugal home, he had a concubine, his adultery caused public scandal, or his lover abused or insulted the wife. Civil law then legitimized and thus strengthened the sexual double standard that had persisted in the form of cultural practice. (Also, within a few years the national government issued instructions for regulating prostitution, thus legitimating that practice and perpetuating sexual inequalities by race, class, and gender.) The 1870 code did allow a couple to seek divorce by mutual consent, thus codifying another liberalization of divorce. Finally, in 1917, during the Mexican Revolution, Mexican women won the right to absolute divorce and remarriage. Until then, men and women both found ways around the strictures of divorce by cohabitation, concubinage, or by remarrying in another place.

Changes in the divorce laws also brought some changes in the custody of children, for although the rights of fathers and the obedience of wives to husbands remained paramount, the 1870 Civil Code expanded women's authority over their children. But decades before in divorce cases, and probably in cases of informal separation, women often retained custody of children, and for the same reasons that women sought divorce more than men: because of abandonment or abuse. By the middle of the nineteenth century, it is clear that alcohol often was involved in cases of abuse, which spurred organization and publications by women against drinking. Mexican women, like women elsewhere in North America and Europe, used problems of drinking and its relation to family abuse to liberalize divorce laws. It seems that profligate males among the rising middle class precipitated women's temperance activities, for it was from the middle class that the increasingly literate and activist women who organized against alcohol came.

Family property laws departed significantly from previous legal tradition in the 1870 and 1884 Civil Codes by lifting spousal and parental restrictions on designation of their property through community property and equal, partible inheritance (including the suppression of dowries for daughters). After 1870, upon marriage a couple could choose to participate in community property or to maintain their property separately. The 1884 Civil Code ended guaranteed inheritance to children. These changes, made with a clear economic motive of allowing individual choice in the use of one's property in order to encourage free movement of wealth, varied in their impact on individuals and on parental authority. On the one hand, the changes eliminated the legal economic safety-net that community property and dowries provided for married women and that equal, partible inheritance had given to both daughters and sons, just as the earlier Ley Lerdo had diminished the economic safety-net of Indian communities. On the other hand, the laws undermined the authority of husbands by assuring women control over their separate property and income without their husbands' interference, and potentially that of parents over children if children knew that they would not inherit. In most cases, the practice of giving daughters part of their inheritance at marriage through the dowry already had declined. Children, especially sons, could seek independence from parents by taking advantage of expanding educational and economic opportunities that developed in the nineteenth century. Women, however, especially those from propertied families, were left the most vulnerable by changes in inheritance laws. Parents had the option of channeling most of a family's wealth to the potentially most productive members: their male offspring. Unlike sons, daughters had fewer opportunities for education, jobs, and investment, and thus fewer opportunities for seeking economic independence from parents or family. The changes in family property law potentially undermined a fundamental function of the Mexican family: that families had the responsibility of providing for all family members throughout their lives.

Family Strategies and Kinship Relations

Family law provided a framework for family relations in eighteenth- and nineteenth-century Mexico but did not necessarily determine the behavior and experience of individual families or their members. Furthermore, some changes in family law were responses to transformations in society that already had taken place. Families responded to the upheaval in politics and the economy of this period by continuing to rely on consanguineous (blood relative) and affinal (marriage) kinship relations, on surrogate kin, and on ties of patronage, as part of the diverse strategies families relied upon to help them survive difficult times or to take advantage of opportunities as they presented themselves.

Family strategies and the obstacles families faced as they approached and moved through the nineteenth century can be discerned by following the life courses of family members through the family cycle of birth, upbringing, marriage, and death. Family strategies often depended on having offspring to perpetuate the family as a lineage and kin groups, help support family members, preserve or enhance social status and wealth, and carry cultural values and tradition to succeeding generations.

Within a year of marriage, a Mexican couple generally had their first child. Fertility was high and depended on the age at marriage. Indian couples tended to marry for the first time very young, at around 16 for women and 18 for men, and they had during the women's childbearing years seven or eight children, on the average. Those of mixed race and whites married somewhat later and had about five to seven children. Most mothers nursed their own children for about a year, making the interval between births about two years. Military officers and bureaucrats—who tended to be mostly white until the mid–nineteenth century, when the composition of both occupations became more diverse—married much later. By the beginning of the nineteenth century, the age discrepancy between spouses was decreasing substantially, probably leading, at least among some groups, to more companionate marriages. Also, among all groups the age at first marriage rose slightly during the nineteenth century. Infant and child mortality, however, was very high, and thus only about two to four children survived to have children of their own. Child mortality declined some in the nineteenth century because of the implementation of public health measures such as the use of smallpox vaccine and improvements in hygiene in some of Mexico's cities. A decrease in child mortality may have been one factor in the increase in Mexico's population in the nineteenth century.

Children, or *hijos de familia*, were under their father's or their family's authority from infancy to young adulthood, and they relied on parents and family for upbringing, security, sustenance, and affection. Children owed parents respect and obedience, and testimony from a variety of documents indicates that most social and ethnic groups valued this respect for parents. In return parents cared for and taught their children the skills needed to survive as adults, and children often followed in their parents' footsteps, the boys doing what their father did and girls generally taking on the domestic role of their mothers. By their midteens, most youths were shouldering adult responsibilities, even though they did not yet have adult rights. Until public education became widely available, it was parents, then, who were the most important educational agents in the lives of children. Kin, neighbors, and even strangers sometimes stepped in when parents were absent and intervened when they were remiss, but the alternatives did not always fulfill a child's need for sustenance and guidance. The loss of parents often compromised a child's well-being and disrupted the socialization process that was important to the child's future livelihood. Parents also bore the major responsibility for their offspring by tradition and law. Other family members were not always available, and the lack of a developed system of social services left children to depend on parents. Even parents were not always dependable; thus, many needs of the minor population went unanswered. Families were not always supportive institutions. Children suffered abuse, abandonment, incest, rape, and harsh punishments.

Nevertheless, Mexican parents, family, and society in general valued children, although some suffered abuse or exploitation. Mexican parents credit the Virgin of Guadalupe with caring for their dead children on their journey to heaven and nursing them upon arrival there. Furthermore, the legal tradition that Mexico inherited from Spain in both secular and canon law, although in disagreement on specific points, reflected an ideology that valued children and sought to protect them. Neither parents nor others charged with carrying for children were supposed to use harsh punishments.

Because the period from the mid–eighteenth to mid–nineteenth centuries in Mexico, as in the rest of the Americas and Europe, was a period of reform, crisis, and change, children increasingly received attention as the means to change society. In particular, the productivity and well-being of society was seen as a product of the health, well-being, and education of its children. In Mexico, much of the literature of this period promoted improving the education, in the larger sense of upbringing, of children. Mexico's most noted author of the early nineteenth century, José Joaquín Fernández de Lizardi, wrote often about the upbringing of children. Two of his best-known novels, *El Periquillo Sarniento* (1816) and *La Quijotita y su prima* (1818), were meant to show parents the right and wrong way to raise children and the consequences of bad upbringing. Mexican newspapers addressed similar issues, and some didactic periodicals directed toward children and youth appeared as well. Journalist Juan Sánchez de la Barquera advocated that mothers nurse their own children and that women have access to education in order to instill morality into their children in his newspaper *Diario de México*. Barquera also founded the first Mexican periodical for children in 1813, *El Correo de los Niños*. A publication advocating better education for Mexican women written by a young Mexican woman was *Cartas sobre la education del bello sexo* (1824). All of these publications wanted Mexican society to enjoy the progress that could be attained through proper education and upbringing of children.

As a result of this attitude toward children, public policies gave more attention and resources to social, educational, and health services for children, especially school-age children and youths. The purpose, of course, was to organize a more obedient and skilled workforce for a more economically productive society, but improving human potential of society was seen as the means to this end. As a consequence, after Independence, states began to organize public school systems to provide schooling, mostly at the primary level, for both boys and girls. They also established programs to train teachers, for as numbers of schools increased substantially in the nineteenth century, the demand for teachers, both male and female, also increased, contributing to greater opportunities for both men and women. Public schooling reduced dependence on parents for training. Public policy toward children, however, was more effective in urban areas.

Household size and structure in Mexico during this period varied considerably. Elite families, who had the greater access to political and economic resources, tended to have larger households because they could afford more servants and their children tended to live longer. But at any one point in time, the majority of households (50 to 80 percent) of most social and ethnic groups had only about four to six people, and the related family in the household was usually parents, or a parent, and children. If we look at households over time, however, we see constant movement in and out of them as family and kin were born, died, or moved, as others married into the family, were adopted, or were taken in as wards, borders, clerks, apprentices, or servants.

The most common household arrangements involving extended family were those in which a parent lived with a married child or a young unmarried child lived with an older married sibling. In both cases, we see the effect of demographic factors. The parent had been widowed and the child orphaned. In fact, few teenaged children had a grandparent living in the same household with them. Unmarried adult women also tended to live in households with other kin. These included both widowed women and single adult women who had not married. Census records and wills at several points in time throughout this period indicate that as much as 30 to 40 percent of the adult female population was widowed. Widows, especially widows with children, were much less likely to remarry than widowers, and they were also more vulnerable to become impoverished because of more limited economic opportunities for women; thus, these women were forced to live with or depend on relatives more often than men.

Some working families engaged in occupations that required the cooperation and cohabitation of an extended family. The families of the mostly mulatto and mestizo muleteers, for example, lived in extended family compounds that included parents, married children, and unmarried children. The father, the older sons, and often the sons-in-law drove the mule trains and thus were often away from home. Meanwhile, the women and young children kept the home and cared for the extra animals that the family used in its business.

In fact, with the large-scale disruptions from 1760 to 1870 caused by riots, famine, epidemics, war, and economic stagnation that brought death and impoverishment to families, many individuals and families were often on the move trying to escape these problems or looking for a better way to make a living. Frequent migration helps explain why some communities had at least 20 to 30 percent of households headed by women. While women remained to care for the home and children by taking in laundry, sewing, or cooking, by renting rooms to boarders, or by selling food or other items as peddlers or in the markets, men migrated to other areas to find work. Family members, as part of a family's strategy, often worked in a variety of occupations that often required some of the members, usually the adult males and sometimes the young single females, to migrate from place to place. As the United States took control of the northern part of Mexico after 1848 and as Mexico's own population grew during the nineteenth century, migration continued not only within Mexico but also across the border, but the family strategy involved was essentially the same. An important consequence was, and is, that in communities that relied on male migration for income, the women developed a keen sense of autonomy and self-reliance. In some communities, too, legal traditions and family strategies that became cultural practice allowed women significant control over a family's real property. We find nineteenth-century women acquiring real estate specifically for their daughters

as a hedge against debt. Other women leased family real property to provide themselves with income.

Families relied on kin beyond the household. Certainly the precarious economic condition of many families that existed from the middle of the eighteenth century made kinship ties important for survival of many members of society, especially women and children. Consanguineous and affinal ties helped families secure and protect social status, jobs, and resources. Bureaucratic, merchant, landowning, and mining families developed extensive family networks for this purpose. Godparentage and co-parentage also cemented or extended ties of kinship. Reliance on kin continued to be an integral part of strategies that Mexican families devised as the country accelerated industrialization and urbanization during the last decades of the nineteenth century.

Select Bibliography

Anderson, Rodney, *Guadalajara a la consumación de la Independencia: Estudio de su población según los padrones de 1821–1822*, translated by Marco Antonio Silva. Guadalajara: Gobierno de Jalisco Secretaría General Unidad, 1983.

Arnold, Linda, *Bureaucracy and Bureaucrats in Mexico City, 1742–1835.* Tucson: University of Arizona Press, 1988.

Arrom, Silvia M., *The Women of Mexico City, 1790–1857.* Stanford, California: Stanford University Press, 1985.

_____, "Changes in Mexico Family Law in the Nineteenth Century." In *Confronting Change, Challenging Tradition: Women in Latin American History*, edited by Gertrude M. Yeager. Wilmington, Delaware: Scholarly Resources, 1994.

Balmori, Diana, Stuart F. Voss, and Miles Wortman, *Notable Family Networks in Latin America.* Chicago: University of Chicago Press, 1984.

Brading, David, *Miners and Merchants in Bourbon Mexico, 1763–1810.* Cambridge: Cambridge University Press, 1971.

_____, *Haciendas and Ranchos in the Mexican Bajío: León, 1700–1860.* Cambridge: Cambridge University Press, 1978.

Calderon de la Barca, Fanny, *Life in Mexico.* Berkeley: University of California Press, 1982.

Carroll, Patrick J., *Blacks in Colonial Veracruz: Race, Ethnicity, and Regional Development.* Austin: University of Texas Press, 1991.

Chance, John K., and William B. Taylor, "Estate and Class in a Colonial City: Oaxaca in 1792." *Comparatives Studies in Society and History* 19 (1977).

Deans-Smith, Susan, *Bureaucrats, Planters, and Workers: The Making of the Tobacco Monopoly in Bourbon Mexico.* Austin: University of Texas Press, 1992.

Gutiérrez, Ramon, *When Jesus Came, the Corn Mothers Went Away: Marriage, Sexuality, and Power in New Mexico, 1500–1846.* Stanford, California: Stanford University Press, 1991.

Harris, Charles H., III, *A Mexican Family Empire: The Latifundio of the Sánchez Navarros, 1765–1867.* Austin: University of Texas Press, 1975.

Kicza, John E., *Colonial Entrepreneurs: Families and Business in Bourbon Mexico City.* Albuquerque: University of New Mexico Press, 1984.

Ladd, Doris M., *The Mexican Nobility at Independence, 1780–1826.* Austin: University of Texas Press, 1976.

Lavrin, Asunción, editor, *Latin American Women: Historical Perspectives.* Westport, Connecticut: Greenwood Press, 1978.

____, editor, *Sexuality and Marriage in Colonial Latin America.* Lincoln: University of Nebraska Press, 1989.

Lomnitz, Larissa Adler, and Marisol Perez-Lizaur, *A Mexican Elite Family, 1820–1980: Kinship, Class, and Culture,* translated by Cinna Lomnitz. Princeton, New Jersey: Princeton University Press, 1987.

Seed, Patricia, *To Love, Honor and Obey in Colonial Mexico: Conflicts over Marriage Choice, 1574–1821.* Stanford, California: Stanford University Press, 1988.

Smith, Raymond, editor, *Kinship Ideology and Practice in Latin America.* Chapel Hill: University of North Carolina Press, 1984.

Thompson, Angela T., "To Save the Children: Inoculation, Vaccination, and Public Health in Guanajuato, Mexico." *The Americas* 49:4 (April 1993).

____, "Children and Schooling in Guanajuato, Mexico, 1790–1840." In *Molding the Hearts and Minds: Education, Communications, and Social Change in Latin America,* edited by John A. Britton. Wilmington, Delaware: SR Books, 1994.

Yeager, Gertrude M., editor, *Confronting Change, Challenging Tradition: Women in Latin American History.* Wilmington, Delaware: SR Books, 1994.

—ANGELA T. THOMPSON

Family and Kinship: Twentieth Century

During the twentieth century, changes in Mexico's society and economy and their complex interrelationship with demographic change exerted a profound influence on Mexican family life. The accelerated process of urbanization and industrialization, as well as advances in health and education throughout the twentieth century, contributed to the transformation of the family environment. Among the more notable changes affecting family life were changes in the structure of production, which led to the gradual loss in importance of family kinship as the basis of production; the waning of patriarchal power structures and the increasing economic independence of individual members of the family group; and finally, the disappearance of the ideologies and practices that reduced the exercise of human sexuality to the task of reproduction.

The beginning of the twentieth century was characterized by high and fluctuating levels of mortality. Life expectancy averaged 30 years in 1920, increasing to 70 years in 1990. The consequences of this drop in the mortality rate were numerous and tended to have repercussions in different areas of family life. These included the increase in the duration of a marriage before termination by the death of a spouse; the postponement of the experience of widowhood; the proportional reduction in the number of minors having to deal with the death of one or both parents, which has meant a drastic decline in the numbers of orphans; and the increased survival of grandparents during one's childhood and early adolescence, thereby increasing the potential for interaction between various successive family generations.

The drop in the mortality rate eventually was accompanied by a marked decline in fertility. In the last three decades of the twentieth century, the global birthrate declined from an average of 7 to 2.7 offspring per woman. This reduction originated in changes in attitude and behavior toward reproduction, initially adopted by a small group of urban-based women born during the 1930s. The modification observed in the reproductive behavior of spouses led to a decrease in family size, changing norms in the age difference between children, and a marked reduction in the time dedicated to procreation in terms of the time elapsing between the first and last born.

The changes in the levels and patterns of mortality and birth were followed by a greater complexity in the norms respective to the formation and dissolution of marital ties. At the end of the century, a small increase in the number of single people was observed, especially among the male population. Nevertheless, matrimony continued to be practiced by almost all Mexicans prior to reaching 50 years of age. At the same time, there was an increase in sexual relations before marriage among young people, a phenomenon largely provoked by greater sexual freedom and the loss of cultural values attributed to female virginity. Marriage sanctioned by the church and state increased as the most common form of union. By the 1990s, three out of every four women began their married life with a civil or religious wedding. At the same time, there was a slight rise in the age of first marriages among women (from 21.5 in 1930 to 22.2 in 1990), while the male average remained more or less constant (24.8 in 1930 to 24.7 in 1990). These tendencies reduced the age difference between spouses.

Family life was affected by notable changes in the means by which matrimony is dissolved (widowhood, separation, and divorce). With the gradual increase in life expectancy, widowhood gave way to separation and divorce as the predominant means of ending a marriage. Indeed, the annual rate of separation and divorce for unions of less than five years' duration and among women who married prior to 18 years of age proved higher among more recent generations than previous ones. The explanation as to why separation and divorce became more frequent is to be found in numerous factors related to wide social changes, particularly more tolerant social, familial, and personal attitudes, the instilling of more permissive guidelines on the theme of matrimonial breakup, as well as the controversy over double standards with regard to sexual mores.

Demographic changes in the country, interacting with other economic, social, and cultural processes, contributed not only to a significant increase in the number of households but also influenced a reduction in their average size and transformed the composition and internal dynamics of the family structure. Among the numerous examples in Mexico of change and continuity in this regard were (1) the continued existence of households on a low subsistence level and the worsening of the absolute and relative number of families in a state of poverty, a fact of prime relevance in the context of the family; (2) the plurality of lifestyles within the home and family, especially the preponderance of nuclear households, and the continuance of those of large and complex type whose increase in the 1980s and 1990s has been interpreted by some authors as a family response to two decades of crisis and economic adjustments; (3) the decline in the relative importance of children within the family structure, a change associated mainly with the drop in the birthrate; (4) the high percentage of elderly in the home, which reflected increases in life expectancy; (5) the high percentage of households consisting of married spouses without children and the decreasing proportion of homes made up exclusively of a married couple with unmarried children (conjugal nuclear families); (6) the increasingly greater percentage of nuclear households made up of one spouse and his or her children; (7) the increase in reconstituted households, made up of individuals who have separated from their previous partners; (8) the growing relative importance of households headed by women; and (9) the large proportion of households made up of people living alone. Various of these changes were reflected in the evolution of the civil codes that governed family life during the twentieth century.

The Legal Context of Family Relations in the Twentieth Century

Mexican families are channels for numerous influences that have operated since the colonial period. These are basically derived from some indigenous customs, transmitted and adapted principally by mestizo (mixed-race) and criollo (Spanish descended) families. The legacy of the African culture, established in several states of the Mexican Republic through the slave trade, was added to this varied and complex mix of influences. The family developed from this original foundation, under the protection of traditions and rules hallowed by custom, influenced by codes and norms derived from Christian morality, and legitimated by the state.

In the twentieth century diverse changes gradually were introduced into the Mexican civil code governing family life, reformulating the dispositions present in various codes of the nineteenth century. These nineteenth-century codes include that promulgated by Benito Juárez on December 8, 1870, which became law on March 1, 1871; and that of 1884, enacted by Manuel González and which came into operation on June 1 of that year. These two codes included restrictions on women, placing them on an inferior level with respect to the male in various spheres of civil life. Only males were allowed to exercise parental authority over children, and marital separation was not accepted nor adoption recognized.

Fundamental changes in this traditional concept of the family came with the Mexican Revolution. In 1916 Venustiano Carranza declared to the Constituent Congress that he would promulgate laws to establish the family on "more rational and just foundations that would elevate spouses to the lofty mission that society and nature have placed in their care." The following year the Ley de Relaciones Familiares (LRF, or Law on Family Relations) was enacted, on the basis that "modern ideas of equality, widely spread and accepted in almost all social institutions, had not achieved a convenient measure of influence on the family." This law, which postulated bases for equality and reciprocity between spouses, despite its lacking a federal character, was adopted in the Federal and Territorial Districts and in various states of the Republic. The LRF took into consideration that "the woman and especially the Mexican woman ... has frequently been the victim of exploitation ... that the state should prevent." It arranged, in contrast to previous legislation, that inheritance should be administered according to mutual agreement, that each spouse should maintain control over the administration and ownership of his or her personal property and the profits thereof, and complete freedom with regard to contracts and obligations. The law made it understood "that both spouses had rights to consider themselves as equals within the home," from which followed several rights for the woman. Nevertheless, a rigid sexual division of labor was assumed in a clause stating that the husband was obligated to support the family even if the woman cooperated in this matter. But is also warned that the work of a married woman should not draw her from the fulfillment of her prime obligation: the direct care for the house and children. Parental authority was understood as a collection of obligations that nature imposed on the marital pair for the benefit of their offspring. This law renewed the requisites for the entrance into matrimony and established adoption as a means whereby a child belonging to neither of the married pair could enter a family, thereby crystallizing the aspirations of those matrimonies that had not succeeded in procreating children. The situation of illegitimate children improved with the suppression of the qualification of bastardy within the codes to facilitate these children's recognition and legitimation and give them the right to bear the surname of the individual by whom they were recognized and to receive nourishment and their hereditary portion under the same conditions as any other child.

One highly novel measure that radically changed the dispositions of 1874 on the durability of matrimony was the establishment of divorce, included in Section 6, Article 75 of the LRF. This stated that "divorce dissolves the marriage link and leaves the couple in a fit state to contract another." Thus it was specified that a marriage could be dissolved during the lifetime of the spouses by mutual and free consent or as the result of grave provocation as established by local laws, thereby freeing both to contracting a new legitimate union.

A new civil code was expedited by Plutarco Elías Calles in 1928, becoming common law on October 1, 1932, for the Federal and Territorial Districts and federal law for the entire Republic. The legislation of March 31, 1884, and the LRF of 1917 were abrogated on the appearance of this latter ruling. The new civil code established the equality of both sexes before the law in clearer terms. The second article specified that "opportunity under the law is equal for men and women; as a result a woman does not remain in a subordinate position for reasons of gender and is not restricted in the acquisition and exercise of her civil rights." From 1917 a legislative tendency in the LRF had been in agreement with this new law. Equality between the sexes had

wide-reaching effects: women had authority and legal considerations equal to those of their husbands; they could organize all matters connected with education and the establishment of the sons on the basis of mutual agreement; it was determined that a woman, without requiring marital authorization, could take a job or exercise a profession to the extent that it would not prejudice her attention to her work in or the running of the home. The code established equal rights in the motives for divorce in that these referred to both sexes and confirmed the legality of separation through mutual consent. Additionally, the thesis of the equality of legitimate and illegitimate children before the law was restated. The law also protected the concubine (the mistress of or a woman married only by the church to a single man) and the offspring of the relationship. As a result of this code, a woman did not lose parental authority over the children of previous marriages, even when she married again. Syphilis, tuberculosis, or any chronic or incurable illness, and the excessive and habitual use of alcoholic beverages or debilitating drugs, were established as an impediment to matrimony. The marital couple were obliged to establish community or separation of goods, attempting through this measure to guarantee the woman's interests.

As of the mid-1990s, family life in Mexico was still ruled by the Civil Code of 1932, although with some reforms. It is well known that while family codes frequently have a long duration, family life depends on flexible arrangements and contingencies experienced on a day-to-day basis. The relative short-term effectiveness of the codes in the context of the reality they seek to normalize creates disparities between law and actual practice in family relations. Mexico has experienced profound social change; over time the diverse social movements that have taken place have consolidated, thereby revindicating the extension of human rights and constitutional guarantees. Within this framework the feminist movement has played an important role in its fight for the improvement in the condition of women, questioning the institutional guidelines that have directed and formed family relations. Various changes suggested by Mexican women have been placed in an international context sensitive to feminist aspirations. From the 1970s various reforms were introduced into the Civil Code of 1932. These include those established during the presidential term of Luis Echeverría Álvarez, especially the reforms of 1974 referring to the rights and obligations that arise from matrimony. Article 162 is most important in this context since it established on one side the mutual obligation of assistance by both spouses, and on the other the rights to decide on the number and age difference of the children.

The 1974 reforms established the domestic equality of the spouses, independently of the economic contributions of each one. The husband's previous obligation to support the family had led to his being considered to have greater prerogatives within the marriage. The economic power that the husband still exercises in many Mexican homes where he continues to fulfill the role of sole provider determines relationships and family life. Meanwhile, in December 1974 Article 4 of the Mexican Constitution of 1917 was reformed, establishing that both spouses are equal under the law.

Democratization within the Domestic Sphere
These reforms imply important changes in legislation, but as of 1996 many essential features of the 1932 Civil Code remained operative. As a result, organized actions have been taken up to organize legislation in conformity with new familial realities. The stability and viability of their social functions have increasingly depended on the progressive consolidation of a context that aids the democratization of family relationships between genders and generations and promotes a fairer division of tasks in the domestic sphere. Codes referring to this theme could help create conditions adequate for families to make the best of their material, human, and cultural resources, moving them toward the crystallization of family relations based on the equal distribution of rights and responsibilities of its members.

— VANIA SALLES AND RODOLFO TUIRÁN

Fernández, Manuel Félix

See Victoria, Guadalupe

Foreign Policy

This entry includes four articles that trace the development of Mexican foreign policy since Independence:

Foreign Policy: 1821–76
Foreign Policy: 1876–1910
Foreign Policy: 1910–46
Foreign Policy: 1946–96

See also Migration to the United States; Military; Nationalism; Petroleum; U.S.-Mexican Border

Foreign Policy: 1821–76

Most observers have described Mexican foreign relations in the first half-century after Independence as a never-ending tale of nightmares. Between 1821 and 1876, Mexico endured four major foreign interventions, at least three of which threatened the country's existence as an independent nation. Moreover, Mexico lost half of its territory to the United States, and the country was constantly in debt to European creditors. Nevertheless, Mexican foreign relations in the so-called National period contributed to the consolidation of the Mexican state. The manifold instances of foreign intervention helped warring factions rally behind national leaders, and Mexican responses to these interventions strengthened a nationalism that had remained weak even by Latin American standards. Ultimately, Mexico's international history of the early and mid–nineteenth century laid the groundwork for the foreign policy during the rule of the dictator Porfirio Díaz and the subsequent Revolutionary regime. While Mexican foreign relations in the National period showed the country's vulnerability to foreign intervention, they also demonstrated the value of a principled policy of nonintervention and respect of international treaties, and they highlighted the nation-building potential of foreign policy.

When Mexico achieved its independence from Spain, its rulers faced a daunting task in their attempt to establish effective central authority. The country paid for the decade of violence that had preceded Independence with a prolonged state of chaos. During the Wars of Independence, rival caudillos had carved out spheres of power. After 1821, their armies upheld their bosses' claims to both regional and national influence, defying the authority of the central government. The only one of these caudillos to remain a national force throughout the next few decades, General Antonio López de Santa Anna, occupied the presidential chair many times but usually returned to his hacienda after a few months in Mexico City. Not surprisingly, the state of the Mexican economy resembled that of the country's political order. The wars had devastated Mexico's granary, the Bajío; the mining industry lay in ruins; the national treasury was empty; and commerce had declined precipitously.

Furthermore, the country's northern frontier remained unsettled and undefended. This region was

Mexico's "Wild North," a vast expanse of mostly barren terrain inhabited by some 200,000 people, most of whom belonged to nomadic Indian tribes. To be sure, small towns such as San Antonio and Santa Fe dotted the landscape as tiny islands of Hispanic presence. But on the whole, this region's ties to Mexico were little more than juridical in character—and were threatened by dynamic U.S. expansionism. Much like the fellow Spanish American republic of Gran Colombia, Mexico faced imminent disintegration. Central America's secession in 1823 appeared to prove the point.

As a consequence, Mexican foreign policy after Independence, inasmuch as the government could pursue one, regarded the defense of the country's territory as its paramount goal. To remain master of the vast expanses that it had inherited from the viceroyalty, the Mexican government needed to tackle two difficult tasks: extending central government control into the entire country (and thus preventing secessions), and forestalling the encroachment by U.S. settlers.

In 1823, only two years after independence, Mexico seemed to fall woefully short in achieving the first of these goals, as the new government of Guadalupe Victoria stood idly by while Central America seceded. That year, however, a problem surfaced that demonstrated that in spite of its weakness, Mexico could act to prevent a further loss of territory in the south: the Chiapas question. Using superior political, diplomatic, and military force, Mexico incorporated the former Central American province and even increased its territory at the expense of Guatemala.

Meanwhile, foreign intervention and continued instability repeatedly threatened Mexico's own sovereignty. Spain's attempt at reconquest in 1829 led to the exodus of more than 25,000 Spaniards, among them many of the leading merchants and intellectuals of the former colony. In 1837, Britain and France used military force to obtain payment of overdue debts in the "Pastry War." A few years later, the planter elites in the Mexican state of Yucatán attempted to secede and applied to enter the United States. Even though the U.S. government rejected the overture, notice had been served that further secessions in the Mexican southeast remained a possibility.

Mexico's greatest problem, however, was the proximity of the United States—a country whose settlers pushed ever westward in search of their "manifest destiny." From the beginning, the Mexican leadership expressed concern about U.S. expansion, a concern that grew in proportion to the U.S. territorial acquisitions of the first half of the nineteenth century. In particular, the Mexican government feared the de facto annexation of the region of Texas through an unbridled migration of Anglo-Saxon farmers and fortune seekers. To prevent this scenario, President Victoria invited U.S. farmers of Catholic faith to settle permanently in Texas. As a condition, Victoria made these settlers promise to respect the sovereignty of Mexican law.

This scheme ultimately proved futile. In 1836, the settlers rebelled and succeeded in wresting Texas from Mexico; nine years later, the "Lone Star Republic" joined the United States. But Texas only whetted U.S. appetite for more Mexican territory. In 1846, complications resulting from a dispute over Texas's southwestern boundary led both countries into a war that ended with the U.S. Army in Mexico City and the loss of half of Mexico's territory. A deeply traumatic experience, the war with the United States demonstrated that the country faced either disintegration or further U.S. annexations unless political stability and economic growth could be achieved. Central America, the unity of which had been shattered in the 1830s, served as a lurid example of what could happen to Mexico in the event that further attempts at political centralization were not successful.

The experience of foreign occupation led to a surge in nationalism of both the popular and elite variants, and it contributed to the formation of national political parties. Earlier, so-called Conservatives and Liberals had gathered in the York and Scotch Masonic lodges in Mexico City, respectively. As Santa Anna's own vacillations between factions illustrate, these labels often were covers for personal ambitions. In the wake of the U.S. occupation of Mexico City, however, the influential statesman and historian Lucas Alamán headed a genuine Conservative Party, while Liberals coalesced around leaders such as Miguel Lerdo, Benito Juárez, and Ignacio Comonfort. Conservatives and Liberals disagreed fundamentally on the lessons that could be drawn from the lost war with the United States.

In Alamán's view, Mexico (mainly criollo—or Spanish-descended—Mexico, of course) represented the best of Catholic Europe: a fear of God and a stable society based on hereditary privilege. The Protestant United States, he thought, threatened this idealized Hispanic Mexico, both by its push for land and by its espousal of liberty and juridical equality. Not only did Alamán deem such ideas inapplicable to Mexico; he also realized that they attacked the existing social order in his home country. To minimize both U.S. political influence and the threat of future annexations, the Conservatives urged the Mexican elites to preserve the country's Hispanic heritage. They also sought to restore the short-lived Mexican monarchy of Agustín de Iturbide by offering the Mexican throne to a Catholic scion of a European dynasty. In addition, Alamán favored the retention of the *fueros,* special immunities enjoyed by the nobility, the Catholic Church, and the army, and he called for the veneration of the Jesuits and conquistador Fernando (Hernán) Cortés as heroes of an Ibero-Mexican tradition.

For their part, Liberals admired the rapid industrial development of Great Britain, Mexico's main trading partner, and opposed protectionist trade barriers and the paternalistic *fueros.* They regarded the United States as a society to be admired, not just to be feared. Mexico, the Liberals maintained, needed to emulate the Anglo-Saxon nations to avoid being swallowed up by the United States. Had the U.S. success in the war, they asked, not been brought about by a superior political and economic system? In the view of the Liberals, Mexico's captivity in tradition and privilege had been its major weakness in the war with the United States. In contrast to the Conservatives, the Liberals feared Spain: as early as the early 1850s, Juárez favored Cuba's independence as a means of removing the principal Spanish "springboard" into the western hemisphere.

Liberalism, however, lacked the cohesiveness of Alamán's Conservatives, as the Liberals remained divided in two camps: the *puros,* or radicals, and the *moderados,* or moderates. While *puros* such as Lerdo were more anticlerical than *moderados* such as Comonfort, the *puros* also distinguished themselves from their rivals in that they favored a radical capitalist transformation as a prerequisite for political reform. Seeking (at least in theory) the complete juridical equality of all Mexicans, the *puros* advocated the primacy of privately over corporately held property and favored unfettered individualism as the engine of economic growth.

Thus, the Mexican elites, apart from a few radical Liberals who flirted with the idea of annexation by the United States, shared a deeply rooted fear of U.S. territorial and political expansion, but they disagreed profoundly on how to prevent further annexations. In short, the Conservatives wanted Mexico to survive by turning to Spain and isolating itself from influences from the north. The Liberals dreamed of borrowing from Anglo-Saxon models to beat the United States at its own game.

During the immediate postwar period, Mexican foreign policy attained a noticeably Conservative touch. Having failed time and again to entice a European prince to occupy the Mexican throne, Alamán sought to enhance relations with the European powers and to increase diplomatic contact with the other Latin American republics. Alamán's ultimate Bolivarian dream—to situate Mexico in an international web of Hispanic culture to safeguard against both the real external threat posed by the United States and the potential internal threat of an uprising against the criollo elites—remained elusive. Naturally, protection of the country's sovereignty remained the primary goal. Many Mexicans still worried that the United States ultimately might annex more or all of their country, and Alamán feared U.S. expansionism into Central America. This fear was justified: many politicians from the southern United States openly advocated further annexations in order to obtain slave territories.

In 1853-54, the very anti-Yankee feelings espoused by Alamán contributed to the downfall of the Conservatives. Santa Anna's sale of a strip of Sonora to the United States in the Gadsden Purchase resulted in widespread outcry over this further loss of territory, and rumors of plans to sell even more of the Mexican north helped end Santa Anna's reign. A year later, the Revolution of Ayutla ousted the Conservatives. The era of chaos had invited U.S. annexation of half of Mexico, and further U.S. territorial gains appeared likely. The task in which Conservatives thus far had failed so dismally—political centralization—had, in the minds of many Mexicans, become a matter inextricably intertwined with the survival of national sovereignty.

It was not surprising, then, that the Reforma of 1855 to 1858 concerned itself with foreign policy as much as with domestic reform. Directed by *puro* Liberals such as Lerdo and Juárez, the Reforma was backed by a large and diverse coalition, including landowners, merchants, army officers, and peasants. This coalition agreed on one fundamental issue: to achieve political stability, Mexico required economic modernization through the promotion of private capital accumulation. In the view of the *puros,* the attraction of foreign immigrants and investment as well as the disentailment of the Catholic Church holdings were necessary steps to that end. Ideally, the Reforma would have created a capitalist yeoman class; the fact that large commercial estates ultimately benefited most from the redistribution mattered little to the program's original appeal.

In matters of foreign policy, the ruling *puros* were friendly to the United States, wary of the European powers, and hostile toward Guatemala. They did not fail to recognize the danger of further U.S. expansionism; nor did Juárez, provisional Liberal president after 1858, want to sell more Mexican territory. But they did believe that a "special economic relationship" with the United States could help Mexico build its infrastructure and attract immigrants, and thus make the country strong enough to prevent further foreign invasions and annexations.

The abortive 1857 Montes-Forsyth Treaties provide a good illustration of this strategy. In these agreements, the Liberal government accorded U.S. investors a dominant position in exchange for a buyout of Mexico's foreign debt. Whether the goal was a U.S. economic protectorate or a milder form of economic hegemony, the Liberals pursued a difficult strategy with these treaties. They intended to give U.S. business interests free rein to develop Mexico "from without" in order to blunt both U.S. territorial expansion and European debt collection *à la* the Pastry War. This Liberal plan, however, had the backing only of U.S. minister John Forsyth, not of his superiors. The administration of President James Buchanan did not demonstrate a great interest in intimate economic ties with Mexico, and the U.S. Senate rejected the Montes-Forsyth treaties.

Despite the enormous U.S. territorial gains of the past decades, Juárez soon found Buchanan to be as aggressive as many of his predecessors. Pressed by southern expansionists, the U.S. president sought territorial concessions from Juárez in exchange for diplomatic recognition and assistance. Yet even when the Mexican Conservatives came close to defeating the Liberals in the civil war known as the War of Reform (1858–61), Juárez would not sell territory. The Liberals proved more flexible on the subject of awarding other strategic advantages, however: at the nadir of their fortunes in the War of Reform, they agreed to give the United States free commercial transit rights across Sonora and the Isthmus of Tehuantepec in exchange for assistance. Fortunately for Mexico (and the patriotic image of the Liberals), the U.S. Senate rejected the proposal known as the McLane-Ocampo Treaty.

Soon after Juárez's victory in the War of Reform, the French Intervention afforded the Liberals a chance to demonstrate their patriotism. In 1862, Emperor Napoleon III, backed by Britain and Spain, sent an invasion force into Mexico. Two years later, the French emperor installed Maximilian von Hapsburg on the throne of a recreated Mexican empire. Helped by the French-Conservative coalition, the Mexican federal army brought Juárez to the brink of disaster. But Maximilian's waffling on key political issues and the departure of the French army in March 1867 gave Juárez an opportunity to seize the momentum. Deserted by its erstwhile allies, Maximilian's regime collapsed. The French Intervention bestowed nationalist credentials upon the Liberals

and thus strengthened their rule. The Conservatives, who earlier had criticized the Liberals for the McLane-Ocampo Treaty, now found themselves discredited as collaborators of a foreign power.

Because the futile French takeover further heightened awareness of Mexico's vulnerability to foreign intervention, the country's foreign relations once again influenced the course of domestic politics. If distant France had been able to impose and sustain a monarch in Mexico, how could Mexicans hope to resist another foreign invasion that might signal the end of their country as an independent nation? Thus, the specter of foreign aggression strengthened Juárez's case for creating a strong presidency in Mexico and helped allow the Mexican president to strengthen government authority in the late 1860s. The Juárez regime created a rural police force, the *rurales;* it smoothed out differences with the Catholic Church; it strengthened a burgeoning executive apparatus at the expense of the legislature; and it began to negotiate with regional caudillos to obtain their allegiance. Ultimately, the construction of the "Restored Republic" entailed the co-optation of many of the Conservatives. Frightened by social unrest and the prospect of foreign intervention, and influenced increasingly by European positivist ideas, many Liberals had begun to embrace the type of authoritarian rule long deemed indispensable by the Conservatives. As a result, "conservative liberalism" became a dominant doctrine in post-1867 Mexico. Under the motto of "order and progress," conservative liberalism embraced both modernization and authoritarian rule. The final result, consummated by the regime of Porfirio Díaz, was the construction of a political "machine" that brokered power at the local, regional, and national levels.

These changes in Mexican politics in turn influenced the formulation of Mexican foreign policy. By the end of the Restored Republic, three different major factions had emerged within the governing elite: the militarists, the reformed *puros,* and the positivists. Together, these groups not only represented different perspectives within a larger "Conservative-Liberal" consensus; they also expressed different ideas about Mexican foreign policy.

The militarists were in essence "reform Conservatives." Many of them had fought against the Liberals and only recently had reconciled themselves with the new order. Free from Alamán's infatuation with Spain, the militarists cast an admiring glance at newly unified Germany and Italy as models for national integration. Both Germany and Italy had been unified by "blood and iron": while the militarists conceded the significance of economic development, they thought that true national integration only could be achieved by military means. Concentrated within the army, and characterized by strong anti-Yankee sentiments, the militarists advocated the building of a strong military to counter threats from abroad. Future president Manuel González, who had fought for the Conservatives in the beginning of the war against the French, numbered among the most influential militarists in the Restored Republic.

The reformed *puros,* by contrast, continued to advocate the adoption of Anglo-Saxon political and economic models. Tempered by political realism and sobered by Buchanan's aggressive diplomacy, reformed *puros* such as Juárez and Porfirio Díaz had given up on the more radical versions of a "special relationship" with the United States. Despite their declining enthusiasm for the United States, however, they were easily the least anti-American of the three factions, and the only one that still entertained the notion that republican democracy was feasible in Mexico.

Dominated by Mexico City elites, the positivist faction emphasized the need for a strong, authoritarian state. Most positivists argued that a type of "democratic Caesarism" was a necessary step in the country's evolution from a backward to a progressive nation. Most of them were more impressed with European than with U.S. models, and some of the positivists even viewed the United States as barbarian and plebeian. Examples of prominent positivists, who later influenced the development of the Científico faction, included Juárez's justice secretary Gabino Barreda.

Led by the reformed puro Juárez, the early Restored Republic enjoyed good relations with the United States. Since the French Intervention had disrupted Mexico's relations with the major European powers, Juárez depended on good relations with the United States. Moreover, U.S. secretary of state William H. Seward reassured Mexican minister Matías Romero that the era of U.S. territorial acquisitions in Mexico was over. Therefore, relations with the United States soon became cordial.

Assured of U.S. goodwill, Juárez refused to negotiate with the European powers on the subject of the exorbitant claims made by their nationals against the Mexican government—a subject on resolution of which the reestablishment of diplomatic ties depended. The clearest manifestation of this stance came during the inauguration of the Mexican Congress in December 1867. Rather than proposing an active agenda for reestablishing diplomatic ties with Britain, France, and Spain, Juárez cast his remarks in distinctly negative tones. He claimed the Europeans had "voluntarily" broken diplomatic relations. Mexico would reestablish relations with these countries only if these powers assumed the initiative. Juárez also demanded that his former enemies forfeit all treaties signed prior to 1862, and that new accords be negotiated on "just and fair" premises. With this principled stance, he gained many admirers in Mexico. Inevitably, however, he thrust his country into the embrace of the United States: the three European powers refused to renew diplomatic relations.

Juárez had reason to believe that this gamble was well worth it. The onset of large-scale industrialization in the United States offered a chance to revive the Liberals' old quest for a "special economic relationship" that would bring "all the fruits of annexation without any of the dangers." Indeed, with the victory of northern industrial over southern agricultural interests in the U.S. Civil War, the goals of U.S. diplomacy had shifted. While plans for further territorial growth remained immobilized, access to Latin American raw materials and an end of European intervention in the hemisphere attained a crucial importance. Mexico, with its proximity to the United States, its hostility to the European powers, and its great diversity in agricultural and mining products, seemed the best Latin American candidate for a close partnership. Even though U.S. capitalists initially had little money to spare, Juárez hoped that the lure of the rich mines in northern and central Mexico eventually would induce them to fund the construction of a railroad system.

Thus, Juárez instructed Romero to promote Mexico as a target for U.S. investments. In particular, he sought the assistance of bankers and railroad magnates to promote the development of Mexico's desert north. Juárez envisioned the construction of railroads linking Mexican mining centers with North American markets. This project represented the old *puro* strategy of using economic development as a shield against U.S. invasions.

This strategy, however, entailed a pronounced Mexican dependence on its relationship with the United States, accentuated by the scarcity of contacts to the rest of Latin America and the absence of diplomatic relations with Britain, France, and Spain. In the end, such a unilateral dependence only could bring harm to Mexico. For that reason—and because the Juárez regime incorporated a growing number of militarists and positivists nervous about U.S. power—the Mexican government slowly moved away from its exclusive reliance on U.S. goodwill. Juárez's successor, the positivist-leaning Sebastián Lerdo de

Tejada, gave a voice to these concerns when he criticized the railroad project with the words "between strength and weakness, [let there be] the desert."

By the time of Lerdo's presidency (1872–76), old problems with the United States had resurfaced. While the U.S. expansionist fever had subsided, two nagging problems led to a deterioration of relations: Apache attacks on the United States from Mexican territory, and a number of (partially frivolous) U.S. claims. Some of these claims antedated the 1848 Treaty of Guadalupe Hidalgo that had expressly relieved the Mexican government from all old claims; others dealt with U.S. damages during the War of Reform and the French Intervention. Even though Lerdo enjoyed full U.S. diplomatic recognition, most potential U.S. investors held off investing in Mexico while a joint commission studied the issue. Having first convened in 1869, this commission did not finish its work until 1877. It did not help Mexico that U.S. president Ulysses S. Grant eschewed the relatively cautious and tactful approach of his two predecessors in favor of a blunt and aggressive policy.

Nevertheless, by 1876 direct European and U.S. aggression appeared a thing of the past. The leaders of postwar Mexico had realized that the United States would henceforth play a dominant role in their country. They had disagreed on how to confront that role: whether to reject it through alliances with European powers or whether to embrace it, in the hope of leading U.S. influence into constructive channels. The faction that had advocated the latter course had won out against the determined resistance of the Conservatives, the Catholic Church, and the European powers, even if much of its program had fallen victim to expediency and compromise.

Mexico's position toward the great powers was well defined. As Porfirian diplomacy would show, the country would seek the economic benefits of its proximity to the northern colossus, but it would not give up its political sovereignty. As long as the United States sought economic gain, its presence was welcome. But if U.S. expansionism should once again threaten Mexico, the U.S. government could count on determined opposition. European political influence, on the other hand, was on the wane, a casualty of the French Intervention.

As this discussion has shown, one cannot separate foreign relations from domestic politics in the National period: the interplay of both presaged future Mexican policies and predicaments. Between 1821 and 1876, the country's political stability was so tenuous, and foreign intervention in Mexican internal affairs so frequent, that Mexico's relationship with foreign powers created realities of domestic politics. The Pastry War, the U.S.-Mexican War, and the French Intervention all highlighted the importance of constructing a central government and ultimately contributed to the creation of a stronger state. These foreign wars stocked an incipient pantheon of Mexican patriotic heroes; Mexicans even today venerate the young cadets who died defending Chapultepec from U.S. troops as Niños Héroes (the Boy Heroes), and the names Ignacio Zaragoza and Benito Juárez stand for the Liberals' patriotic war against the French invaders. The turbulent domestic scene also affected Mexican foreign policy. While some of the political programs and debates of the time may not have reflected significant social or political realities, the debates about Mexico's position in a dangerous world belied the supposedly monolithic nature of Mexican foreign policy. As in the twentieth century, for example, some nineteenth-century Mexican leaders advocated an isolationist policy in order to stave off U.S. aggression, while others favored an attempt to "ride the tiger" so as to extract benefit from the country's vicinity to the United States. Thus, as Mexico struggled for its survival, the country lived through experiences that proved formative for subsequent foreign policy.

See also French Intervention; Guadalupe Hidalgo, Treaty of; Texan Secession; U.S.-Mexican War; Wars of Independence

Select Bibliography

Bazant, Jan, "Mexico from Independence to 1867." In *Cambridge History of Latin America,* edited by Leslie Bethell. Cambridge: Cambridge University Press, 1985.

Benson, Nettie Lee, "Territorial Integrity in Mexican Politics, 1821–1833." In *The Independence of Mexico and the Creation of the New Nation,* edited by Jaime E. Rodríguez O. Los Angeles: University of California, Los Angeles, Latin American Center, 1989.

Brack, Gene M., *Mexico Views Manifest Destiny, 1821–1846: An Essay on the Origins of the Mexican War.* Albuquerque: University of New Mexico Press, 1975.

Hale, Charles A., *Mexican Liberalism in the Age of Mora, 1821–1853.* New Haven, Connecticut: Yale University Press, 1968.

———, *The Transformation of Liberalism in Late Nineteenth-Century Mexico.* Princeton, New Jersey: Princeton University Press, 1989.

Knight, Alan, "Peasants into Patriots: Thoughts on the Making of the Mexican Nation." *Mexican Studies/Estudios Mexicanos* 10:1 (Winter 1994).

Olliff, Donathon C., *Reforma Mexico and the United States: A Search for Alternatives to Annexation, 1854–1861.* Tuscaloosa: University of Alabama Press, 1981.

Perry, Laurens B., *Juárez and Díaz: Machine Politics in*

Mexico. DeKalb: Northern Illinois University Press, 1978.

Pletcher, David M., *The Diplomacy of Annexation: Texas, Oregon and the Mexican War*. Columbia: University of Missouri Press, 1969.

Reed, Nelson, *The Caste War of Yucatan*. Stanford, California: Stanford University Press, 1964.

Scholes, Walter V., *Mexican Politics During the Juárez Regime, 1855–1872*. Colombia: University of Missouri Press, 1957.

Schoonover, Thomas D., *Dollars Over Dominion: The Triumph of Liberalism in Mexican–United States Relations*. Baton Rouge: Louisiana State University Press, 1978.

Vázquez, Josefina Z., and Lorenzo Meyer, *The United States and Mexico*. Chicago: University of Chicago Press, 1985.

—JÜRGEN BUCHENAU

Foreign Policy: 1876–1910

The regime of Porfirio Díaz often has been described as one of the most pro-foreign in Mexican history. In particular, historians and contemporaries alike have condemned it for its allegedly single-minded pursuit of foreign investment and its preferential treatment of foreign workers and investors. While conceding that these measures led to great improvements in infrastructure, a balanced budget, and the creation of an incipient middle class, most scholars agree that Mexico's commercial opening gave wealth to only a relatively small group of people, increased the country's dependence on the United States, squandered national resources, and accelerated the process of disentailment of Indian village land. Not for nothing did the famous dictum "México: madre de los extranjeros y madrastra de los mexicanos" (Mexico: mother of foreigners and stepmother of Mexicans) gain currency during the long Díaz dictatorship. Thus, most of the existing scholarship contends that the Porfiriato was a time of cordial relations with the United States and the European countries (as an example, see the work of Josefina Z. Vázquez and Lorenzo Meyer, 1985).

This tale of willing subordination and cordial relations, however, does not contain the entire story. Instead, the historical evidence reveals that Díaz often promoted a nationalist and independent foreign policy. A veteran and decorated hero of the war against the French, Díaz made frequent reference to his own role in the struggle against foreign invaders. His government sought to inculcate an "official nationalism" in its subjects—a nationalist vision fraught with imagery hostile to foreigners, and especially Spanish, British, French, and U.S. citizens. This nationalism did not limit itself to a two-faced rhetoric that would have cloaked the regime's supposed role as a broker for foreign interests. For instance, Díaz refused to pay more than a token compensation for decades-old European claims against Mexico, a stance that delayed British diplomatic recognition until 1884 and cost the Mexican government much-needed credit from its main source of investments at the time. The perennial dictator did not favor the United States with deferential treatment, either. The Díaz government frequently asserted Mexican interests in the face of aggressive U.S. policies toward Mexico and other Latin American countries. Even as regards foreign investment, Díaz and his associates belatedly recognized the limits of laissez-faire individualism: near the end of their rule, they adopted a number of measures aimed at giving the Mexican state a greater degree of control over the country's enormous mineral resources.

The case of Porfirian foreign policy thus presents an apparent paradox. On the one hand, the Porfirians, disciples of the modernizing philosophies of the nineteenth-century West, believed that closer ties to the burgeoning North Atlantic industrial nations would create a strong Mexican state and thus end the political instability and foreign invasions of decades past. Hence, just like many of their Latin American contemporaries, they agreed to hand over significant privileges to propertied foreigners. On the other hand, the Porfirians continued to fear encroachments on Mexico's political sovereignty and consciously acted to oppose it. Therefore, Díaz occasionally played the part of the cranky nationalist dictator that historians have usually reserved for personages such as Venezuela's Cipriano Castro and Nicaragua's José S. Zelaya.

The early years of the Porfiriato (1876–84) provided the Díaz regime with a number of historical lessons that influenced the development of such a seemingly Janus-faced policy. When he came to power in 1876, Díaz faced an immediate standoff with U.S. president Rutherford B. Hayes. Hayes not only loathed the overthrow of Sebastián Lerdo's constitutionally elected government; he also intended to use Díaz's lack of legitimacy as a point of leverage to obtain concessions in a number of border and financial disputes. To make his point, the U.S. president dispatched troops to the Mexican border and threatened military action; Díaz, on the other hand, ordered General Gerónimo Treviño to resist a possible invasion at all costs. Just when it appeared that this impasse might bring down the Mexican government, Díaz found the help of U.S. railroad and industrial interests. Impatient with the lack of economic opportunities caused by the absence of diplomatic recognition, a number of influential investors and bankers induced the U.S. Congress to appoint a committee to investigate the Mexican situation. In April 1878, Hayes awarded diplomatic recognition with no strings attached and subsequently withdrew U.S. forces from the border. This spat with Hayes had important repercussions for Porfirian foreign policy.

First, the crisis offered Díaz a chance to employ foreign policy as a nationalist cement for his regime. Mid-nineteenth-century Mexican nationalism had centered around a fear of foreign invasion, which gave rise to popular notions of *patria*. Mexico's social and regional divisions made the meaning of the term contested: in some instances, it referred to the *patria chica,* or region; in others, it denoted the *patria grande,* or country. Díaz now launched an effort to promote the *patria grande* in order to strengthen central control and thus crush the *patrias chicas.*

In this effort to foment an official nationalism as an aid in the larger project of state building, Díaz often pointed to his foreign policy. Long after the crisis had passed, he used the conflict with Hayes to show himself as a patriotic leader, an image that built on his earlier heroics facing the French Intervention. The significance of Díaz's principled position vis-à-vis the United States thus had transcended the strictly diplomatic realm. A foreign policy attuned to questions of "national honor," duly applauded by the loyal press, had allowed Díaz to tap into an important well of Mexican nationalism: the fear of foreign invasion.

Díaz made sure that Mexicans would not forget his newfound nationalist credentials: his supporters began to propagate a Liberal patriotic cult that insinuated strong continuities from Benito Juárez's nationalist posture to that of Díaz. With his tribute to Juárez, Díaz not only portrayed himself in Juárez's footsteps; he also extended an olive branch to the old Juaristas, some of whom still resented don Porfirio's seizure of power by force. This effort at constructing an official nationalism became ever more important as Porfirian modernization created a "national ruling class" in Mexico.

How did the Porfirians propagate this official nationalism? They lacked modern means of propaganda, such as radio, television, or even the dissemination of printed information to a large literate public. But the Porfirians did employ important media to spread their agenda outside their small ruling

circle: newspapers, anniversary commemorations, schools, and public works projects. History textbooks, street names, plaques, and statues soon reminded Mexicans of the Liberals' nationalist deeds.

It is difficult to measure the actual effect of this official nationalism for the political cohesion of Porfirian Mexico. The radical Liberal opposition venerated its own version of the nationalist Juárez, and many Conservatives still viewed Díaz as a pro-Yankee iconoclast. But despite the Porfirians' predictable failure to monopolize the nationalist discourse in Mexico, they had provided a set of readily identifiable symbols that promoted the "imagining" of a national community and thus strengthened their rule. The Revolutionary governments—and to a greater extent, those of the Partido Revolucionario Institucional—would only refine this strategy.

Second, Díaz came to understand that foreign investors could be better allies of his regime than foreign governments. As diplomatic relations with the United States remained volatile over the next five years, Díaz and his successor, Manuel González, increasingly relied on foreign investors to smooth out differences with the powerful "northern colossus." González in particular counteracted the occasionally hostile policies by promising U.S. businesses generous concessions in Mexico. During his rule (1880–84), the Mexican Congress passed a slew of legislation amending the old colonial-era agricultural and mining codes that considered land and subsoil the property of the Mexican nation. Henceforth, foreign proprietors could operate as owners rather than concessionaires of mining enterprises, and an 1883 law lifted most restrictions on foreign ownership of land. González also began the practice of appointing foreign investors as confidential Mexican government agents in Washington, and he reorganized the Foreign Ministry (Secretaría de Relaciones Exteriores) to reflect this greater emphasis on economic ties. Never a puppet of Díaz, González thus completed the construction of the legal framework of the Porfirian program of externally driven modernization begun during La Reforma (1855–58). In the process, he created the conditions for better relations with the United States.

As Díaz and González moved toward closer ties with the U.S. economy, they also improved diplomatic relations with a group of old enemies: Great Britain, France, and Spain. The Porfirians regarded at least the first two of these nations as important sources of investment capital, and they also sought to forestall the realistic danger of an excessive dependence on U.S. capital. Therefore, Díaz opened negotiations with France and Spain and won the unqualified diplomatic recognition of his government. González, for his part, negotiated a settlement with Great Britain, the most recalcitrant of the old enemies. In both efforts, investors played a key role in persuading their governments to normalize relations with Mexico.

After Díaz's return to power in 1884, Mexican foreign policy sought to balance the desires of foreign investors against those of Mexican nationalists. Two experienced advisers helped Díaz with this balancing act: the secretary of foreign relations, Ignacio Mariscal, and Matías Romero, the chief Mexican diplomatic representative in the United States. Even though both of these two former associates of Benito Juárez hailed from the state of Oaxaca (as did Díaz), they held widely different views of Mexican foreign relations. While the nationalist Mariscal (who remained close to military circles around González) held a profound mistrust of U.S. intentions and advocated stronger efforts to attract European capital, the pro-business Romero (a former radical Liberal) regarded the United States as the main potential source of the capital needed to build up Mexico's infrastructure. Whereas Mariscal feared that the flow of U.S. investments might one day amount to a "Pacific Conquest" no less dangerous than the U.S.-Mexican War, Romero thought that the existence of strong economic links would make U.S. aggression much less likely. Díaz used the advice of both of these politicians to construct his foreign policy: Mariscal shaped Mexico's inter-American and European diplomacy, and Romero handled most of the negotiations with U.S. investors from his office in Washington, D.C. During the next 14 years, the Oaxacan triumvirate of Díaz, Mariscal, and Romero confronted international issues with a relatively great degree of success.

U.S. diplomacy continued to be capricious and unpredictable: on various occasions, including the famous case of the arrest of newspaper editor Augustus K. Cutting in 1886, the U.S. government assumed an unreasonable position regarding the rights of U.S. citizens in Mexico. Moreover, the government in Washington did not approve a single Mexican extradition request, in the southwestern United States, politicians talked about the possible annexation of Sonora and Baja California, and President Grover Cleveland even warned Díaz to accommodate his government lest he desired to risk losing the flow of U.S. capital. To add to these problems, the two governments haggled over the territory of El Chamizal, a small area near El Paso. Not

surprisingly, Mariscal felt vindicated in his opinions about the United States; nevertheless, he asserted Mexico's positions with great prudence.

In terms of hemispheric issues, Central American conflicts and the First Inter-American Conference demanded constant Mexican attention. In March 1885, Guatemalan President Justo Rufino Barrios declared the forcible unification of Central America —a step that threatened Mexico because of consistent Guatemalan desires to recover Chiapas. In keeping with the Mexican tradition of weakening Guatemala, Díaz helped the eventually victorious alliance against Barrios: by sending troops into the border state of Chiapas, he diverted a large part of the Guatemalan army that stood poised to invade El Salvador. Held in Washington, the Inter-American Conference constituted another type of threat: the United States had placed on the table a proposal for a hemispheric customs union that would have seriously jeopardized the ongoing efforts to prevent unilateral dependence on the United States. Fortunately for Díaz, many other Latin American governments were similarly unwilling to concede advantages to U.S. investors over their European rivals, and a majority of Latin American delegations including the Mexican representative defeated the proposal.

One of Díaz's finest hours as a critic of U.S. hegemonic pretensions came in the wake of the formulation of the so-called Olney Corollary to the Monroe Doctrine. In 1894, U.S. secretary of state Richard Olney had intervened in a long-standing dispute concerning the exact boundary between Venezuela and British-held Guyana. Olney had defended the Venezuelan position by arguing that any revision of the boundary in Great Britain's favor would violate the Monroe Doctrine's prohibition of new European colonization. As the British acquiesced without a fight, Díaz had seen no reason to criticize Olney for his remarks. A few months later, however, Olney boasted that the United States was "practically sovereign" in the hemisphere and that its "fiat" was law, and he enjoined all Latin American nations to accept U.S. protection against European imperialist designs. These remarks ultimately prompted Díaz's 1896 speech on the Monroe Doctrine:

> [I am a] partisan of Monroe's principles, if well understood. ... But we do not think ... that the responsibility for helping the other republics of the hemisphere against the attacks of Europe ... should be solely incumbent on the United States. ... Each one of those republics ought to ... proclaim ... that every attack ...

of a foreign power . . . would be considered an attack upon itself (González, 1966).

The Díaz Doctrine—the belief that the Monroe Doctrine should be multilaterally enforced by all countries in the Americas—has since formed an important cornerstone of Mexican foreign policy. On the surface, the doctrine appeared evenhanded in its rejection of both European and U.S. intervention. But the wording and timing of Díaz's address suggest that it was primarily directed against U.S. interventionism. The Díaz Doctrine, in fact, marked the coming of a new era in the history of Mexican foreign policy. With European intervention and problems on Mexico's southern border remote threats, U.S. expansion grew in importance among Mexican foreign policy concerns.

It soon became clear, however, that Díaz commanded a limited radius of action for initiatives designed to slow the U.S. drive for a greater political and military role in the Caribbean. Having attempted to mediate between the United States and Spain, for example, Díaz could only watch idly as the two countries clashed to decide the future of Cuba and Puerto Rico. The resultant U.S. control over Cuba infuriated both Díaz and many Mexican nationalists who wished to see the Mexican government at the vanguard of a Latin American anti-imperialist league. In 1903 and 1904, U.S. interventions in Panama and the Dominican Republic likewise met with widespread criticism in Mexico, but virtually no word of official protest.

This "Cuba Shock" following the Cuban-Spanish-American War helped set in motion a shift in Porfirian diplomacy. After many years of fostering nationalist expectations in the Mexican public, Díaz found himself unable to deliver on these expectations. As successfully as his government had defended Mexican political sovereignty against aggressive U.S. policies, the Porfirian balancing act now teetered on the brink. Díaz's stance became even more difficult owing to the growing perception that foreigners enjoyed a privileged status in Mexico. Anti-Yankee conservatives soon joined liberals on the radical fringe in demanding more opportunities for Mexicans, and a more assertive diplomacy toward the United States.

To add to these developments, Romero's death in 1898 (the same year that ended with U.S. gunboats in Havana) shifted the balance of power within the Porfirian governing elite toward Mariscal's more nationalist position. The man who replaced Romero as a key foreign-policy adviser, Treasury Secretary José Y. Limantour, was no friend of Mariscal's, but he desired to increase European investments in Mexico as a way of lessening the country's dependence on capital from the United States. To be sure, Limantour played his role intelligently, avoiding at all costs the alienation of U.S. investors. Nevertheless, the 1903 signing of Mexico's largest petroleum contract to date with the British entrepreneur Weetman Pearson signaled the growth of Limantour's influence, and that of the Científico camarilla in general. This ascendancy of the Científicos —and the parallel rise of a much more nationalist camarilla around General Bernardo Reyes—made the Díaz regime ever more wary of U.S. intervention in Latin America.

Between 1904 and 1905, Díaz forestalled an effort to drag Mexico into this rising tide of U.S. intervention: on several occasions he rejected U.S. overtures to make Mexico a regional peacemaker by the grace of Uncle Sam. First, U.S. president Theodore Roosevelt offered Mexico a free hand in the annexation of Cuba, Puerto Rico, the Dominican Republic, and the Central American countries (an offer that was no doubt insincere). When Díaz would not be baited, Roosevelt proposed that Mexico assume a police function in the area. The Mexican president, however, saw through this overly transparent scheme as well. The U.S. president desired to lend a veil of legitimacy to his own intervention by joint action with major Latin American countries. Therefore, even though the plan promised to increase Mexico's prestige, Díaz rejected the idea, terming it vague and injurious to the interests of the smaller nations. As his ambassador to the United States commented, "it was not decorous to offer our share to [U.S.] foreign policy." The creation of virtual spheres of secondary imperialism could give Mexico only the vacuous privilege of acting as Roosevelt's enforcer in the Caribbean.

In the years 1906 to 1908, good fortune and a measure of diplomatic skill allowed Díaz to continue his balancing act. Díaz established a good relationship with President Roosevelt and his second secretary of state, Elihu Root. This relationship—buttressed by continued cooperation on matters of foreign investment—allowed Porfirian foreign policy to register some impressive successes. Most significantly, the successful co-mediation of Central American disputes added to Díaz's stature abroad and prevented direct U.S. military intervention. Mexican delegates on the program committee for the Third Inter-American Conference held in Rio de Janeiro in 1906 helped forestall the presentation of U.S. initiatives similar to those of 1889. In 1907, the Díaz regime agreed to renew an old U.S. lease on the coaling station of Bahía de la Magdalena in Baja California, but it limited the new contract to three years. Even though none of these successes derailed the overall growth of U.S. influence in Mexico and the country's neighborhood, Díaz did make full use of the leeway that his international prestige, Mexico's political stability, and a friendly U.S. government accorded his regime.

During Díaz's last years in office, however, all of these conditions for a successful foreign policy evaporated. The global recession of 1907 sent the Mexican economy into a tailspin and highlighted the privileged role of foreigners: while hundreds of thousands of Mexicans lost their jobs, most white-collar foreign employees continued to earn their paychecks. Moreover, the publication of the famous Creelman Interview, an interview in which Díaz announced his intention not to stand for reelection, ended the so-called "pax porfiriana" and woke up Mexico's sleepy political scene. Díaz's subsequent change of heart caused the organization of strong opposition movements that ultimately coalesced around Francisco I. Madero. Finally, the November 1908 elections in the United States brought to power William H. Taft, a president who did not share his predecessor's willingness to accommodate Díaz in matters of foreign policy.

During the following years, the aging Porfirian regime responded with the time-honored method of "bread or the stick" *(pan o palo)* to the growing outcry of the many Mexicans who felt that their government had failed them. As demonstrated in the brutal suppression of the 1906 miners' strike at Cananea, Sonora, and the 1907 massacre of textile workers in Río Blanco, Veracruz, Díaz used force against the mounting labor protests of the time. But he also ordered the Mexican Congress to reconsider the agricultural and mining legislation of the 1880s and 1890s. Of course, the Díaz regime could not revoke existing concessions to foreign investors without risking serious international repercussions. Nevertheless, the Mexican Congress prepared laws on subsequent concessions that contained many of the provisions of the Revolutionary Constitution of 1917 in nuclear form. For instance, a 1909 law prohibited foreign mining activities close to the border, and the Porfirians created the nationally owned Ferrocarriles Nacionales de México, or National Railroads of Mexico.

As the Porfiriato approached its demise, U.S.-Mexican relations grew more turbulent in several areas. In particular, the activities of anti-Díaz rebels north of the border proved a major irritant in U.S.-Mexican relations. Taft (like Roosevelt) fully cooperated within the scope of his country's neutrality laws, but Mariscal and his successor, Enrique C. Creel, viewed these actions as insufficient. In Porfirian Mexico, authorities arrested and shot troublemakers with nary a hint of due process of law; thus, Mariscal and Creel simply could not understand why U.S. officials spent months and even years fighting legal challenges by Mexican rebels. Moreover, the inception of Dollar Diplomacy damaged U.S.-Mexican relations. As the U.S. State Department increasingly acted as a promotional agency for U.S. investors, Díaz's favoring of Europeans to offset the growing North American economic presence became a political issue. Secretary of State Philander C. Knox regarded U.S. economic ties with Mexico—which by now surpassed those between Great Britain and Mexico—as a security asset. Finally, the cooperation in Central American issues broke down. In April 1909, when Knox attempted to gain Mexican help for bringing down the Nicaraguan regime of José Santos Zelaya—a key ally of Díaz's in Central America, Mariscal declared that Mexico no longer would enforce peacekeeping measures jointly with the United States. Later that same year, Díaz and Knox faced off over Zelaya again. After Zelaya resigned in the face of a revolt supported by the United States in December 1909, the Porfirians gave him asylum and supported his handpicked successor against the continuing rebellion. Ultimately, however, Díaz could not prevent the triumph of the pro-U.S. faction.

All of these problems contributed ultimately to the overthrow of Díaz. To be sure, one cannot accuse the Taft administration of active collusion: his government may have been lukewarm in the application of the neutrality laws to Madero and his followers, but there is little evidence that it desired Díaz's removal. Nevertheless, the existence of the border, and the fact that the Mexican rebels could move relatively freely in the United States, played a great role in facilitating the Madero rebellion. Moreover, with the publication of John K. Turner's *Barbarous Mexico* and other essays critical of Díaz, U.S. public opinion had turned against the Porfirians. Books such as *Barbarous Mexico* gave verbal ammunition to Madero and his followers, and the growing U.S. opposition to Díaz made it impossible for Taft to crack down on Madero the way his predecessor had disposed of the Flores Magón brothers. Many of the Porfirian confidential agents in the United States now deserted the regime and directly or indirectly supported the opposition.

It was no coincidence that Madero made Díaz's foreign policy a key point of attack in his pamphlet

La sucesión presidencial en 1910 (The Presidential Succession in 1910). From Madero's propagandistic vantage point, both aspects of Porfirian foreign policy had failed. On the one hand, Díaz's practice of attracting foreign investments had increased foreign influence in Mexico and brought about the economic crisis of the previous few years. On the other hand, Mexican anti-imperialist measures had failed to stop U.S. encroachments on the sovereignty of Latin American nations.

Modern historians, however, need to guard against the dangers of teleology. Eager to ascribe significance to each one of Díaz's failings in order to explain the coming of the Mexican Revolution, too few historians have undertaken to understand Porfirian foreign policy on its own terms. The fact that the Porfirian balancing act failed in the end should not distract us from the observation that it registered modest successes for many years.

In sum, the Díaz era was hardly one of strident nationalism or unlimited servitude. Instead, the Díaz regime—prodded in different directions by opposing camarillas, foreign investors, and public opinion—remained caught in the same contradictory position that the vicinity of the United States has always imposed on Mexican governments. The modernization of Mexico with the help of foreign capital had allowed the Díaz regime to play a significant international role and to defend Mexico's political sovereignty. In that regard, the Porfirians had successfully followed the national project begun under La Reforma. But the growing economic linkages with the United States and the revival of U.S. hegemonic aspirations in the 1890s and 1900s had made the Porfirian balancing act increasingly difficult, to the point that growing nationalism and xenophobia contributed to the outbreak of the Mexican Revolution. Any analysis of Mexican foreign relations from 1876 to 1911 must thus recognize their essential continuity with those of the regimes preceding and succeeding the rule of Mexico's modernizing nationalist dictator, Porfirio Díaz.

Select Bibliography

Anderson, Benedict, *Imagined Communities: Reflections on the Origins and Spread of Nationalism*. London: Verso, 1983.

Buchenau, Jürgen, *In the Shadow of the Giant: The Making of Mexico's Central America Policy, 1876–1930*. Tuscaloosa: University of Alabama Press, 1996.

Coerver, Don M., *The Porfirian Interregnum: The Presidency of Manuel Gonzalez of Mexico, 1880–1884*. Fort Worth: Texas Christian University Press, 1979.

Cosío Villegas, Daniel, *The United States versus Porfirio Díaz*, translated by Nettie Lee Benson. Austin: University of Texas Press, 1964.

Deger, Robert J., Jr., "Porfirian Foreign Policy and Mexican Nationalism: A Study of Cooperation and Conflict in Mexican-American Relations, 1884–1904." Ph.D. diss., Indiana University, 1979.

Katz, Friedrich, "The Liberal Republic and the Porfiriato, 1876–1910." In *Mexico Since Independence*, edited by Leslie Bethell. Cambridge and New York: Cambridge University Press, 1991.

Knight, Alan, "Peasants into Patriots: Thoughts on the Making of the Mexican Nation." *Mexican Studies/Estudios Mexicanos* 10:1 (Winter 1994).

Langley, Lester G., *America and the Americas: The United States in the Western Hemisphere*. Athens: University of Georgia Press, 1989.

Schell, William B., "Integral Outsiders, Mexico City's American Colony, 1876–1911: Society and Political Economy in Porfirian Mexico." Ph.D. diss., University of North Carolina at Chapel Hill, 1992.

Vázquez, Josefina Z., and Lorenzo Meyer, *The United States and Mexico*. Chicago: University of Chicago Press, 1985.

Weeks, Charles, *The Juárez Myth in Mexico*. Tuscaloosa: University of Alabama Press, 1987.

—JÜRGEN BUCHENAU

Foreign Policy: 1910–46

At the beginning of 1910 it seemed as if Mexican foreign relations would continue as in previous years of the Porfirio Díaz regime. Díaz's balancing act had deadlocked the interests of various European powers against each other and against those from the United States. In spite of the frustrations that this approach caused, another presidential term for Díaz promised what all foreign powers desired most in Mexico: political continuity and stability for future economic activity.

Thus, when the Revolution of 1910 began, it was perceived by foreign observers as just another normal Latin American uprising. When it continued, U.S. oil interests used the opportunity to weaken the English position in the Mexican petroleum sector by reinforcing Revolutionary leader Francisco I. Madero's reservations toward British business. Suddenly, British and French interests found themselves isolated from Madero, whereas German financial houses enjoyed unexpected access to the newly elected president.

By 1912 diplomatic game playing became more serious. Suddenly, all foreign powers recognized that Mexico stood at the beginning of a new historical period. In the words of scholar Friedrich Katz, all foreign powers agreed that the Madero Revolution had unleashed undesirable social forces that needed to be tamed.

But solutions to the "problem" differed sharply. European powers desired violent repression of social uprisings and, therefore, backed the successful counterrevolution led by Victoriano Huerta and Félix Díaz (nephew of Porfirio). The new U.S. president Woodrow Wilson finally paid more attention to the unauthorized conspiratorial activities of his ambassador Henry Lane Wilson (no relation), who had joined the European efforts to remove Madero from office. While the ambassador favored Félix Díaz as future Mexican president, the idealistic President Wilson wanted to put an end to traditional Great Power politics. Mexico became a testing ground for his new foreign policy ideas. he envisioned Mexico as a parliamentary democracy that later could serve as model for all Latin American countries. Thus, U.S. policy soon supported the Constitutionalists in the Mexican north against the Mexico City regime now led by Huerta alone. In addition, the U.S. Navy occupied Veracruz and imposed an arms embargo on Huerta. The counterrevolutionary had to go.

The outbreak of World War I in 1914 once again changed foreign attitudes about events in Mexico. Suddenly, all sides tried to enlist and exploit Mexican Revolutionary movements to serve their geopolitical global strategies. Previous issues-oriented or regional policies seemed no longer appropriate. Domestic and external forces alike began to exploit each other mutually for the benefits of the changing military situations in Mexico and the battlefields of the world. The immediate need for victory by each Revolutionary faction and its foreign supporter became more important than long-term considerations.

Victoriano Huerta was forced out of office by an interplay of domestic and foreign factors. Historian Alan Knight portrayed changes in Mexico during this period largely as a result of domestic pressures. Friedrich Katz, however, has provided overwhelming evidence of the direct and indirect foreign interventions into Mexican affairs between 1914 and 1917. Each faction of the northern Constitutionalists tried to gain U.S. support for its leader. In turn, the United States tried to gain control over the outcome of the Revolution by arranging a Pan American conference between Argentina, Chile, Brazil, and the Revolutionary factions, hoping to pick a desirable successor for Huerta.

President Wilson's decision to abandon Pancho Villa set off a course of events that helped Venustiano Carranza to gain the presidential chair against the original intent of U.S. players. Villa reacted to his rejection by the Wilson administration with an attack on the small border town of Columbus, New Mexico, on March 9, 1916. His goal was to provoke a U.S. invasion into Mexico that would humiliate Carranza and force him out of office. Indeed, U.S. popular nationalism caused Wilson to dispatch General John Joseph Pershing with 10,000 men deep into Mexican territory with the mission to catch Villa. Ironically, this U.S. invasion evoked a strong Mexican nationalist reaction that bolstered President Carranza's resolve to firmly reject U.S. pressures to install a more pro-U.S. president or to turn Mexico into a protectorate, as had been done with Cuba. In the end Carranza won. President Wilson withdrew the Pershing expedition without any concessions from Carranza. Carranza had avoided being drawn into a war with the United States.

Carranza's opposition to Wilson, however, also cost him access to U.S. government or private funds for the reconstruction of the war-torn Mexican economy. By 1917, the only way out seemed to be closer economic cooperation with Germany. When Carranza approached the Germans to explore the issue, the Germans responded with their megalomaniac Zimmermann Telegram, which offered Mexico the return of lands lost to the United States in the War of 1846-48 in exchange for a German-Mexican alliance—thus assuming that Germany would not merely defeat its enemies on the battlefields of Europe, but actually would conquer the United States as well. Again, Carranza realized that the German proposal was not to Mexico's advantage. Until the end of World War I he kept the Germans engaged in discussions, thus avoiding an unfriendly rupture of German-Mexican relations. It also protected the Mexican petroleum industry from possible German sabotage, an event that certainly would have caused the next U.S. invasion of Mexican territory. When World War I ended, Carranza could look back to major foreign policy achievements. His skillful tactics had kept Mexico's territory united and free from foreign occupation. In addition, his diplomatic skill had prevented Revolutionary Mexico from becoming a victim of Great Power designs during the war.

In addition, he used a series of speeches and announcements to formulate a distinct post-Revolutionary Mexican foreign policy doctrine, later coined the Carranza doctrine. It demanded the rejection of the U.S. Monroe Doctrine; foreign respect for and obedience of Mexico's law; the elimination of foreign privileges or monopolies in Mexico; Mexican solidarity with other Latin American nations based on mutual respect and absolute non-intervention; and the negotiation of alliances with

European and other Latin American countries. Later, in 1930, Mexican foreign minister Genaro (Félix) Estrada added the Estrada Doctrine to Carranza's directives. It demanded recognition for all Latin American government, regardless of whether they had come to power by the ballot or by the bullet.

Carranza's assassination in 1920 once again changed the focus of Mexican foreign relations. From 1920 until 1923, the U.S.-Mexican relationship dominated Mexican foreign relations. During these very frustrating years President Álvaro Obregón defended his government against pressure from U.S. minister of interior Albert B. Fall and the by-now-familiar schemes of U.S. oil companies. In the end, like Carranza, he protected Mexico's economic sovereignty, gained the essential U.S. diplomatic recognition, and refused to put in writing any statement that limited Mexico's future economic development. Ironically, recognition brought not only access to international financial markets but also U.S. military support to defeat the substantial threat of the rebellion led by Adolfo de la Huerta in 1923. For once, proximity to the United States helped the Mexican government.

After U.S. recognition in 1923, European countries followed suit. Newly elected president Plutarco Elías Calles developed a strong foreign policy that was accommodating and compromising with U.S. interests inside Mexico, while at the same time confrontational in Central America and the Pan American Conference system, the predecessor of the Organization of American States. In addition, Mexicans employed a sophisticated propaganda campaign inside the United States that aimed at protecting the rights of Mexican Americans who were increasingly victimized as a result of resurgent U.S. nativism. When the pro-Catholic Cristero Rebellion tossed Mexico into its next major crisis in 1926, pressure by U.S. Catholics became a new factor in U.S.-Mexican foreign relations.

A critical change in U.S.-Mexican relations occurred with the dispatch of U.S. ambassador Dwight Morrow to the Mexican capital in 1928. From then on, major U.S.-Mexican issues were handled behind the scenes, directly between Mexican presidents and U.S. ambassadors. This relationship continued with U.S. ambassador Josephus Daniels and Mexican president Lázaro Cárdenas (1934–40), as well as with Ambassador George S. Messersmith and President Manuel Avila Camacho (1940–46). The special relationship between U.S. ambassadors and Mexican presidents proved critical to more constructive bilateral relations and the creation of U.S.-Mexican interdependence during the 1930s.

The worldwide economic depression that shook the capitalist system from 1928 on became the critical impulse for the United States to end its interventionist policies in Latin America. U.S. president Herbert Hoover laid the foundation for Franklin Delano Roosevelt's Good Neighbor policy, which was based on nonintervention. From that moment on, Mexican policy makers decided to move from the limited Pan-American Conference system to the League of Nations in Geneva, which still recognized the U.S. Monroe Doctrine. But unlike the Pan American Conference system, the League of Nations was not dominated by the United States, and the most serious threat of foreign intervention was beginning to come from the rise of fascist states in Europe and Asia.

Under Cárdenas, Mexican delegates used the League of Nations as a platform against international war and intervention. Mexican diplomats acted as mediators in the Chaco War between Bolivia and Paraguay, and condemned vehemently the interventions by Italy into Ethiopia, by Germany into the Ruhr area, and by Japan into China. The Cárdenas administration also was the only government besides the Soviet Union to provide military aid to the Republican forces during the Spanish Civil War. While European powers and the United States stood idly by, Cárdenas's convictions led him to try to prevent a victory of fascist forces in Spain, which he feared might spill later into Latin America.

At the same time, behind the scenes in Mexico City, a crucial professionalization of Mexican foreign relations occurred that added another dimension —technocratic foreign policies—to the more traditional diplomatic initiatives of prior administrations. The 1920s had been the decade when the growth of the post-Revolutionary state had revived the institutionalization of foreign relations within the Ministries of Foreign Affairs and Hacienda (Treasury). The aftermath of the Great Depression professionalized the Mexican foreign service from a traditional diplomatic service into a modern intelligence-gathering bureaucracy. After an administrative reform in 1933, Mexican consuls and diplomats were ordered to act as the government's eyes and ears in the world of continuing international economic depression and growing violence. From 1934 on, these "diplomatic scouts" received the added task of finding markets for Mexico's state-sponsored agricultural modernization and Mexico's petroleum industry after the expropriation in 1938. In addition, the newly founded Ministry of National Economy, the Ministry of War, and the Ministry of Communication and Public Works all pursued contacts with foreign governments and companies, often without oversight from the presidential palace. In the 1930s Mexican foreign policy was diversifying. Some policy areas such as the U.S.-Mexican relationship and the League of Nation policy were supervised by the Mexican president himself; others were developed and executed by bureaucratic technocrats whose central loyalty was to national economic development, not political ideals. The president no longer was the alpha and omega of Mexican foreign relations.

In 1937 the coming together of Cárdenas' fiscal policies, the imperialistic behavior of U.S. and British/Dutch foreign oil companies, the policy of Mexican petroleum syndicates, and a bad harvest triggered an unexpected economic crisis that changed the course of Mexican foreign relations forever. During 1937 the technocrats of the Ministry of Hacienda tried to prevent an economic and political collapse of the Cárdenas administration with the help of diverse and mutually opposing foreign support: the despised British/Dutch oil conglomerate received extensive new drilling rights, a German government agency was used to bring the Tehuantepec oil region into accelerated production, and the U.S. Treasury provided massive support to the fledgling Cárdenas government. When these measures failed, the Cárdenas government expropriated and nationalized the oil industry in 1938 in a desperate attempt to regain governmental control over the national economy and budget and to ensure the survival of the Cardenista agenda.

Initially, the oil expropriation ushered in a foreign policy of survival that focused on circumventing and eliminating the economic boycott of the foreign oil companies and their associated suppliers. But by the time the Mexican state had reestablished some firm ground under its feet, World War II had begun. The new international situation convinced the technocrats in the Mexican ministries to abandon their current developmental policy. Between 1938 and 1940 this policy was replaced with one that used the economic stimuli of the world war as a new engine for Mexico's economic development. Scholar Steven Niblo has demonstrated how a wholesale change in Mexican economic accounting, suggested by U.S. economists, established a new vision of Mexican economic development that was free of any social or political concerns. In 1939 the victory of the Allied powers in World War II was by no means certain. And yet outgoing president Cárdenas, his successor Avila Camacho, and the majority of Mexican technocrats decided that no immediate threat to Mexico existed until Great Britain was defeated. And while these men were using the war to develop their country, they also prepared for a variety of outcomes of the war. Still, Cárdenas allowed the U.S. Federal Bureau of Investigations (FBI) to build a Mexican counterintelligence service that eliminated all dangerous Axis subversive activities by 1941. Under his presidency a very close consultation and cooperation between U.S. and Mexican military forces was initiated that became the official U.S.-Mexican Military Commission at the end of 1941. Cárdenas spent his last months in office defending Mexico against the formation of any unnecessary or hasty military alliance with the United States. A military alliance could open the door to U.S. troops on Mexican soil, which, it was feared, might continue once the war was over. After the end of his presidential term, Cárdenas continued to strengthen Mexico's self-defense capabilities as commander of the Pacific Coast and again later as Avila Camacho's minister of war.

The war added transnational labor issues to the agenda of Mexico's foreign relations. Whereas in the 1930s the Cardenista state had acted to protect Mexican Americans and Mexicans in the United States from nativism, in the 1940s the Avila Camacho administration engaged the Roosevelt administration in the actual management of Mexican labor in the U.S. agricultural and industrial sectors. The outcome was the Bracero Program, through which 300,000 Mexicans obtained permits to work in United States.

Steven Niblo and Blanca Torres Ramírez examined the economic impact of the war from a social perspective. Indeed, the majority of Mexico's population experienced the war as imposed economic hardship owing to inflation, a lack of available consumer goods, as well as food shortages that caused hunger. Niblo demonstrated how these sacrifices for the policies of the Mexican government and the Allied war effort failed to translate into the expected broad developmental benefits for Mexico's population.

But for the administration, the war proved advantageous. Until November 1941, the Avila Camacho administration maintained some limited channels of communication with Nazi Germany and Hispanistic anti-American groups in Latin America, just in case Mexico would have to trade with a Hitler-dominated Europe after the end of the war. Eventually the defeat of the Germans in Stalingrad and their failure to conquer England gave the pro-U.S. faction within the Avila Camacho government enough strength to conclude their move toward a historically unprecedented close economic, political, and military cooperation with the United States and the Allied powers. The Japanese attack on Pearl Harbor generated enough momentum to justify this cooperation to the

Mexican public. Even then, Mexico only ruptured diplomatic relations with Axis powers; it did not yet declare war on them.

This tactic paid off. Mexican negotiators were able to extract from U.S. interests critical concessions that they never would have achieved during peacetime: weeks before Pearl Harbor an agreement with U.S. oil companies in the nationalization dispute had been reached. Thereby Cárdenas's intent to assure national control over Mexico's petroleum sector had been achieved. Furthermore, the United States agreed to buy all Mexican raw materials for the war period, providing Mexico with a guaranteed market. A Lend-Lease agreement provided the Mexican military with modern equipment and revived the fledgling Mexican Air Force. Later, Minister of Hacienda Eduardo Suárez was able to renegotiate Mexico's foreign debt and reduce it by 90 percent, a dramatic repositioning of Mexico for the international financial markets during the postwar period. The Avila Camacho administration also was able to settle agrarian and water rights issues and gained funds for critical street infrastructure projects. In addition, the U.S. government paid for the complete overhaul of the desolate Mexican railway system. The creation of a special U.S.-Mexican industrial commission gave the Mexican leadership special access to U.S. industrial technology. No other Latin American country enjoyed similar preferences during the war. Finally, U.S. pressure was critical for the renewal of British-Mexican diplomatic relations, thus further weakening the position of expropriated British oil companies vis-à-vis the Mexican government. In short, the policies of the Mexican leadership achieved unprecedented gains for the Mexican state, but it failed to translate them into significant gains for Mexico's citizens.

The nationalists in the Avila Camacho administration regained importance once the U.S. victory at Midway and the German retreat in the Soviet Union proved that the Western Hemisphere would not be invaded militarily by Axis forces. Immediately, Mexico renewed diplomatic and economic relations with the Soviet Union, Great Britain, and the French de Gaulle faction and positioned Mexico as an important Latin American player in the postwar international system, organized by the United Nations.

In the end, the Mexican military also found a way to participate actively in World War II, overcoming strong opposition from U.S. military planners. Mexico sent its air force to fight in the Philippines in 1945. In addition, 250,000 Mexicans served in the U.S. military, 14,000 saw combat as part of the U.S. Army, and 1,000 received the Purple Heart. German submarine attacks on Mexican tankers in 1942 also allowed President Avila Camacho and Foreign Minister Ezequiél Padilla to declare war on the Axis powers on May 22, 1942. This move allowed the Mexican government to confiscate the production sites and patents of the German chemical industry in Mexico, which had enjoyed a monopoly in dyes, pharmaceuticals, and fertilizers. Thus the Mexican government added another critical industrial sector to its petroleum industry without resorting to expropriation. These very selective anti-German acts allowed Mexico to claim after 1945 that, unlike during World War I, it had been a staunch supporter of the Allied cause.

By the time the war ended, Mexico had been engaged in close cooperation with the United States without surrendering its territorial sovereignty or signing agreements that would allow the continued presence of U.S. troops in Mexican territory during the Cold War. Once again, the Mexican leadership had shuttled its nation through a Great Power conflict and exploited its circumstances for domestic gains. Mexico had reinvented itself as proud supporter of the western democracies and the United Nations project. It was uniquely prepared to participate in the reconstruction of the international political and economic system alongside the victors of the war.

Select Bibliography

Cronon, Edmund David, *Josephus Daniels in Mexico.* Madison: University of Wisconsin Press, 1975.

Herman, Donald L., *The Comintern in Mexico.* Washington, D.C.: Public Affairs Press, 1974.

Katz, Friedrich, *The Secret War in Mexico: Europe, the United States and the Mexican Revolution.* Chicago: University of Chicago Press, 1981.

Knight, Alan, *U.S.-Mexican Relations 1910–1940: An Interpretation.* La Jolla: Center for U.S.-Mexican Studies, University of California, San Diego, 1987.

Meyer, Lorenzo, *Mexico and the United States in the Oil Controversy 1917–1942.* Austin: University of Texas Press, 1977.

Niblo, Stephen, *War, Diplomacy and Development: The United States and Mexico 1938–1954.* Wilmington, Delaware: Scholarly Resources, 1995.

Powell, T.G., *Mexico and the Spanish Civil War.* Albuquerque: University of New Mexico Press, 1981.

Schuler, Friedrich E., *Between Hitler and Roosevelt: Mexican Foreign Policy in the Age of Lazaro Cardenas 1934–1940.* Albuquerque: University of New Mexico Press, 1997.

Smith, Robert Freeman, *The United States and Revolutionary Nationalism in Mexico, 1916–1932.* Chicago: University of Chicago Press, 1972.

—FRIEDRICH E. SCHULER

Foreign Policy: 1946–96

A rapidly changing world brought about momentous shifts in Mexican foreign policy between 1946 (the wake of World War II) and 1996 (the first year of the North American Free Trade Agreement). The Cold War, Mexico's growing links with the United States, and the country's urbanization and industrialization all produced important changes in the formulation and implementation of Mexican foreign policy. While the superpower conflict and increasingly intimate relations with the United States imposed significant limits on Mexican foreign policy, urbanization and the growth of a middle class pushed the Mexican government in the opposite direction. Nevertheless, much of the framework of Mexican foreign policy persisted through all these innovations. As it had done since the mid–nineteenth century, the Mexican government attempted with limited success to reap the benefits of U.S. dominance without suffering the drawbacks. At least between 1958 and 1988, it also continued the balancing act between limited possibilities and growing nationalist expectations that had characterized Porfirian, Revolutionary, and post-Revolutionary foreign policies alike.

The transition from President Manuel Avila Camacho to Miguel Alemán Valdés in 1946 marked the adjustment to a postwar economy and society. Mexico had helped the Allied effort primarily through its function as a source of much-needed raw materials. Alemán (Mexico's first civilian president since Madero) faced a United States no longer in dire need of Mexican resources. With the Cold War far from heating up to full intensity, the United States turned its back on promises to repay the Latin American countries for their wartime collaboration. As had become evident during the Inter-American Conference on War and Peace Problems held in Mexico City in 1945, the administration of Harry S. Truman refused to heed calls for a Latin American version of the Marshall Plan. Meanwhile, U.S. businesses turned away tens of thousands of Mexican workers hired under the Bracero Program in the early 1940s, and the influx of hundreds of thousands of undocumented aliens (dubbed "wetbacks") caused much ill will in the southwestern United States. Moreover, a growing supply of U.S.-made agricultural and mining products amounted to reduced opportunities for Mexican exporters. As a result, Mexican export revenue declined, and inflation and an ever greater gap between the rich and the poor initially belied the expectations of a postwar economic boom.

Faced with this slump, the Mexican government turned to the advice of the Argentine economist Raúl Prebisch, the president of the United Nations' Economic Commission for Latin America. Prebisch had diagnosed the reliance on externally driven development, that is, the export of raw materials to pay for imported industrial goods, as the cause for most of the economic problems of the region. According to Prebisch's analysis, trading raw materials for manufactured products constituted an "unequal exchange," as the prices of raw materials tended to decline in relative terms over a long period of time. To offset this trend that resulted in a continuous flow of capital from "Third World" to industrialized countries, Prebisch proposed government-assisted import substitution industrialization (ISI) programs accompanied by a protectionist trade policy. Picking up on the beginnings of such a program under Avila Camacho, who had fomented import substitution in order to compensate for the wartime shortage of imported industrial goods, Alemán decided to join other Latin American leaders in a strong push toward state-assisted modernization.

In the late 1940s, Mexican foreign policy played a significant role in assisting the industrialization project. Most importantly, the state sheltered the new industries by imposing new protectionist tariffs on imported manufactured goods, and it took advantage of the existing links between the U.S. and Mexican private sectors to assist in the creation of joint industrial ventures. This policy particularly benefited the Monterrey Group, a faction of wealthy northern industrialists. The Monterrey Group had risen to key status in the Avila Camacho years and enjoyed close ties with investors in Texas and other U.S. states. In addition, Alemán's diplomats continued Avila Camacho's policy of friendship with the Truman administration and worked on assuaging U.S. misgivings about their country's industrialization. As Mexican demand for imports, and particularly for expensive capital goods necessary for industrialization, increased, the former U.S. critics of the Mexican government fell silent. Finally, in 1947, Truman and Alemán exchanged visits to each other's capital cities in an unprecedented show of goodwill. During his visit, which roughly coincided with the centennial of the U.S.-Mexican War, Truman paid homage to the *niños héroes,* the cadets who had died defending Chapultepec Castle, and he even returned some of the Mexican banners seized during that war.

Afraid of relying exclusively on U.S. investments, Alemán also moved to normalize relations with Mexico's wartime enemies. In the absence of commercial and diplomatic relations with Germany and Japan until the 1950s, this normalization primarily affected the treatment of confiscated Axis property in

Mexico. Having opposed the expropriation of the holdings of Mexican citizens of German, Italian, and Japanese descent as Avila Camacho's secretary of Gobernación (the interior), Alemán returned more than 60 percent of confiscated property to its former owners. In the process, he collected handsome kickbacks from proprietors eager to recover their businesses, farms, or real estate from years of neglect and mismanagement. The appropriately named president especially favored German- and Italian-Mexicans in the resolution of their claims. However, he disappointed many Japanese-Mexicans, most of whose property had been sold by the Avila Camacho administration during the war.

In the 1950s, the so-called Mexican Miracle dominated the direction and formulation of foreign policy. Characterized by rapid industrialization and economic growth, the Mexican Miracle brought new opportunities to educated and propertied Mexicans. The upper and middle classes—in other words, those most interested in foreign policy—benefited disproportionately from these new opportunities. Mexican investors realized enormous profits during these years, and a burgeoning service sector offered relatively high-paying jobs to doctors, lawyers, and teachers. Meanwhile, many workers and peasants saw at best a marginal improvement in their living conditions despite the government's insistence that the *desarrollo estabilizador* (stabilizing development) would improve the lives of all. Many workers continued to subsist on minimal wages, agriculture remained in a state of virtual neglect, and most peasants who moved to the cities found that industrialization had not created as many well-paying jobs as the government had promised. The Mexican Miracle thus served the material interests of the elites and middle classes. Even though Alemán and his successor, Adolfo Ruiz Cortines, continued to claim the heritage of Mexico's epic Revolution, their policies marked a return to the Porfirian program of development from without, with the new twist that foreign capital flowed primarily into industry rather than agriculture or mining. In fact, had the Porfirians lived to see the 1950s, they might well have advocated much more caution in embracing U.S. investments than the helmsmen of the Institutional Revolution.

The diplomacy of the Mexican Miracle distinguished itself in its solid support of the United States in Cold War issues and in its anticommunism. Mexico backed the United States in the United Nations on a variety of matters ranging from Korea to Eastern Europe, and it maintained chilly relations with the Soviet Union. Alemán's and Ruiz Cortines's anticommunism resulted in part from personal conviction, in part from ceaseless U.S. radio and press propaganda in Mexico, and in part from the presidents' desire to accommodate and exploit the shrill tones coming out of Washington. In the fall of 1949, the communist triumph in China had heightened the U.S. fear of a world revolution. By the summer of the next year, the U.S. involvement in the Korean War had led to a complete military mobilization. As mobilization again promised lucrative contracts to Latin American mineral exporters, tough anticommunist talk could help procure these contracts for Mexico. The victory of World War II hero Dwight D. Eisenhower in the November 1952 presidential elections in the United States made an anticommunist diplomacy even more important. As the CIA-assisted coups in nationalist Iran (1953) and revolutionary Guatemala (1954) demonstrated, Eisenhower did not continue Truman's relatively flexible policies toward economic nationalism and socialism in the Third World. In this context, even a more left-leaning Mexican government could not have professed friendship for socialist experiments around the world.

As the case of Guatemala revealed, however, this anticommunist attitude found its limits in the matter of U.S. aggression in Latin America. To avoid U.S. hostility, Mexico—as it often had done in prior instances of U.S. intervention—presented its objections at an international diplomatic forum. At the occasion of the Tenth Inter-American Conference held in Caracas in March 1954, U.S. secretary of state John F. Dulles presented an ambiguously worded resolution against communist subversion. Recognizing this resolution as a cloak for future aggression against Guatemala, the Mexican delegation at the conference introduced a number of motions designed to rephrase and weaken the resolution. When a majority defeated most of these motions in Caracas, Mexico joined Costa Rica and Juan Perón's Argentina in abstaining on the final vote (Guatemala cast the only negative vote). This meek protest, however, was all the Mexican government could do to criticize U.S. aggression. As the CIA mercenaries deposed the democratic government of Jacobo Arbenz, Ruiz Cortines remained silent. This stance constituted a compromise between the demands of business leaders and the nationalist left. While business leaders criticized Ruiz Cortines for his cautious challenge to the Eisenhower administration, the left led by ex-President Lázaro Cárdenas deplored the president's failure to condemn the U.S. intervention.

By the late 1950s, conditions were ripe for a more assertive foreign policy. Most importantly, Mexico's international prestige had grown immensely, and the recovering European and Japanese economies took notice of its potential as an investment target. Furthermore, international issues played an increasingly important role in political discourse. Labor and peasant unrest prompted the Mexican government to display a nationalist foreign policy that recalled the days of Cárdenas in an effort to mask the shortcomings of the Mexican Miracle for a majority of the people. The Cuban Revolution left a great initial impact on Mexican public opinion, and the Mexican government found itself between an anti-Castro business community and largely pro-Castro popular organizations. The mass media had created a sizable foreign-policy constituency (the group of people that cares about foreign policy) among the burgeoning middle classes, a constituency that expected Mexico to play a greater role in world affairs. Lastly, as decolonization reached Africa and as Egyptian president Gamal Nasser led Arab countries onto a more nationalist course, these developments weakened the dominance of NATO and the Warsaw Pact in the United Nations General Assembly in favor of the "Third World."

Presiding over the apex of the Mexican Miracle—a time when Mexico appeared to be on the brink of joining the exclusive club of "developed" nations—Adolfo López Mateos inaugurated a much more assertive diplomacy. The election of this young leader, a self-proclaimed champion of land reform and labor unions, represented the decline of Alemán's camarilla and the ascent of neo-Cardenista politicians. Strikingly, the new diplomacy did not come at the cost of a deterioration in U.S.-Mexican relations. Indeed, López Mateos maintained cordial relations with the U.S. government, and particularly the new president, John F. Kennedy. In 1961, Mexico became one of the signatory members of the Alliance for Progress, a program designed to forestall Castro-type revolutions in Latin America with a U.S.-sponsored array of social and economic reforms. A year later, Kennedy proclaimed during a visit to Mexico City that the goals of the Alliance for Progress were identical with those of the Mexican Revolution. Nevertheless, López Mateos was not content with limiting his country to an intimate relationship with the United States; instead, he sought to open up new economic and political partnerships in Europe, East Asia, and the Third World. His government gravitated toward the nascent Non-Aligned Movement, and Mexico became one of the founding members of the Latin American Free Trade Association (LAFTA). The new president toured the globe in an effort to attract new foreign investment and to foster his country's prestige, so much so that Mexicans nicknamed him "López Paseos" because of his frequent travels. At the end of his term, López Mateos could point to a few impressive successes: the United States had returned a strip of disputed border territory (the Chamizal) to Mexico, and Mexico City had become the first Latin American city to be chosen as a site for the Olympic Games.

Fidel Castro's revolution in Cuba revealed both the nature and the limits of this more assertive foreign policy. Initially, López Mateos enthusiastically welcomed Castro's triumph. When the United States opposed the nationalist direction of the revolution and Castro proclaimed himself a socialist, however, the Mexican government ceased to praise the Cuban leader. Instead, López Mateos defended Cuba's right to national self-determination and maintained that posture in the face of enormous U.S. pressure after the April 1961 Bay of Pigs invasion. Not even the Cuban Missile Crisis of October 1962 could make a dent in this Mexican opposition to U.S. intervention. While López Mateos joined Kennedy in condemning Castro for requesting Soviet nuclear missiles, he cautioned that his action did not imply an acquiescence in a U.S. invasion of Cuba. Nevertheless, his government would go no further than this time-honored support for the principle of nonintervention, a principle that enjoyed the support of Mexican conservatives and leftists alike. By the end of his administration, what had been a heartfelt friendship between the Mexican and Cuban governments had cooled to a distant relationship, the existence of formal diplomatic ties notwithstanding.

The administration of Gustavo Díaz Ordaz (1964–70) continued the outlines of López Mateos's foreign policy on a smaller scale. Díaz Ordaz became the first Mexican president to visit Central America; he continued his predecessor's efforts at economic integration; and in 1965, he condemned the U.S. intervention in the Dominican Republic. But the new, much more conservative president, a member of Miguel Alemán's clientelist network, did not share López Mateos's interest in global diplomacy. Conscious of the fact that large sectors of the Mexican middle class had opposed López Mateos's brief flirtation with Castro, he sought to reestablish the focus on economic development only. Bilateral problems with the United States took center stage, including immigration, border troubles, and the continuous relative depreciation of Mexican exports. Indeed, issues concerning "Mexamerica" (the area on both sides of the border that has since taken on a distinctly binational identity) steadily grew in importance. To offset the effects of the termination of the second Bracero

Agreement—an action that produced widespread un-employment in Mexican border towns and increased undocumented entry into the United States—Díaz Ordaz and U.S. textile, toy, and electronics manu-facturers promoted the Border Industrialization Pro-gram. As a result, the Mexican north became the area of *la maquiladora,* the assembly plant for U.S. industry.

By the end of Díaz Ordaz's rule, the Mexican government had enough domestic problems on its hands to turn away from activism in international affairs. In particular, middle-class unrest and run-away population growth accompanied a gradual decline of Mexico's economic indicators. In addition, as Mexican-Americans won small victories in their civil rights movement in the United States, their own relative success highlighted the authoritarian nature of the ruling Partido Revolucionario Institucional (PRI, or Institutional Revolutionary Party). In Octo-ber 1968, the Tlatelolco Massacre, during which authorities killed hundreds of student protesters on the eve of the Olympic Games, revealed the stress of the Mexican political system and the political bank-ruptcy of the unpopular Díaz Ordaz regime. The bloodshed registered an impact far beyond Mexico's boundaries: it unmasked the hollow myth of the Institutional Revolution to even the most casual observer, and it shook the international credibility of the Mexican government. Luis Echeverría Álvarez, the former secretary of Gobernación and the puta-tive "henchman of Tlatelolco," thus inherited a volatile situation when he became president in 1970.

Echeverría decided to confront the unrest with a two-pronged strategy used since the days of Por-firio Díaz: the carrot and the stick. In the neo-Cardenista mold, he used deficit spending to meet some of the most immediate demands, launching a new land reform program and putting people to work in ambitious public projects. The new presi-dent also displayed a strong economic nationalism. He nationalized Mexico's small copper and tobacco industries, he toughened existing requirements that stipulated Mexican co-ownership in many economic sectors, and his government bought the majority of the shares of the national telephone company. He also encouraged greater openness in political debate, less government interference in universities, and the strengthening of opposition parties. But the new president also ruthlessly cracked down on guerrilla movements and protesters, an effort that culminated in the Corpus Christi Massacre of June 1971.

An activist foreign policy, motivated in part by the realization that U.S. demand could never be the main engine for sustained economic growth, played a key role in the "carrot" part of Echeverría's strategy. Echeverría resumed López Mateos's travel diplo-macy, traveling to a total of 36 countries during his six years in office. While continuing to nurture the relationship with the United States, he aggressively courted the European Economic Community and Japan as trading and investment partners. Together with Venezuelan leader Andrés Pérez, he created the Latin American Economic System (SELA), a trade bloc that included Cuba while it excluded the United States. In his frequent meetings with Central Ameri-can presidents, he inaugurated what came to be known as the "guayabera diplomacy," a diplomacy named after the colorful Mexican peasant shirts that the president gave out at these opportunities. To the chagrin of U.S. president Richard Nixon, with whom he maintained a good working relationship, the Mexican president also improved relations with the communist and socialist nations of the world. Taking advantage of the atmosphere of détente (lessening of tensions) that existed between the superpowers, he visited both the Soviet Union and Cuba. Subse-quently, Echeverría negotiated a commercial, scien-tific, and cultural treaty with COMECON, the economic organization of the Soviet Union and its satellite states. Finally, Echeverría made himself into a champion of the "Third World" and presented the Charter of Economic Rights and Duties of States to the UN General Assembly. Designed to stop the exploitation of "Third World" countries, the measure passed, but the United States and the major countries of Western Europe disregarded it. A high-light of this effort was Echeverría's April 1972 visit with the socialist president of Chile, Salvador All-ende Gossens, a visit that culminated in a joint com-muniqué stressing the right of every country to control its natural resources and determine its own internal structures.

This new foreign policy was a made-for-television publicity show with limited practical results. Photo opportunities with Palestinian leader Yasser Arafat and anti-Israeli votes in the UN General Assembly made for good press coverage and met with applause from many left-leaning intellectuals. Eminent social scientists—scholars who otherwise might well have stood at the forefront of opposition to his govern-ment—lauded Echeverría's "new foreign policy" that "opened the country to the outside world." Eche-verría's foreign policy, however, did not reduce Mex-ico's dependence on the United States. Even though the U.S. share of Mexico's foreign trade declined from 66 to 59 percent between 1969 and 1974, U.S. investors still held the same percentage (62 percent) of direct foreign investment that they had owned five years earlier. More Mexican jobs than ever were tied to the U.S. economy. In addition, Echeverría lived on borrowed time: his lavish spending more than quadrupled the debt of the public sector, inflation rose sharply, and the peso lost half of its value in 1976 alone. By the end of his rule in 1976, the IMF (International Monetary Fund) watched the Mexican economy closely and threatened to impose conditions for future lending. As the squalor of many rural dwellings and the growing ring of shantytowns around the capital and other cities attested all too well, neither the social programs nor diplomacy succeeded in narrowing the gap between the upper and middle classes and the average Mexican. As the crisis deepened, Echeverría's activist foreign policy therefore lost credibility both at home and abroad.

Mexico's next president, José López Portillo, began his tenure with a piece of good news that restored the verve of the first four years of his predecessor's administration. In 1976, geologists had discovered vast new oil reserves offshore in the Gulf of Mexico that increased the country's known oil reserves by 1,200 percent. Almost immediately, the news restored much investor confidence in the Mexican economy. As a result, López Portillo, a close associate of Echeverría and the first in a long line of technocrats to ascend to the presidency, presented a refurbished version of his predecessor's populist policies. Of course, the subsequent quadrupling of Mexican oil production could not solve the country's deep social and economic problems. Nevertheless, in a decade of rapidly rising oil prices, Mexico's newfound subsoil wealth rid the López Portillo administration of many of the IMF strictures. The new oil also allowed the government to borrow freely from international lenders giddy about the exorbitant interest rates prevalent during the era; it led to a new phase of corruption and recklessly irresponsible behavior with public finances; and it permitted the financing of more social programs and public works than Mexico could afford.

Relations with the U.S. government initially resulted in further encouragement to the López Portillo administration. During a trip to Washington in February 1977, the Mexican president learned that his U.S. counterpart, Jimmy Carter, intended to accord Mexico a special position in U.S. foreign relations. Carter classified both Mexican oil and the Mexican economy as issues of vital national interest: the former was a key mineral resource, and a breakdown of the latter could have severe implications for the United States in general and the southwestern states in particular. Notwithstanding a series of subsequent spats, López Portillo knew that Carter regarded Mexico as an important strategic partner in Latin America. Carter's own good disposition toward Mexico, however, could not prevent a deterioration of relations in the late 1970s produced by conflicts about a pipeline delivering natural gas to the United States that offended nationalist sensibilities on both sides of the border.

These developments enabled López Portillo to pursue a scaled-down version of Echeverría's global diplomacy. Like his predecessor, the Mexican president acted under pressure from the left, as many Mexicans felt that the export of oil and natural gas would only increase their country's dependency on its northern neighbor. Unlike Echeverría, however, López Portillo concentrated his energy on a few crucial areas. In that respect, no area was more important than Central America, Mexico's southeastern neighbors.

In May 1979, López Portillo started his Central American offensive with a bang when he became the first head of state to break off diplomatic relations with the dictatorial regime of Nicaraguan president Anastasio Somoza Debayle. After the Sandinista triumph in July of that year, the Mexican government became one of the principal supporters of the new, socialist-leaning Nicaragua. López Portillo also attempted to mediate in the civil war between the repressive, right-wing government of El Salvador and two bands of Marxist guerrillas. In August 1981, he and French president François Mitterrand issued the now-famous joint communiqué that recognized the rebels as a representative political force. Finally, when the Sandinistas ran into the rock-solid resistance of Carter's successor, Ronald Reagan, the Mexican leader offered himself as a mediator between the conservative U.S. administration and the Nicaraguan revolutionaries. The Mexican government gained international prestige with these endeavors, and even the Reagan administration accorded it a grudging respect. López Portillo's assertive Central American initiatives, however, in no way constituted a sharp departure from previous foreign policies. Instead, they followed the twin objectives of encouraging political factions friendly to Mexico and limiting the U.S. political and military influence in Central America that both the Porfirians and the Revolutionary governments had pursued during much of the previous century. Like previous initiatives in Central America, they found their limit in the U.S. resolve to achieve policy ends by military force: the Mexican government backed off from its assistance to the Nicaraguan government when Reagan decided to wage an undeclared war on the Sandinistas by means of the Contra rebels.

As had been the case with Díaz Ordaz and Eche-verría, however, economic crisis, scandals, and corruption undid López Portillo's diplomacy. Toward the end of his reign, reports of an economic slow-down and massive graft within the Mexican government resulted in an enormous capital flight from Mexico. During a 12-month period ending in June 1982, more than US$20 billion left the country. Even as López Portillo attempted to prevent further capital flight by nationalizing all major national banks in July of that year, the damage had already been done. At the same time, oil prices fell precipitously, the Mexican economy ran up an enormous balance-of-payments deficit, and foreign debt skyrocketed. Finally, in August 1982, Mexico declared that it no longer could pay the interest on its debt, an announcement that caused a ripple effect throughout Latin America. Thus began a debt crisis that shook the world financial system and ultimately resulted in the imposition of IMF austerity rules on the Mexican government, measures that included price hikes for basic commodities as well as a sweeping devaluation. By May 1983, real wages had plummeted to less than 50 percent of their 1981 level. The country's currency told an ever sadder tale. While a dollar had fetched 25 pesos in 1980, it bought as many as 2,500 only six years later.

By the time Miguel de la Madrid took office in December 1982, Mexico was mired in a deep economic slump that made ambitious diplomatic initiatives unlikely and refocused the country's foreign policy on the United States. As service on the foreign debt consumed almost half of Mexican export revenue, the government had to cut its social expenditures as well as its modest oil-for-credit shipments to the Sandinistas, shipments that already had been curtailed in the face of Reagan's aggressive policies. De la Madrid's first job as president, then, was to placate the IMF and the foreign investment community. He did so by making Mexicans swallow the harsh austerity measures prescribed by the IMF. Protests remained limited, as many Mexicans realized that their government could not oppose the dictates of an international lending organization, however much they justifiably vilified that organization as an instrument of U.S. economic policy. Nevertheless, the crisis had done what U.S. policy had not been able to accomplish: it forced Mexico to adopt neoliberal economic precepts. After all the spending and corruption of the López Portillo years, the Mexican state now found itself unable to influence the country's economy through budget policy. With deficit spending no longer an option and economic policy a captive of IMF advice, the country's leadership increasingly turned to solutions that combined Margaret Thatcher's austere monetarism in Great Britain with Reagan's nod to supply-side economics.

Indeed, the crisis propelled de la Madrid onto a course that must have made his two predecessors cringe. Not only did he patch up relations with the Reagan administration and abandon all populist economic rhetoric; he also initiated steps toward reducing the state's extensive role in the Mexican economy. In particular, he began to decrease tariffs, limit government regulation, and to sell some of the numerous state-owned enterprises. In the process, de la Madrid paved the way for the eventual destruction of the post-Revolutionary model of state-mediated capitalism. These measures accelerated the ever greater integration of the U.S. and Mexican economies. Viewing López Portillo's assertive policies as impractical and detrimental to the vital relationship with the United States, de la Madrid also limited the Mexican role in Central America. In 1983, the foundation of the Contadora Group permitted a graceful withdrawal from what had become a difficult situation for the Mexican government. While de la Madrid discontinued material aid to the Sandinistas, the opportunity to co-mediate the Central American crises with the leaders of Colombia, Panama, and Venezuela offered him an opportunity to participate in an honorable international peacekeeping effort. This attempt rescued him from charges from the left that he was selling out the Sandinistas to the United States, and it also led to some progress in the peace negotiations.

De la Madrid's new, more cautious course proved prudent, as new problems with the United States came to the fore. In particular, undocumented immigration further complicated relations. The immigration issue had long been a sensitive topic in both the United States and Mexico. During the preceding two decades, the number of undocumented Mexicans in the United States had grown exponentially; after 1982, the economic crisis added significantly to these numbers. Reagan, a former governor of California, made "illegal" immigration a focal issue in his administration. As a result, he helped state governors beef up border patrols, and the U.S. Congress debated several versions of an immigration reform bill. The debate pitted the beneficiaries of immigration, which included farmers and other entrepreneurs that employed undocumented workers, against a diverse anti-immigration alliance that included the ultra-conservative Senator Jesse Helms along with the American Federation of Labor–Congress of Industrial Organizations (AFL-CIO) and the United Farm Workers of America. Known as the Immigration

Reform and Control Law, the final compromise granted amnesty to all undocumented workers with at least two years of continued residence in the United States, but it imposed harsh penalties on employers hiring new arrivals without immigration papers. Waged with a number of emotionally charged and even racist arguments, the immigration debate upset many Mexicans. As most Mexicans saw it, the undocumented workers put up with conditions that would be unacceptable for virtually all U.S. citizens in order to earn a fraction of the minimum wage. Moreover, immigrants who crossed the border illegally frequently endured human-rights violations and indignities at the hands of border patrols, criminal gangs, and the notorious coyotes, guides that were not always trustworthy in selling their services for border crossings. Thus, de la Madrid was in a difficult position. During the legislative debate, he lobbied for the civil rights of Mexican citizens in "El Norte," but he consistently manifested his respect for the right of the United States to determine its own immigration policy.

The increasing trafficking in illicit drugs constituted another newly explosive issue between the United States and Mexico. In 1985, the assassination of a Drug Enforcement Agency (DEA) official in Mexico and the subsequent Mexican failure to apprehend suspects led to widespread U.S. charges that the de la Madrid administration was, at best, not serious about the so-called war on drugs, and at worst, engaged in drug trafficking of its own. Frustrated, the Reagan administration assumed the arrogant attitude of demanding that U.S. law enforcement agents be permitted to make arrests in Mexico. Predictably, the Mexican government rejected this imposition on national sovereignty. It did not feel that it should shoulder most of the responsibility for the increasing U.S. drug imports. Even though de la Madrid wholeheartedly cooperated with the Reagan administration in intercepting shipments of controlled substances —shipments that led to increased drug use in Mexico and a surge in drug-related violence—he viewed the drug problem as one of demand rather than supply. As Mexican officials argued persuasively, drugs would come into any country as long as consumers were willing and able to pay large amounts of money to purchase them.

In the face of all these difficulties, the next president, Carlos Salinas de Gortari, decided to cast Mexico's lot firmly with the United States. Yet another technocrat at the helm of the Mexican government, Salinas had many reasons to seek a new departure in international relations. As a neoliberal economist trained at Harvard, Salinas shared the faith of the Reagan administration in free trade and reducing the role of the state in the economy. Even more importantly, the highly questionable outcome of the 1988 presidential elections had undermined his political legitimacy even before he took office. Under the leadership of the charismatic Cuauhtémoc Cárdenas (the son of the popular former president), the Echeverría wing of the PRI had joined smaller leftist parties in the Frente Democratico Nacional (FDN, or National Democratic Front). Attracting widespread support in the Mexican south as well as in the capital, the FDN had mounted a strong challenge to Salinas, the official candidate of the PRI. At the same time, the austerity measures and government repression had alienated the middle class, which helped Manuel Clouthier, the candidate of the conservative Partido de Acción Nacional (PAN, or National Action Party), challenge Salinas in northern Mexico. In the end, official results declared Salinas a narrow winner over Cárdenas, with Clouthier finishing a distant third. A three-week delay in posting the results as well as numerous irregularities, however, had given substance to widespread charges that electoral fraud had deprived Cárdenas of victory. In this situation, Salinas desperately needed political allies. By 1989, he had found them in the PAN, the constituency of which favored closer links with the United States and much less government intervention in the Mexican economy.

Salinas made radical and unprecedented moves to improve relations with the new U.S. administration of George Bush, an administration that combined the pursuit of Reagan's objectives with a more pragmatic approach to achieving them. The Mexican president agreed to crack down on drug rings operating in Mexico, he promised to cooperate with U.S. border authorities on the matter of illegal immigration, he sold many state-owned businesses to private investors, and he added Mexico to the list of members of the General Agreement on Tariffs and Trade (GATT). While he continued to pay lip service to Mexican nationalism, Salinas also moved into formerly sacrosanct territory: he began to revise the post-Revolutionary legislation designed to protect Mexico from foreign exploitation. First, he amended the 1973 Law on Foreign Investment to allow for full foreign ownership of property. Then, he even undermined the hallowed Article 27 of the 1917 Constitution, the article that declared land and subsoil the patrimony of the Mexican nation. Thus, in a span of only five years, Salinas had accommodated important U.S. foreign-policy goals that dated to the nineteenth century. Most importantly, he had abridged two important prerogatives of the Mexican state: to steer and manage the flow of capital, and to regulate foreign ownership of strategic resources in Mexico.

The final objective of Salinas's strategy was the negotiation of the North American Free Trade Agreement. The NAFTA negotiations led to acrimonious debate in all three countries. In Mexico, Salinas's supporters portrayed economic integration as both wecome and inevitable, and they reiterated the nineteenth-century argument that the free-trade agreement would bring "all the fruits of annexation without any of its dangers." Salinas hoped that NAFTA would give Mexican exporters unlimited access to U.S. and Canadian markets. Further, he expected that low wages would lure many North American companies to move their assembly plants south of the border and thus create jobs in Mexico. The younger Cárdenas, on the other hand, denounced the treaty even as it sailed smoothly through the Mexican Congress. As Cárdenas correctly observed, the treaty would make Mexico an economic appendage of the United States, and it would end the right of the Mexican government to protect national sovereignty and the well-being of its citizens. These critiques, however, paled in comparison to the response of a guerrilla group in Chiapas. On January 1, 1994, the day that NAFTA took effect, the Ejército Zapatista de Liberación Nacional (EZLN, or Zapatista Army of National Liberation) began its uprising, in large part to protest the adverse effects that the agreements could bring to the Mexican countryside. In Canada, proponents lauded the potential increase in exports to the United States, while opposition leaders raised the specter of a virtual loss of national independence. In the United States, two strange alliances opposed each other. Led by new president Bill Clinton and ex-president Bush, the NAFTA supporters argued that the treaty would bring new opportunities to U.S. exporters and thus create jobs in the United States. On the other side, labor leaders, self-styled populists, environmentalists, and xenophobic conservatives opposed the treaty. While the former two groups feared that millions of U.S. jobs would be lost to Mexico, the environmentalists warned against the imminent dumping of U.S. hazardous waste in Mexico, a country with lax environmental laws. The conservatives, finally, could not stomach the idea of perpetually granting free-trade privileges to a "Third World" country. This coalition brought together individuals as diverse as presidential candidate Ross Perot (who anticipated a "giant sucking sound of jobs going south"), U.S. House of Representatives majority leader Richard Gephardt, and the fire-breathing Senator Helms. Ultimately, the supporters

prevailed in all three countries, and a vast experiment in international economic relations began.

Despite Salinas's move toward integration with the North American economies, he did not forget the rest of the world. In fact, during the early 1990s, Mexico again made its presence felt in Latin America. In 1991—long before the signing of NAFTA—Salinas negotiated a free-trade agreement with Chile. His Central America policy strikingly resembled George Bush's approach to Mexico on a smaller scale. Hoping to make Mexico a nexus between the United States and the Central American countries, he offered to extend free-trade privileges to Mexico's southern neighbors, who reacted warily to the prospect of increased commerce with their own "colossus of the north." Salinas also began a series of bilateral negotiations with the government of Guatemala to tackle his country's own immigration dilemma: that of Guatemalan refugees in Chiapas. Finally, the Mexican president made significant overtures to Japan and the European Community. His hopes of attracting significant new investments, however, were disappointed. With the end of the Iron Curtain, Eastern Europe became a new primary investment target for the industrial powers of Western Europe, and Japan invested heavily in the rest of East and Southeast Asia. The end of the Cold War, then, had brought no peace dividend to Mexico, and it instead had highlighted the country's dependence on the United States.

While it is too early to assess the effect of Mexico's most recent crisis of 1994 to 1995 on foreign policy, a few observations deserve mention. The economic and political crisis has further eroded the legitimacy of the PRI while undermining international and domestic confidence in the Mexican economy. Salinas's successor, Ernesto Zedillo, has never been able to make Mexicans forget the slain heir-apparent to Salinas, Luis Donaldo Colosio, who had promised to complement NAFTA with a new economic and political arrangement that would benefit all Mexicans instead of a privileged few. At the same time, another devaluation of the Mexican peso, rampant corruption at the highest levels in the last years of the Salinas regime, and yet another round of high inflation have more than eroded the modest gains of the middle class registered in the early 1990s. As a result, Zedillo now faces the same choice that his predecessors faced at the outset of their terms in office: whether to turn toward the United States for support (and a bailout of outstanding loan payments), or whether to embrace populist, nationalist rhetoric to shore up crumbling support at home. Thus far,

Zedillo, like the two presidents before him, has made a clear choice for the former option. In the process, he has raised the question of whether the other option remains a viable one in today's world. If it is not, Mexican foreign policy will seek an ever closer approximation with the United States rather than the time-honored compromise between international realities and domestic expectations. The track record of the last 50 years of the twentieth century, however, indicates that more twists and turns may still lie ahead, and that nationalism has not yet disappeared as an important factor of Mexican foreign policy.

See also Drug Trade; General Agreement on Tariffs and Trade (GATT); Maquiladoras; North American Free Trade Agreement (NAFTA); Peso Crisis of 1994

Select Bibliography

Langley, Lester D., *Mexico and the United States: The Fragile Relationship*. Boston: Twayne, 1991.

Niblo, Stephen, *Diplomacy and Development: The United States and Mexico, 1938–1954*. Wilmington, Delaware: Scholarly Resources, 1995.

Rodrigo Jauberth, H., et al., *The Difficult Triangle: Mexico, Central America, and the United States*. Boulder, Colorado: Westview, 1992.

Roett, Riordan, editor, *Mexico's External Relations in the 1990s*. Boulder, Colorado: Lynne Rienner, 1991.

Vernon, Raymond, *The Dilemma of Mexico's Development: The Roles of the Private and Public Sectors*. Cambridge, Massachusetts: Harvard University Press, 1964.

—JÜRGEN BUCHENAU

French Intervention

The French Intervention or "Second Empire" was one of the most bizarre and tragic episodes in Mexico's history. From 1862 to 1867 French troops occupied the nation in support of the puppet emperor Maximilian. These years brought repression, guerrilla resistance, and countless deaths and abuses. But they also were a watershed. The presence of foreign invaders heightened Mexican nationalism, hardened the resolve of political elites, and ultimately set the stage for the dictatorship of Porfirio Díaz.

Origins

The French invasion had numerous causes. Mexican prelates and Conservatives, unwilling to accept their defeat in the Reform Wars of 1857 to 1861, escaped to France, where they circulated stories of a Mexico pining for the monarchical Catholic rule of colonial times. Mexican president Benito Juárez inadvertently played into their hands when, on July 17, 1861, he declared a two-year moratorium on payment of the Mexican foreign debt. His announcement lent credence to reports that Mexico was suffering under the heel of an immoral and incompetent regime.

In Paris, Emperor Napoléon III dreamed of the profits to be gained in Latin America. In 1846, some years before seizing power, he had written a pamphlet advocating a transoceanic canal for Nicaragua. But in Mexico the overriding economic goal of the imperialists was to revive the nation's fabled mining industry. In the eighteenth century the silver mines of the Bajío had been the greatest in the world; and they would be great again, when vast sums of foreign capital revived them during the reign of Porfirio Díaz. They had fallen into disrepair during the violence of the Wars of Independence and had resisted subsequent attempts to revive them. But their promise remained strong.

At the same time, Napoléon III wanted France to assert itself in Europe's growing competition for global dominion, a sort of colonialism for its own sake. A combination of buffoon and canny dictator, Napoléon III thrived on spectacle and understood the political value of grandiose national undertakings such as foreign wars. France had successfully invaded Algeria in 1830 and Saigon in 1859. Mexico now seemed a vulnerable target. Not only were dissident Mexicans inviting him in, but the area was politically chaotic, and a French empire offered the prestige of containing an expansive U. S. society on behalf of a culture that was monarchical, Iberian, and Catholic. Indeed, the moment seemed right. Seven days after the Mexican moratorium declaration, the first Battle of Bull Run signaled that the United States had embarked on a long civil war, and that the Union, an opponent of European interference in the Americas, would offer only muted protest.

France's government also was susceptible to the influence of bond speculators. Although French lenders held only $2.8 million of Mexico's total $81.5 million foreign debt, these individuals enjoyed special access to Napoléon III. Lacking any direct experience with Mexico, and without the benefit of a British-style foreign service, the French emperor relied upon the speculators as his main source of information. Together with the Mexican exile community, they painted a picture of a nation ready for French-sponsored monarchy.

Only too aware of the international disapproval that would result, Napoléon masked his intervention in an elaborate plot. He prevailed upon Britain and Spain to accompany France in a multinational occupation of the Veracruz customs house as a means of collecting on Mexico's foreign debt. The operation began in December 1861. Within a few months, however, the adventure's real intentions became clear, and the other two nations pulled out. France was now alone in the field.

The first attempt to seize Mexico City met unexpected resistance. On May 5, 1862, Mexican soldiers at Puebla dealt the invaders a stunning defeat. The French attempted an ill-planned uphill attack on the city's fort and were surprised by heavy rains, artillery, cavalry charges, and above all by daring resistance: Miguel Negrete, one of the Mexican commanders, wisely had kept his soldiers behind a high wall until the last minute, so that they would not be intimidated by the sight of French sabers and uniforms. Some 460 French soldiers perished, while Cinco de Mayo became a national holiday and the Mexican commanders—Negrete, Ignacio Zaragoza, and Porfirio Díaz—became national heroes. With General Zaragoza's untimely death from typhus, command passed to Jesús González Ortega, who heavily fortified and garrisoned Puebla. But within a year the French returned in force. On May 17, 1863, Puebla surrendered after a siege of 62 days. A month later French forces marched directly to Mexico City itself. With the old capital now lost, Juárez relocated his government to San Luis Potosí in order to lead a guerrilla resistance against the invaders. For the next five years, two governments ruled Mexico.

Imperial Mexico

The French soon discovered that circumstances in Mexico differed considerably from those described by the Conservative exiles. The actual amount of Conservative support had been wildly exaggerated; any serious attempt at government would have to include Liberals as well. Moreover, the French generals were disgusted by the presumptions of the Mexican church, which was among the Conservatives' strongest supporters. Three centuries of colonialism had shielded the church from reforms and from the struggles with state power that had characterized European history. For all its purported Catholicism, France was now a secular nation, and its military officers had no intention of sharing power with an almost medieval clergy. The generals refused to restore confiscated clerical properties or to revive the church's lost political rights. Chances for a purely Conservative regime thus perished from the onset.

While the invasion was in progress, Napoléon arranged for a neutral figure to serve as emperor: someone neither French nor Mexican, a man removed from the raging ideological quarrels. The first candidates wisely turned down his offer. But he eventually managed to interest Archduke Ferdinand Maximilian von Hapsburg, brother to the Austro-Hungarian emperor Franz Josef. Maximilian was second-rate royalty who dreamed of power and popular adulation, and he quickly realized that without Mexico he would be destined to a life of idle entertainments and minor ceremonial functions. He arrived in Veracruz on May 28, 1864, with his Belgian wife Charlotte—now to be known as Carlota—and began a three-year reign as emperor of Mexico.

The royal couple immediately embraced their new country. They added Spanish to their already extensive repertoire of languages. In the winter of 1863–64 the French army under the iron fist of General Achilles Bazaine had staged a ruthless pacification campaign throughout Mexico; with these many towns now under occupation, they staged a referendum that naturally supported imperial rule. Thus convinced that the people loved him, Maximilian came to relish *lo mexicano* and was fond of appearing in the ostentatious costumes of rural Mexican dandies. He immediately set about planning an imperial makeover for the clothing, architecture, and social protocol of the Mexico City elite. The emperor himself designed the broad Calzada del Emperador (later renamed the Paseo de la Reforma). Maximilian also imposed the metric system, a lasting contribution. Like the kings of medieval Europe, he delighted in touring his realm, reveling in the exotic sights and sounds and occasionally taking a hand in the sugarcane harvest. Above all, he dreamed of railroads.

In other aspects, the empire remained perched halfway between its Conservative collaborators and its Liberal enemies. Maximilian, like the French generals, had no interest in placating Mexico's anachronistic prelates. He refused to overturn the reforms enacted under Juárez and Sebastián Lerdo de Tejada. Political ambivalence was the hallmark of the Second Empire, and it ultimately antagonized all sectors.

Nowhere was this more true than in Maximilian's attempt to construct a base of peasant support. The indigenous peasantry was the soul of the nation, and it had suffered greatly under the Liberal assault on communal property. The emperor's plan was to establish a body known as the *junta de protectores* to review and redress agrarian grievances. In Yucatán, the system took the form of an itinerant defense attorney known as the *abogado defensor de indios*. In theory the idea was sound; after all, this was how Mexico's Revolutionary government would establish itself one-half century later. But imperial efforts were too brief and too few. As the experiences of those later Revolutionaries revealed, real agrarian reform could come only through years of patient and often dangerous investigation, through peasant mobilization, and through organic links between peasants and the state. Maximilian's empire had none of these. His *juntas* and *defensores,* like his decrees against debt peonage, did little more than antagonize the propertied class.

Alliances with regional strongmen were thus inevitable. The best example came from the Monterrey area, which acquired new economic vitality in the early 1860s. Its growth had less to do with imperial policy than with the U.S. Civil War, which had resulted in a Union blockade of Confederate shipping to Europe. In response, the Confederates began to ship cotton south across the border, stockpiling it in a Matamoros tent city known as Bagdad. From there it was shipped to foreign purchasers. The entire district was under the administration of a purported Liberal, Santiago Vidaurri. But in 1862 Vidaurri changed loyalties to the empire rather than surrender the power and the lucrative profits of his situation. An inadvertent consequence of the empire, then, was to contribute to Monterrey's capital accumulation and subsequent industrialization. The prodigious flow of cotton through Tamaulipas and Nuevo León enriched the Monterrey merchants who, under the leadership of the Garza and Sada families, came to control the nation's largest industrial concerns.

A second important stage for imperial power was the southeast. This was particularly true of Yucatán, where rural rebellion and factional wars had raged for nearly two decades. Desperate to get the upper hand with their rivals, certain Yucatecans welcomed in the invaders. As imperial commissar, Maximilian appointed the capable José Salazar Ilarregui, a former engineer and college professor who had helped survey the U.S.-Mexican border after the treaty of Guadalupe Hidalgo. Carlota herself came here in 1865 and entertained representatives from all sectors of the society, from the landed elite to rural Maya caciques. But practicalities proved more difficult than social protocol. Salazar Ilarregui discovered that the Yucatecan propertied classes accepted the empire as long as they themselves ruled at home. Reaction was overtly hostile in neighboring Tabasco, where nationalists, mobilizing around the caudillo (strongman) Gregorio Méndez, took advantage of the lively arms business that had grown around Yucatán's separatist territory of Chan Santa Cruz. They purchased guns and ammunition in Belize, then smuggled them across the relatively open territory of northern Guatemala.

The imperial passions and persuasions amused Mexican urbanites. But for all its comedy, the Second Empire was cruel, bloody, and unsparing. French troops killed or executed some 40,000 to 50,000 Mexicans, not to mention countless others who were imprisoned, tortured, or harassed. Under pressure from the imperial army, Juárez relocated his government ever northward, until he reached El Paso del Norte, the border town later renamed in his honor. In October 1865 the French generals, frustrated by the continued resistance, pressured Maximilian into signing what became known as the "Black Decree," an executive order authorizing the army to shoot armed Juaristas within 24 hours of their capture.

The Empire's End

From 1865 onward the tide of events turned against the empire. General Achille Bazaine's army captured the old Liberal stronghold of Oaxaca City on February 9, 1865, capturing its commander Porfirio Díaz (who soon escaped). But it was to be the last imperial victory. Mexican resistance remained tireless and effective. While imperialists occupied key cities, the guerrilla fighters persisted in the countryside. The rural towns, pacified and then abandoned by the invaders, soon returned to Liberal hands. Moreover, the French had difficulty holding Caribbean coastal areas because of Europeans' susceptibility to tropical disease. Tamaulipas and northern Veracruz in particular remained scenes of guerrilla raids.

The resistance government also maintained a viable political posture. Juárez avoided crossing the border for reasons of political prestige: he did not want to take on the shadowy status of government-in-exile. Indeed, the resistance movement endowed the Liberals with a national popularity that they had not previously possessed. In earlier years the Liberal policies had been bitter and divisive, but now Juárez and his generals became the defenders of national sovereignty. Despite rivalries and lean times, they endured and gradually began to reclaim territory.

The end of the U.S. Civil War brought increased foreign pressure. The imperialists initially tried to turn the situation to their advantage by courting Confederate expatriates as a class of loyal settlers. After all, Confederate colonies were springing up throughout Latin America. In Mexico, the most successful colonies formed in mountainous west Veracruz. The colonies boasted such lofty names as "Villa Carlota" and "New Virginia." They included key Confederate figures such as Jubal Early, notorious for his daring raids on Pennsylvania. It would be Confederate engineers who surveyed the land for the railroad line between Mexico City and Veracruz. Maximilian finessed the slavery issue by allowing the white settlers to keep their black servants in "apprenticeship" for a period of 5 to 10 years.

Eventually, however, the victorious Union government brought full pressure against the interventionists. General Philip Sheridan ended the Confederate exodus by closing the Rio Grande border in 1866. Moreover, Union officers continued to funnel arms and supplies to Juárez's forces in the north. This assistance also acquainted nationalist generals such as Porfirio Díaz with military and economic connections in the United States, a knowledge that later would prove instrumental in constructing Díaz's 35-year dictatorship.

Imperial prospects further deteriorated in 1866, when Napoléon III found himself confronting an expansionist Prussia. In preparation for the coming war, he began to withdraw troops from Mexico in November. Attempts to replace the French legionnaires with Mexicans proved impossible. The Mexican soldiers were poorly trained and even more poorly paid, and unlike the nationalists they had no ideological commitment to their cause. The withdrawal of French troops resulted in bloodbaths of reprisals against collaborators throughout the country. Carlota herself returned to Europe to plead for help from Napoléon and the pope, but her efforts were in vain.

Simultaneously, the empire's southeastern outpost collapsed in the wake of a disastrous campaign against the Maya rebels of Chan Santa Cruz. The effort to mobilize Yucatán in an all-out crusade merely antagonized property holders; soldiers deserted by the hundreds, and the army itself narrowly escaped annihilation by the rebels in October 1866. By this point Tabascan Liberals were pressing from the west. An army rebellion led by Colonial Manuel Cepeda Peraza toppled the regime in June 1867, although the empire's former collaborators —some in exile, others scattered throughout the countryside—continued to cause trouble throughout the year.

For Maximilian the end came swiftly. With the French soldiers now gone, the emperor had only a handful of loyal Conservative generals and a collection of international adventurers. The last imperialists fought on; from April to June they held out in the city of Querétaro. In his spare moments on the battlefield, Maximilian played chess with his officers. After a series of losing battles he was forced to surrender. Pleas of clemency flowed in from Europe, but Juárez knew that he risked an army rebellion if he spared the former emperor. Moreover, he believed

that imperialism needed to be graphically repudiated. On June 19, 1867, Maximilian, together with Conservative Mexican generals Miguel Miramón and Tomás Mejía, died before a firing squad at Cerro de Campanas, "Hill of the Bells." His body eventually was returned to Europe and buried in the Hapsburg family crypt.

Many protagonists in the intervention faired poorly thereafter. Napoléon III lost his war with Prussia in 1870 and went into exile, dying shortly thereafter. Salazar Ilarregui escaped to New York City, while Santiago Vidaurri was executed in a barnyard. Another Conservative general named Leonardo Márquez, "the Tiger of Tacubaya," fled to Havana, where he operated a pawn shop for many years; in the 1890s Márquez, who once had executed prisoners without compunction, returned to Mexico to die a forgotten old man. Carlota went completely mad and, until her death in 1927, remained confined to her Belgian family castle. She never again spoke of her Mexican experiences.

For Mexico itself the imperial occupation had enormous political consequences. The restored Juárez administration inherited pure chaos. The war had exhausted the nation's economic resources and left many Mexicans hungry for stability and growth. Moreover, the collapse of imperial power sparked local bloodlettings and a wave of lawlessness as gangs of former soldiers preyed on the countryside. Initially the restored Liberal government exiled, imprisoned, and even executed former collaborators. However, the persecutions soon ended, as the need to fill the political bureaucracy compelled Juárez and later Porfirio Díaz to employ former imperialists. As one minister later put it, "In Mexico there has not been treason, only mistakes."

The imperial war also set the stage for future authoritarianism. The Liberals long had advocated more democratic practices for Mexico, but conditions now forced Juárez to adopt a form of machine politics that segued into the dictatorship of Porfirio Díaz. The general from Oaxaca emerged from the war with strong national credentials and a reputation for honesty. But he also nursed powerful ambitions, and after 1873 entered into his own alliances with foreign capital in order to realize them. Under the hand of don Porfirio, the railroads and powerful state that had been the fascinations of Emperor Maximilian became a reality, and in the process transformed Mexico forever.

Select Bibliography

Dabbs, Jack A., *The French Army in Mexico, 1861–1867: A Study in Military Government*. The Hague: Mouton, 1963.

Hanna, Alfred Jackson, and Kathryn Abbey Hanna, *Napoleon III and Mexico: American Triumph over Monarchy.* Chapel Hill: University of North Carolina Press, 1971.

Perry, Laurens Ballard, *Juárez and Díaz: Machine Politics in Mexico.* DeKalb: Northern Illinois University Press, 1978.

Ridley, Jasper, *Maximilian and Juárez.* New York: Ticknor and Fields, 1992.

—TERRY RUGELEY

Fuentes, Carlos 1928–

Writer

Carlos Fuentes is the son of Rafael Fuentes Boettiger, a career diplomat who as a cadet had fought against the U.S. invasion of Veracruz, and Berta Macías Rivas. Born in Panama City on November 9, 1928, during one of his father's diplomatic assignments, Fuentes spent his childhood in Quito, Montevideo, Rio de Janeiro, and finally Washington, D.C., where he lived from 1934 to 1940.

Fuentes's early life in Washington left a profound mark on him, making him feel at once at home in and alienated from U.S. culture. Attending elementary school in Washington, Fuentes learned English as his first formal language. He was an avid reader, devouring the works of Mark Twain, Robert Louis Stevenson, and Emilio Salgari. He discovered the difficulty of being a Mexican in the United States following the nationalization of the petroleum industry by the administration of Lázaro Cárdenas in 1938, when Mexicans collectively were condemned as Communists. Fuentes's exposure to Mexican culture was through his family, in that imaginary territory created by an embassy trying to replicate the homeland. He also spent summers with his grandparents in Mexico City so that he would not forget the language and history of Mexico. Fuentes's childhood experience of living between cultures, languages, and nations would repeat itself throughout his life, becoming one the key principles that would inform his work.

In 1940 Fuentes's family moved to Santiago de Chile, where it remained until 1944. Fuentes published his first stories in the *Boletín del Instituto Nacional de Chile.* Defined by the radical experience of Chile's Popular Front government and the tensions of World War II, the literary culture of 1940s Chile was characterized by neo-Romanticism and political poetry, particularly the work of Gabriela Mistral and Pablo Neruda. Taking advantage of the relative tolerance of the diplomatic world, Fuentes's literature teachers, Pedro Aguirre Cerda and the Spanish exile Alejandro Tarragó, introduced him to the work of the Argentinian writer Jorge Luis Borges and the authors of the Generation of 1929.

In 1944 Fuentes returned to Mexico, finishing high school. Entering law school at the national university, Fuentes quickly abandoned his formal studies to frequent the bordellos, cabarets, and other haunts of the Mexico City demimonde, which continued to figure prominently in his writing throughout the 1950s and 1960s. The Spanish exile community also had considerable influence on him, and he later studied with the Spanish philosophers Eduardo Nicol and José Gaos. In the *Revista memorias y ideas de México*, Fuentes published a series of short stories and essays that drew on his meticulous reading of the genre that since has come to be called "the novel of the Mexican Revolution." He also sought to formulate a critique of the "philosophy of *lo mexicano*" then in vogue. He also wrote news articles and analyses for the magazines *Hoy, Novedades,* and *Voz.* From the first he was a dissident from official policy and a severe critic of the Cold War and U.S. policy toward Latin America. The house of Fuentes's parents was frequented by the architects of a Mexican foreign policy based on national autonomy and nonintervention, familiarizing him with a vision of the world that married nationalism with a critique of imperial domination.

The 1950s were a defining period for Fuentes. In 1950 he entered the Mexican diplomatic corps, where he served in posts tightly linking him to the world of the arts and literature in Mexico and abroad. He also returned to law school and helped run the journal *Medio Siglo. Medio Siglo* became a nucleus for writers and thinkers of Fuentes's generation, including such figures as Salvador Elizondo, Sergio Pitol, Marco Antonio Montes de Oca, and—in the early stages of their careers—José Emilio Pacheco and Carlos Monsiváis. Fuentes also formed ties with key political players of his generation, including Mario Moya Palencia, Porfirio Muñoz Ledo, and others. However, this period was particularly fertile for Fuentes's own writing. From 1954 to 1962 Fuentes published four books that—together with Octavio Paz's *Labyrinth of Solitude*—would help determine the shape of contemporary Mexican literature.

Los días enmascarados (1954) brings together a series of short stories that seek to represent "the distinct voices of history" coming together in Mexico City during the 1950s, ranging from a Chac Mool —one of the Maya sculptures of reclining figures— to an attorney wavering about whether he should enter politics to advance his career and fortunes. Fuentes established himself as one of the most important writers in Latin America with *La región más transparente* (1958), the saga of a Mexican family in twentieth-century Mexico from the Revolution through 1950s. In both books Fuentes developed what would become a trademark of his narrative, his intimate engagement with the urban space of Mexico City. "Mexico," he wrote, "is a three-story country" —but he also might have been writing of the three stories of the city in his narrative: at the base, the "profound city" of streetwalkers, indigenous peoples, and historical identities; in the middle the "ambiguous city" of *mestizaje,* the search for identity, the deracinated middle class, and folkloric stereotypes; and at the top the invulnerable, totemic city of elites. In *La muerte de Artemio Cruz* (1962) the last 12 hours before a political cacique's death unfold in a narrative of countless voices. Perhaps Fuentes's most accomplished work, *La muerte de Artemio Cruz* develops many of the technical innovations, motifs, and themes that later would become hallmarks of the Latin American "boom" literatures—the dissolution between narrator and narrative, the shredding of the national myth of *mestizaje,* and the use of urban rather than rural speech. *Aura* (1962), *Cantar de ciegos* (1965), *Líneas para Adami* (1966), *Zona sagrada* (1967), and *Cambio de piel* (1967) further refine these innovations.

If most Mexican literature—as well as the social sciences and humanities—had been characterized by an insular concern with Mexican realities or by submission to western models, Fuentes's broader interest in Latin America as a whole made him something of a *rara avis* in Mexican letters. In his essays and lectures Fuentes sought to represent Latin American literature as a coherent literary and cultural movement. After reading *La nueva novela hispanoamericana* (1969), in which Fuentes coined the term "magic realism" to define the new narrative style that had emerged in Latin American literature, Gabriel García Márquez called him the inventor of the "boom." This concern with Latin America also was a touchstone of his political work. Traveling to Havana for the first time to support the Cuban Revolution in 1959, Fuentes frequently returned in subsequent years, developing a close friendship with the Cuban writers Alejo Carpentier, Lezama Lima, and Cintio Vitier. Expelled from the cultural supplement of the daily newsmagazine *Novedades* for their support of the Cuban Revolution, Fuentes and other writers joined the cultural supplement of *Siempre.* In 1962 Fuentes resigned from the diplomatic corps and joined the Movimiento de Liberación Nacional (MLN, or National Liberation Movement), which united the populist former president of Mexico, Lázaro Cárdenas, with various groups on the Mexican left. Supporting the Cuban Revolution, criticizing United States policy toward Latin America, and seeking to democratize Mexico, the MLN eventually was defeated and forced to dissolve. In 1963 and 1964 Fuentes traveled to Europe, beginning his close association with such other writers of the Latin American "boom" as Julio Cortázar, Gabriel García Márquez, and Mario Vargas Llosa.

In 1965 Fuentes broke with the Cuban Revolution when its cultural bureaucracy launched a campaign against Pablo Neruda. He also became increasingly critical of Soviet authoritarianism, although he never shied from his fierce defense of the right to self-determination and his criticism of U.S. Cold War policies. In 1968 he wrote an account of the Paris uprising, *Paris: La revolución de Mayo,* and later that year he traveled to Prague with Cortázar and García Márquez to support the Czechoslovak writers and intellectuals who were protesting the Soviet invasion of their country; they were hosted by Milan Kundera. On his way back to Mexico in 1969, he was refused entry into the United States for "Communist sedition." Norman Mailer and the Pen Club launched a campaign in his defense, which was later taken up by Senator J. William Fulbright. Fuentes continued his political engagement in the 1970s. His first two plays, *El tuerto es rey* (1970) and *Todos los gatos son pardos* (1971), were biting critiques of authoritarian power structures in Mexico. Fuentes established close ties with the administration of Luis Echeverría, and in 1975 he was named ambassador to France. In one of the most controversial moves of his career, however, he resigned in 1977 to protest the naming of former president Gustavo Díaz Ordaz, who had assumed responsibility for the massacre of hundreds of student protesters in October 1968, as the first Mexican ambassador to Spain since the fall of the Republic.

The Massacre of Tlatelolco and the death of Fuentes's father shortly after sparked a creative crisis that led Fuentes to experiment with new literary models and new ideas. This period of experimentation culminated with the publication of *Terra Nostra* in 1975. Taking Fuentes's concern with the loss of the narrative subject to its greatest extreme, *Terra Nostra* is a history of a people without a history—a people who only can see themselves in alien mirrors. Fuentes seeks to destroy these mirrors, creating characters who are seen in language itself and in their immediate otherness. Fuentes's attempt to construct an epic of Latin America (unsuccessful in the opinion of many critics) won him the Xavier Villaurrutia prize in 1977.

The final years of the 1970s saw a reconciliation between Fuentes and the United States. Teaching and lecturing at several U.S. universities, in 1987 Fuentes was named to the Robert F. Kennedy chair at Harvard University. Fuentes continued to remain a sharp critic of U.S. foreign policy and a defender of Latin American sovereignty, publishing frequently in U.S. newspapers and magazines. Many of these concerns are played out in *Gringo Viejo* (1985), which later was made into a film starring Jane Fonda and Gregory Peck. In *Latin America: At War with the Past* (1985), Fuentes proposes a reinterpretation of the United States' role in Latin America. Fuentes continued to refine his thematic concerns and his experiments with language in *Una familia lejana* (1980), *Agua quemada* (1981), *Cristóbal nonato* (1987), and *La campaña* (1990). He also continued his study of Latin American history, literature, and identity in *Valiente mundo nuevo* (1990), *Geografía de la novela* (1993), and *El naranjo* (1993), "an interiorized history of our language." In 1991 he traveled extensively in Spain, Argentina, Mexico, and California filming *The Buried Mirror,* a cultural history of Spanish-speaking countries prepared for the British Broadcasting Corporation.

In 1994 Fuentes returned to political essay writing in Mexican newspapers and magazines, criticizing neoliberal policies, the administration of Carlos Salinas de Gortari, and a foreign policy that weakened Mexico's political autonomy vis-à-vis the United States. In one of his most telling phrases, he described the 1994 Chiapas uprising as "the first postmodern guerrilla movement" founded "more in the stories of [Mexican writer Carlos] Monsiváis than in the theories of Marx." He continues to participate in the Grupo San Angel, a group of prominent dissident writers and intellectuals that promotes the democratization of Mexico.

Select Bibliography

Brody, Robert, and Charles Rossman, editors, *Carlos Fuentes: A Critical View.* Austin: University of Texas Press, 1982.

Durán, Gloria, *La mágia y las brujas en la obra de Carlos Fuentes.* Translated as *The Archetypes of Carlos Fuentes: From Witch to Androgyne.* Hamden, Connecticutt: Shoestring Press, 1980.

Durán, Victor Manuel, *A Marxist Reading of Fuentes, Vargas Llosa, and Puig.* Lanham, Maryland: University of America Press, 1993.

Faris, Wendy, *Carlos Fuentes.* New York: Ungar, 1983.

González, Alfonso, *Carlos Fuentes: Life, Work, and Criticism.* Fredericton, New Brunswick: York Press, 1987.

Ibsen, Kristine, *Author, Text and Reader in the Novels of Carlos Fuentes.* New York: Peter Lang, 1993.

—ILÁN SEMO

G

Gálvez, José de 1720–87

Visitador

The main architect of the Bourbon Reforms in New Spain, José de Gálvez was born in the town of Macharaviaya in the southern Spanish province of Málaga in 1720. The son of a noble but impoverished family, Gálvez was forced to become a shepherd at a young age following the death of his father. It is reported that when Gálvez was around 12 years old, however, the Bishop of Málaga was so impressed by his abilities that he took him to the city of Málaga and took charge of his education. Under the bishop's sponsorship Gálvez obtained a scholarship to the seminary of San Sebastián, an institution open exclusively to the nobility. When the bishop died, Gálvez was able to find other patrons, and he began his law studies at the University of Salamanca. He finished his studies in Alcalá and subsequently moved to Madrid to practice law.

The public career of José de Gálvez began under the reign of the Bourbon monarch Carlos III. After the death of his first wife Gálvez married an upper-class French woman with excellent connections to French residents at the Spanish court. Through his wife Gálvez was able to make the acquaintance of much of the high nobility and eventually was appointed secretary to Carlos III's prime minister. In 1764 Gálvez was appointed mayor of house and court, enabling him to make the acquaintance of influential members of the Castilian court. Gálvez gained a reputation as a honorable, energetic, and learned man.

In 1765 Gálvez was appointed *visitador* (roughly, royal inspector general) of New Spain, after the king's first and second choices were unable to assume the post. Gálvez's mission was a delicate one, including the inspection of the viceroyalty's tribunals and assuming personal command of the Spanish fleet based in the Americas. Gálvez's most important mission, however, was to maximize tax and tribute remittances to Spain, as endemic warfare with England had forced the Spanish Crown to maintain a standing army in the viceroyalty and to use funds from New Spain to subsidize its colonies in the Caribbean, particularly Cuba.

Gálvez almost immediately clashed with the viceroy of New Spain, the Marquis of Cruillas, as the arrival of the *visitador* to a great extent signified a suspension of the viceroy's political power. Cruillas soon was replaced by the Marquis Carlos Francisco de Croix, who worked quite closely with Gálvez. Nonetheless, the royal *audiencia* (high court) viewed them both with hostility, and they consequently developed many enemies.

Gálvez implemented a number of important reforms in New Spain, most notably the establishment of a new sales tax code that increased royal tax revenues by 9 percent. He also increased support for the mining industry—improving supplies, obtaining a decrease in the price of mercury (an import from Spain needed for processing ore)—and established the Real Tribunal de Minería (Royal Mining Tribunal), which sought to increase production and the recovery of ores for the royal treasury. Perhaps his most famous measure was the establishment of the Real Estanco de Tobaco (Royal Tobacco Monopoly), which earned millions for the Spanish Crown. He also established royal gunpowder, saltpeter, and sulfur factories, and established a profitable viceroyal monopoly on the production and sale of playing cards.

Together with de Croix, Gálvez was a key figure in the expulsion of the Jesuits from New Spain in 1767, and he was responsible for putting down the various uprisings that followed in outlying areas of Mexico. Personally commanding troops sent against rebels in San Luis de la Paz, San Luis Potosí, Guanajuato, Valladolid, and other areas, Gálvez ordered the execution of many rebels and imprisoned many others in distant locations.

Gálvez also was the author of a far-reaching administrative reform in Mexico, dividing the viceroyalty into 11 large provinces called intendancies. The *alcaldes mayores* and *corregidores,* local administrators who purchased their offices and tended to use them to enhance their commercial ventures, were replace by intendants, Crown appointees whose increased salaries where thought to be a hedge against corruption. These reforms were not actually implemented, however, until Gálvez was appointed minister of the Indies; moreover, they first were established in other Spanish colonies and were not actually implemented in New Spain until 1786.

One of Gálvez's least successful ventures was his attempt to increase mining production in California and consolidate Spanish control over the so-called Provincias Internas of northwestern New Spain, which comprised the provinces of California, Sinaloa, Sonora, and Nueva Vizcaya. He also hoped to pacify the Seris and Pimas in Sonora and the Apaches of Chihuahua, who had been resisting Spanish rule. In 1768 Gálvez traveled to the Provincias Internas, taking with him a group of townspeople from San Luis Potosí and Guanajuato. He improved record keeping, established a provincial militia, lowered prices for mercury and gunpowder, and distributed land to the Indians, but his project of establishing new towns and pacifying the region was for the most part a failure. Gálvez suffered a nervous breakdown, taking several months to recover.

An important consequence of Gálvez's expedition to the northwest was the creation of a Comandancia General (General Command) for the Internal Provinces, which would govern the region independently of the viceroy. The Comandancia General would have supreme political and military authority over the region, and would defer to the Audiencia of Guadalajara in judicial matters. The Comandancia General was not established until 1776, however, after Gálvez had been appointed minister of the Council of the Indies. De Croix's nephew was appointed the first commander of the region.

Gálvez concluded his *visita* in 1771, arriving in Cádiz in May 1772 to serve in the Council of the Indies, to which he had been appointed in 1765. In 1773 Gálvez was in charge of the Archive of the Indies and the General Archive of Simancas. Organizing the archive of Simancas, Gálvez also searched for documents that would support the beautification of the former viceroy of New Spain, Juan de Palafox. In 1774 Gálvez was named a member of the Junta General de Comercio, Moneda y Minas (General Junta of Trade, Currency, and Mines); he also served

as superintendent of court regalia. In 1776 he was minister of the Indies; he later was named governor *pro tempore* of the Council of the Indies. In 1777 he was named governor of the council, and in 1780 he was named a member of the Council of State.

As a member of the Council of Indies, Gálvez promulgated a series of ordinances establishing free trade between Spain and its overseas possessions, abolishing the trade monopoly of the fleet system, and opening free traffic to 33 ports between Spain and the Americas. As a consequence Spanish customs receipts quadrupled. Prompted by the royal family, Gálvez helped reestablish the Royal Company of the Philippines, although the Philippine trade remained tightly regulated to protect Spanish producers. He also encouraged the slave trade with the Americas.

In 1785 Gálvez was named Marquis of Sonora and Viscount of Sinaloa. Although he was criticized for obtaining plum assignments for family members, most of them distinguished themselves on their own. Gálvez's brother Macías and Macías's son, Bernardo, were both viceroys of New Spain. His brother Miguel was named ambassador to Prussia and another brother, Antonio, field marshal in the royal navy.

Gálvez and his brother Miguel had a lifelong concern for their home province and were named aldermen for life. They both supported charitable causes in the episcopate of Málaga, and they also lobbied successfully for the creation of a Consulado y Junta de Comercio (Trade Council) in Málaga. A playing card factory was established in their birthplace, Macharaviaya, which under the royal monopoly produced cards for all of Spain's American possessions. Because of his distinguished service in Mexico, Gálvez was able to draw pensions from the Real Tribunal de Minería of New Spain as well as from the Royal Treasury of Mexico. He also was named Caballero Gran Cruz de la Real y Distinguido Orden de Carlos III.

Gálvez died in Aranjuez in 1787. Many whispered that he had been poisoned and that he had fallen out with the king, who had accused his nephew Bernardo, viceroy of New Spain, of favoring the cause of Mexican Independence.

Select Bibliography

Priestly, Herbert Ingram, *José de Gálvez: Visitor General of New Spain (1765–1771)*. Berkely: University of California Press, 1916.

—CLARA ELENA SUÁREZ ARGÜELLO

GATT

See General Agreement on Tariffs and Trade (GATT)

Gender

This entry includes two articles that discuss the social construction of gender and sexuality:

Gender: Overview
Gender: Gender and Mexican Spanish

See also Family and Kinship; Malinche and Malinchismo; Women's Status and Occupation

Gender: Overview

Along with generational, ethnic, and class differences, gender is one of the major social divisions running throughout the twentieth century in Mexico, although, to be sure, gender identities and relations in modern Mexico emerge in remarkably varied ways. This diversity is the reason why making useful generalizations with respect to gender for all regions of Mexico in the twentieth century as a whole is difficult if not impossible, except in the sense that gender is consistently one of the key social axes around which society is understood, organized, divided, and contested. Only in the final three decades of the century in Mexico was gender in its own right established as a major field of scholarly research, beginning with systematic studies on women as wage earners and family networkers, as political activists and sexual partners, as victims of domestic violence, single mothers, and domestics. As to the study of men, masculinity, and of gender and sexuality in the most inclusive sense, this work had barely begun as the century closed.

Gender and sexuality in twentieth century Mexico is a topic with society-wide ramifications and implications, and it is a subject that must be described and explained as well at the more immediate levels of neighborhoods, *ranchos,* and households. Beginning with the participation of women in the Mexican Revolution, continuing with an expanding presence of women in the labor force, and ending the century with the spiraling immiseration of households throughout the country, the modern history of gender and sexuality in Mexico manifests profound changes in relations of power and inequality at every level of society, transformations that have been marked by a process challenging a variety of arrangements in political, economic, and cultural citizenship for Mexican society as a whole.

End of the Porfiriato, the Mexican Revolution, Cardenismo: 1900–40

With the close of the nineteenth century, various factors significantly transformed gender relations in Mexico, among them the consolidation of land holdings, migration, and the encouragement, within the context of relative political stability, of industrial development. Regional and ethnic differences in gender identities and relations were especially conspicuous in this era when Mexico was still predominantly rural in terms of the economy and population. Among Zapotecos in the Tehuantepec Isthmus, for instance, and in marked contrast to most other parts of the country, women dominated in mercantile activities—not that such activities implied, then or later, any form of matriarchal society on the isthmus. In the Sierra Nahua region it was customary early in the century for children to sleep with their fathers and not their mothers between infancy and puberty, whereas in other regions it was unusual for a father to even carry a child much less have such regular bodily contact for hours each night. As subsequent scholarship clearly has shown, distinct cultural values in different indigenous communities were an important factor in shaping diverse ideas and activities relating to gender and sexuality throughout the twentieth century in Mexico.

Industrial development during the Porfiriato (the rule of Porfirio Díaz) drew large numbers of *campesinos* (peasants) into the cities, especially Mexico City, with women constituting more than half the migrants in the years between 1895 and 1910. At the same time that women's participation in wage labor in urban areas increased dramatically between 1890 and 1910, women continued to be largely responsible not only for housework and the care of their own children but often the care of other dependent relatives as well. Nor were single women heads of households uncommon in the capital or other industrial hubs.

The first decades of the twentieth century witnessed the entry of women of all social classes into arenas of social life previously considered more exclusively male preserves, an illustration of overall changes in the meanings and activities associated with femininity. For women in the upper and middle classes, opportunities opened in education and in selected professions like book-binding and printing, although the majority of women from these strata continued to regard work outside the home as a secondary priority at this time. But controversy about women's participation in public activities, including paid work and politics, did develop into an important subject of social debate among the better-off strata in the late nineteenth century and continuing early in the twentieth. As to the working class, employment patterns were highly segregated, with women dominating in service trades like *tortillerías,* in waged domestic labor, in food packaging and processing, and in cigarette manufacture.

The Revolution of 1910 challenged gender relations at several levels. The military mobilization and uprooting of people throughout the country destabilized domestic life and redefined the domestic sphere for many households. As camp followers in the battles of the Revolution, and in the absence of an official commissary corps, women filled the crucial role of feeding the male soldiers. The soldiers and officers in combat were primarily men, although women also joined in the actual fighting, and popular perceptions about women changed as a result of this participation. The realities of the *soldaderas'* contributions to the Revolution, for example, as reflected in many *corridos* (popular songs) and folk tales of the time, were clearly at odds with persistent representations of women as prostitutes, self-sacrificing patriots, or fierce women who were being effectively tamed by male prowess. Yet from the beginning there was disagreement within the ranks of the Revolution regarding women's contributions, and with the professionalization-masculinization of the military forces beginning in 1914, camp followers were forbidden and very little of what women had done for the cause was recognized by the Mexican government in the form of officer commissions or veterans' and widows' pensions.

After the violence of the Revolution subsided, women in areas such as Mérida and the Federal District took to heart the campaign slogans "Effective Suffrage. No Reelection," and began their long struggle for women's suffrage. Revolutionary leaders at the time complained that women were controlled by priests and conservative religious values that were antithetical to the government's liberal political project. When women fought and gained the right to vote in state and municipal elections in the 1920s and 1930s, this was done with the tacit understanding that granting such rights represented an extension of the recognition of women's important *domestic* duties rather than a redefinition of femaleness to include nondomestic and political activities. Indeed, as part of the suffrage movement of this time women were compelled to dispute the latest "scientific" findings that "revealed" irremediable biological differences between men and women that in turn were utilized to argue that, for the best of the Mexican nation, women should exploit their nurturing and emotional strengths and devote themselves to child rearing and the home.

In legislative terms, 1917 was a watershed year in which the legal rights of women were changed. Venustiano Carranza passed the *Ley sobre relaciones familiares* that year, thereby allowing couples limited rights to divorce. How these rights were held to differ for men and women is revealing with respect to distinct legal definitions of male and female conjugal responsibilities. Although adultery on the part of women, for instance, was seen as a legitimate cause for divorce, male infidelity was a justification only in certain instances, such as when male adultery caused public scandal or occurred inside the conjugal home. If a woman did not give cause for a divorce, she had the right to the provision of food and housing by the husband, providing she lived an honest life and did not enter into a new marriage. In a major campaign led by the newspaper *Excelsior* in 1922, and explicitly modeled after a holiday in the United States that served a similar purpose, women's roles as mothers and housekeepers were reinforced as well through the establishment of May 10 as El Día de la Madre, Mother's Day.

Controversy concerning women's sexuality was widespread in intellectual circles during this period, and policies were proposed to deal quite broadly in Mexican society with issues like prostitution early in the century and sex education in the 1930s and 1940s. How to control women's sexuality became the focus of sociological, criminological, medical, and hygienic studies. In part, of course, these debates regarding the Mexican female body denoted the latest chapter in a centuries-old public debate over the Virgin of Guadalupe and la Malinche. Just as the symbolic importance these icons has constantly shifted according to divergent historical exigencies in Mexico, so too in the early twentieth century the Virgin and Malinche were treated as particularly Mexican embodiments of female virtue and traitorous women, respectively.

The 1930s were a golden age of women's public political organizing in Mexico, a time when the boundaries of what was considered feminine were expanded. During the Cárdenas administration women organized in the Frente Único Pro Derechos de la Mujer, most active between 1935 and 1938, which in turn contributed to cross-class alliances among women, and, among upper- and middle-class women, an extension of their concept of womanhood to include working-class women and *campesinas*. A social backlash of sorts developed as well during this time, when various male organizations protested women's entrance into employment and public administration, testifying to the contentious nature of official gender politics, the persistence of publicly proscribed behavior for women, and the incipient conflation of Mexican nationalism and masculinity that would erupt in the mid-century years in Mexico.

"The Dead Time": 1940–70

With a growing dependence on national and international markets, and a consequent decline in independent *campesino* household economies in even the tiniest *pueblos* in Mexico, there occurred in the twentieth century an accelerated transformation of the domestic sphere as issues previously regarded as private and individual became increasingly public and social. With respect to gender and sexuality, for instance, it can be said fairly that the twentieth century has been marked by reproduction "going public." Certain activities have been defined as "women's issues," and such concerns as domestic violence, child care and other domestic work, and reproductive freedom have been socialized. The twentieth century also has seen a trend toward the "denaturalization" of sexuality altogether.

The period following the populist waves of Cardenista reform in the 1930s spelled a temporary lull in women's widespread participation in political campaigns, if not necessarily women's activities in labor outside the home, ushering in what some scholars such as Esperanza Tuñón Pablos have referred to as a "dead time" in the history of Mexican women. Therefore, when women were finally granted the right to vote in 1953—making Mexico one of the last countries in Latin America to grant women suffrage—this marked less a concession to a powerful movement for women's equality in the country at the time than an attempt by the ruling Partido Revolucionario Institucional (PRI, or Institutional Revolutionary Party) to capture and co-opt an enormous new voting bloc in an era of relative social calm. The earlier suffrage movement had significantly expanded the scope of women's activities in the public sphere; at the same time, in many respects women's public political influence remained severely circumscribed.

Beginning in the late 1930s and gathering momentum in the 1940s, Mexico's quest for its own national identity acquired an ever more profoundly gendered and sexual tone. In the cinema, newspapers, and the belles-lettres of the period, images of daring macho men and passive self-sacrificing women—*las mujeres abnegadas*—were increasingly popularized as indicative of the special qualities that made up what was "typical" about Mexican culture. Mexican male identities in the twentieth century were consistently associated with the prestige and politics of the Mexican nation, in particular with the very modern image of the Mexican macho. Beginning with the virile cinematic presence of *charro*-cowboy hero Jorge Negrete, Mexico came to be seen, both internally and internationally, as the consummate land of self-confident, independent, and oftimes violent masculinity, typified by the Negrete standard, "Yo soy mexicano":

I am a Mexican, and this wild land is mine.
On the word of a macho, there's no land
   lovelier and wilder of its kind.
I am a Mexican, and of this I am proud.
I was born scorning life and death.
And though I have bragged, I have never been
   cowed.

In this period and subsequently, changes in Mexican masculinities, and in what it meant to be a man, were consistently insinuated in changes in Mexican national identity overall. No ubiquitous form of Mexican manhood existed during this or any other historical era, any more than were the women of the time uniform in their beliefs, desires, and actions. Nonetheless, widespread literary, psychological, and sociological interpretations of Mexican men and women, of potent Mexican machos and of self-sacrificing Mexican *abnegadas*, took on an authority that was to last for the remainder of the century, an official history of gender in Mexico challenged only in the closing decades by feminist scholarship that documented widespread diversity and change among women and men along the lines of class, ethnicity, generation, and region.

With industrialization in a boom period beginning in the 1940s, migration to the cities from the countryside, still home to four out of five Mexicans, spelled an increasing separation of home from work for men entering the newly built factories, and brought about a concomitant increase in child care responsibilities in the cities for women, who now more often were expected to single-handedly raise all their children, female and male. Mortality rates, especially for infants, continued to fall during this time, and women's responsibilities in the home increased as families had more children.

In the 1950s, when capitalist development in the countryside intensified and rural families became still more vulnerable to the vicissitudes of larger economic forces, the erosion of relations of reciprocity in rural areas was dramatically accelerated. Indeed, the most important factor affecting gender relations in the Mexican countryside through the 1960s was women's entry into the rural labor market. This led to severe disruptions in families throughout the *campo* (countryside), both in terms of labor patterns outside the home, as well as child-rearing practices within. For example, no longer were men nearly as able or expected to train their sons in farming techniques, nor, with the increasing separation of domicile and workplace, could they participate as actively in raising their children in general.

Migration to urban areas of Mexico and to the United States as a result of the increasingly socialized economy of the *campo* led to other new situations for men and women. When migrants from certain communities were primarily men, mothers and older women often were left alone in the *pueblos* and forced to work the fields as well as to continue their previous chores. In other communities during the years after World War II, young women, frequently those from indigenous ethnic groups, traveled to the capital and other cities to seek employment as domestic servants for the expanding middle class. As a result of rural-urban migration overall, and perhaps paradoxically, women played a key role in extending kinship and household ties in the cities as recent migrants there became increasingly dependent upon the utilization of such family and social networks to meet their daily needs such as housing and employment. The impact of migration in this period on gender relations in Mexico is thus extremely mixed, part of larger developments toward economic globalization and integration, as well as ongoing cultural contention over household divisions of labor, class and ethnic inequalities, and intellectual concerns within the Mexican nation.

The Millennium Closes: 1970–96

The last three decades of the twentieth century were marked by the emergence in Mexico, as elsewhere, of a feminist movement with broad influence, albeit often indirect, among the middle and lower strata of society. Simultaneously, paid work for women, in the countryside and especially in the cities, drew more and more mothers and sisters out of their homes and threw women onto assembly lines, into the streets as *vendedoras ambulantes,* and throughout the service sector across the country. Further, beginning in the early 1970s, a dramatic drop in fertility rates occurred, in part due to Mexican government programs designed to lower the average of almost seven

babies per woman. Within 20 years this figure was cut nearly in half, suggesting not simply demographic transitions, but also dramatic changes in cultural attitudes and behavior associated with sexuality, child rearing, and family.

In addition to more demographically traceable transformations, in the late 1970s and 1980s there was an explosion of popularly based movements for social services, for instance, in squatter settlements around older urban cores, in land-rights struggles in the *campo,* among the *damnificados* (loosely, "victims") of the 1985 earthquake in Mexico City, and in the Chiapas Zapatista uprising of 1994, whose stated aims included confronting gender inequalities in immediate ways. Within these popular struggles, women in particular played a prominent role as militants and sometimes leaders, and women's participation in such political organizing activities became part of debates regarding preexisting gender identities and relations. At the same time, this period witnessed the initiation of feminist publications, some appearing as supplements to daily newspapers, centers for battered women, and campaigns to legalize abortion.

The consequences of feminism and women's activities in social movements were mixed, and did not simply result in the extension of gender equality in Mexican society: simultaneous with these demographic and political transformations affecting women and men there occurred an increase in domestic violence, divorce, and child abuse. Though far from indicating uniform or permanent responses to these changes, in part these problems seemed connected to negative reactions on the part of husbands and fathers to women's increasing independence from them in political arenas and in the home. And the domain of official politics seemed particularly resistant to change: it was not until 1974, with the reform of Article 4 of the Constitution of 1917, that women were guaranteed equal rights under the law; as for elected officials, in 1995 women still made up less than 14 percent of the representatives and senators in Mexico's national Congress.

Women's work increasingly came to include remunerated employment during the final three decades of the century. In 1990, nationally over 20 percent of women over 12 years old worked for money, whereas the figure for women in Mexico City was over 30 percent. In addition, unlike women in the rural areas, women in Mexico City continued to labor for wages far longer: over 40 percent of women in the capital worked for money through their early 40s; only slightly more than 20 percent of women in the country as a whole did so in 1990. Certain sectors of the economy, such as the assembly plants situated largely along the Mexico-U.S. border, employed a majority of women as workers, although by the mid-1990s the number of women in these factories had dropped to 60 percent, at least partially as a result of increased mechanization of the plants and the preferential hiring of men to work the new equipment.

In spite of the fact that the figures were debated as to the precise number of women working in various sectors of the economy, in this period, as throughout the twentieth century, it was beyond dispute that women's income was crucial to the survival of most urban families and many rural ones. More controversial was the impact of women's labor activities with respect to household gender relations and gender divisions of labor, and specifically whether women's participation in the labor market and in the generation of income had given women any significantly greater share of control, power, and authority overall in society. Similarly, although girls' attendance in schools continued to increase in this period —by 1975 there was parity of boys and girls in elementary school, by 1989 parity in junior high school, and by 1989 around 42 percent of those enrolled in Mexican universities were women—the exact implications of these figures for equality of men and women in society more broadly continued to be debated hotly in official and popular circles.

One outcome of what some scholars referred to as the "privatization of the crisis" in Mexico, beginning especially in the late 1970s, was the growing number of *madres solteras* (single mothers) whose vulnerabilities owing to more acute levels of poverty may have been offset, in part, by lower levels also of violence, greater equitable distribution of income and consumption, and more attention to children's nutrition than in many households in which men were at least nominally present. Thus, creative and alternative strategies of survival among the poor in Mexico in the last quarter of the century depended in good measure on the specific nature of gender relations as they developed and were changed (or not) within specific households.

In keeping with official Catholic doctrine, and certainly revealing a closer practical relation between church and state than was required by Mexican law, abortions of any kind remained illegal throughout the twentieth century, although they certainly were readily available for women of wealth. As a partial reflection of the gendered influence of Catholicism, in most churches in Mexico in the twentieth century

women made up the strong majority of parishioners. Yet it is also important to recognize that attitudes about and practices relating to sexuality changed during this period, at least as marked by the increasing utilization of birth control (few would argue that the fall in birthrates was a result of lessened sexual activity) and, to a lesser extent, to the increasing openness of homosexuality as a social phenomenon in Mexico.

With respect to birth control, from the beginning this was viewed broadly by women and men in Mexico as mainly a female responsibility. In practice this meant that the most common contraception methods employed were tubal ligations for women who would no longer bear children, and intrauterine devices for younger women. As to homosexuality, a Movimiento de Liberación Homosexual (MLH) emerged in the late 1970s in Mexico City, Guadalajara, and a few other locations, and this together with a more general *"salida del clóset"* (coming out of the closet) in Mexican society contributed to a somewhat greater permissiveness regarding sexual tolerance and interpersonal relations in the country as a whole. Although AIDS cases have not been numerically as widespread in Mexico as in many other countries since the disease first appeared in the 1980s, the epidemic nonetheless had a chilling effect on the openness of cultural practices such as homosexuality in Mexico.

Both the increased use of birth control and the MLH contributed to altered perceptions concerning sexuality on the part of many in Mexico, as captured in the growing belief that sexuality should be regarded as more of an option and a matter of individual proclivities and less as an issue of innate and natural drives. This process can be termed the "denaturalization" of sexuality in Mexico. Nonetheless, double standards regarding sexuality between men and women certainly persisted, and men far more than women were "allowed" their sexual peccadilloes, despite the fact that adultery among women, many scholars believe, was on the rise in Mexico at the end of the twentieth century.

Finally, concerning health care in general, here too gender differences were apparent throughout the twentieth century in Mexico. In terms of life expectancy, for instance, by 1993 the figures were 76 years for women and 69 years for men. More specifically, cervical cancer was the leading cause of death for women aged 30 to 44, and, of course, illegal and botched abortions were the cause of female deaths alone; incidence of alcoholism and alcohol-related deaths—directly from cirrhosis of the liver and alcoholic psychosis, and indirectly from accidents and homicides—were the leading causes of death among men in the so-called productive ages in Mexico at the end of the century.

Conclusion

In households, marketplaces, factories, and *milpas* (maize fields), in education, politics, reproduction, and play, gender and sexual relations have been at the very heart of the modern Mexican experience. Whether couched in terms of common goals or uncontrollable antagonisms, general questions relating to cultural citizenship in Mexico have received concentrated expression throughout the century in the form of the issues of gender and sexuality, in particular the conspicuous chasm between official claims to equality and the myriad realities of inequalities large and small in every corner of the society.

Reproduction is central to social life, and it is anything but stagnant. Whether in terms of the relation of men to the Mexican state, in regard to marital relations within families, or with respect to the impact of paid work on women's authority in society, factors such as education, migration, mass media, fertility rates, and the powerful participation of women in political struggles in the 1970s and 1980s are more than mere statistics. They must be seen in their convergence in order to perceive more clearly a portrait of Mexican society undergoing enormous transformations in the twentieth century, including, and in many respects especially, as concerns gender and sexuality.

Select Bibliography

Fowler-Salamini, Heather, and Mary K. Vaughan, editors, *Women of the Mexican Countryside, 1850–1990.* Tucson: University of Arizona Press, 1994.

González de la Rocha, Mercedes, *The Resources of Poverty: Women and Survival in a Mexican City.* Oxford and Cambridge, Massachusetts: Blackwell, 1994.

Gutmann, Matthew C., *The Meanings of Macho: Being a Man in Mexico City.* Berkeley: University of California Press, 1996.

Macías, Ana, *Against All Odds: The Feminist Movement in Mexico to 1940.* Westport, Connecticut: Greenwood, 1982.

Stephen, Lynn, *Zapotec Women.* Austin: University of Texas Press, 1991.

—MATTHEW C. GUTMANN AND SUSIE S. PORTER

Gender: Gender and Mexican Spanish

Whether found in the sounds of language, grammar, vocabulary, or even daily conversation, gender distinctions are found in all languages worldwide. Indo-European languages such as Spanish offer a particular variation on a theme, a particular array of grammatical genders, phonemes (elementary units of sound), morphemes (elementary units of meaning), and sociocultural contexts. What most distinguishes Mexican Spanish from other versions of Spanish with regard to gender and language is the cultural and social institutions within which phonetically, grammatically, and lexically gendered discourses are spoken and interpreted by native Mexican speakers.

Spanish is composed of grammatical genders—words or parts of words that are classified or marked as feminine (f.), masculine (m.), or both feminine and masculine. Grammatical genders are a property of nouns that requires syntactical agreement on the part of other nouns, adjectives, and articles. For example, in the Spanish translation of the phrase "the red house"—*la casa roja*—both the article *(la)* and the adjective *(roja)* must agree with the feminine gender of the noun *(casa)*. Spanish words can be of two types: double-form and single-form words. Double-form words have both a masculine and a feminine form, such as *amigo* (a male friend) and *amiga* (a female friend). Single-form words only have a masculine, feminine, or androgynous form despite the sex of the referent. For example, *la persona* and *la gente* are feminine grammatically, but refer generically to person and people respectively; *el personaje* is masculine grammatically, but refers generically to a personage; *el/la juez* is androgynous grammatically, and refers generically to a judge.

Spanish words that refer to animate beings (people and animals) as opposed to inanimate things (objects and concepts) do so in three ways: by explicitly or implicitly referring to men, women, or both men and women. *Amigo* is explicitly masculine and *amiga* is explicitly feminine owing to their clearly marked syntactic properties (the suffix *o* versus the suffix *a*), and the sexes of their referents correspond directly to their grammatical genders. *Amigo* refers to a male friend, *amiga* to a female friend. In contrast to double-form words such as *amigo/amiga*, single-form words have an implicit or indirect (rather than an explicit or direct) relationship to the sex of the referent. In these cases qualifiers are required to determine the sex of the implied referent. For example, *la persona* is grammatically feminine but semantically of either or both sex; *la persona* may refer to a man, a woman, or generically to a person, depending upon the context or the qualifiers used by the speaker. In such cases, the speaker must explicitly state the referent's sex if the speaker wishes to convey this information. Ways of doing this are numerous. For example, one may state *"Él es una persona buena"* (he is a good person), emphasizing the subject as male with the pronoun *él* (he). For nouns with ambiguous syntactical endings, an article before the noun is sufficient to make the distinction explicit (e.g., *el* juez or *la* juez, *el* artista or *la* artista, *el* periodista or *la* periodista).

For centuries scholars have wondered whether grammatical genders convey any semantic message of femininity and masculinity. Despite the fact that *el hombre* refers to mankind, does its grammatically masculine form carry any intrinsic meaning of masculinity? In a study of Mexican Spanish, Toshi Konishi found that grammatical gender categories affect meaning and correlate with social and cultural ideas about femininity and masculinity. Significantly, he also found that speakers of Spanish perceive these correlates to have unequal values. Konishi discovered that words in the masculine gender were consistently perceived as higher in potency than those in the feminine. "Gender stereotypes," he writes, "played a role in the choice of he vs. she since antecedents of he tended to be strong, active, brave, wise, and clever, whereas antecedents of she tended to be weak, passive, and foolish." For example, in children's literature, the sun *(el sol)* is referred to as "he" and is thought of as more powerful than the moon *(la luna),* which is personified as "she" and thought of as less potent. Work by other scholars has shown that this phenomenon is not limited to Mexican Spanish.

There is another aspect of the gender-sex relationship worth noting. To explicitly signify men/males there is one gender, the masculine gender. In contrast, to signify women/females there are two genders: one that is feminine *(amiga)* and the other that is masculine/generic *(amigo)*, which linguistically, if not psychologically, includes women/females. In other words, the masculine gender in double-form words has two possible referents; *amigo* can refer explicitly to the sex (a male friend) or implicitly to the general class of friends (male or female, friend as a category of person) just as the word *man* in English has traditionally stood for the sex (a person who is male) as well as the generic (a person/mankind, male or female). *Amiga* has only one referent, and it is explicitly female. While *amigos* is the plural for friends and includes both men and women, the plural *amigas* includes only women. Semantic asymmetry such as this, where the masculine gender dominates over the feminine in the generic as the plural form, requires Spanish speakers to make leaps in their understanding. It is also the reason many women listeners rely heavily on context to determine whether or not they are included when the masculine form of a noun is in use. Recent studies such as Konishi's demonstrate that when the generic term is chosen by a speaker—*amigo(s)*—few speakers think of anything other than male referents. To remedy this discrepancy scholars of the Spanish language such as García Meseguer have suggested that speakers employ the generic only as the generic and make use of qualifiers when referring to the specific sexes; thus, *hombre* unqualified refers only to mankind (to both men and women) but never exclusively to men/males. With qualifiers, however, *hombre* may refer specifically to males if stated specifically as *hombre macho* and to females if stated as *hombre hembra.*

Unlike grammatical genders, which show gender with grammatical markers, the lexicon, or vocabulary, creates gender distinctions with words and meanings. For example, the proper term of address for a man is *señor,* which may be used on its own or with a surname. It is a term of address applied indiscriminately to adult males. There is no equivalent term in Spanish to signify an adult woman. Instead there are two terms to address a woman, *señora* and *señorita,* each of which discriminates two categories of women, married and unmarried. A *señorita* is an unmarried woman or girl; a *señora,* a married one. *Señor* makes no such distinction. In Mexico there are numerous occasions when it is more polite to address a woman whose marital status is unknown as *señorita* than *señora,* despite her age, not so much for the youth but the virginity the former implies. The categorization of women, but not men, along such lines occurs in many other semantic domains. The term *hombre público* is a man in the public eye or sphere, but a *mujer pública* is a prostitute; an *hombre honrado* is an honest man, but a *mujer honrada* is a chaste woman. Words that describe the sexuality of men do so in celebratory tones as *viril* and *potente.* Those same traits in a woman are considered negative. Not surprisingly, words for coitus almost always are cast in phallocentric terms, focused on *penetración* by the male; terms for the female role are passive, unless negatively described. The colloquial terms for sex in Mexico are based on metaphors of conquest: striking, causing harm, even killing; penises are sticks, clubs, and guns, which men, depending often but not always on their class, either put into *(meter)* or throw at *(echar)* a woman. While married men commonly refer to their spouses generically by their sex and in the possessive as *mi mujer,* "my woman," women have no such equivalent available to them, only words for husband *(marido* or *esposo)* or personal names. And finally, while a *señora* does not change her name to that of her husband, as is common practice in English-speaking countries, she often adds her husband's name to hers by using the possessive *de* (of), as in "Señora García de Bustos."

In Mexico and around the world, cultural codes and social conventions have an enormous impact on the shaping of language and its messages. *Padre* and *madre* are two words that provide an example of culturally encoded gender difference in Mexican Spanish. Literally, *padre* is a noun and means "father." When part of the expression *que padre,* however, *padre* is an adjective that translates as "that's terrific." It is a mundane expression, as common as its counterpart *me vale madre,* which literally translates as "it's worth a mother." While *madre* means mother, both as a noun (e.g., the mother of children) and an adjective (e.g., the mother country), idiomatically *madre* is used to describe any number of bad experiences, objects, or circumstances. *Me vale madre* stands in contrast to *que padre.* Instead of referring to greatness, it refers to uselessness. In free translation *me vale madre* renders into something like "it's worthless" or "I don't give a damn." Yet mothers are revered in Mexico, in both the religious (the Virgin Mary, the Mother of God) and secular spheres.

According to Alan Riding there are many words in Mexican Spanish filled with multiple meanings rich in "psychosexual and religious connotations." However, few are as complex in meaning and abundant in variation as *madre.* For example,

> *Nuestra madre* refers to the Virgin Mary, yet, puzzlingly, the word usually is used negatively. The insult *chinga tu madre* can be reduced to *tu madre* with little loss of intensity, while *una madre* can signify something that is unimportant, and *un desmadre* converts a situation into chaos. A *madrazo* is a heavy blow, a *madreador* is a bouncer or hired thug, and *partir la madre*—to "divide" the mother—means to shatter someone or something. ... A son will use the diminutive form *madrecita* to address his own mother, but *mamacita* is a vulgar street comment to a passing girl or a term of endearment for a mistress.

According to A. Bryson Gerrard's handbook of everyday spoken Spanish, *madre* "should need no entry but Mexican usage makes one essential; insults connected with mothers are so common . . . and so offensive that in Mexico [that Mexicans] have steered off the word altogether when it is a matter of referring to immediate relatives." It is better to ask friends about the health of their *mamás* than it is to ask about their *madres,* the handbook warns. "In contrast," Riding notes, "the father figure—*el padre*—plays a lesser linguistic role. A *padrote,* or big father, is a pimp, while something that is excellent is *muy padre.*" The list of idioms deriving from *padre* are all but exhausted by these few expressions, not one of which connotes worthlessness.

The inconsistencies that surround the cultural meaning of the term *madre* are intriguing. Along with *me vale madre* there are expressions such as *a toda madre* and *de poca madre.* The former literally translates into "a total mother," the latter into "of little mother." Yet both are as powerful in their reference to greatness as is *que padre.* The gender-blending of common Mexican names like María José for a girl and José María for a boy or Jesús for a boy and Jesusa for a girl offers some hint of the complexity of gender difference and maintenance with regard to mother-father issues. They suggest that the linguistic construction of gender difference is more than a simple black-and-white matter.

It is quite possible that gender differences may be encoded in the most elementary units of sound in Mexican Spanish. In 1954 Roman Jakobson suggested that there might be biological and psychological roots to the phonology of the terms mother and father. Based on a study by George Peter Murdock of unrelated languages from around the world, Jakobson observed a correspondence in the structure of parental terms used by infants. Words for mother *(mama)* more often than not begin with a nasalized consonant (/m/, /n/, /ng/), and those for father *(papa)* frequently begin with a bilabial or palatal stop (/p/, /b/, /t/ or /d/). Jakobson traced the sounds for mother to the nasalized murmur that children make while sucking at a mother's breast. In Spanish, sounds associated with sucking *(mamar,* to suck) also begin with a nasalized sound. Jakobson did not explore the possible biological and psychological roots to the /p/ of papa, but if he had he might have noted that the sound [p] is forceful whether aspirated as it is in English or unaspirated as in Spanish. It may be that the forcefulness of a consonantal stop such as /p/ or /t/ as opposed to a nasalized murmur such as /m/ was not an arbitrary choice by the infant to signify her/his father any more than the choice of a nasalized murmur to represent the mother was arbitrary. Approximately 30 percent of men's names in Spanish begin with a consonantal stop, but only 4 percent of women's names do. Despite these provocative general data, however, there have been no studies of the phonetic encoding of gender in Mexican Spanish.

Over the past 15 years sociolinguists have demonstrated that in addition to language itself, other nonlinguistic factors have a large impact on the perception and perpetuation of gender difference in language, particularly conversational contexts. Class, culture, ethnicity, and gender (meaning in this case the cultural construction of one's sexuality) can each influence the message conveyed by a language. Gender-specific speech styles, for example, affect the way men and women interact and interpret one another. Confusing linguistic genders (masculine and feminine words) with sexual difference (male and female) on the one hand and socioculturally constructed genders (e.g., masculinity and femininity) on the other is a common occurrence among speakers of a language filled with gender-encoded sounds, syntax, and semantics. Making this confusion conscious is a central activity of many Mexican Spanish speakers, particularly in marked situations such as joking sessions, musical lyrics, and other out-of-the-ordinary performances.

In Mexico there is a social form of discourse found primarily among men, a particular kind of joking called *albur*. Men of all classes and in almost all parts of Mexico outside the indigenous populations engage in these joking sessions. *Albures* are always about sex and sexual conquests that, while stated in male-female terms, are contests between two men, the speakers themselves. There are many circumstances that might spark an *albur*: food at the dinner table, a word, a color. But most commonly *albures* center around women: a passing woman on a street, someone's grandmother, sister, and only on rare occasions, mother. *Albures* are often but not always set pieces, which a boy learns growing up. Just as an English speaker might follow someone's "see you later" with "alligator" so a Mexican man might follow someone's *chico* or *pequeño* with *pásame el plato grande*, thereby initiating a contest that will appear competitive only to someone educated in the craft. While "see you later, alligator" is a simple rhyme without contest, an *albur* always has a winner and a loser so that the initiator in the case above must respond quickly with some sexual reference or he loses. He asks ¿*cómo?*, which might on the surface translate into "what did you say?," but is quickly interpreted by his contestant to be the first person singular of the verb *comer*, to eat, thereby making it easy for the respondent to win by feminizing his contestant with the retort *Siéntate que te veo cansado* (sit down [on me], you look tired). Although the contestants in *albures* are generally men, on occasion women will participate in them. Nonetheless, women's participation in *albures* is limited.

The women's movement in Mexico has sought to change the perception and position of women in Mexican society by several means, including cultural and sociolinguistic ones. Mexican women writers, playwrights, performance artists, and songwriters such as Elena Poniatowska, Jesusa Rodríguez, Astrid Hadad, and Gloria Trevi have in their novels, plays, performances, and songs challenged the sexual biases in Mexican Spanish and society. In addition the Chicanisma movement in the United States, which includes such Mexican American women writers as Sandra Cisneros and Gloria Anzaldúa, has through its written poetry, poetry slams, short stories, and novels challenged the social construction and linguistic usage of Mexican Spanish that subordinate women. All these verbal artists have as their ancestor Sor Juana Inés de la Cruz, the seventeenth-century nun who left a legacy of poetry and letters she had written about sex discrimination. For Sor Juana it was colonial society and the Catholic Church that regulated women's behavior, including what they had to say. Much has changed since the seventeenth century, although some Mexican women argue that the continuities are more striking. What becomes of Mexican Spanish in the days ahead will depend on the work of feminist linguists and verbal artists, as well as such individuals as the young married Mexican woman who responded to the inquiry "Do you use *de* García after your name to indicate you are married?" with "No, I occasionally use *con* (with) or *contra* (against) but never *de* (of)".

Select Bibliography

Frank, Francine Harriet, and Frank Anshen, *Language and the Sexes*. Albany: SUNY Press, 1983.

Gerrard, A. Bryson, *Cassell's Beyond the Dictionary in Spanish: A Handbook of Everyday Usage*. 2nd edition, New York: Funk and Wagnalls, 1972.

Hill, Jane H., and Kenneth C. Hill, *Speaking Mexicano: Dynamics of Syncretic Language in Central Mexico*. Tucson: University of Arizona Press, 1986.

Jakobson, Roman, "Why Mama and Papa?" In *Perspectives in Psychological Theory*. New York: International Universities Press, 1960.

Konishi, Toshi, "The Semantics of Grammatical Gender: A Cross-Cultural Study." *Journal of Psycholinguistic Research* 22:5 (1993).

Riding, Alan, *Distant Neighbors: A Portrait of the Mexicans*. New York: Knopf, 1985.

—Elizabeth Bakewell

General Agreement on Tariffs and Trade (GATT)

Mexico's admission to the General Agreement on Tariffs and Trade in 1986 and its participation in the Uruguay Round negotiations (finalized on April 15, 1994) represented a crucial part of the outward-oriented development strategy that the nation adopted in the mid-1980s. Mexico's participation in the multilateral forum of international trade contributes to the consolidation of the outward-oriented development strategy and the diversification of export markets. GATT/WTO (World Trade Organization) membership also reduces the power of rent-seeking protectionist groups that previously flourished because the commitments accepted by Mexico constrain the state's capacity to reverse the opening of its trade and investment policies. Accordingly, inclusion in the World Trade Organization contributes to the durability, stability, and predictability in Mexico's liberalization reforms.

In addition to solidifying domestic reform, Mexico's participation in the Uruguay Round provided it with more instruments to counteract global protectionist trends, while WTO membership grants Mexico with a clear and transparent set of rules for its export activities, reducing the likelihood of facing unilateral trade restrictions.

However, while membership in the trade forum will facilitate Mexican trade in general, GATT/WTO commitments will also constrain Mexico's ability to develop an industrial policy. The Uruguay Round diminished Mexico's ability to use economic instruments, such as subsidies or production and export requirements to promote industrialization. While Mexico has tried to integrate into the world economy to achieve growth, the result has been a two-tiered industrial structure, in which conglomerates are able to export significantly.

Mexico's participation in the multilateral trade negotiations will yield benefits in terms of market access, market diversification, and international trade rules. However, in order to take full advantage of GATT/WTO membership Mexico must find mechanisms to adjust its productive structure to make its outward-oriented model a successful one. Mexico will have to rely on external sources of financing and technology transfer to close the breach between an inefficient inward industrial sector and a small competitive outward-oriented one.

Mexico's First Attempt at Entering GATT

Since the 1940s, Mexico had followed a policy of import substitution industrialization (ISI), which sought to promote industrialization by substituting domestic manufactures for imports. ISI had allowed the country to experience annual Gross Domestic Product (GDP) growth rates of 6 percent during the so-called era of stabilizing development. Mexico had remained skeptical of the multilateral forum because GATT was considered a threat to the capacity of the state to implement development policies and generally inconsistent with ISI. Through the 1970s and under two different presidents, Mexico twice attempted to introduce trade liberalization reforms but was unsuccessful. First, there was a lack of political support for an outward-oriented model within the administration, the bureaucracy, and domestic groups that had flourished under protection. Second, other short-term solutions available at that time, such as foreign indebtedness and oil exports, were easier to implement and politically less costly. At the same time, international banks needed to lend the oversupply of OPEC "petrodollars"; Mexico's ability to borrow massive amounts of money at reasonable interest rates made liberalization unnecessary.

For these reasons, although GATT was created in 1947, Mexico first attempted to become a member in 1979, when the seventh round of multilateral trade negotiations (the Tokyo Round) was about to come to an end. Since the Luis Echeverría Álvarez administration (1970–76), it had become increasingly evident that relying on a closed domestic market would be insufficient to promote economic growth. During the José López Portillo administration (1976–82), following a trade liberalization effort (1977–79) Mexico solicited GATT membership in January 1979. Policy makers sought an export-oriented development strategy based on a gradual reduction of protection, industrial export promotion, and access to foreign markets.

As a result of GATT changes that responded to developing countries' concerns, such as special and differential treatment, Mexico became interested in joining the organization. Likewise, the failure of the 1979 negotiations for a Mexican trade agreement with the United States made Mexico realize that the alternative to secure market access for its exports was through the multilateral forum, which also provided some legal recourse against a growing trend of U.S. protectionism. The Protocol of Accession that let in Mexico was negotiated during the Tokyo Round and was ready in October 1979. A public debate immediately followed.

The terms of the Protocol were very favorable, as the country was permitted to obviate GATT rules when they threatened domestic policies such as subsidized industrial programs, thus guaranteeing Mexico's capacity to implement a targeted industrial policy. Notwithstanding the favorable conditions, on March 18, 1980, the date that commemorates Mexico's 1938 oil expropriation, President López Portillo announced his decision to decline membership. This resolution coincided with the end of Mexico's trade liberalization.

What accounts for this reversal? Mexico's decision to "postpone" its accession to GATT can be explained by a combination of domestic and international factors: a deeply entrenched inward-oriented model, the 1979 oil boom, the opposition of small- and medium-sized industrialists, and free-trade ambivalence on the part of the president and Mexico's trade policy makers.

Domestic producers that had enjoyed high rents as a result of protection adamantly opposed any attempt to liberalize the economy, even though Mexico's 1979 Protocol of Accession guaranteed these groups protection from competition for a lengthy period. In fact, during the negotiation, Mexico made concessions on only 328 products, which represented less than 10 percent of its total imports. In addition, tariff reductions were accorded for just 21 items, and the elimination of import permits would only affect 34 items. Mexico also obtained other favorable concessions, such as the capacity to use export subsidies and grant tax incentives to industry, the right to protect its industry and agriculture, and permission to utilize quantitative restrictions that were inconsistent with GATT. Such concessions could hardly be considered a radical move toward the opening of Mexico's economy.

However, business associations such as the Cámera Nacional de la Industria de la Transformación (CANACINTRA, or National Chamber of Transformation Industry) and the National College of Economists, which had close ties with the ruling party (the Partido Revolucionario Institucional—PRI, or Institutional Revolutionary Party) became vociferous opponents to GATT's accession. Other associations such as the Confederación Patronal de la República Mexicana (COPARMEX, or Employer's Confederation of the Republic of Mexico), and ANIERM (National Association of Mexican Importers and Exporters) and informal business groups such as the Monterrey Group supported GATT membership but were unable to make their position prevail. Given the lack of consensus among the business community, President López Portillo ultimately decided to maintain the status quo.

Mexico's decision to postpone GATT accession also resulted from bureaucratic conflict between an "inward-oriented" group led by budget minister Carlos Tello and industrial promotion czar José Andrés de Oteyza, on one hand, and the "outward-oriented" faction headed by finance minister Julio Rodolfo Moctezuma Cid and trade minister Héctor Hernández Cervantes. López Portillo initially supported the internationalist group. However, when massive oil reserves were discovered, Mexico's supposed new economic independence tilted the balance against liberalization in general, and GATT in particular. In 1979 the international price of oil soared to record highs. Mexico sought to replace GATT with oil as a means of securing foreign market access and attracting foreign capital; for example, the 1981 Franco-Mexican trade agreement gave Mexico the equivalent of Most-Favored-Nation (MFN) status in the French market in exchange for oil. Thus, the "petrolization" of the Mexican economy seemed to obviate the need to promote exports of manufactures through free trade, because oil provided Mexico with a strong negotiation position. However, this state of affairs would prove short-lived.

Mexico's Unilateral Trade Liberalization

In 1982 the international price of oil collapsed while Mexico's foreign debt had reached almost US$100 billion, resulting in a debt crisis that threatened not only Mexico's economy but also the stability of the international financial system. Mexico had to negotiate a rescue package with the International Monetary Fund (IMF) that required a stabilization program and the introduction of deep economic reforms, among which trade policy was a fundamental component. The moderate unilateral trade liberalization that Mexico initiated in 1983 gradually eliminated official prices, quotas, licenses, and import permits and was accelerated in 1985 when oil prices collapsed again. President Miguel de la Madrid was convinced that going back to ISI would only deepen the crisis. In June 1985 Mexico instituted a set of reforms to rationalize its imports and eliminated import permits for 2,000 tariff items (around 20 percent of the import tariff schedule).

President de la Madrid openly pursued an outward-oriented strategy in which export activity was to become the backbone of Mexico's development strategy. In contrast with the 1979 process, almost no public discussion took place, although business organizations such as the elitist CCE (Business Coordinating Council) and the ANIERM were clear enthusiasts; most public and private organizations acted only as advisers. Ultimately, in the context of an enduring crisis affecting all business interests, the decision to make Mexico a GATT member came from the president.

Mexico's 1986 Protocol of Accession established a tariff ceiling of 50 percent and the elimination of official prices. Mexico was the first acceding country that agreed to bind all of its tariff schedule. As in 1979, Mexico's concessions were rather small; only 5 percent of total import categories were negotiated (373 out of 8,143 import items), which represented 15 percent of the value of imports in 1985. Agriculture and industrial integration programs (automotive, electronics, and pharmaceutical) received a waiver from GATT obligations. Mexico also became a signatory to four of the six Tokyo Round Codes of Conduct—antidumping, customs valuation, import licenses, and technical barriers to trade—which contained special provisions for developing countries.

Domestic macroeconomic reforms led Mexico to go far beyond its GATT commitments. In 1987, just one year after Mexico acquired GATT membership, a bold unilateral trade liberalization reduced the highest tariff level from 100 percent to 20 percent as part of a national stabilization pact including business and labor. By the late 1980s, Mexico had become one of the most open economies among developing countries.

The Uruguay Round

GATT's Uruguay Round, the eighth round of multilateral trade negotiations, was finalized after eight years on April 15, 1994. The Final Act establishes the WTO that comprises 28 different agreements signed by 125 countries. The Uruguay Round Agreements entered into effect on January 1, 1995, and are the result of the most ambitious and comprehensive effort of multilateral trade liberalization.

Mexico's participation in the Uruguay Round marked the country's entrance into the multilateral trade forum. For Mexico, the Uruguay Round was the first step toward the consolidation of what had been a unilateral liberalization process and an outward-oriented development strategy; GATT membership allows Mexico the possibility of using the international trade regime to guarantee export market access and to counteract any possible surge of protectionism. Mexico had a number of objectives: to guarantee the consistency between its regional trade agreements and the WTO rules, avoid

manipulating environmental measures for trade protection, secure market access for its exports, and reduce the use of unilateral measures and unfair trade practices. To analyze Mexico's role in the multilateral trade negotiations as well as those benefits it received, trade issues can be divided into three main areas: market access, institutional framework and rules, and new areas.

Market Access

The most important area for developing countries in general, and Mexico in particular, was that of market access. In addition to tariff reductions, the incorporation of the textile and agricultural sectors into GATT was key for Mexico, given these sectors' weight in trade activities. Mexico and other newly industrializing countries demanded that the developed economies open these markets in return for liberalization in services, intellectual property rights, and investment.

Although liberalization in manufactures already had progressed significantly in GATT negotiations before the Uruguay Round, market access concessions were important for Mexico because industrial goods have become the most significant component of its exports. Between 1985 and 1990, Mexico's growth of manufactured exports showed an annual growth rate of 24 percent. By 1995, the trade-to-production ratio represented 17 percent of GDP, compared with 11 percent in 1980. The Uruguay Round ensured market access for manufactures by reducing tariff rates, tariff escalation, and tariff peaks. Mexico committed to a linear tariff reduction from 50 percent to 35 percent ad valorem, to grant duty-free access to 1 percent of its imports, and to apply quantitative restrictions to less than 2 percent of its import tariff items. Mexico retained the capacity to require import licenses for agricultural products, oil and oil products, weapons and ammunications, certain vehicles, and, on a temporary basis, pharmaceutical products.

Through the gradual dismantling of the protectionist Multifiber Agreement quota system, liberalization in textiles is expected to stimulate Mexico's exports. In the short term, multilateral liberalization will not translate into increased access to export markets. The benefit derives more from the principles and rules established to liberalize trade in textiles than from immediate market access.

Mexico's outward-oriented strategy has been supported through the liberalization of the domestic market because Mexican producers can buy cheaper imports. As a result of the Uruguay Round, Mexico accomplished substantive market access benefits given tariff reduction and nontariff barrier elimination. But liberalization does not automatically mean increased competitiveness in the world market for all firms or sectors. Since Mexico started its process of unilateral trade liberalization in 1985, firms in traditionally inward-oriented manufacturing sectors (e.g., toys, garment, footwear, electric appliances, and electronics) have been unable to gain a competitive position, and many already have disappeared. In contrast, a group of large multinational export-oriented firms involved in sectors such as automobiles, electronics, glass, cement, and textiles have shown their ability to take advantage of the benefits acquired under the Uruguay Round.

Although policy makers hope that export-oriented firms will make inward-oriented firms more competitive through technological and management "spillovers" as well as subcontracting opportunities, it is unclear how inefficient firms will improve if Mexico relies just on market access benefits. Indeed, access to foreign markets will be meaningless without international levels of competitiveness among Mexican industry, something that GATT membership does not guarantee.

Mexico's two-tiered industrial structure also has had political economy implications. Business organizations such as CANACINTRA, which had been very protected although silent during the accession to GATT in 1986, have become open critics of liberalizing policies. Thus, it has been necessary to build political support for economic reforms among those groups that will reap the benefits of liberalization.

With respect to agriculture, liberalization was a major feat of the Uruguay Round. Mexico initially opposed agricultural liberalization because around 40 percent of its population survives on the consumption of maize, most of which was produced by small, inefficient farmers. In addition, Mexico supports domestic production through direct payments to the producer. In fact, Mexico's Protocol of Accession had excluded the agricultural sector from its GATT commitments.

Liberalization means that trade-distorting domestic subsidies will be phased out and export subsidies regulated while quantitative restrictions will be tariffed. Mexico was not enthusiastic about the "tarrification" of all its agriculture nontariff barriers but ended up agreeing to it in all products under the general rules, even those products that were considered "sensitive" such as maize, kidney beans, and dairy products. Mexico, however, bound its tariffs for rice and coarse grains at higher levels than its previous tariff ceiling of 50 percent (to more than 100 percent in some cases). A minimum tariff reduction

of 10 percent on all agriculture products and an average of 24 percent over a 10-year period was agreed.

Mexico's agriculture is not homogeneous, and policies in this sector have reflected social demands dating from the 1910 Revolution. Given the disparities in this sector, market access benefits will help those fruit and vegetable producers that have targeted the export market. Most liberalization in agriculture focused on temperate products as opposed to tropical ones, such as coffee, tea, cocoa, spices, cut flowers, and live plants, because the latter already enjoyed duty-free access or preferential treatment through the unilateral Generalized System of Preferences (GSP). Mexico expects to obtain increased access for its exports of honey, lemons, mangoes, orange juice, rum, cut flowers, unprocessed coffee, avocados, beer, and tequila. The concessions obtained in these products allowed Mexico to obtain reciprocity for its unilateral liberalization and aimed at supporting the efforts to diversify exports to the Japanese, European, and Southeast Asian markets.

Mexico sought to improve access for its key exports (i.e., tropical products, fruits, and vegetables) to generate the income required to compensate for an expected price increase on imports of agricultural commodities with the reduction or elimination of subsidies. Liberalization of trade in agriculture poses a political economy challenge for Mexico given the traditional protection granted to peasants and the subsidies transferred to consumers. Small agriculture producers are now facing open competition from imports, while consumers are having to pay international prices for agriculture products. Opening trade in agriculture implied removing protection and transforming land property rights that involved the termination of land redistribution and the development of a new legal framework that primarily affected the *ejido,* a form of communal land ownership sanctified under the Revolution. Traditional Mexican farmers in the officialist Confederación Nacional Campesina (CNC, or National Peasant Confederation) have questioned the traditional alliance with government as protection and subsidies to this sector are eliminated.

Agriculture not only has been protected but also widely subsidized among developed and developing countries, and Mexico had not been the exception. As a result of the Uruguay Round, Mexico will reduce subsidies (domestic support) from 29 billion pesos to around 25 billion pesos in the period between 1995 and 2004. Mexico, however, is not obliged to eliminate the rural income support program (PROCAMPO) introduced in 1993, which has become the only source of assistance for Mexican peasantry. This program provides farmers twice a year with fixed acreage payments. The program replaces the previous system of guaranteed prices for grain and oilseed producers. In the case of export subsidies, Mexico had already eliminated them, but it registered export subsidies for maize, beans, wheat, sorghum, and sugar to keep the flexibility to grant in the future such subsidies consistent with the provisions of the agreement. Nonetheless, Mexico has committed to eliminate subsidies, and the challenge will be to create the economic conditions that will allow displaced groups to adjust to import competition or to relocate in other areas of production.

Institutional Framework and Rules

For Mexico, the changes to international trade rules regarding such issues as safeguards, antidumping, and subsidies, as well as the strengthening of the dispute-settlement mechanism, were significant to the extent that they are expected to increase transparency and reduce the likelihood that Mexico's major trading partners will use unilateral trade rules to restrict market access. Mexico's participation in the Uruguay Round aimed at achieving access to legal instruments with which to counteract protectionist trends among industrialized countries.

Of particular importance to Mexico was the Agreement on Safeguards, which prohibits the establishment of "gray area measures" such as voluntary export restraints (VERs) and orderly marketing agreements (OMAs), which in the past have been imposed to provide relief to import-competing domestic industries. Mexican exports of iron and steel, footwear, and consumer electronics have faced U.S. VERs, while its tomato exports have been subject to U.S. OMAs. Mexico considers these Uruguay provisions as a step forward in introducing discipline to neo-protectionist behavior.

Antidumping and countervailing duties have become very popular instruments of protection and pose a threat to the international trading system. Mexico wanted stricter discipline on antidumping actions because such measures have been widely used by its trading partners in very competitive exports such as cement. Mexico itself also has developed strong antidumping legislation. Between 1985 and 1993, Mexico initiated 131 cases of dumping against GATT members, while 25 investigations were initiated against Mexican exports.

The Agreement on Subsidies strengthens existing rules. The Uruguay Round defined subsidies for the first time and recognized three categories: prohibited, actionable, and nonactionable. Mexico has already eliminated its export subsidies, but it sought to obtain nonactionable status for certain environmental subsidies, including those for environment-related research and development. Mexico also obtained similar status for certain regional subsidies that will be used to move economic activity away from Mexico City and other industrial centers. Mexico was a proponent of granting a "credit" for those developing countries that phase out their export subsidies ahead of the scheduled time limit of eight years.

Mexico limited its own ability to pursue an industrial policy because changes to trade rules imply a prohibition against subsidies or other forms of industrial incentives and requirements. GATT/WTO has curtailed Mexico's credit and subsidy instruments and its ability to support industrial activities. In addition, the capital scarcity that Mexico has persistently suffered puts it in an extremely vulnerable position because industrial development will depend on foreign capital inflows whose levels are largely determined beyond Mexican borders. Unlike countries such as Korea or Taiwan, which successfully managed to direct foreign investment toward targeted areas and achieved technology transfer through joint ventures, Mexico will have limited policy-making discretion to influence the kind of industry that may develop.

The Uruguay Round was successful in strengthening GATT's mechanism of settling disputes; it set a six-month limit for panels' decisions, expedited panel proceedings, and unified the previously fragmented procedure. Panel decisions no longer depend upon the approval of the parties to a dispute because a party will no longer have the capacity to refuse the establishment of a panel or its obscure term composition. For Mexico such improvements were crucial given the number of trade disputes, particularly from the United States, that it has taken to GATT. It is expected that the new dispute-settlement procedures will translate into the actual implementation of panels' decisions.

In terms of institutional reforms, the creation of the WTO as a peak institution aimed at granting a permanent character to the multilateral trade organization and constraining the capacity of governments to unilaterally impose trade restrictions that are inconsistent with GATT. Mexico along with Canada and the United States was the first participant to submit a concrete proposal to establish the World Trade Organization. Thus, GATT was subsumed under the WTO as one of those agreements.

New Areas

As a result of the increasing importance of services in the international economy, the Uruguay Round incorporated new areas of negotiation such as services, trade-related investment measures, and intellectual property rights. Trade in services represents 25 percent of world trade (around US$1 trillion annually) and almost 60 percent of foreign direct investment.

The General Agreement on Trade in Services (GATS) establishes a benchmark level of market access based on existing national regulations. It is based on the principles of national treatment and reciprocity; future negotiations will address areas where agreement could not be reached, such as financial services. For Mexico, liberalization of services was not something totally new because its own process of economic reform and the North American Free Trade Agreement (NAFTA) negotiations had set the context for negotiating this sector multilaterally. Mexico agreed to allow 100 percent foreign participation in the case of certain professional services, scheduled distribution services, and certain tourism and trade-related services.

Since market access in services is closely linked to investment rules, trade-related investment measures (TRIMs) became part of the negotiation. The Uruguay Round did not go far in liberalizing investment; it only established the framework to initiate consultations toward establishing disciplines on the effects of investment measures on trade. The list of TRIMs includes instruments that Mexico has used to encourage industrialization, such as local content requirements, trade balancing requirements, foreign exchange balancing, and export limits. As part of its economic reforms, Mexico has eliminated almost all of its TRIMs, although some are still in place in the automotive sector, for example. Mexico will eliminate the remaining TRIMs within a five-year period unless an extension is granted. This type of commitment reduces Mexico's capacity to target industrial development through these instruments, which although not economically optimal, have been used worldwide to attain international competitiveness and domestic protection.

Among the new areas, the Agreement on Trade-Related Intellectual Property Rights (TRIPs) is the most comprehensive and reflects the areas of importance to industrialized countries. This agreement covers minimum standards for copyright, trademarks, geographical indications, industrial design, patents, layout designs of integrated circuits, and protection of undisclosed information. Under NAFTA, Mexico had already accepted standards of protection similar to those in the TRIPs Agreement.

For Mexico, participation in the negotiation of these new areas was significant, even though NAFTA would eventually become more important than the WTO in service trade. As an importer of services and technology, it was in Mexico's interest to define the terms of its liberalization to be able to encourage domestic as well as foreign participation in the sector. Mexico's economic growth cannot be tied only to manufacture production or agriculture exports; Mexico has the potential of becoming a strong supplier of services such as construction and tourism. Thus, trade in services may well support Mexico's economic growth.

Conclusions

With Mexico's formal accession to GATT, the likelihood of a sudden reversal of its liberalized trade regime was dramatically reduced while such reforms became more predictable and sustainable. GATT/WTO membership reflects a shift in Mexico's economic model equilibrium from protection and rent-seeking to the support of outward-oriented sectors that benefit from an open economy. Mexico's international commitments forced a distance from groups within business, agriculture, and the bureaucracy that saw their political and economic privileges fade away. The new political economy is still in the process of consolidation, and there exists the risk that this dramatic reform will provoke destabilizing opposition from those groups that refuse or are unable to adjust to the new competition conditions.

Trade liberalization and access to export markets will not automatically translate into increased industrialization, economic growth, and development. Mexico will reap the benefits of its unilateral trade liberalization process and of its deregulation policies by receiving reciprocity from other GATT members. However, Mexico faces the challenge of promoting competitiveness of all its manufacturing, agriculture, and service sectors to take full advantage of the Uruguay Round Agreements. The country's dependence on foreign capital and multinational corporate strategies severely limits the extent to which GATT membership will help strengthen Mexico's outward-oriented industrialization.

Select Bibliography

GATT, *Trade Policy Review of Mexico.* Geneva: GATT, 1993.

Mares, David R., "Explaining Choice of Development Strategies: Suggestions from Mexico, 1970–1982." *International Organization* 39:4 (Autumn 1985).

Newell, Roberto G., and Luis Rubio F., *Mexico's Dilemma: The Political Origins of Economic Crisis.* Boulder, Colorado: Westview Press, 1984.

Rubio, Luis F., Cristina Rodríguez D., and Roberto Blum
V., "The Making of Mexico's Trade Policy and the
Uruguay Round." In *Domestic Trade Politics and the
Uruguay Round*, edited by Henry Nau. New York:
Columbia University Press, 1989.

Story, Dale, "Trade politics in the Third World: A case
study of the Mexican GATT decision." *International
Organization* 36:4 (Autumn 1982).

_____, *Industry, the State and Public Policy in Mexico*.
Austin: University of Texas Press, 1986.

Rajapatirana, Sarath, "Latin America and the Caribbean
after the Uruguay Round: An Assessment." World Bank
Internal Document (July 20, 1995).

World Bank, *World Development Report 1987*.
Washington, D.C.: World Bank, 1987.

—LUZ MARÍA DE LA MORA

Great Depression

The panic of October 1929 on Wall Street unleashed
a series of depressive forces in the world economy
that had been latent for several years. The general
effect was an enormous economic contraction in the
United States, which rapidly spread to many other
countries. Between 1929 and 1933 the gross domestic product of the United States declined at an annual
rate of 8.2 percent, diminishing demand for goods
and services from other countries. These countries
in turn responded by raising protectionist trade barriers to keep employment and economic activity
inside the country, causing a drop in the volume of
international trade.

The impact of the Great Depression, then, was
keenly felt throughout Latin America, particularly
in Mexico. The drop in the national income of the
United States diminished demand for goods and services from Mexico, starting a three-pronged depressive process in the Mexican economy. First, the
volume and value of Mexican exports to the United
States declined dramatically. Between 1929 and 1932
the value of exports contracted almost 65 percent
and the terms of trade dropped 20.8 percent, reducing Mexico's capacity to import by half. This enormous contraction in the external sector reduced the
export activity and thus employment levels in this
sector. The balance of trade suffered grave deterioration as commercial surplus declined from US$97
million in 1929 to only US$39 million in 1932.

The external economic crisis also resulted in a
deterioration in Mexico's balance of trade and a consequent reduction of more than 53 percent in the
Bank of Mexico's reserves between 1929 and 1931.
The money supply also contracted 60 percent during

this period, contributing to the economic depression
in Mexico. In other words, the contraction in international trade brought with it a strong monetary
restriction, hindering economic transactions and
raising the cost of money. Thus, general economic
activity was reduced and the crisis that had begun in
the external sector spread to the rest of the economy.

The third important impact of the international
economic crisis was in public finances, since taxes on
the external sector had represented more than half of
the government's income. As the external sector contracted, government revenues also declined, dropping from 322 million pesos in 1929 to only 179
million pesos in 1932. Moreover, during the depression taxation was the only possible source of government income, as a moratorium was imposed on
external lending and as the government was unable
to find a source for domestic lending. The drop in
state revenues brought with it a decline in public
spending, which in turn contributed to the contraction in aggregate demand in Mexico.

The only factor that dampened the impact of the
depressive forces was the depreciation of the exchange rate as a result of the deterioration in the balance of payment. Although the peso officially was
based on a gold standard and thus had a fixed
exchange rate, the generalized use of silver currency
as a means of exchange meant that the decline in the
price of silver would constitute a depreciation in
the value of the peso. Thus, the depreciation of almost
22 percent between 1929 and 1931 helped mitigate
the drop in demand over the short term. Nonetheless, Mexico's gross domestic product contracted
dramatically, falling at an average rate of 4 percent between 1929 and 1931 with an attendant
decline in employment levels and the overall well-
being of the population. Moreover, the Great Depression in the United States led to the deportation of
approximately 300,000 workers, aggravating the
already difficult situation in Mexico.

The crisis began to ease in the second trimester of
1932, more than a year before it did in the United
States. Mexico's recuperation was spurred by two
factors. On the one hand, the export sector began to
return to life with the recovery of export prices, particularly for petroleum and silver, and the depreciation of the peso, which accelerated after 1932. On
the other, from December 1931 almost through the
end of the following year the Mexican government
implemented a radical change in the economic policy,
which permitted a rapid recovery for the economy.

Most notably, the Bank of Mexico abandoned the
gold standard in July 1931 as international reserves
were exhausted, and a few months later it cautiously

adopted the silver standard. This permitted the Bank of Mexico to begin printing significant quantities of money, since up to that point the bank could only print bills that were backed fully by gold reserves. The Mexican public naturally was chary of these measures, since it remembered the hyperinflation that had accompanied the government's decision to print excessive amounts of paper money during the Revolution; however, as the government began to pay its employees in paper money rather than coins, paper money increasingly was accepted. The increase in the money supply began to reverse the effects of the monetary contraction of the Great Depression; indeed, the reversal was quite rapid as the number of bills in circulation climbed from approximately 100,000 in November 1931, to more than 42 million in December 1932. The Mexican treasury also was able to obtain extraordinary earnings through seigniorage, minting silver coins with less expensive metals during the initial contraction in world silver prices. This permitted the government to engage in public spending over and beyond its fiscal income.

The changes in the Mexican economic policy helped spur a rapid recovery in the export sector. First, starting in 1933 the increase in export prices increased the value of the export sector. Second, the abandonment of the gold standard allowed the peso to drop to levels the market could support; the devaluation of the peso accelerated starting in 1932. These two factors spurred exports and thus aggregate demand, also contributing to the resolution of the broader crisis that had begun in the export sector.

The consequence of these changes was the rapid recovery of the gross domestic product (GDP) starting in the second trimester of 1932, which would continue almost through the end of the decade; between 1932 and 1934 the real GDP increased 18.8 percent. Nonetheless, the reaction was not uniform in all sectors of the Mexican economy. In the agricultural sector the recovery was relatively slow. In part this slow recovery was owing to the fact that the decline in the agricultural sector had been relatively small, since the consumption of basic goods such as food had not fluctuated radically with the population's level of income. Industrial product, however, grew by a staggering 46.7 percent. Indeed, during the 1930s industry was the leading sector of the economy and grew far more rapidly than all other economic activities. Moreover, industrial development was stimulated by a vigorous process of import substitution as imports became relatively expensive. In other words, import substitution was generated by the very mechanisms of the market and not by a premeditated protectionist policy. Such a

trade policy was not put into place until the very end of the 1940s.

Another important, albeit indirect, effect of the Great Depression was the maturation of diverse mechanisms of economic policy. Most notably, the scarce means of payment in 1931–32 spurred growing acceptance of paper money from the Bank of Mexico. The acceptance of paper money, together with the affiliation of most Mexican banks with the Central Bank, constituted the first instruments of monetary policy: the printing of paper money, the possibility of modifying legal reserves, and later the opening of a line of credit for the Central Bank of the Federal Government, which would be abused in subsequent decades. The introduction of an income tax in 1926 permitted the government to count on an additional instrument of fiscal policy in the 1930s. Moreover, the abandonment of the gold standard in 1931 was much more than a simple devaluation, since—at least during the 1930s—it would allow policy to become much more flexible and become a true instrument of economic policy. These new fiscal tools and increased room to maneuver gave economic policy a far more important and effective role. More important, however, was the new activist agenda of the state in determining economic policy, not only in Mexico but throughout Latin America.

Select Bibliography

Haber, Stephen H., *Industry and Underdevelopment: The Industrialization of Mexico, 1890–1940*. Palo Alto, California: Stanford University Press, 1989.

Thorp, Rosemary, editor, *Latin America in the 1930's: The Role of the Periphery in World Crisis*. London: Macmillan, 1984.

—ENRIQUE CÁRDENAS

Guadalupanismo

See Virgin of Guadalupe and Guadalupanismo

Guadalupe Hidalgo, Treaty of

Named after the small village near Mexico City where it was signed, the Treaty of Guadalupe Hidalgo formally ended the U.S.-Mexican War on February 2, 1848. With this agreement, Mexico affirmed the U.S. possession of Texas including all areas north of the Rio Grande (Río Bravo in Mexico). The country also ceded to the United States most of the California and New Mexico territories. Following the 1853 Gadsden Purchase, that area ultimately came to comprise all of the current U.S. states of Arizona, California, New Mexico, Nevada, and Utah, as well as parts of Colorado, Oklahoma, and Wyoming. The total cession amounted to more than half of Mexico's territory; in return, the U.S. government made a cash payment of US$15,000,000 and assumed Mexican debts totaling US$3,250,000. The U.S. government also promised to respect life, liberty, and property of the Mexican residents of the new U.S. territories, and it vowed to help prevent Indian incursions against Mexico.

As Mexican and U.S. goals in the war had diverged widely, the negotiation and ratification of the treaty was a long and arduous process. The Mexican government insisted on respecting the old borders of the 1819 Adams-Onís Treaty, minus Texas northeast of the Nueces River. On the other hand, U.S. president James K. Polk sought the annexation of a wide swath of territory including Baja California, as well as the granting of transit rights across the Isthmus of Tehuantepec.

When U.S. armies penetrated into the Mexican heartland, however, the Mexican position became more difficult to maintain. In September 1847, the presence of General Winfield Scott's troops just outside Mexico City prompted Mexican negotiators to soften their stance. When the resultant armistice agreement failed due to the intransigence of both sides, the U.S. forces occupied Mexico City. With a protracted guerrilla war as the only alternative, the Mexican government agreed to terms among the harshest that the winner of an international war have ever imposed upon the losers. Apart from the Baja California cession and the demand for transit rights, U.S. negotiator Nicholas P. Trist reached all of the significant goals of what had constituted an extreme U.S. position. All the same, the U.S. Senate almost derailed ratification; the northern Whigs feared the expansion of slaveholding territory, while many southern Democrats desired the annexation of more or all of Mexico. In Mexico, ratification was even more difficult. Even though, as the late-nineteenth-century thinker Justo Sierra put it, the Mexican representatives "did as much as they could; they accomplished as much as they should have," influential opposition figures decried the treaty. Only the potential cost of a prolonged occupation in both political and economic terms convinced the Mexican Congress to approve the agreement.

The Treaty of Guadalupe Hidalgo was one of the most traumatic events in post-Conquest Mexican history, and it brought important consequences. First of all, the alienation of a scarcely populated, yet vast part of the national territory constituted an unprecedented act of national humiliation. This humiliation helped bring about a reorientation of Mexican politics, away from caudillismo and toward the formation of true national parties. The Conservatives and Liberals both developed strategies to attempt to prevent further U.S. landgrabbing. In addition, the agreement spurred a widespread fear of further U.S. expansion, a fear that would resonate much later in Mexican foreign policies. The Treaty of Guadalupe Hidalgo came to exemplify not only national shame but also the fundamentally avaricious nature of the "gringos" to the north. In the long run, the treaty brought the United States and Mexico closer together, for better and for worse. For Mexico, the settlement and economic development of the new U.S. Southwest created new opportunities for export-led development. When it became clear during the late Porfiriato that many aspects of this close relationship were less than benign, many Mexicans blamed the "Peaceful Conquest" by U.S. economic penetration on the "Violent Conquest" exemplified by the Treaty of Guadalupe Hidalgo.

Even today, in the age of the North American Free Trade Agreement, the Treaty of Guadalupe Hidalgo remains on the minds of many Mexicans. In recent decades, many millions of Mexicans have taken up residence in the territories lost to the United States in 1848. Most of these territories today form part of *la frontera,* the bicultural border region that is neither exclusively part of the United States nor exclusively Mexican. In that sense, the borders drawn by the Treaty of Guadalupe Hidalgo have begun to lose some of their significance.

Select Bibliography

Griswold de Castillo, Richard, *The Treaty of Guadalupe Hidalgo: A Legacy of Conflict.* Norman: University of Oklahoma Press, 1990.

—JÜRGEN BUCHENAU

Guerrero, Vicente 1782–1831
General and President

Vicente Guerrero was born on April 4, 1782, at Tixtla, in the province (now state) of Mexico. His parents, Juan Pedro Guerrero and María Guadalupe Saldana, were peasant farmers. Vicente Guerrero had mestizo and African bloodlines. As an adult, he was tall and robust, strong-willed, and physically powerful. His complexion was dark and reflected his mixed heritage. "El Negro," as he was called, was intelligent, insightful, shrewd, and persuasive as well as personally committed to ending racially defined caste distinctions. He was more conversant in the indigenous dialect of his region than in Spanish. He claimed to be a descendant of King Nezahualcoyotl of Texcoco.

Until 1810 Guerrero spent his young adult life as a laborer and muleteer. Then in 1810, Miguel Hidalgo y Costilla proclaimed a revolt in Guanajuato against the colonial authority. The revolution spread quickly, and the same year José María Morelos y Pavón raised an army in the south in support of the revolution. Hidalgo and Morelos demanded sweeping social and political changes that would redress the worst grievances of the masses. Guerrero agreed with their cause and enlisted in Morelos's army on December 15, 1810.

Guerrero proved quickly to be a resourceful and brave leader. A captain by 1811, he received promotion to lieutenant colonel a year later. In 1812 he participated in the capture of Oaxaca and commanded forces raiding the western harbors of Tehuantepec, Puerto Escondido, and Santa Cruz. On February 8–9, 1813, he took part in the victory against royalist forces at Santa Cruz; Guerrero was cited for his bravery. While Morelos assaulted Acapulco, Guerrero protected the rebels' southern flank and repulsed a royalist attack at Quantepec on July 1, 1813. During the next few months, the southern insurgents consolidated their gains; the army elected Morelos as *generalísimo,* and the insurgents created a government with a congress to rule over their territory.

However, in late 1813 and early 1814, the insurgents suffered disastrous defeats and had to withdraw into the mountainous interior. During the summer of 1814, Guerrero became a colonel and insurgents concentrated on rebuilding their armies. A dispute over regional command temporarily left Guerrero with 500 men armed with only three rifles. Showing his courage and resourcefulness, Guerrero launched this force against a royalist detachment on the Tacachi River. The surprise night assault routed the enemy, and Guerrero captured 400 rifles and other military supplies.

1815 was another difficult year for the insurgents. Despite various successes, the rebels retreated, and on November 6, 1815, Morelos himself was captured; the royalists executed him in December 1815. Most of the insurgent leaders had now been captured or killed, and there was some confusion as to who should become the insurgent commander. On March 20, 1816, Guerrero achieved the rank of general. Guerrero stressed that he was doing so only to continue Morelos's cause for the underprivileged classes. Guerrero realized that standard attacks were now impossible, so instead he quickly crossed the Mescala River and began large raids and ambushes in the Acapulco area.

Despite this new strategy, the insurgency weakened. In August 1816 a new viceroy, Juan Ruíz de Apodaca, attempted to stamp out the revolution. He initiated aggressive military campaigns that shattered most of the insurgent forces and even worse, offered generous pardons that enticed many insurgents to quit the cause. In 1816 Guerrero was almost captured, and in March 1817 his fortress at Xonacatlan was besieged and then overrun. Despite numerous appeals to surrender and accept a pardon —one such appeal delivered by Guerrero's father— Guerrero continued to fight. At the battle of Calavera, Guerrero was defeated soundly and lost most of his remaining men and equipment. Until later in 1818, he was forced to avoid any large royalist forces. In September 1818, however, Guerrero defeated several viceregal units and dominated the Balsas Valley. He established his own civil government— modeled after Morelos's previous government led by a junta and a congress. Although it dispersed later in 1819 and Guerrero suffered another severe defeat at Aguazarca on November 5, 1819, he continued to mount significant attacks. By 1820 the situation was a stalemate. The insurgents could no longer threaten important areas of New Spain, but the royalists were unable to destroy the insurgent bases.

When the conservatives and church officials of New Spain finally agreed to create an autonomous government, they backed Agustín de Iturbide's compromise. Meanwhile, the viceroy appointed Iturbide as the commander of the southern royalist forces. On November 16, 1820, Iturbide left Mexico City to crush Guerrero's insurgents. Instead, Guerrero defeated the royalists at Zapotepec on January 2, 1821, and at Cueva del Diablo on January 27, 1821. On January 20, Guerrero had urged Iturbide to support Independence and offered to place himself under Iturbide's command in return for such a pledge. Iturbide realized quickly that he could not destroy the insurgents. Therefore he arranged a meeting with Guerrero and offered the rebels a place in his new, independent government. Guerrero agreed formally to Iturbide's Plan de Iguala on February 24, 1821. The plan protected the lives and property of the Catholic Church and the elites and maintained their privileges under a constitutional monarchy. It also created an Independent Mexico and offered all races civil liberties and abolished the caste system. Although Guerrero objected to some of the plan's details, he accepted it and hoped for improvements. As commander of the first division of Iturbide's army, Guerrero issued a manifesto proclaiming Iturbide's "magnanimous," heroic qualities while emphasizing his subordination to the "Father of the Nation." Insurgent and royalist forces alike joined the cause, and on September 27, 1821, Guerrero marched victoriously into Mexico City with Iturbide.

Iturbide soon alienated Guerrero and his new insurgent allies. He appointed a governing junta of 38—none of whom were insurrectionaries—and they named Iturbide president of the interim regency (which was to rule until the selection of an emperor). Iturbide organized the empire into five districts headed by military officers known as captains general. Guerrero became captain general of the south and received promotion to field marshal. But Iturbide humiliated Guerrero by ordering him to Mexico City so that "El Negro" could carry the imperial insignia in the coronation ceremony. In May 1822, Iturbide persuaded the new Congress to elect him emperor. Later Iturbide dismissed the Congress and imposed forced loans to finance his government. Insurgent leaders began a new insurrection, and on January 5, 1823, Guerrero joined the first phase of the movement that eventually toppled Iturbide. On January 25, 1823, Guerrero was shot in the lungs at the battle of Cerro de Almolonga. His severe wound forced Guerrero to spend the rest of the revolt convalescing. He never fully recovered, and the wound plagued him the rest of his life. The forces arrayed against Iturbide swelled, and on March 19, 1823, Iturbide abdicated in the face of increasing demands that Congress be reestablished. In May, Iturbide left the country.

As Guerrero recuperated from his wound, the imperial system disappeared from Mexico. An executive commission of three was created and alternates were elected. After refusing several offers of military command—due to poor health—Guerrero agreed to accept one of the executive alternate positions. As part of the *poder ejecutivo,* Guerrero proved to be a crucial harmonizer and was instrumental in uniting various factions. In June 1824, a national election was held and Guadalupe Victoria was elected president, Nicolás Bravo was elected vice president, and Guerrero received the third-largest number of votes (thus losing). Guerrero retired from public life and tried to improve his health. Unfortunately, the Victoria administration suffered from a worsening financial situation and the increasingly bitter federalist-versus-centralist conflict. Despite his ill health, Guerrero accepted the position of supreme tribunal of war and marine on May 17, 1827. In August, he

left Mexico City to restore order in Veracruz. Then in December, an antifederalist rebellion demanded the dismissal of the ruling officials. Vice President Bravo and several other generals joined the rebellion. Guerrero was sent to quell the rebellion, and on January 7, 1828 he killed or captured the entire rebel force at Tulancingo. Guerrero returned a hero, but the rebellion heightened tensions as the 1828 elections approached.

Guerrero decided to run for president and at first seemed certain to win. A symbol of resistance to Spanish colonial rule, Guerrero became the nominal leader of the federalists. However, conservative centralists and the Mexican upper class supported General Manuel Gómez Pedraza. The campaign became bitter as newspapers on both sides smeared the opposing candidates. When the elections took place in September, Gómez Pedraza won with eleven states to Guerrero's nine. Gómez Pedraza thus won the presidency and Guerrero the vice presidency. Guerrero's supporters refused to accept the results and raised accusations that the election had been fixed. Guerrero himself refused to accept the vote. The spreading sentiment in favor of rebellion then became reality as Antonio López de Santa Anna and other Guerrero supporters began to revolt. On November 30, a revolt began within Mexico City. The lame-duck Victoria government vacillated and tried to negotiate a compromise. Support for Guerrero intensified, especially after Guerrero publicly joined the revolt. Gómez Pedraza realized that his cause was becoming hopeless; he renounced his election victory and soon left Mexico. Guerrero's supporters marched in victoriously but then lost discipline and looted the Parián market—a visible symbol of Hispanic, elite culture. Although Congress validated Guerrero's subsequent election "victory," the illegality of his triumph and the looting of the Parián market convinced the conservatives and elites that Guerrero could not be trusted.

When Guerrero became president on April 1, 1829, he faced immense problems but his populist approach angered the elites. The government was bankrupt, the economy was in shambles, few sources for further revenues existed, the threat of a Spanish invasion loomed, and Guerrero now had enemies among the upper class, the government, and the army. Furthermore, the end of African slavery, which Guerrero supported and legalized in 1829, angered Anglo settlers in Texas. Guerrero's enforcement of the second Spanish expulsion law on March 20, 1829, further alienated the Hispanic community, while his leniency in issuing exemptions upset the radical nativists. Guerrero supported Secretary of the Treasury Lorenzo de Zavala's efforts to gain revenue, including a graduated income tax and property taxes. Spanish merchants particularly hated Guerrero's attempts at tariff protection when he prohibited imports of all but the most expensive cloth.

When the long-awaited Spanish invasion began in July 1829, Guerrero responded firmly. During a short-lived burst of national unity, Santa Anna gathered military forces and, despite bitter resistance, Congress granted Guerrero special war powers. This was the first of many occasions when presidents would be given such authority. Zavala came under heavy criticism when he enacted forced loans, reductions in pensions and salaries, wide-ranging new taxes, and property confiscations, all to fund the war effort. Mexican forces bottled the Spanish army up in Tampico, and Spanish ineptitude as well as yellow fever forced them to surrender in September 1829.

The Spanish invasion had temporarily breathed new life into Guerrero's regime but the added burdens of war proved to be Guerrero's undoing. In August, the Jalisco legislature called for a northern confederation. Their main grievances included accusations that de Zavala's new taxes encroached upon provincial domains and that Guerrero was misusing his emergency powers. In order to appease the opposition, de Zavala agreed to resign on October 12, 1829. But more of Guerrero's opponents forced many of his supporters out of government. Then in December, officers in charge of a reserve army—created to fight the Spanish invaders—drew up an insurrectionary plan at Jalapa. Vice President Anastasio Bustamante "consented" to lead the rebels. Guerrero resigned voluntarily his war powers and attempted to gain congressional support. When this failed, he personally led an army to quell the revolt. Within a week, the capital fell to the conspirators, who established a new regime. Guerrero's army deserted him, and on December 25, 1829, Guerrero promised to abide by the will of the new government.

The oppressive Bustamante government soon triggered a new revolt. Efforts to centralize power and fear of permanent national army garrisons in the interior but controlled by the central government created most of the unrest. By March 1830, the insurrection had spread to the south, and Guerrero decided to lead the revolt because of the persecution of his indigenous allies and because he suspected that Bustamante had sent assassins to kill him. But in January 1831, General Bravo decisively defeated the rebels near Chilpancingo, and on January 14, Guerrero's supposed friend, Francisco Picaluga, betrayed him by turning Guerrero over to Bustamante's troops. The government court-martialed and executed Guerrero in Oaxaca on February 14, 1831. It is more than likely that the upper class wanted Guerrero shot as a warning to those of mixed blood who aspired to mobilize the masses against the Hispanic social order.

Select Bibliography

Anna, Timothy E., *The Mexican Empire of Iturbide.* Lincoln: University of Nebraska Press, 1990.

Bazant, Jan, "From Independence to the Liberal Republic, 1821–67. In *Mexico Since Independence,* edited by Leslie Bethell. New York: Cambridge University Press, 1991.

Green, Stanley, *The Mexican Republic: The First Decade 1823–32.* Pittsburgh: University of Pittsburgh Press, 1987.

Sims, Harold, *The Expulsion of Mexico's Spaniards, 1821–1836.* Pittsburgh: University of Pittsburgh Press, 1990.

Sprague, William, *Vicente Guerrero, Mexican Liberator: A Study in Patriotism.* Chicago: Donnelley, 1939.

—DOUGLAS W. RICHMOND

H

Hapsburg, Ferdinand Maximilian von

See Maximilian (Ferdinand Maximilian von Hapsburg)

Hidalgo Revolt

The insurrection that Miguel Hidalgo y Costilla sparked on September 16, 1810, marks the beginning of the armed struggle for Mexican Independence. The origins of the Hidalgo Revolt can be found as much in Napoléon Bonaparte's invasion of the Iberian Peninsula as in events in the viceroyalty of New Spain. Nonetheless, one also must look for origins in the long-term processes that began in the mid–eighteenth century.

In the latter half of the eighteenth century, a series of laws were enacted that since have come to be known as the Bourbon Reforms. Although these reforms were designed to improve Spain's administration of its overseas empire, by and large they had a negative impact on New Spain. The criollos (Mexicans of Spanish descent)—or "Americans," as they now preferred to be called—felt that they had been displaced from positions of power and prestige by European Spaniards, or *peninsulares*. Moreover, the local offices of *alcalde mayor* and *corregidor* were replaced with directly appointed intendants more accountable to the viceroy and Spanish Crown but less accountable to the local criollo population. Nonetheless, criollo dissidents tended to support local or regional autonomy, not outright independence. Although many had been exposed to Enlightenment ideals of liberty and republican government, they did not question the system of government imposed in New Spain, only the amount of control the Spanish Crown exercised over it.

If many criollos were alienated by the administrative reforms of the late eighteenth century, *peninsu-lares* were angered by the Consolidación de Bienes Reales of December 26, 1804. An attempt by the Spanish Crown to use colonial revenues to underwrite its political and military adventures in Europe, the Consolidación ordered the sequestration of charitable funds in America and their remission to Spain. As the charitable funds were the basis of an informal system of credit in New Spain, the Consolidación had a severe effect not only on the charitable institutions themselves, but also on the entire financial infrastructure of the viceroyalty. The Consolidación also was seen as an attack on the income of the Catholic Church, and many lower-level clergy were impoverished. Protests from all sectors fell on deaf ears, reinforcing autonomist sentiments.

If the Consolidación created some degree of consensus among the peninsular and criollo elites of New Spain, however, this consensus evaporated with the French invasion of the Iberian Peninsula and the resignation of Fernando VII. In the absence of a legitimate monarch, the *ayuntamiento* (city council) of Mexico City became a mouthpiece for the criollos, promoting autonomist interests and declaring the equality of Spain and its American colonies before the law. In the name of all of New Spain, it proposed a meeting of a "junta of authorities" from Mexico's cities and towns, which would fill the vacuum left by the king's departure and defend the kingdom against the French. As the city council's proposals for all practical intents and purposes would create a legitimate, representative, and autonomist government, the *audiencia* (judicial council) of Mexico opposed the *ayuntamiento*'s proposals, becoming the mouthpiece for those interests (primarily peninsular) that felt threatened by any change from the status quo.

The viceroy of New Spain, José de Iturrigaray, sympathized with the *ayuntamiento*'s proposals, convoking a number of meetings to discuss them. Nonetheless, he was unable to patch together any sort of consensus, and the divisions among New Spain's elites continued to widen. These conflicts reached their climax in a coup d'état orchestrated by the peninsular merchant Gabriel de Yermo on September 15, 1808, with the approval of Spanish authorities. The coup and subsequent imprisonment of the viceroy and principal criollo leaders not only created serious doubts about regimes that followed, but also radicalized both the criollo and peninsular factions; indeed, following the coup the terms "peninsular" and "criollo" or "American" took on an additional political connotation: for or against the colonial regime. Moreover, the coup convinced dissident and autonomist criollos of the necessity of conspiracy—and later of armed force—to achieve their political ends.

In December 1809 Spanish authorities uncovered an autonomist conspiracy in the important urban center of Valladolid de Michoacán (present-day Morelia), in which various members of the militia and the clergy had taken part. The conspirators, who had sent envoys to other cities, proposed a junta or congress composed of delegates of the principal cities of New Spain, which would govern in the name of Fernando VII. In order to bring the junta to power they called for an uprising by key parts of the army and militia as well as by a number of Indian governor and their subjects. Various members of the conspiracy went over to the authorities, and its principal leaders were imprisoned, although they were treated leniently by the current viceroy, the archbishop Francisco Xavier de Lizana y Beaumont.

A second conspiracy grew out of the first, the so-called Conspiracy of Querétaro, which also included officers in the militia and clergy. The conspiracy met under the cover of an Academy of Literature, which was permitted to hold meetings and conferences, and with the support of the *corregidor* of the city of Querétaro, Miguel Domínguez, and his wife, Josefa Ortiz de Domínguez, *"la corregidora."* The conspiracy was able to form cells in various other cities, including Celaya, San Miguel el Grande, and Guanajuato. One of the most active conspirators, Ignacio de Allende, was captain of the Queen's Regiment in San Miguel and had been in contact with the conspirators in Valladolid. As a military man, Allende had formed part of the canton of troops established in Jalapa years before by the deposed viceroy Iturrigaray, and like many of his companions he admired Iturrigaray and was disgusted by the people who had overthrown him. The priest of the nearby village of Dolores, Miguel Hidalgo y Costilla, joined the conspiracy at the behest of Allende and became one of its principal leaders.

When the conspiracy was discovered in September 1810, it still did not have a defined plan. One of the conspirators, Manuel Iturriaga, had proposed to organized revolutionary juntas in the principal cities of New Spain to propagate hatred of the *peninsulares*. The juntas would call for Independence in order to prevent New Spain from falling into the hands of the French and imprison the authorities. The *peninsulares* would be arrested and expelled from New Spain, and their goods would finance the Independence movement. The government would remain in the hands of a junta of representatives of the provinces and would govern in the name of Fernando VII.

When Epigmenio González, one of the conspirators, was arrested, a second plan was discovered. This plan called for the establishment of an empire with feudal kingdoms and elector princes. The lands of the criollos would be rented to the Indians, and the haciendas of the *peninsulares* would be seized and granted to the Indians outright. This plan called for a general insurrection not simply of the criollo militias, but of all the people of New Spain. Various conspirators reported this plan to the authorities, forcing Corregidor Miguel Domínguez to crack down. Nonetheless, his wife was able to pass word to Allende, who was able to alert Hidalgo.

On the morning of Sunday, September 16, Hidalgo issued his famous call to arms against the Spanish colonial regime, the so-called Grito de Dolores. He called the villagers of Dolores to mass and informed them of his decision to launch an insurrection to prevent the *peninsulares* from turning New Spain over to the French; the Spanish authorities and peninsular population of Dolores was thrown in prison. Hidalgo's forces included elements from the Queen's Regiment, prisoners who had been liberated from the town jail, and many inhabitants of the region around Dolores. Although the rhetoric of the leaders of the movement was basically the same as that of other criollo autonomists, Hidalgo's movement also sought to unite peasants and workers around such basic issues as land tenure and working conditions, and it sought redress for grievances dating back to the Conquest.

The insurgent movement found broad support among the inhabitants of the prosperous Bajío region of north-central Mexico, a densely populated region where the traditional separation of Indians and Spanish had begun to break down. In the early stage of Hidalgo's revolt the bulk of his troops were composed, on the one hand, of hacienda workers, who formed a cavalry unit under the direction of their foremen; on the other hand were Indians who grouped themselves into an improvised infantry with their bows and arrows, lances, and spears. Relatively few soldiers from the militia accompanied Hidalgo's insurgent army. The army was followed by a large number of women and children with very few arms and little discipline.

After sacking a few stores in Dolores, the insurgents made their way to Atotonilco, where they adopted for their flag the image of the Virgin of Guadalupe, the Indian virgin so deeply venerated by criollos. They entered San Miguel el Grande and Celaya without resistance, and there they were able to find additional support for their forces. In Celaya some degree of organization was imposed on the inchoate insurgent army, and Hidalgo was named "General of America;" Allende also was named general.

On September 28 the insurgents won their first victory over Spanish forces in Guanajuato, the center of silver production in New Spain and the richest city in the viceroyalty. Guanajuato was attacked by nearly 50,000 insurgents and taken after a prolonged and bloody battle. Commanded by the intendant Juan Antonio Riaño, the meager Spanish forces and the *peninsulares* who remained in Guanajuato took refuge with their families in the Granaditas granary, leaving the city at the mercy of the attackers. The local population felt abandoned by the local authorities; taking the side of the insurgents, they helped them sack the granary and massacre of its defenders. The insurgents and the local population then proceeded to sack the city.

The violence of the insurgent forces in the sack of Guanajuato provoked the Spanish regime and its partisans to conduct a war without quarter. Viceroy Francisco Xavier de Venegas, who had arrived from Spain only a few days before the insurrection erupted, took personal charge of counterinsurgency operations. Venegas was a skilled military commander, having participated in the Peninsular Wars against the French, but he also was a skilled politician, winning the support of the high clergy. The bishop elect of Michoacán, Manuel Abad y Queipo, excommunicated Hidalgo and his companions for sacrilege and disturbing the peace, and he prohibited under pain of excommunication that anyone help them; Abad y Queipo's decree later was ratified by the archbishop of Mexico, Francisco Xavier de Lizana y Beaumont. Throughout Mexico priests who were sympathetic to the colonial regime denounced Hidalgo's movement from the pulpit. The press of New Spain, which was completely under the control of colonial authorities, published a veritable flood of material attacking the insurrection. Venegas offered 10,000 pesos for the heads of the principal revolutionary leaders, and throughout the viceroyalty colonial authorities condemned the revolt and threatened the rebels and their supporters with the most severe punishments.

After the taking of Guanajuato the war radicalized. Not only did Europeans abandon towns threatened by the insurrection, but many autonomist criollos allied themselves with the colonial regime, as the insurgents did not always clearly distinguish between criollos and *peninsulares*. If the insurgents had lost much of their elite support, however, they also had gained important resources: men, matériel, and funds. Concerned about the violence their movement had unleashed, the insurgent leaders organized a government in Guanajuato. They also established a mint and a forge for cannon, and they managed to organize their numerous and undisciplined troops.

From Guanajuato the insurgents proceeded to Valladolid, reorganizing the government of the intendancy of Michoacán. Determined to take the capital of the viceroyalty, they proceeded first to Acámbaro, where Hidalgo, in addition to being designated commander-in-chief, named a minister of police and "good order," José María Chico. On the Monte de las Cruces, near the city of Mexico, the insurgents defeated royalist troops under Torcuato Trujillo, but at a very high cost. The rebels remained camped outside Mexico City for three days, demanding that Venegas surrender. They received no answer, however, and over Allende's protests, Hidalgo decided to withdraw to Querétaro without attacking Mexico City.

Hidalgo's decision to fall back was based on a number of factors: lack of munitions, meager support in the central part of the country, and fear of the royalist troops under Félix María Calleja del Rey and Manuel de Flon, which were already close on the insurgents' heels. On November 7 the insurgents suffered a major defeat with great loss of men and matériel. Hidalgo retreated to Valladolid, while Allende returned to Guanajuato to organize its defense.

Meanwhile the conflict had spread to other parts of the viceroyalty, carried both by Hidalgo's own envoys and local leaders, particularly members of the lower clergy. Friar Luis de Herrera launched a rebellion in San Luis Potosí, while José Antonio "El Amo" Torres took Guadalajara. Torres linked up with José María Mercado, who organized the revolutionary movement in Nayarit, taking Tepic and San Blas. Ignacio Jiménez occupied Saltillo, and Texas remained in the hands of Juan Bautista Casas. José María Morelos, who had spoken with Hidalgo in Charo and Indaparapeo, ably fulfilled his commission to launch a rebellion in the southern part of the viceroyalty and take Acapulco.

Nonetheless, the royalists began to recover the cities and towns that had been taken by the insurgents. Guanajuato fell on November 25. Hidalgo

retreated to Guadalajara, where the insurgent movement had become quite strong, and united with
Allende, attempting to reorganize his movement politically and militarily. Chico was named minister of
"mercy and justice" and president of the *audiencia*.
Ignacio López Rayón, who had been his personal secretary, was named secretary of state, and Hidalgo's
brother Mariano was named treasurer. Hoping to
obtain recognition and aid from the United States,
Hidalgo named Pascasio Ortíz ambassador to the
United States. Hidalgo also addressed many of the
land and labor issues foremost on the minds of his
followers, abolishing slavery and community chests
(which had required ever-increasing contributions
from the inhabitants of communal villages), and
established that communal lands were inalienable
and for the exclusive use of indigenous villagers.
Hidalgo's movement also gained use of a printing
press, which they used to publish proclamations and
a few editions of the first insurgent newspaper in
Mexico, *El despertador americano*. Finally, Hidalgo
attempted to impose some degree of order and discipline on the recruits he had been able to add to his
force in Guadalajara.

Hidalgo was unable to consolidate his movement,
however. He continued to clash with Allende and
ordered the indiscriminate massacre of numerous
Europeans, in most cases without any justification
whatsoever. The insurgent movement was defeated
decisively at Puente de Calderón on January 17,
1811. The insurgent troops, by that time numbering
more than 100,000, left Guadalajara to meet the well
organized, disciplined, and supplied troops of Brigadier José de la Cruz, who had just taken Valladolid.
In a bloody battle the insurgents suffered enormous
losses, and the leaders of the movement fled to the
north, heading first to Aguascalientes and later to
Zacatecas. At the Hacienda del Pabellón, Allende
replaced Hidalgo as commander-in-chief, and in a
meeting in Saltillo it was decided that the principal
leaders of the insurgent movement should go to the
United States to seek help, leaving Ignacio Rayón as
the head of the movement in New Spain. On March
21, 1811, Hidalgo, Allende, and their companions
were captured in Acatita de Baján by a former insurgent leader, Ignacio Elizondo. They were taken to
Monclava and then to Chihuahua, where they were
tried and condemned to death. Allende, Aldama, and
Jiménez were shot on July 26, and Hidalgo was
defrocked on July 29 and executed the following day.
Their heads were placed on the four corners of the
granary of Granaditas.

The death of the first insurgent leaders marked the
end of the first stage of the Wars of Independence.

The armed struggle against the colonial regime would
be conducted in a more systematic and organized
fashion by Rayón and Morelos. The insurgent cause
also would be pursued, in many cases without the
least order or coordination, by innumerable smaller
groups who often only were seeking redress for local
grievances. The movement begun by Hidalgo never
did achieve independence, and even once Independence was achieved Hidalgo's specific proposals were
not accepted. Nonetheless, the Hidalgo Revolt helped
make eventual Independence a certainty.

Select Bibliography

Anna, Timothy, "The Independence of Mexico and
    Central America." In *The Independence of Latin
    America,* edited by Leslie Bethell. Cambridge and New
    York: Cambridge University Press, 1987.
Farriss, Nancy M., *Crown and Clergy in Colonial
    Mexico, 1759–1821: The Crisis of Ecclesiastical
    Privelege.* London: Athlone, 1968.
Flores Caballero, Romeo, *Counter-revolution: The Role of
    the Spaniards in the Independence of Mexico, 1804–38,*
    tranlated by Jaime E. Rodríguez O. Lincoln and
    London: University of Nebraska Press, 1974.
Hamill, Hugh M., Jr., *The Hidalgo Revolt: Prelude to
    Mexican Independence.* Westport, Connecticut:
    Greenwood, 1981.
Hamnett, Brian R., *Roots of Insurgency: Mexican
    Regions, 1750–1824.* New York and Cambridge:
    Cambridge University Press, 1986.
Lynch, John, *The Spanish American Revolutions,
    1808–1826.* 2nd edition, New York and London:
    Norton, 1986

— VIRGINIA GUEDEA

Hidalgo y Costilla, Miguel 1753–1811

Priest and Leader of the Independence Movement

Miguel Hidalgo y Costilla, the "father of his
country," was descended from an old criollo family.
He was born on May 8, 1753, in the hacienda of
Corralejo in the jurisdiction of Pénjamo,
Guanajuato, where his father worked as an administrator. He was the second of five children from the
marriage of Cristóbal Hidalgo y Costilla and Ana
María Gallaga Mandarte y Villaseñor. Intelligent and
interested in learning, for which he could count on
the support of his father, for many years Hidalgo
was able to enjoy the possibility of satisfying his
intellectual curiosity and the advantages of a high
level of education. Together with his older brother
José Joaquín, he studied Latin grammar and rhetoric

in the Jesuit College of San Francisco Xavier of Valladolid, Michoacán (today the city of Morelia).

In 1767, the year the Jesuits were expelled from Spanish dominions, he moved to the College of San Nicolás Obispo in the same city, one of the most important educational centers of the viceroyalty, distinguishing himself in courses on philosophy, theology, and the liberal arts. In 1770 he gained his baccalaureate in arts and three years later a baccalaureate in theology from the Real y Pontifica Universidad de México, the most important institution of higher education in New Spain. He decided on a career in the church, receiving four minor orders in 1774; the following year he was made a subdeacon. In 1776 he was ordained as deacon and as priest in 1778.

Hidalgo taught philosophy, theology, Latin grammar, and arts in the College of San Nicolás, where he was nicknamed "the Fox" by both fellow teachers and pupils. Interested in education, he was concerned with revising teaching methods. In 1785 in his capacity as professor in scholastic theology, he won a competition organized by the dean of Valladolid Cathedral in which he showed evidence of his reformist enthusiasm. He was appointed treasurer of the College of San Nicolás Obispo in 1787, its secretary a year later, and rector in 1790. By this time he was also owner of three haciendas: Santa Rosa, San Nicolás, and Jaripeo. In 1792 the ecclesiastical authorities decided to banish him from Valladolid because of the enmity he had stirred up in the college, particularly on account of his keenness for innovative teaching practices, but also for his irregular handling of some funds, his passion for gambling, and the fact that he had two children, Agustina and Lino Mariano, with Manuela Ramos Pichardo. In 1789 another child of his, Joaquín, was born to Bibiana Lucero.

Hidalgo thus abandoned his studious way of life to take up a career as a minister of the church. His new activities allowed him to both practice and develop his sense of social justice while continuing to cultivate his intellectual interests and social activities. The bishop first sent him to serve as interim curate in Colima, where he bought a house that on his departure for San Felipe de los Herreros, or Torres Mochas, in 1793 he gifted to the city hall in order to establish a public school. Apart from attending to his new parish, Hidalgo organized some social and cultural events, including literary and gambling evenings in his house and, the result of his interest in music, dances. He translated and interpreted, among other works, Molière's *Tartuffe*. During this time Hidalgo was reading historical and theological

works as well as volumes on political economy and literature; by this time his library was large and well stocked. As a result of these cultural and social activities and his enlightened attitudes, but most of all because of his way of treating everyone as his equal, Hidalgo's house became known as "Little France." By this stage he had two daughters, Micaela and Josefa, with Josefa Quintana, who acted in the theatrical works that Hidalgo directed. The royal directive on consolidation of royal promissory notes, which seriously affected the credit system in New Spain, proved problematic for Hidalgo, who already owed money on his haciendas.

In 1807 he was denounced for the first time by the Tribunal of the Inquisition for speaking against Catholic orthodoxy and the monarchical government, but no proceedings were taken against him. A year later similar charges were made against him by Manuela Herrera, a one-time lover, and in 1809 Father Diego Miguel Bringas denounced him for possessing prohibited books, but nothing came of these indictments either. In 1803 Hidalgo took over the curacy of Dolores Hidalgo on the death of his eldest brother, Joaquín, the former incumbent. There he concerned himself more with promoting agriculture and industry than the spiritual administration of his congregation. This task was relegated to the priest Francisco Iglesias. Hidalgo encouraged viticulture (which was controlled and indeed prohibited by the authorities to protect the wine trade of Spain), the cultivation of silkworms, and apiculture. He also established a ceramics factory, another for brick making, and various workshops as well as tanks to cure skins. His progressive and innovative approach, his sense of social justice, and his openhandedness with money won him the favor of a large number of his congregation. Keen on music, he started a small orchestra. The curate also held salons at home, where themes of cultural and political interest were discussed. An avid reader, Hidalgo knew Latin, Italian, French, and several indigenous languages. A man of the Enlightenment, as were many of his colleagues, he was a friend of some of the outstanding individuals of his time who shared his enlightened attitudes: men such as the bishop-elect of Michoacán, Manuel Abad y Queipo; Doctor Antonio Labarrieta; José Antonio Rojas; and the intendant of Guanajuato, Juan Antonio Riaño. He also knew the French general Octaviano D'Almivar, sent by Napoléon Bonaparte and imprisoned by the Spanish authorities in Nacogdoches, who passed through Dolores en route for Mexico City.

After a conspiracy was uncovered in December 1809 in Valladolid that attempted to establish a governing junta in New Spain in the name of Fernando VII by force of arms, some of the conspirators moved to Querétaro. There they held meetings under the cover of a literary academy, relying on the support of the *corregidor* (mayor by royal appointment) of the city, Miguel Domínguez, and his wife Josefa Ortíz de Domínguez. Although their plans never were defined clearly, the conspirators had projected a popular uprising in various areas for the purpose of arresting peninsular Spaniards (those born in Europe), whose property would help them to finance the movement. They also discussed the formation of a governing junta to rule in the name of Fernando VII. Hidalgo joined the plot through his friendship with Ignacio Allende, a captain in the regiment of Dragoons of New Spain. As well as attending some of the reunions of the conspirators in Querétaro and San Miguel el Grande, Hidalgo started to find others of the same persuasion and manufacture lances in Dolores and the hacienda of Santa Barbara. This plot also was denounced to the colonial authorities, and Corregidor Domínguez was obliged to imprison various of the conspirators. Warned by Josefa Ortiz, Allende went to Dolores to discuss with Hidalgo what decision to take.

When Juan de Aldama arrived at dawn on September 16, 1810, Hidalgo decided to enter the armed struggle against the colonial authorities. He freed the prisoners, armed them, and secured the support of part of the regiment quartered in Dolores. In his celebration of the mass held later that day, he incited those attending to join his uprising against the colonial regime. The *grito* or "shout" (the word for a call to arms) given by Hidalgo included *vivas* for America and death to bad government. He then imprisoned the subdelegate and the *peninsulares* of the town, and the insurgents sacked some European shops.

In his appeal to and securing of the support of the masses, Hidalgo brought together two very different movements that were largely contradictory. On one side were the urban criollos (those of Spanish descent born in the Americas), who sought greater participation in decision making; on the other side were the *campesino* (peasant) groups and workers, who sought to improve their work conditions. In Atonilco, Hidalgo took an image of the Virgin of Guadalupe, the most venerated in colonial Mexico, and converted it into the flag of the revolt.

Even though he was joined by some troops, such as the regiment in San Miguel el Grande, Hidalgo's forces were badly armed and even less disciplined. On September 19, having entered Celaya without

resistance, Hidalgo was named General of America and Allende Lieutenant General. The insurgents went on to attack and capture the wealthy city of Guanajuato on September 28 after the bloody combat of the Alhondiga de Granaditas, the city granary where the Intendant Riaño and the *peninsulares* had taken refuge. Hidalgo managed to stop the sacking of Guanajuato and the murder of Europeans, and he organized the government of the city, appointing various authorities. He also established a mint and a cannon foundry and attempted to marshal his disorganized troops. The violence of the capture of Guanajuato provoked the colonial government to organize a equally violent counterinsurgency. Thus a war without quarter was declared, in which not only weapons of war but also sermons and the press played important roles. This brutality also prevented many who supported Independence or were discontented with the regime from backing the insurgents, fearful of the disorder and violence that accompanied the movement.

The bishop-elect of Michoacán excommunicated Hidalgo and his followers, an edict that was ratified by the archbishop of Mexico City, Francisco Xavier de Lizana y Beaumont. The Tribunal of the Inquisition reopened the case against Hidalgo, and the Council of the University asked (without success, since Hidalgo had not taken his doctorate) for his name to be removed from the list of those so honored. Viceroy Francisco Xavier Venegas offered a handsome bounty for the head of each of the leading insurgents. A number of aggressive propaganda pieces were written against the movement.

Hidalgo himself decided to move from Guanajuato to Valladolid. En route men continued to flock to his army, including some corps of militia. As they drew close to their objective, the Europeans left the city, and Valladolid was handed over to Hidalgo's army without a fight. Hidalgo took advantage of his stay in the city to regroup his troops, which were increased by some colonial troops, and organize the political control of the Intendency of Michoacán. He also responded to the edict of the Inquisition with his own manifesto. Hidalgo marched on to Mexico City. In Acámbaro he was nominated commander in chief. Here he appointed José María Chico as minister of police and public order. On the march through Michoacán two individuals joined the movement who would be key to the revolt in its second stage: Ignacio López Rayón, who would shortly become Hidalgo's personal secretary, joined in Maravatío; the curate José María Morelos y Pavón, interviewed by Hidalgo in Charo and Indaparapeo, was put in charge of inciting the south to take up arms and capturing the port of Acapulco.

On October 30 at the Monte de las Cruces, on the road between Toluca and Mexico City, the insurgents confronted the royalist militia led by Torquato Trujillo. The latter were defeated but at a great loss of life. From Cuajimalpa, in sight of the capital, Hidalgo demanded the surrender of Viceroy Venegas, but received no response. He could not decide whether or not to march on Mexico City despite the favorable response of Allende. They lacked munitions, had little support in the region, and the royalist forces of Brigadier Félix María Calleja del Rey and the intendant of Puebla, Manuel de Flon, Conde de la Cadena, were drawing closer. The insurgents fell back to Querétaro and began to desert. They met up with Calleja's army in San Jerónimo Aculco and were soundly defeated on November 7, losing a large number of troops on the battlefield and through the taking of prisoners and desertion; equipment and military supplies also were lost. Allende marched to Guanajuato to put the city on defense alert, and Hidalgo went to Valladolid.

Despite these setbacks, the revolt began to gather more adherents and take hold in various areas of the New Spain, largely owing to the forces deployed by various of Hidalgo's agents, such as in New Galicia. As a result, he decided to move on to Guadalajara, which had been taken by José Antonio "The Master" Torres, where he was received with every honor. Here the disagreements that had for various reasons emerged between the two leaders of the movement became clear. Allende wanted Hidalgo to defend Guanajuato; the city was subsequently lost on November 25. He also showed his disgust at the maladministration and disorder, the lack of precision in formulating the objectives of the movement, and the lack of discipline among the troops.

Hidalgo tried to establish a government in Guadalajara and nominated two ministers, Rayón as secretary of state and Chico as minister of justice and president of the Audiencia. He also appointed various other functionaries, including his brother Mariano as treasurer and Pascasio Ortiz de Letona as ambassador to the United States to secure the support and recognition of that country. On the other hand, he dictated important decrees, such as the abolition of slavery, tribute, and state monopolies, and he established the communal lands of the Indians as being for their own exclusive use.

In control of a printing press, Hidalgo published various documents, including proclamations and edicts and the manifesto against the Inquisition that he had written in Valladolid. He was acting as representative of the nation that had elected him to defend its rights. He founded the newspaper *El Despertador Americano*, which published several issues at the same time that he was also marshaling and organizing troops. Nevertheless, he committed various excesses such as surrounding himself with a guard of honor and giving himself the titles of Excellency and Serene Highness. He also ordered the indiscriminate killing of numerous European prisoners. When Calleja drew close to Guadalajara, the insurgent forces, by this time numbering some 100,000 men led by Hidalgo and Allende, marched out of the city to do battle only to be defeated at the Calderón Bridge after a bloody contest on January 17, 1811.

This action marked the beginning of the end of the movement. The rebel army disbanded, and Hidalgo was obliged to retire. He traveled to Aguascalientes toward Zacatecas, and in the hacienda of Pabellón he was divested of his post of commander in chief. In a meeting held in El Saltillo, it was agreed that the main leaders would travel to the United States to seek help while Rayón stayed at the head of the movement in New Spain. Hidalgo, Allende, and his companions were taken prisoner on March 21, in Acatita de Baján by an ex-insurgent, Ignacio Elizondo. Hidalgo was taken to Monclova and from there to Chihuahua, where he instructed the administrator of the post office in Zacatecas, Angel Abella, to plead his case. The legal process was carried out by the military and the church, and Hidalgo was condemned to be executed by a firing squad. During this time Hidalgo showed evidence of repentance for some of his acts and dictated a manifesto in which he condemned the excesses of the movement. This document was later published by the colonial authorities. Defrocked on July 29, he was shot the following day. His head and those of Ignacio Allende, Juan Aldama, and José Mariano Jiménez were set up on the four corners of the Alhondiga de Granaditas.

Select Bibliography

Anna, Timothy, "The Independence of Mexico and Central America." In *The Independence of Latin America,* edited by Leslie Bethell. Cambridge and New York: Cambridge University Press, 1987.

Farriss, Nancy M., *Crown and Clergy in Colonial Mexico, 1759–1821: The Crisis of Ecclesiastical Privelege*. London: Athlone, 1968.

Flores Caballero, Romeo, *Counter-revolution: The Role of the Spaniards in the Independence of Mexico, 1804–38,* tranlated by Jaime E. Rodríguez O. Lincoln and London: University of Nebraska Press, 1974.

Hamill, Hugh M., Jr., *The Hidalgo Revolt: Prelude to Mexican Independence*. Westport, Connecticut: Greenwood, 1981.

Hamnett, Brian R., *Roots of Insurgency: Mexican Regions, 1750–1824*. New York and Cambridge: Cambridge University Press, 1986.

Lynch, John, *The Spanish American Revolutions, 1808–1826*. 2nd edition, New York and London: Norton, 1986.

—VIRGINIA GUEDEA

Huerta, Victoriano 1854–1916

General and President

Despite recent attempts to portray Victoriano Huerta as a reformer, there is little question that he was a self-serving dictator. Huerta had little in common with the rebels who sought either reform or revolution during the civil war years of 1910 to 1920.

Victoriano Huerta's background soon brought him into prominence as a military figure. Born in a small Jalisco village in 1854, Huerta's mestizo father and indigenous mother provided him only a rudimentary education. When a federal general passed through his community, however, Huerta took up with the soldier and became his personal secretary; ultimately, Huerta's patron obtained his admittance into the Colegio Militar. Huerta became commissioned as an officer in 1877, upon his graduation from the corps of engineers.

Huerta soon demonstrated his skills as a military commander. Huerta participated in the Tepic and Sinaloa pacification campaigns from 1878 to 1879. Then he helped organize the general staff by supervising geographic studies in Puebla and Jalapa for nine years as part of a plan to prepare a new military map of Mexico. Huerta's cartographic work carried him to nearly every state until his recall to permanent membership on the General Staff in 1890.

It soon became clear that Huerta excelled in ruthlessly crushing domestic opposition. In October 1893, the dictator Porfirio Díaz sent Huerta to snuff out a revolt in Guerrero. Huerta executed several rebels despite an amnesty. After more cartographic and staff work, Huerta fought Yaqui rebels in Sonora and then fought in the Yucatán campaign of 1900. During the defeat of the Maya, Huerta devised fairly successful antiguerrilla tactics. He was promoted to general in 1901.

As the Porfiriato came to a close in the early years of the new century, Huerta supported Bernardo Reyes. Huerta particularly was grateful when Reyes recommended that Huerta be appointed undersecretary of war. But the Científicos (prominent advisers to Díaz) stopped Huerta's nomination. Angry, Huerta obtained an indefinite leave of absence and worked as an engineer in Monterrey, where Reyes again had assumed the state governorship.

Despite his anger with the Científicos, Huerta had no intention of supporting the insurrection of Francisco I. Madero in 1910. The uprising led Huerta to apply for active military duty. The federal army welcomed Huerta back, issuing him orders to fight in Morelos. In April 1911, he prepared to defend Cuernavaca before being recalled to Mexico City. There, he and other officers consulted with Díaz on the president's decision to resign on May 25, 1911. Díaz feared an attack might be made on his life as he departed for Europe; therefore, Huerta commanded the railroad convoy that escorted the dictator to Veracruz.

Following Díaz's departure, Provisional President Francisco León de la Barra sent Huerta to Morelos in order to speed the demobilization of the 2,500 troops under the command of Emiliano Zapata. Huerta arrived on August 10, 1911; the following day, Zapatistas ambushed his troops. Huerta became frustrated when Zapata demanded the federal troops be withdrawn despite the government's demands that Huerta maintain order. Huerta overreacted several times and pursued Zapatista forces unsuccessfully.

After Madero's electoral victory, the new president ordered Huerta removed from the army because the general supported the ambitions of Madero's political rival, Bernardo Reyes. Huerta fought back but remained inactive as revolts erupted against Madero. When Reyes attempted to revolt, Huerta had no troops under his command and thus could offer no assistance. But when another of Madero's political rivals, Pascual Orozco, revolted in March 1912, the Madero cabinet convinced a reluctant president to allow Huerta to lead government forces against the rebels. Huerta triumphed at the Second Battle of Rellano on May 23, 1912. Orozco retreated, but Madero recalled Huerta to Mexico City, where his prestige among conservatives soared.

But Huerta also attempted to execute Francisco "Pancho" Villa—who had been fighting under his command—for the alleged theft of an expensive Arabian mare after its owner complained to Huerta after the Rellano triumph. Only the intervention of Madero's brothers prevented Villa from being shot, which helps explain Villa's long loyalty to Madero and his passionate hatred of Huerta.

It was only a matter of time before Huerta moved against Madero. Although he agreed that Madero should resign, Huerta initially refused to join the conspiracy led by Félix Díaz (nephew of Porfirio) and Bernardo Reyes; nevertheless, Huerta did not tell Madero about the fatal plot being planned against his presidency. When the revolt finally broke, Madero named Huerta interim commander of loyal troops. Huerta's sympathies lay with the Felicistas, but he wanted a commanding position in a new regime. Therefore, a military stalemate resulted from Huerta's discussions with Félix Díaz about what to do after the fall of Madero. Once the Mexican Senate and U.S. ambassador Henry Lane Wilson favored Madero's resignation, Huerta's forces arrested Madero, and Félix Díaz agreed that Huerta should be provisional president.

Initially, Félix Díaz did not approve of Huerta's appointing himself chief executive on February 18, 1913 (before Madero had had a chance to resign). But Henry Lane Wilson brokered a compromise so that Huerta became provisional president with a Felicista cabinet. It was understood that Huerta then would support Félix Díaz in upcoming elections. Madero and his vice president, José María Pino Suárez, resigned on February 19; according to the 1857 Constitution, the minister of foreign relations, Pedro Lascuráin, now was supposed to assume the presidency. Lascuráin performed only one act as chief executive; he appointed Huerta as minister of the interior, next in line for the presidency, and then resigned. By this maneuver, Huerta became interim president in a technically legal sense. Fearing the presence of Huerta's troops, Congress accepted this charade as the archbishop of Mexico offered a Te Deum.

Huerta's role in the death of Madero remains controversial. At one point, Huerta intended to send Madero out of the country but learned that an attempt would be made to free him. Therefore, he jailed Madero in the National Palace and requested the advice of Henry Lane Wilson, a key supporter. Wilson simply advised Huerta to do "what was best for the peace of the country." Madero and Pino Suárez were executed on the night of February 22, 1913, the day after a Huerta cabinet meeting; circumstantial evidence strongly indicates Huerta's guilt in planning the murders.

The new president received strong backing from foreign diplomats and their governments. Wilson introduced Huerta to his colleagues as "the savior of Mexico" and ordered all U.S. consuls to do everything possible to aid the Huerta regime. Eager for Mexican oil to fuel their new petroleum-powered navy, the British extended recognition to Huerta, and other Europeans followed suit. Meanwhile, Huerta gradually began a process of dismissing Felicista cabinet members as he consolidated power.

Huerta's seizure of power convinced Venustiano Carranza, the governor of Coahuila and a former supporter of Madero, to revolt. He became the first governor to reject Huerta's February 18 circular telegram, a message declaring that the Senate had authorized Huerta to assume executive authority. Carranza disputed the legality of Huerta's status; on February 19, Carranza called upon all of Mexico to join him in armed revolt against Huerta.

Its narrow political focus limited the early phase of Carranza's movement. His followers called themselves Constitutionalists because their general concern became defeating Huerta and holding new elections. Despite his record as a proven reformer, Carranza's Plan de Guadalupe said little about social or economic reform. Initially, Carranza insisted upon unconditional victory, but the federal army soon forced him to retreat from Coahuila. After a 79-day horseback journey, a bedraggled Carranza arrived in Sonora while Pancho Villa, Álvaro Obregón, Jesús Carranza, and Pablo González battled Huerta's offensive. These leaders offered a much more reform-oriented, populist brand of Revolution, and the uprising soon drew widespread support.

Huerta's war measures were extensive. War on two fronts weakened Huerta, who had to send troops to Morelos after Zapata rejected the dictator's offer to become governor. Zapata's peasant army became a formidable opponent because the Zapatistas distributed land wherever they operated. Furthermore, revolts erupted in 13 other states as civil war coincided with increased social revolution. Huerta generally responded with military reflexes. He quickly dismissed Maderista governors and convinced Pascual Orozco to serve in the *rurales* (the rural military police force). Huerta declared that he would win at whatever cost, and his federal army campaigned ruthlessly. Huerta also tried to militarize society. Nearly everyone had to wear a uniform as thousands were drafted. Schools provided military instruction, and war production increased. Although the army numbered 200,000, many of these troops deserted at first opportunity. Defeats in Chihuahua by the fall of 1913 made Huerta's situation quite serious.

By now, U.S. president Woodrow Wilson had grown vehemently opposed to the Huerta regime and was determined to topple the dictator one way or the other. President Wilson dismissed Ambassador Henry Lane Wilson (no relation) and sent a series of emissaries to obtain Huerta's resignation. John Lind, a Minnesota governor who knew little about Mexico, became the first envoy. In August 1913, Lind demanded an armistice, free elections, and that Huerta not be a presidential candidate. Huerta became angered even more when Lind offered him a loan to stay out of the election. Once Huerta publicized the notes of the "peace" mission, Wilson temporarily backed the Catholic Party to succeed Huerta. Wilson's attempt to ally with the Constitutionalists also collapsed. By clamping an arms embargo upon the Huerta regime, Wilson sought sympathy from Carranza. But Carranza refused to accept Wilson's proposal for armed U.S. intervention on a joint basis and for northern Mexico to separate itself from the rest of the country. Although lifting the embargo in February 1914 enabled the Constitutionalists to unleash a spring offensive, Carranza decided to win with minimal foreign aid.

Meanwhile, Huerta's European foreign policy failed as well. Huerta had decided to maintain the Porfirian policy of supporting European capital to provide a check against U.S. investments. Initially, his approach appeared successful. In return for favored treatment, the Europeans quickly extended diplomatic relations. In order to improve their position in Mexican oil fields, the British opposed Woodrow Wilson. But when the British admiralty discovered that Mexican oil was of too low a quality for their fleet, British policy began to slacken in its backing for Huerta. As World War I approached, the British needed U.S. support. The Germans initially backed Huerta as strongly as the British, but the German determination to avoid war with the United States made Berlin back off from outright alliance with Huerta as well.

In his domestic policy, Huerta was a ruthless dictator. The government shut down critical newspapers as a vast network of secret agents spied on the population. The Huerta regime is responsible for dozens of assassinations, including those of Deputy Serapio Rendón and Senator Belisario Domínguez. When legislators protested publicly, Huerta closed Congress and marched the lawmakers to jail.

To tighten his grip, Huerta sent former ally Félix Díaz out of the country. Díaz represented the only legal opposition in presidential elections. Even though Huerta did not conduct a political campaign and had promised that he would not be a candidate during the October 1913 elections, the government declared Huerta the winner. His hand-picked deputies and senators also "won."

Generally a conservative restoration, the Huerta regime lasted longer than Madero's partially because the military and landowners knew that they faced the loss of land and the end of the traditional military if the insurgents won. Nevertheless, Huerta was not as reactionary as traditionally portrayed. He tripled petroleum taxes and discussed nationalizing Mexican oil, he modestly increased educational opportunities in a few areas, and he redistributed small amounts of land. It must be noted, of course, that the latter measures took place toward the end of Huerta's tenure, by which point the end of his regime was in sight. Huerta's bloody counterinsurgency already had cost him much of his popular support, and the Constitutionalists effectively controlled most of the country.

The reasons for Huerta's fall are numerous; not the least was the dictator's personality. Although a brave and disciplined soldier, he was given to egotism, stubborn impatience, and temper tantrums. There is no question that he was an alcoholic, and he reportedly smoked marijuana as well. He also was corrupt; he apparently stole 1.5 million pesos during the Orozco campaign, and after he ousted Madero, Huerta stuffed his pockets with 500-peso notes given him by conservative Mexican supporters and U.S. businessmen.

Such a personality would not tolerate independence among subordinates. As a result, Huerta constantly shuffled his cabinet members, leading to great instability in the government. Over his 17 months in power, Huerta used 32 different ministers. To make matters worse, he often met with them in taverns and restaurants, further disrupting any sense of ministerial authority or administrative continuity.

Fiscal problems also weakened Huerta's regime. European banks that controlled Mexican finances became angered when Huerta seized customs revenue committed to previous loans. Printing an excessive supply of paper money that rapidly lost its value, the government operated with a deficit that amounted to 6 million pesos monthly. Fiscal crises resulted when foreign governments called in debts; forced loans added to Mexico's miseries. Meanwhile, the Constitutionalist rebels occupied key production centers, particularly once they defeated the federal army in the cotton-producing region at Torreón on April 2, 1914. The same month, Carrancista troops probed Tampico's defenses in the oil-producing northeast.

In states such as Coahuila, Huertista policy alienated virtually everyone. Heavy taxes upon cattle ranchers reduced the size of herds while the Huertistas seized horses and cattle in exchange for worthless promissory notes. Municipal taxes increased by as much as five time the original assessments. Huerta continually demanded more taxes and diverted these funds to Mexico City instead of local authorities.

After Huerta centralized the Coahuila school system rigidly and withdrew funds, the Coahuila government closed all its schools by May 1914. An increase in vice, repression of civil liberties, and the reintroduction of the hated *jefes políticos* (local political bosses) angered many.

Nor could Huerta prevent U.S. intervention. The pretext that Woodrow Wilson used was the brief detention of a U.S. officer and six sailors by a Huertista garrison during their defense of Tampico on April 9, 1914. The U.S. Navy lodged a strong protest, and the Mexican commander apologized, ordering the arrest of the unfortunate officer. But the U.S. State Department claimed that the whaleboat from which the shore party had arrived flew a U.S. flag. Wilson demanded that the flag be hoisted on the shoreline with the Mexicans obliged to fire a 21-gun salute to it. When Huerta refused to submit to all these demands, Wilson obtained congressional approval to intervene in Mexico.

The intervention—an attack upon Veracruz—is immortalized in Mexico's national memory as one of the ugliest deeds ever inflicted upon the country by its neighbor to the north. When Wilson learned that a large cargo of U.S. armaments purchased by British and French investors would arrive in Veracruz aboard a German vessel from Hamburg, U.S. forces invaded the city on April 21. With no warning, the fleet shelled the port and inflicted many civilian casualties. The cynical Huerta withdrew federal troops, but enraged inhabitants fought U.S. sailors and marines. Young Mexican naval cadets became some of the bravest defenders until literally blown out of their fortifications by point-blank shelling from U.S. naval guns. Many women died in the streets, and U.S. troops executed those suspected of resistance.

Huerta, however, tried to use the tragedy at Veracruz to strengthen his position. Huerta claimed falsely that Spanish war vessels fought for him against the U.S. fleet in Veracruz. Huerta also attempted to induce Carranza to join him in defending the country, but Carranza refused. Despite Carranza's protests, Huerta ordered his governors to convince the public that Villa and Zapata would march on Veracruz. The saddest aspect of Huerta's opportunism is that many citizens flocked to join the federal army in burst of anti-U.S. patriotism only to be sent north to battle the Constitutionalists. Meanwhile, the German vessel that had caught Wilson's attention sailed from Veracruz with its deadly cargo and unloaded the armaments at a southern port.

As domestic opposition to this fiasco mounted in the United States, Wilson agreed to mediation but once again failed when he attempted to use the peace table to impose a government to his liking in Mexico. By this time, however, Huerta could no longer hold out. As the Constitutionalists marched toward Mexico City, they shattered federal units at Zacatecas in June 1914. Huerta resigned on July 15 and sailed to Spain on a German cruiser. There he plotted to return with German aid in conjunction with Orozco. After arriving in the United States, judicial agents arrested Huerta and jailed him in Fort Bliss, Texas. In January 1916, while under the care of a U.S. doctor in El Paso, he passed away, possibly as a result of cirrhosis of the liver.

Select Bibliography

Katz, Friedrich, *The Secret War in Mexico: Europe, the United States and the Mexican Revolution.* Chicago: University of Chicago Press, 1981.

Meyer, Michael C., *Huerta: A Political Portrait.* Lincoln: University of Nebraska Press, 1972.

Richmond, Douglas W., "Factional Political Strife in Coahuila, 1910–1920." *Hispanic American Historical Review* 60 (February 1980).

—DOUGLAS W. RICHMOND

Human Rights

The notion of human rights in Mexico dates back to the colonial period, when a famous polemic between Bartolomé las Casas, then bishop of Chiapas, and the theologian Ginéz de Sepúlveda, over the rights of the vanquished Indians, led to legislation, the Leyes de Indias, granting Indians basic rights deserving of protection by the Spanish Crown.

During the Wars of Independence from Spain, the Constitution of Apatzingán, whose first version was drafted by the insurgent priest José María Morelos y Pavón in 1814, specified in very clear terms that such rights as popular sovereignty and representation, universality of the law, freedom from slavery and torture, and the obligation of Congress to pass laws ensuring just wages and education for the poor were among the fundamental natural rights of the *americanos,* or people of the former colony of New Spain. Upon achieving independence, individual rights were protected by the Constitution of 1824, and this protection expanded in the Constitution of 1857.

The constitutional history of Mexico is linked closely to the notion of human rights, to the point that one of the provisions established by Mexico in the Treaty of Guadalupe Hidalgo of 1848, in which possession of its northern territories was ceded to the victorious United States after the U.S.-Mexican

War, was that slavery not be reinstated in those lands. The Constitution of 1917, the result of the Mexican Revolution, became the first to establish the protection of social rights, two years before the Constitution of the Weimar Republic did the same in Europe.

During the first part of the twentieth century, post-Revolutionary Mexican governments developed a foreign policy consistent with the principles of peace and nonintervention. This facilitated Mexico's adherence to the League of Nations, its endorsement of the United Nations Charter, and, in 1948, its endorsement of the Universal Declaration of Human Rights drafted by the United Nations and its regional counterpart, the American Declaration of Human Rights, by the Organization of American States (OAS). By the mid-1990s, Mexico was a party to 38 binding international human rights treaties and conventions, both of a regional and universal scope, designed to protect the full range of human rights: individual, civil, political, social, economic, and cultural, as well as the rights of minorities. These conventions were, by virtue of Article 133 of the Constitution of 1917, to be incorporated into domestic legal provisions.

However, the profusion of constitutional provisions and international treaties does not mean that human rights have been respected or systematically promoted in Mexico. In fact, there are really very few domestic legal remedies available to ordinary citizens, and rights proclaimed in international treaties rarely have been upheld by Mexican courts. On closer examination, many abuses have even been encouraged by legal practices. Thus, Supreme Court rulings establishing confession as the most valuable source of evidence in criminal proceedings had the perverse effect of endorsing the use of torture of detainees in order to force them to declare their guilt.

Protection of human rights always has been a constitutionally enshrined goal more than a fact in Mexico. The challenges posed by the complex political and economic issues facing the country made the numerous rights embodied in its succeeding constitutions more a desired objective than a reality. Even this tradition had deteriorated by the mid-1990s, however, especially after the entrance of Mexico into a free trading zone with the United States and Canada, formalized in 1993 by the North American Free Trade Agreement (NAFTA). In the process of instituting a free market economy, Mexican governments modified the Constitution and, as a result, curtailed both social and individual rights. Articles 16, 19, and 20 were reformed in 1996, restricting protection of defendants during criminal proceedings. Article 27, which established land rights, was modified in 1992 in order to allow the privatization of *ejido* (communal village) land.

The Struggle for Political Rights in an Authoritarian Regime

The political system, which emerged from the Mexican Revolution and prevailed as of the mid-1990s, has demonstrated an authoritarian and corporativist nature and has fostered a political culture that emphasizes loyalty and obedience to those in power, rather than the assertion of rights. Its political machinery has been characterized by U.S. social scientist Roderic Camp as "secretive, centralized, uninnovative, discontinuous, arbitrary, uncoordinated, and personalistic."

The Mexican political regime has existed in a class by itself for several reasons, not least among them its resilience and durability. Although by no means a democracy, it has been quite successful in adopting several policies associated with democratic governments, such as formally guaranteed civil and political rights as well as regular elections and opposition parties. However, in practice, the regime has institutionalized human rights abuse and protected its perpetrators. This abuse has been exercised through a complex mixture of co-optation and repression of members of opposition movements. The regime has exercised political domination through a high degree of institutionalization and corporativization of the political process. The political system was founded on a strong presidential figure and an official ruling party that "represents" the interests of society through its sectors: workers, peasants, business, and middle classes.

As of 1996, the country suffered from the effects of an intense but uncertain political transition as a result of the emergence of new political actors demanding a democratic political process. From the late 1960s through the mid-1990s, the political regime underwent a protracted and agonizing crisis of legitimacy, resulting in sporadic, but ever more frequent incidents of serious political violence and repression. This process began with the challenge to the regime posed by the students' movement in 1968, which ended in a massacre of demonstrators in the square of Tlatelolco, a few days before the inauguration of the Olympic Games that were held in Mexico City that year.

In 1996, the ruling Partido Revolucionario Institucional (PRI, or Institutional Revolutionary Party), in power since 1929, controlled the majority of both houses in the Federal Congress along with 28 governorships and 84 percent of municipal governments. Political rights consistently have been violated both legally and in practice until very recently and, as of 1996, still had virtually no constitutional protection. As a rule, elections have been neither free nor fair, although beginning in the 1980s, and thanks to intense citizen mobilization, more overt forms of electoral fraud were eliminated in some regions of Mexico, allowing opposition parties to control 4 governorships of a total of 32, and 325 municipalities of a total of 2,395.

Postelectoral strife always has been a major cause of political violence, and more consistently after 1988, when a belligerent opposition took to electoral politics in the hope of defeating the PRI. This strategy partly was successful, but it also resulted in the assassination of several hundred members and supporters of the center-left party, the Partido de la Revolución Democrática (PRD, or Party of the Democratic Revolution), and the harassment and detention of many members of the main opposition party, the right-of-center Partido de Acción Nacional (PAN, or National Action Party).

The tide of violence also caught the PRI when its reformist candidate for the presidential election of 1994, Luis Donaldo Colosio, was assassinated in a campaign rally by hired gunmen and members of a still obscure plot. Months later, José Francisco Ruiz Massieu, PRI general secretary, was shot in his automobile after leaving a meeting with elected members of Congress. Prominent members of the government of Carlos Salinas de Gortari, including the president's brother, Raúl Salinas, have been implicated in both crimes, although the investigations still are inconclusive.

The period between 1988 and 1994 was marked by the emergence of a vocal and highly organized civil society that took it upon itself to ensure free and fair elections, as well as the full protection of political rights. Hundreds of social and civil organizations joined in the effort to monitor local and federal elections and to report on the numerous irregularities and fraudulent practices that they registered. By the time of the presidential election in 1994, these organizations had acquired considerable expertise as well as international standing, which enabled them to observe the election closely. There is a general consensus that Ernesto Zedillo Ponce de León, who replaced PRI candidate Colosio, was elected in a relatively clean contest in August of 1994. The election was monitored closely by more than 10,000 national and international observers organized by several civic organizations. Alianza Cívica, the most important coalition of observer organizations, reported that although it was clear that Zedillo was undoubtedly the winner, the election had not been a fair competition, since the PRI candidate had a virtual monopoly of the media and many times more resources than the other candidates. Upon taking office, President Zedillo promised a definitive electoral reform that would, once and for all, put an end to conflict and uncertainty.

Social, Economic, and Cultural Rights

The struggle with issues of inequality has defined Mexican political history. This state of affairs led to a social revolution and the reiteration of social justice as the basis of legitimacy of government, proclaimed in the Constitution of 1917. However, the country never has been able to reach its goal of social justice.

For the three decades following World War II, Mexico enjoyed high economic growth and broad-based development giving rise to an extensive middle class, a new industrial working class with steadily rising wage levels, and a rural sector that also increased its income thanks to the opening of new lands, rising productivity, and government-sponsored irrigation projects.

This inward looking, state-led model of development did not mean that income was being distributed evenly, however. Tripartite negotiations under the auspices of PRI labor and peasant organizations, business, and government ensured that a portion of this expanding national wealth trickled down to the lower reaches of society. An aggressive extension of medical and educational services by the government during this period of "stabilizing development" provided the illusion that welfare and social mobility were on the increase. Nevertheless, Mexico never was able to break the pattern of highly skewed income distribution.

The facade began to crumble in the 1970s, when the development model openly began to show its flaws. In 1982, Mexico suffered a severe economic crisis caused by a spiraling foreign debt and the fall of oil prices (its main export) in the international market. The economy under the government of President José López Portillo (1976–82) had been borrowing heavily from foreign banks to finance the rapid development of the nationalized oil industry. In actual fact, very little of this money actually was used in productive investments; according to James Henry, "billions were squandered on noncompetitive steel plants, a $6 billion nuclear plant that still doesn't function, a gas pipeline to nowhere, wasteful development loans, arms and payoffs to contractors and public officials."

In August 1982, the Mexican government announced that it could not meet its debt payments for lack of foreign reserves. The international banking community and the U.S. Treasury came to the rescue with fresh money. Payments were stretched out and new loans were written with the result that Mexico became socially and economically dominated by the debt problem. In order to face the monumental payments on the debt, severe austerity measures recommended by the International Monetary Fund (IMF) and the World Bank were adopted. Thus, wages were slashed, government services and subsidies cut drastically, state-owned industry privatized, and inflation restricted at the cost of higher taxes and interest rates and less credit. The impact of this recovery program preserved the stability of the international trading and finance system, but it caused a dramatic slowing of development. Succeeding administrations continued and increased the breadth and scope of these economic policies with a net loss of economic sovereignty.

At the end of the twentieth century, Mexico seems farther than ever from reaching its desired goal of a more equitable and inclusive social structure. The economy never fully recovered after 1982 and was subjected to periodic bouts of currency devaluation, massive capital flight, and increased dependency on foreign lending. Economic restructuring under the auspices of the international financial community led to the implantation of a free market economy based on exports of a few goods, mainly to the United States and Canada, its major trading partners. The social cost of this policy was devastating. Inequality increased, producing a highly polarized society with rampant unemployment.

Social welfare policies and their legal provisions, which provided subsidized food, health, and education for the majority of the population, were dismantled. Consumption per capita of corn, beans, and wheat dropped more than 35 percent in the 10 years following their price increase at double the rate of the minimum wage. Malnutrition, coupled with a decline of the health budget to almost half of what it had been in 1980, caused a tripling of infant deaths in 1992. Overall spending on education declined from 5.5 percent to 2.5 percent of Mexico's Gross Domestic Product.

In 1992, the Salinas government promoted a bill to reform Article 27 of the Constitution, encouraging the privatization of the *ejido* land ownership in the countryside by a series of measures that included the termination of agrarian reform and of government subsidies and credit loans to small farmers. Mexican agriculture plummeted as a result: as of 1996, almost one-third of the populace still lived in rural areas, but agriculture accounted for only 8 percent of the gross domestic product. Less than 1 percent of rural producers were competitive in the international market, and more than half of Mexican *campesinos* (peasants) and farmers were excluded totally from the formal economy.

Undoubtedly, the Indian population of Mexico was the most negatively affected by these economic policies. As of 1993, approximately one-third of all the municipalities in the country were populated by Indians, and in these, 43 percent of the population was illiterate, more than three times the national average. Six out of ten Indians were unemployed, and the average wage when they found a job was half the national average.

Mexican society had become far more unequal than ever before, with a related increase in violence and a general loss of legitimacy of the political regime. The increase of social protests was dramatic. In Mexico City alone there was an average of six public demonstrations a day in 1995, making a total of 2,522 for that year. In many regions, migration to the United States and Canada became the only hope for employment. Unable to protect the social and economic rights of its population, especially of women and children, and unwilling to concede full recognition of civil and political rights, the Mexican government also became a consistent violator of the right to life, justice, and security.

The Rights to Life, Justice, and Security

Torture, arbitrary detention and imprisonment, forced disappearances, extrajudicial executions, usually for political motives, abysmal prison conditions, repression of the labor movement, and abuse of indigenous and rural populations have been the most persistent violations of the rights to life, justice, and security in Mexico. The perpetrators overwhelmingly have been members of the security forces: police and military, or hired thugs with close connections to the former. These violations have occurred in the context of a society striving for change and democratization. Redress would entail promoting social justice and electoral reform, including truly free elections and an independent Congress and judiciary system.

In rural areas, abuses have been more widespread, especially in the southern states where there is an acute conflict over land between indigenous *campesinos* and landowners. *Guardias blancas,* or vigilantes, have murdered peasant squatters, and in some regions large landowners have maintained private militias to protect their property from invasions. Local and federal authorities have closed their eyes to these militias, which often have employed police or military personnel. Rural violence became more widespread after an armed rebellion of Maya peasants of the Ejército Zapatista de Liberación Nacional (EZLN, or Zapatista Army of National Liberation) erupted in the southernmost state of Chiapas on January 1, 1994.

In addition to the state of Chiapas, the state of Guerrero has witnessed extreme violence against peasants and indigenous populations. State police killed 17 peasants in Aguas Blancas on June 28, 1995, while they were en route to protest against failure of the local government to provide them with fertilizer and herbicides. The police alleged self-defense as the motive for the massacre, but subsequent investigations by official and unofficial bodies established that the unarmed peasants were ambushed by several hundred security personnel under orders from higher state officials. Receiving much pressure from the press and civil society groups, the local government detained and prosecuted several lower-level state officials, but the higher-level authorities were never prosecuted for ordering the killings. In the name of restoring order, various rural areas have been militarized, and human rights groups have reported much increased human rights violation.

Torture has been frequent according to estimates by such organizations as Amnesty International, the Comisión Mexicana de Defensa y Promoción de los Derechos Humanos (CMDPDH, or Mexican Commission for the Defense and Promotion of Human Rights), and the U.S. State Department. Criminal procedures in Mexico consider confessions of detainees as the primary source of evidence in convictions. This fact, when combined with an ill-trained and underpaid police force, has rendered torture and similar abuses an integral part of criminal proceedings. False accusations and undue process of law have become two of the most generalized human rights abuses in the country, affecting all sectors of the population.

Criminal activity in Mexico has reached alarming proportions. According to research by the CMDPDH, the crime rate increased by 47 percent in Mexico City for the first half of 1995, as compared to the same period in 1994. The protracted economic crisis may have been a cause for this rise in criminal activity, since there is a direct relationship between falling income levels and the rise of criminality. Ironically, the large number of police also may have played a role. Mexico has more police per capital than the United States and most European countries, but these forces historically have been riddled with corruption and home to a great number of criminals. According to a high-ranking official in the Ministry

of the Interior, in 1995, 30 percent of all "highway robbers" were or had been policemen. Attorney general of the republic, Antonio Lozano García, estimated in the same year that 80 percent of all federal judicial policemen had engaged in criminal activity.

The failure of the government to protect the population from criminal assaults, especially in the urban areas, is a major human rights problem. In Mexico City, only 3.8 percent of reported crimes from 1990 to 1995 were resolved by the authorities. This fact, coupled with increased pressure from the U.S. government for the prosecution of drug-related crimes, has resulted in a dangerous tendency to rely on the military for public security.

Police impunity and that of politicians has been an established pattern in Mexico. Traditionally, few reported crimes are investigated, and when these crimes are committed by public officials—turning them into human rights abuses—prosecution and punishment are doubly difficult.

The government-sponsored Comisión Nacional de Derechos Humanos (CNDH, or National Commission on Human Rights) has recommended punishment by dismissal or censure of more than 2,000 public servants, most of them members of the security forces, but it has been unsuccessful in bringing criminal or civil charges against the more serious perpetrators of abuse, especially those in the security forces. In some cases, police officers dismissed in one state have found law enforcement employment in another. In other instances, they simply have continued to act in criminal activities.

Impunity has been absolute in the case of members of the military involved in gross and systematic human rights abuses. Aerial attacks on civilians, summary executions, illegal detentions and torture, as well as the rape of alleged EZLN women in Chiapas have gone unpunished. The army has denied any responsibility for these abuses, which have been documented carefully by both official and independent human rights groups, both national and international.

The Defense and Promotion of Human Rights
The defense and promotion of human rights has become a social movement in Mexico. Despite its novelty compared to other forms of collective action, this movement has had a considerable impact on the prevailing political culture as well as a partial institutionalization of its claims. It began in the 1970s with the quest of a group of women, under the leadership of Rosario Ibarra de Piedra, for their disappeared children and husbands held in clandestine prisons by army and security forces as a consequence

of guerrilla activity. Twenty years later, in 1994, some estimates put the number of civil organizations devoted to human rights at 239, the second-largest group of nongovernmental organizations at the time.

The movement has been committed to the expansion of a culture of civility, stressing the notion that citizens have rights and that these must be defended by civil society. In addition to mobilizing thousands of election observers, the human rights movement played an essential role in peace-keeping activities, both by deflecting violence resulting from postelectoral conflicts as well as in advocating for a peaceful solution to the armed conflict in Chiapas.

Human rights organizations have flourished all over the country, despite the fact that many have been harassed and their members threatened and, in some cases, even killed by the police, as was the case with Norma Corona Sapiens, president of the Sinaloa nongovernmental human rights group in May 1990.

In 1990, in an unprecedented acknowledgment of the gravity of human rights violations, the government of Carlos Salinas de Gortari created a governmental institution to address the problem. Thus, the Comisión Nacional de Derechos Humanos came into existence. Its creation was almost simultaneous with the announcement that Mexico and the United States would begin negotiations on NAFTA. This was no coincidence; the Mexican government was already under scrutiny for serious human rights abuses that had come to light. The CNDH was vested with very little prosecutorial powers and virtually no independence. Electoral and labor rights also were excluded from its mandate, despite the fact that abuses arising from these two areas represented a substantial percentage of all reported violations.

In 1992, the Constitution was amended to establish a national system of state-sponsored human rights commissions in the 32 federal entities. These commissions were to function separately from the CNDH. Their performance has been variable, and dependent on many factors, not least of them their degree of autonomy from local governments.

Several years of severe criticism and continual prodding of these official commissions by nongovernmental organizations resulted in an increased effectiveness of their efforts, especially at the national level. They also legitimized the claim for respect of human rights and helped to open the political space for their defense. In its annual report for 1995, the CNDH claimed to have received a total of 9,488 complaints, and it dealt with 2,660, referring the rest to other government agencies. The majority of the former were handled by a process that the CNDH referred to as amicable agreement. Only when this proved impossible was greater pressure exerted in the form of public recommendations. As of July 1996, 1,053 recommendations had been issued, dealing with very serious violations, and 66 percent had been complied with fully.

The EZLN uprising in 1994, with its demands for work, land, justice, and freedom, brought the issue of human rights to the fore. In the 10 days of actual fighting that took place in Chiapas, at least 145 people were killed and hundreds wounded. More than 200 were arbitrarily detained, tortured, and forced to confess their involvement in the movement by members of the Mexican army and security forces. Several cases of aerial bombings of civilians, disappearances, and extrajudicial executions by the military were reported, and 25,000 people were displaced forcibly from their villages.

The nongovernmental human rights community in the country reacted immediately to this situation after the first news reports reached the public. An immense effort to mobilize national and international public opinion ensued. In three weeks, more than 140 nongovernmental organizations from across Mexico, accompanied by their counterparts from other countries (mainly the United States, Canada, and Spain), visited the area of conflict in Chiapas.

A few days after the EZLN had declared war on the Mexican government, more than 200,000 demonstrators marched in Mexico City, in sympathy with the cause of the rebels, demanding a negotiated settlement of the conflict. The main speaker at the peace rally was Miguel Concha, a Dominican friar and prominent human rights activist closely associated with Bishop Samuel Ruiz García of the San Cristóbal de las Casas, Chiapas diocese.

On January 12, 1994, shortly after the rally, President Salinas announced a unilateral cease-fire with the rebels and called for peace talks, which soon began under the auspices of the Congress with the mediation of Bishop Ruiz. Over the ensuing two years, more than 300 prominent intellectuals and leaders of social and civil organizations would participate as advisors to the EZLN on the issues of Indian rights, democracy, justice, social development, and women's rights, which are the agenda for the negotiation. In fact, the EZLN peace talks would produce a blueprint for a new, more inclusive social pact. In principle, the government pledged to honor the outcome of these negotiations, still ongoing in 1996.

Conclusion

The gap between constitutional proclamation of human rights and its enforcement in Mexico began to close in the mid-1990s. This does not mean that the immediate future for human rights is promising. The steady evaporation of social consent for the legitimacy of the prevailing economic and political systems predicts a period of great instability and coercion. However, the long period of crisis and the insertion of Mexico in the global economy has spawned social forces that have pushed the country toward a more open political system. Human rights undoubtedly have played an important part in the national debate, and pressure for their full recognition and protection will increase.

In July 1996, the Inter-American Human Rights Commission (IAHRC) of the Organization of American States (OAS) visited Mexico at the request of President Zedillo Ponce de León; it was the first such visit in 37 years. For a period of 10 days, the commission investigated the general situation of human rights in the country and visited Chiapas, Guerrero, and Baja California. Its members met with the president and his government; members of Congress, the Supreme Court, and the armed forces; religious officials, the EZLN, politicians, businessmen, and more than 100 nongovernmental human rights organizations. In its preliminary report, the IAHRC was impressed by the existence of a large, multifaceted, and diverse civil society, expressed in a number of nongovernmental organizations involved in multiple activities of national relevance. It also stressed the importance and need for an ongoing dialogue between them and the government in order to further human rights and democracy in Mexico.

For more than 20 years, civil society slowly constructed an agenda for justice and democracy in Mexico. Recognition for it has come from the international community. Widespread claims for the reform of the justice system, demilitarization of the police forces, an end to impunity for government and military officials, and the full observance of Indian people's and women's rights were supported by the IAHRC as valid and in accordance with Mexico's obligations under the American Convention for Human Rights adopted in 1978. This acknowledgment by the OAS legitimized society's struggle for human rights and issued a strong signal for change to the Mexican government.

Select Bibliography

Americas Watch, *Human Rights in Mexico: A Policy of Impunity.* New York: Human Rights Watch, 1990.

Amnesty International, *Human Rights Violations in Mexico: A Challenge for the Nineties.* London: AI, 1995.

Barry, Tom, *Mexico: A Country Guide.* Albuquerque, New Mexico: Inter-Hemispheric Education Center, 1992.

Collier, George, *Basta! Land and the Zapatista Rebellion in Chiapas.* San Francisco, California: Food First Books, 1994.

Kotler, Jared, *The Clinton Administration and the Mexican Elections.* Albuquerque, New Mexico: Resource Center Press, 1994.

Olson, Eric, *The Evolving Role of Mexico's Military in Public Security and Antinarcotics Programs.* Washington, D.C.: Washington Office on Latin America, 1996.

Partido de la Revolución Democrática, Human Rights Commission, Parliamentary Group, *The Political Violence in Mexico: A Human Rights Affair.* Mexico City: Congreso de la Unión, 1992.

Rochlin, James, "Redefining Mexican Security during an Era of Post-Sovereignty." *Social Transformation and Humane Governance* 20:3 (July–September 1995).

—MARICLAIRE ACOSTA

I

Independence Wars
See Wars of Independence

Industrial Labor

This entry contains three articles that discuss industrial labor:

Industrial Labor: 1876–1910
Industrial Labor: 1910–40
Industrial Labor: 1940–96

See also Industry and Industrialization; Migration to the United States; Politics and Government; Women's Status and Occupation

Industrial Labor: 1876–1910

By holding onto power so long, Porfirio Díaz did a disservice to the scribblers of professional history as well as to his country. Adopting a much maligned but long-honored tradition, historians label the 35 years of his rule as the "Porfiriato," as if the mere presence of don Porfirio at the head of the country lent a unity to what otherwise were nearly four decades of vast and disparate changes. For example, tracking the labor movement of those years, one uncovers not one but three distinct eras within the urban labor movement. Although its roots clearly predate the 1860s, the first era was born somewhere in the decade prior to Díaz's commandeering of the presidency in 1876. If this first era certainly was affected by the ideological and financial forces accompanying Emperor Maximilian's French-backed ruler, it was more fundamentally a product of the Liberal reforms and the preindustrial economy they fostered.

After several decades of contentious activities and brave hopes, the first phase of Porfirian labor ends somewhere in the early 1880s, a victim of state hostility, its own fragmentation, and economic hard times. The second phase lasts until the middle of the first decade of the new century, characterized by major reordering of public policy and vast economic and social changes. Strongly affected by both the international recession of 1900–01 and the return of prosperity in the following years, the final phase opens in 1906 with the "year of the strikes." Although this phase of the labor movement appears to culminate in the infamous 1907 massacre of textile workers during "la huelga de Río Blanco," in fact the labor movement and the controversies it spawned continued to play a significant role in national affairs until Díaz's resignation in 1911.

Phase One: 1876–80s
As General Porfirio Díaz led his triumphant army into Mexico City in the late fall of 1876, the Mexican labor movement looked very much alive. In the previous half decade at least 32 strikes had disturbed the nation's industrial peace, encouraged in part by an aggressive mutualist movement.

Mutualist organizations (worker benevolent societies) first had appeared in Mexico in the 1850s, and by the mid-1870s the number of members in Mexico City alone is estimated at 8,000 to 10,000 workers. In 1872 prominent Mexico City artisan leaders proposed to establish a national labor confederation. Called the Gran Círculo de Obreros de México, its purpose was to further the "moral and economic" interests of the nation's "working class." By 1875 the Gran Círculo had established 28 branches in 12 states and the Federal District, including locals in several cotton textile mills. Encouraged by its successes, the Gran Círculo called a national labor congress to meet in Mexico City in the spring of 1876. Attending were 173 delegates representing 90 labor groups.

Going beyond the traditional mutualist goals of protecting the artisan and his family from the expenses of accident, sickness, and death, the Congreso Obrero issued a *manifiesto* to "the artisan associations and all the working classes of the country." It called for educational opportunities for adult workers and compulsory education for children, establishment of cooperative shops and markets, working-class representation before the authorities, categories of wages fixed by the state, and better conditions for working women. It recognized no higher authority save the laws of the Republic and the Mexican state, and took an apolitical stance, disavowing affiliation with any political party. It was a brave and farsighted proposal, but one that masked the many divisions and factions within the Congress. The *manifiesto* itself had been the product of angry contentions between moderates and the more radical anarchists. Although the more progressive elements appear to have written the *manifiesto,* the Congress was implacably divided over many issues, including national politics.

Despite its formal apolitical stance taken in the *manifiesto,* in fact the Congress was divided between the anarchists (who warned against taking sides) and the supporters of Díaz or the partisans of his two opponents, Miguel Lerdo de Tejada and José María Iglesias. Indeed, the Gran Círculo's support of Lerdo proved an unfortunate political choice. Díaz's soldiers occupied its Mexico City offices, and subsequent official hostility crippled its activities.

The Gran Círculo lingered into the early 1880s, but economic hard times and open repression by Díaz's handpicked president, General Manuel González, led to its final demise. Mutualist organizations survived throughout much of the rest of the century within the umbrella of the Congreso Obrero, which counted 73 Mexico City affiliates and 46 branches elsewhere. By then, however, the Congreso was solidly a Porfirista organization and functioned as little more than a sinecure for its leadership, including some who had been among the radicals of the 1870s.

Yet ideological differences and political preferences explain only the means of the decline, not the reason for it. The rapid demise of the once-promising labor movement of the 1870s reflected more fundamental weaknesses. For one thing, the nature of Mexico's preindustrial economy created a weak craft economy, forcing the labor movement into contradictions from which it could not emerge. Capitalist profits were made through wholesale control of urban food markets and luxury imports, by speculation in real estate mortgages or other forms of public and private paper, and through control of credit. Industrial production was limited, for the most part,

to small-scale textiles and mining. The traditional craft economy's major competitor came from merchant/capitalist-operated sweatshops and various forms of cottage ("putting out") manufacturing. Moreover, the urban market was limited by the extensive poverty, favoring low-cost sweatshop production vis-à-vis artisan crafts. The labor movement, understandably, reflected those conditions.

The most obvious impact was widespread impoverishment without proletarianization, creating a journeymen class with little hope of shop ownership, yet encouraging no development of a separate social identity beyond traditional hierarchical ranks— apprentice, journeyman, master. During the revolutions of 1848, German journeymen alarmed their masters by calling themselves workers rather than artisans. In Mexico workers who by the work they did should have been called *"obreros"* (manual laborers) were more likely to refer to themselves as *"artesanos."*

It is true that some historians have professed to find the roots of modern class consciousness and conflict within nineteenth-century labor conflicts, a view most recently and cogently argued by Carlos Illades. Others have argued the contrary, however. The scholars Juan Felipe Leal and José Wolenberg point out the inherent "contradictions" within the mutualist movement between its urban artisan and industrial proletariat members, and between master shop owners and journeymen. Such contradictions in fundamental economic interests, Leal and Wolenberg maintain, led to "discrepancies with respect to strategy, tactics, and means of action."

Take the example of Francisco Bañuelos. Bañuelos was the Guadalajara correspondent for the Mexico City newspaper *El Socialista* and at the same time the president of the city's local small businessmen's organization, Las Clases Productoras. He did not consider his situation contradictory, noting that the *"la clase obrera"* and *"la clase productora"* were the same. Yet his organization was quick to condemn agitation by journeymen against shop-owning masters, labeling them as "communist." Emphasizing artisan cooperatives, the French "utopian" socialism, which was common in Mexico at the time, facilitated acceptance of such contradictions.

More importantly, such contradictions were not always apparent because the main "class enemies" of the wage-earning journeymen artisans and shop-owning masters alike were often the merchant *agiotistas* (loan sharks) who controlled the flow of expensive credit, or the merchant-capitalist sweatshop and cottage industry owners who engaged in ruinous competition with the small producers, or the large merchant wholesalers who even before the completion of the railroads controlled the interstate movement of imports.

In other words, the nature of the preindustrial economy itself conditioned the character of the nineteenth-century labor movement. An example is the Mexico City's hatters strike in the summer of 1875. Wage-earning masters, journeymen, and apprentices struck the city's large hat-making sweatshops and could count on the support of a number of the city's small shop-owning masters. In other words, both wage earners and small shop owners saw their economic interests in the same terms. Although one can understand the logic of that arrangement, and even note its short-term benefits, by combining masters and journeymen in a single organization, mutualist societies faced unavoidable long-term contradictions between ownership and wage earner.

Mutualist societies survived well into the twentieth century, but (mirroring the historical experience of other twentieth-century Latin American labor movements) the origins of Mexico's twentieth-century labor movement spring from the more combative, militant industrial labor force after 1900, rather than its mutualist predecessors. Faced with a large pool of unskilled labor continually being augmented by rural victims of agrarian commercialization, and forced to confront an intransigent bourgeoisie stiffened by its friendly relationship with the state, labor's successes prior to 1900 were few and often short-lived.

Phase Two: 1880s–1905

Throughout much of the last three decades of the nineteenth century, the nation's economy stagnated. However, after 1895, stimulated by the building of the railroads, the commercialization of agriculture, the expansion of the urban population, and major revisions in public policy, the nation's economy grew rapidly through the end of the century. Both stagnation and prosperity created their own special problems for Mexican labor.

Strike activity peaked in the mid-1880s (with 17 strikes in 1884 alone), only to explode again after 1905. The issues during the 1880s were overwhelmingly over wages or regulations that affected wages, as owners in those often bad years sought any means possible to reduce wages or raise productivity. Although the Constitution of 1857 technically granted the workers the right to organize, and did not specifically forbid the right to strike, the wording was vague enough to permit most states to pass laws providing fines and jail sentences for those who "impede

the free exercise of industry or labor." Occasionally, however, Porfirian authorities would support workers' actions, as they did in the 1884 Puebla textile strike and the 1887 Mexico City tobacco strike. More often than not, authorities refused to intervene. Given their scarce resources, workers found that without official intervention their ability to successfully carry out strikes against their employers was minimal.

Interestingly, although the number of strikes declined in the 1890s compared to the previous decade, the number of grievances per strike actually increased. Moreover, the nature of those grievances began to change. Relative to wage grievances, issues of hiring and firing, questions of discipline, changes in shop floor practices—in other words, issues of job control and working conditions—were increasing. Longer hours of work were being imposed as electricity made extension of working hours possible. Managers attempted to force changes in traditional practices, such as refusing to allow cotton mill hands to drink pulque for lunch. New regulations were introduced, including a wide-ranging system of fines for anything from misconduct to tool breakage.

In other words, the nature of work was changing, and Mexican workers were responding to those changes. In the past, both left-wing and right-wing scholars labeled such resistance to economic modernization as a "traditional" response by artisans defending their way of life against the inevitable victory of western capitalism. Beginning in the late 1960s and led by such scholars as E. P. Thompson and Eric Hobsbawm, historians have been more likely to argue that traditional cultural norms and values may be exercised in a modern way, creating new consciousness born of old social institutions. In this case, Mexico's workers may be defined as "modern" in that they sought to challenge traditional managerial authority from being exercised arbitrarily, and they did so in a way that if successful would have given them some control over their workplace, rights that workers would demand and many receive in the next century.

A different perspective, however, is offered in a recent work by Stephen H. Haber. Haber concludes that "the low productivity of Mexican workers in the [Porfirian] textile industry was largely the result of workers' resistance to running more machines than they had historically been accustomed to." Whether or not Haber is correct on this issue, his work, which investigates such issues as firm profitability, worker productivity, market share, regional market development, and firm size and source of capital, is an important source for the management side of Porfirian labor relations.

The most extensive labor organization took place on the railroads; by 1905 nearly one-half of the nation's railroad workers were unionized. Labor's strength, however, was weakened by discrimination against Mexican workers in the U.S.-controlled brotherhood that dominated the better-paying jobs. Mexican workers founded a competing brotherhood, often at odds with the former. Prior to 1906, major strikes took place among the mechanics of the Mexican Central (1894), American engineers (1901), Mexican firemen, and American and Mexican engineers on the Mexican National lines (1902). Although most brotherhoods were apolitical craft unions, James Cockcroft (1968) claims to find syndicalist ideological influences, a belief that labor organization should be directed toward a revolutionary general strike.

The largest number of individual industrial actions prior to 1906 took place in the volatile cotton textile industry, particularly in the older, generally Mexican-owned mills of the Federal District and the states of Puebla and Tlaxcala. The complaints increased after 1900, as the owners who survived the 1900–02 recession sought to maintain their competitiveness against the larger, more modern Veracruz mills through new machinery and more stringent labor discipline. Despite the hardships those policies brought to workers, the threat of unemployment in an uncertain economic climate reduced strikes to a mere handful between 1900 and 1906.

Phase Three: 1906–10

The years after 1902 saw a slow return to prosperity, although the sluggish demand for consumer goods encouraged management to dedicate considerable efforts to improve labor efficiency and reduce labor costs. Statistically, as late as 1910 manufacturing workers accounted for only 11.6 percent of the nation's labor force. Yet the figures are misleading, for the strategic location and visibility of the modern sector greatly multiplied its importance. Moreover, nearly all industries and businesses underwent transformation in workplace conditions, occupational structure, and market organization. Even the most traditional craft occupations underwent some measure of de-skilling, as small-scale production increasingly came under competition from imports and larger-scale producers. Finally, while the industrial sector's overall percentage of the nation's labor force changed little over 1900, in fact the modern industrial sector's share had increased significantly.

It was from within this modern sector, and particularly an increasingly militant cotton textile labor,

that the "labor question" emerged. "The year of the strikes," as 1906 would later be called, began with the organizing of a militant textile workers union, the Gran Círculo de Obreros Libres, among the mills of the Federal District and the states of Mexico, Puebla, Tlaxcala, and Veracruz. In the large, modern mills of Orizaba, Veracruz, a revolutionary cadre tied to the exiled Partido Liberal Mexicano (PLM, or Mexican Liberal Party) was expelled, but agitation continued to grow under less politically motivated but determined leadership.

While events simmered in Orizaba, they exploded in Cananea, Sonora, in June 1906, when a spontaneous strike erupted in violence, fueled by Mexican miners' frustration over a double standard whereby U.S. miners were paid twice what Mexican miners earned for the same work. Repressing the miners with excessive force, the state administration inflamed public opinion by permitting armed U.S. marshals and private citizens to cross the border to Cananea on the pretext of protecting American lives.

Publicly the Díaz regime charged that a PLM conspiracy had incited the miners. The regime's motives were several. It hoped to distract the nationalist anger and convince Mexicans that no labor problem existed. It also hoped to provide additional evidence for the U.S. government's case against the exiled PLM leaders then on trial in the United States for violation of U.S. neutrality laws. (The PLM leaders eventually were convicted but for their role in the abortive uprisings of 1906 and 1908, rather for any presumed connection to the labor strife. The U.S. courts also refused extradition of Manuel Sarabia, the only PLM leader formally charged with conspiracy at Cananea.) Publicly and privately, PLM leader Ricardo Flores Magón maintained that the PLM had not been involved in Cananea or in the subsequent strike at Río Blanco.

Despite the furor over U.S. involvement, Díaz refused to chastise the state governor for his role in permitting what many Mexicans saw as a violation of national sovereignty. While the scholar Alan Knight is correct that Cananea did not "lay the groundwork for revolutionary movements in the mines of Sonora," he may be drawing too strong a conclusion when he asserts that Cananea and the labor events to follow were of little significance for the Revolution that would bring down the Díaz government in 1911. More likely, the administration's continual failure to resolve the noisy labor problems more than slightly weakened the Díaz regime's previous aura of supremacy, and thereby both signified and contributed to its political weakness in dealing with later political crises. Cananea specifically is an important benchmark for the Porfirian labor movement as well as the regime. It raised the social question in a dramatic fashion, and at the same time fused it with Mexican nationalism. In the Revolution that eventually replaced Díaz, these two powerful forces would play their role.

A less violent but nonetheless important strike took place that summer on the Mexican Central Railroad. Striking mechanics shut down the line for two weeks while appealing to the governor of Chihuahua (Enrique Creel) and the president himself to arbitrate the crisis. Díaz received the workers' delegation but refused to intervene.

Despite his reluctance to get involved publicly in labor matters, Díaz quietly encouraged his governors and local political chiefs to investigate workers' complaints. When certain governors counseled a hard line, Díaz demurred, suggesting instead that they establish contact with moderate labor leaders. Events, however, quickly moved beyond the government's modest efforts to defuse labor unrest.

In the late fall of 1906 a series of failed strikes in the cotton mills of central Mexico created an atmosphere of bitter frustration. In December Puebla and Tlaxcala locals of the Gran Círculo de Obreros Libres struck some 30 area mills, followed by a Christmas Eve owners' lockout of most of Mexico's remaining cotton mills. On the request of the union and responding to a national press's increasingly negative coverage of the owners' actions, Díaz agreed to act as arbitrator. His *laudo* (finding) made some concessions to the workers' grievances but instituted a blacklisting procedure and failed to deal with the divisive issue of the company store.

Most dissatisfied with the *laudo* were the Orizaba workers, who had not struck but had been locked out by the owners and then had been made even more destitute by being refused credit at the company stores. On January 7, the day workers were supposed to return to work, violence erupted at the huge Río Blanco textile mill near Orizaba. The tragic events that followed are well known, although interpretations differ.

Díaz ordered the troops in and workers died, shot down in the streets or, as were five union leaders, executed on the burned ruins of the company stores. It was a shocking atrocity and, as with Cananea, the image of Mexican soldiers shooting down workers on behalf of foreign capitalists did not so much begin the revolutionary process that would eventually overthrow Díaz as it did undermine the regime's political legitimacy.

Surprisingly, such a show of force did not quell workers' agitation. Only as an economic recession took hold after mid-1907 did textile strikes begin to decline. Despite the decrease in strike activity, the years after 1906 were active ones for the Mexican labor movement. Labor organization increased, not only in textiles, but on the railroads, in the tobacco industry, among electricians and printers of Mexico City, and among many other craftsmen of the Mexican capital. Moreover, workers were making their grievances public in the weekly working-class "penny-press" publications such as *La Guacamaya, El Diablo Bromista, El Diablo Rojo,* and in such older oppositionist papers as *El Paladín, El Diario del Hogar,* and *El País.* They also found a voice in *México Nuevo* and other newspapers that supported the Democratic Party's Bernardo Reyes's bid for power after Díaz's declaration to U.S. journalist James Creelman that he would not seek reelection.

Many of those letters to the editor as well as private letters written to public officials exhibited the bitter sentiments that Alan Knight has called "moral outrage," the sense that while things always had been difficult for workers, the early years of the twentieth century witnessed "new, arbitrary, unjustified exploitation." There are many examples of such outrage, but one of the most eloquent was a March 1909 letter to President Díaz from striking mill hands at La Hormiga cotton mill near Mexico City: "It seems to us that in the land which saw our birth there are no longer any honorable men left who know how to enforce respect for the laws and guarantees for all the people. . . . It just seems to us that everything is becoming a farce, and all that matters is who you know, and how easy you can make it for yourself. We have come to believe that the Republic of the Mexicans is playing out its final moments and in terrifying agony."

Díaz was sufficiently concerned with the mounting uneasiness to encourage the reformist governor of the Federal District, Guillermo Landa y Escandón to set up a new mutualist organization designed to discourage more radical solutions. Indeed, by early 1909 Díaz had given the signal to state and local authorities to once again look into labor complaints, clearly responding to the increased working-class tensions amid the renewed post-Creelman political agitation.

One of the most thorny and persistent labor problems faced by the Díaz government was that of the railroads, two-thirds of which now were controlled by the Mexican government, which had acquired majority stock ownership beginning in 1906. Nonetheless, management labor policy remained essentially unchanged, clearly favoring foreign workers for the better-paying jobs, most of which required a knowledge of English. A series of strikes, conflicts, and ugly incidents involving foreign workers (coupled with editorials and letters to the editor of many newspapers) kept the issue alive. Opposition politician Francisco I. Madero thought it significantly political to offer an Anti-Reelectionist Party platform pledge (Article 6) to accelerate the "Mexicanization" of railroad personnel.

At this point several historiographic controversies warrant discussion. First, were Mexican workers radicalized by their situation, eventually disposed to overthrow Díaz and perhaps even the capitalist structure that oppressed them? If so, what role did the anarcho-syndicalist PLM play in guiding their actions and setting their ideological agenda? The question of the PLM surfaces in the Cananea copper mine strike of June 1906 and the Río Blanco strike of January 1907, as discussed above.

Although the PLM certainly had some influence on the Mexican labor movement and the era's conflicts, the central role that many historians have assigned the PLM is doubtful. Essentially, the PLM was better known in the north than in the industrial center of Mexico, and the earlier influence of the PLM in the Orizaba textile mills had waned by the time of the Río Blanco strike. Further, most industrial workers were not anti-Díaz per se prior to 1909, and certainly not intent on overthrowing the Díaz regime, but would rather see the regime use its influence and power to better their situation. Many Mexican workers became anti-Díaz only after the failed political maneuvers of 1908–09, and by then (as will be seen) they were active in the Anti-Reelectionist cause of Franciso I. Madero, not the PLM. They were not anti-PLM, whom most knew to be a sympathetic if distant group. They simply had little direct contact with the PLM. The Mexican government compiled a list of 51 PLM supporters in Monterrey, only 13 of whom were from the working class, and of those, only 4 individuals were industrial workers; the others were identified with an artisan occupation, perhaps small shop owners rather than journeymen.

Moreover, the overwhelming majority of Mexico's industrial workers were reformist not revolutionary, desiring to improve their material position, to have a voice within the emerging industrial system, and to be treated with respect. The latter is documented in the increasing significance of "dignity" grievances after 1900, and in much of their writings.

That they were reformist can be seen not only in their actions, demanding that government intervene on their behalf, but in their writing. Their

political frame of reference constantly held up the "Constitution of Benito Juárez" as their goal. That the Constitution of 1857 (and Reform liberalism for that matter) was no friend of the labor movement is obvious enough to our contemporary eyes. But to workers of the Río Blanco generation, the Constitution of 1857 and the Reform era itself were social myths, seen as a quest for social justice within the framework of national independence.

Working-class reformism, however, was not simply a naive belief in nineteenth-century liberalism. Rather it fell quite squarely in the reformist stream of contemporary social democracy with which Mexican workers were quite familiar. The PLM, of course, categorically condemned working-class efforts to obtain government support, but for most Mexican workers, seeking government support seemed justified if they were to confront such powerful adversaries as foreign capitalists. That most owners (and many supervisors) were foreign added a strong dose of nationalism to most worker pronouncements, and whether this is tactical or inherent in their ideological Juarism is difficult to judge. But pervasive it certainly was.

In the end, frustrated in their efforts to reform their situation, the Mexican labor movement came to favor the removal of Porfirio Díaz by whatever means necessary and played an active role in accomplishing just that.

Mexican Workers and the Revolution of 1910

What role did the working class play in the Revolutionary events that led to the overthrow of Porfirio Díaz? Although Alan Knight considers that urban workers "contributed little to the overthrow of the old regime," it seems likely that they contributed much, certainly far beyond their small numbers. First, as Knight acknowledges, workers' involvement in the urban riots that preceded the fall of Díaz was "among the most significant expressions of urban, working-class resentment during the Revolution." Such riots often took place in the decaying industrial centers of the Bajío, where workers suffered most from factory competition or were forced into cottage industry by the merchant-turned-petty-entrepreneur. Unorganized though such violence was, its linkage to the urban working classes and their grievances is one role labor played in the Revolution.

There are other examples of direct working-class involvement in the Mexican Revolution. Even before Madero called for revolution, textile workers from Tlaxcalan mills and the huge Metepec mill in Atlixco, Puebla, attacked the Tlaxcalan village of San

Bernadino Contla. Indeed, the Tlaxcala/Metepec textile workers would be active throughout the revolt against Díaz, and they proved worrisome to local officials, killing Rurales (the rural police force), attacking mills, and harassing state forces.

More worrisome still were the Orizaba textile workers who answered Madero's call to arms with an immediate attack on the federal army's Orizaba barracks on the night of November 20. Although after this incident Orizaba textile workers remained out of the fray, the issue should not come down simply to workers shooting soldiers. For one thing, Orizaba mill hands remained potentially disloyal and were a constant cause for alarm for the Orizaba authorities and for the military head of the Veracruz sector, General Joaquin Maass. Even where workers did not take up arms, their political unreliability played a role in the Revolution by forcing federal troops and Rurales to garrison industrial towns, pinning down badly needed troops.

At least as important, if the Revolution began in the regime's political failures, then we must consider labor's role in those failures. For one thing, among the most publicized political controversies during the last five years of the Díaz regime were labor-related disputes: the angry nationalist response to the Cananea "invasion" by U.S. "rangers," the shock of Mexican troops shooting and executing workers of the Río Blanco strike, and the continuing railroad disputes involving Mexican workers' efforts to obtain equal treatment on Mexican national railway enterprises.

Further, Mexican workers played a large role in the contest for the presidency and vice presidency of 1910. Although Bernardo Reyes attracted certain labor support for his brief and abortive run for the presidency and then vice presidency, the Anti-Reelectionist campaign of Francisco I. Madero drew widespread support from a wide cross section of urban and industrial workers.

In the Federal District, in the mines of Zacatecas, the textile mills of Tlaxcala, Puebla, and Veracruz, in Jalisco and Aguascalientes, at least 30 working-class organizations were actively supporting Madero's presidential candidacy. A majority were textile workers, but typographers, electricians, commercial workers, and railroad workers were also among the enthusiasts. When pro-Madero supporters were arrested, they were often identified as workers.

While numbers are difficult to compute, we know that from the militant Santa Rosa textile mill workforce, 489 workers voted in the April 1910 caucus

of the Anti-Reelectionist Party, a figure that amounts to one-fourth of all the mill's employees. (The workers at Santa Rosa had been heavily involved in the events at Río Blanco on January 7, 1907, and two of their leaders had died on the ashes of the company stores, executed by the regime's soldiers.)

When pro-Madero rallies were held in the industrial cities of Puebla and Orizaba (May 1910), in Guadalajara (December 1909), in Mazatlán and Culicán (January 1910), or when 25,000 Anti-Reelectionists converged on Mexico City (May 1910), many were artisans or other urban workers, the kind of people the press called *"gente popular."* In one particularly telling incident, the pro-Díaz daily, *El Imparcial,* attempted to counter working-class support for Madero's May rally in Mexico City by publishing a series of articles elaborating the advantages that the president's economic policies had provided for Mexico's workers. The ploy backfired. For nearly two weeks workers swamped friendly newspapers (especially *México Nuevo*) with letters decrying those so-called advantages. It was an awesome example of bad press for the government, forcing it to compound the error by closing down *México Nuevo* in order to prevent the continued working-class attacks on the Díaz government.

Governments do not rule only from the barrel of a gun, nor fall only because they are outshot. Mexican urban workers, their grievances, and their political choices played a role in the overthrow of Porfirio Díaz that far outweighed their numbers, that overshadowed their armed commitment to revolution, and that, while it did not defeat Díaz, made it difficult for him to survive the crisis.

Select Bibliography

Anderson, Rodney D., *Outcasts in Their Own Land: Mexican Industrial Workers, 1906–1911.* DeKalb: Northern Illinois University Press, 1976.

——, "Guadalajara's Artisans and Shopkeepers, 1842–1907: The Origins of a Mexican Petite Bourgeoisie." In *Five Centuries of Mexican History,* edited by Virginia Guedea and Jaime E. Rodriguez O. Mexico City: Instituto de Investigaciones Mora, 1992.

Haber, Stephen H., *Industry and Underdevelopment: The Industrialization of Mexico, 1890–1940.* Stanford, California: Stanford University Press, 1989.

Hart, John M., *Anarchism and the Mexican Working Class, 1860–1931.* Austin: University of Texas Press, 1978.

Keesing, Donald B., "Structural Change Early in Development: Mexico's Changing Industrial and Occupational Structure from 1895 to 1950." *Journal of Economic History* 29 (December 1969).

Knight, Alan, *Porfirians, Liberals and Peasants,* vol. 1,

The Mexican Revolution. Cambridge: Cambridge University Press, 1986.

La France, David G., *The Mexican Revolution in Puebla, 1908–1913: The Maderista Movement and the Failure of Liberal Reform.* Wilmington, Delaware: Scholarly Resources Books, 1989.

—RODNEY D. ANDERSON

Industrial Labor: 1910–40

Mexico's industrial labor movement acquired many of its most characteristic features during the first three decades following the start of the Mexican Revolution. The consolidation of the Revolutionary state, the legal frameworks that issued from it (above all the 1917 Constitution and the Federal Labor Law of 1931), and the emergence of corporativist ties that bound the state to rural and urban popular movements and created the basis of mass politics, powerfully shaping the ways in which the industrial labor force intervened in Mexican political and economic life.

The historiography of the 1980s and 1990s, however, has de-emphasized the formative role played by governments and the state. Revisionist historians of the late 1960s and 1970s exaggerated the scale, strength, and farsightedness of the state in the pre–World War II period. It is no longer possible to argue that the labor movement was simply "the creation of a Leviathan state." Industrial workers themselves reshaped the projects and scripts developed by the national state. Although governments pacted with strong unions, it is important to remember that members of the same unions frequently contested the state's efforts to dominate and regulate labor.

The history of industrial labor, therefore, needs to be considered against the backdrop of the national political drama of the three decades that span the modest reforms of the Francisco I. Madero presidency (1911–13), the bolder efforts at social and political engineering associated with the governments of the Sonoran Dynasty of the 1920s, and the more explicitly radical economic and political reorganization initiated during the term of President Lázaro Cárdenas (1934–40).

Labor's capacity to maneuver was constrained by certain characteristics of the industrial labor force itself. Mexico was still predominantly an agrarian society in 1910; in that year 68 percent of the labor force worked in agriculture. Approximately 800,000 people were involved in extractive industries, manufacturing, railroad transportation, and gas and electricity production, although the vague and excessively broad occupational classifications employed by the census takers make it difficult to distinguish between "industrial" and artisan and handicraft workers, especially within the manufacturing sector.

With the exception of some important mining centers in Mexico State, Querétaro, and Jalisco, most of the 104,000 workers employed in the extractive sector were concentrated in the northern half of the country (in Chihuahua, Guanajuato, Hidalgo, Zacatecas, Coahuila, Sonora, and Tamaulipas). Manufacturing industry, however, was predominantly concentrated in central Mexico, and particularly along the Mexico City–Puebla–Veracruz axis. The textile industry employed 32,000, with most textile production centered in Orizaba, the Atlixco district of Puebla, and the state and city of Mexico. Other industries employing significant numbers of men and women were jute manufacture, cigarette and cigar making, beer and soft drink production, paper manufacture, boot and shoe making, and a small but growing metallurgical sector. The 18,000 railroad operating and maintenance workers active in 1910 were concentrated at the major termini and junction points: Mexico City, San Luis Potosí, Orizaba, Toluca, Veracruz, and numerous settlements in northern Mexico.

Despite the labor insurgency that punctuated the last years of Porfirio Díaz's long reign (the strikes at Cananea and Río Blanco in 1906 and 1907 are the best known examples), Mexico's industrial workers played a modest role in the rebellion that brought Francisco I. Madero to power in 1911. The worker cells of the anarcho-syndicalist Partido Liberal Mexicano (PLM, or Mexican Liberal Party) participated in some actions against the ancien régime, but the ideological stance of the group's leadership encouraged a policy of isolation and overt hostility toward the modest reformism of Madero. Industrial workers in many industrial towns (Puebla and Orizaba, for example), nevertheless, were active in Maderista anti-reelectionist clubs; mine and railroad workers, especially in the northern states, joined the Maderista insurrection in 1910 and 1911.

The Madero presidency did not pay much attention to courting industrial labor; there were no signs of an embryonic *política de masas* (mass politics). The government's achievements in the labor area were limited to the establishment of a Department of Labor and the negotiation of a new labor contract for the textile industry. Nevertheless, workers were now free to organize. There was a flurry of union organization throughout the country, with skilled workers and artisans in Mexico City, Veracruz, and

Puebla States taking the lead. Railroad workers and stevedores organized, and in July 1911 coal miners in the northern state of Coahuila founded one of the earliest and largest industrial unions, the Unión Minera Mexicana. The newly formed *sindicatos* launched strikes on an unprecedented scale. By the middle of January 1912, there were over 40,000 workers out on strike.

The Casa del Obrero Mundial was the first successful attempt to set up a cross-sectoral and national federation linking trade unions and labor groups. The early Casa, founded in September 1912, acted as a center for the dissemination of information and tactical advice on labor organization. Many of the unions already in existence affiliated with it and many more were formed under its auspices. A creation of the activities and genius of skilled workers and artisans, the Casa by the middle of 1914 had won the support of artisan trades (printing workers, tailors, bakers, chauffeurs, stonemasons, and carpenters) workers in the service sector, tramway workers, and intellectuals and students. Its links with industrial workers in the metropolitan area (for example, in the large textile factories of the Federal District) were much weaker. Moreover, it was not until late 1914 that the Casa made its first serious efforts to establish contact with the large working-class nuclei of Jalisco, Nuevo León, San Luis Potosí, Puebla, and Veracruz.

The predominantly anarchist and anarcho-syndicalist-influenced Casa survived the increasing hostility of the Madero government, and it managed to continue even after the reactionary coup carried out by Victoriano Huerta in February 1913, although the Casa was banned a year later. The years of the Victoriano Huerta interregnum (1913–14) and of the war of the Revolutionary factions (1914–16) transformed the operating environment for industrial workers. As part of the effort to mobilize groups to defeat Huerta and then secure dominance within the "Revolutionary" camp, the military factions competed with each other to win support of workers. The Zapatista-Villista camp (the Convention) had its sympathizers and supporters among workers, but it was Venustiano Carranza's Constitutionalist movement, and in particular its radical or Jacobin wing, that forged the closest links with labor.

The pact signed between the Casa and the Constitutionalists in February 1915 symbolized the new kind of relationship developed between labor and the embryonic Revolutionary state. Seven thousand of the 52,000 members claimed by the Casa fought on the Constitutionalist side in Red Battalions, and the relative immunity from government harassment enjoyed by the Casa between February and July 1915 enabled it to found new unions in areas under Constitutionalist control. Nevertheless, the pact also revealed the limits of this early "alliance." After the Constitutionalists' triumphant reentry into the capital, the Casa was unable to withstand the ever more frequent Carrancista attacks on it, and it was finally crushed in the general strike of July 1916.

Workers learned different lessons from this defeat. A majority tendency explored new ways of cementing a state-labor alliance. The Confederación Regional Obrera Mexicana (CROM, or Regional Confederation of Mexican Workers), founded in 1918, embraced the path of reformist trade unionism. The CROM and its national leader Luis Napoleón Morones found a warm reception from a group of northern Revolutionaries centered around the Sonoran caudillos (regional strongmen)—Álvaro Obregón, Plutarco Elías Calles, and Adolfo de la Huerta. The Obregón-Morones pact of August 1919 marked the CROM's definitive entrance into the political arena. Together with the foundation of the Labor Party in December 1919, it inaugurated a long period of close relations between labor and the Sonoran caudillo coalition during the 1920s.

The bulk of the organized working class at this period, however, still operated within the ideological framework of mutualism or libertarian ideas. Large numbers of workers were alienated by the CROM's orientation and, in particular, its embracing of the strategy of *"acción multiple,"* a combination of direct industrial action with intervention in the political arena. Independent and "Red" workers founded separate organizations, the short-lived Gran Cuerpo Central de Trabajadores (at the end of 1918) and then the Confederación General de Trabajadores (CGT, or General Confederation of Workers) in February 1921. Mostly centered in Mexico City and drawing support from skilled artisans (bakers) and communications and manufacturing workers (streetcar employees, chauffeurs, telephone company employees, and a portion of the textile labor force of Mexico City), the "Red" unions enjoyed a brief and tempestuous relationship with the young Partido Comunista Mexicano (PCM, or Mexican Communist Party) until the Communists and anarcho-syndicalists went their different ways at the end of 1921.

In the benevolent atmosphere of the Obregón government, union membership increased rapidly. The largest union federation, the CROM, claimed an increase in members from 50,000 in 1920 to 1.2 million in 1924, and an extraordinary (and almost certainly grossly inflated) figure of 2 million in 1928. During the 1920s the CROM established a veritable empire. Although the CROM failed to win cabinet appointments under Obregón, several of its leading figures occupied important political and administrative positions, including governor of the Federal District. Leading CROMianos also secured positions within the Department of Labor of the Ministry of Industry, Commerce, and Labor. This gave the CROM considerable authority in the resolution of labor conflicts, strengthening its position against both business interests and rival labor organizations. The CROM enjoyed the full support of the repressive organs of the state in its drive to eliminate rivals and establish hegemony in the labor movement.

The de la Huerta Revolt of 1923 demonstrated to President Obregón the value of a firm political and military commitment from labor in times of crisis. For the second time in 10 years Mexican workers (aided by *agraristas*) armed themselves for the defense of the government. Internationally, the CROM lobbied the U.S. government on behalf of the Obregón administration to close the border to arms shipments for the rebels. The rebellion served to cement the close relations between Calles and the CROM leadership. During the Calles presidency CROM figures headed state governments, Labor Party deputies filled the national legislature, and Luis Morones, a cabinet minister, exercised an influence rivaled by no one except the president himself.

The CROM did have an agrarian presence— during most of the 1920s over 60 percent of its membership was made up of agricultural workers and peasants. But its strength lay in its involvement in small-scale industry; well over half of Mexican workers were artisans or worked in small-scale workshops and plants and government services. The sociological profile of the CROM, therefore, influenced the organization's interest in developing a state-labor pact. The limited bargaining power of many of the CROM's unions and their dependence on state patronage made the search for reliable allies in the state apparatus a necessity.

The CROM, it must be emphasized, did not successfully penetrate many core areas of the industrial working class. Although it had some success in organizing mine workers at the national level (its first large affiliate was the Unión Minera), its efforts to hegemonize railroad, petroleum, and electrical workers failed, and it had only partial success in the textile industry, mainly in Puebla and Veracruz States. Many of these sectors—the electrical, railroad, and petroleum workers are the best examples—enjoyed a relatively strong bargaining position with private capital and could function successfully with less state support.

It is important not to reduce the history of the CROM to the history of its often corrupt national leadership and global project. It is true that during the peak of its influence (1925–28) there was a dramatic decline in strike action undertaken by CROM-affiliated unions. This development reflected the emphasis given to economic reconstruction by Calles and Luis Morones and the CROM's commitment to identify its membership with class peace, social harmony, and the "national" and "revolutionary" aspects of the Calles administration's project; "we are not the enemies of capital but its collaborators" was the proud boast of the CROM's Mexico City union federation at the end of 1927.

In practice, though, the CROM's centrality has been exaggerated. The organization was never able to achieve total dominance over the unionized labor force. In spite of the corruption and reputation for violence enjoyed by many of its labor bosses, many *cromianos* gained a reputation for honesty at the local level. In some regions (in Veracruz State, for example) CROM unions cooperated with the Communist left in spite of the strident anti-Communism practiced by the national organization, which threw in its lot with the American Federation of Labor and its ambitions to build a Pan-American federation of "business" unions.

The political crisis that followed the assassination of Álvaro Obregón in 1928 revealed how vulnerable the CROM had become as a result of its dependence on the patronage of the political class. President Emilio Portes Gil (1928–30) was a longtime opponent of the CROM and used the power of the state to undermine the CROM's privileged position. Although the CROM maintained its strength in east-central Mexico, the confederation lost much of its membership, especially when one of its leading lights, Vicente Lombardo Toledano, broke with the organization in 1933 and formed the Confederación General de Obreros y Campesinos de México (CGOCM, or General Confederation of Workers and Peasants of Mexico) in October of that year.

The establishment of the CGOCM initiated an important new phase in the history of the labor movement. In less than a year it had become the largest single labor federation in Mexico, establishing a tradition of militancy and independence that contrasted sharply with the sycophancy exhibited by the CROM's national leadership. More significantly, the new labor federation emerged at the same time as the most proletarianized segments of the labor force—in the mining, railroad, electricity, and petroleum sectors—and began to consolidate and unify its forces with the establishment of national industrial unions (NIUs) in the first half of the 1930s. The first of these to emerge was the Mexican Railroad Worker's Union (STFRM) in January 1933, an organization that finally succeeded in breaking with the tradition of craft unions that had blocked unification for two decades. The railroad workers, with the help of the Communists, quickly helped mining and metal workers to form their own national union in April 1934. In August of the following year, the petroleum workers, another group with a long history of sectoral division, often built around individual oil companies, also created a unified national industrial union.

The emergence of the national industrial unions, whose status had been legalized by the 1931 federal Labor Code, was a watershed in the history of industrial labor. For the first time the central dynamic of organized labor in Mexico began to be moved by a solid core of industrial workers, many of whom labored in strategically sensitive industries. The new national unions occupied a position to the left of the older union movement. Their radicalism was seen in several areas. The NIUs were strong advocates of Revolutionary nationalism, anticipating the direction in which the Lázaro Cárdenas administration would soon move after taking office in late 1934. More importantly, their members, recalling the painful struggles to resist the CROM's effort to gobble them up in the 1920s, were committed to maintaining a high degree of organizational autonomy vis-à-vis the national state and political parties.

The recomposition of the labor movement took place against the background of the Great Depression. Although officially recognized strikes fell sharply during the Maximato (1929–34, the period when Calles controlled events from behind the scenes after the end of his presidential term), the pace of class conflict accelerated in the industrial and agrarian sectors, a development signaled by a fourfold increase in the number of grievances filed before arbitration and conciliation boards between 1928 and 1932. More significantly, the political and industrial weight of organized workers grew rapidly with the arrival of Lázaro Cárdenas in the presidency at the end of 1934. As the pro-labor sympathies of the new president and the Federal Labor Board became clearer, labor-capital conflict sharpened, with major strikes being declared against a series of largely foreign-owned corporations, including Standard Oil's Huasteca Petroleum Company, the U.S.-owned telephone and telegraph company, and the Canadian-controlled Mexico City tramways company. Labor mobilized in support of Cárdenas's stand against the anxious capitalists (especially in the northern city of Monterrey) and the increasingly reactionary coterie surrounding former president Calles. The CGOCM led several impressive general strikes in 1934, and in the middle of 1935 it joined with other independent and left-wing unions to create a labor body to defend the beleaguered new government: the National Committee for Proletarian Defense. The scene was now set for the emergence of the Confederación de Trabajadores de México (CTM, or Confederation of Mexican Workers) in 1936, which incorporated the CGOCM, several national industrial unions, and the small but highly politicized industrial worker base of the Mexican Communist Party.

A comparison between the new national labor federation CTM and the CROM is revealing. As in the case of the CROM, a major role in the new organization was played by networks of small unions. These constituted the bulk of the unionized workforce in the Federal District and most of the 400,000 workers belonging to the regional confederations who affiliated with the CTM. But unlike the CROM, the CTM from the very beginning incorporated national organizations representing key sectors of the industrial working class. The largest contingent of industrial workers was provided by the 100,000-strong mining and metalworkers union, followed by the railroad workers (58,000 workers), sugar industry workers (45,000), and petroleum workers (30,000).

The Cárdenas years saw the consolidation of a qualitatively new relationship between labor and the state. The first attempt to nationalize a regionally fragmented political system, provide a peaceful way of resolving conflict among military and political caudillos, and secure a smooth presidential succession had been made in 1929 when Calles created the Partido Nacional Revolucionario (PNR, or National Revolutionary Party). But this national party had been unable to anchor itself within the massively fragmented labor movement. The unification drive that culminated in the founding of the CTM and the national industrial unions allowed the state to build a mass base among industrial workers. The CTM became the core of the labor sector of the new revolutionary party—the Partido de la Revolución Mexicana (PRM, or Party of the Mexican Revolution), which the Cardenistas formed out of the PNR in 1938. Together with the peasant sector, urban and industrial labor provided the social base of Mexico's version of the popular front.

The pro-labor policies of the Cárdenas government facilitated a sharp increase in the size of the unionized workforce. In the sectors under federal labor jurisdiction alone, unionized workers increased by 45 percent. However, Cárdenas also placed sharp limitations on the development of the labor-state corporativist pact. The state would tolerate and even encourage labor assault on private capital—insofar as labor cooperated with the task of smashing "feudalism" and creating a framework for the development of national capitalism. Sometimes, this even led to experiments like the introduction of worker administration—in the railroads and newly nationalized oil industry—that stretched capitalism to its limits.

But Cárdenas also limited the CTM's power. He discouraged CTM efforts to organize agricultural workers and peasants, and his efforts to block the creation of a worker-peasant organizing alliance met with success in 1938 when the Confederación Nacional Campesina (CNC, or National Peasant Confederation) became the organizational focus of agrarian workers and peasants. Cárdenas also prevented federal government employees from joining the CTM by supporting the creation of a separate Federation of Public Service Workers' Unions. In the last years of the Cárdenas presidency—especially after 1938—the administration significantly moderated its support of labor militancy when confronted with signs of military and private sector nervousness at the pace of social and economic change.

Moreover, the state-labor pact tolerated and occasionally even encouraged the development of undemocratic practices and social relations within the union movement. The first signs of labor bossism and gangsterism, a phenomenon that would later become labeled *charrismo,* began to surface, especially within the union fiefdoms controlled by Fidel Velázquez and his allies (Fernando Amilpa, Jesús Yurén, Alfonso Sánchez Madariaga, and Blas Chumacero)—who became known as the *cinco lobitos* (five little wolves). The economic base of the *lobitos* lay in the smaller enterprise unions formed in small-scale industry and in the government services rather than in the large national industrial unions. But even the powerful national unions of rail, mine, and petroleum workers, in which the Marxist and Communist left enjoyed a substantial support base, contributed to these negative trends. Both the Marxist labor leader Vicente Lombardo Toledano and the union cadres of the Mexican Communist Party put the building and preservation of trade union unity ahead of radical economic and political projects and the development of democratic processes.

This pragmatic tendency became clear in the early months of the CTM when the Lombardistas and the PCM reluctantly agreed to accept Fidel Velázquez as secretary of organization, a strategically sensitive position within the new confederation. The important national union of miners and metalworkers withdrew from the CTM in disgust. In April of the following year, the tension between the pragmatic and more collaborationist position of the *cinco lobitos* and the left flared up again. When the industrial worker core of the CTM (including the railroad and electrical workers unions) resigned from the confederation in protest over undemocratic governance, Lombardo and the Communist International secured a rapid reversal of the walkout and a humiliating return of the rebel unions to the CTM. The Mexican Communist Party justified its about-face with the Comintern-inspired policy of "Unity At All Cost."

The state-labor pact developed during the Cárdenas presidency undoubtedly delivered major benefits to the labor movement. By 1940 nearly 15 percent of the nonagricultural labor force was unionized. Conflicts between labor and capital were more often or not resolved in labor's favor, at least during the first half of Cárdenas's term. Moreover, the sectoral reorganization of the official party appeared to guarantee a permanent place for industrial labor (and the land reform peasantry) in the post-Revolutionary political organization of Mexico. Nevertheless, the costs of the corporativist pact were also substantial. Inflation in the last years of the administration had eroded a large part of the wage gains achieved by industrial workers. Strikes against "the national interest," such as the railroad strike of 1936, were declared "nonexistent" by federal courts, and a large part of the costs incurred by the experiments in worker administration of the nationalized railroads and petroleum industry were carried by the workers themselves.

A more dangerous by-product of the unification of the industrial labor movement was the way in which the state-labor pact enhanced opportunities for verticalism and co-optation. The extent of labor's subordination to the increasingly undemocratic PRM was seen in the way in which Lombardo Toledano and Fidel Velázquez marshaled the CTM's unions behind the candidacy of Manuel Avila Camacho in the presidential elections of 1940, overriding the opposition of the electricians, railroad workers, and petroleum workers. Paradoxically, the overtly conservative platform of General Juan Andreu Almazán received the support of significant nuclei of industrial workers angered by the widening gap between the anticapitalist rhetoric of the PRM's labor sector and the undemocratic and bureaucratized processes visible within the CTM and other national labor confederations.

See also Partido Revolucionario Institucional (PRI)

Select Bibliography
Collier, Ruth Berins, and David Collier, *Shaping the Political Arena: Critical Junctures, the Labor Movement, and Regime Dynamics in Latin America.* Princeton, New Jersey: Princeton University Press, 1991.
Hamilton, Nora, *The Limits of State Autonomy: Post-Revolutionary Mexico.* Princeton, New Jersey: Princeton University Press, 1982.
Middlebrook, Kevin J., *The Paradox of Revolution: Labor, the State, and Authoritarianism in Mexico.* Baltimore: Johns Hopkins University Press, 1995.

—BARRY CARR

Industrial Labor: 1940–96

Within the Latin American context, the relationship between labor and the Mexican state is quite exceptional. Both actors have created a complex and durable relationship that, at least since the 1940s, can be characterized as mutually beneficial. Since the beginning of the 1980s, when Mexico began to experience the economic problems that typify other Latin American countries (most notably inflation, monetary devaluation, and developmental instability), one may note that the appearance of relatively autonomous labor organizations—so-called independent unionism—has not changed the fundamental relationship between organized labor and the political system.

Historical Origins of Labor-State Relations
When the Casa del Obrero Mundial (the House of the World Worker) was created in 1912, Mexican labor acquired representation within the process of the Revolution. During the struggle against General Victoriano Huerta, the Casa became an active supporter of the Constitutionalist forces and of General Álvaro Obregón, one of its leaders. This support eventually led to the agreement signed in 1915 whereby the Casa committed its support to the Constitutionalists in exchange for economic and social benefits for workers. This instance was the first indication of an alliance that was to be pursued when the Confederación Regional Obrera Mexicana (CROM, or Regional Confederation of Mexican Workers) was created in 1918. In many ways, the CROM was the prototypical modern Mexican labor organization in that it represented an explicit commitment of labor to the objectives of the Mexican state. Two political leaders closely associated with the CROM, Luis Napoleón Morones and Vicente Lombardo Toledano, were instrumental in the passage of a series of labor laws, with the 1931 Labor Code being the most important. As a result of such political gains, the CROM saw its membership grow from less than 10,000 workers in 1918 to over 500,000 by 1927. Political ties between labor and the state strengthened as the Revolutionary regime became more and more institutionalized, culminating under President Lázaro Cárdenas (1934–40) with the creation in 1936 of the Confederación de Trabajadores de México (CTM, or Confederation of Mexican Workers). Lombardo Toledano was central in the creation of this new labor confederation, not only of its organizational structure but also of its ideology. Indeed, his position as both a labor, political, and intellectual personality contributed to the emergence of a series of CTM commitments that continue to this day to be important in shaping the relationship between organized labor and the Mexican political system.

It is important to mention here that from 1912 to 1936, Mexico's social structure did not change as rapidly as did its political sphere. The agricultural sector continued to employ more than two-thirds of the total economically active population, while jobs in the industrial and service sectors increased very little in relative terms. After 1940, however, both total employment and its distribution changed dramatically. In political terms, the 1930s marked a deepening of the Revolution. Serious agrarian reform and the constitution of the ruling Partido Nacional Revolucionario (PNR, or National Revolutionary Party) institutionalized social change at the national level. From 1936 onward, Mexico began to industrialize within the political structure that had been consolidated during the Cárdenas presidency.

During this time, the CTM was ideologically on the left, despite its explicit commitment in support of the Mexican state. The presence of Lombardo Toledano, the existence of many high-level political leaders in the Cárdenas government who adhered to a Marxist perspective, and the then-radical nature of the regime contributed to the development of a special type of relationship between the unions and the state where each coexisted and supported mutual projects. A good example of this alliance is the oil nationalization controversy of 1938, which began as a labor conflict between the foreign oil companies and the various unions representing the workers. The refusal of the companies to negotiate forced the government to intervene and, eventually, to decree the nationalization of the oil industry. At this point, Cárdenas explicitly gave his support to the petroleum unions, thus ratifying the alliance that had emerged two years before with the creation of the CTM. As was true throughout the period from 1912 to 1940, this alliance between the state and the labor movement permitted a certain ideological commitment by the unions to Revolutionary nationalism.

The turning point for this relationship came during World War II, when Mexico intensified its industrialization as a response to difficulties in importing manufactured goods from the United States. Private and public investment increased markedly, as did output in electricity, steel, cement, communications, oil, and housing. With the resulting growth of the industrial labor force, the national industrial unions consolidated their power in the area of railroads, mining and metallurgy, oil, and electricity. Labor conflict also increased, especially in 1944.

But such conflict was not allowed to continue. In 1945, the CTM signed the Pacto Obrero Industrial (Worker Industrial Pact), in which the labor movement committed itself to support the official strategy of national industrial development. At the same time, divisions began to appear within labor leadership. A new generation of leaders, headed by Fidel Velázquez, increasingly questioned the role of Lombardo Toledano. Ultimately, in 1950, Velázquez succeeded in winning the elections for the head of the CTM executive committee, a post which, as of 1996, he still held.

The Velázquez election should be seen as one consequence of President Miguel Alemán Valdés's offensive against labor radicalism. This offensive resulted in the state's consolidation of control of the national industrial unions where some supporters of Lombardo Toledano still remained. The Alemán government's intervention to exclude leaders of leftist tendencies in the railroad workers (1948) and the petroleum workers unions (1951) demonstrated that the state would not allow the existence of an autonomous labor leadership. What is usually referred to as *charrismo,* or rule through corporatist labor bosses, began at this time. Although allowing the continued presence of the labor movement within the government alliance, the state sought to subordinate the unions to the interests of its bourgeois faction, a bourgeoisie increasingly in command of a clearly defined project of capital accumulation.

This structure for controlling politics within the national industrial unions, as well as the demands of rank-and-file workers, paid off with high rates of economic growth. The Mexican Gross Domestic Product (GDP) grew at a rate of 6.1 percent from 1941 to 1946, at 5.7 percent from 1947 to 1952, and at 6.4 percent from 1953 to 1958. But if per capita distribution was slower, it permitted reinvestment in productive facilities. Real salaries actually decreased: the rural minimum salary fell 46 percent from 1939 to 1950, and the average salary in 35 industries declined approximately 26 percent over the same time span. Real salaries surpassed prewar figures only after 1959, and salaries continued to rise only until 1971, when they resumed a downward trend as a result of increasing inflation.

Such income data demonstrate that the existing relationship between organized labor and the state was highly beneficial to the process of capital accumulation. For the sake of completeness, however, one ought to mention that despite the decline in real salary, worker benefits in housing, education, health, and social security experienced substantial improvements in the same period. What labor did not obtain in salaries it obtained collectively through benefits provided directly by the state rather than by entrepreneurs. Such improvements help to explain the continued alliance between labor and the state, where an intensification of labor conflict otherwise might have been expected.

The previous mechanism could be identified as a "trade-off" in which Mexican labor maintained a relationship with the state that relied not only on the satisfaction of economic demands, but also on the satisfaction of the collective needs of the country's workers. The Mexican labor movement and its bureaucratized leadership integrated itself into the larger political system in a way that guaranteed that system's efficient operation while promoting the general welfare of the working class. The high rates of growth, in part, were the result of union quiescence. The considerable decline in the intensity of strike activity and the practice of trade-offs of economic and political demands between labor and the state reinforced the process of capital accumulation.

Linkages between the State and Labor

The preceding historical overview of the period from the Revolution to the early 1950s described the process whereby the unions integrated themselves with the Mexican political system. What this overview did not provide, however, was a structural explanation of how that system functioned in regard to organized labor. This section addresses that question, focusing in particular on three basic aspects: the legal provisions governing union activity, the national union structure itself, and an analysis of strike activity.

Legal Provisions

Article 123 of the 1917 Constitution, the basic statement regarding what labor can and cannot do in the Mexican context, distinguishes two major categories of unions. Section A of Article 123 refers to unions of "industrial workers, agricultural day laborers, domestic employees, artisans, and in general . . . all [covered by private] labor contracts." Such private sector unions are, in turn, subdivided, depending on whether they fall into federal or local-level jurisdiction. Section B pertains to all public sector workers employed by the national government, the various Mexican states, and all municipalities. Each type has a separate specified type of bargaining procedure. Defining labor unions as "associations formed for the study, betterment, and defense of the interests of workers and their employers," the law recognizes five distinct types that, with the exception of the final category, must group a minimum of 20 workers: 1) *gremiales,* or those of the same profession; 2) *de empresa,* or those of a single company; 3) *industriales,* or those in two or more companies located in the same industry; 4) *nacionales de industria,* or those in one or more companies of the same industry located in two or more states; and 5) *oficios varios,* those including less than 20 workers of the same profession, but located in the same municipality. It is also necessary to distinguish between national industrial unions—the fourth category above—where the various sections share a common charter, and the more decentralized national federations where each section has its own separate charter.

The National Union Structure

Mexican labor, through the CTM, is one of the three official components of the present dominant political party, the Partido Revolucionario Institucional (PRI, or Institutional Revolutionary Party), along with the Confederación Nacional Campesina (CNC, or National Peasant Confederation) and the amorphous popular sector. The CTM is a part of the Congreso del Trabajo (CT, or Congress of Work), an umbrella organization that groups all major labor confederations, including those not affiliated with the PRI, national industrial unions not part of the CTM, and the confederation of unions representing government workers, Federación de Sindicatos de Trabajadores al Servicio del Estado (FSTSE, or Federation of Unions of Civil Servants), regulated by Section B of Article 123 of the Constitution. The CT is a kind of forum where labor organizations present common positions to the state, going beyond the bounds of what strict PRI membership might allow. The CT is the heir to a number of earlier similar groupings, many of which also reflected CTM sponsorship. Indeed, Fidel Velázquez encouraged the formation of such a broad-based grouping so as to widen the scope of his organization and, thus, to allow for some diversity

of opinion within the official labor movement. In the 1960s, the Bloque de Unidad Obrera (BUO) played a similar role.

The decision-making process in organizations such as the CTM, the CT, and the national industrial unions is cloaked in secrecy. While it is not clear how election procedures for the higher posts actually function, reelection is typical. The case of the secretary general of the CTM, Fidel Velázquez, is indicative: he occupied the post continuously for more than 45 years after first being elected in 1950. If CTM internal organs such as its National Congress and National Council have clear-cut formal functions, much of their power appears to exist largely on paper. At lower organizational levels, action is taken to persuade or force those unions departing from the CTM line to conform.

In general, the CTM fulfills a fundamental role in the capital accumulation process by maintaining wages at levels acceptable to the owners of capital, by supporting the government in critical situations, and by controlling the rank-and-file members through clientelistic means and with the aid of corrupt union officials. Until now, the CTM has been successful in making it possible for the political system to rely upon it to provide a relatively quiescent labor force. This pattern was consolidated at the end of the 1940s and has been in operation ever since.

Very few unions questioned such control, and those that did have done so only quite recently. What is most significant is the high degree of integration between the labor movement and the government. For each type of worker—blue collar, white collar, and peasant—there is a specific organization said to represent that worker's interests in the larger political world. These labor organizations are incorporated into other broader entities for the purpose of reconciling conflicting group interests. Thus, the PRI interacts with business and with government officials to discuss labor demands. The active presence of many public officials at labor congresses and, reciprocally, the presence of the CTM secretary general at many government functions, illustrates the close relationship that exists among these actors. Such multigroup integration through the political system permits a high degree of flexibility in the negotiation of mutual demands. Of necessity, labor officials, political leaders, and government officeholders must maintain steady contact in their efforts to reconcile the wishes of various groups. The presence of federal deputies in parliament recruited from the labor sector and their increasing relative weight among the PRI delegation is one indication of the importance of labor representation in the governing coalition.

In any overall evaluation of how the highly centralized Mexican political system functions, it is undoubtedly necessary to emphasize the importance of the PRI's role in overseeing the interaction of the various union groups (as in the case of the Congreso del Trabajo) as well as the reality of the interplay of interests among worker, peasant, and popular sectors. One might even assume from this depiction that the political system is not so much a place where control is imposed as the source of important political benefits for those groups so incorporated.

The usefulness of the labor movement to the political system, and vice versa, is only one aspect of their mutual relationship. At other levels such as in collective bargaining negotiation, the importance of the state is critical. The collective contracts signed reflect the political wishes of the state leadership as much as the economic realities of particular businesses. Salary increases, for example, relate directly to general development strategies defined by the government rather than to the profitability of particular companies. In recent years, the so-called *tope salarial,* or maximum salary limit set by the government, fixes the absolute level that unions cannot exceed. In cases where a union has gained what is deemed an excessive concession from management, the Labor or Budget Ministry has intervened to stop its implementation. The consequence is that official salary policy has resulted in negotiations where salary increases are not the central point of contention; instead, discussions have centered on the extent of fringe benefits, or *prestaciones,* where state control is not exerted to the same degree. One important result of the government decision to fix limits on salary hikes has been the serious undermining of union capacity to bargain at the plant level; as a result, the real negotiations are transferred to the highest political level within the government itself.

Strike Activity

An important indicator of the way the state-labor relationship functions in Mexico is the overall tendency for a decrease in the average number of strikers from the 1940s to the present, something surprising given the rising share of industrial workers in the workforce and the intensification of industrialization and urbanization in that same time span. The general decline in strikers is evidence in support of the thesis of increased state control over labor demands in recent years.

During the Cárdenas presidency, but especially in its first three years, strike activity was intense. The average number of strikers in the entire period was the highest of any moment in recent Mexican history. Such labor activism took place in an economic context of little inflationary pressure; strikes seemed more a response to political mobilization than to economic problems.

During the Manuel Avila Camacho presidency (1940–46), strike activity tended to decrease. It was during this time that the CTM signed two agreements with the administration in which it committed itself to support government economic policy. As a result, labor peace tended to prevail during the war years, while import substitution industrialization (a set of policies implemented by an activist, interventionist state designed to encourage the domestic production of previously imported manufactured goods) was intensifying. So-called national unity was the ideological message that Avila Camacho directed toward all social organizations in his attempt to reverse the confrontational politics that had prevailed under Cárdenas. The central government focused on ways to stimulate private investment and to conciliate divergent interests.

At the end of the war, when Miguel Alemán Valdés took power, the more repressive stance adopted by the government toward labor resulted in an actual overall decrease in strike activity and in the specific efforts to gain control over the railroad and oil national industrial unions where dissidents had begun to appear. On the basis of the average number of strikers per strike, one can infer from the data that strikes took place more in large enterprises than in small- and medium-sized factories. Such figures statistically reflect the influence of the very large oil and railroad workers' unions. The pro-business views of Alemán's minister of labor were reflected in his hostile attitudes toward worker demands. While the basic parameters of the relationship were not broken, it was clear that the state consolidated the subordination of labor it had been seeking to attain since 1940. The process of control was represented by the election of Fidel Velázquez as CTM secretary general and the rise to prominence of such leaders as Francisco Pérez Rios and Napoleón Gómez Sada in the electrical workers and mining unions, respectively. The phenomenon of *charrismo* had become institutionalized. After 1952, labor relations would be part of a structure where labor was still strong, but where it could not challenge state decrees.

Under President Adolfo Ruiz Cortines (1952–58), strike activity increased slightly in relation to the level attained under Alemán. The frequency of conflict increased, reaching an average of 24 strikes per year, although the average number of strikers increased slightly less; as a result, the average number of strikers per strike decreased in relation to the earlier period. Such an exclusive focus on aggregate data, however, overlooks important events like the large-scale mobilization of railroad workers that occurred at the end of the Ruiz Cortines administration.

In 1957, labor-management disagreement resulted in a long and bitter rail strike. The overlapping of the strike with the PRI presidential nomination process may have been influential in the choice of Adolfo López Mateos as the PRI's candidate. As the minister of labor in the Ruiz Cortines government, López Mateos had had a lot to do with the development of the railroad conflict. Once he assumed the presidency in December 1958, he decided to resolve the strike through the temporary militarization of the railroads. The resulting government repression against the strike leadership succeeded in finally consolidating state power in a union that had sought to challenge official authority.

After its initial show of force, the López Mateos government moved away from anti-union repression. In the entire period from 1958 to 1964, the average number of strikers and strikes sharply increased to levels not seen since the Cárdenas years. One explanation for this subsequent toleration of strikes may be found in an effort by López Mateos to seek to relegitimate his government with labor after the confrontation of 1958–59. Another relates to the sharp improvement in economic conditions as inflation decreased, nominal and real salaries reversed their previous decline, and the country experienced general economic growth. The combination of greater official toleration and better material conditions, in turn, seemed to have led to a noticeable worker mobilization marked by new strikes, an increase in union membership, and a renewed union presence in the political sphere.

The events of the López Mateos years are indicative of the particular characteristics of state-labor relations in Mexico. Here one can argue that the assumption of control by the CTM over worker demands could transform such petitions in the eyes of the state, making them more acceptable for presentation at a later time when economic conditions were more opportune. The resulting strike activity that followed should be seen as a safety valve for accumulated worker pressures, the release of which is facilitated by the political linkage of organized labor and the state. The overall labor process is oriented toward containing worker demands within official structures like the CTM rather than allowing them to be spontaneously released in the economy at large. The political opening represented by

reduced repression permitted an increase in demands from accepted labor leaders operating within the ruling coalition. Responding to such labor pressure, the state provided material benefits such as salary hikes and the creation of a social security system for government workers in the Instituto de Servicios Sociales y Seguridad Social de los Trabajadores al Servicio del Estado (ISSSTE, or Institute of Social Services and Social Security for Workers at the Service of the State).

Indeed, for the entire six years of Gustavo Díaz Ordaz's presidency, strike activity decreased to very low levels. Such a decline is especially apparent in terms of the number of strikers, which averaged less than 8,000, or not even one-sixth of that seen during the López Mateos presidency. If one assumes that good economic conditions facilitate strike activity given low unemployment and high employer profits, the decrease observed in strikes during the continued economic expansion of the Díaz Ordaz years is likely to be more a response to political than to strictly economic conditions. Under such a political interpretation, the labor leadership is seen as capable of mobilizing or not mobilizing the union rank and file according to the momentary needs of the political system.

Starting with the election of Luis Echeverría Álvarez in 1970, a new labor situation appeared, characterized by continued deterioration of the national economy and the appearance of the so-called independent unions in the automobile industry and elsewhere. Both factors help explain the intensification of strike activity in this recent period, as measured by the number of strikes and of strikers. Worsening inflation, the promotion of "real prices" with the elimination of government subsidies, and the establishment of salary limits led to increased pressure for salary hikes. For the first time since Cárdenas, the demands of the labor movement were now responding to economic causes as workers sought to recover losses in their standard of living.

The same kind of economic motivation clearly continued as the cause of strikes during the presidency of José López Portillo (1977–82). The number of strikes averaged 886 per year, and the number of strikers per strike rose above 50,000, both much higher figures than those experienced under Echeverría. Such militancy was the result of the kind of economic deterioration that long had been the case in many other Latin American countries. Indeed, with price increases of 98.8 percent in 1982 and 80.8 percent in 1983, the limited salary hikes permitted by the state led to consecutive drops in real salary of 4.3 percent and 2.3 percent in those years. During this period, the relationship between labor and the state experienced considerable tension owing to the un-yielding stand taken by the latter. The López Portillo presidency ended with a dramatic rise in strikes and in *emplazamientos a huelga,* the official notice given by unions to employers that a strike will occur unless worker petitions are accepted.

Events from 1982 to 1995 suggest how much the special relationship between labor and the state suffered as a result of the worsening inflation and unemployment and the drop in the standard of living. The state, in turn, sought to moderate some of these effects with new food subsidies, permission to grant fringe benefits not directly affecting salaries, and policies geared to the maintenance of existing employment levels. Additional measures included low-interest loans from the social security system to ease the short-term financial needs of workers and government employees, and loans for house construction and car purchases for middle-level technicians and professionals linked to the state sector. While not fully compensating for real salary losses, such official responses permitted at least part of aggregate economic demand to continue to rise. It is worth noting that these measures were implemented through agreements between the unions and the state where the political commitment of both to Mexico's development was always publicly emphasized. These agreements took place within the political alliance between labor and the state and were perceived as such by Mexican workers.

The Labor Market

In the mid-1990s, the Mexican labor market was characterized by stable levels of unemployment and by an increase in the levels of informalization, especially in the service sector. The economically active population also had grown as a result of the increase in the number of people in households searching for remunerated work and of the higher percentage of women in the workforce (23.5 percent in 1990). Women comprised more than 40 percent of public employment in low-paying occupations, such as secretaries or primary school teachers. In the *maquiladora* (assembly plant) industry, more than 275,000 women worked in nonunionized factories with precarious working conditions. Women's employment also was related to family-based industrial activity in the garment sector, self-employment of women in food preparation or knitting and sewing activities for the national and international market, as well as domestic employment. In general, because occupations do not require formal training nor high levels of education, skill levels in the female workforce proved to be low.

Public employment stagnated at the beginning of the 1990s after having been an important buffer for unemployment for more than two decades. From intense rates of growth of this population in the 1970s and most of the 1980s (8 percent a year from 1975 to 1985), the growth rate became more modest, and public employment actually decreased from 2,097,200 persons in 1989 to 2,056,500 persons in 1991. In addition, in some of what had been or still were state-owned enterprises, employment levels decreased as a result of the process of restructuring that these companies underwent before being privatized.

Industrial employment tended to become concentrated in small- and medium-sized companies, and the composition of employment by firm size in manufacturing, retail sales, and services gave way to a highly atomized industrial structure. Industrial employment concentration decreased; indeed, the average size of manufacturing plants and the absolute decrease in manufacturing employment after 1982 resulted in an atomized industrial sector in which medium- and small-sized companies were increasing their participation in the employment of the productive structure of the country.

The spacial distribution of the working population changed, and new concentrations of industrial employment appeared in states such as Aguascalientes, México, Sonora, Coahuila, and Chihuahua; this had resulted from the relocation of production to "greenfield" sites, geared essentially to production for export. By the mid-1990s, a new economic space was being formed, with important effects in the composition of the labor force, which had become younger, with relatively higher educational levels but not necessarily higher skill levels, and was less aware of the traditions of union organization.

The number of people benefiting from social security mechanisms stagnated, especially from 1989 to 1994, when the number held steady at around 55 percent of the employed population, considering both the institutions that provide services to public employees (the ISSSTE) and for workers in private employment (Instituto Mexicano del Seguro Social —IMSS, or Mexican Institute of Social Security). One can conclude from this figure that the other 45 percent of the employed population did not benefit from social security, health services, and other facilities that ISSSTE and IMSS provide for the Mexican working people. In absolute numbers, there were about 11.5 million people covered by social security and 9 to 10 million people not covered by any kind of benefits. Given the dynamics of the labor market, it is likely that the inserted fraction tended to stagnate after 1991 as well.

Some of these trends within the national labor market caused an intensification of migration toward the northern border and the United States. Some depressed areas of Mexico, such as the south and central areas, home to high concentrations of Indians and the poor, experienced outward migration toward the north in increasing numbers. Migrants found jobs in the *maquiladora* industry at a very high rate: thus, total *maquiladora* employment went from 369,489 persons in 1988 to 580,498 persons in 1994, a 57.1 percent increase in the six-year period; most of these jobs were located in the electrical and electronics industry.

Such trends had a blocking effect on the process of proletarization that took place between 1940 and 1970. Therefore, the rate of unionization stagnated: indeed, when there are fewer and fewer blue- and white-collar workers with formal employment, there will inevitably be less and less unionized workers, especially if the legal framework for the constitution of unions remains the same.

The Situation in Official Unions

In 1983, the CTM and the government operated in the context of a "solidarity pact," where each of them committed to sacrifices in order to limit the effects of the crisis on the workers. For its part, the state proposed the relocation of some of the unemployed, price controls, and the creation of new jobs in the public sector. It also proposed to facilitate the creation of stores selling low-priced goods and to extend lines of credit for small- and medium-sized enterprises (traditionally flexible in matters of employment). In exchange for these concessions, organized labor promised to limit its salary demands.

Nevertheless, in parts of the private sector such as automobiles, steel, and metalworking, conflict erupted. Discontent among workers in these sectors was not only economic; it also derived from rank-and-file refusal to accept proposals that the labor leadership frequently had accepted without a fight. In their desire for a union democracy that associated demands for the renovation of the leadership with those for increased worker participation in union life, reformers never really questioned the entirety of the established union structure. Conscious of the risks entailed in such an extreme position, most limited themselves to issues relating to the particularities of their individual companies. Union democracy, as an issue, was raised within the framework of official labor law, thus making it more difficult for the state to reject it out of hand. Reformers sought merely to put into practice rights that existed on paper, but which never had been implemented.

Ironically, in the public sector where relations should have been running smoothly (as in unions representing government workers, especially the FSTSE), important manifestations of unrest surfaced, linked to the particularly strong effects of the economic crisis felt there. State-sector salary increases fell far behind inflation, while many fringe benefits—worker health care, for example—deteriorated in quality, bringing strong criticism from recipients. The ISSSTE particularly experienced such worsening service. State-sector workers, accustomed to special yearly salary increases announced in the annual presidential state of the union message every September 1, found this form of favoritism discontinued; salary policy for the bureaucracy now reflected that of the rest of the working class. Another area of discontent was among school teachers belonging to the Sindicato Nacional de Trabajadores de la Educación (SNTE, or National Union of Education Workers). Unhappy with the way the national SNTE leadership was dealing with membership problems, dissident locals organized the Coordinadora Nacional de Trabajadores de la Educación, or CNTE, which became quite active in challenging the official union. Given the sheer size of the 650,000 teachers involved, such a conflict would have major national ramifications.

The Situation in the Independent Unions

Private-sector unions not part of the official labor sector account for some 420,000 workers, found principally in the automobile, aviation, and metalworking industries. Rather than seeking to promote a radical ideology seeking fundamental changes in Mexican society, these unions have restricted their activities to local-level concerns such as improved salaries or the reform of internal union affairs, both of which they have militantly pursued. In contrast to the general passivity of the official unions in relation to salary increases, the independent unions have asked for amounts exceeding the maximum limits set by the state. Within the automobile industry, Volkswagen, Nissan, and General Motors have had to deal with such demands, as well as those of more democratically run union locals. In the course of much of the 1970s, the Unidad Obrera Independiente (UOI) played a major role in channeling demands by automobile workers for higher wages and in elaborating proposals for union democracy. Having learned from the violently repressed strikes of 1947–48 and 1958–59 that the state could not be challenged frontally, the UOI concluded that independent unionism in Mexico had to act within the limits of an official labor law that the state already accepted as legitimate. The state was faced with labor mobilization not seeking radical political ends, but limiting itself to questions of worker salary and local union democracy. The independent unions almost never questioned the political system itself; when they were initially so inclined, as in issues related to worker layoffs at the factory of Diesel Nacional (DINA), they reconsidered almost immediately.

In the public sector, a new type of independent unionism similar to the UOI appeared at various institutions of higher learning such as the Universidad Nacional Autónoma de México (UNAM, or the National Autonomous University of Mexico). The salary demands made in excess of the state-imposed limits benefited from the high visibility of union members who were both columnists in newspapers as well as university instructors. Strikes were frequent. Usually headed by unofficial leaders, these unions could go beyond what those in the private sector sought, not confining themselves to economic matters but directly challenging the state ideologically. On balance, they were not particularly successful in either regard, which eventually led to a serious internal crisis in 1984 and 1985.

Independent unionism has been a new force in the Mexican labor movement, contributing to the renovation of labor-state relations by both challenging the subordinate behavior of the official union leadership and making demands for internal union democracy. The leaders of the official unions have responded to this external competition by becoming more active in the promotion of worker interests and, at times, attempting to co-opt some of their rivals with offers of positions in the mainline union hierarchy. One case of the latter was that of the telephone workers' leader, Francisco Hernández Juárez, who was at various occasions an official in the national-level Congreso del Trabajo. He and Elba Esther Gordillo (from SNTE) played an important reformist role from 1989 to 1993 (during Carlos Salinas de Gortari's presidency) by organizing a new confederation, the Federación de Sindicatos de Bienes y Servicios (FESEBES, or Federation of Unions of Goods and Services).

Conclusion

It is impossible to believe that the present situation with regard to organized industrial labor evident in the mid-1990s will continue indefinitely. Indeed, as labor advocates remain unable to limit real salary decreases and as the state progressively distances itself from group support for its policies and becomes immeshed in defining the country's problems in a strictly technical fashion, the political integration of state and labor will be increasingly challenged. In the future, it will not be as easy as it has been to maintain labor's allegiance to the political system if significant benefits are no longer forthcoming to the union rank and file. As the official unions encounter more difficulties in limiting worker demands, the independent unions will gain greater worker support; these official unions, in turn, will be under greater pressure to support more radical positions in their efforts to maintain their support. Ultimately, the official unions may be forced to seriously question their alliance with the state if they are to retain their legitimacy. Any change of this nature would fundamentally alter one of the basic conditions under which the Mexican political system has been operating for decades. Such a change would contribute to the elimination of the Mexican paradox of mobilization without conflict and conflict without mobilization.

See also Partido de la Revolución Democrática (PRD); Partido Revolucionario Institucional (PRI)

Select Bibliography

Cook, María Lorena, *Organizing Dissent: Unions, the State and the Democratic Teacher's Movement in Mexico.* University Park: Pennsylvania State University Press, 1996.

Foweraker, Joe, *Popular Mobilization in Mexico: The Teacher's Movement, 1977–1987.* Cambridge and New York: Cambridge University Press, 1993.

Miller, Richard, "The Role of Labor Organizations in a Developing Country: The Case of Mexico." Ph.D. diss., Cornell University, 1966.

Roxborough, Ian, *Unions and Politics in Mexico: The Case of the Automobile Industry.* Cambridge and New York: Cambridge University Press, 1984.

Thompson, Mark, and Ian Roxborough, "Union Elections and Democracy in Mexico." *British Journal of Industrial Relations* 20:2 (1982).

Zapata, Francisco, "Social concertation in Mexico." In *Participation in Public Policy Making: The Role of Trade Unions and Employer's Associations,* edited by Tiziano Treu. Berlin: Walter De Gruyter, 1992.

—FRANCISCO ZAPATA

Industry and Industrialization

The great majority of scholars who have studied the industrialization of Mexico agree that it started during the long administration of Porfirio Díaz (president 1876–80 and 1884–1911), better known as the Porfiriato. In fact, even though it is possible to point out an evolution that starts in the crafts shops and textile mills of colonial times (some of which employed hundreds of workers who completed the whole manufacturing process under the same roof), the political and economical instability that characterized the first decades of Mexican Independence during the nineteenth century prevented full industrial development. It should be remembered that between 1821 and 1861, Mexico changed presidents 56 times, in addition to being invaded by the United States in 1847 and by France in 1862.

The first Mexican administrations trusted more in mining, agriculture, and trade as sources of national wealth, thereby neglecting almost completely the growth of manufacturing. The initiative of a group of industrialists to create a loan bank (Banco de Avío) in 1830, which would foster the textile industry, collapsed owing to the bank's necessity to finance some of the political groups fighting for power, while imported machinery deteriorated in port, unable to reach the factories.

The Porfiriato: The First Industrialization

It was not until the administration of Porfirio Díaz that the groundwork for industrial development was laid. The contributing factors were the country's political stability, as well as a series of measures directed, on the one hand, at creating an infrastructure of energy and transportation and, on the other, at opening the borders to U.S. and European capital. Starting in 1870, this foreign capital began flowing into the country, mainly to mining and railroads, but also to trade and manufacturing. In 1910, foreign investment reached between 67 and 73 percent of the country's total capital investment.

In those years, the most significant growth was seen in the railways; the amount of rail track in the country increased from 400 miles (640 kilometers) in 1877 to more than 3,000 miles (5,000 kilometers) in 1883, finally reaching 12,000 miles (19,000 kilometers) in 1910. This growth decreased transportation costs, which fostered mining, expanded commercial agriculture, and unified the internal market. Several scholars indicate that the growth of mining and agricultural exports also facilitated the growth of the internal market, which developed manufacturing.

Industrialists multiplied during the Porfiriato. In Chihuahua, Eduardo Creel gave an impulse to the flour industry, while in Monterrey the Garza family started its business empire with the founding of the Cuauhtémoc brewery. In Puebla, Tlaxcala, and Orizaba the textile industry grew, and local businessmen fostered the creation of electrical power plants, which not only supplied their factories but also neighboring cities. By 1910 Mexico produced cotton fabric, wool, linen, jute, leather goods, sugar, pasta, canned goods, wine, liquor, beer, cigarettes, cigars, paper, some chemical products (sulfuric acid and explosives), oils, soaps, candles, matches, stoneware, glass, and cement. In 1903, the country's first iron and steel mill was built with a starting capital of 10 million pesos, contributed by the most prominent industrialists of Monterrey. The plant had Latin America's first blast furnace, which was used to supply the railway and construction industries. By 1911, the manufacturing sector produced 12.1 percent of the gross national product (GNP) and employed 11.5 percent of the workforce.

Despite this spectacular growth of manufacturing, in the early years of the twentieth century the Mexican population was still predominantly rural, and the largest share of industrial investment was made in extractive industries (e.g., mining and oil) owned primarily by U.S. and British concerns.

Industry during the First Revolutionary Administrations

The armed conflict of 1910 to 1917 did not significantly affect manufacturing production, but the nation's economic structure suffered greatly. Thus, while the manufacturing sector's production decreased only 1 percent between 1910 and 1922, mining, agriculture, and livestock diminished by 4, 5.2, and 4.6 percent, respectively. In 1917 the banking industry was nationalized, and the currency's instability discouraged investment in all industrial sectors other than oil and mining, where foreign companies took advantage of the opportunity created by World War I to increase their production and exports.

The Constitution of 1917 also caused distrust among Mexican businessmen, who opposed Articles 27 and 123. Article 27 determined that the Mexican soil and subsoil were the nation's property, which in the opinion of businessmen meant that the principle of private property had been violated; Article 123 regulated working conditions by reducing the number of hours in the working day and creating a series of demands to employers that would lead, years later, to the Federal Work Law of 1931. Lacking a clear concept of industrial development, President Venustiano Carranza chose to invite the country's leading businessmen to discuss the issue in a national convention of industrialists and merchants, which gave rise to two large confederations: the Confederación de Cámaras Industriales de los Estados Unidos Mexicanos (CONCAMIN, or Confederation of Industrial Chambers of the United States of Mexico, established in 1917) and the Confederación de Cámaras Nacionales de Comercio (CONCANACO, or Confederation of National Chambers of Commerce, established in 1918).

The recognition of these confederations and the creation in 1925 of the Bank of Mexico, responsible for the issue of the nation's currency, allowed the gradual recovery of Mexico's credit rating and monetary stability. The Bank of Mexico, initially composed of 51 percent state capital and 49 percent private industrial capital, created the conditions for economic recovery. The interest shown by the administration of President Plutarco Elías Calles (1924–28) in creating a better road system and greater political stability than in previous years favored the recovery of the GNP, which according to some authors reached an annual growth rate of 5.8 percent between 1925 and 1928. In those years, the relative importance of the oil and mining industries decreased (owing, among other things, to the discovery of oil in South America), while the textile and electrical industries grew. More growth also was seen in the food and drink industries, and later in the manufacturing of simple consumer goods, such as cigarettes, paper, and shoes, and the processing of raw materials (sisal and cotton, which were destined for export markets). This growth was unexpectedly interrupted by the international financial crisis in 1929, which severely decreased the demand for exports of raw materials, thereby affecting the whole economy. Between 1930 and 1934, the nation's GNP not only stopped growing but even declined by 0.5 percent.

Under the administration of Lázaro Cárdenas (1934–40), the groundwork was laid to change the nation's economic model (which until then had been based on the export of raw materials) to a different model based on the state as chief promoter of economic development and on the industrial policy of import substitution (import substitution industrialization refers to a set of policies implemented by an activist, interventionist state designed to encourage the domestic production of previously imported manufactured goods). The nationalization of the railways and of the oil industry guaranteed, in the subsequent decades, the transportation of goods and a low-cost fuel supply, starting a subsidy that would last several decades and that would increase in magnitude in the coming years with the nationalization of the power and light industry and of other basic industries, such as steel. These state-owned companies provided cheap production parts to the Mexican industry and fostered its development during many decades. Likewise, the creation of the Mexican labor movement, as evidenced by the Confederación de Trabajadores de México (CTM, or Confederation of Mexican Workers), gave legal rights to the unions and at the same time provided adequate channels to the public and the industrial sectors to negotiate workers' demands in a peaceful way. Subsequently, such development neutralized potential union conflicts, thereby shaping a climate conducive to investment.

The Industrializing Project: From Import Substitution to Stabilizing Development

Starting in 1940, Mexico formally started a new economic orientation based on the need of rapid industrialization in order to become a member of the so-called developed countries. The demands created by World War II fostered industrialization in Mexico, where manufactured goods were produced for the internal market as well as for export to the United States.

In order to promote industrialization, the administrations of Manuel Avila Camacho (1940–46) and Miguel Alemán Valdés (1946–52) established a series of successive measures designed to strengthen Mexican industry during the war years and, later, to protect it at the end of hostilities when the United States once again would start full production of manufactured goods that would compete with Mexican goods. There also arose a new generation of young businessmen who, with relatively little capital, had started small businesses with growth potential that, in the coming years, would benefit from public policies.

A first step was the Law of Industries of Transformation, issued in 1941, which granted large tax breaks to those Mexican businessmen who could prove that their companies were "new" or "necessary." At the same time, the Bank of Mexico underwent restructuring, and the actions of the National Financing Institution (created in 1934 by the Lázaro Cárdenas administration to channel federal resources to different public works) were reoriented toward selective financing of industries and the creation of infrastructure for its development. Industries considered "new and necessary" received federal financing, tax breaks for up to 10 years, permits to import machinery, and other benefits. At the same time, a protectionist policy was consolidated that closed the nation's borders to those products that could be locally manufactured and that imposed restrictions on the establishment of foreign companies, all of which helped the development of a new, protected industrial base, which has been dubbed "the greenhouse industry."

Once the first industrializing effort passed, the nation's economic strategy focused on the so-called stabilizing development, which not only maintained the protectionism of the first decade of industrialization but reinforced it with the establishment of a stable exchange rate (the peso remained at US$12.50

between 1954 and 1976). The new strategy also maintained a highly favorable tax policy to private capital, and foreign investment was curtailed. This allowed the establishment of companies of mixed capital participation, which, being part Mexican, allowed foreign investors to benefit from the protection that the Mexican government granted to the national companies. Aided by U.S. president John F. Kennedy's Alliance for Progress, foreign capital flowed to Mexico and triggered manufacturing growth. It was in this period that the large multinational corporations established many subsidiaries in the country and benefited from Mexican protectionism. Some protests from nationalist businessmen who opposed foreign competition were heard, but these protests were silenced by measures such as the nationalization of the electric industry, which guaranteed the supply of low-cost energy, and by President Adolfo López Mateos's decree requiring local car manufacturers to include at least 60 percent domestically manufactured parts in all vehicles.

The policy of import substitution, based on protectionism, was preserved for four decades. This was a period of important changes: numerous companies were founded and prospered; simultaneously, aided by state protectionism, considerable capital was accumulated, while the nation's GNP started to increase until it reached a 6 percent annual rate. Between 1940 and 1960, manufacturing activity increased its participation in the GNP from 17 to 26 percent.

Mexican industrial structure underwent a relatively fast transition from simple manufacturing (as defined by its organization, technology, and distribution channels) to more complex manufacturing, which also meant the shift from perishable goods to intermediate, nonperishable, and capital goods. Thus, while in 1950 the subsector of foods, drinks, and tobacco comprised 38.5 percent of the total value created by the manufacturing sector, in 1958 it had decreased to only 29.3 percent; such was also the case of the textile subsector, which decreased from 15.6 to 10.3 percent during the same period. In contrast, the chemical industry increased its share from 9 to 13 percent, and the machinery industry went from 2.7 to 11.9 percent of the total value created by the manufacturing sector.

At the same time, the state-controlled oil and electricity sectors grew with lightning speed, maintaining low-cost energy to Mexican industry. By 1970, Mexico was almost self-sufficient in the production of food, oil and oil-derived products, steel, and many consumer goods. Not in vain, some observers called this period of growth "the Mexican Miracle."

The Crisis of Protectionism

At the start of the 1970s, a decrease in the growth rate of industrial investment and production and a declining output in the agribusiness sector forced the government to import growing quantities of raw materials. These tendencies exposed the crisis of the protectionist model, leading decision makers to look for new alternatives.

During the administrations of Luis Echeverría Álvarez (1970–76) and José López Portillo (1976–82), the slowdown of private investment led to an increase of public investment in the manufacturing and oil industries. Owing to a decrease in oil production, however, public investment gradually meant higher foreign debt. The increase of oil prices starting in 1976, on the other hand, promoted heavy government investment in the expansion of the oil industry under the assumption that hydrocarbon exports would foster general industrial development. In this period, strong investments were made in roads and other forms of transportation, and the growth of the petrochemical industry was given priority. In 1981, the state-owned Mexican oil monopoly (Petróleos Mexicanos, or PEMEX) generated almost half of the nation's total investment.

The unexpected decrease in international oil prices made evident the decay of the old economic model of import substitution. Rapid capital flight caused a severe decrease in industrial production and justified the nationalization of the private banks in 1982. The worldwide increase of interest rates worsened the nation's external debt, and the process of economic recovery also was blocked by a series of instabilities caused by protectionism, such as the concentration of industrial production centers in a few places, geared exclusively to the internal market; disorder among industrial sectors; high production costs that prevented effective international competition; and transformation of the country's export structures.

In response to this crisis, the administration of Miguel de la Madrid (1982–88) started the implementation of a new "neoliberal" development model (that is, a model adjusted to the guidelines of the International Monetary Fund, which stressed the payment of the external debt, the reduction of direct public economic activity, and the reorientation of national production toward external markets). These policies were consolidated during the presidency of Carlos Salinas de Gortari (1988–94), characterized by faster privatization of state-owned industries, the sale of the recently acquired banks, the opening of new investment areas traditionally reserved for the state (among them the petrochemical industry, as well as the management of highways, ports, and public services).

In compliance with the new economic policy oriented toward external markets, Mexico joined the General Agreement on Tariffs and Trade (GATT) in 1985, an international organization created to foster free trade among nations and accelerate the elimination of tariff barriers. In less than three years, Mexico went from being a protected country to part of a large worldwide market of diverse consumer goods, which put many Mexican manufacturers at a disadvantage. The North American Free Trade Agreement (NAFTA) among Mexico, the United States, and Canada, which went into effect on January 1, 1994, tried to reduce protectionist policies of Mexico's two most important foreign markets, apart from establishing a series of rules for trade exchange, not only concerning industrial production but also agricultural products, communications, and services. Mexico partially closed its borders to some countries (for example, by imposing higher tariffs to Chinese products) and became part of the North American trading block.

The Limitations of the Modernizing Project

The difficulties of the plan to modernize the Mexican economy became apparent with the crisis that marked the end of the presidency of Salinas and the beginning of the new administration of Ernesto Zedillo Ponce de León in 1994. Some of these difficulties had been anticipated by scholars such as Adam Przeworsky, who repeatedly warned about the risks of an economy that relied a great deal on the regulatory capacity of the market that, inevitably, would create regional imbalances or would cause the collapse of industrial sectors. Apart from the inequality of economic development among negotiating partners and the persistence of protectionism in many countries, it is important to point out that an important limitation of the export model of economic development has been the large domestic imbalance that characterizes the nation's industrial structure; this imbalance is seen, first of all, in the concentration of capital in a very small number of companies, and, second, in the large numbers of medium-sized, small, and "micro" businesses that have low quality control and low competitiveness.

Estimates based on a number of census data show that, by 1990, there were only 2,400 industries (1.95 percent of the nation's total) that employed more than 250 workers. These same industries, according to other data, dominated 66 percent of industrial production and 49.5 percent of all industrial jobs. These industries were followed by about 3,300 "medium-sized" businesses that employed between 101 and 250 workers and that comprised 2.62 percent of the total, whereas businesses with less than 100 workers formed the other 95 percent. Generally speaking, approximately 75 percent of the nation's businesses had fewer than 15 employees. Therefore, the latter belonged to the category of "microcompanies."

The leaders among the large industrial corporations (whose number in 1990 did not exceed 130) were PEMEX and the nation's five automotive companies, which were responsible for the largest increase in exports. To a lesser extent, export also grew in the following sectors: shoes, textiles, beer, paper, glass, and products for the construction industry. By the same token, in the late 1980s and early 1990s, the importance of the *maquiladora* industry grew enormously. The *maquiladoras*, established along the U.S. border, are intermediate or final assembly plants for industrial products. In many cases, the *maquiladoras* not only include large companies, but also medium or small companies that have been able to find a market niche and therefore have taken advantage of demand for certain products in the world market.

However, the new trade climate has had a negative impact on many medium, small, and "micro" companies. Their problems have included poor organization, lack of appropriate technology, and low adaptability to market forces. Often, these companies are family-owned and characterized by the owner's lack of vision and avoidance of risk. The small company is also hampered by the lack of credit, lack of personnel to comply with tax requirements, red tape, or union matters.

Throughout the late 1980s and early 1990s, several federal programs to help the micro, small, and medium companies were implemented, but these businesses complained of a lack of a broad economic policy that would allow them to overcome their problems so that they could export. In 1996 the administration of Ernesto Zedillo launched the Program of Industrial Policy and Foreign Trade, aimed at reconciling the opposition of large corporations to government controls with necessary help to small and medium companies in such forms as technological and administrative help and tax breaks so they can survive the market's unfavorable conditions. In order to achieve this, the Zedillo administration proposed, among other things, better business training, the strengthening of production chains and industrial zones all over the country, and finally, the improvement of technological infrastructure and federal help in all export activities.

See also Ecology; Industrial Labor; Maquiladoras; Mining; Petroleum; Women's Status and Occupation

Select Bibliography

Anderson, Rodney D., *Outcasts in Their Own Land: Mexican Industrial Workers, 1906–1911*. DeKalb: Northern Illinois University Press, 1976.

Haber, Stephen H., *Industry and Underdevelopment: The Industrialization of Mexico, 1890–1940*. Stanford, California: Stanford University Press, 1989.

— CRISTINA PUGA

Inquisition

The Inquisition was a special ecclesiastical and political institution created to combat or suppress heresy and crimes against the colonial church and the Hapsburg viceroyalty. This institution evolved in Mexico from its early European origins, developing a complex bureaucracy and system of procedures. The Inquisition served the important function of endeavoring to maintain social, religious, and political order by the use of coercive power in enforcing religious and political orthodoxy in New Spain. The Inquisition's religious and philosophical influence on various aspects of colonial Mexican life has been abundantly researched, but the very institutional structure, functioning, and jurisdictional conflicts of the Holy Office in Mexico have, to date, received little scholarly attention. Previous studies of the Inquisition were concerned with polemics over its relative cruelty or lenient nature, and the extent of atrocities committed by officials of the Holy Office. The Inquisition's cruel and coercive methods and juridical use of torture were unarguably inhumane, and the institution itself must be condemned as a sad comment on human history. Furthermore, the Inquisition's reprehensible censorship of literature and ideas through its published "Index of Prohibited Books" hindered the development of cultural and intellectual life in New Spain. Nevertheless, early Inquisition historiography focused too much attention on those horrors and spent little time analyzing the Inquisition's impact on society and its effects upon the social and ethnic groups that made up the intricate colonial milieu of New Spain.

Modern revisionist studies, however, have moved beyond the salutary or condemnatory agendas of earlier scholarship to focus on the role the Inquisition played in the formation of the society of New Spain. Recent historical work also has drawn on the rich documentation produced by the Inquisition's complex bureaucracy to reconstruct the moral, ethical, and religious life of colonial Mexico.

Origins, Functions, and Officials of the Inquisition in Mexico

Pope Gregory IX established the Inquisition in 1233 as a permanent tribunal to combat several dissident movements during the Middle Ages. Before that time the job of punishing crimes against the faith belonged to the bishops. Pope Gregory IX, seeing the bishops burdened with their pastoral duties, created tribunals throughout France, Germany, and Italy. Spain, busy in its "reconquest of territory" from the Moors, was left without a formal Inquisition. In 1478, at the request of Fernando V and Isabel I, Pope Sixtus IV established an independent Spanish Inquisition, which served as the model for the Inquisition in the Americas.

From its founding, a unique aspect of the Spanish Inquisition was its virtual independence from papal control. The pope conceded to the Spanish Crown the privilege of royal patronage *(patronato real)*, giving the Crown control over the nomination of all ecclesiastical personnel in Spain and America, including inquisitorial personnel. Although in theory the Inquisition was an ecclesiastical institution, the appointment of inquisitors and other functionaries of the Holy Office became the privilege of the secular monarch.

King Felipe II did not officially create the Tribunal of the Inquisition in New Spain until the royal decree of January 25, 1569. Another royal order dated August 16, 1570, removed the Indians from its jurisdiction and gave the Tribunal of Mexico authority over all of New Spain, including the Philippines, Guatemala, and the Bishopric of Nicaragua. The Inquisition in New Spain functioned from 1570 until its final abolition in 1820 upon Mexico's Independence from Spain, although it changed over time in its focus and primary functions.

From 1522 to 1569, before the official founding of the Tribunal of the Inquisition in New Spain, the monastic orders and the early bishops assumed apostolic powers as inquisitors in a primitive form of Inquisition. This primitive Inquisition attempted to correct the spiritual crimes of the early conquerors and reprimand "erring" Indian neophytes and pagans. From 1571 to 1700, with the removal of its jurisdiction over the Indians, the Mexican Inquisition had as its main function the prosecution and punishment of all acts contrary to the Catholic faith, including apostasy, heresy, and the continued practice of the Jewish religion by newly converted Jews (called *conversos* or "New Christians"). Similarly, the Inquisition often was occupied in the punishment of actions contrary to Christian morality, including blasphemy, bigamy, sodomy, bestiality, fornication, concubinage, and the solicitation of sex in the confessional by priests. The Inquisition further stifled intellectual development by the publication of an alphabetical index of prohibited books, which it sent to its inquisitors and commissaries in the Americas. The Inquisition's agents in New Spain, with this "Index" in hand, made routine visits to ships *(visitas de naos)* in order to search for prohibited books, and they investigated book dealers and private collectors. The final period of the Mexican Inquisition, from 1700 to 1820, saw the growing political use of the Inquisition for the punishment of all dissidents with respect to Catholic dogma and teaching (including Lutherans and other Protestant sects) as well as those who held or stated propositions contrary to the church or the king. Hundreds of residents of New Spain faced Inquisition trials during this period, including two of the most famous leaders of the Mexican Independence movement, Father Miguel Hidalgo y Costilla and José María Morelos y Pavón.

Institutional Hierarchy

Atop the hierarchy of the Holy Office of the Inquisition (also known as the Tribunal) of New Spain sat two to three superior ecclesiastical judges. These inquisitors were aided by a *promotor fiscal* (prosecutor), who brought the initial accusation of the prisoners before the Tribunal, and a *secretario* (secretary), who authorized all of the documents, edicts, and dispatches of the Holy Office. Two *notarios del secreto* (notaries) certified the declarations and testimony of witnesses before the Tribunal and cared for the archive of the Inquisition.

The inquisitors relied on the help of six *consultores* (councillors), who gave them legal advice. These councillors included two theologians and four doctors of canon law. Along with these councillors there were eight *calificadores* (qualifiers—all doctors in theology or canon and civil law), who weighed the evidence presented in each case to decide if there was sufficient cause to proceed in a formal trial. Twelve *alguaciles* (constables) saw to the apprehension of the prisoners. Officials called *alcaldes* served as guards at the various jails used by the Inquisition, including the *carcel secreta* (secret prison for incarceration during the trial until sentencing), the *carcel de penitencia* (for short prison sentences), and the *carcel perpetua* (for those condemned to life in prison). There

also were several *proveedores*, entrusted with the feeding of prisoners. The other lesser officials of the Tribunal included many doormen, several surgeons and doctors required by law to be present during the interrogation and torture of prisoners, and even a barber for the prisoners.

A separate system of secular or lay persons formed an elite group of constables or policemen of the Inquisition, called *familiares*. All those nominated to these positions had their family histories investigated to ensure that they were "old Christians of good faith and customs." These *familiares* of the Inquisition held privileged positions that gave them exemption from prosecution in civil cases. They aided the officials of the Inquisition in the discovery, apprehension, and arrest of suspects. The numbers of these *familiares* varied, but by law there were 12 *familiares* in Mexico City, 4 *familiares* in the seat of each bishopric, and 1 *familiar* in each Spanish town.

A subsidiary institution controlled by the Tribunal of Mexico was the *Real Fisco* (Royal Fiscal Office of the Inquisition), entrusted with the management of the confiscated property and goods of those convicted by the Inquisition. This branch of the Holy Office had the power and duty to oversee the finances and pay for salaries and various fees that the Inquisition incurred during its proceedings. It counted on the services of a *contador* (accountant), several lawyers, and two *notarios del secuestro,* who testified to everything relative to the confiscation of goods.

Throughout the rest of the provinces there were commissaries of the Inquisition who were nominated by the inquisitors and approved by the viceroy and the Crown. Each province held one commissary *(comisario)* of the Inquisition who operated a minor tribunal of the Holy Office, investigating crimes against the faith and then conducting the initial arrest and trial of the accused. In some cases commissaries even passed preliminary sentences, but they could not pass the definitive sentences unless ordered to do so by the Tribunal in Mexico. The commissariats of the Inquisition employed at least one notary, a constable, and a jailer.

Many of the fees and salaries of the Inquisition in New Spain were paid from the fines and confiscated goods of those convicted by the Holy Office. Interpretations of the Inquisition as a corrupt institution bent on the confiscation of as much property as possible emerged from the study of the finances of the Inquisition. Although this extreme interpretation has been disproved, the payment of the officials' salaries exclusively from the sequestered goods of the accused lent itself to corruption. In order to ensure a more secure source of revenue and eliminate corruption,

Pope Urban VIII in 1627 ordered that in each cathedral seat of the Inquisition, one of the prebends or canonries funded by tithe revenues was to be suppressed and its rents applied to the payment of the Inquisition salaries. Scholars such as Henry Lea nevertheless argue that the finances of the Inquisition in New Spain remained precarious as the Holy Office continued to clash with the king and treasury officials concerning salaries.

Trials and Procedures

According to civil and canon law, all Inquisition trials had to follow a standard procedure established since the founding by the publication of Tomás de Torquemada's *Instrucciones* in 1484. The procedure usually began with an *edicto de la fé*, a proclamation requiring, under pain of excommunication, the denunciation of all offenses against the faith. These edicts were periodically placed in all parish churches and often began the process of the Inquisition by urging people to denounce themselves or others of crimes committed against the faith.

Induced by the warnings of the *edicto de la fé*, many people came forward denouncing themselves or giving testimony of crimes committed against the faith by their neighbors. Those who denounced crimes against the faith were summoned before the Inquisition to give testimony to the case. During the investigation each witness declared what he or she knew about the crime and the individual was then sworn to secrecy. Several days after taking the testimony, the witnesses would be recalled to reaffirm their testimonies. Those discovered giving false testimony were tried for the crime of perjury (*téstigo falso*).

After the testimony was taken and reaffirmed, the *calificadores* examined the documents. If they deemed the evidence of the testimony or denunciations sufficient, they authorized the inquisitors to proceed in the formation of a case. The inquisitors then ordered their *alguaciles* or the *familiares* of the Holy Office to arrest the accused. The accused remained incarcerated in the secret prison throughout the trial until sentencing. Not infrequently, prisoners would spend years in jail waiting for their trial. Many perished in jail before the completion of their trials. The Royal Fiscal Office inventoried the prisoner's estate and embargoed his or her goods for the duration of the trial. The accused paid the cost of imprisonment from the revenues of their estate, or if they were poor the Inquisition provided for their sustenance.

The Tribunal seldom informed defendants about the nature of their alleged crimes. It instead told the accused to "examine" their conscience and make a declaration of anything that they found to be "contrary to the faith." The court instructed defendants to make a list of their enemies, whose testimony and denunciations were disregarded in the case. The accused then petitioned and presented their own witnesses, who testified to the defendants' good Christian nature.

The inquisitors and their *consultores* examined the evidence in the case and either insisted on the confession of the accused or continued the examination of witnesses. If torture were inflicted upon the prisoner, the Tribunal administered it once at this point in the trial's proceedings. Torture was used in many cases, but not all of the Inquisition's prisoners were tortured. Strict guidelines were established for the administration and duration of torture, but the process itself led to abuses. The law required that torture only be applied once, but many inquisitors and their aides "suspended" the torture sessions and resumed them over a period of several days. Perhaps more horrifying is the fact that the tortures meted out by the Inquisition and its ministers were equaled or surpassed in rigor by those administered by the civil authorities of the same period in both Spain and the Americas.

After the conclusion of a case, the inquisitors decided upon an appropriate punishment, according to the gravity of the crime. Prisoners who confessed or denounced themselves, showing repentance for their crimes, often received lighter sentences. They were given sentences of reconciliation (*sentencia de reconciliación*), including the wearing of penitential garments called *san benitos* during an *auto de fé* as a mark of shame for their crime. This punishment was combined with short- or long-term imprisonment, a pecuniary fine, forced pilgrimage, or the necessity of hearing masses with other penitents, as well as the prohibition of holding any dignity or public office.

Prisoners pronounced guilty, but who did not confess or repent, were sentenced to death (*sentencia ordinaria o de muerte*). This sentence also entailed excommunication and the total confiscation of the prisoners' estate, which went to the Royal Fiscal Office of the Inquisition. Since the inquisitors could not carry out a corporal sentence themselves, they ordered the prisoner to be "relaxed" to the secular authorities (*relajado al brazo secular*), who executed the prisoner.

The Inquisition and the secular authorities publicly administered all punishments at a formal function called an *auto de fé*. These *autos de fé* were public spectacles undertaken at great cost and attended by all major functionaries of the ecclesiastical and civil governments of New Spain. They were intended to serve as a deterrent to religious heterodoxy and were a major didactic tool of the Inquisition. The public display and humiliation of those condemned served as the Inquisition's cruelest and most degrading weapon against what it considered to be immorality and heretical movements.

Inquisition Studies and the Use of Inquisition Sources: A Historiographical Review

The formal study of the Inquisition did not begin until after the middle of the nineteenth century. Before that time the institution and its documentation were jealously guarded; even its procedures were mired in secrecy. The earliest studies of the Inquisition were tainted by the controversy over the "Black Legend" of Spanish cruelty during the Conquest. Early historians of the Inquisition in New Spain either followed their own political or religious convictions in their analyses or dedicated themselves to the publication of documents and brief institutional sketches.

The Chilean historian, José Toribio Medina, was the first serious scholar to study the Inquisition in the Americas. Following in the Germanic tradition of Leopold von Ranke, Medina limited himself to the publication of primary documents with little serious analysis. Soon after, Henry Charles Lea polemicized the history of the Inquisition in his famous book on the Inquisition published in 1908. He contributed to the "Black Legend" by naively attributing the entire failure of the Spanish Empire on the Americas to the existence of the Inquisition. Lea argued that the Inquisition retarded the political and economic development of the colonies owing to its "malignant influence" on following generations. Although Lea perhaps overstated the Inquisition's negative influence on the politics and economics of nineteenth-century Latin American nations, he was not wrong in stating that the Inquisition had a negative impact on the intellectual development of the pre-Independence period.

Nevertheless, this early historiography was deficient because it focused more on the condemnation or defense of the Inquisition, rather than on a critical analysis of the institution and its impact on colonial society. Lea and other early scholars of the Inquisition continued to focus their efforts on describing the cruel and repressive nature of the institution. This trend in the literature began to change during the late 1970s, however, with the publication of important analytical and interpretive works by scholars both in the United States and Mexico. This new approach to the critical use of Inquisition sources in the study of colonial society and religion added an exciting and progressive dimension to the study of colonial history. The new historiography focused more on the people and actors in the "procesos" of the Inquisition than upon the institution of the Inquisition itself. Following new trends that emphasized the necessity of regional studies, these authors focused their examination upon the analysis of the Inquisition in various geographical regions. Medina's and Lea's emphasis on continental and institutional examinations of the Inquisition were left behind as modern scholars focused their attention on the impact of the Inquisition upon the people and societies of colonial America. The focus on "Black Legend" approaches and the emphasis on political objectives in the study of the Inquisition was abandoned as scholars focused more on its impact on colonial beliefs, religious practices, and philosophy.

Inquisition trial records are now used as a rich source of information on almost every facet of life in colonial Mexico, from the examination of purported mental illnesses in the colony to the study of the impact of the French Enlightenment upon eighteenth-century New Spain. Inquisition documents have enabled historians to better understand and enrich the study of the philosophical and intellectual history of Mexico, which is difficult to trace from civil documentation alone. Ethnohistorical and social histories of the role of women and minorities during the colonial period have used Inquisition sources in order to reveal the nature of these understudied groups and their significance to colonial Mexican society. Similar studies of Inquisition documents by scholars such as Noemí Quezada, Asunción Lavrin, Laura Lewis, and Ruth Behar have added interesting interpretations of colonial and pre-Conquest witchcraft, magic, sexual mores, and gender conflicts. Soriano Ramos and José Abel's study of the Inquisition's censorship of prohibited books puts to good use the Inquisition's ominous "Index" in order to reconstruct colonial attitudes towards marriage, family, and sexuality. Stanley Hordes has examined the relationship between colonial Jews and the Inquisition in New Spain, with an emphasis on revisionism and the interpretive problems caused by previous studies' moralistic approaches to the study of Judaism. Colin Palmer's work with African slave societies in New Spain similarly employed Inquisition documents in order to describe the survival of African folk religious practices.

These exciting advances in the historiography illustrate the creative use of Inquisition documentary sources in the recreation of colonial society, the nature of colonial gender relations, sexual mores, racism, and religious beliefs. Still, more work can be done in reconstructing various facets of colonial history through the use of Inquisition materials. The Inquisition's documents offer modern historians the possibility of recreating aspects of colonial society that otherwise would have been lost to history.

Select Bibliography

Behar, Ruth, "Sex and Sin: Witchcraft and the Devil in Late Colonial Mexico." *American Ethnologist* 14 (1987).

_____, "The Visions of a Guachichil Witch in 1599: A Window on the Subjugation of Mexico's Hunters-Gatherers." *Ethnohistory* 34:2 (Spring 1987).

Greenleaf, Richard E., *The Mexican Inquisition of the Sixteenth Century*. Albuquerque: University of New Mexico Press, 1969.

_____, "Historiography of the Mexican Inquisition: Evolution of Interpretations and Methodologies." In *Cultural Encounters: The Impact of the Inquisition in Spain and the New World*, edited by Mary Elizabeth Perry and Anne J. Cruz. Berkeley: University of California Press, 1991.

Hordes, Stanley, "Historiographical Problems in the Study of the Inquisition and the Mexican Crypto-Jews in the Seventeenth Century." *AJA* 34:2 (November 1982).

Lavrin, Asunción, *Sexuality and Marriage in Colonial Latin America*. Lincoln: University of Nebraska Press, 1989.

Lea, Henry Charles, *The Inquisition in the Spanish Dependencies*. New York: Macmillan, 1908.

Lewis, Laura, "The 'Weakness' of Women and the Feminization of the Indian in Colonial Mexico." *Colonial Latin American Review* 5:1 (1996).

Liebman, Seymour, *The Jews in New Spain: Faith, Flame and the Inquisition*. Miami, Florida: University of Miami Press, 1970.

Plaidy, Jean, "The Inquisition in Mexico." In *The Spanish Inquisition*. New York: Barnes and Noble, 1994.

Schons, Dorothy, *Book Censorship in New Spain*. Austin: University of Texas Press, 1950.

—JOHN F. CHUCHIAK IV

Iturbide, Agustín de 1783–1824

Leader in the Wars of Independence and Emperor of Mexico

The rule of Agustín Cosme Damian de Iturbide represents a transition between the last years of the viceregal regime and the attainment of full independence. The limitations of an empty treasury, a ruined rural economy, a swollen bureaucracy, and a large military precluded any rapid merger of the diverse political entities seeking to guide Mexico at the time. Convinced that such circumstances justified the need for a strong ruler, Iturbide attempted to rule as a constitutional monarch (1822–23). Although he failed as an emperor, Iturbide does not warrant the demonization he received from his contemporary enemies as well as most historians.

Iturbide reflected the views of upper-class criollos (those of Spanish descent born in the Americas), who were determined to preserve the status quo. Iturbide came from a noble Basque family that emigrated to Michoacán in the middle of the eighteenth century. After failing at college, Iturbide began managing his father's hacienda. Like many criollos, Iturbide became an officer in a viceregal regiment at the age of 14. After his 1805 marriage to an upper-class criolla, Iturbide supported the Mexico City revolt that dumped Viceroy José de Iturrigaray in favor of the hard-liner Pedro Garibay. The Iturbide family was so conservative that they sent the new Spanish junta funds. Satisfied with this new order, Iturbide purchased a hacienda worth 93,000 pesos.

The Hidalgo Revolt of 1810, as historian Brian R. Hamnett has demonstrated, responded to myriad local and regional socioeconomic tensions that broke out during a period of imperial confusion and viceregal weaknesses. The radical nature of the Hidalgo insurrection affected Iturbide quickly. Miguel Hidalgo y Costilla's followers sacked Iturbide's property as well as his father's hacienda. Not surprisingly, Iturbide fought the Hidalgo rebels that headed for Mexico City. Iturbide performed well, and the viceroyalty promoted him to the rank of colonel after Iturbide crushed guerrillas in the Bajío area. By the end of 1813, Iturbide had been named overall regional commander of this area.

But Iturbide also became dissatisfied with Spanish rule of Mexico. His frustration resulted from his personal ambitions. Obviously a gifted military leader, Iturbide grew resentful when Spanish officials blocked his promotion because he was a criollo. According to the research of scholar William S. Robertson, the Spanish received many complaints about Iturbide, who was accused of being agnostic, jailing women, torturing prisoners, and seizing haciendas as well as reselling their crops for personal profit. The last charge resulted in the Spanish commander, Félix María Calleja del Rey, removing Iturbide from his troop command.

At this point, Iturbide was still too conservative to consider joining the rebels. In fact, according to

Robertson, Iturbide dreamed of knighthood and traveling to Spain. Frustrated, the vain but ambitious Iturbide sulked in Mexico City, often spending large sums on gambling and prostitutes. As his bitterness increased, Iturbide began to reconsider his loyalty to Spain.

Meanwhile, the rebellion continued. Regional insurgency often was directed at local Spanish merchants to whom the rebels owed high debts. Fighting often was fierce, and people changed sides with alarming frequency. Often, local caciques joined the conflict, setting the stage for regional caudillos who would prevail in various regions after 1821. No one controlled the regional rebels well. At the same time, the viceroy's counterinsurgency tactics could not bring about victory. The insurgency was organized through a network of priests, muleteers, and bandits that became impossible to crush. Guadalupe Victoria emerged as a prominent rebel leader in the Puebla-Veracruz region, while Vicente Guerrero directed insurgents in Oaxaca.

Iturbide's fortunes changed when Viceroy Juan Ruíz de Apodaca gave him a chance to capture Guerrero by appointing Iturbide royal commander to defeat the resistance in Oaxaca. Iturbide's main task was to persuade Guerrero to accept a pardon. By now, however, Iturbide had begun to question the durability of Spanish power, and he considered an opportunity to join in securing Mexico's independence. Iturbide soon began negotiating with Guerrero, various generals, and bishops so that he could take power by means of a brilliant compromise. The rebel leaders were desperate to break the stalemate. Although Spain was weakening, the royalist forces had gained the upper hand over insurgent activity by 1816 or 1818. Many insurrectionaries had accepted the amnesty offer made by Viceroy Juan Ruíz de Apodaca in 1817. Later, Apodaca claimed that the rebellion could be considered finished, despite stubborn resistance in some regions.

Iturbide announced his compromise measure, the Plan de Iguala, from his Cocula headquarters on February 23, 1821. It brought together liberals and conservatives, rebels and royalists, criollos and Spaniards, under broad provisions. The most important assurances of the 26 articles in the Plan de Iguala were its "Three Guarantees": first, Catholicism would be the state religion and other faiths would not be tolerated; second, Mexico would be independent as a constitutional monarchy; finally, there would be equal treatment for Spaniards and Mexicans.

The plan called for the establishment of a monarchy, for Iturbide and the criollos believed that only this form of government could preserve order. King Fernando VII of Spain was invited to come to Mexico as its emperor; if Fernando refused, other members of the Castilian royal family or another reigning dynasty in Europe would be solicited. The plan established a provisional governing body known as the Sovereign Provisional Governing Junta, headed by Iturbide himself. The junta would name a regency to exercise executive power until a monarch arrived. Meanwhile, the junta would govern until the country elected a new congress. Therefore, the junta became an interim legislature, and the regency functioned as an interim executive. Congress would designate the new monarch if Fernando VII, his brothers, and nephews refused invitations to rule as Mexican monarch. The new congress would also write a new constitution to replace the 1812 Spanish Constitution.

The Plan de Iguala was moderate, but Iturbide skillfully played to demands everywhere for peace. Although the upper class maintained its privileges, the news that caste distinctions would be abolished excited many among the masses. The Plan de Iguala was a clever settlement that satisfied criollo army officers, church leaders, and most insurgents, partially because most Mexicans assumed Fernando VII would not leave Madrid. Spain's desperate European situation contributed as much to independence for Mexico as Iturbide's arrangements.

The Plan de Iguala received virtually universal acceptance after Vicente Guerrero, the major rebel in the southern district, accepted it. Once Guerrero placed himself under Iturbide's orders, remaining groups joined quickly. Other veteran rebel leaders, such as Guadalupe Victoria and Nicolás Bravo, accepted Iturbide's leadership because the Plan de Iguala seemed to be the best way to obtain independence. The insurrectionaries themselves simply had not been able to decide upon the most suitable form of government that could appeal to the majority. Aside from negotiations with Guerrero, therefore, Iturbide needed to conduct few face-to-face discussions with the heads of other insurgent forces. The rapid speed with which the masses and the church accepted the Plan de Iguala precluded any serious disagreements with Iturbide.

With 1,800 troops and a seized silver shipment intended for export from Acapulco, Iturbide quickly rallied Mexico to his cause. He offered land and oxen to those who would volunteer to join his Trigarantine Army. The royal army began to desert to Iturbide's forces quickly as General Antonio López de Santa Anna won key victories for Iturbide's cause in Veracruz. Iturbide treated surrendering royal forces kindly, a policy that added to his momentum. By July 1821, Iturbide controlled all of Mexico except the capital, the port of Veracruz, and Perote.

Ultimately, Spain sent a veteran liberal, Juan O'Donojú, to arrange autonomy for New Spain. Iturbide accepted O'Donojú's offer to negotiate, and they met in Córdoba. In August 1821, O'Donojú quickly accepted Iturbide's conditions, known as the Treaties of Córdoba, which mirrored the provisions of the Plan de Iguala. Spain now committed itself to recognize the new Mexican Empire as an independent monarchy. O'Donojú then resigned as Spain's last viceroy as Iturbide entered Mexico City triumphantly in September 1821.

Initially, Iturbide ruled Mexico as president of the regency. To his credit, Iturbide divided the 12 members of the junta equally between conservatives and liberals. Wide support existed for Iturbide to become emperor. Because of its regional nature, the 11-year war for independence did not unify Mexico completely, but Iturbide's victory mandated him to exercise power as Mexico's first leader after Independence. Iturbide enjoyed support from the army, and no nationwide opposition rose against his authority. When it became clear that no European monarch would assume the Mexican throne, the aggressive Iturbide usurped power. Although Congress elected Iturbide emperor on a legal basis in May 1822, the voting took place under threat of army bayonets. As scholar Timothy Anna asserts, Congress preferred Iturbide over a Bourbon monarch because the legislature could dictate the terms of his oath of office.

Iturbide's rule as monarch was characterized by a string of unsettling mistakes, such as his extravagant inauguration, a court emulating those in Europe, and an expensive palace remodeling. After he began to clash with Congress, Iturbide exercised press censorship, jailed opponents arbitrarily, militarized justice, and chose personally members of the new supreme court. Amid steadily mounting debts and bad economic conditions, the government resorted to forced loans from the Catholic Church and various merchants.

Iturbide had promised a limited monarchy, but his rule turned out to be authoritarian. The emperor's power base appears to have been built on unwarranted hopes rather than real benefits. Moreover, the monarchy became too expensive during a time of fiscal and economic crisis. The belief that a republic would bring about faster economic growth by now had become pervasive.

Iturbide's response to the growing political opposition soon sealed his fate. When deputies protested his decisions, Iturbide labeled all his critics as foreign spies. Becoming testy and impatient, Iturbide finally dissolved Congress and appointed another junta to take the place of the legislature in October 1822. Many Mexicans now viewed Iturbide as a despot, and sentiment for a republic continued to increase.

Timothy Anna alleges that Iturbide stepped down magnanimously from his throne in order to avoid civil war, but a better explanation is that the caudillos simply threw Iturbide out. Meanwhile, the Spanish garrison in Veracruz revolted at about the same time that General Santa Anna rose against Iturbide. With the support of Guadalupe Victoria and other Independence forces, Santa Anna called for the establishment of a republic. By February 1823, the emperor held little more than the Mexico City area. After promising to reconvene the legislature, Iturbide found that he could no longer continue and abdicated in March 1823.

Iturbide departed Mexico for Europe in May 1823 after accepting a handsome sum of money in return for a promise never to return. Insecure after the republic did not send him his pension, Iturbide believed that his life was in danger. Because the emerging Holy Alliance on the European continent considered Iturbide a danger, Iturbide took up residence in Britain, which opposed the other European monarchies' hostility to constitutional rule. Despite the attempts of Argentine exile José de San Martín to persuade him not to return to Mexico, Iturbide claimed that the masses wanted him back and imagined that only he could stop a feared invasion of Mexico by the Holy Alliance powers.

Iturbide's decision to return proved fatal. Six days passed after he sailed from Southhampton in May 1824 before anyone noticed that Iturbide had left. On board his ship, Iturbide wrote pamphlets stating that he came not as an emperor but as a soldier who would defend and unify Mexico. What Iturbide did not know was that the Mexican Congress already had declared that should he reenter, he would be placed outside the law and condemned as a traitor. Iturbide finally landed in Tamaulipas. Despite Iturbide's disguise, a soldier recognized his style in mounting a horse and reported him to local authorities. By almost unanimous vote, the Tamaulipas state legislature condemned Iturbide to death. Iturbide was captured and shot; he died at the age of 41. Iturbide's significance quickly faded from the minds of his countrymen. Later, in 1838, the republic brought his remains to Mexico City and gave his relatives financial security.

Iturbide experienced a strange fate for a leader who brought about Mexico's Independence, ending a bloody civil war with an imaginative plan acceptable to all. But although he was a great soldier and a skilled leader in his early days, Iturbide never truly united the country; he merely persuaded the criollo upper class to expel the Spanish overlords while maintaining their own oppressive hold on the poor. The failure of his monarchy strengthened the republic and opened the door for the liberals to take power.

Select Bibliography

Anna, Timothy E., *The Mexican Empire of Iturbide*. Lincoln: University of Nebraska Press, 1990.
Hamnett, Brian R., *Roots of Insurgency: Mexican Regions, 1750–1824*. Cambridge and New York: Cambridge University Press, 1986.
Robertson, William Spence, *Iturbide of Mexico*. Durham, North Carolina: Duke University Press, 1952.

—Douglas W. Richmond

J

Juárez, Benito 1806–72

President

Benito Juárez, who held the presidential office from January 1858 until his death in July 1872, has been the object of so much mythology that it is almost impossible to uncover the actual facts of his life. Official symbolism has transformed him into the immovable stone figure that stands in countless Mexican plazas. By way of reaction to the hagiography, a counter-mythology has developed that attributes to him all manner of failings, treasons, and abuses. Perhaps the best way to approach Benito Juárez is through the five most controversial actions of his career: the negotiation of the McLane-Ocampo Treaty with the United States in 1859; the extension in November 1865 of the presidential term for the duration of the War of the French Intervention; the execution of the Interventionists' puppet emperor, Maximilian von Hapsburg, in June 1867; the proposed plebiscite for reform of the 1857 Constitution in August 1867; and his second reelection in 1871. The first stemmed from his admiration for the United States as the model of republican liberal democracy, which he wanted Mexico to follow. The second originated from a determination not to relinquish leadership of the Liberal cause during an unfinished war against foreign intervention. The third action constituted a warning to European monarchies not to interfere with Mexican sovereignty and the republican tradition. The fourth resulted from a long-held belief that the 1857 Constitution had enabled state governors and the legislative power to gain the upper hand in the political struggle between region and center, legislature and executive. The fifth may well have been a serious miscalculation born of a belief that his work, interrupted by the French Intervention (1862–67), had not been completed.

Benito Juárez was born a Zapotec Indian in the Oaxaca highland village of Guelatao (near Ixtlán) in 1806, and he rose to become a qualified, practicing lawyer in the state capital during the 1830s and 1840s. Originally destined for an ecclesiastical career, he abandoned the Oaxaca City Seminary in 1828 and matriculated at the newly founded (1827) secular Institute of Science and Arts of the State of Oaxaca, of which he became secretary in 1832. There, he came under the influence of a leading local Liberal professor of logic, mathematics, and ethics, Miguel Méndez, another Zapotec from the highlands.

Juárez's political consciousness dawned with the presidential campaign of 1828, in which he supported the candidacy of the former insurgent chieftain, Vicente Guerrero. In 1832, Juárez became a member of the city council and in the following year a deputy in the state congress. Juárez's political position in support of the Valentín Gómez Farías administration of 1833–34 clearly identified him as a prominent provincial Liberal. During the rule of the centralists (1836–46), Juárez experienced a temporary political eclipse, but he was able to reenter political life by 1838. In 1843, he married Margarita Maza. He became secretary to state governor Antonio de León in 1844.

The collapse of Centralism in 1846 and the restoration of the Federal Constitution of 1824 opened the way for Juárez's accession to the Oaxaca state governorship in 1847 and his subsequent election to that office for the term 1848 to 1852. In spite of efforts to develop primary public education, his first term as governor was marred by the ongoing crisis in the southern sector of the Isthmus of Tehuantepec, which involved disputes of land ownership and salt collecting rights between private interests and indigenous communities, rivalry between Tehuantepec and Juchitán, and the polarization of provincial capital and subregion. Local and national conflicts combined to undermine the state Liberal regime in 1853. Juárez, along with other leading Liberals, was arrested in 1853 by the dictatorship of Antonio López de Santa Anna, and he went into exile in New Orleans. Juárez's family remained in Oaxaca under the protection of his two associates, Miguel Castro and Ignacio Mejía.

The national career of Juárez began with the triumph of the Revolution of Ayutla, which ousted Santa Anna in 1855. Juárez gained his first ministerial appointment as secretary for justice and ecclesiastical affairs under the interim presidency of Juan Alvarez (October to December 1855). From this position, on November 23, 1855, Juárez issued the decree known as the Ley Juárez, which intended to restrict the application of the *fuero eclesiástico,* or clerical exemption from civil jurisdiction, and was condemned by the archbishop of Mexico. For most of the presidency of Ignacio Comonfort (December 1855 to January 1858), Juárez was absent from Mexico City as governor of Oaxaca for the second time from January 1856 to October 1857. In this second term as governor, he implemented the Ley Lerdo of June 25, 1856, which mandated the divestment of lands belonging to the Catholic Church, and the Federal Constitution of February 1857, which in addition to codifying many Liberal reforms, gave Mexico its first real bill of rights. He returned to the national capital as president of the Supreme Court, a position that gave him the constitutional right of succession to the presidency in default of the incumbent. Juárez disapproved of Comonfort's executive coup d'état of Tacubaya on December 17, 1857, against the Constitution and the radical wing of the Liberal Party. Conservative officers' removal of Comonfort on January 11, 1858, opened the Civil War of the Reform. Within the Liberal camp, the interim presidency devolved upon Juárez, sustained by the state governors of the center-north (such as Manuel Doblado, Jesús González Ortega, and Anastasio Parrodi) and the geographical peripheries. For much of the Civil War and French Intervention period (1858–67), Juárez strove to assert executive authority and make himself independent of the state governors, who were acting in advance of administration policy on church-state relations and were holding onto federal revenues. From May 1858 until January 1861, the Liberal administration remained in the port of Veracruz under the protection of state governor Manuel Gutiérrez Zamora, an intimate associate of Miguel Lerdo de Tejada, another Veracruzano, author of the Ley Lerdo, and a leading proponent of the Reform Laws of July 1859, which severely restricted the powers of the Catholic Church. During the following year, Lerdo became an increasingly vocal critic and political rival of Juárez.

The Juárez government in Veracruz defined its position in the Manifesto to the Nation of July 7, 1859, which preceded the issue of the Reform Laws. The manifesto reaffirmed the principles codified in the Constitutions of 1824 and 1857 and declared the government's intention to subordinate the Catholic clergy to civil power, to separate church and state, and to advance the secularization of society. Such a program aroused great opposition from Conservative critics; the Conservatives' position was only strengthened by Liberal attempts to secure a U.S. loan with nationalized ecclesiastical properties as collateral, and the negotiations of the McLane-Ocampo Treaty of December 1859, which ceded to the United States right of transit across the Isthmus of Tehuantepec and along the northern border from the Gulf of Mexico to the Sea of Cortés. Nevertheless, the treaty secured U.S. recognition on April 6, 1859, which Liberals regarded as a major gain for their cause. The Reform Laws became national law after Juárez returned to the capital city in January 1861.

Juárez was elected president for the first time in March 1861, with a convincing majority over rival candidates. However, his election did not end intrigues within the Liberal camp designed to remove him in favor of González Ortega (architect of the final military victory over the Conservatives in the Civil War) or Manuel Doblado (who had made and then broken Comonfort). On September 15, 1861, a group of 51 deputies called for Juárez's removal from office, but the votes of a further 52 deputies sustained him. From May 1861 until May 1863, Juárez encountered strong congressional opposition to his call for a renewed presidential style of government. Radical deputies, in particular, argued that the 1857 Constitution had opened the way for a parliamentary type of government, while state governors continued to behave as if they were sovereigns within their own territories. With Conservative guerrilla bands operating in the countryside and deteriorating external relations over the foreign debt, the Juárez government found itself seriously constrained. On July 17, 1861, Juárez unilaterally suspended external debt payments for a two-year period; in response, Great Britain, France, and Spain formed the Tripartite Convention of London in October 1861 and embarked upon an armed intervention in Mexico, designed to enforce payment. French political designs, however, ensured that the other two powers would abandon Mexican territory by the spring of 1862.

On December 11, 1861, Juárez secured from Congress the concession of extraordinary powers to defend national sovereignty in the face of foreign intervention. Further decrees in October 1862 and May 1863 ratified this earlier decree. The draconian law of January 25, 1862, which stipulated capital punishment for collaboration with Interventionist forces, expressed Juárez's determination to resist and reverse foreign designs on Mexican sovereignty. (Under this law, Emperor Maximilian was tried by court martial in 1867 and executed by firing squad.) Juárez's decrees of October 1862, May 1863, and March 1865 defined the nature of treason.

The French advance toward Mexico City in late May 1863 obliged the Juárez administration to regroup in San Luis Potosí. From there, Juárez continued directing efforts to sustain the republic. In November 1865, Juárez's presidential term was extended until the French could be expelled. Juárez's minister in Washington, D.C., Matías Romero, a fellow Oaxacan, attempted to influence public opinion in the United States in favor of the Mexican republican cause. In the meantime, Juárez sought to take advantage of divisions within the Imperial camp. Juárez had no intention of ever abandoning national territory, in spite of considerable personal hardship during his peregrination across the northern states and unbridgeable distance from his wife, Margarita Maza, in exile in New York at a time when they both were shaken by the deaths of their two young sons (five of Juárez's children died in early childhood). He remained the personification of the embattled republic, driven to the very extremity of Paso del Norte in Chihuahua on the Río Bravo border with the United States. Despite notable defections, Juárez could count upon the support of the state governors of Michoacán, Jalisco, Zacatecas, Sonora, Sinaloa, Durango, and Chihuahua. The principal Liberal commanders, Mariano Escobedo and Porfirio Díaz, finally achieved military victory over Interventionist forces in the first half of 1867.

Juárez, supported by his principal ministers, Sebastián Lerdo de Tejada and Ignacio Mejía, was determined to bring Emperor Maximilian to trial and secure punishment for the European intervention. He intended Maximilian's execution to be a powerful deterrent to the European monarchies to refrain from further involvement in the affairs of American republics. In this sense, the long resistance of Juárez to the French during the War of the Intervention acquired an international, rather than a purely Mexican, dimension, which was recognized at the time both within the Americas and by European republican opponents of the dynasties. Even so, the execution of Maximilian remained controversial within Mexico and abroad.

Victory over the Europeans led to Juárez's first reelection in October 1867, provoking the split with General Porfirio Díaz. Thereafter, Porfiristas, a diffuse array of provincial and radical deputies and army commanders, became vocal opponents of the Juárez administration, which they repeatedly accused of constitutional violations. Juárez's abortive attempt to reform the 1857 Constitution in August 1867 to allow himself a third term in office and increase the power of the executive appeared to lend credence to these claims. A series of military-led rebellions broke out in Puebla, San Luis Potosí, Zacatecas, and other states between 1868 and 1870. These rebellions reached their climax with Díaz's Rebellion of La Noria of November 1871 to March 1872, which challenged the second reelection of Juárez in October 1871. The second reelection initially provoked a split with Sebastián Lerdo, who also aspired to succeed Juárez at the expiration of his elected term of office; however, the Porfirista rebellion threw Lerdo and Juárez back into cooperation to defeat an attempt within the military to annul a presidential election by armed force. All opposition groups in Congress and the press accused the Juárez administration of managing elections and thereby rendering them imperfect expressions of the popular will. Military rebels justified the use of armed force on those grounds. Díaz himself argued in the Rebellion of La Noria that only armed intervention could restore the purity of the 1857 Constitution. Juárez countered by branding Díaz a latter-day Santa Anna. Juárez was able to survive the crisis brought about by the Rebellion of La Noria through retaining the loyalty of the majority of army commanders, such as Ramón Corona and Sóstenes Rocha. Even so, Juárez had lost considerable political support in the period after 1867, as the presidential election results of 1871 demonstrated: Juárez collected 5,837 electoral votes, Díaz 3,555, and Lerdo 2,874. In effect, the two rival opposition candidates formed the majority. Congress, acting in its constitutional capacity as an electoral college, determined the outcome of the election in Juárez's favor. With the disintegration of the Rebellion of La Noria, Juárez once again proposed reform of the Constitution, which, as in 1867, included the reestablishment of the Senate (abolished in 1853). On April 1, 1872, Juárez argued that a senate would moderate the actions of the legislative power. Congress again rejected constitutional reform, an objective that Juárez never attained in his lifetime. The presidential term begun on December 1, 1871 would have terminated on November 30, 1875, thus ensuring Juárez 17 unbroken years in office. That prospect in itself was sufficient to concentrate the minds of members of the younger generation.

However, President Juárez died of angina on July 18, 1872. No doubt his death was hastened by the stress of his long political struggles; furthermore, his wife, Margarita Maza de Juárez, had died only five months earlier at the age of 43.

The period of Juárez's predominance was particularly difficult for Mexico, beset by deep-rooted internal divisions and also external pressures. In the half-century immediately following Independence from Spain, Mexico still struggled to find its national identity and assert itself as a sovereign state. Among Juárez's strengths was his ability to understand the significance and complexity of this historical moment. Juárez defined Mexico, in opposition to Catholic and Conservative thought, as a secular and federal republic with a liberal political system in which the civil power was to be supreme. For that reason, he remained opposed throughout his career to the Spanish colonial inheritance and to contemporary European monarchies. He consistently sought to align Mexico with the United States in a common defense of representative government. During the Mexican Civil War of the Reform, Juárez fought to defend the Constitution of 1857 and sought to embody republican virtues as articulated in the Reform Laws and his own Manifesto to the Nation of 1859. During the War of the Intervention, he portrayed himself as the personification of the republic, the moral embodiment of legitimacy, in opposition to the attempt by Napoléon III to reduce independent Mexico to the status of French dependency. Throughout the Civil War in the United States (1861–65), Juárez unswervingly sympathized with the federal forces, the cause of Abraham Lincoln, and the emancipation of the slaves. He resolutely opposed the Confederacy, primarily because it was sustained by the same southern interests that had promoted expansionism at Mexico's expense during the 1840s and 1850s.

Juárez was neither one of the intellectual stars of the Reform constellation nor a leading ideologist of Liberalism. Although, like so many other political figures of his generation, he was trained in law (and, by contrast with them, actually practiced it), he was preferentially a consummate and ruthless politician not averse to the exercise and retention of power. Unlike almost all of his predecessors, he would not be removed from office by a rival politician or army general. By character, Juárez was aloof and obdurate, acerbic and tenacious, of great personal courage and capable of survival in the com-plex society of mid-nineteenth-century Mexico. He retained a belief in the principles of liberal constitutionalism, even if political struggles prevented their literal application. He stood for the depersonalization of political life, but by the end of the War of the Intervention, he himself had become the focus of a personality cult. Certainly, his own personality became the subject of contention during the early part of the Restored Republic, from 1867 to 1872. In that period, three defining issues emerged that would dominate Mexican politics thereafter: presidentialism, centralism, and reelectionism; he stood as a strong proponent of all three.

Events and issues, combined with the personalist tradition of Mexican political life, obliged Juárez to adopt a blend of constitutionalism and authoritarianism and a balance between principle and pragmatism. Faced with intractable ideological divisions within the country and within the Liberal movement, and with entrenched local and regional bases of power, Juárez aligned temporarily with one Liberal faction or another and tacked warily between provincial Liberal cadres. His object was always to insert the authority of the national government into the provincial milieu and, where possible, assert the supremacy of the central power and the primacy of national objectives. After 1867, these tactics earned him widespread opprobrium throughout the radical and provincial wings of Liberalism.

Select Bibliography

Cadenhead, Ivie E., *Benito Juárez*. New York: Twayne, 1973.

Hamnett, Brian R., *Juárez*. London: Longman, 1994.

Perry, Laurens Ballard, *Juárez and Díaz: Machine Politics in Mexico*. DeKalb: Northern Illinois University Press, 1978.

Roeder, Ralph, *Juárez and His Mexico: A Biographical Study*. 2 vols., New York: Viking, 1947.

Weeks, Charles A., *The Juárez Myth in Mexico*. Tuscaloosa: University of Alabama Press, 1987.

—BRIAN R. HAMNETT

K

Kahlo, Frida 1907–54

Artist

Frida Kahlo is one of Mexico's most important twentieth-century figures, well known for the life she suffered and the wrenching self-portraits she painted. Although during her short life she was a recognized figure outside Mexico, her international reputation receded to her own country after her death. In the 1980s a number of important biographies and traveling art shows catapulted her once again into the international mainstream. The large prices her canvases command today at New York and London auction houses is evidence of her growing reputation. Frida Kahlo's legacy—her paintings and life history —has inspired self-portraits, sculptures, short stories, plays, operas, movies, and even fashion shows. In academia she has entered standard art history survey courses, scholarly journals, and the covers of many books, even those having little to do with her or Mexico. During her lifetime Frida Kahlo, the person and the personage, was a symbol of human suffering and emotional strength. Today she is honored and reproduced in various guises worldwide as a patron saint of the post-1968 generation. And, like other saints in their posthumous lives, she is known and invoked by her first name, Frida. Among her followers there can be no doubt to whom they are referring.

Frida Kahlo was born to a German Jewish father of Hungarian descent and a Mexican Catholic mother of European and Indigenous background. She was the third in a family of four daughters. Two other daughters from her father's first marriage joined the family periodically when on vacation from their home in the convent to which they were sent when their parents divorced. Kahlo was raised Catholic, attending church daily as a child with her sisters and devout mother. However, she was not a typical Mexican Catholic girl. When she was not in church or school she was seen romping in the streets outside her house with the neighborhood boys, often in boys' attire. According to those who remember her childhood, she was an accomplished rascal, a cheerful tomboy, until she was six years. From that time onward Kahlo's life was to be a life of illness, operations, recovery and setbacks until her body and soul would expire 40 years later. First polio struck Kahlo, leaving her with a deformed right leg. Twelve years later she suffered from a trolley-car accident on her way home from high school. Her back was broken in three places, her collarbone and pelvis were crushed, her right leg and both feet suffered numerous fractures, and she was impaled by a metal rod through her stomach and vagina. Finally, based on contemporary readings of her x-rays, it appears that Kahlo suffered from spina bifida, a congenital and debilitating condition in which the spine is left partially open at birth. For the rest of her life Kahlo was to have dozens of operations and eventually a leg amputated. She would suffer several miscarriages and abortions. She would spend many months in a body cast in bed, others in a wheelchair and in pain. Despite all this, Kahlo was remarkable for her ability to rise to innumerable occasions.

Kahlo's reaction to her own handicaps and the teasing she received from her cohorts was to foster her strong personality. Kahlo became an extrovert, building friendships in the most public of circles, while simultaneously becoming an introvert, retreating into herself through her writing and her painting. With two half-sisters in a convent, an older sister preparing to be a nun, and a pious mother, Kahlo could have turned to religious devotion for comfort and inner strength. However, Kahlo found herself dissatisfied with the church and turned toward her nonreligious father for a role model. Guillermo Kahlo was an accomplished photographer, which is how he made a living, as well as an amateur painter and pianist. He was well read and had a substantial library. Frida admired all of this about him. But, it may have been his epilepsy that contributed most to the bond that grew between them. Soon after her recovery from polio, it was Frida's father who encouraged her to excel in sports. She took his advice seriously. Before the age of ten and despite her withered leg Kahlo became an accomplished runner, boxer, wrestler, bicyclist and tree climber. While recuperating from the trolley-car accident her father along with her mother brought her paints, canvases, and brushes while she lay for months on her back. From this time onward Kahlo painted her world of pain, which never subsided; indeed, it only grew worse with age.

Frida Kahlo came of age when the newly formed Revolutionary government set up programs to integrate Mexican Indians into mainstream society through public education. She also came of age when the Revolutionary *políticos* and their artistic comrades presided over the Mexicanization of several bourgeois art forms. Long before her accident Kahlo had admired the famous Mexican painter Diego Rivera, who was a central figure in this effort. He had created a mural in her high school while she was a student there, and it was then that she first caught glimpses of him while he painted. After her accident, when she was back on her feet, she met him at a party; from that time onward he would figure prominently in her life. They married in 1929 shortly after their fateful meeting—she was twenty and he forty-two—and they stayed married until her death in 1954. It was not always a smooth relationship, and it included periods of separation and even a tumultuous year of divorce and remarriage to each other. Both Kahlo and Rivera had lovers, but Rivera had a reputation for his philandering; it was almost a second occupation for him that at one time even included Frida's sister Cristina. Although Rivera's philandering hurt Frida enormously, she did her best to overlook it. In the early stages of their marriage she was a devoted wife; she regularly fixed his meals; she joined his artistic circles; she embraced his revolutionary ideologies. In addition, she joined the Communist Party of which her husband was president, and she readily embraced Mexican indigenous identities, as did her husband, casting the European pre-Revolution aesthetic aside in life as much as in art.

With Kahlo's marriage to Rivera, the most vocal and celebrated of all the Mexican muralists, Kahlo placed herself quite literally in the center of the political avant-garde. Owing to Rivera's close friendship with José Vasconcelos, the secretary of public education and architect of the Mexican Mural Renaissance following the Revolution, he was considered *the* man responsible for creating the visual vocabulary of the Revolutionary government. Kahlo and other women who on occasion modeled for Rivera found themselves scripted into the master narratives of his epic paintings that festooned the walls of the Revolutionary government buildings. Through Rivera Kahlo met the Parisian surrealist André Breton, the Russian revolutionary Leon Trotsky, the Italian-American photographer Tina Modotti, and the U.S. industrialists Edsel Ford and Nelson Rockefeller, among others. She traveled across the United States with him, as he painted murals commissioned by wealthy U.S. businessmen. Kahlo managed to use the international settings in which Rivera shined as platforms for her own self, earning a separate reputation in her own right, testimony to the power of her art. By 1938 Kahlo found herself in New York City with her first one-woman show, on the cover of *Vogue* magazine that same year, invited to numerous fancy parties as the guest of honor, and a year later with a one-woman show in Paris, at the invitation of Breton.

Rivera was Kahlo's greatest admirer and most active mentor. He promoted her painting career, encouraged her own style, and had much to do with the construction of her own identity as an artist and as an independent "Mexican" woman. It was Rivera who brought Kahlo her first Tehuana outfit from one of his trips to the Isthmus of Tehuantepec in southern Mexico. These non-tailored, brightly colored outfits with their embroidered shirts and long flowing skirts worn traditionally by the Tehuanas became Kahlo's hallmark both in her life and in her self-portraits. They suited her physical needs, her political agenda, and her strong personality. They made it possible for her to hide her polio-stricken leg and her ailing feet and troubled back; they underscored her allegiance to the nationalistic rhetoric of the Revolution and its ideologies of *Indigenismo* and Mexican-made aesthetic traditions; and, they associated her with the Tehuana women who were known and continue to be known in Mexico as matriarchs of their society. Submerging her body in Tehuana fabrics, Kahlo gave to herself an aura of empowerment and other-worldliness, especially when she traveled to New York and to Paris; they were neither of her class nor of her time. On Kahlo the Tehuana outfit traveled to worlds far beyond its home—to the art worlds of Mexico City, New York, and Paris, to the political worlds of Mexico City, New York, and Los Angeles, to the social worlds of the Rockefellers and Fords and the André Bretons and the Claire Booth Luces. She appeared dressed in this garb in many of her self-portraits, in photographs taken of her, and in the fashion magazine *Vogue*. The Tehuana clothing contributed enormously to making Kahlo a symbol *of* Mexico as well as an advertisement *for* Mexico. On Kahlo the colorful fabrics did not hang quietly as they do today in her home. Instead they were always part of a grand performance.

Although Kahlo was an ardent supporter of the mural tradition and all it claimed to be and do—she promoted it at parties; she marched in political parades—in her painting she rejected it. Her narrative was personalistic, rooted not in the Italian Renaissance and the Beaux-Arts traditions of historical painting, nor in the Mexican school of Russian socialist realism, nor in the historiographic tradition of third-person narration, all of which characterized Rivera's work. Instead Kahlo's artistry drew upon the Mexican traditions of religious folk art known as ex-votos, with their first-person narration of human tragedy and upon the European traditions of portraiture as practiced in Mexico by the church. Kahlo also drew upon images of Christ and Mary for inspiration, but she did so in her own way, challenging the gender-specific conventions of ecclesiastical representation. In Kahlo's paintings women's bodies are as naked and bloody and fully embodied as those of Christ and as clothed and emotionally stoic and disembodied as those of Mary.

Kahlo's verisimilitude, particularly her bloody and fragmented bodies, led André Breton to declare her a surrealist. Surprised, Kahlo claimed that she painted because she needed to do so and painted what came into her head. Kahlo's paintings had little in common with the French surrealist imagination. There were many homespun reasons why she constructed her portraits from the pieces of her life; not one of them connected her to war-torn Europe or to the many phallocentric manifestos of the surrealist movement. Kahlo's fragments mirrored her own personal life, especially her physical life, to her crumbling spine and her ailing foot. However, the awareness of her fragmented body was exaggerated by the conflicting character of post-revolutionary Mexican identity. What was it to be Mexican?—modern, yet pre-Columbian; young, yet old; anti-Catholic, yet Catholic; Western, yet New World; developing, yet underdeveloped; independent, yet colonized; *mestizo*, yet neither Spanish nor Indian. Kahlo identified herself with the contradictions of her *mestizaje* and through the assemblage of disparate objects, through her identity with church and national icons, and through the exposure of her own fragmented materiality she constructed a subjectivity for herself. Her

pictorial honesty came less from something dream-like and imaginary than real. And the bloody Christs of Mexico, the ex-votos and their tragic tales, and her father's documentary approach to photography offered important precedents.

Although Kahlo was upper-middle class and supported many ruling-class constructions of nationhood, in her painting and private life she was at odds with them and their elitist constructions of gender, race, and class differences. She demonstrated her discomfort in various ways. She decorated her house not with European and American imports but with Mexican *artesanías,* a common practice among her artist friends. Her collections of paintings were not the easels of "great" artists, rather the ex-votos of everyday people. When she married Diego Rivera, she wore not a fancy, expensive dress, but a dress belonging to her housekeeper who lent it to her for the occasion. In 1952 she had her photograph taken with all her servants, not common practice among Mexican elites. In the pictorial as well as actual construction of her own *mestizaje* (mixed-race status), Frida Kahlo mixed Indian with European, art with craft, high with low, crossing from one strata to the other with little regard for such elite constructions of difference. Kahlo not only traversed the sacred domains of gender, constructed and preserved by church and state, but she ignored the sacred domains of high and low art and high and low social status, crossing from one level to the other. Rather than mask her racial and cultural hybridism, as other members of the elite did, Kahlo openly acknowledged hers.

As an art teacher at La Esmeralda (1943–53), Kahlo not only refused the hierarchical role of *Maestra* and asked her students to address her with the familiar, second-person *tú* instead of the formal *usted*. She also rejected the tendency to take students to the country to paint the outdoors, popular among teachers then. Instead she took them to see Francisco Goitia, an artist who retreated from the Mexico City art scene to live a peasant—not bohemian—life in Xochimilco, a town south of Mexico City. She also took them to drink at local bars and to visit slums, marketplaces, convents, and churches. "*Muchachos*," she would announce, "locked up here in school we can't do anything. Let's go into the street. Let's go and paint the life in the street." She once had her students paint a mural, but not as the other art teachers at La Esmeralda had their students do, her husband among them. Instead, she chose the wall of a *pulquería* (a type of popular bar) on which to do it. This is what she meant by "life in the street." When she and her students were not outdoors, she encouraged them to paint what was in her house: popular art, traditional Judases, clay figures, popular toys and hand-crafted furniture.

It is not surprising that Frida Kahlo is at the center of contemporary identity politics in and outside Mexico. The insistence of many young painters and writers to credit Frida Kahlo with being a heroine in an otherwise male-dominated landscape and with achieving this recognition by public admission of her personal life helps to explain her popularity among young artists today—men and women—who seek ways to construct their own identities. Her followers are numerous and varied. For women artists in Mexico City, most all of whom grew up in upper-middle-class homes where the Virgin is held as the role model for young girls, Kahlo's rejection of the self-abnegating woman introduces the possibilities of a self-awareness that is profoundly rooted in the flesh and blood of female experiences. Reconstructing womanhood by women on their terms, indeed reconstructing a sexuality that runs contrary to those advocated either by church or state, has few precedents, since historically the representation of female —not to mention male—sexuality was exclusively a male prerogative. Kahlo, through the self portrait, operationalized the psychology of being a woman as she did of being a Mexican. Her imagery is unique in the history of art. As Rivera himself put it; "This is the first time in the history of art that a woman expressed herself with utter frankness."

Select Bibliography

Bakewell, Elizabeth, "Frida Kahlo: A Contemporary Feminist Reading." *Frontiers: A Journal of Women Studies* 14:3 (1993).

Billiter, Erika, *The Blue House: The World of Frida Kahlo.* Seattle: University of Washington Press, and Houston: Museum of Fine Arts, 1993.

Herrera, Hayden, *Frida: A Biography of Frida Kahlo.* New York: Harper and Row, 1983.

Lowe, Sarah M., *The Diary of Frida Kahlo: An Intimate Self-Portrait.* New York: Abrams, and Mexico City: La Vaca Independiente S.A. de C.V., 1995.

Mulvey, Laura, and Peter Wollen, *Frida Kahlo and Tina Modotti.* London: White Chapel Art Gallery, 1982

Zamora, Marta, *Frida Kahlo: The Brush of Anguish,* translated by Marilyn Sode Smith. San Francisco: Chronicle Books, 1990.

—ELIZABETH BAKEWELL

Kinship

See Family and Kinship

L

Las Casas, Bartolomé de 1484–1566
Dominican Friar, Bishop, and Advocate for Indians' Rights

Bartolomé de Las Casas was born in 1484, in Seville. His father was a merchant with maritime inclinations, his mother or stepmother was a well-to-do peasant. A precocious student, he earned a degree in canon and Roman law. In 1502, at the age of 18, Las Casas traveled to the Antilles, settling on the Island of Hispaniola (now the countries of Haiti and the Dominican Republic), where he won recognition as a friend of the Indians. Five years later, he returned, first to Rome, where he was ordained, and then to Spain, where he continued his studies. In 1509 he returned to Hispaniola, where he studied native languages and cultures and served as an Indian catechist.

Invited to Cuba for his expertise with the Indians, he achieved an almost peaceful acceptance of Spanish rule and, with a lay partner, organized a successful *encomienda* of "contented" Indians (*encomiendas* were native settlements "commended" to the care of a Spanish trustee—an *encomendero*—who in return for receiving the Indians' labor had the duty to protect them, maintain missionaries, and contribute to the military defense of the region). But Las Casas was increasingly sickened as he watched the cruel oppression by his fellow Spaniards and the mounting decimation of the native peoples, especially rapid in Cuba. His was not the only voice to attack the *encomienda* system. The first Dominicans had preached against the exploitation. In Cuba, Las Casas himself preached in the same vein, but to no avail. In 1514, after considerable soul-searching and reading, he resolved to return to Spain to tell the king how to correct the situation. Like a Biblical prophet, Las Casas would spend the rest of his life, more than 50 years, pleading and writing on behalf of the Indians.

Las Casas's first six years, from 1514 to 1520, spent in these endeavors, generally are described as a failure, but they actually produced a delayed success. His initial reform plan was based on his own experience. He proposed replacing Indian forced labor for Spanish *encomenderos* with free Indian communities, organized for farming, mining, and barter, as Las Casas himself had done on his own plantation. He wanted the brutal conquistadors to be replaced by peaceful farmer-colonists, and the Indian communities to be organized into peasant cooperatives.

His proposals were partially enacted, but later were totally sabotaged. After the death of the regent and the ascent of young King Carlos I (Emperor Charles V), Las Casas was able to air his views at court. With encouragement from Carlos's tutor, Adrian of Utrecht, he won a contract to found his own colony on the Pearl Coast of Venezuela. The venture was a disaster. His colonists deserted and joined in slave raids; slaving atrocities on the mainland drove those Indians to force of arms, and they wiped out his fledgling outpost.

In a state of deep depression, Las Casas joined the Dominican order in 1522. Fray Bartolomé later wrote that for the next dozen years on Hispaniola, he "seemed to sleep." In fact, during these years he honed his skills with his greatest weapon—the pen—compiling material for a history of the Conquest and sending a series of powerful exposés and pleas to Spain. By 1530 a Reform Commission had recommended his proposals and a reformed Council of the Indies had enacted them: the abolition of future Indian enslavement and the gradual introduction of an alternate institution to the *encomienda*—free Indian towns under the Spanish Crown. In 1534, however, the antislavery law was revoked, as Cardinal Loaysa returned to head the Council of the Indies; his absence in Rome had permitted the reform to be enacted initially. From Mexico the head of the *audiencia* (high court) wrote letters of protest, and in Hispaniola Bartolomé de Las Casas once again saw his work crumble.

That same year an armada arrived from Spain to end the war with Chief Enriquillo, the Indian guerrilla who had been active militarily on the island of Hispaniola for years. However, local authorities warned the captain to avoid combat. They feared that Enriquillo would seize their weapons and take over the island. Accordingly, the captain went in alone and signed a formal peace; but Enriquillo stubbornly refused to leave his mountains. At this point, Fray Bartolomé hastily obtained permission to go with a single companion and visit Chief Enriquillo. Las Casas stayed a month in the guerrilla camp, interviewing the chief (who had been educated by the Franciscans). Subsequently, he brought Enriquillo to the capital and persuaded him to settle with his people. Through this interaction with Enriquillo, Fray Bartolomé had found his answer to the defamation of the Indians and the revocation of the laws protecting them. Two friars alone had accomplished more than 15 years of war parties.

Las Casas's first book—*The Only Way to Draw All People to a Living Faith*—is a reflection of both his early experiences and his successful negotiation with Enriquillo. The book is a description of Indian capacity for the faith; a declaration that peace and friendship and respect for other cultures was the only way prescribed and followed by Christ and the Apostles to spread the Gospel; and a denunciation of conquest and its damnable consequences as mortal sin that required restitution.

Fray Bartolomé sent this treatise to a friend at court and arranged to set out himself as a missionary to Peru. But the ship was becalmed, and he and his small contingent of friars changed vessels and landed in Central America instead. From there Las Casas traveled to Mexico City to the headquarters of a new Dominican province, to which he agreed to transfer. In the meantime, he briefly started mission work in Nicaragua (attached to his old province), but he soon encountered hostility from the Spanish conquistadors and prudently returned to the capital. His new province promptly named him vicar of Guatemala, where he did indeed start a mission according to his beliefs in peaceful conversion—the method he had used with Enriquillo and earlier in the "peaceful reduction" of Cuba. The work was interrupted, however, when he was called back to Mexico City for a Dominican chapter meeting.

On these visits to the capital, Las Casas took part in ecclesiastical conferences. The three resulting resolutions of 1536 were officially carried to Rome by the Dominican Bernardino de Minaya along with three supporting treatises. In Rome, Pope Paul III issued his three famous pro-Indian decrees based on these three resolutions. The encyclical bull *Sublimis Deus* follows the first version of Las Casas's *Only Way* point by point, proclaiming the full humanity and rationality of the Indians (i.e., their capacity to understand and accept the Catholic faith), and the correct means of converting them by preaching and good example. The implementing brief automatically excommunicated all who robbed, oppressed, or enslaved the Indians. Nonetheless, this implementing brief was revoked the following year, at the direct request of Carlos I. Paul III agreed in order to achieve a truce between Carlos I and the king of France—temporary peace in Europe, at the price of Indian freedom.

In 1542, Las Casas helped the emperor put together a Reform Commission to draft new legislation for the colonial administration, and in particular the welfare, care, and survival of the Indians. The result was the New Laws for the Indies. These laws established a regular inspection process of colonial governments to eliminate the rampant corruption. The status of Indian communities gradually was to be changed, from the *encomienda,* which essentially bound Indians to the land as indentured workers, to free Indian towns. Slavery also was abolished. The implementation of the laws produced mixed results. Several colonial administrators were removed for corruption. The status of Indians gradually improved, but the practice of debt peonage never was eliminated. And although slavery officially was abolished among Indian populations, some African slaves were imported.

There is a persistent misconception that Las Casas encouraged the importation of African slaves to ease the lot of the Indians. In his early years at court he had, indeed, transmitted a suggestion from some wealthy *encomenderos* that they would liberate 10 Indians for every black slave they could import duty-free. Dominican friars, reforming officials, and Flemish courtiers recommended the large-scale importation of African slaves, but Las Casas did not. A slave trade license was issued around that time, but it was sold and resold at such a high price that it actually halted the importation of African slaves for almost two decades. Only when the Indians had been nearly exterminated in the Caribbean, and the gold in the rivers was gone, did the large-scale importation of African slaves begin, to man the sugar mills. Writing later, Las Casas regretted that at first he had not protested the suggestion of importing African slaves, but he then believed the lie that these blacks were captives from the "just" defensive war Europe was waging against Islam. Upon learning the truth about the nefarious traffic, he condemned black slavery in the same terms as Indian slavery.

Las Casas wanted to stay at court to ensure that the New Laws would not be undermined by the Council of the Indies, which was still headed by Cardinal Loaysa, who opposed the reforms. The emperor had offered Las Casas the bishopric of Cuzco, the capital of the Inca Empire, but he refused. The next offer was to return to his own mission that he had founded with the Dominicans. Las Casas returned to Mexico in 1544 as the bishop of Chiapas and privy counselor to the emperor. During the next three years he was able to promote the implementation of the New Laws in the area under his influence. By 1547, faced with growing resistance, Las Casas returned for the last time to Spain, where he served as the general advocate of the Indians. This was the position that he had hoped for in 1542. Now the Council of the Indies was required to set aside time on a regular basis to listen to his concerns.

First, however, he needed to repair the damage that had occurred in his absence. The emperor, crushed by debts to Flemish bankers, was tempted by a donation of several thousand ducats to repeal the prime New Law, the Law of No Inheritance that would have extinguished the *encomienda*. Once again Las Casas's life work was crumbling—the antislavery laws surely would be next. Even before he reached Spain, his adversaries had recruited an erudite champion for the conquistadors. Juan Ginéz de Sepúlveda, translator of Aristotle and an accomplished sycophant (witness his laudatory chronicle of the *Deeds of Emperor Charles V*), was the shrillest voice opposing freedom for the Indians. To Sepúlveda, the native peoples of the Spanish colonies belonged to the Aristotelian category of *servos a natura*, or slaves/servants/serfs by nature, to be ruled by superior beings. Even before Las Casas returned to Spain in 1547, Sepúlveda was encouraged by Cardinal Loaysa, by now the grand inquisitor, to write a justification along these lines for conquering and enslaving the Indians. The resulting Latin dialogue, *Democrates alter*, claimed that the pope practically had ordered a holy war against the Indians. Las Casas responded by having publication of the work blocked. Sepúlveda then wrote a "defense" of his work, which Las Casas promptly had censored and banned. Las Casas also had the newly reformed Council of the Indies reinforce the antislavery laws with a provision that conquest could not legitimate slavery, as the Indians had been "free" people. In addition, he persuaded the emperor to convoke a special commission on conquests and slavery, which heard Sepúlveda for a few hours and Las Casas's rebuttal for five days. But the matter did not end there.

In 1552 Las Casas wrote his most famous works: eight tracts addressed to the emperor and Prince Felipe. One of these, the *Brevissima relación*, denouncing the atrocities of the Spanish Conquest, was widely circulated in Europe by critics of Spain in subsequent centuries. Other tracts criticized the practice of *encomienda* and defended the antislavery provisions of the New Laws, demanded restitution to the Indians, and castigated Sepúlveda. Enraged, Sepúlveda called the tracts "rash, scandalous, and heretical," and he denounced Las Casas to the Inquisition. But by then Loaysa was dead, and the groundless accusations were dropped.

In 1556 Carlos I abdicated. The new king, Felipe II, inherited a mountain of debt and looked to the colonies as a way to raise money. When the gold from the Indies proved insufficient, he decided to tighten the screws on the Indians of the Viceroyalty of Peru. The rights of *encomienda* to control the Mexican Indians had been granted to last for one lifetime. Now Philip proposed to sell perpetual *encomiendas*, essentially a form of slavery, for the Indians of Peru. Las Casas strongly opposed the proposal.

Part of his response involved the presentation of a counteroffer from the Peruvian Indians to buy their own freedom. In the process, he wrote his most daring works, openly warning Felipe of the mortal danger to his salvation if he "alienated" (sold) his vassals. Las Casas received powers of attorney to represent chiefs on both continents, and with a Dominican provincial from Peru he actually represented an offer from the Peruvian Indians to pay more than whatever the *encomenderos* could assemble, along with provisions for restoring the native rulers.

Drawing on the experience of blocking the sale of the Indians, Las Casas wrote his two final treatises: *Who Owns the Treasures in the Inca Tombs?* and *Twelve Doubts on the Conquest of Peru*. His culminating offer to Felipe was literally dazzling: the promise of Inca tomb treasures for the right course; or the threat of eternal damnation for the wrong decision. With mounting courage as his strength ebbed (he was nearly 80), he was defying an implacable monarch.

His greatest work, *History of the Indies*, was never finished. He had started it in 1527 as a prior in Hispaniola. The book was to tell the story of the first six decades of the Conquest, but by the time of his death he had only covered the first 30 years. This history is the only contemporaneous account of both the Indian and Spanish versions of the encounter, based on Las Casas's own experiences plus a wealth of eyewitness interviews and key legal documents. In the process of creating this epic work, Las Casas read and transcribed the abridged log of Christopher Columbus's first voyage, creating the only surviving version of this priceless work.

Las Casas died in 1566 in Madrid. What had he ultimately accomplished in 50 years of labor? Although he could never obtain true freedom for the Indians, he had corrected the worst abuses and enabled many indigenous people to survive. The blazing finale to his life struggle on behalf of the Indians is a startling contrast to the accepted picture of him as a nonagenarian without influence. But even more remarkable is the persistence of his influence in Spain and the Americas for some 60 years after his death, in spite of the Inquisition and censorship: a counteroffer by Indians in New Spain, presented by his friend, the bishop of Verapaz; the negotiations to restore the sovereignty of native lords in Peru; his influence on the writing of the Peruvian "prince and chronicler" Guaman Poma de Ayala; and the publication of a large part of one of his later works, *Defense of Indian Civilizations,* under someone else's name and with the aid of a friendly censor. The New Laws that he drafted remain a legal landmark, the most sweeping bill of rights ever issued by a conquering nation on behalf of conquered peoples.

Las Casas's influence in modern times is even more significant. His vision of humanity and respect for Latin America's Indian peoples has found a new voice in contemporary struggles. The "preferential option for the poor" articulated at the 1968 conference of Latin American bishops in Medillín, Colombia, draws heavily on many of Las Casas's most important ideas. The author of the final report of the Medillín conference, Gustavo Gutiérrez, was a lifelong student of the ideas of Las Casas and has played an instrumental role in defining the movement of Liberation Theology that has swept Latin America and revitalized the church in the process. A move underway in the 1990s for the canonization of Las Casas represented a fitting acknowledgment of his great contributions.

Select Bibliography

Gutiérrez, Gustavo, *Las Casas: The Search for the Poor of Jesus Christ.* Maryknoll, New York: Orbis, 1992.

Parish, Helen Rand, editor, *Bartolomé de Las Casas: The Only Way,* translated and restored by Francis Patrick Sullivan. Mahwah, New Jersey: Paulist Press, 1992.

Sanderlin, George, editor and translator, *Witness: The Writings of Bartolomé de Las Casas.* Maryknoll, New York: Orbis, 1992.

Sullivan, Francis Patrick, editor and translator, *Indian Freedom: The Cause of Bartolomé de Las Casas, A Reader.* Kansas City, Missouri: Sheed and Ward, 1995.

Wagner, Henry Raup, and Helen Rand Parish, *The Life and Writings of Bartolomé de Las Casas.* Albuquerque: University of New Mexico Press 1967.

—HELEN RAND PARISH

Lerdo de Tejada, Sebastián 1827–89
President

According to the historian Frank Averill Knapp Jr., "No Mexican president has been more maligned, misunderstood, and misrepresented," than Sebastián Lerdo de Tejada. From his ascension to the interim presidency in July 1872, through the four years he served after his own election to the presidency, until the insurgent forces of Porfirio Díaz drove Lerdo from Mexico City in November 1876, libelous epithets were heaped upon him. History treated the deposed president somewhat more kindly. Lerdo was largely forgotten, his career and reputation eclipsed on one side by his predecessor, Benito Juárez, and erased on the other by the image-makers of the long-serving dictator Porfirio Díaz. Yet Lerdo's doomed efforts to implement the ideals of liberal, democratic, republican government in a Mexico bloodied and impoverished by decades of war were important, preliminary steps in the creation of the modern Mexican state.

Lerdo was born in Jalapa, Veracruz, to a Spanish father and Mexican mother. He was educated in theological colleges and enjoyed a prize-studded educational career. At the National College of San Idelfonso, he studied law and rose from student to professor to, eventually, rector during the turbulent end of the dictatorship of Antonio López de Santa Anna and ensuing Wars of the Reform. Although the rectorship of that prestigious institution provided Lerdo with contacts to most of the influential Mexicans of the day, it seems Lerdo then harbored no political ambitions. His legal studies did prepare him to serve as attorney *(fiscal)* and then magistrate of the Supreme Court between 1855 and 1857, but it was his election as a congressional deputy in 1861 that thrust Lerdo into a political arena from which only force of arms eventually would expel him.

During his congressional career in Mexico City, Lerdo stood out for his unyielding defense of national sovereignty against treaties and foreign claims that would in any fashion compromise the territorial integrity of the nation. When Juárez was forced to take his government to the harsh northern frontier as French troops occupied Mexico, Lerdo accompanied him as the vice president of the permanent delegation of Congress in recess. Juárez soon called upon Lerdo to perform still additional governmental functions, and he appointed Lerdo minister of foreign relations and minister of government. Lerdo rejected French efforts to negotiate a quick end to the Republic, which at times seemed to consist only of Lerdo, another principal minister (José María Iglesias), Juárez himself, and a small group of loyal guards and soldiers unable to decisively alter the military realities of foreign occupation. But the three men and their scattered allies labored heroically to maintain the legal existence of the Republic, until the withdrawal of French troops allowed resurgent Mexican forces to topple the French-imposed emperor Maximilian and restore Juárez in Mexico City in 1867.

When Juárez was reelected to the presidency in 1867, Congress elected Lerdo president of the Supreme Court and, thereby, next in line for succession to the presidency. Lerdo also assumed the offices of minister of foreign relations and chief of Juárez's cabinet. Lerdo thus enjoyed, in addition to his pronounced influence over Juárez based upon long years of mutual labor and risk during the French Intervention, a significant measure of both judicial and executive power. Even before Juárez's reelection, Lerdo penned and circulated a program of constitutional reforms that, if adopted, would significantly strengthen the powers of the executive branch of government at the expense of the Congress. In his controversial August 1867 circular to the nation's governors, Lerdo noted that "the despotism of a convention can be as bad, or worse, than the despotism of a dictator," and that "the peace and well-being of society depend on the convenient equilibrium in the organization of public powers." That call to revise by the unusual means of plebiscite the Constitution of 1857 provoked a storm of opposition, and Juárez eventually dropped the program, although its major provision—the creation of a senate—was finally adopted during Lerdo's term as president. In the meantime the forces in opposition to Juárez already had begun to focus upon Lerdo as a principal object of their rancor.

Restoring peace and order to Mexico after so many years of revolts, invasions, and warfare was the Herculean task of the Juárez administration. It was Lerdo's view that progress toward that end could come only from the pursuit of seemingly contradictory policies: the strengthening of the central government on the one hand, and vigorous opposition to the use of force to overthrow local authorities on the other. Lerdo understood that the project

of centralization required his continuance in power, and insofar as the ability of his party to remain in power depended upon the cooperation of state governors as managers of state elections and chiefs of state militias, Lerdo found himself intervening evermore in state affairs in order to build and maintain the political machine that would construct the stable, centralized, liberal government that he envisioned. It seems inevitable now that Lerdo's project would expose him to the charges subsequently levied against him: subverter of the liberal cause, enemy of states' rights, tyrant.

Lerdo resigned from the Juárez cabinet in 1871 and competed for the presidency against Juárez and Díaz in the elections of that year. Juárez won reelection, Díaz came in second, and the weakness of Lerdo's popular and political support was exposed by his third-place finish. Lerdo remained president of the Supreme Court and, hence, next in line to succeed Juárez. Once Díaz's revolt against Juárez's reelection (the Plan of La Noria) was crushed, and with the death of Juárez in July 1872, the way was clear for Lerdo legally to assume the interim presidency. The nation apparently greeted the legal transfer of power and absence of any ongoing political revolt as promising the dawn of a new era of peace and progress. Lerdo declared his intention to govern as president of the nation, not head of any party, and much to the astonishment of his contemporaries, he retained the Juárez cabinet and many other officials appointed by his predecessor, while offering few immediate spoils to self-avowed Lerdistas. He declared a general amnesty for Porfirian rebels, all of whom, Díaz included, accepted. When Lerdo was elected without opposition in October 1872, the prospects, finally, for peace and unity throughout Mexico seemed truly bright, indeed.

According to Lerdo's principal biographer (Frank Averill Knapp Jr.), peace, order, and respect for law was Lerdo's "religion of state." In that triumvirate, peace and order would take some precedence over law, it seems. Lerdo authorized brutally effective suppression of rebellious local chieftains, sought the suspension of civil liberties in rebellious states, and ushered through Congress the renewal of the highly controversial Law of Highwaymen and Bandits, which gave local authorities power, under certain circumstances, to conduct summary examinations and executions of suspects caught in the act. While for Lerdo and many others the suppression of violence justified temporary suspensions of civil liberties, in other realms Lerdo championed civil liberties and civil tolerance to degrees only dreamed of before. At Lerdo's insistence the Laws of the Reform, only laxly enforced during Juárez's reign, were enacted as constitutional provisions. Congress was moved to pass the legislation that finally would put these reforms into effect, and Lerdo enforced these reforms (many of them drafted in the first instance by his deceased brother, Miguel Lerdo de Tejada) vigorously.

The creation of a senate was key to Lerdo's plan to centralize the power of the federal government and to provide the federal government with a secure, legal basis for intervening, forcefully if necessary, in state affairs. Lerdo managed to complete that project, which had been begun but postponed under the Juárez presidency. According to the final legislation, the 50-seat Senate would function partially as a check upon a Congress that a president otherwise might find difficult to control. Furthermore, the Senate could declare that the executive and legal power of a state had ceased to exist (in the case of armed rebellions or disputed elections, for example) and empower the president to appoint a provisional governor. Finally, the Senate could resolve disputes between the executive and legislative powers of a state and, again, authorize the federal executive to intervene. These were legal powers that would prove very useful to a president like Lerdo, who highly valued legal form but who understood as well the federal executive's need at times forcefully to influence power struggles at the state level. While Lerdo had little time to take advantage of these powers (the first Senate convened for the fall term of 1875), his successor, Porfirio Díaz, would exploit them to full advantage.

Historians have noted that little of interest can be said of Lerdo's foreign policy. As foreign minister under Juárez, Lerdo had established the policy that Mexico could not recognize the official status of representatives of foreign governments that had recognized the regime of Maximilian and had adopted a hostile stance toward the government of the Republic. European nations that fell into that category and that, after the triumph of the Republic, wished to resume normal diplomatic relations would have to take the first steps toward mending the wounds of the past. Some did, but relations with Great Britain and France were not renewed during Lerdo's tenure in office, and Mexico's access to the most important European capital markets was correspondingly limited. Lerdo's relations with the United States were cordial. Lerdo concluded the work of the U.S.-Mexican Mixed Claims Commission of 1868. Although Indian and bandit depredations on both sides of the Rio Grande, as well as occasional violence against U.S. citizens in Mexico, soon added again to the roster of claims each country held against the other, both Lerdo and the U.S. administration desired commercial relations between the two countries to expand unimpeded by such irritations. The United States sought rapid expansion in commercial relations; Lerdo envisioned a more cautious growth.

Lerdo's foreign policy had consequences for his policy of domestic economic development. His vigorous defense of national sovereignty and national honor dictated that relations with England and France would not soon be renewed. Without such relations, access to European capital markets would be restricted, and Mexico would have to rely more heavily on U.S. capital. However, Lerdo understood that in the future, U.S. capital would pose the greater threat to Mexican sovereignty, and he would not allow himself to throw wide open the doors to U.S. investment in Mexican economic infrastructure. Lerdo's administration promoted the development of railroads and communication (the completion of the Mexico City–Veracruz railroad being the principal economic trophy of Lerdo's administration), but it did so only warily, earning the criticism from many quarters that his administration neglected the pressing development needs of the country. Those who came violently to oppose Lerdo did so partly in the name of material progress and economic renovation. The great expansion of U.S.-Mexican commercial relations depended on the expansion of a transportation network connecting producers and consumers in each nation, and Lerdo's successor, Díaz, pursued that task with historic abandon.

Lerdo's task of making liberalism a practical, working political system for a Mexico at peace was far from completed by the conclusion of his first elected term as president. Much had been accomplished: steps had been taken to centralize federal power, codify reforms, and chart the future direction of a cautious policy of economic development that would not endanger national sovereignty. Further, Lerdo had labored consistently to construct an alliance of state governors (with the considerable monopoly of power and resources that they enjoyed at the local level) to support him in these endeavors. It was a seemingly inevitable, although also ill-fated decision, that Lerdo took, then, when he announced that he would seek a second term of office as president in elections scheduled for the summer of 1876. A powerful tendency of liberal thought held that reelection of high officials was inimical to the growth of liberal, democratic institutions, and that only a policy of no reelection would check the timeworn impulses of high officials to concentrate power and wield it ruthlessly for the benefit of themselves and their closest allies. So when Porfirio Díaz revolted against Lerdo in January of 1876, his Plan of

Tuxtepec proclaimed the cause of "No Reelection" as central to the goals of his rebellion.

Lerdo faced many obstacles in his effort to suppress the Díaz rebellion. Lerdo's reelection, although probably no more fraudulent than that of his predecessors, was not above reproach. Lerdo's passion for respecting individual liberties and the rule of law led him to refrain from restraining a press that quickly moved from libel and scandal to open advocacy of rebellion. The still-poor state of Mexican finances hindered full, timely, effective military mobilization against the guerrilla forces of Porfirio Díaz. Finally, Lerdo faced in Porfirio Díaz a master rebel whose guerrilla war in the north drew federal forces in that direction, even as Díaz and his supporters prepared to deliver the government a death blow on a different field of battle in the south. When the president of the Supreme Court, José María Iglesias, declared Lerdo's reelection to be illegal and claimed to be the legal successor, and with the decisive victory of Díaz in battle in Tecoac in November 1876, Lerdo's fate was sealed. Several days after Tecoac, Lerdo fled the capital and headed to exile in New York.

Lerdo died in exile in New York in 1889. His body was returned to Mexico and accorded state honors under President Porfirio Díaz. As Knapp relates, only one of those who spoke at the funeral reflected upon the causes of Lerdo's downfall. Lerdo's failure, that one pointed out, was that he had not understood that bread was the "inseparable companion of peace." Lerdo governed a nation long ravaged by war, whose political and economic edifice was in ruins. Lerdo had believed that the economic development and prosperity of the nation could only be constructed upon a foundation of social peace, the rule of law, a vigorous defense of national sovereignty, and a strong, centralized government. He labored powerfully to the end of creating such a foundation, and under his rule Mexico had enjoyed a then-unprecedented degree of domestic tranquillity and tolerance. Yet when the call to rebellion was sounded again, many decided that the prosperity and progress of the nation required one last resort to arms, altering profoundly the course of modern Mexican history.

Select Bibliography

Knapp, Frank Averill, Jr., *The Life of Sebastián Lerdo de Tejada, 1823–1889: A Study of Influence and Obscurity.* Austin: University of Texas Press, 1951.

Perry, Laurens Ballard, *Juárez and Díaz: Machine Politics in Mexico.* DeKalb: Northern Illinois University Press, 1978.

—PAUL SULLIVAN

Liberalism

Liberalism had a large impact on nineteenth-century Mexico, much as it influenced the United States, Great Britain, and France in the same period. A broad current of ideas that swept across western Europe and the Americas in the eighteenth and nineteenth centuries, liberalism carried various meanings in different political contexts. At the most general level, liberalism was a rejection of traditional strongholds of power for privileged groups such as merchant guilds, religious orders, and special military courts. Liberals typically called for the abolition of these organizations—often called corporations—in order to open opportunities for energetic and ambitious individuals who formed an early version of a loosely structured middle class. Beyond this overview, it is difficult to generalize about liberalism because it followed different patterns in specific countries and time periods. In Mexico, liberal leaders adjusted their ideas and methods throughout the nineteenth century, sometimes disagreeing among themselves, so that the reader is well advised to accept the notion that change was among the most prominent characteristics of liberalism in this era.

Liberalism was probably the most dynamic political movement in nineteenth-century Mexico. With its emphasis on individual freedom and its opposition to the traditional centers of power and influence such as the Catholic Church, liberalism had a controversial impact in a nation only recently separated from the Spanish Empire, in which the Catholic Church, the military, guilds, and other privileged corporate groups had held dominant positions during the colonial era (1519–1821). The advocates of liberalism wanted to break the hold of these corporate structures on property, politics and government, and the educational system in order to clear the way for individual initiative and private enterprise, which they hoped would usher in a new era of economic prosperity. The liberals, therefore, envisioned a thorough transformation of Mexico's national life that reached from propertied wealth to the school classroom. In their pursuit of these goals, however, Mexican reformers often abandoned another basic assumption of liberalism: the call for constitutional limitations on the power of the central government. Such large-scale changes usually required a very active national government led by an assertive chief executive.

The first major confrontation between liberalism and its conservative opponents took place during one of the presidential administrations of General Antonio López de Santa Anna. The general, less interested in the pressing issues of politics than the pomp and pageantry of leadership, in 1833 left the responsibilities of governance to Vice President Valentín Gómez Farías, who was a dedicated liberal reformer. Gómez Farías and most Mexican liberals of his day drew inspiration from the writings of José María Luis Mora, a gifted essayist who placed his talent for persuasion at the service of the liberal cause. In particular, Mora argued in a widely read 1831 essay that the government should require the Catholic Church to surrender all of its property not directly related to its religious functions. This assertion was like a thunderbolt in Mexico's heated political atmosphere of the 1830s because the Catholic Church had accumulated a large portion of the nation's agricultural and urban real estate through wills and donations over the three centuries of the colonial period. Mora's proposal threatened the basic underpinnings of Mexico's economic, social, and religious structure. Vice President Gómez Farías, left in charge of the national government by Santa Anna, acted quickly across a broad front. He nationalized the Franciscan missions in the northwest province of California in an apparent first step in his efforts to secularize church property. He also closed the University of Mexico, an institution dominated by the clergy, and began to reduce the size of the army and to restrict its special privileges.

The bold actions of Gómez Farías aroused the Catholic Church, the army, and their conservative allies who moved to defend the existing hierarchy. These powerful groups appealed to Santa Anna, who, as a military officer as well as politician, decided to remove Gómez Farías from the government in order to foil the liberal reform program. Santa Anna's return to the presidency in 1834 brought an end to this short-lived effort to implant liberalism in Mexico.

Liberalism moved to the periphery of Mexican politics for the remainder of the 1830s and into the 1840s while the nation underwent the excruciating pain of war and territorial dismemberment. The distant province of Texas won its independence from the government in Mexico City in 1836. The expansionist United States annexed Texas in 1845, and soon border disputes led the two nations into a war (1846–48) that proved disastrous for Mexico. The United States invaded Mexico's capital city, defeated the nation's army, and took approximately half of the national territory, including the valuable lands that stretched from Texas to the Pacific coast of California. During this difficult period, liberalism was plagued by internal divisions. The *puros*, radical liberal followers of Gómez Farías, were more

stridently anticlerical than the opposing liberal faction, the *moderados*, who tended to favor gradual methods. This division reduced the impact of liberalism on national politics in these years.

A new generation, led by Benito Juárez, managed to establish a degree of unity within the liberal movement and gained control of the national government in the 1850s. Juárez, a Zapotec Indian who first rose to prominence as the governor of his home state of Oaxaca, challenged the authority of the Santa Anna regime and its conservative supporters. Forced into exile, Juárez took refuge in New Orleans, where he and other liberals began to organize against Santa Anna. Juárez established himself as one of the foremost liberals of his generation during these difficult years. Encouraged by the success of a revolt based in the state of Guerrero, Juárez and other New Orleans exiles returned to Mexico in 1854 and 1855 to take part in a large movement, the Revolution of Ayutla. This movement brought to power a Liberal government that enacted legislation soon known as the Reform Laws. Juárez himself wrote the law that stripped the military and clergy of the right to be tried for serious crimes in special courts run by their own organizations. The Ley Juárez was the first of a series of liberal actions directed against the main strongholds of the conservatives. The second law, written largely by Miguel Lerdo de Tejada, required the Catholic Church to sell or otherwise dispose of its property not directly essential for religious practices (for example, farmland as contrasted with a church sanctuary). The stated intention of the liberals was to break loose property from the control of the Catholic Church for more productive use in the free enterprise economy. Taken together, the Ley Juárez and the Ley Lerdo went beyond the Gómez Farías reforms of the 1830s to strike at the power bases of conservatism in the military and the church. The liberals, in control of the government, also organized a constituent convention that wrote the Constitution of 1857, a document that included the Ley Juárez and Ley Lerdo and extended liberal reforms into other areas.

These sweeping reforms were intended to create a modern economy that would follow the pattern of free enterprise that had brought prosperity to Great Britain and the United States. With church property moving into the market economy and religious and military leaders deprived of their special courts, the liberals were confident that economic prosperity and social change would spread their benefits throughout Mexico. These liberal leaders miscalculated, however. The Ley Lerdo not only deprived the church of its property, it also forced native American villages (legally considered to be corporate entities like the church) to sell their traditional communally held land to individual owners. These transactions did not result in the liberals' goal of a middle class made up of small-to-middle-sized farms in the hands of yeoman farmers (as they were called in the United States). Instead, most church and village properties moved into the grasp of large landowners and speculators, two groups that had the capital necessary to make the purchases. The agrarian ideals of nineteenth-century liberalism did not find fertile ground in Mexico.

Other sources of frustration for liberal reformers came from civil strife and foreign intervention. Conservatives, supported by large segments of the military, fought a bloody war (1857–60) against the liberal government. The victory of the liberals in this conflict brought only temporary respite; conservatives next made an alliance with the French emperor Napoleon III. The result was five years of monarchy under the French-imposed leadership of the ill-fated emperor Maximilian. After the withdrawal of the French army and the defeat and death of Maximilian in 1867, Juárez returned to Mexico City to begin the difficult process of rebuilding his nation.

Juárez finally had control of the national government, but, unfortunately for him and his cause, liberalism as an ideology seemed as exhausted as the nation itself. Juárez, the Mexican president during most of these years, rode out the turmoil of war and intervention to become the symbol of the liberal movement that defended the nation against the conservatives and their imperialist collaborators. Liberalism thereby became linked with Mexican patriotism. While Juárez rose to heroic status among his followers, however, liberals began to realize that their hopes for an agricultural economy made up of a new class of prosperous, independent farmers were doomed to failure. The sale of church lands had weakened Catholic institutions, but the major beneficiaries were wealthy landowners who simply added more property to their already large estates.

Faced with the challenge of trying to govern Mexico while his fellow liberals turned against each other and some even against him, Juárez resorted to autocratic methods, thereby violating the liberal ideal of restricted executive power functioning within a limited central government. The Juárez administration expended much of its energy in dealing with the revolts of dissatisfied liberal politicians, who had expected the rewards of political office, and disappointed peasants, who had seen village lands lost to aggressive hacendados.

The last five years of the Juárez presidency were a time of change for liberalism. In his search for a new approach to Mexico's persistent and burdensome problems, Juárez turned to Gabino Barreda, a Mexican intellectual who had studied with the French philosopher Auguste Comte, the founder of positivism. Barreda returned from France with a new formula for understanding the nation's troubled half-century of Independence and a prescription for progressive political and social change that soon became integral elements in late-nineteenth-century liberalism. Juárez placed Barreda in charge of reforming the nation's educational system, which was to be based in government—not church—schools. Barreda set up the National Preparatory School to train the nation's young elite for their university education. His program became the focal point for the spread of positivist ideas, which emphasized the importance of the hierarchy of knowledge and also a hierarchy in the political and economic life of the nation. Under Juárez and Barreda, liberalism, heavily influenced by positivism, acquired an elitist tone that, coupled with an increasingly autocratic government, laid the basis for the dictatorship of Porfirio Díaz. Juárez's plans for Mexico did not reach maturity because he died of heart failure in 1872 after serving only one year of his final term of office.

Porfirio Díaz dominated Mexican politics from his seizure of power in 1876 until his resignation in the face of the Mexican Revolution in 1911. His standing in history largely has been determined by his image as the tough-minded, often cruel dictator who tamed Mexico; in the first three decades of his public career, however, Díaz earned his reputation as a champion of the liberal cause, particularly his heroic contributions to the defeat of the invading French Army in the Battle of Puebla on May 5, 1862. For the next five years Díaz continued as a loyal liberal general in the struggle against Maximilian's empire. After Juárez and the liberals emerged triumphant in 1867, Díaz turned from a military career to politics, where he encountered a series of disappointing defeats. He became a political opponent of his former mentor and fellow Oaxacan, Juárez. Although his electoral campaigns (which called for no reelection to presidency as a slap at Juárez) and political revolts consistently failed from 1867 to 1872, the hero of the Battle of Puebla gained an understanding of the nation's political system at both the state and national levels. Hardly a liberal thinker like Mora, Gómez Farías, or Juárez, Díaz became skillful in the political tasks of persuasion, image-building, and intimidation.

Liberalism completed its basic transformation in the early years of the Porfirian era. Building upon the changes initiated by Juárez in his last years in the presidency, Díaz in his first term (1876–80) and President Manuel González (1880–84, the only person other than Díaz to hold the presidency during this period) abandoned anticlerical and antimilitary policies and achieved an appreciable reconciliation with the Catholic Church and the army. Díaz and González turned their attention to what became perhaps the central component of late-nineteenth-century liberalism in Mexico: the use of the national government to promote economic development. Both Díaz and González sought and obtained contracts with firms from the United States to build railroads to connect central and northern Mexico with the rapidly expanding railroad system north of the Rio Grande. The resulting improvements in the nation's transportation system connected agricultural lands to urban markets not only in Mexico City, Monterrey, and Guadalajara but also in Denver, Kansas City, St. Louis, Chicago, and other metropolitan centers in the United States. The new Mining Code of 1884 stimulated a revival of mineral extraction as foreign investors began to find value in Mexico's lead and copper reserves as well as the legendary silver and gold mines. Liberalism thus became associated with the expansion of the modern economy.

The economic arrangements reflected the ideological refinements of the Díaz period, which originated with a group of politicians, entrepreneurs, and government ministers widely known as the Científicos. Their name derived from the "scientific" study of politics and society as devised by French positivist philosopher Auguste Comte and advocated in Mexico by Gabino Barreda during the Juárez presidency. This new political/intellectual group coalesced around Manuel Romero Rubio, the minister of the interior and also Díaz's father-in-law. Younger Científicos included educator and historian Justo Sierra, finance expert and later minister of the treasury José Yves Limantour, and agribusiness magnate Enrique Creel. The Científicos transcended regional and state political groupings that had splintered Mexico's political history in the first half-century of Independence to form a national elite of government officials and business leaders. Their national scope along with their modifications of the ideas and practices of liberalism gave them a vital role in the Porfiriato.

Justo Sierra was one of the most outspoken members of this generation to seek a new formulation of ideas and institutions to turn Mexico away from its troubled past toward a more stable and prosperous future. Sierra cited positivism's emphasis on order and hierarchy to justify the acceleration of the trend already under way in the Juárez years: the growth of the national government and the strengthening of the

presidency as its primary agent. A key element in this process was the practice of "scientific politics," through which the methods of research and analysis that had yielded such impressive results in the natural sciences would be applied to the political and social realm to provide Mexico's national leaders with definitive guidelines for the achievement of stability and prosperity.

Sierra and his fellow Científicos put forth their modifications of the liberal ideology because they were convinced that Mexico had to solve the problem of its political instability before other components of progress could take hold. According to historian Charles Hale, the Científicos called for a more powerful nation-state headed by a strong chief executive in order to rectify the flaws of early-nineteenth-century liberalism that placed unrealistic limits on governmental authority. Obviously Díaz turned this executive authority into a dictatorship, but in the 1870s and 1880s, Sierra and other members of the liberal-Científico group were preoccupied with the danger of returning to the chaos of the past.

As Díaz continued in the presidency through the 1890s and into the early twentieth century, however, some liberal elements began to object to this concentration of power. Several members of the Científico elite, led by Sierra, began to propose reforms to balance the increased presidential power with a broader distribution of authority to the judiciary and legislature. In 1893 and again in 1903, they called for such changes, but in both instances the reform effort failed. Groups within the lower classes also became disillusioned with the Díaz regime. Many peasants clung to a combination of ideology and mythology—often called popular liberalism—in which Benito Juárez was the central figure, a legendary champion of patriotism and the common people. Although they did not pose an open threat to the Díaz dictatorship, these peasants created an underlying tension in their celebrations of the collective memory of Juárez through public festivals that, at least by implication, served as expressions of grassroots discontent. The reality of Díaz's official authority and his public image as the benevolent strongman of Mexico overrode these dissident tendencies within liberalism. Díaz who, as an aspiring politician had campaigned against Juárez on the slogan "no reelection" a few decades earlier, now retained an iron grasp on the presidency.

The excesses of Porfirian liberalism also extended into the economic sphere. One of the main goals of the Díaz government, the stimulation of business activity, was accomplished as the construction of railroads and the revision of the mining code enticed foreign entrepreneurs to Mexico. Both foreign and Mexican businessmen also turned their attention to rural villages and, employing the advantages of superior knowledge of the law and close connections with the nation's political leaders, stripped these communities of their best agricultural lands. In the early nineteenth century, around 40 percent of the arable land in central and southern Mexico was held by villages; by 1911 only 5 percent of this type of land remained under their control. The vast majority of Mexican peasants were landless by the last years of the Porfiriato. During this period, some of the more avaricious Científicos ignored liberal concerns about dictatorship and concentrated on their own material gains. The 74-year-old head of state selected a Científico favorite, Ramón Corral, as his vice president in 1904, thereby giving a symbolic endorsement of this grab for property and profits.

Liberalism experienced some dramatic changes in response to the excesses of Porfirian greed and corruption. Sierra's calls for reform and the public celebrations of popular liberalism remained within the parameters of traditional ideas and symbols, but in the first decade of the twentieth century, a new political party, the Partido Liberal Mexicano (PLM, or Mexican Liberal Party) developed a coherent challenge to the Porfirian power structure and the expanding free enterprise system associated with it. Led by Ricardo Flores Magón (and his brothers Jesús and Enrique), the PLM went beyond liberalism's customary emphasis on anticlericalism and individual freedom to call for legislation to end abuse of factory workers, to abolish debt peonage, and to begin a land reform program. The bold pronouncements of the PLM, heavily influenced by anarchism, marked a major break in the history of Mexican liberalism. Ricardo Flores Magón and his small group of followers rejected the Porfirian formula for national advancement based on government support for private business expansion and instead moved their wing of liberalism toward the ideological formulations that were to have an important presence in the Mexican Revolution.

While greed and material gain were primary motives for the Porfirian elite, the public image of Mexican liberalism, both at home and abroad, contained a much more appealing character. The Científicos' mixture of liberalism and positivism found expression through cleverly written speeches and carefully orchestrated demonstrations. For example, Díaz and other government officials cultivated a sense of identification with Benito Juárez as the patriotic defender of a vague, almost mythical liberalism, thereby conveniently neglecting the rivalry between the two men

from 1867 to 1872. Díaz also took advantage of the sophisticated manners of diplomat and cabinet officer Matías Romero to build a favorable reputation for his policies in the United States. Díaz perfected his own abilities in public relations through personal contacts with the large American community resident in Mexico and also through personal acquaintances with the likes of U.S. mining engineer John Hays Hammond and British construction engineer Weetman Pearson (Lord Cowdray). The Mexican president made a point of sending impressive commercial exhibits to international trade fairs in Paris, Berlin, New Orleans, and Chicago and by staging his own demonstrations of Mexico's entry into the world of modernity through the annual reviews of the highly publicized *rurales* (rural mounted police who brought law and order to the nation's roads). His government encouraged and, in some cases, sponsored the publication of articles and books—often in English—that featured Mexico's potential for progress.

The nineteenth-century evolution of Mexican liberalism contains a heavy component of irony. The ideology of Mora, Gómez Farías, and the early Juárez that identified the privileges of the Catholic Church and the military as impediments to national progress by the end of the century had become a complex set of ideas that justified the privileged position of a new elite, the Científicos. The liberalism of the late nineteenth century, however, contained considerable variety and flexibility. Liberals advocated ideas that stretched across a wide range: from the acceptance of dictatorship to bring an end to political instability, to Justo Sierra's calls for a return to the ideal of a limited executive authority based on scientific politics, to the Flores Magón brothers' potent mixture of reformism and anarchism. By the last years of the Díaz period, however, most liberals accepted the calculated, propagandistic appeals of the commercially minded elite to the international business community. Mexican liberalism, like most influential ideologies, contained an internal dynamic of its own that both reflected and changed the life of the nation.

See also Ayutla, Revolution of; Conservatism; Constitution of 1917; Nationalism; Popular Liberalism; Reform Laws; Wars of Reform

Select Bibliography

Bazant, Jan, *Alienation of Church Wealth in Mexico: Social and Economic Aspects of Liberal Revolution, 1856–1875.* Cambridge: Cambridge University Press, 1971.

Berry, Charles R., *The Reform in Oaxaca, 1856–1876: A Microhistory of the Liberal Revolution*. Lincoln: University of Nebraska Press, 1981.

Coatsworth, John, *Growth against Development: The Economic Impact of Railroads in Porfirian Mexico*. DeKalb: Northern Illinois University Press, 1980.

Coerver, Donald M., *The Porfirian Interregnum: The Presidency of Manuel González of Mexico, 1880–1884*. Fort Worth: Texas Christian University Press, 1979.

Costeloe, Michael P., *Church and State in Independent Mexico: A Study of the Patronage Debate, 1821–1857*. London: Royal Historical Society, 1978.

Hale, Charles, *Mexican Liberalism in the Age of Mora, 1821–1853*. New Haven, Connecticut: Yale University Press, 1968.

_____, *The Transformation of Liberalism in Late Nineteenth Century Mexico*. Princeton, New Jersey: Princeton University Press, 1989.

Olliff, Donathon C., *Reforma Mexico and the United States: A Search for Alternatives to Annexation, 1854–1861*. University: University of Alabama Press, 1981.

Perry, Laurens B., *Juárez and Díaz: Machine Politics in Mexico*. DeKalb: Northern Illinois University Press, 1978.

Schoonover, Thomas, *Dollars over Dominion: The Triumph of Liberalism in Mexican–United States Relations, 1861–1867*. Baton Rouge: Louisiana State University Press, 1978.

Sierra, Justo, *The Political Evolution of the Mexican People*. Austin: University of Texas Press, 1969.

Sinkin, Richard, *The Mexican Reform, 1855–1876: A Study in Liberal Nation-Building*. Austin: Latin American Institute, University of Texas, 1979.

Tenenbaum, Barbara, *The Politics of Penury: Debts and Taxes in Mexico, 1821–1856*. Albuquerque: University of New Mexico Press, 1986.

Wasserman, Mark, *Capitalists, Caciques, and Revolution: The Native Elite and Foreign Enterprise in Chihuahua, Mexico, 1842–1911*. Chapel Hill: University of North Carolina Press, 1984.

Weeks, Charles, *The Juárez Myth in Mexico*. University: University of Alabama Press, 1987.

—JOHN A. BRITTON

Limantour, José Yves 1854–1935

Politician and Economist

Considered the very embodiment of scientific administration, José Yves Limantour was undoubtedly the most significant minister in the government of Porfirio Díaz, in which he served as secretary of Hacienda (Treasury Department) from 1893 to 1911. Some of his contemporaries even contended that if Limantour had possessed less talent, less knowledge, and less serenity, the ruin of the country would have been inevitable. Nevertheless, once he left office, Mexico's renowned financial wizard became an obscure historical figure. In fact, modern academic research has yet to produce a full-fledged biography of Limantour despite his undeniable importance in the life of Porfirian Mexico.

While the legitimacy of his birth still remains in question, many facts of Limantour's early life can be discerned despite the legends that previously clouded them. Both his parents, Adèle Marquet and Joseph Yves Limantour, were French immigrants. His father gained a fortune as a ship captain in the Pacific trade during the 1830s and 1840s, until the war between Mexico and the United States nullified California as a source of income. Subsequently, in 1858, U.S. courts denied the elder Limantour's questionable claim to extensive tracts of land in the San Francisco area.

Already one of the richest men in Mexico City by the time of the birth of José Yves, Joseph Limantour expanded his fortune during the Wars of Reform and the French occupation through money lending, arms sales, the acquisition of disentailed property, and other real estate dealings. José Yves's childhood seems to have been defined by social privilege, physical illness, and intellectual precociousness. His higher education consisted of the positivism of the Escuela Nacional Preparatoria and the Escuela Nacional de Jurisprudencia, followed by training in economics in France. In the midst of his grand tour of Europe, Limantour stopped at Mexico's diplomatic mission in Rome in order to choose Mexican, rather than French, citizenship after his 21st birthday.

From the beginning, José Yves Limantour's political career was closely tied to Porfirio Díaz, the leader he later called "the greatest statesman of our country's history." Joseph Limantour's financial support for Díaz helped José Yves obtain teaching positions upon his return from Europe in 1876. During the next few years, he gained recognition as an authority in public administration. From 1877 to 1882, he edited *El Foro*, a journal founded by Justo Sierra and Pablo Macedo to promote the scientific study of law. Limantour moved within a circle of young positivists and supporters of Díaz, many of whom would later become known as Científicos. His closeness to Manuel Romero Rubio and the Díaz political machine made him a city councilman in the capital and a federal deputy. Socially as well as politically, Limantour was firmly linked to don Porfirio. His wife, María Cañas y Buch, the daughter of a longtime Díaz ally, was a childhood friend of Díaz's second wife, Carmen Romero Rubio.

In 1892, Limantour, along with 10 others, signed the Liberal Union manifesto calling for Díaz's reelection and giving priority to orderly material progress over the civic freedoms of traditional liberalism. Limantour's writings during the previous 15 years had argued that Mexico's backwardness required a strong central government to guide the country's economic advance. He had called for a strong—even dictatorial—president who would allow a cadre of capable, scientific administrators to construct the financial, statistical, and institutional apparatus of modern government. Limantour had described the Secretariat of Hacienda as the leading ministry of the executive branch, called upon to set Mexico's economic policies and to oversee other parts of government.

After briefly serving as chief clerk of Hacienda under his longtime ally Matías Romero, Limantour ascended to the leadership of the ministry in 1893. Recent bad harvests, burdensome railroad subsidy payments, and the steady depreciation of the silver-based Mexican peso had left the treasury in dire straights. Aided by new foreign and domestic bond issues, Limantour rapidly reorganized Mexico's finances. By the 1895–96 fiscal year, he had consolidated domestic debt and brought federal income and expenditures into balance. In 1896, legislation proposed by Limantour resulted in the abolition of the *alcabalas,* or internal customs taxes, thereby removing a long-standing obstacle to the formation of a national market. By 1898, the size of the federal budgetary surplus enabled the government to devote funds to debt reduction and to special public investments.

Limantour worked to stabilize the Mexican peso domestically and internationally. Backed by an 1896 law governing credit institutions and the printing of money, Limantour oversaw the emergence of a private banking system across Mexico. By the end of the Porfiriato, the country held some 34 banks of different types. Currency in circulation tripled between 1897 and 1911, while deposits rose almost eightfold. In 1903, following inconclusive international negotiations over the declining value of silver, Limantour sponsored legislation to put the Mexican peso on the gold standard. Since his entry into Hacienda, the exchange value of the silver-based peso had fallen by more than 40 percent in New York and London. The depreciation of the peso constituted a serious burden for import-intensive enterprises such as railroads and for the government's obligation to service the foreign debt. Limantour's monetary reform fixed the worth of the peso in 1905 at 75 centigrams of gold or 50 U.S. cents.

Yet not all of his measures were unqualified successes. Despite the expansion of banking, for example, the availability of credit remained a severe and unresolved problem. During the agricultural drought and recession of 1907–08, short-term credit actually fell 0.2 percent, aggravating existing recessionary conditions. Limantour's top-down financial reforms could not eliminate many of the internal limitations and external vulnerabilities of the Porfirian political economy. The secretary of Hacienda managed to balance Mexico's national finances, but he failed to construct a domestic fiscal regime that would keep pace with economic expansion. While overall government revenues accounted for 11.2 percent of the country's gross domestic product in 1877, they totaled only 7.2 percent in 1910. The federal government's share in 1910 constituted a meager 4 percent, woefully insufficient for coping with the inflation, weakened exports, and economic slump that resulted from the monetary reform of 1905.

Limantour's economic strategy placed a higher priority on the Díaz regime's international credit worthiness than on its capacity to extract domestic revenue. In 1899, the finance minister negotiated a conversion bond issue at 5 percent that enabled the government to reduce interest payments on its gold-denominated foreign debt. In the midst of the elections of 1910, he negotiated a similar conversion issue at 4 percent (only half of this transaction was finalized before the Maderista rebellions changed foreign bankers' minds). Limantour remained convinced that a steady influx of foreign capital would create a modern, prosperous, and ultimately more autonomous Mexican economy. He reported to Congress in December 1905 that

> the day will come, as has been exemplified by the history of other modern nations, when the population, increased by the multiplication of the means of livelihood and trained in more laborious habits, will by degrees redeem itself from indebtedness, and when that happens, the bonds, shares, and other securities of our most flourishing enterprises will be held at home and will not be allowed again to leave the country.

As the unofficial leader of the Científicos, Limantour exemplified what scholar Alan Knight has called the "new economic nationalism" that emerged in Porfirian-Científico circles early in the twentieth century. He stood behind the Porfirian state's circumspect assertion of Mexican sovereignty in the face of U.S. capital. In the words of historian Friedrich Katz, Limantour and the other Científicos believed that "American predominance was inimical to the . . . concept of what Mexico's economic development should be." The finance minister played an important part in official encouragement of British oil investment as a means of avoiding U.S. control over that nascent industry. Even more prominent was his role as the architect of the Mexicanization of the country's rail system, an effort that illustrated the precariousness of Porfirian economic nationalism in the context of limited state resources and presidential succession politics.

Ever since taking charge of Hacienda, Limantour had regarded government railway subsidies as a crucial financial issue. They formed a significant share of Mexico's foreign debt. In 1898 he presented a plan for rationalizing Mexico's rail investments by limiting future subsidies to certain major routes that would connect central and northern Mexico with both the Pacific coast and the southeast. A new railroad law the following year incorporated these ideas and set the stage for more active government rail regulation.

Mexico's improved financial position constituted the foundation for Limantour's assertiveness. Although the country's debt service payments rose by more than 50 percent between the fiscal years 1895–96 and 1910–11, they declined as a share of normal government revenues from 38 to 24 percent. Events after 1900 soon provided Limantour with opportunities to execute his vision of a comprehensive national railway grid to promote development. New rate wars among Mexico's major carriers threatened to upset the stability of the transportation system. At the same time, the financial weaknesses of the Central and Nacional Railways posed the dangerous possibility of a U.S. monopoly over the principal trunk routes between central Mexico and the country's northern border. Limantour intervened quickly, transforming the Mexican government from rail regulator to rail owner.

In 1902–03, Limantour negotiated government stock control of the Interoceánico and the Nacional Railways, thus averting the threat of U.S. monopoly. Subsequent dealings after 1906 with the Central culminated in the formation of the Ferrocarriles Nacionales de México in 1908, a government-controlled partnership with foreign investors that operated over two-thirds of the country's rail system by 1910 and employed over half of all rail workers. Limantour claimed that the creation of the Ferrocarriles Nacionales eliminated undue foreign influence while simultaneously creating the means to operate a more efficient rail system that could be extended to previously untapped areas of the country. In fact, the Nacionales did operate profitably between 1909 and 1911, attaining favorable cost-revenue ratios, adding new lines, and meeting its

obligations to creditors. Limantour later argued from exile that this success would have continued if "disgraceful deeds" of the Revolution had not undermined "one of the most beautiful railway systems in the world."

Contemporaries and later historians have disputed Limantour. The improved operations of the Nacionales between 1909 and 1911 owed less to the efficiencies of consolidation than to cheaper fuel costs derived through the conversion from coal to petroleum. In a remarkably durable analysis carried out in the midst of the Revolution, Fernando González Roa noted that Limantour's 1898 report had actually worked to constrict rail expansion in Mexico, particularly the growth of feeder lines needed to make the rail system more accessible to local economic forces. Few of Limantour's priority routes had reached completion by the end of the Porfiriato. At considerable cost, González Roa contended, Limantour's creation of the Nacionales had accomplished nothing in the national interest not already achieved by his earlier prevention of U.S. monopoly in 1902–03.

The creation of the Ferrocarriles Nacionales manifested dilemmas characteristic of nationalist economic policies under dependent capitalism. To maintain the country's standing among international creditors, Limantour had to assure foreign capitalists of the future profitability of their previous investments in the Central and other consolidated lines. Thus, from its foundation, the new national railway enterprise was overcapitalized and the Mexican government saddled with a precarious level of financial guarantees to external investors. In 1910, the Nacionales devoted 35.2 percent of their gross revenues to bonded debt and dividend service payments, a financial cost that impeded both cheaper local operations and heavy further investments in the system's expansion. "The chief beneficiaries of the Mexicanization," argues historian John H. Coatsworth, "were foreigners: the foreign owners of Mexican railway bonds and the mainly foreign-owned export sector of the Mexican economy," whose operations were spared the potentially disruptive impact of U.S. railroad speculators.

González Roa questioned whether Limantour would have committed such serious errors without some personal conflict of interest. Many Científico functionaries used their influence to enrich themselves during the Porfiriato. Unlike other Científicos, however, most of whom were of lower-middle-class origin, Limantour was born into wealth. Early-twentieth-century scholars remained divided over his possible role in official corruption. Some writers absolved him of illicit conduct, while others accepted his opponents' accusations of secret financial manipulations. While an accurate historical account of the actions of the Porfirian elite remains hampered by the paucity of personal papers from the leading figures of this era, it seems clear that profiteering constituted neither the essence of Limantour's bureaucratic drive nor his purpose in establishing the Ferrocarriles Nacionales de México.

Ultimately, Porfirian Mexico's most exalted *técnico* was never able to shield his accomplishments from the overriding issue of presidential succession. As a member of a narrow elite based in Mexico City with little connection to the rest of the country, Limantour, like his fellow Científicos, overestimated the ability of the Porfirian state to manage Mexican society from the top. He was ill-equipped to cope with the processes of regional consultation that the politics of succession required. Nor could he break from his dependency upon Díaz. It is possible that the president may have forced Bernardo Reyes to resign the vice presidency in 1902 as part of a scheme to establish Limantour as his successor. Nevertheless, Díaz then backed away from the idea. Limantour's public disavowal of the vice presidency in 1904 certainly stemmed more from acquiescence to don Porfirio's will than from a personal reluctance to leave the government bureaucracy that he claimed. Díaz's selection of the unpopular Científico Ramón Corral as vice president in 1904 and his retention of Corral in 1910 blocked both Reyes and Limantour, the two rival choices for an orderly succession.

Limantour spent most of 1910 abroad. Even as late as December of that year, he failed to appreciate the deteriorated position of the regime. He wrote to Díaz from France: "The relative success obtained by the malcontents is an unfathomable mystery to me." Until the end, Limantour remained a loyal instrument of don Porfirio. He helped to negotiate the exit of the aging ruler and, despite his long friendship with the Madero family, refused to continue n his post. He left Mexico, never to return, a few days following the resignation and departure of General Díaz. Although the Revolution destroyed Limantour's work, his state-building approach to government would influence the views of post-Revolutionary elites.

Select Bibliography

Aston, B. W., "The Public Career of Don José Ives Limantour." Ph.D. diss., Texas Tech University, 1972.

Crosman, Herbert A., "The Early Career of José Ives Limantour, 1854–1886." Ph.D. diss., Harvard University, 1949.

Katz, Friedrich, *The Secret War in Mexico: Europe, the United States, and the Mexican Revolution.* Chicago: University of Chicago Press, 1981.

Knight, Alan, *The Mexican Revolution.* 2 vols., Cambridge: Cambridge University Press, 1986.

Schell, William, "Money as Commodity: Mexico's Conversion to the Gold Standard, 1905." *Mexican Studies* 12:1 (Winter 1996).

Turlington, Edgar, *Mexico and Her Foreign Creditors.* New York: Columbia University Press, 1930.

Turner, John Kenneth, *Barbarous Mexico.* Austin: University of Texas Press, 1969.

—ARTHUR SCHMIDT

Literature and National Identity, 1910–96

From the Revolution of 1910 to social developments in the aftermath of the North American Free Trade Agreement, the configuration of Mexican identity has been a major topic of the Mexican literary enterprise, for nationalism is as much a cultural process as a political ideology.

In a multicultural society such as Mexico, the creation of a politically and culturally homogeneous nation—defined as a mestizo nation—was an apparent political necessity in order to keep the country from being torn apart by its internal contradictions. Post-Revolutionary nationalism in the 1920s and 1930s was based on autonomy and self-determination. Thus, nationalism was the result of the assertion of a unique identity as opposed to the inauthentic image promoted by the westernized dictatorship of Porfirio Díaz. At first, the novelty of creating the idea of a new nation caused optimism among the elite, and they worked actively on the project of national reconstruction. Under the cultural nationalism stimulated by José Vasconcelos, secretary of education from 1920 to 1924, a Mexican nation was formed based on characteristics derived from a popular tradition and an indigenous past.

In the same manner that painting and music were affected, the narratives produced after the Mexican Revolution were marked by a strong nationalist expression. In *La raza cósmica* (1925), for example, Vasconcelos had envisioned the "fifth race," a people who were composed of a synthesis of European and indigenous Americans, who would fight against the influences of the United States. Vasconcelos echoed the fears and hopes of such precursors as "the Great Liberator" Simón Bolívar and the Uruguayan essayist José Enrique Rodó, and he thus imagined a unified Mexico; Vasconcelos defined this unified nation only as middle class, mestizo, cultured, and cosmopolitan, however, thus ignoring the large masses who were poor, illiterate, rural peasants, or Indians of multiethnic backgrounds.

At the same time, the historical circumstances that led to the representation of the armed struggle in print also promoted the use of a language that was caustic, anti-intellectual, and popular. Despite certain characteristics that today we consider limitations— linearity, a simplicity of character development, obsessive moralism, Manichean philosophy—new literature began to reflect the specific reality of Mexico. Instead of an urban scene, the narrative drama (the battles and daily events) took place in the rural area and were acted out by the new heroes of the national epic: the peasants, the Revolutionary soldiers, the *soldaderas* (female soldiers or camp followers), and the Indians. The rural and provincial locale that provided the setting of these narratives was in great measure home to the writers themselves, born and raised in the small villages of the Republic. Such writers include not only Mariano Azuela, whose name is linked to the novel of the Revolution with the production of *Los de abajo*, but also José Rubén Romero, Nellie Campobello, Rafael F. Muñoz, Gregorio López y Fuentes, Mauricio Magdaleno, Martín Luis Guzmán, and Vasconcelos himself.

After *Los de abajo* (first serialized in a newspaper in 1915 and republished as a book in 1916, 1920, and 1925) had captured the excitement of the initial Revolutionary tumult, thus initiating the well-known novels of the Mexican Revolution, a current of profound disillusion took hold. Although the armed revolt ended in 1920, the state of anarchy and the political energy of *caciquismo*, or "bossism," persisted, criticized by the disillusioned intellectuals. In some of those novels, such as *Los fracasados* (1908), *Mala yerba* (1909), *Andrés Pérez, maderista* (1911), *Los caciques* (1917), *Las moscas* (1918), *Domitila quiere ser diputado* (1918), and *Las tribulaciones de una familia decente* (1918), Azuela presented an ethical perspective of a Revolution betrayed by opportunism, theft, and economic devastation.

Martín Luis Guzmán in *La querella de México* (1915) and especially Samuel Ramos in *El perfil del hombre y la cultura en México* (1934)—important precursors to *El laberinto de la soledad*, which Octavio Paz published in 1950—offered in their essays a new psychological profile of a nation they considered to be affected by an innate weakness. Although Guzmán depicts all the collective atavisms of a people who appear irredeemable in their attraction to intrigue, dishonesty, and violence in his political

novel *La sombra del caudillo* (1929), other writers, such as Gregorio López y Fuentes in *Campamento* (1931), Muñoz in *Vámanos con Pancho Villa* (1931), and Nellie Campobello in *Cartucho: Relatos de la lucha en el norte de México* (1931), tried to convey another image of a people whose social realities they knew well.

For the novelists who lived the dark reality of the violence and uncertainty of this period of national upheaval, there were no gray tones, only categorical contrasts: the city was corrupt; the countryside, idyllic; the evildoers, ugly; the populace, barbarous. This polarity became even more accentuated and militant in the narratives that focused on the plight of the indigenous populations. In the best novels to reflect the ideals of Cardenismo, such as *El indio* (1935) by López y Fuentes and *El resplandor* (1937) by Mauricio Magdaleno, the Indian still appears disconnected from the mainstream of the Mexican nation. Despite the denunciatory tone of these works, the writers, still motivated by the philosophy of Positivism, presented indigenous society as an exotic world in which the inhabitants, because they were victims, were poetic and pure.

The elite now lacked a common message. Not all writers seemed interested in the Revolution, and some of them of a more aristocratic bent came to form a new vanguardist group. They reacted to the kind of overt and often declamatory nationalism that marked the literature of the 1930s. Through their varied cultural enterprises, such as drama, essays, poetry, and to a lesser degree, novels, intellectuals such as Salvador Novo, Xavier Villaurrutia, Jorge Cuesta, and Jaime Torres Bodet sought to analyze Mexican national identity from an international perspective, which was considered high treason by the more populist sectors who favored a strictly "homemade" literature. They came to form the "Contemporaneos" group. Novo, Cuesta, and Villaurrutia played an important role in cultural journalism and in creating the beginnings of Mexican drama through the activities of Teatro Ulises.

Despite the reforms under President Lázaro Cárdenas (1934–40), the military and political violence of the era tempered the enthusiasm of the intellectuals. Nevertheless, the nationalization project that the Revolution was supposed to bring to Mexico did not yet reflect the multiple identities of the country, but benefited the mestizo who was educated and cultured.

During the 1930s the unified, optimistic vision was soon criticized for its omissions by many intellectuals as they attempted to analyze the nature of *mexicanidad* (Mexicanness). By the 1940s, a new generation of authors (Agustín Yáñez, José Revueltas) reacted against the stark realism and the simple dualism of the previous generation's perspective. The 1940s also brought a new political agenda, and the bourgeoisie were eager to develop a new nation in peace and stability after the previous era of turbulence. The novel benefited from the new stability and reflected a period of great national debate concerning the nature of Mexican identity initiated by Samuel Ramos in 1934.

Al filo del agua (1947) by Agustín Yáñez and *El luto humano* (1943) by José Revueltas were among the first novels to entwine the nationalist agenda with an exploration of innovative narrative techniques: interior monologue, changes in point of view, stream of consciousness. In the renunciation of the previous bipolar perspective, a new complexity was introduced to the depiction not only of provincial life, but of national identity. Nevertheless, the obsession with land and the dialectic of national destiny and the community remained. A new mestizo nation seemed to have emerged; indeed, the mestizo had transformed the identity of the Mexicans and their religious beliefs. But for Revueltas—and for other writers, such as Nellie Campobello, who were more sensitive to cultural diversity—the Revolution's failure had led to the imposition of an artificial *mestizaje* (ideology of race mixing) that distorted their beliefs and individual characteristics. Campobello depicts the agony of the nation from the perspective of the peasants and the oppressed groups of the northern provinces. Hers is one of the alternative voices of the period in the way *Cartucho* and *Las manos de mamá* (1937) tried to demystify the nationalist projects of the founding fathers and expose rather than veil the contradictions between the past and present, universality and locality, tradition and modernity.

At midcentury a modicum of social stability prevailed as Miguel Alemán Valdés was ending his six-year presidency and promulgating the image of being the "First Worker" of the nation, a gesture to the change in emphasis from agrarian reform to industrialization. Perhaps the search beyond the national borders undertaken by Mexican business may be paralleled with the ontological vision expressed by Octavio Paz in his essay collection, *El laberinto de la soledad* (1950). Following the lead of Samuel Ramos, who examined the psychology and the historic roots of Mexican identity, Paz attempted to discover national identity through a focus on differences, since his essay was motivated in part by his travels in the United States and his confrontations as a Mexican with other, expatriate Mexicans, Mexican

Americans, and Anglo citizens of the United States. His essays posit the idea of a pyramid of power influencing the social system of Mexico, the same image Rodolfo Usigli used in his play *Corona de sombra* (1943) to describe the hierarchy of power that reflects the stratified social and ethnic system of Mexico. Paz points out the importance of betrayal as an ongoing motif in Mexican culture, the appearance of which often is linked to the actions of la Malinche, the indigenous female guide and confidante of Fernando (Hernán) Cortés. As an acculturated Amerindian, she was called doña Marina, and the child she bore Cortés has been designated as the first mestizo. Doña Marina may be called the "Mother of the mestizo nation," the Mexican Eve, but she is also judged the traitor to the Indian peoples for having aided Cortés and the invading Spanish soldiers. Her willingness to embrace the foreigner has led to the use of her name to designate a behavior trait, called *malinchismo,* in which Mexicans are said to reject anything native to Mexico in favor of anything foreign. Paz argues that the relationship of doña Marina to Cortés is a root paradigm in Mexico. As the scholar Sandra Messinger Cypess has observed in her study of doña Marina, Paz reads her acceptance of the foreigner from a patriarchal perspective, as if she reacted to the conqueror out of love for Cortés, rather than as a response of the slave that she was to the demands of the conquerors. Paz describes the Mexican as the product of an illegitimate union, as a fatherless child whose parents are the violated "mother Malinche" and the oppressor Cortés. Disinherited by his father, the Mexican mestizo endures a solitude that is related to his "accidental" birth, to his abandonment in a hostile world in which he must hide behind a mask in order to survive. Since Paz's sociological observations, which focus on the male perspective alone, may be considered outmoded, he attempts in *Posdata* (1970) to rectify some of his earlier ideas; still, one must acknowledge the impact of his sociopsychological questioning of the roots of "Mexicanness."

The sparse narratives of Juan Rulfo have been read as a psychological study of the Mexican psyche as a closed space of silences where murmurs may terminate a life more rapidly than give it sustenance. His volume of short stories, *El llano en llamas* (1953), and the masterpiece *Pedro Páramo* (1955) continue both the dark vision of the legacy of the Mexican Revolution and the vernacular language associated with Azuela. His characters are not described specifically as Indians, nor is the Mexican Revolution openly specified, but Rulfo portrays the physical and moral disintegration of rural life in

Mexico that develops as a result of governmental neglect and unbridled power and corruption. In *Pedro Páramo*, the cacique, or local strongman, is able to reduce the entire town to the wasteland that his name suggests because of his uncontested power. But *Pedro Páramo* is much more than a study of the failure of the Mexican Revolution to integrate the diverse ethnic groups and classes into a modern Mexican society; it is a complex novel of mythic power that, at the same time as it echoes the speech patterns of rural Mexico, uses a sophisticated narrative technique with an evocative, lyrical style.

The pervasive interest in Mexican history as a way to understand the present coupled with a strong conviction in cyclical time has characterized the work of many of the writers of the 1960s onward, as well as being reminiscent of Mexica (Aztec) temporal beliefs. Thus, as Elena Garro suggests in *Los recuerdos del porvenir* (1963), patterns of behavior, such as military violence (whether by Spaniards or *federales*), ethnic slaying, and gender oppression seem to repeat in each generation. Set in a small, rural town during the time of the Cristero Rebellion, the novel adds both religious and gender issues to the narrative discourse that explores Mexican national identity. Ostensibly depicting the historical reality of the period in the 1920s when the government engaged in open conflict with the Catholic Church and organized religion, the narrative also has a mythic quality in the way it refers to underlying subtexts and recreates the subtexts or root paradigms that infuse ethnic and gender relations in Mexico. The invading military leader Francisco Rosas invokes the image of the original conqueror Cortés, and Rosas's relation to the women protagonists and the townspeople's reactions to these characters recall the archetypal relationship between Cortés and doña Marina. Garro shows that from the Conquest period on, there has been a historical tendency to blame women for the problems of the nation, to engage in excessive violence, and to ignore or mistreat the Indian population. Garro's work not only offers a powerful description of multiple facets of women's roles in Mexican society, but she deepens the examination of cyclical time and memory, history, and destiny. As her title seems to indicate, the remembrance of the future is a paradox only if one conceives of the future as offering a new reality, a new pattern of behavior.

While Garro, like Yáñez and Rulfo, focused on the rural spaces of Mexico, it is Carlos Fuentes whose first novel, *La región más transparente* (1958), moves the reader to the urban center of Mexico City. Fuentes is one of the first writers to attempt to depict the numerous social classes that coexist in the meta-phoric jungle of post-Revolutionary, mid-twentieth-century Mexico, to highlight the masks of the Mexican psyche that Paz describes in *El laberinto de la soledad* and Usigli depicts in his play *El gesticulador* (1937). Fuentes shows how Mexico City is composed of layers of behaviors, attitudes, and customs from North American and European cultural patterns that have been superimposed over pre-Hispanic cultural practices. In his many narratives, including *La muerte de Artemio Cruz* (1962), *Cambio de piel* (1967), *Terra Nostra* (1975), and *Cristóbal Nonato* (1986), Fuentes articulates a vision of Mexico as a violently contentious, fragmented nation whose indigenous past continues to influence the contemporary period. The chaotic life and death of his most famous character, the opportunist Artemio Cruz, has become an emblem of post-Revolutionary Mexico and symbolizes a nation whose body politic is decaying beyond repair.

Rosario Castellanos is another writer who has critiqued Mexican national identity. Both her first novel, *Balún-Canán* (1957), and *Oficio de tinieblas* (1962) are set in Chiapas and speak of the ethnic struggles that have continued there through the 1990s. A reading of Castellanos's work enables one to appreciate the multiple reasons why Mexico's indigenous populations feel left out of the traditional project of nationalism. The novel is set in the 1930s, in Chiapas during the presidency of Cárdenas. Castellanos's analysis of Mexican national character ranges beyond the ethnic study to encompass racial attitudes in general in Mexico and the way gender issues intersect at all levels of race and class consciousness. In her fiction, essays, poetry, and the provocative farce *El eterno femenino* (1975), Castellanos has clearly examined how categories such as "Indian," "mestizo," and "woman," have shaped Mexican history and literature.

Vicente Leñero (1933) has written a number of novels and plays that also examine a sector of society that had been neglected, the working class and their conditions of life as urban poor, as noted in such novels as *Los albañiles* (1964), which he recast also as a play, *A fuerza de palabras*. Leñero also examines the nature of Mexican Catholicism in such narratives as *Redil de ovejas* (1973) and *El evangelio de Lucas Gavilán* (1979). His play *Martirio de Morelos* (1983), which was considered sacrilegious in its treatment of the national hero, the priest José María Morelos y Pavón, reveals his attack of deference to official history, no matter the sensitivity of the subject matter. Like Leñero, Emilio Carballido, also a novelist but more famous as a dramatist, has been daring in his criticism of official history. His work also recreates the presence of workers, peasants, and simple people from the provinces, often with a lively and keen sense of humor.

Critics such as Luis Leal consider Fernando del Paso's novels to be important in the evolution of the contemporary Mexican novel. Although linked generationally with Gustavo Sainz, José Agustín, Juan de Tovar, and members of "La onda"—that group of writers, as described by Margo Glantz, who came on the scene in the 1960s and broke with traditions, writing about the generation gap in a colloquial vocabulary and iconoclastic style—del Paso, rather, is heir to Revueltas and a disciple of Juan Rulfo in his treatment of conditions of marginality within a complex literary construction. *José Trigo*, published in 1966 before the student massacre of Tlatelolco, anticipates the events that took place there. The narrative spans events from the Mexica Empire of the early sixteenth century to the government's violent repression of the organizers of a railroad strike in 1960. The location of the workers' demonstration becomes historically significant, for the Plaza de las tres culturas, or Tlatelolco, is the very site of the fierce battles that terminated Mexica resistance to the conquistadors and that would witness the clashes between the students and the armed government forces in 1968. Del Paso's second novel, *Palinuro de Mexico* (1977), was inspired in part by the events of Tlatelolco, and beyond its mythological references is a satirical piece that attacks the corruption and injustices that plague Mexico. The repetition of clashes at the Plaza de Tlatelolco reinforces the fatalistic belief of the cyclical nature of Mexican history, as if the blood sacrifice of the Mexica influence the present violence. Del Paso thus also anticipates Fuentes's play *Todos los gatos son pardos* (1970), which begins in the Conquest period and ends with references to the massacre at Tlatelolco, since both offer a variation on the theme of cyclical time that Fuentes had already examined in *La región más transparente*. While del Paso's novel is prophetic, and Fuentes's play is highly allusive, many works have openly used the student uprising as subject matter to explore the impact of historical forces on Mexican actions. So powerful is the meaning of the events of Tlatelolco that even Paz was not permitted the opportunity of using it as a metaphor. Jorge Aguilar Mora, for example, writes in *La divina pareja* (1978) that the tragedy was too real, too historically rooted, to be convert into a mythic, timeless topos, or an interesting metaphor.

Perhaps one of the most famous and explicit of the Tlatelolco pieces is Elena Poniatowska's collage, *La noche de Tlatelolco* (1971). Poniatowska is known for her testimonial narratives, that is, works that document the actual voices of the varied and numerous distinct individuals who compose the body politic but whose interests and values are not always represented in the "heroic" view of the "nation." Whether in *La noche de Tlatelolco* or *La "Flor de Lís"* (1988), with its semiautobiographical focus, Poniatowska has contributed to a revisioning of official history. In *Hasta no verte, Jesús mío* (1969), the testimonial novel based on the life of Josefina Bórquez, the heroine Jesusa Palancares narrates her experiences during the grand sweep of modern Mexican history. Jesusa impresses the reader as a strong and self-reliant woman who negates all the established conventions about typically female traits and their relations to the formulation of national identity for women in Mexico, that they either are sexually accessible, like la Malinche, or as virtuous and maternal as the Virgin of Guadalupe. As she compares herself to her interviewer, a white, upper-class, cosmopolitan intellectual, Jesusa views herself as an outsider—that is, she does not consider herself Mexican because she is poor and illiterate. Her definition reiterates, thus, the mode projected by Vasconcelos in *Raza cósmica*. It is not surprising, perhaps, that Poniatowska, in *La "Flor de Lís"*, presents the other side of this cultural dilemma. In her exploration of the experiences of Mariana, an upper-class, educated, blond woman—a character similar to Poniatowska herself—she shows that Mariana is also at odds with the traditional representation of Mexican national identity. Poniatowska makes clear, then, as Mariana seeks to identify herself as Mexican, the pluralism of the "real," as opposed to the "represented" Mexico.

A comment must be included, too, about the democratization, not only of the characters of fiction, but of the audiences who read literature in Mexico. For example, Sara Sefchovich in the prize-winning novel *Demasiado amor* (1990) makes use of popular forms of fiction—the epistolary novel and the romance—to express serious social concerns. As part of what has been called "Literatura Light," she explores the questions of how to appeal to a larger and more diverse audience.

The reader of contemporary Mexican fiction no longer may think that Mexico is a country preoccupied with its Indian-Spanish heritage alone and the conflicts between Catholic and Indian customs; just as the multiplicity of the indigenous ethnic groups has been recognized in the narratives of such writers as Rosario Castellanos and Carlos Montemayor, for example, a number of narratives have begun to address the growing visibility of the other ethnic and religious groups that now inhabit the country. José Emilio Pacheco, for example, offers one vision of difference in *Morirás lejos* (1967). Known as a major poet, he is also a chronicler of Mexican culture in the mordant style of the essayist Carlos Monsiváis and a representative of the *escritura,* or writerly style. Pacheco's fiction echoes some of the themes of his poetry when he addresses the problems of modern Mexico, from air pollution (not a minor problem as any resident or visitor to Mexico knows) to political corruption. In *Morirás lejos,* a complex, brilliantly structured novel, the allusions to the Holocaust and Nazism emphasize that absolute power corrupts wherever and whenever it functions, from ancient times, to the European Holocaust, to contemporary Mexico.

Pacheco's use of Nazism serves as another way of exploring the political immorality and racial persecution that has distorted Mexican experiences. His work thus points to a new stage in Mexican literature, in which writers deal with Mexico's problems—from political corruption to environmental pollution to racism—in a new vocabulary that eschews provincialism. Although Mexicanness is still a major topic in Mexican literature, the many silent voices that the Mexican Revolution had hoped to release are finally being heard.

The scholar Jean Franco in *Plotting Women* reminds us of the impact of the "master narratives" that have conditioned the representations of nationhood in Mexico with regard to religion, class, and gender throughout its history. Yet in the last half of the twentieth century, a Mexican identity defined within a dominant social ideology solely in terms of religious conviction or ethnic and racial identity, or party affiliation for that matter, is no longer customary or accepted. Many narratives tell the stories, in plural, of the Mexican people, whether in the masculinist voice of Paz or Fuentes, or a feminist one like Angeles Mastretta's revision of macho power in *Arráncame la vida* (1985), or an immigrant voice—whether Jewish, as in Sabina Berman's *La bobe,* or Spanish, as in Luis Arturo Ramos's *Intramuros* (1983)—or as gay Mexicans, as in Luis Zapata's *El vampiro de la colonia Roma* (1979), or lesbian, as in Rosamaría Roffiel's *Amora* (1989). The varied accents that come from Mexican novelists are distinctive and resonant and persuade the reader of the multiple realities they incorporate and the vitality of their work.

See also Corridos; Gender: Gender and Mexican Spanish; Malinche and Malinchismo; Modernism; Nationalism; Virgin of Guadalupe and Guadalupanismo

Select Bibliography

Burgess, Ron, *The New Dramatists of Mexico: 1967–1985.* Lexington: University of Kentucky Press, 1991.

Cypess, Sandra Messinger, *La Malinche in Mexican Literature: From History to Myth.* Austin: University of Texas Press, 1991.

Dauster, Frank, *The Double Strand: Five Contemporary Mexican Poets.* Lexington: University of Kentucky Press, 1987.

Duncan, J., *Voices, Visions, and a New Reality: Mexican Fiction since 1970.* Pittsburgh: University of Pittsburgh Press, 1986.

Foster, David William, *Mexican Literature: A History.* Austin: University of Texas Press, 1994.

Franco, Jean, *Plotting Women: Gender and Representation in Mexico.* New York: Columbia University Press, 1989.

Pupo-Walker, Enrique, and Roberto González Echevarría, editors, *Cambridge History of Latin American Literature.* Cambridge: Cambridge University Press, 1996.

Steele, Cynthia, *Politics, Gender, and the Mexican Novel.* Austin: University of Texas Press, 1992.

—SANDRA M. CYPESS AND SOPHIE DE LA CALLE

Lombardo Toledano, Vicente

1894–1968

Labor Leader and Intellectual

The career of Vicente Lombardo Toledano is also the history of many of the central themes in the intellectual and political trajectory of twentieth-century Mexico. As dean of Mexican Marxism, Lombardo was the best-known link between Mexico and the international world of Marxism and socialism and, therefore, a protagonist in struggles that frequently challenged the legitimacy of the capitalist state consolidated by the governments of Revolutionary Mexico. But Lombardo, more than any other intellectual, also became the key left-wing ideologue of the Mexican Revolution. While aiming to subvert and transform the character of Mexican capitalism, Lombardo's theoretical prescriptions and political action served in crucial ways to strengthen the targets of his criticism. Above all, Lombardo was the chief intellectual architect of the leftist-nationalist political project initiated during the government of Lázaro Cárdenas (1934–40) and defended with varying degrees of enthusiasm by governments and important currents of opinion within and outside the ruling Partido Revolucionario Institucional (PRI, or Institutional Revolutionary Party) until well after Lombardo's death in 1968.

The vision of the Mexican Revolution as a "progressive" nationalist and anti-imperialist experience that could serve as a model for the rest of the Americas was developed with consummate skill by Lombardo. Through his writings and energetic activity in anti-imperialist and trade union organization throughout Latin America, the Maestro, as he was known, worked unceasingly to propagate the leftist credentials of the Mexican Revolution, especially in the 1940s and 1950s.

The essence of the Lombardista project was the urgent necessity of building, and then consolidating, an alliance between the state and worker organizations. This fascination with the potential of state–social movement alliances was born early in Lombardo's career. During the presidency of Plutarco Elías Calles (1924–28), the Confederación Regional Obrera Mexicana (CROM, or Regional Confederation of Mexican Workers) labor organization, in which Lombardo was an active member, enthusiastically collaborated in the government's task of national economic and political reconstruction.

Between 1933 and 1940 the leftward shift in the balance of political and class forces in Mexico encouraged Lombardo to reformulate his concept of an alliance between the popular classes and the state. This project also drew on the Communist International's (Comintern's) idea of the Popular Front (a broad antifascist alliance between communist and bourgeois democratic parties) and exploited the opportunities opened up by Cárdenas's presidency. Now the goal was to assist in modernizing capitalism by eliminating feudal social and economic forms in agriculture (via land reform), promoting industrialization (on the assumption that industrialization would guarantee economic and political independence), and establishing the leading role of the state (rectoría económica del estado) in setting the framework for economic development.

The qualitatively new element in this second stage of the Lombardista state project was the formal incorporation into the ruling party of organized labor and, to a lesser extent, the peasant beneficiaries of land reform. The Confederación de Trabajadores de México (CTM, or Confederation of Mexican Workers), which Lombardo had founded in 1936, became the labor hub of the new corporativist structure established by the Partido de la Revolución Mexicana (PRM, or Party of the Mexican Revolution). Lombardo expected that a strong labor and peasant anchorage would guarantee "national unity" and force capitalist development along a path that would permanently favor the urban and agrarian masses.

By the mid-1930s Lombardo had become an enthusiastic Marxist. But his commitment to "scientific" socialism had taken a long time to develop. In his youth Lombardo's intellectual profile had been shaped by the liberal-humanism, idealism, spiritualism, and antipositivism of Antonio Caso and the Generation of 1910. The Ateneo de la Juventud, not Mexico's anarchists and early socialists, attracted his admiration. Lombardo's shift to the left, it is generally argued, flowed from early contacts with the Mexico City working class. In 1917 he became secretary of the Universidad Popular, a working-class education initiative launched by members of the Ateneo. While a representative of the Universidad Popular, the young intellectual made his first contact with the organized labor movement when he attended the founding conference of Mexico's first national labor organization, the CROM, in 1918. Over the next few years he made a decisive commitment to working-class politics. By 1923 he had become secretary of education and a member of the CROM's Central Committee.

The CROM was a staunchly anticommunist organization, and it was only in 1932, after his break with the now decisively weakened organization, that Lombardo declared himself a "non-Communist Marxist." First, within the so-called Purified CROM and the Confederación General de Obreros y Campesinos de México (CGOCM, or General Confederation of Workers and Peasants of Mexico), and then in the National Committee of Proletarian Defense that he organized in 1935 to rally support behind the embattled new president Lázaro Cárdenas, Lombardo moved steadily to the left. A visit in 1935 to the Soviet Union consolidated Lombardo's Marxism and his commitment to the newly emerging concept of the Popular Front. His growing identification with the young Soviet state did not make Lombardo an automatic ally of the Partido Comunista Mexicano (PCM, or Mexican Communist Party), with which he already had clashed numerous times. Always immensely critical of the PCM, whose intellectual shallowness and political naiveté he resented, Lombardo never accepted the communists' claim to be the authorized interpreter of Marxism in Mexico. His power base in the CTM and the prestige he enjoyed in Mexico and later in Latin America were, nevertheless, immensely attractive to the Comintern and the Soviet Union, which generally supported Lombardo in his many disputes with the Mexican and Latin American communist parties.

A classic example of how Comintern and Soviet support for Lombardo overrode the position of Mexican communists occurred in 1937. Opposition to the

increasingly antidemocratic and anticommunist policies of Lombardo Toledano and his ally Fidel
Velázquez led the Communist Party to support
the withdrawal of its important union allies from the
labor confederation during the Fourth Council of
the CTM. With the help of Earl Browder, leader of the
Communist Party of the United States (CPUSA) and
a major figure within the Comintern, Lombardo managed to reverse the Mexican communists' decision.
The CTM was reunified—around the slogan of Unity
at All Cost (Unidad a Toda Costa)—but on terms dictated by the most conservative sections of the national
labor confederation. The long-term consequences
of the decision were substantial—the consolidation of
an increasingly bureaucratized and corrupt camarilla
of union leaders at the helm of the CTM and the
beginnings of the marginalization of the left—a
process that, ironically, would eventually cost Lombardo his position as general secretary of the CTM
in 1941.

The close relations between Lombardo and the
Soviet Union also vividly manifested themselves in
the fierce opposition that Lombardo and the CTM
mounted against the decision to grant Trotsky exile
in Mexico and in Lombardo's creation and leadership of the Confederation of Latin American Workers (CTAL), founded with Mexican government
financial support in 1938. During World War II
and the period from 1945 to 1948, the CTAL,
under Lombardo's energetic direction, extended the
Cardenista project of revolutionary nationalism
throughout the Caribbean and Central and South
America. The promotion of antifascist national
fronts in Latin America during the war years closely
followed the strategy of the ailing Comintern and the
Soviet Union and succeeded in building an extensive
network of progressive labor organizations throughout Latin America on the basis of the Popular Front's
principles. While Lombardo was increasingly marginalized within the CTM, the dean of Mexican
Marxism became the most successful hemispheric
labor figure in the Americas. It was only with the
onset of the Cold War and the emergence of U.S.
plans to create a Western Hemispheric labor organization that the prestige and grip of the CTAL and
Lombardo began to disintegrate.

The waning of Lombardo's domestic influence
dates from his decision to create a new, broad,
united-front party in the late 1940s. This was not
Lombardo's first foray into party politics. During
his years as the CROM's leading intellectual he had
been a member of that organization's Labor Party
(Partido Laborista) and for a few months, in 1923–
24, served as interim governor of his home state of

Puebla after the elected incumbent joined the de la
Huerta rebellion. But it was the Comintern-inspired
notion of the Popular Front that captured Lombardo's political imagination. He first proposed the
idea of a Popular Front party in the late 1930s, and
the project reemerged with greater energy in 1947
and 1948 during discussions that Lombardo held
with left intellectuals and the leaders of the left of the
labor and peasant movement.

Lombardo's proposal was for the creation of a
party that would support the national democratic,
antifeudal, and anti-imperialist goals of the Mexican
Revolution. Its platform supported rapid industrialization, economic independence, and a deepening of
the agrarian reform. It saw its historic task as combating the Mexican right, which Lombardo identified with the *sinarquista* movement and the newly
established Partido de Acción Nacional (PAN, or
National Action Party) and to a much lesser degree,
conservative forces within the PRI. The Partido
Popular (PP, or Popular Party), established in 1947
by Lombardo, was careful not to confront the PRI
too openly, and when this was not possible, Lombardo always was careful to distinguish between
the actions of "reactionaries" within the PRI and the
figure of the president himself. Thus, during the late
1940s Lombardo had few problems in expressing
loyalty to both President Miguel Alemán Valdés and
Joseph Stalin.

In spite of this cautious stance, the PRI and its sectoral affiliates such as the CTM did not warmly
embrace Lombardo's Popular Party, seeing the new
formation as a threat to the mass base of the ruling
party and its affiliates. But the weakness of the Popular Party can also be attributed to the authoritarian
style of Lombardo himself. He ruled the PP with an
iron fist, and the first 10 years of the new party's life
were punctuated by a series of intraparty quarrels
that peaked between 1956 and 1958 in a major
fracas in which Lombardo lost the support of key
allies such as Enrique Ramírez.

Although Lombardo stood as a presidential candidate of the PP in 1952, for most of its life, the
Partido Popular, which became the Partido Popular
Socialista (PPS, or Popular Socialist Party) in 1960,
expressed almost unqualified political and electoral
support for the PRI. Lombardo, in the last stage of
his life, became a bitter opponent of attempts by
unionists to break down the authoritarian controls
imposed by labor bosses, or *charros*. He opposed the
teachers' reform movement that emerged in Mexico
City during 1957 and played an equivocal role in the
great railway worker mobilizations of 1958–59.
During the student-popular movement of 1968, his

denunciations of the subversive actions of the young protesters were shrill and unforgiving.

The students' bitter critique of the failings of the Mexican state clashed with one of the most distinctive features of Lombardismo—its glorification of the state and its progressive nationalizing and anti-imperialist pretensions long after the radical reformism of the Mexican Revolution had run its course. While the students of 1968 and their allies practiced the libertarianism and anti-authoritarianism of the new left, Lombardismo still represented the more authoritarian strains in the culture of Marxism. Of all the currents within Mexican Marxism, it was Lombardismo that was most intimately bound up with the image and practice of the caudillo, the authoritarian populist.

The legacy of Lombardismo has been very extensive. A Mexican version of British Fabianism, it owed its strength in part to the ideological and political alliance established between its practitioners and the state bureaucracy in whose ranks an extraordinarily large number of Lombardistas and ex-Lombardistas worked. In spite of the political opportunism exhibited by Lombardo and the PPS, Lombardismo also managed to develop a substantial base among Mexican intellectuals in the 1950s and 1960s, which has not been extinguished. The links between the PPS, students, teachers, and teacher trainees meant that at the local level the Lombardistas were closely in touch with popular struggles, particularly among peasants and rural workers. Consequently, the followers of Lombardo often diverged quite strongly from the cautious line articulated by the Maestro himself. Nowhere was the enduring appeal of Lombardo's ideas seen more vividly than in the impressive mobilizations organized by the neo-Cardenista opposition during the presidential election campaign of 1987–88. The electoral earthquake of 1988 and the emergence of the center-left Partido de la Revolución Democrática (PRD, or Party of the Democratic Revolution) convincingly demonstrated the enormous convocatory power of Revolutionary nationalism two decades after the death of the Maestro in 1968.

Select Bibliography

Carr, Barry, *Marxism and Communism in Twentieth Century Mexico*. Lincoln: University of Nebraska Press, 1992.

Millon, Robert, *Mexican Marxist: Vicente Lombardo Toledano*. Chapel Hill: University of North Carolina Press, 1966.

—BARRY CARR

López de Santa Anna, Antonio

See Santa Anna, Antonio López de

M

Madero, Francisco I. 1873–1913

Revolutionary Leader and President

Francisco I. Madero was born on October 30, 1873, into a family of wealthy landowners, cattle ranchers, mine owners, and industrialists in northern Mexico. In 1886, at the age of 13, Madero was sent to study in the United States, and from 1888 to 1892 he attended the École des Hautes Études Commerciales in Paris. In 1893 he entered the University of California at Berkeley to study agriculture.

Madero's thinking matured while he was studying abroad. He saw how the U.S. electoral system worked and developed an admiration for French and U.S. democracy. He also was exposed to spiritism in France in 1891, acquiring a huge library of books on spiritism and beginning a lifelong involvement in spiritist teachings and movements. In 1893 Madero returned to Mexico to manage one of his father's cotton plantations in San Pedro de la Colonias, Coahuila. He introduced irrigation and other agricultural improvements and set up hostels, schools, and homeopathy centers for the poor. In 1903 he married Sara Pérez. Rather than continuing to work on family properties, however, Madero decided to concentrate on politics.

Madero long had been concerned about national and regional problems in Mexico, writing articles for a variety of journals in Coahuila and Mexico City and using his family's wealth to subsidize opposition political clubs and newspapers. In 1904 Madero, various friends, and members of his family organized the Benito Juárez Democratic Club in San Pedro de la Colonias to elect a candidate in the municipal elections; Madero was its first president. Through the newspaper *El Demócrata* they persuaded people in other municipalities in Coahuila to form affiliated clubs. In 1905 delegates from each club met to name a candidate for governor. Madero played a pivotal role in the campaign, financing part of the costs himself, finding other contributors to fund the balance, proposing candidates, and drawing on a vast network of editors, journalists, friends, and relatives to develop a coordinated plan of action and to disseminate political propaganda. Nonetheless, during the elections the incumbent governor violated national electoral law by standing for reelection. The clubs demanded that the elections be nullified, to no avail. This experience helped Madero solidify his ideas about universal suffrage and nonreelection.

In 1908, for reasons that still are not entirely clear, longtime Mexican dictator Porfirio Díaz announced in an interview with a U.S. journalist that he would not stand for reelection, spawning a flood of opposition political activity. In 1909 Madero published *The Presidential Succession of 1910: The National Democratic Party*. Madero demanded that the electoral provision of the Constitution of 1857 be honored, allowing free and fair elections to take place with no incumbents allowed to stand for reelection. He criticized the government of Porfirio Díaz for being absolutist and centralist, keeping a closed network of cronies in power, creating a lapdog press, and preventing the formation of opposition parties. Madero also found much to praise in the Porfirian regime, however, particularly Díaz's administrative acumen and the apparent social peace and material progress of his decades-long rule. Nonetheless, Madero insisted that Mexico needed political change and proposed that a National Democratic Party (later called the Partido Anti-Reeleccionista, or Anti-Reelectionist Party) be created. He suggested that anyone sharing his ideas should organize political clubs, spreading anti-reelectionist ideas through the press and eventually creating a national club. Each state would name a delegate to a national convention, which would propose candidates for president, vice president, and the judiciary.

In 1909 Madero, together with other figures such as the philosopher José Vasconcelos, founded the Centro Anti-Reeleccionista de México (Mexican Anti-Reelectionist Center) in Mexico City. Madero traveled throughout the country on behalf of the center, converting to the anti-reelectionist cause former followers of potential candidate Bernardo Reyes, middle-class voters, and wavering supporters of Díaz (who by now had decided to seek reelection despite his previous declaration that he would not). In gathering this support, however, Madero also helped catalyze a network of opposition to his candidacy among supporters of Porfirio Díaz's regime.

In April 1910 an order went out for Madero's arrest on the grounds that he was an accomplice in a theft of *guayule* (a valuable, rubber-producing crop) from a hacienda in Coahuila. He managed to evade arrest and attend the Anti-Reelectionists' national convention, however, where he was named the party's candidate for president. Madero traveled throughout Mexico, but on the eve of the election he was arrested and imprisoned. Porfirio Díaz was reelected as president and Ramón Corral vice president.

After the elections Madero was freed on bail and returned to the city of San Luis Potosí, where he wrote the Plan de San Luis Potosí. Madero declared the June 1910 elections null and void, calling on the nation to protest the government's conduct. He announced that he was provisionally assuming the presidency until a national plebiscite could be held, and he called on the Mexican people to take up arms on November 20, 1910, to reestablish the principles of universal suffrage and nonreelection.

Madero showed less acumen as a military commander than as a political organizer. When Madero crossed from the United States into Mexico with a small military force, he was defeated quickly and forced to flee back across the border. The largely urban, middle- and upper-class Anti-Reelectionist cells were crushed. The real work of making a revolution was left to a broad collection of local and regional forces. If they all had some general loyalty to the principles of anti-reelectionism and to Madero himself, they also were seeking redress for a wide variety of local, regional, and class grievances; many also had ties to traditions of resistance and rebellion quite at odds with Madero's. Madero never had anything more than nominal control over his own forces, and several of the most important military leaders resented what they saw as Madero's meddling in key tactical and strategic decisions. When Madero refused to allow Revolutionary troops to attack Federal troops cornered in the border city of Ciudad Juárez, Pascual Orozco and Francisco "Pancho" Villa countermanded Madero's orders, sending their troops into Ciudad Juárez and delivering a final, decisive blow to the Porfirian regime. In the Treaty of Ciudad Juárez, Díaz's representatives agreed that Díaz should step down and leave the country. Nonetheless, the treaty only heightened many of the divisions among Madero's followers. If the treaty effectively ended the civil war, it also required that the Revolutionary army be disbanded while allowing the Federal army to continue intact. Although many Revolutionaries (such as Francisco Villa) retired to private life, others refused to lay down their arms.

Francisco León de la Barra was named provisional president so that Madero could run for president legally in a democratic election. Madero devoted most of his energies to the presidential campaign, but he remained quite active in de la Barra's government, alienating two of his most important early supporters. Madero's 1910 running mate, Francisco Vázquez Gómez, and his brother, Interior Minister Emilio Vázquez Gómez, clashed with Madero over his plans to demobilize Revolutionary troops. In response, Madero dismissed Emilio, and at a meeting of the Anti-Reelectionists—now renamed the Partido Progresista Constitucional (Progressive Constitutional Party)—Madero replaced Francisco with José María Pino Suárez as his candidate for vice president. Madero and Pino Suárez handily won the national elections of October 1911, but the break with the Vázquez Gómez brothers only heightened tensions between Madero and many of the popular forces that first had put him into power.

As president Madero promulgated a series of reforms that would have been unthinkable under Porfirio Díaz. He freed political prisoners, abolished the death penalty, and lifted restrictions on the press, even though this last measure increased party factionalism. Madero's most notable reform was the abolition of the *jefaturas políticas,* the hated system of political bosses, which were replaced with independent municipal authorities. These authorities were responsible for restoring the peace, demobilizing Revolutionary troops, and ensuring that local and state elections be conducted in a free and fair manner. Madero also created a department of labor, set up schools and workshops, reduced the workday to 10 hours, and introduced labor regulations for women and children. He also permitted industrial workers to unionize and required railways in Mexico to reverse their practice of giving preference to U.S. workers in hiring, promotion, and wages.

Nonetheless, Madero's reforms did little to address important regional, local, and class grievances, and his agrarian program fell well short of the more radical demands of other Revolutionaries such as

Emiliano Zapata in the state of Morelos; in November 1911 Zapata took up arms against Madero, promulgating a far more far-reaching agrarian program in his Plan de Ayala. Moreover, Madero was unable to check abuses by federal troops against former Revolutionaries. If many Revolutionaries felt that Madero had not gone far enough in his reforms, however, many elite interests felt that he had gone altogether too far; many also sought to use the instability following the Revolution of 1910 to jockey for political and economic advantage. Elite and foreign interests also felt that Madero had not done enough to guarantee stability in Mexico. Drawing on a combination of elite and popular grievances, a series of revolts broke out throughout Mexico in 1912–13. Félix Díaz (nephew of the former dictator) revolted in October 1911, Bernardo Reyes in December 1911, and Pascual Orozco in January 1912.

Madero also faced opposition from within the government. The old Porfirian civil service was intent on maintaining its old privileges, and elements in the federal army resented changes Madero had instituted in the military hierarchy. In February 1913 army troops led by General Victoriano Huerta overthrew Madero following 10 days of bloody street fighting known as the Decena Trágica (Ten Tragic Days). Shortly after his surrender, Madero was murdered by Federal soldiers.

Despite its collapse, Madero's anti-reelectionist movement helped spawn a generation of political leaders who would lead Mexico into the world's first major revolution of the twentieth century. Despite considerable discontent with his administration, Madero enjoyed broad popular support, and he continues to be revered in the popular memory. In the summer of 1914, Revolutionary troops closed on the Mexican capital, dealing the federal army a final and irrevocable defeat. Madero today is lauded in official history as the "apostle of democracy," the man who helped bring the decades-old dictatorship of Porfirio Díaz to an end and spark the revolution whose uncertain legacy continues to shape Mexican political life.

Select Bibliography

Beezley, William, "Madero, the 'Unknown' President and his Political Failure to Organize Rural Mexico." In *Essays on the Mexican Revolution: Revisionist Views of the Leaders*. Austin and London: University of Texas Press, 1979.

Cockroft, James Donald, *Intellectual Precursors of the Mexican Revolution, 1910–1913*. Austin: University of Texas Press, 1968.

Cumberland, Charles, *Mexican Revolution: Genesis under Madero*. Austin: University of Texas Press, 1952.

Ross, Stanley, *Francisco I. Madero, Apostle of Mexican Democracy*. New York: Columbia University Press, 1955.

—YOLIA TORTOLERO CERVANTES

Maize

The plant known commonly as corn or maize is known scientifically as *Zea mays ssp. mays;* it is a gigantic domesticated grass of tropical Mexican origin and produces grain and fodder that are the basis of a number of food, feed, pharmaceutical, and industrial manufactures. Cultivation of maize and the elaboration of its food products are bound inextricably with the rise of pre-Colombian Mesoamerican civilizations. Owing to its adaptability and productivity, the culture of maize spread rapidly around the globe after Spaniards and other Europeans exported the plant from the Americas in the fifteenth and sixteenth centuries. Maize currently is produced in most countries of the world and is the third most planted field crop (after wheat and rice). The bulk of maize production occurs in the United States, the People's Republic of China, and Brazil, which together account for 73 percent of the annual global production of 456.2 million tons. Mexico, the world's fourth-largest producer of maize, currently produces approximately 14 million tons of grain annually on 6.5 million hectares (3 percent of world production on 5 percent of the world's land devoted to maize production).

Biology

Currently, major maize production areas are located in temperate regions of the globe and primarily produce animal feed and industrial materials. In Mexico, however, the culture of maize remains predominantly a subsistence enterprise. Industrial maize varieties are hybrids that tend toward uniformity owing to the requirements of mechanized production and their common ancestry (in almost all cases related to strains developed in the maize belt of the north-central United States). Because most maize produced in Mexico is for direct human consumption, and because it is produced by self-provisioning farmers in small-scale settings, the expensive, uniform, high-yielding "dent" hybrids (so-called because of the characteristic dent in the crown of their kernels) of the north-central United States are not suited to the highly variable production conditions or nutritional requirements of most Mexican producers. Although important niches of hybrid production exist in various areas, notably in the western states of Jalisco and Sinaloa, almost all Mexican maize production is based on small populations of open pollinates. These populations are maintained by peasant farmers and are under constant selection pressure for adaptation to the microclimates of the myriad mountain valleys where these farmers live.

Consequently, there is high genetic biodiversity in the Mexican maize pool, a factor of great importance for the breeding of current and future maize cultivars. In a classic study of this variability conducted during the 1940s, 32 races grouped in 5 racial complexes were identified. Subsequent work has refined this characterization to at least 42 races in 3 great racial complexes. Mexican and international organizations have expended major effort to preserve this rich genetic treasury against the genetic erosion caused by decreased maize cultivation associated with the introduction of hybrids and Mexico's rapidly industrializing economy. The world's major collections of Mexican maize germplasm are maintained by the International Center for Maize and Wheat Improvement (CIMMYT), the Mexican National Institute for Agricultural, Forestry and Livestock Research (INIFAP), and the United States Department of Agriculture's North Central Regional Plant Introduction Station in Ames, Iowa.

History

Maize is the domesticated form of a strain of teosinte *(Zea mays ssp. parviglumis)*, a wild grass occurring naturally in isolated patches currently restricted to elevations between 1,300 and 5,600 feet (400 and 1,700 meters) in the Mexican western Sierra Madre (Michoacán and Jalisco). Both social and plant scientists regard maize agriculture as a prime example of the coevolution of a plant and its domesticators: as the plant and human society evolved, they each exerted strong influence on one another. The Mexican anthropologist and maize historian Arturo Warman has referred to maize as a thoroughly cultural artifact in that it is truly a human invention, a species that does not exist naturally in the wild and can survive only if sown and protected by humans. Likewise, the domestication and improvement of maize is correlated strongly with the development of cultural complexity and rise of the high civilizations of pre-Hispanic Mesoamerica.

The domestication of teosinte predates the historical Mesoamerican period, with most extant oral traditions alluding to this cultural milestone in highly encoded mythical tales and folklore. Lacking a reliable historical record, the issue of maize origins long has been a controversial ethnobotanical problem. Recently, a number of new techniques have been applied to this question. These methods include, in addition to traditional archaeological excavation, numerical taxonomy (cladistics), analysis of chromosome and allozyme homologies, and accelerated mass spectrometry dating techniques. Application of these procedures has permitted scientists to narrow the general date and location of teosinte's domestication between 4000 and 3000 B.C. in Michoacán's Balsas River drainage. However, there is still uncertainty regarding whether this momentous achievement was, in the words of scholar Hugh Iltis, "a process or an event."

In pursuit of evidence for Mesoamerican agricultural origins, archaeologists Richard McNeish and Kent Flannery led various interdisciplinary teams in excavating a number of highland arid caves throughout the central Mexican plateaus. From the 1940s to the 1960s, these researchers documented the transition from hunter-gatherer lifestyle to that of early agriculturists occurring during the fourth and third millennia B.C. in the present-day states of Tamaulipas, Puebla, and Oaxaca (these dates are those assigned by current researchers and are more recent than originally estimated by McNeish and Flannery, who were limited by the dating methods available to them). The picture that emerged was of small migratory bands following the seasonal patterns of plants and animals, subsisting on antelope, deer, rabbits, and similar small prey, gathering piñon nuts, hackberry, and other species, and experimenting with parched grains and cereal meal.

The first cereal domesticated by early Mesoamericans was evidently not maize, but *Setaria geniculata,* a relative of today's grain millets. However, by 2,700 B.C. maize had been introduced from Michoacán to Puebla's Tehuacán Valley, the residents of the Coxcatlán caves in the southern fringes of the valley were utilizing a small-eared variety of maize (six to nine kernels per cob) and had innovated the process for grinding maize grain with stone mortars and baking flat bread. Over a period of 2,000 years the residents of Coxcatlán and of Guila Náquitz, Oaxaca, gradually began to depend more on their cultivars and less on their hunting and foraging. Indicators of social stratification and complexity, such as irrigation works and the manufacture of pottery, textiles, and woven products, increased. By 1400 B.C. maize cultivation had reached both Mexican coasts, and the cultural rise of peoples in the central highlands, southern Gulf Coast and Chiapas-Guatemala lowlands was underway.

It is instructive to compare the history of teosinte's domestication as deciphered by contemporary scientists with oral traditions surviving among native Mesoamerican peoples. In the most common Mesoamerican myth of maize origins, a fox follows an ant and discovers a stash of maize enclosed within a large mountain or boulder, partakes of the grain, and later betrays in his flatulence that he has found a wondrous new food. In most accounts the maize trapped within the mountain or boulder is initially accessible to small animals but not to humans, and it eventually is released to humans by divine intervention. Some interpret this myth as a cultural memory of a time when the foliage or grain produced by the ancestor of maize was edible only by animals and not humans. Alternately, this myth may refer to a sudden set of mutations that instantaneously "liberated" maize.

In these stories, the maize-liberating deity blasts open the mountain encasing maize with a thunderbolt. This explains why maize grain occurs in various colors ranging from black (scorched from having been on the exterior of the stash) through red to blue, yellow, and finally pure white (maize that was at the center of the stash and therefore protected from the bolts of thunder).

There are stories that deal more directly with maize origins. Significantly, the best examples of these are the creation myths that detail the structure and meaning of the universe. A good source of such traditions are the Maya peoples, who maintain the most ancient and continuous cultural relationship with maize among extant indigenous peoples of Mesoamerica, and for whom the major constellation visible in the heart of the night sky is in fact a sacred maize plant about which the universe is ordered.

J. E. S. Thompson collected a large number of Maya maize/creation myths and provided a useful comparative analysis. An important theme is that found among the Mam, Quiché, and Cakchiquel peoples, who believe that in ancient times there was no maize, but people fed on the roots of a plant called "mother maize," *txetxina*, which had a large root and a single stalk. This observation may be of relevance in dealing with the riddle of what aspect of ancestral teosinte attracted the attention of its domesticators as a food source. These traditions tell how people "discovered" maize by noting the presence of grain in dung of the *uech* wildcat. Thompson reports that when asked directly where maize originated, most informants in Maya lands point to the northern boundaries of their territory.

Maya creation myths tell of three gradual improvements of creation. First, men were made of mud, followed by wood and corn dough successively, with maize dough proving to be the ideal human flesh. This idea is further developed in the much later creation myths of the Mexica (Aztecs) of central Mexico, which tell of the present world having been created after a succession of four previous eras, or "suns."

In the accounts of the distinct eras of creation that we have from both the Maya and Mexica, the idea permeates that the creation was persistently improved with each successive era. The myths explain how various beings and features of the world came to be. So, in the First Sun, imperfect giants (they were foragers, not agriculturists, and they were too large for the dimensions of the world) were devoured, save for those who themselves became jaguars. In similar fashion, throughout each of the eras of creation the earth was populated gradually by different organisms. In the Maya account, the failed organisms of the first creation were fashioned from clay and became birds and deer. In the second era humans were fashioned from wood, but it was not until the third attempt (the Fourth Sun for the Aztecs) that the gods made maize dough and mixed it with their own blood to produce present-day humans, literally "maize people," the best possible beings. The Nahuatl word for maize dough is in fact "our flesh" (*toneuhcayotl*).

In like fashion, the food that human beings consumed improved during each iteration of creation. In the First Sun, those beings who did not sow or till ate acorns and fruits. In the Second Sun humans progressed to pine nuts. In the Third Sun it was millet. In the Fourth Sun it was *teocentli* or *cencocopi*, suggestively also known as "Madre de Maíz" (Mother of Corn) in some parts of rural Mexico. The very name *teocentli* is of interest because its literal meaning is "great grain" or "divine grain," revealing that the fruit of the immediate ancestor of maize was known and recognized by maize peoples as a grain. Finally, during the Fifth Sun the food provided by the gods was *centli*, modern cultivated maize. It was integral to the beliefs of the Mesoamericans that not only had the creation been improved at each step, but also its beings, plants, and foods, so that present-day humans, "maize people," were the best possible creature, and maize the best possible food.

Mesoamerican agricultural systems evolved over a period of approximately 4,500 years prior to arrival of the Spaniards in the early sixteenth century. While such systems were highly variable, they unequivocally were centered on the culture of maize. In general, indigenous production systems featured intensive plant polycultures in small plot settings. Species such as beans, peppers, cucurbits, tomatoes, amaranth, and an assortment of greens shared the same production field with maize. Specific agroecological management techniques were related to local climatic, topographic, and cultural features. In arid zones irriation by diversion of spring and river water, as well as the use of artificial water catchments, was common. On hill slopes terraces were employed. In forest zones agroforestry systems were practiced that simulated or fit natural successional stages. In humid zones techniques such as raised-bed agriculture, field drainage, and the *chinampa* system (artificial islands built from lake-bottom silt) were devised. All labor was provided by humans (no draft animals were available), implements consisted of fire-hardened wooden digging sticks and hoes, and few animal domesticates existed (turkeys and a species of edible dog were notable exceptions).

In general, land tenure systems were communal, with rights to parcels of land earned and maintained by working a given parcel and maintaining good social standing. When the Spaniards arrived in the central Valley of Mexico, land was measured by the *quahuitl,* a unit equivalent to 8.2 linear feet (2.5 linear meters), which was squared to express area (67.24 square feet or 6.25 square meters). Indigenous records of parcels cultivated by individual family heads have survived, and these show that land was registered officially by area as well as soil type. Analyses by Barbara Williams of pre-Hispanic codices show that a typical family unit of six individuals might cultivate 4.4 acres (1.8 hectares) of land spread across four different parcels of varying soil quality, and that this land could produce an excess of 17 percent maize grain above the annual dietary needs of the family. This excess production was the family's buffer against poor production seasons, or a potential commodity for sale or barter. It clearly signified an economy beyond subsistence. In addition to each family's communal land, most heads of household contributed a minimal number of labor hours annually to maize production on parcels that supplied the needs of theocratic lords.

The conquering Spaniards introduced new agricultural techniques and species into Mesoamerica, just as they also introduced Mesoamerican species to Europe. Among practices introduced by the Spaniards were extensive plantation agriculture, extensive livestock raising (hogs, cattle, and sheep), monoculture, plowing, broadcast seeding, and lumbering, in addition to a number of new plant species (sugarcane, wheat, and olive trees). Many Mesoamerican crops were introduced into Europe as novelties and

curiosities, but maize spread quickly wherever Spaniards traveled, in large part because of its broad adaptability and high productivity. Although Spaniards themselves tended to regard maize as an inferior grain that produced coarse foodstuffs best suited for animal consumption, many peoples contacted by the Spaniards (and Portuguese) in their expanding global trade routes quickly adopted maize as a source of human food. Thus, maize quickly penetrated Africa, India, and China during the sixteenth century. A Chinese drawing of an apical-eared maize has been dated to 1597.

The Spanish Conquest strongly impacted the social and agricultural systems of Mesoamerica. Initially, the ratio of Spaniards to indigenes in the region was small, and the Spanish population was focused on extracting mineral wealth for transport to Spain. This allowed for parallel economies to develop, where native production systems coexisted with those of the conquerors. Wheat, leavened breads, pork, mutton, and Mediterranean fruits were produced and consumed by the Spaniards, while the natives continued to produce maize and beans in traditional ways. However, the interaction of the parallel economies was detrimental to the native Mesoamericans in that they were the primary source of forced labor for the Spanish mining industry, and increasingly for the Spanish agricultural enterprises. A number of legal structures successively were put in place by Spanish authorities to sanction the appropriation of native labor and property.

Several additional trends aggravated the precarious position of the native population. First, colonial Spaniards appropriated prime agricultural land surrounding major settlements for the production of their own introduced food crops, relegating the natives to marginal areas. The forced labor demands of the Spaniards during the early colonial period, as well as a series of epidemics, severely reduced the native population, impacting both general labor availability as well as the ability of the natives to produce enough to pay tributes, tithes, and feed themselves. As the mining boom subsided in the 1580s and Spanish colonists looked for substitutes to generate capital, they increasingly turned to agriculture. The form of agriculture they adopted (plantation agriculture and grazing) required extensive tracts of land, and the colonists displaced natives and their agricultural systems into remote, mountainous hinterlands and other undesirable locations. The cumulative effect of these trends was to force the indigenous population's retrenchment to a subsistence lifestyle. Economic depression in Spain during this time fueled an immigrant wave to Mexico (New Spain), and, paired with the decimation of the native population, the ratio of Spaniards to indigenes increased dramatically. A famous estimate by Sherburne F. Cook and Woodrow Borah places the native population of Mexico at 1.4 million in 1595, compared with 25.2 million in 1518, when the Spanish arrived. Together with its cultivators, maize became a subsistence crop, identified with the poor and dispossessed (both rural and urban) and used by the Spaniards primarily to feed their livestock.

During the colonial period Spain played an important part in the evolution of mercantile economies into global capitalist economies. The wealth Spaniards generated by extracting labor, land, agricultural produce, and minerals from New Spain was cycled through an expanding trade web that embraced Asia, America, Africa, and Asia. However, the boom and bust cycles characteristic of incipient capitalism raged throughout New Spain, with a disproportionately negative effect on the poor. Between 1560 and 1578 the "official" price of maize grain increased by more than 400 percent. In an attempt to stabilize prices, colonial authorities devised a number of mechanisms, including requirement of payment of tributes in maize grain, in order to stimulate supply. Ultimately, these measures resulted in the creation of an official granary (alhóndiga) in Mexico City, intended to buffer large fluctuations in supply and demand by becoming the central depository for all grain to be sold and by selling this grain at controlled prices. By eliminating intermediaries and speculation the alhóndiga was meant to eliminate fraud and sudden swings in prices. However, in order to function the official granary needed to pay top prices during scarcity and then sell the grain below market price. A royal subsidy compensated for this operating deficit. Although the scheme worked, it was opposed by large landowners.

By 1630 Spanish grain producers had taken over commercial production of the crop. The Indian population producing maize for their own subsistence had become irrelevant to the growing national economy. Although the export of colonial commodities (minerals, furs) to the Spanish motherland was subject to unpredictable market turns and the local market for wheat was relatively fixed by the number of Spaniards in the population of New Spain, the growing mixed-race populace represented a sure market for the capitalist enterprise of maize grain production. Within one century after the Conquest, the Spanish economy successfully had appropriated the best agricultural land and produce of Mesoamerica. However, as Enrique Florescano has observed

> To control the regional market, eliminate its most dangerous competitor, and assure a permanent labor force at its disposal, the large landholding expanded territorially, absorbing the small landholding. Toward the end of the eighteenth century this process had produced at its apex a small "society" of landholders who dominated the country and the city; at its base, a mass of the disinherited, continuously persecuted by hunger and misery. As did no other economic phenomenon, the distortions caused by the large landholding summarized the contradictions that tore at colonial society.

Florescano argues that such centrifugal forces contributed to the dissolution of the Spanish colony in New Spain. During the intervening century between Independence in 1821 and the Revolution of 1910, the dynamics of concentration of wealth in the class of large landholders at the expense of the forced labor of the underclass scarcely seemed to be altered by the fact that Spain was no longer colonial master. Although large-scale landholding eventually was outlawed and the rights of Indian peasants to communal landholding were recognized officially, it was not until the post-Revolutionary land reform programs that serious efforts to were enacted to empower the peasantry. However, even the accelerated land expropriations of Lázaro Cárdenas in the 1930s, intended to redistribute land to the largely indigenous population of dispossessed, had but a fleeting effect.

With few exceptions the best agricultural land in Mexico is devoted to crops other than maize, which is viewed by an increasingly urban population as food of the poor. The top income category of Mexicans obtains less than 13 percent of its dietary protein from the traditional maize-and-bean diet, whereas 84 percent of the protein consumed by those at the lowest income level comes from this source. Steven E. Sanderson has calculated that although 59 percent of total cultivated area in Mexico is devoted to maize, this is more reflective of the number of subsistence farms than it is of actual maize productivity. The importance of the crop is inversely proportional to farm size. While 85 percent of peasant cultivators grow maize, they typically do so in plots of 7.4 acres (3 hectares) or less, under limiting rain-fed conditions. Such farmers typically have limited access to the technical or economic assistance readily available to large-scale agricultural entrepreneurs.

Furthermore, the feasibility of providing effective technical assistance to such farmers is diminished by their limiting ecological and climatic situations. The small plots, marginal lands, and highly variable environments in which peasant farmers produce do not lend themselves to the economies of scale that make intensive hybrid maize production feasible.

Sanderson estimates that Mexican maize cultivation has grown neither in extension nor productivity since the 1950s. Although yields increased from 0.7 tons per hectare in 1950 to 2 tons per hectare by the mid-1990s, these gains represent increased productivity of large-scale farms located in federal irrigation districts, having access to credit, hybrid seed, and synthetic fertilizers. While Mexico was self-sufficient in maize for a brief period prior to 1960, since that time per capita production has fallen to 231 pounds (105 kilograms) annually. Maize imports have risen steadily from none in 1960 to 5 million tons annually.

Through successive policies such as the Sistema Alimentario Mexicano (SAM, or Mexican Food System) and PROCAMPO, the Mexican government attempted simultaneously to support the peasantry and urban wage earners by setting minimum prices to farmers and subsidizing the price of tortillas to consumers. The government's most recent policy has been to abandon such tactics in favor of free market economics. Reversing the long-term official recognition of communal land ownership for the peasantry, the government amended the constitution to allow for private ownership of communal land. The effect of this move will be once again to allow large-scale landholding, which the government and external providers of credit believe will favor the economies of scale necessary to make intensive, industrial agricultural systems profitable. If the policy produces the results envisioned by its drafters, free market dynamics will create economic opportunities for peasants who will be displaced from their land. By comparative advantage, national maize production will decline and a greater proportion of the national maize needs will be met by importing from major producing nations such as the United States (yellow maize for animal feed) and South Africa (white maize for human consumption).

Cultural and Economic Importance

A fundamental value transmitted and preserved through thousands of years among all maize-based groups with links to the pre-Columbian past is a deep reverence for maize as the source of life. Among the descendants of Mesoamerican natives, this belief is expressed even today in words very similar to those collected by Friar Bernardino de Sahagún from a Mexica informant of the sixteenth century:

> If they saw dry grains of maize scattered on the ground, they quickly gathered them up, saying "Our Sustenance suffereth, it lieth weeping. If we should not gather it up, it would accuse us before our Lord. It would say 'O, Our Lord, this vassal picked me not up when I lay scattered upon the ground. Punish him!' Or perhaps we should starve."

This reverence, embodied in the cult of maize deities in the pre-Hispanic past and of agricultural patron saints in the present, reflects the central role of maize in Mesoamerican material subsistence and culture. Most Mexican meals are founded upon maize in one form or another and would be incomplete or inconceivable without the traditional flat bread known as the tortilla. Current annual per capita consumption of tortillas in Mexico is about 410 pounds (186 kilograms), or 1.1 pounds (0.5 kilogram) per day, and in rural areas it is estimated that tortillas provide approximately 70 percent of all caloric intake.

Although maize can supply the minimum daily caloric requirement for humans, alone this grain is a poor source of the essential amino acids lysine and tryptophan. A diet in which maize predominates can lead to serious deficiency diseases such as pellagra and kwashiorkor. The traditional Mexican diet based on maize as a staple avoids such health consequences by two means: first, complementarity with *Phaseolus* bean, also an essential component of the traditional diet (together these two products provide an amino acid profile similar to that of milk), and second, preprocessing of maize grain in an alkali bath, resulting in greater availability of niacin that otherwise is bound and unavailable. It is thought that this alkali treatment originally was devised to separate the fruit case (pericarp) of maize kernels from the endosperm to produce hominy, a step preceding grinding, with the original alkali being wood ashes or slaked lime.

Although tortilla manufacture has been mechanized, the process remains essentially the same as originally prescribed by early Mesoamericans. Mexican Spanish abounds with native words intimately related to the processing of maize for production of tortillas (e.g., *tequisquite, nejayote, nixtamal, metate, testal, comal, tenate*), not to mention the names of the various food products that can be produced from basic corn dough (e.g., *tamal, pozole, tlacoyo*). A 1996 report in the Wall Street Journal indicated that the world market for tortillas is worth about

US$5 billion. According to this report, even though Mexicans consume about 10 times as many tortillas per capita as U.S. consumers, the Mexican tortilla market is still dominated by small *tortillerias*. In Mexico, packaged tortillas account for only 5 percent of sales. However, large flour-producing industries, such as Maseca and Bimbo, are predicting that the end of tortilla subsidies in Mexico will transform the Mexican market, giving an advantage to U.S.-style marketing of plastic-bagged tortillas in supermarkets.

The North American Free Trade Agreement (NAFTA) will have a marked effect on Mexican maize production; traditional government subsidies designed to support cheap tortillas will be reduced gradually until they are eliminated completely in or before the year 2009. It is expected that the quantity of maize produced within Mexico will decrease, with Mexican agriculture specializing more in the production of tropical species and vegetable crops with export value. This will threaten the viability of maize land races that until now have been preserved by Mexican peasants. It has been estimated that at the time of Spanish contact, between 200 and 300 land races of maize were cultivated in Mexico, compared with 42 land races currently. In addition, reduction of internal maize production will affect the diet of rural and urban Mexican residents alike because maize products based on white floury maizes will be replaced by those produced with imported yellow dent grain, or expensive imported white flour maizes, and may be priced beyond the reach of the poor. The phased transition to market-based pricing of maize grain built into NAFTA was allowed specifically to prevent the large-scale social destabilization that almost certainly would result from a sudden rise in the price of this important staple, and to allow for the purported accumulation of wealth that is to result from free market policies and that will allow Mexicans to afford costlier foods.

Policy makers should remember, however, that important social upheavals have resulted from the lack of physical and economic access to maize throughout Mesoamerican and Mexican history. In the year 1450 a series of five consecutive years of crop failures struck the Valley of Mexico, caused by disease, frost, and drought. According to Mexica chronicles, epidemics broke out when people began consuming inedible plants. Children were sold into slavery in exchange for maize. Royal reserves helped feed the population of 200,000, but lasted only for the first year of the disaster. Some students of Mexica history speculate that this event spurred the expansion of the empire under the emperor Moteuczoma Ilhuicamina, whose conquests might have been motivated by a search for more land to ensure a stable food supply. The *petlacalco,* or royal reserve, was thence stocked with a 20-year supply of maize. By the time of the Spanish Conquest, the amount of grain extracted from tributaries each year by Tenochtitlan was enough to feed 50,000 people, a potent effect of maize crop failure, inflicted upon many people across a broad geographic range.

Enrique Florescano documented a series of social and economic crises in colonial Mexico that he showed were directly tied to the rise of maize prices, and which he argues were an important contributor to the political instability that, among other effects, resulted in the revolutionary war against Spain in 1810. Whether the current perturbations of trends in maize production and prices will have similar effects on contemporary Mexican society, or whether the free-market strategies of the present Mexican administrations will successfully allay such catastrophic consequences, remains to be seen. Also in the balance is the possibility that current economic and agricultural policies that reduce traditional maize production in Mexico may decimate the genetic treasury that is the Mexican maize germplasm pool, an important and recurrent contributor to the key hybrid germplasm of the U.S. maize belt. Whatever the final outcome, it is clear that rarely in the history of human societies have the fates of a plant and a people been so intimately intertwined.

See also Cuisine; Rural Economy and Society

Select Bibliography

Doebley, J. F., "Morphology, Molecules and Maize." In *Corn and Culture in the Prehistoric New World*, edited by S. Johannessen and C. A. Hastorf. Boulder, Colorado: Westview, 1994.

Dowswell, C. R., R. L. Paliwal, and R. P. Cantrell, *Maize in the Third World*. Boulder, Colorado: Westview, 1996.

Rooney, L. W., and S. O. Serna-Saldívar, "Food Uses of Whole Corn and Dry-Milled Fractions." In *Corn: Chemistry and Technology*, edited by S. A. Watson and R. E. Ramstad. St. Paul, Minnesota: American Association of Cereal Chemists, 1987.

Sanderson, S. E., *The Transformation of Mexican Agriculture: International Structure and the Politics of Rural Change*. Princeton, New Jersey: Princeton University Press, 1986.

Smith, B. D., *The Emergence of Agriculture*. New York: Freeman, 1995.

Wellhausen, E. J., L. M. Roberts, and E. Hernández X., *Races of Maize in Mexico: Their Origin, Characteristics and Distribution*. Cambridge, Massachusetts: Bussey Institution, Harvard University, 1952.

—RICARDO J. SALVADOR

La Malinche and *Malinchismo*

The documented details of the life of doña Marina are starker than the mythology that has been constructed around her since the sixteenth century. The woman given the baptismal name of Marina and who came to be known as Malintzin (in Nahuatl) and la Malinche (in Spanish) was given to Fernando (Hernán) Cortés in a group of 20 women by Chontal Maya on the Tabasco coast in the spring of 1519. She served as interpreter for Cortés in the Conquest of Mexico. Thereafter, in 1522, she gave birth to a son by Cortés. In 1524 she accompanied him as interpreter on an expedition to what is present-day Honduras. During this period she was married to Juan Jaramillo, and Cortés endowed their union with a labor grant (*encomienda*). At the conclusion of the expedition, she and Jaramillo had a daughter, and Marina died soon thereafter, in 1527.

Subsequent to her death, Jaramillo immediately married a Spanish noblewoman. The child Martín, son of Cortés, was taken to Spain, where his father successfully petitioned for his legitimation. Don Martín was invested as a knight of Saint James and became a soldier of the Spanish king. He returned to Mexico in middle age and was implicated with his half brothers, other sons of Cortés, in a plot to overthrow Spanish rule there. Having escaped back to Spain, he reputedly died in service to his king against the Moors in the War of Granada. Doña María, daughter of Jaramillo, remained with her father and stepmother in Mexico and throughout her adult life engaged in litigation with her stepmother over the dowry that Cortés had bestowed on doña Marina.

The depositions in this case reveal that doña Marina survived less than a decade after falling into Spanish hands. Contrary to legend, she did not travel to Spain to be presented at court. She did not occupy a palace in Mexico City or a house in Cuernavaca. Her two mestizo children, one by Cortés and one by Jaramillo, were not the first mestizo children born on the mainland. She neither raised them nor suffered having them taken from her, and she was no longer living when Cortés married the Spanish doña Juana de Zúñiga, who bore him four children. Nor was don Martín the only mestizo offspring of Cortés; according to his secretary Francisco López de Gómara, Cortés also sired three mestiza daughters, each by a different Indian woman.

Cortés mentions doña Marina just twice in his reports to Spain and only once by name. Her presence and services are acknowledged, however, in the biography written decades after the Conquest by López de Gómara, who—not having been present himself—apparently relied principally on Cortés for information. In a yet later account of the Conquest, Bernal Díaz del Castillo, who had been present, gave her a heroic central role. Other references to doña Marina's part in the Conquest are to be found in requests for pensions (*probanzas*) submitted to the king of Spain by her daughter and grandson and by aging conquerors and their children. These documents maximize doña Marina's services and the petitioners' proximity to her by descent or attachment.

Indigenous artists of the sixteenth century created a pictorial record of her career. She appears in nine illustrations in Book 12 of the *Florentine Codex*, a bilingual Nahuatl-Spanish encyclopedia of indigenous Mexico compiled under the direction of Bernardino de Sahagún. Short of time, the artists were unable to complete their work and left blank spaces toward the end. Otherwise they might have drawn her yet again, because the concluding chapter recounts her interrogation of the surviving defeated Mexica (Aztec) leaders on behalf of Cortés.

The city council of Tlaxcala commissioned a pictorial record, known as the *Lienzo de Tlaxcala*, of their alliance with Cortés against Moteuczoma and his allies. In its 87 scenes doña Marina appears repeatedly. The fragmentary earliest version consists of just four scenes, in all of which she interprets for Cortés in Tlaxcala. Other early indigenous drawings of doña Marina and Cortés are to be found in the *Codex Azcatitlan*, the *Relación de Michoacán*, the *Tepetlan Codex*, the *Coyoacán Codex*, and the *Libro de los gobernadores de Cuauhtinchan*.

Indigenous artists invariably represented doña Marina dressed in *huipilli* and *cueitl* (decorated blouse and skirt), the Nahua woman's proper clothing. Although she appears with loose hair in the Tlaxcalan drawings, she is represented with the distinctive horned hairstyle of Mexica matrons in the *Florentine Codex*. In neither visual representation nor text is moral disapproval expressed. On the contrary, doña Marina's name is unfailingly accorded the honorific suffix *-tzin*, Malin*tzin* being the Nahuatl equivalent of *doña* Marina.

There is no evidence that prior to her Christian baptism she bore a calendrical name including the day sign *Malinalli* (a type of grass), as often is assumed. The form *Malin-tzin* follows naturally from the assimilation of Spanish *Marina* to Nahuatl pronunciation, in which *l* typically replaces *r*. The word *tenepal*, sometimes asserted to have been her lineage name, appears to be a Nahuatl translation of her Spanish designation as *lengua* (interpreter): *tentli* (lip); *tene* (lip-possessor, one who speaks vigorously); *-pal* (by means of); *tenepal* (by means of having lips, of being a vigorous speaker). Hence the elements of the Nahuatl *Malintzin tenepal* correspond to those of Spanish *doña Marina la lengua*.

Spanish speakers, perceiving Nahuatl *tz* as *ch* and entirely missing the Nahuatl whispered final *n*, borrowed *Malintzin* back as *Malinche*, a term they understood the indigenes to use in addressing Cortés and doña Marina alike. Bernal Díaz del Castillo explains this usage with reference to Cortés as an abbreviation of "Marina's Captain" because of their inseparability during the Conquest. However, an instance of the term being used for yet another member of Cortés's company, Juan Pérez de Arteaga, suggests that Nahuatl speakers may have perceived them all to be agents of some heretofore unknown entity with the unfamiliar name *Malintzin*, which was speaking through them.

Doña Marina's utility to Cortés was her multilingualism. When given to him, she spoke both Nahuatl, the language of the Mexica and many other peoples of central Mexico, and Maya, the language of the peoples of the Yucatán Peninsula. Moreover, she knew the conventions of a register of Nahuatl called *tecpillatolli* (lordly speech), a difficult and indirect rhetorical style used among the Nahuatl-speaking elite. Without these special skills, she would have been unable to negotiate successfully for Cortés or counsel him about the intentions of the people with whom he was dealing.

Her command of *tecpillatolli* supports the assertions of López de Gómara and Díaz del Castillo that doña Marina's parents had been Nahuatl-speaking rulers of a city in the area of the present-day state of Tabasco—geographically far from Tenochtitlan, the Mexica's center in the Mexican central highlands, but sharing a common language with the Mexica. A child of Nahua nobility would have received rigorous education in polite speech and proper deportment, but because of the closely guarded life of daughters of noble families, a girl would not have had occasion to become bilingual. This atypical capability of doña Marina had come about through her passing, while still very young, into the hands of Maya in the area east of her original home. Sources differ about whether she was stolen or was given away by her parents. In any case, by the time the Chontal Maya presented her to Cortés, she apparently had acquired the competence of a childhood Nahuatl-Maya bilingual.

Cortés had rescued a Spaniard, Jerónimo de Aguilar, from the northeast coast of Yucatán, where, after surviving a shipwreck, he had been immersed in Maya language and culture for several years. Aguilar served as Maya interpreter for Cortés but knew none of the languages the Spaniards encountered after they left the Yucatán Peninsula. On the Veracruz coast doña Marina revealed her bilingualism and the fact that communities throughout Mesoamerica either were Nahuatl speaking or employed Nahuatl-language interpreters *(nahuatlatos)*. Because of this, she was able to interpret wherever they went, translating into Maya for Aguilar, who translated to Spanish for Cortés and then translated Cortés's Spanish to Maya for doña Marina. In the course of the Conquest years, doña Marina herself acquired Spanish and on the Honduras expedition functioned without Aguilar, interpreting between Spanish and both Nahuatl and Maya, each in numerous regional varieties. Her services were valued highly by both sides according to López de Gómara, Díaz del Castillo, and the authors of various reports to the Spanish Crown.

Prior to learning of her bilingualism, Cortés had given doña Marina to one of his lieutenants, Alonso Hernández de Puertocarrero. When Cortés soon took her back as his interpreter, he gave Puertocarrero another Indian woman in her place and shortly afterward sent him to Spain with a shipment of treasure for the Spanish king. That three years passed and the work of the Conquest was completed before doña Marina gave birth to a child suggests that Cortés not only guarded her from sexual contact with others but also refrained himself, because she was too valuable as an interpreter to be hampered in mobility or around-the-clock availability by pregnancy.

In post-Independence, nineteenth-century Mexico, 300 years after her portrayal in both Spanish and indigenous sources as a powerful woman commanding respect, doña Marina began to be portrayed quite differently. These new depictions focused on her sexuality and condemned her role in the Conquest; the portrayals gave rise to the concept of *malinchismo*, which may be defined broadly as the pursuit of the novel and foreign coupled with rejection and betrayal of one's own.

The modern focus on doña Marina's "willful betrayal" centers on the events leading to the Spanish massacre of the people of Cholula prior to the Spanish occupation of Tenochtitlan. According to both López de Gómara and Díaz del Castillo, doña Marina was offered an opportunity to leave the Spaniards for the protection of the Cholulans, even to the point of entering into marriage with a Cholulan nobleman, but she chose instead to inform Cortés of the Cholulans' plans to ambush the Spaniards. Her role in interrogating Cuauhtemoc, the last ruler of the Mexica, during his imprisonment and interpreting his confession prior to execution during the expedition to Honduras is considered confirmation of her treachery. Whatever her personal history and circumstances with respect to the Spaniards, these acts have been considered ones of free and reprehensible choice.

A novel entitled *Xicoténcatl*, published anonymously in 1826, portrays her as sexually voracious. She beguiles both the Spaniard Diego de Ordaz and the Tlaxcaltecan Xicotencatl while pregnant with the child of Cortés and receives condemnation from all sides for her wantonness and the betrayal of her people. Two decades later a Yucatecan essayist, V. Calero, wrote of her as a wily enchantress who brought about the conception of the child Martín by overwhelming a helpless Cortés with her feminine charms. Twenty-five years later a novel, *Los mártires del Anáhuac*, by another Yucatecan, Eligio Ancona, added a further potent detail to the myth, that her role in the downfall of indigenous Mexico was foretold at her birth. This serves to explain her childhood abandonment and also the overwhelming desire for Cortés that leads to her complicity with the Spaniards against the indigenes. Two novels by Ireneo Paz, *Amor y suplicio* (1873) and *Doña Marina* (1883), assert doña Marina's (and other indigenous women's) preference for European men as lovers and fathers of their children, hence the creation of the mestizo Mexican nation.

Through this nineteenth-century literature, a complex set of depictions of doña Marina arose, offering insights into the development of Mexican nationalist ideologies: la Malinche as Eve, the woman to blame for the despoilation of the American paradise; the child stained by birth prophecy; the indigenous woman burning with desire for the white man; the ambitious schemer using men for her own egotistical ends; the whore; the scapegoat for centuries of colonization. The most influential literary contribution of the twentieth century to the theme of *malinchismo* has been the treatment of doña Marina as *"la chingada"* (the violated one) by Octavio Paz, grandson of Ireneo, in *El laberinto de la soli-dad*, first published in 1950. She has come to be universally identified as lover *(amante)* and mistress *(concubina, amada)* of Cortés.

La Malinche's redemption has been seen in her role as the mother of the first mestizos, although this too is problematical, insofar as Mexicans alienated from their past suffer as *los hijos de la chingada*, products of a mother who has yielded to violation. At some point in the development of the myth, la Malinche also became the American Medea, a woman grieving inconsolably for her lost children—young Martín supposedly was wrenched away from her and taken to Spain by Cortés—and all those who lost their lives to Spanish Conquest and colonialism. In this guise she has been identified with la Llorona, a dangerous female ghost whose laments are heard in the night. La Llorona appears already in the sixteenth-century *Florentine Codex* as an omen of the coming Conquest. The indigenous writers and illustrators of the *Florentine Codex*, however, did not merge the historical doña Marina with the supernatural weeping woman, both of whom they portrayed in Book 12. That identification, pervasive today, is a modern construct.

Postcolonial sexualization and romantic trivialization of doña Marina is reflected in visual as well as literary productions. One of the most striking twentieth-century representations of her is José Clemente Orozco's 1926 painting in which Cortés and Malinche, both naked, rest their feet on a corpse. Her breasts, belly, and thighs are emphasized, while her eyes appear dull beneath a low forehead. Cortés holds one of her hands in his while making a negating gesture across her body with his other arm. An avalanche of paintings, drawings, chapbook and comic book illustrations, and calendar art featuring la Malinche has followed, much of it baring a provocative female body.

Although *malinchismo* portrays indigenous Mexicans as victims of Spanish aggression facilitated by Malinche's lasciviousness and treachery, indigenous conceptualization remains ambivalent. Whereas generally the association of la Malinche with snakes (as the Mexican Eve or as a dangerous serpent herself) is negative, historically snakes have had a positive function in an indigenous belief system that has not been entirely lost. In addition to snakes, Malinche often is associated with lizards and frogs, symbols of water. The volcano that occupies part of the state of Tlaxcala has come to be known as Malinche, and indigenous communities on its slopes perceive Malinche as the source of rain for their crops. Association of cultural figures with mountains is pervasive in indigenous Mesoamerica, and in addition to the Malinche volcano, the snow-covered mountain Iztaccihuatl (the white woman) also is said to be Malintzin, who in her eternal slumber protects humble folk and their domestic animals. In *zazanilli* (Nahuatl folk tales) Malintzin also is said to be an avenger who, having once aided the conquerors, now smites enemies of the common people. In indigenous dance dramas portraying the Conquest, resistance is spirited, but in the end Cortés and Malintzin bring the True Faith to the unenlightened, and in this endeavor, she is a force for good.

In its broadest sense of selling out to foreigners, *malinchismo* tars all with the same brush, but at base the concept is profoundly misogynistic. In a revictimization of the girl child who was treated as disposable property in the sixteenth century, the elements of *malinchismo* have become set in the twentieth. La Malinche is perceived as cursed at birth, driven by ungovernable sexual appetites, unprincipled in pursuit of her own ends regardless of the incalculable price that others must pay for her actions, culpable for bloody deeds carried out by Cortés and his forces. Recently, however, women writers and artists, especially but not exclusively Mexicans and Mexican Americans, have begun a revaluation of doña Marina, seeking in her a positive model. The moral outrage of a violated, abandoned, vengeful Medea/Lilith/Llorona remain, but the themes of strength, intelligence, and will to survive are coming forward.

Select Bibliography

Cypess, Sandra Messinger, *La Malinche in Mexican Literature: From History to Myth*. Austin: University of Texas Press, 1991.

Díaz del Castillo, Bernal, *Historia verdadera de la conquista de la Nueva España*. 2 vols., Mexico City: Porrúa, 1955; as *The Discovery and Conquest of Mexico*, New York: Farrar Straus, 1956.

Fuentes, Patricia de, editor and translator, *The Conquistadors: First Person Accounts of the Conquest of Mexico*. New York: Orion, and London: Cassell, 1963.

Luz, Jimenez, *Porforio Díaz a Zapata: Memoria nahuatl de Milpa Alta*. Mexico City: UNAM, Instituto de Investigaciones Historicas, 1968; as *Life and Death in Milpa Alta: A Nahuatl Chronicle of Díaz and Zapata*, translated and edited by Fernando Horcasitas, Norman: University of Oklahoma Press, 1972.

Karttunen, Frances, *Between Worlds: Interpreters, Guides, and Survivors*. New Brunswick, New Jersey: Rutgers University Press, 1994.

——, "Rethinking Malinche." In *Indian Women: Gender Differentiation and Identity in Early Mexico*, edited by Susan Schroeder, Stephanie Wood, and Robert Haskett. Norman: University of Oklahoma Press, 1996.

Lockhart, James, *We People Here: Nahuatl Accounts of the Conquest of Mexico*. Berkeley and London: University of California Press, 1993.

Pagden, Anthony, editor and translator, *Hernán Cortés: Letters from Mexico*. New Haven, Connecticut, and London: Yale University Press, 1986.

Paz, Octavio, *El laberinto de la Soledad*. Mexico City: Cuadernos Americanos, 1950; 2nd edition, Mexico City: Fondo de Cultura Económica, 1959; as *The Labyrinth of Solitude: Life and Thought in Mexico*, New York and London: Grove, 1961.

Simpson, Lesley Byrd, editor and translator, *Cortés: The Life of the Conqueror by His Secretary Francisco López de Gómara*. Berkeley and London: University of California Press, 1964.

—Frances Karttunen

Maquiladoras

In Mexico, export-led industrialization fueled by foreign investment and technology is beginning to displace other available development strategies, such as import substitution industrialization (the substitution of imported manufactured goods with domestically produced goods), varying degrees of autarky (national economic self-sufficiency), and the traditional reliance on primary product export. This economic trend has led to the creation of increasingly large numbers of *maquiladoras,* or assembly plants owned by foreign companies, located mainly along the Mexico-U.S. border.

To better understand the rise of the *maquiladora,* (or *maquila*) industry, one must examine the recent trend toward industrialization throughout the world. Since the 1960s the rapid and dynamic growth of the so-called Newly Industrializing Countries (NICs), such as the "four dragons" of East Asia (Hong Kong, Singapore, South Korea, and Taiwan), has convinced economic policy makers, academics, journalists, and even some voters that the road to prosperity lies in the export of manufactured goods to the markets of the United States and Europe. Thus, many former colonies that had been rather hostile to transnational corporations (TNCs) began to open their doors, cautiously at first, and to enlist the help of these TNCs to assemble and manufacture clothing, shoes, toys, household goods, auto parts, electronic components, and eventually complete cars and final consumer electronic products. This industrialization was made possible on a large scale by the increasing mobility of capital and by new technologies that unbundled the production process so that component parts for almost any product could be made, assembled, packaged, and sold virtually anywhere. In this way a genuinely global economy began to emerge, and what formerly had been considered to be the nonindustrial parts of the world began to be incorporated into a global system of assembly, production, and marketing.

Mexico has for at least a century been a prime location for foreign investment, mainly but by no means exclusively from the United States. Until the 1970s, most of this foreign investment was in the traditional TNC sectors such as automobiles, petroleum, and pharmaceuticals, which combined import substitution with exporting. But from the 1970s, and increasingly in the 1980s, the balance began to swing to the more specifically export-processing assembly industries—such as electronics, machinery, auto parts, apparel, furniture, sporting goods, and toys—operating under *maquila* rules.

The origin of the term *maquila* derives from colonial times, when the *maquila* was the portion of flour that the miller kept after grinding the corn. The modern *maquila* industry began in the mid-1960s, when the Mexican government introduced the Border Industrialization Program, which permitted Mexican and foreign-owned factories to operate along the U.S. border duty-free, on condition that they exported all their products. These *maquilas*, often termed "in-bond" or "twin" plants (Mexican *maquilas* supposedly "twinned" with supplier plants in the United States), were owned mainly by U.S.-based corporations and thus were able to take advantage of U.S. tariff regulations covering the re-import of assembled unfinished goods using U.S.-manufactured components. After a relatively slow start, the industry grew rapidly, and by the mid-1990s there were more than 2,000 *maquilas*, employing in excess of half a million workers.

In the typical *maquila*, corporations provide the cut cloth, electronic components, or the like; the *maquila* industry receives monetary compensation for assembly work (U.S. dollars are changed into pesos for wages and other production costs); and the assembled goods are returned to the United States, sometimes for sale to *maquila* workers who regularly spend part of their wages there. The *maquila* rules encourage foreign firms to build factories along the border. For U.S. companies, this simplified the logistics of supplying U.S. equipment, materials, and components. The Mexican government had expected (or hoped) that the *maquilas* would buy local materials and components when available, and that the *maquilas* therefore would stimulate Mexican industry. In general, this has not happened. *Maquilas* spend, on average, only about 2 percent of their purchasing budgets on Mexican inputs. The earnings of the employees and the value-added of the industry are largely dependent on the U.S. dollar–Mexican peso exchange rate, and times when the peso has weakened dramatically against the dollar (1975–76, 1982, 1986–88, 1994–95) have been times of rapid expansion of the *maquila* industry.

The nature of *maquila* work always has been politically controversial. U.S. opponents of the *maquilas* assert that U.S. employers increasingly will prefer low-paid Mexican workers to higher-paid U.S. workers; supporters argue that these low-paid jobs would be lost whatever happens, and that the *maquila* industry, through its massive use of components and materials made in the United States, actually protects the high-wage, high-skill jobs of U.S. workers. There is some truth in both these positions, although the documented fact that the real wages of U.S. workers have been declining for some time is of relevance.

Mexican *maquila* promoters always have held out the promise of upgrading *maquila* jobs in Mexico. Some commentators argue that a new type of high-tech *maquila*—for example in the automobile, electronic components, and computer industries—is beginning to characterize the industry, and there always have been some *maquilas* that have done more than simple assembly. Mexican opponents of *maquilas* take exception to the types of jobs created by the *maquilas* and the conditions of the workers, particularly in the overcrowded and infrastructure-poor Mexican border cities.

Although *maquila* industry was initially promoted as a border industrialization program, since the 1970s successive Mexican governments have tried to encourage investors to establish *maquilas* in the interior to relieve infrastructural and labor pressures along the border. From the mid-1980s to the mid-1990s, the proportion of plants and employees located in off-border sites rose from approximately 15 percent to almost 30 percent. The main differences between border and nonborder *maquilas* are the lower wages and generally poorer infrastructure in the interior, and the somewhat greater propensity of some interior *maquilas* to purchase local inputs. Some of these in-terior *maquilas* are, in fact, under-utilized Mexican factories subcontracting under the *maquila* rules.

The label "*maquila* industry" is something of a misnomer, for there are many industries represented in the *maquilas* of Mexico. INEGI, the official Mexican statistical institute, distinguishes 12 industrial sectors in its *maquila* database. In recent years two sectors, electronic components and auto parts, have accounted for approximately half of the total value-added and workforce of the *maquila* industry, and a smaller proportion of the plants. Electrical and electronic equipment and furniture *maquilas* also have shown substantial growth in the 1990s.

While most *maquilas* are wholly owned subsidiaries of foreign corporations or closely related subcontracting associates of them, a significant proportion of *maquilas* are run through shelter companies based on the U.S. side of the border. These "facilitators" provide a variety of services for companies wishing to use the *maquila* system, including handling legal matters, finding premises, hiring and training labor, and organizing customs clearance and transportation. On the Mexican side there are several large *maquila* industrial park operators, the most important being the Bermúdez organization based in Chihuahua, who also provide services for the *maquila* industry.

The *maquila* industry is a Mexican version of the export-oriented industry found all over the world.

Like its counterparts elsewhere, the *maquila* industry thrives through the use of components that are assembled in a highly routinized, standardized, and simplified fashion by low-paid workers doing the same things hundreds or thousands of times every day. The industry traditionally has employed mainly female workers, although the proportion of males has been rising in recent years. By the mid-1990s about 4 out of every 10 shop floor workers were men. Eighty percent of all employees in the *maquilas* work on the shop floor; the failure of the proportion of technical employees and salaried staff to rise very much—indeed this proportion may have fallen slightly in the 1990s—suggests that the much-heralded technological upgrading of the *maquila* industry may not be happening. Nevertheless, there certainly are some *maquilas* owned by or subcontracted to major global corporations that operate state-of-the-art production systems. The point at issue is not their existence but their significance for the *maquila* industry as a whole and, more importantly, their wider significance for the Mexican economy and culture.

The creation of the North American Free Trade Agreement (NAFTA) among the United States, Canada, and Mexico in 1993 formally established the conditions for the progressive elimination of tariffs by the beginning of the twenty-first century. Although these tariffs provide the rationale for the *maquila* industry, it is entirely possible that the *maquilas,* under this or another name, will survive for a considerable period of time for the same reason that they have prospered since they were introduced in the mid-1960s, namely cheap labor for mainly U.S. corporations producing labor-intensive goods and, increasingly, services.

NAFTA has heightened the controversy surrounding the *maquila* industry's impact on jobs, both in the United States and in Mexico. NAFTA has also intensified the debate over *maquila's* environmental impact. While Mexico has had substantial environmental legislation in place since the early 1980s, serious doubts have been expressed about the capacity and the will of national and local authorities to enforce this legislation where it interferes with business.

There have been many attempts to evaluate the contribution of the *maquila* industry to Mexican development, but the difficulty of this task is compounded by the fact that, as in *maquila*-like industries all over the world, some people and communities win and some lose. The most common criteria used to evaluate the developmental impact of the *maquila* industry are jobs created, linkages with local industries, value-added, foreign currency earnings, upgrading of the workforce, technology transfer, conditions of work, and environmental consequences.

The total job count of the *maquila* industry passed the 500,000 mark in mid-1992 and is estimated to have reached 600,000 in 1996. Some commentators predict 900,000 *maquila* jobs by the end of the twentieth century. All these jobs are badly needed, and it is unlikely that they would have been created in the absence of the *maquila* industry, especially along the border.

Linkages between the *maquilas* and local firms in Mexico are marginal, and the value of Mexican components, materials, and other inputs has been stagnant at about 2 percent of the total for many years, despite increasing efforts of Mexican federal and local governments and *maquila* associations to promote local linkages. There has been considerable *maquila*-related industrial and services growth in the U.S. border states, however, particularly in California and southern Texas. One consequence of this is that foreign currency earnings by Mexico have been disappointing. Furthermore, because the peso has lost value against the U.S. dollar, the Mexican share of the profits has not increased in accordance with the growth of the industry.

The upgrading of the workforce—the transmission of administrative skills to managerial staff and technical skills to production staff and workers—is, perhaps, the single greatest contribution of the *maquila* industry. However, it is difficult to assess the extent to which these improvements are a direct result of the *maquila* industry, rather than a result of the general industrialization of Mexico in recent decades.

Genuine technology transfer has happened only in a few isolated cases. There are some well-publicized cases of high-tech *maquilas* and of Mexicans who have acquired skills in the *maquilas* and created their own businesses, sometimes becoming suppliers to their former assembly plants, but in general the industry still earns its reputation for cheap labor and unskilled assembly work.

Work conditions in the *maquilas* are neither significantly better nor worse, sector for sector, than in domestic industry, with cases of disgraceful *maquila* sweatshops countered by model *maquila* workplaces. Unionization of *maquila* workers is uneven. The highest levels are found in the eastern state of Tamaulipas, declining as we move westward along the border to Baja California. Along the border and in some of the more remote interior locations, the entry of large numbers of *maquilas* into previously nonindustrial sites has led to the creation of a new industrial culture supported by local governments, official unions, *maquila* operators, and their organizations.

The environmental impact of *maquilas* is highly controversial. In the campaign against NAFTA, images of extreme environmental degradation and hazard were disseminated around the world. There are legions of press stories and a growing volume of academic research documenting the bad environmental practices of sections of the *maquila* industry, and despite strenuous efforts by some responsible elements in the industry to put this right, the *maquilas* are left with a poor image on this issue in the mid-1990s. It is, however, often difficult to disentangle the culpability of individual *maquilas* from the infrastructural deficiencies of Mexican communities.

The *maquila* industry was created in the mid-1960s to compensate for the end of the Bracero Program (which gave Mexican farmworkers and other laborers employment in the United States), reportedly on the model of Asian export-processing zones that were growing at that time. It has developed into an industry employing mostly young women in unskilled and low-paid work, and at some periods it has been the only growth sector in the Mexican economy. In the 1990s it can be seen as one of the mechanisms through which Mexican workers, factories, and services are integrated into the global economy, a reality that has important political and cultural consequences both locally and globally. Although it is uncertain whether the specific *maquila* model will survive into the next century, similar ways of integrating Mexico into the global economy, polity, and culture can be expected.

Select Bibliography

Sklair, Leslie, *Maquiladora: Annotated Bibliography and Research Guide on the Mexican "In-Bond" Industry*. La Jolla: Center for U.S.-Mexican Studies, University of California, San Diego, 1988.
_____, *Assembling for Development: The Maquila Industry in Mexico and the United States*. 2nd edition, La Jolla: Center for U.S.-Mexican Studies, University of California, San Diego, 1993.
Tiano, Susan, *Patriarchy on the Line*. Philadelphia: Temple University Press, 1995.
Wilson, Patricia, *Exports and Local Development: Mexico's New Maquiladoras*. Austin: University of Texas Press, 1992.

—LESLIE SKLAIR

Marina, Doña

See Malinche and Malinchismo

Massacre of Tlatelolco

The student movement of 1968 burst onto the streets of Mexico City like a social explosion, but the conditions that precipitated it go back much further than the brief time that the protests endured. What began harmlessly enough as a dispute between rival high school students in July of that year swelled into a series of massive street demonstrations to pressure the government of president Gustavo Díaz Ordaz for basic political reforms. It was the first time since the bloody aftermath of the 1910 Revolution that Mexicans challenged the very substance of their government. The tumultuous events culminated in tragedy on October 2, when army troops killed an estimated 300 people who had gathered for a peaceful demonstration at Tlatelolco, the Plaza of the Three Cultures, in the heart of Mexico City.

What happened that summer, in the weeks before Mexico was scheduled to become the first developing nation to host the Olympic games, amounted to a short-lived public trial of the one-party system that had ruled the nation since the wake of Mexican Revolution. Tens of thousands of people in those weeks took to the streets of Mexico City in a seemingly spontaneous social movement, calling for democratization and posing the most serious challenge ever to the authoritarian regime. "They were not the spokesmen of this or that class," Octavio Paz later would write about the students of 1968, "but of the collective conscience." The events of 1968 were a watershed in modern Mexican history that would have an enduring effect on Mexico's political future.

Mexico at the time, and for many more years, would be a paradigm of stability in troubled Latin America, an anomaly in a hemisphere ensnarled in social and political turbulence. The political party that would become the Partido Revolucionario Institucional (PRI, or Institutional Revolutionary Party) was formed in 1929 as a way to end the fratricidal violence that had continued after the Revolution. But the arrangement at first did not resolve the political discord among factions, and stability would not come for nearly a decade. The political system that was consolidated under President Lázaro Cárdenas's tutelage laid the political foundation for three decades of sustained growth that, buoyed by World War II and the beginning of Mexico's industrial revolution, lasted through the 1960s. It was an era of remarkable, sustained growth, rivaled only by the three decades of the Porfirio Díaz dictatorship that preceded the Revolution. To be sure, the political arrangement came at a high price and was not without its detractors. But since 1940, the party provided the forum for a unique convergence of political, economic, and social interests that allowed the ruling elites to barter the terms of political and economic engagement. Mexico's post–World War II industrial boom gave birth to a middle class that grew and prospered.

By the mid-1960s, however, social mobility was curtailed drastically as potential markets for employment became saturated. "The ingredients for widespread unrest had long existed, yet the fatalism of the masses, disarray among the opposition and an efficient security apparatus had helped to preserve stability. But the system proved ill prepared to deal with such a seemingly spontaneous movement," wrote Alan Riding in 1984. The strategy of the one-party government formed in 1929 went hand in hand with a form of state capitalism that allowed Mexico decades of sustained growth. The political system and economy alike were closed, but there were jobs. Mexico also had stability unrivaled in Latin America owing to the PRI's remarkable ability to meld political alliances, co-opt opponents, and when necessary, use repression to preserve power. But by the late 1960s economic expectations diminished as the model faltered. The society, which had shifted from a rural to a more urban-based population, also had become more sophisticated. And in a climate of eroded expectations, an authoritarian system was simply less tolerable. Also, growth had not come for all Mexicans. The poorest Mexicans had seen their share of the country's wealth deteriorate. Mexico to date still has one of the most skewed income distributions in the hemisphere, despite the fact that it had a social revolution. The discontent of the summer of 1968 clashed with the image the Mexican government had put forth to host the Olympics.

"At the very moment in which the Mexican government was receiving international recognition for 40 years of progress, a swash of blood dispelled the official optimism and caused every citizen to doubt the meaning of that progress," Octavio Paz later wrote. On July 22, 1968, a dispute between rival groups of high school students turned into a confrontation with police. A few days later, on July 26, a march by students to protest the earlier police repression and another march by leftist sympathizers to commemorate the fifteenth anniversary of the assault on the Moncada Cuartel that marked the beginning of the Cuban Revolution both became the target of police attacks. That same day authorities occupied the offices of the central committee of the Mexican Communist Party and the workshop where they published *La Voz de Mexico*, the official party organ. The next day students occupied several schools in Mexico City and called for a general strike beginning July 29.

Within days a movement opposing the authoritarian government and calling for democratic change swelled to unprecedented dimensions. The seething social discontent surfaced, and support spread rapidly from students to housewives and bureaucrats. The staggering amount of money the government was spending to host the Olympics exacerbated public discontent. Unlike their French counterparts who had taken to the streets that same year, the Mexicans did not call for revolutionary change. Nor was their agenda as radical as that of the Americans whose protests illuminated the national conflict over the Vietnam War. The Mexican students made a profoundly democratic plea for basic reform. But in the view of the ruling elite, it would have paved the way for the end of the one-party system.

On July 28 the first meeting of the Coordinating Strike Committee was held, and students drafted a list of demands to present to authorities. On July 29 police thwarted an attempt by student to gather in the Zócalo in the heart of Mexico City. At about 1:00 A.M. the following morning the army took over several campuses, firing a bazooka through the door of one. On August 1 the rector of the Universidad Nacional Autónoma de México (UNAM, or the National Autonomous University of Mexico) led a march on behalf of the student victims and in protest of the violation of university autonomy. One of the notable events of those frantic weeks was a "silent demonstration" that drew an estimated 400,000 people, an unprecedented event. Mexico's nascent civil society had outpaced the system with a vision of more open nation. In August a coalition of student leaders petitioned the government with a series of demands, including the elimination of the Granaderos riot police unit that had carried out much of the repression, indemnification for injuries in police confrontations, and freedom for those imprisoned. In one futile response to the social revolt, Díaz Ordaz summoned public employees to a rally in support of the system. In the traditional manner, the workers were *accareado* (hauled) to the Zócalo, the heart of Mexico City and symbolic seat of national power. The event turned into a riot when the employees opted to denounce the government they had been summoned to support. Government officials tried to blame the unrest on "outside forces," but to date there has been no persuasive evidence to support that claim.

Meanwhile, the pressure of the impending Olympic games and international focus on Mexico were a source of enormous preoccupation for the government. An effort to bring students and government representatives together to negotiate a resolution came too late. On the evening of October 2, more than 10,000 people gathered in Tlatelolco for what was to be yet another protest against the regime. Tlatelolco was the spot where, on August 13, 1521, Fernando (Hernán) Cortés defeated the Mexica (Aztec) leader Cuauhtemoc, marking the Conquest of Mexico. "It was neither a triumph not a defeat: it was the painful birth of the mestizo nation that is Mexico today," reads the inscription on a plaque at the site. The crowd had gathered in the plaza while student leaders stood on the third-floor balcony of the Chihuahua apartment building. A helicopter hovered over the Colonial Santiago Church, and shortly after 6:00 P.M. two green Bengal flares dropped, pierced the twilight, and briefly illuminated the crowd. Hundreds of troops emerged from behind austere pre-Hispanic ruins and opened fire with automatic weapons on the crowd. A squad of plainclothes soldiers, members of the Olympic Battalion, each with a white glove or handkerchief on his left hand and a revolver in his right, converged on the third-floor balcony of the Chihuahua apartment building where student leaders had addressed the crowd. They ordered the students to the floor, witnesses say, and began shooting from the balcony into a crowd of hundreds rushing to the defense of the leaders.

Tanks ringed the plaza, and thousands of people were trapped amid a barrage of gunfire that continued sporadically throughout the night. The Italian journalist Oriana Fallaci, who was wounded in the Tlatelolco Massacre, described the horrific assault as she stood on the third-floor balcony of the Chihuahua building: "A shell hit the apartment above us. A second struck the floor below, heavy machine gun fire smashed windows, and the helicopters now started firing their machine guns." She described feeling as if she were "watching the scene from the Russian film *Potemkin,* when the crowd flees down the steps and gradually, as the people rush down, they are hit and their bodies roll down the steps headfirst, and lie there with their heads dangling and legs up." By the next morning an estimated 300 people, among them children, were dead and more an 1,000 were arrested, some of whom were tortured. The government officially reported 32 dead. "The plaza was covered with bodies," said Raúl Álvarez Garín, a student leader who witnessed the massacre. Physicians later would report that some victims had been run through with bayonets. Álvarez was among those arrested. He and scores of others protest organizers later would be convicted on a series of trumped-up charges and sentenced to prison terms ranging from 3 to 17 years. With one huge blow the movement was crushed. In his remarkable reflections on 1968, Octavio Paz wrote, "The Massacre of Tlatelolco shows us that the past we thought was buried is still alive and has burst out among us."

Ten days after the massacre the Olympic torch was lit in Aztec Stadium. Outside the stadium troops and tanks were poised beyond the view of television cameras. There were no international protests, no delegations withdrew, and some, notably the Soviets, praised the Mexican government for its handling of the crisis. The Tlatelolco Massacre—the worst bloodshed in the country since the Mexican Revolution—was a fleeting news item in the international press, one more social scar of that turbulent year. To this day, the 1968 Olympics are more likely remembered internationally for African American athletes' protests. The Mexican regime never addressed the underlying causes of the social discontent of 1968, and the repression triggered a crisis of legitimacy that only worsened over the years. To date the government has thwarted any serious investigation into what happened in 1968. On the twenty-fifth anniversary of the massacre, a group of distinguished Mexican intellectuals and representatives of several human rights groups formed what they called the Truth Commission. Their goal was to pool their collective moral weight to pressure the government to open official files on the events of 1968. The group was denied access to government records and ultimately disbanded, demoralized.

Only two years later, however, on a balmy evening in Jalapa, Veracruz, a few hundred people assembled in the plaza outside the city's lofty cathedral to mark the twenty-seventh anniversary of the massacre. What was remarkable about this gathering and others like it throughout the country were the participants themselves. The majority had not even been born when the Mexican army opened fire on the crowd in Tlatelolco Plaza. But the threads between Jalapa and Tlatelolco were still palpable. "Then Díaz Ordaz," one sign read, "and now [President Ernesto] Zedillo." The youth in Jalapa and elsewhere were to have been the prime beneficiaries of a decade of arduous economic change that was capped by the North American Free Trade Agreement (NAFTA) in 1994. By the end of that year, however, Mexico had plunged into economic crisis. What was clear in Jalapa and in subsequent October 2 commemorations was that Mexico's economic troubles could not be separated from the thorny issue of political legitimacy. The specter of Tlatelolco would not lie still.

Select Bibliography

Fallaci, Oriana, *Nothing, and So Be It.* Garden City, New York: Doubleday, 1972; as *Nothing and Amen,* London: Joseph, 1972.

Newell, Roberto G., and Luis Rubio F., *Mexico's Dilemma: The Political Origins of Economic Crisis.* Boulder, Colorado: Westview, 1984.

Paz, Octavio, *The Other Mexico: Critique of the Pyramid.* New York: Grove, 1972.

Riding, Alan, *Distant Neighbors.* New York: Knopf, 1984.

—SUZANNE BILELLO

Maximilian (Ferdinand Maximilian von Hapsburg) 1832–67

Emperor

Son of Archduke Franz Karl, Ferdinand Maximilian von Hapsburg was born at Schönbrunn Castle in Austria on July 6, 1832. He was the younger brother of Franz Josef, who would reign over the Austro-Hungarian Empire from 1848 until 1916. At age 18 Ferdinand Maximilian enlisted in the basically ornamental Austrian navy. He traveled throughout the Mediterranean and Asia Minor, and in 1860 visited the Brazilian empire. He later recorded his impressions in a two-volume book of poetry and prose, *Memories of My Life* (Paris, 1869). After three years in the navy he had attained the rank of admiral and commanded a 14-battleship squadron. Worried about Austria's apparent decline following the Crimean War, in May 1865, Franz Josef sent Maximilian on a friendship mission to Paris. Maximilian found Napoléon III's empire impressive for its administrative efficiency, but he was struck by the court's lack of dignity: the French Empire, he wrote, is that of the parvenu (newly risen upstart).

In July 1857, Maximilian married Charlotte (Carlota), daughter of King Leopold I of Belgium. The same year Franz Josef named him governor general of Lombardy-Venice. Maximilian and his wife sought to appease the Italian push for independence, suggesting to his brother that he institute much-needed fiscal, military, and administrative reforms, and that Lombardy be governed by an autonomous bicameral legislature. Perhaps jealous of his brother's popularity and prizing imperial unity above all, Franz Josef was unwilling to give the Italians any concessions, and he placed the provinces under the military rule of Count Gyulai. Following defeat in the Austro-French Piedmontese War in 1859, Franz Josef surrendered Lombardy to Sardinia. Scapegoated for the Austrian defeat, Maximilian and Carlota retired to Trieste, where the archduke's main occupation was designing the building and grounds of his residence, Miramar.

Meanwhile in Mexico, in the summer of 1863 a largely Conservative *asamblea de notables* met and resolved that the nation should become a monarchy, and that the throne should be offered to Archduke Maximilian. Although the assembly met under the protection of the French army, which had occupied the capital, it was no puppet government. As early as 1840 the Conservative José María de Estrada had argued that a monarchical system governed by a European prince was the only possible hedge against internal chaos and the rapacity of Mexico's northern neighbor. The defeat of the Conservatives in the War of Reform in 1861 and the Liberal's project of abolishing all vestiges of colonial corporate privilege, however, gave new urgency to the monarchist cause, and prominent Conservatives lobbied the governments of Great Britain, Spain, and France to intervene militarily in Mexico. They found a particularly sympathetic ear in the French court. Napoléon III believed that it was France's mission to save the Latin race in the New World by creating a barrier to U.S. expansionism, which also would create a new market for European goods. In the spring of 1863 French troops moved from the port of Veracruz—which they had been occupying jointly with the British and Spanish armies—into the interior of Mexico. On May 31, 1863, the Liberal government of Benito Juárez fled Mexico City for five years of exile and guerrilla resistance in northern Mexico.

Maximilian and Carlota seemed to be particularly propitious choices for the Mexican throne. Austria was not a maritime power and had not participated in the occupation of Veracruz, so his ascension to the throne would not seem like an attempt at colonization. As a descendant of Spanish King Carlos I (Emperor Charles V), he could make certain symbolic claims on the Mexican throne. Moreover, the young, ambitious couple, who seemed to be doomed to spend the rest of their lives watching the Adriatic, would be ready and willing to participate in a new, exciting project. In October 1863, a Mexican delegation went to Miramar to inform Maximilian of the assembly's decision and formally offer him the Mexican crown. Maximilian said he would accept only if the majority of the nation would confirm the assembly's decision and if France could assure its military and economic support. He promised to establish constitutional rule, supported by institutions that would be both "free and stable."

By early 1864 the archduke's conditions seemed to have been met. The towns and cities under French occupation—arguably representing the majority of the Mexican population—apparently had rallied to the empire. The Treaty of Miramar stated that 25,000

French troops would stay in Mexico until they could be replaced by a reliable Mexican imperial army; the French foreign legion would stay an additional eight years. The financial terms imposed by the French, however, were quite harsh. All expenses of the occupation were to be paid by Maximilian's government, and it would also have to recognize Mexico's national debt, including money owed to private French citizens. Nonetheless, Maximilian defended the territorial integrity of Mexico, refusing to grant France mineral rights in the northeastern state of Sonora. There was still unresolved business for Maximilian in Europe—he was involved in a bitter dispute with Franz Josef for the Austrian throne—and many European rulers warned against his adventure in Mexico. Maximilian accepted the Mexican crown, however, and sailed for Mexico on April 14, 1864.

Maximilian took the reins of the Mexican government from the three-man regency of Juan Nepomuceno Almonte, Mariano Salas, and Archbishop Pelagio Antonio de Labastida in June 1864. His was to be a strong, centralized government—the former states disappeared. The country was divided into departments, governed by political prefects named by the emperor. There were to be no representative bodies at a national level; only municipal councils were to be elected. In 1865 he published an eight-volume collection of laws that were to organize all aspects of Mexican public life—there even was a section on rules and regulations for a practically nonexistent Mexican navy. Rule of law would ensure order, liberty, and equality. His motto was *"Equidad en la Justicia"* (Equity in Justice).

Both Maximilian and Carlota tried hard to be as Mexican as possible: they ate Mexican food, spoke only Spanish—even to the members of the foreign diplomatic corps—and the emperor wore the traditional *charro* outfit—to the horror of some Conservatives, who did not understand why he would want to dress up as a bandit. Maximilian's government was also meant to be one of national reconciliation: the emperor wanted to surround himself with all the capable men interested in consolidating the nation-state and put behind the political hatreds that had driven the country to its bloodiest civil war. His cabinet and state council were made up of both Liberals (José Fernando Ramírez, Pedro Escudero y Echanove, José María Cortés Esparza, Manuel Silicco, Santiago Vidaurri, Jesús López Portillo, José López Uraga) and Conservatives (Teodosio Lares, Hilario Elguero, Joaquín Velázquez de León, Francisco Ramírez). Although the emperor initially favored the Liberals (from 1864 to the summer of 1866) and then turned to his original supporters, the Conservatives (in 1866), he managed to ensure the collaboration of members from both groups throughout his reign.

Maximilian's nation-building project, if complex, was not reactionary: like Napoléon III, Maximilian believed he was emperor by the will of the people. Even though the empire drew from the monarchical traditions of Europe and New Spain, Maximilian was, in some ways, a modern ruler: he published the letters to his ministers so that his plans for government would be publicized, and he traveled throughout the country, trying to turn the national government into a visible entity for the people. He meant for legislation to guarantee "modern" individual rights, such as liberty, property, and freedom of movement and religion. He wanted to pull Mexico out of the cycle of violence and anarchy into which it had fallen since Independence, so it could benefit from "the century's progress." To many Conservatives' dismay, after fruitless discussions with the papal envoy, on June 26, 1865, he ratified the reform disentailment laws against the pope's will. His Indian policy—applied at a national level, which was an innovation for the nineteenth century—ultimately aimed at the same result as the one the Liberals had hoped to accomplish in 1857: the integration of the Indian to the modern, national society and markets, through individual ownership of land. Nevertheless, through laws to protect the hacienda laborers and to ensure that municipal lands were divided among members of the community, the empire, in a way, tried to ease their way into modernity.

Putting aside Maximilian's projects, what was the empire's real impact? It is difficult to say. Despite the imperial couple's apparent popularity, the regime never solidified during its four years of existence. Many Conservatives, objecting to his ideas and angered by their exclusion from government, quickly withdrew their support. Local authorities often went on with business as usual, ignoring all imperial legislation they disagreed with. The treasury, despite the bonds issued in London and Paris, was constantly bankrupt. The emperor, more often than not, was at odds with Marshal Bazaine, commander of the French troops. More importantly, the country never was pacified. Juárez, despite dissension within his camp, stood steadfastly in his refuge of Paso del Norte. The French army controlled most of the country, but disorder and guerrilla warfare were endemic. Even the harsh October 2, 1865 law, which ordered that all men belonging to armed bands—even under a "political pretext"—were to be put to death, was ineffective in putting an end to the unrest. The empire was unable to establish an effective administrative and gubernatorial machine.

By early 1866, under pressure from his legislative assembly, which condemned the expensive, unpopular "Mexican adventure," and from the U.S. government, recently victorious over the rebel Southern Confederacy and able to return its attention to the events in Mexico (where it always had favored the republicans and looked upon the French-supported monarchical regime at its border with utmost distaste), Napoléon III had decided to limit his support to the Mexican Empire. The Prussian triumph over Austria at Sadowa (July 3, 1866) sounded the death knell for the French Intervention in Mexico: the emperor of the French needed his army in Europe. Carlota went to Paris to ask that the Treaty of Miramar be respected. Her pleas were to no avail. In February 1867, the last French troops left Mexico. After visiting the pope in Rome, the empress lost her mind. She never again would see her husband nor return to Mexico. She died in 1927.

Maximilian, abandoned by the French, unable to consolidate his rule over the country and menaced by the advancing republican army, thought of abdicating. Discouraged from this by his mother and wife, who considered it would be dishonorable for him to abandon his post, he submitted his abdication to the vote of his council, in the city of Orizaba, on November 25, 1866. The council rejected the emperor's abdication. On February 13, 1867, Maximilian left Mexico City at the head of the imperial army and set up headquarters in Querétaro. The city fell under siege by republican forces commanded by General Mariano Escobedo on March 6, 1867. On March 15, Maximilian surrendered and was taken prisoner along with Generals Miguel Miramón and Tomás Mejía. The three men were judged by a military tribunal according to the law of January 25, 1862, "for crimes against the independence and security of the nation." Despite his defense by Liberal lawyers Mariano Riva Palacio and Rafael Martínez de la Torre, the intervention of the Prussian government, the pleas of Mrs. Miramón, and personal letters from Victor Hugo and Giuseppe Garibaldi to Benito Juárez, Maximilian was condemned to death. On June 19, 1867, Maximilian, Miramón, and Mejía were executed. His remains lie in the Capucìn crypt in Vienna.

— ERIKA PANI

Mesoamerica

This entry includes 14 articles that discuss ancient Mesoamerica, the cultural and linguistic region occupying the temperate zone south of the Tropic of Cancer and parts of Central America. The first article is a general definition of what scholars mean by the term Mesoamerica, followed by seven articles discussing individual cultural groups and city-states, and finally six articles discussing traits these cultures shared in common.

Mesoamerica: Introduction
Mesoamerica: Maya
Mesoamerica: Mexica
Mesoamerica: Monte Albán
Mesoamerica: Olmec
Mesoamerica: Teotihuacan
Mesoamerica: Toltec
Mesoamerica: Veracruz, Classic and Postclassic
Mesoamerica: Agriculture and Ecology
Mesoamerica: Calendrics
Mesoamerica: Population
Mesoamerica: Religion
Mesoamerica: Warfare
Mesoamerica: Writing

Three other entries include articles that focus on ancient Mesoamerica: Music; Visual Arts; Women's Status and Occupation. See also Conquest; Mexican Spanish

Mesoamerica: Introduction

When scholars use the term *Mesoamerica,* they are referring to a vast and geographically varied territory unified by a set of cultural traits not shared by peoples living immediately beyond its boundaries. There is some disagreement over the exact limits of this territory, which also changed over time. But the northern boundary can be viewed as a U-shaped line ranging from the Sinaloa River to the northwest to the Soto la Marina River on the Gulf of Mexico, with a dip in the middle reaching south to exclude the desert areas of central Mexico. At the south, the border extends from the Ulúa River in Honduras to the Gulf of Fonseca in El Salvador. Thus a large portion of modern-day Mexico, all of Guatemala, Belize, and El Salvador, and part of Honduras comprise ancient Mesoamerica.

The idea of Mesoamerica as a cultural area was developed by the scholar Paul Kirchoff, among others. They observed that the inhabitants of this area, although ethnically and linguistically diverse, could on one level be viewed as a single, homogeneous culture. All Mesoamerican peoples, for example, subsisted on a triad of crops—beans, squash, and especially maize—that they cultivated using regionally distinct farming techniques. Neither the wheel nor metal tools were ever developed for practical use in Mesoamerica, and draft animals were absent. Most people lived in highly stratified societies ruled by elites from urban centers featuring monumental architecture, most notably stepped pyramids. Extensive trade networks and a market system tied diverse regions together over a wide area.

At least four different Mesoamerican civilizations developed hieroglyphic writing, with information recorded in deerskin or bark books as well as in other media. A complex calendrical system meshed the solar year and a 260-day sacred cycle and is still in use in some areas. The Mesoamericans also were accomplished astronomers. Religion, centering on a complex pantheon of deities, was intimately tied to statecraft. Human sacrifice as well as individual penitential bloodletting were thought to be essential to maintaining harmony in the universe. Ritual games, most notably the rubber ball game, were played over a widespread area, even beyond the traditional boundaries of Mesoamerica.

These traits developed over 3,000 years, from the beginnings of settled agricultural life around 1500 B.C. until the Spanish overthrew the Mexica (Aztec) Empire in A.D. 1521. As noted, some of these traits persist today, particularly in rural areas where indigenous agricultural practices, dress, ritual behavior, and religious beliefs remain largely untouched by the outside world.

Select Bibliography

Kirchoff, Paul, "Mesoamerica." *Acta Americana* 1 (1943).

—VIRGINIA E. MILLER

Mesoamerica: Maya

Maya culture is defined by the boundaries within which Maya was spoken in pre-Hispanic times (i.e., much of southern Mexico, Belize, Guatemala, and parts of Honduras and El Salvador). Unlike the Olmec, however, Maya culture is still viable, with 6 million speakers of nearly 30 extant Maya languages inhabiting large portions of the above region.

The Maya region traditionally has been divided into three ecological zones: the southern lowlands, the northern lowlands, and the highland/Pacific slope region. The southern lowlands, the home of many of the great Maya cities, is a blanket of monsoon forest interspersed with savanna grasslands. The occasional river cuts through this vast area, while swampy depressions called *bajos* fill with water during the rainy season. Although the Maya were

farmers, the forest also provided them with a great diversity of plant and animal life, including rubber and avocado trees, deer, tapirs, turkeys, and the elusive jaguar, whose pelt was coveted by Mesoamerican elites. The northern area, essentially a continuation of the south, comprises the Yucatán Peninsula, a great limestone shelf bordered by the Gulf of Mexico on the west and the Caribbean on the east. Moving north, however, rainfall decreases, vegetation becomes shorter and denser, and surface water sources disappear, replaced in pre-Hispanic times by *cenotes,* or natural sinkholes, as well as *chultuns,* small man-made cisterns. Although it has thinner soil and fewer resources than the southern lowlands, the Yucatán Peninsula was an important source of salt production. The entire lowland area had abundant supplies of limestone, from which the Maya constructed their cities and carved their sculptures.

The highlands, a largely volcanic mountain chain stretching from Chiapas through southern Guatemala, have peaks ranging from 3,300 to 13,100 feet (1,000 to 4,000 meters) and are interspersed with fertile valleys, some containing large lakes. The narrow tropical coastal plain ends at the Pacific in broad estuaries, lagoons, and mangrove swamps. Although heavily populated both now and in the past, the highland/Pacific slope region is largely peripheral to developments in Maya culture after the Late Formative period. Nevertheless, the highlands continued to provide materials unavailable in the lowlands, such as obsidian and basalt, while the coast was a rich salt- and cacao-producing area.

In all these areas, the basic subsistence pattern was, and continues to be, slash-and-burn agriculture, a system dependent on burning vegetation, planting maize, and leaving plots fallow until they regain their fertility. In pre-Conquest times, however, shifting agriculture was supplemented in certain areas by intensive methods of cultivation such as raised fields in seasonally flooded land, the use of irrigation canals, and hillside terracing. These more sophisticated agricultural techniques may well be related to the great spurt in population growth that occurred during the Classic period (A.D. 200–900), peaking at perhaps 8 to 14 million people toward the end of this era.

History

While the beginning of Maya civilization is difficult to determine, archaeological discoveries continue to push it back further in time, to at least the Middle Formative, making the dawn of Maya culture contemporaneous with the end of the Olmec. Olmec-style artifacts have even been discovered at Copan,

Honduras, during this period, a find perhaps explained by the presence of jade sources nearby, which the Olmec may have exploited. The first monumental architecture appears as early as 750 B.C. at Nakbe, in the northern Petén region of Guatemala, where an early carved stela also has been found. During the Late Formative, at Nakbe and other Petén sites (Mirador, Tikal, Uaxactun), as well as Cerros and Lamanai in Belize, great stucco deity masks flank the staircases of increasingly larger masonry pyramid-platforms. In Mexico during this period, there are fewer impressive remains, but they include a canal system at Edzna, Campeche, and in Yucatán, a large platform at Yaxuna near Chichen Itza and a human figure carved at the entrance to Loltun Cave.

Around the same time, in highland Chiapas and Guatemala and on the Pacific coast, parallel developments include the carving of great boulders, stelae, and altars, recalling both Olmec precedents and prefiguring lowland Classic Maya sculpture. But the diverse styles of these sculptures are unique to the area, and it is not known whether their makers were Maya-speakers or of some other ethnic or language group.

In any case, by the Late Formative period, those traits that we have come to identify as quintessentially Maya begin to appear in the lowlands: hieroglyphic writing, calendars, vaulted stone architecture, roof combs, and a naturalistic art style expressed in vase and wall painting as well as relief sculpture. The beginning of the Classic period (A.D. 200–900) in the Maya area originally was defined by the earliest written dates. With the discovery of older texts, as well as earlier manifestations of Classic culture such as monumental architecture and elaborate tombs, the initial date of the Classic period eventually may prove to be earlier.

The Classic period is further subdivided into early and late periods, the former ranging from A.D. 200 to 600. Profound changes occurred in the Maya area in the sixth century. First of all, the influence of Teotihuacan, prevalent throughout the Maya region in the preceding two centuries, waned when that great central highland Mexican city collapsed. Secondly, the Maya themselves seem to have been embroiled in internecine warfare: most notably, Caracol, Belize, records its victory over Tikal in 562. Although lowland cities do not seem to have been abandoned, many in the central Petén stopped erecting dated stelae, and in some cases existing public monuments were defaced or destroyed. How all these events relate to one another is still unknown, but after this hiatus, most Maya cities regrouped and entered their era of greatest florescence.

Although the end of the Classic period still is thought to occur around A.D. 900, when most of the southern Maya lowland sites were abandoned, archaeologists have added another period to the traditional chronology, the Terminal Classic. Not a sharply defined period, it encompasses most of the ninth century and the first half of the tenth, when the southern Maya sites were in the throes of collapse. The northern cities, such as Uxmal and Chichen Itza, were in the meantime enjoying their apogee. The causes of the collapse are still unclear, but overpopulation, drought, and the deterioration of the environment appear to have been important factors, leading to increased warfare and perhaps open revolt. Great defensive works were built in the Pasión River area of Guatemala, but to no avail, as eventually almost every lowland city was abandoned.

A complicating factor is the arrival in the Pasión River area of a Mexicanized Maya group, possibly Putún Maya from the Gulf of Campeche, in the mid-ninth century. These merchant-warriors left their mark at Seibal, Guatemala, in particular, in the form of stelae portraits with foreign features accompanied by non-Maya glyphs. They may also have been relatives of the Itza, who around the same time apparently settled at Chichen Itza. This northern site's history is still very unclear but probably bridges the Terminal Classic–Early Postclassic period (c. 800–1200). Chichen Itza displays strong similarities with the Toltec capital of Tula, north of Mexico City, which collapsed in the mid–twelfth century. However, the archaeological, epigraphical, and early colonial records of this period are confusing, and scholars continue to debate the nature of the relationship between the two cities.

The Postclassic, then, begins sometime in the late tenth century and continues until the Spanish Conquest of the Maya area, beginning in the 1520s. After Chichen Itza's fall, Mayapan enjoyed a 200-year reign as capital of Yucatán, only to collapse in the mid–fifteenth century. After this, small independent Maya states flourished both in Yucatán and in highland Guatemala, while the southern lowland cities were largely vacant. The best-known site of this Late Postclassic period (1200–1528) is Tulum on the Caribbean coast of Mexico, probably the first Maya city viewed by the Spanish, who sailed near it in 1518.

In 1528 the Conquest of Yucatán under Francisco de Montejo began, with the founding of the Spanish capital Mérida occurring in 1542. The Itza, who had fled Chichen Itza for Lake Peten-Itza in Guatemala, founding a new capital called Tayasal, were not subdued until 1697.

Social Organization

The archaeological and epigraphical record clearly indicates that no later than the beginning of the Early Classic, Maya cities were governed by hereditary kings. Women occasionally ruled or acted as regents, but Maya society was essentially male-dominated and patrilineal. An aristocratic court surrounded the ruler and included secondary leaders known as *sahal* (or *cahal*), who sometimes served as governors of subordinate sites. Below the nobility were artisans and entertainers, then skilled laborers, and finally the vast stratum of peasant farmers whose endeavors supported upper-class urban life. At all levels of society, but most importantly at the top, ancestors were highly revered and often invoked to lend legitimacy to royal claims.

Unlike Teotihuacan, the Maya were not a unified state with a single dominant capital. Instead, it appears that several city-states jockeyed for power over the centuries, forging relationships through intermarriage and political alliances, as well as engaging in incessant warfare with one another. Neither the nature nor the goals of Maya warfare are well understood, and the propagandistic content of both images and texts often may obscure or distort the outcome as well. Nevertheless, it is clear that the Maya took prisoners for sacrifice, and that the higher ranking the captive, the greater the honor for his captor.

At Chichen Itza, the pattern of rulership seems to have changed from the Late Classic model. Instead of naming single rulers in lineal descent, the site's few inscriptions seem to refer to several important contemporaneous individuals, suggesting some form of joint rule. This system, known as *multepal,* or "govern together" in Maya, was in operation in some parts of Yucatán at the time of the Conquest.

Maya Thought

Although not the originators of writing, the Maya developed the most complex of the various writing systems that flourished in pre-Contact Mesoamerica beginning in the Late Formative period. Largely undeciphered until the 1970s, Maya texts finally have begun to yield the names of cities and rulers as well as recounting significant events in the lives of the elite such as accessions, conquests, and deaths. Long before it became evident that the content of much of Maya writing was historical, however, the calendrical portions of Maya texts had been read. What sets the Maya calendar apart from those of other Mesoamerican groups is that they tied it to a fixed starting point, which in the European system corresponds to August 13, 3114 B.C. As a result, Maya dates (known as the Long Count) can be tied into our own calendar. The Maya used a positional notation system not unlike our own, except that it was vigesimal (based on 20) instead of decimal (based on 10). They also invented the concept of zero, a necessary adjunct to the recording of the Long Count.

The Maya were also accomplished astronomers, observing and recording the movements of the moon, Venus, and possibly of Mars, Mercury, and Jupiter, as well as predicting eclipses. Some buildings may have served as observatories, and windows and doors often were aligned to celestial movements.

Cities

The most impressive remains of Classic Maya civilization are the great cities of the southern lowlands, which include Tikal in Guatemala, Caracol in Belize, Copan in Honduras, Palenque in Mexico, and many others. Although the plan and monumental architecture of each can be strikingly different, certain features appear at almost every major site. These typically include a north-south orientation, a paved ceremonial plaza surrounded by pyramids with small temples on top, palace structures on lower platforms, and at least one ball court. Raised causeways known as *sacbes* (Maya for "white road") may join outlying parts of the site to the center, or even occasionally different cities.

The interiors of masonry Maya buildings invariably were roofed with overlapped stones forming a vault finished with a flat capstone. Although long believed to be a Classic Maya invention, recent discoveries in Guerrero indicate that these corbel vaults may have originated in western Mexico during the Middle Formative period. Maya temples and palaces sometimes were topped by roof combs, huge decorative masonry, and plaster vertical projections that served no functional purpose except to act as giant billboards proclaiming the power of the site and its ruler.

The massive Maya temple-pyramids—some close to 230 feet (70 meters) high—usually served as monuments to the rulers buried within or beneath the pyramidal base. The function of the so-called palace structures is unclear, but they are generally believed to have been the homes of the elite or administrative centers. All of these masonry buildings were often embellished on the exterior with brightly painted stucco reliefs, while the interiors might display murals or carved stone wall panels.

Although the northern Maya area was occupied as early as the Middle Preclassic, it was during the Terminal Classic and Early Postclassic periods that the greatest cities were at their height. Many of these cities are located in the Puuc Hills, a low range in the fertile southwestern part of the Yucatán Peninsula. Northern sites share many characteristics with contemporaneous southern sites, but there are important differences. For example, instead of walls made of masonry blocks, the northern architects built rubble core walls and covered them with slabs of veneer. These walls supported double-chambered, corbel-vaulted rooms with the roof weight concentrated on the central wall, allowing for more open exterior walls. Round columns sometimes were used to support outer door lintels. The upper (and sometimes the lower) facades of buildings were ornamented with stone mosaic decorations, often in geometric designs. Doorways are occasionally in the form of great open monster mouths, a feature particularly characteristic of the Chenes region of northern Campeche. Although not completely absent, texts tend to be laconic with few dates, most of these written in an abbreviated system known as the Short Count. Carved stelae are relatively rare as well. Scholars long have struggled to reconcile the Maya calendar, ceramic sequences, radiocarbon dates, and ethnohistorical accounts in the northern lowlands.

Chichen Itza shares many features with Puuc sites, but in addition displays new traits that also can be seen at Tula. Among these are large colonnaded interior spaces, *chacmools* (reclining stone human figures often placed at the entrances to important structures), reliefs depicting processions of warriors, particularly on daises, and increased ball game and sacrificial iconography. The image of Quetzalcoatl, the feathered serpent known as Kukulcan in Maya, also is prominent here: both central Mexican and Maya legends refer to the overthrow of a Toltec ruler named Quetzalcoatl who, according to one version of the legend, subsequently traveled to Yucatán.

Arts

Most southern Maya sites are dotted with carved stone stelae and accompanying altars, which probably served as daises or thrones. Stelae were erected every *katun* (20 years) or more often to commemorate the deeds of rulers. Most are naturalistic, but idealized, portraits of the ruler in elaborate attire, often holding accoutrements of office such as scepters and large ceremonial bars and sometimes using a crouched prisoner as a footstool. Occasionally he is accompanied by a subordinate or family member, but narrative scenes involving several participants are rare on stelae. More often, such scenes are confined to interior surfaces such as broad stone panels set into the walls, as at Palenque, or the carved lintels of Yaxchilan, Mexico, which served the same commemorative purpose as stelae. The accompanying

texts (or occasionally, a text alone) usually describe events in the ruler's life or recount his genealogy, which is sometimes stated as having begun in mythological times.

Like the Olmec, the Maya valued jade, carving it into beads, pendants, and plaques or forming mosaic masks and vessels over wooden armatures. They also worked flint, obsidian, shell, bone, and wood, although the humid tropical climate has preserved few wooden objects. The elaborate tropical bird feather headdresses and intricately woven cotton textiles that are depicted in more permanent media also have rarely survived.

The Maya modeled in plaster, creating architectural reliefs—often nearly in three dimensions—to flank pyramid staircases or to ornament doorjambs and roofs. Palenque in particular is noted for such stucco reliefs, as the local limestone is too fragile for freestanding stelae. Clay, too, was modeled and molded into lively figurines, the most engaging of which were found on the island necropolis of Jaina, off the coast of Campeche.

Consummate painters, the Maya treated tall cylinder vessels as curved pages, painting scenes of court life and the underworld in a bewildering variety of styles. Long believed to be undecipherable, the texts surrounding the rims of such pots are now known to record such mundane information as the vessel's form and contents and the name of its owner. Of great interest is the presence on a handful of such pots of the painter's name, a departure from the anonymity of all other pre-Columbian art.

Of the few surviving Maya murals, the best-preserved and spectacular are those of Bonampak, Mexico, discovered in 1946 and currently undergoing cleaning and computer-aided reconstruction. Painted at the end of the eighth century, they illustrate the events surrounding the accession of a young heir apparent to the throne, including a vivid battle scene, the most comprehensive documentation of Maya warfare extant.

Although traces of fragmentary bark paper codices or books occasionally have turned up in Maya tombs, the only surviving painted manuscripts all appear to date from the Postclassic period and probably come from Yucatán. None of the four are overtly historical in content, but tend to contain astronomical and ritual information.

Religion

To the Maya, the world's surface was a crocodile floating in a pool of water and the sky was a great double-headed serpent arching overhead. Four deities known as *bacabs* held the sky and the earth apart at four corners, while a sacred tree, the *ceiba* (cottonwood) reached from the sky down to the underworld, joining the three cosmic realms. Like other Mesoamerican peoples, the Maya envisioned the sky as a thirteen-layered dome and the underworld as having nine layers, each governed by a different deity and related to different colors, directions, and the like. Much of our knowledge of the underworld is based on the sixteenth-century highland Quiché Maya epic, the Popol Vuh (Council Book). In this tale, the protagonists, known as the Hero Twins, must travel to the underworld realm and vanquish its lords in order to avenge the deaths of their father and uncle. Not only did the dead go to this cold and unpleasant place, but the sun and moon also had to travel there daily as well.

Although the Maya appear to have worshipped a large and complex pantheon of gods, we know very little about them. Identified in the codices long ago, some have counterparts in Classic Maya art and hieroglyphs. They include long-nosed Chac, the rain god, whose visage is repeated in stone on many Puuc-style facades, as well as Ix-Chel, the moon goddess who was patron of weaving and childbirth. Ancestor veneration also seems to have played an important part in religious life. The Maya may have believed in spirit companions, called *uay*, but the term also means "sorcerer" in modern Maya languages. Whatever its meaning, a Classic Maya hieroglyph for *uay* has been identified in conjunction with both rulers and gods.

Almost all of our information about religious practices and ritual is based on the Postclassic codices and Spanish eyewitness accounts, particularly those of Bishop Diego de Landa. The most important of the late Yucatec rituals were new year's ceremonies, supplemented by rites associated with agriculture and other professions. Studies of earlier Classic Maya hieroglyphs and iconography indicate that autosacrifice, as well as the shedding of captives' blood, was an important complement to significant events in the lives of the elite. While the setting for these rituals is not known, caves seemed to have played a significant role in Maya ritual life during all periods: paintings, offerings, and sacrifices have been found in them.

Select Bibliography

Culbert, T. Patrick, editor, *Classic Maya Political History*. Cambridge: School of American Research–Cambridge University Press, 1991.

Fash, William L., "Changing Perspectives on Maya Civilization." *Annual Review of Anthropology* 23 (1994).

Freidel, David, Linda Schele, and Joy Parker, *Maya*

Cosmos: Three Thousand Years on the Shaman's Path. New York: Morrow, 1993.

Reents-Budet, Dorie, *Painting the Maya Universe: Royal Ceramics of the Classic Period*. Durham, North Carolina, and London: Duke University Press, 1994.

Sharer, Robert J., *The Ancient Maya*. 5th edition, Stanford, California: Stanford University Press, 1994.

—Virginia E. Miller

Mesoamerica: Mexica

The Mexica were one of several ethnic groups to occupy the Valley of Mexico in late pre-Hispanic times. This group also was known as the Culhua-Mexica in recognition of its kinship alliance with the neighboring Culhua, descendants of the revered Toltecs, who occupied the fabled city of Tula from the tenth through twelfth centuries. The Mexica were additionally referred to as the "Tenochca," a term associated with the name of their *altepetl* (city-state), Tenochtitlan, and/or Tenochtitlan's founding leader, Tenoch.

The term "Aztec" frequently is applied to the Mexica of Tenochtitlan, although there is no evidence to indicate that these people called themselves by that name. This was a name devised by Alexander von Humboldt in 1813, its logic deriving from *Aztlan + tec(atl)*. Aztlan (Place of the Herons) was the mythical homeland of the Mexica, and *-teca(h)* literally means "people of." It is currently customary to use this more general term "Aztec" to refer collectively to the Nahuatl-speaking peoples of the Valley of Mexico, or, more extensively, to the Nahuatl-speaking peoples of the Valley of Mexico and neighboring valleys. The term "Aztec" also is used broadly to denote the Aztec Empire, also known as the Triple Alliance Empire, which dominated large areas of central and southern Mexico in the fifteenth and early sixteenth centuries. A further distinction also is made: it is usual to apply "Aztec" to the culture and people of pre-Spanish Mexico, and the term "Nahua" or "Nahuas" when referring to the Nahuatl-speaking peoples of Mexico in post-Conquest times.

The Mexica were the last in a long progression of tribal groups to migrate from northern desert regions into the central Mexican valleys. Accounts of their long and arduous trek range from pictorial codices to textual accounts in the Mexica language (Nahuatl); some of these latter were translated into Spanish in the early years of Spanish colonial rule. The records, numbering around 20, range from mythical accounts to historical itineraries. While the stories vary, there is general agreement on the high points of the journey.

The migration began at Aztlan, an island community surrounded by a lake. Although the lake resources (including fish, waterbirds, and reeds) were abundant, their god Huitzilopochtli (Hummingbird on the Left or Hummingbird of the South) ordered them to seek a more significant destiny. The precise geographic location of Aztlan is unknown and indeed hotly disputed: some researchers place it as distant as the modern-day southwestern United States, others locate it a mere 60 miles northwest of the Valley of Mexico, while still others place it somewhere between those two extremes. Whatever the exact location of this elusive site, it most likely was situated in an arid region northwest of their final destination. Their departure probably occurred sometime early in the twelfth century A.D.

In an early stage of their migration the Mexica stopped briefly at a mountain site called Culhuacan or Teoculhuacan, constructing a temple there to their patron god. This means of venerating Huitzilopochtli was followed throughout the migration. Leaving (Teo)Culhuacan they arrived at nearby Chicomoztoc (Seven Caves). This was reputedly a departure point for many migratory groups, including the Tlaxcallans who settled to the east of the Valley of Mexico and became bitter enemies of the Mexica, and the Tepanec, Chalca, Xochimilca, and others who settled in choice locations in the Valley of Mexico. While Chicomoztoc may have been an actual site where these many migratory groups congregated before continuing their journeys, its name is heavily charged with mythological symbolism: the emergence of human groups from the bowels of the earth through caves is a widespread and surely ancient motif in Mesoamerica. The Mexica were reportedly the last to leave this hallowed site and journey south into the realms of already-established cities and states.

The nomadic migrants collectively were called, by themselves and by others, Chichimeca. This term encompassed many ethnic groups (like the Mexica) who undertook a hunting and gathering way of life in the desert regions north of the areas of settled agriculture. However, this generalization masks the considerable cultural and social variation among these nomadic groups. At one extreme were the Teochichimeca, (True Chichimeca), exclusively hunters and gatherers who hunted with bows and arrows, wore animal skin clothing, used peyote, and fashioned objects from feathers and stone. The actions of the Mexica on their long migration suggest a more complex and "civilized" variety of Chichimec: they built temples wherever they stopped, they were well aware of luxury goods such as jade and cacao, and they cultivated crops such as maize and chilies. They marked time according to the sophisticated Mesoamerican calendars, and practiced human sacrifice. Their social order was heterogeneous and hierarchical; factional disputes occurred, and powerful priests obviously exercised considerable authority over the group. While the Mexica hailed from the northern deserts, all of these traits were well established among the settled agriculturalists of Mesoamerica and suggest that the Mexica were already quite assimilated to Mesoamerican ways before their arrival in the Valley of Mexico.

Chichimeca reaching the fertile central valleys in Mexico encountered much of the territory already settled by peoples tracing their claims and heritages back many centuries. These peoples were organized into city-state polities led by traditional dynasties and exhibiting distinctive ethnic identities. Some early Chichimec migrants, such as the Tlaxcallans and Acolhua, settled in relatively unoccupied areas and apparently met little resistance in claiming their lands. Other migrants, like the Tepanec, became absorbed into existing city-states through intermarriage. The Mexica, however, encountered a densely occupied Valley of Mexico with little available in the way of territorial or social niches.

By the end of the thirteenth century the Mexica were situated tenuously at Chapultepec (Hill of the Grasshopper), where they were attacked by warriors from the powerful city-state of Culhuacan. The Mexica pleaded with the Culhuacan ruler for asylum and a land of their own. In response, the Culhua ruler granted them occupancy of Tizapan, a dreary, snake-infested place rejected by other peoples of the valley. But the Mexica impressed the Culhua ruler by thriving in this inhospitable environment, and they became at least marginally accepted as military mercenaries in Culhua wars. But this relationship was short-lived, as the Mexica sorely offended the Culhua ruler by asking for the ruler's favorite daughter in marriage and subsequently sacrificing her. This specific event prompted a hasty Mexica retreat into the marshes of Lake Texcoco to a small uninhabited island, where at last they spied the symbol heralded by Huitzilopochtli: an eagle with a snake in its beak, perched on a prickly pear cactus. They took refuge on the island, naming their settlement Tenochtitlan (Among the Stone-Prickly Pear Cactus Fruit). It generally is accepted that the year was 1325, although some researchers suggest 1345. In less than two centuries it would become the largest and most powerful city in Mesoamerica.

In these early wanderings the Mexica had become both renowned and feared as fierce and aggressive warriors. From 1325 until the formation of the Triple Alliance in 1430, the Mexica applied their martial skills to serving the neighboring Tepanec city-state of Azcapotzalco as military mercenaries. As successful warriors they gained lands and other material rewards from their overlords. They became so favored that their established tribute payments in products from the lake were moderated. During those initial 105 years they also forged clever political alliances through strategic marriages into established and powerful dynasties, especially those of Culhuacan and Azcapotzalco. These attachments to a now-friendlier Culhuacan also bestowed some political legitimacy by virtue of Culhuacan's hereditary link to the revered and idealized Toltec culture. The Mexica also busied themselves with building and expanding their settlement, a difficult process given the paucity of arable land, the lack of readily available building materials, and the general absence of potable water on the small island.

The tide of history turned for the Mexica in 1428, when the powerful ruler of Azcapotzalco died without leaving a clear line of succession. This placed the Tepanec domain in some political disarray. The alert and aggressive Mexica moved promptly to fill the power vacuum; allied with the Acolhua (their eastern neighbors), they attacked the vulnerable Tepanecs of Azcapotzalco. By 1430 the Mexica of Tenochtitlan and the Acolhua of Texcoco had emerged victorious. They invited the Tepanec of Tlacopan to join them as junior partners in a political and military alliance; this Triple Alliance was to dominate central and southern Mexico for the next 90 years.

Scholarly understanding of Mexica culture during the 90 years of its imperial expansion is based on an abundance of documentary sources and on an increasing amount of archaeological data. Written documents were prodigiously produced by the Mexica and their neighbors; these took the form of pictorial codices. While virtually all of these books were destroyed during and following the Spanish Conquest, abundant textual and pictorial sources were written and copied during the early Spanish colonial period. At the hub of imperial rule, Tenochtitlan served as a center of official recorded history and bureaucratic documentation; Mexico City succeeded Tenochtitlan in this regard. As a result, information on the sixteenth-century Mexica before and after the Spanish Conquest is particularly rich. Recent archaeological investigations in downtown Mexico City have greatly enhanced the written word; excavations from 1978 to 1982 at the Mexica Templo Mayor (Great Temple) have uncovered seven complete building periods and over 100 offertory caches

(collectively containing more than 7,000 artifacts). The rich documentary and archaeological records combine to reveal a dynamic and complex urban culture.

The Mexica proper resided in Tenochtitlan, which grew to a metropolis of 150,000 to 200,000 people by 1519. In size and power it far outstripped its neighbors; even the Acolhua capital city of Texcoco could boast only some 30,000 inhabitants. Following established urban planning traditions in Mesoamerica, the central part of the city was essentially a ritual precinct, in this case a walled one with numerous temples and other religious buildings within. Dominating the urban landscape was the massive dual temple dedicated to the war god Huitzilopochtli and the rain god Tlaloc. Nearby sat the palaces of rulers and other elite officials. These centralized arrangements reflect the Mexica emphases on religion and dynastic power. Relatively small markets were located centrally and scattered about the city, but the major island marketplace was just north at Tlatelolco. While Tlatelolco's citizens were close relatives of the Tenochtitlan Mexica, it was nonetheless a competitor of Tenochtitlan for many years. Tlatelolco finally was conquered by the Mexica in 1473.

Tenochtitlan as a whole was laid out in quarters, each quarter divided into territorial divisions called *calpulli* or *tlaxilacalli*. These divisions were more than just residential suburbs; they served as social and political foci with their own temples, schools, internal leadership, and collective military and tribute obligations. Some *calpulli* served to concentrate craft specializations such as stone working or gold working, or the renowned feather workers of Tlatelolco.

The tiny island was clearly inadequate to serve the settlement needs of the rapidly expanding Mexica population. The Mexica therefore applied a known technique of land reclamation to expand the land area of their small island. The shallow lake bed surrounding the island provided an ideal setting for the creation of *chinampas,* currently misnamed "floating gardens." These were stable plots of land built by piling up alternating layers of mud and vegetation, and situated in the shallow lake bed. They first were secured with posts and later with the roots of willow trees planted along their edges. The plots ranged from 100 to 850 square meters (1,000 to 9,000 square feet), and were constructed in an orderly geometric fashion yielding a systematic network of canals and footpaths throughout the outer reaches of the city. The canals themselves served as arteries for transportation and communication, as well as a source of water and nutrients for the *chinampas*. Well-established *chinampas* also provided house sites for much of the urban population. These agricultural plots were extremely fertile, producing several crops a year even at the Valley of Mexico's elevation of over 7,000 feet. However, it is generally agreed that yields from the *chinampas* and surrounding lake sides would not have been sufficient to feed the large urban populations. Staple foods and other supplies entered the city daily and passed from sellers to buyers in the bustling marketplaces. Additional needed goods were obtained by the Mexica through their imperial tribute system, whereby a wide range of products and materials arrived in Tenochtitlan on a regularized schedule from outlying conquered regions. The Mexica, therefore, drew on a variety of sources for their necessities and luxuries. Nonetheless, they were not immune to nature's calamities; drought, famine, and flood all occasionally struck the island city over its short history.

The guiding principles of Mexica social and political life were hierarchy and heterogeneity. Social arrangements were castelike, although there was apparently some mobility for high achievers on the battlefield. Society was divided fundamentally into two castes, nobility and commoner, with rather unstable intermediate statuses of professional merchants and luxury artisans. Birthright and wealth defined individual placement in any of these categories. The nobility were themselves arranged hierarchically, with the ruler or *tlatoani* at the apex of the hierarchy. As with other city-states in Mesoamerica during the fifteenth and early sixteenth centuries, the Mexica of Tenochtitlan were ruled by a dynasty of hereditary rulers. In this case the preferred succession was from brother to brother before it passed to sons, but in Texcoco sons were preferred over brothers. The hereditary nature of succession was somewhat muted by imperative elections that were designed to choose the most capable among the legitimate heirs. The ruler was responsible for the well-being of his city-state and its citizens; this included undertaking worldly tasks such as establishing alliances and conducting wars, as well as fulfilling ritual obligations such as fasting and sacrifice. Other nobles occupied such prestigious and richly compensated positions as judges, tax collectors, governors, military officers, priests, scribes, and teachers.

Professional merchants *(pochteca)* and luxury artisans *(toltecca)* occupied a vague, unstable position in the social scheme; they were wealthy but lacked noble birthright. Their services and skills were in great demand by the nobility. Elegant symbols of noble status were flaunted eagerly and ostentatiously by those with the right to do so; merchants obtained shimmering feathers and polished stones, while artisans manufactured clever adornments for noble display. These merchants and luxury artisans tended to be concentrated in exclusive *calpulli* throughout the urban centers in the Valley of Mexico, allowing them some internal control over membership, training, resources, rewards, and professional knowledge.

Commoners comprised the bulk of the population. They were the primary producers among the Mexica, working as cultivators, fishermen, and artisans of utilitarian wares such as baskets and pottery. The weaving of cloth was a particularly time-consuming occupation of all women, regardless of social status. Some commoners *(macehualtin*; singular, *macehualli)* resided in *calpulli* and enjoyed rights to lands associated with the *calpulli*. Other commoners *(mayeque,* singular and plural) were attached to the landed estates of nobles, much in the manner of serfs. All commoner men were trained as warriors and expected to perform in battle. There was, however, no standing army. Courageous deeds on the battlefield, defined by the capture of enemy warriors, were rewarded with material goods and enhanced social status. This applied to both nobles and commoners.

Slaves occupied the bottom rung of the social ladder. Slavery among the Mexica largely resembled a system of social welfare: a person in extreme poverty could sell his labor to another for a year's (or more) sustenance. Alternatively, persons with uncontrollable gambling urges could wage (and lose) all their material possessions, finally gambling away themselves (i.e., their labor). Battlefield captives were numerous, but rarely ended up in a slave status; instead, they were destined for ceremonial sacrifice.

Religion and ritual were of paramount importance to the Mexica and were a highly visible component of their daily lives. Their solar and astrological calendars were crammed with rituals, some requiring participation by specialized retinues of priests, others involving participation by the entire populace. Ritual activities ranged from fasting and feasting to ritual bloodletting and human sacrifice. The actual form of these activities varied somewhat according to the demands of the god or goddess venerated; the sun and war gods, for instance, required heart sacrifice, while the rain god demanded children sacrificed by drowning. Blood sacrifice, whether by drawing blood from fleshy parts of the body or by removal of the heart, was grounded in a constellation of beliefs linking life and death in a continuous cycle, life and the continuation of the universe forever contingent on sacrifice and death.

The Mexica of Tenochtitlan were conquered by the Spanish conquistadors under Fernando (Hernán) Cortés in 1521. While the death toll of the Mexica from warfare and disease was enormous, many Mexica and their Nahuatl-speaking neighbors survived. Some significant aspects of Nahua culture thus became integrated into (or existed alongside) the Spanish colonial regime; these ranged from foods to place-names to language to weaving to religious beliefs and rituals. Many such features continue to persist today.

See also Nahua Rulers, Pre-Hispanic; Triple Alliance

Select Bibliography

Berdan, Frances F., *The Aztecs of Central Mexico: An Imperial Society*. Fort Worth, Texas: Harcourt Brace, 1982.
Boone, Elizabeth, *The Aztec World*. Montreal: St. Remy, and Washington, D.C.: Smithsonian, 1994.
Davies, Nigel, *The Aztec Empire: The Toltec Resurgence*. Norman: University of Oklahoma Press, 1987.
Durán, Diego, *The Aztecs: The History of the Indies of New Spain,* translated by Doris Heyden and Fernando Horcasitas. New York: Orion, and London: Cassell, 1964.
Sahagún, Bernardino de, *Florentine Codex: A General History of the Things of New Spain,* translated by Arthur J. O. Anderson and Charles E. Dibble. 14 vols., Santa Fe, New Mexico: School of American Research, and Salt Lake City: University of Utah Press, 1950–82.
Townsend, Richard F., *The Aztecs*. London and New York: Thames and Hudson, 1992.

—FRANCES F. BERDAN

Mesoamerica: Monte Albán

The Zapotec civilization had its origins in the Valley of Oaxaca sometime around 500 B.C. The most famous and enduring monuments of that civilization are the ruins known today as Monte Albán. With a history stretching some 2,000 years before the arrival of Europeans, Monte Albán was a strategically located settlement that quickly became a city and is regarded by many experts as the first in Mesoamerica. Its impressive location on a mountaintop reshaped by human hands to form an acropolis is among the most stunning in the Americas.

In many ways, Monte Albán represents a peripheral part of the Mesoamerican chronology. The areas to the north and south have been more widely studied and commented upon. Situated between the areas associated with the Mexica (Aztec) and the Maya civilizations, Monte Albán was a relatively

early settlement and was contemporary with Teotihuacan, its much larger neighbor to the north. Monte Albán's development was characterized by the growth of interregional trade, specialization in the crafts, and the emergence of city-states. For this reason it is important as a transitional site, foreshadowing the shift from dispersed and simple agricultural settlements to more complex societies and the growth of monumental ceremonial centers.

The name Monte Albán is relatively modern, and its use can be traced only to the seventeenth century, shortly after the Conquest. It seems likely that the name came from an early European settler in the area. The Spanish names Montalván or Monte Albán were not uncommon among the colonizers of Mexico, and this seems the most likely source of the current name. The ancient or indigenous name of the site is unknown. Among local Zapotec speakers, the ruins sometimes are referred to as Danibaan (Sacred Mountain). Local natives who speak the Mixtec language refer to the site as the "Hill of the Jaguar." Both possibilities seem unlikely as specific place names since they serve as general references to centers of power. Furthermore, throughout Mesoamerica jaguars were used as a symbol of power. It is even possible that the site had a number of different names during successive periods.

While it is the Zapotec civilization that is most closely associated with Monte Albán, there is clear evidence of other influences. Over its long history, the site was most likely in contact with other important power centers throughout the region, and that contact is reflected in the art and architecture of the ruins. In its early development, the art of Monte Albán was similar to that of the Olmec culture; the Classic period at the site (c. 100 B.C.–A.D. 650) was Zapotec; and the later eras show evidence of domination by the Mixtec and Mexica cultures.

While the immediate area surrounding the ruins is of limited agricultural value, the Valley of Oaxaca contains rich and fertile land that supported the rise of Monte Albán. Considerable agricultural surplus was necessary for the development of the administrative center populated by craftsmen and the elite. The long history of Monte Albán is a chronicle of the changes and complications taking place in the societies of Mesoamerica. The organic pattern of growth, flowering, and decline, used so commonly to describe the course of empire, can be traced through the archaeological evidence from Monte Albán and seems an appropriate metaphor for the Zapotec culture.

The commonly accepted method for dating and describing the history of Monte Albán is based on ceramic fragments and figures that have been excavated at the site. The standard chronology is generally divided into five periods. Monte Albán I (700–300 B.C.) was characterized by monumental architecture and distinctive low relief sculpture that shows the influence of the Olmec culture. Among the earliest structures is the temple platform known commonly as the Temple of the Danzantes, or dancing figures. The unusual and stylized figures on this structure have elongated heads and drooping mouths, similar to the sculpture of the Olmecs. The figures are accompanied by glyphs that appear to indicate names and dates. This evidence has led some to believe that the Zapotec may have been among the first in Mesoamerica to develop writing and calendrics. Originally, the figures on the temple were thought to be dancers, but experts now agree that, because of their distorted poses, they probably represent corpses, most likely of conquered enemies. Thus, the images would be a show of the political and military power of the Monte Albán elite.

Study of Monte Albán II (300–100 B.C.) has revealed increased military activity and the possible conquest of Monte Albán. Stone slabs from this period show upside-down human heads with closed eyes, as well as glyphs showing places and dates—often indicative of military events. These slabs come primarily from a structure known as Mound J, a fact that has led many to believe that the structure served as some type of war memorial. More recently, however, astroarchaeologist Anthony Aveni has argued that Mound J, with its elaborate tunnel system and arrow shape, may have been a type of observatory; he even claims to have found a zenith sighting line for the star Capella.

In the schema of development at Monte Albán, these first two periods are referred to as late and terminal formative. The third period is divided into Monte Albán IIIA (100 B.C.–A.D. 650) and Monte Albán IIIB (A.D. 650–800). It is often further subdivided by scholars to differentiate the various changes taking place over such a long time span. Monte Albán reached its height between 200 B.C. and A.D. 200 and probably achieved a population of around 15,000 during that time. Trade and commerce were an important element in the daily life of Monte Albán, and evidence exists that it was a major trading partner with its expanding neighbor to the north, Teotihuacan.

Monte Albán developed into the site we know today during the Classic period. Although substantial reshaping of the mountaintop to form an acropolis already had taken place, the major structures of the main plaza date from this era. During the Classic period the plaza itself was enclosed by the construction of walls and ballcourts. Stelae, similar to those of the Maya, also were erected during this period in apparent honor of Zapotec leaders. Perhaps the most characteristic artifacts from Monte Albán are the ceramic urns used in burial chambers—they, too, date from the Classic period.

Earlier ceramic artifacts had been hollow vases, but by the Classic period these had become urns, presumably used for interring food and drink with the deceased. These urn-figurines have the distinctive oversized headdresses of Zapotec deities and appear primarily to represent the gods Yopi and Cocijo. However, recent scholarship has argued that the urns may be a type of portraiture and represent actual people, presumably those buried along with the urn. The urns are ornate and elaborately detailed; many have been retrieved from burial chambers in very good condition. The art historian George Kubler has written this of the amazing artistic ability of Zapotec artists:

> No other American potters ever explored so completely the plastic conditions of wet clay, or retained its forms so completely after firing. The Zapotec never forced the clay or plaster to resemble stone or wood or metal; he used its wet and docile nature for fundamental geometric modelling, and he cut the material, when half-dry, into smooth planes with sharp edges of an unmatched brilliance and suggestiveness of form.

Monte Albán IV dates from A.D. 800 to 1325. This period is characterized in the early centuries by continued vitality but diminished growth as the area came under the strong influence of Teotihuacan. By this time the population is estimated to have grown to 25,000 in the area immediately surrounding Monte Albán. There followed, however, a rapid decline in population at about the same time as the collapse of Teotihuacan. Many scholars believe that these two problems, population growth and the demise of Teotihuacan, are related to the collapse of Monte Albán. Population growth may have pushed the resources of the agricultural lands to their limit, and reduced yields would have placed enormous pressure on the artisans and elites living in Monte Albán, as they had depended on some type of tribute from the agricultural surplus. The demise of Teotihuacan may well have eliminated any threat from the north and thus the very need for Monte Albán. Or, more simply, it may have caused a collapse of the interregional trading that had become an important part of Monte Albán's economy. Whatever the causes for the collapse, the inhabitants of the city were scattered into smaller communities, and Monte Albán faded as a center of power.

The final period, Monte Albán V, dated from 1325 to 1521. Early in this period the central structures became nothing more than a pilgrimage site and necropolis. The practice of burying nobles and elites at the ruins appears to have continued for the next 500 years. Archaeological excavations during the twentieth century have uncovered tombs dating right up to the Spanish Conquest.

Some archaeologists have proposed a special purpose for Monte Albán since it does not fit the typical patterns of development during the same period. Most settlements that developed at about the same time were towns adjacent to agricultural areas or villages near important water sources. Monte Albán does not fit either of these models. Its iconography is devoid of ritual and religious symbols, making it somewhat unlikely that it was a major religious center. Archaeologist Richard Blanton proposes that because of this evidence it is possible that Monte Albán was some type of neutral administrative headquarters for a confederation of different groups. Another bit of archaeological evidence supporting this hypothesis is the settlement pattern surrounding the center of Monte Albán—separate neighborhoods terraced into surrounding hillsides seem to indicate that the area was indeed inhabited by distinct groups. At the heart of Blanton's argument is the fact that the competing groups practicing agriculture in the Oaxaca Valley would have had need for both a political capital and fortress from which to defend themselves against common enemies. Others have argued that Monte Albán and the surrounding areas were never seriously threatened from outside attack and that Monte Albán was simply the Zapotec proclamation of their power and domination in the valley.

Select Bibliography

Bernal, Ignacio, *Official Guide: Oaxacan Valley*, translated by Helen Jones-Perrot de Mandri. Mexico City: INAH, 1988.

Blanton, Richard E., *Monte Albán: Settlement Patterns of the Ancient Zapotec Capital*. New York: Academic Press, 1978.

—MICHAEL D. PHILLIPS

Mesoamerica: Olmec

Around 1860 villagers in Veracruz unearthed a colossal stone head unlike any other pre-Columbian monument known at that time. By the turn of the century, a number of beautifully worked jade figurines of unusual physiognomy and unknown provenance also had attracted the attention of leading Mesoamericanists of the era. Gradually it became clear that all of these artifacts had been produced by a culture as yet unidentified but apparently centered in the Gulf Coast region. Dubbed the Olmec (Nahuatl for "rubber people"), the Mexica word for the later inhabitants of the area, their real name and their language remain unknown. Recent evidence, however, suggests that they spoke a language of the Mixe-Zoque linguistic group.

Olmec culture flourished between approximately 1200 and 400 B.C. within a crescent-shaped area on the Bay of Campeche encompassing southern Veracruz and western Tabasco. It is a hot, humid, riverine environment, rich in fauna and flora that supplemented the Olmec diet of cultivated crops, particularly maize. The Olmec presence, however, has been recognized throughout Mesoamerica, from Guerrero all the way to El Salvador and Honduras, in the form of public architecture, petroglyphs, cave paintings, ceramics, and worked jade. It even has been argued that the origins of the Olmec lie beyond the traditional heartland boundaries, but the antiquity and number of Olmec sites in this area lend strong support to its primacy.

Some scholars also have moved away from the earlier model of the Olmec as the "mother culture" of Mesoamerica from which all later cultures are descended, believing that the Olmec were simply one of several advanced groups in the Formative period (1200–200 B.C.), or that Olmec traits are too widespread to be attributed to a single culture. Nevertheless, it is hard to dispute that many enduring features of Mesoamerican civilization make their first appearance among the Olmec. These include complex settlement systems, bilaterally symmetrical ceremonial complexes, pyramidal structures, the practice of erecting monumental carved stone monuments, the ball game, the extensive use of carved jade and divinatory mirrors, ritual caches, and possibly even the calendar and writing.

Social Organization

We know almost nothing about Olmec social organization, but it obviously took a highly organized and hierarchical society to harness the human energy needed to move tons of earth and stone and to construct the great public works that characterize Olmec centers. Specialists must have been required to direct many activities, including the carving of the great stone heads, which are presumed to be portraits of the elite, as well as the tabletop altars that may have served as their thrones. Finally, the quantities of iron ore, obsidian, mica, flint, jade, and other exotic materials found in the Olmec heartland point to a well-established network of trade with other areas of Mesoamerica, some of which may even have been colonized by the powerful Olmec.

Sites

The Olmec heartland is dotted with sites, of which only a handful have been excavated, most notably San Lorenzo and La Venta. The former appears to have the most important Olmec center between 1200 and 900 B.C. Located on a plateau on a branch of the Coatzacoalcos River, it was enlarged by the addition of artificial projecting ridges on three sides, laboriously constructed by hand-carrying 2.4 million cubic feet (67,000 cubic meters) of earth in baskets. The scholar Michael Coe believes they were added to transform the whole site into a giant bird flying east, but whatever their purpose, the great platform supported many mounds. These were aligned along a north-south axis at 8 degrees west of north, the standard Olmec orientation. Stone is a rare building material at lowland Olmec sites: most structures at San Lorenzo were built of earth, colored clay, and presumably perishable materials such as wood and thatch. Elite residences incorporating stone columns and other elements recently have been excavated, however. A possible ball court has been identified. Artificial lagoons also were constructed here, connected and drained by 650 feet (200 meters) of lidded stone canals buried beneath the surface.

Basalt, used almost exclusively for sculpture, came from the Tuxtla Mountains, 43 miles (70 kilometers) away. The stone was quarried, then apparently dragged down to the nearest waterway and floated from there on rafts along the Gulf Coast and up the Coatzacoalcos River to San Lorenzo, where it was carved into its final form. Despite the difficulties inherent in acquiring stone, an impressive number of monumental sculptures, including ten colossal heads, three altars, and numerous figures in the round, were found here and at nearby satellite sites. Many sculptures were discovered mutilated and may have been systematically buried, either as a final act of violence as the site was destroyed and abandoned or perhaps merely to mark the end of successive rulers' reigns. Others have argued, however, that the monuments merely were recarved and recycled.

In any case, after 900 B.C., La Venta succeeded San Lorenzo as the primary Olmec site. La Venta is located on a low ridge in low-lying wetlands near the Tonalá River in Tabasco, 9 miles (15 kilometers) from the Gulf of Mexico, and covers at least 500 acres (200 hectares). The site is dominated by an extremely eroded 100-foot-high (32-meter) earthen pyramid. Its original form is debated: some see it as a fluted cone, perhaps built in imitation of a volcano, but recent work at the site suggests it may have been a radial structure not unlike some early Maya pyramids. To the north of the pyramid (known as Complex C) is a plaza flanked by low earthen mounds and a smaller court enclosed by basalt columns (called Complex A).

One of the most unusual features of La Venta's ceremonial center is the presence of buried offerings beneath its mounds and plazas. For example, archaeologists found three deep pits filled with massive deposits of serpentine blocks, covered with abstract mosaic pavements and then with multicolored clays. Caches of polished mirrors and jade also were uncovered, most notably an offering of figurines surrounded by celts (chisel- or ax-like instruments), arranged as if the group were conversing within the basalt colonnade above. As at San Lorenzo, large stone heads were set up in close proximity to public architecture. But in addition to heads and altars, at La Venta the Olmec also carved stelae in relief, some of which surely portray their rulers in full regalia and perhaps commemorate rituals or historical events.

Other important heartland Olmec sites include Tres Zapotes, where the first Olmec head was found, Laguna de los Cerros, an unexcavated site whose plan resembles that of La Venta, and El Manatí, where a muddy bog has recently yielded a number of well-preserved wooden busts.

Expansion

During the Early Formative period (1200–900 B.C.), characteristic Olmec pottery was found in burials in tandem with local ceramics in villages in the Valley of Mexico, most notably at Tlatilco and Tlapacoya. The Olmec forms include large white-slipped hollow ceramic babies that also occur at Las Bocas in Puebla, and which may originate in San Lorenzo.

Jade, which appears for the first time in the Olmec heartland at La Venta, may have come from the Río Balsas in Guerrero, the Motagua River in Guatemala, or some unknown source. But its presence at La Venta clearly indicates that the Olmec were expanding to areas in which the mineral is found. During the Middle Formative period (900–500 B.C.), Olmec influence is particularly strong in Guerrero as well as in the Valley of Morelos. Although poorly known archaeologically, Guerrero has long been the source of fine portable Olmec objects in jade and other stones. Furthermore, the recently discovered site of Teopantecuanitlan has ball courts, masonry architecture, and sculpture in Olmec style. Olmec cave paintings also have been found at Juxtlahuaca, Oxtotitlan, and most recently at Cacahuaziziqui.

Chalcatzingo, located at the foot of a cliff at the beginning of a pass into the Morelos Plains, was originally a small village, but between approximately 700 and 500 B.C., Olmec-style carvings appear on the exposed rock walls above the settlement, and monumental sculptures reminiscent of La Venta were erected below.

While the Olmec clearly sought jade and other minerals unavailable in the heartland, what they offered in return is uncertain: perhaps perishable goods such as crocodile meat and jaguar skins, tropical foods and feathers, as well as finished products such as carved jade and ceramics. Given the widespread diffusion of their symbols throughout much of Mesoamerica, the Olmec may have been exporting their ideology as well as simply engaging in trade. Whether the Olmec expansion was accompanied by conquest and subsequent colonization is still debated. Some believe that the Olmec-style monumental art and architecture of sites such as Chalcatzingo indicate long-term occupation by Gulf Coast elites, while others see them as independent developments.

Other areas in which the Olmec left their mark include Oaxaca, the Pacific coast of Guatemala and Chiapas, the middle Grijalva region of Chiapas, and to a minor extent, the Maya area, which eclipsed the Olmec in the Late Formative period (500 B.C.– A.D. 200). Unlike later Mesoamerican civilizations, whose collapse usually was tied to cataclysmic events, the Olmec demise seems to have been gradual, or at least unmarked in the archaeological record as currently understood. However, the Olmec had a far-reaching impact on subsequent cultures, particularly in terms of religion, cosmology, and ritual.

Religion

The Olmec were the first Mesoamericans to systematically record their rulers, their cosmology, and their gods. Olmec iconography has proven notoriously resistant to interpretation, however. The large serpentine mosaic masks buried at La Venta, for example, have been variously construed as stylized jaguar masks and diagrams of the world tree. The former interpretation was that of Matthew Stirling, the first archaeologist to work in the Olmec heartland, who surmised that the Olmec saw themselves as the offspring of a mythical human-jaguar union. The second, more recent hypothesis, is derived from Maya iconographic studies and involves a reading of

the whole site as a cosmogram in which the mosaics are part of a larger, buried underworld landscape.

The "were-jaguar" deity first identified by Stirling can be recognized in the large number of Olmec figures that seem to combine the features of a human and a snarling jaguar. However, further research has indicated that if the Olmec had a pantheon of deities, it included a broader range of composite creatures, including snakes, caimans, raptorial birds, and sharks. Some have proposed that these Olmec supernaturals are the progenitors of the better-known Maya and highland Mexican gods, particularly a crying baby/jaguar deity who may have evolved into the ubiquitous Mesoamerican rain god. Others, however, view these figures as shamanistic: that is, powerful persons in the act of transforming themselves into animals or back into human form, possibly under the influence of hallucinogens. The typical Olmec features of slanting eyes and flaring, downturned upper lip appear on polished stone masks that may have been worn in ritual performances, perhaps of a shamanistic nature.

Like the later Maya, Zapotecs, and Mexica, the Olmec elite sought divine sanction, portraying themselves as gods or shamans. In both monumental art and on portable objects of jade and other materials, they hold or wear elaborate emblems of authority and are shown seated upon the enormous carved thrones found at heartland sites. Incised designs on their faces or bodies may allude to Olmec supernaturals with whom they wished to identify themselves, and to their power to control natural forces such as rainfall and agricultural fertility.

Select Bibliography

Benson, Elizabeth P., and Beatriz de la Fuente, editors, *Olmec Art of Ancient Mexico*. Washington, D.C.: National Gallery of Art, 1996.

Coe, Michael, and Richard Diehl, *In the Land of the Olmec*. 2 vols., Austin: University of Texas Press, 1980.

Coe, Michael, et al., *The Olmec World: Ritual and Rulership*. Princeton, New Jersey: Art Museum, 1995.

Sharer, Robert J., and David Grove, editors, *Regional Perspectives on the Olmec*. Cambridge: School of American Research–Cambridge University Press, 1989.

—VIRGINIA E. MILLER

Mesoamerica: Teotihuacan

Teotihuacan (Nahuatl for "Abode of the Gods") was Mexico's first true urban civilization, and it influenced cities throughout Mexico and beyond to Guatemala. Scholars have found remains of more than 2,600 major structures there. Teotihuacan was founded during Mesoamerica's upper preclassic period, which spanned 600 to 150 B.C. In 100 B.C. a cluster of villages in the valley grew to form the great city. No one knows for sure how long Teotihuacan was occupied, but most archaeologists agree the city thrived for about 1,000 years, that its main building phase occurred by A.D. 100, and that it was abandoned around A.D. 750. Teotihuacan's culture is divided into four archaeological periods:

Teotihuacan I, or *Tzacualli* (600 B.C.–200 B.C.). This Preclassic culture was influenced by three other Mexican cities: Ticoman, Chupicuaro, and Tlapacoya. Figurines of this era were crude and handmade.

Teotihuacan II, or *Miccaotli* (200 B.C.–A.D. 250). Figurines from this period were more carefully made, and transitional pottery appeared, along with black pottery. It was during this period that the great Pyramid of the Sun was built, likely around A.D. 100. Also created during this time were the Street of the Dead, frescoes of the Superpuestos, and the Temple of Quetzalcoatl.

Teotihuacan III, or *Tlamilolpa-Xolalpan* (A.D. 250–650). The village of Tlamilolpa to the east of the sacred ground of Teotihuacan was occupied, and the people traded with the Petén Maya people. Plaster cloisonné has been unearthed from this period. The population reached its height during this time, with a minimum of 75,000 people, probably 125,000, and possibly 200,000. Mold-made figurines depict the contemporary theology: Tlaloc, the rain god; Xipe, a god thought to have human skin and called Our Lord the Flayed One; and the "fat god" often were shown. Frescoes depict jaguars, priests, and rain gods. The city was reconstructed, and the nearby village of Oztoyahualco was again occupied, having been abandoned during the previous period. This phase ends with the desertion of Teotihuacan, for reasons unknown.

Teotihuacan IV, or *Ahuizotla-Amantla* (A.D. 650–900). The late phase of the culture continued in the nearby towns of Portezuelo, El Risco, Calpulalpan, and other sites. Figurines show great ritualistic development, and there is evidence of an increase in human sacrifice. The people of Tajín, Cholula, and Xochicalco carried on Teotihuacan's traditions, modified them, and brought them eventually to the Toltec capital of Tula.

Teotihuacan was a carefully planned city. It was built in several districts, radiating southward from the Pyramid of the Moon. Two rows of buildings extend south of the Moon Plaza. At its height in A.D. 600, Teotihuacan included avenues, markets, plazas, temples, palaces, apartment compounds, a grid system of streets, slums, waterways, reservoirs, and drainage systems. Springs and canals, along with a channeled San Juan River, fed water to the city.

Of the 2,600 major structures found in Teotihuacan, at least 2,000 are apartment buildings. They all have in common clusters of rooms around several patios, common outer walls around the whole group, and the grid system on which they are laid out. Archaeologist René Millon estimates that about 100 people lived in the biggest of the buildings, 20 in the smallest. Each apartment had its own kitchen, may have had cisterns for storing rainwater, and had below-floor ducts for draining rainwater from the patios.

The most common construction material used on Teotihuacan homes was a mix of porous chunks of volcanic stone *(tezontle)* and clay, gravel, and mortar. Polished plaster covered the interior surfaces, and a large number of wooden beams were used for structural support. The high wood content made these building highly flammable, and when Teotihuacan was finally destroyed, a great fire left a blanket of ash over the entire city.

The Pyramid of the Sun makes other Teotihuacan buildings look tiny by comparison. Its base measures 700 feet on each side and it stands 200 feet tall. As is the case with most Mexican pyramids, the Pyramid of the Sun served as a huge, grand base for the temple that once stood atop it. It had no inner chambers, although tunnels have been discovered beneath the structure, and it is filled with 1 million cubic yards of sun-dried bricks and rubble. The pyramid's exterior was composed of stone and faced with plaster. Fragments of pottery, figurines, and tools of the first Teotihuacan period have been found inside, fashioned by the Oztoyahualcoans, the people of a northwest village who are thought to be Teotihuacan's founders and the builders of the two pyramids.

At a certain point in the city's development, every building was rebuilt, with new facades and even new stairs on the two great pyramids. The reason seems to have been a religious shift from one cult to another, not a military conquest by another society.

There were several social classes among Teotihuacan citizens. A city this size needed many farmers, some of whom lived in the city itself or just outside; others lived in neighboring towns and provided agricultural specialties. They sold their produce in the city's large, central market.

The city also had numerous craft specialists. As many as 25 percent of the population were craftsmen, working with obsidian, stone, pottery, and murals; there were couturiers to make the elaborate costumes used in many of the religious ceremonies, sandal makers, masons, plasterers, quarrymen, and a host of other tradesmen. Their goods were exported via traders throughout Mesoamerica. Four hundred workshops have been uncovered in the city.

At the top of Teotihuacan society was the religious, political, and military elite; long-distance traders might also have belonged to this ruling class. There was a constant presence of foreigners in Teotihuacan, probably because of its religious significance and sheer size. Two areas of residences seem to have been permanently dedicated to foreign visitors, as evidenced by tombs, pottery, obsidian blades, and weaving implements found in the ruins.

The Citadel is a group of bases, platforms, and staircases that were probably a priests' and governor's residence. At the rear are the remains of the Temple of Quetzalcoatl. A central staircase leads to its six graded sections; serpents' heads are a predominant decorative theme. The temple contained 366 sculptures, probably corresponding to the solar calendar.

The Street of the Dead (Calle de los Muertos) is 2.5 miles long and 150 feet wide, and lies between the two great pyramids. The two pyramids themselves and the squares that surround them are probably the city's greatest tourist attractions. Along the Street of the Dead lie the remains of more than 75 smaller temples, grouped around small courtyards. Low platforms in the patios and courtyards probably served as dance halls, where ornately outfitted warriors danced intricately choreographed dances. A mural depicts dancers following footprint diagrams on the platform floor while holding curved knives with bleeding human hearts impaled on them.

The Palace of the Jaguars features zoomorphic drawings of the jaguar, an animal which held great significance for the Teotihuacanos. Small holes in the floor are part of the drainage system, in working order for more than 1,000 years.

The Temple of the Plumed Snails can be reached via a tunnel beneath the Palace of Quetzalpapalotl (the butterfly god) and is well preserved by the earth in which it is buried. The palace includes several deep porches, surrounded by an arcade and three large rooms, most likely used for administrative audiences. Surrounding them are other rooms intended for living quarters. It is larger in size, more complex, and

bears special features not found in the more ordinary residences.

No one knows for certain why Teotihuacan was abandoned. Theories range from a major earthquake, a violent invasion, a drastic change in the climate, sudden soil exhaustion, massive crop failure, a dreadful epidemic, or a rebellion of the agricultural people against dictatorial rulers. Whatever the cause, a great fire raged through the city before it was abandoned. The only thing we do know is that after A.D. 650 Teotihuacan was no more.

Select Bibliography

Manzanilla, Linda, "The Economic Organization of the Teotihuacan Priesthood: Hypotheses and Considerations." In *Art, Ideology, and the City of Teotihuacan,* edited by Janet Berlo. Washington, D.C.: Dumbarton Oaks Research Library, 1992.

_____, and Luis Barba, "The Study of Activities in Classic Households: Two Case Studies from Coba and Teotihuacan." *Ancient Mesoamerica* 1:1 (1990).

Miller, Arthur, *The Mural Painting of Teotihuacan.* Washington, D.C.: Dumbarton Oaks, 1973.

Millon, René, *Urbanization at Teotihuacan: The Teotihuacan Map.* Austin: University of Texas Press, 1973.

_____, "The Last Years of Teotihuacan Dominance." In *The Collapse of Ancient States and Civilizations,* edited by N. Yoffee and G. L. Cowgill. Tucson: University of Arizona Press, 1988.

Storey, Rebecca, *Life and Death in the Ancient City of Teotihuacan: A Modern Paleodemographic Synthesis.* Tuscaloosa: University of Alabama Press, 1992.

—LISA COLLINS ORMAN

Mesoamerica: Toltec

Toltec civilization emerged after the fall of Teotihuacan in A.D. 650 and predated the civilization of the Mexica (Aztecs). Its capital was known as Tollan (Place of the Reeds), believed to be the archaeological site known today as Tula. At its height, the Toltec influence reached from what is today the southwestern United States into the Yucatán Peninsula. The cultural impact of the Toltec can be found in art, architecture, military history, mythology, and religion.

The term *Toltec* comes from the Nahuatl word *toltecatl,* which implies a certain sophistication and learnedness as well as skill in the arts and crafts. It also refers simply to an inhabitant of the ancient city of Tollan. In the later Mexica civilization the term was used to identify the highly esteemed artisan class.

The foundation myth of the Toltec tells of a ruler named Mixcoatl (Cloud Serpent), who first led his people to a place called Colhuacan. Later his son moved the people to Tula, and it was he who adopted the cult of Quetzalcoatl (Feathered Serpent). It seems likely that the cult of Quetzalcoatl had existed within Mesoamerica for some time before it was adopted by the Toltec. They, however, are widely credited with spreading the influence and mythology associated with this deity.

Shortly after the destruction of Teotihuacan, nomadic people from the north begin to settle in the central plateau. Known as Chichimecs (Sons of Dogs), these people began to live a more settled and agricultural existence. Their cultural and religious center was Tula. The archaeological record indicates that Tula existed as early as A.D. 650, but at that time it was but a small village. Accompanying Tula's growth and settlement was the adoption of the cult of Quetzalcoatl. This deity represented light and good and did not demand human sacrifice of his followers. At the other extreme, and representing the conflict in Mesoamerican cosmology, was Tezcatlipoca (Smoking Mirror), who stood for evil, darkness, and sorcery. The more violent practices of the Toltec were products of their veneration of Tezcatlipoca.

It seems likely that the Toltec were made up of many different ethnic groups who spoke a variety of languages. Current research proposes that the Toltec came primarily from the northern parts of Mexico and developed a sedentary agricultural existence that replaced their earlier nomadic lifestyle. The Toltec are credited widely with advancing the use of irrigation as part of their political and military organization. With additional arable land, the Toltec were able to inhabit an area outside the fertile Valley of Mexico. Their effective government soon incorporated other nomadic peoples from the north, forming an ever larger and increasingly militant confederacy. The collection of tribute by the Toltec from the people who settled near Tula established a pattern that was to be adopted successfully by both the Mexica and the Spaniards. The Toltec did not become a military power and cultural influence until the ninth century, some two centuries after the establishment of Tula. During those 200 years the city grew to a population of some 30,000, and the Toltec gained control of the Valley of Mexico's green obsidian deposits.

Thus began a period of conquest that saw the Toltec expand their influence from the confines of the central plateau both north and south to the borders of present-day Mexico. Scholars still debate the details of the Toltec expansion, but it is clear that it was a militaristic enterprise driven in part by the need to secure prisoners who would serve as sacrificial victims. The clearest influence of the Toltec in an area far distant from Tula is at the Maya site of Chichen Itza in the Yucatán Peninsula.

The militaristic themes of Toltec life are recorded in their art and architecture, as well as in the histories of a vast region extending thousands of miles from its center at Tula. The complete mixing of military and religious life was something new in the central plateau of Mexico and may have reflected the increased competition for land and resources in an area prone to drought and political instability.

The architectural remains at Tula provide a wealth of information about the Toltec. Quetzalcoatl is widely represented in the art and architecture of Tula as the great feathered serpent. Other characteristic elements in the art and architecture of Tula are realistic anthropomorphic sculptures and enormous four-sided columns depicting male warriors. Perhaps more than for any other single motif, Toltec art is known for its representation of Chacmool, a male deity, reclining with his head and knees raised and a bowl resting on his stomach. The bowl is believed to have been used to hold the hearts of sacrificial victims captured in war. Statues of Chacmool can be found not only in Tula but also at Chichen Itza.

The actual ruins that exist today are of a ceremonial center and not the dwelling places of the Toltec. Small simple homes certainly surrounded the ceremonial center but those structures are long since gone. The site itself is made up of two clusters of structures known generally as Tula Grande and Tula Chico. It is at Tula Grande that most archaeological work has taken place. Ball courts, pyramids, and other structures have been excavated and partially restored at Tula, but perhaps the most interesting artifacts are the immense columns and caryatids that dot the ruins and are believed to have once supported roofs. If this was indeed the case, it would represent a significant development in the architecture of Mesoamerica, since most previous ceremonial structures had been predominantly solid with little or no usable interior space.

Another unique structure at the Tula site is known as the Coatepantli (Serpent Wall). It is a free-standing wall, 131 feet long, with relief sculpture on both sides. The central scene was either destroyed or removed before modern excavations of the site began, but other interesting elements of the wall include low relief sculptures of rattlesnakes devouring human skeletons. Themes of death, destruction, and military strength predominate in the architectural decorations at Tula. Images of the warrior are to be found everywhere. This is in stark contrast to the more geometric decorations found at Teotihuacan.

Like many other pre-Columbian Mesoamerican civilizations, Toltec culture experienced a mysterious collapse. By the end of the twelfth century Tula was in a state of complete decline, and the Toltec had been dispersed throughout Mexico. The various accounts of the demise of the Toltec are often contradictory. Some are based almost purely on the mythological of Mesoamerica, and others are the result of archaeological and ethnographic work done only in recent years.

The most fanciful and interesting account comes from the Mexica and is preserved in the work of Franciscan missionary Bernardino de Sahagún. In the Mexica mythology, Quetzalcoatl is tricked by Tezcatlipoca into drinking pulque, an alcoholic beverage made from fermented sap. After becoming drunk he sleeps with his sister. With these two acts Quetzalcoatl falls from his lofty position, and his followers desert him; thus ends Tula's golden age. With the fall of his opponent, Tezcatlipoca is free to create such havoc among the Toltec that they are either killed or forced to flee Tula. In different versions of this story, Quetzalcoatl is presented either as a great ruler who took upon himself the name of the deity or as the deity himself. In those accounts adhering to the latter version, after his disgrace Quetzalcoatl sets himself on fire and rises from the ashes as the Morning Star.

Archaeological evidence confirms that Tula met a violent end. The excavations undertaken by Jorge Acosta revealed evidence of fire and destruction throughout the site. Most scholars now agree that the fall of Tula was a combination of internal pressures on the subsistence system and external threats from many sources. An additional important stress on the social fabric may have come from the fact that Tula was made up of a very heterogeneous population. Yet another unproven hypothesis concerns a climatological change that may have brought about a reduction in precipitation in the surrounding area. It is unlikely that a single factor brought about the demise of Tula and the Toltec civilization. Some simultaneous combination of events appears to have occurred after 1100 to bring about the decline.

In the struggle to control the Valley of Mexico after the fall of Tula, the Mexica succeeded in part because they were able to take upon themselves the mantle of the Toltec. Through Mexica glorification, Toltec civilization became greater in myth and memory than it ever had been in reality.

Much of what we know of the Toltec comes from the monumental 12-volume work *General History of the Things of New Spain* by Sahagún. In his research with the Mexica shortly after the Conquest, he sought to record the history and culture of the people of the Valley of Mexico. Important in that history is the Mexica veneration of the Toltec. The Mexica looked to the ruins of Tula and the works of the Toltec as the great example of what art could be—in large part accounting for the style of Mexica sculpture. The Mexica looted the site of the ancient city, and many Toltec artifacts have been found among the Mexica ruins. Because of the fanciful blend of history and mythology in Sahagún's work and especially because of the hyperbolic rhetoric of the Mexica concerning the Toltec, identification of the actual site of ancient Tollan was not an easy task.

Prior to World War II it widely was believed that Teotihuacan was ancient Tollan. Modern archaeological innovations and dating techniques generally have discredited this belief. However, there is not complete unanimity among scholars of Mesoamerica that Tula is indeed ancient Tollan. Among the many questions and criticisms concerning the identification of this site as the capital of the Toltec is that Tula is not sufficiently grand and that its artwork is inferior to that found at many other sites. Furthermore, its location in an arid plain is somewhat troubling considering the purported size of the city at its height—it is uncertain that this environment could have supported sufficient production of foodstuffs even with the widespread use of irrigation. Nonetheless, it seems likely that archaeologists' preconceptions about Tollan have been tainted by the Mexica's veneration of the Toltec. Objective and scientific work during the last half of the twentieth century appears to confirm that Tula was indeed the site of Tollan and that the Toltec were perhaps not the larger-than-life heroes depicted in Mexica legend.

See also Quetzalcoatl

Select Bibliography

Davies, Nigel, *The Toltecs until the Fall of Tula.* Norman: University of Oklahoma Press, 1977.

Diehl, Richard A, *Tula: The Toltec Capital of Ancient Mexico.* London and New York: Thames and Hudson, 1983.

Healan, Dan M., editor, *Tula of the Toltecs.* Iowa City: University of Iowa Press, 1989.

—MICHAEL D. PHILLIPS

Mesoamerica: Veracruz, Classic and Postclassic

Despite its strategic location on the Gulf of Mexico between the Maya and the highland cultures of central Mexico, Veracruz remains almost terra incognita archaeologically. When the Spanish landed near the present-day city of Veracruz in 1518, there were numerous ethnic groups living in the area, including historic Olmecs, Huastecs, Totonacs, and Nahuas. Much of the area was under the control of the Mexica, and as a result some groups were eager to cooperate with the new arrivals in order to escape the heavy burden of tribute. Rubber, cacao, and cotton flourished along the hot humid coast and were highly valued in the central highlands.

Most of the important pre-Columbian sites are located on the narrow coastal plain that rises abruptly inland, culminating in the high mountain peaks of the eastern Sierra Madre. After the demise of Olmec culture, the most important center in Veracruz was Cerro de las Mesas. Although the site may overlap with the Olmec, the evidence linking Cerro de las Mesas with the earlier civilization is still tenuous. An Early Classic cache of 782 jade and stone pieces found here, for example, included some Olmec pieces, but many were from Oaxaca and the Maya area. Cerro de las Mesas is otherwise best known for its carved stelae with Long Count dates in the fifth and sixth centuries. Other earlier dates have been found on artifacts in the area, including the Tuxtla Statuette with a date of A.D. 162 and Stela C at Tres Zapotes, dated at 32 B.C. The recent find of the La Mojarra stela in southeastern Veracruz has excited interest not only for its long text with two dates in the second century and writing in a language ancestral to Mixe-Zoquean, but also for its figure carved in a style reminiscent of the sculpture of distant Kaminaljuyu in Guatemala City.

Massive but largely unexcavated Classic period sites dot central Veracruz. Cuajilotes, for example, lying on a riverbank about 37 miles (60 kilometers) south of El Tajín, may have served as a commercial port controlling traffic between the Gulf Coast and the Central Mexican Plateau. Its history spans A.D. 300 to after 1100. The site of El Pital, not far from the coast, was a large (over 100 major structures) and densely populated city supported by extensive raised fields. Contemporary with Teotihuacan, it must have been an important source for the Gulf Coast pottery and other Veracruz features found at the highland city. Matacapan, a long-distance trading center in southern Veracruz, may even have housed a Teotihuacan colony.

Northern Veracruz was dominated in the Late Classic period by the best-documented site in the region, El Tajín, whose existence has been known since the late eighteenth century. Although it flourished during the entire Classic period, it was at its height after the collapse of many of its contemporaries, from about A.D. 900 to 1100. Located in a narrow mountain valley, El Tajín was not only a major political and trade center but was also the focus of important ritual activities. Chief among these was the ball game: 17 ball courts have been found there so far.

Although much remains to be explored and excavated, the core of the site currently consists of two areas. Tajín Chico is a series of terraced hills largely supporting residential buildings, while the main civic structures occupy a flat area to the south and east. The core is dominated by the Pyramid of the Niches, rising 60 feet (18 meters) in six tiers in an elaborate talud-tablero style. The name derives from the deep square niches that surround all four sides, 365 in all, suggesting a symbolic connection to the solar year.

A unique feature of El Tajín's architecture is the use of concrete poured into wooden molds to construct the upper floors and to roof masonry palace-type buildings. Some structures were stuccoed and brightly painted blue or, more often, red. Fragments of elaborate murals have been found here and at other sites, most notably at Las Higueras on the central coast.

The reliefs of El Tajín are executed in what has become known as the Classic Veracruz style. It is characterized by the use of linked intertwined scrolls with a raised double outline. Variations of these scrolls may form the bodies of fantastic creatures or serve as borders for narrative scenes such as those that occur on the walls of El Tajín's South Ball Court. These relief panels seem to form a sequence involving ball playing, ritual human sacrifice, and events involving both human and supernatural actors. A column carved in relief at El Tajín appears to describe a ritual involving a local ruler named 13 Rabbit, in which captives are brought to him for sacrifice. Although his name is clearly calendrical, little else is known about this ruler and his times, as only a few name glyphs and numerals are recorded at El Tajín. The city seems to have suffered a violent end in which sculpture was destroyed and buildings burned, perhaps by invading Totonacs. El Tajín was largely abandoned, and the remnants of the population may have moved south.

The Classic Veracruz style also is represented by a trio of stone implements, all of which seem to be associated with the ball game. These are the *yoke*, the *palma*, and the *hacha*. The *yoke* is a U-shaped stone object, either open or closed at one end, that either represents a ball player belt or actually was worn. Veracruz *yokes* are carved in complex designs representing extended human figures or animals such as toads. *Palmas* are tall, narrow stones, often fan-shaped at the top, that may have been worn with *yokes*. They may be carved in elaborate relief with scroll motifs or human figures, or may take the form of hands or raptorial birds. The *hacha,* or ax (so named because of its shape rather than its function), most often was carved in the form of human heads. Some may have been attached to ball court walls as markers, while others may have functioned in tandem with yokes.

Other important Late Classic centers include Las Remojadas in central Veracruz, known for its hollow clay figurines, some almost life-size, as well as small clay animals on wheels whose function is unknown. Also found here are mold-made figurines with a distinctive smile, perhaps indicative of ecstatic ritual involving pulque or other intoxicants. Some were designed to sit on swings, while others have articulated limbs. The "smiling faces" are widespread in Veracruz, occurring, for example, at Nopiloa in the south, where eggshell-thin fine kaolin (white clay ceramic) examples have been discovered. At nearby El Zapotal, monumental terra-cotta figures, mostly female, as well as smiling figurines, were excavated in association with a mass burial. A large modeled clay shrine featuring a skeletal death god also was found here. A distinctive trait of many of these Veracruz ceramic figures is the use of black asphalt to highlight details, particularly on the face.

The ethnic identity of the occupants of these Classic period sites is not clear, as the current inhabitants are not necessarily their direct descendants. Furthermore, at the time of the Conquest, multiethnic, multilingual communities were common throughout the Veracruz Plains. The Huastec of northern Veracruz and neighboring states speak a form of Maya, but were culturally more like central Mexicans, with whom they maintained strong ties from Teotihuacan times on. Their most significant contributions occurred after A.D. 900 and include a strong tradition of monumental stone sculpture and large numbers of round structures. Such structures, which are also found among the Totonac of central Veracruz, usually are associated with a cult to Quetzalcoatl in his wind god aspect. Cempoala, a large walled city with five temples and an extensive irrigation system, was the major Totonac center and the first Mesoamerican city to be viewed by the Spanish. It was here, in fact, that Fernando (Hernán) Cortés signed the papers authorizing the Conquest of Mexico in 1519, setting in motion a chain of events that eventually would obliterate almost all traces of the Totonac and other Mesoamerican civilizations.

Select Bibliography
Goldstein, Marilyn, editor, *Ceremonial Sculpture of Ancient Veracruz.* Brookville, New York: Long Island University, 1988.
Proskouriakoff, Tatiana, *Varieties of Classic Central Veracruz Sculpture.* Washington, D.C.: Carnegie Institute, 1954.
Stirling, Matthew, "Stone Monuments of the Río Chiquito, Veracruz, Mexico." *Bureau of American Ethnology Bulletin 164, Anthropological Papers* 53 (1955).
Wilkerson, S. Jeffrey K., *El Tajín: A Guide for Visitors.* Xalapa: Museum of Anthropology, 1987.

—VIRGINIA E. MILLER

Mesoamerica: Agriculture and Ecology

The enormous biodiversity of the Mesoamerican territory is one of its most notable characteristics. The culture area defined as Mesoamerica corresponds approximately to an extensive vegetational transition zone called the Neotropical region, situated between north-central Mexico and the Depression of Nicaragua (Map 1). The transitional nature of this zone, together with its broken topography, mainly in Mexico, is the reason for such broad diversity in biological species and their adaptation to particular conditions.

A general way to refer to this environmental diversity is through the use of the concept of natural areas. The scholar R. C. West has differentiated three broad natural areas (Map 2) that summarize the environmental characteristics of Mesoamerica:

1. *Extra-tropical dry lands and adjacent sub-humid areas* of northern Mexico, with clearly differentiated seasonal temperature regimes, large plant "assemblages" needing little water, and landforms associated with arid conditions. This area falls within the Neotropical region.

2. *Cool-tropical highlands,* including the Sierra Madre Occidental and Oriental of Mexico. Oak-conifer forests of North American affinity dominate the area from Mexico to Nicaragua. This area is transitional between the Holartic and Neotropical regions.

3. *Warm-tropical lowlands* of Mexico and Central America, where climate is characterized by high temperatures and year-round frost-free conditions. Tropical plant assemblages vary according to local topography, climate, and soils, ranging from true

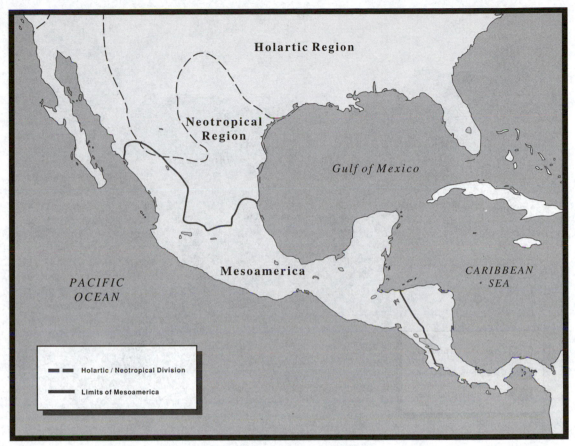

Map 1

lowland rain forest to tropical deciduous woodlands, savanna, and tropical scrub. This division pertains to the Neotropical region.

The northern frontier of the Mesoamerican culture area as originally conceived by the scholar Paul Kirchoff referred to the limit at which rainfall-based agriculture could be successfully practiced, beyond which human communities were dependent largely upon nomadic hunting and gathering of seasonal plant resources. This ecological boundary undoubtedly varied as local climatic conditions fluctuated in response to global trends. It coincides roughly with the division between the extra-tropical drylands and cool-tropical highlands previously defined and with the division between the Holarctic and Neotropical regions.

The southern limit of the culture area coincides approximately with the division between the cool-tropical highlands and the warm-tropical lowlands in the western portions of modern-day Honduras and Nicaragua, where cultural differences among agriculturalists rather than ecological factors provided the basis for differentiating the boundary between Mesoamerican and non-Mesoamerican cultures.

Nonsedentary human groups as well as settled communities occupied and exploited all of the suitable ecological zones available in the temperate or semiarid highlands, tropical lowlands, and coastal, river, and lake habitats. However, archaeological evidence for the specific nature of such adaptations is usually partial and biased, favoring semiarid environments, where preservation conditions are generally better. The independent domestication of plants in Mesoamerica, leading to the origin of agriculture

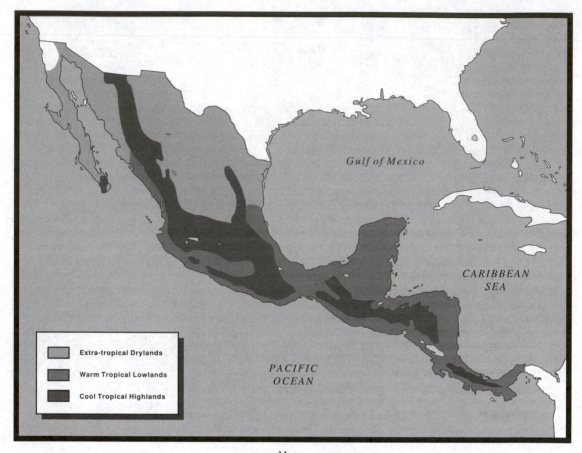

Map 2

and related cultural developments, was undoubtedly a product of such biodiversity.

The concept of symbiosis has been used by some investigators as a way of explaining how the localization of specific resources, available only in certain Mesoamerican subregions, fostered regional specialization and exchange among prehistoric peoples, which in turn propitiated the cultural unity that is the basis of the concept of Mesoamerica as a culture area and the evolution of complex societies in Mesoamerica. In fully developed complex urban societies where a large proportion of the population specialized in nonagricultural activities, local food production was supplemented by additional resources obtained from neighboring regions. Some interregional exchanges may have been strictly "commercial" enterprises, whereas other products came to the urban centers as tribute.

Viewing the environment as a limiting factor, some researchers have attributed the collapse of many spectacular centers in the Maya lowlands, such as Tikal and Uaxactun, to population growth beyond the capacity of the surrounding regions to sustain such large socially stratified communities based on simple agricultural systems. Population growth and consequent resource stress also were invoked as an explanation for the fall of highland centers such as Teotihuacan, where irrigation and other intensive agricultural techniques were thought to be insufficient to provide for a large population, resulting in deforestation and alteration of the hydrological cycle. Regional and even global climatic changes also were invoked periodically as a cause for the decline of Mesoamerican centers.

The results of archaeological research throughout Mesoamerica starting in the late 1960s revealed that the relationship between prehistoric human populations and the natural environment was complex. Archaeological evidence recovered from several regions contributed to the picture of the transition from a hunter-based economy largely dependent upon Pleistocene fauna (i.e., animals present 1.8 million years to 10,000 years ago) to the exploitation of smaller mammals, together with plant gathering, in response to Late Pleistocene climatic change and consequent warming during the Early Holocene (which started 10,000 years ago). In general terms, there appears to have been a long transitional period, perhaps as long as 5,000 years or so, following the adaptation of human groups to modifications in available fauna and flora after the beginning of the global warming that marks the Holocene. During this period dependence upon vegetal resources gradually increased, culminating in the earliest attempts to cultivate certain preferred plants. Some plants ultimately were domesticated, rendering them dependent upon human intervention in order to reproduce successfully. Maize (known scientifically as *Zea mays*) is one of the most well-known examples of this process. Although archaeological data for this transformation are not complete at any of the sites where certain steps in these processes have been documented, it is evident that formerly nomadic groups became increasingly sedentary and experienced population growth as well. The evidence does not necessarily imply that sedentarization is an immediate consequence of plant domestication or the inverse, that sedentary communities were necessary for plant domestication to take place. However, the archaeological record for Mesoamerica does indicate that an increasing number of sedentary communities developed as agricultural activities became increasingly more significant contributors to the subsistence base.

This process suggests that as the exploitation of subsistence resources gave way to their production, ever more intensive demands came to be made on the natural environment. From this early period, human activities had a significant impact on ecological relationships, among biological species and the physical environment. The extent to which this impact was necessarily destructive requires continued investigation.

Domestication of Plants

Mesoamerica is one of several areas in the world where plants were cultivated and domesticated independently, thus providing the basis for the development of agriculturally based societies. It is important to distinguish between cultivation and domestication on the one hand, and agriculture on the other. Cultivation is used here to refer to the intentional planting, care, and harvesting of specific plants that go beyond merely tolerating their presence. It is usually undertaken in order to increase the productivity and, perhaps, the availability of plants that are deemed useful to a society. It does not necessarily imply an attempt to select plants based on favorable characteristics, although such preferences may be a consideration. Cultivation is also appropriate when referring to many plants that are propagated by means of vegetative reproduction. In both cases offspring are genetic replicates of the previous generation, although mutations may occur that, once observed, can be perceived as beneficial to the user. Domestication is used to refer to the conscious process of selecting specific plants with preferred traits and fostering their reproduction in order to produce new generations in which the preferred trait is perpetuated. This process results in plants that ultimately depend upon human intervention in their reproductive cycle (harvesting and subsequent planting) in order to produce the next generation. To use examples from Mesoamerica to illustrate the difference, maguey (the century plant, known scientifically as *Agave* spp.) is cultivated on the basis of manipulation of its vegetative reproductive mechanism that produces offspring essentially identical to the previous generation, whereas domesticated *frijol* (the common bean, or *Phaseolus vulgaris*) manifests certain characteristics not present in its wild progenitors, requiring intentional planting and later harvesting in order to propagate. Finally, agriculture refers to an activity in which cultivated plants are the major component of a society's subsistence base.

A linear progression from plant cultivation to domestication and, finally, to agriculture is too simplistic to explain how these processes developed in prehistoric Mesoamerican societies. However, it is clear that agriculture as the basis for subsistence depends upon the cultivation of specific domesticated plants. Most models describing early agriculture in Mesoamerica and elsewhere usually consider one or sometimes two main domesticated plants as the basis of a society's subsistence economy. Even though diversity in plant use in both regional and seasonal terms has been noted by some researchers, such data are rarely taken into account when the cultural developments associated with early agriculture are considered.

Earlier investigations shared the assumption that the prehistoric communities represented by archaeological vestiges, especially the remains of structures, were fully agricultural societies; however, organic materials indicating what cultivated plants were in fact being used and to what extent agriculture provided subsistence components were seldom visible in archaeological deposits. Most of the archaeological evidence for early plant cultivation and domestication has been found in dry cave sites, where excellent preservation conditions favored organic remains. It was during the late 1960s that suitable techniques for the systematic recovery of plant remains from archaeological soil samples came into use, thus demonstrating the feasibility of comparing frequencies of cultivated and noncultivated wild plants.

Plant cultivation and domestication are considered significant processes for the development of Mesoamerican societies because the inception of such food production is related to a series of sociocultural and economic transformations that are themselves related to increased sedentarism and population growth. Although the botanical evidence currently available from various prehistoric sites suggests that the transition from hunting-gathering to agriculture took place gradually over several millennia, other evidence from isotope analyses of bone collagen from burials dating to the same period may be interpreted as indicating a rather short transitional span between the introduction of domesticated plants, especially maize, and their incorporation into the human diet. As the limiting factors discussed below suggest, more research involving radiocarbon dating of botanical materials as well as additional isotopic studies of early human remains undoubtedly are required in order to clarify this issue.

On the basis of archaeological data from several cave sites in the Mexican states of Tamaulipas, Puebla, and Oaxaca a general scheme for the earliest appearance of certain plants in the prehistoric record can be constructed. However, the following limitations to the interpretation of these data must be kept in mind. First, archaeological plant remains are generally well preserved in exceptionally dry microclimates such as the caves. However, the information from these contexts is not necessarily representative of other kinds of habitation sites (open, semisedentary, or sedentary settlements, for example). The only open site from which early Mesoamerican plant remains have been recovered is Zohapilco, in the southern Basin of Mexico, and there are notable differences in the quality of preservation as well as the genera and species reported as compared to the cave sites. Furthermore, the evidence from cave deposits represents resources available or produced in semiarid highland areas. Plant remains representing subtropical and tropical habitats that were undoubtedly occupied as well by early prehistoric populations are not well known. While it is assumed that root crops were significant food resources, they have left few archaeological traces in Mesoamerica. Finally, it is important to emphasize that the appearance of

domesticated forms of plants in the cave sites should not be interpreted as evidence that the domestication process took place in the same region where such botanical remains have been recovered. Only when clear botanical evidence is present for the transition from specific wild to domesticated forms over time can this process be localized in geographic terms. Archaeological botanical remains representing all of the stages in this process have not been found to date in Mesoamerican sites.

The earliest evidence for hunter-gatherer occupations consists of open campsites, identified on the basis of surface concentrations of particular types of artifacts and, occasionally, hearth remains, and caves or rock shelters where artifacts have been detected together with hearths and floral and faunal materials. Examples include the El Riego Cave in Tehuacán, Puebla (Ajuereado phase, c. 10000–7000 B.C.), Guilá Naquitz in Oaxaca (Naquitz phase, c. 8900–6700 B.C.), as well as caves in southeastern Tamaulipas (Infiernillo phase, 7000–5000 B.C.) and southern Puebla (Texcal I phase, 7000–5000 B.C.).

Gradual population increase is suggested by an increase in the number of sites of this type in addition to specialized camps presumably associated with the seasonal or regional exploitation of specific resources (butchering sites, for example). Cultivated plants and grinding tools begin to make their appearance in the archaeological record around 5000 B.C. in small but apparently semipermanent occupations in rock shelters. Examples of reduced seasonal movements, indicated by faunal and floral remains spanning more than one season, are found in Coxcatlan Cave in Tehuacán (Coxcatlan phase, c. 5000–3400 B.C.) and Gheo-shih in Oaxaca (Jícaras phase, c. 5000–4000 B.C.). In the southern Basin of Mexico during the Playa phase (5500–3500 B.C.), an open site called Zohapilco appears to indicate an incipient sedentary community dependent upon lake resources, hunting, and exploitation of migratory waterfowl as well as plant gathering. None of these areas has revealed evidence for habitational structures before approximately 3000 B.C.

The earliest reported habitation structure in Mesoamerica was uncovered in the Tehuacán Valley and dates to approximately 3000 B.C. (Abejas phase). It consists of a single small oval subterranean feature; no additional structures were located in the area. The period from approximately 3400 to 1500 B.C. is generally considered to be one of increased sedentarism, but seasonal occupation of campsites continued. Zohapilco, which apparently had been abandoned following a volcanic eruption, was resettled around 2500 B.C. (Zohapilco phase) by sedentary agriculturalists who complemented food production with gathered lake resources. Numerous hearths have been associated with this phase, but no clearly defined structures were detected.

Full-fledged villages with rectangular habitational structures appear in the Valley of Oaxaca during the Tierras Largas phase (1400–900 B.C.). The use of cultivated plants and storage facilities suggests an agriculture-based economy by this time. After 900 B.C., grouped villages were established in the Tehuacán and Oaxaca Valleys, with civic ceremonial architecture and an intensified agricultural base supplemented occasionally by irrigation.

Food Production

Although food production does not necessarily involve the cultivation of specifically domesticated plants, these usually are preferable because of their greater yields and other benefits such as sturdier parts that facilitate harvesting by reducing breakage and consequent seed loss. Domesticated grains (such as maize) and so-called pseudo grains (amaranth, for example) also adapt better to storage conditions.

In Mesoamerica food production may have begun very early, as a logical consequence of tolerance of certain edible plants that adapted well to habitats disturbed by human activities. Certain plants may have been brought into settlements, where they were intentionally sown for food or for medicinal or ornamental uses; others found their own way.

The principal plant species that formed the basis of Mesoamerican agricultural systems include maize *(Zea mays)*, beans *(Phaseolus* spp.), squash *(Cucurbita* spp.), chili peppers *(Capsicum* sp.), ground cherry *(Physalis* sp.), and avocado *(Persea americana)*. Different species or varieties were adapted to particular regions. Plants needing little water, such as prickly pear *(Opuntia* spp.) and maguey *(Agave* spp.), were important as well. A large number of additional species also were cultivated, depending upon regional availability and preferences, including amaranth *(Amaranthus* spp.), goosefoot *(Chenopodium berlandieri* spp. *nuttalliae)*, purslane *(Portulaca oleraceae)*, chía *(Salvia* sp.), and numerous fruit trees such as the so-called Mexican cherry *(Prunus capuli)*, hawthorn *(Crataegus mexicana)*, ciruela *(Spondias mombin)*, ramón *(Brosimum alicastrum)*, and palm *(Acrocomia mexicana)*, among many others.

Botanical remains from archaeological sites suggest that regional specializations may have been present from early times. For example, squash (c. 7000 B.C.) and beans (c. 4000–2300 B.C.) seem to have been cultivated before maize in Tamaulipas, whereas maize was earlier in Tehuacán (c. 5000 B.C.) than

elsewhere. On the other hand, squash (specifically *Cucurbita pepo,* c. 8000 B.C.) may have been a very early cultigen (cultivated plant) in the Valley of Oaxaca. The group of plants considered to be basic components of the prehistoric Mesoamerican diet all were represented by cultivated or domesticated forms by around 2000 B.C., although in some cases particular species or varieties were domesticated much later. Our understanding of the chronology of early plant domestication in Mesoamerica (Table 1) undoubtedly will change greatly once the results of ongoing reanalyses of specific botanical materials are available.

In the 1960s scholar R. S. MacNeish attempted to reconstruct the diet of inhabitants of the Tehuacán Valley, Puebla, from the end of the Pleistocene through the beginning of the sixteenth century, using botanical and faunal evidence obtained from radiocarbon-dated archaeological sites. Human coprolites (fossil excrement) provided specific information regarding food consumption, supplemented by historical and ethnographic analogies. According to MacNeish's calculations, these Mesoamericans replaced a large proportion of meat resources with vegetal products over time. This change was related to the decrease in the dependence upon large Pleistocene fauna, in favor of smaller animals (such as rabbits and deer) together with the consumption of gathered wild plant resources. Later the proportion of animal resources declined together with a reduction in wild plants as domesticated species gradually increased in the diet. This process took place over a period of several millennia, and although hunting-gathering activities never ceased completely, agricultural products eventually dominated. Such changes in consumption patterns were associated with archaeological evidence for the change from small nomadic bands to semisedentary and finally sedentary groups within the framework of regional population growth, presumably stimulated by the availability of more reliable food sources and the possibility of sustaining larger, less mobile human groups. Similar patterns are suggested by data from caves in Tamaulipas and Oaxaca, although neither region has produced such a long cultural sequence as Tehuacán.

Agricultural Technology

The distribution of archaeological sites in relation to types of land and their potential agricultural suitability suggests the use of particular techniques, although a large part of the information available about pre-Hispanic agriculture is based on descriptions from sixteenth-century documents. (Some ethnographic examples still exist that substantiate the long

Table 1

Plant Genera	Region			
	Tehuacán Valley	Valley of Oaxaca (Guila Naquitz)	Tamaulipas	Basin of Mexico
Setaria	c. 7000 B.C. (poss. domestic by 6000 B.C.)		c. 3500 B.C.	
Zea mexicana (teosinte)		pollen c. 7400–6700 B.C.		kernels c. 5000 B.C.
Z. mays	c. 5050 B.C. (cobs)		c. 2500 B.C.	pollen c. 5200–2000 B.C.
Cucurbita pepo (squash)	c. 5200 B.C.	c. 8000 B.C.	c. 7000 B.C.	
C. mixta ("cushaw")	c. 5000 B.C.			
C. moschata ("butternut")	c. 4500 B.C. (?)			
Cucurbita sp.				c. 5200–2000 B.C.
Phaseolus sp. (wild runner bean)		c. 8700–6700 B.C.	c. 7000–5500 B.C.	
P. coccineus (scarlet runner bean)	c. 200 B.C.			
P. vulgaris (common bean)	c. 5000–3500 B.C.		c. 4000–2300 B.C.	
P. acutifolius (tepary bean)	c. 3010 B.C.			
Persea americana (avocado)	c. 7200 B.C.			
Capsicum annuum (chile pepper)	c. 6500 B.C. (wild) domestic by c. 4121 B.C.			
Amaranthus sp. (amaranth)	c. 4500 B.C.			c. 5200–2000 B.C. (also Cheno-ams pollen)
Lagenaria (bottle gourd)	c. 5050 B.C.	c. 7000 B.C.	c. 7000 B.C.	
Chenopodium sp.				c. 5200–2000 B.C. (also Cheno-ams pollen)
Sechium sp. (chayote)				c. 5200–2000 B.C.

Source: Emily McClung de Tapia, "The Origins of Agriculture in Mesoamerica and Central America." In *The Origins of Agriculture: An International Perspective*, edited by P. J. Watson and C. W. Cowan. Washington, D.C.: Smithsonian Institution, 1992.

tradition reflected in colonial period descriptions.) Often, archaeological remains of drainage or irrigation canals, dams, or terrace retaining walls would seem to be of pre-Hispanic origin but cannot be dated with confidence as a result of continual reuse or cycles of abandonment, erosion, and subsequent reuse over centuries. In some regions, modern land divisions (such as the household lots or *solares* in Yucatán) may be prehistoric in origin; in most cases such evidence is obscured.

The technology associated with soil preparation, planting, and harvesting was simple, based on the use of a digging stick *(coa)* and a hoe. Human and animal fertilizers were employed in addition to composted vegetal material. Specialized systems such as the *chinampas* (so-called floating fields) also incorporated elements that included mud and vegetation from adjacent canals. Crop rotation may have been practiced in some cases, although the simultaneous planting of complementary species that replaced nutrients depleted from the soil by other plants at the same time was probably more frequent.

The use of more specific technology such as draft animals or the plow did not develop in Mesoamerica, partly because of the absence of animal species of a size and behavior adequate to be domesticated for that purpose, as well as the absence in many areas of large extensions of flat agricultural lands that could be exploited successfully by such techniques. Climatic conditions often favored sloped piedmont plots and simple terraces as more suitable for cultivation, particularly among small self-sufficient communities. This was especially true in higher elevations, where both unpredictable frosts and torrential seasonal rains represented significant threats to crop yields. In some areas, however, irrigation systems or other drainage techniques permitted more effective exploitation of lower elevations.

The social organization of prehistoric agricultural activities is only briefly described in sixteenth-century sources, although some references mention the participation of both men and women and the assistance of children; labors related to land preparation were generally male activities, while planting, weeding, harvesting, and seed selection could be divided or shared depending upon local traditions. Rites were performed in association with different stages of the agricultural cycle to ensure productivity, and these are amply described. The mythical beliefs surrounding human origins and the roots of particular cultural groups also were related closely to critical domesticated plants such as maize. Finally, organized collective labor was undoubtedly required for some kinds of community activities, such

as the construction of terraces or irrigation systems, in addition to civic-ceremonial structures, but there is no clear archaeological evidence beyond the extension of historical analogies to earlier periods.

Ecological Characteristics of Agricultural Systems

Piedmont and forested areas generally were cultivated using different variants of itinerant slash-and-burn cultivation depending upon the climate. Land was cleared and excess vegetation usually burned off, followed by planting. The annual cycle of agricultural activities was programmed according to the variability of factors such as local soil characteristics, potential humidity, slope, temperature, and isolation. Several years of annual planting were followed by a longer period during which the plot was left fallow. In tropical areas, regeneration of vegetation is more rapid, but soil nutrients are not restored until several stages of succession have been completed. Thus, a large area is necessary in order for a farmer to allow enough time for specific plots to recover their fertility. In temperate zones, similar procedures were followed, differing mainly in the number of years during which cultivation was alternated with fallowing. In alluvial plains or suitable flat deep-soil areas, cultivation was continuous, on an annual basis or at more frequent intervals in zones where irrigation could be employed to increase productivity.

In addition to extensive maize plots *(milpas)*, household gardens were undoubtedly important sources of fruits and herbs as well as other edible plants, particularly in dispersed communities and villages. In dense urban settlements, intensive as well as extensive agriculture systems were developed in the surrounding territories.

Slash-and-Burn (Swidden, Milpa, Roza)

This form of cultivation is practiced in tropical areas and consists of cutting down the vegetation within a defined plot, which is then allowed to dry and later burned off. The plot is cultivated for several seasons, after which it is abandoned for a number of years during which the vegetation is allowed to regenerate and natural fertility is restored. Meanwhile, the same process is repeated in another plot. The length of the cultivation period is usually short (1 to 4 years) relative to the amount of fallowing required (10 to 20 years), depending upon specific local conditions. The system requires that a broad area be available for each farmer in order to harvest sufficient maize and other products. It is highly efficient and quite productive when the optimal ratio of cultivation and fallowing is respected and when sufficient land is available to the population.

In ecological terms this technique emulates the biological diversity characteristic of the tropical forest in Mesoamerica through the cultivation of numerous species in a single plot and the succession of vegetative communities during the fallow period. Although it has been branded as a highly destructive practice in modern times because of its relationship to deforestation in tropical areas and the increase of atmospheric carbon dioxide produced as a result of burning off the vegetation, these are largely consequences of modern social, economic, and political factors external to the agricultural system as traditionally practiced.

Barbecho, or Tlacolol
This is similar to slash-and-burn agriculture to the extent that it also involves cutting down the trees, shrubs, and other vegetation in a designated plot, which then are burned off, followed by planting. It is typically employed in cool or temperate zones and differs from the tropical variant insofar as the amount of time required for fallowing. This period is generally shorter in the highlands, and the forest does not regenerate. This type of cultivation is normally rainfall dependent. Like tropical slash-and-burn, it is also extensive in that at any given time most of the total amount of land available to a farmer will be in different stages of fallowing and a large amount of land is necessary in order to sustain each family. The major problem this system has faced is increased population growth, which leads to reductions in the fallowing period and the consequent decrease in soil fertility. Frosts are problematic at higher elevations, and torrential seasonal rains also may pose risks for crops at certain stages of their development. In general terms, *barbecho* is characterized by a lower level of diversity than swidden agriculture, mainly because it is employed primarily for the cultivation of maize at the expense of other crops; however, this practice may be a reflection in part of changes in indigenous agricultural practices following the Conquest.

Many forms of intensive agriculture developed in specific zones where the combination of suitable soils and humidity permitted. In the Río Candelaria Basin and the Río Bec region of Campeche, and the Río Hondo of Quintana Roo, evidence of raised fields and other variants are additional examples of specific agricultural systems designed by the ancient Maya for humidity control in order to maximize productivity. Humidity control undoubtedly was practiced in areas where runoff from rains or nearby seasonal streams could be diverted to hillside plots or terraces. Terrace systems also were utilized widely throughout Mesoamerica, extending from the central highlands to the Maya lowlands.

Irrigation
Irrigation was employed in Mesoamerica as a means of intensifying agricultural production as early as the Formative period (1500 B.C.–A.D. 250). Irrigation took many forms. Its manifestations during pre-Hispanic times varied from the simplest technique that involved directly watering individual plants using jugs filled from wells dug in the fields in Oaxaca or the seasonal divergence of rainwater, to complex systems incorporating permanent canal networks with secondary channels and check dams. Irrigation techniques were dependent upon available water sources including the presence of permanent or seasonal streams, soil characteristics, requirements of particular crops, and the population's needs.

The development of complex irrigation systems in Mesoamerica has been attributed to the need to increase food production as a response to population growth, the need to sustain increasing numbers of nonagricultural specialists in complex societies, and the need to provide surplus agricultural produce to be redistributed as deemed suitable by the society's authority. However, the most important consequence of irrigation is the increase in crop productivity that goes hand in hand with a reduction in the risk of crop loss. In some cases irrigation only provided supplemental humidity for the timely germination of seed, with seasonal rains providing the complement during growth. In other cases, it was employed to facilitate multiple harvests of short-term crops.

Other forms of humidity control, often employed to manage an overabundance of water, also were employed, such as raised fields or drained plots. The *"chinampas"* in the southern Basin of Mexico are one of the most highly specialized examples of humidity control. These rectangular plots at the edges of the lakes were constructed by building up alternating layers of mud and aquatic vegetation from the lake bed itself, anchored by willow trees around the perimeter. Fertility was maintained by periodically dredging the adjacent canals and spreading the mud on the surface of the plot. Similar although not identical procedures were developed in other lake zones such as the Valley of Toluca, the Teotihuacan region, and possibly southwestern Tlaxcala.

The development of several agricultural systems by prehistoric Mesoamerican groups, intensive as well as extensive, reflected a profound familiarity with the natural environment and its diversity. Extensive practices such as slash-and-burn cultivation in the tropical lowlands or its highland variants were used widely throughout the culture area. Intensification took the form of terraces, raised fields, drained fields, and different forms of irrigation adapted to specific regional conditions. The survival of many of these techniques to the present time is a testimony to their success in ecological terms, although their effectiveness has been compromised seriously by socioeconomic factors not directly related to the agricultural systems themselves.

The agricultural techniques developed by pre-Hispanic populations reflect careful management of the components that together constitute the ecological balance of the different regions that were exploited. Although some indications exist of possible overexploitation or inappropriate exploitation of natural resources, their cultural consequences can only be hypothesized. However, most of the available archaeological, ecological, ethnohistorical, and historical data suggest that prehistoric agriculturalists managed to expand and intensify production within the rational limits of total ecological potential, based on their level of technological development.

Perception of the Natural Environment

Archaeological evidence is insufficient for providing a clear view of how prehistoric societies perceived the natural environment, primarily as a source of sustenance but also in more profound ideological terms. With reference to Mesoamerica and, particularly, the central highland region, sixteenth-century historical records document some aspects of this relationship, at least insofar as it was expressed by the Mexica (Aztecs) just prior to the Spanish Conquest. Although these views and associated practices cannot be simply attributed to earlier societies, they probably reflected a long period of cultural development.

Several interrelated beliefs contributed to the perception of humans as an integral part of nature, while simultaneously establishing a sense of recognition and maintenance of an appropriate position with respect to other beings. Every being, animate or inanimate, was believed to possess an essence or internal albeit invisible force. All human action that involved the use of or interaction with other beings or materials invoked their participation as though they, too, were persons. This essence or invisible force, akin to will, possessed by each object or being was personified and viewed as a deity. Thus the relations of humans to other beings and objects constituted an order that guided their conduct toward nature and the rest of society. It was believed that the will of each being or object could be influenced. Therefore offerings, pleas, and prayers were directed to these deities in order to obtain their favor—rain, fertility, fortune, etc. Human perception of all facets of the surrounding environment was based on this order.

Prehistoric populations recognized their dependence upon the products of the earth through their religious beliefs. Agriculture and, particularly, rainfall were major elements of Mesoamerican religion. Many of the agricultural rites mentioned in historical sources attest to a firm recognition of the basic role of domesticated plants (in creation myths, for example), mediated via sacrifices and other offerings to a complex pantheon of deities whose function was to provide fertility and rain and to protect the crops from harm (such as by pests). Similar traditions persist among some modern indigenous groups in Mexico, who associate their ethnic identity with the earth that provides their sustenance through the crops that they tend, and who take great care to offer sacrifices to the appropriate spirits at different stages of the agricultural cycle.

Environmental Alteration in Mesoamerica

All of the agricultural systems previously mentioned represent intentional modifications of the natural landscape and the biological habitats originally present. It is difficult, however, to evaluate the degree of alteration attributable to pre-Hispanic Mesoamerican societies, particularly in the central highland region, mainly because of the significant impact on the landscape that resulted from the introduction of more technologically advanced agricultural techniques after the Spanish Conquest.

During the three centuries of the colonial period, indigenous Mesoamerican society was completely transformed. In spite of the persistence of certain traits tightly linked to pre-Hispanic culture, sooner or later the native population adapted to a new form of organization dictated by the interests of the Spanish Crown and its representatives in the New World. This included the substitution of the native subsistence economy by new crops and agricultural techniques, the introduction of extensive cattle herding, changes in architectural forms, and, especially, different settlement patterns. Colonial authorities did not perceive indigenous practices as logical consequences of adaptive processes, such as plant cultivation and domestication, and intensification on the one hand, and, on the other hand, of the biological relationships among plants (such as the exchange of nutrients among certain cultigens and the symbiotic relations resulting from millennia of associations first as wild species and later as cultigens). The indigenous agricultural systems were overrun in the face of the Spaniards' commercial interests and specific food preferences. New forms of cultivation and distribution of the fruits of the land led to the transformation of the landscape. Many plant species unable to compete with new cultigens or cattle were eliminated, and wild fauna was reduced greatly as a result of the destruction of their habitat.

There is no way of knowing whether indigenous agricultural activities would have ultimately had a similar effect on the landscape in the long run. The difference probably rests in the velocity and, above all, the apparent lack of consciousness on the part of the Spaniards of the impact of colonial modes of exploitation and use of natural resources. The intimate man-nature relationship that characterized the pre-Conquest world, together with the absence of more sophisticated technology (such as metal plows and draft animals) and reinforced by ideology, provided the means by which potentially abusive exploitation of the natural environment was held in check.

See also Cuisine; Maize

Select Bibliography

Byers, D., editor, The Prehistory of the Tehuacán Valley, vol. 1, Environment and Subsistence. Austin: University of Texas Press, 1967.

Farnsworth, P. J., E. Brady, M. J. DeNiro, and R. S. MacNeish, "A Re-Evaluation of the Isotopic and Archaeological Reconstructions of Diet in the Tehuacán Valley." American Antiquity 50 (1985).

Flannery, K. V., "The Origins of Agriculture." Annual Review of Anthropology 2 (1973).

_____, editor, Guilá Naquitz: Archaic Foraging and Early Agriculture in Oaxaca, Mexico. New York: Academic Press, 1986.

_____, K. V., A. V. T. Kirkby, M. J. Kirkby, and A. W. Williams Jr., "Farming Systems and Political Growth in Ancient Oaxaca." Science 158 (1967).

Joyce, A. A., and R. G. Mueller, "The Social Impact of Anthropogenic Landscape Modification in the Rio Verde Drainage Basin, Oaxaca, Mexico." Geoarchaeology 7:6 (1992).

Kirchoff, P., "Mesoamérica." Acta Americana 1:1 (1943).

Long, A., B. Benz, D. Donahue, A. Jull, and L. Toolin, "First Direct AMS Dates on Early Maize from Tehuacán, Mexico." Radiocarbon 31:3 (1989).

MacNeish, R. S., "A Summary of the Subsistence." In The Prehistory of the Tehuacán Valley, vol. 1, Environment and Subsistence, edited by D. Byers. Austin: University of Texas Press, 1967.

McClung de Tapia, Emily, "The Origins of Agriculture in Mesoamerica and Central America." In The Origins of Agriculture: An International Perspective, edited by P. J. Watson and C. W. Cowan. Washington, D.C.: Smithsonian Institution, 1992.

O'Hara, S., F. A. Street-Perrott, and T. P. Burt, "Accelerated Soil Erosion around a Mexican Highland Lake Caused by Pre-Hispanic Agriculture." Nature 362 (1993).

Sanders, W. T., "The Central Mexican Symbiotic Region." In Prehistoric Settlement Patterns in the New World, edited by G. Willey. New York: Viking 1956.

Sanders, W. T., and B. J. Prices, Mesoamerica: The Evolution of a Civilization. New York: Random House, 1968.

Smith, C. E., Jr., "Plant Remains." In The Prehistory of the Tehuacán Valley, vol. 1, Environment and Subsistence, edited by D. Byers. Austin: University of Texas Press, 1967.

West, R. C., "The Natural Regions of Middle America." In Handbook of Middle American Indians, vol. 1, edited by R. C. West. Austin: University of Texas Press, 1964.

—EMILY McCLUNG DE TAPIA

Mesoamerica: Calendrics

A complex calendrical system was one of the most central features of early Mesoamerican culture, continuing even today. Its importance cannot be overemphasized. Calendrical specialists still live in many parts of Mesoamerica, calculating the needs of their patrons with a system that is probably over 26,000 years old. In earlier times, the calendrical system calculated more than the passing days; it also ruled much of life. One did almost nothing important without first determining its calendrical meaning; the system calculated every ritual, major and minor, and helped shape one's actions, even one's personality. Calendrical calculations wove the fiber of existence.

The earliest recorded calendrical date may be an Olmec glyph from Cuicuilco (Valley of Mexico), which in the Julian calendar probably is September 2, 679 B.C. Other early dates from the sixth century B.C. have been found in the Zapotec area (Oaxaca), and the Maya Long Count may have been inaugurated by the Olmec (in the Gulf region) in 355 B.C. All these dates must be considered provisional, since correlating Mesoamerican calendars with European is made problematic by an often incomplete record; such correlations are hotly debated for good reason.

From these very early beginnings, several basic calendrical patterns emerged. All were based on a count of 20 days, although each had many local variations. Every city or area developed its own version because the calendar was governed by the movements of celestial objects as they appeared above the distinctive geography of an area's horizon. The conquering Spanish destroyed certain calendrical rounds because they regulated state rituals; local versions remained in use in communities across Mesoamerica, allowing many to function today. Briefly exploring the calendar's significance and mechanics will help weave an introduction to this amazingly intricate tapestry.

The Calendar's Significance

To understand calendrical systems, one must understand the worldviews underlying them. Mesoamerican cosmoses were inhabited by a huge variety of beings. Everything—deities, people, animals, plants, even cities, mountains, and ages—was considered alive because everything embodied multifarious powers that animated existence, giving each being its particular identity and purpose. Calendars ordered and controlled the motions of these embodied powers according to a logic born from life itself. If things are alive, they move; if they move, they are timed; and if they are timed, they can be calculated. Calendars shaped existence because, by carefully calculating the motions of the cosmos's living things, one could account for and, with some skill and luck, even control life.

Transformative change governed much of existence. Beings were born, grew, aged, died, and decayed; all these temporal transformations created new moments and circumstances. Calendrical systems helped control such transformative changes. Hence everything from the changes a birth thrust upon a family to the transforming of a dead ruler's power into that of his successor was shaped by calendrical forces. Calendars gave people a way to manipulate life's events.

As the tools that controlled transformation, calendars served multiple purposes. These ranged from a farmer's need to calculate the seasons to a ruler's desire to manipulate the most propitious moments for battle or diplomacy. Events both large and small—birth, illness, death, earth's fertility, the sky's motions—all were calculated and ordered by calendrics. People's personal identities were tied to these temporal calculations, for a calendrical name given at birth gave a child positive and negative personality-forming powers. These powers could be altered by numerous forces, including the child's own deeds, things that happened to the child on certain potent days, and various calendrically linked rituals that might enhance the child's abilities.

A special sense of historical time also was calendrically manipulated. Sequential year counts kept track of a city's official history. Such records were tied directly to elite ancestry and began with deities who created and blessed the line, giving it special powers. Sometimes, a history was not recorded when another city controlled it; such was the case with the Maya Long Count. This count recorded Maya mythic origins, elite ancestry, their deeds, and cities'

events. All Long Counts disappeared when those cities collapsed at the end of the Classic period (A.D. 250–900); they no longer were needed, for the calendrical powers of royal lineages also had collapsed.

Computing time could control tremendous powers affecting existence. One used calendrics to structure a child's future. If Maya royal lineages could not record their history, they could not draw on the calendrical forces animating their hegemony. Mexica royalty rewrote their history by reformulating their calendar; they did this to manipulate calendrical powers better. This was more than checking past calculations; by changing how they coordinated historical with celestial events, they altered their past, present, and future realities.

Full knowledge of the complex calendrical mechanics probably was held only by specialists. Today the Maya Ixil (in Guatemala) have three such specialists: an elected priest, who determines the time for communal and civil ceremonies; prayer-sayers, who intervene on behalf of the sick; and day keepers or diviners, who help people determine life's path. In earlier times, even the most humble peasants comprehended rudimentary calendrics. Like the elite, they needed to manipulate their lives' events. Calendrics both accounted for and offered control over all existence, from a child's personality to a ruler's hegemony.

The Calendar's Mechanics

One must recognize how different Mesoamerican calendrics are from Western ones to understand them. The familiar European calendar is a simple affair that stresses uniformity. First, only one calendar round governs all activities from train departures to geological ages and from marriages to the creation and demise of the solar system. Second, this calendar is calculated by the motions of only one celestial object, the sun. Third, because the European calendar tracks only the sun's motions, it counts the moments linearly, as though they were beads on a rope. Everyone rises, eats, works, plays, and sleeps according to the sun's moments: its seconds follow seconds, days upon days, years upon years, and so on. Moment by moment, time irrevocably marches on, never turning back, never doubling over or overlapping. The sun was born once many moments ago and eventually will wear out and die many moments from now. In the meantime each person's life ticks on in the span of moments allotted it. Often, one can ignore the clock ticking away. On Saturday mornings, one may not set the clock. By concentrating on one's youth, one can pretend one's own clock is not set. And by meditating on eternity or beautifully timeless values, one might even eliminate the clock.

But mathematics structured almost everything in Mesoamerica. Its clocks were neither simple nor uniform, and they demanded attention. First, Mesoamerican calendrics calculated life's events according not only to one but numerous calendar rounds. The 365-day solar count often governed high state rituals and elite histories. A divinatory calendar of 260 days, which functioned similarly to Western astrology, governed everyday events such as marriages and business deals. Second, Mesoamericans accounted for not just one or even two, but numerous celestial cycles. The sun's was most important because it gave the days. Intertwined with the 365-day count were also counts of Venus, Mars, constellations, probably the moon, and perhaps other celestial objects now lost to the modern world.

Third, because numerous calendars functioned simultaneously, their moments of conjunctions and disjunctions were key. Moments did not simply line up like beads on a rope. Instead they arranged themselves more like the rope itself in which various fibers of differing lengths are spun together, now some overlapping and others not, now others overlapping that had not. Calendrical time spirals around and around, like the rope turning back or doubling over on itself, its fibers now meshing, now not. No sector of the rope was ever exactly like a previous sector. Calendrical mathematics was like a complicated musical round spinning out its song with many parts in ever-changing harmony. At one time the sopranos and tenors sang their particular lines; at another, the tenors, altos, and basses; later, sopranos, contraltos, and tenors; and so on. Each voice repeated its simple tune as though it were singing alone, yet all these tunes merged and diverged in complicated patterns, each according to the same, never faltering metronomic beat of the days.

Many scholars describe Mesoamerican calendrics as cyclical, but they probably were more complex than that. Time did not just move around until it came back to its beginning; that shape is not very different from European time, for it is like a rope of beads joined into a circle. Instead, time moved in simultaneously progressive and repetitive patterns, more like the many-fibered spiraling rope. During rituals, one collapsed many particular past moments (or fibers) into a single moment (or rope sector) in order to activate all those moments' powers in the present, which then could affect the future. When a child was named at a propitious moment after birth, she or he gained all the powers of the various calendrical strands converging at that point in time. For a Nahua baby, these would include the powers of her or his birth year; one or more deities governing the

13-day week of the divinatory round in which it was born; that week's cardinal direction, color, tree, and bird; the forces of the week's divinatory signs; and those of the day's and night's lords. All these calendrical powers helped the child shape its personality and future by suggesting things like possible characteristics (weak, brave, nervous, honest) or occupation (weaver, warrior, ruler).

Mythically, present moments stretched back, picking up all the powers of those particular years, deities, and days of times past; this was like tying all the same points together on a coil of rope. The binding constituted a unique meshing of numerous past moments, just as the binding of all those points on the rope's coil bound a number of unique sets of fibers. The present moment contained past moments but was identical to no other moment that ever existed or would exist. And because the present could be picked up by future moments, it could affect what would come.

Maya Calendrics

A count of 20 days founded all Mesoamerican calendrical rounds. Each day bore a name and was associated with a deity. The most basic calendrical round was the divinatory calendar. Called the Tzolkin in Yucatec Maya, its age is long and its origin obscure; suggestions range from a lunar cycle, to childbirth, the length of the rainy season, or the period between zenith passages of the sun. The Tzolkin consisted of 20 "weeks" of 13 days each ($20 \times 13 = 260$). The 20 days spun with a count of numbers from 1 to 13. Maya numerical notations used dots for single numbers (one dot for 1, two dots for 2, etc.) and bars for counts of five. Hence a bar and two dots meant seven ($5 + 2 = 7$). In the Tzolkin, the 20-day count and the 13-number count meshed as follows: 1-Imix (day 1 of the 20-day cycle) might be the first day of a week; 2-Ik (day 2), the second; 3-Akbal (day 3), the third; and so on until 13-Ben (day 13) is reached. Then the numbered count starts over but the 20-day count continues with 1-Ix (day 14). When the 20-day count finishes with 7-Ahau (day 20), it starts over with 8-Imix (day 1). After 20 weeks pass, the Tzolkin begins again.

The Haab, or solar round, is the second most basic. This round determined a yearly series of state rituals focused on the agricultural and warring seasons. It is made up of 18 "months," each consisting of one 20-day count, plus an additional period of 5 days, which was considered dangerous and not officially noted ($[18 \times 20] + 5 = 365$). As with the 20 days, each month was identified by a name. A larger cycle of 18,980 days, called the Calendar Round, consisted of the Tzolkin and Haab spinning together (73 × 260 or 52 × 365 = 18,980).

While all of Mesoamerica used some version of the 20-day count, 13-number count, and divinatory and solar calendars, only the Maya used the Long Count. It consisted of 5 counts: *kin* (1 day); *uinal* (20 days); *tun* (18 *uinals* or 360 days); *katun* (20 *tuns* or 7,200 days); and *baktun* (20 *katuns, 400 tuns,* or 144,000 days). The Long Count used these units to record the number of days that had elapsed since the beginning of a Great Cycle, a count of 13 *baktuns.* Dates were carved into monuments from top to bottom and are conventionally written like so: 9.0.19.2.4.

9	baktuns:	9 ×	144,000 =	1,296,000
0	katun:	0 ×	7,200 =	0
19	tuns:	19 ×	360 =	6,840
2	uinals:	2 ×	20 =	40
4	kins:	4 ×	1 =	4

$$1,302,884$$

This date occurred 1,302,884 days after the beginning of its Great Cycle.

Because a date could be fixed so absolutely, the Long Count was used for the Maya elite histories. An abridged version of the Long Count was used after it disappeared with the Classic elite. This round, the Short Count, measured time's passing only in terms of *katuns.* A round of 13 *katuns* lasted approximately 256 vague years (13 × 7,200 days).

Central Highland Calendrics

The calendrical systems from the central Mexican highlands included variations on all but the Long and Short Counts. Instead of bars and dots, Nahua peoples marked the 13-number count with only dots. The divinatory calendar was called the Tonalpohualli. Two additional counts were calculated in this version of the 260-day round, 13 Day Lords and 9 Lords of the Night. The Night Lords apparently held preeminence in Nahua calendrics not accorded them by the Maya. Lacking a Long Count to fix dates, the Nahua Night Lords may have stepped in to fill the gap. Although this theory is still contested, they appear to have been the odd count that always countered all the Calendar Round's other perfectly even counts, causing their calculations never fully to mesh. This meant that each date might be pinpointed exactly.

The Calendar Round gained extreme importance in the Postclassic period (A.D. 900–1521). Every 52 years when the solar round, the Xiuhmolpilli, and the Tonalpohualli ended together, the Binding of the Years ceremony occurred. This sacrificial rite took place on a hill overlooking Tenochtitlan, the Mexica capital. Because it occurred in November when the Pleiades were at their zenith, the ceremony marked both the beginning of the dry season and the approaching nadir of the sun. All fires were extinguished in the entire domain, houses swept clean, and old clothing and household goods thrown away. At midnight, a fire was sparked on the chest of a human offering. His heart was cut out and fed to the fire, which consumed his whole body. It was believed that, if the fire were lighted, a new sun would rise; if not, all would disappear into darkness.

The Calendar Rounds accumulated to create five ages called suns. Although there were five suns, together they were calculated in four rounds of 676 years each (13 × 52 = 676). Each sun was named for the agent of its destruction: 4-Jaguar, 4-Wind, 4-Fire Rain (volcanic action), 4-Water, and 4-Movement (earthquakes). The Mexica lived in the fifth. A failed Binding of the Years would herald its end. But in spite of calendrics' apparent precision, the end might not be imminent, for calendrical history could be reformulated.

Manipulating life's events by restructuring how human events coordinated with temporal was what calendrics were all about. If the purpose of Mesoamerican calendrical systems was to control multifarious powers, thereby controlling the quality of existence, calendrical calculations were the tools for doing that. Calendars were not rigid, fating people to unchangeable existence. They not only provided maps used as guidance through life's journey, manipulating calendrics even could shape the very terrain through which one traveled.

Select Bibliography

Aveni, Anthony F., *Empires of Time: Calendars, Clocks, and Cultures.* New York: Basic Books, 1989.

Caso, Alfonso, "Calendrical Systems of Central Mexico." In *Handbook of Middle American Indians,* vol. 10, edited by Robert Wauchope. Austin: University of Texas Press, 1971.

Durán, Fray Diego, *Book of the Gods and Rites and the Ancient Calendar,* translated by Doris Heyden and Fernando Horcasitas. Norman: University of Oklahoma Press, 1971.

Edmonson, Munro S., *The Book of the Year: Middle American Calendrical Systems.* Salt Lake City: University of Utah Press, 1988.

Sahagún, Fray Bernardino de, *The Florentine Codex: A General History of the Things of New Spain,* translated by Arthur J. O. Anderson and Charles E. Dibble. Santa Fe, New Mexico, and Salt Lake City: School of American Research and University of Utah, 1953–82.

Satterthwaite, Linton, "Calendrics of the Lowland Maya." In *Handbook of Middle American Indians,* vol. 3, edited by Robert Wauchope. Austin: University of Texas Press, 1965.

Tedlock, Barbara, *Time and the Highland Maya.* Albuquerque: University of New Mexico Press, 1982.

—KAY A. READ

Mesoamerica: Population

The peopling of Mexico is one of the most complex phenomena in Mexican prehistory. Perhaps because of this it is also one of the most prolifically studied and controversial. When did humans first appear in the Mexican subcontinent? Did the emergence of agriculture spark demographic revolution? What was the role of demographic pressure in the decay and collapse of many of the great cultural centers, such as La Venta, El Tajín, Cuicuilco, Teotihuacan, Tula, and elsewhere? At first contact with Europeans, were native populations under a Malthusian threat of exceeding the limits of the carrying capacity of the land, or had they achieved harmonious balance with the environment? Answers to these questions are fundamental for understanding the evolution of ancient Mexican culture, politics, society, and economy.

The Asian origins of the first humans in the Americas is universally accepted among Mesoamerican archaeologists, but considerable disagreement persists over the date of first origins—ranging from 20,000 to 70,000 years ago—as well as whether there were one, two, three, or even more migration "waves." The dating of ancient habitational sites is also highly speculative. Human habitation at El Cedral in San Luis Potosí has been placed at 30,000 years ago. Sites at Valsequillo and Tlapacoya are dated to 22,000 years ago. An intensive study of the Tehuacán Valley reveals continuous human occupation from 12,000 years ago.

The Tehuacán Valley site offers a fascinating sequence, however speculative, of habitational densities from remote antiquity to the moment of European contact. From 9,000 to 7,000 years ago demographic densities in the valley averaged some 2.2 inhabitants per 100 square kilometers (39 square miles). Later, as squash seeds and tiny cobs of corn first appear in the archaeological record—2,000 years after the emergence of corn pollen in the Valley of Oaxaca—densities drift upward, increasing sixfold over the next 3,000 years (averaging 14 inhabitants per 100 square kilometers from 5,400 to 4,300 years ago). Millennia pass, as the agricultural revolution continued. With the development of irrigation (2,900 to 2,100 years ago), population growth slowly accelerates and densities swell, from 43 inhabitants per 100 square kilometers (3,000 years ago) to 165 (2,500 years ago) and 1,100 (2,100 to 1,300 years ago). Two thousand years were required for a 25-fold increase in population. In the final phase (1,300 to 500 years ago), in the 800 years preceding contact with Europeans, population densities expanded threefold to some 3,600 inhabitants per 100 square kilometers, fortified towns developed, and "despotic primitive states" took root.

The greatest demographic success in Mesoamerica is found in the Central Mexican Basin. The scholars W. T. Sanders, J. R. Parsons, and R. S. Santley studied more than 3,600 habitation sites to develop a valuable series of population estimates stretching over three millennia. They show the population of the Teotihuacan Valley growing from fewer than 5,000 inhabitants 3,500 years ago to some 1 to 1.2 million in the year 1519. Three long cycles of growth stand out (3,500 to 2,100 years ago, 1,850 to 1,250 years ago, and 850 to 500 years ago), punctuated by two periods of decline (2,100 to 1,850 years ago and 1,250 to 850 years ago). Region-wide decline is explained at times by exogenous factors—a cooling climate or severe seismic activity—and at others by endogenous developments or lack thereof, such as population pressure, economic decay, or political disintegration.

Population estimates by Sanders and colleagues are displayed in Figure 1. If one discounts the most recent and as yet incomplete phase, the graph exhibits three growth cycles at intervals of roughly 1,000 years: 2,500 years ago, 1,500 years ago, and 500 years ago. The graph also shows how—before the cataclysm of 1519—tiny rates of change, averaging less than plus or minus 0.4 percent per year over many centuries, yield substantial shifts in population size and density. Thus, the agricultural "revolution," a multi-millennial process beginning 5,000 years ago, led to a quickening of population growth in Tehuacán, Teotihuacán, Oaxaca, Pátzcuaro, and elsewhere, but no "demographic revolution," although archaeologists interpret the same data to mean a "demographic explosion." Even when prehistoric growth rates reach their peak in the Central Mexican Basin, just 750 years ago, the increase scarcely averages 0.75 percent per year. Figure 1 shows that this region has had only one demographic revolution and it occurred in the twentieth century, when annual growth exceeded 2 percent. As of the mid-1990s, revolution already had begun winding down. By the middle of the next millennium, the twentieth-century growth spurt may resemble one of the demographic swells of the Paleolithic past.

Regional trends summarize myriad local experiences, fruitfully documented in the Teotihuacan Valley study. They show how difficult it was to win at demographic roulette in ancient Mexico. The pioneering bioarchaeologist Frank Saul suggests that we may be asking the wrong question about the decline of Mesoamerican cities, cultures, or peoples. The question should be "not *why* they declined, but rather, *how* they managed to survive for so long." The bioarchaeological record discloses that Mesoamerican populations (indeed, most ancient populations) were fragile, weakened by stress, poor nutrition, and ill-health. The old notion of strong, healthy populations in Mesoamerica—a pre-Columbian paradise—is poorly supported by the evidence. Ethnohistorical interpretations highlight the success stories, but ethnohistorical sources still await demographically informed skeptical scrutiny.

Physical and physiological stress seems ubiquitous in Mesoamerica, although somewhat less so than among most peoples in northern North America. Osteoarthritis (degenerative bone disease), likely the result of extreme physical exertion, is present in adult skeletal remains from 5,000 years ago in the Tehuacán Valley. High rates of healed fractures, severe dental wear, and advanced osteophytosis (the formation of bony extrusions) are common in the earliest skeletal remains. Tuberculosis and treponemal infections (forms of syphilis and yaws), date from 3,000 years ago. Also common are coral-like lesions on the crania (porotic hyperostosis and cribra orbitalia), severe physiological responses to acute or chronic anemia resulting from nutritional deficiencies, extreme parasitic infestation, debilitating infection, blood loss, or some combination of these. The architectural grandeur of Chichen Itza contrasts starkly with the physiological poverty of its population, which suffered from hard labor, illness, infections,

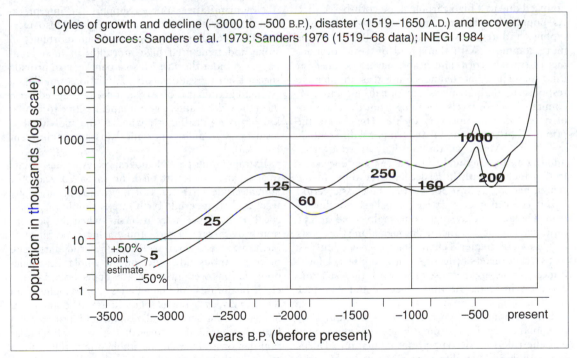

Cyles of growth and decline (−3000 to −500 B.P.), disaster (1519–1650 A.D.) and recovery
Sources: Sanders et al. 1979; Sanders 1976 (1519–68 data); INEGI 1984

Figure 1
Population of the Basin of Mexico across the Millennia

To take error into account, point estimates have been bracketed by smoothed curves at ±50%. The logarithmic scale is used to accurately portray rates of growth and decline for each period. To place colonial and postcolonial figures in perspective, Sander's estimates from historical sources for population decline in the Central Mexican Basin from 1520 to 1568 have been added to the graph, pieced with estimates of total population from a nadir in 1610, followed by recovery to 1793, 1900, and 1990.

and severe malnutrition. A tally from a group of 752 adult Mesoamerican skeletons reveals women with higher rates of facial fractures than men (gender abuse?) and more degenerative joint disease of the wrists (repetitive stress from the arduous labor of preparing tortillas?). Spines of adults of both sexes show severe degenerative wear, averaging 40 percent or more at Jaina, Tlatilco, Cholula, and Copan. The lesson learned from these skeletons is that whenever the human body was the principal means of moving heavy burdens, it paid a strenuous biological cost. Hard, repetitive work exacted severe wear on Mesoamerican bodies of both sexes, particularly joints required for mobility, manipulation of objects, and bearing loads.

Conditions scarcely improved with the multimillennial agricultural "revolution." From Black Mesa Pueblo in the arid northwest to Copan in the humid southeast, the emergence of agriculture reduced dental degeneration caused by the wear and tear of consuming foraged foods, but life-threatening caries, abscesses, and tooth loss became more pronounced due to a high carbohydrate corn-based diet. As populations became more sedentary, diarrhea, typhus, and region-wide famine probably became more common. With the spread of a monotonous diet of squash, corn, and beans, stature declined, at least for males. Shortening stature was an adaptive response to malnutrition, undernutrition, and concomitant disease levels, resulting from the adoption of a settled, neolithic way of life. These were the primary causes of regional and temporal differentials in stature. Males in the north, subsisting from hunting and gathering, averaged 165 centimeters (5 feet, 5 inches) with little decline over time. In the center, average stature for men in the classic period fell to 160 centimeters (5 feet, 3 inches). Southward from Oaxaca, the average adult male stood at 155 centimeters (5 feet, 1 inch), although along the coasts heights were greater. Female stature, averaging 145 to 155 centimeters (4 feet, 9 inches to 5 feet, 1 inch) is more perplexing because there was little systematic variation in space or time (McCaa and Marquez Morfín, 1995).

Paleodemography corroborates the findings of paleopathology. Extraordinarily low life expectancy was the rule for Mesoamerican populations. Paleodemographers favor life expectancy at birth as the measure of choice, but this indicator should be discounted because only extraordinary burial practices and exceptionally thorough recovery techniques will yield representative samples of infants and young children. At most sites (Teotihuacán is an important exception), too few skeletons of infants and children

are recovered to be credible, and paleodemographers' estimates of life expectancy at birth are greatly inflated. The ethnohistorian B. R. Ortiz de Montellano puts life expectancy at birth for the Mexica (Aztecs) at 38 years. A more somber picture emerges when we examine life expectancies at older ages (see Table 1). At age 15, Mesoamerican life expectancies are extremely low, ranging from 13 to 29 additional years of life. In other words, for those surviving to age 15, death came at age 28 to 44. These estimates are well below national figures for Mexico in 1940 (when a 15-year-old could expect an additional 43 years of life, or death at age 58) or 1980 (when a 15-year-old could expect an additional 56 years of life, or death at age 71), even below the worst conditions in model life tables (which contain mortality patterns that cover the range of experiences of historical populations with life expectancies at birth from 20 to 80 years), such as Coale and Demeny's Region South level 1 (in which a 15-year-old could expect to live an additional 34 years, to age 49, and the life expectancy at birth is only 20 years).

Nonquantitative sources support the interpretation that mortality was extremely high in Mesoamerica. The Mexica sculpted signs of high morbidity in stone and structured high mortality in their language. Consider the vast Mexica pantheon to provide succor from a great diversity of afflictions and illness. Nahuatl grammar is obsessed, indeed burdened, with mortality. Why add a grammatical suffix to affinal kin terms to distinguish whether the individual is dead or alive unless mortality was an omnipresent hardship?

Extrapolating paleodemographic estimates points to life expectancies at birth of 15 to 20 years, or annual crude birth rates of 67 to 50 (demography teaches that the crude birth rate is simply the reciprocal of life expectancy at birth—when the population growth rate is zero, thus, a life expectancy at birth of 20 becomes $1/20 = .05$, or a crude birth rate of 50 per thousand). Since on the whole these paleopopulations were growing, the upper bound of the crude birth rate could be set a few points higher than 67, at, say, 75 births per thousand population. Students of modern populations would dismiss these figures as impossible. Nevertheless, a simple simulation demonstrates that the stable population with a crude birth rate of 70 and a growth rate of 0.5 percent per year corresponds to a total fertility rate (TFR, the synthetic mean for mothers who survive to menopause) of 8.8 children. According to the 1990 Mexican census, women aged 50 to 54 with no schooling averaged 7.5 children (computed from the 1 percent national sample). This figure is not the

Table 1
Mean Age at Death from Selected Ages:
Mesoamerican precontact populations and others at various economic-technological levels

	Mean age at death (years)		
From Age:	0	15	50
Tlatilco (2930–3250 BP)[1]	32	37	54
La Ventanilla (350–950)[1]	36	40	54
Cholula (850–1560)[1]	29	35	54
Copán rural (700–1000)[1]	25	44	60
Copán urban (700–1000)[1]	36	41	57
Teotihuacan (early Classic)[2]	24	42	58
Teotihuacan (late Classic)[2]	16	34	66
Teotihuacan (1580–1620)[2]	13	28	52
Cholula (1325–1520)[1]	25	34	51
North American Indians[1]	22	35	55
Hunter-gatherers[1]	22	37	63
Primitive agriculturalists[1]	26	45	68
Model life table (South level 1)[1]	20	49	65
Mexico, 1939–41[1]	40	58	70

Note: Calculations are based on conventional paleodemographic assumptions: skeletal remains are a random sample of deaths for the population studied; the population is closed (migration is nil) and static (crude birth and death rates are balanced, and the rate of population change is zero). Under these conditions, the mean age at death from age x is equivalent to life expectancy at that age.

Sources: [1]McCaa and Marquez Morfín, 1995; [2]Storey, 1992.

maximum because many of these women were not in stable unions nor did they begin child-bearing at the youngest possible age. We need look back only to the nineteenth century to find women meeting this standard, or nearly so. An average total fertility rate of 8.5 children was found by two carefully documented studies of Tzeltal-speakers of Amatenango (Chiapas) and the Euromestizo elite of Mexico City (cited in McCaa, 1993).

Even with a life expectancy at birth as low as 16 years, a high-fertility paleopopulation could grow at 0.5 percent per year. The age structure would be young, with 40 percent of the population under 15 years of age and 90 percent under 50. No paleodemographer or population historian has ever proposed such a frightful scenario for Mesoamerica. Yet these conditions are possible, in fact plausible, given the mortality evidence. To reach an 8.8 total fertility rate, assuming birth intervals averaged 36 months, 26.4 years of child-bearing are required (with the first birth occurring three years after copulation begins). Since menopause occurs near age 40 or 45, girls would have to marry close to the age of puberty, at say 15 years. This is exactly what we find in the earliest extant documentary evidence.

Europeans were surprised by the custom of child marriage among the indigenes. Viceroy Martín Enrí-

quez de Almanza's observation, written in 1577, is typical: "being the custom in the time of their paganism to marry almost at birth because no girl reached the age of twelve without marrying." The extraordinary life histories in the *Codex Mendoza* depict marriage occurring at age 15 and babies being weaned at age 3 (rationed to one-half tortilla, rising to one whole tortilla at age 4, and two from age 13). In "natural fertility" populations, weaning typically anticipates conception—when not actually precipitated by the birth of a new baby to be suckled. In the 1530s and 1540s, for rural Nahuas in Huitzillan and Quauhchichinollan near Yautepec, Morelos, average female age at marriage (defined as co-residing couples) is estimated at 12.7 years (McCaa, 1996). Data for this population of 2,500 reflect authentically indigenous practices because the "spiritual conquest" scarcely had begun in this region. Only one Catholic marriage (versus almost 800 native unions) appears in this manuscript written on fig bark "paper" in Nahuatl by native scribes. The document divulges an obsession with fertility, or better infertility, with scribes noting not only the names and ages of offspring but also, for each couple who had no offspring, the number of years of marriage. The ancient Nahuas were passionate pronatalists. Sterility was a truly deadly sin, leading to the sacrifice of infecund couples, who "served only to occupy the world and not increase it."

Mexica civilization, the most successful in Mesoamerica, survived, indeed thrived, by means of a high-pressure demographic system—high mortality and higher fertility with growth rates triple those of most paleopopulations, but less than one-third post-Revolutionary Mexico's pace of 2 to 3 percent per year (1930–90). The Mexica demographic logic can be seen as the triumph of many unconscious population experiments leading to a system of reproduction that worked over the long run. The fate of most small paleopopulations was extinction (or migration, which in the archaeological record looks much alike). The loss of a reliable water supply, an outbreak of botulism, hemorrhagic fever or life-threatening diarrhea, a lengthy period of sterility or a low birth rate, an out-of-kilter sex ratio, the exhaustion of food resources—paleodemographic roulette was unforgiving.

The agricultural revolution improved the odds of winning, allowed for greater demographic densities, and led to the growth of towns, cities, and city-states. Paradoxically, mortality may have worsened with higher urban densities, but opportunities for successful mating probably improved—thanks to a greater range of possible pairings. Population pressure was not the inevitable outcome. Although by 1500 demographic densities around Lake Pátzcuaro probably exceeded the long-term carrying capacity of the area, in the Central Basin technological innovations, the expansion of *chinampa* agriculture, improved grain transport and storage, and even warfare provided relief from the Malthusian threat. From 1519, with the intrusion of European aliens, catastrophe ensued with the death of millions from disease, exploitation, and warfare. Although the Mexica demographic regime was destabilized, it was not destroyed. Three centuries later, as the Spanish colonial regime expired, the demography of native people was more akin to pre-conquest than to post-colonial conditions.

Select Bibliography

MacNeish, R. S., *The Prehistory of the Tehuacan Valley.* Austin: University of Texas Press, 1967.

_____, "Social Implications of Changes in Population and Settlement Patterns of 12,000 Years of Prehistory in the Tehuacan Valley of Mexico." In *Population and Economics,* edited by P. Deprez. Winnipeg: University of Manitoba Press, 1970.

_____, *The Origins of Agriculture and Settled Life.* Norman: University of Oklahoma Press, 1992.

McCaa, Robert, "The Peopling of 19th Century Mexico: Critical Scrutiny of a Censured Century." *Statistical Abstract of Latin America* 30 (1993).

_____, "Marriageways in Mexico and Spain, 1500–1900." *Continuity and Change* 9:1 (1994).

_____, and Lourdes Marquez Morfín, "Paleodemography, Nutrition and Health in Ancient Mexico," unpublished paper presented at the Social Science History Association annual meeting (November 16, 1995).

Ortiz de Montellano, B. R., *Aztec Medicine, Health and Nutrition.* New Brunswick, New Jersey: Rutgers University Press, 1990.

Sanders, W. T., J. R. Parsons, and R. S. Santley, *The Basin of Mexico: Ecological Processes in the Evolution of a Civilization.* New York: Academic Press, 1979.

Saul, Frank, *The Human Skeletal Material of Altar de Sacrificios: An Osteobiographic Analysis.* Cambridge, Massachusetts: Papers of the Peabody Museum 63:2 (1972).

Storey, R., *Life and Death in the Ancient City of Teotihuacan: A Modern Paleodemographic Synthesis.* Tuscaloosa: University of Alabama Press, 1992.

—ROBERT MCCAA

Mesoamerica: Religion

A giant solar stone shines like the setting sun from the western wall of Mexico City's Museum of Anthropology. The sun was often a key player in Mexica (also known as Aztec, c. A.D. 1350–1521) cosmic visions, although it may not have been quite the religious epitome that the museum's creators thought it was, for other forces were equally important. Its carved counterpart presents an instructive map, however, for it offers the Mexica version of several important Mesoamerican religious themes: cosmic topography, power-filled inhabitants, calendrically determined transformation, and sacrifice.

First, a cosmic topography is presented on the stone's surface: its arrow-like solar rays map the cardinal and intercardinal directions; a sky band and fire serpents encircling its outer edge depict celestial realms; and jaguar-claw mouths framing its central face mark terrestrial realms. *Second,* various power-filled inhabitants dwell in this topography, from the snakes with little deity heads poking out from between their fearsome fangs, to precious jade stones, the underworld's jaguars, and the godly countenance staring out from the stone's center. *Third,* these beings transform according to calendrical schedule. A ring of the 20 days founding the Mexica calendrical system temporally joins celestial and terrestrial space. The four ages or "suns" (ages were called suns in Nahuatl, the language of the Mexica and other Nahua peoples) appear inside the boundaries of the glyph for the fifth sun, which was called "4-Movement." Each sun transformed into the next, and the fifth was the Mexica's own sun of transformative motion. *Fourth*, dead center sits the enigmatic face of what some believe is the daytime sun as it traveled through the sky, the nighttime sun as it traveled through the earth, or both. Its toothy mouth is slavering in thirst; the equally toothy mouth and staring eye of a sacrificial blade emerges from its tongue's surface. These four themes structured many religious visions from Mesoamerica's earliest Indians to the Mexica living on the eve of the Spanish Conquest.

Four Religious Themes

Mesoamerican religions share a great deal, but each people, period, and geographic location had its own version of religious realities. These four themes, therefore, should be understood as no more than brief sketches.

Cosmic Topography

Most Mesoamerican cosmoses were divided into squares, the cardinal and intercardinal directions marking their sides and corners. This common horizontal map of cosmic topography seems clear to most scholars, but a vertical plan is less so. Many have described early Mesoamerican cosmoses as structured by thirteen (or nine) celestial layers extending upward from the earth's surface and nine terrestrial layers extending down. Unfortunately, the evidence for this is slim, drawn from two main sources: 1) several lists (recorded primarily in Spanish after the Conquest) that enumerate different sets of "sky-waters" (*ilhuicatl* in Nahuatl) and "lands-of-the-dead" *(mictlan)*, which have no reference to any topographical locations; and 2) a single pictorial codex (Spanish commissioned) that arranges one such set in vertical layers. This codex also calls the sky-waters and lands-of-the-dead "heavens" and "hells" and makes explicit comparisons to a medieval Dante-like worldview. One might ask whether the thirteen sky-waters and nine lands-of-the-dead ever were arranged vertically or if this was a Spanish misunderstanding that attempted to bridge two different cultures.

What seems more clear than this medieval-like configuration is that, from early times, most Mesoamerican cosmic topographies were divided into a dry upper and a wet lower realm; the four-sided earth's surface spread out between them. Above, the arched sky provided a sometimes watery wall through which the sun, moon, and stars traveled on their daily and nightly paths. Below extended the moist, rotting underworld into which the sun disappeared every evening, lighting it as it traveled through its dank caverns and passageways. At dawn, the sun reemerged to light the upper world just as the moon and stars entered the lower. Four great trees stood at the cardinal points of earth's surface, their branches supporting the celestial walls and their roots reaching deep into the world-of-the-dead's fertile loam. Four great rain gods also often stood there, directing the flow of water from the underworld to the upper.

Power-filled Inhabitants

Many different beings inhabited these worlds, for everything was animated by a variety of diverse powers. All—people, animals, corn, trees, cities, fields, mountains, even rocks—lived, changed, and ate their appropriate food because they embodied powers allowing them to effectively do things, to be what they were meant to be. Some of these living entities, such as people, animals, spirits, deities like the rain gods, and celestial objects like the sun moved from place to place on their own accord. Others could not; rocks, corn, and trees were rooted to particular spots. As circumstances demanded, one interacted with these power-filled beings both on a daily basis and in special rituals. Forests, for example, were filled with spirits that could trip one. To keep a tree from falling on him, a Nahua woodcutter might ask it to not "eat him" before he forcibly moved it from its spot. Not all powers were malevolent. Good ancestral names had powers to shape a child's personality. And shortly after birth, a Mexica baby received a calendrical name that gave him/her both good and bad potencies. Also according to calendrical schedule, Maya rulers offered their own life-giving powers to cosmic beings by drawing blood in state ceremonies. Names and royal blood were important because the energies flowing through ancestral lineages were especially potent.

Calendrically Determined Transformation

Transformation characterized reality because all things were timed. All living beings (which was everything, including the spaces in which they lived) constantly changed; people, plants, animals, cities, fields, and forests all transformed. This meant that Mesoamericans saw no difference between space and time, for no space existed that was not timed. All things, because they were alive, were born into a particular space, grew through time, aged, died, and decayed through time in a particular space, which also grew, aged, and died.

This sense of transformative impermanence is expressed in many rich natural metaphors such as corn. For the Mexica, corn grew from seed into a plant, eating the underworld's rotting loam. People then ate corn's mature fruit, digested it, and used the excremental results to fertilize new corn. In the Maya myth, the Popol Vuh (Hero Twins) lived and died in the underworld at the same moments in which their alter egos, two corn plants, lived and died in their mother's house on earth's surface. When the boys sacrificed themselves below, their corn died above. Their bones then were ground like cornmeal from which the twins regenerated themselves in new forms, and their corn grew again. Eventually, they rose as the sun and the moon.

"Nothing [was] forever" in this world of "fleeting moments" where even "jade shatters" and one journeys through life for "just a short time." These words, attributed to the fifteenth-century Nahua poet, Nezahualcoyotl, accurately describe the timed impermanence of Mesoamerican existence. A living being, like a person (moving through space) or a cornstalk (rooting itself to its spot), underwent transformative growth and death according to its appropriate life schedule. Even suns' transformations were timed. Many Nahua saw themselves inhabiting a short-lived fifth sun that had been preceded by four earlier suns. After a set period, each sun found itself changed into the next sun by means of some sort of violent destruction. The first sun was eaten by jaguars, thereby becoming the second. The second was blown to bits by wind, becoming the third. The third was destroyed by volcanic action to become the fourth, which, after being destroyed by flood, became the fifth. The Nahua's own sun, the fifth, was doomed to future destruction by earthquake and famine. No mention of a sixth is ever made, and no moral messages are ever implied in the many different versions of this Nahua story.

But for the Quiché Maya, moral messages did structure five sequential ages in which the gods repeatedly attempt to transform various substances into appropriate beings. The Popol Vuh tells how the gods first created the animals. But animals could not properly speak the names of their creators; they only squawked and howled, so they were condemned to being killed for food. Second, the gods made beings of mud. But they crumbled away and could neither walk nor multiply, so they were taken apart. The gods carved the third from wood. But these beings had neither heart nor memory, so a flood killed them, and their own dogs, turkeys, and griddles ate them. Fourth, after many exploits of the Hero Twins in which numerous beings are transformed over and over again to create the things of the known world, men were created. They were created by sacrifice alone, for no women yet existed; yellow and white corn became their flesh and water their blood. But these men were too smart, equal in knowledge to the gods, so they were blinded. Fifth, the gods created

women; and because of these "ladies of rank," the tribes great and small finally came to be as they should: mobile, caring, smart but not too smart, ever mindful of their duties to the gods, and of good ancestry.

Calendrical patterns structured all these transformations. Both the tales about the Nahua five suns and the Popol Vuh are filled with obscure calendrical references. The stories describe not only how the world came to be, but also how one calculates its existence according to the motions of celestial beings. The importance of calendrical calculations cannot be overstated; they were seen as extraordinarily ancient, and they have permeated all aspects of life for centuries. Not only did things change and transform according to some calendar, but much of daily life was ruled by a calendrical system. One did almost nothing important without first determining its calendrical meaning. The system calculated every ritual, great and minor. It even controlled the boundaries of life itself, for all the diverse beings living in the cosmoses lived for particular spans of time that could be counted calendrically. Even the earthquakes that would end the Mexica cosmos would not come until the fifth sun's calendrically calculated life was finished.

Sacrifice

Sacrificial rituals were integral to Mesoamerican religious life from early times. Many are aware of the Mexica high state rites in which warriors offered their hearts to the sun. But fewer are aware of sacrifice's variety and complexity, its integration into daily life, or that many offerings were not human. Most rites were not nearly as dramatic or gory as the warrior rituals. Ritual bloodletting was one of the most common and widespread practices; small quantities were offered on numerous occasions, from the naming of Nahua newborns to the state ceremonies of Maya rulers. Often human blood was not used. The first corn tortilla eaten at dawn, for example, was considered a sacrifice to the sun, and quails, jaguars, crocodiles, ducks, fish, snakes, salamanders, and amaranth cakes were among the many nonhuman offerings used in a wide variety of rituals. Sacrificial techniques varied widely as well. Extreme forms of human sacrifice included heart extraction, decapitation, drowning, and shooting the offering with arrows. Rituals involved both willing and unwilling participants from many segments of society. Males and females of all ages were sacrificed; sometimes they were foreigners, but often not. Ritual foci were equally diverse; sacrifice was associated with both war and the agricultural cycle, and offerings were given to both celestial recipients like the sun and terrestrial ones like the Earth Monster. In other words, sacrifice permeated all existence from one's daily tortillas to warfare, and it was performed in many different ways for many different reasons.

The diversity of these rites and their occasional high drama have spawned a host of scholarly theories. The sixteenth-century Spanish tended to over-emphasize sacrifice's numbers and violence. Spanish authors variously explained indigenous sacrificial rituals as misguided and ignorant practices originating with the devil, as similar to Christian penance, or as mere superstition, depending on the author's own background, the context, and the nature of the specific rite in question. Modern scholarly explanations have varied even more. Some have seen Mesoamerican sacrifice as a stage in a unilinear evolutionary process. Others, by focusing on its environmental, biological, political, social, or psychological functions, have suggested it served as a means of population control, a dietary supplement providing protein, a way for the elite to maintain power, and an effective or maladaptive route to political expansion.

By seeking to uncover the religious logic that might structure these rituals, still others have focused on sacrifice as a coherent system of beliefs. Many of these scholars have agreed that sacrifice involved the ritual sharing of a variety of plant, animal, and human comestibles. Most believe that sacrifice included an exchange between human and nonhuman entities, which sustained the inhabitants of the cosmos in an ordered state of existence. If one wanted the cosmic beings to provide food, one had to feed the cosmic beings.

A number have noted the close sacrificial bond between death and destruction and life and creation, a bond that also correlates with concepts of transformation. The fact that one cannot live without eating (an act that necessarily destroys living things) and the idea that all things are timed are two concepts that mesh nicely. For things must constantly be destroyed if life's transformative processes are to continue; old things are "eaten" to create new things. Just as this transformative reality saw no difference between time and space, so, too, those hungry beings saw no difference between life and death or creation and destruction, each necessitating the others.

Some theories on sacrifice fail to account for enough data, and none alone is sufficient to explain adequately such a complex, widespread, and ancient phenomenon. For understanding basic tenets of Mesoamerican religion, it is probably most helpful to see sacrifice as those exchanges that sustain and nourish the many beings inhabiting the various Mesoamerican cosmoses. Sacrifice creatively transformed things by destructively feeding some beings to other beings. This sustenance allowed deities, people, animals, plants, fields, and mountains to grow and transform. Calendrically determined rituals gave order to this transformative process of eating, for they regulated when sacrificial transformation would take place. Hence the Mexica Sun Stone joined celestial and terrestrial space with calendrical time, all of which encircled the central hungry face with its slavering mouth and sacrificial blade-tongue. The beings of the Mexica cosmos, like other Mesoamerican beings, needed to eat on time if transformation were to be controlled.

A Historical Sampling of Religious Settings

Throughout Mesoamerican history from the Paleoindian period (beginning approximately 40,000 to 35,000 years ago) to the Postclassic (ending A.D. 1521), versions of these four themes appear at different times and places. A short sampling of historical sites can help illustrate some of the different variations Mesoamerican religious themes have taken.

Early History

Little remains from Mesoamerica's early history to give a clear picture of cultural life much less of those aspects that were specifically religious; however, a few intriguing hints exist. During the Paleoindian era (c. 40,000–35,000 years ago to 7000 B.C.), bands of hunters and gatherers roamed a cool and moist Ice Age landscape that was rich in game and good for foraging. At one campsite near Puebla (Valsequillo), someone left behind an elephant bone incised with pictures of mammoths. At Tequixquiac in the Basin of Mexico, a Pleistocene camelid bone was carved in the shape of a doglike figure. One can only surmise their religious significance; they may have involved hunting rituals, or perhaps some tired band member was only relaxing at the day's end.

During this period, one of Mesoamerica's long-standing topographical themes appears at Loltún (Yucatán): caves and the underworld. Pocked by caverns, festooned with stalactites and stalagmites, and honeycombed with channels once filled by underground rivers, Loltún Cave looks like the dark, moist underworld described many centuries later in the Popol Vuh. Used for an extraordinarily long period of time, some of Loltún's occupations may not have been strictly for purposes of shelter, opening the possibility of ritual use.

Archaic Period (7000–1500 B.C.)
The Archaic period ushered in a warmer, much drier climate, and incipient agriculture slowly led people into settled life. Corn, which later becomes such a central cosmological symbol, made its first appearance. But evidence about its use is sketchy, and corn was so nutritionally insignificant at this point that it seems to have warranted little religious attention.

Preclassic Period (1500 B.C.–A.D. 200)
With the growth of sedentary life, religious life became more identifiable. The central plaza of the Maya town Cuello (in Belize, 400 B.C.–A.D. 250) orients itself toward the four directions; a small stepped pyramid rises toward the sky from its western side. As with almost all Mesoamerican pyramids, this was rebuilt several times, each new construction covering the old. Buried beneath the plaza's floor lie what may be an ancestral grave and three sacrificial caches, two with numerous human remains and one with deer mandibles. The cardinal directions and upper and lower realms appear to have structured the Cuello cosmos. Moreover, after the ancestor had been buried, the buildings around the plaza were destroyed and burned; the pyramid was built for the first time, and the first sacrificial cache buried. This suggests that themes of sacrificial creation and destruction were present. As in later times, each new building layer nested over the previous, thereby transforming it. It was not unusual in Mesoamerica to damage or burn old monuments before building new ones, especially when a new ruling line took power. Sustenance also might have been a symbolic factor in Cuello's sacrificially transformative processes for, beside the deer teeth, ordinary cooking pots lie near the heads and mouths of the human offerings, possibly linking images of food and eating.

The Olmecs (c. 1200–600 B.C.) offer a far richer array of religious imagery, producing at least two major urban centers, San Lorenzo and La Venta (in the Gulf region), which served as pilgrimage sites long after their collapse. Olmec religious "influence" was felt in far-reaching sectors of Mesoamerica to such a degree that some have suggested intentional missionary activities. Caves and the underworld again appear, this time as the source of moisture and ancestors. At Chalcatzinco (in Morelos), a petroglyph depicts an ancestor seated within a cave whose opening is shaped like a mist-breathing mouth. Above, clouds sprinkle the upper world with raindrops. At La Venta, an ancestor emerges from another cavernous mouth carved on what was probably a throne. Holding a cord binding him to his lineage, he will use his powers to transform his society. In later times, royal lineages emerged from such caves to do just that. Although a controversial interpretation, some have suggested that child sacrifices occurred at Olmec caves for, in a few cases, the emerging ancestor carries an inert baby whose face is jaguarlike. Children sometimes were sacrificially offered to cave-dwelling rain gods and, throughout Mesoamerica, jaguars were associated with the underworld.

Classic Period (A.D. 200–900)
The great central highland center of Teotihuacan (Valley of Mexico, 150 B.C.–A.D. 750) controlled much of Mesoamerica in the Early Classic period. The city was oriented to 15°25′ east of north and aligned with particular motions of the sun and Pleiades. Its grid pattern was constructed around a centrally located north-south avenue. A river was diverted to intersect this avenue at right angles, creating northern and southern sectors. A gigantic pyramid crowns the northern end of the avenue, and another rises majestically to the sky about halfway down this sector's eastern side. Underneath this second pyramid lies a cave that once held a spring. The cave was modified to contain four chambers, like a four-petaled flower. An excavator in the nineteenth century is supposed to have located sacrificial burials of children at the four corners of each of this pyramid's levels. In the southern sector, a smaller pyramid rises whose sides are graced with feathered serpents and seashells. Also graced with seashells, the monument's depths hold the bodies of around 200 sacrificial offerings probably captured in war. These pyramids were constructed according to calendrically significant dimensions and, as with other monuments, they were built through time in nesting layers. Teotihuacan richly displays its cosmic topography. The cave may mark the Teotihuacaner's place of emergence. Sky's motions coordinate with monuments on earth's surface to mark other key transformative moments in Teotihuacan's life. And its moist underworld holds the fertile powers of sacrificial offerings, some given to rain, others to the sea and war.

In the Late Classic period, the buildings of the Maya city of Palenque (in Chiapas, A.D. 600–800) charted their rulers and sun as they moved like the Hero Twins through the sky and underworld. Both their transformations were celebrated simultaneously on the winter solstice in a dramatic event that still can be witnessed today. Between the hours of 2:30 and 5:30 P.M., the sun slowly sinks behind a ridge on which stands a temple containing the tomb of Lord Pacal, sending a shadow creeping across the valley toward another temple dedicated to a new ruler on the opposite ridge. At 3:30, the sun dips into the underworld through Pacal's tomb, an event shown on his carved sarcophagus lid; an offering of food and the sacrificial remains of four men and a woman lie buried near its foot. At 5:30, the sun's final dying light spotlights a carved frieze depicting the ascension of the new ruler, Chan Bahlum, and God L, a major deity of the underworld. At the moment of death, the sun is reborn as the newly empowered ruler in an event linking a royal lineage's potencies with Palenque's power-filled cosmic topography. And sacrifice nourishes the journey.

Postclassic Period (A.D. 900–1521)
Tenochtitlan, capital city of the Mexica (c. 1350–1521), apportioned itself into four clear sectors crossed by four roads aligned with the cardinal directions. A kinship group occupied each quarter; their patron deity was housed in a temple in each quarter's center. The central temple district stood at the city's crossroads. Buried in the nested foundations of the main temple (the Templo Mayor) are numerous sacrificial caches containing hundreds of animals, seashells, pottery, some cremated remains of elite burials, and a few human offerings (including children sacrificed to the rain gods).

Facing east, the Templo Mayor had a dual staircase leading to two small temples on top. The northern one housed Tlaloc, the ancient god of rain and agriculture, the southern Huitzilopochtli, the Mexica's patron war god. The space between them marked the sun's equinoctial risings on the eastern horizon; the sun marked the boundary of the Mexica cosmos; in summer it moved north along the horizon to its solstice rising, pausing before turning toward the south and the winter solstice. Thus, the solstices marked the cosmos's four corners, while the equinoxes marked the centers of the eastern and western sectors. Each evening the sun was swallowed by the Earth Monster, digested and emitted as excrement at dawn, but only after a group of warriors who had died as sacrificial offerings battled to capture it. At noon, the same warriors battled female warriors, women who had died in war and childbirth. Winning, these women nourished the Earth Monster with this solar "corn" at dusk. At the far eastern and western reaches lay the sea, which rose to form the walls of the cosmic house whose roof was the skies. This house also formed one giant hydraulic system continually recycling its life-giving water.

From Paleoindians to Postclassic peoples, Mesoamerican religious traditions describe cosmoses divided into upper and lower realms. For many, the underworld was the cavernous source of water, food, and royal lineages. The sun often traveled through these realms on its daily journeys, marking the cosmos's four sides with its yearly motions and timing the transformation of these spaces and their royal inhabitants. Sacrifice's powers kept the sun and rulers moving and water flowing. By so doing, it kept food on the table and all the world's diverse beings growing and dying according to their proper schedules.

See also Day of the Dead; Popular Catholicism; Quetzalcoatl

Select Bibliography

Adams, Richard E. W., *Prehistoric Mesoamerica*. Norman: University of Oklahoma Press, 1991.

Aveni, Anthony, *Skywatchers of Ancient Mexico*. Austin: University of Texas Press, 1980.

Carrasco, David, *Religions of Mesoamerica*. San Francisco, California: Harper and Row, 1990.

Codex Chimalpopoc. Reproduced in *History and Mythology of the Aztecs: The Codex Chimalpopoc*, translated by John Bierhorst. Tucson: University of Arizona Press, 1992.

Durán, Fray Diego, *The History of the Indies of New Spain*, translated and annotated by Doris Heyden. Norman: University of Oklahoma Press, 1994.

Heyden, Doris, "An Interpretation of the Cave underneath the Pyramid of the Sun at Teotihuacan, Mexico." *American Antiquity* 40:2 (April 1975).

López Austin, Alfredo, *The Human Body and Ideology: Concepts of the Ancient Nahuas,* translated by Thelma Ortiz de Montellano and Bernard Ortiz de Montellano. 2 vols., Salt Lake City: University of Utah Press, 1988.

——, Leonardo López Luján, and Saburo Sugiyama, "The Temple of Quetzalcoatl at Teotihuacan: Its Possible Ideological Significance." *Ancient Mesoamerica* 2:1 (Spring 1991).

Morley, Sylvanus G., George W. Brainerd, and Robert J. Sharer, *The Ancient Maya*. 4th edition, Stanford, California: Stanford University Press, 1983.

Pasztory, Esther, *Aztec Art*. New York: Harry N. Abrams, 1983.

Popul Vuh: The Definitive Edition of the Maya Book of the Dawn of Life and the Glories of Gods and Kings, translated and annotated by Dennis Tedlock. New York: Simon and Schuster, 1985.

Sahagún, Fray Bernardino de, *The Florentine Codex: A General History of the Things of New Spain,* translated by Arthur J. O. Anderson and Charles E. Dibble. Santa Fe, New Mexico, and Salt Lake City: School of American Research and University of Utah Press, 1953–82.

Schele, Linda, Mary Ellen Millar, and Justin Kerr, *The Blood of Kings: Dynasty and Ritual in Maya Art*. Fort Worth, Texas: Kimball Art Museum, 1986.

Townsend, Richard F., *The Aztecs*. London: Thames and Hudson, 1992.

—KAY A. READ

Mesoamerica: Warfare

Warfare in Mesoamerica was not an unusual or unexpected event. Rather warfare permeated Meso-american society and was intimately linked to polit-ical, social, economic, and religious organization, structuring the lives of commoners as well as nobles. Nowhere was this more evident than among the Mexica (Aztecs), the group for which by far the best documentation exists.

For the Mexica, a typical dawn battle was signaled by the commander's drum or trumpet. The assault began with an arrow and sling stone barrage from about 200 feet, covering the troop advance, during which the soldiers cast atlatl darts. These had great striking force at close range, and their use was in-tended to disrupt and penetrate the opposing for-mations. The barrage continued until the two sides closed—which occurred rapidly—and combat be-came hand-to-hand, with swords and thrusting spears.

The knightly orders led the advance, followed by veteran soldiers who led organized units, and then novice warriors. Movements into and out of battle were orderly, aimed at maintaining a solid front the enemy could not breach and exploit. Once in com-bat, units followed the towering feather standards worn by their leaders; spoken commands could not be reliably heard.

Because the main combat was conducted with hand-to-hand weapons, allowing only the first few ranks to engage the enemy effectively, the Mexica typically broadened the front to take advantage of their greater numbers. The goal was to penetrate the opposing line, to cut the enemy off from reinforce-ments and resupply, or to extend the front until they could turn their opponents' flank and envelop them.

In addition to conventional battles, the Mexica also lay ambushes, especially where the advantage lay with the attacker, such as at narrow mountain passes. Feigned withdrawals were also employed, with the Mexica seeming to flee under pressure. Once the enemy had been drawn into a compromising position, the Mexica would turn on them with the aid of troops that lay in hiding.

Siegecraft was not well developed in central Mex-ico at this time. Although some towns and cities had walls, extensive fortifications were uncommon, and threatened cities more often met their opponents in the open, since walls could be breached or scaled, and remaining behind walls left the city's fields and dependent towns open to assault and destruction. Without these the city was effectively lost anyway. Only by meeting and defeating an attacker before he could lay waste to the region could a city guarantee its safety.

Despite some social and religious goals in war-fare, the Mexica's primary objective was to acquire tributaries. Although they utterly destroyed some towns as lessons to future opponents, the Mexica typ-ically sought capitulation rather than destruction. They usually accomplished this with their numerical advantages. The basic Mexica army was the *xiquip-illi,* a unit of 8,000 men, and many such units were marshaled in their campaigns, guaranteeing not only an absolute numerical superiority over most oppo-nents, but also an even greater qualitative one. Re-gardless of size, only half of the population of any city-state was male, and of those, only about 40 per-cent were of military age (20–45), and of those, only the 10 percent who were elites were likely to have had substantial military training. So even cities larger than the forces arrayed against them were at a dis-advantage against experienced Mexica soldiers, all of whom had undergone formal military training. But beyond the Mexica's numeric superiority and univer-sal military training, perhaps the most important feature of their warfare was not how they conducted battles, but how they projected force at a distance.

The Mexica used their *calpolli* (ward) officials and organization to muster troops and to gather supplies. But because there were no wheeled vehicles or draft animals in Mesoamerica, the simple act of moving large numbers of men posed enormous problems. Like all preindustrial armies, the Mexica moved slowly, probably averaging only one and one-half miles per hour or about 12 miles per day. Relying on existing roads that permitted only double columns over all their length, each army stretched out over great distances—up to seven and one-half miles. To minimize the time needed to reach the target, the Mexica often sent armies along several alternative routes simultaneously.

Logistics drove this concern for speed. Food was carried by accompanying porters *(tlamemes)* in amounts of 50 pounds each. Since each man con-sumed over two pounds of corn per day and there were at least two warriors for every porter, the army carried food for only eight days. This produced a combat radius of 36 miles—three days going, one day fighting, one day recuperating, and three days returning. Most Mesoamerican polities could not overcome these limitations, so their wars were typi-cally fought with neighboring cities. But the Mexica were able to harness their tributary empire to extend their range.

Tributary towns en route supplied additional food-stuffs, allowing the Mexica to project their forces much farther than city-states. Nevertheless, the cost of supplying stationary armies was crushing, so prolonged sieges were avoided. Logistics not only affected the nature of specific battles, but altered the entire course of conquest in Mesoamerica.

The Mexica could reach and fight individual cities, but confederacies and empires presented serious obstacles. Given the time involved and the public marshaling of troops, strategic surprise was impossible, and large polities could march through their own substantial dependent hinterlands to meet the Mexica at their borders. Even if the Mexica won the battle, they could not exploit their advantage because, once inside enemy territory, the Mexica lacked logistical support. And without resupply they had little hope of pursuing their enemies. Thus, while city-states could be reconquered outright, resisting empires and confederacies could not. They required prolonged conflict, in which their borders were chipped away until they were ultimately reduced in size enough to be decisively crushed—a process that could take years or even decades. Thus, the loss of a battle meant very different things to city-states and to empires.

Once having conquered a city-state, the Mexica did not structurally integrate it into their empire. The cost of maintaining distant administrative personnel was too great, and the troops needed to enforce their dictates would have quickly dissipated, exhausting the military strength of the empire. So the Mexica left local rulers in place in exchange for tribute. This system was self-sustaining as long as the conquered rulers believed the Mexica were able to force compliance.

While this imperial system was remarkably cost-effective, it did have an Achilles heel. Anything that weakened or appeared to weaken the Mexica could lead to rebellion. And this, in turn, affected Mexica military patterns. If the Mexica confronted a powerful opponent, they did not always engage in an outright war of conquest, even though they could win, because such a victory might nevertheless leave them so weakened that tributaries elsewhere might be tempted to rebel. Thus, to balance their strategic interests, the Mexica engaged in "flower wars" *(xochiyaoyotl)* in this situation.

Although they had ritual aspects, including taking sacrificial captives, flower wars were essentially an alternative strategy for dealing with major powers. Flower wars were not single clashes, but part of a longer, strategic conflict. They began as demonstrations of individual military prowess with relatively few participants, and an impressive display could lead to capitulation with no need for further conflict.

But if no surrender followed these regimented clashes, the flower wars escalated in ferocity over a period of years, involving more and more men, including commoners as well as nobles. Beginning with swords and thrusting spears to demonstrate individual prowess, indiscriminate killing accompanied the addition of slings and bows, and captives were no longer released but were taken for sacrifice. Thus what began as low-cost exercises in military intimidation escalated into wars of attrition.

A flower war avoided a costly immediate conflict that could undermine imperial control elsewhere and allowed the Mexica to pin down strong opponents, to reduce their offensive threat, and gradually to encircle them, cutting them off from allies and external support. Thus, the initial flower war battles were only the most salient features of a strategy aimed at chipping away at the enemy territory at a relatively low cost in men and matériel, and without endangering imperial expansion or control elsewhere.

Although the Mexica had inherited or evolved an effective imperial and military strategy in light of the material constraints of their world, this system bore the seeds of its own destruction. Because the Mexica's hegemonic strategy was not concerned with conquering all adversaries immediately, disarming any of them, or pushing back nearby competitors, their enemies, the Tlaxcallans, were ready and able to assist in the Conquest of Mexico by the Spaniards. Moreover, because their empire was not structurally integrated, none of their tributaries outside the Valley of Mexico aided the Mexica against the Spaniards. Thus, the imperial strategy that served the Mexica so well in the absence of a major competing power failed to do so when they were confronted by a major, new challenger.

Systematic warfare did not begin with the Mexica, but was common among city-states and persistent in empires. The nature of warfare did change, of course, from its first sophisticated emergence among the Olmecs until the Conquest of Mexico as population numbers and densities increased, military technology improved, tactics altered, and what were considered important resources shifted. Nevertheless, much the same pattern evident among the Mexica probably prevailed in earlier empires.

While warfare's purposes in Mesoamerican society are debated, it did have religious and cosmological underpinnings; captives for ritual sacrifice were needed to propitiate the gods in order to perpetuate the world. But war also had broad social appeal, with military prowess promising social mobility, at least among the Mexica and presumably in earlier empires as well. Moreover, the economic benefits of conquest and the creation of a tributary empire are also apparent, and these advantages permeated the Mexica political system.

Thus, at least some of the purposes of warfare are apparent. And it cannot be considered a blight on Mesoamerican civilization for, indeed, it was the successive imperial expansions that created Mesoamerica as the culture area we recognize. Without the cultural ties and concepts pulled in the wake of conquest, Mesoamerica would have been much less developed and much more heterogeneous.

Select Bibliography

Armillas, Pedro, "Mesoamerican Fortifications." *Antiquity* 25 (1951).

Bandelier, Adolf F., "On the Art of War and Mode of Warfare of the Ancient Mexicans." *Reports of the Peabody Museum of American Archeology and Ethnology* 2 (1880).

Cogwill, George L., "Teotihuacan, Internal Militaristic Competition, and the Fall of the Classic Maya." In *Maya Archaeology and Ethnology,* edited by Norman Hammond and Gordon R. Willey. Austin: University of Texas Press, 1974.

Elam, J. Michael, "Defensible and Fortified Sites." In *Monte Albán's Hinterland, Part II: Prehispanic Settlement Patterns in Tlacolula, Etla, and Ocotlan, The Valley of Oaxaca, Mexico,* edited by Stephen A. Kowalewski, Gary M. Feinman, Laura Finsten, Richard E. Blanton, and Linda M. Nicholas. 2 vols., Ann Arbor: University of Michigan, 1989.

Follett, Prescott H. F., "War and Weapons of the Maya." *Middle American Research Series* 4 (1932).

Hassig, Ross, *Aztec Warfare: Imperial Expansion and Political Control.* Norman: University of Oklahoma Press, 1988.

_____, *War and Society in Ancient Mesoamerica.* Berkeley and Los Angeles: University of California Press, 1992.

Healy, Paul F., and Nancy A. Prikker, "Ancient Maya Warfare: Chronicles of Manifest Superiority." In *Cultures in Conflict: Current Archaeological Perspectives,* edited by Diane Claire Tkaczuk and Brian C. Vivian. Calgary, Alberta: University of Calgary, 1989.

Hirth, Kenneth G., "Militarism and Social Organization at Xochicalco, Morelos." In *Mesoamerica after the Decline of Teotihuacan A.D. 700–900,* edited by Richard A. Diehl and Janet Catherine Berlo. Washington, D.C.: Dumbarton Oaks, 1989.

Peterson, David A., and Thomas B. MacDougall, *Guiengola: A Fortified Site in the Isthmus of Tehuantepec.* Nashville, Tennessee: Vanderbilt University, 1974.

Puleston, Dennis E., and Donald W. Callender Jr., "Defensive Earthworks at Tikal." *Expedition* 9:3 (1967).

Redmond, Elsa M., *A Fuego y Sangre: Early Zapotec Imperialism in the Cuicatlán Cañada, Oaxaca.* Ann Arbor: University of Michigan, 1983.

Webster, David L., "Defensive Earthworks at Becan, Campeche, Mexico: Implications for Maya Warfare." *Middle America Research Institute Series* 41 (1976).

_____, "Lowland Maya Fortifications." *Proceedings of the American Philosophical Society* 120:5 (1976).

_____, "Warfare and the Evolution of Maya Civilization." In *The Origins of Maya Civilization,* edited by Richard E. W. Adams. Albuquerque: University of New Mexico Press, 1977.

_____, "Three Walled Sites of the Northern Maya Lowlands." *Journal of Field Archaeology* 5 (1978).

—ROSS HASSIG

Mesoamerica: Writing

Early definitions of the Mesoamerican cultural region (such as that by Paul Kirchoff) stressed, among other features, a common system of hieroglyphic writing. Although the archaeological record and more recent research has revealed that this is not entirely correct, Mesoamerican writing systems remain an important topic of scholarly discussion. Did writing exist in Mesoamerica? If so, how many systems of writing were created? Where did they originate? How did they evolve? There are no unitary answers for these questions, since the question of what constitutes "writing" remains a contentious issue in anthropological and linguistic research.

Although it is not known when people began to communicate, grunts most probably gave way to elementary sounds (phonemes) during prehistoric times. The ephemeral nature of spoken communication, however, forced many cultures to develop crude systems of written signs. The evolution of writing systems does not always follow the same pattern, but the earliest written signs generally have been stylized visual representations of objects and have been called "pictograms." The second stage generally consists of "ideograms" or "iconograms," images of objects that signify a concept. An arrow, for example, could mean "hunt" or "war." Similarly, a sign for a woman with a special attribute could indicate "goddess." The shift to the third stage usually is quite rapid, especially in syllabic languages such as Sumerian. "Phonograms" are created, representing the sound of an object's name without being a visual representation of the object itself. Thus, *ti,* the sign for "arrow" in Sumerian, is employed to write *ti,* meaning "life." The last phase in the development of writing systems is the alphabet, in which signs represent elementary units of sound.

Not every culture has reached this level, and those that have reached it always have attributed this development to a god or culture hero. The power of the written word is so great that anthropologists define it as marking the difference between archaeology and history, and between so-called primitive and civilized peoples. This has certainly been the case with Mesoamerica. Despite the written testimony of the Conquistadors, who were amazed that the inhabitants of the so-called New World had writing, books, and even libraries, researchers in the nineteenth and early twentieth centuries did not acknowledge the development of writing in Mesoamerica except in the case of the Mexica (Aztecs).

The Gulf Coast

The Olmec culture, which developed on the southern coastal plain of the Gulf of Mexico, produced the first Mesoamerican works of art between 1,500 and 900 B.C. They also created a system of ideograms that was transmitted to other cultural groups throughout the Mesoamerican region and beyond. These signs have been found on Olmec pottery, human and zoomorphic figures and masks, personal ornamentation, and axes. They generally consist of stylized figures: humans, animals, and representations of the landscape and local environment (plants, clouds, mountains, caves, and water). There also are such geometric shapes as circles, crosses, rhomboids, the Olmec "V" or cleft, and scrolls.

Whether governors, ball game players, or ordinary individuals, human beings were the focus of Olmec imagery, organizing the universe and creating a particular worldview in their own likeness. As one of the most ancient cultures in the area, the Olmec laid the foundation for what would become the religion, society, and consequently the economy and polity of the Mesoamerican region. The Mesoamerican worldview that grew out of Olmec culture is made up of three planes, the celestial, terrestrial, and underworld. The center is occupied by the World-Tree, whose roots go deep into the underworld, whose trunk occupies the terrestrial level, and whose branches belong to the heavens. The earthly image of the cosmic tree was incarnated in the figure of the ruler, who was responsible for sustaining the universe and society and who could move between the terrestrial and sacred planes. Knowing the movement of the stars and how to gain the sponsorship of the gods, he could bring their favors down to the community, a form of protection that only could be obtained through sacrifice. In Olmec and other later Mesoamerican writing systems the gods were represented through hybrid figures that combined serpents with birds, crocodiles with plants, or human beings with animals or plants.

Although many authors attribute the development of a numerical and calendrical system to the Olmecs, there is to date no evidence to support this claim. Various Olmec-style inscriptions using the so-called Long Count system, attributed to the Maya, have been found several centuries after the disappearance of the Olmec. To date there has been no explanation for this diaspora, but it is worth noting that some of these inscriptions include graphic signs similar to the Mayan writing that was to emerge later.

Oaxaca

The earliest Mesoamerican inscription that combines a writing system with a Mesoamerican calendar is on Stelae 12 and 13 from the Danzantes Monument (Monte Albán I, 500 to approximately 100 B.C.), although doubts have been raised about its antiquity. One of the inscriptions studied by Alfonso Caso, gives the date in which the event occurred and is made up of the year glyph (the Rain God Cocijo) with the day sign, as well as the day number and the vigesimal number, which make up between them the so-called Mesoamerican calendar. This system, unique in the world was made up of 20 "god days" associated with the 13 "god numbers," which made a total of 260 combinations (13 x 260). This cycle is known by its Nahuatl name, Tonalpohualli, but there is no doubt that it was the same throughout Mesoamerican history and in some areas continues to be used for divinatory purposes. The best evidence for the homogeneity and continuity of the 260-day cycle in Mesoamerica is the fact that the date of the arrival of the Spaniards in Tenochtitlan is recorded as occurring on the same day throughout the area.

The communications of Monte Albán, which are just beginning to be interpreted, seem to refer to the conquest of other sites, migrations, and distinct rituals, especially those associated with death, that are engraved in tombs. The first historical Mesoamerican documents seem to be Zapotec, dated to the Monte Albán I and II horizons (700–300 B.C., 300–100 B.C.), and include the slabs of the Danzantes Monument, various stelae and slabs from Building J. These appear to refer to sites annexed to the regional capital during these two phases. The texts written by the inhabitants of Monte Albán IIIA (100 B.C.-A.D. 650) and B (A.D. 650–800) also have not been deciphered completely but the most recent research suggests that they also deal with historical texts with a genealogical emphasis. This emphasis could lead one to interpret this period as one of change, in which enthronements and alliances were a theme of special interest, although genealogies also are linked with religious information in tomb inscriptions.

The original writing system survived until Monte Albán IV (A.D. 800–1325), when the Mixtecs, another group from the mountain region, conquered the Valley of Oaxaca. Despite Mixtec military domination, the Zapotecs managed to impose their culture through strategic alliances and marriage and through intellectual conquest, which can be seen in the Mixtec Monte Albán V (A.D. 1325–1521).

The Maya

According to the conquistadors, the Mexicans placed great value on their writings "to register everything," whether history, religion, geography, lineage, or scientific knowledge. Unfortunately the only examples to have survived deal with religion and history. Maya writing achieved the highest development in all America and was found on public buildings, on stelae and altars in the great plazas, on temples (lintels, thrones, hieroglyphic stairways, *tableros*), and on ceremonial objects (ceramic, carved jade ornaments, shells, obsidian, turquoise). The system was a mixed one based on pictograms, many of which later took the form of hieroglyphics with a syllabic phonetic value and logograms (whole words), reinforced by affixes (lesser signs) that functioned as phonetic complements to clarify the reading of the sign and by semantic determinatives that indicated the specific meaning of the inscription. The deciphered texts narrate events in the life of each governor: his birth, designation as heir apparent, enthronement, alliances, lineage, battles, anniversaries, and rituals for the community.

The Maya combined the Mesoamerican calendar round of 260 day with a Long Count of 360 days, which later was adopted by neighboring groups in Chiapas and Guatemala. The Maya developed an error-free calendrical system that was used to note astronomical details, the lunar cycle and its eclipses, the planetary cycles (Venus, Mars, Jupiter, and Saturn), and constellations. Periodically the Maya performed rituals linked to astronomical events of importance to the community (conjunctions, aphelions of Venus, eclipses). Numbers were written using dots (each with a value of one) and bars (with a value of 5), which increased according to position, except in the second place, by 20 times the previous number. For example the point in the first or day position *(kin)* has a value of one, extending up to the number 19. A dot put in next vertical position has a value of 20 *(uinal)* extending to the number 17 (there are 18 months or *uinals* in this system). In the third position

the units have a value of 360 (*tun:* 20 × 18). The fourth has a value of 7,200 (*katun:* 360 × 20), and the fifth 144,000 (*baktun:* 7,200 × 20), successively. This great achievement was obtained thanks to the creation of a symbol to designate completion and that acted as an equivalent to zero.

After the fall of Teotihuacan, the Maya cities of the central area gradually declined (A.D. 900). Those of the Yucatán Peninsula, notably Chichen Itza, Uxmal, and Mayapan (A.D. 900–1500), flourished in their stead but did not make inscriptions for public consumption. From this moment knowledge of writing may have begun to be lost. By the time of the Conquest, few possessed the requisite knowledge. The only written documents surviving from the Maya Postclassic period are codices.

Codices consist of lengths of paper made from *amate* paper derived from the *ficus* and covered with a layer of lime on which characters were written and then folded into pages like a screen. Three survive from this period: the *Dresden Codex,* the *Madrid* or *Tro-Cortesiano Codex,* and the *Paris Codex* (the authenticity of a fourth, the *Grolier,* is in doubt). These three codices contain religious texts, based on the cycle of 260 days (numbers 1 through 13 are associated with each of the 20 day signs) that were used by the priests to make auguries and record astronomical data. From what little is known of their meaning, the codices all had a profound religious content. One would suppose that there must have been more, given that the Spanish chroniclers mentioned the diversity of written material that they themselves were responsible for destroying. The oral traditional continued to be quite important, however, and later accounts of Maya history, mythology, song, and ritual were set down in the Maya language using the Latin alphabet.

Central Plateau

From the end of the Late Preclassic (A.D. 200) to the end of the Classic Period (A.D. 700), the inhabitants of Teotihuacan flourished as the great trading society of Mesoamerica, exchanging ideas as well as merchandise. Mural painting was one of the great achievements of Teotihuacan society, and Teotihuacan "communications" are painted on the walls, columns, and floors of buildings, as well as on such minor objects as pottery, urns, and incense burners. Like the Olmecs, however, Teotihuacan never developed a true writing system but relied on a system of ideograms. Similarly, there is little evidence of a Teotihuacan calendrical system; although a number of scholars believe that Teotihuacan left calendrical registers, their analyses seem somewhat specious. In one case the majority of identified "dates" are in fact the calendrical names of deities.

There is considerable divergence among scholars about how Teotihuacan texts should be interpreted, although there is a consensus that texts generally seem to be linked to Tlaloc, the god of rain. Nonetheless, revisionist scholarship has attempted to view Teotihuacan iconography in more of a social and historical light. The famous Tlalocan murals, for example, have been reinterpreted as a representation of the city of Teotihuacan itself, in which the mountain behind the city becomes the Pyramid of the Sun. At the base of the mountain lie the *chinampas* (floating gardens) and seedbeds with products known to have been cultivated at the site, as well as small human figures engaged in the activities of the city.

Teotihuacan long was considered to be basically pacifist, but new findings have challenged this interpretation. The Temple of Quetzalcoatl and the Tetitla murals, which show jaguars and coyotes carrying hearts in their jaws, have led some authors to identify these images as symbols of war and sacrifice. In this instance it is worth noting that the Tlaloc headdress was one of the symbols adapted by the Maya rulers both to indicate triumph over their enemies and to demonstrate that they had performed a sacrifice.

The fall of Teotihuacan affected the entire Mesoamerican economic system as commercial routes were broken up. Although many cities declined in this so-called collapse of the Classic civilizations in Mesoamerica, many other cities expanded to fill the vacuum.

The Postclassic

During this period Xochicalco (in the present-day state of Morelos) and Tula (in the present-day state of Hidalgo) emerged in the Central plateau and Tajín on the Veracruz coast. In Oaxaca the Mixtecs took over Monte Albán and developed a new society. The previously acquired knowledge evolved and developed in a new form. In Oaxaca writing continued to be used on monuments and buildings. Cities such as Mitla, Monte Albán, and Zaachila registered genealogies in tombs as well as on ceramic objects and codices.

During the Oaxacan Postclassic the presence and influence of the Mixtecs is evident. Their dominions occupied the western region of Oaxaca and part of the present-day states of Guerrero and Puebla. Thanks to their codices, Mixtec history has been reconstructed from the seventh century onward in works such as the *Vindobonesis* or *Vienna Codex*, the *Bodley*, the *Zouche-Nuttall*, the *Colombino*, *Becker I* and *Becker II*, *Selden I* (roll), *Selden II*, and the *Gómez de Orozco* fragment. Their content is focused on the narrative of wars and conquests, the succession of rulers, their lineages and marriages, and astronomical events, local events, and plagues of note.

The Mixtec codices (painted onto skin or paper) have a historical-religious content that goes back to the creation of the world and from there to the founders of the local genealogy *(Vindobonensis, Selden Roll)*, a characteristic that has been detected in other Mesoamerican texts. In these the historians "wrote in some characters with such abbreviation that one sole page gives information on the place, site, province, year, month, and day with all the names of the gods, ceremonies and sacrifices or victories that have been celebrated" (Burgoa, 1934).

Among the surviving religious texts are those of the Borgia group from the Puebla-Tlaxcala region, which include the *Borgia*, *Vatican B* or *3,773*, the *Cospi*, *Féjérváry-Mayer*, *Laud*, and *Aubin* fragment. The religious codices were for the use of the priests responsible for preaching, healing, and organizing the life of all the inhabitants of Mesoamerica. Their lives were ruled by the daily presence of the day gods and the number gods, and this information was noted in the religious codices. These dealt with a never-ending future. Life began when the sun was born, the moment when time and heat came into being, and led in turn to the birth of human beings, the "sons of the maize plant."

The Mesoamericans gave their texts this dual temporal quality and thereby indicated if the theme was mythic or historic. In contrast to religious texts that were marked by the 260-day cycle, historical ones had the year glyph of the 365-day year, with the sign of the tutelary rain god of the group, represented by Cocijo in Monte Albán, the Tlaloc headdress among the Mixtecs and Mexica, and the glyph for rain among the Maya. There are other examples such as the square with a knot in Xochicalco and Teotenango in the Postclassic, and the square with a blue background in the Mexican codices, the last documents written in Mesoamerica before the arrival of the Spaniards.

Mexica communications are found on buildings and monuments, mural paintings, and minor objects (ceramics, decorations), as well as codices. Among these are the *Tira de la Peregrinación* (or *Tira del Museo* or *Codex Boturini*) created after the Conquest and of mythic-historical character, and the *Matrícula de Tributos* that according to Víctor

Castillo Farreras refers to "the territorial extension and economic power of Mexico-Tenochtitlan and its allies. It contains toponyms of the conquered peoples, organized into districts and representations of the articles of tribute." The number of themes covered by the codices meant that their number increased to the point of creating repositories to house them, the *amoxcalli,* among which the most outstanding was that of Texcoco. Unfortunately, owing to Spanish zeal, only 21 codices survive to this day.

The Mexica texts present a mixed system that combines pictographs simplified principally to create the toponyms (fields, buildings, hills); ideograms to indicate concepts such as the "scroll" to indicate speech, sun for "day," which also meant "god", and the combination of fire and water meaning "war"; and phonetic-syllabic signs in which one reads the root or first syllable of the object represented. Thus a jar *(comitl)* is read as *co,* and a tooth *(tlantli)* indicates *tlan* or place. This kind of writing was used on monuments, ceramic pieces, and decorative objects, even though the former also carried other kinds of symbols. If some of these bear historical texts, such as the Stone of Tizoc, the majority (the Coatlicue sculpture and the Coyolxauqui and the Sun Stone reliefs, among others) seem to refer to religious thought.

It seems obvious that to sustain these systems, a group of people were required to learn, preserve, and transmit this knowledge. The Spanish Conquest led to the destruction of the system, but the old scribes, the *tlamatinime* and the *Ah Tzib,* valued the oral transmission and used the new writing system, the alphabet, to rescue some of their past. A large part of the information currently relied upon to reconstruct the Mesoamerican past has been derived from such documents.

Select Bibliography

Benson, Elizabeth, *Mesoamerican Writing Systems: A Conference at Dumbarton Oaks, October 30th and 31st, 1971.* Washington, D.C.: Trustees for Harvard University, 1973.

Boone, Elizabeth H., and Walter D. Mignolo, editors, *Writing without Words: Alternative Literacies in Mesoamerica and the Andes.* Durham, North Carolina, and London: Duke University Press, 1994.

Kirchoff, Paul, "Mesoamerica." *Acta Americana* 1 (1943).

Miller, Arthur, *The Mural Painting of Teotihuacan.* Washington, D.C.: Dumbarton Oaks, 1973.

—MARICELA AYALA FALCÓN

Mestizaje

Mexico today is populated primarily by mestizos, people of mixed Spanish and Indian descent. Throughout most of the twentieth century the mestizo has been considered the embodiment of the Mexican nation. But in colonial times most mestizos found themselves marginalized, impoverished, and mired near the bottom of New Spain's hierarchical "caste" pyramid. Beginning in the eighteenth century, as the rigid caste system gradually gave way to more fluid socioeconomic class distinctions, the mestizo began to experience more possibilities for upward mobility. In the nineteenth century, several decades after Mexico achieved its Independence and expelled the remaining Spaniards, Mexican intellectuals began to laud the strength and patriotism of the mestizo. In the 1920s José Vasconcelos would champion the "cosmic race" and equate Mexican national identity with the mestizo. As head of Mexico's Ministry of Public Education (SEP), Vasconcelos was charged with "mestizo-izing" Mexico's still-numerous indigenous population. In recent years, indigenous groups throughout Mexico have challenged the notion that Mexico is a solely mestizo nation. Time will tell whether the Mexican nation-state is capable of accommodating the 56 ethnic groups that reside within its borders and forging a nation that is inclusive and truly national.

Although miscegenation in Mexico also has involved people of African and Asian descent, this discussion will focus on the mixture between the Spanish and Indian populations. The process of miscegenation began with the Conquest in the early sixteenth century. It proceeded apace between 1520 and 1540, when it is estimated that only 6 percent of the Spanish immigrants to New Spain were female. Indigenous women were taken as wives or concubines either by choice or by force. During the course of the sixteenth century a colonial "caste" hierarchy emerged; the conquerors, peninsular Spaniards, naturally placed themselves at the top. Next came children that they had with Spanish women in the New World, or criollos. Next came the mestizos. Near the bottom of this pyramid were the Indians, who were to some measure protected by the Spanish Crown, followed by the blacks. The colonial authorities tried to preserve the colonial order by discouraging miscegenation and attempting to keep the "castes" physically and socially separated from one another. Despite their efforts, however, miscegenation continued, and "racial" subtypes proliferated. Although historical records suggest that 16 different ethnic classifications were used with some frequency, colonial artists had names and rankings for the outcome of dozens of "racial" combinations.

Power and privilege correlated closely with one's "caste." For example, the right to carry a weapon and ride a horse in colonial society was restricted to those at the top of the societal pyramid. As the offspring of Spanish and Indian parents, mestizos were caught between two worlds. Don Martín Cortés, mestizo son of captain Hernán Cortés and his mistress, doña Marina (la Malinche), was considered a Spaniard and was granted every honor except that of inheriting his father's estate, which went to his younger, legitimate criollo brother. Most mestizos, though, were much worse off. During the early colonial period most were illegitimate, and the word mestizo became synonymous with bastard. These children were unrecognized by their Spanish fathers and were raised by their Indian mothers. Culturally they were more Indian than Spanish. In the 1570s the Crown excluded mestizos from the positions of Protector of Indians and Notary Public, and they were prohibited from living among Indians and becoming caciques. In 1643 they were deprived of the right to become soldiers, and at various points throughout the period they were prohibited from becoming ordained as priests.

Rampant miscegenation made the caste system increasingly unviable by the end of the colonial period. This system, which was closed and assigned membership by birth, gave way to a class system, which placed no legal restrictions on vertical social mobility and was based primarily on socioeconomic differences. Late colonial documents refer to the ease with which people "passed" into categories immediately above or below their own. Indians, for example, often passed as mestizos in order to avoid paying tribute, while the inverse occurred when mestizos sought to escape the jurisdiction of the Inquisition.

In 1810, on the eve of the Wars for Independence, New Spain was still 60 percent Indian. Indomestizos made up an additional 10 percent, as did Afromestizos. When mestizo insurgent José María Morelos y Pavón abolished caste distinctions in 1811 and declared that henceforth all inhabitants of New Spain would simply be known as Americans, he was reacting to a de facto situation since the caste system had been eroding for some time. Morelos' insurrection lost steam and he was executed in 1815; Mexican Independence was eventually consummated by criollos in 1821 bent on preserving socioeconomic hierarchies and imitating European and U.S. models of governance.

Caste classifications broke down further during the decades following Independence. Liberal reformers in the 1850s and 1860s abolished corporate privileges for the Church and the military and placed corporate landholdings (of the Church and indigenous communities) on the market. These same Liberal laws technically gave all Mexicans equal rights before the law regardless of their position in the race/class/culture hierarchy.

Yet late in the nineteenth century the political and economic elite in Mexico still looked to Europe for its ideologies, its fashions, its diversions, and its models for economic development. After a snooty French guest to Mexico City's exclusive Jockey Club ridiculed the traditional Mexican rodeo, or charreada, in 1884, Club members vowed to never again to host such an event where Mexican costumes and working horses were on display. To promote the image of a modern, "civilized" Mexico, the Porfirian elite attempted to hide cock and bull fights from the disapproving eyes of European and U.S. visitors, and passed dress codes in high-profile cities. Porfirio Díaz himself was a mestizo who applied white powder to his face to hide his Mixtec Indian features. Throughout the Porfirian dictatorship the dominant class shunned popular Mexico, the Mexico of the mestizo and the Indian.

In the waning years of the Porfiriato, the mestizo population (including now Afromestizos) composed roughly one-half of the Mexican population; indigenous Mexicans composed another 35 percent, criollos and foreigners the remaining 15 percent. These classifications were more social than racial, more behavioral than biological. A relatively well-off Indian who spoke the Spanish language, dressed like a mestizo, and moved with ease in mestizo society might be able to "pass" as a mestizo, and would likely be considered such in his/her community of origin. Indigenous people who migrated to the cities from the countryside tended (or attempted) to lose the behavioral attributes of "Indianness" within one or two generations. In Porfirian Mexico, one's language, dress, culture, social organization, and consciousness was more determinant than the shade of one's skin, even if Indians tended to be darker-skinned than mestizos, who in turn tended to be darker than criollos.

In the years preceding the Mexican Revolution, even as the Porfirian elite continued to ape European culture and embrace European pseudo-scientific racial ideologies, two prominent writers rescued the mestizo from obscurity and declared that Mexico's future lay with its new, vigorous majority. One of these works was written by a member of the Porfirian clique—Justo Sierra. His monumental work, *The Political Evolution of the Mexican People,* published between 1900 and 1902, equated Mexican national identity with the mestizo: "We Mexicans are the sons of two countries and two races. We were born of the Conquest; our roots are in the land where the aborigines lived and in the soil of Spain. This fact rules our whole history; to it we owe our soul." However, Sierra was also a man of his time. Like many other political elites in turn-of-the-century Latin America, he believed that further European immigration was needed to "whiten" Mexico if it were to continue evolving politically. Only then could the nation counteract the influence of the Indian.

The other major late-Porfirian work to exalt the mestizo was *Los grandes problemas nacionales* (The Great National Problems), published in 1909 by Andrés Molina Enríquez. Although this classic is best known for the author's indictment of the Mexican hacienda, it also developed a provocative argument for the historical role of the mestizo. During the Porfiriato, he argued, mestizos occupied the vigorous middle strata in society. Mestizos were the political and military directors, the professionals and intellectuals, the civil bureaucrats, the "labor aristocracy," the struggling small-scale landowners, and the ranchers. Most military men and the infamous rurales were also mestizos. Like Sierra, Molina Enríquez believed that each of Mexico's ethnic groups had discernible characteristics. He argued that mestizos comprised the bedrock of the future Mexican nation because they were the most numerous and strongest component of the population (because they had Indian blood). They were also the most patriotic, because they alone possessed unity of language, religion, origin, desires, and aspirations. This is not to say that the mestizo was perfect in the eyes of Molina Enríquez; he described them as "vulgar, crude, distrustful, restless, and impetuous." But they were also "loyal, generous, and patient . . . and inclined to the sensual pleasures."

While the mestizo was undergoing a rehabilitation of sorts, Mexican intellectuals began to turn their attention to the Indian. If Mexico's future lay with the mestizo, how would its ethnic minorities fit into this future? Throughout his lengthy and illustrious public life Sierra maintained that obligatory primary instruction was the key to incorporating indigenous populations into the Mexican nation, and he vigorously defended a Spanish-only policy in the classroom. When the First Congress of the Indianist Society (Primer Congreso de la Sociedad Indianista) in 1910 manifested its opposition to this policy, Sierra declared that the destruction of indigenous languages was a necessary step toward national integration. The thesis of indigenous "incorporation" gained strength

in 1910, when it was endorsed by Comtean positivist Agustín Aragón, and in 1916, when Manuel Gamio called for a fusion of "races" in *Forjando patria,* his classic call to Mexican nationhood. After the Revolution of 1910–1920 mobilized the country's indigenous and mestizo peasantry as never before, state- and nation-builders after 1920 came to an ideological consensus concerning the "Indian problem." There would be no room for the defenders of indigenous languages and culture in the post-Revolutionary Mexican state. "Incorporation" became gospel.

After nearly a decade of fighting, the Revolution's victors were keen to build a new Mexican state and nation that might prevent future outbreaks of violence and mayhem. They placed much faith in the role that education could play in forging a new national identity. Once Mexicans felt that they shared a common heroic past, common obligations as citizens, and a common destiny, it was thought, they would subsume their local, regional, clientelist, class, and ethnic identities to a common Mexican national identity and a lasting peace could be achieved. Populist education would also help incorporate into the state those popular forces that the Sonorans had been unable to soundly defeat on the battlefield. As concerns Mexico's indigenous population, the state- and nation-building Secretaría de Educación Pública (SEP, or Secretariat of Public Education) was given a great mandate—indeed, a responsibility— to "mestizo-ize" Mexico's indigenous populations. Mexico's official Indian policy, or indigenismo, would be almost entirely in the hands of the SEP from 1921 to 1948.

Mexico's SEP was founded in 1921 by none other than José Vasconcelos, the enigmatic philosopher and critic who championed the mestizo, "the final race, the cosmic race." In an age when imperialist powers the world over embraced pure-race racism, Vasconcelos celebrated racial miscegenation. With indigenous, Spanish, and African blood coursing through its veins, he argued, the "cosmic race" enjoyed all of the benefits of hybridization. Like Molina Enríquez, Vasconcelos equated Mexican national identity with the mestizo character. He believed the mestizo represented the future for not only Mexico, but for the rest of Latin America as well:

> [W]hether we like it or not the mestizo is the dominant element of the Latin-American continent. His characteristics have been pointed out many a time: a great vivacity of mind; quickness of understanding, and at the same time an unsteady temperament; not too much persistence of purpose; a somewhat defective will. . . . I

doubt whether there is a race with less preju- dice, more ready to take up almost any mental adventure, more subtle, and more varied than the mestizo, or half-breed. I find in these traits the hope that the mestizo will produce a civi- lization more universal in its tendency than any other race of the past. (Vasconcelos in Vascon- celos and Gamio, 1926)

Yet Vasconcelos' rejection of pure-race racism and his celebration of the mestizo implied a negation of Mexico's substantial indigenous population. The "cosmic race" was a racial and cultural melting pot which practically ignored the contributions of con- temporary indigenous culture. The thesis of incorpo- ration professed to include the Indian in the Mexican nation, but it denied the Indian his/her language, culture, and personality. Furthermore, "incorpora- tion" was conceived in purely cultural terms; politi- cal and/or economic incorporation would have required major structural transformations that pres- idents Obregón and Calles were loathe to undertake in the 1920s. Indigenous peoples were expected to accept the reality of their own cultural impotence and cede to the benefits of "civilization." Vascon- celos was interested in indigenous Mexico for its glo- rious pre-contact achievements, not for the potential contributions of living, breathing Indians. Ironically, at the same time that Vasconcelos and the SEP spon- sored major archeological expeditions and commis- sioned muralists such as Diego Rivera, David Alfaro Siqueiros, and José Clemente Orozco to glorify Mex- ico's popular, indigenous past, it pursued a policy of ethnocide in the classroom.

Although he served as Director of the SEP for less than three years, Vasconcelos charted the intel- lectual course of public education in Mexico for decades to come. His most enduring legacy was his commitment to rural education. Beginning in 1922 he sent "missionaries" to rural and indigenous re- gions throughout Mexico. Their task was to train teachers, establish schools, and study how best to incorporate Indians into the national (read: mestizo) mainstream. Vasconcelos explicitly rejected the U.S. practice of establishing separate schools for Indians, believing instead that national unity was only possi- ble when all national groups attended the same school together. Spanish was the only language spoken in the classroom. Rafael Ramírez, the SEP's Director of Rural Education in the early 1930s, emphatically cautioned Mexico's rural school teachers that

if you speak to [the Indians] in their language, we will lose the faith that we had in you,

because you run the risk of being the one who is incorporated. You will begin to habitually use the language of the children, later without realizing it you will adopt the customs of their ethnic group, later their inferior ways of life, and finally you yourself will become the Indian, that is, one more unit to incorporate. (In Aguirre Beltrán, 1968)

While the SEP's policy of indigenous incorpora- tion won enthusiastic applause in Mexico City, its reception in rural Mexico was downright frosty. Vasconcelos' "missionaries" generally failed to inter- est indigenous people in a monolingual, monocultural curriculum that was utterly detached from their real- ity. The schools that the missionaries founded, known as the Casas del Pueblo, were poorly attended and usually folded after one or two years of operation. In 1926, the SEP altered its strategy and launched a major experiment in indigenous education and incor- poration in Mexico City. The Casa del Estudiante Indígena was an indigenous boarding school which represented the apogee of the SEP's incorporation- ist project. SEP officials called the Casa a "psycho- logical experiment" designed to prove that Mexico's indigenous population could be incorporated and could perform on par with mestizos when given the chance. As related by Gonzalo Aguirre Beltrán, "The failures of the ... Casa del Pueblo and the rural school in monolingual indigenous communities caused many to have serious doubts about [the Indians'] intellectual capacity." Success at the new Casa would vindicate the incorporationists' position. Failure, warned the director of the Casa in 1927, "would damage terribly, profoundly, the SEP's peri- pheral policy of indigenous incorporation ... it would postpone for dozens of years any new attempt at regeneration by similar institutions."

During its first two years the school merely aimed to "incorporate" its students into the mestizo main- stream. To this end it was hugely successful—too suc- cessful, in fact. In addition to a core curriculum consisting of Spanish, history, math, and civics, stu- dents took advantage of other course offerings at the Casa and in nearby schools catering to Mexico City's mestizo population. While many of the skills learned could be applied in their home villages, like soap- making, hide-tanning, and carpentry, courses in auto repair, electrical work, plumbing, metallurgy, and iron-working not only lacked applicability in rural, indigenous Mexico in the 1920s and early 1930s, but provided the students with the means to remain in the urban environment they had come to call home. The Casa's first graduating class went so far as to petition

Corona, Rafael Ramírez, and the director of the SEP for permission to continue studying in the secondary schools, high schools, and technical schools of the Federal District. "The type of incorporation achieved by the Casa del Estudiante went far beyond what was desirable," noted Director of the Department of Rural and Primary Schools Rafael Ramírez in 1930. Most students did not return to their places of origin "because they felt repugnance for rural life and repulsion at the thought of living with their brothers." Most Casa graduates internalized the assumptions underlying "incorporation" and the Casa's mission. They believed that indigenous peoples had to shed their "Indianness" and join mestizo Mexico in the inexorable march toward progress and modern civilization. Those who did not "incorporate" were considered Mexico's ball and chain. Nothing in the Casa's curriculum taught students to value their indigenous roots. Casa graduates were caught between an identity which they were taught to shun and one which to a large extent refused them.

If the Casa failed to send enlightened missionaries of civilization back to their home communities, did it at least prove that Indians were as competent as mestizos? Official SEP publications took pains to publicly confirm this thesis. Aguirre Beltrán, the late grandfather of Mexican indigenismo, claimed that the students obtained "brilliant results" compared with mestizo students throughout the Republic. Internal documents, however, show Casa employees at a loss to explain the students' apparent inability to perform on a par with mestizos. They were quick to conclude that the scholastic under-achievement of Casa students was more a social problem than an intellectual or genetic one, a conclusion which suggests the degree to which the SEP tried to distance itself from the belief, once widely held, that behavior and performance was determined by "racial" make-up.

In 1932 the Casa was closed, and late in the presidency of Lázaro Cárdenas (1934–40), it appeared that the thesis of indigenous "incorporation" was under siege. The inadequacies of the Casa del Pueblo, the Casa del Estudiante Indígena, the federal rural schools, and the indigenous boarding schools had made it abundantly clear that SEP indigenismo had its limits. In 1940, after much infighting, Mexican delegates at the Interamerican Indigenist Conference held in Pátzcuaro, Michoacán signed on to a declaration endorsing bilingual bicultural education and declaring that "[t]he old theory of the incorporation of the Indian to civilization—a pretext used to better exploit and oppress the aboriginal peoples—has been discarded" (in Aguirre Beltrán, 1983).

Yet the years following the Pátzcuaro conference were disastrous for Indian education. During the presidency of Manuel Avila Camacho (1940–46), the failed policy of "assimilation through education" was revived, especially after Mexico's entry into World War II in May 1942 placed a new emphasis on national unity. Octavio Véjar Vázquez, Avila Camacho's archconservative director of the SEP from September 1941 to December 1943, declared that "The new school is inseparably linked to the idea of nationality, and since the cohesion of the fatherland can only rise from an identical spiritual formation, it is indispensable that the school be the same for all Mexicans regardless of their political or religious affiliation, their race or class . . ." (in Aguirre Beltrán, 1983). After 20 years of evolving toward a curriculum that appreciated difference, the SEP reverted back to the failed incorporationist project championed by Vasconcelos.

Mexico essentially had no official Indian policy again until 1948, when the National Indigenous Institute (INI) was created with the goal of "integrating" indigenous society with mestizo society, and vice versa. The key to "integration" would be the two elements most reviled by the incorporationists: bilingual education and a curriculum specifically tailored to the needs of indigenous Mexicans. While this approach represented an improvement over the SEP's limited policy of monolingual cultural "incorporation," it still failed to attack the overriding structural factors which kept indigenous Mexico in a subordinate, vulnerable, and desperately impoverished condition. Indigenous Mexico would still not be incorporated into the "national mainstream." In the late 1970s, the INI formally abandoned assimilationism, and indigenous groups began to demand pluralism and autonomy with the Mexican state. Still, despite recent attempts to write culturally sensitive, bilingual texts for each of Mexico's 56 linguistic ethnicities, the SEP's main texts continued to show the promestizo bias of José Vasconcelos. As explained in a 1988 textbook, "the indigenous and Spanish people mixed among themselves, and from them the mestizos were born, that is, we, the Mexicans."

In recent years, the mestizos' sole claim to Mexican national identity has begun to erode, at least rhetorically. In response to pressures from national and international indigenous groups and human rights observers, the Salinas administration in 1992 reformed Article 4 of the Constitution of 1917. The first paragraph now reads as follows:

The Mexican Nation has a pluricultural composition, originally based on its indigenous peoples. The law will protect and promote the development of their languages, cultures, uses, customs, resources and specific forms of social organization and will guarantee their members effective access to the jurisdiction of the State.

Never before had the post-Revolutionary state admitted that nonmestizos also have a claim to Mexican national identity. Yet while this reform appears to represent a major shift away from mestizo revolutionary nationalism, it remains nothing more than a symbolic gesture; the Mexican Constitution is more a statement of principles than a binding legal and political document. Until regulatory laws are passed that specify how the Article is to be implemented, the reformed Article 4 has no force. Despite recent indigenous mobilizations and uprisings, the post-Revolutionary state still refuses to accomodate the land's original inhabitants. In all likelihood, the once-maligned Mexican mestizo will remain the embodiment of the Mexican nation for the forseeable future.

See also African Mexicans; Malinche and Malinchismo; Nationalism

Select Bibliography

Díaz Polanco, Héctor, *Indigenous Peoples in Latin America: The Quest for Self-Determination*. Boulder, Colorado: Westview, 1997.

Hindley, Jane, "Towards a Pluricultural Nation: The Limits of Indigenismo and Article 4." In *Dismantling the Mexican State?*, edited by Rob Aitken, Nikki Craske, Gareth A. Jones, and David E. Stansfield. New York: St. Martin's, 1996.

Knight, Alan, "Race, Revolution, and Indigenismo: Mexico, 1910–1940." In *The Idea of Race in Latin America,* edited by Richard Graham. Austin: University of Texas Press, 1990.

Mörner, Magnus, *Race Mixture in the History of Latin America*. Boston: Little, Brown, 1967.

Sierra, Justo, *The Political Evolution of the Mexican People*. Austin: University of Texas Press, 1969.

Vasconcelos, José, and Manuel Gamio, *Aspects of Mexican Civilization*. Chicago: University of Chicago Press, 1926.

—STEPHEN E. LEWIS

Mexica

See Mesoamerica: Mexica

Mexican American Communities

As of the mid-1990s, nearly 18 million Mexican Americans lived in the United States, representing one of the fastest-growing population groups and accounting for the largest share of the 27 million Latinos living in the United States. For purposes of this essay, Latino will refer to the combined Spanish-speaking population of the United States. Latinos include Mexican American, Cubans, Puerto Ricans, Salvadorians, Guatemalans, and other groups from Latin America. The growing numbers of Mexican Americans are not a surprise to social scientists, who noted that this population nearly doubled from 1970 to 1980. Already by the mid-1990s, in the school districts of Los Angeles, San Diego, Houston, Dallas, San Antonio, Laredo, El Paso, Tucson, and Albuquerque, Mexican Americans represented the majority of students in the primary and secondary schools. It is anticipated that over the next generation, Mexican Americans will move from minority to majority status in several southwestern U.S. states.

In the decade of the 1980s, the Latino population grew by 53 percent, nearly 10 times the rate of the "Anglo" (English-speaking, European-descended) population, and at significantly higher rates than the African American population, which registered a 13 percent increase. Comprising 63 percent of the total Latino population, Mexican Americans accounted for the largest share of this group in the United States, followed by Puerto Ricans at 13 percent; Central and South Americans at 12 percent; and Cubans, comprising 5 percent. New Mexico had an estimated 600,000 Mexican American residents, but this state had the highest proportion of Latinos group in the United States, with this group comprising 38.2 percent of the total New Mexican population.

The majority of Mexican Americans live in the southwestern states of Arizona, California, Colorado, New Mexico, and Texas. Two states, California and Texas, with a combined total of 12 million (according to the 1990 census) accounted for more than 50 percent of the total U.S. population of Mexican origin. As of 1996, California had the largest concentration of Mexican Americans, with estimates of nearly 8 million, while Texas accounted for nearly 5 million Mexican Americans. In both California and Texas, Mexican Americans accounted for slightly more than one-quarter of the total population. Mexican communities outside of the southwest region also grew significantly in the 1980s and 1990s. Chicago, Kansas, Miami, Washington, New York, and Philadelphia reported large increases of Mexican Americans in this period.

1521–1821

Contrary to popular belief, Mexican American communities are not new to the United States. Mexicans have lived in the region for nearly four centuries, having settled the region between present-day El Paso and Santa Fe, New Mexico, in 1598. For the first three centuries following the Spanish Conquest of Mexico, Mexicanos settled a broad region of territory extending from San Francisco Bay in northern California to Nacogdoches in eastern Texas. During the Spanish colonial period, Mexicans founded pueblos and developed ranching, farming, and mining industries. Over time, they evolved principally into classes of peasants, ranchers, and merchants, while a small number gained elite status through extensive land ownership, trade with Anglos, and cattle and sheep holdings. Their status in American society is unique because they can claim both indigenous origins (being among the first in this land) and large populations of recent immigrants.

In the aftermath of sixteenth-century exploration and settlement, colonial Mexico's northern provinces provided the majority of the new colonists for their communities to the north. Over the next 200 years, citizens of Nuevo León, Sinaloa, Sonora, and Coahuila ventured north to seek opportunity in the vast frontier outposts. The movement north frequently resulted in the establishment of many hinterland pueblos, including Santa Fe, El Paso, San Francisco, Los Angeles, Tucson, San Antonio, and Corpus Christi. Because Spaniards virtually ceased migrating from the motherland after 1600, we can characterize most of this population as mestizo, a mixture of Spanish and Indian heritage. Over a period of 300 years, then, colonial Mexico and its people transformed, culturally and economically, a vast region of what is today the United States but was then a portion of New Spain.

By the time of the American Revolution, Spanish-speaking communities, including missions and presidios, dotted the landscape of the southwest. Initially, the Spanish Crown and the Catholic Church subsidized the establishment of frontier settlements in what would later be California, Arizona, New Mexico, Colorado, and Texas. The aftermath of Mexican Independence from Spain in 1821 brought renewed governmental pressures on Mexicans to migrate north. Officials in Mexico City at first encouraged but later feared the growing immigration of Anglo-Americans into Texas throughout the region west of the Sabine River and south of the Red River. In an attempt to curtail Anglo-American migration, Mexico sought to promote European settlement by offering generous land grants to settlers. But Europeans came in very small numbers. By contrast, Americans, especially southerners, came in droves, lured by both the prospect of cheap land and the possibility to expand slavery. The Mexican government's immigration policy was a miscalculation that resulted in a disastrous set of events.

1821–1910

The incorporation of Mexicans in Texas took on a new meaning when Texas became an unofficial American colony in the 1830s. In the early 1820s, Mexican officials had given Stephen F. Austin a generous grant of land in the Brazos region of Texas. Austin encouraged American immigration and in just 10 years his "American" colony grew to over 30,000. By 1830, Anglos outnumbered the Mexicans in the territory by more than five to one. In 1835, Anglo-Texans successfully pushed for independence and a year later established the Republic of Texas. Many Mexicans fled south to Mexico to escape the violence that followed the war for an Anglo Texas. The 1836 Texas Constitution did grant Mexicans full rights as Texas citizens, although it maintained the enslavement of blacks.

With the Texas Republic established, the political and social standing of Tejanos (Mexican Texans) changed dramatically. Stephen Austin, who once had been friendly to the Mexicans and had benefited tremendously from the generous Mexican land grants, now changed his attitude. He described Mexicans as a "mongrel Spanish-Indian and Negro race, [posed] against civilization and the Anglo-American race." Since the Anglo Texans also were involved in exterminating the Indians, referring to Mexicans as Indians entailed serious consequences. Not surprisingly, some members of the upper-class Tejanos, such as Lorenzo de Zavala, a former Mexican senator; Jose Navarro, a signer of the Texas Constitution; and Juan Seguin, mayor of San Antonio, tried to maintain ties to the Anglo leadership, hoping that they would not be victimized by the new rulers of their homeland. But they were mistaken. Seguin, for example, fled to Mexico in fear for his life during the turbulent years of the Republic of Texas. Not until Texas joined the Union in 1845 did Tejanos officially become American citizens.

One consequence of the war fought between Mexico and the United States on Texas's soil was that for the Mexican people of Texas, as scholar David McComb pointed out, "the war cast seeds of prejudice that still bear bitter fruit—Mexicans became a despised and distrusted minority." McComb goes on to emphasize that "the terms *spik* and *greaser* became a part of the Texas vocabulary in the 1850s" as Mexicans became second-class citizens.

When the U.S. Senate ratified the Treaty of Guadalupe Hidalgo that ended the war between Mexico and the United States in 1848, they granted citizenship to Mexicans living in the conquered territory. While the Indian treaties of that period did not allow Native Americans to vote, or to participate in the judicial process, the 1848 Treaty did specify that Mexicans would enjoy "all rights as citizens." The treaty also stipulated that Mexicans would be "protected in the free enjoyment of their liberty and property, and secured in the free exercise of their religion without restriction." That equality was only a promise, however; socially they remained second-class citizens in the land of their ancestors. The first conflict over incorporation followed the discovery of gold in northern California. Mexican American miners from southern California were among the first to arrive to "the gold rush" region. But their elation over reaching the gold fields early was short-lived, as Anglo-Americans used violence to drive the Mexicans away. Indeed, Californians treated the region's Mexican American population as if they were a foreign group. Anglos who were racially prejudiced toward Native Americans and African Americans extended their prejudices to Mexican Americans. The philosophy of Manifest Destiny was based on these sentiments.

Uneven economic development and political instability largely account for the vast differences in the unification efforts of Mexicans and Anglos. In some New Mexican counties, for example, Mexican Americans were able to retain their land and managed by their sheer numbers to influence the political process. During the 1870s and 1880s, Mexican Americans relied extensively on ranching and farming to support their families. As the men joined the work gangs on the large ranches, they faced long periods of isolation and monotony. Women worked alongside men doing subsistence agriculture, but they, too, found the frontier life harsh. Cattle ranching and small family farms dominated the southwest region. These industries grew slowly owing to a lack of irrigation, unskilled labor, and poor transportation networks. The small Mexican American communities depended on limited water supplies; they often barely survived by using canal irrigation, ditches, and flooding techniques long applied by Indians and Mexicans in northern Mexico.

In the 50 years after the U.S.-Mexican War, the border region attracted only small numbers of newcomers. With the exception of Los Angeles and San Francisco, this region in 1900 had no cities with a population over 100,000. The population of the entire border states at this time comprised less than 10 percent of the total national population, and urban growth in the area reached merely 50 percent of the level found in the east and midwest. The region's largest metropolitan areas—Los Angeles, San Francisco, San Antonio, El Paso, and San Diego—did not experience rapid growth until after 1900.

At the turn of the century, Texas had the largest Mexican-origin population, nearly 69 percent of the total, while only 2 percent lived in California. In many instances, proximity to Mexico meant that the new migrants were able to encourage other family members to emigrate. Many of the barrios were settled by neighborhood clusters of extended family and friends from the same hometown, south of the border.

Prior to 1910, the majority of Mexicanos living in the southwest labored outside the urban-industrial job markets. Even when they lived in cities, steady factory employment was scarce, forcing thousands to rely on casual agricultural employment in surrounding rural communities. In Texas, for example, many Mexicanos who lived in the cities of San Antonio, Austin, Houston, and Dallas migrated to work the crops in south Texas, but when work was scarce there, they ventured as far north as Wisconsin and Minnesota. Labor experts reported that it was not unusual for south Texas farmers to recruit Mexican pickers from the lower Rio Grande valley, Laredo, San Antonio, and the Winder Garden District and sometimes from as far as Del Rio and Houston.

In all these southwestern enclaves, Mexicanos lived in isolation, often maintaining little contact with the political and economic mainstream. No doubt, their isolation increased because of the desire of Mexicanos to live near factories and construction sites. However, industries such as mining and railroads promoted isolation by segregating workers in company-owned homes. In both small and large communities, segregation was also a consequence of limited housing opportunities created by restrictive real estate covenants. When not excluded by legal policies, Mexicans found themselves restricted from housing outside of the barrio by threats of violence. Such intimidation kept Mexican American residents in enclaves long after European immigrants had begun integrating into American society.

1910–40

The migration of the Mexican Revolutionary era, 1910 to 1930, gave rise to many new Mexican American barrios. More than a million Mexicans, mainly but not exclusively unskilled workers, moved into the U.S. southwest during these tumultuous decades. As the scholars Alejandro Portes and Ruben Rumbaut have underscored,

> contrary to the conventional portrait of Mexican immigration as a movement initiated by the individualistic calculations of gain of the migrants themselves, the process had its historical origins in North American geopolitical and economic expansion that first restructured the neighboring nation and then proceeded to organize dependable labor flows out of it.

Many rural and isolated communities grew as a result of the labor camps created in the southwest during this period. The communities began when the large industrial companies sent their *enganchistas* (labor recruiters) into the interior of Mexico to locate workers. Mexicans came to California, for instance, by train directly from Mexico through the northern Mexican border communities of Nogales, Tijuana, or Mexicali, or indirectly from other southwestern points such as El Paso, Douglas, Laredo, and Del Rio. A few came to California by ship, landing at San Diego, San Pedro, and San Francisco. Before World War II, a smaller number traveled by automobile. When the men, women, and children arrived at the U.S.-Mexican border, they quickly contracted for work in mining and railroad constructions camps between California and Texas. In time these labor camps, or *colonias,* became some of the small towns of California, Arizona, New Mexico, Colorado, and Texas. During the first half of the twentieth century, most workers returned to the homeland after three to six months of work in the United States.

To combat problems of discrimination, Mexican Americans created their own community organizations. These institutions, particularly the ethnic newspapers and mutual-aid societies, were common in every region of the southwest by the early 1930s. Spanish-language schools and labor associations were regional in nature, but they, too, were created as a response to the racial barriers to incorporation into the mainstream society. These barrio institutions survived well beyond the traditional second and third generation patterns commonly found among the European ethnic communities. Their longevity was largely owing to the persistence of class and racial discrimination in the host society when Mexicans attempted to enroll their children in Anglo schools or sought to trade in all-white retail establishments.

Cultural persistence can be attributed to several factors, however. In the first place, the southwest had been solely Spanish-Mexican for three centuries and, as such, native customs and language remained long after the U.S. annexation. Second, the southwest had been absorbing new Mexican immigrants in substantial numbers for several generations. These new immigrants constantly reinforced all aspects of Mexican culture, enabling the Spanish language and Mexican customs to thrive. Third, the proximity to the homeland enabled the Mexican-origin population to visit Mexico frequently and inexpensively. This constant interaction gave Mexican Americans added reason to maintain their Spanish language skills. However, the desire to maintain homeland customs and language acquired new meaning during the Great Depression of the 1930s, when the economic crisis once again would test American attitudes toward the Mexican community.

The advent of the Great Depression in 1929 forestalled the full evolution of Mexican American communities. During the two previous decades, most Mexican communities had grown substantially, and, attendant to the economic opportunities created by World War I, Mexican American workers had made inroads into better-paying urban jobs in construction, manufacturing, and service industries. With the stock market crash of 1929, followed by massive bank closures, every community in America saw large-scale shutdowns of factories and businesses and a subsequent loss of jobs. Faced with a large unemployed Mexican population and dwindling welfare resources, public officials in California, Arizona, and Texas communities decided to repatriate, or deport, Mexican residents.

Arguing that Los Angeles needed its jobs for needy citizens, public officials in that city initiated a massive roundup of Mexican immigrant families in the region. County authorities staged dramatic neighborhood raids designed to uncover those Mexicans thought to be in the United States illegally. Officials who participated in these raids often ignored the citizenship status of those whom they deported. Those apprehended were given only a short notice to pack and leave. Officials provided free railroad transportation to the border, so as to clear Mexicanos out of Los Angeles County. Thousands of children born in the United States were taken to Mexico with parents who did not have citizenship, even though their children were qualified to remain in the United States.

In Texas, where almost 50 percent of the one-half million deportees resided, one scholar, Reynolds R. McKay, found that the civil rights violations included "not permitting returnees to dispose of their property or to collect their wages, deporting many not legally subject to deportation because of their length of Texas residency, separating family, and deporting the infirm." Communities that only a few years earlier praised the diligent work of Mexican laborers turned their backs on assisting them in time of need. This deportation of "aliens" heightened the hostility between the Anglo and Mexican American communities.

1940–96

The unemployment crisis dwindled after 1940 when industry and agriculture began to supply the United States's allies in Europe with food and weapons during World War II. As U.S. soldiers went overseas following the bombing of Pearl Harbor, a domestic labor shortage was created. Although women workers filled many of the vacant jobs, farmers and industrialists were quick to plead their case for cheap labor replacements. At the urging of U.S. employers, the governments of the United States and Mexico signed an international agreement to allow Mexican contract laborers *(braceros)* to enter the United States for a six-month period to work in agriculture, railroad construction, and maintenance. The conditions under which the *braceros* were to work and live were specifically outlined in the agreement: the *braceros* were to receive free transportation and food, guaranteed wages, safe working conditions, and sanitary living quarters. With these protections, Mexican workers flocked to participate in the program.

Responding to increasing opposition from Mexican American workers, unions, and religious groups, the Lyndon B. Johnson administration allowed the Bracero Program to lapse in 1964. With the termination of the Bracero Program, agricultural labor in California was finally able to organize effectively for higher wages and better working conditions.

America's involvement in World War II overshadowed the nation's internal race problem. The war served as an occasion for Mexican Americans to demonstrate their loyalty to the United States, as one-half million Mexican Americans joined the armed forces. Men and women from the barrios also contributed to the combat effort by entering the industrial workforce. In some instances, those who returned home safely found new opportunities that raised their chances for incorporation into the middle class. Thousands of Mexican Americans entered high schools, colleges, and universities with support from the "G.I. Bill," the Veteran's Entitlement Act. Many others bought their first homes with the assistance of the G.I. Bill veteran's benefits. In the post–World War II years, a number of Texas-Mexican veterans organized the League of United Latin American Citizens (LULAC) for the purpose of improving the social and political standing of the Mexican American people. Likewise, one of the most significant changes following the end of World War II was the establishment by these veterans of new political organizations, such as the Community Service Organizations in California, and the American G.I. Forum, founded in Texas by Hector Garcia.

Mexican immigrants entering the United States during the last half of the twentieth century also contributed to the economic development of the southwestern and midwestern regions, as well as to the enlargement of *colonias mexicanas*. After the 1970s, immigrants took up residence in communities settled by an earlier wave of Mexican immigrants, and for the most part they sought housing where there was a satisfactory presence of Mexican businesses, churches, and schools. Over time, these ethnic communities grew into large urban sectors. The tremendous development and growth of ethnic enclaves were especially aided by the rapid growth of urban jobs in construction, light manufacturing, and maintenance and service industries. These newer immigrants had a pronounced loyalty to Mexico, and while they despaired at the segregation and discrimination they encountered, they were unable to do much to combat the racial attitudes of the dominant population.

Mexican American communities of the west have been in a state of flux for the past 150 years. Migrations from the east coast and the southern states, set in motion by the gold strike and augmented by military activity and the construction of the railroad, converted old Mexican-origin pueblos into American cities. By the turn of the century, Spanish-speaking communities of the southwest were inhabited by both descendants of a conquered population and recent immigrants. The incessant flow of migrants from Mexico into the borderland states contributed to the Spanish-speaking communities' ability to preserve Mexicano characteristics. In Los Angeles, San Diego, Tucson, and Santa Fe, Mexican Americans represented a sizable proportion of the population, and in El Paso and San Antonio, Spanish-speaking people became the majority. Today's Mexican communities are ethnic centers with growing political and economic power.

Conclusion

The war between Mexico and the United States forever changed the process of political integration for people of the southwest. In the aftermath of the political change 150 years ago, the new group of U.S. citizens of Mexican-origin sought to develop cultural and economic relations with their fellow Americans. But full incorporation into American society was delayed for most Spanish-speaking residents of the southwest. Nearly a century after the Mexican citizens joined the U.S. community as citizens, they still were faced with virtual exclusion. Nonetheless, exclusion and inequality could be contested in the courts. While the Constitution protected racial and ethnic minorities from discrimination, segregation practices prevailed in most parts of the southwest. With the passage of the Civil Rights Act of 1964 and the 1965 Voting Rights Act, Mexican Americans finally achieved full rights as citizens.

In the coming decades, the United States will be greatly influenced by changing demographics and population shifts. For example, as a result of the wave of migration from 1980 to 1990, the old Mexican communities of the border region, particularly those in California and Texas, gained more than 4 million new residents from Mexico. Likewise, the number of Latino residents more than doubled in sections of California's Orange County, the San Francisco Bay area, San Diego, and Dallas, Texas. These population increases and shifts have already begun to translate into increased economic and political incorporation as Mexican Americans create new businesses, move into management positions in industry and retail markets, and as more Spanish-speaking public officials are elected to public office. As Andy Hernandez, a prominent political organizer, reminds us: "As America becomes more Hispanic, much of its future will be determined by the extent to which its Hispanic population is integrated into the nation's economic, social, and civic life."

See also Guadalupe Hildago, Treaty of; Migration to the United States; Texan Secession; Urbanism and Urbanization: Border Urbanism; U.S.-Mexican Border

Select Bibliography

Acuna, Rodolfo, *Occupied America: A History of Chicanos.* 3rd edition, New York: Harper and Row, 1988.

Chavez, John R., *The Lost Land: The Chicano Image of the Southwest.* Albuquerque: University of New Mexico Press, 1984.

Cruz, Gilbert R., *Let There Be Towns: Spanish Municipal Origins in the American Southwest, 1610–1810.* College Station, Texas: A&M Press, 1988.

De Leon, Arnoldo, *They Called Them Greasers: Anglo Attitudes toward Mexicans in Texas, 1821–1900.* Austin: The University of Texas Press, 1983.

Galarza, Ernesto, *Merchants of Labor: The Mexican Bracero Story.* Santa Barbara, California: McNally and Loftin, West, 1964.

McComb, David G., *Texas: A Modern History.* Austin: University of Texas Press, 1989.

McKay, Reynolds R., "Texas-Mexican Repatriation During the Great Depression." Ph.D. diss., University of Oklahoma, 1982.

Montejano, David, *Anglos and Mexicans in the Making of Texas.* Austin: University of Texas Press, 1987.

Portes, Alejandro, and Ruben G. Rumbaut, *Immigrant America: A Portrait.* Berkeley: University of California Press, 1990.

Romo, Ricardo, "The Urbanization of Southwestern Chicanos in the Early Twentieth Century." In *New Directions in Chicano Scholarship,* edited by Ricardo Romo and Raymund Paredes. San Diego: University of California Press, 1977.

_____, *East Los Angeles: History of a Barrio.* Austin: University of Texas Press, 1983.

San Miguel, Guadalupe, Jr., *"Let All of Them Take Heed": Mexican Americans and the Campaign for Educational Equality in Texas, 1910–1981.* Austin: University of Texas Press, 1987.

Southwest Voter Research Institute, *1988–1989 Biennial Report.* San Antonio, Texas, 1991.

Vigil, James Diego, *From Indians to Chicanos: The Dynamics of Mexican American Culture.* Prospect Heights, Illinois: Waveland Press, Inc., 1980.

Weber, David, editor, *Foreigners in Their Own Land.* Albuquerque: University of New Mexico Press, 1973.

—RICARDO ROMO

Mexican-American War

See U.S.-Mexican War

Mexican Revolution

This entry includes five articles that discuss the Mexican Revolution, focusing on the years 1910 to 1920, the period of greatest popular mobilization and the period that continues to play a central role in the mythology of the Revolution:

Mexican Revolution: Causes
Mexican Revolution: October 1910–February 1913
Mexican Revolution: February 1913–October 1915
Mexican Revolution: October 1915–May 1917
Mexican Revolution: May 1917–December 1920

Mexican Revolution: Causes

The Mexican Revolution erupted in 1910 amid worldwide political violence that saw major upheavals in China, Iran, and Russia and less far-reaching uprisings in Morocco, the Balkans, and South Africa. As in the other sites of major upheavals,

Mexico saw divergent economic, social, cultural, and intellectual currents join together to create revolutionary forces that overwhelmed the political landscape.

In Mexico, as in Iran, Russia, and China, self-interested members of the provincial and local elites joined peasants and workers who shared their aspirations to gain better representation in national polity. Each group sought to redress different grievances, and although the groups that joined in revolution shared nationalist sentiments, these sentiments derived from their particular and widely differing experiences.

The uprising in Mexico stemmed from deepening conflicts between popular forces and more specialized but powerful interests supported by the national government. Specifically, the state supported the owners of great estates in their continuing land conflicts with the peasantry; supported factory and mine owners in their disputes with industrial workers; and supported the metropolitan elites, foreigners, and provincial strongmen allied closely with the regime against the growing demands for broader political and economic participation from the increasingly estranged local and regional elites. The peasants, workers, *pequeña burgesía* (petty bourgeoisie), intellectuals, and local and regional elites shared the belief that the government not only should have done more to serve their interests, but that it had become the source of their discontent.

The economic downturn in the first decade of the twentieth century helped intensify these conflicts. The sugar complex in the state of Morelos, for instance, suffered a drop in output from 115 million pounds (52,230,155 kilograms) in 1908 to under 107 million pounds (48,531,600 kilograms) in 1910. The failure of the Mexican sugar industry to maintain its foreign markets and financial supporters was a major setback, especially in Morelos where it led to the layoffs of thousands of hacienda workers who swamped the town of Cuautla and neighboring settlements. In the last half of the nineteenth century the agrarian working class of the state had lost its land to the estate owners. Now many of them lost their jobs and soon joined the Zapatista agrarian revolution. But the sugar debacle was only one important part of the wider crisis.

Throughout the country, industrial capacity failed to expand enough to absorb peasants displaced by the changing rural economy. Economic crises combined with famine struck in the northern states of Coahuila, Nuevo León, Chihuahua, and Tamaulipas, where property also had been reorganized. At La Laguna, the principal center of commercial cotton production in the nation, output fell from 300,000 to 80,000 tons. The public in the north, no longer self-supporting but still living in small towns, required 200,000 tons of low-grade corn imported by the government in order to survive. In Mazatlán the death rate reached an astronomical 4.4 percent. Unrelieved famine stalked Zacatecas and neighboring Aguascalientes. Meanwhile, the foreign-owned estates in the north, which covered more than one-third of the surface of Chihuahua and comparable percentages of the other northern states, continued to export cattle and vegetables to the United States. Beyond the emergency imports of corn, the government did little to solve the problem. Government officials believed development such as new irrigation projects to be the province of private enterprise; hence, they did nothing. Riots broke out in several northern cities.

Even if the government had been willing to act, its overextended budget limited its options. It had spent large sums on infrastructure projects—such as the port at Veracruz and roads throughout the country—to attract foreign capital. The government also had purchased 50 percent of the national railroad system's stock at inflated prices. By 1910 the debt totaled over 500 million pesos and the government's income had dropped to only 20 percent of that figure. Mining production also slumped across the north, throwing miners out of work. The International Railroad that ran from Durango across important mining and livestock areas reported double-digit declines in tonnage carried.

In the face of so many economic and social problems, the more sophisticated members of the provincial population joined the intellectuals of the cities in demanding a more responsive and participatory government. President Porfirio Díaz reacted with draconian measures, however, arresting the participants at a political convention in San Luis Potosí, including local luminaries. Francisco I. Madero, a wealthy landowner from Coahuila, capitalized on the public's anguish by calling for a more democratic political system.

Given the complexity and depth of the processes that brought about the Revolution, the most useful method of explaining them is in terms of the four identifiable social groups that produced revolutionary actors: the peasantry, industrial workers, petty bourgeoisie and intellectuals, and the overlapping local and regional elites of the provincia. One must bear in mind, of course, that the majority of the members of these groups remained passive or at least did not participate openly in the armed struggles that swirled around them. Nevertheless, the widespread discontent described above led the majority of people not to support the government. The removal of that support made the actions of the revolutionaries viable.

The alienation of the petty bourgeoisie and regional elites played a crucial role in the coming of the Mexican Revolution. Between 1821, when Mexico won independence, and 1910 elements of these two groups frequently challenged the ruling class of Mexico City. They decried efforts at centralization and advocated federalism in order to bolster their position on the periphery. In the course of these disputes a political agenda developed around the themes of "no reelection" of the president, the return of political and administrative authority to the states and localities, the opposition to excise taxes in order to stimulate trade, and the protection of a free press and democratic electoral processes. General Porfirio Díaz endorsed all of these ideas during his rise to power between 1869 and 1876, when he was an insurrectionary leader supported by important figures in Coahuila, Nuevo León, Tamaulipas, Puebla, Oaxaca, and other outlying states.

Once in the presidency, however, Díaz concentrated the power of his insurrectionary allies, established further ties with provincial and local elites from Chihuahua and Sonora to Chiapas and Yucatán, and defeated his federalist opponents, the most dangerous of whom challenged him from their strongholds in Zacatecas, Querétaro, and San Luis Potosí. After crushing the last major rebellions led by the provincial elites in the early 1880s, Díaz consolidated his regime and held it for another quarter of a century. However, the early successes of the regime in directing the economic growth created an ever more articulate and demanding public.

The intellectuals, using newspapers, books and public speeches, played a major role in discrediting the regime and bringing a large portion of the Mexican public to accept its removal. The most important newspapers—*Regeneración,* published by the radical Partido Liberal Mexicano (PLM, or Mexican Liberal Party), and *El Hijo del Ajuizote*—denounced the government for corruption, dictatorship, and the betrayal of national interests. A new genre of critical authors also emerged. The most important of the critical books were Francisco I. Madero's *La sucesión presidencial* (The Presidential Succession) and Heriberto Frías's *Tomochic.* The latter work protested the suppression of the efforts of the mestizo and Indian townspeople in the pueblo of Tomochic in the Sierra Madre Occidental of Chihuahua to save their lands and jurisdiction. American railroad interests had sent a surveying team to the site shortly

before violence erupted. The townspeople, however, fought for more than just land. Through their remoteness, they had long enjoyed cultural as well as political and economic autonomy.

Tomochic capsulized the national crisis between centralization and the continuing popular desire for local rule. Madero's book capsulized the political protest. During the 1890s Mexican novels had protested the hardships experienced by the masses under industrialization and the transition to capitalist agriculture; they had urged reforms and more sympathy for the victims of that process. After 1900 the writers became ever more strident, and by 1905 they openly were advocating rebellion and revolution to end the suffering of their protagonists.

By 1910 the clamor for self-government once again got out of hand, but this time it was far more profound than the political revolutions of the nineteenth century. The number of challengers advocating regional rights had been enhanced by the country's economic growth. The percentage of affluent and educated people now excluded from political power and authority was larger than ever before in the nation's history. Many of these people also were threatened by the new modernizing economy, which had grown increasingly dependent on a steady flow of foreign investments and imports, especially from the United States. When the economy faltered, this affluent but economically threatened and politically excluded segment of the Mexican public turned to revolutionary politics and sought the support of the long suppressed rural and industrial working classes.

By now, the peasants and workers already were rebelling. The peasantry—which comprised an estimated 80 percent of the Mexican population—had a long history of uprisings to redress injustice. The peasantry successfully occupied many disputed areas during the Wars of Independence from 1810 until 1821. However, the *campesinos* (peasants) failed to gain representation in the national governments that emerged after Independence. From the 1820s through the early 1850s a series of state and national government measures enabled the wealthy landowners to regain a considerable portion of their lost estates. Yet, in the early 1850s the peasantry still held some 25 percent of the nation's arable land and the Catholic Church retained a considerable portion of its original 48 percent.

When the Liberals came to power in the 1850s, they provided the initiative for the land privatization program that again turned the peasants against the government. The Liberals began in 1856 with the Ley Lerdo and Article 27 of the 1857 Constitution, which provided the legal basis for the reorganization of the nation's church and *pueblo* (communal village) properties. The Liberals had a twofold purpose in privatization: first, to increase agricultural output and thereby save the nation's moribund economy, and second, to take advantage of the land denunciation powers granted by their legislation. Many in the Liberal leadership became owners of great landholdings, initially through the outright purchase of nationalized church properties and more gradually by means of the alienating of pueblo lands. By 1876, when President Porfirio Díaz came to power, the privatization program already had finished with the church properties. Díaz pushed it forward against the *campesinos* and effectively crushed all resistance. The peasantry attempted periodic rebellions during the rest of the nineteenth and the early twentieth centuries, resisting tax increases and losses of land, water rights, and *pueblo* political autonomies. But without the support of other sectors of society, the *campesinos* had no chance of success. By 1910, when Díaz finally lost his grip on power, the peasantry held only 2 percent of the nation's arable tracts in common.

The large amount of commercially productive land held by foreigners and the attacks on Mexico by the U.S. government in 1914 and 1916 caused the agrarian leaders to attack them as they previously had attacked the Mexican hacienda owners and government. The revolutionaries in Morelos labeled the sugar estate hacendados "Spaniards," while the Chihuahuenses who expelled the Latter Day Saints from their farming communities called them "Yanquis" and "Gringos."

Where these developments in the agricultural sector undercut the peasants economically, the enclosure of communal lands circumscribed their political rights. This political marginalization was occurring at the very moment that the peasantry—the nation's largest demographic group—was claiming the right to participate more directly in local, state, and national affairs.

The industrial working class also had grown increasingly alienated in the late 1890s and first decade of the twentieth century. The heirs of a militant organized labor movement in the 1870s, with a strong anarchist presence, the industrial workers shared the growing sense of citizens' rights expressed by the peasantry. Beginning in 1899 they undertook a series of strikes. In that year they resisted layoffs and wage reductions by shutting down a number of the textile factories in the state of Puebla. Other strikes and unrest followed and grew in seriousness, protesting such issues as abominable working and living conditions and caste-like discrimination.

In 1906 the strikers and their opponents resorted to the use of firearms at the Cananea silver mines in Sonora near the Arizona border. The workers complained that the American management discriminated against workers who were not U.S. citizens —paying them lower salaries, forcing them into segregated housing, and abusing and overcharging them in the company store. The government blundered when it allowed American vigilantes to cross the border, enter the town, and take part in the intimidation of the workers. The vigilantes arrived after the gun battles had subsided, but they turned a serious incident into a major political crisis for the regime. The resulting nationalist outcry did not cease until the government was unseated.

In early 1907, the crisis between the industrial working class and the regime deepened. The textile workers at three mills in the Río Blanco area on the border between the states of Veracruz and Puebla staged a virtual rebellion over such issues as complaints about the French factory owners and the Spanish operator of the company store. The government used the army to repress the workers, who already had forcibly seized the town of Río Blanco. The soldiers killed almost 200 workers and wounded countless others in a day-long battle that included the use of machine guns. President Díaz's actions scandalized the nation. His critics portrayed the event as a massacre undertaken on behalf of foreign owners.

Between 1907 and 1910 worker unrest escalated, encouraged by the articulate and popular opposition to the regime manifested by the PLM. Recurring layoffs and wage reductions in the mining, textile, and sugar industries combined with income stagnation to heighten the crisis. The cost of living continued to rise while the value of the peso declined.

Nationalism played no small role in the workers' and the peasants' unrest. The strikers at Cananea complained of discrimination against them by the American management. At Río Blanco they identified Spaniards and Frenchmen as their principal antagonists. Their feelings had been shaped by repeated national humiliations over the preceding 65 years. Struggles against the foreign armies of Spain, France, and the United States in the nineteenth century were followed by the overwhelming and seemingly unbearable presence of foreign capital in Mexican industry in the early twentieth century. By 1910 foreign investors, including some of the leading companies of the United States and Europe, controlled 130 of Mexico's 170 largest business concerns, of which the Mexican National Railways was the largest. After 1900 an influx of land development companies (many of them directly or indirectly associated with the railroads) led to the purchase of approximately 130,000,000 acres of the nation's 485,000,000-acre surface. In many cases, embittered local citizens accepted jobs from the foreign owners of what once had been their lands. This history created a deep and enduring sense of Mexican nationalism, which by 1910 had become revolutionary. Working-class nationalism would continue to be a critical element in Mexican polity for the remainder of the twentieth century.

As the economic crisis deepened between 1900 and 1910, important sectors of the Mexican public increasingly demonstrated their dissatisfaction with the alliance of government, Mexico City elites, and large foreign companies that dominated them. The ruling alliance included banking, industry, and a major share of ranching and agriculture, especially in the sugar producing areas of the south and the timber stands and cattle ranges of the north. Groups of workers and peasants joined highly variable leaderships, often comprised of local figures, and at other times taken from the petty bourgeoisie, intelligentsia, and provincial elites of the nation, to sweep away the government by the spring of 1911 and launch a civil war that lasted 10 years.

Select Bibliography

Hart, John Mason, *Revolutionary Mexico: The Coming and Process of the Mexican Revolution*. Berkeley: University of California Press, 1987.

Katz, Friedrich, *The Secret War in Mexico*. Chicago: University of Chicago Press, 1981.

Knight, Alan, *The Mexican Revolution*. 2 vols., Cambridge: Cambridge University Press, 1986.

Tutino, John, *From Insurrection to Revolution in Mexico: Social Bases of Agrarian Violence, 1750–1940*. Princeton, New Jersey: Princeton University Press, 1987.

—JOHN MASON HART

Mexican Revolution: October 1910–February 1913

A mood of optimism and national pride possessed the citizens of Mexico City as they took to the streets and parks in July 1910. In less than two months Mexico would be entering its hundredth year of Independence, and judging by the green, white and red ribbons that had begun to adorn the city's buildings, the Republic intended to celebrate the centenary in style. Among the city's elite there were some who had further reason for an extra spring in their step.

The results of the recent presidential election had swept Porfirio Díaz back into office with a resounding majority. For them, there was no better person than Díaz to provide the strong leadership necessary to deliver Mexico from the spate of social unrest that had afflicted the country in recent years.

It mattered little that accusations of fraud surrounded Díaz's victory over his opponent Francisco I. Madero. Similar charges had clouded previous elections, and none of these had managed to dislodge Díaz from his place at the helm of the Republic. In any case, the results had never been in any doubt, since one month earlier Madero had been thrown in jail on spurious charges of fomenting rebellion. Indeed, early signs seemed to suggest that Madero's supporters were resigned to the situation. Prominent figures within Madero's campaign were urging their supporters to accept the election results in the interests of national unity.

Nor did there appear to be any imminent danger of the results intensifying the existing degree of popular unrest. Admittedly, when Madero first moved into the political limelight with his demand for *sufragio efectivo, no reelección* (effective suffrage, no reelection), he seemed to capture the mood of a nation that was tired of Díaz's authoritarian rule. Yet Madero's affluent family background hardly made him an obvious representative of all those who suffered under the incumbent regime. Indeed, his political agenda was limited to the particular problems of the provincial elite class to which he belonged. The more Díaz had resorted to brutality, corruption, and the imposition of outsiders to retain control of the provinces, the more he had clashed with a brand of liberalism shared by Madero and many from the middle classes. Such people abhorred the overbearing nature of the centralist state, and they felt that only by removing Díaz and his cronies could they run their regions in accordance with their own aspirations. It was with this ultimate objective that Madero had launched his electoral challenge.

Such motives were unlikely to have made Madero a popular hero, far less a political extremist. He did not seek major structural change of the political system, merely adjustments that would facilitate greater political and economic freedom. It was to others that the more radical political agenda belonged. Throughout the 1900s, for example, anarchists within the Partido Liberal Mexicano (PLM, or Mexican Liberal Party) had sought to mobilize the workers and peasants and turn them against local representatives of the existing order. In 1906 and 1908 the PLM had orchestrated armed uprisings against Díaz. Although both attempts were suppressed, the PLM's strategy at least appeared to recognize the potential for social change that lay within the growing discontent of the poorer classes. Nonetheless, broader trends and events conspired to create a groundswell of popular support for the Maderista cause.

A recent deterioration in the plight of Mexico's poor had done little to soothe social tension. Under Díaz, the rural economy had undergone a transformation. The elite had become increasingly profit-oriented, and the introduction of new technology made large-scale farming attractive. As never before, the rural elites exploited federal laws to expropriate local peasant community lands. The traditional, if often uneasy, balance of interests between the large estate and the community was swept aside in the name of Porfirian progress. As Indian lands fell into private hands, the deployment of federal troops and officials to crush local resistance became increasingly common. With the rural economy exposed to the vagaries of international markets, the livelihood of those working on plantations and haciendas became less stable. A tolerable existence could quickly turn to hardship when land-owners reacted to falls in market prices by cutting wages and increasing working hours.

Northern states began to pay a high price for the economic development that had attracted foreign investment and economic migrants during the Porfiriato. The local elite and middle classes became frustrated as they saw their opportunities for advancement blocked by Díaz's imposition of governors and by the favorable concessions granted to foreign companies. At the same time, the labor force showed signs of its increasing political awareness and displayed a willingness to consider the revolutionary approach proffered by some within the PLM. Workers organized demonstrations and strikes to protest against the deterioration of their working conditions and discrimination in favor of foreign employees. The brutal suppression of such protests only served to aggravate the situation. The economic slump of 1907 curtailed a worker's freedom to move from one job to another to avoid exploitation. Mass unemployment had brought widespread insecurity, while food shortages caused by poor harvests added to the feeling of discontent. The ever-present phenomenon of banditry in the northern states became increasingly common as individuals and whole communities sought alternative solutions to their problems.

It is from this perspective that the nature of Madero's pre-election support should be viewed. Despite the limited nature of his political agenda, Madero attracted support from other quarters. A vote for Madero was, first and foremost, a vote against the status quo. Such a situation made for odd bedfellows, ranging from the old elites that sought to restore their former privileged positions, to those who sought the more radical solutions favored by the PLM. So when news came of Madero's electoral defeat, few would have been surprised, but the extent of disappointment would have reached far beyond Madero's natural constituency. The prospect of democracy, that only two years before had seemed so bright, once more appeared to have moved into the shadows as the Porfirian political machine settled down to business as usual.

Perhaps the biggest surprise in the summer of 1910 was that Madero escaped with his life and that his affluent associates managed to secure his release from jail. Yet as the diminutive figure of Francisco Madero emerged from his prison cell onto the streets of San Luis Potosí, any sense of relief must have been tempered by a feeling of despondency. It was precisely at this low point in Madero's political career that he began to plan the next battle in a war that many had thought was over. Defying the conditions of his bail, which confined him to the city of San Luis Potosí, Madero stole across the U.S. border on October 7, 1910. From here, Madero and a small group of his supporters began to draft a response to recent events in Mexico.

When Madero's response came, the Plan de San Luis Potosí expressed the fundamental concerns of his natural supporters. This was no charter for social revolution: its demands were essentially political and proposed little to address the everyday anxieties of the majority of Mexican people. Nonetheless, only with hindsight can the Plan be viewed as conservative: at the time it appeared much more radical and, indeed, by departing from a previously non-violent posture, it caught many Maderistas by surprise. The Plan denounced the elections as fraudulent, the Díaz presidency as illegal, and named Madero as provisional president until new elections could be arranged. In order to bring about new elections, the Plan urged Mexicans to take up arms against the incumbent regime. The uprising was to begin on Sunday, November 20. In the interim, Madero called upon all Anti-Reelectionists within the Republic to mobilize local support.

In the event, the Maderista rebellion suffered an inauspicious start. In Puebla City, Aquiles Serdán and his associates had been secretly distributing Maderista propaganda and accumulating arms in readiness for the uprising. On November 18, however, local police launched a raid on the Serdán family home. A bloody siege ensued with heavy casualties on both sides. Serdán was killed, and his sister, Carmen, was thrown in prison awaiting execution. As Madero crossed the border into Mexico on the night of November 19, he was met not by the large rebel army that he had envisaged, but by a small cluster of faithful followers. News from Puebla only compounded the disappointment. Madero had little choice but to return to the United States and await developments. As reports of other failures reached Madero, hopes of an organized, relatively bloodless transition to democracy appeared to have fallen at the first hurdle.

Given such an unpromising beginning, it appears remarkable that within six months the Díaz regime would be over and Madero would be preparing for government. As the old dictator left Mexico for the last time and headed for European exile, he is reported to have commented, "Madero has unleashed a tiger. Now let us see if he can control it." It is unlikely that Díaz was referring to any urban, middle-class solidarity. Rather, he was alluding to the dynamic force that the PLM had sought to recruit, that he himself had fought hard to contain, and that the Plan de San Luis Potosí had barely recognized: the released frustration and anger of the poorer classes.

Just as Madero's electoral campaign had attracted diverse support, so the Plan de San Luis Potosí had resonance far beyond the audience for which it was primarily intended. Artisans, shopkeepers, factory workers, miners, peasants; indeed, all those who identified the local agents of Porfirian rule as the cause of their woes, moved to gain control of their own destiny. Whether they considered themselves to be supporters of Madero, the PLM, or any other cause, it was the mobilization of these groups that conveyed Maderismo from its chaotic beginnings to the National Palace.

In the state of Chihuahua, for example, politics had long been monopolized by members of the wealthy Terrazas-Creel family. Through its connections with central government, the family ran Chihuahua as its own estate, alienating peasants and urban middle classes alike. Pascual Orozco Jr., a local smallholder with a particular grudge against the Terrazas's authority, needed little persuasion to heed Madero's call to arms. While there is no firm evidence to prove that he was, or had been, a member of the PLM, Orozco was at the very least willing to join forces with local members of the PLM in the fight against federal troops. He quickly amassed an army, and their successes against federal troops encouraged others in the region to form rebel units and join the movement. Among these was Doroteo Arango, alias Pancho Villa, whose previous experiences as a bandit quickly secured a place for him and his followers in the annals of Revolutionary history. Orozco soon became recognized as overall commander of a northern rebel army comprising individuals, small groups, and entire rural communities. The motives of his followers varied: some were driven by political conviction, others by opportunism or adventurism. But many more merely sought to redress local injustices.

While the focus of Porfirian concern was drawn toward Orozco's movement, it would be wrong to portray the Revolution as a struggle limited to the northern states. In response to the Plan de San Luis Potosí, a rash of uprisings broke out throughout the Republic as groups seized the chance to force solutions to long-standing grievances. Just as Orozco had risen to prominence in Chihuahua, so leaders in the central states of Veracruz, Tlaxcala, and Guerrero took up arms against the over-bearing centralism of Porfirian power. In the state of Morelos, peasant communities had become increasingly embittered as the local elite used its control of the judiciary to frustrate attempts to settle land disputes. Yet when the villagers of Anenecuilo turned to their municipal president, Emiliano Zapata, to lead the armed struggle, their appetite for social revolution was no greater than that of Madero. In its early days, Zapatismo merely sought to restore a balanced relationship with the elite, not its annihilation. Only later would the movement assume broader significance.

This move to the left emphasizes an important point in understanding the Revolutionary movement as a whole. At its outset, and arguably throughout the Revolution, the challenge to central authority was essentially a local affair. The two prominent foci of popular resistance, headed by Orozco and Villa in the north, and Zapata in the south, were not coordinated: they did not share motives or specific objectives. Throughout the Revolution, peasants took up arms in response to local grievances, rather than universal ideologies. Although Zapata's uprising in March 1911 did draw federal troops away from the northern campaign, any help this afforded Orozco was coincidental to the Zapatistas' primary concern for agrarian reform in Morelos.

The military successes of the popular forces that fought in Madero's name could not disguise the fact that they were only united in their common desire to remove Díaz. Tensions clearly were exposed in May 1911 when, against Madero's orders, Orozco led his forces in an attack against the federal garrison in Ciudad Juárez. Orozco's troops had postponed the offensive for several weeks while Madero unsuccessfully tried to negotiate a peace settlement that would result in Díaz's resignation. Madero's inability to control the actions of Orozco's army emphasized his limited authority over the Revolutionary popular forces. Underlying this impotence lay the differing motives for challenging Díaz: Madero desired a "civilized" transition of political power, while many who fought for him wanted to avenge their previous suffering at the hands of the regime's forces of coercion.

Ironically, the fall of Ciudad Juárez was a crucial factor in persuading Díaz to step down. This pivotal military defeat forced Díaz into a hastily negotiated settlement in which he agreed to resign the presidency in return for safe passage out of the country. The pillar of strength at the heart of Mexican politics for more than 30 years was swept aside by a tide of change. On June 1, 1911, Madero began his journey south to the capital, where he was greeted in triumph by those who thronged the city's colonial streets.

As events in Ciudad Juárez showed, Madero had his own reasons for bringing the military campaign to a swift conclusion. If he found it difficult to contain Orozco's troops locally, he would have even less authority over the myriad of armed groups elsewhere in the Republic. In the event, the removal of the common enemy only served to aggravate the differences between the various anti-Porfirian groups. With Díaz's resignation secured, Madero made moves to prevent the radicalization of the uprising. He endorsed the federal army as the only legitimate armed force under the new regime and instructed all rebel units to demobilize. In addition, Madero excluded Orozco from his provisional cabinet and named the former Porfirian minister, León de la Barra, as interim president. For many who had fought in his name, Madero's early actions were disappointingly conservative. Having removed Díaz, it appeared that Madero was trying to contain the Revolutionary tiger before it had time to enjoy its liberty.

A more ominous development emerged following Zapata's journey to Mexico City to talk with the triumphant Madero. If Orozco had doubts about his political ally, Zapata, too, was quick to realize that Madero was not the panacea for *campesino* (peasant) problems. Stressing the need to establish peace before attempting reform, Madero advocated patience and instructed Zapata to disband his rebels. Interim president de la Barra, however, took a firmer line and instructed General Victoriano Huerta to oversee the restoration of a form of peace in Morelos that favored the local oligarchy. Consequent clashes between Huerta's troops and the Zapatistas set the rebel leader permanently against the Madero administration.

Although Madero enjoyed a sweeping victory in the October 1911 presidential elections, his problems were far from over. The main opposition candidate, the Porfirian general Bernardo Reyes, withdrew from the race prior to the elections and sought refuge in the United States. In August 1911, Madero's decision to favor José María Pino Suárez for the vice presidency in place of his former running mate, Francisco Vázquez Gómez, had caused division within the Maderista ranks. Faced with the mounting resentment of former rebel leaders and a strong contingent among the military and civilian elite harboring Porfirian sympathies, Maderismo needed to display a universality it had never purported to possess. In restricting its aims to seeking democracy through political change, Maderismo appealed to a specific audience. It offered little to the elite of the old order and less to those wanting social change. Challenges to Madero's presidency would come from both quarters.

The limitations of Maderismo soon became apparent. Any moves Madero made toward repaying his debt to the popular classes were more gestures than actual attempts at social reform. Neither the newly formed Department of Labor nor the National Agrarian Commission introduced measures that fundamentally would change the conditions of factory laborers or *campesinos*. Zapata's response was swift and direct. In the very month that Madero became president, Zapata issued the Plan de Ayala. The main thrust of the Plan was the demand for agrarian reform that had been at the heart of Zapatismo since its inception.

Yet the liberal intellectuals who helped draft the Plan transformed it into a document of much broader appeal; Zapata became the popular figure-head of agrarian discontent wherever it arose. The Plan withdrew recognition of Madero's presidency and urged Orozco to lead an army of liberation that the Zapatistas would support. Singling out the excesses of the former oligarchy, the Plan put forward a comprehensive program of agrarian reform that sought to return all the land illegally taken from rural communities during the Porfiriato. Because the Plan addressed a problem shared by many *campesinos,* it was not long before rural communities throughout the central states of Mexico took up arms in its support.

In separate developments, Bernardo Reyes and Emilio Vázquez Gómez, brother of the former vice presidential candidate, compounded Madero's problems by launching their own rebellions against his government. For a while it appeared that Madero would ride out the storm. Reyes failed to attract sufficient support from the federal army and was imprisoned in Mexico City. The simmering resentment between Madero and Orozco appeared to have subsided when the latter agreed to quell a Vazquista rebellion that sought a more comprehensive adoption of the Plan de San Luis Potosí proposals. Yet, even as he did so, Orozco must have been fully aware of Zapata's pledge to support him should he decide to challenge Madero. Finally, Orozco's frustration at the lack of social reform prompted him to declare his own nonconformity with Madero. On March 25, 1912, the Plan Orozquista not only addressed Zapatista grievances, but proposed a comprehensive set of measures designed to improve urban and rural working conditions.

Orozco again proved to be an inspirational leader and he quickly mustered a significant fighting force. His victorious march from Chihuahua to Mexico City was only prevented by the military superiority of federal troops under General Huerta (the same officer who months earlier had stirred up a hornet's nest when clashing with Zapatistas in Morelos). Suffering heavy defeat on the battlefield, Orozco joined the growing number of vanquished Mexicans who took refuge across the U.S. border.

Yet the military challenge to Madero's presidency remained. Zapata's rebellion continued in Morelos and Puebla, while in October 1912, Felix Díaz, nephew of the old dictator, launched a rebellion in Veracruz. Counter-revolutionary in nature, the Felicistas sought to attract support from all those groups who yearned for a return to the halcyon days of the Porfirian past. Like Reyes before him, however, Díaz failed to attract sufficient support from the federal army, and by the end of the month he, too, languished in a military prison in Mexico City. It is an ironic twist that Madero's respect for justice would eventually lead to his downfall. In refusing to resort to barbarism by having Reyes and Felix Díaz executed, Madero kept alive the two men whose actions would later cause more bloodshed than he ever could have envisaged.

From their respective prison cells, Díaz and Reyes used intermediaries to plan Madero's downfall. Their offensive was launched on February 9, 1913, when sections of the federal army under the command of General Manuel Mondragón released Reyes and Díaz and mounted an attack on the National Palace. Reyes was killed in early exchanges and, under heavy fire, Díaz was forced to take refuge in the Ciudadela, an old fortress some two miles away. Once more, Madero turned to General Huerta for military support. Heavy fighting ensued in the narrow colonial streets of the capital city as Huertista and Felicista troops clashed. Many thousands of civilians and troops were killed, and damage to property was widespread; shops remained closed, and few dared venture onto the streets. Until this point, much of the Revolutionary struggle had been played out in the provinces; the citizens of Mexico City had never witnessed such scenes of violence. The period became known as the Decena Trágica, the Tragic Ten Days.

The most curious aspect of this chapter of the Revolution was how the Felicistas were able to hold their own against the vastly superior number of Huertista forces. Events soon provided the answer: Huerta had his own agenda that was not best served by a swift victory against Díaz. Rather, Huerta ordered units loyal to Madero into suicidal attacks, while holding his own forces in reserve. Madero refused to accept persistent rumors of Huerta's disloyalty and continued to place faith in his general. This lack of judgment would be punished brutally when the ten days of tragedy were followed by one act of treachery.

Although there is little firm evidence to implicate President Taft's administration itself, it is accepted that the U.S. ambassador to Mexico, Henry Lane Wilson, took an active role in removing Madero from office. Wilson lobbied hard to gain the support of other diplomats, which resulted in the Spanish ambassador visiting the National Palace to urge Madero to step down. At the same time, Wilson maintained regular contact with both Huerta and Díaz in an attempt to broker a peace deal acceptable to the U.S. government. Such an arrangement depended upon Madero's removal from office, and the installation of a U.S.-recognized administration led by Díaz and Huerta to restore stability. Assuming U.S. recognition to be a formality, and with Madero refusing to resign, Huerta seized the initiative. On February 18, he instructed his troops within the National Palace to arrest Madero and Pino Suárez. The sporadic exchanges of fire between Huertista and Felicista troops ceased while Huerta and Díaz withdrew to the U.S. embassy to carve out Mexico's political future. In accordance with the Mexican constitution, Madero's most senior remaining minister, Pedro Lascuráin, assumed executive control. After naming Huerta as his secretary of the interior, Lascuráin promptly resigned, handing the presidency to Huerta. By a cynical manipulation of the Constitution, Huerta became Mexico's third president within a day.

The final chapter in the failed Maderista experiment took place six days later, when Huerta made arrangements to transfer Madero and Pino Suárez from the National Palace to the Federal District prison. Confusion continues to surround the exact events of the February 22, 1913: what is certain is that as the cars conveying the captives approached the prison gates, a sudden hail of bullets left Madero and Pino Suárez dead. Huerta accounted for the incident as a failed Maderista attempt to free the two men. Such an explanation was a common euphemism during the Revolution for a summary execution. If few believed the story, fewer still were in a position to question it.

Irrespective of the true sequence of events, as the citizens of Mexico City woke up on February 23, 1913, their nation had entered a terrifying new stage in its history. The struggle to replace dictatorship with democracy had resulted in two years of brutal Revolution: thousands lay dead; many had lost their properties and livelihoods; the once prosperous economy was in ruins; and, in recent days, the dying embers of imperfect democracy had been smothered by the emergence of yet another era of conservative, brutal leadership.

Yet stability in Mexico was far from assured. The new U.S. administration of President Woodrow Wilson backed away from the promises made to Huerta by its ambassador in Mexico City. As Huerta seized dictatorial powers, U.S. foreign policy turned against Huerta and refused to recognize his authority. Meanwhile, the tiger of the Revolution remained at large. If the Zapatistas had distrusted Madero, they loathed Huerta. For them, the future was clear: the armed struggle for agrarian reform would continue. Throughout the Republic, communities would have to make their own choice between accepting peace at any price or continuing the struggle. Events would show that the tiger had developed an appetite for *libertad* and was determined to savor it.

Select Bibliography

Benjamin, T., and W. McNellie, *Other Mexicos: Essays on Regional Mexican History, 1876–1911*. Albuquerque: University of New Mexico Press, 1984.

Brading, D.A., *Caudillo and Peasant in the Mexican Revolution*. Cambridge: Cambridge University Press, 1980.

Cockcroft, James D., *Intellectual Precursors of the Mexican Revolution, 1900–1913*. Austin: University of Texas Press, 1976.

Gruening, Ernest, *Mexico and Its Heritage*. New York: Century, 1928.

Katz, Friedrich, *The Secret War in Mexico: Europe, the United States and the Mexican Revolution*. Chicago: University of Chicago Press, 1981.

Knight, Alan, *The Mexican Revolution*, vol. 1. Cambridge: Cambridge University Press, 1986.

LaFrance, David G., *Francisco I. Madero and the Mexican Revolution in Puebla, 1911–1913*. Wilmington: University of Delaware Press, 1989.

Rutherford, J., *Mexican Society during the Revolution: A Literary Approach*. Oxford: Oxford University Press, 1971.

Womack, John, Jr., *Zapata and the Mexican Revolution*. New York: Knopf, 1969.

—KEITH BREWSTER

Mexican Revolution: February 1913–October 1915

On February 9, 1913, the government of Francisco I. Madero, trapped between the peasant armed revolt that demanded more land and the powerful oligarchy determined to maintain its privileges, finally collapsed after 15 months, a victim of a complex alliance of several groups masterminded by the military high command.

Opposition to Madero had been widespread almost from the earliest days of his administration. For some time (at least since January 1913) it had been an open secret that a coup d'état was in the works. According to the rumors, General Manuel Mondragón would command the troops loyal to Félix Díaz, Gregorio Ruiz those loyal to General Bernardo Reyes, and Alberto Garcia Granados the troops of Pascual Orozco. It had been planned that the troops that would orchestrate the taking of the National Palace would come from the academy of Tlalpán and from the gunnery of Tacubaya.

On the appointed day, the attack on the National Palace saw unexpected opposition from loyal commander Lauro Villar. Generals Reyes and Ruiz lost their lives, and the rebel forces, led by Mondragón and Félix Díaz, took refuge in the Ciudadela, a fortress in the center of Mexico City, and successfully resisted Madero's troops. Thus, the infamous Decena Trágica began, the "Ten Tragic Days" in which much of downtown Mexico City was devastated by artillery barrages and street fighting. General Victoriano Huerta, the new commander named by Madero to replace Lauro Villar (who had fallen in combat) and put down the rebellion, became, in effect, the nation's only strongman.

The ability of Victoriano Huerta unlawfully to retain the high command of the federal army and to decide not to quell the rebellion allowed him to fill the power void during the 10 days of fighting in the capital. Chaos reigned everywhere; stores were closed, prices inflated, looting generalized, and public transportation paralyzed.

During those chaotic 10 days, Huerta consolidated his political position, allowing the rebels to consolidate their positions in the Ciudadela. He met with a group of senators, who on February 15 had asked Madero and Vice President José María Pino Suárez to resign. Afterward, Huerta also made contact with a group of congressmen who pressured the House of Representatives to recognize him as the next president. Their proposal was rejected by the liberal majority, however, which insisted that the imprisoned Madero and Pino Suárez still held their constitutional posts.

At the same time, Huerta negotiated for peace with the rebel general Félix Díaz, and through a confidential contact (Enrique Zepeda, later rewarded with the post of governor of Mexico City), he met Henry Lane Wilson, U.S. ambassador and president of the foreign diplomatic corps in Mexico, who from this point forward played an important role in the conflict.

Henry Lane Wilson had many reasons to be dissatisfied with Madero's presidency; what especially irritated him was Madero's inability to achieve internal stability, particularly in northern Mexico, where Pascual Orozco's troops threatened U.S. investments. It came as no surprise, then, that as president of the diplomatic corps he demanded the resignation of Madero and Pino Suárez (he was helped in his task by the Spanish ambassador).

With the so-called Pact of the Embassy, the newly formed alliance between Huerta and Félix Díaz was created formally with the approval of the U.S. embassy. Huerta was named provisional president, and Félix Díaz was given the right to name most members of the cabinet. Despite the enormous power Díaz wielded under this arrangement, the Pact was a triumph for Huerta because he remained the country's military strongman. The liberal majority of the House only accepted the resignation of Madero and Pino Suárez as a way of saving the two men's lives. Nonetheless, the two were murdered shortly after stepping down. The secretary of foreign relations of the Madero government, Pedro Lascuráin, by law successor to the presidency, named Victoriano Huerta secretary of the interior and resigned 45 minutes later, leaving the presidency to Huerta.

Huerta's coup d'état was the result not only of discord within the ruling elite but also of the contradictions between Madero and the lower classes, particularly the peasants. Although Huerta was supported by the leading members of the oligarchy and by the U.S. embassy, he did not "generally" represent the interests of the upper classes; in reality, he can be regarded as the best possible solution to the problems of a fraction of the bourgeoisie harassed by armed peasant revolts, especially the owners of the large sugar-producing haciendas of the state of Morelos threatened by the forces of Emiliano Zapata.

Huerta's Early Regime

In order to consolidate his power, Huerta showed the utmost concern with maintaining his legal status, as shown in his support of those senators and representatives fighting for his recognition as de facto president and in his meetings with all high ranking members of the diplomatic corps. Huerta's pursuit of "legality" would allow him the easier pacification of the country and the gradual displacement of Félix Díaz and his sympathizers in his cabinet, who owed their positions of power to the Pact of the Embassy.

Huerta's regime can be divided into two periods: the first one, from February 19 to October 10, 1913, was characterized by his need to legitimate his government and by an intense political struggle to develop significant social, agricultural, and labor policies. During this period, Huerta came close to being a "constitutional dictator." Starting with his second period, from October 1913 to July 1914, his rule became fully dictatorial.

Throughout the first period Huerta did not exceed his presidential powers, not even when he named Félix Díaz ambassador to Japan, nor when he pressured his vice president's cabinet members to resign, filling those posts with his own men. Huerta still ruled within the law when he suspended, in October 1913, the Senate and the House of Representatives under the excuse that they had transgressed their powers. In fact, Huerta initially had cordial relations with the judicial and legislative powers. During Huerta's first period, the House of Representatives had a liberal majority (most of its members had been elected during Madero's administration) that effectively served as a true counterweight to conservative members José María Lozano of Jalisco, Nemesio García Naranjo of Nuevo León, Francisco de Olaguiberri of the Mexico State, Querido Moheno of Chiapas, and the Catholic minority, so the liberals were able to put obstacles before the executive powers.

During this first period Huerta's social policies reflect an attitude of reconciliation to workers and peasants. Huerta continued Madero's policies of disentailing nonproductive plots of land by imposing very high taxes on them and establishing agricultural schools in several parts of the country. Furthermore, he sold and distributed public plots of land in San Luis Potosí, Michoacán, Veracruz, Tabasco, Chiapas, Baja California, and the Federal District. He also created a system of mortgage bonds to foster the class of small shop owners, an old liberal dream. A war tax on cotton was introduced with the clear intention of guaranteeing the supply of the fiber to the near-paralyzed textile mills of Puebla, Veracruz, and the Federal District.

Huerta's relations with the labor movement were good; he respected the most important labor union in Mexico, the Casa del Obrero Mundial (COM, or House of the World Worker), the right to strike, and allowed, for the first time in Mexico, the celebration of the anniversary of the martyrs of Chicago: the country's first May Day Parade on May 1, 1913. He channeled worker-employer conflicts to the Department of Labor, giving it more powers and a larger budget; he also proposed to improve the existing but rudimentary labor legislation and established the Law of Sunday Rest. Finally, he tried to improve manufacturing facilities affected by the chaos of war.

When Huerta assumed power, he found an almost empty treasury. At the same time he desperately needed to obtain more resources to continue with the war effort and supply the cities most affected by the armed conflict. Devastated lands proved unable to feed the urban population; factories were damaged; public transportation was in ruins, owing to the fact that the railways were the prime target of rebel groups; a huge black market existed; and the masses of the unemployed grew ever larger. Huerta was forced to seek foreign help, but this proved to be difficult. The recently elected Democratic president of the United States, Woodrow Wilson, denied Huerta diplomatic recognition and other possible sources of aid; the European powers, preparing for the coming of World War I, followed suit. Within this framework, the Banco Nacional de México and the Banco de Londres y México raised interest rates, reduced credit, and announced that they would not be able to pay their debts in silver currency, which caused many smaller and provincial banks to close their doors. Owing to the growing lack of financial confidence, large sums of capital left the country and were deposited in U.S. and European banks.

Faced with such a bleak situation, the peso saw drastic devaluation in a very short time. To avoid national bankruptcy, Huerta authorized the minting of new currency with only one-third silver per weight, a strategy copied by resistance leader Venustiano Carranza and several industrialists, hacienda owners, and mining corporations. The Real del Monte Mining Company, based in the state of Hidalgo, printed hundreds of peso bills in early 1914. Toward the end of 1913, the U.S. consul in Durango reported that in Durango alone there were 25 different kinds of currency. Inevitably, inflation soared.

Faced by such a lack of financing and the need to fight the enemies of the regime (especially the

advancing Constitutionalists of Carranza and the Zapatistas approaching the capital), Huerta imposed forced loans on important sectors of the population and on national and state banks. Through complex negotiations, he obtained a loan from the European Bank de París et des Pays Bas.

Resistance to the Huerta Regime

The same groups that started the 1910 Revolution, the peasantry and the anti-oligarchic landowners, once again united to fight the Huerta regime throughout the country. The governor of Coahuila, Venustiano Carranza, was the first to organize the armed resistance by becoming the leader of the *puro* (radical) large landowners of the region of Guaymas, Alamos, and Ures in Sonora, who were against the continuous interference of the federal government in their affairs. The need for land reform interested them less.

Another strong resistance movement was the so-called Sonora Group based in that northern state and led by Álvaro Obregón, Plutarco Elías Calles, and Benjamín Hill. They represented the interests of the middle-sized landowners of the fertile valleys of the Mayo and Yaqui Rivers, who were clamoring for more capital to invest in irrigation works and modern machinery.

These two northern opposition groups joined forces under the Plan of Guadalupe, whose purpose was the reestablishment of a legal government, and soon their forces were fed by the ever-growing masses of dissatisfied and landless peasants on the one hand, and those opposed to Huerta's excesses on the other. Nevertheless, owing to their profound differences, Obregón and Carranza eventually split several years later.

It was easy for Carranza and the other northerners to be the self-proclaimed "defenders of legality," because they were not identified by the people as being part of the dictatorial regime, nor did they participate in the discords of the bourgeois factions of Morelos, the Federal District, or Mexico State. On the other hand, those forces that most tenaciously fought Huerta belonged to Emiliano Zapata in Morelos, Francisco "Pancho" Villa in Chihuahua (who remained staunchly independent despite recognizing Carranza as political leader), and Obregón in Sonora (still relatively independent). There also were a large number of guerrilla groups who, between March and June, 1913, spontaneously joined in the fight against Huerta in Tamaulipas, Zacatecas, Durango, Sinaloa, San Luis Potosí, Tepic, Veracruz, Oaxaca, Tabasco, Chiapas, Michoacán, and Guerrero. Most of these groups did not coordinate their efforts with the national opposition movement and soon disappeared, but a few gained strength and joined the Constitutionalist Army, as was the case of Lucio Blanco in Tamaulipas and Panfilo Nateras in Zacatecas. Many of these military leaders acquired, owing to their military victories and the subsequent social reforms they implemented, a deep-rooted popularity among the general population. It soon became the objective of the Constitutionalist Army (Carranza's faction) to influence and control the numerous fighting peasants and subsequently promise them social reforms that later, once in power, the Constitutionalists were forced to implement, for fear of losing control.

Huerta's Late Regime

Huerta's regime soon abandoned its quest for legitimacy and applied dictatorial methods to remain in power, the culmination of a chain of events that included the military advance of the Constitutionalist and the Zapatista Armies, the Huerta regime's financial failure, its political isolation in the capital, and the continuing hostility of the U.S. government. Thus, starting in October 1913, Huerta's government changed in a radical way, starting with the assassinations of Chihuahua governor Abraham González, Representatives Edmundo Pastelín, Adolfo Gurrión, and Serapio Rendón, and Senator Belisario Dominguez. Huerta's new approach continued with the suspension of the legislative and judicial chambers and the introduction of forced conscription in order to augment the federal troops. Needless to say, the second Huerta period was characterized by rule with an iron hand.

This sudden turn of events provoked discussion in the U.S. Congress of an armed intervention to protect U.S. interests and investments. The future of Mexican oil production and the imminent beginning of World War I were important factors in the implementation of this plan. While the plan was being discussed, an important event took place: Huerta, denied most external financing by the U.S. refusal to recognize him, sought help from Germany and England, and especially from Sir Weetman Pearson (Lord Cowdray), founder of the nation's most important oil company, the Compañía Petrolera El Águila (which controlled more than half of Mexico's oil production), who negotiated a loan in England on behalf of the Mexican government, a fact that infuriated the White House. The U.S. president soon issued an ultimatum, declaring that the United States would not tolerate a European outpost in Mexico and would intervene militarily to stop it. England offered neutrality under the condition that the United States eliminate discriminatory tariffs directed against foreign vessels

in the Panama Canal, which would allow the British to keep obtaining Mexican oil for the imminent conflagration. Ultimately, the British discovered that the Mexican oil was of too low a quality for their fleet.

U.S. president Wilson applied further pressure to the Huerta regime by ordering U.S. companies in Mexico to suspend fiscal payments to the government. He then offered financial support of Carranza, giving him cash in lieu of future taxes. On February 3, 1914, Wilson finally decreed the free flow of arms into Mexico, and the states of Sonora and the border city of Ciudad Juárez became supply centers for the Constitutionalist Army.

Wilson found his pretext for military intervention after the brief detention of a U.S. officer and six sailors by a Huertista garrison during their defense of Tampico on April 9, 1914. The U.S. Navy lodged a strong protest and the Mexican commander apologized, ordering the arrest of the unfortunate officer. But the U.S. State Department claimed that the whaleboat from which the shore party had arrived flew a U.S. flag. Wilson demanded that the flag be hoisted above the shoreline with the Mexicans obliged to fire a 21-gun salute to it. When Huerta refused to submit to all these demands, Wilson obtained congressional approval to intervene in Mexico.

The landing at Veracruz took place on April 21, 1914, and involved 2,000 soldiers supported by 65 ships with almost 30,000 marines on board, and it fully achieved the objective of provoking and dispersing Huerta's troops that until then had been confronting the simultaneous advance of the Villistas and Constitutionalists toward Mexico City. Huerta tried, unsuccessfully, to call for national unity to repeal the foreign invasion, but the armed struggle in the interior did not come to a halt; on the contrary, the Constitutionalists proclaimed themselves defenders of the national territory in case of a declaration of war. One of the main objectives of the U.S. invasion was the attempt to stop the advance of the peasant movement within Carranza's troops (the effects of which were being felt in the United States), rather than bring about the downfall of the Huerta regime. This motivation became evident when the marines did not abandon the country after Huerta left the presidency (July 1914), but only four months later, on November 22, 1914, when a new stage of the Revolution had already begun, after Obregón's and Carranza's entry into Mexico City (August 15 and 20, respectively).

The Convention of Aguascalientes

On August 14, 1914, under the Treaties of Teoloyucan, Mexico City fell under the control of the

Constitutionalist forces. Early on, however, differences between the leaders arose, centered on the provisional presidency and the future of the leadership of the Constitutionalist troops. The Treaties of Teoloyucan called for the organization of a national junta, and this implied the hard work of achieving conciliation and planning a national convention where fundamental decisions regarding the political future of the country would be made. Carranza's conception materialized in the first convention that took place on October 1, 1914; the conference was unrepresentative, for it included only the Revolutionary leaders, and not the Zapatistas or representatives of other social groups.

By contrast, in the Sovereign Revolutionary Convention of Aguascalientes, which took place from October 10 to November 13 of the same year, all movements, ideas, and philosophies of all national and provincial groups and social classes were well represented. The convention's early calls for unity soon gave way to an irreconcilable split between the Carrancista (whose spokesman there was Obregón) and the more radical factions of Villa and Zapata. Ultimately, the Carrancistas lost control of the proceedings, and Eulalio Gutiérrez was chosen as provisional president, an office Carranza himself assumed he would possess. When news of the events reached him, Carranza withdrew his forces from Mexico City and set up a separate Constitutional government in Veracruz. The convention then followed an erratic course as a result of additional schisms; it moved to Mexico City (January 1915), Cuernavaca (February), back to Mexico City (July), Toluca (August), and finally back to Cuernavaca (October).

As the months passed, the convention gradually was dominated first by Villa's forces, and eventually by Zapata's, so that toward the end the convention lost the original popular representation it had possessed, a fact mirrored by the irrepressible advance of the Constitutionalists throughout the country. The triumph of the Revolution's bourgeois wing over the popular armies showed the difficulties of transferring the Revolutionary power as embodied in the convention to effective political power; these difficulties were symbolized by the failure of Villa and Zapata to assume legal executive powers after their triumphant entry into Mexico City in December 1914. Before Villa and Zapata eventually abandoned the capital and retreated to their respective areas of influence, Villa expressed the problem very clearly when, inside the executive office in the National Palace and alternately sharing the presidential chair with Zapata, he exclaimed, "This chair is too big for us."

Indeed, the many different ideas and social backgrounds represented in the Conventionalist forces differed greatly. Villa in his reforms thought of his troops and their families, and also of those peasants whose lands had been taken by the large landowners, but he never included the poor landless peasants, nor did he think of incorporating the laborers in manufacturing processes or even in the administration of the haciendas. One could say that his reforms were based on methods of redistribution of wealth. On the contrary, Zapata's Plan of Ayala demanded immediate possession of all land, water, and hills usurped by the large hacienda owners and recognition of land ownership to the individual who works on it, both of which ideas created an unbridgeable gap between poor peasants and landowners. At the core of their differences was the composition of the troops: whereas Zapata's army was formed mostly of poor, landless peasants, Villa's consisted of former hacienda workers, day laborers, and even miners and railway workers.

Their differences are significant even in the military field. Villa could plan large-scale battles and move his troops and their families throughout the wide open spaces of the northern states, thereby imposing his reforms to those territories that came under his control; Zapata remained localized and sheltered in the central-southern states of Morelos, Guerrero, Puebla, and a part of Veracruz, where he led a highly effective guerrilla war ideally suited to those mountainous regions, and even allowed a rotation of his troops, so that the fighter became a producer and vice versa, thereby guaranteeing the food supply. Neither one offered a viable political alternative to the nation's future.

Meanwhile, Carranza made great progress in the political and military future of his forces, consolidating his provisional government in Veracruz and making moves to gain the support of the lower classes, who soon would follow his commands. An example was the Red Battalions, who, promised better labor legislation and the creation of national unions, fought the Villistas in El Ebano, the Zapatistas in Jalapa and Orizaba, and joined Obregón's troops in El Bajío.

In October 1915, a radically different panorama from the one seen in December 1914 emerged: defeated Villistas, isolated Zapatistas, and strengthened Constitutionalists with full legal powers under the leadership of Carranza, who then went on a six-month political tour of the country, returning to Mexico City to give it back its status of political capital. A new stage in the history of Mexico had begun.

Select Bibliography

Hart, John M., *Revolutionary Mexico: The Coming and Process of the Mexican Revolution*. Berkeley and London: University of California Press, 1989.

Joseph, Gilbert, *Revolution from Without*. Cambridge: Cambridge University Press, 1982.

Katz, Friedrich, *The Secret War in Mexico: Europe, the United States and the Mexican Revolution*. Chicago: University of Chicago Press, 1981.

Knight, Alan, *The Mexican Revolution*. 2 vols., Cambridge: Cambridge University Press, 1986.

Meyer, Michael C., *Huerta: A Political Portrait*. Lincoln: University of Nebraska Press, 1972.

Womack, John, '"The Mexican Revolution 1910–20." In *The Cambridge History of Latin America*, vol. 5, edited by Leslie Bethell. Cambridge: Cambridge University Press, 1986.

—ESPERANZA TUÑÓN PABLOS

Mexican Revolution: October 1915–May 1917

By October 1915, Venustiano Carranza's Constitutionalist forces effectively had driven a firm wedge between the ideologically allied forces of Emiliano Zapata in Morelos and Francisco "Pancho" Villa north of Mexico City. After the crushing defeats of Villa's Division of the North at the two main battles of Celaya in April, the armies of Carranza and Álvaro Obregón controlled the center of the country, paving the way for a Constitutionalist takeover of the capital. In less than a year after the fractious Convention of Aguascalientes, Carranza's supporters had superseded all their opponents and choked them off into more and more isolated sections of Mexico. Yet, three months still remained in what the scholar William Weber Johnson has described as "perhaps the bloodiest year since the Conquest" in Mexico's history.

On October 11, 1915, a portion of Carranza's government transferred to Mexico City from Veracruz, where it had been in exile since its falling out with Provisional President Eulalio Gutiérrez and his agrarian reformers and the Villistas and Zapatistas in November 1914. This enabled the U.S. administration of Woodrow Wilson to extend de facto recognition of the Carranza faction as the official government of Mexico. With this recognition came a prohibition by Washington on the sales of arms or provisions to any other group waging war in the countryside. This decision, too, eventually would wear down any political or military opposition to Carranza.

The Zapatistas in the south remained strangely passive in reaction to "Mister Wilson's" actions. To the scholar John Womack Jr., this attitude is explained as a native skepticism grounded in five years of witnessed desertions and treacheries; simply put, the Zapatistas doubted that Carranza "could retain the loyalty of the genuine revolutionary generals around him." But a more practical reason may be offered: cut off and isolated in the state of Morelos, consistently rebuffed by U.S. authorities as socialists and bandit rebels who would dare to redistribute commercial estates into holdings for peasant villagers, and now denied any access to U.S. arms, Zapata and his chiefs had nowhere to go and no means by which to break out. For the most part, the Zapatistas continued to raid the south but were no longer considered a serious threat to stability by the Constitutionalists and their foreign allies. What Zapata could not clearly see as yet was the reconsolidation of Mexico with Carranza as First Chief. Although the Carranza forces, in Womack's words, "could not yet dominate the whole nation, they could prevent any other factions from displacing them. Henceforth they would rule." Ultimately this would also mean that those who fought "in the interests of the rural poor" would never "become the Mexican state." The glorious unifying visions of Zapata's Plan of Ayala, steadily dimmed by Carranza's elitist regime, never would be realized.

With more territorial leverage, Pancho Villa could fight on, harassing the Constititionalist generals Álvaro Obregón and Plutarco Elías Calles in Sonora and other northern states while trying to rebuild his Division of the North. This seemed highly unlikely; for all intents and purposes, the once apparently invincible army of 22,000 mounted men had been ripped to shreds by Obregón's barbed wire and machine guns at Celaya; the Division of the North with a total loss of over half its forces had ceased to exist as a formidable combat entity. Yet, Villa was able to recover enough of his materials and recruit additional reserves (including several fighters among Yaqui allies in Sonora) to stage fresh attacks from November 1 to 4, 1915, on Calles's forces based in Agua Prieta on the Arizona border. Dismayed by the U.S. government's recognition of the Constitutionalists, Villa was further outraged by the knowledge that Carranza had secretly negotiated a deal with the United States to permit his troops to travel by railway through Texas and New Mexico from Piedras Negras, Coahuila, to Douglas, Arizona. From Douglas, the troops snuck back to reinforce Calles's men. Once again, the Villistas were pummeled by Constitutionalist guns and nearly eradicated. Later,

Pancho Villa would complain bitterly that U.S. searchlights across the border in Douglas had shone upon his troops, denying him the advantage of night attack. In his deep-seated resentments toward the Americans, this was an outrage he could not forget or forgive. With two other major defeats in the same month, at Hermosillo and San Jacinto, Villa was compelled to abandon any hopes of controlling Sonora. As further humiliation of the once great "Centaur of the North," Constitutionalist forces even managed to occupy Ciudad Juárez, Chihuahua, on December 20; on December 24 they controlled Villa's own capital, the city of Chihuahua. Isolated from his sources of support, Villa had no option but to return to his tried and true bandit ways to keep his men fed and outfitted.

The first part of 1916 was witness to tragic events that drew the Wilson government back into the Mexican Civil War in an active way reminiscent of its military intervention at Veracruz in 1914. Debate continues as to Pancho Villa's motives and deliberateness in provoking another intervention by the United States in 1916, but he did successfully create an ambiance of confusion in the borderlands, thus buying him valuable time to rebuild his forces and cleverly maneuver between the Constitutionalist and U.S. invaders of his beloved Chihuahua.

The first of these provoking events took place on January 10, when two Villista commanders, José Rodríguez and Pablo López, stopped a train near Santa Isabel, Chihuahua. They ordered their men to shoot to death 15 American passengers. Villa would later deny sanctioning or blessing this act, but the response across the border was equally violent. Four days following the massacre, mobs in El Paso rioted and attacked the Mexican quarter of the city; General John J. Pershing was forced to deploy his troops to reinstate order. A massive state of alert went up all along the border. Although the killing of Americans (including mining officials) had generated a strong anti-Mexican sentiment in the United States, no response was immediately forthcoming—guerrilla attacks on U.S. citizens had been a routine occurrence since the start of the Mexican Revolution.

Still, Villa had one more card to play. Branded an "outlaw" by decree of Carranza, he began maneuvers that would carry him close to and eventually across the U.S. border on March 9. In an early morning raid on the town of Columbus, New Mexico, approximately 500 Villistas swept down upon the sleeping community and killed 18 Americans, including 10 civilians and 8 soldiers connected to the Thirteenth Cavalry Detachment stationed there. In the resultant chaos of darkness, swirling dust, sporadic gunfire, screaming children and their mothers, and shouts of "Viva Mexico!", the Villistas were able to secure money, arms, and additional horses. By 7:30 that morning, the attackers had withdrawn, fleeing for the Chihuahua wilderness.

Although the standard explanations for Villa's attack on Columbus remain fixed in historic literature—revenge for the U.S. support of Carranza, the desperate act of a regressed bandit, and an attempt to distract his Constitutionalist pursuers and confuse the political alliances between Wilson and Carranza—one other factor is worth noting. With the direct involvement and support of U.S. forces in ensuring Carranza's advantage against Villa (especially support that so flagrantly had come from across the border in repulsing Villa's siege of Agua Prieta), the United States had opened up and expanded the battleground of the Revolution into Mexico's former territories in Arizona and New Mexico. With his back effectively blocked by the armies of Carranza, the most logical arena for Villa's operations now lay north in the relatively calm and open U.S. ranchlands and towns. The attack on Columbus now ushered in the most aggressive intervention of yet another ad hoc "faction" in the Revolution: the Wilsonistas and their so-called Punitive Expedition.

After receiving a call for action from the Wilson administration, Carranza issued a fateful cable giving permission to U.S. forces to intervene if a similar attack "is unfortunately repeated on any other point of the border." Under pressure from the American public, the United States deliberately misinterpreted this message (and possibly applied the five-year-old experience of incessant attacks by many factions across the border) and decided to send troops from Fort Bliss into Chihuahua to pursue and capture Pancho Villa. Under the command of General John J. "Black Jack" Pershing, approximately 5,000 troops of the Punitive Expedition crossed into Mexico on March 15, six days after the raid on Columbus. The real chances of success were slim—as a longtime guerrilla in the Chihuahua wilderness, Villa practically melted into the landscape. One aide to Pershing, Lieutenant George S. Patton Jr. (who would see his first "blood and guts" fighting in Mexico, which thus helped shape the arrogance and brilliant audacity of the later World War II general), wrote with a prescient awareness of the futility of the operation:

I think we will have much more of a party than many think as Villas [sic] men at Columbus fought well and the country [in Mexico] is very bad for regular [U.S.] troops. There are no roads and no maps and no water for the first 100 miles. If we can induce him [Villa] to fight it will be all right but if he breaks up [i.e., fights a guerrilla war] it will be bad, especially if we have Carrenza [sic] on our rear. They can't beat us but they will kill a lot of us. Not me though.

The U.S. soldiers had indeed entered a hostile landscape. Just about every Chihuahuan citizen seethed with rage at the expedition's presence. It was not long before stray patrols were attacked by angry mobs. On April 12 the people of Parral (assisted according to some reports by Carranza's forces) pursued one U.S. detachment, killing two and wounding seven. Pershing demanded the right to officially occupy Chihuahua; Washington refused, ordering the commander to limit activities to "our immediate surroundings." Peace negotiations started on May 2 in Ciudad Juárez to end the Punitive Expedition. The tentativeness of the negotiations (which would not be resolved until January 5, 1917) irked many of the troops to observe cynically, "We rather think that Carranza wants us to stay for a while as our presence keeps Villa out of this part of Chihuahua. . . ." Confined to an ad hoc camp at Colonia Dublan, the troops would face one more harassing attack at Carrizal on June 30, resulting in the deaths of 50 men. When they withdrew February 1917, the last U.S. troops symbolically exiting through Columbus, the singers of Revolutionary *corridos* (ballads) did not fail to sarcastically salute them:

Los soldaditos que vinieron desde Texas
los pobrecitos comenzaron a temblar,
muy fatigados de ocho horas de camino,
los pobrecitos se querían ya regresar.

. . .

Cuando entraron los gringos a Chihuahua
todos pensaban que nos iban a asustar;
pensarían que iban para Nicaragua;
muy asustados pudieron regresar.

(The little soldiers that came from Texas
the poor little tykes started to tremble,
so very tired from eight hours of walking,
the poor babies just wanted to go home.

. . .

When the gringos came to Chihuahua
everybody thought they'd frighten us;
they would think they'd head for Nicaragua;
so very scared they were able to make it
   home.)

Ironically, the Punitive Expedition did seem to keep Pancho Villa at bay, allowing the Carranza government to focus on constitutional concerns. In the fall of 1916 Carranza began to mobilize his plans for a new constitutional convention to be held in Querétaro, a place associated with the creation of the Constitution of 1857 and thus dear to his hero and role model, Benito Juárez. On September 19 Carranza called for the elections of representatives to serve at the Querétaro Congress.

Following the call for a meeting at Querétaro, on September 29 Carranza issued decrees that prohibited the reelection of the president, fixed a maximum of four years for holding the presidential office, and eliminated the office of vice president.

On October 26 the general elections for delegates to the Constituent Congress at Querétaro were held. The winners were expected to create a new constitution, basing their judgments, of course, on a "projected constitution" submitted by Carranza. According to the scholar Robert E. Quirk, the elections were designed to elect only those "who had not opposed Carranza's revolution. . . . There would be no Porfiristas or Huertistas, no Catholics, no Zapatistas, no Villistas, no supporters of the Convention" of Aguascalientes. In essence, it would be a "highly unrepresentative body." Effectively eliminating moderation in debate, the elected Congress would lay the groundwork for a radical social revolution. Opening in November 1916 and closing in January 1917, the Constituent Congress institutionalized many of the anticlerical and xenophobic bigotries of the nineteenth-century Mexican intelligentsia. These actions would continue to feed the flames of factional resentments, betrayals, and bloodshed until the end of the decade.

The constitutional reforms enacted by Carranza and shaped by the Constituent Congress followed in the wake of two other key political events in 1916. In July the economy of the Mexico City area was shut down when various workers' syndicates under the leadership of a group called the Casa del Obrero Mundial (COM, or House of the World Worker) initiated the largest strike the nation had ever seen. With more than 100,000 members, the COM called for workers' control over all capitalist industries. Carranza had dissolved the last elements of the radical Red Battalions in January 1916, but this had stiffened resistance in the other factions of labor. With Mexico City in disarray and thousands roaming the streets in angry protest, martial law was declared August 2. As in the countryside, the Constitutionalists now were dissolving working-class initiatives in the cities. If the city workers protested Carranza's special relations with elitist investors and foreigners, they, too, were finding it fruitless to resist the First Chief by means of either arms or pickets.

The second development was a renewed resistance to Constitutionalist encroachments on Morelos by the Zapatistas. By the end of 1916, 5,000 Zapatista guerrillas were beating back 30,000 Constitutionalist troops. By January 1917 Carranza's campaign to occupy Morelos had collapsed. Although energized by their apparent victory, the Zapatistas succumbed to wishful thinking. Carranza's consolidation of power continued unabated and a new constitution was about to be implemented. The attrition of perpetual isolation eventually would swallow up the sweetness of any feeling of a "free" Morelos.

On February 6, 1917, Carranza called for general elections for the national assembly and the president, to be held on March 11. On February 13 the First Chief named Ignacio Bonillas as ambassador to the United States. On April 26 the Mexican Congress declared Carranza constitutional president for the period December 1, 1916, through November 20, 1920. On May 1 the First Chief entered Mexico City and officially ruled a "united" Mexico under the Constitution of 1917.

It is curious to note that on the day of Carranza's swearing in as president, Obregón, his successful field commander and war minister, resigned for "reasons of health" and retired to his farm in Sonora. In the tradition of Mexican caudillos (strongmen) who aspire to power, this action's symbolic value boldly announced his intention to be president in 1920. Like Agustín de Iturbide, Vicente Guerrero, Antonio López de Santa Anna, and Porfirio Díaz before him, Obregón retired temporarily to await his moment to become the leader of Mexico, the next First Chief.

The period of October 1915 to May 1917 is one particularly defined by the extremes of chaos and order. At the conclusion of this period, it may be true that Zapata and Villa continued to fight, but the tide of an all-pervasive authority was sweeping them away from any base of serious opposition. Within two years Emiliano Zapata would be assassinated and Pancho Villa induced to "retire" to a government-gifted ranch in the state of Durango. Sporadically interrupted by further assassinations and factional disputes, the cooling of the volcanic crust of the Revolution begun in 1917 would continue, hardening and holding in place one Mexico under one constitution and one chief.

Select Bibliography

Azuela, Mariano, *The Underdogs*, translated by E. Munguía Jr. New York: New American Library, 1963.

Bazant, Jan, *A Concise History of Mexico*. Cambridge: Cambridge University Press, 1977.

Blumenson, Martin, *The Patton Papers: 1885–1940*. Boston: Houghton Mifflin, 1972.

Braddy, Haldeen, *Pancho Villa at Columbus: The Raid of 1916*. El Paso: Texas Western College Press, 1965.

Calhoun, Frederick S., *Uses of Force and Wilsonian Foreign Policy*. Kent, Ohio: The Kent State University Press, 1993.

Hart, John Mason, *Revolutionary Mexico: The Coming and Process of the Mexican Revolution*. Berkeley: University of California Press, 1987.

Quirk, Robert E., *The Mexican Revolution and the Catholic Church 1910–1929*. Bloomington: Indiana University Press, 1973.

Tutino, John, "Revolutionary Confrontation, 1913–1917: Regions, Classes, and the New National State." In *Provinces of the Revolution: Essays on Regional Mexican History 1910–1929*, edited by Thomas Benjamin and Mark Wasserman. Albuquerque: University of New Mexico Press, 1990.

Weber Johnson, William, "Modern Mexico Was Formed in the Crucible of Revolution." *Smithsonian* 2:4 (July 1980).

Womack, John, Jr., *Zapata and the Mexican Revolution*. New York: Knopf, 1969.

—JOHN F. CROSSEN

Mexican Revolution: May 1917–December 1920

On May 1, the Constitution of 1917 went into effect, and Venustiano Carranza, the "first chief of the Constitutionalist Army," was inaugurated as president of Mexico. Although Carranza's inauguration had international repercussions, it had little effect domestically: Carranza's enemies cared little about his legal status. Implementing the constitution would be far more of a challenge, as many of its provisions were considered excessively radical by the Catholic Church, merchants and industrialists, landowners, and oil companies.

Pacification

The Constitutionalist Army—now the "Mexican National Army"—had two main enemies: the Division of the North led by Francisco "Pancho" Villa and the Liberating Army of the South led by Emiliano Zapata. There were also other, less important, adversaries whose activities were more localized, such as Saturnino Cedillo in San Luis Potosí.

Carranza's government also was plagued by counter-revolutionary groups. Manuel Peláez's well-armed troops harried the oil camps of the Huasteca region of northeast Mexico, and Félix Díaz, the nephew of the former dictator Porfirio Díaz, operated out of southern Veracruz, supported by many officers from his uncle's defeated Federal Army. In Oaxaca a state's rights movement opposed the 1917 Constitution, while Chiapas saw the creation of two counterrevolutionary groups, the *mapaches* (raccoons) of Tiburcio Fernández Ruiz and the Felicistas under Alberto Pineda Ogarrio. Juan Andrew Almazán attracted followers throughout Mexico, from the north down to Chiapas, and in the state of Michoacán the troops of Inés Chávez García, a former Villista, left ruin in their wake; much the same happened in the neighboring state of Jalisco with its strongman, Pedro Zamora.

In sum there were huge areas in Mexico where the new government simply did not have the power to enforce its laws. Carranza's most urgent priority was military policy. He reorganized the national army, sending its best-armed and most experienced troops and commanders to zones of conflict. In the north, Francisco Murguía was sent to Chihuahua and Durango to pursue Villa, who still moved freely between the city of Parral and the Laguna region, sometimes reaching the state capital of Chihuahua (Murguía later was replaced by Manuel M. Diéguez); Cesáreo Castro hammered at Villa from the other direction in la Laguna. Pablo González was dispatched to pursue Zapata, and Salvador Alvarado left his post of governor of Yucatán to pursue *revoltosos* in southeastern Mexico. Carranza also established an arms and ammunition factory to wean the Federal Army from dependence on foreign producers, who were glutted with orders during World War I.

Results were relatively positive (at least for Carranza). The rebellion was contained if not defeated. Two prominent fighters fell in 1919: Zapata was the victim of an ambush, and Felipe Ángeles, Villa's master strategist, was captured and summarily executed by Diéguez. The *soberanistas* of Oaxaca suffered a series of defeats, and one of their leaders, José Inés Dávila, was killed. By and large, Carranza had every reason to be satisfied as 1919 drew to a close.

Domestic Politics

The Revolution's most radical legislation had been put in place by state governors even before 1917, and for the most part the spirit of the laws continued after the promulgation of the Constitution of 1917. In Jalisco, for example, Governor Manuel M.

Diéguez clashed with the Catholic Church over laws quite similar to article 130 of the Constitution, which limited the number of priests per capita. The archbishop of Guadalajara, Francisco Orozco y Jiménez, was forced to abandon the country for several years.

Although there were relatively few conflicts on a state level, there were a number of clashes over gubernatorial elections. In both Sinaloa and Coahuila the loser in the gubernatorial election fought the winner, and in Tabasco the two front-runners established separate governments, neither of which was recognized legally. The states of Nayarit and Hidalgo saw protracted disputes between the governor and the state legislature, and Mexico City was wracked by a long dispute over municipal representation. A different kind of problem was the political autonomy imposed by some governors, such as Esteban Cantú, who managed to keep Baja California del Norte virtually isolated from the rest of Mexico. Governor Gonzalo Enríquez of Chihuahua faced pressure from the chief of military operations in the region, general Francisco Murguía.

On a national level, reactions to the new constitution were immediate and volatile. The Catholic Church hierarchy condemned restrictions on religious freedom, most notably Articles 3 and 130. Article 3 forbade the clergy from participating in public education, and Article 130 limited the number of priests per capita and restricted the number of foreign priests who could reside in Mexico. Although these articles were implemented in only a few instances (such as in Jalisco), the posturing of the Catholic Church and the Mexican state boded future conflicts.

Merchants and industrialists protested the pro-labor provisions of Article 123. In a conciliatory move, the secretary of industry, commerce, and labor convoked a national congress of merchants and another of industrialists. At the congresses, employers' representatives attempted to have Article 123 abrogated. They also formed a national confederation of chambers of commerce and a confederation of chambers of industry to press their demands in the future.

Article 27 was the most controversial aspect of the Constitution of 1917, however; it affected both national and foreign interests, regulating surface and subsoil property rights. The government began hearing peasant communities' petitions to have lands restored or simply granted to them. In 1917 71 plots of land were distributed, 86 in 1918, 119 in 1919, and 87 by April 1920. Between 1917 and April 1920 101,863 people received a total of 914,000 acres (377,000 hectares). Although later governments distributed far more land, Carranza's government did pay close attention to one key provision that was particularly important for national interests—the regulation of subsoil rights, which would have an enormous impact on the petroleum industry in Mexico. A new registry of property owned by petroleum companies was drafted, and new tax rates were established. Although the oil companies initially refused to pay the new taxes, in the end they had to capitulate. World War I left U.S. interests with scant room to maneuver.

U.S. Pressure

The end of World War I in 1919 was a turning point in U.S.-Mexican relations. During World War I the United States had wanted Mexico to declare war on the Central Powers, but Carranza had opted for neutrality. Both the United States and Germany jockeyed for influence in Mexico. Mexico's neutrality was convenient for Germany, and the U.S. and Great Britain were concerned that Mexican oil could fall into German hands. After the war, U.S. policy became openly aggressive. Senator Albert B. Fall opened hearings against the Carranza government, and Carranza's enemies leaped at the opportunity to testify against him. An enormous file of grievances was assembled, and Fall continued his pressure on Mexico even once President Woodrow Wilson was ill and about to leave the White House.

Events played into Fall's hands. In a naval incident much like the one that had precipitated the invasion of Veracruz in 1914, a boat belonging to the USS *Cheyenne* was stopped in Mexican waters, sparking diplomatic protests and threats of military intervention. Later that year a punitive expedition was sent in pursuit of a bandit who had attempted to kidnap pair of U.S. airmen who had gone down on Mexican soil. The most serious incident was the kidnapping in Puebla of the honorary consul William O. Jenkins. It later turned out that Jenkins had arranged the abduction himself so that he could recover money he owed to the Methodist Church, among other creditors. Carranza remained firm despite U.S. diplomatic pressure, and Wilson had the prudence to ignore the interventionist ranting of Senator Fall and the Republicans. Jenkins was liberated, but he immediately was put on trial by the Carranza government. The U.S. ambassador was recalled to Washington. Relations between Mexico and the United States were at a nadir.

Carranza and Sonora

Despite Carranza's recommendation that the 1920 presidential campaign be postponed, on June 1, 1919, general Álvaro Obregón published a manifesto in Sonora accusing Carranza of having betrayed the ideals of the Mexican Revolution and announcing his candidacy for president. In his campaign against Obregón, Carranza sought to couch the election as a fight between civil ideals and the militarism personified by the generals Obregón and Pablo González, another candidate for president. Carranza's candidate was Ignacio Bonilla, a former ambassador to Washington, an engineer by trade, and—like Obregón—a native of Sonora. By the time Bonilla was able to start his campaign in March 1920, however, Obregón already had completed a whirlwind campaign tour covering nearly half the country.

Relations between the federal government and the state of Sonora were already tense owing to the Carranza administration's insistence on putting the waters of the Sonora River under federal jurisdiction. Obregón's campaign only heightened the tensions. In February Plutarco Elías Calles, Carranza's secretary of industry, commerce, and labor, resigned and returned to his native Sonora to help direct Obregón's campaign. February and March were difficult months. Carranza tried to get military control of Sonora with the help of General Manuel M. Diéguez, and he also accused Obregón of being in league with the Felicista general Roberto Cejudo, putting him under police surveillance. In April Obregón managed to elude his guards and fled to Guerrero. On April 23 Calles and Adolfo de la Huerta, the governor of Sonora, announced the Plan de Agua Prieta. The Plan de Agua Prieta sparked a broad national movement of not recognizing Carranza or the governors of the states that supported him. In what has been termed a "generals' strike," the majority of officers in the Mexican army refused to support Carranza; Diéguez, one of Carranza's last military supporters, was taken prisoner in Guadalajara. Carranza attempted to move his government to Veracruz as he had done in 1915, but railway lines had been cut and Carranza and his entourage were forced to retreat on horseback into the Sierra of Puebla. On May 21, 1920, he was ambushed and killed near the village of Tlaxcalatongo. On June 1 de la Huerta was named interim president until Obregón could assume power.

The Sonorans had formed alliances with several armed groups that had opposed Carranza. In the May 1920 military parade the troops of Emiliano Zapata, Manuel Peláez, and the majority of the Federal Army marched together. Old enemies such as Pablo González, who had commanded Carranza's counterinsurgency against Zapata, and the Zapatista commander Genevevo de la O. had to share positions. Nonetheless, if the new administration could not throw its weight entirely behind the Zapatistas, it could eliminate its most hated enemies. González was court-martialed for sedition; after his case was remanded to a civilian court, he wisely chose to leave for the United States. Jesús Guajardo, Zapata's assassin, had no such luck: tried for murder, he was found guilty and executed. Peláez had supported the Plan de Agua Prieta and was no longer a threat to the government. Félix Díaz entered negotiations with the de la Huerta administration and went into exile in New Orleans, where he unsuccessfully tried to reenergize his movement. The most interesting case, however, was the new government's relationship with Pancho Villa. Although Obregón was not inclined to grant Villa amnesty, de la Huerta granted Villa the hacienda of Canutillo in the state of Durango so that he could retire there to work the land, protected by 50 of his own soldiers.

Oaxaca's sovereignty movement had weakened, so negotiations there were easy; the leader of the *soberanistas,* Guillermo Meixeiro, died a short time later. The leaders of the counterrevolutionary movement in Chiapas, Alberto Pineda Ogarrio and Tiburcio Fernández Ruiz, also laid down their arms. Pineda went into retirement, and Fernández later would be elected governor of Chiapas. The Michoacano strongman Chávez García died of influenza, and Pedro Zamora was harried so intensely by government troops that he ceased to be a real threat. The only Carrancista governor to offer any resistance to the new administration was Esteban Cantú of Baja California del Norte. Troops were sent into Baja California under general Abelardo Rodríguez, and Cantú fled to the United States. By the time Obregón was sworn in as president on December 1, 1920, the armed stage of the Mexican Revolution was effectively over.

Select Bibliography

Beals, Carleton, *Mexican Maze.* Philadelphia and London: Lippincott, 1931.

Brading, David, *Caudillo and Peasant in the Mexican Revolution.* Cambridge and New York: Cambridge University Press, 1980.

Katz, Friedrich, *The Secret War in Mexico: Europe, the United States and the Mexican Revolution.* Chicago and London: University of Chicago Press, 1981.

Knight, Alan, *The Mexican Revolution.* Lincoln and London: University of Nebraska Press, 1986.

Richmond, Douglas W., *Venustiano Carranza's Nationalist Struggle, 1893–1920.* Lincoln and London: University of Nebraska Press, 1983.

Tannenbaum, Frank, *The Mexican Agrarian Revolution.* New York: Macmillan, 1929.

—ÁLVARO MATUTE

Mexican Spanish

With a population of more than 80 million, Mexico is now the largest Spanish-speaking country in the world. The influence of Mexican variant of Spanish which we call "Mexican Spanish" extends far beyond the national borders of Mexico. Although the output of Spain's publishing industries is greater, Mexico's radio, television, and telecommunications industries are the most important in Spanish America.

Cultural Antecedents of Mexican Spanish

Mexico today is a country of enormous contrasts, not only in terms of its landscape, climate, flora, and fauna, but also in the diversity of its indigenous cultures. It is difficult to imagine how life could have been prior to the arrival of the conquistadors. There were two great linguistic and cultural divisions in the territory which today comprises Mexico. The Mesoamerican cultures occupied the temperate and fertile zone south of the Tropic of Cancer through the northern part of Central America. Despite the size and linguistic diversity of the Mesoamerican region, the peoples of Mesoamerica shared a great cultural unity. Five hundred years after Spanish conquest of Mexico, there still remain eleven separate linguistic families in Mexico: Chinantecan, Oaxacan, Huave, Tlapanecan, Totonacan, Mixe-Zoque, Mayan, Uto-Aztecan, Tarascan, Algonquin, and Chiapanecan-Mangue. Although they are quite different from each other, they share a common cosmogony, religious sensibility, conception of social life, and approach to language which continues to help define the elemental features of Mexican culture to this day.

The second group were the hunter-gatherers who inhabited the arid regions north of the Tropic of Cancer. Disparagingly referred to by the Mexica as Chichimecs or "barbarians," these peoples stopped the advance of the Mesoamerican and later Spanish peoples. They have exercised an important but indirect influence on the Spanish population that eventually extended from Mexico City to Guadalajara, east to Monterrey and the northeastern bank of the Rio Grande (Rio Bravo), and north to New Mexico, Texas, and the southern half of present-day California. The Spanish-speaking population of northern Mexico took with it the *mestizaje* (racial mixture) of central New Spain and Spanish language and culture. By not mixing with the indigenous peoples of northern Mexico, this population helped foster a linguistic and social homogeneity which helps explain the considerable linguistic and cultural unity which persists in present-day Mexico.

The Population of Mexico

Debates regarding how many people inhabited the American continent in 1492 will never be resolved since the data on which different demographers and historians base their findings naturally depend on interpretation. In the majority of cases this is limited to extrapolating the quantity on a basis of diverse lists of tributes, pre-Hispanic and Spanish, which are the only accessible documents for demographic research. In the worst examples this extrapolation is slanted by a Hispanicist bias or the reverse, by an tendency to favor the indigenist point of view. Examples of these tendencies would be Ángel Rosenblat on the Hispanicist side and on the indigenist, Woodrow Borah. According to William E. Denevan, who presents the most up-to-date and reliable calculations, even though they could be categorized as being "over the top" (as was done by Nicolás Sánchez de Albornoz) describes the group of hypotheses that tend to increase the population count for America prior to the Conquest), the pre-Hispanic population of Mexico numbered around 21,400,000. Around 1605, scarcely 65 years after the arrival of the Spanish in Mesoamerica, this number had dropped to 1 million. The conquest was responsible for provoking this demographic catastrophe, by decimating the indigenous population through war and via the spread of contagious diseases brought from Europe. Other secondary causes included the exhausting work in the mines and the sugar cane fields, voluntary abortion, and what Sánchez de Albornoz calls *desgano vital* (loss of the will to live). Thus many languages disappeared and those which survived ended up becoming local, losing a greater part of their functional capacity and fragmenting into multiple dialects, many of which now cannot be understood between one local group and another.

The Spanish population (which also included the Negroes who came as servants of the colonial authorities and whose important role in terms of the Conquest as much as the racial composition of Mexico has not been sufficiently studied) was never very high. Peter Boyd Bowman has managed to show, with glimmerings of verisimilitude, that the Spaniards mainly originated from west Andalucía (Seville), Castilla la Vieja and Extremadura. According to the details of the 10,000 Spaniards that populated America until 1600, 30 percent of the colonizers in Mexico were Andalucian, 13 percent from Extremadura and 20 percent from Castilla la Vieja. Nevertheless, the Spanish population never went beyond 1 percent of the total. The mestizaje with the Indians on the other hand, began immediately and increased rapidly. Since Spanish women did not come to New Spain in the initial years of colonization and when they did it was in proportion of one woman for every eight men, the legitimate and illegitimate procreation of the colonizers with Indian women produced a number of mestizo children which grew year by year. From 1.1 percent of the total population around 1570, this percentage grew to 25 percent in 1646 and continued through to 87 percent in 1910 (today the percentage is similar to that of 1910, although such a distinction has no value for contemporary Mexicans).

Spanish domination over the recently conquered territories in Mesoamerica placed under the jurisdiction of New Spain and the phenomenon of mestizaje ensured that the Spanish language predominated within a short time. Indian women, made pregnant by the Spaniards and subsequently rejected by their own people, preferred to teach Spanish to their children. Despite the efforts of the missionaries, particularly the Franciscans headed by Fray Pedro de Gante, to preserve Nahuatl as the lingua franca, Spanish was imposed as the language of administration and commerce (Heath, 1972).

The expansion of Spanish dominion over the territory of New Spain was organized from Mexico City. Once the Aztec dominions of the central plateau were under control, expeditions were sent south to the frontiers of Mesoamerica as far south as Nicaragua and northwards, firstly via Zacatecas and Nuevo León, towards New Mexico and later to Jalisco and the length of the Pacific Coast to San Francisco. These were composed of a reduced number of Spanish soldiers, some friars and a good number of Indians, mestizos and women. It is to be imagined that the language they spoke was a Mexican variant of Spanish, which included an important lexical contribution from Amerindian languages, particularly Nahuatl.

Language and Society in New Spain

Mexican Spanish shares many of the general characteristics of Spanish in the rest of the Americas. First, Mexican Spanish and American Spanish in general share the characteristics that Castillian Spanish acquired in Andalucía—and particularly the city of Seville—after the kings of Castille reconquered Seville from the Moors in the thirteenth century; by the end of the fifteenth century, the letter <s> and the soft <c> were pronounced the same way in Andalucía, as were the letters <ll> and <y>. Second, Spanish throughout the Americas was influenced by the particular shape the Spanish language took in the Caribbean, where colonizers mingled and developed what might be termed a "pioneer Spanish." Finally,

Spanish in the Americas was influence by Amerindian languages. Mexican Spanish was particularly influenced by the Nahuatl language, not only in terms of vocabulary but perhaps also phonetics.

Nonetheless, the evolution of Mexican Spanish possibly also was unique in two important ways. The first was the determinant role played by Mexico City. The political, economic, and cultural center of New Spain, Mexico City was the driving power behind the dispersal of the Spanish language throughout Mexican territory and sought to codify social relations among the Spanish colonizers, mestizos, and indigenous peoples. Mexico City therefore also could have been the driving force behind the evolution of Spanish in Mexico. If so, Mexican Spanish quickly would have acquired a certain unified standard.

The second possible unique factor in the evolution of Mexican Spanish was role played by the viceroyalty of New Spain. The presence of Castilian officials and their court produced two results. On the one hand, there was a Castilian modernization of Spanish, oriented toward the Spanish spoken in the Spanish court in Madrid and Toledo and away from the "vulgarity" of Seville (the best example of this is the disappearance of the *voseo* to indicate the second personal familiar singular and its replacement with the *tuteo*). On the other, there also was a conservation of a literary character that prevented the generalization of the implosive s- or end of the word, as occurred in a large part of the rest of Spanish America, including the coastal areas of the Gulf of Mexico. Although there have been a number of important studies, there still needs to be more sociolinguistic study of the Spanish colonization and expansion in the Americas; social explanations of the uniqueness of Mexican Spanish remain unconfirmed by empirical research.

Dialects of Mexican Spanish

The polity of New Spain rapidly acquired its own linguistic physiognomy. The interior regions, divided into "kingdoms" and later intendancies, evolved according to various factors. These included the characteristics of the indigenous peoples surviving in these areas, the interests involved in the exploitation of mines and agricultural production, the trade routes oriented toward Mexico City and thence to the port of Veracruz, where goods and tribute produced in the colony where sent to Spain, and finally the necessity to avoid attacks by various indigenous groups, particularly in the north of Mexico; the indigenous groups of northern Mexico were not subdued until the beginning of the twentieth century.

According to Juan M. Lope Blanch's *Atlas lingüístico de México*, there seem to be sixteen dialects in present-day Mexican Spanish. Every one of these dialectical variations has its own phonetic, syntactical, and lexical foundations, although the phonetic provides the clearest divisions. Nonetheless, there is a clear unity among the various dialects of Mexican Spanish. All of them are for the most part mutually intelligible, and the phonetic differences are experienced as local and regional accents. Where lexical differences occur, they are usually linked to Amerindian languages, different moments in the colonial process, or differences in systems of production; cattle ranching, mining, agriculture, and fishing, for example, all have their own specialized vocabularies. There is a considerable range of "linguistic loyalty" among the various dialects of Mexican Spanish. That is, dialectical divisions are particularly important in areas with strong regional personalities (such as Nuevo León, northern Veracruz, and Yucatán and Campeche) or where the dialect has especially clear phonetic markers. Most Mexicans will immediately recognize the characteristic intonation of people from northern Mexico, the particular way the *jarochos* (people of southern Veracruz) aspirate the phoneme /s/ when it appears at the end of a word, and the "damaged consonants" of the Yucatecans and Campechans; other dialectical divisions, however, can for the most part only be discerned by the trained ear.

There still needs to be far more nuanced study of the local and regional dialectical variations in Mexican Spanish and their origins. Nonetheless, the dialectical mosaic of contemporary Mexican Spanish has not simply been the preserve of linguists, ethnographers, and historians: it has been a problem of communication among all Mexicans. It has therefore also been a political problem, and from the very beginning of the colonial period Mexico City, the center of political power and communications in Mexico, has been the principal unifying factor in Mexican Spanish.

Standard, "Cultured," and Popular Language

Over and above its dialectical divisions, Mexican Spanish remains relatively stable and unified. A single standardized form of Mexican Spanish is used in the communications media, law and the constitution, education (including for speakers of Amerindians languages), and communication with the rest of the Spanish-speaking world. This "standard language," however, can be broken down into to broad divisions, "cultured" and "popular" language. The "cultured" language of most Mexican literature, scientific texts, and university courses carries far more prestige and is the fruit of the evolution of high culture in Mexico.

Standard language is spoken throughout the country. Because Mexican dialects do not have their own strength or system as did the historical dialects of Europe. Rather, standard language acts as a transmission belt between the dialects and the unique system (in the linguistic sense of the term) of Mexican Spanish. "Cultured" Spanish is transmitted by the national educational system, which uses a standard set of textbooks throughout the entire country. Popular Spanish is transmitted by Mexico City's power to attract migrants, travelers, and economic resources. Mass communications complete the unification of "cultured" and popular language; popular language in particular has been transmitted by the influence of film, radio, and television.

In comparison with international Spanish, Mexican Spanish has the following characteristics. In Mexican Spanish the Castillian distinction among the letters <c, z> and <s> and between the letters <y> and <ll> have been lost; the letter <c> (when it precedes the vowels <e> and <i>) and the letter <z> both are pronounced as <s>, and the letters <ll> and <y> also are pronounced the same, as is the case in most of Spain and some regions of the Andes. Mexican pronunciation tends to be slower than Spanish or Caribbean pronunciation; all consonants are clearly pronounced. In Mexico the word *cansado* is not heard as "cansao," for example, but "cansado." In the southern plateau of Mexico, which includes Mexico City, posttonic vowels (i.e., vowels occurring after the accented syllable) are relaxed. "tl" is pronounced as if it were a single phoneme (as it is in the Amerindian Nahuatl language); *atlántico* is not pronounced "ad-lán-ti-co" or "at-lán-ti-co" as it is in Castillian, but rather as "a-tlán-ti-co." Finally, in many words of Amerindian origin (such as *mixiote, uxmal, Xola*) the letter <x> is pronounced as "sh."

In writing most Mexicans conform to the guidelines laid down by the Spanish Royal Academy, but with two important differences. First, the spelling of Amerindian spoken words tends to reproduce their original phonology—"cenzontle" and not "sinsonte," "México" and not "Méjico." Second, there is a preference for keeping original spelling in foreign languages instead of adapting them to Spanish as the Royal Academy demands ("whisky" and not "güisqui," "film" and not "filme," "diskette" and not "disqueto").

As in the rest of Spanish America, the second person plural pronoun *vosotros* has been replaced with *ustedes,* and second person plural verb conjugation *(amáis, coméis, subís)* has been replaced by the third person plural *(aman, comen, suben).* The etymological direct object pronoun is preferred over the Spanish usage. In Mexico "I saw him" would be rendered as "lo ví," while in Spain it would be rendered as "le ví"; similarly, in Mexico "I called her" would be rendered as "la llamé" rather than "le llamé." Finally, the simple past tense *(amé, comí, subí)* is preferred over the composite past tense *(he amado, he comido, he subido),* which in Mexico is used more to signal duration.

The use of prepositions is somewhat different from the guidelines laid down by the Academy. Sentences indicating the entrance to some place always use the preposition *a* rather than the academically prescribed *en;* for example, "to enter the movie theater" would be rendered "entrar al cine" rather than "entrar en el cine," and "to enter the house" would be rendered "entrar a la casa" rather than "entrar en la casa." As in some Caribbean regions, the preposition *hasta* in Mexican Spanish can mean both the initial limit of an action as well as its final limit. Thus, if in most of the Spanish-speaking world *venden boletos hasta las cinco* would be understood as "they sell tickets until five o'clock," in Mexico it also could be understood as "they sell tickets beginning at five o'clock"; this ambiguity must be resolved through the context of the sentence or through questions that specify the sentence's meaning. Nonetheless, there have not been the sorts of broad, systematic studies of preposition usage which would allow us to determine if there are important differences between Mexican and academic Spanish.

The creation of words uses the same repertory of affixes employed in the rest of the Spanish speaking world. Nonetheless, the resulting word combination vary a great deal from country to country. A bicycle lane in Mexico is called a *ciclopista,* while in Argentina it is called a *bicisenda* and in Peru a *ciclovía.* A speed bump in Mexico is a *tope,* while in Spain it is called a *banda sonora* or a *guardia dormido* ("sleeping policeman"). A chauffered car which can be contracted for special trips or days at a time is called a *taxi turístico* in Mexico, and in Argentina a *remís.*

Although the vast majority of words in standard Mexican Spanish are of Spanish origin, a small fraction of the lexicon is composed of words from foreign languages, particularly French and English (another small fraction comes from Amerindian languages). If during the nineteenth century Gallicism was considered the accursed manifestation of foreign influence over the Spanish language, this role now is played by borrowings from English. Due to the United State's considerable economic and political influence, Anglo-American culture also has considerable influence in contemporary Mexico. Anglicisms can be found everywhere in Mexican Spanish, although the absolute number is probably negligible.

The use of Spanish in Mexico still is characterized by it openness to other languages and its respect for the necessity of all Spanish speakers to understand each other. Until very recently translation of foreign-language works in Mexico was internationally respected. The decline of the publishing industry over the past twenty years, however, has greatly diminished this prestige. The number of translations done in Mexico has fallen (Spain now dominates the market), and many publishing houses have neglected translation.

See also Gender: Gender and Mexican Spanish

Select Bibliography

Boyd-Bowman, Peter, *Patterns of Spanish Emigration to the New World, 1493–1580*. Buffalo: Council on International Studies, State University of New York, Buffalo, 1973.

_____, *Índice geobiográfico de más de 56,000 pobladores de la América hispánica*. Mexico City: UNAM–Fondo de Cultura Económica, 1985.

Canfield, Lincoln D., *La pronunciación del español en América: Ensayo histórico descriptivo*. Bogotá, Colombia: Instituto Caro y Cuervo, 1962.

Denevan, William E., editor, *The Native Population of the Americas in 1492*. Madison: University of Wisconsin Press, 1976.

Heath, Shirley Brice, *La política del lenguaje en México: De la colonia a la nación*. Mexico City: Instituto Nacional Indigenista, 1972.

Lapesa, Rafael, *Historia de la lengua española*. Madrid: Gredos, 1981.

Lara, Luis Fernando, "Activité normative, anglicismes et mots indigènes dans le diccionario del español de México." In *La norme linguistique*, edited by J. Maurais and E. Bédard. Quebec: Conseil de la Langue Française, 1983.

_____, editor, *Diccionario del español usual en México*. Mexico City: Colegio de México, 1996.

Lope Blanch, Juan M., "El léxico de la zona maya en el marco de la dialectología mexicana." *NRFH* 20 (1971).

_____, editor, *Atlas lingüístico de México*. Mexico City: Colegio de México, 1990.

Manrique, Leonardo, *La población indígena mexicana*. Mexico City: INAH, 1994.

Menéndez Pidal, Ramón, "Sevilla frente a Madrid: Algunas precisiones sobre el español de América." In *Miscelánea homenaje a André Martinet*, edited by D. Catalán. Canarias: Universidad de La Laguna, 1962.

Moreno de Alba, José G., *La pronunciación del español en México*. Mexico City: Colegio de México, 1994.

Perissinotto, Giorgio, *Fonología del español hablado en le ciudad de México*. Mexico City: Colegio de México, 1975.

Roesenblat, Ángel, *La población de América en 1492: Viejos y nuevos cálculos*. Mexico City: Colegio de México, 1967.

Sánchez de Albornoz, Nicolás, *La población de América Latina: Desde los tiempos precolombinos al año 2000*. Madrid: Alianza Universidad, 1973.

Zamora Munné, Juan C., and Jorge M. Guitart, *Dialectología hispanoamericana: Teoría, descripción, historia*. Salamanca, Spain: Almar, 1982.

—LUIS FERNANDO LARA

Migration to the United States

This entry includes two articles that discuss migration from Mexico to the United States:

Migration to the United States: 1876–1940
Migration to the United States: 1940–96

See also Foreign Policy; Mexican American Communities; Urbanism and Urbanization; U.S.-Mexican Border

Migration to the United States: 1876–1940

Prior to 1880, migration from Mexico to the United States was practically nonexistent. While there were people of Mexican origin within what are now the boundaries of New Mexico, Texas, Arizona, and California, most had not migrated from Mexico to the United States; rather, residents and their families had come to what is today the southwestern United States when this region was part of New Spain, and then, after the country achieved its Independence in 1821, of Mexico. One notable exception to this were miners from Sonora who migrated to California in the 1850s.

The first large wave of immigrants from Mexico began arriving in the United States in the late nineteenth and early twentieth centuries, pushed primarily by structural, economic, and social transformations that took place as a result of the rule of General Porfirio Díaz (1876–80 and 1884–1911). Of the many projects that Díaz encouraged to promote economic growth and modernization, his renewed emphasis on the importance of private property and the construction of a railway system, which by 1884 connected Mexico City to the United States border, were the most important factors leading to a rise of Mexican migration north. The changes in land tenure brought by the Porfirian government resulted in a large-scale displacement of small landholders, as entire villages lost their lands because they had neither the financial resources nor the knowledge to defend their claims. Railways exacerbated this land struggle by changing property values and pushing peasants into new market economies based on the production of cash and export crops such as sugar and henequen. Some scholars have estimated that by 1910 over 90 percent of all rural families were landless as a result of the increased land concentration and the displacement of peasants and indigenous people during the Porfiriato. Railways provided these landless rural peasants with a fairly inexpensive and quick way to move from their native land to Mexico's urban areas and the north.

At the same time that these changes were taking place in Mexico, an economic transformation in the southwestern United States influenced the movements of these displaced peasants. The completion of the transcontinental railway in 1869 integrated the southwest with the rest of the United States and contributed to booming mining and agriculture industries, both of which required a large number of unskilled workers. Since the U.S. takeover in the 1840s, the region had been too sparsely populated to provide its own workers, and immigration from Asia previously had been an important source of unskilled labor. With the passage of the Chinese Exclusion Act of 1882 and the signing of the "Gentlemen's Agreement" with Japan in 1907, many southwestern employers, particularly the railways, mines, and agricultural interests, could not meet their labor needs. In dire need of workers, they turned to Mexico.

To attract Mexican workers, various companies opened contracting offices in border towns, particularly El Paso, which was the point of entry for many immigrants during this period. Employment agencies specializing in recruiting workers for the railways also sprang up along the border. Furthermore, although the Immigration Act of 1885 forbade the contracting of workers outside the United States, companies hired or made use of agents who traveled to the interior of Mexico, telling people of the job opportunities and high wages that could be obtained in the United States. Given the loss of land, high inflation, and low wages that characterized the Mexican countryside during this period, Mexican men undoubtedly viewed laboring in the United States as an attractive option. This was especially true of the peasants in the densely populated region of central Mexico, particularly the states of Jalisco, Guanajuato, Zacatecas, and Michoacán.

Although it is impossible to provide an accurate figure on the immigration flow north during the late nineteenth century, scholars estimated that by 1900 at least 100,000 Mexicans had migrated to the United States. Many Mexican immigrants first experienced work in the United States on the railways. The continued construction of rail lines in the southwest required a large number of unskilled workers, and Mexicans were hired for many of the most difficult and low-paying jobs, particularly laying track. Mexicans also worked maintaining the track and in many of the railway companies' shops. A 1909 investigation into the status of immigrants in the United States found that Mexicans did the majority of the railway work in Nevada, New Mexico, Arizona, and southern California.

But railways also introduced Mexican immigrants to other employment opportunities in the United States. As scholar Lawrence Cardoso notes, "it was the railroads more than any other single factor that pulled Mexican workers over the border and spread them over the Southwest and beyond as a mobile, cheap labor force available for all types of unskilled work." Many immigrants left the railways to take on jobs in local agriculture, mining, and industries that often offered higher wages. As a result, many Mexicans soon were found working in the mines throughout the Southwest, particularly Arizona, in the cotton fields in southern Texas and the Imperial Valley, in the citrus orchards of southern California and the lower Rio Grande Valley, and in sugar beet farms of northern Colorado. Although most Mexicans remained in the southwest, by the early twentieth century Mexican immigrants also worked in railways throughout the midwest, in coal mines in Oklahoma, and in smelters, packing houses, and auto assembly plants in midwestern cities. By the turn of the century, therefore, Mexicans had become an important sector of the labor force in mining, railways, and agriculture of the southwest and were beginning to fan across other sections of the United States.

The deteriorating living conditions in Mexico and the burgeoning labor opportunities in the southwest intensified northern migration by the first decade of the twentieth century. Whereas in 1890 the number of Mexican citizens living in the United States was probably under 78,000, it increased to 103,000 in 1910 and then doubled to 222,000 by 1920. These figures, of course, underestimate the flow of Mexicans to the United States by not taking into account the men who came to work and then returned to their native country.

The eruption of the Mexican Revolution in 1910 affected both the quantity and the composition of the immigrant stream. While prior to 1910 the men who migrated to the United States primarily had been landless peasants and rural workers, the

Revolutionary chaos encouraged hacienda owners, middle-class professionals, intellectuals, railway workers, and miners to seek both work and protection north of the border. Groups loyal to Porfirio Díaz also moved to such places as San Antonio and Los Angeles. The Revolution, furthermore, resulted in a rise in the number of families, as opposed to single men, who migrated north. Having lost much of what they had as a result of Revolutionary strife, immigrants who had belonged to very different sectors of society while in Mexico now found themselves working alongside each other in unskilled jobs throughout the southwestern United States.

As the conflict and violence of the Mexican Revolution uprooted thousands of Mexican families, the demand for labor continued to increase as a result of the continued prosperity of the southwest and the outbreak of World War I. In addition, the passage of the Immigration Act of 1917 now restricted immigrants from southern and eastern Europe, who previously had worked on western railways, mines, and farms. Mexicans were left out of U.S. quota regulations in 1917 and 1924 and even after. Southwestern interests, particularly growers and sugar beet processing companies, responded to the passage of the 1917 law by launching a campaign complaining of their severe labor shortages and informing the government of the dire consequences that the new legislation's literacy test would have on their labor supply. The growers' efforts paid off quickly; on May 23, 1917, the U.S. secretary of labor initiated a new program that waived the literacy test, head tax, and contract labor clause in the 1917 Immigration Act for temporary agricultural workers from Mexico. Eventually, exceptions also were made for Mexicans coming to work temporarily in railroads, mines, and even government construction work. According to employers, Mexicans were suitable workers because they would stay only temporarily and would then return to their native country. In addition, the Labor Department also tried to set rigid standards to keep the Mexicans admitted under this exception from becoming permanent residents. By the time this program was terminated in early 1921, a total of 72,862 Mexican workers had participated over the course of four years.

Despite the end of this temporary admission program, southwestern employers continued to look to their southern neighbor for workers and Mexicans continued to find migration north an attractive option. The pro-Catholic, peasant-based Cristero Revolt (1926–29) provided a strong incentive for many in Jalisco, Michoacán, and Guanajuato to look north. Even though Mexicans received the lowest wages of any immigrant group and were for the most part prevented from joining labor unions, by the 1920s, approximately 49,000 Mexicans were migrating to the United States per year. Mexicans could easily cross the border when they could not obtain legal permission; the Border Patrol, established in 1924, with its small number of officials was unable to enforce the border effectively before World War II. By the 1920s, Mexicans also were forming large enclaves in large industrial cities such as Los Angeles, San Antonio, and Chicago, which held the largest concentration of Mexicans outside the southwest. This period also witnessed the rise of Mexican and Mexican American urban culture, particularly in radio and print.

The stock market crash in 1929 and the subsequent Great Depression shut off Mexican migration to the United States for more than a decade. Anti-Mexican rhetoric had been circulating in Congress for more than a decade, and now Herbert Hoover blamed Mexican workers, in part, for the southwest's economic troubles. The few existing jobs were now reserved for American citizens, and local governments began a highly organized effort to return Mexican immigrants to their native country. Whereas during the previous 30 years Mexicans had been heavily recruited to work in the United States, they now were rounded up at work, on the street, and in shops, put into boxcars and shipped to Mexico. Government pressures, the lack of employment opportunities and relief, and the rising anti-Mexican sentiments throughout the southwest also encouraged many Mexicans to "voluntarily" repatriate themselves to their native land. The Mexican government, through its consular offices in the United States, provided other incentives, such as free transportation and the promise of access to land and labor, to return Mexicans home. As a result of these local and national efforts, an estimated 500,000 Mexicans, some of whom were U.S.-born children of immigrants, returned to Mexico.

The Great Depression thus marked the end of the first long wave of continuous Mexican migration to the United States. While estimates vary, many scholars believe that between 1 million and 1.5 million Mexicans entered the United States between the 1880s and 1929. Repatriation briefly reversed this long migratory long flow, but the onset of World War II and its concomitant demand for workers would soon lead the United States to once again look to Mexico to fill its labor needs.

Select Bibliography

Cardoso, Lawrence, *Mexican Immigration to the United States, 1897–1931*. Tucson: University of Arizona Press, 1980.

Galarza, Ernesto, *Barrio Boy*. South Bend, Indiana: University of Notre Dame Press, 1971.

Garcia, Mario, *Desert Immigrants: The Mexicans of El Paso, 1880–1920*. New Haven, Connecticut: Yale University Press, 1981.

Gutiérrez, David G., editor, *Between Two Worlds: Mexican Immigrants in the United States*. Wilmington, Delaware: Scholarly Resources, 1996.

Hoffman, Abraham, *Unwanted Mexican Americans during the Great Depression: Repatriation Pressures, 1929–1939*. Tucson: University of Arizona Press, 1974.

Massey, Douglass, et al., *Return to Aztlan: The Social Process of International Migration from Western Mexico*. Berkeley: University of California Press, 1987.

Reisler, Mark, *By the Sweat of their Brow: Mexican Immigrant Labor in the United States, 1900–1940*. Westport, Connecticut: Greenwood Press, 1976.

Sánchez, George J., *Becoming Mexican American: Ethnicity, Culture and Identity in Chicano Los Angeles, 1900–1945*. Oxford: Oxford University Press, 1993.

Vargas, Zaragosa, *Proletarians of the North: A History of Mexican Industrial Workers in Detroit and the Midwest, 1917–1933*. Berkeley: University of California Press, 1993.

— Martín Valadez

Migration to the United States: 1940–96

The migration of people between Mexico and the United States is profound and enduring. Migration, in part, involves the permanent or very long-term resettlement of persons from Mexico to the United States; it likewise includes the repetitive, cyclical movement of persons between permanent homes in Mexico and temporary homes and jobs in the United States. In the Bracero Program (1942–64) such cyclical migration was done under legal auspices of the U.S. and Mexican governments. But the same pattern continued even when considered illegal by the U.S. government, thus creating undocumented immigration. The process of migration, finally, includes the impact of returnees on home regions in Mexico. No single effort to understand or change migration from Mexico to the United States suffices. One can look at migration from the point of view of U.S. intentions: the categories of law, the immigration interests, and policies. But one also learns from the enduring organization of immigration among Mexicans themselves, including economic changes that motivate

Mexicans to depart home communities. Finally, one ought to understand, with empathy, the experience of migration itself, the perils of crossing the border, and the rewards of forming new communities.

Mexican migration to the United States had halted during the 1930s because of the Great Depression and the mass repatriation of Mexicans. When migration resumed after 1940, stimulated by the booming war economy, many "migrants" were returning U.S. citizens who had been swept up in the repatriation. There was a trickle of new legal immigrants and, after 1942, of Bracero contract workers. Importantly, when migration resumed after 1940, it drew on older historical patterns. The same west-central Mexican states contributed immigrants, and they resumed the typical paths and destinations in the United States. California, Texas, and the western United States were important, as was Chicago; however, other cities such as Detroit did not recover as destinations after the repatriation. The evidence indicates that Mexican communities retained their knowledge about U.S. target jobs and residential areas across the divide of the 1930s. Mexican migration to the United States has endured in its basic form for nearly a century.

Legal immigration is the core of the migratory flow from Mexico to the United States, although undocumented immigration has a higher profile. Legal permanent residents (LPRs) are persons admitted to live and work in the United States without restriction. They remain citizens of Mexico and may be deported under U.S. laws, such as for felony violations. After five years, LPRs may, if they choose, apply for naturalization as U.S. citizens, with full political rights. They may not be deported. The proportion of immigrants of Mexican origin who naturalize is relatively low, however. In the decade 1940 to 1950, 61,000 persons of Mexican origin legally immigrated to the United States; from 1951 to 1960, 300,000 persons did; from 1961 to 1970, 454,000 did; from 1971 to 1980, 640,000 did; and in the incomplete decade 1981 to 1989, 975,000 did.

Although the United States severely restricted Asian and European immigration from 1924 to 1965, Mexico, as part of the Western Hemisphere, was not subject to numerical restrictions. Instead, immigrants were admitted from Mexico by means of a petition to the Immigration and Naturalization Service (INS) from U.S. relatives or employers. It often included an offer of work waiting in the United States. This favored the prior connection of immigrant to employer by Bracero or undocumented work, or among immigrants through personal networks. In 1965, U.S. immigration law opened a moderate-sized door to the rest of the world. Again, Mexico, as part of the Americas, was limited only by a hemispheric ceiling of 120,000 persons per year. In 1976, American nations were included in the system of national quotas, 20,000 per nation, supplemented by certain close kin who are not limited by this ceiling. A system of visas requires either specific family relations to citizens or legal residents, or employer petitions approved by the Department of Labor and certifying that immigrant workers will not negatively affect domestic workers. Few Mexicans today enter by employer petition, so legal Mexican immigration involves a subtle coordination of kinship petitions with labor markets, centered on networks of relatives getting jobs for new family members. In 1990 the United States again reconfigured its immigration laws, raising Mexico's annual ceiling to 25,620, and altered the rather arcane system of visas. The overall pattern remains similar, however.

LPRs shape the migratory process of temporary and undocumented immigrants. LPRs often hold key jobs in migrant-utilizing enterprises. They act as labor contractors or informal job brokers. U.S. employers thus depend on legal Mexican immigrants for the renewal of their labor force. When migration occurs in such a chain, LPRs provide critical links of help with housing, border crossing, and other needs. The United States periodically expels accumulated Mexican migrants, but LPRs form enduring beachheads in the United States that permit renewal of Mexican cyclical immigration. In turn, many LPRs of the period between 1960 and 1977 were former Braceros whose patron employers petitioned for their legal entry. Other LPRs were former undocumented immigrants who established kin and other ties sufficient to utilize the U.S. legal framework.

The figures for Mexican legal immigration between 1987 and 1989 temporarily rose through legalization of formerly undocumented persons. This one-time admission was part of the Immigration Reform and Control Act of 1986 (IRCA), a law that otherwise sought to slow undocumented immigration. The IRCA provided two systems for legalization of undocumented immigrants. Persons in the United States without documents continuously since January 1, 1982, were eligible to apply to the main legalization program. Approximately 1,162,000 persons of Mexican origin had their status legalized in this manner. In addition, Special Agricultural Workers (SAWs) could apply for legalization on the basis of 90 days of illegal seasonal agricultural work between 1983 and 1986 or between 1985 and 1986.

The unusual double design of the IRCA legalization indicates something of U.S. politics. The main legalization derived from U.S. notions that a clandestine immigrant population may be legislated out of existence. However, the SAW provisions indicated the continuing power of agribusiness as it seeks a surplus and desperate labor force. Ironically, the combined legalization provisions of the IRCA altered Mexican-origin immigrant communities in ways that defy the plans of legislator and agribusinessman. Legalization permitted diversification of jobs out of agricultural labor, indicating a modest but important expansion in the control that immigrants exercise over their own lives. Legalization has lead to some recomposition of split Mexican-U.S. families, involving permanent resettlement of families in the United States and concomitantly the cyclical commitment to Mexico.

The principal form of cyclical migration from 1942 to 1965 was the Bracero Program. Mexican working men were contracted for up to six-month periods under U.S. government sponsorship. They worked legally but without any rights to immigrate to the United States. Braceros principally worked in farm labor. The program began with a 1942 binational agreement for the importation of agricultural laborers during World War II. The wartime program ended in 1947, two years after the war ceased. In spite of the program's termination, the United States unilaterally admitted temporary Mexican laborers under the exceptional parole authority of the attorney general. In the meantime, Mexico and the United States struggled over a new agreement. Mexico sought to eliminate direct grower contracting of Braceros in favor of government-to-government contracting, a provision meant to reduce contract abuses, as well as other modifications of U.S. unilateral practice. In 1951, the U.S. Congress passed Public Law 78, threatening a massive unilateral program. The two nations soon came to an agreement based on government-to-government contracting. Public Law 78 continued until the United States ended the Bracero Program in December 1964. Overall, approximately 4,650,000 Mexicans were admitted as temporary laborers. The peak years lasted from 1954 to 1960, during which time over 300,000 people were admitted annually.

U.S. agribusiness controlled the political and regulatory arrangement of the Bracero Program throughout its existence. Through farm bureaus and other agricultural associations, farmers exercised profound influence on the local movement and supply of labor, and on the application of contractual obligations. Legal protections were rarely enforced, except through some appeals to Mexican consulates. Workers were not unionized, and Bracero labor suppressed the unionization of U.S. farmworkers during the period. Between 1942 and 1954, especially 1947 to 1954, undocumented immigration coexisted with Bracero contracting, and many Braceros were former undocumented migrants simply recategorized by the INS. Agribusiness alternately battered the INS in Congress and dictated its actions in the field. In 1954, however, General Joseph Swing reshaped the way that farm interests interacted with the U.S. government. He strengthened the border policing image of the INS and closed the back route of undocumented migration, but he rewarded growers by replacing the lost undocumented workers with increased contracting levels and by making the INS the scourge of Mexican workers who left farms and skipped their contracts. As a by-product of this political realignment of U.S. capital and state, over 1 million undocumented Mexicans were driven from the United States in 1954's Operation Wetback.

The Mexican popular experience of the Bracero Program differed, however, from this bleak picture. In part people could not see the politics above them, and in part they viewed the migrant experience through their own goals in life. They sought money to support families, to buy land, and to advance small enterprises. The Bracero work was understood as burdensome, but also as fulfilling such needs. Thus, the Bracero era reinforced the need in rural Mexico for labor sojourning in the United States.

When the Bracero Program ceased in 1964, the conditions for undocumented immigration returned. Undocumented immigration gradually grew from 1965 until the late 1970s. Evidence from arrest statistics of the INS is to be used with caution. They represent events of capture, not numbers of persons who get into the United States; they can be compared among themselves to see trends but definitely should not be used to indicate the undocumented persons residing in the United States. In the following statistics, over 90 percent of arrests are of Mexicans: in 1965, 110,000 undocumented aliens were arrested; in 1970, 345,000; in 1975, 766,000; and by 1979, over 1 million. From 1979 to the present, the number of arrests has remained stable, ranging from several hundred thousands over, to just under, 1 million. Since most persons who enter the United States without documents also leave, and since a fair number of people were legalized in the IRCA, the reasoned estimates of the resident undocumented population of Mexican origin are surprisingly low, approximately 1 million in 1992 (representing only 31 percent of the resident total, according to Michael Fix's and Jeffrey S. Passel's *Immigration and Immigrants* [1994]). These numbers tell a story. In the post-Bracero period, Mexicans gradually learned about undocumented entry in the United States and then consolidated the process, without migration ever being explosive. They developed increasingly effective information about how to cross the border and where to find jobs, and they diversified locations and employment until undocumented networks were indeed an integral part of American society.

U.S. law has never halted undocumented immigration. While work in the United States was illegal for undocumented immigrants themselves, for many decades it was not illegal for the employers. In the 1986 IRCA law, employment of undocumented immigrants was made illegal. The law has not been effective. First, relatively few INS workers are assigned to enforce employer sanctions, and they develop cases with great caution about penalizing businesses. Second, the law absolves firms if the undocumented job applicant provides documents that ostensibly indicate legitimate citizenship or residence inside the United States. A vast market in forged documents has arisen. In lieu of real documents, subtle understandings among firms, managers, existing workers, kin, and friends from the same hometown guide the acquisition of false documents and real jobs. Finally, INS boundary enforcement has proven ineffective against Mexicans. The INS (especially its Border Patrol branch) aggressively arrests undocumented persons. However, when undocumented Mexicans are arrested, they are not held for deportation trial, but rather rapidly released into Mexico without charges (termed "voluntary departure"). From there, they find ways to return to the United States, perhaps with some suffering, but nevertheless able to continue their undocumented presence. This system may appear arbitrary, but realistically the United States cannot afford nor is it willing to impose lengthy imprisonment of hundreds of thousands of Mexican nationals at the border.

The continued presence of voluntary departure, and thus the covert toleration of undocumented migration, is a major fact of U.S. political life requiring explanation. The patterns of employment and geography of undocumented Mexican workers provide an interesting map of domestic U.S. interests in undocumented immigration. Undocumented workers shifted, from 1965 to 1990, from agricultural employment to urban services (restaurants, landscaping, et al.) and secondarily manufacturing and construction. During the same period, undocumented residence shifted from principally rural western locations toward metropolitan areas, the most important still in the west (California, especially). But Mexican residence also expanded throughout the entire United

States. The new sectors pay undocumented immigrants low wages, but in most cases wages at or above the legal minimum. They are generally characterized by small firm size and competitive or high-risk market position. Undocumented workers in a case noted by Robert J. Thomas in *Citizenship, Gender, and Work* (1985) were relatively exploited. They produced more at a faster pace than did U.S. citizens and legal residents working at their sides. This was attributable to the very fact of illegal immigration: migrants maximized earnings before being arrested and deported, or leaving on their own. In some cases, undocumented workers owed their jobs to informal brokers who were connected in turn to smugglers. However, undocumented workers are not necessarily passive; they resist by jumping jobs and occasionally by unionization.

Cohesive agribusiness elites who directly influenced congressmen from southern and western states dominated the older political economy of undocumented and Bracero migration to the United States. The influence of this bloc continues, just as agricultural employment has not disappeared; and because agribusiness is cohesive, it influences even the recent politics of labor supply (e.g., the SAW provisions). The new service and small manufacturing sectors are less politically capable. Rather than openly making immigration policy, they are sheltered by its incompleteness, such as the continuing flaccidity of employer sanctions. Their interests are also facilitated by the quiet networks of migration, which perpetuate and amplify patterns of labor supply without as active a political touch as in the past. In the realm of overt immigration debates, the period from 1975 to 1995 witnessed an accelerating symbolic politics of immigration restriction and xenophobia. We note its roots in areas such as southern California that, ironically, receive the labor benefits of immigrants in services. Study of this contradictory politics has hardly begun, but its analysis must look into realms of conceptual citizenship, race, and power, as well as direct economic interests. The new politics of immigration restriction mobilized support for nominal laws such as the IRCA but through 1995 has not truly reversed the policies protecting employers of undocumented immigrants. The result, so far, is massive law enforcement (the INS employs approximately 5,000 Border Patrol officers) that burdens undocumented immigrants but not those who benefit from them.

Undocumented crossing is risky, disorienting, and transformative for Mexican immigrants. Intensive enforcement against undocumented immigration creates a profitable underworld, with the attendant harms of illegality and clandestinity. Nearly half of Mexican undocumented entrants use smugglers. Dangers, such as vehicles hitting pedestrian immigrants, are rife. The INS makes over 1 million arrests per year, many routine, but some involving fights and human rights abuses. Once inside the United States, new arrivals live with relatives or hometown friends, in marginal industrial districts, older cores of Mexican-origin city neighborhoods (barrios), or unincorporated farmworker settlements *(colonias)*. Housing is crowded, sometimes polluted, and may require outrageous rents. Undocumented residence groups, though predominately male, do include large numbers of women and children. Women come both to sojourn for paid work and to reunite households within the strong Mexican gender division of labor. U.S. migrant households tend to be large, capable of mutual support, flexible, and easily expanded. Fundamentally, Mexican migrant households rely on their own community resources to deal with the United States: seeking housing, finding income, and reducing loneliness and boredom. Undocumented immigrants do use governmental services, though sparsely; they do send children to public schools and will, at extremes, use public hospitals. Debates about whether undocumented immigrants pay more taxes or use more services are inconclusive. Migration to the United States involves more than merely crossing the international border; it entails a complex passage from social and cultural ties in Mexico to a relatively committed settlement and identity within U.S. society. Many immigrants, "sojourners," deliberately exit U.S. society before they build strong ties; for example, most undocumented Mexicans depart the United States without INS arrest. Gradually some persons settle in the United States, becoming social members of U.S. life whether or not the United States accords them political rights and recognition.

We may turn to Mexican folk expressions—*corrido* ballads and painted tin *retablo* religious offerings—to see the popular perspective on immigration. The United States is depicted, first, as a place of promise. Though this may seem to glorify the United States, the emphasis lies as much on social and economic critique of life inside Mexico. Second, the United States is depicted as a place of peril. In their nature as spiritual thanks, *retablos* especially emphasize rescue from perils, whether arrest at the border or serious illness treated in a hospital far from home. This provides a palpable sense of the anxiety —realistic, one might add—induced by immigration. Finally, ballads express anger about job exploitation and racial prejudice, and they enact imaginary scenarios of defiance toward INS arrest. This reveals that immigrants do not internalize their powerless and constrained illegal status, although they may subordinate their feelings in situations calling for caution and deference.

Emigration from Mexico does not result from stagnation and massive rural impoverishment. It actually occurs within two dynamics: the incomplete, but still extensive, redistribution of land and the modernization of agriculture (its technology and commercialization) since the 1940s. These combined forces of uneven development favor capitalist brokers and large farmers, yet they also sweep vast numbers of tiny farmers into the cash economy. The newly commercial peasants have large families, launching the Mexican demographic expansion that also powerfully drives emigration. Moderately well-off peasants often are first to emigrate. They cannot provide land or economic opportunities for all their children, but they can front the money to go to the United States. Once these migrants establish a hometown network, even poorer families can follow the chain. U.S. migration during the period from 1940 to 1980 was strongest in rural towns in the west-central Mexican states of Jalisco, Guanajuato, Michoacán, Zacatecas, San Luis Potosí, and Chihuahua. However, since the debt crisis of 1982, emigration to the United States has proliferated to the entire Mexican nation. It involves emigrants from Mexico City and from southern states such as Oaxaca. Some of the new emigrants are indigenous peoples, such as the Mixtec. Indigenes are a new, doubly exploited segment inside Mexican migration; but in being exploited together, U.S. Mixtecs (and others) create ethnic-national identities more comprehensive than those they had while divided among hometowns in Mexico. All in all, Mexican emigration is becoming wider, deeper, and more diverse.

Sojourning in the United States is usually undertaken as a work role within an obligatory household economy. The amount of money that goes back ("remittances") is difficult to estimate, but a reasoned figure cited by Jorge Durand and Douglas S. Massey in "Mexican Migration to the United States" (1992) was US$2 billion in 1984. Remittances support routine household maintenance, housing, health care, and the like, all of which, in turn, renew continued outmigration of labor power. However, remittances are sufficiently large that they may also be invested in longer-term economic and political projects. Remittances may be applied toward the purchase of land and such agricultural inputs as seed, fertilizer, and implements; migrants may be leading contributors to community public works, schools, and roads. At its best, migration may be understood as permitting Mexicans to cope with underdevelopment, and

at its worst, as contributing to decline in the countryside (e.g., fueling unproductive, status-seeking purchases of land). Such worst-case scenarios occur, however, in regions and times providing few opportunities for small-scale investment. When good land is available, agricultural inputs are realistic, or small-scale industrialization is viable, migrants do make productive use of remittances. Mexico thus shows a complex pattern of social and economic outcomes of migration to the United States. One recent study, for example, compared short-term, low-earning, low-investment migration from northern Coahuila with longer-term, higher-earning, and higher-investment migration from central Zacatecas. This perspective views migration not as a uniform phenomenon, but as being shaped—both in its initiation and results —by land access, rural class structure, and overall economic trajectory.

Interpretations of Mexican-U.S. Migration

Scholarly approaches to Mexican-U.S. migration began with "push/pull" models. Push factors are reasons why Mexicans leave, such as new needs for income; pull factors are opportunities that immigrants find in the United States, such as low-wage service jobs. Push and pull approximate the classical economic categories of supply and demand. Push/pull models tend to assume a rational, solitary decision maker, and thus lead to studies of aggregated individual characteristics (such as educational distribution among migrants) that shape the choice to migrate.

An important criticism of push/pull models is that they artificially separate Mexico and the United States. Many scholars have broadened their perspective to examine broad changes in the global capitalist economy that affect U.S.-Mexican migration. For example, some scholars have looked at the effect of support for large-scale mechanized agriculture. In Mexico, small-scale peasant producers of basic grains have been displaced by large-scale mechanized agriculture and have seen their produce undervalued, increasing migratory supply. At the same time, similar changes in agricultural investment, technology, and cost structures have increased demand for low-wage labor in U.S. agriculture.

Although global development models have been able to document many of the broad changes that increase migration on a regional or global scale, they have done little to explain the formation of specific migratory circuits. Much recent scholarship has sought to address this imbalance, looking at specific migratory networks—the information transfers, assistance, and ties of mutuality that facilitate the movement of people. Networks link specific sending areas in Mexico with specific job markets and residential areas in the United States, requiring modification of push/pull models. A migrant leaving his or her home community in Mexico may have his or her trip financed by family, friends, and neighbors who have already found work in the United States, and she or he may be able to count on their help in finding housing, work, and other resources upon arriving in the United States. Similarly, employers of migrant labor in the United States often do not draw on a broad, undifferentiated labor pool but will choose to hire friends, family, and neighbors of current and past employees. Seen through the lens of network models, migrant labor does not seem to be strictly subject to supply and demand, but segmentary and socially controlled.

Nonetheless, network models are simply too local to conceptualize the broad economic and political changes that lead to the formation of networks in the first place. Many of these broad changes are illuminated by global development models, which look at Mexico and the United States in the context of a changing global capitalist economy. Other models of migration, however, have examined the United States and Mexico as a single system, emphasizing the structural inequalities between the two countries. These models factor in the cost of supporting a workforce in two ways: first, the daily cost of supporting actively employed workers; and second, the "social cost." That is, capitalists must not only pay for the subsistence of current employees, but they also must pay the social costs of bringing current workers to full productivity, raising a new generation of workers, and retirement. In a nonmigratory system workers and their households survive over the long run only when current and lifetime costs are supported in wages or by governments. However, migration permits employers to select a labor force in which the costs of upbringing are borne by another society (Mexico) and another economic order (the peasant household). If push/pull and network models tend to see migration as mitigating inequality, this model sees migration as reinforcing structural inequalities, transferring wealth from relatively poor Mexicans to U.S. employers and their national economy as a whole. Nonetheless, models emphasizing structural inequalities have been criticized for reproducing a static notion of Mexico as a traditional, subsistence peasantry that unproblematically supports an advanced capitalist United States. We need studies that estimate the actual transfer of wealth and a reconsideration of structural inequalities in more adequate historical terms.

Transnationalist models also posit a single system combining Mexican and United States locations, but they usually emphasize questions of identity rather than transfer of wealth (Roger Rouse has combined a transnationalist approach with elements of other models, however, looking at transformation of migrant class identities—how Mexican migrants learn to be and resist being U.S. workers). Transnationalism contends that migrant identities are historically binational and complexly developed; migrants are not simply proprietors of an unambiguous Mexican culture that is assimilated into U.S. society. Nonetheless, we need to be careful to differentiate between migration networks and specifically transnational identities. Some migrant groups emphasize transnational identities over specific national identities (such as the Oaxaca-California Mixtec), while other migrants make decidedly one-sided claims to national identity (such as Mexican applications for permanent residence and, five years later, naturalization in the United States).

Despite the apparent fragmentation of the scholarly literature, there is a broad consensus on a number of questions. Scholars emphasize the power of politically organized capital in deliberately initiating migratory systems (as happened during the Bracero Program) and the subsequent shift to resilient and informal migration relying on networks. Many scholars inquire into the role of the U.S. government in labor regimes, hoping to shed light on the strange legal category of "illegal" immigrant. They now know that models positing a strict division between Mexican and U.S. society are inadequate, and that both economies and identities may be transnational. They remain aware that migration is potentially a transfer of wealth from crisis-ridden Mexico to the relatively comfortable United States. The challenge for scholars is to convert their critical stance into positive paths toward a more just and humane transnational labor regime.

Migration from Mexico to the United States has developed in its own fashion, not easily subject to design by either nation. The United States has seen the development of profound xenophobia, expressed publicly and tactfully in two major reports (1981, 1994) that propose a bureaucratic system of job control and physical border enforcement. Voters in the state of California have passed Proposition 187, a referendum to deny undocumented immigrants schooling, medical care, and other government services. These actions would reduce the quality of life for undocumented families, yet the enduring history of Mexican migration gives no reason to believe that they would halt the movement of people. The United

States, in reality, faces limited options: the status quo, tolerating a clandestine people inside a democratic society; a serious bureaucratic effort to stop immigration by means of a national identification card to control both jobs and movement around the nation; or legal temporary migration—a new Bracero Program—combined with a permanent residence mechanism for settlers out of that migrant stream. Mexico, too, places its designs for migration on the line in the 1990s. The North American Free Trade Agreement (NAFTA) supposedly will create employment in Mexico, but the liberalization of imports, market speculation, and development of capitalized agriculture may have the opposite result, especially in the short run. Likewise, the free market in *ejido* land may expand rural employment, or it may lead to displacement from the countryside. When we acknowledge the urgent interests, demographic pressures, and binational skills of the Mexican people, we realize that migration likely will continue; we then come to ask what conditions—humane or inhumane—and with what results—destructive or constructive—it shall follow.

Select Bibliography

Commission for the Study of International Migration and Cooperative Economic Development, *Unauthorized Migration: An Economic Development Response.* Washington, D.C.: Government Printing Office, 1990.

Durand, Jorge, and Douglas S. Massey, "Mexican Migration to the United States: A Critical Review." *Latin American Research Review* 27:2 (1992).

Fix, Michael, and Jeffrey S. Passel, *Immigration and Immigrants: Setting the Record Straight.* Washington, D.C.: Urban Institute, 1994.

Huddle, Donald, *The Cost of Immigration.* Washington, D.C.: Carrying Capacity Network, 1993.

Select Commission on Immigration and Refugee Policy, *U.S. Immigration Policy and the National Interest: The Final Report and Recommendations.* Washington, D.C.: Government Printing Office, 1981.

Thomas, Robert J., *Citizenship, Gender, and Work: Social Organization of Industrial Agriculture.* Berkeley and Los Angeles: University of California Press, 1985.

U.S. Commission on Immigration Reform, *U.S. Immigration Policy: Restoring Credibility. 1994 Report to Congress.* Washington, D.C.: Government Printing Office, 1994.

—Josiah McC. Heyman

Military

This entry includes three articles that discuss the armed forces of New Spain and Mexico:

Military: Bourbon New Spain
Military: 1821–1914
Military: 1914–96

See also Conquest; Foreign Policy; Human Rights; Nationalism; Rural Economy and Society; U.S.-Mexican Border

Military: Bourbon New Spain

When eighteenth-century military planners in New Spain perceived the need for organized armed forces, they focused upon three potential areas: first, defense of the Gulf Coast, especially near Veracruz, against foreign raiders or invaders; second, protection of northern frontier provinces against bellicose migratory indigenous tribes; and third, internal security against urban uprisings and rural bandit gangs. From the sixteenth century there were attacks and wartime assaults against the coastal cities, towns, and fortifications such as Veracruz, Campeche, and Acapulco. French, British, and Dutch raiders and buccaneers posed chronic threats and interrupted commerce. However, by the time the Bourbons came to power in Spain at the beginning of the eighteenth century, the threats of raids, occupations of towns, and naval blockades gave way to a potential for more ominous invasions. England, the traditional enemy of the French and Spanish Bourbons, now possessed the capacity to launch larger expeditionary forces against Spanish America by employing bases in Jamaica, the West Indies, or the North American colonies. European conflicts of the century invariably produced theaters of naval warfare in the West Indies, amphibious attacks against island possessions, and increased dangers to the walled city of Veracruz and guardian fortress of San Juan Ulúa.

Eighteenth-century wars posed threats that compelled the Spanish Crown to focus upon the enlistment of Mexican armed forces. The British expedition led by Admiral Edward Vernon against Cartagena (1740–42), during the War of Jenkins' Ear, although unsuccessful, also threatened the Panama Isthmus, Cuba, and projected a palpable danger to the mineral wealth and commerce of New Spain. In the Mexican north, the sparsely populated frontier provinces bordering on French Louisiana posed complex military problems. The Comanches, Apaches, and numerous other migratory tribes obtained firearms and raided southward into Mexican frontier mining and stock-raising districts. When France departed Louisiana, Spain's North American territories including the Texas Gulf Coast bordered upon the expansive and acquisitive British colonists and later the equally aggressive Americans.

In the central provinces of New Spain, some cities, towns, and districts resisted central control and sometimes resorted to violence against local officials, unfair taxes, or high prices. Nervous civil and military authorities recalled the 1692 uprising in Mexico City, when shortages and high food prices provoked rioters to attack shops and market stalls. The small viceregal guard of halberdiers and untrained urban militiamen lacked the will to suppress the rioters. Shocked by the extent of property damage, merchants and shopkeepers took up arms themselves to restore peace. Convinced that the *consulado* (merchant guild) of Mexico could fund a permanent militia regiment, in 1693 the Crown authorized the enlistment of the Regimiento Urbano del Comercio, Mexico's oldest militia unit.

Protected only by the viceregal halberdiers, a few understrength companies of regular soldiers garrisoned at port fortifications and in frontier posts and some poorly trained provincial militias, observers in New Spain by midcentury, recognized the need for greater military capability to resist external and internal dangers. When war broke out against Britain in 1761, toward the end of the Seven Years' War, fear of an invasion at Veracruz impelled Viceroy Marqués de Cruillas (Joaquín de Monserrat) to enlist new militias. He requested the imperial government to dispatch European reinforcements, arms, and artillery. Although Cruillas instructed his regional officials to mobilize existing militias and to raise new units, the results were chaotic. Some militia units from Puebla and other interior cities actually reinforced Veracruz, but many provincial administrators simply misplaced their orders or found multiple excuses why they could not comply. Mexicans were indifferent to or actively resisted the prospect of military service that threatened to reduce their earnings and remove them from their homes, and even jeopardized their lives. Men from the temperate highlands expressed pure horror and panic when confronted with the prospect of military duty at Veracruz or other tropical locations where endemic *vomito negro* (yellow fever), malaria, and other diseases awaited them. While Cruillas traveled extensively to animate his subordinates and increased budgets to repair coastal defenses, his efforts produced unsatisfactory results that underscored the existence of entrenched antimilitary attitudes.

The siege and occupation of Havana by British forces in 1762 compelled the Spanish imperial government to rethink defense issues in the Americas and to consider the formation of much stronger permanent armed forces. In Madrid as well as Mexico City and elsewhere, royal officials first had to overcome their nagging anxieties that it was dangerous to arm, equip, and train colonial forces. Notwithstanding many reiterations of the negatives and efforts to limit Mexican participation in any permanent military structures, there were no other practical alternatives. For the remainder of the Bourbon era, invasion threats against New Spain and Spanish preoccupation with other theaters of war made the enlistment of Mexican armed forces absolutely essential.

In 1764 the Crown adopted a plan for colonial armies that would be led by regular infantry, dragoon, and cavalry regiments supported by artillery and engineering companies. To guard against heterodox political thinking in the Americas, peninsular (i.e., Spanish) regiments or battalions were to serve on rotational duty. Although most new units would enlist local men, Spanish-born officers and soldiers were expected to maintain their influence and watchfulness by occupying key posts in leadership cadres assigned to train the new regular and militia units. For an enormous province such as New Spain, it was understood that the great majority of the army would be composed of part-time provincial officers and militiamen drawn from the different social classes. Essentially, the model developed in Cuba and used in New Spain followed the basic organization used by European Spanish provincial militias.

To initiate military reform, in 1764 the Crown dispatched Lieutenant General Juan de Villalba y Angulo to Mexico as *comandante general* and *inspector general*. Accompanying Villalba was a strong leadership cadre including 4 field marshals, 6 colonels, 5 lieutenant colonels, 10 majors, 7 adjutants, 109 lieutenants, 16 cadets, 228 sergeants, 401 corporals, and 151 specialized soldiers including drummers and fifers. In addition, the imperial regime authorized the recruitment at Cádiz of the skeleton of a new infantry regiment, the Infantería de América, which was to be completed in New Spain with Mexican-born officers and soldiers. Villalba's royal instructions reminded him to employ the European cadre to instill Spanish martial values among the Mexican regular soldiers and militiamen.

As might be expected given his broad powers, Villalba challenged Viceroy Cruillas, who as captain general of New Spain was proud of his own wartime record of raising forces and defending his province against potential invasion. At Veracruz, Villalba moved quickly to disband or totally reorganize existing militias. From this point forward, the two senior commanders slowed the implementation of the military reform program by quarreling over jurisdiction, exchanging acrimonious letters, and debating about the structure and purpose of the army. Many of the conflicts between Villalba and Cruillas foreshadowed future debates about the composition of the army of New Spain, the roles of Mexicans, and about different defense strategies.

Villalba and his subordinates completed the Infantería de América and raised two regular dragoon regiments, the Dragones de México y España, which served in Mexico for over 50 years. The Spanish officers traveled to Mexican cities and provinces, where they attempted to enumerate the populations. Based on the nature of a district economy and the social composition of the population, they recommended the enlistment of provincial infantry, dragoon, or cavalry regiments. They consulted with regional administrators and the urban *cabildos* (city and town councils), which identified and recommended members of the wealthy regional elites for militia commissions. In populated provinces and districts within some proximity to Veracruz, Villalba raised six provincial militia regiments of two battalions, each named after its home jurisdiction: Mexico, Puebla, Toluca, Tlaxcala, Córdoba-Orizaba, and Veracruz. Puebla landowners also enlisted a dragoon regiment in nearby towns and villages, boarding the horses at local haciendas. At Querétaro, Celaya, and San Juan del Río, hacienda owners and stock raisers combined to organize a provincial cavalry regiment, the Caballería de Querétaro. A few older units such as the Regimiento Urbano del Comercio, the Cuerpo de (Lancers) of Veracruz, and some coastal defense companies continued unaltered from the earlier period.

From the outset, the militias and regular units recruited almost all of the racial mixtures in the Mexican population, exempting only Indians and blacks who paid the *tributo* (capitation tax). Other racial mixtures of the so-called *castas* were to be enlisted without special distinctions. An early regulation restricting company membership to one-third non-whites could not be enforced in most jurisdictions. The only exception was in the case of the Afro-Mexican *pardos* and *morenos*, who made excellent disease-resistant soldiers but lacked social standing in the racial hierarchy. As anticipated, Villalba received protests from whites about *pardo* and *moreno* participation in the militias. To solve this difficulty, he enlisted special *pardo* battalions in Mexico City, Puebla, and Veracruz, and he reorganized *pardo* and *moreno* companies raised earlier in smaller towns and coastal locations.

Following Villalba's return to Spain in 1766, Viceroy Carlos Francisco de Croix and, later, his inspectors general, Colonels Marqués de la Torre and Francisco Douché, established militia regiments in Valladolid (Morelia), Guadalajara, Pátzcauro, Oaxaca, and a coastal battalion at Tampico and Pánuco. During the riots and protests associated with the expulsion of the Jesuits in 1767, Visitador General José de Gálvez enumerated the populations of Guanajuato and San Luis Potosí districts, enlisting two mixed regional infantry and cavalry units called the Legiones de la Príncipe y San Carlos. Although New Spain now had a defense system based on regular forces and provincial militias, neither Gálvez nor a succession of inspectors general expressed enthusiasm for an army dominated by Mexican provincials. Violence during the expulsion of the Jesuits underscored chronic fears that militiamen might one day turn their weapons against the regime. Expressing a general feeling among senior army officers, Viceroy Croix argued that he trusted regular soldiers more than part-time militiamen even if they were Mexicans. With this in mind, Croix detached the third battalion from the Infantería de América to establish a new regiment called the Infantería de la Corona.

Clearly, many senior Spanish army officers—haughty, intolerant, and schooled in the harsh disciplinary methods emulated from Frederick the Great's Prussia—could not easily accept the unmilitary demeanor, relaxed attitudes, and casual lifestyle of many Mexican soldiers. Europeans complained constantly about indolent vagabonds, drunkenness, thievery, "debauched races," and other vices that they claimed to perceive. The Marqués de Torre, who arrived from Spain in 1768 in command of three Spanish battalions drawn from the Infantería de Savoya, Ultonia, and Flandes, described a rapid decline in discipline among Spanish regular officers and noncommissioned officers. He believed that European soldiers assigned to the training cadres of militia units married Mexicans, developed local interests, and communicated their own noxious vices and laziness to their pupils. Torre declared that many of the European regulars had been recruited directly from peninsular prisons or conscripted from the lowest sectors of society. They failed to keep regimental muster roles, essential service records *(hojas de servicio)*, and neglected militia training assemblies. The cavalry of Querétaro was found to own no horses, and the large Legión de San Carlos, with over 3,500 cavalry and infantrymen enlisted, had a regular army training cadre of only one junior officer, a sergeant, and three corporals.

Torre concluded that most militia regiments were "imaginary" and that the only solution would be to raise regular army infantry battalions in Mexico that would exclude the racially mixed population. Major Pedro de Gorostiza, later subinspector general during the 1790s, recommended the expansion of the regular army and the reduction of all disciplined militias to the status of untrained holding companies *(compañías sueltas)*. In wartime crises such units could supply necessary recruits for the regular regiments. For Spanish officers and other observers who criticized the military potential of Mexican soldiers and the high costs associated with militias, the logical solution was to defend New Spain with metropolitan troops and regulars raised in the viceroyalty. The hard reality that the mother country lacked surplus forces to garrison overseas territories or the ability to pay large regular colonial armies had little impact. In different forms, this debate dragged on until the outbreak of the Hidalgo Revolt in 1810.

On the other side, some military leaders such as Viceroy Antonio María de Bucareli and Inspector General Pascual de Cisneros during the 1770s recognized that the formation of Mexican units required much broader cooperation between recruiters and regional *alcaldes mayores* (mayors) and urban officials. Cisneros believed that with better training and discipline, Mexican militiamen could play significant roles in defense. In 1783, Viceroy Matías de Gálvez commissioned Colonel Francisco Crespo, acting subinspector general of the army of New Spain, to prepare a thorough report analyzing defense needs and the types of soldiers that might be raised in New Spain. Unlike many former military planners, Crespo possessed intimate knowledge of the country and its peoples. He had served as *corregidor* (local Crown representative) of Mexico City, traveled to many provinces, and he was an active member of the intellectual community in the Real Academia de San Carlos. Proposing compromise that reflected the different issues and interests, Crespo outlined a plan for a regular army of four infantry regiments (Corona, Nueva España, Mexico, and Puebla), an oversize battalion of disease-resistant troops stationed permanently at Veracruz, some specialized companies, and the two existing regular dragoon regiments of Spain and Mexico. For an annual cost to the treasury of over 1 million pesos, a peacetime strength of about 5,800 regular army troops could be expanded to a respectable wartime force of 9,300 men.

Regarding the militias of different types that in theory totaled almost 40,000 men, Crespo concluded that the actual value of most existing units was negligible. After examining the hardships of army duty for artisans, agricultural workers, miners, and other segment of the population, Crespo redesigned the system of regiments, battalions, and companies according to differing defensive needs and available populations. There were to be about 11,000 provincial troops enlisted into regional regiments and battalions of infantry, dragoons, and cavalry; 6,700 militiamen in urban and coastal units; and over 22,000 men assigned to untrained reserve companies of infantry and cavalry. The total pool of 40,000 men included mestizos, *pardos,* and *morenos,* exempting only those Indians and blacks who paid capitation tax. Crespo's plan restored dependence upon Mexicans to command and to serve in the regular and militia forces.

While the Spanish Crown approved the outline of Crespo's defense system in 1788, no one foreshadowed the dramatic changes that in the succeeding two decades transformed Mexico's military needs. With the backdrop of the American, French, and Haitian Revolutions, Spaniards who suspected separatist tendencies in the American provinces had good reasons for their doubts. Some European Spanish officers in Mexico, such as Viceroy Conde de Revillagigedo (Juan Vicente de Güemes Pacheco y Padilla), continued to reject the idea of arming the general population. Although Revillagigedo is recognized by historians as a major reformer and backer of the system of provincial intendances, he and his subinspector general, Brigadier Pedro Gorostiza, opposed a Mexican army based upon a small regular force leading a larger number of disciplined provincial militia regiments and battalions. They opted for a much stronger regular army of European Spaniards manned by energetic officers, noncommissioned officers, and soldiers. Revillagigedo viewed Mexicans of mixed race as lazy and prone to vagabondage, while he believed criollo (Spanish-descended, American-born) officers lacked European vigor and discipline. In essence, Revillagigedo wanted to keep arms and military command out of criollo hands. Depending upon the rotation of officers and full regiments from the peninsular army, the viceroy dissolved the existing *pardo* battalions and began to disband the provincial regiments and battalions. With war an increasing likelihood in Europe, Revillagigedo's approach was completely unrealistic. Moreover, the Crown eroded the Mexican regular army by transferring the regular infantry regiments of Nueva España, Mexico, and Puebla to bolster the defenses of more exposed frontline Cuba, Louisiana, and Florida. With most of the regular army stationed overseas and many Mexicans alienated by the unexpected disbandment of their provincial units, Revillagigedo's reforms cannot be said to have improved the military in any respect.

When Viceroy Miguel de la Grúa Talamanca y Branciforte arrived in New Spain in 1794, he discovered an army in total disarray. The remaining force totaled only 4,767 troops, of whom almost 2,000 garrisoned the port city of Veracruz. This left only 2,767 troops to form an army of operations. Although historians often criticize Branciforte for his connections with the corrupt royal favorite Manuel Godoy, he moved quickly and efficiently to rebuild the Mexican provincial militias based on Crespo's plan. In addition, Branciforte solidified effective working relationships with the prestige-hungry criollo elites. In exchange for militia commissions, recognition, and the *fuero militar* (the right to judicial process in military courts), many wealthy criollos donated large sums of money that funded the purchase of arms, uniforms, and equipment and paid much of the operational costs of their regiments, battalions, and companies. Branciforte's recognition of criollo aspirations allowed him to raise an army supported by wealthy merchants, miners, hacendados, administrators, and other members of the elites. Using the *terna* (a list of three potential candidates), urban *cabildos* nominated regional *magnates* (the titled nobility) for senior commands and put forward other officer candidates for commissions as captains and lieutenants in the restored provincial regiments and battalions.

In order to make militia duty prestigious and to give the impression of privileged incentives, Branciforte offered the *fuero militar* to attract recruits. Under normal conditions, this privilege permitted regular army officers, soldiers, and some dependents to have their legal disputes tried in military rather than civil and criminal courts. Because merchants, miners, clergymen, and some other privileged sectors also possessed separate jurisdictions, the legal situation in cases involving militiamen sometimes became complex. Indeed, when the scholar Lyle N. McAlister studied the *fuero militar,* he concluded that the special privileges awarded to soldiers implanted a praetorian tradition in Mexico that following the Wars of Independence (1810–21) made the army "an autonomous and irresponsible institution." While this conclusion reflected contemporary misinterpretations of royal decrees and post-Independence chaos, some officers did attempt to enhance military powers at the expense of other jurisdictions. Nevertheless, the Crown insisted that military privileges granted to militiamen were meant to be honorific rather than real and that there were to be no exemptions from existing laws. The Crown intended the *fuero militar* for regular army soldiers and for militiamen only when they served on active duty. The regime had no intention of authorizing abuses by delinquents or allowing the evasion of existing laws through extending military privileges. As if to underscore this intention, many judgments handed down by courts-martial were more rigorous than those of other legal jurisdictions. Although the existence of the *fuero militar* became highly controversial among Liberals following Mexican Independence, praetorian attitudes by soldiers and army autonomy must be traced in large part to other causes.

This final form of the Mexican provincial army solidified support for the existing regime from an important segment of the criollo elite, backed by the city and town *cabildos*. Headed by a small regular force of infantry and dragoons, the provincial regiments, battalions, coastal militias, and companies defended New Spain against potential enemy invaders, chased smugglers, and served in police functions to maintain internal peace. Senior colonels, lieutenant colonels, and majors *(sargentos mayores)* donated large sums to the treasury and their units for the high social prestige of their royal commissions and uniforms. Even in themselves, the honorary aspects of the *fuero militar* were sufficient to grant special recognition. In a society where wealth did not automatically open doors to political office or administrative posts dominated by peninsular Spaniards, a wealthy miner, merchant, or hacendado could enjoy the status of military rank. Those without the resources or ambitions to purchase colonelcies could satisfy themselves with less expensive commissions as captains or lieutenants. Senior militia officers recruited their dependents and obtained subaltern posts for their relatives.

Wealthy provincial commanders who were mine owners, hacendados, and leaders in other fields handed over the responsibilities for training and administering their units to the regular army officers who served in the training cadres. Generally, the regimental major, who ranked third in command behind the colonel and lieutenant colonel, was a professional officer and often a European Spaniard. Supported by several adjutants, captains, lieutenants, some noncommissioned officers, and a few specialized soldiers, the major watched over training, recruitment, and the important service records that determined longevity in grade and career progress needed for later promotions. With annual inspections by the subinspector general or his designate and the watchfulness of the provincial intendants and district subdelegates—many of whom were former soldiers—the regime established effective checks upon overly aggressive officers and possible disloyalty.

Although centralized military supervision over the far-flung units of the Mexican army succeeded prior to 1810, both the regular and the provincial forces experienced an accelerating process of Mexicanization. Many officers transferred from Spain to Mexico in the 1760s and 1770s were ready for retirement by the end of the 1790s. Most had lived so long in Mexican provinces that they married local women, developed businesses, owned land, invested in mines, and in every respect adopted criollo or Mexican attitudes. Realizing that they would not escape sedentary provincial service and stagnant careers, other officers lost motivation or even became corrupt. After the 1780s, the pressure of international wars prevented the Spanish army from rotating Spanish regiments for temporary duty in New Spain. Without this source of European officers and soldiers, the numbers of Spaniards serving in both the regular army and the militias declined significantly.

The administration of the Mexican army placed enormous burdens upon the viceroys, subinspectors general, and the few officers assigned to the military secretariat in Mexico City. During the 1790s, inspections of regular regiments became less frequent, particularly when the Crown stationed Mexican regular units in Cuba, Louisiana, and the Provincias Internas. Even in New Spain, shortages of troops required regiments to dispatch companies and squadrons to different locations beyond the reach of senior officers or army inspectors. In some situations, officers ran up huge debts against regimental treasuries, broke regulations, and engaged in illegal activities. Since retirement was not mandatory, old commanders served in the army into their eighties despite chronic decrepitude that prevented some of them from mounting horses or even riding in coaches. When these officers failed to maintain discipline, soldiers engaged in gambling and drinking, frequented prostitutes, and staged bawdy entertainments in their barracks. In regular units, the recruitment of jailed vagabonds, petty criminals, and other unsavory characters did nothing to improve the martial aspect of the army.

The provincial militia units were less susceptible to weaknesses experienced by the regulars. Militia officers belonged to the elites, and most soldiers were solid artisans, tradesmen, hacienda dependents, and laborers conscripted part time from their civilian occupations. By 1800 the regime organized the militias into a system of 10 regionally based divisions that coordinated the different organized and semiorganized forces. Commanded by regional intendants or sometimes by energetic army officers such as Colonel Félix María Calleja del Rey of the Tenth Brigade based in San Luis Potosí, in cases of peril the regime could call up over 25,000 men.

Following Spain's declaration of war in 1796 against Britain, international hostilities continued almost uninterrupted until the outbreak of the 1810 Hidalgo Revolt. Although Mexico was not invaded, the level of real danger increased as the British sought new markets and pondered the invasion of Spanish American possessions. In 1796 Viceroy Branciforte felt sufficiently concerned to tour the dilapidated fortifications of Veracruz. The offshore fortress of San Juan Ulúa was in relatively good repair, but the crumbling city walls and bastions were covered by drifting sands piled up like ramps against the outer parapets. Gun carriages were so rotten that any sustained cannon fire broke them to pieces. Of even greater concern, endemic yellow fever annihilated unacclimatized soldiers from the interior highlands and drove their panic-stricken comrades to desert. The Infantería de la Corona y Nueva España garrisoned at Veracruz lost 1,144 men to disease in two years, and troops from the Infantería Provincial de Puebla sent to reinforce the port suffered similar debilitating losses. Word of these disasters spread throughout the interior provinces. By 1798, only 114 soldiers remained healthy enough to stand daily guard duties at the fortress of San Juan Ulúa.

Concerned by these heavy losses, army commanders rejected demands from the coast for additional reinforcements. Instead, they proposed a cantonment of troops drawn from different provincial regiments and battalions at the interior towns of Jalapa, Córdoba, and Orizaba. High above the disease-infested lowlands, these towns enjoyed sufficient altitude to make the climate relatively healthy. Beginning in 1796, Viceroy Branciforte mobilized about 6,000 troops of the new provincial units, headed by regular forces of the depleted Infantería de la Corona y Nueva España returned from garrison duty in Havana. For the first time, Mexican soldiers from different provincial origins served together, shared experiences, and developed a new cohesiveness.

The problem of defending Veracruz opened a major rift between army commanders, including some viceroys and the powerful merchants, shippers, and the resident population of the port city. Until 1810, the viceroys had to resist demands for strong coastal garrisons and to continue Branciforte's strategy of "defense at distance" from cantonments in the temperate highlands. The idea was to bottle up an invading force at Veracruz and to allow tropical diseases to do their work. If the enemy attempted to break out into the interior, the Mexican army would be prepared. Behind this protective cordon of troops, the Fortress of Perote (constructed 1770–75) presented sufficient obstacle so that an invading army would require a siege train including heavy cannon, howitzers, and mortars. Any wavering from this approach to coastal defense cost numerous lives and further entrenched panic among Mexican soldiers. In 1799–1800, Viceroy Miguel José de Azanza set off new flights of deserters when he authorized the transfer of 1,680 militiamen from the provincial regiments to replace losses in the Veracruz garrison and to establish a small cantonment of 600 infantry and 200 cavalry at Arroyo Moreno two leagues outside of the port city. When yellow fever broke out, almost 50 percent of these men perished and 1,396 soldiers died at the Veracruz army hospital of San Carlos.

Although the Peace of Amiens in 1802 relieved the need temporarily for Mexican forces to repel a possible British amphibious invasion, many commanders recognized that "defense at distance" was the only acceptable solution to save soldiers from yellow fever. Between 1799 and 1803 for example, the Infantería de la Corona y Nueva España stationed at Veracruz reported 1,220 deaths and 1,558 desertions. Despite intense pressures from Veracruz and the renewed outbreak of war against Britain, Viceroy José de Iturrigaray refused to concentrate significant forces at the coast. The viceroy drew angry denunciations and bitter opposition that made him permanent enemies among the merchants and shippers of the port. Notwithstanding intelligence reports that Britain had begun to organize an expeditionary force to attack Mexico, Iturrigaray left a skeleton garrison at Veracruz and concentrated the bulk of the Mexican army of operations at Jalapa, Orizaba, and Córdoba. By 1807, the cantonments totaled almost 16,000 men serving with their provincial regiments and battalions. Young provincial officers such as Captain Ignacio Allende and Lieutenant Juan de Aldama of the Regimiento de Dragones Provinciales de la Reina of San Miguel, who achieved prominence later as rebel chiefs in the Hidalgo Revolt, trained in war games, experienced maneuvers, talked politics, and recognized the latent power of a Mexican army.

The catalyst for change in Mexico was Napoléon Bonaparte's invasion of Spain and the 1808 abdications of Carlos IV and Fernando VII that brought Joseph Napoléon to the Spanish throne. When the Spanish people rose up to resist the French, delegates from the Junta Central and other regional juntas requested recognition and financial support from New Spain. While Iturrigaray prevaricated and discussed the political options such as assembling a governing junta in Mexico City, he appeared to side with Mexican criollo interests against the European Spanish minority. For their part, peninsular merchants, bureaucrats, and army officers demanded cooperation with any vestigial government of Spain. With plots and rumors abounding, on the night of September 16, 1808, a group of merchants in Mexico City supported by troops of the Regimiento Urbano del Comercio overthrew Viceroy Iturrigaray.

At the cantonment and in other garrisons, rumors about angry criollo officers who planned a movement to liberate Iturrigaray came to nothing. The army remained quiet while an octogenarian commander, Field Marshal Pedro Garibay, took over as interim viceroy. The new regime arrested dissenters and transferred some troops from the cantonment to bolster urban garrisons such as Mexico City and Puebla. Through 1809, minor plots and conspiracies disturbed domestic tranquility, while rumors of a French invasion kept the troops at the cantonment focused upon the defense of Veracruz and the routes inland. When Archbishop Francisco Xavier de Lizana y Beaumont replaced Garibay as viceroy, he transferred suspect army units out of the capital and demobilized some militias. Fearing an uprising by unknown elements, he surrounded the viceregal palace with artillery and a cordon of regular army troops. In the provinces, conspiracies at Valladolid, Querétaro, and elsewhere attracted the participation of only a few relatively junior militia officers. Elsewhere, militia troops performed police duties in their home districts, guarded public buildings, escorted shipments of corn in regions such as Guanajuato where there was a shortage, and carried on with monthly assemblies.

On September 16, 1810, the outbreak of revolt in the Bajío region of north-central Mexico led by Father Miguel Hidalgo y Costilla caught the army totally by surprise. With some militia regiments at the cantonment and other units garrisoning cities or demobilized in their home provinces, any early response to a significant internal danger was out of the question. Senior officers looked on transfixed; they could not act quickly enough to prevent the fall of San Miguel, Guanajuato, Valladolid, or Guadalajara. In the districts most directly affected, some provincial militia units—especially those of the Eighth Militia Brigade including the Infantry of Celaya, Guanajuato, and Valladolid and the Cavalry and Dragoons of the Príncipe (Guanajuato), Reina (San Miguel), Querétaro, and Michoacán—were caught up and absorbed into the rebellion. Militiamen with their arms and wearing their Spanish uniforms marched with Hidalgo's masses. Some criollo officers, mostly provincial sublieutenants, lieutenants, and captains, attempted to discipline and organize the inchoate popular movement. Of much greater importance, the bulk of the army of New Spain remained loyal and served as the organizing cadre for the royalist armies that fought the long war from

1810 to 1821. While Hidalgo achieved early momentum that carried his forces almost to Mexico City, the lack of weapons, trained soldiers, and good officers meant that except in unusual circumstances the rebels could not field armies capable of fighting conventional battles against the royalists. From San Luis Potosí, Félix Calleja expanded the Tenth Militia Brigade to organize the Army of the Center, which became an effective operational force. The royalist victories at Aculco, Guanajuato, Puente de Calderón, and even the disputed engagement at Las Cruces as Hidalgo's forces approached Mexico City set a pattern for the succeeding decade. Only when the Mexican insurgents adopted new tactics and unconventional guerrilla warfare did they learn how to erode disciplined forces and the counterinsurgents of the royalist army.

See also Hidalgo Revolt; Wars of Independence

Bibliography:

Archer, Christon I., *The Army in Bourbon Mexico, 1760–1810.* Albuquerque: University of New Mexico Press, 1977.

_____, "Combatting the Invisible Enemy: Health and Hospital Care in the Army of New Spain, 1760–1810." *New World: A Journal of Latin American Studies* 2: 1–2 (1987).

Hamnett, Brian R., *Roots of Insurgency: Mexican Regions, 1750–1824.* Cambridge: Cambridge University Press, 1986.

Ladd, Doris M., *The Mexican Nobility at Independence, 1780–1826.* Austin, Texas: Institute of Latin American Studies, 1976.

McAlister, Lyle N., *The "Fuero Militar" in New Spain, 1764–1800.* Gainesville: University of Florida Press, 1957.

Priestley, Herbert I., *José de Gálvez Visitador General of New Spain (1765–1771).* Berkeley: University of California Press, 1916.

Rodríguez O., Jaime E., editor, *Patterns of Contention in Mexican History.* Wilmington, Delaware: Scholarly Resources Books, 1992.

_____, editor, *Mexico in the Age of Democratic Revolutions, 1750–1850.* Boulder: Lynne Rienner Publishers, 1994.

—CHRISTON I. ARCHER

Military: 1821–1914

In 1821, the sudden transition from colonial possession to independent nation caught both the royalist army of New Spain and the insurgent forces almost by surprise. After over a decade of combat and polarization of New Spain, the restoration of the Spanish Constitution in 1820 eroded the militarized system that had kept the rebels in check. Defense against marauding guerrilla forces required the populations of towns and districts to pay heavy military support taxes, to construct blockhouses and parapets, and to mobilize much of the work force for garrison and guard duties, patrols, and convoys. Although the burdens for local defense fell unequally upon the provinces depending upon the extent of rebel activity, most Mexicans were anxious to reduce the burdens of the military. With the possibility of guerrilla attacks, royalist centers had to maintain continuous vigilance and preparedness. Rebel forces raided outlying haciendas, blocked major routes such as the strategic road from Jalapa to Veracruz, and sometimes insurgent cavalrymen expressed their *machismo* by riding recklessly into heavily garrisoned cities such as Puebla by night simply to cause alarm. Similarly, mobile flying detachments of royalist troops attacked the bases of guerrilla power in Veracruz province, the South (today's Guerrero State), Guanajuato, Michoacán, Nueva Galicia, the Huasteca, and in other regions. The restoration of the Constitution created *ayuntamientos constitucionales* that throughout New Spain exercised their new powers to abrogate special military taxes and to demobilize local armed forces.

For royalist army commanders, the events of 1821 confirmed old fears that the long struggle against the Mexican guerrilla-insurgents could not be won. Many regional commanders had expanded their powers to create veritable provincial satrapies in which they profited from decentralization caused by the breakdown of centralized authority. As governor-intendants at Veracruz, Puebla, Guanajuato, and elsewhere, army commanders combined civil and military jurisdictions. Many other military chiefs served as powerful regional and district subdelegates. They dominated commerce, accumulated land and other assets, engaged in contraband trade along the coast, and became accustomed to wielding exceptional powers. Few civilian bureaucrats dared to challenge officers who employed the devices of charging opponents with treason, manipulating convoys, redistributing rebel property, and manipulating news to create an atmosphere of fear. A few military chiefs such as Agustín de Iturbide got themselves into trouble with the central government for heavy-handed illegal activities, but most were too valuable in office as counterinsurgency specialists. With the sanctity of imperial approval, the Constitution provided the catalyst for change that undermined the military embrace of Mexican society. As the *ayuntamientos* restricted funds and demobilized local and regional defense forces, remaining regular army units failed to take up the slack.

In 1821, the rise of Agustín de Iturbide with the Plan de Iguala and the new Army of the Three Guarantees compelled soldiers outside of the South to make rapid career choices. Recognizing the irresistible appeal of a movement that promised to unite such old foes as Iturbide and rebel chiefs such as Vicente Guerrero, Guadalupe Victoria, Nicolás Bravo, Juan Álvarez, and José Francisco Osorno, both royalists and insurgents clamored to join the victorious cavalcade. The few unwavering royalist commanders watched helplessly as their garrisons deserted and their subordinates hastened to attach their careers to the cause of independence. Many officers and soldiers of all ranks—peninsular and criollo —such as Pedro Celestino Negrete, José Antonio Andrade, Melchor Álvarez, Anastasio Bustamante, Miguel Barragán, Luis Quintanar, José Antonio Echávarri, Luis Cortazar, José Joaquín de Herrera, and Manuel Gómez Pedraza, switched sides to embrace the Plan de Iguala. In some cases, such as that of Negrete, sanguinary former royalists now chased their old superiors—in this case Brigadier José de la Cruz, Captain General of Nueva Galicia—out of the country. Similarly, the youthful counterinsurgency commander, Captain Antonio López de Santa Anna, launched his spectacular career from his base at Veracruz. By September, 1821, Iturbide entered Mexico City in triumph.

The victorious army of the 1820s was quite different than the colonial force that entered the Independence war in 1810. Officers who had been dependent upon a centralized imperial command and patronage system had learned to exercise considerable regional and district autonomy. The war decentralized the country and granted significant patronage powers to the military-political commanders of the Mexican provinces. Everywhere, former royalist officers made the transitions necessary to protect their careers. In some regions, independence meant business as usual and the change of a few words to recognize the Mexican empire or republic. Although the promise of "union" in the Plan de Iguala turned out be insufficient to protect some the gachupín (European) officers against forced deportations, among senior Mexican army generals and colonels in 1840 there were still 25 European Spaniards and 81 criollos of royalist pre-1821 origins, and 12 officers who began after 1810 as insurgents. Nevertheless, the expulsion law of 1827 deported Generals Pedro Celestino Negrete, José Antonio Echávarri and some others whose interventions in political disputes surrounding the conflicts between

escocés and yorkista masons made them high profile targets. However, many senior officers of the Mexican army with experience before 1821 continued to be major participants in national political and military affairs into the 1850s and the beginning of the Reforma.

From the military perspective, the period from independence in 1821 up to the Revolution of Ayutla in 1854 was one of internal and external turbulence. The new nation—empire or republic—commenced its career with unsettled business that made the armed forces central to all major events. Through the 1820s, Spain rejected any negotiated settlement, withheld formal recognition, and plotted actively to restore the colony by force. During the imperial experiment and then the republican governments under the federalist Constitution of 1824, Emperor Iturbide felt constrained to maintain a strong military establishment to protect against a possible invasion. Foreign loans and tax revenues required to restore a postwar economy went instead to equip and pay a bloated military establishment. Until 1825, Spanish forces occupied the fortress of San Juan de Ulúa at Veracruz and occasionally bombarded or raided the port city. Finally, in 1829 Spanish Brigadier Isidro Barradas, known as "El Loco" in Mexico, attacked Tampico from Cuba with an expeditionary force of only 3,700 troops. The participation of a few gachupín former residents of Mexico rekindled demands for the deportation of remaining Spaniards residents including senior army officers such as Lieutenant General Negrete. The most famous military-political leader of the period, Antonio López de Santa Anna, became the heroic victor of Tampico and the savior of the nation.

Internally, conflict raged after 1821 between distinct federalist and centralist visions for the new nation. Although self-described centralists emerged only in the 1830s, most army commanders expressed preference for a strong central administration and continuation of special fueros inherited from the colony that accorded military personnel the status of a special corporation with access to military courts and trial by court-martial separate from the ordinary criminal and civil jurisdictions. In defense of these privileges, army officers found natural allies among clerics who fought for their own fueros and other privileged groups such as hacendados, miners, and merchants. In the uprisings and rebellions of the period, the regular army usually supported centralist and conservative positions. On the other side, federalists viewed local militias as a means to defend regional or state interests against the regular army, the dangers of predatory militarism, and the designs of political centralists based in Mexico City. Debates raged over the roles and powers of state militias that many among wealthy classes argued would weaken the nation. In some states and regions, army commanders such as Santa Anna in Veracruz, Juan Álvarez in the South along the Pacific Coast, and Luis Cortazar in Guanajuato ruled their provincial satrapies and could not be directed or integrated by any government into the normal military command structure.

In many respects, the debates over the form of the new national army followed arguments first enunciated in the late eighteenth century over whether to establish a strong regular army or a much smaller professional cadre supported by a larger force of part-time militiamen. The regular army continued the practices and patterns of the army of New Spain and the metropolitan Spanish army—using the same rank system except for the new grade of *generalísimo,* and the same basic organization, military law, and weapons. The new Mexican uniforms followed the same cut as Spanish designs with slight modifications and new badges. Cost was a particular concern during the 1820s since the military absorbed over 75 percent of national government revenues. Monarchists, conservatives, and almost all senior generals supported the regular army while federalists promoted regional militias. Among most professional officers debates raged about the usefulness of poorly armed and ill-trained militiamen who seldom possessed military discipline, firearms, uniforms, or adequate equipment.

As might be expected, military recruitment was an area of permanent concern both in the regular and militia forces. As in past, the *sorteo* (lottery) system did not work among populations that simply fled their home jurisdictions upon the announcement that recruiting would take place. The regular army continued to depend upon rounding up drunks and vagrants at cockpits, bullfights, and gambling dens. Recruiters toured jails to offer petty criminals the alternative of enlistment to end incarceration and demeaning public duties. In Mexico City which had a large floating population of transients and vagabonds, the authorities sent out agents to detain any unemployed young men who appeared fit for duty. As might be expected in an army recruited by compulsion, desertion was a chronic problem. Men arrived in ragged clothing scarcely able to protect their modesty and deserted in their new uniforms. Since the governments sometimes could not pay soldiers for months, there was an active market for uniform parts, arms, munitions, and other military equipment. The poverty of soldiers and often their previous careers outside the law led to many crimes such as robberies, assaults, and attacks against women near barracks or encampments. Reform proposals to reduce the size of the army through a general demobilization of less useful units and individuals were not implemented under Iturbide before he abdicated or by successive republican governments. Indeed, the only real cutbacks occurred when senior officers suppressed militia units in favor of regulars.

The federal Constitution of 1824, altered the existing military structure to create three basic branches of the army—the regular force, the active militia, and the civic militia. The active militia *(milicia activa)* of 16 battalions (eight regiments) followed the basic format of the old provincial militias raised and maintained in major cities and heavily populated provinces. Later, Yucatán and Chiapas added another six battalions. As in the case of the old colonial provincial militias, recruitment of good men by lottery proved to be difficult, and towns situated distant from battalion headquarters tended to evade their responsibilities. Most professional officers pointed out the weaknesses of depending upon ragtag part-time soldiers and advocated the expansion of the regular army. Oriented even further toward districts and regions, the civic militias fell under local controls and command. These were true home defense forces of infantry, cavalry, dragoons, and artillery paid for by *ayuntamientos* (town councils) with the officers selected or elected from their immediate jurisdictions. Enlistment in civic militias protected men from regular army and active militia recruiters. In the years of internal violence to follow, the civic militias emerged as defenders of the federalist states and regions against the armies of the central regimes. Some states such as Jalisco, Zacatecas, and Yucatán recruited as many as 12,000 to 17,000 cavalry and infantry troops that gave these jurisdictions additional clout in dealing with other regions and the central government.

Despite enormous difficulties, many army officers were fully aware that the army needed to educate soldiers and to provide them with adequate medical care, retirement pensions, and other services. As Minister of War beginning in 1835, General José María Tornel y Mendívil pressed for additional training schools and for the expansion of the military academy earlier established at the fortress of Perote and in 1831 moved to the Bethlehemite monastery in Mexico City. Political instability and a chronic shortage of adequate funding prevented most of these plans from reaching operational successes, and young army officers continued to learn their profession on the job.

Following the administration of Guadalupe Victoria, the elections of 1828 marked renewed struggles that reflected old disputes and unsettled issues from the previous decade. Internal chaos, uprisings, and *pronunciamientos* surrounded the 1828 presidential elections that pitted General Juan Vicente Guerrero for the *yorkista* faction against the Minister of War, General Manuel Gómez Pedraza, the first presidential candidate who was not a war hero of the Independence era. When Gómez Pedraza defeated Guerrero in a close vote, Santa Anna proclaimed the Plan de Perote demanding the elevation of Guerrero and also insisting upon the expulsion of remaining Spaniards in the country. While the uprising failed, another movement in Mexico City on behalf of Guerrero called the Acordada Revolt led to sporadic artillery duels between the Ciudadela (the Mexico City arsenal) and the national palace. The revolt also unleashed rioters including some soldiers who robbed and burned the shops of the Parián, a building housing many Spanish-owned shops with expensive goods situated on the Zócalo (main square). Although struggles such as the Acordada Revolt involved comparatively small forces and produced light casualties, the extreme factionalism that divided the army commander-politicians weakened the ability of the Mexican army to respond to internal and external dangers.

While Santa Anna was successful against the Spanish invasion in 1829 at Tampico, the overthrow of Gómez Pedraza and the installation of Guerrero produced near chaos in the capital. This in turn led to yet another military coup in 1830 led by Anastasio Bustamante, Nicolás Bravo, and other officers who proclaimed centralism to replace discredited federalism. Guerrero fled southward to rally federalist forces, only to be betrayed at Acapulco and executed in 1831 at Oaxaca. In 1832, Santa Anna won the presidency for the first time and due in large part to poor health, he permitted Vice President Valentín Gómez Farías to introduce legislation designed to reduce the size of the army and to curtail the *fuero militar*. In 1833, the enlistment of civic militia battalions in Mexico City produced a rumor that the regular army was to be abolished. This led to new *pronunciamientos* and the war cry by soldiers of *religión y fueros* that became more shrill in succeeding decades as liberal opponents pressed for controls over the military. In 1836, the Santa Anna regime abolished the 1824 Constitution and replaced it with a conservative and centralist national charter.

Often abandoned by bankrupt governments and challenged by liberal politicians, Mexico's military forces during the 1830s and 1840s faced political challenges; regional insurrections in Tabasco, Yucatán and elsewhere; a separatist rebellion in the frontier province of Texas; Indian hostilities on the northern frontier; the intervention of France at Veracruz; and finally the disastrous war against the United States (1846–48). In 1835, the central government had to equip an expeditionary army of 6,000 troops with arms, artillery, and logistical support to suppress the uprising of United States settlers in Texas. Although this expedition tested General/President Santa Anna's abilities, despite difficulties with desertion he led a conscript army northward and for a time overcame equipment failures, disease among his troops, and poor logistical services. The defeat at San Jacinto can be attributed at least partially to political infighting in central Mexico and fiscal weaknesses. In 1838 when the national government halted payments on foreign loans, France sent a fleet to blockade and to occupy Veracruz (the Pastry War). Santa Anna's frontline forces engaged the Texans and then the French, while behind them *pronunciamientos* and struggles between federalists and centralists in Mexico City and states such as Zacatecas continued as though there were no external dangers.

At the outbreak of the war with the United States, the Mexican army claimed a theoretical strength of about 19,000 troops, but many soldiers were unavailable, unsuitable, or untrained for combat distant from the populated centers of the nation. Beyond the chronic political instability that made major military operations difficult to sustain, attempts to reform the system of recruitment and officer training launched in 1838 produced only limited results. Most Mexican soldiers continued to be victims of forced levies, vagabonds, or the off-castings of urban areas and jails. From the moment of their recruitment, many men thought only of when and how to desert. Soldiers lived miserable lives often without regular pay, basic nourishment, and sometimes even without uniforms. Poorly armed infantry with outdated Spanish and British muskets, cavalry with worn out carbines and lances which mounted troops despised, and artillery companies with old guns of different calibers, the Mexican forces were no match for their opponents. Often, shortages of munitions and rotten gun carriages further reduced the effectiveness and mobility of the artillery units.

In combat against much better United States artillery and infantrymen equipped with muzzle-loading rifles using percussion caps, the Mexican troops fought with much more valor than some historians have suggested. Even more remarkable given the precarious state of Mexican logistics, in 1847 Santa Anna was able to move an army of almost 15,000 to the northern front. Following the defeat at the battle of Angostura and retreat south to San Luis Potosí, the disastrous losses at Veracruz, Cerro Gordo, Churubusco, Molino del Rey, and Chapultepec led to the American occupation of Mexico City. At Chapultepec, however, some legendary army cadets among the defenders known to all Mexicans as the Niños Héroes died rather than accepting surrender. Nevertheless, even with the American invaders threatening the capital, *pronunciamientos,* revolts, and uprisings behind the lines weakened the potency of Mexican forces.

The defeat by the United States and loss of almost half the national territory sobered but ultimately did not completely terminate the military revolts and bitter struggles between conservative centralists and liberal federalists. Following the Treaty of Guadalupe Hidalgo, the country recovered somewhat under the federalist governments of *moderado* Generals José Joaquín Herrera and Mariano Arista, who had played important roles during the war. However, a new rebellion in 1852 spread from Jalisco into a broader conflagration as conservatives attacked federalists. In 1853, Santa Anna returned to Mexico from Venezuela to assume power once again. He introduced a conservative program and a plan to expand the regular army to 26,500 troops and the civic militias to almost 65,000 men. However, by this time a new generation of liberals stood in his way. The old Guerrero rebel and federalist leader, General Juan Álvarez rejected Santa Anna and on March 1, 1854, proclaimed the Plan de Ayutla, a revolutionary popular movement that in some respects followed the outlines of earlier guerrilla struggles of the Independence era. By August, 1855, Santa Anna had to flee Mexico City into his last exile abroad. The victory of Álvarez and his peasant troops was not only unwelcome in the capital, but appeared to represent the victory of undisciplined militia forces of the lower social orders over the regular army. However, in support of the swarthy *pinto* troops of Guerrero and the Pacific Coast a new generation of liberal reformers swept to power including Benito Juárez, General Ignacio Comonfort, Miguel Lerdo de Tejada, and Melchor Ocampo.

The Revolution of Ayutla introduced a decade of political change and bloody civil war known as La Reforma. While the thrust of liberal reforms produced many changes that affected the Church and other privileged corporations, the abolition of *fueros* under the Ley Juárez and later enshrined in the Constitution of 1857 was tantamount in the thinking of army officers to a declaration of total war. While Comonfort became president, during the Wars of

Reform (1858–61) his attempts at conciliation left him in a precarious position between two belligerent factions. General Félix Zuloaga, a hard line conservative, proclaimed the Plan de Tacubaya and the army named him president of the nation when Comonfort resigned. Juárez who was second in line for the presidency under the Constitution as chief justice of the Supreme Court, escaped to Querétaro where his followers confirmed him as president. The liberals established their capital at Veracruz where they were able to purchase arms, ammunition, and military equipment to pursue the civil war.

Having inherited most of the army and the officer corps, during the first two years of the conflict the conservatives won most of the battles. Generals Miguel Miramón and Leonardo Marquéz drove the liberals north of San Luis Potosí, captured Guadalajara, and occupied the Pacific Coast. In reply, liberal forces used guerrilla warfare to raid conservative territory and to wreck their economy. Both sides abused noncombatants, shot prisoners, and committed numerous other atrocities. By 1859, Miramón attacked Veracruz, but could not defeat the liberals before yellow fever ravaged his forces. With arms and munitions purchased through their control over customs revenues, by 1860 liberal Generals Ignacio Zaragoza and Jesús González Ortega took the offensive against the interior occupied by the conservatives. At the Battle of Silao, González Ortega commanded an army of 8,000 troops with 38 artillery pieces against Miramón with only 3,300 troops and 18 cannons. After three hours of combat, the green conservative recruits broke and fled. By the end of 1860, Miramón and Marquéz suffered definitive defeats and with their officers fled to fight another day.

In an action designed to compel Mexico to pay its debts and many claims by foreigners caused by instability and warfare, in December, 1861, approximately 6,000 Spanish and 2,000 French troops, and a few hundred British marines landed at Veracruz. When it became evident that the French had invasion in mind rather than debt collection, both Spain and Britain withdrew. Commanding 6,000 French troops, General Charles Latrille headed inland to occupy Puebla. On May 5, 1862, the Mexican defenders under General Zaragoza assisted by Brigadier General Porfirio Díaz, repulsed French attacks and drove the invaders back to Orizaba. Unfortunately, Zaragoza died of typhoid fever the same year. However, for a nation battered by warfare and internal chaos, the victory at Puebla was of such high importance that the Cinco de Mayo became a permanent national holiday. A year later, Napoleon III sent an expeditionary force of almost 30,000 troops to invade Mexico. This time following an artillery bombardment and two month siege, the Mexican garrison at Puebla surrendered.

Unable to mount a defense of Mexico City for lack of troops, President Juárez withdrew to San Luis Potosí to continue the struggle. Pursued by Marshal François Bazaine who enjoyed the support of Mexican conservative forces, Juárez and his army retreated to Chihuahua and finally to Paso del Norte (today's Ciudad Juárez) on the border with the United States. While French and Mexican conservative conventional forces were unbeatable on the battlefield by the ill-equipped Mexican constitutionalist army, Juárez unleashed guerrillas who proved as they had done prior to 1821 against Spanish royalists that territory conquered could not be held. In October, 1865, when Emperor Maximilian was convinced by his advisers that Juárez had gone into exile, he declared the war ended and issued a decree condemning Juaristas to death if captured bearing arms. By this act, Maximilian signed his own future death warrant and that of several leading Mexican conservative generals. For a time the French appeared to have defeated the Mexican liberals, but even with 30,000 troops and conservative assistance, endemic guerrilla warfare eroded morale and made the invaders recognize that they had been drawn into a limitless morass.

By 1865, the tide of war began to turn in favor of the Mexican liberals. With the assistance of weapons, munitions, and equipment from the victorious Union army following the Civil War in the United States, Juárez could contemplate the expulsion of the French and the total annihilation of the Mexican conservatives. By March, 1866, Bazaine retreated from Monterrey, Saltillo, and Tampico, pursued by liberal forces that soon recruited new armies. Porfirio Díaz who had surrendered to the French at Oaxaca, escaped at Puebla to organize new guerrilla forces. When the French committed themselves to abandon Mexico by 1867, Maximilian and his conservative army commanders sought to raise a new army strengthened by Austrian and Belgian contingents. With the departure of the French armies, the emperor and his remaining supporters made a last stand at Querétaro. After a long siege, on May 15, 1867, the conservatives surrendered. With the destruction of the conservative cause, it appeared that the divisive factionalism caused by army officers and their political allies might end. Maximilian, accompanied by Generals Miramón and Tomás Mejía, faced firing squads, while General Leonardo Márquez fled the country into permanent exile as a pawnbroker in Cuba. Now victorious, Juárez returned in triumph to Mexico City.

The Constitution of 1857, the defeat of the conservatives in the War of the Reforma, and the final victory of the republic over the French Intervention eliminated the privileges and dominance of the old Mexican army. Unfortunately, however, victory for the liberals did not end *pronunciamientos* and military revolts. Federal army officers who criticized Juárez even during the war against the French often rebelled and some died as traitors after being suppressed by the forces of liberal General Sóstenes Rocha. Many officers experienced difficulties in the adjustment to civilian society and others such as Porfirio Díaz were ambitious to achieve high political office. In 1871, after being defeated in a contested election for the presidency, Díaz proclaimed the Plan de la Noria, arguing that Juárez had abused the principles of the Revolution of Ayutla and of the Constitution of 1857. Díaz attempted a coup d'état in the capital and his brother Félix Díaz, Governor of Oaxaca, assembled an army that disintegrated against the forces of General Rocha. With the sudden death of Juárez in July, 1872, and an interregnum presidency of Sebastián Lerdo de Tejada, in 1876 Díaz rebelled once again under the Plan de Tuxtepec. After a victorious battle at Tecoac in Tlaxcala won by a hastily assembled and ill-disciplined force over a smaller federal army, Porfirio Díaz captured the capital and political power.

With the exception of the presidency of General Manuel González (1881–85), Díaz ruled Mexico for 34 years. Although rebellions led by opponents and former associates continued at first, from the outset Díaz established policies designed to enforce peace and to modernize the nation. In the beginning senior officers held most state governorships, but the number of military office-holders declined during the regime. While the army continued to play important roles, Díaz controlled ambitious generals by transferring them from one command to another in order to prevent them from establishing permanent roots and alliances in one region. Díaz reduced the size of the officer corps and the total strength of the army from a theoretical 30,000 to 20,000 troops. Police work in rural areas earlier affected by banditry and local insurrections fell into the domain of the Rurales, the colorful rural police who guarded railroads, foreign investments, and protected the Pax Porfiriana.

Accompanying these reforms, the regime improved the level of education and effectiveness of at least a portion of the active military personnel. From the 1880s, Díaz authorized the construction of new military installations, better barracks, and housing for married soldiers. Military education became much more important and the Colegio Militar at Chapultepec turned out some capable officers who were aware of the latest military technology and ideas. The army introduced a professional journal, the *Revista del Ejército y la Marina,* which contributed to the diffusion of military information. Mexican officers visited European military academies and attended maneuvers so that they were up to date on the theory and practice of modern warfare. As might be expected by a regime concerned with modernization, advanced weaponry replaced the old equipment of the French Intervention. In 1882, the government purchased 18,500 Remington rifles and shortly thereafter established a factory to manufacture metal cartridges. By the 1890s, the Díaz regime had the capacity to produce and repair light arms. In 1897, the army purchased 20,000 Mauser rifles and 12 million cartridges from Germany with the machinery needed to manufacture ammunition. Modern artillery and machine guns were purchased from the United States and France. In addition, the military received the assignment of nonbellicose missions such as that of mapping and evaluating the natural resources of the national territory.

Unlike its predecessors, the Díaz regime had no foreign enemies. During the 1880s, however, the Yaqui Indians of Sonora rose up in defense of their lands and liberties against landowners who obtained title to disputed lands. General Bernardo Reyes directed a series of campaigns against the Yaqui leader Cajeme who had served earlier with the liberals. Federal troops fought a series of battles against the Indians until 1886 when many surrendered due to starvation. The army captured and executed Cajeme and many of the Indians were sold by Governor Ramón Corral to the plantations of Quintana Roo where many perished. Despite this action, another Yaqui leader called Tetabiate subdivided his forces into very small groups and where possible used ambushes against settlers and military detachments. Even in 1899, the Yaquis lost 400 men in combat, many wounded, and 834 were taken prisoner. Raids and other acts of rebellion continued into the new century. Similar violence took place in Yucatán reminiscent of the Caste War of the mid nineteenth century. There, Victoriano Huerta and other federal officers who later would fight against the Mexican Revolution earned their field experience.

The reform and educational programs within the army masked a number of chronic problems. First, despite professionalization, senior officers served President Díaz personally and like Bernardo Reyes

and Huerta they earned their promotions through total loyalty. In 1910, most senior serving officers were veterans of much earlier wars and all divisional generals were septuagenarians or octogenarians quite incapable of combat duty. Despite the educational reforms, there was a distinct shortage of young subaltern officers. Below the officer corps, the soldiers of the Mexican army continued to be conscripts recruited by levies, or by police sweeps of urban *pulquerías,* cockpits, and gambling houses. Few men actually volunteered for military duty and if they felt endangered many soldiers deserted at the first opportunity. The population continued to look on the army with traditional abhorrence, fearing that any act of opposition, overt political participation against the regime, or labor manifestation would condemn men to duty in the ranks.

In 1910, the federal army failed to respond effectively to the outbreak of revolution. When multiple trouble spots emerged, old officers were slow to take action and fewer than 14,000 troops were available for combat duty. In the northern states, the fire power of modern artillery, machine guns, and rifles won some skirmishes and battles against lightly armed revolutionaries, but the federal troops were tied to the rail lines and soon abandoned rugged mountainous terrain. The Battle of Casas Grandes in 1911 underscored the fact that the rebels could not meet the army on the conventional battlefield where sheer firepower won the day. However, lacking morale and sufficient numbers, the federal soldiers were overwhelmed by many emerging centers of revolt. Soldiers developed the characteristic "blockhouse mentality" and low morale common among dispirited counterinsurgency forces. By 1912, it was too late to restore long neglected local militia forces and desperation within the regime drove Federal army recruiters to round up petty criminals and other elements that deserted, fled when endangered, and sometimes changed sides to join the rebel forces. Attempts to recruit civilian volunteers failed to generate much support. As in previous Mexican conflicts from the Independence wars forward, in many regions the rebels controlled the countryside and the night. Against Francisco Villa, Pascual Orozco, or Emiliano Zapata, the Federal troops often preferred to remain in the towns behind parapets, trenches, and machine guns.

Frustrated and anxious to discover a scapegoat for their own failures, in February, 1913, a group of senior officers attempted a coup to overthrow the government of President Francisco Madero. Instead of a bloodless event, the plotters turned Mexico City into a war zone during the so-called Decena Trágica

(Tragic Ten Days). The military rebels freed General Bernardo Reyes from prison to take over presidential power, but as Reyes approached the national palace on foot he was shot and killed. In the aftermath, government forces and military rebels opened fire with artillery across the city creating considerable damage and loss of life. In the meantime, General Victoriano Huerta who knew about the first attempts, backed a new plot against Madero. This time soldiers arrested and then assassinated the president and vice president in cold blood. Almost no one accepted the explanations of Huerta who grabbed but could not hold power at the death of Madero. Totally discredited, the old Federal army had come to the end of its run. Unable to control the Zapatistas, the Villistas, and other rebels, following the expulsion of Huerta, the Federalist force disbanded and disappeared.

See also Ayutla, Revolution of; French Intervention; Mexican Revolution; Texan Secession; U.S.–Mexican War; Wars of Independence; Wars of Reform

Select Bibliography

Archer, Christon I., "The Officer Corps in New Spain: The Martial Career, 1759–1821." *Jahrbuch für Geschichte von Staat, Wirtschaft und Gesellschaft Lateinamerikas* 19 (1982).

Fowler, Will, *Military Political Identity and Reformism in Independent Mexico: An Analysis of the Memorias de Guerra (1821–1855).* London: Institute of Latin American Studies, 1996.

Green, Stanley C., *The Mexican Republic: The First Decade, 1823–1832.* Pittsburgh, Pennsylvania: University of Pittsburgh Press, 1987.

Guardino, Peter F., *Peasants, Politics and the Formation of Mexico's National State: Guerrero, 1800–1857.* Stanford, California: Stanford University Press, 1996.

Hale, Charles, *Mexican Liberalism in the Age of Mora, 1821–1853.* New Haven: Yale University Press, 1968.

Hamnett, Brian R., *Roots of Insurgency: Mexican Regions, 1750–1824.* Cambridge: Cambridge University Press, 1986.

_____, *Juárez.* London: Longman, 1994.

Knight, Alan, *The Mexican Revolution.* 2 vols., Cambridge: Cambridge University Press, 1986.

Rodríguez O., Jaime E., editor, *The Independence of Mexico and the Creation of the New Nation.* Los Angeles: University of California, Los Angeles, Latin American Center Publications, 1989.

_____, editor, *The Mexican and Mexican American Experience in the Nineteenth Century.* Tempe, Arizona: Bilingual Press, 1989.

_____, editor, *Patterns of Contention in Mexican History.* Wilmington, Delaware: Scholarly Resources, 1992.

Santoni, Pedro, "A Fear of the People: The Civic Militia of Mexico in 1845." *Hispanic American Historical Review* 68:2 (May 1988).

Sims, Harold D., *The Expulsion of Mexico's Spaniards, 1821–1836.* Pittsburgh, Pennsylvania: University of Pittsburgh Press, 1990.

Stevens, Donald F., *Origins of Instability in Early Republican Mexico.* Durham, North Carolina: Duke University Press, 1991.

Vanderwood, Paul J., *Disorder and Progress: Bandits, Police, and Mexican Development.* Lincoln: University of Nebraska Press, 1981.

—CHRISTON I. ARCHER

Military: 1914–96

With the fall of Victoriano Huerta's government in 1914 and the triumph of Constitutionalist forces under Venustiano Carranza, the development of Mexico's armed forces entered a new phase. The Teoloyucan Treaties of August 1914 called for the evacuation, disarmament, and demobilization of the Federal Army. The victory of the Constitutionalist Army was a decisive event that enabled the armed forces to emerge as the pillar of national life. The 1917 Constitution assigned the executive (Article 89) responsibility over the armed forces to guarantee the "internal security" and the "external defense" of the federation.

In 1917 the victorious army had only 11 generals, and only one of them had pursued a professional career. Despite a personal interest in the professionalization of the armed forces, during the early Constitutional period Carranza faced unfavorable conditions. The requirements imposed by the pacification of the country forced Carranza to delay the professionalization of the armed forces. Moreover, it soon became clear that the pacification strategy deployed by the Revolutionary leader and the professionalization of the Revolutionary forces were mutually exclusive goals. Continued conflict among the main Revolutionary groups between 1915 and 1920 obstructed the reorganization of the army and consequently its professionalization. Notwithstanding these problems, under Carranza the first steps toward the subsequent institutionalization of the armed forces were taken. Although his efforts to transfer power to a civilian proved fruitless, the Military College was reopened, the system of rotation of chiefs of military zones reestablished, the total number of troops reduced, and both the cavalry and the infantry corps restructured.

Adolfo de la Huerta's Rebellion of Agua Prieta paved the way to the "institutionalized revolution." Although the revolt brought to the surface the deep divisions within the army, it also made possible the deputation of the armed forces. By 1923, once

President Álvaro Obregón successfully had repressed de la Huerta's rebellion, the Revolutionary officialdom virtually had disappeared; one year later, once the conditions for the pacification of the country were met, the institutionalization of the national army became possible. Obregón reduced the number of total troops by 50 percent, forced many officers to retire, and increased the number of military districts from 20 to 35.

The goal of the professionalization of the armed forces was established fully under the presidency of Plutarco Elías Calles (1924–28). Joaquín Amaro, his secretary of the army and the navy, played a key role in the transition from Revolutionary to professional armed forces. In contrast to other experiences with the professionalization of the armed forces in Latin America, in Mexico no external actors participated. In 1926 the Organic Law of the Army was issued and the Commission for Military Studies and the General Staff of the War Ministry established. In addition, the promotion law introduced by Calles encouraged discipline and helped regulate the behavior of soldiers within the armed forces. This process was interrupted briefly by the 1928 presidential succession, which again revived the interest of the military in national politics. The assassination of President-elect Obregón produced a vacuum of power that forced Calles to devise an institutional mechanism to limit the participation of the military in politics. As pointed out by the scholar Roderic Ai Camp, Mexico provides a unique example of a military leadership transforming itself into a civilian political elite.

To the extent that the new Partido Nacional Revolucionario (PNR, or National Revolutionary Party) ended the pattern of presidential succession conflicts sparking military revolts, it not only represented a new political party but also a new civil-military pact in which the military would increasingly behave as a separate state actor. Indeed, the 1928–29 pact laid the basis for the demilitarization of political competition and eliminated the armed path to power. The process of demilitarization advanced as the proportion of military men at the highest levels of government declined from the previous peak of 50 percent reached under Obregón to approximately 10 percent under President Miguel Alemán Valdés (1946–52). Although other revolts followed the 1929 Escobarista Rebellion, this was the last insurrection of the Revolutionary cycle. Over the years the normative code derived from the 1928–29 pact not only endorsed civilian supremacy but also helped regulate relations between the party and the armed forces.

The depoliticization and subordination of the armed forces also were assisted by a number of measures deployed by successive governments, including low defense budgets, division of armed services, reorganization of military zones, educational programs emphasizing civilian supremacy, and equally important changes in the relationship between the official party and the armed forces, including limited and regulated political participation. In 1937 President Lázaro Cárdenas established the Ministry of National Defense, and two years later naval activities were reorganized under the Ministry of the Navy. Undoubtedly one of the most important changes was the transformation of the PNR into the Partido de la Revolución Mexicana (PRM, or Party of the Mexican Revolution) in 1938 and the creation of four sectors within the party, including the military, which not only reinforced the role of the party as the main arena for political competition but helped dissipate the influence of the military among four voting groups. Subsequently, the danger of military control over the party was averted with the withdrawal of the military sector in 1940, which further disengaged the armed forces from politics. By 1946, when the first civilian president was elected and the official party was renamed the Partido Revolucionario Institucional (PRI, or Institutional Revolutionary Party), the armed forces had been disciplined, unified, and subordinated to the civilian power. Civilian supremacy became clear six years later with the capacity shown by the Alemán administration to contain the Henriquista Revolt. Moreover, the decision of Alemán to establish the presidential guards in 1952 by reinforcing the division among the armed services prevented a situation in which one could become too powerful. The presidential guards, under direct command of the president, have fulfilled at least two key tasks: to provide protection to the president and to contain the danger of disloyal military forces. In general, the relationship between the Secretariat of National Defense and the Estado Mayor Presidencial has been characterized by tension and resentment.

The consolidation of civilian supremacy over the armed forces in the 1950s established the conditions for a particularly stable pattern of civil-military relations. This stability has been attributed partly to the legacy of the Revolution, in terms of providing a common ideological framework to both the civilian and military elites as well as in the hostility shown by the population toward violence. For decades, the impact of foreign relations also provided an environment conducive to stable relations between civilians and soldiers. During the first half of the twentieth century, the perception of a real external threat favored the rapid professionalization of the armed forces; by the second half of the century, the asymmetry of military power between Mexico and its northern neighbor provided the civilian elite with a powerful justification to limit the size of the armed forces and to contain budgetary demands.

The stabilization of civil-military relations in Mexico took place within the context of an authoritarian regime. As mentioned earlier, this involved finely tuned policies of depoliticization and professionalization of the armed forces, policies that were partially intrinsic to the mechanics of a hegemonic party system and were not necessarily aimed at eliminating the armed forces' role as the guardians of the civilian elite. The armed forces played a "tutelage role" and maintained their position as the potential "center of gravity" of the regime. Not only did the suppression of the military sector of the PRM fail to bring to an end the intimate relation between the armed forces and the hegemonic party (as military representation within the party between 1946 and 1964 remained constant), but in that period four generals, Rodolfo Sánchez Taboada, Gabriel Leyva Velázquez, Agustín Olachea Aviles, and Alfonso Corona del Rosal, headed the party. Subsequently, close links between the armed institution, the party, and the bureaucracy were maintained through the army's advisory role and most importantly through the organization of security in successive presidential campaigns. Only recently has this protection been offered to the candidates of opposition parties.

After the 1950s the tasks fulfilled by the military primarily were internal. The armed forces had helped suppress rail workers' strikes by the end of the decade, the telephone and postal workers' movement in 1960, and student movements in Mexico City in 1961 and most importantly in 1968, fostering tensions in civilian-military relations leading to rumors of a military coup. The dramatic events of 1968 may have encouraged the reform of the 1926 Organic Law, eliminating the previous task of maintaining the "rule of the Constitution" and its laws and replacing it with the duty to assist the civilian population in case of emergencies. Counterinsurgent campaigns followed in the late 1960s and early 1970s, particularly in the state of Guerrero, and in the 1980s the activity of the armed forces mostly focused on drug trafficking, meeting the threats posed by the Central American crisis, and ensuring the safety of oil installations. Beginning in the 1980s, the rapid expansion of the drug trade and increased U.S. pressure on Mexico to cooperate in the war against drugs further altered the roles performed by the armed forces, raising concerns about their loyalty and cohesiveness.

The conflict in Chiapas in the 1990s became a test for civil-military relations in Mexico. The outbreak of the Zapatista Rebellion brought to light myriad factors that motivated civil violence; among these public negligence was particularly important. This uprising uncovered the vulnerable flanks of President Carlos Salinas de Gortari's economic and political reform. An extremely complex dynamic of property claims, exacerbated by unfavorable economic and agricultural conditions, as well as population growth and migration flows, led to the radicalization of popular protest in the early 1990s. The militarization of the state, originally associated with the Central American crisis, gradually contributed to an escalation of violence and repression that finally fostered ethnic protest.

Although military intelligence detected insurgent training camps as early as the late 1980s, the setting created by the North American Free Trade Agreement (NAFTA) played a key role in the evolution of the conflict. The government's response was to downplay the conflict, to contain protest through the combination of "legal engineering" in the state's criminal code, outright repression, and a more vigorous social policy. In August 1993, following the first armed confrontation between members of the armed forces and the rebels, the government announced a special program for the Lacandon municipalities. The radicalization of popular protest and the seizure by the Zapatistas of several municipalities in January 1994 demonstrated the limits of this policy. While the events of 1994 suggested that the armed forces effectively were surprised, the NAFTA vote in Congress led the government to ignore the problem and to transfer responsibility to the military, who became the scapegoat.

While it could be argued that the role of the armed forces in the conflict in Chiapas again demonstrated the subordination of the military to civilian authority, the underlying tensions and military discontent seem to suggest that the cost of such subordination had increased considerably. By mid-January the armed forces became the target of considerable criticism. A series of minor crises throughout Salinas's term in office indicated that, in the new institutional context, the capacity of the executive to come to the defense of the military institution had diminished. Not only was the president forced to mediate among old and new political actors—including the National Human Rights Commission, national and international nongovernmental human rights organizations, the military, and the police corps—but the new context also had altered the traditional insularity of the armed forces.

For decades the hegemony enjoyed by the official party, a hegemony maintained by inhibiting the emergence of opposition parties and the creation of alliances between these and members of the armed forces, isolated the military institution and contributed to civilian supremacy. The discipline developed within the hegemonic party and the degree of civilian unity undoubtedly provided a favorable environment to military subordination. The long-lasting hegemony of the official party not only isolated the armed forces from party competition but may have encouraged a deeper sense of institutional loyalty than has been the case in other competitive systems. If increased professionalization did in fact coincide with military neutrality toward successive six-year presidential cycles, as the 1988 elections demonstrated, elite divisions could exert pressures on the institutional loyalty of the armed forces by fostering regime instability.

Undoubtedly, the official party's victory in the 1994 presidential election made clear both the capacity of the official party to contend in increasingly competitive scenarios and that of the armed forces to maintain an important degree of independence from the turbulence underlying the political system. Yet, it is also true that over the late 1980s and 1990s the gradual dismantling of the hegemonic party system, the consolidation of opposition parties, and the mounting symptoms of instability reduced the isolation of the armed forces, increased their exposure to various pressures, and brought some tension into civil-military relations. Not only did protracted negotiations fail to tackle this issue, but the role of the official party continued to be a contentious issue among students of civil-military relations in Mexico. As mentioned earlier, some of the institutional mechanisms underlying civilian tactics of control had been associated closely to the dynamics of the PRI's hegemonic rule. Notwithstanding this, the acceleration of political liberalization exerted pressure on these mechanisms and also disputed the boundaries that for decades had guaranteed the insularity of the Mexican military. Indeed, this process, together with the internationalization of Mexican politics during the 1990s, increasingly exposed the Mexican military to international pressures. Although these changes challenged the stability of "subjective" civilian control and have introduced some changes that eventually could develop into more "objective" forms of control, the Mexican system of civil-military relations was still far from those in consolidated democracies. There was no sufficient transparency in defense budgets, supervisory control by the legislative power was still lacking, the "civilianization" of the defense

ministry had not yet taken place, and rather than the "discontinuation" of the military's internal security role, during the 1990s the armed institution was the object of significant pressures to assume responsibility over matters related to public order.

The Zapatista uprising, taking advantage of the internationalization of domestic politics, played an important role in bringing about some changes, with significant implications for civil-military relations. First, it fostered a debate about the constitutional role of the armed forces and their participation in a number of difficult political situations, including the 1968 student movement, the handling of powerful social groups and political actors, and electoral surveillance. Second, both the uprising in Chiapas as well as the later events in Guerrero made clear the increased cost of overt repression and the regime's reduced ability to resort to "legitimate violence." The combination of domestic and international pressures first forced the government to declare the ceasefire in Chiapas in January 1994, compelled the armed forces to address charges of indiscriminate bombing and human rights violations, and led to the removal of the state government in Guerrero. Third, although charges of human rights violations long preceded the Chiapas uprising, this event significantly increased national and international pressures on the military institution to respect human rights and to incorporate a human rights code in its military doctrine. Indeed, this context helps to explain the decision of the military both to commit itself publicly with the investigation of the claims made by the National Human Rights Commission and subsequently to organize special tours for diplomats and press attaches. Fourth, changes pointing to an incipient "parliamentary supremacy" also were observed in both the context of Chiapas and that of U.S.-Mexican security cooperation. After 1995 the legislative power became actively involved in the process of negotiations in Chiapas. It participated in the drafting of the Law for the Dialogue, Reconciliation, and a Fair Peace in Chiapas, and through the Defense Commission it performed a useful mediating role with the Ministries of the Interior and Defense on issues closely related to the peace process. Most important, the creation of plural legislative commission, the Comisión de Concordia y Pacificación (COCOPA), in March 1995 was a key decision that provided the peace process with an impartial mediator. Similarly, the uncertainty underlying contacts between the governments of the United States and Mexico on issues related to security was the background to new gestures of legislative supervision. In both the Senate and the Chamber of Deputies, the presidents of their respective Defense Commissions, General Álvaro Vallarta and General Luis Garfias, have asked the executive and the Ministry of Defense to provide Congress with thorough information about bilateral security agreements.

Although these trends are far from resembling the mechanisms that characterize democratic civilian control, they have demonstrated their potential for encroaching upon areas previously restricted by the conventional pattern of civil-military relations. The ultimate outcome of these changes is unlikely to be clear-cut. If it is true that democratic change could reinforce these rudimentary forms of public scrutiny and accountability of the armed forces, as has been the case in other countries, political opening could easily multiply the number of institutional channels by which domestic politics can disturb the civil-military pact. Indeed, rapid political change could not only threaten the insularity of the military, but if accompanied by instability it could increase the risk of politicization of the military institution. Given the degree of penetration of the official party into state institutions, including the military, it is not difficult to imagine how the weakening of the PRI could upset the military's political framework and stimulate its politicization by gearing military activity toward some political end. Moreover, the apparent crisis of the once-powerful Mexican presidentialism and of the most prominent institutions of the center could raise military concerns about the need to preserve central authority and to reestablish order. What is clear is that even if democratization advances in a relatively orderly manner, a strong civilian political leadership will still be needed to bind the military firmly within the emerging democratic framework and to establish the necessary mechanisms for objective civilian control.

As of 1996, total armed forces numbered approximately 175,000 (60,000 conscripts) and a 300,000-man reserve force. The army was the dominant service (130,000 men including 60,000 conscripts). The navy was created in 1939 and in 1996 held 37,000 men. The air force was established in 1944 under the jurisdiction of the Secretariat of National Defense. Power within the armed forces is highly centralized. As of 1996 the organization of the army consisted of 9 military regions and 36 zonal garrisons embracing 1 armored, 19 motorized cavalries, 1 mechanized infantry, 7 artillery regiments, 80 infantry battalions, 1 armored brigade (3 armored and 1 mechanized infantry regiments), 2 infantry brigades, and 1 airborne brigade. Following the 1968 student repression the government created a new zone command, established 3 new battalions—infantry, parachute, and military police—and a new company of combat engineers in the presidential guards. As of 1996 the navy was organized in 6 navy regions and 17 naval zones covering the areas of the gulf and the Pacific. The air force comprised 8,000 elements, including 1,500 airborne brigades, 101 combat aircraft, and 25 armed helicopters.

See also Cristero Rebellion; Massacre of Tlatelolco; Mexican Revolution; Zapatista Rebellion in Chiapas

Select Bibliography

Camp, Roderic Ai, *Generals in the Palacio: The Military in Modern Mexico*. New York and Oxford: Oxford University Press, 1992.

Huntington, Samuel, "Reforming Civil-Military Relations." *Journal of Democracy* 6:4 (October 1995).

Knight, Alan, "Mexico's Elite Settlement: Conjuncture and Consequences." In *Elites and Democratic Consolidation in Latin America and Southern Europe,* edited by John Higley and Richard Gunther. Cambridge: Cambridge University Press, 1992.

Lieuwen, Edwin, *Mexican Militarism: The Political Rise and Fall of the Revolutionary Army*. Albuquerque: University of New Mexico Press, 1968.

Ronfeldt, David, editor, *The Modern Mexican Military: A Reassessment*. La Jolla: Center for U.S.-Mexican Studies, University of California, San Diego, 1984.

Serrano, Mónica, "The Armed Branch of the State: Civil-Military Relations in México." *Journal of Latin American Studies* 27 (1995).

Wager, J. Stephen, *The Mexican Military: Approaches to the 21st Century: Coping with a New World Order*. Carlisle, Pennsylvania: Strategic Studies Institute, U.S. Army War College, 1994.

—MÓNICA SERRANO

Mining: Colonial

As a Spanish colony, Mexico produced about 60,000 tons or 2 billion ounces of precious metals, mainly silver. The Mexican peso, minted from the silver, became a widely circulating coin in the Atlantic economy. It paid for European and Asian imports, replenished the royal coffers, sustained the colonial economies, and laid the foundations for the industrial revolution of the late eighteenth and early nineteenth centuries. Mexico itself underwent little economic transformation, however; it remained a supplier of wealth rather than a beneficiary.

As important as mining was to the Mexican colonial economy, it was not ever the largest of its economic sectors. The agricultural sector employed more people and contributed more to the colony's domestic product than any other sector. At the height of the late colonial mining boom (c. 1800), probably no more than 50,000 out of a total population of 4 million to 5 million were employed in the mines, the smelters and refineries, and related occupations, and one-sixth of the domestic product could be attributed to mining. In contrast, agriculture (farming and ranching) employed hundreds of thousands and generated three to four times the output that mining did. Why, then, was mining so crucial in Spain's imperial goals?

The answer is obvious. Mining was perceived as a quick way for individuals and nations to acquire wealth. In many Atlantic societies ores such as gold, silver, and copper were minted into coins, and presumably the more ores that were discovered the more coins could be minted. Access to large ore deposits did not automatically ensure wealth for individuals or nations. Mining was a business, and like other businesses it required capital investment, intelligent management, and reasonable profitability. Without these ore could not be extracted or processed economically, and coins would not be minted. In addition, some societies did better than others at retaining whatever wealth, including currency, that they created. Despite its rich silver mines Mexico became a major exporter of coins to settle international accounts (including contraband) and to satisfy government transfers. This resulted in chronic shortages of coins for domestic transactions, especially in remote areas and for small purchases. Paper money did not exist, although the commercial and governmental sectors used *libranzas,* a form of a bill of exchange. Barter also continued to be practiced widely.

Because the Aztecs valued the precious metals that they mined for their decorative rather than their monetary use, the Spaniards did not find large mining operations after conquest. From the middle of the sixteenth century to the end of rule by Spain in the early 1820s, the business of mining evolved from small operations of single proprietors or family partners with a few dozen workers into large, complex companies with stockholders and thousands of employees. Mining relied heavily on native labor, at least through the seventeenth century, and it, like other Spanish business activities, had a profound effect on the ability of the native communities to survive and adapt. Not only did mining introduce new and harsh forms of labor, but it also drew these communities more fully into a money-based economy. Mining for the purpose of making money was fundamentally different from mining for decorating the emperor's residence.

Silver, of course, accounted for most of the colony's mineral output. Production data are considerably more plentiful for colonial silver mining than for other mining sectors. Because silver producers paid the *quinto* or *diezmo* (20 to 10 percent tax on all processed silver) to the colonial treasury, the royal ledgers can be used to reconstruct trends and cycles of production for the colony as a whole, as well as for individual silver camps and individual silver producers. These sources are not perfect. Some silver escaped the tax collector—some say as much as 20 percent—and some producers with high costs or good contacts received concessions that waived silver-tax payments. Although the data may not reflect accurately or completely silver output in any given year, they can be useful in charting and analyzing how the industry performed over time.

From the last quarter of the sixteenth century until the first quarter of the nineteenth century, output of silver moved up at an annual rate of about 1 percent. This meant that output doubled about every 70 years. From the accompanying graphs (the first based on actual registrations and the second on logs of registration) it is strongly evident that output was higher at the end of the colonial period than at the beginning. Year-to-year fluctuations were frequent and could be severe; at times they turned into decade-long slides. Given the level of technology and the common risks associated with such underground operations, volatility in output should be expected.

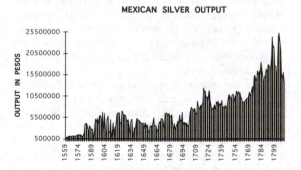

MEXICAN SILVER OUTPUT

MEXICAN SILVER OUTPUT

What needs to be highlighted is that over the long term colonial mining continually staged recoveries that pushed production ever higher.

The most rapid annual growth occurred in the first half-century (up to 1610). Much of the silver was found near the surface and could be mined and refined inexpensively. Registrations (the amount "manifested" before treasury officials for tax purposes) rose from near zero to tens and then hundreds of thousands of pesos (the principal coin), and growth rates are estimated in the range of 2 to 3 percent per year. As miners moved to deeper veins that were less rich in their yields, the cost of mining began to rise. The invention of a new refining process— silver drawn from ore by amalgamation with mercury, rather than by smelting—made it economically feasible to mine low-grade ores. Even so, as illustrated by the trend in the seventeenth century, the amalgamation process did not reduce or eliminate the risks. Output slowed in the seventeenth century compared to the sixteenth or the eighteenth centuries, and this has caused some historians to characterize the period as a "century of depression." During the middle decades, as the log curve (Graph 2) suggests, the upswing had stalled even though over the whole century production increased modestly, at a rate below the 1 percent figure. Production more or less rose in the first third of the seventeenth century, flattened out in the second third, and then resumed its growth in the final third.

In the final century of the colonial period production gained at a rate under 1.5 percent per year. Despite high costs and constant complaints about royal mining policies, miners managed to push silver registrations to their highest levels ever recorded. In the first decade of the eighteenth century, output averaged about 3 million pesos per year; a century later in the first decade of the nineteenth century, it averaged about 15 million pesos. The eighteenth-century curve moved consistently higher, except for a few years in the 1760s. In the late eighteenth century it was estimated that a miner could make money if each ton of ore yielded 2 to 3 ounces of silver. Inventories of mines often reported potentially higher yields, as much as 40 to 50 ounces per ton, but finding such yields were unlikely in camps centuries old. Miners increased production as yields fell not because they introduced new technologies for extracting or processing ore but rather because they invested heavily in rehabilitation (such as drainage systems) that allowed them to recover old but potentially profitable mines. In short, with sufficient capital and skillful management the eighteenth-century yields could make money.

Even though the Spanish Crown theoretically owned all the colony's natural resources, it chose to regulate and tax mining rather than own and operate the mines itself. There were important exceptions. Mercury mining in Spain and Peru remained royal monopolies until the end of the colonial period. Once a claim was registered a miner had to raise the capital, hire the labor, and construct the plant necessary to create a viable business. Access to capital to launch, sustain, and expand their operations always had been an important need for miners small and large. Under the law, merchants, among the wealthiest of the colonists, were prohibited from owning mines. They could own refineries and smelters, and they could advance cash or credit—known as *avíos*—to miners in return for the option to buy their silver. The difference between what they paid the miners and how much they received in coin from the mint became their profit. Moreover, prices of the supplies sold to the miners could be increased to yield profits. In the eighteenth century, with the emergence of mining companies, merchants became stockholders, even though they were still restricted in how much stock they could own. Without a formal banking system merchants performed a vital service as lenders and investors in an ever increasingly costly and risky business. Despite fear and resentment of the merchant elite, this elite provided for mining even in the late sixteenth and early seventeenth centuries the financial wherewithal that both the industry and the government could not or would not provide.

Mining consisted of the extraction of ore from veins and the processing of the ore into silver either by smelting it or refining. Down to the end of the colonial period, camps exhibited two structural patterns. One pattern, dating from the earliest years and surviving until the final years, underscored a split in which refining operations were owned separately from mining operations. By the eighteenth century, however, entrepreneurs came to understand the advantages of combining the operations into what D. A. Brading described as a "vertical" structure. Most of the largest producers in late-colonial Guanajuato or Zacatecas owned one or more refineries to process their ores. Independent refiners *(rescatadores)* did not disappear; they continued to serve the small miners who could not afford to build refineries and large miners whose ore output exceeded their own refinery capacity. Still, the unmistakable trend was for more and more of the mining and refining operations to be concentrated in the hands of a few owners and investors.

Smelters were less expensive to build and run than refineries, which required substantial investment in plant and equipment. On the other hand, smelting was economical only with high-grade ores from which the silver could be "cooked." Refining was a more elaborate process by which the pulverized ore was combined with mercury. First the mercury chemically bonded with the silver and then after being heated it evaporated. What was left was pure silver. As ore grades declined starting in the sixteenth century, refining, which was more efficient at extracting the small amount of silver present in the heaps of ores extracted from underground, constituted 80 to 90 percent of all processing.

Mining remained a labor-intensive industry until the end of the colonial period. Most of the workforce was engaged in underground jobs: extracting the ore, expanding or maintaining the tunnels, or carrying the ore to the surface. The workday was long, hard, and dangerous. On the surface working conditions were not as harsh or severe, and yet they still could be potentially dangerous, especially for those hired to incorporate the mercury, a highly toxic mineral, with the ore. People went to work in the mines and refineries in large part because of wages. Workers were paid a daily wage, and some categories of underground workers earned the *partido*, or a share of the ore that they mined. Studies on wages in mining or across the colonial economy are still sparse, and what we have in the way of data is mainly comparative weekly or monthly wages. From these comparisons we can say that workers in the mining sector could earn more than workers in most other sectors. What we do not know is how they were paid—in cash or some other form—and how far their wages would go in securing a better life. Some owners felt wage pressures from time to time, in particular toward the end of the eighteenth century. They made efforts to reduce or eliminate *partidos* in order to lower their costs, and yet because they needed workers with certain skill levels, underground and aboveground, they were limited to some extent in how much they could modify wage scales. In the end, however, relative to other wages those in the mining sector probably stood at or near the top of the colonial wage scale.

Even though for nearly 300 years Mexico ranked among the world's largest producers of silver, it remained in the economic backwaters. Silver built some magnificent edifices, bought some noble titles, and underwrote royal extravagances, but it contributed little to broadening colonial markets or raising living standards. Being a leader in production of silver did not automatically ensure a transformed economic system.

Select Bibliography

Bakewell, Peter, *Silver Mining and Society in Colonial Mexico: Zacatecas, 1546–1700.* Cambridge: Cambridge University Press, 1971.

_____, "Mining in Colonial Spanish America." In *The Cambridge History of Latin America*, vol. 2: *Colonial Latin America*, edited by Leslie Bethell. Cambridge and New York: Cambridge University Press, 1984.

Brading, D. A., *Miners and Merchants in Bourbon Mexico, 1763–1810.* Cambridge: Cambridge University Press, 1971.

Garner, Richard L., "Long-Term Silver Mining Trends in Spanish America: A Comparative Analysis of Peru and Mexico." *American Historical Review* 93 (1988).

_____, *Economic Growth and Change in Bourbon Mexico.* Gainesville: University Press of Florida, 1993.

—RICHARD L. GARNER

Missions

Acting as agents of both the state and the Catholic Church, the missions of northern New Spain played a crucial role in the extension of the Spanish frontier and the acquisition of new territory. In contrast to other North American colonial powers, Spain followed a policy that attempted to incorporate native peoples into Spanish political and social life. In an arrangement unique to colonial powers in the Americas, the imperial government in New Spain cooperated with the Catholic Church to create a spiritual-cultural frontier that paralleled the military-political frontier.

Two papal determinations provided a foundation for church-state cooperation in New Spain. In 1508, the papal bull *Universalis Ecclesiae Regimini* established the *real patronato*, or royal patronage. In exchange for financial support for the church, the Spanish monarch acquired a set of rights and privileges normally reserved for ecclesiastical authorities. Through this determination, religious establishments in the Americas were incorporated into the imperial administration, under the supervision of the Council of the Indies and the Commissioner General's Office, a new department responsible for ecclesiastical affairs. Many ecclesiastical activities in New Spain required approval from the commissioner general, including the establishment and operation of religious foundations, the appointment of provincials and visitors, and the creation of new provinces. The provincials of religious orders in New Spain were required to send annual reports to Spain, listing the missions in each jurisdiction and the names, ages, and qualifications of all missionaries. In 1537, a second papal bull, *Sublimis Deus,* ended the debate over the nature of the native peoples of America. Although in practice Spaniards often disregarded this determination, it established that Indians were true reasoning men, capable of comprehending Christian principles. The bull created an imperative for the salvation of native souls through conversion to Catholicism. By the early sixteenth century, enslavement of native peoples was officially illegal.

Having been given control of many aspects of church procedure in exchange for financial responsibility, the Spanish civil government entered into a cooperative arrangement with monastic orders that made them the principal vehicle for converting native peoples. The mission system also became an instrument of Spanish political expansion and the primary institution for the introduction of Spanish culture to frontier Indian nations. Missions and presidios, or military outposts, frequently were founded during joint expeditions, in which both military and religious personnel participated. By the early sixteenth century, royal regulations required that a priest, usually a member of one of the orders, accompany all *entradas,* or exploratory expeditions. The extent of financial support depended on the political goals that might be met by the mission in question. Missions in strategically important areas, such as New Mexico or Florida, received extensive financial support because treasury officials believed missionary presence would secure the frontier and that missionary conversion of natives would increase the number of laborers and tax-payers on the rolls. Until the nineteenth century, the royal treasury paid missionary salaries and provided military protection to missions from its fund for "peace and war."

The founding of a new mission required an elaborate series of civil bureaucratic proceedings. The head of the religious order had to submit a petition to the viceroy, the *audiencia* (high court), and the bishop, all of whom were obliged to send reports and documents certifying the necessity for the new foundation to the commissioner general in Spain. The Council of the Indies then selected the new missionaries and the provinces from which they would be taken. Missionaries attempted to locate new missions in areas of concentrated Indian population, with fertile soil, adequate water for irrigation, and easy communication with other Indian pueblos. In addition to the usual soldiers, a new missionary's retinue often included a number of neophytes from an established mission who could assist local Indians in building the necessary structures. In order to secure his position, a new missionary frequently created alliances within the political structure of the tribes in his jurisdiction or allied himself with particular leaders.

Missionaries promptly attempted to reorganize native communities along Spanish lines. On first arrival, they recruited individuals to become ritual assistants: a *temastian,* who served as a catchiest; and a *madore,* or *fiscal,* who worked as an administrator for church affairs. They appointed an Indian governor for civil administration, who maintained order and reported to the missionary, and Indian judges, or *alcaldes,* who administered punishments. A native *maestro de la doctrina* in each pueblo was responsible for overseeing simple religious observances.

The Spanish government considered the mission to be the ideal agent of Spanish culture and used the system to spread selected aspects of Spanish civil life. The government intended that Indian pueblos within the mission system would evolve into Spanish towns, or *villas,* with civil and military officers and a rudimentary Spanish-style administration. To accomplish this, the laws of the Indies prescribed the activities and equipment of missions. Missions were required to have schools, and missionaries were required to learn native languages in order to write catechism and prayer books in native tongues. Neophytes were required to attend morning and evening prayer and were punished for nonattendance. Methods of indoctrination often included gifts of tools, clothing, or decorative items and the presentation of instructional plays. Missionaries gave instruction in Spanish language and social customs, industrial training, agricultural techniques, and the rudiments of Spanish self-governance.

In its ideal conception, the mission was a community of obedient Indians, following the instructions of missionary priests in spiritual and secular matters. Missions became segregated communities for Indian converts, where neophytes could live according to Christian regulations for social behavior. Missionaries made genuine attempts to shield neophytes from influences they considered detrimental to native souls, particularly from the corrupting influence of Spanish settlers, who frequently attempted to exploit native labor. Missionaries preached against social customs unacceptable to Christian values, including plural marriages, sexual relations outside marriage, and drunkenness.

New Spain's mission system was organized into a series of provinces, each of which was subdivided into districts, in which there were several Indian pueblos. Larger Indian towns became mission headquarters, or *cabeceras,* where resident missionaries supervised mission activities for the district. Smaller villages and the *rancherías* of nomadic Indians were designated *pueblos de visita.* Circuit-riding priests visited these smaller settlements on a regular basis, holding religious services in native structures. Until regular ecclesiastical parishes could be established, the recently converted native congregations were organized as *doctrinas,* or native parish districts.

The mission system relied on Indian labor. At each mission, Indian neophytes farmed and raised European stock. Many missions operated ranches, supervised by overseers, with the usual corrals, farm implements, and tools for blacksmithing. The new production systems created new positions, including herdsmen, agricultural overseers, ditch masters, and agricultural laborers. New architecture required adobe makers, masons, carpenters, and a series of specialists in various European crafts. The whole community participated in planting and harvesting, frequently with a soldier or Indian civil official acting as overseer. The missionary retained custody of the harvest and issued provisions on a daily or weekly basis, depending on the degree of responsibility demonstrated by the neophytes. Self-sufficiency and production of surplus were integral parts of the mission program. When a surplus was achieved, it was sold to neighboring presidios or Spanish civilians.

Colonial officials followed a policy of *congregación,* or concentration of native population. This led to the establishment of nucleated mission communities, modeled on the Indian peasant communities of central Mexico, whether or not native groups had a history of living in settled villages. In cases where natives had not lived in pueblos, missionaries established *reducciones,* artificially created pueblos in which influence and control could be exerted with greater ease. Imposition of mission organization through a *reducción* could involve radical changes in settlement and subsistence patterns and sometimes required the use of force. Both government and church policy insisted that the soldiers who accompanied missionaries were present only to ensure the safety of the missionaries, not to force Christianity on unconverted natives. Once missions had been established, however, missionaries often had to rely on the military to prevent converts from leaving and becoming apostates. For nomadic Indian groups, relocation and settlement in the *reducciones* often had devastating effects on native population numbers. Introduced European diseases spread through concentrated mission populations, creating a situation in which death rates exceeded birthrates. In general, missions did not produce self-sustaining populations.

Mission architecture reveals the various functions of the mission. At the center of the pueblo or *reducción,* the church was surrounded by administrative offices, a *convento* (residence for the missionaries),

workshops of various kinds, blacksmith shops, loom rooms, milling rooms, housing for the native population, stockyards, and usually a granary. In hostile territory, a strong defensive wall often enclosed the mission complex. Frequently a native *mayordomo,* keeper of the granaries, lived next to the headquarters or *convento.* Converts lived nearby, sometimes in adobe houses but more often in wattle-and-daub or thatched structures. Mission architecture evolved from simple early structures that utilized existing native architectural styles and building materials to the elaborate Spanish-style missions of the eighteenth century.

Two religious orders, Franciscan and Jesuit, are identified most closely with the missions of Mexico's northern frontier. Although the Franciscan and Jesuit mission systems differed considerably, both followed the same ideal conception and both functioned under extensive bureaucratic systems. The Franciscans, or Friars Minor, were the first members of religious orders to arrive in New Spain. A Franciscan accompanied Christopher Columbus on his second voyage to the New World, and Franciscans arrived in Mexico shortly after the Conquest. Three Franciscan colleges, Santa Cruz at Querétaro (established in 1682), Guadalupe in Zacatecas (established in 1707), and San Fernando in Mexico City (established in 1734), offered special instruction for missionaries and trained most of the Franciscans who worked on the northern frontier. The *crónica* (chronicle) of the Franciscan missionary colleges dictated the methods that could be used for instructing Indian neophytes. Members of the Society of Jesus, or Jesuits, began work in Mexico in 1571. Prior to their expulsion from New Spain in 1767, Jesuits developed extensive educational institutions and established six missionary districts with 99 missions. In each mission province, a Jesuit provincial supervised the work of the missions and sent a visitor to make an annual inspection tour, upon which he reported to the provincial. Both provincials and visitors changed every three years.

Jesuits and Franciscans divided their jurisdiction over the northern frontier, each order usually taking charge of the missions throughout an entire province, or concentrating their efforts on the members of a linguistic or ethnic group. Missionization followed the frontier and generally proceeded from south to north. In 1650 an agreement between the Jesuits and Franciscans set a rough dividing line through western Chihuahua to establish the jurisdiction of each order. Jesuits were responsible primarily for the missions west of the line in Sinaloa, Sonora, the Pimería Alta, Baja California, and the Tarahumara Baja and

Tarahumara Alta districts in western Nueva Vizcaya. Franciscans were responsible for missions east of the line, including the portion of eastern and northern Nueva Vizcaya which became Coahuila, as well as Nuevo México, Tejas, Florida, and Alta California. Outstanding among the pioneer missionaries were the Jesuit Eusebio Kino and the Franciscan Francisco Garcés. Kino worked first in Baja California and after 1686 in northern Sonora, where he often made joint expeditions with Captain Juan Mateo Manje. Prior to his death in 1711, Kino established missions throughout the Pimería Alta. The Franciscan Father Francisco Garcés, who made several joint exploration expeditions with General Juan Bautista de Anza, was killed in 1781 during a Yuman uprising at the mission he established at the junction of the Colorado and Gila Rivers.

Missions were intended to be temporary religious institutions. Secularization, the process of turning the mission jurisdiction into a parish administered by "secular" (non-order) clergy associated with the local bishopric, was the ultimate mission objective. Missionaries were expected to introduce the faith among heathen nations, but as soon as the population was converted and settled, the mission was to be secularized and the missionary replaced by a parish priest. At that time, the common mission lands were to be distributed among the Indians. Initially, both ecclesiastic and civil authorities believed that missions could be turned over to secular clergy within 10 years, but this seldom was accomplished. The process of secularization began in 1753. The Jesuit and Franciscan missions secularized at this time met with a variety of fates. Some were abandoned entirely, others were converted to parish churches. The secularization process came to a sudden climax in 1767, however, with the expulsion of all Jesuits from New Spain. After the expulsion, the former Jesuit missions were either secularized or turned over to the Franciscan order, with its limited supply of missionaries. Although the transition in general was not smooth, most historians agree that the missions fared better under Franciscan control than under secular control. Without missionaries to protect Indian settlements, Spanish civilians increased their incursions onto Indian lands and their misuse of Indian labor. Neophyte populations decreased, and native officials were unable to enforce regulations.

Although their fundamental conceptualization and goals were similar, Jesuit and Franciscan missions differed in organization. Through a special agreement with the viceroy, Jesuit missionaries in many parts of New Spain controlled mission properties and were responsible for mission finances. Franciscans, on the other hand, had less to do with temporalities, although they were entitled to some personal services from the neophytes. When former Jesuit missions were turned over to the Franciscans in 1767, the change in structure caused so many problems that within three years Visitor General Gálvez had to order Franciscans to resume control of mission estates.

The mission frontier was fraught with conflict. Many native nations, including Navajos, Apaches, Utes, and Hopis, resisted conversion and acculturation and were able to maintain independence from Spanish rule. At established missions, neophytes sometimes fled from restrictive living conditions, individually or in small groups. Missionized Indian groups, or factions that had resisted missionization, periodically rose up against Spanish domination and missionary presence. On several occasions uprisings developed into full-fledged rebellions in which missions were attacked and missionaries killed. Uprisings occurred among the Tepehuanes in 1616 and the Tarahumaras in 1648, 1650, 1652, 1690, and 1696. The Pueblo Revolt of 1680, in which all Spaniards were expelled from New Mexico, was the most effective instance of intertribal organization for resistance against the Spanish. Pueblo success initiated a series of uprisings in Nueva Vizcaya, Sonora, and Sinaloa, which broke out periodically from 1684 through the 1690s. In 1740, Lower Pimas, Mayos, and Yaquis participated in uprisings. Again in 1751 rebellions spread throughout Sonora and other parts of the frontier. In 1781, the Yumas cut off contact between the northern frontier and California.

Conflict also occurred between religious orders and other Spanish political factions. Although the mission system was designed to work in conjunction with the military, relations between the two institutions were often acrimonious, missionaries being highly critical of the bad influence that soldiers exerted on neophytes. Spanish settlers in many areas voiced strong criticism of the mission program and even called for its termination. In attempting to mitigate the acquisitive actions of settlers and soldiers, missionaries often found themselves allied with Indians against other Spanish political and economic interests.

The Spanish mission system fell short of its threefold religious, cultural, and political objectives. General agreement exists among historians and anthropologists that missions failed to replace previous religions or fully Hispanicize the native populations in their charge. Native populations themselves frequently determined the degree to which they accepted or dismissed Spanish introductions. Minimally, the mission system provided Amerindians with a new system of magic, which might offer solutions to the ravages of disease, relocation, new methods of warfare, unfamiliar domestic animals, and new agricultural systems brought by the invaders. In political objectives, missions often were unable to perform their defensive function against Indians. Nor were they always successful in their role in European imperial rivalry. Yet, the mission system was crucial to the introduction of European civilization in what is today northern Mexico and the southwestern United States and contributed to Spanish influence on the culture, architecture, laws, customs, agriculture, and language of the region. In contrast to the English frontier in North America, where no similar institution existed, the mission system in New Spain was an institution designed for the cultural transformation and political incorporation of the Indian.

See also Catholic Church; Conquest: Northern Mexico

Select Bibliography

Bannon, John Francis, editor, *Bolton and the Spanish Borderlands*. Norman: University of Oklahoma Press, 1964.

Bolton, Herbert E., *Kino's Historical Memoir of Pimería Alta*. 2 vols., Cleveland, Ohio: Arthur H. Clark, 1919.

Weber, David J., *The Spanish Frontier in North America*. New Haven, Connecticut, and London: Yale University Press, 1992.

Weddle, Robert S., "Cross and Crown: The Spanish Missions in Texas." In *Hispanic Texas: A Historical Guide*, edited by Helen Simons and Catheryn A. Hoyt. Austin: University of Texas Press, 1992.

—Diana Hadley

Modernism

During the last two decades of the nineteenth century, the literature of Spanish America underwent a period of renovation that brought about important stylistic changes in both prose and poetry. In a general sense modernism, as applied to Spanish American literature, denotes change and innovation, a rejection of the excesses of romanticism, but at the same time it conserved the romantic tendencies of exoticism, pessimism, and melancholy. It was part of a general tendency toward renovation of art and literature in western Europe where such movements as nineteenth-century French impressionism, symbolism, Parnassianism, and English Pre-Raphaelitism sought freedom of expression in art and literature.

Modernism, however, is more narrowly applied to a specific Spanish American literary movement that attempted to introduce a subtle beauty and elegance into writing, especially poetry. It rejected mere imitation and frequently delved into the inner states of the writer. Cosmopolitan in nature, the modernists strove to free poetry from didactic ends and rhetorical restraints. Their verse emphasized concision, color, form, and metrical detachment; the result was verse with more emotional sensitivity and a greater visual and musical caliber. The modernists sought to appeal to as many of the senses as possible. In this respect the modernists used many more adjectives than the earlier romantics. They were more precise in poetic expression and in their choice of words. The importance of colors in the whole movement was likewise significant; French Parnassians, symbolists, and impressionists were widely emulated by the early modernists in an attempt to create subjective word pictures, to establish certain moods and emotions, and to explore all possible interrelation of the senses. The French spirit of early modernism was summarized by the undisputed leader of the movement, the Nicaraguan poet Rubén Darío in his poem "Yo soy aquel":

> . . . y muy siglo diez y ocho y muy antiguo
> y muy moderno; audaz cosmopolita
> con Hugo fuerte y con Verlaine ambiguo,
> y una sed de ilusiones infinita.
>
> (. . . and very much eighteenth century and
>   very ancient
> and very modern; a daring cosmopolitan
> with strength from Hugo and an ambiguous
>   Verlaine
> and an infinite thirst for illusions.)

Modernism in Mexico corresponds to the period of the rule of Porfirio Díaz (1876–80 and 1884–1911), an extended period known as the Porfiriato. Díaz was able to transform Mexico into a stable, progressive nation while at the same time attracting a great deal of foreign investment. Opposition was suppressed, especially in rural areas where the mounted police, called the *rurales,* maintained order, often at the expense of personal freedom. Land remained in the hands of the elite, and peasant life was difficult. The peace and stability of the nation, however, permitted modernist literature to flourish, but at the same time these writers rejected a society dedicated to material progress. Their opposition to the Díaz government, nevertheless, was almost totally muted in a search for beauty of expression and freedom both in form and spirit for their verse.

Mexican modernism found an early leader in Manuel Gutiérrez Nájera (1859–95), a journalist of superior talent and founder of the journal *Revista Azul*. Writing both prose and poetry, Gutiérrez Nájera contributed to the principal periodicals of Mexico City until his death in 1895. His entire life was dedicated to letters and to journalism. Although the French influence is always evident in both his prose and poetry, it is his graceful style that distinguishes his literary production. In his verse he communicates a spontaneous feeling of tenderness and skeptical humor. In his elegiac poems he passes through a period of great spiritual doubt and finally achieves a feeling of serenity and resigned melancholy.

The importance of his poetry was great, but it was in his prose writings—chronicles, theater reviews, literary and social criticism, travel notes, and short stories—that Gutiérrez Nájera's contribution to modernism was most decisive. Although a great deal of his writing shows an exotic, even a Parisian verve, Gutiérrez Nájera never traveled outside of Mexico. He often signed his prose writings with the pseudonym "El Duque Job," a sobriquet that revealed both his "noble" ancestry as well as his penchant for physical and mental anguish.

Gutiérrez Nájera was one of the first writers of his generation who professed a special devotion to the use of colors. *Cuentos color de humo* is an early collection of chronicles and short stories that appeared in Mexico City newspapers from 1890 to 1894. Many titles of his poems and chronicles show the same predilection: "Musa blanca," "De blanco," and "Crónica de mil colores." His well-known "La serenata de Schubert" clearly marks his interest in the combination of music and writing, and some of his most frequently quoted verse reveals a dramatic, even a resigned, acceptance of death. With the departure of Rubén Darío from Buenos Aires in 1898, the Argentine capital's importance in modernism began to decline rapidly in favor of Mexico City. Cofounders of the *Revista Azul*, Carlos Díaz Dufóo (1861–1941) and Luis G. Urbina (1864–1934) as well as the poet Salvador Díaz Mirón (1853–1928) were all key figures in the movement's renaissance in the Mexican capital.

The early Mexican modernists considered Justo Sierra their *maestro*. Although he was never considered a genuine modernist, his interest in literary renovation was genuine. Poet, orator, historian, critic, Sierra was one of Mexico's most esteemed figures during one of its most brilliant intellectual periods. In the delicacy of his poetic expression and in the artistic perfection of his prose compositions he heralds the innovations that younger writers were to put into practice.

Many of these same authors later continued to write for the *Revista Moderna*, a review that began publishing in 1898, a year after the *Revista Azul* ceased to exist. The *Revista Moderna* became the herald of the modernist movement throughout all of Spanish America. It was founded by Jesús E. Valenzuela (1856–1911) in close association with Amado Nervo (1870–1919). Valenzuela was instrumental in bringing together the myriad voices of modernism that coalesced around the *Revista Moderna,* and Nervo was to become Mexico's leading modernist after the death of Gutiérrez Nájera.

Death and pantheism are hallmarks of Nervo's mature poetry, but at the same time he cultivates a more simplistic verse; together with Gutiérrez Nájera these two poets are the preeminent figures of Mexican modernism. Despite the modernists' separation, at least in spirit, from the political turmoil that was building in pre-Revolutionary Mexico, it was not possible for the generation of the *Revista Moderna* to withstand the dichotomy of the early revolutionaries, on one hand, and the positivism entrenched in the minds of the so-called Científicos (favored intellectuals and policy advisers) who influenced the Díaz government. In 1910 Francisco I. Madero began a political campaign against Díaz, and in May 1911 Ciudad Juárez fell to rebel forces. The demise of the *Revista Moderna* occurred at the same time.

Mexico, however, produced other modernists who were active well into the twentieth century. One of the cofounders of the *Revista Azul,* Luis G. Urbina is considered a writer of merit during the entire period of Mexican modernism. As was the case with Díaz Mirón and even Gutiérrez Nájera, Urbina began as a devotee of romanticism. His adhesion to modernism is best seen in volumes published in 1910 and thereafter. They reveal a more personal approach to poetry in a period of melancholy as the storm clouds of the Revolution swirled over the nation.

Another modernist who survived the Revolution, José Juan Tablada (1871–1945) was dedicated to the movement from the beginning of his career as a poet. Although he did write nine poems for the *Revista Azul,* he was more closely affiliated with Amado Nervo and the *Revista Moderna* and was one of several modernists who expressed an interest in Japan and Japanese culture. A wealthy friend paid his way to Japan, and the poetry he wrote there appeared in the 1904 volume *El florilegio*. He was a skeptic given to certain periods of sentimentalism together with moments of irony and sarcasm. In the confusion that reigned in Mexico after the fall of Porfirio Díaz and the beginning of the Revolution, Tablada left for Paris where he continued to write both prose and poetry, inspired by his visit to Japan some 10 years earlier. Later he lived, taught, and lectured in Caracas, Venezuela, and in Forest Hills, New York. He did, however, spend his last years in Mexico, where he resided until his death in Cuernavaca.

Efrén Rebolledo (1877–1929) continued the interest in Japanese themes in later modernism. He served in the Mexican diplomatic corps both in Japan and Norway. His prose and poetry convey his deep appreciation of Japan, and his years in Norway produced the novel *Saga de Sigfrida la Blonda* (1922). There were many other Mexican writers who cultivated both prose and poetry during the first decade of the twentieth century. Many of them were associated with the *Revista Moderna* and Amado Nervo. Among them was Balbino Dávalos (1866–1951), whose poetry was outstanding, as were his translations, especially his Spanish versions of the French Parnassian poet Théophile Gautier. Others whose verse he translated included Paul Verlaine, Leconte de Lisle, Pierre Louys, Maurice Maeterlinck, and the American poets John Greenleaf Whittier, Henry Wadsworth Longfellow, Edgar Allan Poe, and Walt Whitman. Of this group Whitman often was cited by the modernists as a primary source of inspiration. Other Mexican writers of this generation were Francisco Manuel de Olaguíbel (1874–1924), a poet with sentimental and sometimes romantic flares in his verse; Rubén M. Campos (1876–1945), whose poetry as well as his fiction were frequently printed in the *Revista Moderna;* Luis Rosado Vega (1873–1958), inspired by both Amado Nervo and Rubén Darío; and Bernardo Couto Castillo (1880–1901), whose promising career was cut short by his untimely death at the age of 21. It should be mentioned that all of the members of this later generation of modernists lived beyond the end of the Mexican Revolution and well beyond modernism as a formal literary movement.

Almost all of these figures were talented prose writers as well as poets, especially Urbina, Nervo, and Tablada. Perhaps the best prose writer of the generation was Jesús Urueta (1868–1920) whose novel *Fresca* appeared in 1903. He was also a scholar of Greek literature and gave a series of lectures collected under the title *Alma-Poesía* (1904). Urueta was an exceptional orator who displayed a certain magnetism in his delivery. Although he was a deputy during the last years of Porfirio Díaz, he was named minister to Argentina in 1919 and died in Buenos Aires. Many of these collaborators of the *Revista Moderna* met on Sundays in the home of Jesús E. Valenzuela, who was in poor health during the first decade of the twentieth century. One of the most prominent members of this group was Manuel José Othón (1858–1906). His poetry painted pictures of rustic solitude and verdant nature and manifested obvious traits of pantheism. Within the circle of the *Revista Moderna,* he was regarded as a poet who cultivated traditional verse, but his prose appeared only in the local press.

One of the most significant cultural initiatives of the young modernists was the formation in 1907 of a series of scholarly lectures under the rubric *Sociedad de Conferencias,* later to be called the *Ateneo de la Juventud* and then baptized with the definitive title *Ateneo de México.* This circle sponsored lectures on such topics as Nietzche, Poe, D'Annunzio, Chopin, José Enrique Rodó, and Sor Juana Inés de la Cruz. Despite the uncertainties brought about during the first years of the Revolution, the *Ateneo* was able to continue its scholarly activities until 1914.

Enrique González Martínez (1871–1952) has been called the last modernist and the first postmodernist. His verse has received universal praise and represents a meditative, pantheistic engrossment. His 1911 volume, *Los senderos ocultos,* reveals a personal metamorphosis that leads to introspection and peaceful serenity. He has frequently been called the poet of silence.

His sonnet "Tuércele el cuello al cisne," however, has come to represent what many believe to be the end of modernism. It rejects one of the classic symbols of modernism, the swan, in favor of the wise owl as a token for new poets. It was never the intention of González Martínez to reject the past but rather to signal an end to elaborate modernist rhetoric and to mark new paths for young writers to explore.

> Tuércele el cuello al cisne de engañoso
>   plumaje
> que da su nota blanca al azul de la fuente;
> él pasea su gracia no más, pero no siente
> el alma de las cosas ni la voz.
>
>   . . .
>
> El [buho] no tiene la gracia del cisne, mas
>   su inquieta
> pupila que se clava en la sombra, interpreta
> el misterioso libro del silencio nocturno.
>
> (Wring the neck of the swan with its false
>   plumage
> that sings its white song to the azure
>   fountain;
> it only flaunts its grace, but it does not
>   perceive

the soul of matter nor the voice of the countryside.

. . .

The owl lacks the grace of the swan, but its anxious
eye that is riveted on the shadow, interprets
the mysterious book of nocturnal silence.)

The Spanish American War in 1898 and the arrival of Darío in Spain in 1892 brought the modernist spirit of renovation to Spain, where the subsequent Generation of 1898 sought new approaches to Spanish literature in the wake of that nation's loss of the final vestiges of its once great empire. Modernism was to continue to flourish in Mexico, however, until the external veneer of progress under Porfirio Díaz crumbled in the wake of the Mexican Revolution. Despite the chaos of war, many of the later modernists continued to write during and after the years of revolution.

After the publication of Rubén Darío's *Cantos de vida y esperanza* in 1905, modernism made significant thematic changes. Interest in regional, social, and political issues, almost totally absent during the movement's early years, began to be explored by younger writers. Some viewed the United States as the Colossus of the North, a power to be reckoned with in the aftermath of the Spanish American War. Others explored regional and indigenous themes or sought to develop an appreciation for cultures that thrived in past centuries. Darío himself changed the thematic course of his writings after 1905 and pointed the way to a more profound focus for his literary production. It has been argued that many of the modernists failed to see the foremost issues of their day and the momentous changes the twentieth century had thrust upon them. The initial events of the new century determined the dissolution of modernism as a formal literary movement, especially in Revolutionary Mexico, and precipitated a reorientation of postmodern literature along different paths. Although many point to the death of Rubén Darío in 1916 as the formal end of modernism as a defined movement in Spanish literature, its spirit of renovation and its search for new avenues of expression continued to shape literature in Mexico as well as in the rest of Latin America throughout the twentieth century.

Select Bibliography

Anderson, Robert, *Spanish American Modernism: A Selected Bibliography*. Tucson: University of Arizona Press, 1970.
Coester, Alfred, *The Literary History of Spanish America*. New York: Macmillan, 1970.
Craig, G. Dundas, *The Modernist Trend in Spanish American Poetry*. Berkeley: University of California Press, 1934.
Davison, Ned J., *The Concept of Modernism in Hispanic Criticism*. Boulder, Colorado: Pruett, 1966.
Henríquez Ureña, Pedro, *Literary Currents in Spanish America*. Cambridge, Massachusetts: Harvard University Press, 1945.
Johnson, M. E., *Swans, Cygnets, and Owls*. Columbia: University of Missouri Press, 1956.
Umphrey, George W., "Fifty Years of Modernism in Spanish American Poetry." *Modern Language Quarterly* 1 (1940).

—HARLEY D. OBERHELMAN

Mora, José María Luís 1794–1850

Lawyer, Statesman, and Social Theorist

José María Luís Mora was the preeminent liberal theorist of Mexico's nineteenth century. Although he supported the initial revolutionary break from Spain as unfortunate but necessary, Mora championed moderate, constitutional change within a stable system as more constructive and ultimately more beneficial in the long run. His ideas had tremendous impact on later generations of Mexican liberals who sought to limit the central government's power and guarantee freedoms for all.

Born in Guanajuato to a prosperous criollo family, Mora had to transcend the regional stigma of his origin to gain access to political power that traditionally was centered in the capital city. Although his family lost everything during the Hidalgo Revolt of 1810, Mora nevertheless worked hard at his studies and earned a reputation through his academic success. In 1819 he completed his degree in theology at San Ildefonso, the most prestigious Jesuit Academy in Mexico, and he remained on the faculty as both teacher and librarian after his graduation. At the same time, Mora's tremendous energy and zest for study allowed him to take his religious orders and join the Archbishopric of Mexico as deacon. In 1821, after failing to advance within the archbishopric's hierarchy, a frustrated Mora turned his attention to problems in the secular world instead.

Although José María Luís Mora's collected works fill only five medium-sized volumes, his thoughts and writing had a disproportionate impact. He began a second career as a journalist and statesman in 1821 and led Mexico's constitutional liberal movement during the early national years. In May 1822 he was sworn in as a member of the province of Mexico's deputation to the Constitutional Congress; his personal inclinations led him to an alliance with José María Fagoaga and others who opposed the short-lived empire of Agustín de Iturbide and any form of monarchism for Mexico. Instead, Mora favored the liberal example of the Cortes of Cádiz Constitution of 1812, which attacked corporate privilege in all its manifestations; at first glance it may seem strange that an ordained and pious man such as Mora would support the dismantling of church privileges, but he had been humiliated by his failure to advance within the archbishopric and also believed in the separation of church and state. In 1824, Mora had gained enough prominence within Mexico State to become the leader of its representative assembly with special responsibility for drafting a new constitution.

By 1824, Mora's interest had shifted from theological matters to the study of law. This should not be surprising considering both the historical links between canon and civil law in the Spanish colonies, and the tremendous intellectual challenge of constructing a new judicial system for Mexico. While serving in the Convention, Mora undertook formal studies in the law and received yet another academic degree. Over the years, Mora had amassed a personal library of over 11,000 volumes, in which history and law titles were the majority. He read French fluently and had a predilection for French authors such as Benjamin Constant.

In May 1824, Mora put his former preaching skills to new use and made his first general address to the Convention on the subject of regional government. He was a powerful orator who used this forum to argue for more local responsibility for people's own affairs, believing that higher echelons of government had greater concerns than dealing with day-to-day details. Part of Mora's greatness as a philosopher of independent Mexico was in his even-handedness; he was able to see many sides of a problem and willing to diffuse power away from the central authorities rather than jealously hoard it for power's own sake. Like others of the liberal constitutionalist group, Mora strongly believed in the separation of powers in order to prevent abuses. Of course, conceiving the idea, drafting a constitution, and promulgating it was one thing; putting it in practice in a still-unstable, newly independent country was quite another.

Like other Spanish Americans of his generation, including Bernardino Rivadavia of Argentina and José Cecilio del Valle of Guatemala, Mora was greatly influenced by European liberal constitutional philosophers Benjamin Constant and Jeremy Bentham. Both men emphasized the importance of laws and constitutions in creating social harmony; there

was the sense that if perfect laws could be written then all would be well. Objective conditions, like freedom of the press or religion, if guaranteed juridically, meant that a society would function seamlessly and the people's happiness and welfare would undoubtedly improve. This optimistic formula obviously had great appeal for Spanish American nations trying to build infrastructure in the wake of the colonial authorities' collapse. It promised a quick fix, the fast track to modernity, wealth, and happiness.

Mora and other Spanish Americans looked to Europe for their models. Mora liked the British system of traveling judges and introduced the mainstay of the British legal system, trial by jury, into Mexico during the 1820s. He also admired Joseph Lancaster's system of mutual teaching and welcomed instructors sent by the British and Foreign School Society to advance the state of public literacy in Mexico. Furthermore, he often quoted Bentham and Benjamin Constant in his many newspaper articles and speeches during the 1820s.

Another important result of Mora's constitutionalism and belief in laws as the supreme authority of the land was his growing alarm at the factiousness of Mexican politics. As the 1820s drew to a close amid civil strife, assassinations of political leaders, and frequent coups, Mora warned Mexicans that "the salvation of the republic does not depend on personal attributes, but on the unquestioned supremacy of the law." He foresaw the danger of letting military power and personalist politics rule Mexico, and tried to alert others. Although his moderating voice was a powerful one, Mora alone could not overcome the various competing interest groups, and he became more disillusioned with competitive politics in general.

Although he earlier had placed his faith in the intelligence and innate goodwill of the Mexican people, by the 1830s Mora began to realize the great problem of constitutional rule in a country with no tradition of popular participation in the institutions of government. This was the difference between Mexico and Britain or France, and it led Mora to authors like Constant, who by now called for government by the best people for the rest of the people. Government was to be led by those who had distinguished themselves or proven themselves fit to serve the people, uphold the constitution, and carry out the business of government; those who were unprepared, ill-educated, or corrupt had no place in this system. After a decade of legal philosophy, Mora turned to more sober social theory.

He has been accused of being fickle because of his ever-changing political alliances, but José María Luís

Mora always had the good of the Mexican nation as his standard and should be applauded for his willingness to reconsider his opinions in the face of contradictory evidence. By the 1830s, following trends in Europe, Mora turned to an examination of the Mexican character and the social realities of its people as a way of determining how it should be governed. He was beginning to realize that laws must spring from social norms if they are to be obeyed, and only then can they begin to modify behavior. In other words, Mexicans might not have been ready for full participatory democracy because it was not in their 300-year-old tradition. And so, Mora the theologian and juridical theorist turned to yet another profession in the 1830s, that of the historian. In his attempt to ascertain the direction for Mexico's future, he had to examine its past.

Mora began to write a survey of Mexican history as a way to trace the development of its culture. He, like others, had to come to terms with the Spanish heritage. Whereas other writers either had denigrated the entire colonial period as one of darkness and brutality or had lauded Spanish cultural achievements, Mora again occupied the unpopular middle ground. He accepted the Spanish legacy as mixed and viewed Independence as a bitter and divisive event but one that was necessary and now to be put behind in an effort to reconstruct the republic. He now recognized the challenges facing a colonial people who had won their freedom by force of arms without having an adequate civil authority ready to assume the reins of government. In Mora's history of Mexico, there are numerous qualifications: Fernando (Hernán) Cortés was a great genius and strategist, but the Conquest was bloody and murderous; Independence destroyed the old power structures, but it had to be done; some Spaniards, such as Gaspar Melchor de Jovellanos, were good, but the Hapsburg kings were bad. Mora's history, stemming from his desire to understand the social psychology of the Mexican people, revealed the profoundly conflicted nature of that society in the years after Independence.

Mora continued to write and reflect for two more decades. His search for a distinct Mexican nationality dominated the rest of his life and became more intense during his last years while resident in Europe as Mexico's minister to England. José María Luís Mora, through his constant study and effort on behalf of the Mexican people, set the agenda for subsequent generations of Mexican writers and thinkers. His balanced examinations of both the colonial and revolutionary independence periods provided starting points for later polemicists, as well as heightened awareness of the political use of history as propaganda. Furthermore, his later studies in Mexican identity highlight the fundamental question of its national history: the definition of what it means to be Mexican. Future generations would argue over this issue, often appealing to Mora's authority, but rarely finding a definitive answer.

Select Bibliography

Hale, Charles, *Mexican Liberalism in the Age of Mora, 1821–1853.* New Haven, Connecticut: Yale University Press, 1968.

—KAREN RACINE

Morelos, José María   1765–1815
Priest and Leader of the Independence Movement

José María Morelos was the most important military commander and politician of the Independence movement in New Spain. He was as successful at organizing an efficient fighting body to defeat colonial troops throughout New Spain as he was at organizing the movement politically and setting up a machinery of government.

Morelos was born in Valladolid, Michoacán (present-day Morelia), on September 30, 1765. He came from a poor family. Although he was registered as a Spaniard in his birth certificate, he belonged to the so-called *castas*—those sectors of New Spanish society made up of people of Indian and African descent. They formed the lowest levels of society. From 1779 to 1790, he worked on the San Rafael Tahuejo estate near Apatzingan, probably as an accountant or bookkeeper. He also may have been a mule driver in Michoacán and Mexico State during this period, and this gave him a good knowledge of both states.

Always passionate about studying, in 1790 he enrolled in the Colegio de San Nicolás Obispo in Valladolid, one of New Spain's most important centers of learning. Miguel Hidalgo y Costilla was then the rector. He took courses in Latin grammar and rhetoric, philosophy, and ethics. Having decided on an ecclesiastical career, in 1795 Morelos entered the Tridentine Seminary in Valladolid, where he studied theology, ethics, and philosophy. In April of the same year, he took the Bachelor of Arts exam at the Royal Pontifical University of Mexico City, and in December he received the tonsure and four minor orders and was ordained subdeacon in Valladolid. In 1796 he went to Uruapan as assistant priest. In September of that same year he was ordained deacon in Valladolid, and in December 1797 became a full-fledged priest. From January 1798 to March 1799 he served as a substitute priest in Churumuco and La Huacana, then went on to San Antonio Urecho, and shortly afterward to San Agustín Carácuaro and Nocupétaro. These were all poor parishes, situated in remote areas with harsh climates, where being a priest was not easy. Nevertheless, he fulfilled his duty.

Despite being a priest, Morelos had three children: Juan Nepomuceno Almonte, who many years later played an important role in establishing Maximilian's empire, was born in Carácuaro in 1803 to Brígida Almonte; José Victoriano was born in Nocupétaro in 1808; and a girl was born in Carácuaro the following year.

When in October 1810 Morelos learned of Miguel Hidalgo's revolt against colonial power in Dolores, he decided to join the movement. On October 20 he caught up with Hidalgo, who asked him to recruit troops in the south and capture the port of Acapulco. He was given the rank of brigadier. The bishop of Michoacán granted Morelos the permission to take on this commission, and he returned to Carácuaro, from where he embarked on his first campaign with 25 men. Unlike Hidalgo and other leaders of the movement who recruited large, disorderly, undisciplined groups of revolutionaries, Morelos trained, armed, and disciplined his troops from the outset and tried to recruit capable men for his command. On his way to Acapulco, he passed through Nocupétaro, Huetamo, Coahuayutla, and Zacatula, where he obtained men and arms, and in Petatlán the local militias joined his army. Pablo, Juan José, and Antonio Galeana brought a canon with them to Tecpan, his first piece of artillery, and in Coyuca he was joined by Juan Álvarez. These were all local leaders with influence in the region. They brought troops and distinguished themselves as revolutionary commanders.

Soon after he joined the Independence movement, Morelos was involved in political and social matters as well as military ones. Dedicated to creating a more egalitarian and just society, without class distinctions, in November 1810 he decreed the abolition of slavery, the caste system, and the "cajas de comunidad" (community chests) in Indian villages.

He fought the Royalists at places such as El Aguacatillo, El Veladero, and Paso Real de La Sabana, where he was joined by Hermenegildo Galeana, later to become his lieutenant. On Hidalgo's orders Morelos continually attacked Acapulco, but without success. He withdrew, therefore, to Tecpan, where he organized the government of the region, establishing it as a province. He then carried on to Chilpancingo,

capturing it in May 1811. On the way he sent two envoys to the United States to ask for help for the movement, and passed the hacienda in Chichihualco belonging to Miguel, Nicolás, Leonardo, Victor, and Máximo Bravo. They joined Morelos with a large number of their workers and became some of the best leaders under his command. Shortly afterward, Morelos took Tixla, where he captured numerous prisoners and ammunition. He defended the town successfully against the Royalists and was joined there by Vicente Guerrero, who was to become another outstanding revolutionary leader. He published an edict proclaiming the introduction of a national copper coin and wrote to Ignacio López Rayón about the need to create a revolutionary governing junta. In August 1811, to support the work Rayón was doing on this score, Morelos sent José Sixto Verduzco to represent him at the meeting called by Rayón in Zitácuaro to create the Suprema Junta Nacional Americana (Supreme National American Junta), consisting of Rayón as president, and Verduzco and José María Liceaga as *vocales* (officials). The junta always had Morelos's support, despite the fact that he did not agree with their governing in the name of Spanish king Fernando VII and the fact that the junta did not always support him when he asked for their help.

Morelos went on to capture Chilapa, which meant that the entire south, with the exception of Acapulco, was now in insurgent hands. In mid-November he went to Tlapa. This was the start of his second campaign, the aim of which was to get near Mexico City and Puebla. He captured Chiautla de la Sal and Izúcar, where he was joined by Mariano Matamoros, the priest at Jantetelco, who later became his second in command and one of the heroes of the Independence war. Morelos went on to Cuautla and then to Taxco and Tenancingo, both of which fell to him. At the beginning of February 1812, he returned to Cuautla, where he was besieged by the most distinguished of the Royalist commanders, Brigadier Félix María Calleja del Rey, at the head of a powerful and well-equipped army. Morelos successfully defended the town for a long time, demonstrating his military skill despite Royalist attacks, shortage of food and supplies, an outbreak of disease in the population, and lack of support from other insurgent groups especially from the junta. The loyalty of his followers and the tenacity of his resistance earned him the name "a second Mohammed" from his adversary Calleja. Morelos was forced to capitulate on May 2, 1812. He went to Chiautla de la Sal, and the following month to Chilapa, where he began his third campaign. In June the junta appointed him commander in chief and its fourth official. After successfully going to the aid of Valerio Trujano, besieged at Huajuapan de León by the Royalists, Morelos carried on to Tehuacán, where he arrived in August. He reorganized his troops and made Matamoros his second in command and Galeana a field marshal.

At the same time, Morelos was involved in the political organization of the revolutionary movement. He was not only in contact with the main insurgent leaders who controlled different regions, but also with those still in areas under Spanish rule who were unhappy with the colonial regime. One of his main contacts was the clandestine society in Mexico City, Los Guadalupes, who supported the various insurgent leaders as well as backing the claims of autonomists within the colonial system. In October 1812, Morelos went to Ozumba, but was stopped by Royalists at Ojo de Agua, and at the end of the month captured Orizaba, where he burned a part of the tobacco crop that provided an important source of funds for the colonial regime. On his return to Tehuacán, in Cumbres de Acultzingo, he was again defeated and lost his artillery. From Tehuacán he went on to Oaxaca, capturing its capital, Antequera, on November 25 and from there controlling the whole province. This gave him the opportunity to organize its government, establish a bank, and publish a newspaper, *El Correo Americano del Sur* (The South American Courier). He wrote to the junta drawing its attention to Oaxaca, where he believed the insurgents had laid the bases for "the conquest of the kingdom."

Morelos had not forgotten the military objective originally given to him by Hidalgo. In February 1813 he began his fourth campaign and went to Acapulco, which he took on April 12. He then laid siege to the fort at San Diego, which did not surrender until August 20, giving the viceregal government enough time to prepare a counterattack. During the siege of San Diego, Morelos was preoccupied by the arguments that for some time had been raging between the three original members of the junta, and which not only damaged the institution itself but also the whole revolutionary movement. Morelos had to mediate between them more than once, and in May he called for the election of a fifth member of the junta, to represent the province of Oaxaca. Influenced by the ideas of Carlos María Bustamante, Morelos was finally convinced that the junta could not be restructured adequately and that a new one had to be created. He called elections in the regions under revolutionary control (which included the recently created province of Tecpan and parts of Michoacán, Mexico, Veracruz, and Puebla) to choose representatives to the Supremo Congreso Nacional Americano (Supreme National American Congress), whose task it would be to lay the foundations of a new nation. The Congress met at Chilpancingo on September 14, 1813. The way it was organized and operated was set out by Morelos in his *Reglamento* (Rules) and *Sentimientos de la Nación* (Sense of Nationhood). It established the separation of powers, although dominated by the legislative; the nature of provincial representation; and while it dispensed with Fernando VII and the monarchic system, it kept Catholicism as the sole religion of New Spain. The Congress, composed of officers of the insurgent army and important personalities from the various regions, elected Morelos leader of its executive body. Shortly afterward, the Congress declared independence from Spain (one of Morelos's aims ever since joining the movement), in a decree written by Bustamante and published in November 1813.

Morelos then embarked on his fifth and last campaign, and in Tlacotepec published his *Rudimientos Militares* (Military Principles). However, the Congress was now empowered to coordinate the revolution's military as well as political activities, and this publication proved detrimental to the movement. On December 23, Morelos was defeated by Ciriaco de Llano and Agustín de Iturbide when, on the orders of the Congress, he tried to take Valladolid. On January 5, he suffered another defeat in Puruarán, and his second in command, Matamoros, was captured by the Royalists. The following February, the Congress removed Morelos from his position as supreme leader in Tlacotepec, where he again was defeated and lost all his belongings and records. The Congress then sent him to Acapulco to save the artillery in the San Diego fort and took him off the executive altogether. After burning Acapulco, where he treated the enemy with uncharacteristic cruelty, Morelos went on to Tecpan, Petatlán, Zacatula, Atijo, and Ario.

The revolutionary movement was beginning to fall apart by then, as much because of the defeats suffered by their leaders as the infighting among them. Morelos caught up with the Congress in Tiripitío, and they all went from there to Apatzingan, where they proclaimed the "Constitutional Decree for the Freedom of Mexican America" on October 22, 1814. Morelos was heavily involved in the writing of the document and was elected onto a new executive body, composed of himself, José María Liceaga, and José María Cos. It became impossible for him to keep his military command, since he had to concentrate on the political organization of a patently disintegrating movement. All through 1815 he was the focal point for the Congress as it was continually pursued by the Royalists. In September he decided the Congress should move to Tehuacán so it would be near the sea, making it possible to ask for help from abroad. He achieved his objective at the cost of his own freedom when Manuel de la Concha captured him in Temalaca.

Morelos was taken to Mexico City, where he was imprisoned by the Inquisition and then taken to La Ciudadela. He was tried, found guilty, defrocked, sentenced to death, and shot in San Cristóbal Ecatepec on December 22, 1815. His imprisonment and death was the final blow for the revolution and marked its end as an organized movement. From then on, the movement was fragmented and without a center from which to coordinate its action.

In 1823 the Mexican Congress declared Morelos "Benemérito de la Patria" (A National Hero), and his place of birth was renamed Morelia in 1828. The state that bears his name was created in 1869.

—Virginia Guedea

Moreno Reyes, Mario (Cantinflas)

1913–93

Actor and Comedian

One of the greatest idols of Spanish-language cinema, Mario Moreno Reyes, better known as Cantinflas, gained international recognition through his rendering of a purely local character, the *peladito*. Cantinflas's creation is a symbol of *mestizaje*, the Spanish-Indian racial mixture that is the Mexican genotype; thus, his persona is very different from that of the country's other major comic, Tin Tan, whose *pachuco* is a hybrid produced by the clash of U.S. and Mexican cultures. Cantinflas defined the *peladito* as

> a prototype of those from poor towns or humble city districts. A man with a superficial education, or none at all, but with much ingenuity, a Mexican characteristic. Practically nonexistent socially, he has great astuteness, and a large, gentle, and open heart. An optimist, he firmly believes that anything is possible. He is like millions of men in Mexico and other Latin American countries.

Cantinflas's *peladito* is the Spanish-speaking world's equivalent of Charlie Chaplin's tramp. However, this invention represents not only the fusion of Indian and Spaniard, but the impact of the unplanned and uncontrolled urbanization that dramatically transformed Mexico from a rural and agricultural society into a conglomeration of unmanageable cities, dominated by the largest of them all, Mexico City. The *peladito* is essentially a shrewd country bumpkin who, streetwise in ways only the powerless learn to become, has discovered how to function in an urban setting. According to Cantinflas, he is a *campesino* who has been turned into a citizen.

The *peladito* had its roots in the search for identity that marked the post-Revolutionary period. In 1934, around the time Cantinflas was developing his personage on stage, the philosopher, Samuel Ramos, produced the first systematic exploration into the Mexican being, *Profile of Man and Culture in Mexico*. There, he described the *pelado* as "the most elemental and clearly defined expression of national character." Literally, *pelado* means "pealed," stripped clean, broke; it is a word used often to refer derisively to the urban poor of Mexico. For Ramos, the effect of being a social pariah is important but not decisive, for he extended the metaphor to turn a class trait into a national characteristic. The *pelado* has two personalities: one, the fictitious entity, is opposed to and dominates the real being. According to Ramos, these warring personalities result in a sense of self-distrust and an insecurity as to his (and his country's) identity.

Mario Moreno Reyes was born August 12, 1913, in Ciudad de los Palacios and began his career around 1930 in the *carpas*, the popular variety theaters, using the name Cantinflas to hide his identity from his family. He described the invention of his personage as a function of the stage panic he once felt there: "Mario Moreno remained paralyzed in front of the crowd until, suddenly, Cantinflas took charge of the situation and began to talk. He desperately babbled words and more words, senseless, foolish words and phrases." Cantinflas's enormous gift for impromptu verbal invention is the very essence of his comedy, and in Mexico, the name has been turned into a verb (something relatively uncommon in the Spanish language as compared to English); to *cantinflear* means to talk a lot and say nothing. The name is also without doubt related to drunkards' nonsensical and sometimes violent verbiage; although the later, moralistic Cantinflas would certainly have denied it, it is clearly a reference to *cantinas*, those Mexican bars that were (and mostly remain) the domain of men. Many sequences in his earlier films take place in this setting.

Up through the 1950s, Cantinflas's humor derived largely from the ways in which the *peladito* turned the tables on the rich and powerful. Language offered an obvious arena; as the instrument of the educated, it is one of the ways the privileged classes maintain their position. Nonetheless, it is a front on which the *peladito* excels. In the face of society's power, Cantinflas explained, "the explanation demanded by the policeman whose hat you stepped on or the boss whose shirt front you just spilled catsup down, the *pelado's* defense is to talk, talk, talk."

A good example is offered in the film *Gran hotel* (1944). Cantinflas's character has just secured a job as a bellboy in a swanky and tightly run hotel. The manager has the staff formed in military files; as their names are called, they leave ranks and stand at attention in front of him while he inspects their uniforms and assigns their tasks. When Cantinflas appears, the manager is appalled at his disarray, and exclaims, "But who dressed you?" The rapid-fire answer is *pura cantinflada*:

> I did it all by myself. You know, what happened is that the pants they gave me, I think they either don't go with the jacket or I don't know what happened, because on one side they're really baggy right?, and on the other side even more so, and they made a sort of a pleat, listen, and I felt very uncomfortable, and going around in uncomfortableness, with something that you don't like, because pants ought to conform to the body and I have fallen hips and the body naturally follows the sense of gravity, according to the anatomical things who are those that study the human body, right?, who see, well, a pleat on one side then that means that on the other side the body is sort of half-fallen, OK, so I said, the problem with adjustments: if the pants are fixed right, I pay and if not, I don't pay, because also, "Why should one pay for an adjustment that one doesn't owe?", or even less. So, that doesn't work out, right? And I say, if they bring the pants and they fit me well and they go with the jacket, then yes. If not, well, I still have two pairs of pants, this one and the old ones, so, I make a little thing like this out of the two so that it's stylish. Don't you think so?

Millions delighted at seeing the tables turned on the punctilious manager, as the *peladito's* guile subtly but tenaciously disarmed him. This technique, though, was transformed over time into something much less subversive. A consideration of Cantinflas's trajectory will enable us to analyze why this key figure of Mexican culture is as reviled by contemporary critics as he was revered by the *pueblo*.

After his cinematic debut in a supporting role in *No te engañes corazón* (1936), Cantinflas teamed up with comedian Manuel Medel to make three films, *Así es mi tierra* (1937), *Aguila o sol* (1937), and *El signo de la muerte* (1939). The first of these was directed by the well-known Russian immigrant, Arcady Boytler, and played off the period's two dominant genres: the Revolutionary epic and the rural musical comedy known as a *ranchera*. Situated in 1916, *Así* begins with the return of a Revolutionary general to his hometown and ends with his leaving to rejoin his army, now accompanied by Cantinflas. The Revolution's presence largely is confined to the film's beginning and end, although the Eisensteinian aesthetics that Boytler incorporates are a cinematic reference to it. The movie is really a musical *ranchera*, although Boytler moved Cantinflas to the foreground, where he eclipsed the love story that was usually the center of this genre. Cantinflas demonstrates his verbal virtuosity most spectacularly in the scene where he escapes from being shot by appearing to assume his aggressor's position as his own. But, he also alludes to the frustration he feels at being unable to articulate his feelings; after hearing an intellectual reflect on the difficulties of life in the country, Cantinflas remarks, "I hear you speak, and it makes me envious because I suddenly feel things and want to explain them, but I explain what I don't feel when I try to say them."

In *Aguila o sol,* Cantinflas and Medel moved to an urban setting, and to a more prominent billing in the credits. After an extensive and irrelevant beginning where children play the actors when young, the film becomes a long series of drunken scenes in which Cantinflas and Medel exchange meaningless phrases and demonstrate the intimate body contact characteristic of inebriated Mexican *machismo*.

El signo de la muerte is the last film in which Cantinflas appeared alongside Medel, as the former sought increasingly to define his own unique comedy form. Although *El signo* included as collaborators important figures such as Salvador Novo and the composer Silvestre Revueltas, the direction by Chano Urueta is weak. The movie is a curious mixture of the news reporter genre together with neo-Aztec ritual sacrifices reminiscent of U.S. films about Egyptian mummies. Most of the action takes place in a museum, where the messianic and fanatical Indianism of the museum director and his followers is an obvious criticism of the period's *indigenista* movement. In one particularly crazy scene, Cantinflas frantically searches for help in order to rescue the heroine, who is about to be sacrificed in the museum's cellar. He encounters Medel, the museum guard who, ignoring his tongue-tied entreaties, makes him imbibe tequila. Cantinflas gets drunk and, the attempted rescue completely forgotten, he becomes the Empress Carlota, appearing in women's clothes for the second time in the film. Medel is transformed into the Emperor Maxmilian, and the two climb into a carriage together as if to sleep, while the screen fades to black.

Such lunacy was typical of Cantinflas's comedy during his most creative period, from 1940 to 1960, and at its center were the *peladito's* constant violations of what was considered acceptable behavior in polite society. The film that marked his definitive rise to stardom was *Ahí está el detalle* (1940), in which he plays a drunken and lecherous glutton, whose nonsensical double-talk confuses a courtroom of lawyers, infecting them with his incoherent verbiage. Here, his comic technique serves to criticize the social control that the legal system maintains over the uneducated through language that often appears to be similar to that employed by Cantinflas himself.

As his character became increasingly defined, he felt that he needed more autonomy to improvise. His following movie, *Ni sangre, ni arena* (1941), was about bullfighting, one of his great passions. During the filming, he quarreled with the well-known director, Alejandro Galindo, but formed a lasting relationship with the assistant director, Miguel M. Delgado, and the writer, Jaime Salvador, who immediately became the mainstays of Cantinflas's movies. The absolute control he gained over his films permitted him to develop his personage, but the lack of association with more demanding directors or writers may have stunted his growth. His enormous popularity and considerable wealth isolated him and made him a prisoner of his own celebrity.

For a number of years, the team of Cantinflas, Delgado, and Salvador made genuinely funny movies, always based on the formula of the *peladito* confronting the powerful and besting them on their own grounds. For example, in *Gran hotel* Cantinflas appeared in a sequence at a fancy night club where he throws his dance partner about as if she were a rag doll (which she becomes in the course of the act), until he finally heaves her into the middle of the dining patricians. Later, as the hotel's bellboy, he makes wealthy tourists carry their own luggage. In *El supersabio* (1948) he is a scientist's assistant who defies the multinational Petroleum Trust Company's executives by telling them a truth that they, corrupt as they are, take to be a lie and thus are fooled by their own mendacity. In *El bolero de Raquel* (1948) he satirizes fancy nightclubs to ridicule the rich and pretentious, as well as their "watchdogs": bodyguards, maids, and managers. These elements of irreverence became increasingly rare as his career advanced.

If one were forced to pinpoint the exact film that marked the start of Cantinflas's creative decline, one might choose *El analfabeto* (1960). There, his character is incarnated as an illiterate who works as a bank guard and eventually learns to read and write, thanks to Mexican public education. However, Cantinflas is not the shrewd, if ignorant, *peladito* of yore; rather, he is a quasi-retarded child-like simpleton who is easily tricked. Gone are the affronts toward the powerful that characterized his former movies: the bank's owner is good while his employees are bad, and the Catholic Church is fundamental to the illiterate's "salvation."

Cantinflas's subsequent films are preachy, tedious, and humorless; his formerly vital attitude toward the uses and abuses of language is replaced with word games that essentially deny the existence of social problems. He takes on social roles he had earlier critiqued in order to lecture from the pulpits of a priest, a doctor, a professor, a diplomat, a politician, and a policeman (the latter role is particularly galling, considering police corruption in reality). He openly encourages a non-political solution to Mexico's problems, suggesting in the *Padrecito* (1964) that entering into politics is a cardinal sin. In *Su excelencia* he offers the Christian doctrine as a solution for the world's problems in an international scenario meant to represent the United Nations.

Given this ideological shift, it is thus understandable that contemporary Mexican film critics and scholars have few positive words for Cantinflas. To the film critic Jorge Ayala Blanco, he incorporates "the worst stereotypes of the Mexican people." Roger Bartra considers that Cantinflas offers a clear example of the ways in which the national culture created by the ruling party (PRI) utilizes and distorts the authentic popular culture. He argues that the slang Cantinflas takes as a jumping-off point is in fact a language profoundly committed with the world from which it comes, but that Cantinflismo empties it of meaning and converts it into a way to avoid commitment and evade responsibilities. For Bartra, the comedian is an excellent metaphor for the peculiar ways in which single-party dictatorship legitimates itself through a labyrinth of contradictions that permits the most radical appearances, knowing that the original meaning of the *pueblo's* demands will inevitably be lost in the maze of corridors, waiting rooms, and offices; he writes, "Cantinflas' message is transparent: misery is a permanent state of stupid primitivism that must be revindicated in an hilarious form."

Writing in 1944, Salvador Novo felt that Cantinflas was the "representation of the Mexican subconscious." But today his *peladito* looks like a stereotype of a people who are lazy and corrupt, twisted and evasive. To be fair to Cantinflas—perhaps better stated, to be fair to his millions of fans—it is important to understand the appeal he had as a representative of those who know how to survive with dignity through quickness of wit in a highly stratified and hierarchical, but ostensibly democratic, society. So his character may speak to something very deep in the nation's subconsciousness: an underdog who carves out his own reality in response to a situation in which he is dominated. It may be significant that Cantinflas was not attacked for corrupting the Spanish language, while Tin Tan received much criticism for incorporating English phrases. Perhaps it could be argued that, though Cantinflas was an appropriate metaphor for the national character at one point, his *peladito* may not have the relevance to today's hybrid culture that Tin Tan's *pachuco* does. Ultimately, Cantinflas's decline followed a natural course: as he became increasingly wealthy from playing a *peladito,* his characterization lost the vital link to the roots that had nourished it, and it became a shell of trappings: old clothes and picturesque prattle. His aping of the *peladito's* words, dress, and mannerisms continued to make many laugh, but he ceased to be a constructive element of Mexican identity long before his death in 1993.

Select Bibliography

Bartra, Roger, *La jaula de la melancolía: Identidad y metamorfosis del mexicano.* Mexico City: Grijalbo, 1987; as *The Cage of Melancholy: Identity and Metamorphosis in the Mexican Character,* New Brunswick, New Jersey: Rutgers University Press, 1992.

—JOHN MRAZ

Morones, Luis Napoleón 1890–1964

Labor Leader

Luis Napoleón Morones was without doubt Mexico's most important union leader of the 1920s. On the one hand, he was the most prominent leader of the Confederación Regional Obrera Mexicana (CROM, or Regional Confederation of Mexican Workers) as well as the so-called Grupo Acción (Action Group) that headed the CROM. He was also the most notable leader of the Partido Laborista (Labor Party) founded in 1919. His influence was felt in political and economic spheres throughout a decade (1918–28) that was undoubtedly decisive in Mexico's post-Revolutionary reconstruction.

Morones was born on October 11, 1890, in Tlalpán, a municipality in the Federal District. His parents were workers and lived in the Barrio Guadalajarita, which was an annex of the San Fernando textile factory. In 1910, when the Revolution erupted, the future labor leader was barely 20 years old. He began working from an early age in the electrical industry. According to scholar J. H. Rettinger, by 1912 Morones was already a member of the Casa del Obrero Mundial (COM, or House of the World Worker), the first labor organization to be created after the outbreak of the Revolution, whose basic objectives were to encourage workers' organization and education. Study groups were created that analyzed the sociology, policy, history, and future strategies of the labor movement as well as the origin and development of European socialism. In December 1914 Morones took part in setting up the Sindicato Mexicano de Electricistas (SME, or Mexican Electrician's Union), an organization that in time joined the COM.

In January 1915 a strike was called against the Compañía Telegráfica y Telefónica Mexicana (Mexican Telegraph and Telephone Company), where Morones worked. The government of Venustiano Carranza seized the business and handed over its administration to the SME. In the subsequent workers' assembly it was decided that Morones and Rafael Castro should take charge of the administration of the company, a proposal approved by the COM. On February 20 the famous pact between the COM and the Carranza government was signed in Veracruz, thereby establishing a political and military alliance between the two forces. In this same year Morones went on to promote the creation of the Unión de Electricistas y Obrereos (Electricians' and Workers' Union) of the Mexican Telegraph and Telephone Company and was elected as its first secretary general.

In February 1916 the Federación de Sindicatos Obreros del Distrito Federal (FSODF, or Federation of Workers' Unions of the Federal District) called a meeting to set up the Primer Congreso Nacional Obrero (First National Workers' Congress) in Veracruz for March of the same year. During the Congress Morones was accredited as a delegate of the SME and made a notable contribution.

The night of July 31, 1916, a strike broke out, led by the SME and seconded by the COM. Carranza, who had declared martial law, ordered the leaders to be arrested. He initially condemned the strikers to death but later modified the sentence. The result of the strike was the dissolution of the COM on August 2 that year.

Luis N. Morones and his closest comrades set up the Partido Socialista Obrero (Socialist Workers' Party) between February 15 and 20, 1917, in a series of meetings held in downtown Mexico City. A large percentage of those attending were cadres of the FSODF. A key document from the assembly explains why this group and party was altering its strategy from one of "Direct Action" to "Multiple Action"—that is, from a strategy based on direct confrontation with the state and capital to a strategy that combined confrontation with legal political activity. The main rationale for this change derived from the experiences of the 1916 strikes and their brutal repression. The new strategy evolved into the explicit intent to participate in the coming electoral contest by submitting its own candidates rather than supporting outside candidates. When the party's candidates for the deputyship were soundly defeated at the polls, however, this new party broke up.

Morones remained unperturbed. The Segundo Congreso Nacional Obrero (Second National Workers' Congress) took place in Tampico, Tamaulipas, in October 1917. Morones, accompanied by Rodolfo Mendoza, attended as head of the Workers' Delegation from the Federal District and the SME. Both leaders also represented the workers of Pachuca, Hidalgo. Given his skill as an orator, Morones was having increasing influence in these congresses. The Tercer Congreso Nacional Obrero (Third National Workers' Congress) was held in Saltillo, Coahuila, in 1918. Morones, as well as promoting his organization during prior meetings, counted on the backing of the FSODF. The congress was notable for the sympathy and stimulus provided by the governor of Tamaulipas, Gustavo Espinoza Mireles. The old members of the COM were in disagreement as to whether or not to attend; Morones was in favor. Despite these and other differences with the diverse groups within the congress, a national workers' central office was created, the first since the outbreak of the 1910 Revolution. Ultimately, the CROM was created, an amalgamation of all groups with representation, the majority from federal organizations. Morones was subsequently nominated as the CROM's first secretary general, with Ricardo Reviño and José Marcos Tristán (both his confidants) as associate secretaries.

During 1918 Morones traveled to Europe to study the organized workers' movement. During a stay of several weeks he visited France, Switzerland, Italy, and Spain. According to Morones, no one had any interest in the labor movement in Mexico. However, the CROM leader was able to observe and experience the European workers' movement firsthand. In November 1918 the Confederación Panamericana del Trabajo (COPA, or Pan-American Workers' Confederation) was founded. Samuel Gompers of the American Federation of Labor (AFL) was appointed president of the organization with Morones (then secretary general of the CROM) as his vice president. In 1919 Morones attended the National Workers' Conference in Washington, D.C., where he specified the objectives of the CROM and asked for the collaboration of the European and American unions to work for international unity. His call met with no response from the delegates.

The year 1919 was crucial for the CROM and its leaders. From May 15 to 18 the Primera Convención del Partido Laborista Mexicano (First Convention of the Mexican Labor Party) was held in Zacatecas. Union leaders and prominent Revolutionary politicians attended. The statutes of the Labor Party corresponded to those of the CROM. The convention also promoted the strategy of Multiple Action. Months later, in view of the selection of candidates for the presidency of Mexico, the CROM leaders and the Labor Party spoke with Pablo González, Álvaro Obregón, and Ignacio Bonilla with a view to establishing an alliance. Only General Obregón accepted the proposals, and he became the "candidate of the working class" for the presidency. This alliance, established in the so-called secret pact or private agreement between Álvaro Obregón and the leaders of the CROM, was accepted on August 6, 1919.

The Labor Party leaders, headed by Morones, were the same as those of the CROM. Together they formed the so-called Grupo Acción, notable for being closed off from other groups within the movement. They called themselves the "high command" with the idea of directing matters by taking a position over and above the CROM and the Labor Party. Morones was appointed "chief of the high command," responsible for steering the helm of the CROM and the Labor Party. The Primer Congreso Nacional Socialista (First National Socialist Congress) took place in the Federal District from August 25 to September 4, 1919. Three currents took part: the reformist, headed by Morones; the anarcho-syndicalist, represented by the Industrial Workers of the World (IWW); and the Marxist, represented by José Allen, Eduardo Camacho, and Manabendra Nat Roy. The different ideas expressed there led the group represented by Morones to abandon the congress.

In December 1920 Álvaro Obregón became president of Mexico. In virtue of the pact established with the CROM, the new president awarded various government posts to union leaders; Morones was nominated director of the Departamento de Establecimientos Fabriles y Aprovisionamientos Militares (Department of Factories and Military Provisioning). In 1922 Morones's request for a visa to visit the USSR was rejected, most probably because of differences expressed in the Socialist Congress of 1919. During Obregón's presidency the CROM leaders were very cautious, focusing on the broadening of their union base through the creation of organizations throughout the country. In 1924 Morones was elected as a federal deputy. On November 12 of the same year there was an attempt on his life in the Chamber of Deputies. Although the would-be assassin's bullet lodged near Morones's heart, he recovered well. The incident was amply reported in the press, and Morones actually gained considerable public sympathy as a result.

Prominent figures of the Grupo Acción were included in the cabinet formed by incoming president Plutarco Elías Calles in December 1924; Morones became secretary of industry, trade, and labor and was responsible for pushing the policy of exercising control over certain industries, petroleum in particular. He also supported the creation of numerous cooperatives as well as that of small- and medium-sized businesses in industry and trade. Grupo Acción figures were to remain in their new posts from December 1, 1924, to July 21, 1928, thus perpetuating the political alliance between the government and the CROM. While the government had the benefit of a powerful sector that guaranteed a broad consensus, the CROM became integrated into the executive and legislative power structures and obtained government support to resolve labor unrest. During this period the CROM also held two governorships and many seats in the Senate and Chamber of Deputies.

In 1925 the CROM leaders achieved the long-awaited official recognition by various European labor organizations on the continent as well as Great Britain. The power of the CROM and the Labor Party was increasing. In April 1928, when the presidential election campaign was at its height, Morones proposed the union struggle as being a return to Direct Action. This declaration surprised many unions, leaders, and political groups.

After Álvaro Obregón had won election to his second term as president in 1928, he was assassinated by León Toral, a religious fanatic encouraged by one "Madre Conchita." In the aftermath of this event, it was pointed out that the Grupo Acción was one of the political groups that had expanded most under Calles's mandate and would have been the most severely affected by Obregón's return to the presidency. Faced with growing pressure from Revolutionaries, politicians, businessmen, and hacendados —and in an attempt to avoid suspicions falling on himself—President Calles decided to ask for the resignation of the CROM leaders. On July 21, 1928, Morones resigned as secretary of industry, trade, and labor.

The fall of the CROM was accelerated by these events, but other factors were weakening it as well. The level of corruption of the CROM leaders had been increasing throughout the 1920s. Wealth derived from their relationship with power and business also had diluted their social convictions. Among the fruits of such relationships, it was said, were the Grupo Acción's large property holdings in Tlalpán in the Federal District. Morones himself had gained possession of the Hotel Mancera, the largest and most luxurious in the metropolis. This group and its leader underwent a great transformation in the 1920s, similar to that experienced by other individuals and groups that had emerged from the Mexican Revolution and by numerous U.S. and European union leaders.

The CROM also was weakened in terms of the relationship between its bases and leaders. As the power of the Grupo Acción increased, so the workers and their unions were treated with increasingly authoritarian and gangster-like methods, very similar to those of the AFL in the United States. The resulting enormous discontent with the leadership of the CROM only was reinforced by the events surrounding the assassination of Obregón in 1928.

The interim president, Emilio Portes Gil, also had a long history of differences with the CROM leadership. Taking advantage of his position, he summoned various union bosses and convinced them to leave the CROM and create another central office. In February 1929 the CROM began to be dismantled. The leader of the Alianza de Obreros y Empleados de la Compañía de Tranvías de México (Workers' and Employees' Alliance of the Mexican Tram Company) decided to resign from the FSODF, one of the pillars of the CROM. Their proposal spread to other organizations in the Federal District. The organizations that abandoned the CROM in February 1929 immediately formed a new membership, that of the Federación Sindical de Trabajadores del Distrito Federal (FSTDF, or Federated Union of Workers of the Federal District), which made its first public appearance on February 25. Similarly, the group set up by Fidel Velázquez, Fernando A. Milpa, Jesús Yerea, Alfonso Sánchez Madariaga, and Luis Quintero was to head the new FSTDF. On April 30 Morones called these leaders "five miserable worms . . . that crawl on their bellies because they don't know how to walk, because they are incapable of doing so." The next day Luis Ariza answered Morones by claiming, "what you describe as 'worms' are five little wolves, that soon, all too soon, will eat all the cocks in your yard." This was but another step in the collapse of the CROM.

In July 1929 Morones left for Europe for six months in an attempt to show that the CROM could survive without him, and also to allow public opinion against him to quiet down. Discontent grew within the CROM until 1932, when two massive desertions occurred. The first was led by Alfredo Pérez Medina, who was followed by the majority of the CROM unions in the Federal District. The second was headed by Vicente Lombardo Toledano, who created a new organization that he called the "purged CROM." As a result the CROM lost all relevance in the Federal District and other federal entities. The collapse of the CROM, the Labor Party, and the Grupo Acción was rapid and decisive. In 1932 the Labor Party tried to resume its political activity by putting forward candidates for deputyships in the Federal District. The result was disastrous; they did not win a single seat. The Grupo Acción and its leader, Luis Napoleón Morones, no longer held any political power.

Morones's final downfall came in conjunction with the power struggle between President Lázaro Cárdenas and former president Calles, who had long controlled events behind the scenes as the *jefe máximo* (maximum chief). In April 1936, after an attempt to dynamite a train on the Veracruz–Mexico City route, responsibility was attributed to Plutarco Elías Calles, Morones, Luis L. León, and Melchor Ortega. On April 10, all four were exiled to the United States by President Cárdenas. Thus the period of *jefe máximo* came to an end along with that of the political life of Morones, the most powerful leader of the CROM. Morones later returned to Mexico to lead an enviscerated CROM. He died in Mexico City in 1964.

—JAVIER AGUILAR GARCÍA

Motion Pictures

This entry is composed of three articles that discuss Mexican cinema and the Mexican motion picture industry:

Motion Pictures: 1896–1930
Motion Pictures: 1930–60
Motion Pictures: 1960–96

Motion Pictures: 1896–1930

From the start Mexican films were influenced by varied expressions of nationalist sentiment. The silent film era can be divided into two parts, the first (1897 to 1915) coincides with the birth and development of the cinematographic "view" while the second (1917 onward) was characterized by narrative film. The original intention of cinema was to capture moving objects. The cameraman "provided a glimpse of the outside world," from whence came the word "view" used to describe films at the time. Later the organization of images became more complex as film technique and narrative input progressively was improved. In 1896 the projection of these films lasted between one and three minutes; 15 years later, during the Revolution, "views" could last three hours. It is notable that Mexico did not develop the art film during this first period to the same extent as film reportage or the documentary recording of events. For various reasons cameramen only filmed objects in movement around them. Evidence of nineteenth-century nationalism in the subjects selected during the first period was conspicuous, particularly in theories that sought to establish a national art in literature and painting to give Mexico prestige abroad. Narrative films would have clear and defined nationalist proposals from the moment they first appeared in 1917.

The Cinematographic "View"
On July 24, 1896, seven months after the first film screening in the basement of the Gran Café de Paris, agents of the Lumière brothers, Ferdinand Bon Bernard, the concessionaire for Venezuela, British and French Guyana and the Antilles, and technical director Gabriel Vayre, arrived in Mexico. Mexico was one point in the vast program that the inventors planned out for their emissaries to conquer the world using images. They were cultural ambassadors, and they knew their job and how to penetrate their markets. The most important part was to obtain the backing of the governing bodies to open the doors of the countries they visited. They were not always well received. In China for instance, the Empress prohibited the spectacle after it was shown, perhaps because she saw it as a powerful instrument of acculturation.

On August 6 the impresarios made their first screening for President Porfirio Díaz in Chapultepec Castle. The show was a success, and the films were projected repeatedly until late in the night. On the fourteenth of that month a further showing was given to journalists and scientific groups in the mezzanine of the Plateros Drugstore at 9 Plateros Street (today Francisco I. Madero Street) in the heart of Mexico City, in the hall which housed the Mexico Stock Exchange. Reports of the time all described the events as wondrous: "it is necessary to attend an exhibition to form a complete idea of the marvelous effect that it produces. It is enough to say that no one is happy just seeing it once, and that is the truth," affirmed one journalist in *El Correo Español*.

On Saturday, August 15, the public saw *Children's Quarrel*, *The Tuileries of Paris*, *The Charge of the Cuirassiers*, *Demolishing of a Wall*, *The Water-sprinkler and the Boy*, *Card players*, *Arrival of a Train*, and *The Child's Meal*. In the handbill the Lumière agents proudly declared that the cinemato-graph was the "only apparatus that during this last year had managed to win over and keep the admira-tion of the most enlightened people of the Old World. The president of the Mexican Republic, General Porfirio Díaz, the president of the French Republic, M. Félix Faure, the Emperor of Germany, the Czar of Russia, the Queen Regent of Spain; indeed all the notables of the world have applauded and praised its success."

Each ticket cost 50 centavos, a high price for that time, equivalent to a seat in the shady side of the bull-ring or the orchestra seats in a theater. The shows' success meant that the impresarios were giving nine daily showings, one every half hour starting at 5:30 P.M. A heterogeneous public invaded the small salon with approximately 40 seats, distributed without the class divisions which different ticket prices imposed in the theater. The audience would have been similar to that seen at church on Sunday, with the exception 12 o'clock mass which the rich usually attended. The social mix was not to the taste of one group who demanded special screenings. On Thursday August 27 the first "gala show" was announced "to satisfy the demand of numerous well-to-do families." The program consisted of 12 films instead of eight, at a charge of one peso rather than the usual 50 centavos.

When the spectacle began to settle into a routine, Gabriel Vayre began to shoot films of various official activities and aspects of Mexico City. President Díaz monopolized attention, being filmed riding in Cha-pultepec, entering the coach that took him from his residence in Chapultepec Castle to the National Pal-ace in the city center, or walking with his ministers. On Sunday, August 23, the first films with a Mex-ican theme were shown to General Díaz in his resi-dence. These included "a moving group of General Díaz again and some members of his family, a scene in the Pane Baths, another in the Colegio Militar, concluding with another film taken in the Viga Canal."

By taking these films the Lumière cameraman satisfied both their curiosity as tourists as well as Mexican nationalism and vanity. They hoped that the people portrayed would come to the cinema en masse to see themselves, accompanied by family and friends, and they were not disappointed. They knew how to flatter different social groups and as a result the cinema penetrated deep into the heart of Mexican society.

In September screenings took place using Edison's Vitascope, which also reproduced scenes from life projected life-size in the Orrin Circus Theater in Villamil Square (a site now occupied by the Blan-quita theater) but with little success. The enormous distance between the lens and the screen meant that the figures appeared blurred. Competition between United States and French studios benefited the public since the prices dropped from 50 centavos to 25 and the gala presentations were suspended. The Vita-scope also featured films on Mexican subjects but unlike those of the Lumière films, the majority were not taken in the open air or in Mexico but put to-gether in the Edison studio known as Black María in Orange, New Jersey. For this reason they lacked depth of field, with the images moving on a dark background. These were presented in public starting in January 1895, through the Kinetoscope, an appa-ratus similar to the cinematograph but which could only be seen by one person at a time. The images were thus not life size, but Lilliputian.

The Lumière representatives left the country at the beginning of 1897, taking with them the Mex-ican films that they had taken and their projectors, except for one that remained with Mexican impre-sario Ignacio Aguirre. Other impresarios presented the new medium in various parts of the country. These included Carlos Mongrand in December 1896, apparently using a Méliès projector in Orizaba and someone else in Mérida in the same year. In 1897 William Taylor Casanova gave screenings in San Juan Bautista (now Villahermosa), Tabasco, Manuel Aguirre in Tepic, the Becerril brothers in Guadala-jara, a member of the family of the future camera-man Jesús Abítia in small isolated villages in the state of Sonora, Romualdo García in Guanajuato and Salvador Toscano opened a salon in Mexico City. Cinema had arrived to stay.

Nationally made films were scarce during the first years of cinema since neither virgin stock nor the chemical ingredients to develop and make copies were made in Mexico, let alone the apparatus to shoot and project films. Mexico had to depend on manufacturers in Europe and the United States. It was not until June 1897 that copies of films made by the Lumière agents arrived along with virgin film stock. According to press reports, two Frenchmen resident in Mexico, Enrique Mouliné and Corrich, began to produce films in the city of Puebla, starting with a film of a bullfight featuring Ponciano Díaz, the most celebrated bullfighter of the time, and later a film of the evening festival in honor of the Virgen del Carmen, also in Puebla. Both shows were very well attended. But the films were not shown immediately, as the agents had to send their negatives to France for processing. Only in December did the inhabitants of Puebla see the results.

National film production began to drop in these first years since few impresarios had 6,000 pesos to buy equipment to take and show their films, a price at that time equivalent to buying a house in the center of Mexico City or a ranch near the city of Monterrey, Nuevo León. Lack of organization within the market also contributed to this reduced film production. Mexico, dependent on foreign input since it lacked technology, first developed film exhibition, followed by their distribution and finally production; the reverse of the developed countries.

The response of the public was enthusiastic. In four years 22 small salons had opened, scattered throughout the popular neighborhoods of Mexico City. The price of entry dropped to between two and three centavos. As every impresario received the same new films, the public soon grew tired of seeing them repeatedly, and the impresarios began to combine cinema with variety shows using impromptu singers. The public was incensed and responded by shouting and throwing objects at the performers. The press protested that Mexico City was not prepared for an abrupt increase in spectacles since there were not sufficient police to keep order. The church joined the fracas when functions were offered for men only showing Méliès films of women in tights. The municipal government initially was reluctant to close down the salons, since violence and alcoholism seemed to decrease in the working-class neighborhoods that boasted small screens. City Hall eventually was forced to crack down, however, and the impresarios fell back on touring the republic, especially those cities that were springing up along the railway network as if by magic.

Few new films arrived. On account of their brevity, one title was not sufficient to cover a whole program. The exhibitors left the number of titles in the same program discretionary, to maintain public interest. On occasions they showed 75 or 100 films at 25 centavos. If they received new films, the quantity was reduced or they showed a new film along with the old. Another trick was to film people in heavily trafficked areas, in the tradition of the Lumière custom of portraying moving objects in front of the camera. The impresarios would announce their proposal in the programs that were handed out in the street and at the entry to the performances with "due warning of the day and the place where shots of the locality will be taken. This company can take views for individuals and family souvenirs such as burials, weddings, baptisms, etc." Announcements would also be shouted by street criers or posted in strategic places in the cities.

The impresarios filmed Sunday walks, people leaving the 12 o'clock mass, workers in factories, weddings, marches, General Díaz attending diverse official functions, popular street dances, the Lenten pilgrimage of Santa Anita, scenes of charrería in a hacienda, and countless other scenes. Films harked back to a *costumbrismo* (a romantic emphasis on pastoral life and customs) that had originated in the concern of the liberal ideologues to find "the soul of Mexico" and markedly influenced the painting of the time. This national expression through art was a characteristic of nineteenth-century nationalism.

Mexican film production during its initial years was similar to that of the Lumière brothers for several reasons. In the first place was the concept of cinema itself. The journalists who attended the first exhibitions had problems in conceptualizing what they saw since a vocabulary to describe film had not yet developed. They also did not know the term "film," describing the works as if they were paintings in an exhibition or associating them with photography, the theater, or "large, life-size" magazine illustrations. The idea that cinema was an extension of the illustrated press seems to have its origin in the Positivism of the Científicos, which had permeated educational circles and power during those years. During 1896, the same year the Científicos established themselves and government subsidized *El Imparcial* was launched, problems arose with a film of Gabriel Vayre that reconstructed a duel in Chapultepec between two members of congress. The newspaper *El Globo*, with its liberal tradition, protested against the "trick" to which the public were about to be subjected and demanded that he insert a few words at the beginning of the film to declare that the piece was reconstruction. The press believed that the cinema should show real, natural scenes, that as a scientific invention it should not lie and trick but show "the truth." One newspaper ridiculed a reconstruction of the Dreyfus trial and another questioned as to how it was possible to see Joan of Arc alive when she had been dead some hundreds of years. The cameramen had an average or higher education; the renowned director Salvador Toscano, for example, studied engineering. Hence his keenness to show the "truth" of events through film.

The year 1906 was a watershed in the history of cinema in Mexico since film distributors started up that were able to satisfy the demand for new material. Quickly more than 30 cinemas opened up and the market was better organized. The distributors signed contracts with exhibitors outside the capital. In 1908 there were to attempts at obtaining a monopoly by the group headed by P. Avelinde and A. Delalande, agents of Pathé Frères, and the Unión Cinematográfica. The attempt ended in disaster since there were no mechanisms to check that their associates fulfilled the conditions necessary for the continuing entry of new distributors. The film business began to stabilize, and more films were produced in Mexico and the first film studios established. These included the American Amusement Company, Lillo García y Compañía, which made only two films with a storyline, *Aventuras de Tip Top* (1907) and *El grito de Dolores* (1907) by Felipe de Jesús Haro. The rest of their work captured real scenes in the style of the Lumière brothers, as did films produced by such other cameramen as Julio Kemendy, Jorge Alcalde, Enrique Rosas, the Alva brothers, Salvador Toscano and Guillermo Becerril. The same guidelines were followed outside Mexico City. Seemingly alone in Orizaba, Manuel Noriega, an impresario with a traveling theater, tried to "construct" a narrative film *El San Lunes del Valedor* (1907). Local conditions determined the characteristics of Mexican cinema in its early stages.

The cameramen developed a peculiar concept of *cine-verité*. Nevertheless, not all aspects of reality were portrayed and to the degree that Porfirismo took hold, so accuracy was avoided in favor of the dream of a society "of peace, order and progress," in the words of the Porfirian dictum. The films made from 1906 portrayed the *belle époque* that began during Díaz's last presidential term (1904–1910). Cameramen did not concern themselves with the Cananea strike in Sonora, nor the worker's strike in Río Blanco, Veracruz, two events with serious political consequences for the country, nor did they record other disagreeable scenes such as the slums of the capital. Indeed, even images of workers leaving the factories or congregations leaving 12 o'clock mass in popular neighborhoods disappeared. Instead the film makers made efforts to show images of "progress." Since films were considered a faithful and exact copy of reality, they became a powerful medium to convince the world that Mexico was on the right track. These cameramen became escapist,

just as did the highest echelons of society. In the time that elapsed between Cananea (June 1906) and Río Blanco (January 1907) more than 30 cinemas opened in Mexico City, thanks to the distributors that offered such escapist dreams in their programs. Political awareness, it seemed was limited by both repression and the cinematograph.

During this time General Díaz was the most popular subject, and he was featured in such events as his journey to the Yucatán, the opening of the railway between Tehuantepec and Manzanillo, and his 1908 interview with U.S. president William Taft in Ciudad Juárez. This last film was the most ambitious to date in terms of narrative, notably for its exceptional length of 45 minutes and the two parallel histories that converged into a finale: the journey of General Díaz from Mexico City to Ciudad Juárez was the first thread, and the last stage of Taft's journey to the same location the second. The film culminated with the interview itself. This dramatic structure, taken from such fiction films as *The Great Train Robbery* (Porter, 1902) and Meliès' productions, was adapted to the Mexican enthusiasm for respecting space and time in the sequence of events—*cine-verité* as it was then understood. Due to ideological and technical limitations, Mexican cameramen developed the informative report with rather different characteristics from those initiated a year later by the Pathé Journal, which in 1909 began to present information on such subjects as the week's events, fashion and sport.

During the rest of the Porfiriato, national film production presented images of escapist complacency: young girls offering flowers in the San Francisco church, an aristocratic wedding, the country excursions of high society, bullfights, army maneuvers in Balbuena fields, the opening of the electric tramline to Xochimilco and the new post office building, a meal "for 5,000 children served by young women from the upper ranks of society" in honor of Ramón Corral, vice president of the republic. This period culminated with images of the Independence Centenary celebrations that revealed the luxury and splendor of the epoch. The Revolution would shake society and force the cameramen to confront reality.

The Revolutionary Documentary
Starting with *Asalto y toma de Ciudad Juárez* in 1911, cameramen began to film political events, becoming increasingly aware of the documentary importance of the image and the need to conserve it in long reportages. They took the cinematograph's particular language to its ultimate consequences, adding the so-called apotheosis to their parallel histories, which in turn observed spatial and temporal

sequence. This approach was first employed in *Asalto y toma de Ciudad Juárez* (the third part of the series *Insurrección en México*), composed of four parts and 36 captions, the last informing that "the people, excited to the point of delirium, acclaim the conqueror, Pascual Orozco." This was the apotheosis, a characteristic that the film makers borrowed from Meliès' ambitious works which in turn had been taken from theatrical tradition. The cameramen knew how films were structured, since they were reproduced in the press and on handbills. The longer duration of the medium obliged their makers to resolve problems of structure, order and rhythm.

Las conferencias de paz en el norte y toma de Ciudad Juárez (1911), which lasted one hour and 15 minutes with 54 captions, ended with the triumphal entrance of the liberating army into Ciudad Juárez. *Viaje triunfal del jefe de la Revolución don Francisco I. Madero desde Ciudad Juárez hasta la Ciudad de México* (1911) repeated the same story but with similar characteristics to *La entrevista Díaz-Taft* (unfortunately for the film makers, Madero ended up entering the country in Piedras Negras, since much of the railway line from Ciudad Juárez had been damaged in the violence of the Revolution. The film began instead with the arrival of Francisco Vázquez Gómez, a well-known Maderista, in San Luis Potosí). The sequential order of the images again indicates the intention of the Alva brothers to narrate two parallel histories that converge in the same finale, since the second caption shows the arrival of Venustiano Carranza in Saltillo prior to arriving in Piedras Negras to greet Madero. The third caption presented the intersection of these two narrative threads with Carranza and Madero walking toward their mutual appointment. From the next caption on the film is a succession of apotheoses, one after another, composed of two captions: "the caudillo of the Revolution acclaimed by more than 200,000 people" and "large turnout in his honor along San Francisco Avenue" in Mexico City.

The next film to emerge with similar features was *Los ultimos sucesos sangrientos de Puebla y la llegada de Madero a esa ciudad* (1911) apparently by Guillermo Becerril, which was divided into 2 parts with 25 captions. Valente Cervantes, an impresario operating in Puebla, contracted Becerril to film the arrival of Madero, at that time presidential candidate, and his wife in the city. On the eve of the visit a confrontation between revolutionary and federal soldiers took place without Madero's permission. When Becerril learned about the fracas and found he had sufficient light, he began to "fix" the images; the film began abruptly, showing without any preamble the "soldiers of the Maderista army, firing on the federal troops; at their feet, cadavers riddled with bullet holes." He portrayed the tragedy from various angles. The first part of the film ended with the public viewing of the dead bodies in the Penitentiary. The second part included scenes of Madero's visit to Puebla, beginning with "the General in Chief of the Atlixco army, Francisco A. García, and his military staff at the station awaiting the arrival of the caudillo of the Revolution" and ending with the well-worn apotheosis: "Mr. Francisco I: Madero and his wife in front of the cinematographic camera."

La Revolución Orozquista o hechos gloriosos del ejército nacional: Combate sostenido por las fuerzas leales contra las revolucionarias en los cerros de Bachimba (1912) brought the revolutionary documentary to its mature expression. The images supported the positivist concepts of objectivity and impartiality to give a fuller idea of the meeting. According to the program, it was divided into three parts, but in fact there were two, one showing the revolutionary side, the other the federal. Initially the Alva brothers, who produced the film, appeared not to be partisan, since they show both armies, thus leading the spectator into becoming a witness to the battle. They did not show the rationale behind the rebel movement, but merely assembled images of various aspects of the conflict. Perhaps the ambiguity of the cameramen regarding these events is the clearest feature of the film and possibly also the most obvious limitation of the documentary films of the Revolutionary period. Despite this, the images shook the public, now hypersensitive as a result of changes in their daily lives, wild rumors, and journalistic reports. Despite its political innocence, the documentary politicized audiences through the power of its images and on more than one occasion provoked violence in the cinemas as well as noisy demonstrations for and against the caudillos.

The next "view of tangible reality," Enrique Rosas' *La Revolución en Veracruz* (1912), was divided into two parts. It consisted of a series of images that showed the federal armies perspective, including scenes taken prior to the conflict, the battle itself, and the aftermath of the defeat of the supporters of Félix Díaz, who had taken up arms against the Madero government. The film did not end with a climax but with scenes showing the effects of a North wind in Veracruz, which had nothing to do with the main story.

The next ambitious productions, three in number, focused on the events of the Ten Tragic Days of 1913. One of them led the spectator to the final climax, "the victorious forces marching from the

Ciudadela to the National Palace." The film contained scenes from the perspectives of both loyalists and rebels, but these were organized differently from those of *Revolución Orozquista*. In fact, the shots of both sides were not grouped separately but alternated. Thus, the spectator saw first "the cannons of Félix Díaz's supporters in Balderas Street" followed by "Government artillery in the Rinconada de San Diego" and "machine gun installed at the axis of Cuauhtémoc and Bolívar Streets." This was followed by an image of the rebels, then portraits of the Generals Mass, Delgado and Rubio Navarrete, active collaborators in the coup d'état. Next came images of violence, followed quickly by the effects of the 10 days' shoot-out in the city that led to the deaths of President Madero and his vice president, José María Pino Suárez. The viewer could see the destroyed buildings on Balderas Street, a house in the Rinconada de San Diego that had acted as a barracks for the soldiers loyal to the president, Madero's house on fire, the Chinese clock on Bucareli Street partially destroyed, and other scenes of devastation. After such dramatic images, the exuberance of those responsible for the coup seemed out of place, but one had to flatter the winners.

The usurping government understood that the restoration of the Pax Porfiriana was dependent on the people forgetting politics. The press therefore was forbidden to discuss the situation of the country. It was by no means extraordinary that the next ambitious film was *El aniversario del fallecimiento de la suegra de Enhart* (1913), based on the daily life of a pair of very popular comedians of the period, Alegría and Enhart, who acted in the Lírico Theater. The potential volatility of film images was vividly demonstrated when news clips were shown with scenes of United States troops preparing to invade Mexico. The public was furious, protesting loudly and marching out of the cinema in a noisy demonstration with shouts of "Long live Mexico" and "Death to the United States." The impresarios suppressed the scenes that provoked the demonstration, and shortly after censorship was initiated that prohibited the making and showing of films that upset civil order.

It was not only the state, however, which was aware of the political power of film. Each caudillo had his own photographers and cameramen to record his deeds. The Alva brothers followed Madero, filming the events that occurred inside and outside Mexico City. Jesús Abítia filmed Obregón's campaigns and the movements of Venustiano Carranza. Villa had at least 10 North American cameramen from the Mutual Film Corporation at his disposal who filmed the capture of Ojinaga, Gómez Palacio and Torreón and in the process made a short film based on his life. Various cameramen portrayed the Zapatistas. The demand for images developed with the cinema and the illustrated press, whose growth up to that point had been parallel.

The Revolution stimulated the visual-historical awareness of photographers, cameramen and caudillos alike. Agustín Victor Casasola expressed this clearly in an exhibition of press photographs in 1911. "We are those who record the impressions of an instant, the slaves of the moment," he declared in the opening address in the presence of the interim president Francisco León de la Barra. Thanks to this awareness of the decisive moment, photographers of the time (film cameramen included), left a visual legacy of the Revolution. The revolutionary documentary oscillated between its structural and propagandist objectives. It offered no novelty from the dramatic point of view except the intrinsic richness of the images in decisive moments of the country's history.

The "view" of Mexican events was exhausted and came to an end. The Soviet cinema achieved something of which the Mexican film makers were incapable, developing arguments with images from reality and making real films, not views, using techniques developed by D.W. Griffith in *Birth of a Nation* (1914) and *Intolerance* (1916). Nonetheless, the ways in which Mexican film makers organized "moving pictures" constituted a real contribution to international cinema.

Post-Revolutionary Nationalism

The next stage was dominated by nationalist propaganda films, which were made during the presidency of Venustiano Carranza. The propagandistic agenda of Mexican film makers during this period imposed a certain homogeneity onto Mexican films. This new nationalist project originated in the deterioration of the country's image due to the Revolution, especially in the United States, whose "Westerns" left no room for doubt on this score. From 1907 on the Mexican in U.S. movies was a drunk, thief, assailant, bandit, and jealous lover. The Revolution sharpened this point of view, particularly the power struggle between the various revolutionary factions, especially after Huerta's defeat.

The first attempts at nationalistic and propagandistic cinema date from April 1915 when the Carrancista rump tried to govern the country and life was hell, characterized by moral crisis, hunger and scarcity of basic necessities—although not of films. Their screenings attracted the terrified inhabitants of Mexico City who found them a palliative as they tried to weather the crisis. As a result of the boom there was talk of "making attempts at cinematographic production ... effective artistic views, of great interest and reality that will rival those produced abroad." Given the unstable political situation of the following months, it is unknown if these plans were carried out.

During these months Mexico's image abroad declined even further, particularly with Villa's attack on Columbus in 1916. The reaction of the United States led to fear of war and the Mexican Government called for an alert to defend the country from invasion. At the end of 1916 there was fresh talk of making films for propaganda purposes to counteract the image propagated by the United States cinema and press. Manuel de la Bandera and Mimí Derba published in *Excelsior* what would be called their "declaration of principles." "I have seen abroad ... films screened that are said to be Mexican in which we are presented to the eyes of the world as savage beasts," De la Bandera affirmed

> In the United States they make an effort to present Mexico as uncultured, bad, and vicious as possible, not doing justice to us by showing the good and the great that is here as well. It is precisely my task, using Mexican actors, to make them understand overseas that cultivated people also exist in our country, that there are things worth seeing, and that this portrayal of savagery and backwardness in dishonest films could, perhaps, be an accident of the revolutionary period we have just experienced, but not a general state of affairs.

Mimí Derba stated that she would form a production company to develop "truly historical themes that show real Mexican customs and stimulate the spirit of the public, encouraging it toward those social tendencies required by our civilization."

Such nationalist concerns were shared by Alfredo B. Cuéllar, who affirmed that he would make films that would bring "renown to Mexico among foreign countries, presenting the attractive side of our national life; our society, salons, walks, clubs, convents, rivers, volcanoes, lakes, landscapes, monasteries, castles and sports." Jacobo Grant announced that he had "now acquired the necessary material ... to make ... national films, to revive historical events, making clear the charm of Mexican soil, and creating dramas that single out the great heart of its people. . . ."

This attitude echoed the ideas of many nineteenth-century liberal ideologues and art critics, perhaps be-

cause the nationalist theories of both were stimulated by the threat posed by foreign powers and the bad image of Mexico spread abroad by travelers' tales. Much as the novel had been used in the nineteenth century, film in the early post-Revolutionary period was used as a proof of loyalty and love for the nation.

The post-Revolutionary Mexican State had a nationalist, educational, economic, indigenist, foreign and cultural nationalistic program, all clearly seen in the policy making of Venustiano Carranza. Cinema was to play an unimportant role in this cultural program; theater, music, literature and, above all, painting took precedence. In 1916 the director of the Escuela Nacional de Bellas Artes (The National School of Fine Arts) insisted that the main objective of the institution was to "educate within the pure environment of Art, without losing sight for a moment of the need for the pupils to seek inspiration in patriotic sources and give life and vigor thereby to our national art." A class of cinematographic mime was added to the curriculum of the Escuela de Arte Teatral (School of Theatrical Art), which was given a "workshop" or cinema studio to practice in. The pupils filmed *Triste crépusculo,* directed by Manuel de la Bandera, as an academic exercise, but the results was less than fortunate. Too many cooks spoiled the cinematic soup.

If the Revolution degraded the image of Mexico abroad, the new cinema ignored it. City dwellers were fed up with the problems provoked by the armed conflict. They looked for escape both from the struggle and their memories through cinema, fortune-tellers or alcoholism. There were several strains of nationalist propaganda in the films of those first years. An initial trend, "cosmopolitan nationalism," clearly was inspired by Italian films, framed within a national backdrop. Such is the case of *La Luz,* the successful first film of this new stage, which showed a bridal pair on a walk that took in the picturesque sites in Mexico City. The leading actress, Emma Padilla, was pronounced the Mexican Pina Menichelli. It was commented that her acting was spoiled by her fondness for imitating the movements, attitudes and costume of the Italian diva. Cosmopolitan nationalism was also evident in the series made by Azteca films, Rosas, Derba y Compañia in 1917: *En defensa propia, La Tigresa, La soñadora, Alma de sacrificio,* and *En la sombra.* These marked the beginning of melodrama and family-based drama that the talking pictures later would take to their limits. Part of this trend was film makers who adapted works of world literature for the screen, such as José Zorrilla de San Martín's *Tabaré,* Giacometti's *La muerte civil,* and *Dos corazones,* which was based on *Helena et Matilde* by Adolph Bellot.

A second current proposed that "truly nationalist" films should show the national landscape, "types," and customs. *Costumbrismo* had two tendencies, a return to the romantic tradition and an offshoot of the *género chico* (playlets on popular themes), which in turn was nourished by Peninsular realism and French naturalism. Following these principles, Manuel de la Bandera tried to show *lo mexicano* in his films *Triste crepúsculo* and *Barranca trágica,* both of romantic *costumbrista* type. The first film contained scenes "truly national, typical, if you like, but far from causing an impression of vulgarity and lack of culture, incarnating in a lively fashion the deepest feelings of the peasants, thereby vesting them with dignity, and the healthiest expression on faces roasted by the sun of the countryside." The plot, nevertheless, did not abandon Italian influence. This is the point of departure for the ranchera genre of comedy, which would develop vigorously in the talking pictures.

Miguel Contreras Torres' *El caporal* (1920) also belongs to this romantic *costumbrismo* vein as do the adaptations of the novels by Ignacio Manuel Altamirano, *Clemencia* and *El Zarco.* Another nationalist trend used Mexican history as a source for its plots, some authors being inspired by the indigenous world, others by the colonial. Among the dramas that took on pre-Hispanic history are *Tlahuicole* and *Netzahualcoyotl, el rey poeta.* The colonial period was covered by *Don Juan Manuel* and *Sor Inés de la Cruz. Fray Don Juan o confésion trágica* (1917) was filmed in the former monastery of Tepozotlán, while the short films inserted in the weekly bulletin *Cine revista México* dealt with legends and traditions attached to the streets of Mexico City.

Mestizaje and the epic of the conquest were the themes of *Cuauhtémoc* and *Tepeyac* in which there also was a concern with praising the indigenous way of life. In *Tabaré* the appreciation of indigenous beauty is the underlying theme. In the list of the characters and the description of their personalities, Luis Lezama, who adapted the work, noted that Tabaré should be "an Indian youth, tall, strongly muscled with an impassive gaze, taciturn, sensitive, and reserved."

The obsession for the landscape was one of the constant production values of those years; landscape and nationalism became equivalent terms. The arguments of the films could be set in the pre-Hispanic, colonial or Independence periods, the nineteenth century or contemporary Mexico. They could describe bourgeois, *campesino* (peasant), or proletarian customs, or they could be adaptations of literary classics. In every one, however, the landscape was an essential element. *La Luz* did not meet with the approval of some for being an imitation of an Italian film, but there was no complaint about Chapultepec, Xochimilco and the Coyoacán nurseries as natural backdrops; the only defect was believed to lie in the incapacity of the camera to capture their beauty. *Santa* was filmed in the sites described in the original novel by Federico Gamboa—in and around San Angel village, the small square of Chimalistac, the Pedregal, a river, and a cemetery. Perhaps the fascination for landscape made Luis G. Peredo, the adapter and director of the work, respect the places and film mostly in the open air. Of particular note was "a beautiful perspective of the metropolis, seen 62 meters up" that was taken from the top of the Independence Monument. In *Dos corazones* this enthusiasm was taken to excess. The cameraman "concerned himself overmuch with landscapes and forgot the most important element: the characters, which on various occasions seemed indistinct." This hunger for landscape continued in the era of talking pictures, where it would be well appeased in the work of Emilio "El Indio" Fernández.

The formal continuity between the concept of the "view" and "film" came from photography, since there were few cameramen from the first stage that stopped working. Almost all became involved in the production of fiction films. Since the portrayal of exteriors had been part of their previous experience, their enthusiasm for landscape satisfied nationalist concerns with interest. The transition, nevertheless, was not without conflict, since the cameramen were unaccustomed to studio work.

A linear narrative about the robberies committed by a band of thieves during 1915, the most difficult year of the Revolution, *El aútomovil gris* (1919) by Enrique Rosas also synthesized the brief history of Mexican cinema up to that time, blending concepts of cinema and the view. It blended the nationalist, journalistic *cine-verité* of the beginning of the century with post-Revolutionary nationalism's interest in landscape and *costumbrismo.* Nonetheless, Rosas also used narrative techniques developed in the United States, including multiple story lines, close ups, tracking shots, and zooms. The story was divided into 12 episodes, grouped into three days, similar to the U.S. serials, in contrast to the "Italian style" of previous films. The film was a flop in the United States, however, especially in New York and Los Angeles, the film makers returned to the study and practice of the new cinematic techniques. The failure of *Santa* in the United States meant the collapse of dreams of nationalist affirmation. The optimism of 1917 became pessimism, and Rosas handed his creation over for domestic consumption only.

The pessimism of the film makers also was due in large part to the difficulty of recuperating their investment, since they generally sold their films to distributors or exhibitors at a fixed and minimal price. If there were any profits they generally went to the distributor. There was no systematic effort in the 1920s to develop a national cinema; rather individual film makers struggled in isolation to make it big. The fundamental reason for the failure of Mexican cinema of this period was due to the entrance of the U.S. films starting in the 1920s. The failure of North American talkies due to the language barrier stimulated the rise of Mexican cinema starting with *Santa* (1932) onward. Despite the problems faced by early Mexican cinema, however, it laid the thematic and ideological bases for Mexican talking pictures. The international success of the films of Emilio Fernández would later fully satisfy the concerns of the early film makers.

Select Bibliography

Mora, Carl J., *The Mexican Cinema: Reflections of a Society, 1896–1988*. Berkeley and London: University of California Press, 1989.

—AURELIO DE LOS REYES

Motion Pictures: 1930–60

On any given Sunday afternoon in the mid-1940s, moviegoers in places as disparate as San José, Costa Rica; Lima, Peru; Los Angeles, California; Havana, Cuba; Caracas, Venezuela; San Antonio, Texas; and even Buenos Aires, Argentina—not to mention Mexico City and all of provincial Mexico—could choose from a number of Mexican films. They would have recognized a multitude of stars, including María Félix, Arturo de Córdova, Pedro Infante, Dolores del Río, Pedro Armendáriz, Jorge Negrete, the Soler brothers (Andrés, Domingo, and Julián), María Antonieta Pons, David Silva, Sara García, and the Argentine expatriate Libertad Lamarque, who had become international icons through Mexican films. These multinational spectators also would have been able to choose from a variety of established genres, including *comedia rancheras, cabareteras,* family melodramas, *indígena* tales, historical epics, slapstick comedies, neorealist social problem works, boxing,

wrestling, and gangster vehicles, and several types of love stories, each associated with noted directors. In addition, audiences throughout the Spanish-speaking world also valued a range of specific artistic characterics, aesthetic signs, and visual styles. For example, Agustín Lara's ubiquitous musical compositions (and frequent on-screen performances), Gabriel Figueroa's cinematography, and the so-called nationalism of his collaborator, director Emilio "El Indio" Fernández Romo, all achieved international recognition. By the early Cold War, added to this regional response was critical acclaim in Eastern and Western European film festivals, such as those at Berlin, Cannes, Venice, Karlovy Vary, and Madrid. But most of all, Latin American movie culture had been Mexicanized; where Bolívar had failed to achieve international unity in the post-Independence period, Cantinflas (Mario Moreno Reyes), arguably, succeeded after World War II.

These qualitative factors went hand-in-hand with quantitative expansion to form a distinctive social epoch, still resonant in contemporary popular culture. From the late-1930s until the late-1950s, Mexican cinema became the world's dominant Spanish-language film industry. Commonly called the golden age of Mexican cinema, this period witnessed the unprecedented international expansion of a developing nation's film industry that, at times, seemed to call into question Hollywood's cultural and commercial hegemony. Despite this prominent development, close historical attention does not reveal a radically nationalist film complex. Mexican cinema presented a national idiom produced by domestic capital and supported (and to some extent controlled) by state intervention, but neither in its economic nor cultural dimensions was it ever entirely sovereign. Much like the country's overall political economy in these decisive, "stabilizing" decades, Mexican cinema represented, ideologically and commercially, the fundamentally conservative, bourgeois orientation of the elites who controlled the nation's institutional development. Moreover, film offered cultural support for the international and domestic project of the national regime, upon whose policies the industry depended. The golden age of Mexican cinema coincided with the triumph of the rightist faction within the post-Revolutionary regime that consolidated power with the onset of World War II and institutionalized itself in the postwar decades. Much like the dissonance between official populist rhetoric and actual reactionary policies during these years, golden age cinema perpetuated nationalist discourse even as its industrial structure and its ideological limits conformed to the dominant political and economic order's mission, based in private-sector accumulation, transnationalized commercial and industrial development, nondemocratic political practices, and pseudonationalist rhetoric.

Yet while the production of Mexican cinema did not represent a radically nationalist moment, in terms of production, it did contain meanings of profound national significance at the level of reception. For viewers, the epoch still resonates in the continuing everyday popularity of golden age films, which appear daily on commercial television, and of the period's stars, who find commemoration in mass-produced books and magazines and in state-sanctioned signs and spectacles such as postage stamps and officially organized public commemorations. The source of this continuing resonance lies in the interplay between the development of Mexican mass society and the rise of motion picture sound technology in the 1930s.

A lumpy mixture of national and international forces combined to form Mexican sound production. Sound films first came to Mexico and the rest of the Spanish-speaking Western Hemisphere from the United States at the end of the 1920s. The early sound-exhibition sector's structure in Mexico, decisive for the development of domestic production, derived from links to U.S. studios, which stimulated the conversion of foreign theaters to their new audio technologies. This derivation, however, did not dictate a simple instrumental, patron-client relationship between Hollywood and Mexican theater owners. Although the U.S. studios had strong contractual relationships with Mexico's major circuits, as well as direct control of several showcase Mexico City movie palaces, this did not constitute total control. In fact, some Mexican exhibitors eventually became important backers of national production. Nevertheless, such contractual relationships and venue control did serve to shape the development of Mexican filmmaking, from its inception, to fit within an international system established by Hollywood. Furthermore, Hollywood stories, styles, and stars decisively reshaped the popular expectations of Mexican moviegoers once again, as they had during the post-World War I silent period.

This early dominance notwithstanding, from the outset of sound production, Hollywood understood the new technology's potential for disrupting the U.S. industry's commercial hegemony in the Western Hemisphere. To prevent this, U.S. producers experimented with Spanish-language sound production throughout the 1930s (a precursor to later attempts at dubbing). For a variety of reasons, most reflecting Latin American audience disapproval, this mode of international production failed. After a burst of such movies in the early 1930s, U.S. Spanish-language production declined dramatically. But in complicated ways, the rubble of its fall contributed crucial material for the foundation of Mexican sound production. Mexico had provided a most pervasive backdrop for original U.S. Spanish-language sound features (one of several types of such films produced). Moreover, future Mexican motion picture talent—including producer-directors Miguel Contreras Torres and (German-born) José Bohr, actor Ramón Novarro, and actress Lupita Tovar, star of the Mexican sound industry's first important feature, *Santa* (1931), among others—gained experience through participation in the U.S. industry's Spanish-language filmmaking.

Although some important early sound filmmakers, such as Juan Bustillo Oro and Contreras Torres, had experience in Mexico's silent movies, most of the leading, early developers of motion picture production in the era rose in the field only after the Mexican Revolution. President Abelardo Rodríguez, for example, became a key early investor in the production company–studio Compañía Nacional Productora de Películas, which had made *Santa,* as well as the operator of an extensive circuit of movie theaters. Alberto Pani Sr., a leading national *político* (who at different times held various key post-Revolutionary ministerial posts), headed a group of similarly connected government and private sector elites to found Cinematográfica Latinoamericana S. A. (CLASA) in 1935. Mexico's most important film studio in the late 1930s and early 1940s, the privately owned CLASA received important government contracts and subsidies to produce political propaganda and entertainment. The early sound film industry's architects often straddled, then, the private and public sectors, representing the opportunities offered by the new enterprise as well as the government's interest in promoting a developing culture industry that would serve national and international mass communication. Films like director Fernando de Fuentes's *¡Vámonos con Pancho Villa!* (1935), CLASA's first feature, crystallized this multifaceted interaction between the new film establishment and the Mexican state. Supported by the government of President Lázaro Cárdenas (1934–40), the film's revisionist interpretation of Villa represented the regime's ambivalence toward the northern Revolutionary as well as its desire to counter Hollywood's denigrating depiction of the nation's recent history (especially Villa).

Official largesse was not, however, the main engine of motion picture development. Mexican production, increasingly concentrated in Mexico City, benefited technically, artistically, and financially from its proximity to Hollywood. A two-way flow of talent took place from the earliest days of sound production. Gabriel Figueroa, soon to be the Mexican film's most important cinematographer, studied under Gregg Toland in Hollywood with the financial assistance of major Mexican producers, including Pani. Similarly, Hollywood expatriates including the cinematographers Jack Draper and Canadian-born Alex Phillips and directors such as Norman Foster, Herbert Kline, and Austrian-born Fred Zinnemann all made important films in Mexico during the 1930s and 1940s, exchanging knowledge with national practitioners as their work, along with that of several other U.S. expatriates, became subsumed in the golden age canon.

In the mid-1930s, as Mexican production grew (rising from one film in 1931 to more than 20 by 1935), labor and capital organized in new ways. In 1934, Mexican producers and studio workers organized themselves respectively as the Asociación de Productores Mexicanos de Películas and the Unión de Trabajadores de Estudios Cinematográficos de México; each would metamorphose into new organizations as the industry and the nation's political economy matured. Significantly, the new groups did not see themselves as opposed to one another. Both were committed to the development of national production and collaborated in their attempts to have the national government coordinate film-sector planning. However, there was no clear consensus about what the Mexican industry's relationship, nor the Mexican state's policies, should be toward Hollywood; some industry leaders advocated collaboration, others resistance. There was agreement on one issue; all motion picture advocates sought to emulate Hollywood's mode of production, even as they hoped to compete with it in the 1930s.

Lázaro Cárdenas's administration brought a more nationalist orientation to government film policies. As Mexican production increased in the mid-1930s, the state sought to foment that growth by enforcing previously neglected protectionist measures as well as instituting new instruments of motion picture promotion. For cultural and commercial reasons, the state initiated measures in 1935 that sought to protect national production through a coordinated system of tariffs and import controls on foreign-language films. Ultimately Cardenista film policies were curtailed by Mexican cinema's economic instability internationally (in spite of its demonstrated popularity). Hollywood's aggressive business tactics, reinforced by U.S. diplomacy, had undone these populist formulas, but they had not undone Mexican production. And in place of protection, the state instituted new policies that served simultaneously to subsidize domestic production and promote Mexican mass communication domestically and abroad.

While ¡Vámonos con Pancho Villa! had lost money, another de Fuentes film was a financial success that fertilized future film markets for Mexico throughout the Western Hemisphere, including the Latino United States. Photographed by Figueroa, Allá en el Rancho Grande (1936) succeeded where U.S. Spanish-language productions had failed. The comedia ranchera's musical motif found favor with foreign audiences and established Mexican cinema as an international force. However, the film reached those far-flung markets via a Hollywood distributor, United Artists. It was a marriage of mutual convenience: in order to exploit international markets more fully, Mexican producers often turned to Hollywood; in order to penetrate the Spanish-language markets it failed to conquer with its own multilingual productions, the U.S. industry co-opted its more successful southern neighbor's productions. But this system was haphazard; it did not produce an international economy of scale upon which Mexican producers could depend. The U.S. industry set the rules, inverting its international business practices for exhibition, where Hollywood offered foreign exhibitors an all-or-nothing proposition by "block-booking" of U.S. productions. When it came to Mexican films, the world's movie metropolis picked and chose.

Changes in business practices brought new production patterns with implications for the form and content of Mexican movies. For example, as it developed domestic and international markets in the mid-1930s, Mexican cinema produced a star system. This form of marketing-led production resembled Hollywood's practices, which had established international motion picture consumption patterns. Mexican producers exploited the mass appeal of individual actors, whose on-screen identities (and, sometimes, offscreen personalities) were linked to specific genres. This pattern reflected the maturation of Mexican film production based on a U.S. industrial model. The development of modern studios was central to this effort. However, while patterned after Hollywood's image factories, these installations never achieved the economic efficiency of their U.S. precursors. They lacked the forward linkages their U.S. precursors established to domestic and international distribution and exhibition networks. Mexican producers often relied on U.S. concerns to market their films not only internationally but also domestically (in order to gain access to screen time).

This lack of vertical integration was derived from the Mexican studios' horizontal limits. Mexican studios were not controlled by single producers, as in the United States. Throughout the golden age, many different companies made films at the ever-fluctuating number (usually between three and five) of major studios operating at any one time. Production companies rented services from studio operators. Although some producers had a more or less regular relationship with a particular studio, at times renting semipermanent office space at a facility, usually they were transients. There were attempts at rationalization. For example, CLASA studios supported an eponymous production company (which, among other films, had produced *¡Vámonos con Pancho Villa!*). But the Mexican industry did not produce rationalized U.S.-style networks despite the ambition of prominent producers to do so. Nevertheless, as Mexican film historian Tomás Pérez Turrent has illustrated, the studios did influence film forms; particular studios were associated with specific genres and styles. So while the rise of Mexican studios, beginning in the 1930s, did not form a coherent industrial system, the studios were central to the emerging shape of national cinema.

By the late 1930s Mexico produced dozens of films annually (over 40 premiered in 1938 alone). But despite this output, the industry's fundamental vulnerabilities were not overcome. By the end of the decade, producers faced a severe distribution crisis. Some blamed 1939's glut of un-exhibited product on Hollywood's domination of international screens, others on the overexploitation of the *comedia ranchera* genre. In response to this bottleneck, the Mexican government instituted a new system of exhibition quotas intended to guarantee minimum screen time for national productions based on a rating system (applied to individual films and matching theaters). These measures were designed not only to safeguard overall production but also to encourage more diverse, high-quality filmmaking. This form of soft protection (regulating exhibition rather than imposing import restrictions) elided direct confrontation with U.S. interests at a moment when, in the wake of the 1938 oil expropriation and the developing antifascist convergence of U.S. and Mexican foreign policies, the Cárdenas administration sought to join forces with the U.S. government to forge links that served its own domestic and international security agendas.

In fact, it would be World War II and in particular U.S.-Mexican relations that would provide the key industrial stimulus for golden age production in the 1940s. Mexico was the United States's chief Spanish-speaking ally in the Western Hemisphere. Even before either the United States or Mexico entered the conflict officially (in 1941 and 1942, respectively), U.S.-Mexican covert economic, military, and cultural cooperation was underway. In fact, Mexican history had served as a symbol of prowar, Pan-American unity disseminated by Hollywood in its depiction of U.S.-Mexican friendship in Warner Brothers' 1939 feature *Juárez* (which the Mexican and U.S. governments jointly promoted). With the outbreak of the war itself, and with the Manuel Avila Camacho administration's declaration of support for the Allies following the sinking of two Mexican oil tankers by German submarines in May 1942, mass media collaboration entered a new phase that served the development of Mexican cinema.

As an international shock, the war created space for Mexican film by erasing the small amount of European film exports to Latin America and by reducing the overall U.S. production (the remaining U.S. production furthermore was concentrated on war themes unpopular in Latin American markets). Flush with expanding revenues, producers and the state combined to organize private capital through the establishment of the Banco Cinematográfico in 1942, which fulfilled unrealized earlier Cardenista plans for a state-run financial institution supporting film production. This concentration of capital streamlined large-scale filmmaking but also focused control in an ever-more-exclusive group of dominant producers. Reflecting the new national identity of film capital and mirroring the broader pattern of private sector industrial nationalism supported by the Avilacamachismo was the establishment in 1943 of the Cámara Nacional de la Industria Cinematográfica as a cross-sector chamber of commerce. To further establish an industrial profile, in 1945 the industry copied Hollywood in establishing its Mexican Academy of Cinematographic Arts and Sciences that began to present the Ariel Awards (Mexico's Oscars) the following year.

But more than the above, the dramatic wartime expansion of production (from fewer than 40 films in 1941 to more than 80 in 1945) was due to the direct intervention of U.S. foreign policy. Recognizing the significant cultural and commercial achievements of Mexican cinema in the 1930s, U.S. media planners sought to exploit the neighboring culture industry for propaganda ends. On the one hand, a friendly film industry in Latin America would counter Axis propaganda, offsetting the influence of Argentine cinema (which was deemed subversive, given that nation's neutralist foreign policies at the start of the war). On the other hand, the

Mexican industry could promote the war with entertainment propaganda that would exceed the limited effectiveness of Pan-American U.S. films like *Juárez*. Just as the Manuel Avila Camacho administration (1940–46) promoted broad private sector industrial development (like the Banco Cinematográfico), it also structurally reoriented Mexican foreign relations toward collaboration with the United States, which was exemplified by future president Miguel Alemán's coordination of U.S. film aid as wartime secretary of the interior.

U.S. intervention took several forms, all with long-term implications for Mexican movie making. In terms of raw materials, the U.S. government's wartime Board of Economic Warfare restricted Argentina's access to virgin film stock while it supplied Mexican producers. More crucially, Nelson Rockefeller's Office of the Coordinator of Inter-American Affairs (an independent government agency that oversaw wartime U.S. commercial and cultural relations with Latin American states) organized Hollywood assistance in order to expand Mexican production. This included the transfer of technology and experts to modernize Mexico's two main studios, CLASA and Azteca, further aggregating Mexican film production. The U.S. intervention also reorganized production and business practices along Hollywood lines. Growing Mexican production found more accessible international markets, often through expanded distribution by Hollywood concerns that sought to co-opt Mexican cinema's popularity. While some Hollywood interests were concerned that the wartime aid facilitated the development of a foreign commercial threat, others attempted to expand their interaction. Most notably, RKO entered into a partnership with a group of investors headed by radio, movie theater, and, later, television magnate Emilio Azcárraga to build Latin America's most important postwar film studio, Estudios Churubusco.

In addition to a significant number of prowar, antifascist propaganda films—such as *Soy puro mexicano* (1942), *Espionaje en el golfo* (1942), and *De Nueva York a Huipanguillo* (1943), to name only a few—the more important impact of U.S.-Mexican collaboration was the overall expansion of national filmmaking. As impressive as the expansion of production, cited above, was the pattern of reception. While Hollywood still exhibited more films than the Mexican industry in Latin America, Mexican movies often commanded more screen time than U.S. productions (a phenomenon that outlasted the war). The war also witnessed the production of some of the emblematic films of golden age Mexican cinema, including Cantinflas's first blockbuster, *Ahí está el detalle* (1940), directed by Juan Bustillo Oro; Joselito Rodríguez's sensational *comedia ranchera ¡Ay, Jalisco no te rajes!* (1941), starring Jorge Negrete and Gloria Marín; and Fernández and Figueroa's iconographic *indígena* classic *María Candelaria* (1943), featuring Dolores del Río and Pedro Armendáriz (one of the team's several important wartime collaborations). Such productions underline the national significance of Mexican cinema's internationalist wartime development: transnational collaboration created space for development of a domestic culture industry.

Generating transnationalization of a different kind, Mexico City's ascendancy as the Spanish-speaking world's film metropolis in the mid-1940s attracted international talent. For example, both Dolores del Río (who returned from Hollywood where her career was on the decline) and Argentine actress Libertad Lamarque (who fled Buenos Aires where she simultaneously suffered the personal animosity of Evita Perón and the decline of her native country's film industry) came to work in Mexico City's thriving studios, and exceeded the considerable success of their prior careers. After working in Hollywood since the 1930s, the nationalist director Roberto Gavaldón returned to his homeland and made his first Mexican film, *La barraca* (1944). Following his wartime sojourn in the United States, Spanish expatriate filmmaker Luis Buñuel also arrived in Mexico City, where, over the next two decades, he produced some of his most enduring international works, including the surrealist *El* (1952), *Robinson Crusoe* (1953), *Nazarín* (1958), *El Angel Exterminador* (1962), and his only English-language work, *The Young One* (1960), which used black-listed U.S. talent in a story that examined U.S. race relations.

Moreover, Mexico City became the setting and, in some cases, subject of increasing numbers of Mexican films, as the capital's nightlife, neighborhoods, and demimonde became the sign of national cinematic culture. This phenomenon had obvious links to the audience. Not only was the nation's metropolis the home to an exploding population of provincial migrants, forming the industry's largest "local" audience, but the area's reach extended far beyond the Valley of Mexico as almost all families had members or friends who had traveled to the country's political and economic center during the 1940s. Demographic change brought new genres, as the city replaced the countryside as the site of national myth making.

Notably the *cabaretera* (set in Veracruz as well as Mexico City) became a staple of 1940s cinema. This formula, raised to an art form by director Alberto Gout, usually featured nightclub musical performances and stories involving Mexico City gangsters, prostitutes, and other marginal types. Plots often revolved around tragic stories of feminine virtue compromised by the corrupt realities of urban life. The melodramas were not only vehicles for musical entertainment—often featuring tropically styled dance routines performed by stars such as María Antonieta Pons or the Cuban-born Ninón Sevilla, and lonesome love ballads sung by Agustín Lara—they also served as public morality lessons and instructional introductions to the modern city for an expanding nation of city dwellers. The 1950s neorealism of Ismael Rodríguez provided urban vehicles for Pedro Infante, who was transformed from a macho *charro* (cowboy) to an urban *galán* (leading man) in this period.

Many of Mexico's leading filmmakers of the 1950s established their credentials as auteurs through urban themes. Gavaldón, collaborating with the leftist writer-intellectual José Revueltas, produced stylish and intriguing urban noires, such as *La Otra* (1946), starring del Río (who played twin sisters) and photographed by Alex Phillips. In films such as *¡Esquina . . . Bajan!* (1948) Alejandro Galindo was perhaps the preeminent chronicler of Mexico City's streets. Even the provincially oriented Emilio Fernández experimented memorably with the urban *cabaretera* in his classic *Salón México* (1948). However, in *Los Olvidados* (1950), Buñuel portrayed the underside of Mexico City's contemporary development through frank (although ultimately nonradical) depictions of the pathology of urban poverty. Shot in a neorealist style by Figueroa, the Spanish director treated the capital in starker terms than most Mexican filmmakers.

Just as Mexico City became an important cinematic backdrop and subject, so did the other area of economic, cultural, and demographic dynamism, the U.S. borderlands. As with the nation's capital, the border entered the national imaginary as an ever-growing number of Mexican families had direct or indirect engagements with the area. The region also had commercial significance for Mexican film production, since the U.S. Latino market had been of prime importance for Mexican producers since the beginning of sound production. golden age Mexican cinema represented these trends. Tin Tan (Germán Valdés) challenged Cantinflas as Mexico's leading cinematic comic. His *pachuco* persona (which brought Los Angeles "Spanglish" and styles to Mexico City and other locales) appealed to transnationalized Mexican and Mexican-American audiences.

The Mexican-U.S. frontier also found more sober cinematic expression. Galindo's masterpiece *Espaldas Mojadas* (1953) stands out. It discouraged undocumented emigration to the United States. Although the film deemphasized the respective responsibilities of the U.S. and Mexican governments for the harsh conditions it portrayed, Mexican officials delayed its release for two years, owing to U.S. government objections (as the U.S. government undertook massive forced repatriation of Mexicans through its Operation Wetback in the mid-1950s).

Some films linked national core and periphery in didactic tales. For example, in Gout's classic *cabaretera* melodrama, *Aventurera* (1949), the heroine, Elena, travels back and forth between Ciudad Juárez and Mexico City as she struggles to overcome misfortune, vice, and deceit before finding safety and happiness with the man of her dreams. Starring the Cuban Ninón Sevilla, shot by the U.S.-trained Canadian Alex Phillips, and written by Gout's frequent collaborator, Spaniard Álvaro Custodio, who supplied a typically Hollywood happy film noir ending, the movie typified the hybridity of so much golden age "Mexican" cinema. Other core-periphery tales had more political messages; *Río Escondido* (1947) exemplified this form. In it, Mexico's reigning screen goddess, María Félix, brings the central government's socially progressive project to a corruptly governed Indian village. Emblematic of the high nationalism of Fernández and Figueroa, the film gained international recognition for postwar Mexican cinema's artistry. In the opinion of Mexican cultural critic Carlos Monsiváis and others, the team's icon making work represented the epitome of Mexico's "cinematic nationalism." But that nationalism never challenged the state's authority nor, more importantly, the increasingly transnationalized political and economic project of the Mexican government. Whether the high aesthetics of Figueroa and Fernández's collaborations or the more popular (and at times intentionally or unintentionally subversive) forms produced in the films of Cantinflas or Pedro Infante, the golden age was built upon and supported a transnational edifice.

Despite the perpetuation of transnational ventures, not only the ambitious undertaking of Estudios Churubusco but also expanded U.S. distribution of money-making Mexican movies (like Columbia's postwar partnership with Posa Films to circulate Cantinflas's films throughout the Western Hemisphere), the dominant pattern was renewed competition between Mexican and U.S. producers after World War II. As the war ended, U.S. aid (including raw film supplies) slowed, creating a new distribution crisis similar to that experienced in 1939, but now more devastating owing to the recent burst of production. Many of the same Mexican producers who had welcomed the U.S. intervention during the war advocated postwar protection through their Asociación de Productores y Distribuidores de Películas Mexicanas. But efforts to impose screen quotas and higher tariffs failed owing to the overall logic of postwar Mexico's political economy and to the particular international vulnerabilities to and dependencies on U.S. factors.

On the macro level, the overall framework of the Mexican state's postwar project prevented decisive confrontation with Hollywood. The industrial nationalism initiated under President Miguel Alemán Valdés (1946–52) and continued under his successor Adolfo Ruiz Cortines (1952–58) was based on U.S.-led transnational development, which contained conflicts with Mexico's northern neighbor. On the micro level, the international structure of Mexican cinema prevented the imposition of the same protectionist policies that served other postwar industries. Not only did the privately owned (and heavily aggregated) exhibition sector continue to depend on U.S. product, but also, despite the vocal economic nationalism of some filmmakers, many producers were aligned with U.S. studios who distributed their films internationally. In addition, all movie-making concerns found themselves vulnerable to Hollywood–U.S. government trade retaliation in key Spanish-speaking markets, including the crucial U.S. Latino audience.

Therefore, while a series of postwar protectionist proposals were made, few were actualized. Instead, new policies aimed to promote more rational business organization. For example, the government organized new domestic and international distributors: Películas Mexicanas (PELMEX) was established in 1945 to cover foreign distribution, and in 1947 the state coordinated Películas Nacionales to distribute movies domestically and reconfigured the privately operated Banco Cinematográfico as the parastatal Banco Nacional Cinematográfico in order to finance private production publicly. In 1949 the government promulgated a new Ley de la Industria Cinematográfica, which created (although never effectively exercised) federal powers to regulate and protect all aspects of the nation's film industry. To oversee the administration of the new regulations (including censorship), a new bureau, the Dirección General de Cinematografía, was established within the Secretariat of the Interior. Despite their ultimate ineffectiveness, collectively these measures reflected not only the economic and sociocultural significance

of film production as an international industry generating great popular demand domestically and abroad, but also its unique importance to the state as a source of national prestige, sign of modernity, and instrument of official ideology and commercial propaganda.

Not all of the Mexican industry's vulnerabilities were external, however, and neither could these be easily solved by tepid state intervention. Labor conflict, oligopolistic exhibition and production practices, and artistic conservatism also contributed to Mexican cinema's postwar decline. With the rise of the Confederación de Trabajadores Mexicanos (CTM) under Cárdenas and the consolidation of its power under its wartime leader Vicente Lombardo Toledano, the earlier coincidence of labor-capital interest ended in the film sector. As the Mexican movie industry grew during World War II, the CTM's Sindicato de Trabajadores de la Industria Cinematográfica, formed at the outset of the war, sought an expanded role in film production, moving beyond its rank-and-file base in the exhibition sector to consolidate its control over the quasi-independent studio workers' sections. The state-linked confederation wanted influence over Latin America's leading culture industry. This 1945 assault, made under the banner of economic and cultural nationalism and directed internationally by Lombardo Toledano, head of the radical international Confederación de Trabajadores de América Latina as the war ended, resulted in new interest-group configurations that underlined some of the inherent national weaknesses in Mexican film production. Regarding labor, STIC aggression led to the formation of an independent union representing feature film artistic talent, the Sindicato de Trabajadores de la Producción Cinematográfica (STPC). Led by some of Mexican cinema's most important male figures—actors Jorge Negrete and Mario Moreno Reyes (Cantinflas) and cinematographer Gabriel Figueroa—the new union fought ferociously and (owing to the celebrity and clout of its leaders) successfully for its own independence from what it labeled the corrupt rule by STIC chiefs.

As far as national capital was concerned, the conflict led to a convergence of interests between U.S. distributors and Mexican producers, who, for separate reasons, each feared the STIC's self-styled "nationalist" moves. Thus, at a critical moment in the development of Mexican film production, as World War II ended, domestic turmoil undermined coordinated attempts to protect wartime gains. Forced into an alliance with the U.S. industry, Mexican producers opposed the radically nationalist cinema policies proposed in the name of anti-Yankeeism by the STIC. Similarly, the presidentially imposed labor settlement resulted in a division of production duties between the rival unions (the STIC gained control of nontheatrical short productions and the STPC received nominal jurisdiction to produce entertainment features). This weakened the organization of the production sector and led to continued conflict between the two unions for years to come, frequently causing chaos in the studios.

Similarly, within the directors' guild, established filmmakers across ideological positions collectively excluded the ascendancy of younger talent in order to preserve the older clique's dominant position. This exclusion applied also to gender. With a few exceptions, such as Matilde Landeta (who produced notable works, including *Trotacalles* in 1951), the directorial league was, as in the United States, male dominated. Such professional conservatism limited artistic innovation necessary for a vibrant national cinema. Financially, too, the monopolization of the Banco Nacional Cinematográfico by a small group of well-heeled and politically connected producers tightly aligned with giant exhibitors further inhibited diverse and competitive filmmaking. These patterns, of course, reflected broader oligopolistic trends, feeding inefficiency that characterized Mexico's political economy during the Alemán Valdés and Ruiz Cortines years.

The postwar decline saw an inversion of the international migration pattern of Dolores del Río and other artists during the war. The actress' frequent partner, Pedro Armendáriz, who successfully, if unspectacularly, crossed over to Hollywood movies. And her rival diva, María Félix, went to make films in Europe. Meanwhile, Mario Moreno transferred his Latin American stardom as Cantinflas to Passepartout in Mike Todd's production *Around the World in Eighty Days* (1956). While Mexico still produced a large quantity of films in the 1950s, frequently surpassing over 100 films per year by mid-decade, they declined in quality and profitability as producers sought quick returns on short-term investments in order to overcome rising production costs and insufficient screen time resulting from the increasing monopolization of the exhibition sector. Owing to this crisis, in 1957 CLASA and Tepeyac Studios each closed their doors.

By the end of the 1950s, the Mexican state under the neopopulism of President Adolfo López Mateos (1958–64) intervened in ways that underlined the inherent contradictions undergirding Mexican cinema's so-called golden age. In 1960, the government nationalized the giant Compañía Operadora de Teatros exhibition chain controlled since the 1930s by the controversial U.S. expatriate businessman William Jenkins and his Mexican partners, who included Manuel Espinosa Yglesias and Manuel Alarcón (both backed by the Avila Camacho clan). At the same time, the government took over operation of Estudios Churubusco, placing Gabriel Figueroa in charge of production. While these moves were symbolically nationalist, their impact was inconsequential. Neither radically challenged Hollywood hegemony, and both established economically inefficient state control over film production. An industry built with a transnational logic could not transcend that trap, derivative of the project of Mexican politicians and capitalists. The rise of television, the neoliberal U.S. trade and communication policies of the Cold War, and the reactionary cronyism of the Mexican postwar political economy combined to undermine national cinema.

In the early 1960s, a new generation of filmmakers and critics—the so-called Nuevo Cine movement—would call for not only radically nationalist industrial practices but also aesthetic and ideological ones. Their analysis tied an indictment of Hollywood cultural and economic hegemony and the Cold War imperialism of the United States to the dominant Mexican filmmaking class, the transnational nexus at the heart of Mexican cinema's golden age.

Select Bibliography

Fein, Seth, "Hollywood, U.S.-Mexican Relations and the Devolution of the Golden Age of Mexican Cinema." *Film Historia* 4:2 (June 1994).

King, John, *Magical Reels: A History of Cinema in Latin America.* New York: Verso, 1990.

Mora, Carl J., *Mexican Cinema: Reflections of a Society, 1896–1988.* 2nd edition, Berkeley: University of California Press, 1988.

Noriega, Chon A., and Steven Ricci, editors, *The Mexican Cinema Project.* Los Angeles: UCLA Film and Television Archive, 1994.

Paranaguá, Antonio Paulo, editor, *Mexican Cinema,* translated by Ana López. London: British Film Institute/IMCINE, 1995.

—SETH FEIN

Motion Pictures: 1960–96

Under the administrations of Adolfo López Mateos (1958–64) and Gustavo Díaz Ordaz (1964–70), Mexico's economic and political contradictions reached unprecedented levels. On the one hand, developmentalist policies resulted in impressive economic growth; on the other, this growth was made possible by protectionist measures that rewarded a small class of politically well-connected capitalists. A small but slowly expanding middle class was concentrated in the large cities while a huge migrant population fleeing rural poverty swelled the urban populations. The people that the cities could not absorb made their way to the northern border towns and into the United States.

Yet such momentous social and political developments were largely ignored by the film industry, which adhered even more tenaciously to genre movies in the face of rising costs and collapsing foreign markets. The Spanish surrealist Luis Buñuel supplied whatever quality there was in Mexican cinema; his *Viridiana,* filmed in Spain but coproduced by the Mexican Gustavo Alatriste, caused an international uproar when it was shown at the Venice Film Festival in 1961. The Vatican denounced it as being anti-Catholic, and the Franco government banned it; such notoriety undoubtedly helped the film become an international hit. In 1962 Jomí García Ascot made the independent feature, *En el balcón vacío,* which was awarded the International Film Critics' Prize at the Locarno Film Festival while the official Mexican entries were ignored.

In an effort to break the industry's impasse and impressed by the work of young university-based independent filmmakers, the Sindicato de Trabajadores de la Producción Cinematográfica (STPC), the union that encompassed the old-line directors, major performers, and technicians who produced full-length features, sponsored the First Contest of Experimental Cinema in 1965. Twelve 35-millimeter full-length films were entered; the first prize was awarded to Rubén Gámez's *La fórmula secreta* and second prize to Alberto Isaac's *En este pueblo no hay ladrones,* adapted by him and Emilio García Riera from a story by Gabriel García Márquez. The STPC contest did not have any immediate repercussions, but a number of the participants became part of the film establishment a few years later.

The conflict in Mexican film circles in the late 1960s was between the entrenched bureaucratic-business groups in the official production agencies and the leftist intellectuals being shaped by the universities. Concerned by Mexico's inequities and the cultural influence of Hollywood, these young filmmakers and scholar-critics longed for an honest, direct cinema that would deal realistically with Mexican life. They were familiar with the best of European cinema, such as Italian neorealism and the French new wave; they also were excited by the frankness and innovativeness of the "new" Latin

American cinema: Brazil's Cinema Novo, the exciting and vigorous Cuban cinema, and the independent filmmakers of Chile and Bolivia.

The administration of Luis Echeverría Álvarez (1970–76) signaled a radical change in official policy toward the film industry. The president saw cinema as a means of projecting a new image of Mexico and supported the admittance of new, young, and often radical directors. He appointed his brother Rodolfo to head the Banco Cinematográfico, which eventually brought all production and distribution under state control. Although the quality of films improved, production declined because credit to private producers had been discontinued. From an output of 72 films in 1970 and 75 in 1972, production fell to 42 films by 1976. The most outspoken film of the period was undoubtedly Felipe Cazals's *Canoa* (1975), a powerful statement on the Tlatelolco Massacre of student demonstrators during the 1968 Summer Olympics. *Canoa* was just one of the many politically and socially outspoken films made by new directors. Some others of note were Luis Alcoriza's *Mecánica nacional* (1971), Paul Leduc's *Reed: México Insurgente* (1971), Alfredo Joscowics's *Crates* (1971), Arturo Ripstein's *El castillo de la pureza* (1972), Alberto Isaac's *El rincón de las vírgenes* (1972) and *Tívoli* (1974), Alfonso Arau's *Calzonzín inspector* (1973), Alejandro Galindo's *El juicio de Martín Cortés* (1973), and the exiled Chilean Miguel Littín's *Actas de Marusia* (1975).

The new administration of José López Portillo (1976–82) reversed the cinematic policies of his predecessor. The new president named his sister, Margarita López Portillo, to head the newly created Directorate of Radio, Television, and Cinema (DRTC). She proceeded to implement the official policy of radically reducing official participation in film production. The new directors that had come into the industry under Echeverría largely were purged or obligated to make low-quality potboilers and *telenovelas,* while Margarita encouraged the return of the commercial producers and their traditional genre pictures. Output increased but quality again suffered.

The outgoing López Portillo administration left Mexico with a devalued peso and a massive debt crisis owing to the collapse of oil prices. It was up to the incoming presidency of Miguel de la Madrid (1982–88) to turn the economy around. The creation of the Instituto Mexicano de Cinematografía (IMCINE) to promote and help produce quality films, and the designation of the respected filmmaker Alberto Isaac as its director, were early causes for optimism among the film community for renewed official support.

In 1985 two films were released that pointed to the continuing potential of Mexican filmmakers to make a quality product that would have both domestic and international appeal. First was Paul Leduc's *Frida,* produced by the respected independent producer, Manuel Barbachano Ponce. Leduc's subject was the flamboyant artist Frida Kahlo, wife of the legendary Diego Rivera. Here was a theme that combined a very Mexican subject with persons and events of international renown, factors that made *Frida* the most successful Mexican film in the international market since Barbachano's own *Nazarín* and Buñuel's films of the 1960s.

Barbachano also produced in that same year Jaime Humberto Hermosillo's *Doña Herlinda y su hijo,* a film that has had practically no distribution in Mexico but was quite successfully internationally. The comedy relates a socially prominent Guadalajara matron's skillful machinations to conceal her gay son's affair with a young music student while also marrying him off, getting a grandson, and keeping everybody happy in the bargain.

The administrations of Carlos Salinas de Gortari (1988-94) and Ernesto Zedillo Ponce de León (1994-) have been clouded by economic instability (the boom under Salinas gave way to bust under Zedillo) and political scandals, including the assassination of Luis Donaldo Colosio, the candidate of the Partido Revolucionario Institucional (PRI, or Institutional Revolutionary Party) to replace Salinas. Filmmakers were also buffeted by the political and economic uncertainty of recent years. In addition to the creation of IMCINE, the secretariat of education founded a Council for Culture and the Arts in January 1989. This took cinematic activity away from the Dirección de Cinematografía, which for decades was under the Department of the Interior (Gobernación), which is more concerned with internal security than culture. Establishing a cultural policy for cinema did not mean that Mexican filmmakers were to benefit from unlimited largesse. They still had to seek out alternate sources of funding: universities, directors' cooperatives, foreign coproducers. For instance, Spain, through its government-owned television network, Televisión Española, was active in coproducing with Mexican and other Latin American filmmakers in the years leading up to the Quincentennial of Columbus's 1492 voyage. A major production in this category was Nicolás Echevarría's *Cabeza de Vaca* (1990), which was coproduced by IMCINE, Televisión Española, the U.S. Public Broadcasting System, and the José Revueltas Film Cooperative.

A significant development in Mexican filmmaking is the number of women filmmakers working in the industry. For decades after the rise of Adela Sequeyro in the 1930s and Matilde Landeta in the 1940s and 1950s, no women filmmakers were able to penetrate the male-dominated directors' guild. In the 1970s, Marcela Fernández Violante broke the barrier with *De todos modos Juan te llamas* (1975), *Cananea* (1977), and *Misterio* (1980). Her career opened the path for the contemporary generation of women directors. Best known is María Novaro, whose *Lola* (1989), *Danzón* (1991), and *El jardín de Edén* (1995) have been well received internationally. Dana Rotberg's first full-length feature was the impressive *Angel de fuego* (1992). Busi Cortés made a feminist period piece titled *El secreto de Romelia* (1988).

A number of Mexican filmmakers have taken on the challenge of entering international markets. Most successful has been Alfonso Arau, who adapted Laura Esquivel's best-selling novel, *Como agua para chocolate* (Like Water for Chocolate), to the screen. This 1991 film became the most successful foreign film ever distributed in the United States, remaining in some major markets for over a year. As often has occurred with other successful foreign directors, Arau was contracted to direct a major Hollywood film, *A Walk in the Clouds* (1995). Another Mexican director who was summoned by Hollywood is Alfonso Cuarón, who wrote and directed the successful and controversial comedy, *Sólo con tu pareja* (1991). In 1995 he directed *The Little Princess*.

The centennial of Mexican cinema in 1996 finds it in a precarious situation, owing to domestic and international economic conditions. The domination of international film markets by Hollywood continues, limiting distribution opportunities for Mexican films as well as those of other countries. Nevertheless, some positive factors existed for Mexican cinema in 1996: since the 1980s Mexican filmmakers steadily had been attracting Mexican middle-class audiences, and several Mexican films were successful internationally. The two official film schools, the Centro Universitario de Estudios Cinematográficos (CUEC) and the Centro de Capacitación Cinematográfica (CCC), continued turning out talented young filmmakers, although their opportunities for steady work were limited. The various political administrations, although struggling with political, social, and economic problems, have managed to continue supporting the film industry, although at times minimally. This unstable situation has impelled Mexican filmmakers to seek new sources of funding, both within Mexico and abroad. With a solid historical tradition and numerous talented filmmakers, screenwriters, and technicians, Mexican cinema has a promising future.

Select Bibliography

Mora, Carl J., *The Mexican Cinema: Reflections of a Society, 1896–1988.* Berkeley and London: University of California Press, 1989.

Ramírez Berg, Charles, *Cinema of Solitude: A Critical Study of Mexican Film, 1967–1983.* Austin: University of Texas Press, 1992.

Reyes Nevares, Beatriz, *The Mexican Cinema: Interviews with Thirteen Directors,* translated by Carl J. Mora and Elizabeth Gard. Albuquerque: University of New Mexico Press, 1976.

—CARL J. MORA

Music

This entry contains three essays that discuss music in Mexico:

Music: Mesoamerica through Seventeenth Century
Music: Eighteenth Century
Music: Nineteenth and Twentieth Centuries

See also Catholic Church; Corridos

Music: Mesoamerica through Seventeenth Century

The indigenous peoples of Mexico used a variety of intriguing musical instruments before their encounter with European culture. The Mexica (Aztecs) meticulously carved inscriptions into many of their instruments and ascribed to them a specific divine purpose, even believing that some of them were fallen gods who had been banished to an earthly life. The two most important instruments in Mexica culture were the *teponaztli* and *huehuetl,* their obligatory pairing reflecting the Mexica conception of the male-female duality of the universe. The *teponaztli* was a type of slit drum, consisting of a hollow wooden barrel placed laterally with an "H" cut into its side. Each of the two tongues of the "H" produced a distinct pitch when struck with mallets *(olmaitl),* resonating much like a large two-note xylophone. The *huehuetl* was a drum whose membrane was stretched over a hollow cylinder that rested on three legs. The player struck the membrane with his fingers, like a bongo.

By striking either in the drum's center or the more taut portion of the membrane near the rim, the player could obtain two different pitches. The ancient *ayacachtli* was a rattle with the hollow chamber shaped of clay or a gourd containing small stones or beads, much like the modern maraca. The Mexica produced the *omitzicahuastli* (a close cousin to the modern guiro) by carving serrated notches into a small bone and then running a stick along the bumps to create a clattering, raspy sound. Vertical flutes held a place of reverence in ceremonies and musical culture. The four-holed *tlapitzalli* had a whistle-like mouthpiece and could be made from almost any small hollow tube, be it clay, cane, or bone. Other instruments include the *atecocoli* and *quiquiztli* (conch shell trumpets), *áyotl* (tortoise shell drum), *chililitli* (clay fife), *coyolli* (jingles), and *huilacapitztli* (five-note clay ocarina). Significantly, other indigenous peoples—such as the Mayas, Purépechas, and Zapotecs—had comparable instruments to those used by the Mexica that were virtually identical except in name. From the earliest times, wind and percussion instruments abounded; stringed instruments, however, largely were new additions brought by the Spanish.

Indigenous rituals and music are treated by most of the early Spanish writers, including Juan de Torquemada, Toribio de Motolinía, Bernardino de Sahagún, Francisco López de Gómora, Alonso de Molina, Diego de Landa, Diego Durán, and Gerónimo Mendieta. Motolinía and Sahagún copiously describe rituals and instruments, and both authors emphasize the professionalism of native musicians and the importance they attached to rehearsal. Performance standards were high: Sahagún relates that an error in performance resulted in the death penalty. Noble youths diligently trained for years to learn the corpus of musical material and also were expected to develop their originality and creativity. New ballads were written to commemorate important events and heroic deeds. Diego de Landa's indispensable accounts of Maya culture reveal remarkable similarities and equivalencies between Maya and Mexica instruments. Diego Durán reconfirms the effort and time needed to master Mexica singing and dancing, and he makes the first known reference to the *sarabanda,* a dance that was to be exported to the European continent and in a mutated form was to become an integral part of the Baroque instrumental suite.

Spanish missionaries saw music as their greatest ally in the conversion of Indian populations, given the prestigious role music played in Mexica culture and the primacy it held in the Christian liturgy.

Motolinía described Tlaxcalan Christian festivities (the Corpus Christi procession of 1538 and Easter procession in 1539) in which the indigenous peoples sang polychoral works along with instrumental accompaniments on trumpets, flutes, drums, and bells. He expressed the delight they had when singing "in their own tongue." The people embraced the new styles with such fervor, Motolinía said, that they habitually filled the courtyard and sang for three to four hours at a time, to the amazement of the Spaniards. He praised their musical memory, quick wits, and uncanny ability to learn new pieces almost immediately. He asserted that they had not only learned to sing but were already directing choirs themselves. This last claim was reconfirmed by Torquemada, who explained that indigenous teachers who had learned music spread it across Mexico, so that even the most remote Indian villages had sophisticated choirs that habitually performed four-part masses and *villancicos* in splendid polyphony. He further noted that they had mastered instrument construction, learned to compose, and amassed huge music libraries through copying choir books brought from Europe by Archbishop Juan de Zumárraga and others.

Unquestionably, these impressive achievements were partly the result of the work of the Franciscan missionaries Pedro de Gante and Juan Caro, who arrived in 1523. Gante established the first church for a native congregation (San José de Belem), and in Texcoco he founded the first school in the Western Hemisphere to teach a European curriculum. His fluency in Nahuatl helped assure his school's success. By 1526 Juan Caro already was instructing the indigenous neophytes the Castilian language and how to sing in four-part harmony. Their contrapuntal skills rose to such a level that by 1530 they were singing polyphony at every Sunday service and on feast days, and Pedro de Gante asserted that his choir could rival the chapel choir of Charles V.

The proliferation of professional musicians among indigenous populations apparently was so rampant that it necessitated a succession of edicts in the futile attempt to limit their excessive number. The First Mexican Council issued a published declaration in 1556 formulating guidelines for the size of musical organizations and their number. It further urged the replacement of "improper" instruments by the organ and forbade dancing the hour before mass. In 1559 choral ensembles were standardized at the level of 12 paid choristers, a number that was to remain the norm through the end of the eighteenth century. Limits were imposed again in 1565 by the Second Mexican Council, implying that the previous edicts

had not sufficiently discouraged Native Americans from pursuing professional careers in music. Gabriel Saldívar studied the records for 123 Indian villages, and his research confirms that the average number of employed musicians for the regional Mexican churches stood at 11.2, although their salary was a pittance compared to the high fees commanded by European-trained performers in the prestigious cathedrals.

Music publishing flourished in Mexico during the sixteenth century; the substantial number of publications and the large press run of many releases dramatically supports Mendieta's, Motolinía's, and Torquemada's claims that Indian choirs had proliferated across Mexico. During the last half of the sixteenth century, 12 liturgical books were printed in Mexico, an impressive number given that Spain only produced 14 during the same time period. The *Graduale Dominicale* of 1576 (an enormous choir book of over 400 folios) went through three impressions in that year, with a combined press run—as carefully estimated by modern scholar Robert Stevenson—of over 1,000 copies. Clearly, there was an urgent need to supply the Indian choirs with the applicable musical literature. Publishing continued into the seventeenth century with the release of Juan Navarro's *Liber in quo quatuor passiones* (1604), which has the distinction of being the first published book of music in the Americas of entirely original works.

The Mexican cathedrals became the seat of the most learned and erudite music making in the New World, far outstripping in magnificence, complexity, and sophistication any of the more modest activities present in the British colonies centuries later. Two cathedrals in particular became the pillars of sacred music composition: Mexico City and Puebla. In 1539 the Mexico City Cathedral appointed its first chapel master, Canon Juan Xuárez, on the basis of his proven success as a music educator of Native Americans since 1535. His next prominent successor was Lázaro del Álamo, an accomplished musician who had been raised in the Segovia Cathedral singing alongside Hernando Franco, who also transplanted himself to the New World and became the most distinguished musician in early Mexican history. Their first teacher at Segovia was none other than Gerónimo de Espinar, who later served as mentor to the youthful Tomás Luis de Victoria, one of the greatest composers of the entire Renaissance. After the death of Charles V, Canon Lázaro del Álamo mounted a magnificent commemorative pageant on November 29, 1559, that left the congregation in awe. The event is detailed by Francisco de Cervantes de Salazar in his *Tumulo Imperial* (1560): he begins with a graphic depiction of 2,000 Indian marchers carrying banners behind the four Indian governors in a two-hour procession. The parade culminated in a musical extravaganza featuring alternating choirs who sang elaborate works by the Spaniard Cristóbal de Morales and the Mexican chapel master, Lázaro del Álamo. The next chapel master, Juan de Vitoria from Burgos, foolishly satirized the viceroy's newly imposed tax policy in a musical play mounted on December 8, 1574, in the cathedral. The text to the evening's entertainment still exists, and it is peppered throughout with instructions for musical performance—making Vitoria the earliest American composer of musical theater. At several points in the skit, a buffoonish tax collector dumped nude, sobbing choirboys out of their bunks to the utter amusement of the audience and outraged amazement of the viceroy. Vitoria soon found himself out of a job, in jail, and thereafter on a ship back to Spain.

After Vitoria's unprecedented gaffe, the Mexico City Cathedral in 1575 hired another talented Spaniard, who was to become the most acclaimed New World composer of the sixteenth century: Hernando Franco. All contemporary accounts praise his artistry and character. He added musicians to the cathedral roster, substantially improved the quality of performance, successfully petitioned for salary increases for his musicians, and brought together musical sources into an impressive and well-maintained music library. Following Franco's death in 1585, Juan Hernández ascended to the top of the cathedral's musical hierarchy. He was a graduate from the University of Mexico and had supplied some additional monophonic chants to the *Graduale Dominicale* printed by Pedro Ocharte in 1576; those pieces constitute the first original works by an American composer to be published in the New World.

The long series of competent chapel masters continues with such artists as Antonio Rodríguez de Mata, Luis Coronado, and Fabián Pérez Ximeno, but it is not until the assumption of the post by Francisco López Capillas that we find a composer of supreme stature. As Franco dominated the musical landscape in the sixteenth century, so López Capillas stands above all rivals in the seventeenth (with the possible exception of Gutiérrez Padilla). López Capillas was born near Mexico City in 1605 and thus is the first chapel master of a major cathedral to be born on American soil. He assumed a post as an organist and bassoonist at the Puebla Cathedral in 1641; one can hardly imagine a better musical influence for him than that of Gutiérrez Padilla, who was chapel master during López Capillas's tenure in

Puebla. López Capilla moved back to Mexico City to assume the dual posts of chapel master and organist in 1654 and remained there until his death in 1674. His stunning mass settings are some of the true gems of the Western art music tradition.

The century closes with José de Agurto y Loaysa and later Antonio de Salazar serving as chapel masters at the Mexico City Cathedral. These two composed exquisite liturgical works that unfortunately are little known today, but their names have entered the history books owing to their collaborations with Sor Juana Inés de la Cruz in setting to music her *villancicos*. (The seventeenth-century *villancico* was a sacred piece in a vernacular language usually for choral resources and instruments that admitted the use of secular elements both stylistically and textually.) José de Agurto y Loaysa—who was known as the "maestro of the *villancico*"—composed five complete *villancico* cycles on Sor Juana texts. Antonio de Salazar succeeded Agurto y Loaysa as chapel master at Mexico City and demonstrated an even more elegant command of musical resources. Before assuming the post in the capital he was chapel master in the other cultural center, Puebla, during which time he, too, had set to music a series of Sor Juana's canonic texts and a handful of her *villancicos*. No other composers' *villancicos* surpassed the charm of Salazar's, nor could their sacred motets approach his in beauty. Additionally, he was a master teacher, as is evidenced by the long list of pupils—including the brilliant prodigy Manuel de Sumaya—who went on to achieve great success across Mexico in the eighteenth century.

The Portuguese immigrant Manuel Rodríguez and his son Antonio Rodríguez de Mesa served as principal organists in the Mexico City Cathedral contemporaneously with Agurto y Loaysa and Salazar. Don Juan de Lienas is yet another significant musician (from the early sixteenth century) who probably resided in Mexico City. The appellation "don" has suggested to some scholars that he was a cacique, a Native American of noble birth. Robert Stevenson has suggested that Lienas was active during the 1630s and most likely was associated with the Incarnation Monastery in Mexico City. Very little else is known of his life except that he was married, which can be gathered from the derogatory asides in the archival manuscripts identifying him as a "cuckolded husband."

Puebla also had an active musical life that was vibrant by the mid–sixteenth century. Francisco de Castillo began serving as organist in 1548, followed by a hodgepodge of minor figures until Juan de Vitoria assumed the chapel master's role in 1566 (after which he was enticed away to Mexico City). Bartolomé de Covarrubias replaced Vitoria, serving from 1571 through 1579, after which Francisco Cairos filled that role through the end of the century.

With Pedro Bermúdez, Puebla saw its first chapel master whose artistry was of the first rank. Born in Granada and surviving a spotty and troubled career at Antequera—where he routinely was fired and rehired—Bermúdez ultimately found his way to the New World in 1597. He was named chapel master at Cuzco in Peru in 1597, moved to Guatemala in 1599, and in 1604 journeyed to Puebla, where he obtained the top spot in the musical hierarchy. As chapel master he wrote engaging compositions that are peppered with more chromatic flavorings and kinetic vigor than those of Franco.

The verve of Bermúdez is even surpassed by that of his successor, Gaspar Fernandes, a Portuguese transplant who was one of the first to truly capture an "American" or "Mexican" spirit in the majority of his works. Much like Bermúdez, Fernandes began his career on the European continent (singing in Évora, Portugal) but soon journeyed across the Atlantic to Guatemala City in 1599, where he made a name for himself as an organist and organ tuner. Appointed chapel master at Guatemala in 1602, he was then asked by the Puebla Cathedral in 1606 to serve them in the same capacity. Fernandes's ability to simultaneously conduct the choir while playing the organ made him a tempting candidate for the Puebla job. He successfully expanded the performing resources at the cathedral, hiring a large number of instrumentalists and choristers. Unfortunately, his tenure at Puebla was blemished by an ever-changing roster of personnel that jeopardized the choir's continuity; there was also the continual bickering between the cathedral chapter and musicians regarding their moonlighting at outside jobs, which often left the cathedral shorthanded for its own musical productions. Additionally, the task of conducting while seated at the organ bench spread Fernandes too thin, and the cathedral resolved the problem in 1622 by hiring Juan Gutiérrez de Padilla as his assistant.

Fernandes's pieces have none of the compositional rigor, architectural scale and magnificence, or craftsmanship of Franco, López Capillas, Lienas, or Gutiérrez de Padilla. But what he lacked in formal craftsmanship he compensated with his by verve and charm. His *villancicos* are spunky and stirring, steeped in the folkloric flavors of Mexico's various ethnic groups. His best works are the energetic and rather raw *negrillos* and *guineos* that imitate or parody the African-influenced music then flourishing in Mexico and the Americas. Although Fernandes's creations are meant for church performance, they clearly derive their inspiration from the popular secular world, especially the *novenario*. African American populations delighted in mounting *novenarios* or *oratorios,* rowdy affairs that were a combination of the religious, superstitious, and festive. They lasted nine days and were held in someone's private patio, where pictures of deceased loved ones were placed on a central, candlelit altar. Singing and dancing resounded to the accompaniment of harp and guitar, and food and drink were plentiful—especially hot chocolate. The repeated unsuccessful attempts by government authorities to forbid them testifies to their popularity.

With Fernandes's death in 1629, Gutiérrez de Padilla became the chapel master in Puebla and directed musical affairs there until his death in 1664. He was born in Málaga and later rose to prominence in the Cádiz Cathedral at Puebla. Padilla petitioned for and received pay raises for his musicians. He was fired mysteriously for an unnamed "misdeed" in 1634, but after six weeks without pay and some additional support in the church hierarchy, he was reinstated. In addition to his duties in the cathedral, he ran an instrument-making shop in the 1640s that employed primarily African American craftsmen. His repertoire and output is unsurpassed in New World archives. He penned at least four splendid polychoral masses now extant in Puebla Cathedral choir books, in addition to a festive four-part mass and various other sacred choral works. Robert Stevenson has compared Padilla's *St. Matthew Passion* favorably with the masterpieces of his European contemporaries. His large number of extended *villancico* cycles —he composed one for each Christmas celebration from 1648 through 1659—stands as one of the greatest contributions to American music history. He actuates their texture with a sparkling rhythmic vigor reminiscent of Fernandes's joyous compositions. These cycles are full of colloquialisms and regional styles. Many have indigenous Mexican attributes, especially those that he labels as *tocotines* or *guastecos.* The rowdy *jácaras* with their infectious energy, the irrepressible fervor of the African American *negrillos,* and the *porto ricos* with their imitation of Caribbean or African American dialects, all share in common a hypnotic rhythmic drive and ethnic flare. Galicia is the butt of the humor in the *gallegos.* Military fanfares, the call-to-arms, and the clamor of battle typify his martial *batallas.* Other secular images arise in the *kalendas, ensaladillas,* and *juguetes.*

With Gutiérrez de Padilla's death in 1664, Juan García de Céspedes was appointed the Puebla chapel master. He had been raised in the cathedral as a child soprano, later gave voice and viol lessons, and ultimately—when Chapel Master Padilla shirked his duties as a music educator—found himself teaching the choirboys counterpoint and singing. As a composer, his work is certainly adequate, and his request to have Palestrina compositions added to the library testifies to his good musical taste. His career was rather lackluster, however; the authorities chided him for not complying with his teaching duties, and he was reprimanded for emphasizing instrumental music at the expense of the choral program. Paralysis tormented his final years. The other principal figures in Puebla for the last half of the century were Juan de Vaeza Saavedra (who was probably a Native American nobleman) and Francisco de Vidales (the nephew of the Mexico City Chapel Master Fabián Ximeno and a superb keyboardist in his own right). Vidales served as the Puebla Cathedral's Principal Organist from his appointment in 1655 until his death in 1702. Puebla's line of distinguished chapel masters closes the century with Mateo Dallo y Lana. Like his predecessors Salazar and Agurto y Loaysa, he was fortunate enough to collaborate with Sor Juana in setting to music some of her *villancico* cycles.

It is clear that instruments were commonplace in the cathedrals from the beginning, and they played an important role in secular life as well. Bernal Díaz de Castillo provides intriguing accounts of the earliest Spanish instrumental music that was brought to Mexico with the conquistadors. He tells of Alonso Ortiz, a musician with Fernando (Hernán) Cortés, who began teaching music and dance following his days as a soldier: when three brothels set up shop next to his business, he moved his business to a better neighborhood. Bernal Díaz also mentions Maese Pedro (a harpist), Benito de Bejel (a drummer and fife player), and five ill-fated wind players who suffered a violent end as part of Cortés's mission to Honduras—four of them were cannibalized. Diego Durán writes in 1579 of a scandalous, licentious dance known as the *sarabanda*. This dance made its way back to Spain, where Spaniards were struck by its sensual and shocking nature; not surprisingly, it became the rage. Once exported to France, it was slowed to a plod and was scrubbed clean of its opprobrious features; it was thus transformed into an unhurried, noble, and stately dance that was to become a respected fixture of the dance suite. The *chacona* had similar origins, beginning in the New World as a "disgraceful" and sensual dance that made it to Europe only to be tamed into a respectable citizen of Baroque musical society.

Select Bibliography

Catalyne, Alice Ray, "Music of the Sixteenth to Eighteenth Centuries in the Cathedral of Puebla, Mexico." *Yearbook of the Inter-American Institute for Musical Research* 2 (1966).

Stevenson, Robert M., *Music in Mexico: A Historical Survey.* New York: Thomas Y. Crowell, 1952.

———, *Music in Mexica and Inca Territory.* Berkeley: University of California Press, 1968.

———, *Renaissance and Baroque Musical Sources in the Americas.* Washington, D.C.: General Secretariat, Organization of American States, 1970.

———, "Puebla Chapelmasters and Organists: Sixteenth and Seventeenth Centuries." Part 1, *Inter-American Music Review* 5:2 (Spring–Summer 1983), and Part 2, *Inter-American Music Review* 6:1 (Fall 1984).

———, "Sub-Saharan Impact on Western Music (to 1800)." *Inter-American Music Review* 12:1 (Fall–Winter 1991).

—CRAIG H. RUSSELL

Music: Eighteenth Century

The rich choral traditions of the previous centuries in New Spain continued to flourish in the eighteenth century, but composers gradually turned their primary interest from charming *villancicos* and modest-scale settings to magnificent polychoral works that were longer and demanded larger instrumental resources. Most sixteenth-century mass settings had been notated for voices alone (although instruments could double and reinforce a vocal line) and by the seventeenth century composers generally added a low-sounding *acompañamiento* or *basso continuo* as a harmonic foundation that would be realized in performance by melodic bass instruments and improvising chordal instruments whose task it was to fill out and enrich the harmonic texture. By the eighteenth century, cathedral performances were generally concerted—that is, they intertwined orchestral parts with the choral melodies. Typically, cathedral performances used twelve singers: for four-part works (soprano-alto-tenor-bass) there would have been three singers on a part. If the work were a polychoral composition, choir one consisted of four vocal soloists (first soprano, second soprano, alto, and tenor), and choir two was a larger group that placed two singers on each part (sopranos, altos, tenors, and basses).

By the eighteenth century the instrumental resources of the cathedrals had greatly expanded and were no longer a jumble of miscellaneous instruments devoted to doubling vocal lines or those confined to the *acompañamiento*. The orchestra became more standardized and its musical function was elevated to such a level that it sometimes rivaled the choir in musical profundity. String sections with multiple violins replaced the previous chamber texture of having violinists play one-on-a-part. Even early in the century violas are mentioned in documents (although labeled viola parts and performance indications are few): they might have been used to double the *acompañamiento* line an octave higher than the cello and bassoon—a practice common in Italy at the time. Whereas the organ had been part of the *acompañamiento* grouping in the seventeenth century, most large-scale Mexican compositions of the eighteenth century give the organ its own labeled performance part. By giving the organ some autonomy separate from the *acompañamiento* grouping, composers were able to assign a specific sonority to each choir through contrasting instruments: choir one is always paired with the *acompañamiento* (i.e., harp plus at least one bass melodic instrument); generally the organ plays whenever choir two is active. Abundant evidence proves that the harp was the preferred chordal instrument of the *acompañamiento* group. In contrast, the harpsichord was used only rarely in the cathedral, and contemporary accounts specifically discourage its use. Documentary evidence also reveals that woodwind and brass players were an obligatory part of a cathedral's musical roster, and they generally were adept at doubling on several instruments. Thus, a pair of flutists could be asked to change to oboes or *octavinos* (high flutes roughly comparable to piccolos) between movements of an extended work. A pair of horn players were employed with regularity; again, the cathedral performance parts suggest that they were capable of shifting to clarion trumpets on demand. Although no specific parts are labeled *atabales* (timpani) in Mexican cathedrals until the nineteenth century, payment records reveal that timpanists were regularly employed throughout the eighteenth century. One can assume that in Mexico, as in Europe, the timpanist was expected to improvise his line by accompanying and reinforcing the trumpets' rhythms.

Mexican mass settings in the eighteenth century are concerted (combining voices and instruments), and most after the 1740s are "numbers masses" in which the lengthy texts are subdivided and set as separate autonomous movements that contrast in key, tempo, meter, mood, and the size of performing resources required. Some movements are imposing, grand polychoral creations; others feature chamber ensembles of duets and trios; and others can feature a single vocal soloist. The Kyrie usually begins slowly, after which it usually embarks on a choral

fugue at the words, "Christ have mercy upon us." The longer texts of the Gloria and Credo are usually subdivided into many separate movements. The Gloria's concluding "amen" is often a thrilling fugue (sometimes related thematically to the Kyrie's fugue) or is in a rollicking compound meter. The Sanctus movement is shorter, a logical result of its brief text. Very often the expected Agnus Dei is altogether missing from the instrumental parts and the score. The mysterious absence of this essential movement is less puzzling if one looks carefully at the choral performance parts of the Sanctus. Repeatedly, the texts for both the Sanctus and Agnus Dei are carefully placed under the vocalists' pitches, implying that both movements are sung to the same music—the choir supplies the appropriate text for each movement while the orchestra plays the unaltered orchestral setting for both.

The Matins service (performed on the evening preceding any major feast day or celebration) was probably the most prestigious compositional genre in eighteenth-century Mexico. It is comprised of three nocturns, roughly equivalent in scale to an act in an opera or oratorio. Each nocturn begins with three psalms framed by short musical snippets called antiphons, followed by three responsories (extended choral works in Latin that are elaborate and often multisectional). Usually, the third nocturn has only two responsories but replaces what would have been the third and final responsory with a setting of the Te Deum. Balance between all three nocturns is thus preserved. Although the responsories usually were choral, some composers occasionally dedicated a responsory or two to a vocal soloist: the sonorities are thus varied through the course of the evening, ranging from rousing polychoral settings to lyrical solo numbers. The Mexican chapel master Antonio de Salazar authored one of the early monuments of the century with his *Responsory Cycle for the Assumption or Christmas* of 1715. Diego Joseph de Salazar plunged into this genre in the early 1730s, followed by Nicolás Ximenes de Cisneros at the decade's end. Midcentury saw the flourishing of this genre as it reached its acme in the hands of Ignacio de Jerusalem, Joseph Lazo y Valero, and Matheo Tollis de la Rocca. Antonio de Juanas, the last chapel master of the century in the Mexico City Cathedral, composed an unfathomable number of these responsory cycles, although they do not approach the imaginative ingenuity, craftsmanship, or distinctive character of his predecessors. During certain feasts such as Christmas or Saint Peter's name-day, the eight Latin responsories of a Matins service could be replaced with eight *villancicos* in a popular and secular flavor and a vernacular language, such as Castilian, Galician, Catalan, Portuguese, or even pseudo-African dialects.

The Vespers service stood close behind the Matins service as the second most important compositional genre. Instead of being divided into three nocturns, it usually had a five-part structure (although the structure of Vespers services varied radically depending on the particular day it was intended and its hierarchy among other feast days). Its five major subdivisions consisted of three concerted psalms, a Marian hymn, and the Magnificat in praise of the Virgin.

Composers authored many smaller works as well in a variety of genres. In eighteenth-century Mexico, a *motete* generally applies to a substantial responsory that was not composed as an integral part of a complete series, but was intended to be substituted for a responsory in a Matins service. The most common place for substitution to occur is the first or eighth responsory, understandably, since the beginning or ending of a cycle would be the best location for added splendor that an awe-inspiring *motet* would bring. The *loa* was a single-movement work in praise of a noble or high church official, almost always written for a special occasion to honor a specific person. As a rule, it is tacked on at the beginning of a larger work or as the opening of an evening's theatrical entertainment. The *solo* is a piece for vocal soloist and chamber ensemble or orchestra that resembles the *villancico's* expected structure *estribillo-coplas-estribillo*. The *cantada* also features a solo voice, but it shuns the Spanish *estribillo-coplas-estribillo* format and instead presents a *recitative* (a style of vocal delivery that imitates the rhythm and natural declamation of speech over a sparse accompaniment) followed by a *da capo aria* (a melodic song in A-B-A form that is tuneful, often florid, rhythmically steady, and full-bodied in its orchestral accompaniment). Also, some composers wrote short instrumental works for organ or for the cathedral orchestra called *versos* (Psalm verses) that were used as substitute passages in Psalm singing: the choir would sing the odd verses in plain chant, interspersed with instrumental *versos* on the even ones. The stacks of uncatalogued orchestral *versos* in the Mexico City and Puebla cathedrals suggest that this was an important orchestral genre, and their abundant presence debunks the assertion that Mexico had no orchestral literature worthy of mention.

Two figures dominate the Mexican cathedral tradition of the eighteenth century: Manuel de Sumaya and Ignacio de Jerusalem. Sumaya was born around 1678, probably in Mexico City, and first appears in the city's cathedral documents in 1694, where he is mentioned as remarkably gifted musician who had been serving as one of the elite choirboys known collectively as Los Seises. His musical talents were honed by the two principal musical artists at the cathedral: Principal Organist José de Ydiáquez and Chapel Master Antonio de Salazar. His play *Rodrigo* (1708) may have contained music—making it one of the earliest examples of original American musical theater—and his opera *Parténope* (1711) holds the distinction of being the first opera composed by an American. In 1715, he replaced Salazar as Mexico City's chapel master, a post he retained until he voluntarily left the capital in 1739 for the provincial city of Oaxaca in order to follow his close friend, Tomás de Montaño, who had been named archbishop of Oaxaca the previous year. Despite the protestations of the Mexico City Cathedral hierarchy, Sumaya remained in Oaxaca until his death on December 21, 1755. Sumaya was succeeded as Oaxaca's chapel master by his own pupil, Juan Mathías de los Reyes, a Native American harpist and singer with considerable compositional talent in his own right. Musically, Sumaya mastered widely disparate styles. On the one hand, he wrote exquisite a cappella vocal polyphony that is reminiscent of the Renaissance masters (although his penchant for augmented chords, secondary-dominant sevenths, and unprepared dissonances would have been far too spicy for his predecessors). His concerted Baroque masterpieces, on the other hand, are full of unflagging rhythmic vigor and spry instrumental figuration.

The Mexico City Cathedral limped along with a series of interim chapel masters, but it was not until the appointment of Ignacio de Jerusalem that the cathedral found a worthy successor. Jerusalem was born in Lecce, Italy, in 1710. As a young man he embarked on a musical theater career in Cádiz, Spain, where he was recruited along with seven other artists by Josef Cárdenas to augment the performing resources of Mexico City's old theater, the Antiguo Coliseo. Once he had arrived in Mexico, his career immediately skyrocketed. In addition to directing the music at the Coliseo and leading as first violin, he soon was composing for the Mexico City Cathedral. In 1750 a poorly run contest was mounted (in which the jurors were incompetent in the skills they were judging) to select the cathedral's next chapel master. Jerusalem's modern tastes made some of his pieces unintelligible to the more conservative jurors, but in spite of the process Jerusalem was approved for the job. In the following years he battled a grave illness (possibly typhoid fever), became estranged from his wife, and was taken to court for alleged embezzlement. Certain court documents also suggest that he was shirking some of his teaching duties. With the arrival in Mexico of a fellow Italian, Matheo Tollis de la Rocca, Jerusalem locked horns and tried to discourage his career. In many ways, Jerusalem must have been rather difficult, even though he clearly was extremely gifted. By the 1760s he had finally put his personal life in order. He was extremely prolific in this final decade before his death on December 15, 1769.

Jerusalem's music is steeped in the progressive traits of the *galante* style: he prefers repetition to sequence; phrases have enormous rhythmic variety where long notes are succeeded by short ones and triplets are interspersed with duple subdivisions. In complete contrast to Sumaya's frenetic and complex chord changes, Jerusalem's work is typified by slow harmonic motion that only infrequently reaches beyond the central defining chords of a given key. He enjoys the Lombardic rhythm or "Scotch snaps" (where a very short note is followed by a long one) and "drumming basses" made of unswerving, repeated bass notes in the *acompañamiento*. Jerusalem ties together the various movements of his mass settings by weaving a unifying motive or two throughout their fabric, much like a Beethoven symphony. Jerusalem's turn toward the *galante* or Classical is developed even further by his successor at the cathedral, Matheo Tollis de la Rocca, who infused his work with theatrical and flamboyant elements of Italian opera. De la Rocca was the first chapel master to prefer the harpsichord to the organ. The century closes with the prolific chapel master Antonio de Juanas, who composed hundreds of works with apparent ease.

Other noteworthy composers outside the capital include the masters whose works are associated primarily with Valladolid (now Morelia). Its cathedral maintained a healthy musical life as can be judged from its impressive archive of eighteenth-century manuscripts. Morelia was also the site of the first music conservatory in the Western Hemisphere, the Conservatorio de las Rosas that opened its doors on August 30, 1743. During the last half of the eighteenth century, there was not a cultural center in the New World that could surpass the talent in Morelia, with composers such as Joseph Gavino Leal, Francisco Moratilla, Gregorio Remacha, Manuel de Zendexas, and Thomás de Ochando. The archives there also contain sophisticated and awe inspiring orchestral works such as the symphonies by Antonio Sarrier and Antonio Rodil.

Secular Music

Plays and musical theater played an increased role in Mexican cultural life in the eighteenth century. The old Coliseo burned to the ground on January 19, 1722, after a performance—ironically—of *The Ruin and Burning of Jerusalem*. To compound the irony, the next evening there was to have been a performance of *Troy Once Stood Here*. A makeshift replacement was thrown together immediately, but the theater was reconstructed with more care in 1725. Performance resources in this old structure were probably small. We safely can assume that the Coliseo's "house band"—as in Spain's theaters—consisted of a harpist and Baroque guitarist who could improvise spontaneously over any of the standard dance tunes. The Baroque guitar (*jarana*) was smaller and lighter than its modern cousin, and had five pairs of gut strings, all in the high register. The glitter and sparkle of this instrument perfectly complemented the deeper resonance of the harp, a fetching combination that has survived unaltered to the present day in the folk music of Veracruz, which combines the folk harp with the *jarana*. With the construction of the larger Coliseo Nuevo in 1752, there was physical space to accommodate larger combos; by 1786 the Coliseo Nuevo employed a permanent chamber orchestra consisting of 12 players: five violins, one viola, one cello, one contrabass, two oboes, and two horns.

Nowhere is the variety of cultural influences in Mexico more intriguing than in eighteenth-century dance music. The Spanish dances that flooded into New Spain varied greatly in style and character. The *bailes* (such as the *jácaras, vacas, canarios, villanos,* and *marizápalos*) were spunky, rowdy dances that allowed movement of the upper body, highly suggestive hand motions, and were generally spicy and sensual. They were accompanied by the strumming of guitars and clatter of castanets. The *danzas* (such as the *gran duque, caballero, gallardas, españoletas,* and *hachas*), in contrast, were more subdued and stately and were meant to convey a noble air. Hand motions and ignoble castanets were considered inappropriate, and dance steps were executed from the waist down. In addition to these two general classes of dances, which had been around for over a century, there were new foot-tapping ones such as the *fandango, seguidillas manchegas, jota,* and *imposibles*. These dances were the progenitors of Mexico's many *zapateados* that feature clicking heels and fancy footwork. They were the dances of choice of those who saw themselves as virile, masculine, and nationalistic.

At the opposite end of the spectrum to the *majos* were the erudite and internationally minded nobles who prided themselves on keeping abreast of European tastes and anything French. These nobles—pejoratively referred to as *petimetres* or *curotacos*—enthusiastically employed dancing masters to learn the steps to the latest *danse à deux* and *danse à bal*. The *danse à deux* was a couple dance in which the dance steps were uniquely matched to a specific piece of music. The male and female pair would trace out symmetrical patterns on the dance floor that were intended more to please the viewers than the actual performers. For each new dance, a new choreography had to be learned; obviously, it was extremely time-consuming for a person of station to keep up with changing fashion. Raoul Auger Feuillet published four to six of these dances each year, and almost immediately after their release in Paris they were in the hands of Mexican musicians and dance teachers. The *danses à bal* were excerpted from French ballets or theatrical works and then published as independent choreographies: they were not necessarily couples dances but could employ a single performer or small group. The Amable (a *danse à bal*) and the Allemanda (a *danse à deux*) were fabulously popular, appearing in nearly every Mexican instrumental music source of the time. Both works were composed by the French opera composer André Campra, but it is unlikely that the Spanish or Mexicans were aware of this attribution at the time. French dance was also the vehicle that popularized much of Jean-Baptiste Lully's music in the New World.

Contredanses overtook the *danse à deux* as the most popular dance fad in Mexico. The *contredanse* was a group dance usually for two couples, four couples, or, less frequently, two lines of dancers of unspecified length. Unlike the *danse à deux,* once the steps to a *contredanse* were learned they could be applied to almost any music in the same meter. This interchangeability and compatibility between choreographies and musical numbers made *contredanses* immensely appealing; individuals were able to dance an evening away without years of laborious study.

Fascinating titles that imply an indigenous Mexican or Caribbean influence begin to appear in the guitar manuscripts of the early eighteenth century. Around the year 1700, Sebastián de Aguirre jots down a few bars of a jaunty, infectious piece called "Portorrico de los negros," which is the earliest known example of notated African American music. His compendium contains other intriguing ditties such as "Tocotín," "El Chiqueador de la Puebla," "Panamá," "El Guasteco," "El Coquís," and a "Corrido" (the earliest example of this genre that was to dominate the nineteenth-century musical landscape

in Mexico). The longest and most engaging examples of African American pieces surface in Santiago de Murcia's guitar manuscript, now called the "Códice Saldívar Number Four." Its stirring rendition of a *cumbé* begins with flurries of syncopated strummed chords with percussive "whacks" between strums to propel this musical piece forward. Friar Steneira at the Monastery of Mercy in Veracruz tried repeatedly (and unsuccessfully) to ban the scandalous *cumbé*. His detailed protestations to the Holy Office provide an image of the events where *cumbés* were danced and the costumes that were worn there. He meticulously records page after page of the *cumbé's* outrageously explicit lyrics (it is little wonder that it was so popular). Murcia's "Zarambeques" provides yet another example of early instrumental music inspired by African American culture.

Murcia's tablature books provide further gems of the Mexican instrumental tradition. His two manuscript books supply a plethora of variation pieces called *pasacalles,* as well as suites, *bailes,* and *danzas,* "battle" pieces, minuets, and a glorious sonata from before 1732 that is in "mature" sonata replete with an exposition, development, and recapitulation. His putative theatrical experience in the Spanish *tea-tros* and Mexican *coliseos* helps explain the presence of certain pieces whose titles match perfectly with theatrical titles of the time. Murcia's mantle passes to another guitarist, Juan Antonio Vargas y Guzmán, who, like Murcia, made the move from Spain to Mexico for the latter half of his career. He draws much of the text for his accompanying treatise straight from Murcia's earlier publications and Joseph de Torres's keyboard treatise, but he then includes 13 sonatas that constitute some of Mexico's best chamber music of the era. Of equal stature are the 28 violin sonatas authored by Joseph de Herrando, which find their way into the back pages of a unique copy of his *Explicación del modo de tocar el violín.* Each explores a different technical problem and different key (going even to the extreme key signatures of seven sharps and seven flats), and collectively they rival the subtlety and virtuosity of Corelli's Opus 5 solo violin sonatas. Several other sources reveal a healthy instrumental tradition that flourished in Mexico. The Morelia Cathedral preserves many important instrumental works by the all-star cast of composers active in eighteenth-century Morelia in conjunction with the cathedral and the Conservatorio de las Rosas. They mark the high point of eighteenth-century orchestral composition in the Americas. A number of splendid orchestral movements known as *versos* survive in many of the cathedrals. Lastly, the chamber music tradition exists (albeit in incomplete sources) in the Eleanor Hague Manuscript of the Southwest Museum in Los Angeles, and in Manuscript 1560 in Mexico City's Biblioteca Nacional. The latter source contains the violin sonatas by Samuel Trent, Bartolomé Gerardo, Antonio, and Ricardo, as well as the Italian master Arcangelo Corelli, who was the most adored European instrumental master in Mexico until the influx of Haydn's creations.

Select Bibliography

Esses, Maurice, *Dance and Instrumental "Diferencias" in Spain During the 17th and Early 18th Centuries*. 3 vols., Stuyvesant, New York: Pendragon Press, 1992.

Russell, Craig H., "Imported Influences in 17th and 18th Century Guitar Music in Spain." In volume 1 of *Actas del Congreso Internacional España en la Música de Occidente*. 2 vols., Madrid: Ministerio de Cultura, 1987.

_____, "Lully and French Dance in Imperial Spain: The Long Road From Versailles to Veracruz." In *Proceedings of the Society of Dance History Scholars*, University of California, Riverside, 1991.

_____, "The Mexican Cathedral Music of Ignacio de Jerusalem: Lost Treasures, Royal Roads, and New Worlds." *Revista de Musicología* 16:1 (1993).

_____, "The *Eleanor Hague Manuscript*: A Sampler of Musical Life in Eighteenth-Century Mexico." *Inter-American Music Review* 14 (Winter–Spring 1995).

_____, *Santiago de Murcia's "Códice Saldívar No. 4": A Treasury of Secular Guitar Music From Baroque Mexico*. 2 vols., Champaign: University of Illinois Press, 1995.

_____, "New Jewels in Old Boxes: Retrieving the Lost Musical Heritages of Colonial Mexico." *Ars Musica Denver* 8 (1995–96).

—CRAIG H. RUSSELL

Music: Nineteenth and Twentieth Centuries

Although the center of musical life in Mexico at the end of the eighteenth century remained Mexico City, important provincial cities such as Puebla, Guadalajara, Durango, Oaxaca, Guanajuato, Morelia, and others also boasted of an advanced musical life. Settlements as far away from the capital as Alta California and Santa Fe to the north and Mérida de Yucatán to the south developed a strong European-based musical life in addition to maintaining strong indigenous musical traditions. The main Mexican musical centers kept in frequent touch with artistic developments in Europe, especially those in Spain, Italy, and France. Likewise, the periphery kept in touch through the center. Organized sacred and secular art music activities around 1800 remained principally sited in the cathedrals, collegiate and parish churches, monasteries and convents, public theaters, the viceregal court, and the salons of the upper class and aristocracy. Informal music making existed everywhere. Until at least 1821 and Independence, except for periods of serious political upheaval, Mexican musical life, based on the European models first established in the sixteenth century, remained essentially unchanged. After 1821, however, changes in social and political life gradually shifted the institutions of musical patronage and learning from the church and viceregal court and its appendages to an increasingly independent public musical and theatrical establishment supported primarily by the middle and upper classes, and governmental officials and agencies. The church's influence on musical life lessened as the century progressed. Before Independence from Spain, music was cultivated to a level of accomplishment in the principal Mexican cities and towns in a manner far superior to that of any settlement in British North America. After Independence, Mexico City maintained a high level of artistic quality in its musical life, certainly on par with New York, New Orleans, Philadelphia, Boston, or Havana.

Turn-of-the-Century Composers

By 1786 composer José María Aldana was performing as second violinist in the Coliseo Orchestra and earning 544 pesos per year (the first violinist was Manuel Delgado); he later advanced to the directorship of this orchestra. In 1807 he played violin in the orchestra in the musical academy of the College of Mines in the capital. The issue for December 18, 1806, of *El Diario de México* extolled Aldana as the "Mexican Lolli" (in reference to the Italian composer Antonio Lolli, whose works were well known in Mexico). He was also called the "Haydn of America" by *El Diario de México* on November 18, 1806. Also active in Mexico City Cathedral (his works are preserved in the cathedral music archive), he composed a number of religious works. On October 9, 1790, Aldana obtained leave from Mexico City cathedral authorities to play violin at Puebla Cathedral during a beatification ceremony. His *Mass in D* was performed under the direction of Carlos Chávez in 1940 at the Museum of Modern Art in New York during a festival of Mexican music as the sole representative of colonial sacred music. Aldana was also the author of five sets of orchestrally accompanied *versos* (four are in the Mexico City Cathedral archives and one in Puebla Cathedral). These *versos* had achieved sufficient popularity to be cited in Aldana's obituary published in the *Diario de México* on February 18, 1810. Besides writing a concerto for his own instrument, the violin, Aldana also wrote keyboard pieces based on dance music forms popular at the time. His *Boleras nuevas* can be found in the music archive of the Conservatorio de las Rosas in Morelia. A minuet with variations by Aldana is found in the *Cuaderno de lecciones con varias composiciones para clave o forte piano* compiled in 1804 by or for María Guadalupe Mayner (in the library of the Secretaría de Hacienda y Crédito Público). Two sonatas of Aldana's for guitar and violin and a *Baile Ynglés* for two guitars are in the *Códice Angulo* (Escuela Nacional de Música, UNAM).

Composer and pianist Mariano Soto Carrillo is known today as the teacher of José Mariano Elízaga and the composer of boleros, *polacas,* and *tonadillas.* An early interpreter of Haydn's keyboard works in Mexico, his performances were praised in the *Diario de México*. He, like Aldana, took part in the academy at the College of Mines and helped to popularize the fortepiano as an instrument of the upper classes at the end of the viceroyalty.

Aldana and Soto Carrillo, as well as younger musicians such as José María Bustamante and José Mariano Elízaga, were among the most important musicians in Mexico at the turn of the century. Bustamante, Mexico City Cathedral chapel master (and director of music in other churches in the capital), premiered on October 27, 1821, at the Coliseo the music he contributed to Francisco Ortega's melodrama *México libre,* in honor of Mexican Independence and the proclamation of Agustín de Iturbide as emperor. Born in Valladolid (Morelia), José Mariano Elízaga as a six-year-old child prodigy won the praise of the editor of the *Gaceta de México* in 1792. Even the viceroy, Juan Vicente de Güemes Pacheco y Padilla, the count of Revillagigedo, was interested in Elízaga's musical precocity; he ordered the youngster brought to the capital at his expense to give public performances. Elízaga entered the Colegio de Infantes in the Mexico City Cathedral, but soon thereafter he returned to his home city. After studies with Morelia cathedral chapel master José María Carrasco, the Morelia cathedral chapter recognized Elízaga's exceptional talents and sent him back to Mexico City to study with Mariano Soto Carrillo, teacher of Carrasco. After Carrasco left Morelia for the organist's post at Puebla, Elízaga returned again to Morelia in 1799 to take up the position of third organist at Morelia cathedral at the age of 13. He taught private piano lessons to Morelia's elite, including doña Ana María Huarte (a student at Morelia's music conservatory, the Colegio de las Rosas), later wife of Augustín de Iturbide. After Independence, his well-placed connections earned him the title of Imperial Chapel Master, a post he abandoned at the fall of the Agustín's empire. His personal connection with government minister Lucas Alamán assured him of patronage during the succeeding political administration. Influenced by the theoretical works of the Spaniards Nassare and Eximeno, Elízaga published his *Elementos de la música* in 1823, one of the first published musical treatises in Mexico, with the help of Alamán. Elízaga established a musical press in the 1820s, one of the first in Mexico and Latin America.

In 1824, Elízaga founded the Sociedad Filarmónica, and in 1825 the Academia Filarmónica (with the support of Alamán and President Guadalupe Victoria), precursors of the present-day Conservatorio Nacional. Elízaga's academy may have been in operation until 1829, by which date he had moved to Guadalajara as cathedral chapel master. However, he remained only a short time there, returning again to Mexico City by 1830, at the request of his friend Alamán. He continued his didactic work, publishing his *Principios de la harmonia* in 1835. Two years before his death in 1842, he returned for the last time to Morelia, to the cathedral chapel mastership. Elízaga cultivated most genres, including sacred music, orchestral music, keyboard music, and other forms. As a composer he was indebted to the Italian musical style. His set of previously unknown piano variations with a humorous slant, *Ultimas variaciones,* was discovered and published in Mexico City.

Elízaga was followed by a group of musicians whose influence was long felt in Mexican musical life, and whose greatest source of inspiration was Italy (and, to a lesser extent, France and Germany). José Antonio Gómez, who began composing as a child, played the continuo part at the keyboard for the performances of Italian opera given by Spanish opera singer Manuel García and his touring company in Mexico City in 1827. Gómez, like Elízaga, and other Mexican composers, wrote musical tutors for use in his teaching, including his *Gramática musical razonada* (1832), as well as harmony, piano, and vocal methods. José Antonio Gómez was one of the first to wed lithography to music printing in Mexico (musical imprints hardly existed before his time in Mexico); his *Gramática musical razonada* contained seven lithographed plates. Gómez was also the editor of an early music journal, the *Instructor Filarmónico,* of 1842.

Music for the Theater

Although Mexican composer Manuel de Zumaya had led the movement toward opera in Mexico in

1711 with *La parténope* (his music is lost but the libretto is in the Biblioteca Nacional), he was not followed by other Mexican composers in this sphere, as opera first was staged in Mexico on a regular basis beginning only in the nineteenth century. However, Italian opera arias or Italianate opera arias by local Mexican composers, with alternate religious texts, sometimes were heard in Mexican cathedrals and probably elsewhere. The Coliseo Nuevo was inaugurated on December 23, 1753, and was the main theater in Mexico City for many years; it was rebuilt in 1806. The first musical genres performed at the Coliseo were of Spanish origin: *tonadillas, sainetes,* and zarzuelas, along with Mexican musical skits and dances. All of these forms were given in Spanish, as were the Italian comic operas performed at the end of the colonial period. Domenico Cimarosa's *Il fanatico burlato* was given in 1805 at the Coliseo as *El filósofo burlado.* Giovanni Paisiello's *Il barbieri di Siviglia* was given as *El barbero de Sevilla* in 1806. Puebla chapel master Manuel Arenzana's two-act opera *El extrangero* and his *Los dos ribales* were presented in Mexico City in 1805, and two of his *tonadillas* were heard in Puebla in 1807. Spaniard-turned-Mexican-resident Manuel Corral's two-act comic opera *Los dos gemelos, o, los tios burlados* with a libretto by Spaniard Ramón Roca was given in 1816 and dedicated to Viceroy Juan Ruiz de Apodaca (the libretto was published by José María de Benavente). The first opera composed in Mexico and given at the Coliseo after Independence was Stefano Cristiani's three-act *El solitario,* given its premier on December 2, 1824 (and heard again in 1825).

A partial sampling of some of the musical, dance, and theatrical events available to Mexico City residents at the beginning of the nineteenth century—taken from the pages of *El Diario de México* —reveals the wide range of entertainment presented at the Coliseo, where Spanish, Mexican, and European dances alternated with theatrical pieces, musical skits or scenes, instrumental music, and songs. On October 4, 1805, Andrés del Castillo sang "*boleras* accompanied on the horn by don Antonio Salot"; on this same occasion "a concert with violin was played in the best taste by the blind don Antonio Ramírez." María Guadalupe Gallardo and Juan Marani performed a *Minue Congó* during intermission on April 6, 1806, at the Coliseo; on that same night Dolores Munguía and Luciano Cortés sang the *tonadilla El Presidiario.* Juan Campuzano was the orchestra director for the 1807–1808 season at the Coliseo (he had been a member of the Coliseo orchestra since at least 1786); the company list for

1808–1809 includes composer José María Aldana as "primer violin de orquesta." *El Diario de Mexico* often lauded the skill and artistry of the instrumentalists employed at the Coliseo:

> In regards to the orchestra, the praises were sung of the following musicians: the expressive don Manuel Delgado, the violinist; the singular don Matías Trujeque, the clarinetist; the incomparable horn player don Antonio Salot; the most able player of the cello and violin known as "El Habanero"; the well-known abilities of don Vicente Virgen; and the contrabassist without equal don Rafael Domínguez.

Ballets accompanied by music were regularly performed at the Coliseo at the end of the eighteenth century and the beginning of the nineteenth. While the musical scores used in operatic performances, musical theater, and ballet at the Coliseo have vanished for the most part, probably owing to the almost wholesale destruction wrought by the ravages of time, fire, and various revolutions, a few pieces of ballet music performed at the Coliseo have been discovered. One of these short pieces is a minuet labeled *Hircana en Yulfa,* undoubtedly from the four-act *Hircana en Yulfa,* presented at the Coliseo on November 4, 1796, in honor of the birthday of Carlos IV. Because of the royal connection, the libretto to the ballet was published in Mexico City in 1796 by Mariano de Zúñiga y Ontiveros, one of the principal publishers of the period. This ballet-pantomime was set to a story by Italian dramatist Carlo Goldoni, from the second part of his orientalist trilogy of 1755–56, the three parts translated into Spanish as *La esposa persa, Hircana en Yulfa,* and *Hircana en Ispahan.* Ballet versions of *Hircana* had been presented in the 1770s and 1780s in Genoa, Mantua, Milan, Palermo, Ferrara, and Venice. It probably also was performed in Madrid about that time, perhaps at the Caños del Peral Theater, for at least one part of the trilogy was printed in Madrid in 1785. This ballet and others were brought to Mexico by dancer and choreographer Juan Medina, a Spaniard who was first recruited to perform at the Coliseo in 1794, and who probably arrived in New Spain in 1796. He was hired by José del Rincón, administrator of the Hospital Real de Naturales, the proprietors of the Coliseo, and Viceroy Revillagigedo. Brought to Mexico as *primer bailarín* (principal dancer) and choreographer, Juan Medina earlier had performed at the Caños del Peral and in Cádiz. Medina brought to theatrical and musical life in Mexico City new dances and music from Spain, Italy, and France that he and his company performed at the Coliseo between 1796 and 1806, and possibly later. Although details about the Coliseo are extremely scarce for the period between 1795 and 1805, it is known that Medina took a six-year lease of the theater in January 1800. In that year he also petitioned the authorities to open a school "of song, drama, and dance" in quarters housed in the Coliseo then occupied by a billiard parlor.

The other piece connected with the Coliseo is entitled *Dido abandonada,* most probably a short musical excerpt by an unidentified composer from the ballet score to Juan Medina's choreographed version of Pietro Metastasio's first original opera libretto, his *Didone abbandonata* of 1724. Based on Virgil's *Aenead* and set by many Italian and German opera composers between 1724 and 1823, Metastasio's libretto also was adapted as a ballet and performed throughout Europe from the 1760s until the 1820s. Like the ballet *Hircana in Yulfa, Dido abandonada* was choreographed by Medina and presented at the Coliseo in honor of the birthday of Carlos IV on November 4, 1805.

During theatrical and musical events given at the Coliseo and elsewhere, and at political rallies and gatherings, patriotic marches sometimes were sung by solists and/or chorus to the accompaniment of full orchestra, often in honor of an important political or military figure. Before Independence, the glory and honor of Fernando VII was acclaimed; after 1821, Iturbide and his successors were lauded in their turn. These ephemeral poetic and musical compositions, almost always by local amateur poets anxious for recognition, frequently were published (text only) in newspapers and preserved in personal memoirs and papers. However, few composers names were ever given. Political observer Carlos María de Bustamante included many of these honorific (and sometimes satirical) panegyrics in his multi-volume personal manuscript *Diario histórico de México.*

Sonecitos del país, popular Mexican songs and dance tunes often performed in a dance context on the stage of the Coliseo, were interspersed between the acts of opera and vernacular theatrical forms at the beginning of the nineteenth century. Popular dance, song, and theatrical forms such as *polacas,* various unidentified *sonecitos, boleras, tonadillas, sainetes,* seguidillas, *contradanzas,* minuets, and fandangos were heard at the Coliseo; before Independence some attracted the attention of the Inquisition as a result of their alleged indecency. The *jarabe* and *chuchumbé* were especially objects of censure by the Holy Office at the end of the colonial period. The dramatic *comedias* (sometimes presented with accompanying music) were closely monitored and

often censored or banned by the ecclesiastical authorities up to the end of the viceroyalty. It is possible that musical pieces such as operas, *sainetes, tonadillas,* and zarzuelas did not attract the same degree of close and diligent attention by censors, possibly because of their musical nature. They were watched with some caution, however. For example, the *sainete Payos hechizados* was banned by the Holy Office in 1804, perhaps because of the idea of witchcraft hinted at in the title.

Arrangements for guitar and keyboard heard at the Coliseo were made by local music teachers and performers during the first half of the nineteenth century for use by both amateur and professional musicians. These arrangements of operatic, theatrical, and dance music for guitar solo and duet, guitar and harp, or piano were often collected into personal copybooks. One important recently discovered manuscript collection includes a potpourri of pieces: the overture to the opera *El tío y la tía* (heard a number of times in the capital in 1824), *Variaciones de [Manuel] Corral, Adagio de Haydn,* the overture to Gioacchino Antonio Rossini's operas *Barbieri di Siviglia, L'italiana in Algeri,* and *Tancredi,* various rondos, solo improvisations on the *jarabe,* and a waltz.

When Spanish tenor and composer Manuel García visited Mexico with his opera company in 1827, he faced strong local audience opposition to singing Italian operas in Italian. In the 1820s, the Mexican public wished to hear the Italian operas of Rossini, Vicenzo Bellini, and Gaetano Donizetti, and other composers sung in Spanish. In the 1840s and 1850s, however, companies singing in Italian visiting Mexico received a warmer welcome. Indeed, midcentury Mexican opera composers such as Cenobio Paniagua, Miguel Meneses, Octaviano Valle, and Melesio Morales, wishing to have their operas staged in their native land, felt obligated to set Italian librettos.

Composer, operatic impresario, and performer Cenobio Paniagua also wrote didatic texts, including *Cartilla elemental de música, Vocalizaciones matinales,* and *Compendio de armonía.* As a youth, Paniagua played second violin in the Morelia Cathedral orchestra. In Mexico City from 1842, he studied with Agustín Caballero, an important local music teachers, and he joined the orchestra of the Mexico City Cathedral, where he assumed the duties of assistant director under Ignacio Trujeque, scion of a distinguished musical family. Paniagua presented the first two acts of his opera *Catalina de Guisa* to a group of friends in 1845 in the house of Agustín Caballero. After much revision, his opera was premiered in 1859 in Mexico City's Teatro Principal by members of the Amilcare Roncari Company, an Italian touring company, and was dedicated to President Miguel Miramón. Like most operas by Mexican composers mounted in Mexico City before 1900, *Catalina* was set to an Italian libretto. The audience was tempted to see in *Catalina* a parallel between the struggle between the opposing factions supporting Benito Juárez and Miguel Miramón and the conflict between the Huguenots and Catholics in sixteenth-century France represented in the plot of the opera. Quite successful for an opera by a local composer, *Catalina* was repeated four times in Mexico City between 1861 and 1863.

After the success of his opera, Paniagua formed a Mexican opera company with his daughter Mariana as principal singer, giving performances of works by Donizetti, Bellini, and Giuseppe Verdi from 1862 to 1864. On May 5, 1863, in celebration of the defeat of the French in 1862, Paniagua presented his second opera, *Pietro D'Abano*. His company also premiered Octaviano Valle's *Clotilde di Coscenza* (1863) and Miguel Meneses's *Agorante rè della Nubia* (1864). Paniagua had many students, some of whom had significant careers as composers and performers, including composer and music critic Melesio Morales, conductor and composer Miguel Meneses, and opera composer Octaviano Valle. Operas by Valle *(Clotilde)*, Ramón Vega *(Adelaida y Comingo)*, and Morales *(Giuletta e Romeo* and *Ildegonda)* were written under Paniagua's guidance.

Four operas by Melesio Morales were performed at the Teatro Nacional in the capital before 1900: *Giuletta e Romeo* (1863); *Ildegonda* (1865), the first Mexican opera to be performed abroad (and the first nineteenth-century Mexican opera to be recorded in its entirety); *Gino Corsini* (1877); and *Cleopatra* (1891); all were written to Italian libretti. However, Aniceto Ortega's opera on a native theme, *Guatimotzín*, was sung in Spanish. Treating the story of the last defense of Mexico by Cuauhtemoc, *Guatimotzín* first was performed at the Teatro Nacional in 1871 with Enrico Tamberlik and Angela Peralta (the "Mexican nightengale") in leading roles. *Guatimotzín* was one of the only Mexican operas of the nineteenth century to deal with a Mexican subject. Ortega incorporated native musical elements in *Guatimotzín*, especially in the "Danza tlaxcalteca," in which he quotes the folk tune "El perico," and in the melody of the dance of the "tzotzopizahuac." Ortega also was involved in expanding Mexican acceptance of European classical forms; he and his musical partner, pianist and composer Tomás León, were among the first Mexican performers to introduce and regularly perform the masterworks of Beethoven in Mexico.

Urban areas outside the capital also promoted opera in the nineteenth century (and continued to do so in the twentieth century). In Guadalajara in the 1860s formal concert and operatic activity began at the Teatro Degollado. Operatic and concert life was chronicled in such local newspapers as *La Unión Liberal* and *La Prensa*, which published reviews, announcements, and notices of touring Italian opera companies, Spanish and Mexican opera and zarzuela troupes, visiting circuses, musical soloists, and local musicians such as conductors Carlos Meneses and Clemente Aguirre and clarinetist Adrián Galarza, all three of whom were founders of the Sociedad Jalisciense de Bellas Artes in 1865.

Puebla audiences were no strangers to opera and music theater. Anna Bishop's touring opera company visited Puebla in 1849 and was followed by other companies, including the José Freixes Troupe presenting zarzuela in 1855; the Domenico Ronzani Italian-Mexican Opera Company in 1864, which gave the Puebla premiers of several Verdi operas (with Jaime Nunó, Catalan composer of the Mexican national anthem, as orchestra director, and Agustín Balderas as chorusmaster); and Mexican soprano Angela Peralta and company in 1866 and 1872. That theatrical life was advanced enough to merit surveillance by civic authorities can be seen from the *Reglamento interior y exterior del teatro* of 1852, in which the Puebla *ayuntamiento*, in regulating *intermedios, sainetes, bailes*, and other theater pieces, wished to avoid "all indecencies with special reference to the dances known as *sonecitos del país* [little dances or tunes of the country]."

The most popular operas and zarzuelas performed in Mexico in the nineteenth century were by European composers, primarily Italian and Spanish. Although Mexican composers wrote operas, most of their commercial success was earned through the lighter forms of zarzuela, musical comedy, and musical review. Spanish-language works that dominated the Mexican stage included Spanish zarzuelas by Joaquín Gaztambide *(Catalina)*, Francisco Asenjo Barbieri *(Jugar con fuego)*, Emilio Arrieta *(Marina)*, Tomás Bretón *(La verbena de la paloma)*, Manuel Fernández Caballero *(El dúo de la Africana)*, Ruperto Chapí y Lorente *(La tempestad)*, and Federico Chueca and Joaquín Valverde *(La gran vía)*, and Mexican zarzuelas such as Carlos Curti's *La cuarta plana*. European works heard in Spanish translation included French opera buffa by Robert Planquette *(Les cloches de corneville*, given as *Las campanas de Carrión* in Spanish-speaking countries), and German operettas such as Franz von Suppé's *Doña Juanita*. These and similar works formed the mainstay of the repertory of the Spanish and Mexican zarzuela troupes that regularly traversed the republic visiting the large cities and small towns. These groups toured throughout Mexico and Central America and traveled as far north as the southwestern United States (especially to Los Angeles, San Francisco, Tucson, Santa Fe, and San Antonio).

The Italian and French operas most frequently performed in Mexico beginning in the second half of the nineteenth century were those that were also the most popular in Europe and the United States. A short list includes the following works: *Il barbieri di Siviglia* by Rossini; *La favorita* and *Lucia di Lammermoor* by Donizetti; *L'Africaine* and *Les Huguenots* by Giacomo Meyerbeer; *Ernani, Il trovatore, Rigoletto, La Traviata, Un ballo in Maschera, Aida,* and others by Verdi; *Faust* by Charles-François Gounod; *Carmen* by Georges Bizet; *La Boheme, Madama Butterfly,* and *Tosca* by Giacomo Puccini; *Manon* by Jules-Émile-Frédéric Massenet; and *Cavalleria Rusticana* by Pietro Mascagni. When Richard Wagner's German operas were introduced in Mexico (sung in Italian)—*Lohengrin* in 1890, *Tannhäuser, Der fliegende Holländer* (with President Porfirio Díaz in attendance), and *Die Walküre* in 1891—they received lukewarm reception. Before the Mexican Revolution and during the Porfiriato, the number of performances of the standard Italian and French operas by resident and touring companies in Mexico surpassed the number of performances of individual nonmusical dramatic works by Mexican or European authors (with some exceptions).

The nineteenth century in Mexico has been called the operatic century because of the domination of opera over all musical forms. Mexican composers in the twentieth century generally have showed less interest in composing operas, especially in comparison to their nineteenth-century predecessors (Paniagua, Valle, Morales, Ortega, Meneses, Felipe Villanueva, Gustavo Campa, Ricardo Castro, and Ernesto Elorduy). However, Mexican audiences have continued to show interest and enthusiasm for opera (except during the general chaos of the Revolution). With some exceptions, the standard nineteenth-century operas remain the most popular today. Although most twentieth-century Mexican composers have concentrated their efforts on concert music, some have been active in writing operas: Miguel Bernal Jiménez *(Tata Vasco,* 1941), Luis Sandi *(Carlota,* 1947), José Pablo Moncayo *(La mulata de Córdoba,* 1948), Eduardo Hernández Moncada *(Elena,* 1948), Carlos Chávez *(Pánfilo y Lauretta,* 1953), Salvador Moreno *(Severino,* 1961), Daniel Catán *(Encuentro en el ocaso,* 1979; *La hija de Rapaccini,* 1990),

Carlos Jiménez Mabarak *(La Güera,* 1981), Mario Lavista *(Aura,* 1988), and Federico Ibarra *(Alicia,* 1990). None of these operas, however, has dominated Mexican stages for long.

Mexican opera singers have distinguished themselves at home and abroad. Angela Peralta, the most important Mexican soprano of the nineteenth century, starred in the first performances of Morales' *Ildegonda* (1866) and *Gino Corsini* (1877), and Ortega's *Guatimotzín* (1871). After an operatic debut at age 15 in Verdi's *Il Trovatore* at the Teatro Nacional, she went to Italy, where she studied voice and appeared in opera. Returning to Mexico in 1865, she was lionized by opera audiences, especially the supporters of the ill-fated Emperor Maximilian. She returned to Europe in 1867, stopping in Havana, New York, Madrid, and elsewhere on the way. After her second return home, she established her own opera company, touring throughout Mexico with operas such as *Lucia di Lammermoor* and *La sonambula.* By Peralta's own count, she appeared in these two operas 166 and 122 times respectively. She also appeared in *Dinorah, La traviata, I puritani,* and other works. She inaugurated the Teatro Degollado (then Teatro Alarcón) in Guadalajara in 1866 with a performance of *Lucia di Lammermoor.* A composer herself, her best-known work was the collection *Album Musical de Angela Peralta.* The vicissitudes of the theatrical life of the time sometimes presented her with unusual performing venues. In La Paz, Baja California, she sang in an enclosed sand pit, and in Veracruz, she sang opera excerpts instead of a complete opera when scenery was not available. She died on tour in Matzatlán in August 1883 of yellow fever and was mourned by the Mexican nation. A number of Mexican singers followed Angela Peralta to national and international fame in operetta and opera. Esperanza Iris and María Conesa appeared in operetta and musical comedy. José Mojica (a tenor turned film star and later a Franciscan monk), Irma González, Gilda Cruz Romo, and, above all, Plácido Domingo (adopted son of Mexico) established international operatic careers, to name but four examples of internationally recognized opera singers.

Music Education in Mexico

During the colonial period the church assumed the major role in the area of formal music education. The schools attached to cathedral foundations provided education in music theory, performance, and composition for boys and men. The religious orders, male and female, also provided for music instruction, in female and male conventual houses and in educational establishments for the laity such as the colegios. An important early musical establishment was the Colegio de las Rosas in Morelia, a well-established music school for girls founded during the colonial period. Music also was performed in and under the sponsorship of the Real y Pontifícia Universidad de México. While music instruction in these locations continued after Independence, secular institutions for music education were established beginning in the 1820s, which over time would result in the formation of a professional conservatory system in Mexico.

The Sociedad Filarmónica established by José Mariano Elízaga in the 1820s was followed in 1838 by the Academia de Música directed by Agustín Caballero and Joaquín Beristáin, and the Gran Sociedad Filarmónica of José Antonio Gómez, founded in 1839. The two short-lived organizations of Caballero, Beristáin, and Gómez, like Elízaga's conservatory, can be seen as forerunners to the Conservatorio Nacional, first founded in 1866 by the Sociedad Filarmónica Mexicana with Caballero as its first director. In 1866–67, the Sociedad Filarmónica Mexicana issued *La armonía,* one of the first musical journals in Mexico. The society counted among its members such important Mexican musicians as Aniceto Ortega, Tomás León, and Julio Ituarte; among its honorary members was Franz Liszt. A few years after its establishment, the conservatory was given quarters in the site of the old University of Mexico. The conservatory was officially named the Conservatorio Nacional in 1877 by President Díaz, and the parent body, the Sociedad Filarmónica, was dissolved. The Conservatorio Nacional de Música has trained generations of musicians, many of whom have made important contributions to musical life in Mexico and elsewhere. After changing sites a number of times from its early home in the Universidad de México, the conservatory currently is located in the new Centro Nacional de las Artes in the Colonia Country Club area of Mexico City, sharing the new center with the research units for music, dance, and theater of the Instituto Nacional de Bellas Artes and other schools for the performing arts.

The most prominent directors of the Conservatorio Nacional include some of the most influential leaders in Mexican musical life. In the nineteenth century, the conservatory was headed by such notables as Agustín Caballero (1866–77), Agustín Balderas (1877–82), and Alfredo Bablot (1882–92). In the twentieth century, Ricardo Castro (1907), Julian Carrillo (1913–14, 1920–23), Eduardo Gariel (1917–20), Carlos Chávez (1929–34), Silvestre Revueltas (1933), Manuel M. Ponce (1933–34), José Rolón (1938), Blas Galindo (1947–60), and Manuel Enríquez (1972–73) led the institution. In this century many of Mexico's most important composers served as its director: Castro, Carrillo, Chávez, Revueltas, Ponce, Rolón, Galindo, Enríquez.

Other important institutions devoted to the professional training of musicians include the Escuela Nacional de Música, founded in 1929 as part of the Universidad Nacional Autónoma de México (it is now located in Coyoacán); the Escuela Superior de Música in Mexico City; the conservatories, academies, music schools, and university music or arts departments in Mexico City (Universidad National Autónoma de México, or UNAM), Aguascalientes, Chihuahua, Durango, Guadalajara, Guanajuato, Hermosillo, León, Mérida, Monterrey, Morelia, Pachuca, Puebla, Querétaro, Saltillo, Toluca, and elsewhere. Although professional-level training in music is currently available in performance, composition, and conducting in Mexico, higher-level postgraduate study in academic areas of music (musicology, ethnomusicology, music analysis, music education) is still in development. Foreign and independently trained Mexican music scholars (and performers) slowly are creating the infrastructure for serious advanced academic musical study within existing Mexican institutions.

Keyboard Instruments and Music

The piano became the keyboard instrument of choice for the salon and home only toward the end of the viceroyalty; harpsichords and clavichords were used before that time. The keyboard music of Joseph Haydn, Wolfgang Amadeus Mozart, Muzio Clementi, and other classical-era composers was imported and sold to amateur and professional musicians. This music was played on pianos that were imported from Europe, and, from at least the 1790s, increasingly were made in Mexico. Piano manufacturers worked in Durango as early as 1793 and in Mexico City from at least 1796. However, the price for imported and domestic pianos was extremely high at the end of the colonial period. As the century progressed, Mexican instrument makers produced more pianos and at a cheaper price. The principal music dealers imported pianos of all price ranges from Europe and the United States. These advances in instrument manufacturing and distribution brought pianos within the reach of the middle class. By the time of the Porfiriato, the piano was nearly as common in middle- and upper-class homes as it was in Europe and the United States.

An avalanche of instrumental salon pieces, primarily for piano, inundated Mexican "polite" society in the capital and throughout the republic during the second half of the century. Operatic paraphrases, operatic potpourris, selections from Spanish and Mexican zarzuelas, and lyric songs with piano accompaniment in Spanish and Italian with Italianate melodies were performed frequently in private salons and public concerts halls throughout the nineteenth century and into the twentieth by resident and touring musicians. Original works and operatic paraphrases for the piano by Franz Liszt, Emile Prudent, Sigismond Thalberg, Henri Herz, and other European composer-pianists flooded the Mexican concert hall, along with works by local composers of art music such as Melesio Morales, Ernesto Elorduy, Julio Ituarte, Felipe Villanueva, Aniceto Ortega, Ricardo Castro, and, later, Manuel M. Ponce and other twentieth-century composers. Nineteenth-century popular salon composers such as Juventino Rosas (author of the world-famous waltz "Sobre las olas"), with less musical training than the aforementioned professional pianist-composers, supplied a seemingly endless list of works based on European dance forms (schottisches, polkas, mazurkas, waltzes, and marches) that reached a large number of amateur performers and a very receptive audience.

Although the compositions for piano performed in Mexico in the second half of the nineteenth century was of mixed artistic value—some were fine works and others trite—Mexican audiences were exposed to the best European works for this instrument. The first performance of Fryderyk Chopin's piano music in Mexico were given in 1854 (of his *Grande Polonaise brillante*, Op. 22) by visiting Dutch pianist Ernst Lübeck. Despite this early performance, Chopin's music was not heard regularly until the 1890s, when foreign pianists such as Eugen d'Albert and Alberto Jonás, and Mexican musicians such as Eduardo Gariel, Carlos J. Meneses, Gustavo Campa, Ricardo Castro, and Felipe Villanueva began to regularly champion Chopin's works in Mexico. These Mexican musicians performed Chopin's music despite the tirades launched against the Polish composer's music by Mexican composer and music critic Melesio Morales.

Like Chopin's music, Franz Liszt's piano works first were performed in Mexico by Ernst Lübeck in 1854. Interest in Liszt's music was recognized officially in 1865, when the Hungarian composer was made an honorary member of the newly founded Sociedad Filarmónica Mexicana. Turning his attention to Mexico, Liszt wrote a "Marche Funèbre En mémoire de Maximilien I, Empereur du Mexique" (Number Six in the set *Années de Pèlerinage, Third Year*) in memory of the death of Emperor Maximilian in 1867. In the 1880s and 1890s, the same foreign and Mexican pianists who championed Chopin's works played Lizst's piano pieces for Mexico City audiences. Internationally known virtuosos such as Ignace Paderewski, Josef Hoffman, and Teresa Carreño played Liszt's music to critical acclaim during their Mexican recitals.

While the piano was the instrument of the home, salon, and concert hall, the organ was the usual keyboard instrument in the church. As in earlier centuries, the need for organs in the performance of sacred music in the nineteenth century in cathedral, church, and convent (before the closure of conventual houses) created a market for these instruments. Before Independence and to a degree after 1821, Mexican organists performed Spanish and European organ music and composed their own works, few of which, unfortunately, still exist. As before 1800, pipe organs were manufactured locally throughout (and after) the nineteenth century. Very important examples from the colonial and early-Independent periods exist today throughout Mexico in many urban and rural areas. Marvelous examples of colonial organs are to be found in both the most logical and unlikely of places in Mexico, in sites as varied as the most obscure rural hamlet to the most famous cathedral. These organs form a significant and precious part of the artistic patrimony of Mexico. Many of these early organs have been restored through the efforts and sponsorship of federal, state, and local governmental authorities and individual Mexican and foreign organ restorers. A number of interesting recordings of these historic colonial Mexican organs recently have been released to an appreciative international market.

Military Music and Wind Bands

Governmental decrees, military reports and records, notices in *El Diario de México* and other early-nineteenth-century journals, and a few examples of manuscript and published music preserve information about the little-known aspect of military music in the late-colonial and early-Independent periods in Mexico. Trumpets, bugles, fifes, drums, and sometimes other wind instruments such as oboes, clarinets, bassoons, and horns were used in Mexico during and after the colonial period. Scattered documentary records (especially in the Archivo General de la Nación and the Biblioteca Nacional) preserve the names of hundreds of military musicians and point to the extensive use of instrumental music in military regiments throughout central Mexico and in presidios on the northern frontier in California, Arizona, Texas, and New Mexico. For example, a 1793 "Reglamento de Sueldos y Haberes" issued by Viceroy Revillagigedo details the instrumentation of some military bands and the annual salaries of military musicians: 1 drum major (156 pesos), 2 drummers of the grenadiers (120 pesos each), 2 first clarinetists (144 pesos each), 2 second clarinetists (120 pesos each), 2 first fifers (132 pesos each), and 2 second fifers (120 pesos each). Some military musicians performed in theater orchestras in addition to serving their military companies. Pablo Musín, musician of the Regiment of Spanish Dragoons, performed theater music in the Coliseo de México in the 1790s and perhaps later; he also sold musical instruments on the side.

Although significant unpublished documentation about military music exists, few musical scores for wind band or wind and percussion instruments from the turn of the century have been uncovered. However, two musical collections provide clues to this area of Mexican musical life. In 1825, Spanish-born Narciso Sort de Sans published in Mexico City his 10-page collection of trumpet calls, *Toques de Ordenanza con la Corneta Para el Ejercito de la Republica de los Estados Unidos Mexicanos* (copy in The Bancroft Library, University of California). Before Independence, Sort de Sans was a musician of the Regiment of Dragoons of the Queen, based in Guadalajara; after 1821 he was a musician at the imperial court of Agustín de Iturbide, and in 1825 he was the captain attached to the Fourth Permanent Battalion. He was expelled in the late 1820s for being a European-born Spaniard. Sort de Sans was also the author of a manuscript music theory tutor, the *Teoría de la música* (probably owned at one time by the waltz composer Juventino Rosas, now in the Saldívar collection in Mexico City).

Composer José Luis Rojas memorialized in music the tumultuous events surrounding Mexican Independence in his *Pieza histórica y militar para fortepiano* of 1822 (manuscript in Tulane University). Rojas describes in musical examples, and in the accompanying rubrics, the battles between the Spanish and Mexican forces during the Wars of Independence. Imitations of military signals appear in this interesting musical battle piece.

The expansion of military bands in the nineteenth century brought wind band music to many areas of Mexico. Wind bands became ubiquitous institutions in most towns and cities of any size throughout the Republic, and they were supported by local, state, and federal governments. They often provided the major and sometimes only form of large-scale musical entertainment for the general population (except for music for staged theatrical performances). The Mexican wind band repertory reflected European and local musical tastes, with a heavy emphasis on popular cultivated dance music and operatic paraphrases, excerpts, and overtures. Although wind music was often published by major publishers in the United States and Europe in the second half of the nineteenth century, Mexican publishers of sheet music only infrequently published wind band arrangements. Musical scores for military bands often were copied by hand or imported from abroad. The advanced musical ability of the later-nineteenth-century bands, such as the Banda de Zapadores led by Miguel Ríos Toledano and the Banda de Infantería, was noted throughout the republic. During the Porfiriato, the principal bands represented federal and state governments on tours throughout Mexico and abroad. Some bands appeared to great acclaim in the United States—especially at international exhibitions in New Orleans and Chicago—and in Europe. Some compositions for wind band by Mexican composers, such as Zacatecas-native Genaro Codina's still-performed *Marcha de Zacatecas*, achieved world-wide fame and came to be seen as representative of Mexican music during the Porfirian epoch.

An open-air concert given in the Alameda in Mexico City by the Banda del Estado Mayor, led by Nabor Vázquez on December 29, 1901 (advertised in *El Imparcial* on that date), gives an indication of the repertory performed by military bands toward the end of the Porfiriato. The works performed included European and Mexican works: March: *Congreso panamericana* (Abundio Martínez), March: *Campo Florido* (Smith), Waltz: *Declaración de amor* (F. Bonbion), *Concert Overture* (Jules Massenet), *Fantasia on Themes from "I Pagliacci"* (Ruggero Leoncavallo), *Divertimiento a la española* (Gabrielli), *Selections from "Tosca"* (Giacomo Puccini), *Vals poético* (Felipe Villanueva), Danzas: *Alma y Corazón* (Ernesto Elorduy).

Musical Imprints and the Dissemination of Musical Scores in Mexico

While music printing was undertaken in Mexico in the sixteenth century by foreign and local printers such as Juan Pablos, Pedro Ocharte, and Antonio Espinosa (thirteen chant collections were printed during the sixteenth century), few musical imprints were issued in Mexico after the sixteenth century and before the nineteenth. Some notable exceptions include the sumptuous *Missa Gothica seu mozarabica* printed in Puebla in 1770 by order of Archbishop Antonio de Lorenzana, and the *Juego Filarmónico* of the Marqués de San Cristóbal of 1794. This paucity of musical imprints was owing to a number of reasons: the cost of music engraving and printing, the regular dissemination of notated music in manuscript form, the regulation of printing and commerce by Spain of its American colonies, and the availability through Spanish intermediaries of printed music from Spain and Europe.

An estate inventory (currently at the Archivo General de la Nación) taken in 1801 of the stock of recently deceased Mexico City bookseller and printer José Fernández de Jaureguí reveals an extensive and impressive range of classical-era printed and manuscript musical scores available for sale in the capital at the turn of the century. More than 1,000 symphonies, along with sextets, string quartets and trios, mixed quartets, duets, sonatas, concertos, serenades, individual pieces for different instruments (especially guitar, cello, piano, flute, and violin), and vocal music selections, are listed in this important inventory. Works by major European composers such as Haydn, Mozart, Johann Wenzel Anton Stamitz, François-Joseph Gossec, Ignaz Joseph Pleyel, Karl Ditters von Dittersdorf, Jan Ladislav Dussek, Karl Friedrich Abel, Johann Christian Bach, Giovanni Battista Pergolesi, Luigi Bocherini, André-Ernest-Modeste Grétry, Giovanni Paisiello, Domenico Cimarosa, Clementi, and Lolli were in Fernández de Jaureguí's bookstore at the time of his death, along with compositions by a host of other minor European composers. The works of Haydn, Pleyel, and Stamitz dominate this list. A surprizing amount of music identified as *música "antigua"* (early music) was also available for sale in Mexico City, including works by Baroque composers such as Corelli, Vivaldi, Locatelli, Albinoni, and Tartini. Also for sale were manuscript copies of sacred and secular music by the peninsular Spaniard Blas de Laserna *(tonadillas)*, the Mexican José Manuel Aldana (a symphony, a concerto, 12 minuets, 12 *contradanzas*, and a duet), and Italian-born Mexico City chapel master and Coliseo violinist and musical director Ignacio de Jerusalem (a set of versos). Spanish and Mexican popular music genres such as *"sonecitos de la tierra," tiranas*, and *boleras* are also identified on this list. Interestingly, a number of instruments are also given on this inventory showing that booksellers sold all sorts of musical goods in Mexico before Independence (the list includes 111 violins, 6 flutes, 2 oboes, 4 horns, 1 German *clave horgano*, 1 small organ, 2 barrel organs, 2 *dulsainas biejas*, and a number of string instruments—2 *octavinos de bandolon*, 1 *bajo maqueado*, 2 *guitarrones de sedro blanco*, 4 *bandolones antiguos*, 1 *guitarron de sedro de la [H]abana*, and 3 *badolines biejos*). The recent discovery of this important document completely changes the notion previously held by some musicologists that classical-era

European music (especially from Austria and Germany) found little favor in Mexico. We now know that Mexican musicians and audiences (at least in the capital but probably elsewhere as well) were current with recent musical fashions and developments in the leading European musical centers such as Vienna, Berlin, Paris, London, and Madrid.

Publications Intended for Teaching Purposes

Because of the regular need for instruction in the performance of plainsong (Gregorian chant) of *canto figurado* ("figured song," or rhythmic versions of liturgical music for one, two, three, or four voices), a number of tutors, treatises, and instruction manuals were written and published in Mexico during and after the colonial period and up to the present century, or were imported from Spain and Europe. Since music printing hardly existed in Mexico in the eighteenth century, plainsong tutors were usually disseminated in manuscript form. Music type scarcely was found in Mexico even at the beginning of the nineteenth century, thus many of the early-nineteenth-century plainsong tutors first were issued with the musical notations written in ink by hand. One example is the anonymous *Compendio de las reglas esenciales del arte de canto llano* of 1822, published for use by the choirboys at Puebla Cathedral. Spanish tutors such as Roman Jimeno's *Método de canto llano y figurado* of 1868, or the *Arte de canto eclesiástico y cantoral* of 1861, for use by the Claretian order, were sold regularly in Mexico City during the second half of the nineteenth century by music dealers such as H. Nagel Sucesores and Murguia.

Music theory treatises intended to teach amateur musicians (especially women) the rules of musical composition, theory, and performance were published from the second third of the nineteenth century onward. Although many Spanish treatises—for example, violinist José Herrando's *Arte y puntual explicación del modo de tocar el violín* of 1756—had been imported in the eighteenth century and earlier, and manuscript tutors were written and collected by Mexicans or resident Spaniards before 1800, publication in Mexico of tutors written by local musicians only began in the nineteenth century. The most famous early published example is José Mariano Elízaga's *Elementos de la música* of 1823 (published by the government press, the Imprenta del Supremo Gobierno), but this text was preceded by Mariano López Elizalde's *Tratado de música y lecciones de clave* of 1821 (published in Guadalajara by Petra Maniares). Elízaga later published his *Principios de la armonía y de la melodía* (Mexico City: Imprenta del Aguila, 1835). These treatises were followed by a succession of music tutors, the most popular and long-lived being those by José Antonio Gómez and José Melchor Gomis Colomer. Gomis was a Spaniard resident in Paris—his *Método completo de canto* was still used in Mexico well into the twentieth century.

Art Music in the Twentieth Century

Like their North American counterparts in Canada and the United States, native Mexican composers struggled throughout the nineteenth century in their own country against the notion that all good art music was imported from or composed in Europe. Some resisted to a certain degree foreign influences and attempted to compose in a nationalistic musical style, based on Mexican folk music traditions and folk themes (for example, Aniceto Ortega's opera *Guatimotzín*). Others capitulated to the overpowering strength of Italian and French (and to a lesser extent, German) styles (Cenubio Paniagua's operas). During the Porfiriato, the Mexican government granted a number of subsidies to local composers so that they might study in Europe with established master teachers and composers. Paris especially was a mecca for Mexican composers such as Ricardo Castro and others, who, at the turn of the century, sought to imbue their music with the latest advances and fashions in European music.

In contrast to this general lack of regard for truly original and native developments in art music in Mexican concert halls and opera houses in the nineteenth century (although there were exceptions), Mexican composers in the early twentieth century benefited from the florescence in the arts in Mexico, especially after the convulsions of the Revolution had ceased. Musicians, and other artists, were the direct beneficiaries of a renewed interest in the arts shown by the Mexican government in the 1920s. Composers such as Manuel M. Ponce, José Rolón, Julián Carrillo, Silvestre Revueltas, and Carlos Chávez benefited alongside their artistic compatriots Diego Rivera, José Clemente Orozco, David Alfaro Siqueiros, and Rufino Tamayo from governmental and individual commissions and support and public presentations of their artistic creations. Mexican composers such as these purposely sought to weave elements of traditional Mexican music and culture into their own compositions and were intensely aware of the need to develop nationalistic musical styles that still could reflect an internationalist outlook. The work that Ponce, Revueltas, Carrillo, Rolón, and Chávez (and a host of others) undertook in creating and maintaining musical institutions (such as orchestras, concert series, formal music education,

and publication activities) in pre–World War II Mexico, and the international visibility they brought to Mexican music, made it possible for succeeding generations of Mexican composers to reap the rewards of increased interest in classical music in Mexico. The past several generations of Mexican composers have benefited greatly from the activities of these earlier pioneers. Their personal compositional styles vary greatly and reflect directly upon their training and personal inclination. They represent all current musical styles and compositional practices: traditional and more experimental uses of tonality; atonality; 12-tone writing and serialism; electronic and computer music developments; the use of jazz, folk, and popular music in a concert music context; the incorporation of improvisation into personal musical langauges; and a mixing of these and many other elements. In addition to Ponce, Rolón, Revueltas, Carrillo, and Chávez, some of the important Mexican composers of this century include Candelario Huízar, Eduardo Hernández Moncada, the Spanish-born Rodolfo Halffter, Blas Galindo, Miguel Bernal Jiménez, José Pablo Moncayo, Carlos Jiménez Mabarak, Manuel Enríquez, Mario Kuri Aldana, Manuel de Elías, Mario Lavista, Julio Estrada, Federico Ibarra, Daniel Catán, and Ana Lara, among a number of others.

In the twentieth century, Mexican conductors increasingly established national and international careers and visiblity A partial list of important musical directors of orchestras, opera companies, and chamber groups includes Carlos Chávez, Silvestre Revueltas, Julián Carrillo, José Pablo Moncayo, Eduardo Hernández Moncada, Luis Herrera de la Fuente, Eduardo Mata, Manuel Enríquez, Manuel de Elías, and Enrique Bátiz. Likewise, the number of Mexican orchestras grew significantly in the last 50 years of the twentieth century. Professional and conservatory orchestras were established and maintained with governmental and private support throughout Mexico; some of the older as well as the more recently established orchestras include Orquesta Sinfónica de México, Orquesta Sinfónica Nacional, the orchestra of the Universidad Nacional Autónoma de México, the groups at the Conservatorio Nacional de México and the Escuela Nacional de Música, and the orchestras in Guadalajara, Xalapa, Puebla, Morelia, Durango, Guanajuato, and Mexico State, among others.

Folk Song, Popular Music, and Dance and Music

A distinction can be made between styles of dance music popular in Mexico in the nineteenth century according to the location in which the dance actually was performed. Dances performed within an aristocratic and upper-class context were of mixed origin, including European importations and native Mexican dances. At and after the turn of the century, the popular dances included European imports such as the contradance (contradanza), waltz, rigodon, alemande, and minuet (often performed with sets of variations). In some instances, some individual dances were heard by the dancers first in a major key followed immediately by a version in the minor key. Spanish and Mexican dances, often with a theatrical origin, included the zapateado, tirana, jarabe, boleras, and polaca. At the end of the colonial period, certain dances attracted the ire of the Inquisition, especially the jarabe and waltz, which were opposed on moral grounds because of their alleged lasciviousness. Despite the efforts of the Holy Office to stamp out the waltz and jarabe, both achieved long-lasting public acceptance. The waltz was taken up by polite society and became one of the principal group social dances, while the jarabe became a representative national dance, especially among the rural working class.

While early jarabes apparently were written or arranged for and performed by guitar (or piano), the form was also adopted by regional folkloric string groups made up of guitars and violins. The jarabe served as an inspiration for early-, mid-, and late-nineteenth-century and twentieth-century composers and music compilers and arrangers. As Gabriel Saldívar has pointed out in his important monograph El jarabe: Baile popular mexicano (1937), the jarabe could be heard in a theatrical context at the Coliseo and elsewhere in Mexico at least since the early part of the nineteenth century. Spanish-born composer Manuel Corral's comic opera Los dos gemelos, o los tíos burlados included a "jarave." Later musicians such as José Antonio Gómez (Variaciones sobre el tema del jarave mexicano, 1841), Tomás León (Jarabe nacional), Julio Ituarte (Ecos de México: Aires nacionales, published before 1890), and Miguel Ríos Toledano (Colección de treinta jarabes, published after 1890), arranged various tunes (sones) from the jarabe complex (a suite of interlocking dance melodies) as piano solos, often for amateur musicians and sometimes for orchestra. The Biblioteca Nacional possesses three important manuscript collections of jarabes that demonstrate the widespread dissemination of this dance: Aires populares, collected by Gergorio Bernal, Colección de jarabes, sones y cantos populares, collected in Jalisco by Aguirre, and Aires musicales del Estado de Jalisco. In the twentieth century the jarabe from Jalisco (the jarabe tapatío) was adopted as a principal representative of Mexican

musical folklore during the nationalist movement in the arts in the 1910s, 1920s, and 1930s.

Folk music from other regions in Mexico also was collected in the nineteenth and twentieth centuries by local musicians. One example of this sort of regional collecting effort is the Miscelanea yucateca: Folklore Maya (now at Tulane University), an interesting collection of folk music from the state of Yucatán, notated and arranged for piano in 1870 by J. Jacinto Cuevas. A notable twentieth-century study and large collection of regional popular and folk music is Francisco J. Santamaria's Antología folklórica y musical de Tabasco of 1952 (with musical arrangements and analysis by Gerónimo Baqueiro Foster).

Small-, medium-, and large-sized songbooks or cancioneros, and single ballad sheets with printed corridos (narrative songs dealing with recent political and historical events) and canciones (lyric songs, often amatory in nature), usually containing only folk and popular song texts and not the corresponding melodies (song tunes were included only sporadically in these ephemeral publications), have been published throughout Mexico and the southwestern United States (especially in Los Angeles and San Antonio) since the nineteenth century. Containing examples of all popular and traditional music forms known at the time in Mexico, these publications often included lithographic and woodblock illustrations designed to attract the attention of the public. These song sheets or song collections usually were accompanied by vivid and often satirical pictorial illustrations designed to illustrate the story of the songs and to aid sales. Illustrators such as José Guadalupe Posada, working for publisher Vanegas Arroyo, illustrated corridos and décimas such as El mosquito americano, Versos de Valentín Mancera, Legítimos versos de Lino Zamora, and El Corrido de los 41. As popular literature, most of these ephermal publications were intended for a quick sale and were related to events of the day. The popularity of well-known songs such as the "Himno Nacional Mexicano" (music by Jaime Nunó), "La golondrina" (music by Narciso Serradell, text by Niceto Zamacois), "La paloma" (music by Sebastián Yradier), and "Perjura" (Miguel Lerdo de Tejada); and corridos such as "La adelita," "La rielera," and others was reinforced by the constant appearance of these song texts in many of these cancioneros.

Twentieth-century Mexican popular songwriters and composers (for example, Agustín Lara, María Grever, José Alfredo Jiménez, and "Tato Nacho") often worked in and on both sides of the divide between the popular or commercial music and folk music traditions. In the nineteenth century, popular composers sought to write romantic songs and dance music modeled on the melodic style of mid-nineteenth-century Italian opera and the European dance forms; at the same time, they alternately adopted a musical style more closely associated with traditional regional folk music styles (often based on the concept of the *son,* or short dance tune). Thus the "polite" music of the Italianate *romanzas* or *canciones* and the European dance forms of the polka, schottische, waltz, lancers, and other popular social dances alternated with local folkloristic genres. These folk music styles were heard in their original forms in rural areas and in arranged or modified versions in urban areas (as in the *jarabe* arrangements mentioned above). As in much of Latin America, popular music in Mexico has been and still is today a mix of all sorts of styles and shows all kinds of influences: mestizo and indigenous folk music traditions, Caribbean and Latin American dance rhythms and forms (habanera, *danzón,* rumba, cha-cha, samba, mambo, *bambuco, cumbia,* merengue, salsa), other dances (bolero, foxtrot, beguine, two-step), Spanish and Mexican musical theater, German marches and Spanish *pasodobles,* Italianate melodies, the use of regional instruments (*guitarrón* and *vihuela* in mariachi music, for example), and distinctly Mexican repertories such as the *corrido, huapango, música ranchera,* and *música norteña.* More recently, the cultural and musical mix has broadened as the influence of African American music styles has been noticed in the Mexican popular music scene. Jazz, blues, rock, and rap have made an impact in Mexico and have influenced local songwriters, popular musicians, and recording artists, record companies, and audiences.

Sacred Art Music

While most published studies of Mexican religious art music have focused on the period up to the mid–eighteenth century, there now exists sufficient documentation to permit a summary of sacred music life at the turn of the century and later. An important letter written in 1785 reveals the continuing importance of sacred music in Mexico toward the end of colonial rule. Exiled Mexican Jesuit Antonio López de Priego, then residing in Bologna, wrote to his sister in 1785, a nun in the Convento de Santa Catarina in Puebla, verifying the high state of sacred music in Mexico in general and in Puebla in particular. As López de Priego pointed out, sacred music in Mexico compared favorably with the Italian and European music scenes.

The Vespers celebrated here [in Bologna] are justly famous, but the first that I heard made me think that I was in a bullring, because everyone kept shouting in a loud voice: bravo! bravo! (which is the Italian for our viva! viva!). Their number of voices and instruments here is large, their compositions very good and exquisite, but not more choice than we have there [in Puebla]. The difference is that what they did here in [17]50 we did there in [17]55, while awaiting copies from Europe. What they perform here with 300 violins we do in Mexico with 10. But we have seen nothing here to rival the organs there in [Mexican] cathedrals, and usually also in other churches as well. . . . So that in overall comparison, we do not come out so far behind.

Until Independence, church authorities continued to maintain extensive, excellent, and well-financed musical establishments (choirs, orchestras, and choir schools). The shifting political winds after 1821 made it increasingly difficult for sacred music to flourish in the same way as before. Cathedral choirs and orchestras gradually evolved after 1821 and up to the middle of the nineteenth century; they sometimes changed from fully staffed resident professional ensembles to freelance groups, and, with the exception of performances on major feast days, were often smaller in size.

Since sacred music in Mexico City, Puebla, and Oaxaca cathedrals has been studied extensively, information about musical life in Durango—a city distant from activities in the heavily populated areas in the center of New Spain—is profiled here in order to illustrate the dissemination of religous music throughout Mexico. At the end of the eighteenth century, chapel master and organist José Mariano Placeres y Nebeda, also an organ builder, repaired the principal organ of the cathedral and left a treatise describing the workings of the Durango organs along with 26 ink drawings of the same. Durango Cathedral's *capilla* (loosely, the chapel's musical establishment) in 1802 was made up of the chapel master (also called on to sing soprano or alto voice parts), an archivist, four violinists, one trumpeter, one bass, two flutes, and three singers. The budget for this musical establishment in that year was 2,215 pesos. In 1820, 13 instrumentalists were employed along with nine singers, the chapel master (who also served as organist), an instrument tuner and repairman, and a librarian. The budget allocation for music in that year had grown to 6,256 pesos. However, Durango's musical *capilla* fell into bad times after Independence owing to lack of funds. Some of the local composers and musicians active in Durango Cathedral starting around 1800 and later include several members of the Meraz family: Durango-native Juan José Meraz, an organist and composer active around 1799 and after, and his sons Juan Nepomuceno *(colegial de beca)* and Atenógenes *(librero de coro)*, who were singers in Durango Cathedral in 1837. Although the Durango Cathedral archive contains musical scores mainly from the eighteenth century by such luminaries as Ignacio de Jerusalem and Manuel de Sumaya, it also retains some nineteenth-century scores.

After 1821, church music, albeit strongly influenced by Italian opera, continued to act as a strong draw for urban audiences, especially on festival occasions. Foreign visitors to Mexico such as Fanny Calderon de la Barca often remarked on the strong appeal and excellence of the music performed in Mexico City Cathedral, various parish churches, and in the many female conventual houses in the capital on major feast days. Huge crowds, sometimes more interested in displays of musical virtuosity than in the actual church service, were attracted to religious observances in these venues. A wide range of music was heard after Independence and before about 1850 on important occasions in Mexico City Cathedral and elsewhere: keyboard works by Beethoven, Henri Herz, Franz Hünten, and others; dance music by Mariano Faliero (a collection of his *cuadrillas* is in the Mexico City Cathedral Archive); European orchestral, vocal, and choral music; arrangements of opera excerpts (with religious texts); and music composed by local Mexican composers such as Luis Baca *(Ave María)*, Cenobio Paniagua (his responsory *Quae est ista* is in the Mexico City Cathedral Archive and his *Mass in C major* is in the Puebla Cathedral Archive), José Ignacio Trujeque *(Ecce quam bonum)*, José María Bustamante (a set of his *versos* is in the the Puebla Cathedral Archive); José María Carrasco (several of his sacred works are in the Puebla Cathedral Archive), and José Antonio Gómez (*Por la llaga que sangrienta en el pie* for Holy Week).

After the appropriation of church properties and the regulation of religious life by the Mexican government during the second half of the nineteenth century, sacred musical life in Mexico fell into decay and decline, a situation never subsequently remedied to any great extent. Nevertheless, during the Porfiriato (the era of Porfirio Díaz, roughly 1876–1910), some Mexican bishops and church musicians attempted to reform and invigorate religious music. Schools of sacred music were established in Querétaro (1892), Morelia (1921), and in other Mexican dioceses. Music instruction in these schools usually centered around the music reforms outlined in the 1903 papal encyclical *Motu Proprio* of Pius X. The importance of plainsong in the liturgy was stressed and the influence of Italiante melodies decreased. However, the activities of these sacred music schools and religious life in general in Mexico were disrupted seriously during the Revolution The anticlericalism of the 1920s further inhibited the cultivation of religious music. This situation gradually changed for the better, such that the school in Morelia achieved important success in the late 1930s under the influence of composer, educator, music historian, and organist Miguel Bernal Jiménez, also the editor of the important journal *Schola Contorum* issued by the school in Morelia for several yeras.

However, despite the many efforts in the twentieth century of ecclesiastical authorities and important figures in Mexico's musical life such as Bernal Jiménez to improve Catholic sacred music, the high quality of music composed and performed in Mexico during the colonial period and the early years of the republic was not recaptured. The religious art music commonly performed in Mexican churches today in most cases pales in comparison with the music of Mexico's celebrated colonial past.

Sacred Folk Music Traditions

The various religious folk music traditions known throughout the republic of Mexico among mestizo and indigenous peoples and in the Spanish-speaking Catholic community in the southwestern United States are of strong musical and religious importance and interest. The quasi-recitational melismatic (several-or-many-note-per-syllable) spiritual songs currently called *alabados* in Hispanic New Mexico are especially sung during Holy Week by members of the fraternal religious paraliturgical (and charitable) groups popularly known as *penitentes* in New Mexico. This New Mexican brotherhood bears a strong resemblance to present-day Mexican parish and local religious organizations and the many *cofradías* (lay brotherhoods) of an earlier period (and are representative of many social classes, occupations, and races). These Mexican *cofradías* can be traced to the sixteenth century. The place of music in the New Mexican groups is similar to that of their Mexican counterparts. Syllabically set hymns and spiritual songs were also sung during Holy Week, during patronal festivals, and throughout the ecclesiastical year within and outside church services, as they still are. Unlike in Hispanic New Mexico, in Mexico and elsewhere in the U.S. southwest (Texas, California, Arizona, southern Colorado), no clear division between these several types of melismatic and syllabic vernacular religious praise songs seems to be made (*alabado* and *alabanza* both derive from the verb *alabar*, "to praise"). These commonplace sacred folk songs are most frequently syllabic in nature, and usually possess melodies typically eight or 16 measures in length. The melodies of these religious songs are frequently sung by high and low voices in parallel thirds or sixths. Harmonic accompaniment, whether provided by guitar, accordion, violin, or, as is currently often the practice, mariachi, is often correspondingly simple. During religious observances, congregational singing alternates with soloists or small groups of singers. The influence of Mexican popular musical styles on this type of vernacular religious song long has been felt.

While these Spanish-language spiritual songs alternated with liturgical music sung in Latin (monophonic chant and polyphonic music—multi-voiced music) in parish church services and monastic and cathedral foundations in Mexico, the official recognition and complete acceptance of vernacular languages into the mass and other Catholic services came only with the Vatican II Council (1962–65). As a result of these Vatican II reforms, the singing of plainsong in Latin in Mexico became less frequent in the 1960s and was supplanted by new Spanish-language settings of the Mass Ordinary and Proper. Local indigenous languages have been incorporated into Catholic religious services, and hymns often are sung in Indian languages in rural communities throughout Mexico.

Among a number of Mexican Catholic hymn books (more properly called collections of nonliturgical devotional spiritual songs) known in the U.S. southwest and in Mexico can be counted the compilation by P. Arzos, *Colección de Cantos Sagrados; Cánticos mexicanos,* compiled by Theodore Labouré, for use in the Oblate missions in Texas; and *Cánticos espirituales* (10 text and three music editions, 1888–1956), originally compiled by Jean Baptiste Ralliere, the French pastor of the village of Tomé, New Mexico. Not often considered worthy of preservation, these earlier Spanish-language hymn books published in Mexico and the U.S. southwest largely have disappeared, making study of this area problematic. Hymns and spiritual songs in honor of the Catholic saints particularly esteemed in Mexico and the U.S. southwest (San José, San Antonio, among many others) are included in these collections, as are *cánticos* (religious songs) in honor of Jesus and Mary in their many guises (Santo Niño de Atocha, la Guadalupana), as well as songs from the Christmas shepherd's plays *Los pastores* (also known as "La pastorela").

Protestant groups increasingly have made converts in many areas of predominantly Catholic Mexico and the U.S. southwest. These include both conservative fundamentalist (especially Evangelical) and other Protestant groups (Methodists, Baptists, Presbyterians, Mennonites, Episcopalians), as well as an increasing number of Mormons. They have brought new singing styles and musical traditions to urban working-class and rural Mexicans. New hymns have been composed for these Spanish-language services, and others have been adapted or adopted from traditional Anglo-American Protestant hymnals. Current popular music styles in white and African-American gospel music, contemporary English-language North American Christian music, and Mexican popular music (especially mariachi music and related forms) have influenced the growing number of Mexican and Mexican-American (and Central American) Protestant congregations north and south of the U.S.-Mexican border. This new evangelization/conversion process has created musical and religious tension and competition with Roman Catholicism, the dominant religious group (still the most politically and socially influential Christian group).

Mexican Music Research

Since the time of the Porfiriato, Mexican investigators have collected and studied a significant body of Mexican folk and popular music. Likewise, Mexican researchers also have investigated national art music styles. Among the earlier generation the most important contributions were made by Alba Herrera y Ogazón, Miguel Galindo, Rubén M. Campos, Vicente T. Mendoza, Gabriel Saldívar, Gerónimo Baqueiro Foster, Otto Mayer-Serra, and Jesús Romero. The individual who has made the greatest and farthest-reaching contribution to the understanding of Mexico's musical history during and since the colonial period is U.S. musicologist Robert Stevenson. With the advent of serious and institutionalized musicological and ethnomusicolgical study in Mexico, Mexican investigators have built upon earlier scholarship and have expanded the scholarly study of traditional, popular, and art music in Mexico.

The destruction visited upon Mexico over the past centuries through war, revolution, foreign intervention, neglect, theft, the ravages of time, and other calamities has hit hard at Mexico's vital musical patrimony. Nevertheless, much documentation remains from Mexico's important musical past. Significant historical collections of manuscript and printed music, and musical documentation of all kinds, can be found dispersed throughout the republic. The cathedral archives in Mexico City, Puebla, Morelia,

Oaxaca, Durango, Guadalajara, and elsewhere, and in collegiate and parish churches (especially the Colegiata de Guadalupe), the holdings of the Archivo General de la Nación (AGN), Biblioteca Nacional (BN), the libraries of the Conservatorio Nacional de Música, Escuela Nacional de Música of UNAM, Conservatorio de las Rosas, Museo Nacional de Antropolgía e Historia (MNAH), and the Centro Nacional de Investigación, Documentación e Información "Carlos Chávez" (CENIDIM) all possess important materials that document the importance of music to daily life in Mexico since the sixteenth century.

Important collections of all varieties of Mexican secular and sacred folk and popular song and dance music collected in Mexico and the U.S. southwest, in the form of wax cylinders, reel-to-reel and cassette tape and wire recordings, shellac, acetate and vinyl discs (7-, 10-, 12-, and 16-inch), and now compact discs and digital audio tape, as well as printed and manuscript textual and musical sources exist throughout Mexico and the United States. The most significant collections include those in Mexico City, at the MNAH, BN (Vicente T. Mendoza Collection), CENIDIM, and the AGN (bawdy or irreligious folk song texts condemned by the Inquisition). Local state governments such as those in Michocán, Veracruz, Jalisco, Tlaxcala, Sonora, and Puebla have sponsored field investigations of traditional music and collecting and recording efforts as well as granting subventions for publication. CENIDIM in Mexico City, with its large number of staff investigators, consistently has maintained the most productive and extensive publication schedule of scholarly musical editions and studies of Mexican music. CENIDIM also has issued luxurious reprints of the principal Mexican music journals of the past *(La armonia, Nuestra música, Música—Revista Mexicana, Revista Musical de México, Cultura Musical,* and *Gaceta Musical).* The contemporary journals *Heterofonía* and *Pauta* for some years have included important studies of Mexican music in all of it various facets. Ediciones Mexicanas de Música, founded by Rodolfo Halffter and others, long has been the principal Mexican publisher of Mexican art music and has issued an impressive number of important works by major composers.

North Americans have also made significant contributions in collecting and studying Mexican and Mexican American folk and popular music. Individuals who have collected, preserved, and published a very large amount of significant Mexican music since the late nineteenth century include Charles Fletcher Lummis, Eleanor Hague, Aurelio Espinosa, John Lomax, Luisa Espinel, Rubén Cobos, John Donald Robb, Jack Loeffler (all active in the U.S. southwest), and Frances Toor, Henrietta Yurchenco, and E. Thomas Stanford (active in Mexico). Especially large and important collections of Mexican folk materials are in the United States at the Library of Congress (American Folklife Center); Indiana University (Archive of Traditional Music); Southwest Museum, Los Angeles (Lummis Collection); University of Texas, Austin (Benson Latin American Library and Barker Texas History Center); University of New Mexico, Albuquerque (J. D. Robb Archive of Southwest Music); Stanford University (Archive of Recorded Sound); Colorado College; and the University of California, Berkeley (Music Library and the Bancroft Library).

Select Bibliography

Koegel, John, "Calendar of Southern California Amusements (1852–1897): Designed for the Spanish-Speaking Public." *Inter-American Music Review* 13:2 (Spring–Summer 1993).
_____, "Mexican and Mexican-American Musical Life in Southern California, 1850–1900." *Inter-American Music Review* 13:2 (Spring–Summer 1993).
Robb, John Donald, *Hispanic Folk Music of New Mexico and the Southwest: A Self-Portrait of a People.* Norman: University of Oklahoma Press, 1980.
Stevenson, Robert, *Music in Mexico.* New York, Thomas Y. Crowell, 1952.

—JOHN KOEGEL

N

NAFTA

See North American Free Trade Agreement (NAFTA)

Nahua Rulers, Pre-Hispanic

Numerous Nahuatl-speaking communities (as well as those populated by other linguistic groups) existed throughout Mesoamerica during the late pre-Hispanic period, and they were governed by a host of different rulers from local lineages. In the widespread communities of central Mexico the structure of rulership, succession practices, and the exercise of power and privilege were not uniform but showed a certain amount of variation. Although in many ways atypical, or at least not universally applicable to other centers, the most documentation on pre-Hispanic Nahua rulership is available for the leading polities in the Basin of Mexico. The most prominent of these were the neighboring Mexica cities located on the western side of Lake Texcoco: Tenochtitlan (the "Aztec" capital and the site of modern Mexico City), and Tlatelolco, site of the city's great marketplace, as well as the Acolhua capital of Tetzcohco (Texcoco) near the eastern edge of the lake. In many ways these cities tended to dominate events not only in their immediate environs but in those towns that came under their sway.

Research on Nahua rulers has traditionally tended to focus on these major centers of power, especially Tenochtitlan, which steadily increased its sphere of influence throughout Mesoamerica from the time of its founding in the early fourteenth century to its final downfall nearly two centuries later. In recent years, however, a more complex picture of Nahua rulership slowly has begun to be pieced together through ongoing field work and archival investiga-

tions directed not only at these renowned power centers but also at local communities, both within the Basin of Mexico and beyond, and to the relationships that existed among them. Also noteworthy are the increasing number of collaborative efforts among specialists trained in different disciplines (archaeology, anthropology, ethnohistory, art history, religious studies, and linguistics, among others), from the colonial as well as pre-Hispanic periods. Their shared efforts are also contributing to a more complete understanding of late pre-Hispanic central Mexico, its rulers, and its people.

The chief ruler of a community or *altepetl* ("water-hill"; town, city, or province) was called a *tlatoani* or "speaker" (pl. *tlatoque*). As head of his city's highly stratified political, military, and priestly hierarchies, the *huey tlatoani* (great speaker) of Tenochtitlan wielded immense power. He controlled tribute, lands, labor, property, and materials inaccessible to others, even members of the royal family, and he held other aristocratic privileges common to the nobility, such as having multiple wives.

The *tlatoani*'s duties were correspondingly weighty. He was responsible for governing the city by overseeing its maintenance and ensuring its economic prosperity. To this end, he undertook such essential civic construction projects as building causeways and canals to provide efficient transportation and aqueducts to ensure fresh water supplies for the population. Aside from collecting and distributing the raw materials and finished products that flowed into the city from periodic tribute levied on conquered territories, he also sustained local and long-distance trade to procure other goods. He also undertook periodic expansions of religious structures such as the Templo Mayor (Main Temple), the city's ritual center.

Highly trained artisans, particularly featherworkers and creators of luxury goods using precious materials such as gold and jade, were at the *tlatoani*'s disposal. Unlike the Maya, the Mexica left surprisingly few overtly historical sculptural artworks commemorating individual rulers. Yet, like the Maya, Nahua rulers utilized visual means to express the aspirations and accomplishments of their reigns, and it seems likely that many of the monumental or highly crafted artworks that have survived—to say nothing of the vast numbers that have perished—were created in connection with *tlatoque* and their manifold concerns.

The *tlatoani* was also the chief commander of the military forces, personally leading his troops into battle to consolidate or expand the Mexica tribute empire. In fact, the newly chosen ruler's first official campaign took place soon after his election. A victorious initial foray not only obtained captives to be publicly sacrificed during his coronation ceremony but also presaged a successful rule by demonstrating his ability to wage war and command tribute from conquered areas. Two of the greatest surviving Mexica historical monuments, the closely related *Stone of Moteuczoma* (Archbishop's Stone) and *Stone of Tizoc,* proclaim in carved relief the victories of these fifteenth-century Tenochca rulers over other cities.

The *tlatoani* also performed priestly functions, such as shedding his own blood in honor of the gods, presiding over sacrificial rituals at major dedicatory ceremonies, and participating in several of the public *veintena* rituals of the solar year. The *Dedication Stone,* for example, which marks the inauguration of the newly renovated Main Temple in 1487, displays the rulers Tizoc and Ahuitzotl dressed in priestly garb and drawing from their bodies sacrificial blood that feeds the stylized image of the voracious Earth Lord, Tlaltecuhtli, below their feet.

Although Tenochtitlan's series of rulers is described as a dynasty, the throne did not pass automatically from father to son. Other qualifications, such as proficiency in battle, were also critical considerations. While candidates were selected from among the members of the royal family, the actual decision was made, or at least affirmed, by a council of elders. A son might well succeed his father, but in other cases a brother, nephew, or other close family member could be chosen.

As among other elites, there was a great deal of intermarriage both among Tenochtitlan's nobility and with the leading families of other Basin of Mexico centers. Tenochca rulers were especially skilled at using marriage as an effective political tool, and part of their success as rulers was based on carefully arranged marriages that reinforced political and military alliances.

Pre-Hispanic Tenochca Rulers

Even before the dynasty of Tenochtitlan was established officially in the late fourteenth century, documents record the presence of leaders whose names became part of the early historical record. The first to be mentioned is the legendary (possibly historical) leader Huitzilopochtli, who led the departure from the island city of Aztlan ("Place of the Cranes" or "Place of Whiteness") and inaugurated the migratory trek that terminated in the Basin of Mexico settlement. At the time, this migratory group, only one of several to set out, was known as the "Azteca," or inhabitants of Aztlan, which they regarded as their ancestral homeland; the name "Mexica" was adopted later while on the migration route.

Among other "founding fathers" at the time of the establishment of Tenochtitlan about 1325, the preeminent leader seems to have been Tenoch, whose personal name was incorporated into the name of the new settlement itself (Tenochtitlan, "Next to the Stone Prickly Pear Cactus Fruit"). Meanwhile, a dissident group of Mexica separated from the main body and settled in a location slightly to the north of Tenochtitlan. Calling their new home Tlatelolco (Place of the Spherical Earth Mound), the Tlatelolca were to become Tenochtitlan's persistent rivals in the Basin of Mexico.

Tenochtitlan's dynasty was established officially with the selection of Acamapichtli (Handful of Reeds), who ruled from about 1376 to 1396. Of mixed Mexica-Colhua ancestry, this young prince apparently was chosen, among other reasons, because of his link to the city of Culhuacan, which claimed to carry on the political legacy of the legendary city of Tollan (Tula) after its collapse. This heritage was the basis of Mexica claims to Toltec descent and legitimate political rule in the Basin of Mexico, where other more well established groups existed; they even began to refer to themselves as Colhua Mexica. During this time, however, the Mexica were not a completely independent people but were tributaries of the Tepanec city-state of Azcapotzalco (Place of the Ant Hill), the dominant polity in the Basin of Mexico under its powerful, shrewd and long-lived ruler Tezozomoc. Meanwhile, forging even closer ties to Azcapotzalco, Tlatelolco chose as its first ruler a son of Tezozomoc, the Tepanec prince Cuacuapitzahuac (Slender Horn) who ruled from 1376 to 1418.

Under Tenochtitlan's second *tlatoani,* Huitzilihhuitl (Hummingbird Feather), Acamapichtli's son who ruled from 1397 to 1417, the Tenochca along with the Tlatelolca continued to pay tribute, including requisite military service, to their Tepanec overlords. Many of the conquests later claimed by the Mexica during this period were actually carried out under Tepanec command. Huitzilihhuitl's marriage to a granddaughter of Tezozomoc illustrates the close relationship that existed between these two Basin polities, one emergent and the other at its political peak.

The rule of the next Tenochca leader, Huitzilihhuitl's son Chimalpopoca (Smoking Shield), who ruled from 1417 to 1427/28, was cut short by the turmoil that erupted upon the death of the aged Tezozomoc about 1426. Tezozomoc's son Maxtla, ruler of the Tepanec center of Coyohuacan ("Place of the Coyotes"; present-day Coyoacán), rashly seized power from the legitimate successor, leading to the outbreak of war between Azcapotzalco and insurgent Basin of Mexico cities. Chimalpopoca perished under mysterious circumstances, as did the ruler of Tlatelolco, Tlacateotl (Divine Lord), who had succeeded his father Cuacuapitzahuac. The heir to Texcoco's throne, the young Acolhua prince Nezahualcoyotl (Fasting Coyote), fled his city after witnessing Maxtla's assassination of his father Ixtlilxochitl.

Inheriting a chaotic situation along with the throne, Tenochtitlan's fourth *tlatoani* Itzcoatl (Obsidian Serpent) led a coalition of Basin cities that defeated the upstart Maxtla and overthrew the yoke of Azcapotzalco. Following the Tepanec War, a coalition formed by Itzcoatl, his grandnephew Nezahualcoyotl, now restored to the throne of Texcoco, and Totoquihuaztli, the dissident Tepanec ruler of Tlacopan ("Place of the *Tlacotl* Plant"; present-day Tacuba), established the Triple Alliance. They proceeded to realign political and military power in the Basin of Mexico and to inaugurate a complex system of tribute distribution from the Tepanec areas brought under their control. Initiating new military campaigns, they further subdued the rich agricultural cities of the Chinampa Zone in the southern area of Lake Texcoco, pushing even further south into Cuauhnahuac (present-day Cuernavaca). Another major participant in these operations was the ruler of Tlatelolco, Cuauhtlahtoa (Speaking Eagle), a grandson of Tlacateotl who ruled from 1428 to 1467. Based on a cryptic passage in the missionary Bernardino de Sahagún's *Florentine Codex* (Book 10), Itzcoatl often is cited for his "rewriting" of Mexica history, which probably only indicates that after their period of subordination to Azcapotzalco, the Tenochca set about to establish an independent identity and to define their own destiny. This able son of Acamapichtli and half brother of Huitzilihhuitl (and uncle of Chimalpopoca) ruled from 1428 to 1440.

The fifth *tlatoani* of Tenochtitlan, Moteuczoma Ilhuicamina (Angry Lord, Archer of the Skies), who ruled from 1440 to 1469, was arguably the greatest of the Tenochca political leaders and military commanders. Son of Huitzilihhuitl, half brother of Chimalpopoca, and nephew of Itzcoatl, he proceeded to extend Tenochtitlan's political compass far beyond the Basin of Mexico, south into the present-day areas of Morelos and Guerrero, east to the Gulf Coast, and southeast into Mixtec territory in the present-day state of Oaxaca. Domestically, Moteuczoma I's long and otherwise successful reign was marred by the catastrophic droughts and famines of the early 1450s. Like his uncle Itzcoatl, Moteuczoma took an active hand in attempting to construct Mexica history, for according to the missionary Diego Durán he is said to have sent out an expedition in search of Aztlan, an account filled with fantastic elements, however. Moteuczoma's prestige was such that Mexica histories began to mythologize episodes in his life, including another fantastic tale about his miraculous conception by a precious greenstone shot by his father Huitzilihhuitl and swallowed by his future mother, a princess of Cuauhnahuac. His associations with Cuauhnahuac and the nearby royal gardens at Huaxtepec (present-day Oaxtepec) suggest that Moteuczoma may have commissioned the carving of an enormous shield of the war and fertility god Xipe Totec, dated to 1469, on a boulder originally located in a barranca outside the city.

Axayacatl (Water Face), grandson of both Moteuczoma Ilhuicamina and Itzcoatl, continued their string of military triumphs during his rule from 1469 to 1481. Aside from his victories over areas in the Toluca and Puebla Valleys and the Gulf Coast, during a civil war with Tlatelolco, Axayacatl decisively vanquished Moquihuix (Drunken One?), who had ruled his city since the death of Cuauhtlahtoa. Having lost its autonomy, Tlatelolco henceforth had its governors appointed by Tenochca *tlatoque*. Axayacatl's string of military successes was marred by his disastrous campaign against the Tarascans of Michoacán, one of Tenochtitlan's bitterest defeats. Also during his reign Nezahualpilli (Fasting Prince) replaced his illustrious father Nezahualcoyotl as ruler of Texcoco, and Chimalpopoca acceded to Tlacopan's throne after the death of his father Totoquihuaztli.

Tenochtitlan's ascendancy stalled under another grandson of Moteuczoma Ilhuicamina and brother of Axayacatl, Tizoc (The Bled One), who ruled from 1481 to 1486. The records on the *Tizoc Stone* to the contrary, during his short and ineffectual reign Tizoc added little to the expansion of the tribute empire, although he did begin a major renovation of the Main Temple.

Ahuitzotl (Water Animal), yet another grandson of Moteuczoma Ilhuicamina and brother of Axayacatl and Tizoc, reversed the military and political fortunes of his sibling. During his reign from 1486 to 1502, he launched a series of impressive military conquests in the Gulf Coast area and the present-day states of Guerrero, Oaxaca, and Chiapas, reaching as far south as the border of present-day Guatemala. An active builder as well, he presided over the dedication of the Main Temple of Tenochtitlan, marked by his relief image (with Tizoc) on the *Dedication Stone* of 1487, and constructed two temples: one in 1502 atop a hill overlooking Tepoztlan dedicated to the *octli* (pulque) deities and commemorated by a plaque with his name sign (the mythical *ahuitzotl*) and the other a rock-cut structure dedicated to the solar cult of warriors carved out of the rugged hillside of Malinalco. Unfortunately, an ambitious project to construct an aqueduct from springs near Coyohuacan ended calamitously, with flood waters inundating Tenochtitlan in 1499. Ahuitzotl also commissioned outstanding examples of monumental art, including the (misnamed) *Stone of Acuecuexatl* of 1499, a possible remnant from a temple to the wind god Quetzalcoatl that depicts Ahuitzotl twice in relief, and the cliff carving of the Toltec ruler Topiltzin Quetzalcoatl on a hillside outside the ancient city of Tollan (Tula), also in 1499. Both monuments probably signal Ahuitzotl's attempt, like his royal forbears, to establish links to the Toltec past.

Moteuczoma Xocoyotzin (Angry Lord the Younger; Moteuczoma II), the son of Axayacatl and great-grandson of Moteuczoma Ilhuicamina who ruled from 1502 to 1520, continued along the same energetic military course as his royal ancestors. With successful forays into the areas of the present-day states of Puebla, Guerrero, Veracruz, and Oaxaca, this ninth *tlatoani* proved to be a capable battlefield commander. By the end of his reign, the cumulative conquests of Tenochca rulers stretched over a huge swath of Mesoamerica, from the Pacific Ocean to the Gulf Coast, from the Tarascan frontier in the north to the Isthmus of Tehuantepec in the south, with the exceptions of Tlaxcallan (Tlaxcala), Metztitlan, Yopitzinco on the coast of present-day Guerrero, and the province of Tototepec in the coastal region of present-day Oaxaca. Like his immediate predecessor, Moteuczoma II commissioned several exceptional monuments, including the multisided *Temple Stone (Teocalli)* that commemorates the New Fire Ceremony of 1507; his life-size image, possibly in 1519, on a rocky cliff in Chapultepec, where a series of carved representations of Tenochca rulers were once visible; and the great *Sun Stone* (Calendar Stone), the most famous of all Mexica artworks. Moteuczoma, nevertheless, undoubtedly will continue to be better remembered as the hapless ruler whose vacillating behavior led to his capture, the unopposed occupation of Tenochtitlan, and the eventual downfall of the Mexica at the hands of invading Spanish forces under Fernando (Hernán) Cortés. The circumstances of his death are in some dispute, with Tenochca sources claiming that he was murdered by Spaniards, and Spanish accounts alleging that he was killed by his own people. The fact that Cacama, Nezahualpilli's successor, and Itzquauhtzin, the appointed governor of Tlatelolco, along with other imprisoned lords were killed by the Spaniards before they evacuated Tenochtitlan during the Noche Triste lends weight to the indigenous version.

Cuitlahuac (Excrement), the ruler of the southern Basin city of Iztapallapan (present-day Ixtapalapa), who was also a son of Axayacatl, was selected to succeed his brother Moteuczoma Xocoyotzin. During his brief reign in 1520, Cuitlahuac achieved one moment of glory: he commanded the combined Tenochca-Tlatelolca forces that ousted the Spaniards and their Indian allies from Tenochtitlan during the tumultuous Noche Triste. Like scores of others, including the ruler of Tlacopan, Totoquihuaztli II, Cuitlahuac succumbed to smallpox, one of the infectious European diseases that ravaged the vulnerable native population and drastically undermined Mexica resistance.

As Cuitlahuac's successor, the young Cuauhtemoc (Falling Eagle), son of Ahuitzotl and cousin of Moteuczoma II, led the desperate Mexica defense against the final Spanish onslaught in 1521. Following the surrender of Tenochtitlan, then of Tlatelolco, Cuauhtemoc was captured and tortured to reveal the supposed whereabouts of "lost" Mexica treasure. Taken as a prisoner on Cortés' expedition to Honduras, Cuauhtemoc was executed in 1525 on the pretext of his involvement in a plot against the conquistador. Despite his tragic end, in Mexico today Cuauhtemoc is revered for his valiant defense of the capital. The Mexican muralist David Alfaro Siqueiros, in particular, has celebrated his heroic if doomed struggle and its meaning to modern Mexico.

After the Conquest of Mexico, indigenous governors, in some cases descendants of pre-Hispanic ruling families, continued to serve the Indian sectors of colonial communities under Spanish oversight. In Tenochtitlan (Mexico City) the first of these Nahua rulers were don Andrés Motelchiuhtzin (1526–30), don Pablo Xochiquentzin (1532–36), don Diego de

Alvarado Huanitzin (1538–41), and don Diego de San Francisco Tehuetzquititzin (1541–44).

Sources for Pre-Hispanic Nahua Rulership

The personalities and circumstances of Nahua rulership have been gleaned from the surviving corpus of documentary sources. These works, painted and written in both Nahuatl and Spanish by Nahua, mestizo, and Spanish authors, record the existence of both legendary and historical rulers for well over 200 years of Mexica history. For example, in its historical section the composite sixteenth-century colonial manuscript, *Codex Telleriano-Remensis*, portrays and comments on Tenochca and Tlatelolca monarchs and their exploits, as well as those from Texcoco and surrounding Basin of Mexico towns. Like other Tenochca manuscripts, the *Codex Mendoza* organizes the contents of its history according to the reigns of rulers and their records of conquest. Mexica rulers also appear notably in the *Codex Azcatitlan, Codex Aubin* of 1576, *Codex Mexicanus,* and *Primeros Memoriales,* compiled by Bernardino de Sahagún and his indigenous collaborators. They are also amply discussed in the works of numerous sixteenth-century chroniclers that treat the history of the Mexica, especially Diego Durán's *History of the Indies of New Spain.*

Among other sources, Tlatelolca rulers appear prominently in the *Codex Cozcatzin* and the *General History of the Things of New Spain* (*Florentine Codex,* Book 8), also produced by Sahagún and his team. Important Acolhua sources include the *Mapa Quinatzin, Mapa Tlotzin, Codex Xolotl, Codex en Cruz,* and Fernando de Alva Ixtlilxochitl's *Relaciones e Historia.* As noted earlier, investigations of other Nahua communities both within and outside the Basin of Mexico are increasingly being undertaken by scholars, utilizing a trove of lesser known Nahuatl and Spanish documents in regional archives.

Although offering indispensable information, central Mexican historical documents do not offer a complete record, individually or collectively, for any ethnic group; there are glaring omissions and confusing inconsistencies. The accounts also tend to be highly partisan, vaunting the accomplishments of the localities that produced them and downplaying those of their rivals. Constructing history presents a challenge to today's researcher, just as, in many ways, it must have to the original compilers of the documents, pre-Hispanic or colonial.

See also Mesoamerica: Mexica; Triple Alliance

Select Bibliography

Berdan, Frances F., and Patricia Rieff Anawalt, *The Codex Mendoza.* 4 vols., Berkeley: University of California Press, 1992.

Davies, Nigel, *The Aztec Empire: The Toltec Resurgence.* Norman: University of Oklahoma Press, 1987.

Durán, Fray Diego, *The History of the Indies of New Spain,* translated, annotated, and with an introduction by Doris Heyden. Norman: University of Oklahoma Press, 1994.

Gillespie, Susan, *The Aztec Kings: The Construction of Rulership in Mexica History.* Tucson: University of Arizona Press, 1989.

Hassig, Ross, *Aztec Warfare: Imperial Expansion and Political Control.* Norman: University of Oklahoma Press, 1988.

Hodge, Mary D., and Michael E. Smith, editors, *Economies and Polities in the Aztec Realm.* Institute for Mesoamerican Studies, the University at Albany, State University of New York, Albany, and Austin: University of Texas Press, 1994.

Nicholson, H. B., with Eloise Quiñones Keber, *Art of Aztec Mexico: Treasures of Tenochtitlan.* Washington, D.C.: National Gallery of Art, 1983.

Quiñones Keber, Eloise, *Codex Telleriano-Remensis: Ritual, Divination, and History in a Pictorial Aztec Manuscript.* Austin: University of Texas Press, 1995.

Sahagún, Bernardino de, *Florentine Codex: General History of the Things of New Spain,* translated and edited by Arthur J. O. Anderson and Charles E. Dibble. 12 vols., School of American Research, Santa Fe, and Salt Lake City: University of Utah, 1950–82.

—ELOISE QUIÑONES KEBER

Nationalism

Of the many "isms" that populate Mexican, Latin American, and even world history, nationalism is the one whose importance is most asserted, but whose character is least understood. Unlike liberalism or communism, it does not reflect any formal doctrine; more than these, it assumes varied forms—policies, attitudes, texts, images—that cover a huge range of phenomena and that are often hard to pin down and impossible to measure. Historians (and others) readily assert the importance of Mexican nationalism; some, such as John Mason Hart, see the Mexican Revolution as a war of national liberation, an essentially nationalist phenomenon. But, compared to the research that has illuminated, for example, regional history or agrarian conditions, studies of Mexican nationalism remain scant and unsatisfactory, not least because students of nationalism have (perhaps unsurprisingly) failed to agree on important questions of definition, theory and causality. Furthermore, studies of Mexican and Latin American nationalism have engaged only sporadically with broader theoretical and comparative analyses of nationalism, while the latter have signally neglected Latin America in general and Mexico in particular. This is regrettable because, as scholar Benedict Anderson notes, Latin America was a crucible of nationalism, its independence struggle anticipating nationalist movements and nascent nation-states that would emerge in subsequent decades. And Mexico is a key case in any discussion of these early nationalist stirrings, not to mention the more thorough and pervasive nationalism of modern mass society.

Any succinct survey must, at the outset, define the area of analysis. The most elementary form of nationalism—which I would as soon term "patriotism"—involves an affective identification with a particular "national" territory (or *patria*), which its inhabitants recognize as distinct, whose existence they value, and whose survival, as a sovereign territorial entity, they seek to promote. (European nationalism often has assumed aggressive, expansionist forms; the Mexican variant usually has been defensive. Either way, the interests of the territorial nation are stressed.) Such *political patriotism* may acquire cultural dimensions: the valorization of a distinct national culture, for example, in the patriotic murals of Diego Rivera or the nationalist writings of Manuel Gamio and José Vasconcelos. It also may involve specifically economic features: *economic nationalism* involves the defense of national resources against foreign influence and penetration, by means of tariff protection, legislation, even expropriation. While economic nationalism focuses on macroeconomic patterns of trade and investment and typically is espoused by policy-making or economic elites, *xenophobia*, in contrast, targets foreign communities resident within Mexico, often assumes popular forms, tends to be more violent, and operates at the microeconomic level. The regulation of foreign oil exploitation by Article 27 of the 1917 Constitution was a classic economic nationalist measure, as was the petroleum nationalization of March 1938; the massacre of Chinese at Torreón in May 1911 or the forced expulsion of Chinese from Sonora in the early 1930s was an example of xenophobia.

Finally, we should recognize an important category of analysis that may relate to each of the above, but that goes beyond them: the phenomenon of modern state building. Whereas traditional dynastic states—including Hapsburg and Bourbon New Spain—rested on divine sanction and caste discrimination, modern states usually have sought a secular, republican legitimacy and have striven to incorporate—therefore, to educate, acculturate, to "rationalize and

nationalize"—a mass of citizens over whom they claim authority. After Independence, therefore, the incipient Mexican nation-state blended patriotism (which arguably had colonial roots) with a new increasingly secular state project. After the Revolution of 1910, this dual effort was renewed, with greater success: the Revolutionary state worked to "nationalize" the divided and dispersed Mexican people, utilizing federal education, new mass organizations (trade unions, communal village landholdings, the dominant party), and "inclusionary" symbols and discourse (*indigenismo;* Revolutionary art; the emotive myths of Francisco "Pancho" Villa, Emiliano Zapata, and Lázaro Cárdenas). Nationalism therefore went beyond a mere defense of the *patria*, of its borders, culture, and economic resources. It now embodied a domestic goal: the incorporation of Mexico's ethnically and regionally divided people into a genuine citizenry owing allegiance to the modern nation-state, a nation-state that, after 1917, additionally claimed a "revolutionary" character. Specific policies therefore responded to dual motives: federal education inculcated sentiments of patriotism, ensuring that Mexicans (Indians included) thought of themselves as Mexican vis-à-vis their neighbors, especially their threatening northern neighbors; but education also served to bolster the Mexican nation-state from within, weaning Mexicans away from local, ethnic, and religious allegiances, making a reality of the state's claims to legitimate authority.

The historical impact of these several strands of nationalism is, of course, complex and variable over time. Furthermore, the starting point of this particular analysis, 1910, is somewhat arbitrary, because—even if the Revolution had important consequences for the development of Mexican nationalism—it is obvious that nationalism existed long before 1910 and, indeed, later Revolutionary nationalism and nation-building drew deeply on pre-1910 precedents, without which the Revolutionary nationalist project would have faced insuperable difficulties.

What were these precedents? First, it is clear that the late colonial period witnessed a growing criollo patriotism that focused on the idea of a distinctive "Mexico," possessed of rough borders, of a specific culture, and of a shared history. The symbol of the Virgin of Guadalupe and, to a lesser degree, Mexico's pre-Conquest heritage afforded a discursive and iconographic basis for this incipient patriotism, to which was added an early economic nationalism, premised on (largely criollo) hostility to Spanish economic power and privilege. These currents flowed into the Independence movement, which also revealed a powerful popular xenophobia directed against the hated *gachupines* (Spanish). However, these sentiments were insufficient to guarantee a stable, integrated, and legitimate nation-state. Nineteenth-century Mexico was plagued by internal conflict and balkanization, by external aggression and territorial loss. Elites, who were hardly blameless themselves, lamented Mexico's lack of patriotism and civic responsibility. If, so it seemed, Mexico remained a precarious and imperfect nation-state, this did not argue an absence of patriotism, even of popular patriotism. Scholars Guy P. C. Thomson and Florencia E. Mallon have shown how, particularly in response to the French Intervention of the 1860s, Mexicans—including illiterate peasant Mexicans—rallied to the defense of the *patria* and, under Benito Juárez's Liberal leadership, contributed to the expulsion of the invader. Liberalism and patriotism thereby achieved a close identity, which the Revolution of 1910 would cement further. Conversely, Catholic forms of patriotism—which possessed their own distinct strengths and cultural manifestations—were somewhat checked by the clerical conservatives' disastrous alliance with Emperor Maximilian and the French.

During this period, economic nationalism was at a discount. The Spanish mercantile elite had been expelled; foreign trade and investment were scant; and there was little foreign immigration to spur xenophobia. During the rule of dictator Porfirio Díaz, things changed. The foreign economic presence swelled, encouraged by Díaz and the Científicos, and foreign immigration increased, albeit modestly. Many observers therefore see the Revolution of 1910 as a nationalist reaction: a political, economic, and xenophobic repudiation of the xenophile policies of the Porfiriato. This is true only to a limited degree; the 1910 Revolution was far from being a fully fledged nationalist revolution (talk of a "war of national liberation" is thoughtless hyperbole). Over time, the chief *nationalist* contribution of the Revolution was less its repudiation of external foreign influence (important though that was) than its decisive acceleration of the process of *domestic* nation-building, of "forging a fatherland," in the words of the revolutionary anthropologist and ideologue Manuel Gamio.

The role of nationalism within the Revolution therefore must be defined carefully and disaggregated. Political patriotism—defense of the *patria*—was a constant element; but it would be truer to say that the Revolution provoked patriotism than that patriotism provoked the Revolution. Critics of the Díaz regime denounced the dictator's patriotic failings—for example, his tolerance of U.S. intervention at the time of the Cananea strike in 1907—but the thrust of the mainstream opposition to Díaz (typified by Francisco I. Madero's anti-reelectionist campaign in 1909–10) was essentially domestic and political: it focused on Díaz's betrayal of democracy, not of the *patria*. More radical critics, such as the Partido Liberal Mexicano (PLM), espoused economic nationalism (and a measure of xenophobia), but their appeal was limited; the notion that the opposition to Díaz was powered by a profound popular antipathy to foreign investment, uniting workers, peasants and the national bourgeoisie, is asserted much more often than it is demonstrated. There were specific flashpoints, such as Cananea, or the Mexicanization of the railroads' workforce. But these were not typical. Most Maderistas, like Madero himself, took a relaxed view of foreign investment: they did not like overt enclaves—company towns like Cananea—but they saw foreign trade and investment as essential and often beneficial. Many workers welcomed such investment and the jobs it brought, while dispossessed peasants, such as the Zapatistas, usually targeted Mexican and Spanish landlords or mayordomos, not U.S. companies. The popular revolution certainly embodied elements of xenophobia—for example, recurrent outbursts directed against Spaniards and Chinese—but its anti-American, anti-imperialist content was quite limited.

The Revolution did stimulate displays of political patriotism, for two principal reasons. First, recurrent U.S. intervention (using the term broadly) provoked Mexican reactions, now as in the past. The biggest example was the U.S. occupation of the port of Veracruz in April 1914 (an intervention, we should note, designed not to subvert the Revolution, but to assist the Revolutionaries in their struggle against Victoriano Huerta). Veracruz stimulated protests, demonstrations, and minor riots, chiefly directed against the physical representations of the United States: flags, statues, consulates. Individual Americans, as well as American business enterprises, suffered relatively little molestation. Lesser U.S. interventions—President William Howard Taft's border mobilization in March 1912, Woodrow Wilson's refusal to recognize Huerta in 1913—generated hostile comment, but little or no violence. Even the Punitive Expedition of 1916–17—the biggest and most sustained intervention of the Revolutionary decade—provoked limited protest.

This case also exemplifies the second important factor: displays of Mexican nationalism depended significantly on Mexican elite reactions; they were not automatic responses to objective conditions. Like most countries (but especially those countries such as

Poland or Ireland confronted by bigger, threatening neighbors), Mexico had a long tradition of politicized patriotism (i.e., patriotism employed in the interests of partisan politics). Nineteenth-century liberals had consolidated their hegemony partly thanks to the conservatives' alliance with Maximilian and the French. During the Revolution, political leaders —conservative and revolutionary, Catholic and anticlerical—tried to turn patriotism to their own advantage and to the disadvantage of their opponents. Critics of Díaz capitalized on the lynching, in Texas, of the Mexican citizen Antonio Rodríguez in 1910. Denied recognition by the United States in 1913, Huerta tried to build support on the basis of a somewhat spurious nationalism, while his Constitutionalist enemies had to evade the charge of conniving with the gringos. Villa's attack on Columbus in March 1916 served the dual purpose of exacting revenge on the United States (which had recognized Venustiano Carranza), while placing Carranza in an awkward bind. Carranza responded, with characteristic acumen, by first damping down news coverage of the expedition, then displaying his own nationalist credentials by confronting the invading U.S. forces. The vicissitudes of the Revolution therefore gave ample scope for displays of rival patriotism (and by referring to "displays" I do not mean that these were purely cynical ploys; sincerity and cynicism no doubt conspired together, in ways we can scarcely unravel). Maderistas, Huertistas, Zapatistas, Carrancistas, and Villistas all felt obliged to demonstrate their patriotism and, wherever possible, question that of their opponents. Nationalism, in the sense of traditional political patriotism, did not therefore provide a valid litmus test of factional allegiance. In the process, however, the Revolution provided new resources for nationalist folklore: the brave resistance of Veracruz's naval cadets in 1914, Villa's attack on Columbus and subsequent eluding of the Punitive Expedition in 1916–17.

Following the high point of revolutionary civil war and the nadir of centralized political authority, a slow, painful process of reconstruction began after 1915. This turn of the tide had important implications for Mexican nationalism. Popular xenophobia—evident in sporadic, local attacks on Chinese or Spaniards—declined as central authority was reinforced (although opportunist politicians, such as the Sonorans, were not above inciting Sinophobia, especially when the Great Depression boosted unemployment and encouraged an ethnicization of economic tensions around 1930). Much more significant, however, reconstruction stimulated economic nationalism: macroeconomic measures designed to

Mexicanize the economy and stem the perceived drain of resources abroad, chiefly to the United States. Economic nationalism had flickered during the late Porfiriato, when critics on the right as well as the left began to question the status of foreign interests and to advocate greater state regulation of foreign railroads, mining, and petroleum production. While both the early liberal revolution (roughly, Maderismo) and its popular counterpart (e.g., Zapatismo) neglected economic nationalism in favor of political and agrarian reform respectively, the later revolution—in particular, the hard-headed, businesslike, realpolitik Revolution of the Sonorans— gave it greater emphasis. The Sonorans and their ideological kin entertained a blueprint of a strong, centralized, progressive nationalist Mexico. Their relationship with the United States, which many of them knew firsthand, was ambivalent: while they feared its power, they sought to emulate its economic achievements. For the Sonorans, the formation of a stable, solvent state involved greater regulation of foreign interests, especially the oil companies, which during the 1910s—and despite the Revolution—had experienced dizzying growth. Article 27 of the 1917 Constitution therefore reserved subsoil deposits to the nation, stripping the oil companies of the freehold property rights they claimed under Porfirian law and opening the door to two decades of sporadic conflict between the state and the companies.

This conflict displayed three dimensions. First, it derived from the efforts of the state—still relatively weak and financially pressed—to extract economic resources from highly profitable foreign companies, in which respect the state was relatively successful. Second, this strictly *economic* nationalism formed part of a broader state-building project undertaken by the Revolutionary leadership, Plutarco Elías Calles in particular. Ruling, as they saw it, a highly imperfect nation, riven by ethnic, regional, class, and political divisions, the Sonorans sought to *forjar patria* (to forge a fatherland), which meant eroding these divisions and fostering Revolutionary and national allegiances. Combating mighty foreigners formed part of this project: Calles therefore confronted not only the oil companies (whose political autonomy was no less galling than their economic wealth) but also the Catholic Church, which similarly represented a state within the state. Revolutionary anticlericalism and nationalism went hand-in-hand and helped provoke the Cristero Rebellion of 1926 to 1929 (during which, we should remember, the Cristeros proclaimed their own popular Catholic variant of patriotism in opposition to the Callista state).

Forging a fatherland, however, went beyond confrontations with foreigners and involved policies of state-building designed to turn wayward subjects into dutiful citizens, parochial peasants into patriotic Mexicans. Such policies—embracing education, agrarian reform, indigenismo, and mass political mobilization—obeyed nationalist motives in the broadest sense. What is more, they were relatively success-ful compared to similar policies pursued elsewhere in Latin America before World War II. "Official" Revolutionary nationalism never established a political monopoly; it faced opposition from die-hard Catholics, doctrinaire liberals, and some extreme elements of both left and right. Nevertheless, the nationalist state-building project, initiated in the 1920s, did serve to break down regional and local boundaries, to involve Mexicans in national organizations (the Partido Nacional Revolucionario, or PNR, and the Confederación Regional Obrera Mexicana, or CROM, in the 1920s; the Partido de la Revolución Mexicana, or PRM; and the Confederación de Trabajardores de México, or CTM, in the 1930s), and to inculcate the ideas and symbols of Revolutionary nationalism, as depicted, for example, in the didactic murals of Diego Rivera and David Alfaro Siqueiros.

The third important dimension was the oldest:traditional patriotism. Premised on the defense of Mexico's sovereignty and independence (especially in the face of U.S. threats), traditional patriotism was much older than the Revolution, but the latter gave it an additional shot in the arm, while expanding both the nationalist repertoire and the state's capacity to mobilize for patriotic causes. The invasion of Veracruz and the Punitive Expedition became the latest chapters in the long history of Mexican resistance to the *coloso del norte;* after 1917, successive administrations resisted U.S. pressure to rewrite the 1917 Constitution, to renege on anticlericalism, and to protect U.S. property rights south of the border. In each of these disputes, which punctuated the 1920s and 1930s, Mexicans could draw upon their old patriotic tradition (or, to put it negatively, they could not afford to forget or traduce that tradition). Meanwhile, the new schools and mass institutions carried the old message to every corner of the country.

The best evidence of successful nation-building came in March 1938, with the petroleum nationalization, which exemplified all these nationalist trends. Lázaro Cárdenas's decision to resolve a long-running labor dispute by expropriating the oil companies and creating the first major third-world state petroleum enterprise was, clearly, a classic example of economic nationalism, which transferred a major resource from private foreign to public Mexican ownership. But, although it may have satisfied long-term economic nationalist ambitions (that is a debatable point), it did not respond to a careful cost-benefit analysis of economic advantage. Rather, it represented a fresh display of political patriotism, premised on the notion that the companies were flouting Mexican law, impugning the honor of the president, and—yet again—acting as a seditious state within the state. (Foreign mining interests, which were economically more important but politically more discreet, suffered no economic nationalist backlash.) In addition, the events of March 1938 revealed the new capacity of the Mexican state to tap patriotic sentiment and to mobilize nationalist demonstrations, even among groups that were not fervently Cardenista. What the events did *not* reveal, we might note, was any significant popular xenophobia: the foreign oil men, virtually unmolested, packed their bags and left; Mexican oil-workers took their place and, despite dire predictions, kept the oil pumping.

If March 1938 was the high point of Revolutionary nationalism, its subsequent trajectory tended to be downhill. The onset of World War II had important but paradoxical results. President Manuel Avila Camacho made national unity and patriotic cohesion the leitmotiv of his administration; but he also encouraged close political, economic, and military collaboration with the United States, which strongly reinforced Mexico's dependence on its northern neighbor. Outstanding U.S.-Mexican disputes (oil and debt) were resolved; U.S. penetration of the Mexican economy forged ahead. What some, especially those on the left, viewed as a wartime exception was, after 1945, revealed as a fact of life: although Mexico clung to its economic nationalist tariff barriers, thus stimulating industrialization, U.S. capital vaulted the fence and participated in the "economic miracle" of the 1950s and 1960s.

U.S.-Mexican détente therefore removed old sources of dispute and dulled the edge of Mexican nationalism, which remained strident only on the extremes of the Communist/Lombardista left and the Sinarquista right. Partly by way of compensation, Mexican administrations displayed both a careful independence of the United States in certain foreign policy areas (e.g., with regard to revolutionary Cuba) and, U.S. critics alleged, a touchy sensitivity to supposed U.S. slights (e.g., the expulsion from the United States of Mexican nationals, known as Operation Wetback). But such distancing, while it appealed to nationalist sentiment in Mexico, did not rupture U.S.-Mexican relations and proved quite compatible with a measure of economic dependency.

Domestically, the increasingly ill-named "revolutionary" regime of the Partido Revolucionario Institucional (PRI, or Institutional Revolutionary Party) maintained its nationalist, state-building efforts. Radio, television, and school texts carried nationalist messages, which received cultural expression in the spectacular National Museum of Anthropology and acquired mass appeal through major sporting events (two soccer World Cups and an Olympic Games). Official nationalism still harked back to the Revolution, but after 1940 it rapidly shed its more militant, socialist and anticlerical feathers in favor of a blander folkloric populism.

After the economic crisis of the 1980s, even bland populism fell into disrepute. Committed to a new "neoliberal" model based on economic liberalization, diversification, and fiscal austerity, the administration of President Carlos Salinas de Gortari dismantled economic nationalist barriers, privatized state enterprises, and took Mexico into the North American Free Trade Agreement (NAFTA). On the foreign policy front Mexico's traditional independence of the United States (evident during the Central American conflicts of the 1980s) gave way to closer collaboration. Domestically, too, Salinas spurned the Revolutionary nationalist tradition. His administration wound up *ejido* (communal land) distribution, made peace with the Catholic Church, and—at the cost of public outcry—rewrote the nation's textbooks along more cosmopolitan, neoliberal lines. In short, the old nationalist legitimacy of the Revolutionary state, premised on a combination of political, cultural, and economic nationalism, gave way to a risky new legitimacy based on the market, globalization, and "modernization." By the 1990s, therefore, the most vocal adherents of traditional nationalism were to be found outside the PRI: in the neo-Cardenista Partido de la Revolución Democrática (PRD) and the Zapatista rebels of Chiapas. A Mexican nation had been forged, but the battle for its soul went on.

See also Conservatism; Gender; Liberalism; Mestizaje

Select Bibliography

Anderson, Benedict, *Imagined Communities*. London: Verso, 1983.
Brading, David, *The Origins of Mexican Nationalism*. Cambridge: Center of Latin American Studies, 1985.
Gellner, Ernest, *Nations and Nationalism*. Ithaca, New York: Cornell University Press, 1983.
Hart, John Mason, *Revolutionary Mexico*. Berkeley: University of California Press, 1987.
Knight, Alan, *U.S.-Mexican Relations, 1910–40*. San Diego: Center for U.S.-Mexican Studies, University of California, San Diego, 1987.
———, "Peasants into Patriots: Thoughts on the Making of the Mexican Nation." *Mexican Studies/Estudios Mexicano* 10:1 (1994).
Mallon, Florencia E., *Peasant and Nation*. Berkeley: University of California Press, 1995.
Meyer, Lorenzo, *Mexico and the United States in the Oil Controversy, 1916–42*. Austin: University of Texas Press, 1977.
Thomson, Guy P. C., "Bulwarks of Patriotic Liberalism: The National Guard, Philharmonic Corps and Patriotic Juntas in Mexico, 1847–88." *Journal of Latin American Studies* 22:1 (1990).

—ALAN KNIGHT

North American Free Trade Agreement (NAFTA)

The North American Free Trade Agreement is a treaty among two industrialized countries (the United States and Canada) and a developing one (Mexico); it is based on principles of equality and full reciprocity despite the vast asymmetries among these nations' economies—the size of the Mexican economy is just 5 percent of the U.S. economy. NAFTA is expected to create the largest single market in the world, with 360 million people and one-third of the world's gross domestic product (GDP), around US$5.5 trillion. However, NAFTA can best be described as an agreement that aims to promote *freer* trade rather than *free* trade. In effect, the treaty provides for a 10-year transition period—with a few exceptions of 15 years—after which all important tariffs will be phased out. Unless a sector is threatened by an emergency situation, by the end of the transition period trade among the three countries will be duty free. Nevertheless, import tariffs are not the only constraint to trade; other kinds of technical restrictions will remain. Thus, NAFTA will not completely liberalize the movement of goods and services among the three countries.

Mexico's decision to negotiate NAFTA resulted from a combination of international economic opportunities and constraints: the 1989 Canada-U.S. Free Trade Agreement, the scarcity of foreign capital outside North America, the creation of regional economic blocs in other parts of the world, and the limited potential for the multilateral trading system under the Uruguay Round of negotiations for the General Agreement on Tariffs and Trade (GATT). Mexico pursued a free trade agreement with the United States as the best strategy to promote its export-oriented economic model, as well as to supplement its unilateral trade liberalization with market access guarantees.

Why NAFTA?

NAFTA was not the first attempt at promoting economic integration between Mexico and the United States. Under the 1942 U.S. Reciprocal Trade Agreements Program, Mexico and the United States entered into a bilateral agreement that lasted only until 1950. In 1980, U.S. presidential candidate Ronald Reagan proposed the creation of a North American common market as a campaign issue. Given Mexico's historical suspicions about excessive U.S. influence in domestic affairs, the project did not go forward; in 1981, a rather ineffective Joint Commission in Trade and Commerce was established instead. More consistent with Mexico's outward orientation, later arrangements leading toward Mexican-U.S. economic integration included the 1985 Bilateral Understanding on Subsidies and Countervailing Duties, the 1987 Framework Agreement on Trade and Investment, and the 1989 Understanding Regarding Trade and Investment Facilitation Talks. Access to foreign capital and export markets was the basis for Mexico's involvement in international trade negotiations with the United States.

Hoping to diversify export markets and reduce the excessive dependence on the U.S. market and to attract foreign investment, President Carlos Salinas de Gortari made a trip to Europe in 1990, during which he realized that the 1989 revolutions in the former Soviet bloc countries had increased competition for foreign capital on the European continent; Mexico was both geographically and politically isolated from European interests. For Mexico, the NAFTA negotiations offered the possibility of securing market access for its exports, as well as attracting foreign capital with which to create jobs, service its foreign debt, and promote economic recovery.

While NAFTA was endorsed by government officials, bureaucrats, politicians, academics, export-oriented business groups, and the financial community in the three countries, there were also vocal opponents among nongovernmental environmental and labor organizations, academics, and politicians that they influenced. In Mexico, the NAFTA debate raised issues of economic growth, political and economic stability, and democratic participation.

NAFTA's Political and Economic Implications for Mexico

The implications of NAFTA's impact on Mexico's political environment and economic progress have been addressed through a number of hypotheses advanced in debates within academic, journalistic, and policy-making circles.

NAFTA supporters have argued that the agreement will lead to economic stability. The treaty enhances certainty and predictability for the Mexican economy because it provides a clear set of rules for trade and investment activities in North America. The Salinas administration conceived of NAFTA as Mexico's best alternative to support the country's new outward-oriented strategy because it would ensure long-term stable market access. NAFTA would give Mexico the instruments to counteract U.S. protectionist practices that in the past had impeded access to Mexican competitive exports.

Domestically Mexico's commitments under NAFTA would provide a stable trade policy agenda because the treaty ties the hands of future Mexican governments; their maneuverability to reverse trade reforms, deregulation, and other liberalizing policies would be dramatically reduced. NAFTA is an instrument that grants a high degree of credibility and permanence to the domestic policy reforms undertaken since the mid-1980s.

A related and even more optimistic assessment of NAFTA is that the agreement would reactivate economic growth through capital inflows. Integrating with a rich country like the United States would yield benefits beyond trade efficiency because it would stimulate direct foreign investment and encourage technology transfer. Mexico's economy has shown severe limitations since the 1970s and has failed to provide the enormous job growth necessary to keep pace with labor market demands. Given the lack of domestic savings and the level of foreign indebtedness, foreign capital has become an indispensable financial source for Mexico's productive activities.

At the political level, it has been suggested that NAFTA would lead to instability. President Salinas's questioned 1988 election demanded building political legitimacy. To do so Salinas proposed NAFTA as part of his broad project of modernization and economic growth. Because prosperity was to be achieved by integrating the Mexican economy to the world market, the political legitimacy of the Salinas administration depended on the fulfillment of Mexican economic growth and stability.

However, this same "neoliberal" project was responsible for the erosion of traditional corporatist support for the Mexican government under the ruling Partido Revolucionario Institucional (PRI, or Institutional Revolutionary Party). During the NAFTA negotiations, labor, agriculture, small business, and much of the bureaucracy—groups that had enjoyed political and economic privileges under a closed and protected market—saw NAFTA as a threat. This fear was deepened by the limited information provided to Mexican civil society and the almost nonexistent debate in the media. Only the export-oriented Mexican business sector, a relatively small proportion of the private sector, became a strong supporter of NAFTA and the Salinas reforms, which they considered to be necessary preconditions for access to foreign capital and markets. Mexico's major industrial groups (e.g., Alfa, Celanese, Cydsa), the Mexican Council of Businessmen, and a number of manufacturing multinational corporations were major NAFTA supporters. Through the Coordinator of Foreign Trade Firms (COECE), which gathered big business representatives from more than 100 productive sectors, the Salinas administration was able to articulate support for NAFTA. Despite numerous and close consultations with top union and peasant leaders, NAFTA never gained domestic consensus and even lacked political support from the PRI's traditional populist bases.

While President Salinas gained widespread support from the United States and the international community, this internationalization only intensified the opposition from economic nationalists and gave the left-wing opposition a new political weapon: if NAFTA failed to reinvigorate the Mexican economy, the PRI would suffer at the polls. As Mexico's economy opens it will be necessary to build and consolidate the new political foundation that will support trade liberalization, and more broadly, macroeconomic reforms.

While NAFTA may threaten political stability, some observers believe that is might also promote a democratic process. Precisely because NAFTA alienates long-time allies, it also opens spaces for more political participation and groups. NAFTA increased Mexico's exposure to the scrutiny of international politics and encouraged a domestic debate with respect to Mexico's economic policy and political reform. The NAFTA negotiations contributed to the mobilization of civil society through Nongovernmental Organizations (NGOs) that built transnational networks within the region with other NGOs such as independent labor unions and environmental groups. Thus, an unintended consequence of NAFTA may be the weakening of Mexico's authoritarian political system.

Areas in Conflict

To understand NAFTA's scope and limits as well as the relevance of some key areas for Mexico, we will examine the negotiation areas that were most problematic and that required keen solutions to avoid a collapse of the talks. Given their economic and political weight in the Canadian, Mexican, and U.S. economies, trade in agriculture, automobiles, energy, and textiles as well as the liberalization of financial services merit special attention.

Agriculture

For Mexico, NAFTA represented the continuation of the liberalization begun in 1988 in order to open Mexican agriculture. The 1992 constitutional reform to Article 27 introduced substantive changes to the land tenure regime in an attempt to promote foreign and domestic private capital participation in agricultural production. However, it also officially ended land distribution, and changed the characteristics of the *ejido*, a form of land tenure in post-Revolutionary Mexico that guaranteed peasants a plot to make their own living.

In the three countries, agriculture was one of the most sensitive and controversial issues. This was the case with corn production in Mexico, a substantial source of employment and income for around 2.5 million rural families. Given the domestic political stakes involved in agricultural liberalization, Mexicans argued that their farmers lagged far behind the productivity levels of Canadian or U.S. producers, and would require years to close the gap, even with private capital. Thus, Mexico sought an exceptional 15-year transition period for very sensitive products such as corn and beans. Likewise, the political sensitivities in each country did not allow a trilateral agreement on agriculture. Mexico negotiated a separate agreement with the United and States and another one with Canada in order to overcome the strong opposition to liberalization from each country's producers, who have benefited from substantial government subsidies.

NAFTA agriculture provisions will serve Mexican exporters of fruits and vegetables, which are well organized in northern and western Mexico and are quite competitive; they will be able to take full advantage of liberalization under NAFTA. These producers have very little to do with traditional Mexican subsistence agriculture, which is concentrated heavily in the central and southern part of Mexico. This dichotomy between subsistence *ejido*-type production and export-led agriculture requires a variety of domestic support policies that go beyond NAFTA to ease the livelihood of Mexican peasantry. Otherwise, the rural exodus will aggravate the already saturated urban labor market.

Automotive Industry

Automotive products form the largest component in trade among the three countries, and represent a clear example of *freer* but not free trade in the region. Rules of origin for the auto sector, which require cars assembled in North America to contain a certain percentage of North American–manufactured parts, are very restrictive and mostly favor producers that already had operations in the region at the time the treaty was negotiated. The minimum North American content defined as 62.5 percent for vehicles in the year 2002 and 60 percent for most auto parts was intended to favor the "Big Three" U.S. producers (General Motors, Ford, and Chrysler) and to a lesser extent regional producers of parts and components. Tracing requirements incorporated to determine the North American content of components and subassemblies such as engines were also part of the strategy to reduce competition from overseas suppliers, especially the Japanese.

The thrust of auto sector liberalization was a 10-year phase-out of Mexico's protectionist automotive policies, which since 1962 had sought to consolodate a Mexican auto industry. NAFTA ended industrial policies that imposed strict production and export requirements on vehicle manufacturing, and had enabled the Mexican auto parts industry to flourish. In 2004 liberalization of the auto industry will completely eliminate the requirements for specific levels of local content and export requirements for manufacturers of autos in Mexico, as well as the conditions for importing foreign vehicles based on sales in the Mexican market as provided in the 1989 Auto Decree.

Opposition to NAFTA targeted auto industry liberalization in particular. Labor unions in the United States and Canada argued that low Mexican wages would act as an incentive for plant relocation and job losses. Such protectionist arguments are simplistic because considerations like access to skilled labor, research and development, access to infrastructure, and financial incentives are more important for location decisions than cheap labor alone. Contrary to the arguments of a number of U.S. congressional lawmakers, labor unions, and citizen groups, the liberalization of the Mexican auto industry will not imply the dismantling of the U.S. auto industry; on the contrary, it will contribute to its strengthening. The NAFTA provisions for this sector will encourage greater rationalization and specialization of production, which will translate into larger shares of intra-regional and intra-industry trade. New plants will enable Mexico to increase its exports of small and compact vehicles to the United States and Canada, while U.S. vehicle producers will integrate their Mexican operations more closely to other plants within the region, making production of other lines more efficient. Mexican auto parts firms that already were suppliers of vehicle assemblers also will benefit from increased production scales. This sector is key for Mexico's future economic growth because of the industry's large potential for both foreign investment and spill-over effects for the rest of the economy.

Energy and Petrochemicals

Trade in energy and petrochemicals was one of the key areas in the negotiation given the strategic importance of strengthening regional energy integration. For Mexico, opening foreign participation in the oil sector was an extremely sensitive issue given that the 1938 nationalization of foreign oil concessions had targeted U.S. oil companies. The negotiation of the oil sector in the NAFTA provoked economic nationalism in Mexico. Left-wing intellectuals, politicians, and organizations such as Cuauhtémoc Cárdenas, the Partido de la Revolución Democrática (PRD, or Party of the Democratic Revolution), and the Petróleos Mexicanos (PEMEX) labor unions raised their voices against the privatization of the energy sector; thus, liberalization was considered a reversal of Mexico's Revolutionary achievements and the loss of national sovereignty.

Given the strategic nature of the oil sector in Mexico, NAFTA did not open foreign investment to oil exploration, production, and refining; standard risk-sharing contracts are not permitted, and open participation of U.S. and Canadian firms in the Mexican gasoline retail market is banned. However, Mexico still committed to this sector's liberalization in specific areas despite the fact that its oil and energy sectors had been highly protected for reasons of security and nationalism.

NAFTA specifies the rights and obligations for trade in crude oil, gas, refined products, basic petrochemicals, coal, electricity, and nuclear energy, and it grants national treatment for these exports. Under certain circumstances import and export restrictions on energy trade may be introduced to conserve exhaustible natural resources, deal with supply shortages, or implement a price stabilization plan.

Although Mexico limits the production of oil, gas, refining, basic petrochemicals, and nuclear and conventional electricity generation to the state, it opened up foreign participation under special conditions. NAFTA investors are entitled to acquire, establish, and operate plants for production of non-basic petrochemical goods and for electricity generating facilities for their "own use," cogeneration, and independent power production. In the case of cross-border trade, NAFTA provides that state firms, end users, and suppliers may negotiate supply contracts. Mexico's Federal Commission of Electricity (CFE), independent power producers, and electric utilities in other NAFTA countries may negotiate power purchase and sale contracts. NAFTA opened opportunities for foreign suppliers to sell to PEMEX and CFE under open and competitive bidding rules.

Textiles

Liberalization in textiles was particularly complex given the international protectionist scheme existing under the Multifiber Agreement and the strong lobbying activity of textile producers to keep the North American market as closed as possible. This sector showed a particular political sensitivity in the United States, where labor unions and textile producers allied to shape very restrictive NAFTA provisions. Their demands reflected a concern for job losses and increased competition from efficient Mexican producers. At the outset of NAFTA's implementation, Mexico granted open access to around 20 percent of U.S. exports of textiles and apparel; all trade restrictions will be phased out after a 10-year transition period.

Rules of origin for the textile industry are highly protectionist, and aim to reduce the likelihood of triangulating goods from third countries (i.e., circumventing import restriction by importing non–North American raw materials or components for final assembly and sale in North America). They also respond to labor demands that feared a massive flood of imports. To avoid alienating support from textile unions and producers, it was established that each NAFTA party may introduce safeguards when textile or apparel producers face serious harm as a result of increased imports from a member country.

Trade in Services

In contrast with the extraordinary liberalization achieved in trade in goods, the service sector was subject to negotiating conflict and the maintenance of protection in such areas as financial services, land transportation, and telecommunications.

The liberalization of trade in services was one of the United States's and Canada's key objectives in the negotiation. Those economies have become net exporters of services and the Mexican market offers a great potential: between 1987 and 1990, the Mexican service sector almost doubled from US$78 billion to US$146 billion. NAFTA built upon the 1989 CUSFTA and GATT's Uruguay Round. This liberalization is based on the principles of national and most-favored-nation treatment. Negotiations focused on domestic regulations addressed to each particular service sector.

Financial Services

Financial efficiency has an important impact on overall economic competitiveness because domestic producers tend to borrow primarily from national financial sources. Consistent with major macroeconomic reforms, since 1988 Mexico started a rapid deregulation of its financial sector to enhance both its efficiency and ability to attract international capital. However, financial opening was severely limited by the newly privatized banks' demands for protection and the Mexican government's priority of keeping the national payments system in domestic hands. The new owners bought the banks at extremely high prices, largely based on the expectations of a growing and insulated market for financial services. Thus, Mexico sought a lengthy transition period to eliminate barriers to access into the Mexican banking system and insisted on strict market-share restrictions on U.S. and Canadian banks.

This negotiation covered the banking, insurance, and securities sector. Liberalization will be carried out based on the principles of national treatment, procedural transparency, and prudential and safeguards measures. Canadian and U.S. banks and securities firms will face market-share limits when acquiring Mexican firms. After January 1, 2000, temporary safeguards provisions will still apply in the banking and securities sectors. Under NAFTA, Mexico did not allow any bank acquisition greater than a 4 percent market share, a ceiling that ensures that Mexico's top three banks remain in domestic hands. Liberalization of financial services also involved insurance services. Mexico agreed to allow the operation of 100 percent foreign-owned firms by the year 2000 in a market that has been valued at around US$3.5 billion.

Other Services

Liberalization of services like land transportation and telecommunications affected domestic regulatory frameworks that Mexico had already started to liberalize unilaterally. Truck, rail, and port deregulation aimed at creating a more efficient transport system in the region. Around 90 percent of Mexican-U.S. trade is shipped by land. Accordingly, to increase production and trade efficiency it was crucial to liberalize land transportation services among NAFTA countries and to establish compatible technical and safety standards. Land transportation liberalization was opposed by the Mexican trucking sector, which feared competition from efficient U.S. competitors. In the United States, the Teamsters Union also protested against granting access to Mexican trucks because they were afraid of losing market share to low-wage truckers. In fact, when the time came to open the border, in December 1995, the overwhelming opposition of U.S. labor delayed it, a move that only benefited alternative forms of transportation (e.g., rail and marine). Politics in the United States played a major role; President Bill Clinton did not want to undermine the support of the Teamsters Union, and of labor in general during the upcoming election year.

In the area of telecommunications, NAFTA liberalized Mexico's market for telecommunications equipment and services valued at US$6 billion, building upon the 1989 reforms that opened the telecommunications service sector to foreign participation. U.S. and Canadian firms expected to benefit from open access to Mexico's market for cellular phones, satellite communications, and fiber optics. Under NAFTA, Mexico's telephone company (Telmex) is supposed to lose its monopoly status for long-distance service (a US$4 billion market) by the end of 1996. U.S. firms such as AT&T, MCI, GTE, Motorola, and Bell Atlantic have separately formed partnerships with Mexican banks and telecommunications companies seeking to satisfy demand in long-distance service. The new competition is expected to lower service rates for consumers, promote the cost efficiency of doing business, and reduce Telmex's revenue.

Deepening Economic Integration

NAFTA went beyond the traditional areas of trade in goods to include liberalization of investment and a stricter enforcement of intellectual property rights. NAFTA eliminates investment barriers and ensures basic protection for NAFTA investors. As part of the deregulation process of foreign investment, Mexico agreed to grant national treatment to U.S. and Canadian firms operating in Mexico. This was consistent with the 1989 reforms to Mexico's 1973 Law of Foreign Investment, which opened foreign capital participation in areas previously reserved to domestic capital or that required Mexican majority participation. The opening of the economy to foreign investment was considered by populist and nationalist groups as a major assault on Mexican sovereignty. Under NAFTA, Mexico committed to eliminate industrial policy instruments like local content and export performance requirements that conditioned the productive activities of foreign investors. However, the Mexican state still exercises exclusive control

over some activities, consistent with its own constitutional provisions.

Opening the economy to foreign capital contributed to the process of privatization of state-owned enterprises, which represented a major blow to a bureaucracy that had enjoyed the rents of protection. Such moves eroded the political support of this group, which was at the core of the state's corporatist structure and had traditionally endorsed PRI governments. Privatization translated into the loss of privileges and in some cases the complete elimination of jobs and inefficient firms that nonetheless had supported an incompetent and corrupt bureaucracy.

A complement to foreign investment liberalization was the strengthening of laws protecting intellectual property rights. Prior to the NAFTA negotiations, Mexico enacted several important related laws (e.g., the 1991 Law for the Promotion and Protection of Industrial Property), which opened most areas of science and technology to patenting and set a 20-year term for patent protection. NAFTA provides a higher level of protection for intellectual property rights (protection for patents, copyrights, trademarks, and trade secrets) than any other previous bilateral or international agreement. NAFTA also provides 50-year copyright protection for producers of computer programs, sound recordings, and motion pictures. Patent protection specifically addressed concerns of pharmaceutical companies operating in Mexico and Canada, as NAFTA eliminated compulsory licensing and extended to at least 20 years the term of patent protection. NAFTA requires enforcement of rights against infringement and piracy, and reduces the threat of piracy of intellectual property rights for authors and inventors. These provisions are expected to act as an incentive for technology transfer and development in Mexico.

The Social Dimension of the Trade Agenda: Environment and Labor

Since the NAFTA negotiations started, nongovernmental groups, politicians, labor unions, and threatened industries expressed their concern over the social, environmental, political, and cultural implications of the agreement. This debate was not limited to the content of the trade agreement itself; it went beyond to raise historical issues that reflected the traditional misgivings that both Mexico and the United States have had with respect to each other. Among the general audience in the United States, there were doubts about the benefits of a partnership with Mexico.

Opposition to NAFTA and the threat to derail its final approval in the U.S. Congress was articulated in concrete arguments in two main areas: labor and environment. Thus, the inclusion of environmental and labor issues on the negotiating agenda responded to demands of groups in society that felt threatened by a U.S.-Mexican partnership.

NAFTA responds to environmentalists' demands by explicitly protecting domestic health, safety, and environmental standards and allowing the establishment of standards that exceed international ones. An innovative element in the regulation of investment in the region is the environmental component that prohibits any country from lowering its own domestic environmental standards to attract investment. Another controversial issue during the 1993 debate about NAFTA's approval in the U.S. Congress was whether the agreement would result in a massive relocation of U.S. jobs in Mexico. Congressional representatives such as Richard Gephardt had a protectionist agenda and fed the fear of U.S. workers who saw in NAFTA a threat to employment rather than an opportunity.

During his 1992 presidential campaign, Bill Clinton established a strong political commitment with those groups that wanted to see a stronger environmental and labor component in the NAFTA. Thus, after NAFTA text was finalized, under the new Clinton administration it became necessary to negotiate two supplemental agreements: the North American Agreement on Environmental Cooperation and the North American Agreement on Labor Cooperation.

For some groups in the three countries, the labor and environmental side agreements were not enough to respond to the threats that corporate capital could raise to the region's social structure. Based on the European experience, some groups wanted to see a social charter for North America in which disparities pertaining to education, democracy, human rights protection, workers' rights, rural development, and environmental protection would be addressed.

Conclusions

The December 1994 peso crisis reflected severe shortcomings in Mexican economic policy. On one hand, such a crisis cannot be attributed to NAFTA's implementation. On the other hand, we cannot consider NAFTA as the device to solve all of Mexico's economic, social, or political problems.

Historically, Mexico has been vulnerable to capital flight, exchange-rate volatility, and high interest rates, all of which damage the environment for conducting business. NAFTA will contribute to improve that environment and thus will contribute to Mexico's economic stability. NAFTA gives a high degree of credibility and permanence to the domestic policy reforms undertaken since the mid-1980s and introduces greater discipline on those economic policies that affect trade and investment. Mexico's membership in NAFTA and in a number of regional trade agreements in Latin America reveals a strong commitment to build the institutional mechanisms required to consolidate an outward-oriented model.

NAFTA has contributed to intra-regional trade and to support of the export productive sector. Although the 1994 peso crisis submerged the Mexican economy in a drastic recession that led to negative GDP growth rates of 7 percent in 1995, NAFTA may help allay the severity and length of the crisis. NAFTA's market access provisions have supported Mexico's export activities, which in turn have been boosted by an undervalued currency. NAFTA is an instrument that can make Mexico's economic recovery less traumatic.

NAFTA is flawed to the extent that it lacks a regional industrial policy framework and ignores the existing economic disparities among the three countries. Not all industrial sectors will benefit from NAFTA. Labor in import-competing industries will be displaced as the three economies open and as liberalization is completed. Labor and industry displacement has the potential of creating political instability. It will be necessary to create adjustment labor programs, as well as to build new political constituencies among the winners from trade liberalization and macroeconomic reforms.

In terms of political participation, the architects of Mexico's economic liberalization process had to take into account domestic groups that articulated specific economic and political interests. Opening the economy meant more competition for resources and market share, a competition that touched on groups with entrenched interests in import substitution and that had been traditional supporters of PRI governments. To become permanent, the outward-oriented model requires of a new political constituency that will only result from increased political participation of other groups in society. In the short term the price of a stronger democracy and the waning of authoritarianism may be instability within Mexico's political system.

See also Maquiladoras; Peso Crisis of 1994

Select Bibliography

del Castillo, Gustavo, and Gustavo Vega Cánovas, *The Politics of Free Trade in North America*. Ottawa: Centre for Trade Policy and Law, 1995.

Grinspun, Ricardo, and Maxwell A. Cameron, editors, *The Political Economy of North American Free Trade*. Ottawa: Canadian Centre for Policy Alternatives, 1993.

Hufbauer, Gary Clyde, and Jeffrey Schott, *NAFTA: An Assessment*. Washington, D.C.: Institute for International Economics, 1993.

Lustig, Nora, Barry P. Bosworth, and Robert Z. Lawrence, editors, *North American Free Trade: Assessing the Impact*. Washington, D.C.: The Brookings Institution, 1992.

Morici, Peter, *Trade Talks with Mexico: A Time for Realism*. Washington, D.C.: National Planning Association, 1991.

Pastor, Manuel, Jr., "Mexican Trade Liberalization and NAFTA." *Latin American Research Review* 29:3 (Summer 1994).

Poitras, Guy, and Raymond Robinson, "The Politics of NAFTA in Mexico." *Journal of Interamerican Studies and World Affairs* 36:1 (Spring 1994).

Russell, Philip L., *Mexico under Salinas*. Austin, Texas: Mexico Resource Center, 1994.

—Luz María de la Mora

O

Obregón, Álvaro 1880–1928
General and President

One of the most prominent figures in the Mexican Revolution, Álvaro Obregón was born on February 19, 1880, on a hacienda in southern Sonora. He was the seventeenth son of Francisco Obregón and Cenobia Salido. His father died while Álvaro was still a child. Álvaro had the practical education of the children of hacendados. Some maintain that he knew the language of the Mayo Indians of the region; others insist that he scarcely spoke it at all. What is certain is that Obregón developed solid agricultural and mechanical skills, a good memory, and an easy wit. Later, he purchased a farm that he called Quinta Chilla. He married young, first to Refugio Urrrea, who died a few years thereafter, and later to María Tapia, with whom he had seven children.

Obregón's political awakening was late. Unlike other Sonorans who would rise to prominence during the Mexican Revolution—most notably Plutarco Elías Calles, Adolfo de la Huerta, and Benjamín Guillermo Hill—Obregón did not support Francisco I. Madero during the initial campaign against the dictatorship of Porfirio Díaz in 1910. Once Madero was in power, however, Obregón was elected municipal president of Huatabampo, and he led a corps of volunteers against the rebel forces of Pascual Orozco, proving himself an able commander. Obregón's military experience was particularly valuable following General Victoriano Huerta's overthrow and assassination of Madero. Like many other Sonorans, Obregón refused to recognize Huerta's military rule and returned to arms, beginning one of the most spectacular military careers of the Mexican Revolution.

According to his own account, Obregón covered 5,000 miles (8,000 kilometers) in his military campaigns throughout Mexico. He first became known for his defeat of the federal general Luis Medina Barrón in the battles of Santa María and Santa Rosa,

Sonora; these were but the first in a long series of victories. Obregón quickly rose through the ranks, from colonel to commander of the Army of the Northwest, moving down the South Pacific Railroad through the state of Sinaloa and the territory of Tepic until he threatened the city of Guadalajara. Supported by the forces of generals Lucio Blanco and Manuel M. Diéguez, Obregón attacked the forces of General José María Mier, defeating them in the battles of Orendáin and El Castillo. With Obregón's victory in the west and Francisco "Pancho" Villa's taking of the city of Zacatecas, the Constitutionalists were able to topple Victoriano Huerta by July 1914. Obregón advanced to Mexico City and participated in the signing of the Treaty of Teoloyucan, in which the Federal Army formally surrendered.

In October 1914 Obregón distinguished himself in the Revolutionary Convention in Aguascalientes, which sought to provide a forum for the various Revolutionary factions to decide the future shape of government in Mexico. He was a frequent rival of Villa—who at one point nearly killed him—and tended to incline toward the faction of Venustiano Carranza. Obregón joined Carranza when he withdrew from the Convention. In April 1915 Obregón prepared his forces to confront the Villistas, who controlled the Bajío region of north-central Mexico. During almost the entire month of April, the forces of Obregón and Villa clashed in the two great battles of Celeya; in the second battle Villa suffered a grave defeat. As Obregón's forces advanced, Obregón was wounded by a grenade, losing his right arm. Benjamín Hill assumed command, defeating the Villistas again at Trinidad Station. With this final defeat the Villistas were nearly crushed, and in 1916 Carranza was able to convoke a constitutional assembly. Obregón played a decisive role in writing the new Constitution of 1917, helping to push through many of its radical measures over the objections of Carranza. Obregón was named minister of war in the interim government, and his defeat of Villa's powerful

Division of the North gave him unquestionable authority over the other Revolutionary generals.

Following Carranza's inauguration as president in May 1917, Obregón retired to private life, dedicating himself to farming and exporting garbanzos (chickpeas) from his native Sonora. Obregón's distance from the capital meant that he could stay outside the constant political infighting of the Carranza administration, preparing himself for his presidential campaign of 1919–20. Shortly before launching his campaign, he published an account of his military experiences, *Ocho mil kilómetros en campaña*. Obregón left his political interests in Mexico City in the hands of Benjamín Hill, who organized Obregón's followers into the Partido Liberal Constitucionalista (PLC, or Liberal Constitutional Party). The PLC included some of the most important members of both houses of the national legislature. Obregón meanwhile toured the United States, announcing that he had left the country to cure his various ills lingering from his military days. In reality, he was seeking U.S. support for his presidential campaign, meeting with President Woodrow Wilson, key generals in the U.S. army, and several state governors.

By 1919 tensions were running high in Mexico, and Carranza had proposed that elections could be postponed. In June Obregón published a manifesto formally launching his political campaign. Obregón made himself noticed with his radical language and his adamant opposition to Carranza. At first Obregón hoped to pitch his bid against that of General Pablo González, whom he thought Carranza would support. However, Carranza instead threw his weight behind a civilian candidate who was virtually unknown in Mexico, Ignacio Bonilla, the former ambassador to Washington. Toward the end of 1919 Obregón began an intense road campaign, following a route similar to the one he had used in his military campaigns, from Sonora to Mexico City, from there traveling to various other parts of the country. His campaign was so successful that Carranza's inner circle became worried and cultivated a network of spies who could report on Obregón's activities throughout Mexico. Obregón formed alliances with many enemies of Carranza, some of which caused him problems. In April 1919, as tensions were reaching their peak, Obregón was subpoenaed in the trial of General Roberto Cejudo, a follower of the rebel general Félix Díaz (the former dictator Porfirio Díaz's nephew), who had been found with documents implicating Obregón. After a last-minute meeting with Pablo González, the other major candidate for the presidency, Obregón managed to elude police

surveillance and escape to the south disguised as a railway brakeman.

A few days after Obregón's escape, his supporters in Sonora published the Plan de Agua Prieta, which called for Carranza's overthrow. As Obregón's followers gained power Carranza fled the capital, which was occupied by Pablo González's forces; Obregón advanced toward Mexico City together with followers of the late Emiliano Zapata. In the Sierra of Puebla, Carranza was ambushed and shot, and the supporters of the Plan de Agua Prieta were able to consolidate their control of the country. Adolfo de la Huerta was named interim president, and Obregón continued his presidential campaign tour, following the same route he had planned before Carranza's crackdown. Pablo González and Ignacio Bonilla withdrew their candidacies, and the only other candidate, the engineer Alfredo Robles Domínguez, was defeated easily by Obregón. On December 1, 1920, Obregón was sworn in as president of Mexico.

Thanks to de la Huerta's peacemaking, Obregón inherited a tranquil country that had overcome the enormous problems of the previous decade. Obregón's cabinet represented many different currents of the Mexican Revolution, including the Sonorans Plutarco Elías Calles, Adolfo de la Huerta, and Benjamín Hill; the former member of the radical Partido Liberal Mexicano (PLM, or Mexican Liberal Party) Antonio I. Villarreal; and the educator and philosopher José Vasconcelos. The cabinet was an efficient team with great loyalty and respect for Obregón.

Tax revenues from the enormous petroleum production of 1921 gave much-needed relief to the treasury's depleted coffers, and de la Huerta, who had been named secretary of the treasury, was able to renegotiate Mexico's external debt. Obregón had a sufficient budget to be able to project a positive image to the world. In September 1921 Obregón presided over celebrations of the centenary of Mexican Independence, celebrations that sought to compete with those that took place in the last days of the dictatorship of Porfirio Díaz marking the centenary of the 1810 Hidalgo Revolt. Far more important, however, was the creation of the Ministry of Public Education, presided over by José Vasconcelos. The pacification of Mexico permitted Obregón to spend more money on education than the military, and Obregón's administration gained prestige through Vasconcelos's imaginative work in promoting education and national culture.

Social upheavals were repressed severely. In 1922 Generals Lucio Blanco and Francisco Murguía independently tried to stage rebellions and promptly were killed. On a much different note, Obregón was able to win considerable support among the Mexican peasantry through an intensified program of land redistribution. Nonetheless, Obregón's land reform did not go entirely smoothly. A U.S. citizen, Rosalie Evans, was killed defending her hacienda when it was besieged by the strongman José María Sánchez, the governor of Puebla. This incident made it even more difficult for Obregón to receive recognition from the United States.

During the Obregón administration the Mexican labor movement also gained strength. Much of this growth was in the progovernment Confederación Regional Obrera Mexicana (CROM, or Regional Confederation of Mexican Workers), whose leader, Luis N. Morones, enjoyed a close relationship with Calles; however, the Confederación General de Trabajadores (CGT, or General Confederation of Workers), inspired by the Third International of the Communist Party, also gained strength. The CGT was repressed severely, particularly during a tram workers' strike in Mexico City; however, in other areas the labor movement won important victories. Although many of his cabinet members tended to support labor, Obregón himself was less than happy about the gains labor made during his tenure.

Political parties also flourished during the Obregón administration. The strongest party was the Partido Liberal Constitucionalista (PLC, or Constitutionalist Liberal Party); after it was dismantled in 1922, it was replaced by the Partido Nacional Cooperatista (National Cooperatist Party). The other important party with seats in the national legislature was the Partido Laborista (Labor Party), which was led by Luis N. Morones, the head of the CROM. A third major party was the Partido Nacional Agrarista (National Agrarian Party), headed by the Zapatista Antonio Díaz Soto y Gama. Relations among the three parties tended to be quite tense and sometimes even violent.

One of Obregón's most intractable problems was the United States's refusal to recognize his government. In the summer of 1923 a series of talks took place between the United States and Mexico to provide the framework for a new treaty of trade, friendship, and cooperation. The final product of the negotiations, the so-called Bucareli Accords, ruptured the fragile peace that had prevailed during the early years of the Obregón administration. The senate refused to approve the accords, and one senator who had opposed the treaty was assassinated. In the chamber of deputies there was a tremendous outcry. The Bucareli Accords implied a series of concessions by the Mexican government that many believed would countervene the fundamental principles of the Mexican Revolution. In September 1923 Obregón was able to announce that he had won recognition from the United States.

Shortly after Obregón's announcement, de la Huerta resigned from his government, allying himself with the Cooperatistas, who had bitterly opposed the Bucareli Accords. De la Huerta and the Cooperatistas were able to gain the support of several of key figures in the Mexican army, who staged a revolt in December 1923. Obregón was able to obtain a ban on arms sales from the United States to the rebel forces, and thanks to his efficient military strategy he quickly was able to defeat de la Huerta's supporters. With de la Huerta's defeat, the way was clear for Calles to succeed Obregón. Although Obregón was able to liquidate his most important opponents in the officer corps, de la Huerta's supporters were able to inflict one important casualty on the Obregón administration in early 1924, when they courtmartialed and executed Felipe Carrillo Puerto, the radical governor of Yucatán. Obregón shuffled the cabinet, replacing de la Huerta with Alberto J. Pani, who was able to renegotiate the Mexican debt; Vasconcelos resigned immediately after the inauguration of the national stadium, which had been constructed by the ministry of education. Obregón stepped down on November 20, 1924, retiring to private life in Sonora.

In 1926 a constitutional reform was approved allowing the reelection of presidents to nonconsecutive terms, opening the way for Obregón to be a presidential candidate in upcoming elections. In 1927 two old allies of Obregón entered the race for president, the generals Francisco R. Serrano and Arnulfo R. Gómez, both of whom attempted armed rebellions against the Calles administration. After a failed coup attempt Serrano was imprisoned and summarily executed together with his supporters; after launching a rebellion in the state of Veracruz, Gómez was caught and shot. By 1928 Obregón was the only candidate for the presidency. Neither his health nor his finances were solid. In the photographs of the period Obregón seems clearly aged, although he was only 47 years old at the time. As Calles's anointed successor he was inheriting a country in upheaval, with a civil war raging against the Cristeros, Catholics who resented the government's radical anticlerical measures. Shortly after his victory in the presidential elections, Obregón survived an assassination attempt while he toured Chapultepec Park in Mexico City in an open car. That afternoon he attended a bullfight to show that he did not fear the Catholics.

On July 17, Obregón was invited to a banquet in the La Bombilla restaurant in the San Ángel district of southern Mexico City. While he listened to a piece of music titled "El limoncito," a young sketch artist approached him to draw a caricature. Once he was close he took a small revolver from his bag and shot the president-elect six times. The name of the assassin was José de León Toral, and he was closely associated with the Catholic activists who previously had attempted to assassinate Obregón. Toral was tried, found guilty, and subjected to capital punishment.

With Obregón's death, the constitution was revised to restore the Revolutionary principle of no reelection. In a presidential address in September 1928, Calles noted that the era of caudillos—military strongmen—had ended. The era of institutions had begun.

Select Bibliography
Hall, Linda, *Álvaro Obregón: Power and Revolution in Mexico, 1911–1920*. College Station: Texas A & M University Press, 1981.

—ÁLVARO MATUTE

Orozco, José Clemente 1883–1949

Painter

José Clemente Orozco is considered one of the three masters, along with Diego Rivera and David Alfaro Siqueiros, of *muralismo*. This national program of mural painting in post-Revolutionary Mexico was an effort to teach history to the illiterate masses. While Orozco is considered a key figure within this artistic movement, his work contrasts with other artists in the way historical events are portrayed. Instead of the idealized vision of the indigenous past and the Mexican Revolution found in the works of such artists as Rivera, Orozco's paintings depict the darker side, reflecting his personal experiences.

Although born in the state of Jalisco, Orozco grew up in Mexico City and was influenced by José Guadalupe Posada's graphic art. Initially Orozco trained to be an agricultural engineer. However, in 1906, at the age of 23, he enrolled at the Academy of San Carlos in Mexico City. Orozco also worked as a caricaturist and illustrator for newspapers in Mexico City, and for one of the Revolutionary armies from 1914 to 1915. While he did not participate directly in the fighting, he supported Venustiano Carranza against Villa and Zapata. It is from this experience in the Revolution that Orozco formed his view of the war. Orozco lost his left hand in an accident, which also damaged his hearing and sight. While he never commented on this accident himself, many believe the injuries Orozco suffered contributed to his darker vision.

While Orozco is known primarily for his murals, his early work consisted of easel paintings. The paintings depict the darker side of life and society. Reviews of his early shows were unenthusiastic. By the 1920s, however, Orozco had begun to experiment with larger-scale art forms. (In the 1922 *Manifesto of the Syndicate of Technical Workers, Painters, and Sculptors*, prominent Mexican artists denounced easel painting as elitist.)

The first murals commissioned as part of José Vasconcelos's national program were painted at the Escuela Nacional Preparatoria in Mexico City. Orozco's frescoes completed between 1923 and 1926 at the ENP focus on the theme of the Mexican Revolution. These murals clearly reject the idealized imagery used by many other artists. Orozco uses dark colors, consisting mostly of browns; his iconography is often religious. The mural *The Trench* depicts the faceless masses of war. The central figure, a soldier, is placed with his back to the viewer. His body is in a pose reminiscent of a crucifixion. The lines and angles are sharp and geometric. The colors are dark browns, reds, and black. In the mural *Cortés and Malinche* the conqueror and his interpreter-guide are seated. A faceless, dark-skinned body lies at their feet. This prone figure often is interpreted as a symbol of the subjugated race, or the offspring of the union of the two cultures. Again, the colors are dark and the shapes geometric.

Orozco, as well as other prominent Mexican muralists, was commissioned for works in the United States in the 1930s. These murals include *Prometheus* (1931, Pomona College, California), and *Quetzalcoatl* (1933, Dartmouth College, New Hampshire). He returned to Mexico in 1934 and went on to paint several murals in Mexico City and in Guadalajara. A series of murals at Instituto Cabañas in Guadalajara is particularly noted for the mural painted on the ceiling of the main dome, *Man in Flames*. Orozco died in 1949 and was the first artist to be buried at the Panteón de Hombres Ilustres.

Select Bibliography
Helm, MacKinley, *Man of Fire: J. C. Orozco; An Intepretative Memoir*. Westport, Connecticut: Greenwood, 1959.

—MONICA I. OROZCO

Orozco Vázquez, Pascual, Jr.

1882–1915

General

Pascual Orozco Vázquez Jr. was born on January 18, 1882, on the Hacienda de Santa Inés, in Guerrero, Chihuahua. He went to school in San Isidro and worked with his father in the fields and transporting minerals. In 1910 Orozco witnessed political upheaval firsthand in Chihuahua, set in motion by the reelection of President Porfirio Díaz. Abraham González, a leader of Francisco I. Madero's rebellion, nominated Orozco's father-in-law, Albino Frías, as military chief of the rebellion. Orozco joined the Maderists with various neighbors from San Isidro, among whom there were a good number of Protestants (including Orozco) who played a prominent role. Elsewhere, the anarchists from the northeast of Chihuahua, in contact with the anarchists in the mines of New Mexico and Arizona and faced with the military incapacity of their leaders, the Flores Magón brothers (who had fled to the United States), took advantage of the moment of Madero's rebellion to take up arms. Beneath a superficial veneer of unity, the Chihuahua revolution was born, but already ideologically split. On one side Madero grasped the idea of democracy, his emblem the colors of the Mexican flag; and on the other the anarchists fought for the more radical ideals of the Flores Magón brothers, with their distinctive red and black flag, and known as the *colorados*. Answering the call of Madero on November 19, the rebels of San Isidro attacked and held Miñaca and the Hacienda de Dolores, where Pascual Orozco was made head of the local Maderista movement.

On November 21, Orozco's band, made up of different groups of Maderistas and anarchists who took up arms from various places in the east of the state, attacked Ciudad Guerrero; not being able to capture it immediately, they retreated and took Pedernales. Orozco, who now commanded 400 men, returned and renewed his attack on Ciudad Guerrero, capturing it on December 4. He also fought against the Federal army in Cerro Prieto, Malpaso, and la Mojina. In Cerro Prieto he was defeated, and the Federal general Juan F. Navarro ordered the execution of 16 prisoners from Orozco's men. These were the first Revolutionary prisoners to be shot in the war, an action with many negative repercussions: in the short term, when Orozco returned to Ciudad Guerrero, after his defeat in Cerro Prieto, he ordered the execution of various political prisoners, among them Urbano Zea, the former political chief of Guerrero. In the long run the old custom of executing prisoners seen in the colonial era and the Apache wars was firmly reestablished in both the Federal army and the Revolutionary factions.

In February 1911, when Madero arrived at Chihuahua from the United States, without counting on any support from the rebel forces available in Chihuahua, he attacked Casas Grandes and was defeated and wounded in one hand. Madero retreated and ordered all the rebel troops to concentrate their efforts on the Hacienda de Bustillos. Orozco joined him with 300 men and was made a general by Madero, the first in the Revolution. After redeploying and organizing the Revolutionary forces, Madero gave orders to return by railroad to the north and reattack Casas Grandes.

En route to this objective, a serious rift developed between Madero and six chiefs with anarchist links: José Inés Salazar, Luis A. García, José C. Parra, Leonides Zapata, Tomás Loza, and Lázaro Alanís. They wrote him a note saying that they did not recognize him as their provisional president in view of the fact that they were members of the Partido Liberal Mexicano (PLM, or Mexican Liberal Party), and they requested that he step down from the Revolutionary army, because they considered him more tyrannical than Porfirio Díaz himself. The head of the Revolution and provisional president of the nation regarded this action as intolerable insubordination and ordered that the six rebel followers of the Flores Magón brothers be disarmed and imprisoned.

Shortly after, and against the wishes of Madero, who was afraid of complications with the U.S. authorities in El Paso, the guerrillas of Orozco and Francisco "Pancho" Villa, the most aggressive, united to attack Ciudad Juárez, forcing General Juan F. Navarro to surrender after a fierce battle. Soon after this Orozco and Villa, who wanted Navarro's head for the executions in Cerro Prieto, planned a revolt because Madero granted the general his life and helped him arrive safely in El Paso.

After the success of the Revolution in Chihuahua, whose indisputable military leader was Pascual Orozco, Madero gave him 50,000 pesos and appointed him head of *rurales* (rural police) in the state. But Orozco aspired to be governor and was annoyed at having to renounce his candidacy because he did not comply with the legal age for this post. His relations with Abraham González, the governor of Chihuahua, were cold but cordial; González was elected by an overwhelming majority of the people of Chihuahua, and Orozco depended upon him for his rural forces. In January 1912, only three months after Madero took over as president of the Republic, Orozco resigned his duties as chief of the *rurales*. The president, still trusting him completely, asked him to continue until March.

Pascual Orozco carefully took stock of his forces. On one hand he had economic and moral support from the oligarchy of Chihuahua, who feared that González was planning to increase taxes on their properties and their industrial and commercial enterprises. On the other hand, he received the support of the Flores Magón brothers and the anarchists of Chihuahua, who wanted to break with Madero, whom they considered an enemy of their class. Just three days after the declaration of peace in Cuidad Juárez, the Flores Magón brothers made public a manifesto pleading with their partisans not to lay down their arms until the radical demands of their party were granted. It was no surprise that there was soon grave disorder in Chihuahua: the uprising in the barracks of Cuidad Juárez and the sacking of the city; the attack on the prison in Chihuahua by a group of rural soldiers who demanded the freedom of the socialists Antonio Rojas and Blas Orpinel, taken there for various reasons; and the insurrection in Casas Grandes of the anarchist leaders José Inés Salazar and Emilio Campa. With the railroad lines under his power in the northeast of the state, Orozco abandoned all his official duties on March 1 and issued a manifesto in which he announced his retirement to private life. On March 2 there was a demonstration in the city of Chihuahua, organized by a member of the oligarchy, demanding the resignation of González. When González refused to resign, on March 3 Orozco finally turned his back on Madero and set himself at the head of the counterrevolution. Ironically, this popular Revolutionary leader had linked up with the state oligarchy, who supported and financed him. He used the Plan de Santa Rosa or de la Empacadora, which contained various radical social hypotheses from the PLM, as his ideological banner.

Orozco pretended that Pancho Villa was on his way to ransack the city in order to make his move. After a few initial successes that gave him control of the major part of the state, and pursuing the Maderistas, he was faced with the Federal army and the guerrillas of Pancho Villa, now his enemy, and was defeated at Rellano, Conejos, and La Cruz. Although he lost the leadership of his faction, he fought as a guerrilla until February 1913, when the Madero government was overthrown in a military coup d'état. When President Madero was assassinated by the army, Orozco proclaimed his loyalty, with an embrace, to the general responsible for the coup, Victoriano Huerta, who rewarded him with the status of brigadier-general. In many ways this alliance was even more ironic than Orozco's previous one. The counter-revolution, begun by Orozco in Chihuahua 11 months earlier, finally succeeded by killing Madero and destroying in its infancy the incipient democratic state of Mexico. Huerta's new military regime brought neither peace nor harmony nor social changes to the country but a new, more brutal, more devastating, and longer war than Madero's. In 1914, owing to the resounding military triumphs of the Northern Division under Villa, which apart from devastating the Federal army relentlessly pursued the troops of Orozco, the anarchists, and the Magonistas, Orozco left Chihuahua and hid in Veracruz, where he rejoined the struggle alongside the dying army of Huerta. Soon after the fall of Huerta and his exile to the United States, Orozco refused to acknowledge Francisco S. Cabrajal, the interim president of the nation, and proclaimed his Plan de Reconstrucción Nacional (Plan of National Reconstruction), which aroused no interest. After capturing the city of León and allowing his troops to ransack it, his forces were destroyed in Gruñidora, Zacatecas. Orozco managed to make his way to the United States, where he finally took refuge in the mountains of Texas. There he hid until 1915, when the U.S. and British intelligence services discovered a plot being hatched by Germany and Victoriano Huerta to attack the United States and prevent its intervention into Europe by provoking a war with Mexico. Huerta traveled to rejoin his old ally Orozco and was stopped by the authorities in El Paso, Texas. A very ill man, he died there soon after. Orozco was found by the U.S. authorities camped out in the Texas mountains with four companions. On August 30, 1915, they were surrounded and surprised by a group of Texan Rangers on a small mountain path near El Paso and shot. In the United States Orozco's death was reported as that of a member of a gang of cattle rustlers in Texas. In 1925 his remains were brought back to the city of Chihuahua and reinterred in the Panteón de Dolores.

Select Bibliography

Katz, Friedrich, *The Secret War in Mexico*. Chicago: University of Chicago Press, 1981.

Hart, John M., *Anarquism and The Mexican Working Class, 1869–1931*. Austin: University of Texas Press, 1978.

Meyer, Michael C., *Mexican Rebel: Pascual Orozco and*

the Mexican Revolution. Lincoln: University of Nebraska Press, 1967.

_____, *Huerta: A Political Portrait*. Lincoln: University of Nebraska Press, 1972.

Raat, Dirk, *Revoltosos: Mexico's Rebels in the United States, 1903–1923*. College Station: Texas A&M University Press, 1981.

—RUBÉN OSORIO ZUÑIGA

P

Partido de Acción Nacional (PAN)

The National Action Party was founded in 1939 by a distinguished lawyer, Manuel Gómez Morín, who during the 1920s had participated with the Revolutionary elite in the setting up of the Banco de México and the Banco de Crédito Agrícola. Nevertheless, he became distanced from the group in power during the presidency of Plutarco Elías Calles (1924–28). In 1929 he supported the campaign of José Vasconcelos (secretary of education from 1921 to 1924) for the presidency in opposition to Pascual Ortíz Rubio, the candidate of the recently created Partido Nacional Revolucionario (PNR, or National Revolutionary Party).

From that moment Gómez Morín championed the need for a permanent political organization that would bring together all those who rejected what they saw as the exaggerated expansion of state power. He also supported a radical interpretation of the Mexican Revolution, one that would link the new regime with Marxism and the socialist trends of the period. Manuel Gómez Morín proposed a modernization program that was both authoritarian and elitist but with a strong commitment to social justice; he foresaw the state playing a tutelary role in the economy and in relation to the popular classes. In a certain way his proposal was not substantially distinct from the model used by the Revolutionaries in power. It differed only in that it explicitly rejected liberalism and individualism, as well as Revolutionary anticlericalism, and defended an organicist vision of society, private property, and the "natural communities" made up of the family, municipality, and trades' union.

The government of Lázaro Cárdenas (1934–40) passed a series of reforms on education, agrarian, and labor matters that aggravated the suspicions of those who feared the Sovietization of the Revolutionary regime. At this time circumstances created a situation favorable to Goméz Morín's project.

During these years he had created a name for himself as an honest academic and competent professional. Between November 1933 and October 1934 he was Rector of the National University in a difficult moment during which the institution was defend-ing itself against infighting between socialist and Catholics, each group trying to impose control.

In these years Gómez Morín established strong connections with militant Catholics that would later provide crucial support in the organization of the PAN. He also secured his reputation as a defender of freedom of education. Having abandoned his career as a public servant during the 1920s, Manuel Gómez Morín dedicated himself to private legal practice, running an office that specialized in commercial law. In this second activity he also forged lasting links with private businessmen, among which the most important were the founder of the powerful Monterrey Group who also would support, although behind the scenes, the founding of the PAN.

The Constituent Assembly of the National Action Party took place on September 14, 1939. It was a time of national crisis, aggravated by the start of World War II and the deepening of ideological antipathies on an international level. Cárdenas's term came to an end amid marked economic deterioration. The agrarian reform had negatively affected agricultural production; the oil expropriation had produced strong pressure on exchange rates; the introduction of socialist education at primary and secondary levels throughout the country had reactivated the tensions between the Revolutionary state and the Catholic Church. Cardenist policies also had provoked important disagreements in the nucleus of the Revolutionary coalition that began to manifest long before the end of his administration. Cárdenas was unable to heal the divisions, despite efforts to maintain Revolutionary unity—for example through the creation of the Partido de la Revolución Mexicana (PRM, or Party of the Mexican Revolution), the successor to the PNR. The most important split was that headed by General Juan Andreu Almazán, who contended against General Manuel Avila Camacho, the candidate of the official party, in the presidential elections of 1940.

Initially the PAN tried to become a kind of general opposition front that absorbed all those in disagreement with the status quo. However, the profile of its founder, a professional whose support base came largely from the then-insignificant middle classes and provincial notables, encountered difficulty in competing with the still-powerful attraction of the Revolutionary generals. In the 1940 elections, in which the PAN had tried to participate as a representative of all currents of anti-Cardenist opinion, Juan Andreu Almazán still drew the strongest opposition to the official party. The PAN did not participate formally in the election, but many PANistas voted for Almazán. The official party put into practice all its usual tricks to ensure the triumph of Manuel Avila Camacho, such as the robbing of ballot boxes and falsification of electoral lists. The election results are still a matter for debate, but the majority of historians agree that the winner, at least in the capital, was General Almazán.

This first experience did not dispirit Gómez Morín, who was determined to form a party that would be an institution distinct from the ephemeral opposition organizations that appeared periodically during election time and were led by personalities of the Revolutionary elite. To achieve continuity, he relied on the support of a large group of university students, the majority Catholic, who in previous years had fought actively in the struggle against Revolutionary anticlericalism and were ready to contribute their organizational experience and militant spirit to the project. Even though Manuel Gómez Morín was a devout believer, he never had belonged to a religious organization and had a secular view of politics. His alliance with the Catholics was based on certain affinities related to the rejection of liberalism and individualism but most of all on their mutual criticism of the Cardenist government.

Efraín González Luna, a lawyer from Guadalajara, Jalisco, well-read in philosophy and with a record of militancy in Catholic groups, played a key role in the alliance between Gómez Morín and the Catholic Church. Versed in Catholic social doctrine, González Luna took responsibility for writing the Doctrina del Partido, a theme that greatly concerned Gómez Morín; he considered that the continuity he sought would be impossible unless the infant organization was supported by a more or less precise compilation of general ideas, principles, and values. Thus the seal was set on an association that was not always free of tensions, between professionals and middle-class Catholic militants. This base membership of the PAN also counted on the discreet support of rising and important businessmen for whom Cardenism had been a bitter experience and who viewed the official party with distrust.

The relative diversity of the groups that participated in the foundation of the PAN disappeared in the 1950s and 1960s when the Catholic presence became more marked; it was also a period when the party experienced its greatest isolation and marginalization within the political system. Until his death in 1972, Manuel Gómez Morín always was opposed to the PAN's identifying itself with a religious creed or being subject to ecclesiastic authority, regardless of its strong Catholic membership. Neither was it convenient for the church to link itself with an opposition party, given its past conflicts with the Revolutionary state. As it happens, the party's link with the church always has been distant and on more than one occasion, tense. It is still possible, in view of the changes to the political system in the 1980s and 1990s, that the links between the PAN and the Catholic Church could change in the future.

Perhaps the most relevant information regarding the beginnings of the PAN that helps to clarify its dynamic in the mid-1990s can be found in its original composition. This latter gave the party a certain flexibility, even when membership proportions (academics, professionals, militant Catholics, and businessmen) were unbalanced, in that the party counted on the necessary groups at different moments throughout its history to be able to take up protests of equally diverse origin. This notwithstanding, and in consonance with its origins, the PAN rarely ceased being the party of the urban middle class.

Functions

From its foundation, the PAN has been identified unequivocally as the independent opposition party whose existence was possible largely because for decades it had very little political relevance. It was not until the 1980s that it acquired the characteristics of a genuine threat to the electoral hegemony of the Partido Revolucionario Institucional (PRI, or Institutional Revolutionary Party), the successor to the PRM. The strength of the PAN's image as an independent opposition is one of its defining characteristics in the Mexican political world and was one of the reasons behind its development in the 1980s and 1990s. Unlike other party groups, the PAN has never been seen as a tool of the state or the official party. The PAN has invariably been a "loyal opposition" party, not in the pejorative sense that some have wanted to attribute the concept, but more in terms of its rejection of violence and commitment to democratic institutions and procedures as the only civilized route to power.

Since its foundation, the PAN has fulfilled various functions within the political system. These changes are a reflection of the evolution of the political system as a whole and of the official party, the PRI, in particular. Thus between 1946 and 1970, the years of the consolidation and increase of the three central elements of Mexican authoritarianism (the post-Revolutionary state, the presidency, and the official party), the PAN played a limited role, since it acted more as a group of particular interests representing a political minority that had neither the possibilities nor the aspiration to take power, but could exercise a certain influence on limited themes such as education and electoral matters. On the other hand, the Mexican regime never committed itself to a one-party model, but rather for decades had distinguished itself from other Latin American countries for its scrupulous respect for the periodic holding of elections at local and national levels. During this long period the participation of PAN candidates in the elections was a testimony to the liberalism of the PRI toward the opposition, toward political pluralism, and also proof that the political system was on the path to democracy. Nevertheless, some considered that the PAN's participation in the elections was serving only to sustain the democratic facade of an essentially antidemocratic regime.

From the beginning of the 1960s, the PAN became the escape valve for a certain kind of political pressure, especially that which manifested periodically between middle-class groups and the state, on the theme of freedom of education. From 1963 other topics began to be included when the electoral reform that created party deputies was introduced. This was a means of representing political minorities in the legislature with the aim of reviving a multiparty state (then almost moribund, given the limited, if not nonexistent, importance of parties and elections in the political system of the time) characterized by opposition minorities and a one-party hegemony. This reform was an important stimulus for the revival of the PAN because it increased its representation in the Chamber of Deputies, which had been practically nil thanks to the PRI majority.

During the populist government of Luis Echeverría Álvarez (1970–76), the PAN experienced very important internal changes under the leadership of José Angel Conchello. He put an end to the Catholic hegemony and proposed to modernize the party so that it could absorb those who wanted a platform from which to criticize the PRI. This "open door" policy provoked very strong tensions within the organization between those who insisted that the PAN was a doctrinaire organization whose immediate objective was not to take power but to educate the electorate and those who proposed a more pragmatic line to push the party completely into a struggle for power the moment that governmental policy provoked social divisions similar to those produced by Cardenism. This internal conflict was so strong that during the 1976 presidential elections the PAN did not put forward a candidate, since none of the aspirants achieved the required majority in the party assembly. This stumbling block provoked a further drop in the already low electoral performance of the PAN in those years, as well as the renunciation of some of the most prominent intellectual leaders who had backed the traditional line of Efraín González Luna. These were short-term losses since internal restructuring that led to the presidency of Conchello prepared the party for the transformation of the 1980s.

From 1983 the PAN acquired an unprecedented importance during the political and financial crisis that set off the nationalization of the banks. This move, decreed by President José López Portillo (1976–82), provoked strong reactions from important groups within the business sector. At the same time, large middle-class groups, who felt that their expectations of economic prosperity had been betrayed when faced with the depressing panorama that augured the mounting of external debt, inflation, the program of economic adjustment of the new government, and the lessening of state intervention, also looked to the PAN as a platform from which to express their frustration. Between 1983 and 1984 the rate of electoral participation increased, and the PAN registered a series of victories in local elections, the most important being the municipal presidencies in the capitals of some important states. These triumphs cannot be viewed apart from the general wave of anti-statism that began to manifest on an international level. Even so, the official party was profoundly affected by austerity programs that notably reduced the negotiating capacity that for years had been the key to their popular support. This economic crisis thus removed the traditional mechanisms used by the PRI to control political participation, while in other sectors of society the organization of the protest vote grew.

The PAN advance in these years was so surprising that many believed Mexican politics to be on the verge of a two-party system. However, the federal elections of 1985 for the Chamber of Deputies gave the lie to these calculations, since the PRI maintained a majority. Even though the expansion of the PAN in these years was originally a local phenomenon, apparently limited to the rich states in the north of the republic, it had a lasting and wide-ranging effect, since from that moment the party became the vehicle for local anger against the centralism of the government, the PRI being simply an instrument of that centralism. Thus the PAN stopped being an escape valve for diverse political tensions and transformed into a real agent of political change whose active existence did not necessarily have a stabilizing effect but could effectively direct and provoke the dismantling of authoritarianism. Thus between 1983 and 1988 the PAN played a very important role in defining the path for political change. As the most influential anti-authoritarian protest group, it followed the democratic route of elections and adhesion to a party system. The new political forces that would activate themselves later would take the same path.

The results of the presidential elections of 1988 were a disappointment for the PAN. Its candidate, Manuel J. Clouthier, did not win a significantly greater percentage of the vote than that obtained by the PAN candidate in 1982, Pablo Emilio Madero, who allegedly captured 17 percent of the vote. The PAN had focused their expectations of triumph in the changes that they had experienced in the intervening six years, derived from the winning of new sympathizers, including in particular numerous business leaders of regional importance that brought both fresh economic and human resources to the party and thereby transformed its appearance. Thanks to this transfusion of new blood, the party had acquired the appearance of a modern organization with a prosperous and relatively young membership accustomed to winning and dealing with power and public opinion in a direct and irreverent fashion. In the past lay the image of the isolated and narcissistic party representing an aging fraction of Catholic militancy whose interest was limited to a kind of long-term spiritual conquest that interpreted politics as a moral crusade.

Manuel J. Clouthier, the successful businessman from Sinaloa who headed the storm of protest of major businessmen against the bank nationalization of 1982, incarnated the new kind of militant that entered the PAN during the 1980s and symbolized what began to be called *neopanismo*. This denomination marked a political style far more pragmatic than that of the traditional PANistas, even though to a certain extent it reflected the 1970s program of José Angel Conchello. The tone was more aggressive, revealing a greater confidence and employing

extraparliamentary means of mobilization that previously had been repudiated. Even though Manuel J. Clouthier did not construct the "new majority" he promised, nor bring the PAN to the presidency, he very significantly broadened the influence of the party, particularly in the north of the country.

From 1988 to 1994, the PAN played a key role in the stabilization of the crisis of legitimacy provoked by the presidential elections for that term. There were grave doubts as to the veracity of the election results that gave the victory to the PRI candidate Carlos Salinas de Gortari; the candidate of the Frente Democratico Nacional (FDN, or National Democratic Front), Cuauhtémoc Cárdenas, claimed he had won. Overcoming their own frustration, the PAN was disposed to take advantage of the fact that Salinas needed the acquiescence of at least one opposition party to assume power. The PAN accepted the electoral results, although under protest, but once the normal process of the change of government was under way, the PAN entered into a privileged form of dialogue with the president, who, taking advantage of the destruction of the Cardenista electorate and their representation in the Chamber of Deputies (an obligatory distribution between all the organizations that had made up the FDN), set up an authentically cooperative relationship with the PAN, which had the declared aim of sweeping electoral reform. The president and the PAN both benefited from this cooperation. The PAN's apparent confidence in Salinas's commitment to political reform boosted his credibility, while the PAN gained influence from its privileged relationship with the president. Even if Salinas benefited, however, the PRI as a whole was a clear loser in this marriage of convenience between the president and the PAN, losing key political offices in the *concertaciones,* or post-electoral accords. The most notable case was the conflict over the governorship of Guanajuato in 1992. After the state electoral commission declared the PRI candidate the victor, a PANista revolt accompanied by strong pressure on Salinas by PAN party leaders forced the PRI candidate to resign. As a compromise, a PANista was designated governor.

In 1989 the PAN won its first governorship in the border state of Baja California. In 1992 it was victorious in Chihuahua, and in 1995 in both Guanajuato and Jalisco, while municipal presidencies and state deputyships increased in a surprising manner. By the mid 1990s the PAN had strengthened its role as the vector for political change in Mexico toward a multiparty and competitive system, since it came to be regarded by many as a real alternative, above all at the local level. This development speaks more of the changes that the Mexican society experienced in the second half of the twentieth century—it became more urbanized, more educated and better informed, with a more complex employment structure and a broad middle-class following—than of the party itself, which to a large extent continued as an organization that carries the protest vote.

Ideology

Throughout its history the PAN has wanted to distinguish itself from the other parties, temporary or permanent, by insisting that it has a doctrine that imbues it with a specificity and individual identity. Traditionally the PANistas have asserted that the PRI is not a true party since it is just a tool of the government and has no ideology. Nevertheless, if one looks carefully at the doctrinal trajectory of the PAN, it is evident that its distinctive characteristics are less than its spokesmen would suggest. Apart from the substratum of Catholic thought that is more or less clear, the identity of the party has been more defined by its function as the party of opposition than by its adhesion to the principles of the Social Doctrine of the Catholic Church or by government programs that, given this affiliation, tend to be similar to those of Christian Democracy. Nevertheless, it is possible to identify certain continuities: antipopulism, antistatism, and the defense of private property, the family, and those social values associated with the morality of the Catholic Church.

The intellectual origins of the party reflect different currents of political thought associated with *Rerum Novarum,* the papal encyclical of Leo XIII. This document served to elaborate religious political doctrines such as those that underpin Catholic parties or democratic Christian parties and nonreligious doctrines that proposed institutional and highly hierarchical democracies. These two kinds of derivations of church social doctrine, one religious and the other secular, are brought together in the PAN and are reflected in the electorate. The Catholic current is solidly based in the center of the country in the states that participated in the peasant-based, pro-Catholic Cristero Rebellion (1926–29), and the nonreligious sector is to be found in the capital and the city of Monterrey.

At the beginning of the 1960s, PANista thought was updated as a result of the changes proposed by the Second Vatican Council. From that time party doctrine began to be reorientated toward the progressive Catholicism of the epoch, which criticized the separation between the church and the poor. Nevertheless, these type of reflections were not welcomed by traditional Catholics nor by the non-religious sector of the party that insisted that one should be more pragmatic and open the organization to middle-and upper-class groups whose support for the party should be based on the rejection of state interventionism and generally on the protectionist politics of the state vis-à-vis the popular classes. The tension between both currents of the PAN exploded in 1977 and culminated with the departure of the leaders of progressive Catholicism.

In its greatest period of growth, the PAN was characterized by pragmatism; even though it continued to talk of doctrine and showed certain affinities with organizations such as the Spanish Partido Popular (Popular Party), it seemed more difficult than ever to talk of an ideology. The party was faithful to its unavoidable commitment to pluralist and competitive democracy, but in economic and social matters its stand was still imprecise and confused. The PAN aspired to win over the largest possible electorate, which, of course, would be heterogeneous. Moreover, by the mid-1990s the position of Catholics inside the party seemed to have reached a fragile point of balance between those who wanted PAN to move toward democratic Christianity and those who were trying to convert it into an ultraliberal party in economic and social terms but conservative with regard to social morality. The PANista governors managed their states on the principle that the best government is that which governs least.

Growth and Electoral Presence

The history of the electoral presence of the PAN is a reflection of that of the PRI. This does not mean that all the voters lost by the official party candidate moved into the PANista opposition, but simply that the weakening of the PRI has benefited all the opposition parties and among them the PAN. Nevertheless, the crucial fact that explains the growth of the PAN has been the great surge in electoral participation. The PAN benefited from electoral politicization and the mobilization of the upper and middle classes, which traditionally have had greater political freedom than the lower classes. An example of the latter are the workers and *campesinos* (peasants) that, until the appearance of the Partido de la Revolución Democrática (PRD, or Party of the Democratic Revolution), were the captive electorate of the PRI.

The PAN participated for the first time with a presidential candidate in 1952, when the party garnered less than 8 percent of the total votes. From that moment until 1982, with the exception of 1976 (when no PAN candidate was presented), the PAN increased its share of the votes in each subsequent presidential election by approximately 2 percent. In

1994 the PAN won approximately 26 percent of the vote, a result which represented 9 percent more than in 1988, assuring it as the second electoral force of the country, in comparison with 50.13 percent for the PRI and 16 percent for the PRD. In the elections for the Chamber of Deputies between 1943 and 1958 the party never obtained more than six deputyships. In the 1960s and 1970s, the PAN increased its representation as a result of the party deputyships system but never to more than 25. In contrast, in 1988 the PAN won 101 deputyships. Even though the number dropped in 1991, a year when the PRI made an extraordinary recovery in these elections, three years later the PAN representation in Congress had increased significantly to 199 deputies and 25 senators.

The electoral growth of the PAN manifested mostly at local levels. The increase after 1985 should be explained principally as an expression of tensions and conflicts between local elites and the federal government. The role of the PAN as a vehicle of state/regional protest against the center explains the fact that in less than 10 years it managed to double and then triple its presence in many states in which it had no showing until the beginning of the 1990s (Coahuila, Colima, Morelos, Oaxaca, Puebla, Quintana Roo, Tamaulipas, Zacatecas) while establishing a stronghold in other states, such as Chiapas, Guerrereo, Nayarit, and Veracruz. This evolution transformed the PAN into an authentic regional force that managed to cross the borders of Baja California, Chihuahua, Coahuila, the Federal District, the Mexico State, Guanajuato, and Jalisco, in which it had concentrated for decades.

In 1996 the PAN governed more than 30 million Mexicans. Apart from four state governorships, it occupied numerous municipal presidencies, some in the most important urban centers of the country, and elected positions in local congresses. It had become the most important opposition party in Mexico and the most powerful adversary confronting the official party.

Select Bibliography

Aguilar Camín, Héctor, and Lorenzo Meyer, *In the Shadow of the Mexican Revolution: Contemporary Mexican History, 1910–1989*. Austin: University of Texas Press, 1993.

Cothran, Dan, *Political Stability and Democracy in Mexico*. Westport, Connecticut: Praeger, 1994.

Levy, Daniel, and Alberto Szekely, *Mexico. Paradoxes of Stability and Change*. Boulder, Colorado: Westview, 1983.

Loaeza, Soledad, "The Role of the Right in Political Change in Mexico, 1982–1988." In *The Right and Democracy in Latin America*, edited by Douglas A. Chalmers, María de Carmo Campobello de Souza, and Atilio A. Boro. New York: Praeger, 1992.

—SOLEDAD LOAEZA

Partido de la Revolución Democrática (PRD)

The Party of the Democratic Revolution is Mexico's largest left-of-center party. Founded in May 1989 in the aftermath of the electoral upheaval of the previous year, the party attempted to capitalize on the 6 million votes obtained by its charismatic leader, Cuauhtémoc Cárdenas, during the 1988 presidential elections. The PRD has attempted to give the broad coalition that supported Cárdenas—the Frente Democratico Nacional (FDN, or National Democratic Front)—a more coherent identity and formal organization, but it has not been able to repeat the FDN's success in 1988.

The PRD is an extraordinarily hybrid party. On the left it draws on the tradition of the independent socialist left, recruiting members of the successor parties and movements to the dissolved Partido Comunista Mexicano (PCM, or Mexican Communist Party) such as the Partido Socialista Mexicano (PSM, or Mexican Socialist Party), as well as from the Partido Mexicano de los Trabajadores (PMT, or Mexican Workers Party), and from certain Trotskyist currents. The centrist forces, which clearly dominate the new party, were recruited initially from dissident members of the ruling Partido Revolucionario Institucional (PRI, or Institutional Revolutionary Party); this dissident wing, the Corriente Democrática, left the government in mid-1986 in protest over the neoliberal economic model pursued by the Miguel de la Madrid government and the blocking of opportunities to democratize the PRI.

The organization therefore sheltered an extraordinary mix of forces and personalities, including iconic figures such as Cuauhtémoc Cárdenas (son of Mexico's most beloved former president, Tata Lázaro Cárdenas); experienced PRI apparatchiks such as Porfirio Muñoz Ledo (president of the PRD in 1996); a former general secretary of the Communist Party, Arnoldo Martinez Verdugo (a PRD deputy); and leftist activists and victims of the repression unleashed by the after the 1968 Tlatelolco Massacre, such as the historian and former Trotskyist militant Adolfo Gilly (a key advisor of Cuauhtémoc Cárdenas) and the architectural engineer and veteran of leftist politics, Heberto Castillo.

The heterogeneous character of the PRD's membership makes it difficult to identify the party ideologically. It certainly is not a socialist party, although a substantial number of the party's members and cadres were formed in various currents of the Marxist and socialist tradition. It would be more accurate to see the PRD as an attempt to preserve and reformulate tenets of what has come to be known as the tradition of Revolutionary nationalism, a key part of the intellectual and political baggage shared by progressive members of the PRI and of large sections of the Mexican left since the 1930s. This tradition incorporates elements of anti-imperialism, emphasizes the need to strengthen Mexico's political and economic sovereignty, and reaffirms the directing authority of the state in economic matters.

The political platform of the PRD calls for the democratization of the Mexican political and electoral system, including an end to presidential despotism and the breaking of the ties that bind labor and peasant organizations to the PRI. It has been a fierce critic of neoliberal economic policies and of the orthodox responses to economic crisis adopted by the government of Ernesto Zedillo Ponce de León. The party also has challenged many of the assumptions sustaining Mexico's incorporation in the North American Free Trade Agreement (NAFTA). Although Cárdenas modified the PRD's early fundamentalist opposition to the free trade agreement, he has been a key figure in the Latin American left's campaign to develop an alternative model of economic integration embracing the entire continent.

The PRD's struggle to create a party of a new type has encountered numerous obstacles. As one PRD member has argued, the PRD is not so much a party as "a collective state of mind." The biggest challenge has been to develop ways of fusing the myriad currents that came together to create the new party. Although some of the founding member organizations of the PRD followed orders and disbanded, others retained their prior organizational loyalties during the first four years of the party's existence. The survival of sectarian behavior based on prior party affiliations has led to noisy disputes over the distribution of positions in the PRD's leadership structure and has contributed to the public perception of the party as a fractious, disunited group. In its Third Congress (August 1995) the PRD resolved to eradicate sectarian abuses.

Electorally, the PRD's first seven years have been disappointing. The party has not been able to repeat the electoral victory achieved by the PSM/FDN coalition in 1988, when even government figures (almost certainly involving gross manipulation of voting tallies) gave the center-left coalition 31 percent of the national vote. Three years later, in the midterm congressional elections of 1991, the PRD obtained only 8.2 percent of the total vote (giving it 41 seats in the Chamber of Deputies). Even taking into account the fact that the PRD in 1991 had lost some of the leftist constituencies active in 1988, the drop in the party's vote was still disappointing. Moreover, in just two years the center-left PRD had ceded its place as the largest opposition force to the right-wing Partido de Acción Nacional (PAN, or National Action Party).

In the presidential elections of 1994, the recovery of the PRI and the advance of the PAN were even more evident. The PRD's vote was disappointingly low. Whereas Cárdenas had won 31 percent of the votes in 1988, his share of the votes in 1994 fell to 17 percent, which gave the PRD only 69 seats in the Congress. Moreover, even though the percentage of Mexicans voting reached a historic high (80 percent) in 1988, in absolute numbers the PRD increased its vote by a paltry 1 percent. In the Federal District, where the center-left had crushed the PRI six years earlier, the PRD's vote actually fell by 45 percent.

The party's experiences in state elections also have been disappointing. In Michoacán, home state of Cuauhtémoc Cárdenas, the PRD has been unable to overturn a long tradition of PRI rule. In the November 1995 gubernatorial election, for example, the PRD's candidate, Cristobal Arias, came second to the PRI candidate (with 31 percent as opposed to 38 percent of votes). In the southeastern state of Tabasco, the party was able to mobilize considerable forces in the 1991 local elections and in the 1994 gubernatorial race. However, on both occasions the local party was unable to secure the governor's seat; the PRD has issued well-substantiated allegations of electoral fraud and financial improprieties by the PRI during both races. In Chiapas, another center of PRD strength, the party has been able to win a substantial number of municipalities. But its fragile and often hostile relationship with the Zapatistas cost it votes when the Ejército Zapatista de Liberación Nacional (EZLN, or Zapatista Army of National Liberation) called on its supporters and sympathizers to abstain from voting in the local elections of October 1995.

In broad terms it could be said that the geographical and sociological profile of the PRD has shifted noticeably since 1989. The party's main support seems to have diminished in the urban, "modern" areas (most noticeably the Federal District, Mexico State, and Baja California Norte), while the party has preserved and strengthened its support in states with a more rural and indigenous character (Tabasco, Guerrero, and Chiapas).

The oil-rich state of Tabasco illustrates this point very well. The state has been a bastion of PRD strength, although the party has twice been cheated of electoral victory, in 1991 and 1994. The PRD's commitment to mass mobilization, direct action, and militant antistate action has been seen nowhere more clearly than in Tabasco, where PRD activists have occupied major towns, organized blockades of PEMEX oil wells, and built a strong following among Chontal indigenous people angered by pollution and soil degradation accompanying oil exploration. Meanwhile, the national standing of the PRD's Tabasco leader, Manuel López Obrador, has grown, and he is considered a possible contender for the position of president of the party.

An examination of the PRD's first years would identify several problem areas. The party's difficulties certainly have not been all of its own making. Repression of the party's activities and members has been especially ferocious. The government has treated the center-left and right-wing oppositions very differently. The contrast in the government's response to the two largest opposition parties became clear as early as July 1989, when the Carlos Salinas de Gortari government recognized the electoral triumph of the PAN in the Baja California gubernatorial elections while simultaneously denying the PRD the victory the party claimed to have achieved in state congressional elections in its stronghold of Michoacán.

The contrast in the government's handling of the PRD and PAN is not surprising in view of the presence of large numbers of distinguished PRI renegades in the PRD and their refusal to cut deals with the Mexican government. The PRI always has taken revenge on defectors. To make matters worse, the PRD's criticism of NAFTA and its often confrontational style have led the PRI to aim its biggest guns at the new party. The publication of a March 1994 letter to the PRI's first presidential candidate in that year's federal elections, Luis Donaldo Colosio, from his campaign manager, Ernesto Zedillo, in which Zedillo vowed to "destroy" the PRD seemed to confirm the existence of a sustained campaign to neutralize the Cardenistas. According to party officials, more than 350 PRD activists had been assassinated by the end of 1995.

Harassment and repression have not been the only government responses to the emergence of the PRD. A series of social mobilization initiatives of the Salinas and Zedillo governments (PRONASOL and PROCAMPO) also have neutralized part of the PRD's popular base; the Comité de Defensa Popular in the important Laguna city of Torreón, for example, accepted PRONASOL funds.

A number of weaknesses in the party's organic development also have contributed to the PRD's failure to engage its potential constituency. Although the new party hoped to build on the broad constellation of forces that had rallied behind Cárdenas in 1988, several important members of the PMS/FDN coalition refused to join the PRD or abandoned the infant organization shortly after its birth.

The basic division within the party has been between the "irredentist" forces associated with Cuauhtémoc Cárdenas and the more conciliatory groups associated with the PRD's national president, Porfirio Muñoz Ledo. The Cardenistas consistently denounced the government of Carlos Salinas as illegitimate; indeed Cárdenas described the PRI's 1988 victory as a "technical coup d'état." The more hard-line group around Cárdenas has frequently demanded the resignation of President Ernesto Zedillo and his replacement by a government of national conciliation. On the other side, the currents associated with Muñoz Ledo have been more prepared to "pact" and negotiate with the government and other forces, especially on the pace and content of democratization. At one level this has been a rhetorical distinction. But it also has been translated into different choices over tactics. The hard-liners sometimes have chosen the path of confrontation and militant street action, the best example being the decision by PRD supporters in Michoacán in 1992 to march on the state capital, Morelia, to protest electoral fraud. The August 1995 Third Congress of the PRD appears to have shifted the balance of forces within the party toward the less intransigent line.

The Zapatista insurrection in Chiapas starting in 1994 also damaged the PRD. The EZLN captured the imagination of broad sections of the center-left's constituency with the bold call for a new politics of democratization. But the Zapatistas stole the clothes of the political left at the same time that they pilloried the "conservatism" of groups like the PRD. On the other hand, the PRD's contradictory response to the EZLN alienated sections of its own constituency. The leadership of the party has tried at times to embrace the Zapatistas, while on other occasions it has distanced itself from the insurrectionary tactics of the EZLN, aware of the public perception of the PRD as a focus of disruption and instability. The poor performance of the PRD in the August 1994 presidential elections reflected, in part, voters' nervousness at the potential for political and economic destabilization created by the reappearance of armed struggle in a strategically sensitive region of the country.

The experiences of the PRD in its first half decade are a measure of both the significant changes and substantial continuities registered in Mexican national politics in the late 1980s and 1990s. The old left has disintegrated but a new, more coherent left has yet to emerge. Meanwhile, the fragile democratization of political life undertaken by the Salinas and Zedillo governments seems to have excluded the PRD, which has made the reformulation of a center-left practice and strategy all the more difficult.

Select Bibliography

Carr, Barry, *Marxism and Communism in Twentieth-Century Mexico.* Lincoln: University of Nebraska Press, 1992.

—BARRY CARR

Partido Revolucionario Institucional (PRI)

The Institutional Revolutionary Party has been one of the most singular political phenomena of the twentieth century. A cornerstone of presidential power for more than six decades, it has given its most important features to the contemporary Mexican state.

Since its foundation as an organ of the Mexican state in 1929, the party has had clear continuity in its institutional role. The party has had three avatars, the Partido Nacional Revolucionario (PNR, or National Revolutionary Party, 1929–38), the Partido de la Revolución Mexicana (PRM, or Party of the Mexican Revolution, 1938–46), and the present-day PRI (1946–). Although the name changes have marked important transitions, the PNR, PRM, and PRI are for all practical intents and purposes a single party. Since 1946 the PRI's candidates have won in all nine presidential elections, and the PRI has never lost the majority in the Mexican legislature, despite an increasingly strong opposition. After the crisis of 1988 the PRI suffered important defeats in state and municipal elections, but its national preeminence remains solid.

Despite its importance, however, academic discussion about the legal and political nature of the PRI has been quite limited. A few theorists have proposed tentative characterizations of the PRI, largely based on its role in the Mexican political system, its relations with other political parties, and its electoral strength. In the 1960s the PRI was characterized as a "strongly dominant party," in the 1970s as a "pragmatic hegemonic state," and in the 1990s as a "single party." More recent analysts have gone beyond these early characterizations and termed the PRI a "state party," examining the relations between the PRI and the Mexican state, the noncompetitive character of the party itself, and the structure and fraudulent practices in the electoral system.

As some critics of this model have pointed out, the PRI is not a "state party" like the Fascist Party in Italy or the Communist Party in the former Soviet Union, whose relationship to the state was constitutionally mandated; the closest analogy is the communist parties of eastern Europe, where the role of the communist parties was not constitutionally defined and the existence of other parties was allowed without offering a real alternative. The PRI is a state party for three reasons: first, it was created by President Plutarco Elías Calles (1924–28) to conserve political power, not to dispute it. Second, the most important organizational changes in the PRI in 1938 and 1946, as well as changes in its principles, programs, and plans, have been imposed by Mexican presidents without any discussion within the party. Finally, the PRI strength comes from the Mexican state and not from the party organization. Indeed, the PRI and the state have been melded to such a degree that in electoral campaigns the PRI has been able to make use of the material, financial, human, propaganda, and logistical resources of the Mexican state.

It has been tempting to exaggerate the PRI's predominance, however, and view it as an all-powerful organization. Nonetheless, the PRI has been sustained by the weakness of the opposition as much as the strength of the PRI—by the incapacity of independent parties to monitor elections and develop a viable alternative. The government has been able to reduce opposition parties with a combination of repression and co-optation, and over the 60 years the PRI has been in power only two alternatives to the PRI have been able to consolidate, the center-right Partido de Acción Nacional (PAN, or National Action Party), founded in 1939, and the center-left Partido de la Revolución Democrática (PRD, or Party of the Democratic Revolution), founded in 1988. Today the PRI is a vast corporatist organization with more than 14 million members. The majority of its members are affiliated with the corporate sectors of the PRI, which the party uses to legitimate official policies and to control voting in elections. Since its founding the PRI has used this corporatist organization as the cornerstone of a political system centered on the executive.

The PRI was formally launched on January 18–20, 1946, during the second national assembly of the PRM. Initially identified with the populism of the administration of Lázaro Cárdenas (1934–40), the PRM had suffered numerous attacks following the electoral fraud of 1940 and the administration of Manuel Avila Camacho (1940–46). In its 1946 assembly the PRM decided to assume a new name and new platform within the framework of the political reforms promulgated in Avila Camacho's new electoral legislation. The project of the new party was defined by the circle of Miguel Alemán Valdés, who was the precandidate of the three "sectors" of the party (labor, peasant, and "popular"). It was the Alemanistas who came up with the new name for the party, amalgamating two contradictory notions, "revolutionary" and "institutional." The Alemanistas intended to present the PRI as a new organization that would no longer be an organism of the state. The PRI would abandon the Cardenista strategy of sectoral organization, drawing its strength from the citizenry as a whole and competing with other parties on equal footing.

Despite its initial intentions, the Alemanistas' project never was implemented. The PRM-affiliated Confederación de Trabajadores de México (CTM, or Confederation of Mexican Workers) already had thrown its weight behind Alemán, vehemently opposing measures that would have marginalized the sectors. In its declaration of principles, the PRI abandoned the thesis that the party's objective was "the preparation of the people for the implementation of a workers' democracy and for the arrival of a socialist regime." Many key agrarian provisions were eliminated (most notably the call for a collective system of land tenure), and the PRM's 1938 motto, *Por una democracia de trabajadores* (For a workers' democracy), was replaced with the more innocuous *Democracia y justicia social* (Democracy and social justice). Many of the PRM's more radical principles were maintained, however, including its contention that "the existence of class struggle is inherent in the capitalist regime of production."

As had happened when the PNR became the PRM in 1938, there was considerable continuity between the PRM and the PRI, and even when the party's principles were substantially modified the internal structure of the party basically remained unchanged. Like the PRM, the PRI maintained a "double" structure: the "direct," "horizontal," or "territorial," which included the various municipal, state, and national party organizations; and the "indirect," sectoral, or corporatist, which included the agrarian, worker, and "popular" sectors of the party that were the real backbone of the party. The new statutes of the PRI sought to weaken the corporatist structure of the party; nonetheless, the corporatist structure of the party continued to be preeminent, since the PRI statutes failed to strengthen the "territorial" structure of the party as a counterweight.

The PRI was presented as a less centralized party than the PRM, but in practice it continued to be as centralized as ever. The statutes of 1946 maintained the language that allowed the Comité Central Ejecutivo (CCE, or Central Executive Committee) almost absolute control over the party. The president of the CCE, who was to be designated by the president of Mexico, was given broad powers within the committee. Indeed, only the state committees and the CCE, which was renamed the Comité Ejecutivo Nacional (CEN, or National Executive Committee) in 1950, maintained any degree of power within the new party organization. The National Assembly, which was supposed to be the "supreme organ" of the PRI, met only two times during the entire Alemán administration (1946–52). The grassroots organizations of the PRI existed only on paper, denying the PRI's rank and file any opportunity to participate in the life of the party. The policies of the Alemán administration further weakened the CTM, separating the national industrial unions from the confederation; other sectoral organizations were similarly weakened. Nonetheless, the CCE, chaired by General Rodolfo Sánchez Taboada, was not able to make the PRI into a "party of citizens," despite a vast membership drive in 1947.

The PNR had been created in 1929 as the party of Plutarco Elías Calles, "the *jefe máximo* of the Mexican Revolution," who over the next six years decided the party's platform and candidates and controlled the next three administrations. After the rupture between Cárdenas and Calles in 1935–36, however, the PNR became the "party of the president," and this presidentialism was only strengthened once it was institutionalized in 1946. In western countries heads of state have a determinant influence over their parties, but in the PRI this influence has become almost absolute. PRI members have not only accepted the president's power over all aspects of the party, but have justified this power as necessary, arguing that a democratic party structure would only divide and weaken the party.

The PRI has consequently been the main support of a regime in which the head of state not only has broad constitutional powers, but also broad meta-constitutional powers derived from his status as the ex oficio head of the PRI. The president's power within the PRI is based on three mechanisms: first, there is no internal democratic structure within the PRI; second, the PRI bureaucracy puts party discipline before individual conscience; and finally, presidents are able to decide the future course of all political careers within the PRI. The PRI permits the president to dominate federal and state legislators as well as state governors and municipal presidents, effectively nullifying the principles of political decentralization—the separation of powers, federalism, and free municipality—set forth in the Mexican constitution.

The increasing power of the presidency in the PRI over the years has only weakened the party. Since the 1950s the PRI has lost much of its democratic potential and its capacity to mobilize and has entered a real identity crisis. This crisis was accentuated during the administrations of Miguel de la Madrid (1982–88), Carlos Salinas de Gortari (1988–94), and Ernesto Zedillo Ponce de León (1994–), when each head of state imposed policies that went against the principles of the PRI and that frequently forced PRI members to support them against their convictions.

One of the most remarkable features of the PRI is the unwritten prerogative of the president to designate his successor (*el dedazo*, "the fingering"), impose him as the PRI's candidate, and ensure that he prevails in national elections through fraudulent electoral practices. (This succession process is called *tapadismo* in popular speech because the president's annointed, *el tapado*, or "the covered one," is a close collaborator of the president who is kept from public view until he is formally designated the PRI's candidate.) Specialists have theorized excessively about the extent to which the president must consult with other PRI powerbrokers before designating a successor. Nonetheless, detailed study of presidential successions has shown that the *dedazo* is a one-person decision. Moreover, the president has considerable room for maneuver, since he is able to advance his closest sympathizers from day one. The opinions of political, labor, and business leaders—or of international organizations—help the president formulate his criteria, but there is no evidence that they ever have been able to impose a candidate. Only once has a group within the PRI been able to veto a possible choice for a sucessor, when in 1951 three ex-presidents opposed Miguel Alemán's choice of a successor.

The president maintains close control over all stages of the succession process. The long-awaited announcement of a successor, the *destape* ("uncovering"), is made by a union leader such as the nonagenarian Fidel Velázquez, one of the sectors, or the CEN. The national convention of the PRI, which is formally in charge of designating a candidate, is relegated to rubber-stamping the president's choice —although the president's annointed is always presented as the choice of the PRI as a whole. Indeed, since 1929 the national conventions have nominated only a single precandidate, the only exceptions being the conventions of 1939 and 1946.

The lack of democratic structures and practices in the PRI has marked its history since its inception and has tended to play into the hands of the party's elites. Nonetheless, the agrarian, labor, and popular forces that joined the party in the 1930s and 1940s have considered the party the only legitimate space for those who sustain the principles of "the Revolution." They have demanded that their leaders be included in the management of the PRI and that a certain number of their leaders be named as candidates for political offices. In 1937 the party established an internal mechanism for selecting candidates, which continued until 1950. In 1937 Lázaro Cárdenas established an "open-door" policy allowing the selection of municipal and legislative candidates through internal plebiscites, with disputes being settled by the party leadership; when the PNR became the PRM in 1938 this form of selecting candidates was incorporated into the party statutes, although an exception was made for the selection of presidential candidates. The plebiscites never were truly democratic. There was considerable manipulation by party leadership, and electoral contests were not between individuals but between party sectors. Despite their flaws, however, these early reforms created a small measure of internal democracy.

When the PRM became the PRI in 1946, union pressure ensured that the selection of candidates in plebiscites remained on the books, despite the determined opposition of the Alemanista managerial clique. Four years later the Alemanistas were able to impose a new centralized party structure. The federal electoral law of 1951 prohibited political parties from having mechanisms for selecting their candidates that resembled "constitutional elections"; anticipating these new laws, the first national assembly of the PRI in 1951 ended the plebiscited system and reestablished the old system of selecting candidates in conventions, which continued for the next four decades. The conventions were profoundly undemocratic, since the rules for attending and voting in them were never specified. Nonetheless, the PRI membership accepted these changes, considering the designation of federal candidates as an unwritten prerogative of the president and the designation of local candidates as an unwritten prerogative of state governors. Conventions never were a forum for openly discussing precandidates; rather, their role was merely to approve official candidates.

The absence of internal democracy weakened the PRI as a whole, but it strengthened Mexican presidentialism. The president of Mexico could impose his policies without the slightest opposition from his own party. If the PRI were free of open dissent, however, it was not free of disputes and divisions—the clash of ideas gave way to the clash of interests, as the centralized process of choosing candidates for political offices sparked conflicts among the leaders of the various sectors of the PRI. Nonetheless, the question of party democracy has refused to go away.

The most significant attempt to democratize the PRI was led by PRI president Carlos A. Madrazo in 1964–65, the early years of the administration of Gustavo Díaz Ordaz. Madrazo had clashed with the party bureaucracy, opposing PRI legislators' attempt to suppress the Revolutionary principle of nonreelection for members of congress during the upcoming elections. This conflict deepened after the fourth national assembly of the PRI when Madrazo made public a plan to democratize the electoral process for municipal candidates, which was immediately opposed by sectoral leaders and local PRI bosses. Madrazo was able to implement his democratic reforms in seven states. In Sinaloa, however, he clashed with local leaders and Governor Leopoldo Sánchez Celis and was forced by Díaz Ordaz to resign.

Madrazo's attempt to democratize the PRI was quickly reduced to a traumatic memory. Later PRI presidents also attempted to foster a limited degree of party democracry but were quickly forced to abandon their efforts. In 1977 PRI president Carlos ("el Negro") Sansores pushed the idea of "transparent democracy," and in 1984 Adolfo Lugo Verduzco also suggested that the PRI democratize. Despite their efforts, their suggestions never ended up being more than irrelevant exercises. During the early years of the Salinas adminstration, however, the drive for party democracy became more intense, and in 1990 the fourteenth national assembly of the PRI approved (in principle) a democratization of internal electoral mechanism. The actual drafting of the reform statutes, however, was delegated to a commission, and the reforms left intact the CEN's prerogative to choose electoral mechanisms.

In 1991 PRI president Luis Donaldo Colosio attempted a "democratic experiment" in various municipal and gubernatorial elections, but the experiment encountered numerous difficulties—ranging from the absence of a PRI membership list to the lack of a democratic culture among PRI members—and ended in failure. The lack of any kind of real will to open the internal electoral process was underscored by the party's prohibition on precandidates campaigning. Moreover, party members always knew in advance who the "annointed" would be. In the selection of a PRI candidate for the governorship of Nuevo León, for example, the official candidate openly campaigned with the support of the party leadership, and in Colima two precandidates clashed not with ideas, but with different mechanisms of electoral fraud. The experiment in party democracy was abandoned, but the demands of many PRI members that the party be democratized did not cease. Toward the end of 1994, when the CEN organized hearings on internal reform, party democracy was one of the principal demands, together with the separation of the PRI from the government.

Authoritarian political parties tend to experience fractures and schisms, and the PRI has not been an exception. During the 1930s and 1940s, many aspirants for political office ended up running as independent candidates and on occasion even managed to defeat the official PRI candidate. Once a law was passed prohibiting independent candidacies, however, dissidents were forced to seek the support of a registered political party. Nonetheless, the practice of dissidents running for office did not disappear. The main electoral opposition to the PRI has come from the ranks of the PRI itself, particularly during presidential elections. The schisms led by General Adalberto Tejeda (1933–34), General Juan Andreu Almazán (1939–40), Ezequiél Padilla (1945–46), and General Miguel Henríquez Guzmán (1951–52) all threatened the PRI's control of presidential elections, but the most important dissident movement was the split led by Cuauhtémoc Cárdenas and Porfirio Muñoz Ledo in 1986–88. In the final years of the administration of Miguel de la Madrid, a group of PRI members known as the Corriente Democrática (Democratic Current) made public their disagreement with official party policies. The Corriente Democrática contended that the government, in adopting neoliberal policies (broadly defined, policies supporting the free market and emphasizing a tight money supply and a balanced budget in the pursuit of manageable inflation rates), had betrayed the ideals of the Mexican Revolution and the PRI itself. The Corriente Democrática demanded a public discussion of the problems of Mexico and of PRI precandidates. De la Madrid signalled his refusal by opening the process of selecting an official candidate to succeed him as president, producing the gravest schism in the 35-year history of the PRI. Cuauhtémoc Cárdenas ran for president as the candidate of an ad-hoc coalition of left-wing and center-left political parties and nongovernmental organizations, and in the elections of July 6, 1988, he was defeated only through a massive electoral fraud.

The electoral fraud of 1988 sparked an institutional crisis in which the very role of the PRI would be questioned. De la Madrid's successor, Carlos Salinas de Gortari, announced shortly after the election that the PRI's days as an "almost single" party were over, but during the six years of his administration he repeatedly refused to accept any real electoral reform or internal reform in the PRI. During negotiations following the 1988 election, Salinas favored the center-right PAN, announcing a strategic alliance with the party in 1993. The internal crisis of the PRI continued to deepen. On the one hand, the party continued to be an arm of the state under control of the executive; on the other, the last few administrations had abandoned the party's founding principles. Despite the gravity of the situation, the party leadership showed no will to change. The fourteenth assembly of the PRI in 1990 refused to listen to demands of party members and ended up being a spectacular failure.

The Salinas administration also decided that the mediation among different interest groups that had been realized by the PRI should be assumed by the government and that the benefits of this mediation should accrue to the presidency. The PRI's power to broker key government services in exchange for political support was severely limited, even when the statutes of 1990 created a new party structure toward this end: the Movimiento Territorial (Territorial Movement), whose primary purpose was to transport voters on election day and (according to the opposition) buy votes. The PRI was reduced to being a mechanism for rigging elections and fell in ever-greater discredit, as the unpopular policies of the Salinas administration were attributed to the PRI. Whereas between 1963 and 1988 the PRI lost 36 percent of its voting strength, during the Salinas adminstration the decline was even more precipitous. The corruption of Salinas's inner circle and its links to drug smuggling, the failure of Salinas's economic policies, and electoral fraud deepened the party's decline, generating increasing opposition to its dominance over Mexican political life. The most important demonstration of opposition to the PRI was the 1994 uprising in Chiapas of the indigenous peasants of the Ejército Zapatista de Liberación Nacional (EZLN, or Zapatista Army of National Liberation). Significantly, a central objective of the Zapatistas was the end of the state party system in Mexico.

The crisis in the PRI has continued to deepen in the past few years, but the nadir was reached on March 23, 1994, with the assasination of the PRI's presidential candidate, Luis Donaldo Colosio, in Tijuana. From the beginning the unsolved murder of Colosio was called a "crime of state," and the selection of a substitute candidate, Ernesto Zedillo, by the CEN rather than the national convention of the PRI was yet another blow to PRI loyalists. On September 28, 1994, the secretary general of the PRI, José Francisco Ruiz Massieu, was assasinated in Mexico City, and the former president's brother, Raúl Salinas de Gortari, was accused of being the intellectual author of the crime. Both the PRI and the delicate marriage between party and state clearly were disintegrating, but the party leadership adopted a defensive posture, rejecting all substantive reform proposals.

Although many European and Latin American leaders have recognized the nondemocratic nature of the PRI, its status as an organ of the Mexican state has given it a degree of legitimacy in international relations. Under the administration of Luis Echeverría Álvarez (1970–76), PRI president Jesús Reyes Heroles embarked on a far-reaching international campaign, meeting with the leaders of the Radical Party in Argentina and European social democratic parties and attending the UDR Congress in Nice. Although Mexican law prohibits political parties from belonging to international party organizations, the PRI was able to be accepted as an observer in the Socialist International, which includes such parties as Britain's Labour Party and France's Socialist Party, increasing the PRI's international presence. The PRI's influence was increased still more during the administration of José López Portillo (1976–82) when in 1979 the PRI joined with other Latin American political parties to form the Conferencia Permanente de Partidos Políticos de América Latina (COPPPAL, or Permanent Conference of Political Parties of Latin America).

As of 1996, it was not clear what the outcome of this political crisis would be. If there is no transition to democracy in Mexican political life, if the PRI is not profoundly reformed and the state party system dismantled, Mexico will not be able to meet the challenges of the twenty-first century. The PRI faces a clear choice. The first option is to stop being a corporatist and authoritarian state party that maintains its hold on power through the fraudulent structures and practices of the electoral system; to become a party of citizens that accepts a profound political reform establishing the rule of law in Mexico; to respect the rights of citizens and end the impunity of public officials. The second option is to continue the current practice of cosmetic reforms that do nothing to change the statist features of the PRI—to continue being an obstacle to the urgently needed reform of the Mexican state. Mexico's transition to democracy depends on the PRI. For nearly 60 years it has sustained a political regime whose end appears to have come.

Select Bibliography

Ames, Barry, "Bases of Support for Mexico's Dominant Party." *American Political Science Review* 64 (March 1970).

Hansen, Roger D., *The Politics of Mexican Development.* Baltimore: The John Hopkins Press, 1971.

McIntire Richmond, Patricia, *Mexico: A Case Study of One-Party Politics.* Berkeley: University of California Press, 1965.

Padgett, Vincent Leon, *Popular Participation in the Mexican "One-Party" System.* Evanston, Illinois: Northwestern University Press, 1955.

Sartori, Giovanni, *Comparative Constitutional Engineering: An Inquiry into Structure, Incentives and Outcomes.* New York: New York University Press, 1994.

Shers, David, *The Popular Sector of the Mexican PRI.* Albuquerque: University of New Mexico Press, 1972.

—LUIS JAVIER GARRIDO

Paz, Octavio 1914–

Writer

Octavio Paz was born on October 31, 1914, in Mexico City. Beginning his studies in Mexico City, he abandoned them, together with his family home, in 1937 to work in Yucatán as a rural schoolteacher. That same year he married Elena Garro (with whom he later had a daughter) and left with her for Spain, where he had been invited to participate in the Second International Congress of Antifascist Writers. In Spain he made the acquaintance of many of the writers who would influence his work and life, including Luis Cernuda, Jorge Guillén, Pablo Neruda, Julien Benda, and Luis Aragon. From 1938 to 1941 he lived and wrote in Mexico, and toward the end of 1943 he began a series of journeys overseas that would have a definitive effect on his work. He spent two years in the United States, receiving a grant from the Guggenheim Foundation in 1944, and in 1945 he began a career in the Mexican diplomatic corps that would last 23 years. His first posting was in Paris, where he remained until 1951. In 1952 he traveled to Japan and India. Between 1953 and 1958 he lived in Mexico City, working for the Department of Foreign Relations. In 1959 he was posted in Paris

once again, and in 1962 he was transferred to India, where he later would be appointed ambassador. In 1964 he married Marie-José Tramini. In 1968 he resigned as ambassador in protest of the Mexican government's massacre of student protesters in the Plaza of Tlatelolco, effectively ending his diplomatic career. Since then he has lived in Mexico City, where he continues to play a key role in the intellectual life of Mexico.

Paz began writing quite early. In 1931 he published his first poem, "Caballera," and participated in the foundation of a student literary journal, *Barrandal.* He later would work with several other journals: *Cuadernos del Valle de México* (1933–34), *Taller poético* (1936–38), *Taller* (1938–41), *El hijo pródigo* (1943–46), *Plural* (1971–76), and *Vuelta* (1976), which is still published.

In 1933 Paz published his first book of poetry, *Luna Silvestre,* which showed the first signs of the lyricism and eroticism that would be constants in his work, and in 1936 he published *¡No Pasarán!,* a collections of poems on the Spanish Civil War. Both books later would be disowned by Paz and excluded from future anthologies. Nonetheless, both books wrestle with an enduring question in Paz's work, the place of poetry in the human enterprise; Paz later would find an adequate way to address this question in the "surrealist revolution." Later books included *Bajo tu clara sombra y otros poemas sobre España* (1937), *Raíz del hombre* (1937)—which received an enthusiastic review from Jorge Cuesta, drawing Paz closer to the Contemporáneos group—and *Entre la piedra y la flor* (1941) and *A la orilla del mundo* (1942).

Libertad bajo palabra (1949) is a milestone in Paz's poetry, marking the influence of two new traditions on Hispanic poetry: on one hand, the English-language poetry of T. S. Eliot, e. e. cummings, and Ezra Pound; on the other, the poetry of the surrealists and especially Stéphane Mallarmé. In *Libertad bajo palabra* synchronicity, typographic play, fragmentarism, and conversational language are combined with sonnets and other fixed forms of versification. Dream images are presented alongside language poetry. Paz experiments with brief poetic forms such as haiku and develops surrealism as a vital attitude, not simply a poetic style, drawing on ideas of love, rebellion, freedom, union of opposites, and reconquest of original innocence. For Paz the value of surrealism did not rest in dream adventures or automatic writing, but in the revolutionary power of poetry as a creator of realities.

After *Libertad bajo palabra* Paz's poetry consolidated what he later would define as "a silent, secret, disenchanted vanguard," experimentation "toward the within of language." *Blanco,* published in 1967, was an accordion-fold book-object, a mandala poem that could be read from four different directions, combining Eastern and Western philosophy, pre-Hispanic motifs, eroticism, the body as text, and the text as body. *Topoemas* (1968) and *Discos visuales* (1971) combined the caligram, concrete poetry, and other combinations of visual and literary art forms. *Renga* (1972), a collective poem in four voices, recreated the Japanese tradition of the *renga,* which seeks the erasure of the individual poetic voice. *¿Águila o sol?* (1950) and *El mono gramático* (1972) challenged the boundaries between poetry and prose. *Salamandra* (1962) included "Homenaje y profanaciones," an exercise in the "transfiguration/disfiguration" of a sonnet of Quevedo, which was linked to his reflections on translation. In *Ladera este* (1969) Paz draws on his contacts in the orient, while *Vuelta* (1976) is a series of poems (among them Paz's celebrated "Nocturno de San Ildefonso") on Paz's reencounters with friendships and places after his return to Mexico. Paz's long poem *Pasado en claro* (1975) also is an exercise in memory, but it is more intimate and profound, a meditation on Paz's relationship with words. In *Arbol adentro* (1987) eroticism, love, and alterity are dominant themes, although there also is a dialogue with literature and the plastic arts (as in *Vuelta*).

The poem, Paz says, is an object of language, a constellation of signs, capable of projecting the reader to experience of poetry, which is a reencounter with the primordial unity from which mankind has been expelled. Primordial time is incarnated in an instant; linear time becomes a pure present that nourishes and transforms the reader. Thus, Paz insists that there is a difference between poetry and poem: there are passages, persons, and deeds in which there can be poetry without being a poem. The poetic experience is at once eminently individual and collective. If the poetic experience occurs in the life of the community as it ritually repeats its foundational myths (a return to its original innocence), it also occurs in the individual's radical encounter with alterity as a revelation, a religious experience. The supernatural, religion, love, and poetry permit the individual to escape himself and become an other.

Paz complements this vision with a poetic existentialism founded in Søren Kierkegaard's "leap of faith" and Martin Heidegger's "being there" with the certainty of death. Poetry, like religion, is part of the original human situation: the knowledge that one has been cast into a hostile, indifferent world and trapped in time and finitude. This vision of Paz situates the poet between the magician and the mystic. From the former he takes his knowledge of the principle of analogy (which puts him in contact with the cosmos, establishing relations among all beings), although he rejects the magician's will to power; from the latter he takes his spirit of communion, although he discards the mystic's quest for solitude. Emphasizing the material aspect of language over anthropocentric concepts of artistic creation, Paz's development has paralleled the idea of Mallarmé and Marcel Duchamp that "the poet is not served by words. He is their servant." Paz's contacts with surrealism—first through the Spanish poets of the Generation of 1927 and later through his friendship with André Breton—have been decisive in the development of his poetry.

The main controversies surrounding Paz's poetry have come from the clash between "pure" and politically engaged poetry. This clash has been played out in various forms: early attempts to efface the "surrealist revolution" in favor of a "surrealism in service of the Revolution"; the social realism of the Spanish Civil War and World War II; the "new realism of *mexicanidad*" during the 1950s that viewed surrealism as an anachronistic, hermetic, xenophile indulgence; and accusations during the 1960s and 1970s that Paz's poetry indulged in utopian elitism or that it was an exercise in the banalization of Mexican myths and stereotypical "natives." Nonetheless, Paz's poetry continues to be a touchstone for young Latin American poets, as well as poets writing in Spanish, English, and French throughout the world.

Paz also has produced a body of essays that is characterized by its use of paradox and word play. The essays have been criticized roundly by scholars who expect systematic rigor, order, hierarchy, and definition of terms. Paz prefers to view the essay more in terms of the creative aspect of language and its capacity to suggest rather than demonstrate; indeed, Paz defines modern criticism as "critical passion," "something more than opinion and less than certainty."

El arco y la lira (1956) is particularly important in the definition of Paz's poetics; the 1967 edition adds "Los signos en rotación," a key chapter that includes Paz's reflections on Mallarmé. *Los hijos del limo: Del romanticismo a la vanguardia* (1974) defines the modern poetic tradition as a "tradition of rupture" and "critical passion," two concepts founded in the clash of analogy and irony. *La otra voz: Poesía y fin de siglo* (1990) continues Paz's examination of the modern tradition, calling for a "poetry of convergence" to follow the "decline of the avant-gardes."

In *Sor Juana Inés de la Cruz o las trampas de la fe* (1982), Paz examines the life, work, and times of Sor Juana, making an important contribution to the study of the Latin American Baroque.

Paz's first important essay, *El laberinto de la soledad* (1950), has become a classic in Mexican literature. Attempting to find an answer to his inquietudes regarding the Mexican character, Paz examines Mexican customs, daily life, and cultural production, as well as making an interpretive survey of Mexican history. Paz continues these reflections in *Posdata* (1970) following the Massacre of Tlatelolco, underscoring the persistence of the Mexica (Aztec) theocracy and its bloody sacrifices beneath modern Mexico. Other essays on political and historical questions include *El ogro filantrópico: Historia y política 1971–1978* (1979), *Tiempo nublado* (1983), and *Pequeña crónica de nuestros días* (1990). Paz discusses such themes as the critique of totalitarian systems; the crisis of imperialist capitalism; the defense of the democracy, pluralism, and freedom; and the problems of modernization in Latin America.

Literary theory, art criticism, and political discussion are combined in *Las perlas del olmo* (1957), *Cuadrivio* (1965), *Puertas al campo* (1966), *Corriente alterna* (1967), *El signo y el garabato* (1973), *In/Mediaciones* (1979), *Sombras de obras* (1983), *Hombres en su siglo y otros ensayos* (1984), *Al paso* (1992), and *Convergencia* (1991). *Claude Lévi-Strauss o el festín de Esopo* (1967) analyzes structuralism, refining his perception of the world of signs. *Marcel Duchamp o el castillo de la pureza* (1968), a book object designed by Vicente Rojo, and *Aparencia desnuda: La obra de Marcel Duchamp* (1973) focus on the work of Marcel Duchamp, who has been an important influence on Paz's ideas regarding artistic creation. *Conjunciones y disyunciones* (1969) discusses eroticism, sexuality, and Eastern and Western religion. *La llama doble: Amor y erotismo* (1993) traces the connections among sex, eroticism, and love, particularly in the Western tradition. *Intinerario* (1993) and *Vislumbres de la India* (1995) are autobiographical essays. In *Traducción: Literatura y literalidad* (1971) Paz discusses the creative work and limitations of the translator: "when writing, the poet does not know how the poem will turn out; when translating, the translator knows that his poem must reproduce the poem under his eyes." Paz has done many translations of his own, including anthologies of Bashô (1957), Fernando Pessoa (1962), William Carlos Williams (1973), and Apollinaire (1979).

Paz's work has received considerable international recognition, including the Premio Miguel de Cervantes (Madrid, 1981) and the International Grand Prize in Poetry (Brussels, 1963). In 1990 Paz received the Nobel Prize in literature. His work has been translated into numerous languages.

Select Bibliography

Fein, John M., *Octavio Paz: A Reading of His Major Poems, 1957–1976*. Lexington: University Press of Kentucky, 1986.

Krauze, Enrique, "Octavio Paz: Facing the Century. A Reading of *Tiempo nublado*," translated by Sonja Karsen. *Salmagundi* 70–71 (Spring–Summer 1986).

Phillips, Rachel, *The Poetic Modes of Octavio Paz*. London: Oxford University Press, 1972.

Wilson, Jason, *Octavio Paz*. Boston: Twayne, 1986.

—RODOLFO MATA

Peso Crisis of 1994

In early January 1995, Mexico was on the verge of defaulting on its foreign obligations; following a devaluation announced in December, investors—foreign investors, in particular—were reluctant to roll over (defer payment on) the country's short-term debt. The panic this caused in international capital markets began to spread to other countries in and outside Latin America. The liquidity crisis was solved by an international financial rescue package led by the U.S. government and the International Monetary Fund (IMF), whose terms were finalized in February. The rescue package was successful not only in solving Mexico's liquidity crisis but also in helping Mexico regain access to capital markets as early as April of that year. Also, in the course of a few months the situation in the other countries returned to normalcy. The only important exception was Argentina, for which the shock waves triggered by the Mexican crisis had a more lasting and profound effect. For all its virtues, however, the rescue package was not able to avoid a major drop—the largest since the Great Depression—in Mexico's economic output in 1995; in that year, gross domestic product (GDP) fell by close to 7 percent from its level in 1994.

This article presents an analysis of the causes of Mexico's liquidity crisis and how it was solved. To most analysts and observers, the Mexican liquidity crisis came as a surprise and proved much more expensive to solve than anticipated.

The Mexican Liquidity Crisis
After the debt-reduction program known as the Brady Plan was signed with commercial banks in 1990 and, particularly, after the passage of the North

American Free Trade Agreement (NAFTA) in 1993, there was a widespread perception that Mexico was unlikely to face a debt crisis of major proportions again. In its macroeconomic policy, the federal government was not repeating the mistakes that led to two previous crises in 1976 and 1982. In particular, the main source of the previous crises, namely, a large fiscal deficit, was not a problem anymore: in 1992 and 1993 the government's accounts were in surplus.

The events in December 1994 proved optimism mistaken. Market-oriented reforms notwithstanding, a relatively small departure from fiscal and monetary conservatism—especially when compared to that of 1981—led Mexico to a liquidity crisis of unprecedented magnitude. The liquidity crisis that followed the devaluation of the Mexican peso in December 1994 left many analysts, investors, and observers bewildered by its magnitude. Early on several economists had been saying that the peso was overvalued (i.e., the dollar was too cheap, which resulted in Mexicans buying large quantities of imported goods, thereby diminishing exports). If left uncorrected, these economists warned, the overvaluation could lead eventually to a speculative attack at a time when international reserves held at the Bank of Mexico were too low.

These analysts were right in one respect. A flight of investors from the peso when reserves were already too low is what led to the forced devaluation in December 1994. However, what followed *after* the December devaluation was in fact quite different from predictions. Far from calming the markets, the devaluation resulted in a financial crisis with significant spillover effects on other countries, particularly in Latin America. This crisis went far beyond a standard speculative attack. What originally was intended as a 15 percent increase in the exchange rate band's ceiling (i.e., the maximum intended level for the value of the dollar) in a matter of days put Mexico on the verge of default. The flight of capital not only from Mexico but also from other so-called emerging markets in Latin America and elsewhere took governments and international financial institutions by surprise. Hence, an analysis of Mexico's 1994 crisis has to address two separate questions: what caused the devaluation in December, and why did the devaluation turn into a financial crisis? We now turn to the first question.

Higher U.S. Interest Rates and Political Shocks

Although some analysts viewed the situation of an appreciating peso, low and declining domestic savings, and a high external imbalance with concern, the predominant view at the end of 1993 was that these imbalances were transitory and that Mexico was on its way to prosperity. The source of greatest concern was that the counterpart of these imbalances was Mexico's reliance on rather volatile capital inflows. If for whatever reasons market sentiment changed and these inflows slowed, the country could be forced to make a major adjustment. However, given the prestige enjoyed by Mexico's government, the program of economic reforms, the commitment to price stability, and the boost to credibility given by the passage of NAFTA, the presumption was that foreign investors would continue to favor Mexico as a destination of their capital.

Then came the year of 1994. It started with the guerrilla uprising in Chiapas on January 1. In February, the U.S. Federal Reserve announced the first of a series of increases in interest rates to reduce the chances of higher inflation. In March, the presidential candidate of the ruling Partido Revolucionario Institucional (PRI, or Institutional Revolutionary Party), Luis Donaldo Colosio, was assassinated. In September came another assassination: that of the PRI's secretary general, José Francisco Ruiz Massieu. Interestingly, the Chiapas uprising in early January did not translate into capital flight. Perhaps because fighting was halted after 10 days, when the uprising started to give way to negotiations, foreign investors remained rather unconcerned. This optimism is reflected in the fact that Mexico's international reserves increased by about US$4 billion in the following two months. The increase in U.S. interest rates in February did not have an immediate negative impact either. The first sharp impact on confidence was felt with the assassination of Colosio. In the course of three days, international reserves fell by about US$3 billion, and within a month they declined from US$28.3 billion to US$17.5 billion.

At this point, the government had two options: to change its exchange rate policy, or make no change in the exchange rate policy and instead raise domestic interest rates, make use of international reserves, and issue more of the short-term government debt instruments indexed to the dollar, known as Tesobonos. The authorities chose the second option and decided to wait it out, until expectations were reversed. Interest rates on the bellweather 28-day CETES (Treasury Certificates) rose from about 9 percent per year in March to 16 percent in April 1994, and outstanding Tesobonos began to increase by leaps and bounds.

The economic policy measures taken in April appear to have received the tacit support of the U.S. and Canadian governments, as indicated by the fact that both put in place swap arrangements (which if activated were the equivalent of short-term loans) for a total of close to US$7 billion. The United States's contribution was equal to US$6 billion, and Canada added $1 billion of Canadian dollars. These swap arrangements were subsequently made permanent and formalized in the North American Framework Arrangement (NAFA) signed on April 26, 1994. However the funds pledged under the NAFA turned out to be too small to stop markets from panicking at the end of 1994.

After April 1994, the dollar often was at the maximum value permitted by the existing policy, and the information available indicated that international reserves stayed at around US$17 billion throughout most of the period until November. The Bank of Mexico (Central Bank) later argued that the relative stability of international reserves during this period was a sign that the peso was not under unmanageable pressures. However, the huge change in the amount of Tesobonos held by the public was sending the opposite message. Between March and June 1994, the sum of Tesobonos increased from US$3.1 billion to US$12.6 billion; the figure rose to US$19.2 billion in September and to US$29.2 billion in December. Throughout the year, the composition of the government's debt held by foreigners had changed radically: in December 1993, 70 percent was in CETES and 6 percent in Tesobonos; in December 1994, 10 percent was in CETES and 87 percent in Tesobonos. Clearly, many investors feared a devaluation of the peso and preferred to hold Mexican debt that was indexed to the dollar.

The systematic increase in Tesobonos held by the public ought to have been seen as an unequivocal sign of the lack of credibility of the exchange rate policy. It also implied that the Mexican government was undertaking a large portion of the exchange rate risk given that these short-term obligations were indexed to the dollar. This "dollarization" of the internal public debt probably explains the surprising stability of international reserves from April onward in the face of rising external interest rates and internal political uncertainty. The Tesobonos, in fact, gave a false sense of security both to the creditors and to the government. As we shall see, the enormous value of Tesobonos held by foreigners was one of the principal causes of the liquidity crisis that followed the December devaluation: given the large magnitude of the short-term debt indexed to the dollar in relation to available reserves, investors feared a default and refused to roll over Mexico's short-term debt.

Unfortunately, the assumption that the slowdown in capital inflows was temporary led to a monetary policy—especially in the last quarter of 1994—that proved incompatible with the exchange rate policy. The monetary authorities compensated the capital outflows by injecting more domestic credit. This led to a fall in the domestic interest rates beginning in July, a trend contrary to the interest rate in the United States. The expansion of domestic credit and the relaxation of the fiscal stance—through the net credit provided by the development banks—exacerbated the pressures on the peso.

Confronted with the panorama of falling domestic interest rates while the U.S. rates were rising, a current account deficit of 8 percent of GDP in 1994 and a similar deficit expected in 1995, and the memory that approximately every six years since 1976 the government abandoned its vows not to devalue, investors—in particular, those who were more acquainted with Mexico's history—increasingly began to flee, especially in November and early December. On December 16 international reserves had dropped to approximately US$11 billion.

Faced with the situation of dwindling international reserves, the government called for an extraordinary meeting of the "Pacto" (composed of representatives of workers, agricultural producers, and the business sector) on the evening of December 19. At this meeting it was agreed to raise the ceiling of the band within which the dollar was allowed to fluctuate to 4 pesos to the dollar (a rise of about 15 percent in its value). This new ceiling was announced and took effect on the morning of December 20.

Following the announcement, the value of the dollar reached the 4-peso ceiling almost immediately, and it is estimated that in the course of two days US$5 billion left the country. The markets were sending a clear message: the new exchange rate ceiling was not credible. On December 22, the monetary authorities had no other option than to switch to a floating exchange rate (i.e., the Bank of Mexico no longer would intervene to maintain the dollar within a prespecified band). A couple weeks later the peso went into a free fall, with enormous effects on other countries, particularly in Latin America.

Undoubtedly, the policy decision to avoid a devaluation in 1994 at almost any cost had a political rationale. First, there was the fact that following Colosio's assassination Carlos Salinas de Gortari unveiled a new presidential candidate, Ernesto Zedillo Ponce de León, who was not popular in the PRI. Second, there were the presidential elections in August. The decisions to allow the massive conversion of CETES to Tesobonos and to resist a change in exchange rate policy probably were driven by the upcoming elections. Once again the industrialized world appears tacitly to have supported the decision to keep the exchange rate regime unchanged. In the wake of the August elections, the Bank of International Settlement (BIS) quietly put together an additional US$6 billion in order to back the peso in this difficult period. However, neither the United States nor the international financial institutions appear to have been concerned by the risks entailed in the large conversion of peso-denominated government securities into the dollar-denominated Tesobonos.

The central question remains: if the main objective of the government was to maintain the exchange rate policy, why did the authorities not take all the necessary steps to make macroeconomic policy congruent with this goal? Why did the government decide not to adopt the most conservative line and assume that—given the trend in external interest rates and the nervousness generated by the political assassinations—it was advisable to follow a more restrictive monetary policy and allow the domestic interest rate to climb? Perhaps the Bank of Mexico was concerned with the potentially destabilizing effect that higher domestic interest rates would have on a fragile banking system. But it seems that the main reason behind the chosen policy course was the perception that the slowdown in capital inflows was a temporary reaction to the series of political shocks of 1994. The market was expected to return to "normalcy" once confidence was restored. This perception was wrong on at least two counts. First, the slowdown in capital inflows was not only the result of political shocks but of economic circumstances as well: for example, the higher U.S. interest rates and the concern over the sustainability of Mexico's exchange rate regime in the face of low domestic savings and large current account deficits. Second, even if capital flows were reacting to extraordinary political events, Mexico was in the middle of a political transition. Financial authorities should have been advised to play on the safe side and be ready for a period of greater political uncertainty and its implication for market confidence.

Erring on the optimistic side turned out to be very costly. For one thing, the Mexican government was forced to devalue when it had lost control, inflicting a terrible blow on its reputation. When it became clear that reserves were too low, the situation unraveled so quickly that the new economic team did not have enough time either to prepare a macroeconomic program to be announced at the time of the devaluation or to address the foreign portfolio investors' concerns. Moreover, given the large amount of Tesobonos, a devaluation meant a substantial increase in the peso-value of the government's short-term

obligations. Low reserves, the unpreparedness of the Mexican financial authorities, and the large size of short-term dollar debt turned out to be a deadly combination. In a panic, market agents refused to roll over Mexico's short-term debt, and a liquidity crisis ensued.

The Markets Panic

Why did the devaluation turn into a liquidity crisis? The events that followed the devaluation of the peso in 1994 indicate that there was a serious misjudgment of the potential reaction of financial markets to a peso devaluation. Those investors who had their funds in the stock market or in other instruments denominated in pesos interpreted the devaluation as a breach of contract. Their immediate reaction was to remove Mexico from the list of recipient countries; those who could withdrew their capital as soon as possible.

Scarcely a week after the initial devaluation, the Mexican government faced difficulties in rolling over the Tesobonos coming due. This was an ominous sign. Contrary to what many analysts in and outside the official sector had predicted and expected, the devaluation did not bring calm to the markets. Quite the opposite, the devaluation actually caused a major loss of confidence among foreign investors. Foreign investors, as Ted Truman from the U.S. Federal Reserve put it, "realized that their investment strategies had been based on one or more false premises concerning the nature of Mexico's exchange rate regime or the probability that they could liquidate their holdings before any crisis hit." They realized that the Mexican government would not be in a position to service the short-term claims without incurring a massive depreciation of the peso; hence, the risk of default was as real as ever.

By the end of the first week of January, the refusal to roll over Mexican debt began to affect other instruments such as dollar-denominated certificates of deposit. Mexico was on the verge of default, and the financial markets of Latin America and other regions began to be affected. The rush to the door by many investors was the result of a combination of anger, fear, and uncertainty. Investors were angry for a very simple reason. The devaluation caused them substantial losses, at least on paper. According to Truman, "the Mexican stock market dropped by two-thirds (68 percent) in dollar terms between December 19, 1994, and its low in March 9, 1995, and as of the end of June was still about 45 percent its level prior to the peso devaluation." Foreign and domestic holders of CETES suffered losses as well when their instruments matured in the course of

1995. These investors felt that they lost money because the Mexican government "tricked" them. They resented the government's repeated denial that there would be a devaluation, the fact that it did not realign the exchange rate when it was "natural" (for example, when the "Pacto" was renewed in September 1994), or alternatively, raise domestic interest rates to defend the existing exchange rate policy. Investors also were upset by the lack of competence with which the government handled the devaluation itself. They were surprised—as were many others—by the absence of a coherent macroeconomic plan at the time the devaluation was announced.

But perhaps the most important contributing factor to the debacle of the peso was the fear of default. Faced with the combination of a high concentration of government debt in short-term instruments, the replacement of almost the entire short-term government debt from CETES to Tesobonos, and the low levels of international reserves shortly after the devaluation, portfolio investors feared that the Mexican government would be forced to declare the peso inconvertible and default. This fear surged when through simple arithmetic calculations investors saw that payments coming due in 1995 were far greater than the estimated resources available. The total short-term debt coming due in 1995, public and private, was estimated at close to US$50 billion; in contrast, international reserves in the Bank of Mexico were about US$6 billion and the swaps available through NAFA were about US$7 billion.

Soon it became evident that to calm the markets and stop the financial meltdown, there had to be a financial rescue package large enough to put the fears of default to rest. Otherwise, the panic selling and the spillover into other markets would not be halted. To stop the panic, it was essential to find a lender of last resort. This led to the two most dramatic decisions of this episode. On January 31, 1995, U.S. president Bill Clinton announced that he would use executive authority to provide Mexico with up to US$20 billion in loans and loan guarantees through the Exchange Stabilization Fund (ESF), the largest use of this facility many times over. At the same time, Michel Camdessus, managing director of the IMF, announced that the IMF would increase the 18-month standby arrangement to US$17.8 billion, the largest ever extended by the IMF both in terms of its value and as a percentage of the country's quota.

In addition to the unprecedented contributions of the U.S. government and the IMF, the package would include US$10 billion from other industrialized nations through the BIS; $1 billion from Canada; US$1 billion in currency swaps from Argentina, Brazil, Chile, and Colombia (which did not materialize); and US$3 billion in new loans from commercial banks (which also failed to materialize). The total projected sum came close to US$53 billion. However, in reality only the US$20 billion from the United States, the US$17.8 billion from the IMF, and the $1 billion from Canada became available, plus loans from the World Bank and the Inter-American Development Bank for US$3 billion in total. Although the BIS loan became available on paper, it was not very helpful because of the stringent restrictions on its use. Ultimately, other industrialized nations viewed Mexico's financial troubles as a problem of the United States and hence were not eager to help; some were annoyed that they even had been asked.

Of the total rescue package, the US$17.8 billion from the IMF program were made immediately available. One limitation of the rest of the funds was that they would not be available all at once but in tranches (bond series), and that their availability would depend on Mexico's strict compliance with a set of economic conditions and targets. In the case of the ESF loans, their availability also would be affected by domestic political factors in the United States. Due to the vehemence of critics of the U.S. rescue package in Congress, the administration became increasingly more cautious in extending the ESF loans to Mexico, particularly when the objective of solving Mexico's short-term liquidity problem was on the whole achieved.

The success of the 1995 rescue package was evidenced by the speed with which the Mexican government was able to return to the international capital markets. As mentioned above, between mid-1995 and early 1996, Mexico was able to raise approximately US$8 billion, with the terms and maturities of the loans improving over the period. Moreover, although there were a few additional incidents of market volatility, the peso achieved an acceptable degree of stability after March 1995. Finally, the possibility of the crisis spreading to other countries in the region and other regions as well was brought to a halt. In contrast to 1982, the liquidity and confidence crisis was limited to one country: Mexico.

Nevertheless, despite all its accomplishments, the financial rescue package was not able to spare Mexico from a major recession, the worst since the Great Depression. During 1995, Mexican output fell by close to 7 percent, unemployment doubled to reach close to 7 percent, and real wages contracted year-on-year by about 21 percent. Although without the financial assistance the situation undoubtedly would have been far worse, it is remarkable that a sizable financial support program did not translate into a softer landing of the Mexican economy.

Select Bibliography

Banco de México, *Report on Monetary Policy: January 1995.* Mexico City: Banco de México, 1995.

Calvo, G., "Comments and Discussion to Dornbusch and Werner 'Mexico: Stabilization, Reform and No Growth.'" In *Brookings Papers on Economic Activity.* Washington, D.C.: The Brookings Institution, 1994.

Dornbusch, R., and A. Werner, "Mexico: Stabilization, Reform and No Growth." In *Brookings Papers on Economic Activity.* Washington, D.C.: The Brookings Institution, 1994.

General Accounting Office, *Mexico's Financial Crisis. Origins, Awareness, Assistance, and Initial Efforts to Recover.* Washington, D.C.: General Accounting Office, 1996.

Kamin, S., and J.H. Rogers, "Monetary Policy in the End-Game to Exchange-Rate Based Stabilizations: The Case of Mexico." Board of Governors of the Federal Reserve System, Washington, D.C. (1995).

Lustig, N., *Mexico: The Remaking of an Economy.* Washington, D.C.: Brookings Institution, 1992.

Oks, D., "Stabilization and Growth Recovery in Mexico: Lessons and Dilemmas." Latin America and the Caribbean Regional Office, The World Bank, Washington, D.C. (1992).

Truman, E. M., "The Risks and Implications of External Financial Shocks: Lessons from Mexico." International Finance Discussion Paper, Federal Reserve, No. 535. (1996).

Wertman, P., "The Mexican Support Package: A Survey and Analysis." CRS Report for Congress, 95-1006 E. (1995).

———, "Mexico: Chronology of a Financial Crisis." CRS Report for Congress, 95-1007 E. (1995).

—NORA LUSTIG

Petroleum

This entry is composed of two articles that discuss the oil industry in Mexico:

Petroleum: Pre-1938
Petroleum: 1938–96

Petroleum: Pre-1938

The existence of petroleum deposits had been known to the pre-Columbian inhabitants of Mesoamerica. They found the pitch in bubbling tar pits *(chapopotes)* and along the beaches of the Gulf Coast, which they used for incense and to patch canoes.

These same oil deposits became a hazard for the early Spanish settlers of the coastal region of Veracruz and Campeche, who lost livestock in the *chapopotes.* Commercial interest in these deposits date from the 1860s. Soon after the beginning of the oil industry in Pennsylvania, Mexican and some American entrepreneurs attempted to set up crude distilleries to convert the exudation of these oil ponds into kerosene for lanterns. Nonetheless, the remoteness of these deposits, the tropic vegetation and the hot climate of the region, and the lack of a domestic market prevented easy commercial development of Mexico petroleum.

However, development of the railway system stimulated both a market and a transportation system for petroleum products. The foreign entrepreneurs who pioneered the Mexican oil industry maintained close ties to the foreign-owned railway lines. The first U.S. marketer of imported petroleum products, Henry Clay Pierce, arrived at the moment that railway building was booming, beginning in the mid-1880s. His firm imported crude oil from Pennsylvania for the Standard Oil Company of New Jersey, then refined it into kerosene and lubricants in small distilleries at Veracruz, Tampico, Mexico City, and Monterrey. In 1904, Edward L. Doheny, who already had oil interests in California, opened up the first producing oil field at El Ebano, San Luis Potosí, astride the right-of-way of the Mexican Central Railway. At the same time, the British engineer Sir Weetman Pearson (later Lord Cowdray) developed an oil field near Minatitlán along the Tehuantepec Railroad that his company was then constructing across the Isthmus. Even before he had sufficient production, Pearson completed a refinery at Minatitlán in 1908 to compete with Pierce's imported products. The railways permitted these early entrepreneurs to transport the latest oil technology such as steam boilers and cable tools to the remote oil deposits. Management of this early industry was exclusively British and American, except in the case of the renowned Mexican geologist Ezequiel Ordóñez, who worked for the Doheny organization. Railways provided the initial markets for domestic oil production, and the railway locomotives were gradually converted to run on domestic oil rather than imported coal. Moreover, railways began to deliver fuel oil and lubricants to mining operations and tar for paving the streets of the country's larger cities.

Until the foreign-owned oil industry began to export petroleum from Mexico in 1911, production was somewhat disappointing. Then, in 1908, a great well blew out in fiery destruction at Dos Bocas, just west of Tuxpan. The great reservoirs of petroleum in this area lay in porous beds of limestone at a depth of 1,800 to 2,000 feet, well below sea level and under great pressure from the underlying salt water. When the first drill bits broke through to the oil deposits, the wells here blew in with a ferocious rush of gas and crude, easily ignited by boiler fires as was Dos Bocas. Although that well was destroyed, oil prospectors directed their attention to this region, which would become known as the Faja de Oro (the Golden Lane) because of the richness of its deposits of "black gold." In 1910, the Pearson interests hired the young American geologist Everette DeGolyer, who brought in the well known as Potrero del Llano No. 4. It was one of the most prolific oil wells in the world, producing some 104.8 million barrels of crude oil in its nine-year existence. In the next year, the Doheny interests drilled several prolific wells at Casiano, also in the Golden Lane. The two fledgling oil concerns quickly borrowed capital abroad to build pipelines and oil terminals at Tampico and Tuxpan, allowing them to gain access to foreign markets. The first shipment of Mexican petroleum was exported from Tampico on May 25, 1911, the day on which President Porfirio Díaz went into exile.

In the next ten years, while the Revolution raged, the foreign-controlled oil companies would make Mexico the world's second-ranking oil producer after the United States. A legion of foreign lease-takers and oil prospectors came during this first Great Mexican oil boom. Hundreds of new companies were established, most of them quite small and speculative. Lord Cowdray took advantage of his pioneering status in making his oil company, El Águila, into the leading producer. His refineries at Tampico and Minatitlán were the largest in the country, and his retailers commanded the domestic market for oil products. Doheny's interests, combined into the Huasteca Petroleum Company, ultimately took over as the leading producer following the discovery of another great oil well at Cerro Azul in 1916. Although both companies supplied large export contracts, eventually they developed their own retailing apparatus abroad, selling in the United States, Europe, and South America. Although it exported to the U.S., the British-owned El Águila itself never directly entered the American wholesale and retail markets.

During World War I, most companies operating in Mexico flourished as production rose at the same time that international prices increased precipitously. Mexican oil, which smoked excessively when burned as fuel oil, did not supply the great battle fleets but was utilized extensively in industry and in the merchant marine. Because it formed an enclave along the Gulf Coast of Veracruz, the oil industry survived the revolutionary fighting then gripping the country. Most oil camps, pipelines, pump stations, and refineries were already on line when the first revolutionary armies arrived in Northern Veracruz in 1914. The oil boom eventually attracted the interest of the largest U.S. and European companies, such as Standard Oil (New Jersey), the Texas Company, Sinclair, and Royal Dutch Shell, each of which had purchased producing and exporting subsidiaries here before the decade was out. However, the Mexico-based producing companies of El Águila and Huasteca remained the largest operators within the country.

Thousands of American and Chinese workers as well as 50,000 Mexicans were to find employment in petroleum during the boom. As the oil industry overwhelmed the relatively unpopulated oil region, most laborers came from other locations. Americans with experience in U.S. petroleum and other industries commanded the better-paying, skilled work. Mexican temporary laborers provided assistance in construction and maintenance jobs that required little prior knowledge of imported technology. Chinese laborers occupied service jobs in the offices, billets, and mess halls of foreign workers. They accepted the lowest pay of all and were regarded with contempt by many Mexicans. In the refineries and terminals of Tampico in the North and Minatitlán and Coatzalcoalcos in Southern Veracruz, an oil proletariat of more skilled Mexican workers developed. They had emigrated from Central and Northern Mexico during the revolutionary unrest, bringing mechanical skills acquired in the mining and railroad industries. As the terminal for the petroleum exports from the Golden Lane, Tampico in particular became a boom town in the 1910s. Foreign managers and workers constructed quality housing in company compounds and hillside neighborhoods, while Mexican migrants built their ramshackle houses along the railway tracks, behind refinery walls, and on the shores of the lagoons.

At first, the native-born semi-skilled laborers were satisfied to be earning a wage, but they soon became disgruntled at the lack of promotion into the better-paying jobs held by the Americans. The racism of their foreign supervisors caused additional resentment. In 1915, when the cost of living rose, the workers organized the first unions to demand wage increases and equal treatment with foreigners. The mechanics, boiler workers, stillmen, and other skilled Mexicans organized along craft lines; their strikes shut down production here and there among the refineries and terminals. The oil companies begrudgingly gave in to union demands for wage increases and a reduced average work-week. But the foreign supervisors refused to recognize unions and accused labor leaders of being in the pay of the Germans during the war and the Bolsheviks after the war. As a result of labor unrest at Tampico and Minatitlán, the ideas and objectives of labor unions would become a part of the ideology of the Mexican Revolution.

The relationship between the foreign oil interests and the Mexican governments was cordial at least until 1915. The government of Porfirio Díaz encouraged the development of the oil industry with tax breaks and changes in the property laws. President Díaz himself took a direct interest in helping the British interests of Sir Weetman Pearson prevent the Americans from completely dominating the nascent industry. However, once established, the industry was expected to yield public revenues to the state. The Díaz government raised tax rates on petroleum in 1910, and Presidents Madero and Huerta did the same when faced with mounting budget deficits during the Revolution. Even before the Constitution of 1917, the state and federal governments under Venustiano Carranza began to see the booming oil industry as a fitting source of revenues. In 1915, the Petroleum Department was formed within the Secretariat of Industry, and the Petroleum Fiscal Agency was created as a part of the Secretariat of Treasury.

The government's regulatory oversight and tax increases were justified in Article 27 of the Constitution of 1917. Article 27 overturned the liberal property laws of 1884 and 1891, which had encouraged investments in mining and oil by giving subsoil property rights to the owners of surface properties; freehold titles and leases had the same legal standing in Mexico as in Great Britain and the United States. Article 27 restored the colonial legal tradition of state ownership of mineral rights. The oil fields became royalty property of the state, and the oil companies became concessionaires, just as colonial miners had paid royalties to the Spanish Crown for the privilege of exploiting the king's mines.

The oil companies and the government came into conflict over how Article 27 was to be interpreted. The oil companies maintained that other articles of the Constitution protected them from the loss of their previously-acquired property rights. Subsequent post-Revolutionary regimes sought to include all oil fields as state property, however, even if they had been developed prior to 1917. With this objective in mind, President Carranza placed a tax on oil production and required companies to register all their wells. The companies resisted and sought the protection of their home governments, making the con-stitutional dilemma a diplomatic problem as well. In the meanwhile, a rebellion in the oil zone complicated relations between the industry and the government. General Manuel Peláez, an oil property owner himself, took up arms against the Carranza government. He extorted money for the rebellion directly from the oil camps, which gave the government an opportunity to portray Peláez "as being in the pay" of the companies. These matters still had not been resolved when Carranza fell from power in 1920.

The year 1921 was a watershed in the petroleum industry in several respects. Under President Álvaro Obregón, the government had been able to reduce endemic rebellion and to restore a modicum of political unity for the first time in 10 years. General Peláez relinquished control of the oil zone. The internal political peace permitted Obregón to increase taxes on the oil industry, upholding a policy shared by all national administrations since 1910. The Obregón government did not succeed without resistance, but a company boycott of oil exports in 1921 failed when the British company, El Águila, broke ranks and negotiated with the government. Thereafter, the government began to renegotiate with foreign bankers, who also looked to the foreign-owned oil industry as a source of tax revenues to pay the restructured debt. Diplomatic pressure forced the oil companies to recognize the fiscal implications of Article 27 if not its theoretical features in the Bucareli accord of 1923 and the Calles-Morrow agreement of 1928.

More important, 1921 also signaled the beginning of several structural transformations within the Mexican oil industry. First, production began to decline as salt-water seeped into the prolific oil reservoirs. Some of the most productive wells became exhausted and had to be shut in. By the end of the decade, total Mexican production amounted to less than 40 million barrels per year, just 20 percent of what it had been in the peak year of 1920.

Mexico's adversity was compounded by an even steeper downturn in the international prices of petroleum as new fields in the United States and Latin America came on line. Nineteen-twenty's high prices dropped by 45 percent to $1.73 per barrel during the succeeding year and to $1.17 by 1928. Shell and Jersey Standard were investing heavily in infrastructure and exploration in the Maracaibo region of Venezuela. Jersey Standard abruptly moved men and matériel from its faltering Mexican fields to its subsidiaries in Peru and Colombia. As Mexican production declined, that of its competitors rose. By 1929, Venezuela had become the third largest producer of petroleum in the world, and Mexico had dropped to seventh.

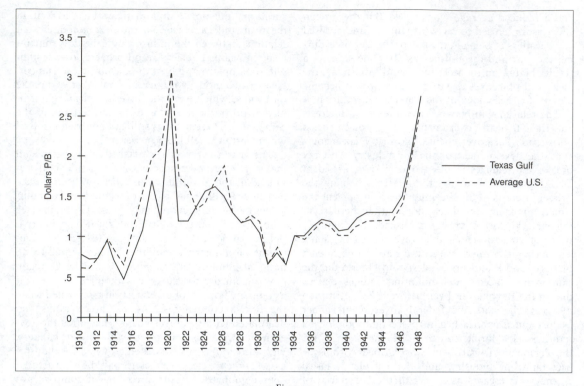

Figure 1
Average Yearly Oil Prices in the United States, 1910–1938, in Dollars per Barrel
Source: Petroleum Facts and Figures, *New York: American Petroleum Institute, 1951.*

The structure of industry ownership responded in a manner designed to minimize Mexico's weakness in an increasingly competitive international marketplace. It consolidated. Lord Cowdray began the process as early as 1919, selling management control of El Águila, Mexico's largest oil firm, to the Royal Dutch Shell. Doheny's considerable assets in Mexico also went on the sales block. In 1925, the Midwestern marketing giant, Standard Oil Company of Indiana, acquired all of Doheny's refining and marketing properties on the East Coast of the United States, his Mexican assets, and the Lago concession in Venezuela. Smaller companies now sold out or abandoned their Mexican properties. By the end of the decade, Sinclair bought out the Pierce refining and marketing group. By 1930, when oil prices slipped once again, Jersey Standard seemed to have withdrawn from Mexico. Not even Standard Indiana could withstand the falling prices. Toward the end of 1932, Standard Indiana reconstituted itself by selling off its Venezuelan and Mexican assets to Jersey Standard. The Huasteca company also fell under the control of the world's biggest oil company.

These realignments within Mexico's oil industry, natural enough given the production and price trends of the 1920s, accompanied a readjustment in the final destination of Mexico's oil production. Still predominantly an net oil exporter, Mexico experienced an economic resurgence following the Revolution. El Águila and Huasteca expanded their domestic marketing, diverting increasing proportions of their production to meet growing domestic demands. Indeed, by 1928, a narrow majority of El Águila's gross sales receipts came from domestic as opposed to foreign sales. Nonetheless, the expansion of the Mexican market for petroleum invited competition. The erosion of Mexico's oil production, combined with the railway bottlenecks across the Sierra Occidental, meant that consumers along the west coast of Mexico had to look to California for oil products. The Standard Oil Company of California built bulk stations at the major ports of Guaymas, Mazatlán, and Acapulco and penetrated inland as far as Guadalajara. As in the United States, gasoline for cars and trucks proved to be the growth market.

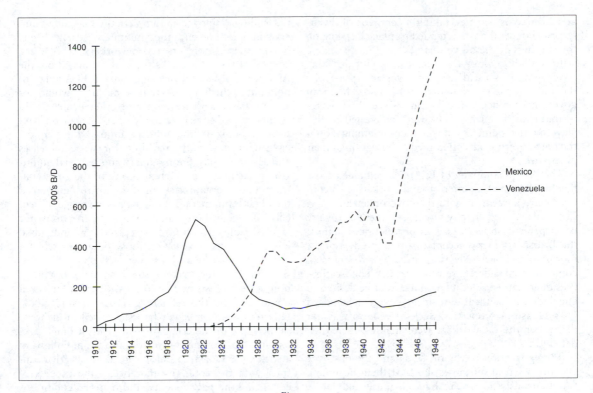

Figure 2
Yearly Petroleum Production of Mexico and Venezuela in Thousands of Barrels per Day
Source: John D. Wirth, editor, Latin American Oil Companies and the Politics of Energy, *Lincoln, University of Nebraska Press, 1985.*

Slippage of its world ranking, however, did not mean the continued decline of Mexican production. Shell introduced the latest technological innovations for oil exploration, including seismographic survey equipment to chart the substrata and select sites for wildcat drilling. Using the new technology, El Águila discovered a new producing field in 1929, Poza Ricá, which eventually would contribute one-third of the nation's total production. However, other potential oil fields escaped discovery. The private companies drilled several exploratory wells in Tabasco and Campeche, the location of today's La Reforma oil fields, but without success.

Mexico recovered relatively early from the world-wide depression. The nation's industrial production and exports by 1934 had returned to their 1929 levels, and the numbers of cars and trucks multiplied. A government road building program—from 695 kilometers in 1928 to 9,929 kilometers at the end of the 1930s—expanded the domestic usage of gasoline. Import-substitution industrialization and renewed foreign investment in Mexico also contributed to the strong domestic demand for energy. By 1937,

domestic consumers were using 70 percent of total Mexican oil production. These developments tended to secure for El Águila, historically the more flexible of the foreign companies, nearly two-thirds of Mexico's total oil industry. El Águila pushed ahead with plans for laying a pipeline from Poza Ricá to Mexico City, where the British company constructed a new refinery.

Even before President Lázaro Cárdenas had taken office, the government renewed its efforts to force the oil companies to conform to Article 123. Even as El Águila was completing its pipeline and refinery at Mexico City, the government delayed the issuance of drilling permits and even granted the small state company, Petromex, production rights at Poza Ricá. Furthermore, the state's power to impose taxes and set prices also grew with the domestic market. In an effort to stabilize the cost of living of workers who depended on urban transportation, the government regulated the price of fuel. In 1934, the taxi drivers of the capital went on strike in protest when El Águila increased gasoline prices to 20 centavos per liter. The state responded by setting the gasoline price at 18 centavos per liter, taking 8 centavos of this as tax. Such federal powers tended to place a ceiling on the earnings of the oil companies.

In actuality, what the Mexican politicians may have viewed as fiscal necessity was interpreted by the oil companies as nationalism. Soon, Mexican government officials too began to see these issues in nationalistic terms. They were converted to this view by the oilmen's constant complaining about the host government's attempted confiscation of their properties.

The British company of El Águila remained more flexible than the U.S. interests and worked out a concessionary agreement with the government in 1937. El Águila agreed to pay the government a royalty of 25 percent on its Poza Ricá production. In effect, the British company accepted the very government interpretation of Article 27 that the North American companies considered retroactive and confiscatory. President Cárdenas let it be known that he desired to conclude an identical agreement covering Standard Oil's Huasteca properties. Such a scenario was not to be, for the oil workers were making their own demands.

The exhaustion of the oil fields and the post-war decline in world oil prices, both of them beginning simultaneously in 1921, had also affected labor. They made work in the foreign-controlled industry quite insecure. From 1920 to 1922, oil companies responded to falling prices and production with massive layoffs. The owners' boycott of 1921 further dislocated the work force, throwing an additional 7,000 laborers out of their jobs.

As prices stabilized and the layoffs ceased, the workers organized to recoup lost income and to gain a measure of security in the industry. The old trade unions of skilled workers in the refineries and oil terminals resumed organizing the less skilled workers at the plant and company level. The first strikes broke out at refineries in Tampico and Minatitlán in 1922, and the Obregón government, which counted on the support of organized labor, showed sympathy. The government expanded its labor bureaucracy in Tampico and Minatitlán and established numerous Federal Boards of Conciliation and Arbitration. Thereafter, union leaders appealed directly to federal bureaucrats, to local and state officials, to fraternal unions, to governors—and inevitably, to the President of Mexico.

By the mid-1920s, the unions had made important gains in the refineries and oil fields of the larger companies. In these efforts, unions were asking the companies to comply with the basic guarantees outlined in Article 123 of the 1917 Constitution. As the leading employer in Tampico, the El Águila refinery could not prevent union militancy. A strike broke out in 1923 among its 1,200 workers, who seized control of the refinery. As the strike dragged on, the Americans pressured British company El Águila "to hold out to the limit," so that labor unrest would not spread. Beset with a number of other problems, El Águila instead gave in to the workers. It signed a contract recognizing the refinery union, granting the eight-hour day, and providing for wage increases and severance pay. Soon refinery and terminal unions won pacts that were carbon copies of the 1923 contract. Labor organizers gained union recognition at the plant level, increases in pay, a wide range of benefits, an eight-hour day, and compensations for layoffs. Collective contracts replaced the individual labor contracts—except on those occasions when a union lost a strike and disintegrated.

The role of the strike in the dynamic of organization is best illustrated by the case of the Huasteca union. Led by the refinery group at Tampico, the Huasteca union in 1925 had succeeded in incorporating most of the company's oil fields around Tuxpan into one company-wide organization. Following a strike, the Huasteca union signed a collective contract with the company that began the process of equalizing the pay, benefits, and material conditions at all the company's installations. The union did not consolidate its power without using strong-arm methods on its rivals. When competing workers killed a member of the majority union, the latter declared a second strike, demanding that the company fire fourteen members of the rival group. Many workers did not support the second strike, and the government was unsympathetic. Both the strike and the union disintegrated after several months. The Huasteca company took advantage of the situation in order to economize, offering to rehire only one-third of the strikers.

Moreover, strikes were as much a result of political and union rivalries as of genuine grievances against the companies. The Confederación Regional Obrera Mexicana (CROM) assisted in the organization of the Huasteca and El Águila refineries, but many oil workers soon became alienated by CROM's tactics and broke with the national leadership. Only several El Águila unions on the Isthmus willingly cooperated with CROM leadership. But the appointment of CROM leader, Luis Morones, to the Calles cabinet tended to mute his inclination to support additional labor demands. In the 1925 refinery strike of CROM's own Minatitlán affiliate, the national labor leadership intervened directly with management in Mexico City. El Águila paid CROM 250,000 pesos that was supposed to have been distributed—but may not have been—among the Minatitlán affiliates. There followed a period of squabbling among disillusioned labor leaders, compounded in 1926 by another break in oil prices.

The oil workers, however, succeeded in gaining some concessions from the foreign companies in the 1920s. The Obregón and Calles governments increased the number of Federal Boards of Conciliation and Arbitration. Therefore, when the companies laid-off workers from 1926 through 1932, the *despedidos* turned to the Federal Boards with their claims for severance pay. Company after company now had to pay two and three-months' wages to workers who were let go. In the hearings before the Federal Boards, the companies lost so many individual claims that they gave up contesting most of them. They still downsized, but those workers laid off in the late 1920s had benefits not enjoyed by those let go in the early 1920s.

Nevertheless, the international depression and the slide in world prices once again weakened the oil unions. Companies responded to sagging prices by laying off workers and cutting wages. At first, workers were disoriented by further decline in the industry, and labor leaders found little support for strikes and work actions in 1930 and 1931. During this period of declining demand for labor—accompanied by layoffs, pay cuts, and extended hours—the unions disintegrated. In 1932, the number of oil workers had reached its lowest point. Perhaps a mere 13,000 laborers remained from the more than 50,000 who had been employed in the industry in 1921.

The modest resurgence in the oil industry beginning in 1933 strengthened the unions, as did the presidential campaign of the following year. The oil companies began to rehire and even replaced some foreign workers with Mexicans as an economic measure. A strike in the Minatitlán refinery of El Águila, uniting six different trade unions, was a crucial test of labor's resolve. President Abelardo Rodríguez mediated the dispute in 1934 and granted the refinery union a number of critical benefits. The settlement equalized pay on the Isthmus between the refinery and the oil fields, workers in the latter always having received fewer benefits. More important, the settlement granted the unions a closed shop. Under the so-called exclusionary clause, labor leaders had the right to nominate workers for all new openings. They could cause veteran workers to lose their jobs in the oil industry simply by expelling them from the union. Union after union soon struck in order to win the same concessions.

When the national labor leadership supported President Cárdenas in his political dispute with ex-President Calles, the oil unions finally acquired the power to organize the entire industry. In 1936, El Águila's refinery union at Tampico brought together some 20 other oil unions to form the Sindicato de Trabajadores Petroleros de la República Mexicana (STPRM, or Union of Petroleum Workers of the Republic of Mexico). It affiliated with the powerful Confederación de Trabajadores de México (CTM), organized in the same year. In order to consolidate their power with a new collective contract, STPRM launched several strikes within the next two years, seeking to equalize pay and benefits throughout the industry. Nonetheless, a problem arose. STPRM had to gain an industry-wide pact superior to any existing contract, meaning that smaller companies would have had to concede pay increases and fringe benefits in excess of those earned by the more privileged workers of Huasteca and El Águila. These demands represented a financial burden that few of the smaller companies could afford.

The Petroleum Workers Union desired to sign a single nation-wide collective contract with all the companies. Labor officials emphasized grievances likely to win popular support against the foreign companies. They demanded parity between Mexican and foreign workers, security for oil workers, union control of most personnel matters, and large pay rises. Most important, under the workers' proposal the companies would lose a large number of its management and supervisory positions to union control. For example, the national collective contract would have allowed El Águila only one confidential employee in its Azcapotzalco refinery, instead of the thirteen who then worked there.

President Cárdenas averted an oil workers' walkout by sponsoring negotiations between the companies and the oil union, but these negotiations broke down in the spring of 1937. The national union then struck the industry for two weeks. Once again, President Cárdenas cajoled the workers back to work, acceding to a union request that a government commission investigate the companies' finances to determine if they could afford the new contract. While a commission headed by the economist Jesús Silva Herzog investigated, there was still much agitation within the oil workers union. The Poza Ricá workers went out on a 57-day wildcat strike. That action caused much disruption in Mexico City, and pressure mounted on the government to settle the labor dispute. By this time, the workers too had became quite adamant about the wage package, as the cost of living in 1937 was increasing. In December, Silva

Herzog's investigative commission decided that the companies could afford the union's administrative demands as well as a 26 million peso wage increase to the workers. The oil executives decided not to compromise because they believed they could not afford the higher wages if they also lost management prerogatives. The companies subsequently appealed to the Mexican Supreme Court, which on March 1, 1938, decided against them.

Still the oil companies resisted. The president offered the oil companies one last compromise that would have permitted them to observe the Supreme Court decision. Among the companies, only El Águila's managers wanted to accept the eleventh hour compromise, but they could not persuade the Standard Oil directors of Huasteca. While Cárdenas waited for the companies to respond, the unions pressed for expropriation, moving to seize the oil fields, loading docks, and pump stations. On March 18, 1938, President Cárdenas nationalized the oil industry.

Following several months of worker administration, the government reorganized the petroleum industry and created the state company known as Petróleos Mexicanos or Pémex. Production problems, overstaffing, and an international boycott plagued the first years of this national company. However, Mexico's cooperation with the Allied powers during World War II gained the diplomatic support necessary to acquire foreign technical assistance. Mexican and American diplomats in 1942 successfully negotiated Mexico's payment to the private American companies for the nationalized petroleum properties. The British Foreign Office concluded a separate agreement for the reimbursement of British-owned oil assets in 1947.

Select Bibliography

Brown, Jonathan C., *Oil and Revolution in Mexico*. Berkeley and Los Angeles: University of California Press, 1993.

———, and Alan Knight, editors, *The Mexican Petroleum Industry in the Twentieth Century*. Austin: University of Texas Press, 1992.

Hall, Linda B., *Oil, Banks, and Politics: The United States and Postrevolutionary Mexico, 1917–1924*. Austin: University of Texas Press, 1995.

Meyer, Lorenzo, *Mexico and the United States in the Oil Controversy, 1917–1942*. Austin: University of Texas Press, 1977.

Philip, George D. E., *Oil and Politics in Latin America: Nationalist Movements and State Oil Companies*. Cambridge and New York: Cambridge University Press, 1982.

Rippy, Merrill, *Oil and the Mexican Revolution*. Leiden: Brill, 1972.

Wirth, John D., editor, *Latin American Oil Companies and the Politics of Energy*. Lincoln: University of Nebraska Press, 1985.

—JONATHAN C. BROWN

Petroleum: 1938–96

The Mexican oil industry has long been a central part of Mexican nationalism, and of the nation's economic model. In Hispanic societies, mineral wealth in the ground traditionally belonged to the Crown and its successor governments. Nationalization of foreign oil concessions was therefore both a return to an earlier economic order and an expansion of the role of the Mexican state in the economy. The creation of the state-owned oil firm, Petróleos Mexicanos (PEMEX), enabled the direct achievement of goals through control of the oil industry but also made the industry more vulnerable to domestic political pressures. The oil industry also was vulnerable to rapid changes in world oil prices. These factors led to rapid shifts in the nominal value of the oil industry. Its contribution to gross domestic product (GDP) varied from almost 3 percent in 1973, to over 13 percent in 1983, and to just over 6 percent in the early 1990s. In 1995 its daily production was 2.2 million barrels of crude oil and 1.6 billion cubic feet of natural gas; annual product was valued at US$13 billion at March 1996 prices. Its share of government tax income ranged from over 3 percent in 1971, to almost 50 percent in 1983, to a little more than 25 percent in 1993, and to 35 percent in 1995. Its contribution to exports was over 70 percent in 1983, falling to 22 percent in 1993. In some years, its contribution to net export earnings was smaller because of the industry's large imports. Its role in foreign exchange availability was larger than immediately apparent because PEMEX's funds from foreign borrowing were passed to the federal government. PEMEX's share of the public foreign debt rose from just over 10 percent in 1970 to a little more than 29 percent in 1981 (and 38 percent of the short-term public foreign debt), falling thereafter. However, PEMEX's export income was used to guarantee the repayment of the 1995 U.S. "bailout" loan to Mexico, highlighting the oil industry's importance in Mexico's international trade and investment policy.

When it was nationalized in 1938, the Mexican oil industry produced crude oil for export. After nationalization, increased attention to domestic needs led to provision of the asphalt that paved the roads needed to create a significant national market and of fertilizer needed to develop commercial export agriculture.

Difficult labor conditions and shortages stemming both from World War II and from the exit of skilled managers and technical staff after the expropriation prevented production from reaching prenationalization levels until 1946. There was little success in exploration, and production therefore was carried out without adequate knowledge of Mexican oil reserves; in the absence of finding new oil fields, oil was produced until the 1950s from existing fields at inappropriately rapid rates that damaged the fields.

In 1947 agreements between Mexico and foreign oil companies led to the resumption of foreign provision of financing and technology to the Mexican oil industry. The largest prenationalization oil companies did not make such agreements. In 1949 risk contracts for exploration were signed with independent oil firms, but not with the large multinationals. Improved drilling methods were introduced; new oil and gas fields were discovered in the northeast and south of Mexico. Lack of imported supplies for gasoline production and Mexico's rapid economic growth resulted in Mexico's inability to supply all of the gasoline demanded within the country. In an attempt to end the resulting black market in oil products, three new refineries were built from 1946 to 1950. Foreign companies designed, inspected, and operated them, using Mexican technicians, materials, and domestic savings. These were the first steps in replacing foreign suppliers of the oil industry, progressing from the simplest tasks and equipment to those requiring increasing levels of expertise.

These postwar developments were carried out by the director general of PEMEX, Antonio Bermúdez (1946–58), who stated that PEMEX's objectives were conserving and developing oil resources; supplying the Mexican market, (exporting only after supplying domestic demand); providing tax revenue to the government; raising the cultural standards of workers; and benefiting communities in oil-producing zones. After 1953, PEMEX was able to shift from exporting crude to exporting more valuable refined petroleum products, but tended to export fuel oil, whose price was less than that of PEMEX's imports of gasoline, kerosene, diesel, and lubricants.

In contrast to the earlier pattern of locating refineries near oil fields to facilitate exports, PEMEX now built refineries close to domestic markets. Pipeline construction enabled it to supply crude oil and oil products to most of Mexico. The demand for oil products was increasing more rapidly than gross domestic product from 1945 to 1960, in part as a consequence of low, subsidized prices for oil

products; in 1958 PEMEX's real prices were one-third their 1938 level. These subsidies went 50 percent to the north and 30 percent to the center of Mexico. From 1946 to 1958, PEMEX's tax payments and subsidies were 7 percent of total capital invested in Mexico. From 1939 to 1959, however, 5 percent of investment went to the oil industry. The net result is that PEMEX subsidized the rest of the economy, breaking the link between PEMEX's efficiency and its income. The government, rather than PEMEX's management, set oil product prices and oil industry wages. For example, President Adolfo Ruiz Cortines in 1954 declared "the role of PEMEX is not one of profit but of social service." Moreover, accounting methods made it difficult to set price on the basis of cost: with a mandate to supply the nation, profitability analysis focused on overall refinery operations, rather than on specific products.

PEMEX needed additional funds for investment. However, multinational oil companies lobbied against U.S. government loans to PEMEX through the early 1950s, when they became more interested in investing in the Middle East and Venezuela than in obtaining favorable investment conditions in Mexico. PEMEX then was able to obtain funds from foreign commercial banks, and, starting in 1958, from domestic sources, through an increase in oil product prices.

Some analysts, however, believe that PEMEX's high internal costs and inefficient operations explained the lack of sufficient funds for self-financed investment. This analysis focuses on the power of the union to determine the number of people employed, pay, and other work conditions. In 1947 the Sindicato de Trabajadores Petroleros de la República Mexicana (STPRM, or Union of Petroleum Workers of the Republic of Mexico) was granted power to hire personnel and admit members, and also was allowed to participate in work contracts between PEMEX and private companies; it could form cooperatives that obtained preferred treatment in obtaining work contracts. In exchange for these concessions, which benefited union leaders more than oil workers, the union limited demands for real wages, although it obtained more than the sums lost in wages in the form of benefits such as financial aid for housing and establishment of schools, hospitals, and scholarships. Moreover, oil industry employment grew 258 percent from 1938 to 1958.

The limits placed on PEMEX's ability to self-finance its investment projects forced it to seek foreign sources of funds for its expansion into petrochemicals. Private investors could invest in "secondary" petrochemicals, in which foreigners could have a 40 percent interest; "basic" petrochemicals were reserved to PEMEX. Nonetheless, the distinction between "basic" and "secondary" petrochemicals was largely arbitrary. Basic petrochemicals were defined as 16 products in 1960, 45 in 1967, and by 1986 production of 70 strategic petrochemicals was reserved to PEMEX. Products were shifted between basic and secondary categories depending on the need for finance. In 1986, in order to reduce the subsidy PEMEX provided on petrochemicals, the government began to withdraw from secondary petrochemical production; moreover, 36 products were moved from the basic to secondary category. In 1989, this number was reduced to 20, and by 1992, only 8 products were so classified. The trend reached a logical conclusion when the government, as part of the reorganization of PEMEX, decided to sell secondary petrochemical plants. In 1996, PEMEX's petrochemical assets accounted for 8 percent of its total assets and 1 percent of its profits. The sale of the plants was opposed by the oil union and various political groups that tried to block the sale in order to obtain broader objectives. The issues involved the role of the oil industry in the nation's political economy, environmental responsibilities of PEMEX, and the relations between oil-producing states and the federal government. PEMEX has, at times, been called the least efficient oil company in the world. Its sales per worker have been one-tenth that of Exxon or Royal Dutch. But this comparison does not take into account PEMEX's operation of hospitals, schools, stores, and other social services, which are expenses undertaken by governments in many other nations. In the long run, PEMEX anticipated shifting from direct assistance to areas in which it operates to assistance through payment of federal, state, and local taxes, and perhaps through federal revenue sharing. Similarly, as in other oil companies in developing areas, it had to provide more training than would be needed in a country with a more highly educated labor force. The increasing share of engineering and technical services provided by Mexican sources, the patenting of processes developed by PEMEX's Mexican Petroleum Institute, and the increased ability of the Mexican capital goods industry—in part as a result of PEMEX's assistance—to supply the oil and other industries indicate the general benefits that accrued to the nation as well as to PEMEX as a result of its activities. The difficulty in determining which expenditures were profitable for PEMEX, which benefited the nation, and which served private purposes led to increasing pressure to reorganize PEMEX, facilitating accountability of executives and transparency of accounts.

Part of PEMEX's high costs resulted from considerable union control of PEMEX and consequent overstaffing. Union opposition to the candidacy for president of Carlos Salinas de Gortari in 1988 and its threats to stop the flow of oil if its wishes were not heeded led to the arrest on various charges of 35 union leaders in January 1989. This made it possible to reorganize PEMEX. In 1992 PEMEX was converted into a holding company and subsidiary companies: PEMEX Exploration and Production, PEMEX Refining, PEMEX Natural Gas and Basic Petrochemicals, PEMEX Secondary Petrochemicals, and PEMEX International (PMI). Each was to pay income tax. Analysts expected the government gradually to transfer gains or losses from changing world oil prices from the government to the company, giving PEMEX an incentive to operate profitably. This transfer would require a change in Mexico's tax system, under which PEMEX's income would be taxed at 67 percent (yielding US$13 billion to the government in 1995), compared to 35 percent for other businesses.

Measures taken in 1995 to increase the efficiency of the newly formed subsidiaries included the formulation of medium-term strategic plans, incorporating three-year investment plans, and the preparation of performance contracts to be signed by PEMEX and each of its subsidiaries. Increasing transparency of operations was indicated when PEMEX published the price it received and the production costs for crude oil. Technical measures to increase short-term profitability included drilling in areas with the highest probability of success using new technology. This implied increasing concentration of drilling in the Gulf of Mexico, off the shore of Campeche.

Some of the reduction in costs reflected the fall in PEMEX's employment from 210,000 in 1987 to about 106,000 in 1993. Similarly, PEMEX divested itself of activities that were not related to its main business activities. The production of lubricants, air transport, and medical services were transferred to joint ventures, with PEMEX retaining only 49 percent participation; its partners were to manage the company. The restructuring of PEMEX in ways that made it more comparable to other oil companies was accompanied by changes in its accounting practices so that they complied with the requirements of the Securities and Exchange Commission of the United States. In the future, this may enable PEMEX to secure capital via instruments other than loans and may facilitate the sale of its secondary petrochemical operations. In a related move, in 1993 PEMEX introduced a new franchise system for gasoline stations designed to modernize them, shortening lines at pumps and cleaning up rest rooms. Sub-franchises, which could be owned by foreigners, were now permitted.

The changing role of foreigners in the Mexican economy resulted from the need for capital, technology, and the belief that foreign competition would force Mexican firms to be more efficient in the long run. These forces resulted in the opening of Mexico to foreign trade in the mid-1980s and its partnership in the North American Free Trade Agreement (NAFTA), which provides for a limited opening for foreign participation in the energy sector. At the time NAFTA was enacted in 1992, Mexican energy trade was more restricted than that of the United States or Canada. NAFTA increased U.S. and Canadian access to petrochemical and gas services and to bidding on provision of oil-related goods and services in Mexico. NAFTA opened to foreign participation PEMEX contracts in excess of US$250,000 for goods and services and in excess of US$8 million for construction services: 50 percent immediately and 100 percent by the year 2003. In 1993, PEMEX contracts were about US$5.5 billion. Mexican procedures were to be made comparable to those of the General Agreement on Tariffs and Trade (GATT), and performance contacts would be introduced under which oil and gas field services companies would be paid a bonus for exceeding contract goals.

The remaining restrictions on PEMEX's operations in 1996 led the energy secretary to request legislation that would remove excessive regulation of the oil industry as well as the special tax regimes that burdened it, so that PEMEX would more reasonably compare to a private firm. The director general of PEMEX said that although refining and marketing might be treated as an ordinary business for tax purposes, a special regime would be likely for exploration and production operations. The oil belongs to the nation, implying royalty payments in addition to income taxes for crude oil. The timing of a shift to a new tax regime depends upon Mexico's ability to increase other tax revenue and foreign exchange. The December 1994 peso devaluation led to an increase in assembly plant exports; that year's drought implied a decreased ability of Mexico to feed itself and increased food imports. PEMEX's revenues guaranteed the 1995 U.S. loan to Mexico, and its direct tax payments in 1995 were equal to the sum of income tax payments of all other firms in Mexico. Better agricultural conditions, involving both improved weather and government policy, were required if the reduction of Mexico's dependence on oil —urged by future president Ernesto Zedillo Ponce de León in his Ph.D. dissertation—was to take place.

Such a reduction was essential, since projected Mexican demand for refined products exceeded PEMEX's ability to finance the exploration and "downstream" activities needed to supply them. One proposed solution was increasing the use of gas in electric power generation. The 1995–2000 Energy Program stated that operations that do not improve competitiveness will be divested and operations that the private sector is capable of supplying at a lower cost will be transferred gradually and selectively. For example, the proposed sale of secondary petrochemicals and the opening of transportation, distribution, and storage of natural gas to Mexican and foreign companies would provide some of the funds PEMEX required. In March 1996, the energy minister said that the terms of the sale would be amended to allow Mexican companies first rights to majority ownership in plants that produce 13 major petrochemicals. The funds from the sale would be used to modernize the oil industry, to meet government expenses, especially for reducing the foreign debt, and to satisfy environmental concerns. However, opposition to the sale by union and political opposition leaders led to its postponement; an alternate way of keeping the petrochemical plants in Mexican hands was begun by the formation of a publicly held corporation that would issue small denomination shares and use the proceeds to buy shares of petrochemical plants. The delay in sale led the government to announce the planned increase in the production of crude oil in the spring of 1996.

Environmental concerns were important during the NAFTA negotiations. Some analysts claim that in order to demonstrate Mexico's environmental concerns in Mexico City as well as along the border, PEMEX closed its refinery in northern Mexico City in March 1991. This entailed an estimated extra expense of US$1.7 billion to supply the capital with gasoline and eventually to build a new refinery. The 1995–2000 Energy Program proposed a shift to higher octane gasoline and low sulfur diesel. On the other hand, Mexico's less-than-stringent environmental rules and enforcement of them reportedly were an attractive condition of the proposed sale of secondary petrochemical plants.

Environmental concerns also were part of PEMEX's difficult relations in oil-producing areas. Many farmers and fishermen state that PEMEX's activities and pollution destroyed the environment and made it impossible for them to earn a living. It was not always clear if the claims were valid or if compensatory payments reached the intended beneficiaries. In 1996 farmers in Tabasco, led by the defeated candidate for governor, blockaded 60 oil wells, demanding compensation for damaged crops. The blockade ended without bloodshed after the government threatened to end oil operations in the area. PEMEX promised to comply with environmental regulations and to pay indemnification when environmental damage was clearly attributable to PEMEX.

It remains to be seen whether Mexico will succeed in the long run in separating issues of ownership of oil and the role of the oil industry in national economic development from those of the efficient and transparent operation of the oil industry.

Select Bibliography

Philp, George, *Oil and Politics in Latin America: Nationalist Movements and State Companies.* Cambridge: Cambridge University Press, 1982.

Randall, Laura, *The Political Economy of Latin American Oil.* New York: Praeger, 1989.

—Laura Randall

Photography

Photography arrived in Mexico a few months after its invention in Europe during 1839. Its uses prior to 1870 were confined largely to portraits made of the wealthy or of "popular types": picturesque occupations, mostly sellers of "exotic" merchandise, and Indians. There was little of the landscape and cityscape photography seen in Europe, but the different governments in power soon found the medium useful for making visual records of prisoners and prostitutes. In what would later be called photojournalism, daguerrotypes were made of the U.S. troops occupying Saltillo during 1847, the first photographs of a war zone taken in the world.

Among the earliest Mexican photographers to acquire recognition were Luis Campa and Antíoco Cruces, who founded their studio Cruces y Campa, in 1862, where they produced the *cartes de visite* (calling cards) that had become popular in Paris. Both had been students of painting and lithography in the Academia de San Carlos, and their studio soon became the place where rich Mexicans went to have their portraits made. Cruces y Campa also signaled the political potential that photography would have for Mexico's rulers. In 1874, the prestigious firm commercialized a photographic album, *Galería de gobernantes con los retratos de los personajes que han ejercitado el poder en México,* which was evidently well-received, for it was immediately imitated by other photographers, who began to include congressmen, clerics, and literary notables among the powerful celebrities. Two years before, when Benito Juárez died, they had demonstrated their politico-economic acumen by selling 20,000 copies of the *carte de visite* they had made of him.

During the late nineteenth and early twentieth centuries, portraiture reached new heights with the work of Romualdo García and Natalia Baquedano, the latter a pioneer woman photographer in Mexico. Commercial-documentary photography was largely the domain of foreigners such as William Henry Jackson, Abel Briquet, and Charles B. Waite, who were contracted by railroad and steamship lines to document the country's modernization under Porfirio Díaz, and thus further stimulate foreign investment. However, the real milestone of this period was the photojournalist debut of the Casasola brothers, Agustín Víctor and Miguel, who took their first press pictures in 1902.

The Casasola archive is best known for its images of Porfirian progress and its antithesis, the social revolution of 1910 to 1917. Agustín Víctor founded the first Mexican photojournalist agency in 1912, and was a collector as well as a photographer. The images of more than 480 photographers can be found in the Casasola Archive, making it difficult to isolate and analyze the work of the different photographers. Further, much research needs to be done on the publications in which the Casasola's photos appeared.

During the Porfiriato, it appears that their photographs in *El Mundo Ilustrado, El Imparcial's* weekly supplement, represented the poles of that society in radically different, although complementary, ways. "Political news" was dedicated to the order and progress wrought under Díaz, focusing on his ceremonies, state appointments, and diplomatic receptions, as well as his official visits and "informal" trips. However, strikes, the resistance of Indian communities, and the activities of dissenting groups were considered antisocial conduct; they were portrayed as a military, not a political problem. The populace was divided along the same lines. Society people appeared in the social chronicles, while the popular classes were represented as picturesque types or relegated to the police columns.

However, there may be photographs taken during the Porfiriato with some implicit criticism of social conditions. There is no evidence of the intentionally denunciatory photography that can be seen in the images of Jacob Riis or Lewis Hine in the United States; and it appears that no such imagery developed in the rest of Latin America. But poignant photographs such as that of teenage prostitutes indicate that there may well have been a heart, as well as an eye, behind the camera. The U.S. reform movements to which Riis and Hine were related had no counterparts in Mexico, but the Casasolas did document the protest movement against Díaz's reelection in 1910. Further, it appears that the Casasolas developed a distinctly modern style of graphic journalism, capturing Díaz in candid photos, as well as working with a view to creating photo-essays.

The Revolution presented photojournalists with the visual manifestations of a constant social ferment for the first time: lines of people awaiting the distribution of foodstuffs in the midst of famine, protests with banners that clamor for "WATER, WATER, WATER," and women who demanded "Work for all." However, photography (as glimpsed through the Casasola Archive) essentially continued to corroborate the political interpretations of whatever regime was in power in Mexico City and to whom the advertising of opposition gains in the countryside was anathema. There are unusual photographs, such as the repression of *The Mexican Herald* for its criticism of Francisco I. Madero's overthrow during the Decena Trágica (Tragic Ten Days), but in general the images of the Revolution that most dominate are the touching farewells between women and federal soldiers in the Mexico City train station, and the different ruling cliques, whether Maderistas, Huertistas, Zapatistas, Villistas, or Carrancistas.

After the armed struggle ended, Agustín Víctor Casasola was employed by the governments of Álvaro Obregón and Plutarco Elías Calles as the photographic coordinator of various state offices. Thus, it comes as no surprise that there are few images of post-Revolutionary Mexico in his archive that focus on the continuing inequalities. His prison photography, like that of the prostitutes, was made for the *nota roja* of tabloid journalism, but the images carry at least an implicit criticism of class injustice. One might find a certain critique of Luis Napoleón Morones's ostentatious corruption: the unscrupulous leader of the CROM (Confederación Regional Obrera Mexicana, the first national, officialist union) is seated beneath the CROM banner and in front of a table laden with rich foods and expensive wines, his double chin oozing over his white collar. However, flattering representations of President Obregón as the heroic mediator between workers and owners are appropriate visual metaphors for their relations in Mexico; perhaps Casasola preferred more, not less, state control of the labor movement.

The arrival of Edward Weston and Tina Modotti in 1923 was a determining influence on Mexican photography. Integrating themselves into the post-Revolutionary scene, they became close friends of the muralists and other cultural figures. Weston was already famous when he came to Mexico, but it was in this country that he effected the rupture with pictorialism that would define twentieth-century photography throughout the world. Eschewing the soft-focus that attempted to imitate painting, he insisted that he was uninterested in the question of whether photography was art or not, his concern was whether a given image was a good photograph. He was wary of the intrinsic picturesqueness of Mexico and battled to avoid it. One result of his search to define the new medium were his 1925 images of a toilet that served to demonstrate photography's power for reproducing the phenomenal.

Tina Modotti was known as his apprentice, and she followed his example of hard-focus photography that revealed thing-in-themselves. However, her commitment to social justice led her to fill Weston's form with a radically different content. What are probably the first examples of published photographs that questioned the new Mexican order can be found in a handful of her images that appeared during the 1920s in the newspaper of the Mexican Communist Party, *El Machete*. There, depictions of social inequities were accompanied by captions pointing out the contradictions between the promises of the Revolutionary regime and the reality of most people's lives. For example, one image—perhaps inspired by Lewis Hine's investigations and denunciations of U.S. child labor—of a little girl carrying water was ironically titled *The Protection of Children*, and the caption stated: "There are millions of girls like this in Mexico. They labor strenuously for 12 to 15 hours a day, almost always just for food . . . and what food! Nevertheless, the Constitution. . . ."

Modotti's powerful photos were an appropriate counterpart to the extraordinary etchings that were placed on *El Machete*'s pages by its founders, the muralists José Clemente Orozco, David Alfaro Siqueiros, and Diego Rivera, and a welcome change from the fuzzy images of Soviet leaders that had been the papers' photographic staple. However, accustomed to carefully planning her images, she did not feel comfortable photographing in the street, and she had no qualms in creating a photomontage such as "Those on top and those on the bottom" to make her point.

Modotti does not appear to have been a major influence on the photojournalism of the period, having published fewer than 10 photos in *El Machete* before the government closed the newspaper in 1929. Rather, visual representations of political culture prior to the founding of a genuinely critical press

Prostitutas, México, D.F. (Prostitutes, Mexico City) *by Miguel Casasola, 1905*
Photo courtesy of Sistema Nacional de Fototecas del Instituto Nacional de Antropológia e Historia

in the 1970s were almost uniformly laudatory of those in power. Perhaps the constraints within which the publications functioned can be appreciated in the guiding dictum of José Pagés Llergo. The founder of the most important illustrated magazines—*Rotofoto* (1938), *Hoy* (1937), *Mañana* (1942), and *Siempre!* (1953)—Pagés said that his journalists had no restrictions, "as long as they don't touch the President of the Republic or the Virgin of Guadalupe." *Hoy* and *Mañana* were far more restrictive than Pagés's relatively pluralistic code in their reverence for the powerful. However, *Rotofoto* offered images that went against the grain. The magazine lasted only 11 issues, from May 22 to July 31, 1938, before it was destroyed by goons from the official labor union; but during its short life it was an agile, provocative, and fundamentally graphic attempt to vindicate the place of photojournalists in Mexican publications.

The legacy of Weston and Modotti in Mexico was inherited by the greatest of that country's art photographers, Manuel Alvarez Bravo, who was deeply influenced by the hard-focus, the studiously arranged lighting, the careful printing, and the rejection of picturesqueness that characterized their photography. He also worked closely with Henri Cartier-Bresson, and one can see many of the same themes in their images from the 1930s. Alvarez Bravo was invited by André Breton, the founder of surrealism, to participate in an exhibit dedicated to this movement, and he there presented one of his most famous images: *La buena fama duriendo.* Alvarez Bravo has been a fundamental force in Mexican photography, and was a definitive influence on the most aesthetically experimental Mexican photojournalists from 1950 to 1970: Nacho López and Héctor García.

In 1939, the "Hermanos Mayo" arrived in Mexico, fleeing from their defeat as members of the Republican forces in the Spanish Civil War. Composed of five "brothers"—Francisco (Paco), Faustino, Julio, Cándido, and Pablo—this photojournalist collective had taken on the "nom de guerre" of Mayo in honor of May Day. Their commitment to the working class was largely co-opted by the mass media, but they revolutionized Mexican photojournalism by introducing the 35mm Leica camera. A direct result of that technological innovation were dynamic photographs taken in the very center of action, such as that of the Red Cross crew rescuing a wounded oil worker during the 1958 strikes. The Hermanos Mayo played somewhat the same role that other refugees from Europe, such as Robert Capa and Alfred Eisenstadt, played in U.S. publications. Since their arrival they provided images for more than 40 newspapers and magazines, and their archive of some 5 million negatives is the largest in Latin America.

Nacho López is a pivotal figure in the development of Mexican photojournalism. He enjoyed the most autonomy within mass-circulation magazines, usually selecting his own themes and, in some cases, being given the power of decision over image choice and layout. His focus on the daily life of the underdogs was an attempt to rescue the importance of the seemingly insignificant, the dignity of the evidently downtrodden, and the significance of the apparently commonplace. His work represents a sharp break with prior Mexican photojournalism, both in terms of his social commitment as well as in the aesthetic explorations that mark him as a true author of images and the foremost practitioner of the photoessay form in Mexico.

López was clearly the chosen photojournalist of *Siempre!,* for his essays appear in the first six issues. The magazine rather quickly moved away from an illustrated format, no doubt because Pagés Llergo realized that television was displacing the printed image, but before it did so López was able to publish the single most critical *fotoreportaje* of this period, *Only the Humble Go to Hell* (1954). For López, hell was the police stations where only the poor were at the mercy of "insolent, insulting, and ill-humored police who are indifferent to the pain they cause the helpless;" the rich paid off the police in the street in order to spare themselves such ignominy. Corrupt and acting with impunity, the Mexican police were as deserving of a critique in 1954 as they are today, but López's indictment was one of very few that can be found in the entire history of the Mexican press.

Although his career as a photojournalist lasted only from 1950 to 1957 (he then began to work in cinema), López's concern for the downtrodden, his aesthetic search, and his insistence on carrying out authorial intent were a pivotal example to later generations of Mexican photojournalists. His reflections on his craft were important guidelines for his colleagues and students: "My profession is the most appropriate to understand dialectically the world of contradictions, to exhibit the struggle of classes, and to comprehend man [sic] as an individual." He left an important legacy in his classes at the National University (UNAM); as Elsa Medina, one of the more important members of the current generation, said: "He taught me to see."

Another important Mexican photojournalist who began to work in the 1950s is Héctor García, whose pictures of the 1958–59 strikes were so damning of government intervention that the newspaper *Excelsior* refused to publish them. Forming the magazine *Ojo, una revista que ve,* García was able to print images of striking railroad and oil workers, as well as of the brutal beating of a male nurse who attempted to aid a woman overcome by tear gas. García embodies contradictions characteristic of the "perfect dictatorship" within which Mexicans live: he produced many official images while working for President Luis Echeverría Álvarez during the 1970s, but was one of the first photojournalists to explicitly critique the country's rulers. In a 1947 photograph, he poked fun at the *acomodados,* showing their foibles in an image where a tuxedo-suited man raises the toes of his shoes to free the long train of the woman's fancy dress on which he has trod. García also made one of the few photos in which the sharp class distinctions characteristic of Mexico are made manifest: it is September 15th and people are strolling near the Zócalo where the "Grito de independencia" (Cry of Independence) will soon take place. In the foreground is a poor *campesino* (peasant) couple, loaded down with bundles of goods they hope to sell in order to eke out their precarious existence. Behind them come a very different couple, wealthy and dressed in evening clothes. The title García placed on the image speaks to the largely silent cries of protest over such an unfair distribution of wealth: *Cada quien su grito* (To Each His Cry).

In another photo, García directly confronted the cultural mechanisms utilized by the governing party to legitimize its rule. A young sugar cane cutter, covered with the filth of his grueling task, stands in front of a typical post-Revolutionary mural showing a Spanish overseer whipping campesinos as they work in a cane field. Murals such as this emphasize the Spanish exploitation of the Mexican *pueblo* and, by extension, legitimize the "Revolutionary" regime by inferring that such oppression is now a thing of the past. By placing the cane cutter against the mural, and submerging him into it through lowering the contrast, García creates a confrontation between history and myth, and exposes the lies of such officialist renditions of yesterday and today.

Delegación, Sólo los Pobres van al infierno (Only the Humble Go to Hell) by Nacho López, 1954
Photo courtesy of Sistema Nacional de Fototecas del Instituto Nacional de Antropológia e Historia

Weekly magazines had provided photographers a place to publish during the first *edad de oro* (golden age) of Mexican graphic reportage from the end of the 1930s to the mid-1950s. During the 1970s that role was taken over by daily newspapers, and a second *edad de oro* was initiated. In 1977 Manual Becerra Acosta, one of those expelled from *Excelsior* in President Echeverría's repression, led a movement to create a cooperative newspaper. *Uno más uno* to this day describes itself as "The pioneer of graphic journalism in Mexico," and in that daily, young photographers were given great latitude; visual experimentation took precedence over the usually monotonous task of "covering" events. The emphasis placed on photojournalism was even more pronounced in *La Jornada,* the newspaper founded in 1984 by dissidents who left *Uno más uno*. From its very inception *La Jornada* was conceived as a graphic medium: the artist Vicente Rojo designed the daily's format to include an image on every page, whether a photograph or a cartoon.

The new generation of photojournalists have published their work and earned their daily bread in *Uno más uno* and *La Jornada*: Pedro Valtierra, Elsa Medina, Marco Antonio Cruz, Francisco Mata

Rosas, Fabrizio León, Aaron Sanchéz, Andrés Garay, Eniac Martínez, Frida Hartz, Jorge Acevedo, Rubén Pax, Luis Humberto González, Angeles Torrejón, Christa Cowrie, José Antonio López, and Raúl Ortega, to mention only some. Far from believing in the objectivity that dissimulated the service prior graphic reporters such as Agustín Casasola or Enrique Díaz provided to the state apparatus, and fundamentally opposed to the use of photographs as either filler or simple illustration, some members of the "New Mexican Photojournalism" summed up their position in a statement that accompanied a 1988 exhibit of their work:

A new generation of image creators now exists that recognizes the ideological, cultural, and symbolic character of their work; who obviously maintain the premise of their duty to inform, but without pretending to be a "faithful" register of reality. . . . They are conscious that what they transmit is their point of view, opinions, and the position they assume in front of the events they see day after day.

The new photojournalism has treated representatives of the state in ways to which they are little accustomed. For example, Marco Antonio Cruz ironically recast props of official symbolism in his photograph of Miguel de la Madrid against the painted backdrop in a political meeting during 1984. In what must surely be the first critical image of a president in office, de la Madrid appears at the very bottom of the photo, with a huge black cloud over his head on which is written "UNEMPLOYMENT" and from which a lightening bolt comes that is aimed directly at him. In another characteristic image, Andrés Garay photographed the then all-powerful *cacique* of the oil workers, Joaquín Hernández Galicia, seated at a table where bottles of rum and brandy define his space in the frame. Though the image nearly cost Garay a beating, and required great finesse in secreting the film from the banquet, *La Quina sí combina* is a faithful representation of the new generation's work. Fabrizio León produced an acidic commentary on the Mexican electoral process, when he pilloried Miguel Bartlett, then president of the Federal Election Commission and architect of the fraud that most likely gave the presidency to Carlos Salinas de Gortari in 1988, by photographing his haughtiness through the smoke of his cigarette.

The political critique is innovative in the Mexican context, but the most unique element of the New Photojournalism is the development of a documentary form within a newspaper format. This is a result largely of the emphasis on daily life, which allows photographers to publish images that have no relation whatsoever to "news". Thus, photojournalists can follow their own personal interests, confident that they will have a space to publish, if their pictures are aesthetically interesting. This is related to the interest in alternative places to publish, such as books, magazines, exhibits, and posters, which has led many of the photojournalists—Francisco Mata Rosas, Eniac Martínez, Marco Antonio Cruz —into extended documentary projects. Finally, the incorporation of women has been an important force in transforming a photographic form usually dominated by men.

Documentary photography that is not photojournalism has had a long history in Mexico, from the German immigrant, Hugo Brehme, who opened a photo studio in the country during 1910, to the most important contemporary practitioners. In general, it has tended to focus on *México Pintoresco* (picturesque Mexico), the title of Brehme's 1923 book. The natural exoticness and cultural otherness of Mexico—against which Weston, Modotti, and Alvarez Bravo warned and struggled—is attractive to foreign purchasers of images, and therefore difficult to avoid. Obviously, there are great variations in

quality among these different image makers. David Maawad and Alicia Ahumada have produced superb documentary studies of Hidalgo and other areas outside of Mexico City; theirs are among the few images completely free from any taint of the picturesque that so haunts Mexican photography. Mariana Yampolsky has made some wonderful photography of the countryside, its inhabitants and architecture. Graciela Iturbide's is a sophisticated and complex, if often grotesque, imagery which has made her the Mexican photographer who has received the most international recognition. Flor Garduño's work is a false and facile exoticism.

Today in Mexico there are few photographers outside of photojournalism or documentary to attract serious interest. Gerardo Suter has produced some constructed images that are provocative, and the work of Humberto Chavez combines an intense intellectualism with an overwhelming sensuality. However, the history of Mexican photography has largely been written in photojournalist and documentary images.

Select Bibliography

Ferrer, Elizabeth, *A Shadow Born of Earth: New Mexican Photography.* New York: Universe Publishing, 1993.

Hooks, Margaret, *Tina Modotti: Photographer and Revolutionary.* London: Pandora, 1993.

Mraz, John, "Mexican Photography." *History of Photography* 20:4 (1996).

———, and Jaime Vélez, *Uprooted: Braceros Photographed by the Hermanos Mayo.* Houston, Texas: Arte Público Press–University of Houston, 1996.

¡Tierra y libertad! Photographs of Mexico 1900–1935 from the Casasola Archive. Oxford: Museum of Modern Art, 1985.

The World of Agustín Víctor Casasola, Mexico: 1900–1938. Washington D.C.: Fondo del Sol Visual Arts and Media Center, 1984.

Ziff, Trisha, editor, *Between Worlds: Contemporary Mexican Photography.* New York: Impressions, 1990.

—JOHN MRAZ

Politics and Government

This entry includes six articles that discuss politics and government in New Spain and Mexico:

Politics and Government: Hapsburg New Spain
Politics and Government: Bourbon New Spain
Politics and Government: 1821–76
Politics and Government: 1876–1910
Politics and Government: 1910–46
Politics and Government: 1946–96

This entry takes a narrative approach, seeking to capture the dynamism, complexity, and strategic battles in the political history of Mexico. For discussions of specific structures, processes, events, and themes in Mexican politics and government, see also Conservatism; Ecology; Family and Kinship; Foreign Policy; Human Rights; Industrial Labor; Industry and Industrialization; Liberalism; Mesoamerica; Mestizaje; Mexican American Communities; Migration to the United States; Military; Mining; Nationalism; Protestantism; Rural Economy and Society; Urbanism and Urbanization; U.S.-Mexican Border; Women's Status and Occupation

Politics and Government: Hapsburg New Spain

On June 28, 1519, Fernando (Hernán) Cortés founded the first Spanish town in Mexico, la Villa Rica de la Vera Cruz. Cortés was well aware of his tenuous position: the Spanish Crown did not permit would-be conquistadors to go exploring on their own. The Crown's administrators in Santo Domingo had authorized the governor of Cuba, Diego Velázquez to send an expedition to the mainland. Velázquez originally authorized Cortés to lead the expedition, only to rescind that order shortly before Cortés set sail. While Cortés managed to slip out of port before officials could serve him formal written documents attesting his removal from the office of *adelantado* (commander), he was technically an outlaw. Once on the mainland, in a move he hoped would provide him legal protection, Cortés gathered his men into military formation and in the presence of a notary announced his intention to found a *município* (town) in the name of the king. Following the ceremony Cortés appointed *alcaldes ordinarios* (municipal magistrates) and *regidores* (aldermen), which together made up the *cabildo* (city council), also known as an *ayuntamiento*. In addition, Cortés selected the other officials that formed the nucleus of municipal government in both Castile and New Spain, including an *alférez real* (herald and standard bearer), an *alguacil mayor* (chief constable), a *fiel ejecutor* (inspector of weights and measures), a *receptor de penas* (collector of fines), and a *procurador general* (municipal attorney and spokesman). After appointing all of the appropriate officials, selected for their loyalty, Cortés resigned as head of the expedition. The municipal officials then elected him captain and *justicia mayor*, with authority in all military matters pending other instructions from the

Crown. In the course of the sixteenth century, however, the Crown was very diligent in undermining the authority of the first generations of conquistadors and their descendants and imposing royal institutions of governance and authority.

Once Cortés founded Vera Cruz, he laid out the town plan. In a pattern that would be repeated throughout Spanish America, he established the rectilinear *plaza mayor* (main plaza) surrounded by the church, the *cabildo* building, shops, the barracks, the prison, and the slaughterhouse. Streets extended in perpendicular lines from the plaza. As the primary unit of territorial jurisdiction in New Spain, the *município* included not only the *fondo legal* (urban center), but also the *término,* which included all land extending to the limits of other *municípios.* Theoretically, in 1519 Vera Cruz encompassed all of Mexico. In 1521 the *cabildo* of Mexico City claimed jurisdiction over all of New Spain except for territory that fell within the limits of Vera Cruz. Outside of the *fondo legal,* the town founder or the *cabildo* set aside an *ejido,* lands for the support of the *município,* and issued *repartimientos* (distributions) of land to the *vecinos* (inhabitants). Earlier, in 1513 in Santo Domingo, the Crown had established that foot soldiers would receive a *peonía,* or enough land to support a *vecino* and his family, generally a hundred acres or less. Horsemen were entitled to a *caballería,* which was about five times larger than a *peonía,* but which might be as large as 1,000 acres. In reality, *repartimientos* were larger or smaller depending on available land and the number of *vecinos.* Policy dictated that land be distributed so that everyone received some of the best and worst land. The *cabildo* distributed land in multiples of the basic units listed above and generally limited an individual to five *peonías* or three *caballarías.* In New Spain, town founders or the *cabildos* issued *encomiendas* rather than *caballarías* and *peonías.* Originating in medieval Spain and coming to New Spain via Santo Domingo, the *encomienda* gave the *encomendero* the right to extract tribute from Indians living in a specific territory outlined in the grant. Conflict over the nature of the *encomienda* dominated politics and society in sixteenth-century New Spain.

After receiving notification of the defeat of the Mexica (Aztecs) in 1522, King Carlos I (Emperor Charles V, ruled 1517–56) appointed Cortés governor and captain general of New Spain. Overall, Cortés proved to be an able administrator. He showed the same cunning and diplomacy that he had demonstrated during the Conquest. He sent out several expeditions of exploration and discovery, searched for mines, introduced European agriculture, promoted commerce, and issued ordinances. In the meantime, Cortés's enemies were campaigning actively against him in court. They charged that he misused the Crown's funds, hid Mexica treasure for himself, and cheated the treasury in general. These charges coupled with other questions about Cortés's character cast doubt on his loyalty to the Crown. In addition, they offered the Crown the perfect opportunity to replace Cortés, just as it had replaced Columbus, and impose royal authority. In 1527 the Crown appointed a committee of four judges to the First Audiencia (High Court) of Mexico City to replace Cortés. Before they arrived, Cortés took his personal defense directly to the king in 1528. Cortés lavished Carlos I with gifts from New Spain. The king seemed charmed and impressed by Cortés and proceeded to grant Cortés an *encomienda* of 22 towns and 23,000 Indian vassals. In addition, Carlos made Cortés the marqués del Valle de Oaxaca and confirmed his title as captain general. In spite of the wealth of the *marquesado* and the power that Cortés wielded within it, he was insulted that he was not made a duke and appointed governor. The Crown genuinely was concerned with preventing any individual, especially a restless conquistador, from gaining to much power in a colony so far from royal authority. As such, only two *adelantados* received titles of nobility in the Americas: Cortés and Columbus. In fact, royal policy throughout the Hapsburg period (roughly 1517–1700) focused on subduing the power of the first generation of conquistadors and the subsequent claim of their heirs.

Two members of the First Audiencia of Mexico City died shortly after arriving in New Spain. Nuño de Guzmán, an ally of Governor Velázquez, joined the surviving two *oidores* (judges), Diego Delgadillo and Juan Ortíz de Matienzo, as president. The Crown modeled the First Audiencia on the successful Audiencia of Santo Domingo, established in the Caribbean in 1511. Unlike their counterparts in Castile, who simply heard judicial matters, the American *audiencias* had a wide range of responsibilities. The *audiencia* was an executive, legislative, and judicial institution. The First Audiencia of Mexico City proved to be disastrous for the Crown, which had hoped to counter the power of Cortés. Instead of remaining above the petty squabbles and factionalism that pervaded post-conquest political life, the First Audiencia became mired in its own self-interests. Guzmán and the other *oidores* ignored royal instructions and used their positions to benefit themselves, their families, retainers, and friends. Reports of the abuses of the First Audiencia streamed back to Spain, where the Crown decided it needed to appoint a

viceroy, who would reflect not only royal policy but the dignity and authority of the monarchy as well. The person who assumed the office of viceroy would have to be a nobleman of competence whose loyalty was beyond question. After three noblemen turned down the Crown's appointment to viceroy, don Antonio de Mendoza, the count of Tendilla, accepted the position in 1530. He did not arrive in New Spain, however, for five years. In the meantime, the Crown appointed the Second Audiencia to rule the colony.

The most vocal opponent of the First Audiencia was the first bishop and archbishop of Mexico, Juan de Zumárraga. The *audiencia* failed to recognize Zumárraga's authority, even though he arrived in New Spain with the title of Protector of the Indians. In fact the First Audiencia attempted to prevent any Indians from seeking the help and protection of Zumárraga or any other clergy. Zumárraga's fiery sermons and numerous letters to the king contributed significantly to the First Audiencia's eventual removal. Zumárraga's involvement in the politics of the colony was typical of high churchmen in New Spain. The Hapsburgs looked to the hegemony of church and Crown as a fundamental power base in the creation of their Spanish empire. While there was frequent conflict between religious and civil officials, the church was fundamentally important not only in the Christianization of native peoples but in their Hispanicization as well. The most direct and frequent contact that the majority of Indians had with Spaniards was with their local missionary or parish priest. The clergy often protected the Indians from the worst abuses of the Spaniards.

The church performed functions vital to the state beyond their religious vocations. The church was the primary institution of education under the Hapsburgs. The first Mexican educator was the Franciscan friar Pedro de Gante. Arriving before the first Franciscan mission in 1524, Gante received permission to come to New Spain from Carlos I, to whom he was related illegitimately. In Gante's famous school of San José, Indian boys were educated in Latin, Spanish, music, and other academic subjects while men learned trades such as masonry, carpentry, sculpting, painting, and blacksmithing. In 1536, Bishop Zumárraga and Viceroy Mendoza founded the School and College of Santa Cruz de Tlatelolco. Aimed at provided the sons of Indian nobles higher education, the college was a center of humanist instruction in New Spain. Students studied Spanish, Latin, rhetoric, logic, philosophy, music, and medicine. One of the most noted instructors at the college was the Franciscan Bernardino de Sahagún, who used his students and other native informants to write *Historia general de las cosas de la Nueva España*, one of the most important studies of Mexica life dating from the sixteenth century. Mendoza and Zumárraga together petitioned the Crown to found a university for the clerical education of criollos (those of Spanish descent born in the Americas). In 1551 the Crown granted the petition to found the Royal and Pontifical University of Mexico. The founders modeled the university on Spain's illustrious University of Salamanca. Throughout the colonial period, the university trained New Spain's leading literary figures, lawyers, scientists, doctors, and theologians. Women were not admitted to the university, nor were they completely ignored by educators either. Beginning in 1534, nuns arrived in New Spain to open a school for girls. Women's educational opportunities were compatible with those in Europe during the same time.

On the heels of the failings of the First Audiencia, the Crown and Council of the Indies were more prudent in their selection of the *oidores* of the Second Audiencia. Sebastián Ramírez de Fuenleal proved to be an extremely judicious selection. Ramírez de Fuenleal had served as both president of the Audiencia of Santo Domingo and bishop of the same island. A stark contrast to his predecessor, Ramírez de Fuenleal demonstrated high ability and loyalty to the Crown. He was joined by equally talented *oidores,* including Vasco de Quiroga, who later would become the bishop of Michoacán. The Second Audiencia imposed the full authority of the Crown on New Spain and was fairly effective in restoring order to the colony. It represented an important shift in the exercise of royal authority in New Spain. The Crown was utterly dependent on the *adelantados* and conquistadors to open territory in New Spain. The adventurous, wealth-seeking, armed, and creative-thinking conquistadors served the Crown well in the initial phase of the colonial enterprise. The talents of the conquistador, however, were undesirable for administrators in an imperial system that stressed loyalty over performance. Cortés himself showed signs that the Crown would not be able to control him. The Second Audiencia marks the transition from the age of *adelantados* and conquistadors to the age of the entrenched imperial system.

The Audiencia of Mexico City was responsible for a wide range of functions. It was a court of first instance within its territorial jurisdiction and it heard appeals from subordinate *audiencias* and other courts. Early in the sixteenth century, all of the *oidores* heard both civil and criminal cases that came before them. By the late sixteenth century, however, as the number of *oidores* increased with the Crown's

sale of political offices and the growth of the colony in general, *oidores* began to specialize in particular aspects of law. Given the shear weight of royal decrees and the heavy caseload, the split of the *audiencia* into civilian and criminal divisions was a practical necessity. In addition to its judicial functions, the *audiencia* issued ordinances and decrees. All ordinances in New Spain technically were passed only temporarily, pending royal approval. In reality, the Crown depended on its bureaucrats in the Americas to pass legislation of local interest for the operation of the colony. In addition, before the arrival of Viceroy Mendoza in 1535, the Audiencia of Mexico City was the primary executive institution of the colony. Once Mendoza arrived, he became the president of the *audiencia* that corresponded with his viceregal capital, the Audiencia of Mexico City. The viceroy also served as president of subordinate *audiencias*. Such was the case when the Crown formed the Audiencia of New Galicia, with the viceroy as its president, in the village of Compostela in 1548. Under normal conditions, the viceroy delegated someone to serve as the president of the *audiencia* in his absence. As president, the viceroy could manipulate the docket, which could be an extremely useful political tool. The viceroy also could send *oidores* on a circuit to hear cases outside of the *audiencia* capital. The Audiencia of New Galicia was subordinate to the Audiencia of Mexico City until the Crown raised it to a *chancillería audiencia* and moved it to the flourishing city of Guadalajara in 1560. As a *chancillería audiencia,* it gained its own president and a significant degree of autonomy, while remaining under the purview of the viceroy.

No other royal official embodied the full dignity and authority of the Crown as did the viceroy. New Spain's first viceroy, Antonio de Mendoza was a prominent member of one of Spain's most powerful and influential families. Throughout the Hapsburg era, the Crown sought to fill the viceroyalty with members of the high nobility, whom the Crown hoped would best represent its interests. Most viceroys were born in Spain. The few American-born viceroys were the sons of Spanish nobles serving posts in the colony, generally that of viceroy. In a tradition that would continue throughout the colonial period, lavish ceremonies celebrated Mendoza's arrival.

The viceregal court offered a wide range of cultural and entertaining events. It was the center of elite social life in the colony, rivaled only by the extravagant entertainment of some bishops and wealthy laymen. The court was home to the latest plays, music, and literature from Spain and the rest of Europe, some presented as private recitals while others were open to the general public. Dancing was another popular activity of the viceregal court, ranging from private formal balls to more popular forms. While some at the court enjoyed games of chess, cards were more common. In fact, gambling was quite frequent. Individuals bet on cards, dice, horse races, cockfights, or just about any other contest. Bullfights attracted a wide following, and the colonial elite enjoyed jousting, hunting, and other games played on horseback.

The viceroyalty was both the institution headed by and the territory ruled by the viceroy. The viceroyalty of New Spain covered a vast amount of territory, stretching from Panama in the south to Oregon in the north and from the Philippines in the west to the Caribbean in the east. The enormity of the viceroyalty alone made ruling it very difficult. First and foremost, the viceroy was the chief executive of the colony. His duties included general administration; the imposition, collection, and disbursement of taxes; public works; maintenance of order; the return of surplus revenue to the Crown; internal and external defense; support of the church; and the protection of Indians. Supervising the economic development of the colony was one of the viceroy's most important functions. He was responsible for ensuring the continual flow of revenue back to the Crown, especially from the silver industry and the numerous royal-levied taxes. The silver industry was particularly important for financing Crown business and servicing the Crown's constantly increasing debt load. A good viceroy enacted policies that ensured a constant flow of silver revenue to the Crown. The decline of silver production and revenues in the seventeenth century was not the result of inefficient viceroys, however, but rather the inability of monopoly companies to provide the constant supply of mercury needed in the amalgamation process. It is also clear that many silver producers kept much of their revenue in New Spain, greatly enhancing the economic development of the colony.

At the same time, the viceroy served as president of various *audiencias* and maintained the title of captain general, making him the principal military officer of the colony. The *audiencia* was supposed to advise and work with the viceroy. Often, however, the interests of the *audiencia* and the viceroy were in conflict. Church officials and other bureaucrats also challenged the authority of the viceroy. In spite of these challenges, most viceroys proved to be competent, although often unremarkable, rulers.

Here again one can see that the colonial bureaucracy was not designed to be extremely efficient.

Officials had overlapping responsibilities and jurisdictions. So many bureaucrats with similar responsibilities and conflicting interests made the colonial government move very slowly. Mendoza's philosophy of administration, "do little and do it slowly," worked well in the colonial environment. Yet, the Crown designed the redundant system intentionally to provide checks and balances for the power of its officials so far away from the mother country. The Crown jealously guarded its prerogatives and authority, stressing loyalty above all else. Administrative distance, however, forced viceroys to act with a degree of autonomy. For most of the colonial period, the fleets sailed once a year, meaning that the viceroy generally waited many months to receive replies from the Crown. Many times, the viceroy simply could not wait that long. Very often correspondence became tied up between the Crown's various councils, making the delay even longer. Occasionally a reply came that the viceroy believed to be contrary to the best interests of the local situation. At such times, he generally noted *Obedezco pero no cumplo* (I obey but do not execute). This practice allowed viceroys to remain loyal to the Crown and still be responsive to local needs. A viceroy who too often refused to executed the orders of the king was at risk during the final review of his tenure in office, the *residencia*. Therefore, the overlapping jurisdictions helped the Crown ensure that no one individual ever could amass enough power and independence to threaten seriously royal prerogatives.

In spite of the checks and balances, an official so far removed still could abuse his authority to the detriment of the Crown's interests. To make individual bureaucrats more accountable, the Crown instituted the *residencia* and *visita*. The *residencia* was a judicial review of an official's conduct at the end of his term of office. A *juez de residencia* (judge of the official's residency) traveled to the principal town or district associated with the *residenciado* and posted notices announcing the day that the *tribunal de residencia* would begin. Anyone, including Indians, was free to come forward and present accusations or give evidence. The Council of the Indies or the Crown provided the judge of residency with detailed instructions. Generally, the judge was not to be satisfied with general accusations but was to obtain facts and work diligently to find the truth. Fines and forfeitures imposed by the judge help to defray the cost of his salary. The *residenciado,* or agents acting on his behalf, often paid bribes to move the procedure along and reduce fines. If fines exceeded an individual's ability to pay, which they often did, then the judge would collect the fines from the *audiencia*'s general expense account. Often the judge of residency was the official replacing the *residenciado*. The fines and bribes that he accepted helped offset the costs of obtaining his office. The *residencia* could go on for months. A decree of 1667 required a viceroy's *residencia* to be completed within six months. The time limit for minor officials was generally 60 days. Like the *residencia*, the *visita* was a judicial review of an official's conduct in office. The *visita*, however, was a surprise inspection that could occur anytime during an official's tenure.

As New Spain expanded, it became impossible to govern outlying areas from the capital. Within each *audiencia*, officials formalized provincial administration into a series of small subdivisions. These subdivisions were called *corregimientos, alcaldías mayores,* and *gobiernos,* and were administered by *corregidores, alcaldes mayores,* and *gobernadores.* The responsibilities and functions of all three were very similar, so a discussion of the *corregidores* will suffice to describe all three. *Corregidores* had quasi-legislative, judicial, and administrative power in their districts. Their principal responsibility was to preserve order and maintain the Crown's presence in the provinces. To prevent *corregidores* from becoming too powerful, the *audiencia* severely checked their legislative and judicial responsibilities. Following the Conquest, the office of *corregidor* often went to conquistadors, their children, or other early settlers as a form of pension during a time when the Crown was attempting to limit the expansion of the *encomienda*. Most *corregidores* had little or no training in administration, the pay was low, and the office brought little esteem to the holder. The *corregidores* began to supplement their income through legal and extralegal means that often included defrauding the Indians and other lower-class groups. Just as it had done for other offices, the Crown began to appoint more qualified, educated men to the post of *corregidor* in an attempt to mitigate their worst abuses of power. Usually lawyers, the new administrators continued to have the reputation as the most corrupt Crown officials, however. The most notorious were the *corregidores de indios,* who had the responsibility of maintaining order in Indian towns that paid tribute directly to the Crown rather than to an *encomendero*. Often acting in collusion with native chiefs, the *corregidores de indios* defrauded Indians in many different ways. When this happened, Indians could and frequently did file suit in the General Indian Court or the *audiencia*. Indians generally were successful in their suits against the abuses of Spaniards, whether private individuals or Crown officials. The checks and balances of the system were successful in mitigating the worst abuses of provincial officials. In spite of abuses, many royal official took their charge of protecting the Indians seriously.

Separate from provincial officials who were under direct royal authority were the municipal governments of New Spain. Drawing on the traditions of medieval Castile, Cortés founded Vera Cruz in 1519. As the Spanish expanded in New Spain, so did the *município*. Cortés appointed the first town council *(cabildo* or *ayuntamiento),* but by tradition, *vecinos* elected local officials annually. The *cabildo* included anywhere from four or five *regidores* (aldermen) in small towns to 15 *regidores* in late colonial Mexico City. The *cabildo* was responsible for local matters such as defending the town, maintaining order, controlling prices, allocating land, cleaning streets, maintaining supplies of food and water, and numerous other local maters. Generally, the *cabildo* represented the interests of the townspeople, which were often in conflict with royal prerogatives. More representative than other forms of government, the *cabildos* were often composed of criollos. In general, however, the *cabildo* represented the interests of the colonial elite. Even Indian communities had their own *cabildos*. Modeled after those of Spanish towns, Indian *cabildos* were made up of the Indians aristocracy. Spanish officials and clergy exerted significant influence on the Indian *cabildos*. Still, the Indian population had direct local representation by their traditional leaders. Pre-Hispanic village alliances and rivalries continued throughout the colonial period, as evidenced by the large number of cases in the General Indian Court in which one Indian village sued another Indian village. The early democratic nature of the *cabildo* was lost as the Crown began to sell *cabildo* seats in the late sixteenth century. The most frequent purchasers of *cabildo* seats were the criollo elite, who bought their positions in perpetuity. As such, local political power rested in the hands of a few very influential families.

From its bankruptcy in 1557 on, the Crown faced a staggering debt and shortage of funds, which proved far more serious than the loyalty of its officials. Thereafter, Felipe II (r. 1556–98) gradually expanded the sale of public offices from Castile to the Americas, starting with municipal offices. The Crown then expanded the number of offices available in order to recover greater amounts of revenue. By 1606 a royal decree allowed for the sale of a wide range of offices, including fee collecting and honorific positions. The Crown stated that officials who purchased their offices could hold them in perpetuity and even pass them to heirs, providing they paid certain taxes. Spain's continuous involvement in European wars further depleted the treasury, leading to the sale of appointments to treasury posts and the tribunal of accounts in 1633. By 1677 the depleted Crown sold positions of provincial administration, and by 1690 it systematically began to sell *audiencia* appointments. Originally, the Crown did not want to sell the most sensitive imperial bureaucratic appointments, especially those concerned with finance and security. As Spain plunged deeper into debt during the seventeenth century, however, it relented to the point of selling even viceregal appointments by 1700.

The sale of public offices severely undermined the philosophy of imperial administration cherished by the Spanish Hapsburgs. The first bureaucrats to take advantage of the sale of offices were native sons, criollos and *radicados* (men born elsewhere who had become rooted in local society), whom the Crown normally forbade from serving in their home districts. Bureaucrats preferred to serve in their home districts where they were not outsiders and could peddle their influence most effectively. As such, they were able to exercise greater autonomy than the Crown would have otherwise tolerated. Many of the office purchasers were young men who lacked the judgment and maturity of more seasoned bureaucrats. In addition to their limited experience, the young men offered decades of service, which both reduced the number of future sales and could prove daunting if the bureaucrat was undesirable for whatever reason. An important legacy of the sale of public offices is its promotion of corruption. Men who paid very high fees to receive positions that themselves paid relatively little looked for extralegal means of enhancing their financial opportunities. It is a legacy that Mexico's bureaucracy both battles and embraces to this day. While the sale of public offices undermined the Spanish philosophy of imperial administration, it led to responsive government in the hands of the criollo elite. American-born politicians acting with relative autonomy from the Crown held offices at many levels. This was especially important in the development of local economies in the seventeenth century, when Spain's troubles often left its American possessions to fend for themselves. The political center of the Spanish Empire may have been in Iberia, but the economic center already had shifted to America. Criollo political, economic, and social advancement in the seventeenth century set the path toward independence as criollos refused to give up their gains in the face of Spanish pressure in the late eighteenth century.

By 1700 two visions of Hapsburg politics emerged. The first is the rigidity of the imperial bureaucracy.

Authority passed from the king to the Council of the Indies to the viceroy to the *audiencias* to the provincial administrators to municipal officials and finally to the people. Royal decrees and regulations clogged the wheels of the imperial machine. The Crown valued loyal, inefficient bureaucrats over innovative and imaginative officials. Upon closer examination, however, one finds an alternative view of imperial bureaucracy: incredible flexibility and the ability to adapt to changing local needs. Viceroys often chose not to execute royal decrees. Institutions had overlapping boundaries. The Crown depended on officials to enact policies in the local interest. Native sons, criollos and *radicados,* gained autonomy that was previously unknown in New Spain. The corruption of the seventeenth century also demonstrated the flexibility of the imperial system. Graft kept the rigid, hierarchical system moving. It enabled government to function. The government in New Spain evolved from rule by *adelantados* and conquistadors to an entrenched imperial bureaucracy that by 1700 was flexible enough to accommodate local desires and interests of an ever-evolving complex society.

The Hapsburg era came to a pitiful end in 1700. After struggling fruitlessly against economic decay and political decline for most of the century, Spain showed signs increasing vitality in the last decades of the seventeenth century. The economy in particular was rebounding in spite of the ineffective policies of the lackluster Carlos II (r. 1665–1700). Among his other failings, Carlos never produced an heir. As he approached death, the question of who would succeed him dominated Spanish political life. On his deathbed, Carlos fought to prevent the disintegration of his Spanish dominions under three rival claimants. Just before dying, Carlos signed his will granting all of Spain's possessions to Philip of Anjou, who later became Felipe V, over the claims of the prince of Bavaria and the archduke Charles of Austria. English fears of the union of Spain and France under a single Crown led to the War of Spanish Succession (1702–1713.) The Treaty of Utrecht ended the war in 1713. Under the terms of the treaty, Great Britain received Gibraltar and Minorca, trade concessions in the Spanish Caribbean, and a guarantee against the union of the Crowns of Spain and France under Felipe. In 1714, another treaty gave the Spanish Netherlands and Spain's Italian possessions to Austria. The succession of the House of Bourbon led to the loss of territory that the Spanish Hapsburgs had fought so hard to maintain. In New Spain, Hapsburg institutions faced little change until the Bourbon Reforms of the late eighteenth century. Even the Bourbon Reforms brought little structural change to

Hapsburg institutions. In fact, the modern nations of Latin America have maintained borders remarkably similar to the *audiencia* and viceregal borders of the Hapsburgs, allowing for subdivisions added by the Bourbons. The history of Hapsburg politics and government is one of outstanding resiliency. In spite of its apparently rigid structure, it was flexible enough to accommodate the changing needs of the evolving colony. It allowed for local development within the context of absolute loyalty to the Spanish Crown. Its legacy lives on in modern Mexico and throughout Spanish Latin America.

See also Conquest; Conquistadors; Inquisition

Select Bibliography

Aiton, A. S., *Antonio de Mendoza, First Viceroy of New Spain*. Durham, North Carolina: Duke University Press, 1927.

Borah, Woodrow, *Justice by Insurance: The General Indian Court and the Legal Aides of the Half-Real*. Berkeley: University of California Press, 1983.

Burkholder, Mark A., and Lyman L. Johnson, *Colonial Latin America*. Oxford: Oxford University Press, 1994.

Fisher, Lillian Estelle, *Viceregal Administration in the Spanish American Colonies*. Berkeley: University of California Press, 1926.

Gibson, Charles, *The Aztecs under Spanish Rule: A History of the Indians of the Valley of Mexico, 1519–1810*. Stanford, California: Stanford University Press, 1964.

_____, *Spain in America*. New York: Harper, 1966.

Haring, Clarence H., *The Spanish Empire in America*. New York: Oxford University Press, 1947.

Haskett, Robert, *Indigenous Rulers: An Ethnohistory of Town Government in Colonial Cuernavaca*. Albuquerque: University of New Mexico Press, 1991.

Liss, Peggy, *Spanish Empire in Mexico, 1511–1556: Society and the Origins of Nationality*. Chicago: University of Chicago Press, 1975.

MacLachlan, Colin M., *Spain's Empire in the New World: The Role of Ideas in Institutional and Social Change*. Berkeley: University of California Press, 1988.

McAlister, Lyle, *Spain and Portugal in the New World, 1492–1700*. Minneapolis: University of Minnesota Press, 1988.

Meyer, Michael C., and William L. Sherman. *The Course of Mexican History*. 5th ed., Oxford: Oxford University Press, 1995.

Parry, J. H., *The Audiencia of New Galicia in the Sixteenth Century*. Cambridge: Cambridge University Press, 1948.

_____, *The Sale of Public Office in the Spanish Indies under the Hapsburgs*. Berkeley: University of California Press, 1953.

Phelan, John Leddy, *The Kingdom of Quito in the Seventeenth Century*. Madison: University of Wisconsin Press, 1967.

—MARTIN V. FLEMING

Politics and Government: Bourbon New Spain

The advent of the Bourbon dynasty in Spain in 1700 began a series of changes in political and economic institutions. Initially these reforms were applied in Spain and only later were implemented its possessions in the Americas. The "Bourbon Reforms," as they came to be known, sought to resolve the intractable financial crisis which had characterized the Spanish state under Hapsburg rule. The Spanish Crown became the main agent of these political and economic reforms, hoping to impose a more uniform and efficient system of taxation and tribute. Traditional privileges and regional *fueros* (legal immunities) that hampered equality before the law (and the tax collector) were weakened or abolished, as was the intervention of corporate institutions in tax collection. Local and regional governments, which had enjoyed considerable de facto autonomy under the Hapsburgs, were replaced by a system of direct rule, or intendancies.

The first initiative to impose the intendancy system in the Americas was begun by José del Campillo y Cossío, secretary of the treasury under Felipe V. On July 20, 1746, the Crown ordered the viceroys of New Spain and Peru to inform it about the possibilities of instituting a political and economic system in the colonies similar to that in Spain. The Crown sought to centralize political, economic, and administrative decision making in the colonies, ensuring that the colonial bureaucracy was dominated by functionaries loyal to Spain. Under these changes the farming and ranching sector in the colonies increasingly was directed toward the export of raw materials to Spain and the consumption of Spanish industrial goods. Tax and tribute collection were streamlined, allowing the Spanish state to capture more of the financial resources of the Americas.

Although intendancies were instituted in Havana (1764), Louisiana (1765), and Caracas (1766), they were largely defensive measures sparked the increased power of England in the Caribbean. Bourbon policy was not systematically applied in New Spain until the *visita* (tour of inspection) of José de Gálvez from 1765 to 1771. As *visitador general* (inspector general) Gálvez attacked the principal political institution of Hapsburg administration, the viceroyalty. To weaken the viceroy's enormous power Gálvez proposed the replacement of local bureaucrats with intendants. If local bureaucrats in Hapsburg New Spain (*corregidores* and *alcaldes mayores*) had bought their posts, used them for their own personal interests, and allied with local elites, intendants would be appointed directly by the Spanish state and subject to the Spanish crown. Although the viceroy would continue to be the nominal maximum authority in New Spain, the financial system would end up in the hands of a superintendent of the royal treasury, while the regional intendants would control the administration of justice, war, treasury, and police in their respective territories. As minister of the Indies from 1776 to 1787 Gálvez was able to implement many of his policy recommendations. In 1782 Carlos III established the intendancy system in the viceroyalty of Rio de la Plata, and in 1786 he promulgated a "Royal Ordinance of Intendants for New Spain." Needless to say, viceregal and local authorities were less than sanguine about the intendancy system. The application of administrative uniformity was not a seamless process; rather it occurred in fits and starts, advancing and retreating as it clashed with the Hapsburg *ancien regime* in New Spain.

Among the most important conflicts sparked by Bourbon reforms in New Spain were territorial rivalries. In the decades following the military and religious conquest, Spanish administration in the Americas was a patchwork of overlapping political, military, civil, and fiscal jurisdictions—viceroyalties, *audiencia* districts, *gobernaciones* and *alcaldías mayores, corregimientos,* and finally Spanish municipalities and *repúblicas de indios.* The viceroyalty of New Spain was divided into two major judicial districts, the *audiencia* of Mexico and the *audiencia* of Guadalajara. The first included the Kingdom of New Spain and the provinces of Yucatán, Cozumel, and Tabasco, while the second included the Kingdom of Nueva Galicia and the provinces of Copala, Colima, and Zacatula; however, these delimitations were never static. By the time of the Bourbon Reforms, the viceroyalty itself was composed of the Kingdoms of Nueva España (New Spain), Nueva Galicia, Nueva Vizcaya, Nuevo México (New Mexico) and Nuevo León; the Provinces of Yucatán, Coahuila, Sinaloa, Sonora, Tejas (Texas), Nayarit, Vieja California, Nueva California, and the colony of Nuevo Santander (Tamaulipas). Local administration in central Mexico was in the hands of *corregidores,* who controlled town councils and administered justice, as well as a variety of *corregidores* for Indian towns. *Alcaldías mayores* were conceded and later sold by the Crown, and were in charge of tribute collection and the promotion of commerce; by the beginning of the eighteenth century *alcaldes mayores* had become traders or mercantile agents as well as agents of the colonial government. In outlying areas such as the province of Yucatán, the Crown was unable to introduce *corregidores* and *alcaldes*

mayores, and the Yucatecan *ayuntamientos* (city halls) resisted Spanish attempts to appoint a governor over the region.

If the intendancy system sought to rationalize the territorial organization of New Spain, the reality on the ground was left much to be desired. Due to the lack of precise geographic and demographic criteria, some districts ended up in more than one intendancy or none at all. In other cases districts' political reorganization had nothing to do with their economic ties. Nonetheless, the *corregimientos* eventually were assigned (such as the *corregimiento* of Bolaños, which was incorporated into the intendancy of Guadalajara in 1793) or reassigned (such as the Tlapa and Quautla Amilpas, which in 1793 were integrated into the intendancies of Mexico City and Puebla, respectively). Moreover, the importance of the intendancies would continue long after the end of Spanish rule. Asserting their territorial integrity in opposition to the later territorial demarcation imposed by the regent Cortes of Cádiz in 1812, the intendancies would form the basis for territorial divisions in independent Mexico.

Corporations that represented the interests of municipal elites, *cabildos* (town councils) tended to be found in the capitals of the old provinces, key ports, and in *pueblos cabaceros* (head towns, or district seats). Their power in the administration of justice, conferred by the Inquisition, allowed them to exercise control over surrounding towns, forming districts or subregions of larger provinces. *Corregidores, alcaldes mayores,* and even the governors who acted as high justices (as was the case in Yucatán) could be called on to enforce the sentences passed down by the council members *(alcaldes ordinarios).*

The fiscal centralization of the Spanish *cabildos* was a gradual but systematic process which began with the introduction of *cajas reales* (royal depositories) in the principal cities and ports of the viceroyalty, causing the first friction with preexisting municipal governments *(ayuntamientos).* In 1746 the Junta de Hacienda (Treasury Council) was created, and a year later the viceroy was named superintendent general of the treasury. In 1753 Viceroy Francisco de Güemes y Horcasitas (first count of Revillagigedo) put the collection of the *alcabala* (internal tariff) under the control of royal authorities, and as inspector general José de Gálvez launched an energetic policy of breaking the power of the *cabildos* by naming honorary aldermen and representatives from the commons to the councils. Gálvez's measures during his tenure as minister of the Indies (1776–86) further sought to weaken the power of traditionally influential groups.

The Ordinance of 1786 established the Junta Superior de Real Hacienda (Superior Council of the Royal Treasury) to increase Crown control over expenditures of city funds. The royal order of September 14, 1788, mandated that municipal authorities only could invest surpluses from municipal taxes and usufruct fees with the approval of the Real Audiencia, which they would need to contact through provincial intendants. The Junta Superior also approved new regulations for city usufruct fees and put the provincial intendants in charge of enforcing them. As intermediate authorities intendants received proposals for extraordinary expenditures, the repair of roads and urban infrastructure, salary increases for *cabildo* employees, and other matters specified by the Junta Superior. One of the most important branches of the municipal administration was its monopoly on the distribution of meat, which was found in the hands of powerful cattle ranchers. Under the intendancy system, however, there were clashes in many cities over the auctioning off of the municipal meat monopoly. In Jalapa two auctions were organized, one of the *alcaldes ordinarios* and the other of the subdelegate of the intendancy. In Mérida, the capital of Yucatán, the *ayuntamiento* resisted the orders of the intendant regarding meat distribution.

One factor in the friction between *cabildos* and the new local authorities was the necessity felt by many cities with little or no grain production to control the planting and circulation of maize and seed from agricultural districts. The *ayuntamiento* of Campeche vehemently protested starting in 1795 against the incapacity of the new local authorities to satisfy the urban population's need for basic foodstuffs. It accused the subdelegates and other lower authorities of the provincial government of promoting large plantings of maize and monopolizing the trade of basic grains, making the effects of agricultural crises much more acute. In 1785 and 1786 the intendancy of Zacatecas was hit by grain shortages and high prices due to the generalized agricultural crisis in New Spain. The new functionaries had the power to intervene in the transit and distribution of grains in their respective districts, but the intendant of Zacatecas, safeguarding mining interests, was able to use extraterritorial powers to direct the grain production of Aguascalientes to his province.

These interventions by provincial authorities in urban centers were decisive in the resistance of local oligarchies. The intendant presided over the *cabildo* of the capital of the intendancy, and in the 1780s and 1790s the capital cities were divided into *cuarteles* (quarters), which in turn were subdivided into *barrios* (neighborhoods), which were administered by *alcaldes de cuartel* and *alcaldes de barrio* under the direct supervision of the intendant. With the introduction of subdelegates of the intendancy in towns, power was turned over to the local elite, limiting the power of the provincial oligarchy. Subdelegations never ceased to be the weak point of the Bourbon Reforms, and the colonial government never was able to resolve the problem of local administration. Nonetheless, the intendancy system also gave rise to confusions and rivalries on the provincial level, which generated attempts by regional elites to recover political space and lost territories. Although *cabildos* regained the power to appoint honorary aldermen in 1794, however, the recovery of lost territories proved to be out of reach.

Article ten of the Ordinance established the military and political governorships of Yucatán, Tabasco, Veracruz, Acapulco, Nuevo Reino de León, Nuevo Santander, Coahuila, Texas, and Nuevo México. If the intendant was given authority over usufruct fees, municipal taxes, and community funds, which he administered under the authority of the Junta Superior de Hacienda, his judicial and police powers tended to be circumscribed. In the jurisdiction of Acapulco the intendant's authority was limited to Ciudad de los Reyes (the present-day city of Acapulco), its port, and the three *cabaceras* which fell under its jurisdiction. Similar limitations were applied to the other governorships and the king's lieutenant in Campeche, with the exception of the intendancies of Yucatán and Veracruz.

Some excessively large jurisdictions were subdivided. The intendant Juan Antonio de Riaño in Yucatán, for example, established subdelegations in all of the towns around the city of Valladolid. Similarly, the old Audiencia of Nueva Galicia was split into two intendancies, one in the city of Guadalajara and the other in Zacatecas. The *alcaldía mayor* of Aguascalientes suffered the loss of Tecaltiche and later of Juchipila; mining interests demanded the annexation of Aguascalientes, and the *alcaldía* was folded into Zacatecas in 1791. These sorts of changes made relations between municipal authorities and the subdelegate and intendant quite tense. In Aguascalientes *alcaldes* had been able to extend their control beyond the outskirts of the city to all of the towns in the *alcaldía* and their resources. The *alcaldes'* judicial authority meant that the merchants who served on the *cabildo* were able to bring debtors who lived in distant towns within the *alcaldía* to court in the city of Aguascalientes. After the Ordinance, however, the authority of the *alcaldes* was restricted to the city of Aguascalientes and its immediate hinterlands. In a clear illustration of how far the old *cabildos* were prepared to go to win back their former hegemony in their former districts, however, Cayetano Guerrero in 1819 held the posts both of *alcalde ordinario* of the city of Aguascalientes and subdelegate, contravening the explicit prohibition in the Ordinance against officials holding both posts. Guerrero later was an active participant in the campaign to make Aguascalientes a department of the Republic in 1835, and in 1857 Aguascalientes was made into a state.

Similar conflicts occurred throughout New Spain. The *ayuntamiento* of Xalapa, for example, also clashed with the local subdelegate. Nonetheless, not all assertions of local power ended in territorial separations. The province of Querétaro, which had been governed by military commandants and *corregidores*, obtained the status of *alcaldía mayor* in 1777, giving its magistrates considerable power over the outlying areas. In 1786, however, it was incorporated into the intendancy of Mexico, provoking serious conflicts between the *cabildo* of the city of Santiago de Querétaro and Viceroy Juan Vicente de Güemes Pacheco y Padilla (the second count of Revillagigedo). Querétaro was one of the cities that most bitterly opposed the intendancy system, defending its municipal privileges, and the *cabildo* demanded the return of its police and judicial authority over the entire former territory. In a partial solution to the conflict, without explicitly recognizing the *cabildo's* demands, in 1793 the Crown approved the establishment of a subdelegation in the former territory of Querétaro whose head had powers similar to those of an intendant.

In 1797 the Junta Superior responded to the these sorts of restorationist demands by increasing the judicial, fiscal, and administrative power of the subdelegates over the towns that had *ayuntamientos*. In 1799 the Junta decreed that the subdelegate would preside over the *cabildos*, and the decree was approved by the Crown over the vigorous objections of such cities as Xalapa and Córdoba. The status of Querétaro as a *corregimiento* was recognized in 1794. Although it was made into a province together with the *alcaldías* of Cadereyta and Escanela in 1812, it was not until after Independence that it received its own representation in the federal government. In the constitutional decree approved by the insurgent Congress of Apatzingán Querétaro appeared as a separate province, and it finally was admitted as a full state into the union in the Constitution of 1824.

A somewhat more extreme case occurred in Yucatán. Until the mid–eighteenth century, Yucatán was divided into three districts controlled by the *cabildos* of Mérida, Campeche, and Valladolid. Even before the Ordinance, Crown authorities had attempted to impose their authority over the *cabildos*. In the mid–eighteenth century the governor-captain general of Yucatán, Melchor de Navarrete, appointed a lieutenant governor in the *cabildo* of Campeche with authority over defense and justice. The resistance of the Valladolid elites was so vociferous that the governor proposed to the Crown that the *cabildo* be dissolved or, at minimum, that its authority be restricted to the city itself and its immediate outskirts.

The establishment of the intendancy system consummated the trend of reducing the power of the *cabildos* in Yucatán. The delimitation of the districts sparked clashes between the first intendant, Lucas de Gálvez, and the governor general. The intendant soon was able to concentrate administrative functions in his own hands in order to reconfigure the territorial organization of the region. Twelve subdelegations were created, and the authority of individual cities was restricted to a circumference of five leagues. The *ayuntamiento* of Campeche, where the king's lieutenant was based, saw its jurisdiction confined to the city itself and its immediate hinterlands. In their constant protests against the subdelegates and what they saw as the intendants' meddling in local affairs, the elites of Campeche sought to restore the old boundaries of the district of Campeche which had existed since the seventeenth century— and which prefigured the borders of the present-day state of Campeche. In 1858 the rivalry between the cities of Campeche and Mérida was resolved when the elites of the two cities reached an accord which would make the old district of Campeche into a separate entity. The division became official on February 19, 1862, and approved formally by the Mexican government on April 29, 1863.

The reduction of the jurisdictions of the *ayuntamientos* was an unfortunate Crown policy which earned the hostility of regional oligarchies together with *alcaldes mayores* and *alcaldes ordinarios*. In some cases the conflict generated movements that in the short term gave rise to autonomous territorial districts. A look at the map of territorial demarcations prior to the Ordinance permits us to visualize some of the territorial units which were subsumed into intendancies only to reappear as states in the Mexican republic decades later, as happened with Querétaro. Other subdelegations, such as Aguascalientes and Campeche, would maintain an identity characterized by an intense localism that was asserted in opposition to intendancy capitals. These rivalries would continue long after Independence until the former territories were admitted as full states into the union.

Under the constitutional regime of 1812 the capitals of the intendancies were subsumed into a new administrative structure, creating a new set of territorial conflicts. The *ayuntamientos* of Puebla, Oaxaca, and Veracruz all sought to restore the regional hegemony that had been reinforced under the intendancy system. Moreover, the administrative changes gave rise to movements to restore municipal autonomy to important cities in the interior of Mexico as well as port cities with strong local identities. These intractable rivalries would have to be resolved by the governments of independent Mexico.

See also Hidalgo Revolt; Inquisition; Wars of Independence

Select Bibliography

Altman, Ida, and James Lockhart, editors, *Provinces of Early Mexico: Variants of Spanish American Regional Evolution.* Los Angeles: UCLA Latin American Center, 1976.
Bakewell, P. J., *Silver Mining and Society in Colonial Mexico: Zacatecas, 1546–1700.* Cambridge: Cambridge University Press, 1971.
Booker, Jackie R., *Veracruz Merchants, 1770–1829: A Mercantile Elite in Late Bourbon and Early Independent Mexico.* Boulder, Colorado: Westview, 1993.
Brading, D. A., *Miners and Merchants in Bourbon Mexico, 1763–1818.* Cambridge: Cambridge University Press, 1971.
——, "Bourbon Spain and Its American Empire." In *The Cambridge History of Latin America,* vol. 1, edited by Leslie Bethell. Cambridge: Cambridge University Press, 1984.
Coatsworth, John H., "The Limits of Colonial Absolutism: The State in Eighteenth Century Mexico." In *Essays in the Political, Economic and Social History of Colonial Latin America,* edited by Karen Spalding. Newark, Delaware: University of Delaware Press, 1982.
Garner, Richard L., and Spiro E. Stefanou, *Economic Growth and Change in Bourbon Mexico.* Gainesville: University Press of Florida, 1993.
Hoberman, Louisa Schell, and Susan Migden Socolow, *Cities and Society in Colonial Latin America.* Albuquerque: University of New Mexico Press, 1986.
Kicza, John E., *Colonial Entrepreneurs: Families and Business in Bourbon Mexico City.* Albuquerque: University of New Mexico Press, 1983.
Lynch, John, *Bourbon Spain 1700–1808.* Oxford and Cambridge, Massachusetts: Blackwell, 1989.
Martin, Cheryl English, *Governance and Society in Colonial Mexico: Chihuahua in the Eighteenth Century.* Stanford, California: Stanford University Press, 1996.
Stein, Stanley J., "Bureaucracy and Business in the Spanish Empire, 1759–1804: Failure of a Bourbon Reform in Mexico and Peru." *Hispanic American Historical Review* 61:1 (1981).
Swann, Michael M., *Tierra Adentro: Settlement and Society in Colonial Durango.* Boulder, Colorado: Westview, 1982.
Taylor, William B., "Between Local Process and Global Knowledge: An Inquiry into Early Latin American Social History, 1500–1900." In *Reliving the Past: The Worlds of Social History,* edited by Olivier Zunz and David William Cohen. Chapel Hill: University of North Carolina Press, 1985.
Thomson, Guy P. C., *Puebla de los Angeles: Industry and Society in a Mexican City, 1700–1850.* Boulder, Colorado: Westview, 1989.

—MELCHOR CAMPOS GARCÍA

Politics and Government: 1821–76

The main problem confronting Mexico from 1821 to 1876, a period linked in many aspects with the creation of the Mexican state, was the country's inability to form a political constitution. Thus while various styles of government were tried and different factions were involved in power struggles, the country grew steadily weaker. There was, however, one important development: the various ideas and their proponent groups grew more precise and defined, until by the middle of the century they were divided between two main groups, Liberals and Conservatives. The clash between the two and the manner of its resolution paved the way for the consolidation of the Mexican state.

The initial contradictions largely derived from the emancipation process. In 1821 Agustín de Iturbide managed to bring together various interests to achieve one object, that of Independence, but this consensus did not respect other issues of political life. Moreover, the recently emancipated Mexicans showed, as they had prior to Independence, equal flexibility in the adjustment of objectives in the short or long term to establish opportune alliances. Thus secret societies such as the Freemasons became the most powerful political organizations in Independent Mexico. There was little hegemony; political power had become widely dispersed.

Another factor that prevented the consolidation of the state was the lack of money. The economic crisis provoked by the war was exacerbated by changes in international trade and capital flight. Moreover, Mexico inherited the colonial debt. Foreign loans had been obtained under unfavorable circumstances, and further loans had to be contracted. Corruption that had been present in the colonial era only grew worse in Independent Mexico, and subsequent governments inherited the colonial dislike of excessive taxation.

Finally, Mexican politics was deeply affected by international issues. It was important for the country to receive not only recognition as an independent country but also foreign investment. Recognition was a slow process, and the limited support that did arrive came at high cost. The first administrations tried to establish the frontier with the United States and obtain recognition and support from their neighbor. But given the latter's now well-known territorial imperative, the United States had no liking for the creation of a Mexican Empire, despite the recognition of Mexican Independence in January 1823. The United States decided to become the most powerful state in America and announced the Monroe Doctrine in December the same year for that very purpose.

Spain did not recognize the Treaty of Córdoba that formalized the Independence of New Spain and for 15 long years tried to stop other countries from recognizing Mexican Independence, thereby frustrating the country's political development. England was the only brake against U.S. and Spanish threats, but England delayed acknowledgment of Mexico's new status until 1825. France took five years longer. And the Bolivar-inspired dream of a continental union crumbled with thanks as much to U.S. and British intervention as to internal problems within the countries involved.

In its transition to becoming an independent country under the guidelines first set out in Iturbide's Plan of Iguala and later formalized in the Treaty of Córdoba, Mexico was to be ruled initially by a Sovereign Provisional Governing Junta. The junta was then to name a regency to exercise executive authority until a monarch was named by the Spanish Crown or, barring that, by the junta itself, which was to function as a provisional Congress until national elections could be held. The junta envisioned itself (and, ultimately, the elected Congress) as the true representation of the Mexican nation, and therefore the most powerful branch of the government. Iturbide, who was named president of the regency, saw the executive as the dominant branch of government.

The Sovereign Provisional Governing Junta was made up of military men and members of the national elite. Integrated by powerful groups that tried to control the political life of the country from the capital, this elite did not manage to unite the popular will. This situation led to political divisions and weakened the center as against the outlying regions. Consensus began to dissipate, and dissension became more apparent in Congress, thus destabilizing the regime. When Spain did not recognize the Treaty of Córdoba, Iturbide's faction declared the latter emperor. Congress, obliged to approve the election under threat of army bayonets, grew increasingly antagonistic to Iturbide; ultimately, the emperor dissolved Congress, thereby adding further problems to a state already in bankruptcy.

Various military leaders pronounced against Iturbide. The Veracruz Movement was initiated by Antonio López de Santa Anna at the end of 1822. His army was strengthened by the support of further military leaders originally sent against him, a practice that would happen repeatedly in Mexican political life. The Acta de Casa Mata proposed a new Congress and made a suggestion that would characterize many later pronouncements, that the nation was represented by Congress but the army constituted the people during congressional deliberations. The army was an important political player, strengthened by 11 years of armed struggle and protected by immunities. But internal divisions and financial problems prevented integration. As a result, the military intervened in politics to promote their special interests and not those of the body politic.

On the abdication of Iturbide, the cry was for federalism. The deputies elected to Congress were largely federalist republicans, unsuitable for the maintenance of the union. Central America, which had become incorporated into the Mexican Empire, declared independence. The new Congress dedicated itself to organizing government, making it very clear that final authority lay in the hands of the legislative. (This arrangement provoked instability in the Mexican political process; the nation-state would not consolidate until it could count on a powerful executive.) On October 4, 1824, the Constitution was promulgated, which established that the states of the federation must be free and sovereign in matters of public administration and government. The Congress also maintained old privileges, recognizing both ecclesiastical and army immunities. With this compromise constitution the first federal republic was born.

The election of the federalist Guadalupe Victoria (Félix Fernández) as president and the centralist Nicolás Bravo as vice president kept the balance. The gulf between federalists and centralists created a rift within the ranks of the Scottish Rite of Masonry (which was very influential in Mexican politics, having many members in the government); ultimately, the federalists decided to establish their own Masonic group. The U.S. minister Joel Poinsett played an important role in these matters as the promoter and founder of the York Masonic Rite in Mexico, which was federalist in its political leanings. York lodges were created in the states, thereby paving the way for a more popular participation.

The struggle between the Scottish (Escoceses) and Yorkist (Yorkinos) Masonic groups deepened divisions and weakened the state. The violence that erupted during the congressional elections of 1826 made the Senate consider legislating against secret societies, but it was unable to do so. Legally proscribed in 1828, these societies had not disappeared. They became true secret societies and continued to be a politically important force.

Political activity was handled through clandestine organizations. One example was the conspiracy of Joaquín Arenas, discovered in January 1827, which aimed to restore the country's sovereignty to Fernando VII and resulted in increased hatred of the Spanish. The affair also proved a useful device for accusing the Scottish Rite Masons of complicity. The latter reacted by championing a revolt that demanded the annulment of secret societies and respect for the Constitution and the law. Nicolás Bravo, grand master of the Scottish Rite and the first of many acting vice presidents who joined with the opposing side, supported this plan. Vicente Guerrero, grand master of the York Rite, was sent against Bravo and succeeded in defeating him.

Despite the Yorkist victory, the elections of 1828 were very hard fought. The candidacy of Guerrero and Manuel Gómez Pedraza illustrated very different concerns. The Yorkists lost the presidential elections, and immediately insurrections started, also sparking the Acordada Riot and the sack of the Parián, whose destructive results and accompanying popular participation left a terrible mark. The masses were incorporated into political life through the electoral process but also through riots, uprisings, uproars, and protest demonstrations. Despite this, their status remained miserable; they had lost the paternalism of the Spanish laws in exchange for a political equality that would never become effective.

Congress agreed to annul the election of Gómez Pedraza and nominate Guerrero as president and Anastasio Bustamante as his vice president. But Guerrero was unable to calm social disquiet during his brief administration. Nor did he have much support, despite the defeat of the Spanish expedition led by Isidro Barradas in September 1829. Moreover, he could not come to an agreement with Congress, and the bad situation of the exchequer had been aggravated by the Spanish defeat. In November of the same year the Campeche garrison declared for centralism, and in December the reserve army in Perote followed suit, offering to support the federal pact and reestablish the constitutional system. It was then that Vice President Bustamante rebelled against Guerrero, who left to fight the rebels. Congress took advantage of the situation to decree Guerrero's moral incapacity to govern, annul his election, and declare

the revolt justified with the result that Bustamante assumed the presidency.

Public administration was organized during Bustamante's term. Lucas Alamán, minister of finance, did his best to revitalize the economy and managed to obtain an increase in income. Various bishoprics were filled—thanks to the kindness of a Vatican that would not see fit to recognize Mexican Independence until 1836—and the army was disciplined. Bustamante's cabinet, made up of the well-heeled, showed signs of authoritarianism. The press was muzzled, and Guerrero, among others, was assassinated.

Bustamente's term was characterized by continual civil war. Once again a garrison took up arms, this time in Veracruz, again demanding the observance of the Constitution and the law. Santa Anna accepted leadership of the movement, rebellions broke out everywhere, and bloody battles took place. The civil war of 1832, which weakened the army, which destroyed the national economy and damaged the states, was brought to an end by Bustamante. His signing of the Zavaleta Agreement in December of the same year made the army commit itself, as usual, to supporting the federal republican system.

In 1833 Santa Anna was elected president and the radical liberal Valentín Goméz Farías as vice president. Santa Anna assumed the presidency on May 16; on June 3 he left office, citing reasons of poor health. Thus Santa Anna began his habit, to be repeated time after time, of leaving his second-in-command in charge of the executive. A group of passionate reformists came to power with Gómez Farías, whose tenure was characterized by military, political, and above all, ecclesiastical reform. The church was another important political player, which, privileged by immunities, had enormous influence on society and tremendous financial resources. Nevertheless, the church's role was questioned by the Mexican state, which sought to control it as had the Spanish Crown before. The church knew how to take advantage of circumstance; in the case of a permanently poor state, its financial support was very important, but it did not exercise any specific political influence. The exile and death of many bishops had left the church without competent leadership, and the division between a hierarchy that handled the resources and numerous priests in a difficult financial situation did not allow for a true esprit de corps.

The clergy and the army reacted against the reforms, which also lacked popular support, hence more conspiracies and rebellions. First antireformists and later centralists clamored for Santa Anna as leader and protector, with the result that he decided to return to the presidency in 1834. Backed by several revolts, he disarmed the militia, a move that annoyed various states, and he suspended the reform laws, a move that set the legislative powers against him. In January 1835 he sought another term, thereby inspiring further rebellions, some centralist.

The new Congress, on the other hand, dedicated itself to reforming the Constitution and named a revisory committee, which declared itself for centralism. The Constitutional Bases were sworn at the beginning of November of the same year. Thus began the first centralized republic.

Given the strength of federalism, it was surprising that centralism could keep going. External threats and the fragmentation of national territory reveal that it was fear that paralyzed the moderate federalists. Centralism sought to restrain popular political participation and establish strong government; while it maintained a powerful legislature, it was unable to reorganize public finance.

From June 1835 the inhabitants of Austin, Texas, had supported the Federal Constitution. The Texan problem was largely the result of settler politics, whose laws were applied as far as they favored the colonizers, ignoring requisites and restrictions. It also resulted from U.S. expansion and the internal U.S. conflict between free and slave states. The separatist aims of the Texans had been clear almost from the beginning. On the breakdown of the federal regime they proclaimed their independence, established a provisional government, and in November 1835 declared war on Mexico.

From the start they counted on the support of the United States and the enemies of Santa Anna, such as Lorenzo de Zavala, who owned land in Texas and would be its first vice president. Santa Anna marched north to overthrow the rebels, but his initial successes were eclipsed by the defeat at San Jacinto and his capture. The unfair and secret Treaty of Velasco in May 1836 ceded victory to the Texans. Even if Congress refused to recognize the treaty, the precarious condition of the army and the difficult internal situation put the war to one side. There were other federalist revolts, and the problematic economy worsened. Copper currency not only was falsified but rejected by means of riots and protests that precipitated several deaths as well as causing damage to several French businesses.

The centralist constitution, the Seven Constitutional Laws enacted on January 1, 1837, kept an executive harnessed to the legislature and established a supreme Conservative government. A little later elections were held, taking Bustamante to the presidency once again. The federalist uprising continued, as did the bad economic situation. Certain payments were suspended, and the idea of mortgaging ecclesiastical goods was put forth, a suggestion that set the clergy against the government and caused divisions within the church itself.

Matters became even more complicated when war with France erupted as a result of Mexico's refusal to recognize exaggerated and offensive demands of the French representative. Among his most outrageous demands was his insistence that Mexico compensate a French pastry chef whose savories had been devoured by a mob of hungry soldiers in 1828. The conflict hence has been dubbed the Pastry War. Nonetheless, the broader impact of the war proved to be less fertile ground for satire. The French blockade of gulf ports seriously affected commerce, while the destruction of the venerable Fortress of San Juan de Ulúa at the mouth of Veracruz harbor was a powerful blow to Mexican national pride; when the Mexican government offered to pay France's 600,000-peso claim, France upped the ante, demanding that Mexico also pay the costs of the blockade. Santa Anna was able to redeem both Mexican national pride and his own public standing, however, when he returned from his retirement to drive back a French amphibious assault on Veracruz, losing his leg in the process (it later was given a state funeral). France agreed to accept the original 600,000-peso claim from Mexico.

The government's call for unity resulted in the backing of the moderates, but federalist insurrections continued. The most serious was the separatist movement in Yucatán, which declared independence until the establishment of a federalist regime and the enactment of progressive religious reform. Centralism had seriously affected the state's economic privileges.

Attempts in favor of military dictatorship and the interests of foreign merchants were instrumental in the coup d'état of 1841. These foreign dealers had become very influential, performing an important role through the importation of articles, fashions, techniques, and ideas. As a pressure group, they blocked fiscal reform and the fight against contraband and corruption. By 1830 these merchants had begun to back rebellions and participate increasingly in political life.

Thus a new uprising against Bustamante in Guadalajara and Querétaro was backed by Santa Anna and his Plan de Tacubaya, which called for the abolition of all state institutions established by the Constitution of 1836 except the judiciary. A military provisional government was established and a new constituent assembly convened. Bustamante agreed to come to an agreement and signed the Tacubaya declaration.

The new Constitutional Congress of 1842 served to bring to light the differing points of view that divided the Mexicans of that decade into two great groups. A new federalist insurrection managed to dissolve Congress and nominate a National Governing Council to write a new constitution. The Principles of the Political Organization of the Mexican Republic, the second centralist Constitution, was published in 1843. The army and the church, conservative strongholds both, were still favored, even if the Conservatives were disappearing from supreme power.

In 1844 Santa Anna was again elected president, and once again he left the reins of power in the hands of another, this time José Joaquín de Herrera. But the postponement of the Texas campaign made for a new military uprising and a fresh popular revolt that led to the fall of Santa Anna. Mariano Paredes y Arrillaga rebelled in Guadalajara, and Congress stripped Santa Anna of his power and imprisoned him before sending him into exile. Herrera, backed by the so-called Decembrists (moderate federalists) tried to organize the administration and straighten out public finances, but was unable to achieve much. Political agitation continued with the various groups, such as the monarchists, championing their particular interests. These latter groups organized a conspiracy from Spain, backed by England and France, that provided funds for Paredes.

Fresh and very serious difficulties now arose. Texas was annexed to the United States at a moment when Congress proposed to recognize Texan independence so long as it did not do precisely that. War was imminent. The U.S. concept of "Manifest Destiny," widespread from the time the United States had achieved independence, crystallized in 1845. The war against Mexico made this ideology the most popular tenet of U.S. nationalism.

In December 1845 Paredes rebelled in San Luis Potosí, declaring both legislative and executive powers as inoperative. Like numerous previous revolts, this proposed to convene a Congress to create a national constitution. Triumphant, Paredes took over the capital, summoned elections, and made an effort to fight corruption. But the most serious problem was the war. With superb coordination that evidenced a well-organized plan, the U.S. forces started a triple campaign: in the north, in the east against the capital, and in a series of naval and guerrilla operations. Political divisions deepened with Mexican defeats. On August 4, when Paredes left to combat the invaders, Mariano Salas and Gómez Farías revolted and Paredes was taken prisoner in Querétaro.

The federalists once again finally took power under the Plan de la Ciudadela. This plan proposed a Constitutional Congress that would choose a model of government in agreement with the national will, so long as it was not monarchism. Santa Anna was elected president and Gómez Farías vice president. The Constitution of 1824 was reestablished and on May 21, 1847, the Act of Constitution and Reform of the United States of Mexico was passed.

Only 7 of the 19 states had helped in the defense of the country. Yucatán asked the United States for help and offered itself for annexation. A U.S. expedition occupied New Mexico and the Bear Flag Republic was declared in California. Mexico City was occupied on September 14, 1847. Santa Anna resigned and Manuel de la Peña y Peña established a government in Querétaro, and negotiations started with the invaders. The Treaty of Guadalupe Hidalgo was signed on February 2, 1848; according to the treaty's terms Mexico lost more than half its territory. The country had reached the lowest point in its fortunes.

The war with the United States was one of the bitterest of experiences, but it had one positive result: it helped to mature a nationalist consciousness. Political camps also were clarified, and true political parties began to make an appearance.

In 1851 Herrera handed over presidential power peacefully to Mariano Arista. Various liberals of a new generation took part in the government through a more clearly defined Liberal Party, and public finance began to be put in order. Despite this the country had to deal with numerous indigenous revolts—most notably the Caste War that began in 1847 in Yucatán and lasted until the 1880s—agrarian discontent, and incursions by foreign freebooters.

In 1852 José María Blancarte headed another rebellion in Guadalajara that called for the return of Santa Anna and proposed the abolition of federalism and the establishment of a strong executive. Santa Anna returned to power in 1853 allied to the Conservatives. His government was authoritarian, imposing extravagant taxes and breaking up opposition groups through imprisonment and deportations. The territory of La Mesilla (now part of southern Arizona) also was sold to the United States.

The old rebel Juan Álvarez took up arms again in February 1854. His Plan of Ayutla, later amended in Acapulco, gained the allegiance of the south. It sought a new social pact and the vindication of individual liberties, which would be exercised to choose a republican government that would be both representative and liberal. The state and public administration would yet again be reorganized in a Constitutional Congress. The movement spread throughout the country, uniting various leaders such as Porfirio Díaz in Oaxaca and Benito Juárez in exile in New Orleans. The revolt lasted some time; Santa Anna did not resign until August 1855.

On October 1 Álvarez set up a government in Cuernavaca, acting as interim president. His cabinet was Liberal: Melchor Ocampo, Juárez, Guillermo Prieto, Ignacio Comonfort, and Miguel Lerdo de Tejada. The importance of this new generation of educated civilians must be emphasized. This was the generation of the Reform, disciples of José María Luis Mora and Valentín Gómez Farías. Álvarez discharged the promises of the Plan of Ayutla, thereby easing this group's climb to power. But diehards and moderates could not come to an agreement, making way for a new balance, or unbalance, of forces.

Reformist resolutions were begun during his brief government. On November 23, 1855, the Ley Juárez abolished clerical immunities and special courts, thereby initiating a clash with the church and privileged groups. The Revolt of Zacapoaxtla started at the beginning of December to the cry of *religión y fueros* (religion and immunities), which had the support of the bishop of Puebla, Pelagio Antonio de Labastida y Dávalos, and soldiers such as Miguel Miramón. When Manuel Doblado took up arms in Guanajuato, Álvarez resigned and Comonfort became the substitute president, continuing with the reform laws and thereby setting off further rebellions. The Ley Lerdo of June 25, 1856, forced the sale of ecclesiastical town and country properties, thereby affecting not only the church but indigenous communities and other groups. This forced disentailment of valuable properties did not succeed, as planned, in creating a class of small proprietors; the lands fell instead into the hands of speculators. The December 1856 Ley Lafragua on the freedom of the press, laws on the civil register and cemeteries passed in January 1857, and the Ley Iglesias of the following April on privileges, all provoked a reaction from the clergy and military sectors and gave rise to various revolts.

From February 1856 a new Constitutional Congress convened, ending the next February, in which the radicals won out. The Ley Lerdo and Ley Juárez were ratified under the Constitution of 1857, which also saw to the protection of individual guarantees with the law of *amparo* (legal protection), as well as establishing freedom of education, of work, thought, the press, and the right to hold meetings. The new code, which instituted that the republic should be representative, democratic, and federal, established a new national project that sought a balance between the center and the states. It also confirmed the hegemony of the civil power and abolished the military and ecclesiastical privileges that had unleashed the Revolt of Zacapoaxtla.

The division between Liberals and Conservatives was made very clear from the Constitution of 1857. The Conservatives stood by the church. The uprisings against the Constitution divided the Liberals: the diehards wanted to maintain it while the moderates sought further reforms or ignored it completely. Comonfort was undecided. As constitutional president-elect he took power on December 1, 1857, and had to govern with extraordinary powers while various constitutional articles on guarantees were suspended. The revolt grew and various conspiracies materialized.

On December 17, the Conservatives' Plan of Tacubaya was declared, which refused to recognize the Constitution but respected Comonfort. Various radicals were imprisoned, among them Juárez, president of the Supreme Court. Comonfort kept to the Plan, but in January 1858 Félix Zuloaga launched his coup d'état. The new revolt against Comonfort drove him into the arms of the Liberals, but a little later he handed over power to Juárez, next in line for the presidency under the Constitution of 1857. Juárez went to Guanajuato, setting up a government on January 19. Three days later a council in Mexico City nominated Zuloaga president of the country. The Liberal government counted on the support of 9 states, while 11 backed the Plan of Tacubaya.

Thus began the War of Reform, which would last three years and drive the church to revolt against the constitutional state. The war polarized society and radicalized positions. There were three stages: that of 1858, when the Conservatives had military successes; 1859, when forces were balanced; and 1860, when the Liberals recuperated and won.

Juárez left Guanajuato for Guadalajara, but on the point of being arrested he fled to the Pacific coast and then to Veracruz, where he set up a government. On July 7, 1859, he expedited a manifesto proclaiming the separation of church and state, the suppression of monasteries, the confiscation of church goods, and the abolition of parish rights. All these elements were covered by various laws, jointly known as the Laws of the Reform.

Career soldiers tended to be Conservative, but they had little political capacity and squabbled interminably over the presidency. Their weakness within Mexico led them to seek international alliances. Hence, in the Mon-Almonte Treaty with Spain the Conservative government agreed to pay indemnity

for damages Spain had suffered following Independence. Facing a virtually bankrupt treasury, however, the Liberals also were forced to look abroad for
assistance, signing the McLane-Ocampo Treaty with
the United States on December 14, 1859. Although
the Liberals were unwilling to cede any more territory to the United States, they did agree to grant U.S.
railroads transit rights across the Tehuantepec Isthmus and from the Rio Grande and southern Arizona to the Gulf of California. Other overgenerous
concessions were granted in the McLane-Ocampo
Treaty, but the U.S. Senate rejected the treaty as
insufficient (to the great relief of Juárez, who had
come under criticism when word of the negotiations
leaked to the public). The difficult financial situation
of both sides also forced them to make illegal expropriations and obtain loans at high cost, such as
Miramón's confiscation of money from the British
Legation and the Jecker loan, which was to increase
French demands.

The Conservatives were defeated in Calpulapan
on December 22, 1860. Miramón fled abroad, and
his forces threw themselves into a guerrilla war. Supported by the United States, Juárez sought recognition; he was elected president in June 1861, although
not without a struggle with various eminent Liberals.
His government was faced with serious problems; in
the middle of a conflict with Congress over the desperate financial situation, he decreed the suspension
of public debt.

Britain, Spain, and France decided to intervene
by force of arms to recuperate their investment
and signed an agreement in London in 1861 to that
effect. They thought to combat U.S. influence, but in
fact France had imperial ambitions in America. The
Spanish squadron docked at Veracruz in December,
the other two in January of the following year. The
British and Spanish retreated in February after the
Treaties of Soledad, despite the fact that Mexico
owed them (Britain in particular) more than it owed
France.

Thus began the French Intervention commanded
by Count Lorencez. The Mexican victory at Puebla
on May 5 greatly stimulated the country's patriotism, but despite resistance on the part of the majority of Mexico, the French troops managed to take
control of a substantial part of the country. The
republican government was forced to abandon the
capital for San Luis Potosí, from where it began to
edge further north. Elías Federico Forey entered
Mexico City in June 1863 and organized a provisional governing council that designated a regency to
take charge of the executive and summoned an
assembly of notables.

The French soon manifested liberal tendencies that
terrified both Conservatives and clergy. Aquiles
Bazaine, who had replaced Forey, had a serious clash
with Archbishop Labastida y Dávalos over approval
of the nationalization and sale of church goods. The
French emperor, Napoléon III, had made it clear
there were to be no concessions to the church. He
wanted to consolidate an imperial state to combat
church power and strengthen a Mexican middle class
to support the new government.

The assembly of notables opted for monarchy. The
Conservatives believed that it was the only viable
form of government, and the church was in agreement. The crown would be offered to Maximilian
von Hapsburg or another foreign prince selected
by Napoléon III, and the assembly would abdicate
the principle of sovereignty. In October 1863 the
throne of Mexico was offered to Maximilian and the
Treaties of Miramar were signed.

The imperial government was faced with serious
problems, including a heavy financial burden and the
enmity of the church. Not only had Maximilian not
managed a concordat with Rome, but he also published his own reform laws in December 1864, as
well as other laws that affected the great landholders, such as the right of laborers to leave employment
at will and the Indians' rights to communal lands.
In Maximilian the Conservatives had gained a liberal emperor instead of a Catholic monarch. When
Napoléon withdrew his support, Maximilian tried
to seek that of the Conservatives but was unsuccessful and eventually defeated by the Liberal forces,
who took him prisoner and shot him in Querétaro in
June 1867.

Once the republic was restored the monarchist option disappeared. Liberalism triumphed over
Conservatism, constitutionalism over rebellion, and
national independence over foreign interference,
while the Mexican state consolidated itself against
the church. Hegemony rested in the hands of a
secular and republican state.

Despite the candidature of General Porfirio Díaz,
who had made his mark in the Liberal struggle and
the War of French Intervention, Juárez was reelected
in 1867. He kept himself busy pacifying the country
by means of a policy of conciliation and promotion
of economic development, while also reforming the
educational system. He decided to remain in power,
presenting himself as a candidate in 1871, again with
Díaz as his opponent. When Juárez won, Díaz
revolted against this reelection with the Plan of La
Noria, which was unsuccessful.

Juárez died in July 1871. Sebastián Lerdo de Tejada, formerly president of the Supreme Court and

candidate for the presidential elections in 1871, took over the presidency. His politics were anticlerical and included the Laws of the Reform in the Constitution. Díaz revolted again in January 1876, with his Plan of Tuxtepec. His triumph opened the way initially for his assumption to the presidency and later his conservation of that power in his own hands.

See also Ayutla, Revolution of; French Intervention; Guadalupe Hidalgo, Treaty of; Reform Laws; Texan Secession; U.S.-Mexican War; Wars of Independence; Wars of Reform

Select Bibliography

Rodríguez O., Jaime E., *Down from Colonialism: Mexico's Nineteenth-Century Crisis*. Los Angeles: UCLA Latin American Center, 1983.

_____, editor, *The Evolution of the Mexican Political System*. Wilmington, Delaware: Scholarly Resources, 1993.

_____, editor, *Mexico in the Age of Democratic Revolutions, 1750–1850*. Boulder, Colorado, and London: Westview, 1994.

— VIRGINIA GUEDEA

Politics and Government: 1876–1910

Camarillas (clientelist networks of amity, family, and interest) were the basis of politics and government in Mexico from the ouster of the French-imposed emperor Maximilian in 1867 to the close of Porfirio Díaz's dictatorship in 1911; management of such networks proved the realpolitik of liberal state-building. Camarillas formed around notables able to arbitrate disputes or grant favors using their own resources or their association with more prominent state and national figures. State and national figures of influence were pushed and pulled by conflicting regional and state interests. Followers were not mere pawns but could initiate action.

In this political culture, centralism was merely the rational management of camarillas in response to the centrifugal tendencies of political particularism that left much power in the hands of regional elites. Elections confirmed rather than conferred the right to rule, and the right of revolt was considered legitimate or even sacred. In order to govern at all, Presidents Benito Juárez (1861–72), Sebastián Lerdo de Tejada (1872–76), and Porfirio Díaz (1876–1911) sacrificed the ideals of the Constitution of 1857—independent judiciaries and legislatures, checks and balances, a free press, and fair elections—to centralist necessity.

These centralizing tendencies reached their apogee in the dictatorship of Porfirio Díaz, who—with one brief interruption—ruled Mexico from 1876 to 1911, a period known in Mexico as the Porfiriato.

The Rise of the Porfiriato

Caricatured as Augustus Caeser by the feisty popular journal *El Hijo del Ahuizote,* Porfirio Díaz was a republican monarch, and his regime a synthesis of pragmatic Bourbon methods and Liberal republican ideals. Díaz followed the letter of the Constitution of 1857, amending it as needed in consultation with a national legislature selected to balance camarillas, and at the same time he consolidated the power of the Mexican state, shifting favor from military authorities (caudillos) to civil authorities (caciques) and responsibility for internal security from the army to *rurales* (rural police) and *jefe políticos* (political bosses). Along with increasing numbers of schoolteachers, the *rurales* and *jefe políticos* served to introduce the Porfirian secular culture of nationalism and modernity to the towns and villages and to the masses. Foreign-led economic growth provided the material basis of order, and order (or the appearance thereof) begat more economic growth. Foreign investors, all personally loyal to Díaz, became integral to the structure of Porfirian camarillas, forging cross-cutting economic ties that lessened divisions between "*los* ins *y los* outs" (those camarillas currently in power and those now on the outside). In Díaz's own words, his regime was based on *mucha administracion y poca politica*—"much administration and little politics." The Porfirian intellectual elite accepted Díaz's "social dictatorship" as legitimate insofar as it was a transition to effective constitutional government.

Díaz made himself the keystone of the Mexican state. He made his birthday coincide with the anniversary of Hidalgo's Grito de Dolores, which sparked the War of Independence. Public celebration of Porfirio Díaz's victory over the French at Puebla, Cinco de Mayo, replaced the humiliating memory of the 1848 defeat by the Yankees as the core of a confident new Mexican nationalism. The Chapultepec cadets martyred by U.S. invaders were still remembered but as members of a pantheon of Mexican heroes—Cuauhtemoc, Miguel Hidalgo y Costilla, Morelos, and Benito Juárez—of whom only Díaz still lived. By 1910, most Mexicans could recall no other president. As much by longevity as by design, Díaz came to embody the nation.

In his first term, Díaz had little effective control of "his" Tuxtepecista camarillas who had helped bring him to power in the 1876 Revolution of Tuxtepe that overthrew the presidency of Lerdo de Tejada. Díaz was their tool, not vice versa. Faced with revolts by former supporters disgruntled by a lack of financial and political rewards, he was firm but rarely harsh. He much preferred conciliation but coercion was ever present: "five fingers or five bullets," as he was fond of saying. Díaz's policy of *pan o palo* (bread or stick) was instrumental in securing Washington's diplomatic recognition, which was delayed until April 1878 by insurrections of those still loyal to Lerdo de Tejada, by cross-border banditry, and by Apache attacks. Immediately after recognition, U.S. president Ulysses S. Grant's visit to Mexico gave confidence to American investors.

Díaz's economic policy was formulated by Matías Romero and Manuel Zamacona, who had both been *puro* (radical Liberal) ministers to Washington under Juárez. Their program of defensive modernization was calculated to make the best of Mexico's tenuous geopolitical position (in Díaz's own words, "so close to the United States, so far from God") by encouraging a "peaceful invasion" of U.S. capital. Díaz's *puro* advisers predicted that Mexico would "naturalize" American capital and colonists "as rivers entering the sea" to provide "all possible advantages of annexation without . . . its inconveniences." Issues of trade, technology transfer, investment, and finance dominated U.S.-Mexican relations: Mexico sought national strength through economic development, while Washington sought markets and geopolitical influence. At first skeptical, Díaz was won over to the *puro's* U.S.-oriented development plan by 1879 and came to personify it. Eventually, opposition to Díaz was expressed as opposition to the *puro* formula of capital and colonists. The most consistent opposition voice was *El Tiempo*, the leading conservative journal, which held that "peaceful invasion" by Yankees in whatever form was invasion nonetheless.

The González Interregnum

In 1880 Díaz surrendered his office to Manuel González, staying in government as minister of *fomento* (development) until May 1881 and briefly serving as governor of Oaxaca. González was no Díaz puppet. His interregnum saw a significant rotation of power at state and local levels. He created political space for Lerdo's former followers (Lerdistas), allowing governorships to prominent "outs" such as Evaristo Madero in Coahuila and Luis Terrazas in Chihuaha. González's *rotativismo* (revolving-door management of camarillas) was a catalyst for marriage alliances that stabilized the ruling elites. Díaz's second marriage in 1881 to Carmen Romero Rubio was the best known. Her Lerdista father, Manuel, was the mentor

of a circle of up-and-coming young positivist technocrats later known as the Científicos, and he also was mentor of Bernardo Reyes and Joaquín Baranda, who later emerged as the Científicos' principal opponents. Doña Carmen civilized and refined Díaz as her father's protégés refined the caudillos' regime, and her well-known piety improved his relations with the Catholic Church (Archbishop Pelagio Antonio de Labastida y Dávalos, an unrepentant imperialist, performed the ceremony). A calculated dynastic alliance, it conciliated the Lerdista camarillas, blurring the distinction between "*los* ins *y los* outs" at the national level.

Díaz and doña Carmen took their honeymoon as Mexico's representatives to the New Orleans World Fair, accompanied by Matías Romero, linchpin of American interests in Mexico, and his American-born wife, Lucrecia "Lulu" Allen (six of Díaz's closest associates had American wives). Together they traveled to St. Louis, Washington, D.C., and New York, where Díaz met powerful capitalists and politicians, including Collis P. Huntington, Jay Gould, and former U.S. president Grant—all Romero's personal friends. The selling of Díaz by Romero's sophisticated press machine persuaded thousands of American capitalists of the safety of Mexican investments.

Meanwhile, President González paved the way for large-scale U.S. investment, granting railway concessions and passing the land law of 1883 to encourage colonization and the mining law of 1884 to guarantee miners' subsoil rights. But González's lax administration of these ambitious programs brought his government to bankruptcy. Riots attended his attempt to introduce a nickel coin, and his recognition of Mexico's debt to the English government and banking interests was equally unpopular. Relentless attacks by the ambitious Manuel Romero Rubio linked these failings to charges of personal corruption, preparing the way for Díaz's second election in 1884.

The Porfiriato at High Tide

Once reelected, Díaz practiced *rotativismo*, ignoring his old followers and selecting instead as his ministers former Juaristas (Matías Romero became minister to Washington), Lerdistas (Manuel Romero Rubio headed gobernacion, and his protégé Joaquín Baranda headed justice), and even imperialists (Manuel Dublán at hacienda). Carlos Pacheco, González's minister of *fomento,* the only Tuxtepecista in Díaz's new cabinet, was soon replaced. American-generated economic growth allowed Díaz to buy off the old Tuxtepecistas and consolidate his rule. Railroads provided cheap fares for tourists and investors, who were herded through Chapultepec palace by American diplomats and greeted by Díaz himself, binding American investors to him as personal patron and protector. Utterly loyal, these outsiders were integral to the Porfirian mode of tributary capitalism that formed in the absence of impersonal, impartial institutions. Ruling elites were approached through personal relations and nepotism, and local or regional caciques treated foreign entrepreneurs as tributaries brokering their political influence for economic favors. For example, a cacique might obtain a railroad or mining concession for American companies in exchange for cash, stock, and a seat on a company's board of directors.

Elites thus acquired vested, economically rational interests in political stability, but force of arms never ceased to be an option in camarilla politics. When breakdowns in public order did occur, Díaz was able to use conflict between powerful caciques to impose outsiders as dependent governors. In late 1884, he arbitrated an end to a virtual civil war in Coahuila and arranged the election of María Garza Galán, undercutting former governor and Lerdista Evaristo Madero. Disorder in the state Nuevo León enabled Díaz to insert General Bernardo Reyes (commander of the critical Third Military Zone) as governor. The displaced caudillos had to content themselves with Porfirian-derived economic prosperity.

Manuel Romero Rubio and his followers were the major beneficiaries of Porfirian conciliation. Rivals Garza Galán and Reyes were both protégés of Romero Rubio. They raised no objection to amending the Constitution in 1888 to allow Díaz's reelection, and Tuxtepecistas had no one but Díaz. Another amendment two years later allowed indefinite reelection, provoking the anti-reelectionist revolt of 1891 to 1893, which briefly enjoyed some sympathy from those now on the "outs."

If financial crisis had returned Díaz to power, the persistence of national bankruptcy threatened his reelection. Sadly lacking financial talent, the Díaz administration turned to Romero Rubio's young positivists protégés (most notably José Yves Limantour). First employed to investigate monetary questions associated with declining silver prices (1884–89) and recommend policy options, they assisted in the work of the 1888 convention to refinance Mexico's debt. In 1892, the technocrats held a convention as the Liberal Union, articulating a philosophy of "scientific" government and linking their endorsement of Díaz's reelection to Liberal reform—the immovability of judges, continued military reductions, freedom of the press, abolition of *alcabalas* (internal tariffs), and establishment of a vice presidency.

After Díaz's reelection, Matías Romero came to the Ministry of Hacienda, bringing Limantour as subsecretary. In 1893 Romero returned to Washington as minister and Limantour put the nation's public finances in good order, becoming Díaz's indispensable finance wizard. The Científicos (taken here to mean Limantour's camarilla, not the entire Liberal Union) had arrived, but as an in-house opposition; Díaz did not share their reformist enthusiasm. He allowed reform only of the bureaucracy, where Limantour met with mixed success in his efforts to eliminate corruption and ensure uniform, impartial application of regulations. Díaz kept firm control of the *rurales* and the judiciary and continued to appoint governors, national legislators, and *jefe políticos*. Some Científicos entered the national legislature (Díaz's herd of tame horses), but only Limantour had real power.

In the north, Bernardo Reyes's Union and Progress Club, excluded from the Liberal Union convention, met on its own to support Díaz's third term. To consolidate his position against his rival, María Garza Galán, Reyes tacitly supported an anti-reelection revolt in Coahuila covertly funded by Evaristo Madero. Reyes maneuvered Díaz into replacing Garza Galán with a Reyista. After quelling another anti-reelection revolt in Guerrero, Díaz implicitly affirmed the political legitimacy of revolt by issuing a general amnesty. Most *revoltosos* disputed Porfirian political hegemony but embraced order and progress. A few rejected entirely Porfirian notions of progress and refused amnesty for their rebellion, choosing annihilation over modernization.

During the 1896 reelection, the Liberal Union was inert. Díaz had blocked all Científico reforms, conceding only a constitutional amendment to designate a successor from his cabinet without creating a vice presidency. To manage his reelection Díaz turned to the Círculo Nacional Porfirista, an umbrella organization for camarillas including those of the foreign colonies for whom Díaz was synonymous with progress and the protection of capital. Díaz also won over Catholic Conservatives by concluding a treaty with the Vatican, ending a 70-year break in relations, but this came at a cost. Relaxation of the anticlerical Reform Laws prompted a wealthy miner, Camilo Arriaga, to found the anticlerical Club Liberal Ponciano Arriaga (named in honor of his impeccably liberal grandfather). The movement spread quickly to 13 states, opening political space for the post-Tuxtepec generation.

The most vocal opposition of 1896 came from students and young professionals born during the Porfiriato who half-seriously supported the candidacy of eccentric lawyer-journalist Nicolas Zuñiga y Miranda. Their discontent troubled the regime, which deemed the emerging middle class indispensable to formation of the state. In 1900 student leader Jesús Flores Magón entered the Porfirian establishment as legal counsel for the Building and Loan Company of Mexico, but he continued to take on causes such as Emiliano Zapata's lawsuit to recover Villa Ayala lands. His more radical brother, Ricardo, split the delegates to Arriaga's First Liberal Congress in San Luis Potosí by proposing a militant stance toward the Díaz regime many found unacceptable. In 1902 Bernardo Reyes's press manager staged a police riot, broke up Arriaga's Second Liberal Congress, and imprisoned him. Reyes himself jailed Ricardo Flores Magón and his younger brother Ernesto for criticizing the army. This heavy-handed repression radicalized the three brothers. In 1903 they founded the Partido Liberal Mexicano (PLM or, Mexican Liberal Party). In 1905 they began publishing the opposition newspaper *Regeneración* in St. Louis, attacking the regime from exile and exposing a sordid reality of peonage, slavery, and state terror beneath the image of a modern Mexico so effectively promoted in the United States by the Porfirian press machine.

The Realignments of 1898

The year 1898 was a domestic and geopolitical watershed for the regime. Matías Romero's death and the threat of American expansionism following the Spanish-American War decisively shifted the balance of power among the regime's three national camarillas: Matías Romero's *puros*, José Yves Limantour's Científicos, and Bernardo Reyes's Reyistas. After Romero's death, the *puros'* decline altered the pro-U.S. orientation of the regime's program of defensive modernization but did not stem the rate of American investment, which increased from some 250 million dollars that year to one billion by 1910. A national *puro* camarilla still existed, headed by such men as Minister of Justice and Education Joaquín Baranda, but it was difficult for Díaz to play his three-sided political game because the *puros'* relative weakness necessitated alliances with the Reyistas to oppose the Científicos. But the *puros* did retain de facto control of Romero's Porfirian press operation. By 1900 much of that operation involved the *Mexican Herald,* a semiofficial, subsidized publication of the Díaz regime, representing the American business establishment (Díaz's camarilla of integral outsiders). American ambassadors routinely forwarded the *Herald's* opinions to the U.S. State Department as their own, making the newspaper a vital back channel to Washington as the Díaz regime

attempted to moderate growing Yankee imperialism as well as promote continued investment.

Nevertheless, Romero's death in 1898, along with the threat posed by the U.S. occupation of Cuba and Puerto Rico, marked the decline of U.S. influence within the regime. As Díaz's new first adviser, Limantour systematically offset U.S. with European direct investment (harking back to earlier conservative desires to challenge the "peaceful invasion" by the Yankees). He established links to European banking houses and required state governments to stop floating bond issues through U.S. banks. He convinced Díaz to pick the British Sir Weetman Pearson over the American Collis P. Huntington to complete the strategic transisthmian Tehuantepec Railway and build its terminal ports—real competition for the United States's proposed Panama canal. In 1906 he awarded to Pearson petroleum concessions designed to turn Mexico into an oil exporter, ending Standard Oil's monopoly and beginning a cutthroat "oil war" in Mexico. In 1909 the Científico minister of *fomento* advanced an amendment to the mining code that again would have vested subsurface mineral rights in the state. All of these moves had the effect of reducing support for the regime within the U.S. business community.

Domestic factors persuaded Díaz to make Bernardo Reyes minister of war. The army, which earlier had proved inept in squelching revolts, now fought simultaneous wars against the Yaqui and the Maya. For some time Díaz had been trying to reconcile Limantour and Reyes. Limantour's Científicos, a bureaucratic banking camarilla linked to European financiers and with little or no popular base, were no threat to Díaz. Reyes's camarilla, on the other hand, potentially were; they commanded popular support in Masonic Lodges, workingmen's mutual societies, and the military. Once Reyes became minister, there was an initial period of goodwill with Limantour, who made sufficient funds available to reform and reequip the army along Prussian lines. But the good feelings evaporated when, over Limantour's objections, Reyes proposed to more than double the army's size to 76,000 men. As the 1900 presidential election approached, Reyes's cabinet ally, fellow Romero Rubio protégé Joaquín Baranda, published attacks on Limantour, declaring him to be the son of a Frenchman, thus ineligible for office. Eventually, Limantour forced Baranda out of the cabinet but, significantly, Díaz supported Reyes's proposal to expand the military, creating the Second Reserve of the Army in October 1900. Patriots such as Francisco I. Madero and Jesús Flores Magón swelled its ranks.

The creation of the Second Reserve was driven by geopolitical considerations: the U.S. intervention in Cuba and its emergence as an imperial power, which upset the internal Porfirian balance of power. Previously, *puro* leader Matías Romero had helped draft the Díaz Doctrine, which proposed that hemispheric security be made the collective responsibility of all American nations, in response to Washington's declaration of a hemispheric U.S. "protectorate." After U.S. president William McKinley's assassination, Rough Rider Teddy, viewed by all in Mexico as an unscrupulous imperialist, became U.S. president Theodore Roosevelt. A cartoon in *El Hijo del Ahuizote* depicted Uncle Sam annexing all of northern Mexico as Díaz vainly cited his regime's accomplishments and compliance "over the matter of Cuba." At the 1901–02 Pan-American Conference in Mexico City, however, Washington seemed to accept the principle of hemispheric arbitration. Temporary anxiety over Roosevelt diminished and criticism of Reyes's military buildup grew. *Regeneración* editors Ricardo and Enrique Flores Magón characterized the Second Reserve as patronage for Reyista political clubs; the two editors were jailed. But Científico Rosendo Pineda, Díaz's private secretary, attacked Reyes in the press with impunity while Limantour questioned Reyes's loyalty, demanding that Díaz choose between them. Reyes's son responded with anonymous attacks on Limantour. After this was revealed, Díaz removed Reyes as minister of war in December 1902 and returned him to Nuevo León as governor and Third Military Zone commander. Díaz expressed full confidence in Reyes but took the precaution of removing from office his de facto ally, the governor of neighboring Chihuahua. The Second Reserve was disbanded. When Díaz next had need of the army in 1910, it was not ready.

In 1903 Reyes linked his Nuevo León reelection campaign to that of Díaz, permitting his opposition, the Gran Convención, to operate openly, anticipating Díaz's democratic initiative by five years. But, unused to political activism and alarmed by a large rally, Monterrey's police fired into the crowd, killing many. Reyes responded not by disciplining his police, but by arresting opposition leaders as provocateurs. Future rebel Francisco I. Madero later marked this as his political awakening. Reyes went to trial, as much for mismanagement as excessive use of force. Díaz then had the Científico-dominated Mexican Congress acquit him, humiliating them and reducing Reyes to dependency.

The Científicos Liberal Union Convention mobilized for Díaz's reelection and was attended by northern caudillos opposed to Reyes, putting the Científicos in the best position in a decade to move Díaz on the issue of succession. The keynote address pulled no punches: "Nothing could be more lugubrious than the proposed reelection of Díaz, unless THE LAW were his successor." Díaz permitted the creation of the vice presidency and, quid pro quo, received a six-year presidential term. Then he imposed the Científico sympathizer Ramón Corral as vice president over the objection of the Reyistas and other "out" factions. *Rotativismo* was no longer possible.

The Close of the Porfiriato

From 1904 to 1909, Limantour worked for key economic and administrative reforms before the aging Díaz's increasingly likely death could test the "organic peace" touted by Mexico's subsidized press. Limantour undertook the nationalization of the railroads and completed Mexico's conversion to the gold standard by 1905, thereby expediting increasingly better terms on the growing national debt. As 85 percent of Mexican silver mines were foreign owned, ending free coinage of silver was a matter of less political consequence than it might otherwise have been. Foreign investors lacked the option of rebellion. But here, the interests of the foreign miners and the masses converged—silver was popular coin, traditional coin. Ultimately, Limantour's elimination of silver coin brought ill effects on silver miners and on business generally. The most severe effects of Limantour's reform were felt by the humble classes—artisans, shopkeepers, factory workers, and miners.

Other events added fuel to the fire of popular discontent. The organizing junta of the PLM in St. Louis published a manifesto in *Regeneración* demanding improved working conditions, an eight-hour day, education, land reform, the abolition of company stores, of payment in scrip, of child labor, and of the death penalty, and the overthrow of the Díaz regime. *Regeneración* was smuggled to workers at the Cananea copper mines in Sonora, who struck the U.S.-owned operation on June 1. On his own authority, Governor Rafael Izabal, a member of vice president Corral's Sonoran triumvirate, allowed a force of Arizona Rangers to cross the border and order was restored. "Treason!" proclaimed *Regeneración*. "Foreign legions trample our soil and crush our brethren." Twelve hours later *rurales* arrived. Shooting then began and continued sporadically for several days. Cananea did the regime considerable damage domestically and internationally. PLM press rumors aimed at fomenting an uprising in September kept the foreign business community on edge and the Porfirian press machine working overtime reminding the world of Mexico's "organic peace" to keep foreign investment flowing.

The wave of labor unrest following Cananea was owing as much to local conditions as to the activities of the PLM. Workers in the modern sectors of the economy wanted the same wage as foreigners, and worsening economic conditions after 1905 dashed rising expectations. The PLM made it harder for established *ligas* (unions) to maintain their hard-won legitimacy, but it also got the regime's attention. An official report to Díaz on labor relations recommended humane reforms to mitigate the worst abuses of the industrial capitalism to prevent revolution. After Cananea there was a noticeable swell of well-publicized acts of private charity by government officials, and following bad harvests after 1907, the regime supplied subsidized imported corn to keep prices down. Díaz reached out to labor organizations, arbitrated labor disputes, and sponsored workers' mutual associations, thus creating working-class camarillas.

After Cananea, the Científicos smeared Reyes in the United States and Mexico, suggesting he was behind the strikes, but Díaz was convinced that the Magonistas were at the root of it all. Díaz set three priorities in U.S.-Mexican relations: the suppression of the St. Louis junta, the extradition of Ricardo Flores Magón, and increased policing of the border by U.S. authorities to deny asylum to PLM revolutionaries. In exchange, Washington wanted a "Greater Mexico" to extend the Pax Porfiriana over Central America as an alternative to direct U.S. intervention. Díaz initially resisted, but after Cananea a new understanding was reached. Roosevelt increased U.S. forces on the border to check the movement of anti-Díaz elements; in return, Roosevelt obtained Díaz's reluctant cooperation in mediating the war between Guatemala, Honduras, and El Salvador. Internationally, the Marblehead Treaty of 1906 was seen as Mexico's entry onto the world stage, but domestically it added to Díaz's problems by giving weight to PLM charges that he was an adjunct of Roosevelt's "big stick."

Díaz also sought a broad interpretation of Neutrality Acts to use against his political enemies in the United States. But efforts to have the Magonistas extradited were stymied by U.S. court rulings that the charges against the PLM were political, not criminal. To break the impasse, Díaz appointed a new ambassador to the United States: Enrique Creel (then governor of Chihuahua), who had directed covert operations against Magonistas in the United States using the Furlong Detective Agency. Creel convinced Washington to agree to a broad interpretation of the Neutrality Acts to combat the anti-Díaz movement in the United States. In exchange, Mexico agreed to dispatch two gunboats to Honduran waters as "moral force" in support of peace. Within weeks of reaching this understanding, Ricardo Flores Magón was on his way to jail, and Mexican cooperation in Central America ended. Díaz recalled Creel, explaining that his duties as governor barred him from serving as ambassador. But there was more to it.

In October 1907, U.S. secretary of state Eliha Root had visited Mexico for a 10-day tour. Many believed the visit was to settle differences over Central America. Although Washington and the Díaz regime billed it as a goodwill tour, Root's mission was to coax Díaz into retirement so that he might preside over the 1910 elections as Mexico's grand elder statesman. In conjunction with Root's visit, Díaz was convinced by Creel, Thompson, and Roosevelt to give an interview to James Creelman of *Peason's Magazine*. In the interview published in March 1908, Díaz reported to Creelman that he would not seek reelection and would welcome the formation of an opposition party. Rumors circulated that Roosevelt wanted Creel to replace Díaz. Officially, Porfirian authorities gave the report no credence, but Creel was recalled nonetheless.

The Creelman interview revived independent political discourse in Mexico. Andrés Molina Enríquez published *Los grandes problemas nacionales*, a devastating analysis of the regime's social and agrarian failings. Francisco I. Madero launched his national anti-reelectionist movement with the publication of *La sucesión presidencial en 1910*, a relatively mild political critique compared to the no-holds-barred attack loosed on the Díaz system by PLM ally, John K. Turner, in his "Barbarous Mexico" series, which appeared in *American Magazine* throughout 1909. Turner actually helped the regime close ranks; Científicos and Reyistas refuted his charges to maintain the security of Mexican investments, and Conservatives considered Turner's book to be an attack on Mexico's national honor.

So effective was the Porfirian countereffort that by the celebration of Mexico's centennial "Barbarous Mexico" was largely discredited abroad, buried under an avalanche of progovernment press reports.

When Díaz told Creelman that he would not run for reelection, the Mexican economy was still healthy, but by the time the interview appeared in early 1908, the global recession had hit Mexico. Díaz's commitment to retirement, never strong, faltered. Despite what was by this time an almost pathological fear of Reyes, Díaz dispatched Reyes to explain away his unfortunate remarks. In an interview published in Heriberto Barron's *La República,* Reyes cast doubt on the Creelman text, indicating that Díaz, under pressure from Washington to retire, had demonstrated his democratic intentions while preserving the option of retaining the presidency, which Reyes urged Díaz to do. Meanwhile, Reyes's supporters created the Centro Organizador del Partido Democrático (COPD), which quickly became a de facto Reyista front.

Faced with a disorderly democracy in which he had little faith, Díaz began to organize his reelection. In June, Madero declared his candidacy. Reyes refused to cross Díaz by openly seeking the vice presidency, repeatedly endorsing Corral to maintain the position. Nonetheless, Reyistas launched press attacks on Limantour and the Científicos and disrupted Corralista rallies. Díaz responded by removing Reyes from his post as Third Military Zone commander. Reyes, withdrawing to his hacienda, was refused an interview by Díaz. Finished, Reyes meekly accepted a mission to Europe, shortly followed by Limantour, who refinanced Mexico's debt at 4 percent, unsecured, even as fighting broke out.

As Madero's anti-reelection campaign picked up steam and won the support of ex-Reyistas, Díaz traveled north to the border in October to meet U.S. president Howard Taft. All seemed friendly but, in fact, relations were strained by Díaz's disapproval of Washington's efforts to oust the president of Nicaragua. Weeks later, openly at cross-purposes with the United States, Mexico landed a gunboat and spirited the Nicaraguan president to safety. U.S.-Mexican relations sank to their lowest point since Díaz had taken office. Indeed, members of the U.S. State Department speculated whether the landing of U.S. Marines in Nicaragua might have a "moral effect" on Mexico.

As the 1910 election approached, Madero's rhetoric grew bolder. Keeping Corral as vice president would mean revolution; "Barbarous Mexico" was mostly true: Díaz was a despot. Madero's followers, emboldened, demonstrated at Díaz-Corral rallies. Díaz resorted to tried-and-true *pan o palo.* On the one hand, in April, Madero and brother Gustavo received a railroad concession; on the other, in June, Madero was arrested for slandering Díaz. In yet another reversal, the Círculo Nacional Porfirista, a key group of Díaz backers, abandoned Corral and drafted puro Teodoro Dehesa for vice president, although Díaz himself stood firm behind Corral (at least outwardly). Madero was released from prison, and his running mate, Francisco Vázquez Gómez, urged him to back Dehesa. Madero refused.

As Mexico prepared for its glittering centennial, Madero sold his rubber plantation lands to U.S. interests associated with Standard Oil, while his brother Gustavo floated a 27 million peso–railroad bond issue in Paris, providing liquidity to finance a revolution. In October, Francisco I. Madero slipped across the border and issued his Plan de San Luis Potosí, a classic example of the traditional rhetoric of legitimate revolt, not unlike Díaz's Plan de Tuxtepec.

It seemed Díaz faced just another rebellion like countless others. This time, however, his intrigues and those of others had destabilized the internal balance of power, and he could not respond effectively—he had no Reyes, no Limantour, no positive commitment from Washington. Geopolitical circumstances had changed. In addition to foreign policy disagreements concerning Nicaragua, personal and financial alliances also led to the evaporation of U.S. support. Two members of U.S. president Taft's inner circle who supported U.S. aid to suppress Madero—the president's brother and the attorney general—were both silent partners in the Díaz-backed oil company of Lord Cowdray. Their influence on U.S. policy was blocked, however, by advocates of Cowdray's rival in Mexican petroleum: Standard Oil. It seems that the U.S. secretary of state was swayed by his longtime associate Sherburne Hopkins, Madero's Washington representative and attorney for the Standard Oil subsidiary in Mexico. Thus, when Díaz requested vigorous U.S. efforts to halt the cross-border arms traffic, the secretary of state's reply so narrowly defined the Neutrality Acts that Madero literally would have had to arm a warship in U.S. waters to trigger their enforcement. Those conducting Revolution in Madero's name did so from the United States with virtual impunity, Taft's mobilization of 20,000 U.S. troops at the border notwithstanding.

After the fall of Ciudad Juárez and Torreón, Díaz authorized Limantour, just returned from Paris, to negotiate with representatives of the Revolution. Neither he nor Madero wished to destroy the Porfirian state. But Díaz knew what appeared to be solid state structures rested, like the grand public buildings in the capital, on soft ground, on arrangements of camarillas now in rapid transition in the chaos of rebellion. Rational camarilla management would have to begin anew. On May 25, 1911, Díaz resigned and departed for exile in Paris. "Madero has loosed the tiger," he said. "Now we'll see if he can ride it."

See also Caste War of Yucatán; Mexican Revolution: Causes

Select Bibliography

Bazant, Jan, *A Concise History of Mexico from Hidalgo to Cárdenas, 1805–1940*. New York: Cambridge University Press, 1978.

Beals, Carleton, *Porfirio Díaz: Dictator of Mexico*. Philadelphia: Lippincott, 1932.

Beezley, William H., *Judas at the Jockey Club and Other Episodes of Porfirian Mexico*. Lincoln: University of Nebraska Press, 1987.

Coatsworth, John, *Growth against Development: The Economic Impact of Railroads in Porfirian Mexico*. DeKalb: Northern Illinois University Press, 1981.

Cockcroft, James D., *Intellectual Precursors of the Mexican Revolution, 1900–1913*. Austin: University of Texas Press, 1976.

Hale, Charles, *The Transformation of Liberalism in Late-Nineteenth-Century Mexico*. Princeton, New Jersey: Princeton University Press, 1989.

Hart, John Mason, *Revolutionary Mexico: The Coming and Process of the Mexican Revolution*. Berkeley and London: University of California Press, 1989.

Knight, Alan, *The Mexican Revolution*, 2 vols., Lincoln: University of Nebraska Press, 1986.

Perry, Laurens B., *Juárez and Díaz: Machine Politics in Mexico*. DeKalb: Northern Illinois University Press, 1978.

Potash, Robert A., *Mexican Government and Industrial Development: The Banco de Avío*. Amherst: University of Massachusetts Press, 1983.

Raat, W. Dirk, and William H. Beezley, editors, *Twentieth-Century Mexico*. Lincoln and London: University of Nebraska Press, 1986.

Rodríguez O., Jaime E., editor, *The Revolutionary Process in Mexico: Essays on Political and Social Change, 1880–1940*. Los Angeles: UCLA Latin American Center, 1990.

Ross, Stanley R., *Francisco I. Madero: Apostle of Mexican Democracy*. New York: Columbia University Press, 1955.

Vanderwood, Paul J., *Disorder and Progress: Bandits, Police, and Mexican Development*. Revised and enlarged edition, Wilmington, Delaware: Scholarly Resources, 1992.

Vernon, Raymond, *The Dilemma of Mexico's Development: The Role of Private and Public Sectors*. Cambridge, Massachusetts: Harvard University Press, 1982.

—WILLIAM SCHELL JR.

Politics and Government: 1910–46

From the beginnings of the Mexican Revolution in 1910, the capacity of state and key social actors to forge and maintain a system of government based on a broad alliance between heterogeneous groups was repeatedly put to a hard test. Consequently, Mexican political stability followed a difficult course fraught with unanticipated crises and problematic recoveries.

During the decade that followed the Mexican Revolution, the most immediate problem was the consolidation of the Revolutionary coalition. A related and equally crucial necessity was to protect the new regime against foreign intervention. Out of the hegemonic struggles, crises, and recoveries that Mexico underwent between 1910 and 1946 emerged a stable one-party regime based on a broadly cast and highly disciplined popular alliance structured by the principle of state corporatism.

The group that brought Francisco I. Madero to his swift military victory over Porfirio Díaz was highly heterogeneous, with little possibility of reconciling its internal differences. In 1910, Mexico was a nation of some 11 million peasants out of 15 million inhabitants. This rural mass was divided regionally between the north—where peasants attached to large haciendas and cattle ranchers dominated—and the center and south—where villagers had been engaged in decades of struggles to retain their small plots of land, which gradually had been absorbed through fraud and force by local sugar plantation owners. While the mass of the rural population remained for the most part immobilized, small ranchers joined Francisco "Pancho" Villa in the north, while the villagers of Morelos followed Emiliano Zapata. Workers, representing a mere 195,000 souls in 1910, were divided between the anticlerical anarchist-syndicalist tradition and the Catholic tradition of cooperativism and mutual aid societies. (Copied from the European model, these mutual aid societies pooled limited funds for sick and disabled workers, and for widows and orphans. They were politically uninvolved, although many of them adhered to a doctrine of gradual revolution achieved through the restructuring of society by these societies.) The cultural and experiential gap between workers and peasants resulted in totally different expressions of political dissent: the peasants who rallied around Zapata and Villa embodied the moral outrage and fervent aspirations for justice of the rural masses, while workers, literate and secularized, wanted the return of the Liberal Constitution of 1857, under which they could organize and bargain.

The dominant classes also were divided between one faction closely associated with the Porfirian state (including most hacienda owners, foreign investors, and the Catholic Church) and another faction opposed to the Díaz regime, including Mexican owners of small industries (alienated by the policies favoring foreign investors), politicians who had fallen from favor, professionals, intellectuals, and liberals who came from different walks of life, including landowners themselves, as in the case of Madero and Venustiano Carranza. Given such divisions, no single group could entirely dominate the insurrectionary movement. Madero's appeal was strongest among disaffected members of the Porfirian upper bourgeoisie and the liberal urban middle sectors. Zapata's Plan de Ayala, which called for wholesale agrarian redistribution, was abhorrent to most liberals, who could not tolerate a total suppression of their acquired rights and privileges of land and wealth. Yet, Zapata's expropriation of the holdings of individual landowners as punishment for their defense of the Díaz regime generally was found acceptable.

The direction of the Revolution was bound constantly to be weakened by such profound internal differences, oscillating among the interests of its various supporters. In particular, the feasibility of the social reforms proposed by Zapatistas, Villistas, and the left-most wing of the Constitutionalist camp (this term referring to the Constitution of 1857, whose reinstitution Madero and his supporters sought) were contingent upon Madero's capacity to make these reforms acceptable to at least a substantial coalition of interests, while successfully resisting the armed rebellions of those opposed.

Unable to retain Zapata's support while responding to neo-Porfirian pressures to deny agrarian reforms, Madero's administration (1911–13) had to contend with three armed rebellions before the victory of the fourth brought it to a quick and violent end barely 15 months after his ascent to power; Madero himself was assassinated following this coup, orchestrated by Victoriano Huerta. The coup opened a period of armed struggles that would last until 1917, during which the country was divided between Constitutionalists and neo-Porfirians, the latter supporting Huerta. The first, made up of dissenting hacienda owners, Zapatistas, Villistas, and anarchist workers, regrouped under the leadership of Venustiano Carranza, the governor of Coahuila. Zapata's southern army and Villa's famous División del Norte advanced on Mexico City and briefly occupied the National Palace, while Álvaro Obregón, Carranza's right-hand man and a popular agrarian figure, reconquered territory from the east, leaving behind his victorious army a trail of social reforms and land confiscations. By 1916, the Constitutionalist camp emerged a clear victor. Despite this fact, however, it remained deeply divided.

Although anti-Porfirian, Carranza was a relatively conservative hacienda owner who had little interest in carrying out a profound land reform, although he was willing to reward the groups that had supported him in the fight against Huerta. In states headed by progressive governors, a limited amount of this redistribution went to peasants. In others, lawful titles were issued in the names of the governors, giving birth to a new class, known as the "revolutionary millionaires." Following the failure of the Aguascalientes Convention of 1914 to reconcile the rift between moderate and radical Constitutionalists, he waged an undeclared war against Zapata, using the famous anarchist workers' Red Battalions against his former ally, and finally ordering his assassination. Nevertheless, he issued a new Law of Agrarian Reform calling for the restitution of all property confiscated in violation of the Law of 1856, and he resolved the conflict over wages with workers, respecting the latter's constitutional right to organize (while simultaneously keeping in jail their most radical leaders).

Arguments for the reformist conviction of the Constitutionalist camp usually center on the text of the Constitution of 1917, especially its Article 123, which set forth a vast program of social and labor reform. Such arguments usually omit the struggles that took place between the victors when the text was drafted. Merely intending to amend the Liberal Constitution of 1857, Carranza presented a text to the Constitutional assembly convened in Querétaro in 1917 that ignored agrarian and worker issues. This draft met with the overwhelming opposition of the General Assembly, allowing the committee in charge of revising the draft (headed by Obregón, a steadfast reformist) to make proposals more in keeping with the new cast of actors.

It is widely recognized that the Constitution of 1917 laid the foundation for a strong central state whose prerogatives eventually would restrict the capacity of peasants and workers to advance beyond the limited terms obtained in 1917. Yet this distant future was far from predictable in Carranza's time. The weakness of the state instituted by Carranza and the importance of the social base of popular support created by the Revolution to consolidate the regime became evident in 1919, when Carranza stepped down in accordance with the Revolutionary rule of no reelection yet prevented the immensely popular Obregón from becoming a candidate to succeed him in power. As a result, Carranza's presidency ended in increased labor insurgency in favor of Obregón and general political chaos. Obregón swiftly assured himself of labor and peasant support before taking power by force in April 1920 and conducting elections after his military victory was assured.

The ascent to power of the so-called Sonoran dynasty—Obregón (1920–24), Plutarco Elías Calles (1924–28), Emilio Portes Gil (1928–30), Pascual

Ortiz Rubio (1930–32), and Abelardo Rodríguez (1932–34)—bore witness to several important trends: the continuation of the political exclusion of large landowners and the Catholic Church, the gradual loss of power of the military, the slow marginalization of peasants, and the increasing importance of the new revolutionary bourgeoisie. Simultaneously, the state was to become both stronger and more centralized as a result of systematic policies of demilitarization, the control of elections, and the creation of central instruments of economic and monetary policy.

Despite such changes, the state was to remain weak in relation to foreign investors as long as it failed to renegotiate the generous terms the latter had obtained from Díaz. Relations with the United States remained tense until Obregón capitulated in the conflict over property of the subsoil. The Bucarelli Agreement, signed in 1924, declared nonretroactive Article 27 of the 1917 Constitution, which established the sovereignty of the state over the subsoil. This concession ensured U.S. collaboration and thereafter strengthened the government's capacity to repel armed rebellions, particularly the attempt in 1924 by Adolfo de la Huerta to use the support of radical labor to succeed Obregón in power in the same way that Obregón had succeeded Carranza. This redirected the regime toward a more conservative course of limited reforms, controlled labor unions, yet continued anticlericalism.

When Plutarco Elías Calles succeeded Obregón in 1924, through the electoral process rather than a military operation, the regime seemed to have reached a point of relative stability. Calles was not personally pro-peasant, but contributed more to the land reform than his predecessors, although he eventually tried to put an end to land distribution in the hope of creating a nation of small farmers. He also successfully reined in the labor movement by incorporating into the government the leadership of the most accommodating union—the Confederación Regional Obrera Mexicana (CROM, or Regional Confederation of Mexican Workers)—giving it a virtual monopoly of representation over the labor movement. During his presidency, Mexico industrialized, reorganized its finances, built its infrastructure, and attracted foreign investors.

Despite these signs of institutionalization, however, the regime was again shaken by a deep political and economic crisis that struck in the summer of 1926; almost simultaneously, Obregón announced his intention of returning to the presidency (thereby violating the Constitutional rule of no reelection), the price of silver (upon whose export Mexican public finances heavily depended) plummeted, and the government faced an uprising by the Yaqui Indians in Sonora and another by religious peasants—the so-called *cristeros*—in the central western states. Obregón was duly elected, but he was assassinated shortly thereafter under mysterious circumstances. The Cristeros Rebellion, although triggered by a religious conflict between church and state, also had strong agrarian overtones and was massive enough to stalemate the government's efforts to put it down until 1929, when church leaders negotiated the end of the conflict.

It is in these traumatic circumstances that the Partido Nacional Revolucionario (PNR, or National Revolutionary Party) was created, more as a last-minute inspiration to solve the political crisis than a calculated strategy to strengthen the regime, as often pictured in retrospect. Rather than a party representing diverse interests in the country, this body was conceived as a machinery to ensure the peaceful transmission of power from one administration to the next, a function it fulfilled until 1934 by making the selection of presidential candidates an unquestioned prerogative of Calles, nicknamed the *máximo jefe* (hence the term Maximato to refer to this period). Inside the party, consensus was fashioned via the systematic expulsion of all those who expressed any doubt regarding the wisdom of Calles's decisions. Agrarian and working-class interests were absent from the PNR. The National Peasant League and the National Agrarist Party expected so little from it that they had initially abstained from joining (although they later were forced to do so).

Although the PNR temporarily was able to control interelite conflict, it had little power over the popular masses excluded from membership. In the early 1930s, as the effects of the Great Depression were added to those of the crisis of 1926 to 1929, Calles steadily lost his capacity to control open demonstrations of opposition to the government or the strengthening of interests potentially dangerous to the group in power. The clearest evidence was the mass desertion by workers from the CROM and the concomitant rebirth of militant labor under the leadership of Vicente Lombardo Toledano, a disaffected member of the CROM.

After 1930, the balance of power within the official party also was changing. Calles's failure to enact the political and social reforms favored by many of those who initially had supported him was thinning the ranks of his supporters. Despite the virtual police methods employed to maintain internal cohesion, a left wing within the party—the Reds—slowly had asserted itself over the Whites (the right wing). Soon the latter rallied behind Lázaro Cárdenas, an avowed proponent of land reform and labor legislation.

In 1933, under pressure from radical agrarian organizations and supporters of Cárdenas, Calles persuaded President Rodríguez to resign and the party to nominate Cárdenas as the party presidential candidate. The latter had the support of the worker and peasant masses, who saw in him a new opportunity for social and economic reforms; the military, who had been marginalized under Calles; and Callistas themselves, who mistakenly thought that he would remain responsive to the *máximo jefe's* directives.

As soon as he was in power, Cárdenas carried out his plan (previously foiled by Calles) to democratize the official party. Rather than let Lombardo Toledano strengthen his position as an independent leader of the industrial and agricultural workforce, he persuaded him to join a reshaped official party—now called the Partido de la Revolución Mexicana (PRM, or Party of the Mexican Revolution)—in which workers and the military would occupy a prominent place. The support of these groups, rather than interpersonal coalitions among leaders of the Revolution, became the basis of presidential power; peasants were incorporated into the Confederación Nacional Campesina (CNC, or National Peasant Confederation), while workers entered the Confederación de Trabajadores de México (CTM, or Confederation of Mexican Workers) under the leadership of Lombardo Toledano. A third sector, the popular sector, focused on state employees; although it existed in principle, it had no legal existence until 1943. This corporatist structure, which simultaneously ensured presidential power and the hegemony of the official party, was to sustain the regime for decades.

To cement the new alliance, Cárdenas embarked upon a vast program of land distribution (distributing 50 percent more land than all his predecessors combined), and he encouraged unionization among industrial workers. Calles was quick to condemn publicly the escalation of strikes that followed, clearly implying that Cárdenas would be removed from office unless he mended his ways. In response, the president reiterated the government's intention to "fulfill the program of the Revolution" and removed all Callistas from key positions in his cabinet, the party, and the military. Calles abruptly left the country but was back the following year, publicly accusing Cárdenas of "carrying the country to communism." This precipitated the final purge of Callistas from the government and the party, accompanied by massive labor demonstrations in support of Cárdenas.

While analysts are divided on their evaluation of these events, all agree that the president's success was not a mere reflection of his formidable personality. Having redesigned the coalition supporting the regime by incorporating new actors, the latter's stability was no longer dependent upon the president's ability to maintain a precarious balance between overlapping interelite alliances (a task in which Calles had excelled). Instead, Cárdenas presided over a solidly entrenched system of corporatist interest representation in which the support of the laboring masses offset the power of the Revolutionary elite.

Cárdenas did not merely aim at redistributing the pie; he also wanted to increase its size. During his administration, industry and commerce were stimulated, vast irrigation dams were built in the northern states where commercial agriculture started developing under the impetus of the Green Revolution, and roads and harbors were built. Industrialists were granted extensive tariff and other fiscal concessions to facilitate the domestic manufacture of previously imported industrial goods. Despite widespread industrial conflict (particularly on the issue of unionization and the government's support of workers in most conflicts), the gross national product grew by over 30 percent between 1934 and 1940, stimulated by the policies of income redistribution that absorbed this growth.

Nevertheless, the atmosphere of social unrest and hostility against capitalists, which culminated in 1938 with the nationalization of the oil industry, did little to assuage the fears of individual businessmen or console those who actually lost money in the bargain. Toward the end of the Cárdenas era, increasing internal opposition to governmental policies was manifested by massive investment cutbacks, capital flight, credit and trade blockage, and even a military revolt (that was quickly repelled). These events, in turn, precipitated an economic crisis that forced a currency devaluation and finally constrained the government to adopt a more conservative posture, as well as seek a less radical successor.

The presidential succession from Cárdenas to Manuel Avila Camacho marked a moment of extreme vulnerability for Mexico's post-Revolutionary regime. In 1939, the government had to contend with a coalition of conservative opposition under the leadership of Juan Andreu Almazán strong enough to win the presidential election, and strong centrifugal tendencies within the official party itself. The PRM's provision of an open vote by each sector to determine the party's choice of a candidate quickly unleashed battles among its different factions, particularly within the labor sector and between labor and the military. In the end, the choice of a presidential candidate bypassed all official channels, and Manuel Avila Camacho was selected as a compromise candidate.

Elected in 1940 among widespread accusations of fraud, Avila Camacho faced a profoundly divided country. The presidential program of "national unity," aimed at reconciling the right and the left, therefore appeared less a clever strategy to consolidate the regime than an absolute necessity to prevent its breakup. To retain the support of the organized working class while curbing its militancy, the president offered a Worker Pact that provided for an end to strikes in exchange for tripartite decision on wages and profits between labor, employers, and the state. To woo business back, however, the government was careful not to enforce the pact (except for the no-strike clause). In the countryside, Cardenista policies that had stimulated agriculture under the *ejido* system of communal village landholding were dropped in favor of capitalist agriculture, and agrarian redistribution reduced to a mere trickle. These policies, in turn, laid the foundations for the peasant trek to the cities and the slow decline of Mexican agriculture.

Following the failure of the Worker Pact to curb strikes, the government adopted a double strategy of ensuring labor cooperation through a new labor code while vigorously pushing a social security bill, eventually adopted in 1943. Finally, the official party was transformed in three ways: first, by excluding the military (suspected of pro-Almazán leanings); second, by suppressing de jure the right of each sector to nominate a presidential candidate, and de facto that of individuals in each sector to vote against the candidates selected by the party; and third, by creating a third sector, the Confederación Nacional de Organizaciones Populares (CNOP, or National Confederation of Popular Organizations), which included government employees as well as the growing (and heretofore politically excluded) mass of the urban poor. In 1946, when the party was renamed the Partido Revolucionario Institucional (PRI, or Institutional Revolutionary Party), it appeared to be but a distant cousin of the PRM. These new institutions and practices laid the foundation for an additional half-century of stable one-party rule, and for what many in Mexico would come to consider the nation's unique form of restricted political democracy.

See also Constitution of 1917; Cristero Rebellion; Great Depression; Mexican Revolution

Select Bibliography

Brachet-Márquez, Viviane, *The Dynamics of Domination: State, Class and Social Reform in Mexico (1910–1990)*. Pittsburgh: University of Pittsburgh Press, 1994.

Cornelius, Wayne, "Nation Building Participation and Distribution: The Politics of Social Reform under Cárdenas." In *Crisis, Choice and Change: Historical Studies of Political Development*, edited by Gabriel A. Almond, Scott C. Flanagan, and Robert J. Mundt. Boston: Little, Brown, 1973.

Hamilton, Nora, *The Limits of State Autonomy: Postrevolutionary Mexico*. Princeton, New Jersey: Princeton University Press, 1982.

Knight, Alan, *The Mexican Revolution*. Cambridge: Cambridge University Press, 1986.

Womack, John, *Zapata and the Mexican Revolution*. New York: Knopf, 1969.

—VIVIANE BRACHET-MÁRQUEZ

Politics and Government: 1946–96

The framework for the postwar period in Mexican politics was established during the administration of Lázaro Cárdenas (1934–40), when the ruling party instituted a system based on corporatism, centralization of power in the presidency, and a system of party discipline and loyalty. If the ruling party formally functioned as a mechanism to ensure electoral victories and to mediate among competing interest groups, it increasingly became an extension of the Mexican state. This system was reinforced during the administrations of Manuel Avila Camacho (1940–46) and Miguel Alemán Valdés (1946–52), which pursued pro-capital policies while using old Cardenista institutions and rhetoric to blunt protests. Alemán, the first civilian president since the Revolution, played a particularly pivotal role in reinforcing the articulation between the party and the state. The power of the presidency was reinforced, state governors played an increasingly important role in national affairs, and the power of the military was attenuated. Military strongmen still could exercise a sporadic influence in national affairs, as when San Luis Potosí caudillo Gonzalo N. Santos decisively quashed Alemán's efforts to perpetuate his power after the end of his presidential term; however, by and large the power of the caudillos was broken.

If the Alemán administration saw the reinforcement of presidential power, it also saw the consolidation of party corporatism. In 1946 the Partido Revolucionario Mexicano (PRM, or Mexican Revolutionary Party; formerly the Partido Nacional Revolucionario, or PNR) was renamed the Partido Revolucionario Institucional (PRI, or Institutional

Revolutionary Party). The PRI included three umbrella organizations representing labor, the peasantry, and an amorphous "popular sector," which included state workers, the military, professionals, and petty entrepreneurs. The party maintained a multiclass structure with mechanisms to incorporate new social groups. Although business was not formally represented within the party, it exercised considerable informal influence over party platforms and government policy.

Each sector within this corporatist system was guaranteed a certain quota of representatives in both houses of Congress, governorships, and key positions within the executive. The labor and peasant sectors were able to produce important benefits for their members, and in exchange they supported the party in elections and participated in ritual displays of national unity and party loyalty. On May 1, for example, labor unions marched before the president; similarly, the president presided over an annual ceremony to commemorate the enactment of the agrarian law and the birthday of Emiliano Zapata. Business interests also received important perks, concessions, and protection; as long as they were able to make money, they would allow the political elite to rule without interference.

Entrepreneurs

Early in the postwar era the government imposed an economic model known as import substitution industrialization (ISI), characterized by activist, interventionist government policies designed to encourage the domestic production of previously imported manufactured goods. The state thus made entrepreneurs dependent upon government protection and secured their loyalty to the political elite. The influential Cámera Nacional de la Industria de la Transformación (CANACINTRA, or National Chamber of Transformation Industry) assumed a nationalist position supporting the PRI. Other organizations, such as those of merchants, transportation entrepreneurs, and bankers, took a similar position, supporting the PRI in exchange for relative impunity in their business operations (such as for fiscal evasion). Such relations between the state and the business sector gave rise to the term "godfather capitalism."

In the 1970s godfather capitalism began to fail. The Revolutionary myth lost validity for entrepreneurs. The old alliance became obsolete to the extent that entrepreneurs started imposing conditions on the government. The creation in 1975 of the Consejo Coordinador Empresarial (CCE, or Business Coordinating Council) almost became a rebellion when its members presented to the president a new governmental plan just before the PRI unveiled it nominee for the presidency, José López Portillo. In light of this contentious relationship with the government, business people starting supporting the Partido de Acción Nacional (PAN, or National Action Party) and in many cases both the PAN and the PRI.

A new policy was designed during the Miguel de la Madrid administration (1982–88) with the rise to power of the neoliberals (broadly defined, those supporting free market policies that emphasize a tight money supply and a balanced budget in the pursuit of manageable inflation rates). The de la Madrid administration (ended ISI policies, lowering protective trade barriers and starting to sell state-owned enterprises. A new class of politically connected entrepreneurs was able to cash in on the sale of state-owned enterprises at fire sale prices, and large consortia also benefited from de la Madrid's neoliberal policies. Small and medium business were devastated, however, and approximately 300,000 business went bankrupt during the administration of Carlos Salinas de Gortari (1988–94) after Mexico joined the General Agreement of Tariffs and Trade (GATT) and signed the North American Free Trade Agreement (NAFTA). The diminishing political capacity of the traditional business organizations to negotiate also produced important changes reformulating corporatist relationships. In the 1980s the leadership began to support the PAN, and in the 1990s the entrepreneurial discourse became openly antigovernment.

Labor

The end of the 1940s saw the beginning of the "Mexican miracle," a period of high economic growth and low inflation. Although public educational and health indicators improved overall, poverty increased. Many intellectuals attempted call attention to this disequilibrium, but the government was able to ignore these warnings: the PRI's tight corporatist organization allowed it to repress political dissent with low political cost. Independent labor movements were repressed, most notably movements of teachers (1957) and railroad workers (1958); the leaders of the railroad workers' strike, Demetrio Vallejo and Valentín Campa, were jailed, as was the prominent Communist muralist José Alfaro Siqueiros. At the same time, the PRI labor federation, the Confederación de Trabajadores de México (CTM, or Confederation of Mexican Workers) increasingly was characterized by antidemocratic and probusiness leadership (generally referred to as *charros*); Fidel Velázquez was reelected as head of the CTM.

Labor conflicts helped determine the PRI's choice of Adolfo López Mateos for the 1958–64 presidential term. López Mateos was the first presidential candidate who did not come from the Secretaría de Gobernación (Department of the Interior); rather, he came from the Department of Labor, where he had gained ample experience in repressing labor dissidents. López Mateos's successor, Gustavo Díaz Ordaz (1964–70), continued his repressive policies. In 1964 he quashed an attempt by medical students to organize outside the corporatist system, politicizing parts of the middle classes and helping to set the stage for the much broader student movement of 1968. He also promoted the formation of the Congreso de Trabajo (CT, or Labor Congress), which grouped the CTM together with the burgeoning unions in newer industrial sectors. Although the creation of the CT allowed the state to deal with a single intermediary, it also required a redistribution of political rewards and power. The opening of in-bond plants known as *maquiladoras* in the northern border region, attracting U.S. corporations and creating a union-free environment, proved to be a long-standing thorn in the side of official labor federations.

The 1970s saw the creation of new independent unions in the service sector, most notably universities, banks, and public corporations, and they aggressively confronted the government and labor establishment. The breakdown of elite consensus within the PRI after 1968 created a margin of political space for the new unions—one independent union apparently was led by a PRI senator—but their increasing strength eventually prompted the CTM and CT to demand a government crackdown. In 1976 military troops occupied electrical facilities, breaking the independent electrical workers' union, and other independent unions were repressed in the coming months and years. Nonetheless, these proved to be equivocal victories for the CTM and CT, and relations between the labor federations and the government increasingly were strained; government efforts to oust Fidel Velázquez further weakened relations between the government and the CTM and other labor federations. Unions steadily lost influence, and Velázquez was shut out of such key political decisions as presidential succession.

The close of the 1970s brought a dramatic end to the "Mexican miracle" as world oil prices plummeted, hampering the government's ability to pay the bloated international debt. In a desperate attempt to regain control of the spiraling economy, the administrations of Miguel López Portillo (1976–82) and Miguel de la Madrid adopted a series of draconian monetary policies, culminating in the nationalization of the private banking industry in 1982. Although technocrats in the government's financial sector blamed high wages for runaway inflation, real wages have been steadily declining since the López Portillo administration, thanks in part to low levels of labor activism. New organizations such as the Frente Amplio de Trabajo (FAT, or Authentic Labor Front) have had an impact on the plant level, but they have not been able to influence national policy. During the de la Madrid administration the CTM signed a pact with the government freezing wages; by 1988 inflation had reach 160 percent, and real wages had declined to 1940s levels.

President Salinas renewed government attacks on labor unions—and against the octogenarian Fidel Velázquez (perhaps because he had opposed Salinas's nomination). Salinas also jailed the leader of the petroleum workers' union, Joaquín Hernández Galicia "La Quina," who had openly supported the leftist opposition candidate Cuauhtémoc Cárdenas in the 1988 election; some also whispered that La Quina's imprisonment stemmed from his having financed a book on Salinas's childhood murder of his family's maid. The government charged Hernández with murder and smuggling weapons, charges that he maintained were completely spurious. The jailing of the head of the powerful petroleum workers' union had a chilling effect throughout the labor movement.

Working with the general secretary of the telephone workers' union, who previously had supported the left, Salinas created the Federación de Sindicatos de Empresas y Bienes y Servicios (FESEBES, or Federation of Unions of Businesses of Goods and Services). Although Salinas hoped that FESEBES eventually would replace the CTM, the new organization competed more directly against the Federación de Sindicatos de Trabajadores al Servicio del Estado (FSTSE, or Federation of Unions of Civil Servants); eventually the FESEBES joined the CT, effectively neutralizing the new union as a counterweight to the older unions. Until his death in 1997, Fidel Velázquez remained in control of the CTM. Even as it awaited his death, the government had no clear plans for his replacement.

Peasants

During the postwar period land distribution continued, but with serious backlogs. As with labor, the government followed a "single interlocutor" policy with the peasantry, using the official Confederación Nacional Campesina (CNC, or National Peasant Confederation) to organize and control the peasantry. The leadership of official peasant organizations was bought off with economic incentives and political sinecures, and independent peasant organizations were marginalized and repressed. The countryside also saw considerable repression, assassinations of dissident peasant leaders, and massacres. As with labor, the peasantry often was used as a pawn in intraparty squabbles. A peasant massacre at San Ignacio de Rio Muerto, Sonora, in 1975 resulted in the ouster of Governor Carlos Armando Biebrich, effectively ending his political career.

When President Luis Echeverría Álvarez (1970–76) announced the suspension of land distribution, official leaders needed to come up with new incentives to ensure peasant loyalty. They now offered regularization of titles, training, seeds, fertilizers, and technical support, reinforcing peasant dependency; these programs to promote peasant agriculture failed, particularly since many resources were siphoned off by corrupt officials and peasant leaders. As traditional *agrarista* demands for "land and freedom" began to lose ground, the government lost the ability to handle disputes peaceably. By the end of the Echeverría administration, violent peasant conflicts and land invasions erupted throughout the country, especially in Sonora, Sinaloa, and Durango. Chiapas presents one of the worst cases of peasant repression. During the 1980s and 1990s peasant leaders systematically were jailed or murdered. The indigenous uprising of 1994 belied the smug declarations by Governor José Patrocinio González Blanco that agrarian conflicts in the state had been resolved.

Even as it repressed independent peasant movements, the government sought to address deteriorating rural living conditions with such programs as government-subsidized stores, health care programs, and food support programs. At best these were piecemeal efforts, however, and did little to ameliorate social conditions or address the real causes of rural poverty. In the late 1980s the Salinas administration established the Programa Nacional de Solidaridad (PRONASOL, or National Solidarity Program), delivering patronage directly to clients and bypassing local *caciques* (political bosses) and the Priistas old guard—the so-called *dinosauros*—who generally were quite hostile to Salinas's technocratic reforms. Although the program initially enjoyed enormous popularity, in the long term it represented little more than a reconfiguration of the old patron-client relationship, serving more to ensure loyalty to the Salinista young hawks than to promote rural development (indeed, many think that Salinas meant Solidaridad to be an embryonic party to replace the PRI). In the end, the program did little except weaken traditional peasant organizations and the PRI.

The growth of cities spurred the sale of previously inalienable *ejido* (village common) lands and urban land invasions. Urbanization also facilitated Salinas's abrogation of Article 27 of the 1917 constitution, officially putting an end to agrarian reform. Previously inalienable *ejido* lands now could act as collateral on loans or as a guarantee to attract private investment. Like PRONASOL, this Salinista initiative has weakened traditional peasant organizations, which now only have marginal strength in states with a majority rural population.

Perhaps the most important organization to move into the vacuum was El Barzón, a debtors' organization of small farmers and *ejiditarios* who had lost their land, machinery, and other property to the banks. The conflict was sharpened by the December 1994 collapse of the Mexican peso, which greatly increased interest rates for credit card and mortgage holders; as of the mid-1990s El Barzón has become a primarily middle-class organization. The administration of President Ernesto Zedillo Ponce de León (1994–) has not been able to produce a viable solution to the crisis.

The Middle Classes

Since 1946 new organizations among all professional disciplines have been incorporated into the PRI. Such professionals gave the government credit for the "Mexican miracle," and they saw professional opportunities in government positions. For many members of the middle classes, however, the political consequence of the exhaustion of the economic model toward the end of the 1960s was an outdated corporatist framework unable to address new challenges. Among the most severe of these challenges were the student conflicts that started in 1966 at the Universidad Nacional Autónoma de México (UNAM, or the National Autonomous University of Mexico) and the Nicolaita University of Michoacán in Morelia. Such conflicts led to the ouster of university presidents and governors, and, most notably, the October 2, 1968, Massacre in Tlatelolco plaza in Mexico City. The killing of approximately 300 peaceful protesters in Tlatelolco plaza left an indelible mark on the Díaz Ordaz administration.

The oil boom in the 1980s helped maintain economic growth and political support for the PRI from the middle classes, but the further downsizing of the government and the consequent limitation of political opportunities produced disillusion. Many from the middle classes turned their back on the PRI and gave their support to the PAN, leading to PAN victories in many big cities.

Political Parties

In the closing decades of the twentieth century, the system of political parties changed rapidly from a hegemonic party system with political party puppets to a system of real competition. Three political parties have a long histories (PRI, PAN, and the Communist Party, PCM), but a loyal opposition of smaller parties, the so-called *satelites* (satellite parties), helped create an image of democracy and ideological diversity. The Partido Popular Socialista (PPS, or Popular Socialist Party) and the Partido Auténtico de la Revolución Mexicana (PARM, or Authentic Party of the Mexican Revolution) shared the scene for decades without relevance. All this changed rapidly with the rise of new, powerful opposition parties. At the federal level in 1994, four political parties were represented in congress: PRI, PAN, Partido de la Revolución Democrática (PRD, or Party of the Democratic Revolution), and Partido de Trabajadores (PT, or Workers' Party). On the state level, local parties held relatively greater influence. The parties created by the state—such as the Partido Socialista de los Trabajadores (PST, or Party of the Socialist Workers, created 1972), later transformed into the Partido del Frente Cardenista de Reconstrucción Nacional (PFCRN, or Party of the Cardenista Front for National Reconstruction)—came to occupy a reduced political space. Extreme right parties such as the Partido Democrático Mexicano (PDM, or Mexican Democratic Party), which was rooted in the fascist Sinarquista movement, made little difference in elections.

The PAN, with frequent help from the Catholic Church, became a viable opposition party, especially in large urban centers, the north, and Yucatán. In 1989 the party won its first governorship, and by the mid-1990s it had become the second largest political force in the country, winning a role as a leading partner in the Salinas reforms. A new type of political negotiation known as *concertación* was inaugurated, in which a negotiation was conducted to give away electoral positions. That was the case in Guanajuato, where a PAN candidate was appointed substitute governor after the elected governor was forced to resign, and the same happened in San Luis Potosí, where the PRI governor was forced to request a leave of absence after a few weeks in office.

Internally, the PAN diversified. Among the new forces were the "neo-Panistas," entrepreneurs who recently had joined the party. Examples of such neo-Panistas are Ernesto Ruffo, governor of Baja California (1989–95); Francisco Barrio, governor of Chihuahua (1993–); and persons who did not join the party but ran under its banner, such as Francisco Villarreal, mayor of Ciudad Juárez (1993–95). This group's strategy of incremental negotiation with the federal government increased the party's number of governmental positions via recognition of victories, such as in Baja California, or political pressure to receive concessions, such as in Guanajuato. This group even succeeded in placing a member in the executive branch when President Zedillo appointed a Panista as attorney general. Within the party the neo-Panistas were fought by the group known as the Foro Doctrinario, which eventually left the party and joined forces with the PRD.

Although it was the oldest political party in the country, the Partido Comunista Mexicano (PCM, or Mexican Communist Party) had to remain underground for many years. The Movimiento de Liberación Nacional (MLN, or National Liberation Movement), created in the 1950s, established communication between the Cardenista left and individual Marxists, but organizations close to the PCM remained marginalized from the political system. In the 1970s the PCM became legal, and new parties inspired by Trotsky, Mao, and the non-Marxist left were created, such as the Partido Mexicano de los Trabajadores (PMT, or Party of the Mexican Workers) and Partido Revolucionario de los Trabajadores (PRT, or Revolutionary Party of the Workers). Other groups emerged that advocated the proletarian revolution but did not become involved in partisan politics, such as Línea de Masas. The PCM gradually moved to the center, eliminating Communism from its name in 1981 and joining with several other parties to form the Partido Socialista Unificado Mexicano (PSUM, or Unified Mexican Socialist Party).

In 1981, for the first time in Mexico's history, a party allied with the communists won a major election: the Coalición Obrera Campesina Estudiantil del Istmo (COCEI or Coalition of Workers, Peasants, and Students of the Isthmus) won the municipal elections in Juchitán, Oaxaca. But this victory by the left was not repeated in other regions because of the left's fragmentation and internal conflict. It took another seven years for the left to get close to a victory, when in 1988 a leftist coalition with former Priistas, the Frente Democrático Nacional (FDN, or National Democratic Front), supported the presidential candidacy of Cuauhtémoc Cárdenas, son of former president Lázaro Cárdenas. Cuauhtémoc Cárdenas lost to the PRI candidate, Carlos Salinas de Gortari, in an extremely questionable election. In 1989, a new recomposition of the FDN coalition created the PRD, which became the third political force in the country. Cárdenas was the party's presidential candidate in

1994 but finished third, receiving far fewer votes than he had in 1988. Since its creation, the PRD has been subject to internal conflict without increasing its share of power (unlike the PAN, the PRD has refused to take part in *concertaciones*). The party could not even win the governorship of Michoacán in 1995, the state where Cardenismo originated.

The PRI's initial advantage was its ability to co-opt dissidents. There were rewards for all to be had from the coffers of the party and state, which created incentives for the development of a loyal national *intelligentsia*. The repression of the 1960s severely damaged this relationship, however, and opened the door for intellectual dissent. Significant were Octavio Paz's resignation as ambassador to India as protest for the 1968 Massacre of Tlatelolco and the leadership of Carlos Fuentes, Luis Villoro, and Heberto Castillo in the foundation of the PMT.

The PRI began losing votes consistently during this period, and it generally is believed that the party in fact lost the 1988 election, when it received its lowest voter support at the polls and lost the absolute majority in Congress. If the opposition had united, the PRI would have lost 39 of the 40 congressional seats in the Federal District. In 1991, although it had lost governorship and a growing number of cities, the party recovered its majority in Congress. The party's challenge in the 1994 presidential election was not just a victory, but also legitimation. The government spent US$1 billion on safeguards to guarantee a clean election, including a voting card with fingerprint and photograph, and accepted foreign observers. With the Chiapas Zapatista insurrection in the background and a strong PRI campaign playing on the fears of the average voter, however, Mexicans were convinced to vote for the PRI to maintain peace, and the PRI maintained the super-majority it needed in Congress to block reform legislation.

Nevertheless, by 1994 the Mexican electoral system was no longer predictable, and the PRI had lost its guaranteed monopoly on political power. In 1995 the PAN ruled 4 states, the capital cities of 11 others, governed 13 of the 20 largest *municipios,* and had 24 senators, 119 congresspersons, and 218 mayors. The PRD ruled over 132 *municipalities* and had 8 senators and 70 congresspersons. The PT ruled over 11 cities and had 10 congresspersons. Of the 2,020 *municipios,* 53 were ruled by members of four other political parties and independent mayors.

The Left and Guerrilla Movements

The repression of popular mobilization and protest in the 1960s eliminated early hopes of transforming Mexico peacefully outside government-controlled organizations. If the student movement had allowed Communists, Trotskyites, Maoists, and Anarchists to emerge from clandestinity, the repression of 1968 divided them into two groups. One group choose to create new political parties; the other created guerrilla organizations.

During the 1960s in Guerrero, the Asociación Cívica Nacional Revolucionaria (ACNR, or National Revolutionary Civic Association) was created under the command of the school teacher Genaro Vázquez. When Vázquez died, the ACNR became more radical, becoming the Partido de los Pobres (PP, or Party of the Poor) under the command of Lucio Cabañas. The party almost disappeared when Cabañas was killed in 1974. In Chihuahua one group attacked a military garrison in Ciudad Madero, with devastating results for the young guerrillas, but from this action there arose a movement advocating land invasions in the north of the country. The name "Liga 23 de septiembre" (23rd of September League) was taken from this group when the decimated remnants of urban and rural guerrillas unified in 1975.

In the 1970s different guerrilla groups started operating in several parts of the country, with spectacular actions such as the kidnappings of General José Guadalupe Zuño (former governor of Jalisco), the U.S. consul general in Guadalajara, and President's Echeverría father-in-law; the assassination of Eugenio Garza Sada, the head of the powerful Monterrey group of industrialists; and the attempted kidnapping of the sister of President-elect López Portillo in Mexico City. Despite isolated spectacular acts, however, by 1975 most guerrilla groups had succumbed to government attack or co-optation. In the words of a former guerrilla: "We felt as if we were tied up by the strings of a puppeteer and those were suddenly dropped. This is how the guerrilla went down." At the end of the decade the group Antorcha Campesina (Peasant Torch) began engaging in terrorist attacks in Puebla. It eventually was co-opted by the PRI, however, and was reduced to a diffuse movement comprising peasant and student movements in Mexico City. Rumors suggest that Maoist groups were incorporated into the government using this group as a front. Some guerrillas received amnesty, and many former guerrillas were among the first to react in the aftermath the 1985 earthquake in Mexico City, mobilizing the groups they had been organizing in the periphery of Mexico City. After a long silence the Party of the Poor (now called PROCUP) executed limited actions in Mexico City, leading to an overblown governmental reaction.

On January 1, 1994, a guerrilla conflict started in the Lacandon jungle in Chiapas, where the Ejército Zapatista de Liberación Nacional (EZLN, or Zapatista Army of National Liberation) rebelled against the government. Actual fighting lasted only a few days, but the political intensity of the conflict continued. The long-standing grievances of indigenous peasant communities joined the movements born in the 1960s with apparent links to personalities very close to the government and the corporatist system. The PROCUP supported the EZLN, placing a bomb in a shopping center and a missile close to a military base in Mexico City.

The Crisis of the PRI

The electoral system has gone through several electoral reform since the end of World War II. Looking to end the appearance of a PRI monopoly, President López Mateos introduced minority representation in Congress. The number of such minority members was determined by the percentage of votes their parties received, and the members themselves were selected from party lists. In 1970 the voting age was reduced to 18 years of age. In 1977 the number of congressional seats was increased to 400, and five "plurinominal circumscription" *(circunscripción plurinominal)* regions were created, each with a mixed system of election, having some congresspersons elected by direct vote and a number of others elected by party list. In 1986 the number of seats in Congress was increased to 500. In 1993 the number of seats in the Senate was increased to four from each state. President Salinas also promoted various other reforms, weakening the patronage base of the "Dinosaurs" of the PRI old guard while strengthening a narrow circle of technocratic loyalists.

In the search for credibility, new institutions to conduct elections were created and electoral tribunals were modified. The meaningfulness of these reforms was called into question, however, by the 1988 presidential election, believed to have been among the most fraudulent in Mexico's history: in the process of tabulating the votes, the computer system shut down for three days, and when it restarted it showed Salinas to be the victor. In 1994, however, the transformations of the system apparently paid off: the victory of Ernesto Zedillo was not disputed, even though the press was controlled and the fabulous amounts spent by the PRI were not reduced from previous campaign levels.

The most important political process in the postwar period was the transformation of the ruling elite. In the 1940s a governmental group resembling classic technocrats became stronger. President Miguel Alemán Valdés modified recruitment patterns and the characteristics of the ruling elite by inviting professionals to join his cabinet, displacing the military from the executive branch, and promoting a new type of politician. Over the years the group increased its power, controlling the financial system. When the group controlled the presidency in the person of Miguel de la Madrid, it further modified the patterns of recruitment and promotion. Political careers became shorter, studies abroad were rewarded, and party activism was discouraged. Nevertheless, an ideological conflict started between this group and those who promoted the defense of the Revolution; the conflict resulted in the most important split in the history of the PRI and the rise of actual oppositions parties.

If earlier presidents had come from all parts of the country, bureaucratic presidents all came from Mexico City. Echeverría and López Portillo were born in Mexico City; de la Madrid left Colima when he was two years old but never came back to the state. Salinas was born and grew up in Mexico City, although he claims roots in Nuevo León. Zedillo was born in Mexico City, but he claims having links with Baja California because he spent part of his childhood in Mexicali. The one candidate who could have ended this trend was Luis Donaldo Colosio, who was born and raised in Sonora and was educated in Monterrey. His election also could have reversed the trend toward bureaucratization because he had been a congressman, senator, and president of the PRI. His assassination in 1994 and replacement as PRI candidate by Zedillo ended such possibilities.

The trend toward political deterioration that had begun in 1968 accelerated during the Salinas administration. A riot in the San Luis Potosí jail was ended when a paramilitary group executed the prisoners. In less than five years, more than 300 PRD members have been assassinated. In March 1994 the PRI presidential candidate, Luis Donaldo Colosio, was shot to death in Tijuana, and in May of the same year Cardinal Juan Jesús Posadas Ocampo was gunned down along with six other people in the parking lot of Guadalajara International Airport. Informal accusations of guilt, as reflected in rumors and jokes, were directed at the presidency. In September of this same year José Francisco Ruiz Massieu, the PRI secretary general, former brother-in-law of Carlos Salinas, and speaker of the house designee, was assassinated in Mexico City. A plot was discovered among the ranks of the PRI, and Raúl Salinas de Gortari, Carlos's brother, was incarcerated and charged with masterminding the assassination.

The assassination of the PRI candidate badly damaged the old arrangement of power and the presidential succession system that had functioned since 1934 and maintained a disciplined political elite loyal to Revolutionary principles. The selection of Colosio's replacement increased the turbulence. The Zedillo campaign started with conflict when he prepared a new list of candidates for Congress and the Senate, replacing the list already agreed upon with Colosio, thus upsetting the local balance of power. The perception of his candidacy best can be summarized when the PAN presidential candidate, Diego Fernández, told him during the first nationally televised presidential debate in Mexican history: "Your candidacy is the result of two tragedies, the death of Colosio and the presidential designation." Although few believed that he merited the office or possessed the necessary political skills, Zedillo won in what was generally conceded to be a fair election. His administration started with serious economic difficulties, including a steep economic decline and peso devaluation. The opposition increased it share of power, and democracy appeared to arrive by default. During the early years of Zedillo's administration instability appeared to open new opportunities for electoral democracy, but it also increased repressive and authoritarian capabilities of the government and PRI.

See also Earthquake of 1985; General Agreement on Tariffs and Trade (GATT); Massacre of Tlatelolco; North American Free Trade Agreement (NAFTA); Student Movement of 1968; Zapatista Rebellion in Chiapas; *and entries on particular political parties, coalitions, and organizations*

Select Bibliography

Aguilar Camín, Héctor, and Lorenzo Meyer, *In the Shadow of the Mexican Revolution: Contemporary Mexican History, 1910–1989*. Austin: University of Texas Press, 1993.
Cothran, Dan, *Political Stability and Democracy in Mexico*. Westport, Connecticut: Praeger, 1994.
Levy, Daniel, and Alberto Szekely, *Mexico: Paradoxes of Stability and Change*. Boulder, Colorado: Westview, 1983.
Newell G., Roberto, and Luis Rubio, *Mexico's Dilemma: The Political Origins of Economic Crisis*. Boulder, Colorado: Westview, 1984.
Schmidt, Samuel, *The Deterioration of the Mexican Presidency*. Tucson: University of Arizona Press, 1991.

—SAMUEL SCHMIDT

Poniatowska, Elena 1933–
Writer

Elena Poniatowska was born in Paris on May 19, 1933. Her father was French with Polish ancestry, and her mother was a Mexican who grew up in France. This heritage gave Poniatowska a distinctive cultural profile; although she was educated within European and U.S. traditions and institutions, she adopted Mexico and its culture as her own and moved there during World War II.

Poniatowska learned Spanish in Mexico, mainly from the women who worked in her home as domestic servants. These relationships had a profound influence on her work as a writer, since it was through them that she established a link of solidarity with everything Mexican, its language, and its culture. Poniatowska became active within Mexican culture and society once she began to work as a journalist on the newspaper *Excélsior*, where she was able to interview important literary and political figures. This experience also was fundamental to her development as a writer, since her literary output was characterized precisely by the incorporation of techniques of new journalism. Her work combines the observation of a journalist with collage of news items, headlines, and interviews. Through her work with U.S. anthropologist Oscar Lewis, Poniatowska learned the contribution of the tape recorder in reconstructing life stories. From this another quality of her oral prose developed—the characters tell their stories to another person. Unlike other actors of journalistic narrative in Latin America, however, in this testimonial conversation Poniatowska often erases her own presence and participation in the interviews.

Another quality of her journalism is to give voice to the most repressed sectors of Mexican society. Her social commitment as a writer has led Poniatowska to portray the problems in those lives that have been silent and marginalized. Her literature contains a profound historical and social stamp, in which she tends to realistic portrayals of the lives of lower-class women and all those who had not been able to express themselves. Examples of this tendency are *Hasta no verte Jesús mío* (1969), whose heroine Jesusa Palancares, a working-class woman living in an overcrowded part of Mexico, tells her life story, which is full of bad luck and oppression. However, her independence, generosity, indomitable spirit, and will to survive shine through despite changes that she has had to negotiate from the Revolution to the present.

Poniatowska critically examines Mexican history and creates a literary space for marginal history, which has no other public or legitimate place. This is where her most famous work belongs: *La noche de Tlatelolco* (1971), an account of the repression perpetrated by the army against a demonstration by students, workers, artists, and housewives in 1968. Among her other publications emphasizing this social aspect of recent Mexican history is *Todo México* (1990), in which the accounts of recent survivors of the Mexican earthquake are compiled. *Ejército Zapatista de Liberación Nacional* (1994) forms a collection of documents and reports from August 1994 on the Zapatista rebellion in Chiapas.

Poniatowska's interest in the position of women has led her to evaluate the epistolary genre as a privileged narrative form of penetrating the feminine existence. In her novel *Querido Diego te abraza Quiela* (1978), the author makes use of the letters that the painter Angelina Beloff sent to Diego Rivera after the end of their long affair. Her long novel *Tinísima* (1992) is based on the life of an Italian American photographer, Tina Modotti, and her membership in various movements of social liberation in Europe and America. Modotti's work exemplifies committed art in the twentieth century, where political activism and art are part of a living, social project. *Patriota y amante de usted: Manuela Saenz y el libertador. Diarios inéditos* (1993) again shows Poniatowska's preoccupation with recreating the intimate life of historical female characters. The letters, diaries, photographs, and paintings are part of the material the author incorporates into her texts, blurring the lines of strict division between literary genres and what we understand by fictional discourse. Her work shows multiple examples of contemporary popular and feminine culture in Latin America.

Select Bibliography

Chevigny, Bell Gale, "The Transformation of Privilege in the Work of Elena Poniatowska." *Latin American Literary Review* 13:26 (1985).

Jörgensen, Beth E., *The Writing of Elena Poniatowska: Engaging Dialogues.* Austin: University of Texas Press, 1994.

Scott, Nina M., "The Fragmented Narrative Voice of Elena Poniatowska." *Discurso Literario* 7:2 (1990).

Starcevic, Elizabeth D., "Breaking the Silence: Elena Poniatowska: Writer in Transition." In *Literatures in Transition: The Many Voices of the Caribbean Area: A Symposium,* edited by Rose S. Minc. Gaithersburg, Maryland: Hispamérica, 1982.

—BERNARDITA LLANOS

Popular Catholicism

Popular Catholicism took shape with remarkable speed during the first generation of Spanish rule in Mexico, quickly assimilating numerous pre-Hispanic elements into the patterns of Spanish Catholicism. The missionaries were from the "regular" orders: Franciscan, Dominican, and Augustinian friars who worked outside the "secular" church structure governed by the episcopacy. Although many of them are notorious today for their intolerance regarding indigenous customs, they distinguished themselves from the seculars by their willingness to serve in remote villages and to learn the indigenous languages. This assidousness may help explain their successes. Another factor in their success was the tradition in Mexico that conquered people should accept their conquerors' gods. From such slight wisps of cultural openness, and from a growing sense that the friars and their flocks would need each other in the ongoing struggles with the state, there developed a new system of beliefs and practices to which the indigenous people remained intensely attached during four centuries of vicissitudes.

The conquered people found in the new religion a way to allay the worst excesses of the conquest. Being Catholic made them immune to enslavement and enabled them to unite within overtly religious brotherhoods and present a coherent and self-respecting response to the continual demands of the state. Through the years the special place of the Catholic Church among the Mexicans made a formidable, if never fully successful, counterweight to the colonial policy of segregating the indigenous population from power. The friars often were steadfast in defending their parishioners against the state and offered a coherent and passionately held spiritual vision that resonated with the old values. In the friars' sculptures of the new god and his saints could be seen a concept of sacrifice that resembled and yet sublimated the blood-giving of the old religion. The most dramatic of these statues represented a bleeding Christ, a San Sebastian pierced by arrows, martyred friars, and the dolorous mother who replaced their mother goddess Tonantzin. For reasons both practical and spiritual, therefore, the friars seemed to have much to offer.

For the first missionary friars, the new converts validated the millenarian vision that had impelled them to seek this land. Although in subsequent generations members of the Spanish church would work to wipe out the holdovers of the old practices, a sense of urgency and belief in the power of baptism led the earliest missionaries to accept symbols and metaphors from the old religion, hoping these eventually would lead to those of the universal faith.

The old religion did offer many elements that seemed usefully similar to Roman Catholicism. There were tales of a great flood, a rainbow (although of ill omen in pre-Hispanic belief), an Eve-like first woman (Cihuacoatl) alongside the virgin mother, holy crosses, the presentation of the children in the temples, baptism, communion (Toyolilacuatl), confession and absolution, days of fasting, demons, heaven and hell, limbo for children, and the final days. The pre-Hispanic religion also resembled Spanish Catholicism in stressing sacrifice for the greater good and service to the community. In the two cultures, people earned honor through their work for neighborhood associations dedicated to the local god or saint, organizing and supporting the religious festivals that marked the liturgical year. It was thus easy for the friars to set up *cofradías* (confraternities) in the barrios of indigenous villages, each dedicated to a saint and each engaged in yearlong activities that supported and culminated in the saint's fiesta. Combined, fiesta and *cofradía* had the double value of imparting a sacral character to the barrio and village and also of creating solidarity through cooperative effort. These two effects have served villages well in their dealings with external authorities and help explain why fiesta and *cofradía* became the defining characteristics of popular Catholicism in Mexico.

Within less than 50 years the friars and their converts developed a complete religious culture in central and southern Mexico. At the same time there was growing alienation between the sacral community and external church authority. The 1574 Ordenanza del Patronazgo ordered the replacement of the friars by secular clergy, who were less dedicated and carried less prestige in the village. Secularization took place only gradually and required 200 years for completion, but it produced an estrangement between popular Catholicism and the regime of the episcopacy. By the time of Independence in 1821, it is estimated that only 4,000 priests were actually at work in Mexican parishes, which now regarded themselves as autocephalous entities whose relation to the clergy was that of a consumer of services. Priests were called upon for baptisms, for Christmas and for Easter Masses. The village had grown used to organizing its ritual life on its own.

Perhaps the most salient and enduring aspect of village religious ritual is the veneration of the *santos*. The Catholic saints are an expression of the unity of all the baptized faithful, living or dead, and of the promise of salvation. They offer help to the living when called on and are a conduit for grace when they intercede before God. The saints serve a purpose in Catholicism parallel to the role of the ancestor spirits *(nagua)* of the indigenous groups. The cult of the *santos,* a word that refers both to the image and to the holy personage, is the most common form of public worship in Mexico.

The idolatrous aspect of *santo* worship did not escape the Spanish church, especially as the Counter Reformation progressed. In the sixteenth and seventeenth centuries, Christian votive figures were made in Mexico, sometimes by indigenous artists. The earliest native works were crucifixes of corn paste. Meant for processions, they were as tall as a man but weighed less than five pounds. These and *santos* of hollow wood were suspected (rightly) of hiding idols that the Indians came from afar to worship. Many were taken down from the altars, and a campaign to exclude native *santeros* was organized by Spanish artisans as well as by the clergy.

Since the sixteenth century, the most popular *santos* have been Christ, Mary, St. Michael the Archangel, St. James (Santiago), Mary Magdalene, St. Francis, St. Dominic, and St. Ann. Christ, bloody and suffering, has numerous forms that serve to teach the principal aspects of his life. Christ crucified is titled *El Señor (El Señor de la Misericordia, El Señor del Veneno, El Señor de Chalma);* the dead Christ in his coffin is usually *Santo Entierro,* and sometimes he has the powers of Tlaloc, god of the underworld; Christ carrying the cross is *Nuestro Padre Jesús.* Mary is venerated as the Virgin of Guadalupe and in dozens of other guises. She is *La Virgen del Rosario,* special to the Dominicans; or *La Virgen de la Soledad,* comfort of the poor, the lonely, and the afflicted; or simply, *Nuestra Madre.* St. Michael and his archangels are powerful forces, warriors against the Devil, witches, and the spirits that roam the fields *(ayres).*

Following Spanish practice, Mexicans choose a patron saint as protector of their town or community. The saint has as a special charge the welfare of the inhabitants. In return, the community provides a personalized devotion to the saint's image, before which it burns candles and incense and offers the fruit of the fields. The *santo* is dressed in finest cloth and real hair and processed through the streets during the fiestas. Other aspects of the veneration of the images include rewarding successful intervention with gifts that represent the saint's specific power. The devout pin silver or tin amulets of legs, arms, children, and hearts to the clothing of the image when cures have been effected. Pictures of family members who have moved away or disappeared are tied to the *santo*. Two-dollar U.S. bills often are pinned to the *santo* when riches have been granted, or as a promise of more if the prayer is answered. Some *santos* receive gifts specific to their work in the community. San Isidro Labrador, patron saint of farmers, often is surrounded by carved oxen. The Virgin may have a collection of *quinceñera* bouquets or tiaras, given when the chaste petitioner marries.

Traditionally, each town and each of its barrios celebrate the annual canonical feast day of its patron saint with a panoply of communal observances. These include services inside the church or chapel, but much of the celebration occurs in public spaces and even in private homes.

Processions are among the most famous of the fiesta's public events. Parishioners prepare for them by erecting arches festooned with fruits and greenery; on the eve of the procession, the streets are swept clean and then are strewn with flowers or colored sawdust. In some communities it is young women who carry the *santo* on its litter. The procession renews the saint's benediction upon the community and engages the saint in continued protection of the faithful.

Fireworks are also popular, and have been the subject of church and state denunciations since the sixteenth century. The climax of the display is the setting off of a grand *castillo*, a structure as tall as 50 feet with whirling fireworks and plenty of color.

Another public event in traditional fiestas is the *auto*, or dramatic presentation. Subjects include the Passion, Cinco de Mayo, the Conquest of Jerusalem, and Santiago's victory over the Moors. The subtext is sometimes the clash between the Spaniards and the indigenous population. Costume and design, for example, associate the Moors with the Spaniards and Santiago's side with the Aztecs. In Oaxaca communities, one traditional dance represents the Conquest in highly symbolic choreography and involves two girls to represent doña Marina (la Malinche, Cortés's interpreter) in her two aspects, European and indigenous. Although such dances are part of the historical popular Catholicism, the migration of many men from the villages has made it more difficult for the old customs to endure.

The intrinsically political as well as religious message of the dances has made them fashionable venues for the official expression of the nation's pre-Columbian identity. In areas of Guerrero, Oaxaca, and Yucatán, intellectuals and sometimes caciques (local leaders) have removed them from the purvieu of the brotherhoods and now present them as their own. The dances are an overt symbol of an apparent unity within the community. Once removed from the fraternities, their organization and presentation have served the needs of politicians who wish to be seen as the conduit of power to the people.

While the dance takes place today outside the *atrio*, devotions to the saint continue inside the church through the day. According to the anthropologist Jeanette Rodríguez, the fiestas represent the celebration of a year's mutually satisfactory devotion between the saint and the people. Those who have asked for help come to give thanks for favors received. Some who might have been disappointed in their petition to another saint come to begin a new relationship with a saint who is rumored to be more sympathetic to their needs. Flowers or other offerings obtained for the church by the fiesta's sponsors are available to all members of the community, who are allowed to take home a share to place on the altar of the family saint. Private homes figure importantly in fiestas. It is on a private altar that a miniature of the community *santo* has been kept throughout the year, where it can be taken care of by its godparents, just as they would a child.

Traditionally, the public-private intersection in community rituals has been a means of rationalizing class differences. In rural areas in the southern states of Mexico, wealthier citizens build oratories or small chapels, sometimes enclosed, sometimes open-air. These are marked by a cross and hold an altar to the saint. Although they are privately owned, they are part of the system of repartition of wealth that is at the heart of public worship in Mexico. The *santo* is not usually kept in the little chapel. The owner selects as the godfather or *padrino* of the *santo* a man of lesser wealth who is honorable and respected in the community. This man and his wife, the *madrina*, are charged with caring for the *santo* in their home and with preparing a fiesta for the saint on the appointed day of the year. Caring for the *santo* provides the *padrino* with some ability to channel the saint's power to cure illness, especially in children. The *padrino* touches the affected part of the body with a candle, flower, or medallion and then offers this object to the saint. On the day of the fiesta, the *santo* is processed from the home of the *padrino* and through the community to the oratory. Men and women who are of the inner circle commonly offer each other *aguardiente* (liquor) throughout the night they spend honoring the saint. Although the statue and the oratory have been made for the special benefit of a single family, on the saint's day all the people on one or more hacienda will come together to pray, light the candles, and shoot off firecrackers. The owner pays much of the cost, and the *compadres* of the *padrino* cover the rest. This creates a socioeconomic balance in the community and allows men of moral worth to gain respect that otherwise would be due only to the man wealthy enough to build the oratory. Such fiestas also provide a fit occasion for restoring public areas and the school to decent repair and order.

Through much of the colonial period, a community's fiscal support of fiestas was mediated by *cofradías*. These brotherhoods took charge of a saint's altar and image, and they managed the communal plot set aside to provide income for the cult. This arrangement fell victim to the Bourbon appropriation of church property, however, and without the communal plots *cofradías* in many villages gave way to new arrangements in which an individual or couple earned prestige by undertaking the sponsorship of a fiesta for one year. The man was called a *mayordomo,* his wife a *mayordoma. Mayordomía* refers both to the institution or practice and to the collectivity of *mayordomos* in a village. The practice usually involved a ranking system whereby individuals rose through steadily more prestigious ritual tasks or *cargos.* Like the godparenthood described above, it helped soften the impact of economic distinctions while encouraging what amounted to surplus production by the *mayordomo* and by those he enlisted to help him. The enlisting of kin and *compadres* also benefited the community by sealing social relations and providing a locus for political planning and discussion.

These advantages were bothersome, however, to nineteenth- and twentieth-century reformers. The liberal creed was that surplus wealth should go into capital formation and not be locked up by the church, so the new regimes endeavored to displace or emasculate *mayordomías* and *cofradías.* Such efforts often failed, and when they did succeed new ritual systems simply arose to replace the old ones. Thus scholars Lynn Stephen and James W. Dow tell of communities where extensive "kin-*compadrazgo*" networks support elaborate celebrations of life-cycle events such as baptisms and weddings, which take place in private homes beyond the reach of the authorities. In some cases these networks have become the basis for community-wide political action. In essence, they do what fiestas have done, validating the people's self-image as a sacral community and channeling individual efforts toward communal ends.

The ritual system of kin-*compadrazgo* can carry a Mexican from the cradle to the grave in the embrace of the larger community. Life-cycle ceremonies include a large number of rituals that mark a young person's Christian development. These begin with baptism, which is followed by the *sacamisa* or "churching" of the mother some weeks after the birth. As elsewhere, Catholic children in Mexico experience first communion and confirmation as important moments in their lives, but every other time of passage also is likely to be marked by serious religious ceremonies. These include special blessings when children are sick, graduation from primary school, and for girls the *quince años.* This marks the girl's passage into young womanhood at 15 and calls for elaborate and costly celebrations, noted even in those expatriate communities in the United States where much else has been abandoned. After a church ceremony, the *quinceñera* appears before her family at home in a bright dress and the heels and jewelry of a grown-up, accompanied by fifteen *damas* and one young man, her *chambelán.* In adulthood, the ceremonies continue when young people obtain a new house, buy a metate (stone for grinding grain) or farm equipment, or enter into any important new venture. For each of these life-cycle ceremonies the parents choose a set of godparents, if not from among their kin then from those who are socially their equals or slightly superior.

A form of superiority is imparted by godparenthood itself. The godparents of one's child are one's *compadres,* and people in this relationship normally treat each other with an increased measure of respect, using the *usted* form of address and exchanging handshakes when they meet in a public place. Usually this *compadrazgo* relationship ripples through a family—affecting, for example, the way the parents of *compadres* relate to each other. The scholar John M. Ingham argues that this respect marks the belief that godparenthood, being spiritual, is on a higher plane than biological parenthood.

Godparents pay for many of the specific costs in life-cycle ceremonies. More important, they become co-responsible for the young person's moral education. It is the godfather of the *quinceñera,* for example, who must take her aside and warn her about the ways of young men. Godparents also have an important role in arranging the young person's marriage and in planning and paying for the wedding. Because the responsibilities in godparenthood are so serious, and because parents must recruit so many *compadres,* the *compadrazgo* network in a community can be very strong. As we have seen, recent developments have in some cases made *compadrazgo* the successor to *mayordomía* and *cofradías* as the key institution undergirding the community's responses to external pressures.

The survival of the *compadrazgo* and of the fiesta dances suggests that there are mythic questions that the Mexicans feel they cannot face alone. Although Catholicism pervades Mexican society physically and spiritually, it never has completely satisfied the believers' need to control all levels of their universe. On a daily basis, orthodox Christianity and its social supports suggest few recourses against the work of the Devil, who may wear the attributes either of the pre-Columbian gods or of the European Satan. He manifests himself principally in those areas not easily controlled by man and perceived to be dangerous for the priest. Throughout Mexico, the Devil lives in caves, in *barrancas* and rivers, and to win men's souls he will transform himself into an animal or into a strange man. Often he is a coyote, a jaguar, a bat, or a cayman. In these guises, he can come in the night and cause sickness or death. He is a *charro* or a Spaniard, and when he wears these faces, he seeks men's labor and their wealth. He can appear as *Culebra de Agua,* the spirit who controls hail and rain.

In much of rural Mexico, pagan practices survive in the pre-Columbian dances during Holy Week, where the community plays out the great battle between death and eternal life, between the Devil and the *cristianos,* as Mexicans refer to each other. The roles are sacred responsibilities and the young men must prepare themselves ritually for the dance. First they are taught the prayers, the offerings, and the meditations that will draw them into the sacred world that the fiesta creates. Then they learn the songs and the steps from old men who carry the rites in their heads. The great clash of cultures often is an acting out of the birth of the Mexican people in which the old gods and Christ and the saints meet on the same field. Processing with their brothers who carry *santos* and crosses are members of the *cofradías* who wear animal and monster masks that represent exactly the Devil's guises as listed above. The Negrito clowns of Oaxaca lead the dance of the Conquest wearing black-painted masks with tusks and fantastic snouts, characteristics of Tezcatlipoca, the god of night, who conquered Quetzalcoatl, the hero of the light. The skull masks seen in October are a symbiosis of the ancient masks of the god of death and of those worn during the Spanish morality plays. In Sonora, the Yaqui and Mayo Indians still dance a rain dance performed as part of the Christian celebrations. While the humanistic masks worn by some of the group reflect the power of Christian spirituality, those made of animal hide and hair are created in an indigenous tradition that is a result of dreamed visions and contact with animal spirits.

Traditionally, a man makes a mask and, when he puts it on, it hides his soul and transforms him into the spirit soul of the mask. The masks, then, indicate that the belief in the duality of human nature has not disappeared from the culture. During the time of the ritual preparation for the fiesta, and while he is dancing, each man has contact with the spirit world. He will use these contacts in the name of the village *santo* to gain some control over the fertility of the land and of the people.

Outside of the sacred time of the fiesta, there may be in the village a man who is a *curandero,* a man whose province is the spiritual world and who on a daily basis channels the power of the saints in the battle against the Devil. The Devil's work is evidenced by disequilibrium in nature. When a child or an adult sickens with a *susto* (deep sadness), it is said that the Devil, in this case called a *nagual,* has disturbed his or her shadow (called a *nagua*). The *curandero* can see the patient's affected spirit and call it back into the proper alignment in the body, so bringing balance and good health. He can do this through prayers to the *santos* or to spirits, with incense, special drinks, and amulets. These varied tools may have an indigenous or a European source. In the central mountains, masked members of special brotherhoods dance at childbirths and when there has been harm from a bull, or jaguar, or a snake, the Devil's incarnations.

The Devil may bring drought or lightning, frost or flood. Then the shaman will build an altar in the fields or in the caves where the evil dwells and fight the Devil with crosses, prayers, and incense. Just as witches work evil by making manikins of the intended victims, it is usual for the shaman to work with dolls that represent the good outcome that he seeks. If these are clay, they will be painted in accord with the role, the sex, and the class they represent. Sometimes the manikins are simple stones that come from magical places, or they are made of vegetables or flowers that are said to have special powers. At times a *santo,* especially St. Michael on his feast day, is the image needed. These figures then are placed in the open field or on the shaman's home altar among the *santos* with whom he has a special relationship. The choice of location depends upon which is more efficacious in attracting the power he wishes to control, whether of the saints, of nature, or of the Devil himself. It is believed that it takes evil to control evil, and the *santos* invoked must be virile enough to take the risk. The favorite *santos* for these rites are Christ, the Immaculate Conception, and Michael the Archangel, all of whom fought the Devil and won.

The religious practices of the Mexican people evidence a syncretism of ancient and Christian beliefs.

It is a religion of an oppressed peasantry that has recreated itself into a sacral community, united to find peace in a chaotic universe. The differences between popular Catholicism and the practices of the universal Catholic Church are perhaps best understood not in terms of "survivals" of tomfoolery that has yet to be scoured out of people's souls but rather as a response by the indigenous communities to 400 years of insults to their self-image as a people who are more than flesh and blood, a sacral nation elevated by divine powers to a status above the everyday cycles of production and reproduction. The offer of Christianization was accepted because of, and to the extent of, the missionaries' willingness to respect this self-image, but to the extent that they and their successors saw the indigenous people merely as objects of evangelism or economic reform there always has been a very stubborn resistance.

See also Malinche and Malinchismo

Select Bibliography

Brooks, Francis Joseph, *Parish and Cofradía in 18th Century Mexico*. Ann Arbor, Michigan: University Microfilms, 1976.

Cordry, Donald, *Mexican Masks*. Austin: University of Texas Press, 1980.

Harris, Max, "*Indigenismo y Catolicidad*: Folk Dramatizations of Evangelism and Conquest in Central Mexico." *Journal of the American Academy of Religion* 8:1 (Spring 1990).

Ingham, John M., *Mary, Michael, and Lucifer: Folk Catholicism in Central Mexico*. Austin: University of Texas Press, 1986.

McKeever, Furst, and Jill Leslie, *The Natural History of the Soul in Ancient Mexico*. New Haven, Connecticut: Yale University Press, 1995.

Parsons, Elsie Clews, *Mitla, Town of the Souls*. Chicago: University of Chicago Press, 1936.

Ravicz, Robert S., *Organización Social de los Mixtecas*, translated by Daniel Cazés. Mexico City: Instituto Nacional Indigenista, 1965.

Ricard, Robert, *The Spiritual Conquest of Mexico: An Essay on the Apostolate and the Evangelizing Methods of the Medicant Orders in New Spain, 1523–1572*, translated by L. B. Simpson. Berkeley: University of California Press, 1966.

Rodríguez, Jeanette, *Our Lady of Guadalupe: Faith and Empowerment among Mexican-American Women*. Austin: University of Texas Press, 1994.

Stephen, Lynn, *Zapotec Women*. Austin: University of Texas Press, 1991.

—Claire T. Stracke and J. Richard Stracke

Popular Liberalism

Nineteenth-century Mexican liberalism is notable both for its constitutional radicalism (in accomplishing, for example, early universal male suffrage, an ample bill of rights, and a federal system of free and sovereign states) and for the success of Liberals after 1867 in monopolizing the political arena. A pantheon of popular patriotic heroes, a leadership of plebeian origin, punitive anticlericalism, and extreme secularism all set Mexico's period of radical liberal rule, the Reforma, apart from its Latin American counterparts (with the exception perhaps of the Colombia of the Rio Negro constitution, 1861–86) in the completeness of its break with the old order. Yet until recently observers generally have accepted that nineteenth-century Mexican liberalism, despite its radicalism and success in reshaping the state, was a minority doctrine formulated by a governing elite distant from, and largely rejected by, a nation composed not of citizens but of members of "traditional collectivities" such as Indian communities. As recently as 1985, the French historian François-Xavier Guerra concluded that popular, democratic liberalism remained a fiction until the Revolution of 1910 finally broke the molds of the ancien régime.

Recently, however, the view that nineteenth-century Mexican liberalism was first and foremost the ideology of a modernizing elite that lacked popular appeal has come under critical scrutiny. This revisionism stems from a methodological shift away from an exclusive focus on national politics toward the study of regions and localities. The new historiography is concerned less with national leaders and intellectuals than with local political leaders (caciques), local intellectuals (such as schoolteachers and evangelical ministers), and nonelite groups (such as peasants, workers, and Indians). Recent scholarship has begun to chart a far more extensive diffusion of egalitarian and democratic ideas, both socially and geographically, than had hitherto been appreciated. As a result, the traditional dichotomy between a modernizing liberal political elite set against a traditional nation lagging behind by half a century has begun to break down. The term "popular liberalism" (not to be confused with the radical liberalism of Jacobin *puros* such as Ignacio Manuel Altamirano and Rafael Ramírez) is now used to refer to this broader, socially more inclusive, "vernacular" liberalism.

Popular liberalism is best understood not as a separate branch of liberalism, but as an eclectic, locally specific variant of the more orthodox national liberalisms, of which three are most commonly identified by historians: moderate, *puro*/Jacobino, and

Conservative-liberal. Popular liberalism refers to initiatives by local leaders and peasant communities to embrace selected aspects of constitutional liberalism, combining the modern, egalitarian language of individual rights with traditional appeals to the paternal responsibility of rulers to subjects. In her pathbreaking *Peasant and Nation: The Making of Post-Colonial Mexico and Peru* (1995), Florencia Mallon uses an analogous expression, "communitarian liberalism," to describe how Indian communities—hitherto perceived either as victims of Liberal Party policies such as the privatization of common lands or, at best, as passive observers of Mexico's civil and patriotic wars—strove to preserve their autonomy and protect their lands by actively engaging with the liberal state (serving, for instance, in the liberal and Republican armies during the Reforma and European Intervention).

Peasant and Nation is one of the first attempts to analyze the process of liberal nation-state building from the bottom up. Mallon's principal subjects are not the national or regional leaders, nor even the local caciques, but the communities themselves. By applying detailed ethnographic knowledge to the politics of the Puebla Sierra between 1854 and 1876, Mallon discerns patterns in the responses of Nahua and Totonac communities of the Puebla Sierra to great regional, national, and even international events. Mallon claims that through a process of negotiation, confrontation, and conditional cooperation with regional and national leaders, Indian communities, with the help of local intellectuals (often bilingual schoolteachers), succeeded in gaining concessions from the liberal state and in modifying the application of the Liberal Party reform program to accord with local needs.

"Communitarian liberalism," as Mallon calls this grassroots movement, appears most clearly in the democratically controlled village National Guard companies and in communal control of the process of land privatization. By analyzing the written correspondence between villages and higher authorities, Mallon demonstrates how communities incorporated modern liberal ideas into an older language that invoked immemorial communal rights and the paternal responsibility of higher authorities to protect obedient and patriotic subjects. This democratic and locally contrived "counter-hegemonic discourse" was sometimes effective at pressing claims of entitlement (to land, tax exemptions, pensions, freedom from military service, etc.).

Popular acceptance of liberal constitutional ideas followed the collapse of royal absolutism with Napoléon's removal of the Spanish monarchy in 1808.

The Constitution of Cádiz (1812) established the right of settlements larger than 500 persons to be represented by elected councils that would exercise autonomous judicial and administrative authority. Indian tribute and compulsory personal services also were abolished. During the insurgency led by José María Morelos y Pavón between 1811 and 1815, such ideas proved attractive to towns and villages throughout central and southeastern Mexico. In spite of the success of the counterinsurgency in 1815 and the suspension of the Cádiz Constitution between 1814 and 1820, a spontaneous process of new municipal foundations continued, especially in the Indian districts of the southeast, where communities had long asserted their independence. Apart from their catalytic impact locally, liberal constitutional ideas also evolved among the intelligentsia and provincial elites, through Agustín de Iturbide's successful revolution of independence in 1821 to make an important impact upon the first federal constitution in 1824. Peter Guardino has shown how beginning in the 1820s, village elders of Indian communities in the southern part of the state of Mexico (now Guerrero) used the traditional language of *común del pueblo* when asserting their new constitutional rights to appoint their own justices of the peace and to establish autonomous municipalities, independent of the mestizo-controlled colonial head towns (*cabeceras*). These villages provided critical support to regional caciques, such as Juan Alvarez and Gordiano Guzmán, who from the late 1830s spearheaded the revival of federalism until the liberal triumph in the Revolution of Ayutla in 1854.

Popular interest in liberal constitutionalism was not confined to rural communities aspiring to greater autonomy from oppressive *cabaceras*. The early introduction of universal male suffrage and frequent electioneering, combined with repeated calls of citizens to arms during *pronunciamientos*, civil wars, and foreign invasions, fostered an important popular urban constituency. Donald Stevens has shown how radical liberals *(puros)* proved more adept at mobilizing this constituency than moderate liberals or conservatives. From the mid-1820s, the spread of Masonic associations, political clubs, cafés, and intellectual circles; the proliferation of popular newspapers and broadsheets; and increasing literacy fostered the beginnings of a secular culture of liberal citizenship among artisans, lawyers, government officials, militia officers, and teachers. Not until the middle of the century, however, is there evidence of any widespread diffusion of a broader liberal discourse beyond Mexico City and the main provincial capitals. The dawning of Mexico's democratic age came following the promulgation of the Liberal Constitution of 1857, with the widespread recruitment of peasants and artisans into National Guard companies during the Three Years War (1858–61) and the French Intervention (1862–67).

The ordinances of the National Guard, formed in 1847 to confront the American invasion, and the Constitution of 1857 made explicit reference to a range of individual rights and guarantees (freedom from compulsory services and forced recruitment, freedom of conscience, and freedom of association and suffrage) as well as to the duties of citizenship (including the obligation of all Mexican males to defend the *patria*). If applied effectively, these two charters would satisfy the desire of peasant communities for reciprocity and equilibrium in their relations with higher authorities. During the 30 years of civil and patriotic warfare in Mexico that followed the U.S. Civil War, especially in regions that experienced intensive military recruitment (such as the sierras of Hidalgo, Puebla, Veracruz, and Oaxaca), villagers became accustomed to negotiating their terms of service to the liberal state, seeing the democratic organization of the National Guard, with its locally elected officers, as the guardian of their constitutional rights. Tax exemption in exchange for military service and the payment of a head tax (*pensión de rebajados*) to avoid forced recruitment were two of the most attractive contracts struck between villagers and liberal leaders. Also attractive to Indian communities was the constitutional proscription of unremunerated compulsory services, compulsory parish dues, corporal punishment, and jails on haciendas. A bedrock of popular liberalism was formed in these Sierra regions, particularly in those district capitals where local Liberal leaders succeeded in applying the Liberal Reform without antagonizing Indian communities, or, in the case of certain villages in the Puebla Sierra, with their active support. This base of support was exploited over a 30-year period by leaders such as Porfirio Díaz and the "Tres Juanes" of the Puebla Sierra (Juan N. Méndez, Juan Crisóstomo Bonilla, and Juan Francisco Lucas) who, after the Revolution of Tuxtepec in 1876, achieved supreme authority on district, state, and federal levels, dividing the spoils among their popular followings; former Nahua guardsmen, for example, were appointed *jefes políticos* (local political bosses) and municipal presidents in the Puebla Sierra between 1877 and 1884.

One such loyal, liberal, National Guard community was Xochiapulco, a municipality of Nahua peasants in the southern Puebla Sierra. Granted municipal status in 1861 for its participation in the Reform Wars, and nationally recognized for the heroic contribution made by its guardsmen to the Republican victory over the French expeditionary force at Puebla on May 5, 1867, Xochiapulco became an exemplary center for the new liberal creed. The community's leaders were no longer village elders and the Catholic priest, as had been the custom in the Puebla Sierra, but younger national guardsmen who doubled as schoolteachers. During the 1870s, village commons and land expropriated by the liberal state government from an unprofitable hacienda were divided among National Guard soldiers and war widows, in accordance with the law of *desamortización* of 1856. Methodist ministers were invited to establish a mission in the municipality. No church was built for the Roman Catholic community, although the images of saints were housed in an unconsecrated chapel. Throughout the reign of Porfirio Díaz, no incidence of consecutive reelection of a municipal president was recorded in Xochiapulco, contrasting with the perpetuity in office commonly found at the state and national levels.

The period from 1854 to 1876 was the high point of popular liberalism. Central authority remained weak. Elites were divided by acute ideological conflict (before 1867 between liberals and conservatives, and after 1867, between centralizing liberals and the eclectic following of Porfirio Díaz). This brought unprecedented competition for popular support and created more space for the satisfaction of popular demands. Florencia Mallon shows how prolonged patriotic resistance against the European Intervention reinforced these demands from communities that had sacrificed their meager resources and native sons in Mexico's Second War of Independence. These three decades have been described by the historian Alicia Hernández Chávez as "a period of expanding citizenship when political representation achieved its strongest popular content ... the strength of the liberal revolution was sustained by this new spirit of collaboration between the people and the elite."

Where Hernández Chávez sees a single, albeit quarrelsome, liberal family, starting to knit together a young nation through common patriotic struggles, a common pantheon of secular heroes, an egalitarian civic vocabulary, and democratic institutions, Mallon observes a fragmented polity consisting of a multiplicity of competing and mutually irreconcilable liberalisms and nationalisms. Whether one sees the conflicts of the Restored Republic (1867–76) as mere family squabbles over spoils or a more profound conflict between a centralizing elite and popular liberal caciques, few would dispute Hernández Chávez's conclusion that the detente between the political elites and the pueblos broke down during the 1880s, as formerly popular leaders such as Porfirio Díaz manipulated the electoral system to ensure their own future power. Dazzled by economic opportunities, elites put aside their differences and distanced themselves from politics, leaving artisans, industrial workers, and villagers without their patrons. Finally, Díaz's successful pacification of the country took away from these groups the lever on power they had exercised through warfare and military service.

The 1876 Revolution of Tuxtepec, which first brought Porfirio Díaz to power, provides a good measure of the popular impact of constitutional liberalism. Porfirio Díaz in 1876 commanded an eclectic following, including many conservatives and former adherents of the French-supported monarchy of Maximilian von Hapsburg. But the core of his support was the state National Guards who embodied the demands of rural communities in the southeast. In exchange for their support for Díaz during the French Intervention and the Revolts of la Noria and Tuxtepec, National Guard companies from the Puebla, Veracruz, and Oaxaca Sierras expected satisfaction of their demands for municipal autonomy and effective suffrage, freedom to divide their communal property as they saw fit, respect for the fiscal immunities of National Guard veterans, and enforcement of other constitutional guarantees, such as the law against compulsory military services. Recent research by Carmen Salinas on the Revolution of Tuxtepec in the state of Mexico reveals that Díaz drew support from a confederation of municipalities enraged by electoral corruption and broken constitutional promises. For a short time after Díaz's victory, there was talk among some *tuxtepecanos* of investing the nation's municipalities with the status of the "fourth power." But once Díaz's generals were in power, neither federal nor state governments showed much interest in a constitutional change that would lessen their control over the unruly territories from which so many of them had recently emerged. In *The Transformation of Liberalism in Late Nineteenth-Century Mexico*, Charles Hale demonstrates how swiftly Jacobin liberalism was displaced nationally by the elitist and positivist doctrine of conservative liberalism, leaving provincial popular liberalisms stranded.

In spite of the authoritarianism and elitism of the Porfiriato, the radical liberalism of Mexico's 1857 Constitution went unaltered, in contrast to the Colombia of Rafael Nuñez, where the radical Río Negro constitution was replaced by a conservative-liberal model in 1886. The survival of Mexico's radical liberal rhetoric was matched by the endurance—indeed proliferation—of pockets of popular liberal mobilization throughout the national territory, often associated with Methodism and working-class radicalism. First identified by the Swiss historian Jean Pierre Bastian, these niches of liberal resistance are the focus of much recent scholarship. The Díaz regime claimed it was still committed to a radical, secularizing, patriotic liberalism that had been forged over the 60 years between the insurgency and the "free suffrage" rebellions of the Restored Republic. These powerful sentiments were continually refreshed through the public patriotic rituals celebrating the birthdays of heroes such as Miguel Hidalgo y Costilla and Benito Juárez and the anniversaries of great events such as the battle of May 5, 1862. This *historia patria* continued to be explained to Mexican citizens and schoolchildren through constitutional catechisms and school texts. Thus, Mexicans needed little justification for rebelling in 1910 against a regime perceived as being unconstitutional and unpatriotic.

The Revolution of 1910 to 1920 produced a new crop of patriotic heroes, reinforced the liberal identity of the Mexican national state, and reinvigorated the myriad of vernacular liberalisms on the local level. Events in Chiapas since January 1994 have confirmed the importance of local perceptions of justice, constitutional rights, and entitlement, the essence of Mexico's popular liberal heritage.

Select Bibliography

Brading, D. A., *The First America: The Spanish Monarchy, Creole Patriots, and the Liberal State 1492–1867*. Cambridge and New York: Cambridge University Press, 1991.

Guardino, Peter, *Peasants, Politics, and the Formation of Mexico's National State: Guerrero, 1800–57*. Stanford, California: Stanford University Press, 1996.

Hale, Charles, *The Transformation of Liberalism in Late Nineteenth-Century Mexico*. Princeton, New Jersey: Princeton University Press, 1989.

Mallon, Florencia, *Peasant and Nation: The Making of Post-Colonial Mexico and Peru*. Berkeley: University of California Press, 1995.

Stevens, Donald Fithian, *Origins of Instability in Early Republican Mexico*. Durham, North Carolina: Duke University Press, 1991.

Thomson, Guy P. C., "Bulwarks of Patriotic Liberalism: The National Guard, Philharmonic Corps, and Patriotic Juntas in Mexico, 1847–88." *Journal of Latin American Studies* 22 (1990).

—GUY P. C. THOMSON

PRD

See Partido de la Revolución Democrática (PRD)

PRI

See Partido Revolucionario Institucional (PRI)

Prints

Since shortly after the Conquest until the present, Mexican artists, politicians, publishers, and clerics have intentionally exploited the unique qualities of printed images to their greatest advantage. In Mexico, perhaps more than in any other country, the identical and reproducible print has been used to address the challenges and needs of the ever-changing society. From mass conversion to the search for national identity and the quest for social justice, woodcuts, engravings, and lithographs have been employed as vehicles for personal and collective expression. Popular devotional images, heraldic devices, portraits, scientific illustrations, and satirical cartoons are just a few of the types of prints that have reflected and molded the society that produced them.

Unlike most European cities, where printmaking grew by accretion rather than by design, the demands of evangelization brought the printed image to Mexico. The earliest works were imported woodcuts brought from Europe by publishers established in Mexico City. Woodcuts were made by the transference of a design onto a block of hard wood, commonly cherry or pear, with the unmarked area cut away, leaving the image standing out in relief. Juan Pablos, Antonio de Espinosa, Pedro Ocharte, and other publishers used the transplanted images primarily to illustrate the early religious treatises written to aid in the conversion of the indigenous population. It is unknown exactly when local production of woodcut book illustrations and single-sheet prints began. Mexican publishers probably turned to local artists to replace worn blocks and to create new images within a period of two decades or less. The first prints that reasonably can be attributed to Mexican artists were those made to commemorate an event celebrated locally, such as the woodcut of the catafalque built in Mexico City for the funeral of King Carlos I (Emperor Charles V), or those that represented the heraldic device of a local figure. In some cases the presence of undeniably Mexican elements, such as the nopal cactus growing out of the hieroglyphic stone in the arms of Archbishop Montúfar in the *Constituciones del Arzobispado de México* of 1556, argues for local execution. Therefore, while the needs of the friars brought the woodcut to Mexico, the recording of local events and the establishment of the political and social institutions encouraged its development and broadened its use in the viceroyalty.

None of the woodcuts made in New Spain during the sixteenth century were signed. The artists who produced these early prints probably came from all sectors of colonial society: immigrant and locally born Spaniards, mestizos, and Indians. The first named *cortador de imágenes* (also called an *imaginero*), or woodcutter, known in Mexico was Juan Ortiz, who arrived from Spain in 1568. In a 1572 Inquisition document, Ortiz was described as a French-born, but Spanish-raised, artist in the employ of publisher Pedro Ocharte. That European printmakers such as Ortiz were joined by indigenous artists is suggested by the mention of a series of woodcuts made by native woodcutters for a book by fray Juan Bautista which, unfortunately, was never published. These native artists were likely trained in the art of woodcutting at ecclesiastical schools, such as San Jose de los Naturales. The education of local non-Indian artists was probably largely informal, as there were no established guilds or academies for the training of printmakers.

Artists contracted with or formed part of the workshops and households of publishers to provide a variety of woodcuts for the book trade. It is believed that most prints made during the sixteenth century in Mexico were intended for this market and few were distributed as single-sheet, loose images. The exceptions were playing cards (which were made locally as early as the 1540s), devotional images, and heraldic devices stamped at the head of official documents. The woodcuts made for books included decorative friezes with vegetal motifs, ornaments to serve as head- and tail-pieces, architectural framing elements for title pages, heraldic devices of individuals and institutions, and representations of saints or other holy figures. Illustrations were sometimes placed within the body of the text, though books with more than a handful of woodcuts were rare. Because the woodcut image stood in relief, it was placed within the typesetter's form along with the typeface and printed as a single unit. Once completed, the woodcuts remained in the possession of the publisher, rather than the printmaker, and frequently were reused for a variety of texts. This system of patronage mirrored the practice in Spain and continued largely unchanged throughout the colonial period and well into Independence.

Much like the architecture of New Spain in the sixteenth century, the style of the early woodcuts defies classification, ranging from Gothic angularity to Renaissance illusionism. The bulk of the prints from this period, however, were made with attention to the naturalistic representation of the human figure and its surrounding space. The debt owed to contemporary late Renaissance aesthetic also was illustrated by the frequent inclusion of classicizing elements, such as acanthus scrolls and putti. This Renaissance spirit sometimes was contradicted by the manner of execution. Line took precedence over modeling, with thick, unvarying hatches and heavy outlines used to describe forms. Volume was created through parallel, arching hatches set against great expanses of uninked paper. Tonal development was only to be found in the work of the most skilled woodcutters. In general, however, the drawing of all but the roughest woodcuts was clean and confident. Though hardly examples of virtuosity, the draftsmanship and technical execution of the Mexican sixteenth-century prints were adequate for the needs of crown, court, and church.

The Flemish artist, Samuel Stradanus, is generally credited with the promotion, if not the introduction, of the technique of copperplate engraving in New Spain. Engraving consists of the incision of a design into a metal plate and was practiced in Europe as early as the mid–fifteenth century. Stradanus is believed to have arrived in Mexico City around the year 1604 bringing with him this more refined printmaking process. Unlike contemporary Mexican woodcutters, but more in keeping with the practice of printmakers in Europe, Stradanus signed his engravings. The works he produced in Mexico City are excellent examples of Baroque printmaking, full of tonal and linear variation, and demonstrating excellent control of the burin used to incise the lines. For the residents of the viceroyalty, the advantage of the engraving lay not only in its elegant and up-to-date character, which was soon exploited for heraldic devices, frontispieces of finer publications and portraits, but also in its ability to create the highly detailed images necessary for scientific and cartographic illustrations. The use of the new technique, however, was slower to catch on when it came to devotional imagery and publications of lesser quality.

Unfortunately, many seventeenth-century engravings of great artistic and historic significance were not signed by the artist. One *abridor de láminas*, or

Anonymous Woodcut of St. Francis from Aqui comienca un vocabulario en la lengua Castellana y Mexicana *by Alonso de Molina (1555)*

Courtesy of the Nettie Lee Benson Latin American Collection, University of Texas, Austin

engraver, who regularly signed his works was Antonio de Isarti, active in the last quarter of the seventeenth century. Isarti designed and engraved the title page and map for the *Crónica de la Santa Provincia de San Diego de México* by Balthasar de Medina, as well as the astronomical illustration of the approach of a comet in Eusebio Kino's *Exposición Astronómica*. The execution of these engravings demonstrated a tentative handling of the burin, but competent draftsmanship and a keen eye for composition. Antonio de Castro, a woodcutter and engraver working between 1698 and 1750, developed a confident treatment of the engraving medium and technical precision approaching that of his European contemporaries. Castro had a number of large and important commissions such as the illustrations for *El sol eclysado,* the 1701 funeral book for Carlos II, and the images of Our Lady of Guadalupe and Juan Diego in the *Poeticum Viridarium* of 1699. Like their

Engraved title page by Samuel Stradanus from Sanctvm Provinciale concilivm Mexici *(1622)*

Courtesy of the Nettie Lee Benson Latin American Collection, University of Texas, Austin

of dense shadows on engraved plates, as etching could be repeated for deeper lines capable of holding more ink. It is also likely that some engraved plates were etched after a run of printing in order to re-cut the lines beginning to lose their sharp edges. For much the same purposes, colonial printmakers may have also used the technique known as drypoint, in which the design was scratched directly onto the plate with a needle.

The seventeenth century also saw the expansion of printmaking beyond Mexico City. The most developed printing center outside of the capital was Puebla de los Angeles. With printing presses established by 1640, Puebla produced fine examples of Baroque printmaking. While some of the images leaving the presses of Puebla may have been executed in Mexico City or made by transplanted artists, several native born engravers are known to have been active. The most talented of the engravers from Puebla were

predecessors a century earlier, Isarti and other printmakers of the seventeenth and early eighteenth centuries continued to be largely self-taught, learning through informal instruction and copying imported prints. In addition to producing book illustrations, engravers of this era made a great quantity of loose, single-sheet prints. These included devotional images and maps, some of which were quite large.

Sometime during the seventeenth century Mexican printmakers began to practice the technique of copperplate etching, in which a design was scratched into an acid-resistant ground allowing only the exposed metal to be etched when the plate was immersed in acid. Though very few pure etchings were made in New Spain during the colonial period, Mexican artists frequently combined the techniques of etching and engraving. In some cases, the more fluid action of the etching needle was used to create curvilinear forms and small designs which Mexican artists found difficult to do with the burin. In other examples, etching was used to create dark tones in areas

Engraved title page by Antonio de Isarti from Crónica de la Santa Provincia de San Diego de México *by Balthassar de Medina (1682)*

Courtesy of the Nettie Lee Benson Latin American Collection, University of Texas, Austin

Miguel Amat, who produced the first engravings in that city in the last years of the seventeenth century, and José de Nava, an extremely prolific artist active between 1750 and 1817.

During the second half of the eighteenth century, the arrival of the first Spanish treatise on the techniques of printmaking helped to improve the quality of printed images produced in New Spain. Manuel de Rueda's *Instrucciones para gravar en cobre,* written in 1761, described the processes of engraving and etching. Perhaps not coincidentally, the second half of the eighteenth century saw a greater degree of confidence and control of the medium in the work of Mexican printmakers. Strong draftsmanship, tonal variety, and greater exploration of the linear possibilities of engraving marked the work of some of the artists of this period, such as Francisco Silverio, José Benito Ortuño, Diego Troncoso, Manuel de Villavicencio, Francisco Agüera Bustamante, and José Mariano Navarro.

Another phenomenon that radically altered the practice of printmaking in Mexico was the establishment of the Academy of San Carlos in 1783. The school was founded by Jeronimo Antonio Gil, an engraver from Madrid sent to Mexico in 1772 by Carlos III to serve as *grabador mayor,* or chief engraver, of the royal mint. Thanks to Gil's background, the academy offered courses in engraving from the outset. In 1788 José Joaquin Fabregat arrived from Spain to serve as instructor of engraving *en lámina,* or copperplate engraving, while Gil continued to teach engraving *en hueco,* or preparation of coins and medals.

The students learned by studying live models in drawing classes and by copying vast quantities of prints imported from Europe. The prints produced by the faculty and students of the academy exemplified the Neoclassical style popular in Europe at the time and technical perfection never seen before in New Spain. The subjects of these works tended to be great events of contemporary or ancient history, portraits, reproductions of famous works of art, and architectural views. Engravers to emerge from the academy during its first years included Tomás Suria, Manuel López López, José María Montes de Oca, Pedro Vicente Rodríguez, Manuel Araoz, and Francisco Casanova. The images produced at the academy were not popular beyond the limited circles of the Mexican elite. This left a large market for traditional subject matter by both academy-trained and self-taught printmakers.

Many of the engravings produced during the last 75 years of the viceroyalty reflected the increasing polarization of Mexican society. The sector of the community that sought the promotion of Mexico as a modern and independent nation spurred an increase in edifying periodicals with scientific and other illustrations, as well as a variety of geographic and architectural studies. Many of these images reflected the criollo interest in the pre-Hispanic past and the promotion of new technologies. On the other hand, a conservative backlash against the enlightened ideas from Europe encouraged the continued production of established themes, such as allegorical images of Spanish imperial ideas, portraits of religious figures, and illustrations of funerals of peninsular dignitaries. Although neither group showed any interest in the state of contemporary Indians, both appropriated the image of the stereotyped native maiden as allegory. Interestingly, artists appear to have had no problem passing between rival camps. For example, Francisco Agüera Bustamante, a self-taught engraver working in Mexico City at the end of the eighteenth century, engraved illustrations for the *Gazeta de México* and its liberal editor José Antonio Alzate as well as for *La portentosa vida de la muerte* by the conservative author Fray Joaquín Bolaños. This ideological neutrality appears to have been owing to the system of patronage, where a printmaker contracted with a publisher rather than directly with the author or editor.

While the economic hardships of the War of Independence reduced the number of commissions for all printmakers, the immediate post-Independence period saw the introduction of the new technique of lithography, in which a design was made with a greasy crayon on a smooth sheet of stone. Lithography was a rapid method for producing great numbers of identical images and, as had happened with the woodcut, the government of Mexico desired the new printmaking technique as a tool in its struggle to create a unified nation. In order to bring this technique to Mexico, the government contracted in 1825 with liberal Italian expatriate, Claudio Linati de Prevost, to establish a lithographic press in Mexico and to instruct local students in the art of lithography. In exchange he received transatlantic passage for himself and his staff, all required materials, and the monopoly on official printing commissions. Linati produced only six lithographs, all for the periodical *El Iris,* during the seven months he spent in Mexico City, but managed to train several Mexican artists, including José Gracida from Oaxaca. Although Linati left the country in 1826, Gracida and other local lithographers worked for studios established in the capital during the 1830s by other foreigners as well as Mexican entrepreneurs. These included the shops of Pierre Robert and Charles

Fournier, Xavier Rocha, Plácido Blanco, and Joseph Antoine Decaen and a series of partners. Ignacio Cumplido, who believed the lithograph to be the most appropriate medium available for illustrating books and other printed materials, established his publishing firm in 1837. Like others, Cumplido saw the grainy quality and tonal potential of the lithograph as the ideal technique for the romantic subjects popular at the time. Also attractive to publishers was the relative inexpense of the lithograph compared to the time-consuming and labor-intensive engraving.

Mexican lithographers working in the nineteenth century produced images mainly for illustrated texts rather than for single-sheet prints. The materials needing lithographic illustrations ranged from calendars and popular magazines to histories and geographic studies of the Mexican terrain. Many of these publications had a decidedly nationalistic flavor and used the lithograph to teach the diverse Mexican populous about their new nation. Hipólito Salazar, working for the studio of Joseph Decaen, produced many excellent works in popular edifying magazines and books, including the twelve illustrations for *Monumentos de Méjico,* published in 1841. Other lithographers who produced illustrations for periodicals and large commissions included Casimiro Castro and Andrés Campillo, who illustrated *México y sus alrededores* (1855–56), and Hesiquio Iriarte, who collaborated with Castro on *Los mexicanos pintados por si mismos* (1854–55). These and other artists worked on a wide variety of topics, from *costumbrista* images of the Mexican people to portraits, landscapes, and cityscapes. Of course, the demand for religious imagery kept many lithographers busy as well.

The quality of the lithographs produced in Mexican studios in the mid–nineteenth century was superb. Excellent draftsmanship combined with a well-developed sense of composition and design to create images of great detail and naturalism. A high degree of care was given to the reproduction of the textures, shapes, light, and colors of the Mexican landscape and people in many of the images. In no way did the reproductive or informative nature of the

Lithograph of the National Theater of Mexico by Casimiro Castro and G. Rodríguez from México y sus alrededores: Colección de monumentos, trajes y paisajes *(1855–56)*
Courtesy of the Nettie Lee Benson Latin American Collection, University of Texas, Austin

Lithograph from La Orquesta *volume 2, number 22 (Saturday, September 12, 1868), plate number 22. In English, the caption says "Quickly, mama, I am freezing." "Have patience, child; I had to warm the clothes for you."*
Courtesy of the Beinecke Rare Book and Manuscript Library, Yale University

prints interfere with their artistry. During this apex of the practice of lithography, it can be said with confidence that the works coming out of Mexican lithographic presses were as fine as contemporary prints from Europe and the United States.

Another role of the lithograph in Mexican society during the nineteenth century was as political commentator. Beginning within two decades after Independence, satire in political periodicals became a tool to inform, educate, and enlighten the public to the corruption and mismanagement of the leaders of the nation. From Antonio López de Santa Anna to Benito Juárez to Emperor Maximilian to Porfirio Díaz, the presidents and dictators of Mexico had their actions analyzed and ridiculed in lithographs and wood engravings circulated in the opposition press. The tradition began in 1842 with *El gallo pitagórico*, which used the lithographs of Joaquín Heredia, Hesiquio Iriarte, and Plácido Blanco to attack the abuses of the dictatorship of General Santa Anna. Later satirical journals, such as *La Orquesta*,

El Padre Cobos, El Ahuizote, and a multitude of shorter-lived newspapers filled their pages with exaggerated and stylized images of politicians, clerics, and military officials. Gradually, these images created a visual language of readily intelligible symbols of Mexican history and politics to represent the different ideas and people that shaped current events.

Because lithographs could not be printed on the presses that produced the text of the periodicals, most editors contracted with outside studios for their illustrations. Even though lithography and wood engraving were taught periodically at the Academy of San Carlos, most printmakers who produced single-sheet images and illustrations for newspapers and other publications were not academically trained. Many of the artists in the lithographic studios in Mexico City felt that the academy and its European instructors were estranged from the Mexican people. Although some artists showed their work at the annual academy exhibition, most eschewed the academic approach and preferred instead compositions with limited space occupied by sketchy figures drawn with expressive distortion.

By the last quarter of the nineteenth century, lithography saw a decline in popularity as new technologies introduced faster and cheaper printed media into Mexico. Artists continued to work in lithography and wood engraving but also produced prints by the processes of lead or type-metal engraving and zinc etching, the latter technique being largely a combination of the principles of etching and engraving in which an acid-resistant ink was used to protect the design during immersion. The images were distributed as loose, single-sheet prints and as book and periodical illustrations. The subject matter ranged from political satire to ladies' fashions. By this date, many at the academy considered printmaking not to be worthy of academic instruction. Few printmakers finished their training at the academy, opting instead for more lucrative employment producing advertisements and periodical illustrations in the opposition or penny press.

The most famous printmaker of the late nineteenth and early twentieth centuries is, by far, José Guadalupe Posada Aguilar, although his fame owes more to his posthumous rediscovery in the 1920s and 1930s and his own remarkable productivity than to any great recognition of his work during his lifetime. Posada began his career as a lithographer in 1868 in Aguascalientes. He worked for the publisher José Trinidad Pedroza producing satirical and religious images as well as illustrations for broadside advertisements. In 1888, he moved to Mexico City, where he worked until his death in 1913 providing illustrations for several periodicals as well as loose, single-sheet images. Although working for any publisher in need of illustrations, Posada produced many prints for the presses of Antonio de Vanegas Arroyo. The subject of his illustrations ranged from strange and sensational happenings in Mexico and abroad to serious news events. Many of his prints have become the enduring images of the Mexico during the Porfiriato and the Revolution. Posada is perhaps best known for the *calaveras* he produced in large part for the Day of the Dead celebrations in Mexico. In these single-sheet broadsides, famous contemporary public figures were pictured as animated skeletons, while the text, frequently in the form of a *corrido* or laudatory song, discussed the *calavera* in the manner of an epitaph or eulogy.

Posada's popular prints, meant for the hands of the masses rather than the salons of the wealthy, set the stage for Mexican printmaking in the post-Revolutionary period. Many of the artists of that era, a majority of whom were communists or adhered to populist ideologies, saw prints as an effective tool through which their programs of education could be disseminated. In 1937, the Taller de Gráfica Popular was founded by Leopoldo Méndez, Raul Anguiano, Luis Arenal, and Pablo O'Higgins. The artists of the Taller worked primarily in woodcuts, lithographs, and linocuts, the latter being a relief image created using linoleum rather than a wood block. According to the artists of the collective, these printmaking techniques, inherited from nineteenth-century popular prints and specifically the work of Posada, were the most appropriate media for communicating Mexican ideas. The goal of the Taller de Gráfica Popular was to educate the Mexican people about the abuses against them. The collective summarized its purpose in its Declaration of Principles. In this document, the group stated that its purpose was the promotion of printmaking as an effective means of helping the Mexican people "to defend and enrich their national culture" by reflecting "social reality of the times." The subject matter reflected contemporary issues, from workers' strikes to anti-fascist propaganda. A popular theme from the outset was the plight of the Indian in Mexican society. The style of the works generally reflected the bold messages through the use of thick lines, reduced compositions for maximum didactic potential, and stark contrasts of light and dark.

Other artistic movements in the twentieth century have continued to use the print as a medium for the dissemination of formal innovations and social commentary. Printmakers in this century have used a wide variety of printmaking techniques, including woodcut, engraving, etching, drypoint, wood engraving, and lithography, as well as screenprinting, in which a design is transferred to the paper through a piece of cloth; monotype or a single impression taken from an inked plate; and aquatint, a process of engraving in which a ground applied to the plate

Skeleton by José Guadalupe Posada Aguilar

creates a chemical reaction and etches a pattern into the metal. A great deal of contemporary work involves the exploration of the unique qualities of the printed medium as art, beyond its capacity as a tool for the dissemination of a social or political message to a wide audience.

Select Bibliography

Ades, Dawn, *Art in Latin America: The Modern Era, 1820–1980*. New Haven, Connecticut: Yale University Press, and London: South Bank Centre, 1989.
Prignitz-Poda, Helga, *El Taller de Gráfica Popular en México 1937–77*, translated by Elizabeth Siefer. Mexico City: Instituto Nacional de Bellas Artes, 1992.
Thompson, Lawrence S., "Book Illustration in Colonial Spanish America." *Book Illustration* (1963).
Tyler, Ronnie C., *Posada's Mexico*. Washington, D.C.: Library of Congress, 1979.

—KELLY DONAHUE-WALLACE

Protestantism

Since the Conquest, Mexico has been primarily a Catholic nation, and Catholicism has informed the totality of social mores and values. Mexican national consciousness has been interwoven with the great symbols of Catholicism, particularly the cult of the Virgin of Guadalupe. All non-Catholic religions therefore have been considered heresy or a penetration of ideas and values that threatened the Mexican nation. Mexicanist historiography has been marked by this legacy, which probably is why the study of non-Catholic religious minorities has interested foreign historians more than Mexican historians. Protestantism in particular always has seemed to be a minor, exotic topic beyond the pale of social history and the sociology of religion. Nonetheless, this has changed in recent years. The exponential growth of new religious movements has forced sociologists and anthropologists to take non-Catholic religions seriously, and a number of historians have been able to demonstrate the importance of Protestant sects in the origins of the Mexican Revolution of 1910.

Lutheranism in the Colonial Imagination

The Lutheran Reform and the Conquest were contemporary events. When Fernando (Hernán) Cortés conquered Mexico-Tenochtitlan in 1521, Martin Luther had just affirmed his definitive break with Rome in the Diet of Worms. The initial Spanish missionary drive in New Spain occurred under the banner of a Catholic reform that sought to construct a renewed Christianity in New Spain. The reformist activity of regular clergy influenced by the ideas of Erasmus of Rotterdam, however, was fought by secular clergy after counterreformist currents in the Catholic Church took the upper hand in the Council of Trent (1545–63). From then on any religious innovation was considered suspect in Spain and its colonies.

The battle against Erasman clergy was prolonged in the systematic repression of other practices and ideas that were considered heretical. In 1571 the tribunal of the Holy Inquisition was established in Mexico City to combat "the sects of Moses, Mohammed, and Luther." The Jews apparently all were converted and Moslems never were present in substantial numbers in Spain's American colonies, however, so the only possible heresy was the "sect of Luther." The struggle against Lutheranism was directed against foreign pirates and corsairs—Huguenot French, Anglican Englishmen, and Calvinist Dutchmen— who had plundered the Gulf coast of Mexico from Veracruz to Yucatán. Toward the end of the sixteenth century a number of foreign pirates were captured and sentenced to die for so-called Lutheran heresy. They were executed or "reconciled" to the Catholic Church in a series of spectacular autos-dafé, which served to inculcate the association between the terms "Lutheran" and "enemy" in the popular imagination.

During the seventeenth century, however, the heretic became more of an internal enemy, particularly with the conviction of Guillen de Lampart, who had been accused of fomenting rebellions against the Crown, of Lutheran heresy in 1649. Nonetheless, the main target of the Inquisition was not men but books. Not only was Protestant theological literature placed on the Inquisition's Index of banned books, but also books written by English and French philosophers whom the Inquisition suspected of promoting Protestant and agnostic heresy. The condemnation of these new ideas helped create an image of the heretic as a non-Catholic as much as a Protestant in the strictest sense of the term.

In the final years of the colonial period, Protestant ideas were condemned hand in hand with ideas from the French Enlightenment, particularly ideas that promoted religious tolerance. This explains why the insurgent priests Miguel Hidalgo y Costilla and José María Morelos y Pavón ended up being condemned as "libertine, seditious, schismatic, formal heretic, Judaizer, Lutheran, Calvinist, suspected of atheism and materialism." In the inquisitorial imagination subversion of the colonial order and non-Catholic ideas were closely related—although in reality Hidalgo and Morelos were faithful Catholics.

By the end of the colonial period, the Inquisition had effectively shut Protestantism out of New Spain. Nonetheless, Protestantism had an important symbolic presence. Protestantism had come to be associated with Spain's political enemies, be they foreign enemies such as England or internal enemies—the partisans of Independence.

Religious Tolerance and the Nation-State

Mexican Independence brought the question of religious tolerance to the fore, but political and religious elites took the hard line adopted in 1812 by the Spanish regent council, the Cortes of Cadiz, which defined Catholicism as a state religion without any tolerance for other religions. For all practical intents and purposes, Catholicism was the only ideological and social force in Mexico capable of maintaining unity in the vast national territory of Mexico, which verged on disintegrating into regional schisms and caste wars that religious pluralism could only reinforce. Nonetheless, the Independent state realized that the question of religious tolerance could not remain closed forever. On the one hand, Mexico was forming commercial ties with primarily Protestant countries, which demanded freedom of religion for their nationals residing in Mexico; after 1830 commercial treaties with England, Germany, and the United States contained clauses stipulating that Protestant services could be conducted for foreigners under the protection of their respective embassies. On the other hand, religious tolerance became a domestic political issue with the publication of *Tratado sobre la tolerancia religiosa* (Treatise on Religious Tolerance), written by Vicente Rocafuerte in 1831. By defending Protestantism Rocafuerte sought to attract European immigration to Mexico, particularly to the sparsely populated north.

Rocafuerte never was able to insert the principle of religious tolerance into the Constitution, despite the interest of a small number of liberal clerics in distributing Spanish-language bibles in Mexico. The most prominent member of this cadre of liberal clerics was José María Luis Mora, a sometime agent of the British Bible Society. In 1827 another member of the society—and a friend of Mora—the Scottish pastor James Thomson, traveled from Veracruz through Puebla and Mexico to Querétaro, distributing bibles and promoting the Lancasterian school, a system of education in which the older and better students teach the younger, less able students. (Thomson also was an agent for the Royal Lan-

castrian Society of London.) Despite their efforts, during the first half of the nineteenth century Mexico remained closed to non-Catholic religions. This situation would not change until the liberal reforms.

Liberal Reform and Protestantism

The 1854 Plan de Ayutla marks a watershed in the history of contemporary Mexico—shortly after the promulgation of the Plan the liberals were able to impose a liberal constitution onto a Catholic country. The Constitution of 1857 was not so radical in terms of religion as it was in terms of politics and economy, still recognizing Catholicism as a state religion and not tolerating any other religion. From 1857 to 1860, however, Mexico was convulsed by a bitter civil war as conservatives and Catholics sought to reverse the liberals' modest gains. The newly radicalized liberal government quartered in Veracruz responded by promulgating its most radical legislation yet, the Reform Laws. The Reform Laws changed the religious face of Mexico, legally secularizing Mexican society and—in the law of December 4, 1860—establishing freedom of religion; in 1873 the Reform Laws were incorporated into the Mexican constitution. For the first time Protestantism legally could be adopted by Mexican citizens.

Nonetheless, Mexicans did not immediately convert to Protestantism in droves. In 1861 and again in 1867 the liberal leaders Benito Juárez and Melchor Ocampo attempted to create a schismatic Catholic Church in Mexico. Approximately 50 schismatic religious societies were established in central and northern Mexico, with a heterogeneous leadership drawn from liberal Catholic clergy, former officers in liberal armies, and artisans. Aside from a few schismatic churches in Mexico City, which tried to follow a non-Roman Catholicism, the schismatic societies were modeled on Freemason Lodges. Nonetheless, the national church enjoyed scant success.

The survival of Protestantism in Mexico would have been precarious indeed if there had not been a convergence between the Mexican schismatics and U.S. Protestant societies that wished to expand their missionary activities in Mexico. The liberal regime of Sebastián Lerdo de Tejada (1872–76) looked favorably on the work of U.S. missionary societies, believing that it was the only way to break the religious monopoly of the Roman Catholic Church. The schismatic Catholic societies regrouped in various Protestant denominations (Methodist, Presbyterian, Baptist, Episcopal, and Congregationalist, among others). The religious dissidents were interested in the economic, organizational, educational, and editorial resources that the missionary societies made available to them, while the Protestant societies were pleased with the relatively rapid spread of a Protestant movement among the anti-Catholic liberal minorities.

The expansion of Protestant societies in Mexico tended to follow the geographical contours of the liberal anti-Catholic minorities, reaching its apogee between 1872 and 1890. Aside from major urban centers and railroad lines, Protestant societies prospered in a number of specific regions where relatively recent colonization, a long liberal tradition, and claims to political autonomy put them in a marginal relationship to their state capitals. The Chalco district in the state of Mexico, the Zitácuaro district of Michoacán, the Huasteca region of Veracruz, Hidalgo, and San Luis Potosí, the northern sierra of Puebla, the mining towns of Zacatecas around the city of Fresnillo, the south-central region of Tlaxcala, the Chontalpa region of Tabasco, the Guerrero district of Chihuahua, and the mining centers of the Sierra Madre Occidental were the principal rural areas in which Protestant ideas and practices were able to make important inroads; there also was a more diffuse propagation of Protestantism in the states of Coahuila, Nuevo León, and Tamaulipas.

By 1892 there were approximately 469 Protestant congregations, compared with approximately 220 Freemason Lodges and 60 Spiritist circles. The Protestant societies had approximately 100,000 members and sympathizers who represented less than 1 percent of the population in 1910. More than absolute numbers, however, it was the networks created by the Protestant societies that reflected the importance of Protestantism in Mexico relative to similar dissident movements. Another feature that distinguished the Protestant societies from other liberal groupings was their important network of private primary and secondary schools, teachers' training schools, and colleges for men and women, which helped form new generations of religious liberals.

Protestantism tended to be adopted by specific occupational categories—agricultural laborers, miners, textile workers, railroad workers, urban white-collar employees, schoolteachers, and small landowners (rancheros); it did not make substantial gains among the criollo (Spanish-ancestry) liberal elites, the traditional urban middle class, and hacienda peons, and it made even less headway among indigenous groups. Converts to Protestantism tended to come from mestizo (mixed-race) social sectors in transition; their economic status generally was precarious and their ideas liberal and anti-Catholic. Indeed,

Protestantism tended to spread in the same areas as Freemason Lodges, Spiritist circles, Mutualist societies (workers' benevolent societies), and liberal political clubs. These "societies of idea," as the French historian François Furet has called them, were a new associative model in a society profoundly structured by traditional religious and political norms. Joining a Protestant society—or any of the other "societies of idea"—was to drop one's inherited corporate identity and become a new type of social actor, the "brother," a member of a society of equals in which part of the sovereignty of every individual citizen had to be expressed by vote.

Religious Opposition to the Porfirio Díaz Regime (1876–1910)

As "societies of idea," Protestant congregations inculcated ideas and practices that anticipated the central political fiction of the conservative liberal elites of the regime of Porfirio Díaz. If the law and the vote were respected formally by the Porfirian regime, in practice they were betrayed and constantly manipulated to assure—under the Porfirian watchwords of "order and progress"—an invidious stability. The Pax Porfiriana became a dictatorship of a small political class that stripped the Mexican people as a whole of their civil rights. The Protestant societies were acutely aware of Díaz's failure to respect the Constitution of 1857, particularly statutes disestablishing the Catholic Church and mandating freedom of religion. Díaz constantly violated the Reform Laws, implementing an active policy of conciliation with the Catholic Church.

The opposition to the Díaz regime grew after Díaz modified the constitution to assure his reelection in 1887. This new opposition would have important consequences for the Protestant societies, which systematically condemned Díaz's policy of conciliating the Catholic Church and his failure to respect citizens' votes. This rejection of Díaz's policies was expressed in the civic-religious holidays (the anniversaries of the signing of the Constitution of 1857, the defeat of the French in the Battle of Puebla, and Mexican Independence, among many others) that were celebrated in Protestant churches, schools, and even the public plazas of the liberal towns that opposed Díaz. Protestantism had become a liberal civic religion.

Protestant religious leaders were quite active in their opposition to Díaz. In 1895 the three most prominent dissident newspapers, *El Monitor Republicano, El Diario del Hogar,* and *El Hijo del Ahuizote,* for the first time pooled their efforts to create the Grupo Reformista y Constitucional (Reformist and

Constitutional Group). The Grupo sought to condemn the visit of the papal nuncio and the consecration of Mexico to the Virgin of Guadalupe and to propose a candidate to run against General Escobedo, who was widely considered to be a Díaz puppet, in the presidential election of 1896. The Grupo failed in these efforts, but its sympathizers helped pave the way for the liberal clubs of 1901. In August 1900 the liberals of San Luis Potosí organized a national congress of dissident liberals, that met in February 1901. Much as the Catholic and the official liberal press accused, many Protestant pastors attended the congress as delegates of local liberal clubs, and the link between political and religious dissent continued to grow in subsequent years.

This link was particularly important during the unrest of 1906, when Protestants became active in anarchosyndicalist labor organizations. In Rio Blanco, the scene of a bloodily repressed textile workers' strike, the Methodist congregation was composed entirely of workers from the textile mill, and the strike was organized from the church. The intellectual authors of the strike were the Methodist pastor José Rumbia Guzmán and the local leader of the anarchosyndicalist Partido Liberal Mexicano (PLM, or Mexican Liberal Party), José Neyra. In 1907 Rumbia Guzmán and Neyra were sent to jail together. Nonetheless, the Protestant minorities generally disagreed with the violence of the PLM and preferred to focus more on instilling democratic ideas in the Mexican public, much as they had done since the mid–nineteenth century. Protestants enthusiastically supported Francisco I. Madero's candidacy for the presidency in 1909, becoming one of the principal social bases of the Maderista cause.

The repression unleashed in the summer of 1910 following Díaz's reelection and Madero's imprisonment in San Luis Potosí seemed to have crushed the anti-reelectionist movement. However, when Madero was able to escape to the United States and called for a national uprising on November 20, the Protestants were among the first to respond. Teachers at the Colegio Metodista were among those arrested in San Luis Potosí, and arms were discovered in the Methodist Institute in Puebla. Liberals and Methodists were arrested throughout the south-central region of Tlaxcala. Madero's revolution seemed to have been stillborn.

In spite of such repression, between November 20 and the early months of 1911, there were two durable foci of resistance. In the Guerrero district of Chihuahua, a more organized armed movement led by the Pascual Orozco Sr. and Pascual Orozco Jr. emerged, and in the Chontalpa region of Tabasco another armed movement was led by Ignacio Gutiérrez Gómez. It was no coincidence that the leaders of both uprisings and much of their network of support were Protestant. The Orozcos had founded the Protestant congregation of San Isidro in 1885, and Gutiérrez Gómez was the pastor of the Presbyterian congregation of San Felipe Río Nuevo. The Protestant affiliation of the Orozcos and Gutiérrez Gómez enabled them to weave broader regional networks and to draw on both liberal and Protestant ideological bases, mobilizing Protestant local intellectuals and members of Protestant congregations.

The social bases of the Revolutionary movement could not be reduced to the Protestant societies, but for more than 40 years Protestantism had formed a specific ideological space for opposition to Díaz's conservative liberalism. As the historian Alan Knight has remarked, "Protestantism could represent the religious face of political dissent: it could chime in with progressive, enlightened liberalism; and it could also reflect, more practically, the educational effort of the Protestant churches, and thus the tendency for the educationally keen and upwardly mobile to turn to Protestantism at the same time as they turned to political opposition." The active participation of Protestants in the Maderista Revolution would not stop growing in the early months of 1911 until the fall of the Díaz dictatorship.

Protestantism and Revolution

The close link between Protestantism and radical liberalism explains the active participation of Protestants in the Maderista democratization. As the Mexican intellectual Francisco Bulnes wrote in 1920 with all the disdain of an educated criollo toward mestizo Revolutionaries, the Revolution had been the fruit of "the anarchist apostalate filled with secondary schoolteachers, Mexican Protestant pastors, penurious journalists, Philadelphia lawyers recently calved from infectious law schools, and greasy, worn out Masons." Although he was a Spiritist and Freemason, Madero was part of the same educated liberal criollo elite and excluded from his government the very new social actors that had put him into power. Indeed, there was a degree of continuity between his administration and the Porfirian regime. The same liberal elites were in power, and the problem of land was not confronted in any substantive manner. Protestants occupied subaltern posts in his government and played a minor role in his administration. (There was a very small number of exceptions on a regional level. In Tlaxcala Governor Miguel Hidalgo and his secretary, José Rumbia Guzmán, were Protestants; both were killed during the military coup against Madero. In Chihuahua the secretary of Governor Abraham González, Braulio Hernández, was a teacher in a Protestant school.)

The military regime of Victoriano Huerta and the Catholic support that he received once again pushed Protestants into the radical liberal opposition, and Protestants took up arms in support of the Plan de Guadalupe led by the liberal governor of Coahuila, Venustiano Carranza. After 1914 Protestants entered the Carrancista Revolutionary movement en masse. As governor, Carranza had developed close ties with Protestant educators and leaders, cultivating the support of Protestant networks, and he continued to make use of these networks in his campaign against the Huerta regime. In 1914 and 1915, Carranza put the Presbyterian pastor and schoolteacher Gregorio A. Velásquez in charge of the Constitutionalist propaganda office. As a Constitutionalist propagandist, Velásquez was able to recruit many of his agents from a regional network of Protestant popular intellectuals, and from 1916 to 1920 he was director of the official newspaper of the Constitutionalist cause, *El Pueblo*. The Carrancista administration filled with Protestant pastors and schoolteachers who represented a new generation of mestizos educated in Protestant schools. Among the most notable was the Methodist Andrés Osuna, whom Carranza put in charge of the Office of Primary Education in the Federal District from 1916 to 1918; the Presbyterian Eliséo García ran the office in 1919. Osuna attempted to reform primary education in Mexico and establish industrial schools, a project that was well ahead of its time. The Presbyterian Moisés Sáenz acted as director of the elite Escuela Nacional Preparatoria (National Preparatory School) from 1917 to 1920, while the Methodist Alfonso Herrera, the former confidential secretary of General Jesús Carranza, was secretary of the National University from 1916 to 1918. It would be impossible to list the numerous Protestants who obtained posts in the Carranza administration. However, in general terms Carranza's moderation in social and religious issues coincided with the liberalism of Mexican Protestants, who generally had little sympathy for the more radical Revolutionary factions of Francisco "Pancho" Villa and Emiliano Zapata.

The Protestants' clientelistic relationship with Carranza meant that after his death in 1920 they lost considerable influence, and they were marginalized during the administration of Álvaro Obregón (1920–24). Nonetheless, they regained their influence during the anti-Catholic *"maximato"* of Plutarco Elías Calles (1924–34), who had business and familial ties with the Protestant Sáenz and Osuna families. Moisés Sáenz was reappointed subsecretary of education and became an important writer on indigenous education and *indigenismo*, a political and intellectual movement that sought a revalorization of Mexico's indigenous peoples. In his books *Carapan* (1936) and *México íntegro* (1939) Sáenz applied the "active pedagogy" of John Dewey and developed a pedagogical method for indigenous education similar to the education he had received in the Protestant school system, a practical pedagogy that emphasized the development of the student's moral sensibility and will. Sáenz opposed José Vasconcelos's pedagogy, which emphasized access to "universal culture" as an integrating force for the Mexican "cosmic race," and the socialist pedagogy of Narciso Bassols, which saw in science the sole salvation of the Mexican people from their religion superstition.

During the 1930s and 1940s the Protestant societies were marginalized by a revolutionary process that had brought profound social and economic changes to Mexico. Their school system was made insignificant by the rapid expansion of public education implemented by the Revolutionary regimes. The social bases of Protestantism had not grown significantly. Many asked whether Protestantism had a future in Mexico. It seemed to have given Mexico all it had to offer, and its associative liberal legacy seemed to have been replaced by narrow religious sectarianism.

The Mutation of Protestantism

From the 1940s on, Protestantism changed drastically, splitting into several different sects. Since the 1920s Pentecostal movements had appeared in Mexico that emphasized glossolalia (speaking in tongues), thaumaturgy (faith healing), and the magical use of the Bible. This type of religiosity had emerged in the U.S. south and from 1906 had spread rapidly among the urban poor. It also reached Mexican migrant farmworkers in the United States, who on their return to Mexico adapted these new religious practices to Mexican ways of thinking. The Iglesia Apostólica de la Fé en Cristo Jesus (Apostolic Church of Faith in Christ Jesus) and the Iglesia de Dios (Church of God) were among the early expressions of this movement, particularly in northern Mexico.

A particularly successful religious initiative was the Iglesia de la Luz del Mundo (Church of the Light of the World) in the outskirts of Guadalajara, which was founded by a migrant farmworker and former soldier with marked indigenous features, Eusebio González, in 1926. Adopting the name Aaron, González built a powerful Pentecostal movement that has

Protestant Population of Mexico, 1900–1990

Year	Total	Percentage
1900	51,796	0.38
1910	68,839	0.45
1920	73,951	0.50
1930	130,322	0.79
1940	177,954	0.91
1950	344,026	1.30
1960	484,489	1.66
1970	728,801	1.82
1980	1,914,919	3.33
1990	3,447,507	4.89

Source: Dirección General de Estadística, *Censos Generales de Población y de Vivienda de la República Mexicana*. Mexico City: Secretaría de Fomento–Dirección General de Estadística, 1900–1990.

continued growing to this day. The Iglesia de la Luz del Mundo has become a transnational religion, winning converts throughout Latin America, the United States, and even Europe and Africa. The church has developed into a typical messianic movement centered on the person of Aaron, who died in 1986 and was succeeded by his son Samuel.

From the 1950s on, Aaron found ample space for his new religion in the outskirts of Guadalajara, the "beautiful province" where the streets were baptized with place-names from biblical Palestine, and was able to gain numerous converts and sympathizers among the newly arrived migrants in the outskirts of major Mexican cities, recreating the traditional rural universe they had lost. Aaron represented the prototypical pastor-patron, an authoritarian religious leader who had emerged from the political culture of corporatism and drew on his charismatic authority to mobilize broad social sectors. With the growing migration to cities and Mexico's northern frontier and the disintegration of traditional rural societies, religious movements of this type had boomed throughout the country, changing the religious face of Mexico.

The decennial statistics from the INEGI are particularly powerful. Whereas in 1960 Protestants were 1.66 percent of the population of Mexico, they had grown to 3.33 percent in 1980 and 4.89 percent in 1990. During the same period the number of people identifying themselves as Catholic declined from 96.48 percent in 1969 to 89.69 percent in 1990. These very broad data tend to obscure a far more complex reality and probably underestimate the number of Protestants in Mexico. The census does not include within the category "Protestant or

Evangelical" the segment of the Protestant population that identifies itself as "none" or "other" to avoid persecution. The census needs to be read more closely, with greater attention to data broken down by state or even by municipality. The percentage of Protestants tends to be above average in three areas: states on the U.S.-Mexican border, the immense conurbation of Mexico City and the surrounding municipalities in the state of Mexico, and southern Mexico, particularly the states of Tabasco and Chiapas. The center-west of Mexico, on the other hand, tends to have far fewer Protestants than other parts of Mexico.

The case of Chiapas is particularly interesting, since according to the 1990 census only 67.62 percent of the population was Catholic and Protestants made up 16.25 percent of the population. If we break the data down by municipality, we see that in three regions of Chiapas—los Altos, la Cañada, and the zone of Mariscal—the majority of the municipalities have less than half of their population defining itself as Catholic and an extremely elevated number of Protestants. This diffusion of Protestantism in these indigenous communities seems significant. Instead of denouncing the "destabilizing penetration" of Protestantism, one needs to understand the proliferation of new religious movements among indigenous groups in Mexico as the expression of an accelerated social differentiation and acute economic inequality. Religious heterodoxy has become a mode of protest against the power of local bosses who use traditional Catholic festivals to legitimate their economic and political power. In many communities indigenous Protestants have been subject to intense persecution and violence ostensibly for not respecting local traditions, showing how threatening religious differentiation is for the caciques who control land and trade. The situation in Chiapas is reproduced with less intensity in other states, where religious dissidence also has marked conflicting political and economic interests.

It is difficult to describe the current situation of Pentecostalism and Protestantism in Mexico. It is composed of dozens of religious societies grouped in broad umbrella organizations such as the Confraternidad Nacional de Iglesias Cristianas Evangélicas (CONFRATERNICE, or National Confraternity of Evangelical Christian Churches). From a sociological point of view, these new churches are religious protest movements that recruit mainly from the poorest sectors of society, which use religion to organize and respond to their economic, psychic, and health problems. At the same time other new religious movements are directed at the urban middle class, which has been affected severely by the economic crisis of the 1980s and 1990s and is attracted to religious models imported from the United States and adapted to Mexican realities. One of these new middle-class religious movements is Nueva Vida para México A.C., founded during the 1980s by the Reverend Armando Alducín. Finding a sympathetic forum in the venerable Mexico City newspaper *Excélsior,* Alducín organized events in major urban hotels. At the same time, to grow numerically the historically middle-class mainline Protestant denominations have adopted many of the features of Pentecostalist and fundamentalist churches, leading to an increased homogenization of Protestant movements in Mexico.

Seeing a possible articulation between marginalized sectors of Mexican society and the disaffected middle class, many Protestant leaders in Mexico have looked to other Latin American countries such as Guatemala, which saw its first Pentecostalist president in 1990, and Peru, which saw a Protestant pastor named vice president in 1991. Since 1992 Evangelical leaders have attempted to create a new political movement, the Grupo Lerdo, and in 1995 the president of CONFRATERNICE announced that he would soon form an Evangelical political party that would compete in the 1997 elections. With more than 5 million Protestants in the country and an additional number of people in non-Protestant sects that respond to the same type of denominational political language, it does not seem impossible that the new political party could gain a degree of political power.

Although it is quite different from the liberal Protestantism of the nineteenth century, Protestantism in contemporary Mexico is also a latent political force. The exponential growth of Protestant churches could serve denominational political ambitions. It also is worth asking if the multiplication of religious denominations could lead to an incipient political pluralism. If this were the case, contemporary Protestant movements would rediscover the fundamental demand for democratization that Protestants fought for during the Porfiriato and that led them to a profound involvement in the Maderista and Carrancista revolutions.

See also Catholic Church; Inquisition

Select Bibliography
Baldwin, Deborah J., *Protestants and the Mexican Revolution, Missionaries, Ministers and Social Change.* Chicago: University of Chicago Press, 1990.
Bastian, Jean-Pierre, "The Metamorphosis of Latin American Protestant Groups: A Sociohistorical Perspective." *Latin American Research Review* 28:2 (1993).
Knight, Alan, "Intellectuals in the Mexican Revolution." In *Los intelectuales y el poder en México*, edited by Roderic A. Camp. Mexico City: Colegio de México–UCLA Latin American Center, 1991.

—JEAN-PIERRE BASTIAN

Q

Quetzalcoatl

Quetzalcoatl is a Nahuatl (Mexica/Aztec) word that means plumage of the Quetzal bird (Quetzalli) snake *(coatl)*. Quetzalcoatl usually is translated as feathered serpent and, given the high value placed on the feathers of the Quetzal bird, can mean precious serpent. In Mexica legends, myth, and artifacts, Quetzalcoatl appears most frequently as the wind god Ehecatl (wind serpent) who brings the rain clouds. Images of Quetzalcoatl abound in codices, carvings, and paintings. He wears his distinctive jewels cut from conch shell, and in his guise as Ehecatl he also wears a conical hat and a projecting mask through which he blows the wind. His temples are round and are associated with the whirlwind.

Images of serpents decked with feathers are ancient in Mesoamerica, the lands of high civilizations stretching from the north of Mexico into Central America. These images appear in the art of the Olmec before 800 B.C., and by A.D. 300 they are ubiquitous at Teotihuacan in the Basin of Mexico. There the serpent of sky water is paired with Tlaloc, the deity of earth and mountain water. Whether all these images refer to the deity known as Quetzalcoatl by the Mexica is difficult to prove.

The cult of Quetzalcoatl emerged at Xochicalco, Morelos, in approximately A.D. 800, and from there it was carried to Toltec Tula in approximately A.D. 900, perhaps by his priest-king and namesake, Quetzalcoatl Topiltzin. With the expansion of the Toltec Empire, the cult of the feathered serpent spread to the south and east of highland Mexico and into the highlands of Guatemala. Representations of Kukulcan, Yucatec Maya for Quetzalcoatl, are abundant in the northern Yucatán Peninsula, particularly at Chichen Itza.

During this militant phase Quetzalcoatl became known as Tlahuizcalpantecuhtli (Lord of the Place of the House of the Dawn), closely associated with warfare and Venus as the morning star. Xolotl, who is associated with Venus as the evening star, served as his animal counterpart, or *nahual*. Quetzalcoatl and the dog-like Xolotl sometimes are considered twins.

By the Late Postclassic period (1350–1521) the god and the priests of the plumed serpent's cult were conflated, a situation that created confusion following the Conquest. In the myths recorded by the Europeans and later written by the survivors of the Conquest, Quetzalcoatl is both the patron of the Toltec priest-king Ce Acatl Quetzalcoatl Topiltzin (One Reed Our Honorable Lord Quetzalcoatl) and a powerful creator-god combining aspects of the sky-dwelling bird with the earth-dwelling snake. He is the *hombre-díos* (man-god) of the Mexica world, tutelary saint of cities and founder of dynasties.

Mythology

In early sources Quetzalcoatl as deity appears as one of the four sons born to the original creator couple. He and his "brother" Tezcatlipoca raise the sky to separate the heavens from the earth. Quetzalcoatl and Tezcatlipoca then play major roles in the four creations and destructions of the living world. Each of these eras was referred to as a "sun."

After the fourth sun was destroyed by floods, and before the fifth sun dawned, the gods met in council to discuss the repopulation of the earth. They agreed that Quetzalcoatl should go to Mictlan, the land of the dead, and bring back the bones of deceased humankind. Although the lord of the underworld tried to stop him, Quetzalcoatl gathered the bones and ran with them to the earth's surface. Having escaped, he took the bones to the earth goddess who ground them in a metate (the traditional stone for grinding corn into meal). He then brought them back to life by offering his own blood.

Once humans had been reborn, the spirits had to determine what they would eat. Quetzalcoatl then changed himself into an ant and brought the gods kernels of maize out of the Mountain of Sustenance.

The spirits found that corn was good, and the Mountain was split, providing all kinds of food for their new creations.

Finally, the gods gathered at the ancient capital of Teotihuacan to create the fifth sun by throwing themselves into a gigantic bonfire. In the version of the five suns creation myth recorded the missionary Bernardino de Sahagún shortly after the Conquest, even after the gods sacrificed themselves and the sun rose, it wobbled about and would not move. Then it was Ehecatl, the mighty wind, who put the sun in motion.

The universal appeal of the myth of Quetzalcoatl probably lies in its promise of rebirth and reincarnation. He is responsible for the resurrection of humankind, is associated with the cycle of maize, and is identified with the cyclical risings and settings of Venus.

Quetzalcoatl Topiltzin

At Tula Quetzalcoatl manifested himself as a priest-king born on the day *"ce acatl"* who took the god's name as his own. He came to symbolize the legitimization of urban power and authority in a world often threatened by the forces of chaos. This phantom person was the leading protagonist in the drama of the rise and fall of the Toltecs and their capital Tollan (Tula).

The historical Toltecs were a heterogeneous amalgamation of peoples representing at least two major ethnic traditions: the nomadic hunters of the northwest (Chichimeca) and the settled agriculturalists of the southeast (Nonoalcas). These two joined forces and ultimately settled on the ridge above Tula de Allende in the present state of Hidalgo. Quetzalcoatl Topiltzin was portrayed as the mediator who bound these two groups together.

The accounts of Ce Acatl Topiltzin's birth are metaphors for the union of warring opposites. In these accounts his father was most frequently named Mixcoatl/Camaxtli, a hero closely related to Tezcatlipoca and the Chichimeca. Mixcoatl was a hunter and warrior who fought his way south and encountered and impregnated a woman named Chimalma, who represents the earth goddesses worshipped by all agriculturalists. Chimalma died in childbirth, and when Quetzalcoatl was a youth, his father was slain. The orphan avenged his father's murder and launched a career that culminated with his call to rule Tollan.

Many tales were told of the sanctity and holiness of Ce Acatl Topiltzin. He was described by the Spanish chroniclers as an honest and temperate man who fasted and preached "natural law." He never married and knew no woman. It is said that he was the first to begin drawing blood from his ear and tongue as penance for sin.

All authors insist that Quetzalcoatl stood against human sacrifice and would only take the lives of such creatures as serpents and butterflies. In fact much of the drama of the events leading to Ce Acatl Topiltzin's departure from Tula lies in his refusal to sacrifice humans despite pressure and demands from sorcerers and demons representing Tezcatlipoca.

The prologue to the defeat of Quetzalcoatl opens with the appearance of Tezcatlipoca at Tula. He changed shape and plotted Topiltzin's downfall by first playing on his vanity and then getting him drunk. Quetzalcoatl, in a happy mood, called for his sister Quetzalpetlatl so that the two of them could drink together. Although she was doing penance she agreed to come to her brother, and when she arrived the demons served her five draughts of pulque. "Having made themselves drunk, they no longer said 'Let us do penance.'. . . No longer did they go out to puncture themselves with thorns."

Quetzalcoatl was so shamed after the night of debauchery with his sister that he immediately prepared for exile from Tula. On leaving he had everything burned and buried, changed the cacao trees into mesquites, and sent away all the precious birds. Then he traveled through the Valley of Mexico and over the volcanoes to become the special patron of the great commercial and religious center Cholollan (modern-day Cholula, Puebla). Finally he arrived at the Gulf of Mexico.

There are two endings to the saga of Quetzalcoatl Topiltzin. In one he cremated himself somewhere on the southern coast of the Gulf of Mexico. The smoke and ashes from his funeral pyre rose into the sky, and he became the morning star. "And they say as he burned, his ashes arose and what appeared and what they saw were all the precious birds rising into the sky." This phoenix-like ending emphasizes cosmology and celestial cycles. Just as the morning star vanishes and then returns, so will the honorable prince.

The second ending of the myth can also be used to predict the return of Topiltzin Quetzalcoatl to reclaim his kingdom. In this version, Quetzalcoatl was swept off to the east on a serpent raft. This version fits rather well with Maya accounts of the arrival of Kukulcán in Yucatán. In fact, the architectural similarities between Tula of the Toltecs and the northern section of the Maya site of Chichen Itza are so strong that some archaeologists have used them to support this ending to Topiltzin's saga.

Given the cyclical concept of time common throughout Mesoamerica, if Quetzalcoatl Topiltzin were born on *ce acatl* then he should reappear on *ce acatl*. In one of the great coincidences of history, Fernando (Hernán) Cortés landed in southern Veracruz on a date *ce acatl*.

This conjunction has been used to explain why Moteuczoma II failed to attack the Spaniards and allowed them to enter Tenochtitlan. Writers reasoned that Moteuczoma II believed that Cortés might be Quetzalcoatl returning to reclaim his rightful place and was duty-bound to receive the Toltec demigod. It is ironic that Toltec Quetzalcoatl, standing for stability and legitimacy and defeated by shape-changer and necromancer Tezcatlipoca, would return to create chaos among the Mexica.

Spanish interpretations of Quetzalcoatl must be disentangled from native sources. It is possible that the myth of the return and the story of Moteuczoma II's belief that Cortés was Quetzalcoatl is sixteenth-century invention. Cortés and his apologists may have had political reasons for bending the Quetzalcoatl legends to their purpose. When the earliest texts and images of the Quetzalcoatl legend are compared with those composed by the later Franciscans, his saintly aspects are considerably diminished.

Quetzalcoatl in the Colonial World

The early missionary priests had religious reasons for adapting the Quetzalcoatl legends to their purpose. These priests were confronted with two problems. The most serious was the question of "the preaching apostles." Christ had sent his apostles into the world to bring the word to all humankind. Had they forgotten the natives of the Americas? Had the devil prevented proselytizing, or more likely, had the archfiend tempted the savages into a second fall?

The second problem was to explain the presence of "Christian symbols" throughout New Spain. In particular the friars thought they saw the Christian cross in depictions of the Mesoamerican world tree. A solution to these problems presented itself: if Quetzalcoatl could be changed from an Aztec dynastic patron with political, military, and priestly aspects to a saintly, pacific, and penitential figure, then he could be transformed into an apostle carrying with him the icons of Christianity.

St. Thomas Apostle became the designated saint, and the apocryphal *Acta Thomae* was studied for evidence that his evangelical mission beyond the Ganges stretched to the Western Hemisphere. It was pointed out that Thomas means twin in Hebrew, and that he was referred to as Christ's twin; this fit well with references to Quetzalcoatl as the precious twin. Finally, since St. Thomas was a sculptor and since the Toltecs were identified as great artisans and crafts-persons, it was likely that Topiltzin would have been

a sculptor, too. The scholar Jacque Lafaye feels that the Quetzalcoatl–St. Thomas conflation is the "most outstanding example of syncretism between the cosmological myths of ancient America and Christianity."

The survivors of the holocaust of Conquest soon were disabused of the idea of Cortés as Quetzalcoatl. However, the belief in the return of a longed-for redeemer remained. For some the mask of Quetzalcoatl became the mask of Christ, the man-god of the Spaniards who sacrificed himself and promised to return. For others new visions and prophecies arose, and miracles occurred in Indian villages where shamans proclaimed new revenants.

As the colonial period moved on, the syncretism that produced St. Thomas–Quetzalcoatl backfired. If the Americas had been visited, proselytized, and saved by a pre-Conquest saint, then what right did the Spanish invaders have to rule in his place? In the late seventeenth century, writer and poet Carlos de Sigüenza y Góngora exalted native histories and the Indian past and called St. Thomas–Quetzalcoatl the Phoenix of the West; he was an American phoenix, equal to any legendary bird of classical mythology.

The criollos' (Spaniards born in the Americas) growing distrust of the *peninsulares* (Spaniards born in Spain) also is exemplified by the Dominican friar Servando Teresa de Mier's 1794 sermon and 1813 dissertation. Mier claimed that the beliefs, the rites, and the codices of the ancient Mexicans proved that Mexico had been evangelized by St. Thomas–Quetzalcoatl before the arrival of Cortés. Such a revolutionary claim could be used to undermine Spain's evangelical mission, its principal justification for the Conquest.

During Mexico's early Independence period (1821–1860), little is heard directly concerning Quetzalcoatl. Some tried to see the midcentury French Intervention and the placing of Maximilian on the throne of Mexico in 1864 as a symbol of the return. Others compared Emperor Maximilian to the false Quetzalcoatl of Cortés and sought instead the return in the triumph of national heroes over foreign "intrusions." However, the cycle was not complete. Three hundred years had elapsed between Conquest and Independence, and another hundred years had to pass before the specter of Quetzalcoatl returned to his homeland.

Quetzalcoatl in the Contemporary World

Following Mexico's twentieth-century social revolution, an artistic revolution exploded. *Indigenismo* triumphed, and the image of the feathered serpent was used to symbolize the true spirit of the Mexican people overcoming centuries of oppression and banishment.

Writers joined with artists in this celebration of *mexicanidad*. For some Quetzalcoatl came to symbolize the tragic human condition; he was transformed into a myth with which Mexicans could easily identify. Others saw Quetzalcoatl as the great moral hero of ancient Mesoamerica and emphasized that the freedom Quetzalcoatl brought to the world was the light of education, in the writer Carlos Fuentes's words, "a light so powerful that it became the basis for legitimation of any potential successor state to the Toltec legacy."

Mexican artists who took the image of Quetzalcoatl to heart made his legend the theme of their paintings. José Clemente Orozco's mural *The Epic of American Civilization* in Dartmouth College's Baker Library illustrates both the coming and departure of Quetzalcoatl. Orozco saw a parallel between the legend of Prometheus and that of Quetzalcoatl. In both cases the hero sacrificed himself for humankind, was punished by the gods, but remained unbroken in spirit.

Better known are Diego Rivera's panels on the staircase of the National Palace in Mexico City. He painted the *Legend of Quetzalcoatl* as a mythic dreamland and contrasted it with the anarchy of the Conquest. In Fuentes's words, "The work of Diego Rivera reflects the theocratic Indian and Hispanic nostalgia for order and symmetry." Certainly throughout the chaotic history of Mexico, the solace of Quetzalcoatl was more than welcome.

A more recent example of the enduring symbolic power of pre-Hispanic myth was painted by Rufino Tamayo on the walls of the National Museum of Anthropology in Mexico City. Here the full cosmic significance of Quetzalcoatl is summarized in a single monumental icon: the feathered serpent and the jaguar Tezcatlipoca locked in eternal combat backed by their day sun and night sun.

Tamayo's image is a reminder of the continuing relevance of the Quetzalcoatl myth. Quetzalcoatl represents the golden age; subsequently he was defeated by Tezcatlipoca and the forces of chaos. However, hope lies in regeneration, in the reestablishment of order despite the recognition that it will ultimately falter. Like Quetzalcoatl in Tamayo's mural, the forces of light are locked in an eternal battle with the forces of darkness. But, as the myth insists, if defeated they shall return and triumph once again.

Select Bibliography

Bierhorst, John, *The Mythology of Mexico and Central America*. New York: Morrow, 1990.

_____, translator, *History and Mythology of the Aztecs: The Codex Chimalpopoca*. Tucson and London: University of Arizona Press, 1992.

Brundage, Burr Cartwright, *The Phoenix of the Western World: Quetzalcoatl and the Sky Religion*. Norman: University of Oklahoma Press, 1982.

Carrasco, Davíd, *Quetzalcoatl and the Irony of Empire: Myths and Prophecies in the Aztec Tradition*. Chicago: University of Chicago Press, 1982.

Diehl, Richard A., *Tula: The Toltec Capital of Ancient Mexico*. London: Thames and Hudson, 1983.

Durán, Fray Diego, *Book of the Gods and Rites and the Ancient Calendar,* translated and edited by Fernando Horcasitas and Doris Heyden. Norman: University of Oklahoma Press, 1971.

Fuentes, Carlos, *The Buried Mirror: Reflections on Spain and the New World*. New York: Houghton Mifflin, 1992.

LaFaye, Jacque, *Quetzalcoatl and Guadalupe: The Formation of Mexican National Consciousness 1531–1813*. Chicago: University of Chicago Press, 1976.

Nicholson, H. B., "Religion in Pre-Hispanic Mexico." In *Handbook of Middle American Indians*, vol. 10, edited by Gordon F. Ekholm and Ignacio Berna. Austin: University of Texas Press, 1971.

Thompson, J. Eric, *Maya History and Religion*. Norman: University of Oklahoma Press, 1970.

—DONALD MCVICKER

R

Radio

Despite the growth of television, radio continues to have the widest reach and greatest penetration of any mass medium in the country. Radio broadcasting in Mexico operates as a marketplace, a vehicle for state propaganda, an educational tool, and a public medium for political and cultural expression. Over its 70 year history, the unique structure and content of the Mexican broadcasting system has been shaped by two key forces: the commercial imperatives of the radio industry and the hegemonic project of the Mexican state. Whether in conflict, competition, or consensus, the interaction of these two social forces has been the most significant influence on the development of Mexican radio.

The Beginning of Broadcasting: The 1920s

From Mexico's first radio transmission in 1908 until the end of World War I, radio remained a means of point-to-point communication or "wireless telegraphy." At the end of the war, engineer Constantino de Tárnava and Dr. Gómez Fernández were among the first to experiment with voice broadcasting. In 1923 the Secretaría de Comunicaciones y Obras Públicas authorized the first nonexperimental broadcasting stations, and by the end of the year four commercial stations and three government stations were on the air; 16 stations were broadcasting by 1926, and 19 by 1929, the year Mexican stations received the "XE" and "XF" call letter designations. As these figures suggest, the broadcasting market remained limited during the 1920s: only an estimated 25,000 radio sets were in operation in 1926, with the majority located in Mexico City and other large urban areas.

Mexico's early broadcasting entrepreneurs financed their stations with capital accumulated in related fields, such as newspaper publishing, electronics, and retail sales. The first commercial station, CYL, was launched by Luis and Raul Azcárraga, retailers of U.S. radio parts and receivers, in partnership with the Mexico City newspaper *El Universal*. Another early station, CYB (later XEB), was started by a cigarette company, El Buen Tono, with French financial backing. From the beginning, broadcasting was dominated by a small group of entrepreneurs who drew on foreign capital and aligned themselves with powerful financial and industrial families in Mexico.

Because of the newness of the medium and the small number of available stations, many radio listeners used their receivers to search the airwaves for distant radio signals throughout the 1920s. As regular radio programming developed on local stations, it assumed a predominantly elite cultural orientation. Content was dominated by "potted palm" orchestral music, consisting largely of fox trots and tangos, along with European art music. By the late 1920s a modicum of Mexican popular music could be heard over local stations, particularly the pioneering state-operated stations that aimed at the broadest base of Mexican listeners. Station CZE (later XFX), run by the Secretaría de Educación Pública, for example, disseminated popular music along with health information, lectures, art music, and "cultural propaganda."

The Regulatory Framework

Mexico's first radio regulations were forged within a complex environment of post-Revolutionary state-building, economic nationalism, and U.S. imperialism. Therefore, the evolution of the Mexican radio system must be situated within the hemispheric struggle over electronic communications that characterized the 1920s. As the European hold on Latin American communications weakened in the years following World War I, the U.S. government and radio interests (especially the newly formed Radio Corporation of America, RCA) began a concerted effort to shape Latin American broadcasting along U.S. commercial lines. At the 1924 Inter-American

Conference on Electrical Communications held in Mexico City, however, this offensive met resistance from economic nationalists and European-oriented Latin American delegates who favored a government-directed broadcasting model. Against U.S. opposition, the delegates resolved that electronic communication media were public services over which national governments held direct control. These resolutions, which also included a pledge to promote free competition whenever feasible, became the basis for Mexico's first radio law of 1926.

The 1926 Ley de Comunicaciones Eléctricas (LCE, or Law of Electical Communications) and the 1931 and 1932 revisions of the Ley de Vías Generales de Comunicación (LVGC, or Law of General Communications) established a mixed system of commercial and state broadcasting. The 1926 LCE declared the airwaves to be a national resource, allowed only Mexican citizens to own or operate radio stations, and prohibited any transmissions that attacked state security, public order, or the established government. The LVGC replaced the system of one-year licenses required by the 1926 LCE with a system of concessions lasting up to 50 years. Concessionaires were required to carry all government broadcasts free of charge, and faced various content restrictions, including a prohibition against political or religious transmissions and a limit on advertising time. Further regulations, established in defense of "the national culture," required stations to broadcast only in Spanish and prohibited radio studios from being located on foreign soil. In practice, the regulatory framework established under the post-Revolutionary regime of Plutarco Elías Calles (1924–34) ensured the rapid development of commercial broadcasting while giving the state a privileged position of access and control within a highly nationalistic broadcasting system.

Commercial Consolidation and State Activism: The 1930s

Radio broadcasting took off in the 1930s. Between 1930 and 1935 the number of radio stations climbed to over 70, and the number of radio receivers grew to an estimated 200,000 sets. By the end of the decade, over 120 radio stations were broadcasting in Mexico, and the number of radio sets was estimated between 300,000 and 600,000. The number of government-operated radio stations reached a peak of 14 during these years.

Although many prominent regional stations began operations during the early 1930s, Mexico City became the undisputed center of commercial broadcasting. At the epicenter of national broadcasting stood radio entrepreneur Emilio Azcárraga, who started radio station XET in Monterrey just months before opening station XEW in Mexico City in 1930. Station XEW, "La Voz de América Latina desde México" (the Voice of Latin America from Mexico), soon became the most powerful, and most popular, radio station in the country. By the late 1930s, Azcárraga and his company, the Mexican Music Company (an RCA subsidiary), had organized an XEW network encompassing 14 regional stations. In 1938 he founded another flagship station in Mexico City, XEQ, and began to build a second national network. Mexican networks were very different from U.S. networks during the 1930s and 1940s, however. Because of the lack of infrastructure and the prohibitive cost of telephone lines, Azcárraga did not regularly use telephone connections to distribute to his affiliates. Instead, he simulated a broadcasting by shipping recorded programs between affiliate stations.

Along with the rise of the Azcárraga group, the late 1930s witnessed the consolidation of the commercial broadcasting industry as a whole. In 1937 a group of powerful regional broadcasters formed the Asociación Mexicana de Estaciones Radiodifusoras in order to improve their representation in the capital. Mexico City broadcasters soon gained influence in the organization, however, and the name was changed to the Asociación Mexicana de Estaciones Radiodifusoras Comerciales (AMERC). AMERC became a powerful lobbying organization for the industry, and the main force behind the establishment, in 1942, of the Cámara Nacional de la Industria de la Radiodifusión (CIR, later CIRT).

In part, the consolidation of the commercial radio industry was a response to the rise of state activism in radio broadcasting. As the federal government worked to broaden its political power during the early and mid-1930s, it became increasingly active in radio as both a broadcaster and a regulator. For example, the number of government-operated broadcasting stations exploded during the 1930s. The most important were run by the ruling Partido Nacional Revolucionario (PNR, later the PRI), the Secretaría de Educación Pública (SEP), and the Departamento Autónomo de Prensa y Publicidad (DAPP). Although not technically state-owned, PNR station XEFO began broadcasting in 1931 with the explicit goal of increasing national solidarity and building party organization. XEFO provided the first radio coverage of a presidential campaign in 1933, and continued as a strong voice for state and party interests until it went commercial in 1939. SEP stations XEFX (XFX) disseminated educational material, government propaganda, and cultural programming from its first broadcast in 1924 (as station CZE) until the mid-1930s. After station XFX went off the air, DAPP station XEDP became the primary government outlet. One of the DAPP's most ambitious efforts was *La Hora Nacional,* which debuted in 1937 as a weekly program of national music, drama, history, and government reports. Transmitted from station XEDP and broadcast over XEW's powerful radio transmitters, every station in the country was required to re-broadcast the program. After the DAPP disbanded in 1939, production of *La Hora Nacional* continued under the control of the Ministry of Gobernación (Interior).

State regulatory activism also reached a peak in the mid-1930s under the Cárdenas Administration (1934–40). In 1936 the state promulgated the Reglamento de las Estaciones Radiodifusoras Comerciales, Culturales, de Experimentación Científica y de Aficionados, which continued the ban on political broadcasts and expanded government control over radio content in two major ways. First, the law increased the amount of government programming that commercial stations were required to broadcast to 30 minutes per day. Second, the state required all stations to include a minimum of 25 percent *música típica*—typical Mexican music of folk or indigenous origins—in every broadcast. Although commercial broadcasters protested this regulation and asked for more flexibility in presenting music of Mexican authorship, officials argued that the regulation was necessary to promote and defend the national culture. The 1942 revision of the Reglamento continued these specific content requirements.

Another major regulatory initiative, the revision of the 1932 LVGC, was spearheaded by the director of the Secretaría de Comunicaciones y Transportes, General Francisco Múgica. Initially, Múgica proposed the creation of a national network of government broadcasting stations financed by a European-style subscription system. His plan to nationalize the radio system was soon modified, however. By the time it reached the Cámara de Diputados (the lower house of the Mexican legislature) in 1937, it had been reduced to a proposal for a federal commission to regulate commercial broadcasting and a tax on radio receivers to help support cultural stations. Indeed, after considerable industry lobbying, the LVGC that emerged from the Cámara in 1939 was quite favorable to commercial interests. The law directly benefited the broadcasting industry by removing import duties on radio parts and equipment, and the Comisión Consultiva de Radio, initially established to examine the problems of commercial broadcasting, became a means of industry influence over the regulatory process.

Overall, the decade was an extremely innovative period for radio content. Beginning in the early 1930s, government stations disseminated a nationalistic musical content consisting of Mexican art music (especially music by Carlos Chávez and Silvestre Revueltas) and the popular music of regional *orquestas* (orchestras) and *conjuntos* (musical groups). The prevalence of government stations, together with the 25 percent typical Mexican music requirement, created a climate that promoted national musical forms over the radio medium. Commercial broadcasters found that Mexican singers and musicians, performing popular Mexican tunes, provided the ideal radio content to satisfy state nationalism and to capture the national broadcasting market. For example, during the mid-to-late-1930s, musical programming comprised over 90 percent of station XEW's prime-time schedule, with Mexican *orquestas* dominating. These *orquestas,* featuring performers such as Jorge Negrete, Agustín Lara, Pedro Vargas, and Toña de la Negra, were conducted by Mexican composers such as Tata Nacho and Alfonso Esparza Oteo. Although dramatic series were less prominent than music during the 1930s, the period witnessed the birth of radio's most important dramatic genre: the *radionovela* (radio soap opera).

By the end of the decade, a combination of commercial initiatives and government activism produced a unique national radio content. While the state's promotion of a nationalistic cultural content clearly was designed to strengthen its hegemonic position in civil society, the project also meshed well with the entrepreneurial undertakings of Mexico's leading broadcasters. By 1940, the state largely had stepped out of radio as a broadcaster in its own right, but it remained a restrictive regulator vis-à-vis political content and a permissive regulator vis-à-vis commercial content.

The Golden Age of Radio: The 1940s

The 1940s were characterized by the hegemony of the Azcárraga group and the increasing popularity of the radio medium. Over the decade, the number of commercial stations climbed from 126 in 1941 to 195 in 1950, and the number of radio sets grew from an estimated 600,000 to almost 2 million. Assuming approximately six listeners for every radio receiver, a 1943 survey indicated that over 90 percent of the populations of Monterrey and Torreón had regular access to radios, compared to 79 percent in Guadalajara, 68 percent in Mexico City, and only 33 percent in Puebla and Morelia. Although the vast majority of radio listeners continued to be located in urban areas, radio penetration varied considerably from city to city.

Commercial broadcasting became increasingly concentrated and centralized during the 1940s. In 1941, Azcárraga and his partner, Clemente Serna Martínez, consolidated the XEW and XEQ networks into one company, Radio Programas de México (RPM). By 1942 the combined RPM networks included over 60 stations—almost half of all the stations in the country. By the mid-1940s, RPM had over 30 affiliates in Central America, the Caribbean, and the northern rim of South America. Crowning Azcárraga's empire was the construction in 1948 of the massive Radiópolis (later Televicentro) headquarters in Mexico City. Radio networks also proliferated outside of the Azcárraga group. In 1942 station XEOY, Radio Mil, organized a network of 25 stations and became a leading competitor to the Azcárraga group. Radio Mil developed a market niche with a focus on sports programming and, in 1949, switched to an all-news format. Other prominent chains were station XEB's 20-station network, and Cadena Radio Continental's 23-station network.

Although several radio scholars contend that Azcárraga's stations were effectively controlled by U.S radio networks during the 1930s and 1940s, available evidence does not support this claim. For example, there is no evidence of specific affiliation agreements until 1940 and 1941, and these agreements were extremely limited. The U.S. Columbia Broadcasting System (CBS) contracts were for five years and required each affiliate to broadcast just one hour of network programming daily, while the National Broadcasting Corporation (NBC) agreements were for one year and had no programming requirement. In addition, regular telephone line links were never established between U.S. networks and Mexico City stations, and shortwave radio connections proved to be undependable and of poor quality. Overall, the available network agreements suggest superficial "prestige" arrangements between U.S. networks and the Azcárraga group, rather than an effort to develop Mexican stations as regular outlets for U.S. radio programming. Other Mexican networks had similar arrangements, including Radio Mil with the Mutual Broadcasting System, and Cadena Radio Continental with the British Broadcasting Corporation (BBC).

Beginning in 1942, the chief organ of the radio industry, the CIR, developed very close and mutually beneficial relations with the central government. The state took steps to protect the radio industry from wartime shortages, and in return the industry promoted the nationwide literacy campaign initiated by President Manuel Avila Camacho (1940–46). In 1946 members of the CIR organized the Asociación Inter-Americana de Radiodifusoras (AIR) with the aim of unifying continental radio legislation in order to strengthen commercial broadcasting throughout Latin America. At the second conference of the AIR in Buenos Aires in 1948, delegates drew up the Bases de la AIR, a set of principles for shaping broadcasting legislation in the region. These principles conceptualized broadcasting as a fundamentally private activity undertaken in the public interest. The main thrust of the document was to limit the powers of the state by invoking the free speech rights of broadcasters. According to the Bases, government regulations should be limited to the technical aspects of broadcasting, and the state should be prohibited from using commercial radio channels except for official bulletins, weather reports, and emergency broadcasts. In addition, the state should be prohibited from competing with private broadcasters for advertising dollars. Perhaps the most important goal of the AIR was less openly articulated: to ensure that the commercial model would be the dominant model for the new medium of television.

The institutionalization and consolidation of commercial broadcasting was favored by the administrations of both Avila Camacho and Miguel Alemán (1946–52). With state controls over the political content of broadcasting firmly in place, government leaders felt content to leave the further development of the radio medium in commercial hands. While the 1939 LVGC and the 1942 Reglamento kept many strong state regulations in place, they also made the system more amenable to the industry. The 1942 Reglamento, in particular, established a new tolerance for non-Spanish language broadcasting. The law permitted up to 50 percent of advertisements to be in foreign languages, and made it possible to broadcast an unlimited number of non-Spanish language programs with special government permission. In particular, the ruling allowed Mexican broadcasters to import recorded programs from abroad, a possibility that would take on new significance with the beginning of the Second World War.

World War II brought several important developments in Mexican broadcasting, with mixed effects. The most significant event was the propaganda offensive aimed at Mexico by the U.S. Office of the Coordinator of Inter-American Affairs (CIAA). Although U.S. networks had begun broadcasting to Latin America by shortwave in the mid-to-late-1930s, these operations were inhibited by the lack of market development, prohibitive regulations, and the limits of shortwave technology. After the outbreak of war in Europe in 1939, however, the U.S. government used the offices of the CIAA to subsidize commercial broadcasting to the region. Under the direction of Nelson Rockefeller, the agency used a combination of shortwave broadcasts, recorded radio programs, and local broadcasts (together with a host of other media) to disseminate unprecedented quantities of pro-US propaganda throughout Mexico and the rest of Latin America.

While greatly strengthening the position of U.S. advertisers in the Mexican broadcasting market, the CIAA also enhanced the position of the Azcárraga group by relying heavily on the XEW and XEQ networks as the most effective channels for reaching the Mexican radio audience. The agency incorporated its propaganda messages into programs of Mexican music and produced short dramatizations for presentation at strategic points in Azcárraga's prime-time line-up. Ultimately, the CIAA found that the best way to convey its pro-U.S., Pan-American propaganda was to assimilate it to Azcárraga's popular programming content. At war's end, the CIAA took over the shortwave radio operations previously run by CBS and NBC. In 1948, the CIAA Radio Division was transferred to the U.S. State Department, where it became the Voice of America broadcasting service.

Ironically, then, the flood of U.S. wartime propaganda, and U.S. dollars, helped to usher in a golden age of Mexican radio broadcasting. During the 1940s, musical variety programs and *radionovelas* of a distinctly Mexican pitch became the institutional and economic mainstay of commercial radio. While entertainment genres solidified and matured, content innovation took place elsewhere. In Mexico and around the world, the war years saw the rise of broadcast news, propaganda, and political commentary programs. Wartime news shows like *La Interpretación Mexicana de la Guerra*, sponsored by the Mexican Committee of the CIAA, became fixtures during the decade. These brief news programs, broadcast every evening during prime time and anchored by a well-respected commentator, inaugurated a new kind of broadcast journalism in Mexico.

The Center Versus the Regions: The 1950s
The decade of the 1950s witnessed steady growth and consolidation in the radio industry. The number of commercial radio stations increased from 201 in 1951 to 332 in 1959, while the number of radio receivers climbed from just over 2 million in 1952 to over 3 million by the late 1950s. A sign of the postwar maturity of the radio industry was the

formation of labor and professional organizations, including the creation of the Sindicato de Trabajadores de la Industria de la Radiodifusión, Televisión, Similares y Conexos (STIRT) in 1947, and the Asociación Nacional de Locutores de México (ANLM) in 1951. At the national and international levels, the CIR and the AIR continued to influence radio regulations and shape the development of the broadcasting industry. The AIR, in particular, stepped up its opposition to government broadcasting in the region and actively intervened in Argentina, Brazil, Cuba, and Guatemala to defend the prerogatives of commercial broadcasters.

Despite the presence of television and frequency modulation (FM) broadcasting, traditional amplitude modulation (AM) broadcasting continued to grow and expand during the decade. Although the first FM station, XHFM Radio Joya, went on the air in 1953, the take-off of FM broadcasting was hampered by a lack of compatible radio receivers; and by 1959 only 8 FM stations were on the air. The Azcárraga group, in particular, continued to build its AM radio empire. Early in the decade, RPM increased its national broadcasting coverage by buying out two independent networks, Cadena Radio Tricolor (XEBZ) and Cadena Azul (XEX). By 1956, RPM's international activities also had increased significantly: its Latin American network had grown to 80 affiliates, and it began exporting programs to Spain. In addition to the vast RPM networks, three new networks emerged during the period: Rafael Cutberto Navarro's 40-station Radio Cadena Nacional; Cadena Independiente de Radio's 25-station network; and the 23-station network of Red México.

As Mexico City–based networks explored new strategies for reaching regional listeners in the early 1950s, the long-standing tensions between central networks and regional broadcasters rose to the surface. The focus of the conflict was the networks' decisions to install *repetidoras* (repeater stations) in several provincial cities, including Guadalajara, Monterrey, Oaxaca, Veracruz, and Jalapa. *Repetidoras* provided no local radio service and supported no local staff, but simply rebroadcast network programs that were received from the center via telephone lines. As such, *repetidoras* were perceived as a serious threat to regional broadcasters' audiences and advertising revenues. Faced with such a challenge, regional broadcasters banded together to form a Comité Coordinador de Radiodifusoras de los Estados. The *comité* conducted letter-writing campaigns to the president, lodged complaints with the CIR, and spoke out at CIR meetings. At a national CIR assembly in Jalapa, convened specifically to address the *repetidora* issue, a sign was hung over the door of the meeting hall declaring: *"Señores Asambleístas: Bienvenidos. No queremos repetidoras"* (Gentlemen: Welcome. We do not want *repetidoras*).

By 1957, however, neither the CIR nor the government had taken any steps to halt the proliferation of *repetidoras*. Following the policies of recent governments, the administration of Adolfo Ruiz Cortines (1952–58) supported commercial broadcasting initiatives and minimized government activism. Indeed, without its own broadcasting outlets, the state was itself dependent on commercial networks to reach a national radio audience. From the perspective of the central government, then, *repetidoras* promised to improve both the reach of government broadcasts and the integration of the regions into the national domain. The CIR, for its part, worked to diffuse the *repetidora* controversy by drawing regional broadcasters' attention away from the *repetidoras* and toward the need for a new national radio law that would clarify and codify current broadcasting practices. The favorable economic environment also served to diffuse the regional challenge: the 1950s were such profitable years for radio broadcasters of all sizes, that the grave economic impact of the *repetidora* stations simply never materialized. Although tensions between the regions and the center continued, industry centralization remained unstoppable.

Regulatory Codification: The 1960s
Overall, the 1960s were a period of tremendous growth for the industry. Radio's potential audience exploded during this period; between 1960 and 1970 the number of receivers increased from almost 3 million to over 14 million—278 radios for every 1,000 inhabitants. The overall structure of the industry did not change dramatically: the industry remained highly centralized, with roughly 68 percent of gross income going to the top 20 percent of broadcasters. However, the makeup of the dominant broadcasting group did change, as new players filled the gaps created when Azcárraga's attention shifted increasingly to television. Important new chains included Sociedad Mexicana de Radio, S.A. (SOMER), Asociación de Concesionarios Independientes de Radio (ACIR), and Organización Impulsadora de Radio (OIR), which would be highly influential for decades. Organización Estrellas de Oro also would begin to flex its provincial muscles. Meanwhile, television posed a growing threat. While still a medium of limited penetration, television was nevertheless disproportionately profitable. By 1968 television's profits had already come close to equaling those of radio.

Regulatory structures established during the administration of Adolfo López Mateos (1958–64) firmly supported industry growth along commercial lines, although the state did not entirely abandon its nationalist cultural project. The promulgation of the Ley Federal de Radio y Televisión (LFRT) in 1960 marked the completion of a decades-long effort to fully institutionalize the commercial model advocated by the broadcasting industry. This regulatory regime, which would remain in place for decades, reflected several of the principles advocated by the AIR in the late 1940s. Of central importance was the LFRT's adoption of the AIR's characterization of radio broadcasting as an activity undertaken "in the public interest," rather than as a "public service" in itself. This redefinition of broadcasting sharply constrained the government's ability to regulate the industry. For example, under the LFRT, the government was no longer allowed to set maximum advertising rates, but only minimum rates. In addition, broadcasters were allowed considerable latitude in balancing programming and advertising, with the only requirement being the maintenance of a "prudent equilibrium" between the two. The industry did not hesitate to take advantage of these permissive regulations, sometimes devoting more than 20 minutes of every hour to commercials.

At the same time, the new regulatory regime did grant a significant degree of power to the state. The LFRT asserted a strong national interest in broadcasting as a form of national patrimony, and placed regulatory power in the hands of the ministries of Comunicación y Transportes (SCT), Gobernación, and Educación Pública (SEP). The state also occasionally sought to pressure the industry via public statements and newspaper advertisements that berated the industry for its failure to promote national morality and culture. Yet, while Article 5 strongly encouraged broadcasters to valorize national culture, protect public morality, and educate the public, it did not actually "require" them to do much more than provide daily news programming. In sum, while the state refused to abandon its nationalist project, the industry retained a great deal of latitude under the LFRT, interrupted periodically by state propaganda campaigns designed to encourage broadcasters to fulfill their public obligations.

Toward the end of the decade, however, deepening political, economic, and social crises seemed to spark renewed state interest in radio as a vehicle for developing social consensus. As the administration of Gustavo Díaz Ordaz (1964–70) began to reassert itself as a broadcaster and regulator, relations between the state and industry appeared increasingly strained. In 1967 the government reopened the SEP radio station as station XEEP, Radio Educación, a move that indicated state commitment to cultural broadcasting. In 1968 commercial broadcasters vigorously protested further government intervention in the form of a new law that imposed a 25 percent tax on radio services. The state responded by offering to subsidize the tax in exchange for increased government control over those radio services deemed to be in the public interest, an offer that the industry rejected. Within a year, however, state and industry representatives were able to negotiate an agreement that allowed stations to pay the tax in time instead of money. Thus, the 1969 agreement apportioned 12.5 percent of the broadcast day to the state, but did not allow that time to accrue if not fully used. The same year, the state renewed virtually all current licenses, in accordance with Article 16 of the LFRT, which required that preference be given to current license holders in renewal decisions.

Conflict and Reconciliation: The 1970s

The industry continued to expand in this period, although market penetration did not increase as dramatically as it had in the previous decade. By the end of the 1970s, the audience grew to 20 million, while the total number of stations increased by over 25 percent. Control over the airwaves remained highly centralized, with 61 percent of all stations in the hands of 6 major consortia. Radio's expansion was also highly uneven in geographic terms; by 1981, almost 70 percent of radio stations and 70 percent of radio audiences were located in only 12 states.

Under increasing pressure from television, radio broadcasters looked to new technologies to increase their markets. One major area of expansion in this period was FM radio. Until the late 1960s, FM was seen as primarily a space for a kind of "cultural" radio, emphasizing uninterrupted and "ambient" music for hotels and restaurants. In 1970 the Association of FM Broadcasters (ARFMB) was formed to advocate a more commercial FM model. The ARFMB promoted FM radio heavily, encouraging the manufacture of FM-receiving radios and simultaneously pitching the medium to advertisers. By 1980 the number of FM stations had more than doubled (from 65 to 174), and the commercial model of FM radio was firmly in place.

The decade also was marked by the state activism that characterized the late 1960s, with resulting clashes between the state and the broadcasting industry. Indeed, the administration of Luis Echeverría (1970–76) publicly challenged commercial broadcasters. Intensive propaganda campaigns were

mounted during his administration, with the state accusing the mass media of consumerism and immorality, and even threatening nationalization. The industry, in turn, accused the state of socialist sympathies and censorship. However, periodic closed-door negotiating sessions between state officials and CIRT representatives suggest that relations between the state and industry were less hostile than public statements would imply. Government campaigns may have served primarily as public relations tools and mechanisms for negotiating with the industry, rather than serious attacks on the commercial broadcasting model.

Actual regulatory efforts were indeed less confrontational, but the state continued to express a strong national interest in broadcasting. In 1971, Echeverría established the Subsecretaría de Radiodifusión within the SCT to act both as a regulatory arm of the state and as a central coordinator of state broadcasting activities. In 1973, the Reglamento de la LFRT was published, a document which reaffirmed the state's position as a regulator while continuing to assure the primacy of the commercial model. In keeping with a renewed commitment to social consensus and "the national culture," the state asserted its power to monitor the morality of the stations, and added a variety of clauses that affirmed the obligation of industry to promote the national interest; for example, by stimulating the consumption of national products. Content controls intended to promote national culture were loosened, however, and the percentage of programming required to be of national origin was decreased to 10 percent from the 30 percent level required in 1961. The law also clarified the "prudent equilibrium" to be maintained between advertising and programming. In radio, 40 percent of air time could be devoted to advertisements, with 12 interruptions per hour permitted for programs of continuity (for example, *radionovelas*) and 15 interruptions per hour permitted for non-continuous programming (for example, music). In sum, the Reglamento was the final plank of the *"formula mexicana,"* creating a combination of state and private ownership, with the state able to claim 12.5 percent of commercial broadcasting time as official time.

The transition to the administration of José López Portillo (1976–82) was one of open reconciliation, as industry leaders publicly expressed their full support for the PRI candidate. This period of calm was short-lived, however, as broadcasters clashed with the state again in response to new media regulations that accompanied the political reforms of 1977–79. Arguing that the mass media needed to recover their educational, social, and democratic character, López Portillo's Plan Basico de Gobierno announced a reorganization of Article 6 of the Constitution of 1917 to include an explicit *"derecho a la información"* (right to information). The parameters of the law remained unclear, however, and by 1980 broadcasters and politicians began to demand clarification of the clause. Did the right to information create a positive state power to improve public access to the airwaves, or did it imply *freedom* from state controls over public expression? Debates raged in the Cámara de Diputados and in the press for several months. In the end, the proposed right was never clearly defined and became, effectively, a "dead letter" law. However, the second aspect of the proposal, which guaranteed access to the mass media for all political parties, went virtually unchallenged. In 1977 the federal electoral code was changed to require that official time be set aside for the use of political parties. Parties also were permitted to buy commercial advertising time, and stations were forbidden from charging higher rates for political advertisements. More than 50 years after the birth of broadcasting, then, the state's moratorium against "politics over the airwaves" finally was broken.

In addition to these political changes, technological developments—from the rise of television to improved recording techniques—had a profound impact on the overall content of radio programming. Recorded programs increasingly displaced live radio, and many radio actors shifted to television. Most notably, this period saw the beginning of decline of one of the characteristic art forms of radio: the *radionovela*. This genre, which infused the U.S. commercial format of the daytime serial with the melodrama of Mexican popular theater, religion, and music, was immensely popular in the 1930s, 1940s, and 1950s. *Radionovelas* usually centered around archetypal melodramatic characters such as the macho male, the fallen woman, the misguided youth, but also included biographical and biblical tales, and even dramatic presentations of contemporary works of literature. Major stars of the genre included Carlos Chacón Jr., José Antonio Cossio, Carmen Madrigal, and Alicia Montoya. Major sponsors included Colgate and Palmolive. Although the story of San Martin de Porres garnered the highest ratings in radio history in 1963, by the end of the decade fewer and fewer *radionovelas* were being produced. In 1977 only 27 percent of stations polled included *radionovelas* in their daily schedule, and a 1981 poll reported that 93 percent of all stations did not broadcast *radionovelas* at all. In part, the decline of the *radionovela* reflects the prohibitive cost of these productions when compared to the costs of recorded musical programming.

Crisis and Response: The 1980s

During this decade, commercial and noncommercial broadcasters began to speak to new audiences, using both old and new technologies. An important industry trend was the use of satellite technology to broadcast both nationally and internationally. In 1986 Organización Estrellas de Oro was the first to solicit a transponder on the Morelos I Satellite, which it used to establish two radio systems: NOTI-SAT, for news and information, and SUPERESTELAR (1988), which emphasized popular music. Other broadcasters quickly followed suit. Some chains also began to target the U.S. Spanish-speaking population. By 1991, 35 stations in 13 U.S. cities received the news programming of Cadena Radio Centro, a U.S.-based network owned by the Aguirre Jiménez family (also owners of Organización Radio Centro and the OIR network).

The administrations of López Portillo and Miguel de la Madrid (1982–88), meanwhile, took steps to significantly increase state presence on the airwaves by establishing two federally sponsored networks: Grupo IMER, sponsored by the Instituto Mexicano de la Radio, and Radio Cultural Indigenista. These networks were part of a tremendous increase in noncommercial radio, as the number of such stations doubled between 1981 and 1991 (from 47 to 100). In addition to the federal government's efforts, several state governments also sponsored radio networks or cosponsored IMER stations, most notably Nuevo León, Tabasco, and Hidalgo.

The IMER was founded in 1983 as part of a group of semi-independent public cultural organizations dedicated to national integration and cultural decentralization. Despite the call to decentralize, Grupo IMER began building its network in Mexico City, taking over operation of XEB, "la B Grande," one of the first stations in Mexico. By 1995 the network comprised 19 stations scattered throughout the country, with each station receiving some programming from Mexico City headquarters. Following a "mixed" economic model, Grupo IMER relied on both public funding and ad sales for support. According to their official mandate, the stations were required to include 32 percent nonmusical programming. In practice, few achieved that goal, although many did endeavor to fulfill their "cultural" obligations by emphasizing traditional Mexican music.

Radio Cultural Indigenista (RCI), an indigenous language network, was sponsored by the National Indigenous Institute. Its first station, XEZV, la Voz de La Montaña, began broadcasting from Tlapa de Comonfort, Guerrero, in 1979. Buoyed by funding from PRONASOL (Programa Nacional de Solidaridad), the network grew to encompass 17 stations by 1995, with broadcasting service in 28 languages, including Spanish. Its stated mission was the promotion of indigenous language and culture, as well as government programs for indigenous peoples. Indigenous participation was also an important goal of the network. In 1995 the staff was composed of approximately 85 percent bilingual indigenous people, although one recent study suggests that they tended to be relegated to lower-level positions. RCI stations were important communication centers within their regions, transmitting messages to and from dispersed family members, coordinating relief efforts in times of natural disaster, and promoting indigenous cultural traditions. However, scholars suggest that the stations sometimes also have served as spaces for the construction of a narrow and rather limited view of indigenous culture. Nevertheless, the network appears to play an important role in valorizing indigenous culture and giving indigenous people a voice.

In addition to government-sponsored stations, Mexico also had a small but vibrant tradition of independent community radio. These stations were either fully funded by listeners or relied on a variety of foundations for support. Most of these stations were committed explicitly to a model of participatory radio and endeavored to make the stations available for discussions of local political and social issues. Station XEYT, Radio Cultural Campesino (RCC) in Teocelo, Veracruz, for example, trained community members in all aspects of running the station and was one of the few stations entirely dependent upon donations, volunteer labor, and minimal paid announcements. But RCC and other community stations were hard hit by Mexico's economic crises. In response to this situation, communication activists in the 1990s began to argue for changes to Mexico's communication law to allow "permissioned" radio to sell advertising. Under the LFRT, radio stations are divided into several major groups: commercial, official, cultural, experimental, and radio schools. Commercial stations receive a "concession" license and are permitted to sell advertising time. The rest receive permits, which may be withdrawn if commercial announcements are transmitted by the station. The "mixed model" stations of Grupo IMER, considered a kind of federal reserve, represent a major exception to this regulation.

University radio was another major source of noncommercial programming and one of the oldest forms of cultural radio in Mexico. Radio UNAM (once XEXX, now XEUN) was founded in 1937, and several others were founded in later years, of which seven remained operational in 1969. The decade of the 1970s was a period of major growth for university radio, as the number of stations doubled during the decade. In the 1980s and 1990s, however, that growth slowed. Several universities have applied for permits, but the state has granted fewer licenses in recent years. The university stations also have come under criticism for their minimal coverage of political and social issues and their general failure to provide a meaningful alternative to commercial radio. On the other hand, budgetary constraints have sharply limited the production options of these stations.

Although the state sharply increased its broadcasting activities, the 1980s saw few significant regulatory changes. As the decade came to a close, however, political activists redoubled their efforts to reform and modernize the LFRT. A major bone of contention was the potential renewal of 421 commercial licenses. The state was legally required to favor license holders, but opponents argued that, given the intense concentration of radio ownership (15 groups then controlled 80 percent of all stations), renewal was tantamount to affirming the oligopolistic structure of the industry. These arguments failed to persuade state regulators, however, and virtually all of the licenses were renewed.

The latter half of the decade witnessed a visible shift in the form and content of radio news programming. News reporting in Mexico often had been constrained by government pressures, practices of self-censorship, and an uncritical reliance on official sources. In the late 1980s, however, critical political voices slowly began to make their way onto the airwaves. The change may have been the inevitable result of the renewed political crisis and political opening of the late 1980s, but analysts also mark the Mexico City earthquake of 1985 as a turning point. Radio played a central role in coordinating relief efforts, and several stations opened their microphones for community announcements, both official and civil. These emergency measures may have been educational both for broadcasters and listeners, reminding them of radio's potential "public" function.

Overall, however, this new openness in news programming remained constrained by a variety of institutional and political practices. Journalistic agendas continued to be set by state activities and coverage of nonofficial sectors remained minimal. In 1986 coverage of government sectors occupied 17 to 20 percent of program time in a survey of six major stations in Mexico City, while labor and "private" activities received 2 to 5 percent and 5 to 8 percent of program time, respectively. As in the past, official statements often met with little critical investigation. In addition, news programs throughout the nation tended to stress national rather than local news. This was due in large part to the traditional use of national and international news agencies as a major source of copy. Principal news agencies included NOTIMEX, INFORMEX, the Associated Press, Reuters, and United Press International. In addition, several chains carried their own national news programs, the most prominent being Radio Red's star news program, *Monitor*. Overall, Mexico City–based news reporting, now broadcast via satellite, dominated the national airwaves and set the tone and agenda for regional programs.

Radio in Transition: The 1990s and Beyond

Radio's penetration remained high in the 1990s, with at least one receiver in over 95 percent of Mexican homes, but the economic crisis of 1994 put tremendous pressure on the industry. Faced with declining revenues (down 15 percent in 1995), owing in part to shrinking advertising budgets and the continuing competition of television, commercial radio has responded with a wave of buyouts, mergers, and consolidations. In 1995 Mexican radio was more centralized than ever, with the majority of the country's 1,977 stations owned by the 10 largest consortia.

The harsh economic climate has prompted renewed interest in technological innovation. Some broadcasters have invested heavily in new technology to increase the reach of already existing stations. Others have continued to explore the potential of satellite technology. Solidaridad I was launched in 1993, followed two years later by Solidaridad II. These satellites were based on improved technology that permitted better and clearer signals with a wider range. Indeed, Solidaridad II allowed broadcasters to reach all of Mexico and 23 other Latin American countries.

Regulatory strategies remained largely unchanged in the 1990s, despite occasional protests from activists and industry executives. Negotiations over the North American Free Trade Agreement, which went into effect in 1994, sparked concerns that Mexican mass media would be overwhelmed by U.S. cultural products. However, in partial response to pressures from Canada, mass media were largely exempted from the agreement. Mexican law reserved the right to broadcast for Mexican citizens. The LFRT remained firmly in place, with minimal changes since

the 1974 Reglamento. It seems likely, however, that the state will eventually be forced to overhaul its regulatory regime in order to reflect recent changes in radio and television.

Major programming innovations during the 1990s included the growth of the talk show format, which became a regular feature on many stations, and ongoing efforts to expand news programming. In addition, the trend toward more critical radio news coverage continued, although practices of self-censorship were still widespread. Overall, recorded music continued to dominate the airwaves, in accordance with what one survey reported to be the preference of 72 percent of the Mexico City audience. The 1990s also saw a rise in English language stations in Mexico City. In 1995 three stations in the capital carried broadcasts in English, including rebroadcasts of U.S. network news.

As the century drew to a close, Mexican radio entered a new period of transition. Although buffeted by economic crises and competition from other communication technologies, radio remained a vibrant medium in Mexico. The major forces shaping its development remained unchanged, as did its fundamentally oligopolistic structure. The Mexican government's more conservative economic policies, combined with broadcasters' efforts to carve a niche within the global economy, suggest that the state may come to play an increasingly minor role in radio's development. Alternatively, increasing political and social challenges from rival political parties, persistent economic crisis, and the influx of foreign culture accompanying free trade policies may prompt the state to renew its activist stance and continue the pursuit of its nationalist hegemonic project within the broadcasting arena.

Select Bibliography

Barbour, Philip L., "Commercial and Cultural Broadcasting in Mexico." *Annals of the American Academy of Political and Social Sciences* 108 (March 1940).

Hayes, Joy Elizabeth, "Early Mexican Radio Broadcasting: Media Imperialism, State Paternalism, or Mexican Nationalism?" *Studies in Latin American Popular Culture* 12 (1993).

—JOY ELIZABETH HAYES AND CORYNNE MCSHERRY

Railroads

During most of the nineteenth century, Mexico had a highly inefficient communications system. The country's difficult topography, the absence of navigable rivers, and the gradual deterioration of the colonial roads proved large obstacles for communication and transportation. Compared to many other countries, Mexico introduced railway technology very late. The first rail concession was granted as early as 1837, but the 264-mile (425-kilometer) railroad was not completed until 1872. The delay put Mexico behind other Latin American countries: around the mid-1870s they already had built 4,000 miles (7,000 kilometers) of track, as opposed to Mexico's 400 miles (600 kilometers).

This situation helps one understand the significance that political elites of the nineteenth century gave to railroad expansion and the excessive hopes they placed on railroads as the tools to economic development. This attitude also explains the special role given to the first rail line, the Ferrocarril Mexicano (Mexican Railroad), which linked Mexico City to Veracruz, the main gulf port. The original concessionaries of this project failed, and it was finally completed by a British firm. Although this firm had been on friendly terms with Emperor Maximilian, President Benito Juárez renewed their concession after the fall of the empire; the president even gave the company subsidies amounting to 30,00 pesos per finished kilometer of track. Once the Ferrocarril Mexicano opened for service, however, it charged such high fares that it barely had an edge over traditional modes of transportation that used muleteers and carriages. Nevertheless, the firm enjoyed a near total monopoly in the region until the 1890s.

The backers of the Tuxtepec Revolt that brought Porfirio Díaz to power in 1876 also fostered railroad construction by promoting federal and state coinvestments. Between 1877 and 1880 at least 30 concessions were granted, although with only limited success. Mexico still did not have anything even remotely approaching an integrated railway network. Only eight of these first concessions—approximately 125 miles (200 kilometers) of track—were even partially completed, and these local and regional networks were never connected. Recent research has underscored the inadequacy of this strategy of internal financing. Capital still tended to be invested in other sectors, and railway development was further hampered by a lack of cost-effectiveness planning.

The only remaining financing alternative, foreign capital, initially was out of the question owing to the nation's instability and nonpayment of the external debt. Two factors, however, changed the situation: the normalization of U.S.-Mexican relations and the competition among U.S. firms whose tracks were advancing toward Mexico. Given the impossibility of turning to European financing in the mid-1880s,

the Mexican government gave U.S. firms important concessions that would determine the future of railroads in the country. The first concession allowed the Mexican Central Railway to build a line between the capital and Paso del Norte (now known as Ciudad Juárez) and a transcontinental line that would end in Tampico, on the Gulf of Mexico. The second concession authorized the Mexican National Construction Company (later Mexican National Railway) to build a second international line between the capital and Laredo, Texas, on the northern border, and also a second track toward the sea, which never prospered. Their competitor, the Mexican Central Company, later acquired the concession of the Sonora Railway, allowing them access to the Pacific by means of the port of Guaymas.

These concessions had more sensible conditions than President Benito Juárez had given to Mexican Railway. Subsidies were limited to 8,500 pesos per kilometer, a cap was placed on train fares, and the railroads and their properties were to revert to the nation in 99 years. These stipulations were approved in 1880, initiating Mexico's true railroad era. In 1884, when the new trunk line of the Central Railway was completed, 3,500 miles (5,700 kilometers) of track had been built, and by the end of the decade, the company had extended its lines to Guadalajara and Tampico, and the National Railway had finished the Mexico City–Laredo Track.

Two other important projects were begun in the 1880s. The Interoceanic Railway was to compete against the Mexican Railway and was finished in 1891 thanks to British investment. The concession for the International Railway was given during the presidency of Manuel González (1880–84), and it was built by the U.S. magnate Collis Potter Huntington from the Mexican-U.S. border to Durango. Although the participation of Mexican investors was marginal, there were two exceptions worth mentioning: in the Yucatán Peninsula, regional capitalists built a dense system of tracks that linked the ports with the sisal plantations, and in the state of Hidalgo, Gabriel Mancera obtained from state authorities the concessions for his Railway of Hidalgo and the Northeast, with more than 125 miles (200 kilometers) of track under his administration. The construction of the railway network continued in the 1890s. In 1894, after many fruitless years, the Interoceanic tracks of the Isthmus of Tehuantepec finally were completed using public resources, although the railway line eventually was leased to a private company in the late 1890s after it had generated less revenue than expected. Rail lines also were completed between Monterrey and the Gulf of

Mexico, and between Pueblo and Oaxaca. In short, by 1898 Mexico had approximately 8,000 miles (13,000 kilometers) of track, the capital had been linked to all main ports and borders, and the most important cities had access to railway service (with the exception of those cities in the southern and Pacific states).

Nevertheless, the railway system had serious deficiencies, the worst being the lack of a uniform system that would enable efficient connections among the different tracks. Concessions did not prescribe a standard gauge, with the result that by the end of the century 36 percent of the lines were of narrow gauge. This disparity was only partially remedied when the National Railway modified the width of their gauges in the early years of the twentieth century.

The publication of the General Railway Law of April 1899 introduced a new stage in the government's railway policies, which became more restrictive. Concessions were limited, and only those lines seen as vital to the system's improvement were subsidized. Under this law a new railroad connecting the Isthmus of Tehuantepec with the Guatemalan border was constructed, the Central line was lengthened to the Pacific port of Manzanillo, and the Sonora Railway was extended to the southern part of the state, financed by the U.S. firm of Southern Pacific.

During the first decade of the twentieth century the Mexican government found it increasingly difficult to regulate competition among railroads in Mexico. Moreover, it feared that the precarious financial situation of some railroads placed them at risk of absorption by U.S. conglomerates. By 1910 the Mexican government had acquired a majority interest in the Central, National, International, and Interoceanic Railways. This process, known as the "Mexicanization" of the railways, completed the integration of the various railway companies into a single corporation under state control known as the Ferrocarriles Nacionales de México (National Railways).

In 1910, the Mexican government had under its jurisdiction almost 12,500 miles (20,000 kilometers) of track, of which 5,300 miles (8,500 kilometers) belonged to the National Railway; however, the old problem of the lack of standardized gauge had not been fully solved, and many tracks considered vital under the criteria of the 1899 law had not been built. Some deficiencies were particularly prominent: there was not a single railroad track in the whole peninsula of Baja California, an area of 54,000 square miles (140,000 square kilometers). The long-standing isolation of the central plateau from the coasts had been solved with the construction of rail links to the Gulf Coast and to the port of Manzanillo on the Pacific Coast. Nonetheless, there were enormous parts of the country, extending from Chihuahua down to Oaxaca, that were still cut off from the coast. Moreover, there still was no overland transport between the Yucatán Peninsula and the rest of the country.

Despite these deficiencies, the railway system had made significant progress over the state of land transportation that had existed as late as 1880. According to the historian John Coatsworth, the existence of a railway system contributed social savings to the Mexican economy of at least 29 percent of the increase in the national revenues and at least 36 percent of the increase in productivity between 1895 and 1910. These figures only take into account railroad cargo. In the year 1910 alone, the social savings derived from cargo transported by railroad represented at least 11 percent of the gross national product (Coatsworth, 1981). Paradoxically, however, this same interpretation minimizes the economic benefits of railroad communication by introducing negative factors: capital flight and growth geared toward the exterior.

Previous critiques of the system, which emphasized its high subsidies and capital flight in the form of dividends and interest payments, have been called into question by recent research that has concluded that federal railroad subsidies contributed only one-fourth of construction costs, and the total amount of capital flight was 10 percent of the value of all Mexican exports between 1908 and 1911 (Riguzzi, 1995). Judging from this perspective, it can be said that the cost of the railway system was relatively small in comparison to its benefits.

The traditional view of railroad-led economic growth also has been a matter of debate in recent years. The opinion that a high percentage of rail cargo was composed of mineral products destined for export has been put in doubt by empirical evidence, which shows that in the early 1900s approximately 80 percent of rail cargo was used to supply internal markets and industries. However, more recent research also has shown that the impact of railroads varied from industry to industry. The industries that benefited most tended to be those with low unit value—such as construction materials, coal, coke, and mineral ores—which could not have been transported economically without railroads; these sectors accounted for almost 50 percent of all rail cargo in 1907. There also was considerable regional variation. One-third of all railway stations on the Central Railway accounted for 92 percent of all rail cargo, while 67 stations did not account for even 3 percent of all tonnage. This variation can be explained in part by railway stations' proximity to forests and mineral deposits, but in many cases the railways themselves helped reinforce demographic, manufacturing, and commercial concentrations.

The outbreak of the Mexican Revolution produced no immediate effects on the railroads. In the case of the National Railway, the fusion of many lines during the "Mexicanization" of the railroads had lowered administrative costs and eliminated redundant lines built for the purposes of competition. The crisis began to be felt only after the fall of President Francisco I. Madero in 1913, when railroads started to play a strategic role in the armed conflict. Military leaders soon learned that control of railroad tracks meant control of the territory they served; in addition, railroads could move troops and their supplies and hold back the enemy. Thus, railroads became the Revolution's favorite vehicle and obeyed the leader who controlled them. Starting in 1914, most railroad companies were confiscated by Constitutionalist forces under Venustiano Carranza, who eventually returned them to private ownership.

Railway service suffered the wartime destruction of tracks, bridges, deposits, and supplies. Gross income on the National Railways, the main railroad company, fell from 61.5 million pesos in 1911 to less than 2 million in 1914. Transportation tonnage fell one-third between 1910 and 1913 and only recovered to its previous levels in 1924. The armed conflict also caused a fragmentation of the territory, reflected in the decrease of the average distance of cargo transportation from 224 miles (360 kilometers) in 1910 to 145 miles (234 kilometers) in 1913.

The Revolution started the deterioration of the Mexican rail system in several ways. The physical destruction of rail lines and the decline in rail service was complicated by the postponement of reconstruction efforts and the political manipulation of the state-controlled railway companies. The Ferrocarril Nacional survived in a state of permanent insolvency and for all practical purposes defaulted on its international credit obligations. Starting in 1920, the political and organizational forces of the unions worsened the company's situation even more because it had to employ more workers than actually were needed. Some positions received disproportionate wages, even higher than wages for similar positions on U.S. railroads. The ambiguous relationship among the railway administration, organized labor, and the state effectively blocked any comprehensive renewal of Mexico's national rail system, opening the way for a breakdown in the chain of command, indiscipline, and corruption.

Nonetheless, the deterioration of the Mexican national rail system ran much deeper than this. After 1910 the rail system was characterized by a lack of growth in almost all sectors. From 1910 to 1990, less than 2,700 miles (6,000 kilometers) of rail lines were added to the more than 12,500 miles (20,000 kilometers) that had been constructed before 1910, and most of these were made up of auxiliary tracks and did not extend the rail network. The ratio between rail track and population dropped from a maximum of 1.45 kilometers for every 1,000 inhabitants in 1920 to less than 0.33 in 1990. The only truly important projects undertaken during this period were the completion of a railway linking the Yucatán Peninsula and Baja California to mainland Mexico, as well as the completion of a rail link between Chihuahua and the Pacific coast. More recently the route between Mexico City and Veracruz has been modified, and two-way tracks have been added between Mexico City and the north-central city of Querétaro.

The rail system also lagged technologically. As late as the mid-1950s Mexican railroads depended largely on obsolete steam locomotives; only 37 percent of Mexico's engines were diesel powered. The rail lines themselves and the support infrastructure also were completely inadequate for higher volumes of traffic. In addition to its long-standing labor problems, the rail system's inefficiency has been attributed to its rigid fare system as well as the broader notion of the railway as a public utility rather than a profitable business. The survival of a company in a permanent state of insolvency has been made possible only by large infusions of state subsidies.

The deterioration of the rail system meant that railways were not able to compete with the trucking industry. By 1930 only 1,000 miles (1,500 kilometers) of highways had been constructed in Mexico, but by 1950 Mexico's highway network had exceeded the rail network in length; by 1975 the highway network was seven times as long as the rail network. Moreover, the layout of the highway network did not complement the rail network but often duplicated rail routes, robbing railways of much of the more profitable short-distance traffic. The meager complementarity that existed between the rail and highway networks did little to ease the deterioration of the rail system.

It would be exaggeration to say that the decline of the railways was part of a deliberate policy of the Mexican state. Until 1960 railways still accounted for a majority of public investment in the transport sector, averaging around 63 percent from 1951 to 1960. Moreover, the government sponsored numerous studies and plans to reform the rail system,

Table 1
Volume and Characteristics of Railroad Service, 1900–90

Year	Passenger Traffic			Cargo Traffic		
	Transported passengers (thousands)	Passengers per kilometer (thousands)	Average distance (kilometers)	Transported tonnage (thousands)	Tons per kilometer	Average distance (kilometers)
1900	10,688	603.5	56	7,118	2,068	291
1911	16,722	1,138,432	68	13,120	3,550,586	271
1921	24,996	2,134,382	85	8,980	2,269,393	253
1930	20,943	1,448,013	69	13,387	4,041,456	302
1940	27,955	1,861,000	66	15,092	5,764,670	385
1950	32,419	3,024,631	101	23,002	9,391,594	365
1960	32,587	4,127,930	127	34,359	14,004,412	408
1970	37,399	4,534,279	121	41,379	22,595,000	546
1980	23,684	5,296,000	224	60,592	41,330,000	682
1990	17,149	5,336,000	311	50,960	36,417,000	715

Sources: Reseña histórica y estadística de los ferrocarriles de jurisdicción federal. Mexico City: SCOP, various years; *Estadísticas históricas de México.* Mexico City: INEGI-INAH, 1990; *Series estadísticas.* Mexico City: FNM, 1992.

although it has not followed up on all of them. In 1937 the government of Lázaro Cárdenas nationalized the National Railway, and from 1937 to 1940 the Mexican government experimented in worker administration of the rail system.

In 1940 the railways received a second shot in the arm, World War II. The cooperation of the United States allowed the railways to respond to wartime demands, but the extremely heavy use of the already depleted rail system further contributed to its deterioration. The investment in the rail sector during and after this period was at best a rear-guard action,

given that the slipshod maintenance of the rail system had led to an accumulation of other problems. Resources tended to be directed at localized quick fixes, even as more systemic problems kept the rail system from operating smoothly.

The government did attempt to address the most visible problems faced by the railways, particularly the state-owned National Railway. In 1954 the government established a national company to construct railway cars, increasing the rolling stock at its disposal and decreasing its reliance on stock rented from U.S. firms. By 1969 the company had manufactured

Table 2
Composition of Railroad Cargo, 1910–90 (%)

Year	Lumber and Forest Products	Agricultural Products	Inorganic Products	Industrial Products
1910	12.9	25.5	50.9	10.7
1920	12.7	32.3	42.4	12.6
1930	9.7	29.7	53.7	6.8
1940	7.7	35.3	46.6	10.3
1950	5.8	30.3	50.0	13.9
1960	2.9	25.2	46.4	25.5
1970	2.4	22.9	45.3	29.3
1980	1.9	21.5	43.0	33.5
1990	.8	23.0	37.3	39.0

Note: Between 1910 and 1930, data refer to the Ferrocarriles Nacionales (National Railways); starting in 1940 the data include all federal railway concessions.

Sources: Annual Reports. Mexico City: FNM, various years; *Anuario Estadístico de los Estados Unidos Mexicanos.* Mexico City: Dirección General de Estadística, various years; *Series Estadísticas.* Mexico City: FNM, 1992.

nearly 20,000 rail cars, mainly boxcars for the National Railway. Nonetheless, in almost every other area Mexico continued to depend on foreign suppliers for its equipment and rolling stock. Despite its incapacity to revive the rail system, however, the Mexican government attached great symbolic importance to state ownership and control of rail enterprises. Between 1946 and 1987 the government nationalized the entire rail system, unifying it in a single state-controlled corporation.

The systemic problems of the rail system are reflected in the service it has provided (see Table 1). The number of passengers traveling by train scarcely tripled between 1900 and 1950, remained stable in the following decades, and entered a marked decline starting in 1980. Freight traffic has not fared much better. The volume transported in 1940 exceeded the total volume in 1911 by scarcely 2 million metric tons; between 1940 and 1980 the tonnage increased four times, but the growth ended in 1990 when tonnage actually decreased by 10 million metric tons. Given that short-distance travel tends to be more economical by highway, average mileage for both passenger and freight transport has steadily increased.

The composition of freight transport is summarized in Table 2. Cattle and agricultural products remained stable from 1910 to 1990, while lumber and so-called inorganic products (minerals, ore, petroleum, and petroleum derivatives) decreased. Industrial products increased, particularly in the last four decades of the century, when industrial freight became the most important sector.

Such data seem to indicate that, despite its deficiencies, the rail system has been able to respond to the changing demands of Mexico's economy, but this has not been the case. The types of freight carried by Mexico's railways over the years has proven less capable of reflecting the dimensions and rhythms of economic activity. By 1952 trucks accounted for 57 percent of domestic freight transport and trains for 41 percent; this gap widened enormously over the following 30 years. By 1982 75 percent of all freight was transported by truck and only 18 percent by train. The ratio of rail mileage to gross national product declined markedly over the same period, falling from 0.18 kilometers per million pesos in 1952 to 0.03 in 1985. Moreover, railways' contribution to "value added" has been less than 4.3 percent of the transport sector in 1995 versus 81 percent from road transport.

There have been many causes for the progressive decline of the railroad system since the Mexican Revolution. No partial remedy has proven effective, and in the closing years of the twentieth century the state deemed it too risky to direct its resources toward the achievement of a radical solution. This can explain the shift toward reprivatization, which was started by the administration of Carlos Salinas de Gortari (1988–94) and formalized by law in December 1995. However, this last project has encountered many obstacles, making it difficult to predict when and how the reprivatization will begin and how long it will take.

Select Bibliography

Coatsworth, John, *Growth against Development: The Economic Impact of Railroads on Porfirian Mexico.* DeKalb: Northern Illinois University Press, 1981.

Grunstein, Arturo, "Railroads and Sovereignty: The Creation of Ferrocarriles Nacionales and Policymaking in Mexico." Ph.D. diss., University of California, Los Angeles, 1994.

—SANDRA KUNTZ FICKER

Reform Laws

The Reform Laws were a series of decrees and laws expressing the ideology of the Reform era (1855–76), a period of Liberal political predominance. Their antecedents lay in previous Liberal legislation of the Valentín Gómez Farías administration (1833–34), in the measures to restrict ecclesiastical influence taken by the Spanish Cortes (regent councils) of 1810 to 1814 and 1820 to 1823, and in the secularizing ideas of the European Enlightenment. The Reform Laws were issued in two phases, the first in 1855–56 under the administration of Juan Álvarez and Ignacio Comonfort, the second in 1859–60 during the Veracruz administration of Benito Juárez. The promulgation of the federal Constitution of 1857 fell between these two phases. In 1873, President Sebastián Lerdo de Tejada incorporated the Reform Laws into the Constitution. Their strict application provoked a series of rebellions in Catholic heart lands of center-western Mexico, which have sometimes been described as prefiguring the pro-Catholic Cristero Rebellion that wracked the region during the 1920s.

The Ley Juárez—the Law for Administration of Justice—issued by decree on November 23, 1855, attempted to restrict within civil law the *fuero eclesiástico*, which granted the Catholic Church broad privileges and immunities. Juárez, the minister of justice and ecclesiastic affairs in the administration of Juan Álvarez, acknowledged the assistance of two younger Oaxacans, Manuel Dublán and Ignacio Mariscal, in preparing the law. Juárez stood for the supremacy of the civil power and sought not to abolish at that time the corporate privilege of the clergy but to restrict it to the internal discipline of the church. The *fuero* had, in any case, been upheld by the Constitution of 1824, then in force. Juárez conceived the law as a compromise measure. Nevertheless, the archbishop of Mexico, Lázaro de la Garza, condemned the law on November 28 as an attack on the institution of the Catholic Church. A clerical rebellion in the Puebla highland town of Zacapoaxtla broke out in December. Two rebellions in the city of Puebla in 1855–56 undermined the Comonfort administration's conciliation policy. At the opening of the Constituent Assembly on February 18, 1856, the Acta de Jacala declared the Juárez Law to be effective in all parts. The Law of April 26, 1856, restored the Gómez Farías Law of November 6, 1833, removing civil recognition of religious vows.

The Ley Lerdo of June 25, 1856, was the most controversial of the Reform Laws passed in 1855–56. Essentially, it provided for the transfer of corporate property pertaining to the church and to Indian communities into individual ownership. The law removed legal recognition of corporate communities' rights to own property. It formed part of a process of disamortization, which already had begun in Spain and the Spanish Empire during the late 1790s. The release of property from ecclesiastical ownership (mortmain) or from Indian community control formed part of the Liberal project of modernization, which was conceived on developmentalist and secularist lines. The overriding objective of the law was to stimulate the market in landed property and thereby encourage economic development. In Mexico City alone, the regular ecclesiastic orders owned property to the value of 11,065,768 pesos, and the secular (non-order) clergy to the value of 1,322,839 pesos. Miguel Lerdo de Tejada, then minister of finance, required the ecclesiastical authorities to transfer their own real estate to private ownership, giving preference to existing tenants. Annual rents would be converted into interest payment on capital value. The state would receive the fees for adjudication and entitlements. If after a lapse of three months nothing had been done, the ecclesiastical authorities would be required to put their properties up for sale at public auction. The Ignacio Comonfort administration (1855–58) saw this law as conciliatory toward the church and hoped to avoid a breach between church and state. The ecclesiastic hierarchy, however, condemned the law. Bishop Clemente de Jesús Munguía of Michoacán on July 26, 1856, declared it an extension of Gómez Farías's attempt in January 1847 to secure money at the expense of the church, and he argued, moreover, that ecclesiastical properties reflected the social nature of the church. Pope Pius IX condemned both the Ley Juárez and the Ley Lerdo in the secret Allocution of December 15, 1856, which became public in the following year.

The Ley Lerdo was complicated and ambiguous: it required a series of clarifying laws to interpret its meaning. The government received repeated requests for interpretation of this law, which departed entirely from traditional practices of village communal landholding. The brunt of the law fell not on the church, which owned mainly urban real estate, but on the indigenous communities, even though it exempted *ejidos* (vacant lands). The government suffered periodic attacks of conscience with regard to the social impact of its policies. Juárez's Regulation of December 10, 1862, for instance, removed the burdensome fees for property transfers, in order to encourage the peasants to take advantage of the privatization process. The law made no provision for the prior division of properties. Some indigenous communities already had a tradition of private or family land use, and accordingly, were able to benefit from the law, especially in cases where their activities were well incorporated into the market economy.

The law was issued at a time of deepening internal tension within the country concerning the policies of the recently installed Liberal regime. Liberal loss of power at the national level between January 1858 and January 1861 (during the Civil Wars of Reform), and then again from June 1863 and July 1867 (during the French Intervention), interrupted the disamortization process, which the federal government resumed after 1867 and the restoration of the Republic. These delays helped to defuse social conflict over the implementation of the law. The full impact of civil disamortization was not really felt, however, until after 1880, with the expansion of the infrastructure and the revival of the market.

Lerdo believed that less than one-half of the value of ecclesiastical real estate fell under the disamortization procedure by the end of 1856; that year, the process involved adjudication and sales to the value of 20,500,000 pesos. The disamortization process created many new interests that strove to prevent the reversal of the Ley Lerdo. The French-imposed imperial government of Maximilian, which recognized the legal status of indigenous corporate communities and their right of land ownership in 1865 and 1866, still did not rescind the disamortization aspect of the law.

The Ley Lerdo was a social failure in that it did not stimulate the emergence of a new class of small peasants identified with the Liberal program. It did, however, enable some merchants to acquire country properties, existing landowners to extend their holdings at peasant expense, and upwardly mobile ranch owners, many of them mestizos, to gain access to former community or church landed properties.

The Ley Iglesias of April 11, 1857, issued by José María Iglesias, minister of justice, deprived the parish clergy of a large range of traditional fees. Juan José Baz, governor of the Federal District, who was a radical liberal yet a member of Comonfort's entourage, considered this Law on Parish Dues to be an unnecessary provocation of the lower clergy.

The Law for the Nationalization of Ecclesiastical Property, issued by Juárez's Veracruz administration-in-exile during the Wars of Reform on July 12, 1859, made explicit the connection between national debt and disamortization. This was first made by Lorenzo de Zavala during his two periods as minister of finance in 1829 and 1833. Reports of the Ministry of Justice and Ecclesiastical Affairs from 1825 onward had regularly contained estimates of church wealth. From the mid-1830s, when the Liberal *pensador* (thinker) José María Luis Mora had begun to estimate total ecclesiastical wealth, this question came to be debated widely in Liberal circles. The general Liberal belief was that the church was rich but the state poor, and that the expropriation and sale of ecclesiastical properties would assist the state, hard pressed by a large internal and external debt, to recover solvency. Church wealth consisted less of real estate than capital. Mora estimated that the church's total productive capital came to 149,131,860 pesos and that its revenues totaled 7,456,593 pesos, including tithes (valued at 2,341,152 pesos). Furthermore, the church, according to the Conservative, pro-clerical Lucas Alamán, held mortgages on over half of the landed properties in Mexico. Mora calculated that the unproductive capital (sacred vessels, church buildings, etc.) reached a further 30,031,894 pesos in value. Much discussion surrounded the extent of church wealth in Mexico, and Mora's estimates were probably too high, as they did not take into account properties and revenues lost by the church since the latter part of the eighteenth century. Miguel Lerdo, however, argued that the value of total church wealth in 1856, the year of the disamortization, stood as high as 250 million or 300 million pesos.

The Veracruz regime's objectives, however, were two-fold: Lerdo saw revenue-raising to fight the civil war against the Conservative regime in Mexico City as the first priority, and he hoped to use the expropriation as collateral for a U.S. loan; Secretary of Exterior Relations Melchor Ocampo emphasized the social dimension of broadening the base of property ownership and encouraging private enterprise. In the context of a civil war, this latter objective took second place. Even so, the Liberal regime neither prospered from these measures nor received a loan from the United States. President Juárez issued instructions for the arrest of any officials refusing to cooperate in the nationalization procedures. Anticlerical state governors in Michoacán, Jalisco, Nuevo León, and Tamaulipas already had anticipated the Veracruz regime's measures against ecclesiastical property. Lerdo criticized Juárez for not acting fast enough on the issue. After the reoccupation of Mexico City in 1861, the Liberal administration discovered that many ecclesiastical properties were difficult to sell. As the external debt question rose to the crisis point in 1862, the Juárez administration recognized that neither the Lerdo Law nor the National Decree had significantly enhanced the prosperity of the state.

Maximilian's imperial government on February 26, 1865, adopted a policy of revision of land transfers under the disamortization and nationalization laws with the objective of ensuring that property had been acquired in accordance with the legal provisions. The imperial government hoped to benefit indigenous communities in this way and also to earn revenue from the regularization procedure. The principle of civil disposal of ecclesiastical properties was upheld in the face of clerical indignation.

The Mexican state received the sum of 1,083,611 pesos from the disamortization in 1856 and the much higher figure of 10,094,184 pesos from both this and the nationalization. Revenue in 1865–66 totaled 2.55 million pesos but fell to 1,027,911 pesos in 1867–68. It remained well under 1 million pesos annually thereafter. The scholar Robert Knowlton has calculated that revenues received by the state by 1910 totaled 23,016,516 pesos. Knowlton estimated the total value of church wealth on the eve of the disamortization and nationalization to have been somewhere between 100 million and 150 million pesos.

In addition to these measures aimed at acquiring church wealth for the state, a host of other Reform Laws were issued to lessen church authority in the country's day-to-day life. The Law of July 23, 1859, declared marriage to be a legally valid civil contract. This law did not provide for divorce but recognized legal separation if the marriage had irretrievably broken down. That did not imply, however, that either estranged party received the right to remarry during the lifetime of the other. The Law of July 28, 1859, established a Civil Registry for births, marriages, and deaths. Juárez duly registered his newly born son in the Veracruz Civil Registry. On July 31, the clergy were removed from any intervention in burial ceremonies and the administration of cemeteries. The Liberal regime on August 11, 1859, restricted the number of religious holidays and established several new secular holidays. Secular authorities were forbidden to assist at religious functions. Religious ceremonies were forbidden outside churches, the use of church bells was made subject to police regulation, and clerical dress was forbidden in public. The clergy were made subject to taxation on the same basis as other citizens. On December 4, 1860, liberty of religious belief was guaranteed by the Liberal state. This was a natural consequence of the disestablishment of the Catholic religion by the Constitution of 1857. Although Maximilian's regime restored the Catholic establishment, it retained the legislation on religious toleration.

The Reform Laws were not designed to destroy either the Catholic Church in Mexico or the Christian religion as such. The overwhelming majority of legislators would describe themselves as Christians. Liberal intentions, however, were to offer an alternative society in which a citizen could live, marry, and die without recourse to Christian symbols. Juárez and other leading Liberals also hoped to encourage the spread of Protestantism in Mexico, which they identified with the democratic traditions and economic progress of the United States.

See also Ayutla, Revolution of; Liberalism; Wars of Reform

Select Bibliography

Bazant, Jan, *Alienation of Church Wealth in Mexico: Social and Economic Aspects of the Liberal Revolution 1856–75,* translated by Michael P. Costeloe. Cambridge: Cambridge University Press, 1971.
Callcott, Wilfred H., *Liberalism in Mexico 1857–1929.* Stanford, California: Stanford University Press, 1931.
Knowlton, Robert J., *Church Property and the Mexican Reform 1856–1910.* DeKalb: Northern Illinois University Press, 1976.
Scholes, Walter V., *Mexican Politics during the Juárez Regime 1855–1872.* Columbia: University of Missouri Press, 1957.
Sinkin, Richard N., *The Mexican Reform, 1856–1876: A Study in Liberal Nation-Building.* Austin: University of Texas Press, 1979.

—BRIAN R. HAMNETT

Reform Wars

See Wars of Reform

Revolution, Mexican

See Mexican Revolution

Revolution of Ayutla

See Ayutla, Revolution of

Reyes, Bernardo 1850–1913
General, Statesman, and Governor

Bernardo Reyes was born on August 20, 1850, in Guadalajara, Jalisco. His father, Domingo, was a colonel whose military career spanned three decades (1830–62) and featured service in Jalisco on behalf of the Liberal cause. His mother was related to powerful regional caudillos (strongmen), including General Pedro Ogazón, who served as minister of war under Benito Juárez in 1861.

It comes as no surprise, then, that young Bernardo was easily attracted to military life at an early age. The French Intervention (1862–67) of Mexico helped as well, prompting him to join guerrillas in Michoacán as an adolescent. Still an unusually young warrior, he participated in the siege of Querétaro that ended the French occupation, suffering a bayonet wound in the hand-to-hand combat. Commissioned as a junior officer, he rose in rank and status as the Restoration slowly began to pacify the countryside. Able to switch his loyalties to Porfirio Díaz after he seized the presidency, Reyes became a brigadier general in 1880 at age 30.

Under the dictatorship of Díaz (1876–1911), Reyes advanced his career as he helped suppress restless segments of the rural populace. In the early 1880s he oversaw military operations in the western states of Sinaloa and Sonora, where he worked to pacify Apaches along the U.S. frontier, as well as monitor relatively peaceful, precrisis relations with the Mayo and Yaqui tribes. In the late 1880s he assumed military command, and soon thereafter the governorship, of Nuevo León, a state critical to Mexico's stability with its growing population and proximity to the United States.

An able administrator, Reyes established order in the state and consolidated its political links to the Díaz government in Mexico City by dismantling the regional political machine of Generals Gerónimo

Treviño and Francisco Naranjo. He did so in the midst of economic depression, but also at the expense of civil liberties, suspending the rule of law and exerting authority by brutality and decree. Dissidents were rounded up and jailed, while intransigent troublemakers experienced *ley fuga*—the famous Porfirian euphemism for the extrajudicial execution of prisoners.

Abiding by the Porfirian maxim that order begat progress, Reyes was able to modernize Nuevo León in the subsequent decade. The transformation of the state's primary city, Monterrey, was quite astounding. What had in many ways been an area languishing in economic development for centuries suddenly became a haven of commerce and industry. Completion of the Mexican National Railroad from Mexico City to Laredo, Texas, had assured significant economic growth, but historians also give due credit to Reyes's business-minded administration. Wooing foreign capital through tax incentives, favorable labor conditions, and an infrastructure built in part by public works, Reyes watched Monterrey slowly become the "Pittsburgh of Mexico," with its beer breweries, glass factories, and mineral smelting and refining operations. The governor pressed ahead with education reforms that provided primary schooling to children and supplied employers with a sufficiently qualified workforce. Public health, sanitation, and policing soon made Monterrey the nation's second-most modernized urban area, behind Mexico City. Economic advances were not matched by political freedoms, however, as the veneer of democratic elections covered over the patronage and repression that made Nuevo León Reyes's political fiefdom. Intransigent dissidents could be housed in the new penitentiary, however, which opened in 1895.

The rising importance of Monterrey and Nuevo León aided Reyes in his quest for national political prominence. In 1900 he was named minister of war by Díaz, a post at which he again introduced noteworthy reforms. Reyes overhauled the army, improving its organization, tightening discipline, and increasing munitions production and supplies. He created a Second Reserve comprised of National Guard units in each state. His efforts increased military efficiency and facilitated a crackdown on Mexico's "uncivilized" Indians, with campaigns against the Yaqui and Maya that featured brutal enslavement.

Reyes's ambition and influence alarmed some prominent Mexico City politicians, especially Díaz partisans known as Científicos because of their adherence to Positivist thought. They saw to his resignation at the bequest of Díaz in 1902, who subsequently dismantled the Second Reserve by presidential decree

as well. Sent packing to Monterrey, where he again assumed the office of governor, Reyes likely would have remained in the shadows of history had Díaz himself not faced unexpected crises. The Porfiriato was a time of dynamic change in the cities, but of growing frustration in the countryside. The tensions of uneven development were aggravated in the first decade of the twentieth century, as inflation and recession (after 1907) troubled Mexico. A small but restless urban middle class also began to agitate for political change by forming Liberal Clubs that peacefully called for reforms.

Recognizing increased discontent, the aged dictator, Díaz, dropped a political bombshell in March 1908, when he announced through an interview with a U.S. magazine that he would not seek reelection in 1910. Immediately forces favoring change coalesced around Reyes, a natural presidential candidate because of his national prominence, coupled with his known animosity for the Mexico City Científicos. Despite the fact that he had sanctioned the massacre of members of the Monterrey Liberal Club in April 1903, Reyes enjoyed the support of much of the politicized middle class, as well as many northern regional elites, who created a new Democratic Party to support him in January 1909. Masonic Lodges also played a prominent role in the Reyista mobilization, which surged nationwide during the spring. The party was augmented by the creation of "Reyes Clubs" in cities such as Guadalajara and Torreón, which staged demonstrations as part of a groundswell of mainstream opposition that increasingly threatened the dictatorship.

Reyes himself shrewdly remained silent about his intentions. Díaz, however, forced him to break his silence in November 1909, when he ordered the governor on a military mission to Europe. The dictator had changed his mind and decided to run for president again, and he would not tolerate competition. Reyes, despite counsel to the contrary from his son Rodolfo and other advisers, obeyed his new orders. But the specter of change put in motion forces not easily quelled in early 1910. A new opponent to the dictatorship emerged in Francisco I. Madero, whose political fortunes soared as those of Reyes declined. It is interesting to speculate what would have happened if Reyes had refused to comply with Díaz's instructions, for popular support forced the government to arrest Madero, who was able to escape to the United States and trigger a successful revolution.

The Revolution's triumph, complete with the departure of Díaz in May 1911, prompted Reyes to return to Mexico and attempt to regain his place at the head of popular forces. Madero almost made his gambit successful: he insisted on an interim presidency and the formality of elections in October. During this time, support for the indecisive and eccentric Madero eroded markedly. Reyes found new allies among Porfirians and conservative sectors of the middle class—all increasingly uneasy about the direction of newly unleashed political forces. Reyes's campaign was rooted in the rhetoric of "law and order." New Reyes Clubs formed throughout Mexico, with particular strength in conservative bastions like Guadalajara. Violent clashes with Madero supporters followed.

Reyes called for a delay in the elections because of the violence, but the Madero loyalists who controlled the process ignored his request, which undoubtedly was inspired by political considerations. Violence did not seriously mar the scheduled vote. Realizing his electoral strategy was doomed to fall short, he left for Texas, where he planned a revolt. The U.S. government, determined to foster stability under Madero by this time, seized weapons and arrested conspirators. Reyes himself had to return to Mexico prematurely in order to avoid arrest, arriving in Nuevo León and launching his insurgency in December. His pronouncements promised land reform to disgruntled peasants in exchange for their support. With his past heavy-handedness well known, however, his attempts to mobilize a large peasant-based opposition failed. He was arrested on Christmas morning and interned in Mexico City's Santiago Tlatelolco Prison.

After the failed revolt, for the fourth time in a decade, Reyes's political career seemed finished. Yet from prison he attempted one last comeback. A sworn enemy of Madero by now, he plotted a coup, through military intermediaries, with Félix Díaz—a nephew of the exiled dictator, whose own attempts to stir a revolt had also landed him in prison. Through the critical participation of General Manuel Mondragón, both men were released from jail on February 9, 1913. Hours later, Reyes took charge of military detachments as they advanced on the National Palace. Attempts to secure the palace were foiled by a loyal Presidential Guard, however. It is said that Félix Díaz had delayed their arrival through his insistence that he make his appearance more presentable with a full toilet; by the time they arrived, the guards who were to have been part of the coup had been replaced by soldiers loyal to the president. Unaware that the plan had fallen through, Reyes mounted a white horse and led a column across the main plaza in apparent victory, only to be greeted by a hail of bullets. With his death Díaz inherited leadership, but lost it to General Victoriano Huerta, who ousted Madero and became president after the chaos of the infamous Decena Trágica (Tragic Ten Days).

The ambitious Reyes probably missed his best opportunity to obtain lasting national power in 1909–10. Instead of possibly becoming a hero of the Revolution, he became one of its traitors. Had his coup succeeded, it likely would have yielded a temporary government, for Huerta's regime lasted only 17 months. Reyes was survived by his children, including his son Alfonso, who became a noteworthy poet.

Select Bibliography

Cumberland, Charles C., *Mexican Revolution: Genesis under Madero*. Austin: University of Texas Press, 1982.

Niemeyer, E. V., Jr., "Frustrated Invasion: The Revolutionary Attempt of General Bernardo Reyes from San Antonio in 1911." *Southwestern Historical Quarterly* 67 (1963–64).

Ross, Stanley, *Francisco I. Madero: Apostle of Mexican Democracy*. New York: Columbia University Press, 1955.

—JOHN W. SHERMAN

Rivera, Diego 1886–1957
Painter

The real name of the artist known simply as Diego Rivera is said to have been Diego María de la Concepción Juan Nepomuceno Estanislao de la Rivera y Barrientos Acosta Rodríguez. True or false, this name epitomizes him: it is monumental, like his body, his imagination, his work. Hundreds of pages have been written about what is, without doubt, one of the most important painters of the twentieth century.

Diego Rivera was born in the city of Guanajuato in 1886. His father was an educator who founded rural schools, and his mother was also a teacher but later went on to study obstetrics. When he was seven years old Rivera's family moved to Mexico City. Rivera studied painting at the Academy of San Carlos and later spent 14 years in Spain, France, and Italy. His career as a muralist began shortly after his return to Mexico in 1921.

The volume of Rivera's work is as monumental as the works themselves. Aside from a brief lacuna from 1935 to 1943—during which Rivera worked almost entirely on easel painting, engraving, and drawing—Rivera devoted his life to mural painting from the time of his return to Mexico until his death in 1957. Rivera's muralistic work covers several thousand square feet of walls. Rivera's most important works in Mexico can be found in the Ministry of Public Education, the Palacio de Bellas Artes, the Palacio Nacional—the seat of Mexican government—the Ministry of Health, the National Institute of Cardiology, the Hospital de la Raza, and the Cárcamo del Rio Lerma. A particularly important mural, *Sueño de una tarde de domingo en la Alameda* (1947), which Rivera had painted in the Hotel del Prado, was relocated to a specially constructed site to one side of the Alameda Central after the hotel had to be demolished following the 1985 Mexico City earthquake. Rivera also created a mosaic in glass for the facade of the Insurgentes Theater. Other important murals can be found in the School of Architecture in the town of Chapingo and in the Palacio de Cortés in Cuernavaca, Fernando (Hernán) Cortés's former residence. Rivera worked in the United States for several years; two of his frescoes are in California and one in Detroit. He began a mural in the Rockefeller Center in New York, but it was destroyed because it included a portrait of Lenin. Rivera simply painted an identical mural in the Palacio de Bellas Artes in Mexico City.

In 1922, shortly after his return from Europe, Rivera joined the Mexican Communist Party. His relationship with the party always was volatile, and eventually he was expelled. Rivera's tensions with the Communist Party originated with his work for the Mexican state painting murals in government buildings. Rivera also was a close friend of Leon Trotsky, who had taken refuge in Mexico following his expulsion from the Soviet Union, and briefly toyed with Trotskyism. Finally, Rivera painted murals in the United States. Nonetheless, Rivera rejoined the Communist Party in 1954 and died a party member, one of the last great satisfactions of his life.

Rivera's relationships with women were one of the most important—and problematic—aspects of his life. While he lived in Paris his two most significant relationships were with Angelina Beloff and Marievna Vorobiev-Stebelska, both women of Russian origin who were interested in being artists. Beloff and Rivera had a son in 1917 who died the following year, and Vorobiev-Stebelska and Rivera had a daughter whom Rivera refused to recognize. On returning to Mexico Rivera fell in love with Guadalupe Marín, married her, and had two daughters with her; however, this tempestuous relationship did not last long, and in 1929 Rivera married another painter, Frida Kahlo. This was the longest, perhaps the most important, and certainly the most volatile relationship of Rivera's life, and it lasted until Frida's death in 1954. Shortly before his own death Rivera married Emma Hurtado, who was legally his widow.

Throughout his life, Diego Rivera devoted himself body and soul to painting. The title of his autobiography, *Mi arte, mi vida* (My Art, My Life), epitomizes his attitude toward his art; his art came before every other aspect of his life. He was the spearhead of the "Mexican" school of painting, which included such masters as José Clemente Orozco, David Alfaro Siqueiros, and later Rufino Tamayo. Rivera always was polemical, and his work—and the mythology surrounding his life—continues to polarize critical opinion to this day. What particularly stands out, however, are the contradictions in Rivera's own life and work. Rivera was considered one of the most important painters of the Mexican Revolution, but during most of the Revolution (including the armed phase of 1910–17) Rivera was in Europe. He considered himself a revolutionary Marxist, but his murals adorn government buildings throughout Mexico, and he is widely praised by Mexican statesmen. He was deeply involved in many of the social struggles of his time, but his art often echoes the narrow positivism of the ancien régime.

Rivera considered his most important masters to be the great landscape artist José María Velasco and the "popular" engraver José Guadalupe Posada. While living in Europe he devoured western art history. He was strongly influenced by cubism, passing through a period of dutifully imitating Picasso and Georges Braque. He also was influenced by fifteenth- and sixteenth-century Italian frescoes; their influence can be seen in the first murals following his return from Mexico, which he painted in the Escuela Nacional Preparatoria in 1921–22.

Nonetheless, even during his cubist phase Rivera still was interested in Mexican themes, most notably in his portraits of Martín Luis Guzmán and Ramón Gómez de la Serna and in his *Paisaje zapatista* (Zapatista Landscape), all painted in 1915. It was during his last years in Europe, however, that Rivera engaged in his most intense search for his own artistic identity and developed his ideas about *muralismo* as public art for and about the Mexican people. As someone who imagined himself to be a revolutionary, Rivera believed that all art was propaganda. He chose mural painting as his most important medium because he believed that this was the best way to reach the Mexican people, who had just lived through the world's first great peasant revolution of the twentieth century. The great theme of his murals was "history," particularly the social and political history of Mexico.

Nonetheless, there are important contradictions between Rivera's written ideas about his work and the actual content of his paintings. Although Rivera imagined that "the masses" were the protagonists of his paintings, they appear in his murals only as faceless, anonymous toilers. Although Rivera sought to portray class struggle as the engine of human history, what comes across in his painting is more of a "great man" conception of history. Only the great heroes and villains of Mexican history have names and faces in his paintings, and it is they who "make" history.

Like "the masses," women are faceless in Rivera's paintings, generally appearing only as mothers with children or as whores. Nonetheless, women are stripped not simply of their individual but also their class identities. For Rivera women were little more than models for his nudes, idealized representations of Mother Earth, or incarnations of "the beautiful"; they are not included among the wretched of the earth who comprised Rivera's anonymous cause celebre. It is largely because of this limited view of history—and not because of his professed Marxism—that Rivera was able to paint murals in the Palacio Nacional and win the praise of the generation of statesmen who emerged from the Revolution of 1910. Rivera's ideology, as expressed in his paintings, was much closer to the official ideology of the bourgeois faction that triumphed in the Mexican Revolution than to any sort of revolutionary Marxism.

Rivera's life and work cannot be considered in isolation from the official ideology and mythology of the Mexican Revolution; however, they also can not be considered apart from broader questions of *mexicanidad* —"Mexicanness" and Mexican national identity. For Rivera, his search for a personal artistic identity was inextricably part of his search for an identity as a Mexican. In a unique, original, and personal form of creative communication, Rivera sought to express Mexico to Mexicans. Rivera's life blood was *lo mexicano,* particularly Mexican popular and pre-Hispanic art. He had a particular predilection for ex-votos, votive offerings left in Mexican churches, and "Judases," the papier-mâché figures (often satirizing contemporary political figures) that are filled with firecrackers and ceremoniously blown up every New Year's Eve. Rivera bought hundreds of Judases and had several others custom-made (on a monumental scale, like his own work). Rivera and Frida Kahlo collected hundreds of ex-votos, perhaps bought, perhaps stolen. He also put together an important collection of pre-Hispanic art that can be viewed in the Anahuacalli Museum, which he designed—although he never lived to see it completed—to be donated to the Mexican people.

Rivera died in Mexico City in 1957. Contrary to his wishes, his ashes were not placed together with those of Frida Kahlo, but rather in the Rotunda de Hombres Ilustres, where Mexico's national heroes are interred.

Select Bibliography

Le Clézio, J. M. G., *Diego and Frida.* Paris: Stock, 1993.
Wolfe, Bertram D., *The Fabulous Life of Diego Rivera.* New York: Stein and Day, 1963.

—Eli Bartra

Ruiz García, Samuel 1924–

Bishop

Born November 3, 1924, in Irupuato, Guanajuato, Samuel Ruiz García was the first of five children born to Maclovio Ruiz and Guadalupe García, migrant laborers who were married in California. Young Samuel grew up in a conservative religious family during a time and in a place greatly affected by Mexico's bitter church-state conflict. He attended religious schools and entered the Seminario Conciliar de León in 1937. Ruiz was chosen by the Bishop of León in 1947 to study at the Gregorian Pontifical University in Rome, and he earned a doctorate in *sagrada escritura* (scripture) four years later. He was ordained in 1949 and returned to Mexico in 1952 to begin what appeared to be a meteoric career in the church. In León he taught theology at the seminary, became its director, and was made a canon. In late 1959 the 35-year-old Ruiz was named bishop of Chiapas. He arrived in San Cristóbal de las Casas in 1960 with a reputation as a brilliant young conservative and anticommunist.

As bishop of Chiapas Samuel Ruiz underwent a profound personal, intellectual, and theological evolution to become by the mid-1990s the leading symbol of the progressive church of Latin America—the church of the poor and the oppressed. His transformation developed as he traveled by car and airplane and on horseback and foot through his diocese, a remote region with an impoverished indigenous—Maya—majority. Ruiz was influenced by the progressive currents and reforms within the church in the 1960s. He attended the Second Vatican Council from 1962 to 1965 and the Second General Conference of Latin American Bishops in 1968. In Chiapas Ruiz worked to create an autochthonous church, what he has called "an authentic church." The diocese under his leadership invited religious orders to establish schools for indigenous catechists as well as grassroots political organizers to assist local communities in forming cooperatives and credit unions. The diocese has established community health-care clinics and provided other forms of social service as well as legal assistance. In 1974 Ruiz organized the First Indigenous Congress of Chiapas. Two thousand representatives discussed the critical problems facing their communities in their own languages and afterward began to create economic and political organizations to help solve those problems. Ruiz took the lead to assist the 100,000 Maya refugees who escaped from the savage military repression in Guatemala in the early 1980s. The bishop and his priests, missionaries, indigenous catechists and deacons, and other pastoral workers attempted to help parishioners build their own church that speaks their language, is respectful of their culture, and supports their peaceful efforts to liberate themselves from systemic poverty and oppression. (In 1965 the diocese was divided into two dioceses, Tuxtla Gutiérrez and San Cristóbal de las Casas. Ruiz chose to remain in the indigenous highlands and San Cristóbal.)

Ruiz's defense of human rights and assistance to "those who are suffering the most" has won him the enmity of certain local, state, and national government officials, members of the military, cattle ranchers and their organizations, conservative evangelical Protestants, and the so-called *coletos auténticos*, the "genuine citizens" of San Cristóbal. Increased violence by private interests and the government in Chiapas in the 1980s against Indians, *campesinos* (peasants), and occasionally church workers prompted Ruiz to form the Fray Bartolomé de Las Casas Human Rights Center in 1989. Those who regard him as an agitator of Indians and worse refer to Ruiz as "the Red Bishop" and "Comandante Sam." He has received death threats from time to time. He also has been criticized within the church for his alleged use of "Marxist analysis," and there have been efforts, most notably by the Vatican's official envoy to Mexico, to remove him from his position and from Chiapas.

The Zapatista Rebellion of January 1, 1994, brought worldwide attention to Chiapas and the bishop of San Cristóbal. His enemies in government and the press blamed the bishop and his pastoral team for the rebellion. No one in Mexico, however, had greater credibility with the indigenous population of Chiapas and the rebels. Ruiz became the mediator between the Zapatistas and the government in February and afterward worked constantly to find common ground for a lasting peace. No one has defended the indigenous people of Chiapas more than Samuel Ruiz García since the first bishop of Chiapas, Bartolomé de Las Casas. "In this diocese,

we serve the poor, who make up 80 percent of the population," Ruiz declared in a 1994 interview. "We have to be on the side of those who are suffering the most."

Select Bibliography

Ross, John, *Rebellion from the Roots: Indian Uprising in Chiapas*. Monroe, Maine: Common Courage, 1995.
Tangeman, Michael, *Mexico at the Crossroads: Politics, the Church, and the Poor*. Maryknoll, New York: Orbis, 1995.

—Thomas Benjamin

Rulfo, Juan 1918–86

Writer

While a small group of friends always admired Juan Rulfo's writings, as they read the manuscripts of the short stories later collected in *El llano en llamas* (1953; The Burning Plain) and his novel *Pedro Páramo* (1955), Rulfo's great international renown came as a surprise, because it was based on only two slim books. Perhaps the surprise was greater for Rulfo, who did not publish any other novel or collection of short stories for more than 25 years after the appearance of *El llano en llamas*. Critics have called this time lapse, "Rulfo's silence," and the paradox is that his renown increased steadily in inverse proportion to his literary productivity, at the same time that readers anxiously expected new works from him. Rulfo's silence is worth considering since it has a correlative in his own prose, which tends to seek the conciseness of poetry, to avoid explicitness, and to manage language as precisely as a poet would do. Implosion rather than explosion would be a key concept to understand his literary system, how he tried to write, and finally his idea of literature. A very private person, introspective and shy but at the same time humorous and witty when he felt comfortable in the presence of other people, Rulfo brought to literature these same personal qualities. And he also brought himself, aspects of his own life to his writings. One of his most read and admired short stories, "¡Diles que no me maten!" (Tell Them Not to Kill Me!) has a close relationship to a family tragedy: the killing of his father, when Juan Rulfo was still a child. It would not be surprising, then, that one of the main themes in his work is the search for the father. And that is the starting point of *Pedro Páramo*, when Juan Preciado relates: "Vine a Comala porque me dijeron que vivía acquí mi padre, un tal Pedro Páramo" (I came to Comala because I was told that my father, a certain Pedro Páramo, lived here). The theme of the presence/absence of the father is fundamental not only in these two examples but throughout his work.

Rulfo came to Mexican narrative when the literary tradition of the novel of the Mexican Revolution was still hegemonic, and when Mexico itself could not yet take some distance from the most belligerent and violent period in its history, the Mexican Revolution. This social and political movement started in 1910 as an uprising against Porfirio Díaz, the dictator for more than three decades, and it did not stop even after institutional accords named a new president, because in 1926 another uprising disturbed the fragile political equilibrium. This second uprising, the Cristero Rebellion, had pro-Catholic and agrarian motivations, and it had a strong impact on Rulfo's imagination. This can be seen in the title story of *El llano en llamas,* in "La noche que lo dejaron solo" (The Night They Left Him Alone), "El hombre" (The Man), and others, together with important passages of the novel, *Pedro Páramo.* The impact of the Cristero Rebellion, as well as autobiographical incidents, helped Rulfo shape his narrative world, introducing violence in a peculiar way: sudden and stripped from any ethical consideration.

The tradition of the Mexican Revolution in the novel is important not only from a historical point of view, but mainly because Rulfo renewed this tradition in terms of both form and style. While almost every novelist of the time was representing the strong influence of French Naturalism in literature, Rulfo developed his writing in a novel fashion and helped transform Mexican narrative in a radical way. As a very disorganized and spontaneous reader, he brought to Mexican literature the distant influences of Nordic writers such as Selma Lagerlöf, C.M. Ramuz *(Derborance),* Sillampaa, Bjornson, Hauprmann, and the first Hamsun. His influences also included the gothic element discovered in love stories such as *Wuthering Heights* by Emily Brontë, and all these stimuli contributed to Rulfo's own gothicism. Rulfo put his literary universe on the borders of the fantastic, creating an almost surrealistic, moon-like space. The town of Comala is "un lugar sobre las brasas" (a place of burning embers). In Pedro Páramo, Juan Preciado arrives in Comala searching for his father, but he encounters only what seem to be ghosts, murmurs, cries emerging from the walls, until he discovers that everybody is already dead: the reader discovers that the story of Pedro Páramo is being told by a dead man, Juan Preciado, from a deep tomb. It has a complex combination of reality and dream, hope and fear, love and hate, which are never separated. This made his narrative most surprising, original, and admired. There are some short stories, such as "Luvina," in which the characters wonder where they are: "¿En qué país estamos, Agripina? . . . ¿Qué país es éste, Agripina?" (What country are we in, Agripina? . . . What sort of country is this, Agripina?), such is the dream-like atmosphere the narrative creates.

Rulfo started writing the novel *Pedro Páramo* in August 1953, while a Fellow of the Centro Mexicano de Escritores. He intended to call this novel *Los desiertos de la Tierra* (The Deserts of the Earth). When he finished it the following year, is bore the title *Los murmullos* (The Murmurs) but between January and March 1954, a fragment of it was published in a magazine, announcing the forthcoming novel as *Una estrella junto a la luna* (A Start Near the Moon). All these titles refer to different aspects of the novel; the spectacular isolated landscape, the ghosts and their murmurs, the love story between *Pedro Páramo* and Susana San Juan. Finally, the book appeared under the title Pedro Páramo, the name of one of the main characters, because the same publishing house had recently published *Los falsos rumores* (The False Rumors), by Gastón García Cantú, and the publishers wanted to avoid any confusion. During the following 40 years, Pedro Páramo would become the best known of all Mexican novels, and it brought its author well deserved recognition.

There has been a "mythic" reading of Rulfo's work, mostly by other writers, like Octavio Paz and Carlos Fuentes, who see universal themes in Rulfo's work, and even classical ones. Juan Preciado, in his search for his father, would then be a modern version of Telemachus searching for Ulysses. But there is also a more historical reading of Rulfo's stories, considering his strong views on social and political issues, and how they were expressed in his literature. In this sense, we can read his novel and short stories as a deconstruction of political power, and also as an unavoidable critique of the economic and social reforms brought about by the new bourgeoisie which benefited from the Revolution. With great irony, "Nos han dado la tierra" (They Gave Us the Land) comments on the agrarian reform that gave the most unproductive lands to the poorest; "El día del derrumbe" (The Day of the Quake) mocks political discourse and political authorities; and *Pedro Páramo* is one of the most powerful portraits of the "cacique" (the local political boss) to have emerged from Mexican literature.

Select Bibliography
Leal, Luis, *Juan Rulfo*. Boston: Twayne, 1983.

—JORGE RUFFINELLI

Rural Economy and Society

This entry contains five articles that discuss rural economy and society in the post-Conquest era, with emphases on land-labor regimes and rural resistance and rebellion:

Rural Economy and Society: Colonial
Rural Economy and Society: 1821–1910
Rural Economy and Society: 1910–40
Rural Economy and Society: 1940–96, Land-Labor
  Regimes
Rural Economy and Society: 1940–96, Resistance
  and Rebellion

For a discussion of rural economy and society before the Conquest, see Mesoamerica, *particularly the subentry* Agriculture and Ecology. *See also* Corridos; Human Rights; Maize; Military; Nationalism; U.S.-Mexican Border; Women's Status and Occupation

Rural Economy and Society: Colonial

Land-Labor Regimes

In an astute, far-ranging analysis of Mexico's social and economic problems published on the very eve of the Mexican Revolution (*Los grandes problemas nacionales*, 1909), Andrés Molina Enríquez made the often-quoted statement, "The hacienda is not a business." By this he meant that the Mexican landed estate was in general not profit oriented, probably not capitalistic, and certainly not modern, but a "feudal" legacy of the Spanish colonial period. At the very moment he wrote, however, capital intensive Mexican- and foreign-owned agricultural interests were in some regions of the country producing tropical crops for export, as well as more traditional agropastoral products (mean, wheat, maize) for domestic markets. Molina Enríquez's characterization proved more accurate in yet other regions of the country, among them large tracts of the arid north, the more isolated zones of the west coast, and the Indian south outside henequen-, coffee-, cacao-, vanilla-, and sugar-producing areas. In those areas the insertion of the hacienda into local, regional, and international markets was much shallower, capital investment and economic rationalization were at much lower levels, and social relations of production largely were untransformed from older practices. To the extent that the Mexican Revolution was an agrarian upheaval, much modern scholarship would ascribe it to the social and economic stresses generated by growing commercialization and modernization in large-scale agriculture, while other scholars would see the Mexican countryside, and the hacienda within it, as "feudal" and backward. These apparent contradictions in the central institution of Mexican rural life did not originate in the nineteenth century, however, but found their origins in the colonial period. It is therefore with the colonial period that one must begin to construct a genealogy of land-labor regimes in Mexican history.

Often still framed in terms of a "capitalist" versus a "feudal" model, the extended debate in recent scholarship about the nature of the Mexican hacienda and its place in rural society has deeply influenced the historiography of Mexico in general and of the colonial period in particular. There remain a number of important questions about colonial land-labor regimes. On the one hand, for example, the hacienda has begun to look a lot less "feudal" as an agrosocial unit than previously imagined. Empirical studies of the colonial hacienda have uncovered in the institution an economic dynamism and a social polymorphism suggesting that it was in fact quite sensitive to changing market, labor, and capital conditions rather than a fly trapped in the amber of a seigneurial tradition. On the other hand, even the most market-oriented haciendas in the late colonial decades often relied in part on coerced labor, retaining a strongly patriarchal social organization and paternalistic labor practices. This is quite apart, of course, from commercial sugar plantations, concentrated in the Morelos lowlands but scattered elsewhere throughout the colony, which relied on a core labor force of African slaves. We thus are faced with the apparent paradox of commercial economic organization and "feudal"/patriarchal social organization, a theoretical anomaly but a manifest historical reality. It also is necessary to keep in mind that the large landed estate did not exist alone in the colonial countryside, in a moon-like landscape devoid of other population concentrations or other types of productive units. Rather, it cohabited—sometimes symbiotically, sometimes conflictually—with small towns, semidependent or independent family holdings (ranchos), and most importantly with indigenous communities. Certainly the terms of the conflict increasingly have been studied, from informal to lit-igated contention over land and other resources (growing in frequency in the eighteenth century), through everyday forms of subaltern resistance (including banditry), to small-scale riot and rebellion, and finally widespread popular insurgency (1810–21). But the terms of the symbiosis are less well understood, particularly on the peasant side, since small-scale rural subsistence economy has to be reconstructed for the most part inferentially.

From an Extractive to an Agropastoral Economy
The Spanish conquerors and colonizers of Mexico brought with them a great deal of cultural baggage, some of it modified by their Caribbean experience, but none more important than their ideas about the relationship among land, labor, and social power. Men of the nobility and gentry were few in the early generations of the Conquest, although the colony eventually generated its own nobility and upper class based upon mining, commercial and agricultural wealth, and high office. But from the very beginning most migrants aspired to the social status and power associated in Europe with large land holdings. These aspirations had been shaped by centuries of Iberian experience with the Roman latifundium—a large-scale, slave-based, agropastoral holding oriented toward urban markets and supporting an absentee landlord lifestyle—and its descendants. By the time the latifundium model was poised to jump the Atlantic with the conquerors, slavery had fallen away to be replaced by a servile labor force, and the declining Castilian economy of the fifteenth century had come to be dominated by extensive pastoralism, especially with sheep. At the same time, one important legacy of the Reconquista (the Christian "reconquest" of the Iberian Peninsula from the Moors) that would acquire great importance in early American colonial land-labor regimes was the *encomienda,* a form of labor exploitation and landholding instituted by the Castilians to control newly reconquered areas of Moorish population in the peninsula.

During the first two generations or so after the Spanish arrived in Mexico (1521–60), in fact, it was primarily the *encomienda*—already a part of their institutional repertoire for dominating conquered peoples—that mediated their relations with the land and the native peoples, rather than the great family-owned landed estate that was to acquire such economic and social importance somewhat later. Certainly the Europeans made some effort to acquire property in land, but initially a direct intervention in the production process and capital formation interested them less than extracting wealth from an existing Mesoamerican peasantry by political means, which is what the *encomienda* amounted to. This structure was of course predicated on the survival of a large native population, since individual peasant household agricultural surpluses were small and the parasitic European population always growing. After the mid–sixteenth century, increasingly, this indirect exploitation of land and other resources was to give way to more direct forms, of which the traditional hacienda was the dominant type. Parallel with this extractive process in labor grew the silver mining economy, but that was not to reach its apogee until the *encomienda* already had begun to decline owing to native population loss (c. 1550).

In the Americas the *encomienda* conferred no title to land, but only the right of the holder (the *encomendero*) to collect tribute and utilize the labor of those under his charge, in exchange for which he was enjoined by crown law to see to the Christianization of the Indians and their minimal physical welfare. Predictably enough these injunctions often were ignored, and the distinction between rights to labor/tribute and land often honored more in the breach than in the observance, so that many *encomenderos* acquired large tracts of land extralegally. Fernando (Hernán) Cortés assigned to his followers scores of these grants, correlated to indigenous "villages" or other population units, awarding to himself holdings in Oaxaca and Morelos ostensibly embracing some 23,000 tributaries, but actually many tens of thousands of individuals. In other areas of Mesoamerica swashbuckling conquistadors such as Pedro de Alvarado and Nuño Beltrán de Guzmán did likewise with their retinues and favorites, so that *encomienda* grants often became a major part of the booty in the factional struggles of the time and their unavailability a motive of resentment among later arriving Spaniards. While there was undeniably a "feudal" element in all this (the political nature of the grant itself, the support of extended *encomendero* household establishments along paternalistic lines), *encomienda* labor also was linked to capital formation and markets, as in silver mining, agricultural and livestock production, urban construction, and so forth. At the same time, the Europeans were implanting their own property system with the full panoply of written documentation, notaries, law courts, and bureaucratic culture that supported it and consummated the commodification of land and labor.

Paralleling the rise of the *encomienda,* however, in areas of Mesoamerica where native population was either too thin or too resistant to sustain its demands, and where other ecologies than the temperate ones of the central Mexican valleys created different host conditions and possibilities for profits, other types of agrosocial units developed. These were characterized less by parasitic extraction and more by direct Spanish intervention in management, technical control, and capital formation. By the late 1520s, for example, Cortés had established large sugar plantations on the Veracruz coast and in the Cuernavaca area, which relied on a combination of African slave labor and indigenous coerced or wage labor, heavy capital investment, and elaborate European irrigation and processing technologies. Initially linked to foreign consumers, these plantations failed to meet the competition of Brazilian (and later Caribbean) slave-based sugar production and shortly were reoriented to supply domestic markets within the colony, continuing to do so throughout the colonial period. On the arid steppes of the near north and north of New Spain, native labor was hard to come by because of the semi- or nonsedentary organization of Indian society and the fierce resistance offered by some groups to the northward advance of Spanish colonization (e.g., the so-called Chichimec Wars of the second half of the sixteenth century). Here the sprawling livestock hacienda developed, with its organizational and social similarities to the Argentine *estancia* and North American ranch, based on markets for hides, meat, and wool in the northern mining zones and cities farther to the south.

The convergence of royal humanitarian and political concerns over the fate of the indigenous peoples (e.g., the propagation of the New Laws of 1542) with native demographic collapse under the impact of European diseases effectively destroyed the *encomienda* by the last third of the sixteenth century, although the nadir of population loss was still yet to come (c. 1650). Although informal and wage-based labor arrangements already had arisen in many parts of the colony, insofar as the intervention of the colonial state was concerned the *encomienda* was followed by a transitional labor form known as the *repartimiento*, which in fact survived in certain areas and was invoked under certain emergency conditions well into the eighteenth century. The *repartimiento* was a form of coerced wage labor *(corvee)* imposed on male indigenous tributaries on a rotating basis, and bore some similarity to the infamous Andean *mita*. The system was employed primarily in grain production in the central areas of the colony, as well as mining labor (e.g., at Real del Monte) and public works (e.g., the *desagüe*, the monumental system of canals and tunnels that drained the Valley of Mexico flood waters). By the late sixteenth century an extensive free wage-labor market had also come to exist in the countryside, often associated with worker indebtedness, although the credit advances involved seem to have been more a reflection of the strong bargaining position of workers in a labor-scarce economy than an effective means of limiting their physical mobility. Furthermore, black slaves, of whom some 200,000 or so were imported into New Spain during the colonial period, still were to be found as the core labor force on sugar plantations or working as cowboys, domestic servants, and even as mule skinners. Slaves' importance as rural laborers tended to decline in the later colonial period, however, as the indigenous population recovery and overall demographic growth replaced at least in part the cataclysmic losses of the first century of colonial life.

As indigenous population plummeted by some 90 percent after 1521, only to stabilize around 1650 for reasons that still remain vague, Spanish landownership flowed in behind it, absorbing the territory of depopulated or relocated villages, advancing into the far north behind a network of silver transport routes, military presidios, and missions, and reaching the remotest parts of the Mesoamerican southern periphery, as in highland Chiapas. Except in the still densely Indian south (e.g., Oaxaca), indigenous villages tended to be compressed to the smallest possible area allowable under royal law (the *fundo legal*) and often relegated to marginal or otherwise inadequate lands. While population continued in decline, this was less of a problem than when demographic resurgence after the first third of the seventeenth century put pressure on productive resources now preempted by Spanish holdings. Meanwhile, although royal law imposed strict conditions on the transfer of indigenous landed property into European hands and hedged the Indians of New Spain around with the juridical protections of minors, royal land grants of "empty" lands, Spanish town foundations, purchase, and de facto occupation facilitated the wholesale transfer of land from indigenous to colonist hands.

The Mature Hacienda

Although the Mexican colony at times exported significant quantities of cattle hides, dye stuffs (especially cochineal), sugar, and other agricultural products, throughout most of the colonial period the overwhelming part of its trade with Europe pivoted on silver. Most estate agricultural production therefore was oriented toward domestic Mexican markets and consisted of the mundane foodstuffs and primary materials—maize, wheat, meat, fiber—that kept Mexicans fed and clothed. The country's strongly regional organization, made up of hinterlands centered on mining zones, provincial cities, and the viceregal capital; the large distances involved; and high transport costs associated with a weak infrastructure and relatively inefficient means of moving goods (mule trains)—all these factors tended to discourage commodity movement over long distances and produced a more or less cellular market structure, at least for agricultural products. By the late colonial period there is considerable evidence that the push of demographic increase had eased the labor scarcity in many parts of the colony, although whether a "neo-Malthusian" situation existed is still subject to some debate. Results of this trend included a probable decline of individual laborers' debts to landowners (i.e., a softening in their ability to demand credit), a drop from 1775 or so of something like 25 percent in real purchasing power for rural wage laborers (owing to a combination of stable nominal wages and mild inflation for basic consumer goods), and a tendency for temporary workers drawn from the free peasant sector to replace large permanent labor forces.

The mature hacienda—as one might have seen it between, say, 1650 and 1800—could vary greatly in size, with the livestock enterprises of the north embracing hundreds of thousands of acres, whereas the more compact mixed agropastoral units of the center and south sometimes comprised only 2,000 or 3,000 acres (800 or 1,200 hectares) or less. Whatever their size they tended to be organized around a central set of living and working buildings (the *casco*) that included the owner's house, and on larger estates perhaps such amenities as a chapel. Material life was simple even on wealthier haciendas, and owners who could afford it lived for all or part of the year in the capital or provincial cities, leaving day-to-day decisions in the hands of salaried managers. Larger estates might have resident laboring populations of hundreds of people, supplemented at planting and harvest times with seasonal workers from surrounding villages. Agricultural technologies (except on the capital-intensive sugar plantations) were simple, and productivity increase unlikely except by the acquisition and planting of new lands.

Sources of agricultural capital and the social location of large-scale ownership overlapped considerably by the late colonial period. The church, through loans, always had been an important source of capital for landowners, and remained so throughout the colonial period; few were the estates that did not bear their load of church debt, whether the funds had been wasted through conspicuous consumption or actually invested in productive improvement. But the regular church orders also owned a large number of rural properties, most famously the Jesuits, as at their magnificent complex at Santa Lucía in central New Spain. Wealthy merchants and mine owners also invested heavily in land for several reasons: as a hedge against the losses inherent in such risky enterprises as large-scale commerce and mining, as a means to vertical economic integration in their businesses (especially among mine owners), as a form of frozen capital that might serve as surety for borrowed capital, and as a social overhead investment to ensure good marriages with other elite families and serve as the foundation for establishment of entails *(mayorazgos)* or even ennoblement.

Other Elements in the Rural Economy

Aside from the haciendas, which came to dominate the landscape in most parts of the colony, other productive units shared the countryside, as well. Almost everywhere to be found were smaller holdings called ranchos, producing modest incomes, and like the haciendas of a mixed livestock-farming economy. These typically were family operated, with little or no hired labor, although they might be owned independently or leased from larger holdings. These smallholdings, typologically somewhere between peasant communal exploitations and haciendas, clustered heavily in certain areas of the country, as for example to the northeast of Guadalajara, in the Altos area, where the ratio of ranchos to haciendas reached approximately 500-to-1 by 1800 or so. The rent rolls of larger rural estates also typically carried numerous names of renters occupying hacienda lands under a variety of arrangements, among them service tenantry, sharecropping, and the payment of money rents, or a combination of these. This practice brought important cash income to large landowners in normal times, stabilized their income levels in hard times, and helped to cement their social power in the countryside.

Of greater importance in the social and economic fabric of rural New Spain in most places were the indigenous and other ethnically mixed villages in which the majority of the farming population lived. Some of these had existed before the arrival of the Europeans, others were created under the early colonial policy of *congregación,* whereby the Spanish state consolidated and sometimes relocated the remnants of earlier settlements depopulated by disease, and still others sprang up spontaneously as the result of population growth or outward migration from parent villages in the later colonial period. Often arranged spatially in the pattern of a central settlement with outlying hamlets (sometimes called *barrios* or *sujetos*), most had their own governments—subject, of course, to regulation or even intervention by powerful outsiders such as non-Indian land-owners, parish priests, or local magistrates—and controlled some form of farming and common lands (respectively *tierras de reparto* and *ejidos*) held communally but worked on an individual family basis. Private indigenous holdings existed alongside these, providing ample basis for social differentiation within communities. In some regions of the colony such villages were drawn into urban and other markets for basic products, but overall the pueblo economy produced for subsistence needs. The main points of contact between such communities and the neighboring haciendas were in contention over land and in the sale of surplus labor through the wage labor system, where a powerful symbiosis bound privately owned estates to the peasant sector.

Conflict and Politics

Although the highly skewed distribution of land and wealth in the colonial countryside was hardly the only point of contention between people of European descent and those of color, between haves and have-nots, or between the powerful and subalterns, it produced virtually continual tension throughout the colonial era. Village riots were common occurrences, often related to disputes over land between communities or between them and neighboring estates. These seem to have reached a crescendo in the eighteenth century as rural population rebounded, the commercialization of agriculture spread, and contention over resources sharpened, particularly between the peasant and commercial sectors. Indian villagers had become very adept at using the colonial legal system (e.g., the *Juzgado General de Indios,* established in 1591), and the late colonial decades saw court dockets in New Spain and New Galicia (the designation for western Mexico, with its own *audiencia* at Guadalajara) jammed with litigation over land, which sometimes went on for many years, with attendant high legal costs and tensions between litigants.

Landlord hegemony and the representatives of colonial church and state in the countryside aimed to curtail this tension, or at least keep it within manageable bounds. Paternalistic labor practices could not finally counterbalance difficult working conditions, low wages, falling purchasing power, personal indignities, and spreading proletarianization, but they did act to dampen overt expressions of stress. Hacendados often paid their laborers' tributes on credit, loaned them sums to see them through family crises and life cycle events, provided some perquisites as part of the wage structure (e.g., rations and access to subsistence plots), and intervened when

necessary to keep their "gente" out of the hands of local law enforcement officials. Such arrangements as *compadrazgo* (ritual kinship) sometimes bound landlord and laborer or tenant, blunting the edge of sensitive ethnic and class relations, and the labor forces of one hacienda were even known to fight against those of another in land disputes. Parish priests often were more allied to local landowners than not, while ritual practice within the church (public festivals on village saints' days, etc.) did much to quicken the rhythms of rural life as it absorbed villagers' emotional energies to some degree. Ironically, in exerting a measure of social control in the countryside, the matrix of ritual life also forged communal solidarities in rural villages that might underwrite collective action when grievances came to a boil.

Resistance and Rebellion

In contrast to the continual political violence and rural unrest of the nineteenth century, or the epic Mexican Revolution (1910–20) or Cristero Rebellion (1926–29) of the twentieth, the colonial era in Mexico often has been characterized as stable and peaceful, even somnolent. Yet upon closer inspection this proves a false picture, although rural resistance and rebellion seem to have touched certain regions of the country more than others. For much of the sixteenth century the northern provinces were aflame with indigenous anti-Spanish warfare, much of it embraced by the general rubric of the "Chichimec Wars" (c. 1550–1600). The southern periphery of the colony, primarily in areas of Maya culture, also was wracked with stubborn rebellion and the sometimes violent rejection of Christian evangelization, Maya resistance in the Peten region was not finally reduced until the end of the seventeenth century. Relatively large-scale episodes of indigenous resistance were indeed more likely to occur in the peripheral areas of far north and south, where new and systematically militarized colonial penetration, open frontier conditions, and native societies still intact enough to have some sense of their own identities made for a thinner Spanish hegemony and greater possibilities for native defiance. The densely settled central valleys of New Spain, the center-west, and the eastern plateau were anything but exempt from violence, however, and hardly a year passed during which some form of unrest did not take place somewhere in the colony.

While lesser, typically localized resistance and rebellion were endemic to New Spain, it is true that with the notable exception of the Tzeltal revolt (1712) the two centuries from 1550 to 1750 witnessed no *large-scale* rural or indigenous revolt. The sixteenth and eighteenth centuries, however, were particularly marked by rural violence, much of it centrally involving indigenous people, whether in the form of riots by peasant villagers, or of concerted guerrilla resistance by non- or semisedentary Indians to militarized missionary penetration and the white settlement that accompanied it. Spectacular episodes of rural rebellion, messianic uprisings, or widespread conspiracies on a regional scale—e.g., the Mixton War (1541–42), the Tzeltal Revolt (1712–13), the Canek Rebellion (1761), or the rebellion of El Indio Mariano (1801–1802)—have tended to overshadow smaller episodes of collective violence and especially quotidian expressions of discontent or resistance to the colonial order. The 120 years between 1700 and 1820, for example, saw more than 150 village riots in central Mexico alone (not including actions directly associated with the Independence movement), accelerating in frequency after about 1765. Concurrent with these episodes there occurred in much of the colony a rising tide of brigandage and contraband activity, as well as continuing instances of religious heterodoxy, mostly concentrated in rural areas. As the scholarly study of ethnohistory and peasantries has advanced over the last two or three decades, so too has the study of all these forms of rural disaffection and resistance, reevaluating them as forms of evidence for the social and cultural history of the colonial era, and of the political agency and ideological thinking of native peoples.

Rural unrest among subaltern groups, particularly Indians, was in large measure itself a reaction to a colonial order whose own foundations were steeped in violence, but which was, paradoxically, often unwilling or unable to suppress violent responses from the colonized. The pervasiveness of violence in colonial society, and therefore the proneness of colonial subjects to respond in kind, was due in large measure to the very ramshackle nature and weakness of the Spanish empire itself. This encouraged indirect forms of rule in which local indigenous and criollo elites extracted resources from the subaltern population, inconsistently regulated by the colonial state and backed up by force. In addition, it has been observed, the colonial justice system tended to rely not on long incarceration but instead on violent forms of corporal punishment or upon sentences at forced labor (which amounted to much the same thing), in the process creating an atmosphere of arbitrary power and simmering resentment that naturally drew forth violent responses.

Everywhere within its vast domain, therefore, the Spanish colonial state was partially based on violence or the threat of it. Although there was no professional standing army in New Spain until the 1760s, explicit or implicit violence was a central technology of colonial power and a daily reality in the Mexican countryside, directed especially at poor people of color.

Landlord hegemony, the forced extension of market relationships, the payment of taxes, subordination to local curates and secular officials, the implantation of Christian belief—all these and other structural elements of the colonial regime were held in place at least in part by force. The Spanish colonial enterprise differed little in this from other societies forged by military conquest and open usurpation of authority, but all states, ancient or modern, have employed this technology of power in greater or lesser degree. Indeed, Max Weber and other social thinkers after him identified a monopoly on the legitimate use of force as central to the very definition of the state. It is also true, certainly, that the remarkable resilience of the colonial regime rested even more upon forms of native acculturation and the construction of a legitimating ideology by the colonizers, its chief prop the wide inculcation of Christianity among the indigenous population. Yet the hegemony of the Spanish state lay unevenly upon the Mexican colony, particularly in the countryside, where in most areas (save certain regions in the north and along the lowland coastal fringes) Indians were in the majority. The vast distances, underdeveloped means of communication and transportation, shallowness of market relationships in some areas, and the negotiated, co-optative, and finally rather passive nature of the colonial regime itself accounted for this, leaving weak points at which forms of "everyday resistance" were always in evidence, and through which rebellion periodically erupted.

Complex and controversial as the notion of resistance is, a brief conceptual discussion may prove a useful prologue to a closer look at empirical cases of resistance and rebellion in the colonial countryside. First, there is a distinction to be drawn between conflict and resistance, the latter being a subset of the former, typically involving a power asymmetry between a superordinate and a subordinate social actor. In the colonial situation, however, conflict between actors situated as peers in the social hierarchy—between two indigenous villages contending over disputed land, let us say—which did not on its face appear to involve "resistance" as such, might also be construed as resistance to a third interlocutor, the colonial state, which set the terms of the competition and fostered conditions under which horizontal conflict became a mode of preserving ethnic, communal, and political identity somewhat intact. Second, there is a far from perfect congruence between "rural" and "Indian." Although forms of indigenous resistance and rebellion are emphasized here and have tended to attract most attention in recent scholarship, Indians were not alone in the countryside, nor did they alone engage in resistant behaviors. It is worth remembering that at the close of the colonial period the ethnic composition of New Spain was roughly 18 percent "white" (1,108,000), 22 percent mixed castes (1,338,000), and 60 percent Indian (3,676,000).

Third, there are many thorny unresolved interpretive questions relating to resistance itself, which has come much into fashion as a way of representing popular culture, ethnic conflict, and rural-urban friction in Mexican history. For example, are suicide or alcoholism to be seen as forms of resistance, escapism, or pathology, or perhaps some combination of these? And then there is the perennial discussion about banditry, whether of the social or garden varieties: under what circumstances is rural brigandage to be viewed as a form of protest against prevailing social or economic arrangements, if at all, or simply as opportunism? Finally, for some purposes it may be useful to view "resistant" behaviors as distributed along a continuum of intensity, organization, and scale ranging from "victimless" or more passive forms such as suicide, alcoholism, foot-dragging, and sabotage on the job, rumor and aggressive language, and so forth, through religious heterodoxy, endemic litigation in the courts, and civic refusal (to pay taxes, for example), to communal land invasions, riots, localized rebellions, messianic movements, and participation in more generalized insurrection. On the other hand, it would seem appropriate to make an important distinction between the often more anomic, individualized activities at the lower end of the continuum and the often larger scale, collective ones at the upper end, on the assumption that not just resistance but the circumstances of its collective expression are important to understanding how common people negotiated or protested the colonial order.

Quotidian Resistance

There has for some years existed a debate among scholars as to whether the advent of the Spanish colonial regime loosed a torrent of alcohol into rural society, especially into indigenous villages, and into the cities that quickly grew up as the bridgeheads of European domination of the countryside. There is little doubt that native access to intoxicants, both the ubiquitous pulque (fermented agave) and the new wines and distillates (rum, brandy, etc.) the Europeans introduced, widened and became

in large measure desacralized, while at the same time the Christian liturgical calendar provided ever more frequent opportunities for celebratory drinking, and the new nutritional regimen even may have encouraged resort to alcoholic beverages as a source of calories. Certainly it became an article of faith in criollo racialist ideology (as it was of elite views of the peasantry in Europe itself) that Indians were not only lazy, libidinous, sullen, stupid, and suggestible, but also extremely prone to drunkenness. The social reality of this stereotype—that indigenous men, especially, regularly drank themselves into stuporous oblivion and while intoxicated unleashed all sorts of aggressive behavior—is of course open to question. But the evidence in criminal and other records of the colonial period, especially of the eighteenth century, even if discounted somewhat, is sufficient to support the conclusion that there was a good deal of non-ritual drinking, and that it may have created a social problem. The question is whether widespread alcohol consumption as a form of self-anesthetization constituted a form of resistance to an oppressive colonial order, or an escape from it; probably it embraced something of both. And when intoxication disinhibited aggressive behavior, whether toward family members, adult peers, or superordinate figures (work supervisors, priests, or officials), it may certainly be viewed as a facilitator of resistance to the demands imposed upon subaltern people by the colonial order, and of externalization of the frustration and impotence experienced on a daily basis, in particular, by humbler men of color. And branching off from alcohol abuse and its associated forms of violence as a type of resistance were banditry and smuggling, by all accounts also endemic in the colonial countryside, although by no means as significant as they were to become in the bandit-ridden nineteenth century.

The colonial labor regime and the demands it placed upon rural people was an obvious arena for resistance, both passive and violent. In the sixteenth century, while the encomienda primarily mediated the labor and tribute claims made upon indigenous villagers by the Europeans, the murder of encomienda holders by "their" Indians was not unknown, as occurred in the killing of encomendero Salvador Martel in western New Galicia in 1540. More common on rural estates was foot-dragging, malingering, modest levels of sabotage, and the ubiquitous Sunday drinking among working people, which often made of Monday (called "San Lunes," or "Saint Monday") a nonproductive day, much to the disgust of property owners and administrators. Sometimes rural people simply refused to come to work despite economic inducements or the threat of force, as occurred over a span of years in the Puebla countryside at the very end of the colonial era. This was certainly resistance of a sort, although the loss of wages might damage the striker as much as the owner, and the explicit political content is often in doubt.

Much less random and individualized, and linked in a more obvious way to identifiable economic and social conditions in the countryside, was the continual litigation supported especially by indigenous communities against neighboring landowners, whether other rural communities or non-Indian property owners. Indians early became adept at the use of the legal system the Spaniards imposed upon them, most notably in the venue of the General Indian Court (Juzgado General de Indios), a specialized organ of the Audiencia of New Spain established in 1591 to handle indigenous legal matters. Since the Spanish Crown recognized Indian community land titles from early on, and since ownership of land became the single most vexed issue in Indian-Spanish relations under the impact of growing rural commercialization and indigenous population recovery in the later colonial period, suits and countersuits over land ownership and boundaries constantly occupied the attention of Spanish officials, villagers, and non-Indian landowners, rising to a crescendo in the eighteenth century. Such litigation was expensive, time consuming (individual suits sometimes lasted for decades and might recur repeatedly between the same parties or their heirs), and on occasion violent. But the behavior was reinforced among rural villages by the fact that suits at law often achieved positive results for them, helping them to confirm title to lands already held, to recover lands occupied illegally by other communities or white landowners, and over the long haul somewhat slowing the drift of land resources from peasant into hacendado hands. This could shore up the social and political integrity of peasant communities threatened by long-term forces of change, although the outcome was not always beneficial to villagers.

Further within the interior of indigenous and country life, and heavy with cultural and symbolic meanings, were forms of religious "heterodoxy." The nature and scale of such resistance is by its very nature harder to detect in the historical record since religious reservations, selective appropriation of orthodox Catholic thinking, or outright rejection of the new moral dispensation and ritual life often did not emerge directly into the public sphere. Still, when they did the results could be spectacular. In the 1530s, for example, before cases of Indian heterodoxy were removed from the jurisdiction of the Inquisition (1570), a number of indigenous caciques and other men (some of them Nahua priests before the coming of the Europeans), among them Martin Ocelotl and Andres Mixcoatl, were accused of fomenting native cults and curing practices, of prophecy and necromancy, of consorting with the Devil to block the Christian mission, and of other crimes against church and state. There is no question that what the colonial secular and ecclesiastical authorities construed as rejection of Christianity or heterodox blendings of Christian and native religious precepts and practices continued throughout the colonial period, often emerging in the ideological component of violent uprisings. But this also went on among ordinary country people on a daily basis. Sometimes rural priests saw their parishioners' failure to attend mass, observe the holy sacraments, or mute the more unbuttoned aspects of celebratory and ritual behavior as the backsliding of ignorant rustics and indigenous converts forever childlike in their understanding. One rural curate commented not atypically of his indigenous parishioners: "[T]hese miserable Indians live and die not like faithful believers in Jesus Christ, but as though they inhabited still the gloomy caverns of paganism."

But sometimes the slippage between official religious belief and practice and its "popular" manifestations took on darker hues. Witchcraft, rural fertility cults, and demonic possession were not unknown even at the very close of the colonial period. For example, very near Mexico City as late as 1820 or so a rural priest stumbled upon a crude altar in a cave on which he found unidentifiable small effigies ("dolls") and other icons he believed linked to a "pagan" fertility cult whose celebration included forbidden dancing by both sexes, offerings of native foods, and nonliturgical music. It is clear that there was an element of resistance in such practices, that is, an attempt on the part of Indians in particular to preserve traditional or even recently "invented" ways of life with meanings peculiar to village culture, and oppositional to officially sanctioned colonial religious sensibilities.

Riot and Rebellion

The colonial authorities were in some ways morbidly sensitive to civil violence, importing from Spain and installing in major Mexican cities public institutions designed to prevent it: municipal granaries and elaborate pricing regulations for meat and bread, for example, whose function was to keep supplies and prices more or less stable in order to forestall the consumer riots so common in early modern Europe. Little of this, or much policing of any sort, could be done in the thousands of small towns, villages, and hamlets dotting the vast Mexican countryside, however, where colonial authority was spread thin and compromised by the connections of local power holders, and where interethnic tensions often infused the relations of Indians and non-Indians. Here "bargaining by riot" became a time-honored method for country people to express their disaffection with the colonial regime or with local power holders, although the person of the Spanish king (and perhaps the larger legitimacy of the imperial state) almost always was held above the fray ideologically through the invocation by rioters and rebels of the traditional formula "Long live the King! Death to bad government!" Although they appeared acephalous as to leadership and were fairly short-lived (lasting a few days at most), such localized riots (or *tumultos,* as they were widely known) often had been simmering for long periods of time, or recurred regularly in the same localities, and just as often did have identifiable leaders, sometimes village women. Village riots might find their origins in disputes over land with neighboring communities or individual landowners (sometimes beginning or ending with land invasions), fiscal extractions deemed excessive or otherwise inequitable, local elections or other sorts of political events, disputes over the disposition of religious icons, or the transgression of implicit or explicit rules of conduct by local power holders such as landowners, priests, or magistrates.

Hundreds of these episodes took place during the colonial period, each with its own natural and social history, although they shared certain characteristics. Perhaps one such *tumulto* will serve as an example, if not exactly a template. In late 1785 the largely Indian town of Cuauhtitlan, a few miles north of Mexico City, erupted in a riot in which the houses of the local priest, the tithe collector, and at least two Spanish merchants were broken into and partially looted, and from which the curate himself barely escaped with his life. The *tumulto* was occasioned by a public argument during a religious observance over the property of a locally venerated effigy of the Virgin Mary housed in the parish church, the Indian parishioners claiming it as theirs, the Spanish citizens of the town (with the priest's backing) as theirs. As it turned out, the violent confrontation over the possession of the statue was only the tip of the iceberg of local conflict, which also involved shifts in the access to land resources over the long term in favor

of local nonindigenous farmers, and within the Indian community from the poor to a more privileged stratum. Here we find conflated, therefore, at least three elements often at work in localized communal violence: religious sensibility, economic pressure, and interethnic tensions. The element of "resistance" here was by indigenous people against the forces of dissolution bearing down upon their community in the form of internal wealth redistribution and social differentiation, ethnic confrontation with powerful non-Indians, and the conflation of religious sensibility with community identity.

Rural (primarily Indian) rebellion on a larger scale erupted periodically throughout the colonial period, sometimes embracing a large segment of a single ethnolinguistic group or a region, but was most likely to occur in the sixteenth or eighteenth centuries. By all odds one of the most spectacular episodes of such indigenous resistance to European encroachment was the Mixton War (1540–41), which occurred within scarcely a decade of the establishment of an effective Spanish settler presence in New Galicia, in the center-west of Mexico. This Caxcan Indian uprising threatened for a time to extinguish Spanish influence in western Mexico, while its suppression cost the lives and enslavement of thousands of Indians, as well as the lives of the redoubtable Pedro de Alvarado and scores of Spanish *encomenderos,* settlers, soldiers, and missionaries. Occasioned by the substantial draw-down of Spanish military strength in New Galicia attendant upon the assembly of Francisco Vázquez de Coronado's expedition to the north in search of Gran Quivira and the Seven Cities of Cibola, indigenous rebellion was motivated in part by resistance to *encomendero* and missionary demands, in part by generalized anti-Spanish sentiments and festering bitterness over the activities in the area a few years previously of the Spanish conquistador Nuño Beltrán de Guzmán. With the partial military vacuum in New Galicia, the unpacified tribal peoples north of the Santiago River, in what is today southern Zacatecas and northern Jalisco, rose in arms against the Spanish settlers, engaging in numerous raids from fortified hilltops in the Sierra del Mixton, eventually threatening the precarious existence of Guadalajara. The major indigenous leaders were the baptized chieftains don Diego el Zacateco and don Francisco de Aguilar, cacique (chief) of Nochistlan. The movement's ideology definitely embraced millenarian elements, including a war of extermination against the Spaniards, the rejection of Christianity, and the return of the old native gods. The uprising eventually was crushed by a Spanish force under the command of Viceroy Antonio de Mendoza himself, giving way to a savage repression including the branding and enslavement of hundreds of captured natives. Other native rebellions in the Mexican north followed in the sixteenth century, and in the seventeenth uprisings by Acaxee, Xixime, Tepehuane and Tarahumara populations, among others.

Large-scale indigenous resistance movements, as in the case of the Mixton War, often invoked religiously inspired ideologies embracing elements of millenarian thinking, anticlericalism, virulently anti-Spanish sentiment, and, paradoxically, elements of Christian doctrine. Programmatically rather vague, these movements typically centered on messianic or prophetic leader figures and rarely achieved significant crossclass or crossethnic alliances. Two of the most interesting of such uprisings occurred in the eighteenth century in the far southeast of the colony. The Tzeltal Rebellion (1712–13) broke out in the Chiapas highlands among rural indigenous communities suffering increased Spanish tribute demands, a demographic crisis, and internal leadership struggles, coalescing briefly around a messianic hermit and an Indian cult to the Virgin. A half-century later (1761) came the turn of neighboring Yucatán. Here the Indian leader Jacinto Canek led a Maya cultural revitalization movement and rebellion centered on the village of Cisteil, ideologically embracing both traditional Maya and Christian elements, and attracting thousands of indigenous followers until defeated by Spanish forces. Nor was central Mexico free of such episodes, although there they often took the form more of religious cults than open rebellion. Exactly contemporaneous with the Canek rebellion arose the religious movement led by Antonio Perez, in the Yautepec and Popocatepetl areas of central Mexico, in which the prophet preached a mixture of traditional Christian apocalyptic and indigenous religious revival.

At virtually the end of the colonial period arose what is unquestionably one of the most intriguing and mysterious of these indigenous conspiracies or rebellions, the abortive indigenous uprising surrounding the almost certainly apocryphal native messianic figure of "El Indio Mariano" in the area around Tepic from 1800 to 1802. The Spanish civil and military authorities uncovered what they believed a widespread Indian conspiracy and rebellious mobilization embracing both coastal and sierra villages in the Tepic area, and including indigenous groups as far away as the sierra of Nayarit, Durango, and even the far northwest. The eponymous Mariano—very probably himself a fabrication of the movement's indigenous leaders—was said to be linked by kinship to the central Mexican indigenous state of Tlaxcala, a symbol of residual native political legitimacy and therefore the locus in several contemporaneous movements of an anti-Spanish native shadow-state. Mariano was said to have received rights to govern "the Indies" from the Spanish king Carlos IV, but he also displayed elements of chiliastic identification with Jesus Christ. The program of the movement included the restoration of indigenous village lands and the abolition of tribute payments. After some months the conspiracy and mobilization came to naught, one or two armed skirmishes were fought with Spanish forces, and several hundred Indian conspirators were arrested, although the pretender Mariano was himself never apprehended.

Marking the end of the colonial period we have the Wars of Independence (1810–1821) and the emergence of the Mexican successor state. The conventional wisdom tends to depict this tumultuous and violent period as a war of national liberation from Spain carried forward by a crossclass and crossethnic alliance in the name of a burgeoning Mexican nationalism, famously represented by the figure of the Virgin of Guadalupe. But the role of popular groups in the countryside is better understood as a continuation of rural people's struggles—particularly the struggles of indigenous villagers—to preserve intact their communities against the forces of agrarian commercialization, ethnic homogenization, and the extension of the late Bourbon state. The Independence movement may thus be seen in large measure as an internal war carrying forward a centuries-old pattern of rural resistance and rebellion into the nineteenth century, which was to be punctuated with frequent episodes of violence in the countryside and marked at its end by the Revolution of 1910.

See also African Mexicans; Conquest: Ecological Impact; Hidalgo Revolt; Missions

Select Bibliography

Beezley, William H., Cheryl E. Martin, and William E. French, editors, *Rituals of Rule, Rituals of Resistance: Public Celebrations and Popular Culture in Mexico.* Wilmington, Delaware: Scholarly Resources, 1994.

Gosner, Kevin M., *Soldiers of the Virgin: An Ethnohistorical Analysis of the Tzeltal Revolt of 1712.* Tucson: University of Arizona Press, 1992.

Gruzinski, Serge, *Man-Gods in the Mexican Highlands: Indian Power and Colonial Society, 1520–1800.* Stanford, California: Stanford University Press, 1989.

Katz, Friedrich, editor, *Riot, Rebellion, and Revolution: Rural Social Conflict in Mexico.* Princeton, New Jersey: Princeton University Press, 1988.

Scott, James C., *Domination and the Arts of Resistance: Hidden Transcripts*. New Haven, Connecticut: Yale University Press, 1990.

Taylor, William B., *Drinking, Homicide, and Rebellion in Colonial Mexican Villages*. Stanford, California: Stanford University Press, 1979.

—ERIC VAN YOUNG

Rural Economy and Society: 1821–1910

Mexico began the national era as an agrarian society, its rural institutions inherited from the colonial past. The decade of insurgency and Independence from 1810 to 1821 started new conflicts and transformations. The remainder of the nineteenth century brought continuing agrarian changes provoked by sociopolitical conflicts, population growth, liberal policies, and Mexico's changing role in the expanding Atlantic economy.

Land-Labor Regimes

Independent Mexico began the new era with three primary rural institutions—peasant communities, haciendas, and ranchos—that developed and mixed differently in diverse regions to create a regionally varied agrarian Mexico. Peasant communities rooted in the distant pre-Hispanic past had been transformed during the colonial era by depopulation, congregation, and the imposition of Spanish legal forms. Yet they adapted and endured to remain the primary social institutions of agrarian Mexico at Independence. The majority of Mexicans, concentrated in the central and southern highlands, lived in landed communities. Most villagers spoke indigenous languages; most maintained local variants of peasant Christianity adapted under colonial rule.

The majority of communities retained land as the national era began, using it to support local government, community religious life, and the subsistence production of resident families. Community lands, however, rarely were distributed equally. Most communities were led by local elites with ample lands for subsistence and limited surplus production. The same elites ruled local government. The majority of villagers held lands insufficient for family sustenance, and a landless minority struggled to survive in most villages.

Community lands allowed most villagers a base of subsistence autonomy. The limits on the availability and distribution of those lands led them to develop diversified family economies. Men controlled most land and engaged in subsistence cultivation; the limits of that cultivation led them to seek additional earnings, usually by seasonal field labor at nearby estates. Women made cloth, pottery, and other craft goods; traded those wares and small family crop surpluses in local markets; and maintained gardens, made clothing, and raised children. Thus, integrated family economies combining subsistence cultivation, craft production, and local marketing sustained the agrarian majority of villagers—and the communities that they maintained.

Haciendas were large landed estates oriented to commercial production, seeking profit in urban markets and supporting landed elites. Haciendas produced European goods such as wheat, sugar, and livestock to sustain the emerging nation's urban population. Estates also produced maize, seeking to profit from periodic droughts and famines among the indigenous majority. And they made pulque (the fermented juice of maguey), supplying the indigenous intoxicant to the urban taverns.

Haciendas concentrated where fertile lands adjoined urban markets. Around Mexico City, the largest urban market in the New World around 1800, numerous haciendas produced wheat and maize in the valleys of Mexico and Toluca, sugar in the Morelos basin just south, and pulque in the arid zones to the north and east. In the Bajío region of north-central Mexico—where multiple cities and towns engaged in mining, textile production, and trade—fertile and often irrigated lands saw haciendas engaged in wheat and maize production to supply local markets, distant regions of the arid north, and Mexico City (when drought brought scarcity there). Across the dry north, vast estates grazed livestock to supply local mining towns, as well as urban areas of the central highlands. Smaller cities like Puebla, Guadalajara, Oaxaca, and Morelia also were flanked by haciendas oriented to profit local elites by supplying urban markets.

Haciendas developed diverse labor regimes depending on their economic activities and the regional societies in which they operated. In central and southern regions, estates inevitably operated among peasant villages. Most estates maintained only small groups of permanent employees there, mostly mestizos and mulattos working as supervisors, craftsmen, and stock herders. Field labor was done by seasonal wage laborers recruited in neighboring villages. Working a few weeks or months each year, villagers produced the commercial maize, wheat, and sugar that generated estate profits. They simultaneously earned the cash essential to sustain families with insufficient lands for subsistence production. Central highland estates could not profit without villagers' labor; villagers could not survive without the wages of hacienda work. Hacienda production and peasant family economies (and thus peasant communities) were inextricably linked. This integration was inherently exploitative, however. Villagers' work at haciendas generated sustenance for urban society and profits for landed elites; villagers, meanwhile, worked long hours for barely enough pay to sustain their families.

From the Bajío region of north-central Mexico, haciendas operated in regions with little indigenous population and few peasant communities. Haciendas there were the primary economic and social institutions of rural society. They included large resident populations, mostly of mestizos and mulattos. Depending on the particular region's lands and economies, estates combined different employment and tenancy regimes to organize dependent populations for profitable production. In the Bajío region of north-central Mexico, where cultivation ruled, estates employed many men as permanent, year-round laborers who were paid wages and allotted maize rations in a relationship of dependent security. Other residents rented marginal estate lands. They became estate-dependent peasants, producing limited subsistence, perhaps marketing firewood and charcoal, and providing seasonal labor to plant and harvest estate crops while raising and educating children. The wives of both employees and tenants at Bajío estates also spun cloth for nearby textile workshops and made cloth for family use.

In drier northern zones estates primarily grazed livestock and nearly all estate workers were resident employees, allotted monthly salaries along with maize rations. Wages were only an accounting device in regions far from towns and markets. Estates supplied residents with cloth, shoes, candles, and varied foodstuffs and then accounted their goods against their annual earnings. To maintain the system, hacienda managers often brought cloth from Europe, diverse goods from across Mexico, and maize from the Bajío. The system often left workers indebted to estates. In isolated regions where workers were most scarce, such debts might become the pretext to hold families at estates.

Ranchos, small landed properties mixing subsistence production with marketing, were the third major agrarian institution inherited from the colonial past. Most ranchos raised maize for consumption and sale or raised livestock for use and market. Many ranchos also kept mule teams to transport produce to market and to earn income by carrying goods for nearby estates or traders. Ranchero economies were also family economies, with women and children engaged in the production of cloth and diverse craft goods, again both for use and sale.

Most rancheros were criollos, mestizos, or mulattos, forming an agrarian middle sector between landed elites and indigenous peasant villagers. They produced sustenance for their families, but most also aimed to profit from market production—simultaneously operating as prosperous peasants and modest commercial farmers. Some ranchos were owned by notable families in small towns. They operated as small haciendas, with a manager and seasonal workers. Many rancheros were resident proprietors, living on their lands and working with family labor, seasonally joined by hired hands. Other ranchos were rented from haciendas. Across the central and southern highlands, many were leased from landed communities, which used the rents to support local government and religious life.

As the national era began, most ranchos were subordinate institutions, dominated by vast haciendas across most of the north and squeezed among haciendas and landed communities in the central and southern zones. They were integral to Mexico's complex and regionally varied agrarian structure, however. Ranchos leased from communities used lands that might have supported peasant families, while paying rents that did support village governments and religious festivals. Rancheros renting estate lands contributed to hacienda incomes while providing seasonal labor in estate fields. And many independent rancheros spent their adult lives as estate employees, seeking the income to begin independent cultivation. Later they might provide transport services to haciendas as muleteers.

If the land and labor regimes inherited from the colonial era were complex and regionally varied, the century after Independence brought new changes, greater complexities, and escalating conflicts. The decades after 1821 brought a long era of agrarian decompression: the commercial estate economy declined and remained uncertain; landed elites struggled financially; and hacienda ownership became unstable. Meanwhile, with landed elites and their haciendas struggling to break even, peasant villagers and rancheros claimed new roles in the agrarian economy. Villagers put pressure on haciendas, often renewing old land disputes. In some notable cases (as in the Toluca Valley in 1826) communities gained substantial new holdings. Villagers also often claimed higher wages for seasonal work at estates after 1821. Other Mexicans responded to the instability of the early national decades by moving into isolated uplands and creating ranchero societies, while still others bought lands from financially weak haciendas, turning colonial estates into new ranchero communities.

There were regional variations in all these developments, but across Mexico by the 1840s, the hacienda economy was struggling, peasant communities newly entrenched, and ranchero societies in rapid expansion. The nature of the changes is clear; the causes are debated. Liberals who aimed to transform Mexico after Independence did propose the privatization of church and peasant community lands. Yet while discussion, debate, and regional legislation began in the 1820s, national legislation was not drafted until the 1850s—and implementation came even later. The agrarian transformations of the post-Independence decades were neither planned nor legislated.

The crisis of hacienda production and profit resulted in part from the destructive Wars of Independence, the collapse of silver mining, and the consequent weakness of the entire commercial economy. The financial problems of landed elites were worsened by the arrival of new immigrant merchants in control of Mexico's international trade—Britons, French, Italians, and North Americans who were much less likely to invest in Mexican haciendas than their colonial Spanish predecessors. Moreover, constant political turmoil made all investment and commercial activity uncertain from 1810 through the 1870s. All these trends weakened landed elites and the commercial economy in which their haciendas struggled to operate.

In that context, peasant villagers and rancheros actively pressed for advantage, seeking local rural societies less dominated by elites and estates and more oriented toward family economies. In the Bajío, the region of most intense and enduring agrarian insurgency after 1810, rebellious estate residents forced shifts from estate production to ranchero economies. After the insurgency, most Bajío estates were limited to collecting rents from ranchero tenants who themselves controlled production. In the central highlands, many villagers renewed land claims, and a few actually won lands. Many more communities used their control over the seasonal labor essential to estate production (and their landed bases and local cohesion) to demand and obtain higher wages. From the 1830s through the 1850s, many central highland estate operators blamed resistant and demanding villagers for their estates' financial woes. They were not wrong. The economic changes and political conflicts of Independence and nation-building contributed to the decline of the hacienda economy, but villagers and rancheros—seeking their own visions of independence and national society—also weakened the commercial economy and the haciendas that sustained Mexican landed elites.

While the primary changes that brought agrarian decompression occurred from 1810 to the 1840s, the middle decades of the century, marked by persistent civil and international wars, saw these transformations continue and deepen. The decades from the 1840s through the 1870s saw the expansion of sharecropping across Mexico. Facing labor difficulties and scarce profits, estates increasingly turned over lands and production to sharecropping villagers seeking additional lands in the central highlands and to rancheros seeking increased holdings across the north. Sharecropping sharply limited the costs, the risks, and the profits of hacienda operation. It increased production by villagers and rancheros and added new costs and risks to their family economies.

The long post-Independence era of agrarian decompression limited the power of landed elites, restricted the economic importance of the great haciendas, consolidated peasant village economies, and rapidly expanded the ranchero sector of society. In this context Liberals promoted land privatization: the alienation of church lands and the transformation of community lands into personal properties of residents. The goal was the mobilization of property and the promotion of commercial production. The community cohesion that enabled villagers to contest estate lands and demand higher wages would weaken, while subsistence lands bought, sold, and mortgaged freely could be concentrated among the prosperous, expanding the population of poor, landless peasants. The liberal program would undermine community power and peasant family subsistence autonomy. Many rancheros would benefit, and those leasing community (or church) lands could become proprietors. These changes were formally legislated on a national level by the Ley Lerdo of 1856, but implementation would be contested for decades. Broad implementation began only after 1867 and was never completed. The liberal agrarian program aimed to reform agrarian decompression. It favored elites (with the significant exception of the Catholic Church), rancheros, and the commercial economy, while attacking the power and autonomy of indigenous peasant communities.

Only the regime of Porfirio Díaz (1876–80; 1884–1911) effectively reversed post-Independence agrarian decompression. State power finally was stabilized; railroads integrated the Mexican economy internally and (along with steamships) linked it to the United States and Europe; and the commercial economy boomed persistently for the first time since the late colonial era. Across rural Mexico, Porfirian development brought new complexities to land and labor regimes. Landed elites and commercial haciendas found new power, peasant communities faced new attacks, and ranchero societies proliferated. These changes inevitably varied from region to region.

With the regime stabilized and new links formed to the international economy, regions little settled and long peripheral to commercial production suddenly developed. The far northern borderlands, linked to Mexico City and the United States by railroads in the 1880s, saw the last indigenous peoples crushed and their lands claimed. The Porfirian program of surveying and distributing untitled lands created new or enlarged haciendas and many more ranchos. Livestock grazing predominated across arid range lands. But where irrigation was possible, as in the Laguna region of Durango and Coahuila, cotton production boomed to supply manufacturers in Mexico and the United States.

In southern coastal zones, coffee emerged as a profitable new export in the foothills of Veracruz, Oaxaca, and Chiapas. There, too, land surveys created both large haciendas and numerous ranchos. On the arid plains of Yucatán, henequen plantations produced fiber to supply the cordage industry in the United States. Where land, climate, and links to markets allowed, the leading agricultural exports of Porfirian Mexico were livestock, cotton, coffee, and henequen, but many other crops—including citrus, tobacco, and vanilla—entered the world market.

Porfirian stabilization, railroads, and commercial expansion also brought rapid and often radical changes to the Mexican highlands, regions in which haciendas, peasant communities, and rancheros had mixed conflict and integration since colonial times. The transformations and adaptations in these regions also were complex and varied. Where railroads linked regions of good lands with expanding urban markets, commercial haciendas and ranchos expanded and pressed peasant communities for land and labor. Thus did haciendas boom and villagers struggle in the sugar zones of the Morelos basin, the wheat fields of Chalco, and the pulque zone of Apan—all linked by rail to the nation's largest market in Mexico City. Parallel, if less intense, developments occurred in the environs of other expanding Porfirian cities, such as Guadalajara, Morelia, and Puebla.

Where lands were marginal, markets distant, and railroads absent, Porfirian commercial development was less intense and less disruptive. In the highlands of Oaxaca or in the isolated ranchero communities where Michoacán bordered Jalisco, traditional community and family economies endured, mixing subsistence production with limited marketing. There, the Porfirian era continued early national-era developments, and change remained limited.

The sum of Porfirian transformations brought new and more complex diversity to agrarian Mexico, as is evidenced by a survey of Porfirian rural labor regimes. Across the borderlands, workers enjoyed great mobility. The boom development of silver and copper mining, of cattle raising, and of cotton cultivation created an escalating demand for workers that could not be met by the small populations of the vast north. To attract workers, hacienda owners increased wages to levels significantly above those in central and southern Mexico. Men and families migrated in growing numbers, seeking work and new communities in the borderlands. Coercion of workers, once common in the north, was not possible in the Porfirian borderlands. Vast spaces, few people, proximity to the unpatrolled U.S. border, and the need to attract migrants precluded forced labor on a large scale. The Porfirian era made the borderlands a region of rapid growth, labor mobility, and high wages.

Very different labor regimes developed in the booming export economies of southern coastal zones. There, established populations of indigenous villagers lived nearby, usually in upland communities that retained significant yet insufficient lands. Export estates aimed to recruit workers and to hold them for a season—or a lifetime. Wage incentives alone would not draw landed villagers into estate labor on a large scale. Instead, export growers generally offered wage advances to bring workers to their fields. Payment included diverse combinations of cash, maize, and other rations. The key was the estates' provision of advance payment and security of sustenance to those who became laborers. This system inevitably created debts owed by workers to estates, as nearly all workers received advances, wages, and rations in excess of prevailing wage levels. Debts in turn created legal pretexts for coercion, and workers who would leave estates could be captured and returned—if they were found. Southern export plantations built a system in which workers were brought to estates by advanced payments and held there by security of sustenance, a system enforced by state-sanctioned coercion.

Regional variations reflected local histories and the demands of different export crops. In Yucatán, henequen created large, year-round labor demands. Workers and their families lived in estate communities, dependent on estate lands and advances for security of sustenance. In the coffee zones, labor demands were intense, but seasonal. Estates in the foothills of Oaxaca and Chiapas used labor contractors to offer advances to force highland villagers to come and labor for several months in exchange for wages and rations. In Yucatán, advances offered security to estate residents, and the pretext for estates to hold them permanently. In the coffee zones, advances were essential to force workers to remain for the entire harvest, but after harvest time workers were able to return to the highland villages.

In the central highlands, Porfirian rural labor developed very differently. Earlier decades of agrarian decompression had brought population growth, and the implementation of the liberals' privatization program after 1867 brought both losses of community lands and new concentrations of holdings within villages. The result—with infinite local variations —was that the majority of highland families were increasingly land poor, while growing numbers were landless, creating a large population of disposable labor. Where railroads offered access to expanding national markets, the expansion of estate agriculture might create labor demands and provide essential income to struggling highland villagers. The booming sugar estates of Morelos attracted workers from local villages and from adjacent regions of Mexico State. Across the highlands, wherever estates offered work, villagers were available seasonally seeking earnings to supplement declining subsistence production. Wages remained low; coercion was rare.

The rancheros that proliferated under Porfirian development experienced that development in the most diverse ways. Some shared in the boom. Many coffee growers were rancheros families, working their own fields and employing a few seasonal workers for the harvest. In the Bajío, rancheros—both smallholders and estate tenants—produced the foods that sustained the region's commercial and industrial development, again combining family labor with limited seasonal employment of hired hands. Other rancheros mixed subsistence cultivation with the provision of nearby mining zones. Finally, rancheros in isolated areas largely remained subsistence farmers, with limited involvement in the Porfirian commercial boom.

By 1900, land and labor regimes across rural Mexico had reached new levels of complexity and diversity. Patterns of involvement in the Revolution that began in 1910 would reflect that history. People locked by combinations of security and coercion into southern export economies would prove least ready to mount insurrectionary challenges to the Porfirian state and its successors. Despite the breakdown of the state and escalating political violence, estate dependents in Yucatán and the villagers of Oaxaca and Chiapas tied to coffee plantations rarely rebelled.

The northerners who enjoyed high wages and labor mobility under Díaz, in contrast, persistently joined Revolutionary insurrections. Along the border, the financial crisis and economic collapse of 1907, followed by drought in 1909 and 1910, undermined the prospects of men and families who had taken the risks of building new lives in the north. When the promise of the borderlands was broken, just as the political system was facing challenges by the elite, the north became a region of widespread and enduring Revolutionary insurrections.

Revolutionary mobilization was regionally intense in the central highlands. Where booming estates pressed hardest on villagers yet offered only limited seasonal employment (often because mechanization allowed production increases without parallel labor demands), insurrection demanding the return to peasant production and village autonomy became intense, particularly in Morelos (Emiliano Zapata's homeland) and in adjacent regions of the states of Mexico, Puebla, and Guerrero. In other regions, highland Oaxaca, for example, limited estate development and limited pressures on villagers and peasant families led to fewer, more sporadic local uprisings.

Rancheros also faced Revolution and responded in diverse ways. Many in the north, having profited from economic boom while being pressured by large estates operated by politically linked oligarchs, became adamant Revolutionaries. In the Bajío, rancheros had profited from Porfirian development without competing with large estates and rarely joined the Revolution. Others in the uplands where Michoacán joins Jalisco had remained isolated from Porfirian developments and ignored the revolution. Rancheros in Hidalgo and Guerrero led Revolutionary movements that challenged landed elites and claimed local political power. The complex transformations of land and labor regimes during the nineteenth century left diverse legacies to Revolutionary Mexico.

Resistance and Rebellion

The creation of the Mexican nation was a long and contested process. Elite visions of a national state and society were challenged in diverse ways by popular alternatives. Elites sought a national state that would serve such elite interests as economic development and national power. The agrarian majority often had alternative priorities, including subsistence production and family and community autonomy. After 1821, growing numbers of influential leaders promoted liberal ideals: they aimed to turn community lands into private property, they worked to limit the role of the Catholic Church and religion in public affairs, and they demanded the education of the Mexican majority to transform peasant villagers into liberal citizens. Many among the agrarian majority, however, preferred communal landholding, held religion as essential to community culture, and resisted any transformation about which they were not consulted. The result was a long era of post-Independence negotiation and conflict, punctuated between 1840 and 1880 by a series of major regional insurrections.

Resistance, of course, takes diverse forms. It may range from ignoring the edicts of the powerful, to hard negotiations over work, to legal challenges, to brief riots, to massive and violent insurrections. All developed in Mexico during the century after Independence, although the historical record privileges the more public and violent challenges to the emerging nation-state and the developing liberal project.

Independence brought new patterns of rural resistance. During the late colonial era, large and enduring insurrections were few and generally confined to peripheral regions. Most resistance took the form of brief local riots, as much demonstrations as uprisings. They claimed the attention of the authorities and brought disputes over such issues as lands, work, and taxes into the colonial courts. The goal was to force judicial mediation by the colonial courts. The Hidalgo Revolt of 1810 began a decade of insurrection. Within the diverse conflicts over Independence, rural Mexicans, ranging from estate residents in the Bajío, to villagers in Jalisco, to rancheros in the Pacific hot country, took arms to demand their versions of justice and independence. The conflicts that began in 1810 added an insurrectionary tradition to the history of resistance among rural Mexicans.

The Independence engineered in 1821 by elites and the military brought only a short-term recession of insurrectionary conflicts. The rural poor did not stop pressing their interests and resisting the designs of those who would rule them. The post-Independence years brought two decades of weak, divided, and disorganized state powers, allowing the pursuit of agrarian goals through more local and less

violent means. In the Bajío region of north-central Mexico, where insurrection had been most intense and enduring after 1810, in the 1820s rural families pressured estates into dividing lands into tenant holdings, effectively decentralizing estate production and creating a family-based ranchero economy. In the Valley of Toluca in central Mexico, villagers around Tenango del Valle went to court and in 1826 won long-disputed lands from the Condes de Santiago Calimaya, among the colony's greatest landlords. That judicial victory—although later reversed—reverberated among villages across the central highlands, leading many communities to reopen old disputes. At Chalco, post-Independence financial difficulties among landed elites allowed villagers to press estates for higher wages and more favorable working conditions. It was in the context of such agrarian pressures that the 1824 Constitutional Convention considered the privatization of community lands. Many delegates supported such a program, but they chose not to implement it, fearing destabilizing resistance.

Many rural Mexicans took advantage of economic disorganization and political instability to leave villages and haciendas and to move into long-isolated upland regions. There they often settled apparently untitled lands and created ranchero communities, escaping the power of estates and the state.

The first decades after Independence brought political instability and economic disorganization, accompanied by a consolidation of village and ranchero production. That change was caused in part by the institutional collapse, disruption in communications, and loss of a reliable market for agricultural exports. Yet changes favorable to the agrarian majority also resulted from pressures by rural villagers, estate residents, and rancheros working within the context of post-Independence disorganization to promote their own versions of independence. The years from 1821 into the 1840s saw few major insurrections; yet agrarian resistance proved persistent and often successful.

The 1840s brought a return to more violent agrarian conflicts. The national state remained weak and in dispute, but provincial governments began to consolidate their powers and to promote more effectively the interests of landed elites. Local conflicts over lands and labor relations emerged across a large area of southern Mexico from Oaxaca, through Guerrero, to Morelos. Yet violent conflicts remained limited until the outbreak of war against the United States in 1846. With state power locked in international conflict, indigenous peoples in several Mexican regions took the opportunity to challenge programs and policies that assaulted their visions of a just society.

The largest, most violent, most enduring, and best known of the wartime insurrections was the Caste War of Yucatán. Maya villagers, long stoic in their subjection to colonial rule, faced a post-Independence state that promoted land privatization and commercial development, while challenging community control of ancestral lands. Local political conflicts had armed many Mayas and promised them gains, only to leave them victims of elite disputes. When international war provided the opportunity, Maya peasants rose in armed protest over land losses that were challenges to a cosmic order built on community landholding and family maize cultivation. The conflict raged intensely for nearly a decade, and when the state finally gained the upper hand, a remnant of Maya rebels retreated into the back country to maintain an independent society and religious culture through the end of the nineteenth century.

Parallel conflicts occurred during the war at the southern Isthmus of Tehuantepec and in the Sierra Gorda, north of the national capital. At Tehuantepec, simmering conflicts over liberal state policies promoting the privatization of valuable salt beds and favoring large estates in land disputes exploded into violent conflict when the Zapotecs of Juchitán and nearby villagers refused to recognize state law during the war years. Governor Benito Juárez responded with force, setting off years of violent conflict. In the rugged highlands of the Sierra Gorda, indigenous peoples had long resisted colonial rule, joined in the Independence-era insurgencies, and in the 1840s again used the context of larger political conflicts to rise against the incursions of large landowners and commercial exploitation.

All these regional uprisings were eventually contained after the war ended. Their number and extent reveal not only indigenous peoples' discontent with the direction of national developments, they demonstrate that many Mexicans did not then identify with the emerging nation-state. Rather than join that state in its conflict with the United States, peoples of Yucatán, Tehuantepec, and the Sierra Gorda saw the war as an opportunity to challenge those who ruled the struggling Mexican nation.

The late 1840s brought Mexico to a critical juncture. Elites had to face both failure in war and failure to forge a national society. The leaders of numerous Mexican states concluded that it was time to legislate a liberal agrarian reform: the privatization of community lands. Expecting resistance, the same states created rural police. Yet most lacked the administrative organization to privatize community lands effectively and the financial resources to create effective police. As a result, the primary outcome of postwar attempts to weaken the power of indigenous communities was to set off waves of rural conflict that began in the late 1840s and recurred in the 1850s, the late 1860s, and again in the 1870s.

Across the central highlands, the conflicts provoked by the agrarian reforms of midcentury took forms that included passive resistance, legal challenges, political support for the Liberals' Conservative opposition, local riots, and regional uprisings that might last several months. These were less massive insurrectionary movements than the uprisings of the war years, yet they proved widespread, enduring, and a real challenge to attempts to implement the Liberal agrarian reform. Such conflicts developed in Mexico State and the Cuernavaca basin in the late 1840s and early 1850s. When Liberals seized national power in the mid-1850s and made the privatization of community lands national policy through the Ley Lerdo of 1856, resistance became widespread.

Such resistance ensured that there was little effective privatization before a decade of civil war postponed the issue. From 1858 through 1860, Mexican Conservatives fought Mexican Liberals for control of the national state. Following the Liberal victory, from 1862 to 1867, Mexican Liberals fought French invaders and the French-imposed empire of Maximilian—allied with surviving Conservatives—for national power. Rural Mexicans faced new conflicts and new decisions in rapid succession.

Their responses were complex and varied, but important patterns emerged. Rancheros, whether small proprietors, squatters, or tenants of estates or communities, tended toward the Liberals—promoters of small property in rural Mexico. Peasant villagers faced more difficult decisions. The Liberals aimed to assault their community lands. Yet Conservatives were often the very landlords with whom they had contested local lands and labor relations for decades. Many chose to avoid entanglement in the Liberal-Conservative conflict of 1858 to 1860. The conflicts with the French after 1862, however, brought new considerations. Now the nation was at risk. In that context, some peasant villagers—notably in the Sierra de Puebla—allied with the Liberals, and their assistance proved critical to the eventual defeat of the invaders.

The responses of rural Mexicans to the War with the United States in the 1840s and the French invasion and occupation of the 1860s differed sharply. When the United States invaded in 1846, the agrarian majority showed little inclination to defend the nation, and substantial numbers took the opportunity to challenge the state, further weakening the war effort. When the French invaded two decades later, few took the conflict as an opportunity for insurrection, and at least in the Puebla highlands, strategic groups of indigenous villagers joined the Liberals in fighting for the national state.

The differing responses of the agrarian majority to the two midcentury invasions of Mexico by external powers are little understood. Why did the U.S. invasion become an opportunity for mass regional insurrections, while the French invasion did not? Why did few rural Mexicans join the fight against the Yankees, while more were ready to resist the French? Had a new nationalism begun to permeate the rural majority? Were U.S. aims—focused on the acquisition of distant and little-populated northern territories—seen as irrelevant to the agrarian majority? Were French designs on internal dominance viewed as a more direct threat to rural villagers?

National resistance led by Liberals and supported by strategic agrarian allies defeated the French in 1867. The national victory, however, did not lead to agrarian peace. Once the Liberals, led by President Benito Juárez, consolidated national power, they returned to their agenda for agrarian Mexico. They pressed for the privatization of community lands and for the secularization of public culture. The privatization program consolidated Liberal support among many rancheros, who could establish ownership of properties leased from traditional communities.

The same policy of privatization provoked widespread resistance among villagers in diverse regions, including many who had been the Liberals' allies in the recent national conflict. And in many communities, resistance to privatization was stiffened by opposition to Liberal attempts to prohibit public expression of community religious cultures. Again, the nature of the resistance varied. Many villagers simply ignored the Liberal edicts, maintaining community lands and staging very public religious festivals. With their allies in the Sierra de Puebla, the Liberals were pressed to negotiate limited privatizations that left most community lands intact. Elsewhere, in regions ranging from Chalco, to the Mezquital and the Puebla Basin in the central highlands, to more distant regions from Chiapas to Tepic and Sonora, the late 1860s brought renewed regional insurrections that challenged the Liberal vision for rural Mexico. Once again, the rebellions eventually were contained. But the broad range of resistance in the late 1860s slowed the implementation of the Liberal program in many regions and made clear the high price Liberals would pay for any rapid assertion of radical reform.

The mid-1870s brought the last nineteenth-century contest over national power, as Porfirio Díaz challenged Sebastián Lerdo de Tejada for control of the Liberal movement and the national state. Simultaneously, the last nineteenth-century era of agrarian insurrections challenged the Liberal vision of the Mexican nation. In part, the uprisings of the 1870s were one more instance of rural poor people taking advantage of elite conflicts to press their demands. Yet Porfirio Díaz also played to rural discontent in his move to claim national power. Earlier he had been active in mobilizing agrarian support for the war against the French in the Sierra de Puebla. He was more sensitive to agrarian grievances than the more urban, ideological Liberals who looked to Lerdo for leadership—and, of course, Lerdo shared the name of the law (named for his late brother) that demanded the privatization of village lands. Díaz never campaigned for village tradition; he never publicly opposed Liberal agrarian policies. However, he did not promote them although he emphasized his support of local and municipal autonomy: an open position that might attract rancheros as well as many villagers. Thus, Díaz's campaign for the presidency both responded to and promoted rural resistance to Lerdo and the ideological Liberals. Díaz's regime, established in 1876, came to power having raised expectations of a new approach to agrarian justice.

With the consolidation of Díaz's rule, rural resistance took new directions. The massive, enduring regional insurrections that seemed to define agrarian Mexico from the 1840s through the 1870s receded. Conflict did not disappear, but became more local, more negotiated, and less threatening to the national state and regime. What had changed? The consolidation of the state inhibited insurrectionary violence. The reduction of political conflict, the acceleration of economic development, and the integration of the nation via railroads and telegraphs all consolidated state power and limited the space for overt rebellion.

In addition, Díaz reoriented the Liberal project for agrarian Mexico. He continued to favor the privatization of community lands, but he left implementation to local initiative. Local elites often promoted privatization, while poorer villagers opposed it. When conflicts developed Díaz tried to mediate negotiated solutions rather than impose ideological programs. Privatization finally was implemented on a broad scale across Mexico in the 1880s, provoking many local conflicts. Few escalated into challenges to the national regime.

While promoting privatization in carefully limited ways, Díaz backed away from the more ideological Liberals' program of cultural secularization. Having reached an accommodation with the Catholic Church on the national level, he understood the risks of forcing rural communities to limit their annual religious festivities. Thus, when communities faced privatization during the Díaz era, conflicts over land were less often linked to challenges to local religious cultures. The result was a tendency for agrarian conflicts to become localized and less threatening to the national state and the Liberal development project.

If the consolidation of the Díaz regime and its moderation of the Liberal agrarian program successfully ended the post-Independence era of agrarian insurrections, Díaz's development project simultaneously brought new pressures to rural Mexico and new patterns of agrarian conflict and resistance. The rapid incorporation of Mexico into the expanding Atlantic economy, and with it the sudden explosion of export development, brought new demands for land and labor across agrarian Mexico. Entrepreneurs seeking profit—with regime backing—often coveted land and water resources customarily used by villagers and rancheros. Such lands might have been obtained through privatization, the surveying of untitled lands, purchase, or a variety of less legal pressures. Porfirian development thus set off a spate of local land and labor disputes, leading to varied negotiations, court challenges, local demonstrations, stealthy violence, and periodic riots. They rarely led to enduring insurrections, except in peripheral regions—Papantla, Veracruz, the Yaqui Valley of Sonora, and Tomochic, Chihuahua—where long-isolated regions faced sudden incursions of state power and economic developments that challenged both the economic welfare and the cultural independence of local peoples. There, the Díaz regime faced major uprisings in the 1890s.

For most rural Mexicans, the Díaz era brought agrarian compression. Among the agrarian majority, population growth intersected with land loss, declining wages, and insecure tenancies to produce widespread economic deterioration. Yet regime stability, coupled with limited mediation of disputes, inhibited insurrectionary resistance. Conflict was generally contained within communities, there to re-emerge as crime and family violence. Yet pressures mounted and conditions worsened. In 1910, when unresolved issues of political succession broke the Díaz regime, beginning a decade of political conflict, the compressed and contained agrarian grievances generated during the decades of Porfirian peace exploded to

fuel agrarian forces within a social revolution that would eventually reconfigure state and society in twentieth-century Mexico.

See also Ayutla, Revolution of; Caste War of Yucatán; French Intervention; Reform Laws; Wars of Independence; Wars of Reform

Select Bibliography

Harris, Charles, *A Mexican Family Empire: The Latifundio of the Sánchez Navarro Family, 1765–1867.* Austin: University of Texas Press, 1975.

Hu-Dehart, Evelyn, *Yaqui Resistance and Survival: The Struggle for Land and Autonomy, 1821–1910.* Madison: University of Wisconsin Press, 1984.

Jacobs, Ian, *Ranchero Revolt: The Mexican Revolution in Guerrero.* Austin: University of Texas Press, 1982.

Katz, Friedrich, editor, *Riot, Rebellion, and Revolution: Rural Social Conflict in Mexico.* Princeton, New Jersey: Princeton University Press, 1988.

Mallon, Florencia, *Peasant and Nation: The Making of Post-Colonial Mexico and Peru.* Berkeley: University of California Press, 1995.

Miller, Simon, *Landlords and Haciendas in Modernizing Mexico: Essays in Radical Reappraisal.* Amsterdam: Center for Latin American Research and Documentation, 1995.

Reed, Nelson, *The Caste War of Yucatán.* Stanford, California: Stanford University Press, 1964.

Tutino, John, *From Insurrection to Revolution in Mexico: Social Bases of Agrarian Violence, 1750–1940.* Princeton, New Jersey: Princeton University Press, 1986.

Wells, Allen, *Yucatán's Gilded Age: Haciendas, Henequen, and International Harvester, 1860–1915.* Albuquerque: University of New Mexico Press, 1985.

—JOHN TUTINO

Rural Economy and Society: 1910–40

In 1910 Francisco I. Madero called for armed revolt in defense of presidential nonreelection. In his Plan de San Luis Potosí Madero included a call for the restitution through legal channels of illegally seized lands. From the first, the Mexican Revolution was the culmination of complex processes in which systems of land tenure helped define social divisions and hierarchies. The Revolutionary process that established the institutional norms for the Mexican state in the Constitution of 1917 also was an agrarian war as differing conceptions regarding the possession and use of land entered the conflict. This explains the central position of Article 27 in the Constitution, which gave the state the authority to implement agrarian reform.

At the outbreak of the Mexican Revolution, five general systems of land tenure helped define the experience and perspective of the Mexican people. The first was the land of *campesino* (peasant) and indigenous villages, a combination of communal lands and family plots that had been handed down since pre-Hispanic times. During the dictatorship of Porfirio Díaz (1876–1910), however, capitalist haciendas grew at the expense of communal landholdings. It has been estimated that at the beginning of the nineteenth century 40 percent of the arable lands in central and southern Mexico were village communal properties, but by 1910 this fraction had dropped to 5 percent. This process of appropriation and dispossession was fresh in memory of the Revolutionary generation. The expectations of communal villagers went far beyond Madero's call for legal restitution and ended up being formally codified in November 1911 in the Plan de Ayala of Emiliano Zapata's Liberating Army of the South.

The second system of land tenure was organized around the military colonies that had been established in northern Mexico, particularly the state of Chihuahua, during the nineteenth-century wars against nomadic tribes. The owner of the land was the armed *campesino* who had taken possession of the land and made it productive. Once the so-called Apache Wars were over, however, the former military colonies lost many of their juridical rights and privileges, and capitalist haciendas grew at the expense of individual and family plots. In 1905 Governor Enrique Creel of Chihuahua promulgated a new law that forced the colonists' lands onto the open market. The opposition to these measures by the colonists and other *campesinos* later found expression in Francisco "Pancho" Villa's Division of the North.

In the northeast, lands also were held by indigenous groups, most notably in the Yaqui and Mayo valleys of Sonora. For the Yaquis and Mayos land and water formed the body of the community in a sacred bond uniting the community and the basis of time as conceived by their ancestors. This relationship of the people with the land was alien to the spirit of capitalist enterprise that in the 1890s inspired Sonoran hacienda owners to appropriate Yaqui and Mayo lands in a prolonged and bloody war.

All of these systems of land tenure were founded on the idea that land belonged to those who cultivate it. They also formed the basis of village autonomy and local *campesino* democracy. However, each also corresponded to different traditions, histories, and worldviews that would help determine different strategies during the Revolution.

A fourth system of land tenure was that of the old haciendas. Here the rent of land and the labor of the *campesino* was a source of profit for the landowner, but the ownership of land also was a source of prestige and power. The old hacienda system might best be termed a symbiosis of traditional seigniory typical of the ancien régime and the new spirit of capitalist enterprise. Porfirian haciendas combined these two elements in varying degrees, just as they found innumerable ways to combine servile labor and salaried work.

A fifth group, that of rancheros and rich *campesinos,* owned medium-sized individual and family properties *(ranchos)* that also had emerged alongside the haciendas. The rancheros had taken advantage of the expropriation of village lands, contracted work, and could rent part of their properties to poor *campesinos*. Members of this rural middle class, whose size is difficult to estimate based on census records, acted as intermediaries between villages and haciendas and, depending on the region, took different sides during the Revolution.

Nonetheless, the power of the Porfirian regime linked tightly to the landowning elites in symbiosis with the new "steam lords" of the emerging industrial sector. In the mentality of this landholding aristocracy, social prestige, political and military power, and investment capital were the sole determinants of elite membership. All three *campesino* groups—communal villages, former military colonists, and indigenous groups of the northeast—fought against this social regime, capturing or destroying haciendas everywhere Revolutionary battles took place.

The initial direction of the Revolution, however, came from a specific sector of the hacendado elite, owners of modern capitalist haciendas, who tended to be concentrated in northern Mexico. If land had not ceased to be a badge of social prestige for this sector, it still was regarded as a business enterprise and investment. Francisco Madero came from a hacendado family from the northern cotton-producing region of La Laguna; similarly, the Sonoran dynasty that controlled the post-Revolutionary state between 1920 and 1934 through the presidents Álvaro Obregón and Plutarco Elías Calles also owned large agroindustrial holdings in the state of Sonora.

The first phase of the Mexican Revolution, then, was an alliance between capitalist hacendados and *campesinos* against the Porfirian oligarchy. The democratically inclined and upwardly mobile middle class that had emerged during the Pax Porfiriana also made common cause against the Porfirian regime. This phase was short-lived: the treaty of Ciudad

Juárez and the resignation of Porfirio Díaz in May 1911 closed the cycle of power of the landholding oligarchy in Mexico much earlier than in any other Latin American country.

Scarcely had the question of land tenure come into the open, however, when conflict broke out among the various Revolutionary factions. The first agrarian rebellion was led by Emiliano Zapata in November 1911. His Plan de Ayala demanded the restitution of lands to villages and called on *campesinos* to take back their lands by force of arms, going well beyond the call for legal restitution in Madero's Plan de San Luis Potosí. If during the Porfirian regime the burden of proof had been on the villages, under the Plan de Ayala the burden of proof was on the hacendados, who could contest restitution only after villagers already had taken back their lands. Between 1912 and 1918 the Zapatista forces gained control of the state of Morelos just south of Mexico City, as well as parts of the states of Tlaxcala, Guerrero, and Puebla. The Zapatista government dictated far-reaching legislation on land, water rights, government, education, and municipal administration.

The fall of Madero and his assassination in February 1913 at the hands of the Federal army under Victoriano Huerta unleashed the second phase of the Mexican Revolution, the Constitutionalist revolt led by the hacendado and former governor of Coahuila Venustiano Carranza. Although Carranza's Plan de Guadalupe failed to mention the agrarian question, the agrarian Revolutionaries of the south made common cause with the Constitutionalists of the north against the Huerta dictatorship. Moreover, an important faction within the Constitutionalist ranks was concerned fundamentally with land distribution—the Division of the North headed by the peasant caudillo Pancho Villa. Villa's forces proved militarily decisive, breaking the Federal forces in the Battle of Zacatecas in June 1914. Soon after the Constitutionalist victory, however, the Villistas clashed with the Carrancista leadership over their differing conceptions of the agrarian question.

In October 1914 the Revolutionary leaders met in the city of Aguascalientes to patch together an agreement regarding the future organization of the country. Far from creating consensus, however, the Convention at Aguascalientes only widened the divsions between the Carranza and Sonorans on the one hand, and the agrarian Revolutionaries under Zapata and Villa on the other. Eventually the Constitutionalists under Carranza withdrew from the convention, once again plunging the country into civil war.

Although Zapata's Liberating Army of the South and Villa's Division of the North were on the same side in conflict, they had divergent ideas regarding the agrarian question, reflecting the quite different organization of peasant communities in the two parts of the country as well as military exigencies. The Villistas eventually hoped to divide the haciendas and reestablish the military colonies and peasant landholdings; however, the actual division of land in Villista territory was to be postponed until the end of the Revolution. Villa feared that if the agrarian reform took place before victory, the Revolutionary soldiers who were fighting far from their home villages would be left out. The Zapatista agrarian utopia, however, hearkened back to the traditional communal village organization of the region; since Zapatista guerrillas tended to remain within their particular region, agrarian reform could take place immediately. In December 1914 the Villistas and Zapatistas took Mexico City, establishing a Conventionist government and forcing the Constitutionalists to retreat to the port of Veracruz, where Carranza established a rump government. The occupation of the capital by agrarian forces was a decisive moment in Mexican history, even though Mexico City was retaken by the Constitutionalist army under Álvaro Obregón in early 1915.

To prepare his offensive against the agrarian revolution, the Carranza rump government in Veracruz promulgated the agrarian law of January 6, 1915. The law called for the distribution of land in areas under Constitutionalist control and the right of *campesinos* to seek restitution before the law. These promises proved decisive in broadening the Constitutionalists' base of support. Between 1915 and 1916, the Constitutionalists won several decisive victories. Between April and June 1915 they destroyed the Division of the North in four battles in the Bajío region of north-central Mexico. Although the Constitutionalists were able to corner the Zapatistas, they were unable to dislodge them from their Morelos stronghold. The United States government recognized the Carrancista government the same year. Nonetheless, innumerable bands of *campesino* guerrillas continue to operating throughout Mexico; one of the result of this dispersed agrarian war was Villa's attack on the town of Columbus, New Mexico, in March 1916.

In 1916 the Carrancistas convened a constitutional assembly in the city of Querétaro, approving a new constitution on February 5, 1917. One of the mainstays of the new constitution was Article 27, which established the authority of the Mexican state over soil and subsoil, creating a juridical foundation for agrarian reform (and, much later, state control of mineral resources). Article 27 recognized diverse forms of land tenure: farmer and *campesino* small-holdings, village *ejidos* (commons), and indigenous communal lands. If the Carrancista leadership hoped that Article 27 would create a legal channel for agrarian demands, however, the article only served to legitimate agrarian mobilizations. Between 1917 and 1920 the Carranza government tried to circumvent Article 27, freezing land redistribution, returning haciendas expropriated during the Revolution to their former owners, and continuing the war against the remnants of the Villista forces and the Zapatistas in the southern part of the country; on April 10, 1919, Emiliano Zapata was assassinated in a government ambush.

Nonetheless, Carranza's policies only served to alienate his agrarian base of support. Drawing on the support of agrarian revolutionaries, the military rebellion of Agua Prieta overthrew the Carranza government in 1920, establishing an interim government under Adolfo de la Huerta; the leader of the revolt, Álvaro Obregón, later was elected president, serving in office between 1921 and 1924. During the revolt Obregón had cut a deal with the Zapatistas, and once in power he acceded to many of their agrarian demands in Morelos. Even after defeat agrarian forces continued to influence the destiny of the Mexican nation.

At the start of the Revolution in 1910 there were 8,431 haciendas and 48,633 *ranchos* in existence, making a total of 57,064 properties; 96.9 percent of the heads of rural families, however, owned no land at all. Historian Frank Tannenbaum cites some examples of this concentration of landed property: three haciendas occupied the 200 miles (300 kilometers) between the cities of Saltillo and Zacatecas; the Terrazas family properties in Chihuahua encompassed as much land as the entire nation of Costa Rica; in the state of Hidalgo the railway ran 100 miles (150 kilometers) without leaving the properties of the Escandón family; foreign companies owned 78 percent of the land in Baja California; and the Hearst family owned 30,000 square miles (77,700 square kilometers) in Chihuahua, the largest latifundium in the country.

Although the Revolution topple the landed oligarchy from power, it did not immediately change land distribution in the country. Carranza distributed 326,000 acres (132,000 hectares); Álvaro Obregón almost 2.5 million acres (1 million hectares) between 1920 and 1924; and his successor, Plutarco Elías Calles (1924–28), 7 million acres (3 million

hectares). Nonetheless, in 1930 only 13.4 percent of cultivated land belonged to *ejidos* and communities. The remainder was private property, which still was concentrated in very few hands. Plots of less than 25 acres (10 hectares) numbered 614,700, accounting for 1.3 percent of Mexico's exploited surface area. There were 11,500 plots of more than 2,500 acres (1,000 hectares); these latifundia, which accounted for only 1.5 percent of the total number of properties, accounted for 82.8 percent of the exploited surface area. The 1,500 properties of more than 25,000 acres (10,000 hectares), 0.2 percent of the total number of properties, encompassed 54.5 percent of the exploited surface area (Tello, 1967). Not only had the concentration of landed property continued after the Revolution, but many of the Revolutionary chiefs had become the new hacendados, having appropriated properties directly or married into old families who sought to protect their possessions.

Nonetheless, the Revolution had destroyed the ancien régime. More important, it had taught the *campesinos* to use the weapons that still were scattered throughout the country, while Article 27 legitimated agrarian ferment. If the early Revolutionary forces had sought to topple the political regime, however, the new agrarian movements sought to force the government to live up to the promise of the constitution. During the 1920s, then, the countryside was overrun by agrarian movements, invasions of hacienda lands, and armed peasant groups. The mobilizations of *agraristas,* as they came to be called, were particularly intense in the states of Veracruz, Michoacán, Guerrero, Yucatán, and Tlaxcala, although Agrarian Community Leagues arose in almost every state in the nation. In 1924 the Liga Nacional de Comunidades (National League of Communities) was organized under the leadership of the Veracruz *agrarista* Ursulo Galván. Nonetheless, many agrarian leaders —most notably Primo Tapia of Michoacán—were assassinated by landowner "white guards" or by the army. In Veracruz *campesinos* organized agrarian guerrilla bands to defend their lands or invade the haciendas whose lands they were reclaiming.

In 1923 Adolfo de la Huerta led a political revolt against the administration of Álvaro Obregón, backed by most of the army. Obregón sought the support of the radical governor of Veracruz, Adalberto Tejada, and his armed *agraristas* in exchange for promises of land, which he only partially honored; the *agrarista* governor of Yucatán, Felipe Carrillo Puerto, was assassinated during the de la Huerta rebellion. In 1929, faced with a similar revolt led by General Escobar, President Emilio Portes Gil gave new but short-lived encouragement to land distribution to ensure peasant loyalty. It seemed that each military chief could count on *campesino* discontent to further his political ambitions, and military power struggles and *campesinos'* agrarian struggles seemed to be intertwined inextricably during those turbulent years.

In 1926 in response to the anti-religious measures of the government of General Calles, the Cristero Rebellion broke out under the leadership of the Liga de Defensa de la Libertad Religiosa (League for the Defense of Religious Freedom). The movement was particularly strong in the rural regions of Guanajuato, Michoacán, Jalisco, and the western part of the state of Mexico. Although the Cristero *campesinos* were defending their right to keep their churches open and freely practice their faith, their movement also was imbued with unsatisfied agrarian ambitions and ended up involving thousands of armed men. To fight the Cristeros the government mobilized the army and *agrarista* peasants of Veracruz and other regions, declaring that the Revolution was threatened by the Catholic Church and the Cristeros. It was a confused and cruel war, favored by a post-Revolutionary agrarian situation in which illegality, discontent, and revolt predominated.

The Cristero Rebellion was pacified in 1929 following and agreement between the government and the Catholic Church hierarchy. The Cristero *campesinos* in the middle believed that their interests had been abandoned in the accord, however, and some continued the fight. In 1934 the conflict erupted again in what has been termed the Segunda Cristiada or la Segunda, this time without the support of the Catholic Church. The agrarian policy and reforms of the Cárdenas period eventually absorbed the movement.

In the early 1930s two currents of thought came to blows over the agrarian question. One side was represented by president Plutarco Elías Calles, who proposed that a limit be set on land distribution to *ejidos*, after which the government should consolidate individual landholdings, spurring the mechanization and modernization of agriculture. This strain of thought saw the ejido as a transitional institution, ensuring a labor supply for industrial agriculture and training *campesinos* to be private farmers or salaried workers for agroindustry. The *agraristas* themselves, however, believed that agrarian reform should continue until all arable land had been redistributed. The *ejido*—the inalienable common lands, water, and woods of village communities—was believed to be the solution to the land problem and the basic structure of agrarian life and production, ensuring peasant control over agrarian resources yet allowing large-scale production of such cash crops as cotton and henequen.

In December 1933, in the midst of continuing agrarian and labor unrest aggravated by the Great Depression and the return of hundreds of thousands of migrant workers from the United States, the ruling Partido Nacional Revolucionario (PNR, or National Revolutionary Party) nominated General Lázaro Cárdenas as its nominee for the presidential elections of 1934. Cárdenas traveled throughout the country during his campaign, promising agrarian and education reform and calling for an alliance between *campesinos* and the government. As president Cárdenas fulfilled his promises. In March 1934 the Mexican government approved the Agrarian Code, fixing the surface area of *ejidos* at 10 to 20 acres (4 to 8 hectares) and imposing a limit on private landholdings of 370 acres (150 hectares) for irrigated land and 750 acres (300 hectares) for seasonal land. The code eased the formalities for expanding *ejidal* grants and permitted peons who worked for a salary in haciendas to request lands to form "population nuclei," a right that previously had been bestowed only on established villages.

The six years of the Cárdenas administration (1934–40) combined *campesino* uprisings, stout resistance by latifundists, and energetic government action in land distribution. The clash between *campesino* mobilization, often led by rural schoolteachers appointed by the government, and hacendado White Guards, who could count on the support of some high-ranking military officers, created a near civil war for the Cárdenas administration. Rural labor unions throughout the country became involved in many of these conflicts, particularly in areas where the work of salaried peons predominated, such as the cotton region of La Laguna in Coahuila and Durango.

These violent conditions did not prevent the distribution of quantities of lands that were without precedent—and without equal in the years following the Cárdenas administration. If between 1915 and 1934 25 million acres (10.1 million hectares) of land had been awarded, between 1935 and 1940 land distribution reached a total of 43.5 million acres (17.6 million hectares). The 7.5 percent of the exploited surface area that belonged to *ejidos* in 1930 rose to 22.5 percent in 1940. If one takes into account the surface area actually under cultivation, 13.4 percent belonged to *ejidos* in 1930 and 47.4 percent in 1940. Following a wage strike organized by the labor union of Tlahualilo (owned by British and U.S. interests) and other haciendas, in October 1936 the government expropriated the Laguna haciendas, responsible for half the cotton production in the country. In 1937 the government expropriated the henequen haciendas of Yucatán, granting them to *campesinos* as a vast collective *ejido*. The Cárdenas administration also restored almost 1.2 million acres (485,000 hectares) of ancestral lands to the Yaquis of Sonora. In 1938 the Confederación Nacional Campesina (CNC, or National Peasant Confederation) was organized with official backing, an instrument both for organizing and controlling *campesino* mobilizations. The Ejidal Credit Bank also was set up along with other organizations to support agricultural production.

Nonetheless, the Cárdenas administration was forced to make compromises. In 1937 a law was passed declaring a 25-year moratorium on the expropriation of lands dedicated to cattle ranching. Moreover, at the close of the Cárdenas administration largeholders continued to have a strong presence in Mexican agroindustry. In 1940 a total of 1,487 properties of more than 25,000 acres (10,000 hectares) existed, and among these 308 latifundia exceeded 99,000 acres (40,000 hectares; Tello, 1967). However, the wide distribution of lands and the multiplication of the *ejidos* as population centers and focuses of *campesino* life and production with their own elected authorities, schools, and administrative organs, gave a concrete response to the old *campesino* demand for local autonomy. At this level the *ejido* broadened the participation of the rural population in the political life of the country. Although the idea of revolt never entirely disappeared, rural resistance increasingly occurred through institutional channels.

See also Cristero Rebellion; Mexican Revolution

Select Bibliography

Bethell, Leslie, editor, *Mexico since Indepenence*. Cambridge: Cambridge University Press, 1991.
Gilly, Adolfo, *The Mexican Revolution*. London: Verso Books, 1983.
Katz, Friedrich, *The Secret War in Mexico*. Chicago: University of Chicago Press, 1982.
Knight, Alan, *The Mexican Revolution: Counter-revolution and Reconstruction*. 2 vols., Lincoln: University of Nebraska Press, 1986.
Tutino, John, *From Insurrection to Revolution in Mexico*. Princeton, New Jersey: Princeton University Press, 1986.
Womack, John, *Zapata and the Mexican Revolution*. New York: Knopf, 1969.

—ADOLFO GILLY

Rural Economy and Society: 1940–96, Land-Labor Regimes

The period from 1940 to 1996 in Mexico was marked by the end of agrarian reform based on the principles of the Mexican Revolution and the stratification of Mexico's rural economy in ways that supported a policy of economic development first through urban industrialization and later through economic restructuring associated with neoliberalism (a macroeconomic policy based on strict monetarism and the promotion of agricultural and other exports). The pact forged by President Lázaro Cárdenas with Mexico's peasantry unraveled quickly in the 1940s and underwent a brief revitalization in the 1970s under the administration of President Luis Echeverría Álvarez, when the central government briefly encouraged the building of regional peasant organizations while simultaneously supporting commercial agriculture. The most important legacy of this period was the emergence of autonomous regional peasant organizations demanding that Mexico's rural and indigenous sectors be included in national development plans and in Mexican cultural identity. In the state of Chiapas, such movements were pivotal in the building and maintenance of the Ejército Zapatista de Liberación Nacional (EZLN, or Zapatista Army of National Liberation). In Chiapas and elsewhere, peasant organizations that built their identity on the legacy of the Mexican Revolution continued to challenge neoliberal restructuring programs that left rural people on the margins of national and international society. Rebellions such as that of the EZLN in Chiapas suggest that the cycle of the Mexican Revolution has yet to be completed.

Agrarian Reform Realized: The Creation of *Ejidos*
Without a doubt, the most enduring legacy of the Mexican Revolution was the agrarian reform constituted under Article 27 of the Constitution (and formally in a 1920 law) that allowed for the formation of *ejidos* as collective entities with a legal stature, specific territorial limits, and representative bodies of governance. *Ejidos* were created to satisfy the demands of landless peasants who had seen their communal village lands eaten up by large agricultural estates and who served as laborers on these estates. An *ejido* is a communal form of land tenure to which members have use rights, usually in the form of an individual plot of land.

The formation of *ejidos* after the Mexican Revolution involved the transfer of over 170 million acres (70 million hectares) from large estates to slightly more than 3 million peasant beneficiaries. By the end of the Cárdenas presidency in 1940, *ejidos* accounted for approximately one-half of Mexico's cultivated area. The number of landless laborers had declined from 68 percent to 36 percent of the rural workforce. In addition to *ejido* lands, another important part of the rural sector was made up of agrarian communities that held indigenous common lands based on historical claims usually dating to pre-Colombian and colonial times.

The impact of agrarian reforms in various parts of Mexico after the 1930s varied with the extent of agrarian reform and the type of agricultural and labor regime coupled with it. The largest and most important *ejidos* dating from the Cárdenas period were in the Laguna area on the border of Coahuila and Durango. There, some 30,000 families received 8 million acres (3 million hectares). The *ejido* was worked cooperatively and dedicated to the cultivation of commercials crops, initially focused on cotton production. While collective *ejidos* were quickly terminated after changes in the agrarian code in 1942 and labeled as socialist and a threat to private property, the north continued to be the site of large tracts of *ejido* land cultivated for commercial purposes.

The amount of land transferred from large estates to *ejidos* varied regionally. In the state of Oaxaca, for example, large landed estates were not the norm. There haciendas were confined to the central valleys and the coast, and indigenous communities had managed to hold onto significant amounts of land, including private land. Nevertheless, in these areas where communities had lost land, the formation of *ejidos* marked a significant improvement in the lives of landless day laborers and sharecroppers.

In other areas of Mexico, such as eastern Chiapas, the Mexican Revolution was tardy in its arrival, and owing to entrenched resistance to land redistribution, fewer *ejidos* were formed through redistribution of land from large estates in comparison to other parts of the country. Most *ejido* land that was redistributed from large estates in Chiapas was transferred in the 1930s and 1940s, but in eastern Chiapas not until after 1960. There the primary source of *ejido* land was colonization of unused forested areas of the jungle. Colonial land, labor, and social relations remained intact in many areas of Chiapas until the 1970s, when a series of forces including Catholic liberation theology, independent peasant organizations, brutal styles of government, and grinding poverty combined to impulse the formation of new *ejidos*, regional organizations of *ejidos*, and regional peasant organizations.

By far, the most important impact of the *ejido* program was its political success. The servitude that had bound hacienda owners and peons for centuries was broken. Most of the former peons who became *ejidatarios*, however, remained on the margins of the agrarian economy. Small private farmers and *ejidatarios* worked on tiny rain-fed parcels and cultivated corn and beans. Commercial agriculture was the province of medium- and large-scale privately held farms with access to irrigation. These two types of agriculture were interrelated, and production and labor relations from one strongly affected the other.

Industrial Modernization on the Backs of Peasants

The presidencies of Manuel Avila Camacho (1940–46) and Miguel Alemán Valdés (1946–52) made it clear that Mexico's modernity would be built on an industrial state. This entailed an abandonment of the countryside and a focus on industrialization. During Avila Camacho's presidency, industrialization became as important to the national self-conception as agrarian reform was to Cárdenas. Textile, food processing, chemical, beer, and cement industries grew rapidly. In the countryside, commercial agriculture was given some importance because of export possibilities to the United States. Before the rise of the petrochemical industry, agricultural products exported to the United States were an important source of foreign exchange. In this scheme of economic modernization, the *ejido* sector never became a nationally important source of capital accumulation. Agriculture played a subservient role to the industrial sector and partly financed the industrialization process. In the 1940s, Mexico also began a population shift toward the cities. In 1930, 66.5 percent of the population was rural. By 1960, the trend toward a predominantly urban population was clearly forecast. In 1960, 49.3 percent of the population was rural, with lower numbers every subsequent year.

Stratification of Mexican Agriculture

While after 1940 the state's rhetoric made continued references to the legacy of Emiliano Zapata, policy shifted to accommodate dependent capitalism. Peasant agriculture provided cheap foodstuffs to the urbanizing nation and also supplied seasonal labor for agro-export agriculture and other commercial operations. Many have labeled the structure of Mexican agriculture as bimodal, with a wide gap between large-scale commercial producers and a majority of farmers depending on family labor. As the scholar Tom Barry has pointed out, the term trimodal is a better description of the three major categories of farmers: "1) capitalist producers, 2) medium- and small-scale farmers who are surplus producing but rely primarily on family labor, and 3) infrasubsistence or subsistence farmers together with the landless, many of whom work regularly as *jornaleros,* or wage farmworkers."

In accordance with the Mexican model of modernization, which relied heavily on mechanization and chemical inputs to increase commercial productivity, the three sectors worked together. Subsistence farmers and landless wage workers supplied seasonal labor for both medium-scale and capitalist producers. Subsistence agriculture also provided a consistent buffer not only for seasonal agricultural workers, but also for laborers and migrants in other sectors as well. While the productivity of export grains, particularly of wheat, was increasing rapidly, little attention was paid to the production of corn and beans.

From 1940 to 1970 the commercialized agricultural sector experienced impressive growth. By the late 1960s, however, problems set in. Production stagnated and Mexico no longer produced enough basic grains to feed itself. In 1975 Mexico was importing 10 percent of the grain it consumed. By 1983 it imported half the grain consumed. Although the establishment of the Sistema Alimentario Mexicana (SAM, or Mexican Alimentation System) in 1980 and the 1980 Law of Agricultural Development strove to shift policy emphasis from livestock and irrigated production of luxury crops to rainfed subsistence crops produced by peasants, the goal of food self-sufficiency never was reached. While corn imports decreased between 1980 and 1982, bean imports declined only slightly, soybean imports doubled, and other food imports also increased. Two years after the SAM's inauguration, the beginning of economic crisis in Mexico in 1982 eliminated the financial basis for the SAM and for other redistributive food policies implemented by the government in the 1970s. In 1995, Mexico had to import a record 10 million tons of grains, more than 25 percent of the total annual grain consumption.

The way Mexico modernized its agricultural sector had major effects on the rural population and the availability of work. Mexico became the Latin American nation with the highest degree of agricultural mechanization. Such techniques were not suitable for most rural farmers and exacerbated problems of underemployment in the countryside. As stated by Barry, "Each tractor put to work on a farm meant three to four workers lost their jobs. Moreover, rather than relying on sharecroppers or *colonos* (as in a traditional *latifundio* system) or hiring permanent wage workers, Mexico's *neolatifundios* relied on temporary farmworkers."

Echeverría's Agrarian Populism and the Creation of Autonomous Regional Peasant Organizations

The 1970s were characterized by a new agrarian populism fomented from the center by the administration of Luis Echeverría Álvarez (1970–76). Echeverría became the first Mexican president since Cárdenas to encourage local and regional peasant organizing. Built on a model proposed by the World Bank to improve conditions for those left behind by the previous model of development, Echeverría's administration emphasized the provision of credit, infrastructure, technical assistance, health care, marketing support, and educational projects to the rural poor and small producers designed not only to improve socioeconomic conditions in the countryside, but also to boost stagnant agricultural economic growth.

In 1971, the agrarian reform code was revised with a new integral vision of the *ejido* as both an economic and political institution. This change in the law as well as renewed peasant militancy focused attention on the rural sector. Hundreds of large-scale land invasions erupted in the highlands in 1972, with the participation of tens of thousands of peasants. Particularly in Guerrero, but elsewhere as well, these invasions acquired what the scholar Jonathan Fox has called an "insurrectional character." Although the mass movement later declined, numerous independent regional movements lived on.

The 1975 Agrarian Credit Law encouraged the formation of regional associations of small producers for the first time since the 1930s. Unions of *ejidos* were fomented through joining together two or more *ejidos.* Often referred to as second-level organizations, unions of *ejidos* also were brought together to create third-level regional organizations called Rural Collective Interest Associations, or ARICs. These new organizational forms attempted, in the words of Jonathan Fox, "to bring community-based producer groups together around some common economic interest (credit, and input provision, processing, marketing)."

Although aided by organizers with government ties, some of the regional groups came to have a semi-autonomous stance in relation to state agencies and agricultural policies. For example, the Unión de Ejidos "Lázaro Cárdenas" (UELC) was created in 1975 with the assistance of a dynamic team of community organizers working under the PIDER's (Rural Development Investment Program) anti-poverty program of the Echeverría administration. *Ejido* unions like the UELC were always in a contradictory position. While the government did not intend for regional organizations such as the UELC to become autonomous, the degree of their independence could clearly be influenced by the politics of those who helped in their organization. Many of the young PIDER organizers who worked in the UELC and elsewhere emerged from the radical student movement of the 1960s and were committed to organizing, consciousness raising, and helping to transform the country from below. The projects of the PIDER were also structured to encourage the participation of rural communities in decision making and in a coordinated set of activities and services that included developing organizational skills, credit, and training in small-scale industry and marketing of rural products. Organizers encouraged *ejido* unions such as the UELC to have an independent identity and tried to foment autonomous regional organizations under the cover of a government agency. In the state of Chiapas, regional independent peasant organizations that formed an ARIC went on to become part of the social base of the Zapatista Army in the late 1980s.

The wave of land invasions in the early 1970s and the subsequent formation of a wide range of regional peasant organizations is not surprising when related to patterns of landholding and labor relations in the countryside. The absolute number of privately held small farms declined 39 percent between 1950 and 1970, and small-holding peasants controlled only 3 percent of cultivated land and contributed 4 percent of agricultural production in 1970. For those holding land in agrarian reform or *ejido* communities, access to land was not a guarantee of survival. While in 1950 about 85 percent of those working on *ejidos* earned more than half their income from farming, in 1985, less than 40 percent did.

By the early 1980s, the expansion of capitalist agriculture in Mexico had resulted in the marginalization of a vast portion of the rural subsistence sectors. The scholar James Cockcroft estimated in 1983 that nearly 80 percent of Mexico's 25,000 *ejidos* and Indian communities could "no longer support themselves on farming alone, even though 'legally' they account for 43 percent of cultivatable land." In 1980, the economically active population in agriculture was more than 5,699,971, of whom approximately 54 percent were landless wage earners and 46 percent were direct producers.

While Echeverría's agrarian populism did assist in promoting the formation of some autonomous regional organizations and paid more attention to *ejido* production, it did not succeed in establishing new economic and political relations in the countryside—nor was that its intention. The focus of the Echeverría government was more on providing services for those peasants producing for the market, while the majority who existed on the margins were ignored. The policies promoted in the 1970s did not challenge land concentration and continued to support agro-export. The stratification of rural Mexico into the trimodal structure described above continued and was the backdrop for the economic crisis of 1982.

Economic Crisis and Agrarian Restructuring: The Age of Neoliberalism

The administration of Miguel de la Madrid (1982–88) paved the way for the implementation of the North American Free Trade Agreement (NAFTA) and foreshadowed future attempts to encourage privatization of Mexico's *ejido* sector through initiatives such as a 1980 law that authorized joint vetures between private investors and the *ejido* sector. From 1989 onward under the administration of Carlos Salinas de Gortari (1988–94), agricultural producers were affected by economic restructuring in many ways. Normal channels through which small- and medium-scale farmers gained access to credit, fertilizer, and production and marketing support were shut down, including the Mexican Coffee Institute (Inmecafé, which, had offered price supports and marketing assistance), the National Agricultural and Livestock Insurance Company, and the state-owned fertilizer distributor and manufacturer Fertimex.

By the early 1990s, the situation of small- and medium-sized producers even in areas of commercial agriculture was not promising. Increasing numbers of families migrated to Mexican cities and to the United States, with the result that U.S. agricultural wages declined and there was a seasonal scarcity of labor in some parts of Mexico. This prompted women to become a growing part of the seasonal labor force in Mexico.

From 1940 through the 1970s, many rural women stayed home and carried on subsistence work in addition to their normal workloads, while men migrated. Beginning in the 1970s, women increasingly became part of the migrant stream and worked as wage laborers in commercial agriculture. Official statistics show that the number of rural women in the wage labor force jumped from 5.6 percent in 1975 to 20 percent in 1985 and continued to grow every year. This entry into the paid labor force was in response to an overall decline in real wages, decreases in guaranteed prices for basic crops, cutbacks in rural services, and increasing commoditization of goods such as firewood, medicines, and basic foods that formerly were collected free or produced through subsistence agriculture. Local labor shortages cemented women's increasing participation in the seasonal agricultural labor force.

Mexico's debt crisis in the 1980s gave international lending agencies such as the World Bank an even stronger position in dictating national policy in all areas, including agricultural development. Instead of encouraging more equitable distribution, bank policy in the late 1980s was focused on privatization and the dismantling of state institutions. In 1989, the World Bank directed Mexico to "promote greater private-sector participation in the modernization of the food-distribution system, support further reductions in interest-rate subsidies to farmers, and to boost agricultural exports." The Salinas administration committed itself wholeheartedly to the neoliberal model, staking the future of all Mexicans on its success. The administration of Ernesto Zedillo Ponce de León, which began in 1994, has followed suit.

In 1991, the World Bank conditioned a loan for Mexican agriculture on the implementation of specific measures such as canceling price controls on basic food items, privatizing state-owned monopolies, and eliminating price guarantees for corn. In 1992, a series of measures aimed at privatization of government enterprises, a loosening of federal regulations to permit and encourage foreign investment and ownership, and the individualization of property and social relations between the state and its citizens found their logical conclusion in agrarian policy that followed in the wake of the reformation of Article 27 of the Mexican Constitution in 1992. The reformation of Article 27 was part and parcel of a series of policies designed to support the accords reached in the North American Free Trade Agreement. This change in the constitution ended the government's obligation to redistribute land to the landless and permitted (but did not require) the privatization of land held in non-alienable corporate status as *ejido* or communal land. The change in the law affected lands making up almost 50 percent of Mexico's national territory.

To facilitate the proposed changes in landholdings in Mexico's 28,058 *ejidos* and indigenous communities, a new government office was created, the Procuraduría Agraria (Agrarian Attorney's Office). An army of new employees invaded Mexico's *ejidos* to offer information, and if *ejidos* agreed to join the program, to measure and map boundaries between communities and between individual plots within one community. This process often generated considerable debate, or gave new life to boundary disputes with long local histories. If and when all disputes were resolved, *ejidatarios* received certificates specifying their use rights to particular plots of land—usually those they had consistently worked over time. In order to convert the certificate into a private title, *ejidatarios* had to receive approval from a majority of the members in their *ejido*.

By the end of 1993, the future was looking bleak for many of Mexico's farmers and rural workers. As stated succinctly by Tom Barry, Mexican farmers faced six major changes by the end of the governing period of Salinas:

> 1) the withdrawal of government-subsidized inputs, 2) high interest rates and lack of access to credit, 3) the end of land distribution and the new status of ejidal land, 4) an increased flow of cheaper food imports, 5) inadequate government measures to upgrade productivity and competitiveness, and 6) a widely criticized new subsidy program called PROCAMPO.

The End of Agrarian Reform and the Return of Zapatismo

In 1994 there was a wide range of responses in Mexico to the reform of agrarian policy, which ended the state's obligation to redistribute land to those who need it. Reactions included armed rebellion in the state of Chiapas by indigenous peasants organized into the EZLN and acceptance by some indigenous and mestizo communities in Oaxaca to government programs designed to map and measure land in preparation for privatization.

In the *ejido* of La Realidad and others in the region of Las Margaritas in Chiapas, for example, Tojolobal indigenous people rejected reforms to Article 27 of the Constitution. This rejection came through armed rebellion by their participation in the EZLN, and through refusing entry to agrarian officials charged with carrying out programs aimed at ending land redistribution and promoting privatization. Eventually the state of Chiapas organized a separate program to satisfy the demands of the Tojolobales and other ethnic groups in Chiapas who refused to participate in the state restructuring program. Instead of ending land redistribution and encouraging privatization, the state initiated a separate program negotiated with indigenous peasant communities and organizations. Unlike the national program, it *did* involve land redistribution as well as development packages designed by local communities. In addition, the Tojolobales of La Realidad were involved in a national movement for indigenous autonomy strongly affected by the peace negotiation process between the EZLN and the Mexican government. Land became a key issue in this movement.

Interviews with officials from the Agrarian Attorney's Office and the Ministry of Agrarian Reform in Chiapas during 1996 made it clear that resistance to agrarian restructuring in eastern Chiapas had had a major effect on policy. Five hundred *ejidos* within the conflict zone of the EZLN were not included in the regular implementation plan for agrarian restructuring of that state. Officials interviewed who attempted to work in EZLN communities had their trucks burned, and some were held hostage. Zapatista sympathizers continued to challenge the end of land redistribution through support for land reclamations and their insistence that the reformed Article 27 of the Mexican Constitution, which now facilitated restructuring and privatization, be returned to its original intent, "land for those who work it." They invoked Emiliano Zapata as a central symbol in their struggle. This is an example of how historical national symbols put in the service of indigenous struggles can alter structures of political and economic power. In Chiapas, the state abandoned implementing its original agrarian reform policy in Zapatista territory.

The outright rejection of the agrarian restructuring program in Chiapas is contrasted by the Zapotec *ejido* of Santa María del Tule in Oaxaca, which complied with the state's program for ending agrarian reform. Through mapping and measuring *ejido* boundaries and individual use plots to pave the way for privatization of *ejido* land, men and women in Santa María del Tule reconnected with the historical legacy of Emiliano Zapata in the formation of their *ejido*. Their relationship to the state was informed by local historical memory that coded state agrarian officials from the 1920s as "the good guys" in contrast to the "the bad guys," who were Zapotec neighbors who contested their receipt of *ejido* land. This community had engaged in an 18-year struggle with a neighboring community in order to take full possession of the 1,500 acres (600 hectares) of land they had been granted as an *ejido* in the 1930s. In the 1990s, they were receptive to agrarian officials in part because of their historical legacy as "helpers" in securing the original *ejido* lands for the community. After completing the mapping, measuring, and certification of their *ejido* lands, men and women from Santa María del Tule maintained contact with agrarian officials. They presented them with a new set of demands focused on the production process. For example, they developed a new women's credit cooperative as well as a project for increasing household animal production.

Agrarian Mexico in the Twenty-First Century

These two examples demonstrate the complexities of Mexican agrarian history in the twentieth century. The responses of rural men and women to the end of agrarian reform in the 1990s were built on a century of contradictory agrarian policies carried out in relation to a stratified rural population with differing stakes, interests, and interpretations of what policy means. While rural Mexico clearly entered a new era in the 1980s and 1990s, the emergence of the EZLN, other guerrilla movements, and a strong national indigenous rights movement with land and rural development issues high on their agendas indicated that the issues that had prompted the Revolution of 1910 persisted, albeit in new forms. The 95 percent of Mexico's population that was landless in 1895 was now found in the shantytowns of Mexico's cities, migrating throughout the country and to the United States as well as scattered throughout the countryside. Hunger, poverty, and lack of work and opportunities continued to plague the majority of Mexicans. While the *agrarismo* of the original Zapatistas might not have resonated with most of Mexico in the 1990s, demands for housing, land, work, health care, education, and democratic political participation did. The steady low-level boil maintained in many parts of Mexico's countryside in the 1990s, was an important signal for what might follow in the twenty-first century.

See also Drug Trade; Ecology; General Agreement on Tariffs and Trade (GATT); North American Free Trade Agreement (NAFTA); Zapatista Rebellion in Chiapas

Select Bibliography

Barry, Tom, *Zapata's Revenge: Free Trade and the Farm Crisis in Mexico*. Boston: South End, 1995.

Cockcroft, James, *Mexico: Class Formation, Capital Accumulation, and the State*. New York: Monthly Review Press, 1983.

Collier, George A., with Elizabeth Lowery Quaratiell, *Basta! Land and the Zapatista Rebellion in Chiapas*. Oakland, California: Food First Publications, 1994.

de Janvry, Alain, *The Agrarian Question and Reformism in Latin America*. Baltimore: Johns Hopkins University Press, 1981.

Fox, Jonathan, *The Politics of Food in Mexico: State Power and Social Mobilization*. Ithaca, New York: Cornell University Press, 1992.

Hewitt de Alcántara, Cynthia, "Introduction: Economic Restructuring and Rural Subsistence in Mexico." In *Economic Restructuring and Rural Subsistence in Mexico: Corn and the Crisis of the 1980s*, edited by Cynthia Hewitt de Alcántara. San Diego: Ejido Reform Research Project, Center for U.S.-Mexican Studies, University of California, San Diego, 1994.

Paré, Luisa, "The Challenge of Rural Democratization in Mexico." *Journal of Development Studies* 26 (1990).

Stavenhagen, Rodolfo, "Collective Agriculture and Capitalism in Mexico: A Way Out or a Dead End?" In *Modern Mexico: State, Economy, and Social Conflict,* edited by Nora Hamilton and Timothy F. Harding. Beverly Hills, California: Sage, 1986.

Stephen, Lynn, *Zapotec Women.* Austin: University of Texas Press, 1991.

_____, "Too Little, Too Late? The Impact of Article 27 on Women in Oaxaca." In *Reforming Mexico's Agrarian Reform,* edited by Laura Randall. Armonk, New York: Sharpe, 1996.

—LYNN STEPHEN

Rural Economy and Society: 1940–96, Resistance and Rebellion

Historically, Mexican peasants have been among the most rebellious and revolutionary in Latin America. Yet their political activism has consistently faced three recurring dilemmas: the problem of autonomy versus alliances with the state, the relationship with political parties of the opposition, and the difficulty of establishing and maintaining alliances between different regional and national peasant organizations. The period between 1940 and 1994 was marked by a constant search for alternative forms of representation during a period of rapid social and economic change that inevitably transformed the goals and character of rural mobilization. Nevertheless, peasant movements in the 1990s still were faced with the persistent problems of defining their relations toward the state, political parties, and each other.

The post-Revolutionary agrarian reform program was a result of the rural mobilization of 1910 to 1917, but it also provided the state with the means to affirm centralized political control. President Lázaro Cárdenas (1934–40) successfully reorganized the regional peasant leagues affiliated to the official party, culminating in the formation of the Confederación Nacional Campesina (CNC, or National Peasant Confederation) in 1938. This state-peasant alliance was an important pillar for the corporatist state in Mexico, but over time it worked to the disadvantage of the peasantry.

The subordination of the CNC to the state was made clear after 1940, when official policy shifted in favor of private agribusiness interests. The shift had begun toward the end of Cárdenas's presidency because of fears of lost investment and landowner support for fascism in Mexico, but the shift was adopted unambiguously by the administrations of Manuel Avila Camacho (1940–46) and Miguel Alemán Valdés (1946–52). Reforms to the Agrarian Code in 1942 and 1946 made protection from expropriation easier to obtain, while public investment in irrigation works and rural infrastructure and preferential credit were targeted on large-scale agro-export enterprises in the northwest. The political weakness of the CNC was revealed by its failure to mobilize effectively against the counterreform measures. At the same time, attempts to organize along independent lines were frustrated by the governments of Miguel Alemán Valdés, Adolfo Ruiz Cortines (1952–58), and Adolfo López Mateos (1958–64).

Starting in the mid-1940s, regional independent movements emerged as grassroots leaders became frustrated with the slow pace of agrarian reform. The most important of these movements was centered in Morelos, where between 1945 and 1962 Rubén Jaramillo led a mass movement against the corruption of local sugar mill owners and in favor of land reform and democratization of municipal and state government. The movement not only fought in the name of agrarian issues, but also on the electoral front as the Partido Agrario Obrero Morelense (PAOM). The two fronts of struggle remained inextricably linked owing to the economic power wielded by those in political office. It was precisely the PAOM's political threat that provoked the intransigence of the authorities, and the Jaramillistas were forced into clandestinity by government repression and established armed self-defense units to protect peasant land against local bosses (caciques). Although Jaramillo won the solidarity of other popular movements in nearby Mexico City, it was not enough to resist the attacks, which were coordinated by local elite groups. Following a brief period of legalized political activity, in May 1962 Jaramillo and his family were captured and executed by troops and judicial police. No one was ever brought to trial.

In the more general context of popular discontent with the reversal of Cárdenas's reforms, dissident labor unions and peasant movements joined the Unión General de Obreros y Campesinos de México (UGOCM) in 1949, which was affiliated with the new Partido Popular (PP).

In the northwestern states the UGOCM and the PP confronted similar responses to those seen in Morelos. When the UGOCM led land invasions in 1958, its principal leader, Jacinto López, was imprisoned along with other important members. Moreover, when the disputed lands were distributed, it was the CNC and not the UGOCM that benefited most, despite the fact that the latter had been at the forefront of the struggle. Whereas in Morelos the party-movement link provoked repression, in the case of the PP-UGOCM the response was more complex. The PAOM was a regionally defined party, and its candidates did not aspire to seats in the national government. The PP, on the other hand, was a national party of the opposition, led by a prominent Cardenista, Vicente Lombardo Toledano. The ruling Partido Revolucionario Institucional (PRI, or Institutional Revolutionary Party) offered some concessions to the PP leadership in exchange for its loyal opposition in the Chamber of Deputies (i.e., the PP technically was an opposition party but avoided confrontations with the PRI and generally voted the PRI party line, thus hindering the development of a real opposition in Congress). This coincided with Lombardo's preferred strategy of avoiding confrontations with the government and seeking incremental gains by getting PP candidates elected and then ratified by the ruling party. Jacinto López saw this strategy as doomed to failure, given the size of the PRI majority. In fact, Lombardo was criticized for putting his personal well-being before that of the party and the UGOCM. A split was avoided until 1967, but relations were inevitably strained. As the PP leadership became divorced from the base, the UGOCM in Sonora and Sinaloa suffered setbacks in its struggle to defend the social sector. As a result, it was unable to resist the offensive of the right in the early 1960s and finally split into an independent and a progovernment faction in 1973.

A third major challenge to the government's agrarian policies came in 1963 with the formation of the Central Campesina Independiente (CCI). This was the largest opposition confederation and brought together some of the most distinguished regional leaders, including Ramón Danzós Palomino from the Yaqui Valley of Sonora, Arturo Orona from the *ejidos* (communal village landholdings) of the Laguna (Coahuila and Durango), and Alfonso Garzón from Baja California. More importantly, the CCI was not an isolated peasant movement but formed part of the Movimiento de Liberación Nacional (MLN, or Movement for National Liberation), a broad left-wing coalition led by Lázaro Cárdenas, uniting the major Cardenista and communist groups displaced from power in the previous two decades. Like the UGOCM, the CCI demanded the revitalization of land reform, an end to repression, democratization, and respect for the right to organize independently of the ruling party and its union confederations.

In 1964 the government again used repression in an attempt to demoralize the CCI, imprisoning its most radical leaders, including Danzós Palomino. In the context of the Cuban Revolution and the anti-communist propaganda from the right, the MLN and the CCI soon were forced onto the defensive, and their offices were ransacked by police. A split emerged in the CCI as the more moderate factions led by Humberto Serrano and Alfonso Garzón restated their support for the government and tried to expel the communist-affiliated faction. Serrano and Garzón gave their support to the administration of President Gustavo Díaz Ordaz (1964–70), while the communists remained independent of the PRI but seriously weakened. Following the release of Danzós Palomino, the latter group in 1975 renamed itself the Central Independiente de Obreros Agrícolas y Campesinos (CIOAC). As its new name suggested, the CIOAC emphasized not only the land struggle but also the need to organize wage workers to protect labor rights and improve conditions. As a result, it had the most success in the more developed northwestern region. In 1977 the CIOAC also began to organize indigenous workers on coffee plantations in Chiapas. Although it remained formally autonomous of political parties, in practice it helped build electoral support for candidates of the independent left.

The lessons of the PAOM, the UGOCM, and the CCI were confronted by the next generation of activists, who sought to maintain the struggle for "land and liberty." This generation included students, schoolteachers, Catholic lay clergy and priests, and the children of agrarian reform beneficiaries. The 1968 student movement and its brutal repression at Tlatelolco led to a break with earlier perceptions of strategy and organization. A central current of the student movement, with links to rural teacher-training colleges, held that the left's strategy of seeking socialism through parliamentary means was mistaken. The renamed Partido Popular Socialista (PPS, or Popular Socialist Party) and the Partido Comunista Mexicano (PCM, or Mexican Communist Party) were criticized for their lack of organic links to the people and for their highly centralized and bureaucratic internal structures. Instead, the task was to turn the model upside down and build democratic mass organizations from the bottom up. In the early 1970s thousands of students went to rural villages and poor urban districts to put the Maoist theory of the "mass line" into practice. This movement developed into two tendencies: Línea de Masas in the urban context and Línea Proletaria, which organized in industrial unions, and in the countryside.

The emergence of new activists coincided with the continuing weakness of the CNC to represent peasant demands of the state. The repression of land claimant groups from 1976 to 1979 and official declarations indicating that agrarian reform was to be wound down led to protests in several states, although the protests remained dispersed and unco-ordinated. It was in response to these limitations that two new national movements were formed in the late 1970s and early 1980s. The two most promin-ent were the Coordinadora Nacional Plan de Ayala (CNPA) and the Unión Nacional de Organizaciones Regionales Campesinas Autónomas (UNORCA).

In 1979 various events were organized to mark the 100th anniversary of the birth of Emiliano Zapata and to discuss agrarian issues. A series of national meetings were held to exchange testimonies, ideas, and proposals for unity. The main point of conver-gence was resistance to the end of land reform. In October 1979 over 20 independent regional organi-zations formed the CNPA.

The CNPA was made up of poor peasants, mem-bers of indigenous communities, land claimants, and agricultural workers. This explains why the most important issues for the CNPA were the defense of the lands and natural resources of indigenous groups and the implementation of agrarian reform. The CNPA also fought for recognition of rural unions and the defense of indigenous cultures. By the end of the 1980s it was giving greater attention to problems of production, credit, and marketing. The CNPA sought to maintain autonomy from all political parties while allowing individual members freedom to affiliate with whomever they wished as long as they did not contradict the principles of the organi-zation. This position was adopted to avoid incorpo-ration into any single party and to promote a truly grassroots movement with a peasant leadership and a more horizontal and democratic internal structure. It criticized the vertical and hierarchical relationships that exist in traditional confederations such as the CNC. The internal structure of the CNPA thus emphasized broad participation from the grassroots and the rotation of leadership positions. Among some of its regional organizations such practices already had been implemented during the 1970s.

By 1983 the CNPA had developed a capacity for mobilization far greater than its capacity for negoti-ation. Its actions succeeded in postponing the end of land reform, although at a great cost in terms of gov-ernment repression. Moreover, the CNPA was unable to put forward a viable alternative to the govern-ment's austerity policies in the wake of Mexico's debt crisis. Instead, there occurred a process of regional-ization of the peasant movement as each group tried to survive the crisis through mobilization and nego-tiations at the local and state levels. It was also at the regional level that the CNPA achieved its greatest

degree of articulation with other social movements, particularly those representing the interests of in-digenous peoples, schoolteachers, students, and the urban poor.

Regionalization was also a result of local differ-ences concerning alliances with political parties. The Trotskyist Partido Revolucionario de los Trabajado-res (PRT) was the most important party in the CNPA leadership, owing to its alliance with local move-ments in Veracruz, Guerrero, Coahuila, and Sonora. In the context of the 1985 federal elections, the PRT was accused of trying to manipulate the CNPA in favor of its candidates, and several organizations decided to abandon the CNPA in protest.

Further divisions followed as the CNPA proved incapable of taking on new demands beyond that of land reform. The increasing importance of electoral contests in the 1980s undermined the unity of the CNPA. The dominant current that remained in a much weaker organization continued to see elections as simply "a bourgeois game" and attacked those who supported parties as reformist. The greatest strength of the CNPA in 1979, its independence from political parties and its clear class position, turned out to be its greatest weakness in a very different political conjuncture, that of the presidential elec-tions of 1988. It failed to appreciate the importance of the changes that had been occurring in the politi-cal system, and most of its member organizations refused to mobilize support for the candidacy of Cuauhtémoc Cárdenas. The radical and confronta-tional tone of the CNPA was out of step with its real capabilities in the context of economic crisis and repression. Discontent within the movement led sev-eral groups to concentrate their efforts in their own regions and abandon national coordination. Still others looked to new alliances with political parties of the left as the electoral struggles became more important. Similarly, the radicalization of the CNPA reduced its capacity for negotiations with the state, impeding the resolution of basic demands.

At its national meeting in August 1989, several member organizations openly expressed their dis-content. The democratic practices that had distin-guished the internal structure of the CNPA had fallen into disuse, participation was not being promoted, analysis of the current national situation was lack-ing, and no strategic plan had been elaborated. The root of the problem was held to be the political immaturity and intolerance of the most sectarian organizations. This critical current called for the recovery of the positive aspects of the CNPA, pri-marily its earlier democratic form of internal organi-zation and promotion of broad participation. It also recognized that the CNPA was now only one among several peasant movements. After its rapid growth between 1979 and 1982, it entered into decline and has since been overtaken by other organizations, particularly the UNORCA, and by the popularity of neo-Cardenismo. The CNPA declined in importance until it, along with the rest of the peasant movement, was rejuvenated by the armed Zapatista uprising in 1994.

Whereas the CNPA has maintained a radical stance in defense of its demands for land reform, most organizations have opted for less confrontational tactics and have instead actively sought support from the government for their proposals. This shift to pragmatism has been clearly illustrated by the development of the struggle to control decisions relating to production and marketing. This shift was the result of a relative opening toward non-PRI producer organizations on the part of the government after 1979 and a correspondingly conciliatory strategy promoted by Línea Proletaria (LP).

The most important experiences to understand the action of LP in the countryside are those of the Coalición de Ejidos Colectivos de los Valles Yaqui y Mayo (CECVYM) and the Unión de Uniones Ejidales y Grupos Campesinos Solidarios de Chiapas (UU). Following the land redistribution in the Yaqui and Mayo Valleys in December 1976, progovernment organizations lost their support when they signed an agreement with the Rural Credit Bank (BANRURAL) to pay compensation to the former landowners. The agreement also stipulated that areas of expropriated land that contained buildings or infrastructure should be returned to their former owners. In response, the new *ejidatarios* protested by occupying the offices of BANRURAL and forced the bank to reverse its decisions. This initial victory gave rise to the formation of the independent Coalition. In subsequent years the CECVYM fought against the corruption, inefficiency, and clientelism that characterized BANRURAL and the state-owned crop insurance company, Aseguradora Nacional Agrícola y Ganadera (ANAGSA). In 1978 dependency on ANAGSA was overcome through the establishment of a common fund into which all member *ejidos* paid. The fund allowed for the creation of departments of technical assistance and seed reproduction, thereby overcoming the problems created by the corruption of government functionaries. BANRURAL threatened to suspend the payment of credit to those who refused to insure their crops with ANAGSA. In its confrontations with BANRURAL, the Coalition saw the need to gain greater financial independence through the establishment of its own credit

union. By October 1980 the Union of Ejido Credit of the Yaqui and Mayo Valleys was established, constituting a further break in the chain of intermediaries. At the same time the Coalition established its own marketing commission to work in conjunction with the credit union toward the objective of taking greater control of decisions relating to production and marketing.

The objective of the LP activists in the Coalition was to build a viable economic organization in which the direct producers would have control over the decisions affecting their lives. The Coalition concentrated on each area of economic decision making, from crop insurance to credit and marketing, and instituted a series of projects in technical assistance, training, social welfare, and housing. Its success attracted the interest of other producer organizations with similar problems, including the Unión de Uniones of Chiapas, which was formed in September 1980.

The experiences of regional organizations such as the CECVYM and the UU were important in the emergence of the UNORCA. The UNORCA was formed in March 1985 following various meetings to unify regional movements that had not found an adequate response to their demands from the existing official or independent organizations. Significantly, the formation and growth of the UNORCA underlined the weakness of the CNPA by this time to articulate demands other than those of land reform. The UNORCA grew from 26 member organizations in 1985 to 73 by 1989, with a presence in 20 states.

Similarly to the CNPA, the UNORCA did not affiliate itself with any single party, instead respecting the autonomy of each regional member organization to support the party of its choice. In 1988 its members voted for both PRI and Cardenista candidates. However, it emphasized social and economic development of the rural social sector (comprised of land reform beneficiaries). It drew on the experience of member organizations by putting the solution of material and economic problems before ideological struggles. Its alliances were similarly limited to the peasant sector. This position was different from the antiparty stance of the CNPA, since it did not explicitly criticize party affiliation. However, it was critical of the vertical and centralized structures of traditional peasant confederations that "belonged" to political parties.

The predominance of economic over political concerns can be interpreted as a response to the effects of the crisis in the countryside. Immediate problems of production and marketing became the priority. At the same time, the withdrawal of the state from its traditional functions meant that new spaces were being left that producer organizations could potentially fill. This helps explain the interest of President Carlos Salinas de Gortari (1988–94) in cultivating good relations with UNORCA leaders and advisers.

In response to the low credibility that surrounded his election in July 1988, Salinas acted quickly to neutralize potential opposition. In the countryside, two strategies were deployed: first, the Ministry of Agriculture and Water Resources (SARH) selectively met economic demands through the signing of *convenios de concertación;* second, Salinas promoted the formation of a new umbrella organization of peasant movements known as the Congreso Agrario Permanente (CAP). At the same time, Salinas made several speeches in which he emphasized the need to respect the autonomy of peasant organizations and to leave behind the traditional paternalism of the state. He also applied pressure on the CNC to reform and modernize its own structures, which led to the rise to prominence of a reformist current headed by a former UNORCA leader.

Since the early 1970s different administrations had attempted without success to unify peasant movements in a common front. These efforts were top-down initiatives and clearly sought to bolster support for the government. If Salinas was to succeed, he had to acknowledge the autonomy of several movements, including the UNORCA. He also had to respond to the independent unification of 10 national peasant movements in December 1988 behind a set of common agrarian and economic demands (CAU, Convenio de Acción Unitaria). These included groups that supported the political left and Cárdenas. They opposed the austerity policies and neoliberal adjustment policies and feared further moves toward trade liberalization.

Salinas was successful in attracting the support of six organizations that had signed the CAU for the new, officially sponsored CAP, which also included the participation of the CNC and four other pro-government peasant organizations. CNPA opted for observer status only and conditioned its participation on guarantees that repression would be brought to an end. During the first three months of the Salinas administration over 30 peasants belonging to independent organizations were murdered, reflecting a darker side of *concertación* and the continued impunity for repressive acts.

Although Salinas invited the CAP to make policy proposals for a National Agrarian Plan, it soon became evident that its real influence was very limited. In particular, the CAP was unable to counter or even significantly modify Salinas's 1991 reforms to Article 27 of the Constitution of 1917, which potentially allowed for the reconcentration of land in private hands. It also argued in vain against the inclusion of corn and beans in the negotiation of the North American Free Trade Agreement (NAFTA), which was signed in 1993.

By 1988 the peasant movements that had evolved since the mid-1970s were in disarray. Weakened by repression, internal divisions, failed alliances and co-optation, neither the CNPA, the UNORCA, nor the CAP offered a viable strategy for defending the rural social sector in the era of globalization. In fact, the main adversary and sometimes ally since the 1930s, the state, was rapidly restructuring itself in ways that obliged peasants to deal directly with the market from a severely disadvantaged position. Unable to compete with cheaper imports and facing increasing indebtedness, in 1993 a new movement of middle-sized farmers emerged in western Mexico, known as El Barzón. The Barzonistas grew rapidly in 1994 and 1995 as more and more producers defaulted in the face of skyrocketing interest rates and depressed agricultural prices. The movement also incorporated large numbers of small businesses and individual citizens who were hit by the collapse of the peso in December 1994 and the subsequent hike in interest rates on their commercial and personal loans.

The peasant movement also was revitalized by the armed Zapatista uprising on January 1, 1994, in Chiapas. The Zapatistas called for the repeal of Salinas's reforms to Article 27, the dismantling of illegal latifundio holdings, and revision of the effects of NAFTA for indigenous peoples in Mexico. Its impact was particularly significant in Chiapas, where a new alliance of independent peasant movements led over 400 land invasions during 1994 and 1995, while expressing solidarity with the armed Zapatistas. The seventh round of talks between the Zapatistas and the government, held in October 1995, led to an agreement that the original spirit of Article 27 would be restored, allowing for the articulation of alternative proposals that would potentially lead to a more acceptable agrarian legislation.

See also Drug Trade; North American Free Trade Agreement (NAFTA); Partido de la Revolución Democrática (PRD); Partido Revolucionario Institucional (PRI); Zapatista Rebellion in Chiapas

Select Bibliography

Barry, Tom, *Zapata's Revenge: Free Trade and the Farm Crisis in Mexico.* Boston: South End, 1995.
Bartra, Roger, *Agrarian Structure and Political Power in*

Mexico. Baltimore: Johns Hopkins University Press, 1993.

Collier, George A., with Elizabeth Lowery Quaratiell, *Basta! Land and the Zapatista Rebellion in Chiapas.* Oakland, California: Food First Publications, 1994.

Fox, Jonathan, *The Politics of Food in Mexico: State Power and Social Mobilization.* Ithaca, New York: Cornell University Press, 1992.

Gates, Marilyn, *In Default: Peasants, the Debt Crisis and the Agricultural Challenge in Mexico.* Boulder, Colorado: Westview Press, 1993.

Harvey, Neil, *Rebellion in Chiapas: Rural Reforms, Campesino Radicalism and the Limits of Salinismo.* La Jolla: University of California at San Diego, 1994.

Hewitt de Alcántara, Cynthia, *Modernizing Mexican Agriculture: Socioeconomic Implications of Technological Change 1940–70.* Geneva: United Nations Research Institute for Social Development, 1976.

_____, "Introduction: Economic Restructuring and Rural Subsistence in Mexico." In *Economic Restructuring and Rural Subsistence in Mexico: Corn and the Crisis of the 1980s,* edited by Cynthia Hewitt de Alcántara. San Diego: Ejido Reform Research Project, Center for U.S.-Mexican Studies, University of California, San Diego, 1994.

Paré, Luisa, "The Challenge of Rural Democratization in Mexico." *Journal of Development Studies* 26 (1990).

Sanderson, Steven E., *The Transformation of Mexican Agriculture: International Structure and the Politics of Rural Change.* Princeton, New Jersey: Princeton University Press, 1986.

_____, editor, *Economic Restructuring and Rural Subsistence in Rural Mexico: Corn and the Crisis of the 1980s.* La Jolla: Center for U.S.-Mexican Studies, University of California, San Diego, 1994.

—NEIL HARVEY

S

Sahagún, Bernardino de c. 1499–1590
Missionary and Linguist

Bernardino de Sahagún most likely was born in 1499; a Franciscan ordained priest by 1529, he joined a group of missionaries under Antonio de Ciudad Rodrigo in their journey to New Spain. There, after 60 years, he died in 1590. Nothing is known of his 30 years in Spain except that as a student at the University of Salamanca he became a Franciscan. In New Spain, where he arrived barely a decade after Fernando (Hernán) Cortés, he joined the "Twelve Apostles"—the first twelve missionaries in New Spain—in their work of converting the natives, mostly in places near Mexico-Tenochtitlan (Tlalmanalco, Xochimilco, Huexotzinco, Cholula, Tlatelolco), took part in founding the Colegio de Santa Cruz in Tlatelolco, taught Latin to young highborn natives, and always was ready to help the school, which was invaluable in providing New Spain with talented young natives educated with the procedures used by Spanish universities.

But it is as a linguist-philologist and for his sympathetic understanding of the native civilization he was helping transform that Sahagún's fame vastly increased during the twentieth century. He soon mastered Nahuatl, the language dominant in central Mexico and understood far beyond its borders, and within a decade he was writing and delivering sermons in that language. He did not merely translate standard repertoire; rather, with the help of the college's alumni he had helped train, he produced original sermons suited to the background and capabilities of his congregations (examples can be found in *Sermones de Dominicas y Santos en lengua Mexicana*, 1540, revised 1563). During this period, he was recognized as one of the two best European experts in spoken and written Nahuatl, and he worked collecting rhetorical texts (such as the *Huehuetlatolli*, admonitions of the elders to those of younger generations, 1547), organizing the natives'

account of the Conquest, approving the 1555 edition of Alonso de Molina's *Vocabulario en lengua castellana y mexicana*, and gaining ever deeper insight into the pre-Conquest Nahua civilization (much of which he admired) along with increasing doubts as to the effectiveness of the earliest missionaries' mass conversions. These doubts led Sahagún, with the support of his provincial, Francisco de Toral, to compile in Nahuatl what eventually became the encyclopedic *Historia general* [or *universal*] *de las cosas de Nueva España* (General History of the Things in New Spain), intended to acquaint the missionaries with all aspects of the pre-Hispanic civilization, concentrate upon what urgently needed change, and introduce them to the native language so that priests could know the deeper meanings of what they were told and adequately preach to and admonish their congregations. Sahagún began the project around 1559 and continued to expand and refine it until around 1570, when a change of administration led to the dispersal of all his papers throughout the province until 1575. Then, supported by Juan de Ovando, president of the Council of the Indies, and by Rodrigo de Sequera, Franciscan general commissary of New Spain, Sahagún was enabled to complete the work in the form we now know it in the *Floretine Codex*. Sequera saved the codex before (with a change in Spanish Crown policies) his papers again were confiscated.

Sahagún's work is invaluable to today's Meso-americanists not only for its subject matter, but for the way it was compiled. Sahagún submitted carefully constructed questionnaires to committees of elder indigenes born well before the Conquest, who responded in written form with the assistance of young highborn alumni of the Colegio de Santa Cruz, Tlatelolco. The method was extraordinarily precocious for its day—it resembles the techniques of modern ethnographers. But invaluable as the finished work is to today's ethnographers and historians, its main purpose when compiled was to help sixteenth-century missionaries to further and firmly base conversion of the indigenes to Christianity.

Equally important to Sahagún and his colleagues were his purely evangelical writings, also produced in Nahuatl. Besides his sermons, which were numerous, original, and fortified by his intimate knowledge of the people he was addressing, there were a number of formal works meant for publication. At the same time that he began the *Historia general,* he also was dictating to his highborn trilingual aids his *Postilla* (1564) and a series of canticles. The latter eventually became his *Psalmodia Christiana* (1583), new song-dance texts for dance ceremonies in traditional style to replace old pagan ones. The *Postilla,* or apostil, was to have been a large work, part of a collection of evangelical works including the *Coloquios y Doctrina Christiana,* a probably authentic reconstruction of dialogues that had taken place in 1524 between the earliest missionaries and surviving Aztec leaders; the *Doctrina* (now lost); a history of the conversions (never written); the *Postilla* proper (presumed lost), with its *Addiciones a la Postilla,* a treatise on the three theological virtues; and an *Apéndice a la Postilla* (a fragment survives) containing exhortatory and admonitory materials, some from the *Florentine Codex. Epístolas y Evangelio en Mexicano* (1561) and *Evangeli: Lectionarium ex Evangelis et Epistolis* (unknown date) perhaps should be included in these writings. There are, besides, the introspective, meditative *Exercicios Quotidianos* (1574) and a *Manual del Christiano* (1578) for guidance of converts, of which a fragment survives. Of two trilingual *Vocabularios,* one survives. An *Arte* [grammar] *y Vocabulario Apéndiz* and various minor works are lost. On the other hand, three manuscripts related to the *Florentine Codex* survive: *Calendario de las Fiestas y Meses de estos naturales* (date unknown) and *Arte Adivinatoria* and *Calendario Mexicano, Latino y Castellano* (both c. 1585).

Of this long list only the *Psalmodia Christiana* was published in Sahagún's lifetime; it remained in use until, in the eighteenth century, the Holy Office denounced it and destroyed most copies. Such works as the *Postilla* with its *Addiciones* and *Apéndice,* the *Coloquios,* and the *Manual,* although licensed for publication, never were printed because the inquisition enforced the Council of Trent's prohibition to translate holy writ into the vernacular because the Crown reversed previous supportive policies, or possibly because Sahagún himself withdrew them. Useful compilations like the *Arte* and vocabularies, circulated as manuscripts, simply may have worn out with use, while other writings may have survived hidden or in archives because of their very controversial nature.

Select Bibliography

Anderson, Arthur J. O., "Sahagún: Career and Character." In *Florentine Codex: General History of the Things in New Spain.* Santa Fe, New Mexico: School of American Research, and Salt Lake City: University of Utah Press, 1950–82.

Nicolau d'Olwer, Luis, and Howard F. Cline, "Sahagún and His Works." In *Handbook of Middle American Indians,* edited by Howard F. Cline and John B. Glass. Austin: University of Texas Press, 1973.

Quiñones Keber, Eloise, "The Sahaguntine Corpus: A Bibliographic Index of Extant Documents." In *The Work of Bernardino de Sahagún,* edited by J. Jorge Klor de Alva, H. B. Nicholson, and Eloise Quiñones Keber. Albany: State University of New York, 1988.

—ARTHUR JAMES OUTRAM ANDERSON

Salinas de Gortari, Carlos 1948–
President

As Carlos Salinas de Gortari, Mexico's sixtieth constitutional president, passed the green, white, and red presidential sash from his shoulder to his handpicked successor on a crisp autumn day in 1994, the cavernous Legislative Palace, packed with foreign and national well-wishers—diplomats, legislators, bankers, industrialists, clerics, and political faithful—burst into cheers and applause.

Lauded in foreign capitals as one of the twentieth century's great statesmen, this would-be modernizer of Mexico stood at the pinnacle of his prestige and power on December 1, 1994. Behind him lay six years of radical transformation of Mexico, which had seen the death of the interventionist state, the privatization of large numbers of state industries, and the North American Free Trade Agreement (NAFTA), enshrining a new era of U.S.-Mexican relations in law. Ahead of the 46-year-old Mexican politician beckoned a prominent international role, since he was Washington's choice to lead the new World Trade Organization, headquartered in Geneva. Widely popular both in the barrios of Mexico City—where he was hailed as an honest president who had "done a lot for the poor"—and in the plusher quarters on Wall Street—where the value of Mexican bonds and stocks was a measure of the esteem in which he was held—Salinas bridged the previously inseparable chasm between his Third World nation and the First World he aspired to join.

Cracks, however, already were apparent in Salinas's model of economic prosperity and social stability as he was being fêted as the first Mexican president in a quarter of a century to leave office without an economic and political crisis. The year had been the most violent in a quarter century, with a peasant uprising, fratricidal political assassinations, and a rash of kidnappings of the business class. The country's financial house was sitting on a time bomb: US$30 billion in short-term bonds were owed to the captains of international finance and were about to come due. Less than three weeks later, the truth behind this carefully crafted facade was revealed by the massive devaluation of the Mexican currency and the panicked flight of capital.

Salinas's popularity in Mexico collapsed as rapidly as the Mexican peso. But not until the arrest on February 28, 1995, of his older brother Raul Salinas de Gortari—known as the "First Brother"—on charges of having masterminded the September 28, 1994, assassination of politician and former brother-in-law José Francisco Ruiz Massieu, did Washington and Wall Street finally quiet their adulation and withdraw their support. A wild-eyed Salinas staged a 36-hour hunger strike. Then after secret negotiations with his successor, President Ernesto Zedillo Ponce de León, the former president boarded a private corporate jet and flew to exile, leaving a rapidly expanding scandal of corruption and violence behind him.

In centers of power around the world, Salinas's economic reforms were still lauded as the most far-reaching of Mexico's modern history. But judged on the goals that Salinas himself had enunciated as he took office, the economic modernization became nothing more than an end in itself, rather than the means to end Mexico's long history of corruption and economic backwardness. "The economic modernization of Mexico will mean more jobs, less inflation, and greater productivity," pledged Salinas on taking office. "No more sacrifices," he promised Mexicans who had seen their standard of living diminish steadily since 1982. "We want to be part of the First World," he announced as he stated his intentions to negotiate a wide-ranging free trade accord with the United States and Canada. Ultimately, while Salinas was able to integrate his country into the global economy through free trade, more liberal investment laws, and privatization, he was unable to achieve his main stated goals. Economic prosperity under Salinas never quite matched Wall Street enthusiasm. Within weeks after Salinas had left office, Mexicans again were being asked to make new sacrifices; over 1 million lost their jobs in 1995; and the severe austerity conditions imposed in exchange for a U.S.-arranged US$53 billion bailout underscored how far from the First World was the space Mexico inhabited.

This rapid meltdown of Mexico's former favorite son underscored what his numerous critics long had held: Salinas was a better salesman than a reformer. With the passage of time, it is even more difficult to separate the carefully crafted myth about him from reality. Image became the essence for Salinas, and he worked hard at it: always on the run, always in motion, always one step ahead of the public and his adversaries, planning his next move. Nimble on his feet, Salinas never lacked for a quick answer. "A moratorium," he warned the U.S. administration about Mexico's crushing foreign debt, "is not an option, it's a consequence." But problems for Salinas were quickly fixed through persuasion, whether working a crowd or turning his charm on one participant. More than the great modernizer, Salinas could be likened to the great seducer.

Scores of Mexico's best and brightest traveled to the United States in the 1970s to study in America's best universities. Many returned to posts in the Mexican government hierarchy where there was ample room for advancement. Armed with a master's degree in public administration from Harvard's Kennedy School of Government, Salinas joined this ambitious pack in 1974. Fourteen years later, at age 40, he was in a class by himself, having broken away from hundreds of qualified government functionaries and reached the top, a stunning political ascent unmatched since Lázaro Cárdenas became president in 1934 at age 39.

Salinas's family and political background made him exceptionally equipped for this role. Salinas was not just any bright young Mexican. He was part of the political elite that had been both the pillars and beneficiaries of the Mexican Revolution. Miles ahead of his rivals, he could draw on the advice, experience, and political connections of his family, from his father, who was industry and commerce minister for six years, to his uncle Antonio Ortiz Mena, who was finance minister from 1958 to 1970.

Carlos Salinas de Gortari was born April 3, 1948, the second son of Raul Salinas Lozano and Margarita de Gortari, both economists by education. His ambitious father, who had master's degrees from American University and Harvard University, worked in government. His mother stayed home to raise the five children: Raul, who was two years older than Carlos; Enrique; Sergio; and Adriana. In Mexico City, the family at first lived in the middle-class neighborhood of Narvarte, where their house, typical of Mexican construction, stretched up for several stories.

Little is known about his family life, although by all accounts Salinas's father traveled frequently, leaving his wife to deal with the difficulties of bringing up the children. But any images of halcyon early years are dispelled by the tragedy that overtook the family on December 18, 1951, when Carlos was nearly four years old, Raul was six, and their father was director of economic studies at the Finance Ministry. The two boys, along with a neighborhood playmate, took a loaded rifle from their father's closet and shot and killed a 12-year-old maid, Manuela N., who apparently had willingly posed as the target. The family did not know the maid's last name at the time of her death. Salinas's mother was out on an errand; the housekeeper was on another floor. An account of that time from the daily *Excélsior* said authorities were unclear which boy actually had pulled the trigger to kill the unwitting Manuela N., but the report in the newspaper, *El Universal,* the next day quoted young Carlos as saying, "I killed her with just one bullet. I am a hero."

The tragedy was ruled an accident. But the drama was significant enough to merit headlines in the local sections of Mexico City newspapers of that day. Although the story circulated in political and diplomatic circles even before Salinas became president, it was suppressed from public opinion while he was in office. Salinas himself never has publicly commented on the incident.

When Salinas was 10, his father became the minister of industry and commerce under President Adolfo López Mateos. In 1964 López Mateos passed over Raul Salinas and chose his interior minister Gustavo Díaz Ordaz as successor. The loss clearly left its mark on Carlos Salinas and his family. When Salinas received the presidential appointment in October 1987, one of the first statements he made was to his father: "It took us more than 20 years, but we made it."

In material ways, the family's fortunes improved considerably after his father's six-year stint at the head of the powerful agency that regulated business in Mexico. The father constructed a vacation compound for the Salinas family in southeastern Mexico City, where they could mount their horses, play tennis, swim, or give parties for their friends at the playhouse equipped with a theater.

As was tradition for the offspring of government officials of the time, Salinas attended public schools and then enrolled in the School of Economics at the Universidad Nacional Autónoma de México (UNAM, or the National Autonomous University of Mexico) where he was known for his imported sports car and his politically connected father.

There is no indication that Salinas took part in the student uprising of 1968 that closed down the National University and led to the massacre of several hundred students at a demonstration in Tlatelolco in October. His comments on this watershed moment in his university experience are notable for their absence. He was an avid athlete, riding with the Mexican jumping team in the 1971 Pan-American Games held in Cali, Colombia.

Salinas lived and breathed politics. He joined the youth movement of the ruling Partido Revolucionario Institucional (PRI, or Institutional Revolutionary Party) when he was 18 and was a member of the political club, named the Revolutionary Policy and Professional Association, with his close friends and older brother Raul. Most of its members would be at his side when he became president. His relationship with Raul was particularly close. The two spent a year traveling through Europe by car before Salinas entered the university, and Salinas's college thesis was dedicated to his elder brother, "companion of 100 battles."

In 1972 Salinas married Cecilia Occelli, the daughter of a Mexico City engineer, whom he met through his sister at a Mexican Rodeo Association event in 1965. Cecilia, who was trained as a secretary, went with Salinas for almost two years to live in Cambridge, while Salinas studied at the Kennedy School, receiving a master's in public administration in 1974. His next master's degree, in political economy and government, from the same school came in 1975, and he received his doctorate in the same subject in 1978, with a dissertation entitled "Production and Political Participation in the Countryside," carried out with research in the poor states of Puebla and Tlaxcala.

At the time he was completing his last degrees at the Kennedy School, Salinas already was working in the Mexican government. In 1974 he began working in the Department of Economic Studies in the Finance Ministry's General Office for International Financial Affairs. Five years later he was named to head the office. It was at the Finance Ministry that Salinas met Miguel de la Madrid, who became the most decisive factor in Salinas's success. In 1979 he added Joseph-Marie Cordoba, a French transplant to Mexico, to his circle. Cordoba, an economist, would become his most powerful behind-the-scenes adviser and operative for the next 15 years.

De la Madrid took Salinas with him when he was named minister of planning and budget in 1979. There Salinas crafted the National Development Plan, drawn up during Mexico's oil boom. When

President José López Portillo tapped de la Madrid to run for president as the PRI candidate, de la Madrid named Salinas to be his campaign director.

After de la Madrid took office in December 1982, Salinas was named to head the Planning and Budget Ministry. Few saw Salinas as the most influential member of the cabinet, but by 1986 Salinas had won a series of internecine fights with rivals for de la Madrid's attention. The boyish commerce minister Francisco Labastida Ochoa was sent to Sinaloa as governor, and the popular finance minister Jesús Silva-Herzog was banished after a bitter battle over the 1986 financial crisis when he threatened international bankers with debt moratorium. In the final leg, Salinas beat Interior Minister Manuel Bartlett Díaz and Energy Minister Alfredo del Mazo as de la Madrid's choice to run for the highest office.

Running for president was Salinas's first experience as a political candidate. Short and prematurely bald, Salinas was not cut in the usual mold of Mexican politicians. He was acutely sensitive about his appearance; he wore elevated shoes on the campaign trail and had his aides establish official camera crews to film his presidency.

The 1988 presidential campaign was the first time in years that popular support actually mattered to the PRI, which had been able to engineer virtually unopposed victories in the past. Salinas's campaign was overshadowed by a worsening economic situation. His candidacy shattered a long-held consensus within the PRI, triggering a party breakaway candidacy of Cuauhtémoc Cárdenas, heir to the legacy of his revered father. Salinas logged 100,000 miles on his campaign, but as a crowd pleaser he was a failure. "He doesn't know his country," said one political commentator. "And what he does know makes him ashamed." On election night, July 6, 1988, early returns showed Cárdenas leading by a wide margin. Salinas sent his aides to take control of the vote tally, setting off a national crisis. The following day, a shaken Salinas declared himself victor. The PRI-controlled National Congress declared him president-elect with 50.7 percent of the ballots. But as political analyst Luis Javier Garrido wrote, "The government was unable to demonstrate its candidate's triumph, it could not make public 24,643 of the [54,642] precinct documents and contrary to the law, refused to allow the examination of the original ballots and precinct tallies."

Lacking a consensus on his election, a beleaguered Salinas took office December 1, 1988. His task was not only to restore his own legitimacy, but also to reclaim a political legacy he believed had been denied his family. His final agenda, openly discussed among the political elite, was to take power and keep it not just for the traditional six-year term, but for at least the four administrations Salinas estimated were needed to restructure the nation.

Throughout his years in the public eye, Salinas revealed little about himself to the public. Even his confidants described him as very tough. "He is like a boxer, he goes for the knockout," said one top political analyst.

But some aspects of his personal life did slip out. Top aides described him as a fan of Milan Kundera and said he had closely studied the writings of Italian Marxist theorist Antonio Gramsci. Salinas broke with political tradition and sent his three children from the marriage with Cecilia—Adriana, Carlos Emiliano, and Juan Cristóbal—to the Japanese School in the Mexican capital. He installed as a top aide a young college graduate named Ana Paula Girard, who had been at his side during the campaign and whom he married after leaving office and divorcing his wife Cecilia.

Salinas's first actions as president were a series of spectacular strikes against powerful labor leaders, who, coincidentally, also had been his fiercest opponents within his party. His simultaneous arrests of the top leadership of the Petroleum Workers Union did little to end union corruption and were legally questionable but earned him instant praise in Washington and on Wall Street. The mass arrests set the hard-line tone of his administration, silencing effective opposition within his own ranks.

Those arrests were just the beginning. Financial tycoons, aging labor bosses, tax evaders, drug traffickers, even the culprits of a spectacular museum heist, all fell before the onslaught of Salinas's enforcers in the first months of his presidency, fulfilling his aides' promise that he would create his legitimacy on the job and earning him the title of "Giant Killer" on a *Newsweek* cover.

International bankers, pressured by Washington, were forced to accept losses on the US$100 billion foreign debt and exchange debt for bonds under a restructuring known as the Brady Plan, named after U.S. treasury secretary Nicholas Brady. The settlement allowed Mexico to return to global financial markets for its financial needs. Soon money began to flow. In six years, the country received hundreds of billions of dollars of foreign investment in stocks and government securities, as well as foreign investment in factories and businesses.

Although the issue never was discussed in the campaign, Salinas's government embarked on a sweeping privatization of state-run companies, from Telefonos de Mexico to the 18 commercial banks. The jewel in the crown—the phone monopoly—was snatched by one of the men who sat on Salinas's campaign finance committee, Carlos Slim Helu. The banks were sold for as much as double their book value to unseasoned financiers, many of whom were among those made newly rich by the economic liberalization. The US$22 billion that flowed into government coffers from the sales—less than 5 percent from foreign investors—was used to pay the country's internal debt. Criticisms of the privatizations from Cárdenas's opposition Partido de la Revolución Democrática (PRD, or Party of the Democratic Revolution) found no echo in society, but after billions were spent in bailouts (US$20 billion for the banks and US$2 billion for toll roads), the handling of the government's giveaway became one of the key scandals of the Salinas administration.

To bolster his popular support, Salinas launched his Programa Nacional de Solidaridad (PRONASOL, or National Solidarity Program), which channeled millions of dollars into roads, schools, and clinics for impoverished areas without any government oversight of the spending. He attempted to reshape the PRI by incorporating the solidarity themes, but his lack of political reforms became a true test of Salinas restructuring. The Mexican president stated publicly that he wanted to reform the economy before instituting democratic changes to avoid the political chaos that brought about the breakup of the Soviet Union. Writer Carlos Fuentes dubbed his policy "perestroika without glasnost."

But conflictive elections would dog Salinas in his six years as president, while the assassinations of more than 200 members of the PRD would continue unchecked.

On January 1, 1994, as Salinas was toasting the beginning of the hard-fought North American Free Trade Agreement, an indigenous uprising in the country's poorest state of Chiapas set the tone for Salinas's last year in office. While the fighting was halted within days, the indigenous demands for equality and justice struck a sensitive chord in the nation.

Chiapas was still overshadowing the campaign when Salinas's handpicked successor Luis Donaldo Colosio was assassinated on the campaign trail on March 23, 1994. Suspicion fell on Salinas because growing tensions between the president and his selected heir were an open secret; however, as of 1996 no real evidence or formal charges had been presented against the former president. Nevertheless, the crime was described as one of the most costly in history. A record US$30 billion in foreign reserves had slipped to US$17 million when Salinas rendered

his final state-of-the-union address. The kidnapping of the billionaire owner of Banamex, Alfredo Harp Helu, that year and the assassination of Ruiz Massieu shortly before Salinas left office helped contribute to a year of unparalleled financial and political unrest that led up to the December 19 currency devaluation.

None of these problems were immediately obvious to the public, foreign dignitaries, or even the new administration when Zedillo took the oath of office and Salinas went on to what was supposed to be a more brilliant future. But Salinas's short history was never one of unparalleled triumphs. Within the confines of backroom politicking that characterizes the Mexican system, with its "written and unwritten rules," Salinas was a master. But in his one attempt at electoral politics, subject to public accountability, Salinas was a dismal failure. And once events no longer allowed him to stage-manage his image, Salinas's shine quickly tarnished.

Within the immediate years after leaving office, moving in exile from Canada to Cuba to Ireland, Salinas tried to piece together his personal and family legacy, which had crumbled thoroughly, with his brother Raul in jail, with the enrichment of the family being viewed as a national and international scandal, and with his own family torn by his divorce and the birth of his new daughter Margarita. From exile Salinas defended himself and his family, demanding that the Zedillo administration admit to mishandling Mexico's finances—what he called their "errors of December"—and blaming the political problems on the actions of the old guard within the PRI. Not surprisingly, it has been to the United States that Salinas turned, serving on the board of directors of Dow Jones and Company and defending his name in private seminars at Harvard.

Select Bibliography

Carlos Salinas de Gortari: Biography. English and Spanish text, Las Cruces: New Mexico: State University Joint Border Research Institute, 1988.

Russell, Philip L., *Mexico under Salinas.* Austin, Texas: Mexico Resource Center, 1994.

—JANE BUSSEY

Santa Anna, Antonio López de
1794–1876

General and President

Antonio López de Santa Anna, soldier and politician, is perhaps one of the most complex, contradictory figures of the Mexican nineteenth-century. During his public life he espoused every political creed and was in turn supported by every group on the political spectrum. According to Robert A. Wilson, Santa Anna was less like a politician than "the hero of a Spanish novel" or, one could say, of an Italian operetta. The general's military career is spotty to say the least: he was considered largely responsible both for the loss of Texas in 1863 and for Mexico's defeat before the invading U.S. Army in 1847. Nevertheless, his contemporaries knew him as the Benemérito de la Patria, the hero of Tampico, Puebla, and Acajete, the victor over the Spanish and the French. He was also known to be profoundly corrupt, a gambler and womanizer who seemed to be overly fond of colorful uniforms, bright medals, and pompous and often ridiculous ceremony. The leg he lost while fighting the French in 1838—during the "Pastry War"—was given public burial with military honors, only to be dragged out and desecrated by an angry mob in 1855. Despite all this, his was the most pervasive presence during the first 30 years of Mexico's independent life. He seemed to be Mexico's providential *hombre indispensable*. President 11 times between 1833 and 1855, he was periodically called back to power—notwithstanding his recurrent falls from grace—time and time again, as the only person who could "save" Mexico.

What, then, is the historical significance of Santa Anna? His personality looms so enormous over the first decades after Independence that, as the scholar Moisés González Navarro has pointed out, many have tried to understand Mexico through Santa Anna, and not the other way around. Santa Anna, says scholar Enríque González Pedrero, was "a broken mirror which reflected the fragmented, oscillating condition of a society." His eventful career does seem to symbolize the instability of the Mexican nation during much of the nineteenth century.

Born in Jalapa on February 21, 1794, into the middle-class criollo family of a minor Spanish government official, he joined the Fijo de Veracruz Infantry Regiment in 1810, attaining the rank of commander in 1821. That same year, he shifted his allegiance to Agustín de Iturbide's Plan de Iguala and its call for an independent Mexican Empire. Under the empire, he was named commander general of the Veracruz province. When Emperor Agustín, fearing that Santa Anna was building an independent regional power base, discharged him, Santa Anna rose up in arms, advocating a federal republic. Describing these events in his memoirs, Santa Anna virtually admitted to the utter lack of ideological principles that seemed to characterize his later actions: in removing him from his command, Iturbide had "given such a violent blow to his military honor" that his eyes were suddenly opened, and he saw "absolutism in all its fierceness and he felt encouraged to fight against it."

According to scholar John Lynch, the years between 1821 and 1832 were ones of preparation for Santa Anna, during which he built his support base, establishing contacts with both a local clientele and national politicians, thus extending his power from a regional to a national level. His adhesion to the Plan de Casa Mata, which contributed to the fall of Iturbide in 1823, his support of Vicente Guerrero against Manuel Gómez Pedraza, and his defeat of Isidro Barradas's attempt at reconquist in 1829, established his reputation as a patriotic general of vaguely populist ideals. In 1832, the time was ripe: he rose against President Anastasio Bustamante, demanding Gómez Pedraza's return to serve out the last remaining months of his presidency. Through a pact with Valentín Gómez Farías, he saw to it that the political machinery of an embryonic Liberal Party would ensure his election to the presidency, with the "radical" Gómez Farías as vice president, in May 1833. Then, arguing health reasons, Santa Anna left for his Manga del Clavo hacienda in Veracruz on June 3.

Thus Santa Anna began what would become his modus operandi for the following years, during which he periodically would reach the presidency and then stand back from the exercise of power: as John Lynch has pointed out, he was interested in leadership in and for itself, not as a vehicle for implementing certain social or political policies. He would abandon the presidency, with his power intact, leaving others to become worn down by the day-to-day affairs of government. Santa Anna was president from May 16 to June 3, 1833; June 18 to July 5, 1833; October 28 to December 4, 1833; April 24, 1834, to January 27, 1835; March 18 to July 9, 1839; October 9, 1841, to October 25, 1842; March 5 to October 3, 1843; June 4 to September 11, 1844; March 21 to 31, 1847; May 20 to September 15, 1847; and April 20, 1853, to August 9, 1855. This coming and going also enabled him systematically to emerge as the mediator between rivals, or as the defender of threatened interests, as he did in 1833, when he reversed Gómez Farías's anticlerical reforms. His return to the seat of power usually implied a momentary truce, the reaching of some sort of compromise: in 1833, with the removal of the radical Gómez Farías government; in 1836, with the sanction of the centralist Siete Leyes, which increased the power of the presidency and imposed financial qualifications to voting and office holding; in 1841, with the adoption of the Bases de Tacubaya, a temporary armistice between federalist and centralists that called for the establishment of a constitutionalist convention; and in 1843, with that of the conservative, centralist Bases Orgánicas.

On the other hand, his reversals of fortune were also momentous: when he was defeated by the Texas separatist Samuel Houston at San Jacinto—which he blamed entirely on General Vicente Filisola, who had retired his troops to the Rio Grande at Santa Anna's orders—popular reaction was such that Santa Anna decided to retire from public life, for faced "with such cruel ingratitude," only "his family deserved his sacrifices." After the Mexican-American War, Santa Anna was seen as a vile traitor. Benito Juárez, then governor of Oaxaca, would not even let him enter his state as he was leaving the country. He was exiled in Turbaco, Colombia, until, in 1853, the leaders of the Mexican political class—both Conservative (Lucas Alamán) and Liberal (Sebastián Lerdo de Tejada)—called to him as the only "link" that could unite all Mexicans and save the country from dissolution. Santa Anna opted for the Conservative proposal, naming Lucas Alamán minister of foreign relations and head of the cabinet. The Conservatives had wanted to implement a strong dictatorial central government that finally, after 40 years of instability, would guarantee order and national unity, and that would rationalize public administration. Their project failed, owing, among other reasons, to the dictator's erratic and arbitrary behavior—Alamán died very early into the new administration—and to the regional resistance to the centralization of power, especially by Guerrero's Juan Álvarez. After 1855, Santa Anna once again had to flee the country. Thereafter, he made periodic efforts to return, first offering his services to the French-imposed emperor Maximilian as a mediator between Maximilian and Juárez, then as an intermediary between the victorious Republicans and the more moderate Liberals. He finally was allowed to return to the country in 1874, dying in relative obscurity in Mexico City on June 21, 1876.

How then can we understand this man, who alternately was seen as the country's greatest hero and its dangerous enemy? Perhaps one should try to understand Santa Anna through Mexico, and Mexico's situation during the first half of the nineteenth century. Santa Anna was, as John Lynch has shown, a typical caudillo (strongman): the "scourge of anarchy" and "protector of elites." But in the complex, transitional nineteenth-century Mexican society with its divided elites, the role of the caudillo was more difficult than in Argentina or Venezuela. It required careful manipulation of the different elements of power. It was impossible to form a powerful, stable alliance that would either reconcile or crush contending interests. Santa Anna, through his apparently bizarre performance—constantly appearing and disappearing from the public scene—was not the unquestioned strongman who held the country's destiny in his hands, but he managed to remain, for the best part of 30 years, "the most famous man in Mexico," the one all eyes would turn to when there seemed to be a vacuum of power. Santa Anna had a strong regional base in the state of Veracruz, consisting both of the popular element that made up his *jarocho (veracruzano)* army and of the clientele of friends and family he had placed in the state's key government posts, especially the customs offices; he had a strong influence in the army, which he rewarded handsomely every time he came to power; and he held strong links to the *agiotistas* (public bond speculators), whose debts he paid preferentially. He also managed to maintain his prestige and reputation as a patriot, born out of his very able manipulation of propaganda rather than of his dismal military record. As his contemporary Lucas Alamán wrote, one could find his name playing the principal role in all the country's political events. But, as scholar Michael P. Costeloe has pointed out, the decisive element in Santa Anna's success was the fact that he was "the supreme . . . negotiator and fixer of deals." Therefore, although the leading politicians of the time recognized him as essentially a man of power, a corrupt opportunist lacking political principles, they also saw him as the only leader who could build a viable government, who could consolidate, at least momentarily, the conflicting, divisive interests of Mexican society.

Select Bibliography

Callcott, Wilfrid H., *Santa Anna: The Story of an Enigma Who Once Was Mexico*. Hamden, Connecticut: Archon, 1964.

Costeloe, Michael P., *The Central Republic in Mexico, 1835–1846: Hombres de Bien in the Age of Santa Anna*. Cambridge: Cambridge University Press, 1993.

Lynch, John, *Caudillos in Spanish America, 1800–1850*. Oxford: Clarendon, 1992.

—Erika Pani

Science

Any attempt to synthesize the history of science in Mexico immediately runs into the problem of how to understand the term *science*. Such modern historians of Mexican science as Elías Trabulse and Roberto Moreno de los Arcos have tended to see the development of science in Mexico as a coherent enterprise: "At no time can we find a decadence of interest in scientific research. . . . There are no gaps due to lack of scientific activity, no regression, at most brief intervals of minimal acceleration, of near-stagnation due to unfavorable political and social conditions" (Trabulse, 1983). However, the idea that science is a coherent, rational, methodical enterprise for the advancement of knowledge has been rejected by many theorists, such as Paul K. Feyerabend. For scientists such as Richard Phillips Feynman, science is simply "knowledge that works"; it is a rigorous skepticism of grand unified theories. Nonetheless, as the scientist H. Georgi has pointed out, grand unified theories "have had a profound effect, for better or worse, on theoretical particle physics."

A second problem is illustrated by a passage included in Trabulse's four-volume *History of Science in Mexico* (1983–85). In 1746 Matías de Escobar, an Augustinian monk, described the autopsy of the late bishop of Michoacán as follows: "Heaven granted that the circulation of his bile was suspended . . . lest its bitterness should disturb the blood of His Highness. . . . [W]hat appeared to be tiny worms were actually fragments of cinnamon, rosmarin, and lavender that were in his blood." Father Matías fits Einstein's observation that a scientist "must appear to the systematic epistemologist as a kind of unscrupulous opportunist"; however, it is quite probable that Matías himself would have rejected that term "scientist"—if he would have understood the category at all. This problem is accentuated if we move our focus to pre-Hispanic cosmologies.

The most common error is the supposition that Mexico is like other countries and that science has developed in a similar manner. Scientific research as a vocation and career is a relatively recent development in Mexico. Distinguished men of science such as Bernardino de Sahagún and Carlos de Sigüenza y Góngora did not consider themselves primarily scientists. For most of Mexico's history, the scientist was seen more generically as an intellectual. The boundary between pure reflection and scientific work was tenuous at best: scientists participated in politics and wrote novels, while writers and philosophers pontificated about science.

Science in New Spain

One of the earliest Spanish thinkers in New Spain to bring a truly scientific systematic rigor to his work was Bernardino de Sahagún, who developed a rigorous ethnographic methodology, pioneering the use of questionnaires. Although Sahagún's work amazes by its range and depth, Sahagún's motivations were humanistic and religious as well as scientific. One of the so-called Twelve Apostles, the original Franciscan missionaries to New Spain, Sahagún was inspired by the Franciscan ideals of humility and service to try to understand the customs, flora, fauna, and way of life of his converts. Concerned about the disappearance of native cultures, Sahagún also established the Imperial College of Tlatelolco for the instruction of young native priests and scientists, and many of his students became adept at his ethnographic techniques, becoming his most important informants. Sahagún persuaded his native collaborators collectively to write down in Nahuatl an account of Mexica (Aztec) culture and the historical events that led to the downfall of the Mexica Empire. One of Sahagún's students, Martín de la Cruz, is renowned for his magnificently illustrated *Herbarium,* which describes hundred of aboriginal plants together with their pharmacological uses; the work later was translated into Latin by another of Sahagún's students, Juan Badiano.

The development of the physical sciences in Mexico was handicapped by a misguided ban on modern astronomy. As late as the 1770s few writers dared admit familiarity with the works of Copernicus, Galileo, and their followers. Newton was accepted but misunderstood, since many of his key ideas were based on Galileo's. A major exception was Carlos Sigüenza y Góngora, a contemporary of Newton, whose *Libra Astronomica* (1690) reveals a working knowledge of Copernicus, Galileo, Tycho Brahe, Kepler, and Descartes. He calculated the orbit of Halley's comet, and he insisted that science ought to bow to no authority save "reason and experience."

After Sigüenza the small, isolated scientific community in Mexico found itself increasingly out of step with the advances of European science. The Royal and Pontifical University of Mexico, chartered in 1547, remained a bulwark of scholasticism, and the works of Hippocrates and Galen were the sole authorized texts in the Chair of Medicine as late as 1825. Jesuit teachers, the main representatives of modern scientific thought in Mexico during the early eighteenth century, were expelled in 1767. One of the few advocates of scientific study in this period was José Antonio Alzate, a prolific teacher, publicist, and polymath who helped popularize modern scientific ideas in the last decades of the eighteenth century. Writing in the *Gaceta de Liberatura,* Alzate debated other scientists, including León y Gama and Velázquez de León. He even took on the French *Encyclopaedia* for sneering at Spanish contributions to science and technology. Nonetheless, Alzate's merits as a research scientist may have been somewhat exaggerated.

Science in Independent Mexico

After Mexico won Independence in 1821 and for most of the remaining years of the nineteenth century, Mexico was torn by foreign wars and civil strife. Science was largely abandoned, with the exception of a few exceptional and dramatically isolated figures, including Leopoldo Río de la Loza and Andrés Manuel del Río (who discovered the element vanadium). During the autocratic regime of Porfirio Díaz (1884–1911), however, there were some conscious attempts at modernization. The influence of the French positivism lent a new prestige to industrial and scientific progress. Major scientific institutes were founded, including the Astronomical Observatory and the Geological Institute. The University, which had been closed during the years of troubles, was reopened in 1910 as the National University of Mexico. The ruling group of intellectuals around Díaz called themselves the Científicos, illustrating the new prestige of science.

The Mexican Revolution, however, devastated the country once more. The new scientific research institutes were left to their own devices, and the Department of Education was closed down. In 1921 the Department of Education was reorganized under the leadership of José Vasconcelos, and the surviving science groups were attached to what became (after 1929) the Universidad Nacional Autónoma de México (UNAM, or National Autonomous University of Mexico). A National Institute of Scientific Research was proposed from time to time, but UNAM alone seemed to offer the long-term stability needed for science to develop.

The early developments in Mexican physics, biology, astronomy, and engineering from the 1930s through the 1960s were mostly the work of heroic pioneers, including Nabor Carrillo (engineering), Manuel Sandoval Vallarta (physics; taught with Richard P. Feynman at the Massachusetts Institute of Technology); Arturo Rosenblueth (physiology; coauthor of *Cybernetics* with Norbert Wiener), Guillermo Haro (codiscoverer of the Herbig-Haro objects), Marcos Moshinsky (theoretical physics), and Ignacio Chávez (biomedicine); after 1936 refugees from the Spanish Civil War made a special

contribution. The number of Mexican scientists began to rise steadily after 1930 and continues to increase at a rate of 13 to 14 percent annually.

Until 1954 there were no full-time academic appointments at the university, but much of the country's scientific research was carried out at university laboratories. According to the Organization for Economic Cooperation and Development, in 1994 UNAM accounted for nearly half of Mexico's research and development output. In 1971 the Consejo Nacional para la Ciencia y Tecnología (Conacyt, or National Council for Science and Technology; later incorporated into the Department of Education) was organized and support for scientific research was explicitly included in annual federal budgets. Conacyt fellowships were financed at a rate of approximately US$100 million a year; half of this was allotted to fellowships for study in the United States (52 percent), Britain (17 percent), and other countries. Altogether 92,000 fellowships were awarded between 1971 and 1995. In recent years 41 percent of the scholarships were at the doctoral or postdoctoral level, but not all returning graduates have been able to find suitable jobs. The demand for doctoral recipients in industry remains especially weak.

International experts have deemed Mexico's support for scientific research inadequate, amounting only to 0.1 to 0.4 percent of the gross national product in 1994. Since around 1990 the federal government has been committed to raising this figure to 1 percent, but other budgetary priorities have kept this commitment on the back burner. Nonetheless, the government has been credited with some vigorous and innovative actions on the behalf of science. In 1984 the Sistema Nacional de Investigadores (SNI, or National System of Researchers) was created, and it continues to provide a monthly stipend to bona fide scientists. In 1996 there were 3,500 full members of the SNI, all admitted under rigorous peer review procedures, and the SNI's output accounted for 0.03 percent of the world's production of scientific papers. More than half of the members of the SNI belong to four state institutions of higher education (UNAM, CINVESTAV, IPN, and UAM), all located in Mexico City. Members of the SNI are supported for up to three years provided they are completing their doctoral requirements.

Mexican scientists enjoy a solid international reputation. Although they publish mostly in U.S. and European journals, frequently in coauthorship with U.S. and European colleagues, approximately 60 Mexican research journals adhere to international standards and are partially supported by grants from Conacyt. Mexican scientists frequently win scientific awards; the 1995 Nobel Prize in Chemistry was awarded to the UNAM alumnus Mario Molina, who currently teaches at the Massachusetts Institute of Technology. All major fields are represented in Mexican science, but fields that depend heavily on local inspiration and support—particularly the social and earth sciences—tend to lag behind.

Since 1990 the president of Mexico has been advised by the Consejo Consultivo de Ciencias (Science Advisory Council), with members drawn from past winners of the National Science Prize; the Consejo publishes occasional policy papers. The Academy of Scientific Research, with approximately 1,000 members, provides coveted annual awards to scientists under 40 years of age. Adequate science libraries exist at all major research institutes, and annual scientific meetings are held by Mexican scientific associations in every discipline, often underwritten by Conacyt.

The Authoritarian Tradition

The historic lag of Mexican science behind literature and the arts is not clearly understood. The most common explanation, the supposedly negative influence of Spain, is rooted in the anti-Spanish prejudice of the French Enlightenment. Some authors also blame social and political upheavals, but the arts and letters seem to have been immune to them; moreover, the three centuries of Spanish rule were relatively free from social and political disturbance, but yielded little scientific output. Religious opposition to Copernicus was an important if not decisive factor; Italian science, for one, progressed in spite of it. An interesting possible explanation is the prestige of hermeticism in early Mexican science. The writings of the Jesuit Athanasius Kirchner, a mystic and illuminist, were widely studied in Mexico and were at least as influential as those of Galileo and Newton during the crucial seventeenth century.

Perhaps the most important explanation for the lag in Mexican science lies in authoritarian intellectual traditions dating from colonial times. If the intellectual climate of colonial Mexico produced some of the world's most enduring artistic and literary achievements, it was not conducive to critical thinking or real scientific inquiry. During most of Mexico's history, people who engaged in scientific research considered themselves intellectuals first and scientists second, and they were governed by a complex of informal sanctions and prejudices. The term *intellectual* was a badge of membership in the educated caste of criollos (those of Spanish descent), which regarded manual work as socially demeaning. Many great painters were mestizos (those of mixed Indian and European heritage) or Indians because art was considered a manual craft. Natural phenomena, however, were not studies through observation but through the works of Aristotle. Laboratory work tended to be done by assistants belonging to the so-called menial classes. The world's first public prize for scientific and technological achievement, awarded by the English Royal Society in the late seventeenth century to a carpenter for the invention of the marine chronometer, would have been unthinkable in New Spain.

This authoritarian tradition has persisted into the nineteenth and twentieth centuries; scientists' social standing has often mattered more than what they were actually saying. The two major figures in Mexican geology, José Guadalupe Aguilera and Ezequiel Ordóñez, for example, fell out with each other because the mestizo Ordóñez refused to submit to the authority of the white Aguilera. Ordóñez, the better geologist of the two, proposed that Mexico's petroleum reserves had commercial value, but as head of the National Geological Service Aguilera took the contrary position, forcing Ordóñez to leave his post. As a result, Ordóñez went to work for the U.S.-owned oil company La Huasteca, helping it become one of the most important petroleum companies operating in Mexico. Aguilera never would forgive him.

Much of this social prejudice has been reflected in—and reinforced by—lack of support for the sciences. Until recently Mexico has had no organized science, scientific societies, or prominent patrons of the sciences among the viceroys or presidents; the university was closed during most of the crucial nineteenth century. Although there have not been official witch hunts of unorthodox scientists, the official indifference to science has been quite damaging. Even today scientists in Mexico tend to be poorly paid, and the funding of scientific projects depends on the whim of government officials and must be renegotiated each year. Until quite recently, Mexican scientists needed to be independently wealthy or belong to old families of the upper bourgeoisie in order to be successful. To this day some preference for theory over experimental practice can be detected in Mexican science, and many university graduates distance themselves from manual work to preserve their social status.

Select Bibliography

Feyerabend, Paul K., *Against Method: Outline of an Anarchistic Theory of Knowledge.* London and New York: Verso, 1975.
Feynman, Richard Phillips, *"Surely You're Joking, Mr. Feynman!": Adventures of a Curious Character.* New York: Norton, 1985.

Georgi, H., "Grand Unifiers in Theories." In *The New Physics,* edited by Paul Davies. Cambridge: Cambridge University Press, 1990.

—CINNA LOMNITZ

Sexuality

See Gender; Women's Status and Occupation

Siqueiros, David Alfaro 1896–1974

Artist

Born in Santa Rosalia (today Camargo), Chihuahua, on December 29, 1896, David Alfaro Siqueiros stands among the three most important painters in modern Mexican culture, together with Diego Rivera and José Clemente Orozco. Nevertheless, political as well as artistic activities dominated his life.

His artistic training began at the Academia de San Carlos, in Mexico City (today the Escuela Nacional de Artes Plásticas), where he helped in 1911 to lead a student strike. In 1914 he became a volunteer in the Constitutional Army, which overthrew the regime of Victoriano Huerta. Leaving the army as a captain, he returned to his art studies. He studied in Europe from 1919 to 1922, able to finance himself by continuing to receive his military salary from the newly elected Carranza government. In Paris he met Diego Rivera and they traveled together in Italy.

With the support of Latin American artists living in Barcelona (including the Uruguayan Torres García), Siqueiros issued a manifesto to the artists of the region for a renewed and popularly focused artistic commitment. Issued in the periodical *Vida Americana,* it formed part of the intellectual foundation for the muralist renaissance in Mexico.

At the request of the vigorous new minister of education, José Vasconcelos, Siqueiros returned to Mexico, participating in a new government program for popular public art. This program inaugurated the Mexican Mural Movement. His most noted work from this period was *Burial of the Martyred Worker* in the National Preparatory School. Veering from artistic to political activities, Siqueiros joined the Communist Party and organized in 1923 the Union of Technical Workers, Painters, and Sculptors, becoming its first secretary general. This organization published the newspaper *El Machete,* which issued various manifestos supporting the Mexican Revolution and populist art.

Arrested for his political activities in 1930, he was allowed to live in the city of Taxco, there painting some of his most moving and poignant easel works such as *Peasant Mother* and *Portrait of a Dead Child.* Going into exile in the United States in 1932, he returned to mural painting in Los Angeles, using innovative techniques for outdoor works that included synthetic paint, stencils, and air gun. From the United States he went to Argentina and Uruguay, then returned to the United States in 1934, residing in New York City. There he set up an experimental workshop, exploring new materials and means for painting. Among the participants was Jackson Pollock. During 1937 and 1938 he fought in the Spanish Civil War, serving as a member of the Republican Fifth Regiment and becoming a lieutenant-colonel. Under the government of Lázaro Cárdenas, he was able to return in 1939 to Mexico.

Siqueiros broke with Cárdenas, however, over the Mexican government's decision to grant Leon Trotsky political asylum. Siqueiros considered Trotsky anti-Soviet and led a failed attempt to assassinate him in 1940. In the trial for this attempt he was acquitted of homicide but went into exile, this time to Chile in 1941. He returned to Mexico in 1944, supported by the U.S. government as part of its wartime policy of attempting to foster Pan-American solidarity by enlisting Latin American artists in the campaign against fascism. At this time Siqueiros received the support of the Rockefeller Foundation for a painting of José Martí and Abraham Lincoln, *Two Mountain Peaks of America.*

In the postwar period there was an increase in construction, giving new life to mural painting. Siqueiros began but did not complete *Patricians and Patrician Killers* and *Monument to General Ignacio Allende* in a former convent in San Miguel de Allende, where he was teaching in an international art student school. He also painted several works on the Aztec hero, Cuauhtemoc. On an exterior wall of the administration building of the national university, he created a striking, three-dimensional "sculpture painting," *The People to the University and the University to the People.* Nonetheless, despite his fame, he was imprisoned from 1960 to 1964 during a period of anti-Communist fervor under the government of Adolfo López Mateos. While incarcerated he continued to paint and had an exhibition of his "prison paintings" several weeks after his release.

Among his final outdoor murals in Mexico City were *From Porfirio to the Revolution, The March of Humanity,* and *Homage to Diego Rivera, José Clemente Orozco, José Guadalupe Posada, Leopoldo Méndez, Dr. Atl.* He even did an easel painting,

Christ, now in the Vatican Museum. He died in Cuernavaca on January 6, 1974. He was married to Angélica Arenal and had one daughter.

The best murals of Siqueiros are memorable for their vivid coloring and sweeping visual impact, dramatically involving the viewer. They often are dominated by his ideological perspective because he always was committed to the idea that revolution required a revolutionary art. Although he considered his murals his most important works, it was through his easel painting that he survived financially. Moreover, these smaller works often reveal a more sensitive, insightful artist, and have significantly contributed to his reputation.

Select Bibliography

Charlot, Jean, *The Mexican Mural Renaissance, 1920–25.* New Haven, Connecticut: Yale University Press, 1963.

Reed, Alma M., *The Mexican Muralists.* New York: Crown, 1960.

Rochfort, Desmond, *Mexican Muralists: Orozco, Rivera, Siqueiros.* NewYork: Universe, 1993.

Stein, Philip, *Siqueiros: His Life and Works.* New York: International Publishers, 1993.

Tibol, Raquel, *Siqueiros.* Dresden: Verlag der Kunst, 1966.

White, D. Anthony, *Siqueiros: A Biography.* Encino, California: Floricanto Press, 1994.

—EDWARD A. RIEDINGER

Sor Juana Inés de la Cruz

See Cruz, Sor Juana Inés de la

Spanish Language in Mexico

See Mexican Spanish

Sports

Sports in Mexico have undergone a profound transformation since Independence in 1821, reflecting broad changes in national history. During the early republic, when politics were unstable and national organization weak, Mexicans enjoyed informal amusements more frequently than organized events. They also preferred traditional Mexican activities such as cockfighting and bullfighting. The influence of the United States increased during the era of Porfirio Díaz (roughly 1876 to 1910), and enthusiasm for U.S. sports such as baseball intensified. Porfirian Mexicans also enjoyed activities that reinforced the values of Positivism: order and progress. The Mexican Revolution produced marked negative effects on Mexico's national image; international sporting competition from the 1920s to the 1960s provided an opportunity for the country to reinvigorate its reputation.

Mexicans during the early republic participated in a variety of leisure activities. While team sports had not yet become popular, people did gamble and attend dances. Cockfights also enthralled the populace, captivating everyone from Antonio López de Santa Anna to common city dwellers. Spectators would place bets on the fowl, who fought each other to death with blades strapped to their legs. Bullfights likewise proved popular, drawing large crowds on Sundays. Mexicans gathered to witness more spectacular events such as balloon ascensions. Hot air balloons had attracted paying crowds since the colonial period, but they became increasingly popular after Independence. Seating at these ascensions divided people according to class. Prohibitive pricing reserved seats in the shade for the most wealthy, while even seats in the sun were too expensive for the average Mexican, who could only afford the one-peso general-admission ticket. An enthusiast of the sport, Santa Anna incorporated it into national celebrations such as Independence Day.

During the era of Porfirio Díaz, Mexican fascination with spectacle continued. People still gathered to witness aeronautical flights that frequently included trapeze acrobats performing under the hot air balloons. More bizarre events also attracted crowds. When the African American boxer Billy Clark could not engage audiences in fights against Mexicans, he began wrestling bears. Robert C. Pate, an American who became Mexico's first modern sports promoter, hosted a fight in which a bull was pitted against a lion. People thronged into the stands to watch the contest, but the bull won too easily, convincing spectators that such displays were not worth the cost of tickets.

Sports from the United States grew increasingly popular during the Porfiriato, and men such as Pate worked tirelessly to promote them. As more U.S. citizens moved to Mexico, their influence on national culture increased. Mexicans observed the economic success of U.S. citizens both in Mexico and the United States and wished to mimic them in business and recreational activities.

But Mexicans did not embrace all activities that Americans introduced, and they transformed others to suit local circumstances. Pate built a racetrack for horses in Mexico City in 1895, confident that the wealthy Mexicans would enthusiastically and frequently wager money at his track. Attendance declined quickly because Mexicans enjoyed races as part of fiestas rather than as a daily event. Members of the foreign community also introduced sculling to Mexicans, organizing regattas at haciendas in the countryside. The Mexicans altered the sport to fit their own tastes, moving the regattas from the serene setting of country estates to the polluted waters of Lake Texcoco, conveniently located nearer to the city. They also began holding the events on Sundays, which dissuaded many U.S. citizens from participating.

Baseball, unlike some other sports, grew in popularity throughout the Porfiriato. The game first appeared in Mexico City in the 1880s; by the 1890s it had replaced the British game of cricket in popularity. This change reflected the decline of British investment and the corresponding rise in U.S. financial activity in Mexico. U.S. engineers, miners, and railroad employees dispersed the game throughout the country, teaching it to Mexicans in their adopted communities. At the same time, Cuban immigrants who had learned the sport in the 1860s introduced baseball to Yucatecans. Mexicans played on company teams in the 1880s, but by the end of the Porfiriato men competed on well-organized teams that traveled the country. Players along the border even participated in international competitions against Texans. Athletic clubs formed teams in Mexico City, providing ample contenders for contests in the capital district.

The economic success of the United States made U.S. activities appealing to Mexicans, but people particularly enjoyed baseball because of its similarities to bullfighting and because it reinforced the Porfirian ideals of order and progress. Both sports were highly structured and governed by authorities, with judges at bullfights and umpires at baseball games. Both also allowed individuals to emerge as heroes, such as the pitcher Valenzuela, who became famous after a spectacular performance in a 1903 game. Many Mexicans believed that the discipline and teamwork that the game required communicated contemporary industrial values to Mexico's agrarian society.

Mexicans also began cycling during the Porfiriato. Bicycles became popular in 1891 when the Columbia Bicycle Company opened for business selling "safety" bicycles—their equal-sized wheels reduced the number of accidents, while their air-filled tires made riding on cobblestone streets easier. Cyclists throughout the nation joined clubs that organized biking excursions in the countryside. By accepting technological development, wheel enthusiasts displayed the attitudes of modern society.

Members of the prestigious Jockey Club even incorporated the sport into its Easter festivities. The club previously had hosted a traditional Mexican folk event, Judas burnings, during which effigies of infamous local officials or clerics were burned. But in 1895 the Jockey Club abandoned the Judas burnings—which government officials feared would instigate disorder—and participated in a bicycle parade in which cyclists dressed in costumes and decorated their bicycles. While the Judas burnings had encouraged freedom of action and criticism of the government, the parade expressed order, discipline, and the recognition of authority.

The catastrophic effects of the Mexican Revolution reduced participation in some sports, but by the 1920s enthusiasm for athletics had increased. People continued to purchase tickets to spectator events such as jai alai, bullfighting, and boxing. These sports attracted foreign professionals, such as the U.S. boxer Jack Dempsey, who won the admiration of many Mexicans. Horse racing had grown more fashionable since Pate's failed venture, and it continued to draw crowds.

Citizens also enjoyed participating in various games, hosted by a variety of organizations. Clubs continued to sponsor many sporting activities, as they had during the Porfiriato, but schools, companies, and newspapers also hosted athletic events. The Young Men's Christian Association (YMCA), for example, organized the first basketball league in 1912. Soon hundreds of squads, including both men and women, competed in basketball games. Cycling races, such as a 1926 contest from Mexico City to Puebla, attracted many participants. Soccer only slowly gained popularity after British miners introduced the sport in 1900. The growth of the game suffered in the 1910s because of endemic Revolutionary violence, but by the 1920s many teams competed throughout the country. In 1921, President Álvaro Obregón even initiated a soccer championship to celebrate the centennial of Independence.

Although the Revolution retarded baseball's growth in the 1910s, the sport attracted fans from a broad popular base for the first time in the 1920s. The sport became more organized with the formation of the semiprofessional Mexican League in 1925; it had evolved into a professional league by 1940.

Players also participated in other national associations such as the Mexican National Baseball League.

In 1946 Jorge Pasquel became president of the Mexican League and began a feud with professional baseball in the United States. He outraged baseball commissioner "Happy" Chandler when he began recruiting U.S. players such as Vern Stephens and Mickey Owen for Mexican teams. Chandler regarded Pasquel's maneuvers as "raids" and complained loudly in the press, despite the fact that U.S. teams previously had signed Mexican talent. Pasquel demonstrated various motives for his actions. When he discovered that the Mexican National Baseball League was being considered for entrance into the U.S. minor league system, he wanted to strengthen his own organization so that it could be accepted as a member of U.S. organized baseball. Nationalism fueled his determination as he fought against the arrogance of U.S. baseball; by signing U.S. citizens, he could build better teams as well as demonstrate equality in negotiations.

Mexicans had become involved with international competition before the baseball incident in 1946. Presidents Álvaro Obregón and Plutarco Elías Calles used sporting events to improve the Mexican national image after the violent carnage of the Revolution. In 1923 Mexican athletes competed at Guatemala City in tennis, soccer, and basketball. The following year a Mexican delegation attended its first Olympics at Paris, participating in shooting and tennis matches, as well as track and field. National leaders planned to host a Central American competition in 1926, hoping it would improve Mexico's international image. Attending the games, visitors would understand that Mexico was not a country of savages, but a civilized nation capable of bringing together athletes to underscore Hispanic unity as well as athletic prowess.

When Mexico hosted the 1968 Olympics, the struggle to bolster its international image continued. The pressure proved extreme; Mexico was the first Latin American or developing nation to sponsor the acclaimed event. Workers built athletic facilities, hotels, housing projects, and a modern subway system to accommodate and impress visitors from around the world. Officials also planned a cultural Olympics, featuring international art, books, concerts, and plays. The administration of President Gustavo Díaz Ordaz spent millions anticipating earning a profit from tourists and hoping that foreigners would regard Mexico as a wealthy and stable republic. Workers finished the numerous construction jobs on schedule, and the Olympics themselves went well, but Mexico's image was seriously marred when the police and army attacked student protesters, killing as many as 300 people at a demonstration held before the games began.

A variety of sports have continued to be popular in Mexico in the closing years of the twentieth century. Exhibition games by teams from the U.S. National Football League and National Basketball League have attracted large crowds every year. Mexicans themselves have participated in these sports: colleges have fielded football teams, which compete against each other, and many schoolchildren have strove to join basketball teams. A few talented adults have crossed the border to play for U.S. teams. During the 1980s, for example, the pitcher Fernando Valenzuela became internationally famous as a member of the Los Angeles Dodgers. Soccer has remained the most popular game. Children throughout the country play in the streets and courtyards of churches, dreaming of becoming renowned stars. During the 1994 World Cup competition, millions gathered to watch the games and celebrated victory over Ireland, rendering it impossible to find archivists at the Archivo General de Nacion or to hail a taxi.

See also Bullfighting

Selected Bibliography

Arbena, Joseph L., editor, *Sport and Society in Latin America: Diffusion, Dependency, and the Rise of Mass Culture.* New York: Greenwood, 1988.

Beezley, William H., *Judas at the Jockey Club and Other Episodes of Porfirian Mexico.* Lincoln: University of Nebraska Press, 1987.

Klein, Alan M., "Baseball Wars: The Mexican Baseball League and Nationalism in 1946." *Studies in Latin American Popular Culture* 13 (1994).

Kuhn, Gary, "Fiestas and Fiascoes—Balloon Flights in Nineteenth-Century Mexico." *Journal of Sport History* 13 (1986).

McGehee, Richard V., "Sports and Recreational Activities in Guatemala and Mexico, Late 1800s to 1926." *Studies in Latin American Popular Culture* 13 (1994).

Schell, William, "Lions, Bulls, and Baseball: Colonel R. C. Pate and Modern Sports Promotion in Mexico." *Journal of Sport History* 20 (1993).

—SHANNON L. BAKER AND WILLIAM H. BEEZLEY

Student Movement of 1968

During the second half of 1968, on the eve of the Mexico City Olympic Games, Mexico was the scene of an enormous social mobilization led by students in secondary schools and universities. In Mexico City alone more than 200,000 students from five public institutions went out on strike. From August 1 to October 2 huge demonstrations converged on the central plaza in front of the capitol, which hitherto had been reserved for official events presided over by the president himself.

The student movement of 1968 transformed daily life in Mexico. Unlike other movements in Mexican history, it was not directed by individual leaders. Rather, the strike was coordinated by a collective body known as the Consejo Nacional de Huelga (National Strike Council), in which decisions were discussed and approved by majority. From the first days of the strike, students defied the narrow rules that had governed behavior for almost 50 years. The strike was not reduced to abandoning classes, passing out broadsheets, or painting graffiti on buses. It was a means for youth to develop new ideas about freedom and new social relations. It was, in the most profound sense of the term, a movement of liberation.

The year 1968 also saw mass student movements develop throughout the world. Nonetheless, in no other country did a student movement permeate political life as happened in Mexico. Contemporary political life in Mexico simply cannot be understood without looking at the student movement and its aftermath. Nonetheless, even as we look at the most proximate causes and consequences of the student movement, it is important to keep in mind that it was not an isolated phenomenon: it also was an expression of the revolutionary spirit that periodically moves the youth of the world to search for new spaces for critical inquiry and freedom.

Context

The first four years of the presidency of Gustavo Díaz Ordaz (1964–68) saw an intensification of repression against peasant and labor organizations. The independent unions that had emerged in previous years were almost totally repressed, and agrarian demands were met with state repression, provoking violent reactions (most notable the guerrilla war that erupted on September 23, 1965, in the state of Chihuahua). The early years of the Díaz Ordaz administration also saw the development of a disperse student movement, as students pressed largely academic demands and, on occasion, expressed their solidarity with the Cuban Revolution and the people of Vietnam. Several student strikes took place throughout the country. In 1967 a student strike in the School of Agriculture in Ciudad Juárez sparked a national movement that spread to the secondary

schools of Mexico City. Students' experiences in the 1967 strike would play a determinant role in the student movement of 1968.

Nonetheless, the level of politicization of Mexican students was quite low. The small nucleus of students who led the strikes increasingly moved toward the more militant positions of the Juventud del Partido Comunista (Communist Party Youth) or the Maoist movement in Mexico, but they never were able to attract a broader base of supporters. By and large, Mexico City students in 1967 were preoccupied largely with professional concerns. Many students feared that they were receiving inadequate professional training and began to question the educational system and curricula. A considerable portion of students in 1968 were children or grandchildren of professionals who had begun their careers in the 1930s and 1940s, when tens of thousands of students entered the Universidad Nacional and the Universidad Politécnica, received an excellent training, and generally could be assured of professional and social success after graduation. For a number of reasons, however, during the 1960s professional work lost much of its earlier prestige. Many college graduates could not find work, and those who did had to contend with much lower salaries. Their experience flew in the face of official boosterism, which proclaimed the success of the Mexican economy. Drawing on their personal experience, students began to assume ever more critical stances toward "authority" and curricula—but also toward the family, social mores, the exaltation of the individual, government policy, and the decades-long rule of the Partido Revolucionario Institucional (PRI, or Institutional Revolutionary Party).

Repression

The halcyon days of the early student movement, when students had enjoyed relative immunity from state repression, came to an abrupt end on July 23, 1968, when antiriot police known as the Granaderos invaded Vocational School Number Five in a neighborhood in central Mexico City. The aim of the police operation was to capture a street gang that was enrolled in the school, but in the process they hit and shoved numerous student bystanders and even some teachers.

In response the Federación Nacional de Estudiantes Técnicos (FNET, or National Federation of Technical Students) called a demonstration for the evening of July 26, which would culminate at the Polytechnic University. A small group of students split from the main demonstration, however, and marched toward the central plaza of Mexico City.

At the entrance to the plaza they were met by a company of Granaderos, who without warning attacked the students. Several of the students were pursued into the Alameda Central, a nearby park, where members of the Juventud Comunista were holding a meeting to commemorate the ninth anniversary of the assault on the Moncada Barracks, which marked the beginning of the Cuban Revolution. Other students took refuge in the three Escuelas Preparatorias (academic-track secondary schools) near the central plaza. In both places there were new clashes with the police. Several shops in downtown Mexico City had their windows broken. Hundreds of students from the National and Polytechnic universities were beaten and many were arrested. Later that evening, near Preparatoria 3, a bus that had been used as a barricade against the police was set on fire. Throughout the night police continued to attack students throughout the old "University neighborhood" in downtown Mexico City.

In the pre-dawn hours of July 30, crack troops were deployed to dislodge student protesters from downtown Mexico City, converging on Preparatoria 3. Preparatoria 3 at that time was located in an almost impregnable colonial building; the only way in was an enormous wooden door. Blasting the door open with a bazooka, troops poured into the school. Many students were injured, hundreds arrested, and for the first time some were killed. The state-controlled mass media began to foment rumors of a Communist-controlled conspiracy against Mexico.

On August 1 the students of the Politécnico and the Universidad Nacional responded by coming together in a march led by the rector of the Universidad, Javier Barrosa Sierra, and accompanied by hundreds of professors. This demonstration marks the formal beginning of the student movement, as hundreds of thousands of students went out on strike. For the firsts time since the national university was founded centuries before, a rector led students in a protest against the government. For the first time the students of the Politécnico and the Universidad Nacional came together in a common cause. The Mexican intelligentsia allied with the students, rejecting a conciliatory call that President Díaz Ordaz had made from the city of Guadalajara.

Freedom

The first days of August were dedicated to organizing the strike. One of the first measures consisted of guaranteeing respect for administrative and faculty offices, workshops, laboratories, and academic installations. Restricted areas were defined and seals placed on the doors. Representatives were named to represent each school in the meeting of the coordinating council, which after the August 1 demonstration became the Consejo Nacional de Huelga (CNH, or National Strike Council). On each campus a place was established where the "Comité de Lucha" would meet and students could collectively decide on the course the strike was to take. The students learned in a few short days what they never had learned in the classroom: the exercise of democracy, freedom of thought, solidarity, respect for the ideas of others, and equal treatment for men and women. At first the student movement limited itself to protesting the actions taken against the students of the Escuelas Preparatorias and the Escuela Vocacional, but as the weeks went on and the students came into close contact with other segments of the population, the students' concerns broadened. Their movement increasingly began to address the profound injustice experienced by most Mexicans in factories, *ejidos* (village farms), and the *colonias perdidas* (shantytowns) on the outskirts of most Mexican cities.

The Comités de Lucha in each school edited their own mimeographed news sheets to inform the public about the movement. "Brigades" of six or more students were formed more or less spontaneously to distribute the news sheets in markets, plazas, and especially bus routes. The *brigadistas* would wait on a corner and stop a bus (almost all of the bus drivers sympathized with the movement). While the rest of the *brigadistas* watched for the police, four of the students would paint slogans on the sides of the bus. The most important task was boarding the bus to tell the passengers about the movement and ask for their support. While one of the *brigadistas* talked to the passengers, the other passed out the news sheets and asked the passengers for contributions, which were placed in a sealed canister. In the early days of the movement the passengers seemed startled or even uncomfortable, but as time went on the presence of the students in the streets, plazas, markets, and other public places became something expected. The students spoke of justice, freedom, corruption in the government, and the antidemocracy of the ruling party; more and more, people openly expressed their sympathy with applause, smiles, looks of admiration, and especially coins deposited in the canister. The funds collected by the *brigadistas* were the best indicator of the increased support for the movement. The *brigadistas* periodically rotated tasks so that everyone would have an opportunity to practice her or his oratory. Both men and women participated in the *brigadas*, and there was never a sexual division of labor. Men tended to predominate in the *brigadas* in the Politécnico, although in some departments—

such as Biological Sciences—women distinguished themselves for their *brigadismo* and other political activities during the strike.

The *brigadas* would leave during the morning and afternoon rush hours and return at a determined time. Once everyone was back, the canisters were brought together and emptied, and the money counted and entered in a notebook. The movement always received the support it needed from the people and never suffered financial difficulties. With the money from the canisters the students bought everything needed for the news sheets, banners, paint, and signs. In some schools the money was used to purchase mimeograph machines and sound equipment, but the most important use for the money was food for the students on strike. In most schools approximately 20 percent of the student body consistently participated in the strike, remaining at the school all day and night. Generally schools cafeterias would be run as private concessions, but during the strike the Comités de Lucha reached an agreement with the concessionaires to continue service free of charge. Where an agreement could not be reached, students often formed committees to prepare food for the *brigadistas* and the "permanent guard" at the schools.

Brigadismo, participation in large demonstrations, and camping out in the schools broke down students' narrow social affinities. If previously one's friends had been determined by membership in a clique, class, or department, during the strike new, less formal ways of interacting developed. Rivalries among schools—even the Politécnico and the UNAM —disappeared. Similarly, new forms of relations between the sexes also developed. The strike activities established equality, friendship, and solidarity between men and women. The old rituals of dating, *noviazgo* (going steady), virginity, pretense, and bourgeois romanticism were replaced by more spontaneous and genuine ways of interacting. Many couples met over the course of strike activities, sharing the ideals of the movement—the ideals that shaped an entire generation that participated in the political ferment of 1968.

The Massacre of Tlatelolco

The month of August was a period of celebration and intensive learning. Mexico City was inundated with students, and for the first time people saw youth in huge demonstrations, raising signs and banners with the face of the Argentina-born hero of the Cuban Revolution, Ernesto "Ché" Guevara. After the mass media attacked the students for making a non-Mexican a symbol of their movement, the students began to include portraits of Zapata, Morelos, and other national heroes on their banners, sparking a reencounter with a Mexican history that ran counter to officialist obfuscation.

What had started out as a student protest against a particular act of police brutality broadened into a mass-based social movement. The students' *brigadismo* had broken the barrier between the students and other segments of the Mexican public, and this was reflected in their demands. On August 27 approximately 400,000 people—students, workers, parents—gathered in the central plaza of Mexico City. The central plaza of Mexico City was the symbolic center of the entire country. In official demonstrations the president would come to the balcony to speak to the party faithful, who often had been bussed in for the occasion. The August 27 demonstration inverted this symbolism. Many people carried signs showing Díaz Ordaz's head on the body of a gorilla. A chant that began somewhere in the crowd soon was taken up by each contingent entering the plaza: "*Sal al balcón chango cabrón . . . Sal al balcón chango cabrón*" (Come to the balcony now, clever bastard!). In a political system in which the president enjoyed near-absolute power during his six-year term and embodied the government, this was more than a challenge to a particular president: it was an attack on the legitimacy of the entire regime.

Students hoped that after the mass show of support on August 27 Díaz Ordaz at least would address their demands in his upcoming state of the union address on September 1. Nonetheless, Díaz Ordaz instead used his speech to attack the student movement for defaming Mexico on the eve of the Olympic games (which the country was to host)—a charge that had already been taken up by the state-controlled mass media. Díaz Ordaz demanded that students return to classes. "Once reasonable means are exhausted," Díaz Ordaz threatened, "I will exercise, as long as it is strictly necessary, the faculty to call on the totality of the permanent armed forces."

On September 13 students organized another enormous demonstration in the central plaza, this time in total silence. Five days later Mexican troops occupied the Universidad Nacional, arresting more than 2,000 students. On September 23, troops moved against the Politécnico. This time the occupation was far more violent, and several students were killed.

On October 2 the Consejo Nacional de Huelga called another demonstration in the Plaza de las Tres Culturas in Tlatelolco, a broad space surrounded by high-rise apartment blocks and public buildings.

More than 10,000 people arrived. Shortly before the meeting was to begin, the army surrounded the area with more than 200 tanks, assault vehicles, and troop transports. According to the press approximately 5,000 soldiers converged on the area, but several hundred other police in civilian dress also participated. At 5:30 P.M. the meeting began, and at approximately 6:30 P.M. members of the Olympic Battalion of the federal police—identified by a white glove on the left hand—moved into position on the first floor of the building that was being used as a stage for the demonstration. The Olympic Battalion had been given the task of isolating the members of the Consejo Nacional de Huelga to arrest them, and they opened fire into the crowd. At almost the same time, shots rang out from the upper stories of the buildings around the plaza, and the soldiers surrounded the crowd and also opened fire. Within seconds the crowd was caught in a withering crossfire, and over the next half hour the plaza reverberated with machine gun and bazooka fire, and the occasional boom of cannon.

Few people managed to escape the army's encirclement. The military headquarters received more than 1,500 prisoners. Almost all of the representatives of the Consejo Nacional de Huelga on the tribune also were detained. According to television news reports in Mexico, students had opened fire on the soldiers and the death toll was only 30—the majority of them men, women, and children who had come to support the students. According to foreign correspondents at the demonstration, however, between 300 and 400 people were killed. It will be difficult ever to say with any certainty how many people actually were killed, since the only people who had an opportunity to stay and count the dead in the Plaza de las Tres Culturas were soldiers and police.

The Generation of 1968

The massacre of October 2 marked the end of the student movement. There were no more demonstrations or mass meetings, and the streets and plazas were under the control of the army. The joy of August gave way to a sullen passive resistance. Many students determined to engage in a sort of academic suicide, refusing to return to classes even if they lost an entire year or even their academic careers. Soldiers occupied secondary school and university campuses, but they remained empty—notwithstanding the appeals of rector of the UNAM, the director of the Politécnico, and the authorities of the ministry of education. Finally, on December 4 student representatives met in the Politécnico to lift the strike. The Consejo Nacional de Huelga was disbanded,

replaced by Comités Coordinadores in the UNAM and the Politécnico to reorganize the movement after the return to classes. A large demonstration was called for December 13, but it was stopped by the police since the organizers "had not obtained the necessary permits."

Classes returned to relative normality in January 1969. Most students continued their opposition to the government and participated in the creation of a more serious movement for democracy in Mexico. On each campus, however, there were dozens of students who formed new Comités de Lucha, working in clandestine groups of *brigadistas* to leaflet factories and form study groups among the workers. They also organized large student meetings at the UNAM and Politécnico, which attracted considerable support.

Nonetheless, the daily demands of academic work limited the success of the Comités. Thugs found their way into the Escuelas Preparatorias, not only extorting from the students but also dealing marijuana. In 1969 a campaign was designed from outside the schools to increase the use of drugs by students, depoliticizing them and detaching them from the experiences of the previous year. The hippie movement, marijuana, psilocybin, pills, and English-language rock music made headway principally in secondary schools.

This was only one of the tendencies after 1968, however. Many students lost interest in their studies after the October 2 massacre and sought only to find an effective way to change the government of Mexico. Some decided that urban guerrilla warfare was the way and began to participate in such clandestine activities as attacking and disarming police, bank robberies, and kidnapping. During the 1970s urban guerrilla groups proliferated in Mexico, almost all of them detected and infiltrated by the police. Hundreds of young people died from torture in police custody, while others were simply shot; a bulletin later would be issued claiming that they had died in a clash with police. Maoism gained currency in many Comités de Lucha, and in a meeting at the Universidad Nacional in July 1970 the most engaged students were exhorted to abandon their studies and "integrate themselves into the people." Following this call, many youth took up new lives as workers, peasants, or residents of one of the shantytowns ringing the largest cities of Mexico.

The student movement of 1968 did not end with the Massacre of Tlatelolco. The students who had been most politicized by the movement became opposition political activists, seeking to unmask the dictatorial government of Mexico and show how it legitimized itself in an "electoral farce" every six years. This type of questioning was generalized throughout the country together with an intense campaign of "active abstentionism," refusing to participate in elections that were clearly fraudulent. Díaz Ordaz's successor, Luis Echeverría Álvarez, attempted to reestablish relations with the intelligentsia and students. José López Portillo went further, introducing the first of a series of electoral reforms. By this point, however, "active abstentionism" had permeated all levels of society, even reaching the right-wing opposition Partido Acción Nacional (PAN, or National Action Party).

The veterans of the movement of 1968 became the carriers of a new culture that extended throughout the educated middle class. Professors, researchers, writers, cartoonists, musicians, journalists, actors, and professionals of every stripe identified themselves with this new culture, which rejected every type of authoritarianism, worked in solidarity with the poorest members of the society, opposed injustice, identified with socialist struggles, opposed US imperialism, supported liberation movements worldwide, demanded equal rights for women and men, rejected repressive moralism and sought sexual liberation, and fought for critical and democratic education. The dictatorship of the PRI, they were convinced, was the principal obstacle to the creation of a new Mexican nation.

See also Massacre of Tlatelolco

—JESÚS VARGAS VALDEZ

T

Telenovelas

Telenovelas are serialized sentimental dramas transmitted by television. Unlike American soap operas, their length is limited—they hardly ever last more than one year. The story usually reaches an end as soon as the protagonists have overcome the main obstacle in their way. This means that *telenovelas* are generally built around a central conflict that creates growing tension until the problem is resolved with a "happy ending." *Telenovelas* usually are aired Monday through Friday in 30- or 60-minute episodes, which are never independent from one another; they are produced mainly in Mexico, Venezuela, and Brazil.

Telenovelas have become a daily staple of television programming, mainly in Latin America and continental Europe (including Russia and other eastern countries), and they have attained significant success also in some Arab and Asian countries (such as China). In Mexico they rank second among the most-watched television programs (the first being soccer matches), but they rank first when one considers that they captivate their audience for months and not only for 90 minutes.

The *Telenovela* as Genre

Their content varies greatly, but certain shared elements are common to *telenovelas*: first, their main protagonists are usually women; second, central plots tend to be love stories; third, the majority of *telenovelas* can be understood better as melodramas than as comedies; and fourth, the degree of fantasy cannot be correlated with a certain *telenovela*'s failure (as a matter of fact, the further from reality, the more a story seems to be liked, as in Valentín Pimstein's and Emilio Larrosa's Televisa-productions). The first trait does not mean that male protagonists are not acceptable—*Gutierritos* (1965) and *El Premio mayor* (1995–96) are good examples of well-received *telenovelas* with male leads—or that all *telenovelas* have to be built around a love story— *Gutierritos* (1965) and *Chispita* (1982) serve to prove the point. As a matter of act, *telenovelas* constitute a good example of a format open to all kinds of content as long as certain basic characteristics are respected.

Successful *telenovelas* offer symbolic (and often simplistic) representations of a society's values and institutions. To achieve such a symbolic image of reality, characters and plots must be constructed to represent values or institutions rather than to reflect human individuals, to be narratively functional rather than realistic, and to be clear-cut rather than vague or ambiguous. These needs explain *telenovelas*' tendency toward farce and the grotesque.

The importance granted to endings (which usually produce a given series' highest audience ratings —sometimes even doubling the average ratings) confirms assumptions of the symbolic quality of *telenovelas*, as far as endings imply a distinct judgment of the values represented by each character: the "good" and the "evil" characters generally are "rewarded" or "punished" according to society's expectations and values.

This simplistic symbolic quality of *telenovelas*, together with the fact that they are designed for mass consumption, rather than for an elite minority, limits them according to the standards of twentieth-century "elite" art. *Telenovelas* belong to popular literature and—outside Brazil—lack cultural prestige, even though they are enjoyed both by the educated and the uneducated, the rich and the poor, young and old, men and women. All efforts to create "highbrow," ambiguous works either have failed or have achieved only moderate success (such as *El Rincón de los prodigios, La Casa al final de la calle,* or the many recreations of the history of Mexico produced by Televisa), seldom reaching average-size audiences for their time slots. With its opinion gauged by various marketing strategies, the audience participates in the creation of successful *telenovelas* (whenever these are subject to an industrial production process in an open-market context), but only as far as governmental regulations, the producing company's policies, and a story's particular production team will allow.

In Mexico, unwritten but effective rules of censorship by the Ministry of the Interior limited sexual, violent, political, and religious content from the beginning of Mexican television until the late 1980s. Paradoxically, this censorship helped Mexican *telenovelas* sell internationally: They were not able to depict local social conflicts that might not be shared or understood by other countries, and they seldom transgressed the limits of what most countries consider to be morally acceptable. When governmental censorship was reduced in Mexico, producers immediately responded by raising sexual and violent content; subsequently audience ratings dropped considerably. Religious elements (depicted from a positive point of view, but usually not as part of the main plot) were introduced in 1995 in an attempt to stop the great audience decline. A politically tinted work, *Nada personal* by Televisión Azteca, did not appear until 1996, and it achieved only moderate success; it increased the company's audience-share but proved unable to compete with a Televisa love story *(Cañaveral de pasiones)*. A linear development and a standardized language (not too regional, not too specialized, not too unusual, not too peculiar), constitute—as well—an essential part of successful *telenovelas*. To adapt the scholar Anne Rubenstein's observation about *historietas* (comic books/strips) to fit *telenovelas*, it can be said that while the length and complexity of a particular story may show great faith in the audience's memory and patience, "the style in which the story [is] told [betrays] a certain anxiety over [that audience's] naïvete." A great percentage of the narrative elements (archetypes, famous scenes, recurrent titles, renown sentences) in successful *telenovelas* are strictly codified; the audience looks upon them as its own property, and dislikes any defunctionalizing alteration of them. The "good" must always remain "good," for example. Furthermore, the audience does not look for an entirely new work; rather, it expects a combination of a series of known elements together with a new element—a different context, perhaps, or a new socially acceptable solution to a world-old problem.

The above-listed "generic" limitations (understanding "genre" as a previously created and well-known literary format), challenge the creators of these stories and have produced, over the long run, certain narrative formulas that the audience has learned to recognize and appreciate (such as the Cinderella plot line).

Origins and Development of Telenovelas in Mexico

When television was born in Mexico in the 1950s, both the cinema and the *historieta* industries were flourishing. It was a decade of political and economical stability, and the progress and modernity promised by the Revolution seemed finally to be coming true for a vast majority. The radio industry was strong and far-reaching, and *radionovelas* were among its most appreciated programs. It naturally followed that television would experiment with the genre and create *telenovelas*. The first drama program produced with a serial format was called *Ángeles de la calle*, and was aired weekly in 1951. The second was *Senda prohibida*, produced in 1957 by Fernanda Villeli (adapted from its previous radio version). The series aired five times a week.

At the time, television programs were produced either by advertising agencies or by their clients (such as Colgate-Palmolive). This accounts for the market-driven orientation of Mexican television, which somehow managed to coexist with the medium's convenient subjection to the Revolutionary ruling party. This phenomenon led to the formation of Televisa, the gigantic communications conglomerate, nearly 20 years later. Televisa, a near monopoly, became the main Mexican *telenovela* producer, and the most prolific television producer in the world (measured in terms of the number of hours produced annually). Thus, Mexican television's (and with it, the *telenovelas*) content and format have been shaped by three coexisting forces: a conservative nation, a liberal-Revolutionary government, and a nearly capitalist economy.

Primitive *telenovelas* were much shorter than today's, but offered greater variety in content. On the other hand, modern works are produced with greater technological and financial resources. In between, the golden years of *telenovelas* (1982 to 1986) brought (along with notable failures such as *Eclipse* and *La Pasión de Isabela*) great successes, such as *Chispita, Gabriel y Gabriela, Bodas de odio, La Fiera, El Maleficio, La Traición, Vivir un poco, De Pura sangre, Tú o nadie,* and *Cuna de lobos.* Most of these drew audience ratings as high as 70 points, with averages between 40 and 51 points (where 1 point equals 1 percent of the viewing households). After 1986, ratings declined sharply. As of the mid-1990s, average audience ratings for *telenovelas* were 33 points for the 6:30 P.M. to 7:00 P.M. time slot, 33 points for the 7:30 P.M. to 8:00 P.M. time slot, and 34 points for the 9:00 P.M. to 10:00 P.M. time slot.

There have been many reasons for the decline in ratings. First, producers have continuously transgressed collective values (for example, "family" programs frequently violate audiences' expectations about appropriate content for family viewing). At the same time, the overall breadth of content variety has, paradoxically, decreased. Furthermore, a vicious cycle began when the drop in audience ratings lowered the advertising rate for commercial time during a *telenovela* broadcast: networks were forced to sell a greater number of these cheaper commercials, thus aggravating viewers and leading to a further drop in audience ratings. During the broadcast of a *telenovela* in December 1995, for example, a 30-scene-long chapter was interrupted by 50 advertisements. Finally, the drop in ratings may be explained by the greater number of television channels now available in Mexico.

Special mention is due to the government-sponsored *telenovelas* that ran from 1976 to 1989: *Ven conmigo, Acompáñame, Vamos juntos, Caminemos, Nosotras las mujeres,* and *Por amor.* The first one, *Ven conmigo,* mainly promoted adult education (together with family planning); it drew average audience ratings of 32 points. *Caminemos* and *Vamos juntos* mainly promoted family planning; they drew average ratings of only 15 points (both below their time-slot averages); the rest reached even smaller audiences. Despite this, these programs generally are accepted to have contributed to the decrease in Mexico's total fertility rate from 6.37 to 3.8 children-per-couple in only 14 years (of course, these *telenovelas* were just one facet of extensive government campaigns).

Select Bibliography

Allen, R., editor, *To Be Continued . . . : Soap Operas and Global Media Culture.* New York: Routledge, 1995.

Katz, E., and G. Wedell, *Broadcasting in the Third World: Promise and Performance.* Cambridge, Massachusetts: Harvard University Press, 1977.

Lopez, Ana, "The Melodrama in Latin America." In *Imitations of Life: A Reader on Film and Television Melodrama,* edited by M. Landy. Detroit, Michigan: Wayne State University Press, 1991.

Rubenstein, Anne, "México sin vicios." Ph.D. diss., Rutgers University, 1995.

—BLANCA DE LIZAUR

Television

The development of television in Mexico raises two fundamental questions. The first issue stems from the monopolistic character of Mexican television, whereby one corporation has dominated commercial broadcasting since its inception in 1955. This company, currently named Televisa, has held its grasp of Mexico's television audience for over 40 years, as estimates in 1995 put Televisa's average audience share at approximately 80 percent. Second, in light of Televisa's powerful position, television in Mexico generates several thorny issues regarding its cultural impacts and political influence. Although the federal government directly supported broadcasting stations and programming, the state never has seriously challenged the commercial television industry.

To a large extent, this pattern in the development of Mexican television reflects the relationship between the state and the private broadcasting industry. The origins of this relationship derive from commercial radio. By the early 1940s, Mexican radio was virtually controlled by Emilio Azcarraga Vidaurreta. At that time, Azcarraga's network encompassed about 60 percent of Mexico's radio stations, and it dominated all of the country's major radio markets. His grip of Mexican radio allowed Azcarraga to spin off into other enterprises, such as recordings, entertainment promotion, film distribution, and eventually motion picture production. Azcarraga's ascendancy in radio was facilitated by his ability to attract Mexico's leading singers, actors, musicians, and comedians to appear in his radio shows. In brief, Azcarraga's hugely profitable radio empire provided him a powerful place in Mexican society, and his hand in the formation of the country's popular culture was similarly important.

Azcarraga's dominance over radio was facilitated by his ties to the two major broadcasting companies in the United States at that time, NBC (the National Broadcasting Company, owned by the Radio Corporation of America, or RCA) and CBS (the Columbia Broadcasting System). Because of his close association with these American broadcasting companies, notably RCA, Azcarraga was well-aware of the new medium called television even before 1940. World War II had delayed television's commercial applications, but the end of the war led immediately to its commercial development in the United States. Azcarraga followed suit; he petitioned President Manuel Avila Camacho (1940–46) at the close of his administration for a commercial television broadcasting license (others also petitioned for licenses in this period). Despite the obvious capacity of Azcarraga to move into television broadcasting, the Avila Camacho administration rejected the petition, largely it seems, owing to the influence of the president-elect, Miguel Alemán Valdés. The evidence clearly suggests that Alemán intended to thwart Azcarraga's bid to extend his media empire through the new medium. The evidence also suggests, however, that Alemán desired to profit from the commercialization of Mexican television.

As president (1946–52), Alemán shunned any public, obvious indication of his intention to invest personally in the new medium. Instead, he searched for a means to delay the commercial development of television, until he could devise a plan to insinuate himself into the television business. Allegedly at the suggestion of the director of the Instituto Nacional de Bellas Artes, the composer Carlos Chávez, in 1947 Alemán commissioned a two-man team to explore options for the development of television in Mexico. The team consisted of the writer Salvador Novo and the brilliant engineer, Guillermo González Camarena, who was the technical chief of the Azcarraga radio empire (he patented the first color television camera). Submitted in 1948, the resultant report essentially proposed two alternatives, one patterned on the commercial, privately owned model of the United States, and the other a government-run, noncommercial model similar to that of the British Broadcasting Company (BBC) in Great Britain.

The Mexican government after the Revolution of 1910 generally had maintained a benign stance toward the private media, relying on censorship when necessary to keep radio, for instance, in line with governmental policies. Even during the populist presidency of Lázaro Cárdenas, the federal government had refused to take a heavy-handed posture toward a radio industry that was basically unsympathetic to the administration. In legal terms, the state clearly possessed the authority to regulate the industry and to produce programming, as legislation before and since the advent of television repeatedly sustained the potent role of the federal government in mass communications. In fact, early on government radio stations broadcast programming of various types, but they abstained from direct, genuine competition with private ownership; government-run radio stations were notably dull and predictably unpopular. Thus, in practice no precedent existed for the BBC model in Mexico. The federal government under Alemán moved to intervene in the film industry in 1952, but it did so to halt the precipitous decline of Mexican cinematic production, to eliminate the monopolistic control over film distribution by the American expatriate, William Jenkins, and to safeguard the monetary interests of a small circle of well-connected movie impresarios. Yet, the government avoided the actual making of movies, again relying on censorship to curb critical political expression on the part of filmmakers.

Alemán was also manifestly pro-business. He had served as the *secretario de gobernación* (secretary of

the interior) in the Avila Camacho administration, where he consistently used his political influence to support private enterprise and to distance himself from the populism of the previous president, Lázaro Cárdenas. Furthermore, the Alemán administration was infamously corrupt, marked by the frequent abuse of presidential privilege to promote the private interests of Alemán and his cabal of friends and business associates. In short, the history of media-state relations in Mexico, or Alemán's political career, offered little evidence to suggest that he would seriously consider a policy of government control over television. Rather, it appears that Novo and González Camarena were used by Alemán in a scheme for him to become financially involved in the nascent television industry.

In 1949 Rómulo O'Farril received the first license to operate a commercial television station in Mexico (Channel 4), and he began broadcasts in July 1950. O'Farril had made his fortune primarily in the automobile business, but his quick entry into mass communications revealed the hand of Miguel Alemán Valdés. Supporters of Alemán's presidential aspirations gained control of the newspaper *Novedades* in 1946, and Jorge Pasquel, an intimate associate of Alemán, assumed editorial control. Once in office, Alemán persuaded O'Farril to take over *Novedades*. Subsequently, O'Farril was also granted the concession to operate radio station XEX, giving the auto tycoon (aided importantly by his son, Rómulo Jr.) the opportunity to learn the broadcasting business and to develop the technical capacity to move into television broadcasting. Given the association with Alemán, O'Farril's successful bid for a television broadcasting license was no coincidence.

Azcarraga finally acquired the second license granted by the Mexican government for a commercial television broadcasting station (Channel 2), beginning transmissions in May 1951. Other licenses were also approved, including one to González Camarena (Channel 5). It was clear from the beginning that the major contestants in this formative period of Mexican television would be O'Farril and Azcarraga, although the auto magnate held the backing of the former president and an operational advantage of nearly a year over his adversary. Nonetheless, after a bitter and extremely costly period of competition, O'Farril approached Azcarraga with a merger offer in early 1955. Financially wounded by the savage contest, Azcarraga accepted the overture, but he was careful to maintain control over the new corporation, named Telesistema Mexicano (TSM). Shortly thereafter González Camarena threw his lot in with the new company and rejoined his former employer, giving TSM an additional technical and engineering asset. By March 1955, TSM essentially controlled Mexican television, as the holding company possessed three stations (channels 2, 4, and 5). The combination of Azcarraga's hold over entertainment talent, his clout among large advertisers, the profitability of his radio holdings, and the political privileges afforded discreetly by Alemán gave TSM an unassailable advantage over the competition for nearly 15 years. Utilizing his radio connections, Azcarraga quickly developed a web of TSM affiliates in the major urban markets that initially overwhelmed potential rivals.

In 1968, a group of businessmen tied primarily to the ALFA corporation of Monterrey, Nuevo León, mounted a challenge to the dominance of TSM over Mexican television. Using videotape technology and imported American shows for much of its early programming, the upstart network, called Television Independiente de Mexico (TIM, channel 8), made significant headway. Financial problems, however, pushed TIM to agree to a merger with Azcarraga's TSM in December 1972, leading to a new corporation whose logo became Televisa (encompassing channels 2, 4, 5, and 8). In the midst of the conclusion of this momentous deal, Emilio Azcarraga Vidaurreta died, leaving his son, Emilio Azcarraga Milmo, to head Televisa.

In the ensuing years, the younger Azcarraga aggressively exploited Televisa's dominant position, as the company spread further into ancillary areas, such as satellite transmission, expansion into international markets, cable television, sports programming, video distribution, syndication, media-related publications, and movie production for television, among other activities. Protected by governmental policies that impeded foreign competition in the Mexican media market, Televisa established its contemporary dominance of Mexican mass communications in the decade following the death of the elder Azcarraga.

The retreat of the Mexican government from state-led development policies after 1982 offered the possibility of a weakening of Televisa's monopolistic position. Initially, the federal government moved slowly to open mass communications to foreign investors. Finally, the appearance in the early 1990s of U.S.-based video and record distributors, rival cable television networks, and foreign-generated television news services eroded Televisa's previous dominance of the Mexican media. On the other hand, much of the competition for Televisa at that time targeted the country's small though growing middle and upper classes, leaving the bulk of Mexico's television audience still dependent on Televisa's programming.

The most serious challenge to Televisa in the 1990s came increasingly from political pressures, rather than from its economic competitors.

The presidential elections of 1988 and 1994 were hotly contested, fueled by a resurgent Partido de Acción Nacional (PAN, or National Action Party) and a surprisingly strong showing by the reformist, left-leaning Partido Revolucionario Democrático (PRD, or Democratic Revolutionary Party). Both elections revealed the evident pro-government bias of television news reporting; such pro-government coverage became the target of much criticism. With its hold over Mexico's television audience, Televisa was at the center of this political storm. (The rebellion in Chiapas in January 1994 greatly intensified the heated debate over Televisa's prejudicial reporting.) In this tense political context, the sale of one of the government's television facilities in 1993 became a major political issue, rather than simply another example of the privatization policy of President Carlos Salinas de Gortari (1988–94). For many critics of Mexican television, the government's decision on the bids held the potential of weakening the monopolistic position of Televisa, and more importantly, of leading to an alternative perspective in television journalism specifically, and programming in general.

The successful bid came from the Salinas Pliego interests (not related to President Salinas), whose fortune derived primarily from his family's chain of consumer electronic stores and other commercial interests. The decision surprised many experts, as some of the competing bids appeared better capitalized and proposed by business groups with much more experience or assets in broadcasting. Time will tell whether this privatized network (channel 13), in conjunction with the opening of the Mexican media market, will in fact break the dominant position of Televisa.

As Mexico faces the twenty-first century, it appears that the house of Azcarraga will continue to exercise an inordinate influence. Political pressures likely will persist for the government to take action to lessen the preponderant place of Televisa in Mexico, and specifically over televised news coverage. Ironically, the public support for privatization policies may work to diminish the state's hand to dismember such a powerful corporation, as was the case in the United States when NBC was forced to sell one of its networks by the federal government, leading to the creation of ABC (the American Broadcasting Company).

Regardless of the future of Televisa's corporate power, its programming has left an indelible imprint on the shape and content of Mexican television with widespread cultural implications. Televisa (and its predecessor, TSM) has been the primary source of television programming for the vast majority of Mexicans. Mexico has lacked a viable alternative to the way that Televisa has presented television to Mexican audiences. Government-subsidized programming has met with meager public reception, failing to alter the tastes of most Mexicans for television fare. The formula for Mexican television developed by the Azcarraga empire has enjoyed a long period of dominance, making any substantial change difficult to achieve in the viewing habits and expectations of Mexican audiences.

For his initial formula, Azcarraga borrowed from the staples of his radio programming. In the pioneering days of the medium, popular music shows, sports events (bullfights, soccer, boxing), comedy, and radio soap operas were essentially transferred to television, and in some cases these early shows were transmitted simultaneously for both radio and television. In this sense, the popularity of the established "mix" of programming from radio laid the foundations for television, as Azcarraga parlayed his powerful position in Mexican entertainment to attract major stars to his programs. Indeed, with Mexican cinema still enjoying the aura of its golden age, early television shows often featured well-known actors, singers, and musical groups drawn from the Mexican motion picture industry. Although Azcarraga produced the occasional serious drama or classical music concert, most of his programming reflected the formula popularized by radio, including adaptations from the United States. In this regard, perhaps the most enduring format was that of the *telenovela*, or television drama series (i.e., television soap operas). Taking plot lines made familiar by Mexican cinematic melodramas and *radionovelas,* this type of show became immensely popular with television audiences.

Basic changes in television fare have been relatively recent and few in number, aside from the introduction of programming available on expensive cable services that have been beyond the modest incomes of most Mexicans. In the 1970s, Televisa's four channels began increasingly to address specific segments of its audience, based in part on the original mix of programming that targeted particular groups, such as older, primarily female viewers. Hence, one channel would focus on older, primarily female viewers, while another channel would tend to attract a younger, more affluent audience. In the 1990s, talk shows modeled on their U.S. counterparts debuted, as well as televised call-in sales programs. Moreover, variety shows for a new generation of viewers seemed to become less formal, if not more crude, than had been the case in the past, as reflected in the program *Sabado gigante*. Programming from the United States remains strongly evident, but productions from other Spanish-language countries also have appeared regularly on Mexican television with great success. This inclusion of foreign programming nevertheless has been selective and generally consistent with the entrenched conservative character of Mexican television. Thus, the pattern of the traditional mix persists, such as the ubiquitous importance of the *locutor,* or emcee (e.g., Raul Velasco, on the popular, music-laden variety show *Siempre en domingo*); slapstick, Cantinflas-inspired comedic routines; and corny, antic-filled game shows.

The weaknesses of the past have also persisted, none more obvious than the impoverished state of television news reporting. The combination of the Mexican state's capacity for censorship and Televisa's pro-government posture has made for a practice of innocuous news programming on domestic issues, although reporting on world events has improved notably in recent years. Beginning in 1970, the program *24 Horas* and its head, Jacobo Zabludovsky, have dominated television news. Still, despite a periodic expose, usually of localized corruption or government ineptness, substantive investigative television journalism rarely appears in Mexico, particularly of a political nature. An incident during the 1994 presidential campaign illustrated the anemic character of Mexican television journalism. When the upstart station of Salinas Pliego broadcast an interview with the leftist opposition presidential candidate, Cuauhtémoc Cárdenas, the event caused a stir in Mexico for days, compelling Televisa's notorious Zabludovsky subsequently to conduct a similar interview. The hyperbole from the press and political observers over the interview incident served to demonstrate the highly conservative approach of Televisa to news reporting and the general absence of serious television journalism in Mexico.

Surprisingly, Mexican television programming for children represents another weakness, with its lack of playful creativity and a heavy reliance on imported programming, especially from the United States. Moreover, Mexican television has seemingly steered away from factually based dramas or controversial issues, except for the occasional and usually patriotic historical epic. Although advertisements for contraceptive devices have appeared on Mexican television (consistent with the government's efforts to lower Mexico's historically high birthrate) in general the medium has carefully avoided controversial issues. And to its credit, Televisa has experimented with socially beneficial programs, such as the encouragement of adult education through a soap opera series. Yet, such efforts have been surrounded with skepticism over their didactic, relatively safe character and criticism for their contrast with the crassness of Televisa's more commercial offerings. Irreverent situation comedies (or sitcoms) of the American sort, or humor in the British style of "Monty Python," for example, rarely make their way onto the television screens of Mexico.

Furthermore, the pattern in programming established by Televisa has extended beyond Mexico. Since the 1960s, the Azcarraga empire had entered the United States in the form of the Spanish International Network (SIN), providing shows produced by Televisa to reach the large and expanding Spanish-language population in cities such as Miami, San Antonio, Chicago, Los Angeles, New York, and San Francisco. The extent of Azcarraga's control over SIN eventually was found in violation of U.S. government regulations regarding foreign ownership of television stations, forcing Azcarraga Milmo to divest himself from SIN in late 1987. In an ironic twist, Televisa reentered the U.S. market through Univision, a company based on the original SIN, although without a controlling interest in keeping with U.S. federal communications law. Televisa's foray into the United States paralleled its penetration into Latin America (where it has interests in stations in Chile and Venezuela, for instance); its reach has incorporated the Spanish-speaking populations of the Pacific, such as Guam and the Philippines, and Europe, where its *telenovelas* have been seen from Madrid to Moscow (in the latter case via translation). In this sense, Mexican television and its characteristic features have become truly global.

It is apparent that the television market in Mexico will continue to move away from its narrowly conceived, conservative origins. This process of change, however, likely will be gradual, as producers will be slow to act boldly in the face of the tenacious influence of the past. If access to alternative programming remains tied to income, mainstream Mexican television will tend toward reworking old formulas and taking few innovative directions. This conservative character of television is, of course, not unique to Mexico, as indicated by the derivative character of much of television in the United States, for instance. As in most countries, the federal government in Mexico will continue to possess wide authority over television, but how it will exercise that authority in the future is unclear.

The presence of foreign programming, if only through cable services, and the further fragmentation of television audiences by age, gender, and class, for example, likely will induce greater diversification of television fare. The large numbers of Mexicans in the United States will also contribute to this effect, given the influence of immigrants on their communities of origin; an effect clearly visible in major binational television markets along the U.S.-Mexico border, such as El Paso/Ciudad Juárez, and San Diego/Tijuana. In sum, television in Mexico will change, but the character of its origins will more than likely continue to mark its future.

See also Telenovelas

Select Bibliography

Rodriguez, A., "Control Mechanisms of National News Making." In *Questioning the Media: A Critical Introduction,* edited by J. Downing, A. Mohammadi, and A. Sreberny-Mohammadi. Thousand Oaks, California: Sage, 1990; 2nd edition, 1995.

—ALEX M. SARAGOZA

Teotihuacan

See Mesoamerica: Teotihuacan

Terrazas Fuentes, Luis 1829–1923

Soldier and Politician

Luis Terrazas Fuentes was born on July 20, 1829, in the city of Chihuahua. He studied at the Chihuahua Seminary and the Instituto Científico y Literario, also in the state capital, which he left on his father's death.

Mexico around 1850 was emerging from a disastrous war with the United States while at the same time being divided between two factions, Liberal and Conservative, that fought for control of the country. Despite Chihuahua's isolation and distance from Mexico City both sides had found prominent leaders in the state. This did not stop Luis Terrazas, a Conservative criollo (native-born American of Spanish ancestry), who at the age of only 22 years launched himself into the turbulent political scene of a state that was virtually devastated and scarcely functioning. The treasuries were empty, the mines inundated, the pasturelands empty, the territory torn apart by war, and the population decimated by cholera. Those haciendas that had not been abandoned were fortified with thick walls to resist Apache attacks, and the people were poverty stricken thanks to the war and internecine struggles.

In 1851 Terrazas, who by this time owned a grocery store, a soap factory, something in the way of cattle, and some urban-based properties (valued at 18,000 pesos), was nominated guard to the state general treasury by the Liberal governor Juan N. Urquidi. In 1854 he was elected councillor to the Chihuahua City Hall. Two years later he acquired control over meat supplies to the city of Chihuahua through public auction. In 1859 he was elected receiver to the Town Hall, and in the same year, Ángel Trías Álvarez, another Liberal governor, threatened with problems from the Conservative faction, nominated Terrazas political boss of the Iturbide District. He also was elected substitute deputy for the two-year term from 1859 to 1861. In May 1860 José Eligio Muñoz, another Liberal state governor, appointed him colonel of the National Guard and speaker for the council of war against the Apaches. That August Juan J. Mendéz and Terrazas were defeated by invading troops under Spanish-born Conservative Domingo Cajén, and the Liberals lost the city of Chihuahua. One week later Terrazas routed Cajén and retook the state capital. Thanks to this triumph, his prestige among the Liberals was tremendous.

In 1860 Muñoz resigned and the local Congress appointed Terrazas as interim state governor. In the midst of strong opposition from Liberal deputies who objected to his youth (he was, in fact, under the legal age to assume the office), he took on the governorship. One month later he resigned, but the Congress not only confirmed him in the post but also rewarded him for the valuable services to the state and the Mexican Constitution of 1857, awarding him a sword of honor with a hilt of gold and the inscription: "(From) the State Congress to the distinguished citizen Luis Terrazas. He freed the State on August 27, 1860." His governorship ratified, he involved himself in actively supporting Liberal doctrines. These included suppressing judicial costs, repealing the law on robbers, publishing the Reform Laws on the nationalization of church goods, secularizing the cemeteries, hospitals, and charitable institutions, and establishing civil registers in all the municipalities of the state. He limited by a ruling the use of bells in all the churches and fined the priest José de la Luz Corral for publicly praising the Conservatives. Nevertheless, his Liberal enemies accused him of not putting into practice the law of

February 5, 1860, which prohibited governors from interfering in the sale of goods confiscated from the church.

In 1861, after having been temporary governor for a year, he won formal election to the post, and on February 4 took possession as constitutional governor for the four-year term, 1861 to 1865. He was once again accused of violating the law in appropriating vacant lands belonging to the nation and selling church properties to friends and relations. Nevertheless, Terrazas did hand over the gains from these sales to the state treasury. Taking into account the poverty of the exchequer, he diverted federal dues, including customs tariffs, to the benefit of the state treasury (and to the tremendous annoyance of the central government). In April 1862 President Benito Juárez ordered Terrazas to provide a contingent of 2,000 cavalry for the war against the French. Arguing that he could not leave the state defenseless and open to Apache attacks, he only sent 500 men. In 1863, when the national government was defeated, Terrazas was one of the governors who remained faithful to Juárez, refusing to second the petition of Generals Manuel Doblado and Jesús González Ortega, who, counting on the support of numerous governors and Federal Deputies, demanded the president's resignation in order to negotiate peace with the French. Despite Terraza's behavior, Juárez believed that Terrazas was going to betray him. Juárez declared a state of siege in Chihuahua, appointing General José María Patoni as military commander and ordering Jesús José Casavantes to assume the governorship. Terrazas resigned, and while the state capital was occupied by Juárez's troops, he took refuge in Paso del Norte. Ángel Trías Álvarez, his Liberal enemy, was made interim governor for 13 months. Nevertheless, in 1864 Terrazas won the elections for the four-year period 1864 to 1868. While the French troops occupied the city of Chihuahua and President Juárez took refuge in Paso del Norte, Terrazas was nominated imperial prefect by French-imposed emperor Maximilian, a post that he never accepted. In a disastrous political, military, and economic position, Juárez was in great need of support and so reconciled with Terrazas in October 1865. Counting on the support of the state of Chihuahua, Juárez began the reconquest of the country, which finally led to the departure of the French troops in 1867.

During his governorship, Terrazas widened his social base and reaffirmed his political power in Chihuahua while gradually, for a variety of reasons, his enemies abandoned the fight. His main opponent, Ángel Trías Álvarez, died of tuberculosis in 1867.

Terrazas won the elections once again for the four-year term 1868 to 1872, but he had to deal with a strong division in the local Congress provoked by Juárez's reelection. When Porfirio Díaz, who desired the presidency, rebelled under the banner of the Plan de la Noria in 1871, Terrazas remained faithful to Juárez. The latter's death the next year briefly put an end to the tense political situation. With the new president, Sebastián Lerdo de Tejada, Terrazas advocated amnesty for the rebels and accompanied Porfirio Díaz, whom he met in Chihuahua, to the state frontier. Thus began a coolness between both individuals that would have long-term consequences.

In 1873 Terrazas lost control of the governorship to Mariano Samaniego, one of his followers and a personal friend. In 1876 a fresh revolt in Tuxtepec led by Porfirio Díaz was successful in the rest of the country but not in Chihuahua. Díaz's troops arrived in the state a year later, and August Ángel Trías Ochoa, son of his old enemy, became interim governor. Terrazas disappeared once again from the state political scene. Nevertheless, Apache attacks, the imposition of loans to fight the Indian invaders, and a bad harvest that ruined the economy between 1877 and 1879 led to Trías Ochoa's demotion after a short revolt under the umbrella of the Plan de Guerrero. The local legislature once again nominated Terrazas as interim governor, but when Díaz's troops arrived in the state the same year, they found the situation was entirely under the governor's control.

When Terrazas was elected constitutional governor again for the four-year period 1880 to 1884, various prominent families from the Guerrero district—the Casavantes, the Gonzálezes, and the Herreras, backed by the strong support of Lauro Carrillo, Juan María Salazar, and Francisco Maceyra—took the offensive. In 1883 they made initial inroads into banking, finance, trade, and urban transport, acquiring vast territories as shareholders in various surveying companies. Terrazas responded by skillfully linking his businesses and his family to the political and economic elites of the Iturbide, Camargo, and Jiménez districts that were closed to his enemies. His support in Paso del Norte came from the wealthy families of Mariano Samaniego and his son-in-law Innocent Ochoa, with whom he associated to create the Banco Minero de Chihuahua. Terrazas sought and found associates and colleagues throughout the state.

In 1883, a serious and bloody labor conflict in the British-owned mine of Pinos Altos broke out, which was quashed at gunpoint. From 1885, when Terrazas was out of power, various disturbances occurred in the west of the state owing to political and religious problems as well as those related to taxation and lands, which provoked violent repressive measures. Díaz's army was responsible for numerous persecutions, arrests, and summary executions among the civil population, and many fled to the United States. Even though the hidden hand of Terrazas was blamed for initiating these disturbances, his participation has not been proved. At the end of 1891 there was a personal rapprochement between Díaz and Terrazas in Mexico City, whereby difficulties between them were smoothed out. Miguel Ahumada won the elections as constitutional governor of Chihuahua; although not a member of Terrazas's own group, neither was he his enemy. It is not surprising, therefore, that Terrazas openly backed Díaz's candidature as president for the fourth time. In 1892 Terrazas even became vice president of the Porfirio Díaz Club.

At the age of 73 and without appearing directly linked to the state political machine, Terrazas dedicated himself to building his vast empire, which brought together a vast gamut of concerns including farming, cattle ranching, banking, industrial, commercial, and mining interests as well as forestry, railways, insurance, transport, and communications. In May 1903 Governor Miguel Ahumada was transferred to Jalisco and Terrazas was appointed interim governor of the state. His triumph was complete and his domination over Chihuahua all-encompassing. Terrazas's possession of such pervasive economic power was the result of his ability to take the maximum advantage of the great opportunities offered by an export economy, the resources he amassed through the sale of cattle, and the opportunities he tendered as an intermediary for foreign investment. Thus Terrazas obtained sufficient capital not only to dominate his regional rivals but also to form a powerful elite that was able to successfully oppose Porfirio Díaz's attempts to centralize rule in the country. Through major banking investments he controlled all state financing, and Terrazas became the proprietor of 2,659,000 hectares (6,570,299 acres) of the best state land and created one of the largest industrial-commercial and financial empires in Mexico. He also adroitly converted the many members of the Chihuahua elite into his partners, employees, or spouses of his numerous sons and daughters.

Terrazas's ascent to the summit of power can be divided into three stages. Initially he emerged from the subregional conflicts of 1860 to 1870 backed by the Conservative members of his family. During the war with France and the Liberal government of Juárez and Lerdo, he stayed firm, meanwhile increasing his political power and his fortune. The second stage saw the struggle between Terrazas and Díaz for the control of the state. Terrazas was in charge prior to 1884, surrendering control to Díaz between 1884 and 1891, the year in which both arrived at on advantageous situation of mutual respect. In the third stage, between 1903 and 1911, Terrazas managed to take over complete political control when Díaz handed him the interim governorship of the state in 1903. The following year his son-in-law Enrique Creel was elected constitutional governor. From then on the Terrazas-Creel clan ruled over the state of Chihuahua as if it was their private property.

The coming of the Mexican Revolution changed all this. Terrazas, who as indisputable leader of the state oligarchy began a counterrevolution in Chihuahua, saw his empire crumble when Francisco "Pancho" Villa captured the city of Chihuahua in December 1913 and declared himself revolutionary governor of the state. Only four days later he ordered the confiscation of all the properties belonging to the Chihuahua elite, seizing lands, industrial companies, banks, finance companies, and insurance companies and thereby breaking the backbone of their economic control. Terrazas, by then 85 years old, had to flee to El Paso, where he stayed until the end of the war. He lived sufficiently long to recuperate his haciendas, businesses, and properties, which were returned by President Venustiano Carranza. Shortly after the signing of the peace treaty between Villa and the new Mexican government, Terrazas finally was able to return to his native land. He died at the age of 94 on June 15, 1923, in the city of Chihuahua and was buried in the atrium of the Sanctuary of Guadalupe.

Select Bibliography

Katz, Friedrich, *The Secret War in Mexico: Europe, the United States and the Mexican Revolution.* Chicago and London: University of Chicago Press, 1981.

Osorio, Rubén, *In Search of Pancho Villa: Pancho Villa's Correspondence: Letters & Telegrams from 1912 to 1923.* Las Cruces: Border Research Institute, New Mexico State University, 1991.

—Rubén Osorio Zuñiga

Texan Secession

When Mexico achieved independence in 1821, Texas was one of the country's least-populated regions. The Mexican population in Texas was confined to three major settlements: San Antonio, the provincial capital; La Bahía (modern-day Goliad), near the coast; and Nacogdoches, in the eastern pine forests. The approximately 3,000 Tejanos (Mexican Texans) who lived there shared the region with a large number of Indian peoples from plains hunter Comanches to woodland agriculturalist Caddoes. Economic activities consisted almost entirely of subsistence farming, open-range ranching, and military service.

Development of the province had been a perennial problem for colonial authorities. Geographically isolated from the mining and commercial centers of the Mexican interior and lacking mineral resources or sophisticated native cultures to exploit, Texas's small military population was the nucleus of settlement. After the Louisiana Purchase, royal authorities attempted to establish a string of settlements to hold the province against U.S. encroachments. Hostilities during the Mexican War of Independence, however, retarded Texas's development as Tejano insurrectionaries were killed or fled to Louisiana, and recently established settlements were abandoned. The U.S. claims to Mexican territory south to the Rio Grande ceased only with agreement to the Adams-Onís Treaty of 1819. By this time the United States had occupied Texas territory to the Sabine River, prime proof to the government in Mexico that the United States coveted the region.

Recognizing the vulnerability of sparsely settled territory, Mexican authorities turned to immigration as the solution to holding Texas against the United States. Early in 1821 they accepted a proposal for settlement of 300 families made by Moses Austin, who died shortly after, leaving his son Stephen to carry out the plan. Aggressively pursuing approval from the newly independent Mexican government, Stephen F. Austin became the first and most successful of the land impresarios to operate in Mexican Texas. He established the pattern for Mexico's policies concerning land grants both at the national and state levels. The federalist Constitution of 1824 gave the states control over land granting matters; Texas was combined with Coahuila to the south in a single state. By 1831 Austin had more than 5,500 Anglo-Americans and their slaves living in his colonies, a number that exceeded the total Mexican population of Texas.

The impresario system, under which men of means contracted to settle a specific number of families in return for large government land grants and the right to collect fees from colonists, proved only partially successful. Aside from Austin, who fulfilled nearly all his contracts, and Martín de León, the only active Mexican impresario, few contractors came even close to fulfilling their obligations. For instance, efforts to recruit European Catholic immigrants, particularly from Ireland, met with very limited success. In East Texas Anglo-American families mostly filtered into the region individually or came at the prompting of the Galveston Bay and Texas Land Company, a New York corporation holding title to three impresario contracts.

Despite requirements that immigrants take an oath of loyalty to the Mexican nation and accept Roman Catholicism, circumstances prevented the integration of the new settlers into the Mexican population. For the most part the Anglo and Mexican populations were geographically segregated. Except for an isolated group at Nacogdoches, the Mexican population was concentrated along the San Antonio River valley from San Antonio to Goliad, and in the vicinity of Victoria. By the early 1830s there were approximately 20,000 Anglo-Americans and only about 4,500 Mexican-Texans. English continued to be the common language among the foreign settlers, who continued to use their own legal forms in the general absence of Mexican officials. Economic activity within the Anglo-American areas gravitated toward New Orleans. American-style slavery quickly took hold in the 1820s and proved impossible to eliminate. In the absence of an effective Catholic Church presence outside San Antonio and Goliad, Protestantism remained at least the formal religion of many settlers.

Official response to the situation in Texas wavered between efforts to stop the immigration flow and enacting reforms to keep the settler population satisfied. Among the authorities who recognized the threat posed by uncontrolled immigration from the United States to Mexican Texas was General Manuel Mier y Téran. As head of the Mexican commission that marked the Texas-Louisiana border in 1828, and later as commandant general of the northeastern region of the country, he witnessed the Americanizing process at work in eastern Texas and warned Mexico City that Texas would soon be lost if governmental authority was not established quickly and effectively. Under the direction of the Conservative Anastasio Bustamante and his secretary of state, Lucas Alamán, the national government finally responded with the Law of April 6, 1830, which attempted to strike at the heart of the problem. The legislation outlawed any further introduction of slaves and canceled all impresario contracts not in execution, curtailing legal immigration. The law also called for the establishment of seven military posts, ostensibly for frontier defense, and a program of settlement based on Mexican nationals. At the same time the national government made itself responsible for approval of settlement along the coastal and border strip and established customs posts following expiration of a seven-year tax exemption granted to Texas. In 1832 the Coahuila y Texas State Legislature increased tensions by limiting to 10 years all indentured service contracts (a ploy through which slaves from the United States continued to be introduced into Texas after the state's official closure of the slave trade in 1827).

Texans, both Anglo-American and Mexican, protested the measures, sometimes in terms that deepened the suspicions of the government. Armed encounters between colonists and Mexican military units, refusals to pay customs duties, the meeting of two extralegal conventions in 1832 and 1833, and memorials by the San Antonio and Goliad town councils all addressed similar grievances: the continued prohibition of legal immigration; the insecurity of slave property in Texas; the absence of an adequate judicial system; the perception that the tariff system was counter productive; and, above all, the continued union with Coahuila, which had nine times the population of Texas, and thus dominated it in the state legislature. As representative of the Anglo-American Texas colonies, Stephen F. Austin traveled to Mexico City in the spring of 1833 with a list of grievances and a copy of a new state constitution to present for action to the national government.

In 1833 and 1834 Texas also became embroiled in the federalist-centralist struggle taking place in the rest of the nation. As supporters of local control, Mexican Texans generally sided with the federalists. The Anglo-American settlers also tended to look not to the political factions involved but to the inviolability of the federalist Constitution of 1824. Federalists managed to wrest control of the state government away from the centralist faction in the state legislature and transferred the capital from Saltillo to Monclova (in present-day Coahuila). The legislature then undertook a series of reforms aimed at undermining the colonists' grounds for seeking separate statehood. Among the reforms were establishment of a circuit court for Texas and trial by jury, the creation of new administrative districts in Texas, and an increase in the number of Texas representatives to the state legislature. Despite the pro-Texas moves, however, they failed to gain the confidence of the Anglo-American settlers because of their reliance on large-scale sale of public lands to finance the government, which the Texans interpreted as corrupt land speculation.

After removing his Liberal vice president, Valentín Gómez Farías, and reversing a series of anticlerical and antimilitary reforms, President Antonio López de Santa Anna attempted to come to terms with the

Texans. Gómez Farías had rescinded the prohibition on U.S. immigration to Texas but had arrested Austin on charges of treason. Santa Anna freed Austin and tried to reassure the Texans that he had no quarrel with them. At the same time his government made a number of moves that increased tensions in Texas, most notably an order to disband state militias, the decision to crush the federalist governor and state militia at Zacatecas, and the arrest of Coahuila's federalist governor. Also, reports arrived in Texas that Santa Anna was preparing to send a large military force there.

Texan opinion was divided but open to being interpreted as largely disloyal. The major camps consisted of war and peace parties and the Tejano federalists. There is little doubt that a vocal and active minority headed mostly by more recent arrivals made up a war party intent on separating Texas from Mexico. The peace party, which included much of the longer-established Anglo-American population, actively sought to promote separation from Coahuila but wished to remain part of Mexico under the terms of the federalist Constitution of 1824, which Santa Anna had annulled. Most of the Tejano elite, which was centered largely at San Antonio, had become involved in the political struggle between federalists and centralists and had chosen to oppose Santa Anna's centralizing measures. From Mexico City's perspective, therefore, Texas was a hotbed of resistance to the national government.

For Mexican authorities, proof of Texan disloyalty came in the summer of 1835. At the end of June, war party members attacked the Galveston Bay garrison at Anahuac and forced its surrender. Texas officials refused to turn over the leaders of the assault along with other individuals accused by the national government of being troublemakers. Soon after, Austin returned from Mexico to proclaim that Texas should separate from Mexico if the federal military invaded the province. Resistance finally became violent on October 2, when colonists at Gonzales fired on a detachment sent by the federal military commander at San Antonio to collect a small cannon on loan to the settlement.

During the fall and winter of 1835–36, the hostilities in Texas were, at least on the surface, resistance against Santa Anna's suppression of the federal system. For instance, the provisional government organized in November issued a declaration in favor of the Constitution of 1824. At the same time, while the insurgents sought assistance from the United States, they shied away from an alliance with Mexican federalists. (One notable Mexican Liberal supporter of the revolt was Lorenzo de Zavala, who had land interests in Texas.) Many Tejanos who initially joined the revolt against Santa Anna would later abandon the field after Texas declared its independence, but José Antonio Navarro and Francisco Ruiz signed the document, and Juan N. Seguín led a Tejano cavalry company through the end of the war. A significant minority of Mexican Texans, particularly in the Goliad area, and a small group of Anglo-Americans in eastern Texas sided with the central government. The evidence makes clear, however, that the overwhelming majority of the Texan leadership favored complete separation from Mexico.

Early successes by the insurgents, combined with a hardening of the Mexican government's position, propelled the secessionists' drive for a formal declaration of independence from Mexico. In December 1835 General Martín Perfecto Cos surrendered San Antonio to one rebel army while another rebel force captured the garrison at Goliad, leaving Texas entirely in the hands of the insurgents. A group of rebels at the latter place went so far as to issue a declaration of independence, which the provincial authorities rejected as premature.

Such military successes prompted Santa Anna personally to lead a force of 6,000 men against the revolt. At San Antonio in late February, he laid siege to the former Mission San Antonio de Valero, which by that point was only a makeshift fort known as the Alamo. Rather than bypass the small (approximately 200 men) isolated garrison and attack the main insurgent army under Sam Houston, Santa Anna brought his entire force to bear on the fort, which fell on the morning of March 6 with heavy casualties. The execution on Santa Anna's order of over 300 prisoners taken following the surrender of a Texan force under James Fannin at Goliad later than month stiffened resistance among the Texans.

Unbeknown to either side at the Alamo, a convention meeting on March 2 to the northeast at the village of Washington on the Brazos had declared independence. According to the delegates, Mexico had broken its compact with Texas on a number of grounds. The Mexican government had acted tyrannically in abrogating the Constitution of 1824, denying the settlers those republican institutions to which they were accustomed in their home country, and rejecting the petition for separate statehood. It had allowed army officers to act arbitrarily, subordinating civil to military authority, and incited the Indians against the settlers. The government also had failed to establish adequate systems of education and trial by jury and denied settlers liberty of conscience. Most of the charges were contrived, considering that they did not represent anything other than differences in

Anglo-American and Mexican cultures or a singling out of immigrants for special treatment. To the contrary, the Mexican government had granted considerable latitude to the settlers in how they conducted their affairs.

Texas independence was won at the Battle of San Jacinto on April 21, 1836. Santa Anna, having outdistanced the bulk of his army, set up camp in a low-lying and exposed field near the northwestern end of Galveston Bay. His 1,400 men, some of whom had arrived just hours before, were at rest and had failed to post adequate guards when Sam Houston led his entire force of 910 men in an assault that took the Mexicans by surprise. The battle lasted just 18 minutes and, according to Houston's figures, resulted in 630 Mexicans dead and 730 captured. Santa Anna, who had fled, was captured the following day. In subsequent negotiations, Santa Anna signed two treaties, one public and one secret, at the Texas port of Velasco by which he ordered the retreat of the Mexican army, promised not to take up arms against Texas, and agreed to work toward recognition of Texas by the Mexican Congress in return for his freedom. Except for the withdrawal of Mexican forces from Texas, neither pact was honored. The Mexican Congress considered Santa Anna's negotiation of these treaties scandalous and nullified them both. Nevertheless, Texan independence was a fait accompli.

In the decade that Texas struggled to survive as a republic, Mexico refused to recognize its independence. At first, the Mexicans rejected outright the idea of Texan separation as well as the upstart government's claim that its border ran from the mouth to the headwaters of the Rio Grande and from there to the Adams-Onís Treaty line. Mexican forces on a number of occasions made raids into the southern fringes of the republic, the most serious of which being General Adrian Woll's occupation of San Antonio for one week in September 1842. For their part, Texans made a number of raids across the Rio Grande and launched a disastrous expedition in 1841 to gain control of New Mexico and divert at least some of the Santa Fe Trail commerce to Texas. The Texans also supported rebels in northern Mexico and the insurgency in Yucatán during this time. Texas gained recognition from the United States in 1837, although its efforts at annexation were rejected by the U.S. Congress. Recognition by France and Britain's promise of support for negotiations with Mexico led President Mirabeau B. Lamar to abandon any effort at annexation to the United States as a gesture toward Mexico. On reassuming the Texas presidency, Houston renewed annexation negotiations with the United States, which ultimately led Mexico to make a belated offer of recognition. In 1845 the Congress of the United States passed a resolution of annexation, the Texas government held a constitutional convention to draft a state constitution, and on December 29 Texas was admitted as one of the United States. The event precipitated war between Mexico and the United States.

In hindsight the futility of Mexico's effort to retain its Texas territory, indeed the whole of what ultimately became the southwestern United States, is clear. Struggling to forge a national state out of the social and political fragmentation that marked the colonial period, Mexico lacked the economic and human resources to develop the region or to mount an adequate military defense of it. In desperation, Mexican officialdom listened to the siren song of Anglo-American frontiersmen who promised to become good Mexican citizens in return for the opportunity to settle the land and make it productive. Too late, the Mexican government discovered that they had turned Texas over to foreigners who intended to recreate the social, economic, and political system they had left behind in the United States, even at the cost of abandoning their oaths of loyalty to their adoptive nation. The ultimate beneficiary of the situation was the United States, which, taking advantage of Mexican turmoil and the groundwork laid by its advancing frontier folk, acquired dominion of the Mexican north.

See also Guadalupe Hidalgo, Treaty of; U.S.-Mexican Border; U.S.-Mexican War

Select Bibliography

Barker, Eugene, *The Life of Stephen F. Austin, Founder of Texas, 1793–1836*. Austin: University of Texas Press, 1969.

Hardin, Stephen L., *Texian Iliad: A Military History of the Texas Revolution*. Austin: University of Texas Press, 1994.

Lack, Paul D., *The Texas Revolutionary Experience: A Political and Social History, 1835–1836*. College Station: Texas A and M University Press, 1992.

Tijerina, Andrés, *Tejanos and Texas under the Mexican Flag, 1821–1836*. College Station: Texas A and M University Press, 1994.

Weber, David J., *The Mexican Frontier, 1821–1846: The American Southwest under Mexico*. Albuquerque: University of New Mexico Press, 1982.

—JESÚS F. DE LA TEJA

Three Years War

See Wars of Reform (Three Years War)

Tlatelolco, Massacre of

See Massacre of Tlatelolco

Toltec

See Mesoamerica: Toltec

Tourism

The tourist industry of Mexico has evolved markedly from its simple origins in the early twentieth century to its highly capitalized and complex contemporary expression. The development of Mexican tourism has been shaped in large part by the federal government, particularly in the critical period between 1940 and 1960, when the Mexican state focused on building infrastructure for tourism, such as the creation and maintenance of costly transportation facilities, advertising, marketing, and the financing of tourist-related investment. The history of the industry in Mexico also has been influenced by shifts in the global tourist economy, however, especially its spread into developing countries at the turn of the century and its subsequent worldwide diversification.

As early as 1925, economic planners recognized the potential benefits for Mexico of a thriving tourist industry. At that time, border tourism emanating from the United States was the main source of tourist revenues; indeed, over the decades American tourists would be a critical force in shaping the Mexican tourist industry. Government statistics have tracked foreign tourists entering Mexico since the early 1920s, and 80 percent on average have come from the United States. Border tourism in the 1920s, however, contained an unsavory undercurrent. Many Americans flocked to Mexican border towns during the prohibition years (1919–34), when liquor production and consumption were barred in the United States. As a result, bars, casinos, racing venues, and red-light districts proliferated in Ciudad Juárez, Tijuana, and other border cities. This type of tourism expanded during World War II. American military personnel stationed near the border made frequent use of the services and goods offered by Mexican businesses, a trade enlarged by wartime rationing of various products in the United States that were available or less expensive across the border.

Prior to the 1920s, visitors to Mexico encountered a poorly organized tourist structure, generally confined to a handful of sites with meager amenities that appealed to adventurous travelers and few others. Rough roads, uneven train service, and a scarcity of appropriate lodging contributed to the low number of visitors to Mexico. Mexico attracted comparatively less attention from international tourists who desired to travel to non-European locales. Moreover, Mexico saw relatively little domestic tourism; only a small number of Mexicans had the means to travel for leisure extensively, and most tended to travel to Europe or the United States rather than brave the rough travel conditions of their native country. Indeed, despite the romanticized reverence for *patria* (nation) in the late nineteenth century, for most Mexicans of means the concept of travel for pleasure rarely included their native country. The Revolution of 1910 and its attendant nationalism would change this attitude among many Mexicans. Still, the driving force behind the development of the Mexican tourist industry was the potential profits from international visitors (see Tables 1 and 2).

Nevertheless, for much of the period after the violence of the Revolution subsided, tourism contributed significantly to the country's economy. Soon it became a major source of foreign currency. As border tourism increased substantially, accelerated by the growing use of automobiles in the United States, the revenues generated by this type of tourism pushed the Mexican government to facilitate the entry and travel of Americans further into the interior of the country. Thus, in 1929 the first formal legislation concerning tourism was passed in Mexico, establishing the role of the state in the promotion of the industry and its regulation. Since then, the federal government has exercised a fundamental role in the regulation of the industry, from the ratings of hotels

Table 1
Tourism as a Percentage of Mexican Exports of Goods and Services

1940	23%
1945	22%
1950	28%
1955	32%
1960	38%

Table 2
Tourism Receipts

Year	Millions of U.S. Dollars
1939	21.7
1941	31.5
1944	42.5
1947	82.8
1950	156.1

to the licensing of tourist agencies, although the government has been careful to include private business representation in the making of policy concerning tourism.

More importantly, the state provided the foundations for the industry with its willingness to fund its development through various measures, from the building and improvement of roads to the creation of government-supported offices in foreign countries to promote travel to Mexico. This trend in state support for the industry eventually led to the formation of the Fondo Nacional para el Turismo (FONATUR) in 1956, a special development fund for the financing of tourist-related projects. To underscore the importance of the industry to Mexico's economy, a cabinet-level ministry was eventually established.

Nonetheless, the government has generally refrained from direct participation in tourist operations, avoiding government-run hostelries, for example. Rather, the Mexican government has allowed the private sector to dominate the profits generated by the industry. Thus, Mexican tourism invites discussion of state and business relations in the formation of the industry, but this issue is complicated by the authoritarian nature of Mexican politics since the 1920s.

From 1929 to the 1990s, the Partido Revolucionario Institucional (PRI, or Institutional Revolutionary Party) in its various incarnations has dominated national politics. Not surprisingly, political privilege has conditioned the state's tourist policy, such as the location and size of government spending in the promotion and construction of tourist sites. As early as 1930, for instance, the secretary of defense at the time (Juan Andreu Almazán) used his position to begin construction of a road to Acapulco, where he had bought properties with the intent of developing their tourist potential. Hence, political considerations have surrounded at times the state's economic calculations in tourist industry decisions.

A crucial figure in this regard was Miguel Alemán Valdés, president of Mexico from 1946 to 1952,

who most forcefully used the power of his office to accelerate dramatically the industry through government support. Alemán was instrumental in the move to promote Mexico vigorously to foreign travelers, and in the construction of a more modern, highly-commercialized approach to Mexican tourism. Using his political privileges after his departure from office in 1952, Alemán remained a central actor in the promotion of Mexican tourism, including a term as the head of the government's agency for tourism. Alemán represented perhaps the most obvious example of the close relationship between the state and the tourist industry. The turn away from state-led development policies after 1982 failed to alter the pattern of mixing politics with tourism. The political weight of the Figueroa family in the state of Guerrero, for instance, clearly influenced the attempt of the federal government to reanimate the dwindling attraction of Acapulco in the 1980s.

Furthermore, the state's powerful position contributed to the creation of the "tourist gaze" of Mexico, that is, the manipulation of the country's image as a means of attracting foreign visitors as well as domestic travelers. The nationalist ideology that emerged and then matured after the Revolution of 1910 formed the initial basis of Mexico's official cultural policy, with crucial implications for tourism. Thus, the Mexican government initially touted the country's folkloric cultural elements, colonial architecture, and monumental indigenous achievements, most notably the pyramids outside of Mexico City. The cultural nationalism evident in government-subsidized promotional publications of the 1920s and 1930s paralleled that seen in contemporary state-sponsored textbooks and murals. The state invested deeply in its official cultural policy, as evidenced by government-supported archaeological excavations, museums, anthropological research, rehabilitation of historic buildings and neighborhoods, arts performance and production, and programs for the maintenance of folkloric and popular cultural expression. The founding of the Instituto Nacional de Antropología e Historia (INAH) in 1938 best signified this aspect of the state's cultural policy. The work of INAH contributed significantly to the celebration of Mexico's cultural past, symbolized in the construction of the heavily promoted Museo de Antropología in Mexico City.

During World War II, however, the state shifted the focus of its tourist promotion—and its infrastructural investment—to emphasize Mexico's beaches, climate, exoticism, and modernized services. World War II dramatically reduced international travel for pleasure in Europe, greatly enhancing Mexico's pull in the United States as a tourist attraction. Furthermore, the social composition of tourism changed, particularly after 1945, as increasing numbers of middle-class people in Europe and the United States found foreign travel more accessible. A major outcome of this shift was the reconfiguration of the spatial organization of Mexican tourism. At the beginning of state-promoted travel, Mexico City was the centerpiece of Mexican tourism. The change in the industry's focus after 1940 lessened the centrality of the capital, as increasing numbers of tourists (including Mexicans) used Mexico City as a conduit or point of departure to other sites. Thus, the infrastructural spending of the state tended to channel tourists to particular places through specific routes and means of transportation. As a result, a disproportionate amount of government expenditures went to a few sites and related ancillary activities. Acapulco, for instance, received enormous in the 1940s, as the government pushed the bay's tourist development with outlays for a modern highway, sanitation system, water works, and airport improvements. In comparison, Oaxaca received scant attention until much later, as other developments patterned on Acapulco garnered the bulk of state-backed tourist investment. As a consequence, certain sites became highly visible and developed for tourists, primarily foreigners, while many interesting parts of Mexico went largely ignored by the government's tourist industry.

Although the industry generated innumerable jobs and businesses, the benefits often have been marred by manifest inequities and lack of concern for the welfare of many tourism workers. The labor needs of tourism have led to a mushrooming of demand for housing, for instance, that frequently outstripped supply, a problem compounded by low wages, high real estate costs, shoddy construction, and a lack of such structural amenities as well-paved roads and adequate transportation between workplace and workers' residential areas. In recent years the government has made an effort to address these problems, but the effort has fallen far short. Moreover, because many tourist sites have been developed in areas with small populations, labor migration to such sites has exacerbated problems of housing, health care, and the schooling of the workers' children.

The tourism labor force has led to a highly gendered workplace, where a large portion of jobs are held by women as maids, waitresses, and related service workers. In addition, women also lace the semiprofessional sector of tourism workers as travel agents, tour guides, and salespersons. Thus, the tourist industry has accelerated the employment of women, but such gains for women usually have been characterized by low incomes, seasonality, meager benefits, and limited mobility. Furthermore, the largely female composition of the workforce has magnified the problems of proper housing, sufficient health facilities, adequate welfare networks, and good schools.

The adverse social implications of tourist development in Mexico has held similar consequences for the environment. Both government and the private tourist industry have recognized this concern, but there has been little response until relatively recently, and even then it was uneven. In older sites, the ecological damage has been severe, made worse by lapses in the enforcement of environmental regulations, corruption, and inept planning. Nowhere is this more obvious than Acapulco, where the lack of appropriate sewage treatment facilities has nearly ruined the once-pristine waters and beaches of that beautiful bay. The growing interest in ecotourism, and in ecological protection generally, has compelled the Mexican tourist industry to address this issue. But the attention is too little and too late for certain sites, and it is conditioned by the steep costs of environmental rehabilitation, competing economic priorities, constrained government budgets, and political considerations.

The contemporary tourist industry has, to some extent, attempted to redress the errors and imbalances produced by postwar policies. INAH, for example, has tried to regenerate the interests of Mexicans in their cultural past through a myriad of activities that clearly reflect domestic concerns, as opposed to focusing primarily on foreign travelers. Mexico City and its environs once again have received needed attention, as the government has rehabilitated much of the historic central downtown area in the aftermath of the devastating earthquake of 1985. There also has been an effort to restore the fading beauty of the gardens of Xochimilco. Still, beachside resort complexes that proliferated explosively in the 1980s continue to be built, for example, along a corridor running from Cancun to Chetumal, although with less aggressiveness and an allegedly greater concern for the environment. Ecotourism also has debuted in Mexico with much promise; the government has initiated such projects in cooperation with the private sector, including a site in the area north of Puerto Vallarta.

Mexican tourism faces severe tests in the future. The "free market" policies of the dominant party, especially since 1988, signal a retreat from state-led expenditures for tourism. Future expansion will, it seems, depend increasingly on foreign investment and private domestic capital. As a result, the deregulation of business in Mexico threatens the government's professed sensitivity to the environmental impacts of tourist development. Given this new vision of government-business relations, any dramatic changes in addressing the social and environmental problems produced by the tourist industry seem bleak.

The drastic economic downturn of December 1994 punctured the heady expectations that followed the passage a year earlier of the North American Free Trade Agreement (NAFTA). Indeed, the deep recession that began at the onset of Ernesto Zedillo Ponce de León's presidency in 1994 revealed both the vulnerability of the Mexican economy and the weakening political grasp of the dominant party. The need for jobs, investment capital, and revenues likely will push government to accommodate rapid tourist development, despite the possible social or ecological costs, and regardless of the party in power. In this light, the tourist industry may become even more important to Mexico's economic future.

Select Bibliography

García Canclini, Nestor, *Transforming Modernity: Popular Culture in Mexico,* translated by Lidia Lozano. Austin: University of Texas Press, 1993.

Jud, G. Donald, "Tourism and Economic Growth in Mexico since 1960." *Inter-American Economic Affairs* 28:1 (Summer 1974).

Nolan, Mary Lee, and Sidney Nolan, "The Evolution of Tourism in Twentieth-Century Mexico." *Journal of the West* 27 (October 1988).

—ALEX M. SARAGOZA

Treaty of Guadalupe Hidalgo

See Guadalupe Hidalgo, Treaty of

Triple Alliance

The Triple Alliance was a pre-Hispanic military confederation of the three city-states of Tenochtitlan, Texcoco, and Tlacopan. The combined political power and military might of these three Valley of Mexico city-states forged an extensive territorial domain often referred to as the Aztec Empire or the Triple Alliance Empire.

At the time of the formation of this alliance, in 1430, the Valley of Mexico was carved into a mosaic of competing city-states, or *altepetl*. Each *altepetl* was characterized by defined territorial bounds, an established rulership with a history of dynastic continuity, and an overt ethnic identity. The individuality of each *altepetl* was highlighted by adherence to recognized variations of general regional customs: while most Valley of Mexico people spoke Nahuatl, each city-state enjoyed its own dialectal expression; all were polytheistic, but each *altepetl* emphasized particular deities over others. Specifics of calendrics, ceremonies, and economic specializations varied from *altepetl* to *altepetl*.

These numerous city-states interacted with one another by establishing political alliances through elite marriages and other negotiations, and engaging in military combat and at times conquest. This latter situation, conquest, resulted in political and economic domination of a successful city-state over its conquered peoples. The political climate in general was one of unstable alliances, uncertain warfare, and opportunistic rebellions. Allies one year could be enemies the next.

The idea of a military alliance among three powerful city-states may not have been novel with the Triple Alliance. The scholar Nigel Davies entertains the possibility of a central Mexican triumvirate of Tula, Culhuacan, and Otompan that held sway in parts of central Mexico during the eleventh and twelfth centuries A.D. Political power probably was not distributed evenly among the three members of that posited triple alliance; Tula would have been the dominant partner. After the fall of Tula, a triple alliance of Culhuacan, Tenayuca, and Xaltocan dominated the Valley of Mexico. As the political fortunes of Tenayuca and Xaltocan waned, these two centers were replaced by Azcapotzalco and Coatlichan, which, along with the stalwart Culhuacan, constituted a new political triumvirate. If such arrangements did exist, as seems probable, then the formation of the later "Aztec" Triple Alliance was not a new invention but rather an institution grounded in established political tradition.

Immediately prior to 1430, the Valley of Mexico was dominated by the city-state of Azcapotzalco, located to the west of Lake Texcoco. Azcapotzalco was a Tepanec kingdom ruled by a particularly powerful king, Tezozomoc. Tezozomoc used his strength to overpower some city-states, such as Texcoco, and his statecraft to co-opt others into service with promises of rewards. The Mexica (Aztecs) of Tenochtitlan fell into this latter category. They served Azcapotzalco as fierce military mercenaries and with specified tribute payments; later, although still vassals, they accumulated considerable lands and other rewards for their military service to Tezozomoc.

When Tezozomoc died in 1428, uncertain succession to his realm led to the usurpation of his rulership by one of his sons, Maxtla. In this process the Tepanec domain was seriously divided and weakened; it was a prime target for the Mexica of Tenochtitlan and the Acolhua of Texcoco, poised to fill the power vacuum. These two city-states, led by Itzcoatl and Nezahualcoyotl, respectively, vanquished the Tepanec of Azcapotzalco and invited a dissident Tepanec city-state, Tlacopan, to join them as a junior partner in a Triple Alliance. This was reportedly in 1430.

The military and political confederation of Tenochtitlan, Texcoco, and Tlacopan (today's Tacuba) encompassed three dominant ethnic groups of the Valley of Mexico, each already in at least nominal control of considerable territory within the valley. The Acolhuas of Texcoco dominated lands to the east of Lake Texcoco, the Tepanec of Tlacopan exercised control to the west, and the Mexica of Tenochtitlan (built on an island) dominated a number of centers geographically between the two other powers. The early years of the alliance were devoted to consolidating the three respective domains, and conquering persistent enemy city-states within the Valley of Mexico. As these events unfolded, the Mexica emerged as the most militarily powerful of the three allies. One obvious goal of the island Mexica in these conquests was the control of extensive agricultural lands that were appropriated to Mexica nobles as rewards for their military service and achievements. Access to suitable building materials and a reliable potable water supply were also stimuli for Mexica military expansion.

Still during Itzcoatl's rule (1426–40), Triple Alliance military forces began conquering city-states beyond the bounds of the Valley of Mexico. Such enterprises gained considerable momentum under the reigns of succeeding Triple Alliance rulers. Some of these conquests were claimed by individual Triple Alliance partners; some were apparently the joint effort of all three powers; and still others enlisted the military support of already-conquered subjects, providing them with commensurate rewards. Quite an array of military combinations could be marshaled to fulfill Triple Alliance expansionist goals.

The Triple Alliance rulers or *tlatoque* (singular, *tlatoani*) sat at the apex of a hierarchy of rulership and imperial political administration. Each city-state throughout central Mexico also was headed by a *tlatoani* who, upon conquest, would be subject to the demands of the imperial, or Triple Alliance, rulers (sometimes called *huey tlatoque*, "big rulers," or "old rulers"). These "supreme rulers" were selected within their respective city-states through genealogical right and election. While this process was essentially an internal affair, it was apparently expected that the other two Triple Alliance *tlatoque* assent to the choice.

Typically, the imperial powers would retain conquered *tlatoque* in their traditional positions; the Triple Alliance power base was maintained primarily through threats of military reprisal and increased tribute demands. Imperial *tlatoque* also would invite rulers of enemy or politically problematic city-states to the imperial capitals for what may be called "rituals of intimidation": opulent accommodations and exquisite gifts and feasts were offered the visitors, and they were required to view flamboyant rituals involving large numbers of human sacrifices. The imperial design was to both impress and unnerve these high-ranking visitors. The imperial rulers also continually consolidated their power relations through marriages with conquered or allied royalty. Nonetheless, these relations of domination and subordination were remarkably unstable.

A main goal of Triple Alliance conquest was the acquisition of tribute in service or kind from vanquished city-states. Documentary sources suggest that imperial-level tribute was divided unevenly among the three powerful partners, with Tenochtitlan and Texcoco receiving equal shares and the smaller Tlacopan allocated half as much. Tenochtitlan clearly controlled such joint tribute payments; these goods were physically delivered to the Mexica capital before being distributed to the other two allies. The tribute from some conquests was claimed not by the triumvirate as a whole, but rather by each individual power. Texcoco claimed dominion over numerous city-states to the east and northeast of the Valley of Mexico. These centers paid scheduled tribute to their Acolhua overlord in the form of specified material goods, labor on agricultural fields, and service in the Texcocan royal palace. A similar pattern held for the Tepanec of Tlacopan in the western Valley of Mexico. Mexica domination appears to have been more geographically extensive; the tribute tally of the Codex Mendoza encompasses 38 provinces stretching from north-central Mexico to today's Guatemalan border. These tributes, ranging from foodstuffs and textiles to precious stones and shimmering feathers, were most likely sent specifically to fill Tenochtitlan's coffers. The Triple Alliance rulers used such payments to enhance their extravagant lifestyles, ensure reliable food stores, and expand their military and commercial control even further.

In all these military and administrative efforts, the Mexica emerge as the most powerful of the three allies. They appear to have controlled tribute deliveries and to have been the driving force in far-flung military ventures. Nonetheless, there are rather peculiar conflicting reports of political jockeying between Texcoco and Tenochtitlan. One version claims an invasion of Tenochtitlan by Texcoco and the resultant domination of Itzcoatl by Nezahualcoyotl. A contrary story relates the burning of Texcoco by Mexica forces, resulting in Nezahualcoyotl's subservience to Itzcoatl. While the veracity of these tales is suspect, their very existence suggests simmering tensions and unstable relations between the two dominant partners of the Triple Alliance.

The three Triple Alliance polities differed not only in terms of relative power, but also in terms of institutional focus. The Mexica of Tenochtitlan were accomplished and aggressive warriors, following the example of their militarily-able rulers. The Acolhua rulers were noted lawmakers, builders, and philosophers, and promoted those activities in their Texcocan realm. Less is known specifically about the Tepanec of Tlacopan, and they consistently appear as junior and less decisive partners in the alliance.

The Triple Alliance, like the empire it loosely controlled, lasted a mere 90 years before succumbing to defeat. Although the conquest was led by a handful of Spaniards under Fernando (Hernán) Cortés, the bulk of the fighting force was drawn from native city-states. Initially these consisted of Triple Alliance enemies such as the Tlaxcallans and disaffected subjects such as the Cempoallans. As the Spanish Conquest progressed, numerous city-states dominated by the Triple Alliance abandoned those overlords for the Spanish option. Ultimately, Texcoco capitulated and the Mexica of Tenochtitlan stood essentially alone in 1521 against a strong Spanish/native army, the Triple Alliance itself shattered.

Select Bibliography

Berdan, Frances F., *The Aztecs of Central Mexico*. New York: Harcourt Brace, 1982.

———, and Patricia Rieff Anawalt, *The Codex Mendoza*. 4 vols., Berkeley: University of California Press, 1992.

Boone, Elizabeth, *The Aztec World*. Montreal: St. Remy Press, 1994.

Davies, Nigel, *The Toltecs*. Norman: University of Oklahoma Press, 1977.

—FRANCES F. BERDAN

U

Urbanism and Urbanization

At the beginning of the twentieth century, Mexico was an overwhelmingly rural country. By 1990, 7 out of 10 Mexicans dwelled in places with more than 15,000 people, while in 1900 it was only 1 out of 10, and in 1950, 3 out of 10. Mexico today has perhaps the largest megalopolis in the world, Mexico City (18 million inhabitants); three metropolitan areas, Guadalajara (3.5 million), Monterrey (3 million), and Puebla (2 million); and three other cities surpassing 1 million, Ciudad Juárez, Nuevo León, and Tijuana. In contrast, in 1900 the national capital had only 350,000 people and the two other big cities (Guadalajara and Puebla) barely reached 100,000. Such astounding urban growth, which entailed both a natural increase of the urban population and massive internal migrations, cannot be explained without understanding the dynamics of capital accumulation and class formation in the country, as well as the consolidation and centralization of the Mexican political system.

The analysis of urbanization also requires paying specific attention to the history of rural-urban relations, the changing labor market, the fate of protectionist industrialization policies from 1940 to 1980, the contradictory intervention of the state in matters of housing and urban land regulation since the 1970s, and the emergence of an open economy dominated by modern services during the 1980s and 1990s. These phenomena conditioned a drastic transformation of the urban landscape. Mexican cities came to combine the remnants of an architectural and urbanistic legacy from the pre-Hispanic and colonial past with audacious modern buildings and commercial malls, spacious middle-class suburbs, and metropolitan highways and trains. But poverty is also a constant presence. Numerous urban dwellers depend on a precarious "informal" economy and lack access to adequate services and democratic participation. High levels of pollution, traffic disorganization, and criminal violence are also signs of the distorted nature of Mexican urban development.

The Dynamics of Differentiated Urbanization until the 1960s

During Porfirio Díaz's dictatorship (1876–80; 1884–1911), both the federal and state governments made explicit efforts to rationalize urban growth and modernize the cities by expanding the railway network, constructing new marketplaces and squares, paving roads, channeling runaway waters, and introducing electricity and public transport. In 1910 Mexico City and several state capitals boasted sewage and drinking water systems for their central districts, not unlike those in the major cities of Europe and the United States. For the elites, new "residential colonies" or "garden cities" were built on the urban peripheries of Mexico City, Guadalajara, and Puebla. The working classes found room in the old Indian neighborhoods, or barrios, which seldom enjoyed modern amenities. During the Revolutionary years (1910–20) and then during the Cristero Rebellion (1926–29) and its aftermath (1930–34), tens of thousands of people fled rural violence and took refuge in towns and cities. In many urban settlements, this accelerated influx of rural migrants allowed for the building of new lower-income neighborhoods by private developers, usually without any kind of state regulation. In Guadalajara, for instance, the provision of urban services for these new areas was organized by the residents themselves, often under the leadership of their parish priests.

The pacification of the countryside after 1934 as well as the massive land distribution mainly promoted by President Lázaro Cárdenas (1934–40) caused many people to return to the rural areas. Vast tracts of land were opened for agriculture—almost 10 million hectares of new fields between 1930 and 1960—providing employment and food for the increasing population. Yet urban growth did not lose momentum. A crucial factor was import-substitution industrialization (ISI), mostly devoted to the production of consumer goods (clothing, shoes, processed food and drinks, and domestic items). Initially stimulated by economic conditions during World War II, ISI took great advantage of protectionist policies and was enhanced by a phenomenal expansion of the road network. Concomitantly, the availability of industrial commodities in peasant villages and the need for money conditioned a process of agricultural commercialization that provided towns and cities with relatively abundant and cheap food. In addition, paternalistic trade union policies devised by the federal government allowed for the control of the emerging urban working class.

Old colonial cities, such as Guadalajara, Puebla, Nuevo León, Chihuahua, and Mérida, which had for centuries provided commercial and government services to large and densely populated rural hinterlands, became privileged sites for the industrial production of consumer goods, sometimes taking advantage of industrial traditions dating from the nineteenth century. This reinforced their role as regional capitals and secured the continuity of their class structures—a dominant class of public and private administrators, merchants, industrialists, and urban speculators, and a working class of artisans and unskilled laborers. In such places, industry was medium- or small-scale and used old-fashioned technology. In contrast, Monterrey, which never had the benefit of a rich hinterland, became the location of a sophisticated, large-scale industry devoted to capital and intermediate goods for the national and international markets, with a modern upper class of entrepreneurs, managers, and financiers; a middle class of technicians; and a skilled industrial working class. Modern industries also were found in towns specialized in certain branches of production (automobiles in Ciudad Sahagún, steel in Monclova, chemicals in Reynosa, refined oil in Salamanca). In turn, Mexico City fulfilled a triple function: lodging the expanding national bureaucracy, providing services and producing consumer goods for its own hinterland, and generating modern industries for the wider market. In fact, by 1970 more than 40 percent of Mexican industrial production was concentrated in the national capital. This was to a great extent a function of financial and fiscal stimuli as well as generous federal expenditure in transport, energy and water supply, and storage facilities for industries in the Mexico City area.

Market towns situated within the hinterlands of the old regional capitals also experienced considerable growth, because of their pivotal role in the organization of modern agricultural enterprises and agroindustries. Some of these towns, such as Zamora in Michoacán, Ciudad Guzmán in Jalisco, and Valladolid in Yucatán, had long urban histories; others, such as Ciudad Obregón in Sonora, Los Mochis in Sinaloa, Ciudad Mante in Tamaulipas, Alamo in Veracruz, Tamazula in Jalisco, and Tecomán in Colima, grew from small peasant villages. All of them attracted rural migrants who stayed for good, but also a cyclical army of workers (called *golondrinas,* or swallows) for the peak periods of harvesting and processing. In contrast, towns in areas of traditional agriculture had a much slower expansion. Most of these traditional towns had a parasitic function, as they dominated over hinterlands of indigenous communities. Anthropologist Gonzalo Aguirre Beltrán has demonstrated that in such interethnic regions, where the division between Indians and non-Indians coincided with the rural-urban distinction, urban centers (e.g., San Cristóbal de las Casas in the Chiapas highlands, Tlaxiaco in the Oaxaca sierra, Coetzalan in the Puebla sierra, and Ixmiquilpan in the Mezquital steppe of Hidalgo) inhibited agricultural change and industrialization, since modern influences would challenge the hegemony of the traditional elites of landowners and commercial middlemen.

The four old major ports (Veracruz, Acapulco, Mazatlán and Manzanillo) modernized to meet the demands of industrialization and became cities of some importance, also benefiting from increasing demands for tourist services. Tampico, Coatzacoalcos, and Salina Cruz emerged as ports closely linked to the oil industry. As for the previously important silver and gold mining cities, only those that were state capitals (San Luis Potosí, Guanajuato, Zacatecas, Pachuca) experienced growth, but mostly as providers of government services. Iron and copper mining towns such as Durango, Cananea, and Nueva Rosita, however, enjoyed a moderate prosperity because of their relevance for metal-mechanic industrial production.

In 1970 there were more than 150 urban localities (with 15,000 people and more) in the country; yet the highest rate of growth was found in the national capital (an annual average of 5 percent from 1940 to 1970) and to a lesser extent in the three emergent metropolises (Guadalajara, Monterrey, and Puebla). This implied a situation of high urban primacy: in 1970 the population of Mexico City (8.4 million) was six times higher than that of Guadalajara (1.4 million) and almost eight times higher than that of Monterrey (1.1 million). Puebla, the fourth city, had one-half million people. These four cities concentrated 22 percent of the national population, whereas middle-sized cities (50,000 to 500,000 people) lodged only 15 percent. In turn, high primacy, a function of the concentration of public and private investment, meant an increasing attraction of big cities for rural migrants, particularly since the agricultural frontier was virtually exhausted after 1970. This led to saturation of urban labor markets, shortage of urban land and services, and the rise of the informal sector.

Migration, the Labor Market, and the Informal Economy

Market towns and regional cities often received migrants who periodically returned to their villages for long periods of time. This kind of circular migration was feasible when the money earned in urban places could be used to supplement rural incomes or even profitably invested in rural enterprises, and when the urban labor market demanded cyclical work (e.g., for agroindustries and construction). Extended families with members both in the village and in town acted as social and cultural bridges, creating links with employers and helping to find housing and services. But many migrants moved to the city permanently when rural resources were meager. Also, people who found jobs in modern industries and services, which demanded formal education or at least training and commitment, tended to settle for good. For these permanent migrants, family and kin continued to be crucial assets in the process of settlement. Whenever possible, extended families and fellow villagers lived in the same *vecindad* (a house divided into many small, badly equipped apartments), or within the same barrio (quarter), or even built contiguous shacks in the shanty towns that mushroomed on empty land.

Even though urbanization and ISI allowed for the emergence of a professional middle class and an established working class, at least 30 percent of the economically active urban population in the 1960s and 1970s depended on precarious self-employment and casual jobs. In the 1960s, the concept *culture of poverty*, coined by anthropologist Oscar Lewis, was used to analyze the way of life of street vendors, market carriers, artisans, domestic servants, and casual workers in construction and small-scale industries. This type of culture supposedly created a vicious circle where lack of education, deficient information, and meager opportunities conditioned pessimistic and fatalistic attitudes and perpetuated poverty. In the 1970s, the fashionable concept was *marginality*, which emphasized the radical inability of Third World industrialization to create employment for people displaced (marginalized) by modern technologies from traditional peasant and artisan economies. However, this concept also was criticized because it suggested that the urban poor existed in a realm separated from the modern economy, while many studies showed that modern businesses made profitable use of them through subcontracting and putting-out work, which reduced production costs and investment risks. Concomitantly, the presence of a "reserve army" of self-employed and casual workers allowed government and businesses to keep salaries low. Thus, the term *informal economy* was coined to emphasize the fact that the activities of the urban poor were different from others mainly because they took place without full compliance of government regulations. Yet this situation was not only characteristic of small manufacturing or repair workshops, where the owner used the labor of relatives and casual workers without paying them minimum wages or providing social security and a safe work environment, but also of big employers who were able to bend regulations by paying bribes to authorities. After 1976, the ubiquitous crisis of traditional industries, caused by technological dependence, saturation of the national market, and lack of international competitiveness, has conditioned a progressive informalization of this economic sector.

However, the urban labor market became much more diversified over the last two decades of the twentieth century. The crisis of traditional manufacture coexisted with expanding investment in dynamic industries and services and with a drastic opening of the Mexican economy to international financing and marketing. Aguascalientes, Saltillo, Hermosillo, and Guadalajara are four cities that are changing their occupational structure as they become sites for new electronic, chemical, and automotive plants, and for entrepreneurial providers of strategic services, such as computer and technological information and design, international transport, international brokerage and insurance, commercial and financial planning, and professional and technical training. A new urban sector of experts and technicians, made possible by the rapid expansion of universities and technological institutes since the 1970s, has become highly visible in most Mexican cities. In 1960, less than 4 percent of the economically active population had more than 10 years of formal schooling; in 1980, the proportion rose to 11 percent, and it is expected to be 20 percent in the year 2000. An index of modernization and adaptability, diversification has at the same time deepened the cleavage between the rich and the poor. In 1980, nearly 40 percent of the working population had less than four years of schooling, and they mostly were left out of the modernizing, export-oriented sector. Correspondingly, the crisis has brought new people—women and children—to the labor market. In the 1990s, informal employment (including domestic service) was estimated at 35 percent of the urban labor force.

In the fast-growing cities of the northern border —Tijuana, Mexicali, Nogales, Ciudad Juárez, and Matamoros—both diversification and social inequality are particularly noticeable. These cities are privileged locations for *maquiladoras* (assembly plants), which exert a powerful attraction both for international capital—mainly from the United States, Canada, Japan, and Korea—and unskilled, cheap labor from all over Mexico. Hoping to find a job in such industries or in the multifarious services of the border, or else to cross to U.S. territory in search of dollars, flocks of poor people from large urban centers and small peasant villages arrive daily to set up residence in neighborhoods of unbelievable squalor. But many highly educated people also are to be found along the border, bidding for well-paid managerial and professional jobs in industries and complex commercial, financial, and tourist enterprises; in international banks and consulting business; and in colleges and research centers. In the age of the North American Free Trade Agreement (NAFTA), it is expected that the northern border cities, where after 1980 the rate of job creation was the highest in the country, will challenge the economic supremacy of the cities of central Mexico in the upcoming century.

Urban Landscapes and Urban Social Actors

The governments of the Mexican Revolution favored the introduction of a new type of architecture. Instead of the art nouveau and art deco styles that predominated during the last decade of Porfirio Díaz's dictatorship, the new elites preferred a "Mexican-neocolonial" style for their houses and for the vast public buildings that lodged ministries, schools, and hospitals. A generation of socially oriented architects and civil engineers promoted policies of rationalization, socialization, and integration of the urban space, designing wider avenues, public parks, squares, and multistoried apartment buildings. Since the 1940s, the Mexican state has promoted the type of building known as *multifamiliar,* inspired by Le Corbusier's ideas, which purported the optimization of space by bringing together housing, commerce, and multiple services within a single block. Concomitantly some local governments decreed the freezing of urban rents for low-income tenants (for instance in *vecindades* and old houses). And yet

the state lacked a comprehensive policy of public housing until the creation in 1959 of the Instituto Nacional de la Vivienda (which later came to be called the Instituto Nacional para el Fomento de la Vivienda de los Trabajadores).

Supposedly inspired by rationalization principles but guided mainly by the market, urban planning deepened spatial segregation not only in terms of function but also in terms of class. Whereas the business districts and luxury *fraccionamientos* (urban divisions) boasted shining skyscrapers and carefully designed mansions in which "neocolonial" architecture combined with influences from the Bauhaus school and all sorts of modern trends, the peripheries were populated by the poor. Since the housing actions of the state never have been able to provide for more than 10 or 15 percent of the demand, most of the houses of the poor are built by the people themselves. However, private urban land for low-cost housing grew increasingly scarce. After 1960, private developers and speculators coveted land for the construction of huge malls and modern market squares *(plazas comerciales),* sports clubs, stadiums, and entertainment halls. These facilities revalued the surrounding areas, which became *fraccionamientos* for the middle and upper classes. Thus, the poor increasingly were confined to public land and inalienable *ejidos* (communal village lands) engulfed by urban expansion.

Mass invasions of private urban land seldom had been tolerated by local governments. In contrast, invasions of public and *ejido* land were not met with outright repression, partly because many of these invasions were organized by agents of the dominant political party, with the purpose of gaining popular support, or by *ejido* holders hoping to make good money by selling their land illegally. In the 1970s new legislation was passed that allowed for the creation of urban reserves as well as for the expropriation and sale of *ejidos* when needed for urban expansion. In addition to a national Ministry of Urban Planning, a federal Commission for the Regularization of Land Tenure (Comisión para la Regularización de la Tenencia de la Tierra, or CORETT) was created in order to control the process of expropriation and the legalization of occupied *ejido* land. In practice, CORETT has had the function of legitimizing post factum the occupation of *ejidos* rather than rationalizing urban growth. However, CORETT's interventions often unchained popular protests, either because *ejidatarios* were unhappy with the compensation they got for their land, or because the new settlers complained about the extreme slow pace of expropriation, the methods of distributing plots, and the lack of urban services. Lack of adequate services was also a cause of massive complaints from the dwellers of the cheapest private urban divisions *(fraccionamientos populares)*, who sometimes even refused to pay pending installments for their plots and organized in resistance against eviction. Thus Mexico City, Guadalajara, Monterrey, and Tijuana, among other cities, witnessed a series of mobilizations staged by opposition parties and independent urban organizations. Some of these organizations united in coalitions and constituted social and political actors capable of successfully negotiating specific benefits for their following with municipalities, federal agencies, and developers. Beyond this, urban mobilizations contributed to the awakening of civic consciousness and the systematic critique of the prevailing situation of social inequality and authoritarianism.

In the 1980s and 1990s, a series of catastrophes in Mexico City (the 1985 earthquake and the explosions in 1984 and 1996 at the San Juan gas and oil tanks) and Guadalajara (the explosion of six miles of sewage lines in 1992) highlighted the contradictory, fragile nature of urban development in Mexico. Again, these catastrophes conditioned the emergence of civil organizations with specific urban demands but also the awakening of demands for political participation. In these and many other cities, as the twentieth century came to its close, associations of neighbors, workers, and women, "green" organizations for the defense of the environment, religious groups, and political parties, gradually opened spaces for a democratic society of true citizens, which would face gigantic challenges, among them the challenge of forging a just and safe urban way of life.

See also Earthquake of 1985; Maquiladoras; U.S.-Mexican Border: Border Urbanism.

Select Bibliography

Balán, Jorge, Harley Browning, and Elizabeth Jelin, *Men in a Developing Society.* Austin: University of Texas Press, 1973.

de Oliveira, Orlandina, and Bryan Roberts, "Urban Growth and Urban Social Structure in Latin America, 1930–1990." In *The Cambridge History of Latin America,* edited by Leslie Bethell, vol. 6, part 1. Cambridge: Cambridge University Press, 1994

Gilbert, Alan, editor, *Housing and Land in Urban Mexico.* La Jolla: University of California, San Diego, Center for U.S.-Mexican Studies, 1989.

González de la Rocha, Mercedes, *The Resources of Poverty: Women and Survival in a Mexican City.* Oxford: Blackwell, 1994.

Roberts, Bryan R., *The Making of Citizens. Cities of Peasants Revisited.* London: Arnold, 1995.

—GUILLERMO DE LA PEÑA

U.S.-Mexican Border

This entry includes three articles that discuss the U.S.-Mexican border:

U.S.-Mexican Border: 1821–1910
U.S.-Mexican Border: 1910–96
U.S.-Mexican Border: Border Urbanism

See also Foreign Policy; Mexican American Communities; Migration to the United States; Military; Nationalism; Urbanism and Urbanization

U.S.-Mexican Border: 1821–1910

In addition to physically delineating the boundary between the two countries, the U.S.-Mexican border has played a central role in the national myths of both Mexico and the United States. For each country, the domination of nature and indigenous peoples in this region has been viewed as a testament to the nation's strength, virility, and moral righteousness. Although the struggle over the territory that now comprises a great portion of the western United States brought Mexico and the United States to open conflict in 1846–47, the battle was not between competing world views, but rather a competition between similar rivals. The United States and Mexico shared a desire to populate their frontier, make it economically productive, and either turn the indigenous inhabitants into workers or eliminate them as a threat. The United States ultimately won in the rush to colonize this region, not because of a superior Protestant capitalist culture, but because of its advantageous position in the early-nineteenth-century world economy.

Within 27 years of Mexican independence from Spain in 1821, it lost one-half of its territory to the United States. Although Mexican government policies increasingly alienated Mexicans living in their frontier states, structural differences between the United States and Mexican economies determined the success of the former over the latter. Even before Independence, the geographical difficulties of maintaining communication and trade with other parts of Spanish North America forced frontier Mexicans to establish trade links to the United States and other countries. Although officially part of Mexico, frontier Mexicans maintained very distinct cultural and economic identities. The inability of Mexico to incorporate their frontier states into a national market economy and a national culture ultimately left the region underpopulated, isolated, and susceptible to attack.

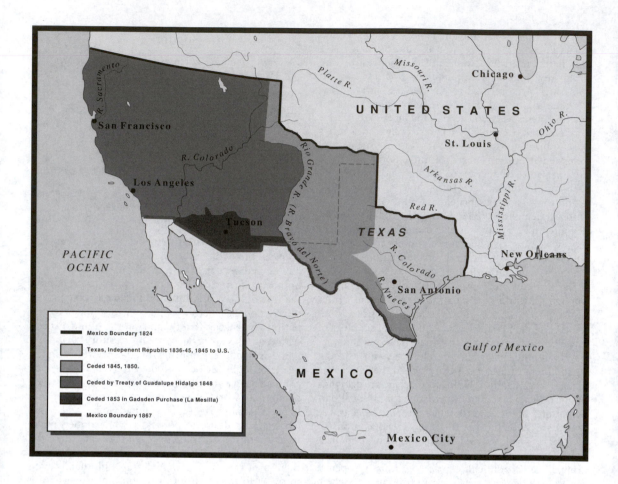

The legend of the map reads:

Mexico Boundary 1824

Texas, Independent Republic 1836-45, 1845 to U.S.

Ceded 1845, 1850.

Ceded by Treaty of Guadalupe Hidalgo 1848

Ceded 1853 in Gadsden Purchase (La Mesilla)

Mexico Boundary 1867

The differing ways in which Mexico and the United States had been inserted into the Atlantic trade economy determined to a large extent the eventual domination of this region by the United States. More than simply a question of having an economic advantage, the conquest of this region was seen as a matter of racial superiority for nations built on the idea of bringing "civilization" to native populations and uninhabited wilderness. The desire to gain economically and defend the nation from rivals cannot in either case be separated from the desire to "civilize the frontier" by either Christianizing indigenous inhabitants, as was the main thrust of the Spanish policy, or removing them altogether from the landscape, as the United States attempted to do.

European imperial competition over the Americas compelled Spain to extend its claims northward, partly to provide a defensive buffer for rich silver mines in northern Mexico and partly to subdue nomadic Indian groups that also threatened the mining regions. By 1821 the British and French no longer

posed a threat, and except for a small Russian foothold in Alta California, the European powers all had been replaced by the United States. Within a few short years the United States thus became the new Mexican nation's most dangerous rival. When Mexico achieved independence from Spain in 1821, the border was that which had been delineated in the Adams-Onís, or Transcontinental, Treaty of 1819. This treaty established the boundary between Spanish North America and the United States as starting in eastern Texas, near the mouth of the Sabine River, and moving northwesterly along the Sabine, Red, and Arkansas Rivers, and then due west to the Pacific at the 42nd parallel.

This legal boundary did not, however, accurately reflect demographic reality, as Anglo-Americans migrated legally and illegally across this border. This flow of Anglo-American immigrants into Texas, beginning before 1821, became a veritable flood in subsequent years. One observer estimated that by mid-1836, just after Texan independence, the population of Texas had surpassed 40,000 inhabitants, with Anglos outnumbering Tejanos 10 to 1. As the Mexican state became more centralist, both Anglo immigrants—who had become Mexican citizens—and their Tejano compatriots began to feel increasingly isolated from the Mexican government. The joining of Coahuila and Texas into one state with its capital in Saltillo several hundred miles away at the southern tip of Coahuila exacerbated sentiments of alienation from the central government. Having to conduct all official government business through a state capital so far away and the passage of a law on April 6, 1830, prohibiting further Anglo-American immigration and slavery in Texas combined to make Anglo-Texans and Tejanos yearn for some form of self-government.

Mexico's president Antonio López de Santa Anna passed reform legislation in 1834 to appease Texans, rescinding the anti-immigration section of the 1830 law and increasing Texan representation in the legislature, but the rift had already set in motion a movement for greater autonomy. Although many Tejanos fought Santa Anna under the banner of federalism, many Anglos already had decided that their goal was the complete independence of Texas from Mexico and even annexation to the United States. The battle at the Alamo, a former mission in San Antonio, on March 6, 1836, although insignificant as a battle, took on great importance as a racially inflected nationalist symbol in both Texas and the United States. "Remember the Alamo" became the battle cry issued by Anglos for over a century to take revenge on Mexicans and Mexican Americans. This mythology ignores that Anglo-Texans and Tejanos fought on the same side at the Alamo, and that the struggle was not a racial or national battle between Mexicans and Anglo-Americans, but an internal Mexican political struggle between federalism and centralism. When Texas declared itself an independent republic on March 2, 1836, the process of Anglo immigration to the region accelerated, ultimately resulting in its annexation to the United States in 1845. Tejanos who had fought for Texan independence along with their Anglo comrades found themselves in an increasingly hostile environment as the Anglo population soared; some Tejanos even abandoned the Texas they had helped create and moved to Mexico.

The other Mexican frontier states of New Mexico and Alta California had, like Texas, grown increasingly isolated from central Mexico and drawn closer to the economic orbit of the United States. The weakening of the two major institutions through which the Mexican government exerted its will on the frontier—the military and the Catholic Church—caused ruptures in the fragile peace that had been constructed. Church missions had played a crucial, if unsuccessful, role in controlling Indian groups by "reducing" them to sedentary lives and putting them to work on missions in agricultural and artisanal production. As the power of the Catholic Church declined and their missions dissolved, settlers in California and Texas gained control of Indians and their production. Indian groups did not succumb to settlers easily, however, and many groups such as the Comanches, the Apaches, the Navajos, and the Utes, some of whom had obtained guns from Anglo traders, were in a better position to conduct raids. As trade shifted from Mexicans to Anglo-Americans, the Spanish policy of buying peace through gifts fell apart, giving way to harsher policies of war and extermination.

The shifting balance of power away from the Catholic Church and toward settlers, together with increasing trade links with the United States, weakened Mexico's fragile hold on these frontier states. Mexico's Byzantine system of tariffs and taxes inherited from Spain made the cost of manufactured goods on the frontier extremely high. Settlers either evaded or underpaid such taxes and increasingly bought goods directly from U.S. traders who made their way into Mexico on routes such as the Santa Fe Trail.

Movements for greater autonomy in the other frontier states followed on the heels of the declaration of Texan independence. Unsuccessful revolts in California in 1836, in New Mexico and Sonora in 1837, and in the Texas lower Rio Grande Valley in 1840 (where the Republic of the Rio Grande existed for a few short months) all demonstrate the dissatisfaction with the central government that existed among Mexicans on the frontier. Although all of these regions within a few years would become part of the United States, these rebellions sought not annexation but to create independent republics or to gain greater autonomy within Mexico.

The political pressures within the United States to gain another slave state, the dictates of Manifest Destiny that propelled the U.S. empire ever westward, and the desires of Anglo-Texans all led to the U.S. annexation of Texas in 1845. Those same forces inspired President James K. Polk to send General Zachary Taylor in 1846 to the contested territory between the Nueces and the Rio Grande Rivers. The provocation had its intended effect: shots were exchanged and the United States declared war on Mexico. Ultimately, the two-pronged U.S. invading force succeeded in sending troops all the way to Mexico City from the port at Veracruz and to the most important city in the north, Monterrey. At the same time, General Stephen Kearny led his Army of the West toward Mexico's other frontier states and occupied Santa Fe, New Mexico. With U.S. troops in their nation's capitol, Mexican officials reluctantly signed the Treaty of Guadalupe Hidalgo on February 2, 1848, thereby ceding the territory comprising present-day Texas, California, New Mexico, Arizona, Utah, Nevada, Wyoming, and a part of Colorado, and establishing the boundary at the Rio Grande, all for the paltry sum of US$15 million. The final piece of the current U.S.-Mexican border fell into place in 1853, when James Gadsden negotiated with a cash-starved Mexican government for the sale of La Mesilla, a piece of land south of the Gila River in Arizona, to allow for the construction of an all-season transcontinental railroad line.

Although settlers on Mexico's northern frontier had experienced dramatic change in the first half of the nineteenth century, nothing could have prepared them for the cataclysmic social, political, and economic transformation that resulted after the U.S. takeover in 1848. Class and racial divisions among the Mexicans as well as distinct regional identities led to a variety of strategies to cope with and in some cases resist the new conditions. Wealthy Mexicans in New Mexico, or Hispanos as they called themselves, maintained their privilege by allying with Anglo bankers, lawyers, merchants, and politicians to form a political boss system known as the Santa Fe Ring. South Texas Mexican elites had a long history of co-operating and even intermarrying with their Anglo-American and European counterparts, and in this way they were able to share political and economic power with newcomer Anglos. In places where the Mexican elite retained some of its power, Anglo-Mexican racial tensions were mitigated, at least until after the first World War when xenophobia reached its apex in the United States. Conflicts in these regions tended to express themselves in terms of class difference or as racial antagonism between white Mexicans and Anglos versus the darker, more Indian Mexicans. However, in areas with only a Mexican laboring class and no Mexican elite, brutal racial hostility reigned.

As well as defining the physical U.S.-Mexican border, the Treaty of Guadalupe Hidalgo and the inconsistent application of its protections for Mexicans exemplify the unequal relationship that characterized Anglo-Mexican relations during the nineteenth and early twentieth centuries. The Treaty gave Mexicans in these territories the opportunity to become U.S. citizens. The U.S. Senate omitted Article 10 of the treaty, which had explicitly guaranteed the

rights of Mexican property holders, but the U.S. government upheld those rights in a Statement of Protocol signed on May 26, 1848. These supposed protections notwithstanding, legal disenfranchisement, the illegal dispossession of Mexicans with the help of paramilitary forces such as the Texas Rangers, and the "voluntary" departure of many Mexicans after the end of the war resulted in the transfer of almost all lands on the border from Mexican to Anglo hands. Complex and costly legal procedures required to obtain definitive U.S. land titles and the market forces that shifted the economy to commercial agriculture and stock-raising resulted in the displacement of many Mexican landowners by the late nineteenth century. In a few notable cases, such as Laredo, Texas, the Mexican elite held onto its land by entering into alliances with Anglo elites and by shifting to commercial agricultural production.

Anglo-Americans seeking land, work, and gold swept westward, especially into California, following quickly on the heels of the U.S. military. Although the push westward by General Kearny has been described by some historians as the "bloodless conquest" because they encountered no immediate overt opposition, Mexicans, particularly those of the lower classes, resisted Anglo domination through banditry, fence-cutting, and occasionally, armed insurrections. In the 1890s, a group calling itself the Gorras Blancas engaged in a war of sabotage in northern New Mexico, cutting fences and tearing up railroad tracks to protest the takeover of their lands by wealthy Hispanos and Anglos. Legends of the mid–nineteenth century Mexican bandits, such as California's Tiburcio Vásquez and Joaquin Murietta, symbolized resistance to Anglo oppression for Mexicans and confirmed Anglo hysteria about barbaric Mexicans.

The Anglo press attempted to portray any armed movement by Mexicans as the work of horse thieves, bandits, and smugglers, but some of these movements had clearly articulated political goals. Juan "Cheno" Cortina, who conducted raids on the Texas-Mexico border from 1859 through the 1870s, issued proclamations decrying the dispossession of Mexican landowners in Texas, which he and his family had suffered. He also noted the unfair treatment received by Mexicans in the Anglo justice system and even conducted one raid to benefit the Union's struggle against the Confederacy. Catarino Garza, who organized an armed revolution from southern Texas to overthrow Mexico's President Porfirio Díaz in 1891, also was characterized by the Anglo press as a bandit and criminal, despite the fact that he fought for liberal principles and the restoration of Mexico's

1857 Constitution. The Texas border continued to be the locus of revolutionary activity into the twentieth century because it provided easy access to guns and enabled would-be revolutionaries to organize their movements out of the reach of Mexican authorities and among a friendly Mexican exile community. This section of the border thus figured prominently in many of Mexico's armed political movements, from Porfirio Díaz's 1876 coup d'état to Francisco Madero's call to rebellion that helped spark the 1910 Revolution.

Beyond its significance as a zone of political ferment since the 1880s, the U.S.-Mexican border has given Mexican agricultural and industrial workers the opportunity to sell their labor in a more lucrative market. Railroad connections from central Mexico to Texas in the 1880s allowed for greater labor mobility and also sparked industrial and agricultural development in both northern Mexico and the southwestern United States. The movement northward in search of economic opportunity that began in the late nineteenth century boomed following the outbreak of the Mexican Revolution in 1910. This influx of Mexican laborers helped to build the railroads, work the mines, and harvest the crops that turned the United States into one of the world's leading industrial powers in the twentieth century.

As well as bringing their labor, Mexicans formed sizable communities throughout the southwestern United States and in cities as far north as Chicago. The close proximity to their home country and the ability to form tight-knit communities north of the border allowed many of these immigrants to maintain cultural ties to Mexico as well as to preserve their native language. By the end of the nineteenth century, Mexicans on the U.S. side of the border began to develop a new consciousness that responded to their condition as an ethnic minority in an Anglo-dominated United States. Although it would not be until the 1920s that Mexican Americans formed national organizations such as the League of United Latin American Citizens (LULAC), by the late nineteenth century Mexicans in the United States already had organized mutual aid societies, fraternal lodges, and even labor unions to gain decent wages, fight racial discrimination, and preserve Mexican culture. Despite racial, economic, and regional divisions, Mexican Americans were united by their common obstacles, primarily Anglo racism in such forms as legal segregation, job discrimination, and physical harassment. It was not until the 1960s, however, that a national Chicano movement emerged in the United States to address the plight of Mexican Americans.

The U.S.-Mexican border always has been a zone of racial and cultural contact, mostly expressed as the aggression of one "race" or "culture" over another, but at moments articulated as an inclusive synthesis of races or cultures. In the early part of the nineteenth century, both the United States and Mexico sought to conquer the frontier by dominating or eliminating the indigenous inhabitants. By the early twentieth century, after continuous wars on autonomous Indian populations in the southwestern United States and northern Mexico, Indians ceased to pose a threat to the advance of "civilization." For whites in the United States, the perceived racial and economic threats posed by Indians were superseded by those posed by Mexicans on the border, along with a whole host of other southern and eastern European immigrants, communists, Jews, and blacks. Meanwhile in Mexico, the Revolution of 1910 glorified an indigenous past but encouraged a mestizo present and future, thereby prophesying an end to the continuation of a living indigenous culture.

By the end of the nineteenth century, the United States had managed to dispossess Mexico of one-half of its territory and had begun to integrate this vast region into a growing national market economy. The ability of the United States to economically link its frontier to the rest of the nation, and thereby to encourage its citizens to colonize the region, allowed the country to succeed where Spain and Mexico had failed. Nonetheless, the U.S.-Mexican border has not been able to halt the increasing Mexicanization of the very region that Mexico ceded in 1848. Ironically, the very market forces that led the United States to dominance are the same ones that have propelled the massive Mexican immigration across the border in the twentieth century. The protection and militarization of the U.S.-Mexican border continue to inspire such heated debate in the United States today because the border played such a central part in the construction of the United States as an imperial world power in the nineteenth century. For most Mexicans, however, the border acts as a constant reminder of their economic and political subordination to their northern neighbor, an obstacle to be overcome, not fortified.

See also Guadalupe Hidalgo, Treaty of; U.S.-Mexican War

Select Bibliography

Bauer, K. Jack, *The Mexican War, 1846–1848.* Lincoln: University of Nebraska Press, 1992.
Brack, Gene M., *Mexico Views Manifest Destiny, 1821–1846: An Essay on the Origins of the Mexican*

War. Albuquerque: University of New Mexico Press, 1975.

Montejano, David, *Anglos and Mexicans in the Making of Texas, 1836–1986.* Austin: University of Texas Press, 1987.

Pletcher, David, *The Diplomacy of Annexation: Texas, Oregon, and the Mexican War.* Columbia: University of Missouri Press, 1973.

Ramírez, José Fernando, *Mexico during the War with the United States,* edited by Walter B. Scholes and translated by Elliot B. Scherr. Columbia: University of Missouri Press, 1950.

Weber, David J., *The Mexican Frontier, 1821–1846.* Albuquerque: University of New Mexico, 1982.

—ELLIOTT YOUNG

U.S.-Mexican Border: 1910–96

In the twentieth century, the U.S.-Mexican border region experienced a dramatic transformation. Economically isolated outposts strung along the international boundary merged into one of the most dynamic regions in the world. A vaguely defined territory in which two sparsely populated frontier areas came into uncertain contact became a region in which two different cultures interacted intensely and ceaselessly. Culturally, the border came both to unite and divide Mexico and the United States and their historical experiences. With the establishment of a North American Free Trade area in 1993, the border region became a major stage in the international economic and geopolitical theater.

The Border Economy

The first 40 years of the twentieth century saw the economy of the border region develop slowly in its traditional sectors: small-scale agriculture, extensive cattle ranching on the vast and arid plains, and mining. In the United States, World War I and the economic boom of the late 1910s led to some stimulation of the economy of the U.S. border states. Large-scale water projects established the U.S. Bureau of Reclamation as one of the main pillars of western economic growth; California and Texas became major producers of petroleum. This boom was followed by bust in the early 1920s, spurring a massive population movement from rural to urban areas. Farmers who remained in agriculture shifted toward more capital-intensive farming to remain competitive. California's Central Valley escaped the economic depression, however, emerging during the 1920s as one of the country's most important centers of cotton, fruit, and vegetable production.

In Mexico the years from 1910 to 1917 were spent in violent revolution as various factions attempted to exert national authority. Peaceful political change was not firmly established until the late 1920s; the threat posed by regional strongmen remained a destabilizing factor until the first official party of the Revolution was organized in 1929. Although the violence of the Revolution did not destroy the Mexican economy of the borderlands, it discouraged long-term investment and reduced confidence in the future. Throughout the 1920s Mexico was led by three men from the border state of Sonora: Plutarco Elías Calles, Álvaro Obregón, and Adolfo de la Huerta. A large portion of federal funds expended in infrastructure projects under these leaders, particularly in roads and irrigation works, went to the border states.

The 1920s saw the first stirrings of economic growth based on tourism along the U.S.-Mexican boundary. Prohibition of alcohol and restrictions on gambling in the United States provided the foundation for Mexican border-town economies based on liquor, gambling, and excitement unavailable north of the border.

The Great Depression and World War II brought momentous and long-lasting changes to the economy of the region. With the New Deal came an enhanced presence of the federal government in the affairs of the western United States, creating a precedent that still stands at the end of the twentieth century. Leaps in federal expenditure during World War II sparked sustained economic growth. The war effort brought the navy to San Diego, San Francisco, and Los Angeles–Long Beach. Other services built large concentrations of men and matériel at Fort Bliss, Fort Ord, Travis Air Force Base, the Presidio in San Francisco, and Camp Pendleton. New industries related to the war effort—particularly shipbuilding and airplane production—created a wartime employment boom and provided a foundation for future growth.

The U.S. government helped turn the border states into a high-tech laboratory during the war, funding research on military technology at advanced western institutions, including the California Institute of Technology, the University of California, and the University of Texas. High-technology industries such as electronics, computers, aviation, and applications of nuclear energy also drew federal investment funds.

The period spanning the 1930s and 1940s also saw important economic changes in the Mexican border states. Beginning with the reforms of Lázaro Cárdenas in the 1930s, and then stimulated by World War II and the Korean War, Mexico embarked on a 50-year period of sustained economic growth. As in the United States, the federal government played a key role in planning and funding infrastructure projects. U.S. involvement in World War II provided two crucial stimuli to Mexico's industrial development: implicit protection from imports and increased wartime demand for Mexican exports. World War II and the Korean War provided rapidly expanding markets for the traditional exports of Mexico's border states in the decade after 1940—particularly minerals, cotton, and oil seeds—fueling a surge in foreign exchange earnings. Free ports, free areas, and free zones were established along the northern border, allowing duty-free imports of consumer goods from the United States.

World War II strongly influenced traditional economic activities in both the United States and Mexico. The war effort increased the demand for the border's extractive products such as petroleum, copper, and uranium, as well as agricultural products such as food, food oils, and cotton. Benefiting from irrigation policies and land reform in the 1920s and 1930s, the agricultural sector saw increased mechanization and greater use of pesticides and herbicides to enhance productivity. As California became the leading agricultural producer in the United States, farmers in northern Mexico turned increasingly to the U.S. market, first for cotton, then for fruits and vegetables.

The war years saw the first large-scale use of immigrant Mexican farm labor in the United States. The Bracero Program (1942–64) provided for the legal, temporary employment of Mexican agricultural laborers in the U.S. border states. Fully half of all the Mexicans contracted as braceros labored in California agriculture.

After the war, the border economy settled into a prolonged period of economic growth. New economic pursuits, stability, and increasing diversity undergirded the pattern of development. The federal governments of both countries continued to facilitate border development through investment in infrastructure.

The nature of regional production changed markedly in the postwar period. By 1990 only 14.3 percent of Mexicans in border states were working in agriculture. In the United States the shift away from primary activities was even more impressive: in 1990 less than 4 percent of the economically active population worked in agriculture.

Manufacturing became the mainstay of the region's economy after 1950. In the U.S. border states, which together outperformed the rest of the U.S. industrial economy after 1970, "clean" industry increasingly led the way. As older U.S. industries—

textiles, automobiles, steel—began to suffer from foreign competition, newer high-tech firms emerged to take their place. These firms kept the U.S. border states relatively strong through the 1970s and 1980s. Mexican industry, in contrast, remained more concentrated in basic industrial sectors such as food processing, mineral refining, and assembly.

The Mexican government established a Border Industrialization Program in 1965 to stimulate the northern regional economies and provide employment for workers displaced by the end of the Bracero Program in 1964. The industrialization program had as its main feature the establishment of *maquilas* (or *maquiladoras*), assembly plants that imported components and raw goods from the United States, assembled them into finished products, and then exported them back to the United States for sale, paying import taxes only on the value added to these goods in Mexico.

The number of *maquila* plants and the number of workers they employed grew rapidly. By 1980 *maquila* production accounted for 25 percent of Mexico's manufactured exports. *Maquilas* produced a wide variety of goods, including electrical and electronic goods, clothing, transportation equipment, furniture, toys, and processed foods. European, Japanese, Taiwanese, and South Korean investors joined U.S. and Mexican entrepreneurs in establishing *maquilas*.

Maquila managers initially preferred employing young, female workers, considering them more efficient than men at assembly tasks requiring manual dexterity and close eye-hand coordination. Struggling to keep unions out of the *maquilas,* they also thought women more docile. One of the unintended consequences of this policy was to encourage the male labor force to look for work on the other side of the border.

The *maquila*-led economic development of the northern Mexican states was much criticized. Critics charged that *maquila* production constituted a U.S. enclave on Mexican soil, that the use of low-wage labor constituted exploitation of Mexican nationals in the interest of the U.S. consumer, and that the *maquilas* brought little long-term benefit to Mexican industrial infrastructure through technology transfer. The impact of assembly plants on the environment and on the health of workers also caused concern. *Maquila* supporters countered these charges, stressing the undeniable benefit of the employment created by the plants.

Some early worries proved unfounded. *Maquilas* did not move on at the earliest sign of opportunity elsewhere (lower wages or less labor agitation); assembly plants expanded their operations and stayed on the border. An increasing number of plants expanded from assembly operations to full-scale manufacturing involving significant wage and technological benefits. And, as Mexico's economic crisis of the 1980s worsened, the number of male *maquila* workers increased significantly. Although women remained in the majority, by 1988 men constituted 41 percent of the *maquila* workforce in Baja California.

Maquila-led development was accompanied by striking growth in high-technology and service industries in areas such as Silicon Valley and Orange County in California, Phoenix in Arizona, and Austin in Texas. The trend also was widespread in Baja California and Chihuahua. Innovation in electronic and computer industries frequently took place in the United States, with assembly being carried out in Mexico. At the same time, a wide range of services—legal, financial, medical, tourist, entertainment, educational, transportation, to name a few—came to employ important portions of the workforce.

Tourism, important to the local economies on both sides of the border, remained a keystone of the border economy after 1950. The number of tourists going to Mexico from U.S. border states grew 24-fold between 1935 and 1970. Tourism was the most important source of foreign exchange in Tijuana and several other Mexican border cities; purchases of goods and services by Mexicans across the border was a major stimulus to the economies of U.S. border cities and states.

The general slowing of the U.S. economy after 1969 affected the border states in different ways. From 1973 to 1981 world oil prices rose dramatically, lifting the Texas economy to new heights. International oil prices began to slide in 1982 and then plummeted in 1986. Texas banks and savings and loans that had invested in real estate during the boom suffered severely. By the late 1980s and early 1990s the Texas bust cycle became evident nationally and then throughout the border states.

The economic coup de grace for the U.S. border states came with the economic and political collapse of the Soviet Union, which led to massive cuts in federal spending. Just as the border states had benefited from federal spending for war and threats of war, they now reeled from the effect of reduced defense expenditures. Unemployment in the four border states went from 5.7 percent in 1989 to 7.2 percent by the end of 1991. Not even California's more diversified economy shielded it from recession; there the rate of unemployment rose to seventh-highest in the nation. In Mexico an economic meltdown triggered by a traumatic devaluation of the peso in December 1994 had a major impact throughout the border economy. Sales plunged, imports slowed, and production declined dramatically; inflation topped 50 percent for 1995.

Life on the Border

In the first 40 years of the century, the population of the border region almost tripled from a total of 6 million in 1900 to approximately 17 million by 1940, an annual rate of 2.5 percent. Most of this growth took place on the U.S. side of the border. Between 1940 and 1980 the pattern was reversed. Growth on the Mexican side was 3.6 percent per year, that on the U.S. side 2.7 percent per year, with yearly growth for the entire region of 2.3 percent. The total population of the 10 U.S. and Mexican border states in 1990 was 65 million. The border region came to claim an ever greater share of the total national populations of both countries. From 6 percent of national total in 1900, the four U.S. border states claimed 21 percent of the national population by 1990. In Mexico the border states accounted for 10 percent of the national population in 1900 and for 16 percent in 1990.

One of the early causes of population growth along the border was the Mexican Revolution of 1910, which between 1910 and 1920 helped push many Mexican migrants north toward the border. Similarly, the U.S. economic boom resulting from preparation for World War I pulled many Americans south with promises of field and factory work. Furthermore, between 1900 and 1930 almost 10 percent of Mexico's population migrated north to the United States. The Great Depression slowed these population movements as hard times fell on the economy of the western United States. Hundreds of thousands of Mexicans lost their jobs in the United States, and tens of thousands returned across the border to Mexico.

The dimensions of the migrant flows to the border grew dramatically after the early 1940s. Large numbers of migrants were pushed out of central Mexico by rapid population growth, declining opportunity in the countryside, and sluggish employment creation in industry. Frequently, they were drawn by significantly greater opportunity in the border region. In the United States, jobs created by World War II drew a great number of people west. In the war years alone, 2 million migrants headed to California, attracted by jobs in industries such as steel, shipbuilding, aircraft manufacture, and services.

Much of the more recent internal migration of Mexicans to the Mexican north can be linked to the development of *maquila* assembly plants along the far northern rim of Mexico. *Maquila* development provided employment at higher wages and with more generous nonwage benefits than available elsewhere in Mexico.

The great migration to the border states was a migration to urban areas. Whereas the Bracero Program led Mexican migrants primarily to rural areas and agricultural occupations, new migrant flows by the 1960s headed for urban jobs in manufacturing, construction, and services. New cities sprouted throughout the borderlands: small towns like Phoenix boomed, and older cities like Los Angeles grew into megalopolises. More than half of all Mexican migrants to California settled in Los Angeles.

Although the U.S. border region already was predominantly an urban society by 1930, 60 years later it was 88 percent urban. Likewise, rapid population growth in the Mexican north was accompanied by the development of urban concentrations in an area previously dominated by small towns and villages. Chihuahua and Hermosillo grew rapidly as they expanded beyond traditional rural economic pursuits into industry and services. By 1990, 85 percent of the population of the Mexican border states lived in urban areas, as contrasted with 43 percent in 1940. The extraordinary postwar growth of two Mexican cities fronting California—Tijuana and Mexicali—led to statehood in 1952 and 1974 for Baja California Norte and Baja California Sur.

By midcentury, a pattern of twin cities had emerged all along the international boundary from Tijuana–San Diego on the Pacific to Matamoros–Brownsville on the Gulf coast. Each twin-city pair shared some growth characteristics and differed in others. San Diego grew with the military bases while Tijuana grew apace as a tourist center not only for military personnel but also for southern Californians attracted initially by the gambling and nightlife. Ciudad Juárez and El Paso grew together as an important commercial hub straddling the lines of communication from northern Mexico to the midwestern United States, a development that made it easy for Ciudad Juárez to become the most important center of the *maquila* industry in the 1970s and 1980s.

The twin-city pairs developed complex interdependencies. Mexican consumers on both sides of the border became an important market for North American businesses. Mexican laborers crossed daily to work in U.S. hotels, restaurants, and private homes. In a reverse flow, thousands of U.S. residents crossed the border to shop, eat, and take advantage of low prices for services such as dental hygiene, automotive repair, and medical consultations. By the mid-1980s, two-way traffic crossing the border, most of it commuters, tourists, and shoppers, exceeded 175 million.

Many disparities exist between border cities. A view from the air from any point over the international boundary reveals a sprawling, partly unpaved Mexican city with thousands of temporary shacks built by recent settlers. Rapid growth outpaced border communities' ability to provide urban services, housing, and social programs to incorporate new migrants. On the U.S. side, smaller urban settlements are characterized by well-established public services and transportation facilities. Underneath the pattern of asymmetry between twin cities, there exist significant difference in wages and rates of unemployment.

The extremely rapid growth of Mexican border cities after 1950 brought with it pressing social problems. In Tijuana the average number of inhabitants in individual housing units increased by one-third between 1960 and the mid-1980s. Most Mexican migrants to Tijuana spent years living in homemade shelters before their neighborhoods were reached by electricity, potable water, or sewage lines.

The lack of basic services created a large public health problem, with waterborne diseases a leading cause of death on the border, particularly among infants. Intestinal infections, respiratory problems, and nutritional deficiencies, which topped the list in Mexican border states, did not appear among the principal causes of death across the border in the United States. The rate of death from all causes was much higher in Mexican border states than in U.S. border states, producing a difference in average life expectancy of five years between residents of the Mexican and U.S. border states.

As Mexico's border states matured socially and economically, they began to demand a greater role in regional and national politics. In the 1980s the conservative Partido de Acción Nacional (PAN, or National Action Party) claimed several major election victories, particularly in Chihuahua, where it won sharply contested offices in Ciudad Juárez in 1983. In 1989 the border area witnessed the first non-PRI (Partido Revolucionario Institucional or Institutional Revolutionary Party) candidate ever to win a gubernatorial election in Mexico when PAN's Ernesto Ruffo, former mayor of Ensenada, became the governor of Baja California Norte. In 1992 another PAN candidate, Francisco Barrio, took the statehouse in Chihuahua. The PAN retained the governorship of Baja California in 1995.

Reflecting social consolidation and political maturity, the culture of the border region grew rich and varied. The border itself, as both barrier and unifying factor, figured prominently in regional cultural expression. Forms of cultural expression ranged from popular music, film, and graffiti to poetry and painting; they shared a complex interchange among popular tradition, the conventions of "high" art, and the influence of the national cultures of Mexico and the United States.

Popular music has perhaps the longest tradition on the border. After World War II, the *corrido,* dating from the mid–nineteenth century, saw a change in its subject matter that reflected the evolving social milieu of the border states: the Mexican avenger was transformed into a helpless victim. In the 1960s, the Chicano movement adopted the *corrido* as a strong mobilizing force, replacing the victim figure with a hero who actively resisted. In the 1980s, popular music of the border made its way into the U.S. cultural mainstream as Los Angeles–based musicians, such as Linda Rondstadt and Los Lobos, found national audiences for explorations of their border roots.

Mural painting, like music a staple of the Mexican artistic tradition, found dramatic expression in the border states during the postwar period. The activism of the Chicano movement inspired many community mural projects such as those in San Diego. Film treatments of border life reached a mass audience by combining popular and high-art expressions. Mexico produced over 200 border films in the postwar period. North American studios also mounted large-scale productions, while in both Mexico and the United States filmmakers working outside the major studios produced some of the most accurate and moving portrayals of border life.

Literature of the border region experienced an exuberant flowering. Many Mexican American writers drew upon the border for both setting and inspiration. On the Mexican side of the border an outpouring of anthologies, short-story collections, poetry, plays, and essays made border literature one of the most dynamic of Mexico's regional expressions. The border region also produced unique currents in critical and feminist theory focusing on the interpretation of works of art produced in the multiethnic, multicultural border states.

U.S.-Mexican Relations at the Border

The border has engendered serious tensions between Mexico and the United States. Beginning in the late nineteenth century, conflict repeatedly came to a head over the shifting of the Rio Grande–Río Bravo boundary. Lost to the United States in the nineteenth century, the Chamizal territory finally was returned to Mexico in 1963 as U.S.-Mexican relations reached a high point.

The flows of the Colorado River became the topic of lasting conflict between the two countries in the 1940s and 1950s as infrastructure investment in agricultural production in both countries boomed. The conflict was resolved finally in 1973 with agreements on the amount of water that would be available to the Mexican side of the border and acceptable salinity levels of the water delivered.

Environmental degradation followed rapid industrialization and population growth in the border region and came to constitute a major challenge for border policy makers. Water pollution led to health threats on both sides of the border. Groundwater quality deteriorated in some areas because of agricultural runoff laden with salts and chemical residues, effluent from leaking industrial storage tanks, and seepage from solid waste disposal sites. Foul air was generated by automobiles, smelting plants and other businesses, and agriculture (burning fields and dust from overtilled soil). More than half of all *maquilas* had toxic-discharge problems. The dumping of hazardous waste and toxic substances south of the border blurred the relevance of the international boundary.

Policy makers were forced by the pressing nature of environmental problems and their political volatility to take action. The construction in 1993 of a long-awaited binational waste treatment plant at the San Diego–Tijuana border constituted an important milestone in transboundary cooperation for environmental planning. In 1992 Presidents George Bush and Carlos Salinas de Gortari formulated an Integrated Environmental Plan for the entire U.S.-Mexican border as part of the proposed North American Free Trade Agreement (NAFTA).

Drug trafficking emerged as a major border problem in U.S.-Mexican relations in the 1980s. Mexican border states served as conduits for large portions of the heroin, cocaine, and marijuana sold in the United States. Mexico argued that its drug interdiction programs were extensive, and that demand in the U.S. market represented the principal stimulant to drug trafficking.

Such bilateral issues have certain traits in common. The nature of the border—long, porous, unmarked, and unguarded for most of its length—makes it difficult to formulate and implement policy. The complex economic and social development of the region, and shifting economic and social borders, preclude simple solutions. Isolation from the centers of national political power makes the resolution of problems in the border region difficult, and residents of the border region feel themselves neglected and misunderstood by federal officials. But the border region attracted increasing attention in the national capitals in the 1980s: an Office of Border Affairs was created in the U.S. Department of State, and groups in the U.S. Congress met regularly to discuss border issues. In Mexico, El Colegio de la Frontera Norte (COLEF) was founded with government support as the northern border's graduate–level think tank. U.S. and Mexican leaders at the highest levels have chosen the U.S.-Mexican border as a site of key meetings and acts of state. Both Ronald Reagan and George Bush met with their Mexican counterparts at the border to discuss issues of international and regional significance. President Bill Clinton's first official meeting with a foreign leader after his election in 1992 was with President Salinas in San Antonio, Texas.

Mechanisms have been developing since the 1950s for dealing with border problems. At many points along the border local officials have created bilateral agreement on such issues as pollution, tourism, transportation, and industrialization. Governors of the 10 border states meet regularly, and over time they have come to discuss substantive matters of concern to inhabitants of the border region. These sorts of regional political processes may provide the best model for managing the bilateral relationship as it is expressed along the border into the twenty-first century.

See also Drug Trade; Maquiladoras

Select Bibliography

Fernández-Kelly, Patricia, *For We Are Sold, I and My People: Women and Industry in Mexico's Frontier*. Albany: State University of New York Press, 1983.

Hansen, Niles, *The Border Economy: Regional Development in the Southwest*. Austin: University of Texas Press, 1981.

Lorey, David E., *United States-Mexico Border Statistics since 1900: 1990 Update*. Los Angeles: UCLA Latin American Center Publications, 1994.

Martínez, Oscar J., *Troublesome Border*. Tucson: University of Arizona Press, 1988.

Ross, Stanley R., editor, *Views across the Border: The United States and Mexico*. Albuquerque: University of New Mexico Press, 1978.

Sklair, Leslie, *Assembling for Development: The Maquila Industry in Mexico and the United States*. La Jolla: Center for U.S.-Mexican Studies, University of California, San Diego, 1993.

—DAVID E. LOREY

U.S.-Mexican Border: Border Urbanism

The phrase "border urbanism" has been an oxymoron for Mexico until recently. Only since 1950 has the northern border territory become one of Mexico's most urbanized regions, with more than 5 million people residing in cities and towns lying along the boundary shared with the United States. For much of the last 150 years, the borderlands region was largely rural in character and sparsely populated. Fifty years ago, there were less than 200,000 people living along the nearly 2,000-mile-long frontier separating the two nations. During the nineteenth century, Mexico's northern border remained isolated and distant from the heartland of urban and industrial life in Mexico, which lie in the valleys etched into the nation's great *meseta central* (central plateau) some 1,000 to 1,500 miles to the south.

Settlement of Mexico's northern frontier occurred in three relatively distinct waves. The first wave actually preceded the formation of the international political boundary. As early as the seventeenth and eighteenth centuries, Spain's colonization of New Spain (Mexico) concentrated in the aforementioned central plateau region, but expeditions in search of minerals and other natural wealth dispersed population and settlements in all directions, including the provinces to the north. Missions, presidios (forts), and pueblos (administrative towns) all were established in the northern territories, near the present-day international border. The most important northern frontier outpost was established at Paso del Norte (modern-day Ciudad Juárez) in 1659; others included Matamoros (1700) and Reynosa (1749).

When the present-day Mexican-U.S. border was created, following the 1848 Treaty of Guadalupe Hidalgo that ended territorial conflict between the two nations, the second period of border urban growth unfolded. Most of the settlements organized at this time functioned as military posts or customs checkpoints along the newly formed international boundary. The best known towns of the period included Tijuana and Nuevo Laredo (both formed in 1848) and Piedras Negras (1849). Several additional "gateways" were formed over the next three decades: Ciudad Acuña (1877), Nogales (1882), and Agua Prieta (1899). A third and final wave of settlements emerged in the early twentieth century. As U.S. capital began to flow south of the border, infrastructure for large-scale agriculture led to the formation of new settlements near the frontier. Examples include Mexicali (1903), San Luis Colorado (1917), and Tecate (1918).

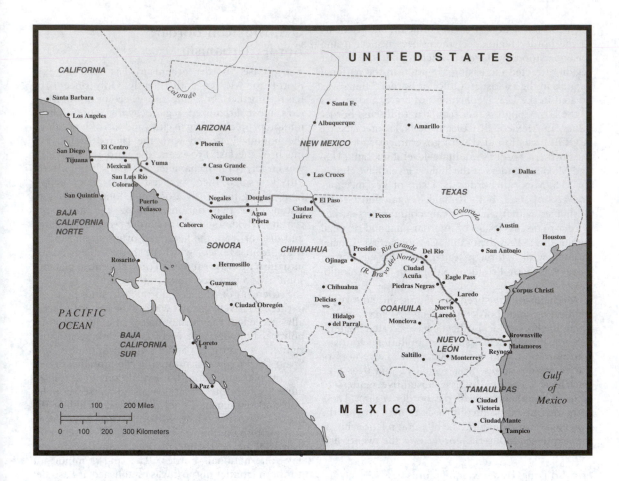

Regional Dynamics: Economic Development and Migration

Two forces mediated the growth of cities in northern Mexico's border zone: the economic development of the neighboring southwestern United States in the period of the late nineteenth and early twentieth century, and the evolution of a geographic strategy of migration dependent upon the border zone as a means to enter the United States. Northern Mexico discovered the economic potential of trade with the United States as early as the 1860s when, during the Civil War, arms were exchanged between Monterrey entrepreneurs and the Confederate States of America, whose coastal shipping lanes were under blockade by the Union navy. Over the next three decades, Mexico began to construct a railroad connection between Mexico City and the northern border. In the 1880s, rail lines were completed between Mexico City and two border points—Laredo and El Paso. President Porfirio Díaz championed foreign investment as part of a program of economic growth for Mexico; the northern border region benefited, as the mining, oil, and agriculture sectors expanded through American capital.

The second half of the nineteenth century was a period of expansion for the economy of the southwestern United States, most notably in the areas of agriculture, mining, manufacturing, and defense. The emergence of important population growth nodes both in the late nineteenth century and early twentieth century, in places like Phoenix, Albuquerque, and El Paso, is evidence of the southwest's enormous transformation in this era. These growing populations would later serve as targets for the service economy of northern Mexico's border towns.

Before that, the expansion of the southwest economy had a more immediate impact on Mexico: it stimulated intensive migration from Mexico's interior to the northern border region, followed by movement to specific geographic zones of high labor demand north of the border. Irrigation projects and massive water projects—like the Roosevelt Dam near Phoenix and the Coolidge Dam in the Gila River valley—opened land for agriculture, but also converted Mexican border cities like Mexicali, Reynosa, Matamoros, and Ciudad Juárez into giant catchments or "sending areas" for seasonal Mexican labor. Equally, the railroads, copper mines, and coal fields of the southwestern United States from the 1880s through the 1920s, generated large Mexican labor migration streams across the border. For example, by 1929 Mexicans accounted for 59.9 percent of the workforce in the nine largest rail companies in the southwestern United States.

Mexican immigration, therefore, became synonymous with southwestern U.S. economic development in the period of the late nineteenth and early twentieth centuries. It is during that period, in fact, that one of the most important elements of Mexico's border urbanism took shape: the emergence of the border towns as systemic Mexican labor migration deployment areas, as well as enclaves for return migrants. One scholar has called this the "springboard-receptacle" function. It is significant that the border towns became, in this period of economic growth, the staging centers for labor migration; much of their twentieth-century character has been built upon this early legacy of cross-border dependency. Border towns became entangled in the shifting fate of the U.S. economy. Although Mexicans had been largely untouched by the first U.S. immigration quotas of 1917, during the 1930s, they were hit hard by the Great Depression. Nearly one-half million Mexican migrants were deported from the United States back to the border towns, which already were suffering from the loss of U.S. consumer spending.

The era of the Bracero Program (1942–64) did more to solidify the role of border towns in the larger migration process than any previous period. When the United States and Mexico established the Emergency Farm Labor Program, or Bracero Program, in 1942, it formalized and accelerated a cross-border labor supply phenomenon that had been building over some five decades. More than 4.6 million labor contracts were issued between 1942 and 1964. During the 22–year period, several million Mexicans permanently settled in the United States, and hundreds of thousands settled in Mexican border towns. Perhaps more significantly, the Bracero Program institutionalized illegal or undocumented Mexican immigration. As U.S. growers began to hire Mexican workers without papers, the Mexicans learned that work in the United States could be found outside the formalities of contract labor. Illegal crossings thus

began to increase. The era of undocumented Mexican immigration had begun. From 1960 to the present, border cities became way stations from which migrants would plan their journeys into the United States. Illegal immigration creates jobs along the border for smugglers and other service providers. In some border towns, like Tijuana and Ciudad Juárez, entire neighborhoods have been built by people who originally were immigrants to the United States.

The termination of the Bracero Program in 1964 was foreshadowed by Operation Wetback (1953–56), a massive U.S. federal government initiative aimed at halting illegal Mexican immigration. More than 1 million Mexicans were deported in the mid-1950s, and many of these were left in Mexican border towns. Not surprisingly, there was a population boom along the northern Mexican border, a trend that, as other economic sectors developed in the region, would continue over the next three decades.

In the last 25 years, undocumented migration has accelerated, and to a great extent it continues to define the modern Mexican border cities. During the 1970s and 1980s, the illegal transshipment of migrants became a lucrative business, with "coyotes" (smugglers) charging as much as US$500 to bring one migrant across the border and deliver them to a "safe house." Illegal immigration also defines the border cities as physical places. The biggest U.S. border cities use fences to try to create a first barrier against illegal entry, but frequently the fences are riddled with holes, or simply torn down. The U.S. border patrol estimates that it apprehends perhaps one of three illegal border crossers or when more sophisticated technology (such as infrared night sensors) is used, perhaps one out of two. Still, more than 1 million people cross the border illegally each year (some are repeat crossers); the largest share of illegal crossings occur in the border cities.

There does not appear to be evidence that illegal border crossings will slow anytime soon. The 1986 Immigration Reform and Control Act (IRCA) passed by the U.S. Congress was supposed to control undocumented migration through four changes: first, the granting of amnesty to all immigrants living continuously in the United States since 1982; second, expansion of the Border Patrol force; third, the issuing of temporary permits to "seasonal agricultural workers" (SAW); and fourth, the enactment of employer sanction laws, which penalize U.S. employers who knowingly hire illegal foreign workers. The sanction laws generated a new cottage industry—the production of phony work documents. Mexico's border residents always have found creative ways to survive in the unique socioeconomic border milieu; once again, they skirted the best-laid plans of IRCA, and through the mid-1990s, undocumented border crossings had not reduced substantially been.

Border Urbanism as a Transfrontier Process: Trade, Tourism, Twin Plants

Early in the twentieth century, scholars believed that international boundaries distorted the spatial behavior of markets, thus creating serious problems for marketing. These scholars could not have foreseen the degree to which cross-border trade became a cornerstone of the economy in Mexico's northern border cities, and subsequently the defining feature in the evolution of transfrontier cities. As early as 1885, under President Porfirio Díaz, the *zona libre* (free zone) program was established to allow duty-free movement of goods into a corridor 12 miles wide along the northern frontier. This program gave Mexican merchants along the border a competitive edge over their northern neighbors in pricing imported goods. The border cities established themselves as marketing centers for imported retail goods (and later for commercial services) for consumers in the United States. The first of many cross-border functional ties was in place. Although the free-zone program was abolished in 1905, under severe pressure from U.S. merchant associations, an economic strategy for Mexico—tapping the U.S. consumer market—had been put in place, and it would resurface throughout the twentieth century. By the 1930s, a limited version of the free zone program once again was constructed. In the 1990s this process reached its logical summit with the North American Free Trade Agreement (NAFTA), which will allow Mexico previously unheard-of access to the lucrative U.S. consumer market.

During the middle of the twentieth century, as the population increased in cities north of the border (San Antonio, El Paso, Dallas, Houston, Phoenix, Tucson, Albuquerque, San Diego, Los Angeles, etc.), the Mexican government recognized that transboundary commerce would be essential to the economic survival of the northern borderlands. By the 1960s, former bracero workers were being repatriated back to Mexico, and many found themselves unemployed in the border towns. In 1961, the Mexican government introduced the Programa Nacional Fronterizo (PRONAF, or National Border Program), designed to invigorate the economy of border towns through expansion of agriculture and industry, as well as physical renovation and beautification. The Mexican government rightly surmised that consumers spend more when the physical setting is pleasing

to them. For too long the border towns had been stereotyped as honky tonk, ramshackle centers of corruption, prostitution, and vice. To change that, most of the large cities were subject to massive clean-up campaigns, especially in the tourist zones.

During the 1970s, commercial development policies concentrated on retaining income within Mexico and building spaces for retail consumers, particularly shopping malls. To achieve the former, the *articulos ganchos* (hook items) program was enacted. The hook item strategy revolved around duty-free import of consumer goods within the original "free zones" of the border. These goods would then be sold to Mexicans as a way of keeping expenditures within Mexico. Even if many of these products were bought wholesale in the United States, retail spending (and thus Mexican income) would remain within Mexico. Meanwhile, Mexican and U.S. capital was recruited for the building of shopping centers and regional malls. The program started slowly but quickened considerably during the real estate boom of the 1980s. While peso devaluations in 1982 and in the 1990s have hurt the economy of border towns, NAFTA has the potential to significantly energize the border cities, especially in the areas of retail trade and professional services.

One specific form of cross-border consumption that emerged along the border early in this century was tourism. When the U.S. Congress passed laws in 1920 prohibiting the sale and consumption of alcohol, the northern Mexican border towns soon moved to fill this niche for the consumer market north of the border. As U.S. border region dwellers became more mobile owing to advances in mass transit and automobile travel, Mexico's border towns converted themselves into service centers for the consumption of "leisure" activities (gambling, health spas and resorts, alcohol consumption, prostitution, etc.). Much of the early tourism infrastructure—roads, bridges, hotels, restaurants, wine and beer factories, casinos —was built with U.S. capital. The secondary effects were considerable, particularly in the areas of new housing and neighborhoods for workers. New commercial areas were built; some became legendary "red light districts" or what some scholars have called *zonas de tolerancia*.

Tourism development acquired new meaning during the administration of President Carlos Salinas de Gortari (1988–94). Like the Porfirio Díaz regime a century earlier, the Salinas administration saw foreign investment as central to Mexico's transformation from a less developed to a modern industrialized nation. The northern border towns had not significantly upgraded their tourism infrastructure in several decades. Salinas's government changed two laws that facilitated the flow of U.S. capital into the border towns: first, previous controls on foreign ownership of business ventures in the tourism sector were relaxed, and second, Americans and other foreigners wanting to purchase land along the coast through lease arrangements saw their lease periods doubled from 30 to 60 years. Riding the wave of the U.S. real estate boom during the 1980s, the first years of the Salinas administration were marked by a crescendo of tourism and commercial building along the border.

The most dynamic economic force in late-twentieth-century transborder urban society has been the "twin plant," or *maquiladora* (assembly plant) sector. One plank in the PRONAF border development strategy was to reduce unemployment by promoting industrial growth. In 1965, the Border Industrial Program (BIP) was created. It was built upon the emerging concept of "off shore" production, whereby U.S. manufacturers moved the assembly stage of the production process to cheap labor zones in places like Hong Kong or Taiwan. The BIP strategy assumed American factories might relocate their labor-intensive assembly operations to the Mexican border. The "twin plant" *maquiladora* concept was built upon the notion that a U.S. factory on one side of the border would produce the parts for manufacturing an industrial commodity (for example, a television set), which then would be shipped south to the assembly plant in Mexico. By agreement, no duties would be paid on the finished products shipped out of Mexico, except on the value added to the original parts. Also, all finished products would be distributed to markets outside of Mexico.

The BIP's impact on Mexican border cities has been gargantuan in the period from 1970 to 1995. In 1970, there were 160 *maquiladoras* in Mexico, employing around 20,000 workers. About 90 percent of these plants were located in border cities. Some 25 years later, there were an estimated 2,000 assembly plants in Mexico, employing about one-half million workers and producing an added value estimated at roughly US$3 billion dollars. About 85 percent of all assembly plants in Mexico remain in the border cities. They have been an important part of the real estate and development boom of the last two decades, manifest in new physical infrastructure such as roads, industrial parks, housing projects; multiplier effects on related economic sectors such as machinery repair, finance, real estate, and services; and additional income earned by workers or through rent collected on the leasing of factory space.

Transfrontier Urban Space

By the 1990s, it is no longer accurate to view Mexico's border cities as separate from their counterpart—U.S. settlements north of the border. So entangled are their economies and social networks that it is appropriate to speak of a "transfrontier metropolis," a single cross-border functional living space within which common daily activity systems (work, shopping, school, and social trips) and environmental features (air sheds, water basins) are shared by U.S. and Mexican urban dwellers. Examples along the frontier (moving from east to west) include: Matamoros-Brownsville; Reynosa-McAllen; Laredo-Nuevo Laredo; Ciudad Juárez-El Paso; Nogales-Nogales; San Luis Colorado-Yuma; Mexicali-Calexico; and Tijuana-San Diego. The transfrontier metropolis is the result of more than a century of symbiotic connections between "twin cities" straddling the frontier.

The border cities exist as part of a transboundary ecosystem, in which the elements of the natural environment—air, water, land—are shared across the humanly constructed international boundary. Environmental policy—air pollution control, water quality management, the administration of water supply, and regulation of toxic waste dumping—must be managed cooperatively across the border. For Mexico and the United States, cooperative management of ecology in the urbanized areas along the border has a history of being an ad-hoc and not terribly efficient process. Serious environmental problems plague the transfrontier cities: these include toxic waste dumping by *maquiladoras*, air pollution, sewage contamination of watersheds, and conflicts over water supply. When NAFTA crystallized in the 1990s, the two nations agreed that the environmental problems of the transborder urbanized regions must be given greater priority in the binational agenda. National and international entities are being formed to define the parameters of the problems. This represents one of the great challenges in Mexico–United States relations for the turn of the century.

The transfrontier metropolis of the Mexican-U.S. border is receiving greater attention from scholars, planners, and policy makers because it is a unique kind of city: a city of two nations and two cultures that is slowly being transformed into a single living space. Urban and environmental planning decisions are elevated to the level of foreign policy making. Daily urban activity systems transcend the border with increasing regularity. Mexican consumers, for example, cross the border frequently either with a border resident card (*mica fronteriza*) or with a legal resident alien card, also known as a "green card." These consumers do not act like outside visitors when they reach their destination *al otro lado* (on the other side of the border). Studies show that Mexican border consumers have considerable knowledge about markets north of the border. For example, research in southern California has shown that Mexican consumers make logical trade-offs between distance traveled to purchase goods, and the price and the importance of the good. Such behavior only comes with intimate knowledge of the city. Another study of border commuters demonstrated that journeys to work have become routinely transborder in nature, with an estimated 250,000 Mexicans crossing the border to commute to work in the United States legally each day. One must also mention the importance of cross-border linkages inherent in the *maquila* program. Assembly plants generate companion facilities on the U.S. side in the form of warehouses, trucking yards, and administrative operations. These plants also create a pool of Mexican workers that tends to cross the border to consumers in the United States. A more negative example of cross-border symbiosis in these emerging metropolises is the activities of narcotics smugglers and others who use the border for illegal transactions. For smuggling, the urbanized border offers an ideal setting. It is crowded with activities that provide cover for smugglers. The border also has a well-entrenched history of smuggling; one might argue that a subculture of smuggling is still in place here. There are enough unemployed and underemployed residents to provide an easy environment in which to recruit "mules" to carry illegal contraband across the border.

Architecture, Art, and the Cultural Landscape

One unfortunate by-product of any unique regional phenomenon such as border urbanism is that those outside the region may seek simplistic rationales or stereotypes as a way of dismissing the region, especially if they are threatened by it. This has been the fate of the Mexican border and its cities to a great extent. In a nation as centralized and politically top-heavy as Mexico, where power, wealth, and prestige traditionally have remained concentrated in the geographic heartland—centered around Mexico City—the growth of the borderlands clearly poses a threat to the social and geographic hierarchy that has been in place for several centuries. The Mexican government supported the growth of the border cities as a way of expanding the national economy. Yet, a regional rivalry between the center of government power, Mexico City, and the new northern border cities is very much in place today.

An excellent illustration of this territorial conflict can be found in the emerging field of border art. Mexican artists in the northern border region suffer two misunderstandings about their work. First, they are viewed by Mexicans as being on the periphery, outside the centers of prestige in art and creativity (Mexico City). The best and most elegant galleries and the high-paying art dealers are all centralized in and around Mexico City. To be a border artist is to be viewed as marginal. Second, Mexican border artists often are understood stereotypically, both in Mexico and the United States, as being part of the Chicano arts, a U.S.-based movement whose iconography draws from nationalism, muralism, and the Mexican American barrio. In fact, most Mexican border artists do not operate within these parameters.

If there has been any cross-border synergy among northern Mexican artists and their counterparts in the United States, it has occurred on two levels: first, as a way of incorporating new ideas and techniques in visual arts, for example, in the use of technology; second as a form of political protest. Northern Mexican artists have been influenced by their southwestern U.S. counterparts working in avant-garde media, for example in performance art incorporating film, video, and other multimedia forms. Artists also have united across the border to protest racism, exploitation, and human rights violations. In 1984, a cross-border art coalition called the Border Arts Workshop/Taller de Arte Fronterizo was formed in the California–Baja California region. The workshop became a social movement that employed art, particularly performance, environmental, and public art, to expose and analyze different forms of regional stereotyping, racism, or anti-immigrant behavior.

There has been considerable stereotyping of both the cultural landscapes and the formal architecture of the border. Before 1970, as noted earlier, many viewed the border as a landscape of urban neglect and decay meshed with images of immorality. Border towns were seen as either ticky-tacky, tasteless, and unimaginative places, or simply corrupt and sleazy. In fact, if one examines both the architecture and vernacular landscapes, a far more complex and fascinating border cultural landscape emerges.

Central to the character of most northern Mexican border towns are the pedestrian-scale tourist districts designed in the 1920s, during the tourism boom along the border associated with the "roaring twenties." The tourism districts evoke a carnival-like, playful, and highly colorful, if eclectic, landscape. The architecture ranges from art deco, streamline moderne, Spanish colonial or Mission Revival, to international style and postmodern. The dominant land uses are commercial, typically curio shops in bright colors, bars with wild neon signs, and back-alley bazaars or arcades, sometimes sunken below ground level. These designs, contrary to the common stereotype of an urban society out of control, are quite deliberately made to be artificial—a sort of Disneyland Mexican exotica for tourists. Such designs may stem from Mexicans' ability to use caricature and irony as a way of poking fun at themselves, so vividly illustrated by the post-Revolutionary muralists. In the end, the tourist districts of Mexico's border cities are quite unpretentiously honky tonk and carefree. Mexican architects on the border speak openly of *la arquitectura del chiste* (the architecture of the joke) in the tourism zone. Such contrived places have been termed by one landscape scholar "other directed," since they are designed for consumption by outsiders. Few places in the world are so meticulously "other directed" as the tourism zones of Mexican border cities.

Near the tourism zones lies another urban district that remains part of the folklore of the northern border towns: the "red light" district, also called the *zona de tolerancia*, or zone of tolerance. Originally conceived as spaces for alcohol consumption and prostitution in the 1920s, these districts survived by redefining themselves over time. During World War II, they became leisure service areas for Americans in the Armed Forces, with strip tease clubs, alcohol, and prostitutes; after 1950, they survived as a curiosity, as much museums as actual zones of prostitution. The original character of these zones—the small nightclubs with exotic signs, neon lighting, hint of sexual transgression—has been maintained, although the neighborhoods have slid into physical decline and taken on the look of skid row districts in the United States. In some cities, the red light districts remain as commercial zones appended to the downtown business district; in others, they have been removed from the downtown and relocated to compounds, or "boys towns," in hidden, isolated locations.

By contrast with the tourism and red light districts, there are other distinctly Mexican landscapes to be found in the border cities. In the construction of commercial spaces, especially the traditional downtown, the commercial streetscapes display the density and spontaneous character of any Mexican city. Public space is ample—on the pedestrian streets and in the ubiquitous *plaza-jardin* (plaza garden) that is so embedded in Mexican tradition. These central plazas anchor the downtown in the tradition of colonial Mexican urban design. If one looks at residential landscapes, there are distinct regional prototypes, such as the adobe or brick blockhouse. Typical Mexican influences on border housescapes include the use of fences and walls to enclose patios and courtyards and the use of exotic, bright colors on the house exterior.

There are also numerous examples of hybridization in the cultural landscapes of the border towns, where U.S. styles and features are combined with Mexican influences to create unique transborder cultural landscapes. In a nation that historically used stone as its principal building material (or reinforced concrete in the modern era), one sees a growing Mexican border cityscape dominated by high-tech, glass-and-steel constructions. These appear in the form of elegant shopping malls, office buildings, banks, or assembly plants (although the latter just as frequently appear as bland, characterless warehouses north). Houses and condominiums copy from styles north of the border. Mexican architects complain that in higher density cities, Mexicans now want the suburban-style houses with dimensions similar to their northern counterparts.

Of course, it is also true that Mexican landscapes spill north across the border into the United States. Professionally, Mexican architects are now gaining commissions to design buildings and urban spaces on the U.S. side of the border. Mission-style architecture dates to the early decades of this century and finds favor in cities such as Tucson, El Paso, and San Diego. Meanwhile, Mexican immigrant barrios along the southwestern U.S. border are shaped by Mexican culture. This is visible in the proliferation of murals, the filling of public places with street vendors, and the ways in which houses and commercial buildings are brightly decorated.

If the old notions of nation-state are fading around the globe, the results are particularly apparent on Mexico's northern frontier. Mexican border residents are influenced by the images of their wealthier American neighbors. In a recent survey, a Mexico City professor found that the images of the city that were most desirable to Mexicans along the border were those associated with the United States —the tourist strip, parabolic antennas, the ruins of the 1920s international-style resorts, or the trails where migrants pass into the United States. Border urbanism, like so many processes of the late twentieth century, has become linked to the global system.

See also Maquiladoras; Tourism

Select Bibliography

Arreola, Daniel D., and James R. Curtis, *The Mexican Border Cities: Landscape Anatomy and Place Personality*. Tucson: University of Arizona Press, 1993.

Bath, C. Richard, "The Emerging Environmental Crisis along the United States-Mexico Border." In *Changing Boundaries in the Americas: New Perspectives on the U.S.-Mexican, Central American, and South American Borders,* edited by Lawrence A. Herzog. La Jolla: Center for U.S.-Mexican Studies, University of California, San Diego, 1992.

Demaris, Ovid, *Poso del Mundo: Inside the Mexican-American Border.* Boston: Little, Brown, 1970.

Garcia Canclini, Nestor, *Culturas Hibridas.* Mexico City: Grijalbo, 1989; as *Hybrid Cultures: Strategies for Entering and Leaving Modernity,* Minneapolis: University of Minnesota Press, 1995.

Gomez-Peña, Guillermo, "A Binational Performance Pilgrimage." In *Visual Arts on the U.S./Mexican Border,* edited by Harry Polkinhorn, et al. Calexico, California: Binational, 1991.

Hansen, Niles, *The Border Economy: Regional Development in the Southwest.* Austin: University of Texas Press, 1980.

Herzog, Lawrence A., *Where North Meets South: Cities, Space and Politics on the U.S.-Mexican Border.* Austin: University of Texas Press, 1990.

House, John, *Frontier on the Rio Grande: A Political Geography of Development and Social Deprivation.* Oxford: Clarendon Press, and New York: Oxford University Press, 1982.

Jackson, John B., "Other Directed Houses." In *Landscapes: Selected Writings of J. B. Jackson,* edited by Ervin H. Zube. Amherst: University of Massachusetts Press, 1970.

Meinig, Donald W., *Southwest: Three Peoples in Geographical Change 1600–1970.* New York and London: Oxford University Press, 1971.

Morales, Rebecca, and Jesus Tamayo-Sanchez, "Urbanization and Development of the United States–Mexico Border." In *Changing Boundaries in the Americas: New Perspectives on the U.S.-Mexican, Central American, and South American Borders,* edited by Lawrence A. Herzog. La Jolla: Center for U.S.-Mexican Studies, University of California, San Diego, 1992.

Sklair, Leslie, *Assembling for Development: The Maquila Industry in Mexico and the United States.* Boston and London: Unwin Hyman, 1989.

Trujillo Munoz, Gabriel, "Art and the Border: A Preliminary Sketch." In *Visual Arts on the U.S./Mexican Border,* edited by Harry Polkinhorn, et al. Calexico, California: Binational, 1991.

Weisman, Alan, *La Frontera: The United States Border with Mexico.* San Diego: Harcourt Brace, 1986.

—LAWRENCE A. HERZOG

U.S.-Mexican War

The year 1996 marked the one hundred and fiftieth anniversary of the war between the United States and Mexico, a conflict that had a dramatic impact on the history of both nations. For the United States, the war with Mexico was a grand exercise in self-identity that helped legitimate its convictions of destiny and mission to the world. On the other hand, Mexico lost nearly 50 percent of its territory and then entered a period of self-examination as a result of the conflict, as leaders sought to identify and address the reasons that had led to such a debacle. Despite the war's importance, several factors have kept the events of 1846 to 1848 shrouded in relative obscurity. In the United States the Civil War overshadows the conflict with Mexico, while Mexican historians, as Josefina Zoraida Vázquez noted in 1977, have proven "incapable of assimilating the war." Her judgment—in part the result of the war's traumatic impact on the national psyche, the partisan bias of Mexican historiography, and the chronic turmoil that afflicted early republican Mexico—remains largely true today.

The roots of the U.S.-Mexican War can be traced to the conflicting national interests and objectives of the United States and Mexico; the westward movement of the U.S. frontier clashed with Mexico's reluctance to relinquish national claims to Texas. The United States coveted Texas, which was no more than a desolate Spanish province with approximately 7,000 settlers in 1800. Spanish colonial authorities believed that populating and colonizing that territory would protect it from the territorial designs of the United States. They granted permission to U.S. families to settle Texas, a policy that Mexico also adopted after winning its Independence. But the colonists that followed Moses Austin and his son Stephen into Texas in the early 1820s did not abide by several provisions designed to foster peaceful integration into the Mexican community. Other factors magnified the perils in this potentially dangerous situation to Mexican territorial integrity. Not only had the number of U.S. colonists in Texas increased rapidly (they comprised a majority of the population by 1830), but the U.S. foreign minister to Mexico, Joel R. Poinsett, had made it clear that he hoped to purchase as much of Texas as possible.

To regain control of Texas and halt U.S. efforts to acquire the province, President Vicente Guerrero abolished slavery throughout Mexico in September 1829. Guerrero hoped to dissuade those settlers who owned slaves from remaining in Texas, but local authorities in Texas did not enforce the decree because they feared it would provoke the settlers into rebelling. Mexico's national legislature then issued the Law of Colonization on April 6, 1830. The decree, among other things, forbade all further immigration from the United States into Texas. The Law of Colonization, however, did not bring forth the anticipated results. Not only did Mexico prove incapable of enforcing its major stipulations, but the decree also heightened resentment among U.S. colonists in Texas. They requested repeal of the Law of Colonization and asked for statehood within the Mexican nation in the fall of 1832. Two years of negotiations between Mexican foreign relations minister Lucas Alamán and Poinsett's replacement, Anthony Butler, made the situation worse. By 1834 Butler was no closer than Poinsett in convincing the Mexicans to sell Texas, and Mexico's distrust of the United States remained unabated.

Any chance for a peaceful settlement disappeared when the government of Valentín Gómez Farías collapsed in April 1834. Supporters of a centralist republic prepared to reinstate Alamán's Law of Colonization and replace the 1824 federal charter with the constitution known as the Siete Leyes. This turn of events horrified U.S. settlers in Texas, and a majority of them had revolted by the fall of 1835. General Antonio López de Santa Anna rushed north and defeated the Texas rebels in March 1836 at the Battles of the Alamo and Goliad, but his victories proved costly. Although the Mexican Congress had decreed that foreigners who attacked the national territory were to be treated and punished as pirates (which meant the death penalty), the execution of the Alamo's defenders and Goliad's prisoners turned these encounters into symbols of barbaric cruelty. Thus, opposition to Mexico in the United States increased, and supplies and men began to pour into Texas. This support provided the Texans with the necessary confidence to make a stand, and they routed Santa Anna's forces at the Battle of San Jacinto on April 21, 1836. Santa Anna signed a treaty recognizing the independence of Texas to avoid being lynched after this embarrassing defeat. Mexico's Congress later repudiated this agreement, but with little practical effect. Texas existed as an independent republic until 1845.

Other events fueled animosities between the United States and Mexico during the late 1830s and early 1840s. Questions related to the nature and payment of claims filed by the U.S. government on behalf of its citizens against Mexico led to charges of bad faith on both sides. Then, the Mexican army made forays into Texas, and captured Texans were treated harshly. Meanwhile, the October 1842 seizure of Monterrey Bay by Commodore Thomas Ap Catesby Jones renewed Mexican suspicions about U.S. expansionism, while the lack of care demonstrated in the selection of the U.S. representatives that followed Anthony Butler to Mexico irritated Mexican sensibilities. Waddy Thompson, for example, was coldly received in 1842 because he had played a leading role in securing U.S. recognition of Texas's independence.

The election in 1844 of James K. Polk as U.S. president further strained the relationship between the neighboring countries. During his campaign Polk declared himself in favor of acquiring Texas, and the U.S. Congress issued the annexation decree in February 1845. Mexico broke diplomatic relations with the United States shortly thereafter, and war seemed imminent. In a last-ditch attempt to halt this turn of events, British diplomats insisted to the Mexican government of General José Joaquín Herrera that recognition of Texas's independence would prevent annexation. Herrera and his advisers pursued this course of action in April and May 1845 and took steps to build a network of support for the policy. In the end, however, their efforts proved fruitless. Texas voted for annexation on July 15.

Three months later, Polk and his cabinet sought to negotiate a solution to the Texas issue and satisfy the U.S. desire for territory. After inquiring whether Mexico would welcome a special commissioner, Polk sent John Slidell to Mexico to negotiate for the Rio Grande as a southern boundary for Texas (the traditional border through Spanish and Mexican rule had been the Nueces River over 150 miles to the north) and to purchase present-day California and New Mexico. The Slidell mission, however, only aggravated matters. There was a serious discrepancy as to Slidell's prerogatives; Mexico had requested a commissioner to solve the pending question of the annexation of Texas, but Polk appointed Slidell minister plenipotentiary and authorized him to solve all pending issues. To admit Slidell in this capacity would have reopened diplomatic relations with the United States, thus weakening Mexico's position in the negotiations. In addition, Mexican citizens became irate when the nature of Slidell's mission became public. As a result, Mexican authorities twice rebuffed Slidell, in December 1845 and again in March 1846.

Mexico's reluctance to relinquish its territory led Polk to create a pretext that would allow him to declare war. On March 8, 1846, following Mexico's second rejection of Slidell, Polk ordered General Zachary Taylor, stationed since July 1845 with approximately 2,000 men in Corpus Christi, Texas, to Point Isabel, located in the disputed area along the Rio Grande. The Mexican government—then headed by General Mariano Paredes y Arrillaga, who in December 1845 had overthrown Herrera and promised to pursue a more belligerent policy against the United States—responded by appointing General Mariano Arista as commander of the Army of the

North; by late April Arista had mustered in Matamoros a force close to 5,200 soldiers. A clash between the opposing armies was all but inevitable, and an April 25 skirmish between U.S. and Mexican troops in the disputed area provided Polk with the excuse he wanted to begin hostilities. Polk, who had written a declaration of war even before news of the encounter had reached him on May 9, was able to claim that U.S. blood had been shed on U.S. soil. Polk asked Congress for a declaration of war on May 11, and the legislature acquiesced to his wishes two days later.

Within a year, U.S. armies had marched into and gained control of northern Mexico, including the present-day states of New Mexico and California, a process facilitated by Mexico's inability to cement relations with its northern periphery and the region's close economic ties to the United States. Colonel Stephen Kearny left Kansas in June 1846 with 1,600 men at the head of the Army of the West. After marching unopposed into Santa Fe, New Mexico (allegedly aided by a bribe paid to Mexican governor Manuel Armijo to withdraw his troops), Kearny split his force into three sections. One remained in Santa Fe, another captured Chihuahua, and Kearny led a third to California, where disgruntled U.S. immigrants already had launched the so-called Bear Flag Revolt to free the area from Mexican rule. Traditional historiography has emphasized the rapid and relatively bloodless U.S. conquest of northern Mexico, but recent research suggests that the occupation of New Mexico and California was not as peaceful as previously believed. A few weeks after the occupation of Santa Fe, Mexicans rebelled and killed the U.S. civil governor, while Mexican Californians under General Andrés Pico defeated the U.S. forces at the Battle of San Pascual. In the end, however, the lack of help from Mexico, the shortcomings of the Mexican military apparatus, and disputes among Mexican leaders brought resistance there to an end.

Meanwhile, the war in northeastern Mexico saw U.S. general Zachary Taylor win several victories —Palo Alto, Resaca de la Palma, and Monterrey— during the late spring and summer of 1846. Despite this turn of events, Mexico did not show any inclination to end the war, so the U.S. government, convinced that it was impracticable to cross the desert, halted Taylor's attack and devised a plan to invade Mexico's heartland. Taylor was ordered to send his best troops to U.S. general Winfield Scott, who was to capture the fortified city of Veracruz on Mexico's eastern coast. From this location the U.S. army would retrace the footsteps of Spanish conquistador Fernando (Hernán) Cortés, march approximately 250 miles inland to Mexico City, and force Mexico to sue for peace.

As the United States was preparing for the campaign in central Mexico, General Santa Anna—who in August 1846 had returned from exile in Cuba and two months later had taken command of the army in San Luis Potosí—took a bold step in an attempt to turn the tide of war. After Santa Anna intercepted a report outlining the new U.S. strategy, he marched his troops northward to the outskirts of the city of Saltillo, where Taylor's depleted army was stationed. The ensuing Battle of Buena Vista (February 22–23, 1847) left Taylor's forces in no condition to assist in the campaign against the Mexican capital. But Santa Anna, in a controversial decision, claimed that his troops were too exhausted to strike a decisive blow on the morning of February 24 and withdrew from the battlefield under the cover of darkness.

Even if Santa Anna's army had prevailed at Buena Vista after another day of fighting, however, it is doubtful whether such a triumph would have been more than a moral victory for Mexico. Over the next few months, as the war shifted to central Mexico, Mexican politicians and army leaders failed to devise a plan capable of stopping the invaders. On April 18, 1847, a few weeks after bombarding Veracruz into surrendering, Scott crushed another Mexican army (led by Santa Anna) at the Battle of Cerro Gordo. The defeat so demoralized the Mexican government that little was done to prevent U.S. troops from occupying the city of Puebla in mid-May 1847, and Scott's army reached the outskirts of Mexico City two months later.

Mexican patriots, however, did not allow U.S. troops to march unopposed into their capital. Over the course of the summer Santa Anna mustered yet another army and helped direct preparations so the city could withstand a siege. The capital's corps of national guardsmen spearheaded resistance at Churubusco (August 20) and Molino del Rey (September 8), while legend has it that at Chapultepec (September 13) six cadets from the Colegio Militar leaped to their deaths rather than surrender to the attacking forces. Despite the heroics of Mexican defenders, however, Scott's soldiers overran the Mexican positions and on September 14, 1847, entered the capital. The invaders withstood three days of popular resistance by the city's beggars and scattered pockets of resistance elsewhere, but the fall of Mexico City meant that the war, for all practical purposes, was over.

Given the commonly held military axiom that nothing unifies a nation as the threat of foreign invasion, why did Mexico fail to offer a more stubborn resistance to the United States? As the specter of war loomed over the country in the spring of 1846, far-sighted Mexicans had begun to discuss how best to carry on such a conflict. Some believed that Mexico possessed several advantages that boded well in case hostilities erupted. The Mexican army appeared to be in superb condition, Mexico had the advantage of being the defensive party, and Great Britain and France were expected to lend international support. Additional factors in Mexico's favor, according to such thinking, included the perceived U.S. military weaknesses, the vulnerability of U.S. shipping, the internal dissension over slavery, and the immorality and injustice of the war.

The real picture, however, was not so favorable. As the scholar David Brading has written, between Independence and the mid-1850s, the turmoil that plagued Mexico submerged the new nation in a "system of institutionalized disorder" that propelled it "from crisis to crisis." The country did not have a suitable framework of political and economic institutions by 1846 and thus was ill prepared to undertake a major military effort. Mexico experimented with an empire, a federal republic, and various forms of centralism, but none provided stable government. In addition, freedom from Spanish rule scarcely altered Mexico's economic and social patterns. At midcentury most of the country's approximately 7 million inhabitants were ill-assimilated Indians who performed manual labor. Factors such as high transportation costs obstructed industrial development. Agriculture remained the predominant economic activity, but the goods produced lacked market outlets. In addition, the army was in disarray; generals (especially Santa Anna) were not skilled in the art of war, soldiers were recruited by force and did not receive adequate military training, and the troops lacked modern weaponry and ammunition. Finally, Mexico misjudged the outside world; no assistance came from England or France, while in 1845–46 Spain tried to capitalize on Mexico's troubled situation to set up a monarchy there.

These conditions, which made fighting the U.S. troops all the more difficult, were aggravated by Mexico's acerbic political rivalries. The three principal groups that had vied for power in early republican Mexico—radical liberals (or *puros*), moderate liberals (or *moderados*), and conservatives—could not set aside their differences over a multitude of political, economic, and social issues critical to the route that Mexico should follow. In addition, personal enmities exacerbated hatreds between the various factions and hindered the organization of cohesive resistance against the United States, particularly

when the *puros,* the only group that genuinely desired war with the United States, seized power between August 1846 and March 1847. As the nineteenth-century Mexican thinker José María Luis Mora put it, politically conscious Mexicans "were not yet over the antipathies caused between them by the mutual attacks on each other that earlier revolts had brought about." On several occasions in the fall of 1846, *moderado* statesman Manuel Gómez Pedraza, his deep-seated antagonism toward *puro* leader Valentín Gómez Farías no doubt exacerbated by the unmerciful tirades to which *puro* newspapers had subjected him during the preceding year, refused Gómez Farías's overtures to effect a rapprochement. Santa Anna's machinations also helped sabotage the Mexican war effort. He left no stone unturned to break his ties to Gómez Farías and the *puros*—who had helped engineer his return from Cuba—and establish a dictatorship.

But the episode that best illuminates how Mexico's lack of domestic solidarity hindered the country's military preparedness during the U.S.-Mexican War is the February 27, 1847, "rebellion of the *polkos.*" On January 11, 1847, Vice President Gómez Farías, who had become acting chief executive owing to Santa Anna's absence at the head of the army in San Luis Potosí, issued a decree that authorized the government to raise 15 million pesos by mortgaging or selling ecclesiastical property. Designed to finance the war against the United States, the law instead fostered public animosity toward Gómez Farías. *Moderado* politicians, senior army chiefs, and high-ranking clerical leaders began to plot against him, and they relied on the civic militia battalions (known as the *polkos* because the polka had become the most popular dance of elite society) organized in the fall of 1846 by Mexico City's well-to-do. The revolt, which erupted just a few days before General Scott's army landed in Veracruz, prevented the Mexican government from assisting that port city or strengthening the city of Puebla or the fortifications near the coast.

These rivalries continued to affect the course of the war after the fall of Mexico City. At that time the *moderados* took control of the government and appointed negotiators to discuss the terms of a peace settlement. Peace, however, was not the only alternative available to Mexican leaders. While a splinter group of *puros* advocated the establishment of a U.S. protectorate to rejuvenate Mexico's social, political, and economic development, the majority of the *puro* bloc, led by Gómez Farías and Michoacán governor Melchor Ocampo, urged the government to adopt guerrilla tactics and continue hostilities. The proposal was not far-fetched. Given the success of insurgent guerrilla forces during Mexico's struggle for Independence and the growing opposition to the war in the United States, a guerrilla war may have given Mexicans additional leverage at the bargaining table.

The *moderados,* however, were bent on peace and agreed to the Treaty of Guadalupe Hidalgo, signed on February 2, 1848. Scholars generally have regarded the efforts of U.S. peace commissioner Nicholas P. Trist as the most important element in the signing of the pact, but other factors helped induce *moderado* leaders to come to terms with Trist. One was the *moderados'* fear that a guerrilla war, which would require arming the populace, would bring further chaos and anarchy to Mexico. In addition, the Catholic Church, Mexican moneylenders *(agiotistas),* and the British diplomatic corps (whose arguments proved most persuasive) pressured the government to settle for peace. High-ranking clerical leaders feared that the church might lose its possessions if war continued, while British agents believed that the anticipated U.S. monetary indemnity would allow the Mexican government to reimburse *agiotistas* and pay those debts to British bondholders outstanding since 1827.

Peace with the United States, however, did not bring immediate unity to Mexico. The shock of military disaster left a deep impression on Mexican society. Thinkers of the day feared that national existence was in jeopardy. The United States could take over at any moment, and ethnic conflict—the Caste War of Yucatán and the Sierra Gorda Rebellion—threatened the country as well. Pundits pressed for a more refined understanding of the ills that affected the republic, but they agreed upon little. A new generation of *puro* and *moderado* statesmen concluded that Mexico's main problem had been the failure to extirpate the Spanish colonial legacy. The military and the church became two of their favorite targets. They held that the army's complete decay, especially the cowardice and incompetence of its officers, and the church's lack of patriotism had been largely responsible for the recent debacle. Conservatives, led by Lucas Alamán, took exception to this position. They blamed the adoption of republican institutions for the tragedy of 1847 and advocated adoption of a monarchical government as the only means of restoring the national well-being.

In the end, the antagonistic nature of the two positions made it all but impossible for Mexican leaders to halt the republic's unsteady course. Intellectual debate grew increasingly rancorous after 1848 and turned to open conflict shortly after Santa Anna returned from yet another exile in 1853. Only in 1867, after overcoming yet another round of civil war and a foreign intervention by the French Bourbons, did the *puros,* under Benito Juárez, consolidate themselves in power and establish a national consensus.

See also Guadalupe Hidalgo, Treaty of; Texan Secession

Select Bibliography

Alcaraz, Ramón, et al., *The Other Side: Or Notes for the History of the War between Mexico and the United States,* translated by Albert C. Ramsey. New York: Burt Franklin, 1970.

Bauer, K. Jack, *The Mexican War, 1846–1848.* Lincoln: University of Nebraska Press, 1992.

Brack, Gene M., *Mexico Views Manifest Destiny, 1821–1846: An Essay on the Origins of the Mexican War.* Albuquerque: University of New Mexico Press, 1975.

Pletcher, David, *The Diplomacy of Annexation: Texas, Oregon, and the Mexican War.* Columbia: University of Missouri Press, 1973.

Ramírez, José Fernando, *Mexico during the War with the United States,* edited by Walter B. Scholes and translated by Elliot B. Scherr. Columbia: University of Missouri Press, 1950.

Robinson, Cecil, editor, *The View from Chapultepec: Mexican Writers on the Mexican-American War.* Tucson: University of Arizona Press, 1989.

Santoni, Pedro, *Mexicans at Arms: Puro Federalists and the Politics of War, 1845–1848.* Forth Worth: Texas Christian University Press, 1996.

—PEDRO SANTONI

V

Vasconcelos, José 1882–1959
Writer, Philosopher, and Educator

One of the most distinguished Mexican intellectuals of the twentieth century, José Vasconcelos was born on February 28, 1882, in the city of Oaxaca. He spent part of his childhood on the U.S.-Mexican border, daily crossing to Eagle Pass, Texas, to attend primary school. His family later moved to Campeche during a period when there were widespread fears that the U.S. invasion of Cuba would shift to Mexico. These tensions later would be reflected in Vasconcelos's idea of the Cosmic Race and his rejection of Anglo culture.

Vasconcelos hoped to study philosophy, but there were no universities that included departments of philosophy in Mexico, since the positivist ethos of late-nineteenth-century Mexico dictated that education should focus on the sciences. He instead studied law, but he also joined a group of radical young scholars knows as the Ateneo de la Juventud, which used French spiritualism to formulate a severe critique of positivist philosophy, undermining the ideas used to justify the dictatorship of Porfirio Díaz and articulating a new vision of the relationship between individual and society.

After finishing law school Vasconcelos joined the U.S. law firm of Warner, Johnson, and Galston. Joining the opposition campaign of Francisco I. Madero, in 1909 Vasconcelos became one of the secretaries of the Anti-Reelectionist movement in Mexico City and the director and editor of *El Antireeleccionista,* its newspaper. Vasconcelos is said to have coined the motto of the anti-reelectionist movement, *sufragio efectivo, no reelección* (effective suffrage, no reelection), which is printed on official government documents to this day. Forced to flee to the United States for political reasons, Vasconcelos later returned to Mexico City. He later was dispatched to the United States once again by Madero to explain the goals of the anti-reelectionist movement to the U.S. public.

After the triumph of Madero, Vasconcelos returned to his work as a lawyer.

After the assassination of Madero, Vasconcelos represented the commander of the Constitutionalist Army, Venustiano Carranza, in the Niagara Falls Conferences, which negotiated the withdrawal of the U.S. troops that had occupied the port of Veracruz. He later was named minister of public instruction by provisional president Eulalio Gutiérrez, although once Carranza assumed the presidency he was force to flee to the United States yet again, returning to his studies of philosophy. After the overthrow of Carranza, provisional president Adolfo de la Huerta named Vasconcelos rector of the National University.

In his inaugural address on June 4, 1920, Vasconcelos emphasized the university's responsibility to educate the Mexican people rather than a small elite and insisted on the necessity of creating a federal ministry of education. As rector Vasconcelos tirelessly traveled throughout the country to convince state governments of the importance of a department of education, eventually garnering enough support for a constitutional amendment to be passed authorizing creation of the new department. On October 12, 1921, President Álvaro Obregón put Vasconcelos in charge of the new Secretaría de Educación Pública (SEP).

During his three years as secretary of education, Vasconcelos divided the SEP into three departments: schools, libraries, and fine arts. Congress also put the new ministry in charge of the departments of indigenous culture and the national campaign against illiteracy. Vasconcelos's pedagogy not only focused on the cognitive skills of children, but also their physical, moral, and aesthetic well-being. Vasconcelos opposed the positivism of the ancien regime, but he also rejected the pragmatic pedagogy of U.S. thinker John Dewey. Mexican education, Vasconcelos believed, should move "from Robinson [Crusoe] to the Odyssey," from the practical, exclusively technical man who was the aim of Anglo-Saxon education to the spiritual traveler who would be steeped in the millennial culture. Adopting Dewey's pedagogy would be suicide for Latin American peoples and an advance for United States imperialism.

Vasconcelos also believed that the SEP should take charge of Indian literacy. Opposed to the segregation of Indians into separate schools, Vasconcelos insisted that the "problem of the Indian" stemmed from ignorance rather than the unjust distribution of land and exploitation. Vasconcelos used the model of the Spanish missions for rural schools. The schoolteacher should become a full member of the community, becoming an advocate for productive, "civilized" life. Nonetheless, the continued importance of latifundism prevented Vasconcelos's educational projects from creating a far-reaching transformation of rural life. In the cities Vasconcelos called on all people who knew how to read—ranging from children to society ladies—to participate in his campaign against illiteracy, creating two key bodies for basic education, the honorary schoolteachers and the children's army.

The department of libraries published inexpensive editions of the classics of world literature and printed (under the auspices of the national graphic arts workshop, which had been folded into the SEP) more than 2 million workbooks to teach people to read and more than 1 million reading textbooks. Vasconcelos followed the model to the Russian commissar of culture, Anatoli Lunacharsky.

In addition to providing physical and artistic education to schoolchildren, the Department of Fine Arts sought to make Mexico the "Athens of the Continent." The department sponsored the great muralists Diego Rivera, José Clemente Orozco, David Alfaro Siqueiros, and Roberto Montenegro, who painted some of their most important works on public buildings. Manuel M. Ponce and Julián Carrillo also helped create a musical renaissance in Mexico, every Sunday staging popular concerts in Chapultepec Park in Mexico City and producing festivals dedicated to particular regions of Latin America and Spain.

From the SEP Vasconcelos sought to make possible the unification of the peoples of Latin America and fight against the imitation of Anglo culture. He believed that it was particularly important to give Latin America an ideology that would permit it to resist Anglo imperialism: the theory of the Cosmic Race. According to this theory the Amazon region would produce the synthesis of all the races of Latin America. A "fifth" mestizo race would be born that would bring together the best of the "four" extant races in Latin America. The future would belong to the mestizo, not to the Anglo.

On June 30, 1924, Vasconcelos resigned from the SEP, beginning a long, difficult career in opposition politics. Failing in a campaign for the governorship of Oaxaca, Vasconcelos was forced into exile, traveling to the United States, South America, and the great capital cities of Europe. After the assassination of Obregón and President Plutarco Elías Calles's promise to permit free elections, Vasconcelos returned to Mexico as an independent candidate for president. Vasconcelos presented himself as a civilian candidate who would privilege the ballot box over the military jackboot, a civilizing Quetzalcoatl (to paraphrase a speech he gave in a Mexico City campaign rally) who would rise above the bloody Huitzilopochtli. In what has come to be known as the Campaign of 1929, Vasconcelos garnered considerable support throughout Mexico, particularly from the middle class, which saw Vasconcelos as a successor to Madero. University students were particularly strong supporters of Vasconcelos as they struggled for university autonomy.

The ruling party, the Partido Nacional Revolucionario (PNR, or National Revolutionary Party) eventually had to resort to electoral fraud to defeat Vasconcelos. According to the official count, the PNR candidate, Pascual Ortiz Rubio, received 1,948,848 votes, while Vasconcelos received only 110,979. Once again Vasconcelos crossed the border into the United States, calling for an armed rebellion in his Plan de Guaymas. Disillusioned by the lack of response from the Mexican people, Vasconcelos scolded them for not defending their vote by the force of arms. Vasconcelos grew ever more bitter, abandoning his early progressivism and moving further to the right. After a fruitless 10 years of self-imposed exile, Vasconcelos returned to Mexico. In 1940 he founded *Timón,* an openly pro-German and fascist journal. Vasconcelos hoped that the Axis powers would finally end Anglo imperialism, but after the defeat of Nazi Germany Vasconcelos's fear of Communism and atheism led him to embrace the United States as a Christian people. Thus, by the end of his life Vasconcelos had abandoned the anti-imperialism that had sustained him since his days in the Ateneo de la Juventud. Vasconcelos died on June 30, 1959, in Mexico City.

Vasconcelos was an important presence in the discipline of philosophy, although he never was an academic in the strictest sense of the term. Similarly, he helped spark important debates among professional philosophers, but his work was never accepted as part of the canon of the discipline. Vasconcelos drew on the work of Henri Bergson, a philosophy founded in emotion rather than reason, as well as a melange of occultism, the theosophy of Helena Petrovna Blavatsky, Christianity, Phythagorism, Platonism, elements of contemporary science, and the work of Kant and Schopenhauer. Vasconcelos believed that reason only suppressed the essential unity of all beings. He believed that the work of the philosopher was akin to that of the musician, harmonizing emotion and reason, as well as myth, poetry, science, and religion. Philosophy presented a true image of the world, which had been created by a god-artist rather than a divine author of order and hierarchy.

If it is difficult to excuse Vasconcelos's anti-intellectualism, political errors, Hispanophilia, and fascist sympathies, his trajectory was by no means unique among Latin American intellectuals. More-over, in many respects Vasconcelos's work was a mile-stone in the history of Latin American culture: he spurred education in Mexico, worked in favor of the democratization of Mexico, produced a body of first-rate writing (particularly autobiography), and formulated an ideology of Latin American emancipation. Vasconcelos has been an inspiration for thinkers throughout Latin America. In the 1920s the Peruvian Victor Raúl Haya de la Torre declared that Vasconcelos was the precursor of the Partido Revo-lucionario Antiimperialista Latinoamericano (Latin American Revolutionary Anti-imperialist Party), better known as the Alianza Popular Revolucionaria Americana (APRA, or American Popular Revolution-ary Alliance). In recent years, Chicano theorists in the United States have found in Vasconcelos's ideas of the *Raza Cósmica* and *Indología* an important foundation for their struggles.

Select Bibliography

Da Beer, Gabriella, *José Vasconcelos and His World*. New York: Las Américas, 1966.
Haddox, John H., *Vasconcelos of Mexico, Philospher and Prophet*. Austin: University of Texas Press, 1967.

—Margarita Vera Cuspinera

Velázquez Sánchez, Fidel 1900–97

Labor Leader

Fidel Velázquez Sánchez was secretary general of the Confederación de Trabajadores de México (CTM, or Confederation of Mexican Workers), the largest labor union in Mexico, for more than 50 years. Only two other people held that post, Vicente Lombardo Toledano from 1936 and 1941 and Fernando Amilpa from 1947 to 1950. Few other leaders in Latin America have been in such a position of power for so long. A corporatist leader par excellence, Veláz-quez was politically active since the ruling Partido Nacional Revolucionario (PNR, or National Revo-lutionary Party; later the Partido Revolucionario Institucional—PRI, or Institutional Revolutionary Party) was founded in 1929. He was one of leaders who has most adamantly defended the PRI and the corporatist political system.

Fidel Velázquez was born on April 24, 1900, in the village of Villa Nicolás Romero in Mexico State, where he attended primary school and worked for much of his childhood. In 1916 Velázquez moved de Mexico City, starting work in the dairy industry. In 1924 Velázquez and Alfonso Sánchez Madari-aga founded the Sindicato de Lechero Ambulantes (Union of Milkmen). The milkmen's union later was incorporated into the Federación de Sindicatos Ob-reros del Distrito Federal (FSODF, or Federation of Workers' Unions of the Federal District), an im-portant affiliate of the Confederación Regional Ob-rera Mexicana (CROM, or Regional Confederation of Mexican Workers).

In the final months of 1928 the FSODF faced a crucial election for its executive committee. The CROM at this time had lost considerable prestige owing to its agreements with the government and accusations that its leaders had been responsible for the assassination of president-elect Álvaro Obregón. Fidel Velázquez, Jesús Yurén, Luis Quintero, Alfonso Sánchez Madariaga, Carlos L. Díaz, and Leonardo Flores, who later were known as Los Lobitos (the wolf cubs), were quite critical of the leadership of the CROM. They believed that the candidates for the executive committee, Alfredo Pérez Medina and Salvador Álvarez, had been imposed by the Grupo Acción, the ruling faction in the CROM, and partic-ularly labor boss Luis N. Morones.

Fearing that they would lose control of the FSODF and taking advantage of the crisis in the CROM, Fidel and the other Lobitos broke with the CROM in January 1929. Later that year they helped form the Federación Sindical de Trabajadores del Distrito Federal (FSTDF, or Federated Union of Workers of the Federal District), which grouped together several of the most important Mexico City labor unions that had split from the CROM.

From 1929 to 1932 Velázquez was the labor rep-resentative in the Federal District conciliation and arbitration commission, and in 1932 he already was secretary general of the FSTDF. In that same year he organized a "unity assembly" with the Confedera-ción de Obreros y Campesinos del Estado de Puebla (Confederation of Workers and Peasants of the State of Puebla), the Alianza de Ferrocarrileros (Alliance of Railroad Workers), the Sindicato de Electricistas (Union of Electrical Workers), a faction of the anarchosyndicalist Confederación General de Trabajadores (CGT, or General Confederation of Workers), and a group headed by the prominent dissident labor leader Vicente Lombardo Toledano. The FSTDF became an organization that united numerous dissident unions from the CROM.

In 1933 the Lobitos and Lombardo Toledano's group united to form a new national labor federation, the Confederación General de Obreros y Campesinos de México (CGOCM, or General Confederation of Workers and Peasants of Mexico). In 1935 Velázquez and the other Lobitos, together with the electricians' union, the Lombardistas, and a Communist tendency created a still larger labor federation, the Comité Nacional de Defensa Proletaria (CNDP, or National Committee for Workers' Defense), receiving the support of still more industrial unions. In February 1936 this loose confederation was molded into a new national labor union, the Confederación de Trabajadores de México (CTM).

During the constitutional congress of the CTM from February 21 to 24, two candidates jostled for the post of secretary of organization and propaganda, Fidel Velázquez for the *sindicalistas* (trade unionists) and Miguel Angel Velasco for the Communists. Realizing that they were a majority, the *sindicalistas* threatened to storm out of the assembly, bringing the election to a halt. In the interests of unity Velázquez was named secretary, reducing the strength of the Communist Party in the congress. During this same period the Lobitos consolidated the forces of the FSTDF, later renamed the Federación de Trabajadores del Distrito Federal (FTDF, or Federation of Workers of the Federal District), making it the most important CTM affiliate in the Federal District.

The CTM also sought to unify the international labor movement, and in September 1938 the Confederación de Trabajadores de América Latina (CTAL, or Confederation of Latin American Workers) was founded with Lombardo Toledano as president and Velázquez as secretary general. In January 1939 both participated in the foundation of the Confederación de Trabajadores de Cuba.

In the second national congress of the CTM from February 25 to February 27, 1941, Lombardo Toledano ceded the presidency to Velázquez. Velázquez served as secretary general from 1941 to 1947 (winning a reelection bid in 1944), consolidating the position of the Lobitos, gradually forcing the Lombardistas out of the union, and ensuring "national unity" with the government and ruling party. One

clear example of this "national unity" was the Pacto Obrero Industrial (Industrial Labor Pact) signed with the government in April 1945, which established an alliance between labor, capital, and the state to promote the industrialization of Mexico. Velázquez served as PRI senator for the Federal District from December 1946 to November 1952.

In 1947 Fernando Amilpa was named secretary general of the CTM. During his three-year term the Lobitos broke the CTM's ties with "foreign forces influenced by the Communists," deaffiliating it from the CTAL and the Federación Sindical Mundial (FSM, or Work Union Federation). The CTM increasingly was characterized by *charrismo,* or boss rule, repressing democratic tendencies within the union and independent labor movements in the country at large. The CTM worked with the government to break the Sindicato de Ferrocarrileros (Union of Railroad Workers) in October 1948, the Sindicato de Petroleros (Union of Petroleum Workers) in August 1949, and the Sindicato de Mineros (Union of Mine Workers) from 1950 to 1952. *Charrismo* was not simply a project of Amilpa or president Miguel Alemán; rather it was the product of the Lobitos, an increasingly repressive political regime, and the broader political context of the Cold War. Capital and the U.S. government worked together to dominate labor organizations throughout Latin America.

Velázquez was elected secretary general once again at the fifth congress of the CTM in March 1950. Velázquez continued the policies of Amilpa, reinforcing labor corporatism, consolidating the CTM, and forcing *charro* leadership onto other labor unions. President Miguel Alemán Valdés (1946–52) considered Velázquez a key ally in his drive for modernization, which he saw in terms of industrialization, the formation of a national market, and import substitution industrialization (ISI) policies. Velázquez was reelected yet again at the 1956, 1962, and 1967 congresses, and he helped solidify the alliance of the CTM with the PRI with each successive administration. Indeed, Velázquez played an increasingly important role in the PRI hierarchy itself. Velázquez also played a key role in the Confederación Internacional de Organizaciones Sindicales Libres (CIOSL, or International Confederation of Free Trade Union Organizations) and the Organización Regional Interamericana del Trabajo (ORIT, or Interamerican Regional Organization of Work), two international labor organizations allied with the U.S. government.

In February 1966 the Asamblea Nacional del Proletariado Mexicano (National Assembly of the

Mexican Proletariat), also known as the Congreso del Trabajo (CT, or Workers' Congress), was formed as a "union of unions" from throughout Mexico. One of its most important promoters, Velázquez has held various offices within the CT, including president, vice president, and president of the commission of political affairs.

From 1970 to 1982 the economic model of Mexico began to show serious problems, and the economic, political, and social stability that had been reflected in the CTM began to break down. The CTM leadership increasingly was questioned both by the national government and the rank and file, spurring the development of insurgent movements within the union. During the CTM congresses of 1974 and 1980 the reelection of Velázquez was explained as an attempt to contain the crisis and to keep the political system united during economic crisis. Presidents of Mexico continued to support the Velázquez leadership over all criticism.

In 1986 and 1992 Velázquez was elected president of the CTM once again. In his speeches Velázquez was increasingly critical of the governments' neoliberal response to the economic crises of the 1980s and 1990s, which have brought reductions in real salaries, broken contracts, and drops in government social spending. In practice, however, Velázquez continued to sign agreements that favor capital: the "pacts of solidarity" in 1983–94, the "pacts for stability and growth" in 1987–94, and the "alliance for production" in 1995. Conversely, the CTM continued to be useful for the government, which was unable to find a substitute for Velázquez. The death of Velázquez in 1997 raised serious questions about the future of the PRI regime.

Select Bibliography

Thompson, Mark, and Ian Roxborough, "Union Elections and Democracy in Mexico." *British Journal of Industrial Relations* 20:2 (1982).

— JAVIER AGUILAR GARCÍA

Veracruz, Classic and Postclassic Mesoamerican

See Mesoamerica: Veracruz, Classic and Postclassic

Victoria, Guadalupe 1785–1843

President

The first duly elected president of Mexico (1824–29), Guadalupe Victoria was born on September 29, 1785, as José Miguel Ramón Adaucto Fernández y Félix in Tamazula, Durango, a mining settlement. At age 12 he was sent to Mexico City to study law, which he did until 1811. He finished his preparatory law studies but abandoned the profession, joining the forces of General José María Morelos y Pavón. He participated in the taking of Oaxaca city (November 25, 1812) and, having distinguished himself in that battle, adopted Guadalupe Victoria as his name. In effect, Guadalupe Victoria stood, in its new bearer's mind, as Mexico's triumph over Spain.

Over the next half-decade (1812–17) Victoria became a skilled guerrilla leader, becoming a colonel in 1814 and winning, in the present-day state of Veracruz, the affection and loyalty of many of its inhabitants. His generalship (by acclamation, it seems) dates from 1815. All his biographers concur in noting Victoria's pleasing manner and kindly personality. By 1817, however, the Spanish had offered amnesty, and many former patriots, exhausted by hard living in the wilds, forsook the Independence struggle temporarily, leaving Victoria without his support network. This caused him to retire to a hacienda in Veracruz, where he remained in seclusion until news of Agustín de Iturbide's pro-Independence Plan de Iguala was proclaimed in 1821.

Victoria's support for Iturbide diminished steadily as the latter's imperial ambitions were revealed. Victoria eventually was imprisoned in Mexico City but succeeded in escaping and making his way to the Veracruz backcountry, where he continued his opposition to Iturbide. At the same time, he secured the support of General Antonio López de Santa Anna, who deferred to Victoria. Victoria was a decided partisan of the republican form of government for Mexico, and although he suffered some defeats, he steadfastly continued in his resistance to Iturbide's imperial rule, which ended in March 1823.

On October 10, 1824, Victoria (the duly elected "patriot" candidate) took office as president of Mexico. The new chief executive came to office with little or no administrative experience, nor did he have a coherent set of policies. Rather, Victoria relied on a coterie of friends for advice, ideas, and their implementation. He came to view Great Britain favorably, which antagonized U.S. minister Joel R. Poinsett. The rivalry between Britain and the United States in the mid-1820s was reflected in the early factionalism and party formation within the Masonic lodges of the elites. Buttressed by British loans and investments, the economy seemed to hold its own for most of Victoria's presidency, at least up to 1827.

Ominously for Mexico's future, no effective revenue system was created during Victoria's tenure. A financial crisis began in 1827, adding to increasing political and social destabilization palpable by 1828. Factions arose within the military. The president vacillated; he appeared unable to exercise leadership. The Acordada Revolt on November 30, 1828, and the mob sacking of the Parián market on December 4 both highlighted Victoria's political helplessness. Nonetheless, precisely because he was not perceived as threatening, he was allowed to complete his presidential term on March 31, 1829.

Once out of office, General Victoria served, when his health permitted, in various peace-keeping assignments (1833, 1834, 1837, and 1838) in Oaxaca and Veracruz States. He had established himself in Veracruz, where he purchased lands near Nautla and Tecolutla, as well as a modest hacienda, "el Jobo," in Tlapacoyan. Beset by physical and mental illnesses, Victoria was unable (especially after 1839) to manage his holdings effectively. By the latter part of 1842, his condition had deteriorated substantially, and the former president was taken to Perote, Veracruz, where he died in the military hospital on March 21, 1843. He died a poor man.

As a hero of Mexico's Independence Wars, General Guadalupe Victoria's remains have, since 1925, rested in the victory column of the Monument to Independence in Mexico City.

Select Bibliography

Arrom, Silvia M., "Popular Politics in Mexico City: The Parián Riot, 1828." *Hispanic American Historical Review* 68 (1988).

Costeloe, Michael P., "Guadalupe Victoria and a Personal Loan from the Church in Independent Mexico." *The Americas* 25 (1969).

De Valder, Arthur Leon, *Guadalupe Victoria: His Role in Mexican Independence*. Albuquerque, New Mexico: Artcraft, 1978.

Flaccus, Elmer W., "Guadalupe Victoria: His Personality as a Cause for His Failure." *The Americas* 23 (1967).

Gardiner, C. Harvey, "The Role of Guadalupe Victoria in Mexican Foreign Relations." *Revista de Historia de América* 26 (1948).

Green, Stanley C., *The Mexican Republic: The First Decade 1823–1832*. Pittsburgh, Pennsylvania: University of Pittsburgh Press, 1987.

Victoria Gómez, Felipe, *Guadalupe Victoria: Primer Presidente de Mexico*. Mexico City: Botas, 1952.

—J. León Helguera

Villa, Francisco (Pancho) 1878–1923
General

Pancho Villa was born in Rio Grande, Durango, on June 5, 1878, and died in Hidalgo de Parral, Chihuahua, on July 20, 1923. Although he was registered under the name of Doroteo Arango, son of Agustín Arango and Micaela Arámbula, he often maintained that he was in fact the son of the bandit Agustín Villa; however, the identity of his real father is still unknown. He attended Rio Grande elementary school, barely learning to read and write before he left school to help his mother support her four younger brothers. For reasons still unclear, at the age of 16 he joined a gang that marauded through the mountains of Durango, with whom he learned survival techniques and the finer points of guerrilla warfare. Villa eventually formed his own gang, which operated in the states of Durango, Sinaloa, and Chihuahua, adopting the name Francisco "Pancho" Villa. A man of many talents, Villa gave up banditry for a time and embarked on a variety of professions, including mule skinner, butcher, bricklayer, milkman, and foreman for a U.S. railway company. At one point he was drafted into the Mexican army, only to desert shortly thereafter. Around 1905 he became a resident of the state of Chihuahua, living first west of Parral and then moving to the vicinity of San Andrés, where he became a cattle rustler and cattle dealer.

In 1910 Abraham González, leader of Francisco I. Madero's Anti-reelectionist Party in Chihuahua, invited Villa to join the movement against the dictatorship of Porfirio Díaz. On November 17, 1910, shortly after the outbreak of the Revolution, Villa captured the Chavarría hacienda, and four days later he defeated an army train at the San Andrés railway station and captured the town. He also won victories against Federal troops at Naica, Camargo, and Pilar de Conchos, but was defeated at Tecolote. He joined Madero at the Bustillos hacienda in March 1911.

At Nuevo Casas Grandes Villa was forced to engage a grave threat to Madero's leadership. Six anarchist leaders, Luis A. García, José Inés Salazar, José C. Parra, Leonides Zapata (no relation to Emiliano Zapata), Tomás Loza, and Lázaro Alanís, published a broadside in which they refused to recognize Madero as provisional president because of their affiliation with the anarchist Partido Liberal Mexicano (PLM, or Mexican Liberal Party), a rival Revolutionary group. They asked that Madero step down as head of the Revolutionary army and accused him of being a worse tyrant than Porfirio Díaz. Under Madero's orders, Villa disarmed and arrested the anarchist leaders, and in recognition of his loyalty he was named a colonel in the Revolutionary army. Nonetheless, when Madero refused to attack the border city of Ciudad Juárez, fearing international complications, Pascual Orozco and Villa countermanded Madero's orders, capturing the city. The Battle of Ciudad Juárez marked the end of the Porfirian regime. On May 25, 1911, Díaz resigned and went into exile in Europe.

After the defeat of Díaz the Revolutionary army was demobilized, although the Federal army was not. Villa, who had no particular interest in politics, retired to private life, working with the German businessman Federico Moye in the city of Chihuahua. Villa's retirement proved to be short-lived, however. Three days after the signing of the Treaty of Ciudad Juárez, the heads of the Partido Liberal Mexicano, the Flores Magón brothers, issued a statement in which they refused to recognize Madero's victory and called on their allies to continue the armed struggle. In March 1912, Pascual Orozco, who had commanded the Revolutionary forces in Chihuahua, accepted the leadership of the anarchist *"colorados"* who had responded to the Flores Magóns' call, gaining control of much of the state of Chihuahua. At the behest of his friend and mentor Abraham González, whom Madero had named governor of Chihuahua, Villa captured Parral from the counterrevolutionary forces and imposed forced loans on the population to finance his army. In Torreón Villa linked up with the Federal army under Victoriano Huerta, who named Villa honorary brigadier general. Nonetheless, Huerta was merely attempting to attract Villa for his own ends, and when it became clear that he could not he sought to eliminate him. Calling Villa a bandit, Huerta accused him of having stolen a fine mare belonging to Marcos Russek, a leading merchant from the city of Jiménez. Insisting that Russek was an Orozco collaborator, Villa struck Huerta. Huerta ordered his execution, but at the eleventh hour Raúl Madero contacted his brother Francisco, who cancelled the execution and ordered Villa's transfer to the Federal penitentiary in Mexico City. While in prison Villa learned of a preparation for a coup d'état against Madero, but Madero refused to listen to Villa's warnings. Villa also received death threats, and on December 1912 he escaped to save his own life an took refuge in El Paso, Texas. Six weeks later he learned of Huerta's coup and the assassination of Madero. Shortly after he received news of the murder of Abraham González.

Although Villa did not organize any kind of response to the assassination of Madero, he reacted violently to the news of the murder of his friend Abraham González. Without resources and accompanied by only eight men, Villa crossed the Mexican border and headed toward western Chihuahua, bastion of the Orozquistas and anarchist forces, who had opportunistically united with Huerta. Soon he was able to attract hundreds of Chihuahuenses to his cause. Using the guerrilla tactics he had learned in his youth, Villa inflicted defeats on Federal and Orozquista forces at Casas Grandes, Pearson, Bustillos, and San Andrés. In September 1913 a meeting of Revolutionary leaders named Villa general of the Division of the North, and on October 2 he defeated Federal forces at the strategically important railway hub at Torreón. Shortly after he unsuccessfully attempted to capture the city of Chihuahua, which was defended by the Orozquista Salvador Mercado. Apparently retreating to the north, Villa captured a freight train north of the city and, in a latter-day variant of the Trojan Horse, hid his soldiers inside and surprised the sleeping Federal garrison at Ciudad Juárez, taking the city almost without a fight on the morning of November 15.

Opposed to street fighting and hoping to avoid problems with U.S. authorities in El Paso, Villa left Ciudad Juárez to engage the Federal army, which was coming to attack him. On November 25, in Tierra Blanca, Villa crushed Jesús Mancilla and the Orozquista José Inés Salazar, and on December 8 he captured the capital of Chihuahua without firing a shot; refusing to fight with Villa, Salvador Mercado and Pascual Orozco had retreated to the border town of Ojinaga. The Revolutionary chiefs named the victorious Villa governor of Chihuahua.

Villa had only been governor for four days when he signed a decree decisively breaking the economic power of the oligarchy that had supported Orozco, confiscating virtually all of its goods and property. He declared publicly that once the Revolution had triumphed, land would be divided in three parts: for pensions for widows and orphans, for Revolutionary soldiers, and for landholders who had lost their lands. He promulgated a general amnesty, created a state bank capitalized at 10 million pesos to support small farmers and business, and lowered the price of meat to 15 centavos per kilogram. He also distributed rations to the unemployed, opened the U.S.-Mexican border to allow foodstuffs and other basic goods to enter, cut all back taxes by 50 percent, and instituted a program of public works to create employment. Finally, Villa opened the Scientific and Literary Institute, reconstructed and funded schools, paid back wages to teachers, and paid the medical bills of enemy soldiers in Chihuahuan hospitals.

Villa was able to attract thousands of men to his new army, and he mercilessly tracked down Orozquistas, anarchists, and members of the oligarchy who had supported Huerta. In order to gain the funds to organize, arm, and provision the Division of the North and turn it into an efficient fighting machine capable of defeating the Federal army, Villa exported huge quantities of cattle and minerals to the United States and obtained credit from businesses in El Paso. He resigned the governorship on January 10, 1914, and inflicted a final blow to the troops of Mercado and Orozco at Ojinaga. Just as the Division of the North was ready to march south, General Felipe Ángeles, the former director of Mexico's military college, put himself under Villa's command and took charge of its artillery. In 15 trains Villa transported his cavalry, artillery, and infantry—a well-equipped army of 8,000 men. The army was followed by a hospital train with the latest medical equipment and staffed by expert surgeons and nurses. Villa's troops captured Torreón on April 2 and defeated the remaining Federal forces at Paredón and San Pedro de las Colonias.

Villa's rapid military success proved unwelcome to Venustiano Carranza, commander in chief of the Revolutionary forces. Carranza ordered Villa to turn away from Zacatecas, gateway to Mexico City, and instead attack Saltillo to the northeast. After a brief standoff, Villa and Ángeles decided to attack Zacatecas on their own authority. Villa's capture of Zacatecas proved a fatal blow to the Huerta government, and Huerta fled the country shortly after. Nonetheless, Carranza prevented Villa from entering Mexico City. Toward the end of 1914, at the convention of Revolutionary forces at Aguascalientes, Carranza and Villa split, and the country was wracked by a new armed conflict: the Constitutionalists, with Carranza and General Álvaro Obregón on one hand; and the Conventionists of Villa and Emiliano Zapata on the other. After a series of skirmished throughout the country, Villa decided to engage the Constitutionalist army in the Bajío region of north-central Mexico. After three bloody defeats at the hands of Obregón, Villa was forced to retreat north. In Chihuahua Villa regrouped his forces and attacked Agua Prieta, Sonora, with 13,000 men and 42 heavy caliber cannon. However, U.S. president Woodrow Wilson, who had promised not to intervene further in the conflict, suddenly recognized Carranza as the de facto government of Mexico and permitted 5,000 Carrancista troops to pass from Eagle Pass, Texas, to Douglas, Arizona, to reinforce Agua Prieta, resulting in a decisive defeat for Villa. Villa was forced to retreat from Sonora across the Sierra Madre in the thick of winter, losing many men to cold and hunger. Shortly after his return to Chihuahua, he was forced to abandon the capital and withdrew to Bustillos, where he decided to continue the war.

In the first days of 1916 Villa wrote to Zapata informing him of his difficult military situation and of a secret pact that, according to his sources, Carranza had signed with the United States to make Mexico a protectorate. In his letter Villa invited Zapata to join him to "attack the Americans in their own dens and make them know that Mexico is the land of the free and the grave of thrones, crowns, and traitors." On January 10, 1916, a Villista detachment attacked a train just north of Santa Isabel and executed 17 U.S. citizens, and on the morning of March 9, 1916, with 480 men, Villa attacked the U.S. town of Columbus, New Mexico.

A week later a punitive expedition of 10,000 men under the command of General John J. Pershing was dispatched south into Chihuahua to find Villa "dead or alive." Villa ordered his guerrilla forces to disperse and hid himself to recover from a wound he had received in combat. Nonetheless, Carranza also viewed the punitive expedition as a violation of Mexico's national sovereignty, and after U.S. and Carrancista forces clashed in El Carrizal, Wilson called up the National Guard. War appeared imminent.

Nonetheless, Carranza was able to negotiate an unconditional withdrawal of U.S. troops, and a frustrated General Pershing withdrew from Chihuahua in February 1917. Villa was still alive, having survived both the punitive expedition and an assassination attempt by the U.S. State Department, and continued his guerrilla resistance to Carranza's government. As the war deepened, the execution of prisoners and other atrocities became routine on both sides. Villa was a born guerrilla leader, and Carranza was not able to inflict a decisive blow against his forces, let alone contain the conflict; indeed, the Defensas Sociales, paramilitary forces created to destroy the guerrilla forces, were not able to win a single victory.

In May 1920 Carranza was deposed and assassinated by the very forces that had brought him to power, and Villa, in control of the coal-producing region of Coahuila, began peace talks with the new president, Adolfo de la Huerta. From this position of strength Villa was able to obtain favorable terms and a peace treaty was signed in June 1920. Villa's forces received four haciendas—San Salvador de Horta and Canutillo in the state of Durango and San Isidro and El Pueblito in Chihuahua—to form agricultural colonies and a year's salary, and they were allowed to retain their arms and horses and, if they wished, to enter the Federal army. Villa maintained the rank of general and was allowed to form a personal guard of 50 soldiers, who would be paid by the government. After three years, Villa had made Canutillo, where he resided, into a highly profitable business. In a country still sunken in poverty, unemployment, and underdevelopment, Canutillo had become a flourishing community with its own electricity; carpentry and saddle maker's shops; textile mill; mill for grinding corn; machine shops; mail, telephone, and telegraph service; street lights; and a public school for 50 children. Moreover, Villa had distributed the land at Canutillo among his soldiers, financed public works in neighboring communities, and opened a bank to provide credit to small farmers.

Although he clearly had withdrawn from political life, Villa was falsely accused of wanting to take up arms against Obregón and opposing the candidacy of Plutarco Elías Calles to the presidency. On July 20, 1923, Villa was assassinated in the city of Parral. Although his murder was officially written off as an act of personal vengeance engineered by Jesús Salas Barraza, a congressional representative from the state of Durango, the whispering campaign that preceded his murder suggests much wider involvement. Three years later Villa's tomb was profaned by unknown persons, his cadaver decapitated, and his head stolen. During the following decades Villa was vilified or simply ignored by the Mexican government. It was only in 1966, during the administration of Gustavo Díaz Ordaz, that the Mexican Congress declared Villa a national hero and ordered that his name be inscribed in gold letters in the halls of Congress. In 1979 his remains were moved to the Monument of the Mexican Revolution in Mexico City.

Select Bibliography

Beezley, William H., *Insurgent Governor: Abraham González and the Mexican Revolution in Chihuahua.* Lincoln: University of Nebraska Press, 1973.

Braddy, Haldeen, *The Paradox of Pancho Villa.* El Paso: Texas Western Press, 1978.

Harris, Charles H., III, and Louis R. Sadler, *Termination with Extreme Prejudice: The United States Versus Pancho Villa.* Las Cruces: New Mexico State University Press, 1988.

Katz, Friedrich, *Villa: Reform Governor of Chihuahua.* Arlington: University of Texas at Arlington, 1979.

_____, *The Secret War in Mexico.* Chicago: University of Chicago Press, 1981.

—RUBÉN OSORIO ZUÑIGA

Virgin of Guadalupe and Guadalupanismo

According to a legend first published in 1648, the Virgin Mary appeared to a native neophyte, Juan Diego, at the hill of Tepeyac, outside Mexico City in December 1531, and instructed him to deliver a message to the bishop-elect of Mexico, fray Juan de Zumárraga. It was her desire to have a church built on the site. When the bishop demanded a proof of the apparition, the Virgin had Juan Diego collect a bundle of flowers from the hill and take them in his cloak *(tilma)* to Zumárraga. When the Indian unfolded the *tilma,* the Virgin's picture was imprinted on it. The devotion to Our Lady of Guadalupe is probably the most single most important factor in Mexican religious and national life. Since the seventeenth century, but in a special way in the past 200 years, it has played an increasingly important role in the development of *mexicanidad*, the sense of Mexican national identity. Today the *tilma* is housed in a large, modern basilica that is the focal point of pilgrimages and national veneration.

The name Guadalupe is of Arabic origin but of uncertain meaning. It was the name given to a village and shrine in Extremadura, Spain. From the end of the thirteenth century it was the center of a popular cult directed toward a small, wooden image of the Virgin Mary. During the Moorish invasion (711–718), it was hidden but was recovered at a later date by a shepherd, sometimes called Gil Cordero. Guadalupe quickly became a center of pilgrimage and devotion. The devotion was brought to the New World by Columbus and after him by the conquistadors, many of whom were from Extremadura.

According to available evidence the chapel or *ermita* (chapel of ease) of Our Lady of Guadalupe at Tepeyac dates from the years 1555–56, although some have argued that it was the site of a preHispanic Mexica (Aztec) devotion. In 1556 the Franciscan provincial, Francisco de Bustamante, spoke of the devotion as being new. On January 10, 1570, the vicar of the chapel, Antonio Freire, wrote that the *ermita* had been founded 15 years earlier by Alonso de Montúfar, the second archbishop of Mexico. A letter written by the Viceroy Martín Enríquez de Almanza on September 21, 1575, said that the chapel had been founded about the year 1555 or 1556. It was originated dedicated to the Nativity of the Virgin Mary (feast day September 8), an invocation that endured until the eighteenth century. At a very early date it was given the popular name of Guadalupe because of the resemblance between the image venerated in the chapel and the one in the choir of Guadalupe in Extremadura.

In the period between 1555–56 and 1648 the shrine and the devotion to the Virgin were mentioned many times in letters and officials records but never with a clear reference to any apparition to an Indian neophyte. Juan de Zumárraga, the first bishop and archbishop of Mexico, never mentioned the apparitions or the chapel in his correspondence or will, even though later tradition would have him play a key role in both. A group of Franciscans who met at Cuauhtitlán in 1532 to write a letter to King Carlos I made no reference to apparitions or the shrine and its devotion. The story of the apparitions never appears in the works of Toribio de Motolinía, Gerónimo de Mendieta, Bartolomé de las Casas, Cervantes de Salazar, nor in the *acta* of provincial councils nor the correspondence of bishops. Some of the native annals written in Nahuatl in the sixteenth century make vague or ambiguous references to an apparition about the years 1555–56, but this may refer only to the placing of the image in the chapel.

The first most important reference is in the Montúfar-Bustamante controversy of 1556. In September of that year the Franciscan provincial Francisco de Bustamante delivered an impassioned condemnation of the devotion of Guadalupe as renascent idolatry and claimed that the image had been painted by an Indian named Marcos. Archbishop Montúfar ordered an investigation of the sermon, which eventually proved fruitless. None of the many witnesses questioned ever referred to an apparition. Antonio Freire, in his report of 1570, made no mention of an apparition tradition. In 1575 Viceroy Martín Enríquez de Almanza wrote a report on the chapel to the Council of the Indies in which he said that the devotion had arisen from a claim by a herdsman to have been cured there. However, he made no reference to the apparition. About the year 1576 the famed Franciscan ethnographer Bernardino de Sahagún condemned the devotion as a revival of worship of the Mexican goddess Tonantzin ("Our Revered Mother") but said nothing either about an image or apparitions. His association of Guadalupe with a pre-Conquest deity is commonly repeated, although the evidence for it is questionable.

The story of the apparitions was first made known by a Mexican priest, Miguel Sánchez, in a book published in 1648. It was directed, however, not to the Indians but to the criollos (persons of European descent born in the Americas), with whom it struck an immediate, sympathetic chord. In the following year the vicar of Guadalupe, Luis Laso de la Vega, published a Nahuatl-language version of the apparitions (now known as the *Nican mopohua*), with the Indians as its intended readership. It seems, however, to have had little impact. From that time until the mid–eighteenth century the devotion was a criollo one, giving criollos a strong, almost messianic sense of identity. It was the first Marian devotion that was not strictly local in character.

From the mid–eighteenth century onward, there is more evidence of a propagation of the devotion among the natives. It was with Miguel Hidalgo's revolution of 1810, however, that the devotion took root among the indigenous peoples as a sign of liberation and nationality. Hidalgo adopted the image of Guadalupe for his standard, just as the royalist Spaniards adopted that of Our Lady of Remedies (Remedios). After Independence the ruling and intellectual classes cultivated Guadalupe as a symbol of *mexicanidad*. Emperor Agustín Iturbide instituted an order of Guadalupe, as did French-imposed emperor Maximilian at a later date. Even anticlerical politicians such as Benito Juárez respected the symbolism and the chapel. In the latter part of the nineteenth century rationalists, anticlericals, and intellectuals were hostile to the devotion, seeing it as a means whereby the clergy kept the natives under their control.

In the last quarter of the century there was an acrimonious dispute over the historical authenticity of the apparition story. In 1875 the priest Vicente de Paúl Andrade published the letters of Servando Teresa de Mier, which offered a strong, if confused, critique of the devotion. The debate intensified in 1881, when Mexico's premier historian, Joaquín García Icazbalceta, published a biography of Archbishop Zumárraga that contained no reference to Guadalupe. In 1883, in response to a request by the archbishop of Mexico, García Icazbalceta wrote a lengthy critique of the tradition. Although the letter was confidential, word of its contents spread, and in 1888 Andrade published a hurried Latin translation of it, in an attempt to influence the Vatican against a formal recognition of the validity of the apparitions. The ensuring years saw a plethora of publications for and against the authenticity of the apparition story, culminating in 1896 with the publication of García Icazbalceta's letter. The controversy had so discouraged the great historian that he abandoned his studies prior to his death in 1894.

The discussions of the apparition/devotion were more subdued in the twentieth century. In 1922 the Mexican Jesuit historia Mariano Cuevas popularized the idea that the *Nican mopohua* was an eyewitness account that went back to the very time of the apparitions. However, his theory that the original manuscript was looted by Winfield Scott during the U.S.-Mexican War and carried to Washington, D.C., has been discredited. In 1926 Primo Feliciano Veláz-quez published a translation of the *Nican mopohua* and in 1931 a reasoned and scholarly defense of the apparition tradition. In recent times this tradition has been defended by Cuevas, Lauro López Beltrán, Xavier Escalada, Ramiro Navarro de Anda, and Ernesto de la Torre Villar. Strong attacks have come in works by Francisco de la Maza and Edmundo O'Gorman. This same period has also seen more dispassionate and scholarly studies of the Guadalupan phenomenon by Jacques Lafaye, Xavier Noguez, and Stafford Poole.

Despite its feeble historical basis the Guadalupe devotion continues to be a supremely important factor in Mexican religious and national life. Originally, it was a monopoly of the criollos, who saw in it a legitimation of their national aspirations. In the eighteenth and nineteenth century it was appropriated by the criollos' descendants, the rulers of the newly independent republic, and embraced by the Indians. For the former, however, it was as a symbol of national identity, a unifying element in an otherwise fragmented nation, while for the latter it was more a popular and deeply personal devotion. Today many scholars, especially anthropologists, interpret it as a symbol of both change and continuity between the pre-Hispanic past, symbolized by Tonantzin, and the post-Conquest present. Guadalupe is commonly viewed as a maternal symbol, offering comfort and solace to the natives in their spiritual orphanhood. A contrasting view is that it was a symbol manipulated by elites, especially in the church, to keep the natives docile and passive. Both views rely on the concept of "guided syncretism"—that is, that the missionary friars' conscious substitution of Guadalupe for a Mexica deity as a means of weaning the natives from their paganism. Guadalupe has also been interpreted as a symbol of both passivity and liberation. In the latter sense it has been adopted by some liberation theologians. Some feminists have rejected it as embodying the subjugation of women, while others have seen it in the opposite sense. Throughout its history Guadalupe has been a malleable and manipulated symbol, and it continues to be so today.

Select Bibliography

Lafaye, Jacques, *Quetzalcoatl and Guadalupe.* Chicago: University of Chicago Press, 1976.
Poole, Stafford, *Our Lady of Guadalupe: The Origins and Sources of a Mexican National Symbol, 1531–1797.* Tucson: University of Arizona Press, 1995.

—STAFFORD POOLE

Visual Arts

This entry includes seven articles that discuss the visual arts in Mexico:

Visual Arts: Mesoamerica
Visual Arts: Sixteenth Century
Visual Arts: Seventeenth Century
Visual Arts: Eighteenth- and Nineteenth-Century Academic Art
Visual Arts: 1910–37, The Revolutionary Tradition
Visual Arts: 1920–45, Art outside the Revolutionary Tradition
Visual Arts: 1945–96

See also Architecture; Malinche and Malinchismo; Nationalism; Photography; Prints

Visual Arts: Mesoamerica

It has long been apparent that what we call "works of art" were of utmost importance in pre-Hispanic Mesoamerica. Although there is no evidence that any Mesoamerican language possessed a word for "art" as we define it, native Mesoamerican artifacts of impressive technical refinement, aesthetic appeal, and deep symbolic content abound in the archaeological and ethnohistorical record. Across time and space, regardless of social and economic class, Mesoamericans seem to have had a passionate interest in creating expressive forms that were—and still are—visually satisfying.

From sixteenth-century, post-Conquest written sources, we know that Mesoamericans, like contemporary peoples, appreciated well-worked artifacts made of precious materials. The Postclassic period (A.D. 900–1521) Mexica (Aztecs) of central Mexico spoke admiringly of a slightly earlier people called the Toltecs, whom they regarded as consummate artists. According to the Franciscan Bernardino de Sahagún, who wrote the multivolume source now called the *Códice florentino* (Florentine Codex), the word "Toltec" signified, for the Mexica, not only the wisdom and good works of these people, but also artfulness and ingenuity in general. From the Toltec capital at Tula, Hidalgo, the Mexica carried back to their own capital, Tenochtitlan, a number of stone and clay sculptures, while making copies of others. From Sahagún's interviews with descendants of the Mexica elite, we can deduce that it was evidence of technical skill, innovativeness, and "wisdom" that the Mexica most revered in these artworks.

According to the Dominican Diego Durán, the responsibility for ordering and conceptualizing these projects largely fell to the Cihuacoatl, the man who held the second-highest office in the Mexica government. The labor and materials that went into them were a form of tax payment, or tribute, to the state and were overseen by the heads of the urban residential districts, or *calpultin* (singular, *calpulli*), who were responsible for their timely and satisfactory completion. Some artisans were housed in the royal palace, where they produced goods for use by the ruler himself. The materials they worked were probably collected as tribute demanded of subject polities within the Mexica empire.

Among the Mexica, women dominated the textile industry, participated in some crafts, such as feather working, and at least occasionally took on the prestigious role of *tlacuilo,* or scribe. The vast majority of painters, stoneworkers, and builders, however, were men. This appears to have been the case among the Classic period (A.D. 200–900) lowland Maya as well. Not only were the patron deities of Classic Maya scribes male, but the skeletons found in burials of individuals who practiced that profession have been identified as male, as well. The high social status that these men enjoyed is evident in the richness of those burials, as well as the fact that they sometimes signed their names on painted Maya ceramic vessels and stone carvings. In several instances they identified themselves as sons of local rulers who were not in line for the throne. Similarly, among the Mexica the roles of manuscript painter and lapidary craftsman were, within the capital at least, usually reserved for the children of the nobility. Future Mexica scribes and painters were educated by priests in a special school, called the *calmecac,* reserved for the children of high-ranking families, where they also learned about historical traditions, philosophy, calendrical reckonings, music, and the stars.

There is considerable evidence that many Mexica crafts were monopolized by specific families or *calpultin,* and that these artists passed their skills on to their descendants. These occupational groups were organized in guilds, each with its own patron deities and its own ritual practices. The most prestigious art form, feather working, for example, was essentially the exclusive province of the Amanteca, a highly esteemed group who lived in the *calpulli* called Amantlan. The Mexica situation seems to have had ample precedents, since there is clear archaeological evidence that groups of individuals and their descendants, probably related through kinship ties, lived and worked together at a common craft within the large apartment compounds of Classic Teotihuacan. Obsidian workers, for example, lived and worked to the north, near the Pyramid of the Moon, while ceramicists had their own residential workshops in other sectors of the city. Ethnicity was a factor at Teotihuacan as well, as two compounds have been identified on the basis of ceramics found there as residential workshops of Zapotec and Maya immigrants. Whether similar arrangements characterized the Classic Maya city is unknown, but there is clear evidence that Maya ceramicists and vase painters were congregated in workshops that specialized in particular vessel forms and decorations.

Why was art so important in Mesoamerica? Scholar Esther Pasztory pointed out that art, for preindustrial peoples who explained and tried to manage the world differently than we do, often took on the role that technology plays for us. Art not only is a way of materializing the invisible, of giving structure to the intangible, but is also an instrument, or tool, that can be used to gain some control over those unseen forces. In Mesoamerica, what we regard as inanimate objects—including both unworked and worked materials—were, like visual images, believed to be alive. Like living people, they had souls and wills and, as such, they possessed tremendous power. Mesoamericans believed that by materializing these forces in the form of objects and images, and then treating them in certain ways, they could persuade the entities encapsulated in the forms to assert their power on their behalf. Accordingly, it is likely that objects and images made of the best materials and reflecting the best workmanship and design were regarded as especially powerful and efficacious. Far from being perceived as "nonutilitarian" and "frivolous," as art so often is perceived today, well-crafted, appropriately designed objects were seen by Mesoamericans as essential to the maintenance of the universe and, by implication, humankind.

The power of the visual image was enhanced by the relatively minimal dependence on writing in Mesoamerica, where some peoples seldom if ever utilized graphic signs to represent language. Only among the Classic Maya were graphic signs extensively used to evoke in the viewer certain sounds, such as syllables and phonemes, which alone or together formed a spoken word. Where these "hieroglyphs" accompanied imagery, they relieved the images of the need to communicate concepts best expressed in written form. This freed the image to emphasize the way things actually or ideally looked. Classic Maya art, in contrast to the imagery of other Mesoamerican groups, was therefore relatively naturalistic, often employing such illusionistic techniques as extensive overlapping, foreshortening, and color shading.

This was not the case elsewhere in Mesoamerica, where use of glyphs to represent sounds was far more sparing. The Mixtecs and the Mexica, in particular, employed what has been called ideographic writing, in which pictorial signs represent things directly, without reference to spoken language. The Mexica, at the time of European contact, were using some logograms and a few phonetic glyphs. These pictorial signs and glyphs were so restricted in number, however, that they seldom formed a lengthy verbal text. Instead, they served largely nominal functions, identifying a place or figure by name or a depicted act or event by date.

Art and the Body

Since writing played a relatively minor role in Mesoamerica, pictorial images bore the primary burden of communication. Author Elizabeth Hill Boone argued that Mesoamerican imagery followed its own rules, or "grammar," deriving meaning from the objects it directly referenced, from the relative placement of its constituent parts, and by the contexts in which it operated. The pictures, in other words, *were* the texts. In view of this, it is not surprising that the most common referent in Mesoamerican imagery was the body. The body, as the scholar John Monaghan has pointed out, readily lends itself as a vehicle of communication, serving as a logical basis for the encoding of all kinds of information. Mesoamerican pictorial manuscripts therefore recounted elaborate stories almost exclusively in terms of painted figures whose poses, orientations, gestures, and costumes not only identified them, but also specified their actions and significance. Mesoamerican art, in other words, was characteristically figural, and bodies constituted the majority of signs.

Since the human body was the primary signifier in Mesoamerica, it is not surprising that the most common form of visual communication was performance. The writings of Sahagún and Durán show that among the Mexica performative acts were the staple of an almost continual succession of elaborate rituals that marked both important points within the various calendrical cycles that structured social life and key political events. During these rituals large numbers of lavishly costumed people congregated in designated spaces, walking or dancing in procession, singing, chanting, or playing musical instruments. Everywhere in Mesoamerica, dancing most likely played a role comparable to language. Among the Yucatec Maya, for example, the words for "dance" and "pray" are almost identical, while the Mixtec verb for "dance" means "to sing with one's feet." From colonial accounts of Mesoamerican rituals, it is clear that they were carefully orchestrated, dramatic, truly multimedia performances in which bodily movements such as posture and gesture carried much of the burden of communicating meaning.

Art objects played a significant role in these staged movements of the pre-Hispanic human body. Some of these objects have survived, but, like the ceremonies themselves, many of the garments, ornaments, and accoutrements used in them were short-lived. The material apparently most often used for Mexica ceremonies—and presumably other peoples' ceremonies as well—was *amate*, a paper made from the pulverized inner bark of the mulberry tree. Bark paper was, to judge from manuscript paintings, cut, folded, pasted or stitched, and sometimes painted to form elaborate headdress ornaments, pleated bows, streamers, sashes, rosettes, and back panels. The man who impersonated the Mexica patron god, Huitzilopochtli, carried a huge torch made of paper in the form of the mythical Fire Serpent, Xiuhcoatl. Because paper is notoriously fragile, however, no Mesoamerican paper garments or accoutrements have survived.

Other festive regalia was made of similarly fragile or perishable materials. Bird costumes and headdresses, back panels, war standards, and the fabulously decorated war shields carried only by the highest-ranking warriors during Mexica military ceremonies, for example, were made with brightly colored feathers that had been knotted or pasted onto a stable ground. A few Mexica feathered shields have survived, the best known being one currently in the Museum für Völkerkunde in Vienna. It is thought to have been owned by the ruler Ahuitzotl (1486–1502), whose name sign represented a mythical animal that looked like a feathered dog. The image on the face of the shield in Vienna represented just such a feathered canine, which is formed of tiny blue cotinga feathers that have been carefully outlined with thin, phalanged plaques of gold. Small pieces of sheet gold mark the eyes, claws, and teeth, and a gold-bordered war glyph *(atl-tlachinolli)* emerges from the mouth. The same museum also possesses the upper part of a large war standard made of the iridescent green tail feathers of the tropical quetzal bird. At the bottom, rows of red and blue cotinga feathers are overlaid with rows of gold disks. This standard, a copy of which can be seen in the National Museum of Anthropology in Mexico City, is usually mistakenly identified as a royal headdress, but its real use is evident in battle scenes painted on the colonial cloth known as the Lienzo de Tlaxcala.

Not only was much Mesoamerican art produced *by* and *for* the body, some was literally made *of* the body as well. Corporeal substances, we know from colonial texts—and increasingly from archaeological findings—often were used as raw materials for hand-crafted works of art. Perhaps the best-known examples are the face masks made from human skulls that have been found in certain Mixtec burials as well as in dedicatory offerings placed in the foundations of the Mexica's main temple (Templo Mayor), in Tenochtitlan. In the Mexica case, these skull masks were enlivened substantially by the addition of inlaid disks of shell and jet in the eye sockets and large flint knives that project from the mouths like giant tongues. A skull mask now in the British Museum is covered on the outside with wide bands of lignite that alternate with bands of turquoise mosaic. The eyes are shell overlaid with iron pyrite, and the nose socket is lined with pieces of pink shell. Such masks, according to Spanish conquistadors such as Bernal Díaz del Castillo, originally were worn by triumphant warriors in dances celebrating their victories and were made from the bodies of the warriors' slain enemies. Throughout Mesoamerica the skull clearly assumed special importance as a signifier, serving as a natural medium for elaboration. Many Mesoamerican peoples, for example, elongated their children's craniums as a means of enhancing their beauty. For the lowland Maya during the Classic period, the results of this custom were recorded in stone reliefs, where portraits of the highest-ranking men and women showed off their elegant profiles.

Some victory masks were made of skin flayed from the faces of victims. In the case of the Mexica month festival called Tlacaxipehualiztli, "Flaying of Men," certain individuals donned entire bodysuits made of the skin of ritually sacrificed and flayed prisoners. This practice of wearing human skins did not originate with the Mexica; clay statues of men dressed in such costumes have survived from diverse places in Mesoamerica. More common was the wearing of animal skins. A stone statue from the late Preclassic period (1500 B.C.–A.D. 200) Olmec culture of southern Veracruz and coastal Tabasco represents a seated man with the skin of a crocodile thrown over his head and back. In a poorly preserved cave painting at the Olmec outpost at Juxtlahuaca, Guerrero, a bearded figure wears gloves and leggings made of jaguar skin; the animal's tail hangs down between his legs.

We lack archaeological evidence of the practice of decorating the skin of living persons, but pre-Hispanic artworks and colonial period texts indicate that it was common and widespread. Clay and stone figurines from the Classic Maya area, for example, show clear evidence of scarification practices. Colonial sources state unequivocally not only that the Maya had themselves tattooed but also that they painted designs or images on their bodies. Alteration of the color or surface of the skin, including painted designs on the torso and limbs, is documented for the Mexica as well. Sahagún's descriptions of the numerous calendrical rituals held in Tenochtitlan include references to the application of paint, feathers, and pyrite flakes to the skin. In some cases the major function of these modifications was probably aesthetic, but body paint also had symbolic meaning. The faces of war captives about to be ritually sacrificed during the month festival of Panquetzaliztli, for example, were painted in bands of blue and yellow to represent the blue and yellow striped face paintings of the legendary Centzonhuitznahua, or "400 Brothers," of the Mexica patron god, Huitzilopochtli, who had long ago slain them when they tried to usurp his authority. Just as the body decorations and costumes of sacrificial victims identified them with their mythic predecessors, so, too, did the priests who participated in these rites dress up as and impersonate the gods.

As the skull masks reveal, Mesoamericans also regarded bone as a suitable medium for artistic expression. From Preclassic times to the present Mesoamericans singled out the femurs of their most distinguished war captives and ancestors and altered their shape with the help of a stone blade. Occasionally these reworked thigh bones served as musical instruments: bone flutes, drumsticks, and rattles all have been retrieved archaeologically. Two such "longbones" were found in a first century B.C. Maya burial at Chiapa de Corzo, Chiapas. One may have been a drum beater, the other a flute stopper. Both femurs were covered with carved depictions of half-human, half-animal supernaturals. A group of more delicately engraved femurs created centuries later were found in the tomb of Hasaw-Ka'an-K'awil, a ruler of the Maya site of Tikal. Some of these were decorated with glyphs, others with figural images. In the famous Mixtec Tomb 7 at Monte Albán, Oaxaca, excavators found elaborately carved weaving battens of bone. The scenes rendered there apparently recorded the origins of the local populace. Sahagún told of Mexica warriors who kept the femora of their dead captives, wrapping them in articles of their own clothing and providing them with a mask for a "face." The warriors' wives kept these personified bones in their homes and petitioned them to protect their husbands while away at war.

Ornaments made of teeth have been found in graves in several cultures, the best known being Teotihuacan. There, at the early first millennium Pyramid of Quetzalcoatl, excavators unearthed several mass burials of what appear to have been sacrificed warriors who died wearing huge necklaces strung with what look like human teeth. In some cases these teeth are indeed human, still rooted in disembodied maxillae presumably extracted from the warriors' vanquished foes. Other maxillae are imitations, the teeth embedded in them being made of carved shell. Among the nobility of many Mesoamerican groups, teeth were sites for adornment while still in the mouths of the living. Maya men of the nobility, like men of means in other parts of Mesoamerica, sometimes notched the edges of their front teeth or inlaid them with disks of greenstone or pyrite. In central Mexico, Mexica women stained their teeth red with cochineal as a means of enhancing their beauty.

Metal and Stone Objects

Many of the objects made by Mesoamerican artists were intended to be worn *on* the body. This is especially true of metal objects, which usually took the form of jewelry. Although the Mexica attributed the origins of metalworking to the Toltecs, it initially appeared in western Mexico and in the Maya area, where it apparently was introduced by people in contact with Central America. During the early Postclassic period, metalwork became increasingly popular and spread throughout Mesoamerica. Gold, bronze, copper, tumbaga (a gold-copper alloy), and silver were the favored materials. Large quantities of worked metal were dredged from the natural well, known as the Sacred Cenote, at Chichen Itza in Yucatán, where it apparently had been thrown in as a form of offering. Many of these objects were copper bells and finger rings; most were imports from Panama and Costa Rica. A few pieces had been overworked, however, by the Maya. The best-known examples of this process are the 17 gold disks, probably once worn as breastplates, reworked by Maya craftsmen with intricate *repoussé* scenes.

The earliest known gold objects in Mexico were found in Guerrero. The technology was simple: embossed sheet gold. More sophisticated metalwork was produced in copper by the Purépucha of Michoacán, whose techniques included *cire-perdue,* or lost-wax casting, filigree, and gilding. The most skilled metalworkers in Mesoamerica, however, lived in southern Mexico, in Oaxaca and Puebla, where the lost-wax casting process was well developed. The apogee of this technique is usually attributed to the Mixtecs, who worked primarily with gold and silver, both of which were available locally. Their favorite forms were necklaces, pectorals and pendants, rings, brooches, ear spools, bells, and labrets. These ornaments were often technical *tours de force,*

constructed of a number of separately made and then carefully linked parts. Many of these were covered with fine, but false (that is, cast) filigree intricately outlining complicated supernatural figures and occasionally Mixtec glyphs. One pectoral, retrieved along with a number of spectacular Mixtec metal objects from Tomb 7 at Monte Albán, consists of four separate, iconographically rich panels, suspended vertically, one from the other, and terminating in a row of stylized feathers from which hang two additional rows of bells.

The Mexica greatly esteemed gold and silver, for which there were no natural sources in the Valley of Mexico. These metals were considered to be the sun's bodily excretions, gold being the sun's excrement and silver—which was worked much less frequently—its urine. The Mexica particularly envied Mixtec metalwork and made a point of acquiring as much of it as they could. Many of the finest metal objects acquired from the Mexica by the Spaniards, who unfortunately melted it all down to make bullion, probably were made by Mixtec craftsmen, some of whom were living in the Mexica capital. Nonetheless, the Mexica had their own gold workers, who probably learned their craft from the Mixtecs. Whether they always reached the level of technical virtuosity of their neighbors to the south is uncertain, but raw materials for them to work were constantly coming into the capital from the south in the form of tribute. The designs used by Mexica gold workers, according to Sahagún, were first drawn for them by the feather workers, suggesting that they closely collaborated. This is supported by the presence of the gold trim found on the feathered shield and war standard discussed earlier.

Gold also was set with stones, suggesting that Mixtec and Mexica metalworkers also collaborated with lapidaries. A now lost shipment of gifts sent to Carlos I included a number of large collars of gold that were set with colored stones, as well as a headdress of turquoise mosaic with 25 beaded gold bells. The best lapidaries in Mexico were the Mixtecs and their southern neighbors, who were the Mexica's principal source of turquoise. The Mexica no doubt learned the craft but also imported worked objects from the south as tribute. A sixteenth-century Mexica tribute list, the Codex Mendoza, lists turquoise mosaic masks as tribute items owed to the Mexica government by a Mixtec community in Guerrero. The Mexica theoretically reserved such masks for their gods, placing them over the faces of their statues, and called the best turquoise *teuxiuitli,* which mean's "divine turquoise." Sahagún stated that the word connoted "the property, the lot of the god" and that it was "much esteemed." These valuable masks belonged to the Mexica supreme ruler, who wore them both in sickness and in death. The same seems to have been true of the Purépucha, as an illustration in the *Relación de Michoacán* shows the bundled corpse of a Purépucha ruler being carried to the funeral pyre wearing a turquoise mask.

Turquoise, however, does not appear to have been as greatly valued as jadeite, or greenstone, from which masks and items of jewelry were also made. Among the Preclassic and Classic lowland Maya, as with the Mixtecs who buried their lord or mistress in Tomb 7 at Monte Albán, jadeite mosaic was favored for funerary masks. In the Maya area, these masks have turned up in the course of excavations of lavish royal tombs, suggesting that, as in central and southern Mexico, the most valuable Maya masks were kept in the hands of ruling families. Similarly, it was these highest-ranking individuals who could afford jade jewelry and ornaments. Hasaw-Ka'an-K'awil of Tikal was buried with 16.5 pounds of worked jadeite, including an 8.5-pound jadeite collar, jadeite earplugs, and a lidded jadeite mosaic cylinder vase with a mosaic handle in the form of a royal portrait. Similarly, in 1952 the remains of Pakal II, a seventh-century dynast of Palenque, were found undisturbed in his carved stone sarcophagus surrounded by a jadeite mosaic funerary mask, a jadeite necklace and breastplate, jadeite wristlets and anklets, a jadeite headband, jadeite figurines, and several large jadeite beads that apparently had been placed in his mouth and hands. The beads are explained by the Maya belief that greenstones contain a sacred essence, or "soul," that has the ability to instill breath and life into the dead in the afterworld. Among the Mexica jadeite symbolized water, breath, and all that is precious and life-giving; indeed it encapsulated the very essence of life itself.

Textiles

By far the most important form of body covering, however, was woven fabric, which was worked into a variety of garments. Some were merely draped over or around the body; others were cut and then slipped over the head; and some were seamed to be worn like sleeveless vests or tunics. Only in rare cases were sleeves or pant legs created; most limb-encasing garments appear to have been made of animal skins.

All woven materials were made on back-strap looms using plain or dyed thread that, in the latter case, could be worked into intricate designs. By the time of the Conquest, the techniques employed in textile manufacture and decoration were numerous: plain, compound, and double-cloth weave; twill; warp-float patterning; gauze; knotted looping stitches; twining; braiding; linking; tapestry; embroidery; tie-dye; batik; pile; brocading; and possibly stamped painting. The majority of the textiles used for clothing were made of bast fibers drawn from a variety of plants. The best-known source in central and southern Mexico was the maguey plant, which also provided a variety of medicines as well as the whitish, slightly intoxicating beverage known as pulque. Garments made from such vegetal fibers were worn primarily by commoners. The Mexica state theoretically banned commoners from wearing cotton cloth, although textiles of all kinds were available in the markets, where they served as a standard measure of value and hence as a form of currency. Nobles, on the other hand, usually wore only the most finely woven and elaborately decorated cotton fabrics, reserving some to use as gifts and rewards for allegiance to the state. At the time of the Conquest, the Mexica state was importing as tribute large quantities of heavily decorated cotton textiles from the Gulf Coast region of what is today Veracruz, whose weavers they especially admired. Most of these textiles were probably retained by the elite.

The Mexica patron deity of the maguey plant, as well as the primordial source of pulque, was a goddess named Mayahuel. The patron deity of weavers in Mexica times, Xochiquetzal, also was female, while among the Postclassic Maya it was the moon goddess Ix Chel. In eastern and central Mexico, the patron deity of raw and spun cotton was the goddess Tlazolteotl. That the deities who presided over spinners and weavers were female reflects women's role as the primary producers of cloth throughout Mesoamerica. Weaving was so closely associated with femininity that baby girls were presented with tiny battens and spindles. When women died they were buried with the weaving instruments they had used as adults. A Mexica creation myth tells of five primordial goddesses who, having sacrificed themselves so that the sun would move, returned to earth years later as *mantas,* or textiles.

Mesoamerican textiles have not easily survived the wet climates in which they were produced and used, but enough fragments have survived to show a preference for allover, largely geometric designs. Stone relief carvings and vase paintings of Classic Maya rulers suggest that some, if not many, of these designs had symbolic significance. Similar designs are woven into textiles made by Maya women today, who identify some of them with various cosmic themes. Throughout Mesoamerica, fibers and textiles seem to have provided a model for the structure of the various parts of the universe, as well as moral behavior. The upper world, or sky, was described as "woven," the underworld and immoderate behavior, as "tangled" and "twisted." The spinning process was further identified with pregnancy and gestation, loom weaving with sexual intercourse and creation in general. The tremendous importance of textiles and the symbolism of their designs underscore their contribution to the semiotic function of the Mesoamerican human body.

In the many ceremonies and rituals staged through time across the Mesoamerican landscape, then, the decorated body served to communicate often-complex messages about social identity and felt needs and was used to help individuals and groups augment their own power. That the multimedia costumes were at times so elaborate that they practically obscured the wearer can be surmised from the thousands of sculptures and paintings produced throughout Mesoamerica over time. Although some of these images depicted animals or often hybridized supernaturals, it was the human body, almost always clothed, that constituted the favorite subject of representational art.

Sculpture

Mesoamerican sculpture was made of many materials, including, as we have seen, human bone and skin. In the Maya area, so-called eccentric flints reveal the Classic Maya ability to shape the brittle edges of large pieces of flint, chert, and obsidian to create silhouetted forms such as profile heads of individuals wearing elaborate hairdos and headdresses. In north-central Veracruz, ancient artists engraved complicated figural scenes on pieces of shell, while at the Classic Maya site of Palenque, in Chiapas, life-like portraits of local dynasts and their family members were modeled in stucco over stone armatures anchored in the walls and roofs of temples and then painted. The practice of polychroming sculpture was widespread in Mesoamerica, being especially popular in the Preclassic and Classic Maya lowlands, where colors were chosen for their symbolic value rather than from a desire to approximate natural appearances.

The earliest and most naturalistic figural sculptures, however, took the form of clay figurines. These were hand-modeled, mold-made, or constructed using a combination of these techniques. Many of these sculptures were fairly small and were found in the home or rubbish heap, suggesting a domestic function. In middle and late Preclassic west Mexico, however, clay figurines up to two feet in height were placed in large shaft tombs, apparently to be used by the deceased in the afterlife. In time, clay figure sculptures appeared in public, ceremonial contexts and took increasingly elaborate forms. Among the early Classic Zapotecs, for example, hand-molded and mold-made ceramic effigy urns have turned up in elite tombs, the figures on their fronts representing heavily dressed, often masked men and, less often, women, who seem to represent either deities or individuals impersonating them. The Zapotecs, like the clay workers of Classic central Veracruz, and later the Mexica, whom they apparently inspired, also produced roughly life-size, hollow ceramic figures in which the arms and legs were shaped like contoured tubes. In Veracruz, at sites like El Zapotal, these figures wore elaborate costumes, including distinctive headdresses, that identified them as religious, perhaps priestly, figures. Probably the most refined and naturalistic Mesoamerican clay figurines come from the Classic Maya island of Jaina, off the coast of Campeche. Seldom taller than one-to one-and-a-half feet, these figurines, most hand-modeled and painted, represented a wide range of supernatural and historical figures, the latter often as elaborately dressed as the deities they honored.

It was, however, in stone that urban sculptors preferred to work. The best-known stone carvers were the Maya, who produced thousands of largely life-size carvings of men—and occasionally women—in full round and relief. Most of these were commissioned during the Classic period by rulers who needed to legitimate their rule, and they typically portrayed those rulers. Other statues represented deities important to the community or the state. As elsewhere in Mesoamerica, Maya stone sculptures-in-the-round almost always represented a single figure, although smaller, subsidiary figures may have appeared in their clothing. By the end of the eighth century, when lowland Maya civilization was on the wane, these costumes at times seemed to overwhelm the wearers, whose face, hands, and parts of their legs were the only parts of their bodies that could be seen. The Mexica, on the other hand, often placed real clothing on their statues, making it unnecessary for the carver to depict the figures' costumes.

Regardless of size, Mesoamerican sculptures-in-the-round tended to be volumetric and compact; the forms seldom opened up or assumed sharp changes in depth and angle. The more monumental forms tended to be symmetrical and static, in contrast to the more lively and naturalistic clay figurines. Horizontals and verticals generally were preferred to diagonals. Artists appear to have respected the integrity of the subject's surface, forcing the viewer to "read" a form like a pier or column. At Tula, where carvers

Colossal Olmec stone head at San Lorenzo
Photo courtesy of Marcela Uribe, Biblioteca Nacional de México

Toltec statue at Tula
Photo courtesy of Marcela Uribe, Biblioteca Nacional de México

may have been inspired by earlier architectural statues at Teotihuacan, costumed lords literally took the form of giant columns, the four sides of the original blocks still evident in their blocky forms. The faces of these men, like most figural representations in central Mexico, bore no expressions of emotion and portrayed little individualization. The latter contrasts with the Maya interest in physiognomy, which at sites like Palenque and Yaxchilan resulted in true, albeit often idealized, royal portraiture.

Like stone sculpture-in-the-round, relief carving is characteristic of the larger, more centralized societies, where it, too, often served the interests of the rulers and the state. Classic Maya relief sculpture tended to the pictorial, depicting sometimes complex scenes with at least several figures arranged in what was occasionally, as at Piedras Negras, a realistic architectural (or landscape) setting. Nevertheless, as in painting, these settings were usually minimal and there is no evidence of true linear perspective beyond some foreshortening and overlapping of forms. Relief-carved and painted figures in southern and central Mexico were usually located against a vacant background, with at most only a place sign to situate them geographically.

In all two-dimensional renderings, the proportions of the head to the body tended to be based on either ideals of beauty or conceptual principles. In central and southern Mexico, where headdresses and jewelry played an important semiotic role in identifying persons, the head typically was much larger in relation to the body than nature would have it. In the Maya area, in contrast, where people seem to have admired long, graceful torsos and legs, it was often much smaller than in nature. Among the Zapotecs, Mixtecs, Teotihuacanos, Toltecs, and Mexica, two-dimensional figures also were normally presented in isomorphic form—that is, with each section of the body rendered in its most easily recognizable form. The head and legs were almost invariably in profile, while the torso was frontal. Entirely frontal figures were quite rare in all areas, where they tended to be reserved for earth and death figures or to arrest the viewer's gaze at a point marking the end or beginning of a sequence or narrative.

Relief carvings usually appeared in an architectural context, especially at doorways, on staircases and roofs, and on piers and pillars. Some relief-carved stone blocks, however, were apparently made to be freestanding; the so-called Acuecuexatl Stone found in Tenochtitlan, which is carved on all sides, is an example. Paintings, on the other hand, appeared in several forms. The three most common were painted manuscripts, wall murals, and ceramic vases, with ceramic vase paintings being the best represented today.

Painting

Unfortunately, almost all of the painted manuscripts were destroyed in the sixteenth century by zealous Spaniards anxious to replace indigenous religions with Christianity. Today there are only four painted manuscripts that predate the Conquest in the Maya area and virtually none for central Mexico. The greatest number of extant manuscripts—11 in all —come from Postclassic southern Mexico, where many can be attributed to the Mixtecs. They exemplify the so-called Mixteca-Puebla style, a pictorial style characterized primarily by a repertoire of symbols popular throughout much of Mesoamerica from the middle Classic period up to the Conquest. Some of the extant Mixteca-Puebla–style manuscripts are historical in nature, but others, like the Maya examples, are calendrical and divinatory. All were used by specialists, some of them in the employ of government officials, who were drawn from the elite and trained in special schools. No examples of pre-Conquest tribute lists or maps have survived.

At the time of the Conquest, Mixtec kings were hanging the historical manuscripts on the inside walls of their houses to document their royal lines of descent as a means of legitimating their rule. Francisco de Burgoa reported that these paintings were consulted during "assemblies," suggesting that they served as mnemonic prompts, or scripts. This impression is reinforced by the fact that the Mixtec word for a singer, *"tutuyondaayaa,"* means "he who holds the songbook." The scholar John Pohl has suggested that the paintings seen on the exteriors of fancy Mixtec ceramic vessels were excerpts from the same narratives that were rendered in detail in the manuscripts, and that they served a similar function: to aid in public recitations of dynastic claims. In the Maya area as well, the outer surfaces of vessels often looked like pages from a painted manuscript and are thought to have been painted by the same class of professionals. One style of Maya vase painting, thought to be the product of a workshop at Nakbé, is actually called codex-style. Since Burgoa stated that the stories depicted in the Mixtec manuscripts were actually acted out at major religious festivals, it seems likely that at least some painted manuscripts and ceramics were important props in public performances.

Extant Mesoamerican manuscripts were made of either animal hide (probably deerskin), the material favored by the Mixtecs, or bark paper, which was used for all extant Mexica and Maya examples. Both materials were covered with a calcium carbonate coating prior to being painted. A few have wooden boards attached at front and back to serve as covers. Although it is known that scribes also painted on cloth prior to the Conquest, no pre-Hispanic *lienzos* have survived. The bark paper manuscripts were usually screen-folded—that is, they were made of a series of sheets glued together to form a single strip and then folded back and forth like an accordion. Some manuscripts were apparently single sheets, either laid flat or simply rolled up when not in use. Those manuscripts that were painted on both sides were arranged chronologically to begin at one end of the strip, continue to the other end, wrap around to the other side, and continue back to the point where they began. In the Mixtec area, the portrayed events tended to be arranged sequentially in a kind of meandering pattern that moved either horizontally or vertically across one or more pages. The paints used were largely vegetal and mineral and, to judge from Classic Maya depictions of scribes, were applied with fiber or animal hair brushes and occasionally sharp tools that functioned like a pen.

At Teotihuacan pigment was sometimes inlaid into recessed areas of clay vessels in a kind of cloisonné technique. As in southern and central Mexico, painted forms were defined by black outlines that separated broad areas of flat color. In the Maya lowlands, these lines were cursive and the contours of the forms, fluid and organic. In Mexico, in contrast, the outlines were more even in width, tended to be straighter, and changed direction more abruptly. Mexican paintings thus featured relatively stiff and blocky figures in contrast to Maya examples, where human, animal, and supernatural forms were relatively dynamic and naturalistic. In both the Maya area and southern and central Mexico, however, there was a tendency to use lines or other means to divide the picture plane into zones, or registers.

The Mesoamerican custom of shearing and overbuilding important edifices, combined with the ravages of time and weather, accounts for the relative paucity of intact murals today. In the Maya area, in particular, where muralism was once a major art form, most of the known wall paintings were partially, if not completely, destroyed. Intact murals in a relatively good state of preservation, such as those found in three rooms of a small building at Bonampak, in Chiapas, were quite rare there. In central and southern Mexico preservation tended to be better, particularly in Oaxaca, where murals have been found primarily in subterranean tombs. At Teotihuacan, where during the fifth to seventh centuries in particular brightly colored murals were painted on almost every available interior wall surface—and sometimes on the exteriors as well—we get our best glimpse of the importance and visual impact of Mesoamerican mural painting. Remnants of tens of thousands of murals testify to their role as Teotihuacan's primary form of expression, depicting everything from cult icons to religious and military rituals, to mythological scenes, to what appear to be everyday events in the lives of the people. Here, as at most other Mesoamerican sites where murals have been found, the technique employed was *buon fresco,* the pigments having been applied to a damp plaster surface. Light red outlines were applied first, then broad areas of color, followed by final dark red outlines. Teotihuacan is unusual in having many murals of repetitive, allover design, as well as a late phase of monochromatic wall paintings executed entirely in varying shades of red. The images were typical of Mexican murals, however, in featuring fairly static compositions with short, blocky, isolated figures set against monochromatic backgrounds. The Classic Maya murals at Bonampak, in contrast, are famous for their pictorial space filled with large numbers of figures engaged in a variety of activities that in places crowd the picture plane as twisting, overlapping, dynamic forms.

Architecture and Urban Centers

Such paintings surely embellished Mesoamerican buildings in order to enliven and give special meaning to the built environment. Whole cities, in fact, are known to have been completely covered with paint. During the Classic period a number of Mesoamerican cities—most of them Maya—were completely painted in red, the color of life itself. These cities were perceived as projections of the power of the state and of the ruler, who was believed to embody that power. The Mexica word for city, *"altepetl,"* actually referred to a ruler's entire political sphere: to his place of residence and to all the people and territories under his control. The word translates as "water mountain" and reflects the Mexica belief that a community was defined by its relation to a place where life-giving waters from the earth's interior flow over the earth's surface from a mountain of sustenance. An *altepetl* represented the power of the polity and its ruler and as such was itself alive.

Like living organisms, all Mesoamerican cities had a "heart," or center; some in the Maya area had more than one. These centers contained the most important religious, administrative, commercial, and residential structures in the city and accordingly usually reflected careful planning. Sometimes—as at Teotihuacan and Tenochtitlan—the inner city was

The Maya city of Uxmal
Photo courtesy of Mexican Government Tourism Office

The Zapotec city of Monte Albán
Photo courtesy of Mexican Government Tourism Office

organized on a grid, while at other times—as at Monte Albán and Tikal—the largest and most important buildings were simply arranged along a major axis, usually defined by a rectangular plaza. This axis was almost always oriented slightly east of north and effectively divided the city into halves. At Teotihuacan, the main axis was marked by a wide, three-mile-long paved avenue known as the Street of the Dead. The Street of the Dead further aligned with a mountain to the north, reflecting an interest in geomantics that is evident at other sites as well. It may have been intersected at a right angle by a second, east-west road, or axis, that further subdivided the city into quarters. In Tenochtitlan, four quadrants corresponding to administrative districts were demarcated by raised causeways that led into the city roughly from the cardinal points. The causeways converged at the gates of the main ceremonial precinct, which was surrounded by administrative buildings and royal residences. Roads and causeways were major features of most Mesoamerican urban landscapes. At the late Classic Maya site of Cobá,

Quintana Roo, 16 causeways radiated out from the center like the spokes of a wheel, connecting the city with other centers some distance away.

In cities such as Tenochtitlan and Teotihuacan, it was only well beyond the core area, where the commoners lived and worked, that roads and houses ceased to conform to the grid. The average Mesoamerican lived in a cluster of three or four small, one- or two-room buildings that shared a common courtyard or patio. In the larger urban centers these houses were made of masonry, with flat roofs, and were normally single story. Larger compounds have been excavated at Teotihuacan and Tula. Teotihuacan was unique in having had as many as 100 or more people living together inside its largest apartment compounds, where rooms were grouped around small sunken patios, each with a drain to handle the rain and a small altar at the center. Porticos, their roofs supported by square columns, allowed sunlight to penetrate the otherwise dark interiors. In the less crowded compounds at Teotihuacan, where the living standard was clearly higher, the interior walls were

Classic-era Maya pyramid at Tikal (Petén, Guatemala)
Photo by Felipe García, courtesy of Guatemala Tourist Commission

often covered with finely painted murals. Elsewhere, especially at lower elevations and in the rural areas of Guatemala, most people probably lived in single-room, wattle-and-daub dwellings with thatched roofs.

In Mesoamerica, the largest and most elaborate structures were typically religious in function, a reflection of the importance of religion to the identity and maintenance of the political unit. By far the most common religious structure was the temple pyramid, which is the hallmark of the Mesoamerican-built environment. Hundreds of temple pyramids lined the main avenue at Teotihuacan; some Maya sites have dozens of them. Each site had its own variant of the building type, but almost all temple-pyramids were steep-sided, tiered, had a rectangular or less often square ground plan and supported a small, one- to three-room structure on top. In Mexica and certain highland Maya cities, two temples shared a single platform. In the deepest recesses of all temples, there was usually an altar, a bench, or both, as well as one or more statues of a deity.

The Mexica called their temples *teocalli,* which translates as "god house," and identified their main temple with a mythical place called Coatepec, or "Snake Mountain." It was at Coatepec that their patron god Huitzilopochtli first had asserted his supremacy by defeating his sibling rivals. To confirm the main temple's identification with Coatepec, Mexica architects had the pyramid base decorated with projecting stone serpent heads. The Maya did something similar: they referred to the pyramid as *witz,* or "mountain," and decorated some pyramids with rows of huge faces, or "masks," of supernaturals who identified their temples and subterranean tombs as mountain caves that served as cosmic portals to the underworld. Throughout Mesoamerica, the entries of certain buildings were designed as giant open mouths representing a mountain cave or the earth itself. When one entered these sacred spaces, he or she entered the body of the earth, where it was believed a person could make direct contact with the ancestral deities.

Accordingly Mesoamerican buildings, like the earth, were treated as living entities. At the time of their construction great caches of symbolically, if not materially, valuable objects were deposited in their foundations as offerings. In the case of the Pyramid of Quetzalcoatl at Teotihuacan, itself covered with tenoned stone heads of mythic creatures, such deposits included groups of sacrificed men and women. Upon completion, important buildings received dedicatory offerings and, when no longer needed, in the Maya area were ritually "terminated."

As told by Sahagún, during the month festival of Panquetzaliztli, the primordial triumph of the Mexica patron god Huitzilopochtli at Coatepec was reenacted annually, amid much pomp and fanfare, on the steps and platform of the main temple. From this we gain the suspicion that a major function of Mesoamerican religious architecture was to serve as a stage for ritual performances. Indeed, it is fair to characterize the Mesoamerican-built environment as largely an architecture of exterior and open spaces, since most temple interiors were not only small, but visually and physically inaccessible to all but a few. There were no windows. Throughout Mesoamerica, roofing techniques were largely based on the post-and-lintel system, although the occasional round temples were covered with thatched conical roofs. The Maya developed a type of vault known as the corbel arch, but it was capable of spanning only relatively small and cramped interior spaces. In Classic north-central Veracruz, at the site of El Tajín, Huastec builders took advantage of the Maya technique of using concrete to create stronger ceilings, but their temples remained fairly small.

Indeed, the most impressive architectural decorations were placed on the outside, not the inside, of structures, where they could be viewed by the public. The famous Pyramid of the Niches at El Tajín is a case in point; its four sides were covered with rows of deeply recessed square niches that created a dramatic effect. The giant carved and modeled architectural masks are another prime example. At Teotihuacan's Pyramid of Quetzalcoatl, masks were tenoned into cantilevered, framed rectangular panels that overhung a short, recessed, sloping panel largely hidden in the shadows. This dramatic combination of a sloping panel with a vertical, overhanging panel, known as the *talud-tablero* system, was adopted by a number of Mesoamerican cities, each of which developed its own distinctive variant. In the Maya area, as in Tenochtitlan, sculpted and painted mansard roofs added height to elevated temples. The Maya extended these heights even further by crowning the roofs with tall, lacy, sculptured roof combs.

During the late Classic period, many cities outside of central Mexico began to decorate pyramid bases and other buildings with their own versions of geometric designs created in stone mosaic. The most popular motif was the step fret, or *greca,* which most scholars think represented the Fire Serpent. At Mitla, in Mixtec territory, the buildings decorated with mosaic step frets faced inward onto a common patio, much as temple pyramids at larger sites fronted vast plazas on a much grander scale. It is these plazas, like the vast causeways, large patios, and other open spaces, that dominated the Mesoamerican-built environment. The soaring temple pyramids and raised platforms that lined and punctuated these open spaces functioned like raised stages, allowing large groups of people to better take in—and be appropriately awed by—the dramatic proceedings. The scholar Andrea Stone argued that these structures often recreated the sacred landscape outside the city, much as the Mexica's main temple represented the distant mountain Coatepec, "capturing" and bringing it into the heart of the city where members of the elite could demonstrate their power and control over it.

According to Burgoa, the histories depicted in Mixtec-painted manuscripts were reenacted during major religious festivals. At Mitla these rites no doubt took place in the patios bordered by *greca*-ornamented buildings. It was at these times that the painted manuscripts and painted ceramic vessels would have been used to prompt oral recitations, songs, and serve as scripts for dances and a variety of rituals. These performers were surely dressed in elaborate regalia. As they moved about the patio, their every sound, gesture, and detail of dress laden with meaning, the boundaries, cosmic identity, and sacredness of the space and the event taking place in it would have been simultaneously communicated by the surrounding buildings and their decorations.

In such situations, architecture can be seen as having collaborated with many of the other major art forms in this part of the world to simultaneously direct and frame the movements of the human body. By creating the setting for and channeling those actions, as well as by specifying and heightening their meaning, architecture worked together with the visual arts to empower people in their ongoing struggle to control the visible natural world, its invisible forces, and each other.

See also Mesoamerica

Select Bibliography

Anawalt, Patricia, *Indian Clothing Before Cortés.* Norman: University of Oklahoma Press, 1981.

Berrin, Kathleen, and Esther Pasztory, editors, *Teotihuacan: Art from the City of the Gods.* San Francisco: The Fine Arts Museums of San Francisco, 1993.

Boone, Elizabeth Hill, "Pictorial Codices of Ancient America." In *The Ancient Americas: Art from Sacred Landscapes,* edited by Richard F. Townsend. Chicago: Art Institute of Chicago, 1992.

_____, "Introduction: Writing and Recording Knowledge." In *Writing without Words: Alternative Literacies in Mesoamerica and the Andes,* edited by Elizabeth Hill Boone and Walter D. Mignolo. Durham, North Carolina: Duke University, 1994.

Bray, Warwick, "Maya Metalwork and Its External Connections." In *Social Process in Maya Prehistory: Studies in Memory of Sir Eric Thompson,* edited by Norman Hammond. London: Academic Press, 1977.

Coe, Michael D., et al., *The Olmec World: Ritual and Rulership.* Princeton, New Jersey: The Art Museum, 1995.

Emmerich, André, *Sweat of the Sun and Tears of the Moon.* Seattle: University of Washington Press, 1965.

Freidel, David, Linda Schele, and Joy Parker, *Maya Cosmos: Three Thousand Years on the Shaman's Path.* New York: Morrow, 1993.

Heyden, Doris, and Paul Gendrop, *Pre-Columbian Architecture of Mesoamerica,* translated by Judith Stanton. New York: Abrams, 1973.

Hosler, Dorothy, *The Sounds and Colors of Power: The Sacred Metallurgical Techology of Ancient West Mexico.* Cambridge, Massachusetts: MIT Press.

King, Mary Elizabeth, "The Prehistoric Textile Industry of Mesoamerica." In *The Junius B. Bird Pre-Columbian Textile Conference: May 19th and 20th, 1973,* edited by Anne Pollard Rowe, et al. Washington, D.C.: The Textile Museum and Dumbarton Oaks, 1979.

Kubler, George, *The Art and Architecture of Ancient America.* 3rd edition, Harmondsworth, Middlesex: Penguin Books, 1984.

Marcus, Joyce, "On the Nature of the Mesoamerican City." In *Prehistoric Settlement Patterns: Essays in Honor of Gordon R. Willey,* edited by Evon Z. Vogt and Richard M. Leventhal. Albuquerque: University of New Mexico Press, 1983.

Miller, Arthur G., *The Mural Painting of Teotihuacán.* Washington, D.C.: Dumbarton Oaks, 1973.

Miller, Mary Ellen, *The Murals of Bonampak.* Princeton, New Jersey: Princeton University Press, 1986.

Pasztory, Esther, *Aztec Art.* New York: Abrams, 1983.

_____, "The Function of Art in Mesoamerica." *Archaeology* 37:1 (1984).

Pohl, John M., "Mexican Codices, Maps, and Lienzos as Social Contracts." In *Writing without Words: Alternative Literacies in Mesoamerica and the Andes,* edited by Elizabeth Hill Boone and Walter D. Mignolo. Durham, North Carolina: Duke University Press, 1994.

Reents-Budet, Dorie, *Painting the Maya Universe: Royal Ceramics of the Classic Period.* Durham, North Carolina: Duke University Press, 1994.

Schele, Linda, and Mary Ellen Miller, *The Blood of Kings: Dynasty and Ritual in Maya Art.* Fort Worth, Texas: Kimbell Art Museum, 1986.

Schele, Linda, and David Freidel, *A Forest of Kings: The Untold Story of the Ancient Maya.* New York: Morrow, 1990.

Umberger, Emily, "Antiques, Revivals, and References to the Past in Aztec Art." *Res* 13 (1987).

—CECELIA F. KLEIN

Visual Arts: Sixteenth Century

The art of sixteenth-century New Spain constitutes a rich visual archive. Architecture, paintings, and works of art in other media evidence the institutions and societal relationships that emerged in the transformative years following Fernando (Hernán) Cortés's campaigns of conquest. Early colonial art production flourished in central Mexico, where the Spanish superimposed New Spain's capital city on the ruins of the Mexica (Aztec) imperial capital, Tenochtitlan. Sixteenth-century artists were, for the most part, native Mexicans who worked at the behest of mendicant missionaries in the colonial cities. In addition, some European-trained artists from Spain and Flanders arrived in sixteenth-century Mexico, where they formed a guild and began to produce religious art for the new churches.

Sixteenth-century Mexican art communicated various kinds of information to its different audiences. Pictorial manuscripts and the painted maps of the *Relaciones geográficas* recorded history and land claims, presenting Mexico's native inhabitants and geography to Europeans—including the Spanish king. In contrast, a host of religious art works served devotional and didactic purposes for missionaries and native catechumens in early Mexican churches and mission complexes. Frescoes and murals, stone and wood sculptures, and woodcut illustrations all depicted Christian iconography derived from art works by Albrecht Dürer and other European artists. Likewise, panel paintings and canvases represented conventional religious themes.

Whereas much sixteenth-century art utilized imported European techniques, representational genres, and Christian iconography, other forms of colonial visual expression clearly referenced the pre-Hispanic past in medium, style, and/or subject. Early colonial artists continued to produce dazzling feather work images, pre-Conquest–style paintings served as evidence in colonial legal proceedings, and some Mexica ceramic styles persisted well into the sixteenth century.

Painted Manuscripts

The hundreds of sixteenth-century painted manuscripts (codices) in library and museum collections worldwide are invaluable sources of pre-Conquest and early colonial Mexican history. Scholars believe that some of the early colonial manuscripts mimic pre-Conquest documents, almost all of which were burned by Spaniards in early colonial times. Central Mexican artists and scribes produced most of the sixteenth-century manuscripts. Art historical studies

have focused chiefly on deciphering their imagery and interpreting the ways in which their painting styles suggest the encroachment of European representational conventions. In such studies, pictorial style and technique frequently are taken as indices of the artist's acculturation to a European world view.

Some early manuscripts utilized materials, formats, and compositions that originated in the pre-Conquest period. The *Tira de la peregrinación*, an early pictorial document that recounted Mexica history, utilized the *tira* (paper strip) format, its glyphic images painted in black on a long sheet of *amate* (fig) paper. Manuscripts such as the *Codex Borbonicus* and the *Codex Fejéváry-Mayer* contained many colorful divinitory, calendrical, and cosmological images and employed the "screenfold" format, in which long sheets of *amate* paper or animal hide were glued and folded to produce a series of separate but connected pages.

The Codex Mendoza and the *Florentine Codex* are examples of another manuscript type—the bound book. Approximating the European medieval illuminated manuscript in format, these books described for a European audience Nahua (native central Mexican) history, institutions, and practices of everyday life. They contained a wealth of painted images as well as written texts in Spanish and Nahuatl, the native Mexican language.

The first viceroy of Mexico, Antonio de Mendoza, probably commissioned the *Codex Mendoza* (hence, its name) from a Nahua artist or artists who likely composed it in the 1540s. The 71-page document was divided into three distinct sections: a recounting of the territorial conquests of Moteuczoma, a pre-Conquest style tribute list, and descriptions of Nahua daily life. The first section of the manuscript contained a vividly painted, full-page map of Tenochtitlan. The tribute lists depicted, enumerated, and labeled objects such as textiles, shields, and costumes that various native communities offered to the Mexica imperial capital in pre-Conquest times.

Under the supervision of the Franciscan friar Bernardino de Sahagún, a team of highly skilled Nahua artists and scribes produced the *Historia general de las cosas de la Nueva España* (Florentine Codex), an abundantly illustrated encyclopedia of sixteenth-century New Spain. The painted images in the codex appear as bordered, medieval-style vignettes positioned within the two columns of text and as smaller decorative borders and grotesque embellishments. Some of the images probably were drawn in imitation of woodcut illustrations in printed books that missionaries brought to New Spain, indicating the native artists' awareness of European pictorial

Map of Tenochtitlan from the Codex Mendoza *(c. 1540s)*
Illustration courtesy of Archivo Fotográfico, Instituto de Investigaciones Estéticas de la UNAM

conventions and perspective. Other images have no apparent European antecedents and exhibit what are thought to be pre-Conquest glyphs, painting styles, and compositions.

Its authors divided the *Florentine Codex* into 12 books with distinct categories of visual and written information. The first book cataloged Mexica deities; subsequent books treated subjects such as Nahua ceremonies, occupations, plants, and animals, and the history of the Conquest. Book Nine contained descriptions and images of Nahua artists, including stone carvers, feather workers, and precious-metal workers. The detailed images and texts in Nahuatl and Spanish explained the techniques and tools with which those artists worked.

Maps

Rural communities of sixteenth-century Nahuas produced over 150 *Relaciones geográficas*—reports to the Spanish Crown on the geography and natural resources of New Spain. Typically, the reports contained maps made by Nahua artist-scribes. These maps and others produced in the sixteenth century form a corpus of visual representations of early viceregal cities and of indigenous conceptions of the rapidly changing world in which Nahuas lived.

Studies of maps have centered on many of the same questions as those of manuscripts. For example, scholars have looked to sixteenth-century maps for visual evidence of a surviving pre-Conquest Nahua worldview as well as invasive Spanish cartographic conventions that would suggest that native mapmaker's acculturation. Maps also constitute important evidence for studies of early colonial transformations in city planning and attest to early colonial community self-definition.

The earliest maps depicted expansive territories and used pre-Conquest conventions such as the footprint to indicate movement through the mapped territory. In using the footprint device, such maps suggest historical narratives. For example, the *Map of Cuauhtinchan* and surrounding areas from the *Historia Tolteca-Chichimeca* (c. 1545–65) employed the footprint convention as well as other glyphic conventions to record the founding and geographic boundaries of the city.

Many later sixteenth-century maps focused on a particular city or pueblo in aerial perspective, emphasizing features such as important roads and churches. Attributed to Gabriel de Rojas, the *Map of Cholula* from the 1580s depicted the grid plan of that city, picturing and labeling its numerous churches in association with glyphlike images of low, rounded hills. The artist painted the plan in black ink

Images of artists from Book 9 of Historia general de las cosas de Nueva España *(Florentine Codex; c. 1559–c. 1570)*

Illustration courtesy of Archivo Fotográfico, Instituto de Investigaciones Estéticas de la UNAM

on light paper, highlighting some buildings in shades of brownish-yellow and hills in shades of green.

Architecture

While pictorial manuscripts and painted maps conveyed information abut Mexico and its history to European audiences, other works of art functioned in the arenas of Christian worship and religious conversion. Churches and mission complexes comprised the bulk of large-scale, sixteenth-century building campaigns, although the largely Nahua workforces also constructed elite residences and civic architecture as well. Many of these structures are still standing today, and Mexico has invested significant resources in recent architectural restoration projects.

Studies of sixteenth-century Mexican architecture have focused predominantly on its formal innovations and its medieval and Renaissance European antecedents. The sixteenth-century cathedral in Mexico City is known through drawings on maps of the early colonial capital and from written sources. Scholars claim that this early church (c. 1525) had a basilican plan with three naves, the central one being the widest. Other important early churches in Mexico, such as the cathedral in Puebla, had similar plans. As pictured and described in the *Florentine Codex,* Nahua stonemasons made up the labor force for church and mission construction projects in central Mexico, and the materials for the early structures often came from the ruined Mexica temples and sculptures. The undersides of some stone column bases associated with early phases of the Mexico City cathedral reveal the remains of Mexica stone sculptures.

In contrast to the basilican plan, many other churches, such as those associated with mendicant missions, appear to have had a single nave. At the Franciscan mission of Huejotzingo, for example, the single nave took the place of the earlier wood and adobe basilican church that preceded it. The mid-sixteenth-century mission there incorporated its single-nave church into an agglomeration of other architectural forms, including an interior courtyard around which were located rooms for cooking, eating, and sleeping; a vast, walled churchyard bounded by stone walls and *posas,* or small temples; and an "open chapel," an innovative three-sided room that opened onto the churchyard and that formed the locus for outdoor celebrations of the liturgy. The Augustinian and Dominican monasteries featured similar plans. An image in Diego Valadés's *Retórica Cristiana* (1579) depicts a prototypical mission as the architectural complex within which a variety of activities took place, including ceremonial processions, the religious instruction of Nahua catechumens, and the administration of sacraments. Missionaries erected similar complexes in other parts of Mexico, including several in and around San Cristóbal de las Casas, Chiapas.

Architectural sculpture on the mission buildings' exteriors typically made reference to the missionaries' religious order. At the Huejotzingo complex, the church facade and the exterior walls of the *posas* incorporated stonework details such as the Franciscan rope, shield, and stigmata. In keeping with the millenarian spirit of early colonial missionaries, Franciscan architectural sculpture often depicted apocalyptic themes such as the Last Judgment.

Murals and Frescoes

The mendicant missions in sixteenth-century Mexico housed works of art in a variety of genres. The evangelical complex featured walls painted with murals and frescoes of various Christian subjects, including the Crucifixion, the Last Judgment, the Immaculate Conception, the Mass of St. Gregory, and images of St. Francis and other saints. Other subjects for wall paintings included the lavish vegetal and floral iconography at the Augustinian mission in Malinalco and depictions of ceremonial processions at Huejotzingo. Art historical studies of early colonial wall paintings have focused predominately on stylistic analyses and the search for their iconographic sources.

Native artists probably used woodcuts in European books as the pictorial models from which they worked. In fact, at the Augustinian mission at Actopan and elsewhere, the extensive, predominately black and white wall paintings took on the appearance of book illustrations, using color only sparingly. Nahua artists generally composed the wall paintings as a series of rectangular images bordered with registers of complex patterns of intertwined animal and vegetal imagery. At the Augustinian monastery of Ixmiquilpan in Hidalgo, the large, colorful nave murals incorporated narrative iconography with the grotesque border design, combining huge acanthus vines with images of native warriors doing battle. While a wide audience, including missionaries and Nahua catechumens, would have had access to some of the mission wall paintings, other murals were located in restricted areas where only the mendicant brothers could have viewed them.

Most works of art by Nahua artists cannot be associated with individual artists. On the basis of stylistic evidence, art historians have suggested individual schools of muralists and have identified the characteristics of individual "hands." Juan Gerson is the only Nahua artist whose name can be associated definitively with specific paintings. His images on the vault of the Franciscan mission church at Tecamachalco, Puebla (c. 1560), depicted apocalyptic scenes and the emblems of the four evangelists.

Religious Paintings and Sculptures

In addition to their elaborate mural and fresco programs, sixteenth-century churches typically housed religious oil paintings on canvas and huge, gilded wooden altarpieces *(retablos)* with painted panels and polychrome figural sculptures in niches. The authors of these works were, in most cases, Spanish artists who had come in the middle of the sixteenth century to New Spain, where they soon established an artists' guild. Later sixteenth-century European painters and sculptors in Mexico followed the directives of the Council of Trent (1563) in choosing conventional religious subjects for their panels, canvases, and figures.

Attributed to Nicolás Tejeda de Guzmán and Pedro de Brizuela, the 1570 *retablo mayor* from the Church of John the Baptist in Cuauhtinchan, Puebla, consisted of eight large, painted scenes from the lives of the Virgin Mary and Christ framed by painted and gilded ionic columns and other architectural forms. Smaller painted panels at the sides and bottom of the *retablo* depicted saints and apostles, and a central niche held a gilded sculpture of the Virgin and

Altarpiece (retablo) *at the Franciscan mission at Huejotzingo, attributed to the painter Simón Pereyns and the sculptor Pedro de Requema*

Photo courtesy of Colección Luis Márquez, Archivo Fotográfico, Instituto de Investigaciones Estéticas de la UNAM

Los Angeles Encadenados al Eufrates (c. 1560) by Juan Gerson, from the vault of the Franciscan mission church at Tecamachalco, Puebla

Illustration courtesy of Instituto Nacional de Antropología e Historia

Child. The sixteenth-century *retablo* at Huejotzingo similarly combined painting, figural sculpture, and architectural forms. Attributed to Flemish painter Simón Pereyns and the sculptor Pedro de Requema, the *retablo* integrated painted scenes from Christ's life with gilded columns, architraves, and niches containing sculpted images of saints. The *retablo's* three central panels housed a sculptural crucifix, a relief sculpture of St. Francis receiving the stigmata, and a sculpted image of St. Michael the archangel.

European-trained artists generally produced the *retablos* and oil paintings, whereas Nahua artists carved the sixteenth-century stone baptismal fonts and *atrio* (churchyard) crosses at early colonial missions. Stylistically similar to early mission architectural sculpture, the massive stone baptismal fonts featured iconography such as rope borders, missionary insignias, flowers, vines, and figures of angels. Paint often colored the sculpted font imagery.

Imposing *atrio* crosses—carved stone crosses erected in mission churchyards—typically exceeded 10 feet in height. The crosses were replete with complex imagery carved in high and low relief and did not depict the Crucifixion in a conventional way. Rather, they represented the instruments of Christ's Passion as well as skulls, symbols for blood, and, occasionally, faces of Christ and the Virgin Mary.

Feather Work

A series of images in Book Nine of the *Florentine Codex* and their accompanying text described the Mexican technique of making images from feathers. This pre-Conquest form of artistic expression particularly interested invading Spaniards, who commissioned religious works in this medium and sent examples of feather work to Europe. Feather work objects in pre-Conquest formats included circular shields with images of animals and geometric symbols.

Early colonial feather work objects typically took the form of rectangular religious paintings in which differently colored feathers created the picture in a mosaic-like fashion. A sixteenth-century feather work image of St. Peter in Zacatecas depicted the haloed saint in an outdoor setting with flowing robes and his attribute, a key. Early colonial artists also created religious vestments with feather work elements. A feather miter from Michoacán depicted a Crucifixion scene and a tree of Jesse.

Book Illustrations

In his *Memoriales e historia de los indios de la Nueva España* (1540s), the friar Toribio de Benavente (Motolinía) noted that Nahua artists were very skilled in making woodcut images from printed prototypes that originated in Europe. Studies of colonial printing suggest that illustrated books with engravings and woodcuts from Germany, Italy, Flanders, and Spain circulated in New Spain beginning in the sixteenth century. Europeans established Mexican printing houses and began to publish works such as Alonso de Molina's *Vocabulario en lengua castellana y mexicana y mexicana y castellana* beginning in the late 1540s.

Sixteenth-century published works often included at least one woodcut image. A few such images appear with great frequency in the archive of early colonial printed books. For example, an image of St. Francis receiving the stigmata from a winged crucifix in the sky appears in several sixteenth-century editions of Molina's dictionary and other dictionaries and grammars. Another frequently reproduced woodcut image represents the Crucifixion.

Arts in Pre-Conquest Styles

Sixteenth-century images painted by Nahua artists in what is considered to be a pre-Conquest style functioned to convey information other than Christian doctrine and encyclopedic data. One such series of paintings on *amate* paper from the *Huejotzingo Codex* (c. 1530) accompanied the records from a lawsuit that Cortés brought in defense of lands that he claimed to own. Nahua witnesses testified by means of reading the images to the court; the pictures depicted quantities of objects represented glyphically in the format of a tribute list. One of the paintings depicted a "picture within a picture": a brightly colored painting of the Virgin and Child stands among a variety of other objects.

Another painting in what is thought to be a pre-Conquest style accompanied a sixteenth-century Inquisition case in which a Nahua man was charged with idolatry. His accusers believed that he had removed and hidden a group of carved, stone images from the Mexica Templo Mayor in the center of Tenochtitlan; the accusers wished to destroy them. The painting testified to the stone images' movement through time and the hands of various parties, including the accused. The artist represented the stone sculptures as wrapped and bound objects whose appearance is not readily discernible to the viewer.

The *lienzo* is a pre-Conquest genre of representation in which images painted on a large, rectangular piece of cloth recorded historical and cartographic information. Native Mexican artists continued to produce *lienzos* in the sixteenth century. Like many colonial maps, the *Lienzo of Zacatepec* (1550–1600) integrates historical events and geographic features, depicting them in a characteristically Mixtec style.

The central Mexican *Lienzo of Tlaxcala* (c. 1550), now known only through eighteenth- and nineteenth-century copy drawings, may have been intended as a gift for the Spanish king. It recorded history as a series of 87 painted events, such as battles and ceremonial meetings, arranged in rows beneath a larger, main scene with heraldic elements. The *Lienzo* emphasized the role that Cortés's Tlaxcalan allies played in the defeat of Moteuczoma and his empire. A series of now-destroyed, painted murals in the Tlaxcalan *cabildo* (Spanish-style municipal council) depicted the same historical events in similar manner, as do the line drawings accompanying Diego Muñoz-Camargo's *Descripción de la ciudad y provincia de Tlaxcala* (1585).

Select Bibliography

Boone, Elizabeth Hill, and Walter D. Mignolo, editors, *Writing without Words: Alternative Literacies in Mesoamerica and the Andes*. Durham, North Carolina: Duke University Press, 1994.

Farago, Claire, *Reframing the Renaissance: Visual Culture in Europe and Latin America, 1450–1650*. New Haven, Connecticut: Yale University Press, 1995.

Gruzinski, Serge, "Colonial Indian Maps in Sixteenth-Century Mexico." In *Res 13* (Spring 1987).

Klor de Alva, J. Jorge, et al., editors, *The Work of Bernardino de Sahagún: Pioneer Ethnographer of Sixteenth-Century Aztec Mexico*. Austin: University of Texas Press, 1988.

Kubler, George, *Mexican Architecture of the Sixteenth Century*. New Haven, Connecticut: Yale University Press, 1948.

McAndrew, John, *The Open-Air Churches of Sixteenth-Century Mexico: Atrios, Posas, Open Chapels, and Other Studies*. Cambridge, Massachusetts: Harvard University Press, 1965.

Mundy, Barbara E., *The Mapping of New Spain: Indigenous Cartography and the Maps of the Relaciones Geográficas*. Chicago: University of Chicago Press, 1996.

Peterson, Jeanette, *The Paradise Garden Murals of Malinalco: Utopia and Empire in Sixteenth-Century Mexico*. Austin: University of Texas Press, 1993.

Robertson, Donald, *Mexican Manuscript Painting of the Early Colonial Period*. New Haven, Connecticut: Yale University Press, 1959.

Toussaint, Manuel, *Colonial Art in Mexico*, edited and translated by Elizabeth Wilder Weismann. Austin: University of Texas Press, 1967.

— MICHAEL SCHREFFLER

Visual Arts: Seventeenth Century

Traditionally viewed as an uneventful time for New Spain, the seventeenth century was in reality a period of great change defined by shifts of peoples, goods, and ideologies. During this period the colony achieved great economic stability, a phenomenon that stimulated art production in a variety of manifestations, ranging from painting to architecture. Several developments contributed to this economic upswing. The most notable were the boom in gold and silver mining in areas such as Zacatecas and successful commercial ventures, such as textile production in major urban centers and the profitable trade route between Acapulco and Manila in the Spanish-controlled Philippines. The latter forged a link through which Asian arts migrated to the colony and influenced subsequent viceregal tastes and styles.

The seventeenth century saw a dramatic rise in immigration to New Spain from Spain and other European nations, as well as from Asia and Africa. Within the colonial territory itself, alarming decreases in indigenous populations prompted searches for new sources of labor, such as the increased importation of African slaves. In addition, Indians migrated in great numbers to Spanish-occupied urban centers despite efforts by the mendicant orders and state officials to maintain a clear division between Spanish and Indian communities.

The commingling of diverse ethnic groups produced a miscegenated, pluralistic society in which the white elites, both peninsular (Spanish-born) and criollo (native-born American of Spanish decent), attempted to construct a rigidly stratified, race-based hierarchy in which they occupied the apex. This endeavor produced an environment replete with social tensions vulnerable to social unrest. After a number of race- and class-based riots—as early as 1612 and later in 1692, the most notable riot documented by Sigüenza y Gongora—criollo and peninsular paranoia of potential insurrections increased. Serious divisions also existed among the white populace as well, fractures that were to produce significant repercussions for all viceregal inhabitants. A divisive gap between criollos and peninsulars exacerbated the colony's dissatisfaction with Spanish authority in the appointment of state and church officials.

Through the conflict and change, colonial seventeenth-century culture took form, producing distinctive cultural expressions indicative of its lived and imagined experience. This dimension of the colonial mise-en-scène is most salient in the arts. Institutional and social ideologies found pictorial concretization in the production of images. Through their immediate, visual nature, painted and sculpted images served as ideal didactic tools with contents easily accessible to their audiences.

Colonial artists utilized pictorial elements drawn from European artistic traditions—initially derived from late medieval aesthetic concerns, mannerism, and later Baroque trends—as well as integrating Asian and local influences. Artists combined these diverse artistic elements in various ways through the alteration of proportions, repetition of details and patterns, and reconfiguration of space and surface, in the process constructing a colonial artistic canon referencing yet quite distinct from its multiple sources.

A fundamental factor that in many ways determined the artistic modifications that occurred in the colony was the establishment of artists' guilds to evaluate artistic skill and regulate artistic practice. In 1552 viceroy Luis de Velasco, the elder, established the first such juridical system that specifically addressed the training of Indian artists and the appropriateness of their artistic production. During this early period, ecclesiastical authority shaped religious iconography. The church's input on acceptable subjects and their representation interfered with painters' artistic license, motivating them to more closely consider protecting their professional interests. As a result, artists formed the first official guilds protected by civil authority, with the resulting creation of the Ordenanzas de Pintores. The Ordenanzas outlined the steps an artist had to follow in order to progress from apprentice to master. Additionally, these edicts established guidelines delineating artists' functions and the types of practices artists were expected to follow. Guild practices continued through the middle to late sixteenth century and then appear to have disappeared; the last mention of guilds was in 1595.

Unlike the sixteenth century, which saw the emergence and authoritative influence of guilds, the seventeenth century witnessed their absence. With the disappearance of the original Ordenanzas and guild organizations in the late sixteenth century, artistic production through the 1600s proceeded unregulated. In the latter part of the seventeenth century, however, a new set of Ordenanzas resurfaced to counter what had been interpreted as the decadent fall of painting, a process of supposed degeneration greatly influenced by the multiplication of Indian and Spanish artists painting in a popular, primitive style. Concerned artists reestablished new guidelines and guilds to monitor artists' output, with the improvement of artistic quality an overriding objective. In 1681 Juan López de Pareja presented a list of known artists to the viceroy, who subsequently reissued the original guidelines. In 1687 the Ordenanzas de Pintores y Doradores were published, utilizing the old regulations as a template but adapting to the contemporary setting. The examination of apprentice artists remained intact with guild leaders as overseers of all processes relating to the evaluations.

A major difference in the new guidelines was that artists were no longer categorized by the different roles of the painter—the first Ordenanzas in the sixteenth century outlines four classes of artists: *imagineros,* responsible for designing, drawing, and painting images; *doradors,* who applied gold onto pigments applied on canvas or sculptures; *pintors al fresco,* who painted in both dry and wet fresco; and *sargueros,* who prepared pigments and unstretched canvases but were treated as one category due to the general method of painting in oils on canvas, a method in which everyone was supposedly trained and thus familiar. The individual guidelines were numerous and addressed a variety of issues. They stipulated, for example, what kinds of materials were not to be used, such as canvases imported from China. Three separate roles were defined for sculpture: *sculptors; doradors;* and *painters.* The Ordenanzas forbade one artist from trespassing onto another's territory. The guidelines and guilds were instituted to exert control over the artists, the work they produced, the techniques and materials used, and the money they earned. However, as in the earlier period, the new guidelines also began to fall into disuse by the middle of the eighteenth century.

To understand what informed the artistic development in the colony, it is important to consider what segments of the colonial population were requesting works of art and thus, through their commissions, determining what was being constructed as a colonial body of work. The three ruling sociopolitical bodies in New Spain—the church, the state, and the elite—were the major sources of patronage and determined the institutional boundaries for artistic production. The boundaries used to define these sociopolitical bodies were not impermeable; consequently, overlaps existed in terms of objectives, functions, constituents, and the kinds of artwork commissioned. For example, members of various segments of the church, the state, and the elite commissioned portraits, thus this genre was not particular to one social group.

Religious Art

Religious painting constituted the main body of colonial art. Motivated by Protestant attacks on the Catholic Church in the late sixteenth century, the Counter-Reformation and the Council of Trent of 1545 to 1563 initiated reforms that strictly outlined the type of iconography artists were allowed to paint. These reforms mandated that religious art represent "realistic" scenes of pious devotion easily comprehensible to its viewers. Consequently, from that time on through the next century, orthodox subject matter and styles dominated the religious art of the colony.

Relics played an important role in stimulating the production of images. Relics shipped to Mexico City were highly prized and venerated; consequently, paintings of the saints with which these sacred objects were affiliated were commissioned and executed to publicize their existence and significance to the faithful. Certain aspects of the late Renaissance-mannerist style predominated in New Spain, impacting both sculpture and painting as evidenced by elongated figures, wide-eyed gazes, delicate hands, and angular features, a style that imbued images with a supernatural quality.

During this period, the emigration of European, trained artists and architects to the colony facilitated the major cathedral construction projects motivated by the ratification of the Council of Trent by the Third Provincial Council of 1585. In tandem with this building exercise, the expanded population in New Spain necessitated the construction of additional churches to fulfill its spiritual needs. This architectural program greatly impacted art production in the colony through the commissioning of numerous artists by church officials and other wealthy patrons to produce the great quantities of didactic visual material needed to adorn the interiors of the multiplying sacred spaces; significantly, the church was one of the primary institutions for learning in addition to the university.

Working within the parameters set by the Counter-Reformation's emphasis on a clearly defined, pious art, artists from Flanders, Italy, and Spain—then living and working in the colony—integrated painting and sculpture in the construction of *retablos* or altar screens. A fundamental characteristic of seventeenth-century art was the amalgamation of disparate media—painting, sculpture, and architecture—into a synthetic whole, for example, richly painted canvases embedded in gilded altar screens housed within the monumental, architectural superstructure. Consequently, cathedrals, churches, monasteries, and convents served as the primary sites housing the finest examples of colonial art.

The work of Andrés de la Concha, dating from the end of the sixteenth century and into the start of the seventeenth, exemplified many of the emergent traits in painting of the early 1600s. Although very little is known about his Spanish origin and early activities, his earliest known work in the colony is the *retablo* for the Dominican church in Yanhuitlan. The altar screen is believed to have been executed at the time of the church's completion, around 1578. The *retablo* included de la Concha's paintings, which were produced earlier in the late sixteenth century. The altarpiece appears to be physically divided into a series of vertical panels forming a screenlike structure. Pictorially and thematically, however, the altarpiece is arranged in horizontal registers consisting of multiple panels representing a number of scenes from Christ's life, such as *La Anunciación, La Adoración de los Pastores, La Adoración de los Reyes,* and *La Circuncisión.* Biblical figures and saints are also depicted, including *Mary Magdalene, St. Dominic, St. Lucas,* and *St. Jerónimo.* An amalgamation of styles marked the state of colonial painting toward the end of the 1500s and into the early decades of the seventeenth century. Scholars have interpreted de la

Concha's artwork as demonstrating such an eclectic character as defined by a synthesis of varying pictorial styles; an Italianizing trend in the simplicity of his composition and in the elegance of his figures; a Spanish influence in the sobriety and restrained drama of the scenes; and a Flemish affect in the treatment of certain figures, possibly stemming from the influence of Simon Pereyns, a Flemish painter who emigrated to the colony in the sixteenth century.

Luis Juárez lived and worked through the middle of the seventeenth century and is perceived by many contemporary art historians as being quite representative of his time and place. He was a disciple of Baltasar de Echave Orio and became the first of a long dynasty of Mexican painters continuing into the eighteenth century. His earliest work, dated 1610, is a painting of *La Aparición del Niño Jesús a San Antonio* commissioned by the religious community of San Diego and cited by José Bernardo Couto—a nineteenth-century scholar credited with writing the first treatise on colonial Mexican art—as a work belonging to the Academia de San Carlos. Juárez produced a number of works during the seventeenth century, many of which survive today and are well known. He painted many images for various convents and monasteries, such as those of the Carmelites, Mercedarians, Franciscans, and Jesuits. *La Oración del Huerto* is considered by many scholars to be one of his most magnificent paintings. It depicts Christ in the garden of Gethsemane before he is tried by Pontius Pilate and crucified. Juárez's style demonstrated mannerist tendencies in its graceful treatment of figures and gestures and in the emphasis on emotional and spiritual expressiveness that illustrates the mystical qualities that characterize Juárez's work. Baroque influence also can be seen as indicated by the expressive qualities in his images, such as his figures' gestures and the golden-haired, childlike angels hovering in a celestial limbo. His work, like that of many other artists at this time, exemplified an art guided by a typical European style in its blending of various national pictorial styles; for example, an evident Dutch influence in his backgrounds and landscapes and an Italian influence in his handling of figures.

Toward the end of the seventeenth century, the European Baroque influence made its presence felt in the colony and subsequently motivated the movement of colonial painting from the graceful mannerist style to the exuberant Baroque. Exemplifying this trend was Cristóbal de Villalpando (c. 1649–1714), an artist commissioned to execute paintings for the sacristy of the cathedral in Mexico City. Those images, representing *La Iglesia Militante* and *La*

La Oración del Huerto *by Luis Juárez*
Illustration courtesy of Archivo Fotográfico, Instituto de Investigaciones Estéticas de la UNAM

Iglesia Triunfante, were completed in 1684–85. Villalpando was greatly influenced by Peter Paul Rubens, whose stylistic influence comes through in the colonial artist's work. The two sacristy paintings, while compositionally reminiscent of Raphael's High Renaissance piece, the *Disputa* (1509), exhibit a Baroque tendency in the artist's depiction of triumphs, the delicate treatment of flowing robes, majestic angels with childlike faces and graceful wings, the abundance of jewels and reflective metals, and in the expression of grandeur. He left a sizable pictorial legacy in the realm of colonial art; in the viceregal capital alone are numerous paintings of his, such as *Escenas de la Pasión* (situated in the cloisters of San Francisco), *La Muerte de Tobías, Santa Teresa recibiendo su Hábito de Manos de la Virgen,* and *El Sermón de la Montaña,* to name a few.

Sculpture during this period was intimately integrated with its immediate environment to such an extent that it cannot be separated from the architectural structure of which it is a part. Sculpture took three main forms: *retablos* or altarpieces; freestanding figural sculptures; and reliefs. The *retablo* in the late sixteenth century through the early seventeenth century exhibited a Renaissance character through its incorporation of classical columns, architectonic structures, and subdued ornateness. In the seventeenth century, the Baroque esthetic became evident in the altarpiece through the modification of the column from one possessing a clean classical form to one composed of a helicoidal or spiral form entwined around the length of the shaft. This version of the *retablo* retained its architectonic elements with an increased degree of elaborate decoration, most notably in the addition of a grapevine motif to the already ornate Solomonic column.

Freestanding figural sculptures were most commonly constructed for niches in the altarpiece specifically made to hold figures of saints and biblical characters. Such sculptures were created by a team of artists. The initial step involved the carving or sculpting of the image from wood by the *imaginero*. Next, another individual would paint the costume with bright colors, patterns, and shading. A specialist in the rendering of human skin would paint the hands, face, and other exposed body parts, simulating living flesh. This included the representation of blood and wounds in certain cases. And one other person was responsible for the application of gold on the painted clothing of the figure.

Reliefs are most notable in architectural facades. Facades consisted of statues and reliefs, particularly decorative reliefs framing portals and windows. The figures represented patron saints and occasionally donors. Decorative elements ranged from earlier Renaissance to later Plateresque and Baroque forms, such as columns and colonettes, vegetal motifs, and cherubs, elements not unlike the types seen on *retablos*. Other relief elements included coats-of-arms and the trademark iconographies of specific religious orders. The interior altarpieces can thus be viewed as reflecting the exterior facades in style and content. Additionally, a relationship between sculptural styles and pictorial representation also is occasionally evident. For example, on the facade of the church of La Encarnación in Mexico, the angels in relief have been interpreted as demonstrating the pictorial style of Baltasar Echave de Orio, a renowned painter of the period.

A significant feature of this period was the emergence and development of the cult of the Virgin of Guadalupe and the consequent proliferation of images of the icon. Despite the popular belief in the original myth of the Virgin of Guadalupe as having appeared to the Indian Juan Diego in the mid–sixteenth century, it was in the seventeenth century that her image, originally a criollo construction, became widely known and accepted as the unifying symbol of the Mexican people. Subsequently, her image began to appear in many paintings, ranging from prints to portraits to *casta* pictures.

Throughout the seventeenth century the church commissioned the greatest number of paintings depicting religious, didactic themes. In addition to images of religious subjects, the body of work related to the church included portraits of church officials and other functionaries; from the colonial period, one of the most notable genres of portraiture is seen in eighteenth-century images of nuns. Portraits, as stated earlier, constituted a category of painting that surpassed institutional boundaries as all elite segments of the viceroyalty commissioned such images. In terms of painting, this genre represents a substantial portion of the body of art production related to the state. Like the church, the state was a social entity both as a colonial authority and as a patron of the visual arts.

State-Sponsored Art

By the end of the 1500s and into the early 1600s, the colony was being led by its ninth viceroy, Gaspar de Zúñiga y Acevedo. His term, from 1595 to 1603, opened the seventeenth century into what was to become the most prosperous epoch for the colony, a period seen by many scholars as representing the economic and cultural apogee of the viceroyalty.

From the beginning of the viceregal period, it was customary for the viceroys to commission portraits of themselves, a tradition appropriated from the Spanish court. Each viceroy had at least one portrait executed commemorating his term in the colony. Portraits of various kings were commissioned to memorialize enthronements and deaths. The portraits provide a wealth of pictorial documentation concerning not only the appearance of each official but contemporary aesthetic styles as well. Through these likenesses, the personages cease to simply be names in a text and adopt a visual life by providing a static image that can be attached to titles, actions, and events.

Portraiture had always been linked to the upper echelons of social hierarchies, with royalty occupying an especially significant position. A major sociopolitical function of portraiture was to establish the king's presence in the council chambers, public assemblies, nobles' palaces, and eventually to the distant viceroyalty in his physical absence. New Spain, modeling its courtly society along the lines established in Spain, took great pains to recreate European norms in terms of dress, ceremony, and customs. This attempt at imitation resulted in the positioning of portraiture as one of the numerous yet most salient social requisites demanded by an aristocratic society, a factor that had wide influence among the greater elite social realm.

The artist Nicolás Rodríguez Juárez produced numerous portraits in the late sixteenth and early seventeenth centuries, many of which survive to this day and are known to be by his hand. One of his portraits, housed within the Cathedral of Mexico, depicts Felipe V. The National Museum holds three other portraits of his in its collection.

Nicolás's younger brother, Juan Rodríguez Juárez, also a painter of renown, painted several noteworthy portraits including a portrait of the officials don Juan de Escalante y Colombres (1697) and don Manuel de Escalante y Colombres (1697), as well as another portrait of Felipe V (1701). His portrait of Viceroy Fernando de Alencastre Noroña y Silva, duke of Linares, is a prime example of the High Baroque style in its esthetic and content. The Duke is depicted enveloped in a constellation of objects signifying his time and social status, such as his white wig, his blue velvet coat with gold embroidery, and the regal, expressionless demeanor his image projects.

Juan's work, like his brother's, demonstrated a vigorous personality with a keen sense of composition. His work exemplified two artistic tendencies: a severity characteristic of seventeenth-century art and a more colorful, softer style indicative of the burgeoning Baroque trend of the following period. In this sense, these two artists can be interpreted as

El Virrey Duque de Linares *by Juan Rodríguez Juárez*
Illustration courtesy of Pinacoteca Virreinal,
Instituto Nacional de Bellas Artes

bridging the distinct, aesthetic modes of pictorial representation informing the stylistic shift that occurred during the seventeenth and eighteenth centuries.

Sculpture did not play a significant role for the state during this time. The best-known example of a state figure, the equestrian bronze sculpture of Carlos IV by Manuel Tolsá in Mexico City, was not produced until the early nineteenth century. The majority of sculpture at this time consisted of religious figural images.

Architecturally, the presence of the state was manifested in government edifices, such as the Viceregal Palace. Although other cities and regions had official administrative buildings, the Viceregal Palace represented the absolute head of the state, a position augmented by its location in the capital of the viceroyalty. The palace was built in 1562; prior to this time, the Spanish king's representatives were housed in what were called Moteuczoma's old residences. These structures were built by native Mexicans between 1522 and 1529 under the direction of the

Spanish architects Juan Rodríguez and Rodrigo de Pontecillas. The buildings, constructed of plastered walls with roofs of cedar, consisted of three large patios framed by corridors. After purchasing these buildings from Cortés's descendants, the Crown commissioned several architects, including Claudio de Arciniega, to remodel the architectural structures. Consequently, the National Palace of Mexico, as it came to be called, possessed a changing, irregular design due to its construction in stages over a period of time by a number of designers. In the 1692 riot, the palace—the monolithic, ever-present symbol of the state—was destroyed. *Biombos* or folding screens, from the same time period depict several versions of the National Palace before its ruination. According to these depictions of the palace, the building demonstrated a sober Italianate, Renaissance style in its minimal ornateness, repetitive yet balanced elements, grand portals, and externally defined stories or levels.

A concurrent trend with the less ornate Renaissance style was the Plateresque. The Plateresque style stood in contrast with Spanish Herrerian architectural forms that were intensely sober and completely devoid of any decorative elements. The Plateresque was ornate and most evident in building facades, specifically in public or civic architectural structures. This style gained favor as an expression of luxury and elite taste. Among the aristocracy of the viceroyalty, a self-conscious demonstration of wealth became fashionable as much as being a requirement to provide evidence of one's noble status. Thus, an ostentatious character permeated the aesthetic sphere of New Spain. This taste for sumptuousness was manifested in artwork commissioned by the colonial aristocracy, specifically in portraiture.

Art for the Elite

The elite represented the largest body of the colony, that is, the inhabitants of the viceroyalty not immediately correlated with the church or the state, although members of the latter two entities can also be defined as elite. Among this social group in New Spain, particularly all of those who had amassed great fortunes through commerce, mining, and agriculture, it was not only important to accrue wealth but to acquire the noble title and prestige associated with wealth. Hard work and economic success brought recognition and entry into the aristocracy with all of its rules of proper behavior and appearance. Portraiture, then, played a prominent ideological and symbolic role in the process of legitimating one's position and newfound status in the eyes of an intensely scrutinizing elite society. This objective was accomplished through the pictorial construction and representation of individuals as members of a noble class.

A significant factor motivating this process was the peninsular response to the criollo elite. Although criollo fear of revolts by Indians, blacks, and *castas* (those of mixed ancestry) was not completely misplaced, their greatest threat came from their supposed equals, the European aristocracies. Although Europeans did not threaten the criollos' general power in the colony in relation to the rest of that society, they substantially restricted it. Due to the conflict between peninsulars and criollos, criollo elites attempted to use their wealth to construct a privileged position for themselves within a waning social hierarchy that had traditionally placed them as inferior to European-born Spaniards. The criollos' objective in acquiring such a status undeniably included reclaiming authority and control over their own homeland.

Portraiture became a social requisite demanded by an aristocratic society modeled on the image of the Spanish court. Motivations for commissioning a portrait involved both perpetuating the sitter's memory and, most importantly, elevating his or her social worth. Portraits represented not individuals but actors in a social drama. High social position did not consist of accruing economic wealth alone; one had to demonstrate that wealth thereby providing evidence of one's high social status. After reaching the ranks of nobility, one received a title obligating that person to maintain a particular lifestyle at great expense. This included building a sumptuous home, maintaining a team of servants, hosting elaborate ceremonies, and patronizing schools, convents, hospitals, and churches. Portraits, then, functioned as one of many markers of high status typically displayed in one's reception room to greet guests and announce the identity and status of its owners.

A famous portrait from this period is the *Retrato de una Dama* by Baltasar de Echave Ibía, son of Baltasar de Echave Orio. Echave Ibía's painting is believed to be a portrait of his mother as well as part of a larger scene. The style of clothing she wears, specifically her collar, places the fashion and possibly the portrait in the early seventeenth century. This image appears to have been a recurring motif in other works by Baltasar de Echave Ibía, as evidenced in the similarity between his mother's image and the *Virgen del Apocalipsis* of 1620, as well as in the faithful reproduction of the same figure as the Virgin in his later work of 1622 depicting the immaculate conception. The *Retrato de una Dama* seems to be an orant or donative work depicting the figure in a kneeling, praying pose indicating that this image

Retrato de una Dama *by Baltasar de Echave Ibía*
Illustration courtesy of Pinacoteca Virreinal, Instituto Nacional de Bellas Artes

may have been part of a larger piece. This posture illustrates the traditional actions a devout donor performed in a painted image. The pictorial arrangement in this type of genre can be read as embodying portraiture's function to augment the sitter's social standing thereby marking his or her identity and status. The representation of the individual as an orant donor in the presence of a sacred figure such as the Virgin Mary reflected that individual's obligations as an elite to sponsor building projects—best exemplified in the construction of churches and cathedrals—and to commission the works of art that would adorn their interiors.

Portraits in seventeenth-century New Spain exhibited quite different stylistic elements from the sensual Baroque characteristics expressed in other kinds of painting. Colonial painters rendered the human form in portraits with the greatest economy, especially facial features. Viceregal portraiture projected an illusion of restraint and tranquillity, obscuring the profoundly conflicted fabric of colonial society. The known portraits from this period possess an air of artifice in the posed aspect of the models, their static faces, and vacant gazes. Viceregal paintings juxtaposed contemporary coloring and composition with accepted artificial poses and formulaic pictorial arrangements. An anachronistic character pervaded the aesthetic sphere of the viceroyalty in their portraits and through the continued presence of earlier pious paintings and furniture adorning the homes of the elite. In contrast to the softening and simplification of physiognomies, artists rendered jewelry, fabrics, and other objects in great detail. Evidently, this painting process emphasized the material trappings of social status; possessions spoke for the person (as a social construct) and not the individual (as a human being).

Colonial portraiture consisted of several categories: society portraits of upper-class men, women, children, and families; patron portraits of donors or benefactors located at the bottom of a religious themed painting; self-portraits executed by the artists themselves; oral/spoken or posthumous portraits of exemplary individuals commonly done many years after that person's death based on literary and oral sources; memento portraits commissioned to serve as personal mementos often intended to be sent to distant friends and relatives; portable portraits that could be rolled up and moved with an itinerant owner; and church portraits of church officials and most notably of nuns at the time of their profession and at their deaths. Two other portrait categories —religious portraits and portraits of kings, viceroys, and various governmental officials—have been discussed above. Additionally, many portraits included a cartouche located in the upper or lower part of the picture space that presented a written text identifying the represented individual, his or her family, and various other items of information that distinguished the depicted person.

A category of painting almost wholly restricted to colonial Mexico is images representing miscegenation or racial mixing. Scholars such as Teresa Castelló Yturbide have suggested that these images may date as early as the late seventeenth century. Beginning then as early as the late 1600s and on through the eighteenth century and the early years of the nineteenth, various artists in New Spain produced series of paintings representing the hybridized products of miscegenation. From the initial confrontations between the "Old World" and the "New" and throughout the colonial period, racial mixing among the Spanish, Indian, and African elements in New Spain played a central role in the social and ideological development of the colony. The peninsular and criollo elites of colonial Mexico constructed a hierarchized classification system that defined distinct racial types, with whites at the apex of the social structure and the rest of the society's ethnic elements below them. The deviation from "pure" white Spanish blood determined the placement of racially mixed individuals within that social system. Each of the categories additionally was circumscribed by a set of socioeconomic and behavioral parameters deemed characteristic of the individuals pertaining to it.

The *casta* paintings referenced this racialized, conceptual framework by pictorially representing its visually identifiable features. Typically arranged in a series of 16 images, either as separate panels or in a chartlike arrangement on one panel, each *casta* painting depicted an adult male belonging to one ethnic group, an adult female of differing ethnicity, and their offspring, whose racially blended status produced a racial category different from either one of the parents' categories. Thus, each series began with the mixture of white/Spanish and either Indian or black/African, with subsequent products intermixing and producing yet more differentiated categories. A significant aspect of these paintings is the integration of word and image in their compositions through the presence of equation-like labels; for example, white and black produce mulatto, identifying the race of the represented subjects. This is similar to the presence of identifying texts in secular, viceregal portraits.

During the seventeenth and eighteenth centuries, paintings encrusted with shell (called *enconchados*) —demonstrating an affinity with Asian lacquered images—became fashionable vehicles for historical and religious narratives. Miguel González and Juan González, two artists believed to have been of Asian derivation, are known to have produced shell paintings. The second half of the seventeenth century saw the greatest production of such images. Many of these ended up in Spain in private collections. A substantial number of shell-encrusted paintings depicted religious subject matter, specifically images of the Virgin Mary. Several known shell pieces representing the Virgin in one form or another include a *Retrato de Nuestra Señora de México* and a series of 12 panels depicting scenes from the life of the Virgin, both owned by Carlos II, and a panel representing *La Familia Sagrada,* owned by Juan de Soto Noguera, a wealthy Spaniard from Seville whose extensive art collection included many objects from New Spain.

Today, the best-known examples of *enconchados* are located in the Museo de América in Madrid. One such image illustrates a scene from the life of Christ, specifically what appears to be the *Flagelación de Cristo*. The picture consists of a central group of five figures that surround the blindfolded, seated Christ. One man kneels before Christ and appears to be placing a branch in his hand. Another figure stands to the side and observes while the other three standing figures strike Christ. Two other figures leaning on a rail stand to the far left and observe the scene. The setting is the interior of a palacelike architectural space. In this painting, shell encrustations are utilized to highlight certain areas of the picture. Shells are placed on clothing, armor, and on certain architectural elements, creating a shimmering effect on certain surfaces scattered throughout the picture field. The entire image is surrounded by an elaborate frame adorned with painted and shell-encrusted flowers and birds. Beyond producing a visually appealing decorative effect, the shells reflect light, appearing to animate the picture space.

Another theme in this medium was the Conquest of Mexico. Several panels depicting various episodes from this historical event belonged to the collection of the Dukes of Moteuczoma and now are part of a private collection in Madrid. One particular panel depicts the *Conquista de Tenochtitlán,* the capital of the Mexica (Aztec) Empire. The Spaniards, dressed in armor with lances and shields, some on horseback but most on foot, attack the Mexica, who appear to be no match with their simple clubs or macanas to the superior weaponry of the Europeans. The central image in the foreground appears to be Cortes on horseback defeating the Mexica emperor, who lies prone on the ground. In the distance appears an inaccurate interpretation of a pyramid and various buildings evidently representing the sacred precinct of the imperial capital. Once again, shell encrustations are carefully arranged on the armor and clothing of certain figures, highlighting the areas where significant actions take place. A similar animating effect is present in the shells' placement and light reflective qualities.

The Conquest narrative also was represented in another Asian-derived medium that utilized shells, namely, pictorial representations on *biombos*. A screen entitled the *Biombo de la Conquista,* attributed to Miguel González, depicted scenes from that event. Depictions on shell-encrusted paintings, through their discrete panels, determined the representation of separate episodes in a narrative. The *biombo* format of a series of hinged panels forming one long picture surface, however, allowed both the construction of discrete scenes on separate panels and the representation of a panoramic scene whose narrative flow could be followed as the eye moved from one end to the other. The picture of the Conquest is composed of battle scenes taking place amid buildings surrounded by thousands of fighting figures. As in the shell-encrusted paintings, the placement of shells on the screen panels also highlight specific areas, specifically armor, shields, rocks, and architectural structures.

In the seventeenth and eighteenth centuries, *biombos* were extremely popular furnishings in elite homes. They served as partitions dividing interior spaces; as barriers to light, sound, wind, and sight; and as ornate decorations. In addition to representing historical narratives, screens depicted other subjects, such as genre themes of hunting scenes or leisurely walks in the countryside, illustrations based on classical literature such as Ovid's *Metamorphosis,* and Renaissance allegorical figures, for example, Juan Correa's *Biombo de las Artes Liberales* of 1670, which depicts the personifications of the liberal arts, such as Grammar, Astronomy, Rhetoric, and Geometry, painted in a lively, Baroque manner.

Most visual art production was commissioned by and for the elite. However, visual art exists that was produced for both elite and common patrons, as well as certain types of images solely produced by and for commoners. A prime example is the *relicario. Relicarios* are small pendants that occasionally contained actual relics of saints; however, more often their reliquary designation was symbolic and based on a miniature painted or sculpted image of a saint. The sacred figure or saint's image was protected behind glass or encased in a small frame of silver or gold with a ring through which a chain could be threaded.

These pendants were worn by devotees and given to family and friends as keepsakes and protective good luck charms. Other types of hagiographic badges included scapulars—cloth badges with holy images worn as protective amulets—and *escudos de monjas,* or nuns' coats-of-arms, which represented a nun's particular order as well as possessing similar protective functions. A seventeenth-century relicario in the Metropolitan Museum's collection depicts *La Anunciación* carved in relief out of rock crystal and surrounded by gold, enamel, and precious gems, such as rubies, diamonds, and pearls. In contrast to that pendant is another fine relicario, although not as luxurious as the first but still as precious, dating from the same time period and housed in the Museo Franz Mayer collection. It represents two saints carved in low relief out of white stone and framed by silver.

Commoners undoubtedly produced their own visual arts. Although little is known about nonelite pictorial art from the first half of the viceregal period—with the exception of pre-Conquest style manuscripts from the middle to late sixteenth century, such as the Techialoyan codices produced by indigenous communities wanting to acquire or maintain property rights—one class of religious image exemplifies a probable type of artistic production from the lower social strata of New Spain in the seventeenth century, that is, the folk *retablo* and/or ex-voto. Although the earliest documented examples are approximately dated from the late eighteenth to the early nineteenth century, the kinds of images produced may reflect an ongoing tradition begun earlier. Folk *retablos* are small oil paintings executed on tin, sometimes on other materials such as wood, by untrained artists. Individuals and families may have commissioned them or purchased them from peddlers who sold them at churches or from door to door. They were placed on home altars where they were venerated and used to request remedies for ailments or solutions to social problems. Normally, ex-voto offerings, small painted images depicting accidents or disasters, were produced and placed in churches or personal altars as a form of propitiation to patron saints or the Virgin Mary in gratitude for sparing a family member. Such images served as contracts promising the holy figure a pilgrimage or some type of recompense for miraculous intercession. Perhaps due to the perishable quality of the materials used, to the instability of life in the lower classes during the colonial period, or to the perceived worthlessness of such unrefined objects, they may have been destroyed or lost.

There is no evident sculptural trend at this time that represents a commission not of a religious nature. Architecture, however, did possess a unique style most notable in residential structures. The aristocracy owned huge parcels of land upon which they built large mansions consisting of elaborate facades that protected the interior living spaces, which typically consisted of a reception room, study, dining area, kitchen, bedrooms, servants' quarters, and the central courtyard. During this period, the homes of the middle class acquired a distinctive form. There were three types: the *casa sola,* the *casa de vecindad,* and the cup-and-saucer variation of the *casa de vecindad.* The *casa sola,* home to the affluent merchant middle class, was constructed in pairs; that is, a rectangular or square patio was divided in half by a wall that separated two homes. These homes usually had smaller rooms or buildings facing the streets, which contained small businesses. The servants' quarters also were located on the first floor. A grand staircase led to the second floor where the inhabitants' living quarters were located, such as the reception/living room facing the street, the din-ing area, and the bedrooms in the rear. A corridor ran the length of the interior patio's perimeter but maintained the wall division separating the two residences.

The *casa de vecindad* consisted of a great corridor along whose length on either side were situated small apartments. Each of these units was formed by two rooms, a kitchen, and occasionally a small patio. Normally, the central corridor would contain a small fountain at the far end; however, in the case of a two-story building, the staircase would be located at the end of the corridor. A variation of this kind of residence was the cup-and-saucer design, which basically was a small space built within a larger one. The first-floor space would open out to the street and normally hold a business, with the living area on the second floor, hence the name.

Conclusion

The majority of visual art during the seventeenth century was commissioned by the church and consisted of religious images and portraitures, both religious and secular. Genres imported and established in the sixteenth century developed in the 1600s and continued into the eighteenth century, such as the *casta* paintings that may have been introduced in the seventeenth century and expanded in the following period. The seventeenth century saw the production and consolidation of genres of painting—despite changing styles based on a shifting sociopolitical structure and cultural aesthetic—that served as the basis for the continued developments lasting throughout the viceregal era. In many ways, this century could feasibly be considered the apogee of colonial culture, not because the eighteenth century witnessed the decline of art and society into a decadent state as has been traditionally opined by scholars, but because the seventeenth century saw the emergence of a relatively stable society and a distinct style evincing a unique Mexican identity and experience.

Select Bibliography

Armella de Aspe, Virginia, and Mercedes Meade de Angula, *A Pictorial Heritage of New Spain: Treasures of the Pinacoteca Virreinal*. Mexico City: Fomento Cultural Banamex, 1993.

Cope, R. Douglas, *The Limits of Racial Domination: Plebeian Society in Colonial Mexico City, 1660–1720*. Madison: University of Wisconsin Press, 1994.

Egan, Martha J., *Relicarios: Devotional Miniatures from the Americas*. Santa Fe: Museum of New Mexico Press, 1993.

Giffords, Gloria F., *Mexican Folk Retablos*. Albuquerque: University of New Mexico Press, 1974.

Israel, Jonathan I., *Race, Class, and Politics in Colonial Mexico 1610–1670*. Oxford: Oxford University Press, 1975.

Motten, Clement G., *Mexican Silver and the Enlightenment*. Oxford: Oxford University Press, 1950.

Palmer, Gabrielle, and Donna Pierce, *Cambios: The Spirit of Transformation in Spanish Colonial Art*. Albuquerque: University of New Mexico Press and Santa Barbara Museum of Art, 1993.

—RAYMOND HERNÁNDEZ-DURÁN

Visual Arts: Eighteenth- and Nineteenth-Century Academic Art

A useful point of departure for the discussion of nineteenth-century Mexican art is not only the late-eighteenth-century establishment of the Royal Academy of Fine Arts (the Academy of San Carlos), but also the tension among competing constructs of *mexicanidad* (Mexican national identity), which were linked inextricably to concepts of race and heritage (e.g., the European, indigenous, and mestizo), partisan politics, and gender.

The Foundation of the Academy

Desirous of reaping the benefits of eighteenth-century New Spain's increased economic prosperity, the Bourbon kings Carlos III (1759–88) and Carlos IV (1788–1808) engineered a reorganization of the colonial administration that strengthened the Spanish Crown's hold on centralized power and its ability to collect revenues. This economically effective bureaucratic reorganization also included the establishment of several important educational institutions, namely, the Botanical Garden, the School of Mines, and the Academy of Fine Arts. The establishment of the academy allowed the colonial administration to control cultural education, thus diminishing the control of the Catholic Church and the guilds, which had been directing art production since the sixteenth century. By 1813, the guilds were effectively destroyed. The academy was established originally as the School of Engraving in 1778 and was housed in the Casa de Moneda, the Royal Mint. There, academic artists produced medals, stamps, and other objects connected to the all-important silver industry, which required skilled engravers. Carlos IV's administration granted a royal charter to convert the School of Engraving into the Royal Academy of Fine Arts of San Carlos in 1783. It was the first such institution in Latin America.

In 1790, the Bourbon Reforms also indirectly yielded a significant archaeological discovery that came to have profound resonance for the interpretation of the pre-Hispanic past, a key concern of nineteenth-century Mexico. During the repaving of the central plaza of Mexico City, laborers found the Mexica (Aztec) Calendar Stone and the relief of the deity Coatlícue; neither object had been visible since their Conquest-period burial. In a lengthy treatise published in 1792, Mexican astronomer Antonio León y Gama interpreted them to have vastly different contributions to make to a construction of the pre-Hispanic past. He interpreted the Mexica Calendar Stone as a remarkable monument to Mexica scientific ingenuity, creating of it a solar clock. It was mounted to the base of the east tower of the cathedral for all to view. By contrast, the serpent-skirted Coatlícue was presented as a horrible, pagan image, capable of stirring up old religious practices. This statue was removed from public view and buried beneath what was then the beginning of Mexico's modern National Museum of Anthropology. It is no coincidence that the Academy of Fine Arts, which would for years regard pre-Hispanic material culture as a source primarily of decorative, historicizing motifs, was established in the same epoch that the Mexica Calendar Stone took on its Enlightenment incarnation.

The Bourbon regime certainly envisioned the academy as a site of enlightened education and art production. The academy's professors were Spaniards trained primarily at the Royal Academy of San Fernando in Madrid or the Academy of San Carlos in Valencia, where training was founded on the study of drawing and the veneration of the classical model. The language of academic classicism in which

Mexican students were thus trained signified high culture and enlightenment. The academy provided for Mexico's elite the possibility for the transformation of a baroque and parochial culture into a more progressive and universal one; written descriptions of the period suggest that this transformation was understood in subtly gendered terms: the feminine, ornamental, and decorative baroque facades of the pre-Bourbon period were to be replaced by the sober, classical, and masculine facades that European-trained academicians could provide.

Beginning with the late-eighteenth-century foundation of the Royal Academy of Fine Arts, the art production of nineteenth-century Mexico revolved heavily around the rise of academic standards, as opposed to guild practices of the colonial period. This included work produced by artists trained at the academy as well as other artists who exhibited works in the public exhibitions that began in 1849. Exemplary of academic art at the turn of the eighteenth century is the work two Spaniards: architect and sculptor Manuel Tolsá and his colleague, easel and mural painter Rafael Ximeno y Planes. Tolsá assumed the directorship of sculpture at the academy, as well as director of works for the Mexico City Cathedral; Ximeno y Planes assumed the directorship of painting. Both artists transformed interior and exterior spaces, particularly those of the metropolitan cathedral. Ximeno y Planes's work ranges from the spare and elegant portraits of academic colleagues to the dramatic, large-scale murals and wall decorations for major public spaces. These spaces include an 1810 tempera mural of the *Assumption of the Virgin* in the octagonal dome (designed by Tolsá) of the cathedral and the 1813 mural-sized wall painting of *Miracle of the Spring*, in which the Virgin of Guadalupe appears at the moment a spring miraculously erupts from the ground at her shrine site of Tepeyac to the north of Mexico City. This work is set in Tolsá's vast building designed for the Mining Tribunal and the School of Mines, known as the Palace of Mines. The representation of two different aspects of the Virgin (of the Assumption and of Guadalupe) underscore the tension between the European and the indigenous in Mexican culture; the Guadalupan, dark-skinned virgin, unlike the European Virgin of the Assumption in the cathedral, was not associated with Spain or the monarchy. She was, in fact, a sufficiently flexible figure to be tied to Mexico and commerce, especially mining, in the late eighteenth century, and then during the early nineteenth century, to be associated with the indigenous and mestizo supporters of Mexico's independence from Spain.

Miracle of Spring *(1813) by Rafael Ximeno y Plane*
Illustration courtesy of Patrimonio Universitario

Tolsá's equestrian statue of Carlos IV, known as *El Caballito*, exemplifies the interconnection between royalist partisanship and academic art, subtly reaffirming Spain's conquest of indigenous Mexico. Inaugurated with great pomp and circumstance in 1816, Tolsá's statue depicted Carlos IV riding his horse in antique armor, symbolically linking the Spanish monarch to Julius Caesar (a detail specifically declared in a 1796 pamphlet describing the sculpture). The statue of the king originally "observed" his distantly placed subjects of the realm from behind a wrought iron balustrade in the Central Plaza. What the viewer could not see was the horse stepping on a quiver of arrows—symbol of the New World.

Independence and the Early National Period

By the turn of the eighteenth century, the complex class, racial, and political antagonisms within New Spain itself, as well as between New Spain and Spain, had intensified dramatically, ultimately erupting into the struggle for Independence. During the first two decades of the nineteenth century, political battles and war itself engaged the major opposing factions of insurgent criollos (those of European descent born in New Spain) and royalist *peninsulares* (those born in Spain). By 1821, after a decade of violence, the independent nation of Mexico had officially emerged.

Of the imagery produced about the Wars for Independence between 1810 and 1821, much was the work of anonymous guilds rather than identifiable academic artists. Beginning in 1810, artists produced numerous portraits commemorating the figures who had come to represent the epoch of Independence. Father Miguel Hidalgo, for one, was represented in ceramic, as well as in paintings on tin, wood, canvas, and wax. His black frock coat, white hair, and banner with the Virgin of Guadalupe became standardized features of his image throughout the nineteenth and twentieth centuries. Allegorical depictions of Mexico's victory over Spain also abounded, and included a vocabulary of cardinal virtues, time, and fame. In addition, the phrygian cap, a broken chain, or a lion being stepped on often visually proclaimed Mexico's Independence.

The art production of the period of Independence signals how important the government and elite private patrons considered the educational power of imagery in public spaces. Ephemeral art such as triumphal arches, and even a small temple covered in allegorical images, helped transform the colonial city. Tolsá's statue of Carlos IV, an affirmation of royal power, was covered for Independence festivities and later removed to the university, so that, as a contemporary document claimed, it would not offend the citizens of the newly independent nation. Numerous projects designed to commemorate the *benemeritos* (Mexico's national heroes), the great benefactors of Mexico, were proposed and carried out by both government and private sponsors; these included outdoor placement of statues and sepulchral monuments as well as the inscription of names in the Mexican Chamber of Deputies.

After Independence, Mexico became an attractive site for foreign visitors as well as foreign investors. Numerous foreign artists, moreover, came to Mexico, individually, or as part of government or commercial enterprises. These artists included the Italian, Claudio Linati, who brought the first lithographic press to Mexico in 1825. Among Linati's graphic contributions was the illustrated compendium *Costumes Civiles, Militaires, et Religieux du Méxique* (1828), first published in Brussels in 12 illustrated installments. Historical figures from the Mexica ruler, Moteuczoma II to contemporary Mexican clerics, contemporary political figures, urban laborers, and country ranchers were represented and described by Linati, whose progressive politics always were

intertwined with his description of social types. Lithography also became a primary medium for Mexican artists, especially for political cartoons, published in midcentury papers and pamphlets, and for book and magazine illustration. Major lithographic artists Casimiro Castro and Hesiquio Iriarte contributed to a wide range of publications. The turn-of-the-twentieth-century artist José Guadalupe Posada, known for his satiric images of grinning *calavera* (skulls) would work not only in lithographs but also in type-metal and zinc engravings.

Other foreign artists visiting Mexico included Germans Johann Friederick Waldeck and Karl (Carlos) Nebel, both of whom worked in lithography. Waldeck was one of a number of nineteenth-century foreign artists who contributed to the popularizing of Mexico's pre-Hispanic ruins in his large illustrated albums; another artist depicting pre-Hispanic sites was the Englishman Frederick Catherwood, who illustrated John Lloyd Stephen's *Incidents of Travel in the Yucatán* of 1843. Painters of the Mexican landscape included the English artist Daniel Egerton, the French artist J. L. B. Gros, and the German artist Johann Moritz Rugendas. Indeed, through the work of both Mexican and foreign artists of the first half of the nineteenth century, the popular conception of Mexico and the Mexican landscape began to take shape.

Throughout the first half of the nineteenth century the federal government held the academy to be a key educational institution with the means to help form new citizens out of former royal subjects. Particularly significant were the liberal reforms of the 1830s established and legislated by the government of Valentín Gómez Farías. The Ley del 21 de Octubre, 1833, for example, established government control of all facets of public education, including the Academy of Fine Arts, as well as depositories of art, antiquities, and natural history. The academy thus was understood to be part of the state's bureaucracy and effective in educating its citizens. The legislation and reforms enacted by the various governments of the nineteenth century demonstrate the academy's value to the state across partisan political lines.

In 1843, for example, the conservative regime of Antonio López de Santa Anna enacted a profoundly significant set of academic reforms. Chief among these was the requirement that directors of the different areas of teaching in the academy (i.e., painting, engraving, sculpture, architecture, and landscape painting) were to be chosen "from among the best Europe has to offer." Within a decade, two Spaniards, two Englishmen, and two Italians had arrived to direct Mexican students' careers in art and architecture. Pelegrín Clavé, a Catalonian trained primarily in Italy, assumed not only the directorship of painting, but also the general directorship of the academy. The staffing of the academy's major posts—whether administrative or pedagogical—with Europeans continued the colonial practice of barring criollos from exercising power in the upper echelons of institutions that had been created with the Bourbon Reforms of the eighteenth century.

A second of the 1843 reforms had a dramatic effect on the public display and criticism of art, namely the establishment of the public academy exhibition, the first one of which was held in 1849. These public exhibitions displayed works by students of the academy, faculty, and artists trained outside of the academy, as well as the works collected by private patrons. Works could range from drawings of plaster casts to architectural projects, to history paintings submitted by faculty, to examples of popular paintings from outside Mexico City. In addition to providing a social space for the display and viewing of art, these exhibitions stimulated the writing of art criticism, particularly in Mexico City newspapers. By midcentury, it was very clear that members of the major political parties agreed that the public should be educated about art as a sign that Mexico was part of the universal fraternity of "civilized" cultures. Particularly important was the discussion of a national art as a correlative to the question of national history: Who could represent Mexico? Which heroes were worthy of representation? Did Mexican history begin with the Spanish Conquest? Did it have its origins in pre-Hispanic culture? Not surprisingly, the answers to these questions frequently fell along partisan political lines. Conservatives, who tended to be pro-European or Spanish and who favored, for example, centralized if not monarchical governmental authority, found Emperor Agustín de Iturbide, rather than the more incendiary José María Morelos or Miguel Hidalgo y Costilla to be the better representative of Independence. They saw the Spanish Conquest as the beginning of Mexico. Liberals, supporters of mestizos, criollos, and the indigenous, as well as a federal democracy, often held up Vicente Guerrero, Hidalgo, and Morelos as truly heroic. They preferred a construction of history that acknowledged the pre-Hispanic past as well as the European one. By the 1850s, academic history painting itself began to resonate with responses to these critical debates.

Art and Politics at Midcentury

The education of academy students was structured by the typical academic hierarchy of history painting,

The Holy Family *(exhibited 1857) by Rafael Flores*
Illustration courtesy of Museo Nacional de Arte

portrait painting, landscape painting, and genre painting. History painting became increasingly important within the context of the public discussion of national history. Landscape painting, traditionally regarded as less prestigious than history painting, grew in stature rapidly. Contributing to this was Italian artist Eugenio Landesio's academic curriculum, but also the increase in patronage of views of private property, particularly of haciendas. Artists often turned to portraiture and sometimes to wall decoration—both in private spaces as well as occasionally in the dimly regarded spaces of *pulquerias* (taverns that sold the traditional alcoholic beverage of central Mexico, pulque)—to make a living. Additionally, artists also were contracted to paint murals in churches; these works included Mexican Juan Cordero's *Christ among the Doctors of the Church,* finished in the Church of Santa Teresa in 1857, and Spaniard Pelegrín Clavé's *The Seven Sacraments and the Adoration of the Cross,* finished in the Templo de la Profesa in 1867. However, within

Columbus in the Court of the Catholic Kings *(exhibited 1851)* by Juan Cordero
Illustration courtesy of Museo Nacional de Arte

a decade of the promulgation of the liberal Reform Laws of the 1850s and the creation of the Constitution of 1857, which included the separation of church and state, church mural commissions effectively ceased.

Religious and classical themes dominated much of academic history painting and sculpture through the 1860s. Recent scholarship argues that academic history painting easily could accommodate partisan political battles. For example, Rafael Flores's *The Holy Family* and Felipe S. Gutiérrez's *The Oath of Brutus,* exhibited in the 1857 academy show, respectively inscribe the conservative and liberal positions on the Constitution of 1857, and its effective separation of church and state. Flores's painting encodes the conservative, Catholic, and familial unit; Gutiérrez's work encodes the public discourse of sacrifice for the state and republicanism.

Midcentury criticism registered a growing interest across the political landscape in the construction of Mexican art, and specifically imagery that could represent Mexican history. Juan Cordero's *Columbus in*

the Court of the Catholic Kings, exhibited in the 1851 academy show, initiated one of the first public debates about secular history painting as well as the dominance of European faculty in the academy hierarchy. Cordero, a well-known Mexican artist who had studied in Italy in the 1840s, offered to Mexico a scene that linked the New World with the Old by including the Spanish monarchs Fernando and Isabel, Columbus, and most important, a group of Indians. Intertwined with Cordero's innovative subject matter was his bid to impress President Antonio López de Santa Anna into giving him—a Mexican— the directorship of the academy. This position ultimately remained in the hands of Cordero's Spanish rival, Pelegrín Clavé.

The production of secular and national scenes by Mexicans and foreigners increased through midcentury. Such representations contributed to the codification of a written national chronicle, as offered in newspapers, pamphlets, and books for both popular and scholarly consumption. Furthermore, although partisan politics undergirded such national histories, all factions agreed on the importance of a national historical education for Mexico's citizens. Imagery contributing to this goal included representations of the Mexica warrior, *Tlahuicole,* by Manuel Vilar, José Obregón's *Young Columbus,* and anecdotal landscapes such as José María Velasco's pre-Hispanic scene, *The Hunt.*

The pictorial representation of the national also included less elite forms of art such as that produced around midcentury by a number of provincial and less formally trained artists, particularly from Puebla and Guanajuato. These artists cotributed to a growing market in portraits, still lives, and genre or *costumbrista* (idealized provincial) scenes. Representative of this tradition are Hermenegildo

Bustos, Agustín Arrieta, and José María Estrada. The academy catalogues list numerous paintings of street scenes, festivals, and social types done by these artists. Such works were often in the collections of well-known members of Mexico's cultural and political elite.

The conflicted field of national art and history is well illustrated by art displayed in the 1865 and 1869 academy shows. The 1865 show, dominated by the presence and patronage of the French-imposed Emperor Maximilian von Hapsburg, was both a paean to imperial power and political savvy. Maximilian, installed as a result of collaboration between Napoléon III of France and Mexican conservatives, was well aware that his foreign presence was

The Discovery of Pulque (1869) by José Obregón
Illustration courtesy of Museo Nacional de Arte

unwelcome both culturally and politically. He commissioned a vast amount of imagery—for private and public spaces—including the Castle of Chapultepec and the National Palace. Resonant of the Parisian urban reforms enacted under Napoléon III, Maximilian ordered the creation of the wide, ceremonial boulevard linking the once-more publicly displayed equestrian statue of Carlos IV by Manuel Tolsá and the Castle of Chapultepec. Ironically, among his painting commissions was a series of life-size portraits of heroes of Independence, including the heretofore symbolically antagonistic Hidalgo, Morelos, and Iturbide. These were displayed in his new Hall of the Ambassadors in the National Palace.

The politically tumultuous period of the 1850s and 1860s—including the War of the Reform and the Liberals' battle to rid Mexico of both foreign and conservative power—culminated in the profoundly symbolic execution of Maximilian in 1867. Although executed according to Mexican law as a traitor to the state, Maximilian's death caused an international furor, contributing to a view of Mexico as barbaric and uncivilized, not unlike the picture of the Mexica created by the Spaniards at the moment of Conquest. Significantly, when the liberals, under the Zapotec Benito Juárez regained power in 1867, culture again became a major field of public discussion and debate. Nineteenth-century discourse indicates that the support and discussion of the arts took on an ever more important role in reconfiguring Mexico's national and international image at this crucial moment.

This intensified interest in art, and specifically the representation of national history, is suggested by the official declaration of a national history painting competition in 1869. Academic representations of national history grew dramatically through the end of the nineteenth century. The range of national historical themes includes well-known episodes and figures primarily from the pre-Hispanic and Conquest periods as well as the national period; rarely were colonial scenes represented. In general these scenes constructed an orderly and hierarchical past; battles were relatively bloodless; heroes were posed to embody power, order, and civility. The most striking images are those that represent the figure of the Indian, the dark-skinned sign of "authentic" culture. History paintings often celebrated this figure, while at the same time placing him/her in cultural and symbolic constructs that demanded assimilation. Assimilation was a key political issue in the nineteenth century, effected by statutes allowing European migration and colonization, as well as the (ideal) development of a universal and secular educational system that would "de-Indianize" and "civilize" those Indians still outside the control of the state, whether through cultural practice or willful political resistance.

History paintings of the Indian, the figure claimed by the victorious liberals of the nineteenth century as the basis of national culture, contributed to this process of assimilation through simultaneous celebration and erasure. Constructs such as the transformation of a pre-Hispanic governing body into a Greco-Roman senate, or the representation of the legendary Toltec priest, Quetzalcoatl, as Jesus, exemplify the pictorial devices used to make indigenous culture in Mexico parallel to, yet unique from, ancient European history. Exemplary is José Obregón's *The Discovery of Pulque* of 1869, a celebrated pre-Hispanic drama orchestrated as Europeanized throne scene, shows a mestizo maiden handing over the natural cactus liquor to a prince of the realm, an enthroned figure who receives/takes both luscious young woman and profitable drink. Similarly, the religious martyr's presence, resonant of Saint Lawrence on the grill, is strong in Leandro Izaguirre's *Torture of Cuauhtémoc* of 1892. Here the artist supplies a dark-skinned indigenous figure, valiant and unrelenting in his resistance to the torture of Cortés and the Spaniards. His weaker Mexica counterpart whimpers in the darkness as the two noble enemies, Cuauhtemoc and Cortés, confront one another. By the end of the century, academic artists routinely painted scenes of ancient and modern Mexican history.

Academics and Modernism at the End of the Century

As a sign of culture and a weapon against international cultural slander, art clearly was important to official Mexico, and continued to be part of a transformation of Mexico in image and in fact. Particularly during the reign of Porfirio Díaz (1876–1911), the display of high culture took place both abroad in international expositions (beginning with the Philadelphia Exposition of 1876) and at home in the streets of Mexico City itself.

During this epoch of positivist-Liberal rule under the decorated war hero Díaz, major sculptural commissions were awarded for the decoration of the very "Boulevard of the Emperor" built by Maximilian and later renamed the Boulevard of the Reform. From the 1870s to 1910, architects and sculptors designed what in its entirety might be seen as a three-dimensional victorious, liberal history. Projects for the Reforma included the casting of life-size bronze statues of representatives from various states of the

Republic, each a heroic figure whose national contributions are detailed in a plaque on the base. It goes without saying that although there were several important women involved in the struggle for Independence, official history disallowed their representation among their male counterparts. Today, in the center of the boulevard, primarily in the traffic round-abouts, or *glorietas,* there are monumental figures constructed in the vocabulary of academic classicism, each with its own complex history of design and sponsorship; these are Cuauhtemoc by Miguel Noreña and Gabriel Guerra (1878–87), Columbus (designs by Manuel Vilar and later Ramón Rodríguez Arangoity, inaugurated in 1892), and a victory monument to Independence (Enrique Alciati and Antonio Rivas Mercado, inaugurated in 1910).The Reforma project as a whole, and especially the Angel of Independence, a draped column on whose base stands the figure of Hidalgo and other allegorical and historical figures, as well as a winged victory at the top, indicates a shift from the city's ceremonial center. Virtually 100 years earlier, the academic classical monument of Tolsá's Carlos IV marked the colonial center of the central plaza, flanked by the cathedral and the National Palace. Commerce, politics, and the consolidation of a nation-state converged to prompt a shift in this center to the Reforma, a reclamation of the Imperial Boulevard itself.

A survey of nineteenth-century Mexican art, and especially academic art, generates a picture of the masculinity of public representations. Although women artists, most of them having received private training by academic artists or in the limited classes they could take at the academy, displayed their work in academy exhibitions as well as international expositions, their work always was regarded as decorative and unoriginal. The mainstay of women artists was the copying of academic works, as well as the production of domestic scenes and portraiture. Contemporary criticism patronizingly devalued the works women exhibited with precious adjectives or spoke more about the "original" that they had copied. Among these artists were Juliana San Román, Luz Osorio, Pilar de la Hidalga, and Carmela Duarte.

The question of gender is important not only in terms of the practitioners of art or who is represented in the visual chronicle of Mexican history. It is also significant in terms of a basic category of western imagery, namely, the nude, or more precisely the female nude. Contrary to European art of the same period, the female nude rarely was seen in Mexico. Interior decorations, such as classically derived wall painting, were among the few sites for partial nudity; contrary to its European counterpart, Mexican academic art rarely provided artists this opportunity. The proscription against the presence of the female nude in the academy may help explain this in part.

Remarkably, in the 1891 academy exhibition, a special room was constructed for the display of the nude both in finished paintings and in studies. This included the work of well-known painter Felipe Gutiérrez, whose *Huntress of the Andes* caused a great deal of controversy. This starkly foreshortened figure is "native" only by virtue of the spear she carries and rouged face as sign of her dark "indigenous" skin. This metaphoric rationale of the mythological Amazon did little to assuage outraged contemporary viewers. And, yet, within a few years, the public presentation of erotic sculptures was taking place in Mexico City's oldest public park, the Alameda. Here, among the other sculptures of natural topiary, marble, and bronze, could be found by about 1900, Jesús Contreras's *Malgré Tout,* a female nude in white marble, awkwardly posed in a crouch, chained but striving to rise from her bondage.

Contreras's French title indicates the trend of late-nineteenth-century artists now studying in Paris, rather than Rome, as their earlier counterparts had done. The center of culture had shifted to France, despite the anti-French sentiment following the mid-century French invasion and the execution of Maximilian. The *afrancesamiento* of Porfirian elite culture was profound; writers and artists alike studied in France and looked there for a modern art outside of what was coming to be regarded by many as a withering academic manner. Mexican artists would refract in their own works French Realism, Impressionism, and Symbolism. As a testament to an aging Mexican academicism, the newspaper *El Ahuitzote* published a satiric lithographic cartoon in 1897 entitled "Professor of Painting at the Academy in Perpetuity." In it, José Pina, trained as a student under Spanish artist Pelegrín Clavé and later, first Mexican painting director of the academy, sits trapped in a cobweb. This cartoon indicates the growing rift among Mexican artists in general; academic classicism was on the decline and a multifaceted modernism was on the rise.

In the 1890s, Mexican artists and writers collaborated in short-lived journals, confronting academic painting that they saw as too centered on the realist object. "Modernism" in Mexico was, as true elsewhere in Latin America, primarily a literary movement. Modernist writers and poets such as Manuel Gutiérrez Nájera, Carlos Díaz Dufoo, and Amado Nervo wrote for illustrated journals such as the

La Crítica (1906–07) by Julio Ruelas
Illustration courtesy of Museo Nacional de Arte

Revista Azul (1894–96) and the *Revista Moderna* (1891–11). Perhaps most best known for his modern, or, more precisely, symbolist works is Julio Ruelas, whose small-scale works were characterized by emotional plays on esoteric subjects and reliance on color, type, design elements, and photography. His etching, *La Crítica* of 1906–07, is a self-portrait that confronts the viewer with a strangely disembodied head with a sharp-beaked bird poking at the top of his skull. As Ruelas himself would have claimed, it was a publicly inaccessible image, an image of the interior.

The Porfirian elite's courting of foreign investors, its concessions to the Catholic Church and large landholders, as well as its the enactment of general political repression catapulted Mexico into revolution by the end of 1910. Díaz's last contribution to Mexican culture emphasized the profound connection he established to the erstwhile political and cultural enemy of the republic. In 1910, the year of Mexico's centennial celebration of Independence and the year of the inauguration of the Monument to Independence in the Paseo de la Reforma, the Díaz government sponsored a major exhibition of Spanish painting. Díaz was an enthusiastic supporter of the dazzling, photographic, and historicist works of Spanish painter Antonio Fabrés, whose work bore the dramatic impact of the more well-known Mariano Fortuny. Fabrés assumed the role of court painter to Díaz and produced large classical decorations for him.

The antagonisms within cultural politics began to emerge at this moment. Gerardo Murillo, better known by his assumed name, Dr. Atl, along with other intellectuals, oversaw a counter-exhibition of art entitled "The First Exhibition of National Art." Included were Saturnino Herrán and Jorge Enciso, artists known for their indigenous scenes, both contemporary and historical. Also among the young artists showing works were Diego Rivera and José Clemente Orozco, whose works were then quite unlike the public murals sponsored by the revolutionary government in the 1920s. In 1911, students at the Academy of San Carlos rioted, demanding the institution's reorganization; Porfirio Díaz was in exile in Paris. This date often is given the burden of signaling an inexorable shift from academic, private, and elite-driven art to the public and political art of muralism. But even after this crucial year, and into the "institutional" phase of the Revolution in the 1920s, artists and patrons accommodated different, if not antagonistic, styles and media, which, despite some claims to the contrary, continued to exist even after the Revolution. And although produced under different conditions and for different patrons and audiences, the issues and conflicts of Mexican national art, especially within an official and institutional context, continued to be profoundly important, and often negotiated around images resonant of those central to the issue of nineteenth-century national art: the chronicle of history—both European and indigenous, the land, the social type, and above all, around the figure of the Indian.

Select Bibliography

Brown, Thomas A., *La Academia de San Carlos de la Nueva España,* translated by María Negrete Deffis and Emilia Martínez. 2 vols., Mexico City: SepSetentas, 1976.

Charlot, Jean, *Mexican Art and the Academy of San Carlos, 1785–1915.* Austin: University of Texas Press, 1962.

Widdifield, Stacie G., *The Embodiment of the National in Nineteenth-Century Mexican Painting.* Tucson: University of Arizona Press, 1996.

—STACIE G. WIDDIFIELD

Visual Arts: 1910–37, The Revolutionary Tradition

The revitalization of Mexican arts in the 1920s, known as the Mexican Renaissance, generally has been attributed to the transformative power of the Mexican Revolution. While artistic and social change in this period are clearly linked, the absolute centrality of the Mexican Revolution to the Mexican Renaissance may be questioned. Indeed, we may find that the arts were as much or more an agent of the change experienced in post-Revolutionary Mexican society as they were a product of the change initiated by the military and political consequences of the Revolution. Moreover, the artistic community sought social change before the Revolution even started. Many factors contributed to the resurgence of Mexican culture in the early part of the twentieth century. Artists and intellectuals held a general disdain for what was considered the "decadence" of industrialized, materialist, European culture. Although it had been developing since the turn of the century, the ultimate justification for this disdain was the atrocities of World War I. In Mexico, as in Latin America in general, artists and writers believed they were in a position to renovate Europe's decadent civilization, primarily by constructing a New World avant-garde on the spiritual strength of native traditions. Nativism had emerged earlier in the late nineteenth century's patriotic interest in historical paintings that depicted indigenous populations. This trend showed itself more prominently in the exhibition of Mexican art for the 1910 centennial of the Mexican Independence movement. Such anti-European, pro-native sentiments dovetailed with anti-aristocrat, pro-peasant, pro-working class politics; artists dedicated themselves to the ideals of the Revolution: they fought on the battlefield, wrote revolutionary manifestos, and established new ways of teaching art in a general effort to create a guiding aesthetic for the new society under construction.

Rather than spontaneously being born of the fighting between 1910 and 1917, this new Revolutionary society was conscientiously built by a partnership of the government and the arts beginning in the 1920s. Together, artists and politicians worked to build a modern Mexico, with the potential to surpass their former European colonizers, who were in a state of social and spiritual exhaustion after the ravages of World War I. Educational projects provided the forum for the joint work of Mexican intellectuals and government officials. The considerable continuity between the use of education and the arts for national unity, in both pre- and post-Revolution Mexico, becomes apparent by considering the parallels between President Porfirio Díaz's educational precepts and the artistic celebrations of the 1910 centennial, as well as the mural and graphic arts of the post-Revolutionary governments.

1910 Centennial Celebrations

Always interested in encouraging foreign investment, Díaz orchestrated this commemoration of the beginnings of the Mexican Independence movement in a way that would impress visiting journalists and dignitaries with the future profitability of a more modern Mexico. As scholars Colin M. MacLachlan and William H. Beezley have noted, public building projects were ceremoniously inaugurated one after the other. A Mexico City parade recounted Mexican history from pre-Columbian societies on: the procession culminated in a show of contemporary businessmen, civil servants, and other professionals. The message of stability and progress was well received by U.S. industrialist Andrew Carnegie and U.S. president Theodore Roosevelt, both of whom praised Díaz's accomplishments for Mexico. This type of effort to marshal Mexican history and culture in order to present the image of a modern nation, as well as to bolster domestic and international support of the president, repeated itself in the state-sponsored, post-Revolution mural projects.

The official centennial festivities also included an exposition of Spanish and Japanese art. When it was learned that no Mexican work was to be included, the artist Dr. Atl (Gerardo Murillo) led an effort to address this strange omission. Many artists gathered together to help Dr. Atl put together an exposition of national art; they included Francisco de la Torre, Roberto Montenegro, José Clemente Orozco, Saturnino Herrán, Francisco Romano Guillemin, Jorge Enciso, Sóstenes Ortega, Alfonso Garduño, and Joaquín Clausell. However, these artists did not select the works for display; instead, crowds of people from the street served as the jury, shouting opinions as objects were held up for their judgment. This egalitarian spirit carried over into the hanging of the show. Beginning students and established artists were placed side by side. Rather than emphasizing the artist, theme and format guided display. The open space of the courtyard was reserved for more "ambitious" works, meaning larger-scale historical subjects. Inside rooms were grouped by theme and media such as landscape, drawing, and graphics. Appropriate to the character of the show, the numerous visitors came from all strata of Mexican society, providing a strong contrast to the more typically elite attendance at cultural events.

While the art on display seemed to have touched on a wide variety of subjects more or less related to national themes, a number of objects addressed the class consciousness that was reflected in the organization of the display. Many works stressed the suffering of the poor, foreshadowing the concern for the worker and peasant in the Revolution and in the art it inspired in the 1920s and beyond. Exhibited examples included José Natividad Correa Toca's *The Orphans*, Herrán's *Pot (Olla) Seller*, Guillemin's *Eternal Martyr*, and Arnulfo Dominguez Bello's sculpture *After the Strike*. Furthermore, other works by well-recognized artists addressed Mexico's indigenous population. This, too, contradicts the impression that indigenism in the arts arose with the Revolution. For example, Enciso was awarded a prize by the newspaper *El Heraldo* for his painting of an Indian offering an olive branch to the eagle of Anáhuac; contemporary critics recognized this as an image of indigenist patriotism. Indigenous themes also were taken up by Herrán, the current darling of the national art academy. *The Legend of the Volcanoes* depicts an indigenous legend of love between a white princess and an Indian prince that ends tragically when the princess's disapproving father turns his daughter into white snow to prevent their union. Herrán's sympathies lie with the brokenhearted Indian prince. This and other works by Herrán had been shown in February at the academy exhibition, revealing the intimacy of the European-oriented establishment and its detractors, who sought a local, Mexican style.

The closeness between the establishment and those who sought to renovate it is exemplified further by the man who led the effort to organize the Mexican art exhibition. Dr. Atl's effectiveness as a liaison between the future generation of young artists then being educated in the national art school and the administration, which had the power to either facilitate or block the changes sought by the young artists, is revealed by the success of this show. Although Dr. Atl did not have an official position in the school at the time, the administration did permit him to give extracurricular workshops in which he discussed his ideas about creation of a national art with the students. In addition, his personal artistic style also reflected the intimacy of the nineteenth-century art that was coming under fire and the development of a nationalist aesthetic to replace it. Dr. Atl is known primarily for his volcanic landscapes executed in an Expressionist manner. Landscape was a popular subject in the nineteenth-century academy; Dr. Atl selected geographic formations that invoked Mexico, and he depicted them with a particularly modern, twentieth-century style, using vibrant colors and strong brush strokes typical of Expressionism— a mode not permitted by the academic standards.

Like Dr. Atl's organizational and artistic activities, the national art exhibition was not truly independent of the establishment it sought to criticize. The Ministry of Public Education lent financial backing, although it was 10 times less than what the organizers of the Spanish art show received. The Díaz administration lavished attention on the art of Mexico's former colonizer, completely ignoring the national effort in the official program of the centennial activities. Not only was Mexican art ignored in the program, but no catalogue seems to have been published. Díaz's secretary of education, Justo Sierra, publicly heralded the Spanish for all they had taught Mexican artists, revealing the persistence of the colonial relationship. Although the "collective character" of the Mexican art exhibition was unusual, one should not ascribe it a more strident character of rupture than it actually possessed. National painters generally did not challenge the superiority of European artists. This is proven not only by the central role of Spanish art in the centennial festivities, but also by the high degree of competition among Mexican artists for European travel scholarships.

In the 1910 Exhibition of Mexican art were found elements central to post-Revolutionary culture and politics: the attention to the worker, the Indian, and the peasant, as well as the collective approach, and the close ties between the establishment and the vanguard. For instance, it is relatively little known, but the first mural projects were proposed by Justo Sierra to Mexican artists after visiting this exhibition. This is odd given Sierra's often-quoted admiration for Spanish art and the general preference of the Díaz administration for things European over things Mexican. Nevertheless, Dr. Atl seized the secretary's suggestion, proposing the theme of human evolution and a collective approach to the work.

Dr. Atl's humanist, collective orientation implies that the seeds of Mexican muralism lie as much in the turn-of-the-century call for spiritual renovation via a return to the communal spirit of the medieval and Renaissance eras, related to more general concerns about the decadence of western civilization in the industrial age, as to the political force of Marxism in Revolutionary Mexican politics. Artists on both sides of the Atlantic shared a sense of disenchantment with modern industrial life and consequently turned toward the spiritual. In late-nineteenth-century France this was expressed in part through symbolism and then art nouveau. In both attitude and style these movements found resonance

The Tree of Life *(1921-22) by Roberto Montenegro*
Illustration courtesy of Patrimonio Universitario

among Mexican artists such as Montenegro, Adolfo Best-Maugard, and others. Montenegro painted one of the first murals, *The Tree of Life,* in a decorative-symbolist vein, in the former convent of San Pedro and San Paulo in 1921–22. Clearly, the rejection of industrial society and the Mexican Revolution's Marxist critique were intimately related. Muralism was not only driven by politics, but also by debates in the arts that manifested themselves as early as 1910 in the national exhibition of the centennial celebrations.

Open Air Schools

The dissent expressed in the insistence on including national art in the centennial festivities did not settle after the 1910 Mexican show closed. In 1911, just after Díaz's resignation, the students at the Academy of San Carlos went on strike against what they perceived to be the outdated, Eurocentric teaching methods of traditional academicism. More specifically, the students wanted Alfredo Ramos Martínez

appointed to direct the institution; they felt that a Mexican interested in more current styles such as Impressionism was more appropriate to direct the national art school. When the government's response proved unacceptable, Ramos Martínez established an alternative to the national academy. He began an Open Air School in Santa Anita, Ixtalco, where students could learn Impressionist techniques outdoors as the Impressionists themselves had done at Barbizon. The centrality of locally observed subject matter seems to have overridden the fact that Impressionism was imported from abroad. Also, its promotion of a personal vision over adherence to academic standards must have contributed to the sense that adoption of Impressionism constituted an act of insurgency. In her work on the Open Air School, author Sylvia Pandolfi noted the uncanny parallels between the student strikes against the academy and the outbreak of the Revolution, as well as the continuing importance of education and the arts to the expression of Mexico's Revolutionary society.

Concurrent with the Open Air Schools, in 1913 Adolfo Best-Maugard developed a systematic method of drawing from a close study of indigenous design. This method, eventually published in 1923 in a book titled *Creative Design,* was based on Best-Maugard's perception that there existed an affinity between folk, or native, arts and modern design. Use of this local resource in an effort to achieve modern expression proved Mexico's competitiveness in the modern world. Modernism, nationalism, and social transformation merged in Best-Maugard's drawing manual. As opposed to the nineteenth-century positivist model, which required leadership from the top of society, Mexican viability now was based on the inclusion of all; accordingly, anyone could tap his or her creative instincts using Best-Maugard's method. As this method heralded native values, José Vasconcelos, Álvaro Obregón's education minister, was a staunch supporter. He adopted the Best-Maugard method for use in public elementary schools from 1921 to 1924.

Vasconcelos also was a strong supporter of the Open Air School, which had dissolved after its intense activities in 1913 and 1914 for the remainder of the Revolution. It was revived in 1920 by Vasconcelos. When the political climate changed and Plutarco Elías Calles took power in 1925, Vasconcelos's mural projects and the Best-Maugard method suffered, but the Open Air Schools remained in place. In concert with the populism of the Revolution, the schools now expanded to include not only the education of the nation's artists but the artistic training of the nation's people. The semirural areas outside Mexico City as well as the nation's children now received the benefits of artistic training outdoors. In 1926 official policy declared the Open Air Schools responsible for cultivating the innate, pre-Columbian talents of the Mexican population. In a move reminiscent of Díaz's use of art to appeal to the international community, Calles sponsored exhibitions that broadcasted students' talents both nationally and internationally. Shows took place in Mexico City, Los Angeles, Paris, Madrid, and Berlin. The success of these exhibitions in promoting Mexico's modern talents was so great that by 1927 new urban schools —such as Centros Populares de Enseñanza Arística Urbana—complemented peasants' rural opportunities, and the workers of Mexico City enjoyed the instruction of Francisco Díaz de León, Gabriel Fernández Ledesma, Fernando Leal, and others.

Many artists who came to play central roles in the Mexican Renaissance participated in the Open Air Schools at one time or another. Orozco and David Alfaro Siqueiros both had brief experiences with the school in its early period and then, of course, became famous for their murals in the post-Revolution period. With Vasconcelos's support the "heroic group of seven" revived the Open Air Barbizon school in Chimalstac, calling the resurrected facility the "Casa del Artista." Díaz de León, Ramón Alva de la Canal, Mateo Bolaños, Emilio García Chavero, Fernández Ledesma, Leal, and Enrique A. Ugarte were later joined by Leopoldo Méndez and Fermín Revueltas. In 1925 Díaz de León became the director of the Open Air School at Tlapan. Leal also became a director of the Open Air School at Coyoacán, in addition to participating in the mural movement's initiation at the National Preparatory School in 1922. Fernández Ledesma and Méndez were founding members of the League of Revolutionary Artists and Writers (LEAR) in 1934; Méndez went on to establish El Taller de Gráfica Popular (TGP, or the People's Graphic Arts Workshop) in 1937.

The consequent activities of the leaders of the Open Air School suggest that this movement was integral to the growing nationalism in Mexican art, for which a sense of native culture was central. The physical location of the Open Air Schools in the Mexican landscape was a way of immersing the artists in their native land, as well as a way of disassociating from the national art academy. Open Air School founder Ramos Martínez believed that if "true art" were to be generated in Mexico, it must stem from "native values." His view was shared by José Vasconcelos, the driving patron of the mural movement.

Atl's Popular Arts Show
Also aware of the social implications of including contemporary indigenous arts, Dr. Atl organized another show for the 1921 centennial of the success of the Mexican Independence movement. However, his post-Revolution exhibition reflected the changed political atmosphere; instead of paintings, this show displayed Mexican popular arts. As author Karen Cordero Reiman has pointed out, Dr. Atl's catalogue minimized the differences between the various cultural groups of Mexico in order to bring them together in this celebration of the new Mexican nation. Like the 1910 centennial, the 1921 rendition sought to legitimate Mexico in the international sphere; Mexico needed to borrow funds to rebuild the damage done during the Revolution and continue on the road to modernity.

Nativism as a tool for national strength was a strategy that transcended the divide between the nineteenth and twentieth centuries, as well as the pre- and post-Revolutionary orders. In addition to the activity of the nineteenth-century academy and the art, exhibitions, and didactic methods promoted by Dr. Atl, Ramos Martínez, and Best-Maugard, the archaeological pursuits of Manuel Gamio also fostered social change. His excavation of Teotihuacan, about which he published a series of books in 1922, was intended to bring the indigenous populations of Mexico into the national fold. He stated, "When native and middle class share one criterion where art is concerned, we shall be culturally redeemed, and national art, one of the solid bases of national consciousness, will have become a fact." Gamio's comments reflected the leading role of the middle class in the Mexican Revolution, despite the working-class rhetoric, as well as the use of the *indio* as a device to forge national unity via the visual arts.

The importance of art to nationalism put the Mexican avant-garde in a unique position. As with their European and Latin American counterparts, the Mexican avant-garde rallied to overthrow the academy and agitated for visual expression more in tune with the modern sensibility of the new century. However, the Mexican avant-garde was unique in that they fought this battle in alliance with, not against, the Mexican government. This is a highly complex situation, for we have seen that the germ for the fusion between artists, Indian culture, and the government is found before the outbreak of the Revolution.

Muralismo

In the post-Revolution administrations of the 1920s and 1930s, muralism was conceived of as a direct result of the Revolution. This Revolutionary rhetoric was central to the role of this art in the construction of a strong, coherent Mexican nation. The rejection of the national art academy was seen as a rejection of the colonial past; Mexico would no longer be dependent on Europe for artistic inspiration, just as twentieth-century Mexico would resist U.S. ownership of Mexico's natural resources and other foreign interference in domestic economics and politics. The vanguard and the current status quo were engaged in a battle against the status quo of the past, as well as for current international respect. The central position of muralism to the development of Mexican nationalism is revealed by the close alignments of the fluctuations of this art movement with the whims and cycles of the government. Nevertheless, this is not to say that government policy entirely determined the character of Mexican muralism. The ideological and stylistic differences of the three most famous practitioners of muralism—Diego Rivera, Siqueiros, and

Orozco—show that individual artists influenced muralism's portrait of Mexico as much as their presidential patrons did.

José Vasconcelos, the influential liaison between the artists and their presidential patrons, was decisively shaped by the activities of the years before the Revolution, rather than the Revolution itself. One of the several institutions significant to Vasconcelos's development was the Ateneo de la Juventud. This group of intellectuals met regularly for philosophical discussions, to organize conferences, and to publish the journal *Savia Moderna*. Vasconcelos was a leading member of the Ateneo, which also included Pedro Henríquez Ureña, Antonio Caso, and Alfonso Reyes. Although the group began meeting in 1906, they became known as the "Generation of 1910"—a date that tied their censure of the Eurocentric Díaz administration to the commemoration of the 1810 initiation of the Mexican Independence movement. The Ateneo's program of self-education was influenced by the Greek humanism and the pan-American, anti-Yankee-imperialist-materialism of José Enrique Rodó's *Ariel* (1900). Together they actively criticized scientific positivism, the banner of the Díaz government, and advocated the adoption of a general liberal humanist education for both the workers and the general public. Artists such as Herrán, Germán Gedovius, Rafael Ponce de León, de la Torre, the Garduño brothers, Rivera, and Dr. Atl collaborated with the Ateneo in its journal and exhibition projects, attracted by its goal of infusing Mexico's philosophic, literary, and artistic productions with the new "renovating spirit." Cordero Reiman has noted that the Ateneo also promoted a racially and culturally mixed model of Mexican identity. Indeed, all addressed *mestizaje*; for example, Caso's archaeological projects, Reyes's 1917 book *Vision of Anahuac*, and the art of Herrán, Gedovius, Dr. Atl, and Rivera.

The focal site of the advent of muralism, the National Preparatory School, reveals further continuities between Vasconcelos's pre- and post-Revolutionary thinking. The school was founded in 1867 by Gabino Barreda, Mexico's premier positivist, and was meant to instruct the leaders of Mexico's elite to carry out the tenets of a positivist society. This ideology held that a scientifically ordered society could evolve toward perfection. Positivism's promise of progress required a dictatorship to instill the prerequisite order; it was Porfirio Díaz's dictatorship, as well as its positivist justification, that the Revolution sought to overturn. Vasconcelos's selection to visually mark the Revolution's social change in this place was an adept political choice. At once he marked the overthrow of the past order, which had been maintained in part through educational institutions, while also declaring a new type of education for a different society. The visual arts were a major force in the move for revision of the Mexican educational system. In fact, one of the primary purposes of the murals was to instruct the illiterate masses—80 percent of the population—on the history of Mexico. The visual arts were clearly meant to be tool for social change.

Vasconcelos once had been a student at the National Preparatory School; his mural commissions reflected this past as well as his skepticism of it. The primary example of this is his 1922 commission of Rivera for the Anfiteatro Bolivar, an auditorium in the National Preparatory School. Rivera's mural, *Creation,* gave Vasconcelos's humanist orientation center stage by inserting Mexican figures into the structure. *Mestizaje,* a dominant theme of this mural, heralds the future benefits of integrating Mexico's native and European heritages. Accordingly, Rivera depicted figures emblematic of the native tradition, the Judeo-Christian ethic, and the intellectual legacy of Hellenic civilization. Seated on opposite sides of the mural are Adam and Eve, depicted as a mestizo couple. A succession of figures depicted above Adam and Eve represent a philosophic, evolutionary view in which society progresses from a materialist to intellectualist phase and culminated in the aesthetic phase. As Mexico had recently achieved the racial fusion and national unification of the intellectualist phase, it was poised to enter the aesthetic phase. Vasconcelos believed only aesthetic intuition could unify the opposing elements in society. The aesthetic stage promised taste and beauty; Vasconcelos hoped to push Mexico into attaining this stage via his art-centered educational projects such as muralism, the Best-Maugard method, and his continuation of the Open Air Schools.

The mural movement has been divided into three phases according to the shifts in power from Álvaro Obregón (1920–24), to Plutarco Elías Calles (1924–34), and then Lázaro Cárdenas (1934–40). Throughout the tenure of these various presidents, artists and the government were allied in their efforts to create an independent, modern, civilized nation both at home and abroad. The muralists used European styles and notions, such as the creation of an image of the nation through painting, as tools for national reconstruction. This new Mexican effort was distinguished by addressing historical subjects ranging from the pre-Columbian past to the more recent events of the Revolution. The very choice to locate the new painting on walls signaled the fusion of Mexico's indigenous and European heritages.

During the early years of reconstruction after the Revolution, Obregón struggled to maintain political and economic stability. As author Mari Ramírez-García argued, the rhetoric of unity along with the populist imagery of the murals helped to satisfy the populace that the promises of the Revolution were being kept by the Obregón administration. The renaissance of Mexican art symbolized the rebirth of Mexican society as a result of the Revolution. Aesthetic ideals depicted in the murals of this period symbolically represented the radical change Obregón sought to create in the minds of those who compared Mexico after the Revolution to the era before the fighting began. Another benefit the Obregón administration reaped from the mural program was the image of social unity and a cultured civilization that was communicated north of the border. The U.S. government initially refused to recognize the post-Revolutionary order. This was an economic blow, for Mexico needed to borrow funds for reconstruction from U.S. banks.

During Calles's presidential administration (1924–28) and his period of rule from behind the scenes (1928–34), the more politically radical artists were forced out of the capital, first to Guadalajara and then to the United States. Only Rivera remained, busy with the project at the Ministry of Public Education from 1926 to 1929. Rivera used the visual language of Christian martyrs to heroize leaders of the Revolution, and his dignified portrayal of the Mexican proletariat served to elevate this group over his caricatures of the Mexican and U.S. bourgeoisie. The irony of Calles's repression of muralism in Mexico was that this was the impetus for the muralists' activity in the United States, resulting in the very international recognition for the cultural worth of Mexico that muralism had set as its aim. Conservative U.S. opinion, however, supported Calles, and the muralists were seen as dangerous Communists. For example, Rivera's Rockefeller Center mural in New York was destroyed owing to his inclusion of a portrait of Lenin, and Siqueiros was deported after causing a red scare in California.

Lázaro Cárdenas's more populist administration permitted the muralists' return and a reinvigoration of mural art. Nevertheless, it was at this time that muralism came under fire for the inaccessibility of most of the murals, for the majority decorated official buildings that were seldom used by the common people. In response Secretary of Education Narciso Bassols advocated didactic murals in public schools, and the ceilings of the Abelardo Rodríguez market in Mexico City were painted. Further criticism was aimed at the mural efforts of the

The Creation *(1922–23) by Diego Rivera*
Illustration courtesy of Archivo Fotográfico, Instituto de Investigaciones Estéticas de la UNAM

early 1920s. Siqueiros condemned Rivera's folkloric style, saying: "Mexican mural painting, owing to the inadequate and defective ideological-political preparation of the painters, in some cases served the demagogic interests of the Mexican government more than the interests of the working class and *campesinos* (peasants)."

The "Tres Grandes" (Orozco, Rivera, and Siqueiros) differed in their attitudes toward the intimacy between the mural movement and the government. In contrast to Rivera's intimacy with both the Communist Party of Mexico and a succession of presidents, Orozco avoided clear political alliances. However, Orozco always remained critical of the failure of the state to live up to the aims of the Revolution. At the same time Orozco was adamant that art should not service propaganda. Although Orozco and Rivera both exploited Christian imagery of martyrdom to depict the suffering of working-class Mexicans, Orozco also criticized the fusion of folk art and painting that was so typical of Rivera's work. However, Orozco's criticism of Rivera may have been due to an aesthetic preference for the separation between "high art" (painting) and "low art" (folklore).

Of the three great muralists, Siqueiros seems to have been the most interested in developing new techniques and new ways of painting consistent with the assertion of a new aesthetic for a modern, revolutionary Mexico. Siqueiros may be best known for his experiments with industrial paint and the spray gun, as this was the seed of Jackson Pollock's abstract innovations. Siqueiros's experiments were an effort to forge a modern art that utilized modern inventions rather than the Renaissance encaustic and fresco techniques that Rivera resurrected from the past.

Artists' Manifestos

Artists wishing to express an alternative viewpoint to that permitted by government-controlled commissions used manifestos as vehicles to call for change in artistic practices. In his 1921 manifesto "Three Appeals for a Modern Direction to the New

Generation of American Painters and Sculptors," Siqueiros outlined the way he imagined Mexico could generate a new, vital aesthetic. Spurred on by the decadence of Spanish art, Siqueiros wrote from Barcelona, calling for a combination of lost values and new values. He advocated artists of the Americas building upon the achievements of the old masters, using the advances of the contemporary age. The new generation should look to the Indian for inspiration, but not in order to create "Indianism, Americanism, or primitivism"; he suggested, rather, that the universal should take precedent over national. Perhaps this is why he thought the Open Air Schools were academic and therefore dangerous. In his 1922 manifesto, "Declaration of Social, Political, and Aesthetic Principles," Siqueiros used Marxist language and openly attacked "bourgeois society." He repudiated easel painting because it was aristocratic and praised monumental painting because it was owned by the public at large. He reasserted the spiritual value of the noble Indian, calling him a national "treasure."

The Indian also was heralded in *El Machete*, the newspaper of the workers and peasants. Muralism's initial humanist character soon was taken over by the more radical political agenda of the Union of Technical Workers, Painters and Sculptors, founded in 1922. Its 1923 manifesto holds Indians to be a creative source due to their communal lifestyle. This text again condemns bourgeois individualism and elevates popular taste over bourgeois taste. Cities come under particular attack for the most extreme corruption. Signatories included Siqueiros, Rivera, X. Guerrero, Fermín Revueltas, Orozco, Ramón Alva Guadarrama, Germán Cueto, and Carlos Mérida.

Liga de Escritores y Artistas Revolucionarios

In 1934, amidst criticism regarding the inaccessibility of murals, a group of militant artists banded together to form the League of Revolutionary Writers and Artists (LEAR). The founding members, Leopoldo Méndez, Pablo O'Higgins, and Juan de la Cabada, had previously been a part of the Proletarian Intellectual Struggle, a group whose purpose was to produce art accessible to and representative of the proletariat. After the imprisonment of Cabada, the group disintegrated, and then reemerged a few years later as the LEAR. The LEAR continued the social confrontation that the Proletarian Intellectual Struggle had begun in accordance with the recommendations of the Sixth Congress of the Communist International. As author Francisco Reyes Palma has reported, the league set out to use art to fight fascism, imperialism, war, and reactionary forces within Mexico.

In contrast to the muralists, the LEAR declared its independence from the government from the outset. In the first issue of its journal, *Frente a Frente* (Face to Face, November 1934), the LEAR stated this openly, calling the government "social-fascist." Méndez in particular characterized the 1934 opening of the Palace of Fine Arts as a "fascist parody"; he pointedly included Rivera's and composer Carlos Chávez's works as targets of his scathing critique. Opposed to the pseudocollectivism of the muralists who, with the exception of Siqueiros, worked with a team of artists but only signed the principal artist's name, the LEAR was more self-consciously egalitarian. Its central aim was educating the working class in artistic techniques by giving the workers the ability to assume the tools of cultural expression.

The LEAR expressly selected a form of expression and distribution that would be accessible to the working class; it primarily published broad sheets that were posted in the streets. These sheets had images as well as graphically intriguing layouts of manifestos. The league also published pamphlets in reproducible forms that permitted many copies to circulate. It was thought that this medium would be more likely to reach the hands of the workers as opposed to the images created by the muralists, whose work was restricted to seldom-seen government offices. This distinction, however, did not prevent members of the LEAR from working on the Rodríguez market murals. This public site of daily living accorded with the LEAR's ideals; its murals there addressed public health and nutrition, as well as the international problems of fascism and war.

LEAR did not remain immune to the power of government funding to consume independent cultural voices. In 1937 Cárdenas added an offer of an annual government subsidy to the free radio time that LEAR already enjoyed. The offer was in part a recognition of the role LEAR had been playing in the official promotion of education. Not surprisingly, the solidification of this relationship coincided with the expansion of LEAR's membership base and activities.

El Taller de Gráfica Popular

In 1937 various art leaders of the LEAR broke away and formed their own group, El Taller de Gráfica Popular (People's Graphic Arts Workshop). This split was not a complete break, as both groups occasionally worked together on joint projects. Méndez, O'Higgins, and Arenal were the principal leaders of the Taller. Their activities included printing posters

Piñata política (1935) by Leopoldo Méndez
Illustration courtesy of Archivo Fotográfico, Instituto de Investigaciones Estéticas de la UNAM

and pamphlets covering international threats such as the Spanish civil war and the rise of the Nazis, or religious strife and caudillismo at home. The Taller also produced portfolios of prints covering subjects such as Franco's Spain and native Mexican costumes in order to generate some income for the group. Linoleum blocks were used in order to ensure the least expensive means of producing the maximum volume. This sort of self-reliance served the Taller well, ensuring its survival into the late 1950s.

Like the advent of muralism, the germ for the graphically expressed social critique of both the LEAR and the Taller may be located, in part, in the nineteenth century. José Guadalupe Posada's satire of Mexican society during the Porfiriato set the precedent for these post-Revolution activities. Indeed, Posada's legacy was claimed by the graphic artists and the muralists alike, and his *calaveras* (skeletons) graced both the painted and postered walls of post-Revolutionary Mexico.

Posada was but one figure mobilized in the state's effort to exploit art as a vehicle for the dissemination of the Revolutionary legend in order to generate a modern image of Mexico, worthy of respect on both domestic and foreign levels. Despite the debates as to the driving force behind the Mexican Renaissance—was it Vasconcelos's mural project or the work of his predecessors?—it is possible to conclude that the spiritual renovation of Mexico was a continuation, in part, of Díaz's nineteenth-century liberal positivism that used education as a tool to forge a modern country. The difference between Díaz's effort and the post-Revolutionary efforts is the twentieth century's ostensible attempt to include the rural poor.

Select Bibliography

Ades, Dawn, *Art in Latin America*. New Haven, Connecticut: Yale University Press, 1989.

Billeter, Erika, editor, *Images of Mexico: The Contribution of Mexico to 20th-Century Art*. Frankfurt: Schirn Kunsthalle Frankfurt, 1987.

Charlot, Jean, *The Mexican Mural Renaissance, 1920–1925*. New Haven, Connecticut: Yale University Press, 1963.

Cordero Reiman, Karen, "Constructing a Modern Mexican Art, 1910–1940." In *South of the Border: Mexico in the American Imagination, 1914–1947*. Edited by James Oles. New Haven, Connecticut: Yale University Art Gallery, 1993.

Edwards, Emily, *Painted Walls of Mexico*. Austin: University of Texas Press, 1966.

Fauchereau, Serge, "The Stridents." *Artforum* 24 (February 1986).

Helm, MacKinley, *Mexican Painters: Rivera, Orozco, Siqueiros and Other Artists of the Social Realist School*. New York: Dover, 1941.

Hennessy, Alistair, "Artists, Intellectuals and Revolution." *Journal of Latin American Studies* 3:1 (May 1971).

MacLachlan, Colin M., and William H. Beezley, *El Gran Pueblo: A History of Greater Mexico*. Englewood Cliffs, New Jersey: Prentice-Hall, 1994.

Oles, James, "South of the Border: American Artists in Mexico, 1914–1947." In *South of the Border, Mexico in the American Imagination, 1914–1947*, edited by James Oles. New Haven, Connecticut: Yale University Art Gallery, 1993.

Pandolfi, Sylvia, "The Mexican Open-Air Painting Schools Movement (1913–1935)." In *Images of Mexico: The Contribution of Mexico to 20th-Century Art*, edited by Erika Billeter. Frankfurt: Schirn Kunsthalle Frankfurt, 1987.

Ramírez-Garcia, Mari Carmen, "Nationalism and the Avant-Garde: Ideological Equilibrium of Mexican Muralism, 1920–1940." In *Images of Mexico: The Contribution of Mexico to 20th-Century Art*, edited by Erika Billeter. Frankfurt: Schirn Kunsthalle Frankfurt, 1987.

———, "The Ideology and Politics of the Mexican Mural Movement: 1920-1925." Ph.D. diss., University of Chicago, 1989.

Rodríguez, Antonio, *A History of Mexican Mural Painting*. London: Thames and Hudson, and New York: Putnam's, 1969.

Reyes Palma, Francisco, "Workshop of Popular Graphics during the Times of Cárdenas." In *Images of Mexico: The Contribution of Mexico to 20th-Century Art*, edited by Erika Billeter. Frankfurt: Schirn Kunsthalle Frankfurt, 1987.

Schwald Innes, John, "Revolution and Renaissance in Mexico: El Ateneo de la Juventud." Ph.D. diss., University of Texas, 1970.

—Ingrid Elliott

Visual Arts: 1920–45, Art outside the Revolutionary Tradition

While the Revolution of 1910 triggered an artistic renaissance in Mexico, interest in Mexico among artists, writers, and intellectuals of the United States also flourished. Although U.S. fascination with Mexico dates back to the nineteenth century, several factors intensified this interest during the 1920s and 1930s. First, precisely because the U.S. government refused to recognize the new Mexican government in the wake of the Revolution, Mexican intellectuals engaged in activities designed to foment support for Mexico among U.S. citizens.

The Mexican Vogue

Traveling exhibitions were one means of achieving recognition of Mexico's cultural richness. The 1922 exhibit "Mexican Popular Arts," for example, which was held in Los Angeles, was ostensibly organized by American Katherine Anne Porter, who wrote the catalogue essay for the exhibit, but was organized primarily by archaeologist and anthropologist Alfonso Caso with assistance from painters Adolfo Best-Maugard, Jorge Enciso, Robert Montenegro, Miguel Covarrubias, Manuel Rodríguez Lozano, Carlos Mérida, and Diego Rivera. Many U.S. venues refused to show the exhibit on the grounds that it was Mexican political propaganda. The show, which attempted to demonstrate the cultural traditions of Mexico and their relevance to contemporary Mexican artistic practices, provided an example that was followed by other exhibits of Mexican art in the United States. In 1928 the Art Center of New York hosted "Applied Arts of Mexico," organized by writer Anita Brenner and Mexican artists, including Covarrubias. This show also presented examples of folk art alongside the works of modern painters. The Museum of Modern Art in New York held the 1940 exhibit, "Twenty Centuries of Mexican Art," which was divided into four sections, each organized by a different Mexican artist, including Covarrubias, Antonio Castro Leal, Montenegro, and archaeologist Caso. These and other exhibits were intended to draw attention to the ongoing cultural renewal in Mexico in order to curry favor for the Álvaro Obregón and following administrations.

A second reason behind the "Mexican vogue" lay in the international arena. During the 1930s, as political events in Europe made the threat of war increasingly real, the United States and Mexico drew closer and the "Mexican vogue" grew. One result of this was the increased presence of Mexican artists in the United States. The muralists in particular benefited from U.S. interest in Mexico. Each of the "Tres Grandes," including Rivera, José Clemente Orozco, and David Alfaro Siqueiros, obtained commissions to execute murals at various sites in the United States. Not only did these commissions provide artists with the opportunity to convey Mexican nationalist ideology to a U.S. audience, but they also led to the adoption of mural painting among artists employed by the U.S. Works Progress Administration (WPA) during the Great Depression.

The "Mexican vogue" did not manifest itself only in the presence of Mexican art and artists in the United States. U.S. writers and artists also were drawn to Mexico, where they sought fertile subject matter based both on their own preconceived notions and the realities of Mexico. Artists, such as painter Marsden Hartley and photographer Edward Weston, found inspiration in the Mexican landscape, pre-Columbian art, the Revolution, and the Mexican people. Writers, including Hart Crane, Paul Bowles, Tennessee Williams, and John Reed, came to Mexico for similar reasons. Anita Brenner, a North American who spent the early years of her life in Mexico, wrote *Idols Behind Altars* in 1929, perhaps the most influential book on Mexico among North Americans during this period. This book, along with magazines aimed at U.S. audiences, such as *Mexican Folkways,* published in Mexico by expatriate Frances Toor, sought, like many of the art exhibits that traveled to the United States, to convey an image of cultural continuity in Mexico—to suggest the presence of the pre-Columbian past in contemporary Mexico and thus to mirror the indigenist ideology of Mexican nationalism.

The "Mexican vogue," the product of both the United States's primitivizing fantasies of "old Mexico" and of Mexican nationalist programs, in many ways answered the needs of both sides. It made Mexican nationalism a presence in the United States, furthering support for official U.S. recognition of the Mexican government, and allowed U.S. artists, writers, intellectuals, and collectors to indulge their often stereotypical ideas of Mexico, whether rural, archaic, primitive, or Revolutionary.

Movements outside the Vogue

Despite the almost exclusive association, only furthered by the "Mexican vogue," of the mural movement with Mexican art of the 1920s and 1930s, many artists in Mexico worked successfully outside of this tradition. Several avant-garde movements emerged, each approaching art from a different philosophic viewpoint. One of the better-known groups, the Estridentistas, was primarily a literary movement of the 1920s whose ideals also were expressed visually. The Estridentistas published several manifestos outlining the ideology of its movement. The first, written by poet Manuel Maples Arce, exalted the cosmopolitan and urban and rejected the art and literature of the past. Despite the Estridentistas's protests to the contrary, the influence of Italian futurism was evident in this manifesto. Unlike the futurists, however, who were engaged with fascist ideology, the Estridentistas's work was rooted in the socialist ideals of the Mexican Revolution. Led by poets Germán List Arzubide and Maples Arce, the Estridentistas called for an urban, internationalist, utopic art. Its first exhibit, held in a cafe in 1924, included literature, plastic art, and music, reflecting the dynamic interdisciplinary qualities of the movement. Diego Rivera and José Clemente Orozco were associated with the group, but other artists, including Leopoldo Méndez, Ramon Alva de la Canal, and

Germán Cueto, perhaps are more representative of
the movement. Their work, primarily used as illustrations for the magazines and poetry volumes of
Estridentismo, reflected the idealization of the city
presented in their manifestos. Somewhat cubist in
nature, the Estridentistas's images often represented
utopic cityscapes, depicted in stark contrasts of black
and white and heightened by the frequent use of
woodcut prints. Their work represents an alternative
approach to the ideals of the Mexican Revolution.

The Contemporáneos, another literary avant-
garde movement of the 1920s and 1930s with ties
to the visual arts, also provided artists with an alternative to muralism. The Contemporáneos published
several journals, including *Falange* (1922–23), *Ulises*
(1927–28), and *Contemporáneos* (1928–31), which
functioned as sites for the expression of its poetry,
art, and ideas. The poets and artists who claimed
membership in this group adopted a far less political
approach to art than did the muralists. They advocated an approach to Mexicanism based on formal
aesthetics rather than literal, nationalist themes. Artists associated with the movement include Rodríguez
Lozano, Julio Castellanos, Agustín Lazo, Antonio
Ruiz, Abraham Angel Card, and Rufino Tamayo. Although these artists were heterogeneous in their aesthetic approaches to art, many taught art in the early
1920s utilizing Adolfo Best-Maugard's art education
program, and Best-Maugard's stress on formal elements rooted in pre-Columbian and folk art as the
basis of *lo mexicano* remained essential to many of
these artists' works. Several of these artists also produced public murals. Their murals, however, tended
to fulfill their personal aesthetic programs rather
than the nationalist agenda associated with the Mexican Renaissance. Like the Estridentistas, the Contemporáneos provided Mexican artists with an
alternative to muralism—an alternative rooted in
formal, rather than nationalistic, possibilities. Artist
Antonio Ruiz founded his own school of art education, La Esmeralda, which ensured that the legacy of
the Contemporáneos would continue in the work
of many artists who came of age during the 1950s
and 1960s.

Women Artists

While the Estridentistas and the Contemporáneos
offered artists membership in artistic communities,
many Mexican artists worked on the margins of
avant-garde movements. Women artists, in particular, were rarely full participants in the vanguard
groups of mid-twentieth-century Mexico. Muralism,
for example, seems to have been an exclusively male
project, and thus women artists often worked more

La Mulita *(1923) by Abraham Angel Card*
*Illustration courtesy of Archivo Fotográfico, Instituto de
Investigaciones Estéticas de la UNAM*

Madona *(1932) by Julio Castellanos*
*Illustration courtesy of Archivo Fotográfico, Instituto de
Investigaciones Estéticas de la UNAM*

independently, developing a sometimes private or personal artistic vocabulary. Among the better-known women artists in mid-twentieth-century Mexico were Frida Kahlo and María Izquierdo. Kahlo, who was married to Diego Rivera and, like Rivera, highly involved in Mexican politics, often produced autobiographical works referring to her childhood and family, her life as an invalid after a tragic bus accident as a teenager, and her relationships with others, including Rivera. Her art, however, must also be understood within the framework of nationalist ideology that dominated much of muralism and other art. Like the muralists, Kahlo's art engaged in the production of *lo mexicano* through references to nationalist concepts. For example, she often referred to the process of *mestizaje,* a nationalist ideal and part of her family heritage through her emphasis on both the European and indigenous elements of her background. She also, like the muralists and others, found aesthetic inspiration in Mexican pre-Columbian and folk art. Kahlo's art, although often intensely personal in subject matter, utilized her own biography as the basis for the expression of nationalist sentiments.

Izquierdo, like Kahlo, engaged in the production of nationalist images outside of the didactic, historicist tradition associated with muralism. Izquierdo taught art for the Departamento de Bellas Artes in the 1930s, and she was a member of the Liga de Escritores y Artistas Revolucionarios. Although her art never was overtly political in nature, her emphasis on Mexican spirituality represents an expression of nationalist ideas. She frequently painted, for example, household altars filled with religious objects or archetypal Mexican women posed as the Virgin. Like Kahlo and others, Izquierdo admired pre-Columbian and folk art such as the tiny votive paintings known as *retablos.* Although her work often has been linked to surrealist thought, it also can be understood as participating in the construction of Mexican national identity through an imaginative exploration of Mexican religious and spiritual themes.

Indigenismo

Women were, of course, not the only artists to work outside of definable avant-garde movements. Several painters, including Mérida, Covarrubias, and Tamayo, produced art that is not easily categorized. These three artists, however, shared an interest in indigenous cultures that was manifested in their art in ways that differed from the indigenism of the muralists. Mérida, who was originally from Guatemala and of Maya ancestry, participated in the mural

movement early in his career. In 1922 he assisted Rivera with a mural in the Escuela Nacional Preparatoria, and later he painted his own mural in the Secretaría de Educación in Mexico City. He also was among the founders of the Sindicato Revolucionario de Obreros Técnicos y Plásticos in 1922. His mature works, however, evolved away from the clarity of muralism in favor of a more abstract, experimental, and decorative style. His works frequently referenced the Maya sacred text, *Popol Vuh,* through the inclusion of stylized figures modeled on the figures in the text. Mérida produced a portfolio of lithographs inspired directly by *Popol Vuh* in which fragments of the written text appeared as overlays to the images. He often included these Maya figures, however, in his other works as well. His engagement with Maya culture ran contrary to that of his Mexican contemporaries, many of whom stressed a belief in the primacy of central Mexican cultures, including the Mexica, over the Maya, as a part of their nationalist approach to indigenism. Mérida's participation in this debate perhaps was best represented in his 1945 exhibit at the Galería de Arte Mexicano in Mexico City in which his paintings depicted themes of both the Mexica and the Maya. The Maya, in these abstracted images, were represented as a poetic, peaceful, utopic people, while the Mexica were aggressive, fierce, and violent warriors. Mérida also expressed his interest in indigenism through the use of colors and papers made with the same materials as those used by the Maya in their codices. Despite his divergence from nationalist versions of indigenism, Mérida's interest in the recuperation of the indigenous past situated him among his contemporaries in the production of a national identity rooted in indigenist thought.

Mérida's work on the behalf of Mexican nationalism manifested itself in other media. He was active, for example, in the production of guidebooks and magazines, including *Mexican Folkways,* that were aimed at a U.S. audience with the intention of drawing attention to the "new" Mexico and winning favor for the Mexican government among influential North Americans. Here, he utilized his interest in and knowledge of pre-Columbian, folk, and modern art in order to project the Mexican national identity abroad.

Like Mérida, Covarrubias's career had many facets. His engagement with indigenous cultures initially sprang out of an anthropological, as well as an artistic, interest. Covarrubias's professional career began in 1921 when, along with Tamayo, Ruiz, Rodríguez Lozano, Angel Card, and Castellanos, he worked as a teacher of Best-Maugard's drawing

Plastic Invention on the Theme of Love *(1939) by Carlos Mérida, casein and watercolor, 75 × 55 cm*
Illustration courtesy of The Art Institute of Chicago; gift of Katharine Kuh, 1955.818; photograph © 1996,
The Art Institute of Chicago,

curriculum. Initially Covarrubias, like many Mexican artists who later diverged from the "Mexican style," participated in the mural movement. He worked with Montenegro on the *Mapa de América* (Map of America) in the Biblioteca Iberoamericana. This mural, particularly in the representation of waves on the ocean, reflected the influence of Best-Maugard's method, which emphasized stylized, linear, and decorative motifs.

In 1923 Covarrubias left Mexico for New York City, where he began to work primarily as a caricaturist. His caricatures and cartoons, particularly those depicting nightlife in Harlem during the age of the Harlem Renaissance, were quite popular, and he contributed regularly to *Vanity Fair, Vogue,* and *The New Yorker.* While in New York Covarrubias also participated in the organization of several exhibits of Mexican art, including the 1928 "Applied Arts of Mexico" held in the Art Center of New York and the

1930 exhibit "Mexican Art" in the American Federation of the Arts. His experiences in museum work had a significant impact on his later work in Mexico as one of the organizers of the new Museo Nacional de Antropología. By 1933 Covarrubias was ready to leave New York and embarked on a new phase in his career.

Covarrubias and his wife, Rosa Rolando Covarrubias, traveled to Bali where they pursued an anthropological and ethnographic study of the island. Their work was published in 1937 in a book titled *Island of Bali.* In 1935 Covarrubias returned to Mexico where he continued his anthropological studies, turning to the indigenous cultures of Mexico. He published one broad anthropological study of the Isthmus of Tehuantepec, *El Sur de México* (Mexico South). His later books focused specifically on the art of indigenous peoples; he wrote one on the art of Native Americans of North America, including Canada and Alaska, and one on the art of Central America and Mexico.

Covarrubias's interest in the material culture and art of the people he studied led him to the field of anthropology, where he also achieved a great deal of success. As an anthropologist and archaeologist, Covarrubias produced his own illustrations of both the objects and peoples he studied for his books. He studied indigenous art extremely thoroughly and learned to reproduce exactly the designs of Mexico's indigenous cultures. Covarrubias, like many other Mexican artists, including Rivera and Montenegro, also was an active collector of pre-Columbian and folk art. He was involved in the excavation of several important sites, including Olmec sites in southern Mexico and Tlatilco, which he felt demonstrated Olmec influence and proved that the Olmec was the oldest Mexican culture, from which many others developed. Covarrubias also was interested in making his research available to the Mexican public. He was a central figure in the reorganization of the Museo Nacional de Antropología between 1947 and 1954, a museum that contributed to the absorption of indigenous cultures into Mexico's national identity. During the course of Covarrubias's highly varied career, his interest in indigenism transcended the production of art as he eventually took a scientific approach to the native cultures of Mexico.

Painter Rufino Tamayo also became interested in the aesthetic possibilities offered by indigenous art through exposure to anthropology and archaeology. After attending the Escuela de Artes Plásticas (the Academy of San Carlos), Tamayo was appointed head of the Departamento de Dibujo Etnográfico at the Museo Nacional de Arqueología in Mexico City in 1921. This experience shaped the indigenist qualities of his work. Although he painted still lifes and figural works on canvas much like those of Izquierdo, with whom he shared a studio from 1929 to 1933, Tamayo also painted murals throughout his career. Tamayo was met with antagonism by many of the muralists who found his aesthetic too European and apolitical in its modernist qualities. A collector of pre-Columbian art, he drew inspiration from the mythological and mystical aspects of this art, utilizing its cosmic symbols and themes in his own work. Like Mérida, Tamayo's work evolved away from realism toward a stylized, abstracted, and fantastic approach to his subject matter. Tamayo's painting is often associated with the ideas of surrealism, although his interest in pre-Columbian art may better explain the dreamlike surrealist qualities of some of his works. One artist clearly influenced by Tamayo's work is Francisco Toledo, who came to prominence as a painter during the 1960s. Toledo, like Tamayo, engaged indigenous themes in an abstracted, expressionist style.

Surrealism

During the late 1930s and early 1940s, Mexico became a site of refuge for many European surrealists fleeing World War II. The surrealist movement drew heavily on the psychoanalytic work of Sigmund Freud and emphasized the importance of dreams and dreamworlds as an alternate reality as well as the role of the subconscious in everyday life. The surrealists advocated attempts to represent dreams and subconscious thoughts artistically, particularly through "automatism," the process of writing or painting automatically, without pause or conscious thought. The surrealists also claimed an internationalist, revolutionary Marxist political perspective.

Surrealist interest in Mexico had begun before the war with the 1936 visit of Antonin Artaud, who visited the Tarahumara Indians and participated in their peyote ritual, about which he later wrote several essays. In 1938 poet André Breton arrived in Mexico, sponsored by the French government, intending to deliver several lectures on surrealism. Although he met resistance from nationalist Mexican artists who felt surrealism was not truly revolutionary, he became friends with Rivera and Kahlo, who were his hosts, as well as with Russian exile Leon Trotsky, who was living with Rivera. Together, Breton, Trotsky, and Rivera wrote a manifesto titled "Towards a Free and Revolutionary Art," and Rivera and Breton planned an international league of revolutionary artists. Rivera, who called Mexico *el lugar surrealista por excelencia* in an interview, found the country fascinating and brought a small collection of pre-Columbian and folk art along with several paintings by Kahlo and photographs by Manuel Alvarez Bravo to Paris for an exhibit, "Mexique." He also published an essay illustrated with Alvarez Bravo's photos and folk art titled "Souvenir du Mexique" in the surrealist journal *Minotaure*.

Rivera's experiences in Mexico drew others to live there as exiles during the war. A small community of surrealist artists developed, including painters Remedios Varo and Leonora Carrington, poet Benjamin Péret, and photographers José Horna and Kati Horna. These artists lived and worked relatively isolated from the Mexican community and from a second group of surrealists that included Wolfgang Paalen, César Moro (a Peruvian who had been living in Paris), Gordon Onslow Ford, Alice Rahon, and Jacqueline Johnson. Paalen, in particular, became active in the Mexican artistic community. Shortly after his arrival in 1940 he organized along with Moro and Breton (who was still in France but helped choose works) the Exposición Internacional del Surrealismo. This exhibit featured the paintings of European surrealists along with the work of contemporary Mexican artists, including Mérida, Rivera, Kahlo, and nearly all the artists associated with the Contemporáneos movement, as well as Mexican folk art and pre-Columbian objects from Rivera's collection. This huge event drew both positive and negative interest in surrealism and made Paalen a central figure in the Mexican art world.

In 1942 Paalen founded the journal *Dyn*, which he published until 1945. *Dyn* reflected Paalen's interest in non-Western arts, particularly pre-Columbian art, as well as in avant-garde developments. Contributors included the surrealists Moro, Onslow Ford, Johnson, and Rahon, as well as many Mexican artists and anthropologists such as Covarrubias, Caso, and Manuel Gamio. Articles on contemporary artists and poets and on the excavations at Tlatilco, Northwest Coast totems, and Mexica codices appeared side by side in the pages of this journal. *Dyn* reflected both the surrealist interest in the "primitive" worlds of non-Western cultures and the Mexican nationalist interest in the restoration of the pre-Columbian past.

A great deal of scholarship on surrealism in Mexico has focused on the degree to which European surrealists influenced the work of their Mexican contemporaries. While the presence of prominent surrealists in Mexico clearly had some impact on certain artists, including Izquierdo, Tamayo, and perhaps some of the Contemporáneos, the surrealist tendency to claim Mexican artists as members of their movement, including Kahlo and Alvarez Bravo, has been seen by some as a colonialist appropriation. Kahlo, in particular, resented Breton's naming of her as a surrealist, claiming instead that the marvelous or fantastic qualities of her work were inspired by the realities of Mexico, not surrealist thought. What is not often considered is the degree to which Mexican artists influenced their surrealist colleagues. The surrealists shared with many Mexican artists an interest in pre-Columbian and Mexican folk art. The surrealists, in fact, incorporated this interest in many of their artistic projects, including exhibits such as the Exposición Internacional del Surrealismo, the journal *Dyn*, and their personal collections of art. The Mexican artists who collaborated on these projects with them probably influenced the surrealist perception of indigenous Mexico and its representation in their art.

One Mexican artist who clearly was engaged with the surrealist movement was painter Gunther Gerszo. Gerszo, although born in Mexico in 1915, spent much of his adolescence and early adulthood in Europe and the United States. In 1941 he returned permanently to Mexico where he met many of the surrealist exiles, including Carrington, Varo, Péret, and Paalen. Inspired by Yves Tanguy, he worked in a surrealist style during this period, painting dreamlike canvases, including the 1944 *Los días de la calle Gabino Barreda* in which he depicted the surrealist residents of that street such as Varo, Carrington, Péret, Esteban Frances, and himself in coded, fantastic guises. Although surrealism played an important role in his work during this period, other artists, including Castellanos and Carlos Orozco Romero, were influential throughout the course of his career, and Gerszo's work evolved toward a geometric abstraction during the 1950s. He shared with many of his contemporaries an interest in pre-Columbian art and began introducing motifs from this art in his work during the early 1960s.

Gerszo, along with artists of the Estridentista movement, the Contemporáneos, women artists, and indigenists such as Mérida, Covarrubias, and Tamayo were all artists working beyond the strict ideological and stylistic boundaries associated with the muralist movement. These artists provided an alternative history to mid-twentieth-century Mexican art and demonstrated the ways artists took varied approaches to the contemporary issues surrounding Mexican nationalism and the indigenist recuperation of the pre-Columbian past and Indian present.

Select Bibliography

Cordero Reiman, Karen, "Constructing a Modern Mexican Art, 1910–1940." In *South of the Border: Mexico in the American Imagination, 1914–1947.* Edited by James Oles. New Haven, Connecticut: Yale University Art Gallery, 1993.

Delpar, Helen, *The Enormous Vogue of Things Mexican: Cultural Relations between the United States and Mexico, 1920–1935.* Tuscaloosa: University of Alabama Press, 1992.

Fauchereau, Serge, "The Stridentists." *Artforum* 25 (September 1986).

Ferrer, Elizabeth, "María Izquierdo." In *Latin American Artists of the Twentieth Century,* edited by Waldo Rasmussen with Fatima Bercht and Elizabeth Ferrer. New York: Museum of Modern Art, 1993.

Herrera, Hayden, *Frida: A Biography of Frida Kahlo.* New York: Harper and Row, 1983.

Hurlburt, Laurance, *The Mexican Muralists in the United States.* Albuquerque: University of New Mexico Press, 1989.

Miller, Mary Ellen, and James Oles, "Introduction." In *South of the Border, Mexico in the American*

Imagination, 1914–1947, edited by James Oles. New Haven, Connecticut: Yale University Art Gallery, 1993.

Traba, Marta, *Art of Latin America: 1900–1980*. Baltimore: Inter-American Development Bank, distributed by the Johns Hopkins University Press, 1994.

Williams, Adriana, *Covarrubias*. Austin: University of Texas Press, 1994.

—COURTNEY GILBERT

Visual Arts: 1945–96

Beginning in the early 1940s the political climate in Mexico underwent a dramatic change. Many of the socially progressive policies implemented under the Lázaro Cárdenas regime (1934–40), such as extensive land redistribution, "socialist" oriented educational reform, and an active support for organized labor, were redirected in favor of economic stability and probusiness concerns. This official shift toward economic modernization gave legislative priority to industrial development at the expense of the various social reforms that were perceived as fundamental goals of the Mexican Revolution. The government, nevertheless, continued to identify itself with the populist and collectivist myth of the Revolution, cultivating its image through the official patronage of social realist muralism, as well as through the manipulation of mass media by the newly established Department of Press and Publicity (1937). In light of these developments the practice of socially committed art for the masses as sanctioned by the state had become largely academic, betraying the nationalist and populist ideology espoused by the art intelligentsia of the 1920s and the 1930s. For artists contemplating the role of art after World War II, the Mexican mural movement had become an empty gesture, firmly established within the curriculum of the art academies and ardently preserved by the patronage of the Mexican government.

La Ruptura

The term "la Ruptura" was originally used by Mexican poet-essayist Octavio Paz in 1951 to describe a group of artists working in the 1920s in conscious opposition to the politically minded Mexican muralists. The expression was later appropriated by art critic Luis Cardoza y Aragón to describe an emerging generation of artists working in the 1950s who were interested in pursuing new methods of expression and in achieving freedom to exhibit modern and contemporary artwork. The movement known as la Ruptura was not a strategy employed by an organized group of artists, but rather a response by several individuals rebelling against government support of ideologically aligned art and advocating an adoption of cosmopolitan and avant-garde artistic techniques. Many of these artists rejected the notion that artwork should serve a utilitarian and political mission; instead they saw art as inspired by the vision and the experience of the individual artist.

The objectives embraced by these artists often were frustrated by advocates of the Mexican mural movement who sought to eliminate the need for commercial art galleries and museums by promoting the idea of publicly accessible artwork and denouncing all other forms of art, such as easel painting and small-scale sculpture, as capitalist and elitist art for private consumption. David Alfaro Siqueiros, one of the founding members of the Mexican mural movement and a vocal advocate of socially responsive art, accused the new generation of artists of being "abstractionists" and of selling out to the U.S. imperialists and labeled them the "whores of Paris." Due in large part to these efforts, as well as to the support of successive government administrations receptive to the benefits of public muralism, there was great resistance to the exhibition of contemporary Mexican and international avant-garde art. The period between 1955 and 1965 was marked by increasing tension between those championing the cause of socially oriented realism and those endorsing the exploration of abstract stylistic tendencies.

Lacking official recognition and facing formidable adversaries, independent artists were able to survive in this climate largely as a result of the changing character of post–World War II Mexican society. The country's hopes of building a modern industrial nation had produced a burgeoning urban middle class, creating a growing private market for easel paintings, graphics, and sculpture. In addition, U.S. interest in suppressing Mexican social realism during the Cold War took the form of support and patronage of select artists who were willing to openly denounce muralism and, most importantly, who were free of any Communist agenda. These circumstances, combined with an increasing spirit of rebellion against art espousing a nationalistic content, provided the impetus for a new generation of artists, art galleries, and art museums to come to the fore.

Stylistically the artwork of this period was quite varied and ranged from lyrical and geometric abstraction to neofiguration. Many artists, however, shared an interest in the liberation of painting techniques through an experimentation with the unconventional use of materials and media. International art movements such as European *informalismo* and U.S. abstract expressionism became important models for artists connected with la Ruptura, both for their association with a spirit of revolt, self-determination, and freedom of expression as for their international acceptance and recognition. Artists such as Lilia Carillo, Enrique Echeverría, Gabriel Aceves Navarro, Fernando García Ponce, Manuel Felguérez, and Vicente Rojo, among several others produced a type of gestural abstraction that emphasized the material-textured qualities of the application of paint on the canvas. Color, shape, and form became the vehicle for expressing meaning in these works.

García Ponce, one of the abstract artists associated with la Ruptura, was an early proponent of *tachisme*, an expressionistic style characterized by a spontaneous application of irregular marks or dabs of colored paint onto a canvas. In the late 1950s García Ponce began to experiment with collage and incorporated printed images and found objects together with paint drips and splashes, textured impastoed surfaces, and geometric motifs. García Ponce's abstract forms and expressionistic technique produced a tension between the perceived underlying geometric order of his paintings and the relative chaos of accidental drips, collaged materials, and the textured surfaces of his canvases.

Other artists associated with la Ruptura, such as José Luis Cuevas, Alberto Gironella, Rafael Coronel, Francisco Corzas, and Francisco Toledo, became known for their neofigurative style. These artists imbued their works with psychologically charged figurative imagery that at times rendered their portraits disturbing and unsettling. Although they employed modern techniques such as a use of expressionistic gestural line and, in the case of Gironella, assemblage and collage, the dominant literary style of these individuals resisted the modernist tendency of eliminating the human figure entirely from the composition.

Cuevas's role as a polemicist and spokesperson for the generation of artists associated with la Ruptura began in 1956 when he issued a personal manifesto entitled "La cortina de nopal" (The Cactus Curtain), condemning what he perceived as the propagandistic nature of the Mexican muralist movement while bringing attention both to his cause and his artwork. By 1957 he had achieved international prominence, showing his work at the Gres Gallery in Washington, D.C., the Metropolitan Museum of Art in New York, and the Edouard Loeb Gallery in Paris, where Picasso purchased two of his drawings. Cuevas's neofigurative watercolors, engravings, and pen-and-ink illustrations of cadavers, bloated and disfigured prostitutes, zoomorphic monsters, and the like explored themes related to human misery and suffering. In contrast to many of the heroic and affirmative images of the human figure painted by the Mexican muralists, Cuevas's prints and drawings alternatively sought to demythologize the achievements of modern man. His exaggerated lines and distorted shapes rendered a world of spiritual and physical decay, and it was Cuevas's characteristic concern with the depiction of the alienated figure in the modern world that later linked him to a new group of artists that emerged in the early 1960s, known as the Nueva Presencia (New Presence).

The Nueva Presencia was formed in Mexico City in 1961 by Arnold Belkin and Francisco Icaza and included Coronel, Corzas, Cuevas, Ignacio "Nacho" Lopez, Artemio Sepúlveda, and Antonio Rodríguez Luna. The group put forth a manifesto and published five issues of a poster-like journal that called for the rejection of academic art, intellectualized criticism, and "art of good taste" and appealed to artists to create humanized imagery accessible to individuals in contemporary society. Its first exhibition took place in 1961 at the Galerías CDI under the heading "The Insiders." This label was based on the title of a book by Seldan Rodman, who portrayed "insiders" as artists who were concerned with the psychological state of the human condition and rejected the artistic conventions of abstract art in order to present portraits of human emotion and bodily experience.

The imagery of the Nueva Presencia members was characterized by a shared concern for the reinsertion of the human figure in artwork. Depictions of lone beings situated in unidentifiable landscapes articulated a search for meaning in the face of personal isolation, a theme influenced by existentialist writers such as Jean-Paul Sartre, Fyodor Dostoyevsky, and Albert Camus, as well as by the Mexican poet Octavio Paz in his celebrated work, *The Labyrinth of Solitude*. The paintings of Nueva Presencia artist Corzas depicted a melancholic and shadowy world filled with alienated and disquieted beings. In a series of works entitled *Las Trashumantes* (The Nomads, 1960), Coraza's itinerant circus personages represented the rootless wandering of figures who occupy a peripheral position in society. Painted in a neoexpressionistic style that relied heavily on the technique of chiaroscuro to create an atmospheric effect, Corzas's motionless and ghostly apparitions depicted the psychological loneliness of estranged human relationships and the spiritual alienation of the individual in contemporary society. By the close of 1963 the Nueva Presencia had dissolved its formal alliance; nevertheless, during the organization's short existence the artist's strategic activities had succeeded in refocusing attention on the importance of figurative expressionism as a central idiom of modern Mexican art.

Development of the Mexican Art Market

Private venues for the exhibition of modern paintings, graphics, and sculpture were established in Mexico during the 1950s largely in reaction to the lack of government support for modern and contemporary avant-garde artwork. Among the most influential galleries to open at this time were Galería Prisse, Galería Proteo, Galería Antonio Souza, and Galería Juan Martín. These alternative sites specialized in the exhibition of contemporary Mexican and international avant-garde trends, providing a space for young progressive artists to show their work, as well as supplying a forum for creative discussion of new and experimental methods of expression. In 1955 Galería Proteo became the site for the "International Confrontation of Experimental Art," organized by painter, sculptor, and architect Mathias Goeritz. This event incorporated work by Mexican, European, and U.S. avant-garde artists and was instrumental in developing an interest in *informalismo* and U.S. abstract expressionism among Mexican artists who wanted to experiment with formal aspects of painting. That same year Galería Proteo presented its "Salon of Free Art," an exhibition held in protest of the official selection of academic artwork for the winter "Salon Nacional de Artes Plásticas." By the early 1960s the function of the private art gallery had shifted from merely being a site of opposition to social realist art to becoming a space where artists could self-consciously critique contemporary art-making practices themselves. In 1961 Galería Antonio Souza received international attention when members of a neo-Dada group known as Los Hartos (The Fed-Ups) came together to protest the perceived emptiness of contemporary art. Artists Goeritz, Jesús "Chucho" Reyes Ferreira, Pedro Friedeberg, Cuevas, and Kati Horna participated in a one-day demonstration and exhibited controversial works such as Cuevas's white wall entitled *Panoramic Visions of Art,* Goeritz's "metachromatic messages," and Friedeberg's surrealist furniture. This critique of contemporary artwork signaled a new stage in modern Mexican art, whereby critical focus had moved away from a concern with establishing an alternative to public muralism toward the initiation of an internal dialogue with post-muralist movements and their artistic practices.

By the mid-1960s the growth of the Mexican art market and the proliferation of privately owned exhibition spaces for avant-garde art began to affect patterns of government patronage. The 1964 inauguration of the Museum of Modern Art in Chapultepec Park implied a full endorsement by the Mexican government of the transition from the patronage of public mural art to the promotion of the private sale and consumption of easel painting. Local and international biennial shows and the opening up of art markets in Mexico, the United States, and abroad enable many artists to gain international exposure. The 1965 Esso Salon for young artists, the Confrontation '66 exhibition presented at the Palace of Fine Arts, the Exposición Solar of 1970, the annual Independent Salons of 1969 through 1971 as well as the emergence of numerous inter-American art competitions and exhibitions signaled the increased internationalization of the Mexican art market and an expansion of artistic opportunities that allowed for a plurality of art-making practices to flourish.

The Tlatelolco Massacre and Its Aftermath

The Mexican student movement of 1968 and its fatal outcome aroused a new spirit of social and political awareness among a generation of young artists. Like their counterparts in Paris, Amsterdam, London, and Tokyo, Mexican university students organized a democratic movement, publicly demanding civil liberties and human rights from the authoritarian Gustavo Díaz Ordaz regime. With the upcoming Olympic Games scheduled to begin in Mexico City in mid-October, the administration was eager to contain the political agitation and social unrest plaguing the capital. A series of clashes between students and riot police precipitated the violence of Tlatelolco in which hundreds of student demonstrators were murdered, wounded, and imprisoned by the Mexican military. The student massacre created an irreparable break between the state and the Mexican intelligentsia, inspired a new genre of literature on the subject of Tlatelolco, and stimulated the formation of several art associations advocating the production of public and popular artwork.

Artistic production during this period was characterized by the introduction of conceptual art-making practices and a revitalized interest in the conceptualization of artists as instruments for social change. Student groups associated with San Carlos University and the La Esmeralda art school sought to create collective artwork while at the same time using new visual techniques taken from the international pop and conceptual art movements. The efforts of these independent groups eventually culminated in the creation of an umbrella organization in 1978 known as the Front of Cultural Workers. This coalition of artist associations produced a manifesto that called for regaining control of the production, distribution, and circulation of art by using alternative methods that would make artwork accessible to a mass audience, thereby rejecting the notion of art as the privileged commodity of a wealthy elite. A critical objective of this project was to eliminate the high cost of producing artwork in order to make it accessible to a broader and more diversified public.

One such group, known as Suma, was formed in mid-1976 at San Carlos University by students interested in collective and conceptual art-making practices. These artists viewed the museum as a capitalist institution and sought to critique the art market's power by avoiding the traditional methods of distribution and circulation. Members of Suma painted and stenciled onto public walls, pavement, and fences; produced popular graphics; printed art books; and distributed "mail art" as a means of circumventing the art museum and the art gallery system. These artists appropriated recognizable imagery from popular mass media such as television, photographic comic books, newspapers, and product advertisements and created works that were meant to shock viewers into recognizing their role as passive consumers of products and ideas. An important goal of Suma was to persuade viewers to become critically aware of the power of the mass media, which the group believed had the potential to shape political and cultural beliefs as well as the capacity to distort historical facts.

Another organization of artists working during this same period was the Pentagon Process Group, created in 1976 by recent graduates of the La Esmeralda art school. Felipe Ehrenberg, an artist associated with the collective, popularized the idea of the "multiple," using techniques borrowed from the commercial art world such as photocopying, blueprinting, stenciling, and the use of the mimeograph machine as a means of creating large quantities of printed artwork that was both portable and economical and therefore more available to a general audience. The members also designed interesting and innovative installation pieces. One such work, produced for an exhibition entitled "Muros frente a muros" (Walls Facing Walls, 1978), was conceived as a two-room installation that referenced the massacre at Tlatelolco. In one room stood a desk and an empty chair stenciled with the date October 2, 1968. In the next room old shoes were left haphazardly scattered across the floor, while on the wall was an inscription referencing the military actions taken against student demonstrators in 1968. The empty chair and the unclaimed shoes were reminders of those imprisoned or killed by government forces on that ill-fated day.

Not all artists in Mexico during the 1970s were working in this unorthodox manner; in fact this period can be seen as producing a multiplication of experimental art forms owing to the liberatory legacy of la Ruptura movement. Artists such as Irma Palacios and Francisco Castro Leñero demonstrated the continued vitality of expressionism in Mexico by working with surface texture, color, and form to endow their works with an organic sense of composition. Other artists, such as Gabriel Macotela and Miguel Castro Leñero continued to experiment with gestural abstraction, reducing images of archaic architecture and rustic landscapes into formal geometric structures and abstract linear designs. Various types of realism and hyperrealism also began to surface at this time by painters such as Xavier Esqueda and Alfredo Castañeda, whose surreal visions and supernatural imagery portrayed scenes filled with characteristic wit and irony. By the end of the decade there was a move to repopularize neofigurative painting by individuals such as Arturo Rivera and Rafael Cauduro. Rivera's paintings, combining human figures and painted references to objects culled from everyday life, sought to articulate a tension between the apparent chaos of nature and the ordering processes of human rationality.

Artistic experimentation with various forms of lyrical, geometric, and neofigurative abstraction during the 1970s dominated the Mexican art world until the mid-1980s, at which time a new generation of mixed-media artists began to receive critical attention, making their presence felt by advancing a uniquely Mexican art movement known today as neo-Mexicanism. The term "neo-Mexicanism" characterizes a number of individuals who appropriated and reinterpreted motifs from Mexican folk and popular culture as a means of underscoring personal rather than universal themes. The intimate and self-referential work of Frida Kahlo has been particularly influential upon the artistic production of many of these individuals. Artists such as Rocío Maldonado, Dulce María Núñez, Nahum B. Zenil, Georgina Quintana, Julio Galán, Monica Castillo, and Elena Climent examined cultural archetypes and vernacular motifs in highly personalized ways in order to expose the contradictions implicit in the concept of "Mexicanness." Visual references to the Virgin of Guadalupe, crosses, *retablos*, and skeletal figures *(calaveras)* popularized in the late nineteenth century by graphic artist José Guadalupe Posada, and popular handicraft items such as toys, ceramics, and textiles are common Mexican motifs that have been recast into visual statements concerning issues such as gender, religion, family, and Mexican national-ism. The incorporation of self-portraiture into these works has been a popular method employed by several neo-Mexican artists as a means of stres-sing issues of personal identity that have broader implications within the context of Mexican society.

The private worlds of artists Galán and Zenil are explored in paintings that united self-portraiture and symbols taken from popular Catholic religious prac-tices and traditions. These individuals have exam-ined questions such as the role of religion and family in contemporary Mexican life and have created auto-biographical scenes that challenge and expand con-ventional culture behavioral paradigms. The format of *retablo* painting has been employed by both artists as a means of emphasizing the intimate and personal nature of the compositions. The *retablo*, a small nar-rative panel painted as an offering of thanks for holy intervention by a dedicator who survived a personal crisis, is usually accompanied by a text that explains the "miracle" that has taken place. The practice of making *retablos* dates back to the colonial era and was later utilized by Mexican artists such as Angel Zárraga and Kahlo, reappearing again in the work of several neo-Mexicanists.

Núñez has presented ironic collaged images of the history of national identity that incorporate refer-ences from pre-Columbian, colonial, and contem-porary Mexican culture. Her mixed-media works stand in opposition to the heroic representations of national culture created by Mexican muralists such as Diego Rivera, Siqueiros, and José Clemente Or-ozco, presenting instead a more encompassing view of the nation that includes contemporary popular traditions, mass media representations, past and pre-sent religious iconic symbols, as well as references to the changing role of women in contemporary Mex-ican society. Her work visually underscores the idea that modern Mexico is comprised of multiple eth-nicities and cultural traditions, as well as an expand-ing population maintaining a diversity of social and political interests.

Despite the stylistic affinities shared by many of the neo-Mexicanists, artistic differences have become consistently more pronounced as art-making prac-tices have grown more interdisciplinary throughout the 1990s. The tendency to fuse past and present artistic styles and to combine disparate media in inno-vative and unconventional ways is often character-ized as postmodern, or as Octavio Paz has proposed,

post–avant-garde, perhaps a more appropriate term for the Mexican context. The expressive works of artists Germán Venegas, who combines painting, collage, object art, and wooden sculptural relief, and Javier Marín, who creates fragmented and textured terra-cotta classical bodies in combination with handpainted graffiti, exemplify this approach to mixed-media art making. This trend also is seen in the work of Néstor Quiñones, whose object paint-ings have referenced Baroque mystical and popular imagery, and in the work of painter-sculptor Sergio Hernández, who has employed materials such as ceramic tiles, sand, and wax to make visual references to the Oaxacan landscape, history, myths, and popular folk culture. Installation and technological multimedia work also has been popularized in Mexico by individuals such as Sylvia Gruner and con-ceptual and installation artist Gabriel Orozco. Gruner's installations have incorporated the use of video and super-8 movies with performance art, object art, drawings, and sculpture in origin works that aggressively and often graphically question past societal constructions of women, official propagan-distic images of Mexican history, and the arbitrary nature of societal conventions and traditions.

Since the pivotal years of la Ruptura, Mexican art and the Mexican art market have become increas-ingly more international, both in the manner that artists have looked to outside sources for artistic inspiration, as well as by virtue of the expanding appreciation of modern and post–avant-garde Mex-ican artwork throughout the world. This does not mean, however, that Mexican artistic inspiration has not been derived predominately from Mexican culture and society. The development of local and national styles and schools has unquestionably been influenced by the rich tradition of art making dating from the pre-Columbian era, through the colonial period, and into modern times, and these specific influences have led to distinctive interpretations of modern and postmodern art within the Mexican context. The unique ways in which art in Mexico has developed over the course of the twentieth century, and the original and innovative contributions that artists have made both locally and internationally over the years, can be seen as evidence of the con-tinued importance of Mexican visual arts as a vital force within society and also of its critical position in the history of art.

Select Bibliography

Bethell, Leslie, editor, *Mexico Since Independence*. Cambridge: Cambridge University Press, 1991.

Emmerich, Luis Carlos, *100 Pintores Mexicanos/100 Mexican Painters*. Monterrey: Museo de Arte Contemporaneo de Monterrey, 1993.

Ferrer, Elizabeth, *Through the Path of Echoes: Contemporary Art in Mexico*. New York: Independent Curators, 1990.

Goldman, Shifra, *Contemporary Painting in a Time of Change*. Austin: University of Texas Press, 1981.

____, *Dimensions of the Americas: Art and Social Change in Latin America and the United States*. Chicago: University of Chicago Press, 1994.

MacLachlan, Colin M., and William H. Beezley, editors, *El Gran Pueblo: A History of Greater Mexico*. Englewood Cliffs, New Jersey: Prentice-Hall, 1994.

Sullivan, Edward, *Aspects of Contemporary Mexican Painting*. New York: The Americas Society, 1990.

—CHARMAINE PICARD

W

Wars of Independence

From the military, political, and social perspectives, the outbreak of the Hidalgo Revolt commencing a decade of warfare (1810–21) caught the leadership of New Spain by surprise. While some bureaucrats, clerics, and criollo leaders had warned about internal turbulence or expressed foreboding about foreign invasions from France or Britain, no one—including the actual conspirators—could have predicted the wrenching internal conflagrations that in different forms endured for 11 years. Following Napoléon's invasion of Spain and a coup in Mexico City led by European-born Spaniards on September 16, 1808, that toppled Viceroy José de Iturrigaray (1803–08), the country was awash with rumors. European-born Spaniards (or *peninsulares*, known by the more derogatory term *gachupines*), perceived criollo separatist plots and dark conspiracies for the general expulsion of their minority, backed by even more diabolical rumors of outright genocide. Mexican-born whites, the criollos, circulated similar reports of conspiracies against their class by the *gachupines*, who were said to support foreign invasions by the French, English, or Americans. Everywhere, an undercurrent of wild exaggerations created an atmosphere of disquiet that articulated suspicions and old divisions in Mexican society. With the benefit of hindsight, historians have turned up minor plots, eccentric messianic messages, millenarian tendencies, and some half-baked projects pondered by small groups of individuals who met to discuss the impact of international events.

In this highly charged climate, Spanish officials might have expected violence—riots, rural uprisings, or even some preemptive coup led by criollos. During 1809 and 1810, the regime redeployed some army units away from a cantonment at Jalapa designed to guard against a possible foreign invasion attempt at Veracruz to reinforce the garrisons of Puebla and Mexico City. Fearing some kind of attack, archbishop and interim viceroy Francisco Xavier de Lizana y Beaumont surrounded the viceregal palace in Mexico City with artillery and heavily armed troops. Aware of the rumors, some army commanders considered mobilizing provincial militia regiments and battalions at cities such as Guanajuato, San Miguel, Celaya, Valladolid, and Querétaro to undertake police duties, but nothing was done since suspicions circulated that Mexican officers and soldiers might be untrustworthy. Indeed, when a small group of criollos at Valladolid (modern-day Morelia) met with several subaltern militia officers returning from the Jalapa cantonment, talk soon turned from the dangers of a foreign invasion or a *gachupín* plot to the possibility of outright Independence for New Spain. There was discussion about a revolt headed by the provincial militias of Guanajuato and Valladolid. These units were to lead a force of 18,000 to 20,000 men, including Indians attracted to the cause by promises of exemption from tribute payment and other taxes. While informants denounced the 1809 Valladolid Conspirators, the concept of recruiting a large force of Indian and *casta* (non-white) soldiers resurfaced in other plots and even in loyalist defense proposals.

In the months prior to September 1810, the regime lurched from crisis to crisis, uncertain whether to focus on the danger of an external foreign invasion or some kind of internal uprising. Poor harvests in 1809, rising food prices, and high unemployment concerned provincial authorities such as Intendant Antonio Riaño of Guanajuato, who considered mobilizing militia troops. At Guadalajara, Zacatecas, Querétaro, and in other towns, local authorities detected heightened unrest and reported the presence of unknown enemies who might be planning popular insurrections. Even in Mexico City, gossip and loose talk about plots and conspiracies kept police officials and Inquisition spies at full alert. Bad news from Spain about military defeats, the collapse of the Junta Central government, and reports from Caracas in

May 1810 of the Venezuelan insurrection, exacerbated fears and sent garbled messages resonating outward from the capital.

In the provinces, certain individuals such as the local curates, innkeepers, muleteers, and minor government bureaucrats transmitted and interpreted news, blending regional issues with broader rumors of *gachupín* plots. Conspiracies or at least discussions and apprehensions about future calamities produced a variety of responses. While some criollos considered collective action to advance autonomy or even Independence, the village and rural populace worried more about possible food shortages, defense of religion, and real or imagined abuses caused by the much disliked *gachupines*. In some districts, local curates whipped up an atmosphere of hysteria that helped set the scene for spontaneous uprisings and adherence to revolutionary movements.

Notwithstanding this background and the existence of warning signs, the explosive popular rebellion in the Bajío provinces that spread to other regions of New Spain shook the regime to its foundations. On September 16, 1810, the uprising led by Father Miguel Hidalgo y Costilla of the town of Dolores produced a chain reaction of violence that for a time appeared likely to overrun Mexico City and to overwhelm the Spanish regime. Contemporary observers such as Bishop Manuel Abad y Queipo of Michoacán identified a "mortifying contagion" of insurgency and described normally submissive Indian villagers transformed into "ferocious monsters." Royalist army commander, Brigadier Félix María Calleja del Rey, characterized the rebellion as a "hydra reborn as fast as one cuts off its heads." Other royalist officers portrayed the insurgents as frightful anarchists and condemned provincial clergymen —the "tonsured rogues"—whom they blamed for inciting a pacific people to commit frightful violence.

Father Hidalgo belonged to an opposition group at the margins of the provincial elite centered at Querétaro that included among others clerics, militia officers, bureaucrats, and criollo land owners. With the denunciation of the so-called conspiracy, the wife of the *corregidor* of Querétaro, Josefa Ortiz de Domínguez—today viewed as a great Mexican national heroine—warned Hidalgo, who decided to launch an uprising immediately rather than surrender or flee. Supported by militia captains Ignacio de Allende and Juan de Aldama, Lieutenant Mariano Abasalo, and some other regional dragoon, cavalry, and infantry officers and soldiers, Hidalgo pronounced his famous Grito de Dolores (Cry of Dolores) that initiated a revolt in favor of King Fernando VII and the Virgen of Guadalupe. The rebels leaders condemned bad government and issued slogans directed against the *gachupines*.

After raising a force of 500 to 800 men armed with a few weapons, Hidalgo attracted numerous adherents as he marched on the towns of San Miguel, Celaya, and Guanajuato. Taking up the powerful symbol of the Virgin of Guadalupe, pillaging captured towns, detaining *gachupines*, and dispatching emissaries in every direction to spread the revolutionary message, Hidalgo initially achieved one success after another. The spontaneous popular uprising grew exponentially, soon overwhelming the efforts of Hidalgo and his commanders to establish discipline and organization. In some respects the Hidalgo Revolt became a series of synchronous uprisings presided over by a loose leadership that was more successful as catalyst than as an organizing directorship. Government officials and militia officers who abandoned their posts to join the rebellion, received significantly inflated titles and commissions. On September 28 a horde of 50,000 to 60,000 rebels overwhelmed the defenders of the *alhóndiga* (granary) at Guanajuato, plundered the city, and executed some *gachupín* residents. In many respects, the violence took the form of a grand peasant revolt as the people sought vengeance and lashed out against a variety of real and imagined dangers. Well away from the main force, local chiefs—sometimes former contrabandists and bandits—gathered armed bands to interdict roads, raid haciendas, and to attack symbols of the regime. From Guanajuato, Hidalgo's army moved to Valladolid, appeared ready to attack Mexico City from Toluca until deflected by the punishing Battle of Las Cruces, and then headed west to occupy Guadalajara. Historians often have viewed the rebel force in negative terms as "a horde" or "rabble," and the conservative Lucas Alamán described the insurgent masses as having the appearance of a wandering barbarian tribe.

Behind the charges of treason and treachery that characterize any major revolution, there were many complex factors at work as the wars unfolded. Many criollos desired political power and supported the concept of autonomy for New Spain within the Spanish Empire. Urban in outlook, most of these individuals felt little enthusiasm for popular revolution or for the potential radicalism unleashed by Hidalgo. Indeed, any real possibility of a united front combining the criollo population with the popular mestizo, Indian, and mulatto insurgents ended with growing anarchy and atrocities directed against European Spaniards at places such as Guanajuato and Valladolid. With the rebel masses directing their energies toward looting, confiscations, executions, and to attacking existing institutions, most criollos saw no alternative other than to protect their own interests by supporting the royalist or Spanish cause. Criollo leaders set aside their own political agendas temporarily and fought through the decade in support of the royalist armies.

Given the speed, spontaneity, and confusion of the revolt, the royalist military response took time to organize. At first no one could be certain if Mexico City was safe. Cities such as Celaya and Querétaro wavered as the surrounding country people joined the rebellion. Viceroy Francisco Xavier de Venegas, a senior army commander himself, had only just arrived in New Spain and needed time to apprise himself of the situation. Moving to strengthen urban garrisons and communications, he appointed Brigadier Félix Calleja, the active commander of the Tenth Militia Division based at San Luis Potosí, to undertake the suppression of rebellion. While Calleja's own confidence wilted temporarily as he assessed the popularity of Hidalgo's message, he mobilized his existing forces and recruited new units of mounted vaqueros (cowboys) and townsmen. Without adequate firearms, artillery, or other weapons, Calleja sought without great success to manufacture artillery pieces, muskets, and swords—eventually arming most of his mounted troops with locally constructed lances.

Calleja commanded an operational field force composed of regular troops, provincial militiamen, and new recruits, called the Army of the Center (based upon geographical positions looking at a map of New Spain). Brigadier José de la Cruz, recently arrived from Spain, led a second operational force called the Army of the Right. The immediate problem and one that challenged the royalists for the duration of the war was how to find and keep sufficient troops for active battlefield and campaign duties. As senior royalist army commanders soon discovered, most regional political and military leaders concerned themselves primarily with garrisoning their own immediate jurisdictions, suppressing local violence caused by guerrilla-bandit gangs, and escorting convoys essential to maintain provincial commerce, agriculture, stock raising, and industry. Indeed, if they were to avoid rapid exhaustion caused by overcommitments and the subdivision of available operational forces into hundreds of small garrison forces, royalist leaders had to organize a quite sophisticated counterinsurgency systems. In a word, the wars would take place on a variety of fronts and with the applications of different tactics and strategies by both sides.

At first, the rebel forces attempted without much success to face the royalists on the conventional battlefield. Beginning with the Battle of Las Cruces near Toluca on October 30, 1810, Colonel Torcuato de Trujillo with about 2,500 hastily assembled royalist troops faced Hidalgo's much larger army, including a cadre of former militiamen with some military training and a much larger untrained force of rural and village men. While most rebel soldiers lacked firearms and carried sharpened sticks, slings, and stones, their great numbers, enthusiasm, and bloodthirsty cries intimidated the royalist troops. The battle raged back and forth, eventually exhausting the royalists, who left the battlefield, awarding the rebels an apparent victory. However, accurate royalist musketry and rounds of grapeshot fired at close range by artillery produced high casualties among the massed rebel formations. In the insurgent vanguard, some of the best-trained troops fell in combat as they attempted to rally their green forces. Although Mexico City lay open to invasion, Hidalgo turned his forces to other objectives.

Clearly, conventional battle involving linear infantry tactics, cavalry, and field artillery required disciplined troops and firepower well beyond the capacity of the rebel forces. If doubts lingered about the dominant superiority of the better armed and trained royalist armies, Brigadiers Calleja and Cruz banished them with overwhelming successes against rebel forces that dared to fight on the open field. At the three major Battles of Aculco, Guanajuato, and Calderón (near Guadalajara), Calleja proved that the huge rebel masses were a military illusion. Although the actual casualty rates were much lower than the inflated numbers published in royalist propaganda, it was clear that in the future rebel chiefs would have to adopt new approaches. Battle defeats banished any remaining euphoria, and hard campaigning against royalist firepower caused early supporters of Hidalgo and Allende to reconsider their dedication to the insurgent cause. Many simply deserted to return home, but they carried their arms with them and would rebel again under different leadership. In the future, most rebels eschewed conventional warfare to adopt the more flexible and successful principles of guerrilla warfare.

While Hidalgo and his senior leadership fled northward from Guadalajara following the Battle of Calderón—only to be captured through treachery, tried, and executed—the war began to change its complexion and to spread. In Guanajuato province for example, Albino García operated out of rugged mountain terrain, commanding a rebel force of about 1,000 guerrillas that combined insurgency and banditry. Other bands occupied similar terrain, often in proximity to major roads and towns which they raided to sustain their activities. Although Félix Calleja and other royalist commanders were successful against large rebel formations, guerrilla tactics caused them difficulties that were almost impossible to solve. Brutal punishments, executions, confiscations, and rigorous suppression of towns and villages produced sullen acquiescence while royalist troops were present, but such measures did little to root out guerrillas who blended in with the rural populace.

Before the rebellion in the Bajío provinces could be controlled, the central focus shifted southward to Zitácuaro, Cuautla Amilpas, Oaxaca, Acapulco, and other towns where Curates José María Morelos y Pavón and Mariano Matamoros, and chiefs such as Vicente Guerrero, Guadalupe Victoria, and Ignacio López Rayón posed new threats. In Nueva Galicia, Brigadier Cruz and the Army of the Right occupied Guadalajara and organized royalist forces to take on many large rebel bands. The real danger was that Morelos might occupy Puebla and encircle the capital, cutting it off from communications and commerce with Veracruz. In 1811, Venegas transferred Calleja and the Army of the Center southward away from the still-unpacified Bajío. This new campaign directed against Morelos illustrated military strengths and weaknesses that affected both sides for the duration of the conflict. First at Zitácuaro and then at Cuautla Amilpas, the rebels fortified towns and through the use of defensive warfare challenged the royalist armies to undertake long and arduous sieges. While on the surface such a strategy seemed extremely naive, desertions, poor communications, rebel interdictions, and above all weak logistics reduced the efficiency of royalist forces. Zitácuaro fell without much struggle, but Cuautla Amilpas commanded by Morelos survived a lengthy siege. The royalist besiegers, now including several expeditionary battalions of Spanish troops, suffered dysentery, low morale, and shortages of food and munitions that for a time evened the odds for the rebels. Nevertheless, the besieged garrison suffered such severe starvation that on May 6, 1812, Morelos and his men broke out of Cuautla Amilpas and fled. As a tactic, defensive warfare practiced by rebel forces for the duration of the wars damaged the royalists but in the end did not succeed.

By 1813 Morelos recovered from the defeat at Cuautla Amilpas, recruited a new army, and once again attempted to encircle Mexico City. Veracruz province now became a major zone of guerrilla warfare that reduced royalist military presence to the garrisoned towns and to heavily defended military convoys between the interior and the coast. The countryside fell to permanent rebel control that the royalists simply could not break. On occasion, they dispatched powerful flying cavalry detachments and divisions to ravage rebel communities and to destroy all crops, orchards, and livestock. From time to time a major military initiative might regain temporary control of the roads and bridges, but the royalists could not defend their advances for very long against mobile mounted guerrillas. It was in this environment that Guadalupe Victoria and other rebel chiefs operated against active counterinsurgency commanders such as the youthful captain Antonio López de Santa Anna. In the meantime, Morelos led his forces southward to occupy Oaxaca in December 1813 and to control much of southern New Spain. From the insurgent perspective, this was a time of optimism, as delegates met at Chilpancingo to declare Independence and later at Apatzingan to promulgate a Constitution. Of course, the fact that these significant events took place in small towns rather than in major cities illustrated the predominant military power of the royalists.

While Morelos captured Acapulco after a siege, his move to the distant south probably served royalist interests more than those of the insurgents. After Calleja became viceroy in March 1813, he extended a plan that he had devised in 1811 to regain royalist control through the militarization of New Spain. This plan required the obligatory enlistment and financing through compulsory local taxation of patriot militias in the cities, towns, haciendas, and rural districts. Calleja envisioned a community defense system to defeat the rebels that involved the construction of block houses, forts, and parapets in every town. With the addition of artillery to harden defenses, these militias would be able to repel the lightly armed raiders or at least force them to carry heavy weapons and siege equipment. In the countryside, mounted guards of hacienda workers would patrol roads, guard convoys, and observe any rebel movements. Where there were rebel concentrations, army divisions and flying detachments would move in to assist the local forces. Although this system did not work in provinces such as Veracruz that remained almost completely outside of royalist control, Calleja obliged many jurisdictions to enlist and to pay the full costs of local patriot militias. Town councils and subdelegates established special taxes and levies based on landholdings and incomes. Over time, these onerous taxes became a heavy burden that increased the general level of exhaustion caused by the wars.

In 1813, Calleja reorganized the military structure to create a series of strong royalist divisions that could crush Morelos and other regional centers of insurgency. Puebla, Valladolid, Guanajuato, and Nueva Galicia emerged as strong regional military headquarters commanded by powerful officers such as Brigadier José de la Cruz, Field Marshal Conde de Castro Terreño, Brigadier Juan José Olazabal, Brigadier Diego García Conde, Brigadier Ciriaco de Llano, Colonel Pedro Celestino Negrete, and Lieutenant Colonel Agustín de Iturbide. Most of these officers, except for García Conde (who had been in New Spain for decades) and Iturbide (a criollo), were European Spaniards with established military careers who arrived in New Spain after 1810. Llano, a former naval officer, and Iturbide crushed Morelos's forces at Valladolid, capturing and executing Mariano Matamoros, one of the best rebel commanders. The Congress of Chilpancingo dissolved, and Oaxaca and the port of Acapulco fell to royalist forces. On November 5, 1815, royalist forces at Tesmalaca captured Morelos, who was made to suffer lengthy interrogations, show trials, and finally an execution by firing squad.

Although historians often identify a lull in the war beginning in 1816 following the death of Morelos and the elimination of conventional rebel armies, the guerrilla war continued uninterrupted and gained in intensity. The royalist army controlled the cities and towns, possessed the heavy firepower and troops needed to enter almost any area, and the capability to protect most convoys against bandits and insurgents. The royalists dominated in the areas of artillery, engineering, and disciplined fire power. Despite continuing weak logistics, royalist forces managed to besiege a succession of isolated island and mountain fortresses at Tepiji de la Seda, San Pedro de Cóporo, Sombrero, San Gregorio, Coyoxquihui in Veracruz province, and Mezcala Island in Lake Chapala. In this last campaign (1812–16) the royalists had to build a fleet of armed galleys to besiege the Mezcala Island fortress and to patrol the lake and its littoral. In 1817, royalist divisions defeated the expedition of the Spanish liberal Javier Mina, who had attempted to breath new life into the rebel cause.

At the same time, neither Viceroy Calleja nor his successor Viceroy Juan Ruiz de Apodaca were completely frank in their assessments of the military situation. Sometimes blinded by the fact that many rebels were willing to accept amnesties and even to serve in the royalist forces, the viceroys compiled impressive statistics that pointed to an end to the wars. They neglected the fact that many insurgents compelled to seek royal pardons later returned to rebellion. Indeed, some guerrilla-bandits who mixed revolution with outright criminal activities managed to enjoy the benefits of three, four, or even as many as nine amnesties. In fact, without the physical presence of royalist troops, many regions soon reverted to rebellion. Except for the carefully defended cities and fortified towns or during occasional military sweeps in force, the provinces of Guanajuato, Michoacán, Nueva Galicia, Veracruz, and regions such as the Llanos de Apan, the Dirección del Sur (Guerrero State), and the region south of Lake Chapala remained very much in rebel hands. The insurgent bands controlled territory employing guerrilla techniques, fluid movements to evade the firepower of royalist columns, and set themselves up in isolated fortifications in rugged mountains that continued to test royalist logistics and resolve.

In many respects, the years between 1816 and 1820 represented a period of stalemate during which neither side could deliver a mortal blow. Through fragmentation and the use of small guerrilla forces, the rebels maintained their existence with low-intensity warfare. Remarkably, they were able to raid guard posts on the outskirts of Mexico City, and they sometimes rode at breakneck speed through heavily defended cities such as Querétaro and Puebla to illustrate their bravado and to deprive the royalist defenders of sleep. In the areas of today's Guerrero State and on the Pacific Coast, Vicente Guerrero and other chiefs such as Bernardo Huacal compelled the royalist forces to confine their activities to the towns and to occasional sweeps in strength. In Veracruz, rebel bands attacked Viceroy Apodaca's convoy as he took office in 1816 and proceeded to close vital communications and trade routes for much of the period until 1821. Indeed, the imperial government became so concerned at the paucity of hard news from Mexico City and at the complaints of hard-pressed merchants that it redirected an expeditionary force of 2,000 troops under Brigadier Fernando Miyares y Mancebo from assignment in Peru to New Spain. Miyares attempted with temporary success to build a military road between Veracruz and Jalapa guarded by fortified posts, patrol forces, and signal towers. When this initiative failed and the guerrillas once again sealed off the interior, in 1818–19 Apodaca dispatched Field Marshal Pascual de Liñán into the region with a strong force to beat back the mobile bands. During these years, Antonio López de Santa Anna advanced his career as a counterinsurgency leader in command of militia companies of amnestied former rebels. He pursued Guadalupe Victoria and resettled the uprooted villagers of Veracruz province in new military-dominated communities.

Many royalist officers recognized the impossibility of ever ending the guerrilla insurgency. Instead, some commanders made do with the situation and created veritable satrapies within their jurisdictions. They became wealthy through the sale of insurgent properties and possessions, taxes upon merchants who needed army convoys, and by skimming whatever resources fell under their control. Unless they committed egregious malfeasance, as in the case of Iturbide at Guanajuato, the regime needed their military skills so much that the viceroys had to put up with numerous irregularities. Brigadier Melchor Álvarez, commander at Oaxaca who arrived in New Spain in 1813 commanding the Infantry Regiment of Savoya and governed Oaxaca following the defeat of Morelos, dismissed all of the serious charges of corruption against him by stating blandly that he lacked a head for numbers. Many of these commanders, including European Spanish officers such as Álvarez; Brigadier Pedro Celestino Negrete; Brigadier Domingo Luaces, commander of the Infantry Regiment of Zaragoza that arrived in New Spain in 1816; and Colonel Juan Horbegoso, transferred from the Infantry Regiment of Granada in 1816 to work directly under Inspector General Pascual de Liñan in Mexico City, in 1821 switched sides to join Iturbide's rebellion. They decided to continue their military careers in Mexico rather than return to Spain.

For many other officers and soldiers, even if they remained loyal to Spain the years of perplexing and hazardous duty without recognition eroded their morale. Following the arrival in 1816 of the Infantry Regiment of Zaragoza, which was to have been part of a much larger expeditionary force, there were no additional Spanish troops dispatched to New Spain. Until 1816 the role of the expeditionary troops in bolstering the royalist cause with fresh military talent and purpose had been highly significant. Once they saw themselves abandoned in an unwinnable war surrounded by enemies, royalist officers and soldiers developed what might be described as a "blockhouse mentality." They avoided risky operations and preferred to remain within the protected confines of their parapets and fortified garrisons. To further destroy morale and military effectiveness, after 1816 the regional royal treasuries lacked the funds to pay the army on time. Some soldiers suffered as their pay was in arrears for months, and they began to prey upon civilians for their sustenance. In many garrisons, royalist troops ceased to function effectively as men thought more about survival than completing their military obligations. Everywhere, the burdens of financing the war and maintaining the royalist army rested heavily upon a damaged economy and a fatigued population. Since the royalists had to divide many regiments into small garrison and occupation forces, financial irregularities, loss

of discipline, and other abuses became common features.

The military stalemate ended in 1820 not in a battlefield defeat but through the restoration in Spain of the Constitution and with elections throughout New Spain of new constitutional *ayuntamientos* (town councils) in most communities over 1,000 inhabitants. Noting that under the Constitution towns possessed controls over taxation and that armed forces were to be paid by the central government, almost unanimously the new *ayuntamientos* suspended obligatory taxation to support local royalist militias and defenses. Army officers who had imposed and maintained the militia system to support their counterinsurgency programs now found themselves without the authority to tax or to exercise compulsion. The town councils refused to pay local troops for operations outside of their home districts, demobilized existing militias, and stacked their weapons in the local barracks. Without these forces, the royalist army could not maintain pressure upon the hundreds of rebel bands, including those led by old insurgents such as Guadalupe Victoria, Miguel Serrano, and Vicente Guerrero.

Given this background, the successful 1821 rebellion of Colonel Agustín de Iturbide is easy to comprehend. Even within regular regiments, officers and soldiers now recognized that the war was lost. European Spanish and Mexican criollo royalist troops insulted each other and fought in taverns and barracks. Some soldiers met to discuss the Constitution and supported Mexicans who proclaimed a new era of peace. Without militia support, royalist units abandoned more isolated posts where they had been in direct contact with rebel forces to coalesce in the larger cities. These events coincided with Viceroy Apodaca's appointment of Iturbide to enter the guerrilla territory of Vicente Guerrero and other chiefs to negotiate amnesties or to launch yet another military offensive in the rugged Dirección del Sur. Having suffered a long period of inactivity in Mexico City caused by corruption charges at Guanajuato, Iturbide returned to service with more on his mind than purely military matters. He met with Guerrero and on February 24, 1821, they issued the Plan de Iguala, proclaiming the Independence of New Spain. Forming a new army called the Ejército de las Tres Guarantías (Army of Three Guarantees) after the guarantees of independence, religion, and union, Iturbide set out to seduce the royalist commanders and soldiers into joining his new cause.

Accepting a project from an army commander who reflected their own special interests, many royalist officers—both criollos and European Spaniards

—decided to forsake their old loyalties to Spain. Even the expeditionary troops of the Regiments of Zamora, Extremadura, Zaragoza, and other units at major cities such as Guadalajara, Querétaro, and Puebla changed sides and loyalties. There were some skirmishes and a few lives sacrificed, but the process was peaceful in most places. Some royalist commanders woke up one morning to find that their soldiers had disappeared. Others could not prevent spontaneous celebrations of Independence, including much firing of guns by their troops that left them speechless and bereft of any means to enforce their old authority. On Iturbide's side, Brigadier Negrete was soon in business at Guadalajara selling passports at high prices for Spanish merchants who wished to flee the country. In Mexico City, where the rump of the old army commanders gathered, the garrison deposed Viceroy Apodaca and replaced him with the Inspector of Artillery Francisco Novella. However, by this point most soldiers had defected, and Spain had lost the war and its most valuable American possession.

The heritage of the Wars of Independence left the new nation with deep problems and controversies that mere plans and constitutions could not solve. It was not that so many people had perished in combat or from starvation, diseases, or the abuses of the military. Indeed, the total casualty rate mentioned by some historians including up to one-half million deaths is impossible to sustain. There were not that many pitched battles, and in most cases even the counterinsurgency programs of the royalists involving concentration of the population and fire-free zones failed to function efficiently. Nevertheless, the war left an indelible imprint in that it decentralized and fragmented the country, leaving powerful army commanders and many aspirant officers who would continue their search for political and military power through uprisings. Army commanders of the generation of Antonio López de Santa Anna held power as presidents, senior politicians, soldiers, and regional bosses at least until midcentury. Spain refused to recognize defeat, continuing to occupy the fortress of San Juan de Ulúa at Veracruz for several years. Although reconquest was an impossible dream, in 1829 the Spanish government dispatched a quixotic invasion force that the climate and Santa Anna defeated at Tampico. Some former royalist European Spanish officers managed to avoid deportation laws directed in the 1820s against the *gachupín* minority. In the Mexican regions, many issues remained unresolved, and the entrenched guerrilla tradition presented one alternative for dissidents and those who felt that they had no other recourse. Without understanding the Wars of Independence, the chaos and complexities of the Mexican nineteenth century cannot be comprehended.

See also Hidalgo Revolt; Virgin of Guadalupe and Guadalupanismo

Select Bibliography

Anna, Timothy E., *The Fall of the Royal Government in Mexico City*. Lincoln: University of Nebraska Press, 1978.

Archer, Christon I., "The Royalist Army in New Spain: Civil-Military Relationships, 1810–1821." *Journal of Latin American Studies* 13:1 (May 1981).

_____, "The Army of New Spain and the Wars of Independence, 1790–1821." *Hispanic American Historical Review* 61:4 (November 1981).

_____, "La Causa Buena: The Counterinsurgency Army of New Spain and the Ten Years' War." In *The Independence of Mexico and the Creation of the New Nation*, edited by Jaime E. Rodríguez O. Los Angeles: UCLA Latin American Center, 1989.

_____, "Bite of the Hydra: The Rebellion of Cura Miguel Hidalgo, 1810–1811." In *Patterns of Contention in Mexican History*, edited by Jaime E. Rodríguez O. Wilmington, Delaware: Scholarly Resources, 1992.

_____, "Insurrection-Reaction-Revolution-Fragmentation: Reconstructing the Choreography of Meltdown in New Spain during the Independence Era." *Mexican Studies/Estudios Mexicanos* 10:1 (Winter 1994).

_____, "New Wars and Old: Félix Calleja and the Independence War of New Spain, 1810–1816." In *Military Heretics: The Unorthodox in Policy and Strategy*, edited by B. J. C. McKercher and Hamish Ion. Westport, Connecticut: Praeger, 1994.

Guardino, Peter F., *Peasants, Politics, and the Formation of Mexico's National State: Guerrero, 1800–1857*. Stanford, California: Stanford University Press, 1996.

Hamill, Hugh M., *The Hidalgo Revolt: Prelude to Mexican Independence*. Gainesville: University of Florida Press, 1966.

Hamnett, Brian R., "Mexico's Royalist Coalition: The Response to Revolution, 1808–1821." *Journal of Latin American Studies* 12:1 (May 1980).

_____, *Roots of Insurgency: Mexican Regions, 1750–1824*. Cambridge: Cambridge University Press, 1986.

Katz, Friederich, editor, *Riot, Rebellion, and Revolution: Rural Social Conflict in Mexico*. Princeton, New Jersey: Princeton University Press, 1988.

Rodríguez O., Jaime E., editor, *The Mexican and Mexican American Experience in the 19th Century*. Tempe, Arizona: Bilingual Press, 1989.

_____, editor, *The Evolution of the Mexican Political System*. Wilmington, Delaware: Scholarly Resources, 1993.

Taylor, William B., *Magistrates of the Sacred: Priests and Parishioners in Eighteenth-Century Mexico*. Stanford, California: Stanford University Press, 1996.

Timmons, Wilbert H., *Morelos of Mexico: Priest, Soldier, Statesman*. El Paso: Texas Western College Press, 1963.

Tutino, John, *From Insurrection to Revolution in Mexico: Social Bases of Agrarian Violence, 1750–1940*.

Princeton, New Jersey: Princeton University Press, 1986.

Van Young, Eric, "Islands in the Storm: Quiet Cities and Violent Countrysides in the Mexican Independence Era." *Past and Present* 118 (February 1988).

—CHRISTON I. ARCHER

Wars of Reform (Three Years War)

The Civil War of the Reform (1858–61) resulted from the intense polarization of the last months of the administration of the moderate Liberal Party president Ignacio Comonfort (1855–58), in which the "church question" (as the Liberals defined it) played a central part. The future of the corporate properties of both the Catholic Church and the indigenous communities became a leading issue in the political background to the conflict. The immediate causes, however, were the two coups d'état of December 17, 1857, and January 11, 1858. In the first of these, Comonfort and a small group of moderates, with the support of General Félix Zuloaga, commander of the Mexico City Garrison, acting together under the terms of the Plan of Tacubaya, nullified the Constitution of 1857 and closed the Constitutional Congress elected in accordance with its provisions, on the grounds that excessive radical influence was driving the country toward civil war. Comonfort's failure to establish a moderate regime in Mexico City undermined his position there. The president's decision to go outside the constitutional system established earlier in the year alienated not only radical Liberals intent upon pushing the Reform movement further and faster, but also many moderates, most state governors, and virtually all popular Liberal groups at the local and provincial levels, which saw in the Reforms Laws and the 1857 Constitution the means of advancing their material interests and their position in society. When Zuloaga pronounced against the remnants of the Comonfort administration on January 11, 1858, with the support of clerics, Conservative Party members, and the official army, Comonfort sought in vain to uphold the original principles of the Revolution of Ayutla (1854–55), which had first brought the Liberals to power. Zuloaga, aware that the two leading Conservative generals, Miguel Miramón and Luis Osollo, were in the vicinity of Mexico City, wished to salvage his own position by removing Comonfort.

The formation of a Conservative Party regime in Mexico City, supported by church and army, made the outbreak of civil war inevitable. Zuloaga nullified the Constitution of 1857 and the Reform Laws. His regime was recognized by the diplomatic corps, including initially by the United States. The administration of President James Buchanan (1857–61) defined its relations with Mexico in terms of further territorial concessions and transit rights. When the Conservative regime refused to negotiate on these issues and then imposed a 1 percent tax on all residents, including foreigners, U.S. minister John Forsyth left Mexico in October 1858.

Zuloaga's regime included well-known Conservative figures, such as Luis G. Cuevas (minister of foreign affairs) and Hilario Elguero (minister of the interior). The Council of War included the monarchist F. J. Miranda and the Conservative polemicist J. J. Pesado, noted for his editorials in *La Cruz* (1855–58). The Liberal Party regrouped in the center-north, first in Guanajuato and subsequently in Guadalajara, around the person of Benito Juárez, who, as elected president of the Supreme Court of Justice under the terms of the 1857 Constitution, claimed the constitutional right to complete Comonfort's term of office. The powerful Liberal state governors of the center-northern states gave Juárez their support on the understanding that he would work in their interests. Juárez owned his position to the 1857 Constitution and proclaimed defenses of constitutional principles as the central platform of the Liberal cause. He sought not only the moral high ground by contrasting Liberal legitimacy with the regime in Mexico City, which had seized power in a coup d'état, but also a broad popular base that would enable him to rise above the state governors' tutelage. The Conservative regime took defense of the church and the Catholic religion as its central platform. At the same time, the Conservatives sought to counterbalance European support against the evident attachment of the Liberals to the United States.

The Conservatives had the better generals, most of whom had risen through the army of Antonio López de Santa Anna during his last regime of 1853 to 1855. Although the Liberals controlled most of the geographical periphery, the ports, and the principal customs revenues, the Conservatives won a series of striking victories that nearly extinguished the Liberal cause in the central zones of Mexico. Osollo, with the support of Miramón and Tomás Mejía (the Indian general from the Sierra Gorda of Querétaro), defeated the Liberal generals Anastasio Parrodi (governor of Jalisco) and Leandro Valle at Salamanca (in the Bajío region of north-central Mexico) on March 10, 1858. The Liberal withdrawal to Guadalajara exposed Guanajuato. Governor Manuel Doblado negotiated the capitulation of Silao with Osollo on March 12, 1858, which opened the city to Conservative forces. Between March 13 and 15, 1858, Juárez and his ministers were trapped and nearly executed by a brief military coup engineered by a section of the Guadalajara garrison. On March 19, Juárez and his ministers retreated to Colima and thence on April 7 to the port of Manzanillo. Four days later they departed by sea for Veracruz. In the meantime, Guadalajara fell to Osollo and Miramón on March 23, and Miramón took Zacatecas on April 10; the city ultimately was recovered by Liberal forces on April 27. Miramón took San Luis Potosí on April 17. By the time the Juárez administration reached Veracruz by way of Panama on May 4, 1858, Conservative forces had taken Morelia and Orizaba. Mejía occupied Tampico on May 14, but Liberal forces regained the port on August 17. Their attempt to regain Guadalajara, however, was frustrated by the indecisive battle at the Barranca de Atenquique (near Ciudad Guzmán) on July 2, 1858, in which Miramón drove off Valle and Santos Degollado, the Liberal commander of western Mexico. Osollo in the meantime had died of illness in San Luis Potosí on June 18, depriving the Conservatives of one of their most distinguished commanders. Liberal forces recovered Durango on July 7, 1858. Miramón defeated Santiago Vidaurri at Ahualulco (San Luis Potosí) on September 29, 1858, with the assistance of Mejía and Leonardo Márquez. This victory enabled him to recover San Luis Potosí on September 30. Márquez entered Zacatecas on October 24. Liberal forces under Degollado and Valle, however, managed to break into Guadalajara—they had been in the vicinity of the city since September 26—during the night of October 27.

In Veracruz, the Juárez government fell under the protection of state governor Manuel Gutiérrez Zamora, close friend of Miguel Lerdo de Tejada, finance minister from January 1859 until June 1860 and leading force in the cabinet. Conflict between Lerdo and the more radical Secretary of Exterior Relations Melchor Ocampo divided the cabinet. The majority of ministers were favorably disposed toward the United States and argued for a U.S. loan even at the cost of territorial concessions. Lerdo in fact favored U.S. protection of Mexico as the only effective guarantee, in light of repeated Liberal military failures, against what he saw as Conservative designs to involve the European powers in Mexican internal affairs. At this time, a breach occurred between Juárez and Santiago Vidaurri over control of Liberal forces, which the latter wished to take from Santos Degollado. Juárez appointed Governor Manuel Doblado commander of the army in mid-1859. In consequence, on September 5, 1859, Vidaurri proclaimed the independence of the state of Nuevo León and Coahuila, which he unilaterally had joined together in 1856 in spite of Comonfort's opposition. Juárez proclaimed Vidaurri an outlaw and sent Doblado's forces into Nuevo León, forcing Vidaurri across the Texas border.

The Conservative regime in Mexico City proved neither stable nor united. As a result of the Plan de Navidad, a junta of notables appointed General Miguel Miramón president on January 2, 1859, thereby removing former president Félix Zuloaga, whose conduct of the war they criticized. Realizing his position was untenable, however, Miramón withdrew and Zuloaga was restored on January 24. Miramón issued a notorious decree on February 16, 1859, providing for the death penalty for collaboration with Liberal forces or for spreading rumors or conspiring against the Mexico City regime. The implications of this decree were graphically underscored in the killings of wounded Liberal prisoners of war and the hospital staff who were attending to them; the massacre was carried out by Leonardo Márquez's forces (acting on Miramón's instructions) at Tacubaya on April 11. This followed the Conservative victory there over Degollado's forces. Henceforth, Márquez became known as the "Tiger of Tacubaya." In June and July 1859, Miramón opened the unsuccessful first siege of Veracruz.

In the Liberal camp, state governors such as Zacatecas' Jesús González Ortega pushed forward the Liberal reform measures in advance of the Juárez administration in Veracruz. González Ortega on June 16, 1859, imposed the death penalty for conspiracy against the Liberal cause and for ecclesiastics who in front of one or more witnesses required retraction of the oath to observe the 1857 Constitution or denied the sacraments to those who had taken it or who had taken advantage of the Ley Lerdo of June 1856 for the disamortization of corporate properties. A notorious anticlerical, González Ortega seized the silver of Durango Cathedral on January 6, 1860. From July 12, 1859, the Veracruz administration began the issue of Reform Laws for the nationalization of church properties, the separation of church and state, and the establishment of civil marriage and civil registry.

The Conservative regime, in its search for European support, authorized the signature of the Mon-Almonte Treaty in Paris of September 26, 1859, designed to restore diplomatic relations between

Mexico and Spain, ruptured since the murder of two Spanish nationals in Mexico during the presidency of Juan Alvarez in 1855. The treaty, negotiated by Juan Nepomuceno Almonte (illegitimate son of Independence leader José María Morelos and a leading Conservative) and Alejandro Mon (Spanish minister in Paris), ratified the Convention of 1853 in accordance with which Santa Anna's last regime agreed to pay outstanding debt obligations to Spain. The Zuloaga regime also agreed to pay compensation for the murdered Spanish nationals. The Juárez administration roundly condemned this treaty and declared Almonte a traitor.

Shortly after Conservative general José María Cobos occupied Oaxaca on November 5, 1859 (he held it until August 9, 1860), Miramón defeated Degollado, Doblado, and José María Arteaga (governor of Querétaro) at Estancia de las Vacas (in the vicinity of Querétaro) on November 13. This proved, however, to be the last major Conservative victory. Nevertheless, Conservative forces published captured correspondence between Melchor Ocampo, then secretary for external relations, and Degollado concerning Finance Minister Lerdo's attempt to secure a U.S. loan. This dealt a particularly embarrassing blow to the Veracruz regime. Juárez attached priority to U.S. recognition of his administration as the sole legitimate government in Mexico. President Buchanan sent Senator Robert McLane of Maryland to Mexico to negotiate new frontiers and transit rights and offer US$10 million for the purchase of Baja California. The Liberal administration secured U.S. recognition on April 6, 1859. Although territorial concessions were not forthcoming, Lerdo proceeded to the United States to negotiate a loan. Juárez himself, Ocampo, and Lerdo were strong partisans of a close association between the United States and Mexico as defenders of the republican system in opposition to the European monarchies. The first Conservative siege of Veracruz made U.S. aid urgent.

The Liberal administration, in its anxiety to secure financial support from the United States, exposed itself to easy Conservative criticism by the negotiation of the McLane-Ocampo Treaty of December 14, 1859. Although the Juárez cabinet resisted traditional U.S. pressure for further territorial concessions from Mexico, ministers were prepared to concede the principle of transit rights across Mexican territory by three routes, two in the north (from Arizona to Guaymas, and from Texas to Mazatlán) and the other across the Isthmus of Tehuantepec, while preserving Mexican sovereignty. The treaty permitted U.S. intervention to protect transit, albeit only at the invitation of the Mexican government. The reputation of the Juárez cabinet was saved when the U.S. Senate declined to ratify the treaty, whereupon Juárez in November 1860 repudiated it.

Miramón's second siege of Veracruz by land in February and March 1860 was intended to coincide with a naval blockade by two ships purchased from the Spanish-controlled part of Havana. The intervention of U.S. ships on March 6, however, prevented General Tomás Marín from imposing the naval blockade; instead, he was escorted to New Orleans as a pirate on March 27 and imprisoned with his associates. This episode, which came to be known as the Anton Lizardo Incident, was used by Conservatives to underscore Juárez's dependency on the United States. Nevertheless, Miramón abandoned the siege on March 21.

In March and April 1860, the breach between Juárez and Lerdo over the pace of reform and the debt question widened. Lerdo's resignation on May 30, 1860, signified the beginning for his opposition campaign for the forthcoming presidential elections of 1861. Lerdo recommended the suspension of payment of the external debt for a specific period, a measure that would provoke the hostility of the European Powers.

On May 9 and 10, 1860, tensions in Mexico City between President Zuloaga and General Miramón rose to a climax. Opposition among Conservative leaders to Miramón led to the latter's abduction of Zuloaga and his transportation with Miramón to Guadalajara. However, on August 3 Zuloaga escaped from captivity in León and proceeded to Mexico City, where he withdrew into private life. Accordingly, the Council of Government declared Miramón to be president. On August 10, however, Governor Jesús González Ortega of Zacatecas and General Ignacio Zaragoza (who in 1862 would distinguish himself in the defeat of French troops in the Battle of Puebla) defeated Miramón in the Bajío at Silao. The latter withdrew to Mexico City, while Guanajuato, Celaya, and Querétaro fell to the Liberals.

Miramón formed a cabinet in Mexico City on August 15, 1860, in which the principal figure was the moderate, Teodosio Lares (minister of justice, ecclesiastical affairs, and education), who had held office under Santa Anna and would again hold office under Emperor Maximilian (1864–67). In the meantime, the new Spanish minister to Mexico, Joaquín Francisco Pacheco, who had been granted safe-conduct through Veracruz by President Juárez on May 23, arrived in the capital. In common with other European diplomatic representatives and several prominent Conservatives, Pacheco favored an armed

European intervention in Mexico, with the possibility of the introduction of a monarch chosen from one of the principal European reigning houses. Even within Liberal Mexico, Doblado and Degollado advocated mediation by the diplomatic corps (which almost in its entirety had recognized the Conservative regime) to end the civil war. Degollado contacted the British minister on September 18. The implications of mediation, however, was the removal of Juárez from the presidency, on the grounds that he was the principal obstacle to a negotiated peace. The military situation put an end to such a scheme.

The collapse of the Conservative regime began with the opening of the Liberal siege of Guadalajara on September 26, 1860, which finally fell to González Ortega on November 3. The Miramón regime, desperately in need of funds, had contacted the dubious Jecker House on October 14 to receive a loan of 700,000 pesos and recognized bonds to the value of 15 million pesos guaranteed against one-fifth of the federal tax revenues. Owing to fiscal pressures on British nationals living in the capital, the British minister severed diplomatic relations with the Conservative regime on October 17 and withdrew to Jalapa. This provided Miramón with the pretext on November 16 to break into the British Legation and appropriate the sum of 660,000 pesos from the safe. The Miramón regime appeared to gain a new lease on life with the defeat of General Felipe de Berriozábal and Degollado at Toluca on December 9, 1860. However, González Ortega appeared in the Valley of Mexico shortly afterward with 16,000 men from the north-central states and routed Miramón's forces of 8,000 men definitively at Calpulalpan on December 22. Two days later, Miramón relinquished power to the City Council of the capital which appointed Berriozábal to await the arrival of González Ortega and the transfer of authority to the Liberal administration still in Veracruz. The Liberal commander entered the capital on Christmas Day with a section of the army. Three days later he promulgated the Reform Laws there. On January 1, 1861, the rest of the army arrived. The Juárez administration arrived on January 11. The formal fighting of the Civil War of the Reform had ended, but Conservative guerrilla bands, sometimes associated with General Leonardo Márquez, remained active in the country and were responsible for the murder of Melchor Ocampo and Santos Degollado in June 1861.

The civil war gave rise to a broad range of popular participation. Defense of state sovereignty, municipal autonomy, and the republican, representative, federal system drew responses in many peasant villages and small towns across the republic. The National

Guard, originally established in the war with the United States (1846–47) and coordinated by President José Joaquín de Herrera's Regulation of 1848, became a central expression of local resistance to the Mexico City regime. In notable instances a locally recruited guard became an instrument for the pursuit of popular causes, in the forefront of which was defense of the principles of the Revolution of Ayutla. In Morelos, for instance, the guard sided with villages in their struggles with local haciendas. The civil war produced the largest popular mobilization since the Insurgency of the 1810s. Popular action frequently originated from below with the masses, and was not necessarily dependent on mobilization or inspiration by the elite. Even so, such mobilization tended to take place around locally recognized chieftains or persons of eminence.

This was the case in the northern sierra Oaxaca, where the cáciques Miguel Castro (state governor from December 1858 to December 1859), Francisco Meijueiro, and Fidencio Hernández formed the core of Liberal opposition to conservative forces in 1859 and 1860. They worked closely with Porfirio Díaz, who was *jefe político,* or district administrator, of Ixtlán in 1859. Díaz trained guerrillas in Ixtlán to fight the Conservative army, and the town became the Liberal state capital during the occupation of Oaxaca City. The National Guard often became the focus around which local leaders built popular support. Governor Marcos Pérez commissioned Fidencio Hernández to organize the sierra National Guard in 1860. Similarly, in the northern sierra of Puebla, local chieftains, who had risen to prominence with the Revolution of Ayutla, took control of a highly effective local National Guard, which became the focus of resistance to Conservative control in the state capital. The leading figure was Juan Nepomuceno Méndez, who dominated the sierra through subsequent decades.

Important as popular mobilization was, it should not be overstated, since no radical and popular Liberal movement developed on a national scale, and no united program of structural reform emerged. Instead, strong Liberal groups, conscious of the reasons for their mobilization, were able to influence national events in response to a combination of local and national issues.

Popular mobilization, moreover, was not confined to the Liberal camp. In Nayarit, Indian resistance to private landlord encroachments on their properties antedated the Reform era, but the civil war conditions after 1858 enabled what would prove to be a long-lasting peasant movement to take shape there under the leadership of Manuel Lozada. Liberal disamortization policies increased resistance to the Comonfort administration. Between 1856 and Comonfort's execution in 1873, Lozada ("el Tigre de Alica") led full-scale resistance to Jalisco state government, then under Liberal control.

The Civil War of the Reform also reopened the struggle between the center and outlying regions (organized as states once more under the terms of the 1857 Constitution). The Conservative regime was centralist and dismantled the state structure of federalism. This conflict was exactly the type that appealed to Liberal state governors and provincial cadres looking to increase the power of the outlying regions. Control of the states on Mexico's geographical periphery gave the Liberal cause access to the coasts and to revenues from trade. This factor proved to be decisive in the outcome of the war.

Of course, this increased strength of the periphery would prove problematic for Juárez as he tried to form a national government. The war had allowed state authorities to retain control over many revenues earmarked for the federal government, and Juárez was to encounter great difficulty in regaining control of these funds. This situation was just one of the many ways in which the war had worsened Mexico's external debt position, increasing the likelihood of conflict with European powers.

Select Bibliography

Bancroft, Hubert Howe, *History of Mexico*, vol. 5, *1824–1861*. San Francisco: Bancroft, 1885.

———, *History of Mexico, vol. 6, 1861–1887*. San Francisco: History Company, 1888.

Berry, Charles R., *The Reform in Oaxaca, 1856–76: A Microhistory of the Liberal Revolution*. Lincoln and London: University of Nebraska Press, 1981.

Dabbs, Jack Autrey, *The French Army in Mexico, 1861–1867: A Study in Military Government*. The Hague: Mouton, 1963.

Hanna, Alfred Jackson, and Kathryn Abbey Hanna, *Napoleon III and Mexico: American Triumph over Monarchy*. Chapel Hill: University of North Carolina Press, 1971.

Ridley, Jasper, *Maximilian and Juárez*. London: Constable, 1993.

—Brian R. Hamnett

Women's Status and Occupation

This entry is composed of five articles that discuss the status and occupation of women:

Women's Status and Occupation: Mesoamerica
Women's Status and Occupation: Indian Women in New Spain
Women's Status and Occupation: Spanish Women in New Spain
Women's Status and Occupation: 1821–1910
Women's Status and Occupation: 1910–96

See also Family and Kinship; Gender; Malinche and Malinchismo; Virgin of Guadalupe and Guadalupanismo

Women's Status and Occupation: Mesoamerica

It is impossible to generalize about the social status of women in pre-Conquest Mesoamerica because we do not have adequate information for many regions and time periods. The best pre-Conquest data on women's status come from the stone carvings, painted manuscripts, ceramic figurines, and utilitarian artifacts of the larger, more centralized groups, such as the Mayas of southeastern Mesoamerica, the Zapotecs and Mixtecs of Oaxaca and Guerrero, and the Nahuas living primarily in central Mexico. Of these groups only the Mayas ever included extensive hieroglyphic captions in their imagery; the others added, if anything, only occasional dates and the names of certain persons and places. For many other peoples who lived and worked in Mesoamerica, we have only images unaccompanied by glyphic inscriptions, or virtually no surviving visual representations of people at all. For these groups we are largely dependent on archaeological traces of settlement and habitation patterns and whatever artifacts they may have left behind.

Fortunately, additional evidence on women's status comes from the pens of post-Conquest conquistadors, clergy, and mendicants. These authors, for the most part, wrote about the same groups that have bequeathed us the richest visual imagery, but they wrote about the period immediately prior to European contact. The best colonial source for our understanding of the status of Nahua women is Bernardino de Sahagún, a Franciscan who arrived in Mexico City in 1529. His many years of interviews with Nahua informants and his numerous writings culminated in the 1570s with a lengthy study of indigenous Nahua culture, the *Codice florentino*

(Florentine Codex). In Yucatán, around 1566, Bishop Diego de Landa compiled our best source on contact period Maya culture, a volume titled *Relación de las cosas de Yucatán*. In contrast to Landa, Sahagún had his work extensively illustrated, apparently using Nahua artists trained in European pictorial techniques. These illustrations, despite their clear evidence of cultural hybridization, have proved invaluable to scholars investigating the status and occupations of pre-Conquest Nahua women. The artists who produced these illustrations, however, like those native artists who painted genealogical, cartographic, and economic manuscripts for other Spanish patrons, were urban descendants of the local aristocracy and, like their patrons, invariably male. Having at least nominally converted to Catholicism, moreover, they may have shared with Europeans a contempt for indigenous religion and may have acquired from them certain Old World fears and dislikes of women. The result is that we have no colonial prose or pictorial sources on the status of Mesoamerican women that are not significantly colored by cultural, gender, and class biases, regardless of whether they were produced by Europeans or natives. None of our sources represent the voice of women.

For this reason, scholars today are divided in their assessments of the status of pre-Conquest women. There are those who conclude that women, relative to men, generally held low social status and little power—that they were, in fact, socially oppressed. These studies tend to be rooted in basic Marxist premises, in particular that which posits that female status and power steadily decline when a society centralizes power and becomes increasingly hierarchic. In opposition to these studies are those that find that pre-contact Mesoamerican women enjoyed relatively high status and exercised considerable power, if not at a political level, then certainly in the domestic, legal, and economic realms. Many of these studies reflect the tenets of recent feminist theory, which seeks to locate female positions of power and project a more positive image of women in history.

The first group is more apt to take at face value many of the colonial accounts of native women's status, without overly worrying about the possibility of bias. Most of their work is based on our information on Nahua women, who are mentioned by European sources to have played a minor role outside the home. Sahagún says, for example, that women ideally stayed in or near the house, learning at an early age how to cook, weave, and provide support for their children and husbands. There is some reason to think that having and raising children was normally the principal responsibility of most, if not all, Mesoamerican women; among the Nahuas at the time of European contact, childless women seem to have been pitied, if not disdained and even feared. Mesoamericanists who see child rearing and domesticity in general as restrictive and undervalued thus conclude that native "housewives" could not have enjoyed a prominent place in the political and economic system, and thus would have suffered from low social status. These scholars seldom seriously consider the possibility that they are imposing on pre-Conquest women their own experiences and cultural values regarding domestic labor.

Those who see Mesoamerican women as having occupied an inferior position also note that, in general, women seldom held top political and religious offices. Nor did the vast majority of women ever fight in battle. Since politics and warfare were the main avenues for attaining social status among the Nahua and Maya, this group of scholars has concluded that Nahua and Maya women could not have enjoyed high status. It is also often noted in these studies that women tend to play a subordinate or negative role in Mesoamerican ideologies. According to the Spanish chroniclers, contact-era Nahuas and Mayas, like some of their descendants today, believed in certain dangerous female supernaturals, as well as every woman's capacity to commit adultery or spy on and betray her husband to his enemies. Women are portrayed in native mythohistories as fomenters of discord and warfare, as well as losers; in contests of power with men, they almost never win. Although a number of goddesses figure among the many deities who were honored by the Nahuas, both of the principal deities honored at the main temple-pyramid in Tenochtitlan, the capital of the Nahua Triple Alliance, were male. The scholar June Nash has argued that female deities, who earlier had numbered among the most prominent members of the Nahua pantheon, were increasingly edged out, or demoted, as the evolving state placed more and more power in the hands of males, while Helen Pollard has made a similar argument regarding Purépucha (Tarascan) people of Michoacán. In the Maya area, the goddess Ixchel was the focus of a popular cult in Quintana Roo and Yucatán at the time of the Conquest, but there is no evidence of a female supernatural having occupied an important place in the various state religions of the Classic period (A.D. 200–900). Classic Maya rulers, who were almost always male, appear on stone stelae and lintels bearing the insignia and titles of male, not female, supernaturals. Since Maya figurine traditions in more rural, decentralized areas abound with three-dimensional representations of females, it appears that Maya females, like Nahua and Purépucha females, took a back seat to males in the official religio-historical ideologies of centralized polities.

There was an important Nahua image of a woman placed at the main temple-pyramid in Tenochtitlan, but it can be seen as reinforcing the argument that women were represented in a negative light in state ideologies. A huge circular stone relief of a mytho-historical women named Coyolxauhqui was placed at the foot of the stair of the main temple leading to the shrine of the national patron god, Huitzilo-pochtli. Her bound and bleeding naked body had been decapitated and dismembered. Sahagún relates a Nahua account of how, at a mountain called Coatepec, Coyolxauhqui had led her brothers in an attack on their mother when she learned that their mother had conceived without a man. The child in the mother's womb, who was Huitzilopochtli, emerged fully armed to defend his mother and soundly defeated his rival siblings. Coyolxauhqui was decapitated and her body rolled down the mountain, where, according to Sahagún, it broke into pieces. Thus, the woman depicted in the huge stone carving at the foot of the main temple-pyramid in Tenochtitlan represented evil and sedition, traits obviously unflattering to women. Scholars who argue that Nahua women were socially subordinate to men in pre-contact times claim that Coyalxauhqui's humiliation and death were to be seen as inevitable, her gender itself a sign of the deserved fate of those who dared to challenge male state authority.

It is state-crafted ideological systems such as this that have given some Mesoamericanists the impression that, in the larger polities at least, pre-Conquest women were politically unimportant and relatively powerless. Other scholars, in contrast, denounce these official ideologies as precisely that: as representing political ideals and rationalizations of state power. Such ideologies, they argue, necessarily distort the social reality of women's lives. At the same time, these scholars urge us to expand, if not redefine, our notions of status and power—that is, to avoid evaluating female status in terms of strictly male values. For these scholars the cumulative evidence indicates not that Mesoamerican women were socially oppressed by their men-folk, but rather that, at least among the commoners, they enjoyed roughly equal status with them. Mesoamerican women, from this perspective, should be understood as complementary to men, with each gender constituting an equal part of a single unit that could not have functioned without the other.

These authors argue that we should not focus exclusively on data from the urban centers because they almost always tell us only about the lives of the elite. The degree and kinds of status that women held at the highest levels of the social hierarchy are not likely to inform us of women's status among the lower classes. These scholars also emphasize that it is equally important to examine the status of women living outside the metropolitan centers. In the towns and villages of more rural areas, they caution, women may have played larger roles and been seen in more positive terms. Evidence of women's roles sometimes comes in forms, media, and contexts atypical of city elites, aspects that are equally deserving of our scrutiny. For example, women, as we have seen, are represented frequently in clay figurines from more rural lowland Maya areas, where they usually are found in a domestic rather than public, institutional context. The biological signs of their sex here are more evident than those of historical women depicted in stone at urban centers, who in appearance often closely resemble men, sometimes even assuming male dress and posture. Moreover, in comparison to the stone-carved figures of elite urban women, these ceramic figures tend to represent women as more active and productive. Many are represented as weaving, cooking, or tending children or domestic animals. In this, they recall Landa's report of Yucatec Maya women that:

> They are great workers and good housekeepers, since on them depends the more important and the most work for the support of their houses, the education of their children, and the payment of their tribute. And in spite of all this, if there is need for it, they sometimes carry a greater burden, cultivating and sowing their supplies. They are good managers, working at night in the moments which remain to them from their housework, and going to market to buy and sell their little articles; they also raise fowls for sale and for food...[and] raise birds for their own pleasure, and for the feathers from which to make their fine clothes.

The frequency of female imagery in the Maya countryside, its unabashed reference to the female body, and its emphasis on female production and reproduction suggest that rural lowland Maya women enjoyed a higher status than their city cousins, a status that may well have been complementary to that of men.

Recent scholarship also has tended to emphasize the positive values attached to domestic work, as well as the variety of other, nondomestic occupations available to women. Women's responsibility for textile production and food preparation, for example, has to be seen in light of the social and economic importance of cloth and foodstuffs in Mesoamerica. At the time of the Conquest, within the empire forged by the Triple Alliance of central Mexico, cloth was a major tribute item. It also served as a kind of currency, being used in the marketplace as a form of standard measure, and, made into articles of clothing, often was presented as a gift. The state had a constant need of quality textiles, which it used to reward its supporters. Elaborate costumes were worn by both military, religious, and state officials, particularly during the numerous Nahua calendrical ceremonies held throughout the year.

Although Nahua men, chiefly the sick and elderly, may have helped at times with the tasks of spinning, weaving, and dying, textiles were regarded as quintessentially female. Women in rural areas to the north and east of Tenochtitlan not only monopolized the tasks of spinning and weaving maguey cloth, but helped in the preparation of the maguey fibers. In the warmer climates of the south and Gulf Coast lowlands, women apparently took full responsibility for raising the plants that provided them with the cotton fibers used for the most prestigious garments; a principal patron of Huastec and Nahua women was a goddess named Ixcuina (Lady Cotton). There are other clues from Nahua ideology that weaving was perceived as an empowering act for women. In Nahua mythohistory, for example, five goddesses who died at the time of the primordial creation of the world later reappeared as woven *mantas* (blankets). Weaving implements such as battens and spindle whorls were charged with symbolism that compared spinning and weaving to the acts of creation and procreation, an association still extant among the Huichols.

Women clearly had a hand, as well, in the production of objects decorated with feathers. Featherworkers were the most esteemed group of Nahua artisans in Tenochtitlan; they formed a kind of guild within the aristocratic district called Amantlan. Although the majority of the featherworkers apparently were male, the profession also was open to Amanteca women. Like Maya women, these Nahua women raised many of the birds whose feathers were used for elite war shields, costumes, and other precious objects. Women's importance to the industry is reflected in the fact that two of the patron deities of featherworkers were female.

The textiles woven by Nahua noblewomen were used by their families and the government, as it would have been demeaning for them to sell their products in the market. This was not the case for commoner women, however, who, like the Maya

women described by Landa, could and did exchange their weavings for other goods. Sahagún's artists depicted several Nahua women selling textiles, as well as others selling a variety of plants. We know that Nahua women cultivated certain plants, especially herbs that had medicinal uses. It is usually assumed that such plants were grown in a garden adjacent to the house, but there are some indications that women helped their men work the more distant fields as well. When their husbands were called away on military duty, women almost certainly assumed the job of farming. Wills drafted in Culhuacan in the years following the Conquest show that some Nahua women owned not only agricultural tools, but also cultivated land, and that in some cases they bequeathed these lands to their daughters.

In the Maya area, as we have seen, women raised domesticated animals; the most common were dogs and deer. Deer were an important source of meat in Maya daily life and were used in religious rituals as a form of offering as well. In Conquest-period central Mexico, as presumably in other areas and times, prepared foods were likewise a staple of religious ceremony. Throughout Mesoamerica, vast amounts of tortillas or tamales were presented as ritual offerings and used to feed the people who participated. Recent research emphasizes the role of public feasting at all levels of social life and the role of women in providing the fare at these times. In addition, in those societies that depended on military expansion to finance the state, food to sustain the troops was a major necessity. It is clear that in Tenochtitlan and, presumably, the other cities of the Triple Alliance as well, the job of preparing this food fell to women.

Women also provided part of the "entertainment" at these gatherings, having been trained as children to sing and dance at the Telpochcalli, a school primarily used to train boys as warriors. Young women whom Sahagún describes as "women of pleasure" were selected during certain month festivals to dance with and serve as sleeping partners for distinguished warriors and nobles who requested them. The service was temporary and had to be cleared through the women's "matrons," who also received a "gift" from the suitor. Because they were carefully guarded by these matrons, it is likely that these women had been trained at the Telpochcalli. In several places, Sahagún refers to them as *auianime*, the Nahua plural for the category of women that he translates elsewhere as "harlots." It seems likely, however, that the word *auiani* was reserved by the Nahuas for a member of a different, lower status group of commoner women who sold sexual favors in the markets. These women were roughly equivalent to what Landa called the "bad public women" of the Yucatec Maya. Some of them apparently accompanied their warriors into battle and a few allegedly died trying to assist them. Scholar Margaret Arvey has argued that the pre-Conquest status of the *auianime*, which she thinks was high, was grossly underrated by Europeans, who had been raised in a culture that feared unregulated female sexuality. She also states that it is entirely possible that prostitution as Sahagún described it was introduced to Mesoamericans by Europeans in the aftermath of the Conquest.

Many Mesoamerican women served as physicians, using their cultivated herbs to make medicines. They apparently specialized in reproductive ailments, in particular obstetrics, but Sahagún's artists show them curing men as well. Midwives in Tenochtitlan had their own deities and ceremonies and were ritually honored and addressed as brave warriors bearing arms. The Spaniards feared these women, whom they associated with witches and accused of practicing black magic, but there is no doubt of the efficacy of many of their cures. Some of them treated psychological and social problems, as well, particularly those pertaining to marital problems such as unrequited love, adultery, and impotence. Their power in the realm of reproduction was shared with women who served as matchmakers and those who took care of other women's children. At a time when infant mortality and death in battle were major problems, the importance of all of these women to society would have been substantial. That their services were appreciated by the state is revealed in the fact that one of the annual ceremonies held by the midwives of Tenochtitlan took place in the main temple precinct.

In central Mexico, the daughters of the Nahua nobility could be sent to the Calmecac, the school primarily reserved for sons of the nobility, who were trained there for the priesthood. While there, the boys endured a hard life of religious service and privation that involved daily bloodletting from their ears, temples, and thighs. The young women, while charged with sweeping the temples and other servile tasks, were not permitted to view the statues of the deities and apparently did not engage in autosacrifice. This parallels Landa's report that Yucatec Maya women were not allowed to shed blood to the idols, nor could they go to the temples to attend or perform sacrifices. It seems likely, however, that some Nahua girls were trained at the Calmecac in the prestigious profession of scribe, since a female manuscript painter of royal birth is depicted in the Codex Telleriano-Remensis. We know that Nahua boys at the Calmecac were taught to write and paint, as well as become versed in calendrical matters.

Most girls sent to the Calmecac did not remain there more than several years, eventually returning to their family homes, most likely to get married. The few that stayed behind became either guardians and teachers of future female students at the school or priestesses. Although Sahagún usually mentions only male priests at Tenochtitlan, the native artists of his earliest extant manuscript, the *Primeros memoriales,* depicted a surprising number of women engaged in priestly activities. Landa mentions a group of old women who on certain occasions were allowed inside Maya temples and who may be a counterpart of these Nahua priestesses. The practice of allowing women to enter the priesthood seems to have been an old one; females carrying priestly incense bags flank a central cult image in the Tepantitla Patio mural at Classic-period Teotihuacan. The cult image itself appears to represent a female deity. Similarly, numerous ceramic figurines from central Veracruz represent women not only elaborately dressed in what seems to be ceremonial garb, but assuming poses that suggest that they are singing or chanting. While it is unlikely that the priesthood offered a career for very many women, it seems clear that women were active participants in religious activities and that some of them took these up as a full-time occupation. Curiously, in Tenochtitlan priestesses apparently were not assigned to female deities; instead they attended male gods. The most important of these gods was Huitzilopochtli, and the women who served him were referred to as his "sisters."

While most Nahua and Maya women may well have performed the majority of their duties at home, then, there were a number of extra-domestic opportunities for economic gain. Domestic activities, moreover, seem to have been valued more highly in pre-Conquest cultures than they tend to be in Euro-American societies today. Scholars who wish to emphasize this evidence for female economic power and status add to this the growing evidence that Nahua women were well protected by the law. To judge by colonial legal documents that have come down to us, not only were Nahua women free to inherit and own property, but they could bequeath it to their daughters. Although husbands could divorce their wives for alleged sterility or poor housekeeping, wives could divorce husbands who abandoned or beat them. This situation was roughly parallel to that in Yucatán, where Mayas of both sexes were free to leave their spouses. A Nahua man—like a Yucatec Maya man—who committed adultery was punished along with the offending woman, and abortion, although it was in theory punishable by death, was safely practiced on a regular basis.

Strictures on women's reproductive functions were doubtless more rigorously enforced among the nobility, especially within the ruling lineages, where legitimacy of birth determined membership in the highest social ranks and was prerequisite for political office. Both Nahua and Maya noblemen practiced polygyny, but they could produce legitimate heirs and successors only through their principal wife. When noblewomen, who never were polygamous, violated the codes of sexual behavior, their fate usually was meted out by their husbands or kinsmen rather than submitted to the court. Both commoner and noblewomen, however, appear to have had the right to present their grievances to a judge. The mid–sixteenth century Codex Mendoza shows three women along with three men facing a row of judges. After the Conquest, as presumably before, Nahua women were frequent plaintiffs in legal actions.

Scholars are increasingly drawing attention to the mounting evidence that pre-Conquest Mesoamerican women occupied more politically important positions than formerly had been realized. The best evidence for this comes from the Classic Maya, and the later, Postclassic period (A.D. 900-1521) Mixtec and Nahua peoples. Although most colonial sources state that the rulers of the three Triple Alliance cities always were male, two of them indicate that a woman, Atotoztli, ruled Tenochtitlan in the late 1460s and early 1470s. If Atotoztli did indeed rule for a period, it would have been because her father, Moteuczoma I, had no brothers, fraternal succession being the pattern at the time. She probably served as regent for her son, Axayacatl, who eventually took the throne.

Although women apparently did not hold high political offices in Yucatán, Classic Maya women sometimes did. The best example is Palenque, where royal women twice succeeded to the highest office. The first woman to do so was Kanal-Ikal, a daughter of the preceding ruler, who may have had no sons; she ruled for over 20 years (A.D. 583-605) and was succeeded by her own son, Ax-Kan. The second was Zak-Kuk, a granddaughter of Kanal-Ikal and the mother of Palenque's most famous dynast, Pakal II. At the time that Zak-Kuk acceded to power, Pakal was only nine years old. He theoretically took over governing the site three years later at the tender age of twelve, but it seems likely that his mother continued to wield power from behind the throne until her death. Hieroglyphic inscriptions on some of the most important stone monuments commissioned by Pakal and his son and successor, Chan-Bahlum II, compare Zak-Kuk to a female creator deity who at the beginning of time gave birth to the gods and the first

Palenque dynast. Pakal's sculptors, on the famous Palenque Oval Tablet, depicted his mother handing him the crown of office upon his accession, and represented both her and Kanal-Ikal twice on the sides of his stone sarcophagus.

Scholars Linda Schele and David Freidel suggest that Pakal, and after him Chan-Bahlum, emphasized the maternal line of their family so as to legitimize their right to rule in a society where succession normally passed through the male line. The importance of Maya queen mothers can be seen at other Classic period sites, too, suggesting that their role was often, if not always, judged important. At Piedras Negras, on Stela 14, a woman assumed to be the new ruler's mother attends his accession, looking up to him as he sits in a royal niche above a scaffold. It was the royal women of Piedras Negras who first led scholar Tatiana Proskouriakoff to suggest that a number of figures in Maya art represent not men as was previously thought, but women of considerable political importance. Proskouriakoff later examined the famous stone-carved lintels of Yaxchilan, where she recognized additional women, usually the rulers' wives. A prominent Yaxchilan woman, in turn, is depicted in the famous painted murals at Bonampak, where she attends a ceremony possibly held to designate the Bonampak ruler's heir. At Calakmul and El Perú, a prominent woman is depicted on a stela paired with one depicting a man, and other portraits of important women were found at Cobá.

The most unusual instance of a Maya woman represented as ruler appears at Naranjo, where a Dos Pilas woman named Wak-Chanil-Ahaw arrived in A.D. 682 to marry a Naranjo noble and establish a royal line linked to that of Dos Pilas. Seventeen years later, having produced a son who acceded to the throne in 693 at the age of five, Wak-Chanil-Ahaw was depicted on Stela 24 standing atop a bound, naked warrior from the defeated site of Ucanal. She appears again on Stela 3, which commemorated her son's anniversary. The two most lavish burials at Caracol contained Maya women, one of whom may have been a ruler. These burials add to a growing number of cases in which female skeletons have been found in wealthy burials dating to the Classic and Postclassic periods. Thus, archaeological evidence combines with epigraphic and iconographic analysis to indicate that at least some women of royal birth held political power and prestige in the Maya region.

At the time of the Conquest and in the years immediately following, the Spaniards reported a number of women governing the towns of western, southern, and rural central Mexico. These *cacicas*, as the Spaniards called them, occasionally also led their men in battle. That women could attain such positions in less centralized areas reinforces suspicions that Nahua women originally had easier access to political office than their female descendants. The situation once may have approximated that of the Mixtecs to the south who, like the Nahuas, reckoned descent bilaterally. Mixtec women of high rank could inherit titles like men, as well as the territories of their parents, and pass them on within the matriline. Daughters had the right to inherit from either parent and, to judge by colonial documents, often did.

Mixtec women of property sometimes were married to a man of rank with fewer possessions as a means of forging an alliance. The use of high-born women to cement peaceful relations with other polities was characteristic of the Nahua and Maya as well, as exemplified by Wak-Chinil-Ahaw's strategic marriage to a man of Naranjo. The practice goes back at least to the beginning of the Postclassic period, to judge by the painted manuscripts that chronicle key episodes in certain Mixtec rulers' rise to power. For this same time period, the manuscripts also make it clear that some women actually assumed control of their polity. This is evidenced in the Codex Nuttall, which details certain episodes in the life and ancestry of the famous Mixtec male leader 8 Deer. There, a female ancestor named 6 Monkey is clearly portrayed as the ruler of a town called Belching Mountain. As ruler, 6 Monkey defeated two other towns in the Mixteca and then sacrificed their leaders, for which she received a new nickname that identified her as a warrior. Near the beginning of Codex Nuttall, at the point where Mixtec ancestors battle the primordial "stone men," armed women are depicted as both winners and losers in the conflict.

In other scenes, male candidates for political office seek the approval and advice of a skull-faced woman who sits within a temple of bones. Scholar John Pohl has suggested that this woman, whose name or title was 9 Grass, was an oracle located at Chalcatongo. One of those to consult 9 Grass was 6 Monkey. Sharisse and Geoffrey McCafferty have taken issue with Alfonso Caso's earlier identification of the main occupant of Tomb 7 at Monte Albán as a man, accusing Caso, rightly or wrongly, of the gender bias that they feel was endemic in his time. The McCaffertys argue instead that the principal tomb occupant was a Mixtec woman who may have occupied a position of power similar to that of 9 Grass.

Elsewhere in Codex Nuttall, a woman named 3 Flint and her daughter of the same name are principal players in rituals that appear to initiate major political and military events. Such women frequently are depicted in scenes of marriage and parentage,

illustrating their importance to lineage rights. The concern with the female parent's role first appears in the southern area on stone-carved genealogical registers produced by the Late Classic (A.D. 600–900) Zapotecs who lived to the east of the Mixtecs, as their descendants do today. In these reliefs the primary subject is marriage, but many of them situate the marital couple beneath an approving ancestor and continue the narrative with scenes of the birth and maturation of a child. Although it is always a male child who is depicted, its mother occupies a place of importance in the composition that in every way is equal to that of the father. Female ancestors also appear often on effigy urns found in Zapotec tombs of the Classic period. Female ancestors were equally important to the Maya and Nahuas. Nahuas told Sahagún that their ideal lineage founder was a woman, and descent through the maternal line played a key role in determining who could succeed a Nahua ruler, sometimes mattering more to a man's chances than did his father's lineage.

Since Nahua women usually were ineligible to succeed their fathers or brothers, the male ruler of Tenochtitlan metaphorically assumed the abilities and responsibilities of the female, being addressed as both the Mother and Father of his people. His chief assistant, the Cihuacoatl, not only had the name of a goddess for his title, but appeared at certain public functions wearing her costume. This appropriation of the female gender by male rulers also took place among the Classic Maya, where rulers' portraits are sometimes accompanied by texts identifying them as mothers, or as giving birth to the gods. Some scholars think that the costume worn by some male rulers in monumental Maya imagery is female, since it appears more often on royal women. These cases have been seen as illustrating the tendency for male rulers to appropriate the roles and abilities of women as a means of disempowering them, but it also can be argued that ruling men's very belief that it was necessary to claim female powers reflects the importance of women and their potential threat to male hegemony.

It is to be hoped that further study will elucidate the role and status of Mesoamerican women, allowing a scholarly consensus on the subject to be formed. In the meantime, one can only note the growing evidence that Mesoamerican women had more diverse and potentially lucrative opportunities than we once thought, and that at least some of them had access to economic and political power. Does this mean, then, that Mesoamerican women in general enjoyed a high status comparable to that of men? For those women who lived in urban capitals of evolving city and imperial states, this seems unlikely. As we have seen, both Nahua and Maya women largely were excluded from the most prestigious and lucrative professions, those of politician and warrior, and women who ruled normally did so as regents on behalf of their sons. Noblewomen often were used as pawns in the formation of strategic alliances and, among the Nahuas, their woven products were appropriated by their family and their state, foreclosing their own chances of marketing them for profit. Moreover, those Nahua commoner women who could and did sell their wares—whether in the form of goods or sexual services—were looked down upon by the nobility. While some noblewomen apparently were trained as musicians and scribes, the sources make it clear that the vast majority in these occupations were male. Female priests may have been more numerous than the Spaniards described in their writings, but they usually served for a short time and normally did not hold the highest posts in the religious hierarchy. In the visual monuments of these centralized polities, moreover, real women are on the whole represented far less often than men, and when they do appear, they usually are either subordinate to a man or appear, themselves, as somewhat "manly." Mythohistorical women, as well, often play a secondary or supporting role in native artwork and narratives, and female deities apparently never served as patrons to developed states. Thus, while it is lamentable that we do not have access to women's own perception of their place in these social systems, and while it is clear that our male sources were biased, the preponderance of evidence available at this point suggests that Mesoamerican women, although they enjoyed greater freedom and choice than was previously thought, seldom shared a standing within their own culture that, in terms of economic and political power and social prestige, would have been equal to that of men.

Select Bibliography

Arvey, Margaret Campbell, "Women of Ill-repute in the Florentine Codex." In *The Role of Gender in Pre-Columbian Art and Architecture*, edited by Virginia E. Miller. Lanham, Maryland: University Press of America, 1988.

Berlo, Janet Catherine, "Icons and Ideologies at Teotihuacan: The Great Goddess Reconsidered." In *Art, Ideology, and the City of Teotihuacan*, edited by Janet Catherine Berlo. Washington, D.C.: Dumbarton Oaks, 1992.

Brown, Betty Ann, "Seen but Not Heard: Women in Aztec Ritual—the Sahagún Texts." In *Text and Image in Pre-Columbian Art: Essays on the Interrelationship of the Verbal and Visual Arts*, edited by Janet Catherine Berlo. Oxford: British Archaeological Review, 1983.

Cline, S. L., *Colonial Culhuacan, 1580–1600: A Social History of an Aztec Town*. Albuquerque: University of New Mexico Press, 1986.

Joyce, Rosemary A., "Women's Work: Images of Production and Reproduction in Pre-Hispanic Southern Central America." *Current Anthropology* 34:3 (1993).

Kellogg, Susan, "Aztec Women in Early Colonial Courts: Structure and Strategy in a Legal Context." In *Five Centuries of Law and Politics in Central Mexico*, edited by Ronald Spores and Ross Hassig. Nashville, Tennessee: Vanderbilt University Press, 1984.

Klein, Cecelia F., "Fighting with Femininity: Gender and War in Aztec Mexico." In *Gender Rhetorics: Postures of Dominance and Submission in Human History*, edited by Richard C. Trexler. Binghamton: Center for Medieval and Early Renaissance Study, State University of New York, 1994.

McCafferty, Sharisse D., and Geoffrey G. McCafferty, "Powerful Women and the Myth of Male Dominance in Aztec Society." *Archaeological Review from Cambridge* 7:1 (1988).

———, "Engendering Tomb 7 at Monte Albán." *Current Anthropology* 35:2 (1994).

Nash, June, "The Aztecs and the Ideology of Male Dominance." *Signs: Journal of Women in Culture and Society* 4:2 (1978).

Pohl, John M. D., *The Politics of Symbolism in the Mixtec Codices*. Nashville, Tennessee: Vanderbilt University Press, 1994.

Pohl, Mary DeLand, "Women, Animal Rearing, and Social Status: The Case of the Formative Period Maya of Central America." In *The Archaeology of Gender*, edited by Dale Walde and Noreen D. Willows. Calgary, Alberta: University of Calgary Archaeological Association, 1991.

Pollard, Helen Perlstein, "The Construction of Ideology in the Emergence of the Prehispanic Tarascan State." *Ancient Mesoamerica* 2 (1991).

Proskouriakoff, Tatiana, "Portraits of Women in Maya Art." In *Essays in Pre-Columbian Art and Archaeology*, edited by S. K. Lothrop, et al. Cambridge, Massachusetts: Harvard University Press, 1961.

Schaefer, Stacy B., "Becoming a Weaver: The Woman's Path in Huichol Culture." Ph.D. diss., University of California, Los Angeles, 1990.

Stone, Andrea, "Aspects of Impersonation in Classic Maya Art." In *Sixth Palenque Round Table, 1986*, edited by Virginia M. Fields. Norman: University of Oklahoma Press, 1991.

—CECELIA F. KLEIN

Women's Status and Occupation: Indian Women in New Spain

Native Americans traditionally are regarded as peoples without history. Historians themselves have helped to perpetuate this misperception, overlooking the unique Indian voice in Mesoamerica as it is known through a combination of oral literature, pictographic records, and ritual state oratorical presentation. Some of the accounts trace to the seventh millennium B.C. Indigenous women are very much a part of these ancient histories. Yet popular conceit has relegated them to perpetual conditions of "oppressed," "silent," "lost." Ongoing ethnohistorical and philological scholarship has done much to abrogate the prejudice against Indian females. Indeed, by all indications women can be credited with the vitality and persistence of key aspects of their cultures, whatever the native population or era. Moreover, such continuities span the centuries, well through the colonial period.

Among the numerous historical accounts about Indian Mexico, those recorded by the natives themselves are surely the most perceptive and informative regarding women's experiences. Best known are the few but precious pictorial manuscripts from the pre-Hispanic and early colonial eras, some of which were analyzed by Indian intellectuals and transliterated to indigenous-language alphabetic script. In many instances oral histories and interviews with female and male informants greatly facilitated their interpretations of past events and served to elaborate the subject matter of the manuscripts considerably. It is these native annals that furnish some of the richest information about women during ancient times as well as the period contemporaneous with their production.

The extant pictorial images on paper, bark, and animal skin are most typically ritual-calendric, historic-genealogical, or civil in content. Few have been studied from a gender-specific perspective, yet the graphics vividly reveal the ubiquitous presence of women—as deities, dynastic figures, even interpreters, as well as in their more quotidian roles as wives, mothers, sisters, and daughters.

Of course, equally important are the archaeological stores of stone and ceramic works found all over Mexico, which complement and corroborate the written histories. Again, the full gamut of women's experiences are depicted, from portraiture to village scenes to rulership accounts and hieroglyphs on stone stelae. After association with the Spaniards, indigenous literacy was reflected in a variety of genres that took on a life of their own and contain information about Indian women in a colonial milieu. Examples of such native- and Spanish-language sources are personal testaments, bills of sale and other business transactions, censuses, letters, parish accounts, and court and city council records. Additionally, Spanish conquerors' chronicles, reports and letters by religious, and the plethora of legal and political records from across New Spain document the roles that Indian women played in their societies.

The sources are in greatest abundance for central, south-central, and southeastern New Spain, the areas of the densest populations, which also, not so coincidentally, at one time or another had indigenous traditions of record keeping. In more peripheral regions, information about Indians in general is less abundant, and specifics about women far more difficult to recover. Nonetheless, what is extant regarding their experiences is no less remarkable. What is most evident is that Indian women, whatever the region or ethnic population, cannot be idealized or stereotyped, for their societies were neither static nor were they necessarily changed by virtue of contact with Europeans.

The native populations of North America are known to have a long tradition of accommodation to a range of changing circumstances. Thus, indigenous women's and men's experiences can be understood best with a processual approach to the subject, that is, that these are contemporaneous and parallel histories of peoples in the Americas and from Spain converging at different levels and at different times with varying outcomes.

Yet for all the information about Indians, not one source contains the autograph of a woman. Literacy in itself for native women, if and when it was practiced during the colonial period, can be described as a sub-rosa endeavor at best. In fact, other than Malintzin (doña Marina), Fernando (Hernán) Cortés's interpreter, little is known about the lives of individual women. Hence, women as personalities, per se, are seldom, if at all, found in the historical record (and the same might be said about Indian men). Rather, women are known in the context of their societies, and not unexpectedly, their contributions in the domestic sphere are the most apparent. The importance of the indigenous household in early Mexico cannot be overstated, for the home was the universe in microcosm; as society, as polity, as cosmos—the nucleus of each tribe or ethnic state.

And it is here in the home, whether with a family construct in the form of the smallest unit conceivable or one with the most extended and elaborate of structures, that women were held most accountable for conservation of their family's, or as it were, their community's, way of life. Ideally, real power for women came in the meticulous attention to their gendered assignments, which symbolically transcended the commonplace and ordered their world at large. It was for the household that women perfected both subtle and overt techniques of resistance, adapting what was new, useful, or inevitable, while retaining fundamental cultural practices. Only in recent times has women's resiliency come to be fully appreciated as a critical factor in the continuity and the integrity of the indigenous community.

During the pre-Hispanic period there is evidence that women participated in the production of ancient pictorial texts, a practice that did not continue after the arrival of the Spaniards. But as co-progenitors of their histories, they were thus active participants in influencing the direction those histories would take. As elders and sages, the Nahuas of central Mexico referred to their historians as *totahuan tonanhuan* (our fathers our mothers). These individuals were the repositories of wisdom, values, and experience, and together they were essential to each generation's understanding of the past, present, and future. Typically ethnocentric, female and male elders imparted what was important to know and remember about the social and political particulars of their state or group.

Such micropatriotism catalyzed a common identity for Indian women and men, and issues of individualism and gender not uncommonly were subordinate to pride of patria. Indeed, while class and rank did differentiate individuals within a polity (and there were both male and female specialists, with offices and titles), such features of distinction were critical to the structure and operation of the indigenous corporation, serving to enhance rather than compromise it. Moreover, female and male roles within each group were traditionally complementary, with gendered tasks and assignments considered separate but equal. Women and men had gender-patterned names and wore clothing appropriate to their sex. There was, of course, intersection of social and economic activities, with female-male relations best described as reciprocal.

Gender parallelism among indigenous peoples, however, by no means devolves to arbitrary categories, for some roles were symbolic, others very practical. In Mesoamerica, for example, at birth females and males received gendered weapons; that is, tool kits symbolic of what would be necessary for each child's life experiences (boys were given implements for war; girls received weaving swords and brooms). As children and then as adults, their roles remained distinct but complementary as males and females alike waged war in equivalent spheres.

In all regions, to some degree, women and men shared or divided tasks of food acquisition or production; the manufacture of textiles and other goods for tribute, sale, or exchange; religious obligations; and household-family-related chores. Polygyny, marriage, and divorce practices were strictly regulated among some groups, while others, especially in regions distant from population centers, had less formal arrangements, where situations of incompatibility were resolved by simply moving on to another partner.

Not uncommonly, Indian women as brides played critical roles in establishing and securing political and economic alliances. And their own female descent practices along with their rank as primary or secondary wives strongly influenced the rulership and marriage potential of their offspring.

What is known generally of life cycle concepts reiterates female gendered activities as participatory in world creation; as both benevolent and vengeful deities; as priestesses, teachers, *curanderas* (traditional healers), midwives, and concubines; and most particularly as wives and mothers eternally charged with the careful execution of household duties considered so profound that in large part they served to maintain the equilibrium of the universe. Their power was such that they were associated with *cihuatlampa* ("toward the place of women," where it is cold and dark, i.e., death), "the West" in some cosmic schemata.

During the colonial era, with paternalism and patriarchy institutionalized by means of Spanish politics and religion, gender complementarity was replaced by male authoritarianism, even in the indigenous home. Catholic Church policy weighed heavily on native women, and while the law, at least for a time, provided avenues for both agency and conservatism, females eventually lost their place and influence in certain social and economic spheres.

The church with its ambivalent attitudes toward women—which viewed women as the source of all evil but also primary vehicles for the inculcation of Christianity and Hispanic values in the home—further compromised their options for social mobility by limiting most educational opportunities. Early in the sixteenth century, Indian girls were encouraged to attend primary schools for about a decade. For reasons that are not clear, this program soon was abandoned. Perhaps it was to ensure that females kept to their domestic duties, for efforts at education for young girls thereafter were on an informal basis. Nor was there a secondary school for Indian girls for more than two centuries, until 1753 when the Jesuits opened the Colegio de Indias Doncellas de Nuestra Señora de Guadalupe in Mexico City. Moreover, little is known about this short-lived operation, for there are no extant rosters of students, nor do we know of their careers. It is likely that the expulsion of the Society of Jesus in 1767 was cause enough for closing the Colegio.

Shortly before, in 1724, the only convent in New Spain for indigenous women, Corpus Christi, was established in Mexico City. It is worth noting that even at this late date the principal criterion for admission was *limpieza de sangre* (purity of blood), which kept the convent exclusively for Indians, much to the consternation of their criollo (European-descended) sisters. The girls and women taking the veil at Corpus Christi were daughters of Indian nobility, whose wealth and prestige afforded the opportunity for these women to dedicate themselves to lives of piety and charity. Moreover, in addition to public recognition of their status as elite, there was even more to be gained by entering the cloisters. At Corpus Christi, at least, Indian females were educated, for their literacy and knowledge of Latin becomes apparent in their record books. The names of a few Indian nuns survive, but the saints' biographies and those of one another, the theater pieces, the music scores, and perhaps the poetry and essays that likely were produced, remain anonymous.

In mission regions, like northern New Spain, the combination of congregation, Christian sacraments (especially monogamous marriage), labor *repartimientos* (labor drafts), and new modes of subsistence all but eliminated traditional roles for women. But here, too, resistance as a response to Spanish hegemony was realized in cultural conservatism. The household especially continued to be central to women's activities. But, overall, indigenous women were sorely restricted under mission regimes, and their activities were seldom if at all noted by the priests in their reports. Rather, it was some untoward manifestation that more typically caught the priests' or local magistrates' attention. In the instances that are documented, the circumstances were such that the domestic situation was in jeopardy, and women acted out, either rebelling physically or resorting to less violent, politically sanctioned methods to try to secure their domains.

Indians in most areas of New Spain were notoriously litigious, and women did not hesitate to use the Spanish legal system to protect themselves and their families. Most telling are their last wills and testaments, the lawsuits that they brought to the courts, and Inquisition and other criminal records. Even in these documents, however, while the names of the women appear and much is often revealed about the immediate situation, with Indian females acting as both litigants and witnesses, they inevitably signed themselves with a cross, not a rubric or a full signature—graphic evidence of at least one aspect of indigenous women's position in the colonial social order.

Another example of native women's resistance was in their use of Catholicism. While doubtless many did become pious devotees, there was nevertheless considerable simulation of Christian ritual as overlay to traditional beliefs and practices. As longtime spiritual mediators—priestesses, midwives, *curanderas,* and death mourners—it was not uncommon for women (or men) to conduct rituals to intercede with deities—ancient, Christian, or a combination of both—on the behalf of an individual or the community, especially during periods of great duress. The records show that nearly as many women as men participated in the ancient "idolatrous" rituals, and that both female and male deities were invoked in the ceremonies. Apparently such rituals were a chronic problem according to religious accounts, and the church encouraged local priests to collect information about the Indians' sacred incantations and ceremonies, not only to punish the perpetrators but also, ironically, to incorporate some of the style and content into the sermons and ecclesiastical treatises that the clergy produced specifically to evangelize their indigenous congregations.

Even in the later years of colonialism, the Spaniards' wants and needs for indigenous-produced goods and services did not diminish, and on numerous occasions their exactions became unbearable. The entire household suffered under these burdens, and women and men did whatever was in their power to alleviate the situation. A classic response was to prevail upon local deities for assistance, and women took advantage of their familiar roles as spiritual brokers to rally forces for the community's survival. In southern New Spain, in Chiapas in 1712, a young girl's vision of a visitation by the Virgin Mary resulted in the construction of a shrine and the development of a popular cult that was contemporaneous with a period of great hardship for several Maya communities. Clerical and civil authorities tried to suppress the natives' participation, which only served to provoke preaching at the shrine on the part of the Virgin through the voice of the girl. Ultimately, official reprisals precipitated a major uprising, bringing death and destruction to Indians and Spaniards alike.

Contrary to general understanding, such gendered activity in both public and private spheres was often more the rule than the exception, even during the colonial era. The "household" in a variety of situations easily encompassed women's economic, religious, and even occasionally political activities. Yet much is to be learned about economic entrepreneurship on the part of indigenous women, whether as pulque vendors, innkeepers, or marketers of agricultural products and crafts, to say nothing of their labor in domestic service and in textile and tobacco factories.

Moreover, for all the church's restrictive policies toward Indian women, it was also their salvation, literally. Both urban and rural women could and did go to church. Mass could be a brief respite from domestic chores, and church festivities were grand occasions for family functions and community gatherings. Essentially a church-affiliated lay organization, the confraternity, or *cofradía,* was an especially attractive religious institution, and one that the Indians embraced enthusiastically. *Cofradías* were both sacred and social corporate institutions allowing the natives to reconstitute some fundamentals of indigenous sociopolitical structures and practices as religious enterprises. The *cofradía* could serve as a household writ large, through the provision of food, clothing, shelter, medicine, and even mourning and preparation for burials, most of which was women's work anyway. Women and men were titled and held ranked offices, quite as things were for at least the nobility in the pre-Hispanic era.

In one very interesting *cofradía* officer membership register that covers much of the eighteenth century (1700–67), hundreds of members with their offices are listed, and most often women outnumber men. Assignments were gendered, and women's activities, along with their church duties, included overseeing the health and welfare of their constituents in local neighborhoods as well as in distant towns. Even young native girls *(doncellas, ichpochtin)* were titled. As *tlachpanque* (sweepers), they were responsible for the maintenance of three distinct areas within the church's chapel, in a sense serving as latter-day Aztec priestesses. They also were charged with enlisting the participation of other girls in their communities.

Obviously, indigenous females moved into, out of, and across a range of culture zones. Challenged or even thwarted in certain colonial spheres, like the courts or elementary education, they found or co-opted other institutions or systems that could be fashioned to suit their purposes. Much about indigenous culture was changed by this time, but there were also quite extraordinary continuities.

In terms of physical and cultural space, for administrative purposes the Spanish government in the mid–sixteenth century divided its American colonies into two *repúblicas* (republics), one for the Indians, one for the Spaniards (and all the groups associated with them). Additionally, the Indians were to live in delineated areas apart from the Spaniards. Such policies were, of course, as unpracticable as the gendered barriers for indigenous populations prescribed by Hispanic institutions. By necessity Spaniards and Indians crossed in and out of and shared their respective territories. There is no denying the prevalence of patriarchal structures in New Spain, yet the evidence indicates that gender-connected complementarity in myriad forms did manifest itself in colonial Indian communities even within that framework.

Colonial native women, obviously, had much to do with maintaining the continuity of those corporations by keeping the traditions of the household integral to what was required for the community as a whole. However, no statues of Indian women commemorating their contributions over the centuries have been erected on Mexico City's boulevards. Even proponents of the Mexican Revolution who exemplified Mexico's Indian populations as a political *cause célèbre* failed to see gender as critical to that venerable historical moment. There has been no apotheosis of Mexico's founding mothers. Even Malintzin (doña Marina), the child-woman interpreter-mistress of Cortés and surely the most famous of all of Mexico's Indians, has been vilified rather than celebrated for her linguistic skills, poise, and ability to finesse encounters between numerous groups of Indians and the Spaniards in circumstances that will never be fully understood. Rather, today she is known as la Malinche, Mexico's ideological Eve (La Chingada). Yet Malinche, in a word, is emblematic of Indian women and a complex of tradition and resistance attributes: alliance, accommodation, survival.

Select Bibliography

Berdan, Frances F., and Patricia Rieff Anawalt, editors, *The Codex Mendoza.* 4 vols., Berkeley: University of California Press, 1992.

Carrasco, Pedro, "Royal Marriages in Ancient Mexico." In *Explorations in Ethnohistory: Indians of Central America in the Sixteenth Century,* edited by H. R. Harvey and Hanns J. Prem. Albuquerque: University of New Mexico Press, 1984.

Kellogg, Susan, *Law and the Transformation of Aztec Culture 1500–1700.* Norman: University of Oklahoma Press, 1995.

Sahagún, Bernardino de, *Florentine Codex: A General History of the Things of New Spain,* translated by Arthur J. O. Anderson and Charles E. Dibble. 14 vols., Santa Fe, New Mexico: School of American Research, and Salt Lake City: University of Utah Press, 1950–82.

Schroeder, Susan, "The Noblewomen of Chalco." *Estudios de Cultural Náhuatl* 22 (1992).

_____, Stephanie Wood, and Robert Haskett, editors, *Indian Women of Early Mexico: Identity, Ethnicity, and Gender Complementarity.* Norman: University of Oklahoma Press, 1997.

—SUSAN SCHROEDER

Women's Status and Occupation: Spanish Women in New Spain

In colonial Mexico the status and occupations of women were determined by a number of factors. Women were influenced by the ideals presented to them by moralists through prescriptive literature and by clerics through sermons, pastorals, edicts, and the confessional. These ideas, which pervaded society, affected all classes, but only members of the elite could really hope to live up to these canons. Prevailing ideas of racial and social rankings also formed boundaries as to acceptable occupations, associations, and conduct. The law also provided another framework for the rights and protections afforded to women and also defined the various states within which they existed: virgin, wives, nuns, and widows. Yet, these ideals and formal limitations should not be taken as a reality; often they were honored more in the breach.

As Spanish women began to settle in Mexico, they brought with them cultural baggage that can be gauged most easily by an examination of the prescriptive literature of clerics. Many guides explained the proper conduct for women as they passed through the various stages of life and *estados* (states). It was clear to these moralists that ideally women fell into one of four states: *doncella* (maiden), wife, widow, or nun. Respectable conduct was defined for each *estado*. These guides urged women to remain as much as possible behind the walls of their homes and to occupy themselves between the management of their households and prayer. Women were responsible for the good management of the domestic economy; they were responsible for the cleanliness of home, the good repair and laundering of clothes, the preparation of food, and finally, the good morals of all who lived within its walls. Wealthy women who could employ servants to undertake most of this work were urged to supervise it closely and to occupy their time with prayer and spinning. It was acceptable for women to leave the house to hear mass or to work in charitable institutions. Women derived status from their independence from paid employment, for this allowed them to remain aloof from the disruptive world outside their homes. Whether women were behind the walls of their homes or outside, they were expected to behave with decorum. The values of modesty and demureness were to characterize their conduct. As such, they had to dress according to standards of moderation, they had to avoid communications with men, and they had to walk with tranquility and poise. These norms of behavior were possible only for women of considerable financial means who could depend on servants to accomplish the tasks that would take them onto the streets. Yet, it should not be assumed that even elite women obeyed these prescriptions rigidly. Elite women socialized, attending dances, the theater, and many other kinds of diversions. Women of lesser means were forced out-of-doors to run errands or to earn a living.

In the eighteenth century, enlightened thinkers challenged some of the notions that underlay this conception of women. The Benedictine monk Benito Feijóo claimed in *A Defense of Women,* that the intellectual capacity of women was equal to men's, but he still defended their submission to men. The Count of Campomanes, adviser to the king, saw a greater participation by women in the economy as a boon to productivity. These ideas led to some changes in legislation, notably the opening of more types of work for women in New Spain. King Carlos III altered the restrictions on certain guilds and opened trades that were seen as compatible with women's "more gentle nature."

Women also were affected by the hierarchical notions of the society in which they lived. Spanish women enjoyed the benefit of belonging to the group conquerors, and thus, in terms of race and ethnicity, they had some innate advantages over women of other groups. This ranking was manifested in notions of *limpieza de sangre* (purity of bloodlines) which transcended gender and the concept of honor. Yet, over the course of the colonial period, some women who classified themselves as Spanish lost status economically so that they lived among people of other races and to some extent married into those groups. Anxiety over such cross-racial unions was at the root of the 1776 Royal Pragmatic, which tried to limit exogamous marriages.

In the established colony, the status of women also was regulated by the law. Spanish women were governed by the legal codes in general but special provisions were geared to gender. Two principles guided the Spanish notions of proper laws in regards to women: restriction and protection. Women were assumed to be inherently inferior to men. For this reason, they were prohibited legally from many activities, especially when such occupations would take them into the public, and into particularly male preserves. Because of such concerns, women were prohibited from holding public offices and could not enter such professions as the law. They also were not allowed to serve as a witness for the signing of wills.

These laws were derived from the codes established centuries before in the Iberian Peninsula. For women in New Spain, the Siete Partidas, a thirteenth-century code compiled during the reign of King

Alfonso el Sabio, and the Leyes de Toro of 1505 were the most influential of these codes. While these statutes formed the basis for legal rights and decisions at the beginning of the colonial process, other decrees modified or redefined the rights and protections of women. For example, in the sixteenth century, the Spanish Crown became concerned for the plight of women left behind in Spain as their husbands settled in Mexico. Over the course of the century, numerous decrees addressed this problem and tried to ensure the passage of such wives to New Spain. Canon law also regulated the rights of women, particularly in relation to marriage and their entry into convents.

Throughout most of their lives, women were placed under the authority of a male figure. This began with the *patria potestas* (paternal authority) of their fathers. This right meant that young women needed permission for any legal transaction. Both young men and women were under the *patria potestas* of their fathers and only reached adulthood at the age of 25. Yet, after the age of majority, unmarried women remained under the jurisdiction of their fathers or guardians unless they were specifically emancipated. The bond could be revoked if any abuse was detected or when a woman married. At that time, a wife came under the authority of her husband, although the rights and obligations of a spouse were different from that of a father. A woman who did not marry usually remained under the nominal control of her eldest brother or a male relative. It was only as widows that women were able to enjoy their full and relatively unfettered civil capacities.

Although the law classified women as weak and thus limited their rights, it also provided protection as a compensation. Fathers were required to provide a dowry for their daughters unless they married someone of whom the father disapproved. The dowry remained the property of the wife throughout the marriage and was supposed to protect women financially throughout their years within a couple, and into widowhood. On their wedding day, men usually gave their wives a gift called the *arras,* and which became the wife's property and remained so even if her husband went bankrupt. The law also mandated that legitimate daughters and widows could not be disinherited. Each would receive a prescribed share of their parent's or their spouse's estate. Widows usually were left half of the property of the couple and, if no will existed, the widow inherited everything as long as no other heirs could make a claim. In theory, these laws ensured the financial stability of women throughout their lives. Yet, in practice, many fathers were not able to provide sufficient dowries, and since husbands were allowed to manage their wives' dowries, at times they squandered their spouses' nest eggs.

The sexual vulnerability of women also was acknowledged within the law. Provisions allowed for the enforcement of marriage promises or the punishment of men who refused to honor their engagements. Men who insulted a woman's reputation by jibes in the streets or gossip could be sued and forced to provide financial compensation. Rape was conceived as an insult to the honor of a family and male relatives were empowered to kill the rapist on the spot. The law recognized this as self-defense; in other words, the man killed to defend the family honor. In practice, men often provided a sum of money when they were found guilty of raping a virgin, or they offered to marry their victim. This arrangement was deemed to compensate for the harm to the victim's chances of marriage because of her loss of virginity.

These protections, however, only were afforded to "decent" women and "honest" wives. Women of loose morals and ones who went even further, such as prostitutes, lost the right to such protections. For example, a prostitute was considered "unrapeable." Nor could a prostitute ask for child support. Wives whose conduct breached the norms of purity, modesty, and devotion could lose the right to their dowries. Widows who did not follow the norms by a sober and dignified isolation could lose the guardianship of their children and even the right to their estates. A woman who flaunted the codes of conduct by dressing in a manner considered indecent could not then ask for the courts to punish an individual who insulted her honor.

Despite the assumed inherent inferiority of women within Spanish law, they were considered competent in many fields. Women administered their own legal affairs. As property owners, they bought, sold, rented, inherited, and bequeathed any type of property. They borrowed and lent capital, they could administer estates and enter into business partnerships. They could initiate lawsuits and appear as witnesses in court. Because of the concern to protect women, the law provided for the cancellation of contracts when they harmed a woman's economic security. Yet, the scholar Silvia Arrom argues that these protections were regularly waived by women, and therefore did not really benefit them.

In the same vein, women were held accountable for proper sexual behavior. If they infringed accepted norms of conduct, or even worse, the law, they could not recur to an image of a weak and irresponsible woman. They were punished for engaging in prostitution, for causing an abortion or infanticide, for extra-marital liaisons, for adultery, for incest, and for bigamy. Women frequently lived with men in informal unions. If they were denounced, they could be punished by a period of imprisonment in the local jail or a *recogimiento* (women's detention center).

All Spanish women were governed by these laws and affected by these attitudes. But, as wives, they were regulated by a further set of rules. In return for the financial sustenance and protection afforded by her spouse, a wife had to obey her spouse. Wives were obliged to live under the same roof as their husbands, and they lost control over their legal transactions, their property, their earnings, and even their domestic activities. Married women could own property, but their husbands controlled it. Similarly, the dowry and *arras* remained the woman's, but her husband could administer them and dispose of any earning from its profits. But property acquired during the marriage was considered to be part of the couple's community property. The only goods that a married woman owned and controlled were the *bienes parafernales*—the goods she brought into the marriage other than the dowry (for example, her jewels and clothes). The husband held exclusive authority over the couple's children. He was the guardian of their education, legal transactions, and property.

As wives who did not fulfill their side of the marital bargain could expect censure or even punishment, so husbands who did not support their families or abused them could be castigated; nevertheless, such a scenario was less likely. Canon law specified that wives were to be treated equally and fairly and not as servants. The Catholic Church frowned upon physical mistreatment by husbands, yet the civil law was harsher to wives, and society, in general, condoned a certain amount of physical abuse by husbands and fathers. When women faced such a situation, they often appealed to their families, who at times provided money and food, and also frequently took their children and grandchildren back into their homes. Wives could also appeal to their priests or to the civil officials. They asked these authority figures to intervene to ensure their physical well-being and to chide their spouses into proper conduct. Finally, when such strategies were not effective and when the abuse was long-standing, some wives applied for an ecclesiastical divorce. This allowed husband and wife to live separately, although it did not dissolve the bond of the marriage vows. Wives often went to live in a convent, and their husbands were obliged to provide a pension for their maintenance.

Despite all these legal limitations, women were active in the economy. Notarial records show that they regularly bought and sold property, founded chantries, disposed of their slaves by selling or freeing them, and took part in lawsuits. As widows, many women continued to run the businesses that they inherited from their spouses. Women are recorded as the owners of sugar mills, mines, cattle ranches, textile workshops, wine shops, wax factories, and cigar factories. In the city, women often were the proprietors of houses, plots of land, and stores. For respectable women, many jobs were not suitable, and if they did not own property, their choices were limited. Those who owned slaves often lived off the earnings of these men or women. Some women worked as *amigas,* teachers of very young children. By the mid–eighteenth century, it became more common for women to work in silk spinning or in candle or cigar factories. Many female occupations are no doubt invisible, but the 1753 census indicates that 27.3 percent of the female population of Mexico city worked in the formal economy, and the 1811 census reveals that this percentage had fallen only slightly to 26.8 percent. In both cases, these figures mean that women represented about one-third of the labor force; in fact, these numbers probably underestimate the proportion of women working outside the home. Within this group of working women, Spanish individuals were the largest group in the 1811 census although probably many of the native women who came into town to sell goods daily and who worked as domestics were not counted, and so these figures should not be relied upon too closely. Nevertheless, they do indicate a strong presence of Spanish women in the workforce.

By the end of the colonial period, women's participation in the workforce had become more diversified. They began to enter into trades that once had been closed to them because of the regulations of guilds. Yet, this challenge to the gender separation of work was still in its infancy. For example, although women dominated the food preparation and sale industry, only men could be bakers. Women tended to prepare raw materials for their elaboration by male guild members. Middle-class women often had owned and operated shops, tobacco *estancos* (government licensed tobacconists), illegal taverns, restaurants, dressmakers' shops, cloth and silk stores, and shawl shops. If these were profitable, the female owner could hand over the management to a second party and retire to her home, with its much-vaunted isolation of decorum. Women often were forced by their circumstances—such as widowhood or an impecunious husband—to work outside the home, but those of the middle or upper classes shunned the stigma that this implied. Very few respectable jobs existed for women, but at the end of the eighteenth century, the inauguration of welfare institutions created some spaces. Women were hired in the Foundling Home, the Poor House, and municipal hospitals to supervise the female sections or to teach the female inmates. The creation of the Royal Tobacco Factory in 1769 was another change that affected women particularly. Traditionally, cigars were rolled in an artisanal fashion in homes, but the new system regrouped all these women under one roof and reorganized the labor along more industrial lines. Women accounted for one-third of the people affected by this change, and some found it impossible to move into the factory either because of their domestic obligations or as in the case of Spanish women, the work outside their homes was incompatible with their concern for their reputations. Traditionally, the literature has portrayed women as working because of personal tragedies. Silvia Arrom has shown that it was common for married women to work and also that the image of the male breadwinner was frequently a mirage. Women worked not because they were bereft as widows or orphans, but for many reasons. They did not necessarily depend upon a spouse, and their likelihood to enter into the workforce depended to a great extent upon their class background.

Select Bibliography

Arrom, Silvia M., *The Women of Mexico City, 1790–1857*. Stanford, California: Stanford University Press, 1985.

Boyer, Richard, "Women, *La Mala Vida*, and the Politics of Marriage." In *Sexuality and Marriage in Colonial Latin America*, edited by Asunción Lavrin. Lincoln: University of Nebraska Press, 1989.

Gutiérrez, Ramón A., *When Jesus Came, the Corn Mothers Went Away: Marriage, Sexuality, and Power in New Mexico, 1500–1846*. Stanford, California: Stanford University Press, 1991.

Lavrin, Asunción, "In Search of the Colonial Woman in Mexico: The Seventeenth and Eighteenth Centuries." In *Latin American Women: Historical Perspectives*. Westport, Connecticut: Greenwood, 1978.

Seed, Patricia, *To Love, Honor and Obey in Colonial Mexico; Conflicts over Marriage Choice, 1574–1821*. Stanford, California: Stanford University Press, 1988.

— SONYA LIPSETT-RIVERA

Women's Status and Occupation: 1821–1910

For most men and women in nineteenth-century Mexico, it was very clear that "a woman's place was in the home." Nonetheless, in Mexico City in 1811, women made up roughly one-third of the labor force, and by 1895, when the first national census was taken, women comprised 17.2 percent of the entire national workforce. The state of San Luis Potosí reported the largest number of working women, and Querétaro the largest proportion. In Mexico City, the average held. Even when women were not marginal to the world of paid work, producers of goods for the marketplace, or providers of services, traditional ideas about women and the home persisted.

According to the census of 1895, at least 16.3 percent of the female population could not be classified as *damas* (ladies or gentlewomen). Women who worked outside of the home, manufactured articles at home, or managed a small shop attached to the home could not be considered *damas;* as class and race tended to determine women's occupations, they also determined social status. Nonetheless, nineteenth-century Mexico was very far from being culturally homogeneous, and many women did not even aspire to be *damas*.

The Work of Poor Women

The inferiority of women in Mexican law can be traced back at least to the *siete partidas* of thirteenth-century Spain. Even when the old laws formally were repealed in 1871, important informal restrictions still were placed on women's economic and political activities. Women were assigned separate shifts and work areas in factories, for example, even if there were no laws mandating segregation. Similarly, there were no laws prohibiting women from heading guilds and unions or requiring that they be paid less money, but for reasons of "decorum" they were excluded from positions of leadership in labor organizations, and their wages were considered "complementary" to men's earnings. Women were paid only the lowest wages permitted by law, and children and prisoners were paid even less.

Cigar workers, textile workers, and seamstresses in clothing manufacture made up the most important work sectors for women in nineteenth-century Mexico, but they were not the only ones. According to the 1895 census, there were many other occupations for women, the majority of an artisanal nature. In shops and small establishments, often family-owned, women not only produced goods but also sold them on the street or in public markets (where they traditionally were purchased by female consumers). The specific tasks varied according to the economic activities of each region, but they tended to include match and matchbox makers; typesetters, book binders, and compositors in the presses; hatmakers, tie makers, fashion designers, embroiderers, corset markers, and glove makers in clothing manufacture; shoemakers; saddlers and trimmers; bakers and pastry cooks; makers of tortillas, *atol* (a beverage made from maize flour), and *mole* (a sauce that is a staple in many Mexican regional cuisines); confectioners and butchers in food preparation; rope makers, who wove agave fibers to make rope and cord; mat makers, sack makers, potters, and chandlers.

Factory labor had been open to women since the first factories came on line, particularly after guild barriers were eliminated in the late eighteenth century. In 1775 Pedro Rodríguez, count of Campomanes and a counselor to King Carlos III, proposed the elimination of guild barriers to encourage women in the "sedentary arts" and vocational education. Rodríguez's proposal was not a concession to feminism, however, but an attempt to bolster Spain's aging workforce. He saw poor women as a source of cheap labor, and he imagined them working in the production of exports (lace, fans, tapestries, embroideries) and keeping shops, an extension of traditionally feminine activities. He argued this would free men to dedicate themselves to more complex and "patriotic" tasks.

In 1784 guild restrictions against women were lifted in Spain. In 1790, widows of guild members in New Spain were authorized to continue working in their late husbands' shops, even if they remarried, and in 1792 the administrator of Guanajuato abolished all unions in his jurisdiction. The crowning moment came in 1799, when the prohibition against women joining guilds was lifted throughout New Spain. This final abrogation of guild restrictions was the result of the struggle of a Mexico City widow, doña Josefa de Celis, whom the embroiderers' guild had barred from selling the shoes she had designed. The new regulations stipulated that women could

> occupy any position in keeping with decorum and their strength within the Ordinances of the Guilds or governmental restrictions that had voted to the contrary and that under no circumstances should the guild or any person impede the education of women and young girls or their employment in tasks appropriate to their sex, nor to bar them from selling or having sold for them products they had manufactured.

The first factories to open in New Spain were cigar factories, and it was there that the first female employees were hired. The First Royal Cigarette and Cigar Factory, founded in Mexico City in 1768, was a monopoly of the Spanish Crown, and later that year the Crown established other factories in the cities of Oaxaca, Puebla, and Veracruz; factories were established in 1776 in Orizaba, two years later in Guadalajara, and in 1779 in Querétaro. That year, the Spanish Crown's "factories" employed a total of 17,000 men and women. By 1846 the government workshops employed 30,000. For the poor Spanish women who had previously worked in cottage industries, the opening of the workshops presented dangers. For them, more than for the others, having to leave home to go to a factory that employed the indigenous and mestizo "common people" was equivalent to compromising their reputation or risking a lower status. The women who lived through this change were also subjected to long work days of 12 or more hours, which wrought havoc with their daily lives and their ability to perform household chores. But the experience of working in large groups, even though it was only manual labor performed individually, opened a door to empowerment, the construction of a combative work culture, and collective struggle.

A significant social distance separated other workers in that turbulent century from domestic servants. In public testimony in *El Monitor Republicano* on May 3, 1846, 26 workers in the Tobacco Factory in Mexico City explained their position in the face of layoffs owing to the introduction of automation to replace the cigar makers. Speaking on behalf of the 6,000 families that depended on the factory, they addressed the president of Mexico and asked him to halt the modernization:

> If in the current state of affairs in our society it is true that work is becoming scarce for men, women are being reduced to an even more disgraceful situation. . . . Everything is calculated according a family supported by the [male] head of the family, but when he is lacking, when a mother is responsible for the welfare and education of her children, or because the daughters or sisters must support themselves, in today's state of affairs and due industrial organization, they have no recourse, no means to support themselves, aside from domestic service, so repugnant and humiliating, for the manual tasks they perform, and they find work even scarcer and the pay more pitiful. This is the cause of the astonishing poverty that a multitude of families

is subjected to. Up until now, the cigar factory was an asylum for these unfortunates and a solution to their deplorable state of poverty. The work is not varied nor lucrative, nor up to health standards, nor exempt from the hazards manual occupations are subject to; nevertheless, it is a source of independence and security otherwise not available to us.

Automation was delayed until 1882, but this was owing to foreign invasions and internal wars rather than to the efforts of the female cigar workers. Nevertheless, the appeal to the press to publicly defend their jobs was a brave and unusual action for women to take at that time. Had they been isolated, working at home, or in small shops, it would have been harder for them to gather the strength to raise their voices publicly.

The cigar makers and the textile workers were the most militant, but their battles were not always against the factory owners. Work was scarce for women, but it was far from being plentiful for men, and this was a source of many confrontations. In that century, so full of political, military, international, and regional crises, work was rarely stable, secure, or sufficient. The relative stability of the government of Porfirio Díaz (roughly 1876–1910, the so-called Pax Porfiriana) did little to improve the lives of workers. During the Díaz dictatorship, the plundering of land belonging to the indigenous communities intensified, and many unemployed and dispossessed men and women migrated to the textile factories of Veracruz, Puebla, and Querétaro or toward the more populated north, to the textile factories of Coahuila or Monterrey, which was becoming an industrial center. The railroads helped to move men and women who looked for work and who once had been rooted to their communities, and it also helped to spread the word about where work could be found.

Around 1874 a long period of struggles ensued for the embattled male cigar makers in the Bola Factory in Mexico City. They staged a strike to end the hiring of women, arguing that women were paid less and were more subservient to the boss's orders. They did not achieve their goal, but it was true that women earned less. Until 1900 a seamstress who worked 12 hours could hope to earn 30 to 40 centavos a day. Female textile workers earned 50 centavos a day, as opposed to men, who earned 80 pesos a day. The female cigar makers found themselves in the same circumstances, and by the end of the century, the work day had lengthened to 16 hours. For almost all, it consisted of piecework. The female cigar workers'

"victory" can be appreciated because of their many battles, not all successful, to reduce their workload; shorten the workday; curtail punishments, the docking of wages, and unjust firings; and forestall automation.

In 1877 the cigar makers of La Sultana, El Borrego, La Africana, Los Aztecas, El Negrito, and El Modelo in Mexico City unsuccessfully stuck in an effort to reduce their workload. In 1881 they stuck in El Moro Muza because a group of workers proposed to produce more in less time. In 1882 some workers in several towns in the state of Veracruz created la Sociedad de Ayuda Mutua La Caridad (The Charity Mutual Aid Society). In 1885 the workers in El Faro, Puebla, went on strike. In the last decade of the century, and until the Mexican Revolution, there was a series of strikes in several cities, and some became increasingly aggressive. The cigar workers appealed to the press, stuck posters on walls, and asked for solidarity from workers of both sexes in other industries. On more than one occasion, they stoned the factories. In 1894 during a strike in El Buen Tono in Mexico City, a worker's son died of starvation. One hundred women stoned the factory. They were jailed, but the Gran Círculo de Obreros Libres and the Sociedad Fraternal Militar, two national labor unions, bailed them out. The workers were fired but found refuge in a textile factory in Tlaxcala, which also was on strike.

The workers created ties of solidarity that went beyond the upheavals in the factories. Labor organization meant more than competition and confrontation: it also fostered bonding and mutual support. Between male and female workers, however, relationships remained ambiguous. Generally speaking, men looked down on women as inferior. They made less money, were assigned less technical tasks, and were the first to be fired in a crisis. In Mérida, Yucatán, in 1915, in the midst of the Mexican Revolution, the female cigar makers created the Sindicato de Obreras y Obreros de las Fabricas de Cigarros (Union of Men and Women Cigar Workers) and struck demanding better working conditions. What happened in this case illustrates the tension that always existed between workers of the opposite sex, for aside from taking the initiative to fight for and to create the union, women later helped men create their own union. The men objected to female leadership and insisted on creating an administrative structure for both sexes.

Despite their work and their struggles, women workers in the nineteenth century did not achieve equality in the workplace. Nor were they successful in getting their male coworkers to accept them as equals. In an effort to unify worker's organizations, in 1876 a Workers' Congress was held in Mexico City, and its program included a discussion on the working conditions of women. A very influential radical group led by Plotino Rhodakanaty, a Greek immigrant, tailor, and respected social activist, sent two women as delegates. The male workers did not accept the participation of the two "esteemed misses" in the congress. They knew they could not call them "ladies" because of their social status, but it amounted to the same thing, and their argument ran thus:

> As reason and conscience and decorum opposes women a place in public tasks, perhaps the Congress thinks we refuse their credentials without publicly acknowledging their merits. A women's place is in the home. The essential characteristics of man renders him capable of combat, while the natural properties of woman render her suitable to poetry, love, and to matters of the heart.

Clearly the factory was not a means of social ascent. But it did create two valuable opportunities for poor women: it kept them from sliding to an even lower status, and it was one of the few ways open to them to earn a living. By referring to providing them with "a source of independence," the cigar workers perhaps meant that this work allowed them to escape the confinement that was part of domestic service.

We can begin to trace the status of some of women's work in an article written in 1908 by Luis Lara Pardo, editor in chief of *El Imparcial*, an influential Mexican City newspaper close to the government of Porfirio Díaz. Lara Pardo criticized the inaccuracy of the health inspector's report on prostitution, which was legalized in Mexico City in 1867. According to the report, there were 10,937 prostitutes in Mexico City in 1904; 11,554 in 1905; and 9,742 in 1906. Lara felt that this number was scandalous—according to him, it meant that 50 out of 1,000 women in the capital were prostitutes. Lara also considered the statistic to be an understatement (in reality, many of the "prostitutes" were saleswomen or vendors and were looked upon as prostitutes because they were seen leaving their homes at daybreak on their way to work). He believed a female occupation equivalent to "secret prostitution" existed, in which prostitution resulted from "simple habit, and whose goal was not remuneration." He was referring to domestic service, which in the health report represented the common means of employment for women reported before prostitution. Lara Pardo's comments demonstrate the level of

status and moral value that the Porfirian authorities, the elite, the middle class, and to some extent other classes in general attributed to domestic help. In 1895 the census reported 190,413 women (and 82,887 men) employed in domestic service. The majority were women employed as servants, wet nurses, cooks, chambermaids, and in similar jobs. They were vulnerable to the sexual abuse of their employers, poorly paid, and worked long hours. Many were indigenous peasants separated from their families and their culture.

The limited opportunities for employment and education open to women, especially the poorest women, meant that domestic service was the most important source of paid work for nineteenth-century women. Domestic service was considered suitable work for women (indeed, domestic work was seen as feminizing men, and men who worked as servants were disenfranchised). It is true that many women worked in households where they were appreciated and well-treated, and in effect became family members, but prostitution and domestic service were the lowest rungs on the social scale in the nineteenth century.

Titles, Occupations, Professions

Teachers and midwives were the first women to have access to professional titles during the first part of the mid–nineteenth century. But in both cases, before the Pax Porfiriana, formal education was scarce or simply not available. The formal title of midwife seems to have been created by doctors in the Schools of medicine more as a means of control over births rather than to professionalize midwifery. In 1834 in Mérida, for example, one needed to know how to read, to have a attended a six-month birthing course, and taken an exam in the School of Medicine and Surgery. By 1845 it was ruled that midwives could obtain a certificate by taking an exam in the Schools of Medicine, without ever having taken the course. The only requirements were for the candidate to be from 18 to 30 years old and to pass a simple arithmetic test. After a while, novice midwives also were required to take two classes in obstetrics. Until 1858 in Mexico City several women asked for and received dispensation from age requirements and from the arithmetic test. In Yucatán it took until 1890 for the first woman to graduate, but by then the rules had changed, and the title was *comadrona* (another term for midwife). Three years of study were required in "the anatomy and physiology of the female pelvis and reproductive organs, a practical/theoretical treatise on the art of midwifery, and a written thesis. In Guanajuato, on the other hand, courses in obstetrics were offered in the School of Arts and Professions, founded in 1873. This school was attended by 154 women and 164 men, "properly separated," who also studied drawing, painting, music, bookkeeping, French, geography, carpentry, and goldsmithing.

The status of midwives was ambiguous. With a title, but more often without one, they were powerful and highly esteemed women in their indigenous villages and communities. They possessed a special and necessary skill, but the medical establishment held them in low esteem. Their popular acceptance, based on traditional knowledge, represented a challenge to the doctors' institutions and skills. They were proof that lack of a formal education and not knowing how to read were not obstacles for respect and a paid profession in the community.

For middle-class women, the most common occupation was elementary school teacher, and here status rose from the lower grades to the higher. From the beginning of colonial time and during the first decades following Independence, educational opportunities open to most women were in nearby schools or day nurseries called *amigas* (Friends) or *migas*. They taught the catechism, how to embroider and sew, sometimes to read, and perhaps to write; and the rudiments of arithmetic. This was not always the case, however, because the teachers in *amigas* could not always read and write themselves. In 1790 a woman applied to the Mexico City Hall for a license to open a *miga*. Her request was based not on skill but on need:

> Finding myself without means of support, I have no other recourse than to apply myself to the instruction and education of young girls. I am a sick, elderly woman with no other means of support except to earn a living by teaching the Christian doctrine, reading, and sewing to young girls. My chronically ill father is in my care, as are my older sisters, three other sisters, and since I am unable to support them, I must. . . .

Although a teacher in a *miga* could earn enough to be considered middle class, earning from 200 to 720 pesos a year until 1820 (depending on the level of her pupils), her social status was low. Owing to their low level of preparation, it was assumed that they were not of *sangre limpia* (clean blood)—that is to say, Spanish—but rather *mestizo* or of mixed caste. It was not considered proper for cultured middle-class men with good family relations to be teachers. Rich women had access to a good education in their own homes, with private teachers. They could themselves have been excellent teachers if the cultural barrier had not impeded it. The most educated teachers and those with the highest status during the first part of the nineteenth century were nuns and lay sisters, but in 1863 President Benito Juárez closed the religious orders.

Following Independence, education was reevaluated, first through official proclamation and later through the improvement of the educational preparation of both male and female teachers. Concerned about women's "intellectual inferiority," liberal and conservative thinkers debated the most effective way to "improve the moral condition of the populace and the education of its women." Following Mexico's defeat by the United States in 1848, many thinkers came to view the education of women as a national priority. In 1833 President Valentín Gómez Farías proposed a reform to make all education public and available to all classes throughout the country. Few changes took place before the defeat of Maximilian's Empire in 1867—the government was too busy attending to finances. There were important changes, however, particularly in civil society. In Guanajuato in 1842, the authorities announced that they had opened schools for both sexes in all cities, towns, and villages. What is especially interesting is that they sought additional funds to contract more teachers because there was "a noticeable surplus" of girls.

In the 1870s the picture changed with the opening of the Schools of Arts and Trades, and with more high schools and elementary schools. Between 1878 and 1907 the number of *escuelas normales* (teachers' colleges) increased from 12 to 26. Women's schools took the lead, increasing from 2 to 12; coeducational schools grew from 2 to 8, while men's schools decreased from 7 to 6. At the end of the Porfirian era, the increase in women teachers was evident. Education now was considered a worthy and dignified occupation and a more prestigious one for women. Male politicians issued many declarations that women teachers should be well paid for the "highly meritorious service" they provided, but women continued to be underpaid.

The Porfirian era brought structural changes with it, including new jobs. Opportunities opened for women to study for and become employed as telegraph or telephone operators, typists, stenographers, and shorthand writers in offices. Professions requiring advanced training were late in coming. In Mexico City in 1887, the first woman medical surgeon, Matilde P. Montayo, graduated from medical school, and in 1889 María Asunción Sandoval became the first lawyer. Although there was no explicit legal prohibition against women attending universities, other exclusionary and segregationist forces were at work. Women were not confident and felt that they were intruders in historically masculine spaces.

When a female student named Rosa Toro was called to the stage during the National School's awards ceremony in 1884 in Mexico City, a group of students mockingly chanted her last name (*toro* means bull in Spanish), and Rosa, "in tears, covered her face and refused to approach the stage." The incident was reported in the press, but an argument ensued as to the proper punishment for her classmates' rudeness. As late as 1907 in the School of Pharmacy annexed to the School of Medicine of San Luis Potosí, some "young ladies" requested to be put in a separate class from the men because they claimed that they "felt inhibited."

Middle-class or upper-class women were viewed even more stereotypically. Women who stayed home were seen in poetic terms, while women who went to work were seen as degraded. Elementary school teachers feminized the profession by associating it with maternalism and imbuing it with the traditionally female sense of mission and noble sacrifice. Significantly, women teachers did not rise to fight for improved working conditions as the factory workers had done. It was the poor women who more decisively confronted the pressure and aggression, who took to the streets and got on the trains to look for jobs, to work, to sell their wares, and to fight.

As far as we know—and we still know very little—for nineteenth-century women, home (and its imaginary extensions such as the primary school) continued to be their proper place. From this perspective it is difficult to say when that century drew to a close; perhaps it still is not over. In 1916 the Feminist Congress of Yucatán was held at the initiative of state governor General Salvador Alvarado. Although the congress was the first in the nation organized by and for women, the suitability of educational equality among men and women was still open to discussion. The conclusion was in the affirmative and was reached by majority. But there were some who sided with the teacher who believed, "Teachers do not get married. It is a fact that educated women seldom marry, and they need a lot of luck. That is why I believe they should be educated even more."

The 1916 Feminist Congress can be considered he last symbolic act for nineteenth-century women, their occupations, and their views about social status. Many participants claimed to support the "equality of the sexes," since women not only obeyed laws but also had the right to make them—to vote

and to be elected was the expression of a new era. Nonetheless, the majority were afraid and haunted by old ghosts, claiming that the struggle for equality had nothing to do with them. The equality of the sexes, they insisted, was an issue belonging to "tomorrow's woman."

See also Industrial Labor; Visual Arts: Eighteenth- and Nineteenth-Century Academic Art

Select Bibliography

Arrom, Silvia Marina, *The Women of Mexico City, 1790–1857*. Stanford, California: Stanford University Press, 1985.

Coatsworth, John, *Growth against Development: The Economic Impact of Railroads on Porfirian Mexico*. DeKalb: Northern Illinois University Press, 1981.

Fowler Salamini, Heather, and Mary Kay Vaughan, editors, *Women of the Mexican Countryside, 1850–1990*. Tuscon and London: University of Arizona Press, 1994.

—ALEJANDRA GARCÍA QUINTANILLA

Women's Status and Occupation: 1910–96

Women's presence within diverse economic areas throughout the twentieth century in Mexico shows a drastically descending curve from 1910 to 1930 and a spectacular increase after 1940. These facts coincide with the country's major periods of overall growth and development.

1910–40: The Armed Struggle and the Institutionalization of Power

In 1910 the percentage of women in the total economically active population was 15.6 percent, with 65.5 percent concentrated in the farming sector, 20.7 percent in the industrial sector, and 13.8 percent taking up the remaining third. However, the distribution of women within the labor market was very particular. A total of 54.8 percent of the female labor force was concentrated in manufacturing (mostly in tobacco and textile factories) and 37.8 percent in services (among which 57 percent were occupied in domestic work, which in this period tended to have a more female aspect). These statistics, of course, conceal and underestimate the work undertaken by women in the farming sector. Since such work was considered a part of their domestic responsibilities, it meant that a large number of *campesinas* (peasant women) were catalogued among the economically inactive segment of the female population.

From the beginning of the armed conflict in 1910 there was a marked decline in the rhythm of urbanization (the urban population only managed to reach the levels it achieved in 1910 during the 1940s) and a pronounced reduction of female participation in the labor market. From 15.6 percent recorded for 1910, the figures register 9.5 percent in 1921, 6.9 percent in 1930, and 7.5 percent in 1940.

The main contraction occurred in the manufacturing industry, where the participation of women declined from 53 percent in 1910 to 12.7 percent in 1940. The service sector followed with a reduction from 62.2 percent to 45.3 percent over the same period. Within this sector the 12,000 female teachers that were in evidence in 1910 had dropped to a total of 4,000 by 1940. In contrast, the employment of women by the government increased from 2,000 to 42,000 during the same period, while by 1940 domestic service include 50 percent of those women included within the third sector.

1940–80: Import Substitution and Industrialization

From 1940 the female PEA witnessed sustained and accelerated growth as a reflection of industrial and urban expansion, the spread of education, and the development of the service sector. The latter showed marked growth, climbing from 19 percent of the economically active population in 1940 to 35 percent in 1970, thereby overtaking the industrial sector, which accounted for 25 percent of total employment.

Between 1940 and 1970 the number of women participating in the economically active population increased 5.7 times, at an annual rate of 6 percent, double the population growth rate. This increase nevertheless was not proportionally distributed in all sectors of the economy. The service sector captured 54 percent of the female workforce, within which existed areas that expanded at a more rapid rate; education swelled by 4,225 percent, female participation in the financial sector increased more than 30 times, while transport and communications showed a tenfold growth rate. Domestic service expanded more than three times in absolute terms, but its participation within the service sector dropped from 50 percent in 1940 to 33 percent in 1970.

By 1950 manufacturing had become the most important industry in the country with an annual growth of 8.1 percent, forcing agriculture into second place with a reduced growth rate of 5.8 percent, followed by the mining and petrol industries, whose growth rates averaged 2.5 percent. The GNP rose to an annual rate of 5.9 percent; the population

of the country increased to a total of 25 million, 50.8 percent of which were women, and the female PEA reached 13 percent.

During the 1960s the urban female population was greater than that in rural areas. The service industry accounted for most female employment with 50.2 percent, followed by commerce with 27 percent, manufacturing industry with 16 percent, and agriculture at 10.8 percent.

The involvement of women in the manufacturing industry showed increments from 12.7 percent in 1940 to 16 percent in 1960, rising to 20.6 percent in 1970, and 26.4 percent in 1980. However their participation was mainly limited to those areas that could be labeled as "traditional," such as the making of clothes, foodstuffs, the putting together of electronic apparatus, and pharmaceutical production, all of which require intricate work and in which wage discrimination frequently did not operate in their favor.

From 1970 to 1980 female employment as a whole rose 149 percent, an increase comparable to the 163 percent growth from 1940 to 1950. In 1980 the service sector reported a total of 56.5 percent of the female economically active population and the area of domestic service continued to be the main source of female employment (35 out every 100 in this sector). However, for the first time in 100 years domestic service lost its primacy (83.9 percent female) to the health sector (86 percent female).

It is notable that between 1970 and 1980 women's employment in the farming sector grew threefold, rising from 12 percent in 1970 to 19 percent in 1980. This surely is owing to the fact that, apart from a better census register that recognized women's role in this sector, there was a strong interregional migrational flow that did not necessarily affect the indices of urbanization and that began to favor salaried employment in the agroindustries.

It is important to point out that the spectacular 316 percent growth of the female economically active population over that of men in the last 40 years of the twentieth century indicates that women have become incorporated in the economy as a response to the necessity of satisfying the demand for labor generated by the industrialization of the country and as a means of supporting the family economy in a "direct" way by earning a salary.

Mexican women in general still pursue the least qualified career structures within different branches of the economy, with few taking up managerial posts. Thus, for example, of 16.9 percent of the women in the government sector in the 1990s, 65 percent were secretaries, teachers and technical support, while only between 5 and 10 percent of the total corresponded to women at the managerial level. One of the obstacles that has blocked women's progress in the workplace is delayed access to education. The lack of equality between the sexes revealed in this context is the result mainly of social, economic, and cultural factors that make it common practice for families to give male children the opportunity to study. This explains why matriculation in basic education is the same for both sexes, but as the level of education increases more women drop out or orientate their education to technical areas, or to training and teachers' training, as a response to social pressures. This means that very few women enter higher education, and if between 1970 and 1980 the presence of women in the universities increased by 140 percent, the global picture shows them as only comprising 35 percent of the student total at this level.

1980–94: Economic Crisis and Recession

From 1982, coincidental with the beginning and sharpening of the economic crisis in Mexico and the so-called lost decade in Latin America, new patterns of behavior became evident in female employment and vocational work in urban areas. The impact of the economic crisis differed according to the different branches of production and gender. If in 1983 the rates of open unemployment of women were higher than those of men by 2 or more percent in 7 of the 12 nonborder zones, by 1986 they continued to exist in only two areas, Monterrey and Veracruz, clear evidence that the male labor force has been more affected by the crisis. Distinct types of urban environments also seem to demand and offer employment opportunities to selective groups of women. Urban areas with a very defined industrial specialization, such as the border cities, continue to hire a large quantity of young women for the *maquiladora* (assembly) industry, despite the crisis. Cities with economies based on services and business, heterogeneous in terms of the co-existence of different forms of organization of work, offer young and unmarried women mainly salaried work in manual and non-manual activities; they offer older, married women with less education independent work in the commercial field and in the provision of unskilled work. In the context of diversified and heterogeneous industrial structures, married women also undertake domestic work, subcontracted by large industrial businesses or work in family businesses that employ adolescent labor of both sexes.

Alterations in the generic traditional composition of sectors of the economy also are evident. Women maintain or increase their numbers in the secondary sector of the border areas (because of the *maquiladora* industry) and in those industrial centers where the crisis has had less effect on the local or regional branches of the economy (Chihuahua, Torreón, Tampico, León), while reducing their relative weight in independent activities and in the third sector. These facts seem to indicate that in urban border areas or those with constant manufacturing development, women continue to dominate industrial work while men basically remain with the option of self-employment or contracting themselves as laborers in the United States. Nevertheless, it is important to point out that *maquilas* appear to be increasing their number of male employees. In 1975, 78.3 percent were women, in 1983 only 71.9 percent, dropping again in 1985 to 68.5 percent and in 1988 to 62 percent. Only the electrical components industry has witnessed an increase in male employment, rising from 15.6 percent in 1975 to 24.7 percent in 1986.

In nonborder cities and particularly in the large metropolises (Mexico City, Guadalajara, Monterrey), the use of female labor in nonsalaried or semi-clandestine jobs that operate on the margin of the labor law is becoming predominant. These sectors cover a broad and heterogeneous area: street sellers, those in family workshops or involved in artisanal projects, and domestic workers subcontracted by capitalist businesses, while men increase their relative presence in the third sector. Male workers expelled from the second sector begin to masculinize the services (their increased presence in traditionally women's work such as selling, banking services, and even teaching is marked), while women who are excluded enter the large cities to work in the informal and clandestine economy.

Several behavioral patterns, along with some novel features, confirm the broad trends discerned for the female economically active population in the previous three or four decades. There is a constant increase in the participation of women in economic activity, even if this is related more to independent work and not to the secondary or traditional tertiary sectors. The social division of work according to gender and the impact of the economic crisis (that paradoxically has increased demand) has devalued work and female employment even further. In periods of recession, women seek more remunerative employment and in the provinces find it with relatively more ease than men. The greater economic participation does not necessarily bring an improvement in the social condition of women, however. They still are obliged, in addition to their daily work, to assume traditional roles as mother and housewife. In periods of crisis the population works harder and lives in worse conditions. Families with low incomes elaborate complex strategies of survival, including relying on the low salaries of many family members.

The crisis also has provoked another series of manifestations regarding patterns of female employment in the popular urban sectors, whereby notably less education and greater need correspond in turn with an unstable and erratic level of employment. As the scholar Teresita de Barbieri has pointed out, "today the paid domestic worker; tomorrow the *maquila* worker toiling at home; the day after tomorrow housewife and mother of a family; two months later independent trader. . . ." This general situation is crosscut by two essential variables, the family role of the working women and their stage in life. It seems clear that the most vulnerable group consists of women running a home who, according to Barbieri, evoke "the image of androgynousness that, instead of expressing fulfillment, blends together all the disadvantages of both sexes. They are responsible both within and without their domestic units; that is, they have to earn for the sake of the survival of the family but in the market their domestic requirements devalue them as an element of the workforce."

Among married women can be found one of the modifications that the economic crisis seem to be provoking in general terms: if historically women tend to abandon employment during their childbearing years, this seems to be changing today; women are not leaving all work but rather shifting the kind of work. Thus, for women of limited resources and low education, the option frequently seems to be independent commercial activity, which allows them to generate income while attending to domestic responsibilities.

Women in the rural sector from the 1970s, and increasingly so from the 1980s, have been essential protagonists in two basic processes within Mexican agriculture: rural salaries and the exodus to the cities. With regard to the former, 86.6 percent of agricultural producers in 1970 were *campesinos* working within a family economy, while commercial agriculture was practiced only by 1.8 percent of producers who absorbed the major part of rural income; the remaining 11.6 percent oscillated between both models. Inside the *campesino* units this situation had an impact on the women inasmuch as assignation of work and the responsibility of female tasks was not only determined on the basis of an internal necessity

of work but also the fluctuations in the structure of the exchange of goods and resources according to market forces or external businesses.

Owing to the competition fomented by urban industry, many income-generating activities traditionally carried out by *campesina* women as members of *ejidatario* and *communero* (communal village farms) families were eliminated or marginalized. Faced with this situation, *campesino* units lost revenue that frequently was indispensable for the purchase of raw materials for farming. The women, mainly adult and married, saw the need to adding a day's agricultural work to their basic workload. This occurred more frequently in those productive areas where technical assistance and credit was scarce.

In those units where the sons and daughters and the husband were obliged to migrate or enter salaried work in another area or region, adult women stayed in their communities of origin, took charge of the production, and assumed broad responsibility for feeding, taking care of, and protecting their children and family relations, without relying on any kind of help and in highly precarious economic conditions.

Young girls and single women belonging to semiproletarianized *campesina* units of production, located in regions where commercial agriculture and agroexports had been started, had the opportunity to enter salaried work in local markets, especially in the agroindustry (e.g. horticulture, growing vegetables and fruits for export, such as coffee, strawberry, tomatoes, and grapes).

Another source of paid work taken up by the rural women of semiproletarianized units during this period was so-called rural manufacturing or domestic work, which appeared during the 1960s. Rural manufacturing has found *campesina* women both docile and a source of cheap labor, which has created and allowed the development of an employment market. In an area that is largely dedicated to the manufacture of clothing, the most broadly spread productive sector, preferential employment is given to adult married women who reside in their community or origin and some single women who carry out the work in their own homes.

The exodus of *campesina* to the cities is an uninterrupted process whereby women, in distinct stages of life, contribute to the third sector of urban employment and resent with particular harshness the consequences of social and economic marginalization to which the rural inhabitants have been subjected, as well as the gender marginalization the face as women.

See also Industrial Labor; Maquiladoras; Migration to the United States

Select Bibliography

Fowler-Salamini, Heather, and Mary K. Vaughan, editors, *Women of the Mexican Countryside, 1850–1990.* Tucson: University of Arizona Press, 1994.

González de la Rocha, Mercedes, *The Resources of Poverty: Women and Survival in a Mexican City.* Oxford and Cambridge, Massachusetts: Blackwell, 1994.

Macías, Ana, *Against All Odds: The Feminist Movement in Mexico to 1940.* Westport, Connecticut: Greenwood, 1982.

Stephen, Lynn, *Zapotec Women.* Austin: University of Texas Press, 1991.

—ESPERANZA TUÑÓN PABLOS

World Trade Organization

See General Agreement on Tariffs and Trade (GATT)

Z

Zapata, Emiliano 1879–1919

General

Emiliano Zapata was born and raised in a *campesino* (peasant) family in the southern Mexican village of Anenecuilco, Morelos. During his childhood, the centuries-long struggle for land and water between the villages and the expanding sugar haciendas of the state was becoming increasingly intense. Growing up in such a charged atmosphere, it is not surprising that Zapata was in trouble with the law at an early age; in 1897, for example, he fled the state to avoid arrest for a minor infraction at a fiesta, and he would later trace his personal rebellion back to about this time. By at least 1906, his rebelliousness had acquired greater focus, as he had become involved in the defense of Anenecuilco's land in the courts. Building upon that interest in his community's welfare, in 1909 he was elected president of the village council, and in 1910 he temporarily resolved a local land dispute by gathering together some 80 men to occupy the land in question by force of arms.

Part of the reason that Zapata could get away with such behavior was that, in 1910, national politics were becoming increasingly unsettled. After having been jailed while running for president against long-time dictator Porfirio Díaz, a hacienda-owner from northern Mexico named Francisco I. Madero called the nation to arms in November with the goal of removing Díaz from power. Isolated, rural rebellions erupted in many parts of the country, and after carefully considering the opportunity that Madero's insurrection provided, Zapata helped organize a small guerrilla movement, which joined the fighting in March 1911. Zapata soon attained leadership of this local rebellion, and by May it had grown large enough to capture the important regional center of Cuautla, Morelos.

The taking of Cuautla, which was not far south of Mexico City, was surely an important factor in inducing Díaz to relinquish power in late May. Once Díaz was gone, however, Zapata quickly discovered how complicated the business of revolution could become. Madero and the other new leaders in Mexico City were more dedicated to democracy than to the land reform that Zapata's peasant following expected. Moreover, the plantation owners of Morelos immediately began maneuvers intended to preserve their power and wealth in the state. With their encouragement, Zapata was attacked by the conservative Mexico City press, which began to call him the "Attila of the South" in June for the real and imagined atrocities perpetrated by his followers. Meanwhile, Madero wavered, uncertain of whether he should support the respectable landlords with whom he naturally identified or the peasants who had participated in the Revolution. Under these circumstances Zapata was reluctant to disarm his forces as the new government demanded; after weeks of negotiations, in August 1911 troops were sent against Zapata under the command of General Victoriano Huerta. Zapata returned to the mountains, now to fight against an ostensibly Revolutionary regime.

To explain his cause to the nation and refute charges that his movement was politically illegitimate, Zapata joined in November with a local schoolmaster named Otilio Montaño to compose the Plan of Ayala, the document upon which much of his subsequent reputation has been based. The Plan of Ayala was a powerful expression of many of the central goals of Mexico's rural rebels. It clarified Zapata's demand for land and water rights, calling not only for the return of resources that the haciendas had stolen, but for the expropriation—with indemnification—of a third part of hacienda "monopolies," which were to be given to peasants without title to land. It also provided for the complete confiscation of the property of those who opposed the Zapatistas. The second main thrust of the document was its call for political liberty. It insisted on the rule of law, and on the right of the people to choose their own representatives. Together these provisions added up to a demand for the basics of social justice from a rural, southern Mexican point of view.

Perhaps more important than the mere writing of this program in establishing Zapata's significance is the fact that he stuck to these fundamental positions throughout the tangled history of the Revolutionary decade. The Plan of Ayala accused Madero of betraying the Revolution, and Zapata fought against him until Huerta removed Madero from the presidency in a February 1913 coup. Huerta then sought to make peace with Zapata, but Zapata was not willing to trust his promises, and the warfare continued. As it did so, Zapatismo grew. Peasants from Morelos, Mexico State, the Federal District, Puebla, Guerrero, and farther afield joined Zapata against the Huerta regime, which had reintroduced the hated Porfirian conscription and thus given them a new reason to support the insurrection. As the movement expanded, it became more diverse, and it was Zapata's task to discipline it and shape it into a force on the national scene. Given its grassroots origins in the myriad villages of the region, achieving that level of discipline was a tremendous challenge, but one that Zapata was able to meet. One measure of his success was that by the summer of 1914 he controlled Morelos and large parts of neighboring states and threatened Mexico City. He had become one of the most prominent leaders of the Mexican Revolution.

In July 1914 Huerta was forced into exile, and Zapata's troops came face to face with those of the northern faction, Constitutionalists, who also had opposed Huerta. Having refused to coordinate his operations with the Constitutionalists until this time, Zapata now was confronted with a crucial decision about what kind of alliances, if any, would be most useful in the pursuit of his agenda. The logical choice was between the leader of Constitutionalism, Venustiano Carranza, and perhaps his most powerful subordinate, Francisco "Pancho" Villa, who was increasingly demonstrating that he and Carranza could no longer get along. Consulting closely with Manuel Palafox, his top intellectual advisor at the time, Zapata eventually chose to side with Villa. Like Madero, after all, Carranza was a hacienda owner and gave little indication that he favored meaningful land reform.

By November 1914 the fighting started again, and on December 4 Zapata and Villa met in the village of Xochimilco, in the Federal District, to solidify their alliance. Two days later they made their official entry into Mexico City, which the Zapatistas had occupied in late November. When Zapata captured Puebla on December 16, it looked as though he and Villa would quickly defeat Carranza. Difficulties, however, already had begun to arise. A series of assassinations in the capital strained relations between Zapata and Villa, and the urban intellectuals these two popular leaders had put in charge of their national government were bickering among themselves.

Just before Christmas Zapata returned to Morelos, where land reform already was under way. Indeed, much of the territory that he controlled would be spared from the newest round of civil war until late 1915, and that provided him with the opportunity to fulfill his promises by helping the peasants act on their hopes for change in a way that they have seldom been able to do in Mexican history. All the haciendas of Morelos were confiscated by the fall of 1914, since it was determined that their owners had indeed opposed Zapata's cause. Then, with the help of agrarian commissions that Palafox organized in Mexico City, the claims of various communities began to be sorted out and lines traced—at least provisionally—between enlarged communal village holdings. Ultimately, the land reform process spread beyond Morelos, into areas of neighboring states that also were under Zapatista rule. This was in many respects the high point of Zapata's rebellion, but the land reform process was not without its tensions. Village titles were sufficiently inconclusive that neighboring communities often squabbled over land and other resources, and civilians and Zapatista soldiers increasingly failed to see eye to eye. Furthermore, there was little trust among the peasants for the agrarian engineers with their urban backgrounds.

In any event, Zapata's land reform would prove to be impermanent. Both the shakiness of the alliance with Villa and Zapatismo's internal difficulties weakened the war effort against Carranza, and in mid-1915 Villa lost the biggest battles of the Revolution to Constitutionalist general Álvaro Obregón. In early August Zapata's army was driven from Mexico City, and in the spring of 1916, Carranza's troops invaded Morelos.

Zapata did not give up. With the help of a new chief advisor, Gildardo Magaña, he sought alliances with anyone who might help him fight Carranza. But as the war effort went sour, resources became increasingly scarce in the Zapatista world, and tensions within the movement reached their highest point. The result was an extended period of infighting and defection. The most striking case was that of Otilio Montaño, who was accused of participating in a rebellion against Zapata's authority in May 1917. Zapata ordered Montaño executed to send a message to other would-be traitors, but the combination of persuasion and punishment with which he had previously managed to keep his movement together was no longer sufficient to counter the centrifugal forces at work.

Zapata sought to compensate for the defections from his own ranks by appealing to troops from other Revolutionary camps to join Zapatismo, but his appeals grew more and more desperate as time passed. Finally, he contacted a supposedly disaffected Carrancista colonel named Jesús Guajardo. They exchanged a few letters, and then on April 10, 1919, Guajardo and Zapata met at the hacienda Chinameca in southern Morelos. Zapata rode in through the gate of the hacienda with a handful of men, and Guajardo's soldiers, assembled as if to do him military honors, shot him dead.

Although the surviving leaders of the movement quickly announced their continued defiance of Carranza, Zapatismo now lacked its symbolic center and grew even weaker as a military force. Eventually, in September 1919, some Zapatistas elected Magaña to succeed Zapata as the head of the organization, but Magaña's moral authority was strictly limited. Neither native to the area nor a peasant, he was hardly in a position to hold the movement together when Zapata could not. The Carrancistas began to reconstitute the haciendas of Morelos; many *campesinos* were willing to settle for the return of peace; and the Zapatistas were reduced to small, isolated bands in remote mountain hideouts.

Zapata's death did not, however, mean the end of his significance in modern Mexican life. The remaining Zapatistas were able to form an alliance with the forces of Álvaro Obregón, who won the Revolution in 1920. Although the Zapatistas had little political power within that alliance, there *was* power in Zapata's program of land and liberty, and Obregón and his successors were quick to appropriate it. Zapata's visage appeared in murals and statues, and each year on the anniversary of his death, politicians gave fancy speeches at his burial site. Within the official tradition of the modern Mexican state, he was enshrined as a sort of founding father and credited with inspiring the land reform that took place in the decades after his death.

Unfortunately, this land reform had its shortcomings. Fundamentally conceived as a political tool of a centralizing state, it failed to free Mexico's peasants from their collective poverty and was incompatible with the political liberties that Zapata sought. Perhaps this is why the peasants of Zapata's home region found it necessary to develop their own interpretation of what he represented. In 1919, some of his followers immediately claimed that he was not dead, that a man who looked like him took his place

at Chinameca, and that Zapata was hiding in the mountains—or in Arabia—until the people needed him again. For them he was too smart, too strong, too important, too symbolic of their cause to die, and in a sense they were right, for he lived on in their stories. Of course, not all peasants believed that Zapata had dodged Guajardo's ambush, but the legend of his survival helped create a vision of a Zapata who was not primarily a founding father of the Mexican state, but rather a Christ-like man-god who embodied demands for social justice, demands that were often made against the state that had appropriated his image. The endurance and geographical extension of this peasant vision of Zapata can be seen in the January 1, 1994, rebellion of the Ejército Zapatista de Liberación Nacional (EZLN, or Zapatista Army of National Liberation) in the state of Chiapas.

Select Bibliography

Ragan, John David, *Emiliano Zapata*. New York: Chelsea House, 1989.
Womack, John, *Zapata and the Mexican Revolution*. New York: Knopf, 1968; London: Thames and Hudson, 1969.

—SAMUEL BRUNK

Zapatista Rebellion in Chiapas

On January 1, 1994, the Ejército Zapatista de Liberación Nacional (EZLN, or Zapatista Army of National Liberation) seized San Cristóbal de las Casas in central highland Chiapas along with township centers in eastern Chiapas, proclaiming a revolution on the inaugural day of the North American Free Trade Agreement (NAFTA) and throwing Mexico into crisis in an election year. The Zapatistas, predominantly Maya-speaking indigenous men, women, and children equipped with rubber boots, homemade uniforms, bandannas, ski masks, and weapons ranging from handmade wooden rifles to Uzi machine guns, startled Mexicans by calling on them to depose the "illegal dictatorship" of President Carlos Salinas de Gortari. In printed communiqués, radio broadcasts, and interviews, masked leaders—including "Subcomandante Marcos," a charismatic, urbane, and patently non-Indian spokesman—condemned the monopoly of power held since the 1930s by Mexico's ruling Partido Revolucionario Institucional (PRI, or Institutional Revolutionary Party). They decried decades of government neglect for peasant and indigenous peoples' elemental needs:

land, housing, work, health services, and schools, as well as justice and democratic representation for all of Mexico's citizens. They named themselves after the popular agrarian rebels under Emiliano Zapata who fought for land and liberty during the Mexican Revolution.

The government quickly moved 12,000 troops and equipment into the area—ultimately deploying half of Mexico's military forces in Chiapas to contain the insurgents tactically. Yet even as they retreated, the Zapatistas seized the high ground of media attention, winning international sympathy as the first post-1992 movement of Native Americans to arm themselves to revindicate centuries of injustices while calling on civil society to join them in a broad movement for political and social reform. Unwilling to mar Mexico's modernizing and democratizing image in an election year by crushing the rebels in what would surely strike Mexican and international civil society as genocidal repression, Salinas declared a unilateral cease-fire on January 12, 1994, and initiated negotiations with the Zapatistas in protracted, episodic dialogues, interspersed with troop deployments. As of June 1996, this strategy still had not resolved fundamental differences nor led the Zapatistas to lay down arms but instead exposed the Mexican government to international scrutiny of its political processes, recent projects of neoliberal restructuring, and growing neglect of marginalized citizens.

Peace talks began in San Cristóbal on February 21, 1994, with liberation theologian Bishop Samuel Ruiz García mediating between the EZLN's general command and Salinas's negotiator Manuel Camacho Solís over 34 broad-ranging Zapatista demands for national as well as regional political, economic, and social reform. Made up of 18 masked men and women in ethnic garb representing four Maya-language groups, the EZLN general command (Comité Clandestino de Revolución Indígena, or CCRI) revealed an intriguing and unprecedented organization of "leaders that follow," with military Subcomandante Marcos subordinate to the indigenous commanders, and these in turn to hinterland constituencies, giving women and children equal voice with men. Their organization inverts the vanguardist hierarchy typical of earlier revolutionary movements in the Americas in which urban-intellectual leaders sometimes misjudged peasants' readiness to flare into revolt, indigenous peoples' willingness to subordinate ethnicity to class, or women's willingness to take up arms without revindicating their own gender subordination. Reaching tentative accords on 32 of the 34 points on March 2, 1991, both sides recessed on a note of optimism to consult with their constituencies.

By this time the highly publicized rebellion had called into question Salinas's program to restructure the Mexican economy, as the public debated Zapatista charges of electoral fraud, political corruption, and government dereliction of duty to Mexico's poor. Critics claimed that Salinas had known about the guerrilla army in Chiapas for over a year but had done nothing for fear of jeopardizing U.S. congressional approval of NAFTA. The candidacy of Luís Donaldo Colosio Murrieta, picked by Salinas to succeed him as president, became clouded with speculation that Salinas would replace Colosio with peace negotiator Camacho, or that Camacho might declare a renegade candidacy. Mexicans wondered if the PRI might lose the presidential elections slated for August. Chiapas, meanwhile, tilted toward anarchy as peasants emboldened by the Zapatista uprising ousted PRI authorities in dozens of local governments and began to invade private ranches, while landowners threatened reprisals. Indigenous groups banded together in some areas to demand autonomy.

Public enthusiasm for the EZLN's armed movement chilled abruptly on March 23, when an assassin shocked Mexico by killing PRI presidential candidate Colosio in Tijuana, Baja California (although there is no evidence whatsoever linking the assassination to the Zapatistas). The PRI hastily replaced Colosio with Ernesto Zedillo Ponce de León and put the Zapatista accords on hold, emphasizing the PRI as the party of nonviolence and political continuity to recoup electoral support. Then, on June 12, the Zapatista rank-and-file rejected the tentative peace accord, refusing to lay down their arms and calling instead for a national convention of civil society to revamp the political system. As leading Mexicans worried that the nation might become ungovernable, several thousand Zapatista sympathizers, including left and progressive politicians, intellectuals, and representatives of indigenous, peasant, and labor organizations converged on "Aguascalientes," a convention site that the Zapatistas carved out of the jungle in eastern Chiapas. Meeting August 6 to 9, this Convención Nacional Democrático (CND) formed a broad national front vowing to resist a fraudulent PRI electoral victory.

Under intense international scrutiny, Zedillo won the August 21 elections with 49 percent of the vote, versus 28 percent for the Partido de Acción Nacional (PAN, or National Action Party) and 16 percent for the Partido de la Revolución Democrática (PRD, or Party of the Democratic Revolution). The Zapatistas and the PRD nonetheless disputed the Chiapas gubernatorial election claimed by PRI candidate

Robledo and vowed to install independent candidate Avendaño. But the government, bolstered by its presidential victory and confident of having militarily hemmed the Zapatistas into eastern Chiapas, simply ignored the threat. Very modest attendance at the second CND convention convoked at Aguascalientes November 2 to 4, 1994, seemed to underscore that the Zapatistas could be written off as a sideshow.

Instead, synergy between Chiapas and national events brought the EZLN back to center stage immediately after the December 1 inauguration of Zedillo as president, when Robledo also took office as PRI governor in Chiapas. In reaction, just as Zedillo devalued the peso, the Zapatistas declared the truce broken and raided towns far outside the perimeter of military encirclement. Confidence in Zedillo and the peso plummeted, and international investors began the massive withdrawal of capital from Mexican financial markets that forced the U.S. administration of President Bill Clinton to authorize a $US20 billion loan to shore up the Mexican economy on January 31, 1995, shortly after Zedillo imposed an austerity program of daunting proportions.

Persuaded by hardliners, and perhaps by a Chase Manhattan Bank consultant's advice that Mexico had to crush the Zapatistas to restore investor confidence, Zedillo issued judicial orders on February 9, 1996, for the arrest of the EZLN leadership, identifying "Marcos" as Rafael Sebastián Guillén Vicente, age 37, a native of Tampico and former professor of communications at the Universidad Nacional Autónoma de México (UNAM, or National Autonomous University of Mexico) who once had served as a Sandinista internationalist in Nicaragua. The federal army advanced quickly into Zapatista-held territory in eastern Chiapas, ransacking the villages of Zapatista sympathizers who fled into the wilderness, but failing to arrest the EZLN leadership.

One of the EZLN accomplishments has been to rally national and international support through the CND and through innovative use of media, including the Internet and an EZLN home page on the World Wide Web. The Zapatistas now mobilized international pressure on Zedillo to call the army advance to a halt on February 14, 1995, and to resume dialogues. Talks resumed in April 1995 after the government agreed to respect zones of de facto Zapatista control, but by mid-1996 these talks had led to only one agreement, announced on February 16 of that year, on issues of indigenous rights, proposing amendments to the constitution to allow traditional government in indigenous communities and to grant indigenous representation in the national congress. Five equally thorny issues await negotiation.

In mid-1996, the government and the Zapatistas seemed to be waiting one another out. The government held the high ground militarily and treated the Zapatistas as a marginal, local problem, restricting access to the rebels on the part of journalists, lay and religious and activists, and human rights advocates. While encircled militarily and beset by harsh economic conditions, the Zapatistas held the moral high ground and repeatedly convoked national and international civil society in referenda and in conferences to discuss indigenous rights and to critique neoliberalism (the new internationalized "free market" paradigm that had displaced state-led capitalism in most of Latin America over the course of the 1980s and 1990s). The rebels' fate depended in part on whether Mexico's economic crisis would deteriorate further, destabilizing the government and reopening the national political arena that the Zapatistas had hailed from the outset and laid claim to on January 11, 1996, by establishing the Frente Zapatista de Liberación Nacional (FZLN, or Zapatista Front for National Liberation) as a political force.

The Chiapas uprising poses questions requiring analysis of the movement's origins. How did the EZLN forge an ethnic alliance over differences of language, religion, geography, and competing territorial claims, in a region where the government has historically held influence over indigenous communities? What was the role of nonindigenous leadership in the movement, and was it by inspired Liberation Theology or by movements elsewhere in the Americas? Was the movement known to the government, and if so, why was it tolerated? Why did the Zapatistas protest NAFTA?

Indians have been the bottom rung of Chiapas society since the Spanish Conquest, when native speakers of Maya languages—Tzotzil, Tzeltal, Chol, and Tojolabal—were concentrated in the highlands around the colonial capital, now San Cristóbal de las Casas, and exploited in commerce and ranching by Spanish and mixed-descent "Ladinos." Thus, it is not surprising that indigenous groups of the Chiapas, central highlands welcomed the Zapatista uprising, yet the origins of the movement trace to the frontier lands of eastern Chiapas where recent colonization pitted settlers against ranchers and the government.

Desperately short of land, Indians began to migrate from the Chiapas central highlands into the eastern frontier in the 1950s, petitioning agrarian authorities to protect them from ranchers and loggers by legalizing settlements under land reform provisions of Article 27 of the Constitution of 1917. While Mexico has not always honored this historic covenant with the peasantry, President Luis

Echeverría Álvarez actually encouraged the frontier colonization during his presidency (1970–76) on its basis.

Yet in 1978 the government established the huge Montes Azules Bioreserve, monopolized its timber rights, and stunned settlers by ordering them out. Colonists resisted relocation and allied with growing opposition to the government as the 1988 elections approached, but they found their vote rigged in favor of the PRI. Shortly after taking office, Salinas rewarded PRI supporters with land grants in Montes Azules but dashed opponents' hopes for ever legalizing their settlements by initiating congressional "reform" of Article 27 to bring agrarian reform to an end in 1992. More than anything else, Salinas's abrogation of agrarian reform, which angered peasants everywhere, turned eastern Chiapas colonists away from legal remedies and toward armed rebellion.

Although armed rebellion was unprecedented, settlers in eastern Chiapas, women as well as men, had mobilized for decades around religion and grass-roots politics. Worshiping together helped consolidate frontier colonies, and mixed-gender congregations began to embrace diverse Protestant churches in eastern Chiapas in the 1950s. Catholic liberation theologian Bishop Samuel Ruiz García responded to the Protestant incursions by organizing native catechists to mobilize settlers in eastern Chiapas as Christian base communities built on grass-roots participation and gender equality. At government behest, Ruíz convoked the 1974 Indigenous Congress through his catechist networks, the first time that Tzeltal-, Tzotzil-, Chol-, and Tojolabal-speaking communities mobilized to revindicate demands for land, schools, clinics, and other needs later echoed by the grass-roots organizers who tapped and expanded from catechists' constituencies.

In the wake of the 1974 Indigenous Congress, eastern Chiapas developed strong ties with the Mexican left, which had changed tactics after the government crushed the student movement in 1968 to take up activism for urban and rural poor. The 1974 congress persuaded left and progressive activists that Indians in Chiapas were worth mobilizing to pressure the government for reforms within the framework of Mexican law. Several independent organizations began to mobilize Chiapas's largely indigenous peasantry. OCEZ (Organización Campesina Emiliano Zapata) organized peasants to pressure for agrarian reform under Article 27. CIOAC (Central Independiente de Obreros Agrícolas y Campesinos) advocated ranch takeovers by resident workers to compensate for decades of illegal underpaid work. The Union de Uniones mobilized for

credits and fair marketing. All three organizations had ties with counterpart organizations elsewhere in Mexico. Although the Union de Uniones initially predominated in eastern Chiapas, all three organizations were active there before the Zapatista uprising.

The government initially tolerated the independent organizations as part of the "social" sector, following decades-old PRI policy for pacting with industry, unionized labor, commerce, ranchers, peasants, and Indians by providing each with political access and public resources. During the presidency of José López Portillo (1976–82), the government—flush with petrodollars borrowed to finance oil development—actually financed ranch buyouts, credits, and subsidies for some independent organizations, although it also circumscribed them politically by reserving municipal governments for PRI followers and by buying off organizations' leaders. Oil development was by this time drawing farm labor even from eastern Chiapas into unskilled construction work in Tabasco and at dams being built in central Chiapas. Cultivators used herbicides and fertilizers to free up time for wage work, and they depended on credits to purchase these inputs as well as on government subsidies for production and marketing provided through independent organizations.

But Mexico's 1982 crisis of external debt—triggered when falling oil prices left the country unable to pay interest on funds borrowed for oil development—hardened the government's stance toward the independents in conjunction with profound changes in Mexican economic and social policy. The debt crisis curtailed the development boom and forced austerity on the nation as the price of international bankers' bailout. The government phased out the subsidies that glued together Mexico's social contract. Salinas inscribed the cutbacks in structural adjustment coupled to NAFTA, which moored Mexico's future to modernization financed by international investment. In the countryside, peasant leaders and independent organizations protesting the cutbacks met greater repression. These policies hurt urban poor as well and jeopardized workers and manufacturers in national industries sacrificed to global competition, thus planting deeply rooted resentments across Mexican society that the Zapatistas tapped by protesting NAFTA.

Little is known precisely of EZLN origins. "Marcos" claims that he and a half-dozen compatriots arrived in eastern Chiapas in 1983 to advocate armed revolution. Whether and to what extent they had contact with Guatemalan or other Central American guerrillas is unclear. They won few followers until the already flourishing independent organizations proved unable to hold the government to the law. The outsiders bided their time, learned Tzeltal (the *lingua franca* of the region), embraced frontier grassroots democracy, and committed themselves to the cause of indigenous leaders and followers who had been radicalized in Chiapas's independent movements. The growing movement declared itself nonsectarian (embracing Protestants as well as Liberation Catholics), and inclusive (recognizing impoverished Ladinos as an ethnicity seeking to recuperate its indigenous cultural roots).

After the fraud-ridden 1988 elections, the movement gathered force as Salinas abrogated Article 27 (agrarian reform), and the economic crisis sharpened. Eastern Chiapas was devastated after Salinas disbanded the Mexican Coffee Institute, which marketed the region's peasant-grown coffee, as the world price of coffee plummeted by half in 1989—just when rigged elections and the ending of agrarian reform were persuading frontier settlers to heed the Zapatista call to arms. The movement's general command, the CCRI, grew to some 20 men and women representing each of the region's ethnicities (including Ladinos as one of many), reaching decisions only after having them discussed and voted on by all the Zapatista communities. By 1992, the military component had swelled to several hundred men and women who had acquired arms at their own expense and undergone clandestine military training in the EZLN. Many of the Zapatistas participated in the pan-indigenous Colombian Quincentennial marches and protests. The government knew of the movement in May 1993 (if not before) after it raided a Zapatista training site in eastern Chiapas, but it did not take further action, probably to avoid jeopardizing NAFTA negotiations. Whether and to what extent the movement developed national ties and organization is disputed. What is clear is that the increasingly inclusive Zapatista movement had deep Mexican roots and addressed fundamental national issues arising from Mexico's insertion in a global order.

Select Bibliography

Collier, George A., and Elizabeth Lowery Quaratiello, *BASTA! Land and the Zapatista Rebellion in Chiapas.* Oakland, California: Food First Books, 1994.

Harvey, Neil, *Rebellion in Chiapas: Rural Reforms, Campesino Radicalism, and the Limits to Salinismo.* La Jolla: Center for U.S.-Mexican Studies, University of California, San Diego, 1994.

Katzenberger, Elaine, editor, *First World, Ha Ha Ha!: The Zapatista Challenge.* San Francisco: City Lights, 1995.

Ross, John, *Rebellion from the Roots: Indian Uprising in Chiapas.* Monroe, Maine: Common Courage, 1995.

Subcomandante Marcos, *Shadows of Tender Fury: The Letters and Communiques of Subcomandante Marcos and the Zapatista Army of National Liberation,* introduction by John Ross. New York: Monthly Review Press, 1995.

—GEORGE A. COLLIER

Zapotecs, Mesoamerican

See Mesoamerica: Monte Albán

Zedillo Ponce de León, Ernesto 1951–

President

Ernesto Zedillo Ponce de León, elected president in 1994, came to occupy the presidency at a critical juncture in Mexico's political history. Whether Mexico continues a long tradition of authoritarian rule by the Partido Revolucionario Institucional (PRI, or Institutional Revolutionary Party) since 1929 or enters the twenty-first century on a more democratic footing will depend to a large extent on how President Zedillo's mandate unfolds.

Ernesto Zedillo Ponce de León was born in Mexico City on December 27, 1951. At an early age his parents moved to Mexicali, Baja California, in search of better employment opportunities. At age 14, he returned to Mexico City to commence high school.

Zedillo's formative period was typical of those who came to be known as the *tecnócratas* (technocrats) in Mexico's political system. Like president Carlos Salinas de Gortari and many other technocratic peers, Zedillo studied economics at the university. After completing an undergraduate degree at the National Polytechnic Institute in Mexico City (1969–72), he continued to pursue a master's degree and doctorate at Yale University (1974–78).

Common among the technocrats, Zedillo's professional career advanced successfully through several key financial institutions in the country. Upon completing his doctoral studies in 1978, he entered the Bank of Mexico (BANXICO) under the tutelage of Leopoldo Solís, one of the country's leading economists and former professor of Carlos Salinas de Gortari. Solís was a mentor to a number of officials who later would occupy important posts in the Salinas government (1988–94). Following a successful stint at BANXICO, in 1987 Zedillo was appointed undersecretary for planning and budgetary control at the

Secretariat of Programming and Budget (SPP). When Salinas became president in 1988, he appointed Zedillo to replace him as secretary of the SPP. It is worth noting that Zedillo and his two predecessors—Salinas and Miguel de la Madrid—all served as secretary of programming and budget at some point before becoming head of state. During his time at SPP, Zedillo distinguished himself in the design of the first "heterodox" stabilization program—the Economic Solidarity Pact of 1987—and thereafter in 1989 as the chief architect of Salinas's National Development Plan. In addition, he participated in the formulation of the Programa Nacional de Solidaridad (Pronasol, or National Solidarity Program), the cornerstone of Salinas's social policy. Like his colleagues at the time—de la Madrid, Salinas, Pedro Aspe, Guillermo Ortiz, and Jaime Serra Puche to name a few—Zedillo favored pro-market economic modernization policies, including privatization, deregulation, and trade liberalization. Technocrats were pitted against the more traditional-thinking "politicos" and "dinosaurs" in an ideological battle over the virtues of state versus market and a struggle for political power.

However, in one key aspect he differed significantly from other technocrats. Whereas de la Madrid, Salinas, and many of the others had enjoyed private school education and came from well-to-do families, Zedillo's background was considerably more modest. It is a credit to his talent, perseverance, and hard work that he managed to be accepted and advance within the exclusive, close-knit technocratic elite that came to power first under de la Madrid and then with Salinas.

In 1992, the Secretariat of Programming and Budget then under Zedillo's charge was fused with the Ministry of Finance to form one super-ministry. In the ensuing cabinet shuffle, Zedillo was appointed Secretary of Public Education. In his new role, he initiated an extensive reform of Mexico's public education, embodied in the National Agreement on the Modernization of Basic Education. Educational decentralization was one of the main thrusts of the new policy. Zedillo's tenure as education minister was not free of controversy, however. An historical revisionist initiative to rewrite the educational system's basic textbook on Mexican history evoked considerable criticism. As a result of the public outcry caused by the government's attempt to have Porfirio Díaz's regime reinterpreted in more favorable terms and the Mexican Revolution in a more critical light, the new texts were never published.

Zedillo's shift to education minister—less prominent on the hierarchical scale than the economic cabinet posts—seemed to indicate that his chances were limited for becoming his party's candidate in the 1994 presidential election. But events would take a dramatic turn. On March 23, 1994, Luis Donaldo Colosio, the PRI's presidential candidate, was assassinated. Having resigned his cabinet post in November 1993 to become the general coordinator of Colosio's electoral campaign, Zedillo was the only major official at the time who met the PRI's internal legal requirements to fill the vacant presidential candidacy. With apparent backing from the political groups of Salinas's chief of staff José María Córdoba and agriculture minister Carlos Hank González, he subsequently was catapulted into the presidential race.

It was a most difficult road to victory in the election of August 21, 1994. Like his predecessors Salinas and de la Madrid, Zedillo had never held an elected post and was therefore a novice in the game of electoral politics. Moreover, in contrast to his main opponents, Cuauhtémoc Cárdenas and Diego Fernández de Cevallos, who had been campaigning since the end of 1993, Zedillo had just five months to get his campaign running. In the country's first-ever televised candidates' debate during May 1994, Zedillo came in a disappointing and unconvincing second to Fernández de Cevallos. Campaign slogans such as "bienestar para la familia" (well-being for the family) and "el sabe como hacerlo" (he knows how to do it) also failed to inspire the electorate. It also did not help that right in the middle of the election campaign, the Chiapas's insurrection that began on January 1, 1994, had alerted the populace to the extreme shortcomings in the government's record on human rights and alleviating poverty. Only a combination of massive campaign spending and a "fear vote"—against the unknown alternative of an opposition-controlled government—eventually swayed the electoral tally in favor of Zedillo. Winning approximately 48 percent of the vote, Zedillo obtained the lowest level ever of popular support of any of the PRI's presidential candidates.

Zedillo has faced three formidable challenges since taking office on December 1, 1994. First, he has had to consolidate his power. Thrust unexpectedly and unprepared into the presidential candidacy in the wake of Colosio's death, Zedillo hardly had a political following of his own when he assumed the presidency. He has been struggling ever since both to impose his will and overcome a widespread perception that he is a weak president. On the one hand this has meant confrontation with his powerful predecessor, Carlos Salinas de Gortari, who, in the tradition of Calles, entertained ambitions of extending his influence beyond his own mandate. On February 28, 1995, Zedillo officials had Raúl Salinas, the former president's brother, imprisoned for alleged complicity in the murder of the PRI's secretary general, José Francisco Ruiz Massieu. Shortly thereafter, Carlos Salinas left Mexico for unofficial exile abroad. On the other hand, he has had to look both to more traditional power brokers and beyond his own party to shore up his power base. In terms of the former, Carlos Hank González, leader of the powerful political group Grupo Atlocomulco and former secretary of agriculture under Salinas, is one such source behind Mexico's current president. After the disappointing performance of Zedillo's inexperienced and poorly connected own confident, Esteban Moteuczoma, Hank González's lieutenant, Emilio Chuayffet, now occupies the key portfolio of secretary of the interior. There are also rumors that José María Córdoba, Salinas's chief of staff, has resurfaced in Zedillo's inner circle after a sojourn abroad following Colosio's assassination.

Paradoxically, there is evidence that Zedillo has also sought to strengthen his presidency via a broad, multipartisan reformist coalition. In January 1995 an historic agreement, the National Political Accord, was signed by the three main political parties, establishing the conditions for negotiating political reform.

Consolidating his power has proven most difficult and even dangerous. For instance, there were rumors in the Mexican press of an assassination attempt against Zedillo in the autumn of 1994. Power politics also have led to at least nine significant changes in the cabinet since his taking of office. Furthermore, there have been periodic suggestions of Zedillo's own pending resignation or demise, well into the spring of 1996. For example, on November 3, 1995, a news cable by the U.S. news agency AP Dow Jones reported an imminent coup d'état against Zedillo, causing considerable turmoil in financial markets.

The second major challenge facing Zedillo has been an unprecedented economic and social crisis. In what has come to be known as the "peso crisis," the executive decision by the Zedillo government to devalue the Mexican currency by 15 percent on December 20, 1994, triggered the near financial collapse of the country. Only a timely U.S.$52 billion rescue package assembled under the leadership of the United States and the International Monetary Fund staved off complete disaster. In March 1995, the Zedillo government introduced the most Draconian emergency stabilization program in Mexican history. The impact of Mexico's ongoing economic and social crisis has been staggering. In 1995, real Gross Domestic Product (GDP) fell by almost 7 percent,

while inflation rose to 52 percent. Some 15,000 businesses folded and 1.5 million jobs were lost. According to official estimates, the crisis has exacted a cost of U.S.$70 billion.

Mexico's social fabric has been affected gravely by economic deterioration. Violence, corruption, vandalism, prostitution, and narcotrafficking all are seemingly on the rise. Crisis also has helped fuel the rise of a multitude of new social movements, of which Zapatista rebels in Chiapas and the nationwide debtors' organization El Barzón are the most prominent. On July 6, 1996, a new guerrilla force called the Ejército Popular Revolucionario allegedly emerged in the state of Guerrero. Zedillo's election slogans mentioned above have become the object of scorn and ridicule against the backdrop of the profound economic and social crisis gripping the country. "Well-being for the family" remains at best a hope, while many seriously question whether "he knows how to do it."

Zedillo's third major challenge, political reform, has proven a daunting task. In his inaugural address, President Zedillo committed his government to negotiating a definitive electoral reform with the participation of political parties and social organizations. The democratization process has proven exceedingly difficult given the reluctance of certain elements within the ruling party to forego undemocratic practices. Despite democratic advances in some state and local elections, such as Jalisco, Baja California, Chihuahua, and Guanajuato, in other locations such as Yucatán, Tabasco, and Puebla, fraudulent electoral practices continue as in the past. The resistance that Zedillo has faced in his quest for democratic reform is best captured in the words of Mexico's long-time PRIista labor leader, Fidel Velázquez: "By the force of arms we won power and only by the force of arms will we relinquish it."

To Zedillo's credit and perseverance, Mexico's four major political parties reached agreement on an historic electoral reform package at the end of July 1996. Ratified unanimously by both the Chamber of Deputees and the Senate, it paves the way among other things for the creation of autonomous electoral organisms, the first-ever election of the mayor of Mexico City, and increased oversight of campaign spending. Perhaps most crucially, it represents a first step toward consensus among the parties on a set of mutually accepted democratic rules of the game. Of course, the midterm elections of July 6, 1997, will be the ultimate litmus test for the new reforms.

There is a perception abroad that Zedillo has wavered on his commitment to open, honest government. It is also mirrored internally, where Zedillo developed early on the reputation for being a "zig-zag" president. For example, after pledging at the outset of his presidency to reach a peaceful agreement with Subcomandante Marcos and the Zapatistas, in February 1995 he ordered a military incursion into Zapatista-held territory to arrest Marcos. This action was subsequently abandoned in favor of a resumption of peace talks. Similar vacillation was evident in the handling of the alleged case of massive fraud committed by PRI governor-elect Roberto Madrazo in the Tabasco state elections. After reaching a secret agreement with the opposition Partido de la Revolución Democrática (PRD, or Party of the Democratic Revolution) to oust Madrazo in exchange for the PRD's participation in the electoral reform process, and after launching a criminal investigation by the Federal Attorney General's Office, Zedillo pulled an about-face and was publicly seen embracing Madrazo during an official visit to Tabasco in June 1996. Zedillo also has been criticized for failing to follow through adequately on his promise to get tough on corruption. Moreover, despite significant judicial reforms and the appointment of an attorney general from the opposition Partido de Acción Nacional (PAN, or National Action Party), Zedillo's authorities still have not solved the political murders of Colosio or Ruiz Massieu.

Zedillo's contradictory actions, however, must be viewed in light of the three challenges mentioned above. The lack of a strong political power base of his own, unprecedented economic and social crisis, and internal resistance to political reform from significant sectors of his party, have made the pursuit of coherent policy exceedingly difficult. For the moment at least, Zedillo should be given the benefit of the doubt in his efforts to alter the country's political and economic landscape.

As Mexico continues to endure seemingly endless corruption scandals and socioeconomic crisis, the electoral fortunes of the country's opposition parties, in particular the PAN, grow proportionately. The middle class has voiced its discontent principally at the ballot box. Consequently, the PAN now holds four governorships—Baja California, Chihuahua, Guanajuato, and Jalisco—and occupies the mayorship of eight of the ten largest cities outside of Mexico City. In 1997's midterm elections, Mexico's opposition parties might even possibly win control of Congress for the first time in this century. Taking this trend into consideration, Ernesto Zedillo may possibly go down in history as the last of a long, uninterrupted line of PRI presidents dating back to 1929. It is to be hoped that he will also be remembered as the president that put the country decisively on a democratic course for the twenty-first century.

Select Bibliography

Centeno, Miguel Angel, *Democracy within Reason: Technocratic Revolution in Mexico.* University Park: Pennsylvania State University Press, 1994.

Poder Ejecutivo Federal, *National Development Plan, 1995–2000.* Mexico City: Presidency of the Republic, 1995.

Presidency of the Republic, *Ernesto Zedillo, President of Mexico: Profile.* Mexico City: Presidency of the Republic, 1995.

Schultz, Donald E., "Through a Glass Darkly: On the Challenges and Enigmas of Mexico's Future." *Mexican Studies* 12:1 (Winter 1996).

—THOMAS LEGLER

INDEX

Page numbers in **boldface** indicate subjects with their own entries; page numbers in *italics* indicate illustrations.

NOTES ON CONTRIBUTORS

Acosta, Mariclaire. President, Comisión Mexicana de Defensa y Promoción de los Derechos Humanos, A.C. **Essay:** Human Rights.

Adorno, Rolena. Professor, Department of Spanish and Portuguese, Yale University. Author of *Guaman Poma: Writing and Resistance in Colonial Peru* (1986) and *Transatlantic Encounters: Europeans and Andeans in the Sixteenth Century* (with Kenneth J. Andrien, 1991). Contributor to *Colonial Latin American Review, Hispanic Issues, MLN, Representations, Revista de Crítica Literaria Latinoamericana,* and *Revista de Estudios Hispánicos.* **Essay:** Díaz del Castillo, Bernal.

Aguilar García, Javier. Investigador Titular, Instituto de Investigaciones Sociales; Profesor, División de Estudios de Postgrado, Facultad de Ciencias Políticas y Sociales, Universidad Nacional Autónoma de México. Contributor to *ACTA Sociologíca* and *El Nuevo Estado Mexicano,* vol. 3 (1992). **Essays:** Morones, Luis Napoleón; Velázquez Sánchez, Fidel.

Ahern, Maureen. Professor of Spanish, Department of Spanish and Portuguese, Ohio State University. Editor and translator of and contributor to *A Rosario Castellanos Reader* (1988). **Essay:** Castellanos, Rosario.

Alvarez, Salvador. Coordinador, Programa de Historia, Universidad Autónoma de Ciudad Juárez. Contributor to *Aboriginal and Colonial Mining and Metallurgy in Spanish America* edited by Alan Kraig and Robert West (1994) and *Arte y Coerción* (with Chantal Cramaussel, 1992). **Essay:** Conquest: Northern Mexico.

Anderson, Arthur James Outram. Professor of Anthropology (Emeritus), California State University. Editor and translator of *Florentine Codex: General History of the Things of New Spain* (with Charles E. Dibble, 1950–82), *Sahagún's Psalmodia Christiana* (1993), *Fray Bernardino de Sahagún: Adiciones, Apéndice a la Postilla y Ejercicio Cotidiano* (1993), and *Codex Chimalpahin,* vols. 2 and 3 (with Susan Schroeder, 1997). **Essay:** Sahagún, Bernardino de.

Anderson, Rodney D. Professor, Department of History, and Director, Urban History Workshop, Florida State University. Author of *Outcasts in Their Own Land: Mexican Industrial Workers, 1906–1911* (1976). Contributor to *Hispanic American Historical Review.* **Essay:** Industrial Labor: 1876–1910.

Archer, Christon I. Professor of History and Director of Latin American Studies, University of Calgary. Author of *The Army in Bourbon Mexico, 1760–1810* (1977). **Essays:** Military: Bourbon New Spain; Military: 1821–1914; Wars of Independence.

Arenal, Electa. Professor of Spanish and Women's Studies, City University of New York. Author of *Untold Sisters: Hispanic Nuns in Their Own Works* (with Stacey Schlau, 1988). Editor and translator of *The Answer/La Respuesta* by Sor Juana Inés de la Cruz (with Amanda Powell, 1994). Contributor to *Reinventing the Americas* edited by Bell Gall Chevigny and Gari LaGuardia (1986). **Essay:** Cruz, Sor Juana Inés de la.

Arroyo García, Israel. Profesor-Investigador, Maestría en Ciencias Políticas, Universidad Autónoma de Puebla. **Essays:** Alamán, Lucas; Conservatism.

Ayala Falcón, Maricela. Investigadora, Centro de Estudios Mayas, Instituto de Investigaciones Filológicas, Universidad Nacional Autónoma de México. Author of *El fonetismo en la escritura Maya* (1985). Contributor to *Homenaje a Franz Bloom* (1983) and *Los Mayas, el esplendor de una civilización* (1990). **Essay:** Mesoamerica: Writing.

Baker, Shannon L., Doctoral Candidate, Department of History, Texas Christian University. **Essay:** Sports.

Bakewell, Elizabeth. Assistant Professor, Department of Anthropology, and Director, Project on the Language-Art Interface (PROLARTI), Brown University. Author of *Object Image Inquiry: The Art Historian at Work* (with M. Schmitt and W. O. Beeman, 1988). Editor of *Looking High and Low: Art and Cultural Identity* (with Brenda Jo Bright, 1995). **Essays:** Gender: Gender and Mexican Spanish; Kahlo, Frida.

Bargellini, Clara. Investigadora, Instituto de Investigaciones Estéticas, Universidad Nacional Autónoma de México. Author of *La Catedral de Chihuahua* (1984) and *La arquitectura de la plata: Iglesias monumentales del centro norte de México, 1640–1750* (1991). **Essay:** Architecture: Colonial.

Bartra, Eli. Profesora-Investigadora, División de Ciencias Sociales y Humanidades, Universidad Autónoma Metropolitana, Xochimilco. Author of *En busca de las diablas: Sobre arte popular y género* (1994) and *Frida Kahlo: Mujer, ideología, arte* (1994). **Essay:** Rivera, Diego.

Bastian, Jean-Pierre. Professor and Director, Centre de Sociologie des Religions en Europe, Faculte de Theologie Protestante, University of Strasbourg. Author of *Los disidentes: Sociedades Protestantes y revolución en México, 1872–1911* (1989) and *Protestantism y modernidad Latinoamericana: Historia de unas minorias religious activas* (1996). **Essay:** Protestantism.

Beezley, William H. Neville G. Penrose Chair of Latin American History, Department of History, Texas Christian University. Author of *El Gran Pueblo: A History of Greater Mexico* (with Colin MacLachlan, 1994). Editor of *Rituals of Rule, Rituals of Resistance: Public Celebrations and Popular Culture in Mexico* (with Cheryl English Martin and William E. French, 1994). **Essay:** Sports.

Benjamin, Thomas. Professor, Department of History, Central Michigan University. Author of *A Rich Land, A Poor People: Politics and Society in Modern Chiapas*, 2nd edition (1996). **Essay:** Ruiz García, Samuel.

Berdan, Frances F. Professor, Department of Anthropology, California State University, San Bernardino. Author of *The Aztecs of Central Mexico* (1982), *The Codex Mendoza*, 4 vols. (with Patricia Anawalt, 1992), and *Aztec Imperial Strategies* (1996). **Essays:** Mesoamerica: Mexica; Triple Alliance.

Bilello, Suzanne. Director, Freedom Forum Latin American Center, Buenos Aires. **Essay:** Massacre of Tlatelolco.

Brachet-Márquez, Viviane. Professor of Sociology, Centro de Estudios Sociológicos, El Colegio de México. Author of *La población de los estados mexicanos en el siglo XIX* (1976), *La tecnología en la industria alimentaria mexicana*, 2nd edition (with Kurt Unger, 1983), and *The Dynamics of Domination: State, Class, and Social Reform in Mexico, 1910–1990* (1994). Contributor to *Cahiers des Amériques Latines* (with Diane Davis), *Latin American Research Review*, *The Sociology of Work*, and *World Development* (with Margaret Sheradden). **Essays:** Politics and Government: 1910–46.

Brandes, Stanley. Professor of Anthropology, University of California, Berkeley. Author of *Metaphors of Masculinity: Sex and Status in Andalusian Folklore* (1980), *Forty: The Age and the Symbol* (1985), and *Power and Persuasion: Ritual and Social Control in Rural Mexico* (1988). **Essay:** Day of the Dead.

Brewster, Keith. Assistant Lecturer, University of Warwick. Contributor to *Journal of Latin American Studies*. **Essay:** Mexican Revolution: October 1910–February 1913.

Britton, John A. Professor of History, Francis Marion University. Author of *Carleton Beals: A Radical Journalist in Latin America* (1987) and *Revolution and Ideology: Images of the Mexican Revolution in the United States* (1995). Editor of and contributor to *The Handbook of Latin American Studies*. **Essay:** Liberalism.

Brown, Jonathan C. Professor, Department of History, University of Texas, Austin. Author of *A*

Socioeconomic History of Argentina, 1776–1860 (1979) and *Oil and Revolution in Mexico* (1993). Editor of *The Mexican Petroleum Industry in the Twentieth Century* (with Alan Knight, 1992) and *Revolution and Restoration: The Rearrangement of Power in Argentina, 1760–1860* (with Mark D. Szuchman, 1994). **Essay:** Petroleum: Pre-1938.

Bruhn, Kathleen. Assistant Professor, Department of Political Science, University of California, Santa Barbara. Author of *Taking on Goliath: The Emergence of a New Left Party and the Struggle for Democracy in Mexico* (1997). **Essay:** Cárdenas, Cuauhtémoc.

Brunk, Samuel. Assistant Professor, Department of History, University of Nebraska, Lincoln. Author of *Emiliano Zapata: Revolution and Betrayal in Mexico* (1995). Contributor to *Hispanic American Historical Review.* **Essay:** Zapata, Emiliano.

Buchenau, Jürgen. Assistant Professor, Department of History, University of Southern Mississippi. Author of *In the Shadow of the Giant: The Making of Mexico's Central America Policy, 1876–1930* (1996). Contributor to *The Americas, Hispanic American Historial Review, Jahrbuch für Geschichte von Gesellschaft, Wirtschaft und Staat Lateinamerikas, SECOLAS Annals,* and *South Eastern Latin Americanist.* **Essays:** Foreign Policy: 1821–76; Foreign Policy: 1876–1910; Foreign Policy: 1946–96; Guadalupe Hidalgo, Treaty of.

Bussey, Jane. Reporter, *Miami Herald.* Contributor to *U.S. News & World Report, The Guardian* (London), and *London Independent.* **Essay:** Salinas de Gortari, Carlos.

Campos García, Melchor. Profesor-Investigador, Unidad de Ciencias Sociales, Universidad Autónoma de Yucatán. Contributor to *Liberalismo, actores y política en Yucatán* edited by Othón Baños Ramírez (1995). **Essay:** Politics and Government: Bourbon New Spain.

Cárdenas, Enrique. Rector y Profesor, Departamento de Economía, Universidad de las Américas, Puebla. Author of *La industrialización mexicana durante la Gran Depresión* (1987) and *Historia económica de México: Lecturas, la hacienda pública y la política económica 1927–1958* (1994). **Essay:** Great Depression.

Carr, Barry. Reader in History, La Trobe University. Author of *El movimiento obrero y la política en*

México, 1910–1929 (1981) and *Marxism and Communism in Twentieth-Century Mexico* (1992). **Essays:** Industrial Labor: 1910–40; Lombardo Toledano, Vicente; Partido de la Revolución Democrática (PRD).

Cervantes, Fernando. Lecturer, Department of Hispanic and Latin American Studies, University of Bristol. Author of *The Devil in the New World: The Impact of Diabolism in New Spain* (1994). **Essay:** Conquest: Central Mexico.

Chuchiak, John F., IV. Doctoral Candidate and Instructor, Tulane University. Author of *An Annotated Guide to CRC Resources on Mexico* (1994). Contributor to *Iglesia y Sociedad en América Colonial* (1995). **Essay:** Inquisition.

Cline, Sarah L. Professor of History, University of California, Santa Barbara. Author of *The Testaments of Culhuacan* (with Miguel León-Portilla, 1984), *Colonial Culhaucan, 1580–1600: A Social History of an Aztec Town* (1986), and *The Book of Tributes* (1993). **Essays:** Catholic Church: Bourbon New Spain; Catholic Church: Hapsburg New Spain.

Collier, George A. Professor of Anthropology, Stanford University. Author of *BASTA! Land and the Zapatista Rebellion in Chiapas* (1994). **Essay:** Zapatista Rebellion in Chiapas.

Crossen, John F. Doctoral Student and Associate Instructor, Department of Spanish and Portuguese, Indiana University, Bloomington. Contributor to *Romance Languages Annual* (1996). Associate editor, *Chiricúa.* **Essay:** Mexican Revolution: October 1915–May 1917.

Cuspinera, Margarita Vera. Profesora, El Colegio de Filosofía, Facultad de Filosofía y Letras, Universidad Nacional Autónoma de México. Author of *El pensamiento filosófico de Vasconcelos* (1979). Contributor to *Bolívar y el mundo de los libertadores* edited by Charles Minguet (1993), *Homenaje a Alfonso Reyes* (1981), and *Obras completas,* vol. 10, by Antonio Caso (1985). **Essay:** Vasconcelos, José.

Cypess, Sandra M. Professor, Department of Spanish, University of Maryland. Author of *La Malinche in Mexican Literature: From History to Myth* (1991). Contributor to *The Bucknell Review: Perspectives on Contemporary Spanish American*

Theatre edited by Frank Dauster (1996); *Cambridge History of Latin American Literature* edited by Enrique Pupo-Walker and Roberto González Echevarría (1996); *A History of Literature in the Caribbean*, vol. 1, edited by James Arnold (1994); and *La Malinche, sus padres y sus hijos* edited by Margo Glantz (1995). **Essay:** Literature and National Identity.

de la Calle, Sophie. Doctoral Candidate, Department of Spanish, University of Maryland. **Essay:** Literature and National Identity.

de la Mora, Luz María. Visiting Research Fellow, Center for U.S.-Mexican Studies, University of California, San Diego; Assistant Negotiator, Automotive Sector, Mexican Delegation, NAFTA. Contributor to *Bianuario México–Estados Unidos, 1993–1994* edited by Gustavo Vega (1995) and *Policy Options/Options Politiques.* **Essays:** General Agreement on Tariffs and Trade (GATT); North American Free Trade Agreement (NAFTA).

de la Peña, Guillermo. Director, Centro de Investigaciones y Estudios Superiores en Antropología Social (CIESAS)–Occidente. Contributor to *The Cambridge History of Latin America.* **Essay:** Urbanism and Urbanization.

de la Teja, Jesús F. Assistant Professor of History, Southwest Texas State University. Author of *A Revolution Remembered: The Memoirs and Selected Correspondence of Juan N. Seguin* (1991) and *San Antonio de Bexar: A Community on New Spain's Northern Frontier* (1995). Contributor to *Historia Mexicana* and *Southwestern Historical Quarterly.* **Essay:** Texan Secession.

de Lizaur, Blanca. Facultad de Filosofía y Letras, Universidad Nacional Autónoma de México. Contributor to *Anthropos, La Experiencia Literaria,* and *Oralidad y Escritura* edited by Eugenia Reveltes (1992). **Essay:** *Telenovelas.*

de los Reyes, Aurelio. Investigador Titular, Instituto de Investigaciones Estéticas, Universidad Nacional Autónoma de México. Author of *Vivir de sueños: El cine en Mexico, 1896–1924* (1981), *Los origenes del cine en Mexico, 1896–1900* (revised edition, 1984), and *Con Villa en Mexico* (1985). **Essay:** Motion Pictures: 1896–1930.

Donahue-Wallace, Kelly. Doctoral Candidate, Spanish Colonial Art History, University of New Mexico. Contributor to *Anales del Instituto de Investigaciones Estéticas.* **Essay:** Prints.

Elliott, Ingrid. Doctoral Candidate, Department of Art History, University of Chicago. **Essay:** Visual Arts: 1910–37, The Revolutionary Tradition.

Falcón Vega, Romana. Profesora-Investigadora, Centro de Estudios Históricos, El Colegio de México. Author of *El agrarismo en Veracruz: La etapa radical, 1928–1935* (1977), *Revolución y caciquismo: San Luis Potosí, 1910–1938* (1984), *La semilla en el surco: Adalberto Tejeda y el radicalismo en Veracruz, 1883–1960* (with Soledad García Morales and María Eugenia Terrones, 1986). Contributor to *Historia Mexicana, La Formas y las políticas del dominio agrario: Homenaje a François Chevalier* edited by Ricardo Avila Palafox, Carlos Martínez Assad, and Jean Meyer (1992), *Mexican Studies,* and *Revista Mexicana de Sociología.* **Essay:** Cedillo, Saturnino.

Fein, Seth. Assistant Professor of History, Georgia State University. Contributor to *Close Encounters of Empire: Writing the Cultural History of U.S.–Latin American Relations* (forthcoming); *Film-Historia; Historia y grafía; Nuevo Texto Crítico; Secuencia; Studies in Latin American Popular Culture; México–Estados Unidos: Encuentros y desencuentros en el cine* (1996); and *Visible Nation: Latin American Film and Video* (forthcoming). **Essay:** Motion Pictures: 1930–60.

Fernández, María. Assistant Professor of Art History, University of Connecticut. Author of *In the Image of the Other: A Call for Re-evaluation of National Identity.* Contributor to *Center Design Book Review.* **Essays:** Architecture: Ninteenth Century; Architecture: Twentieth Century.

Fleming, Martin V. Instructor, Department of History, Xavier University of Louisiana; and Doctoral Candidate, Latin American History, Tulane University. **Essay:** Politics and Government: Hapsburg New Spain.

García, José Z. Director, Center for Latin American Studies, New Mexico State University. **Essay:** Bullfighting.

García Quintanilla, Alejandra. Profesora-Investigadora, Unidad de Ciencias Sociales, Universidad Autónoma de Yucatán. Author of *Los tiempos en Yucatán: Los hombres, las mujeres y la* *naturaleza, siglo XIX* (1986). **Essay:** Women's Status and Occupation: 1821–1910.

Garner, Paul. Professor of Spanish and Latin American Studies, Department of European Languages, Goldsmiths College, University of London. Author of *La Revolución en la provincia: Soberanía estatal y caudillismo en las montañas de Oaxaca* (1988). Contributor to *Bulletin of Latin American Research.* **Essay:** Díaz, Porfirio: Interpretive Discussion.

Garner, Richard L. Retired Associate Professor, Department of History, Penn State University. Author of *Economic Growth and Change in Bourbon Mexico* (with Spiro Stefanou, 1993). **Essay:** Mining: Colonial.

Garrido, Luis Javier. Profesor-Investigador, Universidad Nacional Autónoma de México. Author of *El Partido de la Revolución Institucionalizada* (1982) and *La Ruptura* (1993). **Essay:** Partido Revolucionario Institucional (PRI).

Garza, James A. Doctoral Candidate, Department of History, Texas Christian University. **Essay:** Díaz, Porfirio: Biography.

Gates, Marilyn. Associate Professor of Anthropology and Latin American Studies, Simon Fraser University. Author of *In Default: Peasants, the Debt Crisis and the Agricultural Challenge in Mexico* (1993). Contributor to *Current Anthropology, Journal of Developing Areas,* and *Journal of Latin American Studies.* **Essay:** Ecology.

Gilbert, Courtney. Graduate Student in Art History, University of Chicago. **Essay:** Visual Arts: 1920–45, Art outside the Revolutionary Tradition.

Gilly, Adolfo. Investigador, Universidad Nacional Autónoma de México. Author of *Inside the Cuban Revolution* (1964), *La revolución interrumpida* (1972), *La revolución de la madrugada* (1977), *The Mexican Revolution* (1982), and *El Cardenismo: Una utopia mexicana* (1994). Editor of *Cartas a Cuauhtémoc Cárdenas* (1989). Contributor to *El estado en América Latina: Teoría y práctica* edited by Pablo González Casanova (1990). **Essay:** Rural Economy and Society: 1910–40.

Gonzalbo Aizpuru, Pilar. Profesora-Investigadora, Centro de Estudios Históricos, El Colegio de México. Author of *Historia de la educación en la época*

colonial, 2 vols. (1990). Editor of *Familias novohispanas, Siglos XVI-XIX* (1991) and *La familia en el mundo iberoamericano* (1994). **Essay:** Conquest: Spanish Background.

González Oropeza, Manuel. Investigador, Instituto de Investigaciones Jurídicas, and Profesor, Facultad de Derecho, Universidad Nacional Autónoma de México. Author of *El federalismo* (1995). Editor of *Los legisladores de la nación* (1994) and *Archivo inédito de Ignacio L. Vallarta,* 5 vols. (1994). **Essay:** Constitution of 1917.

Guedea, Virginia. Investigadora Titular, Instituto de Investigaciones Históricas, Universidad Nacional Autónoma de México. Author of *Las gacetas de México y la medicina: Un índice* (1991) and *En busca de un gobierno alterno: Los Guadalupes de México* (1992). Editor of *Five Centuries of Mexican History—Cinco siglos de historia de México, Papers of the VIII Conference of Mexican and North American Historians, San Diego, California, October 18–20, 1990; Memorias de la VIII reunión de historiadores mexicanos y norteamericanos, San Diego, California, 18–20 de octubre de 1990,* 2 vols. (with Jaime E. Rodríguez O., 1992); *La revolución de independencia* (1995); and *Prontuario e indice alfabético de causas de varios individuos eclesiásticos y seculares de quienes se habla en ellas y que resultan más o menos indiciados de adhesión al partido de los rebeldes* (1995). Contributor to *Un hombre entre Europa y América, Homenaje a Juan Antonio Ortegas y Medina* edited by Arturo Azuela and Amaya Garritz (1993), *La ciudad de México en la primera mitad del siglo XIX* edited by Regina Hernández (1994), *Mitos en las relaciones México–Estados Unidos* (with Jaime E. Rodríguez O. and María Esther Schumacher) edited by María Esther Schumacher (1994), and *Mexico in the Age of Democratic Revolutions, 1750–1850* edited by Jaime E. Rodríguez O. (1994). **Essays:** Hidalgo Revolt; Hidalgo y Costilla, Miguel; Morelos, José María; Politics and Government: 1821–76.

Gutmann, Matthew C. Assistant Professor, Department of Anthropology, Brown University. Author of *The Meanings of Macho: Being a Man in Mexico City* (1996). Editor of *Culture, Identity, and Empire in the Americas, 1492–1992* (with Rebecca Dobkins, 1992). Contributor to *Alteridades, Annual Review of Anthropology, Blackwell Dictionary of Anthropology* edited by Thomas J. Barfield (1996), *The Cultural Politics of Childhood* edited by Nancy

Scheper-Hughes and Carolyn Sargent (1996), and *Gender, Sexuality, and Culture: A Reader* edited by Roger N. Lancaster and Micaela di Leonardo (1996). **Essay:** Gender: 1910–96.

Haber, Paul Lawrence. Assistant Professor, Department of Political Science, University of Montana. Contributor to *Latin American Research Review, Movimientos sociales y democracia en el México de los 90s* edited by Sergio Zermeño (1995), *The Politics of Economic Restructuring: State-Society Relations and Regime Change in Mexico* edited by María Cook, Kevin Middlebrook, and Juan Molinar (1994), and *Transforming State-Society Relations in Mexico: The National Solidarity Strategy* edited by Wayne Cornelius, Ann Craig, and Jonathan Fox (1994). **Essay:** Earthquake of 1985.

Hadley, Diana. Research Specialist and Senior Editor, Documentary Relations of the Southwest, Arizona State Museum, University of Arizona. Author of *Environmental Change in Aravaipa, 1870–1970: An Ethnoecological Survey* (1991), *El Río Bonito: An Ethnoecological Study of the Bonita Creek Watershed, Southeastern Arizona* (1993), and *Land Use History of the San Rafael Valley, Arizona, 1540–1960* (1995). Editor of *The Presidio and the Militia on the Northern Frontier of New Spain, 1700–1765,* vol. 2, part 2 (1997). **Essay:** Missions.

Hamilton, Nora. Associate Professor, Department of Political Science, University of Southern California. Author of *The Limits of State Autonomy: Post-Revolutionary Mexico* (1982). Editor of *Modern Mexico: State, Economy and Social Conflict* (with Timothy Harding, 1986). Contributor to *Third World Quarterly* (with Eun Mee Kim). **Essay:** Cárdenas, Lázaro.

Hamnett, Brian R. Professor, Department of History, and Director, Latin American Centre, University of Essex. Author of *Roots of Insurgency: Mexican Regions, 1750–1824* (1986). Contributor to *Profiles in Power* (1994). **Essays:** Juárez, Benito; Reform Laws; Wars of Reform (Three Years War).

Hart, John Mason. Professor of History, University of Houston. Author of *Anarchism and the Mexican Working Class* (1978) and *Revolutionary Mexico: The Coming and Process of the Mexican Revolution* (1987). **Essay:** Mexican Revolution: Causes.

Harvey, Neil. Assistant Professor, Department of Government, New Mexico State University. Author of *Rebellion in Chiapas* (1994). Editor of *Mexico: Dilemmas of Transition* (1993). **Essay:** Rural Economy and Society: 1940–96, Resistance and Rebellion.

Hassig, Ross. Professor of Anthropology, University of Oklahoma. Author of *Trade, Tribute, and Transportation: The Sixteenth-Century Political Economy of the Valley of Mexico* (1985), *Aztec Warfare: Imperial Expansion and Political Control* (1988), *War and Society in Ancient Mesoamerica* (1992), and *Mexico and the Spanish Conquest* (1994). Editor of *Five Centuries of Law and Politics in Central Mexico* (with Ronald M. Spores, 1984) and *Treatise on the Heathen Superstitions and Customs that Today Live among the Indians Native to This New Spain 1629* by Hernando Ruiz de Alarcón (translated and edited with J. Richard Andrews, 1984). Contributor to *History Today, Smoke and Mist: Mesoamerican Studies in Memory of Thelma D. Sullivan* (with J. Richard Andrews) edited by J. Kathryn Josserand and Karen Dakin (1988), *Ancient Road Networks and Settlement Hierarchies in the New World* edited by Charles D. Trombold (1991), *War in the Tribal Zone: Expanding States and Indigenous Warfare* edited by R. Brian Ferguson and Neil L. Whitehead (1992), and *The Hernando de Soto Expedition: History, Historiography, and "Discovery" in the Southeast* edited by Patricia Galloway (1997). **Essay:** Mesoamerica: Warfare.

Hayes, Joy Elizabeth. Assistant Professor of Communication Studies, University of Iowa. Author of *Radio Nation: Communication, Popular Culture, and Nationalism in Mexico* (forthcoming). Contributor to *The Communication Review* and *Studies in Latin American Popular Culture*. **Essay:** Radio.

Helguera, J. León. Professor of History, Emeritus, Vanderbilt University; Senior Editor of *The Americas*. Contributor to *La Colmena Universitaria, Encyclopedia of Latin American History and Culture,* 5 vols., edited by Barbara A. Tenenbaum (1996), *León Rotario,* and *South Eastern Latin Americanist*. **Essay:** Victoria, Guadalupe.

Henderson, Timothy J. Lecturer, History and Latin American Studies, Yale University. Author of *The Worm in the Wheat: Rosalie Evans and Agrarian Struggle in the Puebla-Tlaxcala Valley of Mexico, 1906–1927* (forthcoming). **Essay:** Catholic Church: 1821–1910.

Hernández-Durán, Raymond. Doctoral Candidate, Pre-Columbian and Colonial Mexico, Department of Art History, University of Chicago; MacArthur Fellow, Department of Prints and Drawings, Art Institute of Chicago. **Essay:** Visual Arts: Seventeenth Century.

Herzog, Lawrence A. Professor of Geography and Latin American Studies and Director of the Institute for Built Environments and Comparative Urban Research (BECUR), San Diego State University. Author of *Where North Meets South* (1990). Editor of *Changing Boundaries in the Americas* (1992). Contributor to *Geoforum, Habitat International, Natural Resources Journal, Places,* and *Urban Studies.* **Essay:** U.S.-Mexican Border: Border Urbanism.

Heyman, Josiah McC. Associate Professor of Anthropology, Department of Social Sciences, Michigan Technological University. Author of *Life and Labor on the Border: Working People of Northeastern Sonora, Mexico, 1886–1986* (1991). Contributor to *Current Anthropology* and *Journal of Political Ecology.* **Essay:** Migration to the United States: 1940–96.

Karttunen, Frances. Senior Research Scientist, Linguistics Research Center, University of Texas, Austin. Author of *Nahuatl in the Middle Years* (with James Lockhart, 1976), *An Analytical Dictionary of Nahuatl* (1983, 1992), *The Art of Nahuatl Speech: The Bancroft Dialogues* (with James Lockhart, 1987), and *Between Worlds: Interpreters, Guides, and Survivors* (1994). **Essay:** Malinche and Malinchismo.

Keen, Benjamin. Professor Emeritus, Northern Illinois University. Author of *The Aztec Image in Western Thought* (with Juan Friede, 1971), *Bartolomé de las Casas in History: Toward an Understanding of the Man and His Thoughts* (1971), and *A History of Latin America,* 5th edition (1995). **Essay:** Conquistadors.

Klahn, Norma. Associate Professor of Spanish, Board of Studies in Literature, University of California, Santa Cruz. **Essay:** Campobello, Nellie.

Klein, Cecelia F. Professor of Pre-Columbian Art History, University of California, Los Angeles. Contributor to *The Aztec Templo Mayor* edited by Elizabeth Hill Boone (1987); *Current Topics in Aztec Studies: Essays in Honor of H. B. Nicholson*

edited by Alana Cordy-Collins and Douglas Sharon (1993); *Estudios de Cultura Nahuatl, Gender Rhetorics: Postures of Dominance and Submission in History* (1994); and *Smoke and Mist: Essays in Honor of Thelma D. Sullivan* (1988). **Essays:** Visual Arts: Mesoamerica; Women's Status and Occupation: Mesoamerica.

Knight, Alan. Director, Latin American Centre, St. Antony's College, Oxford University. Author of *The Mexican Revolution* (1986) and *U.S.-Mexican Relations, 1910–1940: An Interpretation* (1987). Editor of *Everyday Forms of State Formation* (with Gil Joseph and Daniel Nugent, 1994). Contributor to *Bulletin of Latin American Research, Cambridge History of Latin America,* vol. 7, edited by Leslie Bethel (1990), *Journal of Latin American Studies,* and *Past and Present.* **Essay:** Nationalism.

Koegel, John. Assistant Professor of Music, University of Missouri, Columbia. Contributor to *American Music Newsletter of the Sonneck Society for American Music, Ars Musica Denver, Diccionario de la música española e hispanoamericana* edited by Emilio Casares Rodicio, *Inter-American Music Review,* and *Journal of the American Music Research Center.* **Essay:** Music: Nineteenth and Twentieth Centuries.

Kuntz Ficker, Sandra. Profesora Titular, Universidad Autónoma Metropolitana, Xochimilco. Author of *Empresa extranjera y mercado interno: El Ferrocarril Central Mexicano, 1880–1907* (1995). Contributor to *Historia Mexicana.* **Essay:** Railroads.

Lara, Luis Fernando. Profesor-Investigador, Centro de Estudios Lingüísticos y Literarios, El Colegio de México. Author of *Diccionario básico del español de México* (1986) and *Dimensiones de la lexicografía* (1990). **Essay:** Mexican Spanish.

Legler, Thomas. Doctoral Candidate, Department of Political Science, York University. Contributor to *Etcetera* and *Voices of Mexico.* **Essay:** Zedillo Ponce de León, Ernesto.

Lewis, Laura A. Visiting Assistant Professor, Department of Anthropology, University of Rochester. Contributor to *Political and Legal Anthropology Review* and *Racism and Antiracism in World Perspective* edited by Benjamin Bowser (1995). **Essay:** African Mexicans.

Lewis, Stephen E. Lecturer, University of Wisconsin, Oshkosh. Contributor to *Anthropology and*

Education Quarterly, Canadian Journal of Latin American and Caribbean Studies, MACLAS Latin American Essays 8 (1995), and *Radical History Review.* Essay: *Mestizaje.*

Lipsett-Rivera, Sonya. Associate Professor, Department of History, Carleton University. Contributor to *The Americas* and *Hispanic American Historical Review.* Essay: Women's Status and Occupation: Spanish Women in New Spain.

Llanos, Bernardita. Associate Professor of Spanish and Women's Studies, Denison University. Author of *(Re)descubrimiento y (Re)conquista de América en la ilustración española* (1994). Contributor to *Taller de Letras* and *Torre de papel.* Essay: Poniatowska, Elena.

Loaeza, Soledad. Profesora-Investigadora, Centro de Estudios Internacionales, El Colegio de México. Contributor to *Revista Mexicana de Sociología* and *The Right and Democracy in Latin America* edited by Douglas A. Chalmers, María de Carmo Campobello de Souza, and Atilio A. Boro (1992). Essay: Partido de Acción Nacional (PAN).

Lomnitz, Cinna. Professor of Seismology, Universidad Nacional Autónoma de México. Author of *Fundamentals of Earthquake Prediction* (1994). Essay: Science.

Lorey, David E. Program Officer for Latin American Studies, The Hewlett Foundation, Menlow Park, California. Author of *U.S.-Mexico Border Statistics since 1900* (1990), *The Rise of the Professions in Twentieth-Century Mexico: University Graduates and Occupational Change* (1992, 1994), *The University and Economic Development in Mexico since 1929* (1993), and *U.S.-Mexico Border Statistics since 1900: 1990 Update* (1993). Essay: U.S.-Mexican Border: 1910–96.

Lustig, Nora. Senior Fellow, Foreign Policy Studies, Brookings Institution. Author of *Mexico: The Remaking of an Economy* (1992). Editor of *Coping with Austerity: Poverty and Inequality in Latin America* (1995) and *North-American Free Trade: Setting the Record Straight* (1997). Essay: Peso Crisis of 1994.

Macías Richard, Carlos. Profesor-Investigador, Division de Ciencias Sociales y Humanidades, Universidad de Quintana Roo. Author of *Vida y temperamento de Plutarco Elías Calles* (1995).

Editor of *Correspondencia personal de Plutarco Elías Calles,* 2 vols. (1991, 1993). Essay: Calles, Plutarco Elías.

Mata, Rodolfo. Investigador, Centro de Estudios Literarios, Instituto de Investigaciones Filológicas, Universidad Nacional Autónoma de México. Author of *Octavio Paz y Haroldo de Campos: Contradicciones de la modernidad en América Latina.* Essay: Paz, Octavio.

Matute, Álvaro. Investigador, Instituto de Investigaciones Históricas, Universidad Nacional Autónoma de México. Author of *La Revolución Mexicana: Actores, escenarios y acciones (Vida cultural y política, 1901–1929)* (1993). Editor of *Estado, iglesia y sociedad en México, Siglo XIX* (1995). Essays: de la Huerta, Adolfo; Mexican Revolution: May 1917–December 1920; Obregón, Álvaro.

McCaa, Robert. Professor of History, University of Minnesota. Contributor to *Annales de Demographie Historique, Hispanic American Historical Review, Historia Mexicana,* and *Population Studies.* Essays: Conquest: Demographic Impact; Mesoamerica: Population.

McClung de Tapia, Emily. Investigadora and Directora, Laboratorio de Paleo-etnobotánica y Paleoambiente, Instituto de Investigaciones Antropológicas, Universidad Nacional Autónoma de México. Author of *Ecología y cultura en Mesoamérica* (1984) and *La domesticación prehispánica del Amaranthus* (1996). Contributor to *Historia general de la medicina en México* edited by G. Aguirre Beltrán and R. Moreno de los Arcos (1990) and *The Origin of Agriculture: An International Perspective* edited by P. J. Watson and C. W. Cowan (1992). Essay: Mesoamerica: Agriculture and Ecology.

McDowell, John Holmes. Professor, Folklore Institute, Indiana University. Author of *Children's Riddling* (1979), *Sayings of the Ancestors: The Spiritual Life of the Sibundoy Indians* (1989), and *"So Wise Were Our Elders": Mythic Narratives of the Kamsá* (1994). Essay: Corridos.

McSherry, Corynne. Doctoral Candidate, Department of Communication, University of California, San Diego. Essay: Radio.

McVicker, Donald. Professor of Anthropology, North Central College, Naperville, Illinois; Research

Associate, Field Museum of Natural History, Chicago. Author of *Quetzalcoatl and Tula: Images and Myth* (1995). Editor of *Mexico: La Visión del Cosmos—Three Thousand Years of Creativity* (1992) and *Testimony of the Image* (with Mary Frech McVicker, 1992). Contributor to *Rediscovering Our Past: Essays on the History of American Archaeology* edited by J. E. Reyman (1992) and *Encyclopedia of Latin American Literature,* vol. 3 (1996). Essay: Quetzalcoatl.

McVicker, Mary Frech. Freelance Writer. Editor of *Testimony of the Image* (with Donald McVicker, 1992). Essay: Calderón de la Barca, Fanny.

Melville, Elinor G. K. Associate Professor, Department of History and Faculty of Environmental Studies, York University. Author of *A Plague of Sheep: Environmental Consequences of the Conquest of Mexico* (1994). Contributor to *Comparative Studies in Society and History.* Essay: Conquest: Ecological Impact.

Meyer, Jean. Investigador, División de Estudios Internacionales, Centro de Investigación y Docencia Económica (CIDE). Author of *Les chrétiens d'Amérique Latine* (1992) and *La Cristiada* (1995). Essay: Catholic Church: 1910–96.

Miller, Virginia E. Associate Professor, Department of the History of Art, University of Illinois, Chicago. Editor of *The Role of Gender in Precolumbian Art and Architecture* (1988) and *The Frieze of the Palace of the Stuccoes, Acanceh, Yucatán, Mexico* (1991). Essays: Mesoamerica: Introduction; Mesoamerica: Maya; Mesoamerica: Olmec; Mesoamerica: Veracruz, Classic and Postclassic.

Mora, Carl J. Visiting Scholar, Latin American Institute, University of New Mexico. Author of *Mexican Cinema: Reflections of a Society, 1896–1988* (1990). Contributor to *Historia y Vida.* Essay: Motion Pictures: 1960–96.

Mraz, John. Senior Research Fellow, Instituto de Ciencias Sociales y Humanidades, Universidad Autónoma de Puebla. Author of *Uprooted: Braceros in the Hermanos Lens* (1996). Essays: Moreno Reyes, Mario (Cantinflas); Photography.

Oberhelman, Harley D. Paul Whitfield Horn Professor of Romance Languages, Texas Tech University. Author of *Ernesto Sábato* (1970), *The Presence of Faulkner in the Writings of García Márquez* (1980), *Gabriel García Márquez: A Study of the Short Fiction* (1991), *The Presence of Hemingway in the Short Fiction of Gabriel García Márquez* (1994), and *García Márquez and Cuba: A Study of Its Presence in His Fiction, Journalism, and Cinema* (1995). Essay: Modernism.

Orozco, Monica I. Doctoral Candidate and Humanities Research Assistantship Fellow, Department of History, University of California, Santa Barbara. Essay: Orozco, José Clemente.

Osorio Zuñiga, Rubén. Centro de Investigación Histórica de Chihuaua. Author of *Cruz Chávez, los Tomoches en armas* (1991), *Pancho Villa, ese desconocido* (1991), *La Muerte de dos generales: Felipe Ángeles y Francisco Villa* (1995), *Tomóchic en llamas* (1995), and *Biografía de Francisco Villa* (1997). Essays: Orozco Vázquez, Pascual, Jr.; Terrazas Fuentes, Luis; Villa, Francisco (Pancho).

Pani, Erika. Doctoral Candidate, Centro de Estudios Históricos, El Colegio de México. Contributor to *Historia Mexicana* and *Secuencia.* Essays: Ayutla, Revolution of; Maximilian (Ferdinand Maximilian von Hapsburg); Santa Anna, Antonio López de.

Parish, Helen Rand. Research Associate, Bancroft Library, University of California, Berkeley; Visiting Scholar, Dominican School of Philosophy and Theology, Graduate Theological Union, University of California, Berkeley. Author of *The Life and Writings of Bartolomé de Las Casas* (with H. R. Wagner, 1967), *The Royal File on the Administration of the Indians* (1980), *Bartolomé de Las Casas: The Only Way* (with F. P. Sullivan, 1992), and *Las Casas en México* (with H. E. Weidman, 1992). Essay: Las Casas, Bartolomé de.

Parra, Max. Assistant Professor of Latin American Literature, University of California, San Diego. Contributor to *Siglo XX/Twentieth Century, Revista de Estudios Hispánicos,* and *Journal of Latin American Cultural Studies.* Essay: Azuela, Mariano.

Phillips, Michael D. Instructor in Humanities, Brigham Young University. Contributor to *International Dictionary of Historic Places,* vol. 1, *The Americas,* edited by Trudy Ring and Robert M. Salkin (1995). Essays: Mesoamerica: Monte Albán; Mesoamerica: Toltec.

Picard, Charmaine. Doctoral Candidate, Department of History, University of Chicago. Essay: Visual Arts: 1945–96.

Pilcher, Jeffrey M. Assistant Professor, Department of History, The Citadel. Author of *¡Que Vivan los Tamales! Food and the Making of Mexican Identity* (forthcoming). **Essay:** Cuisine.

Poole, Stafford, C.M. Vincentian Studies Institute. Author of *Our Lady of Guadalupe: Origins and Sources of a Mexcan National Symbol, 1531–1797* (1995). **Essays:** Catholic Church: Colonial Structure, Divisions, Hierarchy; Virgin of Guadalupe and Guadalupanismo.

Porter, Susie S. Assistant Professor, Department of History and Women's Studies Program, University of Utah, Salt Lake City. **Essay:** Gender: Overview.

Puga, Cristina. Profesora, Facultad de Ciencias Políticas y Sociales, Universidad Nacional Autónoma de México. Author of *México: Empresarios y poder* (1993) and *México: La modernización contradictoria* (with David Torres Mejia, 1995). **Essay:** Industry and Industrialization.

Purnell, Jennie. Assistant Professor, Department of Political Science, Boston College. **Essay:** Cristero Rebellion.

Quiñones Keber, Eloise. Professor, Department of Fine and Performing Arts, Baruch College, City University of New York. Author of *Art of Ancient Mexico: Treasures of Tenochtitlan* (with H. B. Nicholson, 1983) and *Codex Telleriano-Remesis: Ritual, Divination, and History in a Pictorial Aztec Manuscript* (1995). **Essay:** Nahua Rulers, Pre-Hispanic.

Racine, Karen. Doctoral Candidate, Department of History, Tulane University. Contibutor to *Encyclopedia of Latin American History and Culture* (1995) and *Historical Encyclopedia of World Slavery* (1997). **Essay:** Mora, José María Luís.

Randall, Laura. Professor and Graduate Adviser, Department of Economics, Hunter College, City University of New York. Author of *An Economic History of Argentina in the Twentieth Century* (1978), *The Political Economy of Venezuelan Oil* (1987), *El papel de las industrias del petróleo en la promoción del desarrollo nacional* (1989), *The Political Economy of Mexican Oil* (1989), and *The Political Economy of Brazilian Oil* (1993). Editor of *Economic Development, Evolution or Revolution* (1964), *The Changing Structure of Mexico* (1996), and *Reforming Mexico's Agrarian Reform* (1996). **Essay:** Petroleum: 1938–96.

Read, Kay A. Associate Professor, Department of Religious Studies, DePaul University. Author of *Binding Reeds and Burning Hearts: Mexica-Tenochca Concepts of Time and Sacrifice* (1991). Contributor to *History of Religions Journal.* **Essays:** Mesoamerica: Calendrics; Mesoamerica: Religion.

Richmond, Douglas W. Professor of History, University of Texas, Arlington. Author of *Venustiano Carranza's Nationalist Struggle, 1893–1920* (1983) and *Carlos Pellegrini and the Crisis of the Argentine Elites, 1880–1916* (1989). Editor of *Essays on the Mexican War* (1986). **Essays:** Carranza, Venustiano; Guerrero, Vicente; Huerta, Victoriano; Iturbide, Agustín de.

Riedinger, Edward A. Bibliographer for Latin America, Associate Professor, University Libraries, and Adjunct Associate Professor, Department of History, Ohio State University. Author of *Como se faz um presidente* (1988), *Where in the World to Learn* (1995), and *Renaissance in the Tropics, Brazilian Culture, 1922–60* (1996). **Essay:** Siqueiros, David Alfaro.

Riley, G. Micheal. Professor, Department of History, Ohio State University. Author of *Fernando Cortés and the Marquesado in Morelos, 1522–1547* (1973). **Essay:** Cortés, Fernando (Hernán).

Romo, Ricardo. Executive Vice President and Provost, University of Texas, Austin. **Essay:** Mexican American Communities.

Ruffinelli, Jorge. Professor, Department of Spanish and Portuguese, Stanford University. Author of *El lugar de Rulfo y otros ensayos* (1980) and *Crítica en marcha*, 2nd edition (1982). Editor of *Texto Crítico* and *Nuevo Texto Crítico.* **Essay:** Rulfo, Juan.

Rugeley, Terry. Assistant Professor, Department of History, University of Oklahoma. Author of *Yucatán's Maya Peasantry and the Origins of the Caste War, 1800–1847* (1996). Contributor to *Ethnohistory.* **Essays:** Caste War of Yucatán; French Intervention.

Russell, Craig H. Professor of Music, California Polytechnic State University; Director of the San Luis Obispo Mozart Akademie. Author of *Santiago de Murcia's "Códice Saldívar No. 4": A Treasury of Guitar Music from Baroque Mexico*, 2 vols. (1995). **Essays:** Music: Mesoamerica through Seventeenth Century; Music: Eighteenth Century.

Salles, Vania. Profesora-Investigadora, Centro de Estudios Históricos, El Colegio de México. Contributor to *Decline y auge de las identidades* edited by María Luisa Tarrés (1994). **Essay:** Family and Kinship: Twentieth Century.

Salvador, Ricardo J. Associate Professor of Agronomy and Director, North Central Institute for Sustainable Systems, Iowa State University. Contributor to *Crop Science* (with T. P. Nepal and R. B. Pearce) and *Maydica* (with R.B. Pearce). **Essay:** Maize.

Santoni, Pedro. Associate Professor of History, California State University, San Bernardino. Author of *Mexicans at Arms: Puro Federalists and the Politics of War, 1845–1848* (1996). Editor of *The Encyclopedia of the Mexican-American War* (1997). Contributor to *Hispanic American Historical Review.* **Essay:** U.S.-Mexican War.

Saragoza, Alex M. Professor, Department of Ethnic Studies, University of California, Berkeley. Author of *The Monterrey Elite and the Mexican State, 1880–1940* (1988) and *The Mass Media and the State in Mexico: The Origins of Television, 1930–1972.* **Essays:** Television; Tourism.

Schell, William, Jr. Assistant Professor, Department of History, Murray State University. Author of *Medieval Iberian Tradition and the Development of the Mexican Hacienda* (1986). Contributor to *Itinerario: European Journal for Overseas History, Journal of Sports History, Mexican Studies/Estudios Mexicanos, South Eastern Latin Americanist,* and *Xi Lam.* **Essay:** Politics and Government: 1876–1910.

Schmidt, Arthur. Associate Professor of History, Temple University. Author of *The Economic and Social Effect of Railroads in Puebla and Veracruz, Mexico, 1867–1911* (1987) and the foreword to *Nothing, Nobody: Voices of the Mexico City Earthquake* by Elena Poniatowska (with Aurora Camacho de Schmidt, 1995). Contributor to *Globalization, Urbanization, and the State: Selected Studies on Contemporary Latin America* edited by Satya Pattnayak (1995). **Essay:** Limantour, José Yves.

Schmidt, Samuel. Associate Professor, Department of Political Science, University of Texas at El Paso. Author of *The Deterioration of the Mexican Presidency* (1991) and *Mexico 2000: Amenaza y oportunidad* (1995). **Essay:** Politics and Government: 1946–96.

Schreffler, Michael. Doctoral Candidate, Department of Art History, University of Chicago. **Essay:** Visual Arts: Sixteenth Century.

Schroeder, Susan. Associate Professor, Department of History, and Director, Latin American Studies Program, Loyola University, Chicago. Author of *Chimalpahin and the Kingdoms of Chalco* (1991). Editor of *Indian Women of Early Mexico* (1996) and *Codex Chimalpahin,* 6 vols. (1997). **Essay:** Women's Status and Occupation: Indian Women in New Spain.

Schuler, Friedrich E. Assistant Professor of History and International Relations, Portland State University. **Essay:** Foreign Policy: 1910–46.

Schwaller, John F. Associate Provost and Professor of History, University of Montana; Director, Academy of American Franciscan History. Author of *Origins of Church Wealth in Mexico* (1985) and *Church and Clergy in Sixteenth-Century Mexico* (1987). Contributor to *The Americas, Estudios de Cultura Nahuatl, HAHR,* and *Sixteenth-Century Journal.* **Essay:** Family and Kinship: Hapsburg Colonial Period.

Semo, Ilán. Coordinador, Programa de Historia Cultural, Departamento de Historia, Universidad Iberoamericana. Author of *Pensar la Revolución Mexicana.* Editor of *La transición interrumpida: Mexico 1968–1988* (1993); *La Revolución Mexicana en la escritura de su historia* (1995). **Essay:** Fuentes, Carlos.

Serrano, Mónica. Profesora, El Colegio de Mexico; Research Associate, International Institute for Strategic Studies. Editor of *Party Politics in an Uncommon Democracy: Political Parties and Elections in Mexico* (with Neil Harvey, 1994), *Mexico and the North American Free Trade Agreement: Who Will Benefit* (with Nikki Craske and V. Thomas Bulmer, 1994), and *Rebuilding the State: Mexico after Salinas* (with V. Thomas Bulmer, 1995). Contributor to *Journal of Latin American Studies.* **Essay:** Military: 1914–96.

Sherman, John W. Assistant Professor, Department of History, Wright State University. Author of *The Mexican Right: The End of Revolutionary Reform, 1929–1940* (1997). **Essay:** Reyes, Bernardo.

Sklair, Leslie. Reader in Sociology, London School of Economics and Political Science. Author of *Assembling for Development: The Maquila Industry in Mexico and the United States* (1993) and *Sociology of the Global System* (1995). Essay: Maquiladoras.

Stephen, Lynn. Associate Professor of Anthropology, Northeastern University. Author of *Zapotec Women* (1991) and *Women and Social Movements in Latin America: Power from Below* (1997). Contributor to *Latin American Research Review, The Reform of the Mexican Agrarian Reform* edited by Laura Randall (1996), *Reinventing the Commons* edited by Peter Wahl (1996), *Rural Reform in Mexico* edited by David Myhre (1996), and *Studies of Cultural Systems and World Economic Development.* Essay: Rural Economy and Society: 1940–96, Land-Labor Regimes.

Stracke, Claire T. Instructor, Foreign Language Department, Davidson Fine Arts School, Augusta, Georgia. Essay: Popular Catholicism.

Stracke, J. Richard. Professor of English, Augusta College. Essay: Popular Catholicism.

Suárez Argüello, Clara Elena. Investigador, Centro de Investigaciones y Estudios Superiores en Antropología Social (CIESAS). Author of *La política cerealera en la economía novohispana: El caso del trigo* (1985). Contributor to *Trabajo y sociedad en la historia de México, Siglos XVI-XVIII* edited by Gloria Artis (1992). Essay: Gálvez, José de.

Sullivan, Paul. Independant Scholar of Mexican and Central American Anthropology and History. Author of *Unfinished Conversations: Maya and Foreigners between Two Wars* (1989). Essays: Conquest: Yucatán; Lerdo de Tejada, Sebastián.

Thompson, Angela T. Assistant Professor of Latin American History, Department of History, East Carolina University, Greenville. Essay: Family and Kinship: Bourbon Colonial Period and Nineteenth Century.

Thomson, Guy P. C. Lecturer in History, University of Warwick. Author of *Franciso Agustín Diegindlo: Un liberal cuetzalteco decimonónido* (1995) and *Popular Liberalism in the Puebla Sigma: Francisco Luiar and Mexican Politics, 1854–1917* (forthcoming). Essay: Popular Liberalism.

Toro, María Celia. Professor-Researcher, Centro de Estudios Internacionales, El Colegio de México. Author of *Mexico's "War" on Drugs: Causes and Consequences* (1995). Contributor to *Drug Policy in the Americas* edited by Peter H. Smith (1992) and *Mexico: In Search of Security* edited by Bruce Michael Bagley and Sergio Aguayo Quezada (1993). Essay: Drug Trade.

Tortolero Cervantes, Yolia. Doctoral Candidate in History, El Colegio de México. Essay: Madero, Francisco I.

Tuirán, Rodolfo. Investigador, Centro de Estudios Históricos, El Colegio de México. Essay: Family and Kinship: Twentieth Century.

Tuñón Pablos, Esperanza. Investigadora Titular, El Colegio de la Frontera Sur. Author of *Mujeres que se organizan, 1935–1938* (1992), *Mujeres en escena, 1982–1994* (1995), and *Mujer y salud en el sureste de México* (1996). Essays: Mexican Revolution: February 1913–October 1915; Women's Status and Occupation: 1910–96.

Tutino, John. Associate Professor of History, Georgetown University. Author of *From Insurrection to Revolution in Mexico: Social Bases of Agrarian Violence, 1750–1940* (1986). Essay: Rural Economy and Society: 1821–1910.

Valadez, Martín. Doctoral Candidate, Department of History, Stanford University. Essay: Migration to the United States: 1876–1940.

Van Young, Eric. Professor of History, University of California, San Diego. Author of *Hacienda and Market in Eighteenth-Century Mexico: The Rural Economy of the Guadalajara Region, 1675–1820* (1981) and *La crisis del orden colonial: Estructura agraria y rebeliones populares de la Nueva España, 1750–1821* (1992). Editor of *Mexican Regions: Comparative History and Development* (1992). Essay: Rural Economy and Society: Colonial.

Vargas Valdez, Jesús. Investigador, Universidad Autónoma de Ciudad Juárez and Centro de Información del Estado de Chihuahua. Author of *Historia mínima de Chihuahua* (1989), *Catedral de Chihuahua: Testigo de la historia* (1992), *Chihuahuismos: Dimes y diretes, modismos y más razones del uso regional* (1994), *Francisco Villa: El agua fuerte de la Revolución* (1994), *Investigación* *y recopilación de recetas de la cocina regional de Chihuahua* (1996). Editor of *Textos de la Nueva Vizcaya* and *Tomochic: La revolución adelantada* (1994). **Essay:** Student Movement of 1968.

Widdifield, Stacie G. Associate Professor of Art History, University of Arizona, Tuscon. Author of *The Embodiment of the National: Politics, Race and Gender in Late-Nineteenth-Century Mexican Painting* (1996). **Essay:** Visual Arts: Eighteenth- and Nineteenth-Century Academic Art.

Young, Elliott. Doctoral Candidate, University of Texas, Austin. Contributor to *Southwestern Historical Quarterly.* **Essay:** U.S.-Mexican Border: 1821–1910.

Zapata, Francisco. Director, Centro de Estudios Sociológicos, El Colegio de México. Author of *Atacama, desierto de la discordia* (1992), *Autonomía y subordinación en el sindicalismo latinoamericano* (1993), and *El sindicalismo mexicano frente a la restructuración* (1995). **Essay:** Industrial Labor: 1940–96.

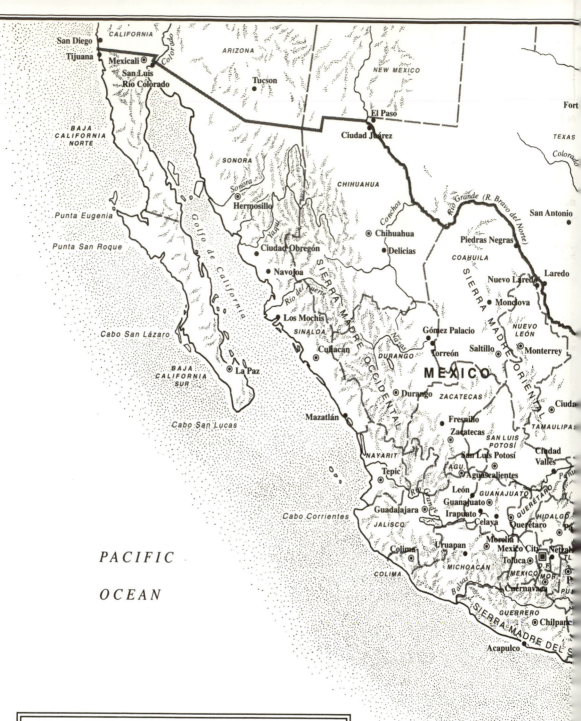

Contemporary Mexico